THOMPSON'S GALLERY

175A HIGH STREET
ALDEBURGH, SUFFOLK

072 885 3743

Alfred John Billinghurst. Oil on canvas.
20ins./24ins. 'Children on the Desert'

We deal in good quality
oils, watercolours and fine antique furniture
and these can be viewed both at
Aldeburgh and at our new London Gallery:

PORTLAND GALLERY

2 HOLLAND PARK TERRACE, PORTLAND ROAD
LONDON W11 TEL. 01-221 0294

guide to THE ANTIQUE SHOPS of BRITAIN 1987

June 1986 — June 1987

compiled by Rosemary Ferguson and Carol Adams

FRONT COVER: *A very fine Queen Anne red lacquer bureau bookcase. Mallett & Son (Antiques) Ltd., 40 New Bond Street, London, W1Y 0BS.*

British Library CIP Data
Guide to the antique shops of Britain. — 1987
June 1986—June 1987
1. Antique dealers — Great Britain — Directories
I. Antique Collectors' Club
380.1'457451'02541   NK1127

Printed in England by Antique Collectors' Club Ltd., Woodbridge, Suffolk.

COTSWOLD ANTIQUE DEALERS' ASSOCIATION
A wealth of Antiques in the heart of England

from a Brass in Northleach Church

Please write to the Secretary
for a free brochure.

FOR ASSISTANCE WITH BUYING, SHIPPING, ACCOMMODATION DURING YOUR VISIT, WRITE TO:

Secretary, CADA, High Street,
Blockley, Gloucestershire.
Telephone (0386)700280

LAMONT ANTIQUES LTD

Architectural Items, Bars, Telephone Boxes, Lamp Posts, Pillars, Panelling, Doors, Fireplaces, Leaded Glass Windows, etc.

Look for the Sign

Confident that our 500 members throughout the country are all elected for their knowledge and integrity.

Confident that all members are experts in their field, that you will obtain the soundest advice and help, that you can both buy and sell with the utmost confidence.

Re-election to membership is reviewed annually.

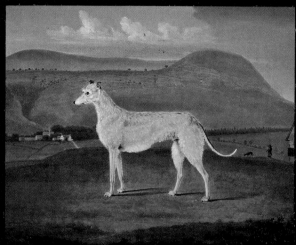

MACLEAN

DUDLEY & MARIE THORPE

Tiradda, Llansadwrn, Dyfed, S. Wales. Tel: 0550-777-509

Period Pine, Oak & Country Furniture

Edward A. Nowell

21-23 Market Place, Wells, Somerset. Telephone 0749 72415

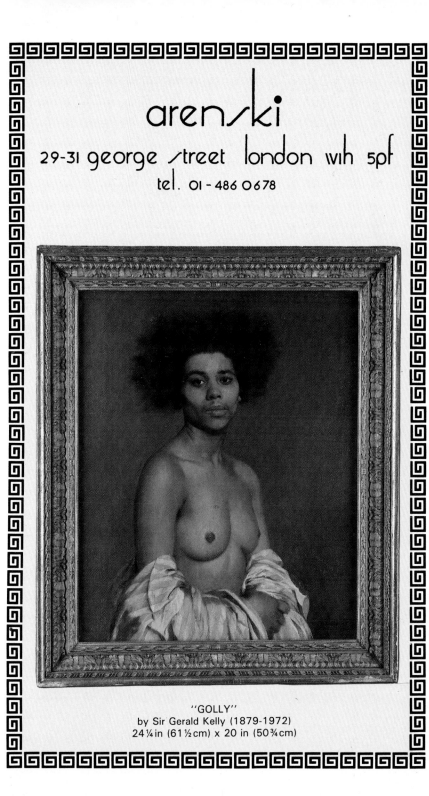

aren/ki

29-31 george /treet london w1h 5pf
tel. 01 - 486 0678

"GOLLY"
by Sir Gerald Kelly (1879-1972)
24¼ in (61½ cm) x 20 in (50¾ cm)

BELINDA COOTE

Specialist in Mason's Ironstone and
19th Century Ceramics, Papier Mâché
and Objet d'Art

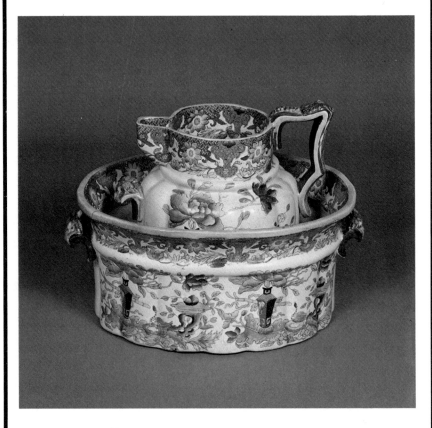

Mason's ironstone jug and footbath, c.1825.

29 Holland Street
London W8 4NA   **Telephone 01-937 3924**

Shop hours 10−6
Saturday 10−1   Resident

VIGO CARPET GALLERY

6A VIGO STREET, LONDON W1X 1AH
TELEPHONE: 01 439 6971

ANTIQUE TABRIZ CARPET
12ft. 10ins. x 9ft. 10ins.

GALLERY ANTIQUES LIMITED

TELEPHONE (0962) 62436/62161

Central Winchester with Own Car Park

All enquiries to 16 Jewry Street, Winchester, Hampshire SO23 8RZ

Large comprehensive stock of Georgian period items in fine 18th Century premises

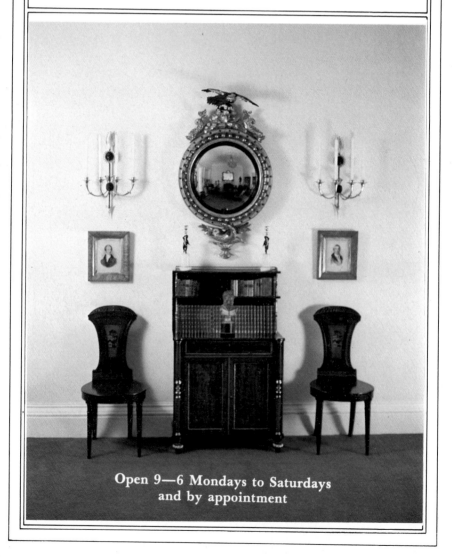

**Open 9—6 Mondays to Saturdays
and by appointment**

LAPADA'S 680 members in the United Kingdom include leading specialists in fine English and Continental furniture, porcelain, silver, glass, paintings, scientific instruments, Art Deco, Art Nouveau, metalware, jewellery, carpets and rugs, clocks, textiles, arms and militaria, pottery, books, barometers, dolls, Orientalia, prints, treen — and many dealing in general antiques and collectors' items.

There are also wholesale warehouse operators specialising in export goods, restorers, fine art packers and shippers, valuers.

All members are committed to a strict code of practice governing their dealings with the public and with members of the trade.

Details of membership requirements and lists of members may be obtained from the Secretary:
London and Provincial Antique Dealers' Association Ltd., 3 Cheval Place, London SW7 1EW. (Tel: 01-584 7911).

LOOK FOR DEALERS DISPLAYING THIS SIGN ▶

LAPADA
Registered Member

Contents

Acknowledgements

Our main sources of information are still trade magazines, papers, catalogues and so on, but we would like to thank the increasing number of antique dealers, private collectors and members of the Antique Collectors' Club who provide much of our information about new shops and passing on comments which go to make our information complete. Without this assistance our job would be more difficult.

We would also like to thank dealers who supported us with advertising and those who sent in information about their own, as well as other, establishments. Each year we include a form at the end of the Guide which dealers can use to update details about their own business. In anticipation of next year's Guide, we are grateful to those dealers who make use of this form.

Finally, thanks must go to the editorial team of The Guide to the Antique Shops of Britain, which carries out the mammoth task of compiling and indexing the entries.

R.F.
C.A.

Joint Editors **Rosemary Ferguson Carol Adams**
Advertisement Sales **David Inman Yvette Patharé**
Editorial Team **Jill Ringrose Chris Simpson Gill Willis**

Madley, Hereford HR2 9NA England

Telephone: Golden Valley (0981) 250244 (3 lines)
Telegrams and Cables: Antiques Hereford
Telex: 35619

Great Brampton House Antiques Ltd

**A superb 18th century, Hepplewhite period, mahogany, commode
of serpentine form. Circa 1780.**

We have one of the largest and finest stocks of period furniture in the country
Specialists in interior design, furniture and furnishings for the period and traditional home
Free delivery in our own vehicles to most parts of the United Kingdom
Goods packed and shipped to any part of the world
We are 7 miles S.W. of Hereford, 15 miles from the M5/50 and 50 minutes from the M4
One hour from Birmingham (M5/50)
Open Monday to Saturday, 9 a.m. to 5 p.m.
Evenings and Sundays by appointment

Price Guides and standard reference works on furniture published by the Antique Collectors' Club.

Send for your free 1986 catalogue.

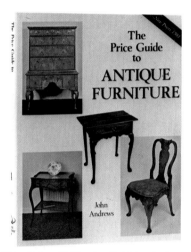

The Price Guide to British Antique Furniture *by John Andrews.* 290pp., 1,043 illus. The most helpful book ever made available to the collector. **£19.50**

The Price Guide to Victorian, Edwardian and 1920s Furniture *by John Andrews.* 218pp., 650 illus. A period where real quality can be found at a reasonable price. **£19.50**

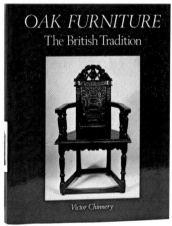

Oak Furniture: The British Tradition *by Victor Chinnery.* 600pp., 2,000 b. & w. illus., 22 col. This excellent book now includes a pictorial index. **£35.00**

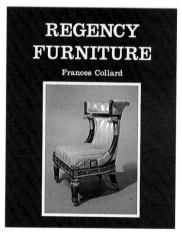

Regency Furniture *by Frances Collard.* 346pp., 304 b. & w. illus., 40 col. The first modern book on the subject and destined to become the standard work. **£29.50**

Available from your local
bookseller or in case of difficulty
from **Antique Collectors' Club,
5 Church Street, Woodbridge,
Suffolk IP12 1DS.**

*All books on this page measure
11 x 8½ in./280 x 216mm.*

19th Century European Furniture *by
Christopher Payne.* 506pp., 1,500 b. & w. illus.,
25 col. The author, an expert from Sotheby's,
covers the period 1830-1910.   £29.50

**Pictorial Dictionary of British 19th Century
Furniture Design,** *an ACC Research Project.*
583pp., 6,200 illus. An invaluable guide to
the dating of 19th century furniture. £35.00

Patrick and Gillian Morley

Antiques and Works of Art

8 Jury Street, Warwick. Tel. Warwick 492963

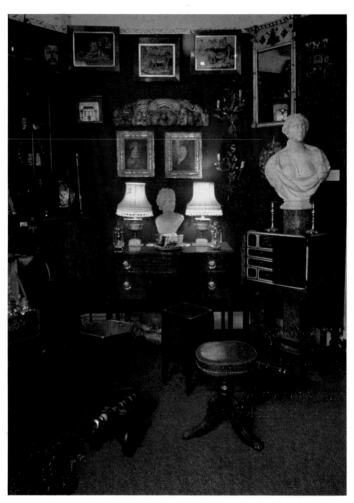

A corner of one of our ten showrooms

ALWAYS SOMETHING RARE AND UNUSUAL IN STOCK

HARLEY
ANTIQUES

Largest collection of selected
antiques and decorative objects
in the West Country.

The Comedy
Christian Malford
Nr. Chippenham,
Wiltshire
Tel. Seagry (0249) 720112

4 miles from M4 Exit 17

Resident on Premises

24

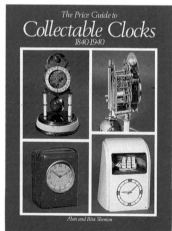

WILLIAM HANDFORD

ANTIQUES

517 KINGS ROAD
LONDON SW10

TELEPHONE
01 351 2768

The Antique Collectors' Club

The Antique Collectors' Club was formed in 1966 and now has a five figure membership spread throughout the world. It publishes the only independently run monthly antiques magazine *Antique Collecting* which caters for those collectors who are interested in widening their knowledge of antiques, both by greater awareness of quality and by discussion of the factors which influence the price that is likely to be asked. The Antique Collectors' Club pioneered the provision of information on prices for collectors and the magazine still leads in the provision of detailed articles on a variety of subjects.

It was in response to the enormous demand for information on "what to pay" that the price guide series was introduced in 1968 with the first edition of *The Price Guide to Antique Furniture* (completely revised, 1978), a book which broke new ground by illustrating the more common types of antique furniture, the sort that collectors could buy in shops and at auctions rather than the rare museum pieces which had previously been used (and still to a large extent are used) to make up the limited amount of illustrations in books published by commercial publishers. Many other price guides have followed, all copiously illustrated, and greatly appreciated by collectors for the valuable information they contain, quite apart from prices. The Antique Collectors' Club also publishes other books on antiques, including horology and art reference works, and a full book list is available.

Club membership, which is open to all collectors, costs £12.95 per annum. Members receive free of charge *Antique Collecting,* the Club's magazine (published every month except August), which contains well-illustrated articles dealing with the practical aspects of collecting not normally dealt with by magazines. Prices, features of value, investment potential, fakes and forgeries are all given prominence in the magazine.

Among other facilities available to members are private buying and selling facilities, the longest list of "For Sales" of any antiques magazine, an annual ceramics conference and the opportunity to meet other collectors at their local antique collectors' clubs. There are nearly eighty in Britain and so far a dozen overseas. Members may also buy the Club's publications at special pre-publication prices.

As its motto implies, the Club is an amateur organisation designed to help collectors to get the most out of their hobby: it is informal and friendly and gives enormous enjoyment to all concerned.

For Collectors — By Collectors — About Collecting

The Antique Collectors' Club, 5 Church Street, Woodbridge, Suffolk

If you've never seen **Antique Collecting**

the monthly journal of the Antique Collectors' Club,

it's probably because it never appears on the bookstall. Certainly if you want detailed information about antiques towards the lower end of the price scale you will be pleasantly surprised at the practical, no nonsense approach typified by a short article published recently on Early 18th Century Walnut Bureaux; two of the bureaux illustrated were examples of what to avoid!

Antique Collecting has been published for 20 years and has a circulation not far short of the antiques magazines on the bookstalls. The differences become obvious when you look at the cumulative index of subjects covered during that time and realise the vast amount of information that has been available to the reader.

If you would like to be kept up-to-date with price trends, learn the important practical aspects of antiques and extend your knowledge, then why not send £12.95 ($25.00) to Antique Collectors' Club, Woodbridge, Suffolk, England and receive the next 11 copies (August excluded) of one of the most interesting Antiques magazines published.

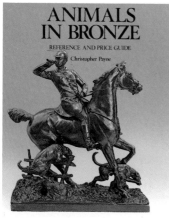
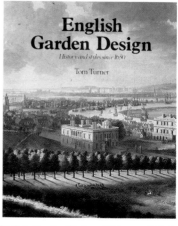
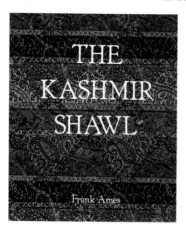

Introduction

This is the 15th edition of the **Guide to the Antique Shops of Britain** which is universally accepted as *the* guide for anybody who wishes to buy antiques in Britain.

Each of the entries is checked annually, which as the reader will readily understand is a colossal task. Increasingly, serious dealers recognise the importance of the Guide and send us very detailed information without having to be reminded that it is due. At the other end of the scale we send hundreds of reminders and make telephone calls, together costing thousands of pounds, to make sure that shops are still there. It is indicative of the high regard in which the Guide is held that dealers are kind enough to tell us about the shops that have opened or closed in their locality and we are most grateful for this unsolicited help.

How has the number of shops changed during the year? This year we have listed 6,477 establishments, which represents an introduction of 752 new establishments, while 599 have departed, a 20% annual change in the composition of shops listed. Please note that all last minute entries are included at the back of the Guide in the Stop Press.

For the price of a few gallons of petrol, the risk of visiting non-existent shops is drastically reduced but perhaps more importantly, time spent in fruitless journeys may be saved. The provision of motorways is very poor by international standards and many foreign visitors tend to underestimate how long it will take to make a visit.

We would stress that quantity of entries is meaningless without detail and here we pride ourselves that the range of information is more detailed and up-to-date than has been available elsewhere. Indeed, much of it is unique giving not only obvious facts — name of proprietor, address, telephone number, opening hours, stock, but also an indication of size of showrooms and price ranges. It is felt that these, although only general, give an indication of the quantity and quality of stock likely to be seen, facts which may well influence a prospective buyer's decision whether to visit a shop or not — in fact a time saver.

Additional information gives details of dealers' trade association memberships, the date the shop was established, and location and parking guidance plus street maps for those towns with over 25 entries. None of these points are necessarily decisive in themselves but, in conjunction with other details, valuable aids which build up a useful picture of the sort of establishment you are likely to find should you decide to visit. However, we strongly recommend that if you know the sort of pieces you want to buy, telephone first and plan the trip accordingly. Dealers questioned this way are normally very honest about their stock.

We start preparing the next Guide in early 1987 and so we should be grateful if dealers would let us know of any changes in their businesses — alterations in type of stock, price range, opening hours are especially important; to assist with this a form appears at the back of the Guide. Notes of changes to other establishments in the area would also be an enormous help.

We are always interested to receive your views about the Guide. How it can be improved or changes that you feel can be made. So please write if you feel that you have something to contribute.

How to use this Guide

The Guide is set out under seven main headings: London, Greater London, England, Channel Islands, Northern Ireland, Scotland and Wales. Counties are listed alphabetically (with the exception of Scotland); within counties there is a listing of towns and within the towns an index of shops, or galleries. London is divided into postal districts. In Scotland, as the majority of shops are concentrated in the central part and some counties have very few, we felt it would be easier for users of the Guide if towns were listed in alphabetical order rather than separated into their respective counties.

To make route planning easier, there is a map at the beginning of each county, coded to show the number of antique shops in any one town, city or village. The roads indicated on the map are only a broad intimation of the routes available and it is advisable to use an up- to-date road map showing the latest improvements in the road system.

Apart from the seven main headings mentioned above, there are further helpful lists; an alphabetical list of towns indicating the counties in which they appear for those not familiar with the location of towns within counties, e.g. Woodbridge is shown in the county of Suffolk. One therefore turns to the Suffolk section to look up Woodbridge. This listing is a valuable aid to the overseas visitor. The second is particularly important to British collectors and dealers, giving an alphabetical list of the name of every shop, proprietor and company director known to be connected with the antique shop or gallery. Thus, if A. Bloggs and B. Brown own an antique shop called Castle Antiques, there will be entries included under Bloggs, A., Brown, B. and Castle Antiques. Listings of specialist dealers, auctioneers, and shippers and packers are also included.

One point that collectors and dealers alike constantly seem to miss is that use of the telephone offers great savings of time and money. Nearly all dealers have to make unscheduled calls during opening hours and the 'back in 5 minutes' notice which has been in the window of a small shop for 20 minutes is a cause of great irritation to the potential buyer. If you have to be a hundred miles along the road in two hours, but there is something in the back of the shop which looks interesting, then the decision to wait or not to wait is even more agonising. A telephone call in advance can forestall such frustrations. When you telephone, it is usually quite acceptable to describe what you are looking for in terms of Antique Collectors' Club books. Increasingly one sees advertisements referring to page numbers. Most dealers have at least some of the books and use them as a basis for communicating information.

All but a handful of dealers are factual and reasonably accurate in describing their stock to us, but there are probably one or two who insist on listing their stock on the basis of what they would like to have, rather than as it is. Information on such dealers from those who use the Guide is greatly appreciated as are any suggestions and ideas; indeed it has been the kindness of so many collectors and dealers who take the trouble to drop us a postcard or telephone (039 43) 5501 and tell us about misleading entries or closures that has helped us to ensure that the Guide has become Britain's premier listing of antique shops and galleries.

Abbreviations in entries

In order to cut the bulk of this book as much as possible without curtailing the amount of information, we have made some very simple contractions in the entries.

BADA: Members are indicated by using a bold type face.

EST: Shows the year in which the shop was established or the number of years the dealer or firm has been trading.

CL: Days when the business is normally closed. It is followed by hours of opening. In some small businesses these may prove erratic, as it is often necessary for the dealer to go out at short notice. Unless otherwise stated, it would be wise to assume that shops are closed on Sundays. If making a long journey, it is advisable to telephone and make an appointment.

SIZE: A guide to the size of the showrooms is given to indicate the quantity of stock likely to be seen. Small is under 600 sq.ft. (60 sq. metres), medium between 600 and 1,500 sq.ft. (60 and 150 sq. metres) and large over 1,500 sq.ft. (150 sq. metres).

STOCK: Dealers are asked to list their stock in order of importance, so that the items listed can be expected to comprise a significant part of the stock. The price range is of very general application and is designed to give some idea to prospective buyers of the type of items to be seen. In an age of inflation the price levels quoted will often be too low, but nevertheless it is felt that they act as a useful general indication of the level of quality. Not stocked items are indicated after those which are stocked. The items listed are not normally to be found in this shop. Advertisements often give extra information on the size of showrooms, etc.

LOC: Location of shop. This is a description given by the owner designed to help the would-be caller. Road numbers in the entries are not necessarily shown on the county maps of the Guide, which are merely general aids to direction.

PARK: This indicates how easy it is for a car to park for 15 minutes outside the shop. Where parking is not easy, alternative suggestions for parking are often given.

TEL: Telephone. Where no exchange or STD code is indicated, this will be the same as for the town or village under which the shop is listed. In addition to their business numbers some dealers have listed their home telephone numbers, so customers can ring for an appointment outside business hours. Clearly callers should use discretion and only make out-of-business calls where they are seriously interested and in any event not late at night or early in the morning.

SER: Additional services which the dealer offers. Where 'buys at auction' is shown in this section, it indicates that if an auction is one which a dealer might normally attend, he may be approached to act as bidder on behalf of someone else. Check the cost of this service, and any others offered, beforehand.

VAT: Indicates which of the two VAT schemes, standard or special, are operated. In some cases both schemes are in operation and some very small shops are not registered.

London

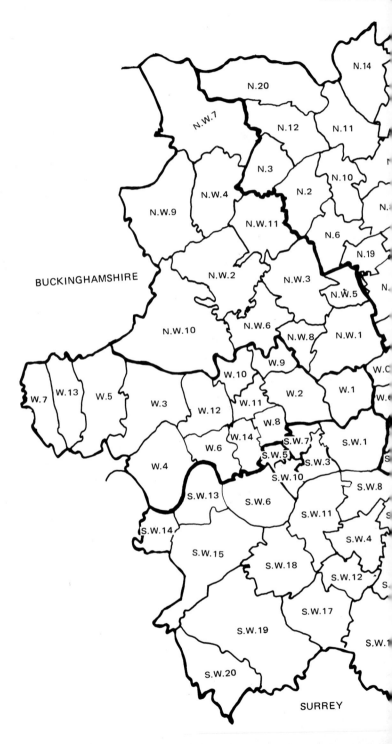

HERTFORDSH

BUCKINGHAMSHIRE

SURREY

London postal districts

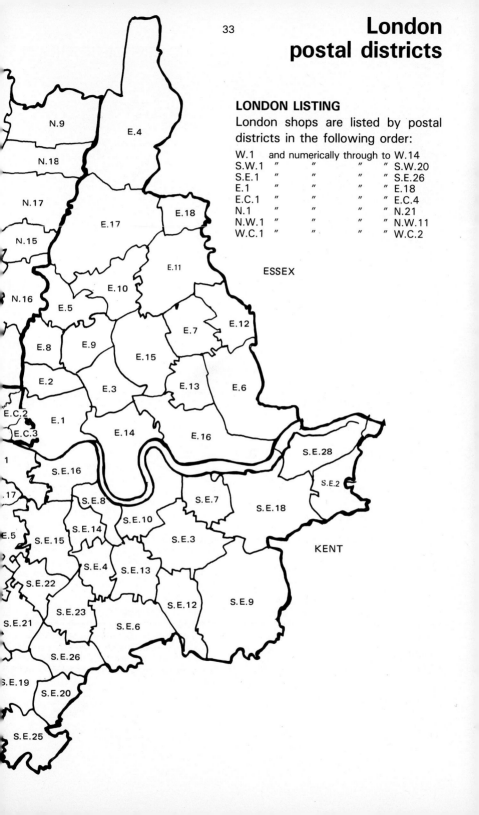

LONDON LISTING

London shops are listed by postal districts in the following order:

W.1	and numerically through to			W.14
S.W.1	"	"	"	" S.W.20
S.E.1	"	"	"	" S.E.26
E.1	"	"	"	" E.18
E.C.1	"	"	"	" E.C.4
N.1	"	"	"	" N.21
N.W.1	"	"	"	" N.W.11
W.C.1	"	"	"	" W.C.2

London W.1

(01)

A.D.C. Heritage Ltd.   LAPADA
2 Old Bond St. (F. Raeymaekers.) Open
10—6, Sat. 10—1. *STOCK: Silver, Sheffield
plate.* TEL: 493 5088.

Aaron Gallery   LAPADA
34 Bruton St. (M. and D. Aaron.) Est. 1910.
CL: Sat. Open 10—6, Sat. by appointment.
*STOCK: Islamic and ancient art, Oriental
carpets.* TEL: 499 9434/5.

Arthur Ackermann and Son Ltd.
3 Old Bond St. Est. 1783. CL: Sat. (some
exceptions). Open 9.30—5.30. SIZE: Medium.
STOCK: English sporting pictures and prints.
LOC: Near Green Park tube station and
Piccadilly. PARK: Meters. TEL: 493 3288/629
0592. SER: Buys at auction. VAT: Stan/Spec.

Adams   LAPADA
2 Royal Arcade, 28 Old Bond St. (Mr. and
Mrs. L. Adams.) CL: Sat. Open 10—6.
*STOCK: European porcelain especially 18th C
Meissen.* TEL: 629 0717.

W.1 continued

Thomas Agnew   BADA
and Sons Ltd.
43 Old Bond St. and 3 Albemarle St. Est.
1817. CL: Sat. Open 9.30—5.30, Thurs.
9.30—6.30. SIZE: Large. *STOCK: Paintings,
drawings, watercolours, engravings and sculptures of all schools.* TEL. 629 6176. VAT:
Spec.

Alexander and Berendt Ltd.
1A Davies St. CL: Sat. Open 9.30—5.30.
SIZE: Large. *STOCK: Fine 17th—18th C
French and other continental furniture and
works of art.* PARK: Meters. TEL: 499 4775.
VAT: Spec.

Antique Porcelain Co. Ltd.
149 New Bond St. (Mrs. R. Beiny.) Est. 1946.
CL: Sat. Open 9—6, Fri. till 5. SIZE: Medium.
*STOCK: Porcelain, faience, French furniture,
18th C.* PARK: Meters. TEL: 629 1254. SER:
Restorations; buys at auction. VAT: Stan/
Spec.

W.1 continued

Philip Antrobus
11 New Bond St. Est. 1815. *STOCK: Jewellery.* TEL: 493 4557.

Arcade Gallery Ltd.
28 Old Bond St. (P. Wengraf.) CL: Sat. and Sun., except by appointment. Open 10—5. SIZE: Large. *STOCK: African tribal art and antiquities; Indian miniatures.* Not stocked: English and Chinese items. LOC: Near Piccadilly. PARK: Meters. TEL: 493 1879. SER: Buys at auction. VAT: Spec.

Arenski
29-31 George St. Est. 1979. *STOCK: Fine furniture, glass, paintings, bronzes, objets d'art, clocks, Fabergé and papier mâché, especially fine 19th C items.* TEL: 486 0678.

Armitage   BADA
4 Davies St., Berkeley Sq. (R. Tadj Saadat.) Open 9.30—5.30, Sat. by appointment. SIZE: Medium. *STOCK: English silver, 16th—20th C.* PARK: Easy. TEL: 408 0675. SER: Valuations; buys at auction.

Armour-Winston Ltd.
43 Burlington Arcade. Est. 1952. CL: Sat. Open 9—5. SIZE: Small. *STOCK: Jewellery, especially Victorian; carriage clocks.* LOC: Off Piccadilly. Between Green Park and Piccadilly tube stations. PARK: Savile Row. TEL: 493 8937. SER: Valuations; restorations. VAT: Stan/Spec.

Asprey p.l.c.   BADA
165—169 New Bond St. Est. 1781. CL: Sat. p.m. Open 9—5.30. SIZE: Large. *STOCK: Furniture, works of art, longcase and bracket clocks, silver, jewellery, objets de vertu, carriage clocks, ships' chronometers, glass.* PARK: Albemarle St., entrance No. 22. TEL: 493 6767. SER: Valuations; restorations (furniture, jewellery, clocks, silver). VAT: Stan/Spec.

Astarte Gallery
Shop 5, Britannia Hotel, Grosvenor Sq. (G.J. and A.G. Davies.) Est. 1956. Open daily, Sat. and Sun. by appointment. SIZE: Medium. *STOCK: Roman, Greek and Egyptian art and artifacts, necklaces and other jewellery, £3—£3,000; medallions, some ancient coins, general antiques; books relating to stock.* PARK: Easy. TEL: 409 1875; hotel — 629 9400; home — 636 5689. SER: Buys at auction (antiquities). VAT: Stan/Spec.

Avakian Oriental Carpets Ltd.
20 Davies St. Open 9—6. Sat. 10—3. *STOCK: Oriental carpets.* TEL: 493 5758.

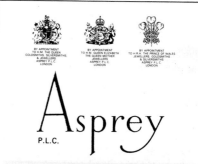

W.1 continued

Gregg Baker Oriental Works of Art
34 Brook St. Est. 1976. Open 10−5, Sat. 11−3, Sun. and other times by appointment. SIZE: Small. *STOCK: Japanese and Chinese works of art and porcelain, mainly 18th and 19th C, £100−£10,000.* LOC: Close to Bond St./Brook St. junction. PARK: Meters. TEL: 629 7926; home − 732 0943. SER: Valuations. FAIRS: Olympia. VAT: Stan/Spec.

Barling of Mount Street Ltd. BADA
112 Mount St. Est. 1946. CL: Sat. Open 9.30−6. SIZE: Medium. *STOCK: European furniture, 15th−17th C; European sculpture and works of art, 10th−15th C; Oriental works of art, to 12th C.* LOC: Between Berkeley and Grosvenor Squares. PARK: Easy, meters. TEL: 499 2858. VAT: Stan/Spec.

K. Barlow Ltd.
27 Conduit St. Open 10−6, Sat. 11−2. *STOCK: Decorative arts, 1900−1950, especially unique designer pieces.* TEL: 629 1653.

C. Barrett and Co.
51 Burlington Arcade, Piccadilly. (S. Freedman.) Est. 1818. CL: Sat. p.m. Open 9.30−5.30. SIZE: Small. *STOCK: European and Oriental ivories, jade, coral, carvings; carved walking sticks, chess and ma-jong sets; Russian silver and enamels.* LOC: Off Piccadilly, between Piccadilly Circus and Green Park Tube Stations, next to Royal Academy. PARK: Nearby. TEL: 493 2570. SER: Valuations. VAT: Stan/Spec.

Baskett and Day
173 New Bond St. CL: Sat. Open 9.30−5.30. *STOCK: Old Master prints and drawings, 16th−19th C; early English drawings.* TEL: 629 2991. VAT: Stan.

John and Arthur Beare BADA
(J. and A. Beare Ltd.)
7 Broadwick St. Est. 1892. CL: Sat. Open 9−12.15 and 1.30−5. *STOCK: Violins, violas, cellos, bows and accessories.* TEL: 437 1449. SER: Valuations. VAT: Stan/Spec.

Brian Beet
3b Burlington Gdns. (B.H. Beet.) Est. 1979. *STOCK: Drink related antiques; colonial silver.* TEL: 437 4975.

Paul Bennett LAPADA
75 George St. (M. Dubiner.) CL: Sat. Open 9.15−6. SIZE: Large. *STOCK: Silver, 1740−1963, £10−£10,000; Sheffield plate.* PARK: Meters. TEL: 935 1555/486 8836. VAT: Stan/Spec.

Bentley and Co. Ltd.
65 New Bond St. CL: Sat. Open 10−5. *STOCK: Jewellery, objets d'art.* PARK: Meters. TEL: 629 0651/0325. VAT: Stan/Spec.

W.1 continued

H. Blairman and Sons Ltd. BADA
119 Mount St. (G.J., M.P. and W.Y. Levy.) Est. 1884. CL: Sat. SIZE: Medium. *STOCK: English and French mid-18th to early 19th C antiques; works of art, mounted porcelain, Chinese mirror pictures; architect designed furniture, 19th C.* TEL: 493 0444; home − 794 9194. FAIRS: Burlington House. VAT: Spec.

Anne Bloom Jewellers
10A New Bond St. Est. 1960. CL: Sat. Open 9.30−5. SIZE: Small. *STOCK: Jewellery, Georgian, Victorian, Edwardian and art deco, from £250; silver, frames and mirrors, 1885−1930.* PARK: N.C.P. and meters. TEL: 491 7728 or 493 0526. SER: Valuations; restorations; buys at auction. VAT: Stan/Spec.

N. Bloom and Son (Antiques) Ltd.
                         LAPADA
40/41 Conduit St. (I. Harris.) Est. 1912. Author of The Price Guide to Antique Silver and The Price Guide to Victorian Silver. CL: Sat. Open 10−6. SIZE: Medium. *STOCK: Silver, 16th C to second-hand; jewellery, 18th−20th C; both £100−£10,000; Russian enamels, animalier bronzes, carriage clocks, 19th C, £100− £5,000.* Not stocked: Furniture, glass, china. LOC: Next to Westbury Hotel. TEL: 629 5060. SER: Valuations; restorations, repairs; buys at auction. VAT: Stan/Spec.

Bluett and Sons Ltd. BADA
48 Davies St. (R.B. Bluett, B.J. St. M. Morgan. A. W. Carter (Canada)) Est. 1884. CL: Sat. *STOCK: Oriental works of art.* TEL: 629 3397 and 629 4018. VAT: Spec.

Blunderbuss Antiques
29 Thayer St. (T. Greenaway.) Open 9.30−4.30. *STOCK: Arms and armour, militaria.* TEL: 486 2444.

Bobinet Ltd. BADA
102 Mount St. (A. Crisford, S. Bull, S. Whitestone.) Est. 1973. *STOCK: Watches, clocks, globes, English furniture, 17th−20th C, £500−£500,000.* TEL: 408 0333/4.SER: Valuations; restorations; buys at auction (clocks, watches, globes). VAT: Stan/Spec.

Bolsover Gallery
Bolsover House, 5−6 Clipstone St. (J. Kyte.) Open 10.30−5, Sat. by appointment. *STOCK: Fine watercolours and oils.* LOC: Near G.P.O. Tower. TEL: 636 7171.

W.1 continued

Bond Street Antique Centre

124 New Bond St. Est. 1970. CL: Sat. Open 10−4. There are 28 dealers selling a wide range of general antiques especially jewellery. Tel: 3515353. Below are listed some of the many specialist dealers at this market.

A. and B. Antiques of London and Henry Block
Stand 17. *Victorian china, silver plate, snuff boxes and modern British pictures.* TEL: 491 3615.

Eli Abramov
Stand 2. *Jewellery, silver and objets d'art.* TEL: 499 1532 and 629 4764.

Accurate Trading Co.
Stand 10. *Jewellery, porcelain, Oriental carpets.* TEL: 402 2689.

Alfano and Bostock
Stand 12. *Jewellery and silver.*

Art-Antica
Stand 16. *Art nouveau and deco, porcelain, objets d'art, glass, bronzes and small furniture.* TEL: 491 2327.

A.S. Beal
Stands 29/30 and 35/37. *Silver and plate.* TEL: 328 7525.

Claudia Beck
Stand 39. *Watercolours.* TEL: 409 2854.

Mrs. J. Beider
Stand 32. *Jewellery.* TEL: 629 3272/2422.

Roy D. Black
Stand 33. *Silver.* TEL: 493 3937.

Collection   **LAPADA**
Stands 8 and 9. *Antique and Edwardian jewellery.* TEL: 629 6777.

Sylvia Collins
Stand 15. *Jewellery.* TEL: 629 9625.

Adele de Havilland
Stand 18. *Oriental porcelain, netsuke, jade, jewellery and hardstone carvings.* TEL: 499 7127.

S. Deacon
Stand 23. *Silver and jewellery.*

Deeva
Stand 31. *Gemstones and Eastern jewellery.*

Mrs. Dowzall
Stand 13. *Jewellery and general antiques..*

K. Edwards
Stands 21 and 22. *Porcelain, general antiques and statuary.* TEL: 629 1670.

Felisa Jewels
Stands 34-43. *Jewellery, objets d'art, pearl, amber, coral and carvings.* TEL: 629 8910.

Folli Follie
Stand 1A. (J. Armstrong.) *Modern bijoux jewellery.* TEL: 629 4298.

Limner Antiques
Stand 25/26. *Portrait miniatures, 16th to mid-19th C.* TEL: 629 5314.

Bond Street Antique Centre continued

Richard Littleton
Stand 7. *Jewellery.* TEL: 491 8044.

Anne Music
Stand 14. *Jewellery and watches.* TEL: 493 5830.

Nonesuch Antiques
Stand 3. *Jewellery.* TEL: 629 6783.

Sheila Poulton
Stand 38. *Silver.* TEL: 493 2185.

Resners'   **BADA**
Stand 1d. *Jewellery to art deco; art objects and silver.* **TEL: 629 4346.**

L. and G. Schaverien
Stand 40/41. *Jewellery.* TEL: 493 3938.

Vinci Antiques   **LAPADA**
Stand 4-6. *Silver, objets d'art, porcelain, glass.* TEL: 499 1041.

Bond Street Carpets

31 New Bond St. (Mrs. M. Schapira.) Open 9−6, Sat. 10−5. *STOCK: Oriental rugs.* TEL: 629 7825.

Bond Street Silver Galleries

Mainly Trade
111−112 New Bond St. CL: Sat. Open 9−5.30. There are 3 floors consisting of 15 shops. *STOCK: Silver, old Sheffield plate.* TEL: 493 6180.

Arthur Black Ltd.
Silver, Sheffield plate. PARK: Meters. TEL: 493 6184. SER: Valuations.

A. and B. Bloomstein Ltd.   **BADA**
Silver, Sheffield plate. **PARK: Meters. TEL: 493 6180. SER: Valuations; restorations.**

John Bull (Antiques) Ltd.
Open 9−4.30. *Silver and plate.* TEL: 629 1251. VAT: Stan/Spec.

Crawford and Pawle
Silver and old Sheffield plate.

Phillip Cull
Silver and Sheffield plate.

Fortunoff Silver Sales Incorporated
Silver including Victorian, plate. TEL: 493 6184.

O. Frydman
Silver, Sheffield and Victorian plate. TEL: 493 4895. VAT: Stan/Spec.

G. Glass and Son   **BADA**
(H. Glass.). *Silver, old Sheffield plate.* **PARK: Meters.TEL: 493 5176.**

W. Kaye
CL: Sat. Open 9−5. SIZE: Medium. *Silver.* PARK: Meters. TEL: 493 5178. SER: Valuations; restorations. VAT: Stan/Spec.

Smith and James
Silver and old Sheffield plate.

E. Swonnell (Silverware) Ltd.
CL: Sat. Open 9−5.20. *Silver, Sheffield plate.* PARK: Meters.TEL: 629 9649. VAT: Stan/Spec.

W.1 continued

Browse and Darby Ltd.
19 Cork St. Est. 1977. *STOCK: French and British paintings, drawings and sculpture, 19th and 20th C.* TEL: 734 7984. VAT: Spec.

Bruford and Heming Ltd.   BADA
28 Conduit St. NAG. CL: Sat. Open 9—6. *STOCK: Domestic silverware, especially flatware, jewellery.* PARK: Meters. TEL: 499 7644, or 629 4289. SER: Valuations; restorations. VAT: Stan/Spec.

Burlington Gallery Ltd.
10 Burlington Gdns. (A.S. Lloyd, N.C. Potter and W.M. Lloyd.) Est. 1980. Open 9.30—5.30, Sat. 10—12. SIZE: Small. *STOCK: Prints and maps, 1600—1860, £10—£1,000.* LOC: Between Bond St. and Regent St. PARK: Old Burlington St. TEL: 734 9228. SER: Valuations; buys at auction (maps and prints). VAT: Stan/Spec.

Burlington Paintings Ltd.
12 Burlington Gdns. (A. Lloyd and M. Day.) Est. 1981. Open 9.30—5.30, Sat. 10—5. SIZE: Small. *STOCK: English and Continental oil paintings and watercolours, 19th to early 20th C, from £200.* LOC: Between Old Bond St. and Regent St., facing Savile Row. PARK: NCP Old Burlington St. TEL: 734 9984. SER: Valuations; restorations (lining, cleaning, reframing oils and watercolours); buys at auction (pictures). FAIRS: Game. VAT: Stan/Spec.

The Button Queen
19 Marylebone Lane. (T. and M. Frith.) Articles on Buttons. Est. 1953. Open 10—6, Thurs. 10—7, Sat. 10—1.30. SIZE: Large. *STOCK: Buttons, antique to modern horn and blazer buttons; buckles, unusual cuff links, mainly 19th C and Edwardian.* LOC: Off Wigmore St. TEL: 935 1505. VAT: Stan.

Cameo Corner at Liberty's   BADA
Liberty & Co. Ltd., Regent St. Est. 1912. Open 9—5.30, Thurs. 9—7, Sat. 9.30—5.30. During December open until 6. SIZE: Medium. *STOCK: Jewellery, to art nouveau and art deco, £100—£10,000.* Not stocked: Furniture, porcelain, pictures. TEL: 734 1234. SER: Restorations (jewellery). VAT: Stan/Spec.

Peter Cameron   LAPADA
at Henry Willis (Antique Silver), 4 Grosvenor St. Est. 1974. CL: Sat. Open 10—6. *STOCK: Silver — novelty, collectors' items, medical, old Sheffield plate, flatware, 17th—20th C, £25—£5,000.* LOC: Just west of Bond St., corner of Avery Row. PARK: Multi-storey 100yds. TEL: 491 8941. FAIRS: Century (Sunday); International Silver and Jewellery, Dorchester Hotel. VAT: Stan/Spec.

W.1 continued

Carrington and Co. Ltd.
170 Regent St. Open 9—5.30. *STOCK: Victorian and Georgian silver, jewellery, watches, clocks.* TEL: 734 3727/8, 493 6123.

Lumley Cazalet Ltd.
24 Davies St. Est. 1967. CL: Sat. Open 10—6. *STOCK: Late 19th—20th C original prints; drawings and prints by Henri Matisse.* TEL: 499 5058.

Rachel Child
1A St. Christophers Pl., Barrett St. CL: Sat. Open 10—5.30. SIZE: Small. *STOCK: Jewellery, £200—£10,000; some silver, £50—£1,000.* LOC: Between Wigmore St. and Oxford St. PARK: Selfridges. TEL: 486 5450. SER: Valuations; restorations (jewellery); buys at auction (jewellery). VAT: Stan/Spec.

J. Christie   BADA, LAPADA
26 Burlington Arcade. (Mrs. M.J. and P.S. Christie.) Est. 1946. CL: Sat. p.m. Open 10—5. SIZE: Small. *STOCK: Silver and plate, objets d'art, animalier bronzes, 19th C.* PARK: Meters. TEL: 629 3070. VAT: Stan/Spec.

Clarendon Gallery
8 Vigo St. (G. Henderson.) CL: Sat. Open 9.30—5.30. *STOCK: Old Master paintings; English and French, 18th—19th C oils, watercolours and architectural drawings.* TEL: 439 4557/8.

Colefax and Fowler
39 Brook St. Est. 1933. CL: Sat. Open 9.30—1 and 2—5.30. SIZE: Medium. *STOCK: Decorative furniture, pictures, lamps and carpets, 18th—19th C.* PARK: Meters. TEL: 493 2231/8. VAT: Stan/Spec.

Collingwood of Conduit Street   BADA
46 Conduit St. Est. 1827. CL: Sat. Open 9—5. *STOCK: Jewellery, silver, objets d'art.* PARK: Meters. SER: Valuations; restorations; clock repairs; buying. VAT: Stan/Spec.

P. and D. Colnaghi and Co. Ltd.
14 Old Bond St. Est. 1760. Open 9.30—5.30. SIZE: Large. *STOCK: European paintings, drawings, prints, 14th—19th C; English paintings, drawings and watercolours; European sculpture, furniture and works of art.* TEL: 491 7408. SER: Valuations. VAT: Spec.

John Crichton
34 Brook St. Est. 1963. CL: Sat. Open 10—5. SIZE: Small. *STOCK: Chinese and Japanese porcelain and works of art.* LOC: Off Bond St. PARK: Meters. TEL: 629 7926; home — 398 1933. SER: Valuations; buys at auction. VAT: Stan/Spec.

W.1 continued

Crowther of Syon Lodge
Old Bond Street House, 6 Old Bond St., Mayfair. Open 10—6, Sat. 10—3. *STOCK: Panelled rooms in pine and oak, chimney pieces in marble, stone and wood; life-sized classical bronze and marble statues; wrought iron gates; garden temples, vases, seats, fountains.* LOC: Near Piccadilly. TEL: 493 8688 and 560 7978. VAT: Spec.

The Curio Shop
21 Shepherd Market. (Mr. and Mrs. J.S. Cotton.) Est. 1948. CL: Sat. Open 9.30—5.30. SIZE: Small. *STOCK: Copper, brass, pewter, Sheffield plate, glass, china, small wood, prints.* PARK: Meters. TEL: 493 5616. VAT: Stan.

Anthony Dallas and Sons Ltd.,
17 Clifford St. Est. 1977. Open 9.30—5. *STOCK: Old Masters, English pictures.* TEL: 734 7127. SER: Valuations; restorations (oils and watercolours); buys at auction (pictures and works of art).

A.B. Davis Ltd.
18 Brook St., (Corner New Bond St.). Est. 1920. CL: Sat. Open 10—5. *STOCK: Antique and secondhand jewellery, small silver items and objets d'art.* TEL: 629 1053. SER: Valuations; repairs (jewellery and silver). VAT: Stan/Spec.

Demas
31 Burlington Arcade. (Mrs. E. Paul.) Est. 1953. CL: Sat. p.m. Open 10—5. *STOCK: Georgian, Victorian and art deco jewellery.* TEL: 493 9496. VAT: Stan.

Denisa the Lady Newborough
1, Whitehorse St., Shepherd's Market. (Lady Newborough.) Est. 1946. Open 10—5. *STOCK: Georgian antiques, Queen Anne, also Charles II and Victorian; antique jewellery.* TEL: 493 3954; home — 493 0854. VAT: Stan.

Denton Antiques
87 Marylebone High St. (M. and M. Denton.) Est. 1923. CL: Sat. Open 10—6. *STOCK: Cut glass, especially chandeliers.* PARK: Meters. TEL: 935 5831. VAT: Stan.

'The Dial' Marylebone
1 Marylebone St., Marylebone. (B. Somerset.) Est. 1948. Open 10—12 and 1—4, by appointment 12—1. SIZE: Medium. *STOCK: Clocks, £500—£3,000; scientific instruments, £100—£200, both 18th C.* LOC: Off New Cavendish St. PARK: Meters. TEL: 935 5143; home — 935 2201. SER: Valuations (clocks); restorations (clock movements, cabinets, gilt and French polishing); buys at auction (clocks, longcase or bracket). VAT: Stan.

W.1 continued

H.C. Dickins
41 Dover St. (F.N. and J.B. Dickins.) CL: Sat. Open 10—5.30. *STOCK: Original 19th—20th C British sporting and landscape paintings, watercolours, drawings and prints.* TEL: 629 9925.

Richard Digby
63 South Molton St. Open by appointment. *STOCK: Jewellery including cameos and intaglios.* TEL: 491 0251.

Anthony d'Offay
9 and 23 Dering St., New Bond St. SLAD. Est. 1969. Open 10—5.30; Sat. 10—1. SIZE: Medium. *STOCK: 20th C British paintings, drawings and sculpture; contemporary international art.* LOC: Near Oxford Circus and Bond St. tube stations. PARK: Meters in Hanover Square. TEL: 499 4100. VAT: Stan/Spec.

A. Douch　　　　　　　　　　*Postal Only*
28 Conduit St. NAG. Est. 1940. *STOCK: Jewellery, silver, coins and medals.* TEL: 493 9413. SER: Valuations. VAT: Stan/Spec.

Charles Ede Ltd.
37 Brook St. Est. 1970. CL: Sat, Mon. Open 12.30—4.30, or by appointment. *STOCK: Greek, Roman and Egyptian antiquities, £20—£4,000.* PARK: Meters. TEL: 493 4944. SER: Buys at auction. VAT: Spec.

Editions Graphiques Gallery
3 Clifford St. (V. Arwas.) Est. 1966. Open 10—6, Sat. 10—2. SIZE: Large. *STOCK: Art nouveau and art deco, glass, ceramics, bronzes, sculpture, furniture, jewellery, silver, pewter, books and posters, 1880—1940, £25—£50,000; paintings, watercolours and drawings, 1880 to date, £100—£20,000; original graphics, lithographs, etchings, woodcuts, 1890 to date, £5—£10,000.* LOC: Between New Bond St. and Saville Row. PARK: 50yds. TEL: 734 3944. SER: Valuations; buys at auction. VAT: Stan/Spec.

Andrew Edmunds
44 Lexington St. CL: Sat. Open 10—6. *STOCK: 18th and early 19th C caricature and decorative prints, books, drawings, period frames.* TEL: 437 8594/439 8066. VAT: Stan/Spec.

Emanouel Antiques Ltd.　　　LAPADA
64 South Audley St. (E. Naghi.) Est. 1974. Open 9.30—6, Sat; 9—1. *STOCK: Important Islamic and fine works of art, 18th and 19th C.* TEL: 493 4350. VAT: Stan/Spec.

W.1 continued

Eskenazi Ltd.   BADA
Foxglove House, 166 Piccadilly. (J.E.
Eskenazi, L. Bandini, P. Constantinidi.) Est.
1960. Open 9.30−6, Sat. by appointment.
SIZE: Large. *STOCK: Early Chinese ceramics;
bronzes, sculpture, works of art; Japanese
netsuke and lacquer.* LOC: Opposite Old Bond
St. TEL: 493 5464. SER: Valuations; buys at
auction. VAT: Spec.

Eyre and Greig
30 Old Bond St. (G. Eyre, C. Greig.) CL: Sat.
Open 10.30−4.30. *STOCK: Indian and S.E.
Asian pictures and works of art.* TEL: 491
1445.

Ted Few   *Trade Only*
6 Wimpole Mews. Est. 1975. Resident. Open
by appointment. SIZE: Small. *STOCK: Paintings, £300−£2,000; sculpture, £150−
£2,000; both 1600−1900; folk art, 1700−
1920, £50−£2,000.* Not stocked: Silver,
jewellery, ceramics, glass, large furniture,
prints, ephemera. LOC: North from junction of
Oxford St. and New Bond St. PARK: Easy.
TEL: 486 4644. SER: Valuations; buys at
auction. VAT: Spec.

Brian Fielden
3 New Cavendish St. Open 9.30−1 and
2−5.30, Sat. 9.30−1. SIZE: Medium. *STOCK:
English walnut and mahogany furniture, 18th
to early 19th C; mirrors and barometers.* LOC:
5 minutes walk north of Bond St. PARK:
Meters. TEL: 935 6912. VAT: Spec.

The Fine Art Society p.l.c.   BADA
148 New Bond St. Est. 1876. Open 9.30−
5.30; Sat. 10−1. SIZE: Large. *STOCK: British
art, paintings, watercolours, drawings, sculpture, decorative arts, 19th and early 20th C.*
PARK: 300yds. TEL: 629 5116. SER: Buys at
auction. VAT: Stan/Spec.

Forman Piccadilly Ltd.
92 Piccadilly. Est. 1962. CL: Sat. Open
10−5.30. *STOCK: Model ships, works of art,
orders, militaria.* TEL: 493 2174 and 499
5648. SER: Valuations.

Fortnum and Mason p.l.c.
Piccadilly. Open 9−5.30. SIZE: Medium.
STOCK: English furniture, 18th C. PARK:
Meters. TEL: 734 8040.

J.A. Fredericks and Son   BADA
Trade Only
Correspondence only to: 99 Hercies Rd.,
Hillingdon, Middlesex. (J.A. and C.J.
Fredericks.) Est. 1938. Open by appointment.
STOCK: English furniture. TEL: Uxbridge
(0895) 55462. VAT: Spec.

W.1 continued

I. Freeman and Son
Simon Kaye Ltd.   BADA
18 Dover St. Est. 1915. CL: Sat. Open
9.30−5. SIZE: Large. *STOCK: Georgian
silver; 18th C Old Sheffield plate; modern and
secondhand silver, medical instruments.* TEL:
493 7658. SER: Valuations; buys at auction.
VAT: Stan/Spec.

Frost and Reed Ltd.   BADA
41 New Bond St. Est. 1808. CL: Sat. p.m.
Open 9−5.30. *STOCK: Paintings and watercolours, 18th−20th C.* PARK: Meters. TEL:
629 2457. SER: Valuations; restorations.
VAT: Stan/Spec.

Sven Gahlin Ltd.
Open by appointment. Est. 1963. *STOCK:
Indian miniatures and Islamic works of art.*
TEL: Bath (0225) 313032.

Galerie George
98 George St. (R. Waterhouse.) Open 10−6,
Sat. by appointment. *STOCK: Fine 18th and
19th C English and European oil paintings and
watercolours, £200−£20,000.* PARK: Meters.
TEL: 935 3322. SER: Valuations; restorations.
VAT: Spec.

Garrard and Co. Ltd.   BADA
(The Crown Jewellers)
112 Regent St. (E.M. Green.) Est. 1723. CL:
Sat. p.m. Open 9−5.30. SIZE: Large. *STOCK:
Silver, clocks, jewellery, from £100.* TEL:
734 7020. SER: Restorations (antique silver
and clocks). FAIRS: Grosvenor House and
Burlington House. VAT: Stan.

Garton and Cooke
9 Lancashire Court, New Bond St. Est. 1967.
CL: Sat. Open 9.30−5.30. SIZE: Small.
*STOCK: British prints, 19th and 20th C,
Haden, Whistler, Palmer, Bone, Cameron,
Nash, Nevinson, Brockhurst, McBey.* LOC:
Between Brook St. and Grosvenor St., opp.
Fenwicks. PARK: Brooks Mews. TEL: 493
2820. SER: Valuations; buys at auction.

Christopher Gibbs Ltd.
118 New Bond St. Est. 1960. CL: Sat. Open
9.30−5.30. SIZE: Large. *STOCK: Pictures of
the major painters of all periods; furniture,
works of art, garden statuary.* TEL: 629 2008.
VAT: Spec.

Thomas Gibson Fine Art Ltd.
9a New Bond St. SLAD. CL: Sat. Open 10−5.
*STOCK: 19th−20th C Masters and selected
Old Masters.* TEL: 499 8572. SER: Valuations.

Attilio Gilberti
70 Wigmore St. CL: Sat. Open 10−5.30.
STOCK: Fine Oriental carpets. TEL: 487 3167
and 935 4339.

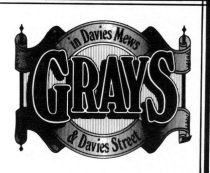
W.1 continued

M. and R. Glendale

9a New Cavendish St. (R. Sands and M.D. Sears.) ABA. CL: Sat. Open 10—6. *STOCK: English children's, illustrated, cookery and wine books; books on women.* TEL: 487 5348.

The Golden Past

6 Brook St. (M. and I. Oppenheimer.) Est. 1938. CL: Sat. Open 10—5. SIZE: Medium. *STOCK: Brooches, necklaces, cultured and natural pearls, guards, rings, ear-rings, bracelets, seals, charms, gold, pinchbeck, £20—£3,000; silver and plate, £20—£1,000.* LOC: From Oxford St., turn into New Bond St., second on left. From Grosvenor Sq. proceed along Brook St., until just after crossing Bond St. PARK: Meters. TEL: 493 6422. SER: Restorations and repairs (jewellery). VAT: Stan/Spec.

Thomas Goode and Co. (London) Ltd.　　　　BADA

19 South Audley St., Grosvenor Sq. Est. 1827. Open 9—5, Sat. 9.30—1.30. SIZE: Large. *STOCK: China, glass, tableware, ornamental.* TEL: 499 2823/4/5. SER: Restorations. VAT: Spec.

A. and F. Gordon　　　　BADA

120a Mount St. Est. 1935. CL: Sat. Open 9.30—5.30. SIZE: Medium. *STOCK: Continental and English furniture, paintings, bronzes, porcelain, marbles.* TEL: 499 5596. VAT: Stan/Spec.

Graus Antiques　　　　LAPADA

125 New Bond St. (E. and H. Graus.) Est. 1948. CL: Sat. Open 9.30—5.30. SIZE: Medium. *STOCK: Watches, jewellery, enamels, objets d'art.* PARK: Meters. TEL: 629 6680. VAT: Stan/Spec.

W.1 continued

Grays Antique Market

58 Davies St. CL: Sat. Open 10—6. TEL: 629 7034. Below are listed the dealers at this market:

A.A.A.
Stand 130. *Automobilia.* TEL: 629 5130.

A. and G. Antiques
Stand 158. *Jewellery.* TEL: 493 7497.

Abacus Antiques
Stand 313. *Jewellery and silver.* TEL: 629 9681.

Alpha Omega
Stand 302/3. *Paintings, watercolours and prints.* TEL: 629 1155. SER: Framing.

Ansari
Stand 331. *Oriental and European porcelain.* TEL: 493 1015.

Antiquarian Prints
Stand 121. *Prints.* TEL: 629 5130.

Antiques Corner
Stand 342. (T. Booth.) *Silver, bronzes, paintings.* TEL: 629 1307.

Arca
Stand 351/2/3. *Ivory, treen, tortoiseshell.* TEL: 629 2729.

Armada Antiques　　　　LAPADA
Stand 122. *Antique Weapons.* TEL: 499 1087.

Armoury Antiques　　　　LAPADA
Stand 123. *Antique Weapons.* TEL: 408 0176.

Osman Aytac
Stand 105. *Islamic ceramics, painting boxes and writing slopes.* TEL: 491 1560.

R. and R. Badir
Stand 144. *Paintings and objets d'art.* TEL: 629 6467.

Bagpuss
Stand 340/1. *Decorators' and collectors' items.* TEL: 629 5011.

Benjamin/Szramko
Stand 127. *Oriental items.* TEL: 499 4340.

Grays Antique Market continued

Peter Binks
Stand 328. *Objets d'art.* TEL: 629 8489.
Donald Bonney
Stand 132. *Oriental and general antiques.*
TEL: 629 5130.
Stanhope Bowry
Stand 104. *Leathers and antique luggage.*
TEL: 629 6194.
Britannia
Stand 101. *Commemorative, Doulton and studio pottery.* TEL: 629 6772.
Patricia Byrne
Stand 321. *Jewellery.* TEL: 629 5011.
Cekay Antiques
Stand 172. *Objets d'art – glass, pictures, walking sticks.* TEL: 629 5130.
Cerberus
Stand 372/3. *Walking canes, silver, watches.* TEL: 499 4340.
Chiltern Collectables
Stand 338. *Collectables.* TEL: 629 5011.
Harry Coleman
Stand 117. *China, porcelain, objects.* TEL: 629 3223.
Joy Continuum
Stand 124. *Oriental and tribal arts.* TEL: 493 4909.
Cozy Sato
Stand 385. *Cameras, lighters and watches.* TEL: 409 0269.
Croesus/Westleigh Antiques   **LAPADA**
Stand 323. *Jewellery and silver.* TEL: 493 0624.
J.M. Davies (Jewellers) Ltd.   **LAPADA**
Jewellery. TEL: 493 0624.
Jacqueline Elicha
Stand 347/8. *Jewellery.* TEL: 408 1129.
Evonne
Stand 368. *Silver and objets d'art.* TEL: 493 9457.
William Ewer
Stand 133. *Antiquarian prints.* TEL: 629 5130.
J. Findlay/D. Mackay
Stand 325. *Art nouveau and art deco, objects and jewellery.* TEL: 629 5991.
J. First
Stand 310. *Silver.* TEL: 629 1307.
Vera Fletcher
Stand 361. *Jewellery, silver.* TEL: 499 3629.
Gaze
Stand 384. *Furniture and works of art.* TEL: 629 3970.
The Gilded Lily   **LAPADA**
Stand 131. *Jewellery.* TEL: 499 6260.
K.N. Grant
Stand 176. *Brass and pewter.* TEL: 629 5130.
Kuniko Gray
Stand 140. *General antiques.* TEL: 629 3223.

Grays Antique Market continued

Solveig and Anita Gray   **LAPADA**
Stand 307/8. *Oriental porcelain, Continental silver, objects.* TEL: 408 1638.
Gres. (David Gill)
Stand 378. *Objets d'art.* TEL: 499 3075.
Henry Gregory   **LAPADA**
Stand 335. *Jewellery.* TEL: 629 0225.
Group 3
Stand 162. *Jewellery.* TEL: 629 5130.
Harlequin, Lancaster, Holland Antiques
LAPADA
Stand 152/3. *Jewellery.* TEL: 629 6502.
Diana Harby
Stand 148/149. *Lace.* TEL: 629 5130.
Hoffman Antiques
Stand 379. *Silver.* TEL: 499 4340.
David Hogg
Stand 142. *Tools, instruments and gadgets.* TEL: 629 3223.
Lynn and Brian Holmes   **LAPADA**
Stands 304/5/6. *Jewellery, silver.* TEL: 629 7327.
Howard Antiques
Stand 374/6. *Silver.* TEL: 408 1550.
Iona Antiques   **BADA**
Stand 107. (S. Joseph.) *19th C animal paintings.* **TEL: 499 2386.**
Eliza Jay
Stand 319/20. *Silver.* TEL: 408 0887.
John Joseph   **LAPADA**
Stand 345. *Jewellery.* TEL: 629 1140.
Kunio Kikuchi
Stand 357/8. *Tobacco jars, pipes, jewellery.* TEL: 629 6808.
Marion Langham
Stand 339/350. *English blue and white, Belleek, corkscrews and metalware.* TEL: 629 5011.
Lazarell
Stand 365/6. *Silver.* TEL: 408 0154.
Pat Lennard
Stand 148/9. *China, glass.* TEL: 629 5130.
Monty Lo
Stand 369. *Meissen and Berlin porcelain.* TEL: 493 9457.
C. Lucbernet
Stand 329/330. *Objets d'art.* TEL: 493 1219.
Peggy Malone
Stand 322. *Jewellery, china, objets d'art.* TEL: 493 7621.
Fiandaca Myers
Stand 386. *Silver.* TEL: 493 0768.
Howard Neville Antiques
Stand 177/178. *European works of art; marine and scientific instruments.* TEL: 493 1148.
Steven O'Donnell   **LAPADA**
Stand 156. *Scientific instruments and general furniture.* TEL: 491 8852.
Omniphil
Stand 110/6. *Antiquarian books, and prints.* TEL: 629 3223.

Grays Antique Market continued

N. Podmore Antiques
Stands 374-6. *Scientific and general instruments and tools.* TEL: 499 4340.

R.B.R. Group
Stand 175. *Jewellery.* TEL: 629 4769.

Ralph and Raymond
Stand 359/360. *Jewellery, silver.* TEL: 409 2937.

A. and I. Ramsay
Stand 327. *Enamel and tortoiseshell.* TEL: 499 4340.

Renate
Stand 333. *Jewellery, silver and coins.* TEL: 408 1059.

Sandra
Stand 301. *Objets d'art and jewellery.* TEL: 629 4340.

Satoe
Stand 161. *Paste and marcasite jewellery.* TEL: 629 5130.

Chris Seidler
Stand 120. *Arms and armour, weapons.* TEL: 629 2851.

Selected Antiques
Stand 362. *European porcelain.* TEL: 499 4340.

Bernard Shapero
Stand 125/137. *Antiquarian books and prints.* TEL: 493 0876.

Grays Antique Market continued

Shapiro and Co.
Stand 380. *Silver, watches and objets d'art.* TEL: 491 2710.

Connie Speight
Stand 108. *Toys, Victoriana, art deco.* TEL: 629 8624.

Surpass Coins
Stand 344. *Coins, jewellery.* TEL: 408 1059.

Talisman   **LAPADA**
Stand 363. *Tribal jewellery.* TEL: 409 2743.

Thimble Society
Stand 134/136. *Thimbles.* TEL: 493 0560.

Trianon   **LAPADA**
Stand 154. *Jewellery.* TEL: 491 2764.

Tugwell and Thomas   **LAPADA**
Stand 109. *Furniture, dog ephemera and animal paintings.* TEL: 499 1337.

Umezawa (M.C.N.)
Stand 126. *Oriental and Japanese porcelain.* TEL: 493 1261.

Ventura-Pauly   **LAPADA**
Stand 354. *Jewellery.* TEL: 408 1057.

Vintage
Stand 371. *Glass and drink related items, English porcelain and objets d'art.*

Grays Antique Market continued

Vitos
Stand 316/8. *Silver, objects, enamel, jewellery.* TEL: 499 0158.

Mary Wellard
Stand 164/5. *Small furniture, objects, glass, pewter.* TEL: 629 5130.

Westminster Group   **LAPADA**
Stand 139/50. *Jewellery.* TEL: 493 8672.

Wheatley Antiques
Stand 106. *Oriental porcelain.* TEL: 408 1528.

Grays Mews

1-7 Davies Mews. CL: Sat. Open 10−6. TEL: 629 7034. Below are listed some of the dealers at this market:

Allison's
J17/18. *Victorian jet, paste and art deco jewellery.* TEL: 629 3788.

Mrs. Angeli
L16. *Jewellery.* TEL: 629 1184.

The Antique Connoisseur p.l.c.
M17/19. *Watches and silver.* TEL: 629 3272.

Apollo Antiques
G16/17. *Oriental ceramics.* TEL: 629 3788.

Armand Antiques
C17/18/22/23. *Oriental works of art.* TEL: 493 6692.

Artifact
J30/31. *Jewellery, ceramics and pottery.* TEL: 493 6053.

E. Assad
A16/17/24/25. B14. *Eastern art.* TEL: 499 4778.

Colin Baddiel
C12/B25. *Toys.* TEL: 629 2813.

Baddiel/Golfiana
B12/A27/8. *Books on golf.* TEL: 408 1239.

Esther Bastasian
J15. *Jewellery, porcelain, silver and pictures.* TEL: 629 3788.

Linda Bee
K19. *Art deco.* TEL: 629 1184.

Bell and Collett
B10/11. *Toys.* TEL: 629 2813.

Francoise Bengue, Mrs. Newman
H24/J14. *Jewellery and paintings.* TEL: 629 1319.

Beslali
K33. *Jewellery and silver.* TEL: 629 1184.

Christine Bridge
K10/12. *English glass, porcelain and paintings.* TEL: 499 3562.

Sue Brown and John Weysom
M14/16. *Jewellery and objects.* TEL: 491 4287.

Circa
H16/17. *General antiques and memorabilia.* TEL: 629 3788.

Teresa Clayton
L24. *Jewellery and Victoriana.* TEL: 629 1184.

Grays Mews continued

Stuart Cropper
L14/15. *Mechanical toys.* TEL: 499 6600.

Barry Davies Oriental Art
E14/17. *Oriental furniture, ivories and netsuke.* TEL: 408 0207.

A. Dolby and S. McGurk
G21. *Samplers and Staffordshire.* TEL: 629 3788.

Donohoe   **LAPADA, BADA**
L25/7, M10/12. *Jewellery, silver and vertu; European needlework, all £50−£15,000.* TEL: 629 5633; home − 455 5507.

Alan Dreezer and Karen Mendelsohn
K32. *Jewellery.* TEL: 629 2371.

Elefantessa
H10/11. *Textiles.* TEL: 629 3191.

Elmarko
H24/J14. *Jewellery, silver.* TEL: 629 1319.

First Impressions
K17/18. *Jewellery, silver.* TEL: 629 3832.

Foley   **LAPADA**
L18/21. *Jewellery.* TEL: 408 1089.

Galerie Harounoff
K20/21. *19th−20th C oil paintings and watercolours.* TEL: 408 0803.

Mr. Gibb
A10/11. *Arms and armour.* TEL: 629 2813.

Trevor Gilbert
G10/11. *Silver.* TEL: 408 0028.

Gordon
J27/K14. *19th C china boxes and decorative items.* TEL: 629 3788.

Patrick and Susan Gould   **LAPADA**
L17. *Art nouveau and art deco glass.* TEL: 408 0129.

C. Anthony Gray
H26/7/8. *Oriental works of art.* TEL: 408 1252.

A. Greaves
B19. *Oriental items.* TEL: 629 3644.

P. Hamilton and Schiff
K15/16. *Jewellery and objets d'art.* TEL: 629 1184.

Brian Harkins
A18/19. *Oriental art, Chinese and Japanese antiques and works of art.*

Heian Gallery
C19. *Oriental ceramics and works of art.* TEL: 629 3644.

Hirsch and Braun
J26. *Silver, jewellery and objects.* TEL: 491 8744.

Howard Hope
L22/23. *Mechanical curiosities and phonographs.* TEL: 499 6600.

Keats
J29. *Silver.* TEL: 499 2382.

Langer and Collins
M13. *Jewellery.* TEL: 629 3596.

Leading Lady
J22. *Theatrical accessories, jewellery bags.*

Grays Mews continued

Leong
A30. TEL: 629 2813.
P.H. McAskie
D10/11. *Toys.* TEL: 629 2813.
Mankowitz/Wilbourg
C31/32. *Tribal antiquities and Oriental works of art.* TEL: 629 2526.
Minoo and Andre
G22/23. *Jewellery, silver and clocks.* TEL: 629 1200.
Namdar
B21/22/C15/6. *Oriental and Islamic works of art.* TEL: 629 1183.
J. O'Callaghan
B23/C14. *Antiquarian and fine books.* TEL: 629 2526.
P. and J. Antiques
J28/K13. *Pewter, ceramics.* TEL: 499 2719.
Madeline Popper   LAPADA
L18-21. *Antique, secondhand and art deco jewellery, including goldwork and cameos; cut steel, Berlin iron, objets de vertu and antiquities.* TEL: 408 1089.
Lily Randall
J16. *Collectors' items, silver and jewellery.* TEL: 629 3788.
Remember When
A29. *Toys, transport ephemera and collectors' tins.*
Reville and Rossiter
L10/13. *Furniture, silver and jewellery.* TEL: 491 8599.
Pat Richardson
G12/13. *Prints.* TEL: 629 1533.
Jonathan Robinson
C22-25. *Chinese porcelain and works of art.* TEL: 629 3644; 493 0592.
Wendy and Alan Robinson —
Tara Antiques
K28/30/31. *Jewellery.* TEL: 408 0909.
J. Romer
B16. *Oriental items.*
Samiramis Ltd.   LAPADA
E18/21. *Islamic works of art and carpets.* TEL: 629 1161.
Lester Saunders
B13. *Toys and dolls.* TEL: 408 1239.
Silv's
J19. *Victorian and art deco, jewellery.*
Simmons and Simmons
K37/38. *Coins and antiquities.* TEL: 629 9321.
Peter and Sara Jane Sloane
B15. *Ancient, Far Eastern and Islamic works of art.* TEL: 408 1043.
Stockspring Antiques   LAPADA
J23/24/25. *English ceramics.* TEL: 629 3788.
Studium
M20/21. *Art deco costume jewellery.* TEL: 408 0131.
John Tan Yan
C20/21. *Oriental art.* TEL: 629 3785.

Grays Mews continued

Tibetan Shop
A14/15. *Tibetan objects.* TEL: 629 2813.
Eugene Tiernan
H18/19. *Furniture and decorative antiques.*
Penelope Uden
H25/J12/13. *Jewellery.* TEL: 493 4843.
Jan Van Beers   BADA
K24/27/32. *Chinese ceramics and works of art.* **TEL: 408 0434.**
Vandekar Antiques
G19/20. H13/14/15. *Oriental works of art.* TEL: 499 0010.
Betty and Vera Vandekar
D13/14/15/16. *Oriental, English and Continental porcelain.* TEL: 493 0701.
Warren
G14/15. *Paintings.* TEL: 629 3788.
Helga Wellingham
A12/13. *Prints.* TEL: 629 2813.
L. Wells
D18/19. *Furniture.* TEL: 629 2813.
D. Wigdor
E11. *Furniture.* TEL: 629 3644.
Michael Willcox
K33/6. *Chinese ceramics, works of art.* TEL: 629 7387.
Willy and Co.
J19/20/21. *Art deco objects and jewellery.* TEL: 629 3788.
Linda Wrigglesworth   LAPADA
A20/21/23. *Chinese textiles.* TEL: 408 0177.
Yesterday
H20/21. *Victorian glass and silver.* TEL: 629 3788.

Richard Green   BADA
(Fine Paintings)
36 and 44 Dover St. SLAD. Est. 1953. CL: Sat. p.m. Open 9.30 – 6. SIZE: Large. *STOCK: Old Masters, British sporting, 19th C French, English landscape and 16th—17th C Dutch and Flemish paintings.* **PARK: Meters. TEL: 493 3939. VAT: Spec.**

Richard Green   BADA
4 New Bond St. Est. 1850. Open 9.30 – 5.30, Sat. 10 – 12.30. *STOCK: Impressionists, marine paintings.* **PARK: Meters. TEL: 491 3277 or 493 3939. VAT: Stan/Spec.**

Simon Griffin Antiques Ltd.
3 Royal Arcade, 28 Old Bond St. (S.J. Griffin.) Est. 1979. Open 10 – 5, Sat. 10 – 12. *STOCK: Silver, old Sheffield plate.* **TEL: 491 7367; VAT: Stan/Spec.**

W.1 continued

Grimaldi
12 Royal Arcade, Old Bond St. (K. Banham and P.A. Belcher.) Est. 1969. CL: Sat. Open 9.30—5.30 or by appointment. SIZE: Small. STOCK: Clocks and watches especially precision, 17th—20th C, £500—£50,000; barometers, 18th—19th C, £500—£5,000; also scientific instruments, 17th—20th C, £500—£20,000. TEL: 493 3953. SER: Valuations; some restorations; buys at auction (clocks, scientific instruments, barometers, furniture). VAT: Stan/Spec.

Hadji Baba Ancient Art
36 Davies St. (R.R. Soleimani.) Est. 1939. Open 9.30—6, Sat. and Sun. by appointment. SIZE: Medium. STOCK: Islamic pottery, ancient glass, bronze, silver, gold, cylinder seals, carpets and rugs. LOC: Next to Claridges Hotel. PARK: Meters. TEL: 499 9363/9384. SER: Valuations.

Hahn and Son Fine Art Dealers
47 Albemarle St. (S. Hahn.) Est. 1897. CL: Sat. Open 9.30—5.30. STOCK: English and Continental oil paintings, 17th—19th C. TEL: 493 9196. VAT: Stan.

W.1 continued

M. Hakim   BADA
4 The Royal Arcade, Old Bond St. CL: Sat. Open 9.30—5. STOCK: Objets d'art, 18th C; jewellery, snuff boxes, English enamels. PARK: Meters. TEL: 629 2643. SER: Valuations; restorations. VAT: Spec.

Halcyon Days   BADA
14 Brook St. (S. Benjamin.) Est. 1950. Open 9.15—5.30, Sat. 9.30—4.30. SIZE: Small. STOCK: 18th to early 19th C enamels, papier mâché, tôle, objects of vertu, treen, Staffordshire pottery figures, prints, small unusual Georgian furniture. LOC: Hanover Square end of Brook St. PARK: Meters and in Hanover Square. TEL: 629 8811. FAIRS: Grosvenor House. VAT: Stan/Spec.

Hancocks and Co. (Jewellers) Ltd.   BADA
1 Burlington Gdns. Est. 1848. CL: Sat. Open 9.30—5. SIZE: Medium. STOCK: Jewellery, 1800—1940, £250—£50,000; especially signed pieces; silver, especially Omar Ramsden, 17th—20th C, £50—£30,000. LOC: Opposite top of Burlington Arcade, off Piccadilly. TEL: 493 8904/5. SER: Valuations; restorations (silver and jewellery); buys at auction. FAIRS: Dorchester. VAT: Stan/Spec.

W.1 continued

Harcourt Antiques   *Trade Only*
5 Harcourt St. (J. Christophe.) Est. 1961. CL: Mon. Open 10—5 or by appointment. *STOCK: English, Continental and Oriental porcelain, pre-1830.* PARK: Easy. TEL: 723 5919. VAT: Stan.

Nicholas Harris   **BADA**
LAPADA
26 Conduit St. Est. 1971. CL: Sat. Open 10—5.30. *STOCK: Fine and collectable jewellery, decorative silver and objets d'art, all periods, £200—£45,000.* LOC: Just off New Bond St., opp. Westbury Hotel. TEL: 499 5991. SER: Valuations; restorations (silver and jewellery; restringing pearls); buys at auction. VAT: Stan/Spec.

S.H. Harris and Son   **BADA**
(London) Ltd.   *Trade only*
17-18 Old Bond St. (B.C. and R.H. Harris.) Est. 1885. CL: Sat. Open 9—5. SIZE: Small. *STOCK: Jewellery and silver.* LOC: 50yds. from Piccadilly. PARK: Burlington St. TEL: 499 0352. SER: Valuations. VAT: Stan/Spec.

Harvey and Gore   **BADA**
4 Burlington Gdns. (B.E. Norman.) Est. 1723. CL: Sat. Open 9.30—5. SIZE: Small. *STOCK: Jewellery, £50—£35,000; silver, £30—£6,000; old Sheffield plate, £30—£2,000; antique paste.* LOC: Near top of Burlington Arcade, off Piccadilly. PARK: 100yds. New Burlington St. TEL: 493 2714. SER: Valuations; restorations (jewellery and silver); buys at auction. VAT: Stan/Spec.

W.R. Harvey & Co. (Antiques) Ltd.   **BADA**
5 Old Bond St. (W.R., G.M. and A.D. Harvey.) Est. 1952. Open 10—5.30, Sat. 10—2. *STOCK: English furniture, clocks and objets d'art, 1690—1830.* TEL: 499 8385. SER: Valuations; restorations. FAIRS: Olympia and Harrogate. VAT: Stan/Spec.

W.1 continued

Brian Haughton Antiques   **LAPADA**
3b Burlington Gdns., Old Bond St. Est. 1965. Open 10—5.30. SIZE: Medium. *STOCK: British and European ceramics, porcelain and pottery, especially Meissen and Belleek, 18th and 19th C, £100—£10,000.* PARK: Nearby, Savile Row N.C.P. TEL: 734 5491. SER: Buys at auction (porcelain and pottery). FAIRS: International Ceramics — Dorchester Hotel (organiser). VAT: Spec.

Jeanette Hayhurst Fine Glass
LAPADA
3b Burlington Gdns. Open 10—5.30, Sat. by appointment. *STOCK: Glass — 18th C English drinking, fine 19th C engraved, table, decanters, scent bottles; Roman and Continental.* TEL: 437 4975.

Heirloom and Howard Ltd.
1 Hay Hill, Berkeley Sq. (D.S. Howard.) Est. 1973. Open 9.30—6, weekends by appointment. *STOCK: Chinese, English and European porcelain, £30—£3,000; seals and dies, £20—£400; Sheffield plate, £5—£200; paintings, coach panels, decorative items, £10—£2,000. All stock has identified coats of arms or crests.* LOC: Green Park underground station 4 minutes walk. PARK: Berkeley Square, Dover St. TEL: 493 5868. SER: Searches for armorial antiques, identifications; restorations; buys at auction. VAT: Mainly spec.

Milne Henderson   **BADA**
96 Mount St. (J. and S. Milne Henderson.) Est. 1970. Open 9.30—5.30, Sat. by appointment. SIZE: Medium. *STOCK: Paintings, £100—£10,000; screens, £1,500—£20,000; prints, £30—£500; all Chinese and Japanese.* LOC: Between Park Lane and Berkeley Square. PARK: Within 3 minutes walk. TEL: 499 2507. SER: Valuations; buys at auction. VAT: Stan.

Hennell Ltd. Founded 1736   **BADA**
(incorporating Frazer and Haws (1868) and E. Lloyd Lawrence (1830))
12 New Bond St. CL: Sat. Open 9—4.30. SIZE: Medium. *STOCK: Jewellery, silver.* PARK: Meters. TEL: 629 6888. SER: Valuations; restorations (silver, jewellery). VAT: Stan/Spec.

Heskia   **BADA**
19 Mount St. Est. 1877. CL: Sat. Open 9.30—6. *STOCK: Oriental carpets, rugs and tapestries.* TEL: 629 1483. SER: Valuations; cleaning and repairs.

G. Heywood Hill Ltd.
10 Curzon St. (D. Bacon.) Open 9—5.30, Sat. 9—12.30. *STOCK: Books, Victorian illustrated, children's and natural history.* TEL: 629 0647.

W.1 continued

Holland and Holland Ltd.
33 Bruton St. Est. 1835. CL: Sat. Open 9—5.30. SIZE: Medium. *STOCK: Guns, rifles and weapons.* PARK: Meters at Berkeley Square. TEL: 499 4411. SER: Valuations. VAT: Stan/Spec.

Holmes Ltd. BADA
29 Old Bond St., also at 24 Burlington Arcade. (A.N., B.J. and I.J. Neale.) CL: Sat. p.m. Open 9—5.30. *STOCK: Jewels and silver.* TEL: 493 1396 and 629 8380. SER: Valuations; restorations. VAT: Stan.

Howard Antiques
8 Davies St., Berkeley Sq. Est. 1957. Open 9—6, Sat. by appointment. SIZE: Medium. *STOCK: English and Continental furniture, objects.* PARK: N.C.P. nearby. TEL: 629 2628. SER: Valuations. VAT: Stan/Spec.

Hudson and Williams
14 Crawford St. (A.E. Gray.) Est. 1976. CL: Sat. Open 10—6, Fri. 10—5. SIZE: Medium. *STOCK: Furniture and pictures, 18th C.* LOC: Just off Baker St. PARK: Easy. TEL: 935 7627; home — same. SER: Valuations; restorations (furniture); buys at auction (18th C furniture). VAT: Spec.

Jadis of London
43 Davies St. (C. Elian and H. Korbon.) Open 9.30—6, Sat. 9.30—1.30. *STOCK: Ancient art, works of art and jewellery.* TEL: 629 2141.

The Jewel House (Mayfair)
23 Lansdowne Row, Berkeley Sq. CL: Sat. Open 9.30—6. *STOCK: Jewellery.* TEL: 499 7936. SER: Valuations; repairs (jewellery). VAT: Stan/Spec.

C. John (Rare Rugs) Ltd. BADA
70 South Audley St., Mayfair. Est. 1947. CL: Sat. Open 9—5.30. *STOCK: Textiles, pre-1800, carpets, tapestries, embroideries.* TEL: 493 5288. VAT: Stan/Spec.

Johnson Walker BADA and Tolhurst Ltd.
64 Burlington Arcade. (B.M. and E. Davidson and J. Agace.) Est. 1849. CL: Sat. Open 9.30—5. *STOCK: Antique and second-hand jewellery, objets d'art.* TEL: 629 2615. SER: Restorations (jewellery, pearl- stringing). VAT: Stan/Spec.

E. Joseph
1 Vere St. Est. 1876. CL: Sat. Open 9.30—5.30 or by appointment. *STOCK: Fine and rare books; watercolours, Victorian to early 20th C.* TEL: 493 8353/4/5. SER: Free catalogues.

W.1 continued

Alexander Juran and Co. BADA
74 New Bond St. Est. 1951. Books and articles on Oriental carpets, rugs, tapestries. CL: Sat. Open 9.15—5.30. *STOCK: Caucasian rugs, nomadic and tribal; carpets, rugs, tapestries.* TEL: 629 2550 and 493 4484. SER: Valuations; repairs. VAT: Stan/Spec.

Kennedy Carpets and Kelims LAPADA
9A Vigo St. (M. Kennedy.) Est. 1977. Open 9.30—6. SIZE: Large. *STOCK: Oriental carpets and kelims, mid-19th to early 20th C, £50—£25,000.* LOC: Off Regent St., up Sackville St. from Piccadilly, left into Vigo St., shop on left-hand side. PARK: Brewer St. TEL: 439 8873. SER: Valuations; restorations and cleaning (carpets and kelims). VAT: Stan.

Robin Kennedy
29 New Bond St. CL: Sat. Open 10—6 or by appointment. *STOCK: Japanese prints and paintings.* TEL: 408 1238; home — 940 3281.

Khalili Gallery LAPADA
15c Clifford St. (off New Bond St.). Est. 1976. CL: Sat. Open 9.30—5.30, or by appointment. *STOCK: Persian, Islamic and other ancient works of art.* TEL: 734 4202.

Richard Kruml
P.O. Box 4LE, 47 Albemarle St. Est. 1966. By appointment. *STOCK: Japanese prints, £25—£10,000.* TEL: 629 3017. VAT: Stan.

D.S. Lavender BADA (Antiques) Ltd.
16b Grafton St. Est. 1945. CL: Sat. Open 9.30—5. SIZE: Medium. *STOCK: Jewels, miniatures, works of art.* PARK: Meters. TEL: 629 1782. SER: Valuations. VAT: Stan/Spec.

Ronald A. Lee (Fine Arts) Ltd. BADA
1/9 Bruton Place. (R.A. and C.B. Lee.) Est. 1930. CL: Sat. Open 10—5. SIZE: Large. *STOCK: Clocks, furniture, pictures, firearms, armour, works of art.* PARK: Meters. TEL: 629 5600 and 499 6266. VAT: Spec.

Lefevre Gallery
30 Bruton St. (A. Reid and Lefevre Ltd.) Est. 1871. CL: Sat. p.m. Open 10—5. SIZE: Medium. *STOCK: Impressionist paintings, 19th—20th C.* LOC: Between Berkeley Sq. and Bond St. PARK: Meters, Berkeley Sq. TEL: 493 2107. SER: Valuations. VAT: Spec.

W.1 continued

The Leger Galleries Ltd.　BADA
13 Old Bond St. (H. Leger, D. Posnett.) Est. 1892. Open 9—5.30, Sat. by appointment. SIZE: Large. STOCK: Old Masters, English paintings, early English watercolours. PARK: Meters. TEL: 629 3538. SER: Valuations; restorations.

Liberty Retail p.l.c.
Regent St. Est. 1875. Open 9.30—6, Thurs. till 7. SIZE: Large. STOCK: General antiques 18th—19th C; Victoriana, Edwardiana, arts and crafts, art nouveau and jewellery. LOC: Regent St. joins Piccadilly and Oxford Circus. PARK: Meters and underground in Cavendish Square. TEL: 734 1234. VAT: Stan.

Libra Designs
82 York St. (M. Gottlieb.) Est. 1980. Open Mon., Wed. and Fri. 10.30—5, other times by appointment. SIZE: Medium. STOCK: Furniture and decorative items, '20s—'30s; art deco, £50—£1,000. LOC: Off Baker St. PARK: Easy. TEL: 402 1976; home — 289 3823. SER: Upholstery; buys at auction (furniture). VAT: Stan.

M. and L. Silver Co. Ltd.　LAPADA
2 Woodstock St. (C. Lasher.) Est. 1952. Open 9—5, weekends by appointment. STOCK: Silver, plate, 1750—1900, £10—10,000. LOC: 100yds. from Bond St. Station. TEL: 499 5392/5170.

Maas Gallery
15a Clifford St., New Bond St. (J.S. Maas.) Est. 1960. Author of 'Victorian Painters' and others. CL: Sat. Open 10—5. SIZE: Medium. STOCK: Victorian paintings, drawings, watercolours. LOC: Between New Bond St. and Cork St. PARK: Easy. TEL: 734 2302. SER: Valuations; buys at auction. VAT: Spec.

W.1 continued

McAlpine Ancient Art
60 Brook St. Est. 1974. CL: Sat. Open 9.30—1 and 2—5, Fri. by appointment only. SIZE: Large. STOCK: Western antiquities. TEL: 629 2247/8. VAT: Spec.

MacConnal Mason Gallery　BADA
15 Burlington Arcade, Piccadilly. Est. 1893. Open 9—5.30. SIZE: Medium. STOCK: Pictures 19th—20th C. PARK: Meters. TEL: 499 6991. SER: Valuations; restorations. VAT: Spec.

Madden Galleries
77 Duke St., Grosvenor Sq. Open 9.30—5, Sat. 9.30—1. STOCK: Paintings, French, Impressionist, post-Impressionist; sculpture. TEL: 493 5854.

Maggs Bros. Ltd.　BADA
50 Berkeley Sq. (J.F. and B.D. Maggs, P. Harcourt, R. Harding and H. Bett.) ABA. Est. 1853. CL: Sat. Open 9.30—5. SIZE: Large. STOCK: Rare books, manuscripts, atlases, autograph letters, and Oriental miniatures. PARK: Meters. TEL: 493 7160 (4 lines). VAT: Stan/Spec.

Mahboubian Gallery
65 Grosvenor St. (H. Mahboubian.) TEL: 493 9112.

SEE
BACK COVER

W.1 continued

Mallett at Bourdon House Ltd.
2 Davies St. CL: Sat. Open 9.30−5.30. SIZE: Large. *STOCK: Continental furniture, clocks, objets d'art; garden statuary and ornaments.* PARK: Meters, Berkeley Sq. TEL: 629 2444/5. VAT: Stan/Spec.

Mallett and Son (Antiques) Ltd.   BADA
40 New Bond St. Est. 1870. CL: Sat. Open 9.30−5.30. SIZE: Large. *STOCK: English furniture, 1690−1835; 17th−18th C clocks; china; needlework; decorative pictures.* PARK: Meters in Hanover Sq. TEL: 499 7411.

D.M. and P. Manheim (Peter Manheim) Ltd.   BADA
69 Upper Berkeley St., Portman Sq. (P. and P. Manheim.) Est. 1926. CL: Sat. Open 10−4.30. SIZE: Large. *STOCK: English pottery, porcelain, enamels.* LOC: Near Marble Arch. PARK: Meters. TEL: 723 6595. VAT: Spec.

W.1 continued

Mansour Gallery
46 Davies St. (M. Mokhtarzadeh.) Open 9.30−5.30, Sat. by appointment. *STOCK: Islamic works of art, miniatures, carpets; ancient glass and glazed wares; also Greek, Roman and Egyptian antiquities.* TEL: 491 7444 and 499 0510. VAT: Stan.

Marks Antiques Ltd.   LAPADA
49 Curzon St. (A. Marks.) Est. 1945. Open 9.30−6 including bank holidays. SIZE: Large. *STOCK: Silver, Sheffield plate.* LOC: Green Park tube, opposite Washington Hotel. PARK: Meters. TEL: 499 1788. SER: Valuations; buys at auction. VAT: Stan/Spec.

Marlborough Fine Art (London) Ltd.
6 Albemarle St. Est. 1946. Open 10−5.30, Sat. 10−12.30. SIZE: Large. *STOCK: Masters, 19th−20th C.* PARK: Meters or near Cork St. TEL: 629 5161.

Marlborough Rare Books Ltd.
35 Old Bond St. Est. 1946. CL: Sat. Open 9.30−5.30. SIZE: Small. *STOCK: Illustrated books of all periods; rare and out of print books on fine and applied arts.* PARK: Meters. TEL: 493 6993. SER: Buys at auction.

MALLETT

MALLETT AT BOURDON HOUSE LTD.
2 DAVIES STREET · BERKELEY SQUARE · LONDON · W1Y 1LJ
TELEPHONE : (01) 629 2444/5   TELEGRAM: MALLETOUS ·LONDON   TELEX: 25692

A very fine and rare pair of early 19th century Russian cut glass vases
with ormolu mounts, by Andrei Nikforowitsch Woronichin, maker to
the Empress Maria Feodrowna. Height: 22ins.

JEREMY J. MASON

Oriental Art

29 NEW BOND STREET
LONDON W.1

Office 01−629−3410
Home 01−874 4173

W.1 continued

Jeremy J. Mason
Oriental Art
29 New Bond St. Est. 1968. Open 11−4, appointment advisable. *STOCK: Oriental art, especially Japanese lacquer; porcelain, works of art, Chinese ceramics and jades.* TEL: 629 3410; home − 874 4173.

Massada Antiques   LAPADA
45 New Bond St. (B. and C. Yacobi.) Est. 1970. CL: Sat. Open 10−5.30, Thurs. 10−6.30. SIZE: Large. *STOCK: Jewellery, 18th to early 20th C, £50−£25,000; small silver holloware, £30−£2,500.* LOC: Near Sotheby's. PARK: Grosvenor Garage. TEL: 493 4792 and 493 5610. SER: Valuations; restorations (jewellery). VAT: Stan/Spec.

Mayfair Carpet Gallery Ltd.
8 Old Bond St. *STOCK: Persian, Oriental rugs and carpets.* TEL: 493 0126.

Mayfair Gallery
97 Mount St. CL: Sat. Open 10−6. *STOCK: Islamic and 18th−19th C works of art; French furniture, 18th−19th C.* TEL: 499 5315.

W.1 continued

Mayfair Microscopes Ltd.
64 Burlington Arcade. (B.M. Davidson.) Est. 1967. CL: Sat. Open 9.30−5. *STOCK: Microscopes, telescopes.* TEL: 629 2616. VAT: Stan/Spec.

Christopher Mendez
51 Lexington St. Est. 1966. CL: Sat. Open 10−5. SIZE: Small. *STOCK: Old Master engravings, etchings, woodcuts, to 1800, £50−£500+; English prints, 18th C, £30−£250; portraits, engraved and mezzotint, £20−£100.* LOC: Lexington St. is at right angles to Brewer St., off Regent St. TEL: 734 2385. SER: Valuations; buys at auction (Old Master prints and 18th C English prints). FAIRS: Europa Book, June. VAT: Stan.

Roy Miles Fine Paintings Ltd.
3 Berkeley Sq. Open by appointment. *STOCK: Major English and high Victorian paintings.* TEL: 491 3611

Nigel Milne Ltd.
16c Grafton St. Est. 1979. Open 9.30−5.30, Sat. by appointment. SIZE: Small. *STOCK: Jewellery, early Victorian to 1930s, £50−£25,000; silver frames, Edwardian, £150−£500.* LOC: Corner Grafton St. and Albemarle St., off New Bond St. PARK: Easy. TEL: 493 9646 and 491 2504. SER: Valuations; buys at auction. VAT: Stan/Spec.

John Mitchell and Son   BADA
8 New Bond St. (1st floor). Est. 1931. CL: Sat. Open 9.30−5. SIZE: Small. *STOCK: Old Master paintings, drawings and watercolours, Dutch, 17th C; English, 18th C; French, 19th C.* LOC: Nearest tube Green Park. PARK: Meters. TEL: 493 7567. SER: Valuations; restorations (pictures); buys at auction.

W.1 continued

Paul Mitchell BADA
99 New Bond St. CL: Sat. Open 9.30—5.30. *STOCK: Picture frames.* TEL: 493 8732/0860.

Sydney L. Moss Ltd. BADA
51 Brook St. (P.G. and E.M. Moss.) Est. 1910. Articles on netsuke, jade, Tang pottery, snuff bottles, marks and I-Hsing stoneware. CL: Sat. Open 9.30—5. SIZE: Large. *STOCK: Chinese and Japanese paintings and works of art, ceramics, 1500BC—1950; Japanese netsuke, 18th—20th C.* LOC: From Grosvenor Sq. up Brook St. to Claridges. PARK: Meters. TEL: 629 4670, 493 7374. SER: Valuations and advice; buys at auction. FAIRS: Burlington House, Grosvenor House. VAT: Spec.

Anthony Mould Ltd.
1st Floor, 173 New Bond St. Open by appointment. *STOCK: Historic portraits, Old Master and English paintings.* TEL: 491 3133.

Mount St. Galleries
125 Mount St. Est. 1966. Open 9—6, Sat. and Sun. by appointment. SIZE: Medium. *STOCK: Furniture, paintings and objects, Continental and Oriental, 18th—19th C.* LOC: 100yds. from Berkeley Sq. PARK: Easy. TEL: 493 5211. VAT: Stan/Spec.

Richard Mundey
19 Chiltern St. Est. 1939. Open 10—5, Sat. by appointment. SIZE: Medium. *STOCK: Antique pewter only, English and Continental, all periods.* LOC: Near Sherlock Holmes Hotel. PARK: Opp. Sherlock Holmes Hotel. TEL: 935 5613. VAT: Stan.

Naxos Art Ltd. Trade only
27 Mount St. Est. 1983. CL: Sat. Open 10—6. SIZE: Large. *STOCK: Archeological objects, works of art and Oriental rugs.* PARK: Easy. TEL: 629 6448/3905. SER: Valuations; restorations; buys at auction. VAT: Spec.

Kenneth Neame Ltd.
25 Brook St. Est. 1925. CL: Sat. Open 9.30—5.30. *STOCK: 18th—19th C English furniture.* PARK: Meters. TEL: 629 0445. SER: Interior decorations. VAT: Spec.

Neptune BADA
99 Mount St. (P. and M. Horsman) Est. 1971. Open 10—6, Sat. by appointment. SIZE: Medium. *STOCK: Early oak and walnut furniture, £500—£20,000; objects £100—£3,000, all 17th—18th C.* LOC: Just off Park Lane. PARK: Easy. TEL: 499 2002; home — Ipswich (0473) 51110. SER: Valuations; restorations; buys at auction. FAIRS: Grosvenor House. VAT: Spec.

W.1 continued

L. Newland
17 Picton Place. Est. 1963. CL: Sat. Open 10—2 and 3.30—6. SIZE: Medium. *STOCK: Secondhand jewellery, £5—£500.* LOC: 1 minute from Selfridges. PARK: Easy, Selfridges. TEL: 935 2864. SER: Valuations; restorations and repairs (jewellery, enamel, ivory, tortoiseshell, antique watches, clocks); testing precious metals and gem stones; buys at auction. VAT: Stan.

Newman and Cooling Ltd. inc. M. Newman Ltd. (Est. 1870) and Cooling Galleries (London) Ltd. (Est. 1797)
38 Albemarle St. SLAD. CL: Sat. except by appointment. Open 9.30—5.30. SIZE: Large. *STOCK: Oil paintings, from £500; watercolours, both 1800—1930.* PARK: Meters. TEL: 930 6068 and 629 5224. SER: Valuations; restorations (oil paintings and drawings). VAT: Spec.

Noortman
40—41 Old Bond St. Open 9.30—5.30. *STOCK: Old Masters, French 19th—20th C.* TEL: 491 7284.

Richard Ogden Ltd. BADA
28 and 29 Burlington Arcade, Piccadilly. Est. 1948. CL: Sat. p.m. Open 9.30—5.15. SIZE: Medium. *STOCK: Antique jewellery, rings.* LOC: Near Piccadilly Circus. PARK: Meters. TEL: 493 9136/7. SER: Valuations; repairs. VAT: Spec.

Osborne Gallery
21 Grosvenor St. (S.J., B.M. and R.W. Fenemore.) Est. 1980. Open 10.30—5.30, Sat. and Sun. and other times by appointment. SIZE: Small. *STOCK: English watercolours, 1750-1950, £500—£3,000; Middle Eastern watercolours, 19th C., £200—£2,500; Malta watercolours, 18th-19th C., £200—£2,000.* TEL: 409 3599. SER: Restorations (watercolours and prints); buys at auction (watercolours). VAT: Stan/Spec.

P. and O. Carpets Ltd. LAPADA
63 South Audley St., other entrance 5a Aldford St. (A. Miles.) Est. 1956. Open 10—6, Sat. 10—1. SIZE: Large. *STOCK: Oriental carpets, £20—10,000.* LOC: Midway between U.S. Embassy and London Hilton. PARK: Easy. TEL: 629 9678. SER: Valuations; restorations. VAT: Stan.

W.1 continued

The Parker Gallery BADA
12A-12B Berkeley St. (Thomas H. Parker Ltd.) SLAD. Est. 1750. CL: Sat. Open 9.30−5.30. SIZE: Medium. STOCK: Historical prints, £10−£1,000; paintings, English, £200− £15,000; ship models, £50−£15,000, all 1700−1950. LOC: Off Piccadilly, opposite Mayfair Hotel. TEL: 499 5906. SER: Restorations (prints, paintings, ship models), mounting, framing. FAIRS: Grosvenor House. VAT: Stan/ Spec.

Partridge (Fine Arts) Ltd.
144−146 New Bond St. Est. 1911. CL: Sat. Open 9.30−5.30. SIZE: Large. STOCK: English and French furniture, silver; paintings of English and Italian School. LOC: North of Bruton St., opp. Sotheby's. PARK: Meters. TEL: 629 0834. SER: Buys at auction. VAT: Spec.

W.H. Patterson Fine Arts Ltd. BADA
19 Albemarle St. (W.H. and P.M. Patterson.) SLAD. Open 9.30−6. SIZE: Large. STOCK: Old Master oil paintings, 18th−19th C. LOC: Near Green Park tube station. PARK: Meters. TEL: 629 4119. SER: Valuations; restorations. VAT: Spec.

Howard Phillips BADA (Antique Glass)
11a Henrietta Place. Est. 1948. CL: Sat. Open 9.30−5.15. SIZE: Medium. STOCK: Glass, pre-Roman to 1830. PARK: Multi- storey. TEL: 580 9844. VAT: Stan/Spec.

Ronald Phillips Ltd. BADA
26 Bruton St. Est. 1952. STOCK: English furniture, objets d'art and porcelain. TEL: 493 2341. VAT: Mainly spec.

S.J. Phillips Ltd. BADA
139 New Bond St. (M.S., N.E.L., J.P. and F.E. Norton.) Est. 1869. CL: Sat. Open 10−5. SIZE: Large. STOCK: Silver, jewellery, gold boxes, miniatures. LOC: Near Bond St. tube station. PARK: Meters. TEL: 629 6261. SER: Valuations; restorations; buys at auction. FAIRS: Burlington House, Grosvenor House. VAT: Stan/Spec.

Piccadilly Gallery
16 Cork St. Est. 1952. CL: Sat; Aug. and Sept. Open 10−5.30, Sat. 10−12.30. STOCK: Symbolist and art nouveau works, 20th C; drawings and watercolours. PARK: Meters. TEL: 499 4632. VAT: Spec.

Portman Carpets
7 Portman Sq. (S., R. and A. Hay.) Est. 1933. Open 10.15−6, Sat. 10.15−1. SIZE: Large. STOCK: Persian, Caucasian and Turkish carpets, rugs and kelims, 19th and 20th C, from £500. LOC: Opposite Churchill Hotel. PARK: Nearby, Gloucester Place N.C.P. TEL: 486 3770. SER: Valuations; restorations (hand knotted Oriental rugs.) VAT: Stan.

W.1 continued

Jonathan Potter Ltd. BADA
1 Grafton St. Est. 1975. Open 9.30−5.30. SIZE: Large. STOCK: Maps, 16th−19th C, £15−£10,000; prints of London, 18th−19th C, £5−£1,000; atlases and travel books, 16th−19th C, £50-£10,000. LOC: Between Berkeley St. and Bond St. PARK: Meters. TEL: 491 3520. SER: Valuations; restorations; colouring, framing; buys at auction (maps and prints); catalogue available. VAT: Stan.

Bernard Quaritch Ltd. (Booksellers)
5-8 Lower John St., Golden Sq. Est. 1847. CL: Sat. Open 9.30−5.30. SIZE: Large. STOCK: Antiquarian books. PARK: Meters, 50yds. TEL: 734 2983. SER: Buys at auction. FAIRS: National, International and New York Book. VAT: Stan.

Rabi Gallery LAPADA
94 Mount St. (R. and V. Soleymani.) Est. 1978. Open 9.30−6, Sat. 10−1. STOCK: Islamic works of art. TEL: 499 8886.

Rare Carpets Gallery
23 Old Bond St. Est. 1963. Open 10−6. SIZE: Medium. STOCK: Persian, Turkish and Caucasian, Belouchis carpets and rugs. LOC: Junction Old/New Bond St. PARK: Burlington Garage. TEL: 491 4315, 499 2374 or 351 3296. SER: Valuations; restorations; part exchange (Oriental and hand-made carpets). VAT: Stan.

William Redford BADA
9 Mount St. CL: Sat. Open 9.30−5.30. SIZE: Large. STOCK: French furniture, works of art, bronzes, some porcelain. TEL: 629 1165.

Anthony Reed
3 Cork St. (Anthony Reed Gallery Ltd.) Est. 1953. CL: Sat. Open 10−5. SIZE: Small. STOCK: Early English watercolours, small English paintings, 18th−19th C, £100− £10,000. LOC: Parallel and adjacent to Bond St. TEL: 437 0157. SER: Valuations; restorations (watercolours); buys at auction. VAT: Spec.

David Richards and Sons LAPADA
12 New Cavendish St. (M., H. and E. Richards.) CL: Sat. Open 9.30−5.30. SIZE: Large. STOCK: Silver, Victorian and old Sheffield plate. LOC: Off Harley St. at corner of Marylebone High St. PARK: Easy. TEL: 935 3206/0322. SER: Valuations; restorations. VAT: Stan/Spec.

The Richmond Gallery
8 Cork St. (T. Pringle, J. Moloney, C. Mayes.) CL: Sat. Open 10−6. STOCK: Impressionist and Post-Impressionist paintings. TEL: 437 9422 (ansaphone).

W.1 continued

Rutland Gallery
32a St. George St. CL: Sat. Open 10−5.
STOCK: British and American primitive paintings, Indian and China trade paintings. TEL: 499 5636.

Sac Freres
45 Old Bond St. (J. Hunger.) Est. 1879. CL: Sat. Open 9.30−5.30. *STOCK: Amber carvings, jewellery, general antiques.* TEL: 493 2333.

Gerald Sattin Ltd.   BADA
25 Burlington Arcade, Piccadilly. (G. and M. Sattin.) Est. 1966. CL: Sat. p.m. Open 9−5.30. SIZE: Medium. *STOCK: English and Continental porcelain, 1720−1880, £55− £2,500; English furniture, 1740−1860, £350−£5,000; English glass, 1700−1900, £55−£2,000; English silver, 1680−1910, £55−£5,000.* Not stocked: Oriental and post-1910 items. LOC: Close to Royal Academy. PARK: 2 mins. away. TEL: 493 6557. SER: Buys at auction. VAT: Stan/Spec.

Robert G. Sawers
P.O. Box 4QA. Open by appointment. *STOCK: Antiquarian books on Far East; Oriental art and Japanese prints.* TEL: 409 0863.

Chas. J. Sawyer   BADA
1 Grafton St. (R.E.B and G. Sawyer.) ABA. Est. 1894. CL: Sat. p.m. Open 9−5.30. SIZE: Medium. *STOCK: English literature, sets and first editions, 18th−19th C, from £10; bindings, colour plate books, original drawings by book illustrators, 19th−20th C, from £50.* LOC: Grafton St. runs west from Bond St. near the point where Old Bond St. becomes New Bond St. PARK: 80yds. in Berkeley Sq. TEL: 493 3810. SER: Valuations; buys at auction. VAT: Stan/Spec.

Scarisbrick and Bate Ltd.
111 Mount St. (A.C. Bate.) Est. 1958. CL: Sat. Open 9−5.30. SIZE: Medium. *STOCK: Furniture, decorative items, mid-18th C to early 19th C.* Not stocked: Glass and china. LOC: By Connaught Hotel (off Park Lane). PARK: Meters. TEL: 499 2043/4/5. SER: Restorations (furniture); buys at auction. VAT: Stan.

B.A. Seaby Ltd.
8 Cavendish Sq. Est. 1926. Publishes monthly bulletin on Numismatics. CL: Sat. Open 9.30−5. SIZE: Medium. *STOCK: Ancient Greek and Roman to modern coins, £1−£20,000; numismatic books and antiquities.* LOC: Coming from Oxford Circus underground, go north towards Langham Place turn left into St. Margaret's St., into Cavendish Sq., premises top right of sq. TEL: 631 3707. SER: Valuations; buys at auction. VAT: Stan/Spec.

W.1 continued

Shaikh and Son (Oriental Rugs) Ltd.
16 Brook St. (M. Shaikh.) CL: Sat. p.m. Open 10−6. *STOCK: Persian carpets, rugs, £100− £10,000.* TEL: 629 3430. SER: Repairing and cleaning.

Sheppard & Cooper Ltd.
35 St. George St. CL: Sat. Open 10−5.30. *STOCK: Glass, works of art, Roman and Greek antiquities.* TEL: 629 6489.

Simeon
19 Burlington Arcade, Piccadilly. Est. 1969. CL: Sat. p.m. Open 10−5. SIZE: Small. *STOCK: Period and estate jewellery, art nouveau, art deco, miniatures, netsuke, inro, small objets d'art, snuff bottles.* PARK: Meters. TEL: 493 3353. VAT: Stan.

W. Sitch & Co. Ltd.
48 Berwick St. (H. Sitch.) Est. 1776. Open 8−5, Sat. 8−1. SIZE: Large. *STOCK: Edwardian and Victorian lighting fixtures and floor standards.* LOC: Off Oxford St. TEL: 437 3776. SER: Valuations; restorations; repairs. VAT: Stan.

W.1 continued

The Sladmore Gallery
32 Bruton Place, Berkeley Sq. Est. 1962. (E.F. Horswell.) Jane Horswell is author of 'Les Animaliers' (Price Guide to Animal Bronzes). CL: Sat. Open 10−6. SIZE: Large. *STOCK: Bronze sculpture, 19th C − Mene Barye; Impressionist, Bugatti, Righetti, Pompon; contemporary, Gill Parker; sporting, polo, wild life paintings and prints − R.D. Digby, E. How, T. Gilbert.* TEL: 499 0365. SER: Valuations; restorations. VAT: Stan/Spec.

Somerville and Simpson
11 Savile Row. CL: Sat. Open 9.30−5.30. *STOCK: Old Masters, prints, drawings, English watercolours, paintings.* TEL: 437 5414. VAT: Spec.

Henry Sotheran Ltd.
2, 3, 4, 5 Sackville St., Piccadilly. Est. 1761. CL: Sat. Open 9−5.30. *STOCK: Antiquarian books and prints.* TEL: 734 1150. SER: Restorations and binding (books, prints); buys at auction. VAT: Stan.

South Audley Art Galleries Ltd.
LAPADA
36 South Audley St. (A.J. Singer.) Est. 1948. CL: Sat. Open 10−6. SIZE: Large. *STOCK: Continental furniture, porcelain; both 19th C; clocks, oil paintings, objets d'art.* LOC: Nr. Grosvenor Sq. TEL: 499 3178 and 3195. VAT: Stan/Spec.

John Sparks Ltd. **BADA**
128 Mount St. Est. 1879. CL: Sat. Open 9−5.30. SIZE: Large. *STOCK: Chinese works of art, B.C. to late 18th C; pottery, porcelain, jade, hardstones.* **PARK: Meters. TEL: 499 1932/2265.** SER: Valuations. **VAT: Stan.**

Alfred Speelman **BADA**
129 Mount St. Est. 1931. Open 10.30−1 and 2.15−5.45. SIZE: Large. *STOCK: Chinese works of art, 7th−19th C; objets d'art, 18th C.* **TEL: 499 5126.** SER: Valuations; buys at auction. **VAT: Spec.**

Edward Speelman Ltd.
175 Piccadilly. Est. 1931. CL: Sat. Open 10−1 and 2−5. SIZE: Medium. *STOCK: Old Master paintings.* PARK: Meters. TEL: 493 0657. SER: Valuations; restorations. VAT: Spec.

Charles Spencer Theatre Gallery
82 York St. Est. 1976. CL: Sat. Open 10.30−5, Thurs. 10−1. or anytime by appointment. SIZE: Small. *STOCK: Prints, portraits and original designs relating to the history of the theatre from 17th C to date, £50−£10,000.* LOC: Between Baker St. and Seymour Place. TEL: 723 5772; home − 286 9396. SER: Valuations; buys at auction (theatrical items.) VAT: Stan.

W.1 continued

H.J. Spiller's Ltd. **BADA**
37 Beak St. Est. 1909. CL: Sat. Open 9−5.30. SIZE: Large. *STOCK: Carved frames, oil master paintings.* **PARK: Meters. TEL: 437 4661. VAT: Stan/Spec.**

Spring Antiques
(B. Snyder.) Est. 1970. Open by appointment. *STOCK: Sporting and decorative prints, mezzotints and aquatints, 18th-19th C, £5−£1,000; Old Master engravings, 15th-19th C, £50−£5,000; oil paintings, 19th C, £20−£500.* TEL: 486 4207. SER: Valuations; restorations; buys at auction; lecturer. FAIRS: Cambridge; Sunday London Hotels. VAT: Spec.

Stair and Co. Ltd. **BADA**
120 Mount St. Est. 1912. CL: Sat. Open 9−5.30. SIZE: Large. *STOCK: 18th C English furniture, works of art, mirrors, chandeliers, barometers, needlework, lamps, clocks, prints.* **LOC: From Park Lane, on right past Connaught Hotel, towards Berkeley Sq. PARK: Meters, and Adam's Row. TEL: 499 1784/5.** SER: Valuations; buys at auction. **VAT: Spec.**

F. Teltscher Ltd.
17 Crawford St. Est. 1956. CL: Sat. Open 10−5. *STOCK: Pictures, wood carvings, works of art.* PARK: Meters. TEL: 935 0525. SER: Valuations; restorations. VAT: Spec.

Tessiers Ltd. **BADA**
26 New Bond St. (C.R.C. Aston, A.L. and R.F. Parsons, P.C. Whitfield.) CL: Sat. Open 9.30−5. *STOCK: Silver, jewellery, objets d'art.* **TEL: 629 0458.** SER: Valuations; restorations. **VAT: Stan.**

Tooley, Adams and Co. Ltd.
83 Marylebone High St. (D. Adams and S. Luck.) ABA. Est. 1981. CL: Sat. Open 9−5. SIZE: Medium. *STOCK: Antiquarian maps, atlases and prints.* LOC: Between Marylebone Rd. and Oxford St. PARK: Moxon St. TEL: 486 9052/935 5855. SER: Valuations; restorations; buys at auction (atlases, printed maps and manuscripts). FAIRS: New York and Chicago. VAT: Stan.

Tortoiseshell and Ivory House Ltd.
24 Chiltern St. Est. 1920. CL: Sat. Open 9−5. SIZE: Small. *STOCK: Oriental hardstones, ivory, jade.* PARK: Meters. TEL: 935 8031. SER: Valuations; restorations. VAT: Stan/Spec.

W.1 continued

Toynbee-Clarke Interiors Ltd.
95 Mount St. (G. and D. Toynbee-Clarke.) Est. 1953. CL: Sat. Open 9−5.30. SIZE: Medium. *STOCK: Decorative English and Continental furniture and objects, 17th−18th C. Chinese hand painted wallpapers, 18th C. French scenic wallpapers, early 19th C. Chinese and Japanese paintings and screens, 17th−19th C.* LOC: Between north-west corner of Berkeley Sq. and Park Lane. PARK: Meters. TEL: 499 4472. SER: Buys at auction. VAT: Stan/Spec.

Tradition — Military Antiques
5a Shepherd St., Mayfair. (R. Belmont-Maitland.) Open 9−6, Sat. till 5. *STOCK: Military uniforms, arms, model soldiers.* TEL: 493 7452. VAT: Stan/Spec.

The Tryon and Moorland Gallery
23-24 Cork St. CL: Sat. Open 9.30−5.30. SIZE: Medium. *STOCK: Sporting and natural history pictures, prints, bronzes and books.* PARK: Meters. TEL: 734 6961/2256. SER: Valuations; restorations; framing; buys at auction. VAT: Stan/Spec.

W.1 continued

Philip Turner (Antiques) Ltd.
16 Crawford St. CL: Sat. Open 10−5. SIZE: Medium. *STOCK: General antiques, especially light fittings.* PARK: Meters or 20 mins. on yellow line. TEL: 935 6074.

Tzigany Fine Arts
28 and 29 Dover St. (A. Cheneviere.) CL: Sat. Open 9.30−6. *STOCK: 18th−19th C furniture and paintings, objets d'art from Russia, Austria, Sweden and Germany.* TEL: 491 1007.

Under Two Flags
4 St. Christopher's Place. (A.C. Coutts.) Est. 1973. CL: Mon. Open 10−5. SIZE: Small. *STOCK: Toy soldiers, old military prints; books, porcelain, bronzes of military interest.* TEL: 935 6934.

Venner's Antiques

(Mrs. S. DAVIS)

7 NEW CAVENDISH STREET
LONDON, W.1
Tel: 01-935 0184

LITTLEWICK GREEN
NR. MAIDENHEAD
BERKS
Tel: Littlewick Green 2588

Three rare pieces of Caughley porcelain: Geranium moulded pickle dish, painted decoration. Miniature teapot, painted decoration. Eyebath, moulded and decorated with the Fisherman pattern. All blue and white, c.1780-85.

W.1 continued

Venners Antiques
7 New Cavendish St. (Mrs. S. Davis.) Open 10.15—4.30, Sat. 10—1. *STOCK: 18th and 19th C English porcelain and pottery.* TEL: 935 0184. SER: Valuations; buys at auction. VAT: Spec.

Vigo Carpet Gallery · LAPADA
6a Vigo St. CL: Sat. Open 9—5.30, Fri. 9—5. *STOCK: Oriental and European rugs and carpets.* TEL: 439 6971.

Vigo-Sternberg Galleries · BADA
37 South Audley St. (V. Roffe and C. Sternberg.) Est. 1920. CL: Sat. Open 9—5.30. *STOCK: European tapestries, 15th C to contemporary; Oriental and European rugs, 1650—1850.* PARK: Meters. TEL: 629 8307. VAT: Stan/Spec.

Wartski Ltd. · BADA
14 Grafton St. Est. 1865. CL: Sat. Open 9.30—5. SIZE: Medium. *STOCK: Jewellery, 18th C gold boxes, Fabergé, Russian works of art, silver.* PARK: Meters. TEL: 493 1141/2/3. SER: Restorations; buys at auction. FAIRS: Burlington House, International Silver and Jewellery. VAT: Stan/Spec.

W.1 continued

Wylma Wayne Fine Art
17 Old Bond St. CL: Sat. Open 10.30—6. *STOCK: Rembrandt and Durer etchings and engravings; 17th-19th C oils and watercolours.* TEL: 629 4511.

The Weiss Gallery p.l.c. · BADA
1b Albemarle St. CL: Sat. Open 10—6. *STOCK: Paintings, furniture and works of art especially early English portraiture.* TEL: 409 0035. SER: Valuations; restorations.

The Welbeck Gallery
18 Thayer St. (D. and S. Spellman.) Est. 1975. Open 10—5, Sat. 10.30—12.30. *STOCK: Prints, topographical, natural history, military, birds, 17th—20th C, etchings, engraving, lithographs.* PARK: Meters. TEL: 935 4825; home — 340 7130. SER: Framing. VAT: Stan.

William Weston Gallery
7 Royal Arcade, Albemarle St. Est. 1964. Articles on etchings, lithographs, drawings. Open 9.30—5, Sat. 10.30—1. SIZE: Small. *STOCK: Etchings, lithographs, drawings, 1800—1960.* LOC: Off Piccadilly. TEL: 493 0722. VAT: Spec.

Wilberry Antiques
32 Crawford St. (R.C. Thornberry and L.G. Oakley.) Est. 1963. CL: Sat. Open 10—6. *STOCK: Staffordshire figures, from £14; unusual collectors' items.* LOC: Between Gloucester Place and Seymour Place. PARK: Easy. TEL: 724 0606. SER: Valuations. VAT: Spec.

Wildenstein and Co. Ltd.
147 New Bond St. Est. 1934. CL: Sat. Open 10—5.30. SIZE: Large. *STOCK: Old Master and impressionist paintings and drawings.* PARK: Meters. TEL: 629 0602.

Wilkins and Wilkins
1 Barrett St., St. Christophers Place. (B. and M. Wilkins.) Est. 1981. CL: Sat. Open 11—5. SIZE: Small. *STOCK: Mainly English 17th to early 19th C portraits, decorative paintings, sporting and marine pictures, £250—£15,000.* LOC: Near Selfridges. TEL: 935 9613. SER: Restorations; framing. VAT: Stan/Spec.

Williams and Son
2 Grafton St. (R.G. and J.R. Williams.) Est. 1931. CL: Sat. Open 9.30—6. SIZE: Large. *STOCK: 19th C, British and European paintings.* LOC: Between Bond St. and Berkeley Sq. TEL: 493 4985 and 5751. VAT: Stan/Spec.

VIGO CARPET GALLERY

6A VIGO STREET, LONDON W1X 1AH
TELEPHONE: 01 439 6971

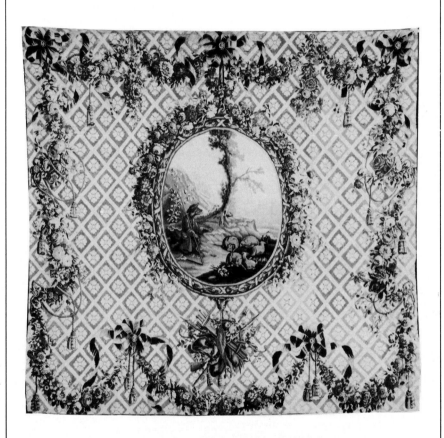

LOUIS XV AUBUSSON TAPESTRY
Scene from La Fontaine's fables after
J.B. Oudry
8ft.10in. x 9ft.11in. (2.63m x 3.02m)

W.1 continued

Henry Willis (Antique Silver)
LAPADA
4 Grosvenor St. Est. 1975. CL: Sat. Open
10−6. *STOCK: Silver, including interesting
items, 16th−19th C, £50−£5,000.* LOC:
Just west of Bond St., corner of Avery Row.
PARK: Multi-storey 100yds. TEL: 491 8949.
SER: Valuations; restorations (silver); buys at
auction. VAT: Stan/Spec.

"Young Stephen" Ltd.   **LAPADA**
1 Burlington Gdns., New Bond St. (Mr. and
Mrs. S. Burton.) Est. 1975. Open 9.30−
5.45, Sat. 10.30−3.30. *STOCK: Edwardian,
art nouveau and art deco jewellery, novelty
silver.* TEL: 499 7927.

Zadah Persian Carpets Ltd.
20 Dering St., (off New Bond St.) Est. 1976.
Open 9.30−5.30, appointment advisable.
STOCK: Oriental carpets and rugs. TEL: 493
2622/2673.

London W.2

Antiquus A.G.   **LAPADA**
17 Pembridge Sq. (J. Fell-Clarke.) Est. 1970.
Open by appointment. SIZE: Small. *STOCK:
Oak and country furniture, £100−£5,000;
tapestries, £1,000−£10,000; objects, £50−
£1,000; all 16th−19th C.* LOC: Close to
Westbourne Grove and Portobello Rd. PARK:
Easy. TEL: 229 0224; home − same. SER:
Valuations; restorations; buys at auction.
FAIRS: Kenilworth, Olympia, Cafe Royal,
Zurich and Lausanne. VAT: Spec.

Peter Bentley   **LAPADA**
22 Connaught St. Est. 1967. Open
9.30−5.30, Sat. 9.30−1. SIZE: Medium.
STOCK: Georgian and Regency furniture. TEL:
723 9394.

Claude Bornoff   **BADA**
20 Chepstow Corner, Pembridge Villas. Est.
1949. CL: Sat. Open 9.30−5.30. SIZE:
Medium. *STOCK: English and Continental
furniture, china, metalware and unusual items.*
LOC: Opposite Coronet Cinema, Westbourne
Grove. PARK: Meters. TEL: 229 8947. VAT:
Stan/Spec.

Connaught Galleries
44 Connaught St. (Mr. Conisbee.) Est. 1966.
Open 9−6.30, Sat. 10−1. SIZE: Medium.
*STOCK: Early Victorian and Georgian furni-
ture, silver plate, porcelain, pictures.* LOC:
Near Marble Arch. PARK: Meters. TEL: 723
1660. VAT: Spec.

W.2 continued

A.B. Davis Ltd.
89/91 Queensway, Bayswater. Est. 1922.
Open 9.30−5.30. SIZE: Medium. *STOCK:
Jewellery, Victorian, to £1,000; silverware.*
LOC: Immediately above Bayswater Under-
ground Station. PARK: Meters or multi-storey.
TEL: 229 2777. SER: Valuations; restorations.
VAT: Stan/Spec.

S. Franses Ltd.   **BADA**
11 Spring St. Open 9−5.30. *STOCK: Decorative tapestries, carpets and textiles.* **TEL:
262 1153. SER: Restorations; cleaning. VAT:
Spec.**

The Holland Press Ltd.
37 Connaught St. Est. 1956. CL: Sat. Open
9.30−5. *STOCK: Books on food, wine, art,
arms, armour including Japanese, maps, bibli-
ographies, reference works on cartography.*
TEL: 262 6184. SER: Buys at auctions.

Hosains Books & Antiques
25 Connaught St. Est. 1979. CL: Sat. p.m.
and Mon. Open 10.30−5.30. *STOCK: Scarce
books, manuscripts, miniatures and prints on
Islamic world, Tibet, Central Asia and India.*
TEL: 262 7900.

Paul Hughes Textiles
3a Pembridge Sq. Resident. Est. 1977. CL:
Mon. Open by appointment. SIZE: Large.
*STOCK: Coptic, pre-Columbian, African and
European items, 14th−20th C; English textiles
and costumes, 17th C.* LOC: Portobello Rd.
PARK: Easy. TEL: 243 8598. SER: Valuations;
restorations; buys at auction (textiles). FAIRS:
Royal Academy. VAT: Stan/Spec.

Leinster Antiques
20 Leinster Terrace, Hyde Park. Open
10.30−6. *STOCK: Oils, watercolours, prints,
silver, porcelain, glass, furniture, dolls, teddy
bears.* TEL: 402 7387.

M. McAleer   **LAPADA**
32A Sussex Place, Hyde Park. (M.J. and Mrs.
M. McAleer.) Est. 1969. CL: Sat. except by
appointment. Open 9−5.30. SIZE: Small.
*STOCK: Small collectable silver, £50−£500;
Irish and Scottish silver, £50−£5,000; all
18th−19th C.* LOC: From Lancaster Gate
underground (Bayswater Rd.) left up Stanhope
Terrace. Near Paddington Station. PARK:
Easy. TEL: 723 5794. SER: Buys at auction
(silver). VAT: Stan/Spec.

W.2 continued

Daniel Mankowitz   *Trade Only*
16 Pembridge Sq. Est. 1970. Open by appointment only. SIZE: Medium. *STOCK: Furniture, English and Continental, 16th—18th C, £100—£10,000; works of art, English and Continental, 15th—19th C, £50—£5,000; tapestries, 16th—18th C, £200—£3,000.* LOC: Between Kensington Church St. and Westbourne Grove. PARK: Easy. TEL: 229 9270; home — same. FAIRS: Olympia. VAT: Spec.

William C. Mansell
24 Connaught St. *STOCK: Gold, silver, clocks, watches and jewellery.* TEL: 723 4154. SER: Restorations; repairs.

The Mark Gallery   BADA
9 Porchester Place, Marble Arch. (H. Mark.) C.I.N.O.A. Est. 1969. CL: Sat. Open 10—1 and 2—6. SIZE: Medium. *STOCK: Russian icons, 16th—19th C; modern graphics.* LOC: Near Marble Arch. TEL: 262 4906. SER: Valuations; restorations; buys at auction. VAT: Stan/Spec.

Orchard Antiques
52 Porchester Rd. (R. Orchard.) Est. 1974. Open 12—6. *STOCK: Glass, china and early kitchenware.* TEL: 221 0154.

S.W. Parry (Old Glass)   *Trade only*
16 Paddington Green. Est. 1975. CL: Sat. Open by appointment. SIZE: Small. *STOCK: Decanters, 19th C, £20—£80; drinking glasses, 18th—19th C, £3—£100.* LOC: From Edgware Rd. turn left into Church St., then left into Paddington Green. PARK: Easy and meters. TEL: 262 7055; home — 740 0248. SER: Valuations; restorations (decanters); polishing; buys at auction (18th—19th C glass). VAT: Stan/Spec.

The Pine House
1 Pembridge Villas. Open 9.30—6, Sun. 10—6. *STOCK: Pine and country furniture.* TEL: 221 7044.

London W.3

Z.J. Okolski
14 Princes Ave. Est. 1973. Open any time by appointment. SIZE: Medium. *STOCK: Oil paintings, 1750—1950.* LOC: ½ mile from Chiswick flyover, off North Circular Rd; ¼ mile from Acton Town underground (Piccadilly line). PARK: Easy. TEL: 992 7032; home — same. SER: Valuations. VAT: Spec.

Woods Warehouse
371 Horn Lane, Acton. (S. Wood.) Est. 1976. Open 9—8, Sat. and Sun. 10—6. SIZE: Large warehouse. *STOCK: General antiques, £50—£1,000.* LOC: A40, junction of Horn Lane. PARK: Easy. TEL: 992 2234. VAT: Stan.

W.3 continued

Yours and Mine
1a King St. (Mrs. B. Barber.) Est. 1967. CL: Wed. Open 11—5. SIZE: Small. *STOCK: Small items, bric-a-brac.* LOC: Main Uxbridge Rd., Acton. PARK: Easy. TEL: 992 3170.

London W.4

Chiswick Antiques
Fisher's Lane, Chiswick. (J.F. Harris.) Est. 1957. CL: Thurs. Open 9—5.30. SIZE: Medium. *STOCK: Small furniture, £50—£100; china, glass, £5—£25; silver, £5—£50, all 18th—19th C.* Not stocked: Large furniture. LOC: Coming from M4 and Great Western Rd. and North Circular, proceed along High Rd., Chiswick, and Fisher's Lane is on left. PARK: Easy, in same road. TEL: 995 2967; home — 994 4915. VAT: Stan.

Chiswick Fireplaces
62 South Parade, Chiswick. (J. Nice.) Open 10.30—5.30. *STOCK: General antiques, Victorian fireplaces with original tiles, lights.* PARK: Easy. TEL: 994 2981.

Goodall and Co. Ltd.
24 and 26 Chiswick High Rd. (C.R. Goodall.) Est. 1905. CL: Thurs. Open 9—5. SIZE: Large. *STOCK: Furniture, maps and prints.* LOC: Via Hammersmith Broadway and King St. shop is 1st left towards London. TEL: 994 1729. VAT: Stan/Spec.

Mangate Gallery   LAPADA
3 Chiswick Lane. (Mrs. S. Beamish.) Est. 1968. Open by appointment only. SIZE: Medium. *STOCK: English and Continental watercolours and oils, 1750—1950, £100—£2,000.* LOC: Off Chiswick High Road., or Hogarth roundabout Gt. West Rd. PARK: Easy. TEL: 995 9867. SER: Cleaning and framing. VAT: Spec.

Moss Galleries
2 Prebend Gdns., Chiswick. (B. and R. Moss.) Est. 1970. Open by appointment. SIZE: Small. *STOCK: Watercolours, 18th—20th C, £50—£3,000.* LOC: Off east end of Chiswick High Rd., near Stamford Brook tube station. PARK: Easy. TEL: 994 2099. SER: Valuations; buys at auction. FAIRS: Olympia, World of Watercolours and Kensington. VAT: Spec.

Strand Antiques
166 Thames Rd., Strand-on-the-Green, Chiswick. Est. 1977. Open Tues.—Sun. 12—5, and other times by appointment. SIZE: Large. *STOCK: Books, kitchen items, glass, furniture, jewellery, paintings, prints, fabrics, china, silver, clothes, and collectors' items, £1—£500.* LOC: Behind Bull's Head Public House, about 400yds. from Kew Bridge. PARK: Easy. TEL: 994 1912.

W.4 continued

Stratton-Quinn Antiques Etc.
164 Thames Rd., Strand-on-the-Green, Chiswick. (N.J. Quinn.) Est. 1980. Open daily including Sun. 10.30−6. SIZE: Medium. *STOCK: Furniture mainly pine, 18th−19th C, £40−£450; mirrors, 18th−20th C, £45−£150; interior decorators' items, 19th−20th C, £5−£150; Victorian beds, £250−£500.* LOC: North side of Thames, east of Kew Bridge, near junction of north and south circulars. PARK: Easy. TEL: 994 3140; home − same.

West London Antiques
The Old Cinema, 160 Chiswick High Rd. (M. Hanness and H. Bonaparte-Wyse.) Est. 1977. Open 10−6, Sun. 12−5. SIZE: Large. *STOCK: Furniture, "gardenalia", decorative and architectural items, 1800−1940, £50−£1,000.* PARK: Easy. TEL: 995 4166. SER: Restorations. VAT: Stan.

London W.5

The Badger
12 St. Mary's Rd. (M. and E. Aalders.) Est. 1967. Open 9.30−6. SIZE: Medium. *STOCK: Furniture, £100−£2,000; clocks, £1,000−£3,000; both 18th−19th C; ceramics, 19th C, £50−£1,000.* PARK: Easy. TEL: 567 5601. SER: Valuations; restorations (furniture and clocks); buys at auction (clocks and watches). VAT: Stan/Spec.

Ealing Gallery
112 Pitshanger Lane. (Mrs. N. Lane.) Est. 1984. CL: Mon. and Wed. Open 10−6. SIZE: Medium. *STOCK: Oil paintings, £100−£2,000; watercolours, £50−£600; both 19th to early 20th C; contemporary paintings, £30−£250.* LOC: Off Hanger Lane, Brunswick Rd. continues into Pitshanger Lane. PARK: Easy. TEL: 997 3108; home − 997 8507. SER: Valuations; restorations (oils and watercolours); framing. VAT: Spec.

Gallery 2
23 High St., Ealing Green. (Mrs. N. Lane.) CL: Wed. p.m. Open 10−6. *STOCK: Oil paintings, £100−£2,000; watercolours, £50−£600; both 19th to early 20th; contemporary paintings, £30−£250.* TEL: 840 7883. PARK: Nearby. SER: Valuations; restorations (oils and watercolours); framing. VAT: Spec.

London W.6

N. Davighi
117 Shepherd's Bush Rd. Est. 1950. Open 9.30−5. SIZE: Medium. *STOCK: Chandeliers, light fittings, general antiques, all Georgian and Victorian.* PARK: Easy. TEL: 603 5357. SER: Valuations; restorations (ormolu, chandeliers and brass).

Questor Antiques
295 King St., Hammersmith. (J.E. Ion.) Est. 1977. CL: Mon. and Sat. Open 10.30−5. SIZE: Small. *STOCK: Small furniture, 18th−19th C, £25−£500; boxes, including tea caddies, writing slopes and toilet boxes, 19th C, £25−£100; general antiques, bric-a-brac and pictures, £5−£50.* LOC: ½ mile along King St. from Hammersmith Broadway towards Chiswick High Rd. PARK: Easy. TEL: 741 3822.

M.L. Waroujian
110−112 Hammersmith Rd. Est. 1959. *STOCK: Oriental carpets and rugs.* TEL: 748 7509. SER: Cleaning, repairs (Persian and Oriental carpets). VAT: Spec.

London W.8

Al Mashreq Galleries
110 Kensington Church St. (J. Mantoura.) Est. 1983. Open 10−6. SIZE: Medium. *STOCK: Islamic art and antiques.* PARK: Meters. TEL: 229 5453. SER: Buys at auction (Islamic and Middle Eastern items). VAT: Spec.

Altfeld Fine Arts
18 Victoria Rd. (B. Altfeld.) Est. 1979. Open by appointment only. SIZE: Small. *STOCK: English watercolours and drawings including Sylvester Stannard, Francis Stevens, George Romney, 18th−19th C, to £2,500+.* LOC: Off Kensington High St. PARK: Behind house. TEL: 937 9920; home − same. SER: Valuations; restorations (paper, foxing); buys at auction. FAIRS: World of Watercolours.

The Antique Home   BADA
104A Kensington Church St. (M. Priestley and B.T.W. Rolleston.) Est. 1950. CL: Sat. p.m. Open 10−1 and 2.30−6. SIZE: Large. *STOCK: English furniture, 18th C, £500−£30,000.* PARK: Easy. TEL: 229 5892. VAT: Spec.

W.8 continued

Eddy Bardawil   LAPADA
106 Kensington Church St. (E.S. Bardawil.)
Est. 1979. Open 9.30—6, Sun. by appointment. SIZE: Medium. *STOCK: English furniture — mahogany, satinwood, walnut; brass
ware, tea-caddies, all pre-1830, £50—£5,000;
prints, 18th C.* LOC: Corner premises,
Berkeley Gardens/Church St. PARK: Easy.
TEL: 221 3967. SER: Valuations; restorations
(furniture); polishing. VAT: Stan/Spec.

Baumkötter Gallery
63a Kensington Church St. (Mrs. L. Baum-
kötter.) Est. 1968. CL: Sat. Open 9.30—6.
SIZE: Large. *STOCK: 17th—19th C oil paintings.* TEL: 937 5171. VAT: Spec.

Anthony Belton   LAPADA
14 Holland St. Est. 1969. Open 10—1 and
2—6, Sat. 10—4.30, or by appointment.
SIZE: Medium. *STOCK: English and European
pottery; decorative and unusual furniture and
objects; primitive, topographical and marine
watercolours and oil paintings; mainly pre-
1830.* Not stocked: Silver, glass, jewellery,
coins. LOC: 1st left going up Kensington
Church St. from Kensington High St. PARK:
Meters or under Kensington Town Hall. TEL:
937 1012; home — same. SER: Valuations;
restorations (paintings, ceramics); buys at
auction. FAIRS: International Ceramic (Dorchester Hotel); Olympia. VAT: Mainly Spec.

Bohun and Busbridge
24 Iverna Gdns. (C. Barker-Mill.) Open by
appointment only. *STOCK: Tribal rugs,
Oriental carpets and woven artifacts;
embroideries, textiles, ikats, woven silks and
brocades, £50—£3,000.* LOC: Kensington
High St. tube. TEL: 937 9145. SER: Repairs;
cleaning.

Bonrose Antiques   LAPADA
172 Kensington Church St. *STOCK: French
clocks; furniture, porcelain and silver.* TEL:
229 5486.

Maurice Braham Ltd.
131 Kensington Church St. (M. Braham and J.
Mitchell.) CL: Sat. Open 10.30—6. *STOCK:
Early European metalwork and works of art;
classical antiquities and ethnographica, early
natural history specimens.* TEL: 727 6878.

David Brower Antiques   LAPADA
113 Kensington Church St. Est. 1965. CL:
Sat. Open 9.30—5.30. SIZE: Medium.
*STOCK: Oriental and Continental decorative
porcelain, £50—£2,000; French and Oriental
furniture, bronzes and clocks.* PARK: Meters
nearby. TEL: 221 4155. SER: Buys at auction.
VAT: Stan/Spec.

Simon Castle   LAPADA
38B Kensington Church St. Est. 1975. Open
10—5.30, Sat. 10.30—3.30. *STOCK: Decorative carvings and treen.* TEL: 937 2268.

W.8 continued

Cathay Antiques
12 Thackeray St. (W. Ying.) Est. 1962. CL: Sat. Open 1—6. SIZE: Medium. *STOCK: Oriental, Chinese and Japanese antiques.* LOC: Behind Barkers. TEL: 937 6066. SER: Buys at auction. VAT: Stan/Spec.

Church Street Galleries Ltd.   BADA
77 Kensington Church St. (Mr. Meyer.) Est. 1954. Open. 9—6, Sat. 10—4. SIZE: Large. *STOCK: Late 17th to early 19th C English furniture.* **PARK: Meters. TEL: 937 2461. VAT: Stan/Spec.**

Coats Oriental Carpets and Co. Ltd.
4 Kensington Church Walk (off Holland St.). (A. Coats.) Est. 1973. Open 11—5, Sat. 11—3 or by appointment. SIZE: Medium. *STOCK: Oriental carpets and rugs, kelims, all £50—£2,000; Oriental textiles and embroideries, £10—£100; all 19th C.* LOC: Small pedestrian alleyway just off Holland St., off south end of Kensington Church St. PARK: Easy. TEL: 937 0983; home — 370 2355. SER: Valuations; restorations (re-weaving); buys at auction. VAT: Stan/Spec.

Aubrey J. Coleman Antiques
     LAPADA
121 Kensington Church St. (G.D. and G.E. Coleman.) Est. 1944. Open 9.30—6, Sat. 9.30—5. SIZE: Medium. *STOCK: Furniture, 1680—1900, £150—£4,000; chess sets, 1750—1880, £100—£4,000; decorative items, arms, pictures, £50—£2,000.* LOC: On corner of Kensington Church St. and Campden St. PARK: Easy. TEL: 221 6228. VAT: Stan/Spec.

Belinda Coote Antiques
29 Holland St. Resident. Est. 1970. Open 10—5.30, Sat. 10—1. *STOCK: Decorative pottery and porcelain, especially ironstone, £5—£5,000; small furniture, papier mâché, tôle peinte, tapestries. Not stocked: Glass, enamel, metalwork.* LOC: 1st left off Kensington Church St. from Kensington High St. TEL: 937 3924. SER: Valuations; restorations (china); buys at auction (pottery and porcelain). FAIRS: Olympia, Chelsea. VAT: Spec.

Mrs. M.E. Crick Ltd.
166 Kensington Church St. Est. 1897. CL: Sat. *STOCK: Chandeliers, 18th C to modern English and Continental, crystal, cut glass and ormolu.* PARK: Meters. TEL: 229 1338. VAT: Stan.

W.8 continued

George Dare
9 Launceston Place, Kensington. Est. 1980.
Open anytime by appointment. SIZE: Medium.
STOCK: *English watercolours and oil paint
ings, mainly 18th and 19th C, £100−£2,500.*
LOC: Turn left off London bound section of
Cromwell Rd., opposite the Forum Hotel.
PARK: Easy. TEL: 937 7072; home − same.
SER: Restorations; framing; buys at auction
(as stock). VAT: Stan.

Davies Antiques   LAPADA
44A Kensington Church St. (H.Q.V. Davies.)
Est. 1976. Open 10.30−5.30, Sat. 10−3.
STOCK: *Continental porcelain, maps and
prints.* TEL: 937 9216.

Delomosne and Son Ltd.   BADA
4 Campden Hill Rd., Kensington. (J.B. Perret,
M.C.F. Mortimer and T.N.M. Osborne.) Est.
1905. Articles on chandeliers, glass and
porcelain. CL: Sat. p.m. Open 9.30−5.30.
SIZE: Medium. STOCK: *English and Irish
glass, pre-1830, £20−£15,000; glass chandeliers, English and European porcelain.* LOC:
50yds. from Kensington High St. PARK:
Municipal garage adjacent. TEL: 937 1804.
SER: Valuations; buys at auction. FAIRS:
Burlington House, Dorchester Ceramics. VAT:
Spec.

Richard Dennis
144 Kensington Church St. Est. 1967. Open
10−6, Sat. 10−2. SIZE: Medium. STOCK:
*English studio pottery, 1870−1950, espec-
ially Doulton, Wedgwood, Moorcroft, Parian.*
LOC: Near Notting Hill Gate tube. TEL: 727
2061. SER: Valuations. VAT: Stan/Spec.

Kay Desmonde
17 Kensington Church Walk. Est. 1964. Open
Sat. 11−3. STOCK: *Dolls, dolls' houses,
dolls' house furniture and accessories.* TEL:
937 2602; home − (04606) 3280.

H. and W. Deutsch Antiques
                        LAPADA
111 Kensington Church St. Est. 1897. CL:
Sat. Open 10−5. SIZE: Large. STOCK:
*18th−19th C Continental and English por-
celain and glassware; silver, plate and enamel
ware, miniature portraits; Oriental porcelain,
cloisonne, bronzes, £20−£3,000.* TEL: 727
5984. VAT: Stan/Spec.

Philip and Bernard Dombey
174 Kensington Church St. Est. 1951. Open
10−4, Sat. 10−2. SIZE: Medium. STOCK:
French clocks. LOC: Near Notting Hill Gate
tube station. PARK: Meters. TEL: 229 7100.
SER: Valuations; restorations. VAT: Stan/
Spec.

W.8 continued

Etna Antiques
81 Kensington Church St. Open 9.30−1 and
2−6, Sat. 10−3.30. STOCK: *Furniture,
English and Continental, works of art, all
18th−19th C.* PARK: Meters. TEL: 937
3754. VAT: Stan/Spec.

Galerie George Kensington
50 Kensington Church St. (R. Waterhouse,
J. Dodd.) Open 10−6, Sat. 10−1. STOCK:
*Fine British and European paintings and
watercolours, especially Impressionist, Post-
Impressionist and Newlyn School, £200−
£20,000, 1870−1920.* PARK: Meters. TEL:
938 3666.

Michael C. German   BADA
                              LAPADA
38B Kensington Church St. Est. 1954. Open
10−5.30, Sat. 10.30−3.30. STOCK: *European and Oriental arms and armour; specialist
in walking sticks.* TEL: 937 2771.

Graham and Oxley   BADA
(Antiques) Ltd.
101 Kensington Church St. Est. 1965. Open
10−5.30, Sat. 10.30−1. STOCK: *18th−19th
C English porcelain, pottery, and decorative
items.* TEL: 229 1850.

Eila Grahame
97c Kensington Church St. Open 9−5.30.
STOCK: *Glass, 17th−18th C; early prints,
needlework; instruments, scientific and medi
cal; pottery, porcelain, 18th C.* TEL: 727 4132.
VAT: Spec.

Green's Antique Galleries
117 Kensington Church St. (S. Green.) Open
9−5.30. SIZE: Medium. STOCK: *Jewellery,
18th C to date, from £25; pre-1930 clothes
and lace; dolls, china, silver, furniture, paintings.* PARK: Easy. TEL: 229 9618/9. VAT:
Stan/Spec.

Grosvenor Antiques Ltd.   BADA
27 Holland St., Kensington. (S.C. and E.
Lorie.) Est. 1950. STOCK: *English and
Continental porcelain and works of art.* TEL:
937 8649. VAT: Spec.

Robert Hales Antiques Ltd.
133 Kensington Church St. Est. 1967. CL:
Sat. Open 10−5.30. SIZE: Small. STOCK:
*Islamic, Oriental and ethnographic arms and
armour; primitive oceanic art, 17th−19th C,
£50−£8,000+.* PARK: Easy. TEL: 229 3887.
SER: Valuations; buys at auction. VAT: Spec.

Jonathan Harris   BADA
54 Kensington Church St. CL: Sat. Open
9.30−6. SIZE: Large. STOCK: *English, Continental, Oriental furniture; works of art.* LOC:
Near Kensington High St. tube station. PARK:
Meters. TEL: 937 3133. VAT: Spec.

W.8 continued
Haslam and Whiteway
105 Kensington Church St. (T.M. Whiteway.) Est. 1969. Open 10—6, Sat. till 1. SIZE: Small. STOCK: British furniture, £50—£10,000; British decorative arts, £5—£5,000; Continental and American decorative arts, stained glass, £5—£500; all 1850—1930. Not stocked: Pre- Victorian items. LOC: From Notting Hill Gate tube station, down Kensington Church St. Shop is approx. 300yds. down on right. PARK: Meters. TEL: 229 1145. SER: Valuations; buys at auction. VAT: Stan.

Hoff Antiques Ltd.   BADA
66a Kensington Church St. (Mrs. R. Hoff.) Est. 1963. Open 10—6, Sat. till 4. SIZE: Small. STOCK: 18th C English and Continental porcelain. Not stocked: Victoriana. LOC: Underground to Kensington High St., Notting Hill Gate. PARK: Meters. TEL: 229 5516; home — 272 6542. SER: Valuations; buys at auction. FAIRS: International Ceramics, Dorchester Hotel; Burlington House. VAT: Spec.

D. Holmes
47c Earls Court Road (in Abingdon Villas), Kensington. Est. 1965. Open 10—6, Sat. 9—2. STOCK: Decorative items and furniture, pre-1920. TEL: 937 6961. SER: Restorations (furniture). VAT: Stan/Spec.

Hope and Glory
131a Kensington Church St. (E.L. Titmuss.) CL: Sat. p.m. and Mon. Open 10—5. STOCK: Royal commemorative china and glass. TEL: 727 8424.

Jonathan Horne   BADA
66b and c Kensington Church St. Est. 1968. CL: Sat. and Sun., except by appointment. Open 9.30—5.30. SIZE: Medium. STOCK: English and Continental pottery, 18th C; early metalwork, wood carvings, needlework and works of art. TEL: 221 5658. VAT: Stan/Spec.

Japanese Gallery
66d Kensington Church St. (Mr. and Mrs. C.D. Wertheim.) Est. 1977. Open 10—6. STOCK: Japanese wood-cut prints; books, screens, netsuke. TEL: 229 2934; home — 226 3347. SER: Buys at auction.

Melvyn Jay Antiques and Objets d'Art   LAPADA
64a Kensington Church St. Est. 1960. Open 9—5.45, Sat. 11—2. SIZE: Medium. STOCK: Mid-19th C French decorative furniture, clocks; Continental porcelain, bronzes and silver, £5—£5,000; English and Continental furniture. LOC: From Marble Arch to Kensington High St. Bus No. 73. PARK: Easy. TEL: 937 6832. SER: Valuations; buys at auction. VAT: Stan/Spec.
W.8 continued

John Jesse and Irina Laski Ltd.
160 Kensington Church St. Open 10—6. STOCK: Art nouveau, art deco, jewellery. TEL: 229 0312.

Howard Jones   LAPADA
43 Kensington Church St. (H. Howard-Jones) Est. 1971. Open 10—5. SIZE: Small. STOCK: Silver, porcelain, bronzes, £20—£5,000. Not stocked: Furniture. PARK: Nearby. TEL: 937 4359. SER: Valuations; restorations. VAT: Stan/Spec.

R. and J. Jones   BADA
137 Kensington Church St. (R. Jones.) Est. 1969. Open 10—5.30, Sat. 10—1. SIZE: Large. STOCK: Dutch, Flemish and Italian paintings, 17th—18th C, £2,000—£20,000; English paintings, 17th—19th C, £500—£15,000; pottery and porcelain, 18th C, £200—£10,000. LOC: Short distance from Notting Hill Gate. PARK: Nearby in side street. TEL: 221 4026. SER: Valuations; buys at auction. FAIRS: Grosvenor House and Burlington House. VAT: Spec.

Peter Kemp
174a Kensington Church St. Est. 1975. CL: Sat. Open 10—1 and 2—5. SIZE: Medium. STOCK: Chinese porcelain, 10th—19th C; Japanese porcelain, 17th—19th C; Continental porcelain, 18th C, Oriental works of art and porcelain, 19th C. LOC: 200yds. from Notting Hill tube station. PARK: Meters nearby. TEL: 229 2988. SER: Valuations; restorations (porcelain); buys at auction (Oriental and Continental porcelain). VAT: Spec.

Kensington Furniture
Troy Court, 214/216 Kensington High St. (Robinson Yates Ltd.) Est. 1967. Open 9—5.30. SIZE: Large. STOCK: Furniture and bric-a- brac. LOC: Near Earls Court Rd. TEL: 937 4973. VAT: Stan/Spec.

Klaber and Klaber   BADA
2A Bedford Gardens, Kensington Church St. (Mrs. B. and Miss P. Klaber.) Est. 1968. Open 10—1 and 2—5; Sat. 10.30—4, other times by appointment. SIZE: Medium. STOCK: European porcelain, 18th C and some early 19th C; English enamels, 18th C. LOC: Turning off Kensington Church St. about half way along. PARK: Meters. TEL: 727 4573. SER: Restoration (porcelain); buys at auction (porcelain, enamels). FAIRS: Burlington House, Grosvenor House, West of England. VAT: Spec.

The Lacquer Chest
75 Kensington Church St. (G. and V. Andersen.) Est. 1959. CL: Sat. p.m. Open 9.30—5.30. SIZE: Large. STOCK: Furniture and unusual items. LOC: Half-way up left-hand side from High St. PARK: Meters. TEL: 937 1306. VAT: Stan/Spec.

W.8 continued

Fiona and Bill Laidlaw Antiques
40 Gordon Pl., Holland St. (Mr. and Mrs. W. Laidlaw.) Est. 1976. Open 10.30—1 and 2—6. SIZE: Medium. *STOCK: Biedermeier furniture, £500—£3,000; English majolica, £25—£5,000; both 19th C. Decorative antiques, 1830—1900, £20—£3,000.* LOC: First left from Kensington Church St. towards Notting Hill Gate. PARK: Easy. TEL: 937 8493. SER: Hire. VAT: Stan/Spec.

Lev (Antiques) Ltd.
97 Kensington Church St. (Mrs. Lev.) Est. 1882. Open 10—1 and 2—5. SIZE: Medium. *STOCK: Jewellery, silver, plate, curios.* PARK: Meters. TEL: 727 9248. SER: Restorations (pictures); repairs (jewellery, silver).

Libra Antiques
131e Kensington Church St. *STOCK: Blue and white pottery, lustre ware.* TEL: 727 2990.

Lindsay Antiques   BADA
99 Kensington Church St. (T. Jellinek and L. Shand.) Est. 1965. Open 9.30—1 and 2.15—5.30, Sat. a.m. by appointment. SIZE: Large. STOCK: *English pottery, 18th C; decorative, unusual objects, 18th—19th C; both £100—£4,000.* PARK: Nearby. TEL: 727 2333. **FAIRS: Olympia and Dorchester Ceramics. VAT: Spec.**

W.8 continued

Eric Lineham and Sons
62 Kensington Church St. Est. 1953. CL: Sat. Open 9.30—5.30. SIZE: Small. *STOCK: English, Continental and Oriental porcelain, English and Continental glass, objets d'art, clocks and watches, art nouveau, chandeliers, enamels.* LOC: Half way along Kensington Church St. PARK: Meters. TEL: 937 9650. VAT: Stan/Spec.

Little Winchester Gallery
36a Kensington Church St. (I. Berge.) Est. 1966. Open 10—1 and 2—6. SIZE: Small. *STOCK: French, Dutch and English paintings, 19th C. 20th C.* PARK: Easy. TEL: 937 8444. SER: Valuations; buys at auction. VAT: Spec.

Lucerne Gallery
7 Kensington Mall, Kensington Church St. Est. 1976. Open 10—6. *STOCK: Paintings, sculpture, furniture, works of art.* TEL: 727 1726. VAT: Spec.

C.H. Major (Antiques) Ltd.
154 Kensington Church St. (A.H. Major.) Est. 1905. Open 9.30—6. SIZE: Large. *STOCK: English mahogany furniture, from 1760, £80—£5,000.* Not stocked: China, glass. PARK: Easy. TEL: 229 1162; home — 997 9018. VAT: Stan.

W.8 continued

David Malik
112 Kensington Church St. CL: Sat. from 1. Open 10—5.30. *STOCK: Chandeliers.* PARK: Meters. TEL: 229 2987. VAT: Stan.

S. Marchant and Son   BADA
120 Kensington Church St. (R.P. Marchant.) Est. 1925. CL: Sat. Open 9.30—5.30. *STOCK: Chinese and Japanese pottery and porcelain, netsuke, ivories, jades, cloisonné, Chinese furniture and paintings.* PARK: Easy, 50yds. opposite and around corner. TEL: 229 5319/3770. SER: Valuations; restorations (porcelain); buys at auction. VAT: Stan/Spec.

J. and J. May   BADA
40 Kensington Church St. Books and articles on commemorative items. Est. 1967. Open 10—1.30 and 2.30—6. SIZE: Small. *STOCK: Commemorative pottery, 1750—1850; commemorative porcelain, enamels, glass pictures, textiles, objets de vertu.* LOC: Underground stations: Notting Hill Gate and Kensington High St. PARK: 25yds. Vicarage Gate. TEL: 937 3575. SER: Valuations; buys at auction. VAT: Stan/Spec.

D. Mellor and A.L. Baxter LAPADA
121a Kensington Church St. Open 10—6.30, Sat. 10—5. *STOCK: Leather bound literary sets; antiquarian books on history, science, medicine, travel and exploration.* TEL: 229 2033.

Michael Coins
6 Hillgate St. (off Notting Hill Gate). (M. Gouby.) Est. 1966. CL: Sat. Open 10—5. SIZE: Small. *STOCK: Coins, English and foreign, 1066 A.D. to date; stamps, banknotes and collectors' items.* LOC: From Marble Arch to Notting Hill Gate, turn left at corner of Coronet Cinema. PARK: Easy. TEL: 727 1518. SER: Valuations; buys at auction. VAT: Stan/Spec.

W.8 continued

D.C. Monk and Son
132—134 Kensington Church St. CL: Sat. Open 10.30—5. *STOCK: Oriental porcelain.* TEL: 229 3727. VAT: Stan/Spec.

Oliver-Sutton Antiques   BADA
34c Kensington Church St. (A. Oliver and P. Sutton.) Est. 1967. Open 10—5.30, Sat. 10—3. *STOCK: Staffordshire pottery; 19th C portrait figures, Walton, Sherratt; pot-lids.* TEL: 937 0633. VAT: Spec.

Peel Antiques
131d Kensington Church St. (corner of Peel St.) (D. and M. Ladd.) Est. 1960. CL: Sat. Open 9.30—1 and 2—5.30. SIZE: Small. *STOCK: Mahogany, 18th C; English and Chinese porcelain, pottery, 18th and early 19th C; household implements, 18th—20th C.* PARK: Easy. TEL: 727 8298. VAT: Stan/Spec.

Henry Phillips   BADA
2 Campden St. Est. 1967. Open 9.30—5.30. SIZE: Small. *STOCK: English furniture, 18th to early 19th C.* LOC: Near Kensington Church St. TEL: 727 4079; home — 937 3448. SER: Buys at auction (English furniture). FAIRS: Grosvenor House.

Robert Pugh
with Constance Stobo, 31 Holland St., off Kensington Church St. Est. 1981. *STOCK: English and Welsh pottery, late 18th to 19th C, £40—£300; treen, 18th—19th C, £50—£200; decorative items, to £500.* TEL: 937 6282; home (0554) 772613. SER: Restorations (ceramics); buys at auction. FAIRS: Olympia; Brighton; West London; Petersfield. VAT: Stan/Spec.

Raffety and Huber   LAPADA
34 Kensington Church St. Open 10—5. *STOCK: Clocks, watches, scientific instruments and furniture, 17th—19th C, £150—£15,000; period and decorative furniture, from £100.* TEL: 938 1100. SER: Valuations; restorations (clocks and watches); buys at auction (horological items, mechanical instruments). FAIRS: Olympia, Park Lane Hotel. VAT: Stan/Spec.

J.S. Rasmussen Fine Arts
5 Logan Mews, Logan Place. Est. 1967. Open by appointment. SIZE: Medium. *STOCK: Netsuke, 18th and 19th C; European furniture.* PARK: Easy. TEL: 373 6527. SER: Valuations; buys at auction. VAT: Spec.

M & D SELIGMANN
Antiques
37 Kensington Church Street, London W8 4LL
Telephone 01 937 0400

Very rare 17th century yew-wood turner's armchair in mint condition.
Illustrated in "Oak Furniture — The British Tradition" by Victor Chinnery.

Fine pair of large 17th century oak figures — 45ins. (114.5cms.) high.

W.8 continued

Paul Reeves
32B Kensington Church St. Est. 1976. Open 10—6. *STOCK: Architect designed furniture and artifacts 1860—1960.* TEL: 937 1594.

John Reid
40a Kensington Church St. Open 10—1 and 2—5.30. *STOCK: Prints.* TEL: 937 3379.

J. Roger (Antiques) Ltd.   BADA
17 Uxbridge St. (J. Roger and C. Bayley.) Open Tues.—Fri., 2.30—5 or by appointment. *STOCK: Late 18th to early 19th C furniture especially small elegant pieces, mirrors, prints, porcelain and boxes.* TEL: 727 2227; home — 603 7627.

Sabin Galleries Ltd.   BADA
Campden Lodge, 82 Campden Hill Rd. (S.F. and E.P. Sabin.) SLAD. Open by appointment only. *STOCK: English paintings and drawings, pre-1830.* TEL: 937 0471.

St. Jude's Antiques   LAPADA
107 Kensington Church St. Open 10—1 and 2—5. *STOCK: English ceramics, 18th to mid-19th C; small period furniture.* TEL: 727 8737. VAT: Spec.

W.8 continued

A.V. and M.R. Santos
1 Campden St. CL: Sat. Open 10—1 and 2—6. *STOCK: Chinese porcelain, 17th—18th C.* TEL: 727 4872. VAT: Spec.

Arthur Seager Antiques Ltd.
25a Holland St. Kensington. (A.A. Seager). Resident. Est. 1972. Open 10—1 and 2—6. Sun. by appointment. SIZE: Medium. *STOCK: Furniture, £200—£2,000; pottery, treen, Mason's ironstone, 18th—19th C; pictures, 19th C, all £100—£500.* LOC: Off Kensington Church St. PARK: Easy. TEL: 937 3262. SER: Valuations; restorations (furniture); buys at auction (furniture). VAT: Stan/Spec.

M and D Seligmann   BADA
37 Kensington Church St. Est. 1948. Open 10—6, Sat. 10.30—2.30 or by appointment. SIZE: Medium. *STOCK: Early country furniture, early English pottery, treen, objets d'art.* LOC: Nearest underground Kensington High St. TEL: 937 0400; home — 722 4315. SER: Valuations; buys at auction. FAIRS: Fine Arts (Olympia), Chelsea (Spring and Autumn), Bath, West of England, and Dorchester Hotel Ceramics. VAT: Stan/Spec.

W.8 continued

Jean Sewell (Antiques) Ltd. BADA
3 Campden St. (R. and J. Sewell.) Est. 1956. Open 10—5.30. SIZE: Medium. STOCK: Porcelain, 18th—19th C, 50p—£500; pottery, 25p—£200; furniture, £20—£500; both 19th C. Not stocked: Silver and china after 1880. LOC: From Notting Hill Gate down Kensington Church St, fourth street on right at Churchill public house. PARK: Easy. TEL: 727 3122. VAT: Stan/Spec.

Sylvia Sheppard
71 Kensington Church St. Est. 1948. CL: Sat. p.m. Open 9.30—5.30. SIZE: Medium. STOCK: Furniture, 1700—1830, £100—£1,500. LOC: Tube to Notting Hill Gate or Kensington High St. PARK: Round corner in Campden Grove and Gloucester Walk. TEL: 937 0965. VAT: Stan/Spec.

Sinai Antiques Ltd. LAPADA
221 Kensington Church St. (E. and M. Sinai.) CL: Sat. Open 9.30—6. STOCK: Carpets, Oriental arts, silver, fine arts. TEL: 229 6190.

Simon Spero
109 Kensington Church St. Est. 1964. Author of 'The Price Guide to 18th C English Porcelain'. CL: Mon. except by appointment. Open 10—5, Sat. 10—1. SIZE: Medium. STOCK: 18th C English ceramics and watercolours. PARK: Meters. TEL: 727 7413. SER: Valuations; buys at auction. VAT: Spec.

Constance Stobo BADA
31 Holland St., off Kensington Church St. STOCK: Small furniture, English lustreware and pottery, 18th—19th C. TEL: 937 6282.

Jacob Stodel BADA LAPADA
116 Kensington Church St. Est. 1949. STOCK: Continental furniture, objets d'art, ceramics, English furniture. VAT: Spec.

Pamela Teignmouth and Son
108 Kensington Church St. (P. Teignmouth and T. Meyer.) Est. 1959. Open 10—6, Sat. 10—4. SIZE: Medium. STOCK: Papier mâché and tôleware, 19th C, £100—£2,000; English furniture 18th—19th C; decorative items. TEL: 229 1602. FAIRS: Olympia and Decorators. VAT: Spec.

Murray Thomson Ltd. LAPADA
141 Kensington Church St. Est. 1966. Open 9.30—6, Sat. 10—1. SIZE: Large. STOCK: General antiques, furniture. TEL: 727 1727. VAT: Stan/Spec.

Traditio Antiques
38a Kensington Church St. (S. Piombo and partners.) Est. 1984. Open 10—6, Sat. 10—1. SIZE: Medium. STOCK: Chinese export porcelain, to £500+; Continental furniture, to £1,000+, both 17th—18th C. TEL: 937 9532. SER: Buys at auction (Oriental porcelain and furniture). VAT: Spec.

W.8 continued

Temple Williams *Postal only*
34 Abingdon Rd. STOCK: Fine Regency furniture. TEL: 937 4677. SER: Valuations.

The Winter Palace
69 Kensington Church St. (N. Lynn and J. Bethge.) Est. 1974. Open 10—5.30, Sat. 11—3. SIZE: Medium. STOCK: Imperial Russian works of art, including paintings, silver, icons, porcelain, Fabergé. TEL: 937 2410. SER: Valuations; restorations; buys at auction. VAT: Spec.

Mary Wise BADA
27 Holland St. Kensington. Est. 1959. STOCK: English porcelain, Chinese ceramics and jade, works of art, bronzes. Not stocked: English pottery, jewellery. TEL: 937 8649. SER: Buys at auction (Chinese and English porcelain). VAT: Spec.

London W.9

Chris Beetles Ltd.
Watercolours and Paintings
104 Randolph Ave. Est. 1975. Open by appointment. SIZE: Large. STOCK: English watercolours, 1750—1930, £50—£25,000; art reference and illustrated books. LOC: 150yds. from Maida Vale tube station, 1 mile from Marble Arch. PARK: Easy. TEL: 286 1404. SER: Valuations. VAT: Spec.

Fluss and Charlesworth Ltd.
1 Lauderdale Rd. (E. Fluss, J. Charlesworth.) Est. 1970. Open 9.30—5.30. STOCK: 18th C. furniture and works of art. TEL: 286 8339.

Robert Hall
36 Formosa St. Est. 1976. Open by appointment. STOCK: Chinese snuff bottles, Ching dynasty; Oriental works of art, jade carvings, 17th—19th C; all £300—£20,000. Chinese contemporary paintings. PARK: Easy. TEL: 286 0809. SER: Valuations; restorations; buys at auction. VAT: Stan/Spec.

Beryl Kendall
The English Watercolour Gallery
2 Warwick Place, Little Venice. Est. 1953. STOCK: English watercolours, 18th—19th C. TEL: 286 9902.

Edward Salti
77 Wellesley Court, Maida Vale. STOCK: Porcelain, Battersea and Bilston boxes, 18th C. TEL: 286 3106.

The Textile Gallery
4 Castellain Rd. (M. and P. Franses.) Open by appointment. STOCK: Textile art, including classical carpets. TEL: 286 1747.

W.9 continued

Vale Antiques
245 Elgin Ave. (P. Gooley.) *STOCK: General antiques.* TEL: 328 4796.

Arnold Wiggins & Sons Ltd. BADA
30—34 Woodfield Place, Harrow Rd. (P. Mason, M. Gregory.) Open by appointment. *STOCK: Picture frames.* TEL: 286 9656.

London W.10

L. and G. Burnett
290 Portobello Rd. Est. 1952. Open Fri. 7—12, Sat. 7—4. *STOCK: Lace and linens, costume and textiles.* TEL: 969 8899.

Clive Loveless BADA
29 Kelfield Gdns., North Kensington. Resident. Est. 1968. Open by appointment. SIZE: Small. *STOCK: Near Eastern tribal rugs, kilims and textiles, 19th C, £500—£10,000; decorative rugs and carpets, 19th—20th C., £300—£10,000.* LOC: Nr. Ladbroke Grove. PARK: Easy. TEL: 969 5831. SER: Valuations; restorations (antique rugs); buys at auction. VAT: Stan/Spec.

London W.11

53 Ledbury Road
(R. O'Connor, D.W. Ellis and R. Cox.) Est. 1951. CL: Sat. Open 9.30—12.30 and 2—5, Wed.—Fri. 10—12.30 and 2—5. SIZE: Medium. *STOCK: Sculpture, metalwork, 16th to early 19th C; decorative and architectural items, 15th C to 1830; all £100—£2,500.* LOC: Off Westbourne Grove. PARK: Easy. TEL: 229 6900; home — 623 3162. SER: Valuations; buys at auction (as stock). VAT: Stan/Spec.

Albion Fine Art
61 Ledbury Rd. (C. Payne.) Open 9.30—1 and 2—6. *STOCK: English and European paintings, 17th—19th C.* TEL: 221 2977. SER: Buys at auction.

Alice's
86 Portobello Rd. (K. Carter.) Est. 1960. Open 9—12.30 and 1.30—5. SIZE: Large. *STOCK: General antiques.* TEL: 229 8187.

Antique Frames and Mirrors
195 Westbourne Grove. *STOCK: Victorian compo and fine carved frames and decorative mirrors.*

W.11 continued

The Antique Textile Company LAPADA
100 Portland Rd., Holland Park (S. Franklyn and J. Wentworth.) Est. 1982. CL: Sat. Open 10—6. *STOCK: Kashmir, paisley, Norwich and French shawls; chintz, period costume, lace, 1600—1850.* LOC: From Notting Hill Gate, 2nd right after Holland Park tube station. PARK: Easy. TEL: 221 7730. SER: Buys at auction.

Axia
43 Pembridge Villas. Est. 1974. *STOCK: Works of art, icons, textiles, metalwork, woodwork and ceramics, Islamic and Byzantine.* TEL: 727 9724.

B. and T. Antiques
79 Ledbury Rd. (Mrs. B. Lewis.) Open 10—6. *STOCK: Furniture, silver, objets d'art, paintings, 18th C to art deco.* TEL: 229 7001.

Serge Baillache
189 Westbourne Grove. Est. 1959. CL: Sat. Open 9.30—5.30. SIZE: Medium. *STOCK: English, Continental and decorative furniture, 18th and 19th C.* LOC: Near Odeon. PARK: Meters. TEL: 229 2270. VAT: Stan/Spec.

Barham Fine Art
83 Portobello Rd. Est. 1954. Open 8.45—6, Sat. 7—6. SIZE: Large. *STOCK: Victorian walnut and inlaid Continental furniture and writing boxes; bronzes, Chinese porcelain, clocks, Victorian and Old Master paintings, Vienna porcelain, marbles, K.P.M. plaques.* TEL: 727 3845. SER: Valuations; buys at auction.

P. R. Barham
111 Portobello Rd. Est. 1951. Open 9—5. SIZE: Medium. *STOCK: Victorian furniture, oriental porcelain, objets d'art, silver, plate.* TEL: 727 3397. SER: Valuations; buys at auction.

David Black Oriental Carpets BADA LAPADA
96 Portland Rd., Holland Park. Est. 1966. Open 11—6. SIZE: Large. *STOCK: Oriental tribal rugs, £250—£10,000; antique kilims, Indian dhurries, Oriental embroideries, 1600—1920, £300—£1,000.* LOC: From Notting Hill Gate, second right after Holland Park tube station. PARK: Meters. TEL: 727 2566. SER: Valuations; restorations; cleaning underfelt. VAT: Spec.

Blake Antiques
216 Westbourne Grove. (G.C. Blake.) Est. 1975. Open 10—5, Sat. and other times by appointment. *STOCK: Period furniture, clocks and decorative items.* TEL: 229 3232. VAT: Stan/Spec.

W.11 continued

Books & Things
Dolphin Arcade, 157 Portobello Rd. (M. Steenson.) A.B.A. Est. 1972. Open Sat. 9—4, Mon.—Fri. by appointment. SIZE: Small. *STOCK: Antiquarian books, £25—£100; posters, £50—£100; both 20th C.* PARK: Meters. TEL: 370 5593. SER: Valuations; buys at auction; catalogues issued. FAIRS: PBFA London, Oxford, Bath.

F.E.A. Briggs Ltd.
73 and 77 Ledbury Rd. Est. 1962. Open 8.30—5.30, Sat. 10—4. SIZE: Large and warehouses. *STOCK: Furniture, £50—£5,000; clocks, music boxes, scientific instruments.* TEL: 727 0909 or 221 4960. SER: Valuations. VAT: Stan/Spec.

John Bull (Antiques) Ltd.
163 Portobello Rd. Est. 1940. Open Sat. only. *STOCK: Silver, plate, jewellery.* TEL: 629 1251. VAT: Stan/Spec.

Helen Buxton Antiques   LAPADA
193 Westbourne Grove. Est. 1975. CL: Sat. Open 10—6. *STOCK: Chinese and Japanese ceramics, works of art and furniture.* TEL: 229 9997.

Caelt Gallery
182 Westbourne Grove. (E.T. Crawshaw.) Est. 1967. Open 9.30—6. SIZE: Large. *STOCK: Oil paintings, 16th—20th C, £100—£5,000.* PARK: Easy. TEL: 229 9309; home — 229 0303. VAT: Spec.

Canonbury Antiques Ltd.
174 Westbourne Grove. Est. 1966. Open 9.30—5.30. SIZE: Large. *STOCK: Furniture, porcelain, bronzes, clocks.* TEL: 229 2786. VAT: Stan/Spec.

Jack Casimir Ltd.   LAPADA
The Brass Shop, 23 Pembridge Rd. Est. 1933. Open 10—5. SIZE: Medium. *STOCK: Brass, copper, pewter.* Not stocked: Silver, china, jewellery. LOC: 2 mins. walk from Notting Hill Gate station. PARK: 100yds. TEL: 727 8643. SER: Exports. VAT: Stan.

Cassio Antiques
68 Ledbury Rd. Est. 1963. Open 10—5.30. SIZE: Large. *STOCK: Furniture.* TEL: 727 0678. VAT: Stan/Spec.

Chanticleer Antiques
105 Portobello Rd. (S. Wilkinson.) Est. 1967. Open Sat. 9.30—5.30 or by appointment. SIZE: Medium. *STOCK: Decorative and collectors items, 18th—19th C, £50—£1,000; European and Oriental works of art.* LOC: Westbourne Grove. PARK: Nearby. TEL: 385 0919. SER: Restorations. FAIRS: Olympia. VAT: Stan/Spec.

W.11 continued

Chantry Galleries
79 Portobello Rd. (Mrs. V. Wellsthorpe.) Open Sat. *STOCK: Isnik objets, Oriental rugs, textiles, Chinese porcelain.* SER: Buys at auction.

William Cleveland
40 Queensdale Rd., Holland Park. Est. 1955. Open 1—5, other times by appointment. SIZE: Medium. *STOCK: Marble mantelpieces, large bronzes, objets d'art, all 18th—19th C.* LOC: Off Holland Park Avenue. PARK: Easy. TEL: 603 5050; home — 727 1620. SER: Restorations (marble mantelpieces). VAT: Stan.

Cocozza Antiques   LAPADA
208 Westbourne Grove. (G. Cocozza.) Open 10—6, Sat. 10—1. *STOCK: Fine furniture, objets d'art, decorative items.* TEL: 221 1535.

Cohen and Pearce (Oriental Porcelain)   BADA
84 Portobello Rd. (M. Cohen and R. Pearce.) Est. 1974. Open Fri. 10—4, Sat. 8—4 otherwise by appointment. *STOCK: Chinese porcelain, bronzes, works of art; Japanese prints.* TEL: 229 9458. SER: Valuations; buys at auction. VAT: Spec.

Frank Collins Antiques   LAPADA
60 Ledbury Rd. Open 9.30—5.30. *STOCK: Fine arts and general antiques.* TEL: 221 7108.

Joan and Clive Collins
Shepherd's Arcade, 153 Portobello Rd. Est. 1959. *STOCK: Art nouveau, art deco.* TEL: 727 6848. VAT: Stan.

The Corner Portobello Antiques Supermarket
282, 284, 288, 290 Westbourne Grove. (W. Lipka Ltd.) LAPADA. Open Fri. 12—4, Sat. 7—6. There are 150 dealers selling a wide range of general miniature antiques, silver and jewellery. TEL: 727 2027. SER: Valuations; restorations.

Curá Antiques
34 Ledbury Rd. (G. Antichi.) Open 9.45—6, Sat. 10.30—1. *STOCK: Continental furniture, sculptures, statues and paintings.* TEL: 229 6880.

John Dale
87 Portobello Rd. Est. 1950. CL: Thurs. Open 9.30—5. SIZE: Medium. *STOCK: Georgian furniture, general antiques.* TEL: 727 1304. VAT: Stan.

Michael Davidson
52 and 54 Ledbury Rd. Est. 1961. CL: Sat. p.m. in winter. Open 9.45—12.45 and 1.15—5. *STOCK: Regency and period furniture, objets d'art.* TEL: 229 6088. SER: Valuations. VAT: Stan/Spec.

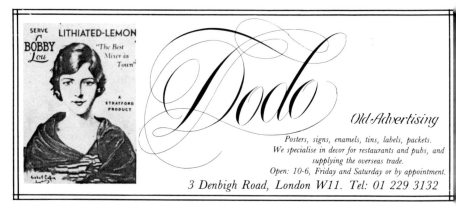

W.11 continued

Barry Davies Oriental Art and Nash Antiques
183 Westbourne Grove. Open 9.30—6, or by appointment. STOCK: Oriental and Japanese furniture; porcelain, bronzes, jade, ivory, netsuke, lacquer work. LOC: Near Portobello Rd. market. PARK: Easy. TEL: 727 3796. SER: Buys at auction. VAT: Stan/Spec.

Delehar
146 Portobello Rd. Est. 1919. Open Sat. 9.30—5. SIZE: Medium. STOCK: Antiques, works of art. Not stocked: Furniture. TEL: 727 9860; or 450 9998. VAT: Stan/Spec.

Peter Delehar
146 Portobello Rd. Est. 1919. Open Sat. 10—4. SIZE: Medium. STOCK: Unusual scientific instruments. TEL: 727 9860 or 866 8659. VAT: Stan/Spec.

Demetzy Books
113 Portobello Rd. (P. and M. Hutchinson.) ABA, PBFA. Est. 1972. Open Sat. 7.30—3.30. SIZE: Small. STOCK: Antiquarian leather bound books, 18th—19th C, £5—£1,000; miniature books, 19th to early 20th C; children's and illustrated books, 18th—20th C, both £5—£200. LOC: 20yds. from junction with Westbourne Grove, opposite Earl of Lonsdale public house. PARK: Meters. TEL: (0993) 2209. SER: Valuations; buys at auction (books). FAIRS: ABA Park Lane; PBFA Russell Hotel, London (monthly); Randolph Hotel, Oxford; ABAA New York and Los Angeles.

Peter and Daniele Dodd
66 Ledbury Rd. Est. 1970. Open 10—6. SIZE: Large. STOCK: Continental and English furniture and paintings; decorative items, 19th C. TEL: 221 4727. SER: Buys at auction; interior design. VAT: Stan/Spec.

W.11 continued

Dodo Old Advertising
3 Denbigh Rd. (E. Farrow.) Est. 1960. Open Fri. and Sat. 10—6 or by appointment. STOCK: English, American and Continental posters, enamels and signs, tins; crate, beer, wine and perfume labels; display figures, pub mirrors, showcards. Not stocked: Furniture, silver, general antiques. LOC: On 15 and 23 bus route, near Notting Hill Gate tube station. TEL: 229 3132.

Dolphin Arcade
155—157 Portobello Rd. Open Sat. 7—5.30. SIZE: Large (34 stalls). STOCK: Jewellery, silver, Oriental porcelain, English pottery, general antiques. TEL: 727 4883. VAT: Stan/Spec.

E. and A. Antiques   LAPADA
36 Ledbury Rd. (E. di Michele.) Est. 1973. Open 9.30—1 and 2—5, resident so usually available. STOCK: Silver and plate, furniture. TEL: 229 1823.

Peter Eaton (Booksellers) Ltd.
80 Holland Park Avenue. Open 10—5. STOCK: Books. LOC: Near Holland Park tube station. TEL: 727 5211. SER: Valuations.

Martin Edwards   BADA
14 Needham Rd. Est. 1980. Open 9.30—5.30. STOCK: Georgian silver, furniture, glass, paintings. Not stocked: Victoriana. TEL: 221 0417. SER: Valuations; buys at auction.

Elgin Antiques
123 Portobello Rd. (A. and B. Bhaduri.) Est. 1950. Open 10—6. SIZE: Medium. STOCK: General antiques, primitive works of art. PARK: Easy. TEL: 727 9852.

The Facade
196 Westbourne Grove. Est. 1973. Open 10.30—6. STOCK: Decorative items, 1900—1930 lighting; Victorian and Edwardian furniture. PARK: Easy. TEL: 727 2159. VAT Stan.

W.11 continued

Jack Fairman (Carpets) Ltd.
218 Westbourne Grove. (D.R.J. and S.J. Page.) CL: Sat. p.m. Open 9.30—6, Sun. by appointment. *STOCK: Persian and Oriental carpets and rugs; tapestries.* TEL: 229 2262/3. SER: Valuations; repairs; cleaning. VAT: Stan.

Keith Finch
187 Westbourne Grove. CL: Sat. Open 9.30—5.30. *STOCK: Walnut and mahogany furniture.* TEL: 229 0267.

Fine Art Association
229 Westbourne Grove. (D. Ewen.) Open 9.30—6. *STOCK: Decorative paintings, 19th—20th C.* TEL: 229 6606.

Judy Fox   LAPADA
81 Portobello Rd. and 176 Westbourne Grove. Est. 1970. Open 10—5. SIZE: Large. *STOCK: Furniture and decorative items, 18th—20th C; inlaid furniture, mainly 19th C; pottery and porcelain.* TEL: 229 8130.

J. Freeman   LAPADA
85a Portobello Rd. Est. 1962. Open 9.30—1 and 2—5.30. Sat. 9—6. SIZE: Medium. *STOCK: Victorian silver plate, 1830—1870, £10—£150, Sheffield plate, 1790—1830, £20—£100, Victorian and later silver, £5—£200.* LOC: Nearest tube station Notting Hill Gate. PARK: Easy. TEL: 221 5076. VAT: Stan.

Philip Garrick Antiques
42 Ledbury Rd. Open 9.30—6. *STOCK: Furniture, bronzes, works of art, 17th—19th C.* Not stocked: Shipping goods. TEL: 243 0500.

The Good Fairy Open Air Market
100 Portobello Rd. (S. Pardoe.) Est. 1978. Open Sat. 6—5. SIZE: Large. There are 80 dealers at this market selling *a wide variety of general antiques including jewellery, silver, general antiques 18th—20th C, £5—£2,000.* LOC: Enter Portobello Rd. at Chepstow Villas, market 150 metres along on right-hand side. PARK: Nearby. TEL: 351 5950.

Gavin Graham Gallery   LAPADA
47 Ledbury Rd. Est. 1973. *STOCK: Paintings, watercolours.* TEL: 229 4848. VAT: Spec.

Grays Portobello
138 Portobello Rd. Open Sat. 7—4. TEL: 221 3069.

Valerie Arieta
Stand 25/26. *American, Indian and ethnographic items and decorative arts.*
David Barker and Jonathan Mankovitz
Stand 14/15. *Antiquities, tribal and Oriental works of art.*
Anne Barlow and Marguerite Harrison
Stand 22. *French faience, Quimper.*

Grays Portobello continued

Pat Bedford
Stand 17. *General antiquities.*
Rob Boys and Roy Clark
Stand 12. *Oriental antiquities.*
Paul Carnell
Stand 8. *Works of art, rare antiquities, treasures and junk, priceless items.*
Reg Clark
Stand 1. *Silver.*
Mrs. Davies
Stand 27/28. *Oriental art.*
Colin Gross
Stand 18. *Ethnography, scientific instruments and weapons.*
Steven Hyder
Stand 21. *Oriental works of art and ceramics.*
Diane Leloup
Stand 10. *Indian and Himalayan art and jewellery.*
Jenny Levine
Stand 23. *English and Continental antiquities.*
Mrs. Liu
Stand 9. *Oriental works of art.*
Lorenz John
Stand 11. (J. Hilliard and L. Denney.) *Oriental and European bronzes.*
Mikado Antiques
Stand 13. *Oriental porcelain, carpets and furniture.*
Jonathan Olliff
Stand 29. *Oddities.*
Guy Robins
Stand 19/20. *Fine art, objets de vertu, antiquities.*
Jorgen Ruben
Stand 3. *Oriental and ethnic antiquities.*
Peter Sloane
Stand 16. *Ancient Islamic and Far Eastern art.*
Tim Soul
Stand 6. *Oriental ceramics and antiquities.*
Thomas Tressler
Stand 24. *Oriental porcelain and pottery.*
Anita Vandenberg and David Barrymore
Stand 7. *Oriental ceramics and antiquities.*
Richard White and Peter Howlett
Stand 4. *Oriental and Continental antiquities.*
Zophie Zwolinska
Stand 5. *Silver and plate.*

L. Guerra Antiques   Trade Only
82 Portobello Rd. Est. 1965. Open 9.30—5.30. SIZE: Large. *STOCK: Victoriana, £20—£1,000; 18th C Continental items, £200—£4,000; ivories and early 20th C items.* LOC: Near Notting Hill tube station. PARK: Easy. TEL: 727 0374. SER: Valuations; buys at auction. VAT: Stan/Spec.

W.11 continued

Hancock Gallery
184 Westbourne Grove. Open 10—6.30, Sat. 10—5. STOCK: Oil paintings. TEL: 229 7827. VAT: Spec.

W. Hildreth Ltd.
137 Portobello Rd. Open Sat. 8—5. SIZE: Large. Over 60 stalls. STOCK: General antiques. TEL: 727 5242.

Hirst Antiques
59 Pembridge Rd. Est. 1963. Open 10—6. SIZE: Medium. STOCK: Oak furniture, 17th—18th C; decorative articles. LOC: End of Portobello Rd., near Notting Hill Gate tube station. TEL: 727 9364. SER: Valuations (oak).

John Hooke and Son
214 Westbourne Grove. Est. 1947. STOCK: General antiques. TEL: 229 1050 and 749 6210. VAT: Stan.

Eric Hudes   LAPADA
142 Portobello Rd. Est. 1946. Open 9—4.15 Sat. only. STOCK: Oriental ceramics, c.900AD—1830; early English pottery, 1720—1830; objets d'art, all £50—£1,000. TEL: Home — 0376 83767. SER: Restorations (pottery and porcelain); buys at auction; worldwide postal transactions. FAIRS: Buxton, Ilkley and Harrogate. VAT: Mainly Spec.

Hyde Park Antiques   LAPADA
191 Westbourne Grove. (G.E. and J.E. Baldwin.) CL: Sat. Open 10—1 and 3—5.30. STOCK: Silver and plate. TEL: 727 1585.

A. Ibba
64 Ledbury Rd. Open 10—7. STOCK: General antiques. TEL: 243 0787.

Olivia Jackson
287 Westbourne Grove. Est. 1959. Open 9—6. SIZE: Large. STOCK: Furniture, prints, porcelain, silver, plate. TEL: 727 2817.

George Johnson Antiques LAPADA
120 Kensington Park Rd. Open 10—5. STOCK: English furniture, walnut and mahogany, 17th—18th C; longcase clocks, barometers. TEL: 229 3119. VAT: Stan/Spec.

Jones
194 Westbourne Grove. (J. and G. Jones.) Est. 1978. Open 10—6 or by appointment. SIZE: Large. STOCK: Lighting 1850—1950 especially art deco and art nouveau. PARK: Easy. TEL: 229 6866. SER: Valuations; prop hire. VAT: Stan.

Krystyna Antiques
190 Westbourne Grove. (K. Kurzelewska.) CL: Sat. Open 10—5. STOCK: English furniture, period to Edwardian; decorative items. TEL: 727 2699.

W.11 continued

Lacy Gallery
38 and 40 Ledbury Rd. Est. 1960. Open 10—5.30. SIZE: Large. STOCK: Period frames, old prints and paintings, decorative, sporting and marine, 18th to early 20th C. LOC: Two roads east of Portobello Rd. PARK: Easy. TEL: 229 9105. VAT: Spec.

S. Lampard and Son Ltd.   BADA
32 Notting Hill Gate. (J.P. Barnett.) Est. 1847. CL: Sat. Open 9.30—4.30. SIZE: Medium. STOCK: Jewellery, silver, clocks. TEL: 229 5457; home — 493 0144. SER: Valuations; restorations. VAT: Stan/Spec.

M. and D. Lewis
1 Lonsdale Rd., 172 and 212 Westbourne Grove. Est. 1960. Open 9.30— 5.30, Sat. 9.30—4. STOCK: Continental and Victorian furniture, porcelain, bronzes. TEL: 727 3908. VAT: Stan.

J. Lipitch Ltd.   BADA
177 Westbourne Grove. Est. 1955. Open 9.30—1 and 2—5.30, Sat. 10—1.30. STOCK: English and Continental furniture, 17th and 18th C; bronze, ormolu and porcelain. TEL: 229 0783. VAT: Spec.

London International Silver Co. Ltd.
82 Portobello Rd. (N. and C.F. Santer.) N.A.G. Est. 1976. Open 9.30—5.30, Sat. 8—6. SIZE: Medium. STOCK: Silver and plate, 17th—20th C, £5—£10,000; cutlery. LOC: Near Notting Hill Gate tube station. PARK: Easy. TEL: 221 1071. SER: Valuations; restorations (silver, silver plate); buys at auction (as stock). FAIRS: Olympia. VAT: Stan/Spec.

London Postcard Centre
21 Kensington Park Rd., (junction Elgin Crescent). (Man. R. Brodrick.) Est. 1968. Open 9.30—6.30. STOCK: Postcards, especially those depicting early South America, photographs, books, posters, advertising matter, £1—£500; topography, art nouveau, art deco and secessionist artists, paintings, watercolours, bronzes, porcelain, bric-a-brac. LOC: Alongside Centrepoint of Portobello Rd., nearest tubes, Notting Hill Gate and Ladbroke Grove. PARK: Easy. TEL: 229 1888 and 727 1900. SER: Valuations; buys at auction; rental facilities.

Peter Loveday Prints   LAPADA
46 Norland Sq. (P.J. Loveday.) Est. 1976. Open by appointment only. STOCK: Prints, drawings, books, British sporting art and topography, 1700—1940. TEL: 221 4479. SER: Valuations; restorations; buys at auction. VAT: Stan/ Spec.

W.11 continued

Robin Martin
44 Ledbury Rd. Est. 1972. Open 10—5.30. SIZE: Medium. *STOCK: General antiques, furniture, pewter, early metalware, scientific instruments.* LOC: Westbourne Grove area. TEL: 727 1301. VAT: Stan.

Mercury Antiques   **BADA**
1 and 1b Ladbroke Rd. (L. Richards.) Est. 1963. Open 10—5.30. SIZE: Medium. *STOCK: English porcelain, 1750—1850; English pottery and Delft, 1700—1850; glass, 1780—1850.* **Not stocked: Jewellery, silver, plate, art nouveau. LOC: Half minute from Notting Hill Gate underground station, turn into Pembridge Rd. and bear left. PARK: In mews at side of shop. TEL: 727 5106. VAT: Mainly spec.**

S. Messim
63a Ledbury Rd. Est. 1960. Open 9.30—1 and 2—6. *STOCK: 18th—19th C English and Continental furniture.* PARK: Easy. TEL: 727 1706. SER: Valuations.

Milne and Moller
35 Colville Terrace. (Mr. and Mrs. C. Moller.) Est. 1976. Open Sat. 9—6, other days by appointment. SIZE: Small. *STOCK: Watercolours and oils, 19th—20th C, £50—£750.* LOC: Near junction of Westbourne Grove and Ledbury Rd. PARK: Easy. TEL: 727 1679; home — same. SER: Valuations; restorations; framing; buys at auction (watercolours). FAIRS: World of Watercolours, Park Lane Hotel. VAT: Spec.

Momtaz Gallery
Persian and Islamic Art
42 Pembridge Rd. Est. 1975. Open 10—5.30. SIZE: Large. *STOCK: Luristan bronzes, Islamic pottery, 9th—14th C; Nishapur, Gurgan, Rayy, Kashan, 9th—11th C; glass and metal work.* PARK: Space 2 mins. away. TEL: 229 5579. SER: Valuations; restorations. VAT: Stan.

Myriad Antiques
131 Portland Rd., Holland Park Ave. (S. Nickerson.) Est. 1970. Open 11—6. SIZE: Medium. *STOCK: Decorative furniture and objects, mostly 19th C, £10—£1,000.* LOC: Between Notting Hill Gate and Shepherds Bush roundabout. TEL: 229 1709. VAT: Stan.

Sylvia Napier Ltd.
32 Ledbury Rd. Est. 1980. Open 10—6. SIZE: Large. *STOCK: Decorative objects and furniture including Oriental, French provincial, and Continental, 16th—20th C, £50—£5,000.* LOC: Parallel to and two blocks east of Portobello Rd. PARK: Easy. TEL: 229 9986/7; home — 221 7247. SER: Restorations; hire. FAIRS: Olympia. VAT: Stan/Spec.

ORMONDE
ORIENTAL ANTIQUES
(Westbourne Antiques Ltd.)

Khymer Buddah carved in sandstone. 110cm. 12th—13th century

ORMONDE GALLERY
156 Portobello Road
London W11
Tel: 01 229 9800

W.11 continued

Pat Nye
Geoffrey Van Arcade, 105 Portobello Rd. Est. 1963. Open Sat. only 7—3.30 or by appointment. SIZE: Small. *STOCK: Needlework samplers, 18th—19th C, £80—£350; brass, £15—£200; snuff boxes and pipe tampers, £15—£150; pottery — gaudy Welsh, Quimper, majolica, £10—£200; all 18th to early 19th C.* LOC: Near Westbourne Grove. PARK: Powys Sq. TEL: Home — 948 4314. FAIRS: West London and Chelsea. VAT: Stan/Spec.

Ormonde Gallery
156 Portobello Rd. (F. Ormonde.) Open 11—5, Sat. 7—5, or by appointment. There are 6 dealers here offering a wide range of Oriental items, textiles, furniture, collectables, porcelain, netsuke, snuff bottles. TEL: 229 9800 and 042482 226. VAT: Stan/Spec.

S.W. Parry (Old Glass)
Stand A4-A5 Westbourne Antique Arcade, 113 Portobello Rd. Est. 1975. Open Sat. 8—4. SIZE: Small. *STOCK: Decanters, 19th C, £20—£80; drinking glasses, 18th—19th C, £3—£100.* PARK: Meters nearby. TEL: Home — 740 0248. SER: Valuations; restorations (decanters); polishing; buys at auction (18th—19th C glass). VAT: Stan/Spec.

W.11 continued

E.S. Phillips and Son   Export Only
99 Portobello Rd. Est. 1962. Open 9.30—
5.30. *STOCK: General antiques, stained glass
windows.* TEL: 229 2113.

Philp   BADA
**59 Ledbury Rd. (R. Philp.) Est. 1961. Open
10—6.** *STOCK: 16th C English portraiture,
medieval sculpture, early furniture, £50—
£10,000.* **PARK: Easy. TEL: 727 7915. VAT:
Spec.**

Pivnick Gallery
40A Ledbury Rd. (S. Pivnick.) Est. 1963.
Open 9.30—6, Sat. 9.30—5.30. SIZE: Small.
*STOCK: Oil paintings, 17th—20th C, £100—
£2,000; watercolours.* LOC: Near Portobello
Rd., off Westbourne Grove. PARK: Easy. TEL:
221 8365; home — 458 2790. SER: Valuations; restorations; buys at auction.

Portland Gallery
2 Holland Park Terrace, Portland Rd. (T.A.
Hewlett & J.A. Thompson.) Est. 1980. CL:
Mon. Open 10—6.30. SIZE: Medium. *STOCK:
British pictures, 1850—1950, £200—£10,000;
British furniture, 1700—1900, £200—£5,000.*
LOC: Corner of Holland Park Ave. and Portland
Rd. PARK: Easy. TEL: 221 0294. SER: Valu-
ations; buys at auction (paintings and furni-
ture). VAT: Spec.

Portobello Silver Company
82 Portobello Rd. (N. Santer.) NAG. Est.
1968. Open 9.30—5, Sat. 8—6. *STOCK:
Silver and silver-plated ware, 1700 to date,
from £2; silver-plated cruets; cutlery, Sheffield
plate, 1770—1840, from £10.* LOC: Near
Notting Hill Gate tube. PARK: Easy. TEL: 221
1071. SER: Valuations; restorations; buys at
auction. FAIRS: International Antiques,
Olympia. VAT: Stan/Spec.

Princedale Antiques
70 Princedale Rd., Holland Park. (G.M. Sykes.)
Est. 1969. Open Thurs.—Sat. 10—6, trade
anytime. SIZE: Medium. *STOCK: Pine and
country furniture, 19th to early 20th C,
£30—£800.* LOC: 300yds. from Holland Park
station. PARK: Easy. TEL: 727 0868 and
workshop 607 6376. VAT: Stan.

W.11 continued

Rabbitz
121 Portobello Rd. (A.C.J. and B.M. Dixon.) Est. 1974. Open Fri. 10−5, Sat. 6−5 other days by appointment. SIZE: Small. STOCK: Oriental ceramics, furniture, £100−£500; European ceramics, £50−£100; all 19th C. LOC: Just south of Westbourne Grove. PARK: Nearby. TEL: 221 9178. SER: Valuations; buys at auction (Japanese ceramics and works of art). VAT: Stan/Spec.

A. Raphael
51 Ledbury Rd. Est. 1948. CL: Sat. Open 10−5 or by appointment. STOCK: Old Master paintings, works of art, general antiques. TEL: 229 6056 and 435 1772. VAT: Stan/Spec.

The Red Lion Market (Portobello Antiques Market)
165/169 Portobello Rd. Est. 1951. Open Fri. and Sat. only 6−6. There are over 200 dealers selling a wide range of general antiques including ethnic antiquities, bronzes, ivory statues, jade, precious metals, dolls, silver and plate, drinking vessels, costumes, Oriental and Western porcelain, furniture, collectables, prints, lace, linen, books, manuscripts, stamps, coins, banknotes, paintings, etchings. TEL: 221 7638; 229 4010 or 834 7649 24-hour service. SER: Valuations; shipping.

Rex Antiques
63 Ledbury Rd. (D. Cura.) Open 9−6, Sat. 9−1. STOCK: Victorian and decorative furniture. TEL: 229 6203.

Rod's Antiques
82B Portobello Rd. (R. Buck.) Est. 1970. Open 9−5. SIZE: Large. STOCK: Barometers, English and European copper, brass, boat models, nautical goods, scientific instruments, interior decorating items. TEL: 229 2544. VAT: Stan.

Roger's Antiques Gallery
65 Portobello Rd. Open 7−5 every Sat. There are 60 dealers selling a wide range of general antiques. TEL: Enquiries − 351 5353.

G. Sarti Antiques Ltd.　LAPADA
186 Westbourne Grove. Open 9.30−1 and 2−6, Sat. 10−3. STOCK: Cabinets, European and English furniture, decorative marbles, 17th and 18th C. TEL: 221 7186.

Schredds of Portobello
107 Portobello Rd. (H.J. and G.R. Schrager.) Est. 1969. Open Sat. 7.30−3.30 or by appointment. SIZE: Small. STOCK: Collectors' silver, 17th−19th C, £10−£1,000; Delft, 17th−18th C; English porcelain, 18th C. PARK: Nearby. TEL: 348 3314; home − same. SER: Valuations; buys at auction. FAIRS: Olympia, West Kensington. VAT: Stan/Spec.

W.11 continued

Shepherd's Arcade
153 Portobello Rd. Est. 1962. Open daily. 1st floor of paintings and frames. SER: Restorations; framing and relining.

Sheraton Antiques Ltd.
192 Westbourne Grove. Open 10−5.30. STOCK: Furniture, especially sets of Chippendale and Queen Anne chairs. TEL: 229 8748. SER: Valuations; French polishing.

David Slater
170 Westbourne Grove. Est. 1961. Open 9.30−1 and 2−5.30, Sat. 10−1. SIZE: Large. STOCK: General antiques, decorative items. PARK: Easy. TEL: 727 3336. VAT: Stan.

Louis Stanton　BADA LAPADA
299 and 301 Westbourne Grove. (L.R. and S.A. Stanton.) Est. 1965. Open 9.30−1 and 2−5.30, Sat. 9−6. SIZE: Medium. STOCK: Early English and Continental oak furniture, walnut, tapestries, clocks, metalware, objets d'art, pre-1750; £20−£10,000; fine English furniture, 18th and early 19th C; unusual decorative items. PARK: Easy. TEL: 727 9336. SER: Valuations; buys at auction. VAT: Stan/Spec.

Stern Gallery
46 Ledbury Rd. (M. Stern.) Est. 1952. Open 10−6, Sat. 10−5.30. SIZE: Medium. STOCK: Oil paintings, 18th−19th C, £200−£1,500. LOC: Off Westbourne Grove near Portobello. PARK: Easy. TEL: 229 6187. SER: Valuations; restorations; buys at auction. VAT: Stan.

L. and M. Sutton
91 Portobello Rd. Open 10−5. SIZE: Medium. STOCK: General antiques. TEL: 727 0386. VAT: Stan.

M. and C. Telfer-Smollett
88 Portobello Rd. Est. 1958. CL: Sun. to Wed. Open 10−5. SIZE: Medium. STOCK: Oriental furniture, fabrics, Middle Eastern screens, tables, natural history specimens. TEL: 727 0117. VAT: Stan/Spec.

Nicholas Thomas Antiques
57 Ledbury Rd. STOCK: Paintings, continental furniture, ormolu, pottery and porcelain. TEL: 243 0669.

Murray Thomson Ltd.　LAPADA
233 Westbourne Grove. Open 9.30−6, Sat. 10−1. SIZE: Large. STOCK: General antiques, furniture. TEL: 221 8174.

W.11 continued

Igor Tociapski
39/41 Ledbury Rd. Est. 1959. CL: Sat. and Fri. p.m. Open 10–5.30. SIZE: Small. *STOCK: Clocks, watches, scientific instruments and mechanical music, 1500–1900.* Not stocked: Tapestries. PARK: Easy. TEL: 229 8317. SER: Restorations (clocks); buys at auction.

Christina Truscott
139 Portobello Rd. Est. 1967. Open Sat. 7.30–3.30. *STOCK: Chinese lacquer, tea caddies, work boxes, small decorative items, late 18th to early 19th C, £100–£500.* TEL: Home – 0403 730554.

Village Gallery
32 Uxbridge St. (T. Malvasi.) Open by appointment. *STOCK: 19th C English and European paintings.* TEL: 229 8928.

Trude Weaver
71 Portobello Rd. Est. 1968. Open 9.30–5. Sat. 9–5. SIZE: Medium. *STOCK: English and Continental furniture, decorative objects, textiles.* PARK: Easy. TEL: 229 8738. SER: Valuations.

A.M. Web   LAPADA
93 Portobello Rd. (J. Donovan.) CL: Mon. Open 10–6. *STOCK: Musical boxes, unusual clocks, automata, old toys and other mechanical antiques.* TEL: 727 1485. VAT: Stan.

W.11 continued

The Witch Ball
206 Westbourne Grove. (L.C.M. Drecker.) Est. 1941. Open 10–6. SIZE: Medium. *STOCK: Victorian furniture, button chairs.* LOC: Near Notting Hill Gate tube. TEL: 229 3908. SER: Restorations; buys at auction.

World Famous Portobello Market
177 Portobello Rd. and 1–3 Elgin Crescent. Est. 1951. Open Fri. and Sat. only 6–6. There are over 200 dealers selling *a wide range of general antiques including ethnic antiquities, bronzes, ivory statues, jade, precious metals, dolls, silver and plate, drinking vessels and costumes.* TEL: 221 7638; 229 4010 or 834 7649 24-hour service. SER: Valuations; restorations; shipping.

The Wyllie Gallery
12 Needham Rd. (J.G. Wyllie.) Open 9–6, Sat. 10–1 or by appointment. *STOCK: 19th–20th C marine paintings and engravings especially works by the Wyllie family.* TEL: 727 0606 or 584 6024.

A rare small size Ridgway teapot, decorated in light and dark blue with gilt and enamelled strawberry border. Pattern 2/36. 3¾ins. high. c.1815. From *Ridgway Porcelains*, by Geoffrey A. Godden, F.R.S.A., published by the **Antique Collectors' Club**, 1985.

W.11 continued

Wynyards Antiques
5 Ladbroke Rd. (Lastlodge Ltd.) Est. 1983. Open 10—5.30, Sat. 10.30—5.30. SIZE: Medium. STOCK: Treen, £5—£500; small furniture, £35—£2,000; objects of art and interest £3—£600, all 17th—19th C. LOC: Near Notting Hill Gate tube station. PARK: Meters. TEL: 221 7936. SER: Restorations (furniture); polishing; caning; upholstery. FAIRS: Ravenscott at Chelsea Town Hall. VAT: Mainly spec.

London W.13

Quest Antiques
90 Northfields Ave., Ealing. (W.A. Turner.) Est. 1979. CL: Mon. and Wed. Open 10.30—5, Sat. 9.30—5. SIZE: Small. STOCK: Furniture, 19th C, to £250; objects and bric-a-brac, 19th—20th C, £5—£300. PARK: Easy. TEL: 840 2349/741 3822; home — same. VAT: Stan.

Rupert's Early Wireless
151 Northfield Ave. (R. Loftus Brigham.) CL: Sat. Open 10—6 or by appointment. STOCK: Early wireless, gramophones, phonographs, telephones and associated items. TEL: 567 1368.

W.13 Antiques
10 The Avenue, Ealing. Open Tues., Thurs., Fri. and Sat. 10—5, or by appointment. SIZE: Medium. STOCK: Furniture, china and general antiques, 18th—20th C. LOC: Off Uxbridge Rd., West Ealing. PARK: Easy. TEL: 998 0390. SER: Valuations. VAT: Stan.

London W.14

Stephen Anson
31a Matheson Rd. Est. 1978. Open by appointment. SIZE: Small. STOCK: English oak and country furniture, 1600—1800, £250—£5,000. PARK: Easy. TEL: 602 5277; home — same.

Charleville Gallery   LAPADA
7 Charleville Rd., West Kensington. (R. and D. Coombes.) Est. 1972. CL: Mon. and Tues. Open 10—5 and alternate Sats. STOCK: Oriental ceramics and works of art, including bronzes, 200BC—19th C, £5—£1,000; Oriental textiles, 18th—19th C. LOC: District Line to West Kensington station or off M4 onto North End Rd. PARK: Easy. TEL: 385 3785. SER: Valuations. FAIRS: West London; Chelsea; British International, Birmingham; Olympia. VAT: Spec.

W.14 continued

Richard Joslin
150 Gordon Mansions. Est. 1971. Open daily, Sat. and Sun. by appointment. SIZE: Small. STOCK: English and Continental oil paintings, 1820—1920, £500—£12,000. LOC: Off Shepherd's Bush Rd., turn into Blythe Rd., 2nd turning on left. PARK: Easy. TEL: 603 6435; home — same. SER: Valuations; restorations (oils and watercolours); framing; buys at auction (oils and watercolours, worldwide). FAIRS: Olympia. VAT: Spec.

Fiona King at the Charleville Gallery
7 Charleville Rd., West Kensington. Est. 1986. Open 10—5 and alternate Sats., Sun., Mon and Tues. by appointment. STOCK: Linen and general textiles, 1850—1920; lace, 1850—1890, all £25—£200. LOC: 2 min. walk from West Kensington station or off M4 onto North End Rd. PARK: Easy. TEL: 385 3785; home — 373 0151.

Picture House
141 North End Rd. (Midasland Ltd.) Est. 1977. Open 10—6, Sat. 10—4. SIZE: Medium. STOCK: English watercolours and oils, 18th—19th C; prints, 19th—20th C. LOC: 200yds. from West Kensington station. PARK: Easy. TEL: 602 2060. SER: Valuations; buys at auction (paintings). VAT: Stan.

Schidlof Galleries
1 Holland Park Court, Holland Park Gdns. Open by appointment. STOCK: Portrait miniatures. TEL: 603 9480.

Simpson Pine Mirrors
17 Girdlers Rd. (S. Yardy.) Resident. Usually available. STOCK: Plain and carved pine mirrors, 18th—19th C. TEL: 603 8625/8635.

London S.W.1

Didier Aaron (London) Ltd.
21 Ryder St., St. James's. Est. 1950. CL: Sat. Open 10—6. SIZE: Large. STOCK: French furniture, 18th C., £5,000—£500,000; Old Master and 19th C pictures, £5,000—£200,000; objets d'art, £2,000—£40,000. LOC: 200yds. from Christie's. PARK: NCP Bury St. TEL: 839 4716/7. SER: Buys at auction (as stock). FAIRS: Burlington House; Biennale de Paris; Winter Antiques Show, New York. VAT: Stan/Spec.

Addison-Ross Gallery
40 Eaton Terrace, Belgravia. (T.C.A. and D.A.A. Ross.) STOCK: Paintings and prints especially sporting and natural history. TEL: 730 1536. SER: Interior design (pictures).

Maurice Asprey Ltd.

41 DUKE STREET, ST. JAMES'S
LONDON, SW1Y 6DF
Telephone 01-930 3921

Three early Victorian silver
sugar sifter spoons.

S.W.1 continued

Ahuan (U.K.) Ltd.
17 Eccleston St. (O. Hoare.) Est. 1975. CL:
Sat. Open 9.30—5.30. *STOCK: Early Persian
and Islamic works of art.* TEL: 730 9382.
VAT: Spec.

Albany Gallery
1 Bury St., St. James's. (W.B. Thomson.) CL:
Sat. Open 10—5.30. *STOCK: English drawings,
watercolours, paintings, decorative items,
18th—19th C.* TEL: 839 6119.

J.A. Allen and Co.
1 Lower Grosvenor Place. Est. 1926. CL: Sat.
p.m. Open 9—5.30. *STOCK: Horse books,
from 1600.* PARK: Meters. TEL: 834 5606.
VAT: Stan.

John Allsopp Antiques
26 Pimlico Rd. Open 10—6, Sat. 10—1, other
times by appointment. *STOCK: Decorative
furniture and objects, 18th—19th C.* TEL: 730
9347.

Albert Amor Ltd.
37 Bury St., St. James's. Est. 1837. CL: Sat.
Open 9.30—4.30. SIZE: Small. *STOCK: 18th
C English ceramics, especially first period
Worcester and blue and white porcelain.*
PARK: Meters. TEL: 930 2444. SER: Valu-
ations; buys at auction. VAT: Spec.

S.W.1 continued

Anno Domini Antiques   BADA
66 Pimlico Rd. (F. Bartman.) Est. 1960. CL:
Sat. p.m. Open 10—1 and 2.15—6. SIZE:
Large. *STOCK: Furniture, 17th to early 19th
C, £200—£7,000; mirrors, 17th—19th C,
£300—£3,000; glass, screens, decorative
items, 18th—19th C, £10—£2,500.* Not
stocked: Silver, jewellery, arms, carpets,
coins. LOC: From Sloane Sq. go down Lower
Sloane St., turn left at traffic lights. PARK:
Easy. TEL: 730 5496; home — 352 3084.
SER: Buys at auction. VAT: Stan/Spec.

Antiques
56 Ebury St. (Gwyneth Antiques.) Est. 1958.
CL: Sat. Open 10—5 or later. SIZE: Small.
*STOCK: Textiles, shawls, Oriental and deco-
rative furniture, some rugs.* LOC: Junction of
Ebury St. and Eccleston St. PARK: Meters.
TEL: 730 2513; home — 352 4864. FAIRS:
West London, Kensington Town Hall (January).

Antiquus
90—92 Pimlico Rd. (E. Amati.) CL: Sat. p.m.
Open 10—1 and 2—5.30. SIZE: Large.
*STOCK: Classical, medieval and Renaissance
works of art, textiles and glass.* LOC: Near
Sloane Sq. underground station. PARK:
Meters in Holbein Place. TEL: 730 8681.

Appleby Bros. Ltd.   BADA
8 Ryder St., St. James's. Est. 1922. CL: Sat.
Open 10—5.30. *STOCK: Fine paintings and
watercolours.* PARK: Meters. TEL: 930 6507.
VAT: Spec.

Artemis Fine Arts (U.K.) Limited
15 Duke St., St. James's. CL: Sat. Open
9.30—5.30. *STOCK: Old Master paintings
and drawings.* TEL: 930 1523.

Maurice Asprey Ltd.   BADA
41 Duke St., St. James's. Est. 1956. Open
9.30—5.30, Sat. during Dec. only 9.30—1.
SIZE: Small. *STOCK: Silver, 15th—20th C,
£100—£75,000; jewellery, 17th—20th C,
£250—£250,000; miniatures, 17th—19th C,
£350—£25,000; objets de vertu, 16th—20th
C, £150—£20,000; Russian works of art,
19th—20th C, £2.000—£15,000.* LOC:
South of Jermyn St. PARK: Meters. TEL: 930
3921. SER: Valuations; restorations, repairs,
restringing; buys at auction. FAIRS: Burlington
House. VAT: Stan/Spec.

Astleys
109 Jermyn St. Est. 1862. CL: Sat. p.m.
SIZE: Medium. *STOCK: Meerschaum pipes,
19th C, £30—£1,500; pottery, porcelain,
primitive and Oriental pipes, £30—£1,500;
smoking accessories, cigar boxes, smoking
cabinets, tobacco jars, 19th C, £20—£200.*
LOC: Near Piccadilly Circus. PARK: Meters.
TEL: 930 1687. SER: Valuations; restorations
(pipes). VAT: Stan.

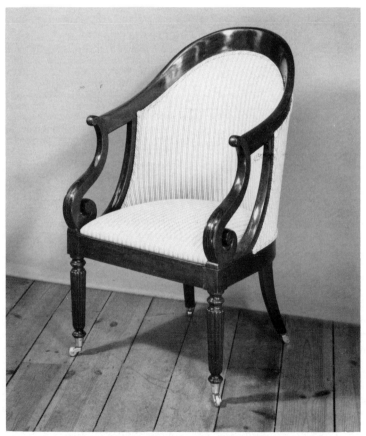

S.W.1 continued

Bayly's Gallery Antiques
8 Princes Arcade, Piccadilly. (P. Anstee.) Open 10−5, Sat. 10−1. SIZE: Small. *STOCK: Collectors items including Staffordshire figures, Valentines, ephemera, pictures and prints, 19th C, £5−£500.* LOC: Near St. James Church. PARK: St. James Sq. TEL: 734 0180. VAT: Spec.

Chris Beetles Ltd. Watercolours and Paintings
5 Ryder St. CL: Sat. and Sun. except by appointment. Open 10−5. SIZE: Large. *STOCK: English watercolours, 18th−20th C, £500−£50,000.* LOC: 100 yards from Royal Academy. PARK: Meters. TEL: 930 8586. SER: Valuations. VAT: Spec.

Belgrave Gallery
22 Mason's Yard, Duke St., St. James's. CL: Sat. Open 10−6. *STOCK: Paintings including British Post-Impressionist.* TEL: 930 0294.

Belgravia Gallery Ltd.
17 Lowndes St. (Mrs. L.G. Awad.) Est. 1982. Open 9.30−6. SIZE: Medium. *STOCK: Oriental and Islamic art, kilims and kilim cushions.* LOC: Off Sloane St. PARK: Easy. TEL: 235 4976. SER: Buys at auction. VAT: Stan.

S.W.1 continued

Raymond Benardout — BADA LAPADA
4 William St., Knightsbridge. Est. 1961. Open 9.30−6, Sat. by appointment. *STOCK: Antique and decorative rugs and carpets, tapestry.* LOC: Next to Park Tower Hotel. TEL: 235 3360. SER: Valuations; restorations (hand cleaning). VAT: Stan/Spec.

Raymond Benardout Antiques Ltd. — BADA LAPADA
5 William St., Knightsbridge. Est. 1979. Open 9.30−6, Sat. by appointment. SIZE: Medium. *STOCK: 17th to mid-19th C English and Continental furniture, works of art.* LOC: Next to Park Tower Hotel. TEL: 235 9588. SER: Restorations. VAT: Stan/Spec.

Bennison
91 Pimlico Rd. Open 10−6 Sat. and Sun. by appointment. *STOCK: 17th− 19th C furniture, pictures, objects and carpets.* PARK: Meters. TEL: 730 8076. VAT: Stan/Spec.

J.H. Bourdon-Smith Ltd. — BADA
24 Mason's Yard, Duke St., St. James's. Est. 1954. CL: Sat. Open 9.30−6. SIZE: Medium. *STOCK: Silver, 1680−1830, £50−£15,000; Victorian and modern silver, 1830 to date, £25−£2,000.* PARK: Meters. TEL: 839 4714/5. SER: Valuations; restorations (silver); buys at auction. FAIRS: Chelsea, British International (Birmingham), Harrogate, Grosvenor House, Burlington House, International Silver and Jewellery (Dorchester). VAT: Stan/Spec.

Bourne Fine Art
14 Masons Yard, Duke St., St. James's. Est. 1978. CL: Sat. Open 10-6. SIZE: Small. *STOCK: Scottish paintings, 1800−1950; decorative arts, 1860−1930.* PARK: Easy. TEL: 930 4215. SER: Valuations; restorations; framing; buys at auction. VAT: Stan/Spec.

Box House Antiques — BADA
105 Pimlico Rd. (J. Maas.) Open 10−5, Sat. 10−1. *STOCK: Furniture, 17th−19th C; needlework, samplers, pictures.* TEL: 730 9257.

Brisigotti Antiques Ltd.
44 Duke St., St. James's. Open 9.30−1 and 2−5.30. *STOCK: European works of art, Old Master paintings.* TEL: 839 4441/2.

Brod Gallery — BADA
24 St. James's St. S.L.A.D. CL: Sat. Open 9.30−5.30. *STOCK: Old Masters; 19th− 20th C French, 18th C and 19th C British paintings.* PARK: Meters. TEL: 839 2606/3871. SER: Valuations. VAT: Spec.

Bury Street Gallery
11 Bury St. Est. 1977. *STOCK: European and English paintings and graphics.* TEL: 930 2902.

S.W.1 continued

Cadogan Gallery
15 Pont St. Open 10—6. Sat. 10—1. *STOCK: English and European oil paintings, 18th—19th C.* TEL: 235 4526.

California Art Galleries   *Trade Only*
15/16 Royal Opera Arcade, Pall Mall. (G. Malmed.) Est. 1973. CL: Sat. and Sun. except by appointment. Open 12—5.30. SIZE: Large. *STOCK: Prints, some hand coloured; London prints; oil paintings, 20th C, from £20.* LOC: Around corner from the Haymarket. PARK: Easy, meters close by. TEL: 930 7679. SER: Valuations; buys at auction. FAIRS: Fine Arts.

Camerer Cuss and Co.   BADA
17 Ryder St., St. James's. (The Cuss Clock Co. Ltd.) Est. 1788. CL: Sat. Open 9.30—5. SIZE: Medium. *STOCK: Clocks, 1600—1910, £250—£30,000; watches, 1600—1930, £100—£35,000.* **TEL: 930 1941. SER: Valuations; restorations (clocks and watches); buys at auction. VAT: Stan/Spec.**

David Carritt Limited
15 Duke St., St. James's. CL: Sat. Open 9.30—5.30. *STOCK: Old Master paintings.* TEL: 930 8733.

S.W.1 continued

Odile Cavendish
14 Lowndes St. Est. 1971. Open by appointment. SIZE: Large. *STOCK: Mainly Oriental, furniture, screens, paintings, works of art.* PARK: Meters. TEL: 235 2491. VAT: Spec.

Cavendish Rare Books
2-4 Princes Arcade, Piccadilly. (B. Grigor-Taylor) ABA. Est. 1974. Open 10—6, Sat. 9.30—1.30. SIZE: Small. *STOCK: Antiquarian books on voyages, travel, mountaineering, polar exploration; also sets.* LOC: Next to Pan-Am Airways office, arcade on south side of Piccadilly. PARK: Burlington Garage. TEL: 734 3840. SER: Valuations; buys at auction (books and manuscripts). FAIRS: ABA, Worldwide.

Chaucer Fine Arts Inc.
45 Pimlico Rd. Open 10—6, Sat. 10—1. *STOCK: Old Master paintings and drawings.* TEL: 730 2972.

Ciancimino Ltd.   BADA
99 Pimlico Rd. Open 10—6, Sat. 10—1. *STOCK: Oriental, English and European fine and decorative works of art, 18th and 19th C.* **TEL: 730 9950.**

S.W.1 continued

Cobra and Bellamy
149 Sloane St. (V. Manussis and T. Hunter.) Est. 1976. Open 10.30−6. SIZE: Medium. *STOCK: Decorative art and jewellery, 20th C, £50−£1,000.* TEL: 730 2823. VAT: Stan.

Edward Cohen
40 Duke St., St. James's. *STOCK: Paintings.* TEL: 839 5180. VAT: Spec.

The Connoisseur Gallery
14/15 Halkin Arcade, Motcomb Street, Belgravia. (M.Z. Irani.) A.B.A. Est. 1966. Open 10−6. SIZE: Medium. *STOCK: Antiquarian books of the Middle East; Oriental paintings, Islamic works of art, 8th−19th C, £50−£10,000+.* LOC: Between Motcomb St. and Lowndes St. PARK: Easy. TEL: 245 6431/2. SER: Valuations; restorations; buys at auction. VAT: Spec.

Mary Cooke Antiques Ltd.   BADA
15 King St., St. James's. Open Mon.−Fri., Sat. a.m. by appointment. *STOCK: Silver.* TEL: 839 6566. SER: Valuations; restorations; buys at auction. FAIRS: Chelsea Spring and Autumn. VAT: Stan/Spec.

Cornucopia
12 Upper Tachbrook St. Est. 1967. Open 11−6. SIZE: Large. *STOCK: Jewellery, 20th C clothing; accessories.* PARK: Meters. TEL: 828 5752.

Crane Gallery
171A Sloane St., 1st Floor. *STOCK: English folk art and 'Americana', furniture, paintings, quilts, weathervanes.* LOC: 2 mins. from Harrods. TEL: 235 2464.

Csaky's Antiques
20 Pimlico Rd. Open 10−6, Sat. 10−1, or by appointment. *STOCK: Early English and Continental oak furniture; carvings, works of art, unusual Oriental items.* TEL: 730 2068.

Peter Dale Ltd.
11/12 Royal Opera Arcade, Pall Mall. Est. 1955. CL: Sat. Open 9.30−5. SIZE: Medium. *STOCK: Firearms, 16th−19th C; edged weapons, armour, 14th−19th C; militaria.* LOC: Arcade behind Her Majesty's Theatre and New Zealand House. PARK: 350yds. Whitcomb St., Public Garage. TEL: 930 3695. SER: Valuations; buys at auction. FAIRS: Arms, spring and autumn. VAT: Spec.

S.W.1 continued

Arthur Davidson Ltd.   BADA
    LAPADA
78/79 Jermyn St. Est. 1962. (A. and L. Davidson.) CINOA. Article on scientific instruments. CL: Sat. p.m. Open 9.30−5.30. SIZE: Medium. *STOCK: Scientific instruments, 17th−19th C, £500−£10,000; curiosities, 16th−19th C, £500−£8,000; early furniture, 16th−18th C, £1,000−£15,000.* Not stocked: China and glass. LOC: Opposite Dunhills. PARK: Easy. TEL: 930 6687. SER: Valuations. FAIRS: Grosvenor House. VAT: Spec.

Kenneth Davis
38 Bury St. Open 9.30−5. *STOCK: Silver and works of art.* TEL: 930 0313.

Shirley Day Ltd.   BADA
91B Jermyn St. Est. 1967. Appointment advisable. *STOCK: Japanese works of art, paintings, screens, sculptures, ceramics, lacquers; early Chinese, Indian and Korean works of art.* TEL: 839 2804. VAT: Stan/Spec.

de Havilland (Antiques) Ltd.
    LAPADA
48 Sloane St. Est. 1964. *STOCK: 18th C furniture, silver and clocks.* TEL: 235 3534.

The Delightful Muddle
11 Upper Tachbrook St., Victoria. (M. and J. Storey.) Est. 1935. Open Thurs., Fri. and Sat. 12−6. SIZE: Small. *STOCK: China, glass, objets d'art, Victorian and Edwardian, £1−£100; lace, £1−£50; linen, general antiques and bric-a-brac, £3−£65, all to Victorian.* LOC: Near Victoria Station, Upper Tachbrook St. runs into Vauxhall Bridge Rd. at Queen Mother Sports Centre. PARK: Meters.

Douwes Fine Art
38 Duke St., St. James's. Est. 1805. CL: Sat. Open 9.30−5.30. SIZE: Small. *STOCK: Old Master paintings, drawings, watercolours, prints.* PARK: Meters. TEL: 839 5795. VAT: Spec.

William R. Drown
41 St. James's Place. Est. 1938. CL: Sat. Open 9.30−5.30. SIZE: Medium. *STOCK: Old Master paintings.* PARK: Meters. TEL: 493 4711. SER: Restorations. VAT: Spec.

Annamaria Edelstein at Robin Symes
94 Jermyn St. CL: Sat. Open 10−5.30. *STOCK: Old Master drawings.* PARK: Meters. TEL: 930 5300.

Owen Edgar Gallery   BADA
9 West Halkin St. Est. 1977. Open 10−6, Sat. by appointment. *STOCK: Paintings, 18th−19th C and major Victorian.* TEL: 235 8989. VAT: Spec.

Arthur Davidson Ltd.
ANTIQUE DEALERS
78/79 Jermyn Street, London, SW1Y 6NB 01-930 6687/930 4643

S.W.1 continued

M. Ekstein Ltd. **BADA**
90 Jermyn St. (L. Ekstein and B. Forster.) Est. 1946. *STOCK: Jewellery, porcelain, enamel, silver, objets d'art, glass.* TEL: 930 2024.

Elmerside Ltd. **BADA**
85—87 Jermyn St. Open by appointment only. *STOCK: Books, prints, paintings and watercolours.* TEL: 730 4753.

Faustus Fine Art Ltd.
Lower Gallery, 90 Jermyn St. Open 9.30—5.30, Sat. 10—1.*STOCK: Old Master paintings, etchings, antiquities.* TEL: 930 1628. VAT: Spec.

Jocelyn Feilding Fine Art Ltd.
8 Duke St., St. James's. Est. 1970. Open 10—5. *STOCK: Old Master paintings, English paintings and watercolours.* TEL: 839 5040 and 930 2902. VAT: Spec.

Fernandes and Marche **LAPADA**
23 Motcomb St. Est. 1956. CL: Sat. and Sun. except by appointment. Open 9.30—5.30. SIZE: Medium. *STOCK: English furniture; giltwood (mirrors, consoles, etc.), both 18th C.* PARK: Meters. TEL: 235 6773. VAT: Spec.

S.W.1 continued

Kate Foster Ltd. **BADA**
9 Halkin Arcade, Motcomb St. (Mrs. K. and C.M.E. Davson.) Est. 1974. CL: Sat. Open 9.30—5.30. SIZE: Medium. *STOCK: European porcelain and ceramics, 18th C.* LOC: Belgravia, behind Carlton Tower Hotel. PARK: Off Motcomb St. TEL: 245 9848; home — (0797) 222661. SER: Valuations; buys at auction. FAIRS: International Ceramic, Dorchester Hotel. VAT: Stan/Spec.

J.A.L. Franks Ltd.
7 Allington St. Est. 1948. *STOCK: Stamps and maps.* TEL: 834 8697.

S. Franses Ltd. **BADA**
82 Jermyn St., St. James's. Est. 1909. CL: Sat. Open 9—5. SIZE: Large. *STOCK: Historic and decorative tapestries, carpets, fabrics and textiles.* TEL: 235 1888. SER: Valuations. VAT: Spec.

Victor Franses Gallery **BADA**
57 Jermyn St., St. James's. Est. 1948. Open 10—5.30, Sat. 11—1. *STOCK: Oriental and European rugs and carpets, tapestries, needlework; 19th C animalier bronzes.* SER: Valuations; restorations. TEL: 493 6284 and 629 1144.

Fry Gallery

58 Jermyn St., St. James's. (C. and S. Fry.) SLAD. CL: Sat. Open 10—5.30. *STOCK: English watercolours and drawings, 18th—19th C.* TEL: 493 4496. VAT: Spec.

Gallery '25

4 Halkin Arcade, Motcomb St., Belgravia. (D. Iglesis and R. Lawrence.) Est. 1969. Open 10.30—6, Sat. 11—3. SIZE: Medium. *STOCK: Art glass, £100—£5,000; signed furniture, £1,000—£10,000; decorative fine art, £50— £5,000; all 1900-1960.* LOC: Arcade between Motcomb St. and West Halkin St. PARK: Easy. Cadogan Sq. TEL: 235 5178. SER: Valuations; buys at auction (as stock). FAIRS: Camden Arts Centre, Decorative Arts. VAT: Stan/Spec.

Gallery Lingard

50 Pall Mall. CL: Sat. Open 10—6 or by appointment. *STOCK: Architectural drawings and watercolours.* TEL: 930 1645.

General Trading Co. Ltd.   LAPADA

144 Sloane St. (E. Barlow.) Est. 1920. Open 9—5.30, Sat. 9—2. SIZE: Medium. *STOCK: English furniture, £100—£2,000; china, pewter, prints, £20—£500; all 18th—19th C.* PARK: 50yds., underground garage (Cadogan Place). TEL: 730 0411. VAT: Stan/Spec.

David Godfrey's Old Newspaper Shop

37 Kinnerton St., Belgravia. Est. 1972. Open 11.30—5, Wed. until 6.30 and some Sats. but appointment advisable. SIZE: Small. *STOCK: Antiquarian newspapers, from 1665.* LOC: Kinnerton St. runs from Wilton Place (off Knightsbridge) to Motcomb St. PARK: Underground nearby. TEL: 235 7788.

Martyn Gregory Gallery

34 Bury St., St. James's. CL: Sat. Open 10—6. SIZE: Medium. *STOCK: English watercolours and paintings, 18th—19th C, £500—£15,000; specialists in pictures relating to China.* TEL: 839 3731. SER: Valuations. VAT: Spec.

IS YOUR ENTRY CORRECT?
If there is even the slightest inaccuracy in your entry, *please* let us know before 1st January 1987.
GUIDE TO THE
ANTIQUE SHOPS OF BRITAIN
5 Church Street, Woodbridge, Suffolk.

Halsey   BADA

Est. 1950. **Strictly by private arrangement.** *Examples of English 17th—18th C oak, walnut, fruitwood and French provincial furniture; carvings, ceramics, tapestries and complementary furnishings.* LOC: Thames Embankment, nr. Pimlico underground station. PARK: Easy. TEL: 828 5529; head office Kingsbridge, Devon (0548) 2440. SER: Commissions undertaken internationally for interiors (individual rooms or entire houses); valuations; antiques purchasing service. All correspondence to Halsey Antiques, Kingsbridge, Devon. VAT: Spec.

Rosemary Hamilton

44 Moreton St. Est. 1985. Open 9.30—1 and 1.30—5.30, Sat. 9.30—1. SIZE: Small. *STOCK: Small furniture, 1840—1890, £500—£1,000; porcelain and fabrics, £100—£500.* LOC: Off Lupus St., Pimlico. PARK: Easy. TEL: 828 5018; home — same. SER: Restorations; gilding; polishing. VAT: Stan.

Charles Hammond Ltd.

165 Sloane St. Est. 1907. CL: Sat. Open 9—5.30. SIZE: Medium. *STOCK: Furniture, upholstered, painted and decorative, from £100.* LOC: Between Knightsbridge and Sloane Sq. underground stations. PARK: Underground in Cadogan Gdns. TEL: 235 2151. VAT: Stan.

Harari and Johns Ltd.

12 Duke St., St. James's. Open 9.30—6. *STOCK: Old Master paintings.* TEL: 839 7671.

M. Harris and Sons   BADA

Gayfere House, 22/23 Gayfere St. (R.M. Harris.) Est. 1868. Open by appointment. SIZE: Small. *STOCK: English period furniture and works of art.* PARK: Meters. TEL: 222 8161. SER: Buys at auction. VAT: Spec.

Harrods Ltd.

Brompton Rd., Knightsbridge. Open 9—5, Wed. 9—7, Sat. 9—6. SIZE: Large. *STOCK: Fine Victorian, inlaid Edwardian, walnut, oak, mahogany, rosewood furniture; paintings, objets d'art.* PARK: Own — Brompton Rd. TEL: 730 1234, ext. 2759.

Julian Hartnoll

Second Floor, 14 Mason's Yard, Duke St. Est. 1968. Open by appointment. *STOCK: 19th C British paintings, drawings and prints especially pre-Raphaelite.* TEL: 839 3842. VAT: Spec.

Hazlitt, Gooden & Fox Ltd.

38 Bury St., St. James's. CL: Sat. Open 9.30—5.30. SIZE: Large. *STOCK: Paintings and drawings, 19th C French and 18th and 19th C English; Italian baroque and rococo paintings.* PARK: Meters. TEL: 930 6422. SER: Valuations; restorations. VAT: Spec.

S.W.1 continued

Heim Gallery
59 Jermyn St. CL: Sat. Open 9.30—5.30. SIZE: Large. *STOCK: Old Master paintings; sculpture.* PARK: Meters. TEL: 493 0688. VAT: Spec.

Thomas Heneage
42 Duke St., St. James's. Est. 1975. Open 9—5. *STOCK: Reference books on the fine and applied arts, archaeology.* TEL: 930 9223; home — 720 1503. SER: Valuations; restorations (bookbinding); buys at auction.

Heraz
Corner of Halkin Arcade and West Halkin St. (M.J. Puttick.) CL: Sat. Open 11—6. *STOCK: Needlework, decorative carpets, tapestries, 17th—20th C, £50—£25,000.* TEL: 235 7416. SER: Valuations; restorations (hand-made carpets and needlework).

Heraz
25 Motcomb St. (M.J. Puttick.) Est. 1974. CL: Sat. Open 11—6. *STOCK: Textile cushions, £50—£25,000.* TEL: 245 9497. SER: Valuations; restorations (hand-made carpets and needlework).

S.W.1 continued

Hermitage Antiques
97 Pimlico Rd. (B. Vieux-Pernon.) Est. 1967. Open 10—6, Sat. 10—1.30, Sun. by appointment. SIZE: Large. *STOCK: Decorative, French provincial and Biedermeier furniture, 17th—19th C, £150—£15,000.* Not stocked: Silver and jewellery. LOC: Off Sloane Square. PARK: Easy. TEL: 730 1973. VAT: Stan/Spec.

Hobhouse Ltd.
39 Duke St., St. James's. (N. Hobhouse.) Est. 1968. CL: Sat. except by appointment. Open 10—5.30. SIZE: Medium. *STOCK: Late 18th and 19th C oils, watercolours, drawings especially Oriental and European natural history, prints, European artists in India/Far East, Oriental and Colonial topography.* TEL: 930 9308. VAT: Spec.

S.W.1 continued

Christopher Hodsall
69 and 50 Pimlico Rd. Open 10—7. *STOCK: 18th—19th C decorative furniture, carpets and rugs, paintings, English and Oriental pottery and porcelain.* TEL: 730 9835.

Hotspur Ltd. BADA
14 Lowndes St. (R.A.B. and B.S. Kern.) Est. 1924. Open 8.30—6, Sat. 9.30—1. SIZE: Large. *STOCK: English furniture, 1690—1800.* LOC: Between Belgrave Square and Lowndes Square. PARK: 2 underground within 100yds. TEL: 235 1918. VAT: Spec.

How of Edinburgh
2—3 Pickering Place, St. James's St. (Mrs. G.E.P. How.) Est. 1930. CL: Sat. Open 9.45—5.30. *STOCK: Silver, to 1800.* LOC: Entry between 3 and 4 St. James's St. PARK: Easy. TEL: 930 7140. VAT: Stan/Spec.

Sally Hunter and Patrick Seale Fine Art
2 Motcomb St. CL: Sat. Open 10—6. *STOCK: British art, 1920 to date.* TEL: 235 0934.

Iconastas BADA
5 Piccadilly Arcade. Open 10—6, Sat. 10—1, other times by appointment. *STOCK: Russian and Greek icons, Russian works of art, Fabergé, 13th to early 20th C.* TEL: 629 1433.

Brand Inglis BADA
9 Halkin Arcade, Motcomb St. CL: Sat. Open 9.30—5.30, or any time by appointment. *STOCK: Silver, all periods.* TEL: 235 6604.

Alan Jacobs Gallery BADA
8 Duke St., St. James's. SLAD. Est. 1970. CL: Sat. Open 10—5. SIZE: Large. *STOCK: Dutch and Flemish 17th C Old Master paintings.* TEL: 930 3709. SER: Valuations; restorations; framing; buys at auction. VAT: Spec.

Michael John Decorative Arts Ltd.
25a Lowndes St. CL: Sat. Open 2—6. *STOCK: English pottery, Continental pottery and porcelain, paintings, furniture, 19th C.* TEL: 235 3154/5.

Oscar and Peter Johnson Ltd.BADA
Lowndes Lodge Gallery, 27 Lowndes St. Est. 1963. CL: Sat. p.m. Open 9.30—5. SIZE: Medium. *STOCK: English paintings, 18th—19th C.* PARK: Meters. TEL: 235 6464. SER: Valuations; restorations. VAT: Spec.

Ruth Joly
32 Moreton St., Pimlico. Open 10—5, Sun. by appointment. SIZE: Medium. *STOCK: Period furniture and decorative items.* TEL: 834 2798.

S.W.1 continued

David Ker Fine Art
85 Bourne St. Est. 1981. Open 9.30—1 and 2—5.30., Sat. and Sun. by appointment. SIZE: Medium. *STOCK: Watercolours, 1780—1950, £30—£1,500; decorative prints, 1780—1930, £50—£250; decorative oils, 1750—1950, £100—£5,000; antique paste jewellery.* LOC: 2 mins. from Sloane Sq. tube station; Bourne St. is parallel to Eaton Terrace. PARK: Easy. TEL: 730 3523; home — 223 6464. SER: Valuations; restorations: cleaning and repair; buys at auction. VAT: Spec.

Khachadourian Gallery
60 Pall Mall. (M. Khachadourian). Est: 1965. Open 9.30—6, Sat. by appointment. SIZE: Medium. *STOCK: Furniture, automobile art and other art deco items, £500—£1,000+.* PARK: Easy. TEL: 930 3333. SER: Valuations; restorations (upholstery, framing); buys at auction. FAIRS: Beaulieu Auto-jumble, Hershes U.S.A. VAT: Stan/Spec.

King Street Galleries
17 King St., St. James's. Open 9.30—5.30, Sat. 9.30—1. *STOCK: Paintings and water-colours, 19th—20th C.* TEL: 930 3993/9392.

Knightsbridge Coins
43 Duke St., St. James's. CL: Sat. Open 10—6. *STOCK: Coins — British, American and South African; medals.* TEL: 930 7597 or 930 8215.

Lane Fine Art Ltd. BADA LAPADA
86/88 Pimlico Rd. (C. Foley.) Open 10—6, Sat. 10—2. *STOCK: Oil paintings 1400—1830; Old Masters, sporting paintings and early portraits, £1,000—£50,000+.* TEL: 730 7374. VAT: Stan/Spec.

Lasson Gallery
34 Duke St., St James's. (Z. Lasson.) Est. 1949. Open 10.30—5.30, Sat. 11—1. *STOCK: 19th—20th C French paintings and Old Masters.* TEL: 930 5950.

S.W.1 continued

Leggatt Brothers
17 Duke St., St. James's. (H. Leggatt.) Est. 1820. CL:Sat. Open 9.30—5. SIZE: Large. *STOCK: Oil paintings, 17th to early 19th C.* LOC: Next to Cavendish Hotel. PARK: Easy. TEL: 930 3772.

Paul Longmire Ltd.
12 Bury St., St. James's. Open 9—5. *STOCK: Antique jewellery, cufflinks, signet rings, objects of art and virtue.* LOC: Coming from Piccadilly, down Duke St., right into King St., first right into Bury St. PARK: Easy. TEL: 930 8720. SER: Enamelling and engraving cufflinks, heraldic seal engravings.

Loot
76—78 Pimlico Rd. and 26 Holbein Place. (Mrs. G. Goldsmith.) Est. 1967. Open 10—1 and 2—6. SIZE: Medium. *STOCK: Decorative and Oriental objects, furniture, 1650—1900.* PARK: Easy. TEL: 730 8097; home — 352 0135. VAT: Stan/Spec.

S.W.1 continued

N.W. Lott and H.J. Gerrish Ltd.
Flat 1, 19 Mason's Yard, Duke St., St. James's. Open by appointment. *STOCK: 19th and 20th C etchings and engravings, some drawings.* TEL: 930 1353.

MacConnal Mason Gallery   BADA
14 Duke St., St. James's. Est. 1893. Open 9—6. SIZE: Large. *STOCK: Pictures, 19th—20th C.* PARK: Meters. TEL: 839 7693 and 499 6991. SER: Valuations; restorations. VAT: Spec.

Rodd McLennan
24 Holbein Place. Est. 1971. Open 9.30—1 and 2—6, Sat. 9.30—1. *STOCK: Biedermeier, Empire, bronze, ormolu, marble accessories.* TEL: 730 6330. VAT: Spec.

The Mall Galleries
17 Carlton House Terrace. Open 10—5 seven days. *STOCK: Paintings.* TEL: 930 6844.

Paul Mason Gallery BADA LAPADA

149 Sloane St. Est. 1969. Open 9—6, Wed. 9—7, Sat. 9—1. *STOCK: Marine, sporting and decorative paintings and prints, 18th—19th C; period and old frames, portfolio stands; ship models.* LOC: Sloane Sq. end of Sloane St. PARK: Easy. TEL: 730 3683/7359. SER: Valuations; restorations (prints, paintings); buys at auction. FAIRS: England and Europe. VAT: Stan/Spec.

Mathaf Gallery Ltd. LAPADA

24 Motcomb St. Est. 1975. Open 9.30—5.30, Sat. by appointment. *STOCK: Paintings, Middle East subjects, 19th C.* TEL: 235 0010. SER: Valuations.

Matthiesen Fine Art Ltd. and Matthiesen Works of Art Ltd.

7-8 Mason's Yard, Duke St., St. James's. Est. 1978. CL: Sat. Open 10—6 or by appointment. *STOCK: Fine Italian Old Master paintings, 1300—1800; French and Spanish Old Master paintings; selected 20th C works; sculpture.* TEL: 930 2437. SER: Valuations; buys at auction.

Mayfair Carpet Gallery Ltd.

91 Knightsbridge. (A.H. Khawaja.) Open 9.30—6.30. *STOCK: Hand-made carpets.* TEL: 235 2541 or 245 9749.

Mayorcas Ltd. BADA

38 Jermyn St. (M.J., J.D. and L.G. Mayorcas.) Est. 1930. CL: Sat. p.m. Open 9.30—5.30. SIZE: Medium. *STOCK: Tapestries, textiles, embroideries, needlework, church vestments, European carpets and rugs.* TEL: 629 4195. SER: Valuations; restorations. VAT: Stan/Spec.

Richard Miles Antiques

8 Holbein Place. Est. 1974. CL: Sat. except by appointment. Open 10—1 and 2—6. SIZE: Medium. *STOCK: Unusual furniture and works of art, 18th to early 19th C, £500—£5,000.* LOC: Between Sloane Sq. and Pimlico Rd. PARK: Easy. TEL: 730 1957. SER: Buys at auction. VAT: Spec.

Lennox Money (Antiques) Ltd.

93 Pimlico Rd. (L.B. Money.) Est. 1964. CL: Sat. p.m. Open 9.45—6. SIZE: Large. *STOCK: Indian, colonial and Oriental furniture; chandeliers.* LOC: 200yds. south of Sloane Sq. TEL: 730 3070. VAT: Spec.

Morton Morris and Co.

32 Bury St., St. James's. (J. Morton Morris.) CL: Sat. Open 9.30—5.30, or by appointment. *STOCK: English paintings and drawings. Old Master paintings, 17th—19th C.* TEL: 930 2825. VAT: Spec.

Guy Morrison

91c Jermyn St. CL: Sat. Open 9.30—5.30. *STOCK: Watercolours and oils, 18th to early 20th C.* TEL: 930 8008.

Murray-Brown

18 Halkin Arcade, Belgravia. (G. and J. Murray-Brown.) Est. 1960. *STOCK: Paintings and prints.* TEL: 235 8353 or Eastbourne (0323) 764298. SER: Restoration and cleaning (oils, watercolours and prints).

Peter Nahum

5 Ryder St. CL: Sat. and Sun. except by appointment. Open 9.30—5.30. SIZE: Large. *STOCK: British and European paintings, drawings and bronzes, 19th—20th C, £500—£500,000.* LOC: 100 yards from Royal Academy. PARK: Meters. TEL: 930 6059. SER: Valuations. VAT: Spec.

Nimrod Dix and Co., Military Antiquarian

17 Piccadilly Arcade, Piccadilly. CL: Sat. Open 10—5. SIZE: Small. *STOCK: British and foreign orders, decorations and medals, late 18th C to date, £1—£10,000.* LOC: Between Piccadilly and Jermyn St. TEL: 493 5082. SER: Valuations; buys at auction (orders, medals and decorations). VAT: Stan/Spec.

Ning Ltd.

58 Cambridge St. (Mrs P. Grant.) Est. 1963. CL: Sat. Open 10—6. *STOCK: Decorative furniture pre-1860; period pine; Spode, Wedgwood, Davenport and blue and white porcelain; small decorative items.* PARK: Meters. TEL: 834 3292. VAT: Spec.

Northfield Antiques (Belgravia)

18 Halkin Arcade, Belgravia. (B. Jackson.) Est. 1959. CL: Mon. and Sat. Open 10—1 and 2—6. SIZE: Small. *STOCK: Porcelain, silver, jewellery and oil paintings.* LOC: Next to Lowndes Hotel. PARK: Motcombe St. TEL: 235 8385. VAT: Stan/Spec.

Old Drawings Gallery

15 King St., St. James's. (G.T. Siden.) CL: Sat. Open 10—5. SIZE: Small. *STOCK: Drawings, 16th—19th C.* TEL: 930 7462; home — 624 9045. SER: Valuations; restorations.

Old London Gallery

15 Royal Opera Arcade, Pall Mall. (Mrs. V. Malmed.) CL: Sat. Open 12—5.30. *STOCK: Prints, 18th—19th C, from £5, some hand coloured and London.* LOC: Near the Haymarket. TEL: 930 7679. SER: Valuations; buys at auction; mounting; framing.

Old Maps and Prints LAPADA

4th Floor, Harrods, Knightsbridge. Est. 1976. *STOCK: Maps, 16th C to 1880; prints, watercolours and oils to 1880; sporting restrikes; Christie's signed, limited edition graphics.* TEL: 730 1234, ext. 2124.

S.W.1 continued

Omell Galleries   LAPADA
22 Bury St., St. James's. Est. 1949. CL: Sat. Open 10—6. SIZE: Large. STOCK: English and Continental paintings, 19th C, £1,000—£15,000. LOC: From Jermyn St. last street on left hand side (coming from Piccadilly to St. James's St.). PARK: Easy. TEL: 839 4274. SER: Restorations. VAT: Stan/Spec.

Omell Galleries   LAPADA
43a Duke St., St. James's. Open 10—6. SIZE: Large. STOCK: Old Master and Continental oil paintings, 19th C, £5,000—£50,000. LOC: Corner of Ryder St. TEL: 930 7744/5. SER: Restorations; framing.

N.R. Omell
6 Duke St., St. James's. Est. 1968. STOCK: 19th C English landscape and marine oil paintings. TEL: 839 6223/4. VAT: Spec.

Hal O'Nians
King St. Gallery, 17 King St., St. James's. Est. 1951. Open weekdays 9.30—5.30, Sat. 9.30—1. SIZE: Medium. STOCK: Paintings, 15th—20th C. TEL: 930 9392/3993. SER: Valuations; framing; restorations. VAT: Spec.

O'Shea Gallery   BADA
89 Lower Sloane St. ABA. Open 9.30—6, Sat. 9.30—1. STOCK: Maps, topographical, decorative natural history, sporting and marine prints; rare atlases, illustrated books, 15th—19th C, £5—£25,000. LOC: Near Sloane Sq. TEL: 730 0081/2. SER: Decorative framing; restorations. VAT: Stan/Spec.

Alec Ossowski
83 Pimlico Rd. Est. 1956. CL: Sat. p.m. Open 9—6. SIZE: Medium. STOCK: Carved gilt, 18th C; mirrors, wood carvings. TEL: 730 3256. SER: Valuations; restorations (gilt furniture). VAT: Stan/Spec.

Michael Parkin Fine Art Ltd.
11 Motcomb St. Open 10—6, Sat. 10—1. STOCK: British paintings, watercolours, drawings and prints, 1850—1950, £50—£10,000. PARK: Easy. TEL: 235 1845. VAT: Spec.

Pawsey and Payne   BADA
4 Ryder St., St. James's. (Hon. N.V.B. and L.N.J. Wallop.) SLAD. Est. 1910. CL: Sat. Open 9.30—5.30. SIZE: Large. STOCK: English and European paintings, 18th—20th C; oils, watercolours. PARK: Meters. TEL: 930 4221. SER: Valuations; restorations. VAT: Spec.

S.W.1 continued

Pickering and Chatto Ltd.
Incorporating Dawsons of Pall Mall. 17 Pall Mall. Est. 1820. CL: Sat. Open 9.30—5.30. SIZE: Large. STOCK: English literature, economics, politics, philosophy, science, medicine, manuscripts and autographs. LOC: 300 yds. on right from Trafalgar Sq. PARK: Easy. TEL: 930 2515.

Polak Gallery   BADA
21 King St., St. James's. Est. 1854. CL: Sat. Open 9.30—5.30. SIZE: Small. STOCK: English and Continental, 18th—19th C oils and watercolours. PARK: Meters. TEL: 930 9245. SER: Valuations; restorations. VAT: Spec.

Pyms Gallery
13 Motcomb St., Belgravia. (A. and M. Hobart.) Est. 1975. CL: Sat. Open 10—6. STOCK: British, Irish and French paintings, 19th—20th C. TEL: 235 3050. SER: Valuations; restorations; buys at auction. VAT: Spec.

J.A. Redmile Ltd.
95 Pimlico Rd. Est. 1965. Open 9.30—6. SIZE: Large. STOCK: Unusual decorative objects and furniture. TEL: 730 0557. VAT: Stan.

Geoffrey Rose Ltd.   BADA
77 Pimlico Rd. Est. 1961. CL: Sat. p.m. Open 9.30—1 and 2—6. SIZE: Medium. STOCK: English furniture, late 18th to early 19th C. TEL: 730 3004.

Ross Hamilton Ltd.   LAPADA
Antiques
73 Pimlico Rd. STOCK: Furniture, pictures and objects, 18th—19th C. TEL: 730 3015.

Barry Sainsbury
145 Ebury St. STOCK: Chinese and Japanese furniture and lacquer. TEL: 730 3393. VAT: Spec.

Saint George's Gallery Books Ltd.
8 Duke St., St. James's. Est. 1948. CL: Sat. p.m. Open 10—6. STOCK: Rare books on fine art. PARK: Meters. TEL: 930 0935. SER: Catalogues available, lists of new titles issued regularly.

Thomas E. Schuster
9 Gillingham St. Est. 1973. CL: Sat. Open 10—5.30 or by appointment. SIZE: Medium. STOCK: Prints, 1600—1890, £30—£1,000; books, 1490—1890, £200—£20,000; atlases, 1570—1780, £1,000—£10,000; some maps. LOC: From Victoria Station into Wilton Rd., then into Gillingham St. PARK: At rear. TEL: 828 7963. SER: Valuations (antiquarian books); buys at auction (rare and valuable books, atlases and colour-plate books worth over £500 each). FAIRS: ABA Park Lane, Hotel Russell. VAT: Stan.

S.W.1 continued

Sims, Reed and Fogg Ltd.
58 Jermyn St. Open 10—6, Sat. by appointment. *STOCK: Rare and out-of-print books on the fine and applied arts; illustrated books.* TEL: 493 5660/0952.

John Carlton Smith BADA
17 Ryder St. St James's. CL: Sat. Open 9.30—5.30. *STOCK: Clocks, barometers, chronometers, 17th—19th C.* **TEL: 930 6622. SER: Valuations. VAT: Spec.**

Peta Smyth — Antique Textiles
42 Moreton St., Pimlico. Est. 1977. CL: Sat. Open 10—5.30. SIZE: Small. *STOCK: European textiles and needlework, 17th—19th C, £5—£500; country furniture.* PARK: Easy. TEL: 630 9898. SER: Restorations (textiles). FAIRS: Olympia. VAT: Stan.

George Spencer Decorations Ltd.
36 Sloane St. Est. 1945. *STOCK: Decorative items, lamps, carpets, pictures, bibelots.* TEL: 235 1501. VAT: Stan/Spec.

Spink and Son Ltd. BADA
5—7 King St., St. James's. Est. 1666. CL: Sat. Open 9.30—5.30. SIZE: Large. *STOCK: English paintings, watercolours, silver, jewellery; paperweights, Chinese, Japanese, Indian; Greek and Roman to present day coins, banknotes, bullion, orders, medals and decorations, numismatic books, Indian, South East Asian, Persian and Islamic art.* **PARK: Meters. TEL: 930 7888. SER: Valuations; buys at auction; commission sales on behalf of private collectors; coin auctions. VAT: Stan/Spec.**

Gerald Spyer and Son (Antiques) Ltd.
18 Motcomb St., Belgrave Sq. Est. 1860. CL: Sat. Open 10—6. SIZE: Large. *STOCK: Furniture, mostly English, pre-1830; gilt mirrors, 18th C; bronze and ormolu decorative items, all £750—£125,000.* LOC: In area between Sloane Sq. Hyde Park Corner and Knightsbridge. PARK: Easy. TEL: 235 3348. SER: Buys at auction. VAT: Spec.

Pamela Streather BADA
The Pink House, 4 Studio Place, Kinnerton St. CINOA. Est. 1964. Open by appointment. *STOCK: Works of art; furniture, 16th—17th C.* **TEL: 235 3450 or (0844) 208859. VAT: Spec.**

Robin Symes Ltd.
3 Ormond Yard, Duke of York St., St. James's and 94 Jermyn St. CL: Sat. Open 10—5.30. SIZE: Large. *STOCK: Antiquities, ancient art,* PARK: Meters. TEL: 930 9856/7 or 930 5300.

William Thuillier
10a West Halkin St. Open by appointment. *STOCK: Old Master paintings and drawings; post Impressionists.* TEL: 235 3543.

S.W.1 continued

Trafalgar Galleries BADA
35 Bury St., St. James's. (B. Cohen and Sons.) CL: Sat. Open 9.30—6. *STOCK: Old Master and 19th C paintings.* **LOC: Just south of Piccadilly. TEL: 839 6466/7.**

Trove
71 Pimlico Rd. (P.S. Roe and J.P.D. Smith.) Est. 1969. CL: Sat. p.m. Open 10—6. SIZE: Medium. *STOCK: Furniture, bronzes, sporting paintings and decorative items.* PARK: Easy. TEL: 730 6514. SER: Restorations (paintings and furniture); buys at auction. VAT: Spec.

Rafael Valls
6 Ryder St., St. James's. Est. 1975. CL: Sat. Open 9.30—6. *STOCK: Old Master, 18th and 19th C paintings.* TEL: 930 0029. VAT: Spec.

Johnny Van Haeften Ltd. BADA
13 Duke St., St. James's. (J. and S. Van Haeften.) Est. 1978. Open 10—6, Sat. and Sun. by appointment. SIZE: Medium. *STOCK: Dutch and Flemish Old Master paintings, 16th—17th C, £5,000—£500,000.* **LOC: Middle of Duke St. TEL: 930 3062/3. SER: Valuations; restorations (Old Masters); buys at auction (Old Masters and other paintings). VAT: Spec.**

S.W.1 continued

Edric Van Vredenburgh
37 Bury St., St. James's. Est. 1961. CL: Sat. Open 10—1 and 2—5.30. SIZE: Small. STOCK: European decorative arts, 1500—1800; sculpture, early objects; Oriental decorative arts, 18th—19th C. LOC: Around corner from Christies. PARK: Easy. TEL: 839 5818/9; home — same. SER: Valuations; buys at auction. VAT: Stan/Spec.

G.B. Vanderkar and Sabin and Vanderkar (Fine Paintings) Ltd.
BADA
43 Duke St., St. James's. Est. 1939. CL: Sat. Open by appointment. STOCK: Dutch, Flemish paintings, all periods. PARK: Meters. TEL: 839 1091. VAT: Spec.

V.C. Vecchi and Sons
23 Great Smith St. Est. 1970. Open 10—6. SIZE: Medium. STOCK: Greek, Roman, Byzantine, medieval and modern coins. Not stocked: Antiques before 500AD. LOC: Close to Westminster Abbey. PARK: Easy. TEL: 222 4459. SER: Valuations; buys at auction (coins); coin auctions. VAT: Stan/Spec.

S.W.1 continued

Valerie Wade
89 Ebury St. CL: Sat. p.m. Open 10—6. STOCK: Decorative furniture including Regency; Victorian paper mâché trays and furniture; textiles, garden urns and lamps. LOC: Ebury St. is a continuation of Pimlico Rd. TEL: 730 3822.

Watts and Christensen
54 Cambridge St. (C.E.H. Watts and H.O. Christensen.) Est. 1979. CL: Sat. Open 9—1 and 2—5.30 but resident so usually available at other times. STOCK: Continental and English furniture, 18th—19th C, £100—£2,000; unusual Continental and English pieces, £50—£1,500. LOC: One minute from Pimlico Rd. over Ebury Bridge. PARK: Easy. TEL: 834 3554. VAT: Spec.

Westenholz Antiques
68, 80 and 82 Pimlico Rd. (P. Von Westenholz.) CL: Sat. Open 10—6. STOCK: Furniture, 18th—19th C. TEL: 730 2151/7004.

MARIA ANDIPA
ICON GALLERY

162 Walton Street, London, S.W.3.
Tel: 01 589 2371.

Icon on panel depicting St. Marina the priestess, holding a cross and a feather, symbolising her martyrdom, wearing a nun's robe of aubergine, brown and ochre on a bright blue background.
Monastic Greek-Macedonian c.1650.
24.5 x 18cm.

S.W.1 continued

David Weston Ltd.
44 Duke St., St. James's. (D.A. Weston.) Est. 1968. CL: Sat. Open 9.30−1 and 2−5.30, appointment advisable. SIZE: Medium. *STOCK: Scientific instruments, 17th−18th C, £300− £25,000; marine antiques.* LOC: Near Christie's. PARK: Meters. TEL: 839 1051/2/3. SER: Valuations. VAT: Stan/Spec.

Whitford and Hughes
6 Duke St. St. James's. (A. Mibus, D. Hughes.) Est. 1972. Open 10−6, Sat. by appointment. *STOCK: Oil paintings £500− £250,000, Belle Epoque, Salon Academy, Vienna Secession, Symbolist, Middle Eastern and Australian.* TEL: 930 5577/9332. VAT: Spec.

Winifred Williams   BADA
3 Bury St., St. James's. (R. Williams.) Est. 1945. CL: Sat. Open 10.30−4.15. *STOCK: Rare European porcelain, English enamels; all 18th C.* PARK: Easy. TEL: 930 4732/0729. VAT: Spec.

Woods Wilson
103 Pimlico Rd. (H. Woods Wilson.) Open 10−6. *STOCK: Japanese lacquer, Oriental porcelain.* TEL: 730 2558.

Christopher Wood Gallery   BADA
15 Motcomb St., Belgravia. Est. 1977. CL: Sat. Open 9−5.30. *STOCK: Victorian paintings, drawings, watercolours, sculpture, studio pottery, photography, illustrated books.* TEL: 235 9141/2. VAT: Spec.

London S.W.3

Norman Adams Ltd.   BADA
8/10 Hans Rd., Knightsbridge. Est. 1923. Open 9−5.30, Sat. and Sun. by appointment. SIZE: Large. *STOCK: English furniture, 18th C, £650−£150,000; objets d'art (English and French) £500−£10,000; mirrors, glass, pictures, 18th C.* LOC: 30yds. off the Brompton Rd. opp. west side entrance to Harrods. TEL: 589 5266. FAIRS: Grosvenor House. VAT: Spec.

Maria Andipa Icon Gallery   BADA
                                    LAPADA
162 Walton St. CINOA. Est. 1968. Open 10.30−6. Sat. till 2. *STOCK: Icons, Greek, Russian, Byzantine, Coptic, Syrian; country furniture, crosses, crucifixes, embroidery, ethnic jewellery.* TEL: 589 2371. SER: Valuations, restorations; buys at auction. FAIRS: Chelsea. VAT: Spec.

S.W.3 continued

Antiquarius Antique Market
135/141 King's Rd. Est. 1970. Open 10—6.
Below are listed some of the many specialist
dealers at this market. LOC: On the corner of
King's Rd. and Flood St., next to Chelsea
Town Hall. TEL: Enquiries 351 5353.
Adrienne
Y2-3. *Clothing, period styles made in
antique materials.* TEL. 351 5171.
Trevor Allen
U2-3. *Jewellery, and objects d'art, rings
18th—19th C.* TEL: 352 7061.
Nigel Appleby — Jarona Antiques
P2. *General antiques, lighting and cork-
screws.* TEL: 352 8882.
Billi Arena
E5. *General antiques, silver plate.* TEL:
352 8734.
S. Artake
V7. *Watches, pens and lighters.* TEL: 352
4739.
Emidia Arzeni
A6. *General antiques.* TEL: 352 7989.
Mr. and Mrs. Bach
E3/E4. *Art deco and art nouveau, glass
and china.* TEL: 352 8734.
Natasha Barbic and Milena Bosch
P7/P8. *General antiques.* TEL: 352 8882.
M. Barham.
Z8. *Clothing.* TEL: 352 4690.
Mrs. B. Barker
Z2. *General antiques, brass, copper.* TEL:
352 7989.
P. Beedles
A13. *Art nouveau and art deco.* TEL: 352
4545.
Miss B. Bental
K3/K4. *Jewellery.* TEL: 351 1102.
Brenda Bentel
Q8. *Jewellery.* TEL: 352 8882.
Sue Biddulph and Sue Banham
Y5. *Clothing.* TEL: 351 9463.
Alexander Bolla
J1. *Jewellery.* TEL: 352 7989.
Joanna Booth
W1-2. *Textiles, furniture and cushions.*
TEL: 352 4739.
William Brown
L5-7. *Prints especially botanicals.* TEL:
352 7217.
Miss K. Brunner
M2. *Tiles.* TEL: 352 7989.
S. Brynolf
D1. *Antiquarian decorative arts and crafts,
glass, porcelain.* TEL: 351 6004.
C. Butterworth
B2/C1/2. *Decorative antiques including
lighting.* TEL: 352 3583.
Bygones
M.12. *Commemoratives.* TEL: 352 4690.
Mrs. M. Campbell
A9/10. *General antiques.* TEL: 352 1460.
Mrs. V. Carroll
P6. *Jewellery and small objects.* TEL: 352
8882.

Antiquarius Antique Market continued

John Cavendish
K5/6. *General antiques.* TEL: 352 7989.
K.L. Chan
V17. *Jewellery.* TEL: 352 4739; 352
7989.
Chelsea Clocks
Z3/Z4. *Clocks, general antiques, brass,
metalware, lighting, early telephones.* TEL:
352 8646.
Nonaka Chizumi
W11. *Jewellery.* TEL: 351 7032.
Eliaho Cohen
Q2. *General antiques, Oriental art.* TEL:
351 7038.
B. Collie
V14/V15. *Jewellery.* TEL: 352 8687; 352
4739; 352 7989.
John G. Connor
V28. *'50s art nouveau and art deco, jewel-
lery and accessories.* TEL: 352 4739.
Mrs S. Cordas
E6. *Furniture and brass.* TEL: 352 7989.
Mrs. M.W. Costiff
W7. *Art nouveau and art deco jewellery.*
TEL: 352 4739.
Jane Course
L1. *General antiques — clocks, boxes,
treen.* TEL: 352 7989.
J. Cowan
M14-15. *Jewellery, pictures, furniture.*
TEL: 352 7989.
Sandie Craine and Ian Torr
U9. *Clothing and accessories.* TEL: 352
4690.
Mr. Crowley
X7. *Clothing and textiles.* TEL: 352 4690.
Mrs. J. Dalby
X2/X3. *Fashion.* TEL: 352 4690.
D. Davies
Q1. *Arms and armour.* TEL: 352 8734.
P. Defresne
t/a Beaubijon. Q9-10. *Costume jewellery.*
TEL: 352 8882.
Mrs. M. Dewenny
V23. *General antiques and jewellery.* TEL:
352 4739.
Anthony Durante and Ephrain Garcia
V26. *Jewellery, art deco and '50s.* TEL:
352 4739.
Caroline Eavis
Z5-7. *Own design beaded dresses.* TEL:
351 5757.
S. Emerson
V20. *Corkscrews.* TEL: 352 4739.
Patricia Evans
M6/U4. *Dolls and accessories.* TEL: 352
2879; 352 7061.
Eves Lace
X5/X6. *Lace and accessories.* TEL: 351
0175.
J. Feleyuska and Mrs. M. Parker
P4/P5. *Antiques and paintings.* TEL: 352
8882.

ABC
antique centres
London's finest centres and busiest markets

135/141 Kings Rd. Chelsea London SW3
Open Monday to Saturday 10am to 6pm

Roger's **A***ntiques Gallery*
65 Portobello Road
London W11
Open every Saturday 7am to 5pm

Bermondsey antique market
& Open Friday mornings 5am to 2pm
Antique Hypermarket
Open Monday to Friday
On the corner of
Long Lane and
Bermondsey St.
London SE1

Bond St.
ANTIQUE CENTRE
124 NEW BOND STREET W1

124 New Bond Street
London W1
Open Monday to Friday
10am to 5.45pm
Saturday 10am to 4pm

Camden antique &
collectors market
Corner of Camden High St. and
Buck St. **Camden Town NW1**
Open Thursday mornings 7am to 1pm

Cutler Street
antique market
Goulston St. (Aldgate end) EC1
for gold, silver, jewellery, gems,
coins and stamps
Open Sunday morning 7am to 2pm

181/183 Kings Rd. Chelsea
London SW3
Open Monday to Saturday
10am to 6pm

Information from the Press Office 15 Flood Street London SW3 01-351 5353 Telex 894638

David Fielden
U1/139. *Antique wedding dresses.* TEL: 351 1745; home — 274 8788.
A. Fothergill
X8. *Period fashion.* TEL: 352 4690.
E. Freestone
J5. *Nautical instruments, artefacts, models.* TEL: 352 4690.
Paddy Frost
P1. *Tiles.* TEL: 352 2203; home — 741 0051.
Mr Garcia and Mr Sulaiman
V24/V25. *Prints, general antiques, jewellery.* TEL: 352 4739.
J. Gendler
E1. *General antiques.* TEL: 352 7989; home — 458 9722.
S.A. Geris
P3. *Watches and clocks.* TEL: 352 8882.
C. Gibson
M10. *Silver and plate, general antiques.* TEL: 352 4690; home — 672 7732.
Mr Gill and Mary Pritchard
A14—A17. *Prints, etchings and lithographs.* TEL: 352 8734; home — 328 6655.
Maurizzio and Loretta Giordani
B4/B5. *Watches.* TEL: 351 4853; 352 7989.
T. Giorgi and Miss S. Dwyer
W4/W5. *Jewellery and bead bags.* TEL: 352 4739.
F. Gonzales
A11/12. *Watches and jewellery.* TEL: 351 2170.
D.M. Green and S. Thorpe
V8. *Silver.* TEL: 351 2911.
W. Green
Q16. *Ivories.* TEL: 352 8882.
R. Gubbins
W3. *Wedding dresses.* TEL: 352 4739.
Mrs. L. Guelfano
L10. *General antiques.* TEL: 352 7989.
Mrs. B. Gunn
N13/N14. *Fans.* TEL: 352 8734.
Micky Hallstroem
P12/P13. *Art deco, jewellery and pewter.* TEL: 352 9471.
Mrs. B. Hamadani
Q14. *General antiques and jewellery.* TEL: 352 8882.
W. Harvey
N6/N7. *Decorative arts, china.* TEL: 352 2203.
Mrs. M.C. Hayman
H3/4, R1/2. *General antiques, frames, treen, scent and ink bottles.* TEL: 351 6568.
J.P. and Mrs. I. Healey
Z1. *Jewellery and general antiques.* TEL: 351 5884.
R. Henson
Q13. *Coins and medals.* TEL: 352 8882.

Maurice Hickley
V16. *Jewellery.* TEL: 352 7989.
Christine Howe
M13. *Postcards.* TEL: 352 7989.
J. Hunter-Smith
N3. *General antiques, art nouveau and art deco.* TEL: 352 2203.
J. and G. Antiques
A7/A8. (Mr. and Mrs. Fefer.) *General antiques, Victorian jewellery and 19th C miniatures.* TEL: 352 7989.
Miss R. Jenkins
V18. *Jewellery and decorative items.* TEL: 352 4739; 352 7989.
Mrs. I.A. Johnson
K1/K2. *Metalware, copper and brass.* TEL: 352 7989.
S. Johnson
T3/4. *Decorative arts.* TEL: 352 8882.
Paul Jones
Y6. *Antique paisleys.* TEL: 352 2117.
Mrs. P.A. Kaskimo
D6. *General antiques.* TEL: 352 7989.
C. Kikas
N1. *Prints.* TEL: 352 8734.
Mrs. B. Kirson
V9. *General antiques.* TEL: 352 4739.
M. Klein
L8/9. *Rare books.* TEL: 351 3820.
R. Lamari
M3/M4. *Jewellery and watches.* TEL: 352 5419.
M. Levy
V13/V19. *Bronzes, art nouveau, glass, porcelain.* TEL: 351 5382/351 7031.
M. Lexton Ltd
G2/G3. *Silver, jewellery, objets d'art, general antiques.* TEL: 352 5980.
A. Lianos and D. Simpson
W10. *Ivory.* TEL: 352 7989.
Andrew Lineham
T5/T6. *Glass, 19th C; English and Continental porcelain, 18th—19th C.* TEL: 352 8882.
Fay Lucas
D2. *Silver and objects.* TEL: 351 6004.
Sue Madden
X9/X10. *Linen, lace, quilts, curtains.* TEL: 351 5767.
Magna Carta Antiques
R3/R4. *General antiques, inkwells, silver, flatware.* TEL: 351 5883.
Henry Man
Q6/Q7. *Art deco, general antiques.* TEL: 352 2099.
John Mansell
N8. *Jewellery.* TEL: 352 2203.
Markov and Beedles
F1/F6. *Jewellery, lighting and watches.* TEL: 352 4545.
G.S. Mathias
R5-8. *Clocks.* TEL: 351 0484; 352 8734.

Antiquarius Antique Market continued

Matthews, Stallbrass and Carter
V5/V6. *General antiques and jewellery.*
TEL: 352 4739.
R. Mee
V11/V12. *Clocks, bronzes, pocket watches.* TEL: 351 7031.
Mrs. E. Mitchell
D3/D4. Silver and plate. TEL: 352 7989.
K. Moffat
V1-4. *Paintings, 19th and 20th C.* TEL: 351 5409.
A. Montilla
V21. *Art nouveau, art deco and 50's items.* TEL: 352 4739.
Mrs. Morrison
J2/J3/J4. *Silver and plate.* TEL: 352 7989.
R.S. and S. Necus
A19/H1/H2. *Silver.* TEL: 352 2405.
Nina
W8/9. (C. Donoghue.) *General antiques, jewellery, masks and fans.* TEL: 351 5999.
Sue Norman
L4. *Blue and white transfer ware.* TEL: 352 7217.
B. O'Brien and H.P. Budhu
A4/5. *Silver, porcelain, furniture and general antiques.* TEL: 352 7989.
Aytac Osman
Q4/Q5. *General antiques, china, from 1900.* TEL: 352 2099.
Louise Packshaw
N12. *Porcelain.* TEL: 352 4690.
H.J. and Miss J. Palmer
M8/M9. *Jewellery and silver.* TEL: 352 4690/7989.
Pamela Furs & Things
Y1 and 4. *Furs and clothing.* TEL: 352 5243.
M. Parker and N. Barbic
Q12. *Paintings.* TEL: 352 8882.
Persiflage
Y8. *Clothing, masks and jewellery.* TEL: 352 4690.
J.H.O. Petkowski
D5. *Watches and jewellery.* TEL: 352 7989.
Miss E. Pollock and Mrs. N. Leon
G1/G4—6. *General antiques, small silver, jewellery and glass.* TEL: 352 8734.
J.J. Proctor, Lucidgate
B1/B6. *Crocodile luggage.* TEL: 352 7989.
The Purple Shop
J6/J9/J10/J11. *Antique and period jewellery and art nouveau.* TEL: 352 1127 or 352 4690.
D. Raynor
N4/N5. *General antiques, china, decorative items.* TEL: 352 2203.
Miss M. Rees
E2. *French faience; English ironstone, Italian majolica.* TEL: 352 8734.

Antiquarius Antique Market continued

K. Reilly
N15/N16. *Art nouveau and art deco.* TEL: 352 8734.
Mrs. G.M. Riley
V10. *General antiques, porcelain and china.* TEL: 352 4739.
J. Roch
M5. *General antiques.* TEL: 352 7989.
Edina Ronay
U7/U8. *Clothing and hand-knitted sweaters.* TEL: 352 1085.
Miss· J. Scott
P9—P11. *General antiques and jewellery.* TEL: 352 8882 or 352 9471.
H. Sedler   **LAPADA**
F2—F5. *Silver, general antiques.* TEL: 351 5000.
Miss S. Shelton
V27. *Jewellery including costume.* TEL: 352 7989.
Mr. and Mrs. Shine
Q15. *General antiques.* TEL: 352 8882.
N. & S. Shorborn
A3. *Antiquities, metalware and treen.* TEL: 352 7989.
D. Shorn
B3. *Jewellery and collector's items.* TEL: 352 8687.
J. Soper
X1. *Silver, plate and general antiques.* TEL: 352 9829.
Paul Steward
M1/M16. *Ethnic jewellery.* TEL: 352 7989.
Jean Terry
Y7. *Clothing.* TEL: 352 4690.
Lt. Col. R.C.W. Thomas
N2. *Silver, china and jewellery.* TEL: 352 2203.
Sue & Alan Thompson
T1/T2 N9—N11. *Jewellery, silver, objets de virtu, enamel and tortoiseshell.* TEL: 352 3494.
Brian Tipping
U6. *Antique pipes.* TEL: 352 3315.
Mrs. J. Tomlin
M7. *General antiques.* TEL: 352 4690.
G. Trotter
Q11. *General antiques.* TEL: 352 8882.
Ursula
P14/P15/P16. *Art nouveau.* TEL: 352 2203.
Salvador Vartuli
V22. *Watches 1900-1950.* TEL: 351 9112.
T.M.V. Viladech
A18. *Militaria, brass, badges, buttons and ephemera.* TEL: 352 8734.
Mrs. T. Walker
L2/L3. *Textiles and jewellery.* TEL: 352 7989.
Mrs. E. Walton
Q3. *Jewellery.* TEL: 352 8882.

Antiquarius Antique Market cotninued

Catherine Williams Antiques
A1/A2. *General antiques and collectors' items.* TEL: 352 7989.
John Charles Wraith
M11. *Jewellery, silver and small items.* TEL: 352 4690.

Apter Fredericks Ltd.   **BADA**
265-267 Fulham Rd. (B. and Mrs. C. Apter.) CL: Sat. Open 9—6. *STOCK: English furniture 17th to early 19th C.* TEL: 352 2188. VAT: Stan/Spec.

H.C. Baxter and Sons   **BADA**
191/193 Fulham Rd. (R.C., T.J., M., J. and G.J. Baxter.) Est. 1928. CL: Sat. Open 8.30—1 and 2.15—5.15. SIZE: Medium. *STOCK: English furniture, 1730—1830, £250— £25,000.* LOC: Next to Royal Marsden hospital, South Kensington nearest station. PARK: Meters. TEL: 352 9826/0807. VAT: Spec.

Joanna Booth   **BADA**
247 King's Rd., Chelsea. Est. 1963. Open 10—6. SIZE: Medium. *STOCK: Wood carvings, sculpture; oak furniture, £50—£5,000; all 17th C; books 17th—19th C, £1—£100; Old Master drawings, fabrics, tapestry.* Not stocked: Silver, glass, pottery, clocks. PARK: Meters. TEL: 352 8998. SER: Buys at auction. VAT: Spec.

The Brotherton Gallery Ltd.
77 Walton St. Est. 1972. Open 10—1.30 and 2.30—5.30. Wed. till 7, Sat. by appointment. *STOCK: Natural history and landscape paintings, English watercolours, 19th—20th C.* TEL: 589 6848. SER: Valuations; restorations; framing; buys at auction; loan exhibitions. VAT: Stan/Spec.

Lorraine Buckland
186 Walton St. Open by appointment. *STOCK: Oils, watercolours, prints and drawings, especially Australian works.* TEL: 584 7268.

Tony Bunzl and Zal Davar LAPADA
344 King's Rd. Open 10—1 and 2—5.30, Sat. by appointment. SIZE: Medium. *STOCK: Furniture, oak and continental, 17th—18th C.* PARK: Easy. TEL: 352 3697. VAT: Stan/Spec.

W.G.T. Burne   **BADA**
(Antique Glass) Ltd.
11 Elystan St. (W.G.T., Mrs. G., R.V. and A.T.G. Burne.) Est. 1936. CL: Thurs. p.m. and Sat. p.m. Open 9—5. SIZE: Large. *STOCK: Glass, collectors' pieces, chandeliers, candelabra, cut glass tableware.* PARK: Meters. TEL: 589 6074. SER: Valuations; renovations. VAT: Stan/Spec.

Butler and Wilson
183-189 Fulham Rd. *STOCK: Jewellery, art deco, crocodile and leather accessories.* TEL: 352 3045.

S.W.3 continued

John Campbell Picture Frames Ltd.
164 Walton St. Open 9.30—5.30, Sat. 9.30—1. *STOCK: Sporting prints, limited editions and lithographs; period and contemporary frames.* TEL: 584 9268. SER: Restorations (oils, watercolours, prints, lithographs); mount cutting; gilding.

Chelsea Antique Market
245A and 253 King's Rd. Est. 1965. Open 10—6. SIZE: Large covered market with approximately 50 dealers. *STOCK: General antiques, especially books and prints.* LOC: From South Kensington underground along Sidney Street to King's Rd., turn right. TEL: 352 5689; stallholders — 352 9695/ 1424. VAT: Stan.

Chelsea Rare Books
313 King's Rd. (L.S. Bernard.) Est. 1968. Open 10—6. *STOCK: Antiquarian books, maps, prints, and watercolours.* TEL: 351 0950. VAT: Stan.

Chenil Galleries Fine Art and Antique Centre
181-183 King's Rd., Chelsea. Est. 1978. Open 10—6. Below are listed some of the many specialist dealers at this market. LOC: Next to Chelsea Town Hall. PARK: Sidney St. TEL: 351 5353. VAT: Stan/Spec.

  G. Accossato
D15. *Small silver, walking sticks and collectables.* TEL: 352 2123.
  A. Acevedo
M1-2 and M5. *Jewellery, objets d'art, watches, 1900—1950.* TEL: 351 0314.
  Nicholas Alloway
U2. *Cameras and photographic works.*
  K. Andrea
E5. *China, glass and collectables.* TEL: 352 8653.
  Antique Martine
E1-2. *Silver and jewellery.* TEL: 352 5964.
  Anthony Barbieri and Daniel Nelson
H1-2/L1. *English and Continental oil paintings, 18th—20th C.* TEL: 352 2123.
  The Box Shop
A13. *Boxes and chess sets.* TEL: 352 2163.
  M. Bristow
C6-7. *Small silver, frames and flatware.* TEL: 352 1285.
  A. Brown
M3-4. *Staffordshire figures and general antiques.* TEL: 352 7384.
  Steven Bubley
G4. *Jewellery, cameras and general antiques.* TEL: 352 2123.
  L. Carter
A6-7. *English drawings and paintings, 18th—20th C.* TEL: 351 2077.
  Chelsea Oriental Carpets
N6-7. *Persian carpets and kelims.* TEL: 351 2123.

Chenil Galleries continued

Cheshire Antiques
B4/5, J1-5. (D. Knight.) *Furniture.* TEL: 351 3901.

B.J. Chilton
A11/12. *Art nouveau, art deco.* TEL: 352 2163.

T. Coakley
D13. *Art deco, art nouveau.* TEL: 351 2914.

John Cox
D3/4. *Decorative art.* TEL: 352 2123.

Judy Daniels
D1. *Art nouveau, deco and jewellery.* TEL: 352 2123.

Jesse Davis
R1-2/R5. *China, furniture, silver, majolica.* TEL: 352 2123.

G. Dewart
C3. *Fine paintings, books and collectables.* TEL: 352 7384.

S. Fields
R3-4. *Watercolours, miniatures, prints, silhouettes, oil paintings, 18th—19th C.* TEL: 352 8653.

Flight of Fancy
D11-12. *Furniture, objets d'art, silver, porcelain.* TEL: 352 4314.

Pauline Fox
K5-7. *General antiques.* TEL: 352 2123.

Chenil Galleries continued

J.P. Gasquet and A. Grant
R6-8. *General antiques, ethnic art, art nouveau, art deco.* TEL: 352 8653.

B. Gordon   **LAPADA**
C4. *Fine silver and Sheffield plate.* TEL: 351 5808; 352 2123.

Barbara Goosens-Berg
G1/2. *General antiques.* TEL: 352 7384.

Grannies Goodies
N1-3/N9-10. *Dolls, small furniture, teddies, toys.* TEL: 352 8653.

Mrs. M. Hayter
D14. *Art nouveau, art deco.* TEL: 351 2914.

D. Howard
B2. *Scientific instruments, nautical and astrological items.* TEL: 352 2163.

Hymore-Hodgson
A8-10. *Longcase and bracket clocks, 18th—19th C.* TEL: 352 9770.

Il Libro
C2 and C8-9. *Books and prints.* TEL: 352 9027; 352 7384.

Mrs. V. Krell
R11. *General antiques, smalls, porcelain, silver, glass.* TEL: 352 2123.

A. Lester, Orientalist
E3. *Oriental paintings, watercolours, works of art.* TEL: 352 0703.

Chenil Galleries continued

O. Lester
B7. *Paintings and prints.* TEL: 352 0703.

Gigi Liliana
B1. *General antiques.* TEL: 352 2163.

Linwick Minerals
G3. (N. Green.) *Minerals.* TEL: 352 2123.

Myra Lustigman
E8. *Victorian jewellery.* TEL: 352 8653.

Agnes McNeill Fine Art
H3. *Oil paintings 18th — 19th C.* TEL: 352 8581.

D. Martin
D5-6. *Small silver, china and glass.* TEL: 352 2123.

Mrs. R. Muggleton
G5. *Furniture, china and bronzes.* TEL: 352 2123.

Nicolaus Antiques
K1-3/K8-10. *Furniture and majolica.* TEL: 352 8790.

Odin Antiques
P1-9/R12-15. *Furniture and accessories, brass, early metalware.* TEL: 352 9066.

Past Times
K4. (G. Hill, C. O'Neill.) *Sporting goods and golfiana.* TEL: 352 7384; 352 2123.

Maria Perez
A5. *Jewellery.* TEL: 351 1933; 352 2163.

Pruskin Gallery
A1-4. (M. and J. Pruskin.) *Art nouveau, art deco, furniture, decorative items, jewellery and watches.* TEL: 352 9095.

Patricia Rhodes and Simon Thorpe
R9-10. *General antiques.* TEL: 352 2123.

St. John's Collection
E6 and E9-10. *Maps and prints, engravings.* TEL: 352 8653.

W.J. Sparrow and B.R. Catley
B6. *Art nouveau and art deco figures.* TEL: 352 7384; 352 2163.

Aubrey Spiers
C5. *English, Continental and Oriental porcelain.* TEL: 352 7384.

N.S. Tullison
N4/5 and 8. *General antiques.* TEL: 352 8653.

Ursula
B3. *Oil paintings, 19th — 20th C.* TEL: 352 2163.

D. Ward
L3-9. *Furniture.* TEL: 351 5881.

Willcocks Antiques
E4/E7. *Books, puppets and general antiques, fans.* TEL: 352 8653.

Clarges Gallery
158 Walton St. (R.J.R. McDougall, E.A. Cruickshank.) Est. 1964. Open 10 — 5.30, other times by appointment. *STOCK: British watercolours, drawings and oils, 19th — 20th C.* TEL: 584 3022. SER: Restorations and framing.

S.W.3 continued

Philip Colleck Ltd.   **BADA**
84 Fulham Rd. (P. Colleck, S.R. Bentley.) Est. 1938. Open 9.30 — 5.30, Sat. 9 — 1. SIZE: Medium. *STOCK: Furniture, English, 17th to early 19th C, £500 — £10,000; works of art.* LOC: Opposite Brompton Hospital. PARK: Easy. TEL: 584 8479. VAT: Spec.

Richard Courtney Ltd.   **BADA**
112 — 114 Fulham Rd. Est. 1959. CL: Sat. Open 9.30 — 1 and 2 — 6.SIZE: Large. *STOCK: English furniture, 18th C, £500 — £20,000.* PARK: Easy. TEL: 370 4020. VAT: Spec.

Colin Denny Ltd.
18 Cale St. Est. 1968. Open 10 — 6. *STOCK: Marine works of art, 19th C.* TEL: 584 0240. VAT: Stan/Spec.

Robert Dickson Antiques Ltd. BADA
263 Fulham Rd. Est. 1969. CL: Sat. Open 9.30 — 5.30. SIZE: Medium. *STOCK: Late 18th and early 19th C decorated furniture and works of art, £500 — £50,000.* PARK: Easy. TEL: 351 0330. VAT: Spec.

Dragons of Walton St. Ltd.
19 and 23 Walton St. (R. Fisher) *STOCK: Mainly painted and decorated furniture; hand decorated children's furniture, decorative items.* LOC: Close to Harrods. PARK: Hasker St. or First St. TEL: 589 3795/0548/5007.

Forty-Eight Walton Street
48 Walton St. Est. 1976. Open 10 — 5.30. SIZE: Medium. *STOCK: English and Continental furniture and decorative works of art, 18th — 19th C, £25 — £5,000.* PARK: Easy. TEL: 581 0213. SER: Buys at auction.

Michael Foster   **BADA**
118 Fulham Rd., Chelsea. Open 9 — 6. *STOCK: 18th C English furniture.* TEL: 373 3636.

C. Fredericks and Son   **BADA**
92 Fulham Rd. (R.F. Fredericks.) Open 9.30 — 5.30, Sat. by appointment. SIZE: Large. *STOCK: Furniture, 18th C, £200 — £10,000.* LOC: Near to South Kensington underground station. PARK: Easy. TEL: 589 5847. SER: Valuations. VAT: Stan/Spec.

Stephen Garratt (Fine Paintings) BADA
146 Brompton Rd. Open 8 — 8 every day, permanent exhibition at Knightsbridge Safe Deposit. *STOCK: Oils and watercolours, 18th — 19th C.* TEL: Home — 603 0861.

Godson and Coles   **BADA**
310 King's Rd. Est. 1978. Open 9.30 — 5.30. *STOCK: English furniture, 18th to early 19th C.* TEL: 352 8509.

Green and Stone
259 Kings Rd. (R.J.S. Baldwin). Est. 1927.
Open 9—6, Wed. 9—7, Sat. 9.30—6. *STOCK:
Writing materials, 18th—19th C, £5—£500;
watercolours, 19th C, £50—£300.* LOC: At
junction of Kings Rd and Old Church St.
PARK: Meters. TEL: 352 0837/6521. SER:
Restorations (pictures and frames). VAT:
Stan.

Robin Greer
30 Sloane Court West. Est. 1965. Open by
appointment. *STOCK: Children's and illustrated books, original illustrations.* TEL: 730
7392. SER: Catalogues issued.

Nicholas Grindley
38 Marlborough, Walton St. Open by appointment. *STOCK: Chinese furniture and Oriental
works of art.* TEL: 584 3473. SER: Valuations; buys at auction. VAT: Spec.

Halliday's Carved Pine
Mantelpieces Ltd.   LAPADA
28 Beauchamp Place. Est. 1948. Open
9.30—5.30. *STOCK: Carved pine and marble
mantelpieces, grates, corner cupboards and
panelling.* TEL: 589 5534. VAT: Stan/Spec.

James Hardy and Co.
235 Brompton Rd. CL: Sat. p.m. Open
9.30—5.30. *STOCK: Silver tableware; silver
and jewellery.* PARK: Meters. TEL: 589 5050.
SER: Valuations.

Heraldry Today
10 Beauchamp Place. (Mrs. R. Pinches.) ABA.
Est. 1954. Open Mon., Tues., and Wed.,
9.30—5. SIZE: Small. *STOCK: Heraldic and
genealogical books, 50p to £1,500.* TEL: 584
1656; home — Marlborough (0672) 20617.

Richard Hewlett Gallery
24 Cale St., Chelsea Green. Est; 1985. Open
9.30—6, Sat. 10—1. SIZE: Medium. *STOCK:
Prints, 16th—19th C, £5—£1,000; maps,
16th—17th C, £100—£2,000.* LOC: Between
Kings Rd. and Fulham Rd., off Sydney St.
PARK: Meters. TEL: 584 8531. SER: Restorations (framing and mounting). VAT: Stan/
Spec.

Michael Hogg Antiques
172 Brompton Rd. Est. 1961. CL: Sat. Open
9.30—6. *STOCK: Furniture, Chinese porcelain.* TEL: 589 8629. VAT: Spec.

E. Hollander   BADA
80 Fulham Rd., South Kensington. (D. Pay.)
Est. 1870. Open 9.30—5.30, Sat. by appointment. *STOCK: Longcase and bracket clocks,
1750—1825; silver, Sheffield plate, English
barometers, 18th—19th C.* LOC: Opposite the
Brompton Chest Hospital. PARK: Easy. TEL:
589 7239 (24 hour answering service). SER:
Restorations (clock mechanisms and cases,
barometers). VAT: Stan/Spec.

Hooper and Purchase
303 Kings Rd., (A.J. Mortimore-Hooper and S.
Purchase.) Est. 1969. Open 9.30—5.45,
Sunday by appointment only. SIZE: Medium.
*STOCK: English and Continental furniture,
chandeliers.* PARK: Meter (Kings Rd.) TEL:
351 3985; home — 352 1391. SER: Valuations; buys at auction. VAT: Stan/Spec.

Stephanie Hoppen Ltd.   BADA
17 Walton St. Est. 1962. CL: Sat. Open
10—6. *STOCK: Prints — botanical, natural
history, architecture.* TEL: 589 3678.

Malcolm Innes Gallery
172 Walton St. Est. 1973. Open 9.30—6 and
some Sats. 10—1. *STOCK: Scottish and
sporting pictures.* TEL: 584 0575/5559. SER:
Restorations; framing. VAT: Special.

Anthony James and Son Ltd.
                                        BADA
88 Fulham Rd. Est. 1949. Open 9.30—6, Sat.
10.30—1. SIZE: Large. *STOCK: Furniture,
1700—1880, £200—£50,000; mirrors, bronzes, ormolu and decorative items, £200—
£20,000.* PARK: Easy. TEL: 584 1120. SER:
Valuations; buys at auction. VAT: Spec.

David James   BADA
(Fine Victorian Watercolours)
291 Brompton Rd. (D. and E. James.) Est.
1980. Open 11.30—6, Sat. 11.30—2.30.
STOCK: Victorian watercolours. TEL: 581
3399.

Jeremy Ltd.   BADA
255 King's Rd. (G., M. and J. Hill.) Est. 1946.
Open 9—6. *STOCK: English, French furniture,
18th C; objets d'art.* TEL: 352 3127/0644.
VAT: Spec.

Lewis M. Kaplan Associates Ltd.
                                       LAPADA
50 Fulham Rd. (L.M. Kaplan and G.D.
Watson.) Est. 1977. Open 11—6. *STOCK:
Art deco and art nouveau glass and furniture,
£50—£10,000; signed art deco and art
nouveau jewellery, £100—£10,000; both
1890-1945.* LOC: At junction of Sydney St.
and Fulham Rd. PARK: Sydney St. TEL: 589
3108 and 584 6328. SER: Valuations; buys
at auction (art nouveau and art deco). VAT:
Stan/Spec.

John Keil Ltd.   BADA
154 Brompton Rd. Est. 1959. CL: Sat. except
by appointment. Open 9—6. SIZE: Large.
*STOCK: English furniture, 18th to early 19th
C, from £500.* LOC: Near Knightsbridge
underground station. PARK: 200yds. TEL:
589 6454. SER: Restorations (fine pieces).
VAT: Spec.

S.W.3 continued

Krios Gallery
305 Brompton Rd. (M. Senior). Est. 1980. Open 10.30—6, Sat. 11—3. SIZE: Medium. *STOCK: English watercolours, 19th C, £100—£500.* LOC: 200 yards from Victoria and Albert Museum. PARK: Meters. TEL: 589 5811. SER: Valuations; restorations; framing; buys at auction (watercolours). VAT: Spec.

Ledger Antiques Ltd.
101A Fulham Rd. (R.M. Donnelly and D.G. Ledger.) Est. 1972. Open 10—5.30, or by appointment. SIZE: Small. *STOCK: Masons Patent Ironstone china, 1790—1850, £50—£2,000; Staffordshire portrait figures, animals, houses and castles, 1800—1860, £50—£1,000; lustreware £50—£500.* LOC: Corner of Fulham Rd. and Elystan St. PARK: Easy. TEL: 581 0922; home — 370 3086. SER: Buys at auction; mail order. VAT: Stan/Spec.

Stanley Leslie
15 Beauchamp Place. CL: Sat. p.m. Open 9—5. *STOCK: Silver and Sheffield plate.* PARK: Meters. TEL: 589 2333.

Michael Lipitch
98 Fulham Rd. *STOCK: 18th C English furniture.* TEL: 589 7327. SER: Commissions undertaken.

Peter Lipitch Ltd.   BADA
120/124 Fulham Rd. Est. 1954. Open 9.30—5.30, Sat. 10—2. SIZE: Large. *STOCK: English and Continental furniture.* TEL: 373 3328. VAT: Spec.

L'Odeon
173 Fulham Rd. (D. Sarel and N. Tovey.) Open 11—6. *STOCK: Art deco.* TEL: 581 3640.

The Map House
54 Beauchamp Place. (Hon. C.A. Savile and Mrs. Savile, Lord Mexborough, Countess of Mexborough, Simon Pointer.) Est. 1907. Open 9.45— 5.45, Sat. 10.30—5, or by appointment. *STOCK: Antique and rare maps, atlases, engravings and globes.* TEL: 589 4325/9821. SER: Valuations; colouring; restorations; framing. VAT: Stan.

Mathon Gallery
38 Cheyne Walk, Chelsea. (Phipps and Co. Ltd.) Est. 1980. Open 9.30—12.30 or by appointment including Sun. SIZE: Medium. *STOCK: British oils, watercolours and sculpture, 19th—20th C, £100—£15,000.* TEL: 352 5381; Malvern (06845) 5606. SER: Valuations; buys at auction (British paintings and sculpture). VAT: Spec.

Monro Heywood Ltd
336 Kings Rd. (J. Monro, E. Heywood). CL: Sat. Open 10—5. *STOCK: Pictures and prints, furniture, china, objects, 18th—20th C, £30—£3,500.* LOC: Opposite Paultons Square. PARK: Easy. TEL: 351 1477. VAT: Spec.

S.W.3 continued

H.W. Newby (A.J. Waller)   BADA and H.C. Mote
15 Walton St. Est. 1949. CL: Sat. Open 9.30—1 and 2—5.30. SIZE: Medium. *STOCK: Porcelain, faience, pottery, pre-1830, £50—£5,000; English and Continental glass.* Not stocked: Silver, jewellery. LOC: Between Ovington St. and Hasker St. PARK: Meters. TEL: 589 2752. SER: Valuations; buys at auction. VAT: Spec.

Pelham Galleries   BADA
163—165 Fulham Rd. (E.W. and A. Rubin.) Est. 1960. *STOCK: Furniture, English, Continental; tapestries; decorative works of art; musical instruments.* TEL: 589 2686. VAT: Spec.

David Pettifer Ltd.   BADA
269 King's Rd. Est. 1963. Open 9.30—1 and 2—5.30. SIZE: Large. *STOCK: English furniture, 18th C; paintings and watercolours, 18th—19th C.* LOC: From Sloane Sq., 11, 19 or 22 bus. PARK: Easy. TEL: 352 3088. SER: Buys at auction. VAT: Stan/Spec.

Prides of London
15 Paultons House, Paultons Sq. Open by appointment only. *STOCK: Fine furniture, objets d'art.* TEL: 586 1227. SER: Interior design.

The Purple Shop
15 Flood St., Chelsea. (A.J. Gardner and O.M. Becker.) Est. 1967. Open 10—6. *STOCK: Antique and period jewellery, especially art nouveau, art deco.* LOC: Near Chelsea Town Hall. PARK: Meter and nearby. TEL: 352 1127. SER: Valuations. VAT: Stan.

Rogers de Rin
76 Royal Hospital Rd., Chelsea. (V. de Rin.) Est. 1950. Open 10—6. SIZE: Small. *STOCK: Wemyss pottery, objets d'art, decorative furnishings, collectors' specialities, all 18th—19th C, £5—£5,000.* LOC: Just beyond Royal Hospital, corner of Paradise Walk. PARK: Easy. TEL: 352 9007. SER: Buys at auction. VAT: Stan/Spec.

Alistair Sampson Antiques   BADA inc. Tobias Jellinek Antiques
156 Brompton Rd. (A.H. Sampson.) Open 9.30—5.30, Sat. 9.30—1. SIZE: Large. *STOCK: English pottery, oak and country furniture, metalwork, needlework, primitive pictures, decorative and interesting items, all 17th—18th C.* PARK: Meters. TEL: 589 5272 and 581 2267. VAT: Spec.

Philip Smith-Carrington
53 Elystan St. Open by appointment. *STOCK: Victorian items — boxes, tea caddies, candlesticks.* TEL: 584 4599.

S.W.3 continued

Andrew Smithson Master Drawings

16 Ovington Sq., Knightsbridge. Est. 1976. Open by appointment only. SIZE: Small. STOCK. *Old Master European drawings, 16th—18th C, £100—£5,000.* PARK: Meters. TEL: 584 4336. SER: Valuations; buys at auction (paintings and drawings).

Louise Stroud F.G.A.　　　　LAPADA

3 Cale St., Chelsea Green. (Stroud's of Taunton). CL: Mon. and Sat. p.m. *STOCK: Jewellery.* TEL: 351 5988; office (0823) 84452. SER: Valuations; repairs. VAT: Stan/Spec.

Oliver Swann Galleries

117A Walton St. Est. 1975. Open 10—1 and 2.30—6, Sat. 10—1, Sat. p.m. and Sun. by appointment. SIZE: Medium. *STOCK: Victorian watercolours, £200—£2,000; marine paintings, £200—£4,000, all 19th C.* PARK: Easy. TEL: 581 4229. SER: Valuations; restorations; buys at auction. FAIRS: C.G.A. Game. VAT: Spec.

Temple Gallery　　　　　　BADA

4 Yeoman's Row. (R.C.C. Temple.) Est. 1960. **Articles on icons. Open by appointment. SIZE: Large.** STOCK: *Icons, Russian and Greek, 12th—16th C, £2,000—£50,000.* **LOC: From Harrods, walk towards Victoria and Albert Museum, fourth turning on left. PARK: Easy.** TEL: 589 6622. SER: Valuations; restorations; buys at auction (icons). VAT: Spec.

Alan G. Thomas

c/o National Westminster Bank, 300 King's Rd. Est. 1956. Open by appointment. *STOCK: Manuscripts, early printing, bibles, literature.* PARK: Meters, opposite. TEL: 352 5130.

David Tremayne Ltd.　　　　BADA

320 King's Rd., Chelsea. (D. Salmon.) CL: Sat. Open 9.30—5.30. SIZE: Medium. *STOCK: Chinese hardwood furniture, Oriental works of art.* TEL: 352 1194. VAT: Spec.

David Tron Antiques　　　　BADA
　　　　　　　　　　　　　　　　LAPADA

275 King's Rd. Open 9.30—1 and 2—6. *STOCK: Furniture, 17th—19th C; works of art. (Also trade department.)* TEL: 352 5918.

Earle D. Vandekar　　　　　BADA
of Knightsbridge Ltd.　　　　LAPADA

138 Brompton Rd. CINOA. Est. 1913. Open 9.30—5.30, Sat. by appointment. SIZE: Large. *STOCK: Porcelain, pottery, faience, glass (English, Oriental, Continental), pre-1830, £100—£40,000.* TEL: 589 8481/3398. VAT: Spec.

S.W.3 continued

Walker Galleries Ltd.

3 Cale St., Chelsea Green. CL: Mon. Open 10—6, Sat. 10—1. SIZE: Small. *STOCK: Paintings, watercolours, Old Master drawings, 16th—19th C, £100—£10,000; Oriental porcelain and works of art, 10th—18th C, £100—£5,000.* LOC: From King's Rd., turn right into Markham St., corner of Chelsea Green. PARK: Easy. TEL: 351 5988. SER: Valuations; restorations (oil paintings and watercolours); buys at auction (oil paintings and watercolours). FAIRS: Chelsea Spring and Autumn. VAT: Spec.

Walker-Bagshawe　　　　　LAPADA

73 Walton St. (C. Walker and N. Bagshawe.) Est. 1975. Open 9.30—6. SIZE: Medium. *STOCK: Paintings, oils, etchings and watercolours, 1870—1930, £2,000—£15,000; arts and crafts furniture, 1900's, £100—£1,000.* LOC: Behind Harrods. PARK: Meters. TEL: 589 4582. SER: Valuations; restorations (oils, watercolours, prints); framing; buys at auction (paintings). FAIRS: Olympia. VAT: Spec.

R. Wearn and Son Ltd.

322 King's Rd. Est. 1928. Open 10—5, Sat. 10—2. *STOCK: General antiques, furniture, 18th and 19th C, £200—£4,000.* TEL: 352 3918. VAT: Stan/Spec.

O.F. Wilson Ltd.　　　　　　BADA
　　　　　　　　　　　　　　　　LAPADA

Queens Elm Parade, Old Church St. (corner of Fulham Rd.), Chelsea. (O.F. Wilson, P. Jackson, M.E. Tushingham.) Est. 1935. STOCK: *English and French furniture, mantelpieces, objets d'art.* TEL: 352 9554. VAT: Spec.

Clifford Wright　　　　　　BADA
Antiques Ltd.

104-106 Fulham Rd. Est. 1964. CL: Sat. p.m. Open 9—6. *STOCK: Period mirrors, giltwood furniture, 1685-1820; polished furniture, 1740-1820.* TEL: 589 0986. VAT: Spec.

London S.W.4

Thomas Heneage

26 Chelsham Rd. Est. 1975. Open by appointment. *STOCK: Reference books on the applied arts; early works of art.* PARK: Easy. TEL: 720 1503; home — same. SER: Valuations; restorations (bookbinding); buys at auction.

London S.W.5

Antique and Modern Furniture Ltd.

160 Earls Court Rd. Est. 1941. CL: Thurs. Open 9—1 and 2.30—6. *STOCK: Furniture mainly 18th—19th C.* TEL: 373 2935.

S.W.5 continued

Beaver Coin Room

Beaver Hotel, 57 Philbeach Gdns. (J. Lis.) Est. 1971. Open by appointment. SIZE: Small. *STOCK: European coins, 10th—18th C, commemorative medals. 15th— 20th C; all £1—£1,000.* LOC: 2 mins. walk from Earls Court Rd. PARK: Easy. TEL: 373 4553. SER: Valuations; buys at auction (coins and medals). FAIRS: International Coin and Coinex, London. VAT: Stan.

Geider

146 Colehern Court, Old Brompton Rd. (D. Geider.) Open by appointment only. TEL: 370 2996.

Kenway Antiques

70 Kenway Rd. (C. and C.P.Boas.) Est. 1950. SIZE: Large. *STOCK: Oriental porcelain; Victoriana; general antiques.* PARK: Meters. TEL: 373 1631. VAT: Spec.

Andrew Kimpton

11 Gledhow Gdns. Open by appointment. *STOCK: Paintings, 18th—20th C.* TEL: 370 1549.

Sanda Lipton   LAPADA

35 Kenway Rd. (Mrs. S. Lipton.) CL: Mon. Open 1.30—6.30, Sat. 9—1. *STOCK: Silver, especially English spoons and flatware, 17th to mid-19th C.* TEL: 373 9625; office — 407 0278.

London S.W.6

20th Century Gallery

821 Fulham Rd. (G. Guest.) Open 10—6. SIZE: Small. *STOCK: Post impressionist from 1900 and contemporary works.* LOC: Nr Munster Rd. junction. PARK: Easy. TEL: 731 5888. SER: Restorations (paintings). VAT: Spec.

634 Kings Road

Chelsea. (J. Thornton and S. March). CL: Sat. Open 10—5.30. *STOCK: Antiquarian books, decorative items.* TEL: 736 6181.

Adams Antiques

53-55 Fulham High St. Open 10—6. *STOCK: Pine, especially Irish and Contiental, 18th—19th C; Swedish rag rugs.* TEL: 736 9136.

Gil Adams Antiques

659 Fulham Rd. (G. Adams and P. Massey.) Est. 1979. Open 10—6, Sat. 10—5. SIZE: Small. *STOCK: General antiques including bookcases, chaises, tables and mirrors, 19th C, £500—£2,000; decorative items, 19th—20th C, £100—£500.* LOC: Near Fulham Broadway. PARK: Easy. TEL: 731 7372. VAT: Stan/Spec.

S.W.6 continued

And So To Bed Limited

638/640 King's Rd. (Mr. and Mrs. K.D. Barnett.) Est. 1970. Open 10—6. SIZE: Large. *STOCK: Brass and wooden beds, complete bedrooms, 19th C, £100—£8,000.* LOC: End of King's Rd., towards Fulham. PARK: Easy. TEL: 731 3593/4/5. SER: Restorations; spares; interior design. VAT: Stan.

Anvil Interiors

55 New Kings Rd., Chelsea. Open 10—5.30. *STOCK: Stripped pine, architectural and oak shipping items.* TEL: 736 5623.

Karin Armelin Antiques

594 King's Rd. Open 10.30—5.30. SIZE: Medium. *STOCK: 18th—19th C English furniture, decorative items, silver and plate.* PARK: Easy. TEL: 736 0375. SER: Valuations. FAIRS: Olympia. VAT: Stan/Spec.

Ashby Antiques

95 Moore Park Rd. (P.J.E. Samuel.) Open 9—6. *STOCK: Oak, mahogany and decorative items; pictures and painted furniture.* TEL: 731 5008; home — same.

Atlantic Bay Carpets

739 Fulham Rd. Est. 1945. CL: Thurs. p.m. Open 9.30—5.30. SIZE: Large. *STOCK: English, Oriental, Persian, Chinese carpets.* TEL: 736 8777. SER: Valuations; restorations. VAT: Stan.

Aubyn Antiques

1 Wandon Rd., King's Rd. (J. and N. Smyth.) Est. 1971. CL: Sun. except by appointment. Open 10—5.30. SIZE: Large. *STOCK: Furniture, £10—£500; oils, watercolours, prints, ceramics, bric-a-brac, £5—£150.* LOC: Between Fulham and King's Rds. at Chelsea football ground. PARK: Easy. TEL: 736 1196; home — 870 8213.

Robert Barley Antiques

48 Fulham High St. (R.A. Barley.) Est. 1965. CL: Sat. Open 9.30—5.30. SIZE: Medium. *STOCK: Decorative furniture, objects, textiles.* LOC: Near Putney Bridge. PARK: Easy. TEL: 736 4429. VAT: Stan/Spec.

Beresford-Clark

558 King's Rd., Chelsea. Est. 1976. CL: Sat. Open 10—5.30. SIZE: Medium. *STOCK: Furniture, decorative paintings, textiles, unusual objects and china.* PARK: Easy. TEL: 731 5079.

Big Ben Antique Clocks

5 Broxholme House, New King's Rd. (R. Lascelles.) Est. 1978. Open 10—5.30. *STOCK: Clocks — longcase, mantel and wall; small furniture and pictures.* LOC: At junction of Wandsworth Bridge Rd. and New King's Rd. TEL: 736 1770. SER: Repairs (clocks); buys at auction.

S.W.6 continued

R. Bonnett
582 King's Rd. Est. 1945. Open 8.30—5. SIZE: Medium. *STOCK: Furniture, 1770—1900, £75—£1,000; Staffordshire figures, £30—£200.* Not stocked: Glass, bric-a-brac. PARK: Easy. TEL: 736 4593; home — 788 2763. VAT: Stan.

Bookham Galleries
164 Wandsworth Bridge Rd. (J.H. and J. Rowe.) Est. 1969. CL: Mon. Open 10—5.30. *STOCK: Furniture, 18th—19th C; Oriental rugs.* TEL: 736 5125.

Audrey Bowley Antiques at Imogen Graham
585 King's Rd. Est. 1960. Open 10—6. SIZE: Medium. *STOCK: General antiques.* TEL: 736 2465. VAT: Stan/Spec.

Erika Brandl — Paintings
758 Fulham Rd. Est. 1976. Open 10—6. SIZE: Small. *STOCK: Original oils and watercolours, British paintings, 1880—1950, £50—£5,000.* LOC: Between Munster Rd. and Fulham Palace Rd. PARK: Easy. TEL: 736 0497. SER: Valuations; restorations (oil paintings); buys at auction (paintings and bronzes). FAIRS: Olympia. VAT: Stan/Spec.

S.W.6 continued

Brandt Oriental Antiques
771 Fulham Rd. (R. Brandt.) Est. 1981. Open daily, until 4 Sat. and by appointment Sun. SIZE: Medium. *STOCK: Oriental furniture, works of art, £200—£5,000.* LOC: Parsons Green end of Fulham Rd. PARK: Easy. TEL: 731 6835; home — 731 6764. SER: Restorations including gilding. VAT: Spec.

I. and J.L. Brown
636 King's Rd. Usually open 9.30—5.30. *STOCK: Country and French provincial furniture including tables and country chairs; metalware and decorative items.* TEL: 736 4141. SER: Restorations.

Arthur Brown's Number Three Ltd.
44 Fulham High St. CL: Sat. Open 9.30—1 and 2—5.30. SIZE: Medium. *STOCK: Furniture, gilt, lacquer and painted, 18th—19th C; decorative and unusual items, especially four poster beds.* PARK: Easy. TEL: 385 4218. VAT: Spec.

C.W. Buckingham   LAPADA
301-303 Munster Rd., Fulham. (Mr. and Mrs. Buckingham.) Est. 1974. Open 9—6, Thurs. 9—1. SIZE: Large. *STOCK: Pine furniture, Windsor chairs.* LOC: Off New King's Rd. PARK: Strode Rd. TEL: 385 2657; home — 385 8475.

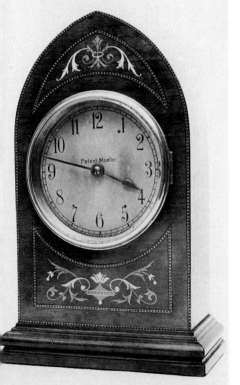

Inlaid mahogany lancet style case, electrically rewound mantel clock with silvered dial signed Patent Moeller. From *The Price Guide to Collectable Clocks 1840-1940* by Alan and Rita Shenton, published by the **Antique Collectors' Club**, 1985.

S.W.6 continued

Rupert Cavendish Antiques
LAPADA
561 King's Rd. Est. 1980. Open 10—6. SIZE: Medium. *STOCK: Empire and Biedereier furniture; watercolours, 19th C; oil paintngs, 17th—19th C.* LOC: Just before New King's Rd. PARK: Easy. TEL: 731 7041/736 6024. SER: Valuations. VAT: Spec.

Hilary Chapman
758 Fulham Rd. *STOCK: Etching, engravings, decorative prints, 18th—20th C.* TEL: 736 0497.

Chelsea Clocks and Antiques
479 Fulham Rd., Chelsea. (P. Dixon and D. Torr.) Est. 1976. CL: Sat. and Mon. Open 12—5.30. *STOCK: Longcase clocks, £450—£2,000; mantel and wall clocks, £50—£450; decorative and collectors' items, £5—£500.* LOC: Opp. Chelsea Football Ground. PARK: Easy. TEL: 731 5704. FAIRS: Olympia. VAT: Stan.

John Clay
263 New King's Rd., Fulham. Est. 1974. Open 8.30—6, Sat. 10—6. SIZE: Medium. *STOCK: Furniture, £50—£5,000; objets d'art and animal objects, silver and clocks, £10—£1,500; all 18th—19th C.* Not stocked: Pine. LOC: Close to Parsons Green, A3. PARK: Easy. TEL: 731 5677. SER: Restorations (furniture, objets d'art). VAT: Stan/Spec.

Fergus Cochrane Antiques
570 King's Rd. (F.V. Cochrane and J.B. Charlick.) Est. 1981. Open 10—6. SIZE: Medium. *STOCK: Decorative furniture and furnishings, 1700—1900, £100—£1,000.* PARK: Easy. TEL: 736 9166; home — 731 5150. VAT: Stan/Spec.

Peter Collins
92 Waterford Rd. Est. 1971. CL: Tues. Open 10—1 and 3—6. *STOCK: Furniture — country woods or painted, 17th to early 19th C; decorative items.* TEL: 736 4149.

The Constant Reader Bookshop
627 Fulham Rd. (G. and A Mullett.) Open 10.30—7. *STOCK: General antiques, second-hand books especially Japan and Far East.* TEL: 731 0218.

J. Crotty and Son Ltd.
74 New King's Rd., Parsons Green. Est. 1945. CL: Sat. p.m. Open 9.30—5. SIZE: Medium. *STOCK: Fire grates, light fittings, fenders, 18th—19th C; marble and pine mantelpieces, fire irons, fire screens.* PARK: In adjacent side street. TEL: 731 4209. SER: Restorations (antique metal fireplace equipment); buys at auction. VAT: Stan.

S.W.6 continued

T. Crowther and Son Ltd.
282 North End Rd., Fulham. Est. 1882. CL: Sat. Open 9—5.30. SIZE: Large. *STOCK: Oak and pine panelling, mainly 17th—18th C; carved wood and marble chimney pieces and Georgian furniture, 1700—1830, £500—£10,000; garden ornaments, 18th—19th C, £500—£5,000.* LOC: Up North End Rd. from Fulham Broadway, on left hand side opposite fruit market, corner of Coomer Place. PARK: Easy. TEL: 385 1375/7. SER: Valuations. VAT: Spec.

Rocco D'Alessandro
610 King's Rd. Est. 1976. SIZE: Medium. *STOCK: English furniture, 18th to early 19th C.* PARK: Easy. TEL: 731 7160; home — same. VAT: Spec.

Teapoy, mahogany, c.1830, taken from a design by Nicholson. From *Regency Furniture* by Frances Collard, published by the **Antique Collectors' Club,** 1985.

RUPERT CAVENDISH
ANTIQUES

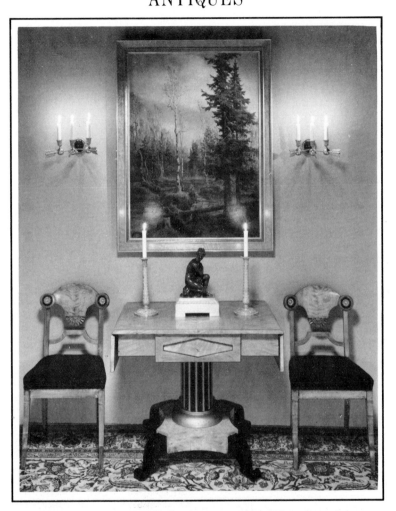

Empire and Biedermeier Furniture
Oil Paintings

561 King's Road, London SW6.   Tel: 01-731 7041.
10 a.m.—6 p.m. Monday—Saturday.

Also trade warehouse—by appointment only.

S.W.6 continued

Zal Davar   LAPADA
Trade and Export Only
26a Munster Rd. Est. 1961. CL: Sat. Open
9.30—5.30. SIZE: Large. *STOCK: Furniture,
19th C.; decorative items.* TEL: 736 2559/
1405. VAT: Stan/Spec.

David Alexander Antiques
102 Waterford Rd. (R.D.A. Robertson and K.
Thurlow.) Est. 1970. Open 10—6, but
appointment advisable. SIZE: Medium.
*STOCK: English and Continental furniture,
16th to early 18th C.* LOC: Turn left at
junction of King's Rd. and New King's Rd.
PARK: Easy. TEL: 731 4644. SER: Valuations;
restorations; buys auction. VAT: Spec.

Peter Evanson
464 Fulham Rd., Fulham Broadway. Est.
1933. Open 9—6. *STOCK: General antiques
and furniture.* TEL: 385 4185.

Fairfax Antiques
568 King's Rd. (J. Fairfax.) Open 10—5.
*STOCK: Fireplaces — cast-iron, marble and
pine.* TEL: 736 5023. SER: Restorations;
metal polishing; fabricating.

Fairhurst Gallery
291 New King's Rd. (M. Fairhurst). Open
10—6. *STOCK: Oils, watercolours, 1880—
1950, £30—£5,000.* LOC: Parsons Green
end of New King's Rd. PARK: In side roads.
TEL: 736 9132. SER: Valuations; buys at
auction.

Five Five Six Antiques   LAPADA
556 King's Rd. Est. 1961. CL: Sat. Open
10—6. SIZE: Medium. *STOCK: General decorative items — early and unusual furniture,
primitive paintings, watercolours, samplers,
needlework cushions, wool and silk works,
decorators' accessories.* TEL: 731 2016;
home — 624 5173. SER: Valuations; interior
decoration. VAT: Stan.

S.W.6 continued

Fleur de Lys Gallery
8 Fulham High St. (H.S. Coronel.) Est. 1949.
Open 10—6. SIZE: Medium. *STOCK: Oil
paintings, 19th C, £200—£2,000; watercolours.* Not stocked: Prints. PARK: Easy but
limited. TEL: 731 7454; home — (0372)
67934.

George Floyd Ltd.
592 Fulham Rd. CL: Sat. Open 8.30—5.30.
SIZE: Large. *STOCK: 18th and early 19th C
furniture and accessories.* TEL: 736 1649.
VAT: Stan/Spec.

Gerald Freedman — Cale Antiques
P.O. Box 458, Fulham. Est. 1961. Open by
appointment. *STOCK: 17th—18th C Chinese
and Japanese porcelain also European
ceramics including Delft, faience and majolica.*
LOC: End of King's Rd., 1 minute from Putney
Bridge railway station. TEL: 736 8666. SER:
Valuations. VAT: Spec.

Galerie 360   *Trade only*
564 King's Rd. (C. Sparks.) Est. 1974. Open
10—6, Sat. 11—5. SIZE: Small. *STOCK:
Objects, 17th—20th C, £50—£4,000.* LOC:
Beyond the "Worlds End", towards Fulham.
PARK: Easy. TEL: 736 5160. SER: Valuations.
FAIRS: Olympia. VAT: Stan/Spec.

Glamour City
336 King's Rd., Chelsea. Est. 1979. Open
10.30—6. *STOCK: Clothes and accessories,
1940—1960; original 1940's pin-up calendars
and graphics.* TEL: 351 5454.

Goodwin and Wadhwa
545 King's Rd. (P. Goodwin and M.
Wadhwa.) Open 10—6, Sat. 11—3. SIZE:
Medium. *STOCK: English and Continental
furniture, 1600—1900, £500—£10,000;
decorative European and Oriental works of art
and paintings, 1500—1900; globes and
scientific instruments, 1650—1880; both
£200—£10,000.* PARK: Easy. TEL: 731
7024. SER: Valuations; restorations; buys at
auction. FAIRS: Olympia. VAT: Stan/Spec.

Imogen Graham
585 King's Rd. Est. 1969. Open 10—5.30.
SIZE: Medium. *STOCK: Furniture, decorative
items, oil paintings, watercolours, samplers.*
PARK: Easy. TEL: 736 2465. VAT: Stan/
Spec.

Alex Grahamslaw
583 King's Rd. Est. 1963. Open 10—6, Sat.
10—5. SIZE: Medium. *STOCK: Furniture,
stripped pine mirrors, objets d'art.* PARK:
Easy. TEL: 731 1245. VAT: Stan/Spec.

Judy Greenwood
657 Fulham Rd. Est. 1978. Open 10—6.
*STOCK: Country furniture, pine, Victoriana,
textiles, quilts.* TEL: 736 6037.

S.W.6 continued

Gregory, Bottley and Lloyd
8-12 Rickett St. Est. 1850. SIZE: Medium. *STOCK: Mineral specimens, £1—£5,000; fossils, £5—£500.* LOC: Behind West Brompton underground. PARK: Easy. TEL: 381 5522; home — 878 5202. SER: Valuations. VAT: Stan.

Guinevere Antiques
574/580 King's Rd. Open 9.30—6, Sat. 10—6. SIZE: Large. *STOCK: General antiques; decorative items.* TEL: 736 2917.

John Hall Antiques and Prints
31 Epple Rd. Est. 1950. Open by appointment. SIZE: Medium. *STOCK: Staffordshire figures, 1760—1860, £40—£1,000; fairings, £30—£600; theatrical items, figures, paintings, prints, playbills, 1760—1900, £1—£200; engraved and lithographed music fronts; greetings cards, postcards, 1800—1900, £1—50.* LOC: Opposite Fulham library. PARK: Easy. TEL: 736 3542. SER: Buys at auction. VAT: Stan/Spec.

S.W.6 continued

Han-Shan Tang Ltd.
717 Fulham Rd. (C. von der Burg and V. Robinson.) Open 10—6, Sat. 10—4 or by appointment. *STOCK: Secondhand and antiquarian books and periodicals on Chinese, Japanese and Korean art and culture.* TEL: 731 2447.

Hollingshead and Co.
783 Fulham Rd. (D. Hollingshead.) Est. 1946. CL: Sat. p.m. Open 10—1 and 2—5. SIZE: Medium. *STOCK: Marble and wood mantelpieces, grates, fenders, fire irons, chandeliers, £50—£20,000.* Not stocked: Furniture. PARK: Easy. TEL: 385 8519. SER: Valuations; restorations (marblework and wood mantelpieces). VAT: Stan.

House of Mirrors
597 King's Rd. (Z. Wigek.) Est. 1960. Open 10—6. *STOCK: Mirrors.* TEL: 736 5885.

P.L. James
681 Fulham Rd. CL: Sat. Open 7—5. *STOCK: Gilded mirrors, English and Oriental lacquer, period objects and furniture.* TEL: 736 0183. SER: Restorations (painted and lacquer furniture, gilding, carving). VAT: Stan/Spec.

Just a Second Antiques Ltd.
40 Fulham High St. (J. Bastillo.) Open 9.30—5.30. *STOCK: Furniture, Georgian, Victorian and Edwardian, silver, china, general antiques, £10—£1,500.* TEL: 731 1919; home — 223 5341. VAT: Stan.

C. Kent (Fireplaces)
167—169 Dawes Rd., Fulham. (C. Kent and J. Gregory.) Est. 1977. Open 9.30—5, Sat. 8.30—4.30 or by appointment. SIZE: Small. *STOCK: Restored cast-iron fireplaces, some marble surrounds, Georgian—Edwardian.* LOC: Between Fulham Broadway and Munster Rd. PARK: Easy. TEL: 385 1494; home — same.

Eric King Antiques
203 New King's Rd. Est. 1966. Open 10—6. SIZE: Medium. *STOCK: Oriental furniture, unusual and decorative items; pine, wicker furniture.* LOC: From Sloane Sq., down King's Rd. and New King's Rd. Shop is opposite Parsons Green. PARK: Easy. TEL: 736 3162; home — 731 2554. VAT: Stan.

M. Lassota
596 King's Rd. Open 10—5. *STOCK: Victorian, Regency, Hepplewhite furniture.* TEL: 736 3932.

Lunn Antiques
86 New King's Rd. (S. Lunn.) Est. 1975. Open 10—6.30. *STOCK: Victorian and Edwardian hand worked linens, sheets, bedspreads, pillowcases, tablecloths, Oriental embroidery, pre-war clothing, some early lace and costume.* TEL: 736 4638. VAT: Stan.

S.W.6 continued

Michael Marriott Ltd.
588 Fulham Rd. Est. 1979. CL: Sat. p.m. and Sun. except by appointment. Open 10—5.30 but appointment preferred. SIZE: Large. *STOCK: English furniture, 1700—1850, £200—£5,000; leather upholstery, £250—£1,500.* LOC: Junction of Fulham Rd. and Parsons Green Lane. PARK: Easy. TEL: 736 3110; home — 381 3455. SER: Valuations; restorations. FAIRS: Olympia, Kensington and Surrey (Heath Bullock), Kenilworth (Spring and Autumn), London Antique Dealers' (Café Royal). VAT: Stan/Spec.

David Martin-Taylor
56 Fulham High St. Open 9.30—6. *STOCK: Furniture and decorative items.* TEL: 731 4135.

Midwinter and Jefferson
479 Fulham Rd. Open 10—6. SIZE: Medium. *STOCK: Period furniture, decorative paintings, works of art and curiosities.* TEL: 731 5704. SER: Valuations; restorations; buys at auction. VAT: Spec.

Ian Moggach Antiques   *Mainly Trade*
723 Fulham Rd. CL: Sat. Open 9.30—5.30. SIZE: Large. *STOCK: 19th C. furniture, including desks, writing tables and bookcases, French marble fireplaces, £200—£1,500.* TEL: 731 4883.

Richard Morris Antiques
142 Wandsworth Bridge Rd. Est. 1960. Open 9.30—6. SIZE: Medium. *STOCK: Pine furniture, complete range, £15—£1,000.* Not stocked: Anything other than pine. LOC: From King's Rd., Chelsea to beginning of New King's Rd. Parsons Green on the right, Wandsworth Bridge Rd. left at traffic lights. PARK: Easy. TEL: 736 1448. VAT: Stan.

Old World Trading Co.
565 King's Rd. (R.J. Campion.) Est. 1970. Open 9.30—6. *STOCK: Fireplaces, chimney pieces and accessories, chandeliers, mirrors.* TEL: 731 4708.

Alec Ossowski
595 King's Rd. CL: Sat. p.m. Open 9—6. *STOCK: Carved gilt, 18th C; mirrors, wood carvings.* TEL: 731 0334. SER: Valuations; restorations (gilt furniture). VAT: Stan/Spec.

Pageant Antiques
122 Dawes Rd., Fulham. (A. Kopriva.) Est. 1974. Open 10—5. SIZE: Large. *STOCK: Architectural fittings, fireplaces, panelling, period architraves and doors, wrought and cast iron staircases.* LOC: Off North End Rd. PARK: Easy. TEL: 385 7739.

S.W.6 continued

Paisnel Gallery Ltd.   LAPADA
768 Fulham Rd., Fulham. (S. Paisnel.) Est. 1976. Open 10—6, Sat. 10—2 or by appointment. SIZE: Small. STOCK: British Post-Impressionist especially Newlyn and St. Ives schools. LOC: Close to Putney Bridge. PARK: Easy. TEL: 736 7898. SER: Valuations; restorations; buys at auction. VAT: Stan/Spec.

Philip Parker
16 Quarrendon St. Open by appointment. STOCK: Oil paintings, 17th—20th C; frames. TEL: 736 2795. SER: Restorations.

M. Pauw Antiques
569 King's Rd. (Ambassador Marketing Ltd.) Est. 1975. CL: Sat. p.m. SIZE: Medium. STOCK: Decorative items, 18th C; woodcarvings, 16th—18th C; furniture, 18th—19th C, all £50—£16,000. PARK: Easy. TEL: 731 4022. FAIRS: Olympia. VAT: Stan/Spec.

Dalton Peett Antiques
610 Fulham Rd., Fulham. (S. and M. Peett.) Est. 1984. Open 10—6. SIZE: Small. STOCK: Furniture, late 18th—19th C, £50—£1,000; pictures, 18th—19th C, £30—£400; ceramics especially 19th C lustreware, £10—£200. Not stocked: Silver, jewellery. LOC: 130yds. west of Parsons Green Lane. PARK: Easy — in side streets. TEL: 731 7481; home — 453 1035/0304. SER: Restorations (upholstery); buys at auction (as stock). VAT: Spec.

The Pine Mine (Crewe-Read Antiques)
100 Wandsworth Bridge Rd., Fulham. (D. Crewe-Read and C. Rolandi.) Est. 1971. Open 9.45—5.45, Sat. till 4.30. SIZE: Large. STOCK: Georgian and Victorian pine, Welsh dressers, farmhouse tables, chests of drawers, boxes and some architectural items. LOC: From Sloane Sq., down King's Rd., into New King's Rd., left into Wandsworth Bridge Rd. PARK: Outside. TEL: 736 1092. SER: Furniture made from old wood; stripping.

The Pine Village
162 Wandsworth Bridge Rd. Est. 1973. Open 10—6 everyday. SIZE: Large. STOCK: Stripped pine furniture, £15—£1,000. LOC: West down King's Rd., into New King's Rd., turn left at Parsons Green, shop about halfway down Wandsworth Bridge Rd. at corner of Beltran Rd. PARK: Easy. TEL: 736 2753. VAT: Stan.

Peter Place Antiques
636 King's Rd. Usually open 9.30—5.30. STOCK: 18th—19th C metalware, decorative items, paintings, folk art. TEL: 736 9945.

S.W.6 continued

Pryce and Brise Antiques
79 Moore Park Rd., Fulham. (N. Pryce and J. Brise). Est. 1983. Open 10—6. SIZE: Small. STOCK: English glass, 18th—19th C; furniture, watercolours, decorative items. LOC: From Kings Rd., going west, turn right before Wandsworth Bridge Rd., into Waterford Rd., shop at junction. PARK: Easy. TEL: 736 1864. SER: Valuations; restorations; buys at auction (glass). VAT: Stan/Spec.

Barrie Quinn Antiques
3 and 4 Broxholme House, New King's Rd. (B.J. Quinn.) Est. 1969. Open 10—5.30. SIZE: Large. STOCK: Furniture, general antiques, glass, clocks, metal, interior decor pieces, £25—£5,000; jardinières, garden statues. LOC: Nr. Parson's Green, Wandsworth Bridge Rd. PARK: Easy. TEL: 736 4747. VAT: Stan.

Rendall Antiques
572 Kings Rd. (R. and L. Rendall.) Est. 1970. Open 9.30—6. STOCK: Furniture, 18th to mid 19th C; decorative objects. TEL: 736 2520. FAIRS: Olympia. VAT: Stan/Spec.

Peter Reynolds
67 New King's Rd. Est. 1974. Open 10—5.30, Sat. 10—4. SIZE: Medium. STOCK: Decorative objects, £15—£500; unusual decorative furniture including wicker, pine and oak, £50—£1,000; all 18th to early 20th C. Not stocked: Jewellery. LOC: Nr. junction of Wandsworth Bridge Rd./New King's Rd. PARK: Easy. TEL: 736 7797. VAT: Stan/Spec.

Paul Richards
16 Fulham High St. Est. 1980. Open 10—6. SIZE: Medium. STOCK: Decorative furniture, light fixtures, 1800—1930. LOC: Off Putney Bridge between end of Fulham Rd. and New Kings Rd. PARK: Easy. TEL: 736 0976. VAT: Stan.

Patrick Sandberg Antiques   BADA
791 Fulham Rd. (P.C.F. Sandberg.) Open 9.30—6, Sat. 10—1.30. SIZE: Large. STOCK: English furniture, 18th to early 19th C; general decorative antiques, clocks, barometers, £100—£10,000. LOC: On the south side of Fulham Rd. between Parsons Green Lane and Munster Rd. PARK: Side streets. TEL: 736 9454; home — same. SER: Restorations (furniture). FAIRS: Olympia, Park Lane. VAT: Spec.

Savile Pine
560 King's Rd. (F.S. Tucker.) Est. 1962. Open 10—5.30. SIZE: Medium. STOCK: Pine furniture. PARK: In side roads. TEL: 736 3625. VAT: Stan.

S.W.6 continued

Sensation Ltd.
66 Fulham High St. (M. Fenwick.) Est. 1958. CL: Sat. and Sun. except by appointment. Open 9—5. SIZE: Large and gallery. *STOCK: English furniture, pottery, porcelain, silver and objets d'art, 17th—19th C; wall decorations.* PARK: At rear. TEL: 736 4135. SER: Valuations; restorations; buys at auction. VAT: Stan/Spec.

David Seyfried Antiques
759 Fulham Rd. Est. 1984. Open 10—6, Sat. 10—1. SIZE: Small. *STOCK: Furniture, 19th C and decorative, £100—£3,000; ceramics and glass, 18th—19th C and decorative, £30—£300.* Not stocked: Silver. LOC: 130yds. west of Parsons Green Lane. PARK: Easy in side streets. TEL: 731 4230; home — 736 6730. SER: Valuations; buys at auction (furniture, glass and porcelain). VAT: Spec.

George Sherlock
588 and 589 King's Rd. Est. 1968. Open 9.30—5.30. SIZE: Large. *STOCK: General antiques, 1650—1900, £20—£5,000.* Not stocked: Glass and china. PARK: Easy. TEL: 736 3955. VAT: Stan/Spec.

Shield and Allen Antiques
584 and 586 King's Rd. Est. 1968. Open 9.30—6. SIZE: Medium. *STOCK: Early furniture, works of art and paintings.* PARK: Easy. TEL: 736 7145. VAT: Spec.

The Singing Tree
69 New King's Rd. (A. Griffith and T. Sanders.) Est. 1975. Open 10—5.30. SIZE: Small. *STOCK: Dolls' houses and accessories, 19th—20th C, 5p—£100.* LOC: Fulham end of King's Rd. PARK: Easy. TEL: 736 4527. FAIRS: All dolls, dolls' houses and doll's house accessories. VAT: Standard.

Spice
2 Wandon Rd., Stanley Bridge. (S. Dix.) Resident. Open 10—7. *STOCK: General antiques, country pine, decorative and unusual items.* TEL: 736 4619. SER: Export; interior design.

Thornhill Galleries Ltd.
76 New King's Rd. (R. Wakefield.) Est. 1880. CL: Thurs. a.m. Open 10—5, Sat. 10—3. SIZE: Large. *STOCK: English and French marble, stone and wooden chimney-pieces, £100—£20,000; English and French panelled rooms, £20,000—£100,000; architectural features and wood carvings, fire grates and fenders; all 17th—19th C. Decorative iron interiors and other fire accessories, 17th—20th C.* LOC: Continuation of King's Rd. Coming from Sloane Sq. shop is on right-hand side. PARK: Easy. TEL: 736 5830. SER: Valuations; restorations (architectural items); buys at auction (architectural items). FAIRS: T.B.A. VAT: Stan/Spec.

S.W.6 continued

Through the Looking Glass Ltd.
563 King's Rd. (J.J.A. and D.A. Pulton.) Est. 1966. Open 9.30—5.30. SIZE: Large. *STOCK: Mirrors, 18th and 19th C.* TEL: 736 7799. SER: Restorations. VAT: Spec.

Ferenc Toth
598A King's Rd. (F. and E. Toth.) Est. 1978. Open 9.30—5.30. SIZE: Medium. *STOCK: Mirrors, £50—£3,000; paintings and furniture, 18th and 19th C.* LOC: Fulham end of King's Rd., Chelsea. PARK: Easy. TEL: 731 2063; home — 602 1771. SER: Valuations; restorations (gilding and frame repair); buys at auction. VAT: Spec.

Francois Valcke
561 King's Rd. Est. 1982. Open 10—6. SIZE: Small. *STOCK: British watercolours, 19th C, £50—£1,500.* LOC: Past World's End. PARK: Easy. TEL: 736 6024. SER: Restorations and framing (watercolours). VAT: Spec.

Meldrum Walker Gallery
27 Filmer Rd., Fulham. (M. and D. Meldrum Walker.) Open 10—6. *STOCK: Victorian watercolours.* TEL: 385 2305. SER: Framing.

Leigh Warren Antiques
566 King's Rd. Open 10—5. *STOCK: General antiques and decorative items.* TEL: 736 2485.

White and Howlett
911 Fulham Rd. (R. White, P. Howlett.) Est. 1978. Open 9.30—5.30, Sun. by appointment. SIZE: Large. *STOCK: Decorative and period furniture, 18th—19th C, £500—£10,000.* PARK: Easy. TEL: 736 1072; home — 673 0373. SER: Valuations; buys at auction (furniture). VAT: Spec.

Whiteway and Waldron Ltd.
305 Munster Rd., Fulham. (M. Whiteway and G. Kirkland.) Est. 1976. CL: Sat. Open 10—6. SIZE: Large. *STOCK: Stained glass, from 1850, £20—£3,000; architectural fittings including panelling, doors, fire surrounds and ironwork, from 1750; carved church woodwork, from 1850.* LOC: At junction of Lillie Rd. and Munster Rd. PARK: On forecourt for loading, otherwise in Strode Rd. TEL: 381 3195. SER: Restorations (stained glass); buys at auction (stained glass and architectural items). VAT: Stan.

Christopher Wray's Lamp Workshop
579 King's Rd. Est. 1964. Open 10—6. SIZE: Large. *STOCK: Replacement shades and parts for oil, gas and early electric lamps.* PARK: Easy. TEL: 736 8434. SER: Restorations (oil and gas lamps). VAT: Stan.

S.W.6 continued

Christopher Wray's Lighting Emporium

600/2/4 King's Rd. Est. 1964. Open 10−6. SIZE: Large. *STOCK: Decorative light fittings of 1880s, brass, antiques, decorative objects.* LOC: From Sloane Square over Stanley Bridge. PARK: Easy. TEL: 736 8434. VAT: Stan.

Christopher Wray's Tiffany Shop

593 King's Rd. Est. 1966. CL: Mon. Open 10−1 and 2−6. SIZE: Medium. *STOCK: Tiffany-style lamps, lampshades and ceiling fans.* PARK: Easy. TEL: 736 8434. VAT: Stan.

London S.W.7

Anglo Persian Carpet Co.   BADA

6 South Kensington Station Arcade. Est. 1910. Open 9.30−6. TEL: 589 5457. SER: Valuations; restorations (carpets and rugs); cleaning.

Benardout and Benardout   BADA

7 Thurloe Place. (N. Benardout.) Est. 1935. CL: Sat. p.m. Open 9−5. SIZE: Large. *STOCK: Persian carpets and rugs, tapestries, needlework.* LOC: Opposite Victoria and Albert Museum. PARK: 50yds. Thurloe Square. TEL: 584 7658 (24hr. ansafone). SER: Valuations; restorations (tapestries, rugs, carpets); cleaning. VAT: Stan.

Aubrey Brocklehurst   BADA

124 Cromwell Rd. Est. 1942. Open 9−6, Sat. 10−1. SIZE: Medium. *STOCK: English clocks.* TEL: 373 0319. SER: Valuations; restorations, furniture and clock repairs; buys at auction. VAT: Spec.

Julie Collino

15 Glendower Place, South Kensington. Est. 1971. Open 11−6, Sat. 12−6, Sun. by appointment. *STOCK: Watercolours, oils, etchings, £25−£1,000; china, £25−£500; both 19th−20th C; furniture, £50−£2,000; card cases, £30−£150.* LOC: Off Harrington Rd. TEL: 584 4733; home − 373 5353. FAIRS: Olympia. VAT: Stan/Spec.

Peter Goodwin   LAPADA

7 Ennismore Mews, Knightsbridge. Est. 1975. Open by appointment. SIZE: Small. *STOCK: Fine scientific, medical and nautical instruments, 16th−20th C, £500−£50,000; furniture, works of art, unusual items.* PARK: Easy. TEL: 581 3873; home − same. SER: Valuations; buys at auction (fine items, 16th−20th C). VAT: Spec.

Robert Hershkowitz Ltd.

94 Queens Gate. Est. 1976. By appointment only. *STOCK: 19th C photographs.* TEL: 373 8994 or Poynings (079 156) 442.

S.W.7 continued

M.P. Levene Ltd.   BADA

5 Thurloe Place. Est. 1926. CL: Sat. p.m. Open 9.30−6. *STOCK: Silver, old Sheffield plate, various, all prices.* LOC: Few minutes past Harrods nr. South Kensington Station. PARK: Easy. TEL: 589 3755. SER: Valuations; buys at auction. VAT: Stan/Spec.

Mrs. Monro Ltd.

11 Montpelier St. Est. 1926. CL: Sat. Open 9.30−1 and 2−5.30. *STOCK: Furniture, 18th−19th C, porcelain, prints.* PARK: Meters. TEL: 589 5052. VAT: Spec.

A. and H. Page

66 Gloucester Rd. Open 9−5.30, Sat. 9−12. *STOCK: Silver, jewellery, objets d'art.* TEL: 584 7349. SER: Buys at auction.

Michael and Margaret Parker Antiques

24 Cheval Place. Est. 1971. Open 10−1 and 2−5; Sat. by appointment. SIZE: Medium. *STOCK: Painted and lacquer furniture and objects, 18th and early 19th C, £100−£3,000; French Provincial furniture, English fruitwood, walnut, 18th C, £1,000−£6,000.* Not stocked: Post-1820. LOC: Off Brompton Rd., opposite Harrods. PARK: Easy. TEL: 589 0133. VAT: Spec.

Period Brass Lights

9a Thurloe Place. (B. Manus.) Est. 1967. CL: Sat. p.m. Open 10.30−1 and 2−5. *STOCK: Brass and gilt reproduction and antique light fittings; general antiques.* PARK: Meters. TEL: 589 8305. SER: Restorations.

John Pope and Hunts Antiques Ltd.   LAPADA

122 Old Brompton Rd. (S. Shamoon.) CL: Sat. Open 10−6. *STOCK: Period furniture, clocks, works of art and paintings.* TEL: 584 2229.

Sheldon's

122 Gloucester Rd. Est. 1951. CL: Sat. Open 9.30−5.30. *STOCK: General antiques, jewellery, silver, watches.* TEL: 373 0038. SER: Valuations; restorations. VAT: Stan.

M. Turpin Ltd.   LAPADA

21 Manson Mews, Queen's Gate. Est. 1946. Open 2−6.30 or by appointment. *STOCK: English and Continental 18th C furniture, mirrors, chandeliers, objets d'art.* PARK: Meters. TEL: 373 8490; messages − 736 3417. VAT: Spec.

London S.W.8

Nicolas Beech
787 Wandsworth Rd. (N.A. Beech). Est. 1981. Open 10—5.30, Sun. by appointment. SIZE: Medium. STOCK: Pine furniture, Georgian, Victorian and Edwardian, £20—£1,000; decorative items, especially kitchen items. LOC: Over Chelsea Bridge (south side), straight over roundabout. At 3rd set of traffic lights turn left, shop 100 yards on right. PARK: Easy. TEL: 720 8552. SER: Restorations (pine); buys at auction (pine and decorative items); pine stripping. VAT: Stan.

Capital Clocks
190 Wandsworth Rd. Est. 1970. Resident. CL: Mon. Open 9.30—4.30, Thurs. by appointment. SIZE: Medium. STOCK: Clocks, pre 1900, £85—£1,000. LOC: ½ mile south of Vauxhall Bridge. PARK: Easy. TEL: 720 6372. SER: Valuations; restorations (movements and cases). buys at auction (clocks). VAT: Spec.

London S.W.9

Scallywag
187—191 Clapham Rd., Stockwell. (J.A. Butterworth.) Est. 1970. Open 9—6, Sat. and Sun. 10—6. SIZE: Large and warehouse. STOCK: Pine, £5—£5,000; architectural fittings, £2—£5,000; both 18th—19th C. LOC: 150yds. from Stockwell tube station, on A3 between The Oval and Stockwell. PARK: Easy, nearby. TEL: 274 0300. SER: Restorations (pine stripping). FAIRS: Lambeth Country and Putney Shows. VAT: Stan/Spec.

London S.W.10

Richard Allan Gallery
20 Park Walk, Chelsea. CL: Mon. Open 11—6, Sat. 11—4 other times by appointment. SIZE: Medium. STOCK: Oils, watercolours and drawings, late 19th—20th C, £100—£3,000. PARK: Easy. TEL: 351 0410.

Balcombe Galleries
7 Stanley Studios, Park Walk. (P. and G. Collins.) Est. 1961. Open by appointment only. SIZE: Large. STOCK: Early oak, pine carvings, bronzes and paintings, 18th—19th C, £25—£1,000; garden furniture, urns, art nouveau, pewter, marble heads. LOC: Fulham Rd./King's Rd. PARK: Easy. TEL: 352 4353; home — 352 9996. SER: Valuations; buys at auction. VAT: Stan/Spec.

S.W.10 continued

John Boyle and Co.
40 Drayton Gdns. ABA. Open by appointment only. STOCK: Antiquarian books — political economy, printing and the mind of Man first editions, science and medicine, English literature. TEL: 373 8247.

T.F. Buckle Ltd.
427 King's Rd. CL: Sat. Open 10—6. STOCK: Fireplaces. TEL: 352 0952.

Chanteau
36 Cathcart Rd. (Madame Y. Chanteau.) Open daily. STOCK: General antiques. TEL: 352 0447. SER: Buys for the overseas trade; import and export.

Furniture Cave
533 King's Rd. (R.I.G. Taylor.) Est. 1967. Open 10—6. SIZE: Large. There are 15 dealers here selling furniture, Victorian, pine, oak, country. PARK: In yard. TEL: 352 2046. SER: Restorations; shipping; forwarding. VAT: Stan/Spec.

William Handford Antiques
517 Kings Rd. (W. Handford and D. Dinitto.) Est. 1974. Open 9.30—6. SIZE: Medium. STOCK: Period and decorative antiques and accessories. LOC: Worlds End, Chelsea. PARK: Easy. TEL: 351 2768. VAT: Stan.

Carlton Hobbs
533 King's Rd. Est. 1975. Open 10—6. STOCK: English and Continental furniture. TEL: 351 3870.

Hollywood Road Antiques
1A Hollywood Rd. (E. Hooberman.) Est. 1972. CL: Sat. Open 10—1 and 2.30—5.30. SIZE: Medium. STOCK: Country and decorative furniture, treen, paintings. PARK: Easy. TEL: 352 5248.

Hollywood Road Gallery
12 Hollywood Rd., Chelsea. (P. and C. Kennaugh.) Open 11—7.30. STOCK: Oils, watercolours, decorative items, 19th—20th C; £50—£1,500. TEL: 351 1973.

Langton Gallery
3 Langton St. (R.S. Stuart and P.G. Bainbridge.) Est. 1970. SIZE: Medium. STOCK: Cartoons, caricatures and illustrations, including W. Heath Robinson, H.M. Bateman, Ronald Searle, Ardizzone, 18th—20th C, £50—£3,500. LOC: Off Kings Rd. at World's End. PARK: Nearby. TEL: 352 9150. SER: Valuations; buys at auction (as stock). VAT: Spec.

**5
1
7
K
I
N
G
S
R
O
A
D**

WILLIAM HANDFORD ANTIQUES

**0
1
3
5
1
2
7
6
8**

S.W.10 continued

Stephen Long
348 Fulham Rd. Est. 1966. CL: Sat. p.m. and Sun. except by appointment. Open 9—1 and 2.15—5.30. SIZE: Small. *STOCK: English pottery, 18th—19th C, under £100. English painted furniture, 18th to early 19th C; toys and games, household and kitchen items, chintz, materials and patchwork, to £400. Not stocked: Stripped pine, large brown furniture, fashionable antiques.* LOC: From South Kensington along road on right between Ifield Rd. and Billing Rd. PARK: Easy. TEL: 352 8226. VAT: Stan/Spec.

The Maclean Gallery
49 Drayton Gdns. Open by appointment only. *STOCK: British, European and erotic art, 1780—1950.* TEL: 373 2867.

H.W. Poulter and Son
279 Fulham Rd. Est. 1946. CL: Sat. p.m. Open 9.30—5. SIZE: Large. *STOCK: English and French marble chimney pieces, grates, fenders, fire-irons, brass, chandeliers.* PARK: Meters. TEL: 352 7268. SER: Restorations (marble work). VAT: Stan/Spec.

S.W.10 continued

Rare Carpets Gallery
496 King's Rd. Open 9.30—6, late on Wed. *STOCK: Persian, Oriental rugs and carpets.* TEL: 351 3296.

Rendlesham and Dark
498 King's Rd. Est. 1970. Open 10—6, Sat. 11—2. SIZE: Medium. *STOCK: English and Continental furniture, objets d'art.* TEL: 351 1442.

Stanley Studios
Park Walk, Chelsea. Est. 1961. Open by appointment. TEL: 352 4353. VAT: Stan/Spec.

Richard von Hünersdorff
P.O. Box 582. ABA. Est. 1969. Open by appointment only. *STOCK: Continental books in rare editions and manuscripts, 15th—19th C; early printing, illustrated books, science and medicine, Latin Americana.* TEL: 373 3899.

S.W.10 continued

Harriet Wynter Ltd.   BADA
Arts and Sciences
50 Redcliffe Rd. Est. 1956. Open by appointment. SIZE: Medium. *STOCK: Early scientific instruments and reference books; garden sundials and decorative items.* TEL: 352 6494. SER: Valuations; restorations (globes, instruments); buys at auction; commissions; hire; catalogues, photograph library. VAT: Stan/Spec.

London S.W.11

Christopher Bangs   LAPADA
By appointment. Est. 1971. *STOCK: Domestic metalwork and metalware, works of art and decorative objects; early lighting and smoothing irons.* PARK: Easy. TEL: 223 5676 (24 hour ansafone). FAIRS: Olympia, Chelsea Spring and Autumn. VAT: Stan/Spec.

Tony Davis Inc.
London and Washington
235/7/9 Lavender Hill, and 23 Battersea Rise. Resident. Est. 1955. Open 10.30—4. SIZE: Large. *STOCK: Furniture, including upholstered; china, glass, books and pictures, Victorian and Edwardian.* LOC: Clapham junction, opposite magistrates court. PARK: Own or nearby. TEL: 228 1370/1. SER: Valuations; buys at auction (Victorian and Edwardian furniture). VAT: Stan.

J.T. Antiques
11 Webb's Rd., Battersea. (J. Chapmann.) Est. 1964. Open 10—1 and 1.30—6, or by appointment. SIZE: Small. *STOCK: Doulton, glass, pictures, porcelain.* LOC: Off A3. PARK: Easy. TEL: 228 7171. FAIRS: East Sheen, Epsom, Dulwich Village, Weybridge.

Number 26
Honeywell Rd., Battersea. (K. Gretton.) Resident. Est. 1979. Open by appointment. SIZE: Small. *STOCK: Advertising figures, jugs, signs, 1890—1939, £5—£200; bottles, 1800—1920, tins, 1860—1950, both £5—£100; stoneware, 1800—1900, £50—£200.* LOC: Near Clapham Junction, just off the south circular. PARK: Easy. TEL: 228 0741. SER: Valuations. FAIRS: Specialist.

Robert Young Antiques
68 Battersea Bridge Rd. Est. 1974. Open 10—6, Sat. 11—5. SIZE: Medium. *STOCK: English oak and country furniture, 17th and 18th C, £100—£3,000; English and European treen and objects of folk art, £15—£2,000; English and European provincial pottery and metalwork, £10—£250.* LOC: Turn off King's Rd. or Chelsea Embankment into Beaufort St., cross over Battersea Bridge Rd., 9th shop on right. PARK: Opp. in side street. TEL: 228 7847. SER: Valuations; buys at auction (treen and country furniture). FAIRS: Olympia. VAT: Stan/Spec.

London S.W.12

The Kilim Warehouse Ltd.
28A Pickets St. (J. Luczyc-Wyhowska.) Est. 1981. Open 10—4, Sun. 11—2. SIZE: Medium. *STOCK: Kilims, £75—£2,000; Berber flat weave tribal rugs, £50—£350.* LOC: Near Clapham South tube station and Nightingale Lane. PARK: Easy. TEL: 675 3122. SER: Restorations. VAT: Stan.

John F.C. Phillips
92 Rossiter Rd. Est. 1978. Open by appointment only. SIZE: Medium. *STOCK: British watercolours, pencil drawings and prints, topography, architecture, landscape and figure subjects, 1750 to late 19th C, £5—£1,500.* LOC: Quite close to Balham railway and underground stations. PARK: Easy. TEL: 673 5150; home — same. SER: Mail order (catalogues issued); buys at auction; topographical research undertaken.

London S.W.13

Abbott and Holder
73 Castelnau, Barnes. Est. 1938. Open Sat. 9—5, weekdays by appointment. *STOCK: Pictures, especially watercolours.* TEL: 748 2416. VAT: Spec.

Beverley Brook Antiques
29 Grove Rd., Barnes. (N. McCormick.) Est. 1976. Open by appointment. SIZE: Medium. *STOCK: Glass, china, silver plate, watercolours.* PARK: Side roads. TEL: Home — 878 5656. SER: Silver re-plating and cleaning.

Campion
71 White Hart Lane, Barnes. (J. Richards.) Est. 1983. Open 10—1 and 2—5.30. SIZE: Small. *STOCK: Jewellery, bric-a-brac, quilts, cushions, some prints, small furniture, £5—£50.* LOC: Along river from Barnes High St., turn left at White Hart public house. PARK: Easy. TEL: 878 6688; home — same. SER: Framing.

Simon Coleman Antiques
40 White Hart Lane, Barnes. Est. 1974. SIZE: Large. *STOCK: Country furniture, oak, fruitwood, pine, French and English farm tables, all 18th—19th C.* PARK: Easy. TEL: 878 5037. VAT: Stan.

The Dining Room Shop
64 White Hart Lane, Barnes. (K. Dyson.) Est. 1986. Open 10.30—5.30, Sun. by appointment. SIZE: Small. *STOCK: Dining room furniture, 18th—19th C, £500—£10,000; glasses, china especially dinner services; cutlery, damask and lace table linen, 19th C; associated small items.* LOC: Near Barnes railway bridge, turning opposite White Hart public house. PARK: Easy. TEL: 878 1020; home — 876 5212. SER: Valuations; restorations; buys at auction (as stock). VAT: Stan/Spec.

Christopher Bangs

01 223 5676   *By appointment only*

Early metalware and metalwork and works of art

S.W.13 continued

Dove Antiques
(D. Emanuel) Est. 1975. Open by appointment. *STOCK: Small furniture, £5—£500; porcelain £5—£200; objets de vertu, bric-a-brac, £5—£100.* LOC: Off Castelnau. PARK: Easy. TEL: 748 5972; home — same. SER: Buys and sells on commission.

Gothic Cottage Antiques
70 Station Rd., Barnes. (N. Marshall.) Est. 1966. CL: Wed. Open 10.30—5.30. SIZE: Small. *STOCK: Stripped pine furniture, bric-a-brac, mainly country items.* LOC: Opposite Barnes Green. PARK: Easy. TEL: 876 2026.

John Haines Antiques Ltd.   BADA
Trade only
59 Elm Grove Rd. (J. and S.D. Haines.) Est. 1960. Open by appointment. SIZE: Small. *STOCK: Furniture and objects, 17th—18th C, £1,000—£1,500.* PARK: Easy. TEL: 876 4215; home — same. SER: Valuations. FAIRS: Olympia. VAT: Spec.

David Loman Ltd.
12 Suffolk Rd. ABA. Open by appointment only. *STOCK: Antiquarian books and manuscripts on Oriental travel, history, culture, linguistics.* TEL: 748 0254

S.W.13 continued

Joy McDonald
50 Station Rd., Barnes. Est. 1966. Resident. SIZE: Small. *STOCK: Furniture, 18th—19th C; pine unusual items, brass, copper.* Not stocked: China, glass. PARK: Easy. TEL: 876 6184. SER: Restorations (furniture); repairs to china.

New Grafton Gallery
49 Church Rd., Barnes. (D. Wolfers.) Est. 1968. CL: Mon. Open 10—5.30. SIZE: Medium. *STOCK: British paintings and drawings, 20th C, £50—£500.* LOC: Off Castelnau which runs from Hammersmith Bridge. PARK: Easy. TEL: 748 8850; home — 876 6294. SER: Valuations; restorations; buys at auction. VAT: Stan/Spec.

Portmeirion Antiques
62 White Hart Lane, Barnes. Est. 1958. Open 10.30—6. *STOCK: Furniture, 1700—1900; china, glass, lamps, decorative items, quilts, rugs.* LOC: Between Thames and Upper Richmond Rd. PARK: Easy. TEL: 876 2367. VAT: Stan/Spec.

Randalls Antiques
46/52 Church Rd., Barnes. (E. Appleton.) Open 9.30—4.30. *STOCK: Decorative items; furniture, 18th—19th C.* TEL: 748 1858; evenings — 948 1260.

S.W.13 continued

Remember When
6 and 7 Rocks Lane, Barnes. (Mr. and Mrs. K. Blore.) Est. 1975. Open 9—7 including Sun. *STOCK: Pine furniture.* TEL: 878 2817.

Wren Antiques
49b Church Rd., Barnes. (M.A. Smith). Est. 1980. CL: Mon. Open 10—1 and 2—5.30. Sun. in summer 11—5. SIZE: Small. *STOCK: Georgian and Victorian furniture, £200— £1,000; silver, Georgian to 1900, £50— £500; books, 17th—20th C, £20—£250.* LOC: Near Barnes High St. (A3003), corner of Grange Rd. PARK: Easy. TEL: 741 7841. SER: Valuations; restorations (furniture).

London S.W.14

Dixon's Antique Market
471 Upper Richmond Rd. West, East Sheen. (J. and R. Dixon.) Est. 1981. CL: Wed. Open 10—5.30 including Sun. SIZE: Large. There are 30 dealers at this market selling *18th and 19th C porcelain; out-of-production Doulton figures, silver, art deco, jewellery and brass, £5—£500; copper, furniture, books and pictures, £5—£1,000; all 1780—1930.* LOC: South Circular Rd. between Richmond and Putney, ½ mile past Bull Hotel. PARK: Easy and side roads. TEL: 878 6788; home — 570 4557. SER: Restorations (porcelain, clocks and furniture). FAIRS: London weekend and 3 day Porcelain.

Helius Antiques   *Trade Only*
487—493 Upper Richmond Rd. West. (Mrs. M. Rowlands.) Est. 1965. CL: Sun. and Wed., except by appointment. Open 10—5, Sat. 10.30—12.45. SIZE: Large. *STOCK: Pedestal desks, bureaux, 18th to early 20th C writing tables, secretaires and bookcases; general antiques, decorative furniture.* LOC: On South Circular rd. PARK: Easy. TEL: 876 5721. VAT: Stan.

Mortlake Antiques
69 Lower Richmond Rd., Mortlake. (C.J. and J.A. Bate.) Est. 1946. CL: Wed. Open 9—6, Sun. 11—4. SIZE: Medium. *STOCK: Furniture, Georgian, Victorian, Edwardian, £5— £600; stripped furniture, especially pine, satin walnut, beech, £10—£500; longcase clocks, 1750—1850, from £450; also wall clocks; small wooden items from £1.* Not stocked: Silver, oil paintings, watercolours, porcelain. LOC: A4, west from Hammersmith; left at first roundabout, A316 towards Richmond, cross river bridge, then left at traffic lights, shop 150yds. on right. PARK: Easy. TEL: 876 8715. VAT: Stan/Spec.

S.W.14 continued

Remember When
138 Upper Richmond Rd., East Sheen. (Mr. and Mrs. K. Blore.) Est. 1975. Open 9—7 including Sun. *STOCK: Pine furniture.* TEL: 876 2100.

Vandeleur Antiquarian Books
69 Sheen Lane. (E.H. Bryant.) Est. 1971. Usually open 12—7, prior telephone call advisable. SIZE: Small. *STOCK: Antiquarian and secondhand books in all subjects, prints and maps.* LOC: Between South Circular and Mortlake Station. PARK: Easy. TEL: 878 6837; home — 393 7752. SER: Valuations; collections purchased. VAT: Stan.

M.S. Wardle
358A Upper Richmond Rd. West, East Sheen. CL: Wed. Open 10—6. *STOCK: Watercolours, oil paintings and prints.* TEL: 878 1100. SER: Restorations; gilding and framing.

London S.W.15

R.A. Barnes Antiques   LAPADA
26 Lower Richmond Rd. Est. 1966. CL: Sat. Open 10—5. SIZE: Large. *STOCK: English, Oriental and Continental antiques and collectables; Wedgwood, ironstone, china, brass, copper, 19th C; art glass, Regency, Victorian and some 18th C small furniture, primitive paintings.* TEL: 789 3371. VAT: Stan/Spec.

J. & R. Bateman Antiques
12 Lower Richmond Rd., Putney. Est. 1975. Open 10—1 and 2—7. SIZE: Small. *STOCK: Furniture, oak and country, 17th and 18th C.* LOC: Across Putney Bridge, turn right at traffic lights. PARK: Easy. TEL: 789 3124; home — 228 9654. SER: Restorations; cabinet making, rushing and caning. VAT: Stan/Spec.

Susan Becker   LAPADA
18 Lower Richmond Rd. Est. 1960. Open 10—5.30. SIZE: Large. *STOCK: English, Continental and Oriental porcelain, glass.* PARK: Easy. TEL: 788 9082. SER: Valuations. VAT: Stan/Spec.

The Clock Clinic Ltd.
85 Lower Richmond Rd. (P.M.L. Banks, R.S. Pedler, F.B.H.I.) Est. 1971. CL: Mon. Open 9—6, Sat. 9—1. *STOCK: Clocks.* TEL: 788 1407. SER: Valuations (clocks); restorations (clocks); buys at auction. VAT: Stan/Spec.

A. and R. Dockerill Ltd.
78 Deodar Rd. Est. 1880. CL: Sat. p.m. Open 8.30—5.15. SIZE: Large. *STOCK: French, English marble and pine chimney pieces; panelling, oak and pine.* PARK: Easy. TEL: 874 2101. SER: Restorations. VAT: Stan.

S.W.15 continued

Foster of Putney
146 Upper Richmond Rd., Putney. (M. and M. Susands.) Est. 1961. CL: Wed. Open 10—6. *STOCK: Antique, Victorian, Edwardian furniture, bric-a-brac, curios.* TEL: 373 5135. SER: Valuations; restorations (furniture). VAT: Stan.

Jorgen Antiques
40 Lower Richmond Rd., Putney. (A.J. Dolleris.) Est. 1960. CL: Mon. and Sat. Open 11—5. SIZE: Medium. *STOCK: English and Continental furniture, 18th to early 19th C, £50—£2,000.* LOC: Between Putney Bridge and Putney Common. PARK: Easy. TEL: 789 7329. VAT: Spec.

A.V. Marsh and Son
Vale House, Kingston Vale. Est. 1960. Open 9—6. *STOCK: Furniture, 18th to early 19th C.* TEL: 546 5996. VAT: Stan/Spec.

Richard Maude Tools
22 Parkfields, Putney. (R.M.C. Maude.) Est. 1977. Open by appointment only. SIZE: Medium. *STOCK: Woodworking tools, 18th—19th C, £5—£1,000; ornamental turning lathes, 19th C, £500—£5,000; books, and old trade catalogues relating to previous items, 18th—19th C, £5—£250; some early ironwork and keys.* Not stocked: Other than stock listed. LOC: ½ mile west of Putney High St., off Upper Richmond Rd. PARK: Easy. TEL: 788 2991. SER: Valuations; buys at auction. VAT: Spec.

Nicodemus
27 Lacy Rd., Putney. (N.P. Ross.) Est. 1942. Open 9.30—6. SIZE: Small. *STOCK: Copper and brassware, 1805—1910, £5—£25; paintings and prints, pre-Edwardian, £10—£150.* LOC: Turn opp. Marks and Spencer, Putney High Street. PARK: Easy. TEL: 789 2838. SER: Hire (furniture).

Michael Phelps Antiquarian Books
19 Chelverton Rd., Putney. Open 10—5 by appointment. *STOCK: Antiquarian books — medicine, science, technology, natural history.* TEL: 785 6766.

Dorothy Rose
32 Lacy Rd. Est. 1967. CL: Thurs. Open 10—6. SIZE: Small. *STOCK: Jewellery, bric-a-brac, objets d'art, general antiques.* PARK: Easy. TEL: 789 1410. VAT: Stan/Spec.

Alan Stone Antiques
3 Wadham Rd., Putney. Open 9—6. *STOCK: General antiques.* TEL: 870 1606 or 642 6877. SER: Restorations.

S.W.15 continued

Taurus Gallery
5 Wadham Rd., Putney. (M. Bull.) Open 12—5.30, Sat. 10—5.30, Mon. and mornings by appointment. *STOCK: Engravings and prints, ephemera, posters, decorative items, greeting cards.* LOC: Off Putney Bridge Rd. opp. ''The Cedar Tree''. TEL: 874 2534. SER: Framing.

Thornhill Galleries Ltd.
78 Deodar Rd., Putney. Est. 1880. Open 9—5.15, Sat. 10—12.30. SIZE: Large. *STOCK: English and French marble, stone and wooden chimney-pieces, English and French panelled rooms, architectural features and wood carvings, fire grates and fenders; all 17th—19th C; decorative iron interiors and other fire accessories, 17th—20th C.* LOC: Off Putney Bridge Rd., at rear of 78 Deodar Rd. (large Georgian house). PARK: Easy. TEL: 874 2101/5669. SER: Valuations; restorations (architectural items); buys at auction (architectural items). FAIRS: T.B.A. VAT: Stan/Spec.

Vaughan
75 Lower Richmond Rd. (M.J. and Mrs. L.M. Vaughan.) Est. 1980. CL: Mon. and Sat. Open 10—5. SIZE: Medium. *STOCK: Decorative 18th—19th C furniture and objects; lamps and lighting fittings.* PARK: Easy. TEL: 789 4245. VAT: Stan/Spec.

London S.W.16

S. Farrelly
634 Streatham High Rd. Est. 1958. CL: Wed. p.m. Open 9—12.30, and 1.30—5.30. SIZE: Medium. *STOCK: General antiques.* PARK: In side roads. TEL: 764 4028. VAT: Stan/Spec.

A. and J. Fowle
542 Streatham High Rd. (A.C. Fowle.) Est. 1962. Open 9.30—7. SIZE: Large. *STOCK: General antiques; Victorian and Edwardian furniture, paintings.* LOC: From London take A23 towards Brighton. PARK: Easy. TEL: 764 2896. VAT: Stan/Spec.

William Reeves Bookseller Ltd.
1a Norbury Crescent. Est. 1871. Open by appointment. SIZE: Medium. *STOCK: Books about music, 1800—1970, £1-£100.* LOC: From station under railway bridge, first left. PARK: Easy. TEL: 764 2108.

Streatham Traders and Shippers Market
United Reform Church Hall, Streatham High St. Est. 1973. Open Tues. 8—3. Varying between 35 and 60 dealers at this market selling a wide variety of small antiques. LOC: Between the ice rink and bus garage. TEL: 764 3602.

S.W.16 continued

Streatham Village Antiques
Est. 1963. Open by appointment. *STOCK: Furniture, bric-a-brac.* PARK: Reasonable. TEL: 769 7833.

Woodstock
1563/1565 London Rd., Norbury. (R. and Mrs. B. Smith.) Open 9−6. *STOCK: Period, country pine and architectural pieces.* TEL: 764 0270.

London S.W.17

Brian R. Verrall and Co.
20 Tooting Bec Rd. Est. 1957. Open 10−6. SIZE: Large. *STOCK: Vintage and veteran motor cycles, motor cars, £50−£50,000; furniture, clocks, and shipping items, 16th− 19th C, £10−£2,000.* LOC: 50yds. from Tooting Bec underground station. PARK: Easy. TEL: 672 1144. SER: Valuations; buys at auction. VAT: Stan/Spec.

London, S.W.18

Rodney Brooke Antiques　LAPADA
27A Elsynge Rd. Open by appointment only. *STOCK: Decorative, rare and unusual furniture, 17th−19th C.* TEL: 870 7055.

Mr. Wandle's Workshop
200−202 Garratt Lane. (D. Taylor.) Open 9−5.30. *STOCK: Victorian and Edwardian fireplaces and surrounds especially cast iron.* TEL: 870 5873.

London, S.W.19

Adams Room Ltd.,　LAPADA
Antiques and Adams Gallery
18−20 Ridgway, Wimbledon Village. Est. 1971. Open 9.30−5. SIZE: Large. *STOCK: Georgian, French furniture; silver, Sheffield plate, glass, porcelain; English landscapes, oil paintings, 18th and 19th C.* LOC: 4 miles from King's Rd., Chelsea; 1 mile off Kingston bypass, M3. TEL: 946 7047 and 947 4784. SER: Export orders arranged. VAT: Spec.

Chelsea Bric-a-Brac Shop Ltd.
16 Hartfield Rd., Wimbledon. (J. and P. Wirth.) Est. 1960. CL: Wed. Open 9.30−6. SIZE: Medium. *STOCK: Furniture − antique, Victorian, pine, and shipping, 1800−1930, £20−£1,500; brass, copper, steel, £1− £500; bric-a-brac, £1−£250; all from Victorian.* Not stocked: Jewellery, weapons. LOC: Left from Wimbledon station, first turning on right, shop 100yds. on left. PARK: 100yds. TEL: 946 6894; home − 542 5509/8112. SER: Valuations; restorations (wood and metal); upholstery; Continental export. VAT: Stan.

Clunes Antiques
9 West Place, Wimbledon Common. Est. 1973. CL: Mon. and Wed. Open 10−5. *STOCK: General small antiques, Staffordshire figures, theatricalia.* TEL: 946 1643.

J.F. Ewing　LAPADA
11 High St., Wimbledon Village. Est. 1969. CL: Mon. Open 10−1 and 2.15−5. SIZE: Small. *STOCK: Jewellery, from 1800, £20− £5,000.* LOC: Continuation south of Wimbledon Parkside, nr. common. PARK: 200yds. TEL: 946 4700. VAT: Stan/Spec.

The Lighthouse Ltd.　LAPADA
67 Ridgway, Wimbledon Village. (Mrs. E. Kingston.) Est. 1969. CL: Wed. Open 10−5. *STOCK: Lighting, chandeliers, small furniture.* TEL: 946 2050.

S.W.19 continued

Richard Maryan and Daughters
177 Merton Rd. Est. 1966. CL: Wed. p.m.
and Mon. Open 10−5. SIZE: Large. STOCK:
General antiques. PARK: Reasonable. TEL:
542 5846.

Mark J. West − Cobb Antiques Ltd.
39B High St., Wimbledon Village. Open
Wed.−Fri. 1−6, Sat. 10−6, other times by
appointment. SIZE: Medium. STOCK: Table
glass, 18th−19th C, £100−£800; decorators' items, glass, ceramics, £50−£1,000;
collectors' glass, small furniture, £100−
£1,000. PARK: Easy. TEL: 946 2811 or 540
7982. SER: Valuations; buys at auction.
FAIRS: Olympia.

Wimbledon Pine Co.
264 Haydons Rd., Wimbledon. (R.A. Clare).
Est. 1978. Open 10−5.30. SIZE: Medium.
STOCK: Pine furniture, 19th C, £10−£1,000.
LOC: Near B.R. station. PARK: Easy. TEL: 540
5032. SER: Pine stripping; pine kitchens.

London S.W.20

Den of Antiquity
96 Coombe Lane, Raynes Park. (O. Clarke.)
Est. 1968. CL: Wed. on sale days. Open
9−6.30. SIZE: Medium. LOC: A3 to Merton,
turn off ¾ mile along Coombe Lane on left.
300yds. from Raynes Park station. PARK:
Easy. TEL: 947 0850; home − 946 4574.
SER: Restorations (furniture and porcelain);
buys at auction. VAT: Stan/Spec.

London S.E.1

The Antiques Exchange (London)   LAPADA
Trade Only
1 Bermondsey Sq. (R.L. Draysey.) Est. 1964.
Open Mon.−Fri. There are 4 dealers here
selling furniture, clocks and small items of
general interest £1−£10,000. TEL: 407 3635.
VAT: Stan.

Antique Hypermarket Bermondsey
Corner of Long Lane and Bermondsey St.
Open Mon.−Fri. STOCK: General antiques
and collectors' items. TEL: 937 1572 or 351
5353.

Nigel A. Bartlett
67 St. Thomas St. CL: Sat. Open 9.30−5.30.
STOCK: Marble, pine and stone chimney
pieces. TEL: 378 7895/6.

S.E.1 continued

Bermondsey Antique Market
Corner of Long Lane and Bermondsey St. Est.
1959. Open Fri. 5−2, or by appointment.
250 stalls. STOCK: General antiques and collectors' items. TEL: 937 1572 or 351 5353.

Bermondsey Antique Warehouse
173 Bermondsey St. (R.J. Whitfield.) Est.
1974. CL: Sat. and Sun. except by appointment. Open 9.30−5.30, Thurs. 9.30−8, Fri.
7−5.30. SIZE: Large. TEL: 407 2040/4250.
Below are listed the dealers at this warehouse:−

Argosy Antiques
General antiques.

D.B. Cater   LAPADA
Est. 1968. General antiques, shipping
goods. VAT: Stan.

P.H. Forrest and Son   LAPADA
Est. 1968. General antiques, shipping
goods. VAT: Stan.

P. Nash   LAPADA
Est. 1973. General antiques, furniture.
VAT: Stan.

Mr. Pickwick Antiques   LAPADA
(J. Sturton.) Est. 1965. Clocks, shipping
goods, general antiques. TEL: Home −
599 6744. VAT: Stan

T. Seal
Est. 1974. Furniture, shipping goods.
VAT: Stan/Spec.

B.G. Watson   LAPADA
Victorian and Edwardian Furniture. VAT:
Stan.

R.J. Whitfield   LAPADA
Est. 1972. General antiques, shipping
goods and chandeliers. VAT: Stan.

Bermondsey Antiques
167 Bermondsey St. CL: Mon. STOCK:
General antiques, Victorian and Edwardian
furniture, shipping goods. PARK: Easy. TEL:
403 2464.

Bermondsey Antiques   Trade Only
245 Long Lane. Open Thurs. 10−6, Fri. 5
a.m.−1 or by appointment. STOCK: General
antiques, Victorian and Edwardian furniture
and shipping goods PARK: Easy. TEL: 407
0309.

Blue Mantle
299-301 Old Kent Rd. (M. Ross.) Open
10.30−6. STOCK: Victorian, Edwardian and
art nouveau fireplaces, furniture, bric-a-brac,
architectural items. TEL: 237 3931.

S.E.1 continued

Lamont Antiques Ltd. **LAPADA**
151 Tower Bridge Rd. (N. Lamont and F. Llewellyn.) CL: Sat. Open 9—5.30. SIZE: Large. *STOCK: Architectural fixtures and fittings, bars and bar furniture, leaded light windows, pub mirrors and signs, shipping furniture, £5—£20,000.* PARK: Own. TEL: 403 0126. SER: Container packing. VAT: Stan.

MacNeill's Art and Antique Warehouse
Newhams Row, 175 Bermondsey St. (MacNeill Press Ltd.) Est. 1978. CL: Sat. Open 9.30—5.30., Thurs. 9.30—8, Fri. 9—5.30 or by appointment. SIZE: Large. *STOCK: Furniture.* TEL: 403 0022. SER: Valuations; restorations; buys at auction.

Oola Boola Antiques London
LAPADA
166 Tower Bridge Rd. (R. Scales.) Est. 1968. CL: Sat. Open 9—5.30, Thurs. 9—6.30, Fri. 9—5.30. SIZE: Large. *STOCK: Furniture, £5—£1,000; mahogany, Victorian and Edwardian shipping goods.* TEL: 403 0794; home — 693 5050.

Penny Farthing Antiques Arcade
177 Bermondsey St. Est. 1976. CL: Sat. Open 10—5, Thurs. 10—6. SIZE: Medium. *STOCK: Furniture, including shipping, £25—£1,000; longcase clocks, £200—£1,000; general small antiques and shipping items, £5—£200.* LOC: 5 minutes from Tower Bridge. PARK: Usually easy. TEL: 407 5171. VAT: Stan.

Tower Bridge Antique **LAPADA** Warehouse Ltd
163 Tower Bridge Rd. CL: Sat. Open 9—5.30. *STOCK: Victorian and Georgian furniture, shipping goods.* TEL: 403 3660. VAT: Stan.

London S.E.3

Berkeley Galleries Ltd.
82 The Hall, Foxes Dale. Est. 1941. Open by appointment. TEL: 852 0586.

Vale Stamps and Antiques
21 Tranquil Vale, Blackheath. (H.J. and R.P. Varnham.) Est. 1952. CL: Thurs. Open 10—5.30. SIZE: Small. *STOCK: Pottery, 3000 BC—500 AD, jewellery, Roman, all £20—£200; bronzes £50—£350; Georgian and Victorian jewellery, £25—£250.* LOC: Village centre, 100yds. from station. PARK: Nearby. TEL: 852 9817. SER: Valuations; buys at auction (antiquities). VAT: Stan/Spec.

London S.E.5

Franklin's Camberwell Antiques Market
161 Camberwell Rd. (R. Franklin.) Est. 1968. CL: Mon. Open 10—6, Sun. 1—6. SIZE: Large. There are five floors at this market offering *a range of general antiques, furniture, brass, copper, silver, clocks, pictures, prints, architectural and garden items.* LOC: 1 mile from Elephant and Castle via Walworth Rd. PARK: 50yds. behind building, outside premises on Sunday. TEL: 703 8089. VAT: Stan/Spec.

Scallywag
The Old Church, Wren Rd., Camberwell Green. (J.A. Butterworth.) Est. 1970. Open 9—6; Sat. and Sun. 10—6. SIZE: Large. *STOCK: Pine, £5—£2,000; architectural fittings, £2—£5,000; both 18th—19th C.* LOC: 150yds. from Camberwell Green, on A2/A20, between The Oval and Peckham. PARK: Easy. TEL: 701 5353. SER: Restorations (pine stripping). FAIRS: Lambeth Country and Putney Shows. VAT: Stan/Spec.

London S.E.6

Silver Sixpence
14 Catford Hill. (D. Clark.) Est. 1968. CL: Mon. Open 10—12 and 12.30—6. SIZE: Large. *STOCK: Clocks, brass fenders, stripped pine.* LOC: 2 mins. Catford Bridge railway station. PARK: Easy. TEL: 690 0046. SER: Stripping (pine).

London S.E.7

Daedalus
43 The Village, Charlton. (L.G. Smith and S. J. Fisher.) Est. 1943. Open 9.30—6, Thurs. 9.30—1, Sat. 9.30—5.30. SIZE: Small. *STOCK: Watches, £25—£700; clocks, £100—£1,000, both 18th and 19th C.* LOC: On B210. PARK: Easy, and opposite. TEL: 858 2514. SER: Valuations; restorations (clocks, watches and jewellery). VAT: Stan/Spec.

London S.E.8

Antique Warehouse
9—12 Deptford Broadway, Deptford. (J. Davison and M. Tillett.) Est. 1976. Open 10—6, Sat. 9.30—6, Sun. 11—4. SIZE: Large. *STOCK: Furniture, 18th to early 20th C, £50—£500.* LOC: A2. PARK: Limited. TEL: 469 0295; home — 319 3469. FAIRS: Wembley. VAT: Stan.

London S.E.9

R.E. Rose, F.B.H.I.
731 Sidcup Rd., Eltham. Est. 1976. Open
9–5. SIZE: Small. *STOCK: Clocks, 1750–
1850, £100–£2,000.* LOC: A20 from
London, shop on left just past fiveways traffic
lights at Green Lane. PARK: Easy. TEL: 859
4754; home – 464 2653. SER: Restorations
(clocks and barometers); spare parts for
antique clocks, watches and barometers.
VAT: Stan/Spec.

London S.E.10

Edward and Victoria Antiques
7 Blackheath Hill, Blackheath. (M. Tillett.)
Open 10–6, Sun. 11–2. *STOCK: General
antiques.* TEL: 691 3062.

The Green Parrot
2 Turpin Lane, Greenwich. (J. Randerson.)
Est. 1971. *STOCK: Porcelain, bric-a-brac,
small furniture.* TEL: 858 6690. VAT: Stan.

Greenwich Antiques Market
Greenwich High Rd. Est. 1972. Open Sun.
7.30–4.30; June–Sept. and every Sat.
There are approximately 80 stalls at this
market selling a wide range of antiques and
bric-a- brac. LOC: Almost opposite railway
station. PARK: Adjacent.

S.E.10 continued

Greenwich Chimes
11 Nelson Rd., Greenwich. *STOCK: Clocks,
furniture, brass and copper fireside accessories, general antiques.*

The Warwick Leadlay Gallery
5 Nelson Rd., Greenwich. Est. 1973. Open
9.30–5.45 and Sun. 11–5. SIZE: Large.
*STOCK: Antiquarian prints, maps and illus-
trated books, 17th–19th C.* LOC: 2 mins.
walk from Cutty Sark. PARK: Nearby. TEL:
858 0317; home – 852 7484. SER: Valuations; cleaning, colouring; mounting, framing.
VAT: Stan.

A. Polly
8 Turpin Lane, Greenwich. *STOCK: Furniture, clocks.* TEL: 858 4048. VAT: Spec.

Relcy Antiques
9 Nelson Rd., Greenwich. (R. Challis.) Est.
1958. CL: Sun. except by appointment. Open
10–6. SIZE: Large. *STOCK: English furniture,
especially bureaux and bookcases, £50–
£15,000; English and Continental pictures,
especially marine and sporting, £20–£5,000;
instruments and marine items, ships' heads,
sextants, telescopes, models, £20–£15,000,
all 18th and 19th C.* Not stocked: Reproduction and art deco. LOC: ¾ mile off A2
towards River Thames. TEL: 858 2812. SER:
Valuations, restorations (furniture and pictures);
buys at auction (Georgian and Victorian
furniture, pictures). VAT: Stan/Spec.

Stool, 'X' frame, rosewood with gilded ornament, c.1825. From *Regency Furniture* by
Frances Collard, published by the **Antique Collectors' Club**, 1985.

S.E.10 continued

Rogers Turner Books Ltd.
22 Nelson Rd., Greenwich. Est. 1975. Open
10—6, Thurs. 10—2. *STOCK: Antiquarian
books especially on clocks and scientific
instruments.* TEL: 853 5271/Paris (010 333)
912 1191. SER: Buys at auction (British and
European); catalogues available.

Spread Eagle Antiques
23 Nelson Rd. (R.F. Moy.) Est. 1954. CL:
Thurs. p.m. Open 10—5.30. SIZE: Large.
*STOCK: Furniture, pictures and decorative
items, 18th—19th C.* PARK: Easy. TEL: 858
9713; home — 692 1618. SER: Valuations;
restorations (pictures, furniture). VAT: Stan/
Spec.

Spread Eagle Antiques
8 Nevada St. (R.F. Moy.) Est. 1954. CL:
Thurs. p.m. Open 10—5.30. SIZE: Large.
*STOCK: China, bric-a-brac, books, prints,
19th C; postcards, costume, pre-1940.* Not
stocked: Weapons. LOC: A202. From London
follow A2, then turn left at Deptford — or
follow riverside road from Tower Bridge.
PARK: Easy. TEL: 692 1618. SER: Valuations;
restorations (furniture, china, pictures). VAT:
Stan/Spec.

Russell Wood Antiques
20 Greenwich Church St. Open daily including
Sun. *STOCK: Furniture, decorative items,
china, glass, lace and linen.* LOC: 200yds.
from 'Cutty Sark' Museum. PARK. Nearby.
TEL: 853 0200.

London S.E.13

Actino Antiques   LAPADA
136 Lee High Rd., Lewisham. (R.T. Jones.)
Est. 1968. Open 10—5.30, Thurs. 10—12 or
by appointment; Sat. 9.30—6. SIZE: Small.
*STOCK: Collectors' items, small furniture,
fenders, lights.* LOC: Leaving Lewisham Clock
Tower on the A20 to Dover, shop 500yds. on
right. PARK: Opposite. TEL: 318 1273. SER:
Valuations. VAT: Stan/Spec.

Morley Galleries   BADA
Robert Morley and Co. Ltd.
4 Belmont Hill, Lewisham. Est. 1881. Open
9—5. *STOCK: Harpsichords, clavichords,
spinets, harps, pianos.* TEL: 852 6151. SER:
Restorations (musical instruments). VAT: Stan/
Spec.

S.E.13 continued

Riverdale Hall Antique and Bric-a-Brac Market
Lewisham Centre, Rennell St. Est. 1981.
Open every Mon. except Bank Holidays
8.30—4.30. SIZE: 50 stalls. *STOCK: General
antiques and bric-a-brac.* LOC: Lewisham High
St. PARK: Easy, next door. TEL: 599 4076.

Whitworth and O'Donnell Ltd.
282 Lewisham High St. (A. O'Donnell.) Est.
1950. Open 10—5, Thurs. 9.30—1. SIZE:
Medium. *STOCK: Jewellery, £10—£500.*
TEL: 690 1282. SER: Restorations (jewellery).
VAT: Stan.

London S.E.15

Peter Allen Antiques Ltd.
World Wide Antique Exporters
17-17a Nunhead Green, Peckham. Est. 1966.
CL: Sat. Open 8—5. SIZE: Warehouse.
STOCK: Victorian walnut and mahogany furniture. TEL: 732 1968.

The Antique Gallery
40 Peckham Rye. (J.H. Yorke.) Open
9—5.30, Sat. 9—1. SIZE: Large. *STOCK:
Furniture, 18th and 19th C; brass, copper,
clocks, pictures, export and shipping goods.*
TEL: 732 7808. VAT: Stan.

G. Austin and Sons Ltd.
39—41 Brayards Rd. Est. 1870. CL: Thurs.
Open 8.30—5.30. SIZE: Large. *STOCK: Furniture, porcelain, silver, pictures.* PARK: Easy.
TEL: 639 0480. VAT: Stan/Spec.

G. Austin and Sons Ltd.
11—23 Peckham Rye. (H., A., D. and V.
Austin.) Est. 1870. D. Austin, book on Old
Sheffield Plate. CL: Thurs. p.m. Open 8.30—
5.30. SIZE: Large. *STOCK: Furniture, silver,
porcelain, pictures, glass, books.* PARK: Easy.
TEL: 639 3163/2725. SER: Free delivery up
to 20 miles. VAT: Stan/Spec.

Butchoff Antiques   LAPADA
48 Peckham Rye. (I.M. Butchoff.) Est. 1962.
Open 9—5.30, Sat. 9—1. SIZE: Large.
*STOCK: Furniture, 18th—20th C, £25—
£5,000.* PARK: Easy. TEL: 639 0736. VAT:
Stan.

A.J. Mangion Antiques
Mainly Trade and Export
1A Philip Walk, Peckham. Open 9—5.30, Sat.
9—1. *STOCK: Furniture and objets d'art.* TEL:
732 6749.

S.E.15 continued

Peckham Rye Antiques
78 Peckham Rye. (T.A. Russell.) Est. 1975. Open 9—5.30, Sat. 9—12.30. SIZE: Medium. *STOCK: Furniture and smalls, 18th C to 1930s, £25—£2,000.* LOC: Main road. PARK: Easy. TEL: 639 9723; home — 732 6201.

F.J. Rutter and A. Fagiani
28—30 Wagner St. Est. 1965. Open 8—1 and 2—6, Sat. 8—1. *STOCK: Bookcases, pedestal desks.* LOC: Off Old Kent Rd. and Ilderton Rd. TEL: 732 7188. SER: Valuatio¡s; restorations (furniture); French polishing. VAT: Stan.

Waveney Antiques   LAPADA
58 and 68 Peckham Rye. (G.E. and R.G. Breeze, R. Behan.) Est. 1971. CL: Sat. p.m Open 9—5.30. SIZE: Large. *STOCK: General antiques.* PARK: Easy. TEL: 732 1251. VAT: Stan.

Ian Wilson Antiques
70-72 Peckham Rye. CL: Sat. Open 9—1 and 2—5. *STOCK: Furniture and effects especially trade and export.* TEL: 639 5068.

London S.E.18

Lawrence Antiques
70 Plumstead High St. Est. 1963. CL: Thurs. p.m. Open 9.30—6. SIZE: Medium. *STOCK: Furniture, copper and brass.* LOC: Near Plumstead station. PARK: Easy. TEL: 854 2380. VAT: Stan.

London S.E.21

Acorn Antiques
111 Rosendale Rd., West Dulwich. (Mrs. G. Kingham.) CL: Mon. Open 10—6.30, Sat. 10—5.30. *STOCK: China, glass, period clothes, pictures, general small antiques and jewellery, some furniture.* TEL: 761 3349.

London S.E.22

Collector's Corner — Militaria
1 North Cross Rd., East Dulwich. (J.H. Joslyn.) Est. 1968. Open 10.30—5.30. SIZE: Small. *STOCK: Wings and insignia; U.S.A. and German military items; helmets, badges, medals, uniforms, reference books.* Not stocked: Guns, firearms. LOC: From Victoria, No. 185 bus. From Elephant and Castle No. 12 to Upland Rd. PARK: Easy. TEL: 693 6285. SER: Film and T.V. hire.

London S.E.23

Oddiquities
61 Waldram Park Rd. and 20 Sunderland Rd., Forest Hill. (Mrs. S.A. Butler.) Est. 1966. CL: Sun. except by appointment and Wed. Open 10—6, Sat. 10—1. SIZE: Medium. *STOCK: Oil lamps, gas and electric light fitments, 1800—1930; fire furnishings, 1780—1920; all £20—£500; general antiques, 1800—1920, £15—£1,000.* Not stocked: Coins, stamps, medals, jewellery. LOC: On South Circular Rd. between Catford and Forest Hill. PARK: Opposite. TEL: 699 9574. VAT: Stan.

The Oddity Shoppe
27 London Rd., Forest Hill. *STOCK: Jewellery, furniture, bric-a-brac.* TEL: 699 9462.

F.E. Whitehart Rare Books
40 Priestfield Rd., Forest Hill. Resident. Est. 1951. Open by appointment only. *STOCK: Books only on medicine, science and technology.* PARK: Easy. TEL: 699 3225. SER: Valuations; restorations (books); buys at auction.

R. Wilkinson and Son
43-45 Wastdale Rd., Forest Hill. Est. 1947. CL: Sat. Open 10—1 and 2—4. SIZE: Medium. *STOCK: Glass, especially chandeliers, 18th C and reproduction, art metal work.* LOC: Turning off South Circular Rd. PARK: Easy. TEL: 699 4420. SER: Restorations and repairs (glass, metalwork).

London S.E.26

Olwen Carthew
109 Kirkdale. Est. 1972. Open 10—5.30, Thurs. 10—3, Sat. 10—4.30. *STOCK: Pine, some handpainted, and country furniture, kitchen items, Lloyd loom.* LOC: ½ mile from South Circular Rd. at Forest Hill. TEL: 699 1363. VAT: Stan.

Denton Antiques
133 Kirkdale Rd., Sydenham. (D. O'Sullivan.) Open 10.30—5.30. *STOCK: Pre-1930s, Edwardian and Victorian furniture and small items.* TEL: 291 2123.

David E. Green Gallery
188 Dartmouth Rd. Est. 1972. CL: Wed. p.m. Thurs. open till 7.30 p.m. *STOCK: Fine early English watercolours and drawings.* TEL: 699 5461. SER: Restorations; framing and mounting, commissions undertaken. VAT: Stan/Spec.

Hillyers   LAPADA
301 Sydenham Rd. Est. 1952. CL: Wed. Open 8.30—4, Sat. 8.30—2. SIZE: Small. *STOCK: Furniture, silver, plate, porcelain, glass, books, bric-a-brac.* PARK: Easy. TEL: 778 6361; home — 777 2506. SER: Valuations. VAT: Stan/Spec.

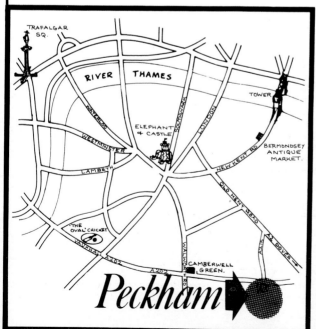

S.E.26 continued

Vintage Cameras Ltd. LAPADA
254 and 256 Kirkdale, Sydenham. (J. Jenkins.) Est. 1968. Open 9—5. SIZE: Large. *STOCK: Vintage cameras, 1840—1950, £50—£5,000; scientific instruments, 18th C to date, £50—£200; general photographica, 1840—1950, £5—£50, images, £5—£500.* LOC: Near South Circular Rd. PARK: Nearby. TEL: 778 5416/5841. SER: Valuations. VAT: Stan.

London E.2

St. Peters Organ Works
St. Peters Close, Warner Place. (J.P. Mander and I. Bell.) Est. 1935. CL: Sat. SIZE: Large. *STOCK: Antique pipe organs.* LOC: Opposite children's hospital, Hackey Rd. PARK: Own. TEL: 739 4747. SER: Valuations; restorations. VAT: Stan.

London E.11

K.N. and P. Blake — Old Cottage Antiques
8 High St., Wanstead. Est. 1920. Open Thurs. and Fri. 10.30—5.30. SIZE: Medium. *STOCK: Furniture, pre 1840; paintings, 19th and 20th C.* LOC: Near Wanstead station and Snaresbrook. TEL: 989 2317 or 504 9264. SER: Valuations; buys at auction. VAT: Stan/Spec.

What the Dickens
19 Cambridge Park, Wanstead. (Mr. Fagin.) Est. 1977. Open Mon. and Sat. 9—1 and 2—5, Tues. 9—5. SIZE: Small. *STOCK: General antiques.* LOC: Eastern Ave. PARK: Easy. TEL: 530 4585; home — same.

London E.15

Lassco Heavy Materials Dept.
Bow Industrial Park, Carpenters Rd. Open 10—5. *STOCK: Salvaged floorboards, oak beams, flagstones, bricks, tiles, slates, English oak and ash boards, mahogany and teak.* TEL: 986 6410.

London E.17

Antique City   Trade Only
98 Wood St. Est. 1978. CL: Thurs. and Sun., except by appointment. Open 9.30—5.00. SIZE Large. *STOCK: General antiques, 19th C, £5—£500.* PARK: In side road opposite. TEL: 520 4032.

E.17 continued

Georgian Village Antiques Market
100 Wood St. 10 shops. Est. 1972. CL: Thurs. Open 10—5. *STOCK: 19th C furniture, clocks, barometers, porcelain, postcards, pottery, jewellery, country items, brass, copper, stamps, silver,* LOC: 50yds. from Dukes Head. PARK: Adjacent. TEL: 520 6638.

J.C. Antiques   Trade Only
12 Warwick Terrace, Lea Bridge Rd. (Mrs. J.R. Wood.) Est. 1965. Open 10.30—7.30, Sun. by appointment. SIZE: Large. *STOCK: Shipping goods, £10—£2,000.* LOC: Roundabout at Lower Clapton, up Lea Bridge Rd. on A104. Last shop on right before Whipps Cross. PARK: Easy. TEL: 539 4275; home — 802 0582. VAT: Stan.

The Junk Shop
101 Wood St., Walthamstow. (K.A.C. Yardley.) Est. 1968. CL: Sun. except by appointment. Open 9—5.30. *STOCK: Trade furniture, small porcelain, jewellery, silver, linen, period costume, pine (unstripped), small glass cabinets, books, art deco.* PARK: Easy. TEL: 521 0014 or 520 5090.

London E.18

Daroch Antiques
138 Hermon Hill, South Woodford. (Mrs. R. Pressman.) Est. 1970. CL: Fri. and Sat. Open 10—3, Sun. 10—1, or by appointment. *STOCK: General antiques.* LOC: A113 Wanstead to Chigwell Rd., near Fir Trees public house. PARK: Easy. TEL: 989 9239.

London E.C.1

Ronald Benjamin Antiques
25B Hatton Garden (entrance in Greville St.). Est. 1948. CL: Sat. Open 10—5.30. SIZE: Small. *STOCK: Jewellery, early Georgian to art deco, from £100; objets d'art, from £200; watches, from £150.* LOC: From High Holborn eastwards, turn left at Holborn Circus into Hatton Garden. PARK: Meters. TEL: 242 6189/9105. SER: Valuations. VAT: Stan/Spec.

City Clocks
Lambs Passage, Chiswell St., Barbican. (J. Rosson.) Est. 1960. Open 7.45—7.15, Sat. and Sun. by appointment. SIZE: Medium. *STOCK: Clocks and some furniture, 19th C, £100—£3,000; watches, 19th and 20th C, £50—£500.* PARK: Easy. TEL: 628 6749; home — 638 3251. SER: Valuations; restorations (clocks); buys at auction (watches and clocks). VAT: Stan.

E.C.1 continued

Cutler Street Antique Market
Goulston St. Open 7 a.m to 2 p.m. every Sun. *STOCK: Gold, silver, jewellery, gems, coins and stamps.* LOC: Aldgate end of Goulston St., close to Petticoat Lane Market. TEL: Enquiries — 351 5353.

Eldridge London and Co.
99-101 Farringdon Rd. (B. Eldridge.) Est. 1953. Open 9—5.30, Sat. 9—1. SIZE: Large. *STOCK: Furniture, decorative items.* PARK: Easy. TEL: 837 0379/0370. VAT: Stan/Spec.

Essie C. Harris   LAPADA
Diamond House, 37/38 Hatton Garden (office). (E.C. and D. Harris.) Est. 1958. CL: Sat. Open 10—5. *STOCK: Jewellery, £50—£20,000.* PARK: Nearby. TEL: 242 9115 and 242 1558. SER: Valuations. FAIRS: Goldsmiths Hall, Basle, Switzerland and Munich, Germany. VAT: Stan/Spec.

R. Holt and Co. Ltd.
98 Hatton Garden. Est. 1948. CL: Sat. Open 9.30—5.30. *STOCK: Chinese artifacts and jewellery.* TEL: 405 0197. SER: Valuations; restorations; gem stone cutting; gem testing; re-stringing.

House of Buckingham (Antiques)
                                LAPADA
113—117 Farringdon Rd. (B.B. White.) Est. 1970. Open 9—6. *STOCK: Boxes, clocks, furniture, brass, nautical goods.* TEL: 278 2013. VAT: Stan/Spec.

Levy Antiques   *Trade Only*
Room 41, 67 Hatton Garden. (J. Levy.) Est. 1950. Open by appointment. *STOCK: Jewellery.* TEL: 405 2426. VAT: Stan.

Priory Antiques
45 Cloth Fair, West Smithfield. (B. Heath and P. Timothy.) Est. 1975. CL: Sat., Mon. Open 10—4. SIZE: Small. *STOCK: Victorian jewellery, £50—£1,000; bric-a-brac, Victorian and later, £5—£100.* LOC: Near St. Bartholomew's Church Hospital and West Smithfield market. PARK: Easy and NCP opposite. TEL: 606 9060. SER: Valuations; restorations (jewellery). VAT: Stan/Spec.

A.R. Ullmann Ltd.
10 Hatton Garden. (J.S. Ullmann.) Est. 1939. CL: Sat. Open 9.30—6. SIZE: Small. *STOCK: Jewellery, gold, silver and diamond; silver and objets d'art.* LOC: Very close to Farringdon and Chancery Lane tube stations. PARK: Multi- storey in St. Cross St. TEL: 405 1877; home — 346 2546. SER: Restorations. VAT: Stan/Spec.

E.C.1 continued

C.J. Vander (Antiques) Ltd.   BADA
                                Trade Only
Dunstan House, 14a St. Cross St. Est. 1886. CL: Sat. Open 9.30—1 and 2—5.30. SIZE: Large. *STOCK: Silver, Sheffield plate.* TEL: 831 6741. SER: Valuations; restorations; buys at auction.

London E.C.2

George Amos and Sons
73 Leonard St. Open 10—5. *STOCK: Architectural joinery, panelled rooms, staircases, doors, carving.* TEL: 739 0448.

London Architectural Salvage & Supply Co. Ltd.
The Mark St. Depository, Mark St. (off Paul St.). Est. 1977. Open 10—5. *STOCK: Architectural relics including doors and door furniture, chimney pieces, flooring, panelled rooms, railings, ironwork, garden and street furniture, glass and ecclesiastical joinery.* TEL: 739 0448/9.

London E.C.3

J. Ash (Rare Books)
25 Royal Exchange. (L. Worms.) Est. 1946. CL: Sat. Open 10—5.30. SIZE: Medium. *STOCK: Books, 1550—1980, £20—£2,000; maps, 1550—1850, £20—£1,000; prints, 1650—1900, £10—£500.* LOC: On the Threadneedle St. side of the Royal Exchange, opposite Bank of England. PARK: Nearby. TEL: 626 2665. SER: Valuations; buys at auction (books and maps); picture framing and mount cutting. VAT: Stan.

Asprey and Co. (City Branch) Ltd.
153 Fenchurch St. Est. 1780. CL: Sat. Open 9—5. SIZE: Small. *STOCK: Silver, clocks, jewellery.* PARK: Meters. TEL: 626 2160. SER: Valuations; restorations. VAT: Stan/Spec.

Halcyon Days   BADA
4 Royal Exchange. (S. Benjamin.) Est. 1950. Open 9.15—5.30. *STOCK: 18th to early 19th C enamels, papier mâché, tôle, objects of vertu, treen, Staffordshire pottery figures, prints, unusual small Georgian furniture.* TEL: 629 8811. VAT: Stan/Spec.

Nanwani and Co.
2 Shopping Arcade, Bank Station Cornhill. Est. 1958. CL: Sat. *STOCK: Precious and semi-precious stones, Oriental items, objets d'art.* TEL: 623 8232. VAT: Stan.

Royal Exchange Art Gallery
14 Royal Exchange. (R. and J. Hadlee.) Est. 1974. CL: Sat. Open 10.30—5.15. *STOCK: Oil paintings and watercolours, 19th and 20th C; especially marine and landscape, etchings.* TEL: 283 4400.

Searle and Co. Ltd.
1 Royal Exchange. Est. 1897. Open 9—5.30. SIZE: Medium. *STOCK: Silver and jewellery.* PARK: Meters. TEL: 626 2456. SER: Valuations; restorations. VAT: Stan/Spec.

London E.C.4

J. Clarke-Hall Ltd.
7 Bride Court, and 22 Bride Lane. ABA. Est. 1934. CL: Sat. Open 10.30—6.30. SIZE: Small. *STOCK: 18th C English literature, especially Dr. Samuel Johnson and his contemporaries; illustrated books and 19th C prints, £3—£2,500; modern first editions.* LOC: Off Bride Lane, which is off bottom of Fleet St., near Ludgate Circus. PARK: Meters. TEL: 353 4116. SER: Restorations (book repairs, rebinding, pictures); framing. VAT: Stan.

London N.1

39 Antiques
39 Essex Rd., Islington. (Mrs. M.S. Ferrant.) Open 9.30—4. *STOCK: Bric-a-brac.* TEL: 359 1639.

Angel Arcade
116—118 Islington High St., Camden Passage, Islington. Open Wed. and Sat. Other days access available to the shops. There are many dealers in this arcade offering a wide range of antiques.

Annie's Antiques and Clothes
10 Camden Passage, Islington. (A. Moss.) CL: Mon. and Thurs. Open 11—5. TEL: 359 0796.

The Antique Trader   LAPADA
357 and 36 Upper St., Islington. (D. Rothera, B. Thompson.) Est. 1968. Open 10—5. SIZE: Large. *STOCK: Furniture, £150—£5,000; brass, copper, china, objets d'art, arts and crafts, £25—£1,000.* LOC: Camden Passage Antiques Centre. PARK: Easy. TEL: 359 2019. VAT: Stan/Spec.

The Ark Angel
14 Camden Passage, Islington. (D. Leroy.) CL: Mon. Open 10—5. *STOCK: Naïve paintings, lacquer, pine, samplers, quilts, unusual and decorative items.* TEL: 226 1644.

As Time Goes By
20 The Mall, 359 Upper St., Camden Passage, Islington. (B. Trenter.) Est. 1981. Open Wed. 9—4.30, Fri. 10.30—3, Sat. 9—5. SIZE: Small. *STOCK: Clocks, 1820—1910, £100—£1,000; small furniture, Victorian and Edwardian, £175—£500.* LOC: Main road through Islington. PARK: Nearby. TEL: 354 3624. SER: Restorations (clocks). VAT: Stan/Spec.

Ian Auld
1 Gateway Arcade, Camden Passage, Islington. Est. 1968. Open Fri. 1.30—5, Wed. and Sat. 10—5. SIZE: Small. *STOCK: Ethnographic items, African, Oceanic, £25—£1,000; antiquities, especially pottery, £25—£250; Coptic and pre- Columbian textiles.* Not stocked: Victoriana. LOC: Near Angel tube station. PARK: Easy. TEL: 359 1440.

Alexander Bailie Antiques
2 Lower Mall, 359 Upper St., Islington. Est. 1966. CL: Mon. Open Wed., Fri. and Sat.; Tues and Thurs. by appointment. SIZE: Small. *STOCK: English mahogany, oak and walnut furniture, 18th—19th C, £500—£1,000; decorative items, clocks, figures and mirrors, 19th C, £150—£500.* LOC: Camden Passage. PARK: Nearby. TEL: Evenings — 354 1739. VAT. Stan/Spec.

N.1 continued

Banbury Fayre
6 Pierrepoint Arcade, Camden Passage, Islington. (N. Steel.) Est. 1985. Open Wed. and Sat. SIZE: Small. *STOCK: Small collectors' items, general antiques, porcelain.* PARK: 200yds. TEL: Home — 852 5675.

David Barklem Ltd.
3—5 Theberton St., Islington. (D.N. Barklem and J.L. Kenyon.) Est. 1979. CL: Thurs. p.m. Open 9.30—5.30. SIZE: Large. *STOCK: Painted and French provincial furniture, 1800— 1920, £5—£3,000; unusual and decorative items; pine.* LOC: Off Upper St. PARK: Easy. TEL: 359 4997. SER: Valuations; buys at auction. FAIRS: Decorative Antiques and Textiles. VAT: Stan/Spec.

William Bedford p.l.c.   BADA
                                   LAPADA
The Merchants Hall, 46 Essex Rd., Islington. (W. and J. Bedford.) Est. 1959. Open 9.30—5.30. SIZE: Large. *STOCK: English period furniture and accessories.* LOC: 100yds. Camden Passage. PARK: Easy. TEL: 226 9648. SER: Valuations; restorations; upholstery. VAT: Stan/Spec.

John Birchmore
23/25 Essex Rd., Islington. Est. 1967. Open 9.30—5. SIZE: Large. *STOCK: General antiques, shipping goods.* TEL: 226 8011. VAT: Stan.

N.1 continued

Boutique Fantasque
13 Pierrepont Row, Camden Passage, Islington. (Mrs. M.A.B. Gates.) Est. 1962. Open Wed. and Sat. SIZE: Small. *STOCK: Watercolours and prints, general antiques, porcelain, jewellery, small collectors' items.* LOC: From Piccadilly, No. 19 and 22 buses. From Marble Arch, No. 30 bus. Tube to Angel station. PARK: 200yds. TEL: Home — Hartley Wintney (025 126) 2287.

Buck and Payne Antiques
5 The Lower Mall and 5 Camden Passage, Islington. (W.M. Buck and M.H. Payne.) CL: Mon. Open 10—5, Wed. 7.30—5. *STOCK: French and English country furniture; unusual and decorative items.* TEL: 226 4326.

Bushe Antiques
52/3 Camden Passage, Islington. CL. Mon. Open 9—5. *STOCK: Longcase and decorative mantle clocks.* TEL: 226 7096/9572. SER: Restorations; spares.

Bushwood Antiques   LAPADA
                              Trade Only
317 Upper St., Islington. (A. Bush.) Est. 1967. Open 9.30—5.30 or by appointment. SIZE: Large. *STOCK: Furniture including Edwardian and Victorian, bric-a-brac, decorator's items, clocks, works of art.* LOC: 100yds. from Camden Passage. PARK: 50yds. TEL: 359 2095. VAT: Stan.

A rare, small, barrel-shaped creamer, painted in underglaze blue, $2^{9}/10$ ins. high, c.1770-5. From *Lowestoft Porcelains* by Geoffrey A. Godden, F.R.S.A., published by the **Antique Collectors' Club,** 1985.

CHANCERY ANTIQUES LTD.

Dealers in fine
SATSUMA · IVORIES
CLOISONNÉ
and other
JAPANESE WORKS
OF ART

357A UPPER STREET ISLINGTON LONDON N.1. TEL. 01-359 9035

N.1 continued

Camden Passage Antiques Centre
357 Upper St., Islington. (J. Friend.) Est. 1960. Open weekdays 10.30—5.30. SIZE: 350 shops and boutiques some of which are listed alphabetically in this section. Also 100 stalls open on certain market days, Wed., general antiques, 8—3, Thurs. books, 9—4, Sat., general antiques, 9—5. LOC: Behind the Angel, Islington. TEL: 359 0190.

Canonbury Antiques
13 Canonbury Place. (A.C. Holyome.) Est. 1965. CL: Sat. p.m. Open 9—6. *STOCK: General antiques, upholstered furniture.* TEL: 359 2246. SER: Restorations (upholstery).

Patric Capon   LAPADA
350 Upper St., Islington. Est. 1970. Open. Wed., and Sat. or by appointment. SIZE: Medium. *STOCK: Unusual carriage clocks, 19th C, £450—£6,000; 8-day and 2-day marine chronometers, 19th C, £850—£4,500; clocks and barometers, 18th—19th C, £400—£6,500.* LOC: Adjacent Camden Passage. PARK: Easy. TEL: 354 0487; home — 467 5722. SER: Valuations; restorations. FAIRS: Olympia. VAT: Stan/Spec.

N.1 continued

Capricorn Antiques Ltd.
76 Upper St., Islington. (F.R. Hudson.) Open 9.30—6 or by appointment. *STOCK: Furniture, 18th C; general antiques.* TEL: 226 4052. SER: Restorations.

Chancery Antiques Ltd.
357a Upper St., Islington. (R. and D. Rote.) Est. 1950. CL: Mon. and Thurs. Open 10.30—5, or by appointment. SIZE: Medium. *STOCK: Oriental works of art especially Japanese Meiji period.* TEL: 359 9035. VAT: Stan/Spec.

Peter Chapman Antiques
                              LAPADA
10 Theberton St., Islington. (P.J. Chapman.) Est. 1971. CL: Sun. and public holidays except by appointment. Open 9.30—1 and 2—6. SIZE: Medium. *STOCK: English furniture, 1700—1900, £50—£5,000; paintings, drawings and prints, 17th to early 20th C, £50—£1,500; stained glass, 1700-1950, £50—£1,000, architectural items.* LOC: 5 mins. walk from Camden Passage down Upper St. PARK: Easy. TEL: 226 5565; home — 348 4846. SER: Valuations; restorations (furniture and period buildings). VAT: Stan/Spec.

Coexistence
17 Canonbury Lane. Open 10—6. *STOCK: Furniture, unusual items, £50—£5,000; decorative objects, including lacquer items, treen, £15—£500; all 16th—18th C.* PARK: Easy. TEL: 226 8382/6831.

Judy Cole at Twenty-Eight Camden Passage
28 Camden Passage, Islington. Open Wed., Fri. and Sat. 10—4.30. *STOCK: Metal items — fireplaces, 18th—19th C, £50—£1,000; spiral staircases, £300—£1,000; balconies, railings, garden furniture, £50—£500, all 19th C.* TEL: 226 4539; home — 226 5913. SER: Valuations; restorations (welding, polishing, sandblasting).

''Commemoratives''
3 Pierrepont Arcade, Camden Passage, Islington. (F. Annesley.) Est. 1971. Open all day Wed. and Sat.; and Fri. p.m. *STOCK: Commemoratives depicting royalty, war, politics, theatre and cinema.* LOC: Northern line underground to Angel. PARK: Meters.

John Creed Antiques Ltd.
3 and 5a Camden Passage, Islington. (C.P.J.J. Creed- Miles.) Est. 1967. Open 10—5.30. SIZE: Medium. *STOCK: Country furniture, stripped pine, £40—£400; metalware, brass, copper, 1600—1850, £20—£200; china, blue printed earthenware, stoneware, 1780—1840, £20—£200.* Not stocked: Silver, pewter, glass, mahogany furniture. LOC: By Angel underground station, Islington. PARK: Easy. TEL: 226 8867. VAT: Stan/Spec.

CAMDEN PASSAGE

London's Antique Village
300 Dealers in Shops
Markets + Arcades

**Camden Passage, Pierrepont Arcade, Gateway Arcade,
The Galleries, Camden Passage Arcade, Pierrepont Row,
Pierrepont Market, Charlton Place Market,
Orange Box Market, The Fleamarket.**
John Friend 01 359 0190

359 Upper St. Camden Passage, London N1

**35 SPECIALIST GALLERIES ON TWO FLOORS SELLING AN
EXTENSIVE RANGE OF ANTIQUES, FURNITURE,
COLLECTABLES.**

01 359 0825

N.1 continued

Davidson Brothers
33 Camden Passage, Islington. (S. and C. Davidson.) Est. 1981. CL: Mon. Open 10.30—5.30, Wed. 8.30—5.30, Fri. 9.30—5.30, Sat. 10—5.30. SIZE: Small. *STOCK. Decorative items, 19th C, £80—£500; unusual furniture, 18th—19th C, £500—£1,500.* LOC: Near Charlton Place. PARK: Meters. TEL: 226 7491. FAIRS: Olympia. VAT: Stan/Spec.

Delaney Antiques
3 The Lower Mall. (W. Delaney.) CL: Mon. Open 10—5, Wed. 7.30—5. *STOCK: Unusual and decorative items.* TEL: 359 0825.

Dome Antiques (Exports) Ltd.
75 Upper St., Islington. (P., A. and P. Woolf.) Est. 1961. Open 9.30—5.30. SIZE: Large. *STOCK: English furniture, 1700—1900, £50—£2,000; desks, library and dining tables.* Not stocked: Silver. LOC: Opposite Islington Green. PARK: Easy. TEL: 226 7227; home — 226 1070. SER: Valuations. VAT: Stan/Spec.

Donay Antiques
35 Camden Passage, Islington. (N. Donay.) Est. 1980. Open 8—5. SIZE: Large. *STOCK: Furniture, game compendiums, £200—£1,000; artists' colour boxes £150—£500; Japanese 19th C textiles, £200—£400; decorative items.* LOC: To the right of Upper St. and near the Angel. PARK: Nearby. TEL: 359 1880.

Dugdale's Antique Warehouse
Mascotte House, 52/54 Islington Park St. (P. and T. Dugdale.) Est. 1980. CL: Mon. Open 10—6, Sat. 8—6. SIZE: Large. *STOCK: Architectural and decorators items, mainly mid 19th C. to early 20th C, £5—£2,500.* LOC: Off Upper St. PARK: Fairly easy. TEL: 354 2265. SER: Valuations; buys at auction (architectural and optical toys, magic lanterns, zoetropes). VAT: Stan.

D.J. Ferrant Antiques
21a Camden Passage, Islington. (J. Ferrant.) Est. 1963. Open 9.30—4. SIZE: Large. *STOCK: Georgian furniture; clocks, bronzes; general antiques.* PARK: Easy. TEL: 359 2597. SER: Buys at auction. VAT: Stan/Spec.

'The Fleamarket'
7 Pierrepont Row, Camden Passage, Islington. 26 Stand-holders. CL: Mon. Open 9.30—6. SIZE: Large. *STOCK: Jewellery, furniture, objets d'art, militaria, guns, swords, pistols, porcelain, coins, medals, stamps, 18th—19th C, £1—£500; antiquarian books, prints, fine art, china, silver, glass and general antiques.* PARK: Easy. TEL: 226 8211. SER: Valuations; buys at auction; weapon repairs.

N.1 continued

Franco's Antique Warehouse
69 Upper St., Islington. Open 10—5. *STOCK: Furniture, 1760—1880.* Not stocked: Pine, jewellery, glass or bronzes. LOC: Near Camden Passage. TEL: 226 7261. SER: Restorations; buys at auction. VAT: Stan.

Franco's Antiques
Shop 49, Camden Passage, Islington. (F.A. Chiodo.) Est. 1970. Open 10—5. SIZE: Medium. *STOCK: English furniture, 1760—1880.* Not stocked: Pine, jewellery, glass and bronzes. TEL: 354 1860. SER: Restorations; buys at auction. VAT: Stan.

Vincent Freeman
1 Camden Passage, Islington. Est. 1966. CL: Mon. Open 10—5. SIZE: Large. *STOCK: Porcelain, glass, clocks, music boxes, Oriental and decorative items, £20—£5,000.* VAT: Stan/Spec.

Furniture Vault
50 Camden Passage, Islington. Open 9—4.30. *STOCK: Furniture, clocks, bronzes and some decorative.* TEL: 354 1047.

Georgian Village
Islington Green. Open 10—4, Wed. and Sat. 7—5. TEL: 226 1571. PARK: Nearby. A wide range of general antiques are available at this market.

Geranium
121 Upper St., Islington. (B. Reeves.) Open 10—5, Sat. 10—6. *STOCK: Victorian pine furniture, especially dressers, chests, tables, storage furniture.* TEL: 359 4281.

Get Stuffed
105 Essex Rd., Islington. (M. St. Clare.) Est. 1975. Open 10—5.30. *STOCK: Stuffed birds, fish, animals; trophies, heads, skins, and rugs; butterflies, insects and natural history specimens. £1—£1,500.* TEL: 226 1364. SER: Restoration; glass domes supplied.

David Graham Antiques
2 The Mall and 7 Lower Mall, Camden Passage, Upper St., Islington. Est. 1973. CL: Mon. Open 10—5, Wed. 8—5, Sat. 10—6. SIZE: Medium. *STOCK: Silver, 1750—1930, £50—£4,000; Victorian silver plate, £5—£500; Sheffield plate, £20—£1,000.* LOC: 2 minutes from Angel Underground. PARK: Easy. TEL: 354 2112. VAT: Stan.

Gordon Gridley
41 Camden Passage, Islington. Est. 1968. Open Wed. and Sat. and by appointment. SIZE: Medium. *STOCK: English and Continental furniture and paintings, decorative objects, metalwork, statuary, scientific instruments, all 17th—19th C, £50—£5,000.* PARK: Nearby, in Charlton Place. TEL: 226 0643; home — 226 9033. SER: Valuations; restorations. VAT: Stan/Spec.

N.1 continued

Rosemary Hart
4 Gateway Arcade, 355 Upper St., Islington. Est. 1980. CL: Mon. and Thurs. Open 11—4, Wed. and Sat. 9—5. SIZE: Small. *STOCK: Silver and plate, £1—£200.* LOC: Near Angel tube station. TEL: 359 6839.

Hart and Rosenberg
2 and 3 Gateway Arcade, 355 Upper St., Islington. (E. Hart and H. Rosenberg.) Est. 1968. CL: Mon. and Thurs. Open 10—5, Wed. 9—5. SIZE: Medium. *STOCK: Chinese, Japanese and European porcelain, works of art, decorative items, some furniture, £25—£5,000.* LOC: Near Angel tube station. PARK: Nearby. TEL: 359 6839. SER: Valuations; buys at auction. VAT: Stan/Spec.

Sheila Hart Antiques   LAPADA
104 Islington High St. Est. 1963. TEL: 226 2315.

Sherry Hatcher
5 Gateway Arcade, Camden Passage, Upper St., Islington. Est. 1966. Open Wed. and Sat. 10.30—5, or by appointment. SIZE: Small. *STOCK: Perfume bottles, sugar shakers, silver, boxes and interesting silver items.* LOC: Near Angel tube station. PARK: Easy. TEL: 226 5679; home — 226 8496. VAT: Stan.

Brian Hawkins Antiques
73 Upper St., Islngton. Open 9.30—5. *STOCK: Furniture, 19th to early 20th C, £50—£1,000+.* TEL: 359 3957.

Heather Antiques
11 Camden Passage, Islington. Est. 1965. CL: Mon. Open 10—4.30, Wed. 9—5; Thurs. 10—1.30. SIZE: Medium. *STOCK: Silver and plate.* TEL: 226 2412. VAT: Stan.

Heritage Antiques   LAPADA
112/114 Islington High Street, Camden Passage, Islington. (A. Daniel.) Est. 1975. Open Wed. 8—5, Sat. 10—5, or by appointment. SIZE: Large. *STOCK: Metalware, £50—£2,000; oak and country furniture, 17th—19th C, £100—£5,000; domestic and decorative items.* TEL: 226 7789. VAT: Stan/Spec.

Highgate Gallery
16 Georgian Village, Camden Passage, Islington. (M. and J. Halsby.) Open Wed. and Sat. 9.30—3.30. *STOCK: Watercolours.* TEL: 226 1571.

N.1 continued

House of Steel Antiques
400 Caledonian Rd. (J. Cole.) Est. 1974. Open 9—5.30, Sat. by appointment. SIZE: Warehouse. *STOCK: Metal items — fireplaces, 18th—19th C, £50—£1,000; spiral staircases, £300—£1,000; balconies, railings, garden furniture, £50—£500; all 19th C.* LOC: Near King's Cross. PARK: Own. TEL: 607 5889; home — 226 5913. SER: Valuations; restorations (welding, polishing, sandblasting). VAT: Stan.

Inheritance
98 Islington High St. and 114 Camden Passage, Islington. (A. Pantelli.) Est. 1969. CL: Mon. Open 10.30—5. SIZE: Small. *STOCK: Jewellery, Oriental and European ceramics, ivories, furniture, cloisonné, clocks, bronzes.* LOC: Travelling north up City Road turn right at the Angel, then first right. TEL: 226 8305. SER: Valuations. VAT: Stan/Spec.

Intercol London
1A Camden Walk, Islington Green. (Y. Beresiner.) Est. 1977. Open 9—5.45, Wed. 8—6, Sat. 8.30—5, Mon. by appointment. SIZE: Large. *STOCK: Playing cards, maps and banknotes including books, £5—£1,000+.* LOC: Camden Passage. PARK: Easy. TEL: 354 2599. SER: Valuations; restorations (maps including colouring); buys at auction (playing cards, maps, banknotes and books). FAIRS: Major specialist European, U.S.A. and Far Eastern. VAT: Stan/Spec.

Islington Artefacts
12 and 14 Essex Rd. (Mrs. C. Hill and D.A. Magee.) Open 9—8. *STOCK: Pine furniture.* TEL: 226 6867.

Japanese Gallery
23 Camden Passage, Islington. Open 9—5. *STOCK: Japanese woodcut prints; books, porcelain, screens, kimonos, scrolls, general Japanese antiques.* TEL: 226 3347. SER: Buys at auction.

Jubilee
10 Pierrepont Row, Camden Passage, Islington. (B. Vosburgh.) Est. 1970. Open Wed. and Sat. 10.30—5 or by appointment. SIZE: Small. *STOCK: Photographic antiques, apparatus and images; magic lanterns, stereoscopic slides, cartes de visite, 10p—£300.* LOC: From Piccadilly Circus, take 19 bus to Angel, Islington. PARK: Meters. TEL: Home — 607 5462. SER: Buys at auction.

Julian Antiques   LAPADA
54 Duncan St. Est. 1964. *STOCK: French clocks, fireplaces, furniture, bronzes, fenders, mirrors.*

Kausmally Antiques
15 Islington Green. (A. Kausmally.) Open 10—6. *STOCK: Victorian and Georgian furniture.* TEL: 359 0741.

N.1 continued

L. Kelaty Ltd.
17—35 Poole St., New North Rd. Est. 1954. CL: Sat. Open 8—6, Fri. 8—5. *STOCK: Rugs and carpets.* TEL: 739 2101.

Thomas Kerr Antiques Ltd.
LAPADA
11 Theberton St. Est. 1977. Open 9.30—6, SIZE: Large. *STOCK: English and Continental furniture, works of art, paintings and decorative objects 17th—20th C, £100—£20,000.*LOC: 5 minutes walk down Upper St. towards Highbury and Islington tube. PARK: Easy. TEL: 226 0626. VAT: Stan/Spec.

Anthea Knowles Rare Toys and Fine Dolls
42 Colebrooke Row. Open by appointment. *STOCK: Tinplate toys, locomotives, dolls, mechanical money boxes, late 19th to early 20th C.* TEL: 354 2333. SER: Valuations; buys at auction.

John Laurie   LAPADA
352 Upper St., Islington. (J. Gewirtz.) Est. 1962. Open 9.30—5. SIZE: Medium. *STOCK: Silver, Sheffield plate.* TEL: 226 0913. SER: Restorations. VAT: Stan.

Sara Lemkow
9 Pierrepont Arcade. Open 10—5. *STOCK: Oil lamps, brass, iron, copper, kitchen utensils.* TEL: 226 2997.

Nellie Lenson and Roy Smith
16 Camden Passage, Islington. Warehouse, 1 St. Peter St. *STOCK: Decorative items, Vienna bronzes, early brass, animalia, French furniture.* TEL: 226 2423.

Michael Lewis Antiques
16 Essex Rd., Islington. Est. 1977. Open 8—6, Sat. 8—5, Sun. by appointment. SIZE: Medium. *STOCK: Pine furniture, 18th—20th C, £10—£2,500.* LOC: 100yds. north of Camden Passage. PARK: Easy. TEL: 359 7733. VAT: Stan.

Wan Li
7 Gateway Arcade, 355 Upper St., Camden Passage, Islington. Est. 1969. *STOCK: Mainly Chinese works of art, porcelain, some European, fans.* TEL: 226 0997. VAT: Stan/Spec.

Finbar MacDonnell
17 Camden Passage, Islington. Open 9—6. *STOCK: Prints, maps, mainly pre-1850.* TEL: 226 0537.

N.1 continued

The Mall Antiques Arcade
359 Upper St., Islington. (Barcbourne Ltd.) Est. 1979. CL: Mon. Open 10—5, Wed. 7.30—5, Sat. 9—6. SIZE: Large. There are 38 galleries on two floors in this arcade selling *a wide range of general antiques including porcelain, furniture, jewellery, silver, pictures, clocks, bronzes and objets d'art, mainly 17th—20th C.* LOC: 5 mins. from Angel tube station. PARK: Meters. TEL: 359 0825 or 349 3111.

J. and J. Mangham
21 The Mall, Camden Passage, Islington. Est. 1975. Open Wed. and Sat. 8.30—4, other times by appointment. *STOCK: Boxes, clocks, barometers, scientific instruments, some gramophones and phonographs.* TEL: Home — Clare (0787) 277563. VAT: Stan/Spec.

Laurence Mitchell Antiques
LAPADA
27 Camden Passage and 6 Gateway Arcade, Camden Passage, Islington. (L.P.J. Mitchell.) Est. 1972. CL: Mon. Open 10—4.30, Wed. 8.30—5. *STOCK: Oriental, European and English ceramics, glass, especially Chinese export; Meissen, Mason ironstone; Oriental and English small furniture.* TEL: 359 7579 or 226 1738. VAT. Stan/Spec.

Pearl Morris
22 The Mall, Camden Passage, Islington. Open Wed. 7.30—4, Sat. 9—5 or by appointment. *STOCK: English and Continental pottery and porcelain, especially Doulton, Lambeth stoneware, and glass.* TEL: 359 8505 or 508 7117.

Number Nineteen
19 Camden Passage, Islington. (D. Griffiths and J. Wright.) CL: Mon. Open 10—3.30, Wed. and Sat. 10—5. *STOCK: Decorative antiques including bentwood, cane, garden and lacquered bamboo furniture; fairground animals and pub fittings.* TEL: 226 1126.

Old Woodworking Tools
288 Upper St., Islington. (T. Barwick.) Open 9.30—6. *STOCK: Woodworking tools.* TEL: 359 9313.

Stephen Orton Antiques LAPADA
72 Upper St., Islington. (S.C. Orton.) Open 9—5. SIZE: Large. *STOCK: Period, Victorian and Edwardian furniture.* LOC: Opposite Camden Passage. TEL: 226 2770; home — 508 1023. SER: Restorations; packing; courier; buying agent. VAT: Stan/Spec.

Kevin Page Oriental Art
2 and 4 Camden Passage, Islington. Est. 1968. CL: Mon. and Thurs. Open 10—4. SIZE: Large. *STOCK: Oriental porcelain, cloisonné, bronzes, ivories, furniture; china, brass.* LOC: 1 min. from Angel tube station. PARK: Easy. TEL: 226 8558. SER: Valuations. VAT: Stan.

N.1 continued

Persian Market   LAPADA
48 Upper St., Islington. Open 10—6, Wed. 9—6. SIZE: 4 floors. *STOCK: Porcelain, bronze, ivory, furniture, carpets and rugs, clocks, glass, silver.* LOC: 200yds. along Upper St. from Angel Underground. PARK: At rear. TEL: 226 7927. SER: Valuations; restorations (porcelain and bronze). VAT: Stan/Spec.

Quaker Lodge Antiques
110 Islington High St., Camden Passage, Islington. (A. Banks.) CL: Mon. Open 10—5. *STOCK: Earthenware and furniture.* TEL: 226 4374 or Wellingborough (0933) 680371.

Rede Hall Antiques
8 Pierrepont Arcade. *STOCK: Pine and country furniture.*

Relic Antiques at Camden Passage
1 Camden Walk, Islington. (M. Gliksten and G. Gower.) Est. 1968. CL: Mon. Open 10—5.30, evenings by appointment. SIZE: Medium. *STOCK: Decorative and collectors items, fairground antiques and animals, shop and pub. fittings, popular and naïve arts, £10—£2,000.* TEL: 359 6755 or 388 2691; home — 586 7648. SER: Valuations. VAT: Stan.

Marcus Ross Antiques
12/14 Pierrepont Row, Camden Passage, Islington. Est. 1972. CL: Mon. Open 10.30—4. *STOCK: Oriental porcelain, general antiques, Victorian walnut furniture.* TEL: 359 8494.

Sekmet Galleries
47 Camden Passage, Islington. (S. Duran.) Est. 1978. CL: Sun. except by appointment. Open 10—6. SIZE: Small. *STOCK: Paintings and decorative furniture, £50—£5,000; decorative china, glass and porcelain, £20—£500; all 19th—20th C.* LOC: Near Angel tube station. PARK: Meters. TEL: 359 1755. SER: Buys at auction.

The Shop on the Corner
12 Camden Passage, Islington. (R. Humphreys and J. Kaye.) Est. 1971. CL: Mon. Open 10—5. *STOCK: Pine furniture, decorative items, brass, general antiques £5—£2,000.* PARK: Nearby. TEL: 226 2444. VAT: Stan.

Robin Sims
7 Camden Passage, Islington. Est. 1970. CL: Mon. Open 10—4, Wed. and Sat. 8—5. SIZE: Small. *STOCK: General antiques, Victoriana, 1840—1920, £5—£1,000.* Not stocked: Large furniture. LOC: Near Angel underground station. PARK: Easy. TEL: 226 2393. VAT: Stan.

N.1 continued

Keith Skeel Antique Warehouse
LAPADA
7-9 Elliotts Place. SIZE: Large. *STOCK: Interesting and unusual furniture.* TEL: 226 7012.

Keith Skeel Antiques   LAPADA
Trade Only
94/96 Islington High St., Islington. Est. 1969. Open 9—6. SIZE: Large. *STOCK: Interesting and unusual items.* LOC: 1 minute from the Angel underground station. TEL: 359 9894. FAIRS: Olympia. VAT: Stan.

Strike One (Islington) Ltd.   BADA
LAPADA
51 Camden Passage, Islington. (J. Mighell.) Est. 1968. Open 9—5 or by appointment. SIZE: Medium. *STOCK: Clocks, pre-1870, especially early English wall and Act of Parliament, £2,000—£15,000; English longcase, 1675—1820, £3,000—£30,000; English bracket, lantern, skeleton and French carriage clocks; Vienna regulators; barometers, early Black Forest clocks, horological books.* **PARK: Easy. TEL: 226 9709; home — 359 6459. SER: Valuations; restorations (clocks, barometers); biannual catalogue available. VAT: Stan/Spec.**

The Studio
2 Charlton Place. Open 10—5.30. *STOCK: Art deco and art nouveau jewellery, fine art; original graphics and sculpture, especially 1920s—1930s.* TEL: 226 5625.

Swan Fine Art
120 Islington High St., Camden Passage, Islington. (P. Child.) Open 10—5, Wed. and Sat. 9—5, Mon. and Thurs. by appointment. SIZE: Medium. *STOCK: Paintings, 18th—19th C, £250—£10,000; 19th C furniture, Regency, Empire and Biedermeier, £200—£2,500+; decorative items, £25—£500+* PARK: Easy except Wed. and Sat. TEL: 226 5335; home — same. SER: Restorations (paintings, frames, furniture). VAT: Spec.

Tadema
10 Charlton Place, Camden Passage, Islington. (S. and D. Newell-Smith.) Est. 1978. Open 10—5.30. SIZE: Medium. *STOCK: Decorative art of the 20th C including bronzes, furniture, glass, ceramics, jewellery, British and Continental paintings.* PARK: Reasonable. TEL: 359 1055 (ansafone). SER: Valuations. VAT: Stan.

Terry Antiques
3 Pierrepont Arcade, Islington. (T.H. Murphy.) *STOCK: Small furniture, objets d'art, £100—£800.* TEL: 226 8211.

'Turn On' Ltd.
116/118 Islington High St., Camden Passage, Islington. Est. 1976. *STOCK: Lighting, 1860—1930.* TEL: 359 7616.

N.1 continued

Leigh Underhill Gallery
100 Islington High St. Est. 1950. CL: Mon. and Tues. Open 9—6. SIZE: Medium. *STOCK: Paintings, drawings, sculpture, etchings, works of art.* PARK: Meters. TEL: 226 5673. VAT: Spec.

Vane House Antiques
15 Camden Passage, Islington. (M. Till and A. Lamas.) Est. 1950. Open 10—5. *STOCK: 18th to early 19th C furniture.* TEL: 359 1343. VAT: Stan/Spec.

G.W. Walford
186 Upper St., Islington. Est. 1951. CL: Sat. Open 9.30—5.30. *STOCK: Antiquarian books.* TEL: 226 5682.

J.V. Webb
16 Pierrepont Row, Camden Passage, Islington. Est. 1948. Open Wed. and Sat. *STOCK: General small antiques; collectors' items.*

Mark J. West — Cobb Antiques Ltd.
15 Georgian Village, Camden Passage, Islington. Open Wed. and Sat., other times by appointment. *STOCK: Glass, including decanters, sets of glasses, 18th—19th C; pottery and decorators' items, 19th C.* TEL: 359 8686; home — 540 7982. SER: Valuations. FAIRS. Olympia. VAT: Stan.

Yesterday Child   LAPADA
24 The Mall, Camden Passage, Islington. (D. and J. Barrington.) Est. 1970. Open Wed. 7.30—3, Fri. 10—3, Sat. 9.30—1.30. SIZE: Small. *STOCK: Dolls, 1800—1925, £25—£5,000.* PARK: Easy. TEL: 354 1601; home (0908) 583403. SER: Valuations; restorations; buys at auction (dolls). FAIRS: April and September Cumberland Hotel International Doll. VAT: Stan/Spec.

London N.2

Amazing Grates
Phoenix House, 61—63 High Rd., East Finchley. (B. Martin.) Resident. Est. 1971. Open 10—6. SIZE: Large. *STOCK: Mantelpieces, grates and fireside items, £200—£1,500; Victorian tiling, £2—£20; early ironwork, all 19th C.* LOC: 100 yds. north of East Finchley tube station. PARK: Own. TEL: 883 9590. SER: Valuations; restorations (ironwork, welding of cast iron and brazing, polishing) VAT: Stan.

N.2 continued

The Antique Shop (Valantique)
9 Fortis Green. (Mrs. V. Steel.) Open 11—6. SIZE: Medium. *STOCK: Small furniture, pottery, porcelain, glass, oil paintings, watercolours, prints, copper, brass, jewellery, light fittings, unusual items, £1—£400.* LOC: 2 minutes from East Finchley tube station. PARK: Easy. TEL: 883 7651. SER: Buys at auction.

Martin Henham (Antiques)
218 High Rd., East Finchley. CL: Thurs. Open 10—6. SIZE: Medium. *STOCK: Furniture, 1710—1920, £5—£1,700; paintings, 1650—1900, £10—£1,000; porcelain, 1750—1910, £5—£450.* PARK: Easy. TEL: 444 5274. SER: Valuations; restorations (furniture and paintings); buys at auction. VAT: Stan/Spec.

Lauri Stewart — Fine Art
36 Church Lane. CL: Thurs. Open 10—5. *STOCK: Watercolours, oils and engravings, 19th—20th C;* TEL: 883 7719. SER: Restorations (oils, watercolours); framing.

London N.3

Park Galleries
20 Hendon Lane, Finchley. Est. 1978. CL: Thurs. p.m. and Mon. Open 9.30—6. *STOCK: English watercolours, 18th—20th C; oil paintings and prints.* TEL: 346 2176.

London N.4

Marion Gray
33 Crouch Hill. (R.J. Orton.) Est. 1955. CL: Sun., except by appointment. Open 10—6. SIZE: Large. *STOCK: Furniture, 17th—19th C, objets d'art.* LOC: Next to Crouch Hill station. TEL: 272 0372. SER: Restorations; upholstery. VAT: Stan/Spec.

London N.5

Elichaoff Oriental
76 Mountgrove Rd. CL: Sat. Open 9—5, or by appointment. *STOCK: Hand knotted Oriental rugs and carpets; furniture.* TEL: 359 2180. SER: Commissions undertaken.

Tony Ellis Antiques
90, 96 and 110 Highbury Park and warehouse at 2B Sotherby Rd. Est. 1967. Open 8—5. SIZE: Large. *STOCK: Furniture, Victorian, £10—£7,000; Edwardian, £5—£5,000; Georgian £50—£12,000; shipping goods.* LOC: Along St. Paul's Rd., first left at Highbury Grove shops, 1 mile to shop, on right. PARK: Easy. TEL: 226 7551; home — 272 0651. SER: Valuations; restorations (furniture, upholstery); buys at auction. VAT: Stan.

N.5 continued

Ester Antiques
88 Highbury Park Rd. (C. De Juan.) Est. 1976. Open 9—12. *STOCK: Victorian and Edwardian furniture, general antiques.* TEL: 359 1573.

Fagin's Phonograph Emporium
189 Blackstock Rd. Est. 1969. Open Sat. 10—4. SIZE: Large. *STOCK: Phonograph equipment; gramophones and spares; early wireless equipment; records.* LOC: Between Highbury and Finsbury Park. TEL: 359 4793. SER: Restorations (phonograph equipment, replacement parts); buys at auction; packing and shipping. VAT: Stan.

Sam Fogg
66 Highbury Hill. Est. 1971. Open by appointment. SIZE: Small. *STOCK: Rare books, manuscripts, all periods.* LOC: Highbury Hill is opposite entrance to Arsenal underground station. PARK: Easy. TEL: 226 0612; home — same. SER: Valuations; buys at auction.

North London Clock Shop Ltd.
72 Highbury Park. (D.S. Tomlin.) Est. 1960. CL: Sat. Open 9—6. SIZE: Medium. *STOCK: Clocks, longcase, bracket, carriage, skeleton, 18th—19th C.* LOC: Turn off Seven Sisters Rd. into Blackstock Rd., continue on to Highbury Park. PARK: Easy. TEL: 226 1609. SER: Restorations (clocks and barometer); wheel cutting, hand engraving, dial painting, clock reconversions. FAIRS: Olympia. VAT: Stan.

London N.6

John Beer
191-199 Archway Rd., Highgate. CL: Thurs. Open 9—1 and 2—5. SIZE: Large. *STOCK: Furniture, 1830—1960s especially English arts and crafts, Gothic and art deco.* LOC: 300yds south Highgate tube station. PARK: Easy. TEL: 340 2183. SER: Valuations; buys at auction. VAT: Stan/Spec.

Centaur Gallery
82 Highgate High St., Highgate Village. Est. 1960. (J. and D. Wieliczko.) *STOCK: 18th to early 19th C oil paintings, watercolours, prints, sculpture, ethnic and folk art, unusual items.* TEL: 340 0087.

Fisher and Sperr
46 Highgate High St. (J.R. Sperr.) Est. 1945. Open daily 10.30—6. SIZE: Large. *STOCK: Books, 15th C to date, 25p—£1,000.* LOC: From centre of Highgate Village, nearest underground stations Archway (Highgate), Highgate. PARK: Easy. TEL: 340 7244. SER: Valuations; restorations (books); buys at auction. VAT: Stan.

N.6 continued

Highgate Gallery
26 Highgate High St. (J. and M. Halsby.) CL: Mon. Open 10—1.30 and 2.30—5.30. *STOCK: English and Scottish watercolours, 1850—1939; Moorcroft pottery.* TEL: 340 7564.

"Stuart Martin"
355 and 355c Archway Rd. CL: Thurs. Open 10—1 and 2.30—6. *STOCK: Victorian, Edwardian and some Georgian furniture; antiquarian books.* TEL: 340 8354 or 723 7415. SER: Restorations; upholstery.

Tempus Antiques Ltd.   LAPADA
P.O. Box 71. (L.D. Lawrence.) Est. 1965. Open by appointment only. *STOCK: Japanese works of art, ivories, bronzes, cloisonne, porcelain, pottery and lacquer.* TEL: 340 4612. SER: Valuations; buys at auction. VAT: Stan/Spec.

London N.7

Keith Harding Antiques
93 Hornsey Rd. (C.A. Burnett, CMBHI and W.K. Harding, FBHI.) Est. 1961. Articles on clocks, musical boxes. CL: Sat. Open 9—6. SIZE: Medium. *STOCK: Musical boxes, clocks, horological books, spare parts.* LOC: Near Holloway Rd. underground station (Piccadilly Line). By road, nr. junction of A1 and A503. PARK: Easy. TEL: 607 6181/2672. SER: Valuations; restorations (musical boxes, clocks); buys at auction. VAT: Stan/Spec.

Princedale Antiques
56 Eden Grove. (G.M. Sykes.) Est. 1969. Open 10.30—6.30. *STOCK: Stripped pine furniture, architectural fittings, decorative items, 19th to early 20th C, £30—£300.* TEL: 727 0868 and 607 6376. VAT: Stan.

London N.10

Barrie Marks Ltd.
5 Princes Ave., Muswell Hill. ABA. Open by appointment only. *STOCK: Antiquarian books — illustrated, private press, colour plate, colour printing; modern first editions.* TEL: 883 1593.

London N.12

Finchley Fine Art Galleries
983 High Rd., North Finchley. (S. Greenman.) Est. 1979. Open 11.30—6.30 including Sun.; Mon. and Wed. by appointment. SIZE: Large. *STOCK: Watercolours, paintings, etchings, prints, mostly English, £25—£1,000; clocks, musical and scientific instruments; furniture, Georgian, Victorian, Edwardian; china and porcelain, Moorcroft, Doulton, Worcester, £5—£1,000; copper, bronze, brass, early photographic apparatus, fire-arms, shotguns, rifles; all 18th—20th C.* LOC: From M.I, left on to North Circular, left at Henlys Corner traffic lights, 2 miles north on left between North Finchley traffic lights and Whetstone traffic lights. PARK: Easy. TEL: 446 4848. SER: Valuations; restorations; framing.

London N.16

W. Forster
83a Stamford Hill. Est. 1952. Open by appointment. *STOCK: Bibliography and books about books.* LOC: Nearest station Manor House (Piccadilly Line) or 253 bus to Stamford Hill Broadway. PARK: Easy. TEL: 800 3919.

B. Hirschler
62 Portland Ave., and 71 Dunsmure Rd. Est. 1958. CL: Sat. and Jewish holidays. *STOCK: Hebraica, Judaica, books, prints, maps on Palestine; Jewish ceremonial objects.* LOC: Nearest underground is Manor House station and Seven Sisters Rd. station. TEL: 800 6395. SER: Valuations.

London N.19

Terry Antiques
175 Junction Rd., Archway, warehouse at 2b Monnery Rd., Archway. (T.H. Murphy.) Est. 1965. Open 9—1 and 2—6, Sat. 9—3. SIZE: Medium. *STOCK: Furniture — mahogany, walnut, rosewood, some oak, mid-18th to mid-19th C, £100—£3,000; objets d'art, grandfather clocks.* PARK: Easy. TEL: 263 1219; home — 889 9781. SER: Restorations (furniture); buys at auction. VAT: Stan.

London N.20

Barnet Antiques and Fine Art
BADA
1180 High Rd., Whetstone. (Mr. Hawkins and Mr. Gerry.) Est. 1959. SIZE: Large. *STOCK: Furniture, 18th C, Regency; pictures, porcelain.* **Not stocked: Victorian furniture. LOC: A1, north of Finchley. TEL: 445 9695. VAT: Spec.**

Frank L. Caira & Co.
20 Coppice Walk, Totteridge. (F.L. and I.D. Caira.) Est. 1946. Open by appointment. *STOCK: Porcelain, furniture, silver, oils, watercolours.* TEL: 445 6126. SER: Valuations. VAT: Stan/Spec.

London N.21

The Little Curiosity Shop   *Trade Only*
24 The Green, Winchmore Hill. (Mrs. H. Freedman.) Est. 1967. CL: Wed. Open 9.30—6. SIZE: Small. *STOCK: Clocks, porcelain, general small antiques, mostly Victorian, bronzes, silver, music boxes, jewellery and diamond items.* LOC: Nearest stations — Winchmore Hill (Eastern Region), and Southgate (Piccadilly Line underground). PARK: Easy. TEL: 886 0925. VAT: Stan.

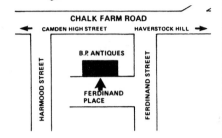
N.21 continued

Rochefort Antiques Gallery
32—34 The Green, Winchmore Hill. (L.W. and Mrs. Stevens-Wilson, Miss W.E. Allam.) Est. 1963. Open 10—1 and 2.30—6. 12 dealers selling:— *Porcelain, English and Continental, 18th—19th C, £1—£1,000; furniture, glass, silver, jewellery, copper, brass, pictures, prints, lamps, books, £1—2,000; lace and linen.* LOC: From London north through Wood Green and Palmers Green — branch off between Palmers Green and Enfield. PARK: Easy. TEL: 886 4779; home — 363 0910. SER: Valuations; silver plating; repairs (clocks and metalware). VAT: Stan/Spec.

London N.W.1

Acquisitions (Fireplaces) Ltd.
269 Camden High St. (K. Kennedy.) Est. 1970. Open 10—6. SIZE: Medium. *STOCK: Victorian and Edwardian fireplaces and fireside accessories, £38—£495.* LOC: 3 minutes walk from Camden Town tube station (Camden High St.). PARK: Easy. TEL: 485 4955. VAT: Stan.

Adams Antiques
47 Chalk Farm Rd. Open 10—6, seven days a week. *STOCK: Pine, especially Irish and Continental, 18th and 19th C.* TEL: 267 9241.

B.P. Antiques
2A Ferdinand Place, Ferdinand St., Chalk Farm. (D. Peston and I. Kammin.) Est. 1984. Open 9—5.30 inc. Sun. or by appointment. SIZE: Large. *STOCK: Furniture, paintings, clocks and barometers, 19th C, £50—£1,000.* LOC: Just off Chalk Farm Rd. PARK: Easy. TEL: 482 4021. SER: Restorations. VAT: Stan/Spec.

N.W.1 continued

Camden Antiques and Collectors' Market
Corner of Camden High St. and Buck St. Open Thurs. from 7. Over 100 dealers selling *a wide range of general antiques.* TEL: 351 5353.

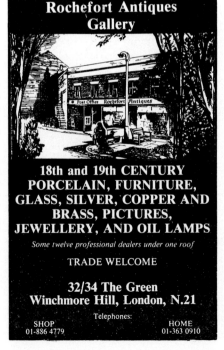

W. R. Harvey & Co (Antiques) Ltd.

FINE ANTIQUE FURNITURE
AND WORKS OF ART

67/70 Chalk Farm Road,
London, NW1 8AN
Tel: 01 485 1504
and at
5 Old Bond Street,
London, W1X 3TA
Tel: 01 499 8385

*A superb, fully fitted, George I period
burr walnut secretaire cabinet,
having its original maker's label
"William Old & John Ody". Circa 1715.*

N.W.1 continued

Country Pine Ltd.
13 Chalk Farm Rd. (Mrs. N. Sacki and B.J. Clark.) Est. 1979. CL: Mon. Open 10—6 inc. Sun. SIZE: Medium. *STOCK: Pine furniture (inc. longcase clocks), 1820—1920, £15—£800; kitchen units in antique pine, 1850—1950, £1—£100.* Not stocked: Jewellery. LOC: Opposite Camden Lock market. PARK: Easy. TEL: 485 9687. SER: Valuations. VAT: Stan/Spec.

Ian Crispin Antiques   Trade Only
95 Lisson Grove. Est. 1971. Open 10—5. *STOCK: Shipping goods, some antiques.* TEL: 402 6845. VAT: Stan.

Dreams
34 Chalk Farm Rd. (L. Amato.) CL: Mon. Open 10.30—6, Sat. and Sun. 11—6. *STOCK: Brass bedsteads.* TEL: 267 8194.

East-Asia Co.
103 Camden High St. Est. 1972. Open 10—6. *STOCK: Oriental antiquarian books on history and culture; Japanese and Chinese paintings and prints; jade, netsuke, objets d'art; books on Oriental art.* TEL: 388 5783.

Galerie 1900
267 Camden High St. (B. Rose, N. Polyviou.) Est. 1970. Open 10—5.30. SIZE: Medium. *STOCK: Glass, pottery, metalware, silver, jewellery, lighting and furnishings, 1800—1950, £100—£1,000.* LOC: Between Camden Town tube station and Camden Lock. PARK: Easy. TEL: 485 1001; home — 969 1803.

W.R. Harvey and Co.   BADA
(Antiques) Ltd.
67/70 Chalk Farm Rd. (W.R., G.M. and A.D. Harvey.) Est. 1952. Open 9.30—1 and 2—5.30. SIZE: Large. *STOCK: English furniture, clocks, objets d'art, 1690—1830.* PARK: Easy. TEL: 485 1504 and 267 2767. SER: Valuations; restorations. FAIRS: Olympia and Harrogate. VAT: Stan/Spec.

Richard Kihl Wine Antiques and Accessories
164 Regents Park Rd. Est. 1978. Open 10—5, Sat. 11—5. SIZE: Small. *STOCK: Wine related antiques — decanters, claret jugs, coasters, glass, decanting cradles, corkscrews, glass funnels, old bottles, 1750—1910, £5—£500.* LOC: Close to London Zoo and Primrose Hill. PARK: Easy. TEL: 586 3838. VAT: Stan.

Laurence Corner Militaria
126—130 Drummond St. (Victor Laurence Ltd.) Est. 1967. Open 9—5.30. SIZE: Large. *STOCK: Uniforms — ambassadorial and court dress, swords, helmets, drums; theatrical costumes.* LOC: From Tottenham Court Rd. — Warren St. end — continue into Hampstead Rd., first turning on right by traffic lights. PARK: Easy. TEL: 388 6811.

N.W.1 continued

Lott — 32
32 Camden Rd., Camden Town. (M. and Mrs. G. Wilkes.) Est. 1975. STOCK: General antiques, curios and stripped pine furniture. TEL: 267 5828. SER: Pine stripping (furniture and architectural fittings).

David Miles
Open by appointment. STOCK: Musical instruments. TEL: 485 1329.

Chas. L. Nyman and Co. Ltd.
Trade Only

230 and 242 Camden High St. Est. 1920. CL: Thurs. p.m., and Sat. Open 9.30—5.30. STOCK: English and Continental 19th C furniture and porcelain. TEL: 485 1907. VAT: Spec.

The Patchwork Dog and The Calico Cat Ltd.
21 Chalk Farm Rd. (J. Zinni-Lask.) Est. 1977. Open Tues.—Sun. 10—6. SIZE: Large. STOCK: American and English patchwork quilts, 1850—1930, £100—£500. LOC: Near Camden Lock. PARK: Easy. TEL: 485 1239. SER: Restorations (quilt repairs). VAT: Stan/Spec.

Regent Antiques
Trade Only

9-10 Chester Court, Albany St. (T. Quaradeghini.) Est. 1983. Open 9.30—5.30, Sat. by appointment. SIZE: Large and warehouse. STOCK: Furniture, 18th C to Edwardian, £50—£5,000+; decorative items and bric- a-brac, 19th—20th C, £10—£1,000. LOC: ¼ mile from Gt. Portland St. station towards Camden Town. PARK: Easy. TEL: 935 6944/7814. SER: Restorations (furniture); gilding. VAT: Stan.

Relic Antiques at Camden Lock and The Camden Lock Antiques Centre
248 Camden High St. (M. Gliksten, G. Gower.) Est. 1968. Open Wed.—Sun., Mon. and Tues. by appointment. SIZE: Medium. STOCK: 9 separate dealers on ground floor — clothes, jewellery, furniture, antiquarian books, ethnic art, toys, art deco and decorators' antiques. Basement warehouse: Decorators' and collectors' items, £1—£200. LOC: Camden Lock. PARK: At Camden Lock or meters. TEL: 485 8072 and 388 2691; home — 586 7648. SER: Valuations.

A. Spigard
236 Camden High St. Open 9—6. STOCK: Furniture. SER: Restorations. VAT: Spec.

W. Tauber
94 Park Rd. Est. 1947. CL: Sat. p.m. SIZE: Medium. STOCK: General antiques. TEL: 723 6143.

N.W.1 continued

This and That (Furniture)
50 and 51 Chalk Farm Rd. (R.P. Schanzer.) Est. 1974. CL: Mon. Open 10.30—6, including Sun. SIZE: Medium. STOCK: Country furniture, stripped pine, oak and walnut, 1880—1900. LOC: Between Roundhouse and Camden Lock. PARK: Easy. TEL: 267 5433. VAT: Stan.

W.E. Walker
277—279 Camden High St. Est. 1930. Open 10—6, weekends by appointment. SIZE: Medium. STOCK: Furniture, 17th—19th C. PARK: Easy. TEL: 485 6210/4433. SER: Valuations; restorations. VAT: Spec.

J. Wolff and Son Ltd.
82 Troutbeck, Albany St., Regents Park. Open by appointment. STOCK: English and French furniture, objets d'art, mirrors, mantel clocks, 18th—19th C. TEL: 388 3588 (24 hours). SER: Restorations (carving, gilding).

London N.W.2

Artinterias
(Cranbourn Antiques) Ltd., 32 Thanet Lodge, Mapesbury Rd. (G. Feuer.) Est. 1940. CL: Sat. Open 9—4, other times by appointment. STOCK: Louis Philippe furniture, porcelain and objets d'art. TEL: 459 0782. VAT: Spec.

H. Baron
136 Chatsworth Rd. Est. 1949. Open by appointment. STOCK: Antiquarian music, musical literature and iconography, autograph music and letters. TEL: 459 2035. VAT: Stan.

The Corner Cupboard
679 Finchley Rd. (M. Fry.) Est. 1950. Open 9.30—6. SIZE: Small. STOCK: Jewellery, 18th—19th C, from £5; silver, china, glass. LOC: Number 2 or 13 bus from Central London. PARK: Easy. TEL: 435 4870. VAT: Stan.

Leon Drucker
25 Dicey Avenue. Est. 1958. Open by appointment. STOCK: First editions, 1850—1940, autograph material, bindings, theatre, cinema and newspaper history. LOC: From central London turn off Edgware Rd., turn left at Cricklewood Broadway. PARK: Easy. TEL: 452 1581. SER: Valuations; buys at auction.

Gunter Fine Art
Trade Only

4 Randall Ave. (G.A. and A.M. Goodwin.) Est. 1977. Open by appointment only. SIZE: Small. STOCK: Watercolours, 18th—20th C, £100—£1,500; oil paintings, 19th C, £200—£2,000. LOC: North Circular Rd., near Brent Cross shopping centre. PARK: Easy. TEL: 452 3997. SER: Buys at auction.

London N.W.3

Patricia Beckman · LAPADA
Est. 1968. Open by appointment. *STOCK: Furniture, 18th and 19th C.* TEL: 435 5050. VAT: Spec.

Tony Bingham · BADA
11 Pond St. Est. 1964. *STOCK: Musical instruments, books, music, oil paintings, engravings of musical interest.* **TEL: 794 1596. VAT: Stan/Spec.**

Michael Carleton
77, 79 and 81 Haverstock Hill. Est. 1966. Open 9—1 and 2—5.30. *STOCK: Antique and decorative furniture, objets d'art, engravings, oils and watercolours.* PARK: Easy. TEL: 722 2277 and 586 4458. SER: Restorations (watercolours, oils); furniture gilding and lacquer; framing.

Chatal Ltd.
457 Finchley Rd. Est. 1964. Open by appointment. *STOCK: Silver, watches, semi-precious jewellery.* TEL: 203 2351. VAT: Spec.

S.A. Cook and Son.
279 Finchley Rd. Est. 1946. Open 9—7, Sat. 9—4. *STOCK: Furniture, silver and plate.* TEL: 435 4543. SER: Valuations; restorations. VAT: Stan.

Clive Daniel Antiques
91A Heath St., Hampstead. (C. and P. Gillinson.) Est. 1977. CL: Mon. Open 10—5.30. SIZE: Small. *STOCK: English furniture, 19th—20th C.* LOC: Hampstead village. PARK: Nearby. TEL: 435 4351. VAT: Stan.

P.G. de Lotz · Postal Only
20 Downside Crescent, Hampstead. ABA. Est. 1967. Catalogue available. *STOCK: Antiquarian books on history warfare — naval, military and aviation.* TEL: 794 5709. SER: Catalogue and search only.

Dolphin Coins
2c England's Lane, Hampstead. (R. Ilsley) BNTA. Est. 1966. Open 9.30—5. SIZE: Medium. *STOCK: British and world coins, early and medieval, from 100BC, £20—£15,000.* LOC: Off Haverstock Lane. PARK: Easy. TEL: 722 4116. SER: Valuations; buys at auction (coins). VAT: Spec.

Stephen Farrelly
152 Fleet Rd. Est. 1948. CL: Thurs. Open 10—6. *STOCK: Pictures, furniture, porcelain, general antiques.* TEL: 485 2089. VAT: Stan/Spec.

The Flask Bookshop
6 Flask Walk, Hampstead. (J. Connolly.) ABA. Est. 1974. CL. Mon. and Thurs. Open 10—5.30. SIZE: Small. *STOCK: Books — modern first editions, art and literature, £5—£100.* LOC: Off Hampstead High St. TEL: 435 2693.

N.W.3 continued

Otto Haas (A. and M. Rosenthal)
49 Belsize Park Gdns. Est. 1866. CL: Sat. Open 9.30—5 by appointment. *STOCK: Manuscripts, printed music, autographs, rare books on music.* TEL: 722 1488.

Hampstead Antique Emporium
12 Heath St., Hampstead. Est. 1967. CL: Mon. Open 10—6. Approx. 25 dealers. *STOCK: Jewellery, clocks, furniture, silver, paintings, prints, metalware, glass, art nouveau, art deco.* LOC: 2 mins. walk from Hampstead underground . TEL: 794 3297. SER: Advice (interior decor). The following are a few of the dealers at the Emporium:—

Hanlin
Original Japanese woodblock paintings and prints.

Haros Antiques
Furniture, 19th C, decorative items, brass, copper, steel. VAT: Stan.

Lee and Stacy
General antiques and paintings.

Mount Gallery
(S.A. Collister.) Est. 1979. *British watercolours, £50—£3,000; oils, £200—£2,000; prints, £25—£500, all 1750—1950.* SER: Restorations; buys at auction; mounting, framing. FAIRS: Olympia and West Midlands.

J.P. and E. O'Dwyer
Porcelain, glass, bric-a-brac, small furniture.

Pickwick Antiques
Scorpio Antiques
Shelagh Antiques
Boutique 2, The Court Yard.

Henry Shelkin
The Court Yard. *Clocks.*

Status Antiques
(S. and J. Taylor.) *Furniture, silver, small collectors' items, 18th C drinking glasses.*

Suzie-Q Antiques
The Court Yard.

The Trio
(Miss S. Mendoza.) *Furniture, porcelain, glass. Also at Woburn Abbey Antiques.* VAT: Stan.

Unicorn Books
Children's illustrated books.

Haverstock Antiques · LAPADA
78 Haverstock Hill. (J. Newton.) Est. 1976. Open 10—5. SIZE: Medium. *STOCK: Restored furniture, mahogany, elm, oak, rosewood, Regency, Georgian and Victorian.* LOC: Near Camden Lock and Chalk Farm tube stations. PARK: Easy. TEL: 267 1627. SER: Restorations. VAT: Stan/Spec.

N.W.3 continued

Just Desks
6 Erskine Rd. (G. Gordon and N. Finch.) Est. 1967. Open 9.30—6 or by appointment. *STOCK: Victorian, Edwardian and reproduction desks, writing tables, davenports, bureaux, chairs, filing cabinets, roll tops.* PARK: Nearby. TEL: 723 7976. VAT: Stan.

Frederick Mulder
83 Belsize Park Gdns. Open by appointment. *STOCK: Prints including Old Master and original; antiquarian illustrated books.* TEL: 722 2105.

Pordes Remainders Ltd.
529B Finchley Rd. Open 9—6. *STOCK: Antiquarian books including scientific and learned.* TEL: 435 9878.

Stanley Smith and Keith Fawkes
1—3 Flask Walk. Est. 1970. Open 10—6. *STOCK: Antiquarian books.* TEL: 435 0614.

Townsends
36 New End Sq. (M. Townsend.) *STOCK: Fireplaces, stained glass, doors and architectural items.* TEL: 794 5706/7. SER: Valuations; restorations.

London N.W.4

Antiques (Hendon) Ltd.
18 Parson St., Hendon. (G. Frankl.) Est. 1960. CL: Wed. p.m. Open 9.30—6. SIZE: Medium. *STOCK: Furniture and paintings, £100—£1,000; china, £10—£300; all 18th—19th C.* LOC: Coming from Golders Green, cross the North Circular Rd. and proceed to the end of Brent St. PARK: Easy. TEL: 203 1194. SER: Valuations; restorations (paintings and furniture); buys at auction. VAT: Stan/Spec.

A. and R.M. Orr Fine Art
38 Downage, Hendon. Est. 1962. Open by appointment only. *STOCK: 17th—19th C paintings.* TEL: 203 0098.

R. & R.'s Gold and Silver Exchange
22 Parson St., Hendon. (A. Randall.) *STOCK: English porcelain, glass, judicial prints, postcards and collectables.* TEL: 203 3971. SER: Export.

Talking Machine
30 Watford Way, Hendon. Open 11—5.30, Sat. 11—5. *STOCK: Mechanical music, old gramophones, phonographs, vintage records and 78's, needles and spare parts, early radio, typewriters, sewing machines.* TEL: 202 3473. SER: Buys at auction. VAT: Stan.

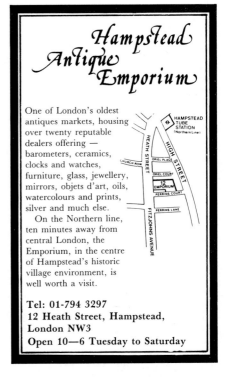

London N.W.5

Abington Books
Ground Floor 'F' Block, I.O.C.C. Complex, 53/79 Highgate Rd. (J. Haldane.) ABA. Est. 1971. By appointment only. SIZE: Small. *STOCK: Books on Oriental rugs, from 1877, £1—£5,000; books on classical tapestries, from 17th C, £1—£1,000.* PARK: Easy. TEL: 267 2701; home — (0223) 891 645. SER: Valuations; book binding; buys at auction (books).

Y. and B. Bolour
53-79 Highgate Rd. CL: Sat. Open 9.30—5.30. *STOCK: Worldwide hand-made tribal and traditional flat weave and pile textile carpets.* TEL: 485 6262.

Game Advice
1 Holmes Rd. (A. and S. Elithorn.) Est. 1976. CL: Mon. except by appointment. Open 10—2 and 3—5.30. SIZE: Small. *STOCK: Games, puzzles, jigsaws, cards, educational toys, chess sets; chess, cookery and children's books, £25—£100; ephemera, £5—£50; all 18th—19th C.* LOC: Just off Kentish Town Rd. PARK: Easy. TEL: 485 2188; home — 485 4226. SER: Valuations; restorations; buys at auction. VAT: Stan/Spec.

N.W.5 continued

M.E. Korn
51 Lady Margaret Rd., Kentish Town. (E. Korn.) ABA, PBFA. Est. 1971. Open by appointment. SIZE: Small. *STOCK: Books — natural history, medical, science, art and literature, 16th—19th C, £10—£100.* LOC: Off Kentish Town Rd., turn into Leighton Rd., then 2nd left. PARK: Easy. TEL: 267 2936; home — 267 5035. SER: Valuations; buys at auction (antiquarian books). FAIRS: PBFA in Russel Hotel monthly, York, Oxford, Cambridge; ABAA in California, Boston, New York and Toronto.

Joseph Lavian
53-79 Highgate Rd. Est. 1950. Open 9—6. SIZE: Large. *STOCK: Oriental carpets, rugs, kelims, tapestries and textiles, 18th—19th C.* LOC: Kentish town Station. PARK: Own. TEL: 485 7955. SER: Valuations; restorations. VAT: Stan.

M. and M. Oriental Gallery Ltd.
53—79 Highgate Rd. (M.A. and M. Karimzadeh.) Est. 1974. CL: Sat. Open 9.30—5, Sun. by appointment. SIZE: Large. *STOCK: Oriental carpets and rugs.* LOC: Kentish Town. PARK: Own. TEL: 267 5973 (24hr.) SER: Valuations; restorations; buys at auction; cleaning. VAT: Stan/Spec.

London N.W.6

Mr. Temple Brooks
12 Mill Lane, West Hampstead. Est. 1936. Resident. Always available. *STOCK: Clocks.* TEL: 452 9696. VAT: Spec.

John Denham Gallery
50 Mill Lane, West Hampstead. CL: Sat. Open 10—5. *STOCK: Paintings, drawings and prints, 17th—20th C, £5—£5,000.* TEL: 794 2635. SER: Restorations; conservation; re-framing. VAT: Spec.

The Diddy Box
82 Mill Lane, West Hampstead. (Mrs. I. Gibbs.) Open Wed. and Fri. 10.30—5.30, Sat. 10.30—1 or any time by appointment. *STOCK: Victoriana, general antiques and bric-a-brac.* TEL: 794 4434. SER: Buys at auction.

End of Day
51 Mill Lane, West Hampstead. (P. St. George.) Open 10.30—6. *STOCK: Lighting and chandeliers.* TEL: 435 8091.

N.W.6 continued

The Furniture Store
Unit 17, 1st Floor, West Hampstead Trade Centre, Blackburn Rd. Est. 1978. Open 10—6, Sun. by appointment. SIZE: Large. *STOCK: Furniture, furnishings and lighting, 1860—1960, £50—£1,000.* LOC: Off West End Lane by West Hampstead underground station. PARK: Easy. TEL: 328 2221. FAIRS: Olympia. VAT: Stan/Spec.

Gallery Kaleidoscope
66 Willesden Lane. (K. Barrie.) Est. 1965. Open 10—6. SIZE: Medium. *STOCK: Oils, watercolours and prints, 18th—20th C.* LOC: 10 mins. from Marble Arch. PARK: Easy. TEL: 328 5833. SER: Restorations; framing. VAT: Stan/Spec.

G. and F. Gillingham Ltd. LAPADA
4 Crediton Hill. Est. 1960. Resident. Prior 'phone call advisable. SIZE: Warehouse. *STOCK: 19th C English and continental furniture, clocks, barometers.* LOC: Off Finchley Rd., N.W.3 and West End Lane, N.W.6. PARK: Easy. TEL: 435 5644. VAT: Stan.

A. Landau
45 Mill Lane, West Hampstead. CL: Mon. Open 10—5, Sat. 2—5.30. *STOCK: Late Victorian and Edwardian items, tiles and stained glass.* LOC: Coming from Marble Arch along Edgware Rd., turn right after Kilburn tube station. TEL: 794 3028; home — 435 0243. VAT: Stan.

Lyons Gallery
47 Mill Lane, West Hampstead. Est. 1968. Resident. Appointment advisable. SIZE: Medium. *STOCK: Art nouveau and art deco, paintings, studio ceramics, art glass.* LOC: Between Edgware Rd. and West End Lane. PARK: Easy. TEL: 794 3537. SER: Buys at auction.

Putnams Antiques
72 Mill Lane, West Hampstead. (Mrs. Allsopp.) Resident. Est. 1977. Open 10—5.30, Sat. 10—5. SIZE: Large. *STOCK: Staffordshire china, decorative furniture, English quilts, rag rugs, samplers.* Not stocked: Jewellery and silver. LOC: From London, up Edgware Rd., Kilburn High Rd., turn right at top of Shoot-Up Hill. PARK: Easy. TEL: 431 2935; home — 435 6869. SER: Valuations.

Scope Antiques
64—66 Willesden Lane. (K. Barrie.) Est. 1966. Open 10—6. SIZE: Large. *STOCK: Furniture, general antiques, decorative items, silver, bric-a-brac.* PARK: Easy. TEL: 328 5833. SER: Repairs (silver). VAT: Stan/Spec.

N.W.6 continued

Robert Stephenson
42 Fairfax Rd. Est. 1983. Open by appointment. SIZE: Small. *STOCK: Carpets and kelims, 19th—20th C, £200—£12,000; textiles and hangings, 18th—20th C, £60—£2,000; objets d'art, 19th C, £200—£1,000.* LOC: Off Finchley Rd. PARK: Easy. TEL: 722 4043; home — same. SER: Valuations; restorations; buys at auction (carpets, textiles and objects). VAT: Stan/Spec.

Eric and Joan Stevens Booksellers
74 Fortune Green Rd. ABA. Est. 1962. Open Sat., other times by appointment. SIZE: Medium. *STOCK: Books, 19th—20th C, £1—£50+.* PARK: Easy, nearby. TEL: 435 7545. SER: Catalogues issued; buys at auction. VAT: Stan.

The Trinket Box
1 Goldhurst Terrace. (M. Fry.) Open 9.30—6. SIZE: Medium. *STOCK: Jewellery, Georgian and Victorian; silver, Victorian and Edwardian; china, bric-a-brac.* PARK: 5 mins. from Finchley Rd. station, 2 and 13 bus. TEL: 624 4264. SER: Valuations VAT: Stan.

Zebra
58 Mill Lane, West Hampstead. (L. Forgione.) CL: Mon. Open 10—6. *STOCK: Bed and table linen; lace and quilts; Victorian nightwear and childrens' clothing.* TEL: 435 3108.

London N.W.7

The Bank House Gallery
8—10 The Broadway, Mill Hill. (R.S. James Ltd.) Open 9.30—5, Fri. 9.30—3, Sat. 9.30—12. *STOCK: Oil paintings, 19th C.* LOC: Close to M1, M25 and A1; 12 minutes by train from Kings Cross. TEL: 906 3124. SER: Restorations; framing; catalogues available.

Gerald Clark Antiques Ltd.
LAPADA
1 High St., Mill Hill Village. (G.J. and J. Clark.) Est. 1976. CL: Sun. and Mon. except by appointment. Open 10—5. SIZE: Medium. *STOCK: Early English and Victorian Staffordshire pottery, porcelain, small furniture, watercolours and plaques, 18th—19th C.* PARK: Easy. TEL: 906 0342. SER: Valuations; buys at auction. FAIRS: Olympia. VAT: Spec.

The <u>Dealers'</u> Market. Over 100 stands and showrooms.

13/25 Church Street, London N.W.8.   01 723 6066

London N.W.8

Alfies Antique Market

13—25 Church St. (B. Gray.) CL: Mon. Open 10—6. More than 100 stands as well as showrooms and craft workshops, selling general antiques, medium price range. TEL: 723 6066.

J. Baker
Stand 768/9. *Radios.*

Barbara Antiques
Stand 227/9. *Old legal documents and porcelain.* TEL: 723 1513.

A. Barragan
Stand 653/4. *Decorative antiques.* TEL: 723 0678.

Beverley
Stand 655/6/7. *Art deco and general antiques.* TEL: 723 0678.

D. Binder
Stand 101/20. *Art deco furniture.* TEL: 723 0542.

Blooms and Blossoms
Stand 212/14. *Pottery and porcelain.* TEL: 723 1513.

Teddy Browne
Stand 201/2. *Bric-a-brac.* TEL: 723 1513.

Gary Brunswick
Stand 711. *Oriental carpets and textiles.* TEL: 723 5731.

Celia
Stand 261/2. *Silver, jewellery, china, porcelain and glass.* TEL: 723 0564.

Robert Cleland
Stand 322/3. *General antiques.* TEL: 402 7448.

De la Fuerte
Stand 606. *General antiques.*

Joe Del Grosso
Stand 841/43. *Books.* TEL: 723 0492.

Annette Dimoch
Stand 821/2. *General antiques.*

Duffy Country Style
Stand 761.

Alfies Antique Market continued

Mark Dunn
Stand 234/5. *Watches, clocks.*

East Gates Antiques
Stand 617. *China, glass, photographica.*

Elena and Peter
Stand 331/33. *General antiques.* TEL: 723 0564.

Ena Antiques
Stand 836/7. *General antiques.* TEL: 723 0429.

T. Erbrick
Stand 239. *Jewellery and general antiques.*

H. Feltz
Stand 402. *Clothing, bric-a-brac.*

Audrey Field
Stand 806/7. *Lace.* TEL: 723 0449.

Jean Fleming
Stand 317/8. *Jewellery, pipes and general antiques.* TEL: 723 5613.

J. Forgioni and Peter Jacques
Stand 713. *Tiles, mirrors, lighting.* TEL: 723 5731. SER: Restorations (china).

Frances
Stand 304. *Jewellery and linen.* TEL: 723 5613.

Fritzi
Stand 219. *Early Mason's Ironstone.* TEL: 723 1513.

Nina Fuller
Stand 320/21. *Furniture and general antiques.* TEL: 402 7448.

The Furniture Store
Stand 501-513. *Furniture.* TEL: 723 9456.

Garry Anne
Stand 401/6/7. *Decorative art 1900—1950.* TEL: 723 0564.

Gloria and Eamon
Stand 327. *Silver, silver plate cutlery, collectors' items and objets d'art.* TEL: 723 0564.

Goldsmith and Perris   **LAPADA**
Silver and plate. TEL: 723 0563.

Alfies Antique Market continued

Roma Goldstein and M. Druks.
Stand 781/4. *General antiques.*
Ena Green
Stand 838/40. *Furniture, china, linen.* TEL: 723 0492.
James Gregory
Stand 772/3. *Rugs.*
Griffiths
Stand 572/3. *Decorators' items.* TEL: 723 3732.
Teresa Grosschild
Stand 203. *Stamps.* TEL: 723 1513.
Carol Hammond
Stand 245. *China and glass.*
Steve Hart
Stand 669/70. *General antiques.* TEL: 723 0678.
Mrs. Heller
Stand 219. *Porcelain, silver plate.* TEL: 723 0564.
Tina Henning
Stand 603. *Paintings.* TEL: 723 8964.
K. Hicks
Stand 671. *Art Deco.* TEL: 723 0678.
Joy Hodgson
Stand 779/80. *Jewellery, beads, general antiques.*
J. and P. Antiques
Stand 208/9. *Pottery and porcelain.* TEL: 723 1513.
Peter Jacques and Jo Jo
Stand 703. *Brass.* TEL: 723 6105. SER: Restorations.
Kersalaers
Stand 832. *Art deco.*
Kim and Elaine
Stand 230. *Oriental porcelain.*
Korniczky
Stand 315/6. *General antiques.* TEL: 723 5613.
L. and M. Antiques
Stand 206/7. *General antiques.* TEL: 723 1513.
Bill and Fiona Laidlaw
Stand 603. *Decorative antiques.* TEL: 723 1370.
S. Lazarus
Stand 401/2. *Country furniture.*
Leni
Stand 242/3/4. *Silver, glass, perfume bottles, jewellery, interior decorating objets d'art.* TEL: 723 3389.
Liz
Stand 258. *Jewellery.*
Lydia
Stand 252. *Jewellery.* TEL: 402 1136.
Marian and Peter
Stand 246. *Jewellery and general antiques.* TEL: 723 3389.
Marie
Stand 254. *Jewellery and small general antiques.* TEL: 723 1513.

Alfies Antique Market continued

Graham Matthews
Stand 651/2. *Art Deco items.*
Sue Mervyn-Jones
Stand 601. *Furniture.*
T. Miall
Stand 232/3. *General antiques.* TEL: 723 0564.
G. Miles
Stand 253. *Silver.* TEL: 723 0564.
M. Miller
Stand 305. *Turn-of-the-century onwards art and decorative objects.* TEL: 723 5613.
Minoo Mog
Stand 256/7. *Jewellery.* TEL: 723 0564.
Mitzi
Stand 224. *Porcelain and glass.* TEL: 723 1513.
Graham Music
Stand 778. *General antiques.*
Mr. N.
Stand 308-312. *Medical and scientific instruments, clocks.* TEL: 723 5613.
Nicholas Antiques
Stand 329/30. *Continental pottery and Oriental works of art.* TEL: 723 0449.
Nello
Stand 701/5. *Collectors' items.* TEL: 723 6105.
Mrs. Otti
Stand 221 and 231-8. *Paintings.*
Paola
Stand 764/5. *Victorian furniture and bric-a- brac.*
Peter
Stand 334. *Brass and bathroom fittings.*
Shaushana Preiss
Stand 313/4. *Paintings and watercolours.* TEL: 723 5613.
Quartlet Art
Stand 616. *General antiques.* TEL: 723 1370.
Robinson
Stand 826/7.
C. Robinson
Stand 812/3. *Art deco, 1950s items.* TEL: 723 0449.
A.C. Rockman
Stand 405. *Bric-a-brac.* TEL: 723 0564.
B.M. Rockman
Stand 403. *Bric-a-brac.* TEL: 723 0564.
Rossu
Stand 247. *General antiques, especially frames.* TEL: 723 0564.
Scholar
Stand 328. *China and glass.* TEL: 723 0449.
Roger Shans-Nia
Stand 255. *Clocks and barometers.* TEL: 723 0564.
Alan Silver
Stand 263. *Paintings.* TEL: 262 3613.

Alfies Antique Market continued

Gloria Sinclair
Stand 204/5/10. *Continental and English porcelain and jewellery.* TEL: 723 1513.
Spafford Art Deco
Stand 814/5. TEL: 723 0449.
Stellas Antiques Art Deco
Stand 801 and 816/7. TEL: 723 0449.
Barbara Stone
Stand 111/13. *Books.* TEL: 723 2829.
Stuff and Nonsense
Stand 408/9. *Pine and kitchen items.* TEL: 723 0564.
Tracey
Stand 757/8. *Art Deco.*
Trevor
Stand 319. *Oriental pottery and china.*
David Tupman
Stand 664/5. *General antiques.*
Valerie
Stand 610-620. *General antiques.* TEL: 723 1370.
John Vickers
Stand 215/16. *Pottery and porcelain.* TEL: 723 1513.
John White
Stand 823-830. *Art deco.* TEL: 723 0449.
Fiona Wicks
Stand 301/2. *Art deco.* TEL: 723 5613.

Bizarre
24 Church St. (A. Taramasco.) Open 10−5. *STOCK: Art deco.* TEL: 724 1305.

China Repairers incorporating Mair and Drayson Antiques
LAPADA
64 Charles Lane, St. John's Wood. (A. Drayson, P. Mair.) Est. 1952. Open 9.30−1 and 2.15−5.30, Sat. by appointment. *STOCK: Early Meissen, English pottery and porcelain, 18th C, £50−£500.* PARK: Meters. TEL: 722 8407. SER: Restorations. VAT: Stan/Spec.

Robert Franses and Sons
5 Nugent Terrace, St. John's Wood. Est. 1969. CL: Sat. Open 9−3 or by appointment. SIZE: Small. *STOCK: European and Oriental carpets, tapestries, needlework, Turkish village rugs, early Chinese rugs.* TEL: 286 6913; home − 328 0949. SER: Restorations. VAT: Stan/Spec.

Furniture Fair
22 Church St. Est. 1964. Open 9.30−5. SIZE: Medium. *STOCK: Victorian chairs, chaises longues.* PARK: Reasonable. TEL: 262 1338. SER: Restorations. VAT: Stan.

N.W.8 continued

The Gallery of Antique Costume and Textiles (Incorporating Topfloor)
2 Church St., Marylebone. Open 10−5.30. *STOCK: European and Eastern textiles including Chinese and Japanese hangings, furnishing textiles, needlework and beadwork items, cushions; Chinese robes, skirts and embroideries; English shepherds' smocks, late 18th to early 20th C; period clothing, 1830−1940; all £5−£10,000.* LOC: 1 mile from Marble Arch, between Edgware Rd. and Lisson Grove. PARK: Easy. TEL: 723 9981 (ansaphone). SER: Valuations; restorations (costume and textiles). FAIRS: Olympia.

The Hugh Evelyn Picture Shop
53 Charlbert St., St. John's Wood. (H. Street.) Est. 1979. CL: Mon. Open 10−6, Sat. 10−2. SIZE: Small. *STOCK: Prints, 17th−19th C, £5−£1,000; watercolours, 19th C, £50−£850.* LOC: From Wellington Rd., past Lords Cricket Ground, turn off down Circus Rd., third on right. PARK: Easy. TEL: 586 5108 (24 hours). SER: Restorations (cleaning and repairs of prints, watercolours and pastels); buys at auction (pictures). VAT: Stan.

Just Desks   LAPADA
20 Church St. (G. Gordon and N. Finch.) Est. 1967. Open 9.30−6 or by appointment. SIZE: Medium. *STOCK: Victorian and Edwardian desks, writing tables, davenports, bureaux, chairs, filing cabinets, roll tops.* PARK: Meters. TEL: 723 7976. VAT: Stan.

Lords Gallery
26 Wellington Rd. (P. Granville.) Est. 1957. Open by appointment. *STOCK: Rare original posters, 19th−20th C, £1−£10,000; Kurt Schwitters; Friedrich Meckseper, £100−£1,000; both 20th C.* LOC: Near Lord's cricket ground. PARK: Easy. TEL: 722 4444. SER: Valuations. VAT: Stan.

Townsends
1 Church St. (M. Townsend.) CL: Mon. Open 10−6. *STOCK: Tiles and door furniture.* TEL: 724 3746.

Townsends
81 Abbey Rd., St. John's Wood. (M. Townsend.) Est. 1972. CL: Mon. Open 10−6. SIZE: Large. *STOCK: Fireplaces, £100−£300; stained glass, £30−£200; architectural items, £10−£300; all 19th C.* LOC: Corner of Abbey Rd. and Boundary Rd. PARK: Easy. TEL: 624 4756. SER: Valuations. VAT: Stan.

Wellington Gallery
1 St. John's Wood High St. (Mr. and Mrs. K. Barclay.) Open 10−5.30. *STOCK: 19th C watercolours, oils and engravings.* TEL: 586 2620.

N.W.8 continued

Wrawby Moor Art Gallery Ltd.
Trade Only
6 St. John's Wood Rd. (J.N. Drummond.) Est. 1972. Open by appointment. *STOCK: English and European oils, 1750—1950, £250— £10,000.* LOC: Pass Lords entrance and next lights, house last bow front on left, facing down Hamilton Terrace. TEL: 286 6452; home — same. SER: Valuations; restorations (oils); buys at auction. VAT: Spec.

London N.W.9

B.C. Metalcrafts Ltd.   *Trade Only*
69 Tewkesbury Gdns. Est. 1946. Open by appointment only. *STOCK: Lighting, ormolu and marble lamps; oriental and European vases; clocks, pre—1900, £5—£500.* Not stocked: Silver. PARK: Easy. TEL: 204 2446. SER: Restorations (metalware); buys at auction. VAT: Stan/Spec.

London N.W.10

Brocantiques   *Trade Only*
31 Linden Avenue. Est. 1974. Open by appointment. *STOCK: Furniture for export.* TEL: 969 7151. VAT: Stan.

London N.W.11

Delieb Antiques Ltd.
31 Woodville Rd. (E. Delieb.) Est. 1953. CL: Sat. Open by appointment only. *STOCK: Collectors' silver and rarities.* TEL: 458 2083. VAT: Spec.

London W.C.1

Atlantis Bookshop Ltd.
49a Museum St. ABA. Open 11—5.30, Sat. 11—5. *STOCK: Antiquarian books on the occult.* TEL: 405 2120.

M. Ayres
31 Museum St. Open 10—6. *STOCK: Antiquarian and illustrated books, etchings, antiquities.* TEL: 636 2844.

Andrew Block
20 Barter St. ABA. Est. 1911. Open 10—4 or by appointment. *STOCK: Antiquarian books, printed ephemera, entertainment material.* LOC: Off Bloomsbury Way. PARK: Bloomsbury Sq. TEL: 405 9660.

Louis W. Bondy
16 Little Russell St. ABA. Est. 1947. Open 10—6, Sat. 10—5. SIZE: Small. *STOCK: Rare books.* LOC: Near British Museum. PARK: Fairly easy. TEL: 405 2733. SER: Valuations. VAT: Stan.

Cinema Bookshop
13-14 Great Russell St. (F. Zentner.) Est. 1969. Open 10.30—5.30. SIZE: Small. *STOCK: Books, magazines, posters and stills.* LOC: First right off Tottenham Court Rd. PARK: Easy. TEL: 637 0206. SER: Mail order. VAT: Stan.

George and Peter Cohn   *Trade Only*
Unit 21, 21 Wren St. Est. 1947. Open 9—5, Sat. and Fri. p.m. by appointment. *STOCK: Decorative lights.* PARK: Forecourt. TEL: 278 3749. SER: Restorations (chandeliers and wall-lights).

Collet's Chinese Gallery
40 Great Russell St. Est. 1952. Open
9.45−5.45. SIZE: Medium. *STOCK: Chinese
and Far Eastern antiquities and works of art,
bronzes, ceramics, coins, jade, snuff bottles,
paintings, calligraphy, prints, block books,
sculpture, £25−£2,000.* LOC: Nearest tube
station, Tottenham Court Rd., turn right into
Great Russell St. PARK: 50yds., opposite
British Museum. TEL: 580 7538. VAT: Spec.

Craddock and Barnard
32 Museum St. (A. Gibbs.) Est. 1914. CL:
Sat. Open 9.30−5.30. SIZE: Small. *STOCK:
Engravings, etchings, woodcuts, 15th−20th
C.* LOC: Near south entrance to British
Museum. TEL: 636 3937. VAT: Stan/Spec.

Sebastian D'Orsai Ltd.
39 Theobalds Rd. (A. Brooks.) CL: Sat. Open
9−5.30. *STOCK: Framed watercolours and
prints.* TEL: 405 6663. SER: Restorations
(paintings and prints); framing; gilding. VAT:
Stan.

E.H.W. and Co.
12 Sicilian Ave., Southampton Row. (Mr.
Woodiwiss.) Est. 1943. CL: Sat. Open
8.30−5. SIZE: Medium. *STOCK: Milled coins,
stamps.* LOC: Near British Museum. TEL: 405
5509. SER: Valuations; buys at auction. VAT:
Stan.

Peter Francis   BADA
**26 Museum St. (P.F. Cheek.) Est. 1949. Open
9.30−1 and 2−5.30, Sat. 10.15−2. SIZE:
Medium.** *STOCK: Furniture, 1760−1860,
£400−£28,000; papier mâché, porcelain,
sculpture, Sheffield plate, glass, tea caddies,
tôle peint, 1760−1860, £20−£2,500.* **LOC:
Continuation of Drury Lane (one way from
Aldwych), close to British Museum (100yds.).
PARK: Bloomsbury Sq. TEL: 637 0165.
FAIRS: Grosvenor House and Harrogate. VAT:
Stan/Spec.**

J.A.L. Franks Ltd.
7 New Oxford St. Est. 1947. *STOCK: Stamps
and maps.* TEL: 405 0274/5.

J.I. Horwit (Henry Faber Ltd.)
94 Southampton Row. (E. Faber.) Est. 1910.
CL: Sat. Open 11−6. *STOCK: Jewellery,
£5−£1,000.* LOC: 3 minutes' walk from
Holborn underground and British Museum.
Next to Bonnington Hotel. PARK: Easy. TEL:
405 0749. SER: Valuations. VAT: Stan/Spec.

Marchmont Bookshop
39 Burton St. (D. Holder.) Open 11−6.
*STOCK: Literature, including modern first
editions.* TEL: 387 7989.

Nihon Token
23 Museum St. (M. and H. Dean.) Est. 1965.
Open 10−5. SIZE: Medium. *STOCK: 6th C
B.C.−19th C A.D.: Japanese swords, fittings,
lacquer, armour, furniture, prints, pottery, porcelain, netsuke, paintings, sculpture, inro,
£3−£4,000.* Not stocked: Non-Japanese
items. LOC: Opposite British Museum.
Nearest tube station − Tottenham Court Rd.
and Holborn. PARK: Meters. TEL: 580 6511;
home − 444 6726. VAT: Spec.

The Print Room
37 Museum St. (A. Balfour-Lynn and J.
Cumming). Est. 1984. Open 10−6, Sat.
10−4, other times by appointment. SIZE:
Medium. *STOCK: Prints, including natural
history, views of London, costume plates and
caricatures, £10−£3,000; antiquarian books
including travel and natural history, £20−
£500, all 1580−1850.* LOC: Off Gt. Russell
St, opposite British Museum. PARK: N.C.P.
Bloomsbury Sq. TEL: 430 0159. SER: Valuations; buys at auction (antiquarian books and
prints).

Arthur Probsthain
41 Great Russell St. Est. 1902. Open
9.30−6, Sat. 11−4. *STOCK: Books, Oriental
and African.* TEL: 636 1096. VAT: Stan.

Shapland
207 High Holborn. (R.S.C. Shapland.) Est.
1837. CL: Sat. Open 9−5. SIZE: Large.
STOCK: Silver, jewellery, Sheffield plate. LOC:
At junction of Kingsway and High Holborn.
PARK: Meters and nearby. TEL: 405 3507.
SER: Valuations; restorations. VAT: Stan/
Spec.

S.J. Shrubsole Ltd.   BADA
**43 Museum St. (C.J. Shrubsole.) Est. 1918.
CL: Sat. Open 9−5.30. SIZE: Medium.**
*STOCK: Silver, late 17th to mid-19th C,
£50−£10,000; old Sheffield plate, mid-18th
to mid-19th C, £10−£1,000.* **LOC: 1 minute
from British Museum. PARK: Easy. TEL: 405
2712. SER: Valuations; restorations (silver);
buys at auction. VAT: Stan/Spec.**

Skoob Books Ltd.
15 Sicilian Ave., Southampton Row, Holborn.
Est. 1978. Open 10.30−6.30. SIZE: Medium.
*STOCK: Books, second-hand literary and
academic, from 19th C, 50p−£50; antiquarian books, pre-1900, £3−£50.* LOC: In
pedestrian arcade, opposite Holborn Underground. PARK: Easy. TEL: 404 3063. SER:
Valuations; buys at auction (books).

'The Stove Shop'
181 Kings Cross Rd. (A. Rodriguez and P.
Crabb). Open 10.30−6, Sat. 11−5. *STOCK:
Original Scandinavian and French stoves and
cooking ranges.* TEL: 833 3534. SER: Restorations; installations; hire and consultancy.

W.C.1 continued

Waterloo Fine Arts Ltd.
40 Bloomsbury Way. (P. and M. Nicholas). Est. 1977. Open 10—5.30, Sun. and other times by appointment. SIZE: Small. *STOCK: Maps, 16th—19th C, £5—£500; prints, 17th—19th C, £50—£100; books, 18th—19th C, £50—£1,200.* LOC: Near British Museum. PARK: 100yds. TEL: 405 9662; home — (0734) 713745. FAIRS: Bonnington Hotel, W.C.1. VAT: Stan.

B. Weinreb Architectural Books Ltd.
93 Great Russell St. CL: Sat. Open 10—5.30. *STOCK: Architectural books.* LOC: Near British Museum. TEL: 636 4895.

B. Weinreb Ltd.
34 Museum St. Open 10—6, Sat. 10—1. *STOCK: Architectural prints and engravings.* LOC: Near British Museum. TEL: 636 4895.

London W.C.2

Anchor Antiques Ltd.   *Trade Only*
26 Charing Cross Rd. (K.B. Embden and H. Samne.) Est. 1964. Open by appointment. *STOCK: Continental and Oriental ceramics, European works of art and objets de vertu.* TEL: 836 5686. VAT: Spec.

W.C.2 continued

A.H. Baldwin and Sons Ltd.   BADA
11 Adelphi Terrace, Robert St. IAPN, BNTA. Est. 1872. CL: Sat. Open 9—5. SIZE: Medium. *STOCK: Coins, 600 B.C.—present; commemorative medals, 16th C to present, numismatic literature.* **LOC: Near Charing Cross. TEL: 930 6879 and 839 1310. SER: Valuations; auction agents for selling and purchasing. VAT: Stan/Spec.**

Bell, Book and Radmall
4 Cecil Court. Est. 1974. CL: Sat. Open 10—5.30. *STOCK: First editions of 19th and 20th C English and American literature including detective and fantasy fiction.* TEL: 240 2161.

M. Bord
(Gold Coin Exchange)
16 Charing Cross Rd. Est. 1969. Open 9.30—6. SIZE: Small. *STOCK: Gold, silver and copper coins, Roman to Elizabeth II, all prices.* LOC: Near Leicester Sq. underground station. TEL: 836 0631 and 240 0479. SER: Valuations; buys at auction. FAIRS: All major coin. VAT: Stan/Spec.

Tea caddy, satinwood inlaid with various woods, c.1800. From *Regency Furniture* by Frances Collard, published by the **Antique Collectors' Club**, 1985.

W.C.2 continued

Clive A Burden Ltd.
13 Cecil Court, Charing Cross Rd. Open 9—5, appointment preferred. SIZE: Medium. *STOCK: Maps, 1500—1860, £1—£1,000; prints, 1720-1870, £1—£100; antiquarian books, pre-1870, £10—£5,000; Vanity Fair prints.* PARK: Nearby. TEL: 836 2177. SER: Valuations; buys at auction (maps, prints or books). VAT: Stan.

Cartographia Ltd.
37 Southampton St. (B. Marsden.) Est. 1976. Open 9—5.30, Sat. 10—5. SIZE: Medium. *STOCK: Maps, world-wide, especially British Isles and North America; topographical engravings especially London; decorative engravings including flowers, fashion and theatre.* LOC: Near Covent Garden and the Strand. PARK: Nearby. TEL: 240 5687/8 (24 hours). VAT: Stan.

Covent Garden Flea Market
Jubilee Market, Covent Garden. (Sherman and Waterman Associates Ltd.) Est. 1975. Open Mon. and Bank Holidays only, 8—4. SIZE: Large. LOC: South side of piazza, just off The Strand, via Southampton St. PARK: Easy and NCP Drury Lane. TEL: 836 2139 or 240 7405.

The Dolls House Toys Ltd.
29 The Market, Covent Garden. Open 10—8. *STOCK: Dolls' houses, miniature furniture.* TEL: 379 7243. VAT: Stan.

Robert Douwma (Prints and Maps) Ltd.
4 Henrietta St., Covent Garden. Open 10—6, Sat. 10—5. *STOCK: Maps, engravings, atlases, to late 19th C, from £10.* TEL: 836 0771. VAT: Stan.

Madame J. Dupont et Fils
1 Cecil Court, Charing Cross Rd. Open Mon. and Wed. 11—5 and by appointment. *STOCK: Antiquarian and secondhand books on travel, costume; prints and maps.* LOC: 1 minute from Leicester Sq. tube station. TEL: 240 1683.

H.M. Fletcher
27 Cecil Court, Charing Cross Rd. Est. 1905. CL: Sat. Open 10—5.30. SIZE: Medium. *STOCK: Books, rare, antiquarian.* LOC: Between Charing Cross Rd. and St. Martin's Lane. PARK: Meters. TEL: 836 2865.

W. and G. Foyle Ltd.
113—119 Charing Cross Rd. Est. 1904. *STOCK: Antiquarian books.*

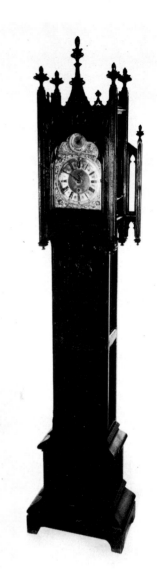

This clock is in the Gothic taste and dates from the late Victorian period. Quality of workmanship in both cases and movement is immediately apparent. from *The Price Guide to Collectable Clocks 1840-1940* by Alan and Rita Shenton, published by the **Antique Collectors' Club**, 1985.

W.C.2 continued

Frognal Rare Books
18 Cecil Court, Charing Cross Rd. (E. Finer.) ABA. Est. 1958. CL: Sat. Open 11—6. SIZE: Medium. *STOCK: Antiquarian books — law (pre-1850) and legal history, banking, currency, economics, history, philosophy, French, German, Italian, 1500—1900, £2—£1,000+; also books on literature, travel, art and topography.* LOC: Between Charing Cross Rd. and St. Martin's Lane. PARK: Meters and nearby. TEL: 240 2815. FAIRS: Park Lane Hotel ABA.

Stanley Gibbons
399 Strand. Est. 1856. CL: Sat. p.m. Open 9—5.30. SIZE: Large. *STOCK: Popular and specialised stamps, postal history, catalogues, albums, accessories.* LOC: Opposite Savoy Hotel. TEL: 836 8444. SER: Valuations. VAT: Stan/Spec.

Grosvenor Prints
28/32 Shelton St., Covent Garden. Est. 1975. Open 10—6, Sat. 10—1. SIZE: Large. *STOCK: Prints, especially topographical and those featuring dogs, 17th—20th C, £5—£1,000.* LOC: Within one-way system near Neal St. PARK: Easy. TEL: 836 1979. SER: Valuations; restorations; buys at auction. VAT: Stan/Spec.

His Nibs
182 Drury Lane. (P. Poole.) Open 10—5, Sat. 11—3. *STOCK: Writing instruments and pen holders, fountain pens.* TEL: 405 7097.

S. and H. Jewell Ltd.
26 Parker St. Est. 1830. CL: Sat. Open 9—5.30. SIZE: Large. *STOCK: Furniture.* PARK: Meters. TEL: 405 8520. SER: Valuations; restorations. VAT: Stan.

Langfords   LAPADA
46—47 Chancery Lane. (L.L. Langford.) NAG. Est. 1941. *STOCK: Silver plate, cased model boats, scientific and marine objects.* TEL: 405 6402. SER: Valuations; restorations; buys at auction. VAT: Stan/Spec.

S. Linden
33 Craven St., Strand. Appointment advisable. *STOCK: Antiquarian and secondhand books.* TEL: 930 3659.

The London Silver Vaults
Chancery House, 53—65 Chancery Lane. Est. 1892. CL: Sat. p.m. Open 9—5.30. *STOCK: Silver, plate, jewellery, objets d'art, clocks, watches, collectors' items.* TEL: 242 3844. The following are some of the dealers at these vaults:—

Lawrence Block
Vault 28 and 65. Est. 1959. *Victorian and Georgian spoons and forks.* TEL: 242 0749. SER: Valuations; restorations; buys at auction.

The London Silver Vaults continued

A. Bloom
Vault 27. TEL: 242 6189.

Luigi Brian Antiques   LAPADA
Vault 56. TEL: 405 2484.

B.L. Collins
Vaults 20. TEL: 404 0628.

R. Feldman Ltd.   LAPADA
Vault 4/6. TEL: 405 6111.

Fine China (London) Ltd.
Vault 24. TEL: 242 6366.

I. Franks   LAPADA
Est. 1926. TEL: 242 4035.

Jules Golding and Co.
Vault 2. (D. Golding.) Est. 1926. TEL: 242 3217. VAT: Stan/Spec.

Hamilton Antiques
Vault 46. TEL: 831 7030.

E. and C.T. Koopman and Son Ltd.   BADA
(The Provincial Antique Silver Co.) Est. 1967. *Silver and jewellery.* TEL: 242 7624/8365. SER: Valuations.

B. Lampert
Vault 19.

Langfords Silver Galleries   LAPADA
Vault 8/10. (L.L. and M.V. Langford.) NAG. Est. 1940. *Silver and plate.* TEL: 405 6401. SER: Valuations; buys at auction. VAT: Stan/Spec.

Leon Antiques Ltd.
Vault 57.

Nat Leslie Ltd.
Vault 21. Est. 1940. TEL: 242 4787. VAT: Stan/Spec.

Linden and Co. (Antiques) Ltd.
Vault 7. (H. Linden, F. Linden and M. Friedner.) TEL: 242 4863. VAT: Stan/Spec.

C. and T. Mammon
TEL: 405 2397.

J. Mammon Antiques   *Trade Only*
Vault 30. TEL: 242 4704.

I.J. Mazure and Co. Ltd.   BADA
Vault 9. *Objects de vertu, Fabergé.* TEL: 242 3470/6264.

H. Miller (Antiques) Ltd.   LAPADA
TEL: 242 7073. VAT: Stan/Spec.

I. Nagioff (Jewellery)
Vault 69. (I. and R. Nagioff.) Est. 1955. *Jewellery, 18th—20th C, £5—£2,000+; objets d'art, 19th C, to £200.* TEL: 405 3766. SER: Valuations; restorations (jewellery). VAT: Stan.

Percy's   LAPADA
Vault 16/17.

H. Perovetz
Vault 13/15.

J. Podlewski and P. Daniel
Vault 51. TEL: 430 1327.

David S. Shure and Co.
Vault 1. (S. Bulka.) Est. 1900. Book on silver. TEL: 405 0011. SER: Valuations; restorations. VAT: Stan.

The London Silver Vaults continued

Silstar
Vault 29. (H. Stern.) Est. 1955. TEL: 242 6740. VAT: Stan/Spec.

B. Silverman   **BADA**
Vault 26. (S. and R. Silverman.) Est. 1927. TEL: 242 3269. SER: Valuations; buys at auction. VAT: Stan/Spec.

Jack Simons (Antiques) Ltd.
Vault 35 and 37. Est. 1955. TEL: 242 3221. VAT: Stan/Spec.

S. and J. Stodel
Vault 34/36/43. TEL: 405 7009.

A. Urbach
Vault 50.

William Walter Antiques Ltd.   **BADA**
Vault 3/5. (R.W. Walter.) Est. 1927. TEL: 242 3248. SER: Valuations; restorations (silver, plate).

A. and G. Weiss
Vault 42/44. TEL: 242 7310. VAT: Stan.

Peter K. Weiss
Vault 42/44/106. Est. 1955. *Watches, clocks.* TEL: 242 8100/7310. VAT: Stan.

Wolfe (Jewellery)
Vault 41. TEL: 405 2101. VAT: Stan/Spec.

IS YOUR ENTRY CORRECT?
If there is even the slightest inaccuracy in your entry, *please* let us know before 1st January 1987.
GUIDE TO THE
ANTIQUE SHOPS OF BRITAIN
5 Church Street, Woodbridge, Suffolk.

W.C.2 continued

Arthur Middleton Ltd.   LAPADA
12 New Row, Covent Garden. Est. 1968. Open 10—6 or by appointment. SIZE: Small. *STOCK: Scientific instruments — navigation, astronomy, surveying, medicine, weighing and measuring, 18th C, up to £5,000; 19th C, £50—£3,500.* LOC: New Row runs between Leicester Square and Covent Garden. Shop 300yds. east from Leicester Square and 3 doors from Moss Bros. PARK: Easy or multi-storey nearby. TEL: 836 7042 and 836 7062. SER: Valuations; buys at auction; prop hire. VAT: Stan.

W.A. Myers (Autographs) Ltd.
Suite 52, Second Floor, 91 St. Martin's Lane. Est. 1889. *STOCK: Autograph letters, documents, inscribed books, manuscripts, catalogues.* TEL: 836 1940.

Avril Noble
2 Southampton St, Covent Garden. PBFA. Est. 1964. Open 10—6, Sat. 10.30—6, Sun. by appointment. SIZE: Large. *STOCK: Maps and engravings of the world, 16th—19th C, £10—£3,000.* LOC: Off the Strand, opposite the Savoy Hotel. PARK: Meters. TEL: 240 1970. SER: Buys at auction. FAIRS: International Map, London; Bonnington Hotel. VAT: Stan.

Old Curiosity Shop
13/14 Portsmouth St. (D. and T. Goldband.) Est. 1780. CL: Christmas Day. Open 9.30—5.30. SIZE: Small. *STOCK: General antiques.* LOC: Off Kingsway, close to Lincoln's Inn Fields. Nearest tube station: Holborn. PARK: Meters. TEL: 405 9891. VAT: Stan.

W.C.2 continued

The Old Drury
187 Drury Lane, Covent Garden. (J. Draycott.) Est. 1977. Open 12—6, Sat. 11—6. SIZE: Large. STOCK: Antiquities — Greek, Cypriot and Phoenician, £15—£1,000, Indian, £30—£1,000, Far Eastern, £20—£200, Egyptian, £14—£5,000, Roman, £10—£500; tribal and ethnic art, African and Oceanic, £10—£1,000; jewellery, Egyptian, pre-Columbian and Roman. LOC: Approx. 300yds. from British Museum entrance. PARK: Nearby. TEL: 242 4939. SER: Valuations; buys at auction.

Pearl Cross Ltd.
35 St. Martin's Court. (D. Strange.) Est. 1897. CL: Sat. Open 9.30—4.45. STOCK: Jewellery, silver, clocks, watches. PARK: Meters. TEL: 836 2814 and 240 0795. SER: Valuations; restorations (jewellery, silver, clocks and watches). VAT: Stan/Spec.

H. Perovetz Ltd.
BADA
LAPADA
50/52 Chancery Lane. Est. 1945. CL: Sat. p.m. Open 9—6. SIZE: Large. STOCK: Silver, Sheffield plate. TEL: 405 8868 or 242 5857. SER: Valuations. VAT: Stan/Spec.

Pleasures of Past Times
11 Cecil Court, Charing Cross Rd. (D.B. Drummond.) Est. 1962. CL: Sat., except first one in the month 11—2.15. Open 11—2.30 and 3.30—6. SIZE: Medium. STOCK: Early juveniles and theatre books; postcards, decorative ephemera (valentine cards); posters and play-bills, 19th C. Not stocked: Coins, stamps, medals, jewellery, cigarette cards. LOC: In pedestrian court between Charing Cross Rd. and St. Martin's Lane. TEL: 836 1142. VAT: Stan.

Henry Pordes Books Ltd.
58/60 Charing Cross Rd. Open 10—7. STOCK: Books including antiquarian. TEL: 836 9031.

Quevedo
25 Cecil Court, Charing Cross Rd. (J.F.T. Rodgers) ABA. Est. 1968. CL: Sat. Open 10—1 and 2—6. SIZE: Small. STOCK: Rare and fine books, 15th—19th C, £10—£5,000. LOC: Off Charing Cross Rd. TEL: 836 9132. SER: Valuations; buys at auction (books). VAT: Stan.

Reg and Philip Remington
14 Cecil Court, Charing Cross Rd. ABA, PBFA. Est. 1979. Open 10—5, Sat. by appointment. SIZE: Medium. STOCK: Voyages and travels, 17th—20th C, £5—£500. LOC: Near Trafalgar Sq. TEL: 836 9771. SER: Buys at auction. FAIRS: Edinburgh Book, Roxburghe Hotel; London Book, Park Lane Hotel. VAT: Stan.

W.C.2 continued

Bertram Rota Ltd.
30/31 Long Acre. Est. 1923. Open 9.30—5.30, Sat. by appointment. STOCK: Antiquarian and secondhand books, especially first editions, private presses, English literature, and literary autographs. TEL: 836 0723.

The Silver Mouse Trap
56 Carey St. (A. Woodhouse.) Est. 1690. CL: Sat. Open 9.30—5.30. SIZE: Medium. STOCK: Jewellery, silver. LOC: South of Lincoln's Inn Fields. TEL: 405 2578. SER: Valuations; restorations. VAT: Spec.

Stage Door Prints
1 Cecil Court, Charing Cross Rd. (A. Reynold.) Open 11—6. STOCK: Prints on opera, ballet and the theatre; topographical, theatre ephemera. TEL: 240 1683.

Peter Stockham at Images
16 Cecil Court, Charing Cross Rd. Est. 1976. CL: Mon. Open 11—6.15; 1st Sat. in month 10—12.30, or by appointment at all other times. STOCK: Early children's books, art and illustrated books, printed ephemera; antique toys, mainly wooden; games and associated items; fine printing. TEL: 836 8661. SER: Buys at auction; catalogue on toys and dolls.

Harold T. Storey
3 Cecil Court, Charing Cross Rd. (T. Kingswood.) Est. 1934. Open 10—5.45, Sat. 10.30—5. SIZE: Small. STOCK: Antiquarian books, engravings. LOC: Between Charing Cross Rd. and St. Martin's Lane. PARK: Trafalgar Square garage. TEL: 836 3777.

Travis and Emery
17 Cecil Court, Charing Cross Rd. (V. Emery.) ABA. Est. 1960. CL: Sat. p.m. Open 10—6. SIZE: Medium. STOCK: Musical literature, music and prints. LOC: Between Charing Cross Rd. and St. Martin's Lane opposite Odeon. PARK: Meters. TEL: 240 2129. VAT: Stan.

Watkins Books Ltd.
19 and 21 Cecil Court, Charing Cross Rd. Est. 1880. Open 10—6, Wed. 10.30—6. STOCK: Mysticism, occultism, Oriental religions, astrology and contemporary spirituality, new and secondhand books.

Zeno Booksellers and Publishers
6 Denmark St. Est. 1944. Open 9.30—6, Sat. till 5. SIZE: Medium. STOCK: Antiquarian books. LOC: From Tottenham Court Rd., into Charing Cross Rd., first turning on left. TEL: 836 2522.

A. Zwemmer Ltd.
24 Litchfield St. Est. 1921. Open 9.30—6; Sat. till 5.30. SIZE: Large. STOCK: Books on fine art. LOC: Just south of Cambridge Circus. TEL: 836 4710.

Greater London

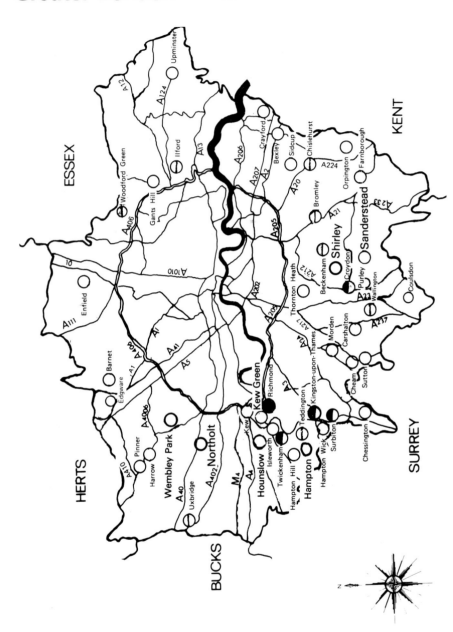

Please note this is only a rough map designed to show dealers the number of shops in the various towns, and is not necessarily totally accurate.

Key to number of shops in this area.

○ 1—2
⊖ 3—5
◑ 6—12
● 13+

BARNET (Herts.)

Barnet Antiques and Fine Art
236 High St. (Mr. Hawkins and Mr. Gerry.) Est. 1959. Open 10—1 and 2—5, Thurs. 9—1. SIZE: Large. *STOCK: George III furniture, 1780—1810; pictures, general antiques, 18th—19th C.* Not stocked: Carpets. LOC: From London follow the A1000 approximately 8 miles. PARK: Easy. TEL: (01) 440 3620 and (01) 445 9695; home — (01) 953 7933. VAT: Stan/Spec.

C. Bellinger Antiques
91 Wood St. Est. 1974. Open Thurs., Fri. and Sat., 10—4, or by appointment. SIZE: Medium. *StOCK: French and English furniure, 18th—19th C; small items.* LOC: Opposite Ravenscroft Park. PARK: Within 100yds. TEL: (01) 449 3467; home — same. VAT: Stan/Spec.

BECKENHAM (Kent)

Beckenham Antique Market
Old Council Hall, Bromley Rd. Est. 1979. Open Wed. only 9.30—2. There are 30 stalls at this market selling *a wide range of general antiques.* TEL: (01) 684 5891.

The Pedlars Pack   LAPADA (Beckenham)
10 Chancery Lane. (Mrs. J. Fell.) Est. 1967. CL: Mon. and Wed. Open 10—5.30. SIZE: Small. *STOCK: Jewellery, bijouterie, silver, copper, brass, small items.* Not stocked: Large items. LOC: Between Shortlands and Beckenham, off main Bromley road. TEL: (01) 658 3848. VAT: Stan/Spec.

Pepys Antiques
9 Kelsey Park Rd. (H. Butler and S.P. Elton.) Est. 1969. CL: Wed. Open 10—5.30. *STOCK: Furniture, paintings, silver, porcelain, copper, brass.* LOC: Central Beckenham. TEL: (01) 650 0994.

Scallywag
22 High St. (J.A. Butterworth.) Est. 1970. Open 9.30—6. SIZE: Large. *STOCK: Pine, 18th—19th C, £5—£5,000.* LOC: 100 yds. from Beckenham Junction station. PARK: Easy. TEL: (01) 658 6633. SER: Restorations; pine stripping. VAT: Stan/Spec.

Norman Witham
2 High St. Est. 1959. Open Fri. and Sat. *STOCK: Porcelain, glass, small furniture, mainly Victorian, £5—£500.* TEL: (01) 650 9096; evenings — (01) 650 4651. SER: Valuations. VAT: Stan/Spec.

BEXLEY (Kent)

Argentum Antiques
18—20 High St. (L.T. Laklia.) Est. 1967. CL: Thurs. p.m. Open 9—5. SIZE: Large. *STOCK: Silver, plate, clocks, porcelain, jewellery, paintings, prints, English and Continental furniture.* LOC: A210. From London take the A2 to Bexley. PARK: Easy. TEL: Crayford (0322) 527915. SER: Valuations; restorations; buys at auction. VAT: Stan.

Emperor Antiques Centre
1 Vicarage Rd. (P.J. Lillicrap.) Open 9—12 and 1—6. There are 6 dealers at this centre selling *a wide range of general antiques.* TEL: Crayford (0322) 524990.

BROMLEY (Kent)

Antica
Rear of 35—41 High St. (L. and P. Muccio.) Open 10—5.30. *STOCK: General antiques.* LOC: Opposite Debenhams. TEL: (01) 464 7661. VAT: Stan.

Bromley Antique Market
United Reformed Church Halls, Widmore Rd. Est. 1968. Open Thursday 7.30—3. There are 70 stalls at this market offering *a wide selection of general antiques, jewellery, books, bric-a-brac, copper, brass and clocks, collectors' items, coins, furs, stamps, postcards.* TEL: (01) 785 2178. VAT: Stan.

Sundridge Antiques
26 Bromley Common. (S.E. Williams.) Est. 1964. CL: Wed. p.m. Open by appointment. SIZE: Large. *STOCK: Furniture, 1680—1920, £10—£1,000; oil paintings, watercolours, 1780—1920, £5—£600; china, glass, 1780—1920, £1—£100.* LOC: Opposite Sundridge Park railway station. PARK: Easy. TEL: (01) 460 8164. SER: Valuations. VAT: Stan/Spec.

Taurus Antiques Ltd.   LAPADA
145 Masons Hill. (P. Quastel.) Est. 1952. CL: Wed. Open 9.30—5.30. SIZE: Large. *STOCK: Furniture, china, glass, boxes, clocks, copper, brass, £5—£2,500.* LOC: 500yds. south of Bromley High St. on A21, corner shop on left. PARK: Easy. TEL: (01) 464 8746. VAT: Stan/Spec.

William Whitfield Antiques   LAPADA
51-53 Beckenham Lane, Shortlands. Open 10—5 or by appointment. *STOCK: Paintings, furniture and silver.* TEL: (01) 466 6506. SER: Valuations.

CARSHALTON (Surrey)

Antiques
314 Carshalton Rd. (E.M. Marshall.) CL: Wed. p.m. *STOCK: General antiques, especially Victorian and Edwardian oil lamps.* TEL: (01) 642 5865.

Carshalton Antique Galleries
5 High St. (B.A. Gough.) Est. 1968. CL: Wed. Open 9—5. SIZE: Large. *STOCK: General antiques, furniture, clocks, glass, china, pictures.* Not stocked: Silver, jewellery, bronze, firearms. PARK: 50yds. opposite, or 60yds. down High St. TEL: (01) 647 5664; home — Dorking (0306) 887187. VAT: Stan/Spec.

CHEAM (Surrey)

Rogers Antiques and Rogers Antique Interiors   LAPADA
22 Ewell Rd., Cheam Village. (M. and C. Rogers.) Est. 1971. CL: Wed. Open 10—5.30. SIZE: Medium. *STOCK: Furniture, 18th—19th C, £100—£2,000; upholstered furniture, Tillman dining tables, boardroom furniture.* LOC: In centre of village, just off Sutton bypass, A217. PARK: 50yds. TEL: (01) 643 8466. SER: Valuations; interior design. VAT: Stan/Spec.

CHESSINGTON (Surrey)

Sybil Hayton Antiques and Crafts
440 Hook Rd. Est. 1960. Open Wed., Thurs., Fri. 10—5.30; Sat. 10—4.30. SIZE: Medium. *STOCK: General antiques, £1—£500.* PARK: Easy. TEL: (01) 397 1646. VAT: Stan.

CHISLEHURST (Kent)

Chislehurst Antiques   LAPADA
7 Royal Parade. (M. Crawley and R. Gosnell.) Est. 1976. CL: Wed. Open 10—1 and 2—5. SIZE: Medium. *STOCK: Furniture, 1760—1900, some porcelain, glass, brass and copper.* LOC: One mile from A20. PARK: Easy. TEL: (01) 467 1530. VAT: Stan/Spec.

Easdens Antiques
4 Royal Parade. (G. and M.H. Easden.) Est. 1925. CL: Wed. p.m. Open 9—5.30. *STOCK: Furniture and upholstery, 18th C; glass, china, brass, copper, silver, porcelain, clocks.* TEL: (01) 467 3352. SER: Restorations. VAT: Stan.

Chislehurst continued

Michael Sim
1 Royal Parade. Open 9—6 including Sun. SIZE: Small. *STOCK: English furniture, Georgian and Regency, £500—£15,000; clocks, £500—£10,000; Oriental porcelain, Ming and Qing, £50—£1,000; pictures, Victorian, £100—£2,000.* LOC: 50 yards from War Memorial at junction of Bromley Rd. and Centre Common Rd. PARK: Easy. TEL: (01) 467 7040; home — same. SER: Valuations; restorations; buys at auction. VAT: Spec.

COULSDON (Surrey)

Knightsbridge Pine
Rear of 5 Lion Green Rd. (M. and M. Sampson.) Est. 1978. Open 8—5.30. SIZE: Medium. *STOCK: English and Continental stripped pine furniture, 19th C, £50—£150.* LOC: Off A23. PARK: Easy. TEL: (01) 668 0148. SER: Restorations; pine stripping, French polishing. VAT: Stan.

David Potashnick Antiques
7 The Parade, Stoats Nest Rd. Open 9.30—6. *STOCK: General antiques.* TEL: (01) 660 8403.

CRAYFORD (Kent)   (0322)

Watling Antiques
139 Crayford Rd. Open 10—6.30. *STOCK: General antiques and shipping goods.* TEL: 523620.

CROYDON (Surrey)

Apollo Galleries   LAPADA
61/65/67 South End. (G.W. Barr.) CL: Sun. except by appointment. Open 9.30—6. SIZE: Large. *STOCK: 19th C oil and watercolour paintings and bronzes, 18th—19th C English and Continental furniture and clocks, porcelain, glass and silver.* LOC: Through Croydon on left on A23. PARK: Own. TEL: (01) 681 3727/680 1968. SER: Restorations (pictures). VAT: Spec.

Keith Atkinson   LAPADA
59 Brighton Rd., South Croydon. Est. 1977. Open 9—6 or by appointment. SIZE: Large. *STOCK: Furniture, Victorian, Edwardian, 1930s', shipping, £50—£5,000.* PARK: Easy. TEL: (01) 688 5559. VAT: Stan.

Brazil Antiques Ltd.   LAPADA
145 Brighton Rd., South Croydon. Est. 1973. *STOCK: Victorian furniture.* TEL: (01) 680 2707. VAT: Stan.

Collectors Corner Antiques
43 Brighton Rd. (R. and A. Pope.) Est. 1980. CL: Wed. and Sun. *STOCK: Dolls, tin toys, dinkies, lead soldiers and animals, furniture, bric-a-brac.* TEL: (01) 680 7511.

Croydon continued

C.P. Florey, A.B.A.
18 Whitethorn Gardens, Shirley Park. Est. 1960. *STOCK: Antiquarian books.* TEL: (01) 654 4724.

G.E. Griffin
43a Brighton Rd., South Croydon. (E.J.H. Robinson.) Est. 1879. SIZE: Large. Open 8—5.30, Sat. 9—5. *STOCK: General antiques.* TEL: (01) 688 3130. SER: Restorations, upholstery.

Peter Howard Books
347 Brighton Rd. Est. 1970. Open 10—5. *STOCK: Antiquarian and second hand books.* TEL: (01) 688 6558; home — (01) 681 1627. VAT: Stan.

Paul Keen Antiques
195—197 Brighton Rd. (P.A. and G. Keen.) Est. 1965. Open 10—5.30. SIZE: Large. *STOCK: Furniture, furnishings, William IV, Victorian, Edwardian, £5—£2,000; Georgian furniture, 1700—1830, £25—£4,000; bric-a- brac, paintings, all periods, £1—£500.* Not stocked: Coins, medals, stamps. LOC: From London take main Brighton Road through Croydon (not by-pass). Shop on left on leaving Croydon. PARK: Easy. TEL: (01) 688 1316. SER: Valuations. VAT: Stan/Spec.

Trengove   BADA
46 South End. Est. 1890. Open 9—6. SIZE: Large. *STOCK: General antiques, Victoriana; oils, watercolours, 18th—19th C.* LOC: On main road through Croydon. TEL: (01) 688 2155. SER: Valuations. VAT: Stan/Spec.

The Whitgift Galleries   LAPADA
77 South End. (A.W.J. Simmons and Son.) Est. 1945. *STOCK: Paintings, 19th—20th C.* TEL: (01) 688 0990. SER: Conservation, restoration, framing. VAT: Stan.

EDGWARE (Middx.)
Edgware Antiques
19 Whitchurch Lane. (E. Schloss.) Est. 1972. CL: Mon. and Thurs. Open 10—5.30. SIZE: Medium. *STOCK: Furniture, pictures, silver and plate, brass and copper, clocks, bric-a- brac, porcelain and shipping goods.* PARK: Easy. TEL: (01) 952 1606; home — (01) 952 5924.

ENFIELD (Middx.)
Enfield Corner Cupboard
61 Chase Side. Est. 1952. Open 9—5.30, Wed. 9-1. *STOCK: Furniture, silver, china.* TEL: (01) 363 6493.

FARNBOROUGH (Kent)   (0689)
Nr. Orpington
Farnborough (Kent) Antiques BADA
10 Church Rd. (J.M. Dewdney and C. Jennings.) Author of articles. Est. 1970. Open Sat. 9.30—5.30, other times by appointment. SIZE: Small. *STOCK: Oak furniture, 1500—1750, £50—£3,000; wood carvings and sculpture, 14th—17th C, £25—£2,000;* Not stocked: Mahogany and post-1750 furniture. LOC: A21 from London, turn right 4½ miles from Bromley into Farnborough village. PARK: Opposite. TEL: 51834. VAT: Spec.

GANTS HILL (Essex)
Antique Clock Repair Shoppe
26 Woodford Ave. (K. Ashton.) Est. 1971. Open 10—5. *STOCK: Clocks, pictures, bric-a-brac.* TEL: (01) 550 9540.

HAMPTON (Middx.)
Ian Sheridan's Bookshop Hampton
Thames Villa, 34 Thames St. Est. 1960. Open 10—7 including Sun. SIZE: Large. *STOCK: Antiquarian and secondhand books; paintings and prints.* LOC: 1 mile from Hampton Court Palace. TEL: (01) 979 1704.

HAMPTON HILL (Middx.)
The Hampton Hill Gallery Ltd.
203 and 205 High St. *STOCK: Watercolours, drawings, prints, 18th—20th C.* TEL: (01) 977 1379/5273. SER: Restorations and cleaning (watercolours, prints and paintings); mounting; framing. VAT: Stan/Spec.

Lady Bountiful Antiques and Objets d'Art
75 High St. (Mrs. J. James.) Est. 1983. Open 10.30—5.30, Sun. 2.30—5.30; Mon., Tues. and Wed. by appointment only. SIZE: Medium. *STOCK: Furniture including gentlemen's linen chests, library tables and chest of drawers, 18th—19th C, £50—£3,000; small items, china, silver and plate, £5—£50.* LOC: From Heathrow, A312 for Teddington or from Sunbury, A308, first left into Church St. PARK: Easy. TEL: (01) 979 8406.

HAMPTON WICK (Surrey)
Discoveries
7 High St. (G.K. Wrathall.) Open 9—1 and 2—5.30. *STOCK: General antiques.* LOC: At foot of Kingston Bridge. TEL: (01) 977 3965.

Hampton Wick Antiques
48 High St. Est. 1957. Open 10—5. *STOCK: General antiques.* TEL: (01) 977 3178.

IS YOUR ENTRY CORRECT?
If there is even the slightest inaccuracy in your entry, *please* let us know before 1st January 1987.
GUIDE TO THE
ANTIQUE SHOPS OF BRITAIN
5 Church Street, Woodbridge, Suffolk.

HARROW (Middx.)
Kathleen Mann Antiques   LAPADA
49 High St. Est. 1973. CL: Wed. Open 9—5.30 or by appointment. SIZE: Medium. *STOCK: Furniture, 18th—19th C, £25—£3,000; decorative items, £1—£1,000.* LOC: Follow Harrow road, or take A40 turning at Greenford roundabout. PARK: Easy. TEL: (01) 422 1892. SER: Buys at auction. VAT: Stan/Spec.

Winston Galleries
68 High St., Harrow Hill. (R and P. Weston.) Est. 1970. CL: Wed. Open 9.30—5.30, or by appointment. *STOCK: Furniture, porcelain, 18th—19th C; general antiques, silver, plate, clocks.* TEL: (01) 422 4470. VAT: Stan/Spec.

HOUNSLOW (Middx.)
The Autograph Shop
68 Staines Rd. CL: Wed. Open 9.30—5.30. SIZE: Small. *STOCK: Framed autographs, £5—£50,000.* LOC: 100 yds. from High St. TEL: (01) 572 2133.

ILFORD (Essex)
Bric-a-Brac
77 Belgrave Rd. (Mrs. M.M. Germain.) Est. 1969. Open 10—2 and 3.30—6.30. *STOCK: Furniture, paintings, bric-a-brac, books.* TEL: (01) 554 8032.

Flowers Antiques
733 High Rd., Seven Kings. (S. Rose.) Est. 1980. Open every day 8—6. *STOCK: Furniture, Edwardian, Victorian; brass, glass, china, jardinieres.* PARK: Easy. TEL: (01) 599 9959. VAT: Stan/Spec.

Gift House Antiques
3 Highview Parade, Redbridge Lane East. (R. and C. Stevens.) Open 9—6. TEL: (01) 550 5168.

ISLEWORTH (Middx.)
Crowther of Syon Lodge Ltd.
Busch Corner, London Rd. Open 9—5, Sat. and Sun. 11—4. *STOCK: Period panelled rooms, in pine and oak; chimney-pieces in marble, stone and wood; life-sized classical bronze and marble statues; wrought iron entrance gates, garden temples, vases, seats, fountains and other statues.* LOC: Just off the A4, half-way between the West End and London Airport. TEL: (01) 560 7978. VAT: Spec.

Isleworth continued

Yistelworth Antiques
1 Thornbury Rd. (C.A. Gibbs). CL: Mon. *STOCK: Samplers, telescopes, clocks, scientific instruments, early oak furniture and general antiques.* LOC: Near Heathrow airport, just off A4. TEL: (01) 847 5429; (01) 560 7793. SER: Valuations.

KEW (Surrey)

Lloyds of Kew
9 Mortlake Terrace. (D. Lloyd.) CL: Wed. Open 10—5.30. *STOCK: Antiquarian books on gardening, botany and general.* PARK: Easy. TEL: (01) 940 2512.

KEW GREEN (Surrey)

Andrew Davis
(formerly Perio Antiques)
6 Mortlake Terrace. Est. 1969. *STOCK: Country furniture, pictures, china, glass, decorative items, from 18th C; architectural fixtures and garden furniture especially ironwork.* TEL: (01) 948 4911. SER: Restorations; stripping (pine); framing.

KINGSTON-UPON-THAMES (Surrey)

Glencorse Antiques　　　　LAPADA
321 Richmond Rd., Ham Parade. (M. Igel, B.S. Prydal). Open 10—5.30. *STOCK: Watercolours, oils and furniture, 18th—19th C.* PARK: Easy. TEL: (01) 541 0871.

Glydon and Guess Ltd.
14 Apple Market. Est. 1940. CL: Wed. Open 9.30—5. *STOCK: Jewellery, small silver, £100—£5,000.* LOC: Town centre. TEL: (01) 546 3758. SER: Restorations; valuations. VAT: Stan.

Kingston-upon-Thames

Kingston Antiques
170 London Rd. (T. and H. Deveson.) Est. 1977. Open 1—6. SIZE: Small. *STOCK: Mahogany, walnut and rosewood furniture, 18th—19th C, £200—£1,500; clocks and objets d'art, 19th C, £300—£1,000; porcelain and bric-a-brac, 19th—20th C, £10—£200.* LOC: At foot of Kingston Hill. PARK: Easy. Tel; (01) 549 5876; home — same. SER: Valuations; restorations (cabinet work and polishing).

Link Gold Ltd.
13 Apple Market. (A.C. Thiele and G.M. Reed). Est. 1981. Open 9.30—5. SIZE: Small. *STOCK: Gold including jewellery, from 1900, £50—£250; silver, from 1800, £15—£200; silver plate, from 1900, £5—£100; general antiques, £5—£100.* Not stocked: Large furniture. LOC: Above Holland & Barrett. PARK: Union St. car park. TEL: 549 5551 or 398 1237. SER: Valuations (jewellery); buys at auctions (as stock). FAIRS: Kempton Park, Sunbury. VAT: Stan/Spec.

Margaret McCloy Pine
49/51 Surbiton Rd. Est. 1969. Open 9—5, or by appointment. *STOCK: Stripped pine furniture.* LOC: Off A307 to Esher. TEL: (01) 549 6423. VAT: Stan.

Warner's Military Specialists
Mail Order Only
2 The Apple Market, Eden St. (G.G. Warner.) Articles on model soldiers, arms and armour. Est. 1962. Appointment advisable. *STOCK: Nazi and Imperial German regalia, 1870—1945, £20—£150; medals, 1900—1960, £20—£500.* Not stocked: General antique furniture. SER: Valuations (swords, arms, armour); restorations (edged weapons and pistols); buys at auction; catalogues available. FAIRS: Arms.

MORDEN (Surrey)
A. Burton-Garbett
35 The Green. Est. 1959. By appointment only. Prospective clients met (at either Morden or Wimbledon tube station) by car. *STOCK: Books on travel, the arts, antiquities of South and Central America, Mexico and the Caribbean, 16th—20th C, £5—£5,000.* TEL: (01) 540 2367. SER: Buys at auction (books, pictures, fine arts, ethnographica). VAT: Stan.

Old Hall Gallery Ltd.
Crown Lodge, Crown Rd. Est. 1949. Open by appointment only. *STOCK: Oil paintings only, 17th—19th C, from £100.* LOC: Near Morden tube station. TEL: (01) 540 9918. SER: Valuations. VAT: Stan.

NORTHOLT (Middx.)
S. and S. Antiques
65a Old Field Circus. (G. Seeley.) Appointment advisable. *STOCK: General antiques.* TEL: (01) 422 5771.

ORPINGTON (Kent)   (0689)
Antica
48 High St., Green Street Green. Open 10—5.30. *STOCK: General antiques.* TEL: Farnborough (0689) 51181.

Clock Investment
Est. 1971. Open by appointment. *STOCK: English and French carriage, longcase, regulator, skeleton, bracket and wall clocks.* TEL: 31431. SER: Buys at auction; investment consultant. VAT: Spec.

PINNER (Middx.)
Artbry's Antiques
44 High St. (A.H. Davies and B.E. Hill.) Est. 1969. CL: Wed. p.m. Open 9—5.30. SIZE: Medium. *STOCK: Furniture, £100—£5,000; crystal, £50—£250; both 18th—19th C; clocks, all types, £50—£3,000; paintings, 17th—19th C, £20—£2,000.* LOC: From Harrow School through Harrow. PARK: Easy. TEL: (01) 868 0834; home — (01) 954 1840. SER: Valuations; restorations (clocks). VAT: Stan/Spec.

Pinner Antiques
24 High St. CL: Wed. Open 10—5.30, other times by appointment *STOCK: General furniture, porcelain, silver, prints.* TEL: (01) 866 5546.

PURLEY (Surrey)
Michael Addison Antiques
28-30 Godstone Rd. (M. and N. Addison.) Est. 1981. CL: Wed. p.m. Open 10—5. SIZE: Medium. *STOCK: Furniture, 1780—1930, £200—£2,000; jewellery, £50—£1,000.* Not stocked: Bric-a-brac. LOC: A22, 1 mile east of Purley. PARK: Easy. TEL: (01) 668 6714. SER: Valuations; restorations; upholstery. VAT: Stan/Spec.

RICHMOND (Surrey)
Antique Mart
72-74 Hill Rise. (G. and Y. Katz.) CL: Wed. Open 10—5, Sun. 2—6. SIZE: Large. *STOCK: Furniture, 18th—19th C.* TEL: (01) 940 6942. SER: Buys at auction. VAT: Stan/Spec.

A rare form of shell-shaped creamer, of a basic type made at several other English factories, most of which employed a dolphin-like handle, instead of this rather skimpy Lowestoft one, 2⁴/₅ins. high, c.1770-5. From *Lowestoft Porcelains* by Geoffrey A. Godden, F.R.S.A., published by the **Antique Collectors' Club,** 1985.

Richmond continued

Antiques Arcade

22 Richmond Hill. Est. 1984. CL: Wed. Open 10.30−5.30, Sun. 2−5.30. SIZE: Medium. There are twelve dealers at this arcade. *STOCK: Fine and general furniture, Staffordshire figures, porcelain, pictures, prints, general antiques and interesting items mainly 18th C to art deco.* PARK: Easy. TEL: (01) 940 2035. SER: Restorations (pictures and china).

Court Antiques (Richmond)

12/14 Brewers Lane and 13 The Green. (A. and L. Coombs.) Est. 1958. Open 9.30−5.30. SIZE: Small. *STOCK: General antiques, jewellery, furniture, silver.* Not stocked: Coins and stamps. LOC: From Richmond station turn left along the Quadrant into George St. Brewers Lane is on the right. PARK: 30yds. turn left. TEL: (01) 940 0515. VAT: Stan.

Mollie Evans

84 Hill Rise. Est. 1965. CL: Mon. and Wed.; Sun. a.m. Open 10.30−5.30. SIZE: Medium. *STOCK: Early country and farmhouse furniture, £50−£2,000; pottery, samplers, some textiles, interesting bygones, unusual bold decorative items, to 1930, £10− £1,000.* Not stocked: Jewellery, coins, medals. LOC: Coming from centre of Richmond, take A307 towards Kingston (Petersham Rd.) Fork left up hill immediately after passing Richmond Bridge on right. PARK: Meters. TEL: (01) 948 0182; home − (01) 940 3720. SER: Buys at auction. VAT: Spec.

Peter and Debbie Gooday

20 Richmond Hill. Est. 1971. CL: Mon. and Wed., except by appointment. Open 11−5.30, Fri. and Sun. 2−5.30. SIZE: Medium. *STOCK: Decorative items and jewellery, art nouveau and art deco; art nouveau metalwork especially Liberty pewter, 1880−1940, £5−£500.* LOC: 100yds. from Richmond Bridge. PARK: Easy. TEL: (01) 940 8652. SER: Buys at auction.

Roland Goslett Gallery

139 Kew Rd. Est. 1974. Open Thurs. and Fri. 10−6, Sat. 10−2, otherwise by appointment. SIZE: Small. *STOCK: English watercolours and oil paintings, 19th to early 20th C, £50−£1,500.* PARK: Easy. TEL: (01) 940 4009. SER: Valuations; restorations; framing. VAT: Spec.

Richmond continued

Hill Rise Antiques   LAPADA

26 Hill Rise. (P. Hinde and D. Milewski.) Est. 1978. CL: Wed. Open 10.30−5.30, Sun. 2.30−6. SIZE: Large. *STOCK: 18th and 19th C walnut and mahogany furniture and longcase clocks, £100−£10,000; silver and plate.* LOC: 1 mile from A316 (M3). PARK: Private. TEL: (01) 948 1140; home − same. FAIRS: Olympia. VAT: Stan/Spec.

Kingabys

15 and 17 Paved Court. (P. Kingaby and A. Glazebrook.) Est. 1960. Open 10−5.30. SIZE: Medium. *STOCK: Jewellery, £20−£1,200; weapons, £20−£200; silver, £10−£750; pictures, £20−£600; small furniture, £40−£750.* LOC: Pedestrian alley leading off Richmond Green. PARK: 150yds. in Friars Lane off Richmond Green. TEL: (01) 940 6533. VAT: Stan.

F. and T. Lawson Antiques

13 Hill Rise. Resident. Est. 1965. CL: Wed. and Sun. a.m. Open 10−12 and 2−5.30, Sat. 10−1 and 2.30−5. SIZE: Medium. *STOCK: Furniture, 1680−1870; paintings and watercolours, both £30−£1,500; clocks, 1650−1930, £50−£2,000; bric-a-brac, £5−£300.* LOC: Near Richmond Bridge at bottom of Hill Rise on the river side, overlooking river. PARK: Further up Hill Rise, and at certain times for loading and unloading. TEL: (01) 940 0461. SER: Valuations; buys at auction. VAT: Stan/Spec.

Layton Antiques

1 Paved Court, The Green. (Lady Layton.) Est. 1967. CL: Wed. and Sun. except by appointment. Open 10−5. SIZE: Medium. *STOCK: 18th and 19th C furniture, silver and decorative items.* LOC: Off The Green at Prince's Head public house. PARK: Easy. TEL: (01) 940 2617. VAT: Stan/Spec.

Le Centre Antiques

20 King St., The Green. (L. Jacomelli.) Est. 1970. CL: Wed. Open 10−5.30. *STOCK: Period and Victorian furniture, clocks, general decorative items.* TEL: (01) 948 1505. VAT: Stan/Spec.

The Richmond Antiquary

28 Hill Rise. (S. Collins.) Est. 1968. CL: Sun. a.m. and Wed. Open 10−5.30. SIZE: Large. *STOCK: Furniture, 19th C; bygones, bric-a-brac; paintings, prints, watercolours, 19th and 20th C, to £400.* Not stocked: Expensive silver, plate, porcelain. LOC: A307 at foot of Richmond Hill, 100yds. from Richmond Bridge. PARK: 200yds. further up the hill. TEL: (01) 948 0583; home − Egham (0784) 37229. SER: Discounts to members carrying guide or magazine. VAT: Spec.

Richmond continued
Richmond Traders
30/32 Hill Rise. CL: Wed. Open 10.30—5.30, Sun. 2—5. There are 16 dealers at these premises selling general antiques. TEL: (01) 948 4638.

SANDERSTEAD (Surrey)
Shirley Warren
42 Kingswood Ave. (Mrs. S. Warren.) Open by appointment only. *STOCK: English and Continental glass, 18th—19th C, £10—£2,000.* TEL: Home — (01) 657 1751. SER: Valuations. FAIRS: Wakefield and other major.

SHIRLEY (Surrey)
Shirley Antiques
574 Wickham Rd. (I. and R. Manzi.) Est. 1976. Open 9.30—5.30. *STOCK: General antiques and shipping goods.* TEL: (01) 777 8335.

Spring Park Jewellers
284 Wickham Rd. (D. Ashton, CMBHI.) Est. 1965. CL: Wed. Open 10—5.30. SIZE: Small. *STOCK: Jewellery, paintings, prints, silver, furniture.* LOC: 2 miles from central Croydon on road to West Wickham. PARK: Easy. TEL: (01) 656 2800. SER: Valuations; clock, watch and jewellery repairs; buys at auction. VAT: Stan.

SIDCUP (Kent)
Bygones
2 Sidcup Hill. (B. Woodcock.) Est. 1964. CL: Mon. Open 10.30—5.30. SIZE: Small. *STOCK: General antiques, bygones, china, £5—£250.* LOC: A20 from London to Ruxley roundabout, 1st exit, north ½ mile, opposite garage. PARK: Easy. TEL: (01) 300 3178.

IS YOUR ENTRY CORRECT?
If there is even the slightest inaccuracy in your entry, *please* let us know before 1st January 1987.
GUIDE TO THE
ANTIQUE SHOPS OF BRITAIN
5 Church Street, Woodbridge, Suffolk.

SURBITON (Surrey)
50's Clothes
107 Brighton Rd. Open 10—5.30, Wed. 10—2. *STOCK: Victorian to 1950s clothes, general antiques and curios.* PARK: Easy. TEL: (01) 399 0706.

House of Mallett
67 and 69 Brighton Rd. (K. Mallett.) Est. 1974. Open Mon., Fri. and Sat. 10—5. Sun. trade only 10—1. SIZE: Large. *STOCK: Mahogany furniture, general antiques and art pottery; art deco.* PARK: Easy. TEL: (01) 390 3796.

B.M. Newlove   LAPADA
139—141 Ewell Rd. Est. 1958. CL: Wed. Open 9.30—5.30. SIZE: Medium and store. *STOCK: Furniture, 17th—19th C, especially early oak and Georgian mahogany, £200—£5,000; china, 18th—19th C, £75—£200; paintings, all periods, £50—£2,000; longcase clocks, Georgian barometers.* Not stocked: Pot-lids, fairings. LOC: Down Kingston by-pass at Tolworth underpass, turn right into Tolworth Broadway, then into Ewell Rd. Shop one mile on. PARK: Easy. TEL: (01) 399 8857. VAT: Stan/Spec.

Quested Antiques
62 Brighton Rd. (A. Quested.) *STOCK: Pine furniture.* TEL: (01) 390 3566.

Surbiton Bookhouse
Rear of 8 Victoria Rd. (G.W. and R.M. Locke.) A.B.A. Est. 1972. Open Thurs.—Sat. 12—6, Mon.—Wed. by appointment. SIZE: Medium. *STOCK: Books, 19th—20th C, £2—£200.* LOC: Near the station. PARK: Nearby. TEL: (01) 390 2552; home — (01) 767 0029. SER: Valuations.

Laurence Tauber Antiques
131 Ewell Rd. CL: Wed. p.m. Open 9.30—5. *STOCK: General antiques, especially for Trade.* PARK: Easy. TEL: (01) 390 0020. VAT: Stan.

SUTTON (Surrey)
S. Warrender and Co.
4 and 6 Cheam Rd. (F.R. Warrender.) Est. 1953. CL: Wed. Open 9—5.30. SIZE: Medium. *STOCK: Jewellery, 1790 to date, £10—£1,500; silver, 1762 to date, £10—£1,000; carriage clocks, 1860—1900, £115—£800.* TEL: (01) 643 4381. SER: Valuations; restorations (jewellery, silver, quality clocks). VAT: Stan.

Whittington Galleries
22 Woodend. (M. Wakely.) Open by appointment. *STOCK: 18th—19th C English and European porcelain, blue and white transferware.* TEL: (01) 644 9327.

TEDDINGTON (Middx.)

Binsted Antiques
21 Middle Lane. (C.J. Wills.) Est. 1968. CL: Sat. and Sun. except by appointment. Open 9—6. *STOCK: General antiques; furniture, 17th—19th C; English and Continental porcelain and pottery, 18th—19th C; Georgian glass and bronzes; oil paintings; restored square pianos prior 1810.* TEL: (01) 943 0626.

Joan Jarman Antiques
81a High St. (Mrs. J.K. Jarman.) Est. 1967. CL: Wed. Open 2—5, Tues. and Sat. 10—1 and 2—5. SIZE: Medium. *STOCK: Furniture, 1760—1860, £200—£2,000; Tunbridge-ware, objets d'art.* Not stocked: Silver, coins, stamps, weapons. PARK: Easy. TEL: Home — (01) 977 4260. VAT: Stan/Spec.

Lanham
76 Broad St. (R. Lanham.) CL: Mon. and Wed. Open 9.30—5. SIZE: Medium. *STOCK: Furniture, 17th to early 19th C, £500—£1,000; bronzes, 19th C, £300—£1,500; 18th—19th C, £200—£3,000.* LOC: Off Kingston to Twickenham road. PARK: Easy. TEL: (01) 977 8198; home — Esher (0372) 62817. SER: Buys at auction (furniture). FAIRS: Guildford. VAT: Stan/Spec.

THORNTON HEATH (Surrey)

Corner Cabinet
446 Whitehorse Rd. (R. Thomas.) Est. 1977. CL: Mon. Open 10—5. *STOCK: General antiques and furniture.* LOC: End of Thornton Heath High St., at junction Whitehorse Rd. and Whitehorse Lane, opposite parish church. TEL: (01) 684 3156.

TWICKENHAM (Middx.)

Rodney Cook Antiques
58 Richmond Rd. Est. 1969. Open 9.30—6. SIZE: Large. *STOCK: Furniture, pre-1900, £5—£500.* Not stocked: Silver, jewellery. LOC: 1 mile from Richmond Bridge on main Richmond-Twickenham Rd. TEL: (01) 892 6884. VAT: Stan.

The Guildhall Bookshop
25 York St. Open 10—5.30. SIZE: Large. *STOCK: Secondhand and out-of-print books on all subjects pre-1900.* PARK: Nearby. TEL: (01) 892 0331.

Anthony C. Hall
30 Staines Rd. Est. 1966. CL: Wed. p.m. and Sat. Open 9—5.30. SIZE: Medium. *STOCK: Antiquarian books.* PARK: Easy. TEL: (01) 898 2638.

A page from William Ridgway's first pattern book which shows wares of the early 1830s, each made in various sizes and different coloured bodies. From *Ridgway Porcelains* by Geoffrey A. Godden, F.R.S.A., published by the **Antique Collectors' Club,** 1985.

Twickenham continued

John Ives Bookseller
5 Normanhurst Drive, St. Margarets. Resident. Est. 1977. Open by appointment at any time. SIZE: Medium. *STOCK: Scarce and out of print books on antiques and collecting, £1—£500.* LOC: Normanhurst Drive is off St. Margarets Rd. near its junction with Chertsey Rd. PARK: Easy. TEL: (01) 892 6265. SER: Valuations (as stock).

Marble Hill Gallery
72 Richmond Rd. (D. and L. Newson.) Est. 1974. Open 10—5.30. *STOCK: Victorian watercolours and fireside furniture, French marble mantels, and pine and white Adam style mantels.* LOC: Richmond-Twickenham rd. PARK: Easy. TEL: (01) 892 1488/8460. VAT: Stan/Spec.

David Morley Antiques
371 Richmond Rd. Est. 1968. CL: Wed. Open 10—5. SIZE: Medium. Not stocked: Large furniture. LOC: Approx. 200yds. from Richmond Bridge. PARK: In side road (adjacent to shop). TEL: (01) 892 2986.

Twickenham continued

Onslow Clocks   LAPADA
48 King St. (M. Onslow-Cole.) Est. 1968. CL: Wed. Open 9—5. SIZE: Large. *STOCK: Clocks, longcase, 17th to early 19th C, £375—£7,000; bracket, 17th to early 18th C, £1,500—£5,000; small bracket, carriage, Vienna regulator, dial French, 18th—19th C, £90—£1,000.* LOC: Town centre. PARK: Rear of shop. TEL: (01) 892 7632. SER: Valuations; restorations (clocks — movements and casework); buys at auction. FAIRS: Olympia. VAT: Stan/Spec.

Phelps Ltd.   LAPADA
Mainly Trade and Export
133/135 St. Margarets Rd. (W.J. and R.C. Phelps.) Est. 1870. Open 9—5.30. SIZE: Large. *STOCK: Victorian and Edwardian furniture and shipping goods.* LOC: Adjacent St. Margaret's station. PARK: Easy. TEL: (01) 892 1778/7129. SER: Restorations. VAT: Stan/Spec.

Rita Shenton   *Mainly postal*
148 Percy Rd. Est. 1973. Open by appointment only. SIZE: Medium. *STOCK: Horological, bell and ornamental turning books, £1—£1,000.* LOC: Continuation of Whitton High St. PARK: Easy. TEL: (01) 894 6888. SER: Valuations; buys at auction (horological books, clocks); catalogues available.

Twickenham continued
York Galleries
34 York St. (D.L. Ferrari.) Est. 1964. CL: Wed. *STOCK: Jewellery, antique and modern, carriage and French clocks, watches, silver and plate, music boxes, china, glass, general antiques, £10—£750.* TEL: (01) 892 9324. VAT: Stan.

Zafer
36 Church St. (R.D. Zafer.) Est. 1971. CL: Wed. Open 10—5.30. SIZE: Small. *STOCK: Clocks, £50—£2,000; furniture, £10—£2,000; silver, £10—£300; jewellery, £10—£500; all from 17th C.* Not stocked: Porcelain and early glass. LOC: Off Twickenham High St., parallel to river. TEL: (01) 891 3183. SER: Valuations; restorations (upholstery). VAT: Stan.

UPMINSTER (Essex)   (040 22)
The Old Cottage Antiques
The Old Cottage, Corbets Tey. (R. Edwards.) Est. 1970. Open 10—5. SIZE: Medium. *STOCK: Furniture, shipping goods, porcelain, silver, general antiques.* Not stocked: Firearms. PARK: Easy. TEL: 22867.

UXBRIDGE (Middx.)   (0895)
Antiques Warehouse (Uxbridge)
34 Rockingham Rd. Est. 1966. Open 9.30—5.30. SIZE: Large. *STOCK: General antiques, shipping items, £1—£2,000.* PARK: Easy. TEL: 56963; 24-hr ansafone. VAT: Stan.

Thomas Barnard (A.B.A.)
11 Windsor St. Est. 1944. CL: Wed. p.m. Open 9—5.30. *STOCK: General antiquarian books; prints, maps, pictures.* TEL: 58054. SER: Book-binding, framing.

John Westley
41—42 Windsor St. (D. and J. Westley.) Est. 1943. CL: Wed. Open 9—5.30. SIZE: Small. *STOCK: Jewellery, second-hand and Victorian, furniture, £5—£2,000; bric-a-brac, from £1.* Not stocked: Musical instruments, books. LOC: Windsor St. is directly opposite Uxbridge underground station. PARK: At rear. TEL: 34933. SER: Valuations. VAT: Stan/Spec.

WALLINGTON (Surrey)
The Attic
7 Parkgate Rd. Open 9.30—5, Sat. 9.30—1. *STOCK: General antiques and shipping goods.* TEL: (01) 669 9656.

Wallington continued
Curiosity Shop
72 Stafford Rd. (Mrs. S. Stokes.) Est. 1938. CL: Wed. Open 9—2, Sun. and afternoons by appointment. *STOCK: Dolls, toys, postcards, collectors' items.* TEL: (01) 647 5267. VAT: Stan.

St. Elphege's Church Hall
Stafford Rd. There are approximately 20 dealers at this market which is open every Wed. 8.30—3. TEL: (01) 642 7378 or 642 4722.

WEMBLEY PARK (Middx.)
Mount Gallery
The Annexe, 18 Mount Drive. (S.A. Collister.) Est. 1979. Open 11—6 Sat. and Sun., weekday evenings by appointment. SIZE: Medium. *STOCK: British watercolours, £50—£3,000; oils, £200—£1,000; prints, £25—£500; all 1750-1950.* LOC: North Circular Rd. going west from M1, by Brent Cross. PARK: Easy. TEL: (01) 904 5184; home — same. SER: Restorations (as stock); buys at auction (as stock); mounting, framing. FAIRS: Olympia and West Midlands.

WOODFORD GREEN (Essex)
P. and K.N. Blake —
Lanehurst Antiques
403 High Rd. Est. 1952. Open Thurs. and Fri. 10—6, Sat. 10—1. SIZE: Medium. *STOCK: Furniture, general antiques.* LOC: A11, close to Castle public house. TEL: (01) 504 9264. SER: Valuations; buys at auction. VAT: Stan/Spec.

Castle Antiques
397 High Rd. CL: Fri. Open 10—5.30. *STOCK: Silver, glass, ceramics, collectors' items, small furniture, to Victorian.* TEL: (01) 506 1007.

Daisy Dawkins Antiques
29 Mill Lane. (L.M. Mulvany.) Est. 1970. Open 9.30—5.30, Thurs. 9.30—12.30. SIZE: Small. *STOCK: Collectors' items, curios, gramophones, 78 records, vintage cameras, 25p—£500.* LOC: Directly off A11, 1 mile from M11 and M25. PARK: Easy. TEL: (01) 505 5030. FAIRS: Alexandra Palace, Harrow, Picketts Lock, Ardingly.

Galerie Lev
1 The Broadway. CL: Thurs. Open 9—1 and 2—5. *STOCK: Oils, watercolours; silver plate, porcelain.* LOC: Near Woodford underground station. TEL: (01) 505 2226. VAT: Stan.

WRAYSBURY
See Berkshire

Avon

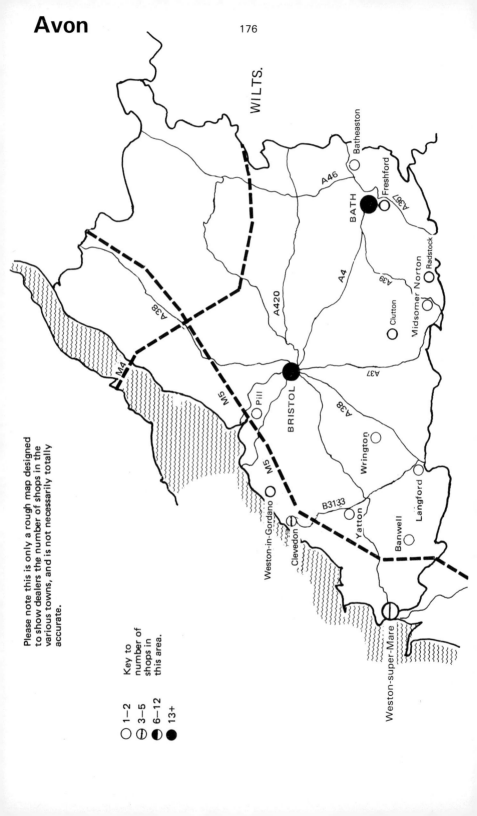

WILTS.

Please note this is only a rough map designed to show dealers the number of shops in the various towns, and is not necessarily totally accurate.

Key to number of shops in this area.

1–2
3–5
6–12
13+

Batheaston

Freshford

BATH

A46

A367

Radstock

A39

Midsomer Norton

Clutton

A4

A420

A38

M4

BRISTOL

A37

Pill

A38

M5

Wrington

M5

Weston-in-Gordano

Clevedon

B3133

Yatton

Banwell

Langford

Weston-super-Mare

BANWELL (0934)
John H. Collings
Antique Village, Knightcott. Est. 1952. Open 9—1 and 2—6. SIZE: Large. *STOCK: Paintings, 1800—1900, £10—£100; furniture, 1760—1850, £25—£200; shipping goods.* Not stocked: Porcelain, fine glass, silver. LOC: Travelling westward, leave M5 by junction 21. Turn left signposted Banwell, West Wick, in one mile first right, then left after one mile, premises 300 metres on right. PARK: Easy. TEL: 823181. SER: Valuations; restorations (paintings). VAT: Stan/Spec.

BATH (0225)
Abbey Galleries
9 Abbey Churchyard. (R. Dickson.) Est. 1930. Open 10.30—5.30. *STOCK: Jewellery, £50; Oriental, £100; both 18th—19th C; silver, 18th C, £100.* Not stocked: Furniture. TEL: 60565. SER: Valuations; restorations (jewellery and clocks); buys at auction. VAT: Stan.

Alderson & Alderson BADA
23 Brock St. (C.J.R. Alderson.) Est. 1975. Open 9.30—1 and 2—5.30. *STOCK: Furniture, 17th—18th C; period metalwork, glass, silver and silhouettes.* LOC: Between the Circus and Royal Crescent. PARK: Easy. TEL: 21652. SER: Valuations; restorations (furniture). VAT: Spec.

Arkea Antiques
10A Monmouth Place. (G. Harmandian.) Est. 1972. *STOCK: Furniture, china, silver, clocks.* TEL: 29413; home — 26653.

Arts of Living
18 Green St. Est. 1972. *STOCK: Persian, Afghan, Russian and Indian rugs, saddle bags, grain bags and jollers, to date.* TEL: 64270. VAT: Stan.

Aspidistra
46 St. James Parade. (J. and J. Waggoner.) Est. 1972. Open 10.30—5. SIZE: Medium. *STOCK: Books and prints, music and musical instruments, curiosities, bygones.* LOC: 2 mins. walk from Bath Abbey, opposite Technical College. PARK: Easy, 20 mins. Multi-storey 1 min.. TEL: 61948. SER: Valuations.

Bartlett Street Antique Centre
7—10 Bartlett St. Open 9.30—5, Wed. 8—5. There are 36+ dealers at this market selling a wide range of general antiques. TEL: 66689, stallholders — 330267 or 310457.

Bath continued

Bath Antique Market
Guinea Lane, Paragon. (Mrs. M. Johnson.) Est. 1968. Open Wed. only, 7—3. There are 90 dealers at this market selling a wide variety of antiques including furniture, porcelain, pottery, glass, pictures, metals, jewellery. TEL: 22510 and 858467. LOC: From London A4 across two sets of traffic lights after entering Bath. Right at third set (Lansdown Rd.) and first right again. PARK: Nearby.

K. Barr
Copper, brass, silver plate, bric-a-brac.

Lee Booker
TEL: Home — (061) 928 7521.

Pat Coleman
General antiques.

R. Cooke and G.J. Dunn
Jewellery, silver, brass, copper, porcelain, small items.

Dennis and Margaret Curtis
Pine furniture, bygones.

Meriel de M. Greg
Collectors' items (especially sewing tools); silver, prints, small furniture.

Helendean Antiques
(E. Frost.) *Silver, porcelain, Tunbridge and Mauchline ware, snuff boxes, silver plate, boxes.* TEL: Home — Broad Hinton (079 373) 465.

Elizabeth Howard
Fans.

Ann King
Period clothes, 19th C to 1960; baby clothes, shawls and bead dresses.

Mrs. March
Porcelain.

Joanna Proops
Linen and lace.

Puzzle House Antiques
Wooden boxes.

Ian Savage Antiques
Pewter, brass, metalware, oak furniture, both 17th—19th C; musical instruments.

Jacqueline Williams
Art glass, nouveau, deco, porcelain, bric-a-brac.

Wye Knot Antiques
(J. Porter-Davison). *Metalware and decorative items, treen, small furniture, scientific and musical instruments.* Tel: Home — (0600) 860577.

Bath Coin Shop
Pulteney Bridge. (H. and A. Swindells.) Est. 1946. Open 9—5.30. *STOCK: Coins (Roman, hammered, early milled, G.B. gold, silver and copper, some foreign); literature and accessories.* PARK: Laura Place; Walcott multi-storey. SER: Valuations. VAT: Stan.

Bath continued

Bath Galleries
33 Broad St. (J. Griffiths.) Open 9.30—5. SIZE: Medium. *STOCK: Furniture, paintings, porcelain, jewellery, clocks, barometers, silver.* LOC: 50yds. from Central Post Office. PARK: Walcot St. multi-park, 30yds. TEL: 62946. SER: Valuations; restorations; buys at auction. VAT: Stan/Spec.

Bath Saturday Antiques Market
Walcot St. (A. Whittingham.) Est. 1978. Open Sat. 7—5. There are 75 stalls at this market selling a wide variety of general antiques, prices ranging from £1—£200. TEL: 60909 any time. LOC: ¼ mile off A4 adjoining Beaufort Hotel. PARK: Multi-storey.

George Bayntun
Manvers St. (C.M. and H.H. Bayntun-Coward.) Est. 1829. CL: Sat. Open 9—1 and 2.15—5.30. SIZE: Large. *STOCK: Rare books. First or fine editions of English literature, standard sets, illustrated and sporting books, poetry, biography and travel, mainly in new leather bindings; also large stock of antiquarian books in original bindings.* LOC: By railway and bus stations. PARK: 50yds. by station. TEL: 66000. SER: Restorations (rare books). VAT: Stan.

Bladud House Antiques
8 Bladud Buildings. (Mrs. E. Radosenska.) CL: Mon. and Thurs. Open 9.30—1 and 2—4.30. *STOCK: Jewellery and small items.* Not stocked: Furniture. TEL: 62929.

Blyth Antiques
28 Sydney Bldgs. (B. Blyth.) Resident. Est. 1971. Open by appointment. *STOCK: Samplers, to 1840, £350—£2,000; ships wool pictures, brass, yew and fruitwood furniture.* LOC: Off Bathwick Hill. PARK: Easy. TEL: 69766. VAT: Spec.

Lawrence Brass and Son
93—95 Walcot St. Est. 1973. Open 8—12 and 1—5, Sun. by appointment. SIZE: Small. *STOCK: Furniture, 16th—19th C, £50—£5,000.* Not stocked: Ceramics, silver, glass. LOC: Main road into town centre. PARK: Easy. TEL: 64057; home — same. SER: Restorations (furniture, clocks and barometers). VAT: Stan.

Bryers Antiques
12a Manvers St. and entrance of Guildhall Market. (S. Bryers.) Est. 1940. *STOCK: Furniture, decorative items, porcelain, glass, silver and Victorian plate.* LOC: Near the bus station. TEL: 66352 and 60535. VAT: Stan/Spec.

Robin and Jan Coleman
27b Belvedere, Lansdown. CL: Thurs. Open 9—6, Tues. 9—8. *STOCK: Interior decorator's items, folk antiques.* TEL: 316216.

Bath continued

Colleton House Gallery
Colleton House Ltd., 8A Quiet St. (Mrs. M.E. Biddle.) Est. 1984. Open 10—1.15 and 2.15—6. SIZE: Large. *STOCK: Oils, £450—£30,000; watercolours, £50— £2,500; both mid 17th to mid 19th C.* LOC: Between Queen Sq. and Milsom St. PARK: Multi-storey under Beaufort Hotel. TEL: 28806; home — (045 383) 4665. SER: Valuations; restorations (oils and watercolours); buys at auction (oils and watercolours). VAT: Spec.

Corridor Stamp Shop
7a The Corridor. (G.H. and S.M. Organ.) Est. 1970. CL: Thurs. p.m. Open 9.30—5.30. SIZE: Small. *STOCK: Stamp and postal history, 1700 to date, 5p—£500; albums, reference books; picture postcards, cigarette cards, 1895—1940.* LOC: Within 200yds. of Abbey. PARK: Walcot St. TEL: 63368; home — 316445. SER: Valuations. FAIRS: Stampex, London, Bristol. VAT: Stan.

Brian and Caroline Craik Ltd.
LAPADA
8 Margaret's Buildings. *STOCK: Decorative items, metalwork, furniture, 18th and 19th C.* TEL: 337161.

IS YOUR ENTRY CORRECT?
If there is even the slightest inaccuracy in your entry, *please* let us know before 1st January 1987.
GUIDE TO THE
ANTIQUE SHOPS OF BRITAIN
5 Church Street, Woodbridge, Suffolk.

Large blue and enamelled mug. Part of "The Nanking Cargo". From **Antique Collecting**, March 1986.

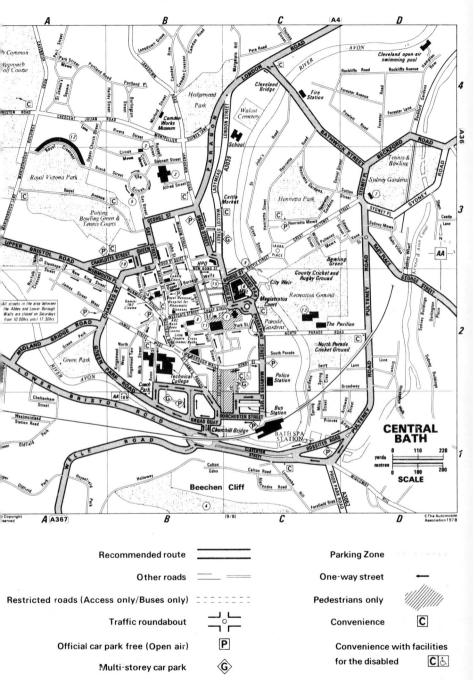

CENTRAL
BATH

SCALE

yards   0   110   220
metres   0   180   200

Recommended route

Other roads

Restricted roads (Access only/Buses only)

Traffic roundabout

Official car park free (Open air)   P

Multi-storey car park   Ⓖ

Parking available on payment (Open air)   Ⓟ

Parking Zone

One-way street

Pedestrians only

Convenience   C

Convenience with facilities
for the disabled   C ♿

Tourist Information Centre   i

Reproduced by kind permission of the Automobile Association

JOHN CROFT ANTIQUES

Fine 18th and early 19th century
Furniture
Decorative Objects

3 GEORGE STREET BATH BA1 2EH
Tel. 0225 66211

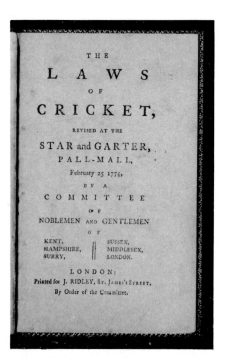

THE
L A W S
OF
C R I C K E T,
REVISED AT THE
STAR and GARTER,
P A L L - M A L L,
February 25 1774,
BY A
C O M M I T T E E
OF
NOBLEMEN AND GENTLEMEN
OF
KENT,   SUSSEX,
HAMPSHIRE,   MIDDLESEX,
SURRY,   LONDON.

L O N D O N:
Printed for J. RIDLEY, St. James's Street,
By Order of the Committee.

Bath continued

John Croft Antiques   LAPADA
3 George St. Open 9.15−5.30. SIZE: Medium. *STOCK: Furniture, 17th to early 19th C; clocks, barometers, decorative objects.* LOC: A4, turn left at top of Milsom St. opp. 'Hole in the Wall' restaurant. PARK: Broad St. 100yds. TEL: 66211. VAT: Spec.

Andrew Dando   BADA
4 Wood St., Queen Sq. (G. Dando.) Est. 1930. Open 9.30−1.15 and 2.30−5.30, Sat. 10−1. *STOCK: English, Continental, Oriental porcelain and pottery, 17th to mid-19th C; furniture, 18th to early 19th C.* LOC: 200yds. from bottom of Milsom St. towards Queen Sq. TEL: 22702. SER: Valuations. VAT: Stan/Spec.

Michael Danny
The Manor House, Wellow. Open by appointment only. *STOCK: British watercolours from 1750.* PARK: Easy. TEL: 832027. SER: Valuations; buys at auction. VAT: Spec.

Gerald Deacon   BADA
2 Wood St., Queen Sq. Est. 1959. CL: Sat. p.m. Open 10−5. *STOCK: English furniture, porcelain, pottery, 18th to early 19th C.* TEL: 25907. VAT: Spec.

Dela-Ware
1 Victoria Buildings, Lower Bristol Rd. (H. Dellow.) Open 9.30−5. *STOCK: General antiques, shipping furniture and bric-a-brac.* TEL: 317350.

Devonshire House Antiques
143 Wellsway. TEL: 312495.

D. and B. Dickinson   BADA
22 New Bond St. (S.G., D. and N.W. Dickinson, Mrs. E.M. Dickinson.) Est. 1917. CL: Mon. and Sat. p.m. Open 9.30−1 and 2.15−5. SIZE: Small. *STOCK: Jewellery, 1770−1900, £10−£1,000; silver, 1750−1900, £25−£1,000; Sheffield plate, 1770−1845, £10−£200.* LOC: Next to Post Office. PARK: 100yds. at bottom of street, turn left then right for multi-storey. TEL: 66502. VAT: Stan/Spec.

Dollin and Daines   BADA
2 Church St., York St. Est. 1968. CL: Thurs. and Sat. Open 10.30−1 and 2−4. *STOCK: Violins, violas, cellos and bows.* TEL: 62752. SER: Restorations (as stock).

''The Laws of Cricket, revised at the Star and Garter, Pall-Mall'', 25th February 1774, published London, full calf and gilt. £600. From an auction feature, **Antique Collecting**, February 1986.

Bath continued

Brian and Angela Downes Antiques
LAPADA
9 Broad St. Est. 1968. Open 9—5.30. SIZE: Large. *STOCK: Furniture, metalware, clocks, paintings, fine English, Chinese and Japanese porcelain, decorators' items, 18th—19th C.* PARK: Easy. TEL: 65352. SER: Valuations. VAT: Stan/Spec.

Gene and Sally Foster (Antiques)
27A Belvedere, Lansdown. Est. 1969. Article on patchwork quilts. Open daily. SIZE: Medium. *STOCK: Decorative and unusual items, 17th—19th C; Continental and English painted furniture, paintings, needlework, prints and metalware, £25—£2,500.* Not stocked: Silver, jewellery, arms and armour. TEL: 28256. VAT: Stan/Spec.

The French Connection
4 Monmouth St. (C. Cooper). Est. 1973. Open 10—5.30, Sun. by appointment. SIZE: Small. *STOCK: Hand-made French and English linen and lace, Victorian, £5—£150; English gold-plated livery buttons, 1860-1880, £8—£35 a set; French kitchen utensils, plate racks and enamel woodburning stoves, 1880-1900, £5—£250.* LOC: Immediately behind Theatre Royal. PARK: Easy. TEL: Home — (0249) 782286. SER: Restorations (metal polishing, wood stripping, decorative paintwork).

The Galleon
33 Monmouth St. (D.L. Gwilliam and M.J. Wren.) Resident. Est. 1972. Open 10—5.30, or by appointment. SIZE: Medium. *STOCK: Furniture, jewellery, silver, general antiques, Georgian to art deco, £5—£1,500.* LOC: Near rear of Theatre Royal. PARK: Easy. TEL: 312330. SER: Buys at auction. VAT: Stan/Spec.

Bath continued

Valentine Gould
33 Belvedere, Lansdown Rd. Est. 1952. Open 9—6. SIZE: Medium. *STOCK: Furniture, paintings, pre-1850.* LOC: From London 3rd set of traffic lights, turn right into Lansdown Rd. PARK: Easy. TEL: 312367. SER: Valuations; restorations. VAT: Spec.

Great Western Antique Centre Ltd.
Bartlett St. Open 9.30—5. There are 60 dealers at this centre with 110 units. LOC: Adjacent to the Assembly Rooms. TEL: 24243; stand holders 310388, 20686 and 28731. There is an additional market every Wed. Below are listed the dealers at this market.

Ancestors
Stand 80-81. (E. Rosser-Rees). *Paintings and small objets d'art.*

Antique Interiors
Stands 53 and 55. (E.A. Gray.) *Furniture, decorative items, objets d'art.*

Avril Antiques
Stands 83 and 113. (A. Brown). *Silver, china and small decorative furniture.*

Ann Bailey & Jill Fausset
Stands 66 and 67. *Small furniture, pictures, ceramics, collectors' items.*

Bennetts
Stands 44-45. (D. and C. Bennett.) *Lampshades, art nouveau and art deco.*

S. Brosinovich
Stands 51 and 52. *Pearls, prints, general antiques and shipping goods.*

Brunel Antiques
Stands 42 and 43. (J. and S. Mildred.) *Art pottery, arts and crafts and furniture.*

Cameo Antiques
Stand 46 and 47. (R. Dougall.) *Jewellery, china, pictures.*

The Collectors Shop
Stand 10. (L.J. Harrison.) *Vintage collectable toys.*

D. Cooper
Stands 31, 32 and 34, *Photographica.*

Great Western Antique Centre continued

Duncan Copeman Antiques
Stand 74. *French provincial furniture and general antiques.*
Crofton Antiques
Stand 25. (R.A. Gresham.) *Prints, Victorian and Edwardian furniture including pine.*
Fairfax Fireplaces
Stand — window. (Miss J. Fairfax.) *Fireplaces.*
Gulliver's
Stands 75-78. *General antiques and pine.*
H. Guymer
Stands 23 and 24. *Brass, copper and treen.*
R. Harris
Stand 63. *Brass and copper, kitchenware, advertising items and collectables.*
The Hope Chest
Stand 3. (J. Watson.) *Bygone linens.*
Sonia House
Stand 30. *Furniture.*
M. Houston
Stand 64. *Objets d'art, pictures and collectables.*
D. Howard and J. Cowell.
Stands 108 and 115. *General antiques.*
Kerry Howard
Stand 106. *Jewellery, silver, Staffordshire, small collectables and general antiques.*
Christopher Jenkins Antiques
Stand 112. *Early furniture and primitives.*
Jessie's Button Box
Stand 17. (J. Partt.). *Collectors' and designers' buttons.*
H. Leigh
Stand 65. *Enamel, pens, watches and jewellery.*
P. Livani
Stand 72. *European and Middle Eastern works of art and furniture.*
Jan and Don Macbeth
Stand 14. *Chesterfields, Victorian and Edwardian suites.*

Great Western Antique Centre continued
Richard McTaggart
Stand 105. *Oriental ceramics and works of art.* TEL: 21505.
Mario Antiques
Stand 8. (M. Zambrzycki.) *Clocks, silver, paintings and furniture.*
Mark's Antiques
Stand 79. (M.P. Nunan). *Music boxes, jewellery, oriental items and silver plate.*
Mendip Antiques   LAPADA
Stands 38-41. (W. Selwyn.) *Furniture, 1760—1860.*

Great Western Antique Centre continued

A. Molano
Stand 73. *General antiques.*
D. Morrell
Stand 48. *Silver, glass, porcelain and small furniture.*
R. and H. Myers
Stand 1. *Bedsteads and Victorian ceramic tiles.*
Nelson and Spurling
Stand 125. *Georgian glass, porcelain and decorative items.*
D. and P. Newlove
Stands 70, 71 and 102. *Furniture, clocks, pine and small items.*
Not Cartier
Stand 94 and 95. (G. Tinne.) *Costume jewellery, beaded trimmings.*
Off the Rails
Stand 22. (S. Relph.) *Antique and period clothes.*
Patina
Stand 21. (P. Biggs.) *Silver including collectables.*
Pineside Studios
Stands 119-120. (G.N. Corke.) *Pine and oak country furniture.*
Pioneer
Stands 18-20, and 27-29. (E.J. Nott). *Period and Victorian pine furniture.*
T. and M. Rivett
Stands 68, 69, 97-99. *Furniture, clocks, brass and copper.*
Roy's
Stands 33 and 121. (N. Girling). *Jewellery and bullion.*
Sedan Chair House
Stand 12. (J. Batley.) *Small period furniture, silver and objets d'art.*
J. Southern
Stand 103-104. *Pine furniture.*
Tassles
Stands 90-93. (K. Jones). *Pre-1960s clothing, accessories and furs.*
Tassles
Stands 87, 96 and 116-118. (M. Adams.) *Pre-1960s clothing, accessories and furs.*
D.H.A. Taylor
Stand 101. *Jewellery, porcelain and general antiques.*
R.C. & L. Tincknell
Stands 59, 61—62. *Victorian silver and plate, glass and furniture.*
Joan Vaughan
Stand 111. *General antiques.*
Vintage Sound
Stand 100. (D. Martin). *Vintage radios (1920-40), gramophones and phonographs.*
Sue Wagstaff
Stand 60. *English pottery, porcelain and small collectors' items.*
William Wagstaff
Stand 114. *China, glass, prints, small Edwardian and Victorian furniture.*

Great Western Antique Centre continued

Winstone Stamp Co. and S.D. Postcards
Stand 82. (D. Winstone). *Postal history, postcards and collectors' items.*
M. Woodford
Stand 127. *Silver and general antiques.*

Great Western Antique Centre Ltd. — The Wednesday Market

Bartlett St. There are approx. 40 dealers on the lower ground floor, selling a wide range of general antiques. Open 7.30—4.30. The market has its own separate entrance. Below are listed the dealers at this market:

M. Bennetta
Stand 52. *General antiques and bric-a-brac.*
M. Blunden
Stands 40 and 45. *China and general antiques.*
D.M. Brinn
Stand 22. *China.*
B. Cooper
Stand 30. *General antiques.*
Jill Cullimore
Stand 9. *General antiques.*
June Davies
Stand 42. *Collectables, prints and antique toys.*
M. Downworth
Stand 46 and 51. *Dolls and general antiques.*
J.L. Duffy
Stand 34. *Jewellery.*
A. Dunn
Stand 41. *Small collectables and general antiques.*
L. Elliott
Stand 29. *General antiques.*
C. Freeman
Stand 5. *General antiques.*
B. Gapp
Stand 48. *Collectors' items.*
L. Garrett
Stand 26. *General antiques.*
K. Goodman
Stand 28. *General antiques and small furniture.*
D.E. Gyles
Stand 44. *Furniture and general antiques.*
Rob Hall Antiques
Stand 8 and 38. (R. and J. Hall.) *Porcelain, silver and jewellery.*
G. Hamilton
Stand 16. *General antiques.*
Harris and Fergie
Stand 3. (R. Harris.) *Metalware.*
V. Holochwost
Stand 57. *General antiques.*
M.K. Holt
Stand 13. *Carnival glass and general antiques.*
J. Jenkins
Stands 4 and 25. *Clothes and accessories.*

Great Western Antique Centre
Wednesday Market continued

E. Kilbane
Stand 7. *General antiques.*

P.E. Martin
Stand 6. *General antiques and 78 r.p.m. records.*

A. Nethercott
Stand 10. *Metalware and primitive furniture.*

R. Prest
Stand 17. *Commemorative items and general antiques.*

A. Roberts
Stand 27. *Books and postcards.*

M.E. Saffell
Stands 11−12. *Metalware.*

Pam Smith
Stand 43. *Costume jewellery, linen and bric-a-brac.*

Pauline Smith
Stands 32 and 33. *Clocks and small furniture.*

Janet Sumner Antiques
Stands 1−2 and 23. (N.J. Sumner.) *Commemorative china.*

R. Tincknell
Stand 53. *Kitchen items, fireirons and brass.*

G. Wall
Stand 39. *General antiques.*

E.N. and M. Whittingham
Stand 14−15. *Furniture and general antiques.*

M. Wilson
Stand 24. *Kitchen items.*

George Gregory
Manvers St. (H.H. Bayntun-Coward.) Est. 1845. CL: Sat. Open 9−1 and 2.15−5.30. SIZE: Large. *STOCK: Books, 1600−1984; engravings.* LOC: By rail station. PARK: By rail station. TEL: 66055. SER: Restorations (fine books). VAT: Stan.

Helena Hood & Co.
3 Margarets Buildings, Brock St. (Mrs.L.M. Hood.) Est. 1973. CL: Sat. p.m. Open 9.30−1 and 2−5.30. SIZE: Small. *STOCK: Decorative items − furniture, carpets, prints, paintings and porcelain, 18th−19th C, £25−£1,500.* LOC: Pedestrian walkway running north from Brock St. PARK: Easy. TEL: 24438. SER: Restorations. VAT: Stan/Spec.

M.A. and D.A. Hughes   LAPADA
11 Pulteney Bridge. Open 10−4.30. *STOCK: Silver.* TEL: 65782. VAT: Stan/Spec.

Bath continued

Mac Humble Antiques   BADA
11 Queen St. (W. Mc A. Humble.) Est. 1979. Open 9.30−5.30, Sat. till 5. SIZE: Small. *STOCK: Mahogany, 18th−19th C, £100−£4,000; metalware, treen, porcelain, decorative items, £20−£200; oak and fruitwood, 17th−19th C, £30−£1,000; needlework, samplers.* LOC: Between Queen Sq. and Milsom St. PARK: Charlotte St. TEL: 62751; home − Limpley Stoke (022 122) 3594. SER: Valuations; restorations; buys at auction. VAT: Stan/Spec.

John Keil   BADA
10 Quiet St. Est. 1955. Open 9−5.30, Sat. 10−1. *STOCK: Mahogany, £250−£5,000; oak, 18th C; metalware and objects, £20−£3,000.* TEL: 63176. SER: Restorations (furniture). VAT: Spec.

"Kimono"
4 Belvedere, Lansdown Rd. (Mrs. K. Page.) Resident. *STOCK: English, foreign and Continental costume; textiles and embroidery, £20−£500.* LOC: Nr. Assembly Rooms and Museum of Costume. TEL: 315987.

"Kimono" Antiques
4 Belvedere, Lansdown Rd. (F. Page.) Resident. Always available to the Trade. *STOCK: European and Oriental decor items; textiles, costume.* LOC: Near Assembly Rooms and Museum of Costume. TEL: 315987. VAT: Spec.

Ann King
38 Belvedere, Lansdown Rd. Est. 1977. CL: Thurs. Open 10−4, Wed. 12−3.30. SIZE: Small. *STOCK: Period clothes, 19th C to 1960; baby clothes, shawls and bead dresses.* LOC: Around corner from Guinea Lane Antique Market. PARK: Easy. TEL: 336245; home − Westbury (0373) 864747.

Stuart King − Piccadilly Antiques
1 and 2 Piccadilly, London Rd. Est. 1967. Open 9−5.30. SIZE: Medium. *STOCK: General country, period painted pine, decorative and humorous items.* LOC: A4. PARK: Easy. TEL: 332779 anytime.

Lansdown Antiques
23 Belvedere, Lansdown Rd. (C.P. and A.M. Kemp.) CL: Thurs. Open 9−6, Tues. 9−8, Sat. 9−5, Sun. by appointment. *STOCK: Furniture, 17th−19th C; metalware, decorative items.* LOC: From A4, across 2 sets of traffic lights, right at 3rd set, shop 350yds. on left. PARK: Easy. TEL: 313417; home − same. VAT: Stan/Spec.

Bath continued

Lantern Gallery   **BADA**
9 George St. (A. Campbell-Macinnes.) Est. 1966. Open 9.30—5.30; Sat. 10—4.30. *STOCK: Old maps, topography, decorative natural history and botanical prints, 1570— 1880.* **TEL: 63727. SER: Restorations;** framing. **VAT: Spec.**

E.P. Mallory and Son Ltd.   **BADA**
1—4 Bridge St. and 5 Old Bond St. Est. 1898. *STOCK: Period silver and Sheffield plate, jewellery, objets de vertu; clocks.* **TEL: 65885. VAT: Stan/Spec.**

Nash Antiques
10 Fountain Buildings, Lansdown Rd. Open 9.30—6. *STOCK: Regency and oak furniture, Oriental and English porcelain, decorative objects.* LOC: Near Great Western Market. PARK: Easy. TEL: 313584. SER: Buys at auction. VAT: Stan/Spec.

No. 12 Queen Street
12 Queen Street. (C. Roberts & K. Stables.) Open 9.30—5.30, other times by appointment. *STOCK: Oak and country furniture, textiles, needlework, samplers, decorative items.* TEL: 62363; home — 314846. SER: Interior decorating. VAT: Spec.

Old Curiosity Shop
33 Walcot St. Est. 1954. CL: Tues. p.m., Thurs. and Fri. *STOCK: Jewellery, lighters, compacts, spectacles, penknives, cut-throat razors, small items.* VAT: Stan.

Paragon Antiques and Collectors Market
3 Bladud Buildings, The Paragon. (T.J. Clifford and Son Ltd.) Est. 1978. Open Wed. 6.30—3.30. SIZE: Large. LOC: Milsom St./Broad St. PARK: 50yds. TEL: 63715.

Pineapple
Fountain Buildings, Lansdown Mews, Lansdown Rd. (N.J. Kemp.) Open 9—6. *STOCK: Pine, architectural and decorative pieces.* TEL: 65223.

Queens Parade Antiques Ltd.
35 Gay St. (S. Isbell, E.A. Quinton, BADA.) Open 9.30—1 and 2—5.30, Sat. till 5, other times by appointment. SIZE: Medium. *STOCK: Furniture, late 17th to early 19th C, £500—£10,000; decorative items, £100— £2,000; pictures, £300—£10,000; architectural items, £500—£5,000.* LOC: Right-hand side of hill leading from Queens Sq. PARK: Opposite. TEL: 20337. SER: Valuations; buys at auction (furniture and decorative items). VAT: Spec.

Quest Antiques and Pine
27 Walcot St. (Mrs. J. Robertson.) CL: Thurs. p.m. Open 10—1 and 2.15—5.30, or by appointment. *STOCK: Furniture, late Victorian and Edwardian, £30—£700; stripped pine, brass, lamps, bric-a-brac.* TEL: 64052. VAT: Stan.

Bath continued

Quiet St. Antiques   **LAPADA**
3 Quiet St. (K. Hastings-Spital and R. Windebank.) Est. 1985. Open 10—6, Wed. and Sat. 9—6. SIZE: Medium. *STOCK: Furniture, 1750—1870, £250—£2,000; objects including bronzes, caddies, some porcelain, 1750—1880, £50—£500; clocks including longcase and carriage, 1750—1900, £150—£2,000.* Not stocked: Silver. LOC: 25yds. from Milsom St., opposite John Keil. PARK: Nearby. TEL: 315727; home — 332399. SER: Valuations; restorations (furniture, clocks, upholstery); buys at auction (furniture and clocks). VAT: Spec.

T.E. Robinson   **BADA**
3 and 4 Bartlett St. *STOCK: Period furniture, glass, unusual and rare items.* **TEL: 63982;** home — 832307. **VAT: Spec.**

Louise Ross & Co Ltd.
1 John St. ABA. Est. 1975. SIZE: Medium. *STOCK: Antiquarian books in fine bindings; prints and maps.* LOC: Facing Queen's Sq. PARK: Beaufort Hotel. TEL: 310332. SER: Valuations; restorations; buys at auction (as stock). VAT: Stan.

M. Sainsbury
35 Gay St. Est. 1930. Open by appointment. *STOCK: Antiquities, pre 1800.* Not stocked: Fine pictures, silver. TEL: 24808. SER: Valuations. VAT: Spec.

Scott Antiques
11 London St. Open 10—5.30. *STOCK: General antiques, Victoriana, bric-a-brac.* TEL: Home — 62423. VAT: Stan/Spec.

Smith and Bottrill
The Clock House, 17 George St. (Mr. McManus.) CL: Sat. p.m. Open 9—1 and 2.30—5.30. *STOCK: Clocks, barometers.* TEL: 22809. SER: Restorations; repairs (clocks).

Sheila Smith Antiques   **LAPADA**
10a Queen St. (S.M. Cooper.) Est. 1967. Open 11—6 or by appointment. SIZE: Small. *STOCK: Fans, needlework tools, accessories, textiles, boxes, treen, glass, bobbins, some lace and collectors' items.* Not stocked: Brass, copper, oil paintings, bronzes, furniture. LOC: From London A4 into City, 3 sets of traffic lights to George St., to end of road, left into Gay St. into Queens Sq. Left at bottom of Sq. to Wood St. Queen St. first on right, shop on right. PARK: Easy. TEL: Home — Frome (0373) 830217. VAT: Stan/Spec.

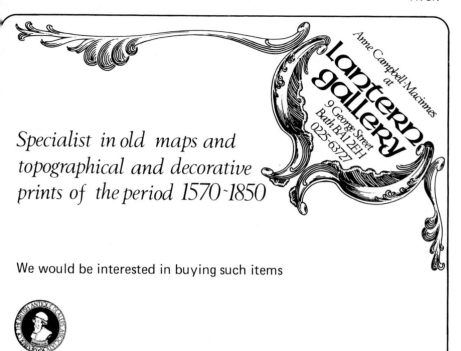
Bath continued

Triangle Antiques
3 Gloucester St., Julian Rd. (E. and C. Sylvester.) Est. 1969. Open Wed. and Sat. 10.30—1 and 2.30—6. SIZE: Medium. *STOCK: General antiques, furniture, decorative items and jewellery.* LOC: Julian Rd. is 3rd left going up Lansdown Hill. PARK: Easy. TEL: 310970. SER: Valuations; restorations (furniture and jewellery).

Trimbridge Galleries
2 Trimbridge. (Mr. and Mrs. A. Anderson.) Est. 1973. SIZE: Small. *STOCK: Watercolours and drawings, £20—£2,000; prints and oil paintings; all 18th—early 20th C.* LOC: Just off lower end of Milsom St. PARK: Easy. TEL: 66390.

R. Vernon
Devonshire House, 143 Wellsway. Est. 1975. *STOCK: Furniture.* TEL: 312495. VAT: Stan.

Walcot Reclamation
108 Walcot St. Est. 1977. Open 8.30—5.30, Sat. 9—5. SIZE: Large. *STOCK: Architectural items and traditional building materials.* PARK: Own and multi-storey nearby. TEL: 66291. SER: Valuations; restorations. VAT: Stan.

Bath continued

Derek and Glenda Wallis
6 Chapel Row, Queen Sq. ABA. Est. 1971. Open 10—5.30. SIZE: Large. *STOCK: General antiquarian, early and Victorian children's books, illustrated; folklore, Canadiana and prints.* LOC: Corner Queen Sq. (city centre). PARK: Easy. TEL: 24677.

Widcombe Antiques and Pine
9 Claverton Buildings, Widcombe. (Mrs. F.J.Winter.) Est. 1972. Open 10.30—5.30. SIZE: Medium. *STOCK: Stripped pine, Georgian and Victorian, £20—£800; brass, copper, especially fenders and fire items.* Not stocked: Books, jewellery and silver. LOC: A36. PARK: Easy at rear. TEL: 28767. VAT: Stan/Spec.

Robert Wilkes Antiques
2 Lansdown Rd. Open Mon. 5 p.m.—8 p.m., Tues. 9—8, Wed. 8—6. SIZE: Large. *STOCK: Small collectable and decorative items, small furniture, 1650—1930, £5—£2,000.* TEL: 315860. VAT: Stan/Spec.

Bath continued

Mark B. Wolfe
2 Nelson Place East. Est. 1962. CL: Thurs. Open 10.30−1 and 2−6. SIZE: Medium. *STOCK: Furniture, Georgian and Victorian, general antiques.* LOC: Top of Walcot St. adjoining London Rd. PARK: Nearby. TEL: 64473. SER: Valuations; buys at auction. VAT: Stan/Spec.

N.S. Woodbridge and C.F. Rogers
15A George St. Open 10−5 Tues. Wed. and Fri. other times by appointment. *STOCK: 18th−19th C paintings and works of art especially topographical works, marine paintings and artifacts, naive and primitive, all subjects.* TEL: 338477 and (02216) 2820.

BATHEASTON
Northend Antiques
The Old Exchange, Brow Hill, Northend. (Mrs. P. Peters.) Resident. Open 10−6. SIZE: Medium. *STOCK: Pottery, porcelain and general antiques.* TEL: Bath (0225) 858206.

BRISTOL   (0272)
Abbas-Combe Pine
4 Upper Maudlin St. (I.R. Sinnott.) Est. 1968. CL: Mon. Open 10−6. SIZE: Medium. *STOCK: Victorian and period English and Welsh pine, £50−£800; toys and clocks.* LOC: Near city centre, at top of Colston St. PARK: Multi-storey nearby. TEL: 299023. SER: Restorations; stripping.

Affordable Arts
76 Colston St. (N. and M. Hankinson.) Open 10−5.30, Sat. 10−4, Mon. and other times by appointment. *STOCK: English watercolours, 1790−1950; contemporary printed and original work by West Country artists, to £400; English oak and country furniture, 1600−1800, £150−£2,000.* TEL: 24838. SER: Framing. VAT: Stan/Spec.

"An Englishman's Home . . ."
56 Stokes Croft. (N. Busek.) Open 9.30−5. SIZE: Medium. *STOCK: Marble and wooden fire surrounds, grates and fenders, bathroom fittings, stained and leaded glass, garden furniture, decorative items.* LOC: City end of Gloucester Rd. 500yds. from Debenhams. PARK: Nearby. TEL: 424257.

Antique Beds
33 Canynge Sq., Clifton. (Mrs. V. Dewdney.) Est. 1973. Open at all times but appointment advisable. SIZE: Small. *STOCK: Four-poster beds, 18th−19th C, £500−£2,000.* LOC: Central Clifton, near zoo. PARK: Easy. TEL: 735134; home − same.

Bristol continued

Belle Vue
48 Alpha Rd, Southville. (A.J. Colley). Open by appointment. *STOCK: Musical boxes, small furniture, metalware, clocks.* TEL: 662010. SER: Musical box restoration, metalware repairs.

Bristol Antique Market
St. Nicholas Markets, The Exchange, Corn St. (M.R. Harper.) Est. 1975. Open: Thurs. and Fri. 9−4. There are 25 dealers offering a wide selection of glass, china, jewellery, metals, porcelain and pottery, furniture. TEL: 20021.

Bristol Guild of Applied Art Ltd.
68/70 Park St. Est. 1908. Open 9−5.30, Sat. 9−5. *STOCK: Furniture, late 19th−20th C.* TEL: 25548.

Bristol Trade Antiques   *Trade Only*
192 Cheltenham Rd. and 451 Bath Rd., Brislington. (L. Dike). Est. 1970. Open by appointment. *STOCK: General antiques.* TEL: 422790 and 717959.

Brunel Antiques
180 Whiteladies Rd., Clifton. (J. Mildred.) Est. 1975. Open 9.30−6. SIZE: Small. *STOCK: Decorative arts, 1860−1930, £50−£500; art pottery and glass, Royal Doulton and Continental figures, art nouveau and art deco, Victorian tiles, arts and craft furniture.* LOC: Main road into city centre from junction 17, M5. PARK: Easy. TEL: 737587; home − same. FAIRS: Victoria Rooms, Bristol and Olympia. VAT: Stan/Spec.

Robin Butler   **BADA**
9 St. Stephen's St. Est. 1978. Open 9.30−5.30, Sat. by appointment. SIZE: Medium. *STOCK: English furniture, 1600− 1820, from £50; wine related antiques, 1750−1880, £10−£2,000; silver, glass, treen and bygones, 1600−1820, £10− £1,000.* **Not stocked: Victoriana, weapons, carpets, shipping goods. LOC: From city centre, St. Stephen's St. is left off Baldwin St. Map showing location sent on request. TEL: 276586; home − 662167. SER: Valuations. FAIRS: West of England. VAT: Spec.**

Cannon Antiques
70 Colston St. (P. Kydd.) Est. 1964. CL: Sun. except by appointment. Open 9−5.30. SIZE: Small. *STOCK: Pewter; brass, especially candlesticks; iron, swords and pistols; copper; all 17th−19th C, £10−£1,000.* LOC: Near Christmas Steps. PARK: Meters. TEL: 299265. SER: Restorations (pewter, brass, weapons, gold and silver); replating. VAT: Stan.

Carnival Antiques   **LAPADA**
'Griffen Court', 19 Lower Park Row. (A.J. Williams.) Est. 1967. Open 9.30−5.30. *STOCK: Glass, china, brass, copper, furniture.* TEL: 297754; home − 835223. SER: Shipping and packing. VAT: Stan/Spec.

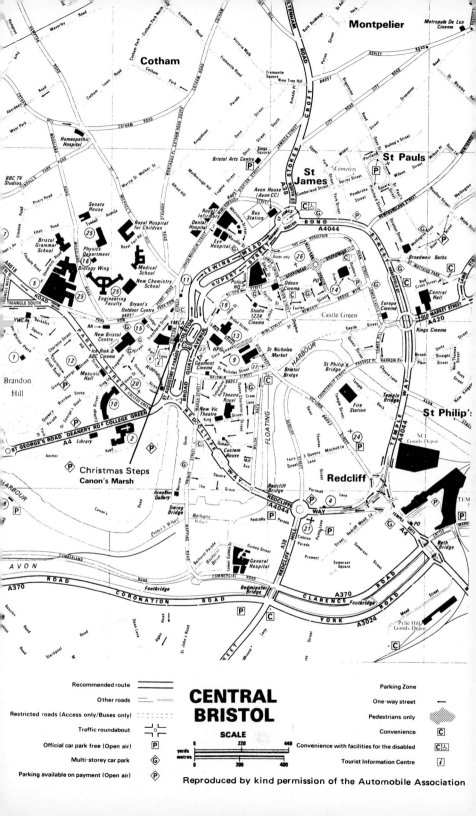

CENTRAL BRISTOL

Bristol continued

Cleeve Antiques
282 Lodge Causeway, Fishponds. (T. and S.E. Scull.) Est. 1978. CL: Wed. Open 9.30—5.30. *STOCK: Furniture and bric-a-brac.* TEL: 658366; home — 567008.

Clifton Antiques Market
26/28 The Mall, Clifton. (A.J.S. Begbie and M.W. Stein.) Est. 1974. CL: Mon. Open 10—6. SIZE: Large. There are 60 dealers at the market offering a wide selection of general antiques and collectors' items, £5—£1,000. LOC: Near Clifton suspension bridge. PARK: Easy. TEL: 741627. Below are listed some of the dealers:—

Ali Baba
Small silver, toys, Victoriana, postcards. TEL: 739429.

Mrs. J. Ball
Porcelain, silver, jewellery. TEL: 734531.

P. Chapman
Architectural items.

Mrs. P. Coles
China, general antiques. TEL: 734698.

S. Coles
Porcelain, brass and copper.

Mrs. M. Durrant
Furniture and small items.

Miss S. Foster
Unusual diamond and gold jewellery. TEL: 734531; home — 738390. VAT: Stan.

Mr. Gibbs
Fine art.

R. Jones
Clocks, watches. SER: Repairs.

Mrs. M. Jubb
General antiques, furniture. TEL: 734698; home — 738520.

Mrs. M.T. Kerridge
Silver, jewellery, small items. TEL: 738504.

Mrs. E. Loud
General antiques. TEL: 734531.

Mac-Smith
(P. Mackenzie-Smith.) *Furniture.* TEL: 735678.

Mrs. M. Middleton
Small items.

Mrs. Morrison
Small items.

Miss O'Sullivan
Period clothing.

Mrs. A. Pluck
Small items. TEL: 734531.

Mrs. M. Potter and Mrs. D. Gregory
China and silver. TEL: 734531.

T. Rawson
Jewellery, coins, medals.

Restoration Workshops
SER: Repairs, restorations, upholstery. TEL: 734738.

Mrs. M. Risdale
Silver, gold, jewellery, china. TEL: 734698.

K. Robinson
Books.

Clifton Antiques Market continued

Mrs. Sharp
Jewellery.

The Silver Stall
Silver frames, silver, general antiques and jewellery. TEL: 734531.

Slade
(Mrs. M. and Miss N. Slade.) *Small general antiques, bric-a-brac, art deco.* TEL: 734698.

Mrs. A. Speight
Art nouveau and art deco. TEL: 734531.

Mrs. Sullivan
General antiques.

Mrs. Tanner
Porcelain and silver.

S. Trickey
Jewellery. SER: Repairs.

Cotham Galleries
22 Cotham Hill, Cotham. (D. Jury.) Est. 1960. Open 9—5.30. SIZE: Small. *STOCK: Furniture, glass, metal.* LOC: From city centre up Park St. into Whiteladies Rd. Turn right at Clifton Down station. PARK: Easy. TEL: 736026. SER: Valuations.

David Cross (Fine Art)
3A Boyces Avenue, Clifton. Est. 1969. Open 9.30—6. SIZE: Medium. *STOCK: Period paintings, marine, Bristol school; drawings and prints, west country, 19th C.* LOC: Between Victoria Sq. and Regent St. PARK: Easy. TEL: 732614. SER: Valuations; restorations (oils, watercolours, frames); buys at auction; framing. VAT: Spec.

Richard Essex Antiques
41 Alma Vale Rd., Clifton. Est. 1969. Open Tues. and Fri. Otherwise appointment advisable. SIZE: Small. *STOCK: General antiques from mid-18th C.* LOC: From Whiteladies Rd. into Alma Rd., 1st right, then 1st left. PARK: Easy. TEL: 733949. VAT: Stan/Spec.

Frocks Antiques
39A Cotham Hill, Cotham. (A.G. Haig-Harrison.) Est. 1977. Open 11—5.30, Wed. 2—5.30. SIZE: Medium. *STOCK: Period clothing, Victoria to 1950s, £5—£45.* LOC: Off Whiteladies Rd., next to antique market. PARK: Easy. TEL: 737461. SER: Costume hire.

Wm. George's Sons Ltd.
52 Park St. Est. 1847. Open 9—5.30. *STOCK: Books, antiquarian and second-hand.* TEL: 276602.

Grey-Harris and Co.   BADA
12 Princess Victoria St., Clifton. Est. 1963. Open 9.30—5.30. *STOCK: Jewellery, Victorian; silver, old Sheffield plate.* TEL: 737365. SER: Valuations. VAT: Stan/Spec.

A.R. Heath
62 Pembroke Rd., Clifton. Open by appointment only. *STOCK: Rare books especially 17th—18th C; English catalogues.* TEL: 741183.

Bristol continued

Michael and Amanda Lewis Oriental Carpets and Rugs
23 Small St. Est.1982. Open 10−5.30, Mon. and weekends by appointment. *STOCK: Oriental carpets and rugs, mainly 19th−20th C, £25−£5,000.* TEL: 24246. SER: Valuations; restorations.

The Mall Gallery
16 The Mall. (C.R.H. Warren.) Est. 1971. CL: Mon; Sat. p.m. Open 10−5.30. *STOCK: Paintings, £300−£2,000; watercolours, £50−£1,000.* TEL: 736263. SER: Buys at auction. VAT: Spec.

The Mall Jewellers
4 The Mall, Clifton. *STOCK: Jewellery, silver, plate.* TEL: 733178. VAT: Stan/Spec.

Michael's Antiques
146 Wells Rd. (M. Beese.) Resident. CL: Sun. TEL: 713943.

Robert Mills   *Trade Only*
16 Clock Tower Yard, Temple Gate. Est. 1969. Open by appointment. SIZE: Large. *STOCK: Furniture, decorative and architectural items, unstripped pine, stained glass, cast iron and church interiors 1780−1900, all £20−£1,000.* LOC: To west of Temple Meads Station, through archway. PARK: Easy. TEL: 556542; home − same. VAT: Stan/Spec.

The Old Curiosity Shop
206 Gloucester Rd., Bishopston. (T. Woodward.) Est. 1964. Open 9.30−1 and 2−5.30. SIZE: Medium. *STOCK: Bric-a-brac, furniture, postcards and cigarette cards, miscellanea, 20p−£150.* LOC: On A38 two miles from city centre. TEL: 48690 or Pilning (045 45) 2448 (any time).

The Oriental Carpet Centre
Maple and Co., 3 Queen's Rd., Clifton. (A.R. Hill). Open 9−5.30, Thurs. 9.30−5.30. *STOCK: Oriental carpets and rugs.* TEL: 290165.

Pelter/Sands Fine Paintings
19 The Mall, Clifton. Open 10−5 or by appointment. *STOCK: Oil paintings, watercolours, 18th−20th C.* TEL: 741830.

Potters Antiques and Coins
14 Park Row. (B.C. Potter.) Est. 1966. Open 10.30−5.30. SIZE: Small. *STOCK: Antiquities; silver, George II to George V, £5−£100; coins, Roman to date, £5−£50; glass, 1750−1870, £5−£75; Georgian brass and copper, commemorative china, fairings, Goss, minerals and fossils.* LOC: Close to Bristol Museum and Art Gallery. PARK: Easy and 50yds. from shop. TEL: 22551. SER: Valuations; buys at auction. VAT: Stan/Spec.

Bristol continued

Quinneys
17 The Mall, Clifton. (B. Richardson.) Est. 1960. Open 10.30−5, Sat. 10.30−1. *STOCK: Jewellery.* TEL: 735877.

Quinneys
54 Park Row. (P. Richardson.) Est. 1960. CL: Sat. p.m. Open 10−4.30. *STOCK: Militaria.* TEL: 273555; home − 730758.

Leigh Rice Antiques   LAPADA
29 The Mall, Clifton. Est. 1975. Open 10−5.30. *STOCK: Furniture, gilt mirrors and decorative items, 18th−19th C.* LOC: Near suspension bridge. PARK: Easy. TEL: 730975. VAT: Stan/Spec.

John Roberts Bookshop
43 Triangle West, Clifton. (J.T. Roberts.) ABA. Est. 1955. Open 9−5.30. SIZE: Medium. *STOCK: Secondhand and antiquarian books, topographical and other prints.* LOC: Just off Queens Rd. shopping centre. PARK: Nearby, multi-storey. TEL: 28568; home − 20600. SER: Picture framing. VAT: Spec.

R.A. Saunders
50 Elmdale Rd., Bedminster. CL: Sun. except by appointment, and Wed. p.m. Open 10−7. *STOCK: Silver, general antiques, jewellery, dolls, prams.* TEL: 662637. SER: Silver and gold plating, bronzing, renovation of jewellery; restorations (furniture, porcelain).

Sedan Chair Antiques
15/19 Portland St., Clifton. (R. Horwood.) Est. 1970. CL: Mon. Open 10−5.30, Sat. 10−1.30. *STOCK: Furniture, general antiques, decorative items.* TEL: 734020.

Triangle Antiques
9 Byron Place, Clifton. (A. Smith, N. Houlton and R. Organ.) Est. 1970. Open 10−5.30. *STOCK: General antiques.* TEL: 292502.

Victoria's Emporium
9 Perry Rd. (V. and L.R. Lewis.) Est. 1966. Open Fri. 1−4. *STOCK: Jewellery.* LOC: Up Christmas Steps and cross road to flight of steps opposite. TEL: 25982. VAT: Stan.

The Vintage Wireless Co. Ltd.
Mail Order Only
Tudor House, Cossham St. Mangotsfield. (T.G. Rees.) Est. 1972. CL: Sat. Open 9−5 by appointment only. SIZE: Medium. *STOCK: Valve radio receivers, vintage valve hi-fi, 1920−1950; radio components, historical and technical data.* LOC: A3174. PARK: Easy. TEL: 565472. SER: Valuations; restorations. VAT: Stan.

Bristol continued

The Wise Owl Book Shop
26 Upper Maudlin St. Open 10.30—1.30 and 2.30—5.30. *STOCK: Antiquarian books especially on music and musicians.* TEL: 22738; evenings — 46936.

CLEVEDON   (0272)
Beech Antiques
Adelaide House, The Beach. (D.A. Coles.) Open by appointment. *STOCK: General antiques, mainly small items.* PARK: Easy. TEL: 876881.

Clevedon Fine Arts Ltd.
(with Clevedon Books)
Cinema Building, Old Church Rd. also at 14 Woodside Rd. Est. 1972. CL: Mon. and Wed. Open 11—5, prior telephone call advisable. *STOCK: Maps, charts, prints, books.* TEL: 875862/872304.

John and Carol Hawley
The Orchard, Clevedon Lane, Clapton Wick. Est. 1972. Open by appointment. *STOCK: Clocks, especially English longcase, bracket, wall and carriage clocks, 1700—1860, £25—£2,000.* TEL: Nailsea (0272) 852052. SER: Valuations; restorations.

CLUTTON
Ian and Dianne McCarthy   *Trade Only*
Arcadian Cottage, 112 Station Rd. Resident. Est. 1958. Open by appointment. SIZE: Medium. *STOCK: Lamps — oil, gas, electric for domestic, industrial, shipping and transport usage; unusual candle lamps; copper and brassware, 17th C to 1920, £5—£500.* PARK: Easy and opposite. TEL: Templecloud (0761) 53188. SER: Valuations; restorations (metalware); cleaning; upholstery; rush seating; spares and lamp-shades; buys at auction (lamps). FAIRS: Birmingham.

FRESHFORD, Nr. Bath
Janet Clarke
3 Woodside Cottages. Open by appointment. *STOCK: Antiquarian books on gastronomy, cookery and wine.* TEL: Limpley Stoke (022 122) 3186. SER: Catalogue issued.

LANGFORD, Nr. Bristol
James R. Cornish
The Old Garden. Est. 1978. Open 9.30—5.30, Sat. and Sun. by appointment. SIZE: Small. *STOCK: Longcase clocks, 1700—1880, £450 —£1,500.* LOC: A38 from Bristol, 4 miles past Bristol Airport turn right to Lower Langford (Yew Tree Motel on corner), the Old Garden is first gateway on right. PARK: Easy. TEL: Wrington (0934) 862704; home — same. SER: Valuations (clocks); restorations (clocks); buys at auction (clocks).
Langford continued

Langford continued

Cottage Antiques
The Old Post Office, Langford Place. (Mrs. M. Hind.) Est. 1972. Open 10—6, Sun. by appointment. SIZE: Small. *STOCK: Oak and country furniture, yew and fruitwood, £25—£1,000; brass, copper, ironwork, £5—£500; porcelain, pottery, treen, country items, £5—£100; all 17th—19th C.* LOC: 12 miles south of Bristol on A38, turn right to Lower Langford, shop 250yds. PARK: Easy. TEL: Wrington (0934) 862597. VAT: Stan/Spec.

MIDSOMER NORTON   (0761)
Somervale Antiques   BADA
                                 LAPADA
6 Radstock Rd. (Wing Cdr. R.G. Thomas.) CINOA. Resident. Open by appointment only. SIZE: Small. *STOCK: English drinking glasses, decanters, cut and coloured Bristol and Nailsea glass, 18th to early 19th C, £10—£2,000; bijouterie, scent bottles.* LOC: On A362 on Radstock side of town. PARK: Easy. TEL: 412686 (24 hrs). SER: Valuations; buys at auction. VAT: Stan/Spec.

PILL   (4 fig. nos.) (027 581)
                 (6 fig. nos.) (0272)
Susan Liddiard Antiques
17 Lodway. Resident. Est. 1970. Open Thurs., Fri. and Sat. 10—5.30, or by appointment. *STOCK: Furniture and clocks, mostly Victorian and Edwardian.* LOC: 1 mile from M5 junction 19. TEL: 2315.

RADSTOCK, Nr. Bath   (0761)
Dela-Ware
1 Waterloo Rd. (H. Dellow.) Open by appointment. *STOCK; General antiques, shipping furniture and bric-a-brac.* TEL: 34628.

WESTON-IN-GORDANO,
Nr. Portishead
Susan Crowe
The Bellows. Usually open but prior telephone call advisable. *STOCK: Porcelain, glass, Staffordshire figures, 18th to early 19th C; small country items, books, pictures, wood engravings.* LOC: Leave M5 at junction 19, A369 for one mile, turn left on to B3124 between Portishead and Clevedon, next to White Hart. PARK: Easy. TEL: Portishead (0272) 843380.

WESTON-SUPER-MARE   (0934)
Clifton House Antiques
67 Clifton Rd. (N.W. & S.M. Adams). Est. 1982. CL: Thurs. Open 10—5.30, Sat. 10—5. Size: Medium. *STOCK: Stripped pine, satin walnut and mahogany, £25—£600.* LOC: Off the seafront. PARK: Easy. TEL: 414415; home — same.

Somervale Antiques

Wing Cdr. R.G. Thomas M.B.E. R.A.F. (Ret'd)
6 Radstock Road
Midsomer Norton, Bath, BA3 2AJ
Tel: Midsomer Norton 412686 (STD 0761)

Shop open daily by appointment. Resident on the premises. 24 hour telephone service. Trains to Bath met by arrangement.

Specialist in 18th and early 19th century English drinking glasses, decanters, cut and coloured Bristol and Nailsea glass, etc. Also, small antique furniture, porcelain, silver, bijouterie, scent bottles, etc.

Member of British Antique Dealers' Association
Member of London and Provincial Antique Dealers' Association

Weston-super-Mare continued

Harwood West End Antiques
LAPADA
13 West St. (A. Harwood.) G.M.C. Est. 1967. Open 9.15—5. *STOCK: General antiques, jewellery, clocks, Victoriana.* TEL: 29874. VAT: Stan/Spec.

Stable Enterprises
The Stables, Clifton Ave. (Mrs. J. Hope.) Est. 1984. CL: Sat. Open 9—5. SIZE: Medium. LOC: Off Clifton/Severn Road. PARK: Easy. TEL: 20906. SER: Restorations (furniture and paintings). Below are listed the dealers trading from these premises:
> **John Butler**
> *Painted chests, paintings.* SER: Restorations (paintings).
> **June Hope**
> *Furniture, 19th C.*
> **David Pike**
> *Furniture, 19th and early 20th C.* SER: Restorations.

Sterling Books
43A Locking Rd. Est. 1966. CL: Thurs. p.m. Open 9—1 and 2—6. *STOCK: Antiquarian and secondhand books, ephemera and prints.* TEL: 25056. SER: Catalogues issued.

Weston-super-Mare continued

Winters' Antiques
LAPADA
Severn Rd. (R.N. and L.B. Winters.) Est. 1967. CL: Sat. p.m. and Thurs. Open 9—12 and 2—4. SIZE: Large. *STOCK: Furniture, clocks and fine art, all periods.* Not stocked: Coins, stamps. LOC: Off sea front. PARK: Easy. TEL: 20118, 23105 and Bleadon (0934) 81460.

WICKWAR see entry under Wotton under Edge, Gloucestershire

WRINGTON   (0934)
Wrington Antiques
Tanners. (P. Kennett.) Est. 1963. *STOCK: Period furniture, country pieces.* TEL: 862200. VAT: Stan/Spec.

YATTON, Nr. Bristol   (0934)
Glenville Antiques
LAPADA
120 High St. (Mrs. S.E.M. Burgan.) Est. 1969. CL: Sun. except by appointment. Open 10.30—5. SIZE: Small. *STOCK: Glass, £5—£150; small furniture, £25—£750; pottery and porcelain, £5—£500, all mainly 19th C; collectors' items, sewing items.* Not stocked: Pewter, guns, antique foreign curios, coins, stamps. LOC: On B3133. PARK: Easy. TEL: 832284. VAT: Stan/Spec.

Bedfordshire

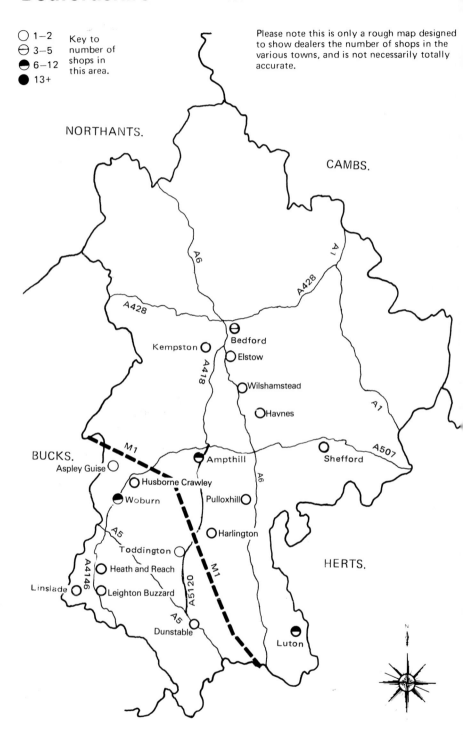

Key to number of shops in this area.
○ 1—2
⊖ 3—5
◐ 6—12
● 13+

Please note this is only a rough map designed to show dealers the number of shops in the various towns, and is not necessarily totally accurate.

NORTHANTS.

CAMBS.

A6

A1

A428

A428

Bedford

Kempston

A418

Elstow

Wilshamstead

A1

Havnes

M1

Shefford

A507

BUCKS.

Aspley Guise

Ampthill

A6

Husborne Crawley

Woburn

Pulloxhill

A5

Harlington

Toddington

HERTS.

A4146

Heath and Reach

A5120

M1

Linslade

Leighton Buzzard

A5

Dunstable

Luton

ROBERT HARMAN ANTIQUES

A trading division of Robert Harman (Fine Art) Ltd

11 CHURCH STREET,
AMPTHILL, BEDFORDSHIRE
Telephone: 0525 402322

*Dealers in fine
Antique Furniture
and Works of Art*

Exhibiting at Café Royal, Chelsea (spring and autumn)
N.E.C. and Olympia.

AMPTHILL (0525)

Ampthill Antiques Centre
Market Sq. (A. and D. Olney.) Est. 1980. CL: Mon. Open 10—5.30 including Sun. SIZE: Large. *STOCK: Furniture, 1700-1950, £20—£1,000; bric-a-brac, £1—£100; copper and brass.* LOC: Town centre. PARK: Easy and at rear. TEL: 403344. VAT: Stan/Spec.

Pat Bently Antiques
7 Kings Arms Yard. Est. 1976. CL: Mon. Open 10.30—4.30; Sun. 2—5. SIZE: Large and barns. *STOCK: Furniture, pine, smalls.* PARK: Easy. TEL: 404939.

Robert Harman Antiques BADA
11 Church St. (R.H. Cannell). Est. 1981. Open 9.30—12.30 and 1.30—5.30, Sun. by appointment. SIZE: Medium. *STOCK: Furniture and works of art, £500—£30,000; papier mâché, tôle, £200—£5,000; all 18th to early 19th C.* PARK: Easy and opposite. TEL: 402322; home — same. SER: Valuations; restorations (furniture); buys at auction (furniture and works of art). FAIRS: Chelsea Spring & Autumn; Olympia; Café Royal; Westminster. VAT: Spec.

Ampthill continued

Ann Roberts Antiques
Kings Arms Yard. Est. 1980. CL: Mon. Open 11—4.30. SIZE: Medium. *STOCK: Furniture, pine, shipping goods, china, brass, early Victorian to 1940; fire accessories including fenders.* Not stocked: Firearms. LOC: Mews off town centre, A507. PARK: 50 yds. TEL: 403394.

Eva Rogers
35 Dunstable St. Est. 1962. CL: Tues. Open 2—5, Sat. all day. *STOCK: General antiques, china, pictures.* PARK: Easy. TEL: Home — Bedford (0234) 854823. VAT: Stan.

S. and S. Timms Antiques Ltd.
LAPADA
16, 18 and 20 Dunstable St. Est. 1976. Open 9—6.30, weekends and other times by appointment. SIZE: Large. *STOCK: Furniture, 1700—1900, £300—£8,000; copper, brass.* LOC: A5120. PARK: Easy. TEL: 403067; home — same. VAT: Stan/Spec.

Ampthill continued

Yesterday's Pine
13 Dunstable St. (N.E. Chesters.) Est. 1975. CL: Mon. and Tues. Open 10—6 and Sun. 2—6. *STOCK: Stripped pine furniture, kitchenalia, decorative ceramics and terracotta.* TEL: 402260. SER: Hand-made furniture from old pine; renovation; stripping; interior and architectural fitments (kitchens, bedrooms, libraries); containers; shipping and packing.

ASPLEY GUISE

Greville Antiques and Design Ltd
The Square. Est. 1970. Open 9—6, Sun. by appointment. SIZE: Large. *STOCK: Oak, 17th—18th C, £250— £5,000; country furniture, decorative items, paintings and carpets, 18th—20th C, £10—£3,000.* PARK: Easy. TEL: Milton Keynes (0908) 584466. SER: Valuations; restorations; buys at auction; interior design. VAT: Stan/Spec.

BEDFORD   (0234)

The Bazaar
96 High St. (F.A. Doyle.) Est. 1970. Open 9.30—5.30. SIZE: Medium. *STOCK: Jewellery, furniture and general antiques, 19th C.* PARK: 100yds. TEL: 54957. VAT: Stan/Spec.

Peter Hill Antiques
193 Goldington Rd. Est. 1965. CL: Sat. p.m. Open 9—1 and 2—6. SIZE: Small. *STOCK: Furniture, walnut, oak, mahogany, 1680—1830; Victorian and Edwardian, all £100—£3,000.* Not stocked: Books, prints, coins, medals. LOC: A428, coming from Cambridge and St. Neots first set of traffic lights on entering Bedford. PARK: Easy. TEL: 52594. SER: Valuations; buys at auction. VAT: Stan/Spec.

Stapleton's Antiques
51 Ford End Rd. (D.H. Stapleton.) Est. 1977. Open 9—5. SIZE: Small and warehouse. *STOCK: General antiques, especially mahogany and oak furniture and clocks, 18th—19th C, £5—£2,000.* LOC: A428. PARK: Easy. TEL: 211087; home — same. SER: Valuations.

DUNSTABLE   (0582)

Chiltern Antiques International
47a High St. South. (J. Hughes.) Open 9.30—5.30. *STOCK: General antiques.* TEL: 602778 and 606751.

Chiltern Jewellery and Coins
47a High St. South. (J. Hughes.) Open 9.30—5.30. *STOCK: Jewellery, coins and medals.* TEL: 606751 and 602778.

ELSTOW

Tavistock Antiques
St. Helena. Est. 1976. Open by appointment. *STOCK: English furniture, 18th—19th C.* PARK: Easy. TEL: Bedford (0234) 44848. SER: Valuations; restorations. FAIRS: Henley-on- Thames, Luton and High Wycombe.

HARLINGTON

Willow Farm Antiques
Willow Farm. (M. and A. Price.) Est. 1974. Open 10—7 every day. SIZE: Large. *STOCK: Country pine, oak and mahogany furniture, £50—£300; bric-a-brac, £5—£50; all 19th C.* LOC: Off Barton Rd. PARK: Easy. TEL: (052 55) 2052; home — same.

HAYNES   (023 066)

Gatward Fine Arts
50 Northwood End Rd. (G.B. Pheazey.) Open by appointment. *STOCK: Mainly 19th C watercolours, some maps and oils.* TEL: Evenings — 348. SER: Restorations; framing.

HEATH AND REACH   (052 523)
Nr. Leighton Buzzard

Charterhouse Antiques
14 Birds Hill. (Mrs. S. Berkeley.) Est. 1978. CL: Thurs. SIZE: Medium. *STOCK: General antiques, £5—£500.* LOC: 1½ miles off A5 on A418 between Woburn and Leighton Buzzard. PARK: 50yds. TEL: 379; home — same. SER: Restorations (metal polishing and repair).

Helton Antiques
26a Birds Hill. (A.H. Cox.) *STOCK: General antiques, shipping goods, collectable items.* TEL: 474.

HUSBORNE CRAWLEY
Nr. Woburn

The Bull Antiques
Open daily, evenings by appointment. *STOCK: Furniture.* LOC: 1 mile from Woburn village. TEL: Ridgmont (052 528) 311.

KEMPSTON

Eva Rogers
Spinney Lodge, Ridge Rd. Est. 1962. *STOCK: General antiques and shipping goods.* TEL: Bedford (0234) 854823; home — same. VAT: Stan.

LEIGHTON BUZZARD   (0525)

David Ball Antique and Fine Art
LAPADA
6—8 Bridge St. (D. and J. Ball.) Est. 1968. CL: Thurs. Open 10—4. SIZE: Large. *STOCK: Furniture, general antiques and watercolours, 17th—20th C, £3—£2,000.* LOC: Bottom of High St. PARK: 100yds. TEL: 382954; home — 210753. SER: Valuations. FAIRS. Luton. VAT: Stan/Spec.

LINSLADE, Nr. Leighton Buzzard

Linslade Antiques and Curios

1 New Rd. (P. and M. Heinsen.) Est. 1978. Open 9.30—6, Sun. 1—5.30. *STOCK: General antiques, bric-a-brac, jewellery, brass, copper, furniture, clocks, fire grates, medals, coins, dolls, pictures.* TEL: Leighton Buzzard (0525) 378348; evenings — Winslow (029 671) 4163.

LUTON (0582)

David Ball Antiques LAPADA

126a Leagrave Rd. SIZE: Large warehouse. *STOCK: General antique and shipping furniture, watercolours, 17th—20th C, £1—£2,000.* TEL: 417560 or Leighton Buzzard (0525) 210753. SER: Valuations. FAIRS: Luton. VAT: Stan/Spec.

Bargain Box

4 and 6a Adelaide St. Open 9—6, Wed. 9—1. *STOCK: General antiques.* TEL: 423809.

Boyle's Furniture

102-104 Hightown Rd. (T. Boyle.) Est. 1974. Open 9.30—6, Wed. 9.30—2. *STOCK: General antiques.* TEL: 32332.

J. Denton (Antiques)

Rear of 440 Dunstable Rd. Est. 1979. CL: Sat. Open 10.15—3, or by appointment. SIZE: Medium. *STOCK: Furniture and small items, Victorian and Edwardian; shipping goods, bric-a-brac.* LOC: Corner of Arundel Rd. and Dunstable Rd. PARK: Easy. TEL: 582726; home — Cheddington (0296) 661471.

Luton continued

Foye Gallery

15 Stanley St. Est. 1960. Open 9.30—5, or by appointment. *STOCK: Engravings, etchings, drawings, watercolours, paintings, maps, books.* TEL: 38487. VAT: Stan.

Knight's Gallery

59—61 Guildford St. (J.C. Knight.) Est. 1973. Open 9—5, Sat. 10—1. SIZE: Small. *STOCK: Watercolours, 19th—20th C, £50—£500.* LOC: Rear of Guildford St. PARK: Easy. TEL: 36266; home — Dunstable (0582) 604142. SER: Valuations; restorations; framing; buys at auction (watercolours). VAT: Stan.

Leaside Antiques LAPADA

44 Gordon St. (T.G. Pepper.) Est. 1968. CL: Wed. p.m. Open 10—6, Sat. till 4. SIZE: Small. *STOCK: Furniture, to 1910; jewellery, silver, porcelain, watches, paintings.* LOC: Opposite old G.P.O. Building behind town hall. TEL: 27957. SER: Repairs (jewellery). VAT: Stan/ Spec.

The Old Pine Loft

Kingham Way, Reginald St. (A. Thompson.) CL: Tues. and lunch-times. SIZE: Medium. *STOCK: Stripped pine including architectural items, to £500.* LOC: Off old Bedford Rd., which runs from the station. PARK: Easy. TEL: 459001. SER: Pine stripping.

PULLOXHILL, Nr. Ampthill

Riches

Unit 2, College Farm. (R.J. Jennings.) CL: Tues. Open 10—1 and 2—4.30. *STOCK: General antiques.* Not stocked: Jewellery, coins, silver. TEL: Flitwick (0525) 717786. SER: Upholstery; framing.

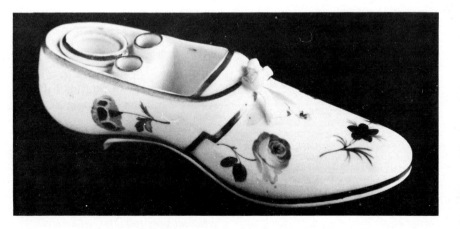

Rockingham porcelain inkstand, 5ins. long. Mark on base in red Cl. 2. Date c.1830. Courtesy the City of Sheffield Museum. From "A Story of Ceramic Shoes", **Antique Collecting,** November 1985.

ATRIUM ANTIQUES

10 minutes from M1 motorway
Leave at exits 12 or 13　　**WOBURN**　　60 minutes from London
5 minutes from A5

Specialising in Georgian and Regency furniture. Small selection of oak and country furniture and decorative items.

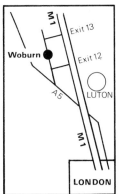

Open Monday to Saturday 9.30 - 5.45, Sunday 2 - 5.45.　Resident on premises.

ATRIUM ANTIQUES LTD 19 Market Place, Woburn MK17 9PZ. Tel (052-525) 444.

SHEFFORD
F. and M. O'Dell
35/37 High St. Est. 1869. CL: Wed. p.m. Open 9–6. *STOCK: English and Continental furniture, clocks and pictures, 17th–19th C, £5–£2,500; general antiques.* TEL: Hitchin (0462) 813940/813132. SER: Valuations; restorations. VAT: Stan/Spec.

Secondhand Alley
2-4 High St. Open 9–5.30, Sat. 9–5. *STOCK: Shipping furniture, bric- a-brac.* PARK: Easy. TEL: Hitchin (0462) 814747. VAT: Stan.

TODDINGTON　　　　　(052 55)
Nr. Dunstable
Cobblers Hall Antiques
119/121 Leighton Rd. (A.G. and N.E. Huckett.) Est. 1974. Open by appointment only. *STOCK: English porcelain, 18th to early 19th C, £25–£250. Georgian and early Victorian writing boxes.* PARK: Easy. TEL: 2890. FAIRS: Bath, Cheltenham, Thoresby Hall, High Wycombe.

WILSHAMSTEAD, Nr. Bedford
Manor Antiques
The Manor House, Cottonend Rd. (Mrs. S. Bowen.) Est. 1976. Open 10–5, Sun. by appointment. SIZE: Large. *STOCK: Furniture, 19th C to Edwardian, £50–£2,000; copper and brass, Georgian to Victorian; lighting and oil lamps, Victorian to 1920s; general antiques.* LOC: Just off A6, 4 miles south of Bedford. PARK: Own. TEL: Bedford (0234) 740262; home – same. SER: Restorations (furniture); buys at auction. FAIRS: Luton. VAT: Stan/Spec.

WOBURN　　(3 fig. nos.) (052 525)
　　　　　　　　(6 fig. nos.) (0525)
Atrium Antiques
19 Market Place (Mrs. A. Fluitman.) Resident. Open 9.30–5.45, Sun. 2–5.45. *STOCK: Georgian furniture, early oak, porcelain including Delft, prints, paintings, rugs and decorative items including Oriental furniture.* PARK: Easy. TEL: 444. VAT: Spec.

George Large Gallery
13/14 Market Place. Open 10–1 and 2–5.30, Sun. 11–1 and 2–5. *STOCK: British art from 1900.* TEL: 658.

"Mary Pickford", date unknown. From "A Year of Romance" in **Antique Collecting,** January 1986.

Woburn continued

Questor
13/14 Market Place. (P. Parkinson-Large.) Open 10—1 and 2—5.30, Sun. 11—1 and 2—5. *STOCK: Furniture, £50—£1,000; porcelain, jewellery, small antiques.* TEL: 658.

Christopher Sykes Antiques   BADA
LAPADA
The Old Parsonage. (C. and M. Sykes.) Est. 1949. Articles on corkscrews, shop signs and sundials. Open 9—6, Sun. 12—6. SIZE: Large. *STOCK: Furniture, 17th to early 19th C, £30—£2,000; scientific instruments, microscopes, sundials, telescopes, sextants, pewter, candlesticks, £20—£2,000; oil paintings (English Schools), watercolours, porcelain, glass, silver, 19th C, £20—£2,000; pottery, wooden boxes, carvings, treen, wine related items and corkscrews, toys, games, metalware.* **LOC: In main St. opposite Post Office on A50. PARK: Easy. TEL: 259 and 467. SER: Valuations; mail order, catalogues available £4 each. VAT: Stan/Spec.**

The Woburn Abbey Antiques Centre
Est. 1967. CL: 25th—26th Dec. (1986) inclusive. Open every day (including Bank Holidays) 11—5 Nov. to Easter; 10—6 Easter to Oct. There are over 50 established dealers at this centre which has 40 shops and 12 showcases, including a Bygones Gallery of 6 shops specialising in Victoriana and Edwardiana. LOC: On A5. Follow signs to Woburn Abbey and after entering grounds, follow signs to Antique Centre. PARK: Easy. TEL: 350. Below are listed the dealers at this centre:

Antelope Antiques
Georgian and Victorian silver.
Beacon Gallery
18th—19th C mahogany furniture.
Blakehall Antiques
19th C mahogany and walnut furniture, light fittings, mirrors and decorative items.
C.K. Antiques
Country furniture, 18th and 19th C; decorative items, brass and copper.
Chapel Antiques
Furniture, 19th C; porcelain, decorative items.
Mary Chaperlin Antiques
18th—19th C English porcelain, miniature and mahogany furniture, prints.
Mrs. E.M. Cheshire   **BADA**
17th—19th C oak and mahogany furniture; decorative items.
Cottage Antiques
18th—19th C oak and mahogany furniture; decorative items.
Martin Cowling
18th—19th C painted furniture, porcelain, mirrors, decorative items, engravings.

The Woburn Abbey Antiques Centre continued

Margaret de Monti Ladds
18th and 19th C oak, mahogany furniture, mirrors and decorative items.
Duncan House Antiques
18th—19th C mahogany furniture; decorative items.
E. and A. Antiques
English and Continental porcelain, 18th and 19th C; watercolours, decorative items.
G.W. Ford and Son Ltd.   BADA
Georgian furniture, decorative items, mirrors.
Sylvia Grant
Small decorative items, silver and boxes.
Granville Antiques
Georgian oak and mahogany furniture, mirrors, decorative items.
Irene Greenman
Victorian and Edwardian furniture; Doulton ware and decorative items.
Robert Harman Antiques
18th—19th C mahogany and walnut furniture, mirrors, boxes and decorative items.
Hereward Antiques
Georgian mahogany furniture, decorative items.
Irene Hollings Antiques
Furniture and decorative items.
Jean Kershaw   LAPADA
17th—19th C oak and mahogany furniture, brass, copper ware and country items.
Lapwing Antiques
18th—19th C furniture and early porcelain.
Lennard Antiques   LAPADA
Furniture, oak, walnut and mahogany, 17th—19th C; prints, 19th C.
Gerald Lewis Antiques
18th—19th C oak and mahogany furniture, clocks and barometers.
Mrs. Jeanne McPherson
Porcelain, decorative items, silver and glass and small 18th and 19th C furniture.
Marling Fine Arts
Oil paintings and watercolours, 19th to early 20th C; Doulton, Moorcroft and art pottery, glass; Edwardian furniture.
Sybil Mendoza
19th C mahogany furniture, paintings and decorative items.
Christopher Perry Antiques
18th—19th C oak and mahogany furniture, mirrors, boxes, decorative items.
Ron Perry   LAPADA
Art nouveau, Victoriana and Edwardian furniture, unusual decorative items, light fittings.
Rosemary Pratt Antiques
Furniture, treen, lignum vitae, 18th and 19th C; decorative items.
John Rapley Antiques
17th—19th C oak and mahogany furniture; decorative items.

The Woburn Abbey Antiques Centre continued

E. Robertson
18th—19th C English porcelain.
Terry Scudder Antiques
18th—19th C oak and mahogany furniture, Delft tiles, porcelain, watercolours.
Sovereign Art
Decorative items, porcelain and unusual items, period furniture and silver.
Sparrow Antiques
17th—19th C oak and mahogany furniture; brass, copper, decorative items and clocks.
Timms Antiques
18th—19th C oak, walnut and mahogany furniture and porcelain.
S. and S. Timms Antiques
Georgian and Victorian oak and mahogany furniture.
Paul Treadaway Antiques
Georgian mahogany furniture, mirrors, engravings, decorative items.
Tudor Antiques
Georgian oak and mahogany furniture, decorative items.
Underwood Antiques
18th—19th C mahogany furniture.
Weaver Antiques
18th and 19th C furniture; Oriental decorative items.
Courtney Wiles
18th—19th C mahogany, rosewood and walnut furniture.
Margaret Williams
18th—19th C mahogany and walnut furniture; brass ware, silver and plate; boxes, decorative items, mirrors.
J. Wolff and Son Ltd.   LAPADA
Mahogany furniture, 18th and 19th C; French furniture, 19th C; mirrors, decorative items.

Woburn Fine Arts
12 Market Pl. (Z. Bieganski.) Est. 1983. CL: Thurs. Open 2—5.30, Sat. and Sun. 11—1 and 2—5.30 or by appointment. SIZE: Medium. *STOCK: Post-impressionist paintings, 1880-1940; European paintings, 17th—18th C; British paintings, 20th C; all £1,000—£2,000.* PARK: Easy. TEL: 624. SER: Valuations; restorations (oils and water-colours).

Yesterdays Pine
Old Chapel, Leighton St. (N.E. Chesters.) Est. 1975. CL: Sat. Open 8—5. *STOCK: Stripped pine furniture, kitchenalia, decorative ceramics.* TEL: 526. SER: Handmade furniture from old pine; renovation; stripping; interiors and architectural fitments (kitchens, bedrooms, libraries); containers; shipping and packing.

WOBURN SANDS
see Buckinghamshire

Woburn Abbey Antiques Centre

One of the largest Antiques Centres under one roof in Great Britain and the most original — with 40 independent shops and over 50 established dealers, many of whom are members of L.A.P.A.D.A. and B.A.D.A. — is situated in the magnificent South Court of Woburn Abbey.

We are pleased to offer the dealer and private collector a wide range of Antiques: Clocks, Lamps, Porcelain and Glass, Paintings, Prints, Georgian Furniture, Jewellery, Georgian Silver, Painted Furniture, Works of Art, etc., at competitive prices.

Within one hour's drive of Oxford, Cambridge, Birmingham and London (via M1, Exit 12 or 13 signposted Woburn Abbey). Trains from St. Pancras to Flitwick or Euston to Bletchley can be met by prior arrangement. Dealers admitted free and their park entrance refunded at the Antiques Centre. Visiting dealers' car park adjacent to the Antiques Centre.

OPEN EVERY DAY OF THE YEAR EXCEPT AS SPECIFIED
Including Sundays and Bank Holidays
Easter to October 10 — 6 p.m. November to Easter 11 — 5 p.m.
Closed for Christmas (1986) 25th–26th December

WOBURN ABBEY ANTIQUES CENTRE, WOBURN ABBEY BEDFORDSHIRE. MK43 0TP

Telephone Woburn (052525) 350

Berkshire

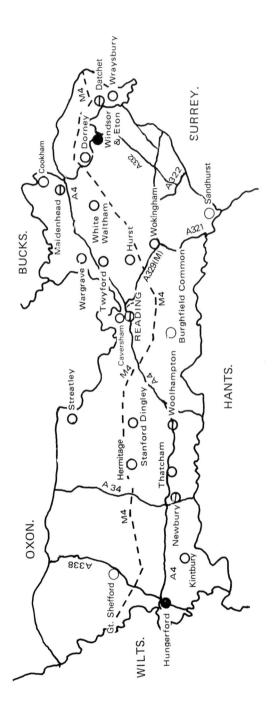

Please note this is only a rough map designed to show dealers the number of shops in the various towns, and is not necessarily totally accurate.

Key to number of shops in this area.

○ 1–2
◐ 3–5
◑ 6–12
● 13+

BURGHFIELD COMMON (073 529)
Nr. Reading
Graham Gallery
(J. Steeds.) Est. 1976. Open by appointment at any time. SIZE: Medium. *STOCK: English watercolours, £20—£300; English oil paintings, £40—£8,000; English prints, £10—£100; all 19th and early 20th C.* LOC: 4 miles from Reading on Burghfield road. PARK: Easy. TEL: 2320. SER: Valuations; restorations (cleaning, framing).

CAVERSHAM, Nr. Reading
Michael G. Baldwin Antiques
36 Silverthorne Drive. Open by appointment only. *STOCK: Small furniture, china.* TEL: Reading (0734) 477868.

The Collectors Gallery
8 Bridge St. Caversham Bridge. (T.B. and H.J. Snook). Open 10—5, Sat. 10—4, Sun. and other times by appointment. SIZE: Medium. *STOCK: Watercolours, £100—£1,000; oil paintings, £100—£1,500; collectables; all 18th—19th C.* TEL: Reading (0734) 483663/8. SER: Restorations (paintings); buys at auction (paintings).

COOKHAM
Phillips and Sons
The Dower House. Open by appointment. *STOCK: British paintings including Staithes group, late 19th to early 20th C, £100—£5,000.* TEL: Bourne End (062 85) 29337. SER: Valuations; restorations (pictures); framing. VAT: Spec.

DATCHET
Datchet Antiques
Silver Cottage, The Green. (Mrs. L.A. Batty.) Est. 1968. CL: Mon. p.m. and Wed. p.m. Open 10—1 and 2.15—5. SIZE: Small. *STOCK: General antiques, Victoriana, collectors' items, furniture, silver, plate, porcelain, pottery.* PARK: Easy. TEL: Slough (0753) 45726.

Datchet continued

Manor House Antiques　　　LAPADA
The Manor House, The Green. (Mrs. J.A. Gibbs.) Est. 1962. CL: Wed. Open 10—5. SIZE: Large. *STOCK: Furniture, 1750—1850, £50—£5,000; general furniture and decorative items.* Not stocked: Jewellery. LOC: Period house overlooking village green. PARK: Easy. TEL: Slough (0753) 42164/41460. SER: Valuations; restorations (upholstery). FAIRS: Olympia, Chelsea, High Wycombe. VAT: Stan/Spec.

Charles Toller　　　BADA
20 High St. (C. and J. Toller.) Est. 1936. Jane Toller — books on papier mâché, miniature furniture, work by prisoners of war, treen, country furniture, and samplers. Open 9.30—5. SIZE: Large. *STOCK: Oak, fruitwood, walnut, yewtree, furniture, 17th—18th C; treen, samplers.* Not stocked: Mahogany furniture, porcelain. LOC: Between the station and river. PARK: Own. TEL: Slough (0753) 42903. VAT: Spec.

DORNEY, Nr. Eton
The Old School Antiques
　　　LAPADA
(Lt. Col. V. and Mrs. A. Wildish.) Resident. Est. 1969. Open 10—5.30 or by appointment. SIZE: Large. *STOCK: Porcelain and English furniture, pre-1850; general antiques.* Not stocked: Items dated post-1850. LOC: On B3026, junction 7 from M4. PARK: Own. TEL: Burnham (062 86) 3247. SER: Valuations; buys at auction. VAT: Spec.

ETON
see Windsor and Eton

GREAT SHEFFORD (048 839)
Nr. Hungerford
Ivy House Antiques
Wantage Rd. (J. Hodgson.) Est. 1972. Open 10—6. *STOCK: Country and pine furniture, kitchenalia, collectors' items, Victoriana.* LOC: A338, 10 minutes from Hungerford towards Wantage.

Richard Barder Antiques
Specialists in Fine Clocks
Fine Longcase, Bracket, Lantern & other antique clocks
(Richard Barder is author of English Country Grandfather Clocks)
Crossways House, Hermitage, Nr. Newbury, Berkshire
Telephone: Hermitage (0635) 200295
We are 3 minutes M4 Junction 13

HERMITAGE, Nr. Newbury (0635)
Richard Barder Antiques
Crossways House. (R.C.R. and P.A. Barder.) Open 9.30−5.30, Sat. 9.30−5, Mon. by appointment. SIZE: Medium. *STOCK: Clocks − English longcase, bracket, lantern, Act of Parliament, regulator and marine chronometers, barometers, 17th−19th C, £150−£15,000; antiquarian and other horological books.* LOC: On B4009. PARK: Easy. TEL: 200295; home − same. SER: Valuations; restorations (clocks); buys at auction (clocks). VAT: Stan/Spec.

HUNGERFORD (0488)
Ashley Antiques
129 High St. Est. 1974. Open 10−5. Appointment advisable. SIZE: Medium. *STOCK: Furniture and general antiques.* LOC: Main street. PARK: Easy. TEL: 82771. SER: Restorations (furniture).

Mary Bellis Antiques BADA
Charnham Close. (E. Willson and D. Gill.) Open 10−5, appointment advisable. *STOCK: Early English and Continental oak furniture and works of art.* PARK: Easy. TEL: 82620. VAT: Spec.

Below Stairs
103 High St. (S. and L. Hofgartner.) Est. 1974. Open 10−6, Sun. 2−6. SIZE: Large. *STOCK: Kitchen items, country and craftman's tools, £10−£100; garden furniture and decorative garden items; stripped and other bedroom furniture and beds, mainly 19th C, £50−£500,* LOC: Main street. PARK: Easy. TEL: 82317; home − same. SER: Valuations. VAT: Stan.

Bow House Antiques
3-4 Faulkner Sq., Charnham St. (L.R. Herrington.) CL: Thurs. p.m. Open 10−5. SIZE: Medium. *STOCK: Small period and 19th C furniture.* LOC: A4. PARK: Easy, own. TEL: 83198; home − 84319. VAT: Spec.

Hungerford continued

The Collectors Shop
27 and 32 Charnham St. (Mrs. V. Lawson) Est. 1977. Open 9.30−5.30. *STOCK: General antiques, pine, furniture, porcelain, collectors' items, including art deco, toys, tins, advertising.* PARK: Easy. TEL: 83519; home − West Hanney (023 587) 536.

The Craftsman
16 Bridge St. (C.J.B. and E.A. Jarrett.) Est. 1965. CL: Thurs. Open 10−5. SIZE: Large. *STOCK: Pine and country furniture.* PARK: Easy. TEL: 82262. VAT: Stan/Spec.

Dolls and Toys of Yesteryear at Bow House Antiques
3-4 Faulkner Sq., Charnham St. (D.M. Herrington.) Open 10−5, Thurs. 10−1. SIZE: Medium. *STOCK: Dolls, £25−£1,600; toys, £5−£250; dolls' houses, £50+; dolls' house accessories, £1−£100; all 19th to early 20th C.* PARK: Easy. TEL: 83198; home − 84319. SER: Valuations (dolls); restoration (dolls). FAIRS: Cumberland (London) Doll; Portman.

The Fire Place (Hungerford) Ltd.
Hungerford Old Fire Station. Charnham St. (E.B. and E.M. Smith). Est. 1976. Open 10−1.30 and 2.15−5. SIZE: Large. *STOCK: Fireplace furnishings and metalware.* LOC: On A4. PARK: Opposite. TEL: 83420. VAT: Stan/Spec.

Thomas Franklin Antiques
28 Charnham St. Est. 1958. Open 9.30−5.30. *STOCK: 18th to early 19th C English and Continental furniture, country items, treen, longcase clocks, oil paintings, pewter.* TEL: 82404.

Hungerford continued

Bibi Harris Antiques *Trade Only*
The Saleroom, Church St. (Mrs. B. Harris.)
Est. 1963. Open 9—6, Sun. and evenings by
appointment. SIZE: Large. *STOCK: Continental and decorative furniture, some smalls.*
LOC: Next to fire station. PARK: Own. TEL:
83382. VAT: Stan/Spec.

Hungerford Arcade
High St. (Wynsave Investments Ltd.) Est.
1972. Open 9.30—5.30, Sun. 10—6. This
arcade consists of over 70 stallholders selling
a wide range of general antiques and period
furniture. PARK: Easy. TEL: 83701.

Roger King Antiques **LAPADA**
111 High St. (Mr. and Mrs. R.F. King.) Est.
1974. Open 9.30—5.30. SIZE: Large.
*STOCK: Furniture, 1730—1880, £50—
£1,000; china, 19th C; oil paintings.* Not
stocked: Silver, jewellery. LOC: Opposite
Hungerford Arcade. PARK: Easy. TEL: 82256.
VAT: Spec.

Derek McIntosh and Company
2 Bridge St. Est. 1977. Open 9—6, Sun. by
appointment. SIZE: Medium. *STOCK: Furniture, £50—£1,000; prints, £50—£300; both
18th—19th C.* TEL: 83777. VAT: Stan/Spec.

Hungerford continued

Medalcrest Ltd.
Charnham House, 29/30 Charnham St. (D.H.
Farrow.) Est. 1981. Open 9.30—5.30, Sat.
10—6, Sun. by appointment. SIZE: Large.
*STOCK: 18th-19th C furniture; barometers,
longcase, bracket and carriage clocks, metalware, small items.* TEL: 84157. VAT: Spec.

The Old Malthouse **BADA**
(P.F. Hunwick.) Est. 1963. Open 9.30—1 and
2—5.30. SIZE: Large. *STOCK: Furniture, 18th
and early 19th C walnut and mahogany.
English porcelain; clocks; barometers.* Not
stocked: Orientalia. LOC: A338, left at Bear
Hotel, shop is approx. 120yds. on left, just
before a bridge. PARK: In front of shop. TEL:
82209. SER: Valuations; buys at auction.
FAIRS: Chelsea, Park Lane, Snape, Brighton.
VAT: Spec.

Pandora's Box
Bridge St. (Mrs. J. Gleave.) Est. 1971. Open
10—4.30. SIZE: Medium. *STOCK: General
antiques, collectors' items, prints, watercolours and Staffordshire figures.* LOC: From
Reading take A4, turn left (A338) — 100yds.
on right. PARK: 100yds. at Bear Hotel.

Hungerford continued

Riverside Antiques
Charnham St. (M. Stockland.) Est. 1976. Open 10—5.30, Sun. by appointment. SIZE: Large. *STOCK: General antiques; furniture, decorative items.* LOC: On A4 just before The Bear Hotel. PARK: Easy. TEL: 82314. VAT: Stan/Spec.

Styles
12 Bridge St. (P. and D. Styles.) Est. 1974. Open 10—5.30, Sun. and other times by appointment. SIZE: Medium. *STOCK: Silver, antique, Victorian and secondhand; silver plate and small collectables.* PARK: Easy. TEL: 83922; home — same. SER: Valuations; finder service. VAT: Stan/Spec.

Trinket Box
1 Bridge St. (R.F. Raisey.) Est. 1972. CL: Mon. and Thurs. Open 10—5. *STOCK: Victoriana, collectors' items, bric-a-brac.* TEL: 83311; home — Kingsclere (0635) 298742.

Victoria's Bedroom
4 Bridge St. (J.A. and M.A. Wallbank-Fox.) CL: Mon. Open 9—5.30; Fri. and Sat. 9—6. *STOCK: Brass and iron beds.* TEL: 82523.

HURST, Nr. Reading
Peter Shepherd Antiques
Penfold, Lodge Rd. Est. 1962. Open by appointment only. *STOCK: Glass, rarities and books.* TEL: Twyford (0734) 340755. VAT: Stan/Spec.

KINTBURY, Nr. Newbury   (0488)
Kintbury Antiques and Fine Art
1 Station Rd. (J.P. Fane). Est. 1984. Open 10—1 and 2.30—5.30, Sat. 10—1 and 2.30—5. Sun. by appointment. SIZE: Small. *STOCK: Watercolours, drawings and prints, 1830—1930, £20—£1,500; porcelain and pottery, 18th—19th C, £5—£500; small furniture, 18th—19th C, £20—£2,000; textiles, 19th to early 20th C, £1—£500.* LOC: In centre of village, opposite garage. PARK: Easy. TEL: 58830; home — Inkpen (04 884) 357. SER: Restoration; framing; cleaning (watercolours, prints).

MAIDENHEAD   (0628)
Jaspers Fine Arts Ltd.
36 Queen St. (T.L. Johnson.) Open 9—6. *STOCK: Maps and prints especially of the Thames Valley; clocks.* TEL: 36459. SER: Repairs (clocks); restorations (paintings, frames).

Maidenhead continued

Lowe and Pomfrett Ltd.
63 Queen St. (D.J. Lowe.) Est. 1950. CL: Sat. May—Oct., and Thurs. Open 9.30—5. SIZE: Medium. *STOCK: Georgian and Victorian jewellery, silver, china, furniture.* Not stocked: Large furniture. LOC: On M4 from London, proceed under railway bridge, round one-way system and take turning on right. Shop is on left. PARK: 75yds. Broadway exit from multi-storey (50yds.) into Queen St.; shop 25yds. on left. TEL: 20759. SER: Valuations; buys at auction. VAT: Stan.

Samman Antiques
71 St. Marks Rd. (F. Daniel). Open 10—5.30. SIZE: Large. *STOCK: General antiques — furniture, porcelain, glass, metalware, period silver and jewellery, nautical and scientific instruments.* LOC: ½ mile off A4. PARK: Easy. Tel: 23058; home — 72974

Widmerpool House Antiques
Boulters Lock. Open by appointment only. *STOCK: English furniture, 18th—19th C; oil paintings, watercolours, prints; porcelain, glass, silver, 19th C.* TEL: 23752.

NEWBURY   (0635)
John Baker Antiques
20 George St., Kingsclere. Est. 1959. Open 9—7, Sat. 10—6. SIZE: Medium. *STOCK: Mahogany, 18th C, £200—£2,000; oak, 17th—18th C, £100—£1,600; desks, Victorian, £240—£800.* Not stocked: Shipping goods. LOC: A339. PARK: Easy (at side). TEL: Kingsclere (0635) 298744. SER: Valuations; restorations (furniture); buys at auction. VAT: Stan/Spec.

Griffons Court
Highclere. (Mr. and Mrs. T.C. Jackson.) Est. 1966. Open by appointment. SIZE: Medium. *STOCK: Fine Georgian furniture, desks, small bookcases, unusual small decorative items, fine paintings.* LOC: 5 miles from Newbury. On A343 at crossroads just inside village boundary. PARK: Easy. TEL: 253247. VAT: Stan/Spec.

Jonathan McCreery
Speen House, Speen. Est. 1967. Open by appointment only. *STOCK: Furniture, 18th—19th C.* TEL: 33680. VAT: Stan/Spec.

READING (0734)

Ann Bye Antiques
88 London St. (F.M. and A. Easton.) Est. 1968. CL: Wed. p.m. Open 9—5.30. *STOCK: Furniture, 18th—19th C; pine and country items, porcelain, small silver, clocks.* TEL: 582029.

S.J. Evans
69 London St. CL: Wed. p.m. Open 10—5.30. *STOCK: General antiques, Victoriana, furniture, glass, silverware, swords, guns, weapons.* TEL: 550968.

P.D. Leatherland Antiques
68 London St. Open 9—5. *STOCK: Furniture including Victorian, china and metalware.* TEL: 581960.

Reading Emporium
1a Merchants Place (off Friar St.). Est. 1972. Open 9—5. There are 13 stalls trading from this address selling *a wide range of items including Victoriana, advertising items, jewellery and bottles.* TEL: 590290.

William Smith (Booksellers) Ltd.
35-39 London St. Est. 1832. Open 9—5.30, Mon. 10—5.30. *STOCK: Antiquarian books.* TEL: 595555. VAT: Stan.

SANDHURST (058 085)
Nr. Camberley, Surrey

Berkshire Metal Finishers Ltd.
Swan Lane Trading Estate. (J.A. and Mrs. J. Sturgeon.) Est. 1957. Open 8—1 and 2—6, Sat. 8—1 and 2—4, Sun. 9—1. SIZE: Large. *STOCK: Brass, copper and steel metalware; silver-plate.* LOC: Off A30 towards Wokingham, 1¼ miles turn left into Swan Lane, estate 1st turning right, last factory near car park. PARK: Easy. TEL: Yateley (0252) 873475. SER: Restorations (metalware polishing and lacquering).

STANFORD DINGLEY, Nr. Reading
Eliot Antiques BADA
(Lady Cathleen Hudson.) Est. 1974. CL: Mon. Open 10.30—1, Sun. and afternoons by appointment. SIZE: Small. *STOCK: English enamels, 18th C, objets de vertu, 18th—19th C, £80—£1,500.* Not stocked: Furniture, pictures. PARK: Easy. TEL: Bradfield (0734) 744649; home — Bradfield (0734) 744346. VAT: Spec.

Guy Bousfield

The Buyer and Vendor of GEORGIAN furniture

58 THAMES STREET, WINDSOR, BERKS.
Tel. Windsor 864575

(Sometimes closed on Mondays)

STREATLEY, Nr. Reading
Vine Cottage Antiques
High St. (B.R. and P.A. Wooster.) CL: Sun. except by appointment. Open 10—5.30. *STOCK: Furniture and general antiques, 18th—19th C.* TEL: Goring-on-Thames (0491) 872425. SER: Restorations; re-upholstery (especially buttoned items). VAT: Spec.

THATCHAM (0635)
Bowman Antiques.
Bluecoats (S.M. Cooke). Open 10—5. *STOCK: General antiques.* PARK: Easy. TEL: 65901.

John Whybrow
The Crown House, High St. Est. 1955. Open by appointment. SIZE: Medium. *STOCK: Furniture, 1760—1850, £20—£500; silver and plate, 1760—1900, £10—£1,000; Persian rugs, 1850—1940, £60—£1,000; violins, £20—£500; porcelain, jewellery.* LOC: From London on A4, turn left into Thatcham Broadway, 40yds. on turn right into High St. PARK: Easy. TEL: 63335.

TWYFORD (0734)
Biggs of Maidenhead BADA
Hare Hatch Grange. (F.R. and M.H. Stamp.) Est. 1866. CL: Mon. SIZE: Large. *STOCK: English furniture, 18th C; clocks, paintings, objets d'art, pre-1830, all from £300.* LOC: Leave M4 junction 8/9, take A423 to A4, turn left 3½ miles on right. PARK: Easy. TEL: Wargrave (073 522) 3281. VAT: Stan/Spec.

Twyford Antiques Centre
1 High St. (G. Spence.) Est. 1980. CL: Wed. Open 9.30—5.30 including Sun. There are 20 dealers at this market selling a wide range of general antiques and furniture. LOC: Centre of Twyford. Just off A4 between Reading and Maidenhead. PARK: 100yds. TEL: 342161. VAT: Stan/Spec.

VIRGINIA WATER
see Surrey

WARGRAVE (073 522)
Millgreen Antiques
84-86 High St. (K. Chate, J. Connell and 12 other dealers) . Open Wed.—Sun. other times by appointment. SIZE: Large. *STOCK: Furniture, Georgian—Edwardian; small items, china, glass, metal.* PARK: Nearby. TEL: 2955. SER: Restoration (furniture); silver plating; metal polishing.

WHITE WALTHAM
Nr. Maidenhead
Braemar Antiques Ltd. LAPADA
Old RAF Mess, Waltham Rd. (J.C. White.) CL: Sat. Open 9—4. *STOCK: Furniture, 18th—19th C.* TEL: Littlewick Green (062 882) 3741. VAT: Stan/Spec.

WINDSOR AND ETON (0753)
This STD code applies to Windsor and Eton

Roger Barnett
91 High St., Eton. Est. 1975. TEL: 867785.

Guy Bousfield BADA
58 Thames St., Windsor. Est. 1958. CL: Some Mon. Open 8.45—5. SIZE: Medium. *STOCK: Georgian furniture, 1720—1800, £100—£2,000.* LOC. Precinct on castle side of Windsor Bridge. PARK: Easy. TEL: 864575. VAT: Spec.

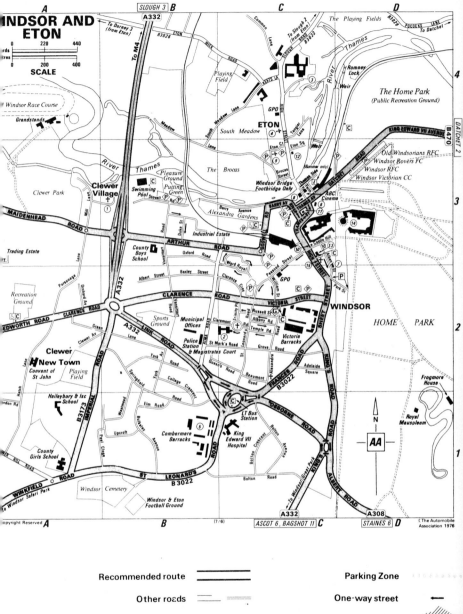

WINDSOR AND ETON

SCALE

Map Legend

Recommended route	————
Other roads	— — —
Restricted roads (Access only/Buses only)	- - - - -
Traffic roundabout	⊥ ○ ⌐
Official car park free (Open air)	P
Multi-storey car park	Ⓖ
Parking available on payment (Open air)	◈P
Parking Zone	
One-way street	←
Pedestrians only	▨
Convenience	C
Convenience with facilities for the disabled	C ♿

Windsor and Eton continued

Eatons of Eton Ltd.   LAPADA
62/63 High St., Eton. (P. and P. Eaton.) Est. 1960. Open 8—5, Sun. 2—6. SIZE: Large. *STOCK: Furniture, 1680—1900, to £4,000; silver, 1730—1900, to £1,500; paintings, £50—£2,000.* PARK: 50yds. almost opposite. TEL: 860337; home — Maidenhead (0628) 27413. SER: Valuations. VAT: Spec.

Eton Antique Bookshop
88 High Street, Eton. TEL: 855534.

Eton Gallery Antiques
116 High St., Eton. (J. Smith.) CL: Mon. and Wed. p.m. Open 10.30—1 and 2—5, Sun. p.m. by appointment. *STOCK: Furniture, 18th—19th C.* TEL: 865147 or 860963.

Gaby Goldscheider
29 Temple Rd., Windsor. Est. 1973. Open by appointment. SIZE: Medium. *STOCK: Books, £2—£150; prints, £1—£8; toys and juvenilia, £2—£150, all 18th—20th C.* LOC: Off St. Leonards Rd. — continuation of Peascod St., near the castle. PARK: Easy. TEL: 861517. SER: Valuations; buys at auction (books and toys).

Derek Greengrass Antiques
                                    LAPADA
34 Frances Rd., Windsor. Est. 1969. CL: Mon. SIZE: Small + warehouse. *STOCK: Furniture, bric-a-brac and collectors' items, shipping furniture.* PARK: Easy. TEL: 865627; home — Bracknell (0344) 50254. VAT: Stan.

Griffin Gallery
89 Grove Rd., Windsor. Est. 1976. *STOCK: Goss and crested china, paintings, watercolours, prints.* TEL: 853658. SER: Restorations.

Windsor and Eton continued

Hoy Antiques
17 Kings Rd., Windsor. CL: Mon. Open 11—6, Sun. 1—6. *STOCK: Pine, mahogany, silver and china.*

Lupin Antiques Ltd.
134 Peascod St., Windsor. Open 9.30—1 and 1.30—5.30. *STOCK: 19th C. Victorian and art nouveau furniture; silver, porcelain and glass.* TEL: 856244. VAT: Spec.

J. Manley
27 High St., Eton. Est. 1891. Open 9—5. *STOCK: Watercolours, old prints.* TEL: 865647. SER: Restorations; framing, mounting.

Peter J. Martin
40 High St., Eton. Est. 1963. CL: Sun. Open 9—1 and 2—5. SIZE: Large and warehouse. *STOCK: Furniture, shipping goods, £5—£2,000; metalware, £10—£500, all from 1800.* LOC: A332. Middle of Eton High St. PARK: 50yds. opp. TEL: 864901; home — 863987. SER: Restorations; shipping arranged; buys at auction. VAT: Stan/Spec.

Mostly Boxes
52B High St., Eton. (G.S. Munday.) Est. 1977. CL: Mon. Open 10.30—5. SIZE: Small. *STOCK: Mainly wooden boxes, caddies, writing slopes, 18th-19th C, £30—£250.* LOC: Centre of High St. PARK: 100 yds. TEL: 850232; home — Ashford (07842) 59304. SER: Restorations (boxes). VAT: Stan.

Mostly Furniture
92 High St., Eton. (G.S. Munday). CL: Mon. Open 10.30—5. SIZE: Small. *STOCK: Victorian and Georgian furniture, boxes.* PARK: Nearby. TEL: 858470; home — Ashford (07842) 59304. SER: Restorations. VAT: Stan.

O'Connor Brothers
59 St. Leonards Rd., Windsor. *STOCK: Furniture and general antiques.* TEL: 866732. VAT: Stan.

Tony L. Oliver
Longclose House, Common Rd., Eton Wick. Est. 1959. Open 9—5 by appointment only. *STOCK: Militaria, medals, badges, insignia especially German 1914—1945; civilian and military vehicles, 1914—1955.* TEL: 862637.

F. Owen
113 High St., Eton. Est. 1959. *STOCK: Military relics.* TEL: 860054.

Windsor and Eton continued

John A. Pearson Ltd.   BADA
127—128 High St., Eton. (Mrs. J.C. Sinclair
Hill.) Est. 1902. Open 9.30—1 and 2—5.30,
but appointment advisable. SIZE: Large.
STOCK: *English furniture, 1700—1850, £50—*
£8,000; oil paintings, 17th—19th C, £50—
£7,000; decorative objects. **Not stocked:**
Items after mid-19th C. LOC: From London
turn off M4, exit 5, past London Airport —
approach only via Datchet/Slough (Windsor
River Bridge closed). PARK: Easy (2 hours).
TEL: 860850. VAT: Spec.

"Roberts"
12a Thames St., Windsor. Est. 1964. Open
9.30—5.30, Sun. 10—6.30. SIZE: Small.
STOCK: *Silver and plate, 18th—20th C, £5—*
£1,000. LOC: Opposite Curew Tower,
Windsor Castle. PARK: Station — Riverside.
TEL: 866268

Studio 101 and Turk's Head Antiques
98 and 101 High St., Eton. (A. Cove.) Est.
1959. Open 10.30—5.30, some Sun. p.m.
SIZE: Medium. STOCK: *Mahogany furniture,*
some 18th C, mainly 19th C, £50—£1,000;
brass, silver plate, 19th C, £10—£200; lace
and jewellery. LOC: Walk over Windsor Bridge
from Windsor and Eton Riverside railway
station. PARK: Public, at rear of premises.
TEL: 863333.

Maurice Taffler Ltd.
17 High St., Eton. Est. 1945. Open 10.30—
5.30. STOCK: *Miniature chairs, decorative*
items, general antiques. TEL: 864711. VAT:
Stan.

Times Past Antiques Ltd.   LAPADA
59 High St., Eton. (P. Jackson.) MBHI. Est.
1970. Open 10—6, Sun. 12—5. SIZE:
Medium. STOCK: *Clocks and watches, £100—*
£3,000; furniture, all 18th—19th C; silver,
19th C, £5—£500. PARK: Reasonable. TEL:
857018; home — same. SER: Valuations;
restorations (clocks and watches); buys at
auction (clocks). VAT: Stan/Spec.

Victoria Antiques
21 Kings Rd., Windsor. Open 11—6. STOCK:
Jewellery, silver, furniture and objets d'art.
TEL: 857611.

Windsor Antique Gallery
45 Thames St., George V Place, Windsor.
Open 10—6, 7 days. STOCK: *General*
antiques especially china and glassware,
Doulton, Gallé pottery and glass, £5—
£15,000. TEL: 852965 and 866445. SER:
Valuations.

Windsor and Eton continued

Windsor Antiques and Design
LAPADA
80 High St., Eton. (A. and H. Procter.) CMBHI.
Est. 1967. Open 10.30— 5.30, Sun. 2.30—
5.30. SIZE: Large. STOCK: *Longcase and wall*
clocks, furniture, 18th—19th C. LOC: Slough
East exit from M4 westbound. PARK: Nearby.
TEL: 860752; home — same. SER: Exporting;
interior design consultants. VAT: Stan/Spec.

Windsor Antiques Market and Fleamarket
Jennings Yard, Thames Ave., Windsor. Open
Wed—Sun and Bank Holidays 11—6. There
are 30 dealers at this market selling a wide
range of general antiques. TEL: 866445.

WOKINGHAM   (0734)
Paul Thomas Fine Paintings
27 Glebelands Rd. Est. 1975. Open by
appointment. STOCK: *Oil paintings and water-*
colours, 19th—20th C. TEL: 794671. SER:
Valuations; restorations; commissions and
finder. VAT: Spec.

WOOLHAMPTON, Nr. Reading
(0734)
The Bath Chair
Woodbine Cottage, Bath Rd. (J.A. Lewzey
and D. Eckersley.) Est. 1980. Open 10—6.
SIZE: Small. STOCK: *Furniture, silver, general*
antiques, £5—£5,000. LOC: A4. PARK: Easy.
TEL: 712225. SER: Valuations; buys at
auction.

The Old Bakery
Bath Rd. (D.R. Carter.) Est. 1969. Resident.
STOCK: *Furniture, objets d'art, collectors'*
items, general antiques. TEL: 712116.

Old Post House Antiques
Bath Rd. (V.A. Liddiard.) Est. 1975. Open
10—6. SIZE: Small. STOCK: *Furniture, 18th—*
19th C, £50—£300; bric-a-brac and brass-
ware, all periods, £2—£100. LOC: On A4.
PARK: Easy. TEL: 712294; home — 713460.

WRAYSBURY   (078 481)
Wyrardisbury Antiques
23 High St. (C. Tuffs.) Est. 1978. Open Tues.,
Wed., Fri. and Sat. 10—5; other times by
appointment. SIZE: Small. STOCK: *Clocks,*
£25—£2,000; small furniture, tea caddies,
boxes and watercolours, £10—£500; por-
celain, £30—£500. LOC: A376 from Staines
by-pass (A30) or from junction 5 M4/A4 via
B470, then B376. PARK: Easy. TEL: 3225.
SER: Restorations (clocks).

Buckinghamshire 212

Please note this is only a rough map designed to show dealers the number of shops in the various towns, and is not necessarily totally accurate.

Key to number of shops in this area.

- ◯ 1–2
- ⊖ 3–5
- ◒ 6–12
- ● 13+

NORTHANTS.

Olney
Stoke Goldington
A509
M1
A422
A422
A413
A422
Tingewick
Buckingham
A5130
Wavendon
A5
Milton Keynes
Woburn Sands
Little Brickhill
Steeple Claydon
Charndon
A413
Whitchurch
A41
Weedon
Waddesdon
A418
Wingrave
BEDS.
Brill
Chilton
Aylesbury
A41
A418
A413
Long Crendon
Haddennam
Wendover
HERTS.
A4010
Monks Risborough
Princes Risborough
Great Missenden
A416
Chesham
OXON.
Naphill
Amersham
A404
A413
High Wycombe
Penn
Chalfont St. Giles
Stokenchurch
Loudwater
Beaconsfield
A40
Chalfont St. Peter
Marlow
Gerrards Cross
Denham
Village
Farnham Common

N

BERKS.

AMERSHAM
(4 & 5 fig. nos.) (024 03)
(6 fig. nos.) (0494)

Benedict Jewellers   LAPADA
37 High St. (W.C. Bennett and K.J. Smith.)
Open 10.30—5.30. *STOCK: Jewellery, silver
plate and glass.* TEL: 22803. SER: Valuations;
repairs (jewellery); re-stringing.

Crispin Antiques
10 The Broadway. (Mrs. S. Newfield.) Est.
1958. Usually open from 9.30 but appointment advisable. *STOCK: Porcelain, 17th—
18th C, including Meissen and Belleek;
furniture, early 18th—19th C, rare pieces.*
PARK: Easy. TEL: 21779. SER: Valuations;
restorations (porcelain and furniture); buys at
auction (porcelain and furniture). VAT: Stan/
Spec.

The Cupboard Antiques
80 High St. (N. Lucas). Open 9—5. *STOCK:
Georgian, Regency and early Victorian furniture.* PARK: Easy. TEL: 22882.

Fantiques
18-20 Hill Ave. (J. Stent, K., M. and P. Raven
and C. McNally.) Est. 1981. Open all day Sat.
and weekday mornings. SIZE: Small. *STOCK:
Porcelain and glass, 19th C to art deco; fans,
prints and maps, 18th—19th C, all £5—
£1,000; small furniture, £50—£1,000;
Victoriana, from £5; mirrors, art deco, £25—
£50.* LOC: In road opposite station. PARK:
Easy. TEL: 5571. SER: Restorations (fans);
framing. FAIRS: Some London hotel.

''Mon Galerie''
49 High St. (A.R. and D.E. Guy.) Est. 1975.
CL: Thurs. *STOCK: Watercolours, engravings,
19th—20th C, £20—£500.* PARK: Outside
shop. TEL: 21705; workshop (0296) 661884.
SER: Valuations; restorations, mounting,
framing.

Michael Quilter
38 High St. Est. 1970. Open 10—5. *STOCK:
General antiques, stripped pine, copper, brass.*
PARK: Easy. TEL: 3723. VAT: Stan.

Sundial Antiques   LAPADA
19 Whielden St. (A. and Mrs. M. Macdonald.)
Est. 1970. CL: Thurs. Open 9.30—5.30.
SIZE: Small. *STOCK: English and European
brass, copper, metalware, fireplace furniture,
18th—19th C, £1—£500; small period
furniture 1670—1870, £25—£1,500; oil
lamps 1840—1914, £10—£350; decorative
items, 1750—1910, £5—£500; weapons
1600—1860, £5—£1,000; pottery, porcelain, £2—£500; curios, pre-1914, £5—
£100.* Not stocked: Jewellery, clocks, coins,
oil paintings, stamps, books. LOC: On A404,
in Old Town 200yds. from High St. on right;
from High Wycombe, 700yds. from hospital
on left. PARK: Easy. TEL: 7955. VAT: Stan/
Spec.

Amersham continued

Town Hall Antiques
25 High St., Old Amersham. (Mrs. D. Krolle.)
Est. 1976. Open 10.30—5, Mon. 2.30—5,
Thurs. 10—1. SIZE: Small. *STOCK: Small
furniture, £25—£400; porcelain, glass, silver
and plate, some Victorian jewellery, £5—
£300; all George IV, William IV, Victorian and
Edwardian; pictures and prints, 18th C and
Victorian, £10—£100.* LOC: By Old Town
Hall. PARK: Easy. TEL: Home — Gerrards
Cross (0753) 882331. SER: Valuations; resto-
rations (silver plating).

Ingram Warwick Ltd. and
Antique Lovers Coterie
20A High St. Est. 1912. CL: Mon. Open
9.30—5.30. SIZE: Medium. *STOCK: Jewellery, £5—£5,000; objets d'art, £5—£500;
maps, prints, and books, £1.50—£350.* LOC:
A413. PARK: Easy. TEL: 21033. SER: Valuations. VAT: Stan/Spec.

AYLESBURY   (0296)

Morton Harvey Antiques
21 Wendover Rd. (J.M. Harvey.) Resident.
CL: Thurs. Open 10—5.30. *STOCK: 18th C
and early Victorian furniture, watercolours;
general antiques.* PARK: Rear of premises.
TEL: 84307.

Weatherheads Bookshop Ltd.
58 Kingsbury. (N.F. Weatherhead.) ABA. Est.
1921. Open 9—5.30. SIZE: Large. *STOCK:
Books, 16th—20th C, 10p—£1,000.* Not
stocked: Other items. LOC: A41. PARK: ½
hour nearby, nearest park 200yds. TEL:
23153. SER: Valuations; buys at auction.

BEACONSFIELD
(4 and 5 fig. nos.) (049 46)
(6 fig. nos.) (0494)

Christopher Cole (Fine Paintings) Ltd.
1 London End. Est. 1975. Open 9.30—5.30.
*STOCK: Oil paintings and watercolours, 19th
and early 20th C.* TEL: 71274.

Grosvenor House Interiors
51 Wycombe End, Beaconsfield Old Town.
(T.I. Marriott.) Est. 1970. Open 9—1 and 2—
5.30. SIZE: Large. *STOCK: 18th—19th C
furniture, especially Victorian; oils and watercolours, fireplaces and accessories.* PARK:
Outside shop. TEL: 77498. SER: Restorations
(marble); metal polishing and lacquering,
interior architectural design, fireplace specialists. VAT: Stan/Spec.

Angela Hone   LAPADA
Open by appointment only. *STOCK: Watercolours, 1850—1920.* TEL: Marlow (062 84)
4170.

Beaconsfield continued

Norton Antiques
56 London End. (T. and N. Hepburn.) Est. 1966. CL: Wed. Open 10−1 and 2−5.30. SIZE: Medium. *STOCK: Furniture 1680− 1850, £25−£1,200; paintings (oil and watercolour), 19th C, £15−£500; clocks, 18th− 19th C, £50−£1,200; woodworking and craftsman's hand tools.* LOC: On left shortly after entering Beaconsfield Old Town from the east. PARK: Easy. TEL: 3674. SER: Valuations; buys at auction; pine stripping. FAIRS: High Wycombe, Oxford. VAT: Stan/Spec.

Old Curiosity Shop
49 Wycombe End. (D. Barker.) CL: Mon. Open 9.45−1 and 2.30−5.30. *STOCK: General antiques, small furniture and interesting items.* TEL: 4473.

Period Furniture Showrooms
49 London End. (E.W.A. and R.E.W. Hearne.) Est. 1965. CL: Wed. Open 9−1 and 2−5. SIZE: Large. *STOCK: Furniture, 1700−1900, £50−£2,000; longcase clocks and others, 1700−1800, £500−£2,000; copper.* LOC: A40 Beaconsfield Old Town. PARK: Own. TEL: 4112. SER: Restorations (furniture). VAT: Stan/Spec.

Charles Sale Ltd.
Crosskeys Gallery, 18 Wycombe End. (W.A. and E.D. Sale.) Est. 1850. Open 9.30−4.30. SIZE: Medium. *STOCK: Furniture, 18th−19th C.* TEL: 4012. VAT: Spec.

The Spinning Wheel
86 London End. (Mrs. M. Royle.) Est. 1945. CL: Wed. Open 10−5. *STOCK: English furniture, 18th−19th C, mahogany and oak items, porcelain, glass.* TEL: 3055; home − Chalfont St. Giles (024 07) 3294. VAT: Stan/Spec.

BRILL, Nr. Aylesbury   (0844)
Brill Antiques
(D. Urch.) Est. 1984. CL: Mon. Open 10.30−5.30, Sun. 2−5.30. *STOCK: General antiques, furniture and books.* LOC: Village centre, off B4011. PARK: Easy. TEL: 237996; home − Long Crendon (0844) 208204.

BUCKINGHAM   (0280)
Aladdin of Buckingham
1 Nelson St. CL: Mon. Open 12−7 including Sun. *STOCK: General antiques, 14th C− 1930.* TEL: 815649. SER: Restorations.

Buckingham Books
20 Market Hill. *STOCK: Architectural books.* TEL: 812800.

Flappers
2 High St. (M. Noone.) Open 9.30−1 and 2−5. *STOCK: Stripped pine, oak and mahogany furniture; lace, linen; 1920s and 1930s costume.* TEL: 813115; evenings − (0604) 740234.

Buckingham continued

Adrian Hornsey Ltd.   Trade Only
Chandos Rd. Est. 1967. *STOCK: General antiques, shipping goods.* TEL: 816363.

CHALFONT ST. GILES   (024 07)
Aquarelle of St. Giles
8 The Lagger. (E. and D. Parkinson.) Est. 1968. Open any time by appointment. *STOCK: Watercolours and drawings, 1750− 1940, £15−£1,000.* Not stocked: Oil paintings. LOC: Take road to Seer Green from village centre, on left hand side shortly after passing Milton's Cottage. PARK: Easy. TEL: 5592. VAT: Spec.

Bucks House
High St. (Mrs. B. Buck.) Est. 1981. Open 10−5. SIZE: Small. *STOCK: Furniture, paintings and decorative art, 19th−20th C, £10− £300.* LOC: On A413. PARK: Nearby. TEL: 5711.

CHALFONT ST. PETER
Paul Jones Antiques
10 Market Place. Est. 1970. CL: Thurs. Open 9.30−5. *STOCK: Furniture, brass and general antiques.* LOC: From A40 take A413, first left at 2nd roundabout, 1st right at shopping centre, up hill on right. PARK: Easy. TEL: Gerrards Cross (0753) 883367. SER: Valuations; restorations (furniture). VAT: Stan/ Spec.

CHARNDON, Nr. Bicester
Courtney Wiles Antiques Ltd.
The Old Longhouse. Est. 1975. Open by appointment only. *STOCK: Furniture.* TEL: Steeple Claydon (029 673) 8045. SER: Valuations; restorations (furniture, clocks, upholstery, caning, porcelain.) VAT: Stan/Spec.

CHESHAM   (0494)
Albert Bartram
177 Hivings Hill. Est. 1968. Usually open, preferably by appointment. *STOCK: Metalwork, 16th−17th C; pewter, small oak furniture, early needlework, pottery, £10− £1,000.* LOC: 1 mile from town centre on the road to Bellingdon. PARK: Easy. TEL: 783271. VAT: Spec.

Peter Farrow
Hillbury House, Missenden Rd. Est. 1976. Open by appointment. SIZE: Small. *STOCK: Victorian furniture, £5−£1,000.* PARK: Easy. TEL: 784138; home − same. SER: Valuations; restorations (furniture); polishing; buys at auction (furniture). VAT: Stan.

For Pine
4 Broad St. (D. Hutchin.) CL: Thurs. Open 9.30−5. *STOCK: Pine.* TEL: 776119.

Chesham continued

Omniphil Ltd.
Germains Lodge, Fullers Hill. (A.R.T. Muddiman.) Est. 1953. CL: Sat. Open 9—5.30 or by appointment. SIZE: Wareouse. *STOCK: Rare prints on all subjects and Illustrated London News from 1842.* TEL: 771851.

Queen Anne House
57 Church St. (Miss A.E. Jackson.) Est. 1918. Open Wed., Fri. and Sat. 9.30—5.30. SIZE: Large. *STOCK: Furniture, decorative and furnishing pieces, porcelain figures, other china, glass, silver plate, copper, brass, Victoriana, clocks, Persian rugs.* Not stocked: Silver, weapons, jewellery. PARK: Easy. 50yds. in same street. TEL: 783811. SER: Buys at auction. VAT: Stan/Spec.

CHILTON, Nr. Aylesbury
Pamela Streather
Stable Cottage. CINOA. Est. 1964. Open weekends by appointment. *STOCK: Works of art; furniture, 16th—17th C.* TEL: (0844) 208859. VAT: Spec.

DENHAM VILLAGE
Antiquities
Est. 1978. Open Tues., Wed. and Fri. 12—5, Sat. 12—5.30, Sun. by appointment. *STOCK: Victorian—Edwardian furniture; pictures, clocks, silver and jewellery.* LOC: Off A40, 1 mile M25. PARK: Easy. TEL: Denham (0895) 833340 or Northwood (092 74) 25125.

Margaret Elmes Antiques
Denham Gallery. (Mrs. M. Elmes.) Est. 1965. Open 10—12.30 and 2.30—5.30 or by appointment. SIZE: Large. *STOCK: English furniture, pottery and porcelain, glass and metal, late 18th and early 19th C.* LOC: Off A40, 2 miles from Uxbridge. PARK: Easy. TEL: Denham (0895) 832244. SER: Restorations (furniture); upholstery. FAIRS: Little Chelsea.

FARNHAM COMMON (028 14)
Noel Gregory Gallery
4 The Broadway. Open 9—1 and 2—6. *STOCK: Victorian watercolours.* TEL: 5522.

A Thing of Beauty
5 The Broadway. (D.M.H. and J.P. Craven.) Est. 1973. Open 10.30—1 and 2.30—5, Wed. and Sat. 10.30—1. SIZE: Medium. *STOCK: English furniture, 1800—1910, £75—£1,000; general antiques, some silver, from 1800, £20—£150.* Not stocked: Maps, books, paintings. LOC: Opposite The Foresters public house in High St. PARK: Easy. TEL: 2099; home — (06286) 61711. SER: Valuations; buys at auction (furniture).

GERRARDS CROSS (0753)
Aristocat LAPADA
19 Packhorse Rd. Est. 1970. CL: Wed. p.m. *STOCK: Silver and plate, jewellery, metalware.* TEL: 888011. SER: Valuations; metal polishing; also commission sales agency. VAT: Stan/Spec.

GREAT MISSENDEN (024 06)
E. and R. Cooper LAPADA
99A High St. Est. 1977. Open 10—1 and 2—5, Mon., Thurs. and Sun. by appointment. SIZE: Small. *STOCK: English watercolours, 1750—1950, £150—£2,000; small English furniture, 1700—1900, £100—£5,000.* LOC: Off main Aylesbury road. PARK: Easy. TEL: 6791; home — (0296) 624783. SER: Valuations; buys at auction (watercolours and furniture). FAIRS: Olympia. VAT: Spec.

Dahl and Son
92 High St. (R. and T. Dahl, Mrs. A. Hansen.) Est. 1982. CL: Thurs. and Sun. except by appointment. Open 9—1 and 2—5. SIZE: Large. *STOCK: Fine furniture, 18th C to Regency; glass, china and decorative items.* PARK: Own at rear. TEL: 6427.

Gemini Antiques
68a High St. (M. Crossley, S. Jordan.) Open 9—1 and 2.15—5. *STOCK: General antiques.* PARK: Easy. TEL: 6203.

Heritage Antiques and Restorations Ltd.
36b High St. (J. and S. Wilshire). Est. 1974. Open 9—5.30, Sun. 10—1. SIZE: Small. *STOCK: Clocks and small furniture, 18th—19th C, £50—£2,500; curios, £5—£100.* LOC: A.413. PARK: Easy. TEL: 5710. SER: Valuations; restorations; buys at auction. VAT: Stan/Spec.

W.E. Hill and Sons BADA
Havenfields. Est. 1762. CL: Sat. Open 10—4. *STOCK: Stringed instruments.* TEL: 3655. VAT: Stan/Spec.

The Pine Merchants
52 High St. (D.J. Peters.) CL: Thurs. Open 9.30—5.30. *STOCK: Pine.* TEL: 2002.

Regency Antiques
Great Missenden Arcade, 76 High St. CL: Thurs. Open 10—5. SIZE: Medium. *STOCK: General small antiques, jewellery, porcelain, clocks, furniture, collectors' items, silver.* LOC: Off main Aylesbury Rd. out of Amersham. PARK: Nearby. TEL: 2330.

M.V. Tooley, CMBHI
The Guild Room, The Lee. Est. 1960. Open Sat. 9—1 and 2—5. *STOCK: Clocks, especially longcase and Vienna.* TEL: 024020 463. SER: Restorations, spare parts (clocks).

Paul Treadaway Antiques
99 High St. Open 10—5. *STOCK: English period furniture, pre-1830; engravings and prints.* TEL: 2171.

HADDENHAM (0844)

Sally Turner　　　LAPADA
Top Barn, Church End. Open by appointment.
STOCK: Period furniture and general antiques.
TEL: 290346. VAT: Spec.

H.S. Wellby Ltd
The Malt House, Church End. (C.S. Wellby.)
Est. 1820. CL: Sat. Open by appointment
9—6. *STOCK: 18th and 19th C paintings.*
TEL: 29036. SER: Restorations. VAT: Spec.

HIGH WYCOMBE (0494)

Beechdean Bygones
The Old House, North Dean, Hughenden.
(Mrs. J. Olink.) Est. 1963. Open 9—6. SIZE:
Small. *STOCK: Victoriana, jewellery, Oriental
items, glass, porcelain, brass, copper; small
furniture, paintings, unusual items.* Not
stocked: Arms, large furniture, coins, longcase
clocks, books. LOC: Coming from High
Wycombe to North Dean, through village,
premises are on left out of village. PARK:
Easy. TEL: Naphill (024 024) 2143.

Browns' of West Wycombe
Church Lane, West Wycombe. Est. Pre-
1900. CL: Sat. Open 8—5.30. *STOCK: Furniture.* LOC: On A40 approximately 3 miles
west of High Wycombe on Oxford Rd. PARK:
Easy. TEL: 24537. SER: Restorations and
hand made copies of period chairs.

R. Tyzack Ltd.　　　*Trade Only*
Kitchener Rd. (R.E.W. and P.A. Hearne, E.R.
Bates.) Est. 1973. CL: Sat. and Sun., except
by appointment. Open 9—12.30 and 1.30—
4.30. SIZE: Large. *STOCK: Furniture, 18th—
19th C, £100—£500; objects, 19th C, £25—
£150.* LOC: West part of town, off Desborough Ave. PARK: Easy. TEL: 23265 and
20993; home — (08447) 205. SER: Restorations (furniture). VAT: Stan/Spec.

Tony Winterburn
41 Castle St. Open 9.30—5. SIZE: Small.
*STOCK: General antiques, Victoriana, china,
glass, collectors' items.* PARK: On forefront.
TEL: 22630. VAT: Spec.

LITTLE BRICKHILL

Baroq Antiques
Watling St. (B. Dawson.) Est. 1968. CL: Mon.
Open 2—5, Sat. 1—5 or by appointment.
SIZE: Small. *STOCK: Pottery and porcelain,
19th C blue and white transfer ware, £3—
£200; silver, £2—£150; clocks, £40—£700,
all 18th—19th C; paintings £10—£300; lace
bobbins; furniture, £50—£1,000.* Not
stocked: Reproductions. LOC: A5. Coming
from Dunstable on right hand side in middle of
village. PARK: Easy. TEL: Gt. Brickhill (052
526) 401; home — Gt. Brickhill (052 526)
561. SER: Buys at auction. VAT: Stan/Spec.

LONG CRENDON (0844)

Crendon Antiques
1 The Square. CL: Mon. and Wed. p.m.
*STOCK: Country antiques, pine; garden stat-
uary and furniture.* LOC: Village centre. PARK:
Nearby. TEL: 208962. VAT: Stan/Spec.

Hollington Antiques
Bicester Rd. (J. and V. Asta.) Est. 1966. Open
seven days a week. SIZE: Medium. *STOCK:
Books, china, glass, curios, militaria, pictures.*
LOC: B4011. Next to 'The Chandos Arms'.
PARK: Easy. TEL: 208294. VAT: Stan.

LOUDWATER

Rudge Books　　　*Mail Order Only*
Swanspool. *STOCK: Secondhand and out of
print books on natural history and gardening.*
TEL: Rickmansworth (0923) 774110.

MARLOW
(4 and 5 fig. nos.) (062 84)
(6 fig. nos.) (0628)

Bishop (Marlow) Ltd.
8 and 10 West St. (P. and L. Bishop.) Est.
1942. Open by appointment. *STOCK: English
furniture, porcelain, 18th—19th C; early
English figures.* LOC: Centre of village. PARK:
At rear. TEL: 3936. SER: Valuations.

David Messum　　　BADA
(Fine Paintings)
The Studio, Lords Wood, Marlow Common.
Est. 1960. Open by apppointment. SIZE:
Large. *STOCK: Pictures, 18th—19th C,
English schools.* TEL: 6565/6. SER: Valu-
ations; restorations (oil paintings). VAT: Stan/
Spec.

MILTON KEYNES (0908)

Jeanne Temple Antiques
Stockwell House, Wavendon. Est. 1968.
SIZE: Medium. *STOCK: Furniture, Regency
and Victorian, coloured glass, oil lamps,
Victorian and Edwardian light fittings, brass
and copper ware.* LOC: Just off main Woburn
Sands to Newport Pagnell road. TEL: 583597.

MONKS RISBOROUGH

Tudor Antiques
(G. and B. Thornley.) Resident. Est. 1962. CL:
Wed., except by appointment. Open 9.30—6.
SIZE: Medium. *STOCK: Furniture, oak and
mahogany, £250—£3,000; decorative prints;
all 18th C.* LOC: On A4010. PARK: Easy. TEL:
Princes Risborough (084 44) 3523. FAIRS:
British International, Birmingham; Olympia,
Kensington and West London. VAT: Stan/
Spec.

NAPHILL   (024 024)
Nr. High Wycombe

A. and E. Foster   BADA
"Little Heysham", Forge Rd. Est. 1972. Open by appointment only. SIZE: Small. *STOCK: English and Continental treen, bygones, metalwork, pre-1830.* Not stocked: Silver, glass, porcelain. LOC: From High Wycombe take the A4128. Take first left after Hughenden Manor; about 2 miles. PARK: Easy. TEL: 2024. FAIRS: Chelsea, Fine Arts Fair, Olympia, Grosvenor House. VAT: Spec.

OLNEY

Antiquarium
Rose Court, Market Place. (C.J. and J. Flack.) Resident. Est. 1970. Open 9—6, Sun. 2—6. SIZE: Small. *STOCK: 19th C and Edwardian furniture, £25—£300; prints, from £6; glass, ceramics, 19th C; books, 19th C to early 20th C.* Not stocked: Militaria, medals, coins. LOC: Leave M1 by exit 14 for Newport Pagnell. PARK: Easy. TEL: Bedford (0234) 712077. SER: Framing. VAT: Stan/Spec.

Olney continued

Market Place Antiques
(J. and A. McGuire.) Est. 1975. Open 10—5.30, Sun. 2—5.30. *STOCK: Furniture, longcase, bracket and wall clocks, silver, jewellery, copper, brass, pewter, pine furniture and porcelain.* PARK: Easy. TEL: Bedford (0234) 712172. SER: Valuations; restorations (clocks, porcelain and furniture — re-caning, re-rushing, upholstery); buys at auction. VAT: Stan/Spec.

Alan Martin Antiques
62 High St. (A.D. Martin.) MBHI. Est. 1978. Open 8.30—12.30 and 1.30—6; Fri. till 7; Sun. 2—5. SIZE: Small. *STOCK: Clocks, £100—£1,500; watches £50—£150; porelain, £10—£100; lacemaking supplies, all 19th C.* PARK: Town square. TEL: Bedford (0234) 712446. SER: Restorations (clocks).

Olney Antique Centre
Rose Court. (A. and J. McGuire.) *STOCK: Furniture, clocks, silver, jewellery, copper, brass, small items.*

Olney Antique Porcelain Company
21 High St. South. (R.F. and Mrs. D.F. Soul.) Est. 1973. CL: Wed. p.m. Open 10—1 and 2.15—5. SIZE: Medium. *STOCK: Porcelain, pottery, English, Continental, 18th—20th C, £5—£200.* LOC: Top of Olney High St. PARK: Easy. TEL: Bedford (0234) 711263 and 711360. SER: Valuations (porcelain).

Olney continued

Rose Court Studio Antiques
Rose Court, Market Place. (C. and J. Overland.) Est. 1977. Open 10—5, Sun. 2—5.30. SIZE: Medium. *STOCK: Furniture, clocks, pine, brass, copper, china, 17th—19th C.* PARK: Market Sq. TEL: Bedford (0234) 712351; home — Oakley (023 02) 4876. VAT: Stan/Spec.

PENN   (049 481)
Nr. High Wycombe
Country Furniture Shop
3 Hazlemere Rd., Potters Cross. (M. and V. Thomas.) Est. 1955. CL: Thurs. p.m. Open 10—1 and 2—5, Sun. 2—4.30. SIZE: Large. *STOCK: Furniture, Georgian, £100—£1,000; Victoriana, £20—£800; also paintings; carved pine mantelpieces.* Not stocked: Weapons. LOC: B474. PARK: Easy. TEL: 2244; home — same. VAT: Stan/Spec.

Penn Barn
By the Pond, Elm Rd. (P.J.M. Hunnings.) ABA. Est. 1968. Open 9.30—1 and 2—5, Sat. 9.30—1; Sat p.m. and Sun. by appointment. SIZE: Medium. *STOCK: Antiquarian books, maps and prints, 19th C, £5—£250; watercolours and oils, 19th to early 20th C, £50—£500.* LOC: B474. PARK: Easy. TEL: 5691; home — 3113. SER: Valuations; restorations; cleaning and repairs. VAT: Stan/Spec.

Francis Wigram   BADA
Cottars Barn, Elm Rd. CL: Wed. p.m. *STOCK: General antiques, furniture, English and Continental porcelain, works of art, decorative items.* **TEL: 3266.**

PRINCES RISBOROUGH   (084 44)
Farrelly Antiques Workshop
The Barns, Old Cross Keys, New Rd. (P. Farrelly.) CL: Sat. Open 9—5. *STOCK: Furniture.* TEL: 7044. SER: Restorations. VAT: Spec.

Vine House Antiques
Vine House, Church St. (Mrs. S.G. Stallabrass.) Est. 1962. CL: Mon.—Wed. Open 10—5.30. SIZE: Small. *STOCK: Glass, porcelain, £5—£100; brass, copper, £10—£100; small furniture, £20—£750, mostly 19th C.* Not stocked: Jewellery, silver and pictures. LOC: Near Market Sq. and opp. library and church. PARK: Easy. TEL: 5485. VAT: Stan.

White House Antiques
33 High St. (M. Amor.) Est. 1961. Open by appointment. *STOCK: Marble, chandeliers and furniture, £1,000+.* LOC: Town centre. TEL: 6976; home — same. SER: Valuations.

STEEPLE CLAYDON   (029 673)
Terence H. Porter, Fine Antique European Arms and Armour
'The Beeches'. Est. 1963. Open by appointment. *STOCK: Spare parts for antique firearms; arms and armour.* TEL: 8255. SER: Restorations (early firearms, including work with gold, silver, mother-of-pearl and ivory); buys at auction.

STOKE GOLDINGTON   (090 855)
Nr. Newport Pagnell
Magpie Antiques
47 High St. (Mrs. J. Mein.) Est. 1976. Open 9—6, Thurs. 9—1. SIZE: Small. *STOCK: English porcelain, 1750—1840, £5—£200; general small antiques, £2—£50.* LOC: Four miles from Newport Pagnell on B526. PARK: Easy. TEL: 220.

STOKENCHURCH
Amend Antiques
Studley Green Garden Centre, Oxford Rd., Studley Green. (B. Amend.) Open daily 12—5. *STOCK: General antiques.* PARK: Easy. TEL: (024026) 2842.

TINGEWICK
The Antique Shop
Main St. (P. E. Whittock.) Resident. Est. 1962. Always open. SIZE: Medium and large warehouse. *STOCK: Stripped pine, 19th C; decorated pine, 18th—19th C; oak, mahogany, copper, brass, ironware, spinning wheels, dairy and kitchen items, tools, carts and wheels; oil paintings and watercolours.* TEL: Finmere (028 04) 334. VAT: Stan/Spec.

Lennard Antiques   LAPADA
The Laurels. Est. 1978. Open Tues, Wed. and Sat. or by appointment. SIZE: Small. *STOCK: Furniture, oak, walnut and mahogany, 17th to early 19th C; accessories.* LOC: On A421 Bicester Rd. — next door to post office. TEL: Finmere (02804) 371.

WADDESDON
Collectors' Corner
106 High St. (Mrs. K. Good and Mrs. V. Grant.) Est. 1967. Open 9—5.30. SIZE: Medium. *STOCK: Silver, 18th—20th C, £5—£200; porcelain, jewellery, mainly 19th C, £5—£100; general antiques.* Not stocked: Coins, militaria. LOC: A41 opp. entrance to Waddesdon Manor. PARK: Easy. TEL: Aylesbury (0296) 651563. VAT: Stan/Spec.

WEEDON, Nr. Aylesbury
Peter Eaton (Booksellers) Ltd.
Lilies. Open 10—5 by appointment. *STOCK: Antiquarian and second-hand books.* TEL: Aylesbury (0296) 641393. SER: Brochure available.

WENDOVER   (0296)
Bowood Antiques
Bowood Lane. (Miss P. Peyton-Jones.) Est. 1960. Open 9—5.30. SIZE: Large. *STOCK: Furniture, porcelain, 17th—19th C, £10— £10,000; textiles, pictures.* LOC: On A413, signposted at Hunts Green turn-off, between Gt. Missenden and Wendover. PARK: Easy. TEL: 622113; home — same. VAT: Spec.

Collectors Treasures Ltd.   LAPADA
Hogarth House, High St. (R.J. and D.M. Eisler, S.D. and R.J. Paessler.) Est. 1964. Open 9.30—5.30. SIZE: Large. *STOCK: Maps, prints, from 16th C, £4—£2,000; antique wallpaper roller lamps.* LOC: A413. PARK: Own. TEL: 624402. SER: Valuations; framing and mounting: mail order available. VAT: Stan.

Wendover Antiques
1 South St. (R. and D. Davies.) Est. 1979. Open 9—5.30. SIZE: Medium. *STOCK: Furniture, £200—£1,000, watercolours and prints, £20—£600, both 18th—19th C; silver, 18th— 20th C, £20—£500; collectors' items including Sheffield plate, £15—£200.* LOC: Near village centre on Wendover—Amersham road. PARK: 100yds. TEL: 622078. VAT: Stan/Spec.

WHITCHURCH
Deerstalker Antiques
28 High St. (R.J. and Mrs. Eichler.) CL: Mon. and Wed. Open 10—5.30. SIZE: Small. *STOCK: General antiques.* TEL: Aylesbury (0296) 641505.

WINGRAVE, Nr. Aylesbury
Peter Arnold Gallery
Knolls Close. Est. 1978. *STOCK: British watercolours and paintings, 1750—1950.* TEL: (0296) 681568.

WOBURN SANDS, Nr. Bletchley
Haydon House Antiques   LAPADA
Haydon House, Station Rd. (G. and M. Tyrrell, D. Missenden.) Est. 1965. CL: Thurs. Open 10—6, Sun. by appointment. SIZE: Large. *STOCK: Furniture (including stripped pine), 18th—19th C, and Edwardian, £25—£1,000; copper, brass, metalware, bygones, prints, £5—£250.* Not stocked: Coins, silver, jewellery. LOC: 2 miles from exit 13, M1 and 2 miles from Woburn Abbey. PARK: On premises. TEL: Milton Keynes (0908) 582447. VAT: Stan.

Neville's Antiques
64—66 Station Rd. (N.K.T. Medcalf.) CL: Mon. and Wed. Open 10—5. SIZE: Small. *STOCK: Furniture and small items, 18th— 19th C, £25—£1,500.* PARK: Easy. TEL: Milton Keynes (0908) 584827.

Cambridgeshire

Key to number of shops in this area.

○ 1–2
⊖ 3–5
⊜ 6–12
◗ 13+

LINCS.

NORFOLK

Wisbech

A47

A47

Outwell

A15

A1

A47

Castor

Peterborough

Wansford

A605

March

Whittlesey

B1040

A141

NORTHANTS.

B660

A15

B660

Doddington

A10

Littleport

Ramsey

A141

B660

Warboys

B1050

A142

Ely

A1

Soham

A604

A141

A1123

Fordham

B660

Godmanchester

St. Ives

A10

Burwell

Brampton

Reach

B1102

Landbeach

A14

A604

Fen Ditton

A45

A45

Cambridge

A45

St. Neots

A45

Trumpington

Comberton

A603

A604

A11

BEDS.

A142

B1040

A14

Orwell

Harston

Little Shelford

Whittlesford

Bartlow

Fowlmere

Duxford

A604

Melbourn

Ickleton

ESSEX

HERTS.

N

Please note this is only a rough map designed to show dealers the number of shops in the various towns, and is not necessarily totally accurate.

BARTLOW, Nr. Cambridge
Rupert Hanbury Antiques Ltd.
The Kennels. (R. and A. Hanbury.) Est. 1983. Open 9.30—5.30. SIZE: Medium. *STOCK: English furniture, 18th—19th C, £50—£1,500; prints, 19th C, £20—£150; general antiques including teacaddies, 18th—19th C.* Not stocked: Silver, jewellery, clocks and pewter. PARK: Easy. TEL: Cambridge (0223) 893535; home — Cambridge (0223) 893200. SER: Restorations; buys at auction (furniture). VAT: Stan.

BRAMPTON
Brampton Mill Antiques
Brampton Mill. (D.E. Clark.) Est. 1955. Open by appointment only. SIZE: Large. *STOCK: General antiques and shipping goods.* LOC: 2 miles from A1. Through Brampton towards Huntingdon, off A604. PARK: Easy. TEL: Huntingdon (0480) 55593. VAT: Stan/Spec.

BURWELL
Peter Norman Antiques and Restorations
Sefton House, 57 North St. (P. Norman and A. Marpole.) Est. 1975. Open 9—12.30 and 2—5.30. SIZE: Small. *STOCK: Furniture, clocks and arms, 17th—19th C, £100—£3,500.* PARK: Easy. TEL: Newmarket (0638) 742197. SER: Valuations; restorations (furniture, oil paintings, clocks, arms). VAT: Stan/Spec.

CAMBRIDGE   (0223)
The Antique Home
15 Gwydir St. (P. Farmar.) CL: Mon. and Thurs. Open 9.30—5. *STOCK: Furniture, 18th to early 20th C.* TEL: 311203.

The Antique Seeker
47 Newnham Rd. (Miss J. Mackinnon.) Est. 1978. Open 9.30—6. SIZE: Medium. *STOCK: Furniture, early Victorian, Edwardian and 1930's, £20—£800; jugs and bowls, china, pictures, £8—£80; linen and lace, £6—£100; jewellery and silver.* LOC: The College Backs, the Fen Causeway, A1132/A603. PARK: Nearby. TEL: 65864; home — 312462. SER: Valuations; restorations. VAT: Stan/Spec.

Antiques Etc.
18 King St. (W. Heffer.) Est. 1970. SIZE: Small. *STOCK: General furniture, silver, china, clocks, watches.* LOC: On the edge of the central shopping district towards Newmarket road. PARK: Multi-storey. TEL: 62825; home — 63634. SER: Valuations; restorations (wood, metalware, silver, china, mother-of-pearl). VAT: Stan/Spec.

Cambridge continued

Jess Applin Antiques   BADA
8 Lensfield Rd. Est. 1968. Open 10—5.30. *STOCK: Furniture, 17th—19th C; general antiques.* LOC: Junction Hills Rd. and Lensfield Rd., opposite church. PARK: Meters and nearby. TEL: 315168; evenings — 246851. VAT: Spec.

Artisan Antiques & Collectables
28 Regent St. (B. Pain and M. Lambourn-Brown.) Est. 1982. Open 9.30—5.30. SIZE: Medium. *STOCK: Metalware, Victoriana, treen, bygones, clocks, prints, pine and country furniture, 18th-19th C, £5—£500.* Not stocked: Jewellery. LOC: Next to Downing College. PARK: Easy. TEL: 355419. SER: Valuations; buys at auction.

John Beazor and Sons Ltd.   BADA
78—80 Regent St. Est. 1870. *STOCK: English furniture, 18th to early 19th C; general antiques.* TEL: 355178. VAT: Stan/Spec.

Benet Gallery
19 Kings Parade. (G.H. and J. Criddle.) Est. 1965. Open 10—5. SIZE: Large. *STOCK: Early maps and Cambridge watercolours, 1575 to date, £3.50—£600; English topography, playing cards.* TEL: 353783; home — 248739. VAT: Stan.

David Bickersteth
38 Fulbrooke Rd. Est. 1967. Open by appointment. *STOCK: Antiquarian books.* TEL: 352291.

The Bookroom (Cambridge)
13A St. Eligius St. (E.A. Searle.) ABA. Est. 1973. Open 9.30—5, Sat. by appointment. SIZE: Small. *STOCK: Science, medicine, natural history, mainly 19th C, £10—£100; military, naval and marine, £5—£50; English literature, mainly 19th C, some private press, £5—£50; Folio Society publications including out-of-print, £4—£10.* LOC: Trumpington Rd. end of Bateman St. PARK: Panton St. TEL: 69694; home — 354566. SER: Valuations; buys at auction (books). VAT: Stan.

Buckies   LAPADA
31 Trinity St. (G. McC. and P.R. Buckie.) NAG, GMC. Est. 1972. CL: Mon. Open 9.45—5.30. SIZE: Medium. *STOCK: Jewellery, silver, objets d'art.* PARK: Multi-storey, nearby. TEL: 357910. SER: Valuations; restorations and repairs. VAT: Stan/Spec.

AA/RAC
****

Egon Ronay

UNIVERSITY ARMS HOTEL
Regent Street, Cambridge

Owned and run by the Bradford family since 1891
Quietly situated near city centre and colleges
115 bedrooms, all with bathrooms
Oak-panelled restaurant overlooking open park
Spacious lounge, three bars
Parkers Bar with lunchtime carved buffet
and specialist Whisky Bar
with over 100 different types of whisky

Tel. (0223) 351241

Cambridge continued

Malcolm G. Clark   BADA
3 Pembroke St. Est. 1947. CL: Thurs. p.m.
Open 9.30−5. *STOCK: English furniture, contemporary items.* TEL: 357117. VAT: Spec.

Collectors Centre
The Old Stable, 10c Hope St., Hope St. Yard.
(R. and A. Warwick.) Est. 1975. CL: Thurs.
Open 9.30−5.15. SIZE: Small. *STOCK: Pine furniture, mid-19th to late 20th C, £50−£100; country items, kitchen bygones, £5−£25.* LOC: Off Mill Rd., opposite Co-op.
PARK: Easy. TEL: 211632. SER: Valuations; restorations (pine). VAT: Stan.

Collectors' Market
Dales Brewery, Gwydir St. (off Mill Rd.). (Mrs.
E. M. Highmoor.) Est. 1976. Open 9.30−5.
There are 10 units at this market *selling a wide variety of collectors' items from 25p−£250,* including bygones, prints, glass, bric-a-brac, kitchenalia, books, furniture. TEL: 66950.

Collins and Clark
81 Regent St. (J.G. Collins.) Est. 1895. CL:
Thurs. p.m. Open 9.30−5. *STOCK: English furniture, English and Oriental porcelain, silver, glass.* TEL: 353801. VAT: Spec.

Cambridge continued

Gabor Cossa Antiques
34 Trumpington St. (J. Eve.) Est. 1948. Open
10−5.15. SIZE: Small. *STOCK: Early English porcelain, pottery and glass; Chinese and Japanese porcelain; Japanese woodcuts; prints and objets d'art.* Not stocked: Furniture and silver. LOC: On main road leading into Cambridge from London. PARK: 400yds. − 2 car parks. TEL: 356049. SER: Buys at auction. VAT: Spec.

Cottage Antiques
16-18 Lensfield Rd. (Mrs. A. Owen and Mrs.
A. Yandell.) Est. 1974. Open 10−5.30. Sun.
by appointment. SIZE: Medium. *STOCK: Glass, china, silver, copper, brass, tiles, Staffordshire figures, Oriental porcelain, boxes, fire-irons, decorative items, country furniture, mainly 19th C, 25p−£1,500.* LOC: Opposite Catholic church. PARK: Nearby. TEL: 316698.

G. David
3 and 16 St. Edwards Passage. ABA. Est.
1896. Open 9−5. *STOCK: Antiquarian, old and out of print books.* TEL: 354619.

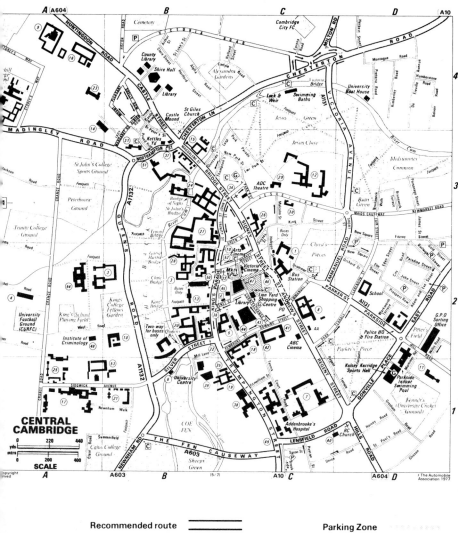

CENTRAL CAMBRIDGE

SCALE

Recommended route	Parking Zone
Other roads	One-way street
Restricted roads (Access only/Buses only)	Pedestrians only
Traffic roundabout	Convenience
Official car park free (Open air)	Convenience with facilities for the disabled
Multi-storey car park	
Parking available on payment (Open air)	Tourist Information Centre

Cambridge continued

Deighton Bell and Co.
13 Trinity St. (Wm. Dawson (Rare books) Ltd.) ABA. Est. 1700. Open 9—5.30, Sat. 9.30—1. SIZE: Large. *STOCK: Antiquarian, rare and fine old books, mainly on English literature, travel, topography, colour plate books; typography, book design. Local prints and maps of all periods and all prices.* PARK: Multi- storey, 300yds. TEL: 353939. SER: Buys at auction. VAT: Stan.

Dolphin Antiques
33 Trumpington St. (R.H. Bramwell and L.J. Aldred.) Open 10—5.30. *STOCK: 18th to early 19th C furniture, metalware and glass. Not stocked: Jewellery;* LOC: Opposite Fitz-william Museum. PARK: Meters or Lion Yard multi- storey. TEL: 354180.

Dove House Antiques
4 New Park St. (A. and L. Scott.) *STOCK: Jewellery and small interesting items.* LOC: Next to Jesus Lane car park. TEL: 316862.

R.T. Firmin
16 Magdalene St. Est. 1974. CL: Mon. Open 10.30—12.30 and 1.30—5. *STOCK: Clocks, English, French, bracket, longcase, carriage, £250—£7,000.* TEL: 67372. SER: Restorations.

Galloway and Porter Ltd.
30 Sidney St. ABA. Est. 1900. CL: Sat. *STOCK: Antiquarian and old books.* TEL: 67876.

Derek Gibbons
The Haunted Bookshop, St. Edward's Passage. Est. 1960. Open 9.30—5.30. *STOCK: Antiquarian and illustrated books.* TEL: 312913.

Lensfield Antiques
12 Lensfield Rd. (P. Farmar and D. Cayley.) Open 9.30—5.30. SIZE: Medium. *STOCK: English furniture, 17th—19th C; collectors' items.* LOC: Opposite Catholic Church. PARK: Meters. TEL: 357636. SER: Valuations; restorations. VAT: Spec.

Michaels Antiques
5 Norfolk St. (M. and J. Smith.) Est. 1978. SIZE: Large. *STOCK: Furniture, £25—£1,500; china, £5—£250; clocks, £50—£1,000; lighting, £25—£300; oils and watercolours, £30—£1,000; all 18th—20th C.* LOC: 5 minutes' walk from town centre. PARK: Nearby. TEL: 357558.

Old School Antiques
Chittering. (S.R. Rumble.) CL: Mon. Open 10—6. *STOCK: Oak, country and 18th to early 19th C mahogany furniture; pottery, porcelain, treen.* LOC: Off A10. TEL: 861831.

Cambridge continued

Jean Pain Gallery
7—8 King's Parade. Est. 1967. Open 9.30—5. SIZE: Medium. *STOCK: Maps and prints including Cambridge, topographical, natural history and caricatures.* LOC: Opposite King's College. PARK: Lion's Yard. TEL: 313970. SER: Buys at auction (prints and maps). FAIRS: Cambridge ABA. VAT: Stan.

Quinto of Cambridge
34 Trinity St. Open 9—6. *STOCK: Maps, prints and art books.* TEL: 358279.

S.J. Webster-Speakman BADA
79 Regent St. Open 10—5.30. *STOCK: English furniture, clocks, Staffordshire pottery, general antiques.* TEL: 315048; evenings — 354809. FAIRS: Spring and Autumn Chelsea. VAT: Spec.

CASTOR (073 121)
Nr. Peterborough
Chapel Collectors Centre
Church Hill. (R.A. and S.D. Shakeshaft.) Est. 1975. CL: Wed. and Thurs. Open 10.30—4.30, Fri. and Sat. 10.30—5, 2nd Sun. each month 2—5. SIZE: Medium. *STOCK: Collectors' items, post and cigarette cards, ephemera, treen and pottery, 1800—1950, £1—£25; prints and books, 1750—1950, £1—£50; stamps, art deco, clothes, 1900—1950.* LOC: Just off old A47, turn at the 'Prince of Wales'. PARK: Easy. TEL: Home — Peterborough (0733) 263328. SER: Valuations (collectors' items); buys at auction. FAIRS: Midlands and E. Anglian.

COMBERTON (022 026)
Comberton Antiques
5a West St. (Mrs. M. McEvoy.) Est. 1980. Open Mon., Fri. and Sat. 10—5, Sun. 2—5. SIZE: Small. *STOCK: Furniture, 1780—1900, £50—£500; bric-a-brac, 1830—1920, £5—£100.* LOC: 6 miles west of Cambridge, 2 miles west of M11. PARK: Easy. TEL: 2674; home — Royston (0763) 60247.

DODDINGTON
A.D. Antiques
34 Benwick Rd. *STOCK: General antiques and Victoriana — jewellery, glass, porcelain (especially Crown Derby and Worcester), brass and copper, clocks and furniture.* TEL: March (0354) 740362.

Doddington continued

Doddington House Antiques
2 Benwick Rd. (B.A. Frankland.) *STOCK: General furniture, stripped pine, mirrors, clocks, pictures and interesting items.* LOC: Near Clocktower. TEL: March (0354) 740755.

DUXFORD
Riro D. Mooney
4 Moorfield Rd. Est. 1946. Open 10—7, Sat. 9—7. SIZE: Medium. *STOCK: General antiques, 1780-1920, £5—£1,200.* LOC: 1 mile from M11. PARK: Easy. TEL: Cambridge (0223) 832252. VAT: Stan/Spec.

ELY   (0353)
Mrs. Mills Antiques
37 Market St. CL: Tues. Open 10—1 and 2—5. *STOCK: General small antiques, porcelain and pottery, 18th—19th C; jewellery, small silver items.* Not stocked: Furniture. TEL: 4268. SER: Restoration (porcelain).

FEN DITTON
Strover Antiques
The Old School, High St. (B.J. and L. Strover.) Est. 1970. Open Fri. and Sat. 9.30—5.30 or by appointment. SIZE: Small. *STOCK: Country furniture and effects.* LOC: 2 miles east of Cambridge on Newmarket road. PARK: Easy. TEL: Teversham (022 05) 5264; home — same. VAT: Spec.

FORDHAM
The Kelterment Antique Centre
5—6 Soham Rd. CL: Wed. Open 9.30—5, Sun. 2.30—5. There are four dealers trading from this centre. *STOCK: Georgian and Victorian furniture and shipping items, copper and brass.* LOC: A142. TEL: Newmarket (0638) 720250.

Phoenix Antiques
1 Carter St. Est. 1966. CL: Wed. p.m. Open normal hours, but appointment advisable. SIZE: Medium. *STOCK: Early European furniture, domestic metalwork, pottery and delft, carpets, scientific instruments, treen and bygones.* LOC: Centre of village. PARK: Own. TEL: Newmarket (0638) 720363.

FOWLMERE,   (076 382)
Nr. Royston
Mere Antiques
High St. (R.W. Smith.) Est. 1979. CL: Tues. Open 10—1 and 2—6, including Sun. SIZE: Medium. *STOCK: Furniture, porcelain and clocks, 18th—19th C, to £5,000; pine furniture, 19th—20th C, to £200.* PARK: Easy. TEL: 477; home — 495. SER: Valuations. VAT: Spec.

GODMANCHESTER
Antiques at The Limes
59 Cambridge St. (R. and R. Lord.) Resident. Est. 1969. CL: Mon. Open from 10, Tues. and Sun. 2—4, Thurs. 2.30—4.30. SIZE: Medium. *STOCK: Small furniture, clocks, rings; automata, music boxes, gramophones.* PARK: Just past shop or by River Ouse. TEL: Huntingdon (0480) 54649. SER: Valuations.

HARSTON
Antique Clocks
1 High St. (C.J. Stocker.) Open every day. LOC: On A10, 5 miles south of Cambridge. PARK: Easy. TEL: Cambridge (0223) 870264.

ICKLETON, Nr. Saffron Walden
Abbey Antiques
18 Abbey St. (K. Wilson.) Est. 1974. CL: Sun. and Mon. except by appointment. Open 10—5. SIZE: Large. *STOCK: General antiques, 17th—20th C, £1—£1,000.* LOC: Turn off at Stumps Cross at Gt. Chesterford, 1 mile to Ickleton, shop is in main street. PARK: Easy. TEL: Saffron Walden (0799) 30637. SER: Valuations; restorations (furniture). VAT: Spec.

Detail of an 1839 taper holder. From "A Touch of Class: Tapersticks", **Antique Collecting,** March 1986.

LANDBEACH
P.R. Garner Antiques
104 High St. Est. 1966. Open by appointment only. SIZE: Medium. *STOCK: China, glass, brass, copper, pewter, unrestored furniture, Victorian and earlier, old gramophones, musical boxes, Victorian and Edwardian, shipping goods.* LOC: Off A10. PARK: Easy. TEL: Cambridge (0223) 860470. SER: Valuations. VAT: Stan/Spec.

LITTLE SHELFORD
Cambridge Fine Art Ltd.   LAPADA
Priesthouse, 33 Church St. (R. and J. Lury.) Resident. Est. 1972. Open by appointment. SIZE: Large. *STOCK: British and European paintings, 1780—1900; British paintings, 1880—1930; portraits, 1650—1930; watercolours, 19th C.* LOC: Next to church. PARK: Easy. TEL: Cambridge (0223) 842866/843537. SER: Valuations; restorations; buys at auction. VAT: Stan/Spec.

LITTLEPORT, Nr. Ely
Richmond Antiques
18 Main St. Est. 1963. Open every day. SIZE: Small. *STOCK: General antiques, 18th—19th C, £50—£500; some early oak.* PARK: Easy. TEL: Ely (0353) 861104.

MARCH   (0354)
Gallery Three
96 and 98 High St. (J. Burn.) Est. 1970. Open Wed. and Sat. 10—4.30, other times by appointment. *STOCK: Porcelain, pottery, glass, silver, small furniture.* PARK: Easy. TEL: 53484 or 52262. SER: Valuations; restorations.

MELBOURN, Nr. Royston
P.N. Hardiman
62 High St. (M. and G.A. Hardiman.) Est. 1933. CL: Sun. except by appointment. Open 8.30—6. SIZE: Medium. *STOCK: English furniture, 18th and 19th C; general antiques.* LOC: A10 between Royston and Cambridge. PARK: At rear. TEL: Royston (0763) 60093. SER: Restorations. VAT: Stan/Spec.

Melantiques
5 Mortlock St. (J.I. Moore.) Est. 1965. CL: Tues., Thurs. and Sun. a.m. Open 10—5. SIZE: Medium. *STOCK: General antiques, furniture, 18th—19th C; silver, brass, copper, stripped pine, porcelain.* LOC: On A10, turn right at traffic lights in Melbourn. On A505 turn at Melbourn signpost 3 miles north of Royston. TEL: Royston (0763) 61538; home — Royston (0763) 61015.

ORWELL
West Farm Antiques   LAPADA
High St. (Mrs. J. Kershaw.) Est. 1964. Open Thurs., Sat. and Sun. or by appointment. SIZE: Large. *STOCK: Country furniture and general antiques, 17th—19th C, £5—£3,000.* Not stocked: Reproductions, silver, clocks, mechanical objects, jewellery. LOC: ½ mile past church on right. PARK: Easy. TEL: Cambridge (0223) 207464. FAIRS: Olympia. VAT: Stan/Spec.

OUTWELL
Langhorn Antiques
Langhorn Lane. (P. Gaunt.) Resident. Est. 1976. Open anytime. SIZE: Medium. *STOCK: Period pine, decorative glass and general antiques.* LOC: Langhorn Lane is next to Esso service station on Downham Market to Wisbech Rd. PARK: Own. TEL: Wisbech (0945) 772668.

PETERBOROUGH   (0733)
Ivor and Patricia Lewis Antique and Fine Art Dealers   LAPADA
Westfield, 30 Westwood Park Rd. Open by appointment. *STOCK: English and French furniture — some signed, porcelain, bronzes.* TEL: 44567.

Old Soke Books
68 Burghley Rd. (P. Clay.) Open Mon., Tues., Fri. and Sat; also Thurs. evening 4.30—8.30. *STOCK: Antiquarian and secondhand books, small general antiques including furniture, paintings, prints and postcards.* TEL: 64147.

G. Smith and Sons (Peterborough) Ltd.
195—197 Lincoln Rd. (M. Groucott.) Est. 1902. CL: Thurs. p.m. Open 9—1 and 2.15—5. SIZE: Medium. *STOCK: General antiques.* LOC: A15. PARK: 50yds. TEL: 43781; home — 71630. SER: Upholstery; restorations. VAT: Stan/Spec.

Studio Antiques
31 Lincoln Rd. (R. Spackman.) Est. 1960. CL: Mon. and Thurs. Open 10.30—5, Sat. 10.30—4. SIZE: Large. *STOCK: Silver, plate, jewellery, glass, china.* LOC: From London on A1, city centre, Boroughbury. PARK: Easy. TEL: 54394. SER: Valuations; restorations (metals); buys at auction. VAT: Stan/Spec.

RAMSEY, Nr. Huntingdon (0487)

Abbey Antiques
63 Great Whyte. (R. & J. Smith.) Est. 1977. CL: Mon. Open 10−5 including Sun. SIZE: Small. *STOCK: Furniture, including pine, 1850−1930, £50−£500; porcelain, Goss and crested china, 1830−1950, £3−£500; brass and copper, 1850−1950, £10−£100.* PARK: Easy. TEL: 814753; home − 812758. SER: Buys at auction. FAIRS: Alexandra Palace, Harrow.

REACH

Dudley's Antiques and Home Interiors
Vine House, Fair Green. (A.F. and J.A. Dudley.) Open 9−5, or by appointment. SIZE: Large. *STOCK: General antiques, furniture, copper, brass, porcelain, pictures, prints, country bygones, curios, collectors' items, clocks, bric-a-brac, from 50p.* LOC: Just off B1102. PARK: Easy. TEL: Newmarket (0638) 741989; home − Newmarket (0638) 742171. SER: Valuations; restorations (clocks, barometers, furniture, silver and metal), caning, rushing, framing, wood carving, turning, French polishing, veneering, uphol-stery and buttoning; design consultant; buys at auction. VAT: Stan/Spec.

ST. IVES (0480)

Adams Antiques   *Trade Only*
Houghton Rd. CL: Sat. Open 8.30−5.30. SIZE: Warehouse. *STOCK: Pine, especially Irish and Continental, 18th−19th C.* TEL: Huntingdon (0480) 300455.

B.R. Knight and Sons   LAPADA
4 The Quay. (Mrs. B.R. Knight and Partners.) Est. 1972. CL: Thurs. Open 10.30−5. SIZE: Large. *STOCK: Porcelain, pottery, silver, pewter, jewellery, paintings, watercolours, etchings, furniture, arts and crafts, art nouveau, art deco.* LOC: On the Riverside Quay, nr. St. Ives bridge. PARK: Market Sq., or south of Bridge. TEL: 68295. SER: Valua-tions. VAT: Stan/Spec.

Timecraft
6 Crown St. Mews. (F.K. Hemmings.) CMBHI. Est. 1950. CL: Tues. and Thurs. Open 9−1 and 2−5. *STOCK: Clocks, watches, baro-meters prints and watercolours.* LOC: Off Crown St. opposite Ketch 22. SER: Resto-rations and repairs (especially longcase and French clocks and barometers). VAT: Stan.

Sydney House Antiques

Gail and Roger Hancox **Est. 1972**
(resident on premises)
Sydney House, 14 Elton Road, Wansford,
Peterborough. Tel. (0780) 782786

We specialise in important British porcelain, pottery
1850-1950, Minton majolica, signed artist Doulton, art
pottery, Worcester, Crown Derby, and 18th and 19th
century furniture, especially marquetry.

WANTED to purchase: Worcester figurines (1880-1940)
Open weekends and bank holidays

Minton jardinières, 6ft.

ST. NEOTS

Crosshall Gallery
171 Crosshall Rd., Eaton Ford. (S. Briggs.)
Est. 1979. Open by appointment. SIZE: Small.
STOCK: Watercolours, mainly 19th C. LOC:
300 yds. from A1/45 crossroads. PARK:
Easy. TEL: Home — Huntingdon (0480)
72400. SER: Buys at auction (watercolours).

Peter John Antiques
38 St. Mary's St., Eynesbury. (K. Smith.) CL:
Tues. Open 10—5.30. *STOCK: General antiques especially jewellery.* PARK: Easy. TEL:
Huntingdon (0480) 216297. SER: Restorations (clocks).

SOHAM

Audraw Ltd.
Staples Lane. (L. Audus.) Est. 1959. CL: Wed.
Open by appointment. SIZE: Warehouse.
*STOCK: Furniture, Georgian, Victorian and
Edwardian £10—£1,000; Victorian glass,
porcelain, £1—£500; brass, copper.* LOC: On
main road between Newmarket and Ely.
PARK: Easy. TEL: Ely (0353) 720342. VAT:
Stan/Spec.

TRUMPINGTON, Nr. Cambridge

Dorothy Radford
Antiques and Interiors
132 Shelford Rd. Est. 1966. Open 11—5.30.
*STOCK: General and decorative antiques
including mirrors, fire items, lighting, objets
d'art, paintings, furniture, needlework, metalwork.* LOC: 2 miles south of Cambridge just
off A10 towards Shelford. TEL: Cambridge
(0223) 840179; home — Cambridge (0223)
357966.

WANSFORD, Nr. Peterborough

Sydney House Antiques
14 Elton Rd. (G. Hancox.) Est. 1972. CL:
Mon. until 1 p.m. and Wed. until 2 p.m., Sun.
2—3. Open Tues. and Thurs. from 8.30, Fri.
from 11.30, Sat. and Sun. from 9. SIZE:
Large. *STOCK: Furniture, including marquetry,
19th—20th C, £150—£2,000; Minton,
1850—1920, £100—£2,000; Doulton and
Lambeth, £50—£1,000; Royal Worcester,
1860—1940, £100—£1,500.* PARK: Easy.
TEL: Stamford (0780) 782365; home —
Stamford (0780) 782786. SER: Valuations;
buys at auction (Minton, Doulton, Royal
Worcester, 19th C furniture).

WARBOYS

'The Golden Drop Antiques'
The Golden Drop, Chatteris Rd. (M. Clarke.)
Open daily. *STOCK: Polished pine, Victorian,
Edwardian, period; shipping goods.* LOC: On
A141, 3 miles from Chatteris towards
Warboys. TEL: Chatteris (035 43) 2990.

WHITTLESEY
Paul Micklin Antiques
1 and 3 Church St. CL: Thurs. Open 9—6.
*STOCK: Victorian and Edwardian furniture,
decorative items.* TEL: Peterborough (0733)
204355.

WHITTLESFORD
Guildhall Antiques
The Guildhall. (M. Finlinson.) Open by appointment. TEL: Cambridge (0223) 833943.

WISBECH   (0945)
Attic Antiques
1 Howletts Hill, Off Norfolk St. (Mrs. S.
Stones.) Est. 1978. CL: Mon. and Wed. Open
10.30—1 and 2—4. SIZE: Small. *STOCK:
General antiques, 19th C to art deco, £5—
£100.* Not stocked: Firearms. LOC: Just off
Wisbech-Downham Rd. PARK: Easy. TEL:
Home — 61802.

Attic Gallery
88 Elm Rd. (D. Ransome.) Est. 1980. Open
anytime by appointment. SIZE: Small. *STOCK:
Signed limited edition prints by Wm. Russell
Flint, Helen Bradley and L.S. Lowry, 1920
onwards, £200—£2,000; porcelain, 19th C,
£20—£1,000; oil paintings and watercolours,
19th C, £150—£1,000.* PARK: Easy. TEL:
583734; home — same. SER: Valuations;
buys at auction. FAIRS: Antiques in Britain at
Norwich, Leicester, Hereford, Bury St.
Edmunds, York, Brecon, Edinburgh, Perth.

B.G.R. Silver
88 Elm Rd. Open anytime by appointment.
STOCK: 18th and 19th C silver. TEL: 583734.
SER: Valuations; buys at auction. FAIRS:
Antiques in Britain at Norwich, Leicester,
Hereford, Bury St. Edmunds, York, Brecon,
Edinburgh, Perth.

Coach House Antiques   LAPADA
55 Elm Rd. (J. Ing.) Est. 1953. CL: Sat. and
Sun. except by appointment. Open 9—5.
SIZE: Large. *STOCK: Silver, Georgian and
Victorian; furniture, Victorian; prints pre-
1820, all to £1,500.* Not stocked: Firearms,
coins, stamps. PARK: Easy. TEL: 583129.
SER: Valuations; buys at auction. VAT: Stan/
Spec

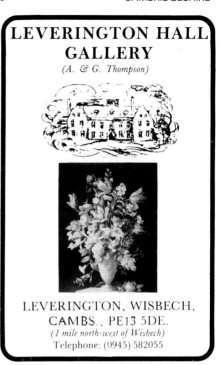

LEVERINGTON HALL GALLERY
(A. & G. Thompson)

LEVERINGTON, WISBECH,
CAMBS., PE13 5DE.
(1 mile north-west of Wisbech)
Telephone: (0945) 582055

Wisbech continued

Peter A. Crofts   BADA
Briar Patch, High Rd., Elm. Est. 1949. CL: Sat.
*STOCK: General antiques, furniture, porcelain,
silver, jewellery.* LOC: A1101. TEL: 584614.
VAT: Stan/Spec.

Eric Golding
12 North Brink. Open by appointment only.
STOCK: Antiquarian books. TEL: 582927.

Leverington Hall Antiques
Leverington. (A. and G. Thompson.) Open
Thurs.—Sat. 11—5 or by appointment. There
are 5 dealers here selling a wide range of
general antiques. PARK: Easy. TEL: 64636.

Leverington Hall Gallery
Leverington. (A. & G. Thompson.) Open daily
by appointment. SIZE: Medium. *STOCK: Oils,
£150—£2,000; watercolours, £25—£1,000;
both 1800—1920; bronzes, 19th C, £100—
£1,500.* PARK: Easy. TEL: 582055; home —
same. SER: Buys at auction (paintings and
bronzes). VAT: Spec.

Cheshire

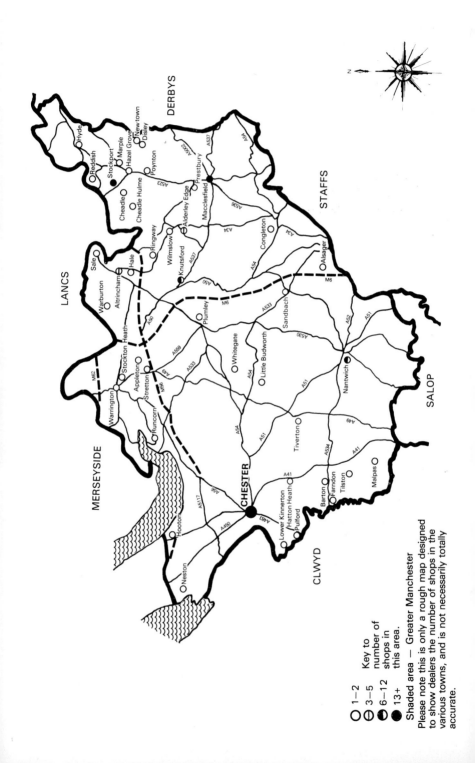

Key to
number of
shops in
this area.

○ 1–2
◐ 3–5
◑ 6–12
● 13+

Shaded area — Greater Manchester

Please note this is only a rough map designed
to show dealers the number of shops in the
various towns, and is not necessarily totally
accurate.

ALDERLEY EDGE (0625)
Alderley Antiques LAPADA
17 London Rd. (G. Bennett and J. Barlow). Est. 1967 Open 10—1 and 2—5. SIZE: Medium. *STOCK: Furniture, £100—£4,000; objets d'art, jewellery, £30—£1,000; paintings, £100—£1,000, all 17th—19th C.* LOC: Town centre, near station. PARK: Easy. TEL: 583468; home — 584819. SER: Valuations. FAIRS: British International, Birmingham. VAT: Stan/Spec.

Anthony Baker Antiques LAPADA
14 London Rd. (G.D.A. Price.) Est. 1974. CL: Mon. Open 10—5.30. SIZE: Medium. *STOCK: Furniture, 17th—19th C, £50—£1,000; barometers, 18th—19th C, £100—£800; glass and pottery.* Not stocked: Jewellery. LOC: A34, village centre. PARK: Easy. TEL: 582674. VAT: Stan./Spec.

Brook Lane Antiques
93 Brook Lane. (M. Goodwin and G.M. Broadbridge.) Est. 1983. CL: Mon. Open 10—5. SIZE: Small. *STOCK: Stripped pine, Victoriana, Edwardiana.* TEL: Wilmslow (0625) 584896. SER: Stencilling.

D.J. Massey and Son
51a London Rd. Est. 1900. Open 9—5.30, Wed. 9—1. SIZE: Large. *STOCK: Jewellery, gold and diamond; silver, all periods.* LOC: On A34. PARK: Easy. TEL: 583565. VAT: Stan.

ALSAGER
Nr. Newcastle under Lyme (Staffs.) (4 & 5 fig. nos) (093 63) (6 fig. nos) (0270)
Stancie Cutler Antique and Collectors Fairs
Alsager Golf and Country Club. Open last Sun. of each month, 10—5. There are 30 stands at this fair selling a wide variety of antiques. TEL: 666802.

Esme's Antiques
Open by appointment. *STOCK: Fine porcelain including Royal Worcester and signed pieces.* TEL: 5603.

ALTRINCHAM
A.C. Antiques
168 Manchester Rd. (A.C. Mortimer.) Est. 1967. Open 9.30—6, Sun. and other times by appointment. SIZE: Small. *STOCK: General antiques, especially art nouveau and decorative items, 18th—20th C, £5—£1,000.* LOC: A556/A56 into Manchester. PARK: Easy and side streets. TEL: (061) 941 4237; home — (061) 928 5627. SER: Valuations; restorations (ceramics, furniture, clocks); buys at auction. VAT: Stan/Spec.

Altrincham continued

L.H. Gilliard
64 and 64A Manchester Rd. Est. 1946. CL: Wed. p.m. Open 10—6, Sat. 10—5. *STOCK: Furniture, 18th—19th C.* TEL: (061) 928 2943. VAT: Stan.

Halo Antiques
97 Hale Rd. (Major and Mrs. P. Oulton.) Est. 1971. CL: Mon. Open 10—5. SIZE: Large. *STOCK: Victorian mahogany, £200—£300; US shipping goods, £50—£100; pine, 19th C, £50—£100.* LOC: A538 from motorway, after 2 miles shop on right. PARK: Easy. TEL: (061) 941 1800; home — same. SER: Buys at auction. VAT: Stan/Spec.

New Street Antiques
48 New St. (Mrs. J. Pearson.) Est. 1968. CL: Mon. and Wed. Open 10.30—1 and 2.15—5. SIZE: Small. *STOCK: Commemorative, Staffordshire, general antiques.* LOC: ½ way along New Street. PARK: Easy. TEL: (0925) 62682 or (061) 904 0636.

Squires Antiques
25 Regent Rd. (Mrs. A. Phillips.) Est. 1977. CL: Wed. Open 10—5. SIZE: Small. *STOCK: Small silver, 1880—1940, £5—£100; small furniture, 1800—1930, £5—£500; brass, copper and bric- a-brac, 1850—1940, £1—£100; jewellery, porcelain, fireplace accessories.* Not stocked: Large furniture, coins and badges. LOC: Adjacent to the hospital, next to large car park. PARK: Own. TEL: (061) 980 4315. SER: Valuations; restorations (porcelain repairs, copper and brass polishing). VAT: Stan.

APPLETON, Nr. Warrington
Lions & Unicorns
Woodside Farm, Green Lane. (Mrs. J.A. Pearson.) Est. 1976. Open by appointment. SIZE: Small. *STOCK: Commemorative china, books and tins.* PARK: Easy. TEL: Warrington (0925) 62682; home — same. SER: Buys at auction; quarterly catalogues; international postal.

BARTON, Nr. Farndon
Derek Rayment Antiques
Orchard House, Barton Road. (D.J. and K.M. Rayment.) Est. 1960. Open by appointment every day. *STOCK: Barometers, 18th—20th C, from £100.* LOC: A534. PARK: Easy. TEL: Farndon (0829) 270429; home — same. SER: Valuations; restorations (barometers only); buys at auction (barometers). FAIRS: Harrogate; British International Birmingham; Olympia. VAT: Stan/Spec.

CHEADLE

Malcolm Frazer Antiques
19 Brooklyn Crescent. Open by appointment.
STOCK: Marine, scientific and decorative antiques. TEL: (061) 428 3781.

D.J. Massey and Son
14 High St. Est. 1900. Open 9−5.30, Wed.
9−1. *STOCK: Jewellery, gold and diamonds.*
PARK: Easy. TEL: (061) 428 6953.

CHEADLE HULME

Allan's Antiques
10 Ravenoak Rd. (C. Allan.) Est. 1979. CL:
Tues. and Wed. *STOCK: Furniture, collectables, general antiques.* TEL: (061) 485 3132.
SER: Buys at auction.

CHESTER   (0244)

Adams Antiques   LAPADA
65 Watergate Row. (B. and T. Adams.) Est.
1973. CL: Sun. except by appointment. Open
10−5. SIZE: Medium. *STOCK: English and Continental furniture, £200−£4,000; English and French clocks, £150−£4,000; oils, watercolours and objets d'art, £10−£1,000;* all 18th−19th C. PARK: Nearby. TEL: 319421.
SER: Valuations; restorations (furniture, clocks, and oil paintings). VAT: Stan/Spec.

Angela Antiques
8 Christleton Rd. Est. 1920. Open Mon.,
Thurs. and Sat., or by appointment. *STOCK: Victorian jewellery, small collectable silver, china and small furniture.* TEL: 336816. VAT: Spec.

Antique Exporters of Chester
                              Export only
Open by appointment only. SIZE: Warehouse.
STOCK: Furniture. TEL: Tarvin (0829) 41001;
home − Chester (0244) 570069. SER: Packing.

Antiques Scheherezade
59 Watergate Row. Est. 1977. Open 10−5.
STOCK: General antiques and bric-a-brac.
TEL: 316733.

Boodle and Dunthorne Ltd.
52 Eastgate St. Est. 1798. Open 9−5.30.
SIZE: Large. *STOCK: Jewellery, watches, silver, 18th−19th C, £50−£10,000; clocks and clock sets, mid-19th C, £250−£2,000.*
Not stocked: Furniture. PARK: Multi-storey in Pepper St. TEL: 26666. VAT: Stan/Spec.

Chester continued

Chester Antique Hypermarket
41 Lower Bridge St. (Antique Forum Ltd.) Est.
1963. Open 10−5. SIZE: Large. LOC: Town centre. PARK: Easy. TEL: (01) 263 4045.

Chester Antiques
49 Watergate Row. (R. and M.D. Davison.)
Est. 1970. *STOCK: Longcase, carriage and mantel clocks; Victorian walnut furniture, oak and mahogany, china and glass, barometers, porcelain, weapons, dolls.* TEL: 311768.
VAT: Spec.

Chester Furniture Cave
97a Christleton Rd., Boughton. (G.A. Hadley.)
Open 10−5. SIZE: Warehouse. *STOCK: Furniture.* PARK: Easy. TEL: 314798.

Farmhouse Antiques
23 Christleton Rd., Boughton. (K. Appleby.)
Est. 1973. Open 10−5.30. SIZE: Large.
STOCK: Copper, brass, farmhouse furniture, longcase clocks. LOC: 1 mile from City centre on main Whitchurch Rd., A41. PARK: Easy.
TEL: 22478; evenings − 318391. VAT: Stan/Spec.

Filkins Antiques
77 Watergate Row. (P. and B. Le Rougetel.)
Est. 1978. Open 10−4.45, Wed. 10−1.
SIZE: Medium. *STOCK: Linen and lace, 19th−20th C, £10−£200; tradesmen's tools and scientific instruments, £1−£300; furniture, £10−£500; all 18th−20th C.* LOC:
Town centre. PARK: Nearby. TEL: 318782;
home − 43259.

Grosvenor Antiques of Chester
22 Watergate St. (Mrs. P. Lloyd.) Est. 1971.
Open 9.30−5.30. SIZE: Medium. *STOCK: Jewellery, Georgian and Victorian; furniture, china, porcelain, shipping goods, dolls, silver, Oriental carpets and rugs.* Not stocked:
Stamps, coins. PARK: Easy. TEL: 315201.
SER: Valuations; restorations; repairs (jewellery). VAT: Stan/Spec.

Guildhall Fair
34 Watergate St. Open Thurs. 10−4. There are 20 dealers at this market selling a wide range of general antiques.

Erica and Hugo Harper
27 Watergate Row. Est. 1964. CL: Wed. p.m.
Open 10−5. SIZE: Large. *STOCK: Victoriana, 25p−£300; furniture, Victorian and Edwardian; copper, glass, china.* Not stocked: Jewellery, militaria, coins, fine furniture. TEL: 23004;
home − 21880. VAT: Stan.

J. Alan Hulme
54 Lower Bridge St. Open 10−5, or by appointment. *STOCK: Maps, 16th−19th C; prints 18th−19th C.* TEL: 44006/336472.

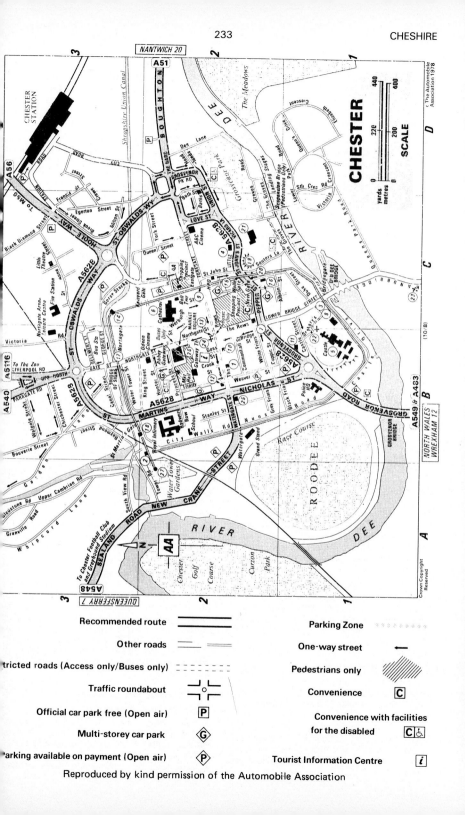

NANTWICH 20
A51

CHESTER STATION

CHESTER

SCALE

yards
metres

Recommended route

Other roads

Restricted roads (Access only/Buses only)

Traffic roundabout

Official car park free (Open air) P

Multi-storey car park G

Parking available on payment (Open air) P

Parking Zone

One-way street

Pedestrians only

Convenience C

Convenience with facilities
for the disabled C &

Tourist Information Centre i

Reproduced by kind permission of the Automobile Association

Chester continued

Jamandic Ltd.
22 Bridge St. Row. Est. 1975. CL: Sun., except by appointment. Open 9.30—5, Sat. 10.30— 1.30. SIZE: Medium. *STOCK: Decorative furniture, porcelain, pictures and prints.* TEL: 312822. VAT: Stan/Spec.

Look Around Antiques
61 Watergate Row. (J. and M. Haywood.) *STOCK: Furniture, 17th—18th C; copper, brass, oil lamps; clocks, longcase and mantel.* TEL: 49826.

Lowe and Sons Ltd.
11 Bridge St. Row. Est. 1770. *STOCK: Jewellery and silver, Georgian, Victorian and Edwardian; unusual collectors' items.* TEL: 25850. VAT: Stan/Spec.

Made of Honour
11 City Walls. (E. Jones.) Open 10—5. *STOCK: General antiques, Staffordshire figures, books.* LOC: Next to Eastgate clock, wall level. TEL: 314208.

Richard A. Nicholson
25 Watergate St. Est. 1961. Open 9.30—1 and 2.15—5. SIZE: Small. *STOCK: Maps, 1540—1840, £1—£1,000; prints, 1650—1890, £1— £300; atlases, £100—£15,000; watercolours and drawings, £4—£200.* LOC: Town centre 100yds. from The Cross. PARK: 200yds. at bottom of street behind church. TEL: 26818; home — 336004. SER: Illustrated monthly catalogue issued. VAT: Stan/Spec.

Christopher Pugh Antiques
LAPADA
68 Waterloo St. Est. 1964. Open 10—5 or by appointment. SIZE: Large. *STOCK: Early English pottery, porcelain, glass, watercolours, maps, 18th to early 19th C furniture, rugs, metalware.* LOC: Next to city walls. PARK: Easy. TEL: 314137; home — 42300. SER: Valuations; buys at auction. VAT: Stan/Spec.

Richmond Galleries
1st Floor, Watergate Buildings, New Crane St. (Mrs. M. Armitage.) Est. 1970. Open 10—5. SIZE: Large. *STOCK: Stripped pine, decorative items.* LOC: Direction of Watergate St., 100 yds. past Race course main entrance. PARK: Own. TEL: 317602; home — 24285.

Sutherland Antiques
1/2 City Walls, Northgate St. (S. New.) Est. 1980. Open daily, Sun. and Mon. by appointment. SIZE: Small. *STOCK: Watercolours, 18th—19th C, £50—£100; furniture, 19th C, £100—£500; silver, all periods, from £50.* LOC: Near Abbey Green. PARK: Easy. TEL: 313400; home — same. SER: Valuations; buys at auction. FAIRS: Monthly Northgate Arena. VAT: Stan.

Chester continued

Bernard Walsh Ltd.
11 St. Michaels Row. Est. 1950. Open 9—5. SIZE: Large. *STOCK: Silver, bijouterie; objets d'art, porcelain; glass, copper, ivory.* PARK: Easy. TEL: 26032.

Watergate Antiques
56 Watergate St. (A. Shindler.) Est. 1968. Open 9.30—5.30. SIZE: Medium. *STOCK: Silver and plate, porcelain and pottery, furniture, militaria, jewellery.* LOC: From Liverpool first set of traffic lights past Waterfall Roundabout, turn left. PARK: At rear. TEL: 44516. VAT: Stan.

Wellesley Wilson
Aldersey Manor, Aldersey. (R.T. Wilson.) Est. 1947. Open by appointment only. *STOCK: Furniture and paintings, 17th—19th C, £50—£5,000.* LOC: ½ mile off A41. TEL: Broxton (082925) 500. SER: Valuations. VAT: Stan/Spec.

CONGLETON   (0260)

Cottage Crafts Antiques
16 Lawton St. (D. Shaw.) CL: Wed. Open 10—5. *STOCK: Pine, shipping goods, Doulton pottery and glass, gold and silver, jewellery, some clocks.* TEL: 274528; home — 275331.

The Old Pine Shop
66a Rood Hill. (Mrs. J.P. Tryon.) Est. 1979. Open 10—5.30, Wed. and Sun. by appointment. SIZE: Small. *STOCK: Stripped pine, £40—£1,000.* LOC: Just off A34. PARK: Nearby. TEL: 279228; home — same.

DISLEY   (066 32)

Crescent Antiques
31 Buxton Rd. (J.P. Cooper.) Est. 1972. CL: Wed. Open 10.30—6, Sun. 12—6. SIZE: Small. *STOCK: General antiques, including furniture, pottery, silver, 19th C, £20—£500.* PARK: 25yds. beyond shop on forecourt of Crescent Inn. TEL: 5677.

Mill Farm Antiques
50 Market St. (F.E. Berry.) Resident. Est. 1968. Open every day, always available. SIZE: Medium. *STOCK: Clocks, mechanical music, general antiques, pianos, shipping goods, £25—£5,000.* LOC: A6 7 miles south of Stockport. PARK: Easy. TEL: 4045 (24 hrs.). SER: Valuations; restorations (clocks, watches, barometers, music boxes). VAT: Stan/Spec.

FARNDON, Nr. Chester   (0829)

Dick Stones Antiques
The Old Bakery, High St. Resident — when closed ring bell. *STOCK: Brass, copper, clocks, porcelain, country bygones and tools, furniture, unusual items.* LOC: A534. TEL: 270243. SER: Restorations and repairs (clocks, barometers); french polishing.

Durham Cathedral, a watercolour by Henry Barlow Carter. From *Understanding Watercolours* by Huon Mallalieu, published by the **Antique Collectors' Club,** 1985.

HALE, Nr Altrincham

Bacchus Antiques — In the Service of Wine

27 Grange Ave. (Mrs. J.A. Johnson.) Est. 1979. Open by appointment only. *STOCK: Corkscrews.* TEL: (061) 980 4747.

Anne Kerr Antiques

191a Ashley Rd. (Mrs. A.B. Kerr.) Est. 1972. CL: Mon. and Wed. Open 10.30—1 and 2.15—5. SIZE: Small. *STOCK: Decorative ware, small silver, 1850—1939, £5—£250; small furniture, 1800—1910, to £450; some Edwardian enamel on silver jewellery.* Not stocked: Large furniture, coins, reproduction pieces, weapons. LOC: Opposite new Ashley Hotel. PARK: Easy. TEL: (061) 928 0091; home — Alderley Edge (0625) 583188. SER: Valuations.

HATTON HEATH, Nr. Chester

Tilston-Woolley Antiques

Hatton Hall Farm. (G. Tilston.) Est. 1961. Open 9—5.30, Sat. 9.30—4.30. SIZE: Large. *STOCK: Mahogany, oak, 18th—19th C, £500—£1,000; country pine, Victorian and Edwardian, £50—£100.* LOC: On A41 4 miles from Chester. PARK: Easy. TEL: Tattenhall (0829) 70003; home — Farndon (0829) 270827. SER: Valuations; restorations; rushing, caning; buys at auction. FAIRS: Buxton, Harrogate and London.

HAZEL GROVE

Gay's (Hazel Grove) Antiques Ltd.   LAPADA
Trade Only

34—38 London Rd. (G.A. Yeo.) Est. 1956. CL: Sat. Open 9—1 and 2—5.30. SIZE: Large. *STOCK: 18th—19th C furniture.* LOC: On A6. PARK: Easy. TEL: (061) 483 5532. VAT: Stan/Spec.

D.J. Massey and Son

177 London Rd. Open 9—5.30, Wed. 9—1. *STOCK: Jewellery, gold and diamonds.* LOC: On A6. PARK: At rear. TEL: (061) 483 5721.

HOOTON

Phillip Courtney and Sons

Oaklands, Oakfield Lane. Est. 1953. *STOCK: Cast iron fire grates, garden ornaments, Victoriana.* LOC: End of Waterworks Lane. TEL: (051) 339 3064. VAT: Stan.

HYDE

W. and I.E. Mann Antiques

270—272 Stockport Rd., Gee Cross. Resident. Est. 1971. *STOCK: General antiques and paintings.* LOC: Centre of Gee Cross village, on main Barnsley/Sheffield road. PARK: Easy. TEL: (061) 368 9196.

Hyde continued

Oxford House — Victorian Skip and Basket Works

Smithy Fold Rd., Gee Cross. (H. Clarke.) Est. 1967. *STOCK: General antiques, shipping goods, old baskets.* TEL: (061) 3382584/ 3683686. SER: Repairs (baskets); caning.

KNUTSFORD   (0565)
Nr. Warrington

David Bedale

5 Minshull St. Est. 1977. SIZE: Small. *STOCK: 17th to early 19th C furniture, metalware, objects.* PARK: 25yds. TEL: 53621. VAT: Stan/Spec.

Cranford Galleries

10 King St. (M.R. Bentley.) Est. 1964. CL: Wed. Open 9.30—5.30. SIZE: Small. *STOCK: Pictures, prints, and Victoriana.* Not stocked: Glass. LOC: Main St. PARK: Easy. TEL: 3646. SER: Framing and mounting. FAIRS: Liverpool, Manchester. VAT: Stan.

John O. Curbishley

19 King St. CL: Wed. Open 9.30—5.30. SIZE: Large. *STOCK: Furniture, 18th—19th C.* PARK: Easy. TEL: 3430; home — 3002. VAT: Stan.

Glynn Interiors

92 King St. Est. 1963. CL: Wed. Open 9—1 and 2—5. SIZE: Large. *STOCK: Furniture, 1750—1900, £50—£2,000; Victorian chairs, £50—£650.* Not stocked: Porcelain. LOC: Ten mins. drive after leaving M6 at Exit 19. PARK: Own. TEL: 4418. SER: Restorations (re-upholstery) and cabinet repairs. VAT: Stan/Spec.

Knutsford Gallery Antiques

12 Princess St. Open Thurs. and Fri. 10—5, Sat. 10—4. *STOCK: Oil paintings, 19th C; prints and watercolours, silver, china, furniture and objets d'art.* TEL: 52778.

Lion Gallery and Bookshop

15a Minshull St. (R.P. Hepner.) Est. 1964. Open Thurs. and Fri. 10.30—4.30, Sat. 10—4.30. SIZE: Medium. *STOCK: Antiquarian maps, prints and books; watercolours; all 16th—20th C; O.S. maps and early directories.* LOC: King St. PARK: Nearby. TEL: 52915. SER: Restorations; binding; cleaning; framing; mounting. VAT: Stan.

Michael Wisehall   BADA

7 Minshull St. Est. 1967. Open 10—1 and 2—5.30. SIZE: Medium. *STOCK: Furniture, 18th C, 19th C and decorative; metalware, decorative and architectural items, 18th—19th C.* PARK: 25yds. TEL: 4901. VAT: Stan/Spec.

LITTLE BUDWORTH (082 921)
Nr. Tarporley
Greenwoods of Oulton Mill LAPADA
Oulton Mill, Park Rd. (Mrs. B. Greenwood.)
Open 9—5, Sat. and Sun. 10—4. STOCK:
Pine. TEL: 282. SER: Hand-made furniture and
kitchens from old pine.

LOWER KINNERTON, Nr. Chester
Brian Edwards Antique Exports
Trade only
Gell Farm. (B.H. Edwards.) Usually open, prior
telephone call preferred. SIZE: Warehouse.
STOCK: Georgian, Victorian and Edwardian
furniture and shipping goods. LOC: 4½ miles
from Chester. TEL: Chester (0244) 660240.
SER: Container packing; courier. VAT: Stan/
Spec.

Old School House Antiques
The Old School House. (M. Melody.) Resident.
Open 10—7 every day. SIZE: Large. STOCK:
Oak, mahogany, shipping goods, 17th—19th
C. TEL: Chester (0244) 660204. VAT: Stan/
Spec.

MACCLESFIELD (0625)
Cheshire Antiques
86—90 Chestergate. (D. Knight.) CL: Sat.
Open 10—5.30. SIZE: Medium. STOCK:
Clocks, from 1650, £500—£1,500; furniture,
18th—19th C, £10—£1,000; porcelain,
pottery, glass, all periods. LOC: From A537,
shop is on right in one-way system 100yds.
from traffic lights. TEL: 23268. SER: Valuations; restorations (porcelain, clocks). VAT:
Stan/Spec.

S.E. Christie Antiques
56 Mill Lane. Resident. Open 10—6. SIZE:
Small. STOCK: Decorative furniture, £100—
£300; decorative items, £25—£150; both
1780—1920. LOC: On Leek road. PARK:
Easy. TEL: 23929.

Robert Copperfield
47-49 Mill Lane. Est. 1960. Open 10—6, or
by appointment. STOCK: 17th—19th C furniture, Oriental rugs, carpets, metalware, textiles, paintings, works of art, ethnographia.
TEL: 26620. VAT: Stan/Spec.

Deja Vu
1 Prestbury Rd. (Mrs. S. Frazer.) CL: Mon.
Open 10—5. STOCK: Clothes and accessories. PARK: Own. TEL: 34834; home —
829514.

Gatehouse Antiques LAPADA
72 Chestergate. (W.H. Livesley.) Est. 1973.
CL: Sun. except by appointment and Wed.
p.m. Open 9—1 and 2—5. STOCK: Small
furniture, silver and plate, glass, brass,
copper, pewter, jewellery, 1650—1880.
PARK: At rear. TEL: 26476; home —
612841. VAT: Spec.

Macclesfield continued
Hidden Gem
3 Chester Rd. (Mrs. P. Tilley.) Usually open
9—5, or by appointment. SIZE: Small.
STOCK: Victorian paintings and general
antiques. TEL: 33884; home — 828348.

Hillman Antiques
60 Mill Lane. (M. Hillman.) Open 9.15—5,
Sat. 11—4. SIZE: Large, and warehouse.
STOCK: Furniture, 18th—19th C; shipping
furniture and Oriental porcelain. TEL: 21227.
VAT: Stan/Spec.

Hills Antiques
Indoor Market, Grosvenor Centre. (D. Hill.)
Est. 1968. CL: Mon. Open 9.30—5.30.
STOCK: Small furniture, jewellery, collectors'
items, stamps, coins, postcards. LOC: Town
Centre. PARK: Easy. TEL: 20777 or 20467.

Deidre King Antiques
124 Chestergate. Est. 1966. Open 10.30—5.
SIZE: Small. STOCK: Decorative English furniture and objects, textiles, samplers, carvings,
sculpture, toys, kitchen items, treen, screens,
lamps, rugs, early prints, folk art, Staffordshire
figures, collectors' items especially unusual
items, 17th—20th C, £5—£2,000. LOC:
Bottom end of Chestergate, through lights,
bear slightly left, next to Chester's restaurant.
PARK: Pinfold St. or opposite. TEL: 25352;
home — 617334.

Macclesfield Antiques
85 Chestergate. (P. Bolton.) Open 10—5.
SIZE: Medium. STOCK: Decorative and small
items, furniture, paintings, 18th—20th C.
PARK: At rear. TEL: 33033; home — 72281.
VAT: Stan/Spec.

D.J. Massey and Son
47 Chestergate. Est. 1900. Open 9—5.30,
Wed. 9—1. STOCK: Jewellery, gold and diamonds, all periods.

Mortens Bookshops Ltd.
Chestergate. STOCK: Antiquarian books,
16th—20th C, £5—£500. LOC: Main St. TEL:
23679 or 22636. SER: Valuations.

Mortens of Macclesfield
54 Chestergate. STOCK: Original prints and
maps. TEL: 25397.

M. and R. Sadler Antiques
97 Chestergate. (R. and Mrs. H. Sadler.) Est.
1948. Open 10—5. SIZE: Small. STOCK:
Jewellery, £1—£250; bric-a-brac, porcelain,
glass, £1—£100, all Victorian and Edwardian;
clocks, watches, 1800—1930. Not stocked:
Large furniture. LOC: 200yds. along main
street facing Town Hall. PARK: Easy. TEL:
23565; home — Bollington (0625) 74431.
SER: Valuations.

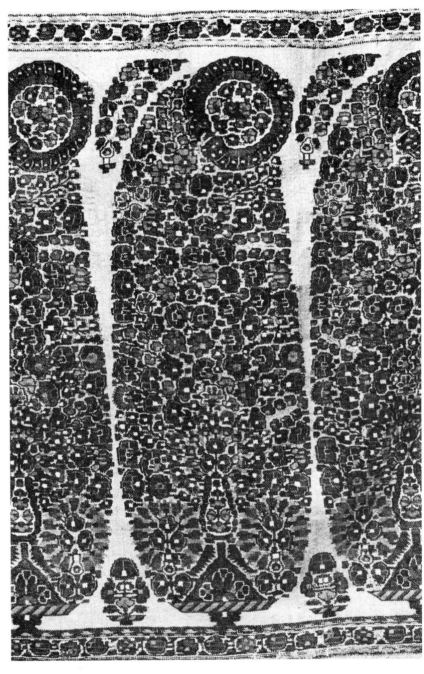

Boteh design from an Afghan period waistband, c.1805. From *The Kashmir Shawl* by Frank Ames, published by the **Antique Collectors' Club,** 1986.

MALPAS (0948)

Stewart Evans *Trade Only*
Church St. Always open. Est. 1955. *STOCK: General antiques; furniture to 1835.* TEL: 860214. SER: Hand-made furniture from old timber; repairs. VAT: Stan/Spec.

MARPLE

Lower Fold Antiques
23 Lower Fold, Marple Bridge. (G. Douglas.) Est. 1974. Resident. Open 10−6. SIZE: Small. *STOCK: General antiques, shipping goods, clocks.* LOC: ⅛ mile from town centre on Compstall Rd. PARK: Easy. TEL: (061)427 4699. SER: Valuations (furniture); restorations (furniture and clocks); clock dial repainting.

J. Milner Antiques *Trade Only*
Poplar Cottage, Windlehurst Rd., Hawk Green. Open anytime by appointment. *STOCK: Early pottery, furniture, old Sheffield plate.* PARK: Easy. TEL: (061) 449 8830. VAT: Stan/Spec.

NANTWICH (0270)

Bridge House Antiques
The Old Police Station, Welsh Row. (L. and V. Tait.) Est. 1950. CL: Wed. p.m. Open 10−5.30. SIZE: Large. *STOCK: Furniture, 19th C, £50−£1,000; china and glass, Victorian, £5−£100; clocks, £100−£500.* Not stocked: Jewellery. PARK: Easy. TEL: 624035. SER: Valuations.

Guy Busby Ltd.
54 Welsh Row. (S.H. French-Greenslade.) CL: Wed. p.m. and Sat. p.m. and Sun. except by appointment. *STOCK: Small furniture, £25−£2,000; porcelain, lamps, decorative items.* PARK: Easy. TEL: 624044 or Tilston (082 98) 332. SER: Interior design. VAT: Stan/Spec.

Chapel Antiques
47 Hospital St. (Miss D.J. Atkin.) Est. 1983. CL: Mon. Open 9.30−5.30, Wed. 9.30−1, or by appointment. SIZE: Medium. *STOCK: Oak, mahogany and pine furniture, Georgian and Victorian, £50−£2,000; longcase clocks, pre-1830, £500−£2,000; copper, brass, silver, glass, porcelain, pottery and small items, 19th C, £5−£250.* LOC: Enter town via Pillory St., turn right into Hospital St. PARK: Easy. TEL: 629508; home − 811437. SER: Valuations; restorations (furniture, clocks); buys at auction.

Nantwich continued

Stancie Cutler Antique and Collectors Fairs
Nantwich Civic Hall. Est. 1975. Open 1st Thurs. of each month, 12−9, trade from 10 a.m. Bank Holidays and New Year's Day 10−6, trade from 8.30 a.m. There are 75 stands at this fair selling *a wide variety of antiques from large furniture to thimbles, mostly pre-1940.* Also 2nd Sat. of each month antique collectors' market, 10−4, trade from 9. There are 70 stands. PARK: Easy. TEL: Home − 666802 (ansaphone).

Farthings Antiques
50/52 Hospital St. (P. and A. Jones.) Est. 1964. CL: Wed. p.m. Open 9−5.30. *STOCK: Furniture, glass, porcelain, silver.* TEL: 625117. VAT: Stan/Spec.

Roderick Gibson
22/24 Hospital St. and The Warehouse, Arnold St. (R.E.L. Gibson.) Est. 1974. CL: Wed. and Sun. except by appointment. Open 9.30−5. SIZE: Large. *STOCK: Furniture, 1700−1920, £50−£5,000; copper and brass, glass, porcelain, silver and pictures, mainly 19th C, £50−£3,000; military, marine and interesting curios, 1800−1920, £20−£300.* PARK: Easy. TEL: 625301; evenings − same. SER: Valuations; restorations (furniture and metalwork); buys at auction. VAT: Stan/Spec.

Mottram Antiques
78 Hospital St. (F. and A. Mottram.) Est: 1965. CL: Mon. and Wed. Open 10−1 and 2−5.30. SIZE: Medium. *STOCK: Furniture, £100−£1,000; decorative objects and instruments; all 18th-19th C.* LOC: In old town, off Pillory St. PARK: Easy. TEL: 628019; home − 661911. SER: Valuations; restorations. VAT: Stan/Spec.

Nantwich Antique Centre
The Old Police Station, Welsh Row. CL: Wed. p.m. Open 10−5.30. There are six dealers at this centre selling *a wide range of furniture, china, glass, art deco and silver.* PARK: Easy. TEL: 624035.

Pillory House
18 Pillory St. (D. Roberts.) Est. 1968. CL: Wed. Open 9−5.30. *STOCK: Hand-carved chimney pieces and oak.* TEL: 623524.

Townwell House Antiques LAPADA
52 Welsh Row. (R. Boyer.) Open 9−6 and by appointment. SIZE: Large. *STOCK: Period furniture.* TEL: 625953. VAT: Stan/Spec.

Wyche House Antiques LAPADA
22 Pepper St. (Miss J. Clewlow.) Est. 1976. CL: Wed. Open 9−5. *STOCK: Furniture, silver, paintings, Worcester, jewellery.* TEL: 626803; home − 628245. VAT: Stan/Spec.

Coppelia Antiques

Valerie and Roy Clements

Holford Lodge
Plumley Moor Road
Plumley, Cheshire

Tel: (056581) 2197   4 Miles M6 (J.19)

8-day brass face showing phases of the moon, chapter ring and spandrels. Very fine quality flame mahogany case in original condition. The collector's choice. Height 90ins. ex finial. Maker JOSEPH TOMLINSON PRESCOT c.1755.

NESTON

Vine House Antiques
Vine House, Parkgate Rd. (P. and M. Prothero.) Est. 1969. Open by appointment. SIZE: Medium. *STOCK: Small furniture, mainly 18th—19th C, £20—£400; silver, from late 18th C, £7.50—£500; glass, 18th—19th C, £1—£80; collectors' items.* Not stocked: Clocks, paintings. LOC: Coming from Chester A540 to West Kirby, 8 miles from Chester turn left to Neston, 50yds. down Parkgate road from village centre. Queen Anne house on right-hand drive in. PARK: Easy. TEL: (051) 336 2423. SER: Valuations; buys at auction.

NEWTOWN

Regent House Antiques
8 Buxton Rd. Est. 1961. Open 9—5, Sat. 2—5. *STOCK: English furniture, clocks, Oriental porcelain, oil paintings, watercolours, general antiques.* LOC: A6, near Disley. PARK: Easy. TEL: New Mills (0663) 42684.

PLUMLEY

Coppelia Antiques
Holford Lodge, Plumley Moor Rd. (V. and R. Clements.) Resident. Est. 1970. Open every day by appointment. SIZE: Medium. *STOCK: Over fifty clocks, £40—£8,000; period furniture, Victorian suites and chairs.* LOC: 4 miles junction 19 M6. PARK: Easy. TEL: Lower Peover (056 581) 2197. SER: Valuations; restorations (clocks). FAIRS: Tatton Park, Chester, British International Birmingham. VAT. Stan/Spec.

POYNTON (0625)

Derbyshire Antiques Ltd.
159 London Rd. South. (R.C. and M.T. Derbyshire.) Resident. Est. 1960. Open 10—5.30, Wed. 10—12.30. SIZE: Large. *STOCK: Early oak and walnut, 16th—18th C; Georgian furniture, mahogany and walnut, to 1820.* LOC: On A523, 1½ miles from A6 Buxton turn-off. PARK: Own. TEL: 873110. SER: Valuations; restorations. VAT: Stan/Spec.

PRESTBURY (0625)

Philip Cowan Antiques
The Village. Open 10—5.30, Sun. 11—5.30, or by appointment. *STOCK: Fine English furniture, 17th—19th C; mahogany sideboards, long sets of chairs, bureaux, secretaire and breakfront bookcases, partners desks, tea, card and dining tables, linen presses, longcase clocks, settees, armchairs; oak dressers, gateleg and refectory tables, ladder and spindle back rush-seated chairs, decorative and small items.* TEL: 828311 or (0860) 311874.

Prestbury continued

Prestbury Antiques
4 Swanwick House, The Village. (M. Rawson-Bridgford.) CL: Mon. and Wed. Open 10—5, Sun. 2—5. *STOCK: Furniture, pictures, silver, glass, ceramics, decorative items and collectables, 18th—20th C.* TEL: Macclesfield (0625) 827966. VAT: Stan/Spec.

PULFORD, Nr. Chester
E. and B. Rushton   *Mainly Trade*
The Old Rectory. Open any time by appointment. *STOCK: Early lighting, porcelain, unusual items, lithophones.* LOC: On A483. TEL: Rossett (0244) 570150.

REDDISH, Nr. Stockport
G.E. Leigh and Son
Houldsworth Sq. (G.E. and J.E. Leigh.) CMBHI. Est. 1947. CL: Wed. Open 9—5.30, SIZE: Small. *STOCK: Jewellery, £10—£300; watches, £10—£500; clocks £20—£1,000; all 19th—20th C.* LOC: From A6 take road to Reddish at Heaton Chapel traffic lights. Turn left in one mile immediately before traffic lights by Clock Tower on Houldsworth Sq. PARK: Easy. TEL: (061) 432 2413. SER: Valuations; restorations. VAT: Spec.

RINGWAY, Nr. Altrincham
Cottage Antiques
Hasty Lane. (J. Gholam.) Est. 1967. SIZE: Medium. *STOCK: Furniture, metalware, ceramics, glass, early 18th—mid 19th C.* Not stocked: Jewellery, jade and ivory. LOC: On main road to Manchester airport. Hasty Lane is off A538, very close to airport. PARK: Easy. TEL: (061) 980 7961. SER: Valuations. VAT: Stan/Spec.

RUNCORN   (5 fig. no.) (092 85)
                        (6 fig. no.) (0928)
B. Braverman
58 High St. CL: Wed. *STOCK: General antiques.* TEL: 72529. FAIRS: Liverpool.

SALE
Eureka Antiques
18 Northenden Rd. (N. Gibson and A.J. O'Donnell.) Est. 1965. Open 10—5. SIZE: Large. *STOCK: Furniture, 17th-19th C, £40—£1,000+; porcelain, 19th C, £10—£100; clocks, 18th-19th C, £100—£750 upwards.* Not stocked: Arms, armour, coins, stamps. LOC: After 3rd set of traffic lights on Manchester to Chester road. Turn left over railway bridge, 300yds. on. PARK: Easy. TEL: (061) 962 5629. SER: Valuations. FAIRS: Harrogate (Spring), West London (Spring, Autumn), Kensington, Brighton, Olympia, British International Birmingham, Buxton. VAT: Stan/Spec.

Sale continued

Trader
68 Washway Rd. (G. Cooper.) CL: Sat. Open 10.30—5 or by appointment. *STOCK: Mahogany furniture.* TEL: (061) 969 9057 (24hrs.).

SANDBACH
           (4 & 5 fig. no.) (093 67)
                        (6 fig no.) (0270)
Peter A. Curbishley
11 Welles St. Est. 1965. Open 9.30—5, Tues. and Sat. by appointment. SIZE: Medium. *STOCK: Furniture and general antiques, 18th—19th C, £5—£1,000.* LOC: 1 mile off Junction 17, M6. PARK: Easy. TEL: 761799.

STOCKPORT
The Antique Shop
23-25 Middle Hillgate. (P. Norgrove.) Open 12.30—5.30, Sat. 10—5 or by appointment. *STOCK: Longcase and wall clocks.* TEL: (061) 477 8970.

Carl Bright Antiques
6 Portland Grove, Heaton Moor. Est. 1972. Open 9—1 and 2—5, Wed. 9—1, Sat. 9—5. SIZE: Medium. *STOCK: Furniture, pottery, glass and curios, 18th C, £5—£100.* LOC: Off Heaton Moor road near A6. PARK: Easy. TEL: (061) 442 9334; home — (061) 431 5685. SER: Restorations.

Chestergate Antiques
145 Buxton Rd. (J.G. Woods.) Open 10—5. *STOCK: Clocks, period and Victorian furniture.* TEL: (061) 456 8050; home — (061) 442 6795.

John S. Curbishley
262 Wellington Rd. South. Open 9—6 or by appointment. SIZE: Large. *STOCK: Furniture, all periods.* Not stocked: Art nouveau. LOC: A6. From Manchester, shop on right on south side of Stockport. PARK: Easy. TEL: (061) 480 3406. SER: Buys at auction. VAT: Stan/Spec.

Curiosity
83 Moorland Rd., Woodsmoor. (L.E. Thompson.) Resident. Est. 1981. CL: Wed. Open 10—6. SIZE: Medium. *STOCK: Furniture, stripped pine; pottery and china, Victorian and art deco; jewellery, linen.* LOC: From Stockport, take 1st right past Davenport Cinema, off A6 2nd left is Moorland Rd. PARK: Easy. TEL: (061) 456 4022.

Flintlock Antiques
28 and 30 Bramhall Lane. (F. Tomlinson and Son.) Est. 1968. SIZE: Large. *STOCK: Furniture, clocks, pictures, scientific instruments.* TEL: (061) 480 9973. VAT: Stan/Spec.

Stockport continued

The Garrick Bookshop
142 Buxton Rd, Heaviley and 20A Wellington Rd. South. (P.S. Aird.) Est. 1969. Open 10—5.30. SIZE: Large. *STOCK: Secondhand books, £5—£100.* LOC: Main A6, 1½ miles from Mersey Square in direction of Buxton, opposite Classic Cinema. PARK: At rear. TEL: (061) 483 6391. SER: Valuations; buys at auction. VAT: Stan.

Grenville Street Bookshop
105 Grenville St., Edgeley. (J.A. Heacock.) Est. 1978. CL: Mon. *STOCK: Secondhand and antiquarian books, some newspapers, magazines, postcards, maps, prints and ephemera.* LOC: Off A6 down Greek St. to roundabout, take second left on to Mercian Way, Grenville St. is at the end on the right. PARK: Easy. TEL: (061) 477 1909.

Hole in the Wall Antiques
Lancashire Hill. (M. and A. Ledger.) Est. 1960. Open 9.30—5.30, Sat. 10—5.30, Sun. by appointment. SIZE: Large. *STOCK: Furniture, 19th—20th C, £100—£400.* LOC: From A6 into Belmont Way, then 4th right at roundabout. PARK: Easy. TEL: (061) 477 3804; home — (061) 480 2656. SER: Valuations; restorations; buys at auction.

Imperial Antiques   LAPADA
295 Buxton Rd., Great Moor. (A. Todd.) Est. 1972. Open 10—5.30, Sun. by appointment. SIZE: Large. *STOCK: Oriental antiques, English and Continental furniture, porcelain, clocks and silver; Persian carpets.* LOC: A6 Buxton Rd., 1½ miles south of town centre. TEL: (061) 483 3322; home — (061) 428 4152. SER: Buys at auction. VAT: Stan/Spec.

Stockport continued

Morris Fine Art   *Trade Only*
1 Newby Rd., Heaton Norris. (J.M. Morris.) Est. 1965. Open by appointment only. SIZE: Medium. *STOCK: Oil paintings, watercolours, English and Continental, 19th—20th C, £50—£500.* LOC: From Mersey Sq., along Heaton Lane to Didsbury Rd., turn right near Orbro, Bankfield Avenue. PARK: Easy. TEL: (061) 432 5459. SER: Valuations; buys at auction. VAT: Stan.

G.R. Naisby and Son Ltd. LAPADA
65—67 Wellington Rd. North. Est. 1955. Open 10.30—5.30, Sat. 10.30—1. SIZE: Large. *STOCK: General items, paintings.* LOC: A6. PARK: Easy. TEL: (061) 480 6445; home — (061) 432 8737. SER: Valuations. VAT: Stan.

Nostalgia
The Victorian Fireplace, 61b Shaw Heath. (D. and E. Durrant.) Est. 1975. Open 10—6, Sun. by appointment. SIZE: Large. *STOCK: Fireplaces, £200—£2,000; architectural items, general antiques, £50—£500; all 19th C.* PARK: Easy and at rear. TEL: (061) 477 7706. SER: Valuations. VAT: Stan/Spec.

Oqyer Antiques
122 Wellington St., Church Gate. (E. Warburton.) Est. 1979. CL: Wed. Open 9.30—5.30, Mon. and Thurs. 12.30—5.30. SIZE: Medium. *STOCK: Cut glass perfume bottles; Victorian glass, blue and white china and pottery, curios, jewellery, kitchenalia, linen, £5—£50.* LOC: Turn into Edwards St. by the Town Hall, at 'T' junction turn left, shop on corner. PARK: Easy. TEL: (061) 429 6646. FAIRS: Deanwater Hotel.

Stockport continued

Page antiques
424 Buxton Rd., Great Moor. Open daily.
SIZE: Large. *STOCK: Victorian and Georgian furniture, brass, copper, silver, plate, stripped pine.* LOC: A6. TEL: (061) 483 9202; home — (061) 427 2412. VAT: Stan/Spec.

Woodford Antiques   LAPADA
382 Buxton Rd., Great Moor (T. and M. Cooper.) Est. 1975. CL: Wed. Open 10—5, Sat. 10—1, Sat. p.m. and Sun. by appointment. SIZE. Medium. *STOCK: Furniture, Georgian to Edwardian, silver plate, brassware and small items.* LOC: On A6, 2 miles south of Stockport. PARK: Easy. TEL: (061) 483 9917; home — Alderley Edge (0625) 582074. SER: Valuations. VAT: Stan/Spec.

STOCKTON HEATH
The Antique Shop
35 Walton Rd. (Mr. and Mrs. M.E. Clare.) CL: Wed. Open 10—5. *STOCK: Furniture, pine, barometers, clocks, instruments and items of interest, £5—£2,000.* TEL: Warrington (0925) 67436.

STRETTON, Nr. Warrington
Antiques Etc.
Shepcroft House, London Rd. (Mr. and Mrs. M.E. Clare.) Est. 1978. Resident, usually available. SIZE: Medium. *STOCK: Furniture, pine, barometers, clocks, instruments and items of interest, £5—£2,000.* LOC: A49, towards Warrington, through Stretton traffic lights, next turning on left. PARK: Easy. TEL: Norcott Brook (092 573) 431.

TILSTON, Nr. Malpas   (082 98)
Well House Antiques
The Well House. (S. French-Greenslade.) Est. 1968. CL: Sun., Mon. and Tues., except by appointment. Open 9.30—5. SIZE: Medium. *STOCK: Small furniture, £5—£2,000; glass, silver, china, 19th C; country bygones.* LOC: From Whitchurch on A41, take B5395 signposted Malpas. PARK: Easy. TEL: 332; home — same. VAT: Stan/Spec.

TIVERTON   (0884)
Mrs. B. Arden   LAPADA
Hulgrave Hall. Resident. Open by appointment only. *STOCK: 18th—19th C oak and mahogany furniture, metalware.* TEL: Tarporley (082 93) 2427.

WARBURTON
Saracens Head Inn
(Hoyles Antiques and Collectors Bazaars.) Open Wed. 2—10, trade from 1.30. There are approx. 40 dealers at this market offering a wide selection of general antiques. PARK: Easy. TEL: (0253) 725788.

WARRINGTON   (0925)
The Magpie's Nest
665, Knutsford Rd., Latchford. (Mrs. V.K. Woolley.) Est. 1967. CL: Sun. a.m., and Mon. and Thurs. Open 10.30—4.30. SIZE. Medium. *STOCK: Furniture, china, glass, silver, copper, brass.* LOC: Main Knutsford-Warrington road, near Manchester ship canal swing bridge PARK: Easy. TEL: 37079.

The Rocking Chair
Unit 3/6 St. Peter's Way. (N. and J. Barratt.) Est. 1971. Open 9—5.30. SIZE: Large. *STOCK: Furniture and bric-a-brac, all periods.* PARK: Easy. TEL: 52409. SER: Valuations; shipping, packing. VAT: Stan.

WHITEGATE, Nr. Northwich
The Antiques Shop
Cinder Hill. (T.H. and B.A. Rogerson.) Est. 1979. CL: Thurs. Open 9.30—6 including Sun., Mon. 2—6. SIZE: Small. *STOCK: Pottery, porcelain, general antiques, jewellery, silver and plate, £5—£500; furniture, clocks, £100—£1,000; all 18th—19th C; paintings, watercolours, 19th C, £25—£500.* LOC: 1½ miles from A556 (Northwich by-pass) near village post office. PARK: Easy. TEL: Sandiway (0606) 882215; home — same.

WILMSLOW   (0625)
Peter Bosson Antiques
10B Swan St. Est. 1965. CL: Mon. and Wed. Open 10—1 and 2—5.30, or by appointment. SIZE: Small. *STOCK: Clocks, 1675—1900, £5—£2,000; barometers, unusual items.* Not stocked: Porcelain, silver. LOC: On A34. PARK: 50yds. away. TEL: 525250; home — 527857. SER: Restorations (repair of clocks); buys at auction. VAT: Stan/Spec.

Knutsford Road Antiques
48 Knutsford Rd. (F.G. and A.P. Casey.) Est. 1969. CL: Wed. p.m. and Mon. Open 10.30—1 and 2.30—5. SIZE: Small. *STOCK: Furniture, £25—£1,000; pottery and porcelain, £5—£200; unusual collectors' items, from £5; small silver, jewellery, glass and metalware.* LOC: B5086. PARK: Easy. TEL: 531829; home — 526043.

Cleverland

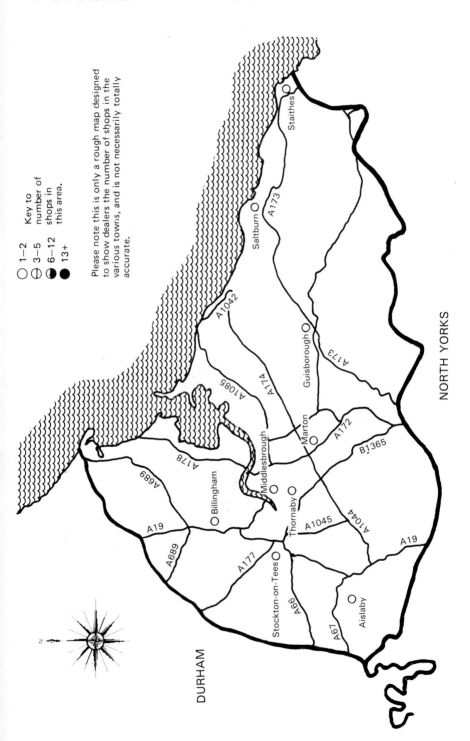

Key to number of shops in this area.

○ 1–2
◑ 3–5
◐ 6–12
● 13+

Please note this is only a rough map designed to show dealers the number of shops in the various towns, and is not necessarily totally accurate.

NORTH YORKS

DURHAM

Staithes

Saltburn

A173

A1042

Guisborough

A173

A1085

A174

Marton

A172

B1365

A178

A689

Billingham

Middlesbrough

Thornaby

A1045

A1044

A19

A689

A19

A177

Stockton-on-Tees

A66

Aislaby

A67

Cleveland

BILLINGHAM
Margaret Bedi Antiques
5 Station Rd. Est. 1976. Open by appointment. *STOCK: Furniture, 1720—1920; metalware; silver and English pottery.* LOC: 300yds. off A19, by village green. PARK: Easy. TEL: Stockton-on-Tees (0642) 607296. VAT: Stan/Spec.

GUISBOROUGH   (0287)
Atrium Antiques
53—55 Church St. (W.L. and M.G. Richardson.) Est. 1967. CL: Sun., Mon. and Wed., except by appointment. Open 10.30—4.30. *STOCK: Furniture, silver, pottery, jewellery, clocks, general items.* LOC: Opposite 12th C priory. PARK: Easy. TEL: 32777 anytime.

MARTON, Nr. Middlesborough
E. and N.R. Charlton Fine Art
and Porcelain   LAPADA
69 Cambridge Ave. Resident. Open by appointment. *STOCK: Fine porcelain, 18th—19th C; Victorian watercolours; small Regency furniture.* TEL: Middlesborough (0642) 319642.

MIDDLESBROUGH   (0642)
Middlesbrough Antiques
109A Marton Rd. (McCrory and Conlon.) Resident. Est. 1973. Open by appointment only. SIZE: Medium. *STOCK: Shipping goods, period and Victorian furniture and effects, 18th—20th C, £50—£1,000.* LOC: Junction of Marton Rd. and Russel St. PARK: Easy. TEL: 240371. SER: Valuations.

Polyera Antiques   LAPADA
8 Oxford Rd., Linthorpe. (M. and A. Moor.) Est. 1974. CL: Sat., Sun. and Wed. except by appointment. Open 10—4.30. SIZE: Medium. *STOCK: Furniture, clocks, shipping goods, small items.* Not stocked: Coins, stamps, firearms. LOC: Close to junction with Roman Rd. PARK: Easy. TEL: 824677; home — 826613. VAT: Stan.

SALTBURN
Endeavour Antiques
The Hollies, Victoria Terrace. (J. MacAuliffe.) Est. 1969. Open by appointment only. SIZE: Small. *STOCK: General and interesting antiques, especially 18th—19th C pottery and porcelain; Victorian and Edwardian jewellery.* TEL: Guisborough (0287) 23557. VAT: Stan/Spec.

STAITHES, Nr. Whitby
The Mariners Antiques
High St. Est. 1967. Open July and August daily. Otherwise open Easter—September 30th Sat. and Sun. only 10—6. SIZE: Small. *STOCK: General antiques, 18th—19th C, £1—£100; oil lamps, £10—£100; jewellery, £2—£200; both 19th to early 20th C.* Not stocked: Coins and firearms. PARK: Easy. TEL: Whitby (0947) 840565; home — Middlesborough (0642) 818377.

STOCKTON-ON-TEES   (0642)
Robin Finnegan (Jeweller)
17 Yarm Lane. Est. 1974. Open 9.30—5.30. SIZE: Medium. *STOCK: Jewellery, general antiques, coins and medals, £1—£2,000.* LOC: 100yds. from Swallow Hotel. PARK: Easy. TEL: 601354. SER: Valuations. VAT: Stan.

THORNABY, Nr. Stockton-on-Tees
Alan Ramsey Antiques   LAPADA
Trade Only
4a Thornaby Place. Est. 1973. CL: Wed. Open 10—3, Sat. and Sun. by appointment. SIZE: Warehouse. *STOCK: Victorian and Edwardian shipping goods, including clocks, ornaments, brass, copperware and pine furniture.* LOC: Follow signs for Stockton, turn left immediately before Stockton bridge. PARK: Easy. TEL: Stockton-on-Tees (0642) 603181; home — Stokesley (0642) 711311. VAT: Stan.

YARM
T.B. and R. Jordan   LAPADA
(Fine Paintings)
137 High St. Est. 1974. Open 10—12.30 and 1.30—5.30. SIZE: Medium. *STOCK: Oil paintings, 19th to early 20th C, £150—£3,000; watercolours, £50—£2,000.* LOC: Town centre. PARK: Easy. TEL: Eaglescliffe (0642) 782599. SER: Valuations; restorations; framing. VAT: Spec.

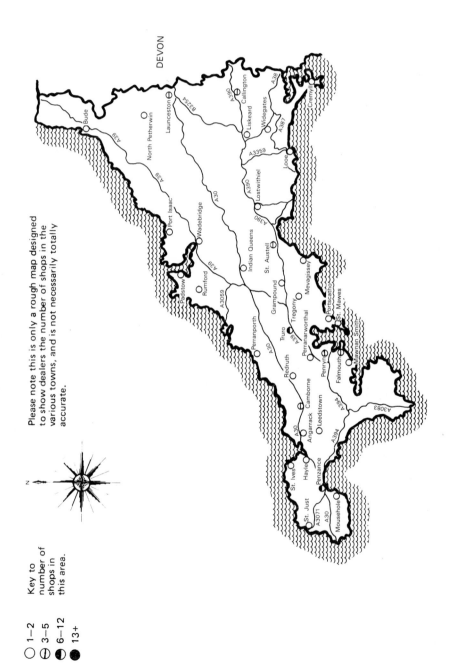

Please note this is only a rough map designed to show dealers the number of shops in the various towns, and is not necessarily totally accurate.

Key to number of shops in this area.

1–2
3–5
6–12
13+

ANGARRACK, Nr. Hayle

Paul Jennings Antiques   *Trade Only*
Millbrook House. Est. 1974. Open by appointment. SIZE: Small. *STOCK: Clocks, furniture, £100—£3,000; watches.* LOC: ½ mile from A30. TEL: Hayle (0736) 754065. VAT: Stan/Spec.

BUDE   (0288)

Bude Antiques
39 Ocean View Rd. (F.G. and H.G. Palmer.) Est. 1962. Open by appointment. *STOCK: General antiques and bric-a-brac.* TEL: 3509.

Cannon Hill Antiques
Fable House, Holnicote Rd. (M.A. Jenkins.) Open by appointment. *STOCK: General antiques, watercolours and oil paintings.* TEL: 4529.

CALLINGTON

Chattels
6 Saltash Rd. (P. Lightbody.) Est. 1968. CL: Sun., except by appointment to the Trade. Open 9.30—5.30. Ring door bell when closed. SIZE: Medium. *STOCK: General antiques.* LOC: A388 crossroads A390 (Tavistock—Liskeard; Saltash—Launceston). PARK: 300yds. TEL: Liskeard (0579) 83184.

Collectors Corner
New Rd. *STOCK: Dinky toys and magazines, motors and model railways.*

Hayloft Antiques
Fore St. *STOCK: Shipping furniture, Victoriana and china.*

Lorelle Art and Antiques
Fore St. (R. Knowles). Est. 1984. CL: Thurs. p.m. Open 10—1 and 1.30—5. SIZE: Medium. *STOCK: Worcester, Doulton, Staffordshire, watercolours, small furniture, glass, 19th C, £5—£100.* LOC: Off main road, opposite Barclays Bank. PARK: 100 yards. TEL: Liskeard (0579) 82783. SER: Valuations; buys at auction (as stock).

CAMBORNE   (0209)

Camborne Junktion
West Charles St. (W. Duncan.) Est. 1975. Open 10—5. Sun. by appointment. SIZE: Warehouse. *STOCK: Lighting and stripped pine, £50—£500; shipping goods.* LOC: 4th turning on left on Helston road out of Camborne. PARK: Own. TEL: 719898; home — Redruth (0209) 211499. SER: Valuations; restorations (French polishing, stripping, metalware repairs and polishing); buys at auction. FAIRS: Ardingly.

Camborne continued

The Old Chair and Wheel Antiques
32 Wellington Rd. (Mrs. N.V. Major.) Est. 1960. Open 10—8. SIZE: Small. *STOCK: Victoriana, china, glass, jewellery, small furniture.* LOC: Road opposite Parish Church in town centre. PARK: Easy. TEL: 713700.

Victoria Gallery
28 Cross St. (J.P. Maker.) CL: Mon. Open 10—5.30. *STOCK: Books, pictures, general antiques.* TEL: 719268.

CREMYLL

Cremyll Antiques
98 Cremyll Beach, Torpoint. *STOCK: Nautical items, small items, jewellery.* TEL: Plymouth (0752) 822934. SER: Repairs (barometers, barographs, watches, clocks, jewellery).

FALMOUTH   (0326)

E. Cunningham Antiques
5 Webber St. Open 10.30—5.30. *STOCK: General antiques.* TEL: 313207.

High Street Antiques and Decor
19 High St. (Cdr. R. Gealer.) Open 9.30—1 and 2—5. SIZE: Large. *STOCK: Maritime antiques, scientific instruments, brass and copper ware, porcelain, jewellery, 18th—20th C.* LOC: From centre of Falmouth (The Moor), turn up High St. — 3 mins. walk. PARK: Nearby. TEL: 319356; home — 317739.

John Maggs
54 Church St. Est. 1900. CL: Sat. p.m. and Wed. Open 10—1 and 2.15—5. SIZE: Medium. *STOCK: Antiquarian prints and maps, all periods to 1850.* Not stocked: Reproductions. LOC: Main street. PARK: At rear of shop. TEL: 313153. SER: Restorations (prints); framing.

Falmouth continued

Packet Quays Gallery
Barracks Ope, High St. (Mrs. A. Rowe.) Est. 1984. Open 10−4.30. SIZE: Small. *STOCK: Small furniture, clocks, copper, brass, marine items, 18th−19th C watercolours and oils, prints and maps, 18th−20th C.* LOC: Just off High St., down steps. PARK: Nearby. TEL: 319336 home − 318279. SER: Buys at auction. FAIRS: Truro, Newton Abbot, Exeter.

GRAMPOUND, Nr. Truro
Radnor House
Fore St. (P. and R. Nosworthy.) Est. 1972. Open 10−6, Sun. and evenings by appointment. SIZE: Medium and store. *STOCK: Mainly 18th and 19th C furniture; decorative items.* Not stocked: Jewellery, coins and weapons. LOC: A390. PARK: Easy. TEL: St. Austell (0726) 882921; home − same. SER: Valuations; buys at auction. VAT: Stan/Spec.

HAYLE   (0736)
W. Dyer & Sons
14 Fore St., Copperhouse. (W.G. Dyer). Resident. Est. 1900. Open 9−1 and 2−5.30, Wed. 9−1. SIZE: Small. *STOCK: Watercolours, some oils, 19th to early 20th C, £25−£250; bric-a-brac, £5−£25.* LOC: Main road. PARK: Easy. TEL: 752787; home − 753362. SER: Valuations; restorations (watercolours and oils).

INDIAN QUEENS, Nr. Newquay
The Collectors Trail
St. Francis Rd. (Mrs. B.M. Hester.) Est. 1979. Open 9−5. SIZE: Medium. *STOCK: Small Victorian and Edwardian furniture, £70−£350; paintings, etchings and engravings, 19th−20th C, £50−£500; copper and brass especially art nouveau, £5−£50.* LOC: A30 from Bodmin, turn right on to A392 to Newquay, shop 100yds. on left. PARK: Easy. TEL: St. Austell (0726) 860338. SER: Valuations; restorations (etchings and engravings cleaned and mounted); buys at auction (small furniture, prints, paintings and copper). FAIRS: Truro, Bristol.

LAUNCESTON   (0566)
The Old Coffee House Antiques
29 Westgate St. (M. Davies and M.D.F. Ward.) CL: Mon. Open 10−5. SIZE: Small. *STOCK: Silver, porcelain and glass, £5−£300.* LOC: Behind town hall. PARK: Opposite. TEL: 3728; home − 4997.

The Pine Shop − Launceston
                                        LAPADA
10 Church St. (B.S. Cooper and R.S. Parsonson.) CL: Thurs. Open 10−5. *STOCK: Pine and general antiques.* TEL: 5605.

The "Royal George" off Dover. Oil painting on canvas signed and dated W.J. Huggins, 1821. Courtesy **Paul Mason Gallery,** 149 Sloane Street, London S.W.1.

Launceston continued

Tamar Gallery
(Antiques and Fine Art)
5 Church St. (Mr. and Mrs. N. Preston.) CL: Thurs. p.m. Open 10−1 and 2.30−5, Mon. by appointment. SIZE: Medium. *STOCK: Watercolours, £30−£1,000; oil paintings, £50−£500; all 18th−20th C; furniture, 17th−19th C, £30−£700; English pottery and porcelain especially 18th to early 19th C blue and white, £10−£200; glass, jewellery, needlework tools, objets d'art, decorative items and bygones.* LOC: Near St. Mary Magdalene Church. PARK: Near Church. TEL: 4233; home − 2740. SER: Restorations (watercolours and oils). VAT: Stan/Spec.

Westward County Pine   LAPADA
Trade Only
The Old Tannery, Newport Industrial Estate. (N.C. Parsonson). CL: Sat. Open 10−5, appointment preferred. *STOCK: Pine and country furniture.* TEL: Canworthy Water (056 681) 309.

LEEDSTOWN, Nr. Hayle   (0736)
A.W. Glasby and Son
Antique Shop. (D.E. Glasby.) Est. 1936. CL: Sat. and Mon. Open 10.15−12.45 and 2.15−5. SIZE: Large. *STOCK: Furniture, porcelain and jewellery, all periods, £10−£1,000.* Not stocked: Coins, medals, scientific instruments. LOC: On main road half-way between Hayle and Helston. PARK: Easy. TEL: 850303. VAT: Stan/Spec.

LISKEARD   (0579)
Antiques and Collectors Fair
Carlton Suite. (Kernow Fairs). Open second Sun. every month 10−4.30. *STOCK: General antiques and collectors' items.* PARK: 100 yards. TEL: Mevagissey (0726) 842957.

Sidbury Galleries
16 Pike St. (J.C. and R.B. Quick.) Est. 1977. CL: Wed. p.m. and Sat. p.m. Open 9.30−5. SIZE: Medium. *STOCK: Furniture, 18th−20th C, £25−£1,500; clothes, £1−£100; collectables, £1−£50, both 19th−20th C.* LOC: Pike St. is the steep hill off The Parade leading to main shopping area. PARK: The Parade. TEL: 46888. VAT: Stan/Spec.

LOOE   (050 36)
Dowling and Bray
Fore St. Est. 1920. *STOCK: General antiques, furniture, pictures.* TEL: 2797. VAT: Stan/Spec.

Looe continued

Tony Martin
Fore St. Est. 1965. CL: Thurs. p.m. Open 9.30−1 and 2−5. Appointment advisable. SIZE: Medium. *STOCK: Porcelain, 18th C; silver, 18th−19th C, both £20−£200; glass, furniture.* LOC: Main street. TEL: 2734; home − 2228. VAT: Stan/Spec.

LOSTWITHIEL
John Bragg Antiques
35 Fore St. Open 10−5. *STOCK: Furniture, mainly Victorian and Edwardian.* LOC: 100yds. off A390. TEL: Bodmin (0208) 872827.

David Patterson Antiques
20 Queen St. Est. 1976. Open 10−5.30. SIZE: Medium. *STOCK: Pine furniture, 19th C, £5−£500; Victoriana, guns, swords, instruments, clocks, watches.* LOC: Opp. Post Office. TEL: Bodmin (0208) 872879.

MAWNAN SMITH, Nr. Falmouth
The Spinning Wheel
The Square. (J.V. Dugdale.) Est. 1965. Open 10−1 and 2.15−5.30. SIZE: Small. *STOCK: Objets d'art and collectors' items.* TEL: Falmouth (0326) 250715; home − (Falmouth (0326) 250584.

MEVAGISSEY   (0726)
J. Barron and Sons
Fore St. TEL: 843405. VAT: Stan.

The Old Curiosity Shop
Olivers Quay. (E. and J. Locks.) CL: Sat. Open 10−5 including Sun., Apr-Oct; Nov-Mar open Wed. and some Sun. *STOCK: General antiques.* TEL: 842957/842117.

MOUSEHOLE
Vanity Fayre
Commercial Rd. (J.L. Gillingham, MPS, DBA.) Est. 1963. CL: Thurs. Open 10−1 and 2−5. SIZE: Medium. *STOCK: Small furniture and clocks, 1800−1900, £10−£500; copper, brass, metals, silver, porcelain, 1700−1900, £5−£500; items of interest, bric-a-brac, from 1800, £1−£250; stamps and coins.* LOC: Main Penzance road through Newlyn and Mousehole. PARK: Nearby. SER: Buys at auction.

NORTH PETHERWIN (056 685)
Nr. Launceston
Pine and Country Antiques
Petherwingate. (W. Herring.) Open 8.30−5.30. SIZE: Medium. *STOCK: Furniture, 19th C including restored and stripped pine, £50−£500; general antiques and bygones.* PARK: Easy. TEL: 381. SER: Restorations; stripping.

PADSTOW (0841)
The Curiosity Shop
West Quay. (Miss S.A. Schofield.) Est. 1982. CL: Sat. Open 10.30−1 and 2−5; also Wed. and Thurs. 7.30−10 p.m.; Sun. 2−5. SIZE: Small. *STOCK: Ceramics, silver and collectables, mainly 19th−20th C, £2−£150.* LOC: Harbour front. PARK: 300yds. TEL: Home − St. Mawgan (0637) 860567. SER: Valuations; buys at auction (ceramics and silver).

Mayflower Antiques
15 Duke St. (Miss C. Hoskin.) Est. 1963. CL: Wed. p.m. and Sun., except in season. Open 10.30−1 and 2.30−5. SIZE: Small. *STOCK: Jewellery, £5−£150; copper, brass, £2−£50, all 19th to early 20th C; commemorative ware, £5−£90; Victorian and later pottery and china, £5−£50.* Not stocked: Weapons, furniture, clocks. LOC: Centre of Padstow. PARK: On Quay. TEL: Home − 532308.

PENRYN
Mainstream
36−40 Market St. (R. Smith.) Open 9−5.30. *STOCK: General antiques.* PARK: Easy. TEL: Falmouth (0326) 75358.

IS YOUR ENTRY CORRECT?
If there is even the slightest inaccuracy in your entry, *please* let us know before 1st January 1987.
GUIDE TO THE
ANTIQUE SHOPS OF BRITAIN
5 Church Street, Woodbridge, Suffolk.

Penryn continued

Penryn Antiques and Pictures
18 Market St. (R.D. James.) Est. 1975. CL: Thurs. p.m. Open 9−5. *STOCK: Small antiques, clocks, prints, maps, oil paintings, watercolours.* PARK: Nearby. TEL: Falmouth (0326) 72229; home − Falmouth (0326) 74978.

Leon Robertson Antiques
7 The Praze. Est. 1972. *STOCK: Furniture and general antiques.* TEL: Falmouth (0326) 72767.

Richard Winkworth Antiques
15 Church Rd. Open 10−5. SIZE: Medium. *STOCK: Pine, satin walnut, brass, copper, china, glass and small antiques.* TEL: Falmouth (0326) 75092.

PENZANCE (0736)
Antron House Antiques
Antron House, Chapel St. (G. and J. Owen.) Est. 1980. Open 9−5; Sat. 9.30−1 in winter, 9.30−5 in summer. SIZE: Small. *STOCK: Edged weapons, £40−£400; militaria, £3−£50, mainly 18th−20th C; Cornish prints and maps, 17th−19th C, £15−£400; shipwreck coins, 16th−19th C, £15−£100.* PARK: Harbour. TEL: 63984; home − same. SER: Valuations; buys at auction (coins and medals).

Attic Antiques
6 The Arcade. (D. Richards.) Resident. Est. 1969. Open daily 10−1 or by appointment. *STOCK: China, glass, small furniture, curios, decorative items, books.* TEL: 61232.

'Bramwell'
3 Old Brewery Yard, Bread St. CL: Wed. Open 10−5. *STOCK: Paintings and collectors' items.* LOC: Top of Bread St., above Mounts Bay Wine Co. TEL: 61160. SER: Restorations (pictures; hand engraving, clock faces re-painted, engraving re- cut).

C.P. and E.M. Frossard
The Store, Belle Vue Terrace. CL: Wed. p.m. and Sat. p.m. except by appointment. Open 9−1 and 2−5.30. *STOCK: Furniture.* TEL: 69292. SER: Restorations.

Brian Humphrys Antiques
1 St. Clare St. Est. 1964. SIZE: Medium. *STOCK: Furniture, clocks, silver, 18th−19th C, £25−£2,000.* PARK: Easy. TEL: 65154. SER: Valuations; buys at auction. VAT: Stan/Spec.

Charles Jackson Antiques
48, 49, 50 Market Jew St. (H.N.B. Jackson.) Est. 1891. SIZE: Large. *STOCK: French and English furniture, oak, glass, porcelain, objets d'art, especially clocks.* TEL: 64388 and 63774. VAT: Stan/Spec.

Penzance continued

Melbourne Antiques
48 Market Jew St. (G.T.M. Jackson.) *STOCK: Jewellery, silver and plate.* TEL: 63774. VAT: Stan/Spec.

New Street Antiques
26 New St. Est. 1975. Open 9.30−5, in summer 9.30−9. SIZE: Medium. *STOCK: Furniture, 17th−19th C, £10−£1,000; brass, china, glass, silver, £1−£300; oils and watercolours, £2−£200.* TEL: 60173. SER: Restorations (furniture, cane seating).

Newton Antiques
85a Market Jew St. (W.N. Newton.) Est. 1956. Open 10.30−5.30. *STOCK: Jewellery, watches, silver, copper, brass, prints and maps of Cornwall, china, glass, coins, small collectables.*

The Old Post House
(Swan Jewellery). 9 Chapel St. (D. Richards). Open 10−5. *STOCK: China, glass, small furniture, curios, decorative items, books.* TEL: 60320.

Tony Sanders Antiques
14 Chapel St. Est. 1972. CL: Wed. Open 9.15−5.30 and evenings in summer 7.30−10. SIZE: Medium. *STOCK: Furniture, 18th−19th C, £10−£500; glass, china, silver, £5−£295; oils and watercolours, 19th and 20th C, £25−£1,500.* TEL: 66620 or 68461. VAT: Stan.

Terry Saunders
Penzance Pine Centre, 13−14 Bread St. Est. 1974. Open 10−5.30, Sat. 10−1. *STOCK: General antiques, pine, silver and plate.* TEL: 64027; home − Penzance (0736) 763658.

PERRANARWORTHAL, Nr. Truro

Old Barn Antiques
(D. Campbell and D. Marsh.) Est. 1960. CL: Sat. Open 10−1 and 2−6, Sat. 10−1. SIZE: Medium. *STOCK: Furniture, 17th to late 19th C; china, clocks, pictures, edged weapons and guns, mainly 18th−19th C.* Not stocked: Books. LOC: A39, midway between Truro and Falmouth. PARK: Easy. TEL: Home − Truro (0872) 863831. SER: Valuations; restorations (wood and metal); buys at auction.

PERRANPORTH

St. George's Antiques
33 St. George's Hill. (J. Holmes.) Est. 1983. CL: Wed. p.m. Open 9.15−1 and 2−5, Sun. in summer 2.30−5. SIZE: Small. *STOCK: Victorian and Edwardian furniture, pottery, porcelain, glass, watercolours, copper and brass, £10−£500.* LOC: B3285, main coast road. PARK: Nearby. TEL: Truro (0872) 572947; home − Truro (0872) 573469. FAIRS: Weston-super-Mare; Carlyon Bay, Truro.

PORT ISAAC

D. Holmes
Pilchards Corner, Port Gaverne. Est. 1965. Open by appointment only. *STOCK: Antique and fine furniture.* TEL: Bodmin (0208) 880254. SER: Restorations.

PORTSCATHO (087 258)
Nr. St. Mawes

Curiosity Antiques
(E. and S. Gale.) Est. 1965. Open 10−5; Oct-Mar by appointment. *STOCK: General antiques, bric-a-brac.* PARK: Easy. LOC: In main square. TEL: 411.

REDRUTH (0209)

Penandrea Gallery
12 Higher Fore St. (W. Dyer and Son F.A.R.G.) Est. 1900. CL: Mon., Thurs. Open 9−1 and 2−5. *STOCK: Watercolours, 19th− 20th C, £5−£1,000; some oils, prints and Victorian items, £1−£100.* LOC: Upper end of main st. PARK: Easy. TEL: 213134. SER: Valuations; restorations; framing (oils and watercolours).

Richard Winkworth Antiques
Unit 6, Station Rd. SIZE: Large. Open 9−5. *STOCK: Pine, oak, satin walnut and mahogany furniture; shipping goods, general antiques.* TEL: 216631.

RUMFORD (3 fig. nos.) (084 14)
Nr. Wadebridge (6 fig. nos.) (0841)

Henley House Antiques
(P. Neale.) *STOCK: Juvenilia, small antiques, bric-a-brac.* TEL: 322.

ST. AUSTELL (0726)

Ancient and Modern   LAPADA
32−34 Polkyth Rd. (P.J. Watts.) Est. 1965. Open 8.30−5. *STOCK: General antiques, paintings, clocks, jewellery, bric-a-brac.* TEL: 73983. VAT: Stan/Spec.

Antiques and Fine Wines
2A East Hill. CL: Thurs. *STOCK: Fine wines, shipping goods, general antiques.* TEL: 67307; evenings − Newquay (06373) 5356.

Mrs. Margaret Chesterton
33 Pentewan Rd. Est. 1965. CL: Sat. p.m. Open 10−5.30, appointment advisable. *STOCK: Victoriana, Edwardiana, 1800−1915; some furniture, porcelain, glass, £1−£500; brass, copper, pewter, jewellery, dolls, automata, musical boxes, watercolours.* LOC: Coming from Plymouth, travel direct to St. Austell. Keep on main by-pass until roundabout for Mevagissey and Pentewan Rd. House is 100yds. on left down this road. PARK: Easy. TEL: 72926.

St. Austell continued

London Apprentice Antiques

Pentewan Rd. (R. and J. Noble.) Resident. Est. 1965. Open 9.30−6. SIZE: Medium. *STOCK: Furniture, 18th−19th C, £25−£800+; Oriental porcelain, furniture and works of art, English porcelain; general antiques.* Not stocked: Coins, jewellery. LOC: On B3273 St. Austell to Mevagissey road. PARK: Easy. TEL: 63780. SER: Valuations; restorations (furniture). VAT: Stan/Spec.

Poldark Antiques

Market House. (Mrs. J. Langran.) Est. 1974. CL: Thurs. Open 9.30−4.30. *STOCK: Jewellery, silver, porcelain, glass, £5−£300; copper, brass, Victoriana, collectors' items; small furniture, £5−£250.* LOC: Opposite parish church. TEL: 72818; home − 63579 (evenings).

ST. IVES

Corner House Antiques

7 Chapel St. (J. West and V.A. Eddy.) Open in winter 9−5, in summer 9−5 and 7−9. *STOCK: General antiques, unusual items, oils and watercolours.* TEL: (0736) 797976.

P.R. Rainsford

1st Floor above Barker & Moore, Chemist, Market Place. Est. 1967. *STOCK: Art books, modern French illustrated bibliography.* VAT: Stan.

St. Ives continued

Mike Read Antique Sciences

Hollies, Talland Rd. Est. 1974. Open by appointment. SIZE: Small. *STOCK: Scientific instruments − navigational, surveying, mining, telescopes and microscopes, medical, 18th−19th C, £10−£5,000.* LOC: Left fork by Porthminster Hotel, left at Talland Garage, then first left, third house on right. PARK: Easy. TEL: Penzance (0736) 796605; home − same. SER: Valuations; restorations. VAT: Spec.

ST. JUST

All Things Bright and Beautiful

Old Sunday School, Cape Cornwall St. (D. and C. Brown.) Est. 1972. CL: Sun. except by appointment. Open 10−6. SIZE: Medium. *STOCK: Stripped pine, mahogany and oak furniture, general antiques and decorative items, £5−£700.* LOC: 200yds. down Cape Cornwall St. from Bank Square. PARK: Easy. TEL: Penzance (0736) 788444.

ST. MAWES (0326)

The Antique Shop

21 Marine Parade. (C. Freeman.) Est. 1970. TEL: 270653/270617.

A fine cast of the 1840s of a learned bear deep into a pile of books, seated casually in a neoclassical armchair in the style of the Louis XVI period. To add to the air of relaxed contentment, Fratin has given the bear one slipper while the other lies discarded underneath the chair. From **Animals in Bronze** by Christopher Payne, published by the **Antique Collectors' Club, 1986.**

TREGONY, Nr. Truro   (087 253)
Clock Tower Antiques
Fore Street. (P.W. Wood.) Est. 1939. Open a.m. and by appointment. SIZE: Large. *STOCK: Furniture, early oak to 19th C, English and Continental, £20—£2,000.* LOC: Between Truro, St. Austell and St. Mawes. PARK: Easy. TEL: 212.

Myrtle House Antiques
67 Fore St. (H.E. Tresidder.) Est. 1953. Open 10—5. *STOCK: Silver, jewellery, clocks, coins, medals, furniture, watches, porcelain, pictures.* TEL: 200. SER: Repair of jewellery, watches, clocks.

TRURO   (0872)
Alan Bennett
15/16 St. Mary's St. Est. 1954. Open 9—5.30. SIZE: Large. *STOCK: Furniture, £50—£3,000; jewellery and porcelain, to 1900, £5—£500.* LOC: Eastern side of cathedral. PARK: 100yds. behind shop. TEL: 73296. VAT: Stan/Spec.

Strickland and Dorling
3 River St. (P. Strickland and T. Dorling.) CL: Thurs. Open 10.30—4.30. *STOCK: Furniture, 18th—19th C; pictures, prints and maps; glass, Staffordshire, pottery, porcelain, collectors' and other items of nautical interest; jewellery, early silver especially spoons.* LOC: Close to Victoria Sq. TEL: 72345.

Trafalgar Gallery
Malpas Rd. (M. Lewis.) Est. 1981. Open 10.30—4.30. SIZE: Small. *STOCK: Small furniture, £50—£100; bric-a-brac, pictures.* LOC: Adjacent to Trafalgar roundabout, on A390. PARK: Easy. TEL: 77888; home — 77979.

Truro Antique Centre
108 Kenwyn St. (M. Pascoe). Open 9.30—5.30. There are 5 dealers at this centre selling *a wide range of general antiques including jewellery.* TEL: 78400.

Village Antiques and Gallery
Peoples Palace, Pydar St. (D. Severn and J. Poole). Est. 1968. Open 10.15—4.15 and by appointment. SIZE: Medium. *STOCK: Early English furniture, 18th C, £500—£1,000; Victorian and Edwardian furniture, £50—£600; silver, plate, porcelain and glass, £5—£150; oils and watercolours, £15—£250.* PARK: Easy. TEL: 70666. SER: Buys at auction (18th—19th C furniture). FAIRS: Truro, Newton Abbot.

Truro continued

Richard Winkworth Antiques
Calenick St. Open 10—5. SIZE: Large. *STOCK: Pine, satin walnut, brass, copper, china, glass and small antiques.* TEL: 40901.

WADEBRIDGE   (020 881)
St. Breock Gallery
St. Breock Churchtown. (Newmark Industrial Securities Ltd.) Open 10—5. *STOCK: Watercolours, 19th C; furniture.* TEL: 2543. LOC: Close to Royal Cornwall Showground.

WIDEGATES   (050 34)
Nr. Looe
Ian Barrett's Furniture Workshop
Pink Cottage. (I. and B. Barrett). Est. 1981. Open 9—5.30, other times by appointment. SIZE: Medium. *STOCK: Furniture, £25—£600; brass and copper, £5—£100; china and glass, £2—£45; all mainly Victorian and Edwardian. Not stocked: Pine, clothing and militaria.* LOC: A387 from Plymouth, 4 miles before Looe. PARK: Easy. TEL: 258; home — same. SER: Restorations (furniture).

John Crome, 'The Shadowed Road', landscape with cottages. Watercolour, 20½ by 16¾ ins. From *Understanding Watercolours* by Huon Mallalieu, published by the **Antique Collectors' Club,** 1985.

THE COTSWOLD ANTIQUE DEALERS' ASSOCIATION

MEMBERS' DIRECTORY

from a Brass in Northleach Church

A Wealth of Antiques in the heart of England

The Cotswolds

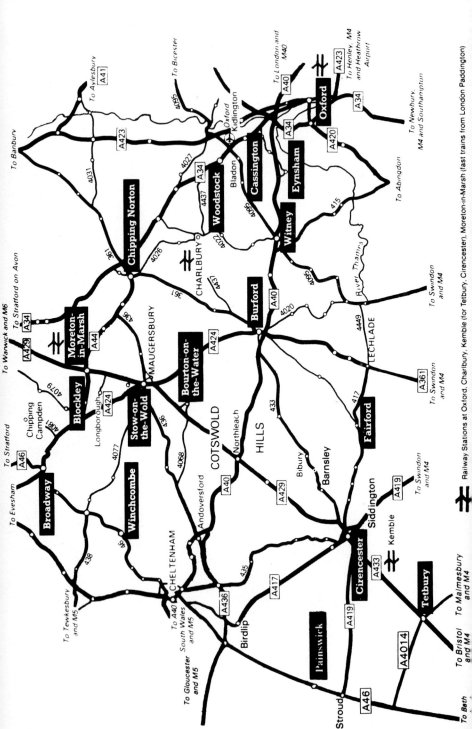

THE COTSWOLD ANTIQUE DEALERS' ASSOCIATION

*Buy Fine Antiques and Works of Art
at provincial prices in England's lovely
and historic countryside*

The Cotswolds, one of the finest areas of unspoilt countryside in the land, have been called "the essence and the heart of England". The region has a distinctive character created by the use of honey-coloured stone in its buildings and dry stone walls. Within the locality the towns and villages are admirably compact and close to each other and the area is well supplied with good hotels and reasonably priced inns. The Cotswolds are within easy reach of London (1½ hours by road or rail) and several major airports.

Cotswold sheep — which inspired the logo of the Cotswold Antique Dealers' Association — a quatrefoil device with a sheep in its centre — have played an important part in the region's history with much of its wealth created by the woollen industry. As for antiques, shops and warehouses of the CADA offer a selection of period furniture, pictures, porcelain, metalwork, and collectables unrivalled outside London.

With the use of the CADA directory on the following pages, which lists the names of its members, their specialities and opening times, visitors from all over the world can plan their buying visit to the Cotswolds. CADA members will asist all visiting collectors and dealers in locating antiques and works of art. They will give you advice on where to stay in the area, assistance with packing, shipping and insurance and the exchange of foreign currencies. They can advise private cusotmers on what can realistically be bought on their available budgets, and if the first dealer does not have the piece which you are selecting he will know of several other members who will. The CADA welcomes home and overseas buyers in the certain knowledge that there are at least fifty dealers with a good and varied stock, a reputation for fair trading and an annual turnover in excess of £15,000,000.

COTSWOLD ANTIQUE DEALERS' ASSOCIATION
MEMBERS' DIRECTORY

BARNSLEY
Nr Cirencester

An extremely pretty and totally unspoilt village. Barnsley House Gardens, which have been much written about, are open to the public all year round.

Denzil Verey

The Close, Barnsley House. Est. 1980. Open 9.30−5.30, Sat. 10.30−5.30, other times by appointment. SIZE: Large. *STOCK: Country furniture, including pine, 18th−19th C; treen, tools, unusual and decorative items.* LOC: 4 miles from Cirencester on A433 to Burford, 1st large house in village, set back off road on the right. PARK: Easy. TEL: Bibury (0285 74) 402; home − (0285 85) 495. VAT: Stan/Spec.

BLOCKLEY   (0386)
Nr. Moreton-in-Marsh

Blockley is a delightful village built into the side of a hill, rising from a clear fast running trout stream, which has such pure water that it was used to wash the silk, which Blockley was famous for in the 18th and 19th centuries. There was such a large output, that five large silk mills were required, which are still standing. Blockley is situated off the A44 between Moreton-in-Marsh and Broadway.

Pamela Rowan   BADA

High St. (M. and P. Rowan.) Resident. Est. 1959. CL: Sun., Mon. and Tues. except by appointment. Open 9−5. SIZE: Medium. *STOCK: English porcelain and pottery, oak and mahogany furniture, all 18th C; copper and brass.* LOC: 1½ miles off A44 between Moreton and Broadway. PARK: Easy. TEL: 700280. SER: Valuations, buys at auction (porcelain). VAT: Spec.

BOURTON-ON-THE-WATER (0451)

Situated on the Windrush river which can be crossed by several stone built bridges dating from 1775, the town boasts some good examples of Cotswold architecture from the 17th and 18th centuries.

Studio Antiques Ltd.

High St. Est. 1933. Always available by appointment. *STOCK: Porcelain, including 1st Period Dr. Wall, Worcester, Nantgarw, Swansea; Georgian silver; English and Continental furniture, all periods including English oak; pewter, brass and copper items.* TEL: 20352. VAT: Spec.

BROADWAY   (0386)

Coming via Fish Hill and the Broadway Beacon, which afford magnificent views across the valley, you enter the town along a wide thoroughfare lined with Cotswold houses. The coaching route on which Broadway was situated was a major boost to the livelihood of its inhabitants.

Gavina Ewart   BADA

60−62 High St. (Mrs. G. and A.J. Ewart.) Est 1964. Open 9.30−1 and 2−5.30. SIZE: Large. *STOCK: Sets of silver cutlery (items matched from stock), 18th−20th C; other silver, teasets, pot-lids and other Prattware, including some rarer items, carriage clocks, 19th C; furniture and porcelain including Worcester, 18th−19th C; oil paintings and watercolours, 19th−20th C; maps, prints and jewellery.* PARK: Easy. TEL: 853371. SER: Valuations; restorations (clocks, furniture and barometers). FAIRS: Buxton, Kenilworth, British International Birmingham. VAT: Stan/Spec.

John Noott, Picton House Gallery

Picton House, High St. Est. 1972. Open 9−1 and 2−5.30, or by appointment. SIZE: Large. *STOCK: Paintings and watercolours, 19th−20th C, £50−£10,000; general antiques, mostly furniture and smalls, 18th−19th C.* LOC: Centre of village. PARK: Easy. TEL: 852787 (ansaphone 24 hrs.). SER: Valuations; restorations, framing. VAT: Stan/Spec.

Silver penannular brooch, Anglo-Saxon, circa 6th/7th century A.D. From **Antique Collecting,** November 1985.

BURFORD   (099 382)

William II granted this former market town a charter to hold its markets. Merchants living in the fine imposing houses dealt in dried fish from Aberdeen, dress materials from France, linen from Ireland, metals from Birmingham and local cider.

The Crypt Antiques

High St. (P. Matthey and M. Schotten.) Est. 1957. Open 9.30—1 and 2—5.30 or by appointment. STOCK: 18th—19th C furniture, antique fishing tackle, golfing collectables. TEL: 2302; home — Shipton-under-Wychwood (0993) 830254. SER: Restorations; stripping (pine).

Jonathan Fyson Antiques

High St. (J.R. Fyson.) Est. 1972. Open 9.30—1 and 2—5.30. SIZE: Small. STOCK: English and Continental furniture, decorative brass and steel including lighting and fireplace accessories; papier mâché, tôle, treen, porcelain, glass, jewellery. LOC: A361. Coming from London on A40 between Oxford and Cheltenham at junction with A361. PARK: Easy. TEL: 3204; home — Oxford (0865) 880943. SER: Valuations. VAT: Spec.

Peter Norden Antiques

High St. Est. 1960. Open 9.30—5.30. SIZE: Medium. STOCK: Early oak and country furniture,, metalware, treen, period mahogany and walnut, 16th—mid-19th C. Not stocked: Silver, bronze, shipping goods. PARK: Easy. TEL: 2121. VAT: Spec.

Swan Gallery

High St. (M. and J. Pratt.) Est. 1966. Open 9.30—5.30. SIZE: Large. STOCK: Furniture — oak, yew, fruitwood and walnut, 17th—20th C, £500—£3,000; oil paintings and watercolours, 19th—20th C, £100—£1,000; metalwork, blue and white pottery and porcelain, small decorative items, 18th—20th C, £50—£500. PARK: Easy. TEL: 2244; home — Edge Hill (029 587) 383. SER: Valuations; restorations (furniture). VAT: Mainly Spec.

CASSINGTON

A quiet village just north of the A40 Oxford to Witney road.

Jonathan Fyson Antiques

The Old School House. (J.R. Fyson.) Resident. Est. 1970. Open 9.30—5.30, Sat. by appointment. SIZE: Medium. STOCK: English and Continental furniture, 17th—19th C, £50—£1,500; pine furniture, metalware, decorative objects. LOC: ¼ mile north of A40. PARK: Easy. TEL: Oxford (0865) 880943. SER: Valuations; restorations. VAT: Spec.

CHIPPING NORTON   (0608)

A charming Cotswold market town situated just off the A34, the main road from Oxford to Stratford-upon-Avon. The name Chipping means trading or dealing, and a weekly market still takes place in the town centre.

The Bugle Antiques   LAPADA

9 Horsefair and warehouse. (M. and D. Harding-Hill.) Est. 1971. Open 9.30—6. STOCK: Mainly country furniture in oak, elm and fruitwood; Windsor chairs, sets of chairs, brass, copper and smalls. TEL: 3322. VAT: Stan/Spec.

C.B. Gardner Antiques

31 High St. Est. 1967. Open 9—6. SIZE: Medium. STOCK; Country furniture, mainly oak, 18th—19th C, £5—£3,000; brass, copper, £5—£75; clocks, £50—£1,500. PARK: Easy. TEL: 3913. VAT: Stan/Spec.

Key Antiques

11 Horsefair. (D. and M. Robinson.) Resident. Open 9.30—6 or by appointment. SIZE: Medium. STOCK: Period oak and country furniture, domestic metalware including kitchenware and lighting, early pottery, paintings, needlework, carvings. LOC: On main road. PARK: Easy. TEL: 3777. VAT: Spec.

Peter Stroud Antiques

Station Yard Industrial Estate. Est. 1971. Open 9—5.30. SIZE: Large. STOCK: 17th—19th C furniture, oak, mahogany; farmhouse tables, armoires. LOC: Just off A44 Moreton-in-Marsh Rd. TEL: 41651. VAT: Stan/Spec.

CIRENCESTER   (0285)

This ancient town, founded in AD75, was called Corinium Dobunnorum, was surrounded by a wall two miles in circumference, and an amphitheatre was developed during the second century. If time permits, take a walk through the old streets of the town, Dollar Street, Thomas and Coxwell Street and then Park Street, past the highest yew hedge in England and back to the lovely Market Square.

Cirencester Antiques Ltd.

Dyer Lodge, 17 Dyer St. (Mr. and Mrs. R.T.G. Chester-Master.) Est. 1959. Open 9—5.30. SIZE: Large. *STOCK: Furniture and works of art, 17th to early 19th C, £50—£15,000.* LOC: Market Place narrows into Dyer St. The shop is 30yds. ahead on the left. PARK: Own at rear. TEL: 2955.

W.W. Holzgrawe Antiques

7 Gosditch St. (W. and A.M. Holzgrawe.) Est. 1952. Open 9.15—1 and 2—5.30. SIZE: Medium. *STOCK; Mahogany, 18th to early 19th C, £100—£8,000; oak, £75—£2,500; walnut, £200—£5,000; both 17th to early 19th C; small items, copper and brass.* LOC: West Market Place, behind parish church. PARK: Limited or Market Pl. TEL: 69351; home — 68625. SER: Valuations. VAT: Spec.

Thomas and Pamela Hudson

At the Sign of the Herald Angel, 19 Park St. Est. 1959. Open 9—1 and 2—5.30. *STOCK: Old Sheffield, small objets de vertu, fans, needlework tools and workboxes.* TEL: 2972. SER: Valuations; buys at auction. VAT: Spec.

Cirencester continued

William H. Stokes   BADA

Roberts House, Siddington. (W.H. Stokes and P.W. Bontoft.) Open 10—6. SIZE: Medium. *STOCK: Oak furniture, 16th—17th C, from £250; brass candlesticks, almsdishes, from £150.* LOC: 1 mile south of Cirencester off A419. PARK: Easy. TEL: 67101. FAIRS: Grosvenor House, Harrogate and Bath. VAT: Spec.

Rankine Taylor Antiques   LAPADA

34 Dollar St. (Mrs. L. Taylor.) Est. 1969. Open 9—5.30, Sun. by appointment. SIZE: Large. *STOCK: Furniture, 17th—19th C, £20—£3,500; glass, 18th—20th C, £3—£250; silver and decorative items, 17th—20th C, £1—£1,000.* Not stocked: Victoriana, militaria. LOC: From Church, turn right up West Market Place, via Gosditch St. into Dollar St. PARK: Gloucester St. (50yds.). TEL: 2529. SER: Valuations; buys at auction (furnishing items). VAT: Stan/Spec.

Thornborough Galleries   BADA

28 Gloucester St. (R. Purdon and A. du Monceau.) Est. 1968. Open 9—5, Sat. 9—1. SIZE: Large. *STOCK: Eastern carpets.* LOC: From town centre towards Gloucester and Cheltenham, shop is about ⅓ mile. PARK: Easy. TEL: 2055. SER: Valuations; restorations (Oriental carpets and rugs). VAT: Stan/Spec.

W.W. HOLZGRAWE, ANTIQUES
17th, 18th & early 19th Century English Furniture
Copper & Brass

7, GOSDITCH ST., CIRENCESTER, GLOS. GL7 2AG
TELEPHONE: (0285) 69351. After hours: (0285) 68625

An example of our moderately priced fine quality 18th and early 19th century English furniture and works of art.

Bower groups, enamel coloured, made in Staffordshire c.1800. From "A Collector's History of English Pottery", **Antique Collecting**, May 1986.

EYNSHAM
Nr. Oxford

If you approach this pleasant village from South Oxford you will cross the River Thames via the Swinbrook Tollbridge. There has been a crossing here for about 700 years. The toll bridge is privately owned and its income is untaxed to this day. Eynsham is also the site of the oldest documented Cistercian Abbey in the country.

David John Ceramics
11 Acre End St. (J. Twitchett and D. Holborough.) Est. 1959. CL: Mon. SIZE: Medium. *STOCK: English ceramics, 18th—20th C, £15—£5,000; small furniture, decorative items.* TEL: Oxford (0865) 880786. VAT: Stan/Spec.

North Parade Antiques   *Trade Only*
2 and 4 Oxford Rd. (M. Bull.) Est. 1959. Open 9—5. SIZE: Warehouse. *STOCK: Furniture and bric-a-brac, 19th C,* LOC: ½ mile off A40. PARK: Easy. TEL: 880923. SER: Restorations. VAT: Stan/Spec.

FAIRFORD

This is the most easterly of the wool towns, developed in the 17th and 18th centuries. Elegant houses from the period stand round the market square today.

Gloucester House Antiques Ltd.
Market Place. (Mr. and Mrs. R. Chester-Master.) Est. 1972. Open 9—5.30. SIZE: Large. *STOCK: English and French country furniture in oak, elm, fruitwood, pine; pottery and decorative items.* PARK: Easy. TEL: Cirencester (0285) 712790; home — Cirencester (0285) 3066. VAT: Stan/Spec.

MORETON-IN-MARSH   (0608)

A thriving market town built on the Fosse Way, the Roman Road running from Bath to Lincoln. The White Hart and the Redesdale Arms were two of Gloucestershire's biggest coaching inns in the era of the stage coach. The 16th century Curfew tower is the oldest building and its bell is dated 1633.

Astley House — Fine Art
Astley House, High St. (D. and N. Glaisyer.) Est. 1974. Open 9—5.30. *STOCK: Oil paintings, 19th—20th C; large decorative paintings.* LOC: Main street. PARK: Easy. TEL: 50601. SER: Restorations (oils and watercolours); framing. VAT: Spec.

Simon Brett   **BADA**
Creswyke House, High St. Est. 1972. Open 9.30—5.30. *STOCK: English and Continental furniture, 17th to early 19th C; works of art, portrait miniatures, old fishing tackle.* TEL: 50751. VAT: Spec.

Franfam Ltd.   **LAPADA**
The Windrush, High St. (J. and S. Franses.) Est. 1974. Open 9—6, or by appointment. *STOCK: Furniture mainly oak and country; metalware, clocks, all 17th to early 19th C; some pottery and paintings.* Not stocked: Silver, coins. LOC: Near junction A429/A44. PARK: Easy. TEL: 50648. SER: Valuations. VAT: Mainly Spec.

David John Ceramics
11 ACRE END STREET
EYNSHAM
OXFORD OX8 1PE
Telephone 0865 880786

One of a fine pair of demi-lune side tables in honey mahogany c.1800 upon which are the Derby ice-pails from the celebrated Barry service c.1810. These were exhibited at The Derby Porcelain International Society's loan exhibition at The Royal Academy in 1985.

Primrose Antiques

High Street,
Moreton-in-Marsh,
Glos. GL56 0LL

Telephone (0608) 50591

*Early Oak, Walnut, Mahogany, Brass,
Copper etc.*

Moreton-in-Marsh continued

Elizabeth Parker
High St. (P.J. King-Smith.) Est. 1975. Open 9—6. SIZE: Medium. *STOCK; Furniture, £50—£3,000; marquetry, satinwood, porcelain, English and Continental £10—£800, all 18th—19th C.; some brass, copper, paintings.* LOC: Opposite Manor House Hotel, on Fosseway junction of A44 from Broadway. TEL: 50917. SER: Buys at auction. VAT: Stan/Spec.

Primrose Antiques
High St. (W.T. and B. Stickland.) Est. 1972. Open 9—5.30. SIZE: Medium. *STOCK: Oak, mahogany, brass, copper, pewter.* PARK: Easy. TEL: 50591; home — (0386) 700119. VAT: Stan/Spec.

OXFORD   (0865)

One of the world's greatest university cities, Oxford is Cotswold in spirit and in the honey-coloured stone with which it is built, if not in fact. Within one square mile alone, Oxford has more than 600 buildings of architectural or historical interest.

North Parade Antiques
75 Banbury Rd. (M. Bull.) (Also warehouse at Willow Bank, Oxford Rd., Eynsham — Trade Only.) Est. 1959. Open 9.30—6. SIZE: Large. *STOCK: Furniture, 1700—1900; bric-a-brac, silver and Sheffield plate, 1800—1930.* Not stocked: Books, coins, stamps. LOC: A40 north to Banbury Road (A423) roundabout, turn towards city, one mile on right. PARK: Own at rear. TEL: 59816; home — 880923 and 514782 (manager). SER: Restoration (as stock). VAT: Stan/Spec.

PAINSWICK   (0452)

A particularly delightful village with close built old houses lining steep streets. It has a famous churchyard with ornate tombs of the wealthy wool merchants and ninety-nine ancient yew trees which form tunnels and avenues.

Painswick Antiques
Beacon House, New St. (J. and H. Hutton-Clarke.) Resident. Est. 1969. CL: Thurs. Open 9.30—1 and 2—5.30, Sat. 9.30—1. Trade welcome any reasonable time. *STOCK: Period furniture, including some highly decorative in oak, walnut, mahogany, yew, fruitwood, and pine.* LOC: On A46 opp. church. PARK: Easy. TEL: 812578. VAT: Mainly Spec.

Stone House Antiques
St. Mary's St. (W.R. Large.) Est. 1936. Open 10—1 and 2—5.30, Sat. 10—1.30, Sat. p.m. and Sun. a.m. by appointment. SIZE: Large. *STOCK: yew, oak and walnut, £500—£3,500; fruitwood, £500—£1,500; all to 19th C; Japanese art and crafts of Meiji period.* Not stocked: Mahogany. PARK: Nearby. TEL: 813540; home — Gloucester (0452) 862343. SER: Buys at auction. VAT: Spec.

"Springtime" by Kate Greenaway, R.I. (1846-1901), 4ins. x 8ins. From "Some 19th and 20th Century Illustrations and Illustrators" in **Antique Collecting,** May 1986.

Plan of

STOW·ON·THE·WOLD

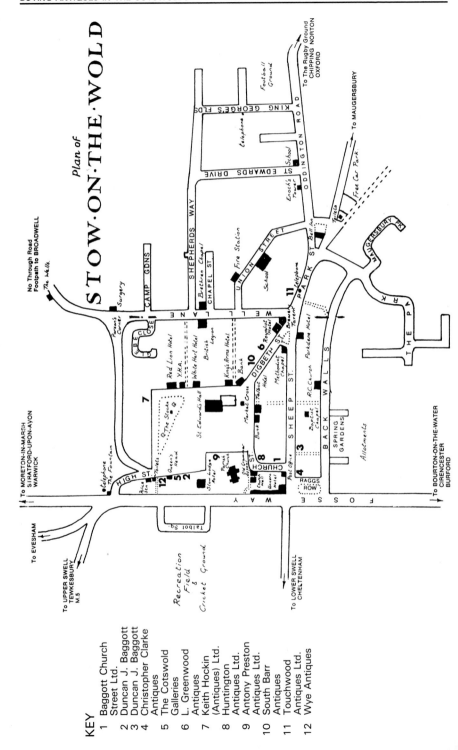

KEY

1 Baggott Church Street Ltd.
2 Duncan J. Baggott
3 Duncan J. Baggott
4 Christopher Clarke Antiques
5 The Cotswold Galleries
6 L. Greenwood Antiques
7 Keith Hockin (Antiques) Ltd.
8 Huntington Antiques Ltd.
9 Antony Preston Antiques Ltd.
10 South Barr Antiques
11 Touchwood Antiques Ltd.
12 Wye Antiques

STOW-ON-THE-WOLD   (0451)

The highest town in the Cotswolds at seven hundred feet, Stow lies to one side of the Fosse Way between Cirencester and Moreton-in-Marsh where the road from Cheltenham to Chipping Norton crosses. The beauty of the town is to leave the main roads and enter the unexpectedly large market square to find impressive yet unpretentious buildings all around.

Baggott Church Street Ltd.

Church St. Est. 1978. Open10—6 or by appointment. SIZE: Large. *STOCK: English oak, mahogany, walnut and yew furniture, 17th—19th C; portrait paintings, metalwork, pottery, treen and decorative items.* LOC: South-west corner of market square. PARK: In market square. TEL: 30370.

Duncan J. Baggott

The Square. Est. 1967. Open 10—6 or by appointment. SIZE: Medium. *STOCK: 17th—19th C. English oak and country furniture, sets of rush-seated chairs, gateleg and farmhouse tables, settles, hanging cupboards, coffers and smaller domestic items; brass, copper and metalwork, fireplace fittings, wall lights, lanterns, samplers and primitive paintings.* PARK: Easy. TEL: 30662. SER: Valuations. VAT: Stan/Spec.

Duncan J. Baggott   *Trade Only*

Huntsmans Yard, Sheep St. Est. 1967. CL: Sat. Open 9—5 or by appointment. SIZE: Large. *STOCK: 17th—19th C. English and Continental oak, mahogany, fruitwood and walnut furniture, large bookcases, dining tables, cupboards, dressers, chairs and small items; portrait and primitive paintings, brass, copper, metalwork, pottery and needleworks.* LOC: Entrance through large gates on right hand side of Sheep Street coming from Fosse Way, just past Church St. PARK: Own. TEL: 30662.

Stow-on-the-Wold continued

Christopher Clarke   **BADA**
Antiques

The Fosse Way. (C.J. Clarke.) Est. 1961. Open 9.30—6. SIZE: Medium. *STOCK: Furniture, 17th—19th C, £300—£15,000; early oak, walnut, mahogany, pottery, 18th C; metalware, 16th—18th C, both £50—£500; also religious and Gothic pieces.* Not stocked: Silver, glass, medals, coins, prints. LOC: Corner of the Fosse Way and Sheep St. PARK: Easy. TEL; 30476. SER: Valuations.

The Cotswold Galleries

The Square. (R. and C. Glaisyer.) Est. 1961. Open 9—5.30 or by appointment. SIZE: Large. *STOCK: Oil paintings, mainly 19th C landscape.* TEL: 30586. SER: Restorations; framing. VAT: Stan/Spec.

DUNCAN J. BAGGOTT

A 17th century oak child's high chair

WYE ANTIQUES

The Square, Stow-on-the-Wold, Gloucestershire, GL54 1AB
Tel. 0451-31004

Antique Staff dalmation c.1850. One of a selection of Staff figures and animals at present in stock. We also stock a large range of furniture.

Stow-on-the-Wold continued

L. Greenwold Antiques   BADA
"Digbeth", Digbeth St. Est. 1973. Open 10—5. SIZE: Medium. *STOCK; Jewellery, English and Oriental porcelain and pottery, silver, decorative items, from £50.* LOC: Just off the south east corner of market sq. PARK: Easy. TEL: 30398. SER: Buys at auction. VAT: Spec.

Keith Hockin (Antiques) Ltd. BADA
The Square. Est. 1968. CL: Sun. except by appointment. Open 9—6. SIZE: Medium. *STOCK: Oak furniture, 1600—1750; country furniture in oak, fruitwoods, yew, 1700—1850; pewter, copper, brass, ironwork, all periods.* Not stocked: Mahogany. PARK: Easy. TEL: 31058. SER: Buys at auction (oak, pewter, metalwork). VAT: Stan/Spec.

Huntington Antiques Ltd.
The Old Forge, Church St. (M.F., S.P. and N.M.J. Golding.) Resident. Est. 1974. Open 9—6 or by appointment. *STOCK: Period oak, walnut and country furniture, medieval to 1740; Eastern carpets and rugs; early metal and treen items; some tapestries and works of art.* TEL: 30842. SER: Valuations; buys at auction. FAIRS: Major dateline. VAT: Spec.

Stow-on-the-Wold continued

Antony Preston   BADA
Antiques Ltd.   LAPADA
The Square. Est. 1968. Open 9.30—6 or by appointment. *STOCK: English and Continental furniture and objects, longcase and bracket clocks, barometers, leather upholstery, all 18th and 19th C.* TEL: 31586/31406. VAT: Stan/Spec.

South Barr Antiques
Digbeth St. (R. Deeley.) Est. 1974. Open 9.30—5.30, Sun. by appointment. SIZE: Large. *STOCK: Clocks, furniture, porcelain, jewellery, 1640—1920, £50—£15,000.* PARK: Market Square. TEL: 30236; home — (0557) 30430. SER: Valuations; restorations. FAIRS: Chipping Norton, Oxford. VAT: Spec.

Touchwood Antiques Ltd. LAPADA
9 Park St. (K.M., L.A., P. and C. Dixon.) Resident. Est. 1880. Open 9.30—5.30 or by appointment. Sun. by appointment only. SIZE: Medium. *STOCK: Oak, walnut, fruitwood, early country and period furniture, medieval to 17th C, £100—£5,000+; treen, metalware and pottery, to 1830.* Not stocked: Late pine. LOC: On A436 just past junction of Digbeth St. and Park St. PARK: Easy. TEL: 30221. SER: Valuations; restorations (wax polishing, esp. large collections and rare items); research medieval to late 17th C furniture; commissions undertaken; finder service. VAT: Stan/Spec.

Wye Antiques
The Square. (C. and S. Wye.) Est. 1960. Open 9.30—6. SIZE: Large. *STOCK: Country furniture, including stripped pine; china including Staffordshire figures, blue and white transferware; decorative bygones, brass and copper.* PARK: Easy. TEL: 31004. VAT: Stan/Spec.

A Soviet Russian peaked cap. £60. From an auction feature, "Police Helmets and Uniforms", **Antique Collecting,** March 1986.

Wain Antiques
Tetbury

45, Long Street
Tetbury
Gloucestershire
GL8 8AA

Tel: Tetbury 52440

Fine English
and Oriental
Ceramics

*A rare late Ming night light in the form of
a recumbent cat c.1640. From the 1st
Hatcher wreck.*

TETBURY   (0666)

An old market town where woolsack races are held each year as a link with the past.

George S. Bolam   BADA
Oak House, 1 The Chipping. Est. 1946. CL: Sat. Open 9.15—5.30. SIZE: Medium. *STOCK: English and Continental furniture, 17th to early 19th C; paintings, Oriental porcelain.* LOC: Turn off main street at Snooty Fox Hotel, then right into Chipping car park. PARK: Easy. TEL: 52211. SER: Valuations. VAT: Spec.

Breakspeare Antiques   LAPADA
Mainly Trade
36 Long St. (M. and S. Breakspeare.) Resident. Est. 1962. CL: Some Thurs. p.m. Open 9.30—5.30, if closed, ring bell. SIZE: Medium. *STOCK: English furniture, mainly mahogany, 18th to early 19th C; longcase clocks, barometers, £50—£3,500.* PARK: Easy. TEL: 53122 or 52192. VAT: Stan/Spec.

Jasper Marsh Antiques   BADA
3 The Chipping. (J. and P. Marsh.) Open 9—1 and 2—5, Sat. 10—4, Sun. by appointment. *STOCK: Mahogany and oak furniture, 18th to early 19th C.* LOC: Off High St. PARK: Easy. TEL: 52832 or Henley-in-Arden (05642) 2088.

John Nicholls
27 Long St. CL: Sat. Open 9.30—5.30, Sat. 10—4. *STOCK: Oak and country furniture, 17th and 18th C.* TEL: 52781; home — Uttoxeter (088 93) 2383.

A 17th century oak tester bed. From "The 17th Century Home: Some topical thoughts", **Antique Collecting,** *April 1986.*

Tetbury continued

Tetbury Antiques
39A Long St. (Caffell Management Services Ltd.) Open 9.30—5.30, Sun. by appointment. *STOCK: English and Continental country furniture and accessories, 18th—19th C.* TEL: 52748; home — Nailsworth (045 383) 3168.

Wain Antiques
45 Long St. (J. and P. Wain.) Est. 1978. Open 9.30—5.30, Sun. by appointment. SIZE: Medium. *STOCK: Pottery and porcelain, European and Oriental 18th—19th C, £5—£1,000.* PARK: Easy. TEL: 52440; home — same. SER: Restorations (ceramics); buys at auction (ceramics). VAT: Spec.

Ian Pout Antiques

99 High Street, Witney, Oxon.

A fast changing stock of affordable antiques
Also a room full of old teddy bears 1902-1950, all for sale

0993 2616

WINCHCOMBE (0242)

An historic town, displaying fine examples of 17th century architecture, huddled along the narrow meandering High Street. Sudeley Castle lies close by, the splendid home of the Seymours.

Kenulf Gallery
Kenulf House, High St. (E. and J. Ford.) Est. 1978. Open 9.30—5.30. *STOCK: Late 18th to early 20th C oil and watercolour paintings and prints; sculpture, and furniture.* TEL: 602124; home — 602776. SER: Valuations; restorations (oils and watercolours); period framing. VAT: Spec.

WITNEY (0993)

To most people the name 'Witney' means blankets which have been made here for upwards of a 1,000 years. The traditional sources of Cotswold wealth, fleece and swift water established the trade. Today its blankets, which are known and sold all over the world, can still be bought in the town.

Colin Greenway Antiques
90 Corn St. Resident. Est. 1975. Open 9—6 or by appointment. SIZE: Medium. *STOCK; Furniture, 17th—20th C; clocks, metalware, decorative and unusual items.* LOC: Along High St. to town centre, turn right, shop 400yds. on right. PARK: Easy. TEL: 5026. VAT: Stan/Spec.

Ian Pout Antiques
99 High St. (I. and J. Pout.) Open 10—5.30. *STOCK: 18th and 19th C country and decorative furniture, metalware, interesting and unusual objects.* TEL: 2616. VAT: Spec.

Anthony Scaramanga Antiques BADA
108 Newland. Est. 1969. CL: Fri. and Sun. except by appointment. Open 10—6. *STOCK: Samplers, 17th—19th C; small furniture, needlework pictures, lace, Staffordshire figures, blue and white pottery.* LOC: From oxford on A40, turn off bypass onto A4002, shop on left before coming to A147 and Witney. PARK: Easy. TEL: 3472. VAT: Spec.

Windrush Antiques
107 High St. (B. Tollett.) Est. 1978. Open 10—5.30. *STOCK: Furniture, especially 17th—18th C, oak, mahogany and country; some metalware and porcelain.* LOC: A40, corner of Mill St. and High St. PARK: Private at rear. TEL: 72536.

Witney Antiques BADA
96/98 Corn St. (L.S.A. and C.J. Jarrett.) Est. 1962. Open 9.30—5. SIZE: Large. *STOCK: English furniture, 17th—18th C; bracket and longcase clocks, mahogany, oak and walnut, metalware, paintings and works of art.* LOC: From Oxford on old A40 through Witney via High St., turn right at T-junction. 400yds. on right. PARK: Easy. TEL: 3902 or 3887. FAIRS: Chelsea. VAT: Spec.

PETER STROUD ANTIQUES

STATION YARD INDUSTRAL ESTATE, CHIPPING NORTON, OXON. OX7 5HX. TEL: 0608 41651

Studio Antiques Ltd

Bourton-on-the-Water, Gloucestershire
Telephone Bourton-on-the-Water
20352 Std 0451

A selection of blue & white first period Worcester & Caughley porcelain.

A view of one of our five showrooms of quality antiques.

KEY ANTIQUES

Danny Robinson
CHIPPING NORTON, OXFORDSHIRE
TELEPHONE 0608 3777

Oak & Country furniture and metalwork always in stock

SEE ADVERTISEMENT UNDER OXFORDSHIRE
FOR FURTHER DETAILS OF STOCK

BAGGOTT
CHURCH STREET LIMITED

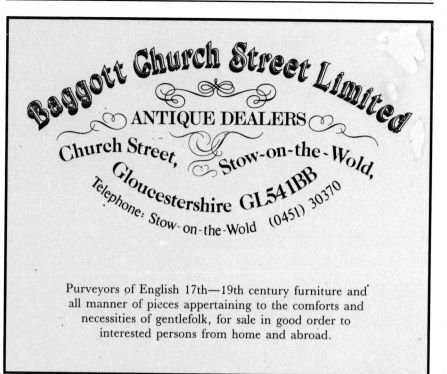

Westerners buying tea at Canton, gouache on paper, c.1820, 28cm x 23cm. From "Chinatrade Paintings, c.1750-1900", **Antique Collecting**, June 1986.

**PORCELAIN
JEWELLERY
SILVER**

L.
GREENWOLD

**DIGBETH STREET
STOW-ON-THE-WOLD
GLOS. GL54 1BN**

Open Mon—Sat. 10—5   **Tel: 0451 30398**

KEITH HOCKIN

**THE SQUARE
STOW-ON-THE-WOLD
GLOUCESTERSHIRE
0451 31058**

Fine 17th and early 18th century Furniture
and objects of the period

ANTONY PRESTON

ANTIQUES LTD.

THE SQUARE
STOW-ON-THE-WOLD
GLOUCESTERSHIRE GL54 1AB ENGLAND

TEL. COTSWOLD (0451) 31586 (HOME) 31406

Superb walnut bureau, having a wonderful colour and original brasses, c.1740.

We have a large stock of 18th and early 19th century furniture, a wide selection of leather upholstery, antique stick and banjo barometers, longcase and bracket clocks all in showroom condition.

Touchwood Antiques LimiteD

Period and Country Furniture

*Specialist Early Timber Wax Polishers to
Museums/Institutions, Country Houses and Private Clients*

9 Park Street, Stow-on-the-Wold, Gloucestershire. Telephone (0451) 30221

*Furniture Research,
Medieval to Jacobean
Period*

*Advice for Interior
Design and Furnishing*

JASPER MARSH

3 THE CHIPPING, TETBURY, GLOUCESTERSHIRE
Telephone Tetbury 0666 52832
Open 9.00—1.00, 2.00—5.00. Sat. 10.00—4.00. Sun. by appointment

Also at

3 HIGH STREET, HENLEY IN ARDEN, WARWICKSHIRE
Telephone Henley in Arden 05642 2088
Open 10.00—5.30 Daily. Sundays 2.15—5.30pm.

We carry a large stock of 17th, 18th and early 19th century period furniture and porcelain at both shops.

John Nicholls

Tetbury
Glos.

Colin Greenway Antiques

90 Corn Street, Witney, Oxon. Telephone: (0993) 5026

17th, 18th, 19th century
**FURNITURE
(IN OAK, MAHOGANY
AND OTHER WOODS)
AND DECORATIVE ITEMS
BOUGHT AND SOLD**

ANTHONY SCARAMANGA ANTIQUES

Newland : Witney
Oxon OX8 6JN
Witney (0993) 3472

Sampler worked by Mary Downing 11ins. x 14ins., dated 1771, with verses, decorative bands and a country scene with a lady, hills, trees, deer and flowers. Colour and condition excellent.

𝔚indrush Antiques

107 High Street, Witney, Oxfordshire
Telephone 0993 72536

18th C Oak crossbanded breakfront dresser. 7ft. wide x 6ft. 6ins. high (c.1820)

Witney Antiques

(L.S.A. & C.J. Jarrett)

96-98 Corn Street, Witney, Oxfordshire OX8 7BU
Telephone Witney (0993) 3902

Fine late 18th century oyster veneered chest of drawers. Circa 1690.

You are invited to visit our spacious showrooms in Witney, where we have on display an important stock of fine furniture, longcase and bracket clocks from the 17th and 18th centuries.

We offer a specialist service for the restoration and conservation of fine and antique furniture. All work is carried out in our own specialist workshops by fully trained and experienced craftsmen.

THE COTSWOLD ANTIQUE
DEALERS SHIPPERS DIRECTORY

THE COTSWOLD ANTIQUE
DEALERS SHIPPERS DIRECTORY

HOTEL ACCOMMODATION

THE FROGMILL, Shipton, **Andoversford,** Nr. Cheltenham, Gloucestershire. Telephone: (0242) 820547	**THE TARA HOTEL,** Upton Hill, Upton St. Leonards, **Gloucester.** Telephone: (0452) 67412
LOWER BROOK HOUSE HOTEL, Blockley, Nr. Moreton-in-Marsh, Gloucestershire. Telephone: (0386) 700286	**THE MANOR HOUSE HOTEL, Moreton-in-Marsh,** Gloucestershire. Telephone: (0608) 50501
THE OLD NEW INN, Bourton-on-the-Water, Gloucestershire. Telephone: (0451) 20467	**COTSWOLD LODGE HOTEL,** 66a Banbury Road, **Oxford.** Telephone: (0865) 512121
THE LAMB INN, Burford, Oxfordshire. Telephone: (099382) 3155	**THE FOSSE MANOR HOTEL, Stow-on-the-Wold,** Gloucestershire. Telephone: (0451) 30354
THE WHITE HART HOTEL, Chipping Norton, Oxfordshire. Telephone: (0608) 2572	**THE SNOOTY FOX,** Market Place, **Tetbury,** Gloucestershire. Telephone: (0666) 52436
STRATTON HOUSE HOTEL, Gloucester Road, **Cirencester,** Gloucestershire. Telephone: (0285) 61761	**THE GEORGE INN, Winchcombe,** Nr. Cheltenham, Gloucestershire. Telephone: (0242) 602331
THE BULL HOTEL, Fairford, Gloucestershire. Telephone: (0285) 712535	**THE FEATHERS HOTEL,** Market Street, **Woodstock,** Oxfordshire. Telephone: (0993) 812291

COTSWOLD ANTIQUE DEALERS' ASSOCIATION

FOR ASSISTANCE WITH BUYING, SHIPPING, AND
ACCOMMODATION DURING YOUR VISIT
WRITE TO: The Secretary, CADA,
High Street, Blockley,
Gloucestershire.
Telephone (0386) 700280

Cumbria

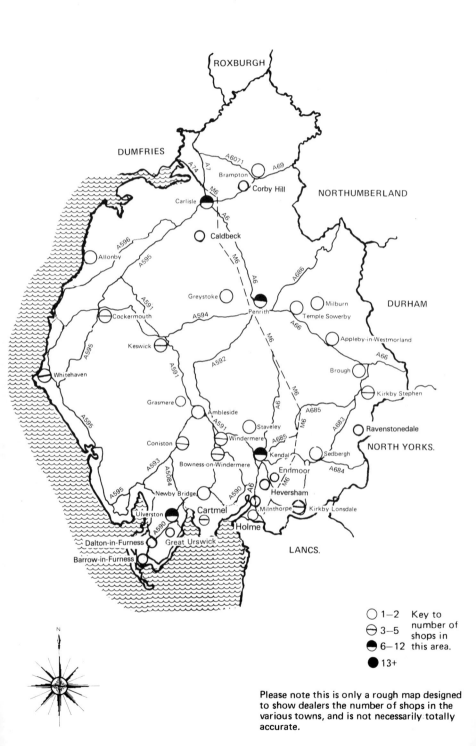

Key to number of shops in this area.

○ 1–2
⊖ 3–5
◐ 6–12
● 13+

Please note this is only a rough map designed to show dealers the number of shops in the various towns, and is not necessarily totally accurate.

ALLONBY (090 084)
Cottage Curios
Main St. (B. Pickering.) Est. 1965. Open daily from 2 p.m.

AMBLESIDE (0966)
Aladdins Cave
Zefferelli's Arcade, Compston Rd. (Mrs. J. Harwood.) Est. 1975. CL: Thurs. Open 10—1 and 2—5. SIZE: Small. *STOCK: Rural antiques, tools and implements, 18th—19th C; coloured glass and general antiques, 19th C; all £5—£500; collectables, linen and kitchen items.* LOC: A591, in shopping arcade under cinema. PARK: Easy. TEL: 33722; home — Grasmere (096 65) 231. SER: Restorations (rush and cane seating). FAIRS: Grasmere.

Beverley Patrick Dennison
LAPADA
Trade only
'Dwarf Hall', Chapel Hill. Open anytime by appointment. *STOCK: Small collectables, domestic lighting, interior decor items, scientific, musical and medical instruments, domestic metalware, all 17th-20th C; ethnographica.* LOC: 200yds. off A591, up Kirkstone Pass Rd., turn right before old church on right. PARK: Easy. TEL: 32651. SER: Finder service. FAIRS: Grasmere. VAT: Stan/Spec.

APPLEBY-IN-WESTMORLAND (0930)
The Black Boy (1677)
1—2 High Wiend. (R. Folder and W. Self.) Est. 1961. CL: Thurs. p.m. Open 9—6. SIZE: Medium. *STOCK: General antiques.* PARK: 100yds. at end of street. TEL: 51491. SER: Valuations. VAT: Stan.

BARROW-IN-FURNESS (0229)
Antiques
235—239 Rawlinson St. (H. Vincent.) Est. 1965. *STOCK: Jewellery, furniture, paintings, weapons, clocks, brass, copperware, silver, bric-a-brac.* LOC: Off A590 (A6). PARK: Easy. TEL: 23432.

Passing Time
221 Rawlinson St. (S.M. and J.A. Silver). CL: Mon. Open 10—4.30. *STOCK: Dolls, toys, pine.* TEL: 35489 or 24349.

BOWNESS-ON-WINDERMERE
Old Curio Shop
Church St. (J. Weightman.) Est. 1960. CL: Thurs. Open March—November 9—4. SIZE: Small. *STOCK: Pottery, porcelain, 18th—20th C, £2—£75; brass, copper, £2—£60; oils.* Not stocked: Large furniture. LOC: Next to Old England Hotel. PARK: In garage forecourt. SER: Buys at auction.

Bowness-on-Windermere continued

Serpentine Antiques
Pinfold, Lake Rd. (M. Worsley.) Est. 1973. CL: Thurs. Open 10—5. SIZE: Medium. *STOCK: General antiques.* Not stocked: Reproductions. LOC: Opposite cinema car park. PARK: Easy. TEL: Windermere (096 62) 4770.

J.W. Thornton Antiques Supermarket
North Terrace. *STOCK: Fine art, general antiques, furniture, shipping items, pine, bric-a-brac, paintings.* TEL: (096 62) 5183/2930 or (0229) 88745. SER: Valuations; buys at auction. VAT: Stan/Spec.

BRAMPTON (069 77)
Mary Fell Antiques
Collector's Corner, 32—34 Main St. Est. 1960. Open Tues., Wed., Fri. and Sat. 11—6, other times by appointment. SIZE: Small. *STOCK: Sheraton and Victorian furniture, porcelain, china, glass, silver and plate, bric-a-brac, early Victorian oil paintings, pictures, prints, jewellery, pot-lids.* Not stocked: Coins, armour and swords. LOC: Town centre, beside public car park. PARK: Easy. TEL: Home — Carlisle (0228) 22224. SER: Valuations; restorations (furniture); buys at auction.

Geoffrey Nanson Antiques
25 Front St. Est. 1977. CL: Thurs. Open 9—12 and 1—5. SIZE: Small. *STOCK: Silver, clocks and watches, £10—£500; carriage clocks, barometers, porcelain, £10—£800; china, glass, brass and copper, small furniture, £5—£600; all 18th—19th C.* LOC: Town centre off A69. PARK: Easy. TEL: 3000; home — Scotby (022872) 650. SER: Valuations; buys at auction. VAT: Stan/Spec.

BROUGH (093 04)
Augill Castle Antiques Ltd.
Augill Castle. (M. Hogarth.) Est. 1966. Open 9—6 or by appointment. SIZE: Large. *STOCK: English and French furniture, 1600—1830, £100—£50,000; Old Master paintings, £250—£75,000; Chinese porcelain, 1400—1820, £50—£25,000.* LOC: From Penrith or Scotch Corner along A66. Take Kendal Rd. (A685) for ½ mile, turn left at road signposted 'South Stainmore', Castle ½ mile up road on left. PARK: Easy. TEL: 412. SER: Valuations; buys at auction. VAT: Spec.

CALDBECK, Nr. Carlisle (069 98)
Croft Head Antiques
Croft Head, Fellside. (N.A. and S.E. McCaw.) Est. 1979. Open by appointment. SIZE: Small. *STOCK: Porcelain, 18th—19th C, £20—£300; prints, watercolours, Victorian glass, £10—£150; small furniture, treen, brass.* PARK: Easy. TEL: 413; home — same.

CARLISLE (0228)

Abbey Antiques
28 Abbey St. (Mrs. R. Hefford.) Est. 1980. Open Mon. 12—5.30, Fri. and Sat. 10.30—5.30 or by appointment. SIZE: Small. *STOCK: Porcelain, glass, silver, collectors' items, furniture, £10—£1,000.* LOC: City centre. PARK: Easy. TEL: 21302.

James W. Clements
19 Fisher St. Est. 1887. CL: Thurs. Open 9—5. *STOCK: Furniture, glass, china, silver Georgian and Victorian, and Victorian jewellery.* TEL: 25565. VAT: Stan/Spec.

Crystal Ball
3 Crosby St. (H. Cain.) CL: Thurs. Open 9—5. *STOCK: Jewellery, silver, brass, furniture and general antiques.* LOC: Opposite Post Office. TEL: 39377.

Maurice Dodd
112 Warwick Rd. (G.W. and V.A. Keates.) Est. 1945. CL: Sun. except by appointment. *STOCK: Books, pictures, prints, general antiques.* TEL: 22087. VAT: Stan/Spec.

Miss Harrison Antiques
16 London Rd. (O.E. Harrison.) Resident. Always open. *STOCK: General antiques.* TEL: 43800.

Ryburgh House Antiques
6 Tullie St. (H. Gale.) CL: Thurs. Open 10—5. *STOCK: General antiques; shipping, Victorian and Edwardian, furniture, small items, Doulton, glass.* LOC: Off Warwick Rd. TEL: 45859.

Saint Nicholas Galleries (Antiques and Jewellery)
39 Bank St. (C. Carruthers.) CL: Mon. Open 10—5. SIZE: Medium. *STOCK: Jewellery, porcelain, silver, plate, pine furniture, bric-a-brac, clocks.* LOC: City centre. PARK: Nearby. TEL: 44459.

Saint Nicholas Galleries (Antiques) Ltd.
28 London Rd. (J., C. and F.E. Carruthers.) CL: Thurs. Open 9.30—5.30. SIZE: Medium. *STOCK: General antiques, 18th C, £5—£500.* LOC: City centre. PARK: Nearby. TEL: 34425; 44459; home — 22249.

CARTMEL (044 854)

Norman Kerr
The Square. Open by appointment only. *STOCK: Transport and engineering books.* TEL: 247.

Cartmel continued

Peter Bain Smith (Bookseller)
Bank Court, Market Sq. CL: Mon, Tues. and Wed. Jan. to Easter. Open 1.30—4.30. In season open every day 10.30—6. *STOCK: Antiquarian books, especially children's and local topography.* LOC: A590 from Levens Bridge, off roundabout towards new Lindale by-pass through Grange-over-Sands. PARK: Nearby. TEL: 369. SER: Valuations.

Jonathan Wood Antiques
Broughton Hall. (J. and S. Wood.) Est. 1982. Open 9.30—6, Sun. and other times by appointment. SIZE: Medium. *STOCK: Furniture, oak, mahogany and walnut, 17th to early 19th C, £30—£3,000; decorative items, £10—£300; paintings, 19th to early 20th C, £10—£1,000.* Not stocked: Militaria, coins and jewellery. LOC: Cartmel turning off A590 at top of Lindale Hill, continue 1½ miles over 2 crossroads, towards Wood Broughton, Broughton Hall signposted. PARK: Own. TEL: 234; home — same. FAIRS: Grasmere. VAT: Stan/Spec.

A faceted teacaddy made of stoneware with an ash glaze on a black slip ground. Fired to nearly 1280°C. Made at the Muchelney Pottery by Jeremy Leach in 1976. 127mm high. From *A Collector's History of English Pottery* by Griselda Lewis, published by the **Antique Collectors' Club,** 1985.

COCKERMOUTH   (0900)

Elaine Bell and Gwenda Davies
5 Station St. Est. 1983. CL: Thurs. Open
10—5. SIZE: Large. *STOCK: General antiques
especially ceramics, furniture, pictures, glass,
books and metalware.* LOC: Just off A66, in
town centre. PARK: Easy. TEL: 826746;
home — 823858 or 826584.

Cockermouth Antiques Market
Main St. Est. 1979. Open 10—5. SIZE: Large.
There are 8 stallholders at this market selling
*Victoriana, art nouveau, art deco, musical
instruments, books, textiles, jewellery, silver
and pictures.* LOC: Town centre, just off A66.
PARK: 50yds. TEL: 824346. SER:
Restorations (furniture); stripping (pine). VAT:
Stan/Spec.

Derwent Antiques
The Old Court House, Main St. (M. Hartley, S.
Ogden.) Est. 1960. CL: Thurs. in winter. SIZE:
Small. *STOCK: Glass, small silver, jewellery,
porcelain, prints, watercolours, small furni-
ture, brass, copper, 19th C, £5—£500.*
PARK: Nearby. TEL: 827197. SER: Buys at
auction (small collectors' items).

Rutherford's Antiques
16 Main St. (Mrs. Rutherford.) Open daily but
appointment advisable. *STOCK: General
antiques.* TEL: 823065.

CONISTON   (0966)

The Old Man Antiques
Yewdale Rd. (R. and Y. Williams.) Est. 1965.
Open daily 10.30—5.30 (later in summer).
Sun. by appointment in winter. SIZE: Medium.
*STOCK: Miscellaneous; also English coins,
1780 onwards, under £5; barometers —
'banjo', from £190 and 'stick' from £220.*
LOC: On Ambleside to Ulverston Rd. PARK:
Easy. TEL: 41389. SER: Restorations
(barometers, barographs and thermographs);
shippers. VAT: Stan.

Fenwick Pattison
Bowmanstead Studio. Est. 1950. CL: Wed.
and Sun. except by appointment. Open
9.30—5.30. SIZE: Medium. *STOCK: Early oak
and country furniture, some mahogany,
£100—£2,500; treen, wood carvings, early
metalware, 16th-18th C, £10—£300.* LOC:
½ mile south of Coniston on A593 to Torver.
PARK: Easy. TEL: 41235. VAT: Stan/Spec.

Coniston continued

Yewdale Antiques
Holywath. (D. Hext.) Est. 1978. Open by
appointment. *STOCK: Silver, porcelain and
brass; oak, 17th and 18th C.* TEL: 41254.

CORBY HILL, Nr. Carlisle

Langley Antiques
The Forge. (D. and Mrs. P. Mather.) Est.
1976. CL: Thurs. Open 10.30—5. SIZE:
Medium. *STOCK: Pine; silver, porcelain, brass
fenders, fire irons, £50—£100; furniture, oak
country, Victorian and Edwardian mahogany
and walnut, all 18th—19th C, £500—£1,000.*
PARK: Easy. TEL: Wetheral (0228) 60899.
SER: Valuations; restorations, buys at auction.
VAT: Stan/Spec.

DALTON-IN-FURNESS   (0229)

Syd Greenhalgh and Son   *Trade only*
Tantabank Farm, Tantabank Rd. Est. 1960.
Open by appointment. SIZE: Large. *STOCK:
General antiques and shipping goods.* LOC:
A590. PARK: Easy. TEL: 62001; home —
same. SER: Collection and packing to U.S.A.
and Australia.

ENDMOOR, Nr. Kendal

Calvert Antiques
Sycamore House. (Mr. and Mrs. N.A.
Hutchinson-Shire, Mr. and Mrs. V.C. Bryan).
Est. 1986. Open 9.30—6, Sun. 10.30—
4.30, Tues. and other times by appointment.
SIZE: Medium. *STOCK: Furniture, 18th to
early 19th C; clocks, 17th—19th C; treen.*
Not stocked: China, silver and jewellery. LOC:
On A65. Leave M6 at junction 36 on to
Skipton/Kirby Lonsdale rd., first exit left to
Endmoor. PARK: Easy. TEL: (044 87) 597;
home — same. SER: Restorations (furniture).
VAT: Stan/Spec.

GRASMERE   (096 65)
Nr. Ambleside

The Stables
College St. (J.A. and K.M. Saalmans.) Est.
1971. Open daily 10—6 Easter—October,
other times telephone call advisable. SIZE:
Small. *STOCK: Brass and copper items, oil
lamps, domestic bygones; pottery, silver,
prints, books.* Not stocked: Weapons, coins.
LOC: By the side of Moss Grove Hotel. PARK:
Easy. TEL: 453; home — same. SER:
Organiser of Grasmere Antiques Markets.
VAT: Stan/Spec.

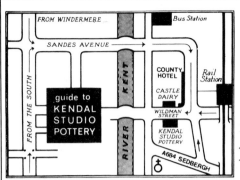

KENDAL STUDIO POTTERY

2/3 WILDMAN STREET
KENDAL, WESTMORLAND
CUMBRIA. LA9 6EN

6 miles from Junction 37 on the M6

**CERAMICS, PAINTINGS
ANTIQUES**

Tel. KENDAL (0539) 23291

10.30am to 1pm/3pm to 6pm Mon—Fri.
10.30am to 1pm/3pm to 5pm Sat.

Access and Barclaycard, Diners and American Express

GREAT URSWICK, Nr. Ulverston

Lilian Wood Antiques
Midtown House. Open by appointment. *STOCK: Furniture, 17th to early 19th C; paintings and decorative items, all periods.* LOC: Off A590 at signpost High Carley Hospital and Urswick. Midtown is second house beyond Derby Arms, turning left. PARK: Easy. TEL: Ulverston (0229) 56297.

GREYSTOKE, Nr. Penrith   (085 33)

Pelican Antiques
Church Rd. (Mrs. J. Kirkby.) Est. 1897. Open daily but phone call advisable. *STOCK: General small antiques, £5—£300.* PARK: Easy. TEL: 447.

HEVERSHAM, Nr. Milnthorpe

Bacchus Antiques — In the Service of Wine
Hawthorn Cottage. (Mrs. J.A. Johnson.) Est. 1979. Open by appointment only. *STOCK: Corkscrews.* TEL: Milnthorpe (044 82) 3337 or (061) 980 4747.

HOLME, Nr. Burton in Kendal

Holme Fires
15 Holme Mills. (T. and S. Smurthwaite.) Est. 1983. Open by appointment. SIZE: Small. *STOCK: Cast-iron fires with tiles, 1850—1930; wooden, marble and slate surrounds, 1800—1930; tiles and fire accessories.* LOC: From A65 into village, turn right, first left for ¾ mile, cottages just after pond. PARK: Easy. TEL: Burton (0524) 781423; home — same. VAT: Stan.

Utopia Antiques Ltd.
Holme Mills. (P.J. and Mrs. J. Wilkinson.) Est. 1970. Open 8.30—6. SIZE: Large. *STOCK: Irish and English pine, 18th—19th C, £25—£2,000.* PARK: Easy. TEL: Burton (0524) 781739; home — (0468) 71867. SER: Restorations (pine); shipping. VAT: Stan.

KENDAL   (0539)

Below Stairs
78 Highgate. (G.M. and V. Ritchie.) CL: Thurs. Open 10—4. *STOCK: Silver, lace, glass, copper and brass, Victoriana.* LOC: Opposite Tesco. TEL: 31456.

Cottage Antiques
151 Highgate. (S. Satchell.) Est. 1974. CL: Thurs. Open 11—4.30, Mon. 1—4.30, Sat. 10—4.30. *STOCK: General antiques and country items, pottery, glass, brass, copper, metalware, treen, kitchen items, tools and craft bygones, small silver, some furniture mainly pine.* Not stocked: Coins. LOC: A6, 300 yards north of church. PARK: At rear. TEL: 22683.

Dower House Antiques
38—40 Kirkland (B. Blakemore.) Open 9.15—6, Thurs. 9.15—1. *STOCK: Pottery, porcelain, paintings, furniture and shipping goods.* TEL: 22778.

Keith D. Edwards Antiques
Crosscrake Farm, Crosscrake. Open anytime, appointment advisable. *STOCK: General antiques, period and shipping furniture, oak.* LOC: Off A65. TEL: (0448) 60313. VAT: Stan/Spec.

Gerrard Antiques
The Old Cottage, 54 Branthwaite Brow. (J. and D.B. Nanson.) Est. 1972. Open Mon., Tues. and Wed. 10—4.30 or by appointment. SIZE: Small. *STOCK: Copper, brass, pottery and porcelain, 18th—19th C, small furniture, Victorian oil lamps.* LOC: Off Market Place. PARK: 50 yds. in Market Place. TEL: 23881; home — Witherslack (044 852) 422. SER: Valuations. VAT: Stan/Spec.

Highgate Antiques
99 and 181 Highgate. (D.J. Jones and P.M. Gunson.) Open 9—5. *STOCK: Clocks, period oak and shipping furniture, 18th—19th C.* TEL: 24527. SER: Buys at auction.

Kendal continued

Kendal Studio Pottery
2/3 Wildman St. (H.P., A.O., and R.A. Aindow.) Est. 1950. Open 10.30—1 and 3—6. Sat. 10.30—1 and 3—5. SIZE: Medium. *STOCK: Ceramics, maps and prints, paintings, general antiques, oak furniture, jewellery, drinking glasses, 18th—19th C; art pottery, 1880—1940.* LOC: Leave M6 at junction 37, follow one-way system, shop on left. PARK: As signposted. TEL: 23291 (24 hrs. answering service). SER: Restorations (paintings and watercolours); finder; shipping. VAT: Stan/Spec.

The Silver Thimble
39 All Hallows Lane. (G.M. and V. Ritchie.) Est. 1980. CL: Thurs. Open 10—4. SIZE: Medium. *STOCK: Jewellery, silver, lace, glass, copper and brass, Victoriana.* LOC: Turn left at first set of traffic lights on main road into Kendal, 200 yds. on right. PARK: Easy. TEL: 31456.

KESWICK   (0596)

Archway Antiques
17 St. John St. (J.M. Wilson). Est. 1985. Open 9.30—5.30. SIZE: Small. *STOCK: Furniture, 19th C, £200—£500; pictures, 19th—20th C, £50—£300; porcelain, glass, china, treen, brass, 18th—20th C, £5—£200.* LOC: In town centre, one mile from A66. PARK: Nearby. TEL: 72842; home — 72986. SER: Valuations; buys at auction (treen).

Holmes Antiques
15 and 26B St. John's St. (C. Holmes.) Est. 1972. CL: Sun. and Wed. in winter. Open 9.30—5. SIZE: Medium. *STOCK: Furniture, paintings, prints, small antiques and collectors' items.* LOC: 50 yds. from George Hotel. PARK: Nearby. TEL: 73605; home — 82364. FAIRS: Grasmere. VAT: Stan/Spec.

John Young and Son (Antiques)
12-14 Main St. Est. 1890. Open 9—5.30. SIZE: Large. *STOCK: Furniture, 1680—1900, £3—£5,000; pottery and porcelain, brass, copperware, pewter, silver, glass, plated ware.* LOC: Town centre. PARK: At rear. TEL: 73434. VAT: Stan/Spec.

KIRKBY LONSDALE   (0468)

Alexander Adamson
Tearnside Hall. Est. 1863. *STOCK: Furniture, £50—£10,000; porcelain, £30—£1,000; glass, £50—£500.* PARK: Easy. TEL: 71989. SER: Valuations; restorations (furniture). VAT: Spec.

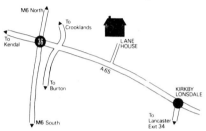

Peter Haworth
Cumbrian Fine Art Galleries
Fine Paintings

Watercolours and Oil paintings
1850—1950

LANE HOUSE is open by appointment at any time. Exhibitions are held regularly and details will be forwarded on request.

LANE HOUSE, COW BROW, VIA CARNFORTH, LANCS.
TEL. CROOKLANDS (04487) 208
LANE HOUSE is ½ mile from junction 36-M6 on the road to Kirkby Lonsdale.

Kirkby Lonsdale continued

Peter Haworth Fine Paintings (Cumbrian Fine Art Galleries)
Lane House, Cow Brow. Est. 1968. Open every day any time by appointment. SIZE: Medium. *STOCK: Watercolours, 18th—20th C, £100—£8,000.* LOC: ½ mile from junction 36 off M6, on road to, and 5 miles from, Kirkby Lonsdale. TEL: Crooklands (044 87) 208. SER: Valuations; restorations. VAT: Spec.

Maggie Tallentire Antiques
8 Market St. Est. 1982. Open by appointment. SIZE: Medium. *STOCK: Period oak and country furniture, metalware, decorative items, textiles, samplers, country pottery.* TEL: 71208/71176. SER: Buys at auction. VAT: Stan/Spec.

David H. Willan
13 Market St. Est. 1983. Open 9—5, including most Sun. SIZE: Small. *STOCK: Pine furniture, brassware, lighting, decorative items and collectables, 50p—£500.* LOC: Opposite Sun Hotel. PARK: Nearby. TEL: 72150. VAT: Stan.

HAUGHEY ANTIQUES
KIRKBY STEPHEN, CUMBRIA CA17 4QS
Telephone 07683 71302
Situated 12 miles from M6 Junction 38
10 minute detour for trade en route to Scotland

Specialising in quality antique furniture.
Extensive stock of 17th, 18th and 19th century furniture, clocks,
barometers, garden statuary and other works of art.

Kirkby Lonsdale continued

David H. Willan — *Trade Only*
Warren House, Burrow via Carnforth. Open by appointment. SIZE: Warehouse. *STOCK: Pine furniture, brassware, lighting, decorative items and collectables.* PARK: Easy. TEL: 34328.

KIRKBY STEPHEN (0930)
Beckfoot Antiques
Beckfoot Hall. (Mrs. R.H. Ford.) Open by appointment only. *STOCK: Silver, jewellery.* TEL: 71348.

Haughey Antiques — LAPADA
Market St. (D.M. Haughey.) Est. 1969. Open 10—5, Sat. 12—5. SIZE: Large. *STOCK: Furniture, 17th—19th C; garden furniture and statuary.* PARK: Easy. TEL: 71302. SER: Valuations. VAT: Stan/Spec.

David Hill
36 Market Sq. Est. 1965. Open 10.30—5.30 in summer. Winter by appointment only. SIZE: Medium. *STOCK: Longcase clocks, £350—£1,500; country furniture, £10—£1,000, all 18th—19th C; curios, £5—£50; shipping goods.* Not stocked: Porcelain, glass. LOC: On A685. PARK: Easy. TEL: 71598. VAT: Stan/Spec.

MILBURN, Nr. Penrith
Netherley Cottage Antiques
(J. and J. Heelis.) Est. 1970. CL: Tues. a.m. Resident at house next door. Open 8.30—8. SIZE: Small. *STOCK: Country cottage pottery, porcelain and ornaments, 18th—19th C, £1—£25; kitchen items, interesting bygones, brass, watercolours, £1—£50; early blue and white plates, and treen; some Oriental items.* Not stocked: Silver and clocks. TEL: Kirkby Thore (0930) 61403. SER: Buys at auction.

MILNTHORPE (044 82)
The Antique Shop
9 Park Rd. Open 10—4.30 Wed. and Fri. SIZE: Medium. *STOCK: General antiques, books, furniture.* LOC: From A6, left at traffic lights in village, opposite Post Office. TEL: 2253.

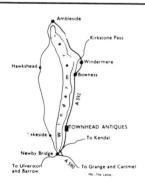
NEWBY BRIDGE   (0448)

Shire Antiques
The Post House, High Newton, Newton-in-Cartmel. (B. and Mrs. J. Shire.) CL: Tues. except by appointment. Open 9.30—5.30, including Sun. SIZE: Medium. STOCK: Early oak furniture, from 16th C; Georgian mahogany, 18th C; Georgian copper, brass, treen. Not stocked: Silver and jewellery. LOC: On A590 to Barrow, house is 50 yds. from main road in village. PARK: Easy. TEL: 31431; home — same. SER: Valuations; restorations (furniture). VAT: Stan/Spec.

Newby Bridge continued

Townhead Antiques
(Mr. and Mrs. C.H. Townley and C.P. Townley.) Est. 1960. CL: Sun. except by appointment. Open 9—5.30. STOCK: 18th—19th C furniture, silver, porcelain, glass, decorative pieces; clocks, pictures, arms, garden furniture. LOC: A592. 1 mile from Newby Bridge on the Windermere road. PARK: Easy. TEL: 31321. VAT: Stan/Spec.

PENRITH   (0768)

Antiques of Penrith

4 Corney Sq. (E. and L. Mildwurf.) Est. 1964. CL: Wed. Open 10—12 and 1.30—4.45, Sat. 10—12. SIZE: Large. *STOCK: Early oak; mahogany furniture, clocks, brass, copper, glass, china, silver plate, metal, Staffordshire figures.* Not stocked: Silver, jewellery, paintings, rugs. LOC: Near Town Hall. PARK: Easy. TEL: 62801. VAT: Stan.

Archer Antiques

58 Castlegate (K. Archer.) Est. 1977. Open 10.30—1 and 2—5, Wed. and Sun. by appointment. SIZE: Medium. *STOCK: Furniture, 18th—20th C, £100—£1,000; small items, 19th C, £10—£250; porcelain, 18th—20th C, £10—£200.* LOC: By Market Sq., on road leading to castle. PARK: 40yds. TEL: 63446; home — Appleby (0930) 51813. SER: Valuations; restorations; buys at auction. VAT: Stan/Spec.

Cornerways

20 Victoria Rd. (P.B. and A.L. Clark.) Est. 1981. CL: Wed. SIZE: Medium. *STOCK: Furniture including Edwardian, £20—£600; collectable items, £2—£200.* LOC: On A6. PARK: Nearby. TEL: 67754; after 6 p.m. 63635. SER: Buys at auction. VAT: Stan/Spec.

Cumberland Pine

Cromwell Towers, Cromwell Rd. (K. and C.M.S. Mills.) Est. 1978. CL: Wed. Open 10—5, Sun. by appointment. SIZE: Large. *STOCK: Stripped pine furniture, £5—£500; fruitwood furniture, £200—£1,000, both 18th—19th C; kitchenalia, Victorian, £1—£50.* LOC: At start of one way system from M6. PARK: Easy. TEL: 66940. SER: Restorations (furniture). VAT: Stan/Spec.

Joseph James Antiques

Corney Sq. (G.R. Walker.) Est. 1970. CL: Wed. Open 9—12.30 and 1.30—5.30. SIZE: Medium. *STOCK: Furniture and upholstery, 18th C and Victorian, £10—£800; porcelain and pottery, £5—200; silver and plate, pictures £2—£500, all 18th—19th C.* LOC: On the one-way system in the town, 100yds. from the main shopping area (Middlegate), 50yds. from the town hall. PARK: Easy (also large car park 100yds.). TEL: 62065. SER: Restorations; re-upholstery. VAT: Stan.

Penrith continued

Penrith Coin and Stamp Centre
37 King St. (Mr. and Mrs. A. Gray.) Resident. Est. 1974. CL: Wed. Sept.—May. Open 9—5.30. SIZE: Medium. *STOCK: Coins, B.C. to date, 1p—£500; jewellery, secondhand, £5—£25; Great Britain and Commonwealth stamps.* LOC: Just off town centre. PARK: Behind shop. TEL: 64185. SER: Valuations; jewellery repairs. FAIRS: Many coin. VAT: Stan.

Jane Pollock Antiques
4 Castlegate. CL: Wed. Open 9.30—5. SIZE: Medium. *STOCK: Georgian and Victorian silver, some 20th C small items; Victorian pottery, blue and white lustre; wooden boxes, some small furniture.* LOC: One-way street from town centre towards station. PARK: Easy. TEL: 67211. SER: Valuations (silver); restorations (silver, blue glass liners); buys at auction (silver, pottery). FAIRS: Buxton, Olympia, Edinburgh, Kensington, Harrogate and Grasmere. VAT: Stan/Spec.

RAVENSTONEDALE, Nr. Kirkby Stephen

The Book House
Grey Garth. (C. and M. Irwin.) ABA, PBFA. Est. 1965. Open every day, appointment preferred. *STOCK: Books, mainly 19th-20th C, £1—£1,000; some prints and maps, 17th-19th C, £5—£500; some postcards, 20th C, 25p—£10.* LOC: Off A685. Square house across road triangle from village school. PARK: Easy. TEL: (058 73) 634; home — same. SER: Valuations. FAIRS: Northern PBFA. VAT: Stan.

SEDBURGH   (0587)

Merlin Antiques
Howgill Lane. (R. Udall.) Est. 1939. Open 10—5, Sat. and Sun. by appointment. SIZE: Medium. *STOCK: Cottage and period furniture, from 1700, £2—£3,000; longcase and wall clocks, brass, copper, stripped pine.* LOC: From M6, junction 37. Turn left at Golden Lyon Hotel, 200yds. up lane. PARK: Easy. TEL: 20301 or 20719. SER: Valuations; restorations; stripping (pine); metal cleaning.

Stable Antiques
Oakdene Country Hotel, Garsdale Rd. Est. 1970. Open every day. *STOCK: Small furniture, brass, copper, silver, china, prints, small collectors' items.* LOC: 6 miles from exit 37, M6. TEL: 20280.

STAVELEY, Nr. Kendal   (0539)
G.J. and M. Laidler Antiques
Trade Only
24 Seedfield. Est. 1973. Phone call advisable. *STOCK: Clocks, interesting metalware, copper, brass, treen.* TEL: 821712. VAT: Stan/Spec.

"The deer were assembled in groups under the fine trees which are always to be found in these parks..." From *Mr. Rowlandson's England* by Robert Southey, ed. John Steel, published by the **Antique Collectors' Club,** 1985.

TEMPLE SOWERBY, Nr. Carlisle
Harpers' Antiques
Sheriff House. (Mr. and Mrs. R.B. Harper.) Est. 1960. Open any time, telephone call advisable. SIZE: Medium. *STOCK: General antiques including furniture, pictures, porcelain, glass, clocks, 18th—19th C, £1—£1,500.* PARK: Easy. TEL: Kirkby Thore (0930) 61359. VAT: Stan/Spec.

ULVERSTON (0229)
A1A Antiques
59B Market St. (J. Thornton.) Est. 1960. Open by appointment. SIZE: Medium. *STOCK: Bric-a-brac, clocks, furniture, shipping items, pictures.* PARK: Easy. TEL: 88745, Windermere (09662) 2930/5183. PARK: Easy. SER: Valuations; restorations; buys at auction. VAT: Stan/Spec.

Ulverston continued
The Antique Warehouse
Lower Brook St. (Mrs. D. Satterthwaite.) Est. 1974. CL: Mon. and Wed. Open 10—3. SIZE: Medium and warehouse. *STOCK: Oak and mahogany furniture, clocks, £100—£500; shipping furniture, 1920s oak and pine, paintings and prints, £50—£100; collectors' items — glass, china, silver, copper, brass, books, £5—£25.* LOC: On corner of main car park. PARK: Easy. TEL: Home — Broughton-in-Furness (065 76) 539. SER: Restorations (chairs re-seated, rush or cane work; clocks and watches). VAT: Stan.

Elizabeth's and Son
Market Hall. (E.A. and J.R. Bevins.) Est. 1960. CL: Wed. Open 9—5. SIZE: Medium. *STOCK: Victorian and Georgian glass, porcelain and silver; 19th C brass, copper, books; Victorian jewellery.* LOC: Town centre. PARK: Easy. TEL: 52763. SER: Buys at auction.

Ulverston continued

Saracen Antiques
4 Soutergate. (Mrs. J. Thompson.) Est. 1984. CL: Sun. and Wed. except by appointment. Open 10—12.30 and 1.30—5. SIZE: Medium. *STOCK: Early oak and mahogany, early 17th to mid 19th C, £30—£2,000; paintings, mainly 19th C, £60—£1,000; longcase, wall and French clocks, early 18th to late 19th C, £100—£2,000; decorative items, mainly 19th C.* Not stocked: Jewellery, textiles. LOC: Junction of King St., Fountain St. and Soutergate. PARK: Easy. TEL: 52745; home — 55403. SER: Restorations (longcase clocks, oil paintings and watercolours). VAT: Stan/Spec.

Soutergate Antiques
1 Soutergate. (B. Johnson.) Est. 1984. CL: Wed. p.m. Open 9.30—12.30 and 2—5. SIZE: Small. *STOCK: Furniture, bric-a-brac, curios, 19th C, £2—£400.* PARK: Nearby. TEL: Home — 56189. SER: Restorations (furniture).

Ulverston Point
The Gill. (Mrs. B. Spendlove.) Est. 1981. Open 10—4.30. SIZE: Medium. *STOCK: Tables and chairs, 17th-19th C, £200—£1,000; watercolours, writing boxes and other small cabinets, 19th C, £50—£150.* LOC: 40yds. off King St. PARK: Nearby. TEL: 56162. SER: Restorations (furniture); buys at auction. VAT: Spec.

WHITEHAVEN   (0946)
Georgian Shop
44 Roper St. (Mrs. M.L.D. Graham.) Est. 1970. CL: Mon. and Wed. Open 10.30—4.30. SIZE: Small. LOC: Beside Whitehaven News Office. TEL: 3760 (evenings).

Owen Kelly Antiques
10—11 New St. (V.C. Kelly.) Open by appointment only. *STOCK: General antiques including china, silver.* TEL: 2879.

Michael Moon
41-43 Roper St. (M. and S. Moon.) ABA, PBFA. Est. 1969. CL: Wed. Open 10—5. SIZE: Large. *STOCK: Antiquarian books including Cumbrian topography.* PARK: Easy. TEL: 62936. FAIRS: PBFA Northern. VAT: Stan.

Whitehaven continued

T. West
44 Market Place. CL: Mon. and Wed. Open 10.30—4. *STOCK: General antiques.* TEL: 4931.

WINDERMERE   (096 62)
The Birdcage Antiques
College Rd. (Miss T.A. Smith). Est. 1983. CL: Thurs. Open 10—5.30, Sun. by appointment. SIZE: Small. *STOCK: General antiques, glass, brass and copper, oil lamps, country bygones, Staffordshire, 18th C to 1920, £10—£500; 19th C pottery.* LOC: From A591 through village, past end of one-way system, turn right after 50 yards. PARK: Nearby. TEL: 5063; home—3041. VAT: Stan/Spec.

Century Antiques and Art Gallery
Victoria Cottage, Victoria St. (D. and R. Hopwood.) Est. 1969. CL: Thurs. Open 9—1 and 2.30—5.30. *STOCK: Furniture, collectors' items, clocks, pictures.* LOC: On main road from station, adjacent to Elleray Hotel. TEL: 4126.

Joseph Thornton Antiques
4 Victoria St. (J.W. Thornton.) Est. 1971. Open by appointment. SIZE: Large. *STOCK: General antiques, especially furniture, £1—£15,000; bric-a-brac, pictures, clocks.* LOC: 50yds. from railway station. PARK: Easy. TEL: 2930/5183 or Ulverston (0229) 88745. SER: Valuations; buys at auction. VAT: Stan/Spec.

H.V. Wilkinson Antiques
Crescent Rd. Hours variable, usually available evenings. *STOCK: General antiques, prints, pictures, watercolours, Victoriana.* TEL: 3815.

Windermere Antiques
The Courtyard, Main Rd. (J. Hopwood). Open 9.30—5.30 including Sun. during holiday season. *STOCK: Clocks — longcase, wall, bracket and carriage, mainly 18th C; small furniture.* LOC: 50 yards from W.H. Smith on same side, through archway. PARK: Easy. TEL: 5810. SER: Restorations (clocks). VAT: Stan/Spec.

Windermere and Bowness Dollmaking Co.
College Rd. Est. 1971. CL: Thurs. and Sun. except by appointment. Open 10—5, out of season appointment advisable. *STOCK: Victoria Church porcelain and wax dolls.* LOC: 100yds. from railway station. TEL: 4785. SER: Restorations (dolls); spare parts (dolls).

Derbyshire

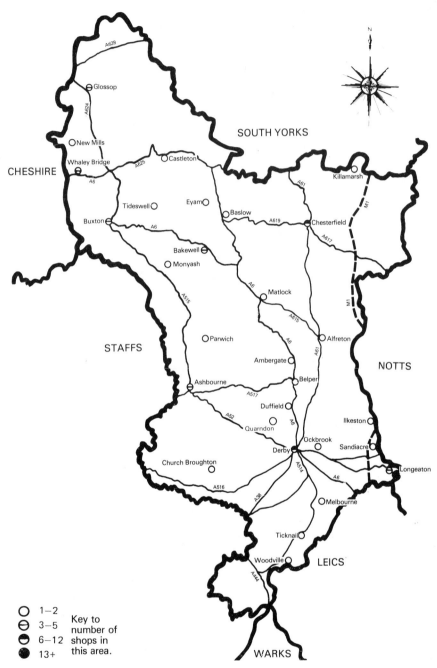

SOUTH YORKS

CHESHIRE

STAFFS

NOTTS

LEICS

WARKS

A628

A624

Glossop

New Mills

Whaley Bridge

A625

Castleton

A6

Killamarsh

M1

Tideswell

Eyam

Baslow

A619

Chesterfield

A617

Buxton

A6

Bakewell

Monyash

A515

A6

Matlock

A615

Parwich

A6

Alfreton

Ambergate

A461

Ashbourne

Belper

A517

Duffield

A52

Quarndon

A6

Ilkeston

Ockbrook

Sandiacre

Church Broughton

Derby

A514

Longeaton

A516

A6

A38

Melbourne

Ticknall

Woodville

A444

Key to number of shops in this area.

○ 1–2
⊖ 3–5
⬤ 6–12
● 13+

Please note this is only a rough map designed to show dealers the number of shops in the various towns, and is not necessarily totally accurate.

ALFRETON (0773)
Curiosity Shop and Alfreton Piano Co.
37 King St. (K. and G. Allsop.) Est. 1969. CL: Wed. Open 9.30—5. SIZE: Small. *STOCK: Stripped pine and pianos.* LOC: A61. PARK: Easy. TEL: 832427. SER: Valuations. VAT: Stan.

AMBERGATE(4 fig. nos.) (077 385)
(6 fig. nos.) (0773)
The Dolls' House
8 Derby Rd. (Mrs. C.M. Stratton-Shaw.) Est. 1968. Open weekends or available at 13 Derby Rd. during week. SIZE: Small. *STOCK: Brass, copper, china, glass, jewellery, curios, £5—£100; country furniture, £10—£400; dolls, toys, children's pictures and furniture.* LOC: On A6. PARK: Easy.

P.W. Gottschald
32 Derby Rd. (P.W., D.J. and C.R. Gottschald). Est. 1948. Open 10—6, Sun. 11—5. SIZE: Medium. *STOCK: European porcelain, £50—£1,000; European furniture, £100—£2,000; both 18th—19th C; paintings, watercolours and drawings, mainly 19th C, £25—£1,000.* LOC: A6. PARK: Easy. TEL: 6428; home — (0629) 4043. SER: Valuations. FAIRS: Buxton, Thoresby Hall, Cheltenham. VAT: Stan/Spec.

ASHBOURNE (0335)
John Brown Antiques
38 Church St. Open 9—5. *STOCK: General antiques.* TEL: 43470.

Ashbourne continued

Pamela Elsom — Antiques
LAPADA
5 Church St. Est. 1963. CL: Wed. Open 10—5. SIZE: Medium. *STOCK: Furniture, £20—£2,000, metalware, both 17th—19th C; period smalls, general antiques, treen, pottery, glass, secondhand book dept.* Not stocked: Coins, militaria. LOC: On A52. PARK: Easy. TEL: 43468. SER: Valuations. VAT: Spec.

Manion Antiques
23 Church St. (Mrs. V.J. Manion). Est 1985. Open Fri., Sat. and Sun. 10—5, other times by appointment. SIZE: Small. *STOCK: Porcelain, silver and jewellery, 19th C, £50—£100.* PARK: Easy. TEL: 43207; home — same. SER: Valuations. FAIRS: Little Chelsea.

Out of Time Antiques
21 Church St. (T. Wardle, M. and G. Bassett and M. Locke.) Est. 1975. Open 10—5, Wed. and Sun. by appointment. SIZE: Small. *STOCK: Decorative and collectable items, £10—£200; metalware, stripped pine, £20—£300; oak and mahogany, £30—£500.* LOC: A52. PARK: Easy. TEL: 42096; home — 42741/43586/42074.

Spurrier-Smith Antiques *Mainly Trade*
28 and 41 Church St. (I. Spurrier-Smith.) Est. 1973. CL: Wed. Open 10—6. Sun. by appointment. SIZE: Large. *STOCK: Furniture, pictures, porcelain, pottery, metalware, instruments, Oriental, bronzes, collectables, pine.* TEL: 43669; home — Cowers Lane (077 389) 368. SER: Valuations. VAT: Stan/Spec.

Kenneth Upchurch
30B Church St. Est. 1972. *STOCK: Oil paintings and watercolours, mainly 19th C. Studio and art pottery, porcelain and pottery, 18th and 19th C.* TEL: Derby (0332) 754499.

BAKEWELL (062 981)

Antiques Coffee House
Buxton Rd. (P. Cassidy.) Est. 1971. Open 10—5, Sun. 2—5, or by appointment. SIZE: Large and warehouse. *STOCK: Furniture, pine, 18th—20th C; shipping goods, £5—£500; smalls, from £1.* LOC: First shop on left on entering Bakewell from Buxton on A6. TEL: 3544 any time. SER: Valuations; buys at auction; containers.

Beedham Antiques Ltd.
Holme Hall. (W.H. Beedham.) Open by appointment. SIZE: Large. *STOCK: English oak furniture, 16th—17th C.* LOC: Off A619. TEL: 3285. SER: Valuations; buys at auction. VAT: Spec.

K. Chappell BADA
Antiques and Fine Art
King St. Est. 1940. Open 9—6. *STOCK: 17th—19th C English furniture, oil paintings, porcelain, pottery, metalwork and clocks.* TEL: 2496 or 4531. VAT: Stan/Spec.

Bakewell continued

Maurice Goldstone and Son BADA
Avenel Court and The Old Town Hall. (M. Goldstone.) Est. 1927. Open 9—6 or by appointment. SIZE: Large. *STOCK: Oak furniture, 16th—18th C, from £100; walnut furniture, brass, 18th C, from £500.* PARK: Easy. TEL: 2487; home — same. SER: Valuations; buys at auction. VAT: Spec.

Water Lane Antiques
Water Lane. (M. Pembery and J. Shaw.) Est. 1967. CL: Thurs. Open 10—1 and 2—5. SIZE: Medium. *STOCK: Furniture, £500—£4,000; metalware, £100—£1,000; objets d'art, £100—£1,500, all 18th—19th C.* LOC: Off Market Sq. PARK: Nearby. TEL: 4161. SER: Valuations; restorations. VAT: Stan/Spec.

BASLOW (024 688)

K. Chappell Antiques and Fine Art
Goose Green. Est. 1940. Open by appointment only. *STOCK: English furniture, 17th—19th C; oil paintings, porcelain, metalwork, clocks.* TEL: 3311.

Maurice Goldstone & Son

(*MICHAEL GOLDSTONE*)

AVENEL COURT
BAKEWELL
DERBYSHIRE DE4 1DZ
TELEPHONE 062981 2487

EARLY PERIOD FURNITURE & DECORATION

A Rising Top Hutch Chestnut, c.1550.

BELPER (4 fig. no.) (077 382)
(6 fig. no.) (0773)

Sweetings (Antiques 'n' Things)
1a The Butts. (K.J. Sweeting and Miss J.L. Bunting.) Est. 1971. CL: Wed. p.m. SIZE: Large. *STOCK: Stripped pine and satinwood furniture, £50—£100; oak, shipping goods, bric-a-brac, £5—£100; all 19th—20th C.* LOC: Off A6, near Market Place. PARK: Easy. TEL: 5930. SER: Valuations; restorations (pine and satinwood); buys at auction. VAT: Stan.

Neil Wayne
"The Razor Man"
High Peak Products, Old Baptist Chapel, rear of 'Riflemans Arms', 72 Bridge St. Est. 1969. Open every day 9.30—6, prior telephone call appreciated. SIZE: Medium. *STOCK: Razors and shaving items, 18th to early 19th C, £20—£300; knives including fruit, pocket, hunting and cutlery, 17th—19th C, £20—£500; optical and medical items, 17th—20th C, £10—£1,000.* PARK: Easy. TEL: 7910/7020; home — same. SER: Valuations; restoration (razors and gentlemen's sets).

BUXTON (0298)

Landau Antiques
"The Knoll", Marlborough Rd. (H. and V. Metcalfe.) Open by appointment. *STOCK: Georgian, Victorian and Edwardian furniture.* TEL: 6062.

Pandora's Box Antiques and Gifts
84 Spring Gardens. (P.F. Wells.) Est. 1978. CL: Tues. and Thurs. Open 11—5 in summer, Fri. and Sat. only in winter. SIZE: Small. *STOCK: General antiques and collectors' items, mainly 19th to early 20th C, £5—£350.* LOC: Next to the cinema. PARK: Side road. TEL: Home — Sheffield (0742) 307913. SER: Valuations. FAIRS: Pandora.

West End Galleries
8 Cavendish Circus. (A. and A. Needham.) Est. 1955. CL: Sat. Open 9—5. SIZE: Large. *STOCK: French, Dutch, English furniture; clocks, paintings, works of art, bronzes.* LOC: A6. PARK: Easy. TEL: 4546. VAT: Stan/Spec.

Slip-decorated dish. The Pelican in her Piety, made by Ralph Simpson in Staffordshire, c.1714. 432mm diameter. From *A Collector's History of English Pottery* by Griselda Lewis, published by the **Antique Collectors' Club,** 1985.

Brian Bingham Antiques

SPECIALISING IN 17th AND 18th CENTURY OAK AND COUNTRY FURNITURE

Half mile from Town Centre on A619

420, CHATSWORTH ROAD,
BRAMPTON,
CHESTERFIELD

TEL.
CHESTERFIELD 201235
HOME 208441

CASTLETON

Ann Capon Antiques
Market Place. (Mrs. A. Capon.) Est. 1960. Open any time. Resident. SIZE: Medium. *STOCK: Furniture, stripped pine, pottery, porcelain, glass, metalware and Sheffield plate.* Not stocked: 18th C glass. LOC: From Sheffield turn left (opp. Bulls Head) off A625. PARK: Easy. TEL: Hope Valley (0433) 20270; home — same.

CHESTERFIELD   (0246)

Brian Bingham Antiques
420 Chatsworth Rd., Brampton. Est. 1964. CL: Wed. p.m. Open 10—4, Sat. 10—5. SIZE: Medium. *STOCK: Oak, 17th—18th C, £50—£3,000.* LOC: A619. PARK: Easy. TEL: 201235; home — 208441. SER: Valuations. VAT: Stan/Spec.

Chesterfield Antiques Centre
195 Chatsworth Rd. (C.B. Sheppard). *STOCK: General antiques, collectors' items, paintings.* LOC: 5 miles from junction 29, M1. TEL: 205614.

F. Hall Ltd.
9-11 Beetwell St. CL: Wed. Open 9.30—5.30. *STOCK: Guns, general antiques.* TEL: 73133. SER: Restorations.

Alan Hill Books
278 Chatsworth Rd. Est. 1980. Open 10—5.30. *STOCK: Antiquarian books.* TEL: 32274.

Chesterfield continued

The Military Shop
103 Markham Rd. (A.D. Goodlad.) Est. 1974. CL: Wed. SIZE: Small. *STOCK: General militaria.* LOC: 100yds. from A61. PARK: Easy. TEL: 38219.

Ian Morris
86 Saltergate. Est. 1967. Open 9—5. SIZE: Medium. *STOCK: Furniture, 19th to early 20th C, £100—1,000; pictures, small items.* LOC: Main thoroughfare, just past town hall. PARK: 100yds. TEL: 35120. SER: Valuations. VAT: Stan/spec.

Tilleys Bookshops
19 and 29/31 South St., New Whittington. (A.G.J. and A.A.J.C. Tilley.) Est. 1977. Open 9—1.30 and 3—5. SIZE: Medium. *STOCK: Magazines, books, postcards, comics, cigarette cards, ephemera.* PARK: Easy. TEL: 454270; home — Sheffield (0742) 656154. SER: Mail order, twice yearly list issued. FAIRS: Leeds, Nottingham, Manchester, Buxton.

IS YOUR ENTRY CORRECT?
If there is even the slightest inaccuracy in your entry, *please* let us know before 1st January 1987.
GUIDE TO THE
ANTIQUE SHOPS OF BRITAIN
5 Church Street, Woodbridge, Suffolk.

Chesterfield continued

Westfield Antiques
Freebirch Cottage, Freebirch. Est. 1968. Open by appointment only. *STOCK: 19th C porcelain especially English, early maps, Chinese embroidery.* LOC: B6050. TEL: Baslow (024 688) 3153. FAIRS: Buxton, Tatton Park, Cheltenham.

CHURCH BROUGHTON, Nr. Derby
Broughton Antiques
The Lawns. (Mrs. G.S. Pratt.) Resident. Est. 1977. Open Mon. Fri. and Sat. 10−4, other times by appointment. SIZE: Small. *STOCK: Furniture, £20−£300; porcelain, brass, silver, collectors' items, £1−£100.* Not stocked: Clocks and militaria. LOC: From Derby first house on right in village. PARK: Easy. TEL: Sudbury (028 378) 428; home − same. SER: Valuations. FAIRS: Local.

DERBY   (0332)
Abbey House
115 Woods Lane. (E. White.) Resident. Est. 1959. SIZE: Large. *STOCK: Furniture, clocks, Victoriana, dolls, shipping goods.* TEL: 31426. SER: Restorations; repairs.

Carousel Antiques
42 Midland Rd. (E. Linnett.) Est. 1960. CL: Wed. Open 10−5. *STOCK: General Victoriana, furniture, collectors' items, clocks.* LOC: 5 minutes from railway station, next to G.P.O. PARK: At rear. TEL: 31371.

Derby Antique Centre
11 Friargate. (D. Foddy and J. Parkin.) Est. 1975. Open 10−5.30, Sun. a.m. by appointment. SIZE: Large. *STOCK: Furniture and clocks, porcelain, 18th−19th C, £25−£1,000; silver and jewellery, 19th−20th C, £5−£500; dolls and toys, cameras, linen, pictures, pine, copper and brass.* LOC: Close to city centre and inner ring road. PARK: Restricted and 200yds. TEL: 385002; home − 671241. SER: Restorations (furniture and clocks). VAT: Stan/Spec.

Derby Antiques Market
52−56 Curzon St. (E.I. Corry.) Est. 1954. CL: Wed. p.m. Open 9−5. SIZE: Medium. *STOCK: Furniture, paintings, china, silver.* TEL: 41861. VAT: Spec.

Friary Cabinetmakers
22 Friar Gate. (G.A. Poyser.) Open 10−4, after hours at workshop at rear. SIZE: Small. *STOCK: Furniture, copper, brass.* LOC: From Derby centre take A52 Ashbourne Rd. PARK: 20yds. away at left side of shop. TEL: 32629. SER: Restorations; buys at auction.

Derby continued

Laura's Bookshop
58 Osmaston Rd. Est. 1969. CL: Mon. and Wed. *STOCK: Antiquarian and secondhand books, antiquarian maps and prints, especially local history and topography.* PARK: Own. TEL: 47094. VAT: Stan.

Charles H. Ward
12 Friar Gate. (M.G. Ward.) CL: Wed. p.m. *STOCK: Oil paintings, 19th−20th C; watercolours.* TEL: 42893. SER: Restorations.

DUFFIELD, Nr. Derby
Duffield Antiques
3/5 Town St. (Mrs. Preston.) Est. 1972. Open 10.30−5.30. SIZE: Medium. *STOCK: General antiques, Victoriana, collectors' items, pottery.* LOC: A6. PARK: Easy.

Wayside Antiques
62 Town St. (Mrs. J. Harding.) Est. 1975. *STOCK: Furniture, 18th and 19th C, £50−£800; porcelain, pictures, boxes and silver.* TEL: Derby (0332) 840346. VAT: Stan/Spec.

EYAM
Oxley Antiques and Fine Arts
Main St. (N.S. Oxley.) Est. 1906. Open Fri., Sat. and Sun. 12−5 or by appointment. SIZE: Small. *STOCK: Cottage furniture, small items, watercolours, paintings, porcelain, copper and brass, 18th−19th C.* LOC: ½ mile off A623, west end of village. PARK: Easy. TEL: Baslow (024 688) 3265.

GLOSSOP   (045 74)
Chapel Antiques
Brookfield. (E. and M. Annal.) Est. 1964. Open Sat.−Tues. 10−5, or by appointment. SIZE: Medium. *STOCK: Furniture, oak, ceramics, from 17th C.* LOC: A57. PARK: Easy. TEL: 66711; home − (0457) 64184. SER: Valuations; restorations; buys at auction.

A small handled-dish, a rare component to a large blue-printed dinner service. Printed initial mark 'J & W R', 5¾ins. long, c.1820-5. From *Ridgway Porcelains* by Geoffrey A. Godden, F.R.S.A., published by the **Antique Collectors' Club, 1985.**

Glossop continued

Derbyshire Clocks
104 High St. West. (J.A. Lees.) Est. 1975. *STOCK: Clocks.* TEL: 62677. SER: Restorations (clocks).

Seymour Galleries
Church St. South, Old Glossop. (P. Seymour.) Est. 1971. CL: Mon. and Tues. Open 10—5.30 including Sun. but appointment advisable. *STOCK: Early oak and country furniture, unusual decorative items.* TEL: 62555; home — same.

ILKESTON   (0602)

Andy's Antiques
35 Alvenor St. CL: Thurs. Open 9.30—1 and 2—6.30. SIZE: Large. *STOCK: Victoriana and bric-a-brac.* PARK: Easy. TEL: 306415; home — same. VAT: Stan.

Durose Antiques
10 Havelock St., Nottingham Rd. (M.D. Durose.) Est. 1965. *STOCK: 18th—19th C furniture, longcase clocks; dolls' houses and miniature furniture.* TEL: 324889.

KILLAMARSH

Havenplan's Architectural Emporium.
The Old Station, Station Rd. Est. 1972. Open 10—5. SIZE: Large. *STOCK: Architectural fittings and decorative items, church interiors and furnishings, fireplaces, doors, decorative cast ironwork and masonry, 18th to early 20th C, £5—£500.* LOC: M1, exit 30. Take A616 towards Sheffield, turn right on to B6053, turn right on to B6058 towards Killamarsh, turn right at Page Feeds Mill. PARK: Easy. TEL: Sheffield (0742) 489972; home — Chesterfield (0246) 433315.

LONG EATON   (0602)

Antique Shop
17 Station Rd. (P. Ledger.) Resident. Est. 1973. Open daily. SIZE: Small. *STOCK: General antiques, dolls, toys.* LOC: 2 miles from the M1. PARK: Nearby. TEL: 729327.

Long Eaton continued

Goodacre Engraving Ltd.
Thrumpton Ave., (off Chatsworth Ave.), Meadow Lane. Est. 1948. *STOCK: Clocks, movements, parts and castings.* SER: Hand engraving, movement repairs, silvering and dial repainting. TEL: 734387. VAT: Stan.

Miss Elany
2 Salisbury St. (D. and Mrs. Mottershead.) Est. 1977. Open 9—5, Sun. by appointment. SIZE: Medium. *STOCK: Pianos, 1900 to date, £50— £500; general antiques, Victorian and Edwardian, £25—£200.* PARK: Easy. TEL: 734835; home — 729651. VAT: Stan.

MATLOCK (0629)
Resonia Antiques
79 Dale Rd. (A. Chapman.) CL: Thurs. Open 10—5. *STOCK: General antiques especially clocks.* PARK: Easy. TEL: 55500.

MELBOURNE (033 16)
Melbourne Treasure Chest
60 Potter St. (Mrs. W. Gee.) CL: Mon., Thurs. and Sat. Open 10.30—4.30. *STOCK: General antiques.* TEL: 3399.

MONYASH, Nr. Bakewell
Mrs. A. Robinson
Chapel St. Est. 1961. Open Sat., Sun. and Mon. 2—6, or by appointment. *STOCK: Oak, mahogany, porcelain, collectors' items, £1— £1,000.* TEL: Bakewell (062 981) 2926.

NEW MILLS (0663)
Regent House Antiques
8 Buxton Rd., New Town. CL: Fri. Open 10.30—5, Sat. 2—5, or by appointment. SIZE: Medium. *STOCK: General antiques, period furniture, clocks; copper, brass, decorative items.* PARK: Easy. TEL: 42684. VAT: Stan/ Spec.

OCKBROOK
Ockbrook Antiques
9 Flood St. (N. Critchlow.) Est. 1967. Open 11—5 or anytime by appointment. SIZE: Large. *STOCK: Furniture, Victorian to 1920s; porcelain and small items, to £150.* LOC: Off A52. PARK: Own. TEL: Derby (0332) 666533; home — Derby (0332) 662899. SER: Valuations; restorations.

Barnacle-encrusted blue and white tureen, cover and stand. Part of ''The Nanking Cargo'', **Antique Collecting,** March 1986.

PARWICH, Nr. Ashbourne
(3 fig. no.) (033 525)
(5 fig. no.) (0335)
Old Farmhouse Furniture
Parwich Lees Farm, Alsop Rd. (R. Beech.) Est. 1977. Open 8−5, weekends by appointment. SIZE: Large. *STOCK: English and Irish pine, 18th−19th C, £10−£500.* LOC: Approx. 1½ miles off Buxton/Ashbourne road. PARK: Easy. TEL: 473; home − same. VAT: Stan.

QUARNDON, Nr. Derby
Friary Antiques   LAPADA
(N.W. Jackson.) Est. 1968. Open by appointment only. *STOCK: Decorative antiques, small collectors' items, silver plate.* TEL: Derby (0332) 552160.

SANDIACRE   (0602)
The Bookshop
4 Station Rd. (I.H.R. Cowley.) CL: Wed. Open 9−5. *STOCK: Antiquarian and academic books, all subjects.* LOC: By Junction 25, M1. TEL: 393379.

TICKNALL
Sam Savage Antiques   LAPADA
Hayes Farm, Main St. (S. and M. Savage.) Resident. Est. 1969. Open 10−5.30, Sun. by appointment. SIZE: Large. *STOCK: Early period furniture, 17th−19th C; decorative items, Oriental rugs, paintings.* LOC: Centre of Ticknall, on A514, 4 miles from Ashby-de-la-Zouch. PARK: Easy. TEL: Melbourne (033 16) 2195. SER: Valuations. VAT: Stan/Spec.

TIDESWELL, Nr. Buxton   (0298)
Yesterday Antiques
6 Commercial Rd. (N.F. Thompson.) Est. 1983. Open 9.30−5.30, Sun. by appointment. SIZE: Medium. *STOCK: Victorian brass, brass and iron beds; 17th−20th C furniture including longcase clocks; silver, paintings, pottery and porcelain.* LOC: Opposite church, off A623. PARK: Easy. TEL: 871932; home − same. SER: Valuations; restorations; buys at auction.

WHALEY BRIDGE   (066 33)
The Antique Home Ltd   LAPADA
3 Lower Macclesfield Rd. Open 10−5, Sat. 11−5, Sun. 12−5. *STOCK: English and Continental furniture, clocks, porcelain, bronzes, objets d'art.* TEL: 3078.
Deane Antiques
131 Buxton Rd. (J. Donelly.) Open Mon., Tues., Thurs. 9.30−4.15 or by appointment. *STOCK: Silver, pottery, furniture.* TEL: 2928; home − 2673.

RICHARD GLASS
Hockerley Old Hall,
Whaley Bridge,
Nr. Buxton.
Tel: Buxton 06633 4320

Stock: Furniture, 17th and 18th century oak from £300; decorative items. Open by appointment.

Whaley Bridge continued
Richard Glass
Hockerley Old Hall. Open Mon., Fri. and Sat. 9−5.30 or by appointment. *STOCK: Furniture 17th−18th C oak, from £300; decorative items.* LOC: ½ mile off A6. TEL: 4320. FAIRS: Buxton. VAT: Spec.

Martin Marsh Militaria
114 Buxton Rd. Est. 1967. Open by appointment. SIZE: Small. *STOCK: British military badges, militaria and weapons.* LOC: Next to school, 50yds. from traffic lights. PARK: Easy. TEL: 3267. SER: Valuations (weapons); mail order badge catalogues available. FAIRS: Major Arms in U.K.

WOODVILLE
Wooden Box Antiques
32 High St. (Mrs. R. Bowler.) Est. 1982. Open 10−5, some Sun. SIZE: Medium. *STOCK: Furniture, Georgian−Edwardian, £75−£400; writing boxes, tea caddies and mirrors, Georgian−Victorian, £50−£150; country pine furniture, Georgian−Edwardian, £30−£450.* LOC: A50, between Ashby de la Zouch and Burton-on-Trent. PARK: Easy. TEL: Burton-on-Trent (0283) 212014; home − same. SER: Restorations (furniture); buys at auction (furniture). FAIRS: Some local.

Devonshire

Key:
- ○ 1–2
- ⊖ 3–5
- ◒ 6–12 Key to number of shops in this area.
- ● 13+

Lynton

Combe Martin

Ilfracombe

SOMERSET

Braunton

Barnstaple

Bradiford

Bideford

A361

South Molton

Meshaw

Bampton

Chulmleigh

Tiverton

A373

Stockland

Iddesleigh

Morchard Bishop

Cullompton

Honiton

Axminster

Winkleigh

Hatherleigh

Sandford

Whimple

Ottery St. Mary

Colyton

Northlew

Okehampton

Exeter

Harpford

Seaton

Chagford

Topsham

Woodbury

Sidmouth

CORNWALL

Moretonhampstead

East Budleigh

Lydford

Budleigh Salterton

A382

Dawlish

Exmouth

A384

Newton Abbot

Teignmouth

Tavistock

Horrabridge

Ashburton

Shaldon

Buckfastleigh

Maidencombe

Dartington

Torquay

Sparkwell

South Brent

Totnes

A385

Plymouth

Harbertonford

A38

Ivybridge

Modbury

Brixham

Dartmouth

Aveton Gifford

Kingsbridge

Salcombe

Please note this is only a rough map designed to show dealers the number of shops in the various towns, and is not necessarily totally accurate.

ASHBURTON (0364)

Ashburton Marbles

6 West St. (A. and A. Ager.) Est. 1976. CL: Wed. p.m. and Sat. p.m. Open 9.30—5. SIZE: Large. *STOCK: Marble and wooden fire-surrounds, decorative cast iron interiors; scuttles, fenders, overmantels, 1790—1910; architectural and decorative antiques.* PARK: Easy, adjacent. TEL: 53189.

Dartmoor Antiques Centre

Off West St. (West Country Antiques and Collectors' Fairs, G. Mosdell.) ABA. Est. 1984. Open Mon. and Thurs. 9—4. There are 20 dealers at this centre selling a wide range of general antiques. LOC: Opposite town centre car park. PARK: Easy. TEL: 52182. VAT: Stan/Spec.

Lisa and Stuart Goddard-Smith

"Wild Goose", East St. Est. 1964. Open 9—5.15, Wed., Sat. and Sun. by appointment. SIZE: Small. *STOCK: Country furniture, metalware, treen, original paintings, unusual items.* LOC: Opposite the Golden Lion. TEL: 53337. VAT: Mainly Spec.

Philip J.L. Thomas   *Trade Only*

80 East St. Est. 1973. Open by appointment. SIZE: Medium. *STOCK: European and Oriental ceramics, 17th—20th C, £25—£1,000; works of art.* LOC: Going south, ½ mile off A38, main road into town. PARK: Easy. TEL: 52330; home — same. SER: Valuations. VAT: Stan/Spec.

AVETON GIFFORD
Nr. Kingsbridge

Aune Valley Antiques

Fore St. (J. and E. Sharpe.) Est. 1976. *STOCK: Furniture, bric-a-brac, dolls.* PARK: Easy. TEL: Kingsbridge (0548) 550240. VAT: Spec.

AXMINSTER (0297)

The Old Curiosity Shop (Antiques)

South St. (N.A. and C. Love.) Resident. Open 8.30—5.30, Wed. 8.30—1. *STOCK: Furniture, Georgian and Victorian; general antiques and curios, clocks, silver, secondhand books.* LOC: In town centre, next to library. PARK: Easy. TEL: 33016; home — same. SER: Restorations (furniture, china and clocks); re-caning and rushing of chairs; picture framing. VAT: Stan/Spec.

W.G. Potter and Son

West St. Est. 1863. CL: Sat. p.m. Open 9—5. SIZE: Medium. *STOCK: Furniture, 17th—19th C, clocks, both £50—£5,000; books, £5—£200; china, £5—£500; silver, £10—£1,000.* LOC: In main street (A35) opposite church. PARK: Easy. TEL: 32063. SER: Restorations (furniture); buys at auction. VAT: Stan/Spec.

BAMPTON, Nr. Tiverton (0398)

Bampton Antiques

9 Castle St. (W.R. Jackson.) Est. 1983. Open 10.30—5, Sun. by appointment. SIZE: Medium. *STOCK: Furniture, silver and porcelain, clocks, 1700—1900; fine art 1800—1900; all £5—£500.* LOC: A361 from Taunton, shop on right entering Bampton. PARK: Frog St. TEL: Home — 31899. SER: Valuations; restorations (clocks); buys at auction. FAIRS: Dulverton.

Bampton continued

Robert Byles
7 Castle St. Est. 1966. CL: Sun. except by appointment. Open 9−1 and 2−6. *STOCK: Early oak, local farmhouse tables and settles, metalwork, pottery, unstripped period pine.* TEL: 31515. VAT: Stan/Spec.

BARNSTAPLE (0271)
Ancient and Modern
Oaklands, Victoria Rd., Barnstaple Rd. (G. Down.) Est. 1966. Open by appointment. SIZE: Medium. *STOCK: Furniture, 18th−19th C, to £2,000; copper, brass, Victoriana, bric-a-brac.* Not stocked: Stamps, coins. TEL: 45642. SER: Restorations (furniture). VAT: Stan/Spec.

William Mayo Antiques
15 Bear St. Est. 1975. *STOCK: Jewellery, watches, clocks, gold and silver.* TEL: 75305. SER: Restorations and repairs (clocks, watches).

Minerva Gallery
123 Boutport St. (P.J. Newcombe.) Est. 1972. CL: Wed. p.m. Open 9.30−5. SIZE: Medium. *STOCK: Maps and prints, photographs, oils and watercolours, £1−£500.* TEL: 71025. SER: Picture framing, mounting. VAT: Stan.

Mark Parkhouse Antiques and Jewellery
106 High St. Est. 1976. CL: Wed. p.m. *STOCK: Jewellery, furniture, silver, paintings, clocks, glass, porcelain, small collectors items, 18th−19th C, £20−£5,000.* PARK: Nearby. TEL: 74504. SER: Valuations; buys at auction. VAT: Stan/Spec.

Porcupines Bookshop and Toy Museum
11 Boutport St. (S. Lowe.) Est. 1963. CL: Mon. Open 10−6. SIZE: Medium. *STOCK: Books, 16th−20th C.* LOC: Boutport St. runs parallel with High St. TEL: 43641.

IS YOUR ENTRY CORRECT?
If there is even the slightest inaccuracy in your entry, *please* let us know before 1st January 1987.
GUIDE TO THE
ANTIQUE SHOPS OF BRITAIN
5 Church Street, Woodbridge, Suffolk.

BIDEFORD (023 72)
Century Galleries
7 Cooper St. (Thomas Williams Antiques Ltd.) *STOCK: General antiques, jewellery, silverware, china.* TEL: 77245. VAT: Stan/Spec.

Chandlers
65 High St. (R.J. Lloyd.) Est. 1955. CL: Wed. Open 9.30−5. SIZE: Medium. *STOCK: Pictures, prints, pots, general antiques and books.* PARK: 20yds. up street. TEL: 72331 and 72435. VAT: Stan.

J. Collins and Son
The Studio, 63 and 28 High St. (J. and P. Biggs.) Est. 1953. CL: Wed. Open 9.30−5, or by appointment. SIZE: Large. *STOCK: General antiques, fine watercolours and oils.* LOC: From Bideford Bridge turn right, then first left into the High St. PARK: Easy. TEL: 73103; home − 76485. SER: Valuations; restorations (period furniture, paintings and watercolours); cleaning and framing. Buys at auction (pictures). VAT: Stan/Spec.

'Farmhouse Furniture'
12 Rope Walk. Est. 1979. Open 9−5, Sat. by appointment. SIZE: Large. *STOCK: Victorian pine and country furniture.* LOC: Into town across bridge, turn right along quay, Rope Walk is left immediately before second set of traffic lights. TEL: 70984/79902. VAT: Stan/Spec.

Minerva Gallery
20 Mill St. (R. Jennings.) Est. 1973. CL: Wed. p.m. Open 9.30−5. SIZE: Small. *STOCK: Maps and prints, photographs, oils, watercolours, £1−£500.* PARK: Easy. TEL: 76483. SER: Picture framing, mounting. VAT: Stan.

Petticombe Manor Antiques
Petticombe Manor, Monkleigh. (O. and M.E. Wilson.) Est. 1971. CL: Wed. except by appointment. Open daily until 7 p.m. SIZE: Large. *STOCK: Furniture including dining tables and chairs, desks and bureaux, bookcases and display cabinets, Pembroke and Sutherland tables; china, glass, brass and copper, oils and watercolours, prints and mirrors, hand-stripped pine, mainly 19th to early 20th C.* LOC: Large manor house on A388 Bideford to Holsworthy road. PARK: Own. TEL: 75605; home − same. SER: Restorations (re-upholstery, French polishing, cabinet work); buys at auction (furniture). VAT: Stan.

BRADIFORD, Nr. Barnstaple
Portobello Antiques *Trade Only*
Anchor Mills. (B. Edwards.) Est. 1969. Open every day. SIZE: Medium. *STOCK: General antiques.* TEL: Barnstaple (0271) 72045. VAT: Stan/Spec.

J. Collins and Son (Est. 1953)

THE STUDIO
63 and 28 High Street,
BIDEFORD
North Devon EX39 2AN
Tel: (02372) 73103

Five extensive showrooms of
antiques and two galleries with a
large selection of over 300
Victorian Oil Paintings and
Watercolours in stock
fully restored and framed.

**Antiques, Uniques,
Period Furniture,
and
Fine Paintings**

BRAUNTON   (0271)

Eileen Cooper Antiques
Challoners Rd. (Mrs. M. Chugg.) Est. 1952.
CL: Usually Wed. p.m., and Mon. Open
10.30—1 and 2—5, or by appointment. SIZE:
Small. *STOCK: General antiques, collectable
items, lace, fine linen, christening gowns,
embroideries, pictures, prints, small furniture,
jewellery, silver including some Exeter hall-
marked.* Not stocked: Coins, medals. LOC:
From Barnstaple, across traffic lights at
Braunton (6 miles), then 200yds. on right.
PARK: Easy. TEL: 813320; home — 816005.

Timothy Coward Fine Silver
Marisco, Saunton. Open by appointment.
STOCK: Silver. TEL: 890466.

BRIXHAM
          **(4 and 5 fig. no.) (080 45)
          (6 fig. no.) (0803)**

Courtney Beer
Milton House, Milton St. SIZE: Large. *STOCK:
18th C furniture.* TEL: 3195.

John Prestige Antiques
1 and 2 Greenswood Court. Est. 1971. CL: Sat.
and Sun. except by appointment. Open
8.45—6. *STOCK: Period and Victorian furniture.*
TEL: 6141; home — 3739. SER: Valuations;
restorations; desk lining. VAT: Stan/Spec.

BUCKFASTLEIGH   (0364)

H.V. Bendon
33 Market St. Est. 1970. CL: Wed. p.m. Open
9.30—1 and 2—6; Sun. 10—1. *STOCK: Furniture, porcelain and general antiques.* PARK:
Adjacent. TEL: 43565.

Drawers
The Old Wheelwrights, 45 Plymouth Rd. (S.J.
and V.J. Bradshaw.) Est. 1978. CL: Wed. Open
9.30—5.30, Sat. 10—5.30. SIZE: Large.
*STOCK: Pine furniture, £50—£1,000;
decorators items, £50—£500; small items and
bric-a-brac, £5—£100, all 18th—20th C.* LOC:
Adjacent A38 mid-way Plymouth and Exeter.
PARK: Easy. TEL: 42848. SER: Restorations
(pine); stripping. VAT: Stan/Spec.

Woodview House
114 Plymouth Rd. (D. and D. Pope). Est.
1973. Always open. SIZE: Medium. *STOCK:
Small furniture, to £3,000; decorative items,
paintings, to £2,000; all 18th—19th C.* LOC:
Just off A38. PARK: Easy. TEL: 43552; home
— same. SER: Buys at auction (silver and
furniture). FAIRS: Many 3 day. VAT: Spec.

BUDLEIGH SALTERTON (039 54)

Robert Barton Antiques
15 Fore St. Est. 1958. Open daily 10—12.30 and 3—5. *STOCK: Furniture, general antiques.* TEL: Home — 2549. VAT: Spec.

New Gallery
Abele Tree House, 9 Fore St. (Major J.G. and Mrs. P. Hull.) Est. 1968. CL: Sun. and Mon. except by appointment. SIZE: Large. *STOCK: Fine art, oil paintings, watercolour drawings, prints from 17th C to modern signed proofs, maps and sculpture.* PARK: Adjacent. TEL: 3768. SER: Valuations; restorations; framing; ultra-violet examination; buys at auction. VAT: Stan/Spec.

Quinney's
High St. (Miss A. Fearfield and Miss S.M. Nevill.) Est. 1947. CL: Thurs. p.m. Open 9.15—12.45 and 2.15—4.30, Sat. p.m. by appointment. *STOCK: Furniture, porcelain, silver, glass.* PARK: Easy. TEL: 2793. SER: Valuations; minor restorations. VAT: Spec.

Budleigh Salterton continued

David J. Thorn   BADA
2 High St. Est. 1950. CL: Thurs. p.m. and Sat. p.m. Open 10—1 and 2.15—5.30. SIZE: Small. *STOCK: English, Continental and Oriental pottery and porcelain, 1620—1850, £5—£2,000; English furniure, 1680—1870, £20—£2,000; paintings, silver, jewellery, books, £1—£1,000.* LOC: From Exeter through Exmouth into Budleigh Salterton or from Honiton. PARK: Easy. TEL: 2448. SER: Valuations. VAT: Stan/Spec.

CHAGFORD   (064 73)

John Meredith
41 New St., and The Square. (J. and A. Meredith.) Est. 1979. Open every day 9—1 and 2—5 or by appointment. SIZE: Large. *STOCK: Mahogany, 18th—19th C, £25—£2,000; country oak, 16th—19th C, £5—£1,000; Oriental brass and copper, swords and weapons, large unusual items and large architectural building items.* LOC: 50yds. right of church. PARK: Easy. TEL: 3405 and 3474; home — 3405. SER: Buys at auction. VAT: Stan/Spec.

Mary Payton Antiques
The Old Market House. (Mrs. M. Payton.) Est. 1968. CL: Wed. and Mon. Open 10—1 and 2.30—5. SIZE: Small. *STOCK: English pottery and porcelain, especially Staffordshire, English glass, 18th—19th C; maps and prints (West Country), 17th—19th C.* Not stocked: Jewellery, firearms, coins, silver, pewter. LOC: Coming from Whiddon Down (A30) by A382, turn right at Easton Court. Shop in the town square. PARK: Easy. TEL: 2428; home — 2388.

CHULMLEIGH

W. Bagnall Antiques
Lingfield. Est. 1965. Open by appointment. *STOCK: Oak, mahogany and walnut furniture, 17th—18th C.* LOC: On Colleton Mills Rd. PARK: Easy. TEL: 80576; home — same.

Chulmleigh Antiques
Rainbow House, Fore St. (R.P. and N.T. Kelly.) Est. 1974. Open 10—4; Sat. p.m., Wed. and other times by appointment. SIZE: Medium. *STOCK: General and country antiques, 17th C to 1950s, £1—£1,000; oil paintings, watercolours and prints, 19th-20th C, £5—£500; curios and bygones, £1—£200.* LOC: Main Street. PARK: Easy. TEL: Home — Chittlehamholt (076 94) 437. SER: Valuations; buys at auction (oil paintings and watercolours).

COLYTON (0297)

Brookfield Gallery
Market Place. (Mrs. J. Campbell.) Est. 1971. CL: Sun., Mon. and Wed., except by appointment. Open 10—1 and 2.30—5. SIZE: Small. *STOCK: Watercolours — English 1880—1940, Continental, 19th C; small antiques, Victorian sentimental prints, door furniture, and furniture fittings.* LOC: Top end of Market Place. PARK: Easy. TEL: 52038. SER: Restorations (ceramics); buys at auction.

Lomas Antique Shop
Gwinear, South St. (W.J. Lomas.) Est. 1870. Open by appointment. SIZE: Medium. *STOCK: English chairs and furniture, 17th—18th C, from £100; pictures, glass and rugs.* PARK: Easy. TEL: 52652 or 52367. SER: Valuations. VAT: Stan/Spec.

COMBE MARTIN (027 188)
Nr. Ilfracombe

Retrospect Antiques
Sunnymede, King St. Est. 1976. CL: Sun. in winter. *STOCK: General antiques, and bric-a-brac.* TEL: 2346.

CULLOMPTON (0884)

Mills Antiques
39 Fore St. Est. 1979. CL: Thurs. Open 9.15—5.30. *STOCK: Furniture, 17th-19th C; bric-a-brac.* TEL: 33266. VAT: Stan/Spec.

DARTINGTON, Nr. Totnes

Home Features
Unit 4, Webbersway. (Home Features Ltd.) Est. 1974. Open by appointment. SIZE: Medium. *STOCK: Marine paintings, oils and watercolours, 18th—19th C, £50—£2,500.* LOC: Main Plymouth road. PARK: Easy. TEL: 866377; home — (054 882) 543. SER: Valuations; buys at auction (marine paintings). VAT: Stan/Spec.

DARTMOUTH (080 43)

Agincourt House (A.D.1380)
Lower Ferry. (Wing Cdr. R.L. Bowes.) Est. 1966. Open 10—5.30, Sun. 2.30—5. SIZE: Large. *STOCK: General antiques, 18th—19th C.* Not stocked: Postage stamps. LOC: From Torbay, cross river by Lower Ferry, (from Kingswear) turn left 10yds. after landing from ferry. PARK: Easy. TEL: 2472. SER: Buys at auction. VAT: Stan.

Anthony Burden Antiques
Duke St. Est. 1963. Open 10—5.30. SIZE: Small. *STOCK: Small furniture, porcelain, silver, clocks.* LOC: Near Boat Pool. TEL: 2723.

DAWLISH (0626)

Dawlish Antiques
1 Beach St. (Mrs. A. Clark.) CL: Thurs. Open 10.30—4.30. *STOCK: General antiques.* TEL: 864999.

EAST BUDLEIGH

Antiques at Budleigh House
Budleigh House. (W. Cook.) Est. 1982. CL: Mon. and Wed. Open 10—5, Sat. 10—1. SIZE: Small. *STOCK: 18th—19th C small furniture and decorative objects, porcelain, glass, silver and metalware, £5—£500.* LOC: Opposite Sir Walter Raleigh public house. PARK: Easy. TEL: Budleigh Salterton (039 54) 5368; home — same. SER: Valuations; buys at auction.

The Old Bakery
(C. Murphey.) CL: Thurs. p.m. *STOCK: Small Victorian furniture, Sheffield plate, porcelain.* TEL: Budleigh Salterton (039 54) 3289.

EXETER (0392)

Wm. Bruford and Son Ltd.   BADA
1 Bedford St. Est. 1894. CL: Sat. p.m. Open 9—5.30. SIZE: Large. *STOCK: Jewellery, Victorian, late Georgian; silver (especially spoons), from 1600, £20—£2,000; occasionally carriage clocks.* Not stocked: China, glass, furniture, metalware. TEL: 54901. SER: Valuations; restorations (clocks, silver and jewellery); buys at auction. VAT: Stan/Spec.

Charles Cox
20 Old Tiverton Rd. ABA. Est. 1974. Open by appointment. *STOCK: 19th C English and American literature.* TEL: 55776.

Exeter Antique Wholesalers
Trade Only
Exeter Airport, Clyst Honiton. LOC: A30. Below are listed the three dealers who are trading as the above.

David Biggs   LAPADA
Stockwell Antiques. CL: Sat. Open 8—5 or by appointment. *STOCK: Trade and export antiques.* TEL: 66279 and (039 54) 5379.

Ian McBain and Sons
(I.G.S. McBain and Sons). Est. 1963. Open 9—6, Sat. 9—2, Sun. by appointment. *STOCK: Furniture, Victorian and Edwardian, £10—£6,000; Victorian dolls, £65—£5,000.* TEL: 66261. VAT: Stan.

Exeter continued

Exeter Rare Books
Guildhall Shopping Centre. (R. Parry.) A.B.A. Est. 1965. Open 10—1 and 2—5. SIZE: Small. STOCK: Books, antiquarian, second-hand and out-of-print, 17th—20th C, £5—£500. LOC: City centre. PARK: Easy. TEL: 36021. SER: Valuations; buys at auction. FAIRS: Exeter.

Fagins Antiques
Unit 16, Airport Rd., Exeter Airport. (C.J. Strong.) CL: Sat. Open 10—5. STOCK: Stripped and painted pine furniture. TEL: 64201 or Exmouth (0395) 266602 (24hrs.).

Gold and Silver Exchange
Eastgate House, Princesshay. STOCK: Jewellery. TEL: 217478.

Ironbridge Antiques
4 St. Davids Hill. (R. Hyde.) Open 10—5. STOCK: Pine and country furniture. TEL: 213673.

Brian Mortimer
87 Queen St. CL: Wed. p.m. STOCK: General antiques, jewellery, porcelain, Victoriana. TEL: 79994. VAT: Stan/Spec.

John Nathan Antiques
153/154 Cowick St., St. Thomas. (I. Doble.) Est. 1950. CL: Wed. p.m. Open 9—1 and 2—5.30. STOCK: Silver and jewellery, £5—£5,000; clocks, £25—£3,000; all Georgian and Victorian; furniture, £50—£2,000. Not stocked: Paintings. LOC: From Exeter inner by-pass over new Exe Bridge, take A30 Okehampton Rd. under railway arch, shop on right. PARK: Easy. TEL: 72228. SER: Valuations; restorations (silver and jewellery); buys at auction. VAT: Stan.

The Original Victorian Furniture Company
144 Fore St. (G. and G. Southard.) Est. 1976. Open 9—5.30. SIZE: Medium. STOCK: Furniture, restored and polished to original condition, late 19th C, £100—£500. LOC: In main thoroughfare into town from the west. PARK: Within 300 yards. TEL: 213680; home — same. SER: Valuations; restorations (furniture). VAT: Stan.

Pirouette
5 West St. (L. Duriez.) Open 10—5. STOCK: Lace, shawls, babywear, linen, 1920's costume, Victorian and Edwardian bridal wear. TEL: 32643.

The Quay Gallery
43 The Quay. (B.A. Ledger and A.W. White.) Est. 1984. Open 10—5. STOCK: Marine artifacts, Victoriana, collectors' items, £6—£1,000; paintings, watercolours, prints, 18th—20th C, £15—£1,000. LOC: By river and canal basin, near city centre. PARK: Easy. TEL: 213283. SER: Buys at auction (paintings).

Exeter continued

C. Samuels and Sons Ltd.
17-18 Waterbeer St. (P.J. and G. Manson.) Est. 1872. SIZE: Large. STOCK: Prints and maps, 17th—19th C, £10—£500. LOC: Behind Guildhall. PARK: Nearby. TEL: 73219. SER: Restorations; picture-framing; mounting. VAT: Stan.

Shiraz Oriental Antiques and Carpets
22 New Bridge St. CL: Wed. and lunch times. SIZE: Large. STOCK: Oriental rugs and carpets, Islamic, Indian, Japanese and Chinese works of art, 19th C and earlier, £50—£5,000. LOC: Bottom of High St., near bridge. PARK: Nearby. TEL: 214206. SER: Valuations.

Peter Wadham
5 Cathedral Close. Est. 1967. Open 9.30—5.30. SIZE: Medium. STOCK: English and some Continental furniture, 1650—1850; general small antiques. LOC: Centre of city, facing Cathedral, north tower. PARK: Own. TEL: 39741. VAT: Spec.

Waterwheel Pine and Antiques
Cricklepitt Mill, Commercial Rd. (P.J. Baldwin and W. Bone.) Est. 1973. Open 10—5. SIZE: Large. STOCK: Pine and country furniture, 18th—19th C, £50—£500; paintings, mirrors, pottery and collectors' items, 19th—20th C, £5—£500; pre-1940 fabrics and clothes, £5—£200. Not stocked: Silver. LOC: 100 yards from Quay and Exe Bridge. PARK: Easy. TEL: 217076; home — Whiddon Down (064 723) 468. SER: Valuations; restorations (pine and upholstery). VAT: Stan.

A.T. Whitton
151/152 Fore St. Est. 1953. Open 9—5. STOCK: General antiques, stripped pine. TEL: 73377. VAT: Stan.

EXMOUTH   (0395)
R.J. Burrough
29 Woodfield Close. Est. 1977. Open at any time but appointment preferred. SIZE: Small. STOCK: Clocks — longcase and bracket, 18th—19th C, £200—£5,000; carriage, £100—£2,000; wall, £50—£500; both 19th C. LOC: Off A376. PARK: Easy. TEL: 279004; home — same. SER: Valuations; restorations (clocks); buys at auction (clocks).

Fagins Antiques
28 Albion St. (C.J. Strong.) Open 10—5. STOCK: China and bric-a-brac. TEL: 266602 or Exeter (0392) 64201.

Treasures
32-34 Exeter Rd. (Z. Jones.) Open 9—5. STOCK: General antiques. TEL: 273258.

Exmouth continued

Michael Vaughan Antiques and Jewellery
5 High St. Est. 1965. Open 10—5. *STOCK: Jewellery, silver and small items for export.* LOC: Town centre. PARK: Easy. TEL: 271528.

HARBERTONFORD   (080 423)
Fine Pine Antiques
Woodland Rd. Est. 1973. Open 8.30—5.30. *STOCK: Stripped pine and country furniture.* TEL: 465. SER: Restorations, stripping.

Tony Hodges Antiques
The Old Store, Woodland Rd. (T.A.R. Hodges.) Est. 1972. CL: Mon. Open 10—5 (Easter to Oct.) Open Tues., Fri. and Sat. 10—5 or by appointment (Winter). SIZE: Medium. *STOCK: Country and cottage furniture, stripped pine, £25—£400; china, glass, copper and brass, mainly Victorian and Edwardian.* Not stocked: Coins, stamps and guns. LOC: Just off A381, behind church. PARK: Easy. TEL: 609; home — 345.

HARPFORD, Nr. Sidmouth
John Lyle (Lyle and Davidson Ltd.)
ABA. Est. 1952. Open by appointment. SIZE: Medium. *STOCK: Old cookery and wine books and prints, 1450-1900.* LOC: 10 miles from Exeter—Dorchester road, near Newton Poppleford. PARK: Easy. TEL: (0395) 68294. SER: Valuations (books).

HATHERLEIGH
Hatherleigh Antiques
51 Market St. (S. and M. Dann.) CL: Wed. and Thus. Open 10—1 and 2—5. SIZE: Medium. *STOCK: Country pottery and furniture, metalware, 17th—19th C.* PARK: Easy. TEL: Home — 810500. SER: Buys at auction (as stock). VAT: Stan/Spec.

HONITON   (0404)
Abingdon House Antiques
136 High St. (M.V. Melliar-Smith and J.J. Butler.) Est. 1985. Open 9.30—5. SIZE: Large. There are approximately 20 dealers at this centre selling *a wide range of general antiques and furniture.* LOC: Exeter end of High St. PARK: Nearby. TEL: 2108; home — 850464.

Honiton continued

J. Barrymore and Co.
73-75 High St. (J. and M. Ogden.) Est. 1979. Open 10—5.30. SIZE: Medium. *STOCK: Silver, 17th—20th C, £50—£5,000; Old Sheffield plate, Victorian electro-plate, £50—£500; jewellery, £50—£2,500; all 19th C to early 20th C.* LOC: Main st. PARK: Easy. TEL: 2244; home — Ottery St. Mary (040 481) 3902. VAT: Stan/Spec.

Roderick P. Butler   BADA
Marwood House. Est. 1948. Open 9.30—5.30. SIZE: Large. *STOCK: Furniture, metalwork, works of art (unusual and interesting items) 17th to early 19th C.* **LOC: Adjacent to roundabout at eastern end of High St. PARK: In courtyard. TEL: 2169. VAT: Spec.**

Christopher J. Button-Stephens (formerly Old Curiosity Shop)
Plympton House, 59 High St. CL: Sat. p.m. and Thurs. Open 9.30—1 and 2—5. SIZE: Large. *STOCK: General antiques including copper and brass, from 1800.* LOC: Main St. PARK: Easy. TEL: 2640. VAT: Stan/Spec.

Fountain Antiques
132 High St. (N. and M. Peache.) Open 9.30—5.30. *STOCK: General antiques and pine furniture.* TEL: 2074.

Honiton Antiques
126 High St. (P. and Mrs. S. Hampshire.) Open 9—5. SIZE: Large. *STOCK: 18th—19th C furniture, mahogany, oak and country; brass, porcelain.* TEL: 3565; home — Ottery St. Mary (040 481) 4540. VAT: Stan/Spec.

The Honiton Lace Shop
44 High St. Open 9.30—1 and 2—5. *STOCK: Lace, textiles, bobbins and associated items.* TEL: 2416.

L.J. Huggett and Son
''Bramble Cross'', Exeter Rd. SIZE: Large. *STOCK: Furniture, porcelain, silver.* TEL: 2043.

Honiton continued

R.E. Martin
176 High St. Est. 1945. CL: Thurs. *STOCK: Furniture, 1750-1820, to £5,000; china, 18th C; silver, 1750-1880.* TEL: 3275. SER: Valuations; buys at auction. VAT: Stan/Spec.

Otter Antiques
69 High St. (G.F. Wilkin.) Open 9—5.30, Thurs. 9—1. *STOCK: Silver and plate including cutlery and flatware.* TEL: 2627.

Jane and Neil Page
Elmfield Farm, Weston. Est. 1961. Open by appointment. *STOCK: Decorative and unusual items, needleworks.* TEL: 2969 or 2416. VAT: Spec.

Geoffrey M. Woodhead
53 High St. Est. 1950. CL: Sat. p.m. Open 9.30—5.30. SIZE: Medium. *STOCK: China, unusual items, books, some furniture.* Not stocked: Coins, stamps, silver, plate. LOC: A30. From London, shop is in main street on the right. PARK: Easy. TEL: 2969. VAT: Stan/Spec.

HORRABRIDGE
Ye Olde Saddlers Shoppe
(R. Howes.) Est. 1970. SIZE: Small. *STOCK: General antiques, furniture, clocks and watches, collectors' items.* LOC: 4 miles from Tavistock on A386. PARK: Easy. TEL: Yelverton (0822) 852109.

IDDESLEIGH, Nr. Winkleigh
Trevor Micklem Antiques Ltd.
BADA
Duke of York Inn. (C.T., S.E.M. and T.J.M. Micklem.) Est. 1952. Open daily, weekends by appointment. *STOCK: Early furniture, delft ware, pottery, pewter, needlework and metalware.* TEL: Okehampton (0837) 810253.

ILFRACOMBE (0271)
W.R. Brown
9 Northfield Rd. Est. 1946. *STOCK: General antiques, trade items.* TEL: Home — 62843. VAT: Stan/Spec.

IVYBRIDGE
Thomson Antiques
Ermefield House, Western Rd. (A.D. and S. Thomson.) Est. 1968. CL: Sat. p.m. Otherwise open but appointment advisable. SIZE: Large. *STOCK: Mahogany, walnut and oak furniture, small collectors' items.* LOC: Opposite main car park. PARK: Easy. TEL: Plymouth (0752) 892304; home — same. VAT: Stan/Spec.

KINGSBRIDGE (0548)
Halsey
BADA
Boffins Boft, Bowcombe Creek. (A. Halsey.) CINOA. Est. 1950. CL: Sat. p.m. and Sun. except by appointment. Open 10—5. *STOCK: Fine English and Continental oak and fruitwood furniture, complementary and period furnishings, 17th to early 18th C, £60— £10,000.* LOC: 1½ miles on A379 Kingsbridge—Dartmouth road. PARK: Easy. TEL: 2440. SER: Commissions undertaken internationally for interiors (individual rooms or entire houses); valuations; antiques purchasing service. VAT: Spec.

Kingswood Pine and Antiques
85 Fore St. (J.A.S. Hawkins.) CL: Thurs. p.m. Open 9—5. SIZE: Small. *STOCK: Pine furniture; pottery, porcelain, £2—£200; small antiques; all 18th—19th C.* LOC: On A379 Plymouth — Dartmouth road, in one-way section, main street. PARK: Easy, nearby. TEL: 6829. SER: Stripping and finishing.

LYDFORD (082 282)
Nr. Okehampton
Skeaping Gallery
Townend House. Est. 1972. Open by appointment. *STOCK: Oils and watercolours.* TEL: 383. VAT: Spec.

LYNTON (0598)
Cantabrian Antiques and Architectural Furnishing
Park St. (I.A. Williamson.) CL: Mon. Open 10—6. *STOCK: Architectural antiques.* TEL: 53282.

Mark Westgarth Antiques
Queen St. (M.W. Westgarth.) Est. 1984. Open 9.30—12 and 1—5, Sat. 9.30—5. SIZE: Small. *STOCK: Furniture, 1600—1870, £50—£1,500; ceramics, 18th—19th C, £20— £1,000; treen 17th—19th C, £20—£500.* LOC: Off Lee Rd. PARK: Easy. TEL: 53619, home — 52253. SER: Valuations; restorations (furniture and ceramics); buys at auction (furniture).

MAIDENCOMBE, Nr. Torquay
G.A. Whiteway-Wilkinson
Sunsea, Teignmouth Rd. Est. 1943. Open by appointment only. *STOCK: General antiques, fine art and jewellery.* LOC: Approximately half-way on main Torquay/Teignmouth road. TEL: Torquay (0803) 39692. VAT: Spec.

ANGELA HALSEY
Boffins Boft, Bowcombe Creek, Kingsbridge, South Devon.

An example of the largest stock of important 17th century English furniture in the West Country. Route 379 Kingsbridge 1½ miles. Valuations for insurance and probate.
TEL. (STD 0548) 2440

MESHAW, Nr. South Molton
Thomas and Dymond   LAPADA
Priestcott. (R.N. Thomas, J. Dymond.) Est. 1970. Open by appointment. *STOCK: English furniture, 18th—19th C, £500—£5,000; Mason's ironstone, blue and white transfer ware, decorative items.* TEL: (076 97) 532. FAIRS: West London Jan. and Aug.; Olympia.

MODBURY   (0548)
Nr. Ivybridge
Country Cottage Furniture
The Old Smithy, Back St. (D.H. Bramhall.) Est. 1963. Open 9—5.30, Sat. 10—5.30. SIZE: Large. *STOCK: Restored pine furniture, 18th—19th C.* TEL: 830888. VAT: Stan/Spec.

Téméraire
63 Brownston St. (J. Jefferies.) Est. 1970. CL: Wed. p.m. Open 10—5.30. SIZE: Large. *STOCK: Scientific instruments, £30—£3,000; period furniture.* LOC: Town centre. PARK: Easy. TEL: 830317. VAT: Spec.

Wild Goose Antiques
34 Church St. (Mr. and Mrs. E. Christopher-Walsh.) Open 10—5 and by appointment. *STOCK: General antiques, pictures, porcelain, chandeliers, silver, jewellery.* TEL: 830715; home — 830238. VAT: Stan.

MORCHARD BISHOP   (036 37)
Nr. Crediton
Morchard Bishop Antiques
Meadowbank Cottage. (J.C. and E.A. Child.) Resident. Open by appointment. *STOCK: General antiques especially copper, brass, iron, treen.* LOC: 8 miles west of Crediton, 2 miles off A377. PARK: Easy. TEL: 456.

MORETONHAMPSTEAD   (0647)
The Old Brass Kettle
2—4 Ford St. (H. Clark.) Est. 1950. CL: Sun. except by appointment, and Thurs. Open 9.30—1 and 2.15—5.30. SIZE: Medium. *STOCK: Pottery, porcelain and furniture, 19th C.* LOC: A382 from Newton Abbot, B3212 from Exeter. PARK: Easy. TEL: 40334. SER: Buys at auction. VAT: Spec.

NEWTON ABBOT   (0626)
Julian Antiques
Aller Vale Buildings, Moor Park Rd., Kingerswell. (J.V.S. Goode.) Open 8.30—5, Sat. and other times by appointment. SIZE: Warehouse. *STOCK: Furniture including Victorian.* TEL: (08047) 2629 or (0803) 24934. SER: Container packing.

Newton Abbot continued

Newton Abbot Antiques Centre

55 East St. (P. and D. Stockman.) Est. 1973. Open every Tues. 9—4. There are 50 dealers at this market offering a wide range of antiques. LOC: 200yds. from clock tower. PARK: Through arch. TEL: 4074. Below are listed some of the dealers at this market:—

Anton Antiques
Furniture, glass, china.
Bennett Antiques
China.
Biggs
Furniture, china, glass and jewellery.
Mrs. Boutell
General antiques, furniture, pictures.
Robin Brice
General antiques, art nouveau, art deco.
Mrs. Brown
Small furniture, china, plate, jewellery.
Camel Antiques
(B. and S. Murphy.) China, glass, brass and copper, small furniture. TEL: Camelford (084 02) 2476.
Clovelly Antiques
Silver, jewellery, china, furniture.
Collectors Corner
Silver, china, Staffs.
Edwardian Antiques
Crown Derby, Royal Worcester, Doulton.

Newton Abbot Antiques Centre continued

Vyvyan Goode
Furniture and silver, pictures, objets d'art, glass, plate.
Hendrika Antiques
Clocks, small furniture, china, Continental items.
Jo Hicks — Bolton Galleries
Furniture, curios, pictures, silver, jewellery.
Mrs. Hill
Linen and lace, small china.
B. Hunt
Silver and china, furniture, period tools.
S. Johnson
Small items, china, pottery, silver.
John Lawrence
Furniture and china, metal toys.
Mrs. Lock
General antiques, china and pottery.
Loft Antiques
Period furniture, china, Staffordshire.
Mrs. Mathews
Silver, jewellery, china and furniture.
Chris. Mitchell — Totnes Antiques
Early silver and flatware.
Mosdell
Antiquarian books and prints.

A good and rare model of an Arab stallion by Fratin, c.1850, who produced comparatively few horse models and groups during his career. This mustang is well detailed and nicely proportioned giving it a friendly realism and making it a desirable bronze. From *Animals in Bronze* by Christopher Payne published by the **Antique Collectors' Club, 1986.**

Newton Abbot Antiques Centre continued

P & D Antiques
Victorian and shipping furniture.
Mrs. Payne
Furniture, china.
Mrs. Peddie
Silver, jewellery, furniture, china and pottery.
Postcard Corner (Mr. and Mrs. Brown)
Postcards and Goss.
Pridham
General antiques and unusual items.
B. Pridham
Furniture, china, collectors' items.
Miss Revell
China, dolls, toys, ephemera.
Mrs. Richards
Furniture, bric-a-brac, Victorian and Edwardian.
J. Ruff
Crown Derby, Doulton, Royal Worcester.
Sadler
Plate, china, glass.
P. Sherman
Furniture, china.
Silver Shop
Silver and plate.
Paul Stockman
Pottery and period porcelain, furniture, flat back, Staffs.
Sheila B. Strange
Porcelain, silver plate, brass and copper, small furniture, glass, objets d'art. TEL: Home — Starcross (062 689) 304.
Alistair Suthurland
Oriental objects.
Talisman
Furniture, pottery, pictures, clocks, watches.
Mrs. Thackray
Dolls, Victoriana, china.
S. Thorpe
Period silver, clocks, china, silver plate.
Union Antiques
Furniture, china.
Village Antiques
Silver, china and furniture.
Mrs. Walker
Jewellery, china, glass.
V. Ware
Coloured glass, jewellery.
Derick Wilson
Jewellery, shipping goods and furniture.
K. Wilton
Furniture, china, smalls, shipping goods.
P. Winchester
Postcards.
Winckworth
Clocks, small furniture, jewellery and china.
P. Wright
General antiques, small items.
Mavis Young
Small general antiques.

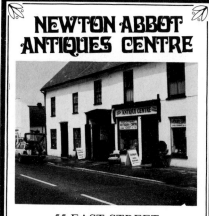

Newton Abbot continued

Old Treasures
126a Queen St. (Mr. and Mrs. J.F. Gordon.) Est. 1971. CL: Thurs. p.m. Open 9.30—4.30, Sat. 9.30—3. SIZE: Small. *STOCK: Jewellery, £3—£800; glass, porcelain, portrait miniatures.* Not stocked: Large furniture, weapons. LOC: On A380, 100yds. from Queen's Hotel. PARK: Easy. TEL: 67181. FAIRS: Snape, Wilton House, British International, Birmingham. VAT: Stan/Spec.

NORTHLEW, Nr. Okehampton
Christopher Drake Fine Prints
The Old Rectory. By appointment only. *STOCK: English and European master prints.* TEL: Beaworthy (040 922) 613 or (01) 629 5571. SER: Valuations; free catalogues available.

OKEHAMPTON (0837)

Alan Jones Antiques LAPADA
Trade Only
Fatherford Farm. Est. 1971. Open anytime by appointment. SIZE: Large warehouse. *STOCK: Furniture — all types.* LOC: On A30, one mile from Okehampton. PARK: Easy. TEL: 2970; home — Black Torrington (040 923) 428. SER: Valuations. VAT: Stan.

OTTERY ST. MARY (040 481)

Georgian House Antiques
13 Silver St. (P. and Mrs S. Hampshire.) Open 10—5.30. SIZE: Large. *STOCK: 18th—19th C furniture, porcelain and collectables.* TEL: 4540; home — same. VAT: Stan/Spec.

Squirrels
2 Cornhill. (Mr. and Mrs. E.W. Cook.) Est. 1984. CL: Wed. Open 10—1 and 2—4. SIZE: Small. *STOCK: Small pine furniture, mainly 19th C, £25—£250; porcelain, 18th—19th C, £25—£100; decorative items, 19th—20th C, £5—£50.* LOC: Town centre near St. Mary's Church. PARK: Church precincts. TEL: 4295; home — same.

PLYMOUTH (0752)

Alvin Antiques
148 Union St. (A.F.H. Gamble.) Est. 1936. Open 9.30—1 and 2—5.30. SIZE: Medium. *STOCK: Furniture, George I to Victorian, £10—£5,000; silver from 1700, £2—£1,500; porcelain, 1750—1918. £2—£5,000.* LOC: From Exeter follow Royal Parade through city centre to join Union St. on way to Devonport. Shop situated half way along Union St. on right. PARK: Easy. TEL: 665628. SER: Valuations. FAIRS: Plymouth. VAT: Stan/Spec.

Barbican Antique Market
82—84 Vauxhall St. (A.F.H. Gamble.) Open 10—5.30. 22 stallholders. *STOCK: Silver, glass, jewellery, clocks, paintings, coins, furniture.* TEL: 667990/266927.

A.E. Barham
13 The Parade. Open 10—5.30. *STOCK: Furniture, glass, china, pictures; general antiques.* LOC: Opposite Customs House. PARK: Easy. TEL: 663886.

N. and P. Bennett
16 Southside St., Barbican. (N.P.J. Bennett.) Est. 1958. CL: Wed. p.m. Open 9.30—1 and 2—6. SIZE: Small. *STOCK: Items of interest, from £5, including art nouveau and art deco.* LOC: From City centre follow signs for Barbican and the Hoe. TEL: 668676. SER: Buys at auction. VAT: Spec.

Plymouth continued

Galaxy Art
38 New St., Barbican. (R.A. Badgery.) Est. 1961. Open 9.15—5.30. SIZE: Small. *STOCK: General antiques especially scientific instruments up to 1930, £5—£1,000.* PARK: Easy. TEL: 667842.

Luella Antiques
40 North Hill. Est. 1964. *STOCK: Furniture, china, objets d'art and jewellery.* TEL: 667536.

M. & A. Furnishers
44 Breton Side. (M. Antonucci.) Open 8—6, seven days a week. *STOCK: Pine furniture and general antiques.* TEL: 665419 or 25818.

New Street Antique Centre
27 New St., The Barbican. (Richard Hills and Partners Ltd.) Est. 1980. Open 10—5, Sun. 2—5 summer months only. SIZE: Medium. *STOCK: Clocks, silver, jewellery, weapons, general antiques.* PARK: Nearby. TEL: 661165; home — 661522. VAT: Stan/Spec.

Colin Rhodes Antiques LAPADA
53 Southside St. Est. 1972. *STOCK: Paintings, period furniture, silver, clocks, general antiques.* TEL: 669079; home — 42761. SER: Valuations. VAT: Spec.

Brian Taylor Antiques
24 Molesworth Rd., Stoke. Est. 1975. Open 9—5.30, Sun. by appointment. SIZE: Medium. *STOCK: Fireplaces and accessories, country furniture, £50—£500; clocks £50—£2,000, all 18th—19th C; gramophones and phonographs, 1885—1930, £100—£1,000.* LOC: 50 yds. from Victoria Park, map sent on request. PARK: Easy. TEL: 569061; home — same. SER: Valuations; restorations (clocks and gramophones). VAT: Stan/Spec.

Sue Young
Open by appointment. *STOCK: 19th and 20th C watercolours.* TEL: 896281.

SALCOMBE (054 884)

A-B Gallery
67 Fore St. (A.S. and J.L. Arnold-Brown.) Est. 1966. Open most days 9.30—4.30, prior 'phone call advisable. SIZE: Medium. *STOCK: Oils, mid 19th to 20th C, £500—£3,000; watercolours, late 19th to 20th C., £50—£300; etchings and prints, 19th—20th C, £10—£100.* LOC: Central, near Whitestrand car park. PARK: Easy. TEL: 2764. SER: Valuations; buys at auction (pictures). VAT: Spec.

ALAN JONES ANTIQUES

Fatherford Farm, Okehampton, Devon.

Telephone 0837 2970
Home 040923 428

One of the largest stocks of Shipping Goods and Period Furniture in the Country, typical of South African, New Zealand, Australian, American and all Continental Markets

Also over 100 oil paintings in constantly changing stock

Containers packed, and all normal services provided
OPEN at any time by appointment

Salcombe continued

Heritage Antiques and Gallery Six
10 Union St. (W. and S.J. Tod.) Est. 1977. Open every day, Spring to Autumn 10—10; mornings only in winter. SIZE: Small. *STOCK: Furniture and objets d'art, mainly 19th C; paintings, 19th—20th C, all £5—£500.* LOC: Lower end of town centre. PARK: Nearby. TEL: 3124. SER: Valuations; restorations.

Normandy House Antiques
Fore St. (Mr. and Mrs. N.W. Neal.) Resident. Est. 1974. Open 10—1 and 2—5. *STOCK: Mason's ironstone, porcelain, nautical instruments, charts, maps and prints.* TEL: 2362.

SANDFORD, Nr. Crediton

Taylor-Halsey Antiques
'Strangs'. (M. & R. Halsey.) Resident. Est 1971. *STOCK: 17th—19th C furniture and associated items; books.* LOC: 3 miles from Crediton. TEL: Home — Crediton (036 32) 3408. FAIRS: PBFA and others.

SEATON (0297)
Etceteras Antiques
Beer Rd. (B. Warren.) Est. 1969. Open 10—4 or by appointment. *STOCK: General antiques.* TEL: 21965.

SHALDON, Nr. Teignmouth (0626)
Tempus Fugit
16c Fore St. (R.C. Walkley.) Est. 1982. CL: Thurs. Open 9.30—5, Sat. 10—1, Sun. a.m. by appointment. SIZE: Small. *STOCK: Clocks, 18th—19th C, £25—£6,000; watches, furniture, paintings, jewellery and porcelain.* LOC: From A379 take left turn over bridge to Shaldon. On bend turn left into Fore St., shop on right. PARK: Easy. TEL: 872752. SER: Valuations; restorations (clocks); buys at auction; export facilities. VAT: Stan/Spec.

SIDMOUTH (039 55)
Copperfields LAPADA
Pepys House, 1 Church St. (H. Halkes and C. Trotman.) Est. 1962. CL: Thurs. Open 10—1 and 2.15—5. SIZE: Small. *STOCK: Silver, jewellery, 1700 onwards, £5—£2,000; old Sheffield and later silver plate, £5—£750; small clocks, especially carriage, £50—£750.* Not stocked: Furniture. LOC: In town centre near church. PARK: Easy. TEL: 2145. SER: Valuations (silver and jewellery). VAT: Stan/Spec.

Fox Antiques
70 High St. (J. and B. Napier-Fenning.) Open 10—1 and 2.15—5, Thurs. and Sat. 10—1. *STOCK: Furniture, porcelain, glass, curios and mirrors, 19th C.* TEL: 3485.

Gainsborough House Antiques
12 Fore St. (K.S. Scratchley.) Est. 1937. CL: Thurs. p.m. except by appointment and Sat. p.m. Open 9—1 and 2—5. SIZE: Medium. *STOCK: Porcelain, silver, copper, brass, pre-1920s, £5—£500; furniture, Georgian and Victorian, £50—£1,000; militaria and medals, 1650 to date, 50p—£500.* LOC: From High St., 100yds. down Fore St. on left. PARK: 75yds. TEL: 4394; home — 5112/3337. SER: Valuations. VAT: Stan/Spec.

Dorothy Hartnell Antiques and Victoriana
38 Mill St. Est. 1974. CL: Thurs. in winter. Open 10—1 and 2—5; Sun. by appointment. SIZE: Medium. *STOCK: China, small furniture, brass, pictures, interesting items, 18th—19th C, £5—£1,500.* LOC: 70yds. off High St., rear Nat. West. Bank. PARK: Nearby. TEL: 2300. VAT: Stan/Spec.

Sidmouth continued

Hilton Antiques
All Saints Rd. Est. 1964. CL: Thurs. p.m. Open 9—5. *STOCK: Furniture, general antiques.* TEL: 6028. VAT: Stan/Spec.

The Lantern Shop
4 New St. (Miss J.M. Creeke.) Est. 1974. CL: Thurs. p.m. and Sat. p.m. Open 9.45—12.45 and 2.15—4.45. SIZE: Medium. *STOCK: Period table lighting, 1750—1950, £45—£1,000; English porcelain, 1800—1915, £5—£1,000; watercolours and oils, 1800—1950, £15—£1,000; small furniture, 1750—1920, £25—£850.* LOC: Town centre, just off Market Sq., behind sea front. PARK: Opposite. TEL: 6320. SER: Valuations; restorations (lamps, oil paintings); framing; lamp shade re-covering; buys at auction (as stock). VAT: Stan/Spec.

The Little Lantern Shop
Old Fore St. (Miss J.M. Creeke.) Est. 1974. CL: Mon. p.m. and Thurs. p.m. Open 10—12.45 and 2.15—4.45. SIZE: Medium. *STOCK: Topographical prints, especially East Devon, 1750—1850, £5—£450; decorative prints, 1750—1940, antiques images, 1700—1900, both £5—£250; maps, especially south-west England, 1600—1850, £10—£400.* LOC: Town centre between Market Sq. and High St. PARK: Opposite. TEL: 78462. SER: Valuations; restorations (cleaning and re-framing prints); buys at auction (as stock). VAT: Stan.

Sefton Antiques for the Country Home
Old Fore St. (A. and A. Miller, and J. Montgomery.) Est. 1976. Open 9.30—6. SIZE: Small. *STOCK: General antiques.* Not stocked: Reproductions. LOC: Between High St. and Market Sq. PARK: Easy. TEL: 2842. SER: Valuations; restorations. VAT: Stan/Spec.

Sidmouth Antiques Market
Blackmore Drive. (B. and L.M. Percik.) Est. 1983. Open Tues., Wed. and Fri. 9.30—4.30. SIZE: Large. *STOCK: General antiques.* LOC: Off main street, top end of town, adjoining library. PARK: Nearby. TEL: 5365.

Sue Wilde
12 High St. CL: Thurs. Open 10—1 and 2.15—5. *STOCK: Textiles, lace, costumes, art deco, art nouveau.* TEL: 77966.

SOUTH BRENT (036 47)
Philip Andrade Ltd. BADA
White Oxen Manor, Rattery. Open 9—6; Sat. 9—1 or by appointment. *STOCK: Furniture, 17th to early 19th C, £50—£3,000; English pottery, porcelain, silver, works of art, 17th to early 19th C.* **TEL: 2454.** SER: Valuations. VAT: Stan/Spec.

PHILIP ANDRADE LIMITED

WHITE OXEN MANOR
RATTERY SOUTH BRENT TQ10 9JX

TELEPHONE: SOUTH BRENT (03647) 2454

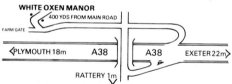

EXTENSIVE STOCK
OF QUALITY ANTIQUE FURNITURE,
ENGLISH AND ORIENTAL PORCELAIN
SILVER, WORKS OF ART

South Brent continued

Fine Pine Antiques
Zeaston Farm, Yellow Berry Lane. *STOCK: Stripped pine and country furniture, general antiques, decorative items.* TEL: 2505.

Larri Clocks and Junk
1 and 2 Church St. (L.G. Wootton.) Est. 1948. CL: Thurs. a.m. Open 9−1, afternoons and Sun. by appointment. SIZE: Medium. *STOCK: Clocks, all periods; small antiques, unusual curios.* LOC: Just off A38. PARK: Easy. TEL: 2553. SER: Valuations; repairs and restorations (clocks, especially longcase).

P.M. Pollak
Moorview, Plymouth Rd. (Dr. P.M. Pollak.) ABA. Est. 1973. Open by appointment. SIZE: Small. *STOCK: Antiquarian books especially medicine and science; prints, some instruments, £50−£5,000.* LOC: On edge of village, near London Inn. PARK: Own. TEL: 3457. SER: Valuations; buys at auction; catalogues issued, computer searches.

SOUTH MOLTON   (076 95)
Architectural Antiques
Savoy Showrooms, New Rd. (A. Busek.) Est. 1978. Open 9−6, Sun. by appointment. SIZE: Large. *STOCK: Architectural fittings, panelling, doors, fire surrounds especially marble, bathroom fittings, pub and shop interiors, garden furniture and decorative items.* LOC: Just off town centre, on A373. PARK: Easy. TEL: 3342; home − 2509. SER: Restorations. VAT: Stan.

Drummer Antiques   *Trade Only*
100 East St. (J.D. Durn.) Est. 1977. CL: Wed. except by appointment. SIZE: Large. *STOCK: General antiques and small items.* LOC: A361. TEL: 2521. SER: Buys at auction. VAT: Stan/Spec.

Drummer's Antique Centre
19 Broad St., Town Sq. Open 9.30−5.30. *STOCK: English furniture and furnishings, porcelain, prints, copper and brass, ironwork.* TEL: 3841 or 2521. VAT: Stan/Spec.

South Molton continued

Golding and Sons   *Trade Only*
Est. 1972. Open by appointment only. SIZE: Warehouse. *STOCK: Pine, mahogany, oak and shipping goods.* TEL: 3401.

Norman Antiques and Decorative Arts
113 East St. (I. and L. Norman.) Est. 1970. CL: Tues. Open 10−12.30 and 2−5, Sat. 10−1. SIZE: Small. *STOCK: China, porcelain, glass, objets de vertu, jewellery, 19th−20th C, £2−£500.* LOC: A361, 100yds. from town centre. PARK: Easy and nearby. TEL: 3055; home − same. SER: Valuations; restorations (jewellery).

South Molton Antiques
103 East St. (D. and W. Nicholl.) Est. 1976. Open 9−5. *STOCK: Shipping goods, oak, mahogany, Victorian furniture, and pine, £10−£1,000; general antiques.* LOC: A361, Taunton side of Town square. TEL: 3478. VAT: Stan/Spec.

SPARKWELL, Nr. Plympton
Alan Jones Antiques
Applethorn Slade Farm. Est. 1965. Resident. Open by appointment. SIZE: Small. *STOCK: Clocks, scientific and marine items, country furniture, primitive and unusual items, 18th−19th C, £5−£500.* LOC: 200yds. from Sparkwell flyover. PARK: Easy. TEL: Plymouth (0752) 338188. FAIRS: Newton Abbot.

STOCKLAND, Nr. Honiton
Colystock Antiques
Rising Sun Farm. (D.C. and S.J. McCollum.) Est. 1975. Open 8.30−6. SIZE: Large. *STOCK: Pine and oak including English, Irish and Continental, 18th−19th C.* TEL: Upottery (040 486) 271. SER: Container packing and documentation courier.

TAVISTOCK   (0822)
Archways
Abbey Arch, Bedford Sq. (C. Mallinson.) Est. 1969. CL: Wed. p.m. and Sat. p.m. Open 10−4. SIZE: Medium. *STOCK: Furniture, paintings, porcelain.* Not stocked: Militaria. LOC: In town centre. PARK: Easy. TEL: 2773; home − Yelverton (0822) 852622.

King Street Curios
5 King St. (T. and P. Bates.) Est. 1979. Open 9−5.30. SIZE: Medium. *STOCK: Pottery, porcelain, collectors' items; art deco, art nouveau, jewellery, up to £100.* LOC: Town centre.

A Regency period mahogany bookcase, c.1815

TEIGNMOUTH (062 67)

Charterhouse Antiques
1 Northumberland Place. (A. and S. Webster.) Est. 1974. CL: Mon. and Thurs. Open 11−1 and 2.15−5, Sat. 10−1 and 2−5. SIZE: Small. *STOCK: Pottery and porcelain, especially commemoratives, 18th C to 1930s, £1− £200; Victorian jewellery and small silver, 1800−1930, £5−£400; weapons, small furniture, paintings, 1780−1900, £10−£500.* LOC: If facing sea, turn right at Post Office, second left, shop round corner on left. PARK: Easy and nearby. TEL: Home − Newton Abbot (0626) 4592. VAT: Stan.

Curio Shop
11 Northumberland Place. (B.C. Wale.) Est. 1976. CL: Thurs. Open 10.15−5. SIZE: Small. *STOCK: Militaria, curios, medals, badges, £3−£500.* LOC: 200yds. off the Exeter − Torquay road, nr. the quay. PARK: Adjacent.

Peter Dryden Ltd. BADA
Teign Court. Open by appointment. *STOCK: English and Continental furniture and works of art.* TEL: 4597.

Extence Antiques
2 Wellington St., also at Triangle Place. (T.E. and L.E. Extence.) Est. 1928. CL: Sun. and Thurs. except by appointment. Open 9.30−1 and 2−5.30. SIZE: Large. *STOCK: Furniture, from Georgian; jewellery, silver, objets d'art, clocks and pocket watches.* PARK: Limited outside shop. TEL: 3353. SER: Restorations (clocks). VAT: Stan/Spec.

The Very Small Shop
19 French St. (Mr. and Mrs. A.M.F. Ritchie.) Est. 1954. Open evenings, 4 p.m. to 8 p.m. or by appointment. SIZE: Small. *STOCK: Jewellery, Georgian to 1930, £10−£150; silver, Georgian to modern, £5−£500; china and glass, 50p−£50.* Not stocked: Furniture, watches and clocks, coins and reproductions. LOC: From town centre take Dawlish road, A379, shop is on left about 100yds. by small green. PARK: Easy. TEL: 2902; home − same. SER: Buys at auction.

TIVERTON (0884)

Bygone Days Antiques
40 Gold St. (N. Park.) CL: Thurs. except by appointment. Open 9.30−1 and 2−5. *STOCK: Furniture, Victorian and Georgian; watercolours and oils.* TEL: 252832.

Tiverton continued

Chancery Antiques
8—10 Barrington St. Est. 1967. CL: Sun. and Thurs. except by appointment. Open 9—5. SIZE: Large. *STOCK: Furniture, stripped pine.* PARK: Easy. TEL: 252416; home — 253190. SER: Export facilities. VAT: Stan/Spec.

Grey House Antiques
8 Newport St. (A. Peters.) Resident. Est. 1984. Open 10—5.30 or by appointment. *STOCK: Period furniture, objets d'art.* LOC: Main route into town from motorway. PARK: Limited or opposite. TEL: 255846.

Town End Antiques
24 Silver St. (J. Marshall.) Open 9—5.45 or by appointment. *STOCK: Ceramics, silver, coins, stamps, cigarette cards, postcards, army badges.* TEL: 254250. VAT: Stan.

TOPSHAM, Nr. Exeter   (039 287)
Allnutt Antiques
13 Fore St. (J. and E. Gage.) Est. 1950. CL: Wed. Open 10—5 or by appointment. *STOCK: Porcelain, 1800—1890; glass, 1780—1890; silver, furniture, 1800—1900.* Not stocked: Pictures. LOC: 1 mile from Countess Weir roundabout (A377) towards Exmouth. PARK: Own. TEL: 4224. SER: Valuations.

The Clock Shop Antiques
40 Fore St. (B. Palmer.) Est. 1976. CL: Sat. p.m. Open 10—1 and 2—5. SIZE: Medium. *STOCK: Clocks, 18th C.* TEL: 5986; home — Exeter (0392) 832124. SER: Restorations; buys at auction. FAIRS: Newton Abbot. VAT: Spec.

Holloway Antiques
41 Fore St. Open 10—5.30, Mon. and Wed. by appointment. *STOCK: 19th C small furniture, porcelain, silver, paintings, glass.* TEL: 4707. VAT: Stan/Spec.

TORQUAY   (0803)
Birbeck Antiques
219 Union St., Torre. (H.S. and K. Birbeck.) Est. 1955. CL: Sat. p.m. Open 10—5. SIZE: Small. *STOCK: Chinese, Japanese, English and Continental porcelain, pottery, glass, furniture and works of art, 17th to early 20th C, to £5,000.* Not stocked: Silver, weapons, rugs. LOC: From Newton Abbot enter Torquay's one-way system at Tom Brown's garage. Fork left, first right past car park, 30yds. PARK: Easy. TEL: 23318; home — 214836. SER: Valuations; restorations (oil paintings); buys at auction. VAT: Stan/Spec.

Torquay continued

Castle Lane Books
Off Market St. (I.E. Smith.) Est. 1975. CL: Sun. and Wed., except by appointment. Open 10.30—5.30. SIZE: Large. *STOCK: Books, especially out-of-print and antiquarian, from 1600s to date, £5—£1,000.* LOC: Off Market St., half way down main shopping centre, in old police station. PARK: Easy — for 1 hour. TEL: 28991. SER: Valuations; restorations (rebinding in cloth or leather); buys at auction (books, pictures and engravings); searches made for specific books not in stock.

Chamberlin Galleries Ltd.
1 Victoria Parade. Est. 1947. TEL: 27626. VAT: Stan.

Derby House Antiques
48 South St., Torre. (B. Ward.) Est. 1976. CL: Sat. p.m. and Wed. p.m. except by appointment. Open 10—1 and 2.15—5.15. SIZE: Small. *STOCK: English and Continental ceramics, £20—£75; small furniture, £25—£100; small silver, glass and collectors' items, £15—£75; all mainly 19th C and early 20th C.* LOC: Bear right from Newton Rd., into Torquay. PARK: Easy. TEL: 212335.

The Devonshire Gallery   BADA
                                 LAPADA
45 Abbey Rd. (H. Birbeck and C. Stodgell.) Est. 1972. CL: Sun. except by appointment. Open 10—1 and 2—5.30. SIZE: Medium. *STOCK: Oil paintings, £100—£30,000; watercolours and drawings, £20—£1,500; all 19th to early 20th C; engravings and prints, 19th C, £10—£500.* **LOC: 200yds. up Abbey Rd. from main street roundabout at Torquay G.P.O. PARK: Easy or 200yds. TEL: 27144. SER: Valuations; restorations; picture cleaning, restoring, re-lining (vacuum press), framing; buys at auction. VAT: Spec.**

Torquay continued

Fortunate Finds
32 Tor Church Rd. (N.E. Lythgoe.) Est. 1971. CL: Wed. *STOCK: General antiques, Victoriana, coins.* TEL: 27495; home — 22076.

Julian Antiques
205 Union St. (J.V.S. Goode.) Open 9.30—5, Sat. 9—1. *STOCK: General antiques.* TEL: 28851.

Laburnum Antique Galleries
3 Laburnum Row. (M. Gordon.) Est. 1960. CL: Sun. except by appointment, Wed. p.m. and Sat. p.m. Open 9—5. *STOCK: General antiques, arms, armour.* LOC: Off Union St. TEL: 26983. VAT: Stan/Spec.

Russells (Antiques) Ltd.
64 Fleet St. Est. 1945. *STOCK: Furniture, jewellery, silver, decorative items.* TEL: 22781. VAT: Stan.

Sheraton House
1 Laburnum Row, Torre. (K. Goodman) *STOCK: Period furniture and decorations.* TEL: 23334.

Torquay continued

Torquay Antique Centre
177 Union St. CL: Sat. p.m. Open 10—6. There are about 20 dealers at this centre offering a wide selection of general antiques. LOC: Follow one-way system from Castle Circus to Union St. PARK: Easy. TEL: 26621. Below are listed some of the dealers:

Cannon Hill Antiques
General antiques.

Peterson Antiques
Furniture, ivories, objects.

Pomeroy Antiques
Jewellery, silver.

The Silver Shop
Silver, plate and jewellery.

Silverdale Antiques
Porcelain and pottery.

Torre Antique Traders
266 Higher Union St. (P. and Mrs. R. Curtis, N. Boulton, J. Morris.) Open 10—5. SIZE: Medium. *STOCK: General antiques.* LOC: Continuation of main shopping area (Union St.). PARK: Easy. TEL: 22184.

"No class of people in England require the superintendance of law more than the innkeepers." From *Mr. Rowlandson's England* by Robert Southey, ed. John Steel, published by the **Antique Collectors' Club,** 1985.

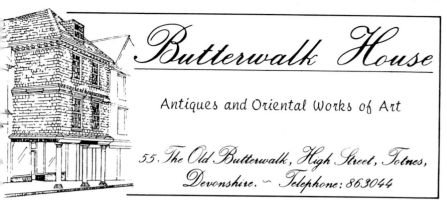

Butterwalk House

Antiques and Oriental Works of Art

55, The Old Butterwalk, High Street, Totnes, Devonshire. ~ Telephone: 863044

TOTNES (0803)

Butterwalk House
55 The Old Butterwalk. (Mrs. S.J. Nixon.) Est. 1978. Open 10—5.30, Thurs. and Sat. 10—1. SIZE: Large. *STOCK: Small furniture, £250—£5,000; decorative items, Oriental art, bronzes, china, silver, treen, paintings, £10—£1,000.* LOC: In town centre. PARK: Nearby. TEL: 863044. VAT: Stan/Spec.

Collards Books
4 Castle St. (B. Collard.) Est. 1970. CL: Thurs. p.m. and lunch hr. in winter only. Open 10—5. SIZE: Large. *STOCK: Antiquarian and secondhand books.* LOC: Opposite castle. PARK: Nearby. TEL: Home — Kingsbridge (0548) 550246.

Country Cottage Furniture
71 Fore St. (D.H. Bramhall.) CL: Thurs. Open 10—5. *STOCK: Restored pine furniture, 18th—19th C.* TEL: 865239.

Fine Pine Antiques
85 High St. Est. 1973. CL: Mon. and Thurs. *STOCK: Stripped pine and country furniture.* SER: Restorations, stripping.

Lamont Antiques
7-9 High St. CL: Thurs. p.m. Open 9—5.30. *STOCK: General antiques.* TEL: 864897.

Hugh Mendl Antiques
Collards Bookshop, 4 Castle St. Open 10—5 during holiday season; otherwise 10—1 and 2.15—5, Sun. by appointment to trade. SIZE: Small. *STOCK: Late 18th—19th C pottery and porcelain, especially nursery plates and blue and white transfer ware; small papier mâché and other objects; Baxter and licensee prints, Valentines.* LOC: Near castle. PARK: North St. TEL: Home — 863970. SER: Buys at auction (as stock).

Totnes continued

Beverley J. Pyke — Fine British Watercolours
The Gothic House, Bank Lane. CL: Tues. in summer, Wed. in winter. Open 10—1.30 and 2.30—5.30 or by appointment. SIZE: Small. *STOCK: Watercolours, 20th C, £50—£600.* LOC: Opposite P.O. in Fore St. PARK: Nearby. TEL: 864219; home — same.

WHIMPLE (0404)

Anthony James Antiques
The Square. (A.J. and F. Mulligan.) Open daily or by appointment. SIZE: Medium. *STOCK: Furniture, 17th—18th C; small items, metalware.* PARK: Easy. TEL: 822146. VAT: Spec.

WINKLEIGH (083 783)

L.R. Ryce
Cottage Antiques, The Square. *STOCK: Brass, copper, porcelain, silver, plate and small furniture.* PARK: Easy. TEL: 244.

Mrs M. Webb
Nine Beeches. Usually open, resident on premises. *STOCK: Furniture, brass, copper, porcelain, clocks, collectors' items.* LOC: On main Torrington road. PARK: Own. TEL: 209.

WOODBURY, Nr Exeter (0395)

Woodbury Antiques
Church St. (H. Jarman.) Est. 1966. Open 10—5.30. SIZE: Large. *STOCK: Victorian —Edwardian furniture and items.* PARK: Easy. TEL: 32727. VAT: Stan/Spec.

Dorset

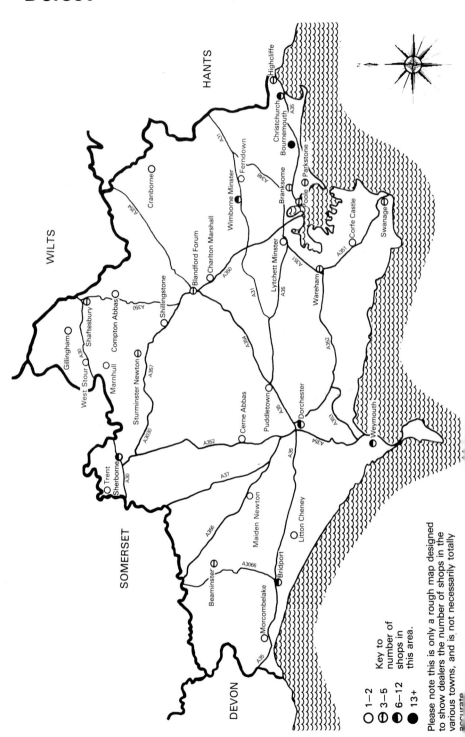

Key to number of shops in this area.

○ 1–2
◐ 3–5
◑ 6–12
● 13+

Please note this is only a rough map designed to show dealers the number of shops in the various towns, and is not necessarily totally accurate.

Dorset

BEAMINSTER (0308)

Beaminster Antiques
4 Church St. (Mrs. T.P.F. Frampton.) Est. 1982. Open 9.30—5.30, Wed. 9.30—1. SIZE: Small. *STOCK: Small furniture, £20—£700; silver, £10—£400; jewellery, £5—£700, all Georgian to art deco; objets d'art, porcelain, boxes, 18th C to art deco, £5—£700; brass and pictures, 18th C to 1920s, £1—£500.* Not stocked: Coins and medals. LOC: Just off square. PARK: Easy. TEL: 862591; home — Corscombe (093 589) 395.

Cottage Antiques
17 The Square. CL: Wed. Open 10—5.30 or by appointment. *STOCK: Furniture, paintings, clocks, prints, decorative items.* LOC: A3066. TEL: 862136.

Daniels House Antiques   LAPADA
Daniels House, Hogshill St. (C. and G.C. Hennessy.) Est. 1977. CL: Sun. except by appointment. Open 10—6 or by appointment. SIZE: Medium. *STOCK: Pine, country and painted furniture, English and Continental, 18th—19th C.* LOC: On A3066, 200yds. north of the Square. PARK: Easy. TEL: 862635; home — same. VAT: Stan/Spec.

Good Hope Antiques
2 Hogshill St. (D. Beney.) Est. 1980. CL: Wed. Open 9.30—1 and 2—5. SIZE: Medium. *STOCK: Clocks, especially longcase and bracket, £500—£3,000; furniture, £200—£1,000; all 18th—19th C.* LOC: Town square. PARK: Easy. TEL: 862119; home — same. SER: Valuations; restorations (clocks, including dials). VAT: Spec.

BLANDFORD FORUM

A & D Antiques
21 East St. (A. and D. Edgington.) Est. 1981. CL: Mon. and Wed. p.m. Open 10—5, Sun. by appointment. SIZE: Small. *STOCK: Drinking glasses, 18th C, £50—£1,000; decanters, 19th C, £15—£100; Goss, 20th C, £3—£35.* LOC: Town centre on main east-west route (one- way system). PARK: Easy. TEL: Blandford (0258) 55643; home — same. SER: Valuations (glass); buys at auction (18th C drinking glasses and decanters).

Blandford Forum continued

Julian Chanter Antiques
15 East St. (J.P. and A.M. Chanter.) Est. 1975. Open by appointment. *STOCK: Early metal, country pottery, needlework and furniture.* TEL: Blandford (0258) 52525; evenings — Fontmell Magna (0747) 811966. VAT: Spec.

Lauretta — Jewellers
7 East St. (Mrs. J.E.L. Trickett.) NAG. Est. 1979. CL: Mon. and Wed. Open 10—1 and 2.30—5. SIZE: Small. *STOCK: Jewellery, 1750—1930s, £5—£5,000; objets d'art, £5—£500.* PARK: Easy. TEL: Blandford (0258) 55455.

Stour Gallery
East St. Gallery, 28 East St. (R. Butler.) Est. 1966. CL: Mon. and Wed. p.m. Open 10—1, and 2—4, Sun. by appointment. SIZE: Medium. *STOCK: Watercolours, oils and pastels, early 19th C to early 20th C, £25—£1,000.* LOC: On right-hand side of road from Shaftesbury, on one way system. PARK: Opposite or behind. TEL: Blandford (0258) 56293; home — Sturminster Newton (0258) 72837. SER: Restorations (oils, watercolours, wash line mounts); framing.

Peter Strowger of Blandford
                                    LAPADA
13 East St. Est. 1962. CL: Sun. and Mon. except by appointment. Open 10.30—1.15 and 2.30—6. SIZE: Medium. *STOCK: Furniture, 17th—19th C, £50—£1,500; porcelain and pottery (Oriental, Continental and English), mid-18th to mid-19th C, £50—£750; oil paintings, watercolours, 18th—19th C, £25—£1,000.* Not stocked: Coins, stamps, medals. LOC: On A354. PARK: Easy. TEL: Blandford (0258) 54374. VAT: Stan/Spec.

BOURNEMOUTH (0202)

Michael Andrews Antiques
914 Christchurch Rd. Est. 1967. CL: Wed. p.m. Open 10—5.30. SIZE: Medium. *STOCK: Furniture, art nouveau, copper, brass, shipping goods.* PARK: Opposite. TEL: 427615. VAT: Stan.

The Antique Centre
837/839 Christchurch Rd., East Boscombe. (C. Williams and R. Hadley.) Est. 1961. Open 9.30—5.30. SIZE: Large. *STOCK: Silver plate, old Sheffield to art deco; porcelain and pottery, 18th—20th C; both £5—£500; writing slopes, caddies, work boxes, £50—£400; bric-a-brac, clothes, Victorian to 1960s, £1—£50; furniture, Georgian to art deco, £10—£500; Oriental items, 1800—1920; dolls, Victorian and Edwardian; both £10—£1,000.* PARK: Easy and at rear. TEL: 421052. SER: Restorations (silver and jewellery repairs, replating); buys at auction.

Antiques and Curios
117 Charminster Rd. (D.J. Atfield.) Est. 1957. CL: Wed. p.m. Open 10—6. SIZE: Medium. *STOCK: General antiques.* PARK: Easy. TEL: 21318.

Antiques and Furnishings
339 Charminster Rd. (P. Neath, T. Boyne.) Open 10—5.30. *STOCK: Stripped pine, lloyd loom, brass; copper, china, linen, lace.* TEL: 527976.

Antiques Trade Warehouse
Trade Only
28 Lorne Park Rd. (Mrs A.L. Williams.) Est. 1978. CL: Sat. SIZE: Large. *STOCK: Victoriana, shipping and period items, bric-a-brac.* LOC: Close to Old Christchurch Rd., Lansdowne. PARK: Easy. TEL: 292944.

Michael Baldwin
1125 Christchurch Rd., Boscombe. Est. 1951. CL: Wed. Open 9—12 and 2—5. *STOCK: English and Continental furniture, 18th—19th C; Dutch marquetry pieces, porcelain, bronzes; silver, pictures.* PARK: Easy. TEL: 428343. VAT: Stan.

Bell of Boscombe
693 Christchurch Rd. Est. 1947. CL: Wed. Open 10—4. *STOCK: Silver and jewellery.* TEL: 34892.

C. Bennett and Sons
646 Wimborne Rd., Winton. Est. 1946. TEL: 527205; home — 765288.

Blade and Bayonet
884 Christchurch Rd., Boscombe. (L.M. Martin.) Resident. Est. 1982. Open 10—12 and 1—5, Fri. 10—12. SIZE: Medium. *STOCK: Militaria, mid 17th to 20th C, £50—£100.* LOC: Near Pokesdown station. PARK: Easy. TEL: 429891. SER: Valuations; restorations (mainly cleaning weapons). FAIRS: Bournemouth, Southsea, St. Leonards.

Bournemouth continued

Commin's Antiquarian Bookshop
Est. 1892. Open 9—6 including Sun. *STOCK: Antiquarian and secondhand books, maps and prints.* TEL: 27504. VAT: Stan.

Peter Denver Antiques
36 Calvin Rd., Winton. (P. Denver White.) Est. 1961. CL: Mon. Open 10—6. SIZE: Small. *STOCK: Furniture, porcelain, pictures, glass, Georgian—Edwardian, £5—£800.* LOC: Off main Wimborne Rd. PARK: Easy. TEL: 532536; home — 513911. VAT: Stan/Spec.

Desire Attire
862 Christchurch Rd., Boscombe. (Mrs. P. Jacques, Mrs. J.C. Freestone.) Open 10—5. *STOCK: Jewellery, general antiques, pre-1950s clothes, interesting items.* TEL: 422407.

Fine Arts
207 Old Christchurch Rd. (G. Russell.) SIZE: Large. *STOCK: English and Continental furniture, porcelain, clocks, Victorian oil paintings.* LOC: Near Lansdowne. TEL: 291054; home — 292547. VAT: Stan.

Gallery 922
922 Christchurch Rd., Boscombe. (M. Howell, R. Peacock.) Open 10—1 and 2—5.30. SIZE: Medium. *STOCK: Furniture, £20—£500; copper and brass, £20—£200; art nouveau, art deco and smalls, £10—£500; all 19th to early 20th C.* PARK: Easy, opposite. TEL: 421095. SER: Valuations; buys at auction (art nouveau, art deco). FAIRS: Local. VAT: Stan/Spec.

Lionel Geneen Ltd.
781 Christchurch Rd., Boscombe. Est. 1902. CL: Lunchtimes. Open 9.15—5, Sat. 9.15—12. SIZE: Large. *STOCK: English, Continental and Oriental furniture, china and works of art including bronzes, enamels, ivories, jades, art nouveau and art deco, all 17th C to early 20th C.* LOC: Main road through Boscombe. PARK: Easy. TEL: 422961; home — 764709. SER: Valuations. VAT: Stan/Spec.

Georgian House Antiques
110—112 Commercial Rd. Est. 1967. CL: Wed. p.m. Open 9—5.30. *STOCK: General antiques, silver, coins, jewellery.* TEL: 24175. VAT: Stan.

H.L.B. Antiques
139 Barrack Rd. (H.L. Blechman.) Est. 1969. SIZE: Large. *STOCK: All collectable items.* PARK: Easy. TEL: 429252 and 482388. VAT: Stan/Spec.

Hampshire Gallery
18 Lansdowne Rd. Est. 1971. *STOCK: Paintings and watercolours, 17th to early 20th C.* TEL: 21211. SER: Valuations; restorations. VAT: Spec.

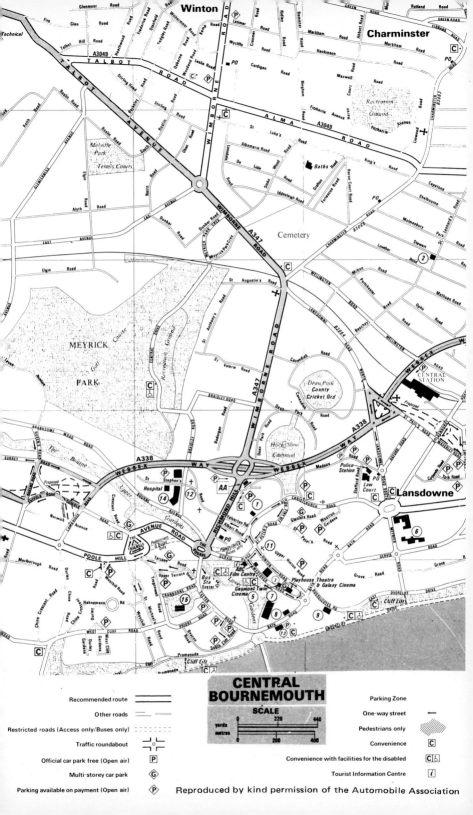

CENTRAL BOURNEMOUTH

SCALE

Recommended route		Parking Zone
Other roads		One-way street
Restricted roads (Access only/Buses only)		Pedestrians only
Traffic roundabout		Convenience — C
Official car park free (Open air) — P		Convenience with facilities for the disabled — C
Multi-storey car park — G		Tourist Information Centre — i
Parking available on payment (Open air) — P		

Reproduced by kind permission of the Automobile Association

Bournemouth continued

King and Hayman
202 Old Christchurch Rd. Est. 1914. Open 9.30—5 Mon.—Fri. from June—Sept; Mon.—Thurs. from Oct.—May. *STOCK: General antiques, silver, medals, coins, jewellery, porcelain, paintings, stamps and furniture.* TEL: 21919.

Lafrance and Weber
112 Charminster Rd. Open 8.30—1 and 2—5.30, Sat. 9—1. *STOCK: Paintings and watercolours, 19th C.* TEL: 511926. SER: Restorations; framing.

Marney's
813 Christchurch Rd., Boscombe. (M. Lumb.) *STOCK: General antiques, furniture, pottery and porcelain.* TEL: 423907.

Moordown Antiques
885 Wimborne Rd. (T.A. Bond.) Open Tues. and Thurs. 10—1 and 2.15—5, Sat. 10—1 and 2.15—4. *STOCK: General antiques.* TEL: 513732.

Kenneth Mummery Ltd.
9 St. Winifreds Rd. Est. 1917. Open by appointment only. *STOCK: Antiquarian books on music in all languages.* TEL: 25170.

G.B. Mussenden and Son, Antiques, Jewellery and Silver
24 Seamoor Rd., Westbourne. Est. 1948. CL: Wed. Open 9—5. SIZE: Medium. *STOCK: Antiques, jewellery, silver.* LOC: Central Westbourne, corner of R.L. Stevenson Ave. PARK: Easy. TEL: 764462. SER: Valuations. VAT: Stan/Spec.

R.E. Porter
2 and 4 Post Office Rd. Est. 1934. Open 9.30—5. SIZE: Medium. *STOCK: Silver (including early antique spoons up to modern), Georgian, £20—£5,000.* Not stocked: Furniture, paintings, arms, armour, carpets, etc. LOC: Coming from the square, take the Old Christchurch Rd. exit from the roundabout, then first turning on left. PARK: 300yds. at top of Richmond Hill. TEL: 24289. SER: Valuations. VAT: Stan/Spec.

Portique
15/16/17 Criterion Arcade. Est. 1971. *STOCK: Silver, jewellery, china, glass including paperweights, cloisonné.* LOC: Coming from the square take the Old Christchurch Rd. from roundabout, arcade entrance is between first and second turnings on left. TEL: 22979. VAT: Stan/Spec.

R.E.M. Antiques
823a Christchurch Rd., Boscombe. (R.E. Morgan.) Open 9—1 and 2.15—5.30. Sat. 9—1. *STOCK: General antiques mainly furniture and clocks.* TEL: 429367. VAT: Spec.

Bournemouth continued

S.H. and W.P. Reynolds
888 Christchurch Rd., Boscombe. Est. 1952. SIZE: Large. *STOCK: General antiques, bric-a-brac.*

Sainsburys of Bournemouth and New World Export Co. Ltd.   LAPADA
23-25 Abbott Rd. Est. 1918. CL: Sat. p.m. Open 8—1 and 2—6. *STOCK: Furniture, especially bookcases and dining tables, 18th C, to £15,000.* PARK: Own. TEL: 529271; home — 763616. VAT: Stan/Spec.

Sandy's Antiques
790 Christchurch Rd., Boscombe. *STOCK: Oriental items; general antiques; shipping goods, pre-1930.* TEL: 301190; evenings — 470787. VAT: Stan/Spec.

Shippey's of Boscombe
15—16 Royal Arcade, Boscombe. Est. 1927. CL: Wed. Open 9.30—5. SIZE: Small. *STOCK: Victorian and later jewellery, objets d'art, silver, china, glass, ivories, £1—£300.* Not stocked: Pictures. LOC: Centre of Boscombe, at Palmerston Rd. end of Arcade. PARK: Within 200yds. TEL: 36548. SER: Restorations (jewellery). VAT: Spec.

Peter Stebbing Ltd.
7 Post Office Rd. (P.M. Stebbing.) Est. 1960. Open 9.30—5. SIZE: Medium. *STOCK: Furniture, £25—£1,000; glass, silver, £1—£100; metalware, jewellery, all 18th—19th C.* LOC: Next to Head Post Office. PARK: 200yds. TEL: 22587. SER: Valuations.

Sterling Coins and Medals
2 Somerset Rd., Boscombe. (W.N. Graham.) Est. 1969. CL: Wed. Open 10—1 and 2—5. SIZE: Small. *STOCK: Coins, medals, militaria, gold, silver.* LOC: Next to 806 Christchurch Rd. TEL: 423881. SER: Valuations. VAT: Stan.

D.C. Stuart Antiques
336 Holdenhurst Rd. Open 9—5.30, Sat. 9—5. *STOCK: General antiques and silver; jewellery by prior request.* TEL: 34218.

R.A. Swift and Sons   LAPADA
St. Andrews Hall, 4c Wolverton Rd., Boscombe. Est. 1904. Open 9—5.30, Sat. 9—4. SIZE: Large. *STOCK: English and Continental furniture, 18th—19th C; porcelain, pottery, paintings, silver, Sheffield plate, glass, clocks.* TEL: 34470; home — 763045. VAT: Stan/Spec.

Victorian Chairman
883 Christchurch Rd., Boscombe. (R. Leo.) Open 9.30—5.30. *STOCK: Furniture, especially chairs, suites.* TEL: 420996. SER: Upholstery.

R A SWIFT & SONS

ANTIQUES AND WORKS OF ART

R A SWIFT & SONS

ST. ANDREWS HALL · 4c WOLVERTON ROAD · BOSCOMBE
(off Christchurch Road)
BOURNEMOUTH BH7 6HT · TEL: (0202) 34470
AMPLE PARKING ON THE PREMISES

Established for over 50 years

Bournemouth continued

Victorian Parlour
1a Parkwood Rd., Boscombe. (D.S. Lloyd.) Est. 1984. Open 9.30−1 and 2−5. SIZE: Small. *STOCK: Small furniture, Victorian, £250−£400; small silver, 18th−19th C, £20−£80; Victoriana, £5−£50.* PARK: Easy. TEL: 433928. SER: Restorations (caning, rush seating); buys at auction.

Christopher Williams Antiquarian Bookseller
23 St. Leonards Rd. Est. 1967. CL: Mon. and Sat. Open 10−1 and 2−5.30, other times by appointment. *STOCK: Books especially on antiques, art, bibliography, cookery, wine, topography.* TEL: 519683.

Sidney Wright (Booksellers)
12−13 Royal Arcade, Boscombe. Est. 1905. Open 9−5.45, Wed. 9−1. *STOCK: Antiquarian and general second-hand books.* TEL: 37153.

BRANKSOME

Allen's (Branksome) Ltd.
447/449 Poole Rd. (D.L. and P.J. D'Ardenne.) Est. 1948. Open 9−1 and 2.15−6. SIZE: Large. *STOCK: Furniture.* TEL: Bournemouth (0202) 763724. VAT: Stan.

Branksome Antiques
370 Poole Rd. (R.E. and L.J. Maskell, B.A. Neal.) Est. 1973. CL: Wed. Open 10−5, Sat. 10−4. SIZE: Medium. *STOCK: Furniture, 19th−20th C, £50−£200; scientific instruments, 19th C, £100−£300; general antiques and bric-a-brac, £5−£50.* PARK: Easy. TEL: Bournemouth (0202) 763324; home − Sturminster Newton (0258) 72296. SER: Buys at auction (as stock). VAT: Stan/Spec.

David Mack Antiques
434−437 Poole Rd. and 43a Langley Rd. Est. 1963. Open 9−5.30 or by appointment. SIZE: Large. *STOCK: 18th−19th C tables, chairs, display cabinets, desks, bureaux, bookcases; later furniture and shipping goods.* LOC: 200yds. from Sainsburys Homebase. PARK: Own. TEL: Bournemouth (0202) 760005. SER: Valuations; restorations. VAT: Stan/Spec.

BRIDPORT   (0308)

Beach and Co. Antiques
9 East St. (F. and J. Blakey.) CL: Thurs. p.m. Open 9.30−5. *STOCK: Furniture, china, glass.* LOC: Town centre, opposite town hall. TEL: Evenings − 22931.

Bridport continued

Chancery Lane Antiques
18 Chancery Lane. (A. and G. Martelli.) Est. 1985. Open daily, Sun. by appointment. SIZE: Small. *STOCK: English country and mahogany furniture, £20−£1,000; oils and watercolours, £20−£5,000; both 18th−19th C; Italian and other Continental furniture, 17th−19th C, £250−£2,500.* Not stocked: Brass, copper, bric-a-brac. LOC: Small alley behind Bull Hotel in West St. (A35). PARK: Easy. TEL: 22373; home − (0297) 89415. SER: Valuations; restorations; buys at auction. VAT: Stan/Spec.

Cox's Corner
40 St. Michael's Lane. (C. Cox.) SIZE: Large. *STOCK: Furniture, pictures.* TEL: 23451.

Croft Antiques
3 and 7 Barrack St. (D. and C. Ross.) Est. 1966. CL: Mon. and Thurs. Evenings by appointment. *STOCK: 18th and 19th C furniture, general antiques, decorative items, porcelain, glass and metalware.* TEL: 22552; home − Broadwindsor (0308) 68352. VAT: Stan/Spec.

Hobby Horse Antiques
29 West Allington. (J. Rodber.) Est. 1948. CL: Thurs. Open 10−1 and 2.30−5. SIZE: Large. *STOCK: Mechanical antiques, toys, small furniture, porcelain, brass, copper, bygones, silver, jewellery.* Not stocked: Oak, weapons, coins. LOC: West of Bridport on south side of A35 between Dorchester and Exeter. PARK: Easy. TEL: 22801.

PIC's Bookshop
11 South St. CL: Thurs. p.m. *STOCK: Books, engravings and prints.*

Tudor House Antiques   LAPADA
88 East St. (P. and V. Knight, A. and D. Burton.) Est. 1940. Open 9−1 and 2−5.30, Sun. by appointment. SIZE: Small. *STOCK: General antiques.* LOC: Left hand side of main A35 from Dorchester. PARK: Easy. TEL: 27200; home − same. VAT: Stan/Spec.

CERNE ABBAS   (030 03)

Cerne Antiques
(I. Pulliblank.) Est. 1972. CL: Fri. Open 10−1 and 2−5, Sun. 2−5. SIZE: Medium. *STOCK: Silver, porcelain, furniture including unusual items, mainly 19th C, £1−£300.* LOC: A352. PARK: Easy. TEL: 490; home − same.

CHARLTON MARSHALL
Nr. Blandford

Zona Dawson Antiques
The Old Clubhouse. Est. 1958. Open 10−6. *STOCK: 18th and 19th C, mainly furniture, clocks.* TEL: Blandford (0258) 53146. VAT: Spec

CHRISTCHURCH (0202)
J.L. Arditti
88 Bargates. (A. and J.L. Arditti.) Est. 1964. CL: Sun. except by appointment. Open 9—5.30. SIZE: Medium. *STOCK: Oriental carpets and rugs, 18th to early 20th C, £250—£4,000; kelims and flatweaves, 19th C, £150—£1,000.* LOC: From town centre take road towards Hurn airport, left side on corner of Bargates and Twynham Avenue. PARK: Twynham Avenue. TEL: 485414. SER: Valuations; restorations (Persian rugs). FAIRS: 'Antiques Weekend', Ringwood. VAT: Stan/Spec.

Christchurch Carpets
55/57 Bargates. (J. Sheppard.) Est. 1963. Open 9—5.30. SIZE: Large. *STOCK: Persian carpets and rugs, 19th—20th C, £100—£500.* LOC: Main road. PARK: Adjacent. TEL: 482712. SER: Valuations. VAT:Stan/Spec.

Hamptons
12 Purewell. (G. Hampton.) CL: Sat. a.m. Open 10—6. SIZE: Large. *STOCK: Furniture, 18th—19th C; general antiques, clocks, china, silver, instruments, metalware, oil paintings, Chinese and Persian carpets and rugs.* PARK: Easy. TEL: 484000.

Hirst Antiques
4 Church St. (Mr. and Mrs. R.B. Hirsbrunner.) Est. 1981. Open 9.30—5.30, Sun. by appointment. SIZE: Medium. *STOCK: Art deco pottery, £1—£500; porcelain and pottery, 18th—19th C £5—£300; furniture 19th C, £100—£1,000.* LOC: A35. TEL: 473981.

Molly Katz
The Old Barn, Millhams St. CL: Wed. Open 10—5. *STOCK: Country furniture, porcelain, pottery, silver, objets d'art, paintings, copper, brass.* TEL: 484307. SER: Interior decorating.

M. & R. Antiques
149 Barrack Rd. (M.I. Lankshear.) Open 9—6. *STOCK: General antiques especially militaria.* TEL: 473091.

Whotnots
77 Bargates. (J. and A. Goddard.) CL: Wed. Open 9.30—1 and 2.15—5. *STOCK: General antiques.* TEL: 475068.

COMPTON ABBAS
Nr. Shaftesbury

David Lane Antiques   LAPADA
The Old Forge. Est. 1965. Appointment advisable. *STOCK: Early oak, mahogany and pine; decorative items, clocks, metalware.* TEL: Fontmell Magna (0747) 811881. LOC: On A350. SER: Restorations (furniture). VAT: Stan/Spec.

CORFE CASTLE (0929)
The Little Shop
East St. (S. Lovell.) Est. 1981. CL: Sat. SIZE: Small. *STOCK: China, pottery, silver, prints, watercolours, £5—£100.* LOC: A351 at foot of castle. PARK: 25 yards. TEL: Wareham (092 95) 6498. SER: Restorations; buys at auction (porcelain, pottery, china). VAT: Stan.

CRANBORNE (072 54)
Nr. Wimborne

Tower Antiques   *Mainly Export*
The Square. (P.W. Kear and P. White.) Resident. Est. 1975. *STOCK: Georgian and Victorian furniture, especially bookcases.* TEL: 552.

The Web
The Square. (Mrs. H.K. Waterfield and Mrs. B. Mathews.) Est. 1968. CL: Mon. Open 10—12 and 2—5. SIZE: Medium. *STOCK: Country furniture, general antiques, trade goods.* Not stocked: Coins, medals, militaria, weapons. LOC: In village square. PARK: Easy. TEL: 222. and Verwood (0202) 822563. FAIRS: Netherbrook, Ringwood. VAT: Stan/Spec.

DORCHESTER (0305)
Antique Market
Town Hall/Corn Exchange. Est. 1979. Open one Wed. each month (dates in local press). There are 35 stands at this market selling a wide range of general antiques. TEL: Stalbridge (0963) 62478.

Colliton Antique and Craft Centre
Colliton St., North Sq. Open daily, Sun. by appointment. There are 8 dealers at this centre selling mainly *18th—19th C furniture, £25—£1,000; ornaments, brass, copper, bric-a- brac, to £200; jewellery, £20—£600.* LOC: By town clock. PARK: Easy. TEL: 69398; home — 62444 and 60115. SER: Valuations; restorations (cabinet work, upholstery and metalware). VAT: Stan/Spec.

Dorchester Antiques
22 High West St. (J.M. Holloway.) Open 9.30—5.30. *STOCK: Furniture, porcelain, copper, brass, pictures, 18th—early 20th C.* LOC: Main St. through Dorchester, next to Royal Oak. TEL: Home — Cerne Abbas (03003) 549.

R.E. Greenland
8 Church St. CL: Thurs. p.m. Open 9—5. *STOCK: Antiquarian and secondhand books.* LOC: Church St. runs parallel to South St. PARK: In Durngage St. or Charles St. TEL: 62517; home — 63853.

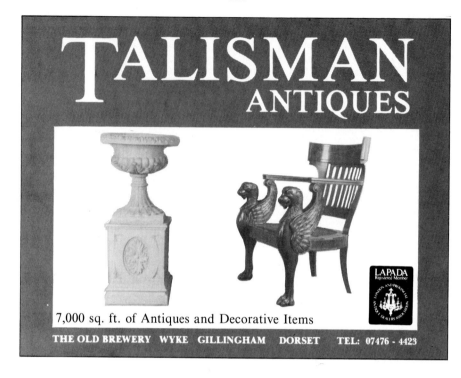

TALISMAN
ANTIQUES

7,000 sq. ft. of Antiques and Decorative Items

THE OLD BREWERY   WYKE   GILLINGHAM   DORSET   TEL: 07476 - 4423

Dorchester continued

Michael Legg
15 High East St. (Showrooms) and Old Malt House, Bottom-o-Town. (E.M.J. Legg.) Open 9—5.30 or any time by appointment. SIZE: Medium. *STOCK: 17th—19th C furniture, porcelain, pictures, silver, glass.* TEL: 64596. VAT: Stan/Spec.

Legg of Dorchester
Regency House, 51 High East St. (W. and H. Legg.) Est. 1930. *STOCK: General antiques, Regency and decorative furniture, stripped pine.* TEL: 64964. VAT: Stan/Spec.

"Plume of Feathers Antiques"
Foremost House, 3 Princes St. (A. Elwin.) Est. 1972. *STOCK: Victorian jewellery, bric-a-brac, small furniture, ephemera.* TEL: 67729.

Tudor Gallery
Acland Rd. (J.R. and I.D. Lake.) Open 9.30—5, Thurs. 9.30—1. *STOCK: Watercolours, engravings and prints.* TEL: 62456.

J. and F. Turbibilles
57 Icen Way. (I.G. Jeans.) Open 9—5. *STOCK: Mainly stripped pine, general antiques.* TEL: 63659.

FERNDOWN,   (0202)
Nr. Wimborne

Old Chapel Antiques and Collectors Centre
552 Wimborne Road East. (L. Fowler and Y. Warner.) Est. 1980. Open 10—4. SIZE: Medium. There are several dealers at this centre selling *a wide range of general antiques including china, linen, brass and copper, pine and other furniture, dolls, mainly 18th—20th C, £5—£400.* LOC: A31 north of Bournemouth at junction with Victoria Rd. PARK: Easy and Queens Rd. TEL: 873422; home — 875167 and 873391. FAIRS: Forest.

GILLINGHAM   (074 76)

Shaftesbury Antiques
Staddleston Hall. (D.M. Hetreed.) Open by appointment. *STOCK: 19th C English and Continental drawings and paintings; fruitwood furniture, objets d'art and European porcelain.* TEL: East Stour (074 785) 363.

Talisman Antiques   LAPADA
The Old Brewery, Wyke. Open 9—6, Sat. 10—4. SIZE: Large. *STOCK: Unusual and decorative items, garden furniture, architectural fittings, 18th—19th C; English and Continental furniture.* TEL: 4423. VAT: Stan/Spec.

HIGHCLIFFE (042 52)
Nr. Christchurch
The Brass Cannon
389 Lymington Rd. (B.G. Greene.) Est. 1969. Open 9—5.30, Wed. 9—12.30. SIZE: Small. *STOCK: Jewellery, paintings, china.* TEL: 5050. VAT: Stan.

D.M. Jewellers Ltd.
251 Lymington Rd. Open 10—5.30. *STOCK: Silver and plate, jewellery.* VAT: Stan.

W.S. Judd
420 Lymington Rd. Est. 1964. CL: Wed. TEL: 5601. VAT: Stan.

M.R. Simpson Antiques
Chewton House, Chewton Farm Rd. Est. 1964. Open by telephone appointment only. *STOCK: English furniture, barometers, tea caddies.* TEL: 77105.

LITTON CHENEY, Nr. Dorchester
Coombe Farm Antiques
(A.N.W. and Mrs. E.M. Percival.) Est. 1960. Open 9—5, weekends and evenings by appointment. *STOCK: 18th—20th C furniture, especially four poster and other beds.* LOC: A35. PARK: In own grounds. TEL: Long Bredy (03083) 248.

LYTCHETT MINSTER (0202)
The Old Button Shop
(T. Johns.) Est. 1970. CL: Mon. Open 2—5, Sat. 11—1. *STOCK: Small antiques, brass, copper, curios, unusual items, and antique Dorset buttons.* TEL: 622169.

MAIDEN NEWTON (0300)
Country Antiques
Dorchester Rd. (Mrs. J. Curtis.) Est. 1975. Open 10—1 and 2—5; Wed., Sun. and other times by appointment. SIZE: Small. *STOCK: General antiques, to 1930s, £5—£100+.* LOC: Dorchester/Crewkerne road. PARK: Easy. TEL: Home — 20881. SER: Repairs.

MARNHULL, (0258)
Nr. Sturminster Newton
Dial House Antiques
Burton St. (Mrs. B. Hart.) Resident. Est. 1974. CL: Sun., Sat. p.m. and Wed. p.m. except by appointment. Open 10—1 and 2—5. SIZE: Small. *STOCK: Small furniture, £50—£1,000; pottery and porcelain, £10—£200; pictures and decorative items, £20—£500; all 17th—19th C.* Not stocked: Coins, medals, weapons. LOC: Next to the Post Office. PARK: Easy. TEL: 820261. TEL: Valuations. VAT: Spec.

MORCOMBELAKE, Nr. Bridport
Little Bric-a-Brac Shop
The Green. (I. Caddy.) Est. 1973. *STOCK: Small furniture, pottery and porcelain, brass and copper, collectors' items.* LOC: A35. TEL: Chideock (0297) 89346.

PARKSTONE (0202)
Nr. Poole
Antiques by Nikki
123a Commercial Rd., Lower Parkstone. (M.N. Medd.) CL: Wed. p.m. Open 10—5 or by appointment. *STOCK: Decorators' objects, pine, country, decorative furniture and porcelain.* TEL: 740939.

D.J. Burgess
116a Ashley Rd. CL: Wed. Open 9—5.30. *STOCK: Clocks, watches, jewellery, some furniture.* TEL: 730542. SER: Restorations (clocks); repairs (clocks).

D.J. Jewellery
166—168 Ashley Rd. (D.J.O'Sullivan.) NAG. Est. 1978. CL: Wed. p.m. Open 9—6. SIZE: Medium. *STOCK: Jewellery, £5—£1,000; small silver, £5—£500; plate, glass and porcelain, £5—£200.* Not stocked: Furniture. PARK: Easy. TEL: 745148. SER: Valuations; restorations (jewellery); buys at auction (jewellery). VAT: Stan.

F.G. Pearce
119 Parkstone Rd. TEL: 743881.

Wiffen's Antiques
97/101 Bournemouth Rd. (C.A. Wiffen.) Est. 1960. Open 9—5.30. SIZE: Large. *STOCK: Furniture, including shipping, porcelain, pictures, silver, plate, clocks, brass and copper, jewellery, bric-a-brac, pre-1950, from £5.* PARK: At rear. TEL: 736567. SER: Valuations; restorations.

POOLE (0202)
Arndale Antiques
99 Arndale Centre. (Mrs. J.M. Anstey.) Est. 1974. Open 9—5. SIZE: Small. *STOCK: Rings, jewellery, porcelain, china, Victorian; silver, small items, £5—£1,000.* Not stocked: Furniture. LOC: Town centre. PARK: Multi-storey. TEL: 677398. SER: Valuations. VAT: Stan.

The Bournemouth Gallery Ltd.
37 Haven Rd., Canford Cliffs. Open 9.30—5.30. *STOCK: Oil paintings and watercolours, 19th C.* TEL: 707628.

Butterchurn Antiques
48 High St. (G.A.J. Hoad and S.M. Wiggs.) Est. 1982. CL: Mon. Open 9.30—5. SIZE: Medium. *STOCK: General antiques and collectables; Victorian and Edwardian furniture.* PARK: Easy. TEL: 670910.

Poole continued
Sheradon Craft Workshop
31/37 Hill St. (W.J. Lovell.) Est. 1977. Open
9—5. SIZE: Large. *STOCK: Furniture,
18th—19th C, from £50.* TEL: 682252. SER:
Restorations (wood); polishing; upholstery;
buys at auction (furniture). VAT: Stan/Spec.

PUDDLETOWN
(3 & 4 fig. nos.) (030 584)
(6 fig. no.) (0305)
Antique Map and Bookshop
32 High St. (C.D. and H.M. Proctor.) Open
9—1 and 2—5. *STOCK: Antiquarian and
secondhand books, maps, prints and engravings.* TEL: 633. SER: Postal.

SHAFTESBURY   (0747)
The Book in Hand
17 Bell St. CL: Wed. *STOCK: Antiquarian, first
editions and general books.*

G.E. Johnson and Son
(Shaftesbury) Ltd.
41-45 High St. Est. 1855. Open 9—5, Wed.
9—1. *STOCK: Furniture.* TEL: 2113.

Sue Ryder
Angel Lane. (S. Ryder Foundation.) Est. 1970.
CL: Wed. p.m. Open 10—1 and 2—5.
STOCK: General small antiques, silver, china.
TEL: Home — Donhead (074 788) 373. VAT:
Stan.

SHERBORNE   (0935)
Antique Market
Digby Hall. Est. 1976. Open one Thurs. each
month (dates in local press). There are 40+
dealers at this market selling a wide range of
general antiques, bygones and collectables.
TEL: (0258) 840224.

Jasper Burton Antiques
23 Cheap St. Est. 1964. CL: Wed. Open 9—1
and 2—5. SIZE: Medium. *STOCK: General
antiques, especially furniture.* PARK: Easy.
TEL: 814434; home — 812322. VAT: Stan/
Spec.

Castleton Country Furniture
Long St. (D. Hamilton.) Open 9—5.30. Sun.
by appointment. *STOCK: Pine.* TEL: 812195.

Country Pine and Antiques
3 The Green. (S. Dodge.) Open 9—5.30.
SIZE: Medium. *STOCK: Finished pine.* LOC:
Off A30, 1st shop on left hand side. PARK:
Easy. TEL: 815216.

Sherborne continued
Dodge and Son
28-33 Cheap St. (S. Dodge.) Open 9—5.30.
SIZE: Large. *STOCK: Period furniture, clocks,
oils, maps, watercolours, silver, porcelain,
ironwork, statuary, fire accessories including
pine mantels.* PARK: At rear. TEL: 815151.
VAT: Stan/Spec.

Greystoke Antiques
Swan Yard, Off Cheap St. (F.L. and N.E.
Butcher.) Est. 1970. Open 9.15—5. *STOCK:
Silver, from Georgian; 18th—19th C pottery
and porcelain, especially blue transfer ware;
furniture and general antiques.* LOC: Off main
street. PARK: Car park adjacent to Swan Yard,
or outside shop. TEL: 812833. VAT: Stan/
Spec.

Johnsons of Sherborne Ltd.
South St. (N.R. and J.J. Johnson.) Est. 1920.
Sun. and Wed. p.m. by appointment. Open
8—1 and 2—5. SIZE: Large. *STOCK: Furniture, 18th to mid-19th C; mahogany and
satinwood furniture, late 19th C; art nouveau.*
LOC: From the west on A30 turn right at
centre of Sherborne. PARK: Easy. TEL:
812585. SER: Valuations; restorations (furniture, also upholstery). VAT: Stan/Spec.

Moira Lord
Open by appointment. *STOCK: Pottery and
porcelain, 18th—19th C.* LOC: Town centre.
TEL: 814874.

Mattar Arcade Antique Centre
17 Newlands. (S. and M. Mattar.) Est. 1965.
CL: Wed. p.m. Open 9.30—5.30. SIZE: 12
shops. *STOCK: Paintings, china, silver,
furniture, carpets, silks, clocks, pewter.* LOC:
From A30 enter the town via Greenhill. PARK:
100yds. TEL: 813464.

The Nook
South St. (H.B. and B.C. Bruton.) *STOCK:
General antiques — furniture, china, glass,
brass and copper.* TEL: 813987. VAT: Stan/
Spec.

Old Mermaid Antiques
South St. (B.A. and G. Banks.) Est. 1963.
Open 9—1 and 2—5. SIZE: Medium. *STOCK:
Furniture, £25—£2,500; longcase, wall and
bracket clocks, £50—£3,000; small items,
£5—£200, mainly 18th—19th C.* LOC: Off
Cheap St. towards station. PARK: Easy. TEL:
815487. SER: Valuations; restorations
(cabinet making, polishing and clock movements); buys at auction (clocks and furniture).
VAT: Stan/Spec.

Sherborne Antiques Ltd.
At the China Gallery, Long St. (E. Roxburgh.)
Est. 1960. Open 9—5.30. SIZE: Small.
STOCK: 17th—19th C furniture and clocks.
TEL: 812978.

SHILLINGSTONE

Ivy House Antiques
The Cross. (A.H.C. and D.C. Juett.) Est. 1972. Open 9.30−5.30, or by appointment. SIZE: Medium. *STOCK: Furniture, from 17th C, £10−£1,000; porcelain, from George III, £10−£200; silver, from George I, £10−£500; china, glass, jewellery, copper, brass, pictures.* Not stocked: Weapons, medals, coins. LOC: A357. PARK: Easy. TEL: Child Okeford (0258) 860278. VAT: Stan/Spec.

STURMINSTER NEWTON (0258)

Quarter Jack Antiques
The Quarter Jack, Bridge St. (H.C. and Mrs. A.B. Neilson.) Resident. Est. 1969. CL: Wed. p.m. Open 9.30−5.30. SIZE: Small. *STOCK: 18th C drinking glasses, decanters and other glass, 18th−19th C, all £5−£400; furniture, 18th−19th C, £40−£700; walking sticks, £2−£60; early English porcelain, copper, brass.* TEL: 72558; home − same.

Frank P. Stonelake. 'The hunting gent, Captain Smart', from a hand tinted lithograph, 5¼ins. x 6½ins. From **The Dictionary of British Equestrian Artists** by Sally Mitchell, published by the **Antique Collectors' Club,** 1985.

Sturminster Newton continued

Toll House
Trade Only

Bagber Lane. (R.E. and L.J. Maskell, B.A. Neal.) Est. 1973. Open by appointment only. SIZE: Warehouse. *STOCK: Furniture, 19th−20th C, £50−£200; scientific instruments, 19th C, £100−£300; general antiques and bric-a-brac, £5−£50.* PARK: Easy. TEL: 72296 or Bournemouth (0202) 763324. SER: Buys at auction (as stock). VAT: Stan/Spec.

Tom Tribe and Son
Bridge St. CMBHI. Resident. Usually open 9−5, Sat. 9−1, but appointment advisable. *STOCK: Longcase clocks.* PARK: At side of shop. TEL: 72311. VAT: Stan/Spec.

SWANAGE (0929)

Bishop's of Swanage
31 Station Rd. and 2 Springfield Rd. (G.W. and N.S. Bishop.) Est. 1950. CL: Thurs. p.m. *STOCK: General antiques, mainly furniture.* TEL: 423245. SER: Buys at auction. VAT: Stan/Spec.

Georgian Gems
28 High St. (B. Barker.) Est. 1971. Open 9.30−1 and 2.30−5 or by appointment. SIZE: Small. *STOCK: Jewellery, £5−£1,500; silver, £5−£500; both from 1700.* LOC: Town centre. PARK: Nearby. TEL: 424697. SER: Valuations; repairs (jewellery); gem testing.

CAPTAIN·SMART

Swanage continued

Barry Lamb
12 Commercial Rd. Open by appointment. SIZE: Small. *STOCK: English porcelain, 19th C, £20—£500; reference books on ceramics, £10—£200.* PARK: Nearby at station. TEL: 424423. SER: Valuations; catalogue available. FAIRS: Wakefield Ceramic; Silhouette.

The Old Forge
273a High St. (D. and J. Ferraris.) Est. 1967. CL: Wed. Open 10—1 and 2.30—5. SIZE: Small. *STOCK: General antiques especially stamps, coins and militaria.* LOC: From town centre just over ½ mile up the High St. PARK: Easy. TEL: 423319.

TRENT, Nr. Sherborne
Old Barn Antiques Co.
Flamberts. (G.W. Mott and T.E. Haines.) Resident. Est. 1959. Open 9—1 and 2—5, appointment advisable. SIZE: Medium. *STOCK: Furniture, 18th—19th C, £300—£3,000.* PARK: Easy. TEL: Sherborne (0935) 850648. SER: Valuations; restorations; upholstery; polishing; buys at auction (furniture). VAT: Spec.

WAREHAM   (092 95)
Eve's Casket
South St. (L.J. and S. Bawden.) Resident. Est. 1968. CL: Wed. Open 9.30—5. SIZE: Medium. *STOCK: Furniture, silver and porcelain, 19th C, £5—£1,000.* PARK: Opposite. TEL: 2810. SER: Buys at auction.

Long Hall Antiques and Design
Long Hall, North St. (J. Brooks-Rex and A. Brooks-Court.) Resident. Est. 1974. Open 10—1 and 2.15—5.30, Mon. and Wed. by appointment. SIZE: Small. *STOCK: Small Victorian and Edwardian furniture, French country bronzes, silver, plate, china, glass, gardenalia, 19th C, art nouveau, art deco, £5—£500.* PARK: Limited and nearby. TEL: 6778 or 51651. SER: Valuations; restorations (metal and ceramics).

Judy Wallington — Antiques
28 South St. Est. 1979. CL: Mon and Wed. except by appointment. Open 10—1 and 2.30—5. SIZE: Medium. *STOCK: Porcelain and pottery, 18th C to art deco, £25—£500; silver and glass, mainly 19th C, £5—£300; jewellery, 19th—20th C, £10—£300.* PARK: Easy and nearby. TEL: 2662; home — 2537. SER: Valuations.

WEST STOUR
Chantry Galleries
The Triangle. (Mrs. V. Wellsthorpe). Open by appointment. *STOCK: Isnik objets, Oriental rugs, textiles, Chinese porcelain.* TEL: East Stour (074 785) 363. SER: Buys at auction.

WEYMOUTH   (0305)
Books Afloat
66 Park St. (J. Ritchie). CL: Mon. Open 9.30—5.30. *STOCK: Rare and secondhand books especially nautical; maritime ephemera, ship models, painting, prints.* LOC: Near railway station. PARK: Nearby. TEL: 779774.

Hunter Antiques
29 Park St. (Mrs. Hunter.) Est. 1966. CL: Wed. p.m. in winter only. Open 10—5.30. *STOCK: Bric-a-brac, Victoriana, small furniture, dolls.* TEL: 774281.

Mad Hatter
11 Trinity St. (L. Drake.) Open 9.30—6. *STOCK: Period clothes, jewellery, bric-a-brac.* TEL: 782819.

Park Antiquities
Park St. (F. and Mrs. J. Ballard.) *STOCK: General antiques, porcelain, small furniture, needlework tools, treen.* LOC: Near Jubilee clock. PARK: Nearby. TEL: 787666.

J.T. and C. Pitman
20 Crescent St. Open 9—5.30. TEL: 783061. VAT: Stan.

The Treasure Chest
29 East St. (P. S. Barrett.) CL: Wed p.m. Open 10—5. SIZE: Small. *STOCK: Maps, prints, general antiques, coins, medals, silver, china.* PARK: Next door. TEL: 772757.

WIMBORNE MINSTER
Antiquatat Antiques   LAPADA
The Old Civic Centre, Hanham Rd. (D.W. Schwier.) Est. 1973. Open 9.—4.30. SIZE: Large. *STOCK: Period furniture, silver, porcelain, clocks, containers.* PARK: Own. TEL: Wimborne (0202) 887496.

IS YOUR ENTRY CORRECT?
If there is even the slightest inaccuracy in your entry, *please* let us know before 1st January 1987.
GUIDE TO THE
ANTIQUE SHOPS OF BRITAIN
5 Church Street, Woodbridge, Suffolk.

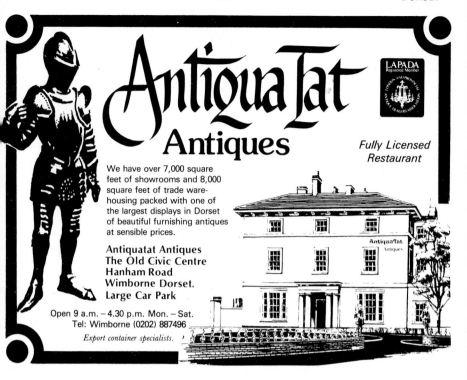
Wimborne Minster continued

Barnes House Antiques Centre

West Row. (A.W. Johnston and 6 dealers.) CL: Wed. Open 10–5. SIZE: Large. *STOCK: Porcelain 18th–20th C; glass, 19th–20th C; furniture, late Georgian–Edwardian; books, antiquarian, secondhand and first editions; scent bottles, boxes, papier mâché, pictures, prints, silver and plate, furnishing items, to 1930.* LOC: Between West. St. and Cornmarket. PARK: Nearby. TEL: Wimborne (0202) 886275.

'Granny's Treasures'

11 West Row. There are several dealers here selling *small and interesting items, curios, bric-a-brac, small furniture, copper, brass, linen, prints and pictures.*

Metcalfe Jackson

Trumpeters, 25 West St. (B.M. Jackson.) Est. 1962. *STOCK: Early English furniture, Oriental rugs, Chinese ceramics, old master drawings.* TEL: Wimborne (0202) 883327.

Wimborne Minster continued

Minster Antiques

12 Corn Market. (A.A. Mason.) Est. 1974. Open 10–5.30. Open Sun. April–October only. SIZE: Large. *STOCK: Porcelain, china, glass, 18th–19th C, £1–£100; furniture, 18th to early 20th C, £5–£500; brass, copper, collectors' items, 18th–20th C, £1–£100.* LOC: 100yds. from main High St., at side of Minster church. PARK: Easy. TEL: Wimborne (0202) 883355. SER: Valuations; restorations; wood repairs and upholstery.

Victoriana

3 Leigh Rd. (Mrs. P. Hammer.) CL: Mon., Wed. and Sat. Open 10–4. *STOCK: General small antiques, glass, jewellery, silver, brass, objets d'art.* PARK: Easy. TEL: Wimborne (0202) 886739.

Wimborne Antiques

46 High St. (J.F. Mason.) Est. 1975. Open 10–1 and 1.30–5, Sun. by appointment. SIZE: Medium. *STOCK: Furniture including pine; paintings, glass, jewellery, china, prints, £5–£500.* LOC: Near Minster church. PARK: Easy. TEL: Wimborne (0202) 887863. SER: Valuations; restorations (furniture); upholstery and polishing.

Durham

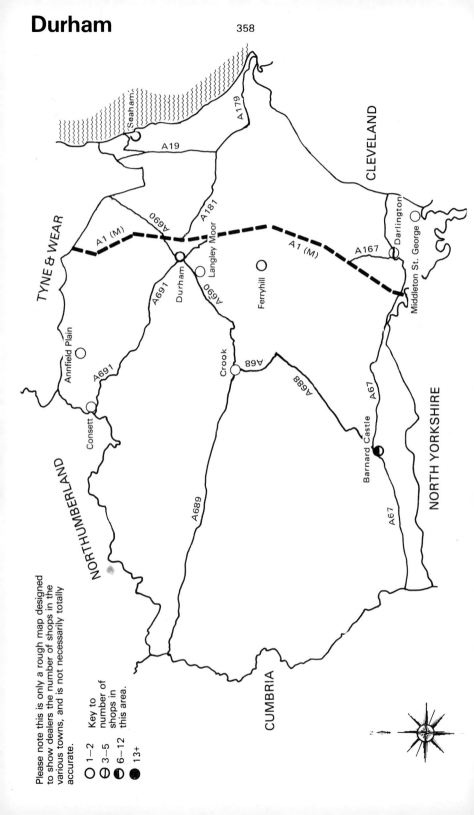

Please note this is only a rough map designed to show dealers the number of shops in the various towns, and is not necessarily totally accurate.

Key to number of shops in this area.

○ 1–2
◐ 3–5
◑ 6–12
● 13+

TYNE & WEAR

CLEVELAND

NORTHUMBERLAND

NORTH YORKSHIRE

CUMBRIA

Seaham

A19

A179

A181

A690

A1 (M)

A691

Durham

Langley Moor

A690

Ferryhill

A1 (M)

A167

Darlington

Middleton St. George

Anfield Plain

A691

Consett

Crook

A68

A688

Barnard Castle

A67

A689

A67

ANNFIELD PLAIN
Nr. Stanley
Emporium of Art and Age ✓
10 West Rd. (Mrs. P.W. Halloway.) Est. 1978. Open Wed.—Fri. 10—5.45, or by appointment. SIZE: Small. *STOCK: Small unusual items, china, glass, silver, books and pictures.* PARK: Easy, opposite. TEL: Stanley (0207) 239808; home — Durham (0385) 63150. SER: Buys at auction. FAIRS: Three Tuns Hotel, Durham and Guildhall, Newcastle-upon-Tyne.

BARNARD CASTLE
The Collector
Douglas House, The Bank. (R.A. Jordan.) Est. 1970. Open Wed. and Sat. or by appointment. *STOCK: Small collectable items, including postcards, prints, watercolours, oils, books, photographs and bottles (cellar); period and Victorian furniture.* TEL: Teesdale (0833) 37783. SER: Restorations (furniture, brass, copper, steel, watercolours, oils and pottery); interior design.

Barnard Castle continued

Gibberd and Grant Antiques
40 The Bank. (M. Gibberd and S.A. Grant.) Resident. Est. 1978. Open 10—6, Sun. by appointment. SIZE: Medium. *STOCK: Period and Victorian furniture, paintings and prints, decorative items.* Not stocked: Coins, medals and bottles. LOC: A67. PARK: Easy. TEL: Teesdale (0833) 37437.

Stephanie Grant Antiques
38 The Bank. Est. 1977. CL: Sun. and Thurs. Nov—Mar. Open every day 10—5 April—Oct. or by appointment. SIZE: Small. *STOCK: General antiques, paintings and prints, to £600; furniture — mahogany, pine and country, copper, brass, cast-iron, pottery.* LOC: A67. PARK: Easy. TEL: Teesdale (0833) 37437.

Horse Market Antiques
27 Horse Market. (P. and P.K. Robson.) Est. 1973. Open 9.30—5.30 or by appointment. SIZE: Large. *STOCK: Pine and country furniture, fireplaces and fittings, collectors' and unusual items.* LOC: Main shopping area. PARK: Nearby. TEL: Teesdale (0833) 37881; home — Bishop Auckland (0388) 528451. VAT: Stan/Spec.

Two rare small mugs painted in underglaze blue, in the early style, 2⅜ins. high. Painter's number '7' on inside of footrim, c.1758-9. From *Lowestoft Porcelains* by Geoffrey A. Godden, F.R.S.A., published by the **Antique Collectors' Club**, 1985.

Barnard Castle continued

The Mudlark (Collectors Shop)
11 Galgate. (E.W. and Mrs. V. Seaton.) Resident. Est. 1977. CL: Sun. except in holiday season. Open 10—5. SIZE: Small. *STOCK: Roman, Greek, Cypriot and Egyptian items in bronze, terra-cotta and glass; ancient jewellery; curios, coins, fossils, minerals, bottles, pot lids, dolls and collectable items.* LOC: A67 main street. PARK: Easy. TEL: Teesdale (0833) 37859.

Newgate Curios
12 Newgate. (E. Sidaway.) Est. 1975. Open 11—5, Wed., Fri. and Sat., or by appointment. SIZE: Small. *STOCK: Furniture, silver and jewellery, china and glass.* LOC: 30yds. Market Cross towards Bowes Museum. PARK: Easy. TEL: Home — Teesdale (0833) 38163.

CONSETT (0207)
Harry Raine Antiques
Kelvinside House, Villa Real Rd. Appointment advisable. SIZE: Large. *STOCK: General antiques.* TEL: 503935.

CROOK
Jo Patterson Antiques *Trade Only*
12a Prospect Rd. Industrial Estate. (J.W.B. Patterson.) Est. 1968. CL: Sat. Open 9—4.30. SIZE: Large. *STOCK: Shipping goods, 19th—20th C.* LOC: 4 miles from A68. PARK: Easy. TEL: Bishop Auckland (0388) 763696; home — Bishop Auckland (0388) 746586. SER: Valuations; restorations; container packing. VAT: Stan.

DARLINGTON (0325)
Judy Brown Antiques
181 Grange Rd. (Mrs. J.A. Brown.) Est. 1982. Open 10—4, Sun., Tues. and Wed. by appointment. SIZE: Medium. *STOCK: Furniture, Georgian and Victorian, £50—£1,500; Georgian silver.* LOC: Mid-way between Blackwell Grange Moat Hotel and town centre on A66 from Scotch Corner into town. PARK: Easy. TEL: 484000; home — 720684. SER: Restorations (furniture and paintings); buys at auction (furniture). VAT: Stan/Spec.

S. Brown and Sons
'The Popular Mart'
26 Hollyhurst Rd. Est. 1976. CL: Wed. p.m. and Sat. p.m., except by appointment. Open 9.30—12 and 1—5.30, Wed. until 1 and Sat. until 2. SIZE: Large. *STOCK: General antiques, from late 19th C, £5—£500.* LOC: From town centre, along Woodlands Rd. to Hollyhurst Rd., shop adjacent to Memorial Hospital. PARK: Easy. TEL: 54769; home — 55490. SER: Valuations; buys at auction.

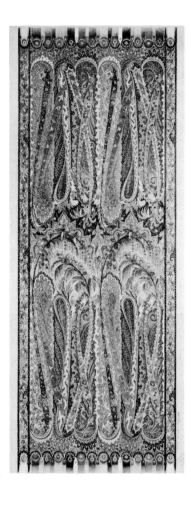

Shawl painting shown at the Universal Exhibition of 1851 by Berrus. From *The Kashmir Shawl* by Frank Ames, published by the **Antique Collectors' Club,** 1986.

Darlington continued
Nichol and Hill
9 Grange Rd. (D. Brown.) CL: Wed. Open 10—5. SIZE: Medium. *STOCK: Furniture, £30—£800; porcelain, £5—£200; silver, £10—£200.* LOC: Opposite Imperial Hotel. PARK: Easy. TEL: 464479. SER: Restorations; upholstery.

Ronald Richardson
28 Post House Wynd. Est. 1852. CL: Wed. Open 9—5. SIZE: Medium. *STOCK: Jewellery, 19th C; silver, Sheffield plate, clocks and barometers, 18th—19th C.* Not stocked: Furniture. LOC: One-way street leading into middle of High Row, opposite town clock. PARK: 200yds. in side streets. TEL: 464860. SER: Valuations; restorations (silver plate, clocks,   jewellery).   VAT: Stan/ Spec.

Stella Rutherford Ltd.
14 Coniscliffe Rd. (Mrs. J. Davidson.) Est. 1959. CL: Wed. Open 10—4. SIZE: Medium. *STOCK: Furniture, £50—£500; silver, jewellery, china, glass, £5—£200.* LOC: A167. From south leave motorway at first Darlington exit. Follow one-way system into Coniscliffe Rd. PARK: 30yds. opposite. TEL: 468934. SER: Valuations. VAT: Spec.

DURHAM   (5 & 6 fig. nos.) (0385)
(7 fig. nos.) (091)
Bridge Antiques
93 Elvet Bridge. (R.A. and M.V. Graham.) Est. 1972. CL: Wed. Open 9.30—5. SIZE: Medium. *STOCK: Musical instruments and general antiques.* LOC: North on A177 turn left at traffic lights, near County Hotel. PARK: Municipal nearby. TEL: 45530. SER: Valuations; restorations; buys at auction. VAT: Stan.

J. Shotton
Antiquarian Books and Prints
89 Elvet Bridge. Est. 1967. Open 9—5, Sat. 9.30—5. *STOCK: Antiquarian books, prints, maps and paintings.* TEL: 64597.

FERRYHILL   (0740)
Robin Shield Antiques
Great Chilton Farm. (W.R. and P.E. Shield.) Est. 1974. Usually open, appointment advisable. SIZE: Large. *STOCK: Furniture, £200—£2,000; works of art, £50—£1,000; paintings, £200—£1,500; all 17th—19th C.* LOC: A689 between Chilton and Chilton Lane. PARK: Easy. TEL: Bishop Auckland (0388) 720237; home — same. SER: Valuations; buys at auction. VAT: Stan/Spec.

LANGLEY MOOR, Nr. Durham
Durham Furniture
12 High St. South. (H. and K. Nelson.) Est. 1977. Open by appointment Tues.—Fri., Sat. 10—5. SIZE: Small. *STOCK: Furniture and antiques, 18th C, £500—£1,000.* LOC: A1 traffic lights, at Neville's Cross near Durham travelling north, turn left, shop 2 miles further on through railway bridge. PARK: Easy. TEL: Durham (0385) 781808; home — Durham (0385) 44191. SER: Valuations; restorations (furniture, boulle and marquetry).

MIDDLETON ST. GEORGE
Nr. Darlington
Carousel Antiques
The Red House, Church Lane. (J. and R. Winram.) Est. 1968. SIZE: Medium. *STOCK: Furniture and general antiques, 18th—19th C, £5—£1,000; porcelain, 19th C, £5—£200.* TEL: Darlington (0325) 332093. SER: Valuations; buys at auction. FAIRS: Most 3 day fairs in major cities.

SEAHAM   (0783)
Lynden Antiques
East Farm, Dalton-le-Dale. (D. Liddell). Resident, usually available. SIZE: Warehouse. *STOCK: General antiques — shipping goods, furniture including pine and desks, some architectural items.* TEL: 816321.

Past and Present
13 Lord St. (E. Patrickson.) Est. 1969. *STOCK: General antiques, books.* TEL: 813888. VAT: Stan.

IS YOUR ENTRY CORRECT?
If there is even the slightest inaccuracy in your entry, *please* let us know before 1st January 1987.
GUIDE TO THE
ANTIQUE SHOPS OF BRITAIN
5 Church Street, Woodbridge, Suffolk.

Essex

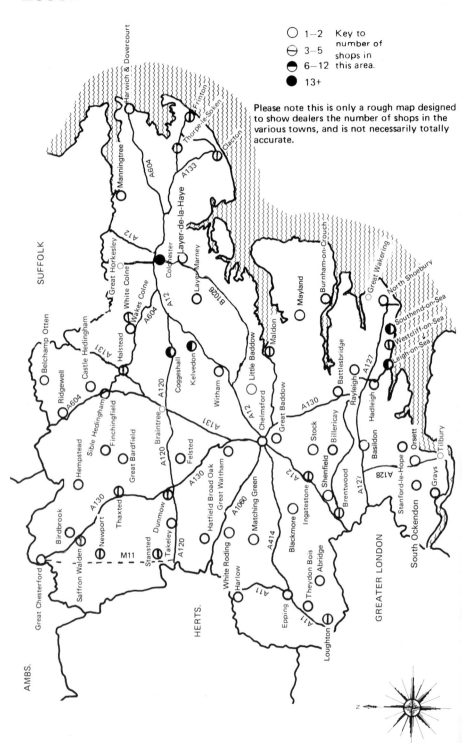

Key to number of shops in this area.
- ○ 1—2
- ⊖ 3—5
- ◓ 6—12
- ● 13+

Please note this is only a rough map designed to show dealers the number of shops in the various towns, and is not necessarily totally accurate.

Essex

ABRIDGE

Abridge Antique Centre
Market Place. (J.S. and F.M. Yewman.) Est. 1960. Open 10—5, Thurs. 10—1. SIZE: Large, nine small shops. STOCK: Clocks, £50—£3,500; furniture, £50—£1,000; both 18th—19th C; small items, china, and porcelain including Doulton, silver, 19th—20th C, £5—£500. LOC: Chigwell—Ongar road opposite The Rodings Restaurant. PARK: Market Sq. TEL: Theydon Bois (037 881) 3113/2107. FAIRS: Local. VAT: Stan/Spec.

BASILDON   (0268)

Bishops Antiques
100 Town Sq. Open 8.30—5.30, Fri. 8.30—6, Sat. 8.30—5.45. STOCK: Jewellery. TEL: 21853.

Victor Hall Antiques
The Old Dairy, Cranes Farm Rd. Est. 1970. Open 9.30—6, Sun. 10—4. SIZE: Large. STOCK: General antiques. LOC: 2 minutes from A127, 10 minutes from M25. PARK: Easy. TEL: 289545/6. VAT: Stan.

BATTLESBRIDGE

Battlesbridge Antique Centre
Some forty dealers with units located in the adjacent premises of Haybarn, Cromwell House, Bridgebarn, the Old Granary and trade warehouse. There are large car parks, furniture restoration workshops and facilities for containers. LOC: A130, mid-way between Chelmsford and Southend. STOCK: Wide range, from large furniture to jewellery with specialist dealers for most items, all periods.
Cromwell House Antique Centre
(F. Gallie.) TEL: Wickford (037 44) 4005. (Office). Ground Floor Dealers — TEL: Wickford (037 44) 62612. First Floor Dealers — TEL: Wickford (037 44) 4030.
Haybarn and Bridgebarn Antique Centres
LAPADA
(J.P. Pettitt.) TEL: Wickford (037 44) 63500/5884.
The Old Granary Antique and Craft Centre
(J.F. Gallie.) Office. TEL: Wickford (037 44) 63344.
Muggeridge Farm Warehouse

BELCHAMP OTTEN, Nr. Sudbury

Leo S. Olschki
Gridleys. ABA. Open by appointment. SIZE: Large. STOCK: Books, mainly Continental 16th—18th C on art, architecture, science, theology and classics. LOC: Sudbury A131 turn right at King's Head public house, right again at Finch Hill, follow signs to Belchamp Otten. PARK: Easy. TEL: Sudbury (0787) 277341; home — same. FAIRS: ABA London.

BILLERICAY
(4 and 5 fig. no.) (027 74)
(6 fig. no.) (0277)
Sheredays Antiques Centre
22 High St. Est. 1970. There are 9 dealers at this centre offering a wide range of general antiques. CL: Thurs. Open 10—4.30. SIZE: Large. TEL: 22323 and 4356. PARK: Easy. Below are listed the dealers at this centre:
Charley Farleys
General antiques and bric-a-brac.
Classic Art
Oleographs, furniture.
Joan Davidson
18th-19th C porcelain, pottery and furniture, small silver, jewellery and collectors' items.
Dress The Part
Costumes, accessories. TEL: 57328. SER: Fancy dress hire.
Sally Grater
General antiques; 18th—19th C furniture, jewellery, silver; porcelain, pottery and glass. SER: Repairs (clocks).
H. and I. Jones
Jewellery, furniture, silver, porcelain, collectors' items. TEL: Home — Southend (0702) 525672. SER: Jewellery repaired, altered and made-to-order.
The Music Centre
Instruments, classical records, jazz, spoken word films. TEL: 56196.
Young Antiques
Stripped furniture, general antiques. TEL: 4341.

BIRDBROOK

I. Westrope
The Elms. Est. 1958. Open 9—6, Sat. 9—12 or by appointment. STOCK: Furniture, bric-a-brac, china, dolls, pine, garden ornaments. LOC: On A604. TEL: Ridgewell (044 085) 365; evenings — Ridgewell (044 085) 426.

BLACKMORE   (0277)
Nr. Ingatestone

Kate Davie
Haygreen Farm. Open Sat. and Sun. 10—5 or by appointment. STOCK: Victorian upholstered furniture and period pine. TEL: 821275.

BRAINTREE   (0376)

Eric Hudes   Postal only
LAPADA
Paigles, Perry Green, Bradwell. Est. 1946. STOCK: Oriental ceramics, 900 AD to 1830; early English pottery, 1720—1830; objets d'art; all £50—£1,000. TEL: Silver End (0376) 83767. SER: Restorations (pottery and porcelain); buys at auction; postal transactions. FAIRS: Buxton, Ilkley, Harrogate. VAT: Mainly Spec.

LOUIS LIPMAN
Antiques and Curios

33-35 Kings Road
Brentwood
0277-222380

OPEN EVERY DAY EXCEPT THURSDAYS
A good trade call

One or more chairs of this Sheraton pattern required for a set

BRENTWOOD (0277)

Brandler Galleries
1 Coptfold Rd. (J. Brandler). Resident. Est. 1973. CL: Mon. Open 10—5.30, Sun. by appointment. SIZE: Medium. *STOCK: British pictures, £25—£2,000; furniture, £35—£300, both 19th—20th C.* LOC: Near Post Office. PARK: Easy at rear. TEL: 222269. SER: Valuations (photographs); restorations (pictures — cleaning, relining, framing); buys at auction (pictures).

David Hollens Antiques
80-82 King's Rd. (D. Hollens and Mrs. P. Stanley.) Est. 1983. CL: Thurs. Open 9.30—5.30, Sun. by appointment. SIZE: Medium. *STOCK: English pottery, porcelain and glass, 1750—1880, £10—£300; oil paintings and watercolours, small furniture, caddies and boxes, 1800—1900, £25—£500.* Not stocked: Coins, medals and weapons. LOC: Near railway station. PARK: Opposite and 50 yards. TEL: 229365; home — same. SER: Valuations; restorations (furniture, clocks and ceramics).

Louis Lipman
33—35 King's Rd. Est. 1969. CL: Thurs. Open 9.30—5.30. SIZE: Medium. *STOCK: Victoriana, bric-a-brac, small decorative furniture, 19th C, £10—£100; oil paintings and watercolours, 18th—19th C, £10—£200; 19th C furniture, especially bookcases, secretaires, £100—£1,000.* LOC: 100yds. from High St. PARK: Easy. TEL: 222380. SER: Valuations; restorations (pictures). VAT: Stan/Spec.

BURES, See Suffolk

BURNHAM-ON-CROUCH

Past and Present
70 Station Rd. (Mrs. E. McKay.) Open 10—5. *STOCK: General antiques.* TEL: Maldon (0621) 782348.

Burnham-on-Crouch continued

Quay Antiques
1 Crouch Rd. (C. McMullan.) Est. 1961. CL: Wed. Open 10—5. *STOCK: Paintings, prints, china, glass, Victoriana, jewellery, small furniture.* TEL: Home — Maldon (0621) 782863.

CASTLE HEDINGHAM

Orbell House Gallery
Orbell House. (E. and I. Greene.) Resident. Est. 1968. CL: Mon. except by appointment. Open by appointment only. SIZE: Medium plus gallery. *STOCK: Oriental, Persian, Anatolian, Afghan and Caucasian rugs and carpets, £200—£4,000.* PARK: Easy. TEL: Hedingham (0787) 60298. SER: Valuations; repairing and cleaning (Oriental rugs). FAIRS: Castle Hedingham, Bury St. Edmunds and Snape. VAT: Stan/Spec.

CHELMSFORD (0245)

G. and J.E. Manfield
28 Broomfield Rd. (G.F. and J.E. Shiner.) Est. 1954. CL: Wed. Open 9.30—5.30. SIZE: Medium. *STOCK: Bric-a-brac, jewellery, books, Victoriana, £5—£250; clocks and pictures; furniture.* Not stocked: Coins and stamps. LOC: On A130. PARK: At rear. TEL: 57985.

CHIPPING ONGAR
See Ongar

CLACTON-ON-SEA (0255)

Patina Antiques
32a Frinton Rd. CL: Wed and Thurs. Open 9.30—4. *STOCK: General antiques and bric-a-brac.*

EDWARD & INKA GREENE
Old & Antique Oriental Rugs & Carpets

ORBELL HOUSE GALLERY
Castle Hedingham, Essex
Telephone: Hedingham 60298 (0787)

Clacton-on-Sea continued

Penny-farthing Antiques
75A Pennyfarthing Old Rd. (D.E. Johnson.) Est. 1966. Books and articles on guns, war medals, militaria. CL: Wed. Open 9—1 and 2—5.30. SIZE: Small. *STOCK: Weapons, militaria, 1790—1800, 25p—£150; coins, ancient and modern, 15p—£100; medals, ancient and modern, 50p—£500.* Not stocked: Furniture. LOC: From Colchester, turn left on A133 down Old Road for approx. ½ mile. Shop is on right opposite cinema. PARK: Easy. TEL: 424962. SER: Valuations.

Shaftesbury Antiques
78-80 High St. (R.W. and E.V. Dewar.) Est. 1977. CL: Wed. p.m. Open 9.30—1 and 2—5.30, Sun. by appointment. SIZE: Small. *STOCK: Militaria — edged weapons and accoutrements, reference books, 18th C to date, £3—£300; small furniture and interesting items, £5—£300; china, pottery and glass, £2—£40; all Victorian and later.* LOC: From A133 left toward town centre, left at Carnarvon Rd. roundabout, left at second lights into High St., premises 300yds. on right. PARK: Nearby. TEL: 428602; home — same.

COGGESHALL   (0376)
Antique Centre
Doubleday Corner. (S. Mabey.) Est. 1977. Open 10—5. SIZE: Medium. There are 12 dealers selling *pottery, porcelain, silver and plate, £10—£300; furniture, 19th—20th C, £20—£2,000; general antiques.* LOC: A120. PARK: At rear. TEL: 62646; home — (0245) 56027. SER: Valuations.

Antique Metals
12 East St. (R.M. and S.V. Chaplin.) Est. 1959. Open every day 9—6. *STOCK: Brass, copper, polished steel, especially fenders; brass beds.* TEL: 62252.

Coggeshall continued

Wilfred Bull
85 West St. Est. 1955. Open 9—1 and 2—6. SIZE: Large. *STOCK: English and Continental furniture, 18th C.* Not stocked: Victoriana, bric-a-brac. LOC: A120 from town centre towards Braintree. PARK: Easy. TEL: 61385. SER: Valuations; buys at auction. VAT: Spec.

Dolphyn
8 Market End. (T.H. and M.G. Disley.) GMC. Open 9.30—5.30; Sun. 11—4. *STOCK: General antiques especially mirrors.* TEL: 61608; workshop — 61661. SER: Restorations, cleaning and framing (pictures); gilding.

Findings
12 Stoneham St. (Mrs. R. Aylwin.) Est. 1973. CL: Wed. Open 10—1 and 2—5, Sun. by appointment. SIZE: Small. *STOCK: Small furniture, all periods, £25—£250; jewellery and silver, £5—£250; bric-a-brac.* LOC: Centre of village. PARK: Easy. TEL: 62351; home — 61537.

Joan Jobson's
6A East St. (J. Corder.) Est. 1974. Open 9.30—5; Sun. 2—5 in Summer. SIZE: Medium. *STOCK: Bric-a-brac, Victoriana, general antiques and shipping furniture.* TEL: Home — 61717.

Lindsell Chairs
11 Market Hill. (T.J.L. Martin.) Est. 1982. Open 10—6, Sun. 2—6. SIZE: Large. *STOCK: Chairs and other seating, mid-18th C to 1914, £30—£2,000+ for sets and suites.* Not stocked: Commode chairs, bergère suites. LOC: Town centre. PARK: Nearby. TEL: 62766; home — Great Easton (037 184) 222. VAT: Stan/Spec.

Lion Antiques

Proprietor: A. C. HOLLINGWORTH

10 Bridge Street, Coggeshall, Essex CO6 1NP
Telephone Coggeshall (0376) 61530

18th & 19th Century Furniture   **Silver and Porcelain**

Coggeshall continued

Lion Antiques   LAPADA
10 Bridge St. Est. 1973. Open 10—1 and 2—5. SIZE: Medium. *STOCK: Georgian and Regency furniture, porcelain, silver plate, paintings and prints.* PARK: Easy. TEL: 61530. VAT: Spec.

Mark Marchant Antiques   LAPADA
3 Market Sq. Est. 1960. Resident. Open 9.30—5, Sun. 2—5. SIZE: Large. *STOCK: Clocks and decorative works, 18th C; general furniture, decor furnishings, all periods.* LOC: A120. PARK: Easy. TEL: 61188. SER: Valuations; restorations; buys at auction. VAT: Spec.

John Smith Antiques
1 Church St. (J.P. Smith.) Est. 1973. Open 9.30—5. SIZE: Medium. *STOCK: Paintings, prints and miniatures, 19th—20th C, £5—£800; furniture, 18th—19th C, £30—£2,000; shipping items, £10—£200.* Not stocked: Coins, stamps. LOC: Town centre. PARK: Nearby. TEL: 62051; home — same. SER: Valuations; restorations (pictures); framing. VAT: Stan/Spec.

Wheelwright Antiques
63/65 West St. (W.T. Newton.) Resident. Open seven days 10—6. *STOCK: Pine, stripped furniture, general antiques.* TEL: 61972.

COLCHESTER   (0206)

Badger Antiques
The Old House, The Street, Elmstead Market. (A. Johnson). Resident. Est. 1977. Open 9.30—5.30, Sun. by appointment. SIZE: Medium. *STOCK: Furniture, lace, linen, Victorian underwear, clocks, china, glass.* LOC: 4 miles from Colchester on old A133 Clacton road. PARK: Easy. TEL: Wivenhoe (020 622) 2044. SER: Valuations; restorations (furniture and clocks).

Colchester continued

Barntiques
Lampitts Farm, Turkeycock Lane, Stanway. (A. Jones and S. Doubleday.) Resident. Est. 1978. Open second and fourth Sat. in each month and by appointment. SIZE: Medium. *STOCK: General antiques.* LOC: Turn left at Eight Ash Green from A604. PARK: Easy. TEL: 210486; home — 577031.

S. Bond and Son
14 North Hill. (M. and R. Bond.) CL: Thurs. p.m. Open 9—5.30. SIZE: Large. *STOCK: Furniture, oil paintings, watercolours.* TEL: 572925. SER: Restorations. VAT: Stan/Spec.

Breton Antiques
18 East Hill. (Mrs. Sandberg.) Est. 1971. CL: Thurs. Open 10—4.30. Sat. 9.30—1. SIZE: Medium. *STOCK: Tea bowls, 18th C, £5—£35; porcelain, 18th—19th C, under £5.* Not stocked: Firearms, knives. LOC: Past Colchester Castle and half-way down East Hill. PARK: Easy. TEL: 867711; home — 574723.

Elizabeth Cannon
85 Crouch St. Open 9.30—5.30. *STOCK: General antiques, jewellery, engravings, silver, glass, porcelain and some furniture.* PARK: Easy. TEL: 575817.

Castle Bookshop
37 North Hill. (A.B. Doncaster.) CL: Thurs. *STOCK: Antiquarian and secondhand books, maps and prints.* TEL: 577520. VAT: Stan.

MARGERY DEAN ANTIQUES
ESTABLISHED 1947

Large stock of 17th, 18th and early 19th century furniture. Also pine and country. Dealers especially welcome.

THE GALLERIES
ALMA STREET, WIVENHOE
NR. COLCHESTER

Telephone Wivenhoe 2523 and evenings Colchester 250485
12 Capacious showrooms

Colchester continued

The Coin and Stamp Centre
1st Floor, 13 Centurion House, St. John's St. (R.B. Field.) Est. 1968. CL: Thurs. Open 9−5. SIZE: Medium. *STOCK: Coins and stamps; medals, postcards, cigarette cards and accessories.* TEL: 41232. SER: Valuations.

Davana
88−97 Hythe Hill. (D.E. Donnelly.) Est. 1963. CL: Thurs. p.m. Open 9.30−1 and 2.30−5. SIZE: Small. *STOCK: Lighting items, Victorian, Edwardian, art nouveau and art deco, hand-stripped satin-walnut and pine furniture, brass, brass and iron beds, fireplace surrounds and all fittings, kitchen utensils, 1800-1930.* PARK: Easy. TEL: 66383. SER: Buys at auction (furniture).

Margery Dean Antiques   LAPADA
The Galleries, Wivenhoe. Book on English Antique Furniture. Est. 1947. Open 9−12.30 and 1.30−5; Sat. 10−12.30 and 2−5. SIZE: Large. *STOCK: Furniture, 17th−19th C; also country and pine.* Not stocked: Reproductions. LOC: From London turn off Clacton Rd., take 1st right by Essex University to Wivenhoe. Shop situated before church in side road on left. PARK: Easy. TEL: Wivenhoe (020 622) 2523; home − 250485. SER: Valuations. VAT: Spec.

John Drury
P.O. Box 77. Open by appointment. *STOCK: Antiquarian books.* TEL: Ramsey (0255) 886260.

Colchester continued

East Gates Antiques
91A East Hill. (J. Latford). Est. 1980. CL: Sun. and Mon. except by appointment. Open 10−6. SIZE: Small. *STOCK: China and glass, 19th to early 20th C, £5−£350; cameras and photographica, pre-1930, £5−£200; general antiques, mainly 19th C.* Not stocked: Jewellery. LOC: 200 yards from Castle, opposite St. James' church. PARK: 100 yards down hill or multi-storey 100 yards up hill. TEL: 564474; home − Wivenhoe (020622) 2712. SER: Valuations (cameras and photographica); restorations (pre-1930 cameras); buys at auction (cameras and daguerreotypes).

Steve Garrard   *Trade Only*
The Warehouse, Lampitts Farm, Stanway. SIZE: Small. *STOCK: Pine.* PARK: Easy. TEL: 212333. VAT: Stan.

Grandad's Photography Museum
91 East Hill. (J. Latford.) Est. 1978. CL: Sun. and Mon. except by appointment. Open 10−6. SIZE: Medium. *STOCK: Cameras and photographica, images, photographic books, stereoscopes.* LOC: Opposite St. James church. TEL: 564474. SER: Valuations; restorations; buys at auction. FAIRS: Covent Garden.

Richard Iles Gallery
10a, 10 and 12 Northgate St. (R. and C. Iles). Est. 1970. Open 10−1 and 2−4. Thurs. 10−1. SIZE: Small. *STOCK: Watercolours, 19th to early 20th C, £75−£700.* LOC: Off North Hill. PARK: N.C.P. nearby. TEL: 577877. SER: Valuations; restorations (oils, engravings and watercolours) framing; buys at auction. VAT: Stan/Spec.

Colchester continued

Partner and Puxon · BADA
7 and 16 North Hill. (S.H., M. and J.G. Partner.) Est. 1937. CL: Thurs. p.m. Open 9−1 and 2.15−5.30. SIZE: Large. *STOCK: English furniture, 16th to early 19th C, £100−£20,000; porcelain and pottery, 18th−19th C, £10−£2,000; period metalware, £50−£1,500; also Continental and country furniture, shipping goods, general furnishing items.* LOC: In town centre; North Hill leads from High St. to Railway Station. TEL: 573317. SER: Valuations. VAT: Stan/Spec.

Scheregate Antiques
3a Scheregate Steps. (H. and R. Francis.) Est. 1974. Open Mon. and Fri. 10−5, Tues. and Wed. 9−5, Sat. 9−1. SIZE: Small. *STOCK: Silver and gold jewellery and pocket watches, medals and coins, £5−£1,000.* LOC: Opposite Scheregate Hotel. PARK: Nearby. TEL: 66474. SER: Repairs (watches).

Trinity Antiques Centre
7 Trinity St. Est. 1976. Open 9.30−5. There are 8 dealers at this centre offering a wide variety of antiques including small furniture, copper, clocks, brass, porcelain, silver, jewellery, collectors' items, Victoriana, weapons, maps and prints, linen, pine furniture. TEL: 577775.

DOVERCOURT
See Harwich and Dovercourt

DUNMOW
Church End Antiques
Church End. (Mrs. S. Bowring, J.M. Black.) CL: Sat. Open 10−6. *STOCK: General antiques.* TEL: Great Dunmow (0371) 3431.

Hammerbeck · *Mainly Trade*
83 High St. Open Thurs. or by appointment. SIZE: Medium. *STOCK: General antiques, mainly furniture.* TEL: Great Dunmow (0371) 820419.

Simon Hilton
Flemings Hill Farm, Gt. Easton. Resident. Est. 1937. Open by appointment. *STOCK: Oil paintings, £100−£10,000; watercolours, drawings, £25−£1,000; fine prints, bronzes, £5−£500; all 17th−20th C.* TEL: Bishops Stortford (0279) 850279. SER: Valuations; restorations (oil paintings, watercolours and drawings); buys at auction. VAT: Spec.

EPPING · (0378)
Epping Galleries
64−66 High St. (P. Hellmers.) Est. 1972. CL: Wed. Open 10−5. SIZE: Large. *STOCK: Furniture, paintings, porcelain, glass, linen, 19th−20th C, £5−£300.* LOC: B1393, (A11). PARK: Easy. TEL: 73023/4. SER: Restorations; upholstery; framing. VAT: Stan/Spec.

Epping Saturday Market
Rear of 64-66 High St. (P. Hellmers.) Est. 1977. Open every Sat. a.m. There are 80 stalls at this market selling general antiques and bric-a- brac. TEL: 73023/4.

FELSTED, Nr. Gt. Dunmow
Argyll House Antiques
Argyll House, Station Rd. (J. Howard and C. Dinnis.) Est. 1978. CL: Wed. SIZE: Medium. *STOCK: Furniture, Victorian and Edwardian, £25−£500; porcelain, 19th C to mid-20th C, £5−£150; collectors' items and ephemera, £1−£150.* LOC: Village centre. PARK: Easy. TEL: Gt. Dunmow (0371) 820682; home − same.

The Venture
Causeway End. (H. Richards.) Est. 1973. CL: Mon. Open 9.30−5.30, or by appointment. SIZE: Medium. *STOCK: Furniture, 18th−19th C; porcelain, silver, brass, copper, glass, pewter.* Not stocked: Medals, coins, stamps. LOC: B1417. PARK: Easy. TEL: Gt. Dunmow (0371) 820248; home − same.

FINCHINGFIELD, Nr. Braintree
Andrew Tate
Great Wincey Farm. Est. 1972. Open 9−5, Sat. 9−1 or by appointment. *STOCK: Stripped pine.* TEL: Great Dunmow (0371) 810004.

FRINTON-ON-SEA · (02556)
The Bow Window
58 Connaught Ave. Est. 1963. CL: Wed. p.m. *STOCK: Jewellery, silver, porcelain, china, oils, watercolours, decorative items.* TEL: 4607.

Dickens Curios
151 Connaught Ave. (Miss M. Wilsher.) Est. 1970. Open Mon. 11−1 and 2.15−5.30, Tues. and Thurs. 9.30−1, and 2.15−5.30, Wed. 9.30−1, Fri. 10.30−1 and 2.15−5.30, Sat. 9.30−1 and 2.15−5.00. SIZE: Small. *STOCK: Victoriana and earlier items, £5−£200; furniture, 18th−20th C, £5−£300; jewellery, £5−£25; coins and cigarette cards.* Not stocked: Firearms. LOC: From Frinton Station ¼ mile down Connaught Ave., opp. Hammond's Garage. PARK: Easy. TEL: 4134.

MARKSWOOD GALLERY
(Eric Goodwin)
Great Bardfield, near Braintree, Essex
*PAINTINGS, WATERCOLOURS, ETCHINGS
STUDIO CERAMICS, SMALL FURNITURE*

*LILLIAN STANNARD (1877-1944)
"Where busy bees in sunshine reap a harvest
for their Hives". Watercolour of a Bedfordshire
cottage garden exhibited Royal Academy 1902.*

*We wish to buy fine paintings and watercolours and small antique furniture
Gallery hours: 11 – 1 and 2.30 – 5 Open Sunday afternoons*
CLOSED each Monday, Wednesday and Friday but appointments made any time.

A telephone call prior to visit always advised.
Tel: (0371) 810106 or 810329 after hours

Frinton-on-Sea continued

Frinton Antiques
5 Old Rd. (K.J. and Mrs. Pethick.) Est. 1952. CL: Sun. and Wed. except by appointment. Open 9.30 – 5.15. *STOCK: Early furniture, silver, glass, porcelain, brass, copper.* PARK: Easy. TEL: 71310 or 71894. VAT: Stan/Spec.

Old Road Antiques Centre
58 Old Rd. (N. Basile and M. Triggs.) Est. 1950. CL: Wed. p.m. Open 9.30 – 5.30. SIZE: Large. *STOCK: General antiques, Victorian and Edwardian, £5 – £2,000.* LOC. Left off Connaught Ave. PARK: Easy. TEL: 5075. SER. Valuations; restorations; French polishing.

GANTS HILL
See Greater London

GRAYS

Lodge House Antiques
17 The Parade, Lodge Lane. (Mrs. A. Henderson.) CL: Wed. Open 9 – 5.30, Sat. 9 – 1. *STOCK: General antiques.* TEL: Grays Thurrock (0375) 76846.

GREAT BADDOW

Baddow Antique and Craft Centre
The Bringy, Church St. Est. 1969. Open 10 – 5, Sun. 12 – 5. The Centre has 22 dealers offering furniture, general antiques, Victorian brass bedsteads, bric-a-brac and shipping goods. PARK: Easy. TEL: Chelmsford (0245) 76159. SER: Restorations; upholstery.

GREAT BARDFIELD

Golden Sovereign.
The Old Police House, High St. (C. and W. Leitch.) Est. 1969. CL: Wed. and Sat. Open 10 – 6. SIZE: Small. *STOCK: Glass, silver, small furniture, small items, 18th – 19th C, from £5.* LOC: B1057. From Dunmow, 100yds. beyond Thaxted turning, .2nd shop on left. PARK: Easy. TEL: Gt. Dunmow (0371) 810507; home — same.

Markswood Gallery   LAPADA
(E. Goodwin.) Est. 1978. CL: Mon., Wed. and Fri. Open 11 – 1 and 2.30 – 5, Sun. 2 – 5, appointment always advisable. *STOCK: Watercolours and oil paintings, all periods; small furniture.* TEL: Gt. Dunmow (0371) 810106; home — Gt. Dunmow (0371) 810329. SER: Restorations; framing; buys at auction.

Bridget Burgess

The Grove
Great Horkesley
Colchester, Essex
Tel. 0206-271277

**Watercolours, Embroideries,
Small Furniture (esp.
Chairs), Looking Glasses,
Decorative Items and
Unusual Bygones
Open daily by appointment**

Services: Framing, picture
cleaning and restoration, textile
restoration and searching for
specific interesting antiques.

GREAT CHESTERFORD
Nr. Saffron Walden

C. and J. Mortimer and Sons
The Sugar House, School St. Est. 1962. Open
Thurs.—Sun. 2.30—5, or by appointment.
SIZE: Medium. *STOCK: Oak furniture, 16th—
18th C, £120—£10,000; oil paintings, mainly
portraits, 16th—17th C, £300—£8,000.*
LOC: From London on B1383 — formerly
A11. PARK: Easy. TEL: Saffron Walden (0799)
30261.

GREAT DUNMOW
See Dunmow

GREAT HORKESLEY
Nr. Colchester

Bridget Burgess
The Grove, Tog Lane. Est. 1972. Open by
appointment only. SIZE: Small. *STOCK: Watercolours, engravings, embroideries, looking
glasses, unusual small and decorative items.*
LOC: A134 through Gt. Horkesley, take 2nd
left after Yew Tree public house. PARK: Easy.
TEL: Colchester (0206) 271277. SER: Valuations; mounting and framing; buys at auction
(pictures, mirrors); finder.

GREAT WAKERING

Books and Things
195 High St. (M. Sherman.) Est. 1976. CL:
Sat. Open 1.30—5.30 including Sun. *STOCK:
General small antiques, china, porcelain,
brass, copper.* Not stocked: Furniture. TEL:
Southend-on-Sea (0702) 219752.

GREAT WALTHAM
Nr. Chelmsford

The Stores
(M. Webster.) Est. 1974. CL: Sun. and Tues.
Open 10—5. SIZE: Large. *STOCK: Pine furni-
ture.* LOC: On A130. PARK: At rear. TEL:
Chelmsford (0245) 360277; home — Braintree
(0376) 26997. VAT: Stan.

HADLEIGH

Shanclare Antiques
374 London Rd. (Mrs. M. Hanreck.) Est.
1973. CL: Thurs. Open 10—6, or by appointment. SIZE: Medium. *STOCK: Furniture,
18th—19th C, £200—£2,000; porcelain,
glass and Oriental items.* LOC: On south side
A13 Hadleigh/Leigh-on-Sea border. PARK:
Easy. TEL: Southend-on-Sea (0702) 558321;
home — same. SER: Valuations.

HALSTEAD   (0787)

Helen Blomfield
Hampers, Little Maplestead. Est. 1958. Open
by appointment. SIZE: Small. *STOCK: Silver
and Sheffield plate, 18th—20th C, £5—
£1,000.* LOC: A131 from Halstead towards
Sudbury, after one mile turn first left to The
Maplesteads. ½ mile further, white-gabled
farmhouse on right. TEL: 472159. SER: Valuations (silver); buys at auction. VAT: Stan/
Spec.

Halstead Antiques
71 Head St. (P. and R. Earl.) Est. 1973.
STOCK: Small antiques, glass, bric-a-brac.
TEL: 473265.

Napier House Antiques
Head St. (V. McGregor.) Open 8.30—5.30 or
by appointment. SIZE: Medium. *STOCK:
General antiques.* TEL: 477346.

Tempus Fugit
c/o Trinity House, Trinity St. (S. and M.
Charles.) Open by appointment only. SIZE:
Small. *STOCK: Clocks, bracket, longcase,
lantern, £200—£5,000.* LOC: Opposite park
in centre of town. Use side door. PARK:
Opposite. TEL: 475409. SER: Valuations;
restorations.

RUNDELLS ANTIQUES

(M. & R. COX)
OPEN 7 DAYS
A WEEK

TELEPHONE:
HARLOW 22906

MAIN LONDON ROAD (B1393)
Nr. HARLOW, ESSEX
LARGE DRIVE-IN CAR PARK

TRADE WELCOME
- *Period Furniture*
- *Victoriana*
- *Silver and Plate*
- *Oil Paintings*
- *Porcelain*
- *Brass and Copper*
- *Persian Rugs*
- *Watercolours*
- *Prints Etc.,*

HARLOW   (0279)
Rundells Antiques
Rundells, London Rd. Est. 1951. Open 9.30−5. SIZE: Large. *STOCK: 17th−19th C furniture, porcelain, paintings, brass, copper.* LOC: B.1393, half-way between Epping and Harlow. PARK: Own. TEL: 22906. VAT: Stan/Spec.

HARWICH AND   (0255)
DOVERCOURT
Mayflower Antiques
2 Una Rd., Parkeston. (J.W. Odgers.) Est. 1970. CL: Sat. Open 9.30−1 and 2.30−5.30. SIZE: Medium. *STOCK: Clocks; furniture, 18th−19th C; polyphons, phonographs, organs, horn gramophones, scientific and marine instruments and general antiques.* LOC: Main road to Parkeston Quay. PARK: Easy. TEL: 504079. SER: Restorations (clocks, watches). VAT: Stan/Spec.

HATFIELD BROAD OAK (027 970)
Tudor Antiques
(R.M. and P.A. Wood.) Est. 1977. Open 9.30−6.30. *STOCK: Furniture, porcelain, glass, unusual items.* LOC: B183, close to M11. TEL: 557. VAT: Stan/Spec.

HEMPSTEAD, Nr. Saffron Walden
Michael Beaumont Antiques
Hempstead Hall. Open every day 10.30−5. SIZE: Large. *STOCK: Furniture − oak, mahogany, walnut, rosewood, 17th−19th C, £50−£2,500.* LOC: On B1054 between Hempstead and Steeple Bumpstead. PARK: Easy. TEL: Steeple Bumpstead (0440 84) 239. SER: Restorations (furniture). VAT: Stan/Spec.

ILFORD
See Greater London

INGATESTONE   (0277)
Cameron Antiques
128 High St. (Mrs. V. Sullivan.) Est. 1983. CL: Mon. Open 10−5.30, Wed. by appointment. SIZE: Small. *STOCK: Stripped pine, kitchenalia; local prints and maps, 19th C.* LOC: B1002, opposite P.O. PARK: Easy. TEL: 354917; home − same.

Meyers Gallery
66 High St. (Mrs. J. Meyers.) Est. 1972. CL: Wed. Open 10−5. SIZE: Medium. *STOCK: Oil paintings and watercolours, 18th−20th C and living artists, £25−£2,000; small Victorian furniture.* PARK: Nearby. TEL: 355335. SER: Restorations; framing. VAT: Stan/Spec.

Catherine Walden Antique Jewellery
58 High St. (Mrs. L. Tredgett.) CL: Mon. and Wed. Open 10.30−4, Sat. 10.30−5. *STOCK: Jewellery, silver and small furniture.* TEL: 352925.

IS YOUR ENTRY CORRECT?
If there is even the slightest inaccuracy in your entry, *please* let us know before 1st January 1987.
GUIDE TO THE
ANTIQUE SHOPS OF BRITAIN
5 Church Street, Woodbridge, Suffolk.

KELVEDON, Nr. Colchester (0376)

Dial House Antiques
High St. (D. Mason.) Open 10—5 or by appointment. SIZE: Small. *STOCK: Furniture, mainly Victorian and Edwardian, £25—£750; china and glass, silver and jewellery, Georgian to Edwardian, to £200.* LOC: Off A12 between Chelmsford and Colchester. PARK: Easy. TEL: 70706. FAIRS: Furze Hill.

Kelvedon Antiques BADA
90 High St. (J. Billings.) Est. 1965. CL: Sun. except by appointment. Open 9.30—1 and 2—5.30. SIZE: Medium. *STOCK: Furniture, 18th to early 19th C.* LOC: From London on right hand side of main street. PARK: Easy. TEL: 70557. VAT: Stan/Spec.

Kelvedon Antiques Centre
139 High St. (D. Mason.) Open 10—5 or by appointment. SIZE: Medium. There are 8 dealers at this centre selling furniture, porcelain, pottery, glass, silver, jewellery, linen, art deco, collectors' items, 18th—20th C. LOC: Off A12 between Chelmsford and Colchester. PARK: Easy. TEL: 70896; home — 70706. FAIRS: Furze Hill.

Millers Antiques Kelvedon
LAPADA
46 High St. Est. 1920. Open 9—6, Sat. 10—4 or by appointment. SIZE: Large. *STOCK: 17th—19th C mahogany, walnut and oak furniture.* PARK: Own. TEL: 70098. VAT: Stan/Spec.

Kelvedon continued

G.T. Ratcliff Ltd. *Trade Only*
Durwards Hall. (D.V. Ratcliff and W.D. Boyd Ratcliff.) Est. 1935. CL: Sat. p.m. Open 9—5. SIZE: Large. *STOCK: Furniture, mainly 18th and 19th C.* LOC: A12. PARK: Easy. TEL: 70234. VAT: Stan.

Thomas Sykes Antiques LAPADA
16 High St. (T.W. Sykes and O.P. Folkard.) Est. 1984. Open 9—5, Sun. by appointment. SIZE: Large. *STOCK: Furniture, 18th—19th C; porcelain, lamps and decorative items.* LOC: Off A12. PARK: Own. TEL: 71969. SER: Valuations; buys at auction. VAT: Spec.

LAYER DE LA HAYE (020 634)

Pughs' Porcelains
Layer Fields House, Field Farm Rd. (J. and J. Pugh.) Resident. Open by appointment. SIZE: Medium. *STOCK: English porcelain, late 18th and early 19th C, £20—£2,500.* LOC: Layer Rd. from Colchester, turn left at The Folly. PARK: Easy. TEL: Colchester (0206) 348170. SER: Buys at auction. FAIRS: Bath, Cheltenham, Wakefield ceramic, Olympia.

LAYER MARNEY

Peter and Audrey Edwick
Little Winters. Est. 1959. Open by appointment only. *STOCK: Porcelain including early Worcester, Derby, Coalport and Welsh; Georgian and early Victorian silver, £5—£1,200; decorative brass items, collectors' boxes.* LOC: Off B1022. PARK: Easy. TEL: Colchester (0206) 330302. FAIRS: Most principal. VAT: Spec.

Left: a Bremen Police shako with cockade. £50. Right: a Berlin Police shako with cockade. £120. From an auction feature, "Police Helmets and Uniforms", **Antique Collecting,** March 1986.

LEIGH-ON-SEA

K.S. Buchan
114 The Broadway. Open 10—5. *STOCK: Furniture and general antiques.* TEL: Southend-on-Sea. (0702) 79440.

Chalkwell Antiques
73 Leigh Rd. (J. Webb and D. Stoker.) Est. 1980. CL: Wed. Open 9.30—5, Sat. 9.30—6. SIZE: Large. *STOCK: Furniture, £50—£1,000; ceramics, general antiques, metalware, silver plate, £5—£500; all Victorian to 1930s.* Not stocked: Bric-a-brac. LOC: Just off A13 in High Rd. PARK: Easy. TEL: Southend-on-Sea (0702) 715615; home — Southend-on-Sea (0702) 231134 and 73012. SER: Valuations; restorations (upholstery and French polishing).

Stephen Charles Antiques
3 Leigh Hill. Est. 1973. Open Mon., Fri. and Sat. 12.30—6, other times (Trade only) by appointment. SIZE: Small. *STOCK: Art deco, Victoriana, collectors' items, small furniture, all £1—£1,000.* PARK: Easy. TEL: Southend-on-Sea (0702) 714649, or Rayleigh (0268) 774977.

Collectors' Paradise
993 London Rd. (H.W. and P.E. Smith.) Est. 1967. CL: Fri. Open 10.30—6. SIZE: Small. *STOCK: Clocks, 1830—1920, from £35; bric-a-brac; postcards, 1900—1930s; cigarette cards, 1889—1939.* LOC: On A13. PARK: Easy. TEL: Southend-on-Sea (0702) 73077.

B. and W. Cutler
109 Rectory Grove. Est. 1974. CL: Wed. Open 9—5.30. *STOCK: Furniture, silver, plate, brass, small china.* LOC: A13 to Southend, turn right into Hadleigh Rd., at end turn left into Rectory Grove, shop 30yds. on right. PARK: Easy. TEL: Southend-on-Sea (0702) 712857.

Pall Mall Antiques
104c and 104d Elm Rd. (M. Sherman.) Open 10—5. *STOCK: Bric-a-brac, curios, brass, furniture, general antiques.* TEL: Southend-on-Sea (0702) 77235.

Past and Present
81 and 83 Broadway West. (R. Banks.) CL: Wed. Open 9.30—4.30. *STOCK: General antiques.* TEL: Southend-on-Sea (0702) 79101.

John Stacey and Sons
86—90 Pall Mall. Est. 1946. CL: Sat. p.m. Open 9—5.30. *STOCK: General antiques.* TEL: Southend-on-Sea (0702) 77051. SER: Valuations; restorations; exporters; auctioneers. VAT: Stan.

J. Streamer Antiques
86 Broadway and 212 Leigh Rd. Est. 1965. CL: Wed. p.m. Open 9.30—5.30. *STOCK: Jewellery, silver, bric-a-brac, small furniture.* TEL: Southend-on-Sea (0702) 72895 and Southend-on-Sea (0702) 711633.

Leigh-on-Sea continued

Richard Wrenn Antiques
113/115 Broadway West. Est. 1950. CL: Mon. and Wed. Open 10.30—5.30. SIZE: Large. *STOCK: Furniture, £85—£5,000; porcelain, glass, £10—£500; jewellery, silver, objets d'art, £40—£2,000; metalware, brass, copper, £20—£500.* LOC: 250yds. west of Leigh church. TEL: Southend-on-Sea (0702) 710745. VAT: Stan/Spec.

LITTLE BADDOW, Nr. Chelmsford

Michael Tubbs (Old Parsonage Gallery)
Parsonage Farm, Parsonage Lane. Est. 1974. Open by appointment only. SIZE: Medium. *STOCK: Early British watercolours and drawings, 18th, 19th and selected 20th C, £100—£2,000.* LOC: From Danbury, Parsonage Lane is to the left just before 'The General Arms'. PARK: Easy. TEL: Danbury (024 541) 3279. SER: Valuations; buys at auction; London exhibitions. VAT: Spec.

LOUGHTON

Chattels of Church Hill
36 Church Hill. (J.H. and J.P. Whitehouse.) Resident. Est. 1976. CL: Thurs. Open 10—5.30. SIZE: Small. *STOCK: Furniture, 18th—19th C, £50—£500; clocks, 19th C, £50—£300; silver, 19th—20th C, £20—£200; Victorian watercolours, £20—£400; objets d'art.* LOC: Continuation of Loughton High St. PARK: Easy. TEL: (01) 508 3307. SER: Valuations; restorations (clocks).

Brian Hawkins Antiques
12 Forest Rd. Est. 1968. Open 9.30—1 and 2—5, Thurs. by appointment. SIZE: Medium. *STOCK: Furniture, 19th to early 20th C, £50—£1,000+.* PARK: Easy. TEL: (01) 508 6044; home — (01) 508 1350. SER: Valuations; restorations (cabinet work and polishing); buys at auction. VAT: Stan.

Loughton Antiques
120 High Rd. (C.J. Anderson.) Open Tues. 10—4, Sat. 10—5. *STOCK: General antiques, bric-a-brac.* TEL: (01) 508 0070.

MALDON (0621)

The Antique Rooms
63D Maldon High St. (P. Southgate, E. Hedley, K. Finch.) Est. 1966. Open 10—5, Wed. 10—1. SIZE: Medium. *STOCK: Furniture, pottery, porcelain, glass and silver, mainly 19th C; costume, linen and lace, Victorian to 1950, £1.50—£150; jewellery, lacemaking equipment, cast-iron fireplaces, fenders, collectors' items.* LOC: Just off High St., in courtyard at rear of Maldon bookshop. PARK: Nearby. TEL: 56985.

Maldon continued

The Antique Warehouse
3rd Floor, Fullbridge Mill, Fullbridge. (D. and I. Vince.) Est. 1972. Open 10—5. SIZE: Warehouse. *STOCK: Furniture, 19th C and some 18th C; shipping, pine, satin walnut and smalls.* LOC: B1019 into Maldon. PARK: Easy. TEL: 55660; home — (0245) 320301. SER: Valuations, buys at auction (furniture, oil paintings and watercolours). VAT: Stan.

Maldon Antiques and Collectors Market
United Reformed Church Hall, Market Hill. Est. 1975. 20 dealers. Open first Sat. every month, 10—5. PARK: Easy. TEL: Earls Colne (078 75) 2826.

Barbara Paul and Daughters
Hazeldean, 105 High St. Est. 1969. CL: Wed. p.m. Open 10—5.30. *STOCK: Furniture, pine, porcelain, pictures, prints, Victoriana, books, jewellery, silver, coins and collectors' items.* TEL: 55405.

MANNINGTREE
"Forty Nine"
High St. (A. Patterson.) CL: Wed. p.m. Open 10—1 and 2—5. *STOCK: General and country antiques.* PARK: Easy. TEL: Colchester (0206) 396170.

F. Freestone
"Kiln Tops", 29 Colchester Rd. Open 9—6, appointment advisable. *STOCK: General antiques, furniture, clocks.* TEL: Colchester (0206) 392998.

MATCHING GREEN, Nr. Harlow
Stone Hall Antiques *Trade & Export Only*
Down Hall Rd. Est. 1971. Open 9—5.30, Sat. and Sun. by appointment. SIZE: Warehouse. *STOCK: Furniture 17th—19th C, £50—£10,000.* LOC: Turning off A1060 at Hatfield Heath. PARK: Own. TEL: Bishops Stortford (0279) 731440; home — same. VAT: Stan.

MAYLAND
John Bailey Antique Clocks
Mayland Hill Cottage. CL: Mon. and Tues. Open 10.30—5.30. SIZE: Small. *STOCK: Longcase clocks, £500—£2,000; clocks, £35—£400; small furniture, £50—£250; books on horology.* PARK: Easy. TEL: Wickford (03744) 62612; home — Maldon (0621) 772139. SER: Restorations; buys at auction (longcase clocks).

NEWPORT, Nr. Saffron Walden
Brown House Antiques
High St. (B.E. & J. Hodgkinson.) Est. 1978. Open 10—5. SIZE: Medium. *STOCK: Pine furniture, Victorian, £50—£500; silver and jewellery, Victorian and Edwardian, £25—£1,000; oils and watercolours.* LOC: B1383, off M11 at Stansted interchange. PARK: Easy. TEL: Saffron Walden (0799) 40238; home — same. SER: Valuations; restorations; buys at auction (furniture). VAT: Stan/Spec.

Galerie Appenzell
High St. (L. Simms.) Open 10—5. *STOCK: Watercolours, prints, oils.* LOC: 2 miles from Saffron Walden on A11. PARK: At rear. TEL: Saffron Walden (0799) 40623; home — Royston (0763) 838146.

Little Shop Antiques
High St. Est. 1979. CL: Mon. and Wed. Open 10—5; Fri. and Sun. 2—5. *STOCK: General antiques including porcelain, glass, brass, pewter, silver, pictures, prints, jewellery.* LOC: B1383.

M11 Antiques Centre
High St. (B. and J. Hodgkinson.) Est. 1970. SIZE: Large. *STOCK: Furniture, 18th C to Edwardian, £100—£4,000; clocks, silver, china, Oriental items, £10—£500.* LOC: Old A11. PARK: Own. Tel: Saffron Walden (0799) 40321; home — Saffron Walden (0799) 40238. SER: Valuations; restorations (mahogany, French polishing); buys at auction (furniture, silver, jewellery). VAT: Stan/Spec.

Regency House
High St. (H.P. Duke.) Est. 1969. Open 9.30—5.30. SIZE: Small. *STOCK: 18th—19th C items, £50—£500.* Not stocked: Glass, oak. LOC: Adjacent to Saffron Walden on A11. PARK: Easy. TEL: Saffron Walden (0799) 40763.

NORTH SHOEBURY
Idler's Alley Antiques
3 Parsons Corner. (I. Fisher and M. Brown.) Est. 1964. CL: Mon. Open most afternoons. *STOCK: Prints, porcelain and furniture.* LOC: On A13 roundabout.

ORSETT
Orsett Hall Antiques Fair
Orsett Hall, Princes Charles Ave. (Stephen Charles Fairs.) Open second Sun. each month 10.30—5. *STOCK: General antiques, Victoriana, art deco, collectors' items.* LOC: Corner of Prince Charles Ave. and A128. PARK: Own. TEL: Southend-on-Sea (0702) 714649/556745 or Rayleigh (0268) 774977.

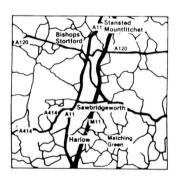

RAYLEIGH (0268)

F.G. Bruschweiler **LAPADA**
(Antiques) Ltd. *Trade Only*
41-67 Lower Lambricks. Est. 1954. Open
9—5, Sat. by appointment. SIZE: Warehouse.
STOCK: Furniture, 18th—19th C. LOC: A127
to Weir roundabout through Rayleigh High St.
and Hockley Rd., first left past cemetery, then
second left, warehouse round corner on left.
PARK: Easy. TEL: 773761; home — (062
182) 8152. VAT: Stan.

Tilly's Antiques
Pearson's Farm, London Rd. (S.T. and R.J.
Austen.) Open 9.30—5. STOCK: General
antiques. TEL: 777405.

RIDGEWELL, (044 085)
Nr. Halstead

Ridgewell Crafts and Antiques
(A.A. and C.M.J. Godsell and P. Crouch.) Est.
1952. CL: Wed. Open 10—6.30 including
Sun. SIZE: Medium. STOCK: Clocks and
watches, 19th C, £5—£500; china, brass,
copper, some furniture. LOC: On A604, 6
miles from Haverhill towards Colchester.
PARK: Easy. TEL: 272. SER: Clock and watch
repairs.

SAFFRON WALDEN (0799)

The Church St. Gallery **LAPADA**
17 Church St. (P.M. Pickard.) CL: Thurs. Open
10—1 and 2.15—5, Sat. 10.30—4. SIZE:
Medium. STOCK: Watercolours, 18th—20th
C; oils and prints, 19th C; sculpture and studio
pottery. LOC: South of church. PARK: Market
Sq. or Common. TEL: 24422. SER: Valuations;
restorations; buys at auction; framing. FAIRS:
British International, Birmingham. VAT: Stan/
Spec.

Lankester Antiques and Books
Old Sun Inn, Church St. and Market Hill. (J.
and P. Lankester.) Est. 1965. Open 9.30—
5.30. SIZE: Large. STOCK: Furniture, porcelain, pottery, metalwork, general antiques,
books, prints and maps. TEL: 22685. VAT:
Stan.

LITTLEBURY ANTIQUES – LITTLEBURY RESTORATIONS
58/60 FAIRYCROFT ROAD   SAFFRON WALDEN   ESSEX   CB10 1LZ
TELEPHONE : SAFFRON WALDEN (0799) 27961
Evenings and Weekends: (0799) 22931; Albury (027974) 530

Barometers, Marine antiques, fine ship models, Chronometers, Walking sticks, Chess sets and other high quality interesting pieces

Expert restoration by craftsmen; barometers, all forms of furniture repair, replacement of marquetry, all inlay work carefully matched.

Business hours 9am – 5pm Monday to Friday, Weekend by appointment only
Railway Station: Audley End (1½ miles away) London to Cambridge line

---

Saffron Walden continued

Littlebury Antiques – Littlebury Restorations Ltd.
58/60 Fairycroft Rd. (N.H. D'Oyly and M.A. Hudson.) Est. 1962. CL: Sat. and Sun. except by appointment. Open 9–5. SIZE: Medium. *STOCK: Marine antiques and paintings, clocks, chronometers, chess sets, walking sticks, barometers and curios.* PARK: Easy. TEL: 27961 weekends and evenings 22931; Albury (027 974) 530. SER: Valuations; restorations; buys at auction. VAT: Stan/Spec.

Norfolk Antiques
16 Market Row (behind Town Hall.) (J. Ryles and C. Goldney.) Est. 1959. CL: Thurs. Open 10.30–1 and 2–5.30. SIZE: Small. *STOCK: Furniture, glass, porcelain and general antiques.* PARK: On the Market Square. TEL: 27633.

Jane Sumner
9 Market Sq. (Mrs. J. Sumner.) SIZE: Medium. *STOCK: Early oak, Georgian mahogany, metalware, jewellery.* TEL: 23611. FAIRS: Organiser.

SHENFIELD
The Chart House
33 Spurgate, Hutton Mount. (C.C. Crouchman.) Est. 1974. Open by appointment only. SIZE: Small. *STOCK: Nautical items.* PARK: Easy. TEL: Brentwood (0277) 225012; home – same. SER: Hire of nautical items and equipment; buys at auction. VAT: Stan.

SIBLE HEDINGHAM, Nr. Halstead
Hedingham Antiques
100 Swan St. (T. and P. Patterson.) Open 10–5 or by appointment. SIZE: Medium. *STOCK: Furniture, 1790–1910; china, glass, silver plate, Victorian to art deco.* LOC: A604, village centre. PARK: Easy. TEL: Hedingham (0787) 60360; home – same.

W.A. Pinn & Sons   BADA
124 Swan St. (K.H. and W.J. Pinn.) Est. 1943. CL: Sun. except by appointment. SIZE: Medium. *STOCK: Furniture, 17th to early 19th C, £100–£5,000; clocks, 18th to early 19th C, £250–£3,500; interesting items, prior to 1830, £10–£1,500.* LOC: On A604 opposite Shell Garage. PARK: On premises. TEL: Hedingham (0787) 61127. FAIRS: Chelsea Spring and Autumn Antiques, Snape, Olympia. VAT: Stan/Spec.

SOUTH OCKENDON   (0708)
Alfred S. Allen and Co. *Mail Order Only* P.O. Box No. 4. Est. 1964. *STOCK: Coins and accessories, coin jewellery.* SER: Buys at auction. VAT: Stan/Spec.

SOUTHEND-ON-SEA (0702)

Atticus Books
Kickshaws, 20 Alexandra St. (F.H. Eddelin.) Est. 1974. CL: Wed. Open 11—1 and 2.30—6. *STOCK: Secondhand and antiquarian books; paintings, maps and prints.* LOC: Centre of town, 50yds. from High St. PARK: Meters and opposite. TEL: 353630.

Kickshaws
20 Alexandra St. (Mrs. A.M. Eddelin.) Est. 1974. CL: Wed. Open 11—1 and 2.30—6. SIZE: Small. *STOCK: General antiques, £5—£500.* LOC: Centre of town, 50yds. from High St. PARK: Meters and opposite. TEL: 353630.

Lonsdale Antiques
86 Lonsdale Rd., Southchurch. (H.M. Clark.) CL: Wed. Open 9—5.30. *STOCK: Jewellery, pictures, porcelain, general small antiques.* TEL: 62643.

Penny Farthing Antiques
18 Alexandra St. (N.S. Cameron.) CL: Wed. Open 9.30—5.30. *STOCK: General antiques.* TEL: 344786. SER: Repairs (clocks and watches).

Southend-on-Sea continued

Powlings
180 London Rd. (L.G. Powling.) CL: Wed. Open 9.30—1. SIZE: Small. *STOCK: Furniture, 1830—1900.* LOC: On A13, midway between High St. and Hamlet Court Rd. PARK: Easy. TEL: 343643.

Reddings Art and Antiques
98 London Rd. (F.H. Redding.) Resident. Open 9—5.30. *STOCK: Oils and watercolours, general antiques.* TEL: 354647.

Southend Pine
468-470A Southchurch Rd. (J. Pitcher.) Open 9—6. *STOCK: Stripped pine furniture.* TEL: 64649.

STANFORD-LE-HOPE (0375)

Barton House Antiques
Wharf Rd. (L. and J. Pigney.) Est. 1973. Open all times but appointment advisable. SIZE: Medium. *STOCK: 17th—19th C furniture; 18th—19th C English porcelain, including English 18th C blue and white, copper, brass and glass.* LOC: Turn off A13 to centre of town, 200yds. on right hand side. PARK: Easy. TEL: 672494. SER: Valuations; buys at auction. VAT: Spec.

A good cast of the 'Charging Senegal Elephant' by Barye. From *Animals in Bronze* by Christopher Payne, published by the **Antique Collectors' Club,** 1986.

Thomas
Ivester-Lloyd.
'Mr. Jorrocks
confronted by a
weritable harm of the
sea'. Pen and wash.
From *The Dictionary
of Equestrian Artists*
by Sally Mitchell,
published by the
**Antique Collectors'
Club,** 1985.

STANSTED

Julia Bennett (Antiques)
The Mill House, 30 Lower St. *STOCK: Decorative items and country furniture.* TEL: Bishop's Stortford (0279) 816066; home — Bishop's Stortford (0279) 850279.

F.J.H. Harris   LAPADA
23 Silver St. (F.J. Harris.) Est. 1956. Open 9.30—5.30. SIZE: Medium. *STOCK: Furniture, 18th to late 19th C; porcelain, silver, plate, 18th—19th C, £5—£2,000.* LOC: On A11. PARK: 500yds. north. TEL: Bishop's Stortford (0279) 813371. SER: Valuations. VAT: Stan/Spec.

Linden House Antiques
3 Silver St. (A.W. and K.M. Sargeant.) Est. 1961. CL: Sun. except by appointment. Open 9—5.30. SIZE: Large. *STOCK: English furniture, 18th—19th C, £100—£5,000; small decorative items, including library and dining room furniture.* LOC: On A11. TEL: Bishop's Stortford (0279) 812372. VAT: Spec.

Stansted continued

Valmar Antiques
Croft House, High Lane. (J., M. and N. Orpin.) Resident. Est. 1960. Open 8—5 or by appointment. SIZE: Large. *STOCK: Furniture and decorative items, £50—£3,500 +.* TEL: Bishop's Stortford (0279) 813201.

Wiskin Antiques
18 Silver St. (K. and M. Wiskin.) Est. 1973. Open 10—5.30, Sun. by appointment. SIZE: Medium. *STOCK: Mahogany, walnut, oak 18th—19th C; pine, £50—£2,000; clocks, silver, small items, £5—£800.* Not stocked: Reproduction. LOC: B1383 (Old A11), one mile from M11, junction 8. PARK: At rear. TEL: Bishop's Stortford (0279) 812376; home — same. VAT: Spec.

STOCK   (0277)

Sabine Antiques
38 High St. (C.E. Sabine.) Est. 1974. CL: Mon. Open 10—5 or by appointment. *STOCK: Furniture, from £50; china and glass, from £5.* LOC: In centre of village on B1007. PARK: Easy. TEL: 840553. SER: Valuations; restorations (furniture); silver plating.

TAKELEY
Country Kitchen Antiques
The Chestnuts, Dunmow Rd. TEL: Bishop's Stortford (0279) 870333.

THAXTED (0371)
Snow's
Watling St. (M. Snow.) Est. 1968. Open 10—1 and 2—5.30. SIZE: Medium. *STOCK: Pictures, pre-1940, £45—£950; furniture, pre-1900, £50—£500; objets d'art, all periods, £25—£500.* LOC: On Dunmow—Saffron Walden Rd. in centre of Thaxted. PARK: Nearby. TEL: 830001. SER: Valuations.

Thaxted Galleries
1 Newbiggin St. (J.E. Sheppard.) Est. 1958. CL: Sun. except by appointment. Open 9— 5.30. SIZE: Large. *STOCK: Furniture, £200— £1,000; oak furniture, £250—£1,500; all 17th—18th C; antique lamp bases.* LOC: On B184. PARK: At rear. TEL: 830350.

Turpin's Antiques BADA
4 Stoney Lane. (J.F. Braund.) SIZE: Large. *STOCK: 17th and 18th C walnut, oak and mahogany, metalware.* **TEL: 830495. SER: Buys at auction. VAT: Spec.**

THEYDON BOIS (037 881)
Nr. Epping
A.F. Allbrook
22 Morgan Crescent. (R.L. and M.F. Allbrook.) Est. 1944. Open by appointment only. *STOCK: English pottery, 17th to early 19th C, £15—£1,500.* LOC: On Central Line underground. By road, turn off A104 at Wake Arms roundabout. TEL: 2344. SER: Valuations; buys at auction. VAT: Spec.

Hillair Antiques
Theydon Galleries, Loughton Lane. (P. Tillbrook.) Open Sat. 10—1 and 2—4, Sun. 10—1 or by appointment. *STOCK: Doulton, Wedgwood, ceramics, glass, silver, jewellery, furniture.* LOC: Behind village green. PARK: In front. TEL: 3770; home — 2108. SER: Buys at auction (Doulton).

THORPE-LE-SOKEN
Country Pine Antiques (Pearce's Pieces)
High St. Est. 1977. *STOCK: Pine.*

Le Soken Antiques LAPADA
High St. Est. 1977. Open Thurs.—Sat. 10—6 or by appointment. *STOCK: 18th and 19th C furniture, metalware, pottery, porcelain, treen, tea caddies, writing slopes, Tunbridgeware, sewing and collectors' items.* TEL: Clacton-on-Sea (0255) 861337.

TILBURY (037 52)
J.L. Rourke
197 Dock Rd. Resident. Est. 1961. CL: Sat. Open 10.30—5 or by appointment. *STOCK: General antiques.* TEL: 2964.

UPMINSTER
See Greater London

WAKES COLNE, Nr. Colchester
Janet Gordon
Wakes Colne House. Resident. Usually open. *STOCK: Furniture, pre-1900, and decorative items.* LOC: A604. PARK: Easy. TEL: Earls Colne (078 75) 2402/2028. SER: Curtains, covers and fabrics.

WESTCLIFF-ON-SEA
David, Jean and John Antiques
Lincoln House Gallery, 587 London Road. Est. 1963. CL: Wed. Open 9.30—5.30. SIZE: Large. *STOCK: Clocks, furniture, £25—£3,000; porcelain, bronzes, weapons, objets d'art, some shipping goods.* LOC: Opposite Classic Cinema. TEL: Southend-on-Sea (0702) 339106; home — Wickford (03744) 3330; evenings — Rayleigh (0268) 743815. SER: Valuations; restorations (clocks, barometers and small furniture). VAT: Stan/Spec.

It's About Time
863 London Rd. (R. and V. Alps.) Est. 1980. CL: Wed. Open 10—5.30, Thurs. and Fri. 9.30—5.30, Sat. 9—5.30. SIZE: Medium. *STOCK: Clocks, 18th—19th C, £100— £1,500; barometers, Victorian and Edwardian furniture.* LOC: A13. PARK: Easy. TEL: Southend-on-Sea (0702) 72574; home — Southend-on-Sea (0702) 205204.

London-West Exports
333 Westborough Rd. (C. Waite.) Open 10—6. *STOCK: General antiques.* TEL: Southend-on- Sea (0702) 337664. SER: Shipping.

Miscellaneous Shop
22a/b Milton Rd. (J. Line.) Est. 1962. CL: Wed. SIZE: Medium. *STOCK: Small furniture, Victorian and Edwardian, £5—£100; shipping goods.* LOC: Follow A12 to within 1 mile of Southend, turn right at Cricketers public house, shop is approx. 300yds. on left. PARK: Next door. TEL: Southend-on-Sea (0702) 344624; home — Southend-on-Sea (0702) 711270. SER: Valuations; buys at auction (paintings and small Victorian furniture).

R. Patten
24 Park St. Open 9.30—5.30, evenings by appointment. *STOCK: General antiques.* TEL: Southend-on-Sea (0702) 330113.

WHITE COLNE, Nr. Colchester

Compton-Dando
(Fine Arts) Limited
Berewyk Hall. (A. and J. Compton-Dando.) Open all reasonable hours. 24 hour answering service. *STOCK: 17th to early 19th C English and Continental furniture.* LOC: B1024. At 'King's Head' take left turn marked 'Bures' and make for White Colne parish church. Berewyk Hall lies just beyond, on left. TEL: Earls Colne (07875) 2200. VAT: Stan/Spec.

Fox and Pheasant Antique Pine
(J. and J. Kearin.) Est. 1978. Open 10—5 including Sun. SIZE: Large. *STOCK: Stripped pine.* LOC: A604. PARK: Easy. TEL: Earls Colne (078 75) 3297. SER: Pine stripping and restorations.

White Colne continued

Greyhound Lodge Antiques
Colchester Rd. (L. and J. Morden.) Est. 1974. Open daily. *STOCK: Period and Victorian furniture.* LOC: A604, 8 miles east of Colchester. PARK: Easy. TEL: Earls Colne (078 75) 2311.

WHITE RODING   (024 976)
White Roding Antiques
'Ivydene', Chelmsford Rd. (F. and J. Neill.) Est. 1971. Open by appointment. SIZE: Medium. *STOCK: Furniture and shipping goods, 18th—19th C, £10—£1,500.* LOC: A1060 between Bishops Stortford and Chelmsford. PARK: Easy. TEL: 376; home — same. VAT: Stan/Spec.

WITHAM   (0376)
Witham Antiques
Open by appointment. *STOCK: Furniture, period and later; silver and gold items, jewellery, porcelain, copper, brass, coins and clocks.* TEL: 512416.

WOODFORD GREEN
See Greater London

Gloucestershire

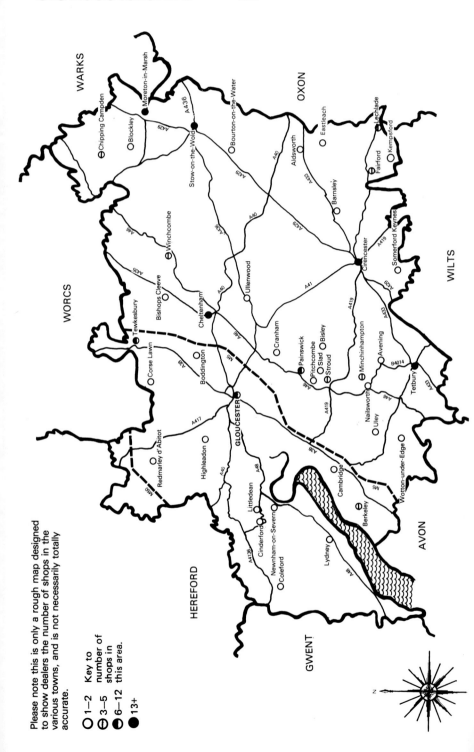

ALDSWORTH,
Nr. Cheltenham
Gerald and Katherine Manus
Antiques
The Old Chapel. Open 10—6, Sun. by appointment. *STOCK: Oak, walnut and mahogany furniture.* TEL: Windrush (045 14) 547. SER: Interior decoration.

AVENING
Upton Lodge Galleries
Avening House. (J. Grant.) Est. 1979. Open by appointment. SIZE: Medium. *STOCK: Oils and watercolours, 1880—1950, £100—£5,000.* PARK: Easy. TEL: Nailsworth (045 383) 4048.

BARNSLEY
Nr. Cirencester
Denzil Verey
The Close, Barnsley House, CADA. Est. 1980. Open 9.30—5.30, Sat. 10.30—5.30, other times by appointment. SIZE: Large. *STOCK: Country furniture, including pine, 18th—19th C; treen, tools, unusual and decorative items.* LOC: 4 miles from Cirencester on A433 to Burford, 1st large house in village, set back off road on the right. PARK: Easy. TEL: Bibury (0285 74) 402; home — (0285 85) 495. VAT: Stan/Spec.

BERKELEY
The Antique Shop
11 High St. (H. Trueman.) Resident. Est. 1976. CL: Sat. p.m. Mon. and Wed. Open 9.30—5.30. SIZE: Small. *STOCK: Small furniture and decorative items, porcelain, glass, needlework and pictures.* LOC: From A38 turn left into High St. past Berkeley Arms Hotel, shop 100yds. on left. PARK: Easy. TEL: Dursley (0453) 811085.

IS YOUR ENTRY CORRECT?
If there is even the slightest inaccuracy in your entry, *please* let us know before 1st January 1987.
GUIDE TO THE
ANTIQUE SHOPS OF BRITAIN
5 Church Street, Woodbridge, Suffolk.

Denzil Verey Antiques

The Close, Barnsley House,
Near Cirencester,
Gloucestershire. GL7 5EE
Bibury (0285 74) 402

18th and 19th century country furniture, pine, treen and unusual items

---

Berkeley continued

Berkeley Antiques   LAPADA
Marybrook St. (P. and R. Dennis.) Est. 1970. CL: Sat. p.m. and Wed. Open 9.30—1 and 2—5.30, Sun. by appointment. SIZE: Large. *STOCK: Brass, copper, 18th—19th C, £5—£200; oak, Victorian rosewood and mahogany furniture, 17th—19th C, £50—£1,200.* LOC: Opposite hospital. PARK: Easy. TEL: Dursley (0453) 810391. VAT: Stan/Spec.

Sylvia Harris
13 High St. (Mrs. S.J. Harris). Est. 1984. Open 10—6, Wed. by appointment. SIZE: Medium. *STOCK: Jewellery, porcelain, silver and plate, £25—£500.* LOC: From A38 turn left into High St., past Berkeley Arms Hotel, shop 150 yds. on left. PARK: Easy. TEL: Dursley (0453) 811120. SER: Valuations. VAT: Stan/Spec.

Berkeley continued

Michael R. Mathews
13 High St. Resident. Est. 1983. Open 10—6, Sat. 10—1, Wed. by appointment. SIZE: Medium. *STOCK: Furniture, 17th—19th C; porcelain and silver.* PARK: Easy. TEL: Dursley (0453) 811120. SER: Valuations; restorations (furniture). VAT: Spec.

Newcomb Antiques
17—19 High St. (J. and W. Newcomb Cryer.) Resident. Est. 1978. CL: Wed. and Sat. p.m. Open 9.30—5.45. SIZE: Medium. *STOCK: 18th and 19th C furniture, general antiques, small silver, porcelain and pine.* LOC: From A38 on B4066 past Berkeley Arms Hotel, turn left into High St., last shop 200yds. on left. PARK: Easy. TEL: Dursley (0453) 810338. VAT: Stan/Spec.

BISHOPS CLEEVE (024 267)
Nr. Cheltenham

Cleeve Picture Framing
Church Rd. (J. Gardner.) Open 9—1 and 2—6, Sat. 9—12. *STOCK: Prints and pictures.* TEL: 2785. SER: Framing, cleaning, restoring (oils, watercolours and prints).

The Priory Gallery
The Priory, Station Rd. (R.M. and E. James.) Est. 1977. Open by appointment only. SIZE: Medium. *STOCK: Watercolours and oils, mainly English, 1870—1930, £500—£20,000.* LOC: A435. PARK: Easy. TEL: 3226. SER: Valuations; restorations (watercolours, prints and oils); framing; buys at auction (watercolours, oils). VAT: Stan/Spec.

BISLEY, Nr. Stroud

High Street Antiques
(H. Ross.) CL: Wed. and Thurs. Open 12—6. SIZE: Small. *STOCK: General antiques, furniture, china, glass, silver, Oriental and Eastern rugs.* TEL: Home — Gloucester (0452) 740275.

BLOCKLEY (0386)
Nr. Moreton-in-Marsh

Pamela Rowan **BADA**
High St. (M. and P. Rowan.) CADA. Resident. Est. 1959. CL: Sun., Mon. and Tues. except by appointment. Open 9.—5. SIZE: Medium. *STOCK: English porcelain and pottery, oak and mahogany furniture, all 18th C; copper and brass.* LOC: 1½ miles off A44 between Moreton and Broadway. PARK: Easy. TEL: 700280. SER: Valuations, buys at auction (porcelain). VAT: Spec.

BODDINGTON, Nr. Cheltenham

The Original Architectural Heritage
Boddington Manor. Est. 1978. Open 9—5, Sat. 10.30—1 or by appointment. SIZE: Large. *STOCK: Period panelling, oak mahogany and pine; chimney pieces in marble, stone, oak and mahogany; garden statuary, fountains, seats and urns; complete shop and pub interiors, ornamental gates; stained, leaded and etched glass; doors, decorative and unusual items.* PARK: Easy. TEL: Cheltenham (0242) 68741. VAT: Stan.

BOURTON-ON-THE-WATER (0451)

Mill House Antiques
The Mill House. (J.S. Cooper.) Est. 1966. Open 9.30—6. SIZE: Medium. *STOCK: General antiques, English and Continental furniture, glass, porcelain, collectors' items.* TEL: 20656.

Studio Antiques Ltd.
High St. CADA. Est. 1933. Always available by appointment. *STOCK: Porcelain, including 1st Period Dr. Wall, Worcester, Nantgarw, Swansea; Georgian silver; English and Continental furniture, all periods including English oak; pewter, brass and copper items.* TEL: 20352. VAT: Spec.

PAMELA ROWAN

High Street, Blockley, Nr. Moreton in Marsh, Glos.
Telephone 0386 700 280

Specialising in 18th century
English porcelain. We also have a
good stock of 18th century English
mahogany oak furniture.

**BLOCKLEY IS OFF THE A44
BETWEEN BROADWAY AND
MORETON IN MARSH**

Open Wednesday to Saturday inclusive
any other time by appointment
Resident on the premises.

Fine pair of early Derby figures, c.1760.

Studio Antiques Ltd

Bourton-on-the-Water, Gloucestershire
Telephone Bourton-on-the-Water
20352 Std 0451

Examples of transfer printed Dr. Wall — Worcester porcelain.

Cheltenham continued

CAMBRIDGE (045 389)
Nr. Gloucester

Bell House Antiques
Bell House. (G. and J. Hawkins.) Resident. Open 11−1 and 2−5 including Sun. SIZE: Medium. *STOCK: General antiques including 19th C pine, £5−£500.* LOC: Near Slimbridge, on main A38. PARK: Easy. TEL: 463. SER: Valuations. VAT: Stan/Spec.

CHELTENHAM (0242)

Antiques (Cheltenham)   LAPADA
22 Montpellier Walk. (J. Turner.) Est. 1950. *STOCK: Furniture, porcelain, silver, fine arts.* TEL: 522939. VAT: Stan/Spec.

Armada Exports   LAPADA
50 Suffolk Rd. (K.J. Shave.) Resident. Est. 1970. Open 9−5.30. *STOCK: General antiques.* TEL: 32615 and 529812. VAT: Stan.

David Bannister, F.R.G.S.
26 Kings Rd. Est. 1962. Open by appointment only. SIZE: Medium. *STOCK: Early maps and prints, 1480−1850, £5−£5,000; decorative and topographical prints; atlases and colour plate books.* TEL: 514287. SER: Valuations; restorations; lectures; buys at auction; catalogues issued. VAT: Stan.

Barrie's Bookshop
4 Montpellier Walk, Antiquarian Dept. 1st floor. (P. and M. Barrie.) ABA. Open by appointment. *STOCK: Antiquarian books including travel; bindings.* LOC: Near the Queen's Hotel. PARK: Easy. TEL: 515813.

Bed of Roses
12 Prestbury Rd. (M. Losh.) Est. 1978. Open 9.30−5.30. SIZE: Large. *STOCK: Stripped pine.* LOC: 200 metres on town side of roundabout, A46. PARK: Easy. TEL: 31918 (24 hrs.). SER: Restorations, pine stripping, metal polishing. VAT: Stan/Spec.

Benson Antiques
13 Suffolk Parade, Montpellier. (H.F. and F. Benson.) Est. 1961. Open by appointment. SIZE: Medium. *STOCK: Furniture, decorative items; table and bedlinen.* LOC: Off Montpellier Terrace. PARK: Easy. TEL: 578366; home − 517739. VAT: Spec.

Bick
5 Montpellier Walk. (J.H. and M.M. Bishop.) Est. 1900. CL: Wed. Open 9.15−1 and 2−5. SIZE: Small. *STOCK: Jewellery, 1800−1900, £5−£150; silver, plate, 1750−1900, £5−£250; clocks, watches; porcelain.* Not stocked: Pewter, brass, copper. LOC: Top of the Promenade, nr. Queens Hotel and Rotunda. PARK: Easy. TEL: 524738. SER: Valuations. VAT: Stan.

Bottles and Bygones
96 Horsefair St., Charlton Kings. (J. and M. Brown.) Est. 1974. CL: Mon. and Tues. Open 10−5.30. *STOCK: Bottles, pot-lids, pipes, dolls' heads, enamel signs, children's books, postcards, general antiques, furniture, collectors' items, cameras and gramophones.* LOC: 1 mile from Cheltenham off Cirencester road. PARK: Easy. TEL: 36393; home − same.

Brocante Antiques
197 London Rd. TEL: 43120.

Brownings Antiques
401 High St. Open 9−5.30. *STOCK: General antiques.* TEL: 527169. VAT: Stan.

Butler and Co.
115 Promenade. (D.J. Butler.) Est. 1968. Open Sat. only. SIZE: Small. *STOCK: English coins, 1st to 20th C and world coins, 19th C, both £5−£25; British campaign medals, 19th−20th C, £50−£100.* PARK: Easy. TEL: 522272; home − 34439. SER: Valuations. FAIRS: Bristol and West of England Coin, July and Oct.

Cameo Antiques/China Doll
31 Suffolk Parade. (R.L. and R.A. Chitty.) Est. 1970. CL: Wed. p.m. Open 10−1 and 2−5. SIZE: Small. *STOCK: General antiques, 19th−20th C, £5−£5,000; Victoriana, from £1; collectors' items, art deco, art pottery, Doulton, Moorcroft; china and wax dolls; furniture, 18th C and decorative; shipping goods in trade warehouse.* Not stocked: Militaria. PARK: Easy. TEL: Home − 33164. VAT: Stan/Spec.

Carlton House Antiques
18−21 Suffolk Parade. (M.J. Blunt.) Est. 1961. SIZE: Medium. *STOCK: English and Continental furniture, 17th−19th C; bracket clocks, 18th and 19th C; copper, brass.* PARK: Easy. TEL: 30834 or 54246. VAT: Stan.

Carrie's Antiques
16 Suffolk Rd. (S. Freeman.) Open Thurs.− Sat. 10−5, other times by appointment. *STOCK: Small decorative antiques including porcelain, glass, jewellery, furniture, Oriental items, late 18th to early 20th C, £2−£250.* LOC: Near Bath Rd. shopping area and Colleges. PARK: Nearby. TEL: 584895; home − 42713.

Castle Antiques   LAPADA
15 Commercial St. (T.C. Germain.) Est. 1953. Open by appointment only. *STOCK: Silver and Sheffield plate, from 18th C, £50−£3,000; barometers, 18th-19th C, £150−£1,000; jewellery, 19th C, £50−£2,000.* PARK: Easy. TEL: 524563; home − same. SER: Valuations; restorations.

Cheltenham Antique Market
54 Suffolk Rd. (K.J. Shave.) Est. 1970. There are 30 dealers trading from this market. Open 9−5.30. TEL: 529812, 32615, 520139 (ansafone).

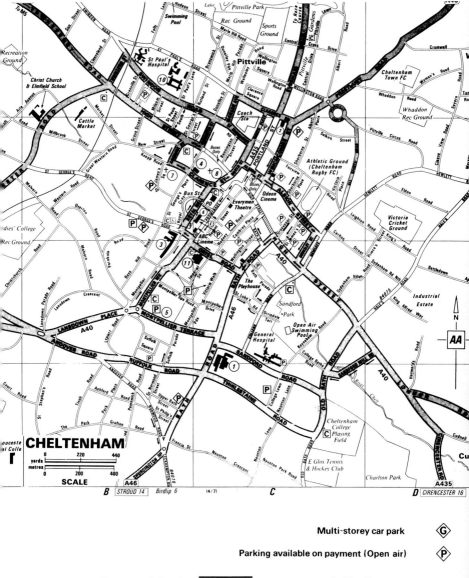

CHELTENHAM

yards 0   220   440
metres 0   200   400
SCALE

B | STROUD 14 | Birdlip 6   (4/7)   C   D | CIRENCESTER 16

Multi-storey car park   ⊙G

Parking available on payment (Open air)   ⊙P

Recommended route

Other roads

Restricted roads (Access only/Buses only)

Traffic roundabout

Official car park free (Open air)   P

Parking Zone

One-way street   ←

Pedestrians only

Convenience   C

Convenience with facilities
for the disabled   C ♿

Tourist Information Centre   i

Reproduced by kind permission of the
Automobile Association

Cheltenham continued

Cocoa
7 Queens Circus. (O.J. Dell.) Est. 1973. Open 10−5. SIZE: Small. *STOCK: Lace clothes, fans, interesting small items and jewellery, 19th−20th C, £5−£500.* LOC: Rear of Montpellier, near Queens Hotel. PARK: Easy. TEL 33588; home − same. SER: Valuations; restorations (period textiles). VAT: Stan.

George Curtis   BADA
                                     LAPADA
14 Suffolk Parade. Est. 1957. CL: Wed. p.m. Open 9−5.30, but any time by appointment. *STOCK: Clocks, 17th−18th C; English marquetry, French and Dutch longcase clocks; also mantel, bracket and unusual carriage clocks.* PARK: Easy. TEL: 513828.

Colin Elliott   LAPADA
4 Gt. Norwood St. Est. 1967. CL: Wed. Open 10−5.30, but appointment advisable. SIZE: Small. *STOCK: Watches, £20−£1,000; clocks, £100−£2,000; musical boxes.* Not stocked: All other items. PARK: Approx. 200yds. on main Bath Rd. TEL: 528590. VAT: Stan/Spec.

Finders Antiques
19 Suffolk Rd. (C. Meadows.) Open 10−1 and 2.30−5. SIZE: Small. *STOCK: Porcelain, pottery, glass, needlework items, small silver and jewellery, collectors' items, small furniture.* LOC: On A40.

Gladys Green
15 Montpellier Walk. Est. 1946. CL: Wed. p.m. Open 9−5. SIZE: Medium. *STOCK: Furniture, 18th−19th C; porcelain, both £100−£5,000; silver and Victorian jewellery, £5−£5,000.* LOC: Conjunction of Promenade and main shopping centre. PARK: Easy. TEL: 512088. SER: Buys at auction. VAT: Stan/Spec.

Homer Oriental Rugs
Stoneleigh, Parabola Rd. (J.P.J. Homer.) Est. 1969. Open at any time by appointment. SIZE: Small. *STOCK: Oriental rugs, mainly Turcoman and tribal, £75−£1,500.* LOC: 200yds. from Savoy Hotel, behind Montpellier. PARK: Easy. TEL: 34243. SER: Valuations; restorations; cleaning.

David Howard
9A Montpellier Grove. Est. 1983. Open by appointment. *STOCK: Fine oil paintings, watercolours and drawings, 19th−20th C, £100−£2,000.* PARK: Easy. TEL: 39887; home − same. SER: Valuations; buys at auction; research (pictures).

H.W. Keil (Cheltenham) Ltd. BADA
129−131 Promenade. Est. 1953. SIZE: Large. *STOCK: Furniture, paintings, 17th−18th C, metalwork, chandeliers.* LOC: Opp. Queens Hotel, at top of Promenade. PARK: Easy. TEL: 522509. SER: Upholstery. VAT: Spec.

Cheltenham continued

Manor House Antiques
42 Suffolk Rd. (J.G. Benton.) Est. 1972. Open 9.30−5. SIZE: Large. *STOCK: Furniture, general antiques, 19th C and Victorian, £50−£1,500; shipping goods.* Not stocked: Small items, china and jewellery. LOC: A40. PARK: Nearby. TEL: 32780; home − Tewkesbury (0684) 293222. VAT: Stan/Spec.

Martin and Co. Ltd.   BADA
19 The Promenade. (I.M. and N.C.S. Dimmer.) Est. 1890. CL: Sat. p.m. *STOCK: Silver, Sheffield plate, jewellery, objets d'art.* TEL: 522821. VAT: Stan/Spec.

Mirrors
8 Suffolk Rd. (S. Watts.) Est. 1977. CL: Tues. Open 10−5.30. *STOCK: Mirrors, 18th−20th C, £20−£1,000.* PARK: Easy. TEL: 45808. SER: Restorations; re-gilding.

Montpellier Clocks
13 Rotunda Terrace, Montpellier. (G. Curtis, B. Bass.) Open 9.30−6. *STOCK: Clocks, 17th−19th C; small furniture.* LOC: Close to Queens Hotel. PARK: Easy. TEL: 42178.

Elizabeth Niner Antiques
53 Gt. Norwood St. Est. 1972. Open 9.30−5. SIZE: Medium. *STOCK: Fourposter beds, mahogany furniture, 18th−19th C; objets d'art, 1700−1900, £10−£800.* LOC: Off Suffolk Rd. PARK: Easy. TEL: 516497; home − 520066. VAT: Stan/Spec.

Patrick Oliver   LAPADA
4 Tivoli St. Est. 1896. SIZE: Large. *STOCK: Furniture and shipping goods.* PARK: Easy. TEL: 513392; home − 519538. VAT: Stan/Spec.

J. and J.D. Pomfret   *Mainly Trade*
188 Bath Rd. Est. 1954. CL: Wed. p.m. Open 10−12.30 and 2−6. SIZE: Large. *STOCK: Furniture, general antiques and shipping items; oil lamps, burners, chimneys, globes, shades, etc.* Not stocked: French furniture. LOC: Up Bath Rd. from town centre, on left. PARK: 100yds. behind other side of Bath Rd., also Exmouth St. TEL: 529239; home − 529579. VAT: Stan/Spec.

Eric Pride Oriental Rugs
Lower Ground Floor, 8 Imperial Sq. GMC. Est. 1980. Open 10−6. SIZE: Medium. *STOCK: Rugs and carpets, £100−£4,000; kilims, £200−£1,000; saddle-bags and horse covers, £150−£800; all 19th to early 20th C.* LOC: Opposite town hall entrance. PARK: Easy. TEL: 580822; home − 521057. SER: Valuations; restorations (cleaning and repairs); buys at auction (rugs from Persia, Caucasus and Central Asia; carpets from Turkey and Persia; kilims and bags). VAT: Stan.

Cheltennam continued

Scott-Cooper Ltd.   BADA
52 The Promenade. Est. 1914. *STOCK: Silver, plate, jewellery, clocks, ivory, enamel, objets de vertu.* **TEL: 522580. SER: Repair and restoration of silver and jewellery. VAT: Stan/Spec.**

David Slade
70 Naunton Crescent. Est. 1973. Open by appointment. *STOCK: Small decorative antiques.* TEL: 510619. FAIRS: Heritage, London, every Sun.

Geoffrey Stead
The Old Rectory, Dowdeswell. Est. 1963. *STOCK: English and Continental furniture; decorative objects, paintings.* Not stocked: Porcelain, glass, silver, shipping goods. LOC: 3 miles from Cheltenham, just off A40. Turn right, signpost to Dowdeswell. 1st house on left up hill. PARK: Easy. TEL: 820571. SER: Valuations; buys at auction. VAT: Spec.

Struwwelpeter
35 Prestbury Rd. (N. and R. Bliss.) Est. 1976. Open 9.30—1 and 2—6. SIZE: Medium. *STOCK: General antiques, 19th to early 20th C, £50—£200; shipping oak, early 20th C, from £25.* LOC: ½ mile from town centre on Prestbury/Winchcombe road. PARK: Adjacent. TEL: 30152; home — same. VAT: Stan/Spec.

Cheltenham continued

R.E. Summerfield
1 and 2 Montpellier Ave. Est. 1950. *STOCK: General antiques, bric-a-brac, Victoriana, decorative items.* TEL: 516101.

Turtle Antiques
29 and 30 Suffolk Parade. (P. Field and W. Forsyth). Open 9—6. SIZE: Medium. *STOCK: Furniture, 18th C to Edwardian; watercolours, oils, prints, all £25—£1,000; china, silver plate and glass.* LOC: Off Suffolk Rd. (A40). PARK: Easy. TEL. 41646; home — same. VAT: Stan/Spec.

CHIPPING CAMPDEN
Pedlars
Lower High St. (M. Fazackerley.) CL: Thurs. p.m. Open 10—5. *STOCK: Victorian furniture, general antiques.* TEL: Evesham (0386) 840680.

Saxton House Gallery   LAPADA
High St. (S.D. and J. Coy.) CL: Thurs. Open 9—5.30. SIZE: Medium. *STOCK: Fine English clocks and barometers, unusual carriage clocks, jewellery, Georgian furniture, paintings and watercolours.* LOC: Centre of village. PARK: Easy. TEL: Evesham (0386) 840278. VAT: Stan/Spec.

Chipping Campden continued

Swan Antiques
High St. (J. Stocker.) Est. 1960. Open 9—1 and 2—5, Thurs. 9—12. SIZE: Medium. *STOCK: Furniture, £150—£2,000; silver, £25—£1,500; china, £35—£500, all 18th—19th C; other decorative items.* LOC: 50yds. from Woolmarket. PARK: Easy. TEL: Evesham (0386) 840759. SER: Valuations; buys at auction. VAT: Stan/Spec.

Woolmarket Antiques
High St. (M.K. Havemann-Mart.) CL: Thurs. p.m. Open 10—1 and 2—5, Sun. by appointment. SIZE: Medium. *STOCK: Sewing and craft tools, workboxes and lace bobbins, £5—£900; small collectables, £5—£50; all 18th—19th C.* LOC: Behind old Market Hall. PARK: Easy. TEL: Evesham (0386) 840827; home — same. SER: Valuations. FAIRS: Newton Abbot.

CINDERFORD

Market Street Antiques
37 Market St. (B. Harris.) Open 9—5.30, Sun. 10—4. *STOCK: General antiques.* TEL: Dean (0594) 22686.

Cinderford continued

Puzzle House Antiques   LAPADA
Trafalgar. Open by appointment only. *STOCK: Writing and other boxes, lap desks, small antiques for the dining room.* TEL: Dean (0594) 60653. VAT: Stan/Spec.

CIRENCESTER   (0285)

Walter Bull and Son (Cirencester) Ltd.
10 Dyer St. Est. 1815. Open 9—5. SIZE: Small. *STOCK: Silver, from 1700, £10—£1,500; china, from 1800, £15—£150; objets d'art.* LOC: Lower end of Market Place. PARK: At rear. TEL: 3875. SER: Restorations (jewellery and silver). VAT: Stan/Spec.

Cirencester Antique Market
Market Place. (Antique Forum Ltd.) Open Fri. There are approx. 60 dealers at this market offering *a wide range of general antiques.* TEL: (01) 263 4045.

Cirencester Antiques Ltd.
Dyer Lodge, 17 Dyer St. (Mr. and Mrs. R.T.G. Chester-Master.) CADA. Est. 1959. Open 9—5.30. SIZE: Large. *STOCK: Furniture and works of art, 17th to early 19th C, £50—£15,000.* LOC: Market Place narrows into Dyer St. The shop is 30yds. ahead on the left. PARK: Own at rear. TEL: 2955.

WILLIAM H. STOKES

W.H. Stokes   P.W. Bontoft

EARLY OAK FURNITURE

ROBERTS HOUSE,
SIDDINGTON,
CIRENCESTER,
GLOUCESTERSHIRE
GL7 6EX
Telephone Cirencester (0285) 67101

Fine Elizabethan carved oak Poster Bed

Cirencester continued

Corner Cupboard Curios
2 Church St. (P. Larner.) *STOCK: General antiques and gramophonalia.* TEL: 5476.

Country Seats
15 Gosditch St. (Mrs. J. Lodge.) Est. 1982. Open 10—5.30. SIZE: Medium. *STOCK: Chairs, all periods, £100—£1,000.* LOC: Just behind main church. PARK: Own. TEL: 67557; home — 4281. SER: Restorations; buys at auction (especially matching sets of chairs).

Jay Gray Antiques
Syrena House, 1 Cheltenham Rd. (Mrs. J. Gray.) Est. 1961. Open 9—6, or by appointment. *STOCK: English and French furniture; English, Continental and Oriental porcelain; all 18th—19th C; pictures, silver, glass, jewellery, collectors' items, objets d'art.* Not stocked: Uniforms, shawls, Goss china. LOC: Junction of A435 and A417. PARK: Easy. TEL: 2755. SER: Buys at auction. VAT: Spec.

W.W. Holzgrawe Antiques
7 Gosditch St. (W. and A.M. Holzgrawe.) CADA. Est. 1952. Open 9.15—1 and 2—5.30. SIZE: Medium. *STOCK: Mahogany, 18th to early 19th C, £100—£8,000; oak, £75—£2,500; walnut, £200—£5,000; both 17th to early 19th C; small items, copper and brass.* LOC: West Market Place, behind parish church. PARK: Limited or Market Pl. TEL: 69351; home — 68625. SER: Valuations. VAT: Spec.

The Hon. Maurice Howard
Frith House, Far Oakridge. Open by appointment. *STOCK: Old English watercolours and marine oil paintings.* TEL: Frampton Mansell (028 576) 586.

Thomas and Pamela Hudson
At the Sign of the Herald Angel, 19 Park St. CADA. Est. 1959. Open 9—1 and 2—5.30. *STOCK: Old Sheffield, small objets de vertu, fans, needlework tools and workboxes.* TEL: 2972. SER: Valuations; buys at auction. VAT: Spec.

Cirencester continued

The William Marler Gallery
36—38 Dyer St. Est. 1975. Open 9.30—5.30. SIZE: Large. *STOCK: Wildlife and sporting paintings and watercolours, £100—£20,000; signed proofs and prints, £20—£1,500; all 19th—20th C.* PARK: Easy. TEL: 68526/7.

Monk Bretton Books
Somerford Keynes House. Open by appointment. *STOCK: Antiquarian and 20th C private press books.* TEL: 860554.

A.J. Ponsford Antiques
51—53 Dollar St. (A.J. and R.L.Ponsford.) Est. 1962. CL: Sat. Open 8—5.30. SIZE: Large. *STOCK: Furniture, 1800—1830, £25—£4,000; furniture, 1700—1800, £50—£5,500; copper, brass.* Not stocked: Silver. LOC: 200yds. from Church on left towards Gloucester at junction of Thomas St. and Spitalgate Lane. PARK: 50yds. opp. TEL: 2355. SER: Valuations; restorations (furniture and oil paintings); rushing, caning, upholstery, picture framing; buys at auction. VAT: Stan/Spec.

John D. Rivers   LAPADA
1 Ashcroft Rd. Est. 1973. CL: Mon. Open 10—5, Sat. 10—4. SIZE: Small. *STOCK: Jewellery, 18th—20th C, £25—£1,000.* LOC: Off Cricklade St. PARK: Nearby. TEL: 67616. SER: Valuations; restorations. VAT: Stan/Spec.

Antony Sidgwick Antiques
25 Park St. Open by appointment only. *STOCK: 18th C creamware and cutlery; decorative items.* TEL: 3628.

William H. Stokes   BADA
Roberts House, Siddington. (W.H. Stokes and P.W. Bontoft.) CADA. Open 10—6. SIZE: Medium. *STOCK: Oak furniture, 16th—17th C, from £250; brass candlesticks, almsdishes, from £150.* **LOC: 1 mile south of Cirencester off A419. PARK: Easy. TEL: 67101. FAIRS: Grosvenor House, Harrogate and Bath. VAT: Spec.**

Cirencester continued

Rankine Taylor Antiques   LAPADA
34 Dollar St. (Mrs. L. Taylor.) CADA. Est. 1969. Open 9—5.30. Sun. by appointment. SIZE: Large. *STOCK: Furniture, 17th—19th C, £20—£3,500; glass, 18th—20th C, £3—£250; silver and decorative items, 17th—20th C, £1—£1,000.* Not stocked: Victoriana, militaria. LOC: From Church, turn right up West Market Place, via Gosditch St. into Dollar St. PARK: Gloucester St. (50yds.). TEL: 2529. SER: Valuations; buys at auction (furnishing items). VAT: Stan/Spec.

Thornborough Galleries   BADA
28 Gloucester St. (R. Purdon and A. du Monceau.) CADA. Est. 1968. Open 9—5, Sat. 9—1. SIZE: Large. *STOCK: Eastern carpets.* LOC: From town centre towards Gloucester and Cheltenham, shop is about ⅓ mile. PARK: Easy. TEL: 2055. SER: Valuations; restorations (Oriental carpets and rugs). VAT: Stan/Spec.

P.J. Ward Fine Paintings
11 Gosditch St. Open 9—5. *STOCK: 17th—19th C paintings.* TEL: 68499. SER: Valuations; restorations; framing. VAT: Spec.

Westwood Antiques
Unit 1 and 2, Ullenwood Court. (H.W. and P.J. Minett-Westwood.) Open 8—5.30 or by appointment. SIZE: Large. *STOCK: Fine art and antiques, 17th—19th C.* TEL: Cheltenham (0242) 578369; home — 3341.

COLEFORD

St. John's Studio
18 St. John St. (A.E. and D.D. Young.) Est. 1947. CL: Thurs. Open 10—1 and 2—5. SIZE: Large. *STOCK: 19th C furniture, pottery, porcelain, glass; clocks, £20—£250; prints, maps, 1700—1889, £3—£25; 18th—19th C Chinese porcelain, watercolours, oil paintings, books, £5—£50.* LOC: In town centre 100yds. from Lloyds Bank. PARK: In Box Bush Rd. opp. TEL: Dean (0594) 32368.

CORSE LAWN

Arthur S. Lewis   LAPADA
Est. 1964. Open by appointment only. SIZE: Medium. *STOCK: Clocks, 18th—19th C, £500—£6,000; musical boxes, £800—£9,000; barometers, £350—£3,000.* LOC: 4 miles from Tewkesbury on B4211. PARK: Easy. TEL: Tirley (045 278) 258. SER: Valuations. VAT: Stan/Spec.

CRANHAM

Heather Newman Gallery
Milidduwa, Mill Lane. Est. 1969. Open every day by appointment. *STOCK: British watercolours and drawings, 18th—20th C, £50—£5,000.* LOC: Near Prinknash Abbey, just off A46 at Cranham Corner. PARK: Easy. TEL: Painswick (0452) 812230. SER: Major exhibitions with illustrated catalogues, May and Nov; valuations; buys at auction. VAT: Spec.

EASTLEACH, Nr. Cirencester

Guy Holland   BADA
Sheepbridge Barn. Est. 1961. Open by appointment only. *STOCK: English furniture, late 17th to late 18th C.* **TEL: Southrop (036 785) 296.** VAT: Spec.

Trouthouse Antiques
Macaroni Wood. (B.D. Cotton.) Est. 1965. Open 8—5, Sat. 9—12 or by appointment. *STOCK: English country furniture especially chairs and tables; French provincial furniture including armoires, buffets, and farmhouse tables.* TEL: Southrop (036 785) 298.

FAIRFORD

Gloucester House Antiques Ltd.
Market Place. (Mr. and Mrs. R. Chester-Master.) CADA. Est. 1972. Open 9—5.30. SIZE: Large. *STOCK: English and French country furniture in oak, elm, fruitwood, pine; pottery and decorative items.* PARK: Easy. TEL: Cirencester (0285) 712790; home — Cirencester (0285) 3066. VAT: Stan/Spec.

William Pelly
Linden House. (W.R.B. Pelly.) Est. 1960. Open by appointment. *STOCK: Oil Paintings, 17th—20th C, £20—£2,000; watercolours, 18th—19th C, £3—£300; 17th—20th C drawings, £3—£300.* Not stocked: General antiques. LOC: Next door to hospital, in the Croft. PARK: Easy. TEL: Cirencester (0285) 712297 or 712356. SER: Valuations. VAT: Spec.

Charles Woodward Antiques
Market Place. Est. 1974. Open 10—5.30, Sat. 9.30—4.30, or by appointment. *STOCK: Furniture, 17th—19th C; brass, small items.* TEL: Cirencester (0285) 712094; home — Kempsford (028 581) 203. SER: Valuations; restorations. VAT: Stan/Spec.

GLOUCESTER (0452)

Douglas J. Bartrick
The Antique Centre, Severn Rd. Est. 1971. Open 9—5, Sat. 9—4.30, Sun. 1—4.30. STOCK: 18th—19th C furniture, clocks, oils and watercolours, maps and prints. LOC: Gloucester dock area. PARK: At side of building. TEL: 29716; home — 68465. SER: Restorations (clocks); insurance and record photography.

J.A. Brown
Shop 8 — Centre Arcade, Antique Centre, Severn Rd. F.G.A. Est. 1980. Open 8.30—5, Sat. 8.30—4.30, Sun. 1—4.30. SIZE: Small. STOCK: Jewellery and silver, 19th—20th C; small furniture, porcelain and ivory, 19th C; all £5—£500. PARK: Easy. TEL: 29716 and 414582. SER: Valuations. FAIRS: Pittville Pump Room, Cheltenham. VAT: Stan/Spec.

E.J. Cook and Son Antiques
At the Antique Centre, Severn Rd. (E.J. and C.A. Cook.) Est. 1949. Open 9—5, Sat. 9—4.30, Sun. 1—4.30. SIZE: Large. STOCK: Furniture, clocks, oils and watercolours, small items, 17th—19th C, £50—£6,000. LOC: On ring road close to dock area. PARK: Easy. TEL: 29716; home — 20911. SER: Restorations (furniture, upholstery and clocks); buys at auction (furniture). VAT: Stan/Spec.

The Curiosity Shop, Military and Curio Supplies
82—84 Southgate St. (J. and B. Williams.) Est. 1964. Open 10—6, Sun. by appointment. STOCK: Medals, badges, coins, govnt. surplus, gold, silver, all £1—£500. LOC: A38, 350yds. from city centre. PARK: Easy, and multi-storey 200yds. TEL: 27716. SER: Valuations, finder service, costume hire.

Farr
At The Antique Centre, Severn Rd. (A. and J. Farr.) Open 9—5, Sun. 1—4.30. STOCK: Silver, watches, clocks, pottery, brass and glass. LOC: Gloucester dock area.

HQ84
Southgate St. (Mrs. B. Williams.) CL: Sat. Open 9.30—5.30 or by appointment. STOCK: Militaria, medals, badges, coins, small general antiques. Not stocked: Furniture. TEL: 27716.

Hayes and Newby Antique Warehouse
The Pit, Hare Lane. (P. and A. Hayes, B. Newby.) Est. 1976. Open 10—6. SIZE: Large. STOCK: American shipping oak, 19th—20th C, £25—£1,000; furniture, Victorian and Edwardian, £25—£500; architectural items. LOC: Off Worcester St. and Northgate St. PARK: Nearby. TEL: 24722/31145; home — 21359. VAT: Stan.

Gloucester continued

David Kent Antiques
300 Barton St. Est. 1967. Open 10—4.30, Sat. 10—12.30. STOCK: Victorian shipping items and books. LOC: Through town, near ring road, east side. PARK: Easy. TEL: 34396; home — 60976. VAT: Stan/Spec.

Lenda Antiques
83 Southgate St. Open 9.30—5.30. STOCK: General antiques especially porcelain and pottery. TEL: 410443.

Pegler's Antiques
2A Carlton Rd. (W.H. Pegler.) Est. 1968. CL: Mon. Open 10—12 and 2—4.30. STOCK: General small antiques; coins, jewellery, clocks. TEL: 20801.

HIGHLEADON
Nr. Newent
Rose Cottage Antiques
Rose Cottage. (C.L. and G.L. Wright.) Est. 1982. CL: Tues. Open 9.30—6. Sun. by appointment. SIZE: Small. STOCK: Porcelain, 1880—1960, £5—£120; glass, 1885—1930, £5—£80. PARK: Easy. TEL: Tibberton (045 279) 296; home — same. SER: Valuations; restorations (furniture).

KEMPSFORD, (028 581)
Nr. Fairford
Corinium Antiques
The Old Vicarage. (Mrs. H. Mahoney.) Est. 1980. Open 10—5, or by appointment. SIZE: Large. STOCK: Country furniture and pine, 17th—19th C; copper, brass, treen, unusual decorative accessories and agricultural items. PARK: Easy. TEL: 370.

LECHLADE
Antiques Etcetera
High St. (Mrs. C.L. Haillay.) Est. 1969. Open 10—5, Sun. and evenings by appointment. SIZE: Medium. STOCK: General antiques, country furniture and artifacts, decorators' items. PARK: Easy. TEL: Faringdon (0367) 52567; home — (0793) 770387. VAT: Stan/Spec.

Peter Bell Fine Arts
High St. (Mrs. P. Bell.) Open 10—1 and 2—5.30. STOCK: Country furniture, 17th and 18th C; early metalwork; English glass, pre-1850; English delft, oils, etchings and watercolours. LOC: North side of High St. PARK: Easy. TEL: Faringdon (0367) 52987; home — Faringdon (0367) 52255. VAT: Stan/Spec.

Lechlade continued

Gerard Campbell
Maple House, Market Place. (J. and G. Campbell.) Est. 1980. Open by appointment. SIZE: Large. *STOCK: Clocks especially Biedermeier, Vienna and regulator, 18th—19th C, £500—£6,000; watercolours, 19th C, £250—£2,500; Doulton, 19th C, £20—£200.* PARK: Easy. TEL: Faringdon (0367) 52267; home — same. SER: Valuations; buys at auction. VAT: Spec.

Peter Whitby Antiques
Ashleigh House, High St. Open 9—5.30. *STOCK: Furniture, metalware, porcelain, scientific instruments, items of interest.* PARK: Easy. TEL: Faringdon (0367) 52347. VAT: Spec.

LITTLEDEAN, Nr. Cinderford

Brayne Court Gallery
High St. (F.J. Grogan.) Est. 1983. Open by appointment. SIZE: Small. *STOCK: Oils and watercolours, 19th—20th C, £200—£3,000.* LOC: Off A48 onto A4151. PARK: Easy. TEL: Dean (0594) 22163; home — same. SER: Buys at auction (watercolours and prints).

LYDNEY

Crossbow Antiques
Bridge House, Newerne St. TEL: Dean (0594) 43662.

MINCHINHAMPTON, Nr. Stroud

Hampton Gallery
Knapp Lodge. Est. 1974. *STOCK: Weapons, arms and armour.* TEL: Brimscombe (0453) 884137.

R.J. Vosper
20 High St. Est. 1952. *STOCK: Furniture, glass, china, silver, brass, plate, bric-a-brac, 18th—20th C.* TEL: Brimscombe (0453) 882480. VAT: Stan.

Mick and Fanny Wright
'The Trumpet', West End. CL: Mon. Open 10.30—5.30. SIZE: Medium. *STOCK: Clocks, watches, silver, furniture, china including Pratt-ware, copper, brass, some toys, pipes, gramophones.* LOC: In road from town centre to the common. PARK: Nearby. TEL: Brimscombe (0453) 883027. VAT: Spec.

MORETON-IN-MARSH (0608)

Antique Centre
London House, High St. Est. 1979. Open 9.30—5.30. SIZE: Large. *STOCK: Furniture, paintings, watercolours, prints, domestic artifacts, clocks, silver, jewellery and plate, mainly 17th—19th C, £5—£3,000.* LOC: Centre of High St. (A429). PARK: Easy. TEL: 51084. VAT: Stan/Spec.

Moreton-in-Marsh continued

Astley House — Fine Art
Astley House, High St. (D. and N. Glaisyer.) CADA. Est. 1974. Open 9—5.30. *STOCK: Oil paintings, 19th—20th C; large decorative paintings.* LOC: Main street. PARK: Easy. TEL: 50601. SER: Restorations (oils and watercolours); framing. VAT: Spec.

The Avon Gallery
High St. (S. Creaton.) Est. 1978. CL: Wed. Open 9.30—5. *STOCK: Prints, especially sporting; maps.* TEL: 50614. SER: Picture framing.

Simon Brett BADA
Creswyke House, High St. Est. 1972. Open 9.30—5.30. *STOCK: English and Continental furniture, 17th to early 19th C; works of art, portrait miniatures, old fishing tackle.* TEL: 50751. VAT: Spec.

Moreton-in-Marsh continued

Paul Cater Antiques
High St. (P.J.C. Cater). Est. 1978. Open 9.30—5.30, Sun. by appointment. SIZE: Medium. *STOCK: Oak, walnut and mahogany furniture, £50—£5,000; carvings and treen, £10—£1,000; metalware, £10—£700; all 17th—19th C.* LOC: Northern end of High St on A429. PARK: Easy. TEL: 51888; home — same. VAT: Spec.

Fosse House Antiques
High St. (K.W. and Y.F. Heath.) Open by appointment only. TEL: 51443.

Franfam Ltd.   LAPADA
The Windrush, High St. (J. and S. Franses.) CADA. Est. 1974. Open 9—6, or by appointment. *STOCK: Furniture mainly oak and country; metalware, clocks, all 17th to early 19th C; some pottery and paintings.* Not stocked: Silver, coins. LOC: Near junction A429/A44. PARK: Easy. TEL: 50648. SER: Valuations. VAT: Mainly special.

Grimes House Antiques
High St. (S. and V. Farnsworth.) Est. 1978. CL: Wed. Open 9.30—1 and 2—5.30. *STOCK: General antiques, Victorian watercolours.* TEL: 51029. SER: Picture framing.

The Little Window
High St. (J.C. Bend.) Est. 1956. Open 10—5. SIZE: Small. *STOCK: Staffordshire pottery, Victoriana, collectors' items.* LOC: Main street. PARK: Easy. TEL: 50380.

Mrs. M.K. Nielsen   LAPADA
Seaford House, High St. Est. 1965. CL: Tues. and Wed. Open 9.30—1 and 2—5. SIZE: Medium. *STOCK: Derby porcelain, £45—£2,000; Worcester, £35—£2,000; furniture, £100—£3,000; brass, copper, glass, pictures, £100—£1,000; general antiques, £15—£1,200.* LOC: A429 Fosseway. PARK: Easy. TEL: 50448. VAT: Stan/Spec.

Elizabeth Parker
High St. (P.J. King-Smith.) CADA. Est. 1975. Open 9—6. SIZE: Medium. *STOCK: Furniture, £50—£3,000; marquetry, satinwood, porcelain, English and Continental, £10—£800, all 18th—19th C., some brass, copper, paintings.* LOC: Opposite Manor House Hotel, on Fosseway junction of A44 from Broadway. TEL: 50917. SER: Buys at auction. VAT: Stan/Spec.

Moreton-in-Marsh continued

Primrose Antiques
High St. (W.T. & B. Stickland.) CADA. Est. 1972. Open 9—5.30. SIZE: Medium. *STOCK: Oak, mahogany, brass, copper, pewter.* PARK: Easy. TEL: 50591; home — (0386) 700119. VAT: Stan/Spec.

Peter Roberts Antiques
High St. Open 10—6 or by appointment. SIZE: Medium. *STOCK: Decorative furniture, objets d'art, garden furniture, mirrors, beds, mainly 19th C, £50—£3,000.* LOC: Fosseway. PARK: Easy. TEL: 50698; home — same. SER: Valuations. VAT: Spec.

Anthony Sampson   BADA
Dale House. Est. 1967. Open 9—1, 2—5.30, Sun. by appointment. SIZE: Medium. *STOCK: Town and country furniture, to 1830; decorative items.* Not stocked: Reproductions. LOC: Main street. PARK: Easy. TEL: 50763. VAT: Spec.

NAILSWORTH   (045 383)
John Barry   BADA
                                 LAPADA
Barton End Hall. Est. 1963. Open 9.30—5.30, Sun. by appointment. SIZE: Medium. *STOCK: Fine English and Continental furniture, paintings, objets d'art, 18th to early 19th C, from £500.* LOC: 1 mile south of Nailsworth on A46 Bath Rd. PARK: Easy. TEL: 3471; home — same. SER: Valuations. FAIRS: Chelsea Spring and Autumn, Olympia, Park Lane Hotel. VAT: Spec.

Bridge Street Antiques
Bridge St. (A.P. Wood.) Est. 1971. Open Wed. to Sat. 10—5. SIZE: Medium. *STOCK: Stripped pine furniture, 19th C, £30—£300; Victorian and Edwardian bric-a-brac, £1—£25.* LOC: A46. PARK: Easy. TEL: 3978; home — same. VAT: Stan.

NEWNHAM-ON-SEVERN (059 455)
Newnham Bookshop
High St. (R. Orman.) Open Thurs. — Sat. 10—1 and 2—5 or by appointment. *STOCK: Antiquarian and secondhand books especially Folio Society.* TEL: (0594) 516324.

Ridgeway Antiques
The Old House, Lower High St. Open by appointment. *STOCK: 19th C furniture, especially upholstered items.* PARK: Easy. TEL: 558.

PAINSWICK   (0452)

Craig Carrington Antiques
Brook House. Est. 1970. Open 9—6, or by appointment. *STOCK: English and Continental furniture and works of art, £50—£15,000.* TEL: 813248. SER: Buys at auction. VAT: Spec.

Greenhouse Antiques   Trade only
Greenhouse Court Lodge, Bulls Cross. (T.G. Stait.) Est. 1986. Open 9.30—5.30, Sat. and Sun. by appointment. SIZE: Small. *STOCK: English walnut furniture, 18th C, £100—£10,000.* LOC: ½ mile outside village. PARK: Easy. TEL: 812487; home — same. SER: Buys at auction (furniture). VAT: Spec.

Hamand Antiques
Friday St. (F.N.L. Chapman.) Est. 1964. CL: Sat. p.m. Open 10—1 and 2—5.30, appointment advisable. *STOCK: Porcelain and glass, 18th—19th C; furniture, 18th C; silver, Sheffield plate, metalware, art nouveau.* Not stocked: Victoriana, bric-a-brac. LOC: From Stroud, turn right by church, from Cheltenham turn left by church. PARK: Easy. TEL: 812310. SER: Valuations. VAT: Spec.

Painswick continued

Painswick Antiques
Beacon House, New St. (J. and H. Hutton-Clarke.) CADA. Resident. Est. 1969. CL: Thurs. Open 9.30—1 and 2—5.30, Sat. 9.30—1. Trade welcome any reasonable time. *STOCK: Period furniture, including some highly decorative in oak, walnut, mahogany, yew, fruitwood and pine.* LOC: On A46 opp. church. PARK: Easy. TEL: 812578. VAT: Mainly Spec.

Regent Antiques   Trade Only
Dynevor House, New St. (Mr. and Mrs. G. Coggins.) Est. 1960. CL: Sat. and Sun., except by appointment. Open 10—5.30. SIZE: Medium. *STOCK: 17th—18th C, oak, walnut and mahogany, £100—£1,000.* LOC: Main road opp. church. PARK: Easy. TEL: 812543. SER: Restorations (furniture). VAT: Spec.

Painswick Antiques

Painswick Interiors

(John Hutton-Clarke)

(Hazel Hutton-Clarke)

FINE QUALITY PERIOD FURNITURE

BEACON HOUSE
Painswick Gloucestershire England   Telephone (0452) 812578

STONE HOUSE ANTIQUES

St. Mary's Street,
Painswick, Glos.
Telephone: Painswick 813540

Early Country Furniture
Craft & Design Gallery

18th century yew-wood highback armchairs; 18th century burr-yew candletable; 18th century tavern clock.

Painswick continued

Stone House Antiques
St. Mary's St. (W.R. Large.) CADA. Est. 1936. Open 10—1 and 2—5.30, Sat. 10—1.30, Sat. p.m. and Sun. a.m. by appointment. SIZE: Large. *STOCK: Yew, oak and walnut, £500—£3,500; fruitwood £500—£1,500; all to 19th C; Japanese art and crafts of Meiji period.* Not stocked: Mahogany. PARK: Nearby. TEL: 813540; home — Gloucester (0452) 862343. SER: Buys at auction. VAT: Spec.

PITCHCOMBE, Nr. Stroud
Joan Silcocks
Pitchcombe View. (Mrs. J.M. Silcocks.) Est. 1979. Open by appointment. SIZE: Small. *STOCK: Watercolours, £50—£1,500, 18th—20th C.* LOC: Just off A46, on A4173. PARK: Easy. TEL: Painswick (0452) 812225.

REDMARLEY D'ABITOT
John Nash Antiques and Interiors
The Coach House, Drury Lane. (J. Nash and L. Calleja.) Est. 1972. Open by appointment. SIZE: Medium. *STOCK: Mahogany, oak and walnut furniture, 18th—19th C, £100—£2,500; decorative items, fabrics and wallpapers.* LOC: Off A417. PARK: Easy. TEL: Bromesberrow (053 181) 616; home — same. SER: Valuations; restorations; buys at auction (furniture, silver). VAT: Stan/Spec.

SLAD, Nr. Stroud
Ian Hodgkins and Co. Ltd.
Upper Vatch Mill, The Vatch. Open by appointment only. *STOCK: Antiquarian books including pre-Raphaelites and associates, the Brontës; 19th C illustrated, children's, art and literature books.* TEL: Stroud (04536) 4270.

SOMERFORD KEYNES
Nr. Cirencester
E.C. Legg and Son
The Old School House. Est. 1902. CL: Sat.
p.m. Open 9−5. *STOCK: 18th−19th C furniture.* TEL: Cirencester (0285) 861420. SER:
Restorations (furniture); caning. VAT: Spec.

STOW-ON-THE-WOLD   (0451)
Baggott Church Street Ltd.
Church St. CADA. Est. 1978. Open 10−6, or
by appointment. SIZE: Large. *STOCK: English
oak, mahogany, walnut and yew furniture,
17th−19th C; portrait paintings, metalwork,
pottery, treen and decorative items.* LOC:
South-west corner of market square. PARK: In
market square. TEL: 30370.

Duncan J. Baggott
The Square. CADA. Est. 1967. Open 10−6,
or by appointment. SIZE: Medium. *STOCK:
17th−19th C. English oak and country furniture, sets of rush-seated chairs, gateleg and
farmhouse tables, settles, hanging cupboards,
coffers and smaller domestic items; brass,
copper and metalwork, fireplace fittings, wall
lights, lanterns, samplers and primitive paintings.* PARK: Easy. TEL: 30662. SER: Valuations. VAT: Stan/Spec.

Duncan J. Baggott.   *Trade Only*
Huntsmans Yard, Sheep St. CADA. Est.
1967. CL: Sat. Open 9−5 or by appointment.
SIZE: Large. *STOCK: 17th−19th C. English
and continental oak, mahogany, fruitwood
and walnut furniture, large bookcases, dining
tables, cupboards, dressers, chairs and small
items; portrait and primitive paintings, brass,
copper, metalwork, pottery and needleworks.*
LOC: Entrance through large gates on right
hand side of Sheep Street coming from Fosse
Way, just past Church St. PARK: Own. TEL:
30662.

Colin Brand Antiques
Tudor House, Sheep St. Est. 1985. CL: Wed.
Open 10−1 and 2−5, Sun. by appointment.
SIZE: Medium. *STOCK: Clocks, small furni-
ture, £200−£2,000; porcelain, £30−£600,
all pre-1900.* LOC: Opposite Post Office.
PARK: Main square. TEL: 31760; home −
same. VAT. Spec.

D. Bryden
Sheep St. Est. 1979. CL: Wed. Open
10−12.30 and 2−5. SIZE: Small. *STOCK:
English silver, 18th−19th C, £20−£3,000;
English porcelain, 19th C, £50−£700; rose-
wood and mahogany furniture, Victorian and
Edwardian, £100−£1,000.* LOC: Off A429.
PARK: Stow Sq. TEL: 30840. VAT: Stan/
Spec.

Stow-on-the-Wold continued
J. and J. Caspall Antiques
Sheep St. Est. 1971. Open 9.30−5.30 or by
appointment. *STOCK: Period oak, elm, fruitwood, 16th C to 1760; early metalwork,
especially lighting and hearth, early woodcarvings, domestic and decorative items.*
PARK: Nearby. TEL: 31160. SER: Valuations.
VAT: Spec.

Chantry House Antiques
Chantry House, Sheep St. (Hon. B.M. Davis,
G. and A.J. Ewart.) Open 9.30−1 and
2−5.30. SIZE: Small. *STOCK: Furniture,
£300−£4,000; porcelain, both 18−19th C;
silver especially cutlery, 19th C.* LOC: From
Fosse Way take road into town, premises are
400yds. on the right before Grapevine Hotel.
PARK: Easy. TEL: 30450; home − same.
SER: Valuations. VAT: Stan/Spec.

The Church Street Gallery
Church St. (J. Davies.) Est. 1971. Open
10−6. SIZE: Large. *STOCK: British paintings
and watercolours, 19th−20th C, £50−
£25,000.* PARK: Next street or in square. TEL:
31698 or 31790. SER: Restorations (cleaning
watercolours and oils, defoxing of watercolours, framing). VAT: Spec.

Christopher Clarke   BADA
Antiques
**The Fosse Way. (C.J. Clarke.) CADA. Est.
1961. Open 9.30−6. SIZE: Medium.** *STOCK:
Furniture, 17th−19th C, £300−£15,000;
early oak, walnut, mahogany, pottery, 18th C;
metalware, 16th−18th C, both £50−£500;
also religious and Gothic pieces.* **Not stocked:
Silver, glass, medals, coins, prints. LOC:
Corner of the Fosse Way and Sheep St. PARK:
Easy. TEL: 30476. SER: Valuations.**

IS YOUR ENTRY CORRECT?
If there is even the slightest
inaccuracy in your entry, *please* let us
know before 1st January 1987.
GUIDE TO THE
ANTIQUE SHOPS OF BRITAIN
5 Church Street, Woodbridge, Suffolk.

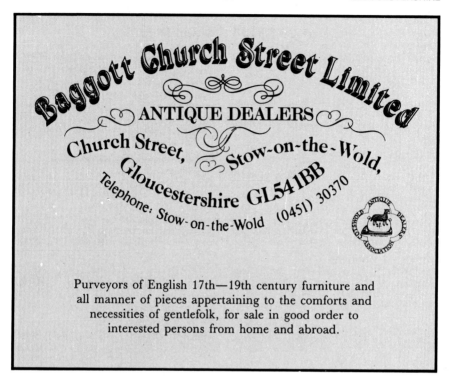

Baggott Church Street Limited

ANTIQUE DEALERS

Church Street, Stow-on-the-Wold,
Gloucestershire GL541BB
Telephone: Stow-on-the-Wold (0451) 30370

Purveyors of English 17th—19th century furniture and
all manner of pieces appertaining to the comforts and
necessities of gentlefolk, for sale in good order to
interested persons from home and abroad.

Stow-on-the-Wold continued

The Cotswold Galleries
The Square. (R. and C. Glaisyer.) CADA. Est. 1961. Open 9—5.30, or by appointment. SIZE: Large. *STOCK: Oil paintings, mainly 19th C landscape.* TEL: 30586. SER: Restorations; framing. VAT: Stan/Spec.

Country Life Antiques
Sheep St. Est. 1972. Open 10—5. *STOCK: Pewter, brass, copper, pine furniture, early metalware and scientific instruments.* PARK: Easy. TEL: 30776.

Country Life Antiques
Grey House, The Square. Open 10—5.30. *STOCK: Furniture, oil paintings, scientific instruments, decorative accessories.* PARK: Easy. TEL: 31564.

Fosse Gallery
The Square. (G. O'Farrell and John Lindsey Fine Art Ltd.) Est. 1979. Open 10—5.30. SIZE: Large. *STOCK: British post impressionist paintings and watercolours, £100—£10,000.* LOC: Off Fosseway, A429. PARK: Easy. TEL: 31319. SER: Valuations; buys at auction. VAT: Spec.

Stow-on-the-Wold continued

Fox House Antiques
Digbeth St. (J. Ward and S. Gilbert.) Est. 1981. Open 10—5.30. SIZE: Medium. *STOCK: Country and kitchen furniture, mostly pine; domestic items and bygones, brass, copper, ironwork, all 18th—19th C.* LOC: Near Market Square. PARK: Easy. TEL: 31609; home — same. VAT: Stan/Spec.

Freeman
4 Park St. (R.H. and E.M. Freeman.) Resident. Open 9.30—5.30, Sun. by appointment. SIZE: Medium. *STOCK: Oriental porcelain, works of art, small furniture, 18th—19th C, £50—£1,000.* LOC: Just off town square. PARK: Easy. TEL: 31184. VAT: Stan/Spec.

L. Greenwold   BADA
"Digbeth", Digbeth St. CADA. Est. 1973. Open 10—5. SIZE: Medium. *STOCK: Jewellery, English and Oriental porcelain and pottery, silver, decorative items, from £50.* LOC: Just off the south east corner of market sq. PARK: Easy. TEL: 30398. SER: Buys at auction. VAT: Spec.

Stow-on-the-Wold continued

Keith Hockin (Antiques) Ltd   BADA
The Square. **CADA. Est. 1968. CL: Sun. except by appointment. Open 9—6. SIZE: Medium.** *STOCK: Oak furniture, 1600—1750: country furniture in oak, fruitwoods, yew, 1700—1850; pewter, copper, brass, ironwork, all periods.* **Not stocked: Mahogany. PARK: Easy. TEL: 31058. SER: Buys at auction (oak, pewter, metalwork). VAT: Stan/ Spec.**

Huntington Antiques Ltd.
The Old Forge, Church St. (M.F., S.P. and N.M.J. Golding.) CADA. Resident. Est. 1974. Open 9—6 or by appointment. *STOCK: Period oak, walnut and country furniture, medieval to 1740; Eastern carpets and rugs; early metal and treen items; some tapestries and works of art.* TEL: 30842. SER: Valuations; buys at auction. FAIRS: Major dateline. VAT: Spec.

Mansfield Antiques
Park St. (A.R. Mansfield.) Est. 1982. Open 10—5.30. SIZE: Small. *STOCK: Oak, elm and pine country furniture, 17th—19th C, £50— £600; kitchen ware, art deco, porcelain, 19th—20th C, £5—£100; pictures, treen, brass, copper, metalware, bottles, 17th— 19th C, £1—£200; antiquities and coins, B.C., £5—£100.* LOC: On left from Chipping Norton, just before branching off to Digbeth St. PARK: Easy. TEL: 31812; home — (0608) 41648. SER: Buys at auction.

Lilian Middleton's Antique Dolls' Shop
Days Stable, Sheep St. CADA. Est. 1977. CL: Wed. Open 9—5.30, Sun. 1—5. *STOCK: Dolls and accessories, including dolls' house furniture.* TEL: 30381. SER: Dolls' hospital and museum.

Macao waterfront, gouache on paper, c.1800, 130cm x 47cm. From "Chinatrade Paintings" c.1750-1900, in **Antique Collecting**, June 1986.

Stow-on-the-Wold continued

William Morris
1 Digbeth St. (T.W. Morris.) Resident. CL: Sun. except by appointment. Open 9.30—1 and 2—5.30. *STOCK: Arts and crafts furniture, from £200; studio pottery, decorative items, from £20, both 1850—1950; illustrated, private press and books relating to arts and crafts movement, 1850 to date, £10—£500.* LOC: The Square. PARK: Easy. TEL: 31542. VAT: Spec.

Richard Moult Antiques
The Square. Est. 1961. CL: Sun. except by appointment. Open 9.30—5.30. SIZE: Large. *STOCK: General antiques, early oak, brass, copper, glass, porcelain, clocks, guns, music boxes, and especially country chairs.* LOC: Coming from north to south, turn into square from main Fosseway. PARK: Easy. TEL: 30377. SER: Buys at auction; shipping facilities. VAT: Stan/Spec.

Simon W. Nutter   BADA
Wraggs Row, Fosse Way. Open 9.30—5.30 or by appointment. *STOCK: Furniture, 17th to early 19th C.* **TEL: 30658.**

Rudolph Otto
The Little House, Sheep St. (R.O. and E.M. Schwager.) Est. 1950. Open 9.30—5.30. SIZE: Medium. *STOCK: Early Georgian mahogany furniture, £50—£2,000; Queen Anne, walnut furniture, mirrors, £250—£3,000; oak furniture, 1600—1680, £80—£1,350.* Not stocked: Victorian bric-a-brac, art nouveau. LOC: Off the Fosseway, opp. the Post Office. PARK: Easy. TEL: 30455. SER: Valuations; restorations. VAT: Stan/Spec.

Park House Antiques
Park St. (N. and J. Kook.) Est. 1981. Open 10—5.30, Sun. 10—5. SIZE: Large. *STOCK: Watercolours, £100—£800; oil paintings, £400—£4,000; both 18th—19th C; furniture, 17th C to early Victorian, £100—£4,000.* PARK: Easy. TEL: 30159; home — same. SER: Valuations. VAT: Stan/Spec.

VANBRUGH HOUSE ANTIQUES
(John & Monica Sands)

Park Street
Stow-on-the-Wold
Gloucestershire
Telephone 0451-30797

*Fine and large 19th century
Singing 'Bird in a Gilded Cage'*

Stow-on-the-Wold continued

Antony Preston Antiques Ltd.   BADA LAPADA
The Square. CADA. Est. **1968.** Open **9.30—6, or by appointment.** *STOCK: English and Continental furniture and objects, longcase and bracket clocks, barometers, leather upholstery, all 18th and 19th C.* TEL: **31586/ 31406.** VAT: **Stan/Spec.**

South Bar Antiques
Digbeth St. (R. Deeley.) CADA. Est. 1974. Open 9.30—5.30, Sun. by appointment. SIZE: Large. *STOCK: Clocks, furniture, porcelain, jewellery, 1640—1920, £50—£15,000.* PARK: Market Square. TEL: 30236; home — (0557) 30430. SER: Valuations; restorations. FAIRS: Chipping Norton, Oxford. VAT: Spec.

Touchwood Antiques Ltd.   LAPADA
9 Park St. (K.M., L.A., P. and C. Dixon.) CADA. Resident. Est. 1880. Open 9.30—5.30, or by appointment. Sun. by appointment only. SIZE: Medium. *STOCK: Oak, walnut, fruitwood, early country and period furniture, medieval to 17th C, £100—£5,000+; treen, metalware and pottery, to 1830.* Not stocked: Late pine. LOC: On A436 just past junction of Digbeth St. and Park St. PARK: Easy. TEL: 30221. SER: Valuations; restorations (wax polishing, esp. large collections and rare items); research medieval to late 17th C furniture; commissions undertaken; finder service. VAT: Stan/Spec.

Van Riemsdijk Fine Art   LAPADA
Digbeth St. (Mrs. B. Van Riemsdijk.) Open 10—1 and 2—5. *STOCK: Oils and watercolours, 19th to early 20th C.* TEL: 30424. VAT: Spec.

Vanbrugh House Antiques
Park St. (J. and M.M. Sands.) Resident. Est. 1972. Open 10—6, or by appointment. *STOCK: Furniture and silver, 17th to early 19th C; early maps, arms, armour, music boxes, square pianos, clocks.* LOC: Opposite the Bell Inn. PARK: Easy. TEL: 30797. SER: Valuations; buys at auction (mechanical music items). FAIRS: Major dateline. VAT: Stan/Spec.

Stow-on-the-Wold

Wye Antiques
The Square. (C. and S. Wye.) CADA. Est. 1960. Open 9.30—6. SIZE: Large. *STOCK: Country furniture, including stripped pine; china including Staffordshire figures, blue and white transferware; decorative bygones, brass and copper.* PARK: Easy. TEL: 31004. VAT: Stan/Spec.

STROUD (4 and 5 fig. no.) (045 36)   (6 fig. no.) (0453)

Cotswold Curios   LAPADA
1 Middle St. (J.T. Smith.) Est. 1969. CL: Thurs. p.m. Open 10—4.30, Sat. and Sun. by appointment, trade any time. *STOCK: Period English and Continental furniture, clocks, paintings.* TEL: 5956; home — Brimscombe (0453) 882564.

A.W. England and Sons
54 Lower St. Est. 1892. Open 9—5. SIZE: Large. *STOCK: General antiques, chairs, furniture, pictures and shipping goods.* TEL: 3262. VAT: Stan.

Gnome Cottage Antiques
55—57 Middle St. (I.A. McGrane.) Est. 1961. Open 9.30—5.30. *STOCK: General antiques, furniture, prints, glass, china.* TEL: 3669.

Shabby Tiger Antiques
18 Nelson St. (S. Krucker.) Est. 1975. CL: Thurs. p.m. and Sun., except by appointment. Open 10—5.30. *STOCK: 19th C furniture, pictures, jewellery, collectors' items, stuffed animals, bric-a-brac, decorator's items and interior accessories.* LOC: Nelson St. is a continuation of High St. close to town centre. PARK: Opp. TEL: 79175. SER: Buys at auction. VAT: Stan.

Ron and Pam Sparrow
Cornermead, Gannicox Rd. Open by appointment. *STOCK: Watercolours, 19th and early 20th C.* TEL: 4379.

ANTONY PRESTON
ANTIQUES LTD.
THE SQUARE STOW-ON-THE-WOLD
GLOUCESTERSHIRE GL54 1AB ENGLAND
TEL. COTSWOLD (0451) 31586 (HOME) 31406

A classic Sheraton period crossbanded mahogany sofa table, c.1790.

We have a large stock of 18th and early 19th century furniture, a wide selection of leather upholstery, antique stick and banjo barometers, longcase and bracket clocks all in showroom condition.

Specialist Early Timber Wax Polishers to Museums/Institutions, Country Houses and Private Clients

Furniture Research, Medieval to Jacobean Period

Advice for Interior Design and Furnishing

WAX POLISH

9 Park Street, Stow-on-the-Wold, Gloucestershire. Telephone (0451) 30221
Period and Country Furniture

TETBURY (0666)

Argent Gallery
49 Long St. (L. Ayliffe and H. Walker.) Open 9.30—1 and 2—5.30. *STOCK: Silver and jewellery.* TEL: 52265.

George S. Bolam BADA
Oak House, 1 The Chipping. CADA. Est. 1946. CL: Sat. Open 9.15—5.30. SIZE: Medium. *STOCK: English and Continental furniture, 17th to early 19th C; paintings, Oriental porcelain.* LOC: Turn off main street at Snooty Fox Hotel, then right into Chipping car park. PARK: Easy. TEL: 52211. SER: Valuations. VAT: Spec.

Breakspeare Antiques LAPADA
Mainly Trade
36 Long St. (M. and S. Breakspeare.) CADA. Resident. Est. 1962. CL: Some Thurs. p.m. Open 9.30—5.30, if closed, ring bell. SIZE: Medium. *STOCK: English furniture, mainly mahogany, 18th to early 19th C; longcase clocks, barometers, £50—£3,500.* PARK: Easy. TEL: 53122 or 52192. VAT: Stan/Spec.

A.M. Breakspeare Antiques
57 Long St. Open 9.30—5.30 (available at 36 Long St. when closed). SIZE: Medium. *STOCK: Mahogany furniture, clocks and barometers, 18th—19th C.* PARK: Easy. TEL: 52192 or 53122.

J. and M. Bristow Antiques BADA
28 Long St. (M.J. and J.A. Bristow.) Est. 1964. CL: Thurs. Open 10—1 and 2—6, but any time by appointment. SIZE: Small. *STOCK: Longcase, bracket and lantern clocks; barometers, 17th—18th C; furniture.* Not stocked: Victoriana, bric-a-brac. LOC: In main street. PARK: Easy. TEL: 52222. VAT: Spec.

The Chest of Drawers
24 Long St. (A. and P. Bristow.) Resident. Est. 1969. CL: Thurs. a.m. Open 9—5.30. SIZE: Medium. *STOCK: Late Georgian, Regency and Victorian furniture; country pieces, 17th—18th C; china and brass.* LOC: On A433. PARK: Easy. TEL: 52105; home — same. VAT: Spec.

Tetbury continued

Colleton House Gallery
22 Market Place. (Mrs. M.E.P. Biddle.) Est. 1979. Open 10—1 and 2—6.30, Mon. by appointment. SIZE: Medium. *STOCK: Oils, £100—£3,000; watercolours, £50—£1,000; both 1825—1950; prints, etchings, mezzotints, 1825 to date, £20—£250.* PARK: Easy. TEL: 52048; home — (045 383) 4665. SER: Valuations; restorations (oils, watercolours and prints); buys at auction (oils and watercolours).

Joane Crarer Antiques
The Fullers Cottage, 18 Long St. Est. 1963. Open mornings or by appointment. SIZE: Small. *STOCK: Small items, 18th C and Victorian.* LOC: Main St. PARK: Easy. TEL: 52660. SER: Valuations.

Gastrell House
33 Long St. (J. Morris.) Open 10—6 or by appointment. *STOCK: Period furniture, 17th to early 19th C; clocks, paintings.* TEL: 52228. SER: Restorations (furniture, clocks and paintings); photography (objets d'art); interior design. VAT: Stan/Spec.

Jasper Marsh Antiques BADA
3 The Chipping. (J. and P. Marsh.) CADA. Open 9—1 and 2—5, Sat. 10—4, Sun. by appointment. *STOCK: Mahogany and oak furniture, 18th to early 19th C.* LOC: Off High St. PARK: Easy. TEL: 52832 or Henley-in-Arden (05642) 2088.

Paul Nash Antiques BADA
Barn House, Cherington. (P.L. and A.S. Gifford Nash.) Resident. Est. 1961. Open by appointment only. *STOCK: English furniture, 1600—1830, £100—£20,000.* LOC: 4 miles from Tetbury. PARK: Own. TEL: Rodmarton (028584) 215. VAT: Spec.

John Nicholls
27 Long St. CADA. Open 9.30—5.30, Sat. 10—4. *STOCK: Oak and country furniture, 17th and 18th C.* TEL: 52781; home — Uttoxeter (088 93) 2383.

JASPER MARSH

3 THE CHIPPING, TETBURY, GLOUCESTERSHIRE

Telephone:
Tetbury
(0666) 52832

We carry a large stock of 17th, 18th and early 19th century Period Furniture and Porcelain

THREE SHOWROOMS

*Open 9.00—1.00, 2.00—5.00.
Saturday 10—4
Sun. by appointment*

Also at 3 High Street, Henley-in-Arden, Warwickshire

John Nicholls

Specialising in 17th and 18th Century Oak and Country Furniture

27, LONG STREET, TETBURY, GLOUCESTER GL8 8AA
TEL. TETBURY (0666) 52781 HOME — UTTOXETER 2383

Dealer in good 17th and 18th century oak and country furniture

Open Mon.—Fri. 9.30—5.30
Sat. 10.00—4.00
Closed for lunch 1—2
Otherwise by appointment

Tetbury continued

Tetbury Antiques
39A Long St. (Caffell Management Services Ltd.) CADA. Open 9.30—5.30, Sun. by appointment. *STOCK: English and Continental country furniture and accessories, 18th—19th C.* TEL: 52748; home — Nailsworth (045 383) 3168.

Wain Antiques   BADA
45 Long St. (J. and P. Wain.) CADA. Est. 1978. Open 9.30—5.30, Sun. by appointment. SIZE: Medium. *STOCK: Pottery and porcelain, European and Oriental, 18th—19th C, £5—£1,000.* PARK: Easy. TEL: 52440; home — same. SER: Restorations (ceramics); buys at auction (ceramics). VAT: Spec.

K.W. and J.E. Watherington (Antiques)   LAPADA
61 Long St. Resident. Open 9—5, or by appointment. SIZE: Medium. *STOCK: Mainly mahogany furniture, 18th to early 19th C.* TEL: 52285, evenings — 52993. SER: Export. VAT: Stan/Spec.

L.A. Woodburn Antiques
42 Long St. CL: Thurs. Open 10—1 and 2—5. *STOCK: Furniture, 17th—19th C.* TEL: 52687.

Yeo Antiques   LAPADA
(B.D. and B.G. Ackrill.) Open by appointment. *STOCK: Furniture, metalware, clocks, porcelain and pottery.* TEL: 52130. SER: Valuations; restorations; interior decor; buys at auction. VAT: Stan/Spec.

TEWKESBURY   (0684)

Abbey Antiques
62 Church St. Est. 1945. CL: Thurs. p.m. *STOCK: General antiques; Victoriana; trade and shipping goods.* TEL: 292378.

Tewkesbury continued

Antiques and Amber
7 The Stables, St. Mary's Lane. (W. and Mrs. A. Metcalfe.) Resident on premises, prior telephone call advisable. *STOCK: Victorian and Georgian jewellery especially amber; objets d'art.* LOC: 100yds off A38, near abbey. PARK: Easy. TEL: 297617.

Gainsborough House Antiques
81 Church St. (A. and B. Hilson.) Open 9.30—5. *STOCK: Furniture, 18th to early 19th C; glass, porcelain.* TEL: 293072. SER: Restoration and conservation.

''The Look-In'' (Antiques)
76 Church St. (Mrs. V.M. Brown.) Est. 1980. Open 10—5. *STOCK: Furniture, bric-a-brac, china, clocks, prints and watercolours, oils, silver and plate, jewellery, glass, books and metalware, £3—£800.* LOC: Opposite Abbey main entrance. PARK: Opp. and at rear. TEL: 292042; home — Elmley Castle (038 674) 588.

F.W. Taylor
71 Church St. Est. 1972. Open 9—5. SIZE: Medium. *STOCK: Period furniture, £100—£1,500; porcelain and pottery, £10—£1,000; Georgian and Victorian glass, small collectable silver and flatware; maps, prints and other decorative items.* LOC: Close to Abbey. PARK: 100 yds. TEL: 295990. SER: Valuations; buys at auction. VAT: Stan/Spec.

Tewkesbury Antiques Centre
78 Church St. (J. Preece.) Est. 1967. Open 9.30—5, or by appointment. SIZE: Large. There are 10 dealers at this centre selling *furniture, 18th—19th C, £25—£500; shipping items, 19th C and Edwardian, £25—£500; brass, silver and china, mainly 19th C, £5—£50.* LOC: From town centre turn into Church St., centre is 300yds. on the right. PARK: Easy. TEL: 294091.

ULEY, Nr. Dursley

Old Chapel Antiques   LAPADA
Mainly Trade
Fop St. and The Street. (B. and L. Narbeth.) Est. 1972. CL: Wed. p.m. Open 9—5. SIZE: Large. *STOCK: Furniture, shipping goods, stripped pine, small items, bygones.* LOC: B4066. PARK: Easy. TEL: Dursley (0453) 860656. SER: Restorations. VAT: Stan/Spec.

ULLENWOOD, Nr. Cheltenham

John Townsend
2 Oxford Cottages. Est. 1969. Open by appointment only. *STOCK: Stripped pine, shipping goods, country furniture.* TEL: Coberley (024 287) 223. VAT: Stan/Spec.

Kenulf Gallery

High Street, Winchcombe, Glos. 0242 602124
on A46 between Broadway and Cheltenham

George Hyde-Pownall. Signed.
Oil on artist's board. 6ins. x 9ins. "Piccadilly"

WINCHCOMBE   (0242)

Kenulf Gallery
Kenulf House, High St. (E. and J. Ford.) CADA. Est. 1978. Open 9.30—5.30. *STOCK: Late 18th to early 20th C oil and watercolour paintings and prints; sculpture, and furniture.* TEL: 602124; home — 602776. SER: Valuations; restorations (oils and watercolours); period framing. VAT: Spec.

Muriel Lindsay
Queen Anne House. Resident. Est. 1965. Open 9.30—1 and 2—5.30, Sun. by appointment. *STOCK: Furniture, 18th—19th C, metalwork, silver, glass, small items.* TEL: 602319. VAT: Stan/Spec.

Prichard Antiques
'Fairview', High St. (K.H. and D.Y. Prichard.) Est. 1979. Open 9—6, Sun. by appointment. SIZE: Medium. *STOCK: Period furniture, £10—£5,000; treen, £1—£500; metalwork, £5—£500, all 17th—19th C.* LOC: On main Broadway to Cheltenham road, opposite turning to Sudeley Castle. PARK: Easy. TEL: 603566; home — 603705. SER: Valuations. VAT: Spec.

WOTTON-UNDER-EDGE

Bell Passage Antiques   LAPADA
38 High St., Wickwar, and warehouse at Arnolds Field Estate, Wickwar. (Mrs. D.V. Brand.) Est. 1966. CL: Mon, and Thurs. Open 8—6, or by appointment. *STOCK: Furniture, 17th—19th C, £40—£1,200; glass, 18th—19th C, £1—£100; porcelain, 18th—20th C, £1—£800; clocks, 18th—20th C, £10—£1,500; prints, oils and watercolours, 18th—19th C, £20—£2,000.* Not stocked: Guns. LOC: On B4060, M5 Junction 14, M4 Junction 18. PARK: Easy. TEL: Wickwar (045 424) 251. SER: Valuations, restorations (furniture, pictures, upholstery); buys at auction. VAT: Stan/Spec.

G.M.S. Antiques
36 High St., Wickwar. (G.M. St. G. Stacey.) G.M.C. Est. 1975. CL: Mon. and Thurs. Open 8—6 or by appointment. SIZE: Large. *STOCK: Furniture, oak, mahogany and walnut, 18th—19th C, £50—£1,000; metalwork and decorative items, £10—£300; glass, jewellery and silver, oils and watercolours, 19th C, £20—£2,000.* Not stocked: Guns. LOC: B4060. PARK: Easy. TEL: Wickwar (045 424) 251. SER: Valuations; restorations (furniture, pictures, upholstery); buys at auction. VAT: Stan/Spec.

Hampshire

Please note this is only a rough map designed to show dealers the number of shops in the various towns, and is not necessarily totally accurate.

Key to number of shops in this area.

○ 1–2
◑ 3–5
◐ 6–12
● 13+

ALRESFORD   (096 273)

Alresford Gallery
Livingstone House, Broad St. (K.E. Bell.) Est.
1973. CL: Wed. p.m. Open 9—5, Sun. by
appointment. SIZE: Medium. *STOCK: Victorian watercolours, £100—£500.* PARK: Easy.
TEL: 3002; home — 3556. SER: Valuations;
restorations (watercolours). VAT: Spec.

Artemesia   LAPADA
16 West St. (D.T.L. Wright.) Est. 1972. SIZE:
Medium. Open 9—5.30. *STOCK: Oriental porcelain, bronze, furniture, works of art, 12th—19th C, £20—£5,000.* LOC: A31. PARK:
Easy. TEL: 2277. SER: Valuations; buys at
auction. VAT: Spec.

De Lucy Antiques
12 East St. (Mrs. B.E. Woods.) Est. 1985. CL:
Wed. Open 10—5. SIZE: Medium. *STOCK:
Fine period furniture, oil paintings, decorative
items, rugs, pewter, brass and copper, porcelain and glass, 17th to early 19th C.* LOC:
A31, opposite National Westminster bank.
PARK: Nearby. TEL: 3932. VAT: Spec.

Evans and Evans
40 West St. (Alresford Clocks Ltd. — D. and
N. Evans.) Est. 1953. CL: Mon. Open 9.30—1
and 2—5.30. SIZE: Medium. *STOCK: Clocks,
watches, 1680—1900, £150—£20,000;
musical boxes, 19th C, £200—£7,000;
Regency and Victorian barometers, £200—£2,000.* Stock only as listed. LOC: A31. Shop
on left going north. PARK: Easy. TEL: 2170.
SER: Valuations; restorations (clocks, musical
boxes); buys at auction. VAT: Stan/Spec.

Alresford continued

Grenville Gore-Langton
Pleasant House, West St. Est. 1955. CL:
Wed. Open 9.30—1 and 2—5. SIZE: Medium.
*STOCK: Furniture, 18th—19th C; furnishing
items.* Not stocked: Jewellery. PARK: Easy.
TEL: 2899; home — Itchen Abbas (096 278)
300. VAT: Stan/Spec.

Rogers of Alresford   LAPADA
16 West St. (T. and V. Rogers.) Est. 1968.
Open 10—5.30. SIZE: Medium. *STOCK:
English country furniture, decorative items,
and works of art, collectors' items including
commemorative ware, Delftware, Sunderland
lustre, Staffordshire blue and other earthenware.* Not stocked: Coins, stamps. LOC:
Town centre, A31. PARK: Easy. TEL: 2862
and 2277. SER: Valuations (specialised collections); buys at London auctions. FAIRS: All
major. VAT: Stan/Spec.

Studio Bookshop and Gallery
17 Broad St. (L. Oxley.) ABA. Est. 1951. CL:
Wed. p.m. Open 9—1 and 2—5. SIZE: Large.
*STOCK: Antiquarian books, £5—£1,500;
topographical prints, £2—£250; maps, £5—£200.* LOC: B3046. PARK: Easy. TEL: 2188.
SER: Valuations; restorations (oil paintings,
prints); framing. FAIRS: Boston, London ABA.
VAT: Stan.

Winchester House Antiques
39 Broad St. (D. and P. Thompson.) Open
9—5 or by appointment. *STOCK: General
antiques.* TEL: 3110.

ALVERSTOKE, Nr. Gosport

Alverstoke Antiques
47 Village Rd. (Dyer and Follet Ltd.) Est.
1960. Open 9—12.45 and 2.15—5.30. SIZE:
Small. *STOCK: Furniture.* PARK: Easy. TEL:
Gosport (0705) 582204. SER: Restorations.
VAT: Stan/Spec.

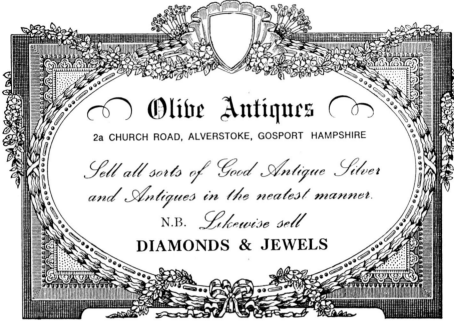

Olive Antiques
2a CHURCH ROAD, ALVERSTOKE, GOSPORT HAMPSHIRE

Sell all sorts of Good Antique Silver and Antiques in the neatest manner.

N.B. *Likewise sell*

DIAMONDS & JEWELS

TEL. (0705) 522812

Alverstone continued

Olive Antiques
2A Church Rd. Open 8.15–5. *STOCK: Gold, silver, clocks, jewellery and porcelain.* TEL Gosport (0705) 522812.

BASINGSTOKE (0256)
Squirrel Collectors Centre
9 New St. (A.H. Stone, Mrs. R.A. Austen and Mrs. K. Woods.) Est. 1981. Open 10–5.30. SIZE: Small. *STOCK: Small items, jewellery and silver, Victorian and Edwardian, £5–£1,500; collectors items, books and stamps.* LOC: Near traffic lights at junction with Winchester St. PARK: Nearby. TEL: 464885. SER: Valuations. FAIRS: Farnham Maltings monthly. VAT: Stan.

BEAULIEU (0590)
Beaulieu Fine Arts
The Malt House, High St. (Mr. and Mrs. F. Cookson.) Est. 1975. Open 9–1 and 2–5.30 including Sun. SIZE: Medium. *STOCK: Watercolours and oil paintings, from £40; drawings and etchings, from £10, mainly 19th–20th C.* LOC: Centre of High St. PARK: High St. TEL: 612089. VAT: Stan/Spec.

BENTLEY, Nr. Farnham (0420)
Enid Farr
Lime House. Resident. Est. 1961. Open 9–6, or by appointment. *STOCK: Furniture, 18th to early 19th C; copper, brass, treen and giltwood carvings.* LOC: A31, 4 miles west of Farnham on Winchester Rd. PARK: Easy. TEL: 22387. VAT: Stan/Spec.

BISHOPS SUTTON, Nr. Alresford
Parrington Fine Art
The Old Post Office. (J. and Mrs. E. Parrington.) Est. 1981. CL: Mon. Open Wed. and Sat., other days by appointment. SIZE: Small. *STOCK: Paintings, 18th–19th C, £100–£2,000.* LOC: From Alresford into village, The Ship public house on the left, next turning left School Lane, shop on the left. PARK: Easy. TEL: Alresford (096 273) 2685; home — same. SER: Valuations; restorations (cleaning and framing); buys at auction (oil paintings).

BISHOPS WALTHAM (048 93)
Elsies Antiques (and Junk)
11 Winchester Rd. (E.M. Starks.) Est. 1961. CL: Mon. and Tues. SIZE: Large. *STOCK: Furniture, bric-a-brac.* Not stocked: Silver, jewellery. PARK: Easy at rear. TEL: 2474.

Bishops Waltham continued

Pinecrafts
4 Brook St. (A. Robinson.) Open 10—5. SIZE: Large. *STOCK: Pine furniture.* TEL: 2878. SER: Restorations; stripping. VAT: Stan.

BORDON   (4 fig. no.) (042 03)
(6 fig. no.) (0420)

Bristow (Antiques)
Lindford. (D.R. Bristow.) Est. 1968. CL: Wed. p.m. SIZE: Medium. *STOCK: Period furniture.* PARK: Easy. TEL: 2301.

BOTLEY   (048 92)
Battersby Antiques
8 Winchester St. Est. 1959. CL: Sun., Wed. and Thurs. except by appointment. Open 10—5. *STOCK: Small furniture, porcelain and collectors' items.* LOC: A3051 to Winchester. PARK: Easy. TEL: 2354. VAT: Stan/Spec.

CADNAM

C.W. Buckingham   LAPADA
Twin Firs, Southampton Rd. Resident. CL: Thurs. Open 9—6 or by appointment. *STOCK: Mainly pine, some period and Victorian furniture.* TEL: Southampton (0703) 812122.

CLANFIELD   (036 781)
Harold Bolwell
The Wagon Wheel, 54 South Lane. Est. 1964. *STOCK: Furniture, Victorian, Regency and some stripped pine.* TEL: Horndean (0705) 593398.

EVERSLEY   (0734)
Airdale Antiques   *Mainly Trade*
Moorcote, Lower Common. (E.J. Andreae.) Est. 1972. Usually open but appointment advisable. SIZE: Small. *STOCK: Period country furniture, £20—£1,500.* PARK: Easy. TEL: 733132. VAT: Spec.

EVERSLEY CROSS
Forster Ritchie   LAPADA
Vann Place. (J.D. and M.W. Forster.) Resident. Est. 1977. Open 9.30—6, Sun. by appointment. SIZE: Medium. *STOCK: Furniture, 17th—19th C, £50—£1,500.* LOC: On A327 adjacent Eversley Cricket Club. PARK: Easy. TEL: Eversley (0734) 733408; shop — Hook (025 672) 2309. SER: Valuations; restorations; shipping. VAT: Stan/Spec.

FAREHAM   (0329)
Elizabethans
58 High St. (Mrs. E. Keeble.) Est. 1961. CL: Wed., Fri. and Sat. p.m. Open 10—4.30. *STOCK: Small general antiques, furniture, jewellery, pictures.* TEL: 234964.

FARNBOROUGH   (0252)
Martin and Parke   LAPADA
97 Lynchford Rd. (J. Martin, N.S. Carter.) Est. 1971. Open 9—5. SIZE: Large. *STOCK: Pre-1940 furniture and shipping goods.* TEL: 515311. VAT: Stan.

FLEET   (4 and 5 fig. no.) (025 14)
(6 fig. no.) (0252)

Robert Alexander
11 King's Rd. (R.R. Alexander.) Est. 1950. CL: Wed. p.m. Open 10—1 and 2—5.30. SIZE: Medium. *STOCK: Furniture, mainly 19th C, £300—£950.* LOC: Near Pearson's sale room. PARK: Own. TEL: 3713. SER: Restorations (furniture). VAT: Stan/Spec.

FORDINGBRIDGE   (0425)
Avon Lodge Antiques
Southampton Rd. (G. and J. Pearce.) Est. 1960. CL: Sat. and Sun. except by appointment. Open 9.30—5.30. SIZE: Large. *STOCK: Furniture, including pine, £5—£1,000; metalware, china, glass, dolls, £5—£250, all 1600—1900.* LOC: B3078. PARK: Easy. TEL: 53275; home — same. SER: Buys at auction.

Mark Collier   BADA
24 High St. Open 10—5.30 or by appointment. *STOCK: Furniture, Oriental and other ceramics, silver.* TEL: 52555.

Duveen Antiques
Burgate. (C.D. and Mrs. I. Aston.) Est. 1972. Resident. Always open. SIZE: Large. *STOCK: Early oak furniture, 16th—18th C, £50—£5,000; longcase clocks, 18th C, £300—£2,000; carvings, 15th—17th C, £20—£1,000; treen, 17th—19th C; brass and copper.* LOC: On A338, adjacent Tudor Rose Inn. PARK: Easy. TEL: 53309. VAT: Stan/Spec.

Jonathan Green Antiques
22 High St. CL: Thurs. Open 10—4.30. *STOCK: General antiques, silver and plate.* TEL: 52898.

Old Dolls House Antiques
Bridge St. (D.S. Gordon.) Open Fri. and Sat. 11—4 other times by appointment. *STOCK: Dolls, dolls' houses and teddies.* TEL: 52450.

FYFIELD, Nr. Andover   (027 785)
Country Cottage Bedsteads
Stable Grange. (S. Wilson.) Est. 1974. Open by appointment. SIZE: Small. *STOCK: Brass and iron bedsteads, 1850—1930, £100—£500.* LOC: A303 from Andover towards Thruxton. PARK: Easy. TEL: Weyhill (026 477) 2608; home — same. SER: Valuations; restorations (re-enamelling and polishing); buys at auction (metal bedsteads).

ANDWELLS

18th and early 19th century furniture
HIGH STREET
HARTLEY WINTNEY
HANTS
Tel. Hartley Wintney 2305

GOSPORT   (0705)
Athena Antiques Centre and Peel Common Stamps
151 Forton Rd. (A.R. and T.A. Tonks.) Est. 1981. CL: Mon. and Wed. Open 10—5, Fri. and Sat. 9.30—5. SIZE: Medium. *STOCK: Furniture including pine, glass and crystal, Victorian—Edwardian, £10—£300; stamps, from 1840, 10p—£150.* LOC: A32. PARK: At rear. TEL: 583597; home — Locks Heath (04895) 84633. SER: Valuations; restorations. FAIRS: Fareham, Sarisbury Green, Millbrook. VAT: Stan.

E.T. Cooper
20 Stoke Rd. Est. 1972. CL: Wed. p.m. Open 9.30—12.30 and 1.30—5. SIZE: Medium. *STOCK: Silver, china, glass, furniture, mechanical music, fairground equipment.* LOC: Main road from Lee-on-Solent through Gosport. PARK: In side road. TEL: 585032. SER: Valuations; buys at auction. VAT: Stan.

Peter Pan's Bazaar
105 Forton Rd. (S.V. Panormo.) Est. 1960. CL: Mon., Tues. and Wed. *STOCK: Vintage cameras, early photographica, images, 1850—1950, £5—£500.* LOC: Main road into town. PARK: Easy. TEL: 524254. FAIRS: Main south of England.

Peter Pan's of Gosport
105c Forton Rd. (J. McClaren.) Est. 1965. CL: Mon., Tues. and Wed. *STOCK: Jewellery, dolls, toys and miniatures.* LOC: Main road into town. PARK: Easy. TEL: 524254. FAIRS: Main south of England.

HARTLEY WINTNEY   (025 126)
Nicholas Abbott
High St. (C. and A. Abbott.) Est. 1962. Open 9.30—5.30. SIZE: Large. *STOCK: English furniture, 18th to early 19th C.* LOC: A30. PARK: Easy. TEL: 2365; home — 3509. VAT: Stan/Spec.

Hartley Wintney continued

Andwells   LAPADA
High St. (P. Heraty.) Est. 1967. Open 9—1 and 2—5.30. SIZE: Large. *STOCK: Georgian and Regency furniture, mainly mahogany.* LOC: Main street. PARK: Easy. TEL: 2305. VAT: Spec.

Cedar Antiques   BADA
High St. (D.S. Green.) Est. 1964. Open 9—6, trade any time. SIZE: Large, and warehouse. *STOCK: Fine English oak, walnut and country furniture, 17th—18th C, £20—£10,000; French Provincial furniture; longcase clocks, 1680—1780, £800—£5,000; steel and brasswork, £10—£500. Not stocked: China, glass, silver.* LOC: A30. PARK: Opposite. TEL: 3252. SER: Valuations; restorations (clocks, period furniture). FAIRS: West of England, Park Lane. VAT: Stan/Spec.

Bryan Clisby at Andwells Antiques
High St. Est. 1976. Open 9.30—1 and 2—5.30. SIZE: Large. *STOCK: Longcase clocks, 1690—1840, £500—£3,000; barometers, 1800—1850, £150—£450.* LOC: A30 village centre. PARK: Easy. TEL: 2305; home — Fleet (025 14) 28041. SER: Valuations; restorations (clocks and barometers). VAT: Spec.

Just the Thing   LAPADA
High St. (S. Carpenter.) Est. 1975. Open 9—5 or by appointment. SIZE: Large. *STOCK: Period mahogany and country furniture; paintings, china, brass, copper, silver and Victorian jewellery.* TEL: 3393; home — 2916. VAT: Stan/Spec.

David Lazarus Antiques
High St. Est. 1973. Resident. Open 9.30—5.30; some Sundays, other times by appointment. SIZE: Medium. *STOCK: 17th to early 19th C English and Continental furniture; objets d'art.* LOC: Main street. PARK: Nearby. TEL: 2272. VAT: Stan/Spec.

Nicholas Abbott

High Street
Hartley Wintney
Hampshire
Tel: 025·126 2365

A good selection of period furniture dating from 1680 to 1830

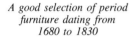

Cedar Antiques

**Hartley Wintney
Hampshire
Tel: (025126) 3252**

Resident 5 minutes distance
Trade welcome at any time

*Queen Anne walnut veneered chest of drawers.
Circa 1710*

*Bracket clock by James Markwick, London,
with movement of 8 day duration having verge
escapement and quarter repeat on 6 bells.
Circa 1695*

J.F. Herring Snr. (1795–1865)

ANTHONY WILLSON
18th Century Furniture
Fine Paintings

22 High Street, Hartley Wintney
Telephone 4499

Hartley Wintney continued

Millon Antiques
High St. (P. and J. Millon.) Open 9.30—5. SIZE: Medium. *STOCK: English furniture, 18th—19th C, including some walnut.* LOC: A30, end of village green. TEL: 3393. VAT: Spec.

Old Forge Antiques
Old Forge Cottage, The Green. (Mrs. M.A.B. Gates.) CL: Wed. and Sat. except by appointment. Open 10.30—5, but appointment advisable. SIZE: Medium. *STOCK: General antiques, watercolours, oils, prints.* LOC: A30. PARK: Easy. TEL: 2287.

Phoenix Green Antiques
London Rd. (J. Biles.) Open 8.30—6 or by appointment. SIZE: Large. *STOCK: English and French country furniture, mahogany, 18th—19th C.* TEL: 4430.

A.W. Porter and Son
High St. (M.A. Porter.) Est. 1844. CL: Wed. p.m. Open 9—1 and 2—5.30. *STOCK: Clocks, furniture, silver, jewellery, pictures, glass.* LOC: Opposite Lloyds Bank. TEL: 2676. SER: Restorations (clocks, pictures). VAT: Stan/Spec.

Anthony Willson   LAPADA
St. Peter's Gallery, 22 High St. Open daily, Sun. and lunch times by appointment. SIZE: Medium. *STOCK: Oil paintings and watercolours, 18th to early 20th C, £300—£5,000; furniture, 18th C, £500—£5,000.* PARK: Easy. TEL: 4499; home — Bramdean (096 279) 445. SER: Valuations; restorations (oil paintings and watercolours); buys at auction. VAT: Stan/Spec.

HAVANT   (0705)
Antiques and Nice Things
40 North St. (M.T. Davis-Shaw.) Est. 1965. Open 9.30—5.30. *STOCK: Paintings, prints, porcelain, copper, brass, silver, Sheffield plate, small furniture, maps, dolls, clocks, jewellery, glass.* LOC: Near station. PARK: Own. TEL: 484935; home — (0243) 372551. SER: Restorations.

HAYLING ISLAND   (0705)
J. Morton Lee
Cedar House, Bacon Lane. Est. 1984. Open by appointment. *STOCK: Watercolours, 19th—20th C, £50—£5,000.* PARK: Easy. TEL: 464444. SER: Valuations; buys at auction. FAIRS: Buxton, Surrey and Kensington. VAT: Stan/Spec.

HOOK   (025 672)
Forster Ritchie   LAPADA
The Acorn, London Rd. (J.D. and M.W. Forster.) Est. 1977. Open 9.30—6, Sun. by appointment. SIZE: Medium. *STOCK: Furniture, and silver, 17th—19th C, £50—£5,000; jewellery and glass, 18th—20th C, £50—£1,000; fashions and lace, 19th C, £25—£50.* LOC: Junction A30 and A32. PARK: Easy. TEL: 2309; home — Eversley (0734) 733408. SER: Valuations; restorations; shipping. VAT: Stan/Spec.

HORNDEAN   (0705)
Goss and Crested China Ltd.
62 Murray Rd. (N.J. Pine.) Est. 1968. SIZE: Medium. *STOCK: Goss, 1860—1930, £2—£1,000; other heraldic china, 1890—1930, £1—£50.* PARK: Easy. TEL: 597440. SER: Valuations, buys at auction (Goss). VAT: Stan.

HURSLEY, Nr. Winchester   (0962)
Hursley Antiques
(S. Thorne.) Est. 1980. Open 10—6. *STOCK: Country furniture, brass, copper, metal.* LOC: 2½ miles from Winchester on Romsey Rd. PARK: Easy. TEL: Winchester (0962) 75488. SER: Restorations (metalware); repairs (metalware).

LISS   (0730)
Simon Darby Antiques
Farnham Rd. Est. 1970. Open 9—5.30. SIZE: Large. *STOCK: English furniture, 18th—20th C, £10—£850; silver plate, metalware, china, glass, 19th—20th C, £1—£100.* LOC: A325. PARK: Easy. TEL: 893922. SER: Restorations (furniture); buys at auction. VAT: Stan/Spec.

J. Du Cros Antiques
Farnham Rd., West Liss. (Mr. and Mrs. J. Du Cros.) Est. 1982. Open 9.30—5.30, Sun. by appointment. SIZE: Medium. *STOCK: Furniture, 1700—1920, £100—£1,500; treen, metalware, pewter, brass, copper, plate, 1800—1920, £5—£200.* Not stocked: Glass and porcelain. LOC: Adjacent Spread Eagle public house on village green, A325. PARK: Easy. TEL: 895299; home — same. VAT: Stan/Spec.

Dunkley Carpets and Pictures
(R.D.J. and L.D.M. Bendall.) Est. 1970. Open by appointment. SIZE: Large. *STOCK: Oriental rugs; 18th—19th C watercolours and oil paintings.* PARK: Easy. TEL: 893104. VAT: Stan/Spec.

Liss Antiques
141 Station Rd. (M. Doe.) CL: Wed. Open 10—5. *STOCK: General antiques.* TEL: 895025.

The Liss Bookshop and Gallery
71 and 73 Station Rd. (O.E.M. Butler and A.E. Gabie.) Resident. Est. 1978. Open 10—6. SIZE: Large. *STOCK: Antiquarian and secondhand books; watercolours and prints, oils, £10—£5,000.* LOC: 1 mile off A3. PARK: Easy. TEL: 892406; home — 893149. SER: Valuations; restorations; picture framing; buys at auction (books and paintings). VAT: Stan.

Liss Pine Warehouse
71 Station Rd. (Floydmist Ltd — P. Head and S. Caesar.) Est. 1983. Open 9—1 and 2—6. SIZE: Large. *STOCK: Pine furniture, 18th—19th C, £60—£500.* LOC: Next to station. PARK: Easy. TEL: 893743; home — 894044. SER: Restorations; stripping, polishing. VAT: Stan/Spec.

J. MORTON LEE
FINE WATERCOLOURS

HMS Warrior
Edouardo de Martino

CEDAR HOUSE, BACON LANE, HAYLING ISLAND
BY APPOINTMENT PLEASE
TEL: (0705) 464444

LYMINGTON   (0590)
Corfield of Lymington Ltd.   BADA
120 High St. and The Old School, Pennington. Open 9.15—5.30. SIZE: Large. *STOCK: English furniture, porcelain, English School watercolours and oil paintings, 18th to early 19th C; militaria.* TEL: 73532, 75359 and 77872. SER: Valuations; restorations (furniture, pictures). VAT: Stan/Spec.

Hughes and Smeeth Ltd.
1 Gosport St. (P. Hughes and S. Smeeth.) ABA. Est. 1976. Open 9.30—5.30. SIZE: Small. *STOCK: Antiquarian and secondhand books, maps and prints.* LOC: At bottom of High St. PARK: Nearby. TEL: 76324. SER: Valuations; restorations (oil paintings), binding, framing. VAT: Stan.

Old Solent House Galleries
Quay St. (Mrs. M. Brook-Hart.) Est. 1967. Open Sat., weekdays by appointment. SIZE: Medium. *STOCK: 19th and 20th C marine paintings, oils, £300—£5,000; watercolours, £80—£450; some glass and small furniture.* TEL: 75511. SER: Restorations (paintings); buys at auction. VAT: Spec.

Lymington continued

## Tara Associates Ltd.					*Mail order*
South End House, Church Lane. (P. and E. Watson.) *STOCK: Antiquarian books including social and economic history, exploration and trade, fashion and manners, feminism, fine bindings.* TEL: 76848.

## LYNDHURST					(042 128)
### Lita Kaye of Lyndhurst			BADA
13 High St. (L. and S. Ferder.) Est. 1947. Open 9.30—1 and 2.15—5. SIZE: Large. *STOCK: Furniture, clocks, 1690—1820; decorative porcelain, 19th C.* LOC: A35. PARK: 100yds. in High St. TEL: 2337. VAT: Stan/Spec.

MATTINGLEY, Nr. Basingstoke
Anna Hoysted
Goodchilds Farm, Chandlers Green. Open by appointment. *STOCK: English watercolours and drawings, 19th—20th C, £50—£1,500.* LOC: Near Stratfield Saye Estate between A32 and A33. PARK: Easy. TEL: Basingstoke (0256) 882355.

MEONSTOKE
W.D. Trivess
Heathfield House. Est. 1936. Open by appointment only. *STOCK: Maps and topographical views.* TEL: (0489) 877326. SER: List available.

MICHELDEVER STATION
Nr. Winchester
Marjorie Clare
The Old Post Cottage, Andover Rd. (Mrs. M. Clare.) Est. 1950. Open 10—5.30, Sun. 11—4, Mon. by appointment but prior 'phone call appreciated. SIZE: Medium. *STOCK: Period furniture, £40—£1,200; Edwardian satinwood, to £850; silver, £10—£500; paintings, signed pottery, Victorian, art nouveau and collectors' items, £20—£1,500.* Not stocked: Pine. LOC: From London, take M3, then left fork A303 (West) Micheldever Station signposted 3 miles on left, showroom next to 'The Dove'. PARK: Easy. TEL: Micheldever (096 289) 242. SER: Valuations. VAT: Spec.

MIDDLE WALLOP
Nr. Stockbridge
### Roger Wilson					*Mainly Trade*
The Old George. Resident. Est. 1956. SIZE: Small. *STOCK: 18th to early 19th C furniture, to £1,000.* Not stocked: Weapons. LOC: On the crossroads of B3084 and A343. PARK: Easy. TEL: Andover (0264) 781422. SER: Restorations (furniture). VAT: Spec.

MILFORD-ON-SEA
Nr. Lymington
Cameo Antiques
27 Keyhaven Rd. (R. Herman.) Est. 1980. CL: Mon., Wed. and lunchtimes. SIZE: Small. *STOCK: China and collectables, £5—£150; furniture and treen.* LOC: Off the village green, shop opp. "The White Horse". PARK: Easy. TEL: Lymington (0590) 45250; home — Lymington (0590) 42972. FAIRS: Ringwood.

## OAKLEY,					(023 02)
Nr. Basingstoke
E.H. Hutchins
48 Pardown, East Oakley. Est. 1933. *STOCK: General antiques.* Not stocked: China, jewellery, ornaments. LOC: B3400. PARK: Easy. TEL: Basingstoke (0256) 780494. VAT: Stan.

## ODIHAM					(025 671)
Woodgoods
High St. Est. 1967. Open 9—5. SIZE: Large. *STOCK: Stripped pine, £5—£400; pine kitchens.* LOC: Centre of main street. PARK: Easy. TEL: 2676. VAT: Stan.

## PETERSFIELD					(0730)
The Barn
Station Rd. (P. Gadsden.) Est. 1956. Open 9—5. *STOCK: Victoriana, bric-a-brac; also large store of trade and shipping goods.* TEL: 62958. VAT: Stan.

Cull Antiques
14 Dragon St. (J. Cull.) Est. 1978. Open 10—5.30 or by appointment. *STOCK: 18th C English furniture and metalwork.* TEL: 63670; home — 63471.

Dragon Antiques
9 Dragon St. (London Rd.). (Mr. and Mrs. L.R. Kirkland.) Est. 1952. Open 9—5.30. *STOCK: Furniture, china, glass, silver, curios, metalwork, general antiques.* Not stocked: Coins, garden ornaments, very large furniture. LOC: A3. Opposite Toby Jug restaurant. PARK: Opposite. TEL: 62570; home — 64427. FAIRS: English and Overseas. VAT: Stan/Spec.

Elmore
5 Charles St. (Mr. and Mrs. L.G. Mortimer.) Est. 1969. CL: Mon., Wed. and Thurs. Open 9.30—5. *STOCK: Small furniture, porcelain, glass, bric-a-brac, pictures and prints.* TEL: 62383.

Folly Antiques Centre
College St. Est. 1977. Open 9.30—5, Thurs. 9.30—1. There are several specialist shops selling a wide variety of antique silver, watercolours, porcelain, glass, furniture, jewellery, brass, copper, period clothes, lace, collectors' items and objets d'art. LOC: On A3. TEL: 64816.

Petersfield continued

Fort Antiques
(House of Antiques), 4 College St. Est. 1971.
CL: Thurs. p.m. Open 9.30—1 and 2—5.
STOCK: Furniture, £50—£1,500; silver, 17th—19th C, £5—£600; glass, china, paintings, 18th—19th C, £5—£400; objets d'art, £5—£200; clocks, £25—£2,500; jewellery, 18th and 19th C, £20—£2,000. TEL: 62172. VAT: Stan/Spec.

The House of Antiques　　LAPADA
4 College St. (C.G. Foord, S.A. Grout-Smith.)
Est. 1979. CL: Thurs. p.m. Open 9.30—5.30,
until 5 in winter. SIZE: Medium. Various
dealers specialising in 18th—19th C furniture
and pine; boxes, porcelain, pottery, glass,
brass, copper, metalware, medals, antiquities,
treen, silver, collectors' items. LOC: On A3
opposite Red Lion Hotel. PARK: Behind shop.
TEL: 62172. SER: Restorations (boxes, furniture, gilding, papier mâché, painted furniture.
FAIRS: London and south of England. VAT:
Stan/Spec.

The Petersfield Bookshop　　BADA
16a Chapel St. (F. Westwood.) ABA. Est.
1918. Open 9—5.30. SIZE: Large. *STOCK:
Books, old and modern, £1—£500; maps and
prints, 1600—1850, £1—£20; oils and watercolours, 19th C, £20—£1,000.* LOC: Chapel
St. runs from the Square to Station Rd. PARK:
Opposite. TEL: 63438. SER: Restorations and
rebinding of old leather books; picture-framing
and mount-cutting. FAIRS: Northern and
Buxton, San Francisco, Boston and London.
VAT: Stan.

PLAITFORD, Nr. Romsey
Plaitford House Gallery
(W.B. Yeo.) Est. 1960. Open most days and
any time by appointment. SIZE: Large.
*STOCK: Oil paintings, watercolours, bronzes,
1800—1950, £5—£5,000.* LOC: 1 mile north
of A36 midway between Salisbury and
Southampton on the road joining Landford and
Sherfield English. PARK: Easy. TEL: West
Wellow (0794) 22221. SER: Valuations; restorations and cleaning of oils and watercolours.
VAT: Spec.

PORTSMOUTH　　　　(0705)
Tony Amos Antiques
239 Albert Rd., Southsea and warehouse at
152 Haslemere Rd., Southsea. Open 9—5,
Sat. 9—12. *STOCK: General antiques and
shipping goods.* TEL: 750152 or 736818.

A.R. Challis Ltd.
95, 97, and 106 Palmerston Rd., Southsea.
Est. 1948. CL: Sat. p.m. Open 9—1 and
2—5. *STOCK: Glass-ware, furniture, china,
pictures.* TEL: 823838. VAT: Stan.

Rodney Dodson Antiques　LAPADA
85 Fawcett Rd., Southsea. Open 8.30—5.30. *STOCK: General antiques.* TEL: 829481
or 262226.

A. Fleming (Southsea) Ltd.　　BADA
The Clock Tower, Castle Rd. Est. 1905. CL:
Sat. p.m. Open 8.30—5. SIZE: Large. *STOCK:
Furniture, silver, china, porcelain, medals;
general antiques, jewellery.* TEL: 822934.
SER: Valuations; restorations. VAT: Stan/
Spec.

The Gallery
11 and 19 Marmion Rd., Southsea. (I.
Murphy.) Open 10—5. *STOCK: At No. 19 —
Victorian chairs and chesterfields, at No. 11 —
furniture, mainly Victorian and Edwardian.* PARK: Nearby. TEL: 822016. VAT: Stan.

Leslie's
107 Fratton Rd. (E. Lord.) Est. 1946. CL:
Wed. p.m. Open 9.30—1 and 2—5.30, Sat.
until 6. SIZE: Small. *STOCK: Victorian and
antique rings, brooches, 1850—1920,
£10—£350.* Not stocked: Furniture, pictures.
LOC: Fratton railway station, or 4 shops from
main Co-op store in Fratton Rd. PARK: Easy.
TEL: 825952. SER: Valuations; restorations
(antique jewellery). VAT: Stan.

IS YOUR ENTRY CORRECT?
If there is even the slightest
inaccuracy in your entry, *please* let us
know before 1st January 1987.
GUIDE TO THE
ANTIQUE SHOPS OF BRITAIN
5 Church Street, Woodbridge, Suffolk.

Pretty Chairs

JOYCE RUFFELL
189/191 Highland
Road
Southsea, Hants.
Tel. Portsmouth 731411

Portsmouth continued

Longporte Antiques
98 Marmion Rd., Southsea. (G. Strickland.) Est. 1972. CL: Sun. except by appointment. Open 10—5.30. SIZE: Small. *STOCK: Furniture, 18th—19th C, £50—£500; oil paintings and watercolours, 19th C, £50—£200.* Not stocked: Jewellery, silverware. LOC: Off Palmerston Rd., main shopping centre. PARK: Easy. TEL: 829279.

Colin Macleod's Antique Centre
159/161 Goldsmith Ave., Southsea and warehouse at 139 Goldsmith Ave. Open 8.30—5.30, Sun. by appointment. SIZE: Large. *STOCK: Victorian shipping items, 1840—1940, £50—£250; general antiques.* LOC: Adjacent Portsmouth Football ground. PARK: Easy. TEL: 734173 and 816278. SER: Valuations; restorations; containers. VAT: Stan/Spec.

Paul Maynard Antiques
23/25 Warren Ave. and 151 Highland Rd., Southsea. Est. 1973. Open 9—5, Sat. 9—1. SIZE: Medium. *STOCK: Furniture, mainly English but also, French, Swedish and Danish, 1800—1920, £50—£1,000.* PARK: Easy. TEL: 861633. VAT: Stan/Spec.

Portsmouth continued

Osborne Antiques and Jewellery
55 Osborne Rd., Southsea. (D. Garcia.) Est. 1960. Open 9—5. SIZE: Small. *STOCK: Jewellery, glass, silver.* LOC: Main shopping centre. PARK: Opposite. TEL: 825101. VAT: Stan.

Portsmouth Stamp Shop
184 Chichester Rd., North End. (G. Coast.) Est. 1967. Open 9.15—5.30, Fri. 9.15—8. *STOCK: Stamps, coins, cigarette cards, postcards, banknotes.* TEL: 663450. VAT: Stan.

Pretty Chairs   LAPADA
189—191 Highland Rd., Southsea. (J. Ruffell.) Est. 1963. CL: Wed. p.m. Open 10—5. SIZE: Large. *STOCK: Victorian chairs, tables, wood boxes, desks, bureaux, sofas, French style furniture and cabriole-legged chairs.* LOC: Off Eastney Rd. PARK: Easy. TEL: 731411. VAT: Stan/Spec.

W.R. Priddy
65 Fawcett Rd., Southsea. CL: Sat. Open 10—5.30. *STOCK: General antiques.* TEL: 826135 or 738906.

P. Tallack
77 Castle Rd., Southsea. Est. 1960. Open 9.30—5. *STOCK: General antiques.* PARK: Nearby. TEL: 820239.

RAMSDELL, Nr. Basingstoke

Ewhurst Gallery   LAPADA
(R. Mayfield.) Est. 1976. Open any time by appointment. *STOCK: Watercolours and drawings, 18th to early 20th C, £50—£2,500.* LOC: ¼ mile off A339, 5 miles from Basingstoke. PARK: Easy. TEL: Basingstoke (0256) 850051. SER: Valuations; buys at auction; finder. VAT: Spec.

RINGWOOD
(4 and 5 fig. no.) (042 54)
(6 fig. no.) (0425)

Stanley Blanchard   BADA
Moortown House, Moortown. (S. and J. Blanchard.) Open 8.30—6.30, weekends by appointment. SIZE: Large. *STOCK: Furniture, pictures and porcelain.* LOC: Main road. PARK: Easy. TEL: 2377. VAT: Stan/Spec.

Barbara Davies Antiques
30A Christchurch Rd. Est. 1965. CL: Tues. and Thurs. Open 10—4.30 (10—4 Oct. to Mar.), Sat. 10—12.30. SIZE: Small. *STOCK: Porcelain, 1760—1930, £5—£100; small furniture, 1850—1935, £20—£150; watercolours and prints, 1850—1930, £10—£150.* LOC: Off A31 into Ringwood, turn off roundabout to Moortown, next roundabout, turn right, shop on left 250yds. PARK: Behind Greyfriars Community Centre. TEL: Home — (0202) 872268. SER: Valuations (pottery and porcelain).

Ringwood continued

Millers of Chelsea Antiques Ltd.
LAPADA
Netherbrook House, 86 Christchurch Rd. Est.
1898. Open 9—5.30, weekends and evenings
by appointment. SIZE: Large. *STOCK: Furniture — country English and French provincial,
English and Continental mahogany and gilt,
military, decorative items, 18th—19th C,
£25—£2,000.* LOC: On B3347 towards
Christchurch. PARK: Own. TEL: 2062. FAIRS:
Ringwood Antiques Weekend. VAT: Stan/Spec.

P.E. Palmer Antiques
The Matchbox, 132 Christchurch Rd. Est.
1961. Open 10—5. SIZE: Large. *STOCK:
Furniture, collectors' items, 17th—19th C;
jewellery, bric-a-brac.* LOC: By the old railway
crossing. PARK: Easy. TEL: 4695. SER: Valuations; restorations (furniture, porcelain, silver);
buys at auction.

Pine Company
104 Christchurch Rd. and Unit 9, Millstream
Estate. (D.R. and G.B. Smith.) Est. 1978.
Open 9.30—1 and 2—5.30. SIZE: Large and
warehouse. *STOCK; Pine and other wood,
18th—19th C, £30—£1,000; model railways,
19th—20th C, from £5.* Not stocked: Silver,
fine china, bric-a-brac. LOC: Almost opposite
fire station. PARK: Own. TEL: 3932/6705;
home — same. SER: Restorations. VAT: Stan.

Tyrrell Bookshop and Gallery
80 Christchurch Rd. (N. Owen.) Est. 1984.
CL: Thurs. Open 9.30—1 and 2.15—5, Sat.
9.30—1 and 2—5, Sun. a.m. by appointment.
SIZE: Small. *STOCK: Antiquarian books,
18th—19th C, £5—£50; prints and watercolours, £10—£100; furniture, £50—£200;
both 19th C.* PARK: 25yds. TEL: 474489;
home — same. VAT: Stan.

ROMSEY   (0794)
Bell Antiques
8 Bell St. (M. and B.M. Gay.) Est. 1979. CL:
Wed. p.m. Open 9.30—5.30. SIZE: Medium.
*STOCK: General antiques including art
nouveau and art deco; furniture, glass, pottery, porcelain, jewellery, 19th and 20th C;
topographical prints.* LOC: Town centre.
PARK: Adjacent. TEL: 514719. VAT: Stan/
Spec.

Cambridge Antiques
5 Bell St. Open 9—5.30. SIZE: Large. *STOCK:
Furniture, clocks, paintings, china, metalware.*
LOC: From the West, Romsey by-pass, left
into Palmerston St., first left then first right,
100yds. on left. TEL: 523089. VAT: Stan/
Spec.

Charles Antiques   LAPADA
101 The Hundred. (T.R. Cambridge.) Est.
1972. Open 9—5.30. SIZE: Large. *STOCK:
Furniture, clocks, small china, shipping goods.*
LOC: From the west, Romsey by-pass, left
into Palmerston St., 1st right into The
Hundred. PARK: Easy. TEL: 512885. VAT:
Stan/Spec.

Cornmarket Antiques
Cornmarket. (Mrs. J.P. Bachmann.) Est.
1970. CL: Wed. Open 9.30—3.30. SIZE:
Small. *STOCK: General antiques, £5—£75;
small furniture, £30—£350; all 1750—1930.*
PARK: Easy. TEL: 512094; home —
Southampton (0703) 735284.

Old Cottage Things
Broxmore Park, Sherfield-English. (M. Hyde.)
Est. 1970. *STOCK: Exterior and interior archi-
ectural items, country furniture, garden items.*
TEL: 8538.

Romsey continued

Romsey Medal and Collectors Centre

112 The Hundred. (T. Cambridge.) Est. 1980. Open 9—5.30 by appointment. *STOCK: Medals, militaria, crested china, clocks, furniture.* LOC: From the west, Romsey by-pass, left into Palmerston St. 1st right into The Hundred. PARK: Easy. TEL: 512069/512885.

Warwick Antiques and Middlebridge Antiques Ltd.

15 Middlebridge St. Est. 1970. CL: Wed. p.m. Open 9.30—5.30. *STOCK: Furniture, general antiques, trade goods; clocks.* TEL: 523405 or 13356. SER: Restorations and repairs (clocks and furniture).

SOUTHAMPTON   (0703)

Mr. Alfred's "Old Curiosity Shop" incorporating James Morris, Fine Art Dealer

280 Shirley Rd., Shirley. Est. 1952. Open 9—6. *STOCK: Furniture, 18th—20th C; paintings, porcelain, bronzes, brass, glass, books, silver, jewellery and general antiques.* LOC: On left of main Shirley road, ¾ mile from Southampton central station. PARK: Outside. TEL: 774772.

Bedford Place Antiques

30 Bedford Place. (A. and T. Wright.) Est. 1977. CL: Wed. Open 9.30—4. *STOCK: Furniture, general antiques, paintings.* TEL: 223642; home — 778257.

Southampton continued

Meg Campbell

10 Church Lane, Highfield. Est. 1967. Open by appointment only. *STOCK: Old English silver, collectors' pieces, old Sheffield plate.* TEL: 557636. SER: Mail order; catalogues available. VAT: Spec.

T.A. Cherrington

67A Bedford Pl. CL: Wed. Open 10—5.30. *STOCK: Antiquarian and secondhand books.* TEL: 224265.

Cottage Antiques

9 Northam Rd. (K.J. Leslie.) Open 10—5.30. *STOCK: General antiques, furniture, Victorian, trade goods.* TEL: 221546; home — 452246. VAT: Stan.

R.J. Elliot

45 Northam Rd. Open 10—5. *STOCK: Silver, plate, small antiques.* TEL: 226642.

H.M. Gilbert and Son

2½ Portland St. (B.L. and R.C. Gilbert.) ABA. Est. 1859. Open 8.30—5. *STOCK: Antiquarian books.* PARK: Easy. TEL: 226420. VAT: Stan.

"...the behaviour of these people was so unlike that of inn waiters, and had so much the appearance of real hospitality..." From **Mr. Rowlandson's England** by Robert Southey, ed. John Steel, published by the **Antique Collectors' Club,** 1985.

Southampton continued

Hingston's
13 Northam Rd. Est. 1963. CL: Wed. and Fri. Open 10—4. SIZE: Large. *STOCK: Large pottery and porcelain, 18th—19th C; furniture, Victorian coloured glass, pot-lids.* Not stocked: Rugs, jewellery. LOC: From Portsmouth take Northam road for Southampton town centre. TEL: 220180; home — 812301.

N. Hingston's
15 Northam Rd. CL: Wed. and Fri. p.m. Open 9.30—4.30. *STOCK: 19th—20th C shipping furniture.* TEL: 812301.

Jubilee Antiques
340 Burgess Rd., Swaythling. (R. Brown.) Open 9.30—6, Sun. by appointment. SIZE: Medium. *STOCK: Furniture including stripped pine and satinwood, 19th C, £5—£500; clocks, 18th—20th C, £5—£1,000; bric-a-brac.* LOC: Just off M27. PARK: Easy. TEL: 551515; home — same. SER: Valuations; restorations (hand-stripping).

R.K. Leslie Antiques
23 Northam Rd. Est. 1961. CL: Wed. p.m. and Sat. Open 10—5. *STOCK: Silver, jewellery, curios, china, clocks, furniture.* TEL: 224784. VAT: Stan.

Lodge Road Antiques
71 Lodge Rd. (C. and J. Griffith.) Est. 1981. CL: Wed. Open 9—5.30. SIZE: Large. *STOCK: Furniture and bric-a-brac, 18th—20th C, £5—£500; pine, 19th C, £50—£200.* LOC: From Winchester by-pass turn into main avenue, left at 3rd set of traffic lights beside Merchant Navy Hotel, shop 500yds. on right adjacent bus shelter. PARK: Easy. TEL: 38086. SER: Valuations; restorations. VAT: Stan/Spec.

L. Moody
70 Bedford Place. (J. and A.H. Gubb.) Est. 1905. CL: Wed. p.m. Open 8—5.30. SIZE: Large. *STOCK: Furniture, 1650—1910, from £25; silver, porcelain, to 1900.* LOC: ½ mile north of Civic Centre. PARK: 50yds. in next block. TEL: 333720. SER: Valuations. VAT: Stan/Spec.

Oldfield
34 Northam Rd. (A. Downes.) Est. 1970. Open 10.30—5. SIZE: Medium. *STOCK: Maps, books, prints, 16th—20th C, £1—£1,500.* LOC: Near Six Dials roundabout on Portsmouth road into city. PARK: Easy. TEL: 38916. SER: Valuations; colouring, mounting and framing of maps and prints. FAIRS: Monthly map and print, Bonnington Hotel, London.

Parkhouse and Wyatt Ltd.
96 Above Bar. Est. 1794. SIZE: Small. *STOCK: Silver, jewellery.* LOC: City centre. PARK: Meters. TEL: 226653 ext. 25. SER: Valuations; repairs.

Southampton continued

Relics Antiques
54 Northam Rd. (R.M. Simmonds.) Open 9—5. *STOCK: General antiques.* TEL: 221635.

STOCKBRIDGE

Douglas Gordon Antiques   BADA
The Old Rectory. (Lord Douglas Gordon.) Open 10—5.30, or by appointment. *STOCK: English and Continental period furniture, 17th to early 19th C; some porcelain, glass, pictures, decorative items.* TEL: Andover (0264) 810662. VAT: Spec.

George Hofman, Antiques
At the Sign of the Black Cat
Brookside, High St. Est. 1973. Open 10—5.30. Sat. 10—4. SIZE: Medium. *STOCK: Furniture, small items, general antiques.* LOC: A30. PARK: At rear. TEL: Andover (0264) 810570; home — same. VAT: Stan/Spec.

Lane Antiques
High St. (E.K. Lane.) Est. 1978. Open 10—5.30, Wed. 10—2, Sun. by appointment. SIZE: Small. *STOCK: English and Continental porcelain, 18th—19th C, £50—£100; French clocks, silver and plate, jewellery, decorative items, glass, small furniture.* PARK: Easy. TEL: Andover (0264) 810435; home — same.

Victor Mahy Ltd.   BADA
Mulberry House, High St. (J.V. Mahy and J.H. Parnaby.) Est. 1963. Open 9—5.30. *STOCK: Furniture and pictures, 18th C.* TEL: Andover (0264) 810466. SER: Restorations (picture cleaning).

Victor Needham Antiques   BADA
High St., Broughton. (B. and H. Fox.) Est. 1880. CL: Wed. Open 9—5.30 or by appointment. *STOCK: Furniture, 17th—18th C; works of art and garden ornaments.* TEL: Broughton (079 430) 205; home — Broughton (079 430) 472.

Pedlar's Pack
High St. (Mrs. P. Melville.) Open 9.30—5.30, Mon. and Wed. by appointment. SIZE: Small. *STOCK: Staffordshire pottery, 19th C, £25—£150; small furniture, Victorian and Edwardian, £25—£500; glass and bric-a-brac, 19th—20th C, £5—£50.* LOC: A30. PARK: Easy. TEL: Andover (0264) 810493; home — same.

Stockbridge Antiques
High St. (Mrs. P. Bradley.) Est. 1960. SIZE: Medium. *STOCK: Small furniture, 18th—19th C, to £2,000; glass, from 18th C; porcelain, small silver, pictures, rugs.* Not stocked: Coins, stamps, weapons. LOC: A30. PARK: Easy. TEL: Andover (0264) 810829; home — same. VAT: Spec.

Stockbridge continued

Elizabeth Viney   BADA
Jacob's House, High St. (Miss E.A. Viney, MBE.) Est. 1967. CL: Sun. and some Mon. and Wed., appointment advisable. Open 9—5. SIZE: Small. *STOCK: Furniture — mahogany, 1720—1825, £75—£5,500; walnut, £125—£6,500; oak and country, 1650—1710, £65—£5,250; treen, brass and copper, 1700—1825, £15—£375.* Not stocked: Victoriana. LOC: A30. Opposite old Post Office. PARK: Easy. TEL: Andover (0264) 810761. VAT: Stan/Spec.

STROUD, Nr. Petersfield
Abacus Antiques
58 Winchester Rd. (J. Crawford.) Est. 1969. Open 10—6, Sun. by appointment. SIZE: Medium. *STOCK: English oak and country furniture, 17th—19th C, £50—£1,000; English Delftware, 18th C, £50—£200.* LOC: 2 miles west of Petersfield on Winchester road. PARK: Easy. TEL: Petersfield (0730) 61935; home — same. SER: Restorations (furniture). VAT: Stan/Spec.

TITCHFIELD, Nr. Fareham   (0329)
Gaylords
75 West St. (D.L. Hebbard.) Est. 1970. Open 9.30—5.30. SIZE: Large. *STOCK: Furniture from 18th C; clocks, shipping goods, £5—£3,000.* LOC: Just off A27. PARK: Easy. TEL: 43402; home — Stubbington (0329) 662606. SER: Valuations; buys at auction (furniture). VAT: Stan/Spec.

Pamela Manley Antique Jewellery
6 and 8 South St. Est.1965. Open Thurs.—Sat. SIZE: Small. *STOCK: Jewellery, 19th to early 20th C, £5—£500; silver and plate, glass, £10—£500; porcelain, bronzes, boxes.* LOC: ¼ mile from A27. PARK: Easy. TEL: 42794. SER: Valuations; buys at auction.

Titchfield Antiques Ltd.
13—15 South St. CL: Mon. Open 10—5.30, Sun. 2—6. *STOCK: Art nouveau, art deco, silver and plate, furniture, 17th C to Edwardian.* PARK: Easy. TEL: 45968. SER: Restorations (as stock).

TWYFORD   (0962)
Jeffery Hammond Antiques
18—19 High St. (J. and E. Hammond.) Est. 1970. Open 9—6 or by appointment. SIZE: Medium. *STOCK: Furniture, 17th to early 19th C, £100—£5,000.* LOC: Village centre. PARK: Own. TEL: 714036 anytime. SER: Valuations. VAT: Stan/Spec.

Twyford Antiques
High St. Open 9.30—5.30. *STOCK: Clocks, furniture, shipping goods.* TEL: 713484. SER: Valuations; restorations (clocks).

UPHAM, Nr. Southampton
Susanna Fisher   *Mainly Postal*
Spencer. Est. 1971. Open by appointment only. *STOCK: Navigational charts and sailing directions, 16th—19th C.* TEL: Durley (048 96) 291. SER: Buys at auction; catalogues available.

WHITCHURCH   (025 682)
Regency House Antiques
Regency House, 14 Church St. (J.W.L. Mouat.) Resident. Est. 1968. CL: Wed. Open 9.30—7. SIZE: Medium. *STOCK: 17th—19th C, oak, mahogany and pine furniture, longcase clocks; metalwork and bric-a-brac.* LOC: B3400. On Newbury road, coming from Winchester, take first turning on left at crossroads in Whitchurch. PARK: Opposite. TEL: 2149. SER: Valuations; buys at auction. VAT: Spec.

Something Particular
23 Winchester St. (Mrs. M. Bevan.) Resident. *STOCK: Furniture, general antiques and bric-a-brac.* LOC: On 1st bridge towards Winchester almost opp. silk mills. PARK: Easy. TEL: 2525.

WINCHESTER   (0962)
Antiques and Interiors
6 Andover Rd. (W. Todd and G. Austin. M.Ins.M.) Est. 1973. CL: Sun. except by appointment. Open 9.30—5. SIZE: Small. *STOCK: Decorative pottery, porcelain, glass, mirrors, clocks, lamps and furniture, 19th—20th C; selected 19th—20th C decorators' and furnishing items.* LOC: Near railway station on main Andover road. PARK: Easy. TEL: 69824.

Joseph William   BADA
Blanchard Ltd   LAPADA
12 Jewry St. Est. 1940. Open 9—1 and 2—5. SIZE: Large. *STOCK: General antiques, especially breakfront bookcases.* PARK: Behind shop. TEL: 54547 and 52041. VAT: Stan/Spec.

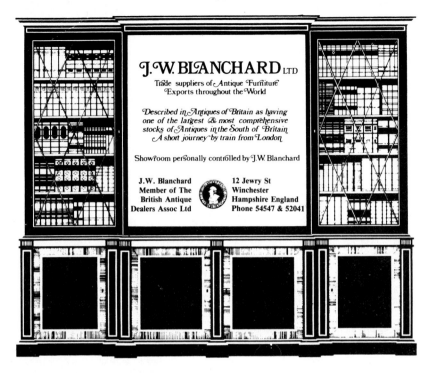

Winchester continued

Michael Bullivant
24 St. Swithun St. Resident. Open by appointment only. *STOCK: Watercolours, 18th to early 20th C, £25—£400.* LOC: Off Southgate St., near the College and Cathedral. PARK: Opposite. TEL: 56675. SER: Valuations; buys at auction.

Burns and Graham
4 St. Thomas St. Est. 1971. CL: Thurs. p.m. *STOCK: Furniture, 17th to early 19th C; decorative items.* TEL: 53779. VAT: Stan/Spec.

Winchester continued

Close Antiques   BADA
19 Little Minster St. (Mrs. C. Baron.) Open 9—5. SIZE: Small. *STOCK: 17th—18th C oak, fruitwood and walnut country furniture; early pottery, Delftware, Staffordshire figures, samplers, early brass, copper, iron and treen.* **LOC: Behind Splinters restaurant in the Square, close to west front of the Cathedral. PARK: Easy. TEL: 64763. VAT: Stan/Spec.**

Winchester continued

Peter Daly
at the rear of Thompson Antiques, 20a Jewry St. Open Wed., Fri. and Sat. 10—5. *STOCK: Rare and secondhand books.* TEL: Home — 67732.

Polly de Courcy-Ireland   BADA
16 Chilbolton Ave. Est. 1972. By appointment only. *STOCK: English and Continental treen; pre-1830 and unusual items in brass and bone.* TEL: 65716.

Gallery Antiques Ltd.
16 Jewry St. (A.P.F. Rothman.) Est. 1981. Open 9—6 or by appointment. SIZE: Large. *STOCK: Furniture especially Regency, 17th to early 19th C, £50—£20,000; paintings, engravings, £50—£10,000; decorative items, £20—£12,000; both 18th—19th C.* LOC: Near public library. PARK: Own. TEL: 62436. VAT: Stan/Spec.

H.M. Gilbert
19 The Square. (B.L. and R.C. Gilbert.) ABA. Open 9—5.30. *STOCK: Antiquarian and secondhand books.* TEL: 52832.

Look
35 Middlebrook St. (R. and M. Cutting.) Est. 1956. Open 12.30—5, Sat. all day. SIZE: Small. *STOCK: General small antiques, porcelain, Victoriana, £5—£25; dolls and curios, to 1930; silver and jewellery, Victorian.* Not stocked: Furniture. LOC: In main car park near Post Office. PARK: Easy. TEL: 63731.

IS YOUR ENTRY CORRECT?
If there is even the slightest inaccuracy in your entry, *please* let us know before 1st January 1987.
GUIDE TO THE
ANTIQUE SHOPS OF BRITAIN
5 Church Street, Woodbridge, Suffolk.

Winchester continued

Gerald E. Marsh   BADA
(Antique Clocks)
32a The Square. Est. 1947. CL: Thurs. p.m. Open 9—1 and 2—5. *STOCK: Clocks, English longcase and bracket, £300—£20,000; French and Continental, £200—£10,000; early watches and barometers, £150—£7,000; all 1680—1800.* Not stocked: Other antiques. LOC: Near Cathedral. PARK: Easy. TEL: 54505. SER: Valuations; restorations (clocks); buys at auction. VAT: Spec.

The Pine Cellars
38 Jewry St. (N. Spencer-Brayn.) Est. 1970. Open 9.30-5.30. SIZE: Large and warehouse. *STOCK: Pine and country furniture, 18th—19th C, £10—£2,000; painted furniture, architectural items, panelled rooms.* LOC: One way street, a right turn from top of High St. or St. Georges St., shop 100yds. on right. PARK: Nearby. TEL: 67014. SER: Stripping and export. VAT: Stan/Spec.

Printed Page
2/3 Bridge St. (J. and C. Wright.) Est. 1977. CL: Mon. SIZE: Small. *STOCK: Antique maps and prints, 17th—19th C, £1—£350.* LOC: Bottom of High St., cross over river and shop is on left. PARK: In Water Lane, adjacent to shop. TEL: 54072; home — 62995. SER: Valuations; picture framing, mount cutting; buys at auction; postal service. VAT: Stan.

SPCK Bookshops
24 The Square. Open 9—5.30. *STOCK: Books including antiquarian.* TEL: 66617.

St. George's Antiques Centre
10a St. George's St. CL: Mon. except by appointment. Open 10—4.30. SIZE: Medium. There are 6 stalls at this centre selling *a wide variety of general antiques including art pottery, boxes, china, art deco, Doulton, fans, glass, jewellery, linen and lace, porcelain, small furniture, silver, watercolours and oils.* LOC: Down passageway between Ladbrokes and Flairs (Drycleaners). PARK: Nearby. TEL: 56317; home — 51650 and 63165. FAIRS: Lyndhurst Park Hotel and Winchester Guildhall.

W.G. Skipwith
5 Parchment St. Est. 1966. CL: Thurs. p.m. SIZE: Small. *STOCK: Prints, some watercolours and oils, 19th—20th C, from £5.* LOC: Near pedestrian precinct. PARK: Easy. TEL: 52911. SER: Valuations; restorations (oils, watercolours, prints, china). VAT: Stan/Spec.

Winchester continued

Thompson Antiques formerly Ships and Sealing Wax

20a Jewry St. Open 9.30–5. SIZE: Large. *STOCK: Victoriana and later furniture, pine, pictures, decorative items, shipping goods.* TEL: 66633; home — 884504.

Todd and Austin Antiques of Winchester

2 Andover Rd. (W. Todd and G. Austin.) Est. 1964. CL: Sun. except by appointment. Open 9.30–5. SIZE: Medium. *STOCK: English porcelain and pottery, 1750–1930; Oriental and Chinese porcelain, to late 19th C; English and Continental glass, 19th to early 20th C; French, English and Bohemian paperweights, mid 19th C, from £100; boxes including writing cases, tea caddies, knee desks, 18th and 19th C; objets d'art; clocks, visiting card cases, snuff boxes, perfume bottles, miniatures painted on ivory, furniture, cabinets, small decorative items and art nouveau, 19th to early 20th C; decorative silver, 19th C; Victorian jewellery.* LOC: 1 minute from Winchester Station. PARK: At station or nearby. TEL: 69824. SER: Restorations (clocks, barometers). FAIRS: Kensington.

Winchester continued

I.S. Trudgett

3 Andover Rd. Est. 1965. CL: Thurs. Open 9.45–12.30 and 1.30–3.30. SIZE: Small. *STOCK: Small and general antiques, collectors' items including glass, pottery and porcelain, jewellery, prints, badges, medals, cigarette cards, sets and rare items, postcards and curios, to 1940.* LOC: Main Andover road. PARK: Easy. TEL: 54132; evening — 62070.

WOODLANDS, Nr. Southampton
Doreen Gardner Antiques

Wealdon, Ringwood Rd. Est. 1970. Appointment advisable. *STOCK: Pottery, porcelain, brass and copper, 18th and 19th C; dolls' houses, tools.* LOC: A336. TEL: Totton (0703) 869991.

Hereford and Worcester

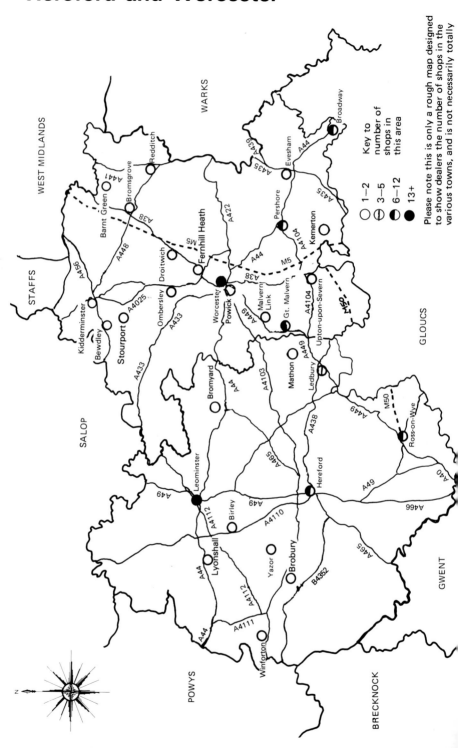

WEST MIDLANDS

WARKS

STAFFS

SALOP

GLOUCS

GWENT

BRECKNOCK

POWYS

Redditch

Barnt Green

Bromsgrove

Kidderminster

Bewdley

Stourport

Ombersley

Droitwich

Fernhill Heath

Worcester

Powick

Malvern Link

Gt. Malvern

Upton-upon-Severn

Pershore

Kemerton

Evesham

Broadway

Bromyard

Mathon

Ledbury

Leominster

Birley

Lyonshall

Yazor

Brobury

Hereford

Ross-on-Wye

Winforton

A441

A448

A456

A38

A4025

A433

M5

A422

A44

A38

M5

A435

A439

A435

A4104

A449

A4104

M50

A449

A44

A4103

A438

A465

A4112

A49

A4110

A4112

A4111

A44

B4352

A465

A49

A466

A40

M50

A449

Key to
number of
shops in
this area

○ 1–2
◑ 3–5
◕ 6–12
● 13+

Please note this is only a rough map designed
to show dealers the number of shops in the
various towns, and is not necessarily totally

Hereford and Worcester

BARNT GREEN, Nr. Birmingham

Barnt Green Antiques
93 Hewell Rd. (N. Slater.) Est. 1965. Open 9−1 and 2−6. SIZE: Medium. *STOCK: Furniture, 18th−19th C, £100−£5,000.* PARK: Easy. TEL: (021) 445 4942. SER: Valuations; restorations (furniture, clocks, oils); framing; buys at auction. VAT: Stan/Spec.

BEWDLEY   (0299)

Gibbons and Co.
89 Welch Gate. (P.H. Gibbons.) Est. 1983. Open Thurs. and Fri. 10−12.30 and 1.30−5, Sat. 10−5. SIZE: Small. *STOCK: Antiquarian and secondhand books, 17th−20th C, £1−£50.* LOC: Near town centre on A456. PARK: Nearby. TEL: Home − 400183. SER: Valuations. FAIRS: Local book.

BIRLEY

Gay Walker
Birley Court. (Miss G. Walker.) Est. 1970. Open Sun., Mon. and Wed. or by appointment. SIZE: Medium. *STOCK: Mahogany, oak, unstripped pine, treen and unusual items, 17th C to Victorian.* LOC: Large house opposite church, ½ mile from the A4110. PARK: Easy. TEL: Ivington (056 888) 238. VAT: Stan/Spec.

BROADWAY   (0386)

Broadway Antique Arcade
13A Leamington Rd. (R.G. Brown.) Est. 1984. CL: Mon. Open 10−5, including Sun. SIZE: Medium. *STOCK: Furniture, porcelain, brass and copper, jewellery and linen, 19th C to art deco, £5−£1,000.* LOC: 400yds. from High St. PARK: Easy. TEL: 853035; home − same and 853138.

Cotswold House
21 The Green. (R. Hagen.) Open 9.30−1 and 2−6, Sun. by appointment. SIZE: Large. *STOCK: Oil paintings, late 19th to 20th C, £100−£25,000.* PARK: Easy. TEL: 853624 or 858561. SER: Valuations; restorations; buys at auction (paintings). VAT: Spec.

Broadway continued

Gavina Ewart   BADA
60−62 High St. (Mrs. G. and A.J. Ewart.) CADA. Est. 1964. Open 9.30−1 and 2−5.30. SIZE: Large. *STOCK: Sets of silver cutlery (items matched from stock), 18th−20th C; other silver, teasets, pot-lids and other Prattware, including some rarer items, carriage clocks, 19th C; furniture and porcelain including Worcester, 18th−19th C; oil paintings and watercolours, 19th−20th C; maps, prints and jewellery.* PARK: Easy. TEL: 853371. SER: Valuations; restorations (clocks, furniture and barometers). FAIRS: Buxton, Kenilworth, British International Birmingham. VAT: Stan/Spec.

Fayme Antiques
Laundry Cottage, 159 High St. (Miss F.M. Philp.) Est. 1974. Open by appointment. SIZE: Medium. *STOCK: Small decorative furniture, painted pine, 18th−19th C, £100−£1,000; treen, wood carvings, brass, copper and ironware, 17th−19th C, £25−£1,000; garden furnishings.* Not stocked: Silver and porcelain. LOC: Cottage is first house in Broadway on left coming from London on A44. PARK: Easy. TEL: 852061; home − same. SER: Restorations (metalware and furniture); buys at auction. VAT: Stan/Spec.

Fenwick and Fisher Antiques
88 High St. Est. 1980. Open 9−6. SIZE: Medium. *STOCK: Furniture, works of art, samplers, boxes, treen, Tunbridgeware, delft, 17th to early 19th C.* TEL: 853227.

Richard Hagen Ltd.
Yew Tree House. Open 9−6. Sun. by appointment. *STOCK: 19th−20th C oils and watercolours.* TEL: 853624. SER: Valuations; restorations; framing. VAT: Spec.

Hay Loft Gallery
Berry Wormington. (Mrs. J.R. and Miss S.A. Pitt.) Resident. Est. 1984. Open 10.30−5.30 or by appointment. SIZE: Medium. *STOCK: Victorian paintings, £250−£8,000; Victorian watercolours, £250−£3,000.* LOC: A46 towards Cheltenham, farm on right hand side. PARK: Easy. TEL: (024 269) 202. SER: Restorations; framing. VAT: Spec.

H.W. Keil Ltd.   BADA
Tudor House, Broad Close, Eadburgha Hall. (V.M. Keil.) Est. 1925. CL: Thurs. p.m. Open 9−5.30. SIZE: Large. *STOCK: Walnut, oak and mahogany furniture and works of art, all 17th−18th C.* TEL: 852408. VAT: Spec.

Broadway continued

John Noott, Picton House Gallery
Picton House, High St. CADA. Est. 1972. Open 9—1 and 2—5.30, or by appointment. SIZE: Large. *STOCK: Paintings and watercolours, 19th—20th C, £50—£10,000; general antiques, mostly furniture and smalls, 18th—19th C.* LOC: Centre of village. PARK: Easy. TEL: 852787 (ansaphone 24 hrs.). SER: Valuations; restorations, framing. VAT: Stan/Spec.

Olive Branch Antiques
80 High St. (P. and S. Riley.) Resident. Est. 1977. Open every day 9.30—6. SIZE: Small. *STOCK: Furniture, to 1900, from £100; clocks, £90—£800; pottery, £5—£150.* LOC: Top end of High St. on A46. PARK: Easy and at rear. TEL: 853440. SER: Restorations (furniture). VAT: Stan/Spec.

Stratford Trevers ABA
The Long Room, 45 High St. Open 9—5.30, Sun. 2.15—5.30. *STOCK: Antiquarian books, maps and prints.* TEL: 853668. VAT: Stan.

BROBURY, Nr. Hay-on-Wye
Brobury House Gallery
(E. Okarma.) Resident. Est. 1972. Open 9—4.30, 9—4 in winter. *STOCK: Old prints, 17th—20th C; watercolours, 19th—20th C.* PARK: Easy. TEL: Moccas (09817) 229. SER: Restorations (framing). VAT: Spec.

BROMSGROVE (0527)
Strand Antiques
158 High St. (D.G. Croucher.) Est. 1977. Open 9—6. *STOCK: General antiques.* TEL: 72686.

BROMYARD (0885)
Lennox Antiques
3 Broad St. (W.A. and E.S. Jones.) Est. 1981. CL: Mon., Tues. and Wed. Open 10.30—5. SIZE: Small. *STOCK: Pottery and porcelain, 19th—20th C, £5—£25; glass, £1—£25; small furniture, £10—£200.* LOC: Town centre. PARK: Easy. TEL: 83432; home — Malvern (068 45) 5684. SER: Restorations (pottery, porcelain and cloisonné).

DROITWICH (0905)
Grant Fine Art
9A Victoria Sq. Est. 1976. Open by appointment only. SIZE: Small. *STOCK: Antiquarian books and golfiana, £5—£500.* TEL: 778155.

Droitwich continued

H. and B. Wolf Antiques Ltd.
128 Worcester Rd. (H.G. and B.J. Wolf.) Est. 1948. CL: Thurs. Open 9.30—5.30. SIZE: Medium. *STOCK: Porcelain, pottery, from 1750, £15—£750; glass from 1725; general antiques.* Not stocked: Coins, stamps, medals. LOC: A38. PARK: Easy. TEL: 772320; home — same. VAT: Stan/Spec.

EVESHAM (0386)
Acorn Antiques
17 Port St. (A. Beszant.) Est. 1972. CL: Wed. and Fri. Open 10—5. SIZE: Small. *STOCK: General antiques, Victoriana, pine, £5—£500; some oak, 18th C; small items.* PARK: 100yds. TEL: 49288.

Magpie Jewellers and Antiques
LAPADA
2 Port St. and 61 High St. (R.J. and E.R. Bunn.) Est. 1975. Open 9.30—5.30, Wed. 9.30—1. SIZE: Large. *STOCK: Silver, jewellery, furniture and general antiques.* TEL: 41631 any time.

FERNHILL HEATH, Nr. Worcester
Edgar Davis Antiques
The Old Bakery. (D. and A. Davis.) Est. 1960. CL: Thurs. Open 9—6, Sun. 10—4. SIZE: Medium. *STOCK: Furniture, 18th—20th C; pictures and clocks, 19th—20th C; all £50—£5,000; porcelain, gold and silver, 19th—20th C, £5—£2,000.* LOC: A38. PARK: Easy. TEL: Worcester (0905) 51787; home — same. SER: Valuations; restorations (furniture, pictures and clocks.) VAT: Stan.

GREAT MALVERN
Aladdin's Cave
83c Church St. (Mr. and Mrs. A. McConnell.) Est. 1984. Open 10—5. SIZE: Medium. *STOCK: Furniture, porcelain and general antiques, mainly pre-1900, £5—£1,500.* Not stocked: Militaria. LOC: Opposite priory church gate. PARK: Nearby. TEL: Malvern (068 45) 60905; home — Malvern (068 45) 61746. SER: Restorations (furniture, re-caning).

Joan Coates of Malvern
26 St. Ann's Rd. Resident. Est. 1969. Open Thurs. and Fri. 10—1 and 2.30—5.30, Sat. 10—1. SIZE: Small. *STOCK: Silver, £5—£250; small furniture, £20—£800; both 18th—20th C; small items.* LOC: From Worcester take A449, in town Foley Arms Hotel on left-hand side, take first right. PARK: Easy. TEL: Malvern (068 45) 5509. SER: Valuations.

Art nouveau slip-trailed tile. Possibly designed by Louis Solon and made by Minton. c.1890. 457mm x 305mm. From *A Collector's History of English Pottery* by Griselda Lewis, published by the **Antique Collectors' Club,** 1985.

Great Malvern continued

Great Malvern Antiques Arcade
6 Abbey Rd. (R.J. Rice and L. Sutton.) Est. 1966. Open 9.30−5.30, Sun. by appointment. *STOCK: Decorative antiques, unusual and non-traditional furniture and paintings, to £2,500.* LOC: 150yds. from Winter Gardens. PARK: Easy. TEL: Malvern (06845) 5490; home − same. FAIRS: Olympia, British International, Birmingham. VAT: Stan/Spec.

The Malvern Bookshop
7 Abbey Rd. (R.A.H. Lechmere.) Est. 1955. CL: Wed. p.m. Open 9.15−1 and 2.15−5.30. SIZE: Medium. *STOCK: Antiquarian and modern books; particularly books on antiques and collecting.* LOC: Next to Malvern G.P.O. PARK: Easy. TEL: Malvern (068 45) 5915; home − Colwall (0684) 40340. SER: Valuations; restorations (books); buys at auction.

Malvern Studios   LAPADA
56 Cowleigh Rd. (L.M. Hall.) Open 9.15−12.45 and 1.45−5.30. Sun. by appointment. *STOCK: Period furniture and general furnishings, Edwardian painted and inlaid furniture.* TEL: Malvern (068 45) 4913. SER: Restorations; woodcarving; polishing; interior design. VAT: Stan/Spec.

Miscellany Antiques
18 and 20 Cowleigh Rd. (R.S. and E.A. Hunaban.) Resident. Est. 1974. CL: Sat. and Wed. p.m. except by appointment. Open 9.30−1 and 2−5, trade any time. SIZE: Medium. *STOCK: Walnut, mahogany, 19th C, £50−£5,000; Victorian, Edwardian and some period furniture; porcelain, silver and plate, jewellery, shipping goods.* LOC: B4219 to Bromyard. PARK: Easy. TEL: Malvern (068 45) 66671. SER: Valuations. VAT: Stan.

Revivals
91/93 Cowleigh Rd. (C. and J. Roebuck.) Est. 1985. Open 10−1 and 2−5, Sun. p.m. and lunch hour by appointment. SIZE: Small. *STOCK: Small furniture, pine and hardwood, 19th C and Edwardian, £50−£500; china, glass, metalware, silver and plate, 19th−20th C, £5−£200.* LOC: Take Worcester road for ½ mile and follow directions for Bromyard for approx. ½ mile. PARK: Easy. TEL: Malvern (068 45) 4894; home − same.

T.J. Antiques
43 Worcester Rd. Est. 1974. CL: Wed. Open 9.30−5. SIZE: Large. *STOCK: Shipping goods, Doulton, art nouveau and general antiques, 18th−20th C, £1−£1,000.* PARK: Easy. TEL: Malvern. (068 45) 3092; home − same. SER: Valuations. VAT: Stan.

Great Malvern continued

Tinderbox
83a Church St. (H.S. Russell.) CL: Mon. and Wed. Open 10−5. *STOCK: General antiques including architectural items and costume.* TEL: Malvern (068 45) 64445.

Whitmore   *Postal Only*
Teynham Lodge, Chase Road, Upper Colwall. *STOCK: British and foreign coins, 1700−1950, £1−£500; trade tokens, 1650−1900, £1−£200; commemorative medallions, 1600−1950, £1−£100.* TEL: Colwall (0684) 40651.

Woodstock Interiors
Unicorn Yard, rear of 6/8 Belle Vue Terrace. (R.P.W. Somers.) Est. 1973. Open 9−5.30. SIZE: Large. *STOCK: Pine furniture, 18th−19th C, £25−£1,500.* PARK: Easy, own. TEL: Malvern (068 45) 60297. SER: Valuations; restorations; buys at auction. VAT: Stan/Spec.

Madley, Hereford HR2 9NA England.
Telephone: Golden Valley (0981) 250244 (3 lines)
Telephone and Cables: Antiques Hereford
Telex: 35619

Great Brampton House Antiques Ltd

We have one of the largest and finest stocks of period furniture in the country. Free delivery in our own vehicles to most parts of the United Kingdom. Goods packed and shipped to any part of the world.

We are 7 miles S.W. of Hereford, 15 miles from the M5/50 and 50 minutes

A large circular, Regency period, mahogany, dining table. Circa 1810.

HAY-ON-WYE
See Powys, Wales

HEREFORD   (0432)

Berrows House Antiques
Bath St. (S. Cousins.) Open daily. *STOCK: Pine, general antiques, shipping goods.* PARK: Easy. TEL: 268822.

I. and J.L. Brown Ltd.
58—59 Commercial Rd. Open 8—5.30 but appointment advisable. SIZE: Large. *STOCK: Matched sets of period country chairs, £100—£2,500; country and general furniture, including farmhouse tables, mahogany, decorative items and brass.* LOC: A465, 300 metres from railway station, 100 metres from city ring road. PARK: On premises. TEL: 58895; home — Carey (0432 70) 674. SER: Restorations; re-rushing chairs; container packing. VAT: Stan/Spec.

Hereford continued

Great Brampton House Antiques Ltd. LAPADA
Great Brampton House, Madley. (F.G. and P.B. Howell.) Est. 1969. Open 9—5 or by appointment. SIZE: Large. *STOCK: English and French furniture and fine art.* TEL: Golden Valley (0981) 250244 (3 lines). SER: Interior design.

Joynt Antiques
25 and 27 St. Owen St. (P.F. and B.F. Joynt.) Open 9.30—5.30. SIZE: Medium. *STOCK: Victorian and Edwardian furniture.* TEL: 56834.

Pierpoint Gallery
10 Church St. (A.G. and H.L. Beaver.) Est. 1969. CL: Thurs. Open 9.30—5.30. SIZE: Medium. *STOCK: Antiquarian books, maps, prints, 1550—1850, £5—£200.* Not stocked: Modern reprints and reproductions. LOC: Off Cathedral Precinct. PARK: Nearby. TEL: 267002. VAT: Stan.

G.E. Richards and Son Antiques LAPADA
57 Blueschool St. Est. 1969. Open 9—5. SIZE: Medium. *STOCK: General antiques, £2—£2,000.* LOC: On ring road by traffic signals. PARK: Opposite, but private loading bay at rear. TEL: 267840; home — 55278 and 268827. VAT: Stan/Spec.

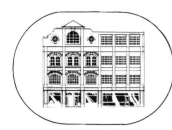

KEMERTON, Nr. Tewkesbury
Upper Court
(H.W. and D.M. Herford.) Resident. Est. 1963. Open by appointment only. SIZE: Medium. *STOCK: Unusual and decorative furniture, 18th—19th C, £500—£1,000; textiles including samplers, patchwork, linen, cashmere; small items, snuff boxes, scent bottles, silver frames, china (services) and toys.* LOC: Georgian manor house behind parish church. PARK: Easy. TEL: (038 689) 351; home — same. SER: Restorations (furniture and upholstery); buys at auction (as stock). FAIRS: Olympia. VAT: Stan/Spec.

KIDDERMINSTER   (0562)
B.B.M. Jewellery and Antiques
8 and 9 Lion St. (W.V. and A. Crook.) Est. 1977. CL: Tues. Open 10—5. SIZE: Medium. *STOCK: Jewellery, 19th C, £50—£3,000; coins, £5—£1,000; general antiques, £5—£500.* LOC: Adjacent Youth Centre, off ring road. PARK: Easy. TEL: 744118; home — Stourport (029 93) 3602. SER: Valuations; restorations (jewellery); buys at auction (jewellery and coins). VAT: Stan.

LEDBURY   (0531)
Holland Bros. Antiquarian Booksellers
Barn House, New St. Open by appointment. *STOCK: Books.* TEL: 2825.

Willow Antiques
Callow Hills Farm, Hereford Rd. (Mrs. H. Gardner.) Est. 1961. *STOCK: Period furniture, porcelain and paintings.* TEL: Trumpet (053 183) 558.

York House Antiques
155 The Homend. Open 9.30—5.30 or by appointment. *STOCK: General antiques, small collectables and jewellery.* LOC: Outskirts of town on Hereford Rd. PARK: Opposite. TEL: 4687.

LEOMINSTER   (0568)
Barometer Shop
25 Broad St. (R. Cookson). Est. 1965. Open 9—5.30, Sun. by appointment. *STOCK: Barometers, clocks, watches, scientific instruments.* LOC: Corner of A49 and Broad St. PARK: At rear. TEL: 3652. SER: Restorations.

J.A. Bishop
Shaftesbury House, Broad St. Est. 1950. *STOCK: General antique furniture.* TEL: 2050. VAT: Stan/Spec.

Leominster continued

Boyne House Antiques
Inc. Lion Antiques, 15 Broad St. (M. Sachser.) Est. 1965. Open daily, Sun. by appointment. SIZE: Large. *STOCK: Furniture, 18th—19th C; stripped pine, architectural items.* TEL: 3361/ 3725. SER: Restorations (furniture and upholstery); dressers and fire surrounds made from old timber; stripping; polishing; buys at auction.

Coltsfoot Gallery
(E. Collins.) Est. 1971. SIZE: Medium. *STOCK: Sporting and wildlife prints, from 1750, £10—£800; watercolours — landscapes, sporting and wildlife subjects, from 1850, £100—£2,000.* PARK: Easy. TEL: Steens Bridge (056 882) 277; home — same. SER: Restorations (prints and watercolours).

Geoffrey Crofts Ltd.
29—31 South St. Est. 1973. Open 9—5.30, Sat. 10—4. SIZE: Medium. *STOCK: Country furniture, 18th—19th C, £100—£3,000; mahogany, Georgian and Victorian, £100—£2,000; decorative items, porcelain and pottery, £5—£500.* LOC: A49, 500yds. from town centre. PARK: Easy. TEL: 611580; home — 5706. SER: Valuations; restorations; buys at auction. VAT: Stan/Spec.

P. and S.N. Eddy
22 Etnam St. Resident. Est. 1951. CL: Sun. except by appointment. Open 9—6. SIZE: Small. *STOCK: General antiques, including oak and mahogany furniture, saltglaze stoneware and blue and white pottery, 18th and 19th C; early metalware, treen and bygones. Not stocked: Arms, armour, coins, medals, jewellery.* LOC: A44. PARK: Easy. TEL: 2813; home — same.

Hubbard Antiques   LAPADA
The Golden Lion, Bridge St. (D. and T. Saunders.) Resident. Open 9—6, otherwise ring door bell. *STOCK: 16th—18th C oak furniture; early metalware, period walnut, country furniture and treen.* LOC: North side of town, junction of A49 and B4361. PARK: Own. TEL: 4362.

Just-a-Living
5 Bridge St. (M. Chappelow, O. James and M. Phillipson.) Est. 1972. Open 10—5, Sat. and Sun. by appointment. SIZE: Medium. *STOCK: Country furniture, 17th to early 19th C, £5—£500; treen, early oak, Staffordshire figures, unstripped pine.* LOC: Edge of town on right-hand side from Ludlow. PARK: Easy. TEL: 611514, Eardisley (054 46) 654 or Kingsland (056 881) 556. VAT: Stan/Spec.

Hubbard Antiques

of

LEOMINSTER

The Golden Lion, Bridge Street, Leominster
on the A49   Tel. 0568 4362

Specialists in:

17th & 18th Century Oak Country Furniture
(comb back chairs always in stock)
Early Metalware:- interesting stock of 19th century
copperware. Carvings and rare treen.

OPEN MONDAY — SATURDAY 9.00—6.00
No half-day or lunchtime closing
RESIDENT — so also available at other times

Private car park for 20 cars or large loading vehicles

Leominster continued

La Barre Ltd.
The Place, 116 South St. (P. La Barre.) Est. 1964. Open 8.30—6, Sat. 10—4, other times by appointment. SIZE: Large. *STOCK: Pine, mahogany, oak furniture, 17th—19th C, £30—£5,000; objects.* Not stocked: Silver, 20th C shipping items. LOC: On main A49, town centre ½ mile. PARK: Easy. TEL: 4315; home — 2434. VAT: Stan/Spec.

Leominster Antiques
87 Etnam St. (J. Hall.) Resident. Open 9—7, Sun. by appointment. SIZE: Large. *STOCK: Country bygones, textiles, decorative items and 19th C furniture.* LOC: A44 Worcester Rd. PARK: Easy. TEL: 3217. VAT: Stan/Spec.

Leominster Antiques Market
14 Broad St. Est. 1973. CL: Sat. Open 10—5. Three floors of showrooms displaying a wide range of general antiques supplied by 12 dealers. TEL: 2189. SER: Restorations (furniture). Below are listed some of the dealers:—
> J.H. Bayliss
> R. Bradshaw
> Mrs. Cox
> Croft Antiques (J.W. Noble)
> **Eardisley Antiques**
> *Royal Doulton, Victorian coloured glass, £10—£100; ceramics, small furniture, 18th—19th C.* TEL: Eardisley (054 46) 310.
> Mr. Bryan Edge (Furniture restorer)
> Hilbery House (Mr. Maund.) *Jewellery.*
> L. Leighton
> S. Walter
> Jeff. Wilson

Michael Stewart Antiques
Lion Yard, 15 Broad St. Est. 1972. Open daily, Sun. by appointment. *STOCK: Period and Victorian pine for export, country furniture some oak and mahogany.* TEL: 4946; evenings — 5484.

Waterway Galleries
25 Broad St. (D. Roberts Antiques.) Est. 1980. Open 9—5.30, Sun. by appointment. *STOCK: Early oak, mahogany, longcase clocks, country furniture, small items, pine, some shipping goods.* LOC: Corner of A49 and Broad St. PARK: At rear. TEL: 2988. SER: Valuations. VAT: Stan/Spec.

LYONSHALL, Nr. Kington (054 48)
Border Bygones
'The Valletts', Forge Crossing. (P.G. Sheppard and M.G. Edwards.) Est. 1983. Open by appointment only. SIZE: Medium and workshop. *STOCK: Collectable items, £5—£1,000; paper items, £5—£500; both 17th—20th C; small items, clocks, pictures, 18th—19th C, £5—£1,000; cigarette and post cards.* LOC: Details given upon appointment. PARK: Easy. TEL: 470; home — same. SER: Valuations; restorations (paintings, prints, clocks); buys at auction.

MALVERN, see GREAT MALVERN

MALVERN LINK
Kimber and Son
6 Lower Howsell Rd. Est. 1956. CL: Sat. and Sun. except by appointment. *STOCK: Furniture, 18th—19th C; general antiques, furnishing items. Warehouse for trade.* TEL: Malvern (06845) 4339; home — 2000. VAT: Stan/Spec.

MATHON, Nr. Malvern
Mathon Gallery
Mathon Court. (Phipps and Co. Ltd.) Est. 1980. Open 9.30—12.30 or by appointment including Sun. SIZE: Medium. *STOCK: British oils, watercolours and sculpture, 19th—20th C, £100—£15,000.* LOC: Approx. 1 mile west of Malvern, off B4232. TEL: Malvern (06845) 5606 and (01) 352 5381. SER: Valuations; buys at auction (British paintings and sculpture). VAT: Spec.

OMBERSLEY, Nr. Droitwich
Stables Antiques
Coach Yard, Crown and Sandys Hotel. (B. and A. Pearce.) Est. 1974. CL: Mon. Open 10—5, any time by appointment. SIZE: Medium. *STOCK: Furniture, 17th—19th C, £100—£7,000; china and pottery, 18th—19th C, £10—£1,000; bygones and early metalwares.* Not stocked: Bric-a-brac. LOC: 6 miles north of Worcester on A449. PARK: Easy. TEL: Worcester (0905) 620353. SER: Valuations; restorations (china, paintings); buys at auction. VAT: Stan/Spec.

The Thatched Barn Antiques
Hawford. (Mr. and Mrs. W. Tremellen.) Open by appointment. *STOCK: Mahogany, oak and rosewood furniture, interesting small items.* TEL: Worcester (0905) 620271.

PERSHORE   (0386)
Carleton House Antiques
20 Bridge St. (V. Wood.) CL: Thurs. Open 10—5. PARK: Easy. TEL: 554235.

LA BARRE LTD.

The Place One One Six SOUTH STREET **Leominster**
Herefordshire

Tel: Leominster (0568) 4315

ANTIQUE FURNITURE 1600 – 1840
VICTORIAN, EDWARDIAN AND COUNTRY FURNITURE
PINE
DECORATIVE ARTICLES

A selection from our 25,000 square feet of stock
Opening hours: Monday — Friday 8.30—6.00pm
Saturdays 10.00am — 4.00pm
Other times by appointment (0568) 4315

Pershore continued

Hansen Chard Antiques
126 High St. (P.W. Ridler.) Est. 1983. CL: Mon. Open 10—5, Thurs. 10—1, but appointment advisable. SIZE: Small. *STOCK: Clocks, pre-1940; longcase clocks, pre-1850, £10—£1,000.* LOC: On A44. PARK: Easy. TEL: 553423; home — same. SER: Restorations (clocks); buys at auction (clocks).

Penoyre Antiques
9 and 11 Bridge St. Est. 1969. CL: Thurs. Open 9.30—1 and 2—5.30 or by appointment. SIZE: Medium. *STOCK: 18th—19th C mirrors and mahogany furniture especially dining; Oriental porcelain, hardwood furniture, chandeliers, glass, Sheffield plate, pictures, prints; £15—£15,000.* PARK: Easy (in main square). TEL: 553522. VAT: Spec.

Perrott House Antiques
17 Bridge St. (M.K. and J.S. Ellingworth.) Est. 1980. Open Wed. and Fri. 9—1 and 2—5; Sat. 10—1 and 2—5.30 and by appointment. *STOCK: Furniture, 17th—18th C; silver, porcelain, clocks, books, general antiques.* TEL: 552801. SER: Buys at auction. VAT: Stan/Spec.

Pershore continued

S.W. Antiques
Newlands. (R.J. Whiteside.) Est. 1978. Open 9.30—5.15, Sat. 9—5. SIZE: Large. *STOCK: Pine, 19th C, £50—£750; general furniture, £25—£500; metalware, £5—£150; both 1800—1930; some shipping goods.* Not stocked: Coins, stamps, postcards and fine china. LOC: Off Broad St. PARK: Own. TEL: 555580. SER: Valuations; buys at auction. VAT: Stan/Spec.

Times Past
84 High St. (J. Pollitt.) Est. 1977. CL: Thurs. Open 10—1 and 2—5 and by appointment. SIZE: Small. *STOCK: Blue and white transferware pottery, pre-1830; needlework tools and accessories; glass, treen, small silver, jewellery and collectors' items, 1680—1930.* LOC: A44, opposite Pershore Garage. PARK: Easy, 100yds. TEL: 554258; home — same. SER: Valuations. VAT: Stan/Spec.

POWICK, Nr. Worcester

The Barn Gallery

Sandpits Farm, Colletts Green Rd. (M.D. Ham.) Est. 1977. Open Thurs. or by appointment. SIZE: Medium. *STOCK: Paintings and watercolours, 1830—1930, £100—£10,000.* LOC: ¼ mile north of A449. PARK: Easy. TEL: Worcester (0905) 830029; home — same. SER: Valuations; restorations (paintings and watercolours); framing; buys at auction (paintings and watercolours). VAT: Spec.

REDDITCH   (0527)

Alan Morris

503 Evesham Rd., Crabbs Cross. Est. 1968. Open 10—6. SIZE: Large. *STOCK: Oil lamps and parts, bric-a-brac, £1—£100; small furniture.* PARK: Easy. TEL: 45084. VAT: Stan.

ROSS-ON-WYE   (0989)

Baileys Architectural Antiques

The Engine Shed, Ashburton Industrial Estate. (M. and S. Bailey.) Est. 1978. Open 9.30—5. SIZE: Large. *STOCK: Architectural antiques including stained glass, fireplaces, bathroom fittings, garden furniture, cast and timber balustrades, 18th—20th C, £10—£1,000.* LOC: A40, follow signs to Gloucester. TEL: 63015.

Fritz Fryer Antique Lighting

1st Floor, 27 Gloucester Rd. (F. Fryer and J. Graham.) Est. 1981. CL: Wed. and Sun. except by appointment. Open 10—5.30. *STOCK: Decorative lighting, original shades, glass chandeliers, Georgian to art deco, £25—£3,000.* LOC: Last shop on right off main Gloucester road. PARK: Easy. TEL: 64738; home — Llangarron (098 984) 512. SER: Valuations; restorations; buys at auction (luminaires). FAIRS: Olympia.

Robin Lloyd Antiques

23/24 Brookend St. Est. 1970. Open 10—5.30 or any time by appointment. SIZE: Large. *STOCK: Oak and country furniture, candlesticks, brass, iron, copper, blue and white, clocks, sporting relics and unusual items.* LOC: 100yds. downhill from Market Hall. PARK: Opposite. TEL: 62123. SER: Copies made in 18th C oak. VAT: Stan/Spec.

Old Pine Shop

Gloucester Rd. (B. Miller.) Est. 1976. Open 10—5.30 or by appointment. SIZE: Large. *STOCK: Pine furniture, especially dressers, chests, settles, coffers, corner cupboards, linen presses, side tables, 1830—1930.* LOC: Last shop on main Gloucester road. PARK: Easy and Cantilupe Rd. TEL: 64738; home — (0594) 543349. SER: Restorations (pine stripping).

Ross-on-Wye continued

Serendipity

Old Railway Inn, Brookend. (R. Brookes.) Est. 1969. Open 9.30—5.30 or by appointment. SIZE: Large. *STOCK: General antiques, 17th—19th C.* LOC: From M50 first left into town, shop on right at bottom of hill. TEL: 63836; home — (053 184) 245. SER: Restorations (furniture); buys at auction. FAIRS: Kensington, Harrogate, British International, Birmingham, Olympia. VAT: Stan/Spec.

Trecilla Antiques

36 and 36A High St. (Lt. Col. and Mrs. I.G. Mathews.) Est. 1969. CL: Wed. p.m. and Sun. except by appointment. Open approximately 9—5.30. SIZE: Large. *STOCK: Furniture, longcase clocks, all periods; arms and armour, £50—£5,000; silver, china, glass, metalware, £10—£1,000; prints, maps, militaria and bygones, £1—£300.* LOC: A40. PARK: Private. TEL: 63010; home — (0981) 540274. SER: Valuations; restorations; buys at auction. VAT: Stan/Spec.

STOURPORT
(4 and 5 fig. no.) (029 93)
(6 fig. no.) (0299)

Antiques and Furnishings

102 Minster Rd. (R. Matthews.) Open 9—6. *STOCK: General antiques.* TEL: 77339.

A model of a recumbent ram. From a "Preview of Sale of Lowestoft Porcelain", **Antique Collecting**, February 1986.

UPTON-UPON-SEVERN (068 46)

The Highway Gallery
40 Old St. (J. Daniell.) Est. 1969. CL: Thurs. and Mon. Open 10.30—5, but appointment advisable. SIZE: Small. *STOCK: Oils, watercolours, 19th—20th C, £15—£2,000.* Not stocked: Prints. LOC: 100yds. from crossroads towards Malvern. PARK: Easy. TEL: 2645; home — 2909. SER: Valuations; restorations (reline and clean); buys at auction (pictures). VAT: Spec.

WINFORTON, Nr. Hereford

Gerald and Vera Taylor
Winforton Court. Est. 1965. Open by appointment. SIZE: Medium. *STOCK: Longcase clocks, 18th—early 19th C, furniture, pre-1880.* LOC: Between Hereford and Brecon on A438. PARK: Easy. TEL: Eardisley (054 46) 226. SER: Valuations; buys at auction. VAT: Stan/Spec.

WORCESTER (0905)

Alma Street Warehouse
Alma St. (J. and D. Venn). CL: Mon. and Thurs. Open 9.30—1 and 2—4.30. *STOCK: General antiques.* LOC: Off Droitwich Rd. PARK: Easy. TEL: 27493.

Andrew Boyle (Booksellers) Ltd.
21 Friar St. Est. 1928. Appointment advisable. *STOCK: Antiquarian and secondhand books.* TEL: 611700. SER: Buys at auction.

Worcester continued

Bygones by the Cathedral
LAPADA
Deansway. (G. Bullock.) FGA. Est. 1946. Open 9.30—1 and 2—5.30. *STOCK: Furniture, 17th—19th C; silver, Sheffield plate, jewellery, paintings, glass, English and Continental pottery and porcelain, especially Royal Worcester.* LOC: Adjacent main entrance to Cathedral. TEL: 25388.

Bygones (Worcester)
LAPADA
55 Sidbury. (G.D. Bullock.) FGA. Est. 1946. Open 9.30—1 and 2—5.30. *STOCK: Furniture, 17th—19th C; silver, Sheffield plate, jewellery, paintings, glass, English and Continental porcelain; pottery, especially Royal Worcester.* LOC: Opposite the public car park in Sidbury and adjacent to the City Walls road junction. TEL: 23132. VAT: Stan/Spec.

Cottage Antiques
15 New St. (S.M. Wall.) CL: Thurs. Open 9.30—5.30. *STOCK: Arms, militaria; country furniture, early lighting; decorative items.* TEL: 24574.

Friars Gate Antiques
19 Friar St. (S.M. Cronin.) Open 10.30—6. *STOCK: Watercolours and oils, Victoriana, collectors' items.* TEL: 24192.

A rare tray, perhaps a spoon tray, from a tea service. Other rare square trays of this type have a more scalloped edge. 4½ins. square. c.1765-8. From *Lowestoft Porcelains* by Geoffrey A. Godden, published by the **Antique Collectors' Club**, 1985.

Worcester continued

Jean Hodge   LAPADA
Peachley Manor, Hallow Lane, Lower Broadheath. Resident. Est. 1969. Open daily including Sunday. SIZE: Medium. *STOCK: Furniture, 18th—19th C; general antiques.* LOC: Off B4204 3 miles N.W. Worcester. PARK: Easy. TEL: 640255.

Sarah Hodge
Peachley Manor, Hallow Lane, Lower Broadheath. Resident. Est. 1985. Open daily including Sun. SIZE: Medium. *STOCK: General antiques, country bygones.* LOC: Off B4204, 3 miles N.W. Worcester. PARK: Easy. TEL: 640255.

Janus Books and Antiques
44 and 47 New St. (R.T. Slim.) Est. 1978. CL: Thurs. p.m. Open 10—4. SIZE: Medium. *STOCK: Antiquarian and secondhand books, ephemera and postcards; small furniture, 19th to early 20th C, £5—£100; linen, to 1930s, £2—£50; curios and unusual collectable items.* LOC: From car park, over footbridge spanning City Wall Road, shops opposite. PARK: Limited and nearby. TEL: 611537; home — 620697 (24 hours). SER: Valuations. FAIRS: Waverley (organiser).

M. Lees and Sons   LAPADA
Tower House, Severn St. Resident. Est. 1955. CL: Thurs. Open 9.15—5.15, Sat. by appointment. SIZE: Large. *STOCK: Furniture, 1780—1880; porcelain 1750—1920.* LOC: At southern end of Worcester Cathedral adjacent to Edgar Tower; near Royal Worcester Porcelain Museum and factory. PARK: Easy. TEL: 26620; home — 427142. VAT: Stan/Spec.

Keith Robinson Antiques
49 Upper Tything. (K.B. Robinson.) Est. 1973. Open 9—5.30, Sun. by appointment. SIZE: Large. *STOCK: Furniture, 17th C to 1930, £10—£5,000.* LOC: A38. PARK: Easy. TEL: 25357; home — Birtsmorton (068 481) 599. SER: Valuations; restorations; buys at auction (furniture and accessories). VAT: Stan/Spec.

T. and D. Taplin
3 Angel Mall. Est. 1970. CL: Mon. Open 10—5. SIZE: Medium. *STOCK: Furniture, £75—£2,000; dolls, 1800—1910; Georgian, Victorian and Edwardian jewellery, samplers and lace, silver, glass, brass and copper, watercolours, porcelain.* LOC: Angel Place, off Foregate St., near multi-storey car park. TEL: 29014. SER: Restorations (dolls and furniture).

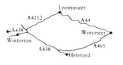
Worcester continued

Tolley's Galleries
26 College St. (T.M. Tolley.) *STOCK: Oriental and general antiques, Eastern bronzes, Oriental rugs, 17th—19th C.* PARK: Easy. TEL: 26632. VAT: Stan.

W.H.E.A.P. Antiques
54 St. Johns. (P. Hooper.) Open 9—6 or by appointment. *STOCK: General antiques and shipping goods.* TEL: 427796. SER: Restorations; waxing and polishing.

YAZOR

M. and J. Russell   *Mainly Trade*
The Old Vicarage. Est. 1969. CL: Tues. and Thurs. *STOCK: Old English furniture, especially oak and country pieces.* LOC: 7 miles west of Hereford on A480. TEL: Bridge Sollars (098 122) 674.

Please note this is only a rough map designed to show dealers the number of shops in the various towns, and is not necessarily totally accurate.

○ 1—2 Key to
⊖ 3—5 number of
◒ 6—12 shops in
● 13+ this area.

ALDBURY, Nr. Tring

Micawber Antiques
14 Trooper Rd. Est. 1973. Open 10—5. SIZE: Medium. *STOCK: Pine, collectors' items, general antiques.* PARK: Easy. TEL: Aldbury Common (044 285) 251. SER: Valuations; pine stripping; clock repairs.

BALDOCK (0462)
The Attic
20 Whitehorse St. (P. Sheppard.) Est. 1977. CL: Mon. and Thurs. SIZE: Small. *STOCK: Small furniture, china, brass and copper, dolls and teddy bears, £5—£100.* LOC: 3 minutes from A1(M). PARK: Easy. TEL: 893880.

Baldock continued

Anthony Butt Antiques
7/9 Church St. Resident. Est. 1950. Usually open. *STOCK: English furniture, 17th—19th C, £100—£2,000; works of art and objects of interest.* Not stocked: Bric-a-brac, shipping goods. PARK: Easy. TEL: 895272. SER: Valuations. VAT: Spec.

Ford Antiques
52 High St. (K.C. and Mrs. Ives.) Est. 1972. CL: Thurs. Open 10—1 and 2—5.30. SIZE: Large. *STOCK: Furniture, 18th—19th C, £20—£1,100; mercurial stick and wheel barometers, £75—£600; clocks, silver, collectors' items, £5—£400.* PARK: Easy. TEL: 893197. SER: Restorations (mercurial barometers). VAT: Stan/Spec.

Mark Shanks

350 High Street · Berkhamsted

Hertfordshire HP4 1HT

Berkhamsted (04427) 4790

〰️

A large selection of Fine Furniture,
Barometers and Works of Art

Baldock continued

Ralph and Bruce Moss   LAPADA
26 Whitehorse St. (R.A. and B.A. Moss.) Est. 1973. Open 9—6. SIZE: Large. *STOCK: Furniture, £50—£5,000; general antiques, £5—£5,000.* LOC: A505, in town centre. PARK: Own. TEL: 892751. VAT: Stan/Spec.

Arthur Porter
31 Whitehorse St. (A.G.R. Porter.) Est. 1969. Open 9—6. SIZE: Large. *STOCK: Pine furniture, 18th—20th C; English, Continental and decorative items.* LOC: Main street. PARK: Easy. TEL: 895351. SER: Valuations: restorations; stripping. VAT: Stan/Spec.

BARNET
See Greater London

BERKHAMSTED
       (4 and 5 fig. no.) (044 27)
       (6 fig. no.) (0442)

Michael Armson (Antiques) Ltd.
Antiques Warehouse, Shootersway. Open Tues., Thurs. and Sat. mornings or by appointment. SIZE: Large. *STOCK: Furniture, 17th—19th C.* TEL: 2241; home — (0296) 61141.

Berkhamsted continued

J. and J. Hutton
123 High St. Est. 1955. CL: Wed. Open 9—5 Oct.—Dec., otherwise strictly by appointment only. SIZE: Small. *STOCK: English table glass, 18th—19th C.* TEL: 5979 or 5576; home — same. VAT: Stan.

Park Street Antiques   BADA
350 High St. (M. Shanks.) Est. 1960. Open 9.30—5.30. SIZE: Large. *STOCK: Furniture, £100—£30,000; barometers, £100—£10,000; both 17th—19th C; works of art, sculpture, £30—£3,000; longcase clocks, rugs and carpets.* **Not stocked: Silver, jewellery, coins.** LOC: A41. PARK: At west end of town. TEL: 4790; home — Cholesbury (024 029) 255. VAT: Stan/Spec.

BISHOP'S STORTFORD   (0279)

The Windhill Antiquary
4 High St. (F.W. and G.R. Crozier.) Est. 1951. CL: Wed. p.m. Open 10—1 and 2—4. SIZE: Medium. *STOCK: English furniture, 18th C; carved and gilded wall mirrors, 17th—19th C.* Not stocked: Shipping goods. LOC: Next to George Hotel. PARK: Up hill — first right. TEL: 51587; home — Ware (0920) 821316. VAT: Stan/Spec.

BUSHEY, Nr. Watford

Circa Antiques
43 High St., Bushey Village. (K. Wildman.) Est. 1978. Open 9.30—5.30 or by appointment. SIZE: Medium. STOCK: General antiques, furniture, porcelain, silver and clocks. TEL: (01) 950 9233.

Country Life Antiques
33a High St. (P. Myers.) Est. 1981. CL: Wed. p.m. Open 9.30—5. SIZE: Large. STOCK Victorian stripped pine, £25—£500; general antiques, china and smalls. PARK: Easy. TEL: (01) 950 8575. VAT: Stan.

Julian Thwaites and Co.
33 Chalk Hill, Oxhey. Est. 1971. Open 9—5, Sat. 9.30—12.30. STOCK: Stringed instruments, from violins to double basses. TEL: Watford (0923) 32412. SER: Restorations.

Yesterdays Antiques   Trade Only
13 Sparrows Herne. (M. Isenberg.) Est. 1973. Open Mon., Thurs. and Sat. 9.15—2.30. STOCK: Furniture, 17th—20th C; interesting smalls. TEL: (01) 950 7600.

CODICOTE, Nr. Hitchin

Wheldon and Wesley Ltd.
Lytton Lodge. Mail order business only. Est. 1921. Open by appointment only. STOCK: Antiquarian books on Natural History. TEL: Stevenage (0438) 820370. SER: Buys at auction.

HARPENDEN
(4 and 5 fig. no.) (058 27) (6 fig. no.) (0582)

Hammersley Galleries   Mainly Trade
12 Roundwood Lane. (S.V. Hammersley.) Est. 1910. Open by appointment. SIZE: Large. STOCK: Paintings, 18th—19th C, £300—£1,500. PARK: Own. TEL: 4053. VAT: Spec.

IS YOUR ENTRY CORRECT?
If there is even the slightest inaccuracy in your entry, *please* let us know before 1st January 1987.
GUIDE TO THE
ANTIQUE SHOPS OF BRITAIN
5 Church Street, Woodbridge, Suffolk.

HATFIELD   (070 72)

The Antiques Book Centre
93 Bradmore Green, Brookmans Park. (J.S. and S.D. Smith.) Est. 1973. CL: Mon. and Wed. Open 10—3.30; Sat. 9.30—12.30. SIZE: Large. STOCK: Reference books on antiques, art, collecting and the antique trade, general antiquarian and secondhand books. LOC: 100yds. from Brookmans Park Railway Station. PARK: Easy. TEL: Potters Bar (0707) 44426. SER: Catalogue sent on request, finder. VAT: Stan.

HEMEL HEMPSTEAD   (0442)

Abbey Antiques and Arts LAPADA
97 High St. (L., E. and S. Eames.) Est. 1962. CL: Wed. p.m. Open 9.30—5.30. SIZE: Medium. STOCK: Silver, plate, jewellery, £5—£2,000; early English watercolours, £100—£5,000; furniture, 17th—19th C. Not stocked: Porcelain. LOC: From London on M1 through main shopping centre to old town. PARK: Easy. TEL: 64667; home — 45078. SER: Valuations; restorations (as stock); buys at auction. VAT: Stan/Spec.

Antique and Collectors Market
Market Pl. (Antique Forum (Birmingham) Ltd.) Open Wed. 9—2. There are 100 dealers at this market selling a wide range of general antiques. TEL: (01) 624 3214.

Antiques
15a High St. (Mrs. R. Dolton.) Est. 1970. CL: Tues. and Wed. Open 10—5. SIZE: Small. STOCK: Victorian and Edwardian jewellery; sets of dining chairs, £180—£350; dining tables, £70—£250; chests of drawers, chairs, £70. PARK: Road parallel with High St. TEL: 64329. VAT: Stan/Spec.

Cherry Antiques
101—103 High St. (A. and R.S. Cullen, J. and M. Payne.) CL: Wed. p.m. Open 9.30—4.30. SIZE: Medium. STOCK: Victorian, Edwardian and some period furniture, general antiques, collectors' and decorative items, bric-a-brac, needlework tools, dolls, linens, some silver, plate, jewellery. PARK: Easy. TEL: 64358. VAT: Stan/Spec.

Georgina Antiques
100 High St. (M.A. Nathan and Mrs. V. Barnes.) Est. 1951. CL: Wed. Open 10—5.45. SIZE: Small. STOCK: Oriental antiquities, £5—£4,000; general antiques and bygones. LOC: From London on A41. Turn off Two Waters up through shopping centre to Old Town. PARK: Easy. TEL: 56957. SER: Valuations.

Hemel Hempstead continued

Linaire Antiques
136 Piccotts End. (P. Lindley.) Est. 1967. CL: Wed. Open 10−5. SIZE: Small. *STOCK: Small furniture, jewellery and collectors' items, bric- a-brac.* TEL: 56729. VAT: Spec.

HERTFORD   (0992)
Beckwith and Son
St. Nicholas Hall, St. Andrew St. (A.K. Loveday, FSVA, G.C.M. Gray, N.P.J. Bunce and P. Chappell.) Est. 1904. Open 9−1 and 2−5.30. SIZE: Large. *STOCK: General antiques, furniture, silver, pottery, porcelain, prints, weapons, clocks, watches, glass.* Not stocked: Fabrics. LOC: A602/B158. PARK: Adjacent. SER: Valuations; restorations (fine porcelain, furniture, upholstery, silver). TEL: 52079. VAT: Stan/Spec.

Georgian House Antiques
42 St. Andrew St. (G.H. Defty.) Est. 1970. CL: Thurs. p.m. Open 9−1 and 2−5.30, Sat. 9−6. SIZE: Medium. *STOCK: General antiques, 18th C, Victorian, Edwardian, Regency, £25−£200.* LOC: Between Hertford North and East stations. PARK: Easy. TEL: 53508; home − 53250.

E. and R. Horton
13 Castle St. Est. 1972. Open 9−5. *STOCK: Clocks, weapons, furniture, general antiques.* TEL: 57546. VAT: Stan.

Hertford continued

Neale Antiques
21 and 21a Old Cross. (A.J. and S.C. Neale.) NAG. Est. 1956. CL: Thurs. Open 9.30−1 and 2−5.30. SIZE: Medium. *STOCK: Furniture, mostly George III to late Victorian, £20−£750; silver, 1750−1900, £10−£300; music boxes, cylinder and disc, 1850−1910, £100−£600.* LOC: From London take A10 and A602 and keep on relief road. Turn right at sign for Wadesmill and Bengeo. PARK: Nearby. TEL: 51347; home − 52519. SER: Valuations; restorations (silver, clocks, watches, furniture, upholstery, music boxes). VAT: Stan.

L. Partridge Antiques
25 St. Andrew St. (P.M. and P.A. Hodgkinson.) Est. 1934. CL: Thurs. and Wed. a.m. Open 10−1 and 2−6. SIZE: Large. *STOCK: Oil paintings, prints, furnishings, silver, jewellery.* PARK: Easy. TEL: 54385; home − Albury (027 974) 257. SER: Valuations; restorations (oil paintings, prints, silver, jewellery); upholstery; buys at auction.

Michael Rochford
8 St. Andrew St. Open 10−6. *STOCK: Trade goods including general antiques, furniture, longcase clocks.* TEL: 51291.

A teabowl and saucer from *Lowestoft Porcelains* by Geoffrey A. Godden, published by the **Antique Collectors' Club,** 1985.

Hertford continued

Romic
4 Evron Place. (R.H. and R.J. Dobbs.) Est. 1982. CL: Thurs. except by appointment. Open 9.30−2 and 2.30−5.30, Sat. 10−2 and 2.30−5.30. SIZE: Medium. *STOCK: Stripped pine, country furniture, 1780−1880.* Not stocked: Bric-a-brac. LOC: Pedestrian way just off Market Place and Maidenhead St. PARK: Market Place or multi-storey. TEL: 552880; home − Welwyn Garden (0707) 335267. VAT: Stan/Spec.

Something Old
1/3 Old Cross. CL: Mon. and Thurs. Open 10−5.30. *STOCK: General antiques.* TEL: 551530.

Village Green Antiques
21 and 23 St. Andrew St. and 6 and 8 Old Cross. (N. and P. Petre.) Est. 1970. CL: Thurs. p.m. Open 10−5.30. SIZE: Large. *STOCK: Furniture, £50−£10,000; porcelain, metalware, works of art, decorative items.* LOC: 200yds. from A414. PARK: At rear. TEL: 57698; home − 56994. VAT: Stan/Spec.

HITCHIN (0462)

Abacus
7 Sun St. CL: Wed. p.m. Open 9−1 and 2.30−5. SIZE: Large. *STOCK: Furniture, Jacobean−Edwardian, £10−£2,000; silver, Georgian onwards, £1−£500; china, barometers, clocks.* Not stocked: Weapons. LOC: From town centre, through Market Place. Sun. St. on left. PARK: 100yds. TEL: 34774. VAT: Stan/Spec.

Acorn Antiques
1 West Alley. (I. Fuke.) Est. 1972. Open Tues. and Sat. 10−4. *STOCK: Pine, general antiques and collectors' items.* LOC: Opposite West Alley antique market, and adjacent Arcade car park. TEL: Royston (0763) 61630.

The Aspidistra
29 Sun St. (M. Plant.) Est. 1971. CL: Wed. Open 9.30−5.30. *STOCK: Victoriana, pine, jewellery, furniture, bric-a-brac.* TEL: 53817. VAT: Stan.

Bexfield Antiques
13 and 14 Sun St. (A.B. Bexfield.) Est. 1962. CL: Wed. Open 9−5.30. *STOCK: Jewellery, silver, porcelain, furniture.* PARK: Nearby. TEL:32641.

Courtyard Antiques
Rear of 23 Bancroft. (Mrs. J.M. Savitsky.) Est. 1965. Open Tues., Thurs. and Sat. 10−5. *STOCK: Furniture, glass, porcelain, silver and plate, brass and copper, jewellery and collectors' items.* LOC: Town centre. PARK: Easy. TEL: Welwyn Garden (0707) 326757.

Hitchin continued

Michael Gander
10 Bridge St. Est. 1973. Open 9−6. *STOCK: Period furniture, metalware.* TEL: 32678.

Hitchin Antiques Gallery
37 Bridge St. (R.J. Perry.) SIZE: Large. CL: Sun. except by appointment. Open 10−5.30. There are 15 dealers at this centre selling *a wide range of general antiques including furniture, watercolours, jewellery, Victorian chimney pots and garden items, to £5,000.* PARK: Nearby. TEL: 34525; home − (0582) 25546. SER: Valuations; restorations (furniture, re-upholstery, clocks and glass). FAIRS: Luton.

Eric T. Moore
24 Bridge St. Open 9.30−1 and 2.15−5.30, Wed. 9−12.30, Sat. all day. *STOCK: Antiquarian books, maps and prints.* TEL: 50497. SER: Picture framing, mount cutting.

R.J. Perry Antiques LAPADA
38 Bridge St. Open 10−5.30. SIZE: 3 floors. *STOCK: Metalware, interior decorators' pieces, small furniture, general antiques.* TEL. 34525. SER: Valuations; restorations (furniture, upholstery, metalware).

Phillips of Hitchin BADA
(Antiques) Ltd.
The Manor House. (M. and J. Phillips.) Est. 1884. Open 9−1 and 2−5.30. SIZE: Large. *STOCK: Furniture, walnut, oak and mahogany, 17th to early 19th C, £500−£20,000.* LOC: In Bancroft, main street of Hitchin. PARK: Easy. TEL: 32067. SER: Books on collecting. FAIRS: Specialist antique exhibitions at the Manor House. VAT: Spec.

Roslyn House Galleries Ltd.
LAPADA
7 and 8 Sun. St. (Mrs. E.A. Rodwell and G.W. Kippax.) Est. 1906. CL: Wed. p.m. Open 9−1 and 2.30−5. SIZE: Large. *STOCK: Furniture, Jacobean to Edwardian, £10−£2,000; silver, Georgian to modern, £1−£500; china, clocks, barometers, jewellery.* Not stocked: Weapons. LOC: Via town centre and Old Market Square, past Sun Hotel. PARK: In Old Market Square. TEL: 34774. SER: Valuations. VAT: Stan/Spec.

Carole Thomas (Fine Arts)
32a Sun St. Est. 1977. CL: Wed. Open 10.30−5, Sat. 10−5.30. SIZE: Large. *STOCK: English watercolours, 1820−1900, £85−£1,000; oils, 1830−1920s, £130−£1,000; etchings, prints.* LOC: Off Market Sq. PARK: Market Sq. TEL: 36077. SER: Valuations; restorations (watercolours, oils).

For 100 years and over three generations discerning collectors from all over the world have come to find carefully chosen English 17th and 18th century furniture displayed in the period rooms of this Georgian manor house only 30 miles (1 hour by car) from London.

PHILLIPS *of* HITCHIN

(ANTIQUES) LTD.

The Manor House

Hitchin, Herts

SG5 1JW
Members of the British Antique Dealers Association

Telephone: Hitchin 32067
STD 0462

Cables: Phillips
Hitchin

KIMPTON (0438)
Annick Antiques
28 High St. (Mrs. Turl.) Open seven days 10−6. *STOCK: Victorian, Edwardian and 1930s furniture, country oak and general antiques.* TEL: 832491.

KING'S LANGLEY (092 77)
Frenches Farm Antiques
Tower Hill, Chipperfield. (I. Cross.) Est. 1972. Open 2−6 or by appointment. SIZE: Large. *STOCK: Furniture, including pine, £15−£350; porcelain, Victoriana, copper, brass, £1−£50; all 18th−19th C.* Not stocked: Silver, jewellery, firearms, paintings. LOC: From Chipperfield take Bovingdon Rd. On right 500yds. from Royal Oak public house. PARK: Easy. TEL: 65843.

KNEBWORTH
The Antiques Shop at Knebworth
10 Station Rd. (J.A. Wright.) Est. 1970. CL: Mon. Open from 10. SIZE: Small. LOC: A1000. PARK: Easy. TEL: Stevenage (0438) 813738. SER: Valuations.

LETCHMORE HEATH, Nr. Watford
Anne Barlow Antiques
1 Letchmore Cottages. (Mrs. Barlow and Mrs. Harrison.) Est. 1952. CL: Mon. Open 10.30−6, weekends 3−6, or by appointment. SIZE: Small. *STOCK: Continental and unusual items, country furniture, faience porcelain, toys, clocks, collectors' items, £1−£500.* PARK: Easy. TEL: Radlett (092 76) 5270/5992. SER: Valuations.

MUCH HADHAM (027 984)
Keith Arden and Clouds Gallery
LAPADA
Morris Cottage (K. Williams and M. Arden-Davis.) Resident. Est. 1977. Open by appointment. SIZE: Medium. *STOCK: Porcelain, 18th−20th C, £100−£2,000; watercolours, £150−£750; small furniture, £150−£300.* TEL: 2297. SER: Valuations; buys at auction. FAIRS: Most major. VAT: Stan/Spec.

Careless Cottage Antiques
High St. (M. Furze.) Est. 1979. Usually open 9.30−5.30. SIZE: Medium. *STOCK: General antiques, country furniture, 17th−19th C, £100−£2,500; china, glass, small and decorative items, 19th to early 20th C prints and watercolours, £1−£200.* LOC: On B1004, at North end of village. PARK: Easy. TEL: 2007.

"Minerva" off Marseilles. Watercolour signed and dated Antoine Roux, 1815.
Courtesy **Paul Mason Gallery**, 149 Sloane Street, London S.W.1.

Much Hadham continued

Stuart Howard Antiques
Gaytons. (M. Howard.) Est. 1977. Open Sat. and Sun. 10−6, or by appointment. SIZE: Small. *STOCK: Furniture, £200−£4,500; clocks, £200−£5,000; both 17th−19th C; Victorian and Edwardian jewellery, small items, brass and copper.* PARK: Easy. TEL: 2152.

PUCKERIDGE

St. Ouen Antiques   LAPADA
Vintage Corner, Old Cambridge Rd. (V.C.J., J., J., and S.T. Blake and Mrs. P.B. Francis.) Est. 1918. Open 10.30−5. SIZE: Large. *STOCK: English and Continental furniture, decorative items, silver, porcelain, pottery, glass, clocks, barometers, paintings.* TEL: Ware (0920) 821336. SER: Valuations; restorations.

RADLETT   (092 76)

J. Foster & Son
21 High Firs, Gills Hill. (W. Johnston.) Est. 1902. Open by appointment only. SIZE: Medium. *STOCK: Paintings, porcelain and silver, 18th−19th C, to £5,000.* LOC: 100yds. from Watling St. PARK: 300yds. TEL: 6012. SER: Valuations; buys at auction (mainly furniture). VAT: Spec.

Hasel-Britt Ltd.
157 Watling St. (Mrs. Britton.) Est. 1962. CL: Wed. Open 10−5.30. *STOCK: General antiques, 19th C; pottery and porcelain.* TEL: 4477.

Old Hat
64 Watling St. (N.G. Rogers.) Est. 1972. CL: Wed. p.m. Open 9.30−5.30. SIZE: Medium. *STOCK: General antiques, furniture, Victoriana, £5−£1,000; oils, watercolours, porcelain, jewellery, 18th−19th C, £20−£500.* LOC: A5. PARK: Easy. TEL: 5753. VAT: Stan/Spec.

REDBOURN,   (058 285)
Nr. St. Albans

J.N. Antiques   LAPADA
86 High St. (M. and J. Brunning.) Est. 1975. Open 9−6. SIZE: Medium. *STOCK: Furniture, 18th−19th C, £5−£1,000; brass and copper, porcelain, 19th C, £5−£100.* PARK: 50yds. TEL: 3603 (24 hrs.). SER: Valuations. VAT: Spec.

Redbourn continued

Tim Wharton Antiques
24 High St. Est. 1970. CL: Mon. and usually Thurs. Open 10−5.30, Sat. 10−4. *STOCK: Furniture, mahogany, oak and elm, 18th and 19th C; copper, brass, ironware and general small antiques.* LOC: On left entering village from St. Albans on A5183. PARK: Easy. TEL: 4371. VAT: Stan/Spec.

RICKMANSWORTH   (0923)

Clive A. Burden
46 Talbot Rd. Est. 1966. Open 9−5, appointment preferred. SIZE: Medium. *STOCK: Maps, 1500−1860, £1−£1,000; prints, 1720−1870, £1−£100; antiquarian books, pre-1870, £10−£5,000.* LOC: In main shopping area. PARK: Nearby. TEL:778097; home − 772387. SER: Valuations; buys at auction (maps, prints or books). VAT: Stan.

McCrudden Gallery
23 Station Rd. CL: Wed. Open 10−5.30. SIZE: Medium. *STOCK: Fine paintings, watercolours, limited editions prints, etchings and engravings.* LOC: Town centre. PARK: Easy. TEL: 772613. SER: Restorations (pictures and frames); buys at auction.

Northwood Maps Ltd.
71 Nightingale Rd. (P. Shires and T. Sparks.) Est. 1977. Open by appointment. SIZE: Small. *STOCK: Maps and atlases, 16th−20th C, £2−£2,000.* PARK: Easy. TEL: 772258. SER: Valuations; buys at auction (maps).

Sheraton Galleries
22 Church St. Est. 1970. CL: Wed. Open 10−5. *STOCK: Furniture, paintings, clocks.* TEL: 720261. VAT: Stan/Spec.

IS YOUR ENTRY CORRECT?
If there is even the slightest inaccuracy in your entry, *please* let us know before 1st January 1987.
GUIDE TO THE
ANTIQUE SHOPS OF BRITAIN
5 Church Street, Woodbridge, Suffolk.

ROYSTON (0763)

Greenbury Antiques
Corn Exchange, Market Place. (I. Cornwell, J. Carr.) Est. 1972. Open Wed., and Sat. 9—5, or by appointment. SIZE: Medium. *STOCK: Furniture, silver, jewellery, porcelain, curios, £1—£600.* LOC: Off Market Hill. PARK: Within 50—100yds. TEL: 45019 or Barkway (076 384) 362.

Market Antiques
Corn Exchange. (J. Colman.) Est. 1979. Open Wed. and Sat. 9—4.30. SIZE: Small. *STOCK: Furniture, £10—£250; jewellery, £1—£200.* LOC: Beside Market Square. TEL: Evenings — 43338.

Royston Antiques
27—29 Kneesworth St. (J. and M. Newnham.) Est. 1965. CL: Thurs. Open 9.30—5. SIZE: Large. *STOCK: Furniture, 1750—1930, £10—£1,000; silver, jewellery, porcelain, books, £5—£500; collectors' items, pine, copper, brass, steel.* TEL: 43876.

ST. ALBANS (0727)

Bernards Heath Antiques
126 Sandridge Rd. (A. Farrant.) Open 9.30—5.30. *STOCK: Collectors' items, dolls, furniture, linen and antique lace, wedding dresses.* LOC: On Weathampstead Rd. opp. Bernards Heath. PARK: In slip road. TEL: 51109.

The Clock Shop —
Philip Setterfield of St. Albans
161 Victoria St. Est. 1974. CL: Thurs. Open 10.30—6.30. *STOCK: Clocks and watches.* LOC: On bridge over city station. TEL: 56633. SER: Restoration; repairs (clocks, watches, barometers). VAT: Stan/Spec.

Dolphin Antiques   LAPADA
13 Holywell Hill. (C. Constable.) Est. 1967. CL: Sat. Open 9—5, or by appointment to overseas trade. SIZE: Large. *STOCK: Furniture, 18th—19th C, £100—£4,000; porcelain, £20—£1,000; glass, brass and copper, £10—£300; pictures, prints, £10—£500.* Not stocked: Coins, medals, weapons. LOC: Turn left at Peahen Hotel. PARK: Cathedral yard or public. TEL: 63080; home — 61941. SER: Restorations (furniture). VAT: Stan/Spec.

Barbara Hudson
Spinney Cottage. Est. 1972. Open by appointment only. *STOCK: Pottery, porcelain, 18th—19th C.* TEL: 53457.

St. Albans continued

James of St. Albans
11 George St. (S.N., W.M. and W. James.) Est. 1957. Open 10—5, Thurs. 10—1. *STOCK: Furniture, general antiques, 18th—19th C.* TEL: 56996. VAT: Stan/Spec.

Christopher Perry Antiques
27 College St. Est. 1975. Appointment advisable. SIZE: Small. *STOCK: Furniture — walnut, mahogany and oak, £50—£2,000; metalware and interesting items, £20—£400; all 1600—1850; prints.* Not stocked: Bric-a-brac, late Victorian and Edwardian furniture. LOC: From Peahen Hotel A5/A6 crossroad into Verulam Rd. Turn left just before pedestrian crossing into Lower Dagnell St., shop 50yds down on right. PARK: Easy. TEL: 32772; home — same. VAT: Stan/Spec.

St. Albans Antique Market
Town Hall, Chequer St. Est. 1978. Open Mon. 9.30—4, including some Bank Holidays. There are 34 stands at this market selling a wide variety of antiques. TEL: 50427.

Stevens Antiques
41 London Rd. (J.E. Stevens.) Est. 1971. CL: Thurs. Open 10—5.30, Sat. 9.30—5, Sun. by appointment. SIZE: Medium. *STOCK: Stripped pine, £25—£400; small antiques — brass, boxes, china, porcelain, £10—£150, all 19th C; Victorian and Edwardian furniture, 19th to early 20th C, £30—£1,000.* LOC: Off Holywell Hill or Chequer St. PARK: Own, at rear. TEL: 57266; home — 50427. SER: Valuations. VAT: Stan.

Thomas Thorp
9 George St. Est. 1883. CL: Mon. *STOCK: Antiquarian books.* TEL: 65576.

SARRATT, Nr. Rickmansworth

Penrose Antiques
The Green. (D. and E. Harriman.) Est. 1976. Open 10—6. SIZE: Small, and barn. *STOCK: Clocks, swords, guns, pictures, furniture, curios.* LOC: Near M25. PARK: Easy. TEL: Kings Langley (092 77) 68632. SER: Valuations; restorations (as stock).

SAWBRIDGEWORTH

The Herts and Essex Antique Centre
The Maltings, Station Rd. Est. 1982. CL: Mon. Open 10.30—6 including Sun. SIZE: Large. There are over 100 dealers at this centre dealing in *a wide range of antiques, from 1780 to date, prices range from 50p—£500+* LOC: Town centre opposite B.R. Station. PARK: Easy. TEL: Bishops Stortford (0279) 725809. SER: Restorations.

Collins Antiques

F.G. & C. Collins, Antiques, Wheathampstead, Herts.

WHEATHAMPSTEAD

Telephone 058—283 3111   25 miles from London
International + 44 58—283 3111   A1 M to Junction 4 then the B653

TRING   (044 282)

Richard Barrow Antiques
83 High St. CL: Wed. Open 9.30—5.30. *STOCK: General antiques.* TEL: 6223; home — Aldbury Common (044 285) 339.

John Bly   BADA
50 High St. (F., N., and J. Bly.) **Books on furniture and silver. Est. 1888. CL: Wed. p.m. Open 9—5.30. SIZE: Large.** *STOCK: English furniture and silver, 18th C.* **TEL: 3030. VAT: Stan/Spec.**

Country Clocks
3 Pendley Bridge Cottages, Tring Station. (T. and J. Cartmell.) Est. 1976. CL: Tues. and Fri. except by appointment. SIZE: Small. *STOCK: Clocks, 18th—19th C.* LOC: One mile from A41, in village, cottage nearest canal bridge. PARK: Easy. TEL: 5090. SER: Restorations (clocks).

WATFORD   (0923)

Copper Kettle Antiques
172 Bushey Mill Lane. (R. and C. Barton.) Est. 1970. CL: Wed. Open 9.30—4.30. SIZE: Large. *STOCK: General antiques, Victoriana, paintings, watercolours, books, prints, clocks, furniture.* TEL: 48877. VAT: Stan/Spec.

WELWYN   (043 871)

Bowden Antiques
Burnham Green. (R. and C. Bowden.) Resident. Est. 1981. CL: Wed., Thurs. and Sat. Open 10—6. SIZE: Small. *STOCK: Furniture, Victorian and Edwardian, £5—£500; silver, £5—£200; porcelain, glass, £5—£50; both Victorian.* PARK: Easy. TEL: Bulls Green (043 879) 265; home — Bulls Green (043 879) 716. SER: Restoration (furniture). FAIRS: Chiltern, Midas.

WHEATHAMPSTEAD   (058 283)

**Collins Antiques
(F.G. and C. Collins Ltd.)**
Corner House. (S.J. and M.C. Collins.) Est. 1907. Open 9—1 and 2—5. SIZE: Large. *STOCK: Furniture, mahogany, 1730—1890, £25—£4,500; oak, 1600—1800, £25—£2,000; walnut, 1700—1740, £75—£2,000. Not stocked: Silver.* LOC: From Hatfield take B653. PARK: Easy. TEL: 3111; home — 3483 or 2531. SER: Restorations. VAT: Stan/Spec.

Humberside

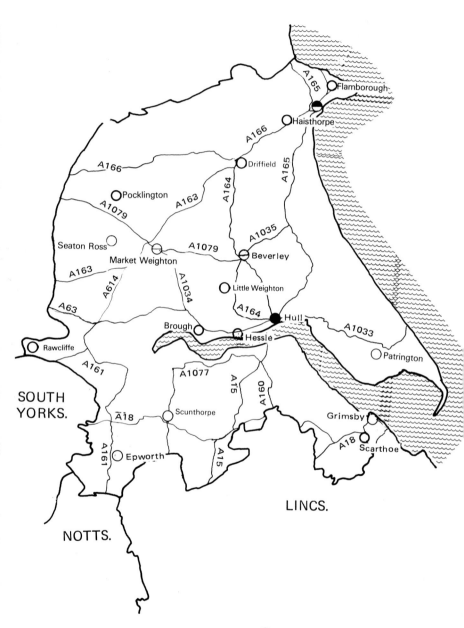

Flamborough

A165

Haisthorpe

A166

A166

Driffield

A165

A164

Pocklington

A163

A1079

A1035

Seaton Ross

A1079

Beverley

Market Weighton

A163

A614

A1034

Little Weighton

A164

A63

Hull

Brough

A1033

Hessle

Rawcliffe

Patrington

A161

A1077

A15

A160

SOUTH YORKS.

A18

Scunthorpe

Grimsby

A161

Epworth

A15

A18

Scarthoe

NOTTS.

LINCS.

Please note this is only a rough map designed to show dealers the number of shops in the various towns, and is not necessarily totally accurate.

○ 1—2   Key to
⊖ 3—5   number of shops in
◒ 6—12   this area.
● 13+

BEVERLEY

Ray Hawley
5 North Bar Within. Open 9—5. *STOCK: General antiques, furniture, pottery, porcelain, glass, oil paintings, silver, arms and armour.* TEL: Hull (0482) 868193. VAT: Stan/Spec.

Ladygate Antiques
8 Ladygate. (P. and L. Goodman.) Est. 1963. Open 9.30—1 and 2—5.30. SIZE: Medium. *STOCK: Furniture, longcase clocks, pottery and porcelain, glass, brass, copperware, pewter, jewellery, maritime relics, silver and plate.* Not stocked: Militaria, coins. PARK: Easy. TEL: Hull (0482) 881494; home — Hull (0482) 882299/868857.

James H. Starkey Galleries
49 Highgate. Est. 1968. Open 10—2, Mon. and Fri. 10—12, Sat. and other times by appointment. SIZE: Medium. *STOCK: Oil paintings, 16th—19th C, £100+; drawings and watercolours, 17th—19th C, from £10.* LOC: Opposite Beverley Minster. PARK: Easy. TEL: Hull (0482) 881179. SER: Valuations; restorations (paintings); buys at auction. VAT: Stan/Spec.

BRIDLINGTON (0262)

Art and Antiques
80 High St. (K. and E. Sweeney.) Open 10—4. *STOCK: General antiques, jewellery and silver.* PARK: Easy. TEL: Home — 850921. SER: Restorations (clock face painting and lacquer work). VAT: Stan/Spec.

Clockcraft Antiques
83 High St. (P.G. Harker.) CL: Thurs. Open 11—4. TEL: 602802.

C.J. and A.J. Dixon Ltd.
23 Prospect St. Est. 1969. Open 9—5.30. SIZE: Medium. *STOCK: Jewellery, gold, silver, medals and coins.* LOC: Town centre. PARK: Easy. TEL: 676877 and 673539. SER: Valuations. VAT: Stan/Spec.

R. and C. McIntyre
2 Lansdowne Rd. Est. 1950. CL: Thurs. Open 10—5 in Winter; Open every day in Summer. *STOCK: Porcelain, glass, silver, jewellery, brass, copper.* TEL: 676575.

Priory Antiques
47-49 High St. (P.R. Rogerson.) Est. 1979. CL: Thurs. Open 10—5. *STOCK: General antiques.* TEL: 601365.

Sedman Antiques
Carnaby Court, Off Moor Lane, Carnaby. (R.H.S. and M.A. Sedman.) Est. 1971. Open 10—5.30, Sun. by appointment. *STOCK: General antiques, period and shipping furniture, Oriental porcelain, Victorian collectors' items.* LOC: Off A165. TEL: 674039. VAT: Stan/Spec.

Bridlington continued

Smith's Antiques
24 Quay Rd. Est. 1968. Open 9.30—6. SIZE: Small. *STOCK: Shipping items, smalls, £5—£300.* LOC: Near level crossing. PARK: Easy. TEL: 675624; home — same. SER: Valuations; buys at auction (shipping items, period furniture).

Sweet's Antiques
24 West St. (Mrs. S.M. Sweet.) Est. 1950. Open 10—6. *STOCK: General antiques, porcelain, glass.* TEL: 677396.

R.W. and E.H.G. Wheeldon
Bessingby Lodge, Bessingby. Est. 1963. Open by appointment. *STOCK: General antiques, furniture, clocks.* LOC: On A166, at entrance to Bessingby Hall. PARK: Own. TEL: 603308.

BROUGH

Boothferry Antiques
66 Station Rd. (P. Smith.) Open by appointment. SIZE: Warehouse. *STOCK: Furniture and shipping goods.* SER: Packing; shipping; courier for N.E. England.

DRIFFIELD (0377)

The Crested China Co.
The Station House. (D. Taylor.) Est. 1983. Open by appointment. *STOCK: Goss and crested china.* TEL: 47042.

FLAMBOROUGH, Nr. Bridlington

Lesley Berry Antiques
The Manor House. (Mrs. L. Berry.) Resident. Est. 1972. Open 10—6 daily but appointment advisable. SIZE: Small. *STOCK: Furniture, 18th—19th C, £50—£750; silver, jewellery, amber, Whitby jet, pre-1914, £10—£400; oils, watercolours, prints, £15—£500; treen, copper, brass, £5—£100.* Not stocked: Shipping goods. LOC: Shop on corner of Tower St. and Lighthouse Rd. PARK: Easy. TEL: Bridlington (0262) 850943. SER: Buys at auction. FAIRS: Antiques in Britain.

HAISTHORPE, Nr. Gt. Driffield

Micheal Bishop Antiques
Breeze Farm. (M. and S. Bishop.) Est. 1972. Open 1—5, Sat. and Sun. 10—5. *STOCK: Shipping goods, from 1900, £50—£500; smalls.* LOC: A166. PARK: Own. TEL: Bridlington (0262) 89393; home — same. SER: Container packing. VAT: Stan.

HESSLE

The Antique Parlour
21 The Weir. (S. Beercock.) Est. 1967. CL: Sun. except to trade. *STOCK: General antiques, Victoriana, bric-a-brac, curios.* TEL: Hull (0482) 643329.

HULL (0482)

'55' Antiques
55 Springbank. (G. Etherington.) Est. 1960. Open 9—5. SIZE: Medium. *STOCK: Furniture, 17th—19th C, £80—£3,000; paintings, 17th to early 20th C, £40—£3,000; Victoriana, from £20; Victorian garden furniture, vases, urns.* LOC: Take Willerby road; crossroads at north end of town is Springbank. Shop 150yds. on left. PARK: First left, first left again. TEL: 224510. SER: Valuations; restorations (furniture, paintings, clocks, china); buys at auction. VAT: Spec.

Bank House Antiques
175 Spring Bank. (B. and M. Taylor.) Open 9.30—5.30. *STOCK: General antiques.* TEL: 227337.

Britannia Antiques
Unit 4, 338 Wincolmlee. (G.T. Able.) Open 9.30—6. *STOCK: Victorian and Edwardian fireplace surrounds, fireside tools and furniture.* TEL: 226364.

Brunswick Antiques
64a Beverley Rd. (P. Allison.) Est. 1976. CL: Sat. Open 9.30—4.30. *STOCK: General antiques, shipping and smalls.* TEL: 20874; home — 847653.

De Grey Antiques
96 De Grey St., Beverley Rd. (G. Dick.) Est. 1962. Open 9.30—1 and 2—5.45. SIZE: Medium. *STOCK: Furniture, clocks, paintings, Georgian, £30—£450; furniture, paintings and watercolours, Victorian, £5—£350; glass, china, pewter, brass, copper and oil lamps, £5—£150.* LOC: Off main Beverley Rd., near overhead railway bridge. PARK: Easy. TEL: 442184; home — 41081. SER: Valuations; buys at auction.

Grannie's Parlour
33 Anlaby Rd. (Mrs. N. Pye.) Open 11—5. *STOCK: Victoriana, dolls, toys, kitchenalia.* TEL: 228258; home — 41020.

Hull continued

Grannie's Treasures
4 Midland St. (Mrs. N. Pye.) Open 11.30—5. *STOCK: Advertising items, postcards, tins, bottles, bric-a-brac, pre-1940s clothing.* TEL: 228258; after hours — 41020.

David K. Hakeney Antiques
LAPADA
64 George St. Est. 1971. Open 10—6. SIZE: Medium plus warehouse. *STOCK: Georgian, Victorian, Edwardian furniture, smalls, shipping goods.* LOC: City centre. TEL: 228190; home — 668634. VAT: Stan/Spec.

The House of Antiques
211 Beverley High Rd. (C. St. John-House.) Est. 1950. Open 10—6. SIZE: Medium. *STOCK: Small general antiques.* LOC: One mile from city centre on left. PARK: Easy. TEL: 43736.

Imperial Antiques
397 Hessle Rd. (M. Langton.) Resident, always open. *STOCK: General antiques and furniture.* TEL: 27439.

Jaycee Antiques
11 Princes Ave. (C. and J. West.) Est. 1978. Open 10—5. SIZE: Small. *STOCK: Furniture, £50—£500; glass, £5—£100; jewellery, £10—£100; all Georgian and Victorian.* Not stocked: Militaria and clothes. LOC: Off A63. From station turn left at traffic lights to 'Y' junction, take right fork, shop on left. PARK: 100 yards side street. TEL: 448632. SER: Valuations; buys at auction (furniture). FAIRS: Local Sunday.

K. Books of Hull
15 and 17 Hepworth's Arcade, Silver St. Open 10—5.30. *STOCK: Antiquarian books, prints and maps.* TEL: 26457.

Lesley's Antiques
329 Hessle Rd. Est. 1967. Open 10—5.30. SIZE: Medium. *STOCK: General antiques, shipping goods; collectors' items, mostly under £25.* LOC: On main Hull to Hessle Rd. PARK: Easy. TEL: 23986; home — 646280. SER: Restorations.

Geoffrey Mole/Antique Exports
LAPADA
Warehouse 400 Wincolmlee. Est. 1974. CL: Sat. p.m. Open 9—5. SIZE: Large. *STOCK: Shipping furniture, 1850—1920, £5—£2,000; general antiques, 19th C.* LOC: ½ mile east off main Beverley Rd. PARK: Easy. TEL: 27858. SER: Packing, shipping and courier service. VAT: Stan.

Hull continued

Padgetts Antiques, Photographic and Scientific
50 Savile St. (G.R. Padgett.) Est. 1965. Open 9—5.30, Sat. 9—5. SIZE: Small. *STOCK: Cameras and photographic miscellanea, £10—£5,000; scientific and ships' instruments, £25—£250; mechanical and domestic machines, £5—£500; all late 19th to early 20th C; clocks, 1770—1850; early photographs and images, 1850—1900.* LOC: Between Queen Victoria Sq. and George St. PARK: Easy. TEL: 25442. SER: Valuations. VAT: Stan.

Pearson Antiques   *Trade Only*
Unit 18, The Warehouse, 4 Dalton St. (W.B.T. Grozier.) Est. 1972. Open 10—5, Sat. by appointment. SIZE: Large. *STOCK: Furniture, pottery, brass, silver and plate, stuffed birds, stone figures, late 17th C to Edwardian, £50—£500.* LOC: Off Cleaveland St. PARK: Easy. TEL: 29647; home — 862927. SER: Valuations. VAT: Spec.

Sandringham Antiques
476 Beverley Rd. (J. and P. Allison.) Est. 1968. *STOCK: General antiques.* TEL: 43013, 847653 or 20874.

Hull continued

Paul Wilson Old, Antique and Reproduction Pine   LAPADA
Perth St. West. Est. 1972. Open 8—5.30, Sat. 9—12 other times by appointment. *STOCK: English, Scottish, Irish, Welsh, German, Austrian and Danish pine.* LOC: Near inner ring road, 10 mins. from Humber bridge. Telephone for further details. TEL: 447923/448607. SER: Export and U.K. delivery; catalogue available. VAT. Stan.

LITTLE WEIGHTON

B.L. Levine LAPADA
t/a Rowley Restorations. Rowley Rd. Est. 1977. SIZE: Large. *STOCK: Victorian mahogany, £50—£2,000.* PARK: Easy. TEL: Hull (0482) 844531. SER: Restorations, polishing, container packing; courier. VAT: Stan.

MARKET WEIGHTON (0696)
Nr. York
Dis & Dat
2 Churchside. (J. Plantenga.) CL: Thurs. Open 9—5. *STOCK: General small antiques and bric-a-brac.* TEL: 73213.

C.G. Dyson and Sons
51 Market Place. Est. 1966. CL: Thurs. p.m. Open 9—5.30, Sat. till 5. SIZE: Small. *STOCK: 18th—19th C clocks, £50—£600; 19th C jewellery; paintings and prints, all £5—£200.* Not stocked: Porcelain. LOC: On main road in centre of town. PARK: Behind shop next door. TEL: 72391. SER: Valuations; restorations. VAT: Stan/Spec.

Grannie's Attic
Kiplingcotes Station. Est. 1964. TEL: Dalton Holme (069 64) 284.

Houghton Hall Antiques
Houghton Hall, Cliffe Rd. (M.E. Watson.) Est. 1965. Open daily 8—4, Sun. 11—4. SIZE: Large. *STOCK: Furniture, 17th—19th C, £5—£5,000; china, 19th C, £1—£600; paintings and prints, £20—£1,000; objets d'art.* Not stocked: Coins, guns. LOC: Turn right in middle of town by garage, signposted Brough. After 200yds. turn right on Cliffe Rd. Hall is 1 mile further on. PARK: Easy. TEL: 73234. SER: Valuations; restorations (furniture); buys at auction. FAIRS: New York (U.S.A.). VAT: Stan/Spec.

Gordon Huetson Antiques
Mount Pleasant Farm, Cliffe Rd. Open 9—6. SIZE: Large. *STOCK: Furniture, 1790—1935.* PARK: Own. TEL: 72872. SER: Valuations; buys at auction. VAT: Stan/Spec.

Pieter Plantenga
Old Brewery. CL: Thurs. Open 9—5. *STOCK: Stripped pine, general furniture.* TEL: 73213.

PATRINGTON (0964)
Clyde Antiques
12 Market Place. (S.M. Nettleton.) Est. 1978. CL: Sun., Mon. and Wed. except by appointment. Open 10—5. SIZE: Medium. *STOCK: General antiques.* PARK: Easy. TEL: 30650; home — Withernsea (096 42) 2471. SER: Valuations. VAT: Stan.

POCKLINGTON (075 92)
In Retrospect
3a Pavement. (I. and R. Barker.) Est. 1978. CL: Mon. and Wed., otherwise open. Sun. by appointment. SIZE: Small. *STOCK: Furniture, mainly 19th C, £50—£500; paintings, 19th to early 20th C, £25—£500; ceramics and collectables, BC—1900, £5—£500.* LOC: In centre of village, opposite church. PARK: Easy. TEL: 304894; home — Melbourne (0759) 318559.

Wilton House Gallery
95 Market St. (J.R. Moor.) ADA. Est. 1978. Open 9.30—1 and 2—5; Wed. 9.30—1, Sat. 9.30—2 or by appointment. SIZE: Medium. *STOCK: Antiquities, 6th C B.C. to 16th C, £5—£3,000; Japanese and Chinese ceramics, 16th—20th C, £5—£1,000; studio ceramics, 20th C, £5—£1,500.* LOC: 1 mile off A1079, between York and Hull. PARK: Own. TEL: 4858; home — 3157. SER: Valuations; buys at auction (as stock). VAT: Stan.

RAWCLIFFE, Nr. Goole
John Waddington Antiques
70-72 High St. Est. 1967. Resident. Open 9—6 including Sun. SIZE: Medium. *STOCK: Furniture, £10—£2,000; silver and plate, £5—£1,000; both 18th—19th C; bric-a-brac, from £5.* Not stocked: Stamps and coins. LOC: A614. PARK: Easy. TEL: Goole (0405) 83802. VAT: Stan/Spec.

SEATON ROSS
Rytham Antiques
Rytham Gate House. (Mrs. M.M. Quirke.) Est. 1981. CL: Mon. Open 10—5, Sun. by appointment. SIZE: Small. *STOCK: Silver, small furniture, 19th C, £50—£500; jewellery, late Victorian, £20—£100.* LOC: Off A1079. PARK: Easy. TEL: Melbourne (0759) 318200; home — same.

EPWORTH   (0427)
Nr. Doncaster
Thorpe's Antiques and Curio Shop
2 and 4 Albion Hill. (T. Thorpe.) Est. 1960.
CL: Sun. except by appointment. Open 9—12
and 1—5, Wed. till 4. SIZE: Medium. *STOCK:
General antiques, bric-a-brac.* LOC: A18, turn
off at sign Epworth, Belton. Shop in market
place. PARK: Easy. TEL: 872210; home —
same.

GRIMSBY   (0472)
Bell Antiques   *Trade Only*
68 Harold St. (V. Hawkey.) Est. 1964. Open
by appointment, telephone previous evening.
SIZE: Large. *STOCK: Pine, especially Scandinavian.* PARK: Easy. TEL: 695110; home —
same. VAT: Stan.

P.K. and R.H. Leigh
42 Friargate, Riverhead Centre. (R.H. Leigh.)
Est. 1920. Open 9—5. SIZE: Medium.
STOCK: General antiques and reproductions.
Not stocked: Large furniture. PARK: River-
head. TEL: 42597. VAT: Stan/Spec.

SCARTHOE, Nr. Grimsby
Scarthoe Antiques
38 Louth Rd. (P. Bridges.) Est. 1975. CL:
Mon. and Thurs. Open 10—5. SIZE: Medium.
*STOCK: Jewellery, silver, porcelain, collectors'
items, maps, prints, linen.* LOC: A16. PARK:
Easy. TEL: 77394.

SCUNTHORPE   (0724)
Guns and Tackle
251A Ashby High St. (J.A. Bowden.) CL:
Wed. Open 9—5.30. *STOCK: Guns and
militaria.* TEL: 865445. SER: Restorations
(guns); repairs (guns).

Mill Antiques
251 Ashby High St. (J. and B. Bowden.) Est.
1954. CL: Wed. Open 9—5.30. SIZE:
Medium. *STOCK: General antiques, militaria,
firearms.* LOC: Off A18. PARK: Easy. TEL:
865445. SER: Repairs (guns).

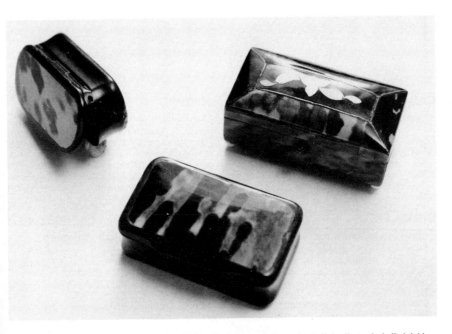

Left and centre. Buffalo horn snuffboxes with blond, deep mottled tortoiseshell (really turtleshell) inlaid on lids. Note recessed Mauchline type hinge with hole, through which the brass pin or horn dowel is fed. Both pieces have recently been repolished. Early 19th century. Right. Shallow domed tortoiseshell pin and needle box with silver strips between small panels, the centre one inlaid with mother-of-pearl; with small ivory feet. Late 19th century. From "Beginners' Corner: Tortoiseshell", **Antique Collecting**, May 1986.

Isle of Man

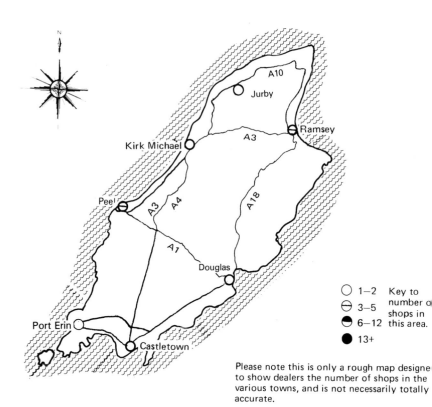

○ 1—2 Key to
⊖ 3—5 number of
◐ 6—12 shops in
● 13+ this area.

Please note this is only a rough map designed to show dealers the number of shops in the various towns, and is not necessarily totally accurate.

CASTLETOWN (0624)
J. and H. Bell Antiques   LAPADA
22 Arbory St. Est. 1965. CL: Tues. and Thurs. Open 10—5.30. SIZE: Medium. *STOCK: Jewellery, silver, china, glass, early metalware, small furniture, 18th—20th C, £5—£500.* PARK: 50 yards. TEL: 823132; home — 822414. SER: Valuations. VAT: Stan/Spec.

DOUGLAS (0624)
John Corrin Antiques
73 Circular Rd. Est. 1972. CL: Some Fri. Open 9—5, Sun. by appointment. SIZE: Medium. *STOCK: Furniture, late 18th—19th C, £50—£700; clocks, some longcase, early 19th C, £50—£1,000; barometers, 19th C, £100—£500.* LOC: From the promenade, travel up Victoria St., this becomes Prospect Hill and Circular Rd. is on left. PARK: Easy. TEL: 29655; home — 21382. SER: Valuations; restorations (barometers, clocks, furniture).

JURBY
Old Bakery Antiques
Unit 212, Jurby Airfield. Open Wed., Sat., and Sun. 12—4. *STOCK: Victoriana, English oak, mahogany, walnut, pine, 1800—1930; shipping goods, 1800—1930s; longcase and other clocks, general antiques.* TEL: Sulby (062489) 7483; evenings — Ramsey (0624) 815919. SER: Export.

KIRK MICHAEL (062 487)
Church View House Antiques
                                    LAPADA
Main Rd. (P.H. Morrison.) Est. 1973. Open 9.30—5.30. *STOCK: Furniture, porcelain, pictures, glass, silver, 18th—19th C.* LOC: Opposite Parish Church. PARK: Easy. TEL: 433. SER: Valuations; restorations. VAT: Spec.

PEEL (062 484)

Bygones Ltd.
12 Market St. (M. Boardley.) Est. 1975. Summer open Tues., Wed. and Sat., Thurs., a.m. and Mon. p.m. Winter open Tues., Wed., and Sat.SIZE: Medium. *STOCK: Small items, silver, plate, porcelain, copper and brass, boxes, art pottery, art nouveau and art deco.* PARK: Easy. TEL: Home — Douglas (0624) 76414.

Castle Antiques
5 Castle St. (F. Quayle.) Est. 1972. Open Mon., Wed. and Sat., other times by appointment. *STOCK: Paintings, watercolours, maps and prints, mostly Manx.* Tel: 3105.

Dorothea Horn At The Golden Past
18A Michael St. Est. 1982. Summer open 10.30—4.30. Winter open 12—4.30, Sat. 10.30—4.30. SIZE: Medium. *STOCK: Jewellery, porcelain, silver, glass, books, paintings and furniture, 1840—1940, £5—£100.* LOC: Main shopping street. PARK: Easy. TEL: 2170; home — St. Johns (062 471) 255. FAIRS: Peel.

A.L. McPherson Antiques
Castle St. Open Wed. and Sat. 10.30—5. *STOCK: Pine, kitchenalia, brass.* PARK: Easy. TEL: 2170/2767.

PORT ERIN (0624)

Spinning Wheel
Church Rd. (I. Miller and D. Keggin.) Est. 1979. Open 10—5. *STOCK: Silver, plate, china, glass, jewellery, pottery, small furniture, linen, brass, bric-a-brac, clocks and watches, flatware.* TEL: 833137. VAT: Stan.

IS YOUR ENTRY CORRECT?
If there is even the slightest inaccuracy in your entry, *please* let us know before 1st January 1987.
GUIDE TO THE
ANTIQUE SHOPS OF BRITAIN
5 Church Street, Woodbridge, Suffolk.

RAMSEY (0624)

P.G. Allom and Co. Ltd.
3 Parliament St. Est. 1965. *STOCK: Jewellery, silver, some secondhand.* TEL: 812490.

Hour Glass Antiques
2 Bourne Place. (Mrs. P. Bourne and Miss V. Corkhill.) Est. 1977. CL: Wed. p.m. Open 10—5. *STOCK: General antiques, silver, furniture, copper and brass.* TEL: 812775.

Quay Antiques
1 West Quay. (E. Huyton and R.W. Courtenay.) Est. 1969. CL: Wed. p.m. Open 10—5.30. *STOCK: General antiques.* TEL: 813599. VAT: Stan.

One of a pair of Wedgwood black basalt griffin candlesticks. Height 34cm. From "English Pottery at Christie's" in **Antique Collecting,** April 1986.

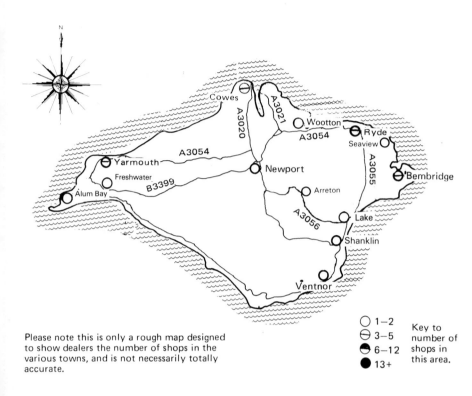

Please note this is only a rough map designed to show dealers the number of shops in the various towns, and is not necessarily totally accurate.

Key to number of shops in this area.

○ 1—2
⊖ 3—5
◓ 6—12
● 13+

Isle of Wight STD code applies to all exchanges unless otherwise stated

ALUM BAY   (0983)

Museum of Clocks
(R. Taylor.) CL: Sat. Open 10—5 including Sun. Easter—Oct. By appointment only in winter. *STOCK: Clocks and watches, 17th C—1900.* PARK: Easy. TEL: 754193.

ARRETON

Kollectarama
Old Railway Station, Horringford. (R. Morgan.) Est. 1969. Open by appointment. *STOCK: Bottles, stoneware, 17th to early 20th C, 25p—£1,000; pot-lids, £5—£250; advertising items, postcards, breweriana, 25p— £200.* TEL: 865306.

BEMBRIDGE

Vectis Fine Arts Gallery
41 High St. (T. Mostyn-Joyner.) Est. 1972. Open 9.30—4.30. SIZE: Large. *STOCK: English watercolours especially marine, 18th to early 20th C, £40—£2,000; antiquarian engravings, books and maps, Isle of Wight only, 18th—19th C, £10—£500; marine oil paintings, 18th to early 20th C.* LOC: Main road. PARK: Easy. TEL: 872316; home — 852848. SER: Valuations; restorations (oil paintings, watercolours); framing and mounting; buys at auction (pictures). VAT: Stan/Spec.

Windmill Antiques   LAPADA
1 Foreland Rd. (E.J. de Kort.) Est. 1970. CL: Thurs. p.m. SIZE: Medium. *STOCK: Furniture, silver, porcelain, jewellery.* TEL: 873666. SER: Valuations; buys at auction. VAT: Stan/Spec.

World's End Watercolours
Open by appointment only. *STOCK: Watercolours, 1850—1950; some oils.* TEL: 872307. SER: Framing; restorations; photography.

COWES

Finishing Touches
42 High St. (M. Scadgell.) Open 9.15—5. *STOCK: Oil paintings, watercolours and prints, 1850 to date; objets d'art.* TEL: 294875.

Galerias Segui
75 High St. Est. 1976. Open 9.30—5. SIZE: Medium. *STOCK: Furniture, £50—£400; silver, porcelain, prints and watercolours, £15—£100; all 18th—19th C.* LOC: Next to Post Office, near Red Funnel Pier. PARK: 200yds. TEL: 292148; home — 852967.

The Marine Gallery
1 Bath Rd. (C. Campbell.) Est. 1955. Open summer months only 10—1 and 2—5. SIZE: Small. *STOCK: Marine oils, watercolours and prints, £50—£5,000.* LOC: Continuation of High St. leading to esplanade and sea. PARK: Easy. TEL: 200124; home — 855300. SER: Valuations; restorations (oils, watercolours and prints); buys at auction (pictures). VAT: Stan/Spec.

Chris Watts   *Trade Only*
Ivy House, Sun Hill. Open by appointment. *STOCK: Furniture, paintings and metalwork, 18th—19th C.* TEL: 298963. VAT: Stan/Spec.

FRESHWATER

Farthings Antiques
10 The Sheilings. (D.E. and Mrs. Farthing.) *STOCK: Porcelain, pottery and figures.* LOC: Heathfield Rd. PARK: Easy. TEL: 752997; home — same. FAIRS: Heathfield Hotel, Freshwater.

LAKE

Lake Antiques
Sandown Rd. (P. Burfield.) Est. 1982. Open 10—5, Wed. 10—1. *STOCK: General antiques, Victorian and Edwardian furniture, clocks.* LOC: On the main Sandown—Shanklin Rd. PARK: On forecourt. TEL: 406888 or 865005.

NEWPORT

The Old Firm
68 Pyle St. (M. and T. Brett.) Est. 1975. Open 9.30—5, Thurs. 9.30—4. SIZE: Medium. *STOCK: Stripped pine, 18th—20th C, £5—£500; Victorian china.* LOC: Opposite Castlehold Lane. PARK: Easy. TEL: 529592; home — Chillerton (098 370) 605. SER: Pine stripping; buys at auction.

Jamawar or gown (long) shawl. Dogra period, late 19th century. From *The Kashmir Shawl* by Frank Ames, published by the **Antique Collectors' Club,** 1986.

Flowers from the Dara Shikoh Album, c.1635. During Jehangir's reign, Western influence in the form of a flowering plant, naturalistic in appearance, became a favourite among Mughal patrons of the arts. From *The Kashmir Shawl* by Frank Ames, published by the **Antique Collectors' Club**, 1986.

Newport continued

Marilyn Rose Antiques
The Parlour, 87 Pyle St. Est. 1979. CL: Thurs. Open 10.30−1 and 2−4.30. *STOCK: Silver, porcelain, jewellery, period clothes and effects, small furniture, copper, brass and bric-a-brac.* LOC: Opposite R.C. Church. PARK: Easy. TEL: 528850; home − 293846.

RYDE

Antiques
9 Royal Victoria Arcade, Union St. (F. Cross.) CL: Thurs. Open 10−5. *STOCK: General antiques, silver, jewellery.* TEL: 64661.

Hayter's
19−20 Cross St. (R.W. and F.L. Hayter.) Est. 1956. CL: Thurs. Open 9−1 and 2−5.30. SIZE: Large. *STOCK: Furniture including Victorian.* LOC: Through main traffic flow from sea front to town centre. TEL: 63795. VAT: Stan/Spec.

E.D. Jones & Son Antiques
63 High St. CL: Sun. and Thurs., except by appointment. Open 10−5. *STOCK: Furniture, general antiques, glass, china, brass, copper, pictures, militaria.* TEL: 66054 or 614394. VAT: Stan/Spec.

The Sedan Chair
11 High St. (P. Nightingale). Est. 1972. CL: Mon. and Thurs. Open 10.30−1 and 2.30−5.30. SIZE: Medium. *STOCK: Period and Victorian furniture, glass, small silver, china, small objets d'art, 1780−1920, £2−£500.* Not stocked: Weapons. LOC: 5 mins. walk from Ryde pier and esplanade. PARK: 100yds. behind shop. TEL: 64237; home − 740337. SER: Valuations (furniture).

The Snuff Box
10 High St. (J. and B. Van Praagh.) Est. 1966. CL: Thurs. p.m. Open 10.30−1 and 2.30−5.30. SIZE: Medium. *STOCK: Period furniture, porcelain, Victorian glass, small silver pieces; Victoriana, small objets d'art, 1780−1920, £1−£500.* Not stocked: Weapons. LOC: 5 mins. walk from Ryde pier and esplanade. PARK: 100yds. immediately behind shop. TEL: 67722; home − 63403. SER: Valuations (silver and porcelain).

SEAVIEW　　　　　(098 371)
Nr. Ryde

Seaview Antiques
West St. Open 10−1 and 2.30−5, Thurs. 10−1, other times by appointment. *STOCK: General interesting items especially lace bobbins and other needlework tools, Victorian jewellery, small furniture and violins.* TEL: 2882.

SHANKLIN

Keith Shotter, Collectors Centre
81 Regent St. Est. 1974. Open 9.30−5. *STOCK: Coins, medals, jewellery, bottles, 50 B.C. to 1930.* LOC: 100yds. from railway station. PARK: Easy. TEL: 862334 or 853620. VAT: Stan.

VENTNOR

A. and S. Keen
19 Pier St. ABA. *STOCK: Antiquarian and secondhand books, small general antiques.* TEL: 853706.

Parasol Antiques
21 Church St. *STOCK: Furniture, jewellery, silver and china.* LOC: Opposite St. Catherine's church in town centre. TEL: 854931; home − 730597.

WOOTTON

A.T. Rowe
Open by appointment. *STOCK: Silver.* TEL: 883772.

YARMOUTH

The Gallery
The Square. (C. Campbell.) Est 1956. Open 10−1 and 2−5, Sun. 11−12.30 and 2.30−5. SIZE: Small. *STOCK: Watercolours, £50−£500; oil paintings, £300−£5,000; both 18th−20th C; maps and engravings, 18th−19th C, £10−£200.* LOC: Opposite church. PARK: Easy. TEL: 760784; home − 855300. SER: Valuations; restorations (oils, watercolours and prints); buys at auction (pictures). VAT: Stan/Spec.

Marlborough House Antiques
86 High St. (P.A. and V.K. Webb.) Est. 1972. *STOCK: Furniture, china, brass, copper, glass.* TEL: 760498.

Marlborough House Antiques
St. James Sq. (P.A. and V.K. Webb.) Est. 1972. *STOCK: Jewellery, watches, silver, glass, prints and maps.* TEL: 760498.

Kent

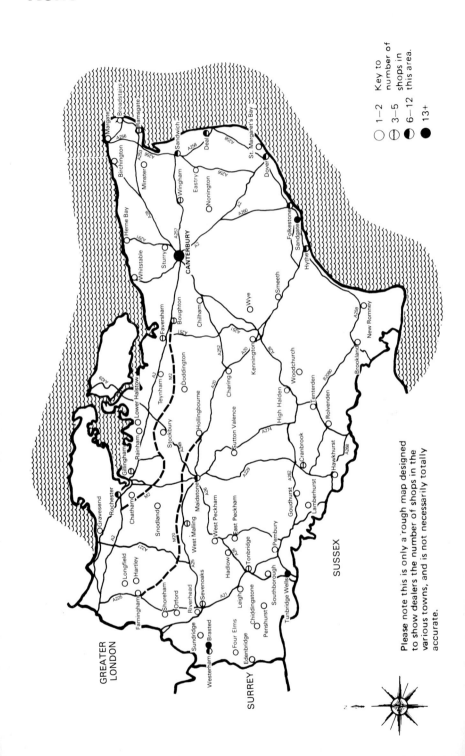

Key to number of shops in this area.

- ○ 1–2
- ◑ 3–5
- ◕ 6–12
- ● 13+

Please note this is only a rough map designed to show dealers the number of shops in the various towns, and is not necessarily totally accurate.

GREATER LONDON

SURREY

SUSSEX

BECKENHAM
See Greater London

BEXLEY
See Greater London

BIRCHINGTON, Nr. Margate
Birchington Antiques
41 Station Rd. (A.S. Fish.) Open Thurs.—Sun. 10—5.30. *STOCK: General antiques.* TEL: (0843) 41302.

Silvesters   LAPADA
Laburnum House, 2 Station Rd. (Mr. and Mrs. G.M.A. Wallis and S.N. Hartley.) Est. 1953. CL: Sat. and Wed. p.m. Open 9.30—5, other times by appointment. SIZE: Medium. *STOCK: Furniture, all periods, £50—£1,750; silver, jewellery, porcelain and curios, £5—£300; pictures, £25—£250; shipping furniture.* LOC: M2 from London — Thanet Way. PARK: Opposite. TEL: Thanet (0843) 41524. SER: Valuations; restorations (pictures and furniture); buys at auction. VAT: Stan/Spec.

BOUGHTON, Nr. Faversham
The Clock Shop Antiques
187 The Street. (S.G. Fowler.) Resident. Est. 1968. Articles on clocks. CL: Sun. except by appointment. Open 10—6. SIZE: Small. *STOCK: Clocks, small furniture, general antiques.* PARK: Easy. TEL: Canterbury (0227) 751258. SER: Repairs.

Jean Collyer Antiques
194 The Street. (Mrs. J.B. Collyer.) Est. 1977. CL: Thurs. Open 10—1 and 2—5. SIZE: Small. *STOCK: Porcelain, glass, furniture, general antiques, 18th to mid-19th C.* PARK: Easy. TEL: Canterbury (0227) 751454; home — same. SER: Valuations. VAT: Stan/Spec.

Peter Dyke Antiques
204 and 206 The Street. Est. 1981. Open 9.15—6, Sun. by appointment. SIZE: Medium. *STOCK: Furniture, mahogany and oak, 18th—19th C, £50—£1,000; watercolours and oil paintings, £50—£1,000; some shipping items.* PARK: Easy. TEL: Canterbury (0227) 750621; home — same. SER: Valuations; restorations (furniture and pictures); buys at auction (furniture). VAT: Stan/Spec.

Philip Faithfull Antiques
202 The Street. Open by appointment. *STOCK: Furniture, curios.* TEL: Canterbury (0227) 750395. SER: Restorations (furniture); French polishing. VAT: Stan/Spec.

Hansen Antiques
119 The Street. (S. Hansen.) Est. 1920. Resident. Always available. *STOCK: Small furniture.* TEL: Canterbury (0227) 751421.

BRASTED, Nr. Westerham
The Attic (Sevenoaks) Ltd.
The Village House. (R. and J. Brydon.) ABA. Resident. Est. 1953. Appointment advisable. *STOCK: Antiquarian books.* TEL: Westerham (0959) 63507.

David Barrington
The Antique Shop. Est. 1947. Open 9—6. SIZE: Medium. *STOCK: Furniture, 18th C.* LOC: A25. PARK: Easy. TEL: Westerham (0959) 62537. VAT: Stan/Spec.

Brasted Antiques
The Old Bakery. (Mrs. R.B. Rowlett.) Open 10—5.30. *STOCK: Furniture and bric-a-brac.* TEL: (0959) 64863.

Nigel Coleman Antiques   BADA
High St. Est. 1969. Open 9.30—5.30. SIZE: Medium. *STOCK: Barometers, £300—£5,000; tea caddies, £100—£500; bureaux, chests, tables — card, tea, work and sofa; secretaire bookcases, £500—£6,000, all 1700—1850.* LOC: A25. PARK: Own. TEL: Westerham (0959) 64042. SER: Restorations (barometers). VAT: Stan/Spec.

Ivy House Antiques
High St. (R. Throp and P. Welsh.) Open 10—6. SIZE: Medium. *STOCK: Furniture, porcelain, paintings, decorative items.* LOC: A25. PARK: Easy. TEL: Westerham (0959) 64581; home — same. VAT: Stan/Spec.

Keymer Son & Co. Ltd.
Swaylands Place, The Green. Est. 1977. Open 9.30—5.30, Sat. a.m. by appointment. SIZE: Small. *STOCK: Furniture, £100—£500; clocks, £200—£1,000; both 18th—19th C.* LOC: A25. PARK: Easy. TEL: Westerham (0959) 64203.

Mandey's Antiques
High St. (P. Poynter and J. Stimpson.) Est. 1957. Open 8.30—5.30, Sat. and Sun. by appointment. SIZE: Large. *STOCK: General furniture, 1600—1840.* PARK: Easy. TEL: Westerham (0959) 62408. VAT: Stan/Spec.

Old Hall (Sphinx Gallery)   LAPADA
The Blacksmiths Shop, High St. (L. Van Den Bussche.) Open 10—5.30, Sun. and other times by appointment. SIZE: Large. *STOCK: Early English and continental oak furniture, 17th—18th C; metalware, statues, delft pottery.* TEL: Westerham (0959) 63114. SER: Valuations.

Old Manor House Antiques
The Green, High St. Open daily. *STOCK: Clocks, watches and general antiques.* TEL: Westerham (0959) 62536.

Brasted continued

Southdown House Antique Galleries
High St. (R. and D. Thomas.) Est. 1978. Open 9.30—5.30. *STOCK: Furniture, porcelain, glass, metalware, 18th—19th C; oils and watercolours, 19th C.* TEL: Westerham (0959) 63522.

Dinah Stoodley
High St. (Mrs. D. Stoodley.) Est. 1965. Open 9—6, Sun. by appointment. SIZE: Medium. *STOCK: Oak and country furniture, 17th—19th C, pewter and metalware, pottery.* Not stocked: Victoriana, jewellery, silver. LOC: A25. PARK: Easy. TEL: Westerham (0959) 63616. VAT: Stan/Spec.

Tilings Antiques
High St. (H. Loveland, L. Matthews and P. Fawcett.) Est. 1974. Open 10—5.30. SIZE: Medium. *STOCK: Porcelain, bronze and glass, £20—£1,000; furniture, £100—£1,000; all 18th—19th C.* LOC: Village centre on A25. PARK: Easy. TEL: Westerham (0959) 64735. VAT: Stan/Spec.

The Village Gallery
High St. (Mrs. J. Key.) Open 9.30—5.30, Wed. 9.30—1. *STOCK: Pine furniture and general antiques.* TEL: Westerham (0959) 62503.

W.W. Warner (Antiques) Ltd.   BADA
The Green. (Mrs. C.U. Warner.) Est. 1957. Open 10—1 and 2—5. SIZE: Medium. *STOCK: English porcelain, 18th—19th C, £5—£1,000; English pottery, 18th to early 19th C, £10—£500; small mahogany furniture, prior to 1830, £30—£1,000.* Not stocked: Silver, Victoriana. LOC: A25. PARK: Easy. TEL: Westerham (0959) 63698. SER: Buys at London auctions. VAT: Spec.

The Weald Gallery
High St. (S.J. and N.V. Turley.) Est. 1972. Open 9.30—5.30. SIZE: Small. *STOCK: Watercolours, 1800—1940, £30—£5,000.* LOC: A25. PARK: Easy. TEL: Knockholt (0959) 32738; Sats. — Westerham (0959) 64041. SER: Valuations; restorations (watercolours, oil paintings and prints). VAT: Stan/Spec.

BROMLEY
See Greater London

BROADSTAIRS
Broadstairs Antiques
49 Belvedere Rd. (P. Edwards.) Est. 1980. CL: Wed. Open 10—5. *STOCK: General antiques.* TEL: Thanet (0843) 61965.

BROOKLAND   (067 94)
Nr. Romney Marsh
Brookland Antiques
(I. and R. Buchan.) Est. 1972. SIZE: Medium. *STOCK: Copper, brass.* LOC: On A259. TEL: 373.

CANTERBURY   (0227)
Antiques Odds & Ends
Thanet House, 92 Broad St. (J. Griffith.) Open 10—5.30. *STOCK: General antiques.* TEL: 67723.

Bell Harry Books
110 Northgate. (J. Hubbard.) Est. 1977. Open 10—5.30. *STOCK: Secondhand and out of print books.* TEL: 453481; home — 67934.

Canterbury Rastro
44a High St. (J. Coppage.) Open 10—5. *STOCK: General antiques.* TEL: 463537.

Canterbury Weekly Antique Market
Sidney Cooper Centre, St. Peter's St. Open Sat. 8—4.

Chaucer Bookshop
6 Beer Cart Lane. (R. Leach and D. Miles.) ABA and PBFA. Est. 1977. Open 10—5.15. SIZE: Medium. *STOCK: Books and prints, 18th—20th C, £5—£100; maps, 18th—19th C, £50—£250.* LOC: 5 minutes walk from cathedral, via Mercury Lane and St. Margaret's St. PARK: Castle St. TEL: 453912. SER: Valuations; restorations (book binding); buys at auction (books, maps and prints). FAIRS: PBFA, London. VAT: Stan.

Cloisters
26 Palace St. (A. De Jaeger.) Resident. Est. 1982. Open 9.30—5.30. SIZE: Small. *STOCK: Prints, especially topographical, birds, flowers and fashion, 19th C, £5—£25; maps and fine prints, 18th—19th C, £50—£150.* LOC: Opposite north gate of cathedral. PARK: Multistorey nearby. TEL: 462729. SER: Restorations; mounting and framing. VAT: Stan.

Coach House Antiques
Duck Lane, St. Radiguns, Northgate. Est. 1975. Open 10—1 and 2—5. SIZE: Large. *STOCK: General antiques, bygones, kitchenalia, small furniture.* PARK: Opposite. TEL: 463117.

Coins of Canterbury
82 Castle St. Est. 1969. Open 9—5.30. *STOCK: Coins, medals, prints, postcards.* TEL: 60518. VAT: Stan/Spec.

Conquest House Antiques
17 Palace St. (Mrs. C. Hill and D.A. Magee.) Open 9—6. *STOCK: General antiques.* TEL: 464587.

Canterbury continued

H.S. Greenfield and Son, Gunmakers (Est. 1805)

4/5 Upper Bridge St. (A.G. and T.S. Greenfield.) Est. 1805. CL: Thurs. p.m. *STOCK: English sporting guns, in pairs and singles; Continental sporting guns, firearms, swords, flintlock and percussion pistols.* TEL: 456959. SER: Valuations; restorations (antique firearms). VAT: Stan.

R. and J.L. Henley Antiques

37a Broad St. Open 9—6. *STOCK: Furniture, brass, copper, clocks.* TEL: 69055. VAT: Stan/Spec.

Hoodeners Antiques and Collectors Market

Red Cross Centre, Lower Chantry Lane. (A.W. Garratt.) Est. 1974. Open first and third Sat. monthly 9—4.30. SIZE: Medium. The dealers at this market are selling *18th—19th C porcelain, silver, jewellery, collectors' items, small furniture, weights, measures, scales, arms and armour, £1—£2,000.* LOC: City centre roundabout take A2 Dover Rd. 1st left at traffic lights, 400yds. from roundabout. PARK: Easy. TEL: Petham (022 770) 437. VAT: Stan/Spec.

Ivy Lane Antique Centre

Ivy Lane. (B. West and J. Cabral.) Est. 1984. Open 9—5.30. SIZE: Medium. There are 16 dealers at this centre selling *mainly Victorian and Edwardian smalls, £5—£300.* LOC: 1 minutes walk from city coach station, Longport. PARK: Nearby. TEL: 60378. FAIRS: Kent.

Juspine

108 Wincheap. (Mrs. C. Hilden.) Open 9—6. *STOCK: Pine.* TEL: 470482.

Leadenhall Gallery

12 Palace St. (A. Greenaway.) Open 9.30—5.30, Sun. 11—5. *STOCK: Prints and maps.* TEL: 457339.

Nan Leith's Brocanterbury

Errol House, 68 Stour St. *STOCK: Art deco, Victoriana, pressed glass, costume jewellery.* TEL: 454519.

Rachel Lloyd Antiques

2 The Borough, Northgate. Est. 1965. CL: Thurs. p.m. Open 10—5.30, but appointment advisable Sat. p.m. SIZE: Medium. *STOCK: Early oak and walnut, 17th—18th C; country Spanish and French furniture; iron work and carvings; mahogany, 18th—19th C.* TEL: 455254. SER: Valuations; restorations. VAT: Stan/Spec.

Canterbury continued

Northgate Antiques

37 Northgate. (M. Chilver.) Est. 1973. CL: Thurs. p.m. Open 9—6. SIZE: Medium. *STOCK: Georgian, Victorian country items, porcelain, silver, shipping goods.* LOC: A28 Margate Rd. at traffic lights. PARK: In side road. TEL: 464773. SER: Restorations (furniture, porcelain).

Parker-Williams   LAPADA

22 Palace St. (L. Parker and E. Williams.) CL: Sun. a.m. and Thurs. p.m. SIZE: Medium. *STOCK: Furniture 18th—19th C; porcelain, silver, bronzes, pictures, copper, brass, clocks.* TEL: 68341. VAT: Stan/Spec.

The Saracen's Lantern

9 The Borough. (W.J. Christophers.) Est. 1966. *STOCK: General antiques, silver, jewellery, clocks, watches, Victorian bottles, furniture, china, pot-lids, jars.* LOC: Near Cathedral opp. King's School. PARK: Municipal park at rear, by way of St. Radigun's St. TEL: 451968.

Staplegate Antiques

20 The Borough, Palace St. (Mrs. E. Botting.) Est. 1984. Open 9.30—5.30. SIZE: Medium. *STOCK: General antiques, furniture and porcelain, Victorian and Edwardian, £5—£1,000; silver, jewellery, objets d'art, kilims, books.* LOC: Between Mint Yard Gate and King's School Shop. PARK: Nearby. TEL: 463009; home — (022 786) 224.

CHARING   (023 371)

Palace Gallery Antiques

Market Pl. (Mrs. S. Tucker.) Est. 1984. CL: Wed. and Thurs. Open 10—1 and 2—5, Sun. and Mon. by appointment. SIZE: Small. *STOCK: Decorative furniture, porcelain, metalware, textiles and silver, mainly 18th—19th C; collectors' items, period clothes and accessories, all £5—£2,000.* LOC: Take turning to church off High St. PARK: Easy. TEL: 2592; home — same. SER: Valuations; restorations; commissions undertaken.

Peckwater Pine and Antiques

17 High St. (F.H. and S.M. Tucker.) Est. 1983. CL: Wed. and Thurs. Open 10—5, Sun. by appointment. SIZE: Medium. *STOCK: Pine and country furniture, 18th—19th C, £5—£1,000; kitchenalia, cast-iron and enamel wares, Victorian.* LOC: Next to Lloyds Bank. PARK: Easy. TEL: 2592; home — same. SER: Valuations; restorations; buys at auction. FAIRS: Ardingly. VAT: Stan/Spec.

CHATHAM

John Chawner
44 Chatham Hill. Est. 1971. Open 9.30—12.30 and 1.30—5.30 or by appointment. STOCK: Clocks and inlaid furniture. LOC: A2. PARK: Easy. TEL: Medway (0634) 30874 or Medway (0634) 811147. SER: Restorations (clocks).

Collectors' Corner Antiques
139 New Rd. (P. Rose.) Open 10—5.30. SIZE: Large. STOCK: General antiques including stripped furniture, jewellery, fairings, Staffordshire figures, glass, pictures, kitchenalia, coins, medals, banknotes, pot-lids, advertising items, badges, bottles, militaria. TEL: Medway (0634) 407795.

CHIDDINGSTONE, Nr. Edenbridge

Barbara Lane Antiques
Tudor Cottage. (Mrs. E.B. Avery.) Est. 1967. Open 10—6. STOCK: General antiques, furniture, silver and plate, porcelain. LOC: Behind Castle Inn. PARK: Easy. TEL: Penshurst (0892) 870577.

CHILHAM, Nr. Canterbury

Chilham Antiques Ltd.
The Square. (Mrs. J. Green.) Est. 1965. Open 9—6, Sun. 12—1 and 3—5. SIZE: Large. STOCK: Oil paintings, English and Continental, 18th—19th C; period furniture, glass, silver, porcelain, objets d'art. Not stocked: Firearms. LOC: Follow A20 from London via Maidstone by-pass. PARK: Easy. TEL: Canterbury (0227) 730250/730565. SER: Restorations (cleaning and framing of pictures). VAT: Stan/Spec.

Peacock Antiques
The Square. (S. Blacklocks.) Open 9.30—6, Sat. 10—6, Sun. 2—6. SIZE: Medium. STOCK: Furniture, 17th—19th C, £200—£4,000; silver, copper and brass, 18th—19th C, £25—£5,000; china, glass, objets d'art, 19th C, £25—£1,000. LOC: ½ mile off Canterbury to Ashford road and 200yds. off Canterbury to Maidstone road. PARK: Easy. TEL: Canterbury (0227) 730219. VAT: Stan/Spec.

CHISLEHURST
See Greater London

CRANBROOK   (0580)

Bridge House Antiques & Jewellery
2 Bridge Bldgs. (Mr. and Mrs. H. Canham.) CL: Wed. Open 9.30—5.30. STOCK: General antiques. TEL: 712573.

Cranbrook continued

Findings Antiques
High St. (M.B. Fairbarns.) CL: Wed. p.m. Open 9.30—5.30. SIZE: Large. STOCK: General antiques, bygones; furniture, porcelain, glass, silver, Victorian jewellery. TEL: 712372. VAT: Stan/Spec.

F.B. Monge
Hundred House. Est. 1971. Open by appointment. STOCK: Period oak. TEL: 712011.

The Old Bakery Antiques LAPADA
The Old Bakery, St. David's Bridge. (Mr. and Mrs. D.R. Bryan.) Est. 1971. Open 9—5.30, Wed. 9—1 and by appointment. SIZE: Medium. STOCK: Period oak and country furniture, some copper and brass. Not stocked: Silver, shipping goods. LOC: Make for Tan Yard car park — off road towards Windmill. PARK: Adjacent. TEL: 713103. SER: Valuations; restorations. VAT: Stan/Spec.

Swan Antiques
Stone St. (R.S. White, M. Fielder.) Resident. Est. 1977. Open 10—1 and 2—5.15, Wed. and Sun. and other times by appointment. SIZE: Medium. STOCK: English country furniture, mainly small oak, elm and pine, £15—£2,000; English pottery, treen, pictures and collectables; all pre-1890, decorative items, painted furniture. LOC: Opposite Barclays Bank. PARK: Nearby. TEL: 712720. SER: Valuations; interiors. FAIRS: Ardingly. VAT: Spec.

CRAYFORD
See Greater London

DEAL   (0304)

Country Style
125 High St. (M. and K. Short.) Est. 1976. CL: Thurs. Open 10—12 and 2—4, Sat. 9—5, Sun. by appointment. SIZE: Small. STOCK: Stripped pine furniture, £30—£350; linen, £5—£50. PARK: Easy and Union Rd. TEL: 366536; home — same. SER: Valuations; restorations.

The Print Room
95 Beach St. (J. Wright.) Est. 1981. CL: Thurs. Open 10.30—1 and 3—5.30 or by appointment. SIZE: Medium. STOCK: Prints and maps. LOC: On seafront, opposite Royal Hotel. PARK: Nearby. TEL: 368904; home — 364515. SER: Valuations; colouring; cleaning; framing; searches undertaken.

Quill Antiques
12 Alfred Sq. (E. Liley and A.R. Young.) Open by appointment. STOCK: General antiques, bric-a-brac. TEL: 372184.

Deal continued

Serendipity
168/170 High St. (M. and K. Short.) Est. 1976. CL: Wed. and Thurs. Open 10—12 and 2—4, Sat. 9—5, Sun. by appointment. SIZE: Small. *STOCK: Oil paintings and watercolours, 1840—1900, £25—£500; Staffordshire figures, 1780—1900, £30—£250.* PARK: Easy and Union Rd. TEL: 366536; home — same. SER: Valuations; restorations.

Trade Winds
123 High St. (W. Martin.) Open 9.30—6. *STOCK: Soft furniture.* TEL: 374483.

Wade Galleries
Globe House, 191 Beach St. (S. Harris and P.J. Pierce.) Est. 1965. Open 10—4 by appointment. *STOCK: Decorators' items, leatherbound books.* TEL: 362856.

DODDINGTON (079 586)
Nr. Sittingbourne

Periwinkle Press
Chequers Hill. (E.R., A., A.L. and J.R. Swain.) Resident. Est. 1967. SIZE: Small. *STOCK: Prints, 18th—19th C, £20—£100; items suitable for framing, prints, watercolours, plaques; books, some secondhand.* LOC: A20. PARK: Easy. TEL: 246. SER: Restorations (prints and oils); framing. FAIRS: Some local. VAT: Stan.

DOVER (0304)

G. Baker Antiques
196 London Rd. Est. 1980. Open 9.30—5.30. *STOCK: General antiques.* TEL: 214003.

Bonnies
18 Bartholomew St. (P. and R. Janes.) Est. 1985. Open 9—5. *STOCK: General antiques.* TEL: 204206. SER: Upholstery; restorations.

Dover continued

Paul Marklew (Antique Jewellers)
19a High St. Open 9.30—5. *STOCK: Jewellery, silver and porcelain; gold bullion.* TEL: 203721. VAT: Stan.

W.J. Morrill Ltd. *Trade Only*
437 Folkestone Rd. (D. Barnes.) Est. 1910. Open by appointment. *STOCK: Oil paintings, 18th—20th C, £50—£1,000.* Not stocked: Watercolours. LOC: 1½ miles from town centre on main Folkestone road. PARK: Easy. TEL: 201989; home — same. SER: Restorations (paintings); relining and framing. VAT: Stan/Spec.

Parks of Dover
4 Park Place. (R. Napier.) Est. 1979. Open 10—4, Tues., Wed. and Sun. by appointment. SIZE: Small. *STOCK: Art nouveau, art deco and Victorian items, £5—£500.* LOC: Town centre, opposite police station. PARK: Easy. TEL: 215389; home — 822730. SER: Valuations. FAIRS: Ardingly, Great Danes, Dover and Sandwich. VAT: Stan.

Stuff
87 London Rd. (R. Bowle.) Est. 1982. CL: Wed. Open 9.30—5.30. *STOCK: General antiques.* TEL: 215405.

EAST PECKHAM (0622)
Nr Tonbridge

Desmond and Amanda North
LAPADA
The Orchard, Hale St. Est. 1971. Open daily, appointment advisable. SIZE: Medium. *STOCK: Oriental rugs, runners, carpets and cushions, 1800—1939, £50—£2,500.* LOC: On B2015, 150yds south of junction with B2016. PARK: Easy. TEL: 871353; home — same. SER: Valuations; restorations (reweaving, re-edging, patching, cleaning).

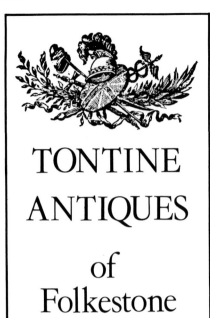

TONTINE
ANTIQUES
of
Folkestone

Telephone: 0303 53077

EASTRY

The Plough
High St. (D.A. Magee.) *STOCK: Stripped pine.* TEL: Deal (0304) 617418.

EDENBRIDGE (0732)

Chevertons of Edenbridge Ltd.
LAPADA
67 and 69 High St. (D. Adam.) CL: Sat. Open 9—5.30. SIZE: Large. *STOCK: Furniture, 17th—19th C, £100—£15,000.* Not stocked: Silver, oil paintings, porcelain. LOC: From Westerham, on B2026 to Edenbridge. PARK: Easy. TEL: 863196 and 863358. VAT: Stan/Spec.

FARNBOROUGH
See Greater London

FARNINGHAM (0322)

P.T. Beasley
Forge Yard, High St. (P.T. and R. Beasley.) Est. 1964. CL: Tues. *STOCK: English furniture, some pewter, brass, Delft, woodcarvings.* LOC: Near the Pied Bull Hotel. TEL: 862453.

FAVERSHAM (0795)

Gunpowder House Antiques
78 Lower West St. (E. Platt.) Est. 1967. Open 9—6, Sun. by appointment. *STOCK: Late 18th—19th C general antiques, £10—£1,000.* LOC: From Ospringe, turn left at Alms Houses, then right into West St. PARK: Opposite. TEL: 534208.

Rebecca's Antiques and Furnishings
The Hollies, Eastling. Open Mon. to Sat. *STOCK: Chairs, sofas, lamps, decorators' items.* TEL: 89392. SER: Restorations; upholstery; caning.

Squires Antiques
3 Jacob Yard, Preston St. (A. Squires.) Est. 1985. Open 10—5. *STOCK: General antiques especially agricultural items.* TEL: 531503.

FOLKESTONE (0303)

Richard Amos
37 Cheriton High St. Open 9.30—12 and 2—5, Wed. 9.30—12. *STOCK: General antiques.* TEL: 75449.

M.P. Glasspole Fine Art
9 Rendezvous St. Est. 1972. Open 10—1 and 2.15—5. SIZE: Medium. *STOCK: Oil paintings and watercolours, pre-1920, £80—£600; gold and silver, £6—£500; shipping furniture, bric-a-brac, £2—£300.* LOC: Near harbour. PARK: Easy. TEL: 45460; home — 43112. SER: Valuations; buys at auction (oils, watercolours, jewellery). VAT: Stan/Spec.

Alan Lord Antiques
71 Tontine St. (A.G. and J.A. Lord.) Est. 1956. CL: Wed. and Sat. p.m. Open 9—1 and 2—4.30. *STOCK: General antiques, £1—£2,000.* LOC: Road up from harbour. PARK: Easy. TEL: 53674. VAT: Stan/Spec.

G. and D.I. Marrin and Sons
149 Sandgate Rd. ABA. Est. 1949. Open 9.30—5.30. SIZE: Large. *STOCK: Maps, early engravings, topographical and sporting prints, paintings, drawings, books, engravings.* TEL: 53016. SER: Restorations; framing. VAT: Stan.

Tontine Antiques Ltd.
75—81 Tontine St. (W. Patrick.) Est. 1968. Open 9—5.30. SIZE: Large. *STOCK: General antiques, pictures, decorative items.* LOC: Shop on left at end of main shopping street running north from harbour. TEL: 53077; home — 893157. VAT: Stan/Spec.

CHEVERTONS

OF EDENBRIDGE LTD

ONE OF THE LARGEST AND MOST VARIED STOCKS OF FURNITURE IN THE SOUTH OF ENGLAND

One hour's drive from London

Car park on premises

Open Monday — Friday 9 a.m. — 5.30 p.m.

TAYLOUR HOUSE, HIGH STREET, EDENBRIDGE, KENT
Telephone (0732) 863196 and 863358

Folkestone continued

Traditional Furniture
248 Seabrook Rd., Seabrook. (M. Hannant). Est. 1977. Open daily. SIZE: Large. *STOCK: Pine, 19th C, £50—£500.* LOC: 1½ miles from end of M20 on A259. PARK: Easy. TEL: 39931; home — 39304. SER: Restorations (pine stripping and repair), buys at auction (pine). VAT: Stan.

Winterdown Books
P.O. Box 106. (G.G. Meynell.) Est. 1979. *STOCK: Medical and scientific books, 18th C.* TEL: Hawkinge (030 389) 3110. SER: Catalogue available.

FOUR ELMS (073 270)
Harvesters Barn
Four Elms Rd. (C. Sanson.) Open 9.30—5, Sat. 9—1. *STOCK: Pine.* TEL: 278.

GILLINGHAM
Coxsmith U.K. LAPADA
Trade Only
96a Shakespeare Rd. (C.D. Cox.) Open 9—5. *STOCK: Shipping goods.* PARK: Easy. TEL: Medway (0634) 575983. SER: Shipping.

Dickens Antiques
42 Sturdee Ave. (G. Peek.) Est. 1979. CL: Wed. Open 9—5, Sat. 9—12. *STOCK: Furniture, jewellery.* TEL: (0634) 50950.

T.H. and J. Mason
46 Jeffery St. Est. 1948. CL: Wed. Open 9—5. *STOCK: China, glass, jewellery, small furniture, militaria, medals, bric-a-brac.* TEL: Medway (0634) 52914.

GOUDHURST (0580)
Old Saddlers Antiques
Church Rd. (S. Curd.) Est. 1969. CL: Wed. Open 9.30—12.30 and 2.30—5.30. SIZE: Small. *STOCK: 18th—19th C, small furniture; porcelain, small silver items, 1750—1870; 19th C pictures, prints, copper, horse brasses, jewellery.* Not stocked: Large furniture. LOC: Opposite Church. PARK: Outside. TEL: 211458. VAT: Spec.

Tattlebury Gallery
Tattlebury Corner, Church Rd. (N. and A. Crowhurst.) Est. 1967. CL: Mon. Open 9.30—1 and 2—5.30, Sat. 9.30—5.30, Sun. by appointment. SIZE: Small. *STOCK: Victorian oil paintings and watercolours, £100—£1,500.* LOC: Approx. 200yds. out of Goudhurst on A262 towards Sissinghurst. PARK: Easy. TEL: 211771; home — same; SER: Valuations; restorations (paintings and watercolours); framing; buys at auction (pictures).

GRAVESEND (0474)
Greg Martin Antiques
116 Wrotham Rd. Est. 1982. CL: Wed. Open 11—6. *STOCK: General antiques.* TEL: 66067.

John Sharp Antiques
Under the Sign of the Blackamoor, 2 Saddington St. Est. 1966. Open 10—12.30 and 2—5, Wed. 10—1. SIZE: Medium. *STOCK: Furniture, mainly mahogany, 18th—19th C, to £500; silver, 18th—20th C, £15—£400; pottery and porcelain, £5—£200.* LOC: Town centre, off Parrock St. PARK: Nearby. TEL: 533232; home — 326764. SER: Valuations; buys at auction.

HADLOW, Nr. Tonbridge (0732)
The Pedlar's Pack (Hadlow)
LAPADA
The Square. (Mrs. N. Joy.) Est. 1976. CL: Sun. except by appointment. Open 10—5.30 Mon. and Wed. 10—1. SIZE: Medium. *STOCK: Country furniture, £50—£400; brass, copper, glass and china, £25—£100; all 18th—19th C; jewellery, objets d'art, small interesting items, 19th—20th C, £25—£300.* LOC: On Tonbridge to Maidstone Rd. PARK: Easy. TEL: 851296; home — same. VAT: Stan/Spec.

HARTLEY, Nr. Dartford
Hartley Antiques
Yew Cottage, Hartley Green. (Mrs. E.E. Lievesley.) Est. 1968. CL: Mon. and Wed. Open 9.30—5. SIZE: Small. *STOCK: Silver plate, jewellery, copper, brass, china, glass, £1—£100.* Not stocked: Furniture. LOC: ¾ mile from Longfield on B260. Between A2 and A20. PARK: Easy. TEL: Longfield (04747) 2330.

HAWKHURST (058 05)
Septimus Quayles Emporium
Ockley Rd. (Mrs. M.R. Brown.) Est. 1971. Open 9.30—1 and 2.15—5, Wed. 9.30—1. Sat. 10—1 and 2.15—4. *STOCK: General, small antiques.* TEL: 2222.

HERNE BAY (0227)
B. and J. Antiques (Curio Corner)
22 Charles St. (W. Philby.) Est. 1962. CL: Thurs. Open 9.30—1 and 2—4. SIZE: Medium. *STOCK: Shipping furniture, collectors' items, £5—£500.* PARK: Nearby. TEL: 363475; home — 366653. SER: Valuations. VAT: Stan.

Wheellock Arms and Armour
54—56 Mortimer St. (P. and I. Law.) Open 9—4.30, Thurs. 9—1. *STOCK: Arms, armour, army cap badges, militaria, guns and shooting accessories, army surplus, furniture, bric-a-brac, china.* PARK: Easy. TEL: 373278; home — 369112.

HIGH HALDEN (023 385)
The White House Antiques
Ashford Rd. (P. Newman.) CL: Wed. Open 10—4. STOCK: Pine. TEL: 562.

HOLLINGBOURNE (062 780)
The Old Forge
Pilgrims Way. (I. Newbury.) Est. 1951. CL: Thurs. Open 10.30—6, Sun., and other times by appointment. SIZE: Medium. STOCK: Furniture, 17th—18th C, £100—£3,000; Prattware, pot-lids, Staffordshire figures, £40—£400; jewellery, £20—£400; copper, pewter, glass, £20—£100; general antiques. Not stocked: Mahogany, Victoriana, pictures. LOC: From London on A20 to Maidstone by-pass. Then take first turning left after motorway ends. PARK: Easy. TEL: 360.

HYTHE (0303)
The Den of Antiquity
35 Dymchurch Rd. (R.A. Chapman.) Est. 1962. CL: Wed. and Thurs. Open 9—5 but any time by appointment. SIZE: Medium. STOCK: Jewellery, silver, pottery, porcelain, glass, instruments, objets de vertu and d'art, rare and limited pieces of Royal Doulton. LOC: A259, main coast road from Folkestone to Hastings. PARK: Easy. TEL: 67162.

The Front Parlour
152a Seabrook Rd., Seabrook. (Mrs. A.G. Douglass.) Est. 1967. Open 10—5. SIZE: Small. STOCK: Antique and collectors' items, carnival glass, £5—£500. PARK: Easy.

Hera Fine Art
252 Seabrook Rd., Seabrook. (J. and C. Hutchison.) Est. 1978. Open 10—6. STOCK: Oil paintings and frames, 18th and 19th C, £50—£1,000. PARK: Easy. TEL: 39046. SER: Restorations (paintings and frames).

Homewood Antiques
7 Dymchurch Rd. (D.C. and R.A. Homewood.) Est. 1984. Open 9—5.30, Sat. 10—4.30. STOCK: General antiques. TEL: 65229.

Hythe Antique Centre
High St. (P. Leath-Butler and H. Van Kuijk.) Est. 1973. Open 10—5.30. SIZE: Large. STOCK: General furniture, china, porcelain, paintings, prints, coins, medals, period costume, linen and lace. LOC: 50yds. from A259 at 1st turning to Hythe town centre. PARK: Easy. TEL: 69643.

Hythe continued
Hythe Galleries
125 High St. (D. Arthy and A. Pratt.) Est. 1974. CL: Wed. p.m. Open 10—5.30. SIZE: Medium. STOCK: Victorian jewellery, copper, brass, porcelain, furniture, art nouveau and art deco, £5—£500; watercolours and oil paintings, Victorian, £30—£500; antiquarian prints, Kent topographical, maps, sporting and natural history, pre-1880, £5—£250. PARK: 200yds. TEL: 69339; home — Canterbury (0227) 720459. SER: Restorations (paintings, especially watercolours, furniture, china, jewellery). FAIRS: Felbridge — East Grinstead, Greenways — West Malling, Chilham. VAT: Stan/Spec.

Malthouse Arcade
High St. (Mr. and Mrs. R.M. Maxtone Graham.) Est. 1974. Open Fri. and Sat. 10—6. SIZE: Large. There are 37 stalls at this market selling a wide selection of antiques and collectors' items. LOC: West end of High St. PARK: 50yds. TEL: 60103; home — Sandwich (0304) 613270.

Radio Vintage
250 Seabrook Rd., Seabrook. (L. Riches.) Open 9.30—6, Sun. by appointment. STOCK: Radios, 1920—1950. TEL: 30693.

Samovar Antiques
158 High St. (Mrs. F. Clutterbuck.) Open 9—5, Wed. 9—1. STOCK: Clocks, Oriental rugs. TEL: 64239.

KENNINGTON, Nr. Ashford
Peter Knight
The Mill House. Est. 1968. Open daily but appointment advisable. STOCK: General antiques. LOC: On A28, near The Golden Ball public house. TEL: (0233) 23009. VAT: Stan/Spec.

LAMBERHURST (0892)
The China Locker
(G. Wilson.) Open by appointment only. SIZE: Small. STOCK: Prints, etchings and watercolours, 18th—19th C; some pottery and porcelain, all £5—£40. TEL: 890555. FAIRS: Monthly — Calverley Hotel, Tunbridge Wells; Greenways Hotel A20, West Malling; Hilden Manor, Tonbridge.

LEIGH, Nr. Tonbridge
Anthony Woodburn   BADA LAPADA
Orchard House, High St. Est. 1975. Open daily, Sun. by appointment. SIZE: Medium. STOCK: Clocks and barometers, 17th—18th C, from £500. LOC: Off A21. PARK: Easy. TEL: Hildenborough (0732) 832258. SER: Valuations; buys at auction (clocks). VAT: Spec.

LONGFIELD (047 47)
Nr. Dartford
Longfield Antiques
11 Station Rd. (Mrs. P. Drury.) Est. 1977. CL: Thurs. Open 9.30—5. *STOCK: Dolls, jewellery, general antiques.* TEL: 5076.

LOWER HALSTOW
Nr. Sittingbourne
Halstow Antiques
Green Farm House. (I.P. Harvey.) Est. 1972. CL: Tues. Open 10—8. SIZE: Small. *STOCK: Oak furniture, 16th—18th C, £100—£1,000; country furniture, £50—£500; copper, silver, brass.* LOC: One mile north of A2 between Rainham and Newington by village green. PARK: Easy. TEL: Newington (0795) 842016.

MAIDSTONE (0622)
Charles International Antiques LAPADA
3 Market St. (Mr. and Mrs. C. Bremner.) Est. 1968. Open 10—5. *STOCK: Victorian, Edwardian and shipping goods.* TEL: 682882. SER: Valuations.

Crescent Antiques
25 Postley Rd. (A.J. Page.) CL: Wed. Open 9—5.30, Sun. 9—2. *STOCK: Victorian fireplaces, bedsteads, gas lighting.* TEL: 682464.

Leadenhall Gallery
6 Puddings Lane. (A. Greenaway.) Open 10—4.30. *STOCK: Old maps and prints.* TEL: 683707

Memory Lane
52 Sandling Rd. (Mrs. J. Marriner.) Open Mon., Tues. and Fri. 11—4, other times by appointment. *STOCK: Bric-a-brac, china and glass.* TEL: 685513.

Salmagundi
63 Charlton St. (B.C. Shillingford.) Est. 1968. Open 9—5.30. SIZE: Small. *STOCK: Victoriana, bric-a-brac, collectables, £5—£50.* Not stocked: Coins, stamps. LOC: From Maidstone, 1 mile up Tonbridge Rd., turn left at Milton St., Charlton St. is second turning on left. PARK: Easy. TEL: 26859; home — same. SER: Valuations.

Sutton Valence Antiques LAPADA
Trade Only
Unit 4, Haslemere, Parkwood. (T. and N. Mullarkey and M. Marles.) Open 9—5.30. SIZE: Large. *STOCK: Shipping furniture.* PARK: Easy. TEL: 675332/843333/843499.

MARGATE
Furniture Mart
Grotto Hill. (R.G. Scott.) Est. 1971. CL: Wed. SIZE: Large. *STOCK: General antiques £1—£1,500; shipping goods.* LOC: Corner of Bath Place and Grotto Hill. TEL: Thanet (0843) 220653. SER: Restorations; stripping; leathering. VAT: Stan.

M. Klein
7 Market Place. Est. 1946. *STOCK: Furniture, bric-a-brac, silver, objets d'art, 18th—19th C.* TEL: Thanet (0843) 292637. SER: Buys at auction. VAT: Stan/Spec.

MINSTER (Thanet), Nr. Ramsgate
Michael Lamb Antiques
The White Horse, 2 Church St. Est. 1967. CL: Sat. Open 9.30—1 and 2—5.30, or by appointment. SIZE: Small with store. *STOCK: General antiques, £5—£500.* LOC: Short distance from M2—A299 roundabout at Thanet Way. PARK: Easy. TEL: Thanet (0843) 821666. SER: Valuations; restorations (furniture). VAT: Stan/Spec.

NEW ROMNEY (0679)
East Kent Antiques LAPADA
Corner of West St. and High St. (R. Massingham.) Est. 1967. *STOCK: 18th and early 19th C English furniture, paintings and porcelain.* TEL: 62630. SER: Valuations.

Meridian Antiques
20—22 High St. (N. Wilson.) Est. 1956. CL: Wed. Open 9.30—5.30. *STOCK: General antiques, small furniture; jewellery, £5—£250; glass, £10—£30; all 1800—1950; porcelain, small Oriental.* Not stocked: Reproductions. PARK: Easy. TEL: 63675. SER: Valuations.

NONINGTON (0304)
Nr. Dover
Southdown House Antiques
(D. and V. Mowatt.) Est. 1977. Open 9—6, Tues. 9—1; Wed. and Sun. by appointment. SIZE: Small. *STOCK: Furniture, £30—£600; china, £5—£100; both 19th C; bric-a-brac, 19th to early 20th C, £5—£30.* PARK: Easy. TEL: 840987. SER: Restorations (general and re-upholstery).

ORPINGTON
See Greater London

OTFORD (095 92)
Darenth Bookshop
8 High St. Est. 1979. CL: Wed. p.m. Open 9—5.30. *STOCK: Secondhand and antiquarian books; prints, maps and watercolours.* TEL: 2430.

Otford continued

Hofmann and Freeman Ltd.
8 High St. Est. 1966. Open by appointment. *STOCK: Antiquarian books.* TEL: 2926.

PEMBURY (089 282)
Nr. Tunbridge Wells
The Old House
30 Hastings Rd. (G.R. Wimsett.) Est. 1946. CL: Sat. except by appointment. Open 9—6. SIZE: Medium. *STOCK: General antiques; furniture, early oak.* Not stocked: Coins, stamps, guns. LOC: A21, in centre of village, 5 miles south of Tonbridge. PARK: Own. TEL: 2807; home — same. SER: Valuations. VAT: Stan/Spec.

PENSHURST (0892)
Bridge House Antiques   LAPADA
Bridge House. (R. Binning.) Est. 1966. *STOCK: Early country oak and elm furniture.* TEL: 870209. SER: Shipping. VAT: Stan/Spec.

RAINHAM
Rainham Antiques
295 High St. (M.G. Hamlyn and A.C. Walker.) Est. 1954. Open 10—5.30. SIZE: Large. *STOCK: Furniture, £10—£3,000; china, silver, metal, general antiques, jewellery, £1—£2,000, all 18th—19th C.* LOC: ¼ mile past Rainham Church on A2. PARK: Easy. TEL: Medway (0634) 31037. VAT: Stan.

RAMSGATE
Ash House
18 Hereson Rd. (P. Wimsett.) Est. 1957. Open Fri. and Sat. 11—5, trade by appointment. *STOCK: Stripped pine, general antiques.* TEL: Thanet (0843) 595480. VAT: Stan.

Rod Hoyle & Son Antiques
Unit 24, Laundry Rd., Minster. CL: Sat. Open 9.30—5.30. *STOCK: Furniture.* TEL: Thanet (0843) 822334.

Patricia Antiques   LAPADA
Mainly Trade
2 Grange Rd. (J. Pratt.) Est. 1960. CL: Sat. and Thurs. Open 10—4. *STOCK: Period furniture and some shipping goods.* TEL: Thanet (0843) 591222. VAT: Spec.

Ramsgate Antiques
121 Kings Rd. (R. Dorosti.) Open 10—2. *STOCK: General antiques, Persian carpets.* TEL: Thanet (0843) 594901; home — Thanet (0843) 580376.

Les Sackett Antiques
75 Hereson Rd. Open 9—6. *STOCK: General antiques.* TEL: Thanet (0843) 596161.

RIVERHEAD
Mandarin Gallery
32 London Rd. (Mrs. M-C. Liu.) Est. 1984. CL: Wed. Open 9.30—1 and 2—5. SIZE: Small. *STOCK: Chinese blackwood and rosewood furniture, 18th—19th C, £200—£2,000; Oriental porcelain, £15—£1,000; Oriental paintings on silk and paper, £10—£500; both 19th—20th C.* Not stocked: Non-Oriental items. LOC: A21. PARK: Easy. TEL: Sevenoaks (0732) 457399; home — same. SER: Valuations; restorations (Chinese furniture).

ROCHESTER
Castle Antiques
88 High St. (S. and A. Smith.) Est. 1975. CL: Sun. except by appointment. Open 9—5.30. *STOCK: English furniture, porcelain, pictures, general antiques.* LOC: Main London Rd., close to A2/M2. PARK: Easy. TEL: Medway (0634) 409148; home — 576565. VAT: Stan/Spec.

Cottage Style Antiques
24 Bill Street Rd. (W. Miskimmin.) CL: Wed. Open 9.30—5.30. *STOCK: General antiques.* TEL: Medway (0634) 717623.

Francis Iles
Rutland House, La Providence, High St. (The Family Iles.) Est. 1960. Open 9.30—5.30, Wed. 9.30—1. SIZE: Large. *STOCK: Watercolours and oils, mainly 20th C, £50—£1,000.* LOC: Off central High St. PARK: 40yds. TEL: Medway (0634) 43081/2. SER: Restorations (cleaning and relining); framing. VAT: Stan/Spec.

Langley Galleries
153 High St. (K.J. Cook.) Est. 1978. Open 9—5.30. *STOCK: Watercolours, oils, 19th—20th C.* TEL: Medway (0634) 811802. SER: Restorations and cleaning (watercolours and oils), framing.

Northgate Antiques
48 High St. (P.C. Hanks.) Est. 1980. Open 10.30—3.30. SIZE: Small. *STOCK: Small items, £1—£100; clocks, £50—£1,000; porcelain and pottery, £1—£250; shipping goods; all 18th C to 1920.* LOC: A2 near Rochester Bridge. PARK: Easy. TEL: Medway (0634) 812179; home — Medway (0634) 65428. SER: Valuations; buys at auction (porcelain and furniture). VAT: Stan.

Rochester Antiques and Flea Market
Corporation St. (Antique Forum Ltd.) Open Sat. 9—2. 100 stalls. TEL: (01) 263 4045. PARK: Easy.

Rochester continued

The Victory
43 High St. (L. Burford and M. Petrie.) Open 10—5. *STOCK: General antiques.* TEL: Medway (0634) 43750.

World of Books
96 High St. Est. 1974. Open 10—6. *STOCK: Secondhand and antiquarian books.*

ROLVENDEN
Nr. Cranbrook

Falstaff Antiques
63—67 High St. (C.M. Booth.) Est. 1964. CL: Sun., and Wed. p.m. except by appointment. Open 9—6. SIZE: Medium. *STOCK: English furniture, £5—£700; china, metal, glass, silver, £1—£200; all periods.* Not stocked: Paintings. LOC: On A28, 3 miles from Tenterden, 1st shop on left in village. PARK: Easy. TEL: Cranbrook (0580) 241234. SER: Valuations; buys at auction. FAIRS: Tenterden. VAT: Stan/Spec.

ST. MARGARET'S BAY, Nr. Dover

Impressions and Alexandra's Antiques
1-3 The Droveway. (J. Cox-Freeman.) Est. 1979. Open 10—1 and 2.15—4.30, Wed. and Sat. p.m. by appointment only. SIZE: Small. *STOCK: Paintings by Victorian and local artists; furniture, porcelain and jewellery.* LOC: Between Dover and Deal at top of hill. PARK: Easy. TEL: Dover (0304) 853102; home — Dover (0304) 852682.

SANDGATE, Nr. Folkestone

Antiques Etcetera
93 High St. (H. and M.F. Brown.) Est. 1964. Open 11—1 and 2—5.30, Sun. 11—1. SIZE: Small. *STOCK: Furniture, £5—£100; bric-a-brac and curios, £5—£25; all late 19th C. to early 20th C; general antiques, 19th C, £30—£150.* LOC: A259. PARK: Easy. TEL: Folkestone (0303) 39389; home — Folkestone (0303) 52683.

Antiquest
21 High St. (C.M. Amos.) Est. 1964. Open 10—5.30. SIZE: Medium. *STOCK: Furniture, prints, paintings, general antiques.* LOC: Main road, between Hythe and Folkestone. PARK: Easy. TEL: Folkestone (0303) 39300.

Beaubush House Antiques LAPADA
95 High St. (J. and F. Winikus.) Open 9.30—5.30. SIZE: Medium. *STOCK: English and Continental porcelain and pottery, 18th—19th C, £50—£2,000; small furniture, £400—£3,000; jewellery, £100—£2,000.* LOC: Main street. PARK: Opposite.TEL: Folkestone (0303) 39099; home — same. SER: Valuations.

Sandgate continued

Mary Brooker Antiques
39 High St. (Mrs. M. Brooker.) Est. 1960. CL: Wed. Open 10—5.30. SIZE: Small. *STOCK: Dolls, toys, 18th—19th C, £5—£500; Japanese items, 17th —19th C, £20—£500; jewellery, 18th—20th C, £5—£500; nurses' buckles, silver, 18th—20th C; early brass, china, collectors items.* Not stocked: Large furniture. PARK: Easy. TEL: Folkestone (0303) 39207; home — same.

The Castle
Castle Rd. Est. 1976. *STOCK: Oils, water-colours, prints and engravings.* TEL: Folkestone (0303) 39465.

Derek J. Cheney Antiques
Grafton Cottage, The Esplanade. Est. 1979. Open by appointment. SIZE: Medium. *STOCK: Furniture, 17th—19th C; longcase clocks.* LOC: A259. PARK: Easy. TEL: Folkestone (0303) 39005. VAT: Stan/Spec.

Clark and Bell Antiques
88a High St. TEL: Folkestone (0303) 39325.

County Antiques
17 High St. (B. Nilson.) Open 9.30—5. *STOCK: General antiques.* TEL: Folkestone (0303) 30291.

Michael File Antiques
13-15 High St. Est. 1974. *STOCK: Furniture, 18th—19th C; general antiques.* TEL: Folkestone (0303) 39574. VAT: Spec.

Michael Fitch Antiques   LAPADA
99 High St. Open 10—6, Sun. by appointment. *STOCK: Georgian, Victorian and Edwardian furniture.* TEL: Folkestone (0303) 39600; evenings — Folkestone (0303) 30839.

Freeman and Lloyd Antiques
LAPADA
44 High St. (K. Freeman and M.R. Lloyd.) Est. 1968. Open 9.30—5.30. SIZE: Medium. *STOCK: English furniture, Georgian and Regency clocks; paintings and period items.* LOC: On main coast road between Hythe and Folkestone (A259). PARK: Easy. TEL: Folkestone (0303) 38986 (any time). SER: Valuations. VAT: Stan/Spec.

Howard Godfrey Antiques   BADA
56—60 High St. Est. 1965. Open 10—5.30. *STOCK: Paintings, furniture, period silver, clocks, jewellery.* TEL: Folkestone (0303) 39133. VAT: Stan/Spec.

Hyron Antiques
86 High St. (R. Welsh.) Open 9.30—5.30. *STOCK: General antiques.* TEL: Folkestone (0303) 30698. SER: Buys at auction.

Sandgate continued

Noble Antiques
59A High St. (F.G. Noble and 4 other dealers.) Est. 1976. Open every day. SIZE: Medium. *STOCK: Clocks, furniture, silver, porcelain, jewellery, bric-a-brac, £5—£1,000.* PARK: Easy. TEL: Folkestone (0303) 39466.

Nordens
43 High St. Est. 1946. CL: Wed. p.m. Open 10—5.30 or by appointment. *STOCK: General antiques, Victoriana, bric-a-brac.* LOC: Main Folkestone to Hythe Rd. TEL: Folkestone (0303) 38443.

The Old Rose Gallery (Antique Market)
152 High St. (V.B. and C.D.P. Gover.) Est. 1966. Open 9.30—6. SIZE: Large. The dealers at this market stock a wide range of antiques, including: *period furniture, Victoriana, silver, brass, pictures, jewellery, stripped pine.* PARK: Easy, at rear. TEL: Folkestone (0303) 39173; home — same.

J.T. Rutherford and Son
55 High St. Est. 1963. Open 9—6; Sun. 9—2, and by appointment. SIZE: Medium. *STOCK: Furniture, 18th—19th C; longcase clocks.* LOC: A295. PARK: Easy. TEL: Folkestone (0303) 39515; home — Hythe (0303) 60822. SER: Restorations (furniture); buys at auction. VAT: Stan/Spec.

Sandgate Antiques Centre
61—63 High St. (J. Greenwall.) Est. 1964. Open 10—6, Sun. 11—6. SIZE: Large. Below are listed the dealers at this centre who sell a wide range of general antiques. LOC: Folkestone—Brighton road. PARK: Easy. TEL: Folkestone (0303) 38987. SER: Valuations.

> Jonathan Greenwall Antiques   **LAPADA**
> Diana Hobson Antiques
> B. and T. Holmes Antiques
> Edward Hutchings Antiques
> P. and D. Jennings
> Judith Antiques
> David Lancefield Antiques

SANDWICH   (0304)

James Atkinson Gallery
38 King St. (R.J. and S.M.R. Atkinson.) Est. 1977. CL: Wed. Open 10—12.30 and 2.15—5 or by appointment. *STOCK: 19th C. oils and watercolours; marine paintings by T.F.R. Thompson.* LOC: Next to Post Office. TEL: 617216; home — 613298. SER: Restorations; framing. VAT: Stan/Spec.

Sandwich continued

Delf Antiques
12 Delf St. (Mrs. P. Wickens.) Est. 1972. CL: Wed. Open 10—1 and 2—4. SIZE: Medium. *STOCK: Cottage furniture, 18th—19th C; decorative items.* Not stocked: Clocks, jewellery. LOC: Behind E. Kent Bus Station, facing Ancient Guildhall. PARK: Behind Guildhall. TEL: 612779.

Empire Antiques
Old Council Yard, Gazen Salts, Strand St. (D.A. Magee.) Open 8—5, Sat. by appointment. *STOCK: Stripped pine and shipping furniture.* TEL: Deal (0304) 614474. SER: Container; import; export; stripping.

Noah's Ark Antique Centre
King St. (Mr and Mrs. R.M. Maxtone Graham.) Est. 1978. CL: Wed. Open 10—5. SIZE: Medium. *STOCK: Staffordshire figures, china, porcelain, antiquarian books, watercolours, oil paintings, prints, small furniture, silver, jewellery, copper and brass.* PARK: Guildhall. TEL: 611144; home — 613270. SER: Valuations.

James Porter Antiques
5 Potter St. Est. 1948. CL: Wed. Open 9.30—5.30. SIZE: Large. *STOCK: Furniture, 18th—19th C.* TEL: 612218.

Nancy Wilson
36 Harnet St. CL: Wed. p.m. Open 10—5. *STOCK: General small clocks, furniture, Victoriana, bric-a-brac, collectors' items.* TEL: 613456, or 612345.

SEVENOAKS   (0732)

The Antiques Centre
120 London Rd. (R. Harrison.) Est. 1964. Open 9—1 and 2—5.30, Sun. and evenings by appointment to trade only. 12 dealers offering a selection of: *mahogany, oak, Oriental and pine furniture, clocks, barometers, paintings, porcelain, dolls, jewellery, glass, silver, copper, brass and decorative items, all 17th—19th C.* TEL: 452104. VAT: Stan/Spec.

Bradbourne Gallery
4 St. John's Hill. (Jane Ross Antiques and Decoration.) Open 9.30—5, Sat. 9—1. There are 6 dealers here selling a wide range of *silver, furniture, ceramics, jewellery, glass, prints and paintings, treen, 18th C to Edwardian.* LOC: 1 mile from town centre, continuation of High St./Dartford Rd. PARK: Easy. TEL: 460756.

Caroline's Pine — Antiques
25 High St. (Mrs. C. Sulford-Smith.) CL: Mon. Open 9.30—5.30, Wed. 10.30—12. *STOCK: Pine and decorative items.* TEL: 451097.

Sevenoaks continued

A.A. Harrison and Son
79 London Rd. (J.E. Harrison.) Est. 1919. CL: Wed. p.m. Open 9.30—5, Sat. 10—4. *STOCK: General antiques, furniture, paintings.* TEL: 453276. VAT: Stan/Spec.

Sevenoaks Furniture Gallery
140 High St. Est. 1976. Open 9.30—5. *STOCK: Pine furniture, all periods.* TEL: 453030.

Sheldon Ward Antiques
57 St. Johns Hill. (S.A. Ward). Est. 1966. CL. Mon. and Wed. Open 2.15—5, Thurs. 10—1 and 2.15—5, Sat. 10—1.15. SIZE: Small. *STOCK: Furniture, and bric-a-brac, from 19th C, £5—£120.* LOC: Main road to Dartford Tunnel. PARK: Easy. TEL: 455311; home — same. SER: Valuations; restorations (inlay, marquetry, rushing and caning); buys at auction (furniture).

SHOREHAM, Nr. Sevenoaks
The Porcelain Collector
The Old Pony Stable, High St. (D. Porter.) Est. 1962. Open daily 10—4 by appointment. SIZE: Medium. *STOCK: English and Continental porcelain especially Royal Worcester, Royal Doulton, Lambeth, Dresden, Sèvres and Royal Vienna; silver, glass, jewellery, metalware, small furniture, toys, clocks, militaria; all from 18th C., art nouveau and art deco.* PARK: Easy. TEL: Otford (095 92) 3416 between 9 a.m. and 9 p.m. SER: Valuations; restorations (porcelain and furniture); buys at auction.

SIDCUP
See Greater London

SMEETH, Nr. Ashford
S.G. Child and Son
Evegate, Water Mill. Est. 1948. Available anytime. *STOCK: Furniture.* TEL: Aldington (023 372) 234. SER: Restorations (furniture).

SNODLAND   (0634)
Aaron Antiques
90 High St. (R.J. Goodman.) Open 10—5, or by appointment. *STOCK: Clocks and pocket watches, paintings and prints, period and shipping furniture, English, Continental and Oriental porcelain; antiquarian books, postcards.* TEL: 241748. VAT: Stan.

SOUTHBOROUGH
Nr. Tunbridge Wells
Henry Baines
14 Church Rd. Est. 1968. Open 8.30—4.30, Sat. 10—4.30. *STOCK: Early oak and country furniture especially sets of chairs.* PARK: Easy. TEL: Tunbridge Wells (0892) 32099. VAT: Stan/Spec.

STOCKBURY
Steppes Hill Farm Antiques   BADA
The Hill Farm. (W.F.A. Buck.) Est. 1965. Always open, appointment advisable. SIZE: Medium. *STOCK: English porcelain, pottery, pot-lids, 18th—20th C, £5—£5,000; small silver; caddy spoons, wine labels, silver boxes, 18th—19th C, to £1,000; furniture, 18th—19th C, £10—£5,000.* LOC: 5 mins. from M2 on A249. Enquire in village for Steppes Hill Antiques. PARK: Easy. TEL: Newington (0795) 842205. SER: Valuations; buys at auction. FAIRS: Chelsea, Dorchester and Burlington House. VAT: Spec.

STURRY, Nr. Canterbury
Guy Defferary
17 Fordwich Rd. Est. 1974. Open 10—5, Sat. 10—1. *STOCK: Furniture and small items, mainly 18th—19th C.* TEL: Canterbury (0227) 711476. SER: Valuations; buys at auction. VAT: Stan/Spec.

SUNDRIDGE, Nr. Sevenoaks
Old Hall (Sphinx Gallery)   LAPADA
(L. Van Den Bussche.) Est. 1963. Open 9—6, other times and Sun. by appointment. SIZE: Medium. *STOCK: Early English and Continental oak furniture, 17th—18th C; metalware, statues, delft pottery.* LOC: A25 between Sevenoaks and Westerham. PARK: Easy, opposite. TEL: Westerham (0959) 62589. SER: Valuations.

Sundridge Antiques   LAPADA
9 Church Rd. (S. and A. Gooseman.) Open 9—5.30. *STOCK: Furniture, porcelain, objets d'art.* TEL: Westerham (0959) 64104.

SUTTON VALENCE, Nr. Maidstone
Sutton Valence Antiques   LAPADA
(T. and N. Mullarkey and M. Marles.) Est. 1971. Open 10—5.30. SIZE: Large. *STOCK: Furniture, porcelain, clocks, silver, metalware, shipping items, 18th—19th C.* LOC: On A274 Maidstone/Tenterden Rd. PARK: Side of shop. TEL: Maidstone (0622) 843333/843499. SER: Valuations. VAT: Stan/Spec.

TENTERDEN (058 06)

Peter and Maggie Cosmos
Little Westwell, Rolvenden Rd. Open by appointment. *STOCK: English Georgian furniture.* LOC: On A28, one mile from town centre. TEL: 2844.

John McMaster BADA
5 Sayers Sq., Sayers Lane. Est. 1847. CL: Sun. except by appointment. *STOCK: Furniture, engravings, silver, small decorative items.* TEL: 2941.

TEYNHAM (0795)
Nr. Sittingbourne

Jackson-Grant Antiques
The Old Chapel, 133 London Rd. (D.M. Jackson-Grant). Est. 1966. Open 10—9, Tues. 10—7, Sat. 10—6, Sun. 12—5, prior telephone call advisable after 4.30 weekdays. SIZE: Large. *STOCK: Furniture, including pine, 19th C; £30—£500; country furniture, oak, 17th—18th C, £100—£1,000; smalls, 19th C to art deco, £5—£100.* LOC: A2 between Faversham and Sittingbourne. PARK: Easy. TEL: 522027; home — same. SER: Restorations (furniture, pine stripping and finishing). FAIRS: Kent Ideal Home. VAT: Stan/Spec.

TONBRIDGE (0732)

Barden House Antiques
1—3 Priory St. (Mrs. B.D. Parsons.) Open 10—5. There are 6 dealers at these premises offering *a wide range of general antiques.* TEL: 350142; evenings — 355718.

Edmund Eldridge Antiques
167 High St. (E.A.W. Eldridge.) Open 9.30—5.30, Sat. 10—1. SIZE: Small. *STOCK: Clocks, £100—£1,000; period furnishings, £5—£1,000.* LOC: A21, north end of High St. PARK: At rear. TEL: 361921. SER: Valuations; restorations (clocks); buys at auction (clocks). VAT: Stan/Spec.

Tonbridge continued

Derek Roberts Antiques BADA
24 and 25 Shipbourne Rd. Est. 1968. Open 9.30—1 and 2.15—5.30 or by appointment. SIZE: Medium. *STOCK: Clocks — bracket, longcase including regulator, skeleton, carriage, wall, £300—£40,000; Georgian furniture, Tunbridgeware.* Not stocked: Porcelain, glass. LOC: A227. From London to Tonbridge turn left 20yds. before first set of traffic lights at Tonbridge. Turn left at T junction; shop is 20yds. further on right. PARK: Easy. TEL: 358986 or 351719. SER: Restorations; clock making; cabinet work; reupholstery. VAT: Spec.

Tudor Cottage Antiques Centre
22—23 Shipbourne Rd. Open 10—5, other times by appointment. SIZE: Medium. There are seven dealers at this centre selling — *furniture, £100—£500; silver and porcelain, £25—£500; all 18th—19th C; objets d'art, copper and brass, 19th C, £25—£500.* PARK: Easy. TEL: 351719; home — 455437 and (0892) 35059. SER: Valuations (silver and furniture); buys at auction (silver and 19th C furniture).

TUNBRIDGE WELLS (0892)

Annexe Antiques
33 The Pantiles (M. Broad.) Est. 1981. CL: Wed. Open 9.30—5. SIZE: Medium. *STOCK: Silver and plate, 1820—1920, £50—£100; glass and porcelain, brass, treen, pictures, toys, clocks, scientific instruments, tapestries, from 1850, £25—£50.* PARK: Nearby. TEL: 47213. VAT: Spec.

Derek Roberts Antiques

24-25 Shipbourne Road, Tonbridge, Kent. TN10 3DN
Tel. (0732) 358986

Antique Clocks
Period Furniture
Tunbridge Ware

Two fine musical clocks, the longcase by Eardley Norton, an eminent maker and the table clock by Manley of London.

We carry a very extensive range of fully restored clocks of all types in our two showrooms in Tonbridge and issue illustrated catalogues either on annual subscription £20 U.K., £24 Europe, £28 Overseas Airmail, or singly £5 U.K., £6 Europe, £7 Overseas Airmail.

Tunbridge Wells continued

Annique Antiques
13 Nevill St. (Mrs. A. Boanas and N. Holland.) Est. 1978. CL: Wed. Open 10—5. *STOCK: 18th—19th C furniture, porcelain, needlework, watercolours, prints.* TEL: 26776.

Castle Antiques
Castle St. (M. Bolton.) CL: Mon. and Wed. Open 10—5. *STOCK: Antique and Victorian pine, oak, painted furniture and small objects.* LOC: Castle St. runs between London Rd. (A26) and High St. PARK: Easy. TEL: 26695; home — (0435) 830338. SER: Shipping.

Chapel Place Antiques
9 Chapel Place. (J. and A. Clare.) Open 11—6 *STOCK: Silver, plate, jewellery, dolls, general antiques, some furniture.* TEL: 46561; home — Horam Road (043 53) 2624.

Clare Gallery
21 High St. *STOCK: Paintings, 19th—20th C.* LOC: 200yds. from Central Station. TEL: 38717. SER: Valuations; restorations; framing. VAT: Spec.

Collectables
53 Colebrook Rd. (J.R. Hickmott.) Open 9.30—6. *STOCK: General antiques.* TEL: 39085.

Tunbridge Wells continued

Corn Exchange Antiques
29 The Pantiles. (B. Henderson.) Open 9—5.30. *STOCK: General antiques, especially Georgian furniture.* TEL: 39652; evenings — Grays Thurrock (0375) 76846.

Cowden Antiques
24 Mount Ephraim Rd. (A. Linstead.) Est. 1970. CL: Sat. p.m. Open 9.30—5. SIZE: Large. *STOCK: Furniture, period oak, pine, mahogany, to late 19th C; decorative items, pictures, 18th and 19th C porcelain.* PARK: Easy. TEL: 20752. VAT: Stan/Spec.

The Cubby Hole
1 Lime Hill Rd. (P.J.K. Sidders.) Est. 1974. CL: Sat. p.m. Open 9—5.30. SIZE: Small. *STOCK: General antiques, some shipping goods, to £1,000.* LOC: Adjacent main shops by Tunbridge Wells 'Five Ways'. PARK: Outside. TEL: 30436.

Franca Antiques
2 Castle St. Est. 1981. CL: Mon. and Wed. Open 9.30—5.30 or by appointment. *STOCK: Furniture and general antiques, classic maps, prints, postal history and stamps.* TEL: 25779.

Tunbridge Wells continued

Frankham Gallery

4 Nevill St. (M.B. Wells.) Open 10–5. SIZE: Large. *STOCK: Paintings, 17th–20th C, £25– £2,500; furniture, 18th–19th C, £25– £2,000; bronze and marble sculpture.* LOC: Last shop on right leaving town (A267), gallery backs on to The Pantiles. PARK: Behind gallery. TEL: 29244. SER: Valuations; restorations; buys at auction. VAT: Stan/ Spec.

Gray Antiques

23 Shirley Grove, Rusthall. (B.D. Gray.) Resident. Est. 1968. Open by appointment. SIZE: Small. *STOCK: Furniture, 18th–19th C, £25–£2,500; Georgian and Victorian silver, china and glass.* LOC: Off Langton Rd. PARK: Easy. TEL: 20288. SER: Valuations; restorations (furniture); French polishing; buys at auction (furniture).

Hadlow Antiques

No. 1 The Pantiles. (M. and L. Adler.) Est. 1966. CL: Wed. p.m. and Sat. p.m. Open 10–5. SIZE: Small. *STOCK: Clocks, watches, 17th–20th C; dolls and accessories, automata, 19th–20th C; scientific and medical instruments, music boxes, singing birds, collectors' items.* LOC: Corner of Nevill St. PARK: Nearby. TEL: 29858. SER: Restorations; buys at auction. VAT: Stan/Spec.

Hall's Bookshop

20 Chapel Place. Est. 1898. CL: Wed. Open 9.30–5. *STOCK: Antiquarian and second-hand books.* TEL: 27842.

Tunbridge Wells continued

Peter Hoare Ltd.

12 Goods Station Rd. Open 9–5.30. *STOCK: General antiques.* TEL: 41508/42760.

Leonard Lassalle (Antiques) Ltd.   BADA

21 The Pantiles. Est. 1968. Open 9–1 and 2–5.30, or by appointment. SIZE: Medium. *STOCK: English and Continental furniture, early ironwork, bronze, brass, copper and pewter, fabrics, needlework, embroidery and tapestry, 16th–18th C; rugs, carpets, pre-1900; early pottery, delftware, faience and majolica; early carvings, works of art and paintings.* LOC: Centre of Pantiles. PARK: In Warwick Park. TEL: 31645; home – (0892 88) 3295. SER: 17th C interior design; valuations; restorations (early oak only). VAT: Spec.

Charles A. Lusted Ltd.

96A Calverley Rd. Est. 1947. Article on medals and coins. Open 9–1 and 2–5. Catalogue by subscription only. *STOCK: Medals, decorations, old militaria, all periods, £2– £5,000.* LOC: Upper end of main shopping street. PARK: 200yds. to the rear. TEL: 25731. VAT: Stan/Spec.

Mission Antique Centre

Old Methodist Church Buildings, Camden Rd. (M. Baldwin.) Est. 1970. There are 6 dealers at this centre offering *a wide range of furniture, 19th C, £50–£100; prints, statues, boxiana, 18th–19th C, £50–£500; collectors' items, 19th C, £5–£200.* LOC: Town centre. PARK: Easy. TEL: 45858. SER: Restorations (furniture); upholstery. VAT: Stan.

a) Tudor Iron buckle with part of the original leather strap. b) Medieval bronze buckle, c.1250-1380. c) Tudor brass strap-end. Pin missing. From "Collecting Buckles", **Antique Collecting**, February 1986.

Tunbridge Wells continued

Angela Page Antiques
Sion House, 15 Mount Sion. Resident. Est. 1973. Open by appointment. SIZE: Small. *STOCK: Oak and country furniture, treen, textiles, objects of folk art, all 17th—19th C.* LOC: Short walk from The Pantiles, on left going up Mount Sion. TEL: 22217. FAIRS: Olympia, West London, Brighton, Chelsea Town Hall. VAT: Spec.

Pantiles Antiques
31 The Pantiles. (E.M. Blackburn.) Est. 1979. CL: Wed. Open 10—5.30. SIZE: Medium. *STOCK: Decorative items, lamps including standard; bronze, copper, brass, furniture, porcelain, pictures.* Not stocked: Carpets. PARK: Easy. TEL: 31291.

Pennink and Owers
23—25 The Pantiles. Est. 1957. Open 9—1 and 2—5.30 daily. SIZE: Large. *STOCK: Mahogany and oak furniture, 18th C, £50—£500; 19th C needlework pictures; curtains, carpets, lampshades, prints, stripped pine.* LOC: Centre of Pantiles. PARK: Reasonable. TEL: 25825 or 35051. SER: Restorations. VAT: Stan/Spec.

Patricia Russell Antiques
43 Mount Ephraim. Est. 1969. CL: Mon. Open 10—5.30, Sat. 10—5. *STOCK: Jewellery, silver, glass, porcelain, small furniture.* LOC: Junction of London Rd., and Mount Ephraim, overlooking the common. TEL: 23719; home — 24855.

Rusthall Antiques
32 High St., Rusthall. (A.B. Stone.) CL: Mon. Open 10—5. *STOCK: General antiques, furniture, collectors' items, jewellery.* LOC: 2 miles off A264. TEL: 21225; home — 20668. VAT: Stan.

Strawsons Antiques   LAPADA
33, 39 and 41 The Pantiles. Est. 1913. Open 9.30—5.30, Wed. 9.30—4. SIZE: Large. *STOCK: Furniture, mahogany, walnut, oak, rosewood, 17th—19th C; silver and plate, Tunbridgeware, jewellery, boxes, glass.* LOC: Follow directions to Pantiles. PARK: Easy, nearby. TEL: 30607. VAT: Spec.

John Thompson
27 The Pantiles. (J. Macdonald and N. Thompson.) Est. 1982. Open 9.30—1 and 2—5.30. SIZE: Medium. *STOCK: Furniture, 17th to early 19th C; porcelain, pottery, glass, decorative items, 18th to early 19th C; paintings and prints, 17th—19th C.* Not stocked: Jewellery, silver and militaria. PARK: Warwick Park/Lower Walk Pantiles. TEL: 47215. SER: Restorations (furniture). VAT: Spec.

Tunbridge Wells continued

Victoria House Antiques
42a Victoria Rd. (A.W. King.) Open 9—5, Sat. 9—6. *STOCK: General antiques.* TEL: 44513.

White Horse Antiques
7 Chapel Place. (B. and J. Dilliway.) Est. 1978. Open Thurs., Fri. and Sat. 10—6. SIZE: Small. *STOCK: Glass, porcelain and pottery, 18th—20th C, £2—£100; works of art, 19th—20th C, £10—£100.* LOC: From bottom end of High St., Chapel Place is a walkway to the Pantiles. PARK: Mount Sion or on common. TEL: 25810.

York Gallery (Tunbridge Wells) Ltd.
6 Castle St. (Mr. and Mrs. D. Alcock.) Est. 1984. CL: Wed. p.m. except by appointment. Open 9—5.30. SIZE: Medium. *STOCK: Oils and watercolours, £50—£2,500; prints, £1—£200; all Victorian and contemporary.* LOC: Off High St., towards Pantiles. PARK: Nearby. TEL: 22326. SER: Valuations; restorations (oils, watercolours, prints, frames); buys at auction.

WEST MALLING   (0732)
The Old Clock Shop
63 High St. (S.L. Luck.) Est. 1970. CL: Wed. Open 9—5. SIZE: Medium. *STOCK: Grandfather clocks, 17th—19th C; bracket and wall clocks.* LOC: ¼ mile from main A20. PARK: Easy. TEL: 843246 or 840345. VAT: Spec.

Victoria Pataky Antiques and Reproductions
2/3 The Colonnade, West St. CL: Wed. *STOCK: General antiques, Victoriana.* TEL: 843646.

Scott House Antiques
High St. (M. Smith.) Est. 1973. CL: Wed. p.m. *STOCK: General antiques, Victoriana, curios, silver, china, furniture, clocks, prints, £5—£1,000.* LOC: Opposite county library. TEL: 841380.

WEST PECKHAM, Nr. Maidstone
Langold Antiques Ltd.
Oxon Hoath. (H.M. Bayne-Powell; the Hon. M. Wyndham; R.W. Baring.) Est. 1967. CL: Sat. Open 9—1 and 2.15—5.30. SIZE: Medium. *STOCK: English furniture, 18th—19th C.* LOC: Coming from A26, turn left at Carpenters Lane on entering Hadlow. Left at T junction, right at crossroads, 400yds. to lodge gates on right. Showrooms at rear of mansion. PARK: Easy. TEL: Plaxtol (0732) 810577. SER: Restorations (furniture). VAT: Spec.

West Peckham continued

"Persian Rugs"
Vines Farm, Matthews Lane. (R. and G. King.) Resident. Est. 1969. Open 9—7, Sun. by appointment. SIZE: Large. *STOCK: Persian rugs and carpets, to 1900, £100—£750.* LOC: A26 from Tonbridge to Maidstone. Just off Hadlow village turn left then right, premises are first on right. PARK: Easy. TEL: Hadlow (0732) 850228. SER: Valuations; restorations (Oriental carpets); buys at auction (Persian carpets). VAT: Stan.

WESTERHAM   (0959)
Cosmo Antiques   *Mainly Trade*
18 Market Sq. (P. Cosmos.) Est. 1972. Open 9.30—5.30. SIZE: Large. *STOCK: Furniture, china, rugs, jewellery.* LOC: On A25. PARK: At rear. TEL: 62080.

Dunsdale Lodge Antiques   BADA
Dunsdale Lodge, Brasted Rd. (A. Scott.) Est. 1967. Open daily 9—7. SIZE: Small. *STOCK: English porcelain figures, 18th C, £100—£900; English pottery figures, 18th—19th C, £35—£1,000; Staffordshire portrait figures, 19th C, £30—£250; Continental figures, 19th C, £50—£300; lustre; cottages and Toby jugs.* **LOC: Shop 500yds. from town on A25. PARK: Easy. TEL: 62160. SER: Valuations; buys at auction. VAT: Spec.**

Henry Hall Antique Clocks
LAPADA
19 Market Sq. Est. 1954. CL: Sun. except by appointment. Open 10—5.30. SIZE: Medium. *STOCK: Longcase and bracket clocks, 1690—1900, £200—£12,000; English regulators, 18th—19th C, £2,000—£9,000.* LOC: A25. PARK: Easy, in Market Sq. TEL: 62200; home — same. SER: Valuations (clocks); buys at auction. VAT: Stan/Spec.

Westerham continued

Anthony J. Hook
3 The Green. Est. 1948. CL: Sat. Open 9—5.30, Mon. 4—5.30. SIZE: Medium. *STOCK: English furniture, 18th—19th C.* LOC: A25. TEL: 62161. VAT: Stan/Spec.

'Jolie'
18 Market Sq. (O.M. Cosmos.) Open 9.30—5.30. *STOCK: Jewellery and porcelain, 19th and 20th C.* LOC: On A25. TEL: 62080.

Manor Antiques
2a High St. (S. Morris.) Open 10—5 and Sun. p.m. SIZE: Medium. *STOCK: Furniture, paintings, china, brass and copper, 19th C; books.* LOC: A25. PARK: Croydon Rd. TEL: 64810.

Denys Sargeant
21 The Green. Est. 1949. CL: Mon. and Wed. Open 9.30—5.30. *STOCK: Glass, especially chandeliers and candelabras, decanters and drinking glasses; lustres.* TEL: 62130. VAT: Stan/Spec.

Twenty-One Antiques
21 High St. (M. Richardson.) Open 10—5. SIZE: Small. *STOCK: General antiques, porcelain, £5—£500; small furniture, £20—£750; silver, pewter, £10—£500; paintings, £50—£500.* LOC: A25. PARK: In side road opposite. TEL: 63055.

Westerham Antique Centre
18 Market Sq. (P. Cosmos.) Est. 1972. Open 9.30—5.30. *STOCK: General antiques.* TEL: 62080.

ANTHONY J. HOOK

3 The Green, Westerham, Kent
Tel. Westerham 62161

Period Furniture and Shipping Goods
Open Monday 4 – 5.30
Tuesday to Friday 9.00 – 5.30

Westerham continued

Westerham Galleries
The Green. (Mr. and Mrs. R.R. Wood.) Est. 1962. CL: Fri. except by appointment. Open 10—6, including Sun. SIZE: Large. *STOCK: Paintings, 18th—19th C, £50—£5,000; bronze, 19th C, £50—£3,000; small furniture.* LOC: A25, opposite village green. PARK: At rear. TEL: 63359; home — same. SER: Restorations; buys at auction (paintings). VAT: Spec.

WHITSTABLE   (0227)
Laurens Antiques
17 Harbour St. (G.A. Laurens.) Est. 1965. Open 9.30—5.30. SIZE: Medium. *STOCK: Furniture, 18th—19th C, £50—£100+.* LOC: Turn off Thanet Way at Longreach roundabout, straight down to one-way system in High St. PARK: 1 min. walk at rear of shop. TEL: 261940; home — same. SER: Valuations; restorations (cabinet work); buys at auction.

Magpie
8 Harbour St. (C. Davies.) Est. 1976. CL: Sun. and Wed. except by appointment. Open 9—1 and 2.30—5.30. PARK: In Sydenham St. opposite. TEL: 273929. SER: Restorations; buys at auction. VAT: Stan/Spec.

WINGHAM
Nr. Canterbury
Bridge Antiques
97 High St. (A. and C. Cripps.) Est. 1968. Resident. CL: Wed. Open 10—6 or by appointment. SIZE: Large. *STOCK: English and Continental furniture, clocks, dolls and toys, books, shipping goods, bric-a-brac.* TEL: Canterbury (0227) 720445.

Lloyd's Bookshop
27 High St. (Mrs. J. Morrison.) ABA. Est. 1958. Open Mon.—Sat. SIZE: Large. *STOCK: Antiquarian and secondhand books, prints, watercolours, ephemera, maps, music.* PARK: Easy. TEL: Canterbury (0227) 720774. SER: Valuations. VAT: Stan.

Wingham continued

The Minstrel Antiques
69 High St. (P. and N. Dharia.) Est. 1982. CL: Wed. p.m. Open 9.30—5 including Bank Holiday Mons. SIZE: Small. *STOCK: Furniture, mainly Victorian, from £50; watercolours, oils, prints, etchings, 19th C, £10—£300; small china, glass, silver, plate, jewellery, 1800 to art deco, £1—£100.* LOC: On A257, next to Post Office. PARK: Easy. TEL: Canterbury (0227) 720331; home — same.

Silvesters   LAPADA
33 High St. (S.N. Hartley, Mr. and Mrs. G.M.A. Wallis.) Est. 1953. Open 9.30—5, other times by appointment. *STOCK: Furniture, Georgian and Victorian; decorative items, silver, porcelain, glass.* LOC: At main junction in town. TEL: Canterbury (0227) 720278. VAT: Stan/Spec.

WOODCHURCH   (023 386)
Nr. Ashford
Woodchurch Antiques
3 The Green. (Mrs. K. Hewson.) Est. 1982. CL: Wed. and Thurs. Open 10—5.30, Sun. by appointment. SIZE: Medium. *STOCK: Pine, oak, country items, domestic collectables, £5—£500.* LOC: At top of green close to church. TEL: 249; home — same.

WYE   (0233)
Millhouse Antiques
George House, Bridge St. (T.E. Fitzgerald-Moore.) Est. 1972. CL: Sun. and Wed. except by appointment. Open 10—1 and 2—5. *STOCK: General antiques, silver, porcelain.* LOC: Village is 4 miles from Ashford. PARK: In courtyard. TEL: 812035. SER: Valuations; buys at auction. VAT: Stan/Spec.

Lancashire

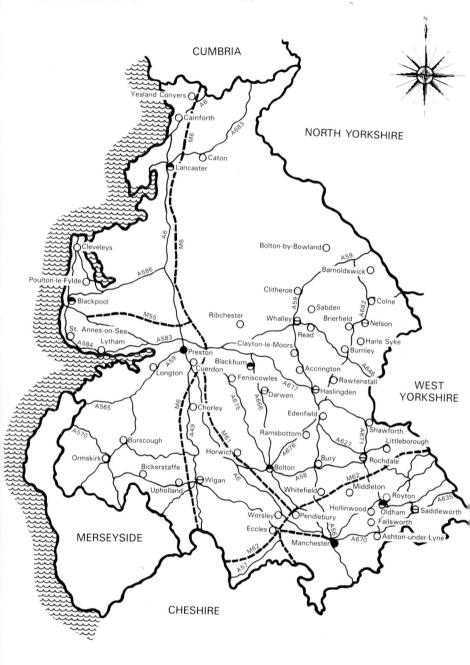

CUMBRIA

NORTH YORKSHIRE

Yealand Conyers
Carnforth
Caton
Lancaster

Cleveleys
Poulton-le-Fylde
Blackpool
St. Annes-on-Sea
Lytham
Longton

Bolton-by-Bowland
Barnoldswick
Clitheroe
Colne
Sabden
Whalley
Brierfield
Nelson
Read
Harle Syke
Burnley
Ribchester
Clayton-le-Moors
Preston
Blackburn
Accrington
Cuerdon
Rawtenstall
Feniscowles
Darwen
Haslingden
Chorley
Edenfield
Burscough
Ramsbottom
Shawforth
Littleborough
Horwich
Bury
Rochdale
Ormskirk
Bolton
Bickerstaffe
Wigan
Whitefield
Middleton
Royton
Upholland
Saddleworth
Hollinwood
Oldham
Worsley
Pendlebury
Failsworth
Eccles
Ashton-under-Lyne
Manchester

WEST
YORKSHIRE

MERSEYSIDE

CHESHIRE

○ 1–2
⊖ 3–5
⬤ 6–12
● 13+

Key to
number of
shops in
this area.

Please note this is only a rough map designed
to show dealers the number of shops in the
various towns, and is not necessarily totally
accurate.

KENWORTHYS LTD

Established 1880   **Jewellers & Silversmiths**   **Tel 061-330 3043-4**

OFFER ONE OF THE LARGEST AND MOST COMPREHENSIVE STOCKS OF ANTIQUE SILVER AND OLD SHEFFIELD PLATE IN THE NORTH

A George III silver coffee pot by G. Smith, London, 1787. 33.05ozs.

**226 Stamford Street
Ashton-under-Lyne OL6 7LW
Manchester**

ACCRINGTON   (0254)

J. Bridgeman Coins
129a Blackburn Rd. Est. 1977. CL: Sun. and Wed. Open 10—5.30. *STOCK: Coins, medals, postcards, cigarette cards and jewellery.* TEL: 384757; home — 382049.

ASHTON-UNDER-LYNE

Kenworthys Ltd.   **BADA**
226 Stamford St. (Mrs. E. Kenworthy and C.J. and M. Collings.) Est. 1880. CL: Tues. Open 9—5.30. *STOCK: Silver and jewellery, all periods, £1—£5,000.* PARK: 50yds. away behind shop. TEL: (061) 330 3043/4. SER: Valuations; restorations; buys at auction. FAIRS: Harrogate, Buxton; International Jewellery, Dorchester Hotel. VAT: Stan/Spec.

Tameside Antiques
Cavendish Mill, 85 Cavendish St. (B. Boyle and D. Downworth.) Est. 1973. Open every day. SIZE: Large and warehouse. *STOCK: Chairs, pedestal tables, longcase and wall clocks, shipping goods, pianos, desks, bureaux, bookcases.* LOC: On roundabout at Ashton. TEL: (061) 344 5477; home — (061) 320 9298; (061) 308 4445. SER: Valuations; re-upholstery, packing and shipping. VAT: Stan.

BARNOLDSWICK   (0282)
Nr. Colne

C. and N. Bardwell
10 Frank St. Est. 1963. CL: Mon. and Tues. Open 10—5, Sat. 10—4. SIZE: Medium. *STOCK: Furniture, glass, jewellery, pottery, silver, plate, all periods.* LOC: Town centre. PARK: Easy. TEL: 813558. VAT: Stan.

BICKERSTAFFE, Nr. Ormskirk

E.W. Webster   **BADA**
Wash Farm, Rainford Rd. Est. 1975. Open anytime by appointment. SIZE: Large. *STOCK: Furniture, early metal, needlework, treen, decorative items, 1650—1850.* Not stocked: Bric-a-brac. LOC: Exit 3, M58 on to A570, turn left 100yds. PARK: Easy. TEL: Skelmersdale (0695) 24322. VAT: Spec.

BLACKBURN   (0254)

Ancient and Modern
56 Bank Top. (D.G. Bennett.) Est. 1952. Open 9—6. *STOCK: Jewellery, Victorian to date, £20—£500.* LOC: One mile from town centre. PARK: Easy. TEL: 63256. SER: Valuations; restorations; buys at auction (gold, silver, stamps, coins); repairs (watches and longcase clocks).

Blackburn continued

T. & D. Brindle LAPADA
8 Lynwood Rd. CL: Sat. p.m. Open 9—5. *STOCK: Decorative items.* LOC: On M6 to Blackburn, left at traffic lights after Moat House, then right before Dog Inn. Warehouse at bottom of hill. TEL: 56185 or 670714; home — 812397. VAT: Stan/Spec.

S. Carysforth
252 Revidge Rd. TEL: 51969. VAT: Stan/Spec.

Duggans
47 Preston New Rd. (J.A. Duggan.) Est. 1959. CL: Thurs. and Sat. Open 9.30—5. *STOCK: Coins, English, European, American and colonial.* TEL: 670113. VAT: Stan/Spec.

Mitchell's (Lock Antiques)
76 Bolton Rd. (S. Mitchell.) Open 9—4. *STOCK: General antiques.* TEL: 664663.

Anthony Walmsley Antiques
93 Montague St. (A. and F.A. Walmsley.) Est. 1968. CL: Sun., except by appointment. Open 10—6. SIZE: Medium. *STOCK: General furniture, clocks.* Not stocked: Guns or weapons. LOC: 2 minutes from town centre. Montague St. links Preston New Rd. and Preston Old Rd. PARK: Easy. TEL: 698755 any time. SER: Valuations; restorations; buys at auction; shipping and packing; courier service.

BLACKPOOL (0253)

Antediluvian and Ark Antiques
46 Grasmere Rd. (C. and Y. Sagers.) CL: Mon. Open 10—5.30 or by appointment. *STOCK: General small antiques especially Doulton and Moorcroft.* LOC: Off Central Drive, near football ground. PARK: Easy. TEL: 20970; home — same. SER: Buys at auction.

De Molen Ltd. *Trade and Export Only*
Moss Hey Garages, Chapel Rd., Marton Moss. Open daily. *STOCK: Pine, rustic, primitive and farmhouse items.* TEL: 696324.

D. Kavanagh and Son
29A Caunce St. Open 10—5, appointment advisable. *STOCK: Dolls.* TEL: 20701.

R.H. Latham Antiques
21 Stanmore Ave. Open by appointment. SIZE: Large. *STOCK: Stripped pine, some Georgian furniture, brass, copper and porcelain.* TEL: Home — 691263. SER: Shipping.

Marton Galleries (Antiques)
8 Hawes Side Lane. (J. and E. Parker.) *STOCK: Furniture, clocks, china, silver, pocket watches, pictures.* TEL: 61432.

Blackpool continued

Oak Tree Antiques
60 Bond St. (R.N. and J. Thomson.) Est. 1968. CL: Wed. p.m., all day Wed. from Nov. to Easter. Open 10—5, or by appointment. *STOCK: Furniture, £50—£500; brass and copper, £5—£100; all Regency, Victorian and Edwardian; porcelain, 1800 onwards, £1—£150.* Not stocked: Coins and medals. LOC: 200yds. from promenade. PARK: Easy. TEL: 43046. SER: Buys at auction. VAT: Stan.

Tom Owen Aquarius Antiques
18 Rawcliffe St. Est. 1965. Open 10.30—5.00. *STOCK: Trade items in wood, brass and copper, bric-a-brac, collectors' items.* LOC: Just off south promenade. PARK: Easy. TEL: 33008. VAT: Stan.

R. and L. Coins
521 Lytham Rd. Est. 1965. CL: Sat. Open 9—5. SIZE: Large. *STOCK: English and ancient coins, gold bullion coins, jewellery and silver, £1—£10,000+.* LOC: Lytham Rd. runs from Central Promenade south to Blackpool Airport main gates. Shop is ¼ mile from airport. PARK: Easy. TEL: 43081/2. SER: Valuations. VAT: Stan/Spec.

BOLTON (0204)

Astley Bridge Antiques
419/421 Blackburn Rd., Astley Bridge. (G. and D. Taylor.) Est. 1970. CL: Sat. and Sun., except by appointment. Open 10—4. SIZE: Large. *STOCK: Furniture and clocks, £5—£1,000; pottery, glass, weapons, pictures, general antiques, shipping goods, £1—£500, all 17th C to Edwardian.* Not stocked: Stamps. LOC: 2 miles north of town centre on A666, 30yds. from the bridge. PARK: Easy. TEL: 51160; home — 53390. SER: Valuations; buys at auction.

Drop Dial Antiques
Last Drop Village, Hospital Rd., Bromley Cross. (I.W. & I.E. Roberts). Est. 1975. Open by appointment. SIZE: Small. *STOCK: Clocks, mainly English and French, 18th—20th C; £50—£2,000; mercury barometers, 19th—20th C., £100—£500; paintings, silver and general antiques, £20—£500.* Not stocked: Stamps and armour. LOC: Beneath Last Drop Collectors Market. PARK: Easy. TEL: 57186; home — Adlington (Chorley) (0257) 480995. SER: Valuations; restorations (clocks and barometers). VAT: Stan/Spec.

Gallery 77
18 Princess St., Bradshawgate. (M. Wayne.) Open 9.—5. *STOCK: Watercolours, oil paintings, 19th to early 20th C.* TEL: 35252. SER: Restorations; framing; buys at auction.

Bolton continued

Last Drop Antique and Collectors Club

Last Drop Hotel, Bromley Cross. Open Sun. 11—4. There are about 40 dealers at these premises offering a wide selection of antiques and collectables.

G. Oakes and Son Bolton Ltd.

160 Blackburn Rd. Est. 1958. CL: Wed. Open 9.30—5.30. *STOCK: Furniture.* TEL: 26587. SER: Shipping and packing; buys at auction. VAT: Stan.

Park Galleries Antiques, Fine Art and Decor

167 Mayor St. (Mrs. S. Hunt.) Est. 1964. Open Thurs., Fri. and Sat. 10.30—5, or by appointment. SIZE: Medium. *STOCK: Furniture, 17th to early 20th C, £75—£2,500; porcelain, 18th—19th C, £5—£450; miniatures, glass, brass, silver, etc., 1800—1900, £5—£485.* Not stocked: Weapons, coins, medals. LOC: On B6202. PARK: Side and rear. TEL: 29827; home — (061) 764 5853. SER: Restorations (brass, porcelain, upholstery, small furniture); buys at auction.

BOLTON-BY-BOWLAND   (020 07)
Nr. Clitheroe

Harrop Fold Clocks (F. Robinson)

Harrop Fold, Lane Ends. Est. 1974. Open by appointment. SIZE: Medium. *STOCK; British clocks, barometers, 18th—19th C, £200—£2,000.* LOC: Through Clitheroe to Chatburn and Grindleton. Take Slaidburn road, turn left after 3 miles. PARK: Own. TEL: 665; home — same. SER: Valuations; restorations (clocks).

BRIERFIELD, Nr. Nelson

J.H. Blakey and Sons Ltd. (Est. 1905)

5 Colne Rd. and showrooms at Burnley Rd., Brierfield Centre. Est. 1905. *STOCK: Furniture, brass, copper, pewter, clocks, curios.* TEL: Nelson (0282) 63593. SER: Restorations; organ and piano repairs. VAT: Stan.

BROMLEY CROSS
See Bolton

BURNLEY   (0282)

Burnley Antiques   BADA
and Fine Arts Ltd.   LAPADA

(Mrs. E. Falik.) Est. 1970. Open by appointment only. SIZE: Medium. *STOCK: 18th—19th C porcelain.* PARK: Easy. TEL: 65172. SER: Valuations. VAT: Spec.

BURSCOUGH   (0704)
Nr. Ormskirk

West Lancs. Antiques   LAPADA

Black Horse Farm, 123 Liverpool Rd. (W. & B. Griffiths.) Est. 1959. Open 9—5.30. SIZE: Large. *STOCK: General antiques.* LOC: A59. PARK: Easy. TEL: 894634; home — 35720. SER: Courier; packing and shipping. VAT: Stan/Spec.

BURY

Newtons

151 The Rock. (C.W. Newton.) Est. 1931. Open 9—5.30. SIZE: Small. *STOCK: General antiques, 18th—19th C, £5—£500.* Not stocked: Continental furniture. LOC: From Manchester through Bury town centre, shop is on left 200yds. before Fire Station. PARK: 50yds. behind shop. TEL: (061) 764 1863. SER: Valuations; restorations (antique furniture). VAT: Stan.

CARNFORTH   (0524)

Wm. Goodfellow (Antiques)

The Green, Over Kellet. Est. 1975. CL: Wed. Open 10.30—6, or by appointment. SIZE: Small. *STOCK: Small period furniture, pre-1830, £50—£1,000; pottery and porcelain, 1750—1870; silver, glass and metalware, pre-1900, £5—£500.* Not stocked: Large furniture. LOC: B6254. PARK: Easy. TEL: 733030. SER: Valuations; restorations (cabinet work and silver repair); buys at auction. VAT: Stan/Spec.

CATON, Nr. Lancaster   (0524)
"Tequesta"

Lancaster Rd. CL: Mon. Open any time by appointment. SIZE: Small. *STOCK: General antiques and bric-a-brac.* LOC: A683. PARK: Easy. TEL: 770488. SER: Valuations.

CHORLEY   (025 72)

Charisma Curios and Antiques

13 St. George's St. (N., Mrs. V.M. and Miss N.S. Langton.) Est. 1977. CL: Wed. and Sun., except by appointment. Open 10—5. *STOCK: General antiques, period furniture, stripped pine, clocks, porcelain, silver, jewellery and shipping goods.* LOC: Off A6, town centre, near St. George's church. PARK: Outside. TEL: 67720; evenings — 76845. SER: Restorations (furniture); upholstery; stripping (pine); caning; rush seating.

The Source   *Export Trade Only*
Enterprises Ltd.

Gillibrand Barn, Mountbatten Rd. Est. 1971. TEL: 78766. VAT: Stan.

CLAYTON-LE-MOORS
Nr. Accrington
Sparth House Antiques
Sparth House, Whalley Rd. (W. and B. Coleman.) Est. 1967. TEL: Accrington (0254) 31746.

CLEVELEYS, Nr. Blackpool (0253)
Mrs. E.N. Robinson
13 Beach Rd. Est. 1960. CL: Wed. p.m. Open 9.30—6. SIZE: Small. *STOCK: Victorian, small furniture, pottery and porcelain; Victorian and Georgian metalware, curios; small silver, jade, jewellery, pictures; all periods.* Not stocked: Large furniture. PARK: Easy. TEL: 854763; home — same.

CLITHEROE (0200)
Castle Antiques
15 Moor Lane. (J. and B. Tomkinson.) Open Tues., Thurs. and Fri. 10—5; Sat. 11.30—4. SIZE: Large. *STOCK: Shipping goods, stained glass windows, pine, Lloyd loom items, clocks, kitchen items.* TEL: 26568; home — Accrington (0254) 35820.

Ethos Gallery
4 York St. (F. and P. Barnes). Est. 1978. Open 9—5. Wed. and Sun. by appointment. SIZE: Medium. *STOCK: Oil paintings and watercolours, 19th C, £100—£5,000; paintings, £100—£2,000; English crystal £5—£100, both 20th C.* LOC: A59 in town centre. PARK: Own. TEL: 27878; home — 22597. SER: Valuations; restorations (oils and watercolours).VAT: Stan.

COLNE (0282)
Ancient and Modern
66 Albert Rd. (C.V. Burton.) CL: Sat. p.m. Open 10—5. *STOCK: Victorian and Edwardian furniture; cut glass.* TEL: 865180.

Enloc Antiques
Old Corporation Yard, Knotts Lane. (J. Cox.) Est. 1978. Open 10—12.30 and 2—5, Sat. 10—12 or anytime by appointment. SIZE: Large. *STOCK: Pine, 18th—20th C, £20—£500; kitchen chairs, 19th C, £10—£35; Lloyd looms, £5—£50.* LOC: Turn into Bridge St. off A56, approximately 100 metres at foot of hill, turn left through iron gates. PARK: Easy. TEL: 861417; home — same. SER: Restorations (pine stripping, repolishing and joinery). VAT: Stan.

CUERDON, Nr. Preston
Susan and James Cook
Dixon's Farm, Wigan Rd. Resident. Est. 1970. Open by appointment. SIZE: Medium. *STOCK: Complete church interiors including pews, panels, pulpits, stained glass.* LOC: A6. PARK: Easy. TEL: Preston (0772) 321390. VAT: Stan/Spec.

DARWEN (0254)
Darwen Antique Exports
St. James 'Old' School, St. James Crescent, Winterton Rd. (M. Manning.) Est. 1968. CL: Sat. Open 8.30—5, other times by appointment. *STOCK: Pine and shipping goods.* TEL: 72283; home — 773688. SER: Export. VAT: Stan.

K.C. Antiques
538 Bolton Rd. (K. Davies.) Open 9—5, Sun. 12—4. SIZE: Small. *STOCK: 18th—19th C furniture, shipping goods and pine.* LOC: A66. TEL: 772252; home — same. VAT: Stan.

Whitehall Antiques *Trade Only*
Earcroft School, Blackburn Rd. (K. Almond.) Est. 1963. Open 9.30—5.30, Sat. 9.30—1. SIZE: Warehouse. *STOCK: Furniture, general antiques and shipping goods.* TEL: 73521. VAT: Stan.

Peter Young Antiques *Trade Only*
Earcroft School, Blackburn Rd. Est. 1967. CL: Sat. Open 9.30—5.30. *STOCK: General antiques, decorative and unusual items, shipping goods.*

ECCLES, Nr. Manchester
Eccles Used Furniture and Antique Centre
325/7 Liverpool Rd., Patricroft Bridge. (G. Rust.) Est. 1953. Open 10—6. SIZE: Medium. *STOCK: Figures, furniture, glass, porcelain.* LOC: On Patricroft bridge. PARK: Opposite. TEL: (061) 789 4467.

EDENFIELD, Nr. Bury
The Antique Shop LAPADA
17 Market St. (R. and Mrs. J. Salisbury.) Est. 1964. Open 10—5.30, Sat. and Sun. 1—5.30. SIZE: Large. *STOCK: General antiques, shipping goods, £1—£1,000.* LOC: On A56. PARK: Easy. TEL: Ramsbottom (070 682) 2351; home — same. SER: Valuations. VAT: Stan/Spec.

FAILSWORTH, Nr. Manchester
John Maloney
497 Oldham Rd. Est. 1956. TEL: (061) 682 0961.

FENISCOWLES, Nr. Blackburn
Old Smithy
726 Preston Old Rd. (R.C. Lynch.) Est. 1967.
Open 9—5. SIZE: Large. *STOCK: Longcase
clocks, 17th—18th C, £100—£1,000;
furniture, £20—£500; brass beds, 18th C,
£50—£500; miners lamps and others,
£15—£100; fireplaces, 18th—19th C, £5—
£500; musical instruments including violins,
17th—19th C, £20—£200; glass, pottery and
silver, 18th C, 50p—£200; shipping goods,
pub and architectural items; Victorian fireplaces, £20—£500; Victorian lace and linen,
20's and 30's clothes.* LOC: Opposite Fieldens
Arms. PARK: Own or nearby. TEL: Blackburn
(0254) 29943; home — Blackburn (0254)
580874. SER: Valuations; restorations (wooden
items); buys at auction. FAIRS: Park Hall,
Charnock Richard.

HARLE SYKE, Nr Burnley
Ralph A. Sutcliffe   LAPADA
Trade Only
Harle Syke Mill. Est. 1962. Open 8—5, Sat.
by appointment. SIZE: Large. *STOCK: Furniture, 19th and 20th C; architectural items and
accessories.* LOC: Main road from Burnley to
Haggate. PARK: Easy. TEL: Burnley (0282)
31412. VAT: Stan.

HASLINGDEN
Clifton House Antiques
Clifton House, 198 Blackburn Rd. (D. Clink.)
Est. 1958. CL: Sat. and Sun. Open 9—6.
SIZE: Medium. *STOCK: General antiques,
£5—£500.* PARK: Easy. TEL: Rossendale
(0706) 214895. VAT: Stan.

Fieldings Antiques
176, 178 and 180 Blackburn Rd. Est. 1956.
CL: Thurs. Open 9—4.30, Fri. 9—4. SIZE:
Large. *STOCK: Longcase clocks, £30—
£2,000; wall clocks and other antiques, sets
of chairs, pine, period oak, shipping goods,
toys and steam engines.* PARK: Easy. TEL:
Blackburn (0254) 63358; or Rossendale
(0706) 214254. SER: Buys at auction.

Speakmans
186 Blackburn Rd. (P. Speakman). Est. 1956.
CL: Sat. Open 9.30—5.30. SIZE: Small.
*STOCK: Furniture, pottery, porcelain, glass,
clocks, pictures and unusual items.* PARK:
Easy. TEL: Home — Rossendale (0706)
224282.

HOLLINWOOD, Nr. Oldham
Abbey Antiques
299/301 Manchester Rd. (D. Mullin.) Est.
1969. Open 10—6, Sun. 11—3. SIZE: Large.
STOCK: Stripped pine and general antiques.
LOC: A62. PARK: At side. TEL: (061) 681
6538. SER: Restorations; repairs (clocks).

Hollinwood continued
David Nuttall Antiques
267 Manchester Rd. Open 10—5 or by
appointment. *STOCK: General antiques and
fine art.* TEL: (061) 682 4702.

HORWICH   (0204)
Nr. Bolton
Alan Butterworth (Antiques) Ltd.
Union Mill, Albert St. Open 9—5. *STOCK:
Furniture, 17th—19th C; art nouveau, pot-
tery, porcelain, brass, copper, shipping goods.*
TEL: 693733; after hours — 68094. SER:
Export; packing and shipping; courier.

LANCASTER   (0524)
Anne Tique — Curio Jewellers
73 North Rd. Est. 1948. Open 10—5. SIZE:
Small. *STOCK: Jewellery.* LOC: Around corner
from bus station. PARK: Nearby. TEL: 65343.

G.W. Antiques
47 North Rd. (G. and J. Woods). Est. 1978.
Open 9—5.30. SIZE: Large. *STOCK: Stripped
pine, 18th to early 20th C, £30—£1,500.*
LOC: A6. PARK: 60 yds. TEL: 32050. SER:
Valuations; restorations (furniture); stripping.
VAT: Stan/Spec.

Lancastrian Antiques
66 Penny St. (S.P. and H.S. Wilkinson.) CL:
Mon. and Wed. Open 10—4.30. *STOCK:
General antiques.* TEL: 37323.

Sun Street Clock Shop
10 Sun St. (J.M. and M.L. Pendlebury, F.J.
Clarke.) Est. 1978. Open 9.30—5.30, Sat. till
3.30. SIZE: Small. *STOCK: Clocks, mainly
19th C, £25—£1,500.* LOC: 1st street on
right off Church St. PARK: Church St. TEL:
39196. SER: Valuations; restorations and
repairs (clocks, watches, barometers). VAT:
Stan/Spec.

Vicary Antiques
18a Brock St. Est. 1974. CL: Wed. Open
10—5. SIZE: Small. *STOCK: Paintings, prints,
works of art, 1850—1950; antique fabrics
and furniture.* TEL: Home — 781425. VAT:
Stan/Spec.

Wishing Well
138 and 140 Greaves Rd. (R. Hardcastle.) Est.
1970. Open 10—6. SIZE: Medium. *STOCK:
Glassware, pottery, bric-a-brac, £1—£250;
jewellery, £1—£1,000; silver and plate,
£5—£1000, all 19th—20th C; brass, copper,
pewter, £1—£250; furniture, £5—£2,000.*
LOC: A6 approx. ½ mile out of city towards
Preston. PARK: Easy. TEL: 381899.

LITTLEBOROUGH, (0706)
Nr. Rochdale
Sandleton-Edwards
Dry Dock Mill, New Rd. (D.L. Elton). Est. 1981. CL: Mon. Open 10—5.30, Sun. 12—5. SIZE: Large. *STOCK: Pine, £100—£1,000; general antiques and shipping items, £50—£200.* LOC: A58. PARK: Easy. TEL: 74626. SER: Restorations. FAIRS: Rochdale and Bury. VAT: Stan/Spec.

LONGTON, Nr. Preston (0772)
Betty Easterby   LAPADA
Trade Only
Longton Hall. Est. 1960. CL: Sat. Open 9—5.30. *STOCK: Furniture, Georgian, Victorian and Edwardian; longcase clocks and barometers.* TEL: 613324. VAT: Stan.

LYTHAM (0253)
Clifton Antiques
8 Market Sq. (Mrs. M.K. Howarth, A.P. and D.A. Allen.) Est. 1975. Open 10.30—5. SIZE: Medium. *STOCK: Small pine furniture, silver, jewellery, £5—£500; brass, copper, crochet work.* Not stocked: Weapons, coins. PARK: Easy. TEL: 736356.

MANCHESTER (061)
A.S. Antiques
26 Broad St., Salford. (A. Sternshine.) Est. 1975. CL: Tues. Open 10—5, Sat. 10—4. SIZE: Large. *STOCK: Art nouveau, 1900—1910, art deco, 1920—1930; furniture, general antiques, to art deco period.* Not stocked: Weapons. LOC: On A6, 100yds. from Salford Technical College. PARK: Easy. TEL: 737 5938. SER: Valuations.

The Baron Antiques   LAPADA
373 Bury New Rd. (Mr. Brunsveld.) Open 9.30—6. SIZE: Large. *STOCK: 18th C mahogany and early oak furniture, Victorian walnut, clocks, porcelain, objets d'art, shipping goods.* TEL: 773 9929. SER: Valuations; restorations.

Constance Bishop
32 Wellington Rd., Whalley Range. (C. Bishop and V.W. Osbaldiston.) Est. 1964. Open 10.30—6. SIZE: Medium. *STOCK: Furniture, including mahogany and walnut, 18th—19th C.* Not stocked: Oak. LOC: Off Withington Rd. — Whalley Range — direct road from south end of Mancunian Way. PARK: Easy. TEL: 226 1672. SER: Valuations.

Boodle and Dunthorne Ltd.
1 King St. Est. 1798. Open 9—5.30. SIZE: Large. *STOCK: Silver, 18th—19th C, £100—£5,000; clocks and clock sets, mid-19th C, £100—£1,000; jewellery, Victorian, £100—£5,000.* Not stocked: Furniture. TEL: 833 9000. VAT: Stan/Spec.

Manchester continued
Britannia Antiques
754 Stockport Rd., Longsight. (G. Zammit and Sons.) Open 9—6. *STOCK: Furniture, shipping goods, general antiques, all periods.* TEL: 224 8350/6425. VAT: Stan.

Browzers
14 Warwick St., Prestwich. (A.E. and M. Seddon.) Open 10—5.30. *STOCK: Second-hand books; prints.* TEL: 798 0626 or 773 2327. SER: Book lists available (S.A.E.).

Bulldog Antiques
393 Bury New Rd., Prestwich. (P. Wordsworth.) Est. 1971. CL: Sun. except by appointment. Open 9.30—6. SIZE: Large. *STOCK: Georgian, Victorian and Edwardian furniture, £25—£1,000; clocks especially longcase and wall clock sets, 18th—19th C, £35—£1,200; militaria, swords, guns, pistols, shotguns, war medals, pottery, prints, pictures, general antiques and shipping goods.* LOC: A56 from Manchester, shop 4 miles along main Bury Rd. PARK: At rear. TEL: 798 9277; home — 790 7153. SER: Restorations (furniture); French polishing, watch and clock repairs. VAT: Stan.

The Connoisseur   LAPADA
528 Wilmslow Rd. (Mr. and Mrs. S. Cohen.) Est. 1950. CL: Wed., and Mon. a.m. Open 10—1 and 2.30—6.30. *STOCK: English and French furniture and paintings, 18th—19th C; Sèvres and Meissen porcelain, 19th C upwards.* Not stocked: Brass, copper, pewter. LOC: From Manchester 4 miles due south down Oxford Rd. — shop situated at corner opp. Withington Fire Station. From south towards city, 150yds. after Christie's Hospital. PARK: Easy. TEL: 445 2504. VAT: Stan/Spec.

Crown Antiques
125 Burton Rd., West Didsbury. (C. and D. Humphrey.) CL: Wed. Open 9—5. *STOCK: Jewellery, pottery and porcelain.* TEL: 445 7374.

Dickinson Deansgreen Gallery
LAPADA
17/19 John Dalton St. (D. Dickinson.) Est. 1976. Open 9.30—5.30 or by appointment. *STOCK: Furniture and decorative items, 18th—19th C.* LOC: Between Albert Sq. and Deansgate. PARK: Easy and multi-storey nearby. TEL: 834 1042. SER: Valuations.

Dutch Connexion
1026/1028 Stockport Rd., Levenshulme. *STOCK: Furniture, pine, shipping goods and Victoriana, bric-a-brac, silver, gold, copper and brass.* TEL: 224 2550.

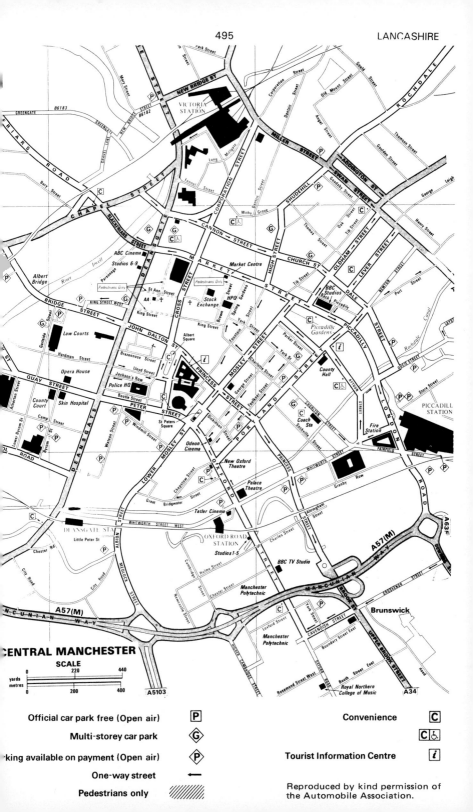

CENTRAL MANCHESTER

SCALE

Official car park free (Open air)	P	Convenience	C
Multi-storey car park	G		C
Parking available on payment (Open air)	P	Tourist Information Centre	i
One-way street	←		
Pedestrians only	////		

Manchester continued

David Friend Antiques
23 Guest Rd., Prestwich. Open by appointment only. *STOCK: Porcelain and works of art.* TEL: 773 1382. VAT: Stan/Spec.

The Fulda Gallery
19 Vine St., Salford. (M.J. Fulda.) Est. 1969. Open by appointment only. *STOCK: Oil paintings, 1600—1930, £100—£6,000; watercolours, 1800—1930, £50—£2,000.* LOC: Near Salford Police Station off Bury New Rd. TEL: 792 1962. SER: Valuations; restorations; buys at auction.

Gibb's Bookshop Ltd.
10, Charlotte St. Est. 1926. *STOCK: Books.* TEL: 236 7179.

The Ginnell Gallery   LAPADA
16 Lloyd St. (Mr. and Mrs. J.K. Mottershead.) Est. 1973. Open 9—5, Sat. 1—4 or by appointment. *STOCK: English 18th—19th C furniture and pottery, early iron and brass.* TEL: 833 9037.

E. and C.T. Koopman   BADA
and Son Ltd.
4 John Dalton St. CL: Sat. Open 10—5. *STOCK: Silver, objets d'art, jewellery, porcelain.* TEL: 832 9036 and 834 2420.

J. Long   Trade Only
915 Stockport Rd., Levenshulme. Est. 1964. Open 10—6. SIZE: Large. *STOCK: Clocks, especially longcase, £50—£6,000; period furniture, to £200,000; shipping goods, £5—£20,000.* Not stocked: Porcelain, silver. LOC: 2 miles from Mersey Square, Stockport, on A6 towards Manchester. PARK: Easy. TEL: 224 7923/8018. SER: Valuations; buys at auction (clocks). VAT: Stan.

Manchester Antique Hypermarket
Levenshulme Town Hall, 965 Stockport Road, Levenshulme. Open 10—5. There are 50 dealers at this market. PARK: Easy. TEL: 224 2410.

Eric J. Morten
2/4/6/8/9 Warburton St., Didsbury. Est. 1959. Open 10—6. SIZE: Large. *STOCK: Antiquarian books, 16th—20th C, £5—£500.* LOC: Warburton St. is off Wilmslow Rd., near traffic lights in Didsbury village. A34. PARK: Easy. TEL: 445 7629 and Macclesfield (0625) 23679. SER: Valuations; buys at auction (antiquarian books).

Manchester continued

Paul Quentin
626 Manchester Rd., Bury. (D. and P. Eccleston.) Est. 1965. Open 9—7 or any time to trade. SIZE: Large. *STOCK: Furniture, 1600—1920; shipping goods, £5—£500; collectors' items, all periods, weapons, jewellery, copper, brass, pewter, lamps.* Not stocked: Fine porcelain. LOC: On A56, 2 miles south of Bury centre. PARK: Easy. TEL: 766 6673. SER: Valuations; spare parts for paraffin lamps. VAT: Stan.

Royal Exchange Shopping Centre
Antiques Gallery, St. Ann's Sq. Open 9.30—5.30. TEL: 834 1427; 834 5765. Below are listed the dealers at this centre:

Adamas Antiques
No.17. *Jewellery.*
Alexander Antiques
No.4. *Furniture, glass and silver.*
The Antique Fireplace
No.12.
Arsenic and Old Lace
No.13. *Silk and lace wedding dresses.*
M. Bailey
No.3. *Stamps.*
Gary Carey
No.7. *Jewellery, pottery and silk.*
Franks Bookshop
No.11. *Books.*
Renee Franks
No.10. *General antiques.*
Grenville Art Gallery
No.8. *Fine paintings.*
Joan Grupman
No.14. *Stripped pine and jewellery.*
Irving Antiques
No.15. *Toys and dolls.*
Jenny Jones
No.5. *Jewellery.*
Linen and Lace
No.2. *Table linens and lace.*
Manchester Coin and Medal Centre
No.9. *Coins, medals and banknotes.*
Old Curiosity Shop
No.1. *Desks, Whitby jet, general antiques.*
Pine Place
No.18. *China, bric-a-brac, porcelain.*
Swan Antiques
No.16. *Jewellery.*

St. James Antiques
41 South King's St. *STOCK: Antique jewellery.* LOC: Off Deansgate, in town centre. TEL: 834 9632.

Shaw's Bookshop Ltd.
11 Police St. Est. 1947. Open 9—5.30. SIZE: Large. *STOCK: Secondhand and antiquarian books, 1500—1970; maps and prints.* LOC: Police St. is off King St., between King St. and St. Ann's Sq. PARK: 200yds. away — Kendal Milne car park. TEL: 834 7587. SER: Valuations; restorations (bindings); buys at auction; framing.

Manchester continued

Shulman of Manchester
41 Brooklands Rd., Prestwich. (H. and S. Shulman.) Est. 1964. Open 9.30−6, Sat. 10−12. *STOCK: Coins, medals, medallions, banknotes, paintings, cricketana, militaria.* LOC: 1½ miles from junction 18 on M62. PARK: Easy. TEL: 740 6190. SER: Valuations.

Tameside Antiques
1092 Stockport Rd., Levenshulme. (B. Boyle and D. Downworth.) Open every day. *STOCK: Furniture, longcase and wall clocks, shipping goods, pianos, coloured glass doors.* LOC: A6. TEL: 432 1619. SER: Valuations; reupholstery; packing and shipping. VAT: Stan.

Village Furniture Co.
58 School Lane, Didsbury. Est. 1978. Open 9−5.30, Sat. 10−4. *STOCK: Pine, 18th−19th C.* PARK: Easy. TEL: 445 4747.

L. Walton
41 Woodland Rd., Levenshulme. Open by appointment only. *STOCK: Maps, prints, photographs.* TEL: 224 6630.

MIDDLETON
Dusty Corner
120 Townley St. (G. Campbell.) Open 11−3.30, Wed. 11−5.30, Sat. 11−5. SIZE: Small. *STOCK: Victorian pottery, clocks, miscellany, £10−£100.* Not stocked: Large furniture. LOC: Follow Oldham sign from Middleton roundabout, turn right at traffic lights (200yds. from roundabout), shop is 200yds. on right. PARK: Easy. TEL: Home − (061) 643 1757.

G.G. Exports   *Trade only*
25 Middleton Rd. (S.J. Goulding.) Est. 1970. Always available but prior telephone call advisable. SIZE: Large. *STOCK: Shipping goods, £30−£200; Victoriana, £50−£400; general antiques.* Not stocked: Pine and expensive furniture. LOC: On main road between Morecambe promenade and Middleton. PARK: Easy. TEL: Morecambe (0524) 51565. VAT: Stan.

NELSON   (0282)
Colin Blakey Galleries
115 Manchester Rd. Est. 1926. CL: Tues. Open 9.15−5.30, Sat. 9.30−5. *STOCK: Fireplaces and hearth furniture, French clock sets, 19th C, £600−£800; porcelain figures, prints.* LOC: Exit 12 off M65. PARK: Opposite. TEL: 64941. SER: Restorations (fire furniture). VAT: Stan.

Britton's Jewellers
36 Scotland Rd. Est. 1970. CL: Tues. *STOCK: Jewellery and watches.* PARK: Opposite. TEL: 697659.

Nelson continued

Margaret's Antique Shop
79a Scotland Rd. (M. Owen.) Est. 1948. CL: Tues. Open 10−6. SIZE: Small. LOC: Town centre. PARK: Easy.

OLDHAM
Ace Antiques
40 Huddersfield Rd. (R. and J. O'Brien.) Est. 1970. CL: Sat. Open 9−5 or by appointment. *STOCK: Furniture, Edwardian and Victorian, shipping goods; general antiques and pianos.* LOC: On main Oldham to Huddersfield Rd. PARK: Own at rear. TEL: (061) 620 5755; home − (061) 626 2062.

Malik Antiques
253 Lees Rd. (S.H. Malik.) Est. 1972. Open by appointment only. *STOCK: General antiques and shipping goods, fine porcelain and furniture.* TEL: (061) 652 2842.

Miss H. Nuttall
269 Manchester Rd., Hollinwood. Est. 1925. *STOCK: Furniture, 18th to early 19th C; pottery, porcelain, decorative and general antiques, especially watercolours.* TEL: (061) 681 3766.

Oldham Antique Centre
1 Retiro St. (R. Butterworth.) Open 9−5. *STOCK: English furniture, leaded lights and doors.* TEL: (061) 665 3861.

H.C. Simpson and Sons Jewellers (Oldham) Ltd.
37 High St. Open 9−5.30. *STOCK: Clocks, jewellery, watches.* TEL: (061) 624 7187. SER: Restorations (clocks).

Waterloo Antiques
16 Waterloo St. (B.J. and S. Marks.) Est. 1969. Open 10−5. SIZE: Medium. *STOCK: General antiques, jewellery.* LOC: Town centre. TEL: (061) 624 5975. SER: Valuations.

ORMSKIRK   (0695)
Oasis Fine Arts Ltd.   LAPADA
Island House, Parrs Lane, Aughton. (Mrs. S. Forbes.) Est. 1978. Open by appointment. SIZE: Small. *STOCK: Furniture, to £5,000; copper and brass, £100−£1,000; decorative items, £100−£2,000; all 18th to early 19th C.* LOC: A570 to Ormskirk, turn left at Scarth Hill to station. PARK: Easy. TEL: 421080; home − same. SER: Buys at auction (furniture). FAIRS: Piccadilly, Kenilworth, British International, Birmingham; Olympia, Park Lane. VAT: Stan/Spec.

Revival Pine Stripping
15 Derby St. (N.F. and M.A. Sumner.) CL: Mon. and Wed. Open 10−4.30. SIZE: Small. *STOCK: Pine furniture.* LOC: Off A59. PARK: Nearby. TEL: 79298; home − 78308. SER: Stripping.

PENDLEBURY

L. Perry
592 Bolton Rd. CL: Sat. Open 9—5.30. SIZE: Small. *STOCK: General antiques.* LOC: A666. PARK: Easy. TEL: (061)794 3735. SER: Buys at auction.

POULTON-LE-FYLDE
Nr. Blackpool

Country Pine
3 Queens Sq. (C. Kinder and A. Heyes.) Est. 1983. Open 9.30—5, Wed. 9.30—12.30. SIZE: Medium. *STOCK: Stripped pine, beech, oak, lace, linen, china, moulded glass, late Victorian and Edwardian, £3—£100.* PARK: Nearby. TEL: Blackpool (0253) 894084. SER: Restorations (furniture); stripping. VAT: Stan.

PRESSTON   (0772)
Ages Ago Antiques   LAPADA
47-49 New Hall Lane. (A.W. and S. Shalloe.) Est. 1974. Resident. CL: Sun. except by appointment. Open 9—5.30, Sat. 9—1. SIZE: Medium. *STOCK: Furniture, 17th—20th C, £50—£5,000; longcase clocks, 18th—19th C, £250—£3,000; silver and plate, 18th—20th C, £20—£500; paintings, 19th—20th C, £25—£2,000; porcelain and china, 18th—20th C, £5—£1,000.* PARK: Easy. TEL: 798606. SER: Valuations. VAT: Stan/Spec.

Donald Allison Antiques   LAPADA
117—119 New Hall Lane. Open 9—5.30, Sun. and evenings by appointment. SIZE: Large. *STOCK: English, European and Oriental furniture, paintings, pottery, porcelain and objets d'art.* PARK: Easy. TEL: 701916. SER: Valuations. VAT: Stan/Spec.

Bow inkpot "made at New Canton" 1750. From "Auction Report" by Simon Spero, **Antique Collecting,** May 1986.

Preston continued

Antique and Reproduction Clocks
73 Friargate. (N.E. Oldfield, FBHI.) TEL: 58465. VAT: Stan.

Richard Bamber and Son Ltd.
102 Friargate. Est. 1909. CL: Thurs. p.m. SIZE: Large. *STOCK: General antiques.* TEL: 54480 and 54352.

Barronfield Gallery
47 Friargate. Open 10-5, Thurs. and Sun. by appointment. SIZE: Medium. *STOCK: Victorian and Edwardian watercolours, £100—£2,500.* LOC: Near Ringway on Friargate. PARK: Nearby. TEL: 563465; home — 690512.

Jack Blackburn
105 New Hall Lane. Est. 1968. *STOCK: Clocks, pocket watches, £7—£300; barometers, jewellery, £10—£120; small furniture, 1800, £20—£150; general shipping goods.* TEL: 791117. VAT: Stan.

W.J. Cowell and Sons
121—123 New Hall Lane. CL: Sat. Open 10—6, or by appointment. SIZE: Large. *STOCK: Victorian mahogany and walnut, Edwardian furniture and shipping goods for Dutch, Italian and Australian markets, stained glass leaded windows.* TEL: 794529 and 715646. VAT: Stan.

Duckworth's Antiques   *Trade Only*
41 and 45 New Hall Lane. (V.K., N. and M. Duckworth.) Est. 1960. CL: Sun. except by appointment. Open 9.30—6. SIZE: Medium. *STOCK: General antiques.* Not stocked: Arms, armour, coins, medals. LOC: Main road leading from M6 motorway. PARK: Easy. TEL: 794336; home — 742720.

Halewood and Sons
37 Friargate. Est. 1867. CL: Thurs. p.m. *STOCK: Antiquarian books.* TEL: 52603.

R.H. Latham Antiques
167 New Hall Lane. Est. 1966. SIZE: Medium and warehouse. *STOCK: Furniture, 1700—1900, £25—£1,000; china, glass, metal goods, 1750—1900, £5—£100; stripped pine.* TEL: 792056; home — Blackpool (0253) 691263.

North Western Antique Centre
New Preston Mill (Horrockses Yard), New Hall Lane. (P. and P. Allison.) Open 8.30—5.30, Sat. and Sun. by appointment. There are over 20 dealers at this centre, selling a wide range of general antiques especially shipping furniture. TEL: 794498. Below are listed the dealers.

C.W. Allison & Sons   LAPADA
(R. Allison.). *Furniture, paintings and porcelain.* TEL: Home — Blackpool (0253) 63054.
Paul Allison
Shipping goods.

North Western Antique Centre continued

Philip Allison
Shipping goods.
Burlington House
Mahogany and oak furniture.
G. Busato
Shipping goods and bric-a-brac.
Peter Charleston
Mahogany, walnut, pine and shipping furniture.
R. Coventry
Victorian furniture.
R. Cummings
Art deco, furniture.
L. Fairclough
Shipping and country furniture.
Fylde Antiques
Shipping and Victorian furniture.
Barry Hudson
Country furniture.
Don Kavangh
Bric-a-brac, dolls and toys.
B. Kelly
Shipping and Victorian oak and mahogany.
John Lambert
Shipping furniture, clocks and paintings.
L. Liberati
Victorian mahogany and walnut.
M.J. Antiques
(J.M. Shuttleworth.) *Shipping and country furniture.*
P. Norris
Shipping furniture.
Ramsay Antiques
(H. and C. Ramsay.) *General antiques, decorative and country items, textiles.* TEL: Home — Bolton (0204) 594681.
K. Rowlands
Shipping furniture, bric-a-brac.
J. Swire
Art nouveau, art deco, bric-a-brac.
Ray Wade Antiques   **LAPADA**
Furniture, including shipping; paintings, objets d'art, collectors' items. TEL: 792950; home — Hambleton (0253) 700715.

Tom Owen Antiques
111 New Hall Lane. *STOCK: Furniture and collectors' items.* LOC: Just off M6. PARK: Easy. TEL: 792950. VAT: Stan.

Preston Book Co.
68 Friargate. Est. 1950. Open 9.30—6. *STOCK: Antiquarian books.* TEL: 52603. SER: Buys at auction.

IS YOUR ENTRY CORRECT?
If there is even the slightest inaccuracy in your entry, *please* let us know before 1st January 1987.
GUIDE TO THE
ANTIQUE SHOPS OF BRITAIN
5 Church Street, Woodbridge, Suffolk.

Preston continued

Swag
24 Leyland Rd., Penwortham. (M. Fletcher.) Est. 1967. CL: Thurs. p.m. Open 9—6. SIZE: Small. *STOCK: Dolls, especially 1830—1920, £5—£250; pottery, porcelain, furniture.* LOC: 3 miles from exit 29, M6, following St. Anne's signs. PARK: Easy. TEL: 744970. SER: Restorations (dolls).

Frederick Treasure Ltd.   LAPADA
The Treasure House, 274—278 New Hall Lane. (J.F. Treasure.) Est. 1908. Open 9.30—5.30, Sat. 10—4. SIZE: Large. *STOCK: Furniture, 1650—1900, £10—£5,000.* Not stocked: Silver, paintings. PARK: Easy. TEL: 700216; home — Lytham (0253) 736801. SER: Valuations (furniture). VAT: Stan/Spec.

Ray Wade Antiques   LAPADA
111 New Hall Lane. Est. 1978. CL: Sat. Open 9.30—5.30. SIZE: Small. *STOCK: Furniture, some shipping; paintings, £5—£1,000; objets d'art, collectors' items.* PARK: Easy. TEL: 792950; home — Hambleton (0253) 700715. SER: Valuations; buys at auction. VAT: Stan/Spec.

RAMSBOTTOM   (070 682)
Pot of Gold Antiques
1 Peel Brow. (R. Palmer.) Est. 1972. Open 9—5.30. SIZE: Medium, and workshop. *STOCK: Stripped pine and satin walnut, late 19th C; painted furniture.* PARK: In side street. TEL: 5534.

RAWTENSTALL
Chesters & Co.
200 Haslingden Old Rd. (B. Chesters.) Est. 1977. Open by appointment. SIZE: Small. *STOCK: Pianolas (player-pianos), and piano rolls.* PARK: Easy. TEL: Rossendale (0706) 224617. SER: Valuations; restorations (pianolas).

READ, Nr. Padiham
Miles Fielding Antiques
Friendship Mill. Open Mon. and Tues. mornings, other times by appointment. *STOCK: Stripped and painted pine, country furniture, shipping goods.* TEL: Clitheroe (0200) 41330.

RIBCHESTER   (025 484)
Nr. Preston
Ribchester Antiques
27 Church St. (Mrs. N. Livesley.) Open 2—5. SIZE: Small. *STOCK: Oriental items, rugs, to £500; English ceramics and glass, 18th—20th C; some jewellery and silver.* Not stocked: Weapons, large furniture. PARK: Easy. TEL: 397.

ROCHDALE   (0706)
S.C. Falk   LAPADA
Open by appointment only. *STOCK: Fine English period furniture.* TEL: 44946. VAT: Stan/Spec.

F. Griffiths
298 Yorkshire St. TEL: 40097.

Owen Antiques
189—193 Oldham Rd. (J.G.T. Owen.) Est. 1891. Open 11.30—7, Sun. 2—6. *STOCK: Clocks and paintings, 17th—19th C, £100— £5,000; early oak and walnut, spinning wheels, silver, pewter, pistols, phonographs, wireless sets, coins, model ships, orreries and gothic clocks, nautical items.* Not stocked: Dolls, large sideboards. LOC: A627 from town centre up hill (Oldham road) for ½ mile. Next block to high level pavement on left hand side past railway bridge. PARK: 30 mins., otherwise in adjoining side streets. TEL: 48138; home — 353270. SER: Valuations; restorations (clocks and furniture).

Anne Taylor
195 Oldham Rd. Est. 1968. CL: Tues. Open 12—5, or by appointment. SIZE: Small. *STOCK: Porcelain, pottery, glass, copper, brass, pewter, furniture, Victoriana, £1— £500.* Not stocked: Weapons, medals. LOC: ½ mile from Rochdale Town Hall. A627. PARK: Easy. TEL: Home — 41151. SER: Buys at auction.

ROYTON, Nr. Oldham
Valley Antiques
151 Oldham Rd. (R. Byron.) Est. 1973. Open 10—6. SIZE: Medium. *STOCK: General antiques including stripped pine, porcelain, pottery, oak furniture, 19th C, £25—£300.* PARK: Easy. TEL: (061) 624 5030. SER: Valuations; restorations (pine stripping, upholstery, clocks).

SABDEN
Walter Aspinall Antiques
Union Mill, Watt St. Est. 1964. Open 9—5, weekends by appointment. SIZE: Large. *STOCK: General shipping goods for U.S.A. market.* LOC: On Pendle Hill between Clitheroe and Padiham. TEL: Padiham (0282) 76311. SER: Export; packing; courier; containers.

SADDLEWORTH   (045 77)
Nr. Oldham
Heyday
Huddersfield Rd., Delph. (H.J. Bell.) Est. 1972. Open most days including Sunday, or by appointment. SIZE: Medium. *STOCK: Furniture, 19th C, £5—£500; art nouveau and art deco items.* LOC: On A62 at road junction to Rochdale. PARK: Easy. TEL: 5849; home — same.

Oldfield Cottage Antiques
Denshaw Rd., Delph. (Mrs. R. Potts.) Est. 1982. Open Fri., Sat. and Sun, other times by appointment. SIZE: Medium. *STOCK: Pine — Victorian and German; kitchenalia, fireplaces and stoves.* PARK: Easy. TEL: 4537; home — same. SER: Valuations; restorations (pine stripping and waxing).

Peter Young Antiques   Trade Only
Friarmere School House, 47 Huddersfield Rd., Delph. Est. 1967. Open by appointment. *STOCK: General antiques, decorative and unusual items, shipping goods.* TEL: 70467.

ST. ANNES-ON-SEA   (0253)
Curios (St. Annes)
12 St. Albans Rd. (Mrs. C.A. Yates.) Est. 1945. CL: Wed. Open 10—5. SIZE: Medium. *STOCK: China, glass, silver and plate, fans, pewter, brass, copper, treen, Victorian curios, 1810—1945.* LOC: From St. Annes Sq. over railway bridge. Turn right at traffic lights into St. Davids Rd., 200yds. on right. PARK: Easy. TEL: 726120.

Spinning Wheel Antiques
16 St. Davids Rd. (Major C.M. Yates.) Est. 1945. CL: Wed. Open 10—5 or by appointment. SIZE: Medium. *STOCK: General antiques, porcelain, mid-18th to 1930, £5—£500; small furniture, silver, early 18th C to 1970s, £5—£2,500.* LOC: From St. Annes Sq. over railway bridge. Turn right at traffic lights into St. Davids Rd., shop 200yds. on right. PARK: Easy. TEL: 724187. SER: Valuations.

SHAWFORTH, Nr. Rochdale
Shawforth Antiques
193 Market St. (J. and E. Bracewell.) Est. 1967. Open 9.30—8, Sun. 9.30—5. SIZE: Small. *STOCK: Victoriana, clocks, bric-a-brac.* LOC: On Rochdale to Bacup Rd. PARK: Easy. TEL: Whitworth (070 685) 3402.

UPHOLLAND   (0695)
Nr. Wigan
Lancashire Bygones
12 Parliament St. (Mrs. M. Rathbone.) Est. 1975. CL: Mon., Tues. and Thurs. Open 10—5. SIZE: Small. *STOCK: General antiques, £5—£500; collectors' items, £2—£100.* LOC: On main road near church. PARK: Easy. TEL: 625624/622458.

WHALLEY, Nr. Blackburn
                                   (025 482)
The Abbey Antique Shop
43 and 45 King St. (A.D. and E. Austin.) Est. 1950. Open 9.30—6. SIZE: Large. *STOCK: Furniture, £10—£450; ceramics, £5—£150; both 18th—19th C; pewter, copper and brass, 17th—18th C.* Not stocked: Coins and stamps. LOC: A59. PARK: Easy. TEL: 3139. VAT: Stan/Spec.

Davies Antiques
32 King St. (G. and E. Davies.) Est. 1971. Open 10—5. SIZE: Small. *STOCK: British country furniture, and longcase clocks, to £3,000; jewellery, to £500.* Not stocked: Coins, weapons, Continental furniture. LOC: A59. PARK: Easy. TEL: 3764. VAT: Stan/Spec.

J.J. and P. Mather
29 King St. Est. 1985. Open 10.30—5.30, Sun. and Wed. by appointment. SIZE: Small. TEL: 2454; home — Great Harwood (0254) 884139. VAT: Spec.

WHITEFIELD, Nr. Manchester
Henry Donn Gallery
138/142 Bury New Rd. Est. 1954. Open 9.30—5.30. *STOCK: Paintings, 19th—20th C, £5—£15,000.* LOC: Off motorway M62; junction 17 — towards Bury. PARK: At rear. TEL: (061) 766 8819. SER: Valuations; framing; restorations (pictures). VAT: Stan/Spec.

WIGAN   (0942)
Jimmy Collins   LAPADA
Antiques Ltd.   *Trade Only*
Mab's Cross House, 136 Standishgate. (J.J. Collins.) Est. 1965. CL: Sat. Open 9—12 and 1—5. SIZE: Large. *STOCK: Furniture, 1650—1930, £5—£500; shipping goods, clocks, pottery, porcelain, glass, metalware, paintings.* Not stocked: Arms, armour. LOC: 100yds. from Central Park Rugby Football Ground. PARK: Easy. TEL: 48180; home — 41484. VAT: Stan/Spec.

L.G. Gough
550 Bolton Rd., Aspull. Est. 1964. Open 9—6. *STOCK: Pine and shipping goods, furniture, £5—£500.* LOC: Junction 6 off M61 then B5239. TEL: 831327. SER: Restorations (rush and cane), chair turning.

John Robinson   *Export and Trade Only*
Antiques
172—176 Manchester Rd., Higher Ince. Est. 1965. Open any time. SIZE: Large. *STOCK: General antiques.* LOC: A577 nr. Ince Bar. PARK: Easy. TEL: 47773 or 41671. SER: Packing for export, etc. VAT: Stan.

E. Sheargold
130—130a Standishgate. SIZE: Large. *STOCK: General antiques.* TEL: 42980.

Standishgate Antiques
110 Standishgate. (W. Hindle and Son.) Est. 1961. CL: Sat. Open 10.30—5. SIZE: Medium. *STOCK: Furniture.* LOC: 200yds. from town centre, opp. St. Mary's Catholic Church. PARK: Easy. TEL: Home — Brinscall (0254) 830552. VAT: Stan.

WORSLEY
H. and M.J. Burke
Oldpacket House Buildings. ADA. Est. 1959. CL: Sat. Open 10—5, appointment advisable. *STOCK: Period English furniture.* TEL: (061) 794 2093. VAT: Spec.

YEALAND CONYERS
Nr. Carnforth
M. and I. Finch
15 Yealand Rd. Est. 1970. Appointment advisable. SIZE: Medium. *STOCK: Brass, copper, treen, scientific instruments, rugs, furniture.* Not stocked: Jewellery, silver. LOC: 2 miles from M6, exit 35, just off A6. PARK: Easy. TEL: Carnforth (0524) 73 2212. SER: Buys at auction. VAT: Stan/Spec.

Leicestershire

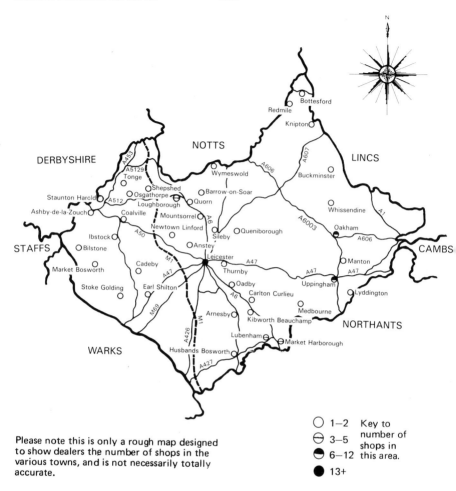

Please note this is only a rough map designed to show dealers the number of shops in the various towns, and is not necessarily totally accurate.

○	1—2
⊖	3—5
◒	6—12
●	13+

Key to number of shops in this area.

ANSTEY, Nr. Leicester

Antiques in Charnwood   LAPADA
68 Bradgate Rd. (B. Whadcock.) Est. 1982. CL: Mon. and Fri. Open 10—5, Sun. 2—5. *STOCK: General antiques including fine period furniture, Georgian—Edwardian.* TEL: Leicester (0533) 350708. VAT: Stan/Spec.

The Charnwood Gallery
24 Albion St. (F. East.) Est. 1974. Open 9—5, Sat. by appointment. SIZE: Medium. *STOCK: Printing and paper trade items — wood printing blocks, printing machines, book-binding equipment, 18th—20th C, £5—£1,000; some print machines, to £5,000.* PARK: Easy, own. TEL: Leicester (0533) 362569. SER: Valuations; restorations (furniture); furniture and wall plaques made from antique wood and copper printing blocks. VAT: Stan.

ARNESBY

Leycester Map Galleries Ltd.
Postal Business Only
Well House. (T. Forster.) Resident. Est. 1978. Open by appointment only. SIZE: Small. *STOCK: World-wide maps and sea charts, 1496-1870, £3—£700; atlases, £100—£3,000.* PARK: Easy. TEL: Peatling Magna (053 758) 462 (24 hour answering service). SER: Valuations; restorations (colouring and cleaning maps); buys at auction (antique maps). FAIRS: Bonnington Hotel, London (monthly). VAT: Stan.

" Ivanhoe Antiques "

(JOHN & ANN MANSFIELD)

Antique Furniture & Fine Porcelain

Tel. Ashby-de-la-Zouch 415424
Evenings 412524

53, MARKET STREET,
ASHBY-DE-LA-ZOUCH,
LEICESTERSHIRE.

This dealer has fine quality Georgian furniture, porcelain, oil paintings, prints, also copper and brassware.

ASHBY-DE-LA-ZOUCH (0530)
Ashby Antiques
51 Market St. (W. and M.E. Allen.) Est. 1965. CL: Wed. Open 10—5. SIZE: Large. *STOCK: General antiques, 1750—1920; early metalware, £2—£2,500.* TEL: 415004. VAT: Stan/ Spec.

Ivanhoe Antiques   LAPADA
53 Market St. (J. and A. Mansfield.) Est. 1976. CL: Wed. Open 10—5, Sun. by appointment. SIZE: Medium. *STOCK: Furniture, £5—£3,000; porcelain, Derby, Worcester and Coalport, £5—£500; all 18th—19th C; metalware and oil paintings, 19th C.* LOC: On A50 in centre of town. PARK: Easy. TEL: 415424; home — 412524. VAT: Stan/Spec.

BARROW-ON-SOAR
Bishop Beveridge House   *Trade Only*
Beveridge St. (T.L. Middleton.) Open 9—6. *STOCK: Furniture and general antiques.* TEL: Quorn (0509) 412270.

BILSTONE, Nr. Nuneaton
John Speed (Maps)
Drove House. Est. 1972. Open by appointment only. *STOCK: Maps, £2—£1,000; atlases, travel and topographical books, £1—£2,000.* TEL: (0827) 880439.

BOTTESFORD (0949)
Thomas Keen
51 High St. (T.E. Keen, FRSA.) Est. 1970. Appointment advisable. *STOCK: Furniture, 17th—19th C; metalwork, oil paintings, decorative items.* TEL: 42177. SER: Restorations, lectures (furniture).

BUCKMINSTER
Buckminster Antiques
Cow Row. (C.T. and M. Wain.) Est. 1975. Open Sat., Sun., Wed. and Bank Holidays 2—5. SIZE: Small. *STOCK: General antiques including pottery, porcelain, copper, brass, furniture, clocks, jewellery and bygones, all £2—£300.* Not stocked: Coins, medals, stamps, firearms. LOC: On B676. PARK: Easy. TEL: Home — Melton Mowbray (0664) 2099.

CADEBY, Nr. Nuneaton
P. Stanworth (Fine Arts)
The Grange. (Mr. and Mrs. G. Stanworth.) Resident. Est. 1965. Open by appointment. SIZE: Medium. *STOCK: Oil paintings, 18th to early 20th C, £100—£8,000.* LOC: Just off A447. PARK: Easy. TEL: Market Bosworth (0455) 291023. VAT: Spec.

CARLTON CURLIEU
Sporting Paintings Ltd.
Carlton Carlieu Manor. (M.J. Brankin-Frisby.) Est. 1980. Open by appointment only. SIZE: Small. *STOCK: Sporting watercolours and animalier bronzes, £100—£5,000.* LOC: Off A6 onto B6047, left at three gates, first right. PARK: Easy. TEL: Great Glen (053 759) 2283; home — same. SER: Restorations (watercolours); framing; buys at auction (watercolours and bronzes).

COALVILLE (0530)
Keystone Antiques LAPADA
9 Ashby Rd. (I. and H. McPherson, FGA.) Est. 1979. CL: Wed. Open 10—5.30, Sat. 10—4. SIZE: Medium. *STOCK: Jewellery, Victorian and Georgian, £25—£500; silver, 1700—1920, £20—£500; small collectable items, 18th—19th C, £15—£200; oil paintings, furniture, cranberry, needlework tools, Victorian and Georgian table glass.* LOC: A50, town centre. PARK: At rear. TEL: 35966. SER: Valuations (jewellery); gem testing. FAIRS: Gamlin Exhibition Services. VAT: Stan/Spec.

Massey's Antiques
26 Hotel St. (Mr. and Mrs. C.A. Irons.) Est. 1969. CL: Wed. Open 9—5. SIZE: Small. *STOCK: Bric-a-brac and bygones, small furniture, militaria, 1850-1945.* PARK: Rear. TEL: 32374; home — 32448.

EARL SHILTON (0455)
Earl Shilton Antiques
98 Wood St. (J.H. Hall.) Est. 1977. CL: Wed. Open 10—5. SIZE: Medium. *STOCK: Longcase clocks, Edwardian tables and chairs, Victorian glass, to £800.* PARK: Easy. TEL: 47117.

HUSBANDS BOSWORTH
Nr. Market Harborough
Past and Present
High St. (Mrs. M. Dalloe). Est. 1965. CL: Tues. Open 10—1 and 2—5, Thurs. and Sat. 10—1. SIZE: Small. *STOCK: General antiques, 19th C, £5—£100.* LOC: A427. PARK: Nearby. TEL: Home — Market Harborough (0858) 34428. SER: Valuations: restorations; cane seating.

IBSTOCK, Nr. Leicester
Mandrake Stephenson Antiques
101 High St. Est. 1979. Open 10—5, Sat. 10—4. SIZE: Small. *STOCK: Furniture, Georgian—Edwardian, £50—£500; pottery, pictures.* PARK: Easy. TEL: 60898; home — Leicester (0533) 549683. SER: Valuations; restorations (furniture).

KIBWORTH BEAUCHAMP
The Kibworth Antique Centre
5 Weir Rd. (R. Wheatley.) Est. 1971. CL: Mon. Open 10—6, Sun. 2—6, other times by appointment. SIZE: Large. *STOCK: Furniture, 18th—19th C, £100—£1,000; paintings and prints, £25—£1,500; Doulton stoneware pottery, £20—£300, jewellery, all 19th—20th C; silver, 18th—20th C, £10—£1,000.* LOC: Just off A6, in village centre. PARK: Easy. TEL: Kibworth (053 753) 2761; home — same. SER: Valuations; buys at auction. VAT: Spec.

KNIPTON
Nr. Grantham
Anthony W. Laywood
ABA. Est. 1967. Open by appointment. SIZE: Medium. *STOCK: Antiquarian books, pre-1850, £20—£2,000.* LOC: 1½ miles off the Grantham—Melton Mowbray road. PARK: Easy. TEL: Grantham (0476) 870 224. SER: Valuations; buys at auction.

LEICESTER (0533)
The Antiques Complex
St. Nicholas Pl. (K.W. Sansom.) Open 9.30—5.30, Sun. 2—5. SIZE: Large. There are 40 dealers at this complex offering a wide range of *general antiques including furniture, collectables, clocks, porcelain, glass, jewellery, paintings and decorative items.* LOC: Adjacent to High St., near Holiday Inn. PARK: Own. TEL: 533343. SER: Container packing.

Antique Emporium *Trade Only*
232 Narborough Rd. (N. Norton and T.M. Egan.) Open 9.30—5.30. SIZE: Large. *STOCK: Shipping goods.* LOC: 1 mile from junction 21, M1 (A46.) PARK: Easy. TEL: 824942. SER: Restorations. VAT: Stan.

Birches Art Deco Shop
15 Francis St., Stoneygate. (C. and H. Birch.) Est. 1978. CL: Wed. Open 10—5.30, Sun. by appointment. SIZE: Medium. *STOCK: Art deco, some Victoriana and kitchenalia.* LOC: 1 mile south of city centre, off A6. PARK: Easy. TEL: 703235; home — 703694. FAIRS: Art Deco, Nottingham, Bob Evans. VAT: Stan.

Corner Cottage Antiques
64 Narborough Rd. (J. and B. Roberts.) Est. 1969. Open 10—5.30 or by appointment. SIZE: Medium. *STOCK: 18th—20th C furniture, porcelain, china, copper, Victorian mahogany furniture for Australian, American, German, French and Italian markets.* LOC: 2 miles from junction 21 M1 (A46.) PARK: Easy. TEL: 548488; home — Sutton Elms (0455) 282583. VAT: Stan/Spec.

Curiotique
27a Wharf St., South. (L. Jefford.) Est. 1960. Open Wed.—Fri. 10—6. SIZE: Medium. *STOCK: Furniture, brass, copper, silver plate, pottery, porcelain, glassware, linen and lace.* LOC: Off Humberstone Gate. PARK: Easy. TEL: 56045.

Leicester continued

Golden Oldies
272 Welford Rd. (C. Chibnall.) Est. 1978. CL: Mon. Open 10—5.30. SIZE: Medium. *STOCK: Period clothes including Victorian 'whites', shawls, evening wear, mens, costume jewellery, books, 1900—1950, £1—£100; art deco, £5—£100.* LOC: A50 Welford road, ½ mile from city centre. PARK: Clarendon Park Rd. TEL: 706999. SER: Costume and fancy dress hire.

Leicester Antique Centre Ltd.
16—26 Oxford St. Open 10—5.30, Sun. 2—5; or by appointment. SIZE: Large. There are approximately 100 dealers at this market selling *period furniture, shipping goods, silver, bric-a- brac and general antiques, 18th to mid-20th C, 50p—£5,000.* LOC: Main ring road. PARK: Own. TEL: 553006/540118. SER: Valuations; restorations (furniture, clocks, porcelain); buys at auction; container loading facilities; courier. VAT: Stan/Spec.

Letty's Antiques Ltd.
6 Rutland St. Est. 1952. *STOCK: Silver, jewellery, china and brass.* TEL: 26435.

Walter Moores and Son
89 Wellington St. (H. and P. Moores and S. Austin.) Est. 1925. Open 8.30—6.30. *STOCK: General antiques, 1680—1820, £5—£500; 17th—19th C English and Continental furniture.* LOC: From London Rd. railway station go up Waterloo Way, first right, then first left and left again. PARK: Easy. TEL: 551402; home — 704992. VAT: Stan/Spec.

Robert Neville Antiques
Trade and Export
The Old Dairy, Western Boulevard. Est. 1974. Open 10—6, Sun. by appointment. SIZE: Medium. *STOCK: Shipping goods, pine.* PARK: Easy. TEL: 541201/542819. SER: Buys at auction. VAT: Stan/Spec.

Quorn Antiques
Mainly Trade
214 Narborough Rd. (Mr. Gough.) Est. 1960. *STOCK: General antiques, shipping items.* TEL: 825917; home — Quorn (0509) 413385.

Chris Roper's Pine Shop
312 Welford Rd. Open 9.30—5.30. *STOCK: Stripped and unstripped pine.* PARK: Easy. TEL: 704553; home — 402981. VAT: Stan.

Ryte Lynes Antiques
4 Shaftesbury Rd., (off Narborough Rd.) (R. Fenn, G. Jones.) Est. 1977. Open 8.30—6. Sat. 9—12. *STOCK: General antiques.* SER: Restorations.

Leicester continued

E. Smith (Leicester) Ltd   LAPADA
The Antiques Complex, St. Nicholas Pl. (K.W. Sansom.) Est. 1888. Open 9.30—5.30. SIZE: Large. *STOCK: Furniture, 18th—19th C and Edwardian, £50—£1,000; clocks, smalls and paintings.* LOC: Adjacent High St., near Holiday Inn. PARK: Own. TEL: 533343. SER: Valuations; buys at auction (18th—19th C furniture and paintings). VAT: Stan/Spec.

Hammond Smith
Beaumont House, 24 Knighton Dr. Est. 1981. Open by appointment. SIZE: Small. *STOCK: British watercolours, 1750—1920, £100—£5,000; British etching, 19th—20th C, £50—£300.* LOC: Off London Rd., Stoneygate, South Leicester. PARK: Easy. TEL: 709020; home — same. SER: Valuations; restorations (watercolours and prints cleaned, mounted and framed); buys at auction (watercolours). VAT: Spec.

Leicester continued

Withers of Leicester
142a London Rd. (S. Frings.) Est. 1860. CL: Thurs. p.m. and Sat. Open 9—5.30. SIZE: Medium. *STOCK: Furniture, 17th—19th C, £10—£1,000; china, 18th—19th C, £10—£300; oil paintings, 19th C, £5—£500.* Not stocked: Jewellery and coins. LOC: Entering town on main London Rd. PARK: Easy. TEL: 544836; home — 708968. SER: Valuations; restorations (furniture). VAT: Stan/Spec.

LOUGHBOROUGH (0509)
Carillon Antiques
64 Leicester Rd. (Mrs. M. Trasler and Mrs. M. Turner). Est. 1982. CL: Wed. Open 10—5. SIZE: Medium. There are 20 dealers at these premises offering a wide range of *jewellery, silver, linen, pottery, porcelain, Dinky toys, kitchenalia and small furniture.* LOC: On A6 on outskirts of town. PARK: Easy. TEL: 237169; home — 261682.

Copperfield Antiques
221a Derby Rd. (Mrs. B. Gardner). Est. 1970. CL: Mon. and Wed. Open 10—5, Sat. 10—1. SIZE: Small. *STOCK: Furniture, £40—£400; porcelain, £5—£100; both early 19th C; brass, copper, china, glass, paintings and boxes, early 19th to early 20th C., £5—£250.* LOC: A6. PARK: Easy. TEL: 232026; home — 239281.

Lowe of Loughborough
37—40 Church Gate. Est. 1846. CL: Sat. SIZE: Large and warehouse. *STOCK: Furniture and period upholstery from early oak c.1600 to Edwardian; mahogany, walnut, oak, £20—£8,000; clocks, bracket and longcase, £95—£2,500; porcelain, pewter, maps, copper and brass.* Not stocked: Jewellery. PARK: Own. LOC: Opposite parish church. TEL: 212554 and 217876. SER: Upholstery; restorations; interior design. VAT: Stan/Spec.

LUBENHAM
Nr. Market Harborough
Leicestershire Sporting Gallery
The Old Granary. When closed apply 87 Lubenham Hill. (R.L. Leete.) Est. 1958. SIZE: Large. *STOCK: Oil paintings, prints including Vanity Fair, cricket, lawyers, golf, jockeys, rowing, nautical; engravings, maps, furniture, including pine, mahogany and oak.* LOC: Centre of village. PARK: Rear of village green opposite. TEL: Market Harborough (0858) 65787. VAT: Stan.

Lubenham continued

Lubenham Antiques and The Brown Jack Bookshop
78 Main St. (R.L. Leete.) Est. 1958. Open 9—6, Sun. 10—12, Thurs. 9—12, Fri. 9—7, prior phone call advisable. When closed call at 87 Lubenham Hill. SIZE: Medium. *STOCK: Model railway engines, general prints, maps, books; clocks, engravings, horse brasses, militaria, oil paintings.* Not stocked: Japanese, Chinese and Oriental items. PARK: Easy. TEL: Market Harborough (0858) 65787. SER: Valuations; picture framing. VAT: Stan.

T.J. Roberts
Manor Farm, The Green. Resident. Open by appointment. *STOCK: Furniture — oak, walnut, mahogany, 18th—19th C; paintings.* TEL: Market Harborough (0858) 31758; home — same.

LYDDINGTON, Nr. Uppingham
Lapwing Antiques
115 Main St. (D.L. Jones Ltd.) Est. 1962. Open by appointment only. *STOCK: Porcelain, 18th—19th C, £5—£200; furniture, 17th to early 19th C, £200—£2,000; watercolours, 19th C, £30—£100.* LOC: Edge of village. PARK: Easy. SER: Valuations; restorations; buys at auction (pottery and porcelain). TEL: Uppingham (0572) 822852. VAT: Spec.

MANTON (057 285)
David Smith Antiques
Old Cottage, 20 St. Mary's Rd. Est. 1953. CL: Sun., except by appointment. Open 9—5. *STOCK: Furniture, glass, silver.* PARK: Easy. TEL: 244. VAT: Stan/Spec.

MARKET BOSWORTH (0455)
Corner Cottage Antiques
5 Market Pl., The Square. (J. and B. Roberts.) Est. 1969. CL: Thurs. Open 10—5. *STOCK: 18th—20th C furniture, pottery, porcelain, glass, brass and copper, general antiques.* PARK: Easy. TEL: 290344; home — Sutton Elms (0455) 282583. VAT: Stan/Spec.

Country Antiques
4 Main St. (M. and A. Boylan.) Est. 1980. CL: Tues. Open 10—5.30. SIZE: Small. *STOCK: Stripped pine furniture, Victorian, £20—£500; chests of drawers, dressers, tables and chairs.* LOC: Off A447. PARK: Easy. TEL: 291303; home — same. SER: Pine stripping.

MARKET HARBOROUGH   (0858)

Abbey Antiques
17 Abbey St. (M.A. Muckle.) Est. 1977. CL: Wed. Open 10—12.30 and 1.30—5. Sat. 9—5. SIZE: Medium. *STOCK: Furniture, 19th C, £50—£1,000; decorative items, bric-a-brac, £1—£150.* LOC: 100 yards off town centre. PARK: Easy. TEL: 62282; home — 64085. SER: Valuations. VAT: Stan/Spec.

Richard Kimbell Antiques
Riverside. CL: Sat. Open 7.30—5. SIZE: Large warehouse. *STOCK: Pine and country furniture, from £5.* TEL: 33444. SER: Shipping and packing; manufacturer.

Nithsdale Gallery
42 High St. (Mrs. A.M. Hutchins.) Est. 1981. CL: Wed. Open 10—5. SIZE: Medium. *STOCK: General antiques, pine, china, prints, furniture, Victoriana.* Not stocked: Coins, firearms, stamps, militaria. LOC: A6. PARK: Easy. TEL: 32277; home — same.

Vendy Antiques
The Paddocks, High St. (D.R., T.W and Mrs. V.R. Vendy.) Est. 1966; Open 10—1 and 2—5. SIZE: Large. *STOCK: General antiques including furniture and smalls, mainly Victorian, £5—£1,000+.* LOC: 12 miles east of M1, junction 20, on A6. TEL: 31085. VAT: Stan/Spec.

MEDBOURNE

E. and C. Royall Antiques
10 Waterfall Way. Open 9—6 including Sun. *STOCK: Furniture, pictures, silver, porcelain, glassware, ivories and oriental bronzes.* TEL: Medbourne Green (085 883) 744; home — same. SER: Restorations (bronzes, ivories, brassware, metalware, woodcarving, upholstery, French polishing.)

MOUNTSORREL

The Collection Antique Centre
34 Market Place. (I. Corrall and Mrs. M. Naylor.) Est. 1972. Open Fri. and Sat. 12—5, Sun. 12—6, other times by appointment. SIZE: Large. *STOCK; Furniture — mahogany, oak, satin walnut, pine; pottery, prints, watercolours and oils, copper and brass, glass, all Victorian and Edwardian; cast and tile fireplaces, Victorian; all £5—£1,000.* LOC: A6. PARK: Easy. TEL: Home — Sileby (050 981) 2128. SER: Valuations; restorations (pine and satin walnut); buys at auction (Victorian and Edwardian items).

The Market Place
50 Market Place. (K. Button.) CL: Mon. Open 10—5. *STOCK; General antiques especially collectables.* TEL: Leicester (0533) 302249.

This example of a Diana swinging clock was manufactured during the 1930s but similar clocks appeared in the Hirst Bros. catalogue for 1910 retailing at 30/-. From *The Price Guide to Collectable Clocks 1840-1940* by Alan and Rita Shenton, published by the **Antique Collectors' Club**, 1985.

NEWTOWN LINFORD, Nr. Leicester

Bradgate Antiques
500 Main St. (Miss S. Brown.) Est. 1984. CL: Mon. Open 10—5 including Sun., Wed. and Thurs. by appointment. SIZE: Small. *STOCK: General antiques, mainly Victorian, country furniture including pine, pottery, prints, water-colours, brass, linen, £1—£500.* LOC: B5327 opposite church. PARK: Easy. TEL: Home — Markfield (0530) 242498. SER: Restorations (chairs re-caned and re-rushed).

OADBY

John Hardy Antique Shop
91 London Rd. Est. 1963. Open every day. *STOCK: Oriental antiques, bronzes, weapons, oil lamps and instruments.* TEL: Leicester (0533) 712862; home — Leicester (0533) 677676. VAT: Stan/Spec.

OAKHAM   (0572)

Flore's House Antiques
34 High St. (M. Kilby.) CL: Thurs. Open 10—5. *STOCK: Furniture.* TEL: 57207. SER: Restorations (furniture); upholstery, french polishing, cane and rush seating.

Grafton Country Pictures
153 Brooke Rd. (F. Gray). Est. 1967. Open by appointment. *STOCK: Sporting, farming, natural history, decorative prints, 18th and 19th C.* TEL: 57266.

Manor House Antiques
The Manor House, 1. Northgate. (C. Dilger.) Resident. CL: Thurs. and Sun. except by appointment. Open 10—5.30, SIZE: Small. *STOCK: Victorian Staffordshire figures, cran-berry, Bristol blue and green glass, collectors' items, Regency, Victorian and Edwardian furniture, prints and engravings.* Not stocked: Clocks and jewellery. LOC: Opposite church. PARK: Nearby. TEL: 55252.

Oakham Antiques
16 Melton Rd. Open 9—5, Sat. by appoint-ment. *STOCK: Brass, glass, small furniture, postcards, lamps, pictures, prints, silver.* TEL: Morcott (057 287) 840.

The Old House Gallery
13—15 Market Place. (R.A. Clarke.) Resident. Est. 1959. Open 9.30—5. SIZE: Medium. *STOCK: Oil paintings, £50—£3,500; water-colours, £25—£500; prints and objets d'art, £5—£500; antiquarian county maps, £15—£250.* LOC: In Market Square. PARK: Easy. TEL: 55538; home — 3130. SER: Valuations; restorations (oils, watercolours, prints, fram-ing).

Oakham continued

Rutland Coins and Antiques
27 Mill St. (W.R. Lynn.) Est. 1967. Open 9—12 and 1—4.30. SIZE: Medium. *STOCK: Furniture, 1650—1850, £25—£3,500; 18th—19th C English furniture, clocks and general antiques.* LOC: A606. PARK: Easy. TEL: 3364; home — 56683. SER: Valuations; buys at auction. VAT: Stan/Spec.

The Rutland Gallery Workshop
Westgate Car Park (R.A. and A.M. Clarke.) Open 9.30—1, Fri. and Sat. 2—5. *STOCK: General antiques, pine, £5—£800; paintings, pots, prints and antiquarian maps.* LOC: Behind Gateway supermarket. TEL: 57661. SER: Restorations; framing.

OSGATHORPE, Nr. Loughborough

Stable Antiques
35 Main St. (Mrs. P. Wilkinson.) Est. 1975. Open anytime, appointment advisable. SIZE: Medium. *STOCK: Prints, mainly sporting, watercolours and Baxters from late 18th C; small furniture, silver, boxes, cut-glass decanters and claret jugs, sporting books.* Not stocked: Brass, copper, weapons. LOC: Off B5324. PARK: Own. TEL: Coalville (0530) 222463. SER: Valuations. FAIRS: Mentmore, Newtown Linford, Haddon Hall, Thoresby Hall.

QUENIBOROUGH, Nr. Leicester

J. Green and Son
1 Coppice Lane. (R. Green.) Resident. Est. 1932. Appointment advisable. SIZE: Medium. *STOCK: 18th—19th C English and Conti-nental furniture.* LOC: Off A607 Leicester—Melton Mowbray Rd. PARK: Easy. TEL: Leicester (0533) 606682. SER: Valuations; buys at auction. VAT: Stan/Spec.

QUORN   (0509)

David E. Burrows   LAPADA
4 High St. Est. 1973. Open 9—6.30, Sun. by appointment. SIZE: Medium. *STOCK: Furni-ture, oak, mahogany and walnut, 1650—1880, £25—£2,000; longcase and other clocks, £50—£1,500; pictures and prints, £10—£500; treen, copper and brass, porcelain, £5—£500.* Not stocked: Bric-a-brac. LOC: On A6, in centre of village. PARK: Opposite. TEL: 412191. FAIRS: Kenilworth and Buxton. VAT: Stan/Spec.

J. Green & Son
Antiques
1 Coppice Lane, Queniborough, Leicester
Telephone Leicester 606682

Quorn continued

Mill on the Soar Antiques Ltd.
1/3 High St. (J. York.) *STOCK: Furniture, 17th—19th C; glass, porcelain, decorative items.* LOC: In centre of village, on A6. PARK: Easy. TEL: 414218.

REDMILE

Evelyn Buckle
The Villa, Main St. (Mrs. R.N. Buckle.) Resident. Est. 1978. Open by appointment only. *STOCK: Furniture, 17th—19th C, £20—£1,000; paintings, metalwork and decorative items, £5—£500.* PARK: Easy. TEL: Bottesford (0949) 42057.

SHEPSHED   **(0509)**
Nr. Loughborough

G.K. Hadfield
Blackbrook Hill House, Tickow Lane. Resident. Est. 1972. Open 9—5. *STOCK: Clocks, longcase, Act of Parliament, skeleton, Black Forest, American and carriage; secondhand and rare horological books.* LOC: 1¾ miles along the A512 west of M1, exit 23. PARK: Easy. TEL: 503014. SER: Restoration materials (antique clocks). VAT: Stan/Spec.

SILEBY,   **(050 981)**
Nr Loughborough

R.A. James Antiques
Ammonite Gallery, 25a High St. *STOCK: Mainly stripped pine, general antiques.* TEL: 2169.

STAUNTON HAROLD

Ropers Hill Antiques
Ropers Hill Farm. (S. and R. Southworth.) Est. 1974. Open 9—5.30 every day or by appointment. SIZE: Small. *STOCK: General antiques, shipping goods, silver and metalware.* LOC: On A453. PARK: Easy. TEL: Ashby de la Zouch (0530) 413919. SER: Valuations.

STOKE GOLDING, Nr. Hinckley

Harper's Hill Farm Antiques
Main St. (Mrs. E.C. Dickinson.) Est. 1975. CL: Mon. and Fri. Open 2—5.30 including Sun. SIZE: Small. *STOCK: Oak, mahogany, walnut and pine furniture, £5—£650; porcelain, pictures and jewellery; all 18th—19th C; brass, copper and iron work.* Not stocked: Silver. LOC: 2 miles north-west of Hinckley. PARK: Easy. TEL: Home — Hinckley (0455) 212418. SER: Buys at auction.

THURNBY
J.A. Morrison Ltd.
43 Grange Lane. Est. 1952. Open daily 9—6. *STOCK: Decorative and collectors' items in militaria.* TEL: Leicester (0533) 413750. SER: Buys at auction. VAT: Stan.

TONGE, Nr. Melbourne
The Spindles
(Mrs. C. Reynolds.) Est. 1972. Resident. Usually available but telephone call advisable. SIZE: Large. *STOCK: Clocks, watches, 17th—19th C.* LOC: 3 miles from exit 24 M1. PARK: Easy. TEL: Melbourne (033 16) 2609. VAT: Stan.

UPPINGHAM   (0572)
Allsorts Antiques
5 Hopes Yard. (Mrs. P. Wake and Mrs. A. Hex.) Est. 1984. CL: Mon. and Thurs. Open 10—1 and 2—4.30. SIZE: Medium. *STOCK: Small furniture including pine, brass, prints, porcelain, glass and bric-a-brac, 19th C, to £100.* LOC: In small alleyway off High St. PARK: Nearby. TEL: Home — 823204 and 821269.

Uppingham continued
Ayston House Antiques
Ayston Rd. (J.A. and K. Langley.) Est. 1980. Open 10—1.15 and 1.45—5, Thurs. and Sun. by appointment. SIZE: Small. *STOCK: Country furniture including pine, £50—£250; bric-a-brac, £5—£50; all Victorian and Edwardian.* LOC: ½ mile off A47. PARK: Easy. TEL: Home — Empingham (078 086) 411.

Bay House
33 High St. East. (G. Todd.) Est. 1983. CL: Mon. and Thurs. p.m. Open 10—1.30 and 2—5, Sat. 9.30—5. SIZE: Medium. *STOCK: Bric-a-brac, jewellery, small furniture, Victorian—Edwardian, £5—£25.* LOC: Near Falcon Hotel, facing town square. PARK: Nearby. TEL: 821045; home — 822574. VAT: Stan.

IS YOUR ENTRY CORRECT?
If there is even the slightest inaccuracy in your entry, *please* let us know before 1st January 1987.
GUIDE TO THE
ANTIQUE SHOPS OF BRITAIN
5 Church Street, Woodbridge, Suffolk.

An Indian elephant, c.1910, unmistakably by Bugatti with his unique sense of poise and balance. Here he has modelled quite simply one of these delightful creatures leaning over the ha-ha at the zoo to take gently a morsel of food from an onlooker. From *Animals in Bronze* by Christopher Payne, published by the **Antique Collectors' Club**, 1986.

Uppingham continued

Clutter
14 Orange St. (M.C. Sumner). Est. 1982. CL: Thurs. Open 10—5. *STOCK: Victorian linen and lace; Victorian and Georgian jewellery; interesting and unusual brass, copper, silver, porcelain, glass, small furniture, kitchenalia, 10p—£1,000.* LOC: Take old A47 from by-pass, shop 25 yards from traffic lights. PARK: Opposite. TEL: 823745; home — Belton-in-Rutland 243. SER: Valuations; restorations (furniture, brass, copper, silver).

John Garner
51 High St. East. Est. 1967. Open 9.30—5.30. Sun. 2—5. SIZE: Large. *STOCK: Furniture, clocks, paintings, bronzes, silverware, picture frames, all 18th—19th C; restrike engravings.* LOC: Just off A47, close to market place. PARK: Easy. TEL: 823607. SER: Valuations; restorations (pictures and furniture); framing; courier; export. Illustrated catalogue available on request. VAT: Stan/Spec.

Gilberts of Uppingham
Ayston Rd. (K. Gilbert). Open Wed. Fri. and Sat. 9.30—5. *STOCK: General antiques.* TEL: 823486.

Goldmark Bookshop
14 Orange St. (M.M. Goldmark). Open 9.30—1 and 2—5.30, Thurs. 9.30—1, Sat. 9.30—5.30. *STOCK: Antiquarian and second-hand books.* LOC: Take old A47 from by-pass, shop 25 yds. from traffic lights, next to Clutter. PARK: Opposite. TEL: 822694.

E. and C. Royall Antiques
Printers Yard, High St. East. CL: Thurs. Open 10—4.30. *STOCK: Furniture, pictures, silver, porcelain, glassware, ivories and oriental bronzes.* TEL: Medbourne Green (085 883) 744.

Uppingham continued

Sutton Antiques
Falcon Hotel Courtyard. (J.A. Sutton.) CL: Mon. and Thurs. Open 10.30—4.30. *STOCK: Small furniture, porcelain, clocks, interior decorating items.* TEL: 821195.

Tattersall's
14b Orange St. (J. Tattersall). Est. 1971. CL: Wed. and Thurs. Open 9—12 and 1—5. SIZE: Small. *STOCK: Mirrors, chairs, tables, 19th—20th C., £50—£500.* PARK: Easy and 200 yards. TEL: 821171. SER: Restorations (rush and cane work).

WHISSENDINE   (066 479)
Nr. Oakham

Old Bakehouse
11 Main St. (E. and W. Stevenson.) Open seven days, prior phone call advisable. *STOCK: Stripped pine furniture.* LOC: Off A606, opposite village school. TEL: 691. SER: Stripping (pine). FAIRS: Local.

WYMESWOLD   (0509)
Nr. Loughborough

N. Bryan-Peach Antiques
28 Far St. Open 10—6 every day. SIZE: Small. *STOCK: Clocks, barometers, watches, furniture, 18th—19th C, £50—£2,000.* PARK: Easy. TEL: 880425. SER: Valuations; restorations; buys at auction. VAT: Spec.

Hornbeam Antiques
London Cottage, 59 London Lane. (Mrs. G.J. Bottomley.) Est. 1979. Open by appointment. SIZE: Small. *STOCK: English porcelain and pottery, 18th to early 20th C, £10—£300; small furniture, Regency to Edwardian, £30—£500; watercolours, 19th C, £10—£200.* LOC: Junction of London Lane with main Rempstone Rd. (A6006) on edge of village. PARK: Easy. TEL: 881102; home — same. FAIRS: Midlands and North.

Lincolnshire 512

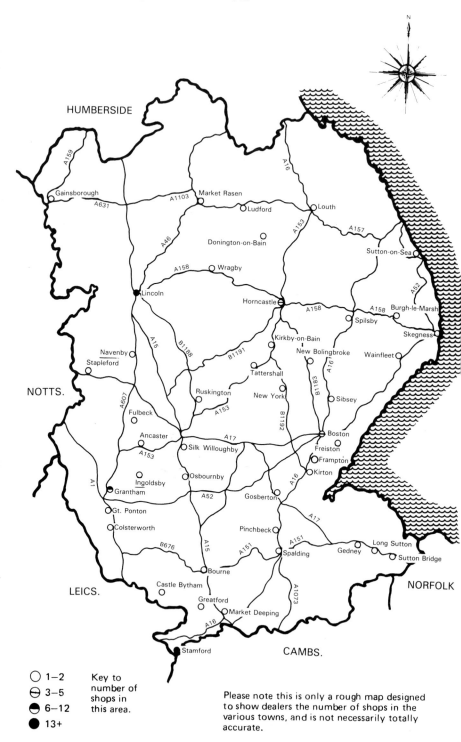

HUMBERSIDE

NOTTS.

LEICS.

NORFOLK

CAMBS.

- A159
- Gainsborough
- A631
- A1103
- Market Rasen
- Ludford
- A16
- Louth
- A157
- A153
- Donington-on-Bain
- A46
- Sutton-on-Sea
- A158
- Wragby
- A52
- Lincoln
- Horncastle
- A158
- A158
- Burgh-le-Marsh
- Spilsby
- Skegness
- A15
- B1188
- B1191
- Kirkby-on-Bain
- New Bolingbroke
- Wainfleet
- Navenby
- Stapleford
- Tattershall
- A161
- B1183
- A607
- Fulbeck
- Ruskington
- New York
- Sibsey
- A153
- B1192
- A1
- Ancaster
- A17
- Boston
- A153
- Silk Willoughby
- Freiston
- Ingoldsby
- Osbournby
- Frampton
- Grantham
- A52
- Kirton
- Gosberton
- A16
- Gt. Ponton
- A17
- Colsterworth
- Pinchbeck
- Long Sutton
- B676
- A15
- A151
- A151
- Gedney
- Sutton Bridge
- Bourne
- Spalding
- Castle Bytham
- Greatford
- A1073
- A16
- Market Deeping
- Stamford

Key to number of shops in this area.
- ○ 1–2
- ◑ 3–5
- ◕ 6–12
- ● 13+

Please note this is only a rough map designed to show dealers the number of shops in the various towns, and is not necessarily totally accurate.

ANCASTER

K. Rawdon
The Old Coaching House, Ermine Way. Est. 1960. SIZE: Medium. *STOCK: Cottage furniture and general antiques.* TEL: Loveden (0400) 30372.

BOSTON   (0205)

Boston Antiques Centre
12 West St. (D. and P. Pilling.) Est. 1965. Open 9—5.30. SIZE: Medium. *STOCK: Jewellery, silver and plate.* LOC: 2 minutes walk from town centre on Spalding side. PARK: 1 minutes walk. TEL: 61510. SER: Valuations; restorations; export. VAT: Stan/Spec.

The Bric-a-Brac Shop
9A Pen St. (Mrs. S.M. Taylor.) Est. 1976. Open Wed., Fri. and Sat. 10—1 and 2—4. SIZE: Small. *STOCK: China, glass, silver and plate, jewellery, 1830—1930, £2—£200.* LOC: 40 metres from 'New England' Hotel. PARK: Easy. TEL: 64118; home — same. SER: Buys at auction (bric-a-brac).

Carousel Antique Centre T/A Goodbuys
45 London Rd. Open 10—6 every day. There are 12 dealers at this centre selling *Victorian furniture, pine, shipping goods, smalls.* TEL: 54515.

Particles of Time
7 Red Lion St. (L.B. Brand.) CL: Mon., Tues. and Thurs. Open 10.30—3.30, Sat. 10.30—4.30. *STOCK: Jewellery and general antiques.* LOC: Behind Woolworths. TEL: Home — Spilsby (0790) 53060.

BOURNE   (0778)

Bourne Antiques
The Mill, North Rd. (G. Burns.) Est. 1975. Open 10—1 and 2—5. SIZE: Medium. *STOCK: Furniture, clocks, small items, period and Victorian, £50—£500.* LOC: A15. PARK: Easy. TEL: 425323; home — 423781. VAT: Stan/Spec.

BURGH-LE-MARSH, Nr. Skegness

Station Antiques
Old Railway Station. (R.I. Hill, C.L. and J.K. Ditheridge.) Resident. Est. 1972. Open seven days in summer, weekends only in winter. SIZE: Small. *STOCK: General antiques including furniture and small items, 19th to early 20th C, £20—£400.* LOC: A158. PARK: Easy. TEL: Skegness (0754) 810161; home — Alford (052 12) 2422.

CASTLE BYTHAM   (078 081)

Greystoke Antiques
15 Castlegate. (R. and S. Dean.) Resident. Open by appointment. SIZE: Small. *STOCK: Oak and country furniture, 17th—19th C, £100—£1,500; carvings, 16th—17th C, £100—£800; metalware, 15th—18th C, £50—£1,500.* LOC: In centre of village. PARK: Easy. TEL: 274. VAT: Spec.

COLSTERWORTH

Clive Underwood Antiques
46 High St. Est. 1970. CL: Mon. Open 9.30—5.30. *STOCK: Furniture, oak, mahogany, 17th—18th C, £15—£3,000; some pictures, glass, porcelain.* Not stocked: Victorian items. LOC: ½ mile off A1 between Stamford and Grantham. TEL: Grantham (0476) 860689. SER: Valuations; restorations. VAT: Stan/Spec.

DONINGTON-ON-BAIN
Nr. Louth

Lindum Antiques
Main Rd. (D.G. and M. Wilby.) Est. 1972. Open by appointment. SIZE: Medium. *STOCK: Pottery and porcelain, 18th—19th C, £30—£1,000; small furniture, £10—£350.* Not stocked: Coins. LOC: Near Belmont television mast. TEL: Stenigot (050 784) 639. FAIRS: Most major. VAT: Spec.

FRAMPTON, Nr. Boston

Robert John Kent
Pinewood, Ralphs Lane. Open daily. *STOCK: Pine and some other furniture.* LOC: B1391. TEL: Boston (0205) 723739.

FREISTON, Nr. Boston

Geoff Parker   *Trade Only*
Antiques Ltd.   **LAPADA**
"The Chestnuts", Haltoft End. Est. 1966. Open 9—5. SIZE: Large. *STOCK: Furniture, clocks, £10—£2,000; silver, plate, glass, porcelain, £2—£1,000; shipping goods.* LOC: 3 miles from Boston on A52 to Skegness. TEL: Boston (0205) 760444; home — same. VAT: Stan/Spec.

FULBECK, Nr. Grantham

Peter Coulson Antiques
Manor Stables. Est. 1969. Open 10—5.30, Sun. 2—5. SIZE: Small. *STOCK: Furniture and clocks, 18th C to 1920, £5—£1,000.* LOC: A607, midway between Lincoln and Grantham. PARK: Easy. TEL: Lovedon (0400) 73172; home — Grantham (0476) 77979. SER: Restorations (furniture and clocks including movements).

GAINSBOROUGH (0427)
Antiques
1, 3 and 5 Spring Gardens and 2 North St. (Mrs. C. Watt.) Open, resident, ring bell. *STOCK: Furniture, smalls, stripped pine.* LOC: Main door on North St., opposite Sun Inn. TEL: 4882. SER: Export (stripped pine).

GEDNEY
Paul Johnston Antiques
Old Red Lion. Est. 1975. SIZE: Small. *STOCK: Early oak and country furniture; treen, metalwork.* LOC: Just off A17 on B1359. PARK: Easy. TEL: Holbeach (0406) 362414; home — same.

GOSBERTON, Nr. Spalding
Craven Hammond Antiques
Trade Only
Ball Hall. (P.M.C. Hammond.) Est. 1975. Open 8.30—5, Sat. and any time by appointment. SIZE: Large. *STOCK: Furniture, especially period walnut, 17th—19th C, £10—£5,000.* LOC: From A17 take A16 to Spalding for 4½ miles. Turn right at Gosberton and immediately on Bourne Rd. B1397 (Belchmire Lane). After ¾ mile turn right into Wargate Way, premises 50yds. on right. PARK: Own. TEL: Spalding (0775) 840784; home — same. SER: Restorations (period furniture). VAT: Stan.

Mary King
Victoria House, 2 Wargate Way. Est. 1965. Open by appointment. *STOCK: Furniture including pine, silver, jewellery, Victoriana.* TEL: Spalding (0775) 840317. SER: Export arranged.

GRANTHAM (0476)
A. Barlow
Heage House, 25 Belton Lane. Est. 1970. Open 9—5.30. *STOCK: Small furniture and objets d'art.* TEL: 68748.

J. Dobie (Antiques) Ltd.
44 North Parade. Resident. Open Tues., Wed. and Fri. *STOCK: Furniture, porcelain, pottery, pictures, prints.* TEL: 78810.

Harold Nadin
109 London Rd. CL: Sat. p.m. Open 9.30—5. *STOCK: Furniture, 17th to early 19th C; general antiques.* TEL: 63562.

J. and J. Palmer Ltd
42/44 Swinegate. Est. 1981. CL: Mon. Open 10—6, Wed. 10—1. SIZE: Large. *STOCK: Pine, 19th C, £50—£350.* LOC: Next to St. Wulframs Church. PARK: Easy. TEL: 70093; home — Loveden (0400) 72570. SER: Valuations. VAT: Stan.

Grantham continued

W. Redmile Antiques
10 Vine St. (T.J. and J.W. Redmile.) Est. 1936. Open 9—6. *STOCK: General antiques, period furniture, silver, porcelain.* LOC: From London turn right at Angel Hotel. PARK: Easy. TEL: 64074. SER: Valuations. VAT: Stan/Spec.

G.D. and Z. Rudkin Antiques
The Old School, Station Rd. CL: Sat. Open 9—6. *STOCK: Stripped pine and export furniture.* LOC: Near railway station. TEL: 61477. VAT: Stan.

GREAT PONTON (047 683)
Nr. Grantham
Roberson Whaley
Trade Only
The Mews, Great Ponton House. (C.J.R. Whaley). Est. 1943. Open daily. *STOCK: Paintings, furniture, silver and jewellery.* LOC: Driveway on A1 north bound carriageway, 2 miles south of Grantham. PARK: Easy. TEL: 311; home — same. SER: Valuations.

GREATFORD (077 836)
Nr. Stamford
The Complete Automobilist
Dept. 1, The Old Rectory. Est. 1965. CL: Sat. and Sun., except by appointment. Open 8.30—5. *STOCK: Hard-to-get parts for older vehicles.* LOC: 5 miles East Stamford. PARK: Easy. TEL: 336. SER: Catalogue available.

HORNCASTLE (065 82)
The Lincolnshire Antiques Centre
Bridge St. Open 9—5. SIZE: Large. *STOCK: General antiques, £5—£5,000.* LOC: To rear of "The Kitchen Range". PARK: Own. TEL: 7794. SER: Container packing and collection. VAT: Stan/Spec.

Milestone House Antiques
Milestone House, 48 North St. (A.M. Heawood.) Est. 1982. Open 9—5. SIZE: Small. *STOCK: Small and unusual general antiques.* Not stocked: Militaria, coins, silver. LOC: From Market Place, turn left up North St., shop 300yds. on right. PARK: Easy. TEL: 2238; home — same.

Laurence Shaw Antiques LAPADA
Spilsby Rd. Open 8.30—5. SIZE: Large. *STOCK: Furniture and general antiques, 17th—20th C, £5—£5,000.* PARK: Easy. TEL: 7638; home — Winceby (065 888) 600. SER: Container packing and collection. VAT: Stan/Spec.

Stowaway (U.K.) Ltd.
2 Langton Hill. (T. and J. Finseth.) Est. 1972. Open 8—5, Sat by appointment. SIZE: Large. *STOCK: Stripped pine furniture.* PARK: Easy. TEL: 7445. SER: Container packing. VAT: Stan.

INGOLDSBY (047 685)
Nr. Grantham
P.D.R. Pine
Oaklands. (D.T. Parkin and D.A. Dobney.) Est. 1977. Open 9.30—6, Sat. and Sun. by appointment. STOCK: Antique and Victorian stripped pine. TEL: 400.

KIRKBY-ON-BAIN
Nr. Woodhall Spa
Kirkby Antiques Ltd. LAPADA
Highfield, Roughton Rd. (J.F., M.F., R. and A.E. Carter.) Est. 1963. Open 8—5 or by appointment. SIZE: Large. STOCK: Georgian and Victorian furniture, shipping goods. LOC: From Horncastle, take Boston Rd. towards Tattershall. Turn right at Major Petrol Station, just through Haltham. Turn left just over bridge, shop is 200yds. on right-hand side of road. PARK: Easy. TEL: Woodhall Spa (0526) 52119 and 53461. SER: Restorations and furniture conversions; container facilities; clients collected from airports and railway stations on request. VAT: Stan.

KIRTON, Nr. Boston
R. Briere Antiques
38 London Rd. Resident. Est. 1968. CL: Sun., except by appointment. Open 9.30—5.30. SIZE: Large. STOCK: Oak, walnut, mahogany furniture, 16th—19th C, £30—£5,000+; pictures, 18th and 19th C, £30—£700. Not stocked: Porcelain. LOC: Centre of village near Church. PARK: Easy. TEL: Boston (0205) 723169. SER: Valuations. VAT: Stan/Spec.

Kirton Antiques LAPADA
Warehouse, 3 High St. (A.R. Marshall.) Est. 1973. Open 8.30—5.30, Sun. by appointment. STOCK: Furniture, shipping goods, bric-a-brac, Georgian, Victorian, Edwardian. TEL: Boston (0205) 722595, 722895, 722134. VAT: Stan.

LINCOLN (0522)
Antiques
Top Lodge, Doddington Rd. (F. Carpenter.) Resident, open daily. STOCK: Furniture, paintings, small general antiques and bric-a-brac. PARK: Easy. TEL: 680192.

Michael Brewer Trade Only
5 Drury Lane. (M.N. Brewer.) Est. 1954. Open by appointment. SIZE: Medium. STOCK: Furniture, oil paintings, silver, porcelain, bronzes, works of art. Not stocked: Coins. LOC: Close to Cathedral. PARK: 20yds. TEL: 45854. SER: Valuations; buys at auction. VAT: Stan/Spec.

Castle Gallery
61 Steep Hill. (A.R. Buchanan.) Est. 1983. Open 10—5.30, Sun. by appointment. SIZE: Medium. STOCK: Oil paintings, 17th—19th C, £500—£3,000; watercolours, 18th—20th C, £50—£1,200; furniture and ceramics, 18th—19th C, £70—£900. LOC: 100yds. from Lincoln cathedral. PARK: Easy. TEL: 35078; home — same. SER: Valuations; restorations (oils and watercolours); framing; buys at auction (paintings and watercolours). VAT: Stan/Spec.

Anthony Cotton
26—27 Steep Hill. Est. 1969. CL: Sun. except by appointment. Open 9.30—1 and 2—5.30. SIZE: Medium. STOCK: English furniture, 16th—19th C; longcase clocks, decorative items, metalware. LOC: 2 minutes from Cathedral. PARK: Nearby. TEL: 25838; home — Welton (0673) 60562. VAT: Stan/Spec.

Designs on Pine
27 The Strait. (R.G. Chesterton-North.) Est. 1965. Open 10—4. STOCK: Pine. TEL: 29252.

C. and K.E. Dring
111 High St., also 43 Steep Hill. CL: Wed. Open 10—5.30. STOCK: Victorian and Edwardian inlaid furniture; shipping goods, porcelain, clocks. TEL: 40733 or 39456.

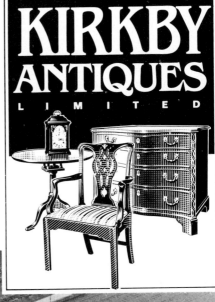

Lincoln continued

Eastgate Antique Centre
Black Horse Chambers, 6 Eastgate. (N. Marris.) Est. 1970. Open 9.30—5. SIZE: Medium. *STOCK: Furniture, 17th—19th C, £50—£2,500+; jewellery and silver, to 1920, £5—£1,000; collectors items, 18th—19th C, £5—£500; barometers and instruments, £100—£500; oils and watercolours, 19th C, £100—£2,500.* LOC: Near Cathedral, in the Uphill area. PARK: Easy. TEL: 44404; home — 754327. SER: Valuations; restorations (furniture and silver smithing). VAT: Stan/Spec.

Golden Goose Books
20 and 21 Steep Hill. (W. West-Skinn and A. Cockram.) Est. 1983. Open 10—5.30. *STOCK: Antiquarian books, bookcases, carpets, decorative items, £1—£5,000.* TEL: Wragby (0673) 858294.

David J. Hansord   BADA
32 Steep Hill. Est. 1972. Open 9.30—1 and 2—5.30. SIZE: Medium. *STOCK: English and Continental furniture, 17th to early 19th C, £100—£10,000; clocks, barometers and scientific instruments, mainly 18th C, from £50.* Not stocked: Later items. LOC: Few yards from Cathedral. PARK: Easy. TEL: 30044; home — 26983. SER: Valuations; buys at auction. VAT: Stan/Spec.

Harlequin Gallery
22 Steep Hill. (R. West-Skinn.) Est. 1962. Open 10—5.30. *STOCK: Antiquarian books, prints, maps, 10p—£12,000.* TEL: 22589; home — Wragby (0673) 858294. VAT: Stan/Spec.

L. and D. Antiques
275 Monks Rd. (L. and D.W. Downes.) Est. 1980. Open 10—5.30. SIZE: Medium. *STOCK: General antiques, furniture, clocks, porcelain, books, postcards, Victorian, Edwardian and Art Deco, £1—£250.* LOC: 1st turning on left off Lindum Hill, along Monks Rd. about ¾ mile past the Monks Abbey ruins. PARK: Easy. TEL: 42897; home — same. SER: Valuations; restorations (furniture); buys at auction. FAIRS: Holycourt.

Lincoln Fine Art
Dernstall House, 33 The Strait. (Mrs. D. Glen-Doepel.) Est. 1974. Open 10—1 and 2—5.30. *STOCK: Oil paintings including decorative portraits, landscapes, marine, watercolours, miniatures, Old Master paintings and drawings, 17th—19th C, £25—£6,000.* LOC: Top of High St., opposite 'Skegness Pottery'. PARK: Nearby. TEL: 33029. SER: Valuations.

Lincoln continued

Richard Pullen Jeweller
28 The Strait. Est. 1979. CL: Wed. Open 10—5. SIZE: Small. *STOCK: Jewellery and silver, 18th—20th C.* LOC: Top of High St. PARK: Easy. TEL: 37170; home — Wickenby (067 35) 541. SER: Valuations; restorations (jewellery and silver).

Rowletts
338 High St. (A.H. Rowlett.) Open 9—5, Wed. 9—1. *STOCK: Coins, gold, silver.* TEL: 24139.

The Strait Antiques
5 The Strait. (F.M. Davies.) Est. 1970. CL: Mon. and Wed. Open 10—4, Sat. 10—5. SIZE: Medium. *STOCK: English pottery and porcelain, 18th—19th C, £25—£200; blue and white transfer ware, early 19th C, £5—£50; general antiques and furniture, 19th to early 20th C; dolls.* LOC: At the start of the ascent to the Cathedral from the top of the High St. PARK: Easy, behind shop. TEL: 23130. VAT Stan/Spec.

R.G. Toogood
44 Steep Hill. Est. 1946. CL: Wed. p.m. Open 9.30—5.30. *STOCK: Small antiques, silver, collectors' items, porcelain, glass, Victoriana, bric-a-brac.* TEL: 28687.

James Usher and Son Ltd.
6 Silver St. CL: Wed. p.m. Open 9—5.30. *STOCK: Silver, jewellery.* TEL: 27547.

E.E. Wallis
24 Steep Hill. Est. 1925. CL: Wed. Open 9.30—5. *STOCK: Furniture, silver, brassware.* TEL: 28996.

LONG SUTTON
E. and J. Northam
15 High St. (Mrs. Northam.) *STOCK: General antiques, glass, oil lamps, silver.* TEL: Holbeach (0406) 363191.

LOUTH   (0507)
Louth Antiques
19 New Market. (D.A. Spindley.) Est. 1974. Open Wed., Fri. and Sat. SIZE: Medium. *STOCK: General antiques.* TEL: 602475.

LUDFORD, Nr. Market Rasen
Country Life Antiques
The Barn. (T.J. Gardner.) Open Sat. 10—6 or by appointment. *STOCK: Pine.* LOC: A631 Market Rasen to Louth. TEL: Market Rasen (0673) 843469; home — Tealby (067 383) 419 (ansafone).

Both paintings by George Wright. Above "Passing the hunt", 11¾ins. x 17¾ins. Below "Full Cry", 10ins. x 18ins. George Wright's distinctive and most competent style speaks for itself. He is a very consistent artist. From *The Dictionary of British Equestrian Artists* by Sally Mitchell, published by the **Antique Collectors' Club,** 1985.

MARKET DEEPING (0778)
Nr. Peterborough
Church Street Antiques
68 Church St. (M. Roth.) CL: Mon. and Tues. Open 10—5, other times by appointment. *STOCK: Jewellery, silver, small furniture, porcelain, prints, lamps.* LOC: A15. TEL: 342660. SER: Picture framing, hand-made lamp shades.

MARKET RASEN (0673)
Bothy Antiques
Queen St. (Mrs. M. Foster.) Est. 1976. Open Tues., Fri., Sat. and Sun. 2—4.30. SIZE: Small. *STOCK: Smalls, 19th to early 20th C, £2—£50; prints, watercolours, engravings and oils, 19th C, £10—£100; small Victorian furniture especially oak, some pine, £25—£250.* PARK: Easy. TEL: Wickenby (067 35) 464. SER: Valuations; restorations (pictures and porcelain); buys at auction (as stock).

Country Life Antiques
Queen St. Passage. (T.J. Gardner.) Est. 1980. CL: Mon. except by appointment. Open 10—12.30 and 1.30—5, Sat. 9—12.30. SIZE: Medium. *STOCK: Pine, 19th C, £50—£375; pictures and prints, 18th—20th C, £5—£600; general antiques, toys and decorative items, 19th—20th C, £1—£140.* LOC: In pedestrian passage between St. John's car park and High St. PARK: Easy. TEL: 843469; home — Tealby (067 383) 419 (ansafone). SER: Restorations (pine stripping, sand blasting, copper and brass polishing, pine, pictures and framing).

Harwood Tate
Church Mill, Caistor Rd. (J. Harwood Tate.) CL: Sat. Open 9.30—5.30, or by appointment. SIZE: Large. *STOCK: Furniture, mahogany, rosewood, oak; clocks, 18th to early 19th C; ornamental items including pictures and prints, 18th—19th C. Not stocked: Shipping goods.* LOC: Take A46 from Lincoln, Church Mill is off town centre, north of church. PARK: Easy. TEL: 843579. VAT: Stan/Spec.

NAVENBY, Nr. Lincoln
The Pedlar
37 High St. (Mrs. P.M. Barter.) Est. 1970. Open Thurs — Sat. 10—6, other times by appointment. *STOCK: Jewellery, porcelain, furniture and general antiques.* TEL: Lincoln (0522) 810922.

NEW BOLINGBROKE, Nr. Boston
Junktion
The Old Railway Station. (J. Rundle.) Est. 1981. Open Wed. 10—12 and 1—3.30, Sat. 10—12 and 1—4, prior 'phone call advisable. SIZE: Medium. *STOCK: Early advertising, decorative and architectural items; toys, automobilia, mechanical antiques and bygones; early slot machines, 20th C collectables. Not stocked: Porcelain and jewellery.* LOC: B1183 Horncastle to Boston road. PARK: Easy. TEL: Boston (0205) 78429.

NEW YORK
A.W. Murfin and Sons   Trade only
Sandy Bank Rd. Est. 1972. Open 8—5, weekends and other times by appointment. SIZE: Medium. *STOCK: Restored period and Victorian furniture.* TEL: Coningsby (0526) 42821.

OSBOURNBY
Osbournby Antiques
Audley House, North St. (S. Wood.) Est. 1948. Open 9—5.30, Sun. 10—3, or any time by appointment. *STOCK: Period and shipping furniture, clocks, pictures, silver, plate, glassware, ornamental items, upholstered Victorian furniture.* LOC: On A15, 10 miles north of Bourne, turn left into village market place, then right into North St. to far end. PARK: Easy. TEL: Culverthorpe (052 95) 251.

PINCHBECK, Nr. Spalding
Bygone Ways
Money Bridge House (J.H. Sneath.) Est. 1979. Open by appointment. SIZE: Medium. *STOCK: Farm and craftsmen's tools, £5—£50; country bygones, £20—£100; horse brasses, £10—£25, all 18th—19th C.* LOC: 1½ miles west of Pinchbeck on B1150. PARK: Easy. TEL: Pinchbeck Bars (077 587) 309. SER: Valuations; restorations (farm and craftsmen's tools).

IS YOUR ENTRY CORRECT?
If there is even the slightest inaccuracy in your entry, *please* let us know before 1st January 1987.
GUIDE TO THE
ANTIQUE SHOPS OF BRITAIN
5 Church Street, Woodbridge, Suffolk.

RUSKINGTON   (0526)

Pinfold Antiques   LAPADA
3 Pinfold Lane. (J. Ballinger, J.D. Harman.) Est. 1981. Open 10—5. SIZE: Medium. *STOCK: Longcase clocks, 17th—19th C, £500—£5,000; period English furniture, weapons, scientific instruments, £50—£3,000.* PARK: Easy. TEL: 832200; home — 832272/832057. SER: Valuations; restorations; buys at auctions. FAIRS: Olympia, Wilton House, Robert Bailey.

SIBSEY, Nr. Boston

Pyrmont Antiques
(Mrs. M. Meyer.) Est. 1969. Open most days but appointment advisable. SIZE: Medium. *STOCK: Longcase clocks, furniture, 1700—1930; porcelain, art nouveau, glass, silver.* Not stocked: Militaria. LOC: Near Chapel. PARK: Easy. TEL: Boston (0205) 750392; home — same. SER: Buys at auction.

SILK WILLOUGHBY, Nr. Sleaford

J. and R. Ratcliffe
The Old Rectory. Est. 1954. SIZE: Medium. *STOCK: Furniture, decorative items, 1600—1830.* LOC: 1 mile south of Sleaford on A15. TEL: Sleaford (0529) 302932. VAT: Stan/Spec.

SKEGNESS   (0754)

G.H. Crowson   *Mostly Trade*
50 High St. Open daily 10—6. *STOCK: General antiques, jewellery.* TEL: 4360.

SPALDING   (0775)

N.V. Baker
23 Commercial Rd. Est. 1957. *STOCK: General antiques, furniture, copper, brass.* TEL: 2568.

Dean's Antiques
"The Walnuts", Weston St. Mary's. (Mrs. B. Dean.) Est. 1969. Open daily. SIZE: Medium. *STOCK: Victoriana, bric-a-brac, general antiques, £1—£100.* LOC: On Spalding to Holbeach main road A151. PARK: Easy. TEL: Holbeach (0406) 370429.

SPILSBY   (0790)

Shaw Antiques
High St. (Mrs. J.M. Shaw.) CL: Tues. *STOCK: Victoriana, silver, glass, general antiques, furniture, pine, oak, mahogany.* TEL: 52317 or 52297.

Spilsby continued

Spilsby Antiques

29 Halton Rd. (D. and Mrs. C. Goodland.) Est. 1980. CL: Tues. Open 9.30–5.30, Sun. by appointment. SIZE: Medium. *STOCK: Jewellery, silver, china, glass, small furniture, 19th C, £5–£500.* PARK: Easy. TEL: 52148. VAT: Stan.

STAMFORD (0780)

Books Etc.

3b Wharf Rd. (A. and B. Schein.) Est. 1978. Open 11–5.30; Sun. 2–5 summer only. SIZE: Medium. *STOCK: Books, 16th–20th C, £1–£2,000; postcards and stamps, 10p–£50; games, prints, jigsaws, ephemera.* LOC: ½ mile off A1. PARK: Easy. TEL: 54980. SER: Valuations; restorations (rebinding); buys at auction.

Jane Cox

5 St. Mary's Hill. Est. 1968. CL: Thurs. Open 9–5. SIZE: Small. *STOCK: Small items, country furniture, needlework, metalwork.* PARK: Easy. TEL: 64159.

O.M. and R.D. Cox

5 St. Mary's Hill. Est. 1954. Open 9–5. *STOCK: 17th–19th C English and Continental furniture; Victorian and earlier jewellery.* PARK: At rear. TEL: 64159.

Stamford continued

Robin Cox Antiques

29 St. Leonards St. Est. 1965. *STOCK: Furniture, oak and country, especially period pine, some mahogany; early carvings, architectural fittings, decorated and decorative furniture, £25–£2,000.* TEL: 64592. VAT: Stan/Spec.

Dawson of Stamford

29 St. Peter's St. (J. Dawson.) CL: Thurs. Open 9–5.30. SIZE: Medium. *STOCK: Furniture, pre-1836, silver, jewellery.* LOC: From centre of Stamford take All Saints Place (opp. All St. Church). St. Peter's St. is a continuation of this street. PARK: Easy. TEL: 54166. VAT: Stan/Spec.

Michael Day Antiques

North St. Est. 1976. Open 9.30–5. SIZE: Warehouse. *STOCK: Period, Victorian and shipping furniture, mahogany, oak, pine, walnut and inlaid.* LOC: Off Scotgate. PARK: Easy. TEL: 56825; home — Peterborough (0733) 40167. VAT: Stan/Spec.

Dickenson and Thomas (Antiques)

Old Granary, 10 North St. Est. 1970. Open 9–6. SIZE: Large. *STOCK: Stripped pine, militaria, architectural pine fitments, ironware.* LOC: From south take old A1 through Stamford. Turn right at second set of traffic lights, large warehouse on right. PARK: Opp. TEL: 62236; home — 55093 or Oakham (0572) 57333. VAT: Stan.

"I must admit to a certain weakness for Farington's drawings, which is not inappropriate since they are generally rather weak." From **Understanding Watercolours** by Huon Mallalieu, published by the **Antique Collectors' Club**, 1985.

Stamford continued

Barbara Hall Antiques
7 High St., St. Martins. Est. 1973. Open 9—5, Thurs. and Sun. by appointment. SIZE: Medium. *STOCK: Porcelain and furniture, 18th—19th C, £50—£1,000; copper, brass, pictures and collectors' items, 19th C, £5—£500.* LOC: Opposite the George Hotel. PARK: Easy. TEL: 52594; home — same. SER: Restorations (porcelain and upholstery).

Timothy Kendrew Antiques
LAPADA
5—8 George Hotel Mews, The George Hotel. Est. 1975. Open 9.30—5.30. SIZE: Large. *STOCK: Porcelain, £50—£1,000+; small furniture, £50—£2,000+; both 18th to early 19th C; silver, £50—£2,000+; jewellery £10—£1,500; oils and watercolours, £50—£1,000; all 18th—19th C.* Not stocked: Coins, medals and shipping items. LOC: Opposite George Hotel Business Centre. PARK: Easy. TEL: 56072; home — (08012) 2325. SER: Valuations; buys at auction (porcelain, silver and furniture). FAIRS: Local and London. VAT: Stan/Spec.

St. George's Antiques
St. George's Sq. (G.H. Burns.) Est. 1974. Open 10—4.30. SIZE: Medium and warehouse. *STOCK: Period, Victorian and shipping furniture, clocks and small items.* TEL: 54117; home — Bourne (0778) 423781. VAT: Stan/Spec.

St. Mary's Galleries
5 St. Mary's Hill. (Mrs. O.M. and R.D. Cox.) Est. 1961. CL: Thurs. Open 9.30—5. SIZE: Medium. *STOCK: Furniture, 1600—1860, £5—£500; carvings, treen, wooden and metal implements and tools; jewellery, Victorian and Georgian, £2—£130; unusual items, 1600—1900, £1—£30; some textiles.* LOC: On old A1 leading south out of Stamford. PARK: Easy, at rear. TEL: 64159. VAT: Spec.

John Sinclair
11/12 St. Mary's St. (F.J. Sinclair.) Est. 1970. Open 9—5.30. SIZE: Large. *STOCK: Oak country furniture, 18th C, £200—£3,000; Victorian mahogany furniture, £100—£1,000; Royal Worcester and Crown Derby porcelain, 19th C, £50—£5,000.* LOC: Near A1. PARK: George Hotel car park. TEL: 65421. VAT: Stan/Spec.

Staniland (Booksellers)
4 St. George's St. (M.F. and M.G. Staniland.) Est. 1973. CL: Tues. in winter and Thurs. Open 10—5. SIZE: Medium. *STOCK: Books, mainly 19th—20th C, 50p—£250; postcards, 1890—1930, 10p—£30.* LOC: High St. PARK: St. Leonard's St. TEL: 55800; home — Greatford (077 836) 559.

Stamford continued

Paul Warrington Antiques
32 St. Paul's St. Est. 1976. Open 9—1 and 2—5. SIZE: Large. *STOCK: Pine, oak and mahogany, 18th—19th C.* PARK: Easy. TEL: 54360; home — 83628. SER: Valuations. VAT: Stan/Spec.

STAPLEFORD
Allens Antiques
Moor Farm. Open 8.30—5. *STOCK: Pine.* LOC: Off A17 Sleaford Rd. TEL: Bassingham (052 285) 392.

SUTTON BRIDGE
Bridge Antiques
30 and 32 Bridge Rd. (A. and R. Gittins.) Est. 1965. Open 5 days a week or by appointment. SIZE: Large and 2 warehouses. *STOCK: Furniture.* LOC: On A17. PARK: Easy. TEL: Holbeach (0406) 350535/350704.

SUTTON-ON-SEA   (0521)
Number Ten Antiques
1A, Marine Ave. (N. Birkinshaw and D. Prosser.) Est. 1984. Open seven days. SIZE: Small. *STOCK: Jewellery, silver, porcelain and furniture.* PARK: Easy. TEL: 42396; home — 42276. SER: Restorations (furniture and jewellery).

TATTERSHALL
Wayside Antiques
Market Place. (G. and Mrs. Ball.) Est. 1969. Open 10—5.30. SIZE: Small. *STOCK: General antiques, £5—£1,000.* LOC: On A158. PARK: Easy. TEL: Coningsby (0526) 42436. VAT: Stan/Spec.

WAINFLEET
The Antique Centre
1 Spilsby Rd. (P. and T. Stevenson.) Est. 1967. Open Mon. 10—5, or by appointment. SIZE: Large. *STOCK: Furniture, general antiques, 18th—19th C, from £20.* LOC: From Boston cross river and go straight past market, with Clock Tower on right. Shop is 300yds. on. PARK: Own. TEL: (0754) 880489; home — same. VAT: Stan/Spec.

WRAGBY, Nr. Lincoln   (0673)
Tealby Pine   *Trade Only*
Goltho Hall, Goltho. (R.G. Chesterton-North.) Est. 1965. Open every day but appointment preferred. SIZE: Large. *STOCK: Pine, 18th—19th C, £5—£500.* LOC: From Lincoln on A158. 1 mile before Wragby, take right turn signposted Goltho. PARK: Easy. TEL: 858789; home — same. SER: Restorations (furniture stripping). VAT: Stan/Spec.

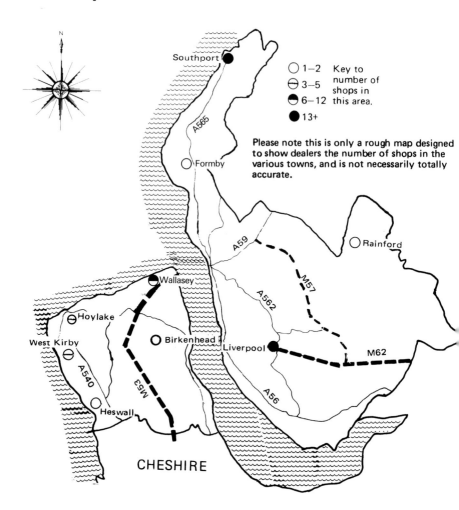

N

Southport

A565

Formby

○ 1—2 — Key to number of shops in this area.
⊖ 3—5
◒ 6—12
● 13+

Please note this is only a rough map designed to show dealers the number of shops in the various towns, and is not necessarily totally accurate.

A59

○ Rainford

◒ Wallasey

M57

A562

⊖ Hoylake

West Kirby

○ Birkenhead ⊖ Liverpool ●

M62

A540

M53

○ Heswall

A56

CHESHIRE

BIRKENHEAD

Abbey Antiques

2 Rose Mount, Oxton Village. (G.P. Duncan.) CL: Thurs. Open 10—4.30. *STOCK: General antiques*. PARK: Easy. TEL: (051) 653 9060; home — (051) 677 3111.

William Courtney and Sons
LAPADA

Cross/Chester St., Tunnel Entrance, Corner premises including 11—19 Cross St. Est. 1893. Open daily, Sun. and Thurs. p.m. by appointment. SIZE: Large. *STOCK: General antiques, shipping goods, display cabinets, carved oak furniture, bureaux; art glass, Staffordshire figures*. PARK: Easy. TEL: (051) 647 8693. VAT: Stan.

FORMBY   (070 48)

Antiques and Heirlooms

4 Ryeground Lane. (Mrs. M. Drayton.) Est. 1984. Open 10—5, Wed. and Thurs. by appointment. SIZE: Small. *STOCK: Silver plate and smalls, from £5; general antiques, furniture, pictures and prints*. Not stocked: Weapons, coins, medals and stamps. LOC: Opposite Grapes Hotel. PARK: Easy. TEL: 78905; home — Southport (0704) 69657. SER: Buys at auction. FAIRS: Park Hall, Charnock Richard; Bingley Hall, Stafford.

Formby Antiques

6 Victoria Buildings, Freshfield. Est. 1970. Open Tues., Thurs. and Sat. *STOCK: Mainly mahogany and walnut furniture, especially desks, 18th C to early 20th C*. TEL: 79116. VAT: Spec.

HESWALL

C. Rosenberg
The Antique Shop, 120—122 Telegraph Rd. Est. 1960. CL: Wed. p.m. Open 10—5.30. *STOCK: Jewellery, silver, porcelain, objets d'art.* TEL: (051) 342 1053. VAT: Stan.

HOYLAKE

The Clock Shop
7 The Quadrant. (K. and D. Whay.) Est. 1969. Open 10—5. *STOCK: Clocks and jewellery.* PARK: Easy. TEL: (051) 632 1888. SER: Restorations (clock and jewellery repairs). VAT: Stan/Spec.

M. Fearn Antiques
124a Market St. Open 10.30—5, or by appointment. *STOCK: Furniture, silver, porcelain, dolls, toys, jewellery.* TEL: (051) 632 3839.

Jon David (Fine Furniture) Ltd.
128—130 Market St. (C.W.R. Atkinson.) Est. 1977. Open 9.30—5.30. *STOCK: Furniture, porcelain, glass, silver, collectors items.* LOC: On main road. PARK: At rear. TEL: (051) 632 4231. VAT: Spec.

Market Antiques
80 Market St. (W. Bateman.) Est. 1969. Open Thurs. and Fri. 10—1 and 2.15—4.30, Sat. 10—5.30, other times by appointment. SIZE: Medium. *STOCK: Furniture, £10—£1,000; trade and shipping goods, silver, glass, china, £2—£250; paintings, prints, £2—£200.* Not stocked: Weapons, medals, coins. LOC: On main street in town centre A563 or A540. PARK: Ship Inn forecourt, or in side streets opp., or at rear. TEL: (051) 632 4059. VAT: Stan/Spec.

Hoylake continued

Olde Englande
1 Cable Rd. South. CL: Wed. p.m. Open 10—5. *STOCK: Furniture, curios and general antiques, Victorian and Edwardian.* PARK: Easy. TEL: (051) 632 4740. VAT: Stan.

LIVERPOOL (051)

The Antiques Gallery
37 Hanover St. Est. 1964. Open 9—5, Sat. 10—1. *STOCK: Furniture, clocks, oriental items, silver, objets d'art.* TEL: 709 9529.

Boodle and Dunthorne Ltd.
Boodles House, Lord St. Est. 1798. Open 9—5.30. SIZE: Large. *STOCK: Silver, 18th—19th C, £100—£5,000; clocks and clock-sets, mid-19th C, £200—£4,000; jewellery, Victorian and Georgian, £100—£10,000.* Not stocked: Furniture. PARK: In Paradise St. TEL: 227 2525. VAT: Stan/Spec.

Philip Cowan Antiques
33 Parliament St. *STOCK: General antiques, especially furniture and clocks.* TEL: 709 1217.

Delta Antiques
175/177 Smithdown Rd. (E.P. Jones.) Est. 1979. CL: Sat. a.m. and Wed. Open 10—12 and 1—5. SIZE: Medium. *STOCK: Stripped pine, 19th C, £50—£100.* LOC: Ring road, city centre. PARK: Nearby. TEL: 734 4277; home — same. SER: Restorations; French polishing.

Liverpool continued

Kensington Tower Antiques Ltd.   *Trade Only*

Christ Church, 170 Kensington. (R. Swainbank.) Est. 1960. CL: Sat. and Sun. except by appointment; and Mon. Open 9—5. SIZE: Large. *STOCK: Shipping goods, general antiques.* LOC: A57. PARK: Easy. TEL: 260 9466; home — 924 6538. VAT: Stan.

Alan Leonard Antiques

503 Smithdown Rd. Est. 1957. Open 9.30—5.30. SIZE: Medium. *STOCK: Furniture, £25—£2,000; pottery and porcelain, silver and plate, oil paintings and watercolours, £5—£1,000; all 18th to early 20th C.* LOC: Main arterial road from city centre (3 miles) to M62 (2 miles). PARK: Easy. TEL: 733 5277. home — 722 4766. SER: Valuations; buys at auction. VAT: Stan/Spec.

Liverpool continued

Liverpool Coin and Medal Co.

70 Lime St. (L.J. Ross.) Est. 1977. Open 10—5. *STOCK: Coins and medals.* TEL: 708 8441.

Lyver & Boydell Galleries   LAPADA

15 Castle St. Est. 1861. CL: Sat. Open 10.30—5.30. SIZE: Medium. *STOCK: Paintings and watercolours, 18th—20th C., £50—£5,000; maps and prints, 16th—19th C., £1—£1,500.* LOC: City centre, opposite Town Hall. PARK: Multi-storey. TEL: 236 3256. SER: Valuations; cleaning; framing; restorations; buys at auction. FAIRS: National. VAT: Stan/Spec.

Maggs Antiques   LAPADA

26—30 Fleet St. (G. Webster.) Est. 1965. Open daily. *STOCK: General antiques, period and shipping smalls, £1—£1,000.* LOC: In town centre by Central station. PARK: Meters. TEL: 708 0221; evenings — Runcorn (09285) 64958. SER: Restorations; container packing, courier.

E. Pryor and Son

110 London Rd. (Mr. Wilding.) Est. 1876. CL: Wed. *STOCK: General antiques, jewellery, Georgian and Victorian silver, pottery, porcelain, coins, clocks, paintings, ivory and carvings.* TEL: 709 1361. VAT: Stan.

Ryan-Wood Antiques

102 Seel St. Est. 1972. Open 9.30—5 or by appointment. *STOCK: Furniture, paintings, china, silver, curios, bric-a-brac, Victoriana, Edwardiana, art deco, clothing and furs.* TEL: 709 7776; home — 709 3203. VAT: Stan.

A typical Lowestoft bottle-shape vase of small size, here turned to show the amusing and so typical Lowestoft prancing bird on the reverse. Painter's number '3', 6¼ins. high, c.1765-8. From *Lowestoft Porcelains* by Geoffrey A. Godden, F.R.S.A., published by the **Antique Collectors' Club**, 1985.

Liverpool continued

Savoy Antiques

Trade Only

7 Bridgewater St. (B. Coleman.) Est. 1960. Open 9—5, Sat. 9—12. SIZE: Warehouse. STOCK: Shipping goods, 19th—20th C, £5—£500; period furniture, 18th—19th C, £100—£2,000. LOC: City centre, near Holiday Inn. PARK: Easy. TEL: 708 9159. SER: Restorations; repairs; packers, export. VAT: Stan.

D. Simpson and Son Ltd.

Yew Treehouse Farm, Broom Way, Off Higher Rd., Halewood. (D. and E. Simpson.) Est. 1976. Open 9—5. SIZE: Large. STOCK: Period Georgian mahogany restored chests of drawers, linen presses and tall-boys; country pine, oak and mahogany shipping furniture. LOC: 5 minutes from Speke Airport. PARK: Easy. TEL: 486 9382; home — same. SER: Restorations (Georgian furniture); shipping and packing; polishing; courier and finder; fine 17th—18th C copies manufactured. VAT: Stan.

Swainbanks Ltd.

50-56 Fox St. CL: Sat. Open 9—5 or by appointment. SIZE: Large. STOCK: Shipping goods and general antiques. TEL: 207 4030 or 924 6538. SER: Containers. VAT: Stan.

Theta Gallery

Trade Only

29 and 31 Parliament St. (J. Matson.) Open by appointment. SIZE: Warehouse. STOCK: General antiques, especially furniture and clocks. TEL: 708 6375.

RAINFORD (074 488)

Richards Antiques

Church Rd. (D.M. Richards) Open 9.30—12 and 2—5 or by appointment. SIZE: Medium. STOCK: Furniture and general antiques. LOC: Opposite village hall. PARK: Easy. TEL: 5588 and (0744) 20804. SER: Restorations (furniture). VAT: Stan.

Colin Stock

BADA

8 Mossborough Rd. Est. 1895. Open by appointment. STOCK: Furniture, 18th—19th C. TEL: 2246.

SOUTHPORT (0704)

Arcadia Gallery

42 Wayfarers Arcade, Lord St. (M. Fryer) Est. 1977. CL: Tues. Open 10.30—5. SIZE: Medium. STOCK: Furniture, including French, 18th and 19th C, £100—£5,000; clocks, £100—£3,000; paintings, fireplaces, decorative items. LOC: Rear entry to Arcade from West St. which runs parallel to Lord St. PARK: Easy. TEL: 42504. SER: Valuations; restorations. VAT: Stan/Spec.

Southport continued

Bobbins

42a Wayfarers Arcade, Lord St. (S.A. Fryer and D.B. Crook.) Est. 1982. CL: Tues. Open 10.30—5. STOCK: Tablecloths, bed spreads and linen, lace, lace curtains, shawls, small silver and collectables, jewellery. TEL: 42504.

C.K. Broadhurst and Co. Ltd.

5—7 Market St. Est. 1926. CL: Tues. p.m. STOCK: Rare books, first editions, coloured plate books, topography. TEL: 32064 and 34110.

Churchtown Antiques

Bow Place, 1 Churchgate, Churchtown. (R.W. and M.V. Burlington.) Est. 1977. CL: Mon. and Tues. Open 11—5, other times by appointment. STOCK: General antiques, jewellery, silver and some shipping. LOC: Close to Botanic Gardens, side of Old Smithy. PARK: Easy. TEL: 36068. SER: Valuations; buys at auction.

The Clock Shop

14 Wesley St. (E.J. and A. Rimmer.) Est. 1979. CL: Tues. p.m. Open 9—5. SIZE: Small. STOCK: Clocks, £50—£1,000. LOC: Opposite Morrison's Superstore, 50yds. from main shopping street. PARK: 50yds. TEL: 31569. SER: Valuations; restorations (clock and watch repairs).

Decor Galleries

92B Lord St. (F. D. Glover.) CL: Tues. STOCK: Decorative items, furniture, 18th—19th C. TEL: 35134. VAT: Stan.

Fine Pine

19/38 Market St. (R. and W. Griffiths.) CL: Tues. Open 9.30—5.30. STOCK: Pine. TEL: 38056; evenings — 35720. SER: Shipping, packing and courier.

Jays, Fine Art Dealers LAPADA

Cambridge Gallery, 4 Cambridge Arcade. (A. and B. Joseph.) Est. 1953. CL: Tues. Open 10—1 and 2.15—5.30. STOCK: Oil paintings, £350—£10,000; watercolours, £45—£5,000; both 18th to early 20th C. Not stocked: General antiques. LOC: From Lord St., Arcade is off Town Hall service road, and adjacent to Southport Arts Centre. PARK: Easy. On Town Hall service road. TEL: 34488 (24 hour answering service). SER: Valuations; restorations (paintings and watercolours); framing; regilding; mounting; buys at auction. VAT: Spec.

Southport continued

Lodge Furniture
98 Zetland St. *STOCK: Shipping goods, bric-a- brac.* LOC: Corner of Hawkshead St., off Manchester Rd. PARK: Easy. TEL: 43441. FAIRS: Park Hall, Charnock Richard; Floral Hall, Southport.

Molloy's Furnishers Ltd.
6-8 St. James St. (P. Molloy.) Est. 1955. Open daily. SIZE: Large. *STOCK: Mahogany and oak, shipping and Edwardian furniture.* LOC: On A570, Scarisbrick new road. PARK: Easy. TEL: 35204 or 48101; home — 32857. VAT: Stan.

Something Old
43 Virginia St. Est. 1968. CL: Tues. Open 10.30—5, other times by appointment. *STOCK: Clocks, furniture, bric-a-brac.* LOC: Up Eastbank St. from Lord St., left at the traffic island. TEL: 33629.

The Spinning Wheel
1 Liverpool Rd., Birkdale. (R. Bell.) Est. 1966. CL: Tues. Open 10—5. SIZE: Small. *STOCK: General antiques, £5—£1,000+.* TEL: 68245; home — 67613. VAT: Stan.

Southport continued

Studio 41
340 Liverpool Rd., Birkdale. (B. Sullivan.) Open by appointment only. *STOCK: 19th and 20th C oils and watercolours.* TEL: 79132. SER: Valuations; buys at auction.

Tony and Anne Sutcliffe Antiques
130 Cemetery Rd. and Warehouse, 37A Linaker St. Est. 1969. Open 8.30—5, weekends by appointment. SIZE: Large. *STOCK: Shipping goods, Victorian and period furniture.* LOC: Town centre. TEL: 37068; home — 33465. SER: Containers; courier. VAT: Stan/Spec.

Union Antiques
1B Union St. (K. Burns.) CL: Tues. Open 10—5. *STOCK: Victorian and Edwardian furniture, silver, porcelain, jewellery, bric-a-brac, paintings, coins and medals.* TEL: 38973.

H.S. Walne
183 Lord St. CL: Tues. Open 10.15—5.30. *STOCK: Diamonds, gold, silver, jewellery, watches and clocks.* TEL: 32469.

A charming portrait of a leopard in playful mood, more akin to our image of its domestic cousins. Thi bronze is recorded as being unsigned but has a lengthy inscription dedicated to two friends killed in 1917 There is a certain naïvety about the modelling but the feel and inspiration are pure Bugatti. From *Animal in Bronze* by Christopher Payne, published by the **Antique Collectors' Club,** 1986.

Southport continued

Weldon Antiques and Jewellery
655 Lord St. (H.W. and N.C. Weldon.) Est. 1914. Open 9.30—5.30. SIZE: Medium. *STOCK: Furniture, clocks, watches, jewellery, silver, coins.* Not normally stocked: Militaria. PARK: Easy. TEL: 32191. SER: Valuations; restorations. VAT: Stan.

The White Elephant
22 Kew Rd., Birkdale. (J. Wajzner.) Est. 1967. *STOCK: General antiques, fine art, ethnographica, collectors' items, weapons, medals, coins, books, postcards.* TEL: 60525. VAT: Stan/Spec.

York Court Antiques
44c Aughton Rd., Birkdale. (M. Gillman and A. Ruane.) Open 10—5, Wed. 10—1. *STOCK: Furniture.* TEL: 66507.

WALLASEY

23 Squadron
Rowson St., New Brighton. (K. Wickham.) CL: Wed. Open 10—4. *STOCK: Victorian and Edwardian lighting, fireplaces.* LOC: Leave M53 at junction 1, take A554 via promenade, turn right into Rowson St. PARK: Easy. TEL: (051) 630 5601.

Arbiter
10 Atherton St., New Brighton. (W.D.L. Scobie and P.D. Ferrett.) Resident. Est. 1983. CL: Wed. Open 11—6, Sat. 2—6, or by appointment. *STOCK: Arts and crafts, art nouveau and art deco, £5—£1,200; Oriental and ethnographic, decorative arts, £60—£800; lithographs and etchings, 20th C, £80—£120.* LOC: Opposite New Brighton station. PARK: Easy. TEL: (051) 639 1159. SER: Valuations; buys at auction.

Arcade Antiques
109 Wallasey Rd., Liscard. Est. 1980. CL: Wed. Open 10—5. SIZE: Medium. *STOCK: Victorian and Edwardian furniture, £50—£1,500; silver, collectables, shipping items, £5—£500.* LOC: Main approach road to Wallasey Precinct. PARK: Easy. TEL: (051) 638 9164; home — (051) 630 2649.

A.M. Duffy Antiques
76 Rowson St., New Brighton. Est. 1976. Open 10—5. SIZE: Small. *STOCK: Pine and country furniture, textiles and decorative items.* LOC: Leave M53 at junction 1, take A554 via promenade, turn right into Rowson St. PARK: Easy. TEL: (051) 639 6905/8728.

Wallasey continued

Falstaff Antiques
Rowson St., New Brighton. (J. Lynch.) Open 9—5. *STOCK: Georgian, Victorian and Edwardian shipping furniture and effects.* LOC: Leave M53 at junction 1, take A554 via promenade, turn right into Rowson St. PARK: Easy. TEL: (051) 638 5433; evenings — (051) 638 3547.

Grove Antiques   *Trade only*
2 Wesley Grove. (A.G. and E.A. Downes.) Open 9.15—1.15, afternoons and weekends by appointment. SIZE: Large. *STOCK: General antiques, 19th—20th C, £25—£500.* LOC: Opposite town hall. PARK: Easy. TEL: (051) 630 2827; home — (051) 638 1214. SER: Buys at auction. VAT: Stan.

Robbies Antiques
140 Seabank Rd., New Brighton. (R. Dalby.) CL: Wed. Open 2—5. *STOCK: Furniture and ceramics, general antiques and collectors items.* TEL: (051) 638 3848. SER: Restorations (furniture); re-upholstery.

WEST KIRBY

Helen Horswill Antiques
62 Grange Rd. Open 10—5 or by appointment. SIZE: Medium. *STOCK: Furniture, 17th to early 19th C; decorative items.* LOC: A540. PARK: Easy. TEL: (051) 625 7111/625 1678/625 6182.

Oliver Antiques
62 Grange Rd. (J. O. Horswill.) Open 10—5, or by appointment. SIZE: Medium. *STOCK: Furniture, 17th to early 19th C; decorative items.* LOC: A540. PARK: Easy. TEL: (051) 625 7111/625 1678/625 6182.

Wirral Antiques
62 Grange Rd. Est. 1965. Open 10—5, or by appointment. SIZE: Medium. *STOCK: 17th, 18th C and Regency furniture, period decorative items, pine furniture.* LOC: A540. PARK: Easy. TEL: (051) 625 7111/625 1678/625 6182. VAT: Stan/Spec.

IS YOUR ENTRY CORRECT?
If there is even the slightest inaccuracy in your entry, *please* let us know before 1st January 1987.
GUIDE TO THE
ANTIQUE SHOPS OF BRITAIN
5 Church Street, Woodbridge, Suffolk.

Norfolk

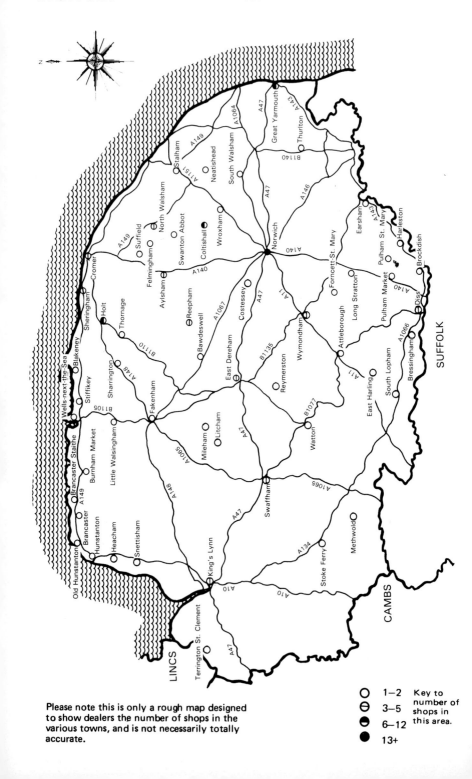

Please note this is only a rough map designed to show dealers the number of shops in the various towns, and is not necessarily totally accurate.

	Key to
○ 1–2	number of
⊖ 3–5	shops in
⊜ 6–12	this area.
● 13+	

ATTLEBOROUGH (0953)
A.E. Bush and Partners
Queens Sq., and London Rd. (A.G. and M.S. Becker.) Est. 1960. Open Queens Sq. 9—1 and 2—5.30; London Rd. Sun. and Wed. STOCK: Furniture — carved oak, mahogany, 19th C. LOC: A11. PARK: Easy. TEL: 452175; home — 453220. SER: Restorations; export and storage; buys at auction. VAT: Stan/Spec.

F. and T. King
High St. Est. 1945. CL. Mon. and Tues. Open 9.30—6. STOCK: Furniture, Georgian and Victorian; glass, china. PARK: In drives on either side of shop. TEL: 453285. SER: Valuations. FAIRS: London and provincial. Organisers of Everyman Antiques Fairs. VAT: Stan/Spec.

AYLSHAM (0263)
Pearse Lukies   Trade Only
Bayfield House, White Hart St. Open preferably by appointment. STOCK: Period oak, sculpture, objects, 18th C furniture. TEL: 734137.

L.W. Pead
20 Sir Williams Close. Est. 1969. Open by appointment. STOCK: General antiques. TEL: 733324.

White Hart Gallery
3 White Hart St. (O.W. Nisbet.) Est. 1965. CL: Wed. Open 10—5. SIZE: Medium. STOCK: Furniture, early 18th C to Edwardian, £50—£800; decorative items, early 19th C to 1930, £15—£200; pictures, 19th C to 1930, £120—£250. LOC: From market square along Red Lion St. to fork in road. PARK: Nearby. TEL: 733461; home — same. SER: Valuations; buys at auction. VAT: Stan/Spec.

BAWDESWELL (036 288)
Nr. East Dereham
Norfolk Polyphon and Clock Centre
Wood Farm. (N.B. Vince.) Open: Weekends. Week days preferably by appointment. STOCK: All types of mechanical music-polyphons, cylinder musical boxes, organs, orchestrions, automata and fine clocks, particularly early English bracket and longcase. LOC: On B1145, 1 mile east of Bawdeswell village and junction with A1067. TEL: 230. VAT: Stan/Spec.

BLAKENEY (059 451)
Providence House Antiques
High St. Resident. STOCK: Clocks, £50—£1,000; furniture, 18th—19th C, £50—£1,500; silver, china. PARK: Easy. TEL: Cley (0263) 740403. SER: Valuations.

BRANCASTER (0485)
Nr. King's Lynn
Steed-Croft Antiques
'Marshlands', Cross Lane. (J.M. Tate.) Open by appointment only. STOCK: Period furniture. TEL: 210812.

BRANCASTER STAITHE
Nr. King's Lynn
Brancaster Staithe Antiques
Coast Rd. (M.J. Wilson.) Open every day during season, weekends and by appointment in winter. STOCK: Victorian tables, chairs; oak, unusual pine, bookpresses, bordalous, art deco. TEL: Brancaster (0485) 210600.

BRESSINGHAM, Nr. Diss (037 988)
David Bateson Antiques
Lodge Farm. (D. and P. Bateson.) Est. 1966. Open by appointment. SIZE: Medium. STOCK: Country furniture. LOC: 1½ miles from Bressingham north of A1066 from Diss. PARK: Easy. TEL: 629. SER: Valuations. VAT: Stan/Spec.

BROCKDISH, Nr. Diss
Brockdish Antiques
Commerce House. (M. Palfrey.) Est. 1975. CL: Wed. p.m. Open 9—5.30. STOCK: Furniture. LOC: A143. TEL: Hoxne (037 975) 498. SER: Restorations; upholstery.

Eekhout Gallery
Rosebrook, Grove Rd. Est. 1964. Open daily by prior appointment. SIZE: Small. STOCK: Rare and out of print books, prints, oils, watercolours. LOC: Off A143 Scole to Bungay road, opposite the Green. PARK: Easy. TEL: Hoxne (037 975) 575. SER: Restorations.

BURNHAM MARKET
M. and A. Cringle
The Old Black Horse. Est. 1965. CL: Wed. Open 10—1 and 2—5. SIZE: Medium. STOCK: Furniture, mainly country items, £50—£500; china, glass, pottery, prints, maps, £10—£200. Not stocked: Large expensive furniture, Oriental and Continental antiques, reproductions. LOC: In village centre. PARK: Easy. TEL: Fakenham (0328) 738456. VAT: Spec.

MARKET HOUSE

BURNHAM MARKET KING'S LYNN, NORFOLK
Fakenham (0328) 738475
J. Maufe

Norwich 35 miles   King's Lynn 25 miles

FINE QUALITY PERIOD FURNITURE AND WORKS OF ART

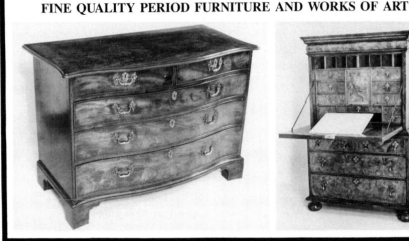

Burnham Market continued

Market House   BADA
(J. Maufe.) Resident. Appointment advisable.
SIZE: Medium. *STOCK: English furniture —
walnut, mahogany, rosewood and some oak,
late 17th to mid-19th C, £25—£20,000;
works of art, mirrors, small decorative items,
some porcelain and Victorian watercolours.*
Not stocked: Clocks, silver, jewellery. LOC:
B1355, large Queen Anne house on green in
village centre. PARK: Easy. TEL: Fakenham
(0328) 738475. SER: Valuations; buys at
auction. VAT: Spec.

COLTISHALL

Elizabeth Allport   LAPADA
(Corner Antiques)
at the Coltishall Antiques Centre. Est. 1967.
Open 10—5, Sun. by appointment. SIZE:
Medium. *STOCK: Objets de vertu, collectors'
items, porcelain, pottery and silver,
18th—19th C; glass, 19th C, all £5—£1,000;
copper, brass, furniture, 18th—19th C,
£5—£2,000.* LOC: B1150 road from Norwich
into Coltishall, shop on left. TEL: Norwich
(0603) 738306; home — Norwich (0603)
737631. SER: Valuations; restorations (pottery and porcelain, furniture); buys at auction.
FAIRS: Norwich (Jan. and Easter.) VAT:
Stan/Spec.

Coltishall continued

The Antique Shop
Church St. (R. Bradbury.) Est. 1967. Open by
appointment. *STOCK: Period furniture.* PARK:
Easy. TEL: Norwich (0603) 737444. VAT:
Stan.

Eric Bates and Sons
High St. Est. 1973. Open 9—5.30. SIZE:
Large. *STOCK: General antiques, Georgian,
Victorian, Edwardian and shipping furniture.*
TEL: Norwich (0603) 738716. SER: Restora-
tions (furniture); upholstery; container pack-
ing. VAT: Stan/Spec.

Coltishall Antiques Centre
High St. (E. Allport.) Est. 1980. Open 10—5.
SIZE: Large. There are several specialists
among the dealers at this centre who sell a
*wide variety of mainly small items including
porcelain and pottery, silver, jewellery, collectors' items, brass and copper, scientific and
medical instruments, craftsmen's tools,
marine items, militaria, maps, prints, postcards, clocks and watches, glass and unusual
items, all 18th C to art deco.* LOC: B1150 on
corner of main street. PARK: Easy. TEL:
Norwich (0603) 738306. SER: Valuations;
restorations (pottery and porcelain, furniture;
objets de vertu, clocks and watches, barometers and upholstery). VAT: Stan/Spec.

Coltishall continued

Gwendoline Golder

The Little Shop. Open 2—5.30. *STOCK: General antiques and bygones, collectors' items, crested ware.* TEL: Norwich (0603) 737404.

Isabel Neal Cabinet Antiques

Bank House, High St. Est. 1968. Open 9.30—5.30. SIZE: Small. *STOCK: Porcelain, pottery, especially blue and white, 17th—20th C; small furniture, watercolours, copper, brass, pewter, collectors' items.* LOC: B1150 towards North Walsham, shop on right. PARK: Easy. TEL: Norwich (0603) 737379.

COSTESSEY, Nr. Norwich

The Coach House

Townhouse Rd., Old Costessey. (J. Hines.) Resident. Open by appointment. *STOCK: 18th—20th C paintings; drawings, Victorian watercolours and post-war artists; original prints, etchings, engravings; Baxter and Le Blond.* TEL: Norwich (0603) 742977. SER: Cleaning prints and watercolours; framing.

CROMER   (0263)

Bond Street Antiques (inc. Jas. J. Briggs)

6 Bond St. and 38 Church St. (M.R.T. and J.A. Jones.) NAG, FGA. Est. 1958. Open 9—1 and 2.15—5.30, Sat. 9—6, Sun. by appointment. SIZE: Medium. *STOCK: Jewellery, silver, porcelain, china, glass, small furniture, 18th—20th C, £50—£1,000.* LOC: From Church St. bear right to Post Office, shop on opposite side on street further along. PARK: Easy. TEL: 513134; home — same. SER: Valuations; restorations (watches and jewellery); gem testing and analysis. VAT: Stan.

Past and Present

28 Louden Rd. (Wing Cmdr. M.H.J. Colman.) CL: Wed. p.m. in winter. Open 10.30—1 and 2.30—4.30. SIZE: Small. *STOCK: Copper, brass, porcelain, clocks, small furniture, bric-a-brac.* LOC: Opposite shoppers' car park. PARK: Easy. TEL: 512894.

Benjamin Rust Antiques

3 St. Margaret's Rd. *STOCK: Furniture, 18th and 19th C, glass, clocks and decorative items.* LOC: Near Norwich Rd. traffic lights. PARK: Own. TEL: 511452. SER: Restorations. VAT: Spec.

Cromer continued

A.E. Seago

15 Church St. (D.C. Seago.) Est. 1937. CL: Sun. and Wed. October to April. Open 9—1 and 2—5.15. SIZE: Medium. *STOCK: Furniture, 1790—1910, £25—£1,000; English coins and medals, 1660—1920, 25p—£150; English maps, 1610—1830, £4—£50.* Not stocked: Silver, garden furniture, oil paintings. LOC: From Sheringham take main coast road, then New St. into High St. PARK: Easy. 50yds. away around Church. TEL: 512733. SER: Valuations. VAT: Stan/Spec.

DEREHAM, see EAST DEREHAM

DISS (0379)

Diss Antiques
2 Market Place. Open 9—1 and 2—5, or by appointment. SIZE: Large. STOCK: Barometers, furniture, clocks, porcelain, copper, brass. PARK: Nearby. TEL: 2213; home — 51369. SER: Restorations (especially barometers); restoration materials; export facilities. VAT: Stan/Spec.

Peter Fox Antiques
5 St. Nicholas St. Est. 1968. CL: Tues. Open 10.30—3, Sat. 9—1 and 2—6, or by appointment. STOCK: Furniture, clocks, pictures, china, glass. PARK: Nearby. TEL: 2948. VAT: Stan/Spec.

Idears of Diss
incorporating Benton Antiques Ltd.
1 Chapel St. Est. 1972. Open 9.30—5. SIZE: Large. STOCK: Furniture, 17th—19th C, £50—£1,000; porcelain, china, prints, and paintings, 18th—20th C, £10—£100; fabrics, upholstery. LOC: In town centre, near church. PARK: Easy. TEL: 51521. VAT: Stan/Spec.

John Oliver and Co.   LAPADA
41 Mere St. Est. 1947. Open 10—5.30. SIZE: Medium. STOCK: Furniture, 17th—19th C; ceramics and jewellery. LOC: In main shopping centre, adjoining the Mere. PARK: Around corner. TEL: 2662, 3414 or 898670. SER: Valuations; restorations.

Robert D. Pearse
26a St. Nicholas St. Open Fri. and Sat. 10—5. STOCK: Small furniture, ceramics and collectors' items.

EARSHAM, Nr. Bungay

John Derham Ltd.
Earsham Hall. Est. 1966. Open by appointment. SIZE: Large. STOCK: Pine furniture. LOC: On Earsham to Hedenham Rd. PARK: Easy. SER: Container service. TEL: Bungay (0986) 3423.

EAST DEREHAM

Anglia Antiques
Old Church School, Cemetery Rd. (S.R. Allison.) Resident. Open Mon. to Fri., or by appointment. STOCK: Furniture, oil paintings, watercolours, ceramics, bric-a-brac. TEL: Dereham (0362) 4828.

Antiques and Collectables
8 Aldiss Court, High St. (L.I. Wells.) Open daily. STOCK: Country and pine furniture, porcelain including Doulton, Derby, Worcester, Spode and Minton, especialy wall plates.

Dereham Antiques
9 Norwich St. (M. Fanthorpe.) Est. 1969. CL: Wed. Open 10—5. STOCK: Jewellery, china, glass, small silver items. PARK: Nearby. TEL: Dereham (0362) 3200. VAT: Stan.

East Dereham continued

Wynyard R.T. Wilkinson — Fine Silver
Bylaugh. Est. 1966. Open by appointment. STOCK: English Scottish, Irish and colonial silver, 17th to early 19th C, £5—£10,000+. LOC: 6 miles north of East Dereham on B1147. PARK: Easy. TEL: Bawdeswell (036 288) 200; home — same. SER: Valuations; buys at auction. VAT: Stan/Spec.

EAST HARLING (0953)

Cheese Hill Antiques
Memorial Green. (R. and J. Crone.) Est. 1971. Open 9—1 and 2—5, Sat. 10—12.30. SIZE: Medium. STOCK: Stripped pine, 1782-1962, £5—£400. LOC: 2 miles off A11. PARK: Easy. TEL: 718142. SER: Restorations (pine); stripping; reproduction pine furniture made to order.

FAKENHAM (0328)

Bygones
6 Norwich Rd. (Mrs. S. Rivett.) Est. 1969. Open 10—1. STOCK: General antiques and bygones. LOC: On Norwich Rd. into Fakenham. TEL: 2924; home — Melton Constable (0263) 860462.

Fakenham Antique Centre
Old Congregational Chapel, 14 Norwich Rd. (B.D. Brewster.) Est. 1972. Open 10—5, Thurs. 9—5. SIZE: Large. LOC: Turn off A.148 towards the town centre, past the Post Office turn left, centre 50yds. on the right. PARK: Easy. TEL: 2941; home — Melton Constable (0263) 860543. SER: Restoration (furniture and clocks); polishing. Below are listed the dealers at this centre:-

Grace Aldiss
Small furniture, plate and porcelain. TEL: Elmham (036 281) 239.

Alexandrena
Victoriana and collectors' items. TEL: Binham (032 875) 517.

Paddy Ashworth-Jones
China, glass and small furniture. TEL: 2390.

Janet Boon
Linen, china, glass and small furniture. TEL: Gayton (055 386) 229.

Avril Brewster
China, glass, plate, small furniture. TEL: Melton Constable (0263) 860543.

Brian Brewster
Furniture, Georgian, Victorian and Edwardian. TEL: Melton Constable (0263) 860543.

Gilbert and Edna Briere
Decorative and ususual items, period furniture and pictures. TEL: Aylsham (0263) 732651.

Elaine Cawthorn
Kitchenalia and collectables. TEL: 4504.

Fakenham Antique Centre continued

Daphne Coleman
Small Victorian furniture and decorative items. TEL: Dereham (0362) 3070.

Leon and Rowena Harris
Country furniture, rugs and pictures. TEL: Norwich (0603) 870628.

Rachael Hay
General antiques. TEL: Kings Lynn (0553) 765432.

Winifred Hunka
Oriental and English porcelain and glass. TEL: Holt (026 371) 2667.

John MacPherson
Clocks, period and Victorian furniture. TEL: Cley (0263) 740403.

John Othen
Books mostly Norfolk fieldsports and countryside; ephemera. TEL: Foulsham (036284) 865.

Keith Wakeham
Porcelain, pictures, small furniture. TEL: Saxthorpe (026387) 837.

Joyce Waymouth
General antiques. TEL: Kings Lynn (0553) 83224.

Jean and Robert Woodhouse
General antiques especially clocks. TEL: Hunstanton (04853) 2903.

FELMINGHAM, Nr. North Walsham

Solus Marketing   *Export Only*
(Norfolk)   **LAPADA**
Cromer Rd. (J.A. Ayers.) Est. 1973. STOCK: Silver. TEL: North Walsham (0692) 402042.

FORNCETT ST. MARY
Nr. Norwich

The Newcomen Gallery
Church Cottage, Low Rd. (Mrs. S. Mansbridge.) Est. 1983. Open by appointment. SIZE: Small. *STOCK: Watercolours, 18th—20th C; oil paintings.* LOC: 2 miles west of Long Stratton on A140. PARK: Easy. TEL: (0508 41) 8273; home — same. SER: Valuations; restorations (oils and watercolours); framing; buys at auction (pictures).

GREAT YARMOUTH   (0493)

David Ferrow
77 Howard St. South. ABA. Est. 1940. CL: Thurs. Open 9.30—1 and 2.30—5.30, Sat. 9.30—5.30. Telephone call advisable. SIZE: Large. *STOCK: Books, some antiquarian maps, local prints, manuscripts.* LOC: From London over river bridge, keep to nearside, turn left and then right to car park. PARK: Easy. TEL: 843800; home — 662247. SER: Valuations; restorations (books and prints). VAT: Stan.

Great Yarmouth continued

The Ferrow Family Antiques
6 and 7 Hall Quay, also 1 George St. Est. 1957. CL: Thurs. p.m. Open 9.15—5.30. *STOCK: General antiques, £1—£2,000.* Not stocked: Guns, medals, coins, jewellery. LOC: Near Haven Bridge, off A12. TEL: 855391; home — 844630. SER: Valuations; restorations; buys at auction; hire. VAT: Stan/Spec.

The Haven Gallery
6/7 Hall Quay. (M. and J. Ferrow and Son.) CL: Thurs. p.m. Open 9.15—5.30. *STOCK: Watercolours, drawings, prints, oil paintings, 19th C, £10—£1,000.* LOC: Near Haven Bridge, off A12. TEL: 855391; home — 844630. SER: Valuations, restorations (framing, collections). VAT: Stan/Spec.

Barry Howkins Antiques   LAPADA
35 King St. CL: Thurs. p.m. Open 9—5.30. SIZE: Large. *STOCK: Barometers, clocks, copper, brass, jewellery, porcelain, Staffordshire china, glass, pictures.* LOC: In main shopping rd. PARK: Opposite. TEL: 842713. VAT: Stan/Spec.

John Howkins   *Trade Only*
Old Hall, 145 King St. Open by appointment only. *STOCK: Sets of chairs, bureaux, bookcases, desks, tables, shipping goods, 1850—1920.* LOC: Main shopping street. TEL: 853620/857065/855533. VAT: Stan/Spec.

Peter Howkins
39, 40, 41 and 135 King St. Est. 1946. CL: Thurs. p.m. Open 9—5.30. SIZE: Large. *STOCK: At 135 King St. — jewellery, Victorian to present day, £5—£5,000; silver, George III to present day, £1—£2,000; at 39 and 40 King St. — furniture, upholstery, Georgian to Victorian, £5—£2,000; at 41 King St. — investment antiques.* LOC: From Norwich through town one-way system to road signposted Lowestoft which intersects King St. PARK: Easy. TEL: 844639. SER: Valuations; restorations (jewellery, special upholstery, silver, furniture). FAIRS: Norwich, Snape and Gt. Yarmouth.

Rodney and Michael Wheatley
16a Northgate St., White Horse Plain; also at 2 Fullers Hill; 3 Caister Rd., and trade warehouse at Kitchener Rd. Est. 1971. Open 9.30—5, Thurs. 9.30—1. SIZE: Large. *STOCK: General antiques.* LOC: 2 minutes walk from Market Place. PARK: Easy. TEL: 857219. VAT: Stan.

HARLESTON   (0379)
Charles Wright Antiques
The Magpie Hotel Yard. (C.W. Wright.) Est. 1973. CL: Thurs. and Fri. SIZE: Small. STOCK: Stripped pine and general antiques, 18th—20th C, £5—£200; country furniture, £20—£200; bric-a-brac including carvings and treen, to £75; all 17th—20th C. LOC: Town centre. PARK: Easy. TEL: 853796. SER: Restorations (furniture).

HEACHAM,   (0485)
Nr. King's Lynn
Peter Robinson
Pear Tree House, 7 Lynn Rd. Est. 1880. Open 9—5. Appointment advisable Thurs. and Sat. SIZE: Medium. STOCK: Furniture, 1600—1870, £10—£1,000; china, 1750—1830, £2—£200; metalwork, 1700—1870, £5—£150. Not stocked: Late shipping goods. LOC: Shop on left on entry to village. PARK: Easy. TEL: 70228. SER: Valuations, buys at auction. VAT: Stan/Spec.

HOLT   (4 fig. nos) (026 371)
(6 fig. nos.) (2063)
Golden Oldies
29 Norwich Rd. (C.A. Wilkins.) CL: Thurs. Open 10—5. STOCK: Victorian and Edwardian furniture, bric-a-brac, clocks, china, glass, silver, brass, copper and collectors' items. TEL: 3614. SER: Buys at auction.

Goodman of Holt
Albert St. Open 9—5.30. SIZE: Large. STOCK: Furniture. LOC: On perimeter of public car park. TEL: 3471. VAT: Stan/Spec.

Simon Gough Books
5 Fish Hill. Est. 1976. Open 9.30—5. STOCK: Antiquarian and secondhand books; bindings. TEL; 2650.

Holt Antiques Centre
Albert Hall, Albert St. Open 10—5. STOCK: Pine, oak, art deco, porcelain, glass, linen, clothes, childrens books, collectors' items. TEL: 733301.

Humbleyard Fine Art
3 Fish Hill. (J.D. Layte.) Est. 1971. CL: Fri. Open 10—5. SIZE: Medium. STOCK: Scientific and medical instruments, 1700—1900, £5—£2,000; paintings, 1850-1950, £30—£500; cabinet makers tools, 1700-1900, £5—£200; nautical and unusual items, non painted pictures. PARK: Easy. TEL: 3362. SER: Valuations; restorations (watercolours, prints); buys at auction (paintings and instruments.) FAIRS: Olympia. VAT: Spec.

New Street Antiques
33 New St. (B.J. Adams.) CL: Sun. except by appointment. Open 10—5.30. SIZE: Large. STOCK: Stripped pine and Victorian furniture. TEL: 3089.

Holt continued
Richard Scott Antiques
30 High St. Est. 1967. CL: Thurs. Open 10—1 and 2—5. SIZE: Medium. STOCK: Pottery and porcelain, rare and unusual objects. LOC: On A148. PARK: Easy. TEL: 2479. SER: Valuations; conservation advice. VAT: Stan.

HUNSTANTON   (048 53)
Delawood Antiques
10 Westgate. (J.E. and R.C. Woodhouse.) M.B.H.I., B.W.C.G. Est. 1975. CL: Mon., Tues., and Thurs. during winter. Open 10—5, Sun. 1—5 by prior telephone call. SIZE: Small. STOCK: General antiques, £5—£1,000; jewellery, £10—£500, Georgian, Victorian and Edwardian longcase, dial, wall and mantle clocks, £20—£1,000; books, furniture, collectors' items. LOC: Near town centre and bus station. PARK: Easy. TEL: 2903; home — same. SER: Valuations; restorations (longcase, bracket, fusee clocks, astrological functions) repairs.

KING'S LYNN   (0553)
Norfolk Galleries
Railway Rd. (B. Houchen and G.R. Cumbley.) Open 9—6, Sat. 9—1, Sat. p.m. by appointment. STOCK: Victorian and Edwardian furniture. PARK: Nearby. TEL: 65060.

The Old Granary Antique and Collectors Centre
King Staithe Lane, off Queens St. Open 10—5. STOCK: China, glass, books, silver, jewellery, brass, copper, postcards, linen, some furniture, and general antiques. PARK: Easy. TEL: 775509. SER: Buys at auction.

Old Granary Studio
King Staithe Lane, off Queens St. (A. Reed.) Est. 1966. Open 10—5.30. SIZE: Medium. STOCK: Pictures and prints, 18th—20th C, £5—£100; clothes, 19th—20th C.. LOC: From Tuesday Market Place to St. Margarets Church, 3rd turning on right. PARK: Easy. TEL: 775509; home — Dereham (0362) 820070. SER: Valuations; restorations (relining and cleaning oil paintings); buys at auction (pictures and prints); picture framing. VAT: Stan.

Tower Gallery
Middleton Tower. (T.H. and J. Barclay.) Est. 1963. SIZE: Large. STOCK: General antiques including furniture, china, glass, silver, prints, pictures. LOC: One mile off A47. PARK: Easy. TEL: 840203 or 840581.

C. Winlove
14 and 17 (workshop) Purfleet St. (A. and H.V.H. Winlove.) Est. 1890. Open 9.30—1 and 2.30—5, Sat. till 4. SIZE: Small. Large workshop. STOCK: Furniture. LOC: Opposite Customs House. PARK: On quay opposite. TEL: 775628. SER: Restorations (furniture).

LITCHAM, Nr. King's Lynn
Priory Antiques
Litcham Priory. (B.J. Jones.) Est. 1964. Open 9.30−5, Sun. 10−5. SIZE: Large. *STOCK: Industrial bygones, pine and cottage furniture, 19th C, 25p−£75.* PARK: Easy. TEL: Fakenham (0328) 701262.

LITTLE WALSINGHAM
Howard Fears
t/a Pilgrims Progress
51 High St. Always available. *STOCK: Antiquarian and secondhand books, ephemera, stamps, prints.* SER: Buys at auction.

LONG STRATTON   (0508)
Old Coach House
Ipswich Rd. Est. 1976. CL: Mon. Open 10−1 and 2−5. *STOCK: General antiques, pine, Victorian and Edwardian export furniture, paintings, copper, brass, china.* TEL: 30942.

METHWOLD   (0366)
Court House Antiques
39 Stoke Rd. (J. Livingstone.) CL: Tues. Open 10.30−5.30 including Sun. *STOCK: Victorian furniture, bric-a-brac and clocks.* LOC: B1106, ¼ mile north of village. TEL: 728644.

MILEHAM, Nr. King's Lynn
Henry Merckel
Est. 1967. Open 9−6. *STOCK: Oak furniture, china, jewellery, 18th−19th C.* Not stocked: Coins, weapons. PARK: Easy. TEL: Fakenham (0328) 701234. SER: Valuations.

A fine portrait group by Frémiet, 1860-1880, of a pair of hounds that must have been favourite hunting dogs. Typically of Frémiet there is a tremendous amount of character in these two animals with their most appealing faces. From *Animals in Bronze* by Christopher Payne, published by the **Antique Collectors' Club,** 1986.

NEATISHEAD
Margaret Corson
Irstead Manor. Est. 1966. Open by appointment. *STOCK: Furniture, oak and mahogany, 17th−18th C; 18th C porcelain, especially Lowestoft, early English pottery, Delftware, glass, watercolours, and treen, £5−£2,000.* TEL: Horning (0692) 630274. VAT: Spec.

NORTH WALSHAM   (0692)
Anglia Antique Exporters
Trade Warehouse, Station Yard, Norwich Rd. (J. Connaughton and P. Keegan). SIZE: Large. *STOCK: Victorian, Edwardian, pine and general shipping goods, £10−£1,500.* TEL: 406266; home − (026378) 568.

Eric Bates and Sons   LAPADA
Melbourne House. Bacton Rd. Est. 1973. Open 8−5.30. SIZE: Large. *STOCK: General antiques, Victorian, Edwardian, shipping furniture.* TEL: 403221. SER: Restorations (furniture); upholstery; shipping and container packing. VAT: Stan/Spec.

North Walsham Antique Gallery
29 Grammar School Rd. (M.B. and I.F. Hicks.) Est. 1970. CL: Wed. Open 9−1 and 2−5. SIZE: Medium. *STOCK: China, glass, silver, collectors' items, small furniture.* TEL: 405059. SER: Valuations; restorations. VAT: Stan/Spec.

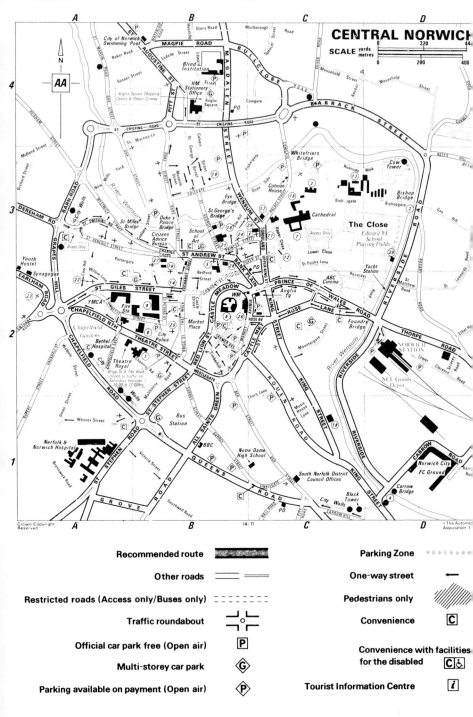

CENTRAL NORWICH

Recommended route	Parking Zone
Other roads	One-way street
Restricted roads (Access only/Buses only)	Pedestrians only
Traffic roundabout	Convenience
Official car park free (Open air)	
Multi-storey car park	Convenience with facilities for the disabled
Parking available on payment (Open air)	Tourist Information Centre

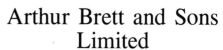

Arthur Brett and Sons Limited

ESTABLISHED 1870

40-44 St. Giles Street, Norwich, NR2 1LW, England

Telephone: Norwich (0603) 628171

OPEN FIVE DAYS A WEEK,
SATURDAYS BY APPOINTMENT

*Dealers in fine English 17th, 18th and 19th Century Furniture
Selected Pieces of Oak Furniture, Treen, Wood Sculpture, Bygones and Decorative Items*

Rare William & Mary Kingwood and Marquetry inlaid Chest on Stand. Height 50ins. Width 39½ins. Depth 25ins.

MEMBERS BRITISH
ANTIQUE DEALERS
ASSOCIATION

Parking facilities for a limited period only
outside our showrooms

NORWICH   (0603)

The Antique Textile Shop
45 St. Benedict's St. (C. St. John-Foti.) Est. 1984. Open by appointment. SIZE: Medium. *STOCK: Shawls and quilts, woolwork, embroidery and beaded items, early costume.* LOC: Close to St. Andrews hall. PARK: Easy. TEL: 54641. SER: Restorations (fabric repair and conservation).

Arthur Brett and Sons Ltd.   BADA
40/44 St. Giles St. Est. 1870. Open 9.30—5, Sat. by appointment. SIZE: Large. *STOCK: Furniture, mahogany, walnut and oak, 17th—18th C; sculpture, metalwork.* LOC: Near City Hall. PARK: Easy. TEL: 628171. FAIRS: Grosvenor House and Harrogate. VAT: Stan/Spec.

Cathedral Gallery
10b Wensum St. (P.R. Crowe.) Open 10—5. *STOCK: Rare books, prints and maps.* TEL: 612428.

Cloisters Antiques Fair
St. Andrew's and Blackfriars Hall, St. Andrew's Plain. (Norwich City Council.) Est. 1976. Open Wed. only 9.30—3.30. There are twenty-three dealers at this fair, selling *a wide variety of general antiques.* PARK: Easy. TEL: 628477.

Norwich continued

Country and Eastern
8 Redwell St. (J. Millward.) Est. 1978. Open daily. SIZE: Large. *STOCK: Oriental rugs, kelims, and textiles, late 19th C to early 20th C, £50—£500; primitive and country furniture, 18th—19th C, £25—£500; woolwork pictures, 17th—19th C, £10—£200; bygones, 18th—19th C, £2—£75.* LOC: Top of Elm Hill. PARK: Nearby. TEL: 623107. VAT: Stan/Spec.

Peter R. Crowe
75 Upper St. Giles St. Open 9.30—6. *STOCK: Antiquarian books, maps, prints.* TEL: 624800.

Thomas Crowe
77 Upper St. Giles St. CL: Sat. p.m. Open 9—1 and 2.15—5.30. *STOCK: Books, prints.* TEL: 621962.

Charles Cubitt
10 All Saints Green. (Mrs. A.B. Cubitt and Mrs. A.E.C. Hunter.) Est. 1863. CL: Thurs. Open 9.30—5. SIZE: Medium. *STOCK: Jewellery, silver, plate, china, glass, antiquarian books.* LOC: Opposite Bond's store. PARK: Behind Bond's store. TEL: 622569.

Norwich continued

D'Amico Antiques Ltd.   LAPADA
20 Highland Rd., off Colman Rd. (J.E. Wrightson and Mrs. P. Mawtus.) NAWCC. Est. 1947. Resident. SIZE: Small. *STOCK: Clocks, 17th—20th C.* LOC: Off Colman Rd. (part of Norwich ring road) near Unthank Rd. traffic lights. PARK: Easy. TEL: 52320. SER: Restorations (clocks). VAT: Stan/Spec.

The Fairhurst Gallery
13 Bedford St. Est. 1951. Open 10—5. SIZE: Large. *STOCK: Oil paintings, 16th—20th C, £5—£5,000; watercolours, 18th—19th C, £5—£2,000; etchings, engravings, colour prints, 18th—20th C, £2—£200; frames, 16th—20th C.* LOC: Behind Travel Australia. TEL: 614214. SER: Valuations; restorations (pictures, furniture, samplers); framemakers. VAT: Spec.

Michael Hallam Antiques
17 Magdalen St. (M.J. Hallam.) Est. 1969. Open 10.30—5. SIZE: Small. *STOCK: Furniture, porcelain, pictures and small items, mainly 19th C, £10—£500.* LOC: Near cathedral. TEL: 621163; home — 413692. SER: Valuations; restorations (porcelain and pottery). VAT: Stan/Spec.

Donna and Jean Hannent
Est. 1980. Open by appointment. SIZE: Small. *STOCK: Jewellery, 1800-1940, £50—£1,500; silver jewellery, 1850-1940, £5—£100; collectors' items including snuff boxes, 1800—1900, £20—£200.* PARK: Easy. TEL: 611197. SER: Valuations.

G. Jarrett
12-14 Old Palace Rd. Est. 1961. TEL: 625847; home — 618244.

Henry Levine and Co.   BADA
55 London St. (D. and L. Levine.) Est. 1865. CL: Thurs. Open 9.15—5.30. *STOCK: Silver, jewellery, Sheffield plate.* TEL: 628709. SER: Valuations (especially Norwich silver). VAT: Stan/Spec.

The Little Gallery
38 Elm Hill. (I. Hook.) Est. 1968. *STOCK: Watercolours, drawings.* SER: Buys at auction. TEL: 625809. VAT: Spec.

Maddermarket Antiques
7 St. John's Alley, Maddermarket. (J.R. and D.A. Callan.) Est. 1955. CL: Mon. Open 10—5. SIZE: Small. *STOCK: Victoriana, £5—£250; jewellery, silverware, general antiques.* LOC: In city centre near to City Hall. PARK: Easy. TEL: 620610.

Norwich continued

Mandell's Gallery   BADA
Elm Hill. Est. 1964. Open 9—5.30. SIZE: Large. *STOCK: Oils, watercolours, specialising in Norwich and Suffolk schools.* LOC: Near shopping centre, close to Cathedral. PARK: Easy. TEL: 626892/629180. SER: Valuations; restorations; framing. VAT: Spec.

The Movie Shop
Antiquarian and Nostalgia Centre, St. Gregory's Alley. Open 10—5. SIZE: Large. *STOCK: Books, magazines and movie ephemera; furniture, porcelain, pre-1940 clothes and textiles, general antiques.* TEL: 615239.

Night and Day Antiques
22-24 St. Benedict St. Est. 1978. Open 10—5. *STOCK: Victorian and Edwardian lighting, brass and iron beds, bathroom fittings, fireplaces and surrounds.* Not stocked: Silver. LOC: Close to St. Andrew's Hall. PARK: Easy. TEL: 660046. SER: Restorations (metal work and polishing). VAT: Stan/Spec.

Ninety-One
91 St. Giles St. Open 9.30—5.30. *STOCK: Furniture including pine and oak.* SER: French spoken.

Norfolk Antiques (Exporters)
51 St. Giles St. *STOCK: Shipping goods.* TEL: 628535.

Norwich Antique and Collectors Centre
Quayside, Fye Bridge. (R.A. Dazeley and I.J. Ford.) Est. 1962. Open 10—5. SIZE: Large. There are 40 dealers at this centre selling *a wide range of general antiques and collectors items, 2p—£1,000+.* LOC: Near the cathedral. PARK: Nearby. TEL: 612582. SER: Valuations; restorations; framing.

Anthony Reed
1 Westwick St. (A. and V. Reed.) Est. 1966. Open 9.30—6, Sat. 10—1. SIZE: Small. *STOCK: Picture frames and prints, 18th—20th C, £1—£100.* PARK: Easy. TEL: 612894; home — Dereham (0362) 820070. SER: Valuations; restorations (cleaning and relining); buys at auction. VAT: Stan.

St. Giles Antiques and Period Fashion
51 St. Giles St. (G. Matthews.) Est. 1976. Open 10—5. *STOCK: Glass, china, silver, jewellery, pre-1960 fashion, linen, lace, furs.* TEL: 628535.

Norwich continued

The Scientific Anglian (Bookshop)
30—30a St. Benedict St. (N.B. Peake.) Est. 1965. CL: Mon. a.m. and Thurs. a.m. Open 10—5.30. SIZE: Large. *STOCK: Secondhand books, old and modern, 30p—£200; antiquarian items, 1500—1900, from £1.* Not stocked: Maps or prints. LOC: 3 minutes walk from City Hall straight down Upper Goat Lane, turn left into St. Benedict's. PARK: 30 minute parking ½ minute due west; multi-storey parking St. Andrew's due. TEL: 624079. SER: Valuations; buys at auction. VAT: Stan.

Oswald Sebley
20 Lower Goat Lane. (P.H. Knights.) Est. 1895. CL: Thurs. Open 9—5.15. SIZE: Small. *STOCK: Silver, 18th—20th C, £15—£2,000; jewellery, Victorian, £10—£4,000.* LOC: 150yds. to right of City Hall, down paved street. PARK: Nearby. TEL: 626504. SER: Valuations; restorations (silver and gold jewellery). VAT: Stan/Spec.

James and Ann Tillett   LAPADA
12 and 13 Tombland. Est. 1972. Open 9.30—5.30. *STOCK: English domestic silver and flatware, from 17th C; mustard pots, collectors' items, barometers, barographs, longcase clocks, jewellery, from 18th C.* LOC: Opposite Erpingham Gate, Norwich Cathedral and Maid's Head Hotel. TEL: 624914. SER: Valuations; restorations (silver); export facilities. VAT: Stan/Spec.

Norwich continued

William G. Wells
20 St. John Maddermarket. Est. 1952. CL: Thurs. p.m. Open 10—5 or by appointment. SIZE: Medium. *STOCK: Furniture, 18th—19th C, £100—£10,000; porcelain, glass, 18th C, £5—£1000; paintings, 18th—19th C, £50—£5,000; clocks, £50—£3,000.* Not stocked: Silver, firearms, swords. LOC: Opposite St. Andrew's multi-storey car park. PARK: Easy. TEL: 621260. SER: Valuations; restorations (clocks, furniture, oil paintings). FAIRS: Norwich, Snape. VAT: Stan/Spec.

Wensum Antiques
20 Wensum St. (K.C. and M.E. Blacklock.) Est. 1976. *STOCK: Glass and china, 19th C; small furniture.* TEL: 616867.

The Whatnot
10 Unthank Rd. (T.J. Watts.) Est. 1967. CL: Thurs. Open 9.15—5. *STOCK: General antiques.* TEL: 625614. SER: Valuations.

Yesteryear
24D Magdalen St. (Mrs. E. Watson.) Est. 1980. Open 10.30—6. *STOCK: General antiques, pictures, oils, watercolours, prints, collectors' items, bygones, bric-a-brac.* PARK: Nearby. TEL: 624260 or 622908. SER: Buys at auction.

Robert Young Antiques   LAPADA
4A Exchange St. (K. and R. Young.) Est. 1970. CL: Mon. Open 10—4. *STOCK: Jewellery 18th—20th C, £5—£5,000.* LOC: Off Market Sq. opposite Jarrolds. PARK: Nearby. TEL: 618605. VAT: Stan/Spec.

A Lowestoft 'Chelsea ewer' creamer painted in slight manner by the Tulip painter, 2¼ins. high, c.1775. From **Lowestoft Porcelains** by Geoffrey A. Godden, F.R.S.A., published by the **Antique Collectors' Club**, 1985.

OLD HUNSTANTON
Irene Poulter Antiques
Neptune House. *STOCK: Small furniture, 18th−19th C; porcelain, boxes, oil paintings, watercolours, prints, objets de vertu.* LOC: A149. TEL: King's Lynn (0553) 2122.

OUTWELL See Cambridgeshire

PULHAM MARKET   (037 976)
Tim Hayes
at Bumbles Hotel. Open 10−5.30 but prior telephone call advisable. *STOCK: Furniture, bric-a-brac.* LOC: On A.140. TEL: 8277 or Diss (0379) 2849.

PULHAM ST. MARY, Nr Harleston
Don Bateman
Home Farm. Open by appointment. *STOCK: Architectural items.* TEL: Pulham Market (037 976) 784.

REEPHAM
The Chimes
Market Place. (P. and E. Elphick.) Est. 1977. CL: Thurs. p.m. Open 9.30−5. SIZE: Medium. *STOCK: General antiques and Victoriana, nautical items and paintings, old farming implements.* PARK: Easy. TEL: Norwich (0603) 870480; home − same.

George and Dragon Gallery
Old George and Dragon, Norwich Rd. (D. King.) Est. 1963. CL: Sat. p.m. Open 9−12.30 and 1.30−5.30. SIZE: Small. *STOCK: Prints, 18th−19th C; maps, 17th−19th C; watercolours, 19th−20th C; all £10−£100.* Not stocked: Oil paintings. LOC: From Norwich Ring Rd. take Reepham Rd. PARK: Easy. TEL: Norwich (0603) 870360. SER: Restorations (prints, maps, watercolours, oil paintings).

Reepham continued

Orchard House, Oriental Rugs
Ollands Rd. (Mrs. S. Aitchison.) Resident. Est. 1975. Open every day. SIZE: Medium. *STOCK: Carpets and rugs.* TEL: Norwich (0603) 870234. SER: Valuations; repairs.

REYMERSTON, Nr. Norwich
Xanthus Gallery
(P. Goodman). Est. 1982. Open by appointment. SIZE: Small. *STOCK: English pictures and drawings, 1750−1950, £100−£4,000.* LOC: 10 minutes from A47. PARK: Easy. TEL: (0362) 850862; home − same. SER: Valuations; restorations (paintings); buys at auction (paintings). VAT: Stan.

SHARRINGTON
Nr. Melton Constable
Sharrington Antiques
(P. Coke.) Est. 1944. CL: Jan.−Mar. Open by chance 9.30−5.00, or by appointment. SIZE: Medium. *STOCK: Small and interesting items, £5−£500; china, pictures, embroideries, treen, papier mâché.* LOC: 3 miles west of Holt. PARK: Easy. TEL; Melton Constable (0263) 861411; home − Melton Constable (0263) 860719.

SHERINGHAM   (0263)
Rose Denis
16 High St. *STOCK: Jewellery, silver, china, furniture.* TEL: 823699.

Dorothy's Antiques
23 Waterbank Rd. (Mrs. D.E. Collier.) Est. 1975. *STOCK: Glass, especially Cranberry, Royal Worcester, Meissen, Sitzendorf porcelain, commemoratives, Goss china, brass, copper, small furniture, clocks, cased birds, ribbon plates, porcelain shoes, collectors' items.* TEL: 822319; home − 823018.

LEO PRATT

OLD CURIOSITY SHOP
SOUTH WALSHAM   NORFOLK
Tel: S. Walsham 204

ANTIQUE DEALERS SINCE 1890

Five showrooms of every kind of antique and bygone art. Furniture, porcelain, glass, pictures, enamel, pewter, brass and copper, treen, collectors' items, clocks and watches.
Stock always changing. 1,000 items to choose from.
Closed Sundays and Mondays all day. Easy parking.

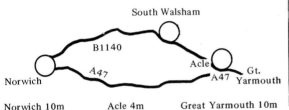

Norwich 10m   Acle 4m   Great Yarmouth 10m

Sheringham continued

Parriss
20 Station Rd. (J.H. Parriss.) Est. 1947. CL: Wed. Open 9—5.30. SIZE: Medium. *STOCK: Jewellery, £30—£2,500; silver, £40—£2,000; clocks, £100—£3,000.* LOC: A1082, in main street. PARK: Within 150yds. TEL: 822661. SER: Valuations; restorations (jewellery, silver, clocks). VAT: Stan.

SNETTISHAM, Nr. King's Lynn
Jasper Antiques
11A Hall Rd. (M. Norris). Est. 1975. CL: Tues and Thurs. Open 10—1, afternoons by appointment, Sat. 10—1 and 2—5. SIZE: Medium. *STOCK: Ceramics, £5—£800; furniture, £50—£1,000, both 18th—19th C; jewellery, 19th C, £5—£250.* LOC: Narrow passageway from Market Sq. to Hall Rd. PARK: Easy and Market Sq. TEL: Dersingham (0485) 41485. SER: Valuations; restorations (jewellery and furniture); buys at auction.

SOUTH LOPHAM, Nr. Diss
The Gallery and Things
The Street. (H. and E. Chalk.) CL: Mon. Open 9.30—5.30 including Sun. and Bank Holidays. *STOCK: 19th C watercolours, some oils and prints, small general antiques, antiquarian books.* LOC: A1066 Diss/Thetford Rd. TEL: Bressingham (037 988) 761. SER: Framing.

SOUTH WALSHAM   (060 549)
Leo Pratt and Son
Old Curiosity Shop. (R. and E.D. Pratt.) Est. 1890. CL: Mon. Open 9—1 and 2—5.30. SIZE: Large. *STOCK: Furniture, from 1700; porcelain, glass, pottery, 1830; shipping furniture, metalware.* PARK: Easy. TEL: 204; home — Great Yarmouth (0493) 750682. SER: Restorations (furniture); buys at auction. FAIRS: Norwich. VAT: Stan/Spec.

STALHAM (0692)
Stalham Antique Gallery
High St. (M.B. and I.F. Hicks.) Est. 1970. Open 9—1 and 2—5. SIZE: Medium. *STOCK: Furniture, Regency to 19th C; some early oak; pictures, china, glass.* Not stocked: Reproductions. PARK: Easy. TEL: 80636. SER: Valuations; restorations. VAT: Spec.

STIFFKEY
Bric-a-Brac Hall
The Old Methodist Chapel. Open by arrangement with Stiffkey Lamp Shop. *STOCK: Furniture, books, china, art deco and art nouveau items, bric-a-brac.* TEL: Binham (032 875) 460.

The Stiffkey Lamp Shop
Townshend Arms. (R. Belsten and D. Mann.) Est. 1976. Open 10.30—6, Sun. 1—6. SIZE: Medium. *STOCK: Lamps, gas, electric and oil, 1800—1920, £25—£2,000; rare lamp fittings.* LOC: Coast road near Wells-on-Sea. PARK: Easy. TEL: Binham (032 875) 460. SER: Restorations (lamp fittings). VAT: Stan.

STOKE FERRY (0366)
Nr. King's Lynn
Farmhouse Antiques
White's Farmhouse, Barker's Drove, off Oxborough Rd. (P. Philpot.) Est. 1969. Resident. CL: Wed. and Thurs., otherwise open. *STOCK: General antiques, especially desks and writing tables.* TEL: 500588.

SUFFIELD, Nr Aylsham
G. and E. Briere
Keepers Cottage. Resident. Est. 1966. Open by appointment. SIZE: Medium. *STOCK: Period furniture, paintings, unusual decorative items.* LOC: First fork left past the garage on Aylsham—North Walsham Rd. TEL: Aylsham (0263) 732651.

SWAFFHAM (0760)
Manor Farm Antiques and Garden Ornaments
Manor Farm. (Mr. and Mrs. P. Ison.) Est. 1959. Open 9—5, weekends and evenings by appointment. SIZE: Large. *STOCK: General antiques, Victoriana, beds, cradles, pine, bamboo, Kings silver plate, marble figures, statuary, urns and general garden ornaments and furniture.* LOC: Take Swaffham turn off new by-pass. Shop 200yds. from traffic lights on Norwich Rd. PARK: Easy. TEL: 21395. SER: Valuations; buys at auction.

The central avenue at St. Paul's Walden Bury, Hertfordshire. From *English Garden Design: History and Styles since 1650* by Tom Turner, published by the **Antique Collectors' Club,** 1986.

Swaffham continued

Swaffham Antiques Centre
'Cranglegate', Market Place. (K.W. Buckie.)
Resident. Est. 1960. Open 10−1 and 2−5.
SIZE: Small. *STOCK: China and collectors'
items, £5−£200; small furniture, some
pictures, £50−£1,000; all 18th−20th C.*
LOC: A47. PARK: In square opposite or in
passage at rear. TEL: 21277; home − 21052.
FAIRS: Local.

Swaffham Antiques Supplies
66−68 London St. (M. and R. Cross.) Est.
1959. CL: Mon. Open 10−5. SIZE: Large.
*STOCK: General antiques, 18th−19th C,
shipping furntiure, £100−£5,000.* LOC: Off
A47. PARK: Easy. TEL: 21697; home − same.

SWANTON ABBOT (069 269)
Nr. Aylesham

Oriental Rugs
Swanton Abbot Hall. (Mrs. G. Riley Smith.)
Est. 1977. Open every day but appointment
advisable. SIZE: Medium. *STOCK: Oriental
rugs, carpets and textiles.* LOC: Take road to
Burgh-next-to-Aylsham, Hall is 4 miles from
Aylsham. PARK: Easy. TEL: 244; home −
same. SER: Valuations; restorations.

TERRINGTON ST. CLEMENT
Nr. King's Lynn

D'Amico Antiques Ltd.
17 Sutton Rd. (Mrs. Watson.) Resident. Est.
1950. *STOCK: Small furniture, china, glass,
silver.* TEL: King's Lynn (0553) 828479. VAT:
Stan/Spec.

THORNAGE, Nr. Holt

Peter Hammond
Church House. Est. 1978. Open 10−5 or by
appointment. SIZE: Medium. *STOCK: Furniture, 17th−19th C, £50−£1,500.* PARK:
Easy. TEL: Melton Constable (0263) 861352.

THURLTON

M.D. Cannell Antiques
2 Sandy Lane. Resident. Always open.
STOCK: Period and Victorian furniture. TEL:
Raveningham (050 846) 441.

WATTON (0953)

Clermont Antiques *Trade Only*
Clermont Hall. (P. Jones.) Resident. Est. 1983.
Open by appointment. SIZE: Large. *STOCK:
Furniture, decorative items, prints, 18th to
early 19th C.* LOC: Down farm track, off
B1108. PARK: Easy. TEL: 882189. VAT: Spec.

WELLS-NEXT-THE-SEA

Marshfield Antiques
51 High St. (Mr. and Mrs. C.R. Waters.) Est.
1967. CL: Thurs. Open 9−12.30 and 1.30−
5.30. SIZE: Medium. *STOCK: Furniture,
porcelain, silver, collectors' pieces.* LOC: At
church end of High St. PARK: Easy. TEL:
Fakenham (0328) 710 552. VAT: Stan/Spec.

'Sailmakers Barn'
High St. (B. Dryburgh.) Open 10−6 by
appointment only. *STOCK: Oriental rugs and
carpets, 19th−20th C; watercolours and oils.*
LOC: Church end of High St. PARK: Easy. TEL:
Fakenham (0328) 710883. SER: Valuations;
restorations; repairs.

WROXHAM (060 53)

T.C.S. Brooke BADA
The Grange. (T.C.S., M.A. and S.T. Brooke.)
Est. 1932. CL: Wed. Open 9.30−1 and
2.15−5.30. *STOCK: English porcelain, 18th
C, furniture (mainly Georgian), silver, glass,
works of art, Oriental rugs.* PARK: Easy. TEL:
2644. SER: Valuations. VAT: Spec.

WYMONDHAM (0953)

King
Market Place. (M. King.) Est. 1969. CL: Mon.
and Wed., except by appointment. Open 9−5.
*STOCK: General antiques, furniture, copper,
brass, silver, jewellery, porcelain.* LOC: In
Market Square. PARK: Easy. TEL: 604758;
evenings − 602427. VAT: Stan/Spec.

M.E. and J.E. Standley
'Waveney', 106 Norwich Rd. and warehouses
at Chandlers Hill. Open Sat., otherwise by
appointment. *STOCK: Furniture, 17th−19th C
and Victorian.* TEL: 602566.

R.C. Standley
197 Norwich Rd. Open Sat., otherwise by
appointment. *STOCK: Furniture, 17th−19th C
and Victorian; small items.* TEL: 602042.

Turret House
27 Middleton St. (Dr. and Mrs. D.H. Morgan.)
PBFA. Est. 1972. Resident. SIZE: Small.
*STOCK: Scientific, nautical and medical
instruments, 18th−19th C, £5−£2,000; antiquarian books, £1−£500; some general
antiques including barometers. Not stocked:
Silver, jewellery and ceramics.* LOC: Corner of
Vicar St., adjacent to War Memorial. TEL:
603462. SER: Buys at auction. FAIRS: London
(monthly) and major provincial PBFA. VAT:
Stan/Spec.

Northamptonshire 546

LEICS

Ashley ◯   Weldon ◯   A43

A427   A427   A605

A6

Desborough   Islip ◯   Oundle ◯

A508   Thrapston ◯

Guilsborough ◯   Kettering ◯   CAMB

A50   West Haddon ⊖   Finedon ◯   A6

Long Buckby ◯   A43   A605

A361   A5   M1   A50   A508   Wellingborough ◯   Rushden ◯

A45

Harpole ◯   NORTHAMPTON

WARKS   Weedon ⊖ ◯ Flore   M1   BEDS

A5   A428

Pattishall ◯

Upper Boddington ◯   A43

A361   Towcester ⊖   A508   M1

Paulerspury ◯

Brackley ⊖   A43   Potterspury ◯ ◯ Cosgrove

A422

OXFORD   Croughton ◯   BUCKS

N

Please note this is only a rough map designed
to show dealers the number of shops in the
various towns, and is not necessarily totally
accurate.

◯ 1–2   Key to
⊖ 3–5   number of
◉ 6–12   shops in
⬤ 13+   this area.

A MOST EXTENSIVE STOCK OF ANTIQUE FURNITURE IN TRADITIONAL SURROUNDINGS

Cosgrove, Milton Keynes MK19 7JB. Tel: Milton Keynes (0908) 565888/Telex: 825203

ASHLEY (063 087)
Nr. Market Harborough

Hoffman **BADA**
Owsley House. (J.E. Hoffman.) Est. 1966. Open by appointment. SIZE: Large. STOCK: English and Continental clocks and barometers, 17th—19th C, from £200; period furniture. PARK: Easy. TEL: Medbourne Green (085 883) 8315. SER: Valuations. VAT: Stan/Spec.

BRACKLEY (0280)

Peter and Heather Jackson Antiques
3 Market Place. CL: Wed. Open 10.30—1 and 2—5. STOCK: English and Continental porcelain and pottery, 18th—19th C; furniture, paintings, silver, jewellery, glass, watercolours prints, arms, coins and Persian rugs. TEL: 703259. SER: Valuations; restorations.

Juno's Antiques
4 Bridge St. CL: Wed. Open 10—1 and 2—5. STOCK: General antiques. LOC: Northampton/Oxford road. TEL: 700639.

Brackley continued

Brenda Nutting Antiques
Hollywood House, 69 High St. Est. 1977. CL: Sun. a.m. Open 10—5.30, Wed. 10—2, Sun. p.m. and Wed. p.m. by appointment. SIZE: Medium. STOCK: General antiques, £1—£1,000. LOC: A43. PARK: Easy. TEL: 703362; home — same.

The Old Hall Bookshop
32 Market Place. (J. and Lady Juliet Townsend.) Est. 1977. Open 9.30—1 and 2—5.30. SIZE: Large. STOCK: Antiquarian, secondhand and new books. LOC: Town centre on east side of Market Place. PARK: Easy. TEL: 704146. VAT: Stan.

COSGROVE, Nr. Milton Keynes

Restall Brown and **LAPADA**
Clennell Ltd.
(S. Brown and A Frazer.) Est. 1905. Open Mon.—Fri. 8.30—5.30, appointment advisable; other times by appointment. STOCK: English furniture, 17th—19th C. LOC: Off A5, trains can be met at Central Milton Keynes Station. TEL: Milton Keynes (0908) 565888. VAT: Stan/Spec.

CROUGHTON, Nr. Brackley (0869)
Croughton Antiques
29 High St. (T. and L. Cross.) Est. 1971. Open Wed.—Sun. 10—6 or by appointment. SIZE: Medium + warehouse. STOCK: General antiques, decorators' items and shipping goods. LOC: B4031. PARK: Easy. TEL: 810203. VAT: Stan/Spec.

DESBOROUGH, Nr. Kettering
Richard Kimbell Antiques   Trade only
Harborough Rd. Est. 1967. Open by appointment. SIZE: Warehouse. STOCK: Pine, £5—£1,500. PARK: Easy. TEL: Market Harborough (0858) 33444. SER: Restorations; stripping (pine); container packing and shipping.

FINEDON
Jean Burnett Antiques
3a Church St. Est. 1967. Open 10—5.30. STOCK: Samplers and other embroideries, needlework tools and accessories, decorative items. TEL: Wellingborough (0933) 680430. FAIRS: Olympia.

Finedon Antiques Centre
3 Church St. (D.H. Burnett.) Open Wed. 10—4.30. There are 10—14 dealers at this centre offering general antiques. TEL: Wellingborough (0933) 680430.

Finedon continued

Noton Antiques
1 High St. Est. 1978. Open 10—6. STOCK: General antiques. TEL: Wellingborough (0933) 680973. SER: Buys at auction; storage.

Quaker Lodge Antiques
28 Church St. (D. and S. Banks.) Resident. STOCK: Period, Victorian and Edwardian furniture and general antiques. TEL: Wellingborough (0933) 680371.

Shadowfax Antiques
9 High St. (R. Hawkins.) CL: Sat. Open 10—5. STOCK: General antiques especially unusual and rare items. TEL: Wellingborough (0933) 681774.

Thorpe Antiques
51 High St. (M.R. Clow.) Est. 1968. CL: Fri. Open 10—5, Sat. p.m and other times by appointment. SIZE: Large and warehouse. STOCK: Large furniture, late Georgian and Victorian; 1920s shipping goods. TEL: Wellingborough (0933) 680196. SER: Buys at auction. VAT: Stan/Spec.

FLORE, Nr. Weedon
Flore House Antiques Ltd.   Trade Only
Flore House. (P.G. Norman.) Est. 1968. Open 9.30—6.30, Sun. by appointment. SIZE: Large. STOCK: Decorative furniture and accessories. LOC: Turn left at bollards into The Avenue for Flore House. PARK: Easy. TEL: Weedon (0327) 40585. VAT: Stan.

GUILSBOROUGH
Nick Goodwin Exports
The Firs, Nortoft Rd. Open every day by appointment. SIZE: Warehouse. STOCK: Oak, mahogany, walnut, stripped and painted pine, smalls. TEL: (0280) 813115 or (0604) 740234. SER: Restorations and pine stripping; export; shipping; packing; courier.

HARPOLE
Inglenook Antiques
23 High St. (T. and P. Havard.) Est. 1971. CL: Thurs. and Sun. Open 10—7. SIZE: Small. STOCK: Jewellery, £1—£75; stripped pine furniture, £15—£175; general antiques, £1—£200. LOC: In main street. PARK: Easy. TEL: Northampton (0604) 830007.

Bower group in earthenware, under-glaze coloured. Made by Geoffrey Fuller, 1985. From "A Collector's History of English Pottery" in **Antique Collecting**, May 1986.

Cave's OF NORTHAMPTON

111 KETTERING ROAD

REGENT HOUSE
ROYAL TERRACE

Hidden away in our Basement Showroom is a large stock full of delightful surprises but mainly 18th Century Furniture in all woods and in condition worthy of your home. Dealers show card and ask to see Warehouse of unrestored goods.

Gillian Cave's Georgian House furnished with Antiques that are for sale — naturally their condition lives up to her own standards. Georgian Furniture, Oil Paintings, Silver and a little porcelain. Dealers show card and ask to see Trader Lots in Basement.

LOOP OFF M1 EXITS 15 and 16 or SHORT DETOUR FROM A5

ISLIP

J. Roe Antiques
The Old Furnace Site, Kettering Rd. (Mr. and Mrs. J. Roe.) Est. 1968. Open 6 days a week. *STOCK: General antiques; Continental and American shipping goods.* TEL: Thrapston (080 12) 2937. VAT: Stan.

KETTERING (0536)

Alexis Brook
74 Lower St. (Mrs. A. Brook.) Est. 1959. CL: Sun. a.m. Open from 10 onwards, appointment advisable. SIZE: Medium. *STOCK: General antiques, £1—£3,000.* LOC: On A6 from Market Harborough. House halfway up hill on left before main shopping centre. PARK: At Collingwood Motors, adjacent. TEL: 513854.

C.W. Ward Antiques
Dene House, 40 Lower St. (C. Mason.) Est. 1912. Open 9—6. SIZE: Small. *STOCK: General antiques, furniture; pottery, porcelain, pewter, treen, glass and bygones.* LOC: 25yds. from GPO on A6. PARK: Opposite. TEL: 513537. SER: Valuations; restorations (furniture, silver, porcelain). VAT: Stan/Spec.

LONG BUCKBY (0327)

R.E. Thompson
17 Church St. Est. 1968. Open 9—7 every day. SIZE: Large. *STOCK: Shipping goods, furniture, 19th—20th C; stripped pine, clocks, £1—£1,000.* PARK: Easy. TEL: 842242. VAT: Stan.

NORTHAMPTON (0604)

F. and C.H. Cave
111 Kettering Rd. Est. 1879. CL: Thurs. Open 9—5.30. SIZE: Large. *STOCK: Furniture, 1700—1914, £30—£10,000; general antiques.* Not stocked: Books and jewellery. LOC: On A43, on left at Kettering Rd., near town centre. PARK: Adjoining side streets. TEL: 38278. VAT: Stan/Spec.

Michael Jones Jeweller
1 Gold St. Est. 1919. *STOCK: Silver, gold and silver jewellery, French and carriage clocks.* TEL: 32548. VAT: Stan/Spec.

Regent House
Royal Terrace. (G. Cave.) Est. 1951. CL: Sat. p.m. Open 9—1 and 2—6. SIZE: Large. *STOCK: Furniture, 1660—1870, £30—£14,000; paintings, 1700—1900, £10—£3,000.* Not stocked: Books, jewellery. LOC: On A508. White detached house near town centre; left hand side just north of Regent Square. PARK: Half-circle drive. TEL: 37992. VAT: Spec.

R.S.J. Savage and Son   LAPADA
Alfred St. (M.J. Savage.) Est. 1905. Open 9—5.15, Sat. 9—12.30. *STOCK: Oils and watercolours, especially local artists, 18th C to date; antiquarian maps and prints, mirrors, framed pot lids.* LOC: Turn at mini roundabout on Billing Rd, into Alfred St. near hospital. Victorian building on left. PARK: Adjoining streets. TEL: 33852. SER: Restorations (paintings); framing; brochure available.

The Wilby Gallery
242 Wellingborough Rd. (G. Southall.) Est. 1974. CL: Thurs. Open 10—5. *STOCK: Oil paintings, furniture, porcelain, jewellery, and general antiques.* TEL: 31118.

Northampton continued

Wootton Billingham
79 St. Giles St. (D.J. Veryard.) Est. 1897. Open 10—5. *STOCK: Antiquarian and secondhand books.* TEL: 34531.

OUNDLE, (0832) Nr. Peterborough
Howard Antiques
46/46A West St. Est. 1964. CL: Mon. Open 10—4.30. SIZE: Medium. *STOCK: Clocks, furniture, £25—£1,000; collectors' items, china, glass, metalwork, £5—£200, all 17th—19th C.* PARK: Easy. TEL: 74239; home — Bedford (0234) 711106.

PATTISHALL (0327) Nr. Towcester
F. King
Fosters Booth Rd. Open by appointment only. *STOCK: Furniture, English and Continental pictures, 18th—19th C.* LOC: Between Towcester and Weedon on A5. TEL: 830326. VAT: Spec.

PAULERSPURY (032 733) Nr. Towcester
The Antique Galleries BADA
Watling St. (M. Cameron.) Est. 1948. Open 9—6. SIZE: Large. *STOCK: English furniture, 1650—1830, £50—£5,000; prints, 1750—1850, £30—£300.* Not stocked: Items not listed above. LOC: From London A5, 5 miles north of Stony Stratford, house on right at the top of a hill. PARK: Easy. TEL: 238. VAT: Spec.

POTTERSPURY, Nr. Towcester
Reindeer Antiques Ltd. BADA
LAPADA
43 Watling St. (J.W. Butterworth.) Est. 1959. Open 9—6. SIZE: Large. *STOCK: Period English furniture, paintings, metal, clocks, garden furniture and statuary.* LOC: A5. TEL: Yardley Gobion (0908) 542407. VAT: Stan/Spec.

This clock was introduced in 1929 when Walt Disney films were making their début and there is a label pasted to the base stating that the design was 'By permission of Walt Disney. Mickey Mouse Ltd.' From *The Price Guide to Collectable Clocks 1840-1940* by Alan and Rita Shenton, published by the **Antique Collectors' Club**, 1985.

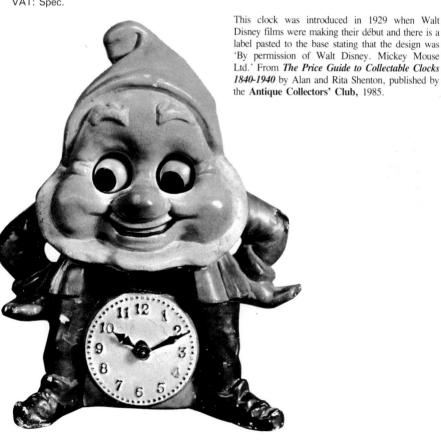

RUSHDEN (0933)
D.W. Sherwood Antiques Ltd.
59 Little St. Est. 1960. *STOCK: General antiques.* TEL: 53265.

THRAPSTON (080 12)
Nr. Kettering
Chancery Antiques
24/26 High St. (R. Andrews.) Est. 1973. Open Mon., Wed., and Fri. 9.30—1 and 2—6, other days by appointment. SIZE: Medium. *STOCK: Furniture, £50—£500; clocks, £10—£500, 1780—1900; decorative items, 1850—1930, £10—£100.* LOC: Centre of High St. PARK: Easy. TEL: 2434; home — same.

TOWCESTER (0327)
Acorn Antiques
The Old Mill, Moat Lane. (I.B. Porter.) Open 9—5, Sat. 10—4. SIZE: Large. *STOCK: Pine and hardwood country furniture, architectural items.* PARK: Easy. TEL: 52788; home — same. SER: Valuations; restorations (pine stripping and repairs, French polishing). VAT: Stan.

Archway Antiques
237 Watling St. West. Est. 1975. Open 10—5, Sat. by appointment. SIZE: Medium. *STOCK: Period furniture, 17th—19th C; Oriental porcelain and rugs.* LOC: On main A5 Watling St. near junction with A43. PARK: Easy. TEL: 50962. VAT: Spec.

Ron Green
209, 227 and 241 Watling St. and 239 Watling St. West. Est. 1952. Open 9am—10pm. SIZE: Large. *STOCK: English and Continental furniture; oil paintings and decorative items.* TEL: 50387.

Towcester continued

R. and M. Nicholas
161 Watling St. Open 9.30—6. SIZE: Small. *STOCK: 18th—19th C porcelain, silver and glass.* TEL: 50639. VAT: Stan/Spec.

Worden Antiques
2 Watling St. (J. Jones.) Est. 1961. Open 9—6, Sat. 9—5, Sun. by appointment. SIZE: Medium. *STOCK: Furniture, 18th—19th C, £200—£750; shipping goods, 19th C, £25—£200; pictures and china.* LOC: A5. PARK: Easy. TEL: 51898; home — 51675. VAT: Spec.

UPPER BODDINGTON,
Nr. Daventry
Archway Antiques
Hill Farm House, Frog Lane. (B.A. and S.A. Robertson.) Est. 1975. Open by appointment. SIZE: Medium. *STOCK: Country furniture, 1750—1840, £100—£1,500, brass, copper and treen, £20—£300.* Not stocked: Clocks, silver and paintings. LOC: 2 miles off Daventry/Banbury road. PARK: Easy. TEL: Byfield (0327) 60803; home — same. SER: Valuations; restorations (furniture). VAT: Stan/Spec.

WEEDON (0327)
Janos Aladics
66 and 66a High St. Est. 1968. Open 10—6. *STOCK: Persian rugs.* PARK: Easy. TEL: 40574.

V. and C. Madeira
The Village, 62 High St. (V.M.R. Madeira.) Est. 1969. Open every day 9—5.30. SIZE: Small. *STOCK: Furniture, 17th—19th C, £50—£1000.* PARK: Easy. TEL: 42015; home — (0926) 25012. SER: Valuations; restorations (furniture and leather linings). VAT: Stan/Spec.

Weedon continued

Thirty-Eight Antiques
25 High St. (E. Saunders.) Open by appointment. SIZE: Large. *STOCK: English and French furniture in pine and fruitwood; decorative small items.* TEL: 40766. VAT: Stan.

The Village Antique Market
62 High St. (E.A. and J.M. Saunders.) Est. 1967. Open 9.30—5.30, Sun. 10.30—5.30. SIZE: Large. There are 40 dealers at this market selling *a wide variety of general antiques and interesting items.* LOC: On A45, just off A5. PARK: At side of market. TEL: 42015. VAT: Stan.

Weedon Antiques
Magpie House, High St. (L. Batsford.) Open every day. *STOCK: Furniture, china, porcelain.* TEL: 40948. VAT: Stan.

WELDON
The Loft — S.F. Oliver and Son
15—17 High St. (S.F. and C.H. Oliver.) Est. 1969. Open 10—5 including Sun. by appointment. SIZE: Large. *STOCK: Mechanical objects, £1—£100; clocks, £5—£300; furniture, £5—£500; radios, fire equipment, lighting fixtures.* LOC: In Village, off by-pass. PARK: Easy. TEL: Corby (0536) 65855; home — Duddington (078 083) 207. SER: Valuations; restorations (metal, wood).

WELLINGBOROUGH   (0933)
W.F. Knight Ltd.
2 Park Rd. Est. 1922. Open 9—5.30. SIZE: Small. *STOCK: General antiques.* LOC: Town centre. TEL: 222463. SER: Restorations (silver); framing. VAT: Stan/Spec.

Wellingborough continued

Bryan Perkins Antiques   *Trade Only*
Finedon Rd. (B.H. and J. Perkins.) Est. 1971. CL: Sat. p.m. Open 9—5. SIZE: Large. *STOCK: Furniture and paintings, 19th C, £200—£2,000; small items.* PARK: Easy. TEL: 228812; home — Kettering (0536) 790259. SER: Valuations; restorations (furniture). VAT: Spec.

WEST HADDON   (078 887)
Antiques
9 West End. Est. 1978. CL: Sun., except by appointment. Open 10—5.30. SIZE: Medium. *STOCK: Country furniture, period metalwork, brass and copper, treen and other domestic items.* LOC: A428. PARK: Easy. TEL: 772; home — Crick (0788) 822330. VAT: Spec.

The Country Pine Shop
21 High St. (S.M. Walters.) Est. 1985. CL: Wed. Open 10—5.30. SIZE: Medium. *STOCK: Stripped pine, £50—£400; china and glass, to £50; all 19th C; linen and lace.* LOC: A428. TEL: 354; home — 711. SER: Restorations (pine stripping). VAT: Stan.

Paul Hopwell Antiques   BADA
LAPADA
30 High St. Est. 1974. CL: Sun. except by appointment. Open 9—6. SIZE: Large. *STOCK: 17th and 18th C oak and walnut country furniture, longcase clocks, metalware, oil paintings and prints mainly sporting and country pursuits.* **LOC: A428. PARK: Easy. TEL: 636. SER: Valuations; restorations (furniture and metalware); buys at auction. VAT: Spec.**

Shoulder mantle (detail). Mughal, late 17th or early 18th century. From *The Kashmir Shawl* by Frank Ames, published by the **Antique Collectors' Club,** 1986.

Northumberland

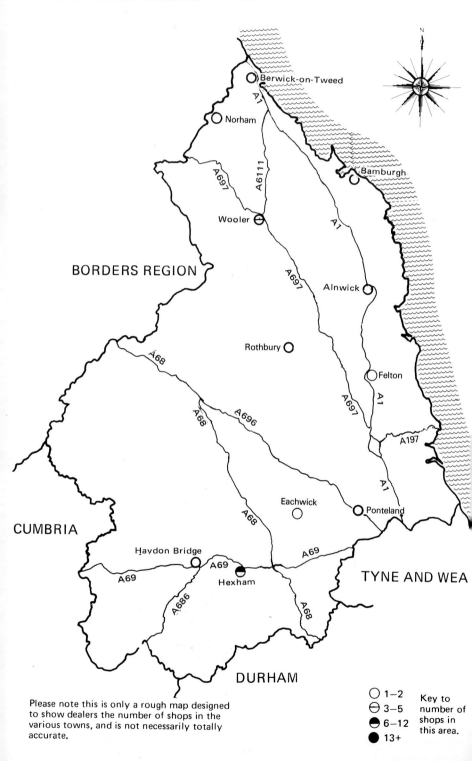

BORDERS REGION

Berwick-on-Tweed

Norham

Bamburgh

Wooler

Alnwick

Rothbury

Felton

CUMBRIA

Eachwick

Ponteland

Haydon Bridge

Hexham

TYNE AND WEA

DURHAM

Please note this is only a rough map designed
to show dealers the number of shops in the
various towns, and is not necessarily totally
accurate.

◯ 1–2	Key to
⊖ 3–5	number of
◐ 6–12	shops in
● 13+	this area.

ALNWICK (0665)

Bondgate Antiques LAPADA
Hill House, 39 Bondgate Within. (P. and B. Marshall.) NNADA. Est. 1947. CL: Wed. p.m. Open 10—12.30 and 2—5. STOCK: General antiques, clocks, silver, plate, glass, china and furniture, £5—£500. LOC: In town centre opposite Lloyds Bank. PARK: Easy. TEL: 603394; home — 602596. SER: Valuations; buys at auction. VAT: Stan/Spec.

Tamblyn
12 Bondgate Without. (Mrs. S.M. Hirst.) Est. 1981. CL: Mon. and Wed. Open 2—4.30, Sat. 10—4.30. SIZE: Medium. STOCK: General antiques including country furniture, earthenware, pictures, to 20th C; antiquities, glass, £5—£150. LOC: Diagonally opposite war memorial at southern entrance to town. PARK: Easy. TEL: 603024; home — same. SER: Valuations.

BAMBURGH (066 84)

T. Crewe Dixon
7 Lucker Rd. Est. 1968. CL: Wed. Open 9.15—4.30. SIZE: Medium. STOCK: Furniture, silver, glass, clocks, pewter, prints and nautical items, £5—£50. LOC: B1341. PARK: Easy. TEL: 229; home — 287. VAT: Stan/Spec.

BERWICK-ON-TWEED (0289)

Bridge End Antiques
8-12 Bridge End. (R. Goodfellow.) Open 10—4.30 or by appointment. STOCK: General antiques and shipping furniture. TEL: 308702; home — (066 84) 433.

Castlegate Antiques
83 Castlegate. (Mrs. R. Fairbairn.) Est. 1973. CL: Sat. p.m. Open 9—1 and 2—5 or by appointment. SIZE: Medium. STOCK: Clocks, furniture, shipping items, general antiques, Victorian, £1—£1,000. Not stocked: Coins, stamps. LOC: A1, at junction to Berwick railway station. PARK: Easy. TEL: 306009.

EACHWICK

Hazel Cottage Clocks
Hazel Cottage. (E. and M. Charlton.) Open every day 9.30—6. SIZE: Medium. STOCK: Clocks, £50—£4,000; also unrestored clocks; small furniture, brass, copper. LOC: Just off Darras Hall to Stamfordham road, opp. Wylam turn-off. PARK: Easy. TEL: Wylam (066 14) 2415. SER: Restorations (longcase clocks). VAT: Spec.

FELTON (067 087)
Nr. Morpeth

Felton Park Antiques
Felton Park. (D. and A. Burton.) Resident. Est. 1973. STOCK: Small Georgian furniture, pottery and porcelain — mainly Sunderland lustre, Newhall blue and white transfer ware. PARK: Easy. TEL: 319. SER: Valuations; restorations; polishing. FAIRS: Most Northern. VAT: Spec.

HAYDON BRIDGE (043 484)
Nr. Hexham

Haydon Bridge Antiques
3 Shaftoe St. (J. and J. Smith.) Est. 1974. CL: Thurs. Open 9—5.30 and by appointment. SIZE: Large. STOCK: Stripped pine, £5—£500; Victorian and Edwardian oak and mahogany, shipping goods, Victorian oils and watercolours. PARK: Easy. TEL: 200; home — 461. VAT: Stan.

HEXHAM (0434)

Robert Archbold—Violins
31 Hencotes. Est. 1970. Open 9—5.30 or by appointment. STOCK: Violins, violas, cellos, double basses. TEL: 604694.

Beaufort Gallery
St. Mary's Wynd, Beaumont St. (Mrs. J. Essenhigh and Mrs. C. Braithwaite.) Est. 1980. Open 10—5, Wed. 2—5, Wed. a.m. and Sun. by appointment. SIZE: Medium. STOCK: Watercolours, 18th—20th C, £400—£2,000; some oils especially Scottish school, 19th—20th C, £900—£2,000. PARK: Easy. TEL: 605808. SER: Valuations; restorations (oils and watercolours); buys at auction (19th C watercolours).

Hexham continued

Arthur Boaden Antiques   LAPADA
27, 29 and 30 Market Place. (R.J. Boaden.) Est. 1948. CL: Thurs. Open 9—12.30 and 1.30—5. SIZE: Large. *STOCK: Small furniture, Georgian, Regency, Victorian, £50—£3,000; Victorian bric-a-brac, £1—£100; paintings, 19th—20th C, £50—£1,000; Victorian jewellery, from £10.* LOC: Opposite Hexham Abbey, off A69. PARK: Easy. TEL: 603187. SER: Valuations; restorations (pictures); jewellery repairs. VAT: Stan/Spec.

Gordon Caris
16 Market Place. Est. 1972. CL: Thurs. Open 9—5. *STOCK: Clocks and watches.* SER: Restorations (clocks and watches). TEL: 602106.

Hexham continued

Colmans of Hexham (Saleroom and Antique Fair)
15 St. Mary's Chare. (J.F. Turnbull.) CL: Thurs. Open 10—5. LOC: South of Market Place. PARK: Easy. TEL: 603812 or 605522. Below are listed the dealers at this Antique Fair:—

Bede Antiques
(W. Bedford.) General antiques, silver, jewellery, furniture, pictures, porcelain, brass, copper.

Colmans
Furniture, including stripped pine.

Meminissi
Silver, small furniture, collectables including medals, militaria, cigarette cards, coins, postcards.

Shenton Antiques
General antiques.

Scarf designed by Couder, Paris, 1834, 3m x 77cm. From *The Kashmir Shawl* by Frank Ames, published by the **Antique Collectors' Club,** 1986.

Hexham continued

Hallstile Antiques

17 Hallstile Bank. (E. Elliott, P. Neumann.) CL:
Thurs. Open 10−5, Sun. by appointment.
SIZE: Large. *STOCK: Stripped pine, 19th C,
£20−£600; Georgian and Victorian furniture
and effects, £50−£1,000; Maling pottery.*
LOC: Just off Market Place. PARK: Nearby.
TEL: 602239; home − 605003 or (0661)
33046. SER: Upholstery.

J.A. and T. Hedley

3 St. Mary's Chare. (D. Hall and W.H. Jewitt.)
Est. 1819. CL: Thurs. p.m. Open 9−5. SIZE:
Medium. *STOCK: 17th C to Victorian furni-
ture; 18th C to Edwardian porcelain, silver,
glass, china, etc.* Not stocked: Reproductions.
LOC: Off Battle Hill (A69). PARK: 400yds.
TEL: 602317. SER: Valuations; restorations
(furniture); buys at auction (furniture). VAT:
Stan/Spec.

Hencotes Antiques and Books

8 Hencotes. (Mrs. J.D. Clayton.) Est. 1972.
CL: Thurs. p.m. Open 10−5. SIZE: Small.
STOCK: Small antiques, books. LOC: Main
A69 through Hexham about 200yds. past
Beaumont St. PARK: In Beaumont St. TEL:
605971.

Hexham Antiques
(Inc. Hotspur Antiques)

6 Rear Battle Hill. (J. and D. Latham.) Est.
1977. CL: Sun. and Thurs., except by
appointment. Open 10.30−4.30, Sat. 9.30−
4.30. SIZE: Large. *STOCK: Furniture, clocks,
pictures, glass, china, boxes and collectors'
items, to art deco.* LOC: Main shopping street,
opposite National Westminster Bank. PARK:
400 metres. TEL: 603851; home − 604813.
SER: Valuations; buys at auction. VAT: Spec.

Trevor-Venis Antiques

13 Hencotes. (P.F. Trevor-Venis.) Est. 1984.
Open 9−5, Sun. by appointment. SIZE:
Medium. *STOCK: English furniture, 19th C,
£100−£3,000; Georgian furniture, £100−
£5,000; paintings, porcelain, prints, works of
art, 18th−20th C, £10−£1,000.* Not stocked: Carpets and silver. LOC: A695. PARK:
Easy. TEL: 607458; home − (0434 71)
2751. SER: Valuations; restorations (furniture
and paintings); buys at auction. VAT: Spec.

Turn of the Century Antiques

8 Market St. (E. Alston and P. Pearce.) Est.
1975. Open Tues., Fri., Sat. 11−5. *STOCK:
Books, country bygones, china, glass, shipping items, furniture; all £1−£200.* PARK:
Market Sq. TEL: Home − 603595 or Bell-
ingham (0660) 30218.

Vindolanda Antiques

29 Hencotes. (S.N. Archbold.) Est. 1972.
Open 9−5.30. *STOCK: General antiques, Victoriana.* TEL: 604694.

NORHAM, Nr. Berwick-on-Tweed
J. and D. Stewart

6 and 8 West St. Resident. Est. 1969. SIZE:
Medium. *STOCK: China, glass, collectors
items, mainly Victorian; some pine.* LOC: 7
miles north of Berwick-on-Tweed. PARK:
Easy. TEL: Berwick-on-Tweed (0289) 82376.

PONTELAND   (0661)
Nr. Newcastle
Ponteland Antiques

10 West Rd. Est. 1961. CL: Mon. Open
10−1 and 2−5. SIZE: Small. *STOCK: Jewellery, £25−£500; silver, porcelain and china,
£10−£500; small furniture, £50−£500; all
Victorian and Edwardian.* LOC: 2 miles north-
west of Newcastle airport on A696. PARK:
200yds. TEL: 71311. SER: Valuations.

ROTHBURY   (0669)
The Jackdaw Antiques

Town Foot, (J.G. Taylor.) Est. 1970. Open
every day 11−6, Easter to Christmas. CL:
Mon. Open 11−5, Sun. 2−4, January to
Easter. *STOCK: General antiques.* TEL: 20785
or 20795 (24hrs.).

WOOLER   (0668)
Border Sporting Gallery

25 High St. (D. and T. Ross.) CL: Thurs. p.m.
Open 9−5.30, Sat. 9−5. SIZE: Medium.
*STOCK: Sporting oils and prints, Snaffles, L.
Edwards, Tom Carr, Thorburn and Strutt,
1925 and earlier, £10−£1,000.* LOC: Main
St. PARK: Easy. TEL: 81872; home − Milfield
(066 86) 271. SER: Valuations; restorations;
buys at auction. FAIRS: Northern and
southern agricultural shows. VAT: Stan/Spec.

Glendale Antiques

Peth Head. (E. and M. Redpath.) Open 10−5.
Available any time to Trade. SIZE: Large.
*STOCK: Furniture, clocks, porcelain, silver,
trade and shipping goods.* TEL: 81396. VAT:
Stan. SER: Buys at auction.

W.J. Miller and Son   *Trade Only*

1−5 Church St. (J. Miller.) Est. 1947. Open
any time by appointment. SIZE: Large, and
warehouses. *STOCK: General antiques for
trade and export.* LOC: A697. PARK: Nearby.
TEL: 81500; home − Wooperton (066 87)
281. VAT: Stan/Spec.

Nottingham

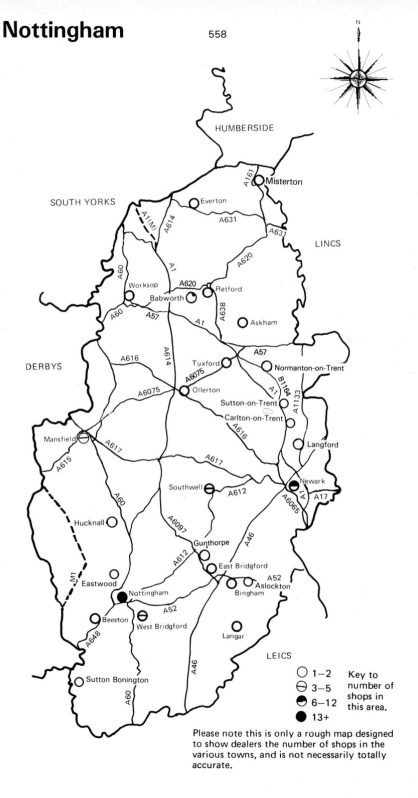

HUMBERSIDE

Misterton

SOUTH YORKS

Everton

A631

LINCS

A1(M)

A614

A1

A620

A60

Worksop

A620

Retford

Babworth

A60

A57

A1

A638

Askham

DERBYS

A616

A614

Tuxford

A57

A6075

Normanton-on-Trent

A6075

Ollerton

A1

B1164

A1133

Sutton-on-Trent

Carlton-on-Trent

A616

Mansfield

A617

Langford

A615

A617

Newark

A60

Southwell

A612

A6065

A17

Hucknall

A6097

A46

M1

Eastwood

Gunthorpe

A612

East Bridgford

A52

Nottingham

Aslockton

Bingham

Beeston

A52

Langar

West Bridgford

A648

LEICS

A46

Sutton Bonington

A60

Key to
number of
shops in
this area.

○ 1–2
⊖ 3–5
◑ 6–12
● 13+

Please note this is only a rough map designed
to show dealers the number of shops in the
various towns, and is not necessarily totally
accurate.

ASKHAM, Nr. Newark
Sally Mitchell Fine Arts
Thornlea. Est. 1967. Author of the Dictionary of British Equestrian Artists. Appointment advisable. SIZE: Medium. *STOCK: Mainly 20th C sporting paintings and prints, some 17th—19th C sporting paintings.* LOC: 5 miles from Retford; 5 mins. from Markham Moor roundabout on A1. PARK: Easy. TEL: Gamston (077 783) 234. SER: Valuations; restorations; framing; lectures; buys at auction.

ASLOCKTON, Nr. Nottingham
Michael Thompson Antiques
Aslockton Grange. (M. and M. Thompson.) Est. 1967. Appointment advisable. *STOCK: Oak and mahogany furniture, £20—£2,000; pine; all 18th—19th C.* LOC: On A52, 1 mile past Bingham between Nottingham and Grantham. PARK: Own. TEL: Whatton (0949) 50204.

BABWORTH, Nr. Retford
Retford Pine   *Trade Only*
Morton Farmhouse. (R.J. Mottishaw and C. Nangle). Open strictly by prior telephone appointment. SIZE: Medium. *STOCK: Unstripped pine furniture; some shipping, £40—£500.* LOC: From A1 take B6420 to Retford, farmhouse 1½ miles on left. PARK: Easy. TEL: Retford (0777) 705557; home — same. VAT: Stan.

BEESTON
Elizabeth Bailey
33 Chilwell Rd. Est. 1966. CL: Thurs. Open 10—5.30, Mon. 2—5.30. *STOCK: Furniture, 18th, 19th C and Edwardian; porcelain, glass, silver, some jewellery, decorative items, hand-stripped pine.* TEL: Nottingham (0602) 255685; home — Nottingham (0602) 259259. SER: Restorations (furniture).

BINGHAM   (0949)
E.M. Cheshire   BADA
                                     LAPADA
The Manor House, Market Place. CL: Wed. p.m. Open 9.30—5.30. *STOCK: Furniture, 17th C oak; 18th—19th C mahogany, early metalware.* TEL: 38861. VAT: Stan/Spec. Also at shop 34 Woburn Abbey.

CARLTON-ON-TRENT, Nr. Newark
Tudor Rose Antiques
Yew Tree Farm. (D.H. and Mrs. C. Rose.) Resident. Est. 1984. Open 9—6 every day. SIZE: Medium. *STOCK: Furniture, 18th—19th C, £10—£1,000; interesting items, 19th—20th C, £1—£200.* LOC: ¼ mile from Sutton-on-Trent turning off A1. PARK: Easy. TEL: Newark (0636) 821841. SER: Restorations (furniture).

EAST BRIDGFORD   (0949)
East Bridgford Antiques Centre
Main St. (M. and M. Thompson.) Est. 1981. Open daily. SIZE: Medium. There are 7 dealers at this centre selling *oak, mahogany and pine furniture, 17th—19th C; treen, collectors' items.* TEL: 20741.

EASTWOOD, Nr. Nottingham
Stonecourt Antiques
20 Mansfield Rd. (D.J. Mitchell and P.W. Miller.) Est. 1980. Open 10—5.30, Sun., Mon. and Wed. by appointment. SIZE: Small. *STOCK: Furniture, £100—£3,000; clocks, £60—£5,000; both 18th—19th C; paintings, porcelain, pottery and metalware, 18th—20th C, £50—£1,500.* LOC: From junction 26 take A610 through Eastwood shopping area, turn right at traffic lights into Mansfield Rd., shop 50yds. on right. PARK: Easy and at rear. TEL: (0773) 760806; home — (0629) 4253 or (0623) 751710. SER: Valuations; restorations (clocks). FAIRS: Buxton.

EVERTON, Nr. Doncaster
The Barnard Gallery
Grange Farm. (F.B. and R. Poynter.) Est. 1956. SIZE: Small. *STOCK: Prints and engravings, antiquarian maps and books, 18th—19th C, £1—£1,000; watercolours, 19th—20th C, £5—£250.* LOC: Left hand side of Brewery Lane, north from A161 Bawtry/Gainsborough road. PARK: Easy. TEL: Retford (0777) 817324. SER: Restorations (prints, paintings, watercolours).

GUNTHORPE, Nr. Nottingham
Witsend Antiques
Main St. (J. Weaver.) Resident. Usually open including evenings. SIZE: Large. *STOCK: General antiques mainly furniture.* TEL: Nottingham (0602) 663360.

HUCKNALL
Curiosity Corner
53a Watnull Rd. (C. Channer). Open 9.15—5; Wed. 9.15—12. *STOCK: General antiques.* TEL: Nottingham (0602) 630789.

LANGAR
Andrew Skirving (Fine Art)
The Hall. Est. 1962. Open by appointment. *STOCK: English paintings, drawings.* TEL: Harby (0949) 60559. VAT: Spec.

LANGFORD
T. Baker   *Trade Only*
Langford House Farm. Est. 1966. CL: Sun. except by appointment and Sat. SIZE: Medium. *STOCK: Victoriana, period furniture and oak.* LOC: A1133. PARK: Own. TEL: Newark (0636) 704026.

MANSFIELD (0623)

The Book Shelf
16 Albert St. (F.B. and S. Payton.) CL: Wed. Open 9.30—5, Sat. 9—5. SIZE: Medium. *STOCK: Antiquarian and secondhand books.* LOC: Town centre. TEL: 648231; home — 640601. SER: Binding; buys at auction (books).

Fair Deal Antiques   *Trade only*
138 Chesterfield Rd. North (D. Lowe.) Est. 1972. CL: Sat. p.m. and Sun. except by appointment. Open 9.30—5.30. SIZE: Large. *STOCK: Shipping goods, £50—£100; furniture, mainly mahogany, Victorian, £100—£1,000; period furniture, metalware and small items.* PARK: Easy. TEL: 653768 and 512419. VAT: Stan.

Mansfield Antiques
49—51 Ratcliffe Gate. Est. 1975. Open 9—5.30. SIZE: Large, and warehouse. *STOCK: Furniture.* LOC: On A617 Newark Rd. PARK: Easy and adjacent. TEL: 27475; home — 32108. SER: Valuations; buys at auction. VAT: Stan/Spec.

Mansfield continued

Rievel Antiques
78 Nottingham Rd. Est. 1940. TEL: 21534.

John B. Sheppard Antiques
122—124 Chesterfield Rd. North. Est. 1970. CL: Wed. Open 9.30—5.30, Sat. 9.30—5. *STOCK: Furniture, period to shipping, some clocks, £10—£2,000.* LOC: 4 miles from M1, exit 29. PARK: Forecourt. TEL: 31691. VAT: Stan/Spec.

MISTERTON, Nr. Doncaster

Antiques and Things
Milton Lodge, Stockwith Rd. (D. and B. Hudson.) Est. 1964. Open 10—5, Sun. 12—5, Wed. and Thurs. by appointment. SIZE: Medium. *STOCK: Furniture, porcelain and china, collectors' items and clocks, 1800—1930, £5—£250.* LOC: From Walkeringham, turn right before village. PARK: Own. TEL: Gainsborough (0427) 890010; home — same. SER: Restorations (upholstery and stripping — not pine); buys at auction (furniture). VAT: Stan.

Samuel John Carter. 'Grey coach horse in a stable', 20ins. x 27ins., signed and dated. The *Dictionary of Equestrian Artists* by Sally Mitchell, published by the **Antique Collectors' Club**, 1985.

NEWARK   (0636)

Allens Antiques
25 Castlegate. (A.T. Cox.) Open 10—5. *STOCK: Furniture, Victorian, Edwardian and pine.* TEL: 702446.

Arrow Antiques   *Export only*
Langton Lodge, Coddington. (A. Dennis.) Open by appointment. *STOCK: General antiques.* TEL: 706607.

Castle Antiques
Warehouse at Bairds Malt, Northgate. (R. Key.) Est. 1974. Open 8—5. SIZE: Large. *STOCK: Pine furniture, 18th—19th C; shipping goods.* Not stocked: Jewellery, watches, small items. LOC: On A46, 1 mile from A1 (Lincoln turn). PARK: Easy. TEL: 704290; home — 707764/73804. SER: Valuations; container packing. VAT: Stan.

Castle Gate Antiques Centre
55 Castle Gate. Est. 1985. Open 9—5. SIZE: Large. There are 12 dealers at this centre selling *18th—19th C furniture including mahogany and country; pottery and porcelain; barometers, jewellery, clocks, oils and water-colours, silver including Georgian and Victorian; rugs and linen, £5—£3,000.* LOC: Nottingham side of town, 250yds. from castle. PARK: Easy. TEL: 700076. SER: Valuations; restorations (furniture including upholstery). VAT: Stan/Spec.

Newark continued

D. and G. Antiques
11 Kings Rd. (Mr. and Mrs. D. Stutchbury.) Est. 1982. CL: Mon. Open 9.30—5. SIZE: Large. *STOCK: Furniture, mainly 19th C, £50—£500; porcelain and glass, 19th C, £5—£100; pictures, Victorian, £20—£150.* LOC: From Market Sq. 500yds., opposite school playing fields. PARK: Easy. TEL: 702 782. SER: Restorations; buys at auction.

D and V Antiques
4A Northgate. (D. and V. Whitehead.) Est. 1982. Open 9.30—5. SIZE: Small. *STOCK: Furniture, Victorian and Edwardian, £50+; small items, clocks, oil lamps.* LOC: A46 before town centre (Lincoln side). PARK: Easy. TEL: 71888; home — 76880.

Newark Art and Antiques Centre
The Market Place, Chain Lane. Incorporating Olde Bank House Antiques, and complex of 30 other separate dealers all trading under one roof. (G. Jacobs.) CL: Thurs. p.m. Open 9.30—5. *STOCK: Georgian and Victorian furniture, pottery, porcelain, glass, swords, militaria, coins, clocks, pictures, books; Victoriana, silver, jewellery and general antiques.* TEL: 703959.

Repind Ltd.
60 Millgate. Open 9—5. *STOCK: Pine.* TEL: 79637.

Newark continued

Jack Spratt Antiques
5, Victoria St. Est. 1976. Open 9—5.30, Sat. 9—2 or by appointment. SIZE: Large and warehouse. *STOCK: Pine*, LOC: Northgate traffic lights. PARK: Own. TEL: 707714 or 74853. SER: Container packing. VAT: Stan.

T.T. Antiques
Warehouse, Hatchett Lane off Lincoln Rd. (T. Tunstall.) Open 9—5 or by appointment. *STOCK: Pine and period furniture, clocks.* TEL: 704030; warehouse — 73553.

Trent Antiques
46-48 Castlegate. (T. Healey.) Est. 1969. Always available. *STOCK: Pine.* TEL: 704148 or 76555. SER: Pine stripping.

NORMANTON-ON-TRENT
Nr. Newark
F.J. McCarthy Ltd.
The Grange. Est. 1946. CL: Sat. *STOCK: Furniture, English and Continental 18th C; works of art.* TEL: Newark (0636) 821382. VAT: Stan/Spec.

NOTTINGHAM   (0602)
Antiques and General Trading Co.
145 Lower Parliament St. (C. and M. Drummond-Hoy.) Est. 1965. CL: Thurs. Open 10—5. SIZE: Large. *STOCK: Furniture, from 17th C, £200—£1,500; decorative furniture, £50—£500.* LOC: A52. PARK: At side. TEL: 585971; home — (0664) 62184. SER: Valuations; restorations (furniture). VAT: Stan/Spec.

Nottingham continued

Breck Antiques
726 Mansfield Rd., Woodthorpe. (P.H.K. Astill.) Est. 1969. Open Sat., other times by appointment. SIZE: Small. *STOCK: Furniture and porcelain, 18th—19th C.* LOC: Main Mansfield road. PARK: Forecourt. TEL: 605263; home — 621197. SER: Valuations.

Heather Cowley's Book Shop
235—237 Mansfield Rd. ABA, ILAB, NBL, FATG. Est. 1962. Open 9.30—5.30. SIZE: Large. *STOCK: Books, topography, heraldry, antiquarian, 16th—20th C, £5—£1,000; scholarly books, 15p—£300; reference books on antiques, maps and engravings, 16th—19th C, £1.25—£150.* LOC: A614. PARK: Private at 240 North Sherwood St. (rear). TEL: 473836. SER: Valuations; restorations (books and oil paintings); picture- framing (hand-made swept frames). FAIRS: ABA, London. VAT: Spec.

Friar Antiques and Collectors Centre
12-18 Friar Lane. Open 9.15—5. There are 44 dealers at this centre selling *a wide range of general antiques.* TEL: 417857.

Gatehouse
100 Friar Lane. (Mrs. S. Butcher and Mrs. C. Layfield.) Est. 1982. Open 10—5, Fri. 10—5.45, Sat. 10—4, Sun. by appointment. SIZE: Medium. *STOCK: Pine, 19th C, £50—£1,000; china and glass, 20th C, £5—£100; jewellery, £5—£100.* LOC: Town centre opposite castle gatehouse. PARK: Easy, multi-storey at rear. TEL: 415451. SER: Valuations; restorations (pine including stripping); buys at auction (pine furniture). VAT: Stan.

The Golden Cage
99 Derby Rd. (J. and D. Pearson and J. Paradise.) CL: Thurs. Open 10—4.30. *STOCK: Beaded dresses, Victorian clothes, linen, yesterday's interesting clothes.* TEL: 411600 or 223329.

Granny's Attic
308 Carlton Hill, Carlton. (Mrs. A. Pembleton). Open Tues., Thurs. and Fri. 9—3.30; Sat. 9.30—4. *STOCK: Dolls miniatures, general antiques and furniture.* TEL: 265204.

Hockley Coins
16 Hockley. (D.T. Peake.) CL: Thurs. Open 10—4. *STOCK: Coins, militaria, postcards, toys, banknotes.* TEL: 507097.

Nottingham continued

Huntingdon Antiques
189 Huntingdon St. (R. Scott.) Open 9—5, Sat. 9—1. *STOCK: General antiques.* TEL: 582771.

Melville Kemp Ltd.
89—91 Derby Rd. Est. 1900. CL: Sat. p.m. and Thurs. Open 9.30—1 and 2—5.30. SIZE: Small. *STOCK: Jewellery, Victorian; silver, Georgian and Victorian, both £5—£5,000; ornate English and Continental porcelain, Sheffield plate.* Not stocked: Furniture. LOC: From Nottingham on main Derby Rd. PARK: Easy. TEL: 417055. SER: Valuations; restorations (silver, china, jewellery); buys at auction. VAT: Stan/Spec.

Lustre, Metal Antiques Ltd.
Canning Circus, Derby Rd. Est. 1957. Open 9—5. *STOCK: Copper, brass, silver, plated and cast iron items.* TEL: 704385; evenings — 268765. SER: Renovations. VAT: Stan/Spec.

Nottingham continued

Matsell Antiques Ltd.
2 and 4 Derby St., off Derby Rd. (B. and P. Matsell.) Est. 1945. Open 10—5, Sat. 10—1, Thurs. and Sun. by appointment. SIZE: Large. *STOCK: Furniture, including decorative, and objects, pre-1830, £100—£10,000; porcelain and glass, £50—£1,000.* PARK: Easy. TEL: 472691; home — 288267. SER: Valuations; buys at auction. FAIRS: British International, Birmingham; Kenilworth. VAT: Stan/Spec.

Nottingham Antique Centre
British Rail Goods Yard, London Rd. (P.G. Murdoch.) Est. 1969. CL: Sat. p.m. Open 9—5, Sat. a.m. by appointment. SIZE: Large. *STOCK: Shipping furniture, Georgian and Victorian, £50—£200; clocks and pottery, Edwardian, £50—£500; bric-a-brac, Victorian, £5—£25.* LOC: From city centre, head south via Lower Parliament St. to Canal St. island. Carry on to London Rd., turn left at 2nd set of traffic lights. PARK: Easy. TEL: 54504/55548. VAT: Stan.

Chestnut basket with intricate pierced decoration. Made in Leeds, impressed 'HARTLEY GREEN & COLLINS POTTERY', 1730, 280mm high. From *A Collector's History of English Pottery* by Griselda Lewis, published by the **Antique Collectors' Club, 1985.**

Nottingham continued

Park Antiques and Fine Arts
170 Derby Rd. (J. Sullivan). Open 9.30—5. *STOCK: General antiques.* TEL: 781194.

Parkside Antiques
138—140 Derby Rd. (Canning Circus). (M. and C. Hufton.) Est. 1983. CL: Thurs. Open 10—5, Tues. and Wed. 2—5. SIZE: Medium. *STOCK: Furniture, especially tables, chairs and other seating, £50—£1,000.* PARK: At rear. TEL: 474416. FAIRS: Stamford.

S. Pembleton
306 Carlton Hill, Carlton. Open Tues., Thurs. and Fri. 9—5, Sat. 10—5. *STOCK: General antiques.* TEL: 265204.

Mike Pollock
110 Derby Rd. Open 10.30—2.30. *STOCK: General antiques, Victoriana, clocks, mechanical and steam models, toys, bygones.* TEL; 474266.

David and Carole Potter Antiques
76 Derby Rd. Est. 1966. CL: Thurs. Open 10—4. SIZE: Medium. *STOCK: Clocks, 18th—19th C, £20—£3,000; period furniture, 17th—19th C; pottery, porcelain and glass, 18th—19th C, £10—£2,000; trade and shipping goods.* LOC: From Nottingham centre, take main Derby Rd., shop on right. PARK: Easy. TEL: 417911; home — 211084. VAT: Stan/Spec.

Station Pine Antiques
103 Carrington St. (J. Budd and E.L. Kingstone.) Open 9.30—5.30. SIZE: Large. *STOCK: Pine.* TEL: 582710.

Top Hat Antiques Centre
66—72 Derby Rd. (Top Hat Exhibitions Ltd.) Est. 1978. Open 9.30—5. SIZE: Large. *STOCK: Furniture, Georgian to Edwardian; small porcelain and metal items, to art deco; oils watercolours and prints, 19th—20th C, £30—£1,000.* LOC: A52 town centre. PARK: Easy. TEL: 419143; home — 258769 and 259841. SER: Restorations (porcelain and paintings). VAT: Stan/Spec.

Trade Wind Antiques
2 Queens Rd. (Mr. and Mrs. M. Storer.) Est. 1965. Open 10—5. SIZE: Large. *STOCK: Clocks and general antiques.* LOC: Opposite Midland Station. TEL: 862850.

Trident Arms
74 Derby Rd. Est. 1970. Open 9.30—5.15. Sat. 10—4. SIZE: Large. *STOCK: Arms, and armour of all ages and nations.* LOC: From city centre take main Derby Rd., shop on right. PARK: Easy. TEL: 474137. SER: Valuations; buys at auction (weapons). VAT: Stan/Spec.

Nottingham continued

Twemlow and Co. Ltd.
17 King St. Est. 1947. CL: Mon. Open 9—5.30. SIZE: Large. *STOCK: Jewellery and silver.* TEL: 472677.

Vintage Pine
113/115 Ilkeston Rd. Est. 1981. CL: Mon. Open 10.30—5.30, Sat. 10.30—3.30. SIZE: Large. *STOCK: Pine furniture, prints, bric-a-brac.* LOC: A609. PARK: Easy. TEL: 702571. SER: Restorations (pine); stripping; pine furniture made to order. VAT: Stan.

Mrs. D. Wise
78 Derby Rd. Est. 1965. CL: Thurs. p.m. Open 10—5. SIZE: Small. *STOCK: Furniture, 18th—19th C, decorative Victorian and Edwardian; carved oak; export goods; also silver, plate, general antiques.* LOC: A52. From town centre take main road to Derby. PARK: Easy. TEL: 472132. VAT: Stan/Spec.

OLLERTON

T.S. Barrows and Son
Hamlyn Lodge, Station Rd. (R., N. and J.S. Barrows.) CL: Mon. Open 10—5, Fri. 10—6.30, Sun. 12—5. SIZE: Small. *STOCK: General antiques, 18th—19th C, £100—£500.* LOC: Off A614. PARK: Easy. TEL: Mansfield (0623) 823600 and Worksop (0909) 485252. SER: Restorations (furniture). VAT: Stan.

Curiosity
Market Place. (S. Dyson.) Est. 1974. Open 9.30—8, Thurs. 4—8. *STOCK: Books, curios, Victorian and later.* LOC: On A614. TEL: Mansfield (0623) 823400.

RETFORD   (0777)
Riverside Lodge Antiques
Riverside Lodge, London Rd. (W.M. Ball.) Est. 1958. Open every day, 10—1 and 2—5.30. SIZE: Medium. *STOCK: Royal Worcester vases and figures, 1862—1930; period furniture.* PARK: Easy. TEL: 705688. SER: Restorations (furniture); buys at auction.

SOUTHWELL   (0636)
Patricia Cragg
56 Church St. Est. 1961. CL: Mon. and Tues. Open 10—5. *STOCK: Furniture, 18th—19th C; English and Continental porcelain; glass, clocks.* PARK: Easy. TEL: 813605; home — same.

King Street Gallery
7 King St. (V.N. and J. Stroud.) Open 10—5, Sun. by appointment. SIZE: Large. *STOCK: Furniture, paintings, objets d'art; prints, 18th—19th C, all £10—£5,000.* LOC: Town centre. PARK: Easy. TEL: 813176; home — 814194. VAT: Stan/Spec.

Southwell continued

Norwell Antiques
Norwell House, 31A Westgate. (Mrs. H. Lewis.) Est. 1978. Open 9.30—5.30. SIZE: Small. *STOCK: Furniture, Georgian, Victorian and Edwardian; general antiques, silver, watercolours and prints.* PARK: Easy. TEL: 814203; home — same.

Strouds of Southwell (Antiques)
3 Westgate. (V.N. and J. Stroud.) Est. 1972. Open 10—5, Sun. by appointment. SIZE: Large. *STOCK: Furniture, pewter and metalware, paintings, 17th—19th C, £50—£5,000.* LOC: Town centre. PARK: Easy. TEL: 815001; home — 814194. SER: Valuations; restorations (furniture). VAT: Stan/Spec.

SUTTON BONINGTON, Nr. Loughborough
Bonington Clocks
2 Marle Pit Hill. (Mrs. J. McVay.) Open by appointment. *STOCK: Clocks — longcase, dial and wall.* TEL: Kegworth (05097) 2900; home — same. SER: Buys at auction.

SUTTON-ON-TRENT, Nr. Newark
Trade Antiques
Linden's Farm, Old Great North Rd. Resident. Open 9—5 every day or by appointment. *STOCK: Pine — tables, chairs, dressers, beds, bureaux, chests.* LOC: B1164 from A1, take first left, farm on right opposite Major's Garage. TEL: Newark (0636) 821825. SER: Containers.

TUXFORD   (0777)
Dukeries Antiques
Newcastle Cottage, 74 Newcastle St. (J. and J. Coupe.) Est. 1972. Resident, usually open. SIZE: Medium. *STOCK: Furniture, 18th—19th C; brass and copper, porcelain.* LOC: Just off A1. PARK: Easy. TEL: 871506; home — same. SER: Valuations. FAIRS: Castle, Robert Bailey and Historic House. VAT: Stan/Spec.

Webster
Westwood, Ollerton Rd. (A. Webster.) Est. 1973. Open any time by appointment. *STOCK: Furniture, Georgian, Victorian and Edwardian; Continental porcelain, £1—£1,000.* LOC: Main Tuxford to Ollerton Rd. 1 mile off A1. PARK: Easy. TEL: 870282. VAT: Stan/Spec.

WEST BRIDGFORD
Berkeleys
Trent Bridge. (C. Prescott and R. Price.) Est. 1974. CL: Sat. and Mon. Open 10—4, Fri. by appointment. SIZE: Large. *STOCK: Furniture, 18th—19th C, £250—£2,500; silver, £30—£1,000; small items, £10—£500; both 18th—20th C; jewellery, 19th—20th C, £20—£2,000.* LOC: 20yds. from River Trent. PARK: Easy. TEL: Nottingham (0602) 820538. SER: Valuations. VAT: Stan/Spec.

Joan Cotton (Antiques)
5 Davies Rd. Est. 1969. CL: Wed. Open 9—5. *STOCK: General antiques, Victoriana, jewellery, silver, china, glass, furniture and bygones.* LOC: ½ mile along Bridgford Rd. from Trent Bridge, in town centre. PARK: On forecourt. TEL: Nottingham (0602) 813043.

Alastair Fraser Antiques
Loughborough Rd. CL: Thurs. Open 10.30—5.30. SIZE: Medium. *STOCK: Pine, mahogany and shipping furniture, general antiques.* LOC: Opposite County Hall. PARK: Easy. TEL: Nottingham (0602) 821835; evenings — Nottingham (0602) 812782. SER: Restorations (furniture).

Moulton's Antiques
5 Portland Rd. (J. Moulton.) CL: Mon. Open 10—5.30. *STOCK: General antiques.* TEL: Nottingham (0602) 814354; home — Harby (0949) 60980.

Nottingham Stamp Exchange
1 Trent Bridge Buildings. (D. and T. Henson.) Est. 1969. Open 9—5.30. SIZE: Small. *STOCK: Stamps, medals and coins.* PARK: Easy. TEL: Nottingham (0602) 819016. SER: Valuations; restorations (medals). VAT: Stan/Spec.

WORKSOP   (0909)
Treasure Trove Antiques
155 Gateford Rd. (Mr. and Mrs. J. Stokes.) Est. 1948. CL: Sun., except by appointment. Open 9—6. SIZE: Medium, plus trade warehouse. *STOCK: Furniture, country and oak, mahogany and stripped pine, Georgian to Victorian, £10—£1,000; general shipping goods; clocks, china, brass and copper, curios, bric-a-brac.* LOC: ½ mile from centre of Worksop, on A57. PARK: Easy. TEL: 472447; home — Gamston (077 783) 612. SER: Restorations; buys at auction. VAT: Stan.

Worksop Antiques   LAPADA
20 Park St. (J.W. Dench.) Resident. Open 10—5. *STOCK: Furniture, English pottery and porcelain, clocks, glass, brass, and copper.* LOC: Town centre. VAT: Stan/Spec.

Oxfordshire

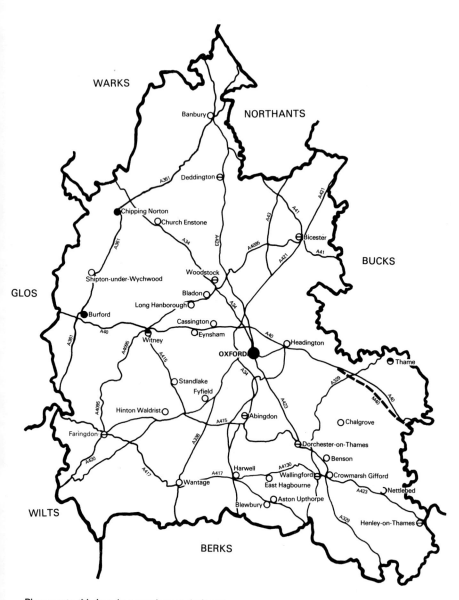

WARKS

NORTHANTS

Banbury

Deddington

Chipping Norton

Church Enstone

Bicester

BUCKS

Shipton-under-Wychwood

Woodstock

Bladon

Long Hanborough

Burford

Cassington

Eynsham

Witney

Headington

OXFORD

Thame

GLOS

Standlake

Fyfield

Hinton Waldrist

Abingdon

Chalgrove

Faringdon

Dorchester-on-Thames

Benson

Harwell

Wantage

Wallingford

Crowmarsh Gifford

East Hagbourne

Nettlebed

Blewbury

Aston Upthorpe

Henley-on-Thames

WILTS

BERKS

Please note this is only a rough map designed to show dealers the number of shops in the various towns, and is not necessarily totally accurate.

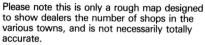

○	1—2	Key to
⊖	3—5	number of
●	6—12	shops in
●	13+	this area.

ABINGDON (0235)
Checker Books
2 Checker Walk. (Weir.) Est. 1955. Open by appointment. *STOCK: Antiquarian books.* TEL: 28172.

Melrose Antiques
45 Stert St. (Mrs. P. Schneider.) Resident. Est. 1969. CL: Wed. and Thurs. *STOCK: Furniture, porcelain, pictures, jewellery and unusual items.* LOC: A415. TEL: 20146.

R.R. Morris Antiques
29 Broad St. Est. 1934. CL: Thurs. Open 9—5.30. *STOCK: Furniture, 17th to early 19th C, general antiques.* TEL: 20766; evenings — 848386. VAT: Spec.

ASTON UPTHORPE, Nr. Didcot
Jean Lathbury Antiques
Edlins House. Resident. Open by appointment only. *STOCK: English pottery, Staffordshire lustre, creamware; English Delft tiles; watercolours and drawings, glass, collectors' items, small furniture.* PARK: Easy. TEL: Blewbury (0235) 850468.

BANBURY (0295)
Banbury Bookshop
White Lion Walk. (N. Mills.) Open 9—5.30. *STOCK: Books.* LOC: Off High St. TEL: 52002.

BENSON
Bygones
Paddock House, Brook St. (M.A. and J.O. Cleland.) Est. 1968. CL: Wed. Open 10—6 +, including Sun. SIZE: Medium. *STOCK: General antiques.* LOC: On B4009 opp. Farmer's Man. PARK: Easy. TEL: Wallingford (0491) 38307. SER: Restorations. VAT: Spec.

Sarum Antiques
23 Castle Sq. (N.J. Hatton.) Resident. Est. 1968. CL: Wed. Open 10—5.30. SIZE: Large. *STOCK: Furniture, 19th C.* LOC: Off main Henley to Oxford road. PARK: Easy. TEL: Wallingford (0491) 38527.

BICESTER (0869)
The Barn
Crumps Butts, off Bell Lane. (E. Latimer.) Est. 1975. CL: Sat. and lunchtimes. SIZE: Medium. *STOCK: Furniture including shipping items, 18th—20th C, £50—£500.* LOC: Town centre. PARK: Easy. TEL: 252958. SER: Restorations; veneering and polishing; buys at auction.

Lisseter of Bicester
3 Kings End. (D. Lisseter.) Est. 1945. Open 9—5.30. *STOCK: Furniture, all periods; Victoriana.* PARK: Easy, opposite. TEL: 252402. VAT: Stan/Spec.

Bicester continued

Original State Ltd.
Trade and Export only
2 Wedgewood Rd., Off Churchill Rd. (R.A. Carter.) Est. 1976. CL: Sat. Open 8—4.30. SIZE: Large. *STOCK: Furniture, to Edwardian, £5—£2,500; general antiques, pre-1840; shipping items.* LOC: Off A41. PARK: Easy. TEL: 243472 (ansaphone). SER: Restorations; packing; shipping. VAT: Stan/Spec.

Tollgate Antiques
31 North St. (D. and M. Palmer.) Resident. Est. 1965. Open 9.30—6 or by appointment. SIZE: Large. *STOCK: Furniture, china, books, pictures, brass, copper, clocks, shipping goods.* LOC: On A41. PARK: Easy. TEL: 241296. SER: Buys at auction.

BLADON, Nr. Woodstock
Blenheim Antiques
Park St. (N. Hurdle.) Resident. Est. 1974. Open 9.30—6. *STOCK: 18th and 19th C furniture, clocks.* TEL: Woodstock (0993) 811841. VAT: Stan/Spec.

Park House Antiques
(C. Harries.) Resident. Est. 1978. Open 9—6 every day. *STOCK: Furniture and paintings.* PARK: Easy. TEL: Woodstock (0993) 812817. VAT: Stan/Spec.

BLEWBURY (0235)
Blewbury Antiques
London Rd. (S. and E. Richardson.) Est. 1973. CL: Wed. Open 10—6; including weekends. *STOCK: General antiques, books, Victoriana, bric-a-brac.* TEL: 850366.

BURFORD (099 382)
Burford Antiques
At the Roundabout. (K.C. Day and Son (Exports) Ltd). Est. 1968. Open 9.30—5.30, Sun. 12—5. SIZE: Large. *STOCK: Furniture, 18th—19th C, £100—£1,000.* LOC: A40. PARK: Easy. TEL: 2552. SER: Valuations; restorations; buys at auction. VAT: Stan/Spec.

The Burford Gallery
Classica House, High St. (B. Etheridge.) Est. 1976. CL: Mon. except by appointment. Open 10—6 and most Suns. SIZE: Medium. *STOCK: British and Continental watercolours, 18th to early 20th C, £40—£2,000.* LOC: 400yds. from A40 roundabout. PARK: Easy. TEL: 2305; home — same. SER: Valuations; framing and mounting; buys at auction (watercolours). VAT: Spec.

HORSESHOE ANTIQUES AND GALLERY

BRIAN AND PAMELA EVANS
HIGH STREET, BURFORD,
OXON OX8 4RJ
TELEPHONE 099 382 3244
099 382 2429 after hours

Fine 17th and 18th century oak
furniture, 18th and 19th century
Staffordshire figures and animals;
Victorian and early 20th century
Watercolours and Oil paintings;
period copper and brass; longcase clocks

*Small Enclosed Dresser, North Wales,
superb colour and patination, early 18th century.*

Burford continued

Clement House Antiques   BADA
**High St. (D. Stevens.) Est. 1971. Open
9.30—1 and 2—5.30. SIZE: Medium.**
*STOCK: Furniture, town and country,
pre-1850, £50—£5,000; decorative items,
glass.* **Not stocked: Reproductions. LOC: A40.
PARK: Easy. TEL: 3172. SER: Valuations;
restorations. VAT: Spec.**

The Crypt Antiques
High St. (P. Matthey and M. Schotten.)
CADA. Est. 1957. Open 9.30—1 and 2—
5.30 or by appointment. *STOCK: 18th—
19th C furniture, antique fishing tackle,
golfing collectables.* TEL: 2302; home —
Shipton-under-Wychwood (0993) 830254.
SER: Restorations; stripping (pine).

IS YOUR ENTRY CORRECT?
If there is even the slightest
inaccuracy in your entry, *please* let us
know before 1st January 1987.
GUIDE TO THE
ANTIQUE SHOPS OF BRITAIN
5 Church Street, Woodbridge, Suffolk.

Burford continued

Denver House Antiques and Collectables
Denver House, Witney St. (T. and B. Radman.)
Resident. Est. 1976. Open 10—5.30, Sun. by
appointment. SIZE: Small. *STOCK: Coins and
medals, B.C. to date, £1—£10,000; stamps
and paper money, 1840 to date,
50p—£3,000; maps, books, small silver,
1500 to date, £1—£800.* PARK: Easy and
nearby. TEL: 2040 (24 hours). SER: Valuations; restorations (maps and bank notes);
buys at auction (coins, stamps, medals,
sovereign and stamp cases, maps, covers and
tokens). VAT: Stan.

Jonathan Fyson Antiques
High St. (J.R. Fyson.) CADA. Est. 1972. Open
9.30—1 and 2—5.30. SIZE: Small. *STOCK:
English and Continental furniture, decorative
brass and steel including lighting and fireplace
accessories; papier mâché, tôle, treen, porcelain, glass, jewellery.* LOC: A361. Coming
from London on A40 between Oxford and
Cheltenham at junction with A361. PARK:
Easy. TEL: 3204; home — Oxford (0865)
880943. SER: Valuations. VAT: Spec.

Burford continued

Horseshoe Antiques and Gallery
LAPADA

High St. (B. and Mrs. P. Evans.) CL: Wed. and Sun. except by appointment. Open 9.30—6. SIZE: Medium. *STOCK: Early oak and country furniture, metalware, Victorian Staffordshire pottery; 19th—20th C watercolours and oil paintings.* LOC: East side of High St. PARK: Easy. TEL: 3244; home — 2429. VAT: Spec.

Jubilee Books

18 High St. Est. 1976. CL: Wed. Open 9.30—5.30. *STOCK: Antiquarian and secondhand books.* TEL: 2209.

Anthony Nielsen Antiques

High St. Est. 1977. Open 9.30—1 and 2—5.30. SIZE: Large. *STOCK: Furniture, mahogany, walnut, rosewood, oak, William and Mary—Edwardian, £100—£10,000; copper, brass and silver plate, £20—£400.* PARK: Easy. TEL: 2014; after hours (0451) 21710.

Peter Norden Antiques

High St. CADA. Est. 1960. Open 9.30—5.30. SIZE: Medium. *STOCK: Early oak and country furniture, metalware, treen, period mahogany and walnut, 16th to mid-19th C.* Not stocked: Silver, bronze, shipping goods. PARK: Easy. TEL: 2121. VAT: Spec.

Mary Phillips

The Hill. Open by appointment. *STOCK: Jewellery.* TEL: 2297.

Brian Sinfield Gallery

High St. Open 10—5.30. *STOCK: Paintings and watercolours from 1750, £200—£18,000.* LOC: Centre of High St. PARK: Easy. TEL: 2402. SER: Valuations; restorations; buys at auction.

Su and Son

High St. (S. Day.) Open 10—5, Sun. in summer 1—5. *STOCK: Furniture and decorative items.* TEL: 2256.

Swan Gallery

High St. (M. and J. Pratt.) CADA. Est. 1966. Open 9.30—5.30. SIZE: Large. *STOCK: Furniture — oak, yew, fruitwood and walnut, 17th—18th C, £500—£3,000; oil paintings and watercolours, 19th—20th C, £100—£1,000; metalwork, blue and white pottery and porcelain, small decorative items, 18th—20th C, £50—£500.* PARK: Easy. TEL: 2244; home — Edge Hill (029 587) 383. SER: Valuations; restorations (furniture). VAT: Mainly Spec.

Zene Walker, Burford   **BADA**

The Bull House, High St. (P. Walker.) Est. 1954. Open 9-5.30. SIZE: Large. *STOCK: 18th C furniture, pottery, porcelain, Delft ware.* TEL: 3284. VAT: Stan/Spec.

JONATHAN FYSON ANTIQUES
THE OLD SCHOOL HOUSE
CASSINGTON, OXFORD, OX8 1DN
Tel: Oxford 880943

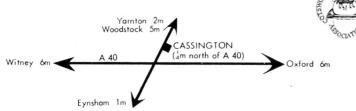

English and Continental Furniture, Pine, Brass and Decorative Items

Resident on premises   *Also in the High Street, Burford*

Burford continued

Frank Williams
The Old Post Office, High St. Est. 1933. Open 9.30—5.30. SIZE: Large. *STOCK: General antiques, furniture, decorative items.* TEL: 2128. VAT: Spec.

CASSINGTON

Jonathan Fyson Antiques
The Old School House. (J.R. Fyson.) CADA. Resident. Est. 1970. Open 9.30—5.30, Sat. by appointment. SIZE: Medium. *STOCK: English and Continental furniture, 17th—19th C, £50—£1,500; pine furniture, metalware, decorative objects.* LOC: ¼ mile north of A40. PARK: Easy. TEL: Oxford (0865) 880943. SER: Valuations; restorations. VAT: Spec.

CHALGROVE, Nr. Oxford

Quadrangle Gallery, Warehouse
Warpsgrove. (P. and R. Hitchcox.) Est. 1957. Open 9—6, Sun. 2.30—6. SIZE: Large. *STOCK: Furniture, 1700—1930.* LOC: 10 miles east of Oxford on B480. TEL: Oxford (0865) 57035 or 890241. SER: Restorations; buys at auction. VAT: Stan/Spec.

CHIPPING NORTON   (0608)

The Bugle Antiques   LAPADA
9 Horsefair and warehouse. (M. and D. Harding-Hill.) CADA. Est. 1971. Open 9.30—6. *STOCK: Mainly country furniture in oak, elm and fruitwood; Windsor chairs, sets of chairs, brass, copper and smalls.* TEL: 3322. VAT: Stan/Spec.

G. and E. Cashmore Antiques
50 West St. Est. 1977. Open 9—7, Sun. 10—5. SIZE: Small. *STOCK; Small country furniture, elm, oak and fruitwood, £50—£450; treen and metalware, £2—£50, all 18th to mid-19th C.* Not stocked: China and silver. LOC: On Churchill road on lefthand side past British Legion. PARK: Easy. TEL: 3441; home — same. VAT: Stan/Spec.

Robert Croot Antiques
16 New St. Open 9-6. *STOCK: Oak and country furniture, sets of chairs, desks, clocks.* LOC: 100yds. down from Town Hall. TEL: 3294 (anytime). VAT: Stan/Spec.

C.B. Gardner Antiques
31 High St. CADA. Est. 1967. Open 9—6. SIZE: Medium. *STOCK: Country furniture, mainly oak, 18th—19th C, £5—£3,000; brass, copper, £5—£75; clocks, £50—£1,500.* PARK: Easy. TEL: 3913. VAT: Stan/Spec.

Chipping Norton continued

Horse Fair Antiques
21 Horsefair. (R.K. Walker.) Open 9.30—6.
SIZE: Medium. *STOCK: English country furniture, 17th—19th C; some Victoriana; barometers.* LOC: Oxford end of main road through Chipping Norton. PARK: Easy. TEL: 3089/3226. VAT: Spec.

Jonathan Howard
21 Market Place. (J.G. Howard.) Est. 1979.
CL: Sun., except by appointment and Thurs. p.m. Open 10—1 and 2—6. SIZE: Small. *STOCK: Clocks — longcase, 18th—19th C, £500—£1,000; wall, 19th C, £100—£200; pocket watches, 18th—19th C, £25—£200.* PARK: Easy. TEL: 3065; home — same. SER: Valuations; restorations (mechanical, dials and cases). VAT: Stan/Spec.

Key Antiques
11 Horse Fair. (D. and M. Robinson.) CADA. Resident. Open 9.30—6 or by appointment. SIZE: Medium. *STOCK: Period oak and country furniture, domestic metalware including kitchenware and lighting, early pottery, paintings, needlework, carvings.* LOC: On main road. PARK: Easy. TEL: 3777. VAT: Spec.

An abundance of quality stock at affordable prices.

BUGLE ANTIQUES
9 Horse Fair, Chipping Norton, Oxon
Tel: (0608) 3322

KEY ANTIQUES

11 HORSE FAIR, CHIPPING NORTON
TELEPHONE 0608 3777

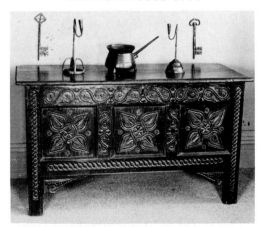

A fine oak chest circa 1660. Keys 15th century. Rushlight holders 18th century. Bronze posnet pot 16th century.

Chipping Norton continued

Packer House Antiques

28 High St. (T. and S. Jones.) Est. 1979. Open 9.30—6. SIZE: Small. *STOCK: Oak country furniture, 17th—19th C; copper and brass, 18th—19th C; writing boxes and tea caddies.* PARK: Opposite. TEL: 3255; home — same.

Keith Platt Antiques

4 West St. Open 9.30—5.30. *STOCK: Pine and country furniture, decorative items, clocks.* TEL: Home — Stow-on-the-Wold (0451) 31188.

Peter Stroud Antiques

Station Yard Industrial Estate. CADA. Est. 1971. Open 9—5.30. SIZE: Large. *STOCK: 17th—19th C furniture, oak, mahogany; farmhouse tables, armoires.* LOC: Just off A44 Moreton-in-Marsh road. TEL: 41651. VAT: Stan/Spec.

Peter Wiggins

Raffles, Southcombe. Est. 1969. Usually available. *STOCK: Barometers.* LOC: 1 mile from Chipping Norton on A34. TEL: 2652; home — same. SER: Valuations; restorations (barometers, clocks, automata); buys at auction. VAT: Stan.

CHURCH ENSTONE
Nr. Oxford

Warrack and Perkins

Rectory Farm House. (Mr. and Mrs. G. Perkins.) ABA. Est. 1964. Open by appointment only. SIZE: Small. *STOCK: Books, £10—£4,000; prints, £10—£500, all 19th—20th C.* LOC: 1½ miles north off A34 at Enstone. PARK: Easy. TEL: Enstone (060 872) 572. SER: Buys at auction. FAIRS: Europa, London. VAT: Stan.

CROWMARSH GIFFORD
Nr. Wallingford

Pennyfarthing

49 The Street. (Sqn.-Ldr. D.L. Mealing.) Open 9—5.30. *STOCK: Mechanical, scientific and curios; horse-drawn vehicles; agricultural items, bric-a-brac, garden furniture.* PARK: Easy. TEL: Wallingford (0491) 37470. FAIRS: Oxford and Reading.

DEDDINGTON (0869)
The Antique Centre

Laurel House, Bull Ring, Market Place. (Mrs. J.P. Hope.) Est. 1972. Open Wed.—Sat. 10—5. SIZE: Large. LOC: Off A423 Oxford to Banbury road at Deddington traffic lights. PARK: Easy. TEL: 38968. SER: Valuations; buys at auction. FAIRS: Chipping Norton, Henley and Oxford. Below are listed the dealers at this centre:

Diana Gates
Silver, commemorative ware, pressed glass; unusual and decorative collectors' items, small furniture.

Patricia Hayward
Jewellery, treen, rugs, furniture and general antiques.

June Hope
Silver, clocks, watches, furniture including 19th to early 20th C stripped pine and satin walnut and related items, general antiques.

Carroll Lymbery
Silver, porcelain, small furniture and collectors' items.

Barbara Martin
Kitchenalia, copper and brassware, 19th C furniture and collectors' items, some jewellery.

Gordon and Muriel Newark
Oils and watercolours, porcelain and furniture.

Sandra Smith
18th—19th C furniture, copper and brassware.

Clare Thomas
Silver plate, small furniture, decorative items.

Deddington continued

Castle Antiques Ltd.
Chapel Sq. (J. and J. Vaughan.) Est. 1968.
Open 10—5. SIZE: Large. *STOCK: Furniture,
£25—£1,000; silver, metalware, £10—£250;
pottery, porcelain, £10—£100; kitchenalia.*
LOC: Off Market Place. PARK: Easy. TEL:
38688. VAT: Stan/Spec.

G. Enstone
Featherton House, Chapel Sq. Est. 1960.
Open 10—6 and Sun. p.m. SIZE: Medium.
*STOCK: Oak and country furniture, clocks,
17th—19th C, £10—£500; Victoriana, bric-a-
brac, shipping goods.* Not stocked: Expensive
furniture and porcelain. LOC: On A423 and
B4031. PARK: Easy. TEL: 38259.

Grove Galleries
High St. (R.A.W. Gregory.) Est. 1970. CL:
Mon. Open daily, Sun. by appointment. SIZE:
Small. *STOCK: Furniture including country
pine, collectors' items, 18th—19th C, £25—
£500; oils and watercolours, mainly 19th C,
£50—£1,000; clocks, longcase, wall and
mantel; Victorian linen.* PARK: Nearby. TEL:
38397; home — same. SER: Valuations
(paintings and collectors' items); restorations;
cleaning (oil paintings); buys at auction
(paintings and furniture). FAIRS: Henley,
Oxford, Upper Heyford. VAT: Spec.

J.P. Antiques
High St. (A. and J. James-Priday.) Open
10—6. *STOCK: General antiques.* PARK:
Easy. TEL: 38743.

DORCHESTER-ON-THAMES

Dorchester Galleries
Rotten Row. (D. Knipe.) Est. 1978. Open
10—6, Sun. and Wed. by appointment only.
*STOCK: Paintings, £35—£900; prints, £10—
£350, both 18th—20th C; glass and china,
19th—20th C, £1—£50; maps, 16th—19th
C, £30—£350.* LOC: Off Henley—Oxford
road, opposite Dorchester Abbey. PARK:
Easy. TEL: Oxford (0865) 341116. SER:
Valuations; restorations; buys at auction (pictures, prints).

Giffengate Antiques
16 High St. (E.M. and S.A. Reily-Collins.) Est.
1978. CL: Sat. lunchtime. Open 9—5. SIZE:
Large. *STOCK: English and Continental porcelain, silver, glass, pictures and furniture,
17th—19th C, £50—£5,000.* PARK: Own.
TEL: Oxford (0865) 341149. SER: Valuations;
restorations. FAIRS: Olympia. VAT: Stan/Spec.

Hallidays Antiques Ltd.   LAPADA
The Old College, High St. Est. 1950. SIZE:
Large. *STOCK: Furniture, 17th—19th C,
£100—£20,000; paintings, 18th—19th C,
£100—£4,000; decorative and small items,
pine and marble mantelpieces, firegrates,
fenders, 18th—20th C; room panelling.* PARK:
At rear. TEL: Oxford (0865) 340028. FAIRS:
Olympia. VAT: Stan/Spec.

Dorchester-on-Thames continued

Mike Ottrey Antiques
28 High St. (M.J. Ottrey.) Est. 1955. CL: Fri.
Open 9.30—1 and 2—5.30. SIZE: Medium.
*STOCK: Oak and mahogany furniture, copper
and brass, unusual items, 17th—19th C.* LOC:
Village centre, next to White Hart Hotel.
PARK: Easy. TEL: Oxford (0865) 340079.
VAT: Stan/Spec.

EAST HAGBOURNE, Nr. Didcot
E.M. Lawson and Co.
Kingsholm. (W.J. and K.M. Lawson.) Est. 1921. CL: Sat. Usually open 10—5 but appointment preferred. *STOCK: Antiquarian and rare books, 1500—1900.* PARK: Easy. TEL: Didcot (0235) 812033. VAT: Stan.

EYNSHAM, Nr. Oxford
David John Ceramics
11, Acre End St. (J. Twitchett and D. Holborough.) Est. 1959. CL: Mon. SIZE: Medium. *STOCK: English ceramics, 18th—20th C, £15—£5,000; small furniture, decorative items.* TEL: Oxford (0865) 880786. VAT: Stan/Spec.

North Parade Antiques   Trade Only
2 and 4 Oxford Rd. (M. Bull.) CADA. Est. 1959. Open 9—5. SIZE: Warehouse. *STOCK: Furniture and bric-a-brac, 19th C.* LOC: ½ mile off A40. PARK: Easy. TEL: 880923. SER: Restorations. VAT: Stan/Spec.

John Wilson (Autographs) Ltd.
50 Acre End St. ABA. Est. 1967. Open 9—6, Sat. by appointment. SIZE: Large. *STOCK: Autograph letters, historical documents, manuscripts, £100—£200.* LOC: From Oxford, off the A40 towards Cheltenham. PARK: Easy. TEL: Oxford (0865) 880883. SER: Valuations; buys at auction (as stock). FAIRS: ABA London. VAT: Stan.

FARINGDON   (0367)
A. and F. Partners   BADA
16-20 London St. Open 9.30—6. SIZE: Medium. *STOCK: English and Continental oak and walnut, £100—£8,000; carvings and treen, £25—£2,000; English delftware, collectors' items.* Not stocked: Victoriana. LOC: A420. PARK: Easy, within 20yds. TEL: 20078. SER: Valuations; upholstery. VAT: Spec.

Peter Campbell Antiques
23 Marlborough St. Est. 1976. CL: Mon. Open 10—5. SIZE: Medium. *STOCK: General antiques, 18th—19th C, £25—£600.* PARK: Easy. TEL: 20264; home — same. VAT: Stan/Spec.

Faringdon Gallery
21 London St. (G.E. Lott.) CL: Thurs. Usually open, appointment preferred. *STOCK: Watercolours, oils, etchings and books, 19th—20th C, £25—£3,000;* LOC: A420. PARK: Market Sq. TEL: 22030; home — same. SER: Valuations; restorations (framing and mounting); buys at auction (paintings and prints). VAT: Spec.

Faringdon continued
Betty Haslam
4 Market Place. Est. 1974. Open 10—5. SIZE: Medium. *STOCK: Oils, watercolours and sporting pictures, 1800—1920; small silver, collectables and interesting furniture.* PARK: Easy. LOC: Town centre. TEL: 21574; home — Lambourn (0488) 71455. SER: Restoration and framing, buys at auction. VAT: Spec.

La Chaise Antique
30 London St. (R. Clark.) Est. 1968. CL: Sun., except by appointment. Open 10—6. SIZE: Large. *STOCK: Chairs, pre-1860; furniture, 18th and 19th C; general antiques, decorators' items.* Not stocked: Silver, porcelain and glass. LOC: A420. PARK: At rear. TEL: 20427. SER: Valuations; restorations; upholstery (leather and fabrics). FAIRS: Oxford, High Wycombe and Henley (organiser). VAT: Spec.

FYFIELD, Nr. Abingdon
Blackwell's Rare Books
Fyfield Manor. Est. 1879. Open 9—5.15. *STOCK: Antiquarian and rare books.* LOC: A420 adjacent to village green. PARK: Easy. TEL: Oxford (0865) 390692. SER: Valuations; binding; buys at auction. VAT: Stan/Spec.

HARWELL, Nr. Didcot
Kings Manor Antiques
Kings Manor, High St. (M. Winterbourne.) Est. 1979. CL: Mon. Open 10—4.30, Fri. and Sun. by appointment. SIZE: Medium. *STOCK: Furniture, Georgian—Edwardian, £50—£1,500; china, glass and collectors' items, 18th C to 1930s, £5—£100; stripped pine, Victorian, £10—£400.* LOC: 1 mile from A34. PARK: Easy. TEL: Abingdon (0235) 835612; home — same. SER: Restorations (furniture).

HEADINGTON
Barclay Antiques
107 Windmill Rd. (C. and B. Barclay.) Est. 1979. CL: Wed. Open 10—5.30. SIZE: Small. *STOCK: Porcelain, silver and jewellery, 18th—19th C, £50—£100; period lamps, 20th C, £5—£100.* PARK: Easy. TEL: Oxford (0865) 69551. SER: Valuations. FAIRS: Oxford.

The Barry M. Keene Gallery

Fine 18th, 19th and early 20th Century
**WATERCOLOURS
PAINTINGS, ETCHINGS,
MAPS & PRINTS**

"The Morning of Life"   Samuel Palmer O.W.C.S.
Etching   (1805-1881)

12 Thameside, Henley-on-Thames, Oxfordshire
Tel: Henley-on-Thames (0491) 577119
Open: Monday to Saturday 9.30 a.m. to 5.30 p.m.
(Master Frame Maker)

HENLEY-ON-THAMES   (0491)

Henley-on-Thames continued

Barry M. Keene Gallery
12 Thameside. Est. 1971. Open 9.30—5.30. *STOCK: Watercolours, paintings, etchings, maps and prints, 18th to early 20th C, £5—£10,000.* TEL: 577119. SER: Restorations; framing, cleaning, relining, gilding. VAT: Stan/Spec.

Richard J. Kingston   BADA
95 Bell St. Open 9—5.30, Sat. 9.30—5 or by appointment. **SIZE: Medium.** *STOCK: Furniture, 17th to early 19th C; silver, porcelain, paintings, antiquarian and secondhand books.* LOC: A423 some ½ mile from town centre traffic lights. PARK: Easy. TEL: 574535; home — 573133. SER: Restorations. FAIRS: Surrey. VAT: Stan/Spec.

Market Place Antiques   LAPADA
35 Market Place. (E. Whittaker.) Est. 1966. Open 10—1 and 2—6, Sat. 10—5. SIZE: Large. *STOCK: French provincial and country furniture, pine, needlework, treen, tools, unusual and architectural items.* LOC: At top of Market Place left of town hall. PARK: Easy. TEL: 572387. VAT: Stan/Spec.

B.R. Ryland
75 Reading Rd. Est. 1945. CL: Wed. Open 9—5.30. SIZE: Large. *STOCK: Furniture, Victorian and later, £10—£300; copper, brass, clocks, £10—£200; china and glass, all periods, £5—£50.* LOC: A4155. From Reading first shop on right on entering Henley. From London M4 turn left after Henley bridge, follow the river past station, then turn left, last shop on the parade. PARK: Opposite. TEL: 573663. VAT: Stan.

Thames Gallery
Thameside. (S. Came.) Open 10—5. *STOCK: Georgian and Victorian English silver; jewellery, objets de vertu; paintings, 19th C.* TEL: 572449.

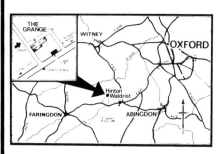

ANTONY DAVENPORT

Good 17th—19th Century Furniture and Decorative Items

THE GRANGE, HINTON WALDRIST
(OPP. THE CHURCH),
NR. FARINGDON, OXON.
TELEPHONE LONGWORTH
(STD 0865) 820227

HINTON WALDRIST
Antony Davenport
The Grange. SIZE: Large. *STOCK: Furniture, 17th—19th C; mirrors, pictures.* LOC: 1 mile off A420 between Kingston Bagpuize and Faringdon, opposite Parish church. TEL: Longworth (0865) 820227. SER: Upholstery; restorations (furniture, pictures). VAT: Spec.

LONG HANBOROUGH
Hanborough Antiques
127 Main Rd. Open 10—5, Sun. 2—5. SIZE: Medium. *STOCK: Furniture, country and period; pottery, porcelain, Victoriana, rural and domestic bygones, brass and copper, collectors' items.* LOC: Going north from Oxford on A34 turn left before Woodstock on to A4095. PARK: Easy. TEL: Freeland (0993) 881484.

NETTLEBED   (0491)
Harvey Ferry and William Clegg Antiques   LAPADA
The Barns, 1 High Street. (H. and S. Ferry, W. and S. Clegg.) Est. 1965. Open 9—5.30, Sat. 10—4. SIZE: Large. *STOCK: English furniture, 1630—1830, £100—£10,000; associated items, 1680—1850, £10—£1,000; trade goods, 1630—1850, £100—£10,000.* LOC: A423, Henley to Oxford, Barns at rear of first house on left in Nettlebed. PARK: Easy. TEL: 641533. SER: Valuations; restorations (furniture); buys at auction. VAT: Spec.

OXFORD   (0865)
The Antiquary   BADA
50 St. Giles St. (P.M. Goodban.) Est. 1890. CL: Thurs. Open 11.30—3. *STOCK: Jewellery, £1—£500; also silver, £1—£400; both 18th—20th C; china, 18th—19th C, £5—£300.* Not stocked: Furniture, arms and armour, carpets, decorative items. PARK: Easy. TEL: 59875. VAT: Stan.

Oxford continued

Reginald Davis   BADA
34 High St. (M.D. Marcus.) Est. 1941. CL: Thurs. Open 9—5. *STOCK: Silver, English and Continental, 17th to early 19th C; jewellery, Sheffield plate, Georgian and Victorian.* Not stocked: Glass, china, pewter. LOC: On A40. PARK: Easy. TEL: 248347. SER: Valuations; restorations (silver, jewellery). VAT: Stan/Spec.

The Desk Shop
41 St. Clements. (J. Devereux.) Est. 1971. Open 9—5.30, Sat. 9—5 or by appointment. SIZE: Medium. *STOCK: Pedestal and partner desks, 1750—1900, £500—£15,000.* PARK: Easy. TEL: 245524. SER: Valuations; restorations; re-leathering; buys at auction (desks). VAT: Stan.

The Farmhouse
The Fourth Avenue, Covered Market. (J.G. Patterson.) Est. 1976. Open 9.30—5. SIZE: Large. *STOCK: Pine furniture, 19th C, £50—£500; country furniture, dressers, tables, desks and coffers, 18th—19th C, £100—£1,500.* Not stocked: Small items. LOC: Town centre, just off High St. TEL: 247084. VAT: Stan/Spec.

Laurie Leigh Antiques
36 High St. (L., D. and W. Leigh.) Est. 1963. CL: Thurs. Open 11—6. *STOCK: English clocks, keyboard musical instruments.* TEL: 244197. VAT: Stan/Spec.

Magna Gallery
41 High St. (B. Kentish.) Est. 1965. Open 10—6. SIZE: Medium. *STOCK: Maps, prints, 1570—1870, 50p—£500.* TEL: 245805. SER: Valuations. VAT: Stan.

Oxford continued

P. Audley Miller
46 High St. Open 9.30—5. *STOCK: General
antiques, glass, china; longcase, mantel and
bracket clocks.* TEL: 247952. FAIRS: Oxford
(organiser). VAT: Stan/Spec.

North Parade Antiques
75 Banbury Rd. (M. Bull.) CADA. (Also warehouse at Willow Bank, Oxford Rd., Eynsham
— Trade Only.) Est. 1959. Open 9.30—6.
SIZE: Large. *STOCK: Furniture, 1700—1900;
bric-a-brac, silver and Sheffield plate,
1800—1930.* Not stocked: Books, coins,
stamps. LOC: A40 north to Banbury Road
(A423) roundabout, turn towards city, one
mile on right. PARK: Own at rear. TEL:
59816; home — 880923 and 514782
(manager). SER: Restoration (as stock). VAT:
Stan/Spec.

Oxford continued

Number Ten
10 North Parade. (Mrs. P. Clewett.) Est.
1979. CL: Sun. except by appointment. Open
10—5 (prior telephone call advisable), Thurs.
and Sat. 10—1. SIZE: Small. *STOCK: English
porcelain, 1780—1920, £1—£150; small
general antiques, 1600—1920, £1—£800.*
LOC: North Parade is second left turning from
central Oxford on Banbury road. PARK:
50yds. TEL: 512816; home — same. VAT:
Stan/Spec.

Oxford continued

Oriental Carpets
25 Oakthorpe Rd., Summertown. (C.T. Legge) Est. 1970. SIZE: Medium. *STOCK: Rugs, various sizes, mainly 19th C, £50—£3,000.* LOC: Near shopping parade. PARK: Easy. TEL: 57572. SER: Valuations; restorations (reweaving). VAT: Stan.

Oxford Antiques Omnibus
The Basement, Omni Store, George St. (S. Vetta and G. Hedge.) Est. 1981. Open Wed. and Sat. 10—4.30, trade from 9 a.m. SIZE: Large. There are 26 stalls at this market selling *a wide range of general antiques including watercolours, books, silver, brass and textiles, jewellery, ceramics and small furniture, £5—£200.* LOC: Near bus station and Apollo Theatre. PARK: Nearby. TEL: Home — 739071 or Didcot (0235) 817076. SER: Valuations (pictures, silver and jewellery); restorations (clocks); picture framing.

Pandora's Bric-a-Brac
59 St. Aldates. Est. 1965. *STOCK: General antiques and bric-a-brac.* TEL: 247925.

D. Parikian
The Old Rectory, Waterstock. Open by appointment. *STOCK: Antiquarian books, mythology, iconography, emblemata, Continental books pre-1800.* TEL: Ickford (084 47) 603. SER: Buys at auction.

Oxford continued

Payne and Son (Goldsmiths) Ltd.   BADA
131 High St. (D.M., G.N., E.P. and J.D. Payne.) Est. 1790. Open weekdays 8.30—1 and 2—5. SIZE: Medium. *STOCK: British silver, antique, Victorian, modern and second-hand; jewellery, all £40—£1,000+.* LOC: Town centre near Carfax traffic lights. PARK: 800yds. TEL: 243787. SER: Restorations (English silver). VAT: Stan/Spec.

Quadrangle Gallery
1 Walton Crescent. (P. and R. Hitchcox.) Est. 1973. CL: Mon. a.m. Open 10—5. SIZE: Large. *STOCK: Furniture and shipping items, 1740—1940, £5—£1,000+; pictures, £5—£350+; objets d'art, £5—£150+, both 1790—1950.* LOC: From St. Giles, turn left down Little Clarendon St., cross over Walton St. into Walton Crescent. PARK: Easy. TEL: 57035; warehouse — 890241. SER: Restorations (cane seating); French polishing; buys at auction. VAT: Stan/Spec.

A. Rosenthal Ltd.
9—10 Broad St. Est. 1936. Open 10—5.30, Sat. by appointment. *STOCK: Continental literature; Judaica; early printed books and autograph letters.* TEL: 243093. SER: Buys at auction.

A fine pair of large tea canisters, of a type which may have fitted into a lockable wooden container. One is turned to show the narrow end and the flat, glazed base with painter's number. 4⁹/10ins. high. Painter's number '5'. c.1763-5. From *Lowestoft Porcelains* by Geoffrey A. Godden, F.R.S.A., published by the **Antique Collectors' Club**, 1985.

Oxford continued

Rowell and Son Ltd.   BADA
115 High St. Open 9—5. SIZE: Medium. *STOCK: Silver, all periods, all prices; also Sheffield plate, late 18th and 19th C, to £150.* PARK: 200yds. TEL: 242187. SER: Valuations; restorations (silver and jewellery); buys at auction. VAT: Stan/Spec.

Sanders of Oxford Ltd.
104 High St. CL: Sat. p.m. SIZE: Medium. *STOCK: Prints, maps, watercolours and antiquarian books.* TEL: 242590. VAT: Stan/Spec.

Serendipity
96 Cowley Rd. (R.D. Davids.) *STOCK: General antiques.* TEL: 721874.

A. and J. Stuart-Mobey and Daughter
Bedford House, Godstow Rd., Lower Wolvercote. Est. 1957. Open by appointment. *STOCK: Furniture, late 17th to early 20th C, £5—£500; bric-a-brac, curios.* Not stocked: Jewellery, coins. TEL: 50170. SER: Valuations; buys at auction.

Studio One Gallery
214 Banbury Rd., Summertown. (B. Clark.) Est. 1974. Open 9.30—5.30, Thurs. and Sat. 9.30—1.30 or by appointment. *STOCK: Watercolours, 18th to early 20th C, £60—£800; 20th C wood engravings, etchings, books.* LOC: 2 miles from city centre. PARK: Forecourt or nearby. TEL: 511637. VAT: Stan/Spec.

J. Thornton and Son
11 Broad St. Open 9—5.30. *STOCK: Antiquarian books.* TEL: 242939.

Titles Old and Rare Books
15/1 Turl St. Est. 1972. Open 9.30—5.30. *STOCK: Antiquarian and secondhand books, general subjects especially literature, agriculture, travel and natural history.* TEL: 727928.

Oxford continued

Robin Waterfield Ltd.
36 Park End St. Open 9.30—5.30. *STOCK: Antiquarian and secondhand books especially academic in the humanities; 17th—18th C English books; modern first editions, literary autographs.* TEL: 721809.

SHIPTON-UNDER-WYCHWOOD
(0993)

Ye Olde Junk Shoppe
St. Michael's College, Milton Rd. (B. Hill.) Est. 1960. Open every day. SIZE: Large. *STOCK: Country pine and oak furniture, brass, copper, curios, pictures.* PARK: Easy. TEL: 830576.

STANDLAKE, Nr. Witney (086 731)
Manor Farm Antiques
Manor Farm. (Mrs. M. Leveson-Gower.) Est. 1964. Open 10—6. SIZE: Large. *STOCK: Beds, brass and iron; Victorian stripped pine, shipping goods, small items and bric-a-brac.* PARK: Easy, in Farmyard. TEL: 303.

THAME   (084 421)
Donald Butler Antiques
16 Park St. Est. 1972. CL: Wed. Open 9.30—1 and 2—5.30. *STOCK: Chairs, especially spoon-backs, Victorian, £200—£450; furniture, £50—£400; small items, £5—£25; both Victorian and Edwardian.* LOC: 4 miles off M40. PARK: Easy. TEL: 3842 (ansaphone). SER: Restorations (re-upholstery). VAT: Stan.

Peter Fell of Thame   BADA
81 High St. (P. and K. Fell.) Resident. CL: Mon. Open 9.30—5.30 or by appointment. SIZE: Large. *STOCK: English longcase, bracket, wall and mantel clocks; and the occasional grand piano.* LOC: On left at start of High St. approaching from Oxford or Aylesbury, near mini-roundabout. PARK: Easy. TEL: 4487. SER: Valuations (clocks); restorations (clocks). VAT: Spec.

Thame continued

Priests Antiques and Fine Arts
60 North St. (M.G. and A.C. Priest.) Est. 1979. Open 10—1 and 2.15—5, Sat. 10—5. SIZE: Large. *STOCK: Mahogany, 18th C; early walnut and oak, 17th—18th C; oil paintings and primitives, Victorian.* PARK: Easy. TEL: 4461. SER: Valuations. VAT: Spec.

Rosemary and Time
42 Park St. Open 9—6. *STOCK: Clocks, watches, barometers and scientific instruments.* TEL: 6923. SER: Valuations; restorations; old spare parts. VAT: Stan/Spec.

H. and D. Smith
Sons and Daughters
1 Upper High St. Est. 1960. CL: Wed. p.m. Open 9.30—5.30. SIZE: Large. *STOCK: Furniture, Victorian and earlier; bric-a-brac, books.* TEL: 2035. VAT: Stan/Spec.

Telling Time Antiques
57 North St. (S. Telling.) Est. 1978. *STOCK: Longcase and bracket clocks, 17th—20th C, £250—£2,000; watches, £5—£2,000; wall, mantel, carriage and French clocks, £20—£1,500; furniture, jewellery, general antiques.* PARK: Easy. TEL: 3007. SER: Valuations. VAT: Stan/Spec.

Thame Antique and Art Galleries
11-12 High St. Open 9—5.30. SIZE: Large. *STOCK: Furniture, 18th and 19th C; Victorian oil paintings and watercolours.* TEL: 2725.

WALLINGFORD (0491)
The Antique Shop
6 St. Peters St. (L. O'Donnell.) Est. 1974. CL: Mon. and Wed. Open 9.30—1 and 2—5. SIZE: Medium. *STOCK: Stripped pine, £20—£200; unrestored furniture, £5—£200; clocks, £20—£300; longcase clocks, from £300; small collectors' items, porcelain, silver and brass, £1—£200.* LOC: Into town over Wallingford Bridge, turn first left into Thames St. then first right. PARK: Easy. TEL: 39345. SER: Restorations (clocks); buys at auction. FAIRS: Organizer of Portcullis Antiques and Collectors Fairs (Oxfordshire).

Eagle House
16 High St. (W.J. Ottrey and Son.) Est. 1932. Open 9—5.30. SIZE: Medium. *STOCK: 17th—18th C English furniture, longcase clocks, and oil paintings.* LOC: A429. PARK: At rear. TEL: 36429. VAT: Stan/Spec.

The Lamb Arcade
High St. CL: Wed. Open 9.30—5.30. TEL: 35048 and 35166. Administration (01) 349 3111. SER: Restoration. Below are listed some of the dealers at this centre:
Jane Albuquerque
Pine and furniture.

The Lamb Arcade continued

Annalicia Antiques
(A. Collins.) *China, silver and collectors' items.* TEL: Warborough (086 732) 8123.
Ann Brewer
Furniture and small items.
Castle Antiques
(R.R. Wright.) *English porcelain to 1835, £10—£300; silver and small items.* TEL: Home —39025.
Toby English
Antiquarian and secondhand books.
Flight and Carr
(J. .and D. Suckling.) *Furniture, porcelain and silver.* TEL: Crowmarsh (049 169) 737.
Heyday Antiques
(A. Halliburton.) *Small furniture, curios, pictures and collectors' items.* TEL: 39909.
Pat Heyward
General antiques.
J.J. Antiques
Furniture.
Jean's
General.
Carol Peacock
Commemorative china and furniture.
Margaret Richmond
Country items including furniture.
Julie Strachie
Pine.
Special Edition
(E. Hornsby.) *Porcelain, silver, small furniture and crafts.* TEL: Clifton Hampden (086 730) 7842 and 7883.
Tags
(T. and A. Green.) *Collectors' items, curios, jewellery, militaria, scientific instruments and furniture.* TEL: Home — Blewbury (0235) 850 676.
Rosemary Toop
Boxes, small furniture, collectors' items, needlework tools and lace bobbins. TEL: Home — Kingston Blount (0844) 52859.
Top Shop
General antiques.

George G. Shand
20 High St. Open 9—6. *STOCK: Period furniture, mostly oak; decorative objects, works of art.* TEL: 39332.

PRIESTS

Antiques and Fine Arts
60 North Street, Thame, Oxfordshire
Telephone Thame 4461

Fine quality mid eighteenth century mahogany serpentine fronted
gentleman's commode, circa 1745

Wallingford continued

Summers, Davis and Son Ltd.
BADA
LAPADA

Calleva House, 6 High St. (M.S. Baylis and G. Wells.) Est. 1917. Open 8—5.30. SIZE: Large. *STOCK: English and continental decorative furniture, 17th—19th C.* Not stocked: Silver, shipping goods. LOC: From London, shop is on left, 50yds. from Thames Bridge. PARK: Easy. TEL: 36284. VAT: Spec.

WANTAGE   (023 57)
Arts and Antiques (Oxford) Ltd.

33 Wallingford St. (J.F.W. King.) Est. 1947. CL: Thurs. p.m. Open 9.30—6 or by appointment. SIZE: Medium. *STOCK: Furniture, oil paintings, watercolours, sculpture, bronzes, general antiques including unusual items, £5—£6,000.* PARK: Easy. TEL: 2676. SER: Valuations; restorations (oil paintings). VAT: Spec.

WITNEY   (0993)
Angela John Antiques

81 Corn St. (P. Broome.) Est. 1975. Open 9—5.30. SIZE: Medium. *STOCK: Mahogany, pine, brass and copper, glass, porcelain and collectables, 19th C, £5—£500.* LOC: From A40 turn right at the green. PARK: Easy. TEL: 4246; home — 72448. VAT: Stan/Spec.

Witney continued

Robin Bellamy   **BADA**

97 Corn St. (P.R.G. and J.M. Hornsby.) Est. 1966. Open by appointment. SIZE: Small. *STOCK: Pewter, metalware, works of art, 15th—18th C, £100—£5,000.* Not stocked: Mahogany, Victoriana, glass, arms. LOC: Off High St. or via by-pass. PARK: Easy. TEL: 4793. FAIRS: Grosvenor House. VAT: Spec.

Colin Greenway Antiques

90 Corn St. CADA. Resident. Est. 1975. Open 9—6 or by appointment. SIZE: Medium. *STOCK: Furniture, 17th—20th C; clocks, metalware, decorative and unusual items.* LOC: Along High St. to town centre, turn right, shop 400yds. on right. PARK: Easy. TEL: 5026. VAT: Stan/Spec.

Ian Pout Antiques

99 High St. (I. and J. Pout.) CADA. Open 10—5.30. *STOCK: 18th and 19th C country and decorative furniture, metalware, interesting and unusual objects.* TEL: 2616. VAT: Spec.

Early Victorian mahogany cased bracket clock by Charles Skinner, London. From *The Price Guide to Collectable Clocks 1840-1940* by Alan and Rita Shenton, published by the **Antique Collectors' Club,** 1985.

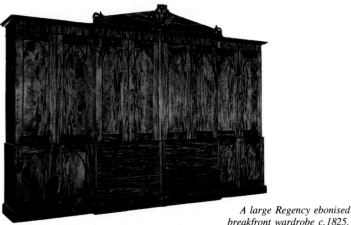

George Fenn. 'Grey horse in a landscape with a dog'. Signed and dated 1835. From *The Dictionary of Equestrian Artists* by Sally Mitchell, published by the **Antique Collectors' Club,** 1985.

Witney continued

Anthony Scaramanga Antiques
BADA
108 Newland. CADA. Est. 1969. CL: Fri. and Sun. except by appointment. Open 10—6. *STOCK: Samplers, 17th—19th C; small furniture, needlework pictures, lace, Staffordshire figures, blue and white pottery.* **LOC: From Oxford on A40, turn off bypass onto A4002, shop on left before coming to A147 and Witney. PARK: Easy. TEL: 3472. VAT: Spec.**

Smithies
35 Bridge St. (I. Smith.) Est. 1978. Open 9—5.30, Sun. by appointment. SIZE: Large. *STOCK: General antiques and shipping items, including stripped pine, Oriental rugs, early metalware, kitchenalia, all pre-1930s, to £500.* LOC: Main road. PARK: Easy. TEL: 4611; home — 850598. SER: Valuations. VAT: Stan/Spec.

Joan Wilkins Antiques
158 Corn St. (Mrs. J. Wilkins.) Est. 1973. CL: Tues. p.m. Open 10—5. *STOCK: Furniture, 18th—19th C, £75—£1,500; 19th C glass, metalware, £10—£500.* LOC: Town centre. PARK: Easy. TEL: 4749. VAT: Spec.

Windrush Antiques
107 High St. (B. Tollett.) CADA. Est. 1978. Open 10—5.30. *STOCK: Furniture, especially 17th—18th C, oak, mahogany and country; some metalware and porcelain.* LOC: A40, corner of Mill St. and High St. PARK: Private at rear. TEL: 72536.

18th C Elm Bacon Settle

Windrush Antiques
107 High Street, Witney,
Oxfordshire
Telephone 72536

William Barraud. Bay hunter and terrier in a landscape, signed and dated 1845. From *The Dictionary of Equestrian Artists* by Sally Mitchell, published by the **Antique Collectors' Club,** 1985.

Witney continued

Witney Antiques
BADA
**96/98 Corn St. (L.S.A. and C.J. Jarrett.)
CADA. Est. 1962. Open 9.30—5. SIZE:
Large.** *STOCK: English furniture, 17th—18th
C; bracket and longcase clocks, mahogany,
oak and walnut, metalware, paintings and
works of art.* **LOC: From Oxford on old A40
through Witney via High St., turn right at T-
junction, 400yds. on right. PARK: Easy. TEL:
3902 or 3887. FAIRS: Chelsea. VAT: Spec.**

WOODSTOCK (0993)
Fox House
30/32 Oxford St. (A. Wilson and J. Coles.)
Resident. Est. 1977. CL: Wed. Open 9.30—
5.30, Sun. 2.15—5. SIZE: Large. *STOCK:
General antiques, interesting items, silver and
plate, Victoriana, furniture.* LOC: A34, next to
Marlborough Hotel. PARK: Easy. TEL: 811377.
SER: Valuations; restorations; buys at auction.
VAT: Stan/Spec.

Woodstock continued

Museum Bookshop
County Museum, Fletcher's House. (Oxfordshire County Council.) Est. 1966. Oct.—April
CL: Mon. Open 10—4, Sat. 10—5, Sun.
2—5; May—Sept. Open 10—5, Sat. 10—6,
Sun. 2—6. SIZE: Small. *STOCK: Books on
antiquities, crafts, archaeology, local history,
original fine art, mainly pictures.* LOC: In town
centre, between P.O. and Barclays Bank.
PARK: Easy. TEL: 811456. VAT: Stan.

Peter La Cave (fl.1789-1816). From *Understanding
Watercolours* by H.L. Mallalieu, published by the
Antique Collectors' Club, 1985.

Witney Antiques

L.S.A. & C.J. Jarrett

96-98 Corn Street, Witney, Oxfordshire, OX8 7BU
Telephone Witney (0993) 3902

*An outstanding red walnut triple top gaming table in fine original
condition. Circa 1740.*

You are invited to visit our spacious showrooms in Witney, where we have on display an important stock of fine furniture, longcase and bracket clocks from the 17th and 18th centuries.

We offer a specialist service for the restoration and conservation of fine and antique furniture. All work is carried out in our own specialist workshops by fully trained and experienced craftsmen.

A rare model by Moigniez, c.1870, of a well detailed male goat in a proud and defiant posture that looks more realistic than most. Every inch of the model is worked on with no smooth surfaces and a lot of chiselling in the long hair of the animal. From *Animals in Bronze* by Christopher Payne, published by the **Antique Collectors' Club,** 1986.

Woodstock continued

Span Antiques
6 Market Place. (H. and M. Haig.) Resident. Est. 1978. CL: Wed. Open 10—1 and 2—5 including Sun. SIZE: Medium. LOC: Near Town Hall. PARK: Easy. TEL: 811332. SER: Valuations. Below are listed some of the dealers selling from these premises:

Arcadia Antiques
European and Oriental ceramics.
Derek Bramwell
Silver and Chinese porcelain.
Doreen Caudwell
Table linen and textiles.
R. and M. Eden
Georgian furniture.
Four Seasons Antiques
English porcelain.
Lis Hall-Bakker
Art nouveau and deco.
Giulia Irving
English porcelain.
Alan Stuart-Mobey
Furniture and small items.
Bret Wiles
Kitchen antiques, iron, copper, brass and farming bygones.

Woodstock continued

Woodstock Antiques
11 Market St. (C. Mason-Pope.) Est. 1979. CL: Mon. Open 9.30—5.30, Sun. 1—5.30, other times by appointment. SIZE: Medium. *STOCK: Staffordshire figures and animals, £50—£1,500; small furniture, £100—£2,000; decorative objects, pictures and prints, £100—£500, all 18th and early 19th C.* LOC: Town centre. PARK: Easy. TEL: 811494; home — same. VAT: Stan/Spec.

Shropshire

590

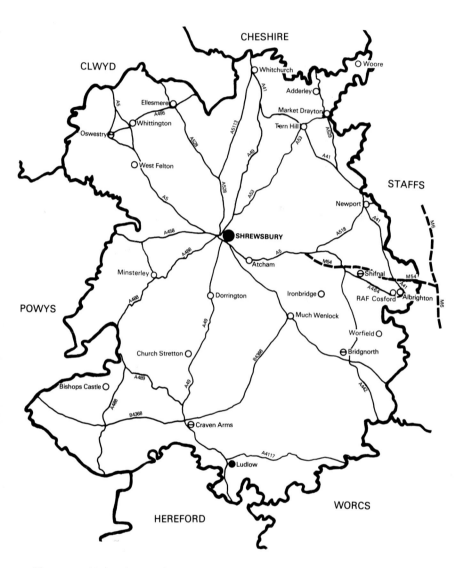

CHESHIRE

CLWYD

Woore

Whitchurch

Adderley

Ellesmere

Market Drayton

Whittington

Tern Hill

Oswestry

West Felton

STAFFS

Newport

SHREWSBURY

Atcham

Shifnal

Minsterley

Dorrington

Ironbridge

RAF Cosford

Albrighton

POWYS

Much Wenlock

Worfield

Church Stretton

Bridgnorth

Bishops Castle

Craven Arms

Ludlow

HEREFORD

WORCS

Please note this is only a rough map designed to show dealers the number of shops in the various towns, and is not necessarily totally accurate.

○ 1–2
⊖ 3–5
⊖ 6–12
● 13+

Key to number of shops in this area.

ADDERLEY, Nr. Market Drayton

Doreen Elkington Antiques

(Mrs. D.E. Elkington.) Est. 1979. CL: Thurs. Open 10—5.30 including Sun, or by appointment. SIZE: Small. *STOCK: Furniture, £70—£500; silver, plate and collectors' items, 18th—20th C; porcelain, glass, 19th C; brass, copper, 18th—19th C; all £5—£150; art nouveau.* LOC: A529 from Market Drayton to Audlem. TEL: Market Drayton (0630) 5433; home — same. SER: Valuations.

ALBRIGHTON (090 722)
(NEACHLEY)

Doveridge House of Neachley
BADA
LAPADA

Long Lane (alongside RAF Cosford). (Cdr. and Mrs. H.E.R. Bain.) Est. 1967. Open 9—6 including Sun. or by appointment. SIZE: Large. STOCK: English and Continental furniture, fine art, clocks, decorative artifacts. LOC: From London M1 to M6. Junction 10A via new M54 for North and Mid Wales. Leave at Junction 3 (A41) in Wolverhampton direction ½ a mile. See Neachley signpost, immediately right into Long Lane, 4th entrance. From the North, M6 Junction 11, A460 towards Wolverhampton. Join M54 at Junction 1 then as Junction 3 above. PARK: Easy. TEL: 3131/2. SER: Valuations; restorations (furniture and oils); interior design; export.

ATCHAM, Nr. Shrewsbury

Mytton Antiques

Norton Cross Roads. (M.A. and E.A. Nares.) Est. 1972. Open 10.30—5 or by appointment. SIZE: Medium. *STOCK: General antiques, especially longcase clocks.* LOC: On A5 between Shrewsbury and Wellington. PARK: Own. TEL: Uppington (095 286) 229 (24 hrs.) SER: Buys at auction. VAT: Stan/Spec.

BISHOPS CASTLE (0588)

The Cobbles Antiques

7 The Square. (R.J. and M.T. Gannon.) Est. 1972. Open Thurs. and Fri. 10—5, Tues. 10—1 and 2—4, Sat. 10—1, or by appointment, anytime to trade. SIZE: Large + warehouse. *STOCK: Victorian and mahogany furniture, pianos, shipping furniture, 19th—20th C, £50—£1,500; decorative items — china, glass, metalware, clocks.* LOC: A49. PARK: Reasonable. TEL: 638040; home — 638240. SER: Valuations; packing; shipping. VAT: Stan/Spec.

BRIDGNORTH (074 62)

John Astill Antiques

4 St. John St., Low Town. Est. 1947. Open 8.30am—9pm. SIZE: Medium. *STOCK: Furniture, Victorian, £5—£150; furniture, oak and walnut, 18th C, £6—£400; furniture, George III, £20—£300; bric-a-brac; glass; porcelain.* LOC: From Kidderminster and Stourbridge enter Bridgnorth by St. John St. PARK: 50yds. and opposite before shop and 10yds. after. TEL: 3440.

Bakehouse Antiques

6 St. John St., Low Town. (C.P. Dixon.) Est. 1971. Open 10—5.30. SIZE: Medium. *STOCK: Country furniture, mostly oak, some mahogany, mainly 18th C, £50—£700; copper, brass, £20—£80; decorative pottery and porcelain, £10—£50; all 18th—19th C.* LOC: In one-way street approx. 100yds. off Cann Hall by-pass. PARK: Easy. TEL: 3227. VAT: Stan/Spec.

English Heritage

2 Whitburn St., High Town. (J.I. White.) Est. 1980. CL: Thurs. Open 9.30—6. SIZE: Medium. *STOCK: General antiques, especially maps and prints.* LOC: Just off High St. PARK: In High St. TEL: 2097. SER: Framing, buys at auction, import/export. VAT: Stan/Spec.

Pauline Norton Galleries *Trade Only*

Bank St. Est. 1963. CL: Thurs. Open 10.30—1 and 2—5.30 or by appointment. SIZE: Medium. *STOCK: Oil and watercolour paintings, 19th C, £5—£3,000; miniatures, 18th—19th C, £50—£1,000.* LOC: Bank St. is opposite G.P.O. in High St. PARK: Listley St. TEL: 4889. SER: Restorations (paintings); framing. FAIRS: Local. VAT: Spec.

CHURCH STRETTON (0694)

Old Barn Antiques **LAPADA**

High St. (Lt. Col. and Mrs. D.W. Witting.) Est. 1980. CL: Mon., Wed. and Sun. except by appointment. Open 10.15—5.15. SIZE: Medium. *STOCK: Furniture, Georgian—Edwardian; general antiques, porcelain, silver. Not stocked: Coins, jewellery, books and militaria.* LOC: Off A49. PARK: Bucks Head car park at rear. TEL: 723742; home — 722294. VAT: Stan/Spec.

Stretton Antiques

5 The Square. (H.A. Davies.) Est. 1967. CL: Tues. and Wed. Open 11—5. *STOCK: General antiques, militaria.* LOC: Off A49 in old town centre square. PARK: Easy. TEL: 723526.

)GE HOUSE
OF
CHLEY

STMENT PIECES, ELEGANT FURNITURE OR
EPTIONAL CONDITION AT DOVERIDGE FOR
D PRICES

ANE, NR. SHIFNAL, SHROPSHIRE TF11 8PJ
S: ANTIQUES, SHIFNAL, ENGLAND
Birmingham International Airport. 2 hours Inter-city
rrangements can be made for private aircraft.
10A via M54 for North (& Mid) Wales. Leave at
CHLEY signpost, immediately right into LONG LANE.
pton. Join M54 at Junction 1 then as Junction 3 above.

CRAVEN ARMS   (058 82)
Cartwright and Co.
Stokesay Antiques, Shrewsbury Rd. CL: Sun. except by appointment. Open 9—5.30. STOCK: General antiques. LOC: A49. PARK: Easy. TEL: 2263. SER: Restorations (furniture). VAT: Stan/Spec.

Pym Antiques
6 Market St. (J. and S. Pym). Resident. Est. 1980. CL: Wed. Open 9.30—1 and 2—5. SIZE: Medium. STOCK: China, glass, jewellery, silver, 19th—20th C, £5—£100. LOC: Off A49. PARK: Nearby. TEL: 2497. FAIRS: Local.

Stokesay Antiques
Shrewsbury Rd. (J.I. and S. Briscoe.) Open 9—6. STOCK: Unstripped pine, shipping goods, treen, country items, bric-a-brac, 19th to early 20th C. TEL: 2263; home — Clun (05884) 374.

DORRINGTON   (074 373)
Nr. Shrewsbury
D.J. Wakeman and Co. Ltd.
                            LAPADA
Grove Farmhouse. CL: Sat. and Sun., except by appointment. SIZE: Medium. STOCK: Furniture up to and including 19th C. LOC: On A49. VAT: Stan/Spec.

ELLESMERE   (069 171)
White Lion Antiques
Market St. (Mrs. D. Wheeldon.) Est. 1966. STOCK: Furniture, clocks, pottery, porcelain, glass. TEL: 2335.

IRONBRIDGE   (095 245)
Bill Dickenson
Tudor House Antiques, 11 Tontine Hill. Open 10—5.30, Sun. 2.30—5.30. STOCK: General antiques especially porcelain, including Caughley and Coalport. LOC: Opposite bridge. TEL: 3783.

Ironbridge Antique Centre
Dale End. (F.G. Cooke.) Est. 1968. Open 10—5, Sat. 10—6, Sun. 2—6. SIZE: Large. STOCK: Porcelain, 1800—1950, £1—£3,000; furniture, £20—£1,000; pictures, jewellery, general antiques and bric-a-brac, 50p—£1,000; all 1700—1930. PARK: Easy. TEL: 3784. SER: Valuations; restorations (cabinet making); buys at auction.

LUDLOW   (0584)
Antique Corner
5 Corve St. (A.J. Sciville and J. Clegg.) Est. 1960. Open 10—6. STOCK: Country furniture, unstripped pine, treen, china, metalware. TEL: 3176; home — Bromfield (058 477) 468.

Ludlow continued
D.W. and A.B. Bayliss
22 Old St. Resident. STOCK: Furniture, 18th—19th C; silver, decorative items. TEL: 3634. SER: Valuations.

Beaker Antiques
29 Corve St. (M. and L. Riley.) Est. 1983. Open 9—5.30, Sun. by appointment. SIZE: Small. STOCK: English oak and country furniture, 17th—18th C, £200—£3,000; treen, 17th—19th C, £50—£500; carvings, 16th—17th C, £200— £1,000. Not stocked: Victoriana. LOC: Opposite Cattle Market. PARK: Easy. TEL: 5793; home — Stoke St. Milborough (058 475) 315. SER: Buys at auction (country furniture). VAT: Spec.

Castle Lodge
(D.G. and H.J. Pearce.) CL: Thurs. p.m. Open 9—5.30, but appointment always advisable. SIZE: Large. STOCK: 16th—17th C oak and walnut furniture. LOC: Nr. the castle. PARK: Easy. TEL: 2833. VAT: Spec .

R.G. Cave and Sons Ltd.   BADA
                                   LAPADA
17 Broad St. Est. 1962. Resident. Open 9.30—6. STOCK: Furniture, 1630—1830; clocks, barometers, metalwork, fine art and collectors' items. PARK: Easy. TEL: 3568. SER: Valuations. VAT: Spec.

Country House Antiques
29 Corve St. Open 9—5.30. STOCK: Furniture, 18th to early 19th C; boxes, glass, metalware and decorative items. PARK: Easy. TEL: 5765; home — (054 73) 684.

I. and S. Antiques
Gravel Hill. (J.I. and S. Briscoe.) Est. 1970. CL: Thurs. Open 9—5. SIZE: Medium. STOCK: Unstripped pine, shipping goods, treen, country items, bric-a-brac, 19th to early 20th C. PARK: Easy. TEL: 5718; home — Clun (05884) 374. SER: Containers. VAT: Stan/Spec.

Ludlow Antiques Centre
29 Corve St. (A.D. Arnsby.) SIZE: Large. STOCK: Furniture, 17th C to Edwardian; ceramics, paintings, clocks, brass, copper, pewter, treen. TEL: 5157, home — Stoke St. Milborough (058 475) 330.

The William Marler Gallery
Dawes Mansion, Church St. Est. 1975. CL: Thurs p.m. Open 9.30—5. SIZE: Medium. STOCK: Wildlife and sporting paintings and watercolours, £100—£15,000; signed proofs and prints, £5—£1,000; all 19th—20th C. LOC: Town centre near church. PARK: Nearby. TEL: 4160. SER: Valuations; restorations (oil paintings, watercolours and prints); framing. VAT: Stan/Spec.

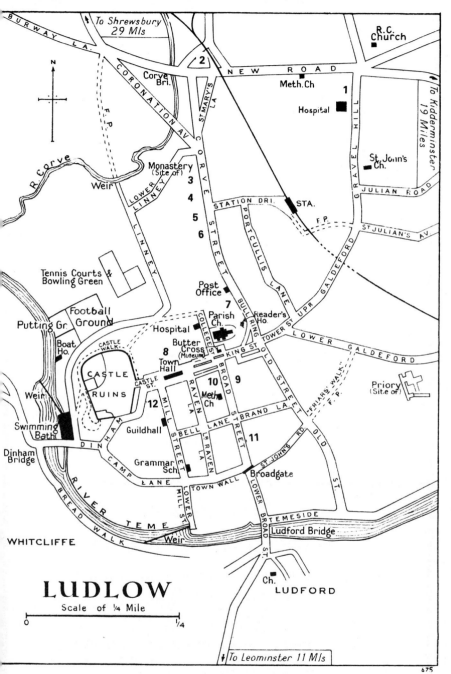

LUDLOW

Scale of ¼ Mile

0   ¼

STREET PLAN OF LUDLOW

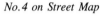

BEAKER ANTIQUES

Specialists in 17th and 18th Century English country furniture

Export services available

Superbly carved 17th Century Oak Coffer

Martyn and Linda Riley
29 Corve Street
LUDLOW

Shop
Ludlow 5793

Home
Stoke St Milborough 315

No.5 on Street Map

Paul Smith

M & R TAYLOR
53 Broad Street
Ludlow
Tel: Ludlow 4169

No.10 on Street Map

17th to 19th century oak, mahogany and walnut furniture, treen and metalware.

Fine Furniture of Old England
Castle Lodge
Ludlow Shropshire Tel. 0584 2873
No. 12 on Street Map

Ludlow continued

Mitre House Antiques
Corve Bridge. (L. Jones.) Open 9—5.30.
STOCK: Clocks, pine and general antiques.
TEL: 2138.

Olivia Rumens   BADA
30 Corve St. Resident. Open 10—5. CL:
Thurs. *STOCK: English and Continental oil
paintings, 17th—18th C.* TEL: 3952. SER:
Restorations. VAT: Spec.

St. Leonards Antiques
Corve St. (A. Smith.) Open 9—5. There are 8
dealers at this centre selling *furniture, silver,
jewellery, porcelain, clocks, pictures, Oriental
carpets, brass, copper and interesting bygones.* TEL: 5573. SER: Restorations (clocks
and furniture).

Paul Smith   BADA
The Old Chapel, Old St. (P. and B. Smith.) Est.
1944. Appointment advisable. SIZE: Medium.
*STOCK: Furniture, mahogany, 1720—1810;
some oak and walnut.* Not stocked: Coins,
weapons, Victoriana. LOC: Town centre.
PARK: Easy, nearby. TEL: ?666. SER:
Valuations. VAT: Spec.

M. and R. Taylor (Antiques)
53 Broad St. (M. Taylor.) Est. 1977. Open
from 9 a.m. including evenings. SIZE:
Medium. *STOCK: Furniture, mahogany, oak
and walnut, Persian rugs, brass and copper,
17th—19th C.* PARK: Nearby. TEL: 4169;
home — same. VAT: Stan/Spec.

Teme Valley Antiques
1 The Bull Ring. (C.S. Harvey.) Est. 1979.
Usually open 10—5.30, Sun. by appointment.
SIZE: Medium. *STOCK: English and Continental porcelain, 18th to early 20th C, £25—
£2,000; furniture, oil and watercolour paintings, 17th to early 20th C, £50—£800; silver,
plate, metalware and glass, 18th—19th C,
£10—£500.* Not stocked: Militaria, coins and
carpets. LOC: Town centre opposite Boots.
PARK: Easy. TEL: 4686. SER: Valuations;
buys at auction (porcelain). VAT: Stan/Spec.

Stanley Woolston   BADA
                                 LAPADA
29 Broad St. Est. 1910. Resident, seldom
closed. SIZE: Medium. *STOCK: Furniture,
Georgian and earlier; general antiques, small
and decorative items, country pieces, fabrics.*
LOC: Very near Broad Gate, south from
Buttercross. PARK: Easy. TEL: 3554. SER:
Valuations; interior decoration. VAT: Stan/
Spec.

MARKET DRAYTON   (0630)

Steve Sutcliffe
20 and 22 Stafford St. CL: Thurs. Open
9.30—5. *STOCK: Maps, prints.* TEL: 2069.

MINSTERLEY

Bryan Bird Antiques
Lower Farm House, Hem Lane, Westley. Est.
1966. Resident, usually available but Sun. and
evenings by appointment. SIZE: Medium.
*STOCK: Clocks — longcase, carriage, Vien-
nese and English fusee, skeletons, American
and German wall, £85—£2,000; country
furniture, oak and pine, 18th—19th C, £30—
£2,000; Victorian and Georgian furniture,
brass, copper, paintings and collectors' items;
shipping goods.* LOC: Take A488 from
Shrewsbury by-pass (A5). Turn off at small
roundabout towards Westbury. Turn left after
1½ miles into Hem Lane, premises (15th C.
farmhouse) on left. TEL: Shrewsbury (0743)
790146. SER: Valuations; restorations (clock
parts made, gear cutting; furniture); buys at
auction. VAT: Spec.

MUCH WENLOCK   (0952)

Adela Johnson Antiques
5 Wilmore St. (Mrs. A. Johnson.) Est. 1977.
CL: Wed. Open 10.30—5.30. SIZE: Small.
*STOCK: Jewellery and general antiques, all
periods to art deco, £1—£300; furniture,
including stripped pine, unusual Georgian and
Victorian, £20—£500; curios, lighting (oil and
electric), objets d'art, £1—£250.* Not stocked:
Weapons and coins. LOC: Opposite church.
PARK: Easy. TEL: 727479; home — same.

Wenlock Antiques
61 High St. (K.C. Howard.) Est. 1965. Open
9—5.30. SIZE: Medium. *STOCK: Country
furniture, mainly 18th C, £50—£750; copper
and brass, £20—£80; decorative pottery and
porcelain, £20—£200, both 18th—19th C.*
LOC: On main Shrewsbury to Bridgnorth road.
PARK: Easy. TEL: Telford (0952) 727271.
VAT: Stan/Spec.

IS YOUR ENTRY CORRECT?
If there is even the slightest
inaccuracy in your entry, *please* let us
know before 1st January 1987.
GUIDE TO THE
ANTIQUE SHOPS OF BRITAIN
5 Church Street, Woodbridge, Suffolk.

NEWPORT (0952)

Worth's
34 St. Mary's St. (G.F.E. Worth.) Resident. Est. 1932. CL: Thurs. and lunch hours. SIZE: Medium. *STOCK: General antiques, 19th C; shipping goods, antiquarian books.* LOC: Opposite church on main A41. PARK: Easy. TEL: 810122. VAT: Stan/Spec.

OSWESTRY (0691)

The Antique Shop
King St. Est. 1963. Open 9—5, Sun. by appointment. *STOCK: General antiques and secondhand goods; Victoriana, bric-a-brac.* TEL: 653011. VAT: Stan.

Little Raven Antiques
11 Albion Hill. (G.A. and B. Fogg.) Est. 1969. CL: Thurs. Open 10—4. SIZE: Small. *STOCK: Jewellery, 18th C, £50—£100; ceramics, 18th—19th C, £25—£50; small furniture, to £300.* LOC: Near market. TEL: 652172.

Willow Antiques
92 Willow St. (J. Weston.) CL: Mon. and Thurs. Open 9.30—5. *STOCK: General antiques, porcelain, glass, Victoriana, furniture, bric-a-brac, china.* TEL: 661640.

SHIFNAL

Broadway Antiques
25 Broadway. (Mrs. E. Onions.) Est. 1968. Resident. SIZE: Medium. *STOCK: Oak and country furniture, 17th—19th C; brass, copper, metalware.* LOC: Town centre on Newport Rd. PARK: Easy. TEL: Telford (0952) 460997. VAT: Stan/Spec.

Nigel Collins (Fine Books) At the Southgate Gallery
20 Market Place. Est. 1973. CL: Mon. and Thurs. Open 10—5, Sat. 10—1. *STOCK: New and out of print books and catalogues on predominately British art, especially 20th C.* TEL: Telford (0952) 460351.

Southgate Gallery
20 Market Place. (J. Constable, N. Collins.) Est. 1968. CL: Mon. and Thurs. Open 10—4.30, Sat. 10—1 or by appointment. *STOCK: Watercolours and oil paintings, 19th—20th C.* TEL: Telford (0952) 460351. SER: Valuations; restorations.

Martin and Ruth Taylor Antiques   LAPADA
Rear of 6 Broadway. Est. 1975. Open by appointment. SIZE: Warehouse. *STOCK: Oak and mahogany, 17th—19th C; Georgian, Victorian, Edwardian and shipping goods.* LOC: Town centre, on Newport road. PARK: Easy. TEL: Telford (0952) 461504. SER: Valuations; restorations. VAT: Stan/Spec.

SHREWSBURY (0743)

Candle Lane Books
28—29 Princess St. (J. Thornhill.) Open 9.30—5. *STOCK: Antiquarian and second-hand books.* TEL: 65301.

Castle Gate Antiques
15 Castle Gates. (E. Birch.) Est. 1963. CL: Thurs. Open 10—4.30. *STOCK: English and Oriental pottery and porcelain, 18th and 19th C; country furniture, 17th and 18th C; general antiques.* TEL: Evenings — 61011.

Hutton Antiques
18 Princess St. (Mrs. P.I. Hutton.) Est. 1978. CL: Thurs. Open 9.30—12.30 and 1.30—5. SIZE: Medium. *STOCK: Silver, porcelain and glass, 18th—19th C, £50—£200; watercolours, 19th—20th C, £80—£200; small furniture, 18th—19th C, £125—£500; Victorian jewellery.* LOC: Off square, near Music Hall. PARK: Easy. TEL: 245810. SER: Valuations.

Lantern Antiques
5 and 6 Milk St. (Mr. and Mrs. A. Love.) Est. 1960. CL: Sat. p.m. and Thurs. Open 9.30—1 and 2.30—5. SIZE: Large. *STOCK: Furniture, pre-1890, £25—£300; china, pre-1930, £1—£100; glass, pre-1900, £1—£70; small silver.* LOC: Town centre up Wyle Cop. 1st turn left to High St., then 1st left again to Milk St. Side door on left opposite Old St. Chad's Church. PARK: 50yds. TEL: 3783. SER: Valuations (furniture, china, glass); buys at auction.

The Little Gem
18 St. Mary's St. (M.A. Bowdler.) Est. 1969. Open 9—5.30. SIZE: Medium. *STOCK: Georgian and Victorian jewellery, Coalport china, maps, watercolours, small silver.* Not stocked: Weapons, coins, medals, furniture. LOC: Opposite St. Mary's Church along from G.P.O. PARK: In side road (St. Mary's Place) opposite shop. TEL: 52085.

F.C. Manser and Son Ltd.
53/54 Wyle Cop. (G. Manser and family.) Est. 1944. CL: Thurs. p.m. Open 9—1 and 2—5.30. SIZE: Large. *STOCK: Furniture, 17th—20th C, £50—£15,000; Oriental items, 15th—20th C, £5—£2,000; silver, plate, copper, 18th—20th, £5—£2,000; jewellery, linen and lace.* Not stocked: Coins, medals. LOC: 150yds. town side of English bridge. PARK: Own. TEL: 51120 and 245730. SER: Valuations; restorations. VAT: Stan/Spec.

Shrewsbury continued

Mill House Antiques
139 Abbey Foregate. (Fine Art Services Ltd.) Est. 1963. Open 9−2 and 3−5.30, Sat. 9−4, Sun. 10−2, or by appointment. SIZE: Medium. *STOCK; English furniture and English and European porcelain, 18th C; silver, jewellery, oriental rugs, firearms, paintings and watercolours, all 19th C.* LOC: From A5 to town centre, just past Lord Hill Hotel. PARK: Easy. TEL: 240327/8; home − same. SER: Valuations; restorations (oil paintings); framing; buys at auction. VAT: Spec.

Nevill Antiques
9−10 Milk St. (R. Nevill.) Est. 1974. CL: Thurs. Open 9.30−1 and 2−5. SIZE: Medium. *STOCK: Furniture, 18th−19th C; ceramics, glass, silver and plate, rugs, topographical books.* LOC: Town centre up Wyle Cop. TEL: 51013. SER: Restorations; polishing; repairs to locks. VAT: Stan/Spec.

Raleigh Antiques
1A Greyfriars Rd., Coleham. (R. and G. Handbury-Madin.) Est. 1971. CL: Thurs. p.m. and Sat. Open 10−1 and 2−5. SIZE: Small. *STOCK: General antiques, £5−£200.* PARK: Easy. TEL: 59552. SER: Valuations; restorations (furniture).

Raleigh House
23 Belle Vue Rd. (R. and G. Handbury-Madin.) Est. 1968. Open 10−5. *STOCK: Furniture, £50−£1,000.* PARK: Easy. TEL: 59552. SER: Valuations; restorations (furniture, clocks).

Michael Robertson
Est. 1974. Open by appointment only. *STOCK: Jewellery including secondhand.* TEL: Bomere Heath (0939) 290612.

Severn Fine Art
77 Wyle Cop. (G. Hancock.) Open 9−5.30, Sun. and evenings by appointment. SIZE: Small. *STOCK: Oil paintings and watercolours, 19th to early 20th C, £250−£2,500.* LOC: Town centre. PARK: Easy. TEL: 247514; home − same. SER: Valuations; restorations; buys at auction (19th−20th C pictures).

Shrewsbury Antique Centre
15 Princess House, The Sq. (J. Langford.) Est. 1978. Open 9.30−5.30 including Sun. SIZE: Large. There are 37 dealers at this centre offering *a wide range of general antiques and collectables.* LOC: Town centre just off the Sq. PARK: Nearby. TEL: 247704. SER: Valuations; restorations (furniture, pictures and silver).

Shrewsbury continued

Shrewsbury Antique Market
Frankwell Quay Warehouse. (Vintagevale Ltd.) Open 10−5.30, Sun. 12−5. SIZE: Large. This market consists of 45 lock-up and open units from which the dealers sell *a wide range of general antiques and collectors' items, £1−£2,000.* LOC: Alongside Frankwell Quay car park. PARK: Easy. TEL: 50916. SER: Valuations; restorations including taxidermy.

Silk Road
23 Wyle Cop. (A. Turner.) Est. 1982. CL: Thurs. p.m. Open 10.30−5.30. SIZE: Medium. *STOCK: Oriental and English porcelain, 18th−19th C, £5−£500; Korean furniture, £150−£2,000; Chinese paintings, embroideries, clothes, ivories and snuff boxes; English carpentry tools, bric-a-brac, linen.* LOC: Town centre. PARK: Nearby. TEL: 67889. SER: Valuations. FAIRS: Century, London. VAT: Stan/Spec.

Michael Smith Antiques
39 St. John's Hill. Est. 1974. CL: Sat. p.m. Open 10−1 and 2−5. SIZE: Medium. *STOCK: Furniture, 17th−19th C, £10−£4,000; decorative and collectors' items.* LOC: Town centre near St. Chad's church. TEL: 56439. VAT: Stan/Spec.

Vintage Fishing Tackle Shop and Angling Art Gallery
103 Longden Coleman. (C. Partington). Resident. Est. 1977. Open Sat. 10−6, other days by appointment. SIZE: Small. *STOCK: Angling items, from 1496 to date, mainly under £100.* LOC: A5, next to cemetery. PARK: Nearby. TEL: 69373. SER: Valuations; restorations (rods, reels); buys at auction. VAT: Stan/Spec.

TERN HILL   (063 083)
Nr. Market Drayton
A.J. and L. Onions − White Cottage Antiques
White Cottage, 8 Tern Hill. Est. 1965. Open 9.30−5.30. SIZE: Medium. *STOCK: 17th−19th C furniture, copper, brass, iron, longcase clocks.* LOC: On A41, 200yds. from traffic lights at Tern Hill. PARK: Easy. TEL: 222. VAT: Stan/Spec.

WEST FELTON, Nr. Oswestry
West Felton Antiques
(H.T.N. Gommers.) Est. 1967. Open 9−6, seven days. SIZE: Large. *STOCK: Furniture, and accessories 18th−19th C.* LOC: 12 miles north of Shrewsbury on A5. PARK: Easy. TEL: Queens Head (069 188) 335. VAT: Stan/Spec.

A.J.Onions & L.Onions

White Cottage — Antiques, 8 Tern Hill, Market Drayton, Shropshire. Tel. — Tern Hill 222

17th C carved oak food cupboard with pierced decorative panels in lower doors.

Early 18th C sectional oak bureau with well compartment.

WHITCHURCH (0948)

Dodington Antiques
15 Dodington. (G. MacGillivray.) Resident. Est. 1978. Always open. SIZE: Medium. STOCK: Oak, fruitwood, walnut and country furniture, mahogany and treen, £10—£1,500. LOC: On fringe of town centre, by Kwik Save. PARK: Easy. TEL: 3399. SER: Buys at auction. VAT: Stan/Spec.

Ellesmere House Antiques *Trade Only*
Dodington. (R. Whitney.) Usually open but appointment advisable. SIZE: Medium. STOCK: Early oak and country furniture, related items. TEL: 4084.

WHITTINGTON, Nr. Oswestry

Trefor-Jones Antiques
The Old Poste House, Three Trees. (P. Trefor-Jones.) Est. 1960. CL: Mon. and Thurs. Open 11—4.30, Sun. by appointment. SIZE: Medium. STOCK: Pot-lids, fairings, Staffordshire figures, £25—£100; dolls, accessories, costume; Oriental porcelain and metalwork, £20—£300; silver, plate, general items. Not stocked: Jewellery, coins. LOC: Shop at junction of A5 and A495. 50yds. from White Lion Inn. PARK: Easy. TEL: Oswestry (0691) 662312.

WOORE, Nr. Crewe

The Mount
12 Nantwich Rd. Est. 1978. CL: Wed. SIZE: Small. STOCK: Bric-a-brac, 19th to early 20th C, £5—£25; local maps, prints and views, £2—£250. LOC: Junction of A51 and A525. PARK: Easy. TEL: Pipe Gate (063 081) 274; home — same. SER: Repairs; buys at auction.

WORFIELD, (074 64) Nr. Bridgnorth

Old Vicarage Gallery
(P. Iles). Est. 1983. Open 9—5 including Sun. SIZE: Large. STOCK: Victorian watercolours and prints. LOC: Between A442 and A454. PARK: Easy. TEL: 497 and 498. VAT: Stan.

Somerset

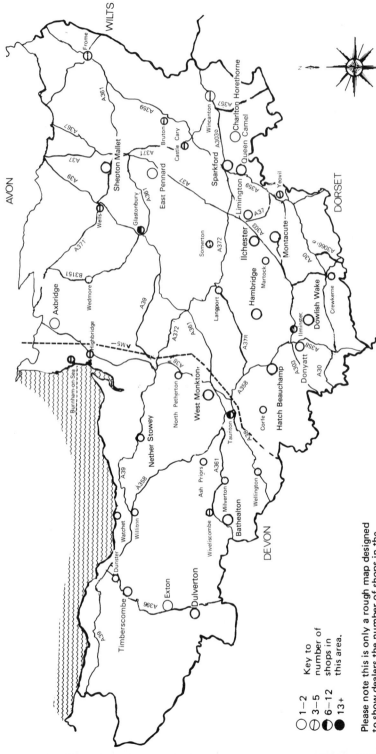

WILTS

AVON

DORSET

DEVON

Frome

A361

A359

A367

A37

A39

A361

Shepton Mallet

Bruton

A371

Castle Cary

Wincanton

A357

Charlton Horethorne

A3030

Queen Camel

Sparkford

Glastonbury

East Pennard

Wells

A371

A37

Somerton

A372

Limington

A359

A37

Yeovil

Ilchester

A303

Montacute

A30

A3066

Axbridge

Wedmore

B3151

A39

Langport

A372

A361

Hambridge

Martock

Dowlish Wake

Crewkerne

Highbridge

A5

Burnham-on-Sea

North Petherton

A38

West Monkton

Taunton

A38

Corfe

Hatch Beauchamp

A358

A37R

Ilminster

A358

A303

Donyatt

A30

Nether Stowey

A39

Watchet

Williton

Dunster

A358

Ash Priors

A361

Milverton

Bathealton

Wellington

Wiveliscombe

Timberscombe

A396

Exton

Dulverton

A39

Key to
number of
shops in
this area.

1–2
3–5
6–12
13+

Please note this is only a rough map designed
to show dealers the number of shops in the
various towns, and is not necessarily totally
accurate.

The Granary Galleries

(RICHARD HALL)

**LARGE STOCK
ENGLISH &
CONTINENTAL
FURNITURE
PORCELAIN
OIL PAINTINGS
SHIPPING GOODS**

**OLD COUNTRY PINE.
DRESSERS, TABLES,
etc.**

Court House, Ash Priors, Nr. Bishops Lydeard, Taunton, Somerset
Route A358 out of Taunton on the Minehead Road
Tel Bishops Lydeard (0823) 432402, private (0823) 432816 after 6.30 pm

---

ASH PRIORS, Nr. Taunton

The Granary Galleries
Court House. (R. Hall.) Est. 1969. Open 8.30—5.30. SIZE: Large. *STOCK: Period items, general antiques, 18th—19th C furniture, some shipping goods.* PARK: Easy. TEL: Bishop's Lydeard (0823) 432402; home after 6.30 Bishop's Lydeard (0823) 432816. VAT: Stan/Spec.

Hall's Antiques
Court House. (A.R. and J.M. Hall.) Est. 1945. CL: Sun. except by appointment. Open 8.30—5.30. SIZE: Large. *STOCK: English and Continental furniture, 18th—19th C; oil paintings, watercolours, 17th—19th C; all £25— £10,000; shipping goods.* LOC: On A358. PARK: Easy. TEL: Bishop's Lydeard (0823) 432402; home — same. SER: Valuations; buys at auction. VAT: Stan/Spec.

AXBRIDGE   (0934)

N.J. Arlidge
The Corner House Gallery, The Square. Est. 1982. Open Sat. a.m. or anytime by appointment. SIZE: Small. *STOCK: Watercolours, 18th—19th C, £100—£750; oil paintings, 1750—1900, £200—£2,000.* LOC: Town centre. PARK: Easy. TEL: 732757; home — same. SER: Buys at auction.

IS YOUR ENTRY CORRECT?
If there is even the slightest inaccuracy in your entry, *please* let us know before 1st January 1987.
GUIDE TO THE
ANTIQUE SHOPS OF BRITAIN
5 Church Street, Woodbridge, Suffolk.

CHARLES READ

Bathealton Court,
Taunton, Somerset
TA4 2AJ

Tel: Wiveliscombe (0984)
23225

*fine eighteenth and early
nineteenth century furniture and
decorative objects, displayed in
this classical Charles II
country house*

Open: By appointment

BATHEALTON, Nr. Taunton

Charles Read
Bathealton Court. Est. 1978. Open by appointment. SIZE: Medium. *STOCK: Period furniture, pre-1840 especially Georgian mahogany; decorative items, both £40—£4,000.* LOC: Off A361 3 miles from Milverton centre. PARK: Easy. TEL: Wiveliscombe (0984) 23225; home — same. SER: Valuations; interior design/decoration. VAT: Spec.

BRUTON   (0749)

Bruton Gallery
(M. Le Marchant.) SIZE: Large. *STOCK: 19th—20th C European sculpture.* TEL: 2205/2697. VAT: Stan/Spec.

Michael Lewis Gallery
17 High St. Est. 1953. Open 9—6, Sun. by appointment. SIZE: Large. *STOCK: Maps, 1575—1850, £20—£500; prints, 1700—1900, £10—£250; rare books, 1500—1980, £5—£500.* LOC: A359. PARK: Easy. TEL: 813557; home — same. SER: Bookbinding and picture framing. VAT: Stan.

Marksdanes Antiques Ltd.
Station Rd. SIZE: Large. *STOCK: Victorian furniture, shipping goods.* TEL: 813267. VAT: Stan.

Bruton continued

Peter Murray Antique Exports
Station Rd. Resident. Est. 1969. Open 8.30—6, weekends by appointment. SIZE: Large. *STOCK: Georgian, Victorian, Edwardian and later furniture, smalls, shipping items.* PARK: Easy. TEL: 812417. SER: Valuations; export; packing; shipping; courier. VAT: Stan/Spec.

BURNHAM-ON-SEA   (0278)

Adam Antiques
30 Adam St. (S. and R. Coombes.) Est. 1977. Open 9—1 and 2—5.30. SIZE: Large. *STOCK: Furniture, clocks, brass, porcelain and shipping goods.* PARK: Easy. TEL: 783193.

C.T. Culverwell
Victoria St. (B.G. and C.P. Blake.) Est. 1920. Open 9—1 and 2—5.30. SIZE: Large. *STOCK: Furniture, £5—£1,000; silver, £1—£1,000; jewellery, £1—£800.* LOC: Next to church and GPO. PARK: Easy. TEL: 782307; home — 784662. VAT: Stan/Spec.

Terence Kelly Antiques
1 Cross St. Est. 1965. CL: Thurs. p.m. and Sat. p.m. Open 9.30—5 or by appointment. SIZE: Medium. *STOCK: Furniture, pottery, porcelain, paintings, metalware, antiquities and primitive art.* PARK: Easy. TEL: 782129; home — 785052. SER: Valuations. VAT: Stan/Spec.

CASTLE CARY   (0963)

Cary Antiques Ltd.
2 High St. (Mrs. J.A. Oldham.) Est. 1977. CL: Wed. Open 10—5.30. SIZE: Small. *STOCK: Furniture, Victorian and Edwardian, £30—£500; china, brass and copper, glass, bric-a-brac, pictures, 18th—19th C, £5—£150.* LOC: Town centre, B3152. PARK: Easy. TEL: 50437. SER: Valuations; picture framing; caning and rushing; repairs (china).

Domus
Woodcock St. (P.S. Pearson.) Est. 1976. CL: Thurs. p.m. and Sun. except by appointment. Open 10—1 and 2—5.30, Sat. 10—1 and 2—5. SIZE: Large. *STOCK: Pine furniture, 18th—19th C, £30—£700; decorative china and glass, 19th to early 20th C.* LOC: Town centre. PARK: Easy. TEL: 50912; home — 50489. SER: Valuations; restorations (pine); buys at auction (furniture). FAIRS: Bath and West Showground. VAT: Stan/Spec.

Longley's Antiques
1 High St. (J. Longley and A. Gregory.) Est. 1959. Open daily. SIZE: Small. *STOCK: General antiques, £5—£500.* PARK: Easy. TEL: 51259.

John Martin Antiques
Woodcock St. Est. 1975. Open 9.30—5.30. STOCK: Clocks, watches, copper and brass, oil lamps, decorative items, jewellery, furniture. TEL: 50733.

CHARLTON HORETHORNE
Nr. Sherborne
Rosemary and David White   LAPADA
Trade Only

The Forge. Resident. Est. 1970. Open daily, Sat. and Sun. by appointment. SIZE: Large. *STOCK: Furniture, 18th—19th C, decorative items.* LOC: B3145, midway between Wincanton and Sherborne. PARK: Easy. TEL: Corton Denham (096 322) 347. SER: Restoration (furniture). VAT: Stan/Spec.

CORFE, Nr. Taunton
Grange Court Antiques
(Mr. and Mrs. P.M. Halliday Hawker.) Est. 1800. CL: Fri., Sat. and Sun. SIZE: Large. *STOCK: Country furniture, stripped pine, oak and elm, treen, £1—£600.* LOC: B3170. From Taunton Grange Court driveway is on right entering village. PARK: Easy. TEL: Blagdon Hill (082 342) 498. VAT: Stan.

CREWKERNE   (0460)
Crewkerne Antique Centre
42 East St. (S. Hallah.) Open 9.30—5.30. SIZE: Large. There are 12 dealers at this centre offering *English and European country furniture and decorative items.* TEL: 76755.

Crewkerne Furniture Emporium
20-22 East St. (J. Wells and A.P. Bucke.) Est. 1974. Open 9—5.30. *STOCK: Furniture, shipping goods, collectors' items, horse-drawn and agricultural bygones.* TEL: 75319.

Oscars
13—15 Market Square and North St. (B.J. and H.M. Hall.) Est. 1966. Open 10—5.30. SIZE: Large. *STOCK: Victoriana, Georgiana, furniture; shipping goods.* LOC: Centre of the square on A30. PARK: Easy. TEL: 72718. VAT: Stan/Spec.

DONYATT, Nr. Ilminster
Something Old
Church Cottage. (Mrs. M.A. Wood). Resident. Est. 1980. Open 10.15—6, Sat. 11—6, Sun. p.m. by appointment. SIZE: Small. *STOCK: Pottery and porcelain, 1765—1875, £5—£75; bric-a-brac, 1880—1930, £1—£15; small furniture, 1870—1900, £15—£65.* Not stocked: Art deco. LOC: From A303, take A358. PARK: Easy. TEL: Ilminster (046 05) 4283.

DOWLISH WAKE, Nr. Ilminster
Dowlish Wake Antiques
(Mrs. G. Estling.) Est. 1973. Open 10—1 and 2.30—5.30, Sun. by appointment. SIZE: Medium. *STOCK: Ceramics only — English porcelain and pottery, late 18th C to early 20th C.* LOC: From A303 or A30 take Ilminster/Crewkerne road and turn off at Kingstone corner, downhill to village. PARK: Easy. TEL: Ilminster (046 05) 2784; home — same. VAT: Stan/Spec.

DULVERTON   (0398)
Dulverton Antique Centre
Lower Town Hall. (D. Gregory.) Open 10—5. SIZE: Small. *STOCK: Furniture, 18th—19th C, £100—£700; silver, 18th—20th C, £5—£500; oil paintings, £50—£250; watercolours, £20—£250; U.K. philatelic items, £1—£250.* LOC: Town centre. PARK: Easy, nearby. TEL: 23522; home — 23843. SER: Valuations; restorations; plating; buys at auction. VAT: Spec.

Rothwell and Dunworth
2 Bridge St. (Mrs. C. Rothwell and M. Dunworth.) ABA. Est. 1975. Open 10.30—1 and 2.30—5, Sat. 10.30—1. SIZE: Medium. *STOCK: Antiquarian and secondhand books especially on hunting and horses.* LOC: 1st shop in village over River Baile. PARK: 100yds. SER: Valuations; book-binding.

DUNSTER   (0643)
Nr. Minehead
Antiques
21 High St. Est. 1968.

"...and think they have reformed religion because they have divested it of all that is cheerful..." From *Mr. Rowlandson's England* by Robert Southey ed. John Steel, published by the **Antique Collectors' Club,** 1985.

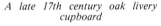
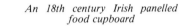
EAST PENNARD
Nr. Shepton Mallet
Pennard House   **LAPADA**
Trade Only
(M. and S. Dearden.) Est. 1979. Resident, always open. SIZE: Large. *STOCK: Pine furniture, 18th—19th C, £100—£2,000; French provincial tables, armoires, buffets, £300—£3,000.* LOC: From Shepton Mallet, 4 miles south off A37. PARK: Easy. TEL: Ditcheat (074 986) 266; home — same. SER: Valuations; restorations (pine and country furniture). VAT: Stan/Spec.

EXTON, Nr. Dulverton
A. Lodge-Mortimer
The Old School House. Open by appointment only. *STOCK: Porcelain and pottery, especially English Delftware and Oriental porcelain, £5—£2,000; small furniture and objets d'art, £5—£1,000; watercolours.* LOC: Just off A396 from Bridgetown on Dunster/Tiverton road. TEL: Winsford (064 385) 358. SER: Valuations; buys at auction; commissions undertaken; author and lecturer.

FROME   (0373)
Georgine Evers   *Trade only*
The Old Vicarage, Buckland Denham. Est. 1969. Resident. Open by appointment. *STOCK: Country, dairy and kitchen items, quilts, samplers, rugs, pottery, pictures and country furniture.* TEL: 61611.

Tom Hickman
10 Bath St. Open 9—6, appointment advisable. SIZE: Medium. *STOCK: Furniture, 17th—19th C; decorative and unusual items, pictures, needlework.* TEL: 73076. SER: Valuations; interior design.

Old Curiosity Shop
15 Catherine Hill. (R. and B. Hackett.) CL: Thurs. Open 10—1 and 2—5. *STOCK: Antiquarian books.* TEL: 64482.

Sutton and Sons
15 and 33 Vicarage St. *STOCK: Furniture, 18th—19th C; clocks, pictures, decorative pieces.* TEL: 62062. SER: Restorations and upholstery. VAT: Stan/Spec.

GLASTONBURY   (0458)
Abbey Antiques
51 High St. (G.E. Browning and Son.) Est. 1952. Open 9—5.30. SIZE: Large. *STOCK: Glass, furniture, longcase clocks, china, objets d'art, firearms.* TEL: 31694. VAT: Stan/Spec.

CHALON

Merchants of 18th and 19th Century European Country & Decorative Antiques

Old Hambridge Mill
Hambridge
Nr. Curry Rivel, Somerset
Tel: (0458) 252374

Please phone for appointment

Glastonbury continued

Abbots House
Benedict St. (Mrs. P. Elliott.) Est. 1973. *STOCK: Jewellery, silver; china, glass.* TEL: 32123.

Antiques Fair
Glastonbury Abbey Car Park, Market Place. Est. 1960. Open 9.30—6, (7 days in summer). *STOCK: Unusual and decorative items; furniture, Georgian and Victorian; jewellery.* TEL: 32939.

The Flintlock
17a High St. (F.W. Laver.) Est. 1965. CL: Wed. Open 9.30—1 and 2—5. SIZE: Medium. *STOCK: Firearms, £50—£500; militaria; both 19th C; medals, general ephemera, books, instruments, small furniture.* LOC: A361. PARK: At rear. TEL: 31525; home — 32813. SER: Valuations; restorations (metal and wood); buys at auction.

Heywood Antiques
67 High St. (J. Heywood.) Est. 1978. Open 10—5. *STOCK: Clocks, period furniture, metalware, glass, porcelain, pottery, pictures.* TEL: 31590 (any time). SER: Valuations; restorations. VAT: Spec.

Monarch Antiques
15 High St. (J.A. Badman.) Est. 1970. Open 9.45—5.45. SIZE: Medium. *STOCK: General antiques and collectors' items, religious items including icons, coins, military items, antiquities and weapons, £5—£1,000.* LOC: On A39. PARK: At rear. TEL: 32498. SER: Valuations; restorations (porcelain and pictures). VAT: Stan/Spec.

The Shop Upstairs
Crescent Antiquities, 15 High St. (C. Cooper.) *STOCK: Mid-Eastern and Oriental ceramics; antiquities of Palestine; small items and African bronze art.* TEL: 31599.

Glastonbury continued

Matthew Willis, Antique Clocks
3 Wells Rd. CL: Wed. p.m. Open 9—5. *STOCK: English, French and American clocks.* TEL: 32103.

HAMBRIDGE, Nr. Langport
Chalon U.K. Ltd.
LAPADA
Old Hambridge Mill. (N., M. and T. Chalon.) Est. 1974. Open by appointment. SIZE: Large. *STOCK: Pine — Continental, Irish, British; architectural and decorative items.* TEL: Langport (0458) 252374; home — Chard (0460) 67715. VAT: Stan/Spec.

HATCH BEAUCHAMP (0823)
Nr. Taunton
Old Forge Antiques
(J.E. and M.G. Cooke.) Resident. Est. 1980. Open every day. *STOCK: Country pine, painted and unusual items.* LOC: Midway between Taunton and Ilminster on A358, signposted to Hatch Beauchamp. PARK: Own. TEL: 480158.

HIGHBRIDGE
Colin Dyte Exports Ltd. LAPADA
Huntspill Rd. Open 8—6, Sat. 8—12, Sun. and Bank Holidays by appointment. *STOCK: General antiques, trade and shipping goods.* PARK: Easy. TEL: Burnham-on-Sea (0278) 788590 and 788605; home — Puriton (0278) 683761. SER: Packing and shipping; transport; documentation; courier.

T.M. Dyte Antiques
1 Huntspill Rd. Open 9—6. *STOCK: Shipping goods.* TEL: Burnham-on-Sea (0278) 786495.

Highbridge continued

Keith Griffiths Antiques/ Highbridge Antique Galleries

Est. 1952. Open 9.30−5.30. SIZE: Large. *STOCK: Trade and shipping goods, general furniture, especially chairs; garden furniture, collectable and small items.* LOC: On A38. PARK: Easy. TEL: Burnham-on-Sea (0278) 784521; home − Weston-super-Mare (0934) 27791. SER: Buys at auction. Courier service. VAT: Stan/Spec.

Terence Kelly Antiques

Huntspill Court, West Huntspill. Open by appointment. *STOCK: Furniture, decorative and collectors' items.* TEL: Burnham-on-Sea (0278) 785052.

The Treasure Chest Ltd.   *Trade Only*

The Jays, 19 Alstone Lane. (R.J. and V. Rumble.) Est. 1964. CL: Sun., except by appointment. SIZE: Medium. *STOCK: Furniture, £25−£1,000; china, glass, watches, £10−£500; all 18th−19th C and Victorian, musical boxes, 19th C, £200−£2,000; clocks, £10−£800.* LOC: Off A38 down lane by Royal Artillery public house, 200yds. on left. PARK: Easy. TEL: Burnham-on-Sea (0278) 787267. SER: Valuations; restorations (pictures and china); buys at auction. VAT: Stan/Spec.

ILCHESTER   (0935)

Ilchester Antique Pine

Church St. (R. Oram.) Open 9−5.30, Sat. 9−1, Sun. and evenings by appointment. *STOCK: Country pine, fruitwood, oak and elm, decorative ironwork, tools.* LOC: Just off A303. PARK: Easy. TEL: 841212.

ILMINSTER   (046 05)

Ray Best Antiques

North St. House. (R. and W. Best.) Est. 1964. Open 9.30−6, Sat. 11−3. Trade any time by appointment. SIZE: Medium. *STOCK: Furniture, £10−£3,000; clocks, £50−£2,000; metalware, £5−£500, all 17th−19th C; porcelain, glass, 18th−19th C, £5−£500; silver, country items, weapons.* Not stocked: Coins, stamps, medals. LOC: A3037. From London on A303 taking 2nd turning into Ilminster on left down one-way street. Shop is on right. PARK: Easy. TEL: 2194. SER: Buys at auction. VAT: Spec.

Country Antiques Centre

21-23 West St. (J. Barnard). Resident. Est. 1979. Open 10−5, Sun. by appointment. SIZE: Medium. There are 8 dealers at this centre selling a wide range of *furniture, including mahogany, ceramics, drinking glasses and general antiques, 18th−20th C.* LOC: On A303 to the west of town, at traffic lights crossing. PARK: Easy, at rear. TEL: 4151 or 2269. SER: Valuations.

Ilminster continued

Moolham Mill Antiques   BADA

Mainly Trade

Moolham Mill, Moolham Lane. (R. Cropper.) Est. 1966. CL: Sun., except by appointment. Open 9−6. SIZE: Medium. *STOCK: Oak furniture, 17th−18th C; mahogany furniture, 18th to early 19th C; Delft, pewter, 18th−19th C; metalwork, treen, decorative items, needleworks, samplers.* Not stocked: Silver, Victorian furniture. LOC: From Ilminster on A303 take A3037 for Chard. One mile from centre of Ilminster take road signposted to Dowlish Wake/Kingstone. Premises 300yds. on right. PARK: Easy. TEL: 2834. SER: Valuations; buys at auction. VAT: Spec.

J.A. Stancomb

Bullen Court, Broadway. Est. 1965. Open any time but appointment advisable. *STOCK: Silver.* LOC: From London A303, 2 miles beyond Ilminster. The Five Dials Inn on right, turn right around inn and 400yds. to river bridge. Gate at left on bridge. PARK: Easy. TEL: 2640; home − same. SER: Valuations. VAT: Spec.

LANGPORT   (0458)

Antique Dealers International

Bow St. (Antique Dealers International plc.) Open 8.30−6, Sat. and Sun. by appointment. SIZE: Large. *STOCK: English and Continental furniture, £200−£20,000; works of art − bronzes, paintings and porcelain, £100−£10,000; all 17th−19th C; designer and decorative items, £100−£5,000.* LOC: A378 adjacent river Parrat. 10 mins. M5, junction 25. PARK: Easy. TEL: 252977. SER: Valuations; restorations (furniture and pictures); buys at auction. VAT: Stan/Spec.

Shirley's Antiques

Bow St. (S.A. Hollard.) Est. 1958. Usually open. *STOCK: Shipping goods, furniture and smalls.* TEL: 250064.

LIMINGTON

Genges Farm Antiques

Genges Farm. (R. and P.M. Gilbert.) Resident. Est. 1965. Always available. SIZE: Large. *STOCK: Pine and country furniture especially Irish and period; French provincial furniture and decorative items; period oak and elm.* LOC: Off A37. PARK: Easy. TEL: Ilchester (0935) 840464.

MARTOCK   (0935)

Martock Gallery

Treasurer's House. (G.I. Palmer.) Est. 1971. *STOCK: Watercolours, 18th−19th C, some oil paintings, prints, £5−£100.* LOC: Opposite church. TEL: 823288. SER: Buys at auction.

MILVERTON (0823)
Nr. Taunton

Heads 'n' Tails
1 Silver St. (D. and A. McKinley.) CL: Tues. Open 10—5.30. *STOCK: Taxidermy including Victorian, pictures, books, general antiques and collectables.* TEL: 400258. SER: Taxidermy.

Milverton Antiques
Fore St. (A. Waymouth.) Est. 1972. Resident, open any time. SIZE: Medium. *STOCK: Pine and oak country furniture, longcase clocks, interesting china, copper, brass and treen.* PARK: 50yds. TEL: 400597. VAT: Stan/Spec.

MONTACUTE, Nr. Yeovil

Gerald Lewis   **BADA**
The Old Brewery, The Old Estate Yard. (G. and B. Lewis.) Open by appointment only. *STOCK: 18th C furniture and clocks.* **TEL: Martock (0935) 825435.**

Montacute Antiques
April Cottage, 12 South St. (Mrs. M.A. Mead.) Open Thurs.—Sat. 9.30—5.30, other times by appointment. *STOCK: Small furniture, porcelain, glass, pictures, metalware, decorative and interesting items.* PARK: Easy. TEL: Martock (0935) 824786.

NETHER STOWEY (0278)
Nr. Bridgwater

Den of Antiquity
St. Mary St. (M.S. Todd.) Est. 1967. Open 10—5 or by appointment. SIZE: Medium. *STOCK: Philatelic literature, world topographical, maps, handbooks, postcards, ephemera.* LOC: A39. PARK: Easy. TEL: 732426. SER: Valuations; buys at auction. VAT: Stan.

NORTH PETHERTON (0278)
Nr. Bridgwater

Kathleen's Antiques
60 Fore St. (K. Pocock.) Resident. Est. 1971. Open 9—6.30. SIZE: Medium. *STOCK: Furniture, clocks, 18th—19th C, £50—£650; oil paintings, watercolours, sporting prints, £10—£250; silver, £10—£250; china, glass, copper, brass, Victorian, £10—£125.* LOC: A38. PARK: Easy. TEL: 662535.

QUEEN CAMEL, Nr. Yeovil

R. Bonnett Antiques
The Thatch, High St. Open 9—5.30, Sun. and other times by appointment. *STOCK: Furniture and smalls including paintings, pre-1900.* LOC: A359. TEL: Yeovil (0935) 850724.

Lieutenant Monroe being carried off by a tiger. Possibly c.1815. 280mm high. From *A Collector's History of English Pottery* by Griselda Lewis, published by the **Antique Collectors' Club**, 1985.

SHEPTON MALLET   (0749)

Peter Coe — English Paintings and Watercolours

The Priory. Open 10—6 by appointment only, except during exhibitions. SIZE: Medium. *STOCK: English paintings and watercolours, 18th to early 19th C, £200—£4,000; early 20th C, £200—£2,500.* LOC: Western edge of town, entry from A371 Wells Rd. PARK: Easy. TEL: 2412; home — same. SER: Valuations; restorations (oils and watercolours); buys at auction (British paintings and watercolours).

SOMERTON   (0458)

The London Cigarette Card Co. Ltd.

Sutton Rd. (I.A. and E.K. Laker, F.C. Doggett, Y. Berktay.) Est. 1927. CL: Sat. SIZE: Medium. *STOCK: Cigarette cards, 1885 to date; sets from £2; other cards, from 10p.* PARK: Easy. TEL: 73452. SER: Mail order.

Market Cross Galleries Ltd.

Town Hall. Open by appointment only. *STOCK: Oils and watercolours, 18th and early 19th C; general furniture.* TEL: 73753.

Old Zion Chapel

Sutton Rd. (A.A. Johnston.) Est. 1961. CL: Sat. Open 9.30—1 and 2—5. SIZE: Medium. *STOCK: Military books, all periods.* LOC: Just off the Triangle. PARK: 100yds. TEL: 72713. SER: Valuations.

Somerton continued

James Ribbons   *Trade Only*

The Bank House, Acre Lane. Est. 1971. Open by appointment. SIZE: Small. *STOCK: Victorian furniture, £50—£1,000; small items, glass and porcelain, £50—£100; light fittings, £50—£1,000; all 19th C.* LOC: 2 miles off A303. PARK: Easy. TEL: 73964; home — same. SER: Valuations; restorations; buys at auction. VAT: Stan/Spec.

SPARKFORD, Nr. Yeovil

Paul Watson

Orchard Cottage. Open by appointment only. *STOCK: Watercolours, 18th to early 20th C, £50—£3,000.* LOC: Private drive on south side of A303 opposite Brains Lane. PARK: Easy. TEL: (0963) 51342; home — (0963) 40259. SER: Valuations: restorations (mounting, framing, cleaning). VAT: Spec.

TAUNTON   (0823)

Deane Antiques

57 East Reach. (Mrs. V.J. Wathew.) Est. 1976. CL: Thurs. Open 9.30—5. SIZE: Medium. *STOCK: Furniture, decorative items, general antiques, pine, shipping items.* LOC: Opposite Rowcliffe's Garage. PARK: Easy. TEL: 76804. VAT: Stan/Spec.

Madelaine of Taunton

12B Bath Place. Open 10—5, Sat. 10—1. *STOCK: Silver, Georgian and Victorian furniture.* PARK: Easy. TEL: 53764. SER: Buys at auction. VAT: Stan.

Rothwell and Dunworth

14 Paul St. (Mrs. C. Rothwell and M. Dunworth.) ABA. Est. 1975. Open 11—5.30. SIZE: Medium. *STOCK: Antiquarian and secondhand books.* LOC: Off A38, opposite Sainsbury's. PARK: Multi-storey opposite. TEL: 82476. SER: Valuations; book-binding. FAIRS: PBFA at Russell Hotel.

Taunton continued

Selwoods
Queen Anne Cottage, Mary St. Est. 1927. Open 9—5. SIZE: Large. *STOCK: Furniture, antique, Victorian and Edwardian.* TEL: 72780.

Staplegrove Lodge Antiques
Staplegrove Lodge. (T. Atkins.) Est. 1958. CL: Mon. Open 10—5; Sat. p.m. and Sun. by appointment. SIZE: Medium. *STOCK: General antiques, furniture, silver, porcelain, pot-lids.* LOC: Pink house just off A361 Taunton/Barnstaple road up No Through Road just before the Cross Keys inn. PARK: Own. TEL: 81153; home — same.

Taunton Antiques Centre
27/29 Silver St. (S.M. Lowe and M. and P.A. Carter.) Est. 1978. Open Mon. 9—4. There are 100 dealers at this centre, selling a wide *variety of general antiques and collectables, including specialists in most fields.* LOC: 1½ miles from junction 25, M5, toward town centre, 100 yds. from Sainsbury Superstore. PARK: Easy. TEL: 89327.

TIMBERSCOMBE, (064 384) Nr. Minehead

Zwan Antiques
(M. van Zwanenberg.) Open Tues., Thurs. and Sun. p.m. or by appointment. *STOCK: Jewellery, 18th—20th C, £1—£2,000; porcelain, 18th—19th C, £5—£300; hunting prints and riding items, 19th—20th C, £1—£100; small items.* LOC: 2 miles out of Dunster on A396. PARK: Outside. TEL: 621 or 608. SER: Valuations; buys at auction.

WATCHET (0984)

Clarence House Antiques
41 Swain St. Est. 1970. CL: Sun. in winter. Open 10—6.30. SIZE: Medium. *STOCK: General antiques, pine, brass, copper, bric-a-brac, upholstered furniture.* TEL: 31389. VAT: Stan.

Battle between lion and crocodile. From "Japanese Okimono" in **Antique Collecting**, June 1986.

Watchet continued

Nick Cotton Antiques and Fine Art
Beechstone House, 47 Swain St. Est. 1970. Open 10—5.30, Sun. by appointment. SIZE: Medium. *STOCK: Paintings, 1750—1950; period furniture.* TEL: 31814 (any time). SER: Restorations; framing; research. VAT: Spec.

WEDMORE   (0934)

Coach House Gallery
Church St. Est. 1976. Open 9—6 or by appointment. SIZE: Small. *STOCK: English watercolours, 19th and early 20th C; small furniture, English porcelain; glass and silver, 18th C.* LOC: Opposite St. Mary's Church. TEL: 712718; home — same.

WELLINGTON   (082 347)

Michael and Amanda Lewis Oriental Carpets and Rugs
8 North St. Est. 1982. Open 10—5.30, Mon. and weekends by appointment. SIZE: Small. *STOCK: Oriental carpets and rugs, mainly 19th—20th C, £25—£5,000.* PARK: 100 yards. TEL: 7430; home — same. SER: Valuations; restorations (as stock).

Oxenhams
74 Mantle St. CL: Thurs. p.m. Open 9—9, Sun. by appointment. *STOCK: General antiques.* LOC: On A38. PARK: Easy. TEL: 2592.

WELLS   (0749)

Shelagh Berryman Music Boxes
15 Market Place. Open 10—1 and 2—5.30 or by appointment. *STOCK: Music boxes, clocks, watercolours and dolls, mainly 19th C, £200—£12,000.* TEL: 76203. SER: Valuations; restorations (as stock); buys at auction.

Cherub Antiques
9 Sadler St. (ground and 1st floor). (Mr. and Mrs. J.O. Newsam.) Est. 1973. Open 9—5.30. SIZE: Medium. *STOCK: Furniture, Georgian and Victorian; clocks, especially longcase and English dial; silver and small decorative items.* Not stocked: Weapons, books, medals, coins. LOC: On A39, 20yds. before Market Place. PARK: In Market Place. TEL: 72503; evenings — 73893. VAT: Stan/Spec.

Bernard G. House (Mitre Antiques)
13 Market Place. Est. 1963. Open 9.30—5.30. SIZE: Medium. *STOCK: Barometers and scientific instruments, furniture including miniatures and apprentice pieces, 18th—19th C; longcase and bracket clocks, metalware, decorative and architectural items.* PARK: In Market Place. TEL: 72607. SER: Restorations. VAT: Stan/Spec.

Houston Gallery
9 Sadler St. (2nd floor). (M.J. Carter.) CL: Wed. p.m. Open 10—5.30. *STOCK: English oil paintings, 19th—20th C.* TEL: 73148.

Wells continued

Edward A. Nowell BADA
21/23 Market Place. Est. 1952. Open 9—1 and 2—5.30. SIZE: Large. *STOCK: Furniture, clocks, barometers, 17th to early 19th C; jewellery, silver, porcelain, English and Continental, all prices.* **Not stocked: Victoriana, bric-a-brac, curios, weapons, books. LOC: From any direction, turn left into Market Place (one-way system). PARK: 20yds. facing shop. TEL: 72415. SER: Valuations; restorations (furniture, silver, clocks and jewellery); re-upholstery. VAT: Stan/Spec.**

WEST MONKTON (0823)
Nr. Taunton
William Morley Antiques
Musgrave's Old Farm. (W.H. Morley.) Est. 1970. Open daily, appointment advisable. SIZE: Medium. *STOCK: Oak furniture, 17th to early 18th C, £250—£1,500; country furniture, yew and fruitwood, 18th C, £200—£750; mahogany furniture, 18th to early 19th C, £200—£1,500; early metalware, brass, treen, country bygones, £5—£200; English glass, 1730—1850; Wemyss ware.* PARK: Easy. LOC: From A38 or A361, second house on right before entering village. TEL: 412751. SER: Valuations; restorations (furniture); buys at auction (furniture). VAT: Spec.

WILLITON (0984)
Edward Venn
52 Long St. Est. 1979. Open 10—5. *STOCK: Country furniture, 18th C; clocks.* TEL: 32631 (ansaphone). SER: Restorations (furniture, barometers and clocks).

Williton continued

Williton Antiques
26 High St. (J. and H. Root.) Est. 1970. Usually open Mon., Wed. and Fri. 9.30—5. SIZE: Small. *STOCK: Metalware, country bygones, small period furniture, china, glass and treen, 17th—19th C, £5—£300.* Not stocked: Coins, stamps and guns. LOC: A358, corner shop on left on approach from Taunton. PARK: Easy, side of shop in Bridge St. TEL: Home — 32393.

WINCANTON (0963)
The Greyhound Gallery Ltd.
Market Place. (D.P. Russell-Funnel.) Est. 1954. Open 9—1 and 2—7.30; Sun. by appointment. SIZE: Medium. *STOCK: English oak and walnut furniture, 17th to early 18th C, £500—£10,000; sporting prints, 18th—19th C, £50—£500.* PARK: Easy. TEL: 33005; home — same. SER: Valuations. VAT: Stan/Spec.

Mattar Antique Galleries
Wincanton Manor House, The Dogs. (S. and M. Mattar.) SIZE: Medium. *STOCK: Paintings, oak furniture, delft, carpets, tapestries.* LOC: From A303 to town centre, turn into South St. PARK: Easy. TEL: 32362/34154.

David and Penny Newlove Antiques
28 High St. Est. 1968. CL: Sun. except to the trade. SIZE: Medium. *STOCK: Furniture, pine, mahogany, oak and walnut, 17th—19th C; clocks, both £20—£850; general small antiques, watches, pictures, prints, £5—£200; all 18th—19th C.* Not stocked: Militaria, stamps and coins. PARK: Easy. TEL: 32672. VAT: Stan/Spec.

Barry M. Sainsbury
17 High St. Est. 1958. CL: Thurs. p.m. *STOCK: Oak and mahogany furniture, china, glass, pictures, decorative items.* TEL: 32289. SER: Restorations; cabinet makers. VAT: Stan/Spec.

White clay cottage decorated with extruded strands of clay to simulate creepers and with large flowers and leaves on the base, 98mm high. From *A Collector's History of English Pottery* by Griselda Lewis, published by the **Antique Collectors' Club**, 1985.

A selection from
our extensive
stock of antiques.

WIVELISCOMBE   (0984)

Brownsells Granary
9 High St. (J. White.) Est. 1960. *STOCK: Country furniture and clocks.* PARK: Easy. TEL: 23117; home — Milverton (0823) 400427.

J.C. Giddings
11 The Square. CL: Thurs. Open 9—5. SIZE: Medium, plus warehouses. *STOCK: Hardwood furniture, especially large items, 17th— 20th C.* TEL: 23829; home — 23703. VAT: Stan.

Peter Lee Antiques
1 Silver St. (P. and A. Lee.) CL: Thurs. and Sat. p.m. Open 9—5. *STOCK: Furniture, china, general antiques, fine arts and unusual items.* LOC: A361, town centre. PARK: Nearby. TEL: 24055.

Wood House Antiques
14 Church St. Resident. *STOCK: General antiques and collectors' items, furniture, glass, jewellery.* LOC: A361. PARK: By church or Croft Way. TEL: 23088.

YEOVIL   (0935)

Brimsmore House Antiques
Brimsmore House, Tintinhull Rd. (W. Rose.) Resident, always available. Est. 1970. *STOCK: General antiques and bric-a-brac.* TEL: 74959.

Fox and Co.
30 Princes St. Est. 1970. *STOCK: Antiquities, coins, medals and militaria, books.* PARK: Easy. TEL: 72323. VAT: Stan/Spec.

Mactaggart Books
Little Brympton, Brympton d'Evercy. Est. 1971. Usually open but telephone call advisable. *STOCK: Secondhand and antiquarian books.* TEL: (0935 86) 2609.

Woodfords Antiques
225 Knapp House, Preston Plucknett. (D. Woodford.) Est. 1965. Always open. SIZE: Medium. *STOCK: General antiques, £1— £1,000; clocks — longcase, wall, bracket and carriage; pictures, porcelain, watches, musical boxes, polyphones, automation.* LOC: Taunton road 1¼ miles on left from Yeovil general hospital. PARK: Easy. TEL: 23391. SER: Valuations; restorations (clocks); buys at auction. VAT: Spec.

Staffordshire

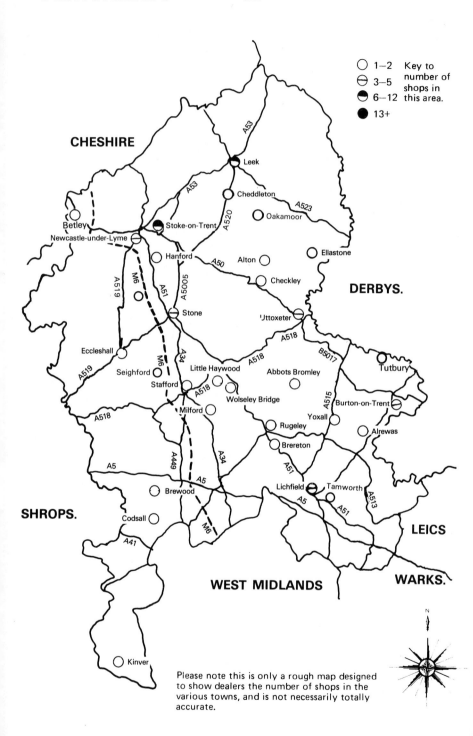

Key to number of shops in this area.
- ◯ 1–2
- ⊖ 3–5
- ◐ 6–12
- ● 13+

CHESHIRE

Betley

Newcastle-under-Lyme

Leek

Cheddleton

Oakamoor

Stoke-on-Trent

Hanford

Alton

Ellastone

Checkley

DERBYS.

Stone

Uttoxeter

Eccleshall

Seighford

Little Haywood

Abbots Bromley

Tutbury

Stafford

Wolseley Bridge

Burton-on-Trent

Milford

Yoxall

Rugeley

Alrewas

Brereton

Brewood

Lichfield

Tamworth

Codsall

LEICS.

SHROPS.

WEST MIDLANDS

WARKS.

Kinver

Please note this is only a rough map designed to show dealers the number of shops in the various towns, and is not necessarily totally accurate.

N

ABBOTS BROMLEY, Nr. Rugeley
Ivy House Antiques
Ivy House, High St. (Mrs. B.A. Hammersley.) Est. 1959. Open 10—6, Sat. and Sun. 2—6. SIZE: Small. *STOCK: General antiques, porcelain, glass, china, small furniture and bygones.* PARK: Easy. TEL: Burton-on-Trent (0283) 840259.

ALREWAS
Nr. Burton-on-Trent
Ashley House Antiques
115 Main St. (P.A. Benton.) Est. 1977. Open Thurs., Fri. and Sat. 11—5 and Sun. 2—5. *STOCK: Furniture, longcase and Vienna wall-clocks, brass, copper, horse brasses, ribbon/lace, plates.* PARK: Easy. TEL: Brownhills (0543) 373655.

Poley Antiques
5 Main St. (D.T. and A.G. Poley.) Est. 1977. Open Thurs—Sat. 10—5.30, or by appointment. SIZE: Small. *STOCK: General antiques, small furniture, silver, jewellery, china, glass, copper, brass, 1840—1940, £1—£300.* Not stocked: Stamps, coins and militaria. LOC: 20yds. from A38, on A513. PARK: Easy. TEL: Burton-on-Trent (0283) 791151.

ALTON
M.J. and I. Cope
Open daily 9—6. *STOCK: Victorian and Edwardian furniture, pottery, brass and copper; pine and shipping items.* LOC: Centre of village, ½ mile from Alton Towers. PARK: Easy. TEL: Oakamoor (0538) 702524.

BETLEY, Nr. Crewe
Betley Court Gallery
Main Rd. (Prof. G.N. Brown and Dr. F. Brown.) Resident. Est. 1980. CL: Mon. Open afternoons or by appointment anytime. SIZE: Large. *STOCK: Oils, watercolours, prints, £20—£5,000; ceramics especially Doulton Lambeth and Wedgwood, £20—£2,500, both 18th—20th C; furniture, Georgian, Regency, Victorian, £20—£2,500.* Not stocked: Militaria, clocks. LOC: Village centre. PARK: Easy. TEL: Crewe (0270) 820652. SER: Buys at auction.

IS YOUR ENTRY CORRECT?
If there is even the slightest inaccuracy in your entry, *please* let us know before 1st January 1987.
GUIDE TO THE
ANTIQUE SHOPS OF BRITAIN
5 Church Street, Woodbridge, Suffolk.

BRERETON, Nr. Rugeley
Rugeley Antique Centre
161/3 Main Rd. CL: Wed. Open 10—5.30 and some Sun. or by appointment to the trade. SIZE: Medium. There are 28 units at this centre offering *a wide range of china, glass, pottery, pictures, furniture, pine, treen, linen and shipping goods.* LOC: A51, 10 minutes north of Lichfield opposite Cedar Tree Hotel. PARK: Own. TEL: Rugeley (088 94) 77166; home — same.

BREWOOD   (0902)
The Antique Shop
1 Stafford St. (I. Follows.) Resident. Est. 1973. CL: Sun. a.m. and Wed. SIZE: Medium. *STOCK: Furniture, clocks, 18th—19th C, £500—£2,000.* LOC: 2 miles south of A5 nr. Gailey Island. PARK: Easy. TEL: 850863. VAT: Stan.

BURTON-ON-TRENT   (0283)
Broadway Studios
127 New St. (F.H. Dyson.) Est. 1969. CL: Wed. SIZE: Medium. *STOCK: Decorative maps, prints, watercolours, oil paintings, £1—£500;* SER: Picture framing and mount cutting. TEL: 41802. VAT: Stan.

Burton Antiques
3 Horninglow Rd. (C.H. Armett). Est. 1977. Open 9.30—5, Wed. 9.30—4. SIZE: Small. *STOCK: Shipping furniture and pine, £25—£100.* LOC: A50. PARK: Nearby. TEL: 42331; home — (053 88) 339. SER: Valuations; restorations (pine stripping); buys at auction. FAIRS: Bowman. VAT: Stan/Spec.

Holloways Antiques
138 Derby St. Open 9—5.30. *STOCK: Mainly 18th—19th C furniture, clocks, pictures, silver plate, porcelain and pine.* VAT: Stan/Spec.

H.J. Richards and Son
Abbey Arcade, High St. Est. 1934. Open 9—5.30, Tues 9.30—5.30, Sat. 9—5. SIZE: Small. *STOCK: Jewellery, mainly Victorian and Edwardian, £50—£1,000; silver.* LOC: Market Place end of main shopping thoroughfare. PARK: Limited and nearby. TEL: 65921. SER: Valuations; restorations (silver, jewellery and clocks). VAT: Stan/Spec.

CHECKLEY
Nr. Stoke-on-Trent
Alpha Antiques
Church Cottage. (M. and D. Harper.) Resident. *STOCK: 18th to early 20th C mahogany and rosewood furniture and decorative items.* TEL: Tean (0538) 722149. SER: Re-upholstery.

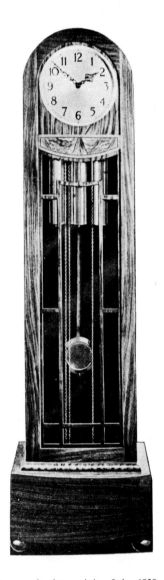

This longcase is characteristic of the 1930s and although for many years totally ignored by collectors it will now be coming into favour with those decorating their homes in period pieces of that date. It has the added advantage of being extremely pleasant to listen to — the chimes are most sonorous. From *The Price Guide to Collectable Clocks, 1840-1940* by Alan and Rita Shenton, published by the **Antique Collectors' Club**, 1985.

CHEDDLETON, Nr. Leek
Jewel Antiques
49 Churchill Ave. Est. 1966. Open most days or by appointment. *STOCK: Jewellery, £50−£1,000, paintings, £50−£2,500, both from 1750; furniture, small items and bric-a-brac, 1850−1920, £25−£1,000.* PARK: Easy. TEL: Churnet Side (0538) 360161/360744. SER: Restorations (jewellery and art); buys at auction. FAIRS: Buxton, Stafford, Sandbach, Nantwich, Uttoxeter, Clayton Lodge, Newcastle and Knutsford.

R.G. Wragg
319 Cheadle Rd. Est. 1970. Resident, usually available. *STOCK: Books, 19th C, £5−£200.* TEL: Churnet Side (0538) 360044.

CODSALL   (090 74)
Dam Mill Antiques
Birches Rd. (G. and H. Bassett.) Est. 1977. SIZE: Small. CL: Tues. and Thurs. Open 10−1 and 2.30−5.30. *STOCK: General antiques, small furniture, china, glass, copper, brass, silver and jewellery.* PARK: Easy. TEL: 3780.

ECCLESHALL   (0785)
The Cottage Antique Shop
14 Stafford St. (J.L. Rutherford.) CL: Wed. and Thurs. Open 9−6, Sat. 9−5. *STOCK: Country furniture, oak, longcase clocks, pottery, porcelain, commemorative ware.* TEL: Home — 850548. SER: Restorations (furniture); pine stripping.

B. Timmis and Son
41 High St. Est. 1945. CL: Wed. Open 10−5. *STOCK: Small antiques, shipping goods, longcase clocks, pine, metals.* LOC: In main street. PARK: Easy. TEL: 850883. VAT: Stan/Spec.

ELLASTONE   (033 524)
Nr. Ashbourne
P.J. Fradley
Ellastone Old House. Est. 1952. CL: Some Sat. Open most days, but any time by appointment. SIZE: Large. *STOCK: Period furniture especially oak, brass, pewter, copper, treen and general antiques.* LOC: B5032 between Ashbourne and Uttoxeter, stone house in village centre. PARK: Easy. TEL: 291. VAT: Spec.

HANFORD, Nr. Stoke-on-Trent
The Little Antique Shop
167 Stone Rd. (P. and S. Lumley.) Est. 1951. Open 10−7.30, Sun. by appointment. SIZE: Large. *STOCK: Georgian−Edwardian, £20−£1,500.* Not stocked: Pine and pre-war furniture. LOC: 1 mile from junction 15, M6. PARK: Easy. TEL: Stoke-on-Trent (0782) 657674. SER: Restorations (French polishing, inlay and small repairs); buys at auction. VAT: Spec.

KINVER   (0384)

Kinver Antiques
55 High St. (L. Blewitt.) Est. 1983. CL: Mon.
Open 10.15—5.30. *STOCK: Period furniture,
bric-a-brac, gold and silver, jewellery.* TEL:
873455. SER: Restorations; French polishing,
upholstery, soft furnishings.

LEEK   (0538)

Antiques and Objets d'Art of Leek
70 St. Edwards St. Est. 1955. CL: Thurs.
Open 10—6. *STOCK: English and Continental
furniture; porcelain, silver, glass, oil paintings.*
TEL: 382587. FAIRS: Buxton. VAT: Spec.

Anvil Antiques
Three warehouses — Old Step Row and The
Old School, Alsop St. (K.L. and J.S. Spooner.)
Est. 1975. Open 9—6. SIZE: Large. *STOCK:
Stripped pine, architectural and oak shipping
items.* LOC: Warehouses — turn off Compton
opposite Catholic church to Cornhill St. Take
left between two car parks, or second on left
down Broad St. PARK: Easy. TEL: 371657.
VAT: Stan.

Aspleys Antique Market
Compton Mill, Compton. (J. Aspley.) Est.
1976. CL: Sun. except by appointment. Open
9—6. SIZE: Large. *STOCK: General antiques,
especially pine, shipping items, bric-a-brac,
mainly Victorian and Edwardian.* PARK: Own.
TEL: 373396. SER: Restorations (mainly
pine); shipping and packing; courier service.
VAT: Stan.

England's Gallery
1 Ball Haye Terrace. (F.J. and S. England.) Est.
1968. CL: Thurs. Open 11—6. SIZE: Large.
*STOCK: Oils and watercolours, 18th—19th C,
£500—£10,000; etchings, engravings, lithographs, mezzotints, £50—£100.* LOC: Buxton
road into Leek, turn right at first traffic lights,
gallery 300 yards on right. PARK: Easy and
nearby. TEL: 373451; home — 386352. SER:
Valuations; restorations (cleaning, relining,
framing, regilding, mount cutting); buys at
auction (paintings). VAT: Stan.

Gilligans Antiques
59 St. Edward St. (M.T. Gilligan.) Est. 1977.
STOCK: Victorian and Edwardian furniture.
TEL: 384174.

Grosvenor Antiques
Overton Bank House. (K. and S. Grosvenor.)
Open 9—5 or by appointment. *STOCK: English
furniture, general antiques.* TEL: 385669.
SER: Buys at auction.

Leek continued

Norman Grosvenor   LAPADA
4—6 Brook St. Est. 1962. Open 9—5.
*STOCK: Georgian furniture, £100—£2,000;
Victorian furniture, £25—£1,000; Edwardian
and later furnishings, £5—£50.* LOC: Near
traffic lights. PARK: At rear. TEL: 384506;
home — 382976. VAT: Stan/Spec.

Jewel Antiques
1A Overton Bank. Est. 1966. Open most days
or by appointment. *STOCK: Jewellery, £50—
£1,000; paintings £50—£2,500; both from
1750; furniture, small items and bric-a-brac,
1850—1920, £25—£1,000.* TEL: Churnet
Side (0538) 360161/360744. SER: Restorations (jewellery and art); buys at auction.
FAIRS: Buxton, Stafford, Knutsford,
Sandbach, Nantwich, Uttoxeter, Clayton
Lodge, Newcastle.

Willott Antiques
1 Clerk Bank. (J. Willott.) Est. 1977. Open
10—4.30. SIZE: Medium. *STOCK: General
antiques, including oak and mahogany furniture and pottery.* LOC: Main Macclesfield road
into Leek. PARK: Easy. TEL: 371519; home
— Stoke-on-Trent (0782) 504609. VAT:
Stan.

Pat Wood
Stanley St. CL: Thurs. *STOCK: Paintings and
prints.* TEL: 385696. SER: Restorations
(pictures); framing.

LICHFIELD   (0543)

The Antique Shop
31 Tamworth St. (Mrs. P.M. Rackham.) Open
9.30—1.30 and 2.30—5.30. SIZE: Medium.
*STOCK: Furniture, pottery, porcelain, silver,
prints, paintings, copper and brass, jewellery,
glass, £5—£700.* PARK: Easy. TEL: 268324.

Corridor Antiques and Perdy's
Junk Shop
53 and 55 Tamworth St. (P.J. Mellor.)
STOCK: General antiques and shipping goods.
TEL: 263223/251489.

Curiosity Shop
45 Tamworth St. (G.H. Howarth.) Est. 1976.
Open 9—5, Wed. 9—12. *STOCK: General
antiques.* TEL: 252563.

Justin Pinewood
2 Pinfold Hill, Shenstone. (S. Silvester.) Open
9—5.30. *STOCK: Stripped pine furniture.*
TEL: Shenstone (0543) 481057. SER: Stripping (doors and furniture).

L. Royden Smith
Church View, Farewell Lane, Burntwood. Est.
1972. Open Wed. and Sat. 10.30—5 or by
appointment. *STOCK: Antiquarian books,
general antiques, bric-a-brac, shipping goods.*
TEL: Burntwood (054 36) 2217. VAT: Stan.

STAFFORDSHIRE 626

LITTLE HAYWOOD (0889)
Nr. Stafford
Jalna Antiques
Coley Lane. (G. and D. Hancox.) Resident. Est. 1974. CL: Mon. Open 12—6. *STOCK: General antiques, Victoriana.* LOC: ½ mile off A51, 3 miles north of Rugeley. TEL: 881381. SER: Re-upholstery and renovation. VAT: Spec.

MILFORD
Milford Lodge Galleries
Milford Lodge. (R.J. Phillips.) CL: Sat. p.m. Open 10—6. *STOCK: English furniture, 17th to early 19th C; porcelain, pottery, paintings, watercolours, decorative items.* TEL: Stafford (0785) 661067. VAT: Spec.

NEWCASTLE-UNDER-LYME (0782)
Antique Market
The Stones. (Antique Forum (Birmingham) Ltd.) Open Tues. 7—2. There are 100 dealers at this market selling *a wide range of general antiques.* TEL: Sandon (088 97) 527.

Errington Antiques
63 George St. (corner of George and Albert St.) (G.K. Errington.) CL: Thurs. Open 10—12.30 and 2—5. *STOCK: General antiques.* TEL: 632822.

Hood and Broomfield   LAPADA
Lyme Galleries, 29 Albert St. (J. Hood and G.H. Broomfield.) Open 10—5.30, Sat. 10—4. *STOCK: Oils and watercolours, 19th and early 20th C.* TEL: 626859. SER: Restorations; framing. VAT: Spec.

Upstairs, Downstairs
54 London Rd. (H. Newport.) Est. 1981. CL: Thurs. Open 9.30—6.30, Sat. 9.30—3.30. SIZE: Small. *STOCK: Furniture, especially couches and chaise longues, dining, occasional and armchairs, 1860—1930, £50—£250; chests of drawers, bureaux, occasional tables and cabinets, 1860—1940s, £25—£250.* LOC: A34, 100 yards from town centre. PARK: Easy. TEL: 612081. SER: Valuations; restorations (re-upholstery, French polishing). FAIRS: Some local.

OAKAMOOR, Nr. Stoke-on-Trent
Directmoor Ltd.   Trade Only
The Coppice Farm, nr. Moorcourt Farley Rd. (D. Johnson.) Est. 1977. Open daily, Sat. and Sun. by appointment. SIZE: Large. *STOCK: Stripped and restored pine furniture, country furnishing items.* LOC: Follow Alton Towers signs from motorways. PARK: Easy. TEL: 702419; home — same. SER: Valuations; restorations; container packing and shipping. VAT: Stan.

RUGELEY (088 94)
Eveline Winter
1 Wolseley Rd. (Mrs. E. Winter.) Est. 1962. Open 10.30—5.30. SIZE: Small. *STOCK: Staffordshire figure, pre-Victorian, from £50; Victorian, £12—£200; also English porcelain, 18th C, £15—£70; copper, brass, glass and general antiques.* Not stocked: Coins and weapons. LOC: Coming from Lichfield or Stafford stay on A51 and avoid town by-pass. PARK: Easy at side of shop. TEL: 3259.

SEIGHFORD (078 575)
C. and J. Mowe   Trade Only
Stockingate Farm, Coton Clanford. Est. 1970. Open by appointment. *STOCK: Shipping goods, pine and general antiques.* TEL: 799. VAT: Stan/Spec.

STAFFORD (0785)
Browse
127 Lichfield Rd. (H. Barnes.) Est. 1981. CL: Wed. Open 9.30—5. SIZE: Large. *STOCK: Furniture, 1860—1940s, £25—£300.* LOC: Outskirts of town. PARK: Easy. TEL: 41097; home — 3345. SER: Valuations; restorations (small upholstery, caning).

STOKE-ON-TRENT (0782)
Ann's Antiques
24 Leek Rd, Stockton Brook. CL: Thurs. Open 10—5. *STOCK: Victorian furniture, brass, copper, jewellery, paintings, pottery and unusual items.* VAT: Stan.

Antiques and Old Lace
512 Hartshill Rd. (Mrs. W. Lowen.) Est. 1968. CL: Thurs. Open 10—5, Mon. 1.30—5. *STOCK: Lace, linen, period clothes, furniture, small items.* PARK: Nearby. TEL: 610194; home — 621716.

Antiques Workshop and Boulton's Antiques
43-45 Hope St., Hanley. (H. and S. Oakes, J. Rowley.) Est. 1974. Open 9.30—5.30, Sun. by appointment. SIZE: Medium. *STOCK: Country pine, 19th C, £50—£400; pottery, 19th—20th C, £5—£25; general antiques.* PARK: Own at rear. TEL: 273645; home — 620358. SER: Valuations; restorations (pine stripping, upholstery, polishing).

Castle Antiques
113 Victoria St., Hartshill. (J. Taylor.) Est. 1965. CL: Thurs. Open 10—5.30. SIZE: Medium. *STOCK: Edwardian and Victorian furniture and clocks, £100—£500.* LOC: 300 yards from main road. PARK: 100 yards. TEL: 625168. VAT: Stan/Spec.

Stoke-on-Trent continued

W.G. Steele
20 Piccadilly, Hanley. Est. 1770. Open 9—6. *STOCK: Victorian and Edwardian jewellery.* Not stocked: Furniture. TEL: 23216.

The Tinder Box
61 Lichfield St., Hanley. (Mr. and Mrs. G.E. Yarwood.) Est. 1969. Open 10.45—5.30, Sat. 10.45—2.30. SIZE: Large. *STOCK: Victorian oil lamps and spare parts; early brass and copper, jewellery, furniture and unusual items.* PARK: Easy. TEL: 261368 or 550508. SER: Cleaning (brass and copper), buys at auction.

Tunnicliffes Antiques
17 Broad St., Hanley. (A.J. Tunnicliffe.) Est. 1959. CL: Thurs. Open 10—4. SIZE: Small. *STOCK: Staffordshire pottery and china, to £100; general antiques.* Not stocked: Weapons. PARK: Nearby. TEL: 272930.

STONE   (0785)

Johnsons of Stone
Unit 8B, Whitebridge Industrial Estate, Whitebridge Lane. (P. and J. Johnson.) Open 9—5, Sat. by appointment. SIZE: Large. *STOCK: Pine and country furniture, decorative items, quilts and samplers pre-1880.* PARK: Easy. TEL: 817466. SER: Restorations (furniture); pine stripping. VAT: Stan/Spec.

Stone Antique Centre
Bridge House, 56 Newcastle Rd. (E. Smith.) Est. 1980. CL: Mon. Open 10.30—5.30. SIZE: Medium. The dealers at this centre offer *a wide range of general antiques including jewellery, silver and glass.* TEL: 818218; home — (0735) 372.

Stone-Wares Antiques
24 Radford St. (G. and S. Wheeler.) Est. 1978. CL: Wed. Open 9—6, Sun. by appointment. SIZE: Medium. *STOCK: Period pine, longcase clocks, mahogany, £5—£1,500.* LOC: A520 north of Stone. PARK: Easy. TEL: 815000; home — same. SER: Valuations; restorations (furniture); stripping; buys at auction. VAT: Stan/Spec.

TAMWORTH   (0827)

Bolehall Antiques
116 Lichfield St. (K.W. and J.M. Plater). Est. 1980. Open 9.30—5, Wed. 9.30—12.30, Sun. by appointment. SIZE: Medium. *STOCK: Stripped pine, metalware, lamps, oak, general antiques, Victorian, £5—£100.* LOC: Town centre. PARK: Easy. TEL: 52911; home — 57505. SER: Valuations; restorations; French polishing. FAIRS: Park Hall, Bakewell Show.

TUTBURY, Nr. Burton-on-Trent

Glenys Rose Antiques
High St. (Mrs. G.E. Rose.) Est. 1982. CL: Wed. and Sun. except by appointment. Open 10—5. SIZE: Small. *STOCK: Furniture, silver, porcelain, jewellery, copper, brass.* LOC: A50. PARK: Easy. TEL: Home — Hoar Cross (028 375) 301.

Tutbury Mill Antiques
6 Lower High St. (F.J. and G.J. Allen.) Open seven days 9.30—6.30. SIZE: Large. *STOCK: General antiques.* PARK: Own. TEL: (0283) 815998/9.

UTTOXETER   (088 93)

Aspleys Antique Market
18 Carter St. Open 9.30—5.30, Sun. by appointment. SIZE: 10 rooms. *STOCK: General antiques including smalls.* TEL: 5291.

Dorothy Franks
The Old Chantrey House, Church Sq. (A. and P.M. Jaggar.) Est. 1971. CL: Mon. and Thurs. Open any time by appointment. SIZE: Small. *STOCK: Paintings and furniture.* PARK: Easy. TEL: 3058.

Pine Antiques
52 Bridge St. (M.A. and A. Groves.) Open 9.30—5. *STOCK: English country pine and satinwood, pottery, linen and kitchenalia.* TEL: 5374; home — 4898.

WOLSELEY BRIDGE

The Old Barn
(G. and D. Hancox.) CL: Mon. Open 12—6. *STOCK: Furniture and smalls.* LOC: A51. TEL: Little Haywood (0889) 881381. VAT: Spec.

YOXALL   (0543)
Nr. Burton-on-Trent

Roger Armson t/a
J.C.E. and N.I. Armson   LAPADA
The Hollies. Est. 1955. Open 9—5, Sat. and other times by appointment. SIZE: Large. *STOCK: Period furniture and shipping goods.* LOC: On A515. TEL: 472352. VAT: Stan/Spec.

H.W. Heron and Son Ltd.
                                       LAPADA
The Antique Shop, 1 King St. (H.N.M., Mrs. J. and Mrs. E.M. Heron.) Est. 1949. Open 9—6, Sat. and Sun. 10.30—6. SIZE: Large. *STOCK: Furniture, porcelain, glass, pictures, all prices.* Not stocked: Coins, books. LOC: On A515, in centre of village, opp. church. PARK: Easy. TEL: 472266; home — same. SER: Valuations. VAT: Stan/Spec.

Suffolk

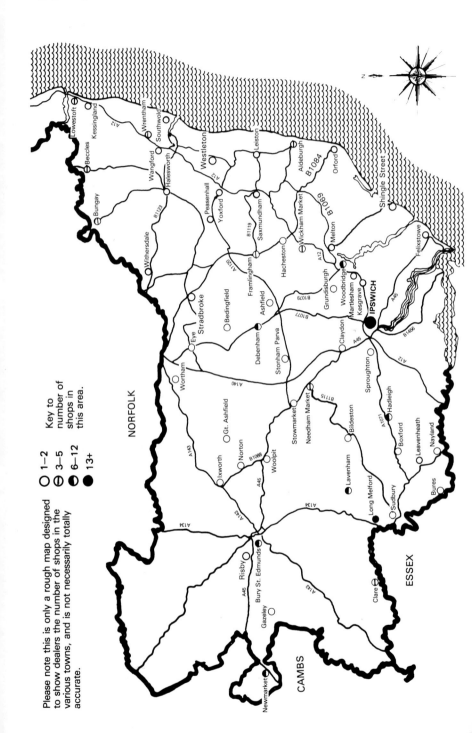

Please note this is only a rough map designed to show dealers the number of shops in the various towns, and is not necessarily totally accurate.

Key to number of shops in this area.

○ 1–2
◑ 3–5
◐ 6–12
● 13+

Suffolk

ALDEBURGH (072 885)

Aldeburgh Antiques
Wentworth Rd. (H. Royall.) Est. 1980. Usually open Fri. and Sat. 10.30−1 and 2.30−5. SIZE: Small. *STOCK: Ceramics, glass, copper, brass, curios, small furniture, oriental items, mirrors, some fabrics, lace, period clothes.* PARK: Nearby. TEL: 2977; home − Southwold (0502) 722201.

Guillemot
134/136 High St. (L. Weaver.) Est. 1973. Open 10−1 and 2−5, Sat. 10−1 and 2−6, Wed. p.m. and Sun. by appointment. SIZE: Medium. *STOCK: Pine, elm and fruitwood country furniture, dressers, tables and treen, 17th−19th C.* LOC: Town centre. PARK: Easy. TEL: 3933. VAT: Stan/Spec.

Mole Hall Antiques
102/104 High St. (P. Weaver.) Est. 1976. Open 10−6, Wed. 10−1, Sun. and other times by appointment. SIZE: Small. *STOCK: Country furniture, 18th−19th C; decoy ducks and unusual carvings, 19th C; both £50−£100; shop and pub signs, art deco lamps, 19th−20th C, £20−£150.* PARK: Easy. TEL: 2361; home − same. VAT: Stan/Spec.

Thompson's Gallery
175A High St. (J. and S. Thompson.) Open 10−5, or by appointment. SIZE: Medium. *STOCK: Oils and watercolours, 18th−20th C, furniture, 18th to early 19th C; both £50−£2,500.* PARK: Easy. TEL: 3743; home − 2488. SER: Valuations; restorations; framing; buys at auction. VAT: Spec.

Ye Olde Curiosity Shope
Oakley Sq. (R.J. and Mrs. Crisp.) Est. 1968. Open 9.30−1 and 2.30−5. SIZE: Medium. *STOCK: Copper, brass, objets d'art, porcelain, paintings, 19th−20th C, £1−£500; furniture, 18th−20th C, £10−£1,000.* LOC: Town centre. PARK: At rear. TEL: 2267 or 2823.

ASHFIELD, Nr. Stowmarket

Mrs. A.M. Ponsonby
Upham House. Est. 1963. Open by appointment. SIZE: Medium. *STOCK: Furniture, 18th to early 19th C, to £4,000; furnishing pieces.* Not stocked: Clocks, firearms. LOC: Off main Ipswich to Framlingham road, 2½ miles short of Earl Soham, on by-road to Cretingham. PARK: Easy. TEL: Earl Soham (072 882) 200. SER: Restorations (cabinet making). FAIRS: Buxton, Kenilworth. VAT: Stan/Spec.

BECCLES (0502)

Andrew's Gallery/Norman Hall
6 Ingate. (A.J. and N. Hall.) Est. 1974. CL: Sun. except by appointment and Wed. Open 9−5.30. SIZE: Medium. *STOCK: English watercolours, art deco china, postcards.* LOC: Beccles−Worlingham Rd., nr. level crossing. PARK: Forecourt. TEL: 713263. SER: Restorations (furniture); buys at auction (watercolours); framing.

Art and Antiques
6 The Walk. Open 10−5. SIZE: Medium. *STOCK: General antiques, silver, bric-a-brac.* LOC: Town centre opp. church. PARK: 2 hours outside shop. TEL: 716447 or 713631.

Beccles Gallery
Saltgate House. (S. and F.T. Abrehart.) CL: Mon. Open 10−1 and 2−5. *STOCK: Prints; oils and watercolours, 19th−20th C.* TEL: 714017. SER: Restorations and cleaning (oils, watercolours); framing.

Frank Collins Antiques   LAPADA
Marlborough Farm, London Rd., Weston. Open by appointment. *STOCK: Fine art and general antiques.* TEL: 714842.

Saltgate Antiques
11 Saltgate. (A.M. Ratcliffe.) Resident. Est. 1971. CL: Wed. p.m. Open 10−5. SIZE: Medium. *STOCK: Furniture, 17th−19th C, £25−£2,000; shipping goods; collectors' items, brass, copper, Staffordshire figures, 19th C bric-a-brac, £5−£300.* LOC: A146 opp. bus station. PARK: Easy. TEL: 712776.

Waveney Antiques Centre
Saltgate. Open 10−5.30. There are 20 dealers at this centre selling *a wide variety of general antiques, antiquarian books, furniture, silver, clocks and collectors' items.* PARK: At rear of premises. TEL: 716147.

BEDINGFIELD, Nr. Eye

The Old Red Lion
The St. Est. 1973. Open by appointment. *STOCK: Early furniture.* LOC: 3 miles from Eye, 2 miles from Debenham. TEL: Worlingworth (072 876) 491. SER: Restorations (furniture, oil paintings, wood carvings).

BILDESTON (0449)
Oswald Simpson LAPADA
Market Place. Est. 1971. Open 9.30—5.30, other times by appointment. SIZE: Large. STOCK: Early oak and country furniture £25— £3,000; brass, copper, pewter and country items, £10—£400, all 17th—19th C; samplers and needlework, 17th—20th C, £20— £1,000. PARK: Easy. TEL: 740030. SER: Valuations; restorations. VAT: Spec.

BOXFORD (0787)
The Corner Cupboard
The Old Bakery. CL: Mon. Open 10—5. STOCK: Victoriana, papier mache, samplers, beadwork and small furniture. PARK: Easy. TEL: 210123.

BUNGAY (0986)
Border Booksellers
40 Earsham St. (P. and H. Morrow, Mrs. E. Barr.) Est. 1977. Open 9—5.30. SIZE: Small. STOCK: Antiquarian and secondhand books, maps and prints 16th—20th C, £1—£500. LOC: Next to Post Office. PARK: Easy. TEL: 3148. SER: Valuations; restorations (cloth and leather restoration and re-binding); buys at auction (books, maps and prints).

Bridge Street Antiques
24 Bridge St. (P.L. and W.B. Foulger.) Est. 1967. Open Tues., Thurs. and Sat. 9.30— 12.30 and 2—5. SIZE: Small. STOCK: General antiques, satin walnut and pine furniture, 19th—20th C, £5—£250. LOC: A144. PARK: Easy. TEL: Home — 4449.

Broad Street Antiques
Broad St. (J. Stamp.) Est. 1971. Open 10—1 and 2—5, Sat. 10—1. STOCK: General antiques, bric-a-brac. TEL: 2960 evenings. VAT: Stan.

Country House Antiques
30 Earsham St. (G.R. Searle). Est. 1979. CL: Wed. Open 10—1 and 2—4.30, Sat. 10.30— 1 and 2—3.30. SIZE: Medium. STOCK: Mahogany, oak and blonde furniture, 18th— 19th C; porcelain, collectables. LOC: Near Post Office. PARK: Easy. TEL: 2875; home — Brooke (0508) 58144 or 50707. SER: Valuations; restorations.

Bungay continued
Cransford Gallery
20 Broad St. (H.M. and V.J. Vincent.) Est. 1978. CL: Sun. except by appointment; and occasionally Wed. SIZE: Small. STOCK: Paintings especially early English watercolours, 1750—1900, £25—£1,000; porcelain, from £25; small furniture, 18th—19th C, to £500. LOC: Near town centre. PARK: Easy. TEL: 2043. SER: Valuations; buys at auction (paintings). VAT: Spec.

BURES (0787)
Bures Antiques
1 Bridge St. (Mrs. J. Way and Mrs. P. Holme.) Est. 1973. Open 9.30—5.30, Sun. by appointment. SIZE: Large. STOCK: General antiques, from 16th C to art deco, furniture, china, glass, metalware, stripped pine, £5—£1,000+. PARK: Own. TEL: 227858; home — Colchester (0206) 210215. SER: Restorations (furniture and metalwork). VAT: Stan/Spec.

Maynscroft Antiques
Church Sq. (P. Chaplin.) CL: Tues. and Thurs. Open 9—6. STOCK: General antiques. TEL: 227395; home — same.

BURY ST. EDMUNDS (0284)
Corner Shop Antiques
1 Guildhall St. Open 10—5. SIZE: Small. STOCK: Victoriana, porcelain, jewellery, silver, clocks and collectors' items. LOC: Corner of Abbeygate and Guildhall St.

Guildhall Gallery LAPADA
1 and 1a Churchgate St. (P.N. Hewes.) Est. 1965. CL: Thurs. Open 10—1 and 2—5.30. SIZE: Large. STOCK: Oil paintings, £100— £5,000; watercolours, £50—£400; sporting prints and others, £10—£250; all 19th C. PARK: Easy. TEL: 62366. SER: Valuations; restorations; framing. VAT: Stan/Spec.

IS YOUR ENTRY CORRECT?
If there is even the slightest inaccuracy in your entry, *please* let us know before 1st January 1987.
GUIDE TO THE
ANTIQUE SHOPS OF BRITAIN
5 Church Street, Woodbridge, Suffolk.

Bury St. Edmunds continued

Guildhall Street Antiques
27 Guildhall St. (Mrs. T. Cutting.) Est. 1965. CL: Mon. a.m., Tues. and Thurs. Open 9.30—5.30. SIZE: Medium. *STOCK: General antiques, bric-a-brac, £25—£2,500.* LOC: From town centre down Guildhall St. to below Churchgate St. junction. PARK: Easy. TEL: 703060 or Horringer (028 488) 278. SER: Valuations.

Peppers Period Pieces
22-24 Churchgate St. (M.E. and Mrs. G.J. Pepper.) Est. 1975. Open 10—5. *STOCK: Country oak furniture, 16th—18th C; some elm, fruitwood, mahogany; English domestic implements in brass, copper, lead, iron, pewter and treen, 18th to early 20th C; some pottery and porcelain, furniture, bygones and collectables, late 19th to early 20th C.* Not stocked: Reproductions. PARK: Easy. TEL: 68786; home — Stanton (0359) 50606. SER: Valuations; repairs and polishing of all types. VAT: Spec.

Bury St. Edmunds continued

The Pine Shop
128 Southgate St. (V. and J. Edmunds.) Est. 1973. CL: Mon. and Thurs. Open 9.30—4.30. SIZE: Large. *STOCK: Stripped pine, £10—£800.* LOC: From Ipswich, A45, turn right at roundabout, shop 600 yds. on corner. TEL: 60103; home — Coney Weston (035 921) 285. VAT: Stan/Spec.

St. Edmunds Antique Centre
30 St. Johns St. (R. Chapman.) Est. 1970. Open 9.30—5.30, Sun. by appointment. SIZE: Medium. *STOCK: Porcelain, £25—£750; decorative furniture, £350—£5,000; books, £1—£200; oils and watercolours, £40—£1,000, all 18th—20th C; maps, prints, cameras, coins, medals, gramophones and collectables, £1—£200.* PARK: Nearby. TEL: 64469. SER: Valuations; restorations (furniture and ceramics); buys at auction. VAT: Stan.

THE CLARE COLLECTOR

**1 Nethergate Street,
Clare (near Long Melford),
Suffolk.
Telephone: Clare (0787) 277909**

*17th, 18th and 19th century furniture,
pictures, porcelain, works of art and curios at
reasonable prices.*

Bury St. Edmunds continued

Trench Enterprises
Open by appointment only. *STOCK: Old and antique jigsaws.* TEL: 60909. SER: Valuations; restorations; subscription stock list available quarterly; searches undertaken.

R.N. Usher
42 Southgate St. Est. 1938. CL: Sun., except by appointment. Open 9—5.30. Ring bell any time. SIZE: Small. *STOCK: Furniture, mahogany (mainly) and painted, 1720—1840, £20— £7,000; china, glass, 18th—19th C, £1— £800; architectural items, mainly mantelpieces, any period, £50—£5,000.* Not stocked: Brass, copper, reproductions. LOC: South side of town on A45 to Ipswich. PARK: Opposite. TEL: 4838. SER: Caning and gilding, repainting furniture; buys at auction. VAT: Stan/Spec.

Bury St. Edmunds continued

Winston Mac (Silversmith)
65 St. John's St. (E.W. McKnight.) Est. 1978. CL: Sun. except by appointment and Sat. Open 9—5. SIZE: Small. *STOCK: Silver tea services, creamers, salts.* PARK: Easy. TEL: 67910. SER: Restorations (silver and plating). VAT: Stan/Spec.

CLARE   (0787)
The Clare Collector   LAPADA
1 Nethergate St. (J. Verney.) Est. 1979. Open 10—1 and 2—5.30. SIZE: Medium. *STOCK: English and continental oak, walnut, mahogany and fruitwood furniture, 17th—19th C; pottery and porcelain, prints and watercolours, Oriental and tribal rugs, unusual items.* PARK: Easy. TEL: 277909; home — 277494. VAT: Spec.

The Clare Hall Co. Ltd.
The Old Court, Nethergate St. Est. 1982. Open 10—5.30 or by appointment. SIZE: Large. *STOCK: Decorative items, upholstered, painted and gilt furniture, ormolu, oil paintings and rugs.* LOC: A1092. PARK: Easy. TEL: 277510. SER: Restorations (all woods and upholstery); desks leathered. VAT: Stan/Spec.

Granny's Attic
22 High St. (M. Sadler.) Est. 1972. Open April—Dec., Tues., Thurs. and Fri. 2—5 Sat. 11—4.30. Dec.—April Sat. only 11—4.30. *STOCK: Cottage bygones, period clothing, linens, collectors' items.* LOC: Off main road, opposite church tower doorway. PARK: Easy. TEL: 277740. SER: Buys at auction.

Michael Moore Antiques
The Old Court, Nethergate St. Est. 1962. Open 10—5.30, or by appointment. SIZE: Large. *STOCK: Georgian and Victorian pine, £25—£800; decorative items, upholstered furniture.* LOC: A1092. PARK: Easy. TEL: 277510. SER: Restorations (all woods and upholstery); desks leathered. VAT: Stan/Spec.

F.D. Salter Antiques
1-2 Church St. Est. 1959. CL: Wed. p.m. Open 9—5. SIZE: Medium. *STOCK: Oak and mahogany furniture, English porcelain, 18th to early 19th C, £100—£500.* LOC: A1092. PARK: Easy. TEL. 277693. SER: Valuations; restorations (furniture). FAIRS: N.E.C. Birmingham; Snape and Bury St. Edmunds. VAT: Stan/Spec.

Trinder's Booksellers
Malting Lane. (P. Trinder). Est. 1975. Open Tues., Thurs. and Sat. 10—1 and 2—5, other times by appointment. SIZE: Medium. *STOCK: Books including British Isles topography, architecture, 19th—20th C.* PARK: Nearby. TEL: 277130; home — same.

CLAYDON, Nr. Ipswich

Brownhouse Antiques
Ipswich Rd. (Mrs. S. Bradley.) CL: Mon. Open 10—5 or by appointment. *STOCK: Stripped pine, Victoriana, curios, collectors' items.* TEL: Ipswich (0473) 830130.

DEBENHAM (0728)

Chancery Antiques
13 Chancery Lane. (A.D.P. Bryant.) CL: Sat. p.m. Open 10—1 and 2—5. *STOCK: Furniture, 18th—19th C; prints.* TEL: 860827.

The Dove Antiques
18 Aspall Rd. (J. Pynn). Est. 1972. CL: Fri. Open 10—5 including Sun. SIZE: Medium. *STOCK: Furniture, to 19th C; porcelain, silver and jewellery, linen, books.* LOC: B1077 on outskirts of town towards Eye. PARK: Easy. TEL: 860001; home — same.

Fleming's Antiques
High St. *STOCK: Furniture, including garden.* PARK: Easy. TEL: 860422. VAT: Spec.

N. Lanchester
21 High St. Open every day. *STOCK: General antiques, shipping goods and smalls.* TEL: 860756.

Debenham continued

Lovejoys Antiques
Forresters Hall, 52 High St. (C. Bigden, R. Frost). Est. 1971. Open daily, Sun. by appointment. SIZE: Large. *STOCK: Period oak, mahogany, decorative items, paintings and clocks.* PARK: Easy. TEL: 860777; home — Ipswich (0473) 59092. VAT: Stan/Spec.

EYE (0379)

A.N. Antiques
Home Farm, South Green. (R.O. and J.I. Norman and T.W. Allen.) Est. 1985. Open Sun. 10—6, other times by appointment. SIZE: Medium. *STOCK: Longcase clocks, 18th to mid-19th C, £300—£4,000; mechanical music including polyphons, 1860—1910, £200—£4,000; small mahogany furniture, 1780—1850, £250—£1,000.* Not stocked: Large and shipping furniture. LOC: From A140 through Eye on B1117 towards Stradbroke for 2 miles. Turn left to Hoxne, after 1 mile turn right on lane marked 'South Green Hoxne, no through road'. Fork right then left, premises at end of lane. PARK: Easy. TEL: 870367 or (0508) 78378; home — same. SER: Valuations (clocks, music boxes); restorations (clocks); buys at auction (longcase clocks). VAT: Stan/Spec.

Eye continued

The Corner Shop
Castle St. (Mrs. O.M. Whalley.) Est. 1969. Open Fri. and Sat. TEL: 870614.

FELIXSTOWE (0394)

John McCulloch Antiques
1a Hamilton Rd. Open 9.30—5, Wed. 9.30—1. *STOCK: Furniture, copper, brass, pictures, clocks and bric-a-brac.* LOC: Main street, sea front end at top of Bent Hill. PARK: Around corner. TEL: 283126; home — 272179.

FRAMLINGHAM (0728)

Bed Bazaar
29 Double St. (B. Goodbrey.) CL: Wed. Open 9—1 and 2—5.30, prior telephone call advisable. *STOCK: Victorian brass and iron beds.* LOC: Up Church St. towards Framlingham Castle. Opposite church gates turn right into Double St. PARK: Easy. TEL: 723756. SER: Restorations (beds); polishing (brass, copper).

Framlingham continued

B.R. Clover Antiques
14 Bridge St. Resident. CL: Wed. p.m.
*STOCK: Oak and mahogany furniture, small
items, glass and porcelain.* TEL: 723159.
VAT: Stan/Spec.

Goodbreys   *Mainly Trade*
29 Double St. (R. and M. Goodbrey.) Est.
1965. Open Mon—Fri. trade only, otherwise
by appointment; Sat. 9—5.30. SIZE: Large.
*STOCK: Furniture, Georgian, £25—£1,500;
William IV decorative, Biedermier, birch and
bird's eye maple furniture, £100—£2,000;
some country and continental furniture;
pictures, mirrors, glass, textiles, £1—£750.*
LOC: Up Church St. towards Framlingham
Castle. Opposite church gates turn right into
Double St. PARK: Easy. TEL: 723756. VAT:
Mainly spec.

Regency House
(T. Fleming.) Est. 1962. Open by appointment. *STOCK: Furniture and oil paintings.*
LOC: Opposite Church. PARK: Easy. TEL:
723553.

Tiffins Antiques
14 Fore St. (P.A. Macgregor.) Est. 1982.
Open daily, Sun. and other times by appointment. SIZE: Small. *STOCK: General antiques
including Victorian and country items, £5—
£500.* LOC: From Market Sq. into Church St.,
turn immediately right into Crown and Anchor
Lane, shop at junction with Fairfield Rd. PARK:
Easy. TEL: 723015; home — same. SER:
Valuations.

GAZELEY, Nr. Newmarket

Gazeley Antiques
2 Moulton Rd. (S.J. Cope-Brown.) Est. 1978.
Open evenings and weekends or by appointment. SIZE: Medium. *STOCK: Studio pottery
and porcelain, pot-lids, Prattware and Doulton,
Victorian to art nouveau and art deco, £5—
£100; furniture, 1800—1930, £5—£500;
copper and brass, from 1800, £5—£100.*
LOC: At T junction of Moulton Rd. and Gazeley High St., next to Gazeley Pond. PARK: At
rear. TEL: Newmarket (0638) 750974. SER:
Valuations; restorations (pottery and porcelain); buys at auction.

GREAT ASHFIELD

Bullivant Antiques
White Gates, Elmswell Rd. (P.T. Bullivant.)
Est. 1977. Open daily, Sat. and Sun. by
appointment. SIZE: Medium. *STOCK: Furniture, longcase clocks, 17th—18th C, £200—
£8,000.* LOC: Turn off A45 at Elmswell, 1½
miles on Gt. Ashfield Rd. TEL: Elmswell
(0359) 40040; home — same. SER: Valuations; restorations (clocks); buys at auction
(as stock). VAT: Spec.

GRUNDISBURGH   (047 335)
Nr. Woodbridge
Bond's Manor Antiques
Bond's Manor. (T.K. and W.E. Hickford.) Est.
1983. Open by appointment. SIZE: Small.
*STOCK: Furniture and accessories, 17th to
early 19th C.* LOC: 1 mile west of village
green. PARK: Easy. TEL: 357; home — same.

HACHESTON
Nr. Wickham Market

Joyce Hardy
Pine and Country Furniture
Resident. CL: Sun. and Wed. except by
appointment. Open 9.30—5.30. *STOCK: Pine
and period furniture.* LOC: B1116. On Framlingham Rd. PARK: Easy. TEL: Wickham
Market (0728) 746485. SER: Hand-made
furniture from old pine.

HADLEIGH, Nr. Ipswich   (0473)
Barn End Antiques and Firearms
(P.M. Skoulding.) Est. 1958. *STOCK: Fire-
arms, guns, swords, ammunition, and allied
items; silver, furniture, clocks, bygones,
Victoriana.* PARK: Easy. TEL: 823164. SER:
Valuations; repairs (guns).

Church Street Antiques
4 Church St. (M. Hart.) Est. 1970. Open
9.30—6, Sun. by appointment. SIZE: Large.
*STOCK: Furniture, clocks, barometers and
decorative items.* LOC: On main Ipswich to
Sudbury Rd. PARK: Easy. TEL: 822418. VAT:
Spec.

The Olde Shoulder Curiosity Shop
126 High St. Est. 1964. Open 9.30—1 and
2—5.30. SIZE: Large. *STOCK: Edwardian
furniture for restoration, fireplaces, books and
general antiques.* PARK: Easy. TEL: 823274.

Hadleigh continued

Randolph   **BADA**
97 and 99 High St. (B.F. and H.M. Marston, V.M. Brett.) Est. 1921. Open 9—5.30, but appointment advisable, Sun. only by appointment. SIZE: Medium. *STOCK: Furniture, 1560—1830, £20—£15,000; brass, copper, porcelain, delftware, some paintings, treen.* Not stocked: Silver. PARK: Easy. TEL: 823789. SER: Valuations; restorations (furniture). FAIRS: Grosvenor House; Harrogate. VAT: Spec.

Isobel Rhodes
69—73 Angel St. *STOCK: Furniture, oak, country, mahogany; brassware.* TEL: 823754; home — Gt. Wenham (0473) 310409. VAT: Spec.

Gordon Sutcliffe   **BADA**
105 High St. Est. 1952. CL: Mon. Open 10—1 and 2—5. *STOCK: Furniture, 1620—1820, £100—£3,000+; porcelain.* Not stocked: Victorian furniture, bric-a-brac, reproductions. TEL: 823464. SER: Valuations. FAIRS: Chelsea. VAT: Spec.

Tara's Hall
Victoria House, Market Place. (B. O'Keefe.) Est. 1977. CL: Wed. Open 10—5. SIZE: Medium. *STOCK: Clothing and linen, mainly 19th—20th C, £1—£150; jewellery, especially Georgian and art nouveau, 18th—20th C, £1—£500; small antiques and bric-a-brac.* PARK: Easy. TEL: 824031. SER: Valuations; buys at auction (jewellery, art nouveau objects, period clothing).

HALESWORTH   **(098 67)**

Ash Tree Antiques
Ash Tree Farm, Wissett. (P.M. and A.M.F.T. Lambert.) Est. 1980. Open Sat. and Sun. 10—5, other times by appointment. SIZE: Medium. *STOCK: Small pine and country furniture, 18th C to date, £5—£100; pottery and porcelain £5—£50.* LOC: 1 mile from Halesworth P.O. on Wissett Rd. PARK: Easy. TEL: 2867; home — same. SER: Buys at auction.

Blyth Bygones
8 Station Rd. Est. 1966. CL: Mon. Open 10—5. *STOCK: General antiques especially pine.* TEL: 3397. SER: Pine stripping.

IPSWICH   **(0473)**

A. Abbott Antiques
757 Woodbridge Rd. (C. Lillistone.) Est. 1965. CL: Wed. Open 10.30—5. SIZE: Medium. *STOCK: Small items, especially clocks and jewellery; Victorian, Edwardian and shipping furniture, £5—£1,000.* PARK: Easy. TEL: 78900; home — same.

Tony Adams Bygones Shop
52 Woodbridge Rd. CL: Wed. p.m. Open 10—5. *STOCK: General antiques and bygones, especially wireless sets and accessories and toy trains, bric-a-brac.* PARK: Christchurch St.

Aprile
29 St. Peter's St. Est. 1926. CL: Sat. *STOCK: Jewellery, Victoriana.* TEL: 51869.

Atfield and Daughter
17 St. Stephen's Lane. (D.A. and Miss S.F. Atfield.) Est. 1920. Open 9.30—5.30. SIZE: Large. *STOCK: Furniture, clocks, metal, pottery, £5—£500; pistols, swords, guns, militaria, scientific instruments, £10—£800; books on collecting, £5—£15.* LOC: Opposite bus station, Old Cattle Market. PARK: Nearby. TEL: 51158. SER: Valuations; restorations (general cabinet work); buys at auction. VAT: Stan.

Mike Bloomfield Antiques
13a St. Peters St. Est. 1972. CL: Sat. Open 9—5. *STOCK: Georgian, Regency and Victorian furniture; clocks, horse brasses and hunting prints.* TEL: 211359; home — 43996.

Pot and cover, famille rose, 6ins. From "Chinese Enamels" in **Antique Collecting**, June 1986.

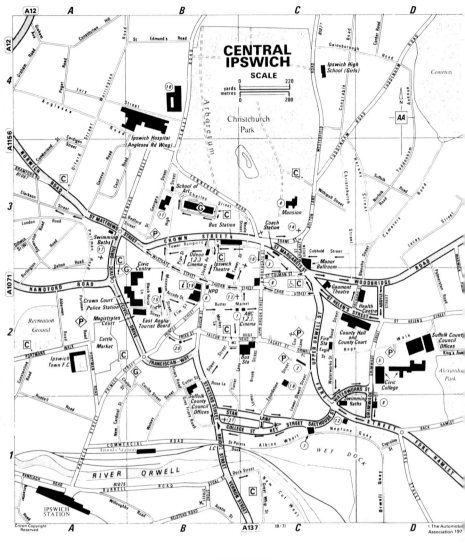

CENTRAL IPSWICH

SCALE

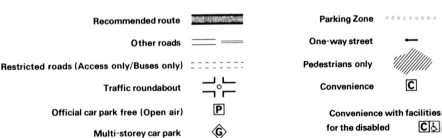

Recommended route		Parking Zone
Other roads		One-way street
Restricted roads (Access only/Buses only)		Pedestrians only
Traffic roundabout		Convenience
Official car park free (Open air)		
Multi-storey car park		Convenience with facilities for the disabled
Parking available on payment (Open air)		Tourist Information Centre

Ipswich continued

Paul Bruce Antiques   LAPADA
25/27 St. Helen's St. Est. 1972. CL: Weekends except by appointment. Open 9—5.30, (also Sat. for pine). SIZE: Medium. *STOCK: Pine, oak and mahogany furniture, paintings, general antiques, £20—£1,500.* LOC: Opposite County Hall. PARK: Own. TEL: 55400 or 212794. VAT: Stan/Spec.

Sonia Cordell Antiques
13 St. Peters St. Est. 1961. CL: Sat. Open 10—4 or by appointment. *STOCK: Small bygone treasures, jewellery, silver, sewing tools.* PARK: Nearby. TEL: 219508; home — Felixstowe (0394) 282254.

Country Bygones and Antiques
13c St. Peters St. (P. Adams.) CL: Sat. except by appointment. Open 10—5. *STOCK: Domestic, country and decorative items, Victoriana, some jewellery.* PARK: Nearby. TEL: 53683; home — Kirton (03948) 392.

Claude Cox at College Gateway Bookshop
3 Silent St. CL: Wed. Open 10—5. SIZE: Medium. *STOCK: Books, from 1470; some local maps and prints.* LOC: Follow Inner Ring Road to end, turn right, then left into Silent St. Shop is first on left. PARK: Nearby. TEL: 54776. SER: Valuations; restorations (rebinding); buys at auction, catalogue available.

Ipswich continued

Croydon & Sons Ltd.
50—56 Tavern St. Est. 1865. Open 9—5.30. SIZE: Large. *STOCK: Silver, 18th and 19th C, £5—£1,000; watches, clocks, 19th C, £30—£1,000.* LOC: Opposite Great White Horse Hotel. TEL: 56514. SER: Valuations; restorations (silver, silver plate, clocks, watches and jewellery). VAT: Stan/Spec.

The Edwardian Shop
556 Spring Rd. *STOCK: 1930s oak furniture.* TEL: 716576; evenings — 712890.

Forte's
27 St. Peter's St. (S. and M. Fortescue.) Est. 1950. CL: Sat. Open 9—6. *STOCK: Furniture, oil paintings.* PARK: Easy. TEL: 51342.

John Gazeley Associates Fine Art
17 Fonnereau Rd. Est. 1966. Usually open but appointment advisable. SIZE: Small. *STOCK: Decorative oil paintings, watercolours and prints, 18th to early 20th C, £5—£500; topographical engravings of local interest.* LOC: Central Ipswich off Crown St., east side of Christchurch Park. PARK: Easy. TEL: 52420; home — same. SER: Restorations (cleaning, re-lining paintings); framing.

Ipswich continued

Hubbard Antiques
16 St. Margarets Green and 47 St. Nicholas St. Est. 1964. Open 9—6. SIZE: Large. *STOCK: General antiques, period furniture, mahogany and oak.* PARK: Easy. TEL: 211344/226033. SER: Valuations; restorations. VAT: Stan/Spec.

Ipswich Paint Strippers
48 Woodbridge Rd. (L.A. Buitenhuis.) Est. 1983. Open 9—1 and 2—5.30, Thurs. 9—1. *STOCK: Victorian pine — dressers, £200—£400, chests, £100—£150, tables, £100—£200.* PARK: Opposite in Christchurch St. TEL: 211667; home — same. SER: Restorations. VAT: Stan.

John's Antiques
3—5 Alston Rd. (J. Burton.) Resident. Est. 1975. CL: Wed. Open Mon. and Sat. 10—6, otherwise 1—6. SIZE: Small. *STOCK: Furniture and bric-a-brac 1900—1940, £5—£100; weapons, 1850—1940, £10—£50.* LOC: 2nd left off Felixstowe Rd. after fork with Nacton Rd. coming from town centre. PARK: Easy. TEL: 210055 or 51723.

Majors Galleries
6 St. Helens St. (D. Briggs.) Est. 1982. CL: Wed. Open 10—5.30, Sat. 11—5. SIZE: Medium. *STOCK: Furniture, 19th C; art deco and art nouveau, £1—£400; decorative small items including clocks, ornaments, plates and pictures, 19th C.* LOC: Opposite Gaumont theatre. PARK: Nearby. TEL: 221190.

Moulin Antiques
167 Spring Rd. Est. 1975. Open 9.30—1 and 2—5, Sat. 9.30—1. SIZE: Small. *STOCK: General antiques, Victoriana, art nouveau, art deco, stripped pine.* TEL: 719252; home — 76147.

R.W. Paul
20a Fore St. (J.J. Duggan.) Est. 1948. CL: Sat. p.m. Open 9.30—5. SIZE: Medium. *STOCK: Furniture, porcelain, Victorian and Edwardian; some silver.* LOC: Fore St. leads out to Felixstowe Rd. PARK: 250yds. (Cox Lane). TEL: 51696.

Tom Smith Antiques
33A St. Peter's St. and warehouse. Est. 1959. *STOCK: Period furniture, accessories, shipping goods, £5—£5,000.* TEL: 210172.

Spring Antiques
436 Spring Rd. (S. Bullard.) Est. 1970. CL: Thurs. Open 9.30—1. SIZE: Small. *STOCK: Clocks, brass, silver and plate, china, jewellery. Not stocked: Coins, stamps.* LOC: From Woodbridge, bear left at 2nd roundabout for town centre then take left fork at Lattice Barn Inn. Shop opp. Inskil school. PARK: 50yds. in adjacent streets. TEL: 75606.

Ipswich continued

Patrick Taylor Antiques
1st Floor, entrance under arch, 13 St. Peter's St. Est. 1963. Open by appointment. SIZE: Medium. *STOCK: English and Continental porcelain, £5—£250; silver, £5—£50; all 18th—19th C.* LOC: From Town Hall pass through Queen St. and St. Nicholas St. to St. Peter's St. PARK: Silent St. TEL: 50774; home — 328351. SER: Valuations; restorations (furniture, silver, pottery and porcelain, clocks).

Thompson's
418 Norwich Rd. (D. and Mrs. S. Thompson.) Est. 1978. CL: Sun. except by appointment. Open 10—5.30. SIZE: Medium. *STOCK: Furniture, mainly late Victorian and shipping, 1870 to date, £10—£400.* LOC: 1 mile from town centre, on corner at traffic lights next to railway bridge. PARK: Own, at side of premises. TEL: 47793; home — 328460. SER: Valuations; buys at auction (shipping items). VAT: Stan/Spec.

Thompson's Antiques
386 Spring Rd. (D. and Mrs. S. Thompson.) CL: Sun. except by appointment. Open 10—1 or by appointment. *STOCK: General antiques mainly bric-a-brac and china, some furniture.* LOC: 1 mile from town centre towards Woodbridge. TEL: 75742; home — 328460. SER: Valuations; buys at auction (shipping items).

Victoria House Antiques
46 Norwich Rd. (R. Pegg.) Est. 1980. Open 9—6. *STOCK: Furniture and general antiques.* TEL: 210306.

C.A. Wall and Co.
11 St. Peter's St. Est. 1972. Open 9.30—5.30. *STOCK: Furniture, porcelain, £10—£500.* LOC: Past Town Hall, down Queen St., St. Nicholas St. to St. Peter's St. PARK: Silent St. TEL: 214366/52572. VAT: Stan/Spec.

Gerald Weir Antiques   LAPADA
7-11 Vermont Rd. Open by appointment anytime. SIZE: Large. *STOCK: Georgian and Victorian furniture.* TEL: 52606 or 55572.

E.W. Cousins and Son

Established since 1910
27 High Street, Ixworth, Near Bury St. Edmunds, Suffolk
Tel. Pakenham 30254

*Specialists in Georgian
and Victorian furniture
Large selection of clocks
and barometers*

*8,000 sq.ft. of selected furniture
Export Trade welcome
Containers packed
Wholesale and Retail Trade*

IXWORTH, Nr. Bury St. Edmunds

E.W. Cousins and Son   LAPADA
27 High St. CL: Sat. p.m. SIZE: Large.
*STOCK: General antiques, 18th—19th C,
£25—£1,500; shipping items.* LOC: A143.
Opposite Methodist Chapel. PARK: Easy. TEL:
Pakenham (0359) 30254. SER: Valuations;
restorations. VAT: Stan/Spec.

KESGRAVE

Mainline Furniture
83 Main Rd. (Mr. and Mrs. R.S. Rust.) Est.
1977. Open 9—6. *STOCK: Furniture, Victorian to 1930s; china and collectables, clocks.*
TEL: Ipswich (0473) 623092.

KESSINGLAND

Kessingland Antiques
36A High St. Est. 1976. Open every day
9—12.30 and 1.30—5.30. SIZE: Large.
*STOCK: Edwardian, Victorian and Georgian
furniture, stripped pine, general antiques,
pocket watches, clocks, jewellery, shipping
goods.* LOC: On A12, 3 miles south of
Lowestoft. PARK: On forecourt and own. TEL:
Lowestoft (0502) 740562. VAT: Stan/Spec.

LAVENHAM   (0787)

R.G. Archer
7 Water St. Est. 1970. Open 9—5, Sun.
10—5. *STOCK: Antiquarian and secondhand
books.* PARK: Easy. TEL: 247229.

J. and J. Baker
12—14 Water St. and 3a High St. (C.J. and
Mrs. B.A.J. Baker.) Est. 1960. Open 9—1 and
2—5.30. SIZE: Medium. *STOCK: Oak and
mahogany furniture, 1600—1830, £20—
£2,000; oils and watercolours, 19th C, £50—
£3,000; English porcelain and metalware,
18th—19th C, £10—£200; collectors' items,
£10—£100.* LOC: Below Swan Hotel at T
junction of B1070 and B1071. PARK: Easy.
TEL: 247 610. VAT: Stan/Spec.

Lavenham continued

Tim Bell Antiques
Maltings Farm, Thorpe Morieux. Open Mon.—
Sat. *STOCK: Furniture including shipping;
small items.* TEL: Bury St. Edmunds (0284)
828843.

Marshbeck Antiques
Lavenham Antiques and Craft Centre, High St.
(S. Marshall and P. Beck.) Est. 1981. Open
every day 10.30—4.30. SIZE: Small. *STOCK:
Silver and jewellery, 1800—1940; china and
glass, 19th C; all £5—£100.* LOC: Main
street. PARK: Easy. TEL: 247548.

Motts of Lavenham
8 Water St. (J.G. and D.M. Mott.) Est. 1980.
Open 10—4.30, Sun. by appointment. SIZE:
Small. *STOCK: Furniture, £20—£1,000;
pottery and porcelain, £5—£350, all 19th C;
metal toys and diecasts, 20th C, 20p—£100.*
LOC: Off High St. by Swan Hotel, shop
200yds. on left. PARK: Easy. TEL: Rattlesden
(044 93) 637; home — same. SER: Buys at
auction (tinplate and diecasts). VAT: Stan.

Tom Smith Antiques
36 Market Place. Est. 1959. SIZE: Large. and
warehouse. *STOCK: Furniture, early Staffordshire figures, rugs.* TEL: 247463. SER: Valuations; restorations. VAT: Stan/Spec.

LEAVENHEATH

Clock House
Locks Lane. (A.G. Smeeth). Est. 1983. Open
by appointment. SIZE: Small. *STOCK: English
clocks, late 18th to early 19th C, £500—
£1,500; French and English clocks, Victorian
and Edwardian, £150—£500.* PARK: Easy.
TEL: Nayland (0206) 262187; home — same.
SER: Valuations; restorations (clocks); buys at
auction (clocks).

LEISTON   (0728)

Leiston Trading Post
21a Cross St. (A.E. Moore.) Est. 1967. CL: Wed. Open 10—12.30 and 2—5, Mon. 10—12, Sat. 10—5, Sun. by appointment only. SIZE: Small. *STOCK: Bric-a-brac, Victoriana, Victorian and Edwardian furniture.* PARK: Easy. TEL: 830081; home — 830281. VAT: Stan.

LONG MELFORD

Ashley Antiques
Belmont House, Hall St. Est. 1965. Open 9.30—5.30, or by appointment. SIZE: Medium. *STOCK: Paintings, watercolour drawings, furniture, porcelain, Oriental rugs.* LOC: A134, opposite Crown Hotel. PARK: Easy. TEL: Sudbury (0787) 75434. VAT: Spec.

Mrs. R. Bell
Coconut House, Hall St. Resident. CL: Sun. and Wed. except by appointment. Open 9—6. SIZE: Medium. *STOCK: Furniture and paintings.* LOC: Opposite Bull Hotel. PARK: Easy. TEL: Sudbury (0787) 79860; home — same. SER: Valuations; restorations (paintings); framing. VAT: Stan/Spec.

Long Melford continued

Carling Antiques
8 Hall St. (R. Carling.) Usually open 10—1, and 2—5.30. *STOCK: General antiques, furniture, metalware, clocks and barometers.* TEL: Sudbury (0787) 312012.

Chater-House Gallery
Foundry House, Hall St. (A. Chater-House.) Open 10—5 including Sun. SIZE: Large and warehouse. *STOCK: Ceramics, clocks, jewellery, late 18th—20th C.* TEL: Sudbury (0787) 79831. SER: Valuations; restorations (furniture, clocks); upholstery.

Compton-Dando (Fine Arts) Ltd.
Hall St. Open 9.30—5.30. *STOCK: Period English and Continental furniture, interesting decorative fixtures and fittings.* TEL: Sudbury (0.787) 312610. SER: Packing, insurance and transport. VAT: Stan/Spec.

DENZIL GRANT
17th and 18th Century Antiques and Tapestries

HALL STREET, LONG MELFORD, SUFFOLK
Telephone Sudbury 75470 or Rattlesden 576

Figured walnut kneehole dressing chest. Circa 1720

Long Melford continued

Country Antiques
10 Westgate St. (Mrs. I. Bury.) Est. 1967. Open 11—5. SIZE: Medium. *STOCK: Cottage and farmhouse bygones, hand tools especially woodworking, ironwork and stoneware, toys, brass, pewter and copper, modest jewellery, treen, pottery, linen, lace, embroidery and Victorian accessories.* Not stocked: Arms, coins, expensive porcelain and silver. LOC: On outskirts of Long Melford, on road to Clare, nr. church. PARK: Easy. TEL: Sudbury (0787) 310617. VAT: Stan/Spec.

Cross Keys Antiques
Little St. Marys. (W.C. Nunn and Son.) Est. 1890. Open 2.15—5.30. SIZE: Medium. *STOCK: General antiques, furniture, 1730—1830; furniture, 1650—1730, both £5—£1,000; Victoriana, 1830—1890.* LOC: A134. From Sudbury shop is on right opp. Theobalds Bus Garage. PARK: Easy. TEL: Sudbury (0787) 75787; home — Sudbury (0787) 74782. SER: Valuations. VAT: Spec.

The Enchanted Aviary
63 Hall St. (C.C. Frost.) Est. 1970. Open 9.30—5.30, but appointment advisable. SIZE: Medium. *STOCK: Cased and uncased mounted birds, animals, fish, mostly late Victorian, £5—£300.* PARK: Easy. TEL: Sudbury (0787) 78814. VAT: Spec.

Long Melford continued

The Goff Galleries
Hall St. (B. Goff Gillings.) Est. 1958. SIZE: Medium. *STOCK: Furniture, 18th C, £500—£25,000; oil paintings, 1580—1830, £350—£5,000.* Not stocked: Victorian items. LOC: On main A134, opp. Bull Hotel. PARK: Easy. TEL: Sudbury (0787) 78228. SER: Valuations. VAT: Spec.

Denzil Grant Antiques
Hall St. Est. 1979. Open 10—5.30 or by appointment. *STOCK: Furniture, 16th to early 19th C; tapestry, metalware.* LOC: On A134 in centre of village. PARK: Easy. TEL: Sudbury (0787) 75470; home — Rattlesden (044 93) 576. SER: Valuations; restorations (furniture, tapestry).

Long Melford continued

Long Melford Antiques Centre

The Chapel Maltings. (Baroness V. von Dahlen.) Est. 1984. Open 10—5.30 or by appointment. SIZE: Large. There are 38 dealers at this centre selling mainly *furniture, Queen Anne, Georgian, Edwardian and Victorian; silver, china, glass and decorators' items, £5—£10,000.* LOC: A134, Sudbury end of village. TEL: Sudbury (0787) 79287; home — Sudbury (0787) 277231. SER: Valuations; restorations (furniture); packing and shipping; buys at auction. VAT: Stan/Spec.

Alexander Lyall Antiques

Belmont House, Hall St. (A.J. Lyall.) Est. 1977. Open 9.30—5.30. SIZE: Medium. *STOCK: Furniture, 18th—19th C.* LOC: A134 opposite Crown Hotel. PARK: Easy. TEL: Sudbury (0787) 75434; home — same. SER: Restorations (furniture); buys at auction (English furniture). VAT: Stan/Spec.

Janice Newman

Old Pharmacy House, Hall St. CL: Wed. Open 10.30—5.30. *STOCK: General antiques especially porcelain and English blue and white.* TEL: Sudbury (0787) 312182.

Long Melford continued

The Old Forge

Bridge St. (C. and I. Chilton). Open 9.30—6 including Sun. SIZE: Medium. *STOCK: Pine, mahogany and oak, 17th—20th C, £5—£1,500; shipping smalls, £1—£50.* LOC: On A134, 2½ miles from Long Melford. VAT: Stan/Spec.

Old George Antiques

Coconut House, Hall St. (W.M. Wild and J.G.R. Tyndall.) CL: Sun. and Wed. except by appointment. Open 9—6. SIZE: Medium. *STOCK: Mahogany and decorated furniture, 18th C, £150—£5,000; Oriental and English lacquer, walnut furniture, 17th C.* LOC: Opposite Bull Hotel. PARK: Easy. TEL: Sudbury (0787) 79860. SER: Valuations; buys at auction. VAT: Stan/Spec.

Pauline Peretz Antiques   LAPADA

Linden House, Hall St. Est. 1969. Open 10—5. *STOCK: Silver, furniture, prints and decorative items, 18th to early 19th C.* PARK: Easy. TEL: Sudbury (0787) 70534. VAT: Stan/Spec.

Seabrook Antiques

Hall St. (D. Edwards and J. Tanner.) Open 9.30—5.30 or by appointment. *STOCK: Oak furniture and unusual items, 17th—19th C.* TEL: Sudbury (0787) 76876/311788.

Sun House Antiques

Hall Street, Long Melford,
Suffolk. Tel: (0787) 78252

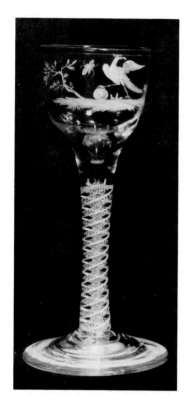

*Wine Glass enamelled by the Beilby family
from Newcastle. Circa. 1770.*

Open: Thursday, Friday, Saturday
or by appointment

Long Melford continued

Sun House Antiques   BADA
**Hall St. (M. Thompson.) Est. 1966. CL: Mon.,
Tues. and Wed. except by appointment. Open
10—5. SIZE: Medium.** *STOCK: Country furniture, 18th and 19th C; glass, pottery, needlework, blue and white, metalware.* **PARK:
Easy. TEL: Sudbury (0787) 78252. FAIRS:
Grosvenor House. VAT: Spec.**

Suthburgh Antiques
Red House, Hall St. (R.P. Alston.) Est. 1977.
CL: Sun. except by appointment. Open
10—5. SIZE: Medium. *STOCK: Furniture,
£300—£6,000; Georgian barometers and
clocks, £400—£5,000; antiquarian maps and
prints, 1600—1850, £25—£450, small collectors' items, boxes, silver, glass, 1760—
1820, £25—£75.* Not stocked: Victorian
furniture and later items. LOC: Opposite Bull
Hotel, A134. PARK: Easy. TEL: Sudbury
(0787) 74818; home — Sudbury (0787)
72667. SER: Valuations; buys at auction.
VAT: Stan/Spec.

Tudor Antiques
Little St. Mary, Main St. (A.H. Denton-Ford.)
Est. 1974. Open 9.30—6, Sun. 2—5. SIZE:
Large. *STOCK: General antiques, 50p—
£1,000; curios, silver, objets d'art, country
furniture, bygones.* LOC: Sudbury end of Long
Melford, shop with yellow blind. PARK: Easy.
TEL: Sudbury (0787) 75950. SER: Valuations; shipping; metal polishing. VAT: Stan/
Spec.

Ward Antiques
Hall St. (S. Cooke, J. Ward). Est. 1982. Open
10—1 and 2—5.30, Sun. by appointment.
SIZE: Large. *STOCK: Furniture, 17th to early
19th C, £50—£5,000.* Not stocked: Silver
and glass. LOC: A134. PARK: Easy. TEL:
Sudbury (0787) 78265; home — Sudbury
(0787) 312549. SER: Valuations; restorations; buys at auction (furniture). VAT:
Stan/Spec.

Westgate Street Antiques
4 Westgate St. (Mrs. J. Harding.) Est. 1982.
Open 10—5. SIZE: Medium. *STOCK: Stripped
country pine, decorative and general antiques.*
LOC: On Clare road, near church. PARK: Easy.
TEL: Sudbury (0787) 310210. VAT: Stan/
Spec.

LOWESTOFT   (0502)

Ann Teak
560 London Rd. South. (Mrs. S. Elwood.) Est. 1967. Open 10.30—12.45 and 2.15—5. *STOCK: Bric-a-brac, bygones, cottage items.* PARK: Easy. TEL: Home — 65574.

Royal Thoroughfare Gallery
6 Pier Terrace (R.H. Sprake.) Est. 1979. Open by appointment. SIZE: Small. *STOCK: Furniture, £10—£500; paintings, £10—£3,000; both 19th C; some small objects of art.* Not stocked: Silver, jewellery and gold. LOC: Close to town centre and harbour bridge. PARK: 100yds. TEL: 82006/61930. SER: Valuations; buys at auction.

W. Taylor Antiques
13 St. Peter's St. (W.D.J. Taylor.) Est. 1965. Open Tues., Fri. and Sat. 10—4. SIZE: Small. *STOCK: Furniture, 1840—1910, £5—£250; pictures, 1830—1920, £3—£100; bygones and bric-a-brac, £1—£100.* LOC: Opposite Market Place, High St., A12. PARK: 100yds. opp. TEL: 3374; home — 730421. VAT: Stan.

Windsor Gallery
167 London Rd. South. (R.W. Glanfield.) Open 9.15—1 and 2—5. *STOCK: Pictures and bric-a- brac.* TEL: 512278.

MARTLESHAM, Nr. Woodbridge

Martlesham Antiques
The Thatched Roadhouse. (C. Bigden, R.F. Frost). Est. 1973. Open daily, Sun. by appointment. SIZE: Large. *STOCK: Furniture and decorative items, 17th—20th C., £25—£3,000.* LOC: A12 opposite Red Lion public house. PARK: Own. TEL: Woodbridge (03943) 6732; home — Ipswich (0473) 59092.

MELTON, Nr. Woodbridge

Melton Antiques
Kingdom Hall, The St. (A. Harvey-Jones.) Est. 1975. Open 9.30—4.30. SIZE: Small. *STOCK: Silver, collector's items, £5—£500; decorative items and furniture, £15—£200; both 18th—19th C; Victoriana and general antiques, 19th C, £5—£150.* LOC: On right hand-side coming from Woodbridge. PARK: Easy. TEL: Woodbridge (039 43) 6232.

NAYLAND   (0206)

Hugh Arnold Antiques
20 High St. Est. 1967. Open 9—5.30. SIZE: Large. *STOCK: Furniture, 17th—19th C, £20—£4,000; metals, glass, bronzes, porcelain, pottery, blue and white, barometers, stoneware, rugs, clocks, pictures, bygones.* LOC: Near Parish Church, opp. Post Office. PARK: Easy. TEL: 262486; home — 262422. SER: Valuations. VAT: Stan/Spec.

Nayland continued

Templar Antiques
The Corner House, 2 Bear St. (P. Wilson.) Resident. Est. 1972. Open 9.30—5.30, otherwise by appointment. SIZE: Small. *STOCK: Porcelain and earthenware 18th—20th C, £20—£500; glass, £25—£300; small furniture, tables, mirrors, chairs, £100—£900; all 18th—19th C; decorative items, rugs.* LOC: Just off A134, village centre. PARK: Nearby. TEL: 262520.

NEEDHAM MARKET   (0449)

Roy Arnold
77 High St. Est. 1974. Open 9.30—5.30, appointment advisable, Sun. by appointment. SIZE: Medium. *STOCK: Woodworkers' and craftsmen's tools, scientific instruments and books, £10—£5,000.* LOC: A45, centre of High St. PARK: Easy. TEL: 720110. VAT: Stan/Spec.

The Old Town Hall Antique Centre
High St. (S. and R. Abbott.) Open 10—5. The dealers at this centre offer a wide range of general antiques. TEL: 720773. SER: Repairs (jewellery and clocks).

The Relic Shop
106 High St. (C. Russell.) Est. 1976. CL: Tues. Open 10—4.30. *STOCK: Jewellery, silver, pine and country furniture, Victoriana.* TEL: 721245; home — Ipswich (0473) 830858.

NEWMARKET   (0638)

Clock Tower Antiques
2 and 12/14 Old Station Rd. (Mrs. W. Thurston.) Est. 1967. Open 10.30—5.45. SIZE: Large. *STOCK: Furniture, porcelain, clocks, brass, copper, paintings, prints and watercolours, Staffordshire, fairings, coloured glass, lamps, dolls, toys, costume, small silver, plate, treen and tea boxes.* LOC: Near Clock Tower in High St. PARK: About 100yds. Turn past shop. TEL: 664915. SER: Buys at auction. FAIRS: Bury St. Edmunds and others.

Dudley's Antiques and Home Interiors
13 High St. (A.F. and J.A. Dudley.) Open 9—5 or by appointment. *STOCK: General antiques, furniture, copper, brass, porcelain, pictures, prints, country bygones, curios, collectors' items, clocks, bric-a-brac, from 50p.* SER: Restorations (clocks, barometers, furniture, silver and metal); caning, rushing, framing, wood carving, turning, French polishing, veneering, upholstery and buttoning; design consultant; furniture made to order. TEL: 662958 or 741989 (ansaphone).

Newmarket continued

Jemima Godfrey
5 Rous Rd. (Miss A. Lanham.) Est. 1968. Open Thurs. and Fri. 10—5. SIZE: Small. *STOCK: Small antiques and jewellery, 19th C.* LOC: Just off High St., nr. clock tower. PARK: Easy. TEL: 663584.

Newmarket Gallery
156 High St. (N.R. Herbert.) Resident. Open 9.30—1 and 2—5, Sun. and Wed. by appointment. SIZE: Small. *STOCK: Sporting prints, drawings, pictures.* LOC: A11 at south end of High St. PARK: Easy. TEL: 661183. SER: Valuations; restorations; buys at auction.

Northwold Gallery
Rear of 30 High St. (C.G. and J.A. Troman.) Est. 1973. CL: Sat. p.m. and Wed. Open 10—1 and 2—5. SIZE: Medium. *STOCK: Paintings and prints, 19th C to contemporary, to £100.* LOC: Behind Waggon and Horses public house. PARK: Easy. TEL: 668758; home — Methwold (0366) 581. SER: Framing; restorations (oils, watercolours and prints). VAT: Stan.

R.E. and G.B. Way
Brettons, Burrough Green. Open 9—5.30, but appointment advisable. *STOCK: Antiquarian books on shooting, fishing, horses, horse racing and hunting.* TEL: Stetchworth (063 876) 217.

NORTON
Nr. Bury St. Edmunds
E. J. Everitt
Long Reach, Ashfield Rd. Open 9—5. SIZE: Large. *STOCK: Georgian, Victorian and shipping furniture.* LOC: Just off A45 between Ipswich and Bury St. Edmunds. TEL: Elmswell (0359) 41581.

ORFORD   (039 45)
Castle Antiques
Market Sq. (B.M. Bennett.) Est. 1969. Open 12—4.30 every day. *STOCK: Furniture, general small antiques, bric-a-brac, glass, china, clocks.* TEL: 388.

PEASENHALL   (072 879)
Peasenhall Art and Antiques Gallery
The Street (A. and M. Wickins.) Est. 1972. Resident. Open every day. *STOCK: 19th C watercolours and oils; country furniture, all woods.* TEL: 224; home — same. SER: Restorations (oils, watercolours, furniture). VAT: Spec.

RISBY
Nr. Bury St. Edmunds
The Barn
(A.W. guy.) Open seven days 10—1 and 2—4. There are 24 dealers at these premises offering *furniture, porcelain, metalware, tools, pine, art deco.* LOC: Just off A45 west of Bury St. Edmunds. TEL. Bury St. Edmunds (0284) 810454.

SAXMUNDHAM   (0728)
Jean Campbell
26A High St. Est. 1982. Open 9.30—5. *STOCK: Country pieces, silver, Victoriana.* PARK: Nearby. TEL: 2895. VAT: Stan/Spec.

Market Place Antiques
Market Place. CL: Thurs. Open 10—5. *STOCK: General antiques.* TEL: 2503.

SHINGLE STREET, Nr. Woodbridge
Peter Downing   LAPADA
Alde House. Open by appointment. *STOCK: General antiques.* TEL: Shottisham (0394) 411873.

SOUTHWOLD   (0502)
David and Dorothy Lee
21 High St. (D.M. and D.L. Lee.) Est. 1965. CL: Wed., except 10—1 July—Sept. Open 10—1 and 2.30—5.30. SIZE: Small. *STOCK: Furniture, china, glass, bygones, treen, from late 18th C.* Not stocked: Coins, stamps, firearms, edge weapons. TEL: 722795; home — 722576. SER: Restoration (furniture).

SPROUGHTON, Nr. Ipswich
Run of the Mill
The Mill. (S. Hughes-Reckitt, A. Jones.) Open first Sat. of each month, or by appointment. *STOCK: General antiques.* TEL: Ipswich (0473) 41454.

STONHAM PARVA
Nr. Stowmarket
E.T. Webster
Mill Barn, Church Lane. Open by appointment. *STOCK: Antiquarian books relating to English literature 16th—20th C; oak for restorations.* TEL: Stowmarket (0449) 711397.

STOWMARKET   (0449)
Chelsea House Antiques
27 Station Rd. (D. Cordon and S. Bates.) Est. 1974. CL: Sun., except by appointment and Mon. and Tues. Open 10—5, Wed. 10.30—1 and 2—5. SIZE: Small. *STOCK: Furniture, £100; decorative items, £1—£75; both 18th—19th C. Victoriana, £5—£100; stripped pine.* LOC: Town centre off A45. PARK: Nearby. TEL: Home — Elmswell (0359) 40895.

STRADBROKE, Nr. Diss (037 984)
Mary Palmer Antiques
The Cottage Farm, New St. (Mrs. M. Palmer Stones.) Resident. Est. 1980. Open 9—9, Sun. by appointment. SIZE: Small. *STOCK: English glass, 1750—1850; furniture, 1700—1900.* LOC: B1117. PARK: Easy. TEL: 8100. SER: Valuations; restorations (furniture).

SUDBURY (0787)
Gainsborough Street Gallery
26 Gainsborough St. (S. Eve, T. Heigham). Est. 1981. CL: Wed. and Fri. Open 10—1 and 2—4. SIZE: Small. *STOCK: Furniture, mirrors, decorative items, silver and plate including flatware and Old Sheffield, 18th and 19th C, £5—£1,000.* LOC: 150yds. from Market Hill. PARK: Nearby. TEL: Home — Lavenham (0787) 247349. SER: Buys at auction (furniture, silver).

D. Rochester
3 and 4 Church St. Est. 1969. *STOCK: Furniture, glass, china.* TEL: 75280.

WANGFORD (0502 78)
Nr. Beccles
Wangford Antiques
'Churchview', 10 High St. (A. and T. Upcraft.) Est. 1983. CL: Mon. and Thurs. Open 10—4 and most Sun. SIZE: Medium. *STOCK: Furniture, 18th C to 1930's, £20—£300; china and glass, Victorian to Art Deco, £5—£50.* PARK: Easy. TEL: 626; home — same.

WESTLETON, (072 873)
Nr. Saxmundham
Lovejoy at Westleton
Ebenezer House, Yoxford Rd. (R. Parr.) Est. 1980. Open 10—5, Sun. 10—2. SIZE: Medium. *STOCK: Victorian and Edwardian furniture, smalls and china.* LOC: 200yds. from junction Blythburgh/Leiston road. PARK: Easy. TEL: 529; home — same.

WICKHAM MARKET (0728)
Crafers Antiques
The Hill (Mrs. E. Davies.) Est. 1970. CL: Lunchtime Tues., and Thurs. Open 9.30—5.30. *STOCK: 18th—19th C porcelain and pottery, glass, silver, jewellery, furniture and collectors items.* LOC: Opposite church. TEL: 747347.

Morris Antiques and Bygones
70 High St. (V. and M.J. Taylor.) Est. 1965. Open Wed.—Sat. 10.30—12.30 and 2.30—4.30 or by appointment. SIZE: Large. *STOCK: Furniture, 18th—19th C; general antiques.* Not stocked: Paintings. LOC: 20yds. north from Market Hill. PARK: Private park at rear. From Market Hill first turning right off Easton Rd. TEL: 746275, home — 747207.

Wickham Market continued
Victoria Pine
87 High St. (L.D. & M.W. Turner.) Est. 1981. Open 9—6. SIZE: Medium. *STOCK: Period and Victorian stripped pine.* LOC: Just off Market Sq. opposite Morris Antiques. PARK: Village sq. TEL: 746654; home — same.

Roy Webb
179 High St. Open Mon., Thurs. and Sat. 10—6 or by appointment. *STOCK: Furniture, 18th—19th C; clocks.* TEL: 746077; home — Woodbridge (039 43) 2697. VAT: Stan.

WITHERSDALE, Nr. Harleston
The Grange Gallery
Withersdale Lodge. (Col. and Mrs. J. Allford.) Est. 1971. Open anytime by appointment. SIZE: Medium. *STOCK: Watercolours; 18th—19th C small furniture.* LOC: 2½ miles from Harleston on B1123 Halesworth Rd. PARK: Easy. TEL: Harleston (0379) 852254. SER: Framing; buys at auction.

WOODBRIDGE (039 43)
Antique Furniture Warehouse
Trade and Export Only
Old Maltings, Crown Place. (H.T. and R.E. Ferguson.) Est. 1976. CL: Sat., Sun. except by appointment. Usually open 9—5. SIZE: Large. *STOCK: Furniture, 17th to early 20th C, £5—£5,000; shipping goods, small items.* LOC: In centre of town, off Quay St. First warehouse in Crown Place. TEL: 7222; home — Eyke (0394) 460237. VAT: Stan/Spec.

Continental pottery faience figure of a seated cat after Emile Gallé, 14ins. high. From "Auction Feature" in **Antique Collecting,** June 1986.

The Simon Carter Gallery

23 MARKET HILL
WOODBRIDGE SUFFOLK
IP12 4LX
Telephone Woodbridge 2242

**DRAWINGS, WATERCOLOURS AND OIL
PAINTINGS OF ALL PERIODS.
ANTIQUE FURNITURE AND DECORATIVE ITEMS.**

**OPEN MONDAY — SATURDAY,
9.15a.m. — 5.30p.m.**

FRENCH, GERMAN AND ITALIAN SPOKEN.

**THE GALLERY IS 1¼ HOURS BY TRAIN FROM
LIVERPOOL STREET STATION, LONDON, AND
LESS THAN 1 HOUR BY ROAD FROM HARWICH.**

David Gibbins Antiques

Member of the British Antique Dealers Association
21 MARKET HILL, WOODBRIDGE, SUFFOLK, IP12 4LX
Tel: Woodbridge 3531

Fine Adam period shield back armchair with painted decoration c.1780 and mahogany wine table of similar period typical of our stock.

Woodbridge continued

Simon Carter Gallery
23 Market Hill. Est. 1960. Open 9.15−5.30.
SIZE: Large. *STOCK: English and Continental oil paintings, 17th−20th C; English watercolours and drawings, 18th−20th C; furniture, oak and mahogany, 17th−19th C; decorative objects, some prints.* Not stocked: Clocks, porcelain, silver. PARK: 60yds. behind gallery in Theatre St. TEL: 2242; home − Shottisham (0394) 411334. SER: Three exhibitions held annually. VAT: Spec.

David Gibbins Antiques   BADA
21 Market Hill. Est. 1964. Open 9.30−5.30, Wed. 9.30−1. *STOCK: English furniture, late 16th to early 19th C, £300−£15,000; English pottery and porcelain, pewter, metalwork, clocks.* PARK: Own in Theatre St. TEL: 3531; home − 2685. SER: Valuations; buys at auction. VAT: Spec.

Hamilton Antiques
8 Church St. (H.T. and R.E. Ferguson.) Est. 1976. CL: Wed. p.m. except by appointment. Open 9.30−1 and 2−5, Sat. 9.30−1 and 2−4.30. *STOCK: Furniture − mahogany, walnut, oak, fruitwood, 17th−20th C, £50−£5,000.* TEL: 7222; home − Eyke (0394) 460237. VAT: Stan/Spec.

Woodbridge continued

Anthony Hurst Antiques   LAPADA
13 Church St. (A.H.B. Hurst.) Est. 1957. CL: Wed. p.m. Open 9.30−1 and 2−5.30. SIZE: Large. *STOCK: English furniture, oak, walnut and mahogany, 1600−1900, £40−£3,000.* PARK: Easy. TEL: 2500. SER: Valuations; restorations (furniture); buys at auction. FAIRS: Snape. VAT: Stan/Spec.

Lambert's Barn
24A Church St. CL: Wed. p.m. Open 9.30−1 and 2−5. SIZE: Large. *STOCK: Mainly Victorian and 20th C furniture, miscellaneous items.* PARK: Easy.

Woolpit Antiques
The Street. Open daily or by appointment. *STOCK: Furniture, including painted, decorative items, Victoriana, beadworks, £5—£500.* TEL: Home — Elmswell (0359) 40895.

WORTHAM, Nr. Diss

The Falcon Gallery
Honeypot Farm. (N. Smith.) Resident. Est. 1974. Open by appointment seven days. SIZE: Medium. *STOCK: Watercolours and oils, 19th C.* LOC: South side of A143 in village centre, 4 miles west of Diss. PARK: Easy. TEL: Mellis (037 983) 312. SER: Valuations; restorations (oils, watercolours); framing. VAT: Stan/Spec.

WRENTHAM,   (050 275)
Nr. Beccles

The Old Reading Room Antiques
(J. and W. Pipe.) Open 10—5.30, Sun. 2—5.30. *STOCK: Bric-a-brac, Victoriana, pre-1940 clothes.* LOC: A12. PARK: Easy. TEL: 376.

Wren House Antiques
1 High St. (J. and W. Pipe.) Open Tues., Thurs. and Sat. 10—5. *STOCK: Clocks, china, glass, maps, prints, jewellery.* TEL: 276. SER: Repairs (clocks).

Wrentham Antiques
40-44 High St. (B. Spearing). Est. 1948. Always open. SIZE: Large. *STOCK: Victorian and decorative furniture.* LOC: A12. PARK: Easy. TEL: 583; home — Lowestoft (0502) 513633. SER: Buys at auction. VAT: Stan/Spec.

YOXFORD   (072 877)

Yoxford Antiques and
Country Things
Old Butcher's Shop and Bank House, High St. (K. Veness.) Est. 1982. CL: Wed. Open 11—5.30, Sun. by appointment. SIZE: Medium. *STOCK: General antiques including small furniture, collectables, bric-a-brac, 18th—19th C, £1—£200.* LOC: Old Butcher's shop — opposite church; Bank House — corner A12/A1120. PARK: Easy. TEL: 661. SER: Restorations.

Yoxford Bazaar
High St. (Mrs. F.R. Rush.) Est. 1952. CL: Wed. and Fri. Open 10.30—5.30 or by appointment. *STOCK: Small decorative items, bric-a-brac, Victoriana, period clothes, jewellery, prints, pictures and needlework.* LOC: Just off A12 on A1120 in main street, beyond church and Griffin public house. PARK: Easy. TEL: 448.

EDWARD MANSON

CLOCKS

8, Market Hill,
Woodbridge IP12 4LP
Tel. No. (03943) 7226

Edward Manson
8 Market Hill. Open 10—5.30, Wed. 10—1. *STOCK: Clocks.* TEL: 7226. SER: Restorations (clocks).

Sarah Meysey-Thompson
10 Church St. Est. 1962. CL: Wed. p.m. Open 9—5.30. *STOCK: General antiques.* PARK: Easy. TEL: 2144.

A.G. Voss   BADA
24 Market Hill. Est. 1965. CL: Wed. Open 9.30—1 and 2—5. *STOCK: Furniture, 17th to early 19th C, from £65; longcase clocks, 18th C, from £400.* PARK: Nearby and at rear. TEL: 5830. SER: Valuations; restorations. VAT: Spec.

WOOLPIT
Nr. Bury St. Edmunds

J.C. Heather
Clandore House. Est. 1946. Open every day 9—8. SIZE: Large. *STOCK: Furniture, 18th—19th C, £20—£1,000.* Not stocked: China. LOC: Near centre of village on right. PARK: Easy. TEL: Elmswell (0359) 40297. VAT: Stan/Spec.

Surrey

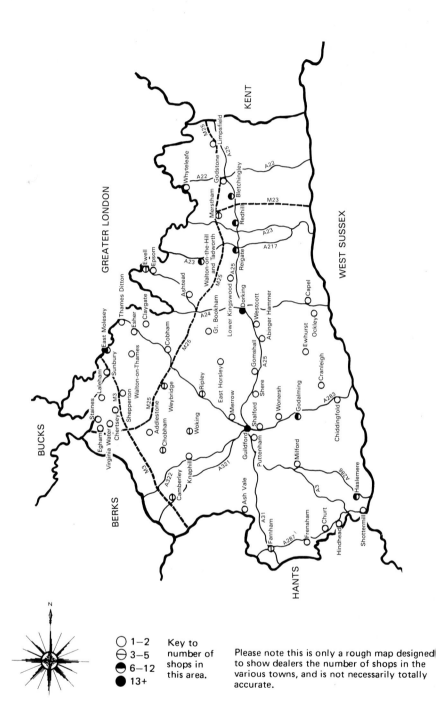

KENT

GREATER LONDON

WEST SUSSEX

BUCKS

BERKS

HANTS

Whyteleafe
Limpsfield
Godstone
Merstham
Bletchingley
Redhill
Reigate
A22
A25
M25
A23
M23
A22
A217
A23

Ewell
Epsom
Ashtead
Walton-on-the-Hill and Tadworth
Lower Kingswood
Reigate
Capel
Dorking
Westcott
Abinger Hammer
Ewhurst
Ockley

Thames Ditton
Esher
Claygate
Cobham
Gt. Bookham
Merrow
Gomshall
Shere
A25
Cranleigh
A24
M25

East Molesey
Sunbury
Walton-on-Thames
Weybridge
Ripley
East Horsley
Wonersh
Godalming
Chiddingfold
A283

Staines
Laleham
Shepperton
Addlestone
Chobham
Woking
Shalford
Puttenham
Milford
Haslemere
A3
A287

Egham
Virginia Water
Chertsey
M3
M25
Knaphill
Ash Vale
Guildford
A321
A322
Camberley

Frensham
Churt
Hindhead
Shottermill
Farnham
A31
A287

M3

N

○ 1–2
⊖ 3–5
◑ 6–12
● 13+

Key to number of shops in this area.

Please note this is only a rough map designed to show dealers the number of shops in the various towns, and is not necessarily totally accurate.

ABINGER HAMMER
Stirling Antiques
Aberdeen House. (V.S. Burrell.) Est. 1968. CL: Thurs. Open 9.30—6.30. *STOCK: Stained glass, furniture, copper, brass, jewellery, silver, curios, dolls.* PARK: Easy. LOC: A25 between Dorking and Guildford. TEL: Dorking (0306) 730706. VAT: Stan.

ADDLESTONE, Nr. Weybridge
Brian Antiques
131 Station Rd. Open 10—5.30. *STOCK: General antiques.* PARK: Easy. TEL: (0932) 57353.

ASH VALE
House of Christian Antiques
5—7 Vale Rd. (A. and I. Bail.) Est. 1970. Open 10—6, Sat. 10—1. SIZE: Medium. *STOCK: Mahogany and oak furniture, 19th C, £100—£150; pine, 19th—20th C, £50—£100.* LOC: Take Tongham turning from A3, first right then left at 2nd roundabout, premises on canal bridge. PARK: Easy. TEL: (0252) 314478; home — same. SER: Valuations; restorations; buys at auction (Victorian or pine items).

ASHTEAD   (037 22)
Gadsby Stores
88/90 The Street. (B.J. Haskins and A.S.R. Dickenson.) Est. 1975. CL: Sun. except by appointment. Open 9.30—6. SIZE: Large. *STOCK: Furniture, 1700—1900, £50—£3,000; silver, 1700—1930, £5—£1,000; glass, porcelain, copper and brass, 1700—1900, £5—£500.* PARK: Easy, at rear. TEL: 72305; home — Bookham (0372) 53265. SER: Buys at auction. VAT: Stan/Spec.

Memory Lane Antiques
102 The Street. (J. Lock.) Est. 1984. CL: Wed. Open 10—5. SIZE: Small. *STOCK: Dolls, toys and general antiques, 19th C, £5—£200.* PARK: Easy. TEL: 73436. FAIRS: Dorking Halls and Seven Hills Hotel.

BLETCHINGLEY
Castle Antiques
Castle Sq. (H. and K. Brown.) Open 9.30—5.30. *STOCK: China, copper, brass, small furniture, pewter, metalware, English pottery and porcelain; decorative furniture, antiquarian books and maps.* TEL: Godstone (0883) 843228.

Bletchingley continued

Cider House Galleries Ltd.
Norfolk House, 80 High St. (D.G. Roberts.) Est. 1967. CL: Sat. p.m. and Sun. except by appointment. Open 9.30—5.30. SIZE: Large. *STOCK: Paintings, 17th—19th C, from £200.* LOC: A25, behind F.G. Lawrence Auctioneers. PARK: Own. TEL: Godstone (0883) 842198; home — Betchworth (073 784) 4439. SER: Valuations. VAT: Stan/Spec.

Elias Clark Antiques Ltd.   BADA
                                  LAPADA
1 The Cobbles, High St. (L.D. and J.M. Clark.) Est. 1978. CL: Mon. Open 10—1 and 2.30—5 other times by appointment. *STOCK: English pottery-figures, plaques, toby jugs, prattware, creamware, pearlware, English delft, 18th—19th C, £20—£2,000; oak and country furniture, naïve and primitive paintings.* **LOC: Village centre. PARK: Easy. TEL: Godstone (0883) 843714. VAT: Spec.**

John Anthony Antiques   LAPADA
71 High St. (J.A. and N. Hart.) Resident. Open 10—6 or by appointment. *STOCK: 18th—19th C furniture especially desks.* TEL: Godstone (0883) 843197.

Simon Marsh
The Old Butchers Shop. High St. Est. 1970. Open 10—6. *STOCK: Grandfather clocks; 18th and 19th C, furniture.* PARK: Easy. TEL: Godstone (0883) 843350. SER: Restorations (furniture and clocks); upholstery.

Post House Antiques   LAPADA
32 High St. (P. and V. Bradley.) Open daily, Sun. by appointment. *STOCK: General antiques, mirrors, fenders, decorative items, shipping goods.* LOC: A25. PARK: Easy. TEL: Godstone (0883) 843317 and Redhill (0737) 69692. VAT: Stan/Spec.

Quill Antiques
The Limes. 86 High St. (J. Davis.) Open 10—5, Wed. 10—1 or by appointment. *STOCK: Furniture, general antiques, Victorian jewellery and clothing, shipping items, copper and fire-irons.* TEL: Godstone (0883) 843755.

CAMBERLEY   (0276)
The Antique House
245/247 London Rd. (R. and S. Campbell.) Resident. Est. 1979. Open 9.30—5.30, Sun. by appointment. SIZE: Medium. *STOCK: Furniture, 18th C to Edwardian, £100—£2,000; porcelain and glass, 19th—20th C, £10—£100; silver and plate, 18th—20th C, £10—£1,000.* LOC: A30, opposite Royal Military Academy. PARK: Easy. TEL: 26412. SER: Restorations (jewellery, silver and furniture); buys at auction (silver, furniture). VAT: Stan/Spec.

Camberley continued

Antiques — Sheila White
Sandhurst Farm House, 207 Yorktown Rd., College Town. *STOCK: General antiques.* LOC: Barn at rear of premises. TEL: Yateley (0252) 873290.

Clarke's Antiques (Camberley)
2 Osnaburgh Parade, 311 London Rd. (J.E. Clarke.) Est. 1963. CL: Wed. p.m. Open 8.30—6. *STOCK: General antiques, 18th— 19th C furniture, jewellery, some secondhand.* TEL: 22677. VAT: Stan/Spec.

CAPEL, Nr. Dorking
The Treasure Chest
Main Rd. (Mrs. A. Holden.) CL: Thurs. Open 9.30—6. *STOCK: Fine porcelain, figures, vases, objets d'art.* LOC: 6 miles south of Dorking on A24. PARK: Easy. TEL: Dorking (0306) 711254.

CARSHALTON
See Greater London

CHEAM
See Greater London

CHERTSEY (093 28)
Surrey Antiques Centre
10 Windsor St. (P.L. Allen.) Open 10—5. There are 10 dealers at this centre selling *ethnic art, pictures, clocks, furniture, jewellery, glass, pottery and porcelain, silver.* TEL: 63313; home — (0932) 41097.

CHESSINGTON
See Greater London

CHIDDINGFOLD, Nr. Godalming
Now and Then Antiques
1 Petworth Rd. (Mrs. J. Robinson.) CL: Mon. Open 10.30—5, Wed. 9.30—1. *STOCK: Furniture, Georgian and Victorian; porcelain, paintings, objets d'art.* TEL: (042 879) 2727.

CHOBHAM (099 05)
Chobham Antiques Market
62 High St. (Danelagh Estates Ltd.) Est. 1984. Open 10—5. SIZE: Medium. *STOCK: Furniture, clocks, porcelain, glass, pictures, curios.* TEL: 6226.

Holly Style Antiques
24 High St. (S. Blackburn.) Est. 1978. *STOCK: Victorian and early oak and pine, £50—£500; porcelain, china, glass, brass and copper, early country pieces, £5—£50; silver, £7—£50; lace, lace pillows, silk flowers.* PARK: At rear. TEL: 6040.

Chobham continued

Penny Farthing Antiques and Pretty Things
The Doll's House, 71 High St. (S. Blackburn.) Est. 1978. SIZE: Small. *STOCK: Victorian and early oak and pine, £50—£500; porcelain, china, glass, brass and copper and early country pieces, £5—£50; silver, £7—£50; lace, lace pillows, silk flowers.* PARK: Easy; behind shop or opposite. TEL: 7718.

The Tarrystone
40—42 High St. (Mrs. D. Hanbury.) Est. 1960. Open 9—1 and 2—5, Sat. 9—1. *STOCK: Furniture, brass, porcelain.* PARK: Easy. TEL: 7494.

CHURT
Horn Antiques BADA
Farnham Rd. (Mrs. P. Hardwick.) Est. 1980. Open Wed.—Sat. 9.30—5.30. SIZE: Small. *STOCK: Horn items and bygones, 16th—19th C; fine oak and country furniture, 17th—18th C; topographical framed prints, 18th—19th C.* Not stocked: Silver, jewellery and glass. LOC: Next to village hall on A287. PARK: Easy. TEL: Headley Down (0428) 714298; home — same. SER: Restorations (small period furniture). VAT: Spec.

CLAYGATE
Keeble Ltd.
22 The Parade. (F.J. Keeble.) CL: Sat. Open 9—5.30. *STOCK: Furniture, late 18th C; light fittings.* TEL: Esher (0372). 68966. VAT: Stan.

COBHAM (0932)
Antics
44 Portsmouth Rd. (K. Needham.) Est. 1967. Open 9.30—1 and 2—5.30. SIZE: Large. *STOCK: Pine furniture, rustic and farmhouse antiques; shipping goods.* LOC: A3. PARK: Easy. TEL: 65505. VAT: Stan.

Cobham Galleries
65 Portsmouth Rd. (Mrs. T.B. Boyle and Mrs. M.F. Pound.) Open 9.30—5. *STOCK: Period and country furniture, watercolours, oils.* TEL: 67909. SER: Buys at auction.

Not Just Silver
7 Church St. (Mrs. S. Hughes.) Est. 1969. Open 9.30—5, Sun. by appointment. SIZE: Small. *STOCK: Silver, from Georgian, £50— £2,000; old Sheffield plate, £30—£400; English and Continental porcelain, 18th— 19th C, £5—£800; objets d'art including bronze, to £1,000.* LOC: In one-way system near church. PARK: Easy. TEL: 68382; home — Weybridge (0932) 51750. SER: Valuations; restorations (re-plating, metalwork, glass and porcelain); buys at auction (English and European silver and porcelain).

HORN ANTIQUES

**CHURT, FARNHAM
SURREY GU10 2JA
Tel. 0428—714298**

Cobham continued

Shepherds Antiques Ltd.
65 Portsmouth Rd. Open 9—5.30. *STOCK: Georgian and Victorian furniture, especially chairs and tables.* TEL: 67909; home — 62034. SER: Restorations.

Alanna Staton Antiques   LAPADA
4 Anyards Rd., High St. (Mr. and Mrs. Staton.) Est. 1967. CL: Wed. p.m. Open 9.30—1 and 2—5. *STOCK: 18th and 19th C furniture, objets d'art, copper, brass, plate, silver, jewellery, glass.* LOC: A3 from London, in village centre. PARK: Easy. TEL: 63407. SER: Valuations. VAT: Stan/Spec.

COULSDON
See Greater London

CRANLEIGH   (0483)

William Hockley Antiques
Kent House, High St. (D. and V. Thrower.) Est. 1974. Open 10—1 and 2—5, Sat. 10—5, Wed. p.m. and Sun. by appointment. SIZE: Medium. *STOCK: English country oak and walnut furniture, 18th and early 19th C; early English pottery including Staffordshire, creamware and cow creamers,· £100—£1,000.* PARK: Own at rear. TEL: 276197; home — Dunsfold (048 649) 331. SER: Valuations; restorations (furniture); buys at auction (furniture). VAT: Spec.

David Mann and Sons Ltd.
High St. Est. 1887. Open 8.30—1 and 2—5.30. *STOCK: Furniture, 17th—18th C; Oriental carpets and rugs; general antiques.* TEL: 273777. VAT: Stan/Spec.

CROYDON
See Greater London

DORKING   (0306)

Madeleine Bilson
47 West St. Open 10—5.30. *STOCK: Furniture, porcelain, glass, brass and copper, silver, jewellery, Oriental items, objets d'art, 18th—19th C.* TEL: 889323 or 880162.

Dorking continued

Roy Breeden Antiques
7 West St. CL: Wed. Open 9—5.30. *STOCK: Furniture and decorative items.* TEL: 882552.

Noel Collins
15 West St. Est. 1975. CL: Wed. Open 10—5. *STOCK: Jewellery.*

J. and M. Coombes
44 West St. Est. 1965. Open 9.30—5.30. *STOCK: General antiques.* TEL: 885479. VAT: Stan.

Dorking Antiques
58 West St. (E. Hutton and P. Norman.) Est. 1947. CL: Wed. Open 9.30—1 and 2—6, or by appointment. *STOCK: 18th—19th C English furniture, clocks, glass, pewter, maps.* LOC: From London on A24, then follow one-way system into West St. PARK: 100yds. in Church St. off West St. TEL: 883777. VAT: Stan/Spec.

Dorking Desk Shop
20 West St. (J.G. Elias.) Est. 1969. Open 8—1 and 2—5.30, Sat. 10.30—1 and 2—5. SIZE: Medium. *STOCK: Desks, especially partners, cylinder bureaux, davenports, knee-hole and pedestal, 18th to mid-20th C, £100—£5,000.* PARK: Nearby. TEL: 883327 or 880535; evenings — 887697. VAT: Stan/Spec.

J.G. Elias Antiques
37 West St. Est. 1969. Open 8—1 and 2—5.30, Sat. 10—1 and 2—5. SIZE: Medium. *STOCK: Furniture — oak and mahogany bureaux and bookcases, pedestal desks and partners, oak, walnut and mahogany, chests of drawers, tables, chairs, bookcases, £50—£5,000; all 17th—20th C.* PARK: Nearby. TEL. 883327 or 880535; evenings — 887697. VAT: Stan/Spec.

Hampshires of Dorking
51/52 West St. (Thorpe and Foster Ltd.) Open 9.30—6. SIZE: Large. *STOCK: English walnut, mahogany and satinwood furniture, 18th C, £500—£25,000.* PARK: At rear. TEL: 887076. VAT: Spec.

Eleanor Hutton
(Jewellers and Silversmiths)
59 West St. Est. 1945. CL: Wed. Open 9—1 and 2—5.30. SIZE: Medium. *STOCK: Jewellery, silver, glass and collectors' items, from 18th C.* LOC: From London on A24, then follow one-way system into West St. PARK: 100yds. in Church St. off West St. TEL: 883777. SER: Valuations; restorations; replating. VAT: Stan/Spec.

Dorking continued

Kennedy and Spooner Antiques
1 Meadowbank Rd. (S.D. Kennedy and P.J. Spooner.) Resident. Est. 1984. Open 10—1 and 2—5.30, Sun. by appointment. SIZE: Small. *STOCK: English furniture, 17th—19th C, £50—£1,000; arms and armour, pre-1860; collectors' items and general antiques.* LOC: Adjacent to car park behind West St. PARK: Easy. TEL: 881773; home — Bookham (0372) 52877. SER: Valuations; restorations (furniture). VAT: Stan/Spec.

Loft Antiques
6 Old Kings Head Court, 11 High St. and rear of 8 West St. (J. Pritchard.) Est. 1977. CL: Wed. SIZE: Small and warehouse. *STOCK: Pine, oak and country furniture, 18th—19th C, £10—£600; brass, copper and writing boxes, 18th—19th C, £10—£300; curios, 18th—20th C, £10—£600.* PARK: Easy and at rear. TEL: 888874. SER: Valuations; buys at auction. VAT: Stan/Spec.

Lyons Court Antiques
1 and 2 Lyons Court, High St. (Mrs. N. Cellier.) Est. 1970. CL: Wed. and Thurs. Open 10—5. *STOCK: General antiques, pine and bric-a- brac.* LOC: Turn up at side of Lloyds Bank, shop is on left. PARK: Easy. TEL: 883582.

Reflections
54 West St. Est. 1970. *STOCK: General antiques and bric-a-brac.* TEL: 881775.

The Stable Antiques
Old King's Head Court, 11 High St. (R. Kenchington.) Est. 1983. Open 9.30—5.30. SIZE: Small. *STOCK: Mahogany and rosewood furniture, 18th to early 19th C, £150—£1,500; oak and country furniture, 17th to early 18th C, £200—£1,200; boxes and unusual items, 18th—19th C, £80—£250.* LOC: Through archway, 20yds. from High St. PARK: Behind courtyard. TEL: 885452.

Swan Antiques
62a West St. (Major and Mrs. R. Grogan, R.M. Douglas.) Est. 1959. Open 10—1 and 2—5. SIZE: Medium. *STOCK: English furniture, 17th to early 19th C, £100—£4,000; decorative objects, £50—£1,000.* Not stocked: Silver, jewellery, arms, coins, Orientalia. LOC: A25. From London A24 to Dorking High St., follow one-way system to West St. PARK: 100yds. TEL: 881217; home — (01) 394 2361. VAT: Stan/Spec.

Thorpe and Foster Ltd.
49 West St. Open 9.30—6. SIZE: Large. *STOCK: English walnut, mahogany and satinwood furniture, 18th C, £500—£25,000.* LOC: On A24. PARK: At rear. TEL: 881029. VAT: Spec.

Dorking continued

Tucker and Langs
Old King's Head Court, High St. Est. 1985. *STOCK: Brass, copper and decorators' items.* TEL: 882203.

Upstairs, Downstairs Antiques
Old King's Head Court, High St. (Mrs. J. Sayer and Mrs. T. Harrison.) Open 9.30—5.30. SIZE: Medium. *STOCK: Porcelain and Staffordshire, to £500; small furniture, to £1,000; jewellery and silver, to £1,500; all 18th—19th C.* LOC: Opposite Nat West Bank, through archway. PARK: At rear in North St. TEL: 888849. SER: Valuations; restorations (furniture and porcelain).

Victoria and Edward Antiques Centre
61 West St. Est. 1972. Open 9.30—5.30. SIZE: Medium. There are up to 26 dealers at this centre selling a wide range of *general antiques.* PARK: Nearby. TEL: 889645.

West Street Antiques
63 West St. (J.G. Spooner and Mrs. K. Small.) Est. 1980. Open 10—1 and 2—5.30. SIZE: Small. *STOCK: Furniture, £100—£5,000; silver, £20—£2,000, both 17th to early 20th C; arms and armour, 18th—19th C, £20—£2,000; brass, copper, pewter, glass, ceramics, collectors' items, pictures, 18th—20th C, from £10.* Not stocked: Jewellery and carpets. LOC: West St. (A25) one-way system. PARK: Nearby. TEL: 883487; home — Bookham (0372) 52877. SER: Valuations; buys at auction. VAT: Stan/Spec.

Patrick Worth Antiques   BADA
11 West St. (B.P. Meyer.) Est. 1967. CL: Wed. Open 9.30—5.30. SIZE: Large. *STOCK: Period furniture, decorative items, mainly 18th to early 19th C.* **Not stocked: Silver, glass and jewellery.** LOC: A25. TEL: 884484. VAT: Stan/Spec.

EAST HORSLEY   (048 65)
A.E. Gould and Sons (Antiques) Ltd.
                                                    LAPADA
Old Rectory Cottage, Ockham Rd. South. (D. and P. Gould.) Est. 1949. Open 9.30—5, Sat. and Sun. by appointment. SIZE: Large. *STOCK: Furniture, 18th C, £200—£3,000; 19th C, £100—£1,000; barometers, clocks, brass and glass, £100—£500.* PARK: Easy. TEL: 3747; home — (01) 949 4251 and (01) 788 7573. VAT: Stan.

EAST MOLESEY
The Antique Centre (East Molesey)
46 Bridge Rd. (R.V. and C. Rumble.) Est. 1980. CL: Wed. Open 10—5. SIZE: Small. *STOCK: Silver and plate, £5—£400; small furniture, £50—£600; porcelain, pottery and jewellery, £5—£500; all 18th—20th C; Staffordshire figures, 19th C, £60—£300.* PARK: Easy. TEL: (01) 979 4969; home — Esher (0372) 64034.

The Antiques Arcade
77 Bridge Rd. (J.L. Abbott.) Open 10—5. There are 11 dealers at this arcade selling *general antiques.* TEL: (01) 979 7954.

Antiques Etcetera
9a Bridge Rd. (J. Busby.) CL: Wed. and Fri. Open 10.30—6. SIZE: Small. *STOCK: Small Victoriana, collectors' items.* TEL: (01) 979 9022.

B.S. Antiques
39 Bridge Rd. (S. Anderman.) Est. 1983. CL: Wed. Open 10—5. SIZE: Medium. *STOCK: Clocks, barometers, prints, some furniture.* LOC: Near Hampton Court. PARK: Easy. TEL: (01) 941 1812. SER: Valuations; restorations (clocks and barometers). VAT: Spec.

The Court Gallery
16 Bridge Rd. (J. Clark.) Est. 1980. CL: Wed. Open 10—5.30. SIZE: Small. *STOCK: Oils, watercolours and drawings, 19th—20th C, £50—£500; Staffordshire pottery, 19th C, £20—£100.* LOC: From Scilly Isles roundabout turn into Hampton Court Way, Bridge Rd. is on left by Hampton Court Bridge. PARK: Easy. TEL: (01) 941 2212. SER: Valuations; restorations (oils and watercolours); framing.

The Gooday Shop and Gooday Studio
48—50 Bridge Rd. (R. Gooday.) CL: Wed. and mornings. *STOCK: Collectors' items, toys, dolls, paintings and prints.* TEL: (01) 979 9971.

Hampton Court Antiques
75 Bridge Rd., Hampton Court. (H. Abbott.) CL: Wed. Open 10—5. *STOCK: General antiques including clocks, furniture, lamps and decorative objects.* TEL: (01) 941 6398.

Hampton Court Revival Antique Market
52 Bridge Rd., Hampton Court. CL: Wed. SIZE: Large. There are approximately 40 dealers at this market selling *a wide range of general antiques including silver, porcelain, jewellery, pictures, decorative items, pine.* LOC: Near Hampton Court Palace. PARK: Easy. TEL: (01) 979 3552. VAT: Stan/Spec.

G.E. DAY
Antiques

*82 West Street
Farnham, Surrey
Telephone Farnham 715043*

East Molesey continued

Lady Bountiful Two Antiques and Objets d'Art

1 Lion Gate, Hampton Court. (Mrs. J. James.) Open 10.30—5.30, Sun. 2.30—5.30; Mon., Tues. and Wed. by appointment. *STOCK: Furniture including gentlemen's linen chests, library tables and chests of drawers, 18th—19th C, £50—£3,000; small items, china, silver and plate, £5—£50.* TEL: (01) 943 1656.

Nicholas Antiques

31 Bridge Rd. CL: Wed. p.m. Open 9.30—5. *STOCK: Furniture, general antiques and decorative items.* TEL: (01) 979 0354. VAT: Stan/Spec.

Yesterdays

21 Bridge Rd. Open 10.30—5. *STOCK: Brass and steel fenders, fire irons; small furniture and pine items; silver plate and Victorian porcelain.*

EGHAM   (0784)

Fishers of Surrey

94 High St. (R. and E.S. Fisher.) Est. 1972. CL: Wed. Open 9—5. SIZE: Medium. *STOCK: General antiques, Victorian and Edwardian.* LOC: Next to Police Station. PARK: Easy. TEL: 32981. SER: Valuations.

Egham continued

Jack's Antiques

89b High St. Est. 1966. TEL: 35444.

R.R. Oliver

25 Runnymede Rd. Open 9—5. *STOCK: Furniture.* PARK: Easy. TEL: 32856.

Stampantique Ltd.

86 High St. (A.S. Carlyon-Gibbs.) Est. 1976. Open 10—6. SIZE: Large. *STOCK: Postage stamps — Aden, Bahamas, Barbados, Egypt, Ghana, Hungary, India, Jamaica, Monserrat, Newfoundland, Great Britain, Australia, Papua New Guinea, Mauritius, USA, Eire, Israel, Germany, France, Hong Kong, Gibraltar, Ceylon, Gold Coast, Canada; watercolours, oils and prints, mainly Victorian, £10—£3,000; longcase, bracket, wall, and carriage clocks, watches; furniture, especially chairs, 17th—20th C; porcelain, copper and brass, cloisonné, silver and gold, £5—£500.* PARK: Easy. TEL: 36290; home — Maidenhead (0628) 39353. SER: Valuations; restorations (pictures and furniture); framing; clock and watch repairs, French polishing, upholstery; buys at auction.

EPSOM   (037 27)

Link Gold Ltd.

95 High St. (A.C. Thiele and G.M. Reed.) Open 9.30—4, Sat. 9.30—3.30. *STOCK: Gold including jewellery, from 1900, £50—£250; silver, from 1800, £15—£200; silver plate, from 1900, £5—£100; general antiques, £5—£100.* TEL: 29970.

ESHER   (0372)

Leon Abbott Antiquarian Horologist

158 Ember Lane. Est. 1970. *STOCK: Clocks and books.* TEL: (01) 398 2984. VAT: Spec.

Kensington Galleries   LAPADA

Badgers Wood, West End Lane. (J.S. Bates). Open by appointment only. *STOCK: Oil paintings especially sporting.* TEL: 64407. SER: Valuations; restorations.

EWELL

A.E. Booth

9 High St. Est. 1932. Open 9—5.30. SIZE: Medium. *STOCK: Furniture, 18th to early 19th C, £50—£2,000; glass, general antiques.* PARK: Own. TEL: (01) 393 5245. SER: Valuations; restorations (furniture, metalwork, clocks and barometers). VAT: Stan/Spec.

J.W. McKenzie

12 Stoneleigh Park Rd. Est. 1971. Appointment advisable. *STOCK: Antiquarian books on theatre and cricket.* TEL: (01) 393 7700.

P. & B. JORDAN
Antiques

90 WEST STREET, FARNHAM　　FARNHAM 716272

Furniture, Porcelain, Oil Paintings, Prints, etc.

Monday-Friday 9.30 a.m. - 1 p.m.　　　*Saturday 9.30 a.m.-1 p.m. and 2 p.m. - 5.30 p.m.*

Ewell continued

Token House Antiques
7 Market Parade, High St. (Mrs. D. Walker.) Est. 1966. CL: Wed. Open 10−1 and 2−5. *STOCK: Furniture, small silver, boxes, collectors' items and general antiques, 18th−19th C.* LOC: Opp. post office. PARK: Forecourt. TEL: (01) 393 9654.

Well House Antiques
11 High St. Est. 1969. CL: Wed. Open 10−5.30. *STOCK: Jewellery, silver, plate, clocks, watches, general antiques.* TEL: (01) 394 0299. VAT: Stan.

EWHURST
Nr. Cranleigh

Cranleigh Antiques
Milkhill, The Street. (R. Hoskin.) Est. 1976. Open 10−5, Sat. 10−1 and Sun. by appointment. SIZE: Medium. *STOCK: Oak and mahogany furniture, 18th−19th C, £5−£1,000; general antiques and bygones.* TEL: Cranleigh (0483) 277318. PARK: Easy. SER: Valuations. VAT: Stan.

Cranleigh Framing Studio
Milkhill, The Street. Open 9−5, Sat. 10−1. *STOCK: Victorian watercolours, prints.* PARK: Easy. TEL: Cranleigh (0483) 271770. SER: Restorations; cleaning.

FARNHAM　　　　　　(0252)

Bits and Pieces
37 West St. (Mrs. C.J. Wickins.) CL: Wed. p.m. *STOCK: Victoriana, bric-a-brac.* TEL: 722355.

Bourne Mill Antiques
Guildford Rd. (Premises shared by 30 dealers.) Est. 1971. Open 9.30−5.30 everyday. *STOCK: Stripped pine, general antiques, bric-a-brac, linen, watercolours, oil paintings, architectural and collectors' items.* TEL: 716663.

Farnham continued

Casque and Gauntlet Antiques Ltd.
55/59 Badshot Lea Rd., Badshot Lea. (R. Colt.) Est. 1957. SIZE: Large. *STOCK: Militaria, arms, armour.* LOC: On Aldershot to Farnham road. PARK: Easy. TEL: Aldershot (0252) 20745, Extension 2. SER: Restorations (metals); re-gilding. VAT: Stan/Spec.

G.E. Day
82 West St. (Miss J.L. Day and Mrs. J.E. Ross.) Est. 1931. CL: Wed. p.m. Open 9.30−1 and 2.15−5 or by appointment. *STOCK: Copper, brass, glass, from 1750, £15−£150; oak furniture, 1700−1850, £70−£1,000; Georgian, Edwardian and Victorian furniture, £70−£3,000.* LOC: Opposite museum and Bits and Pieces. PARK: Adjacent. TEL: 715043. VAT: Stan/Spec.

Farnham Antique Centre
27 South St. (Miss M.A. Stanford.) Est. 1976. Open 9.30−5. SIZE: Large. There are 21 dealers at this centre offering *a wide range of general antiques, including silver, jewellery, porcelain, brass and copper, clocks, dolls, toys, textiles, pine, Oriental items, small period furniture and collectors' items.* LOC: On the one-way system into Farnham, large corner site. PARK: At rear. TEL: 724475.

P. and B. Jordan　　　　　BADA
90 West St. (P.A. and W.E. Jordan.) Est. 1962. Open 9.30−1, Sat. 9.30−1 and 2−5.30 or by appointment. SIZE: Medium. *STOCK: Furniture and ceramics, from 1750, £50−£500; oil paintings, prints, from 1700, £5−£500; glass, brass fenders, from 1700, £5−£50.* Not stocked: Carpets, tapestries. LOC: On main road through town centre. PARK: Round corner, 'The Hart' Rd. TEL: 716272. VAT: Stan/Spec.

Farnham continued

Maltings Market
Bridge Sq. Est. 1969. There are over 150 stalls at this monthly market of which 50% sell a *wide variety of antiques, bric-a-brac, postcards and collectables.* LOC: Follow signs to Wagon Yard car park, Maltings over footbridge. TEL: 726234.

R. and M. Putnam
60 Downing St. Est. 1957. CL: Sun. except by appointment, and Wed. p.m. Open 10—1 and 2—5.30; 5 on Sat. SIZE: Medium. *STOCK: Period pine furniture, 18th—19th C; Staffordshire pottery, 19th C; brass, copper, oil and watercolour paintings.* LOC: Town centre. PARK: Easy. TEL: 715769; home — 715485. SER: Restorations (furniture); buys at auction. VAT: Stan/Spec.

Village Pine
32 West St. (S. McGrath.) Est. 1981. Open 10—4.30, Sat. 10—5. SIZE: Large. *STOCK: Pine furniture including dressers, chests of drawers and boxes, unusual and small items, Victorian, £35—£650.* LOC: On left past Bishops Table Hotel. PARK: Easy. TEL: 726660.

Karel Weijand   LAPADA
Lion and Lamb Courtyard. Est. 1963. Open 9.30—5.30. SIZE: Medium. *STOCK: Oriental and Persian rugs, £80—£10,000; silk rugs, pre-1915.* LOC: Off West St. PARK: Easy. TEL: 726215. SER: Valuations; restorations. VAT: Stan/Spec.

Wrecclesham Antiques
47 Wrecclesham Rd. (A. Vallis and J. Hudson.) Est. 1979. Open daily, Sun. by appointment. SIZE: Medium. *STOCK: Pine, 19th C, £50—£450; clocks, 17th—19th C, £150—£800; Victorian furniture, 19th C, £60—£300.* LOC: A325. PARK: Easy. TEL: 716468; home — same.

FRENSHAM   (025 125)
Douglas Franks
St. Anthony's. Est. 1949. Open by appointment. *STOCK: Furniture and accessories.* TEL: 2467. VAT: Stan/Spec.

GODALMING
(4 and 5 fig. no.) (048 68)
(6 fig. no.) (0483)
Andrew Cottrell Galleries
7/9 Church St. (A. and Mrs. A.E. Cottrell.) Est. 1965. Open 9—5.30. SIZE: Large. *STOCK: General antiques, furniture, small items, to 1940, £100—£500.* PARK: At rear. TEL: 7570. SER: Valuations; restorations; buys at auction. VAT: Stan/Spec.

Godalming continued

P. and J. Goldthorpe
Bicton Croft, Deanery Rd. Open by appointment only. *STOCK: Paintings, mainly English and Dutch, 17th—18th C.* TEL: 4356.

Heath-Bullock   BADA
8 Meadrow. (A.H. and R.J. Heath-Bullock.) Est. 1926. Open 9—5. SIZE: Large. *STOCK: English and Continental furniture, garden ornaments, works of art.* LOC: A3100. From Guildford on the left side approaching Godalming. PARK: Own. TEL: 22562. FAIRS: Exhibitors at and organisers of Buxton, Surrey and Kensington.

Priory Antiques
29 Church St. (P. Rotchell.) Open 10—3, Sat. 9.30—1.30. *STOCK: General antiques.* TEL: 21804.

Surrey Pine
Wharf St. (J. Chappell.) Open 10—5.30. *STOCK: Pine.* TEL: 28991.

David White Antiques
34 Meadrow. (D. and Y. White.) Resident. Est. 1981. CL: Wed. p.m. Open 9.30—5 and by appointment. SIZE: Medium. *STOCK: English country furniture, especially fruitwood and yew and unusual chairs, 17th to early 19th C, £50—£2,000; copper, brass and treen, from £20.* LOC: A3100, opposite Pickfords Depository. PARK: Easy. TEL: 20957. VAT: Stan/Spec.

Ye Olde Curiosity Shoppe
99 High St. *STOCK: Silver, brass, copper, bric-a-brac.* TEL: 5889.

GODSTONE   (0883)
Old Forge Antiques
The Green. Open 10—5.30. *STOCK: Copper, brass, glass, porcelain, silver, jewellery, small furniture and collectables.* TEL: 843230.

GOMSHALL
Gomshall Gallery
(V. Lloyd. Antiques Ltd.) CL: Mon. *STOCK: Oil paintings, 16th—19th C; small antiques and works of art.* LOC: A25 between Guildford and Dorking. TEL: Shere (048 641) 2433. VAT: Stan/Spec.

Vera Lloyd Antiques Ltd.
Gomshall Mill. (C.L. Lloyd and Miss A. Krasine.) CL: Mon. Open 9—5.30, including Sun. *STOCK: Decorative items; 16th—19th C paintings.* LOC: Historic water mill on A25. Between Guildford and Dorking. PARK: Easy. TEL: Shere (048 641) 2433. VAT: Stan/Spec.

GREAT BOOKHAM
Nr. Leatherhead
Bookham Galleries
Leatherhead Rd. (J. Rowe.) Est. 1969. Open by appointment. SIZE: Large. *STOCK: Persian rugs; furniture, 18th—19th C.* LOC: A246. PARK: Easy. TEL: Bookham (0372) 52668. VAT: Stan/Spec.

Roger A. Davis
Antiquarian Horologist
19 Dorking Rd. Est. 1971. CL: Mon. and Wed., Fri. p.m. and Sun. a.m. except by appointment. Open 9.30—12.30 and 2—5.30. SIZE: Small. *STOCK: Clocks, 18th—19th C, £30—£2,000.* LOC: From Leatherhead A246 to centre of village, turn left at sign for Polesden Lacey, shop ¼ mile along Dorking Rd. PARK: Easy. TEL: Bookham (0372) 57655; home — Bookham (0372) 53167. SER: Valuations; restorations (mechanical and case work); buys at auction (antique clocks).

GUILDFORD   (0483)
Ali-baba
134 Worplesdon Rd. (T.J. Smith.) Open 10—6. *STOCK: General antiques, bric-a-brac.* PARK: Easy. TEL: 575429; home — 60847.

Guildford continued

The Antiques Centre
22 Haydon Place, Corner of Martyr Rd. (Mrs. J.S.A. Voke.) Est. 1969. CL: Mon. and Wed. Open 10—5. LOC: Close to Surrey Advertiser. PARK: 100yds. on left from North St. TEL: 67817. The wide variety of goods offered is shown by the principal items of stock which follow the names of some of the dealers listed below:

Eleanor Adams
Sewing tools, lace bobbins, fans, embroideries, samplers, boxes, Baxter prints.
Tony Bathurst
Glass, china, kitchenalia, period clothes and accessories.
Ginette Fournier
General antiques.
Peter Goodall
Prints, engravings, etchings and lithographs.
Beryl Joyce
Oriental and European ceramics, glass, antiquities, pictures and decorative items.
Helen McHugh
Lace, baby gowns and general antiques.
Sylvia Pullen
Silver, jewellery.
Joanna Voke
Dolls, dolls' houses, toys, jewellery and general antiques.

Guildford continued

Denning Antiques
1 Chapel St. Open 10—5. *STOCK: Lace, linen, pre-1930 clothes, textiles, collectors' items, silver and china.* LOC: Off High St. PARK: Nearby. TEL: 39595.

Gillingham Antiques
'Lyndhurst', 148 London Rd. Est. 1920. CL: Sat. Open 9—1 and 2—5.30. SIZE: Medium. *STOCK: Mahogany, oak and walnut furniture, 17th—19th C.* Not stocked: Reproductions or Victoriana. LOC: 3 doors from A.A. Office. PARK: Easy. TEL: 61952. FAIRS: Guildford. VAT: Stan/Spec.

Harper's Antiques
2 Castle St. (Mrs. N.C. Harper.) Est. 1968. Open daily 10—5.30. *STOCK: Jewellery, porcelain, glass, silver, collectors' items.* TEL: 62294. VAT: Stan.

Horological Workshops
204 Worplesdon Rd. (B.R. Ward, M.D. Tooke.) Est. 1968. Open 8.30—5.30, Sat. 9—12.30 or by appointment. *STOCK: Clocks, watches, barometers.* TEL: 576496. SER: Buys at auction.

Odds 'n' Ends Antiques
2 Mill Lane. (L. Webb.) *STOCK: General antiques, bric-a-brac.* TEL: 571640.

G. Oliver and Sons   BADA
St. Catherine's House, Portsmouth Rd. (H.R. Oliver.) Open 9—5.30. *STOCK: Oak, walnut, mahogany furniture, mostly English, 17th—19th C; china, silver, garden ornaments.* TEL: 575427. VAT: Spec.

Rossinyol Antiques
81 Stoke Rd. (Mrs. C. Dunster.) Open 10—5.30. *STOCK: Furniture and bric-a-brac.* TEL: 33081 and 504423.

Geoffrey G. Stevens
26—28 Church Rd. Est. 1950. Open 9—5, Wed. p.m. appointment advisable. *STOCK: Barometers and clocks.* TEL: 504075.

Thomas Thorp Bookseller
170 High St. Est. 1883. Open 9—5, 5.30 on Sat. SIZE: Large. *STOCK: Books including antiquarian and out-of-print.* LOC: At traffic lights at top of High St. PARK: Road running parallel High St. 200yds. away. TEL: 62770. SER: Valuations; buys at auction (antiquarian books). Private collections bought.

Charles W. Traylen
Castle House, 49/50 Quarry St. Est. 1945. CL: Mon. Open 9—1 and 2—5. SIZE: Large. *STOCK: Fine books and manuscripts, 13th C to date.* PARK: 200yds. TEL: 572424. SER: Valuations; restorations (bindings); buys at auction. VAT: Stan.

Guildford continued

Ye Old Curiosity Shoppe
5 The Quadrant. (Mrs. V.G. Trower.) Est. 1946. CL: Wed. Open 9.30—5. *STOCK: China, glass, bric-a-brac, coins, medals and tropical shells.* TEL: 504365. VAT: Stan.

HAMPTON WICK
See Greater London

HASLEMERE   (0428)

Allen Avery Interiors
1 High St. Est. 1971. CL: Sat. p.m. and Wed. Open 9—1 and 2.15—5. *STOCK: English furniture.* TEL: 3883.

Cry for the Moon
11 Lower St. (J.L. Ackroyd.) Est. 1977. Open 9.30—5.30. SIZE: Medium. *STOCK: Jewellery, £10—£5,000; silver, £5—£500; general antiques, £5—£300; all 18th—20th C.* Not stocked: Militaria. LOC: On high pavement. TEL: 51499. SER: Valuations; restorations (jewellery); commissions. VAT: Stan/Spec.

J.K. Glover (Antiques)
Grayswood. Open every day. *STOCK: General antiques, Victoriana, lace.* TEL: 2184.

Julia Holmes,
Antique Maps and Prints
Muirfield Place, Bunch Lane. Est. 1972. By appointment only. SIZE: Medium. *STOCK: Maps, 1600—1850, £10—£1,000; prints, especially sporting subjects, all periods, to £500.* LOC: Off Farnham Lane which is off Weyhill shopping area. PARK: Easy. TEL: 2153. SER: Valuations; restorations (cleaning and colouring of maps and prints, framing); buys at auction; catalogues available. FAIRS: Local and major sporting events. VAT: Stan.

The Jackdaw Antiques
6 Weyhill. (P. Richardson.) Resident. Est. 1972. Open from 10. SIZE: Medium. *STOCK: Brass, copper, other metalware, furniture, collectables.* LOC: A286. PARK: Own. TEL: 53989.

Surrey Clock Centre
3 Lower St. (C. Ingrams and S. Haw.) Est. 1962. Open 9—1 and 2—5. SIZE: Large. *STOCK: Grandfather clocks, 1680—1850, £500—£2,000; carriage clocks, 1790—1900, £150—£2,000; bracket clocks, 1680 and after, from £150.* PARK: Easy. TEL: 4547. SER: Valuations; restorations (clocks, brass and painted dials to the trade); buys at auction. VAT: Stan/Spec.

John L. Williams
12 Petworth Rd. Est. 1960. CL: Mon. *STOCK: Clocks.* TEL: 51120. SER: Restorations (clocks). VAT: Stan.

Haslemere continued
Wood's Wharf Antiques Bazaar
56 High St. (D. Brindle-Wood-Williams.) There
are 14 dealers at this market offering *a wide
selection of antiques.* LOC: Opposite The
Georgian Hotel. TEL: 2125.

HINDHEAD   (042 873)
Albany Antiques Ltd.
8—10 London Rd. (T. Winstanley.) Est. 1965.
CL: Sun. except by appointment. Open 9—6.
*STOCK: Furniture, 17th—18th C, £20—£400;
china (also Chinese), £5—£400; metalware,
£7—£50, both 18th—19th C.* Not stocked:
Silver. LOC: On A3. PARK: Easy. TEL: 5528.
VAT: Stan/Spec.

Peter Borton Fine Arts
Moorlands, Linkside West. Est. 1969. Open
by appointment. *STOCK: Paintings and watercolours, 18th—20th C.* TEL: 5033. SER:
Restorations; framing.

M.J. Bowdery
12 London Rd. Resident, always available.
Est. 1970. *STOCK: Furniture, 18th—19th C.*
TEL: 6376. VAT: Stan/Spec.

Oriel Antiques
3 Royal Parade, Tilford Rd. (J. Gear.) Est.
1974. CL: Mon. and Wed. p.m. Open 9—5.30.
*STOCK: Furniture and pictures, 18th—19th
C.* TEL: 6281.

"Second Hand Rose"
Portsmouth Rd., Bramshott Chase. (S.J.
Ridout.) Est. 1980. Open 9.30—6, Tues.
9.30—8. SIZE: Large. *STOCK: English and
Continental furniture, 18th—20th C; brass,
paintings, bric-a-brac.* LOC: On A3, 1 mile
S.W. of Hindhead. PARK: Easy. TEL: 4880;
home — same. VAT: Stan/Spec.

Wigmores Ltd.
The Golden Hind, London Rd. (P. Gadsden.)
Est. 1965. Open every day 9—5. SIZE: Large.
STOCK: General antiques. LOC: On A3,
200yds. from traffic lights. PARK: Easy. TEL:
6441. VAT: Stan.

KEW
See Greater London

KEW GREEN
See Greater London

KINGSTON-UPON-THAMES
See Greater London

KNAPHILL, Nr. Woking
Knaphill Antiques
38 High St. (P.W. and J.A. Bethney.) CL:
Mon. Open 8.30—6. SIZE: Small. *STOCK:
Barometers, Georgian and Victorian furniture.*
LOC: Off A322 turn right after the Fox Public
House at Bisley towards Knaphill, shop
opposite Crown public house. TEL: Brookwood
(048 67) 3179; home — Guildford (0483)
811616.

LALEHAM, Nr. Staines
Everyday Antiques
21 Shepperton Rd. (J. Ross.) Open 9.30—
5.30, Sun. 10—1. *STOCK: Victorian and
Edwardian furntiure.* TEL: Staines (0784)
61080.

Laleham Antiques
23 Shepperton Rd. (H. and E. Potter.) Est.
1970. Open 10—5. *STOCK: Furniture, pine,
general and trade antiques.* LOC: B376.
PARK: Easy. TEL: Staines (0784) 50353.

LIMPSFIELD
Ann Gray Antiques
The Antique Shop. Est. 1949. Open every
day. SIZE: Large. *STOCK: Furniture, copper,
brass, pictures, ceramics.* PARK: Easy. TEL:
Oxted (088 33) 3836. SER: Buys at auction.

Limpsfield Watercolours
High St. (Mrs. C. Reason.) FATG. Est. 1985.
Open Tues., Fri. and Sat. 9—2. SIZE: Small.
*STOCK: Watercolours, £15—£2,000; prints
and etchings, £5—£200; oils, £200—£500;
all mainly 19th—20th C.* Not stocked: Modern
oils. LOC: B269. PARK: Easy. TEL: Oxted
(088 33) 7010. SER: Restorations (watercolours); buys at auction (watercolours and
prints).

LOWER KINGSWOOD
Tony Davis
inc. London and Washington
Brighton Rd. Open 10.30—4 including Sun.
*STOCK: Furniture, including upholstered;
china, glass and pictures, Victorian and
Edwardian.* TEL: Mogador (0737) 833107.
SER: Valuations; buys at auction (Victorian
and Edwardian furniture). VAT: Stan.

MERROW, Nr. Guildford
The Pine Shop
174 Epsom Rd. (S. Hamilton.) CL: Wed. Open
10—1 and 2—5. *STOCK: Pine furniture.* TEL:
Guildford (0483) 572533.

MERSTHAM (073 74)

Michael and Margaret Baker
4/6 High St. Open 10—5. *STOCK: General antiques, textiles, samplers and decorative items.* TEL: 2658.

Frank Mann Antiques
20 High St. (F.W. Walton.) CL: Wed. Open 10—5. *STOCK: Mainly Georgian mahogany furniture, including long sets of chairs and dining tables.* TEL: 2643.

The Old Smithy Antique Centre
7 High St. (S.N. and I.C. Williams.) Open 10—5. The dealers at this centre offer *a wide range of general antiques.* TEL: 2306.

Rayne Antiques
34 High St. (R. Barr.) Open 9.30—5.30. *STOCK: Furniture, clocks and paintings, 18th—19th C.* TEL: 3443. VAT: Spec.

Showcase
High Street. (Mrs. M. Myland and J. Butler.) Open 10—4. *STOCK: General antiques.* TEL: 2340.

MILFORD, Nr. Godalming

Michael Andrews Antiques
Portsmouth Rd. Est. 1974. CL: Thurs. p.m. Open daily, Sun. by appointment. SIZE: Small. *STOCK: Furniture, 18th to early 19th C.* LOC: Corner of Cherry Tree Rd. PARK: Easy. TEL. Godalming (048 68) 20765; home — same. VAT: Stan/Spec.

The Refectory
Est. 1930. Open most days but appointment advisable. *STOCK: 17th—18th C furniture, mainly oak.* TEL: Godalming (048 68) 21234. VAT: Spec.

The Reid Gallery
Mousehill House. (G. and P. Reid.) Est. 1959. Open by appointment. *STOCK: Watercolours, 19th C.* TEL: Godalming (04868) 6990. SER: Valuations; restorations. VAT: Stan/Spec.

MORDEN
See Greater London

OCKLEY, Nr. Dorking

Stane Street Antiques
Tiquary, Stane St. (M. Pinkerton.) Open by appointment only. SIZE: Medium. *STOCK: Furniture, decorative items, garden furniture, all 19th—20th C.* LOC: A29. PARK: Easy. TEL: Oakwood Hill (030 679) 245; home — same.

PURLEY
See Greater London

PUTTENHAM, Nr. Guildford

Puttenham Gallery Antiques
Winters Farmhouse. (R. Thompson-Bone.) Est. 1983. Open by appointment only. SIZE: Small. *STOCK: Furniture, including country, 18th—19th C, £50—£500; ceramics, small silver.* PARK: Easy. TEL: Guildford (0483) 810226. SER: Restorations (furniture, silver); buys at auction.

REDHILL (0737)

Adams Antiques
Mainly Trade
77 Brighton Rd. Est. 1968. CL: Sat. Open 10—5. SIZE: Medium. *STOCK: Victoriana, bric-a-brac.* LOC: South Redhill. TEL: 62185 (any time).

Dades of Redhill
29 Brighton Rd. (P.V. Dade and R.G. Bartlett.) CL: Sat. Open 9—5. *STOCK: General antiques.* TEL: 64904. VAT: Stan/Spec.

The English Street Furniture Company
Somers House, Linkfield Corner. Est. 1978. SIZE: Medium. *STOCK: Cast iron gas lighting standards; copper street lanterns, £100—£400; both 19th C.* LOC: A25. PARK: Easy. TEL: 60986. VAT: Stan.

Ivelet Books Ltd
Postal only
18 Fairlawn Dr. *STOCK: Old, rare and out-of-print books on landscape architecture, the garden, plant hunting, applied arts, ornithology, European mammals.* TEL: 64520. SER: Catalogues available.

F.G. Lawrence and Sons
89 Brighton Rd. Est. 1871. CL: Wed. p.m. Open 9—1 and 2—5, Sat. 10—1. SIZE: Large. *STOCK: General antiques, Victorian and Georgian.* LOC: On A23. PARK: Easy. TEL: 64196. SER: Valuations; buys at auction. VAT: Stan.

IS YOUR ENTRY CORRECT?
If there is even the slightest inaccuracy in your entry, *please* let us know before 1st January 1987.
GUIDE TO THE
ANTIQUE SHOPS OF BRITAIN
5 Church Street, Woodbridge, Suffolk.

Redhill continued

Wakeman Brothers
43 Woodlands Rd. Est. 1921. Open Fri. a.m. STOCK: Furniture. TEL: 61895. VAT: Stan.

REIGATE   (073 72)
Bourne Gallery   LAPADA
31/33 Lesbourne Rd. (J. Robertson.) Est. 1970. CL: Wed. p.m. Open 10—1 and 2—5.30, or evenings by appointment. SIZE: Large. STOCK: 19th and 20th C oils and watercolours, etchings, £50—£5,000. PARK: Easy. TEL: 41614. SER: Restorations (oil paintings). VAT: Spec.

Heath Antiques
15 Flanchford Rd. (J. and P. Gibson). Resident but prior telephone call advisable. SIZE: Small. STOCK: Porcelain, 18th—20th C, £5—£250; silver, general antiques, small furniture. LOC: Reigate Heath, just off A25 main Reigate-Dorking road. PARK: Easy. TEL: 44230; home — same. SER: Valuations.

Reigate continued

Esmond Holden Ltd.
53a High St. (K.E. Holden). Est. 1983. CL: Wed. p.m. Open 9—5. SIZE: Small. STOCK: Books, 18th C to date; china, £5—£100; furniture, £20—£500; all 19th C. LOC: Town centre. PARK: Behind shop. TEL: 44754. VAT: Stan/Spec.

Lewis and Lloyd   BADA
(Reigate) Ltd.   LAPADA
13 West St. (J.D. and P.C. Lewis.) Est. 1968. CL: Wed. Open 9.30—5. SIZE: Medium. STOCK: English furniture, 18th—19th C, £1,500—£25,000; clocks, £2,000—£10,000. LOC: A25. PARK: Easy. TEL: 21509; home — Redhill (0737) 69589. SER: Valuations (furniture). VAT: Stan/Spec.

Bertram Noller (Reigate)
14a London Rd. (A.M. Noller.) Est. 1970. CL: Tues. and Wed. Open 9.30—1 and 2—5.30. SIZE: Small. STOCK: Collectors' items, furniture, grates, fenders, mantels, copper, brass, glass, pewter, £1—£500. LOC: West side of one-way traffic system. Opposite Upper West St. car park. PARK: Opposite. TEL: 42548. SER: Valuations; restorations (furniture, marble).

J. Hartley Antiques Ltd.

**186 HIGH STREET
RIPLEY
SURREY
TELEPHONE: GUILDFORD
(0483) 224318**

TRADE AND EXPORT

Queen Anne
Georgian and Regency
Furniture
Paintings

Reigate continued

John Powell
45 Church St. CL: Wed. Open 9—5. *STOCK: Arms, armour, militaria, general antiques.* TEL: 44111. SER: Restorations. VAT: Stan.

Reigate Antiques Arcade
57 High St. Open 10—5.30. There are 12 dealers at this arcade selling *general small antiques.* TEL: 22654.

Reigate Galleries Ltd.
45a Bell St. (K.W. Morrish.) Est. 1958. CL: Wed. p.m. Open 9—1 and 2.15—5.30. SIZE: Large. *STOCK: Old prints, engravings, antiquarian books.* PARK: Opposite. TEL: 46055. SER: Restorations (oil paintings); picture framing. VAT: Stan.

Victoriana Dolls　　　　　LAPADA
(Mr. and Mrs. C. Bond.) Open by appointment. *STOCK: Dolls and accessories.* TEL: 49525.

Antony Waley
14 High St. Open 9—5.30. *STOCK: Antiquarian and secondhand illustrated and private press books.* TEL: 40020.

IS YOUR ENTRY CORRECT?
If there is even the slightest inaccuracy in your entry, *please* let us know before 1st January 1987.
GUIDE TO THE
ANTIQUE SHOPS OF BRITAIN
5 Church Street, Woodbridge, Suffolk.

RICHMOND
See Greater London

RIPLEY, Nr. Woking
J. Hartley Antiques Ltd.
186 High St. Est. 1949. Open 8.45—5, Sat. 9.45—2.45. *STOCK: Queen Anne and Georgian furniture.* TEL: Guildford (0483) 224318. VAT: Stan.

Manor House
High St. Est. 1952. SIZE: Medium. *STOCK: Furniture, 18th C; copper and brass, 18th—19th C; clocks.* LOC: A3. PARK: Easy. TEL: Guildford (0483) 225350. VAT: Stan/Spec.

Ripley Antiques　　　　　LAPADA
67 High St. Est. 1960. CL: Wed. p.m. and Sun. except by appointment. Open 9.30—1 and 2—5.15. SIZE: Large. *STOCK: Furniture, decorative items, American shipping goods mainly early 18th—19th C.* LOC: 2 mins. from junction 10 at M25/A3 interchange. PARK: Easy. TEL: Guildford (0483) 224981 and 224333. SER: Valuations; restorations. VAT: Stan/Spec.

Sage Antiques and Interiors
　　　　　　　　　　　　　　LAPADA
The Green Cottage, High St. (H. and C. Sage.) G.M.C. Est. 1971. Open 9.30—12.30 and 2—5.30, Sat. all day. SIZE: Large. *STOCK: Furniture, mahogany, oak, walnut, 1650—1900, £50—£5,000; oil paintings, £50—£1,500; watercolours, £10—£500; china, £2—£200, all 19th—20th C; silver, Sheffield plate, brass, copper, pewter, decorative items, objets d'art, 18th—20th C, £5—£500.* LOC: Village centre, on main road. PARK: Easy. TEL: Guildford (0483) 224396. SER: Restorations (furniture, pictures); interior design. VAT: Stan.

Longford Castle. From *Gardens in Edwardian England* published by the **Antique Collectors' Club,** 1985.

Anthony Welling

Broadway Barn, High Street
Ripley, Surrey, GU23 6AQ
Tel. 0483 225384

**Specialist in C17th and C18th oak
and country furniture**

Ripley continued

Anthony Welling Antiques   BADA
Broadway Barn, High St. Est. 1970. CL: Sun.
except by appointment. Open 9—1 and
2—5.30 and evenings by appointment. SIZE:
Large. *STOCK: English oak, 17th—18th C,
£150—£5,000; country furniture, 18th C,
£100—£3,000; brass, copper, pewter, some
oils and watercolours, 18th C, £20—£500.*
Not stocked: Glass, china, silver. LOC: Turn
off A3 at Ripley, shop in centre of village on
service road. PARK: Easy. TEL: Guildford
(0483) 225384. VAT: Spec.

SANDERSTEAD,
See Greater London

SHALFORD, Nr. Guildford
M. and D. Granshaw
Ye Olde Malt House, The Street. Est. 1895.
Open every day 9.30—5.30. *STOCK: English
furniture, 17th—19th C; stripped pine, metalware and garden ornaments, statuary, glass,
silver, jewellery, general antiques.* LOC: A281.
1 mile from Guildford, opposite Seahorse Inn.
TEL: Guildford (0483) 61462. VAT: Stan.

Shalford continued

Michael Spratt Watercolours
Kingfishers, East Shalford Lane. Est. 1975.
Open by appointment. SIZE: Small. *STOCK:
English watercolours, 18th to early 19th C,
£150—£2,500.* LOC: Off A281 main street.
PARK: Easy. TEL: Guildford (0483) 504607;
home — same. SER: Valuations; buys at
auction (early English watercolours). VAT:
Spec.

SHEPPERTON
Rickett & Co. Antiques
Church Sq. (A.L. Spencer.) Est. 1968. Open
10—5, Wed. 10—1, prior telephone call
advisable. *STOCK: Brass and copper, pine,
18th—19th C, £100—£300; fenders and fire
tools, oil lamps, inkwells, chandeliers.* LOC:
10 minutes from London airport. PARK: Easy.
TEL: Walton-on-Thames (0932) 243571;
home — Walton-on-Thames (0932) 222508.
SER: Restorations (metal repairs and polishing). VAT: Spec.

SHERE   **(048 641)**
Yesterdays Pine
Gomshall Lane. (J. and V. Stuart.) Open
9.30—5.30, Sun. 1.30—5.30. *STOCK: 18th
and 19th C pine.* TEL: 3198.

SHIRLEY
See Greater London

SHOTTERMILL, Nr. Haslemere
Grannie's Attic
Checkerboards, Hindhead Rd. (A.G.J. Buckland.) CL: Sat. Open 9.30—6. *STOCK: Small general antiques, bric-a-brac.* TEL: Haslemere (0428) 4572.

STAINES   (0784)
Antique Market
Oast House, Kingston Rd. (J.Lear and P. Smith.) Open on last Sun. of each month except Dec. 9.30—4.30. There are 30 dealers at this market selling *general antiques.* LOC: Near Police Station. PARK: Easy. TEL: Sunbury (09327) 84480 or Ashford (07842) 53334.

K.W. Dunster Antiques   LAPADA
23 Church St. CL: Mon. and Thurs. Open 9.30—5.30. SIZE: Medium. *STOCK: Clocks, furniture, general antiques, interior decor, jewellery, nautical items.* TEL: 53297; home — Wraysbury (078481) 3146. VAT: Stan/Spec.

Link Gold Ltd.
73a High St. (A.C. Thiele and G.M. Reed.) Open Tues. and Sat. 9.30—3. *STOCK: Gold including jewellery, from 1900, £50—£250; silver, from 1800, £15—£200; silver plate, from 1900, £5—£100; general antiques, £5—£100.* TEL: Head Office (01) 549 5551 or (01) 398 1237.

Margaret Melville Watercolours
11 Colnebridge Close, Market Sq. By appointment only. *STOCK: English watercolours, late 18th C to early 20th C, £70—£1,000.* TEL: 55395.

SUNBURY   (093 27)
Van Broek Antiques
Manor Farm, 128 Green St. (Mrs. J. Puyenbroek.) Est. 1976. Open by appointment. *STOCK: Pine and Victorian furniture, some smalls.* TEL: 80486. SER: Restorations.

SURBITON
See Greater London

SUTTON
See Greater London

THAMES DITTON
Fern Cottage Antique Centre
28/30 High St. Est. 1960. Open 10.30—5. SIZE: Large. There are 20 dealers at this centre offering a wide range of *general antiques, 18th—19th C furniture, maps, prints, porcelain, pine, silver, jewellery.* TEL: (01) 398 2281.

Thames Ditton continued
Elizabeth Gant
52 High St. PBFA. Est. 1981. CL: Wed. SIZE: Small. *STOCK: Antiquarian, secondhand and illustrated books, especially childrens; ephemera, toys, postcards, 10p—£1,000.* PARK: Nearby. TEL: (01) 398 0962; (01) 398 5107. SER: Valuations; restorations (bookbinding); buys at auction (books). FAIRS: Bonnington Book; some PBFA.

THORNTON HEATH
See Greater London

VIRGINIA WATER
Pastiche
16 Station Approach. (Mrs. J. Lamb.) CL: Mon. Open 11—5. *STOCK: General antiques, porcelain, tapestries, stained glass, copper, brass, clocks and decorators' items.* TEL: Wentworth (09904) 3119. SER: Restorations (furniture and porcelain).

WALLINGTON
See Greater London

WALTON-ON-THAMES   (0932)
Boathouse Gallery
The Towpath, Manor Rd. (B.E. Clark.) CL: Mon. *STOCK: Oil paintings, watercolours, engravings.* TEL: 242718. SER: Picture framing, mounting and restoration. VAT: Stan.

Siggi's Antiques Centre
76 Queen's Rd., Hersham. *STOCK: Early Victorian and Edwardian furniture, art deco, Victorian linen, porcelain, silver and jewellery, Oriental pottery.*

WALTON-ON-THE-HILL
and TADWORTH
Ian Caldwell   LAPADA
9a Tadworth Green, Dorking Rd. Resident. Est. 1978. Open 9.30—6. SIZE: Medium. *STOCK: Oak, walnut and mahogany furniture especially Georgian.* LOC: 2 miles from M25, ¼ mile from A217 on B2032 in Dorking direction. PARK: Easy. TEL: Tadworth (073 781) 3969. SER: Valuations; restorations. VAT: Stan/Spec.

William Cooper and Son
Avondale, Dorking Rd., Tadworth. Est. 1945. Open 9—5. SIZE: Small. *STOCK: Furniture, general antiques.* PARK: Easy. TEL: Tadworth (073 781) 3861. VAT: Stan/Spec.

Country Shop Antiques
20 Walton St. (L. Coombs.) Est. 1972. CL: Wed. and Sat. Open 10.30—4. SIZE: Small. *STOCK: General antiques, small furniture.* PARK: Easy. TEL: Tadworth (073 781) 3393.

Walton-on-the-Hill

The Moorhen Antiques
9 Walton St. (Mr. and Mrs. B. Page.) CL: Mon. and Wed. Open 10−1 and 2−5. SIZE: Medium. *STOCK: Pine furniture, collectors' items, needlework, papier mâché, Tunbridge-ware, copper and brass.* LOC: ¼ mile after Burgh Heath take right fork signposted Tadworth. Straight on to Walton. Opp. the Mere Pond in main street. PARK: Easy. TEL: Tadworth (073 781) 2272.

Pond Antiques
11a Walton St. (B. Page). CL: Mon. and Wed. Open 10−1 and 2−5. *STOCK: Victorian stripped pine furniture, general antiques.* LOC: Opposite the Mere Pond in main street. TEL: Tadworth (073 781) 2272.

Scott Antiques   BADA
67 Walton St. (G.P.H. and Mrs. A.E. Graves, A.T. Clarke.) Est. 1972. CL: Wed. Open 10−1 and 2.30−5. SIZE: Medium. *STOCK: Period furniture, oils, watercolours by listed artists.* Not stocked: Glass, silver, jewellery, bric-a-brac. LOC: A217 from London. Take right fork at roundabout on to B2220. PARK: Easy. TEL: Tadworth (073 781) 2097. VAT: Stan/Spec.

WESTCOTT, Nr. Dorking
Westcott Antiques
2 The Green. (R.A. Windley.) Est. 1968. CL: Sun. p.m. Open 9.30−5. SIZE: Large. *STOCK: Oak and walnut furniture, 1600−1800; mahogany furniture, 1700−1820.* LOC: A25. Two miles west of Dorking on road to Guildford. PARK: Easy. TEL: Dorking (0306) 881900; home − Dorking (0306) 882180. SER: Valuations; restorations (furniture); buys at auction. VAT: Stan/Spec.

WEYBRIDGE   (0932)
Church House Antiques   LAPADA
42 Church St. (R.W. Foster.) Est. 1966. Open 10−5.30. SIZE: Medium. *STOCK: Furniture, 18th−19th C, £75−£3,000; jewellery, 18th−19th C, some modern, £10−£2,500; prints, pictures, militaria, musical boxes, glass, copper, brass.* Not stocked: Coins and stamps. PARK: At rear. TEL: 42190. SER: Restorations (furniture). VAT: Stan/Spec.

The Clock Shop Weybridge
64 Church St. Est. 1970. Open 9.30−6. SIZE: Medium. *STOCK: Clocks, 1685−1900, £500−£4,000; French carriage clocks, from £175.* LOC: Opposite Midland Bank on corner. PARK: Easy. TEL: 40407/55503. SER: Valuations; restorations (clocks); buys at auction. VAT: Stan/Spec.

"...at night you perceive that you are in a land of housebreakers..."
From *Mr. Rowlandson's England* by Robert Southey, ed. John Steel, published by the **Antique Collectors' Club,** 1985.

A.J. Saunders

R. Saunders

A.K. Saunders

71, Queen's Road, Weybridge, Surrey.

Genuine Antiques, Curios and Silver

Expert in Restoring
Old English Furniture

Closing Day -- Wednesday

Telephone   -   -   Weybridge 42601

Weybridge continued

Edward Cross — Fine Paintings
128 Oatlands Drive. Est: 1973. Open Fri. 10—12.30 and 2—4, Sat. 10—12.30. SIZE: Medium. *STOCK: Oil paintings and watercolours, 19th—20th C, £500—£15,000.* LOC: A3050. PARK: Opposite. TEL: 51093. SER: Valuations; restorations (watercolours and oil paintings); buys at auction (pictures). VAT: Spec.

R. Saunders   BADA
71 Queen's Rd. (A.J. and A.K. Saunders.) Est. 1878. CL: Wed. Open 9.30—1 and 2.30—5. SIZE: Medium. *STOCK: English mahogany, oak and walnut furniture, wheel and stick barometers, 1650—1830, £50—£5,000; glass, porcelain, silver, watercolours, pewter and brass. Not stocked: Reproductions.* PARK: 150yds. in York Rd. TEL: 42601. SER: Valuations; restorations (furniture). VAT: Spec.

Weybridge Antiques
66-68 Church St. (P. Pocock.) Est. 1974. Open 9.15—5.45, Sun. and evenings by appointment. SIZE: Large. *STOCK: Furniture, 17th—19th C, Sheraton, Regency, Georgian, Victorian and Edwardian, £50—£2,500; oil and watercolour paintings, £40—£3,000; silver, glass, bronze, porcelain and jewellery, £15—£1,000; all 18th to early 20th C.* LOC: 2½ miles off A3 at Cobham turn-off. Almost opposite Midland Bank. PARK: Rear and forecourt. TEL: 52503. SER: Valuations; restorations. VAT: Stan/Spec.

WHYTELEAFE

Round-a-bout Antiques
4 Wellesley Parade, Godstone Rd. (R.J. Morrison, S.A. Dias and J.C. MacLennon.) Est. 1970. Open 10—4, Sat. 10—5, Sun. 2—5. SIZE: Large. *STOCK: Victorian, Edwardian, art deco, general antiques, fireplace furniture including fenders, light fittings.* PARK: In lay- by. TEL: Upper Warlingham (088 32) 5417.

WOKING   (048 62)

Bakers of Maybury Ltd.
42 Arnold Rd. (K.R. Baker.) *STOCK: General antiques.* TEL: 67425.

Barbers Picture Framing
18 Chertsey Rd. *STOCK: Victorian and Edwardian watercolours, £75—£500.* TEL: 69926.

Chattels
156 High St., Old Woking. (J. Kendall.) Open 9—5, Sat. by appointment. SIZE: Small. *STOCK: Clocks, barometers, some small furniture.* LOC: Two miles off A3 at Ripley. PARK: Own. TEL: 71310. SER: Restorations (English clocks, furniture).

The Venture
High St., Old Woking. (D. Wilkins, D. Law.) Est. 1946. Resident. Always open. *STOCK: General antiques, pre-1920, especially pine.* TEL: 72103.

Wych House Antiques   LAPADA
Wych House, Wych Hill. (A. and C. Perry.) Est. 1965. Open 9—6, Sat. 9—1. SIZE: Large + warehouses. *STOCK: Continental and English furniture, decorative items, paintings.* TEL: 64636. VAT: Stan.

WONERSH

M. Odell Foster
Millmead. Est. 1964. CL: Sun. except by appointment. Open 9—5.30, appointment advisable. *STOCK: Roman, Greek, Egyptian and .other antiquities (catalogues available).* TEL: Guildford (0483) 892375 or Chute Standen (026 470) 796.

Sussex East

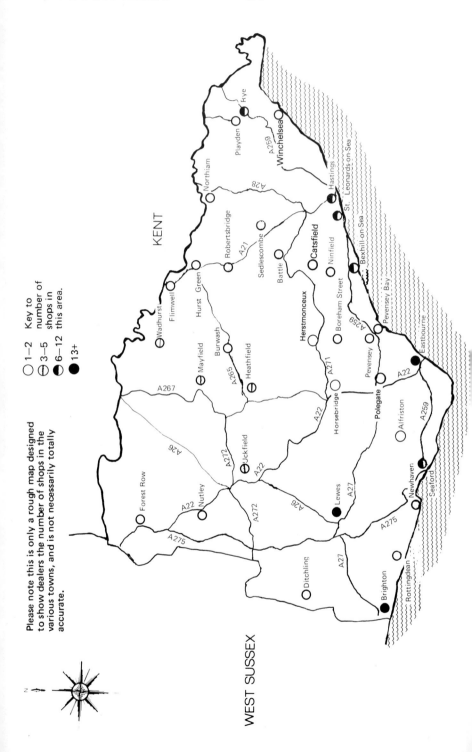

Please note this is only a rough map designed to show dealers the number of shops in the various towns, and is not necessarily totally accurate.

Key to number of shops in this area.

○ 1–2
◑ 3–5
◕ 6–12
● 13+

KENT

WEST SUSSEX

Rye
Playden
Winchelsea
Northiam
Hastings
St. Leonards-on-Sea
Robertsbridge
Sedlescombe
Catsfield
Ninfield
Bexhill-on-Sea
Battle
Wadhurst
Flimwell
Hurst Green
Boreham Street
Herstmonceux
Pevensey Bay
Burwash
Mayfield
Heathfield
Pevensey
Eastbourne
Horsebridge
Polegate
Forest Row
Uckfield
Alfriston
Nutley
Lewes
Newhaven
Seaford
Ditchling
Brighton
Rottingdean

A259
A28
A21
A265
A267
A26
A272
A22
A271
A259
A275
A27

ALFRISTON, Nr. Polegate (0323)
Alfriston Antiques
The Square. (J. Tourell.) Est. 1967. CL: Wed. p.m. and Mon. Open 10—1 and 2.30—5.30, appointment advisable during winter months. SIZE: Small. *STOCK: Collectors' items, boxes, caddy spoons, silver, plate, carriage and other French clocks, jewellery, paintings, pot-lids, a wide variety of books wholesaled, copper, brass.* PARK: Easy. TEL: 870498. VAT: Stan/Spec.

The Old Paint Shop
Twytton House, High St. (Mrs. P.J. Radford.) Open every day 11—5. SIZE: Medium. *STOCK: Metalware, weapons, glass, china, jewellery, prints and maps.* PARK: Easy. TEL: 870440.

BATTLE (042 46)
Chapel Antiques
Whatlington. (M. Browne.) Resident. Est. 1957. Open at all times. SIZE: Medium. *STOCK: 18th C chests of drawers, bureaux; 19th C Persian rugs.* Not stocked: Victoriana. LOC: From Battle proceed up Mount St. to Whatlington. The Chapel has a steeple and is in a very prominent position. PARK: Easy. TEL: Sedlescombe (042 487) 272. VAT: Spec.

Magpie Antiques
38 Mount St. (C. and G. Huckvale.) *STOCK: General antiques, Victoriana, bric-a-brac.* TEL: 2194; home — 2341.

BEXHILL-ON-SEA (0424)
Barclay Antiques LAPADA
7 Village Mews, Little Common. (R. and M. Barclay.) Est. 1971. CL: Wed. Open 10—4.30. SIZE: Medium. *STOCK: Pottery and porcelain especially Worcester, Derby and Coalport, 18th—19th C, £75—£400; small furniture including desks and secretaires; watercolours and oils, all 19th C, £300—£1,500; treen including Tunbridgeware, 19th C, £50—£300; slag glass, £10—£200.* LOC: Coast road. PARK: Easy. TEL: Home — Rye (0797) 222734. SER: Valuations; restorations (furniture and porcelain, exceptional pieces only); buys at auction (porcelain). FAIRS: Kensington, Buxton, Snape, Brighton, Bath, Bury St. Edmunds, Olympia. VAT: Spec.

Bexhill-on-Sea continued

Bexhill Antiques Centre
Quaker's Mill, Old Town. (A. Kingsford.). Est. 1972. Open 6 days a week 10—5.30. *STOCK: General antiques, including furniture, silver, porcelain and jewellery.* LOC: A259 coast road. PARK: Opposite. TEL: 211542. Below are listed some of the 15 dealers at this centre:—

R. Amstad
Clocks.
R. Brown
Furniture.
Sally Campbell
Studio pottery, art nouveau, art deco and collectors' items.
N. Carey
Porcelain.
P. Gardner
Ceramics and smalls.
Norah Green
Small furniture, linen and glass.
Tony Kingsford
General and shipping furniture. SER: Buys at auction.
N. Little
Doll's furniture and smalls.
Pauline Moon
Jewellery.
Ann Naves
Silver and plate, smalls.
Philip Stocker
Jewellery and silver.
B. Watson
Furniture, silver and porcelain.

Coppers
No. 4 Village Mews, Little Common. (Mrs. E. Pinner.) Open 10—5.30. *STOCK: Maps, porcelain, trade signs, glass, boxes.*

Chris Fryer Antiques
10 Sackville Rd. Open 9.30—5.30, Wed. 9.30—1. *STOCK: Furniture, silver, jewellery, small items.* TEL: 221660.

The Gallery
18 Endwell Rd. (Mrs. D. Kelly.) Est. 1980. Open 9—4. SIZE: Warehouse. *STOCK: Furniture, porcelain, glass, from 18th C; shipping goods.* TEL: 212127.

K. and A. Antiques
70 London Rd. Est. 1946. Open 8.30—6. SIZE: Medium. *STOCK: Clocks, £30—£2,000; furniture, £50—£800; small items, £1—£100.* LOC: Off main Hastings to Brighton Rd. PARK: Easy. TEL: 211357; home — same.

Bexhill-on-Sea continued

Martom Antiques
115 London Rd. (M. Smith.) Est. 1977. Open 9.30—1 and 1.30—5, Wed. and Sun. by appointment. SIZE: Medium. *STOCK: Desks, 18th—19th C, £500—£2,500; Victorian, Edwardian, shipping oak, pine, £50—£350.* LOC: Off A259. PARK: Opposite. TEL: 224191. SER: Restorations (leather linings, gold tooling); buys at auction (18th—19th C furniture).

Mews Gallery
8 Village Mews, Little Common. (J.E. Stalker.) Open 10—5. *STOCK: Furniture, glass, silver and plate, pictures.* TEL: Cooden (04243) 5839.

David and Sarah Pullen Antiques
LAPADA
29/31 Sea Rd. SIZE: Large. *STOCK: Clocks and furniture, 18th—19th C, £50—£3,000; decorative items £10—£1,000.* LOC: Town centre near railway station. TEL: 222035; home — 225546.

Tamar Gallery
17 Wickham Ave. Est. 1974. CL: Wed. Open 9—1 and 2.30—5.30. SIZE: Medium. *STOCK: Watercolours and oil paintings, furniture, general antiques, 1780—1940, £5—£500.* LOC: Town centre, nr. library. PARK: Easy. TEL: 221835.

Village Antiques
2 and 4 Cooden Sea Rd., Little Common. (Mr. and Mrs. D. Cowpland.) Resident. Est. 1975. Open 10—5. SIZE: Large. *STOCK: Furniture, shipping goods.* LOC: On A259. TEL: Cooden (042 43) 5214 or Battle (042 46) 2035. SER: Restorations. VAT: Stan/Spec.

BOREHAM STREET, Nr. Hailsham

Camelot Antiques
(Mrs. B.C. Chambers.) Est. 1968. CL: Wed. Open 10—1 and 2.15—5.30. SIZE: Small. *STOCK: Porcelain and pottery, 1800—1930, £5—£300; small furniture, 19th—20th C, £25—£600; silver, copper, brass, glass, Victorian, £5—£100.* Not stocked: Firearms, stamps, medals. PARK: Easy. TEL: Herstmonceux (0323) 833460. FAIRS: Various country.

BRIGHTON (0273)

Adrian Alan Ltd. **LAPADA**
4 Frederick Place. Est. 1963. Open 8.30—5.30, Sat. 9—1. SIZE: Large. *STOCK: English and Continental furniture, clocks, barometers, bronzes and metalware.* TEL: 25277/25015. VAT: Stan/Spec.

Brighton continued

Adrian Alan Ltd
15c Prince Albert St. Est. 1963. Open 10—5 or by appointment. *STOCK: English and continental furniture, clocks, barometers, bronzes and metalware.* TEL: 25277/25015. VAT: Stan/Spec.

Angel Antiques **LAPADA**
16 Church Rd., Hove. (P. Angel.) Est. 1951. CL: Sat. p.m. Open 9—5. SIZE: Medium. *STOCK: Small furniture, china, jewellery.* LOC: In main shopping centre. PARK: Easy. TEL: 737955. VAT: Stan.

Ansells
48 Norfolk Sq., Western Rd. Est. 1934. *STOCK: Gold, diamonds, Victorian jewellery, silver, watches, objets de vertu, general antiques.* TEL: 27973. VAT: Stan.

Antiques, Linen and Lace
32 Holland Rd., Hove. (J. and B.P. Mendes.) Est. 1974. Open 9—1 and 2—5, Sat. by appointment. SIZE: Small and basement. *STOCK: General antiques, linen and lace.* LOC: Brighton sea front towards Worthing turn by Brunswick Hotel to Palmeira Sq. PARK: In nearby streets. TEL: 731574; home — 775978 (ansaphone).

Ashton's Antiques *Mainly Trade*
1—3 Clyde Rd., Preston Circus. (R. Ashton.) CL: Wed. Open 9.30—5. *STOCK: General trade and shipping goods.* TEL: 605253. VAT: Stan/Spec.

Attic Antiques **LAPADA**
Mainly Trade
23 and 32 Ship St. (F.B. and M.J. Moorhead and Son.) Est. 1965. CL: Sat. Open 11.30—1, prior telephone call advisable. *STOCK: General antiques, 1720—1920, £15—£1,500; paintings, clocks, barometers, Oriental antiques, bronzes, English and Continental china, tantalus, Victorian oil lamps, copper, brass, pewter; Imari, Canton, Satsuma and Worcester china; Georgian, Victorian, Edwardian and continental furniture.* TEL: 29464 or 26378. VAT: Stan.

H. Balchin and Son
18—19 Castle St. (C.B. Balchin.) Est. 1930. Resident. CL: Thurs. and Sat. p.m. Open 9.30—1 and 2.30—5.30. SIZE: Large. *STOCK: General antiques 18th—19th C.* LOC: From Western Rd., down Preston St., Castle St. is second turning on left. PARK: Loading only. SER: Valuations. VAT: Stan/Spec.

Ron Beech **LAPADA**
150 Portland Rd., Hove. (R.E. Beech.) Est. 1977. CL: Mon. Open 10.30—1.30 and 3.30—6.30. SIZE: Medium. *STOCK: Victorian Staffordshire figures and pot-lids, 19th C, £25—£500.* LOC: South of A27. PARK: Easy. TEL: 724477 (ansaphone). SER: Valuations. FAIRS: Petersfield, London (West Kensington). VAT: Stan/Spec.

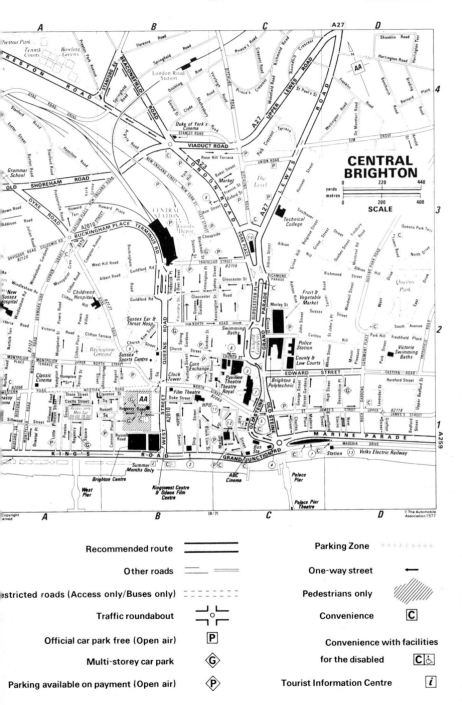

CENTRAL BRIGHTON

SCALE

Recommended route		Parking Zone
Other roads		One-way street
Restricted roads (Access only/Buses only)		Pedestrians only
Traffic roundabout		Convenience
Official car park free (Open air)	P	
		Convenience with facilities
Multi-storey car park	G	for the disabled
Parking available on payment (Open air)	P	Tourist Information Centre

Reproduced by kind permission of the Automobile Association

Brighton continued

John Bird/Annette Puttnam
39 and 44 Upper North St. Est. 1970. Open 9.30—5.30, Sat. and other times by appointment. *STOCK: Furniture — country, pine, oak, fruitwood, painted grained and wicker kitchen, architectural and garden; paintings, needlework, fabric and baskets.* TEL: 739425.

Bits and Pieces
15 Terminus Rd. (Miss D. Clarke.) Est. 1965. CL: Sun. except by appointment. Open 10.30—6. SIZE: Small. *STOCK: Porcelain, small furniture.* TEL: 27021.

Brighton Antique Wholesalers
39 Upper Gardner St. There are several furniture dealers at these premises selling *18th—19th C furniture, £50—£5,000.* LOC: Off North Rd. PARK: Easy. TEL: 695457.

Brighton Antiques Gallery
41 Meeting House Lane. Est. 1975. Open 10—5.30. There are twenty-two stalls at this market selling *a wide variety of antiques including porcelain, paintings, dolls, silver, clocks, glass, jewellery, copper and brass, small furniture, arms, militaria, Victorian paper, unusual collectors' items, coins, ephemera, valentines and toys.* TEL: 26693 and 21059. VAT: Stan/Spec.

Bruton, Brighton   LAPADA
31/32 Meeting House Lane. Est. 1969. Open 10—5. *STOCK: Victoriana, brass, copper, furniture.* TEL: 26591. VAT: Stan/Spec.

Caroline Buxton Interiors
22 Victoria Rd. Open 10—5.30, Sat. 10—4. *STOCK: Decorative items, furniture including painted, lacquered and bamboo.* TEL: 771200.

P. Carmichael   LAPADA
33 Upper North St. (H. Mileham.) Est. 1946. CL: Sat. p.m. Open 9.30—5.30. *STOCK: Barometers, general antiques, 18th—19th C furniture.* TEL: 28072. SER: Buys at auction. VAT: Stan/Spec.

Carroll Bros. Antiques *Trade and Export*
136 Albion St., Southwick. (J.J., J.N. and B.P. Carroll.) Est. 1975. CL: Sat. p.m. Open 9—5. *STOCK: Reveneered furniture, walnut, mahogany, elm; oil paintings, £200—£3,000.* LOC: On A259. PARK: Easy. TEL: 593857. VAT: Stan.

David Crook
16 Bond St. Est. 1957. CL: Sun., except by appointment. Open 10.30—5.30. *STOCK: General antiques, jewellery, Victorian needlework, 1920s items and linens, furniture, glass and china.* TEL: 26040.

Brighton continued

A.F. Dade Antiques
83 Gloucester Rd. Est. 1960. CL: Sat. Open 10—1 and 2—5. SIZE: Medium. *STOCK: English furniture, 1740-1790, £500—£1,000; furniture, 1840-1860, £100-1,000; furniture, 1890-1910, £50—£1,000.* LOC: 300yds. from station, just off Queens Rd. PARK: Easy. TEL: 672043. SER: Valuations; buys at auction. VAT: Stan/Spec.

Graham Deane Antiques
36 Gloucester Rd. CL: Sat. Open 9.30—5.30. *STOCK: Furniture, china, brass, general antiques.* TEL: 609000.

Mike Deasy Ltd.
108—114 Eastern Rd. (M. and P. Deasy.) Est. 1956. Open 8—6, Sat. 8—1. SIZE: Large. *STOCK: General antiques and garden ornaments, £5—£20,000.* Not stocked: Silver. PARK: Own. TEL: 687237 and 688523.

Harry Diamond and Son
26 North St., The Lanes. (R. and H. Diamond.) Est. 1937. Open 9—5. *STOCK: Diamond jewellery, antique silver and 19th C French clocks, £50—£20,000.* Not stocked: Coins, furniture. TEL: 29696. VAT: Stan.

James Doyle Antiques
9 Union St., The Lanes. (J.R. Doyle.) Est. 1975. Open 9.30—6. *STOCK: Jewellery, silver.* TEL: 23694.

Dupont Galleries
33 Grand Parade. (Z. Hodgkins.) Est. 1976. Open 11—6 or by appointment. SIZE: Large. *STOCK: Old and rare Oriental carpets and kilims.* LOC: Near Regency Pavilion. PARK: Easy. TEL: 600932. SER: Valuations; restorations. VAT: Stan.

D.H. Edmonds Ltd
27 and 28 Meeting House Lane, The Lanes. Est. 1965. Open 10—5.30. SIZE: Large. *STOCK: Jewellery, silver, objets d'art, watches, £50—£20,000.* TEL: 27713 and 28871. VAT: Stan.

J.A.L. Franks Ltd.
22 Bond St. Est. 1947. CL: Wed. Open 9—6. *STOCK: Postcards, stamps.* TEL: 686120. VAT: Stan.

Gloucester Road Antiques *Trade Only*
94 Gloucester Rd. (S. Brooke.) Est. 1970. CL: Sat. except by appointment. Open 10—1 and 2—5.30. SIZE: Large. *STOCK: Furniture, 18th and 19th C, to £5,000, shipping items, to 1930.* LOC: From London turn right into Trafalgar St., left into Sidney St., right into Gloucester Rd., shop on right. PARK: Easy. TEL: 691164; home — Haywards Heath (0444) 453589. VAT: Stan/Spec.

Brighton continued

Paul Goble
44 Meeting House Lane, The Lanes. Est. 1965. Open 9.30—5. *STOCK: Jewellery, watches silver, pictures and prints.* TEL: 202801. VAT: Stan.

Golfiana Miscellanea Ltd
13 Gt. College St. Open by appointment. *STOCK: Golf art, books, memorabilia, antiques.* TEL: 672565. VAT: Stan.

Douglas Hall Ltd.
23 Meeting House Lane. (A.M. Longthorne.) Est. 1968. Open 9.30—5. *STOCK: Silver, jewellery.* TEL: 25323. VAT: Stan.

Hallmarks
4 Union St., The Lanes. (L.F. and J.E Jenner and J. Hersheson.) Est. 1966. Open 9—5. SIZE: Small. *STOCK: Silver, jewellery, clocks.* PARK: Meters. TEL: 725477. VAT: Stan/Spec.

Simon Hatchwell Antiques
64/65 Middle St. Est. 1961. CL: Sat. SIZE: Large. *STOCK: Barometers, grandfather clocks, 17th C; English and European antiques, paintings, chandeliers, bronzes and carpets, 17th—20th C.* Not stocked: Jewellery. PARK: Easy. TEL: 27663. SER: Restorations (barometers and furniture). VAT: Stan/Spec.

David Hawkins (Brighton) Ltd.
LAPADA
15B Prince Albert St. The Lanes. Est. 1958. Open 9—5. SIZE: Large. *STOCK: General antiques; fine art, shipping goods, decorative and collectors' items, arms and armour, £10—£7,500.* LOC: Large detached building at south entrance of The Lanes. TEL: 21357. VAT: Stan/Spec.

Holleyman and Treacher Ltd.
21a and 22 Duke St. Open 9—5.30. Est. 1937. *STOCK: Antiquarian books, music, maps and prints.* TEL: 28007.

Brighton continued

J. Hopkins (Antiques) Ltd.   BADA
34 Upper North St. Est. 1959. *STOCK: English and Continental furniture, pictures, glass.* TEL: 730673. SER: Valuations. VAT: Stan/Spec.

The House of Antiques   LAPADA
25 Meeting House Lane and 17 Prince Albert St. (A. Margiotta.) Open 9.30—5.30. *STOCK: Jewellery, works of art, general antiques, glass, porcelain, silver, music boxes, oil paintings, furniture.* TEL: 29960, 27680 and 24961. VAT: Stan.

Dudley Hume
46 and 50 Upper North St. Est. 1973. CL: Sat. and Sun., except by appointment. SIZE: Medium. *STOCK: Period and Victorian furniture, metal, light fittings.* LOC: Parallel to the Western Rd., one block to the north. TEL: 23461. VAT: Stan/Spec.

Jubilee Antique Cellars and Collectors Market
Gardner St. (Sherman and Waterman Assoc. Ltd.) Open 9—5. There are 25 units at this market selling *general antiques.* TEL: 600574 or (01) 836 3186/2136.

Kingsbury Antiques
Hallmarks, 4 Union St. (J.J. Hersheson.) Open 9—5. *STOCK: Old Sheffield plate, silver, glass; small furniture, clocks.* TEL: 725477. VAT: Stan/Spec.

Kingsbury Warehouse
Kingsbury St. (Mrs. L. Watson.) CL: Sat. Open 10—5. *STOCK: China, furniture, jewellery, pictures, shipping items, copper, horse- drawn vehicles.* TEL: 699156.

Kollect-o-Mania
25 Trafalgar St. Open 10—5. There are 18 dealers at this centre selling *a wide range of general antiques, records, books, dolls' houses, miniature furniture.* LOC: Near station. TEL: 694229.

Brighton continued

Don Lancaster Antiques
19, 60 and 60a Middle St. Open 9—6 or by appointment. SIZE: Large. *STOCK: China, glass, caddies, inkwells, metalware, country, traditional and decorated furniture, decorative items.* LOC: Adjoining The Lanes. PARK: Easy. TEL: 727791. VAT: Stan/Spec.

Lennox Antiques
53 Upper North St. (L.P. Cato.) Est. 1975. Open 9—6, Sat. and Sun. by appointment. SIZE: Small. *STOCK: Georgian furniture, £500—£5,000; Victorian furniture, decorative works of art, to early 20th C, £50—£2,500.* LOC: M23/A23. PARK: Easy and York Hill. TEL: 29409; home — 563104. SER: Valuations; buys at auction. FAIRS: West Dean, Chichester, Castle Ashby, Northampton. VAT: Stan/Spec.

The Leopard
35 Kensington Gdns. (A. and A. Leppard.) Est. 1973. Open 9—5, Wed. 9—1, Sat. 8—5. SIZE: Medium. *STOCK: Costume and military uniforms, 19th C, £50—£200; lace, table and bed linen, 19th—20th C, £5—£50; period clothing, early 20th C, £5—£100.* LOC: Pedestrian street at bottom of Gloucester Rd. PARK: Easy. TEL: 695427; home — 507619.

Brighton continued

H. Miller (Antiques) Ltd.   LAPADA
22a Ship St. Est. 1947. Open 10—5, Sat. 9—1. *STOCK: Silver, jewellery, Sheffield silver, plate.* TEL: 26255. VAT: Stan/Spec.

Minutiques
82B Trafalgar St. (Mr. and Mrs. J. Jackman.) Est. 1970. CL: Thurs. p.m. Open 9.30—5.15. *STOCK: Dolls, miniatures, books, doll restoration materials.* LOC: Between railway station and main London Rd. (St. Peter's Church). PARK: Limited in street opposite or 3 car parks behind shop. TEL: 681862; home — 551042. SER: Restorations (antique dolls). Catalogues available. VAT: Spec.

Patrick Moorhead Antiques
59A Ship St. *STOCK: General antiques, paintings, furniture, Oriental art, English and Continental china.* TEL: 28209.

Michael Norman Antiques
17/18 Bond St. (M.P. Keehan.) CL: Sat. Open 9—5.30. SIZE: Large. *STOCK: Furniture, 19th C.* TEL: 697716.

Michael Norman Antiques Ltd   BADA
15 Ship St. Open 9—5.30. Est. 1965. *STOCK: English furniture.* TEL: 29253/4 or 26712. VAT: Stan/Spec.

Brighton continued

Oasis Antiques
39 Kensington Gardens. (I. and A. Stevenson.) Est. 1970. Open 10—5, Mon. 11—5, Sat. 8—5. SIZE: Medium. *STOCK: Lighting and furniture, to 1930, £1—£5,000; oriental items including bronzes, art glass, period clothes, linen and lace, gramophones, art nouveau, art deco.* LOC: Off North Road from railway station, centre of north Lanes. PARK: Nearby. TEL: 683885. SER: Restorations (furniture, metals and ceramics); polishing.

Colin Page Antiquarian Books
36 Duke St. (C.G. Page.) Est. 1971. Open 10—5.30. *STOCK: Antiquarian and second-hand books, especially British topography, travel, natural history, illustrated and bindings, 16th—20th C, £1—£5,000.* LOC: Town centre. PARK: Meters or nearby. TEL: 25954.

Page and Hawkes
30 Trafalgar St. Open 10—5.30. *STOCK: English and continental art nouveau, arts and crafts movement furniture, decorative arts, 1890—1940; Japanese folk crafts and works of art.* TEL: 609310.

Dermot and Jill Palmer Antiques
7 and 8 Union St., The Lanes. Resident. Est. 1963. Open 9—6, Sun. by appointment. *STOCK: Unusual decorative items, screens, lacquer work, toys, primitive pictures, country furniture, needlework, £5—£1,000.* TEL: 28669. FAIRS: Olympia. VAT: Stan/Spec.

Pandora's Box
112 St. George's Rd., Kemptown. (P.J. Crawford.) Open 10—2 or by appointment. *STOCK: Porcelain, pottery, small furniture, Doulton, Moorcroft.* TEL: 603305.

Park Galleries
217 Preston Rd., Preston Village. (S. Fellowes). Est. 1985. Open daily, Sun. by appointment. SIZE: Small. *STOCK: Painted and lacquer furniture, £100—£1,000; Bergere furniture, £500—£2,000; decorative small items, £50—£500; all 19th to early 20th C.* LOC: Main London—Brighton road off Preston Park. PARK: Nearby. TEL: 504057. SER: Valuations; restorations (furniture, china and upholstery). VAT: Stan/Spec.

The Past for Sale
3b Kensington Gardens. (W. Gillett.) CL: Sun. except by appointment. Open 9—4.30. *STOCK: Victorian underwear and night-dresses; table and bed linen; cushions, beaded bags, jet, fans, and accessories; Chinese gowns, embroideries and shawls; collectors' handkerchiefs, collars and lace.* PARK: Church St. TEL: 692609; home — 726037.

Brighton continued

Trevor Philip and Sons Ltd.
LAPADA
2 Prince Albert St. Open 9—5. *STOCK: Medical, marine and scientific instruments, ship models, marine paintings.* TEL: 202119. VAT: Stan/Spec.

Quinto Bookshop
34 Duke St. Open 9—6, Sun. 11—6. *STOCK: Antiquarian and secondhand books, maps and prints.* TEL: 26991.

Robinson's Bookshop Ltd.
11 Bond St. (Mrs. S. Robinson, T.P. and P.M. Brown.) Est. 1958. Open 9.15—5.30. *STOCK: Books on antiques and art; general and technical books.* LOC: Off North St. one street west of Theatre Royal. TEL: 29012.

Rodney Arthur Classics   *Trade Only*
Rear of 64—78 Davigdor Rd., Hove. (R.A. and Mrs. K.A.G. Oliver.) Est. 1979. Open 8.15—12.15 or by appointment. SIZE: Medium. *STOCK: Furniture, mainly Victorian and Edwardian shipping, £35—£850.* LOC: From Seven Dials, Davigdor Rd. is the exit to the west. PARK: Easy. TEL: 551613 or 26550. VAT: Stan.

Clive Rogers Oriental Rugs
22 Brunswick Rd., Hove. Est. 1974. Open Fri. and Sat. 9—6. SIZE: Medium. *STOCK: Oriental rugs, carpets, textiles; Oriental and Islamic works of art.* LOC: Off Western Rd. PARK: Easy. TEL: 738257; home — same. SER: Valuations; restorations (as stock); buys at auction. VAT: Stan/Spec.

Rutland Antiques
48 Upper North St. Open 10.30—5.30, Sun. by appointment. SIZE: Small. *STOCK: Furniture, porcelain, textiles and general antiques.* LOC: North of and parallel to Western Rd. PARK: Reasonable. TEL: 29991.

Semus Antiques
379 Kingsway, Hove. (P. and R. Semus.) Est. 1966. Open 9—6. SIZE: Large. *STOCK: General antiques and Victorian furniture, £50—£2,500.* LOC: Main coast road. PARK: Easy. TEL: 420154. SER: Packing.

Frank Semus Ltd.
20 Middle St. (F. and I. Semus.) Est. 1952. CL: Sat. p.m. Open 9—5. SIZE: Medium, storerooms, workshop at 9 Boyces St. *STOCK: Walnut, mahogany, oak dressers, bow chests, secretaires.* PARK: Meters in Middle St., and West St. TEL: 28883. VAT: Stan.

Robert Shaw Antiques
58 Brunswick Sq., Hove. Est. 1979. Open by appointment only. *STOCK: Pine, rocking animals, painted furniture.* TEL: 202065. VAT: Spec.

Brighton continued

Shelton Frames and Prints
4 Islingword Rd. (D.F. Saw.) Est. 1952. CL: Sat. Open 9—5.30, or by appointment. STOCK: Prints, porcelain, silver, pictures. PARK: Easy. TEL: 698345. SER: Restorations (oils and silks); framing; mount cutting; wash and line work, wet and dry mounting, heat laminations.

Shop of the Yellow Frog
10/11 The Lanes. (J.N. Chalcraft.) Est. 1946. Open 9—6, and Sun. during season. SIZE: Small. STOCK: 19th C jewellery, from £10; 18th—19th C silver, 18th C porcelain, both £5—£500. Not stocked: Large furniture. LOC: Near Brighton Pavilion. TEL: 25497. SER: Valuations; restorations (watches, jewellery, furniture); buys at auction.

S. and L. Simmons   LAPADA
9 Meeting House Lane, The Lanes. (L.M. and S.L. Simmons.) NAG. Est. 1948. Open 9.30—5.30. STOCK: Jewellery and silver, 19th C. TEL: 27949. VAT: Stan.

Raymond J. Smith (Antiques)
96—98 Gloucester Rd. STOCK: Furniture and clocks, 18th—19th C. TEL: 692828.

South Coast Antiques Ltd. LAPADA
3 Kensington Pl. (W.E. Collins.) CL: Sat. Open 10—5. STOCK: General antiques. TEL: 609828.

Cyril Stone
Hove. Est. 1950. Open by appointment only. STOCK: Watercolours, oil paintings, objets d'art, 18th—19th C. TEL: 739523. SER: Restorations (pictures). FAIRS: Chelsea, Kensington and others. VAT: Spec.

The Sussex Commemorative Ware Centre
88 Western Rd, Hove. (R. Prior.) Est. 1974. Open 9.30—12.30, Sat. 9.30—12.30 and 2—3.30, other times by appointment. STOCK: Antique and modern original commemoratives including Doulton and limited editions; Parian. TEL: 773911. SER: Catalogues.

Tapsell Antiques   LAPADA
10 Ship St. Gardens, Coachhouse, 59 and 59a Middle St. and 18 Middle St. Est. 1948. Open 9—1 and 2.15—5.30, other times by appointment. SIZE: Large. STOCK: Oriental and Continental porcelain, English and Continental furniture, clocks, general antiques. TEL: 28341. VAT: Stan/Spec.

Toby Antiques
Dukes Arcade, 32 Duke St. Est. 1970. Open 9.30—5.30. STOCK: General antiques, copper, silver, brass, collectors' items, toys, dolls' houses. TEL: 25800.

Brighton continued

Victorian Interiors
12 Boundary Rd, Hove. (R. Grover.) Open 9.30—5.30. STOCK: Pine furniture. TEL: 423384.

Barrie Ward Antiques and Associates
Trade warehouse 1a Brooker St., Hove. Est. 1975. Appointment advisable. STOCK: Georgian and Victorian shipping furniture, small items, clocks, china, silver. LOC: 500 yds. north of King Alfred swimming pool, next to "Viccaris" in Stirling Place. TEL: 720182. SER: Restorations; polishing; container packing and shipping (especially Australian, U.S. and Continental markets).

Graham Webb
59 Ship St. Est. 1961. CL: Mon. Open 10—5. SIZE: Small. STOCK: Cylinder and disc musical boxes, all mechanical musical instruments, £150—£8,000. LOC: Close to the Lanes. PARK: In Middle St. TEL: 21803; home — 772154. VAT: Stan/Spec.

'Weiner aus Wien' Military Antiques
2 Market St., The Lanes. (G. Weiner.) Est. 1962. Open 10—4.30, Sun. by appointment. SIZE: Small. STOCK: Orders, decorations, badges and insignia of Imperial Germany and Austrian states; pikelhaubes and other head-dress; Third Reich orders, decorations, badges and weapons; firearms and edged weapons; Imperial and Nazi German head-dress and accoutrements; British Victorian and French Napoleonic militaria, including medals and badges, all £5—£2,000. TEL: 729948. SER: Valuations; restorations (edged weapons); buys at auction (militaria); mail order catalogues available. FAIRS: London Arms, London West Hotel; Bedford Arms; Nottingham Arms.

Stephen and Sonia Welbourne
43 Denmark Villas, Hove. Open by appointment. STOCK: Early English watercolours. LOC: Near Hove station. TEL: 722518.

E. and B. White
43—47 Upper North St. and warehouse at 36 Robertson Rd. Est. 1962. CL: Sat. p.m. Open 9.30—5. SIZE: Medium. STOCK: Oak furniture, £50—£2,000. LOC: Upper North St. runs parallel to and north of Western Rd. (the main shopping street). TEL: 28706. VAT: Spec.

David Wigdor
44 Victoria St. Est. 1968. Open 10—1 and 2—5, Sat. and Sun. by appointment. STOCK: General antiques. TEL: 25908. VAT: Stan/Spec.

Brighton continued

J. and S. Williams
Gold and Silversmiths
3 Planet House, 1 The Drive, Hove. Est. 1910. CL: Sat. p.m. Open 9—5. *STOCK: Jewellery and silver.* TEL: 738489.

The Witch Ball
48 Meeting House Lane. (Mrs. G. Daniels and Miss R. Glassman.) Est. 1966. Open 10.30—6. *STOCK: 18th—19th C, cartoons and prints; 16th—19th C, maps.* TEL: 26618. VAT: Stan.

Yellow Lantern Antiques Ltd.
34 and 65B Holland Rd., Hove. (B.R. Higgins.) Est. 1950. CL: Sat. p.m. Open 9—1 and 2.15—5.30. SIZE: Medium. *STOCK: Mainly English furniture, £50—£3,000; French and English clocks; both to 1850; bronzes, 19th C, £100—£1,500; Continental porcelain, 1820—60, £50—£1,000.* Not stocked: Pottery, oak, 18th C porcelain. LOC: From Brighton sea-front to Hove, turn right at Hotel Alexander, shop 100yds. on left past traffic lights (opposite Maples furnishing store). PARK: Easy. TEL: 771572; home — Shoreham (079 17) 5476. SER: Valuations; restorations; buys at auction. FAIRS: Buxton. VAT: Spec.

Zyzyx
42 Clyde Rd. (D.V. Wood.) Est. 1966. Resident. *STOCK: Postcards, cigarette cards, stamps, ephemera, die-cast models.* TEL: 606332.

BURWASH,   (0435)
Nr. Etchingham

Chateau Briand Antique Centre
High St. Open 10—5, Sun. 12—5. There are 8 dealers at this centre selling *lace, linen, ethnic textiles, glass, ivories, bronzes.* TEL: 882535.

Lime Tree Antiques
High St. (S. and A. Vickery.) Est. 1967. Open 9—6, usually open Sun. but appointment advisable. SIZE: Medium. *STOCK: Old oak, silver, clocks, glass, porcelain, firearms, rugs, antiquarian books, prints, oils and water-colours, £5—£5,000.* PARK: Easy. TEL: 882385. SER: Restorations (paintings, prints and furniture). VAT: Stan/Spec.

CATSFIELD

B.B.C. Antiques
Burnt Barn Cottage, Frickley Lane. (B. and J. Morley.) Est. 1972. Open 8—6, Fri. and Sat. 9—1, or by appointment. SIZE: Medium. *STOCK: Windsor chairs, pine dressers, 19th C, £200—£700; oak furniture, 18th C, £300—£450.* PARK: Easy. TEL: (0424) 892036; home — same. SER: Restorations (wood turning). FAIRS: Olympia, British International, Birmingham. VAT: Stan/Spec.

DITCHLING

Dycheling Antiques
34 High St. (E.A. Hudson.) Est. 1977. Open 11—5, Sat. 10.30—5. SIZE: Medium. *STOCK: Furniture, silver, glass and china, Georgian—Edwardian, £5—£1,000.* LOC: Off A23. PARK: Easy. TEL: Hassocks (079 18) 2929; home — same.

Nona Shaw Antiques
4 and 8 West St. Est. 1954. SIZE: Medium. *STOCK: Porcelain, furniture, silver, copper and brass.* VAT: Stan/Spec.

EASTBOURNE   (0323)

Angloam Warehouse   *Trade Only*
2a Beach Rd. (L. Williams and H. Hoevel-mann). Est. 1976. Open 9.30—5, Sat. and Sun. by appointment. SIZE: Large. *STOCK: Shipping furniture, 1850—1920, £50—£300; period furniture, pre 1850, £500+; general antiques.* LOC: Off Seaside Rd. PARK: Easy. TEL: 648661; Tunbridge Wells (0892) 36627; Horam Rd. (043 53) 2126. SER: Restorations. VAT: Stan.

Antique Market
Leaf Hall, Seaside. (R. Evenden.) Open Tues. and Sat. 9—5. 16 stallholders. *STOCK: General antiques.* TEL: 27530.

Douglas Barsley Antiques
                                         LAPADA
44 Cornfield Rd. Est. 1966. Open 9—1.30 and 2—5.15. *STOCK: Small collectors' items, silver, porcelain, small fine furniture.* TEL: 33666.

Douglas Barsley Antiques
                                         LAPADA
214-216 Seaside. Est. 1966. Open 9—5, Wed. and Sat. 9—1. *STOCK: General antiques and shipping furniture.* TEL: 26834.

Wm. Bruford and Son Ltd.   **BADA**
11/13 Cornfield Rd. Est. 1883. CL: Wed. p.m. Open 9—1 and 2—5.30. SIZE: Medium. *STOCK: Jewellery, Victorian, late Georgian; some silver, clocks (bracket, carriage), watches, from 1750, £50—£1,000.* **Not stocked: China, glass, brass, pewter, furniture.** TEL: 25452. SER: Valuations; restorations (clocks and silver). VAT: Stan/Spec.

John Cowderoy Antiques **LAPADA**
42 South St. (J.H., R., D.J. and R.A. Cowderoy.) G.M.C. Est. 1972. CL: Wed. p.m. Open 9.30—1 and 2.30—5. SIZE: Large. *STOCK: Clocks, musical boxes, furniture, porcelain, silver and plate, jewellery, copper, brass, paintings.* LOC: 150yds. from Town Hall. PARK: Easy. TEL: 20058. SER: Restorations (clocks, music boxes and furniture). VAT: Stan/Spec.

Eastbourne continued

Michael Day Antiques
46 Ocklynge Rd. Est. 1969. CL: Wed. p.m. and Sat. p.m. Open 10−12.45 and 2.30−5. SIZE: Medium. *STOCK: Victorian furniture, £50−£500; brass and copper, £50−£100; shipping goods, £50−£250.* LOC: In old town, near St. Mary's Church. PARK: Easy. TEL: 638731; home − 26547. VAT: Stan/Spec.

Roderick Dew
29 South St. Est. 1971. CL: Wed. Open 10−5. *STOCK: Antiquarian books, especially on art and antiques.* TEL: 646206.

Eastbourne Antiques Market
80 Seaside. (C. French.) Est. 1969. Open 10−5.30. SIZE: Large. 35 stalls offering *a selection of general antiques.* PARK: Easy. TEL: 20128. FAIRS: Eastbourne and others. VAT: Stan.

Eastbourne Fine Art
9 Meads St. (R.J. Day.) Est. 1964. CL: Wed. and Sat. p.m. Open 9.30−1 and 2−5. SIZE: Medium. *STOCK: East Anglian paintings, watercolours, English and continental paintings, all 19th C.* LOC: Meads village, west end of Eastbourne. PARK: Easy. TEL: 25634. SER: Restorations; framing (oils and watercolours); gilding.

Elliott and Scholz Antiques
12 Willingdon Rd. (C.R. Elliott and K.V. Scholz.) Est. 1981. Open 9.30−5, Wed. and Sat. 9.30−2. SIZE: Small. *STOCK: Small furniture, £500−£1,000; clocks, £100−£300; bric-a-brac, £50−£100, all 19th−20th C.* LOC: A22. PARK: Easy. TEL: 32200; home − 639063. SER: Valuations.

London and Sussex Antiquarian Book and Print Services
112 South St. (L. Lawrence.) Open 9.30−5, Sun. by appointment. *STOCK: Books, including colour plate, prints and literature, 19th−20th C.* TEL: 30857.

James Ludby Antiques
25 Ocklynge Rd. (G. Ludby.) Est. 1967. Open daily, Wed. p.m., Sat. p.m., lunchtimes and Sun. by appointment. SIZE: Small. *STOCK: Furniture, small items, china, glass and brass, unusual interesting items, 18th C to 1930, £5−£500.* LOC: In 'Old Town'. PARK: Easy. TEL: 32073. SER: Valuations. FAIRS: Brighton.

Ernest Pickering
44 South St. Est. 1946. CL: Wed. p.m. and Sat. p.m. Open 9−5. *STOCK: Furniture, porcelain, grandfather clocks.* TEL: 30483. VAT: Stan/Spec.

Eastbourne continued

Raymond Smith
30 South St. (J.R. and T. Smith). Resident. Est. 1963. CL: Wed. Open 9−5.30. SIZE: Large. *STOCK: Second-hand and antiquarian books, 16th−20th C, to £500; publishers' remainders, 50p−£25; maps and prints, 17th−20th C, 50p−£350.* LOC: 200 yds east of Town Hall. PARK: Easy. TEL: 34128. SER: Valuations. VAT: Stan.

E. Stacy-Marks Ltd. BADA
24 Cornfield Rd. Est. 1889. SIZE: Large. *STOCK: Paintings, English and Dutch schools, 18th−19th C.* **TEL: 20429. VAT: Stan.**

Stewart Gallery
25 Grove Rd. (Gallery Laraine Ltd.) Est. 1970. Open 9−5.30, Sun. 11−5. SIZE: Large. *STOCK: Paintings and ceramics, 19th−20th C, £5−£25,000; onyx and glassware.* LOC: Next to library, 150yds. from station. PARK: Easy. TEL: 29588; home − same. SER: Valuations; restorations (paintings and frames); buys at auction (paintings). VAT: Stan/Spec.

W.H. Weller and Son
12 North St. (D.G. Ricketts.) Est. 1892. CL: Sat. Open 10−12.30 and 2−4. *STOCK: Metalware, brass, silver, bronzes and oil lamps.* TEL: 23592. SER: Restorations (metalware).

FLIMWELL (058 087)

Graham Lower
Stonecrouch Farmhouse. Open 9−6 or by appointment. *STOCK: English and Continental 17th−18th C oak furniture.* LOC: A21. TEL: 535. SER: Valuations. VAT: Spec.

FOREST ROW (034 282)

Crosby Books *Postal Only*
Orlingbury House, Lewes Rd. Est. 1971. Open by appointment only. *STOCK: Books on Oriental rugs and glass collecting.* TEL: 4545.

Forest Row Antiques
The Square. (P. Hall, A. Hardman, R. Monje.) Est. 1971. Open 10−6, Sun. by appointment. SIZE: Large. *STOCK: General antiques especially furniture, from £5.* LOC: A22. PARK: Easy. TEL: 3091. SER: Valuations. VAT: Stan.

HASTINGS (0424)

Abbey Antiques
364-366 Old London Rd. (A.T., Y.M. and S.T. Dennis.) Est. 1960. CL: Sat. Open 10.30−4.30. *STOCK: Period, Georgian, Victorian, Edwardian and shipping furniture, porcelain, brass and copper, glass, linen, lace, curios, clocks, barometers, pictures.* LOC: A21 from Dover. 1 mile before Hastings. PARK: Easy. TEL: 429178. VAT: Stan/Spec.

Hastings continued

Coach House Antiques
44 George St. (L.J. Holden.) Open 9—5.30 every day. *STOCK: General antiques.* PARK: Easy. TEL: 431748.

Galleon Antiques
42 Westfield Lane, Baldslow. *STOCK: Early Chinese and Japanese furniture, carvings, silks, bronzes.* LOC: On A28. TEL: 751686.

Howes Bookshop
Trinity Hall, Braybrooke Terrace. ABA. Est. 1920. CL: Sat. p.m. Open 9.30—1 and 2.15—5. *STOCK: Antiquarian and academic books in literature, history, theology, bibliography.* TEL: 423437. FAIRS: ABA.

Nakota Curios
12 Courthouse St. (D.E. Taylor.) Est. 1964. CL: Wed. and Fri. Open 10.30—1 and 2.30—5. SIZE: Medium. *STOCK: General trade items, decorative china, furniture, Victoriana.* Not stocked: Coins, medals. PARK: Easy. TEL: 438900.

J. Radcliffe
40 Cambridge Rd. CL: Wed. p.m. Open 10—1 and 2—5. *STOCK: General antiques, trade goods.* TEL: 426361.

HEATHFIELD　　　　　　(043 52)

Heathfield Antiques Centre
Heathfield Market. (M.F. Hale.) Open Tues., Wed. and Sat. 10—4 or by appointment. SIZE: Large. *STOCK: Furniture, porcelain, dolls, silver, pictures, miniature items, jewellery.* LOC: Adjoining Heathfield Market, 1 mile east of town centre, near Crown Hotel on A265. PARK: Easy. TEL: Home — (042 482) 387.

Heathfield continued

Heffle Corner Antiques
Station Rd. (Mr. and Mrs. R.F. Willatt.) Est. 1980. CL: Wed. p.m. Open 9.30—1 and 2—5. SIZE: Small. *STOCK: Militaria, arms and armour, medals, documents, uniforms and maps, 1600—1914, £5—£1,000; china, pottery and ceramics, 1800—1930, £2—£100; small furniture, 19th C, £20—£200; coins, ancient to date.* Not stocked: Silver and carpets. LOC: Just off High St. PARK: At rear. TEL: 3381; home — same. SER: Valuations; restorations (arms and armour); buys at auction (militaria).

D.J. Wright Antiques
Burnetts Farm, Cross in Hand. Est. 1973. Resident, always available. *STOCK: Furniture, paintings.* TEL: 4081. SER: Valuations; buys at auction.

HERSTMONCEUX　　　　　(0323)

The New Malthouse
Hailsham Rd. (J. Hunwick.) Est. 1962. Open 10—5. *STOCK: Furniture, 18th C, £50—£5,000; English porcelain, glass, clocks, barometers.* Not stocked: Orientalia. LOC: A271 next to school. PARK: Easy. TEL: 833542. SER: Valuations; buys at auction. VAT: Spec.

HORSEBRIDGE, Nr. Hailsham

Horsebridge Antiques Centre
1 North St. (R. Lane.) Resident. Est. 1978. Open 10—1 and 1.30—5. SIZE: Large. *STOCK: General antiques including furniture, silver, glass, pottery, brass and copper.* LOC: A271. PARK: Easy. TEL: (0323) 844414. SER: Valuations.

A pheasant by Moigniez of the 1860s, and an ideal dining room bronze. The detail in the feathers is a little worn and is typical of casts readily available today. From *Animals in Bronze* by Christopher Payne, published by the **Anique Collectors' Club,** 1986.

Pigeon House
Antiques

52 London Road
Hurst Green, East Sussex

*18th and 19th century furniture
and furnishing pieces.*

HOVE see Brighton

HURST GREEN (058 086)

Delmas
Little Bernhurst. (P.D. Stimpson.) Est. 1973. CL: Wed. Open 10—6.30. *STOCK: English and Continental furniture and paintings.* TEL: 345. VAT: Stan/Spec.

Pigeon House Antiques LAPADA
52 London Rd. (D.K. and R.M. Wiltshire.) Resident. Est. 1974. *STOCK: English and Continental furniture, rosewood, satinwood, maple, mahogany 18th—19th C; decorative items.* LOC: On A21, next to the Royal George. PARK: Easy. TEL: 474. VAT: Stan/Spec.

LEWES (0273)

Bow Windows Book Shop
128 High St. (A. and J. Shelley.) Open 9—5.30. SIZE: Large. *STOCK: Books, natural history, English literature, travel, topography.* LOC: Off A27. TEL: 472839. FAIRS: Antiquarian Book.

Celia Charlottes
7 Malling St. (C.C. Russell.) Est. 1976. Open Thurs., Fri. and Sat. SIZE: Medium. *STOCK: Antique lace, needlework, embroideries, textiles, wall hangings, christening gowns, lace veils, fine bedspreads, lace tablecloths, Victorian nighties, shawls, small miscellaneous items.* LOC: A27, bottom of Cliffe High St. PARK: Easy. TEL: 473303.

Cliffe Antiques Centre
47 Cliffe High St. (Miss P. Harrison.) Est. 1984. Open 9.30—5. SIZE: Medium. There are 16 dealers at this centre selling a wide range of general antiques, £5—£1,000. LOC: Follow town centre signs, turning left at traffic lights. PARK: Easy. TEL: 473266.

Lewes continued

Coombe House Antiques (Georgian Town House)
Malling St. (Mrs. M. Grinling.) Open 10—5 every day. SIZE: Large. *STOCK: Continental and English furniture, 18th—19th C; pictures, small items, papier mâché, garden furniture and ornaments.* PARK: Easy. TEL: 473862.

A.J. Cumming
159 High St. Est. 1976. Open 10—1 and 2—5. *STOCK: Antiquarian and out of print books.* TEL: 472319. SER: Buys at auction.

H.P. Dennison and Son
22 High St. (D.H. Dennison.) Est. 1933. CL: Wed. p.m. Open 8.30—5. SIZE: Medium. *STOCK: Mahogany furniture, early 19th C.* PARK: Easy. TEL: 473665. SER: Valuations; restorations (furniture). VAT: Stan/Spec.

The Drawing Room
53 High St. Open 9.30—5.30. SIZE: Large. *STOCK: Furniture, pictures, objets d'art.* TEL: 478560.

Felix Gallery
Corner of Sun St., and Lancaster St. (W.S.H. and Mrs M.M. Whitehead.) Est. 1981. Open 10—6, Sun 12—6. SIZE: Small. *STOCK: Cats only — pottery, porcelain, enamel, woodcarvings, bronze, jewellery, pictures, English, Continental and Oriental.* LOC: 2 minutes from town centre. PARK: Easy. TEL: 472668; home — same.

Fifteenth Century Bookshop
99 High St. (E. Blundell.) Est. 1938. *STOCK: Antiquarian books.* TEL: 474160.

Friars Walk Antiques
21 Friars Walk. (Mrs. R. Duke.) Est. 1963. Open 9.30—5.30. SIZE: Medium. *STOCK: Furniture, from early 19th C; copper, brass and fenders.* PARK: Easy. TEL: 472549. SER: Valuations; restorations; buys at auction.

Lewes continued

Gimbles
5 Mount Pleasant. Est. 1965. SIZE: Medium. *STOCK: Dining room furniture and ornaments, pre-1900; porcelain.* PARK: Easy. TEL: 473522. SER: Restorations (porcelain).

Renée and Roy Green   BADA
Trade Only
Ashcombe House, Lewes Rd. CL: Wed. *STOCK: Furniture and objects, 17th to early 19th C.* **LOC: From Brighton A27, entrance on left-hand side 500yds. from Lewes (A275) turn-off. TEL: 474794.**

Lewes Antiques Centre
20 Cliffe High St. (R. Brown.) Est. 1968. Open 10—5. SIZE: Large. There are 62 stallholders selling *furniture, china, copper and metalware, glass, clocks.* LOC: A27, from London to Brighton, follow one-way system in town to end of Little East St., continue over Phoenix Causeway, turn right at roundabout, first right to rear entrance. PARK: Own. TEL: 476148. SER: Shipping facilities.

Stephen Moore Ltd.   BADA
103 High St. Est. 1946. CL: Wed. Open 9.30—5, appointment advisable. *STOCK: Furniture, 18th C; pictures, jewellery.* **TEL: 474158. VAT: Spec.**

Southdown Antiques
48 Cliffe High St. (Miss P.I. and K.A. Foster.) Est. 1969. Open Mon., Tues., and Thurs. mornings or by appointment. SIZE: Medium. *STOCK: Small antiques, especially 18th—19th C English, Continental and Oriental porcelain, objets d'art, works of art, glass, papier mâché trays, silver plate, £20—£2,000.* LOC: A27. One-way street north. PARK: Easy. TEL: 472439. VAT: Stan/Spec.

Trevor   BADA
Trevor House, 110 High St. Est. 1946. *STOCK: Furniture, 17th to early 19th C; works of art.* **VAT: Spec.**

Lionel Young Antiques
1 South St., Cliffe Corner. Est. 1920. CL: Wed. *STOCK: General antiques, furniture, china, glass, pictures, prints and plate.* TEL: 472455.

MAYFIELD   (0435)

Croust House
Five Ashes. (D. and D. Onions). Est. 1955. SIZE: Medium. *STOCK: Furniture, 18th—19th C; china, dolls.* PARK: Easy. TEL: Hadlow Down (082 585) 235; home — same. SER: Valuations.

Mayfield continued

Wm. J. Gravener Antiques
High St. (Mr. and Mrs. Gravener.) Resident. Est. 1965. *STOCK: Furniture, longcase clocks.* TEL: 873389. VAT: Spec.

Tandridge Antiques
High St. (Mrs. A.F. Brown.) Est. 1966. CL: Wed., except by appointment. Open 9—6. SIZE: Medium. *STOCK: Furniture, porcelain, pottery, glass, pictures, 1700—1920.* Not stocked: Weapons, firearms. LOC: A267. Between Royal Oak and National Westminster Bank. PARK: 1 car, otherwise in or off High St. TEL: 873275. SER: Restorations (furniture and pictures).

NEWHAVEN   (0273)

Newhaven Antique Market
28 South Way. (R. Mayne, A. Wilkinson.) Est. 1971. Open every day 9.30—5. *STOCK: Victoriana, Edwardian, bric-a-brac.* TEL: 517207.

Newhaven continued

Leonard Russell LAPADA
21 Kings Ave., Mount Pleasant. Resident. Est. 1981. Open by appointment. SIZE: Small. *STOCK: English pottery figures, groups, animals, busts, lustre, 1750—1850, £45—£1,000; English Toby jugs, 1765—1840, £85—£1,250; Prattware including plaques, Toby and serving jugs, money boxes, animals, cow creamers, £200—£800; English silk pictures, 18th and 19th C, £100—£500.* LOC: 500 yards from A259 South Coast Rd., ¾ mile from town centre. PARK: Easy. TEL: 515153. SER: Valuations; restorations (pottery); buys at auction (pottery). FAIRS: Olympia, Kensington; British International, Birmingham; Brighton Petersfield, Bath, Wilton House, Greenway (Kent).

NINFIELD, Nr. Battle (0424)
Martin Hutton BADA
Luxford House, Standard Hill. Est. 1957. Open by appointment. *STOCK: English furniture and porcelain, 18th—19th C.* **PARK: Easy. TEL: 892088. VAT: Spec.**

NORTHIAM (079 74)
Northiam Antiques
Main St. Est. 1973. *STOCK: Country furniture, walnut, mahogany and oak.* TEL: 2182. SER: Restorations.

NUTLEY (082 571)
Three Gables Antiques
High St. Open 9.30—6, Sun. 11—6. *STOCK: Furniture, pine, linen, collectors' items, bric-a-brac.* TEL: 2343.

PEVENSEY
The Old Mint House LAPADA
(J.C. Nicholson.) Est. 1901. Open 9—5, Sun. by appointment. SIZE: Large and warehouse. *STOCK: Furniture, porcelain, clocks, 18th—19th C, £20—£5,000.* LOC: A259 coast road. PARK: Own. TEL: Eastbourne (0323) 762337. SER: Buys at auction. VAT: Stan/Spec.

PEVENSEY BAY
Michael Harmer
21 Richmond Rd. *STOCK: General antiques, especially firearms, works of art.* TEL: Cooden (042 43) 2831.

PLAYDEN, Nr. Rye
Old Post House Antiques
Old Post House. (D. Cooke.) Est. 1957. Open any time by appointment. SIZE: Medium. *STOCK: Oil paintings.* LOC: A268, opp. Peace and Plenty public house. PARK: Easy. TEL: Iden (079 78) 303. SER: Valuations; restorations; packing and shipping. VAT: Spec.

POLEGATE (03212)
John Botting Antiques LAPADA
A27 Antiques Warehouse, Unit 2 Chaucer Industrial Estate, Dittons Rd. SIZE: Large. *STOCK: Furniture, shipping goods and bric-a-brac, antique, Victorian and Continental.* TEL: 5301.

Graham Price Antiques
A27 Antiques Warehouse, Unit 4 Chaucer Industrial Estate, Dittons Rd. Open 9—6. SIZE: Large. *STOCK: Victorian and pine furniture, shipping goods and accessories.* LOC: Between Hastings and Brighton on A27. TEL: 7167; home — Burwash (0435) 882553. SER: Packing, shipping and courier.

ROBERTSBRIDGE (0580)
De Montfort
49 High St. (E.D.and A.A. Sloane.) Est. 1961. Open 10.30—5.30 SIZE: Large. *STOCK: English and Continental furniture, 1500—1800; Islamic and ancient art; Oriental carpets, kelims, and textiles. Not stocked: Any items not included above.* LOC: A21. PARK: Easy. TEL: 880698. VAT: Spec.

ROTTINGDEAN
Trade Wind
Little Crescent. (R. Morley Smith.) Est. 1974. Open by appointment only. *STOCK: Small furniture and English porcelain, prints, watercolours.* TEL: Brighton (0273) 31177.

RYE   (0797)
Bragge and Sons
Landgate House. (N.H. and J.R. Bragge.) Est. 1840. CL: Tues. p.m. Open 9—5. *STOCK: 18th C furniture and works of art.* LOC: Entrance to town — Landgate. TEL: 223358. SER: Valuations; restorations. VAT: Spec.

R. Dellar
Western House, Winchelsea Rd. Resident. Est. 1969. Open by appointment only. *STOCK: Paintings, prints, some decorative items.* TEL: 223419. VAT: Stan/Spec.

Herbert Gordon Gasson
The Lion Galleries, Lion St. (T.J. Booth.) Est. 1909. CL: Tues. p.m. Open 9—1 and 2—5.30. SIZE: Large. *STOCK: 17th—18th C oak and walnut; Staffordshire and Chinese porcelain.* Not stocked: Silver and glass. PARK: Easy. TEL: 222208. SER: Restorations. VAT: Stan/Spec.

Ann Lingard   LAPADA
Rope Walk Antiques. Est. 1972. CL: Sun. except by appointment. Open 9—5.30. SIZE: Large. *STOCK: Pine furniture, kitchenalia.* Not stocked: Jewellery, silver and plate. LOC: Cinque Port St., opp. Conduit Hill. PARK: Own, and public next door. TEL: 223486.

Mint Dolls and Toys
71 The Mint. Est. 1970. Open 10—5 every day. *STOCK: Dolls, toys, Steiff, miniatures.* TEL: 222237 or 225952.

Rye continued
Rye Antiques
93 High St. and Holloway House, 24 High St. (Mrs. D. Turner.) Est. 1966. CL: Sun., except by appointment. Open 9—6. SIZE: Large. *STOCK: Oak, walnut and mahogany furniture, 17th—19th C, £50—£3,000; clocks, longcase, bracket, wall, French, 18th—19th C, £30—£1,500; metalware, jewellery, silver and plate, 17th—19th C, £5—£500.* Not stocked: Glass, coins, bric-a-brac. PARK: Easy. TEL: 222259. SER: Valuations. VAT: Stan/Spec.

Strand Antiques
Strand House. Est. 1975. CL: Fri. Several dealers selling a wide variety of *antiques, from furniture to small collectors' items, especially jewellery.* Below are listed the dealers at this market.
> **Doreen Hughes**
> **Jessica Kay**
> **Frances Reese**
> **Brenda Rodd**
> **Jean Tucker**
> **Kim Tucker**

ST. LEONARDS-ON-SEA,
Nr. Hastings
Aarquebus Antiques
46 Norman Rd. (Mr. and Mrs. G. Jukes.) Resident. Est. 1957. Open 9—6 every day. SIZE: Medium. *STOCK: Furniture, 18th C, £500—£1,000; shipping goods, Victorian to 1930, £5—£500; glass, gold and silver, 18th—19th C, £5—£1,000.* LOC: From London, turn right after main post office on A2100. PARK: Easy. TEL: Hastings (0424) 433267. SER: Valuations; restorations (furniture); pine stripping; buys at auction.

St. Leonards-on-Sea continued

Banner Antiques
56 Norman Rd. (G.M. Schofield.) Est. 1972.
CL: Wed. Open 10—1 and 2.15—5.30. SIZE:
Large. *STOCK: Furniture, porcelain, pottery,
copper, brass, watercolours.* Not stocked:
Jewellery, silver, weapons. PARK: Easy. TEL:
Hastings (0424) 420050.

Barry Dunlinson
38 Coach House Mews, Western Rd. Open by
appointment. *STOCK: Interesting decorative
items.* LOC: Next to Warrior Sq. PARK: Easy.
TEL: Hastings (0424) 426569. SER: Valuations;
buys at auction.

Raymond and Betty Fieldhouse
70 Norman Rd. Est. 1968. CL: Wed. and Fri.
Open 10—1 and 2.15—5. SIZE: Medium.
*STOCK: Victoriana, £20—£100; pot-lids,
1845, £25—£100; Regency items, oak items,
1700, £80—£200.* LOC: Off sea front. PARK:
Easy. TEL: Home — Hastings (0424) 421456.
SER: Valuations. VAT: Stan/Spec.

Galleon Antiques
19 Marina. *STOCK: Furniture, some Chinese.*
LOC: A259 — seafront. TEL: Hastings (0424)
440974. SER: Restorations.

Galleon Antiques
18 Gensing Rd. *STOCK: Furniture.* LOC: Off
Norman Rd. TEL: Hastings (0424) 424145.
SER: Restorations.

St. Leonards-on-Sea continued

K. Nunn
106 Bohemia Rd. Open Mon., Tues. and
Thurs. 9—5. *STOCK: General antiques,
weapons and unusual items.* TEL: Hastings
(0424) 431093. SER: Buys at auction. VAT:
Stan/Spec.

Oracle Antiques
40 Norman Rd. (C. and C.J. Georgiou.) Open
9—5.30, Sat. 9—1, otherwise by appointment. *STOCK: Pine, mahogany and oak furniture.* TEL: Hastings (0424) 422603.

René Antiques and Art
Derek Ashby Antiques
17A Kings Rd. Est. 1975. *STOCK: Furniture,
period and shipping, copper, china and pine.*
LOC: Just off seafront. TEL: Hastings (0424)
715867 or 432610. SER: Export.

St. Leonards Clocks
22 Grand Parade. (P. Abery.) Est. 1968. Open
9—6. *STOCK: Clocks.* TEL: Hastings (0424)
444550. SER: Repairs.

Trade Antiques and
Hastings Antiques   *Trade Only*
59/61 Norman Rd. (P.E. Poole.) Est. 1961.
CL: Sat. SIZE: Medium. *STOCK: General
shipping goods.* LOC: Off London Rd. PARK:
Easy. TEL: Hastings (0424) 428561. VAT:
Stan.

The Porch and Terrace at St. Catherine Court, Bath. From *Gardens in Edwardian England*
published by the **Antique Collectors' Club,** 1985.

SEAFORD (0323)

Molly Alexander
Crouch House, Crouch Lane. Est. 1967. *STOCK: Paintings, watercolours and antiquities.* LOC: Opposite new Constitutional Club. PARK: Opposite. TEL: 896577.

Richard Alexander
Crouch House, Crouch Lane. Est. 1948. Open by appointment. *STOCK: Oriental items, Greek, Roman and Egyptian antiquities, coins, oils and watercolours, £10—£500.* PARK: Easy. TEL: 896577.

The Old House
13, 15, 17 High St. (P.R. and S.M. Barrett.) Est. 1928. Open 8.30—1 and 2—5. SIZE: Large. *STOCK: 18th—19th C furniture, china and glass, £5—£5,000.* LOC: Near Railway Station. PARK: In own yard in South St. TEL: 892091; home — 898364. SER: Valuations; restorations (furniture); shippers. VAT: Stan.

Pepper's Antique Pine
Crouch Lane. (R. Newton and J. Marvin.) Est. 1982. Open 9—12.30 and 2—6, Wed. p.m. and Sun. by appointment. SIZE: Medium. *STOCK: General antiques.* LOC: A259 into Broad St. leading to High St. PARK: Easy and nearby. TEL: 891400; home — same. SER: Restorations; stripping.

Seaford's "Barn Collectors' Market" and Studio Book Shop
The Barn, Church Lane. Est. 1967. Open Tues., Thurs., and Sat., 10—4.30. There are several dealers selling *a wide range of antiques, ephemera, books and collectors' items.* LOC: Off High St. TEL: 890010.

Steyne House Antiques
35 Steyne Rd. (J.R. Deakin.) Est. 1969. Open 10.30—5.30, Sat. 10.30—4, Sun. by appointment. SIZE: Small. *STOCK: Staffordshire figures, pottery and porcelain, copper and brass, 19th C, £25—£100+; furniture, mainly country oak and elm, 18th C, £100—£500; decorative agricultural items, 19th C., £20—£70.* LOC: Off A259 into Broad St., take 2nd right into High St., then 3rd left. PARK: Easy and opposite. TEL: 895088; home — same.

SEDLESCOMBE (042 487)

Holmes House Antiques
The Green (F.J. Fleischer.) Est. 1973. CL: Mon. Open 10—12 and 3—6 including Sun. SIZE: Small. *STOCK: Watercolours and oil paintings, £100—£1,000; small silver, £10—£100; both 19th C; furniture, 19th—20th C, £300—£500.* PARK: Easy. TEL: 450; home — same.

UCKFIELD (0825)

Nicholas Bowlby
Owl House, Poundgate. Est. 1981. Open every day by appointment. SIZE: Medium. *STOCK: English watercolours and drawings, 18th—20th C, £20—£1,000.* LOC: Just off A26, 1½ miles south of Crowborough. PARK: Easy. TEL: Crowborough (089 26) 3722; home — same. SER: Valuations; restorations; buys at auction (watercolours and drawings). VAT: Spec.

Ivan R. Deverall
Duval House, The Glen, Cambridge Way. *STOCK: Maps.* TEL: 2474. SER: Catalogue available; colouring. VAT: Stan.

Georgian House Antiques
222 High St. (Mrs. I. Crouch and P. Hale.) Resident. Est. 1976. CL: Some Weds. Open 10—6, Sun. and evenings by appointment. SIZE: Large. *STOCK: English domestic oak and country furniture and related decorative items, 1600—1860.* Not stocked: Bric-a-brac. LOC: A22. PARK: Nearby. TEL: 5074. VAT: Spec.

Ringles Cross Antiques
Ringles Cross. (C. and J. Dunford.) Est. 1965. Open 7 days a week 9.30—6. *STOCK: Oriental and English country furniture, works of art.* PARK: Easy. LOC: Between junction of A22 and A26 1 mile north of Uckfield. TEL: 2909. VAT: Spec.

W.F. Wilson
244 High St. Est. 1961. CL: Mon. and Wed. except by appointment. *STOCK: Pictures, works of art.* TEL: 3125. VAT: Spec.

WADHURST (089 288)

Art and Antiques (Wadhurst)
High St. (D. Maskell.) Open 10—5 Thurs., Fri., and Sat. *STOCK: Lace, period clothes, brass, pewter, copper, porcelain, old English pottery, dolls.* TEL: 2091.

Aldo Broccardi-Schelmi (Fine Arts) (Belmont Galleries Ltd.)   LAPADA
Dewhurst Lodge. Est. 1976. Open by appointment only. *STOCK: English period furniture; works of art, 1690—1830.* LOC: On Frant to Wadhurst Rd., ¼ mile from Wadhurst Station. TEL: 3519. VAT: Spec.

P.B. Pollington
4 Central Parade, High St. Est. 1949. Open 9—1 and 2—5.30, or by appointment. *STOCK: General antiques.* TEL: 2866.

WINCHELSEA

Thomas Crispin   BADA
The Little Manor. Open by appointment only. *STOCK: English oak.* **PARK: Easy. TEL: Rye (0797) 226699. VAT: Spec.**

Sussex West

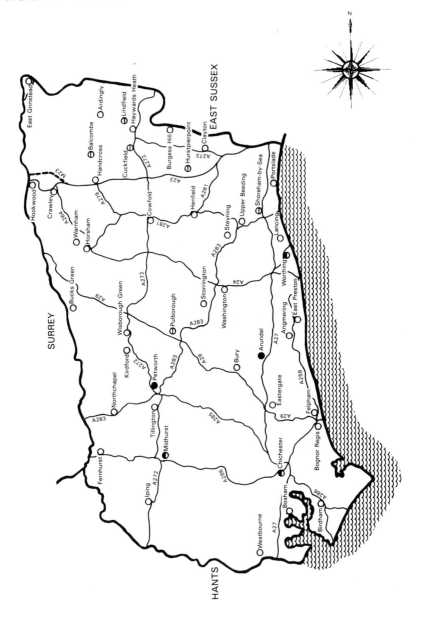

Key to number of shops in this area.

○ 1–2
θ 3–5
◓ 6–12
● 13+

Please note this is only a rough map designed to show dealers the number of shops in the various towns, and is not necessarily totally accurate.

ANGMERING

Bygones
The Square. (R.A. and Mrs. L.R. Whittaker.) Est. 1965. CL: Wed. Open 10—1 and 2.15—5.30, Sat. 10—1. SIZE: Medium. *STOCK: Furniture, £50—£1,000; china, £5—£150; silver, £10—£250; linen, £5—£75; all 1800—1920.* LOC: A280. PARK: Easy. TEL: Rustington (0903) 786152; home — same. SER: Valuations; buys at auction (furniture).

ARDINGLY   (0444)
Nr. Haywards Heath

Ardingly Antiques
64 High St. (Mrs. P. Gordon.) Est. 1972. CL: Mon. and Wed. Open 10.30—1 and 2.30—5.30, Sun. 2.30—5.30 or by appointment. SIZE: Medium. *STOCK: Georgian, Victorian and Edwardian furniture; button back chairs, porcelain, silver and glass, clocks.* LOC: On B2028. PARK: Easy. TEL: 892680.

ARUNDEL   (0903)

Armstrong-Davis Gallery
The Square. *STOCK: Fine sculptures of all periods; original bronze sculptures by 19th—20th C masters.* TEL: 882752. SER: Commissions accepted for sculpture in relation to architectural, industrial and private projects. Represented in Italy and Switzerland.

Arundel Antiques and Collectors' Market
51 High St. (Mrs. A.C. Chadwick.) Est. 1935. Open 10.30—5, Sat. 9.30—5. SIZE: Medium. *STOCK: General antiques, Doulton artists' stoneware and figures; porcelain, glass, silver, dolls, teddy bears, lace, linen, jewellery, thimbles, Goss, postcards, books, coins, brass, copper, militaria, small furniture, collectors' items, £5—£500.* LOC: A27. PARK: Easy.

Arundel Antiques Market
5 River Rd. (T. Miller.) Est. 1963. 30 stalls. Open Sat. 9—5. *STOCK: Silver, jewellery, glass, china, general antiques.* LOC: On River Arun, adjacent to bridge. PARK: Adjacent. TEL: 882012.

Baynton-Williams   BADA
Maltravers House, 49 Maltravers St. (R.H. and S.C. Baynton-Williams.) ABA. Open 9.30—6. SIZE: Large. *STOCK: Maps, views, sporting, marine and decorative prints; atlases, illustrated books.* **LOC: 200yds. from Castle. PARK: Easy. TEL: 882898. VAT: Stan/Spec.**

Arundel continued

Country Life by Bursig
1 Tarrant Sq., Tarrant St. (R.H. Bursig.) Est. 1978. Open 9.30—5, Sun 2—5. SIZE: Large. *STOCK: Furniture, oak, mahogany and walnut, 17th—19th C, £50—£2,000; oil paintings and watercolours, £50—£500; porcelain, pewter and brass, £5—£200, all 19th C.* PARK: Easy. TEL: 883456; home — Bognor Regis (0243) 822045. VAT: Spec.

Pat Golding
6 Castle Mews, Tarrant St. Open 10—4. *STOCK: Ceramics and glass, 18th—20th C.*

Lasseters
8a High St. Est. 1780. *STOCK: Jewellery, silver.* TEL: 882651. VAT: Stan/Spec.

The Old Coach House
Tarrant Sq. (Mrs. B. Driver.) *STOCK: Paintings, prints, unusual furniture for interior decorators, lamps, mirrors.* TEL: 882921.

Serendipity Antiques
5 Tarrant St. (A.G. Brown.) Est. 1972. CL: Sun. a.m. Open 9.30—1 and 2—6. SIZE: Medium. *STOCK: Victorian prints, watercolours, oils and especially maps.* Not stocked: China, glass, brass. LOC: Opposite Norfolk Hotel, turn left for Chichester, first shop on left. PARK: Further up Tarrant St. TEL: 882047. SER: Restorations (oil paintings); colouring (maps and prints). VAT: Stan/Spec.

Spencer Swaffer   LAPADA
30 High St. Est. 1974. Open 9—6. SIZE: Large. *STOCK: Unusual decorative items, traditional items, brass, blue and white, Staffordshire, dinner services, pine, oak dressers, marble tables, bamboo, shop fittings, candlesticks, majolica, French, painted and garden furniture.* PARK: Easy. TEL: 882132. VAT: Stan/Spec.

Taylor Gallery
55 Tarrant St. (H.C.H. Merewether.) Resident. Est. 1972. Usually open every day, prior telephone call advisable. SIZE: Medium. *STOCK: Decorative paintings, 1880—1940, mainly £50—£500.* LOC: Near town centre. PARK: Easy. TEL: 883985. SER: Valuations; buys at auction (paintings). VAT: Spec.

Treasure House Antiques
31 High St. (Mrs. Henderson.) Est. 1969. CL: Wed. p.m. *STOCK: Commemoration china and general antiques.* PARK: Easy. TEL: 883101/882908.

Treasure House Antiques Market
Rear of High St. near Crown Yard car park. Est. 1972. Open Sat. 9—5. *STOCK: Silver, jewellery, clocks, lace, curios, pictures, gramophones, china, Victoriana, domestic bygones, pocillovy, tools.* PARK: Easy. TEL: 883101/882908.

BALCOMBE (0444)
Balcombe Galleries
(P. Collins.) ARCA. Est. 1961. Open 9—5.30. SIZE: Large. *STOCK: Early oak, garden furniture, country furniture, paintings, £50—£100.* PARK: Easy. TEL: 811439; home — 811415. SER: Valuations; restorations (furniture and paintings); buys at auction. VAT: Stan/Spec.

Pine and Design
Haywards Heath Rd. (J.M. Nelson, G. Lindsay-Stewart.) Est. 1974. CL: Sun. a.m. SIZE: Medium. *STOCK: Stripped pine furniture, mirrors, sofas, pictures, lace, 18th—19th C, £25—£500.* LOC: B2036. PARK: Easy. TEL: 811700; home — Copthorne (0342) 715466. SER: Restorations and interior design, hand-made kitchens and furniture from old pine. VAT: Stan.

Woodall and Emery Ltd.
Haywards Heath Rd. Est. 1884. TEL: 811608. VAT: Stan.

BIRDHAM, Nr. Chichester
Meynell's Books ABA
Broomfield, Lock Lane. Open by appointment only. LOC: Off A286 south of Chichester. TEL: Chichester (0243) 512798.

BOGNOR REGIS (0243)
Peter Martin Antiques *Trade only*
Old Cottage, 70 North Bersted St. (G.P. and E. Platts-Martin.) Resident. Est. 1984. Open by appointment. SIZE: Small. *STOCK: Early oak and country furniture, £150—£1,500; early metalware, £50—£250, both 17th—18th C; treen, 18th—19th C, £25—£150.* Not stocked: Bric-a-brac, Victoriana. LOC: A259. Turn left at Royal Oak, thatched cottage 500yds on right. PARK: Easy. TEL: 823298. SER: Restorations (china, quilts). VAT: Spec.

BOSHAM (0243)
Bosham Antiques
(L.M. and M.D. Lain.) CL: Sun. a.m. Open 8.30—6. *STOCK: General antiques, upholstered and shipping goods.* LOC: A27 at Bosham roundabout. PARK: Own. TEL: 572005. VAT: Stan/Spec.

BUCKS GREEN, Nr. Rudgwick
Kings Antiques
Guildford Rd. (M. and P. Larcombe.) Est. 1974. Open 9—1 and 2—5. SIZE: Large. *STOCK: Furniture, £5—£1,000.* LOC: A281. PARK: Own. TEL: Rudgwick (040 372) 2084. SER: Valuations; restorations (furniture). VAT: Stan/Spec.

BURGESS HILL (044 46)
British Antique LAPADA
Exporters Ltd. *Trade and Export Only*
Queen Elizabeth Ave. Est. 1963. CL: Sat. Open 8—5.30. SIZE: Large. *STOCK: General antiques.* LOC: Off Queen Elizabeth Ave. TEL: 45577. SER: Exporters. VAT: Stan.

Military Antiques
42 Janes Lane. (R.J. Hunt.) Est. 1963. Open by appointment. *STOCK: Helmets, militaria, badges, uniforms, swords, guns, models.* TEL: 3516 and 43088.

BURY, Nr. Arundel (079 881)
David Mattey Antiques
The Old Forge, Bury Gate. CL: Mon. and Fri. Open 10—4.30. SIZE: Medium. *STOCK: Pine cottage furniture, Victorian bygones, oil paintings.* LOC: A29. PARK: Easy. TEL: 487.

CHICHESTER (0243)
Antique Shop
Frensham House, Hunston. (J.M. Riley.) Est. 1956. Open 9—6. *STOCK: English furniture, 1700—1830, £200—£3,000; bureaux, chests of drawers, tables, chairs.* LOC: One mile south of Chichester by-pass on B2145. PARK: Easy. TEL: 782660.

Asser Fine Arts
St. Peter's Market, West St. (R. Asser.) Est. 1983. CL: Mon. Open 10—4.30, Sun. by appointment. SIZE: Small. *STOCK: Watercolours, £100—£250; pastels and pencil drawings, £50—£200; oil paintings, £300—£500; all 18th C to early 20th C.* LOC: A renovated church opposite cathedral. PARK: 100yds. TEL: 775488; home — (07983) 3293. SER: Restorations (watercolours); buys at auction (watercolours and oils).

Chichester Gallery
25 Sadlers Walk, East St. (W. and N. Higbee.) SIZE: Medium. *STOCK: Oriental rugs, £50—£2,000.* LOC: Arcade on the north side of East St. PARK: Nearby. TEL: 780037; home — 528739.

Gems Antiques
39 West St. (M.L. Hancock.) Open 10—1 and 2—5. *STOCK: Period furniture, Staffordshire and porcelain figures, books and pictures.* TEL: 786173.

Peter Hancock Antiques
40—41 West St. Articles on coins. Est. 1950. Open 9.30—6. SIZE: Medium. *STOCK: Silver, jewellery, porcelain, furniture, £20—£2,000; pictures, glass, clocks, books, £5—£500; all 18th—19th C. ethnographica, art nouveau, art deco, 19th—20th C, £5—£500.* LOC: From Chichester Cross, 17 doors past Cathedral. PARK: Easy. TEL: 786173. SER: Valuations. VAT: Stan.

INTRODUCTION TO

BRITISH ANTIQUE EXPORTERS LTD.

MEMBER OF: LAPADA, GUILD OF MASTER CRAFTSMEN

£7,500 TO
£10,000
WILL GIVE YOU
VARIETY
SELECTION
VALUE

WHOLESALE
EXPORTERS
CONTAINERS OF
FINE GEORGIAN,
VICTORIAN AND
EDWARDIAN
ANTIQUE FURNI-
TURE AND
DECORATIVE
ACCESSORIES

IF FOR ANY
REASON OUR
CHOICE DOES NOT
COME UP TO
YOUR EXPECTA-
TIONS WE WILL
*REFUND YOUR
MONEY*

QUEEN ELIZABETH AVENUE, BURGESS HILL, WEST SUSSEX, RH15 9RX, ENGLAND
TEL: BURGESS HILL (04446) 45577. CABLES: BRITISHANTIQUES BURGESS HILL. TELEX: 87688

Chichester continued

M.A. Hill
57 Pound Farm Rd. CL: Thurs. Open 9—5.30. *STOCK: Furniture, china.* TEL: 783470.

The Old Stores Antiques
Halnaker. (Mrs. N.P. Pearse.) Est. 1974. CL: Mon. and Sat. Open 10.30—4.30. SIZE: Small. *STOCK: General antiques, 1800—1930, £5—£550.* Not stocked: Militaria. LOC: 4 miles from Chichester on A285. PARK: Easy and at rear. TEL: Home — Selsey (0243) 602540.

Wendy Rowden Antiques
10 Sadlers Walk, 44 East St. Est. 1975. CL: Mon. Open 10—5.30. SIZE: Small. *STOCK: Jewellery, £20—£500; silver, £15—£150; porcelain and glass, £10—£100; small furniture, £50—£350; all Georgian—Edwardian.* LOC: From the market cross on left off East St. PARK: At rear. TEL: 779754; home — Bosham (0243) 572388. VAT: Stan.

CLAYTON, Nr. Hassocks
Steve Powell Antiques
Millbrook, Underhill Lane. Open by appointment. *STOCK: English and French country furniture, brass, copper and decorative items.* TEL: Hassocks (079 18) 2605.

COWFOLD   (040 386)
Cowfold Clocks
The Olde House, The Street. (F.M. Henderson.) CL: Mon. Open 9.30—5.30. *STOCK: Clocks.* SER: Repairs (clocks). TEL: 505.

CRAWLEY   (0293)
Vintage Antiques
37 High St. (B.F. Roe.) Est. 1968. *STOCK: Victoriana, clocks and watches, glass, china, furniture and unusual items.* LOC: In the centre of Old Crawley. TEL: 23732.

CUCKFIELD
Peter Jeeves Antiques   LAPADA
High St. (P. and T. Jeeves.) Est. 1975. CL: Sun. except by appointment. SIZE: Medium. *STOCK: Furniture, 17th—19th C, £50—£3,000; pine, 18th—19th C, £40—£400; objets d'art, treen, china, glass, £5—£300; hand painted furniture and items for interior design.* LOC: 10 minutes from A23, turn off towards Haywards Heath. PARK: Easy. TEL: Haywards Heath (0444) 454420; home — Newick (082 572) 2687. SER: Valuations; restorations (French polishing, inlay, carving); finder; buys at auction. FAIRS: Brighton. VAT: Stan/Spec.

Cuckfield continued

B. and C. Seago
The Shop next to the Ship Inn, Whitemans Green. Est. 1964. Open 10—5.30. *STOCK: Antiquarian and secondhand books.* TEL: Haywards Heath (0444) 456111. SER: Valuations. VAT: Stan.

Richard Usher Antiques
23 South St. Est. 1978. CL: Wed p.m. and Sat. p.m. Open 10—5. SIZE: Medium. *STOCK: Furniture, 17th—19th C, £50—£1,000; porcelain, glass and decorative items.* LOC: A272. PARK: Easy. SER: Valuations; restorations.

EAST GRINSTEAD   (0342)
W.J. Faupel   *Mail order*
3 Halsford Lane. ABA. *STOCK: Maps.* TEL: 27043.

Now and Then
4 High St. (B.R.C. Harrison.) Est. 1975. CL: Wed. p.m. Open 9.30—5.30. *STOCK: Silver, china and objets d'art.* TEL: 21659. VAT: Stan/Spec.

EAST PRESTON
Nr. Littlehampton
Bay Trees Antiques
The Street. (Mrs. M. Endersby.) Est. 1973. Open every day. SIZE: Medium. *STOCK: Furniture, 17th—18th C, £300—£3,000.* Not stocked: Bric-a-brac. LOC: Near Angmering station. PARK: Easy. TEL. Rustington (0526) 771109; home — same.

EASTERGATE,   (024 368)
Nr. Chichester
Granville Antiques   LAPADA
Mount Pleasant Farm, Level Mare Lane. Est. 1979. Open by appointment. SIZE: Small. *STOCK: English furniture, pre-1840, £750—£1,250; glass, silver, porcelain, paintings.* LOC: Off A27. PARK: Easy. TEL: 2293; home — same. SER: Valuations; restorations (cabinet work); buys at auction (period furniture). FAIRS: Olympia; British International, Birmingham; Cafe Royal; Surrey; Kensington. VAT: Spec.

FELPHAM
Antiquarius
45 Felpham Rd. *STOCK: China, porcelain, copper, brass, clocks, silver, small furniture.* TEL: Bognor Regis (0243) 821056.

FERNHURST,
Nr. Haslemere
The Pine Shop
9b Midhurst Rd. (S. Hamilton.) CL: Wed. Open 10—3. *STOCK: Pine.* TEL: Haslemere (0428) 53253.

HANDCROSS   (0444)
Handcross Antiques
High St. Est. 1978. CL: Mon. Open 9.30–3.30; Wed. and Sat. 9.30–1. *STOCK: General antiques.* TEL: 400784.

HAYWARDS HEATH   (0444)
Ramm Antiques
43 Sussex Rd. (R.E. Ramm.) *STOCK: Pine and general antiques.* TEL: 451393.

HENFIELD   (0273)
Alexander Antiques
Post House, Small Dole. (Mrs. J.A. Goodinge.) Est. 1971. CL: Sun. except by appointment. SIZE: Medium. *STOCK: Country furniture, brass, copper, pewter, samplers, small collectors' and decorative items.* LOC: A2037. PARK: Easy. TEL: 493121; home — same. VAT: Stan/Spec.

Norton House Antiques
High St. (J.S. Young.) Est. 1959. CL: Tues. Open (including Sun.) 9.30–6. SIZE: Small. *STOCK: Oak and Victorian furniture, English, 17th–19th C, copper, brass, general collectors' items, £10–£500.* LOC: Centre of High St. opp. public car park. TEL: 492064. VAT: Stan/Spec.

HOOKWOOD, Nr. Horley
The Hinton Gallery   LAPADA
Crutchfield Farm, Crutchfield Lane. (S. and A. Waley.) Est. 1970. Open by appointment. *STOCK: Middle East Orientalist paintings; oil paintings, £100–£10,000; watercolours, £25–£1,000; both 18th–20th C.* LOC: Just off A217. PARK: Easy. TEL: Crawley (0293) 862417/862719. VAT: Spec.

HORSHAM   (0403)
L.E. Lampard and Sons
23–31 Springfield Rd. Est. 1920. Open 8–1 and 2–5. SIZE: Medium. *STOCK: Mahogany and oak furniture, firebacks, grates.* TEL: 54012 and 64332. VAT: Stan/Spec.

HURSTPIERPOINT   (0273)
Magnus Broe and Samuel Orr
36 High St. Est. 1974. CL: Wed. p.m. and Mon. *STOCK: Clocks.* TEL: 832081. SER: Restorations (clocks and furniture).

Chimera Books
17 High St. (R. and J. Lyon.) Open 9–1 and 2–5.30, other times by appointment. SIZE: Large. *STOCK: Antiquarian books especially childrens and Far East.* TEL: 832255.

Julian Antiques
124 High St. Est. 1964. CL: Sat. Open 9–5. *STOCK: French clocks, bronzes, art deco, fireplaces, mirrors, furniture.* TEL: 832145.

Hurstpierpoint continued
Michael Miller
The Lamb, 8 Cuckfield Rd. (M. and V. Miller.) Est. 1880. Open Sat. 9.30–5, other times appointment advisable. *STOCK: Arms and armour, post-1460, from £5; general antiques.* TEL: 834567. SER: Buys at auction; exporters.

IPING, Nr. Midhurst
The Plough
Robins Bottom Cottage. (Mrs. A. Smithells.) Est. 1980. Open by appointment only. SIZE: Medium. *STOCK: Decorative and collectable agricultural implements, including horsedrawn ploughs, wooden harrows, haysweeps, £50–£150; hand tools — saws, hay-knives, wheelwrights, blacksmiths, £3–£20; barn and domestic appliances — mangles, cheese presses, butter workers, pulpers, cake crackers, £50–£150; all mainly Victorian and Edwardian.* LOC: 2 miles off A3 just north of Petersfield, Hants., telephone for directions. PARK: Easy. TEL: Milland (042 876) 323; home — same. SER: Buys at auction (agricultural implements). VAT: Stan.

KIRDFORD   (040 377)
Nr. Billingshurst
Sheila Hinde Fine Art
Idolsfold House. *STOCK: Fine paintings and watercolours; animalier bronzes and early Staffordshire pottery.* VAT: Spec.

Kirdford Antiques
High St. (S. and N. Callingham.) *STOCK: English furniture, 17th−19th C.* TEL: 578. SER: Restorations.

LANCING   (0903)
Curiosites
152 South St. (J.D. Van Dam.) Est. 1968. Open 9.30−1 every day. SIZE: Medium. *STOCK: Paintings, prints, models, toys, cameras, art nouveau, art deco, dolls, postcards, books.* PARK: Forecourt. TEL: 752670; home − Shoreham (079 17) 4669. SER: Restorations; framing.

The Old Pine Shop
33/37 Penhill Rd. (M.J. Procter.) Open 9−5.30. *STOCK: Pine.* TEL: 763869.

LINDFIELD   (044 47)
Alma Antiques
79 High St. Est. 1976. CL: Wed. Open 10.30−5. *STOCK: Small collectable items, porcelain, glass, silver, copper, brass, furniture, watercolours and prints.*

David Burkinshaw
66 High St. Open 9−1 and 2−5, Sat. 9−1. *STOCK: Pedestal and partner desks.* TEL: 2826.

The Corner Gallery
99 High St. (R. Mulcare, N. Schwartz.) Est. 1974. CL: Sun. a.m. Open 10−5. SIZE: Medium. *STOCK: Furniture, 18th−19th C, £75−£100; glass, 19th C, £2−£12; china, porcelain, 17th−19th C, £5−£25.* Not stocked: Books. LOC: A272 Haywards Heath, turn off to B2028. PARK: Nearby. TEL: 2483.

Hillside Antiques   *Trade Only*
Units 12−13, Lindfield Enterprise Estate, Lewes Rd. (P.C. and C.C. Becker.) Est. 1976. Open 9.30−5, weekends by appointment. SIZE: Large. *STOCK: Pine and country furniture, £100−£500, decorative and interesting items, £10−£50, all 18th−19th C.* PARK: Easy. TEL: 3042; home − (0444) 811003. VAT: Stan.

Lindfield Galleries Ltd.   BADA
59 High St. Est. 1972. CL: Wed. Open 9.30−5.30. *STOCK: Oriental carpets, European tapestries, furniture, oil paintings.* **TEL: 3817. VAT: Stan/Spec.**

MIDHURST   (073 081)
Antiques and Market
Old Manor Cottage, Church Hill. (Mrs. L. Simms.) Open 9.30−5.30. SIZE: Medium. *STOCK: General antiques and small items.* PARK: Nearby. TEL: 3891.

Campbell Walchli Antiques
Church Hill. (A. Campbell and S. Walchli.) Resident. Est. 1974. CL: Wed. Open 10−1 and 2−5. SIZE: Medium. *STOCK: Mahogany furniture, Georgian, £50−£2,000; copper, brass, 19th C, £5−£100; Sheffield plate, porcelain, £5−£75.* Not stocked: Jewellery, scientific instruments and Oriental. LOC: Next to Manor House Restaurant. PARK: Easy. TEL: 4233. FAIRS: Petersfield and Goodwood House. VAT: Stan/Spec.

Eagle House Antiques Market
Market Sq. (J.H. Brown.) Open daily. SIZE: Medium. There are 15 dealers selling *general antiques, furniture, silver, porcelain, pictures and glass, £5−£1,000.* PARK: Easy. TEL: 2718.

Gauntlett Antiques
Grange Rd. CL: Sat. Open 9−12.30 and 1.30−5. SIZE: Large. *STOCK: General antiques.* LOC: Corner Grand Rd. and Bepton Rd. PARK: Nearby. TEL: 3101. VAT: Stan/Spec.

Midhurst Antiques Market
Knockhundred Row. (D.M. Brindle-Wood-Williams.) Est. 1974. Open 9.30−5.30. TEL: 4231.

The Pine Warehouse
The Wharf. (S. Hamilton.) CL: Wed. Open 3.30−5.30, Sun. 10−12.30. *STOCK: Pine.* TEL: 5345.

NORTHCHAPEL   (042 878)
Nr. Petworth
D. and A. Callingham Antiques
Est. 1966. CL: Wed. *STOCK: English furniture.* LOC: On A283. TEL: 379. VAT: Stan/Spec.

PETWORTH   (0798)
Majid Amini − Persian Carpet Gallery
Church St. Open 9.30−5. *STOCK: Oriental rugs.* LOC: A272. PARK: Nearby. TEL: 43344. SER: Valuations; restorations; cleaning.

Angel Shades
Angel St. (C.J. and E.C. Stiling.) Open 10−5.30. *STOCK: Mahogany and period furniture, some oak, porcelain.* TEL: 43295.

The Antique Centre
Angel St. Est. 1978. Open 10−1 and 2−5.30. SIZE: Large. *STOCK: Furniture, porcelain, paintings, silver, furnishing and designer items.* LOC: Corner Angel St. and East St. PARK: Nearby. TEL: 43221.

PETWORTH
WEST SUSSEX

Petworth Art & Antique
Dealers Association

Over 25 dealers
within 5 mins. walk

For brochure write or 'phone
Hon. Sec. P.A.A.D.A.
Fairfield House, High St.
Petworth, GU28 0AU
0798-42324

Petworth continued

Ballroom Antiques
Swan House, Market Sq. (N.P. Roberts.) Open 10—5.30. *STOCK: Furniture, copper, bronze, brass, silver and plate, clocks, Oriental items, porcelain, paintings, works of art, all 16th— 19th C.* TEL: 43638.

Boss Antiques
Hell's Bells Corner. *STOCK: Furniture, ceramics and general antiques.*

Lesley Bragge Antiques
Fairfield House, High St. Est. 1974. Open 10—1 and 2—5.30. SIZE: Medium. *STOCK: English, French and garden furniture, brass, copper, ormolu, decorative items, silver and plate, porcelain, 18th—19th C, £50—£3,000.* LOC: Off Golden Square. PARK: Nearby. TEL: 42324. SER: Valuations; restorations; upholstery. VAT: Stan/Spec.

Richard Davidson Antiques   BADA
Lombard St. Open 9.30—5.30. Other times and Sun. by appointment. *STOCK: Fine furniture and decoration.* TEL: 42508; out of hours 43354. VAT: Special.

Petworth continued

Flora Dora Antiques
Lombard St. (J. and P. Waldy). Est. 1978. Open 10—5.30. SIZE: Small. *STOCK: Furniture including mirrors, 18th—19th C, £50— £1,000; copper and brass, 18th—20th C, £5—£500; porcelain, glass and pictures, 18th—19th C, £5—£500.* PARK: Easy. TEL: 43109; home — same. VAT: Stan/Spec.

Frith Antiques
New St. (H.A. and Mrs. M.A. Frith.) Est. 1974. Open 10—5. SIZE: Small. *STOCK: Oak and mahogany country furniture, £50—£1,500; copper, brass, steel and pewter, £10—£300; all 17th—19th C; woodworking tools, 1700— 1920, £5—£250; cut steel jewellery, 1750— 1850, £5—£150. Not stocked: Silver.* LOC: 50yds. Town Square. PARK: Nearby. TEL: 43155; home — Bury (079 881) 606. FAIRS: West London — Jan. and Aug., Olympia, Brighton. VAT: Stan/Spec.

Griffin Antiques
Squires Holt, Church St. (R. and C. Wilson.) Est. 1981. Open 10—1 and 2—5.30. SIZE: Medium. *STOCK: English oak, 17th—19th C, £400—£5,000; English pine, £50—£500, domestic metalware, £20—£500, both 18th— 19th C.* LOC: Town centre. PARK: Easy. TEL: 43306; home — same. VAT: Stan/Spec.

JOHN G. MORRIS LTD.

MARKET SQUARE, PETWORTH, SUSSEX
GU28 OAH

17th, 18th & 19th CENTURY
ENGLISH & CONTINENTAL
FURNITURE, CLOCKS & BRONZES

TELEPHONE: 0798 42305   E.C. WEDNESDAY

Petworth continued

Herman Antiques
High St. (N. and S. Herman). Est. 1974. Open 10−1 and 2−5.30, Sun. by appointment. SIZE: Small. *STOCK: Oak and country furniture, £100−£1,000; treen, metalwork, deocrative items, £50−£500; all 17th−19th C.* LOC: Just off The Square. PARK: Easy. TEL: Home — (0243) 773476. FAIRS: Brighton. VAT: Spec.

William Hockley Antiques   LAPADA
East St. (D. and V. Thrower.) Est. 1974. *STOCK: Country oak and walnut, furniture and decorative items, 18th and 19th C; early English pottery, creamware and cow creamers.* TEL: Home — Dunsfold (048 649) 331. SER: Buys at auction.

Howes Gallery
The Square. (B.K. Wigg.) Est. 1968. Open 10−1 and 2−5.15. SIZE: Medium. *STOCK: Oil paintings, 19th C, £200−£5,000; watercolours, 19th C to early 20th C, £100−£900.* LOC: Town centre. PARK: Easy and 200yds. TEL: 43523. VAT: Spec.

Petworth continued

Humphry Antiques
East St. (J. and M. Humphry.) Open 10−1 and 2−5.30, Sun. by appointment. SIZE: Medium. *STOCK: Mainly English country oak furniture, 17th−18th C; carvings, tapestry, treen, metalwork, unusual and decorative items.* LOC: Between antique market and post office. TEL: 43053; home — 42944.

Rose Lodge
Norworth, East St. (Mrs. R. Lodge.) Est. 1977. Open 10−1 and 2.15−5, Mon. a.m. and Sun. by appointment. SIZE: Small. *STOCK: Linen, 19th C; lace, from 18th C; period clothing; all £5−£100.* LOC: Next door to Antique Market. PARK: Easy. TEL: 43217; home — same. SER: Valuations.

Millhouse
The Square. (E.G. and C.F. Rawnsley.) Open 10−5 or by appointment. SIZE: Medium. *STOCK: Fine period furniture.* PARK: In the Square. TEL: 43080; evenings Lodsworth (079 85) 406. SER: Valuations; buys at auction; antiques search, export. VAT: Spec.

PETWORTH
ANTIQUES WAREHOUSE

UNIT 5 · COLHOOK INDUSTRIAL PARK · NR. PETWORTH · W. SUSSEX
TEL: NORTHCHAPEL (042-878) 667

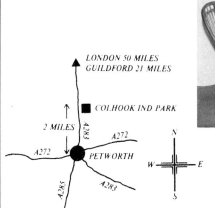

LONDON 50 MILES
GUILDFORD 21 MILES

COLHOOK IND PARK

2 MILES

A283

A272

A272

PETWORTH

A285

A283

N

W — E

S

*specialising in Antique and Decorative
Furniture, Architectural and Garden Items*

Petworth continued

Millhouse Fine Arts
The Square. (E.G. and C.F. Rawnsley). Open 10—5 or by appointment. SIZE: Medium. *STOCK: 18th—19th C oil paintings and watercolours, pastels, gouaches.* PARK: In the Square. TEL: 43080; evenings — Lodsworth (079 85) 406. SER: Valuations; buys at auction. VAT: Spec.

John G. Morris Ltd.   BADA
Market Sq. Est. 1962. CL: Wed. p.m. Open 10—6 or by appointment. SIZE: Medium. *STOCK: Furniture, English and Continental, 1660—1850, from £100; English clocks, 18th—19th C, £800—£6,000; English barometers, £300—£1,200; French animalier bronzes, 19th C, £200—£1,200; some porcelain.* Not stocked: Bric-a-brac, jewellery, porcelain, Edwardian articles. LOC: On A272. PARK: Easy. TEL: 42305. SER: Valuations; buys at auction. VAT: Stan/Spec.

Michael J. O'Neill
Swan House, Market Sq. Open 9.30—5.30. *STOCK: Fine English furniture and clocks, 17th—18th C.* TEL: 42616.

Petworth continued

Pam Antiques
Angel St. (M. Chapman.) Est. 1974. Open 7 days 10—1 and 2.15—5. SIZE: Small. *STOCK: Metalware, 17th—19th C, from £10; oak and country furniture, 17th—18th C, from £20; pictures, treen, decorative items, 18th—19th C, from £5.* Not stocked: Glass and bric-a-brac. LOC: 100yds. east from town centre, opposite antique centre. PARK: Nearby. TEL: 43394; home — Bosham (0243) 572862. SER: Restorations (metalware). VAT: Spec.

Petworth Antique Market
East St. (D.M. and P.J. Rayment.) Est. 1968. Open 10—5.30. SIZE: Large. There are 36 dealers selling *general antiques, books, furniture, brass, copper, pictures, textiles.* LOC: Near church. PARK: Adjoining. TEL: 42073. VAT: Stan/Spec.

Petworth Antiques Warehouse
Unit 5, Colhook Industrial Park. (R. MacWhirter and J. Harris.) CL: Sat. Open 9—1 and 2—5. *STOCK: English period, architectural and decorative furniture and smalls; English and Continental garden furniture, all £5—£5,000+.* LOC: 2 miles from Petworth towards Guildford, A283. PARK: Easy. TEL: Northchapel (042 878) 667. VAT: Stan/Spec.

Petworth continued

Ernest Streeter and Daughter
The Clock House, Lombard St. Est. 1888. CL: Wed. *STOCK: Silver, jewellery.* TEL: 42239. VAT: Stan.

Michael Wakelin and Helen Linfield **LAPADA**
10 New St. Est. 1968. Resident. Open 10—5 or by appointment. *STOCK: English formal and country furniture, Continental furniture, metalwork, wood carvings, treen, primitive pictures, textiles, lighting and mirrors.* TEL: 42417. VAT: Stan/Spec.

Jeremy Wood Fine Art
East St. Est. 1974. Open 10—1 and 2—5. *STOCK: Oils and watercolours, etchings, 1880—1930, £5—£500; art reference books, illustrated art and travel books, £1—£50.* TEL: 43408. VAT: Spec.

PORTSLADE

Peter Marks Antique Warehouse **LAPADA**
1/11 Church Rd. Est. 1965. Open 9.30—6, Sat. 9.30—1. SIZE: Large. *STOCK: General antiques, shipping goods.* TEL: Brighton (0273) 415471. VAT: Stan.

J. Powell (Hove) Ltd. **LAPADA**
20 Wellington Rd. Est. 1949. CL: Sun. and Sat. p.m. except by appointment. Open 9—6. SIZE: Large. *STOCK: Bookcases, display cabinets, £110—£1,500; writing tables and desks, £120—£1,200; longcase and bracket clocks, £50—£2,000; general furniture, shipping goods, 18th—20th C, £5—£1,500.* Not stocked: Porcelain, jewellery, silver. LOC: 150yds. west of Boundary Rd., on seafront. PARK: Easy. TEL: Brighton (0273) 411599; home — Brighton (0273) 593274. SER: Restorations (furniture). VAT: Stan.

PULBOROUGH (079 82)

Roy Barton **BADA**
Myrtle Cottage, Codmore Hill. Est. 1948. Resident. Appointment advisable. SIZE: Medium. *STOCK: 18th to early 19th C mahogany; 17th to early 18th C oak and walnut furniture; 17th—18th C longcase clocks, from £500; paintings and watercolours, from £50.* Not stocked: Victoriana. LOC: A29, 1 mile north of Pulborough. PARK: Easy. TEL: 2730. VAT: Spec.

Hill House, Codmore Hill
(Mr. and Mrs. T.A. Stodart.) Est. 1972. CL: Sun. except by appointment. Open 9.30—6. SIZE: Medium. *STOCK: Furniture, 17th—20th C, £25—£1,500; ceramics, 18th—20th C, £5—£400; pictures, 17th—20th C, £3—£500; bronzes, 17th—20th C, £25—£1,000; copper, brass, metalwork, garden furnishings, £10—£400.* Not stocked: Coins, stamps, fabrics. LOC: On A29, 1½ miles north of Pulborough, opposite 'Rose and Crown'. PARK: Easy opposite. TEL: 2380. SER: Valuations; buys at auction.

Mare Hill Galleries
Mare Hill. (C. and V. Trewin.) Est. 1970. Open 10—5. *STOCK: Furniture, paintings, porcelain, oriental works of art.* Not stocked: Silver, jewellery. TEL: 2006. VAT: Stan/Spec.

Mulberry House Galleries
Mulberry House, Codmore Hill. (M. Scadgell.) Resident. Est. 1974. Open 9—6; Wed. p.m., Sat. p.m. and Sun. by appointment. *STOCK: British oil paintings and watercolours, 1840—1940.* LOC: A29, 1 mile north of Pulborough, opposite Rose and Crown public house. PARK: Own. TEL: 2463. SER: Valuations; restorations, cleaning. VAT: Spec.

Blue-dash charger decorated with a polychrome scene of Adam and Eve. Made in Bristol c.1690. From "Delft Ware in the 17th Century House" in **Antique Collecting,** April 1986.

Pulborough continued

Trade Winds Antiques
42a Lower St. (A.F.M. Chalmers.) Est. 1976. Open daily, Sun by appointment. *STOCK: Pine and country items, 19th—20th C.* LOC: Main road. PARK: Nearby. TEL: 3030; home — Worthing (0903) 208509. SER: Valuations; buys at auction. VAT: Stan/Spec.

SHOREHAM-BY-SEA
(4 & 5 fig. nos.) (079 17)
(6 fig. nos.) (0273)

The Old Warehouse
Western Rd. (Mrs. M. Mills.) SIZE: Large. Open 9—1, other times by appointment. *STOCK: General antiques including clothes.* TEL: 453504.

Tudor Cottage Antiques
Upper Shoreham Rd. (S. and N. Harvey.) Resident. Est. 1967. Open daily including Sun. a.m. (also during summer evenings). *STOCK: General antiques, Victoriana.* LOC: Near Amsterdam Restaurant. TEL: 3554.

Western Antiques
1 Western Rd. (D. and D. Steers.) Est. 1969. CL: Wed. and Sat. *STOCK: Collectors' items; general antiques, small furniture.* LOC: 150yds. south of Shoreham Station. PARK: Opposite and west of shop. TEL: 61311

STEYNING   (0903)
David R. Fileman
Squirrels, Bayards. Open daily. *STOCK: Table glass, £20—£1,000; chandeliers, candelabra, £500—£20,000; all 18th—19th C. Collectors' items, 17th—19th C, £25—£2,000; paperweights, 19th C, £50—£5,000.* LOC: A283 to north of Steyning village. TEL: 813229. SER: Valuations; restorations (chandeliers and candelabra). VAT: Stan/Spec.

STORRINGTON   (090 66)
Storrington Antiques
46 West St. (Mrs. P.M. Bond.) Est. 1967. Open 9.30—5 daily. *STOCK: Furniture and general antiques.* TEL: 2193.

TILLINGTON, Nr. Petworth
Loewenthal Antiques
Tillington Cottage. CL: Wed. *STOCK: 18th C furniture and objets d'art.* LOC: A272, 1 mile west of Petworth. TEL: Petworth (0798) 42969.

UPPER BEEDING, Nr. Steyning
Heritage Interiors
High St. (C. Short.) TEL: Steyning (0903) 812104.

"Masquerade", date unknown. From "A Year of Romance", **Antique Collecting,** January 1986.

WARNHAM
Warnham Antiques
24 Church St. (J.A. Kay.) Est. 1977. CL: Mon. and Fri. Open 10—1 and 2—5. SIZE: Medium. *STOCK: Chests, tables, chairs, bureaux, clocks and pictures, 18th—19th C, to £500.* LOC: Off A24. PARK: Easy. TEL: Horsham (0403) 52802; home — Horsham (0403) 60767.

WASHINGTON
Chanctonbury Antiques
Clematis Cottage. (G. Troche.) Est. 1961. CL: Sun. and Tues. except by appointment. Open 10—5.30. SIZE: Medium. *STOCK: Porcelain, needlework, glass, furniture, objets de vertu.* LOC: Just off A24. PARK: Easy. TEL: Ashington (0903) 892233.

Pine and Country Antiques — Sandhill Barn
Est. 1969. Open from 9.30—5.30. SIZE: Large. *STOCK: Pine and country furniture, bygones, tools, early iron, brass, copper, treen, kitchen items.* Not stocked: Silver, jewellery, mahogany. LOC: At the Washington roundabout (crossroads of A24 and A283), take the Steyning road and turn left immediately into cul-de-sac. PARK: Easy. TEL: Ashington (0903) 892888. SER: Stripping (pine). VAT: Stan.

WESTBOURNE, Nr. Emsworth
Westbourne Antiques
1—3 Lamb Buildings, The Square. (H.J. and V.J. Lain.) Est. 1951. Open 9—5. SIZE: Large. *STOCK: Silver, jewellery, collectors' items, furniture.* PARK: In nearby streets. TEL: Emsworth (024 34) 3711. SER: Valuations; repairs (jewellery).

WISBOROUGH GREEN   (0403)
Nr. Billingshurst
Wisborough Green Antiques
Billingshurst Rd. (A. Hughes.) Est. 1975. Open 10—1 and 2.15—5. SIZE: Medium. *STOCK: Georgian and Victorian furniture, pine, porcelain, sewing items, lace, jewellery, paintings, rugs.* LOC: A272. Next to Three Crowns public house. PARK: Easy. TEL: 700650.

WORTHING   (0903)
7 The Arcade
(J. Law.) CL: Wed. Open 10—5. *STOCK: Dolls, miniatures, juvenalia and collectables.* TEL: 200274.

A. Biscoe
122 Montague St. (R. Byskou.) CL: Wed. p.m. Open 10—6. *STOCK: Furniture, silver, porcelain, 18th—19th C; jewellery, clocks and objets d'art.* TEL: 202489; home — Rustington (0903) 782723.

Broadwater Bookroom
20 Broadwater St. East, Broadwater. Est. 1950. *STOCK: Books, pictures, postcards.* TEL: 39708.

A rare small mug, with typical handle form, 3½ins. high, c.1768 (or earlier). From *Lowestoft Porcelains* by Geoffrey A. Godden, F.R.S.A., published by the **Antique Collectors' Club**, 1985.

Worthing continued

Cameo Corner
163 Montague St. (E. Stanton.) Est. 1952. CL: Wed. p.m. Open 9.30—5.30. SIZE: Small. *STOCK: Jewellery, silver, Chinese porcelain, 1750—1936, £5—£500.* LOC: Montague St. is parallel with Marine Parade. PARK: Easy. TEL: 30533. VAT: Stan.

Cheriton Antiques
21 New Broadway, Tarring Rd. (A.C. Biggs and Mrs. M.D. Edwards.) CL: Wed. Open 9.30—5.30. *STOCK: Mainly furniture.* Not stocked: Jewellery. TEL: 35463.

Chloe Antiques
61 Brighton Rd. (Mrs. D. Peters.) Est. 1960. Open 9.30—12.30 and 2—5. SIZE: Small. *STOCK: General antiques, furniture, jewellery, china, glass, bric-a-brac.* LOC: From Brighton, on main rd. just past Beach House Park on corner. PARK: Opposite. TEL: 202697.

Geoffrey Godden Chinaman   BADA
17 Crescent Rd. (G.A. Godden.) Est. 1900. CL: Sat. Open 9.30—1 and 2.15—5. SIZE: Large. *STOCK: English porcelain and pottery, all periods and all prices.* LOC: Town centre. PARK: Easy. TEL: 35958 and 31901. VAT: Spec.

Worthing continued

Godden of Worthing   BADA
17 Crescent Rd. (G.A. Godden.) Est. 1900. CL: Sat. Open 9.30—1 and 2.15—5. SIZE: Large. *STOCK: Ceramics, 18th—19th C; decorative accessories.* PARK: Easy. TEL: 35958 and 31901. VAT: Spec.

Snoopers Paradise
Bric-a-Brac Market
Over 5, 7, 9 South Farm Rd.

Robert Warner and Son Ltd.
1, 5, 7, 9, 11 South Farm Rd. Est. 1945. CL: Wed. p.m. SIZE: Large. *STOCK: Furniture, bric-a-brac.* TEL: 32710. VAT: Stan.

Whitehouse Antiques Ltd.
87 Rowlands Rd. (G.G. Cross.) Est. 1959. CL: Wed. and Sat. p.m. Open 9.30—1 and 2—5 or by appointment. SIZE: Large. *STOCK: Furniture, shipping goods, china, silver, pewter, brass.* LOC: Near seafront. PARK: Easy. TEL: 30844. VAT: Stan/Spec.

H. Wilson and Son   LAPADA
28 High St. Open 8.30—5.30. SIZE: Large. *STOCK: General antiques, shipping goods, bric-a-brac, £1—£5,000.* LOC: Town centre. PARK: Multi-storey opp. TEL: 202059. VAT: Stan/Spec.

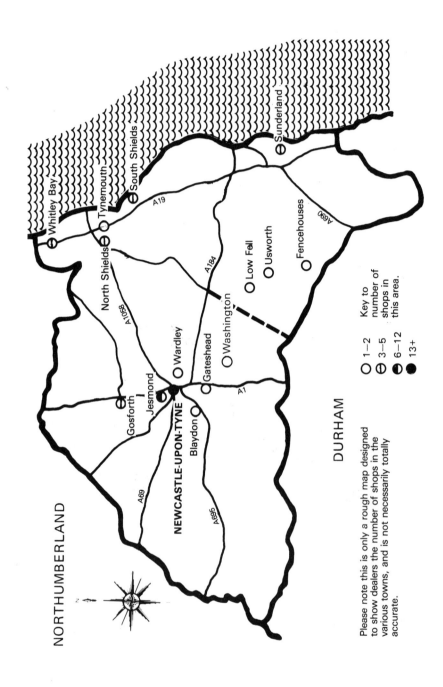

NORTHUMBERLAND

DURHAM

Whitley Bay

Tynemouth

South Shields

Sunderland

North Shields

A19

A1058

A184

Low Fell

Usworth

Fencehouses

A690

Gosforth

Jesmond

Wardley

Gateshead

Washington

NEWCASTLE-UPON-TYNE

Blaydon

A1

A69

A695

Key to
number of
shops in
this area.

○ 1—2
◑ 3—5
◕ 6—12
● 13+

Please note this is only a rough map designed
to show dealers the number of shops in the
various towns, and is not necessarily totally
accurate.

BLAYDON,
Nr. Newcastle-upon-Tyne
Blaydon Antique Centre
10 Bridge St. (Mrs. E. Bradshaw.) Est. 1979.
Open 11—4.30. SIZE: Medium. *STOCK:
Furniture, 18th—19th C, £50—£500; china,
glass, brass and pictures.* PARK: Easy. TEL:
Tyneside (091) 4143535; home — (091)
2363641. SER: Valuations; buys at auction.
FAIRS: Local.

FENCEHOUSES   (0385)
Nr. Sunderland
Antony Clingly Antiques   *Trade Only*
Former Colliery Row Methodist Church, North
View, Chilton Moor. Est. 1977. Open 9—5,
Sun. by appointment. SIZE: Large warehouse.
*STOCK: General shipping goods, Georgian
and decorative American furniture, ornate
stained glass.* LOC: From A1 take A690, turn
off at Houghton, 5 miles before Sunderland.
PARK: Easy. TEL: 852030. SER: Shipping and
documentation; packing worldwide; courier;
buys at auction.

GATESHEAD
The Windmill
223 Coatsworth Rd. (G. Taylor.) Est. 1978.
Open 10—5.30, Sat. 10—4.30. SIZE: Medium.
*STOCK: General antiques — furniture, pictures,
clocks, bric-a-brac, £5—£500.* Not stocked:
Jewellery. LOC: Corner of Whitehall Rd.
PARK: Easy. TEL: (091) 4772300; home —
(091) 4774161. SER: Valuations; restorations
(oil paintings and watercolours); framing; re-
upholstery.

GOSFORTH,
Nr. Newcastle-upon-Tyne
Causey Antique Shop
Causey St. *STOCK: Furniture, 19th C; Victor-
iana and collectors items.*

Anna Harrison Fine Antiques
                              LAPADA
Grange Park, Great North Rd. Est. 1976. Open
10—4.30. SIZE: Large. *STOCK: English furniture, porcelain, oils and watercolours.* LOC:
A6125, 3 miles north of city centre, near
Regent Centre, opposite county rugby ground.
PARK: Forecourt. TEL: (091) 2843202; home
— (091) 2367652. SER: Valuations; restorations. VAT: Stan/Spec.

Gosforth continued
P. and D. Smith Antiques
6 Ashburton Rd. Est. 1970. CL: Wed. p.m.
Open 10—5. SIZE: Small. *STOCK: Silver,
1600—1950, £5—£1,500; pewter, silver
plate, 1750—1900, £2—£150; glass and
Oriental works of art, from £5—£1,000.* Not
stocked: Reproductions. LOC: Turn left at
double traffic lights on A1 in Gosforth. Up
Salters Rd. for ¾ mile, turn left into Ashburton
Rd. PARK: Easy. TEL: (091) 2856455. VAT:
Stan/Spec.

JESMOND
Nr. Newcastle-upon-Tyne
Julie Brenchley Antique Jewellery
                              LAPADA
11 and 12 Clayton Rd. Est: 1976. CL: Mon.
and Tues. SIZE: Small. *STOCK: Jewellery,
18th—19th C, £50—£1,000.* PARK: Easy.
TEL: Tyneside (091) 2810082; home —
(0632) 571800. SER: Valuations; restorations.
FAIRS: N.E.C., Birmingham; Penman's
London; Tatton Park, Cheshire. VAT:
Stan/Spec.

Jesmond continued

Clayton Antiques
15a Clayton Rd., (D. and J. Westle.) Est. 1979. CL: Wed. Open 11—5 or by appointment. SIZE: Small. *STOCK: Small furniture, 18th and 19th C glass, jewellery, metalware and collectables.* LOC: Off Osborne Rd. PARK: Easy. TEL: (091) 2817416. VAT: Stan.

Geoffrey Hugall
19 Clayton Rd. Est. 1970. Open 10—5 or by appointment. SIZE: Medium. *STOCK: General antiques, furniture, china, silver, period and decorative items, paintings.* Not stocked: Weapons, musical instruments. PARK: Easy. TEL: (091) 2818408. VAT: Stan/Spec.

Owen Humble   LAPADA
11-13 Clayton Rd. Est. 1958. Open 6 days. SIZE: Large and warehouse. *STOCK: Furniture, general antiques.* PARK: Easy. SER: Restorations. VAT: Stan/Spec.

Osborne Art and Antiques
18c Osborne Rd. (F.T. and S. Jackman.) Est. 1974. Open 10—5.15. *STOCK: Victorian oil paintings, watercolours, drawings.* TEL: (091) 2816380. SER: Restorations; picture framing. VAT: Stan/Spec.

John Walker Antiques
46 Brentwood Ave. Est. 1972. Open 10—1 and 2—5. SIZE: Large and large warehouse. Open 8—5. *STOCK: Furniture, brass, copper, shipping goods and items of architectural interest at warehouse.* TEL: (091) 2815871. VAT: Stan/Spec.

A Tuareg amulet case. From "Traditional Jewellery" in **Antique Collecting,** April 1986.

Jesmond continued

W. and J. Walker
231 Jesmond Rd. Est. 1976. Open 10—5. SIZE: Medium. *STOCK: Furniture, clocks, bric-a-brac, all 19th C.* LOC: Main road to east coast. PARK: Osborne Ave. — around corner. TEL: (091) 2817286. VAT: Stan.

LOW FELL, Nr. Gateshead
N. Jewett
639/643 Durham Rd. Est. 1948. SIZE: Large. *STOCK: Antique and reproduction furniture, glass, china, £5—£5,000.* LOC: On A1, 3 miles south of Newcastle-upon-Tyne. PARK: On hill opp. TEL: (091) 4877636. SER: Valuations. VAT: Stan/Spec.

NEWCASTLE-UPON-TYNE   (0632)
The Antique Centre
46 Low Friar St. (Bede Antiques Ltd.) Est. 1977. Open 10—5. SIZE: Large. There are approx. 30 dealers at this centre, selling a wide range of general antiques including *furniture, £5—£500; jewellery, £50—£100; china, glass and linen, £5—£25.* PARK: Easy and adjacent. TEL: 614577. SER: Valuations; restorations. VAT: Stan.

J.H. Corbitt (Numismatists) Ltd.
105 Clayton St. (J.H. Corbitt, FRNS.) Est. 1960. CL: Wed. p.m. Open 9—5. *STOCK: Coins, medals, militaria, Victorian jewellery, £1—£10,000.* LOC: City centre. TEL: 324356. SER: Valuations. VAT: Stan/Spec.

Davidson's The Jewellers Ltd.
94 and 96 Grey St. Open 9—5. *STOCK: Jewellery, silver.* TEL: 322551 or 322895.

The Dean Gallery
42 Dean St. (A.P. Graham.) Est. 1970. CL: Sat. p.m. Open 9—5. SIZE: Large. *STOCK: Oils, watercolours, local and national, 18th to early 20th C, £50—£1,500.* LOC: Going north over Tyne Bridge, turn left, and left again. PARK: Easy. TEL: 321208. SER: Valuations; restorations; framing. VAT: Stan/Spec.

Hattam's Antiques
42 Pink Lane. (D., P. and W. Hattam.) Est. 1949. Open 10—5. SIZE: Medium. *STOCK: Silver and plate, Victorian and secondhand jewellery, £5—£3,000; clocks, china, £5—£1,000; art nouveau, art deco, Japanese; brass, pottery, glass.* LOC: From south, through Gateshead over bridge past station and turn right, back into the town. Next to ABC. PARK: 200yds. around opp. block, or outside. TEL: 324459. VAT: Stan.

H. Krolick
83 Quayside. Est. 1947. TEL: 2857916; home — 2856741.

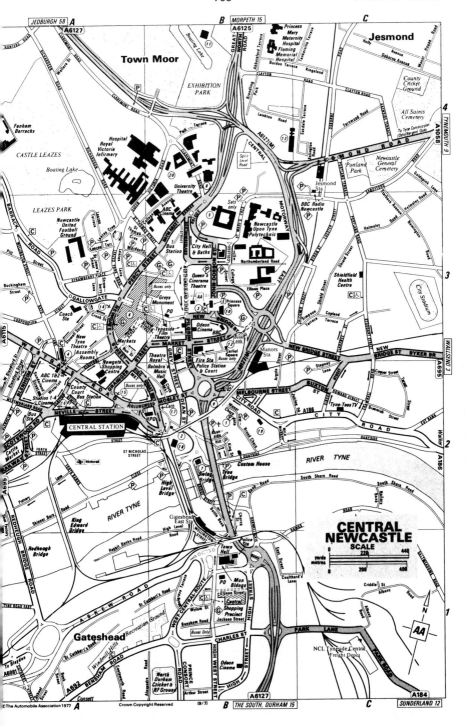

Newcastle-upon-Tyne continued

Owen's Jewellers
14 Shields Rd., Byker. (D.W. Robertson.) Est. 1968. Open 10—5, Wed. 11—1. *STOCK: Jewellery.* TEL: 654332.

Pianoland incorporating Cradle Well Antiques
244 Jesmond Rd. *STOCK: Pianos and general antiques.* TEL: 810691. SER: Restorations (pianos); container and export service.

W. Robinson (Newcastle) Ltd.
49—53 Grainger Market. Est. 1881. Open 9—5.30, Wed. 9—1. *STOCK: Antiquarian books.* TEL: 322978.

Rosalynd and Carole Spicker
75 Grainger Market. *STOCK: Antique, Victorian and secondhand jewellery, curios.* TEL: 325057.

R.D. Steedman
9 Grey St. Est. 1907. CL: Sat. p.m. *STOCK: Rare books.* TEL: 326561.

NORTH SHIELDS   (0632)
Alyn House
8-10 Queen Alexandra Rd. (H.J. Danskin.) Est. 1977. CL: Wed. Open 10—5. *STOCK: General antiques.* TEL: 584868.

North Shields continued

Maggie May's Plantiquity
Incorporating Tynemouth Fine Art, 49 Kirton Park Terrace. (Miss M.L. Hayes.) Open 10.30—6. SIZE: Medium. *STOCK: General antiques, jewellery, art deco, linen, Victorian and Edwardian furniture, china, glass, toys, metalware, stuffed animals and birds; 19th C paintings and watercolours.* LOC: Near Preston Hospital. TEL: 574683.

Dixon Mitchell Antiques
Ye Old Market Place, 101 Howard St. (J.D. Mitchell.) Est. 1976. CL: Wed. Open 9—5. *STOCK: General antiques and shipping goods.* TEL: 595552 (24hr. answering service).

Pattersons Antiques
1 Grey St. (J. and P. Chester). Est. 1978. Resident. CL: Mon. and Wed. except by appointment. Open 10—4. SIZE: Small and shipping warehouse. *STOCK: Small furniture, shipping items, art nouveau, art deco, paintings, clothing, furs and accessories, general antiques, small items, £1—£500.* LOC: Coast road from Newcastle to Tynemouth, follow signs for N. Shields turn left at Linskill High School, white shop on corner. PARK: Easy. TEL: 572118. SER: Buys at auction. FAIRS: Local.

The front of a superb Lowestoft porcelain flask, painted in underglaze blue, by an artist noteworthy for his swirled clouds and dotted ground. This painter was perhaps Richard Powles and the shipbuilding scene is one of the finest examples of Lowestoft underglaze blue painting, 5½ins. high, diameter 4⁴/⁵ins. c.1780. From *Lowestoft Porcelains* by Geoffrey A. Godden, F.R.S.A., published by the **Antique Collectors' Club**, 1985.

SOUTH SHIELDS (0632)

The Curiosity Shop
16 Frederick St. Est. 1969. CL: Wed. p.m.
STOCK: General antiques, paintings, weapons, jewellery. TEL: 565560.

William White
20A Frederick St. Open 9.30—4. TEL: 568461.

R. Willis Antiques and Curios
149 Imeary St. Est. 1970. CL: Sat. Open 10—4.30. *STOCK: General antiques.* TEL: 565987.

SUNDERLAND (0783)

Gladstone Antiques
2 Gladstone St. (T. Robson.) Est. 1939. CL: Wed. p.m. Open 10—5. SIZE: Large. *STOCK: Furniture, clocks, decor, architectural goods.* LOC: Cross Wearmouth Bridge, north side. PARK: Easy. TEL: 659378; home — 641422. FAIRS: Tyneside. VAT: Stan.

Peter Newrick Antiques
1 Derwent St. Est. 1971. Open 9.30—5.30. SIZE: Warehouse. *STOCK: General antiques and American shipping items.* TEL: 41074 or 286412. SER: Container packing (worldwide). VAT: Stan.

Peter Smith Antiques   LAPADA
2 Tunstall Rd. and warehouse at 14 Borough Rd. Est. 1968. Open 9.30—5.30, Sat. p.m. and Sun. by appointment. SIZE: Large. *STOCK: Victorian, Edwardian and shipping goods, £5—£6,000.* LOC: On A690, 9 miles from A1M. PARK: Easy. TEL: 677842; warehouse — 673537; home — 40008. SER: Valuations, restorations; some shipping; buys at auction. VAT: Stan/Spec.

TYNEMOUTH

Renaissance Antiques
11 Front St. (E. and N. Moore.) Est. 1977. CL: Wed.—Fri. Open 10.30—1 and 2—4. SIZE: Medium and trade goods store. *STOCK: Furniture, Georgian to art deco, £50—£1,000; china and porcelain, silver, brass and copper, £5—£100; shipping goods.* LOC: Main coast road from Newcastle. PARK: Easy. TEL: 595555; home — North Shields (0632) 574073. SER: Valuations.

David R. Strain Antiques   LAPADA
66 Front St. Est. 1983. Open 9.30—5.30. SIZE: Medium. *STOCK: Furniture and general antiques, Edwardian, Victorian, Georgian, £5—£2,000.* Not stocked: Weapons, books, silver and jewellery. LOC: Main coast road from Newcastle, 10 minutes from Tyne tunnel. PARK: Easy. TEL: North Shields (0632) 592459; home — North Shields (0632) 590300. SER: Valuations; buys at auction (furniture). VAT: Stan/Spec.

USWORTH, Nr. Washington

Tom Robson   *Trade Only*
East House. *STOCK: Furniture, clocks.* TEL: Boldon (0783) 361868. VAT: Stan.

WARDLEY
Nr. Newcastle-upon-Tyne

Laverick Hall Antiques   *Trade Only*
Laverick Hall, Sunderland Rd. (P. and J. Sampson.) Est. 1961. CL: Sat. Open 9—4.30. SIZE: Large. *STOCK: General antiques and American shipping items.* LOC: Turn right at Sunderland junction top of A1(M), premises second on left. PARK: Easy. TEL: Felling (0632) 697362; home — same. VAT: Stan/Spec.

WASHINGTON

Harry Carr Antiques
Field House, Rickleton. Open by appointment. *STOCK: General antiques and furniture.* TEL: Chester-le-Street (0385) 886442.

WHITLEY BAY

And So To Bed
59-65 Whitley Rd. (W.I. Raw.) Est. 1981. Open 9—5. SIZE: Medium. *STOCK: Brass and iron beds, bedroom furniture, lamps, mirrors, bedding sets and linen, £150—£1,000.* LOC: Cullercoats end of Whitley Rd. PARK: Easy. TEL: (091) 252 4611. VAT: Stan.

The Bric-a-Brac
195 Park View. (C. Rawes.) Est. 1953. CL: Tues. Open 9—5. SIZE: Medium. *STOCK: General antiques.* TEL: (091) 252 6141.

Northumbria Pine
54 Whitley Rd. (Mr. and Mrs. W.I. Raw.) Est. 1979. Open 9—5. SIZE: Medium. *STOCK: Stripped pine, 19th C, £100—£700.* LOC: Cullercoats end of Whitley Rd., behind sea front. PARK: Easy. TEL: (091) 252 4550. VAT: Stan.

Treasure Chest
2 Norham Rd. Est.1974. CL: Wed., and Thurs. Open 10.30—1 and 2—4. SIZE: Small. *STOCK: General antiques.* LOC: Just off main shopping area of Park View, leading to Monkseaton Railway Station. PARK: Easy.

Warwickshire

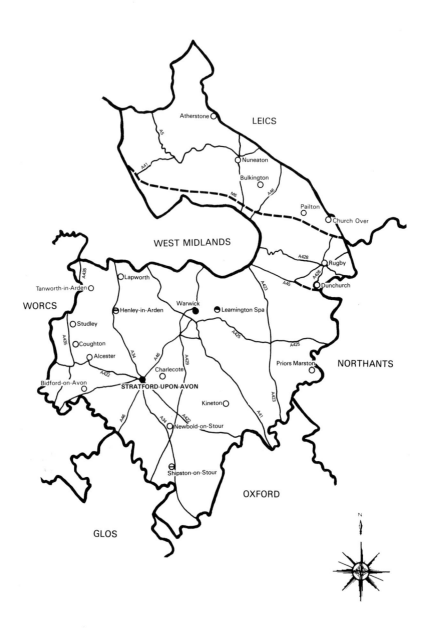

LEICS

Atherstone

Nuneaton

Bulkington

Pailton

Church Over

WEST MIDLANDS

A428

Rugby

Lapworth

A435

Tanworth-in-Arden

Warwick

Leamington Spa

Dunchurch

A423

A45

WORCS

Henley-in-Arden

Studley

A435

Coughton

Alcester

A422

A46

A34

A429

A425

A425

Priors Marston

NORTHANTS

Charlecote

Bidford-on-Avon

STRATFORD-UPON-AVON

A46

A34

Kineton

A422

A423

A41

Newbold-on-Stour

Shipston-on-Stour

OXFORD

GLOS

N

Please note this is only a rough map designed
to show dealers the number of shops in the
various towns, and is not necessarily totally
accurate.

○ 1–2	Key to
⊖ 3–5	number of
◑ 6–12	shops in
● 13+	this area.

ALCESTER (0789)

High St. Antiques
11A High St. (P. Payne.) Est. 1979. Open 11—1 and 2.30—5, prior telephone call advisable. SIZE: Small. *STOCK: Glass and china, 18th—20th C, but mainly 19th C, £5—£200; brass, copper and silver, 19th—20th C, £5—£100+; post-cards and art deco china.* LOC: On left-hand side near church coming from Stratford-on-Avon road. PARK: Rear of High St. TEL: 764009; home — same. SER: Valuations.

Malthouse Antique Centre
Market Pl. (C. Elliott and L. Berry.) Est. 1982. Open 10—5, Sun. 11—5. SIZE: Large. *STOCK: Victorian pine furniture, £25—£300; furniture, from Georgian, £100—£1,000; paintings and prints, £25—£1,000.* LOC: Off High St. PARK: Easy. TEL: 764032. SER: Valuations; restorations; buys at auction. VAT: Stan/Spec.

ATHERSTONE (082 77)

'The Chatelaine'
18—20 Church St., Market Sq. (M. and N. Holmes Field.) Est. 1970. CL: Mon., and Thurs. Open 10—5. *STOCK: Oil lamps, Staffordshire, bargeware, curios, porcelain, furniture, prints.* LOC: Off A5. TEL: 3870.

BIDFORD-ON-AVON (0789)

The Antiques Centre
High St. Est. 1983. CL: Mon. Open 10—5, Sun. 2—5.30. There are 8 dealers at this centre. *STOCK: Furniture, china, glass, jewellery, paintings, bygones, clocks.* PARK: Easy. TEL: 773680.

Crown Antiques
14 High St. (J. and C. Ford.) Est. 1980. Resident. CL: Thurs. Open 10—5.30, Sat. 10—4.30, Sun. by appointment. SIZE: Medium. *STOCK: Victorian mahogany, £50—£2,000+; oak shipping items, £50—£1,000; general antiques, some period furniture, £5—£2,500.* LOC: 100yds. off A439. PARK: Easy. TEL: 772939. SER: Valuations; buys at auction (furniture). VAT: Stan/Spec.

BULKINGTON, Nr. Nuneaton

Sport and Country Gallery LAPADA
Northwood House. (R.M. Hill.) Open by appointment. *STOCK: 19th C and 20th C oils and watercolours of sporting and rural life.* TEL: Bedworth (0203) 314335. VAT: Spec.

CHARLECOTE

Country Furniture
Kingsmead Farm. (Mrs. J. Seccombe). Resident. Est. 1970. Open Sat. and Sun., other times by appointment. SIZE: Medium. *STOCK: Period pine, 18th—19th C, £20—£500; watercolours and prints, bric-a-brac; country furniture.* TEL: Stratford-upon-Avon (0789) 840254. SER: Valuations. VAT: Stan.

CHURCH OVER, Nr. Rugby

Mawby's International
Old Village Hall, School St. Est. 1974. Open 9—5. SIZE: Warehouse. *STOCK: Mainly stripped pine furniture.* LOC: Off A426. TEL: Rugby (0788) 832600 or 75305.

COUGHTON, Nr. Alcester

Coughton Galleries Ltd.
Coughton Court. (Lady Isabel Throckmorton.) Est. 1968. Open 10—5.30 Wed., Thurs., Sat., and Sun. or by appointment. SIZE: Medium. *STOCK: 19th and 20th C English oil paintings, watercolours and prints.* TEL: Alcester (0789) 762642. VAT: Spec.

DUNCHURCH, Nr. Rugby

The Antique Centre
16/16a Daventry Rd. (D. Thompson and Mrs. J. Edwards.) Resident. Est. 1981. CL: Fri. Open 10.30—5. including Sun. SIZE: Medium. *STOCK: General small items, £5—£25; furniture, jewellery, from £5, all pre-1930.* LOC: Opposite Guy Fawkes Cottage. PARK: Easy. TEL: Rugby (0788) 817147. SER: Valuations.

HENLEY-IN-ARDEN (056 42)

Arden Gallery
(G.B. Horton.) Est. 1963. CL: Sat. p.m. Open 12—6. SIZE: Medium. *STOCK: Oil paintings, Victorian, £20—£1,000; watercolours, all periods, to £400; portrait miniatures.* LOC: A34. PARK: Easy. TEL: 2520. SER: Valuations; restorations (paintings). VAT: Spec.

Colmore Galleries Ltd
52 High St. Open 11—5.30. *STOCK: Pictures, 19th—20th C.* TEL: 2938. SER: Valuations; restorations; framing.

IS YOUR ENTRY CORRECT?
If there is even the slightest inaccuracy in your entry, *please* let us know before 1st January 1987.
GUIDE TO THE
ANTIQUE SHOPS OF BRITAIN
5 Church Street, Woodbridge, Suffolk.

Henley-in-Arden continued

Ferneyhough BADA LAPADA

Brook House, Beaudesert. (M.H. and A.R. Ferneyhough.) Est. 1940. SIZE: Large. *STOCK: Period furniture and works of art.* Not stocked: Weapons. LOC: ½ mile north from Henley-in-Arden towards Birmingham on A34. PARK: Easy. TEL: 2451. VAT: Spec.

Lacy Gallery

56 High St. CL: Sat. and Wed. a.m. Open 10—1 and 2—5.30. *STOCK: Period frames; sporting and decorative paintings, watercolours and prints, 18th—20th C.* TEL: 3073.

Jasper Marsh BADA

3 High St. (J.B. and P.R.J. Marsh.) Est. 1967. Open 10—5.30, Sun. 2.15—5.30. *STOCK: English furniture, Georgian, oak and mahogany, 17th to early 19th C, English and Oriental porcelain, Chinoiserie and Oriental art.* TEL: 2088. VAT: Spec.

KINETON (0926)

Chestnuts Antiques

Southam St. (Mrs. J.C. Wiglesworth.) Resident. Est. 1972. Open Mon., Wed., and Fri. 10—5, or by appointment. SIZE: Small. *STOCK: Useful and decorative furniture, silver and plate, porcelain, glass, linen, collectors' items, tiles.* LOC: Next to church. PARK: Easy. TEL: 640574.

LAPWORTH (056 43)

G. Buxton Gooding — Lapworth Clocks

160 Station Lane. Est. 1930. Open 9—5 by appointment. *STOCK: Longcase clocks.* TEL: 3243. SER: Valuations; restorations.

LEAMINGTON SPA (0926)

Antiques and Heirlooms

2 Abbott St. (A. Jackson.) Open 9.30—5.30. *STOCK: Stripped pine.* TEL: 832000. SER: Stripping (pine).

Charltons Antiques

5 Park St. (W. and F. Charlton.) Est. 1956. CL: Thurs. and Sun., and Mon. a.m. Open 10—5. SIZE: Small. *STOCK: General antiques, Victoriana.* TEL: 21026.

Hague Antiques

2 Regent St. (J. Hague.) Est. 1967. Open 9.30—1 and 2—5. SIZE: Medium. *STOCK: Furniture, copper and brass, dolls, unstripped pine.* LOC: One of the main roads which cross the Parade. PARK: Easy. TEL: 37236. VAT: Stan/Spec.

David Hooper Antiques

20 Regent St. Open 9—6. *STOCK: General antiques.* TEL: 29679.

Leamington Spa continued

The Little Shop

2 Warwick St. (P. Powell.) Est. 1967. CL: Mon. Open 10.30—5. SIZE: Small. *STOCK: General antiques, Victoriana, bric-a-brac.* TEL: Home — 23701. SER: Buys at auction.

Spa Antiques

1a Beaconsfield St. West. (A. Jackson.) Open 10—6. *STOCK: Stripped pine.* TEL: 28107. SER: Pine stripping.

Trading Post

39 Chandos St. (B. Morris.) Est. 1949. CL: Thurs. p.m. Open 10—12 and 2—4. *STOCK: Small general antiques, Victorian jewellery.* TEL: 21857.

Percy F. Wale Ltd.

32 and 34 Regent St. (B.A., P.G. and G.S. Barton.) Est. 1918. Open 9—1 and 2—6, Sat. 9—6. SIZE: Large. *STOCK: Furniture, £500—£6,000; clocks, £1,000—£3,000; silver, £250—£3,000, all 1780—1920.* LOC: Regent St. crosses main Parade in centre of town, shop situated at Western end. PARK: Easy. TEL: 21288. SER: Restorations (upholstery, furniture). VAT: Stan/Spec.

Windsor Street Antique Centre

Open 9—5.30. *STOCK: Pine and general antiques.* TEL: 22927.

NEWBOLD-ON-STOUR

B. and C. Antiques

Stratford Rd. (B. and C. Underwood.) Est. 1983. Open 10—6. SIZE: Small. *STOCK: Furniture, £150—£2,000; porcelain, copper and brass, £25—£300; all 18th—19th C.* LOC: A34. PARK: Easy. TEL: Alderminster (078 987) 566; home — same.

NUNEATON (0203)

Nuneaton Antiques Trade Only

Staffa House, 47 Princess St. (R.J. Clarke.) Resident. Est. 1967. SIZE: Large. *STOCK: 17th—20th C, furniture, clocks, paintings and general antiques.* TEL: 340575. VAT: Stan/Spec.

Vivian Antiques

32 Coton Rd. (C. Vivian.) Est. 1973. CL: Thurs. Open 10—5, Sat. 10—1 or by appointment. SIZE: Medium. *STOCK: Furniture, 18th—19th C; shipping goods.* LOC: A444. PARK: Easy. TEL: 381945; home — 346795. SER: Restorations (furniture).

PAILTON, Nr. Rugby

Burton Fine Art

Midsummer Cottage, Rugby Rd. Open by appointment. *STOCK; Oil paintings and watercolours, 19th—20th C.* TEL: Rugby (0788) 833191. SER: Restorations (oil paintings); framing; mounting.

PRIORS MARSTON, Nr. Rugby

Daneby House Antiques
Daneby House. (Daneby Antiques Ltd.) Est. 1965. CL: Mon. and Tues. Open 9—6, or by appointment. SIZE: Small. STOCK: Furniture, Queen Anne to Victorian, £40—£1,000; china, glass, £2—£50; metalware, silver, £2—£100; all Georgian to Victorian. LOC: 6 miles from Daventry. PARK: Easy. TEL: Byfield (0327) 60347. SER: Buys at auction.

RUGBY (0788)

Antiques Etc.
22 Railway Terrace. CL: Tues., and Wed. Open 10—5. There are 18 stalls at this centre selling a wide range of general antiques, small items and furniture, £1—£1,000. PARK: Easy.

Linnets Nest Antiques
50 Church St. (Mrs. L. Windsor.) Est. 1974. CL: Wed. and Sun., except by appointment. SIZE: Medium. STOCK: Edwardian and Victorian furniture, pre-1930, shipping goods, stripped pine, 18th C country furniture, jewellery. TEL: 61393; evenings — 535701. VAT: Stan/Spec.

SHIPSTON-ON-STOUR (0608)

Birmingham House Antiques
8 Church St. (J. and V. Bolton.) Est. 1972. Open 9—5.30 or by appointment. STOCK: Period and Victorian furniture, especially country woods. TEL: 62037 or Tysoe (029 588) 439.

Fine-Lines (Fine Art)
The Old Rectory at 31 Sheep St. (L.W. and R.M. Guthrie.) Est. 1975. By appointment only. SIZE: Medium. STOCK: British watercolours, 1850—1950, £100—£5,000. LOC: On main one-way street. PARK: Easy. TEL: 62323; home — same. SER: Restorations; cleaning; framing; buys at auction (paintings, watercolours and drawings). VAT: Spec.

'Time in Hand'
11 Church St. (F.R. Bennett.) Open 9.30—1 and 2—5.30 or by appointment. SIZE: Medium. STOCK: Longcase and wall clocks, barometers. PARK: Town square. TEL: 62578. SER: Restoration (clocks, watches, barometers and mechanical instruments).

Henry Wigington and Partners
22 New St. Est. 1908. CL: Sun. except by appointment. Open 10—6. SIZE: Medium. STOCK: Furniture and oil paintings. LOC: A34. PARK: 50yds. north of shop. TEL: 61205. SER: Restorations (oil paintings). VAT: Spec.

STRATFORD-UPON-AVON (0789)

Abode
Shrieve's House, 40 Sheep St. (Mrs. A Bannister.) Est. 1975. Open 9—5.30. SIZE: Large. STOCK: Furniture, including pine, 19th C, £100—£500; interior design items, curtains and wallpapers. LOC: Town centre. TEL: 68755. SER: Valuations; restorations (recaning, re-rushing, re-upholstery, stripping and polishing); stencilling, murals; buys at auction (furniture). FAIRS: Decorex International (Interior Design). VAT: Stan.

The Antique Arcade
Sheep St. (D. Chambers.) Est. 1979. CL: Mon. Open 10.30—5.30. There are ten dealers in this arcade selling jewellery, furniture, Oriental items, guns, art nouveau. TEL: 297249.

Antique Gifts
29 Meer St. (M.C. Smith and J.M. Ibbitson). Est. 1972. Open 10—6 including some Sun. SIZE: Small. STOCK: Silver, jewellery, porcelain, furniture, art deco, art nouveau. LOC: Town centre 50 yards from Shakespeare's birthplace. PARK: Easy. TEL: 293522; home — same. SER: Restorations (furniture, jewellery, porcelain); buys at auction.

Arbour Antiques Ltd. BADA
Poet's Arbour, Sheep St. (R.J. Wigington.) Est. 1952. Open 9—6, Sat. by appointment. STOCK: Arms, armour. LOC: From town centre towards Theatre and River, behind Cobweb Cafe through archway at right. PARK: Easy. TEL: 293453. VAT: Spec.

Arden Antiques
7 Greenhill St. Est. 1972. CL: Thurs. Open 9.30—5. SIZE: Medium. STOCK: Copper, brass, Victoriana; small furniture, 18th—19th C. LOC: Near traffic lights. PARK: Nearby. TEL: 67067.

Jean A. Bateman LAPADA
41 Sheep St. Open 9.30—5.30. STOCK: Victorian and Georgian jewellery, objets d'art and vertu, including scent bottles and fans. TEL: 298494. SER: Valuations. VAT: Stan/Spec.

Bow Cottage Antiques
Antique Arcade, 4 Sheep St. (R. Harvey-Morgan.) Open 10.30—5.30. STOCK: English porcelain 18th—19th C, £5—£200; glass and English silver, 18th—20th C, £5—£150+; oil paintings, watercolours; engravings; maps; general antiques, small furniture. TEL: 297249. Messages can be left at 67302 or 205883. SER: Jewellery and silver repairs. VAT: Stan.

Burman Antiques
37 Sheep St. (J. and J. Burman Holtom.) Est. 1973. SIZE: Medium. STOCK: Furniture, £200—£4,000; pictures, prints, maps, £50—£3,000; silver, porcelain, brass and copper, £50—£500; all 18th and 19th C. LOC: Near Shakespeare Memorial Theatre. PARK: Easy. TEL: 293917/295164. SER: Restorations (furniture, porcelain, silver). VAT: Spec.

Stratford-upon-Avon continued

Robert Garrett Antiques
John St. (Robert Garrett (Auctioneers) Ltd.) Est. 1883. Open 9.30—5, Thurs. 9.30—1. SIZE: Large. *STOCK: Furniture, 1600—1900, £200—£5,000.* LOC: Town centre, 50 yards from bus depot. PARK: Own. TEL: 292795. SER: Valuations; restorations (furniture). VAT: Stan/Spec.

Lace
The Courtyard. Ely St. (M. Evans.) Open 10—5.30. *STOCK: Victorian whites, linen, textiles and lace.* TEL: 67776.

La-di-da
7 Union St. (P.M. Barber.) Open 9—1 and 2—5, Sun. by appointment. *STOCK: Stripped pine, £5—£500; architectural items, from £10; both Georgian and Victorian; brass, brass and iron beds, Victorian, £75—£750; period kitchens.* TEL: 67521. SER: Restorations (pine); interior design. VAT: Spec.

Derek R. Lord
1 Wood St. Est. 1959. Open Mon. and Wed. 9.30—5 or by appointment. *STOCK: Weapons, 16th to mid-19th C, £50—£10,000.* LOC: Off Bridge St. PARK: Adjacent. TEL: 297509. SER: Valuations; restorations; buys at auction. FAIRS: All major arms. VAT: Spec.

The Ruskin Gallery Ltd.
11 Chapel St. (Mrs. C. Thomson.) Est. 1940. CL: Thurs. p.m. Open 10—5. *STOCK: Oil paintings, watercolours, 18th—19th C.* TEL: 67940.

Squirrel Antiques
Shop 4, Court Yard, Ely St. Est. 1938. *STOCK: Porcelain, pottery, silver, plate, jewellery, Victorian table linen, small furniture.* TEL: (021) 747 4494. SER: Buys at auction.

Stratford Antique Centre
Ely St. (N. Sims.) Open 10—5.30 every day. There are 60 dealers at this market selling *general antiques.* TEL: 204180.

Robert Vaughan
20 Chapel St. (R. and C.M. Vaughan.) ABA. Est. 1953. Open 9.30—6. SIZE: Medium. *STOCK: Antiquarian and out-of-print books, maps and prints.* LOC: Town centre. PARK: Easy. TEL: 205312. SER: Valuations; buys at auction (books). VAT: Stan.

James Wigington
'Winchester 73', 276 Alcester Rd. Open by appointment. *STOCK: Fishing tackle, 1760—1960; firearms, general antiques.* TEL: 293881.

STUDLEY   (052 785)
Prospect Antiques
Chester House, Alcester Rd. (R.T. Felix.) CL: Sat. p.m. Open 10—5. SIZE: Large. *STOCK: General furniture, porcelain, glass, bronzes, Oriental items.* LOC: A435. PARK: Easy. TEL: 2494. VAT: Stan/Spec.

TANWORTH-IN-ARDEN   (056 44)
Peter Montagu-Williams
Gilberts Green. Open daily or by appointment. *STOCK: Fine paintings, furniture and ornaments for house and garden.* TEL: 2314.

WARWICK   (0926)
Duncan M. Allsop
26 Smith St. ABA. Est. 1965. Open 9.30—5.30. SIZE: Medium. *STOCK: Antiquarian and modern books, topographical prints and maps.* LOC: 50 yards east of Eastgate. PARK: Nearby. TEL: 493266. FAIRS: ABA London.

Apollo Antiques Ltd.   LAPADA
62 West St. (R.H. Mynott.) Est. 1968. CL: Sat. Open 9.30—5.30. SIZE: Large and warehouse. *STOCK: Period, Victorian, Continental and decorative furniture, bronzes, Oriental furniture, works of art, shipping goods.* PARK Easy. TEL: 494746 (24 hr. answering service.) SER: Valuations; restorations; packing and shipping. VAT: Stan/Spec.

H.H. Bray Ltd.   LAPADA
9 Jury St. (B. and I. Harper.) Est. 1929. Open 9.30—5.30. *STOCK: Silver, jewellery, Sheffield plate.* LOC: On main Stratford to Warwick road. PARK: Easy. TEL: 492791. SER: Valuations. VAT: Stan/Spec.

Castle Antiques — Warwick's Art Deco Shop
1 Mill St. (H. and P. Watson.) Resident. Est. 1980. CL: Thurs. Open 10—6 including Sun. SIZE: Medium. *STOCK: Pottery, furniture, lamps, light fittings, jewellery, figurines, 1920—1940, £5—£500.* Not stocked: Militaria, coins, stamps. LOC: A45, opposite gatehouse of Warwick Castle. PARK: Nearby. TEL: 498068. SER: Finder service. FAIRS: Nottingham art deco, Alexandra Palace.

Devon House Clocks   *Trade Only*
Devon House, 4 Charles St. (D.J. Davies.) Resident. Open at any time but appointment preferred. *STOCK: Clocks, mainly longcase, Vienna, dial, some bracket, from 17th, £50—£3,000.* LOC: Off Emscote Rd. PARK: Easy. TEL. 401476; home — same. SER: Valuations (clocks). VAT: Mainly Spec.

Emscote Antiques
148 Emscote Rd. Open 9—5.30. *STOCK: General antiques.* TEL: 491291.

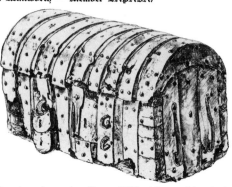
Warwick continued

Goodsons (Ragamuffin) Antiques
19 West Rock, Birmingham Rd. (R. and C. Goodson). Est. 1971. Open 9—6. *STOCK: Furniture, silver, jewellery, bric-a-brac.* TEL: 492079 and 401801.

Tim Harrison
Trade Only
36 Market St. Est. 1974. CL: Sat. and Sun., except by appointment. SIZE: Large. *STOCK: Mahogany and oak shipping furniture.* TEL: 491400. VAT: Stan.

Russell Lane Antiques
8 High St. (R.G.H. Lane.) Open 10.30—5. *STOCK: Jewellery and silver.* TEL: 494494.

Patrick and Gilliam Morley LAPADA
8 Jury St. Est. 1968. CL: Sat. p.m. *STOCK: Fine period furniture, carvings, decorative and unusual items.* Not stocked: Reproductions. LOC: Almost opp. Lord Leicester Hotel in High St. PARK: Own at rear or opposite. TEL: 492 963; home — Kenilworth (0926) 54191. VAT: Stan/Spec.

The Old Pine Seller
35 Smith St. (K. and J. Platt.) Open 9.30—6, Sun. by appointment. *STOCK: Early stripped pine and oak, advertising signs, general kitchen antiques.* TEL: 492151. SER: Stripping, polishing, reedwork.

Warwick continued

Martin Payne Antiques
30 Brook St. Est. 1971. CL: Thurs. p.m. Open 10—1 and 2—5.30. SIZE: Small. *STOCK: Silver, 18th—19th C, £50—£2,000.* LOC: Between High St. and Market Pl. PARK: Easy. TEL: 494948; home — (0608) 61282. SER: Valuations; restorations (silver repairs and re-plating); buys at auction (silver). VAT: Stan/Spec.

James Reeve
at Quinneys of Warwick, 9 Church St. Est. 1865. CL: Sat. p.m. Open 9—5.30. *STOCK: Furniture, mahogany, oak, and rosewood, 17th—18th C, £30—£4,000; furniture, 19th C, £20—£2,000; glass, copper, brass, pewter, china.* TEL: 498113. VAT: Stan/Spec.

Saltisford Pine Antiques
33 The Saltisford. (Mr. and Mrs. I. Taylor.) Est. 1961. Open 9—6.30 every day. *STOCK: General antiques, mainly pine.* TEL: 491885. SER: Stripping (pine).

A.T. Silvester and Son Ltd.
LAPADA
2/4 High St. (S.K., Y.M. and C.A. Silvester.) Est. 1924. Open 9—1 and 2—5.30. SIZE: Large. *STOCK: Furniture, 18th C, £10—£1,000; silver, china, glass, jewellery and unusual items, 18th—19th C.* LOC: Centre of main street. PARK: Easy. TEL: 492972. VAT: Stan/Spec.

Warwick continued

Smith St. Antique Centre
7 Smith St. (E. Brook and W. Mechilli.) Est. 1971. Open 10—5.30. SIZE: Large. LOC: Corner position, Smith St. is an extension of High St. PARK: Easy and at rear. TEL: 497864; home — Leamington Spa (0926) 882060. VAT: Stan/Spec. Below are listed the dealers at this centre:

Erol Brook
Silver and plate, decanters, curios, barometers.
Chaplefield Antiques
Silver, jewellery, glassware.
Eleanor Antiques
(Mrs. E.W.E. Creed.) *Porcelain and glass.*
Joe Hart
Small furniture, samplers and prints.
Chris James
Military medals, furniture, clocks and silver.
Walter Mechilli
Silver and plate, decanters, porcelain.
Janice Paull
Mason ironstone, glass and porcelain.
Eunice Rendell
Silver, jewellery and glass.
Sandy Price Antiques
Small furniture, jewellery and silver.
Joyce Smith
Porcelain, silver, jewellery, small furniture.
Don Spencer
Furniture, clocks, barometers and jewellery.
Turtons Antiques
Jewellery, silver, gold.
Winston Yeates
Silver and plate, jewellery.

Swan Lane Antiques (Antique Centre)
28 Swan St. (J. Jones.) Est. 1983. Open 10—5.30. SIZE: Medium. There are several dealers at this centre selling *furniture, clocks, barometers, porcelain, glass, 18th—19th C, £5—£500; jewellery, silver, plate, £20—£500; crested china, linen, £5—£200, all 19th C; carpets, 20th C, £50—£1,000.* LOC: Near Market Sq. PARK: Easy at rear. TEL: 400040; home — Leamington Spa (0926) 28622. SER: Valuations; restorations; buys at auction. VAT: Stan.

The Tao Antiques
66a Smith St. (Mrs. J. Black.) Open 10—6. *STOCK: General antiques.* TEL: 495029.

Jeremy Venables Antiques *Trade Only*
56 West St. Est. 1977. Open 9—1.30 and 2.30—6, Sat. and Sun. by appointment. SIZE: Large and warehouse. *STOCK: Furniture for Italy, New Zealand and Australia.* LOC: A46. PARK: Easy. TEL: 490025; home — same. SER: Restorations. VAT: Stan.

Warwick continued

Vintage Antique Market
36 Market Place. (R. Thompson.) Est. 1977. Open 10—5.30. Gallery selling *watercolours 1880—1920* and 14 stands selling a wide range of goods including *furniture, pine, clocks, porcelain, bric-a-brac, jewellery.* TEL: 491527.

The Warwick Antique Centre
20—22 High St. Open 6 days a week. There are approximately 30 dealers at this market offering *a wide variety of general antiques.* TEL: 495704/494948/491382.

Warwick Antiques
16—18 High St. (M. Morrison.) Est. 1969. CL: Sat. p.m. Open 9—5.30. SIZE: Large and warehouses. *STOCK: Furniture, mahogany, oak, Chinese; metalware, copper, brass, pewter, glass, china, bygones, curios, statuary, garden furniture, shipping goods.* LOC: Midway between E. and W. Gate clock towers. PARK: At rear. TEL: 492482. SER: Restorations (furniture). VAT: Stan/Spec.

Warwick Desks
20 West Rock. (Mrs. C. Mynott.) Est. 1977. Open 9.30—1 and 2—6, Sat. 9.30—1. SIZE: Small. *STOCK: Office and study furniture.* LOC: Off Birmingham Rd. PARK: Easy. TEL: 494666. VAT. Stan/Spec.

West Midlands

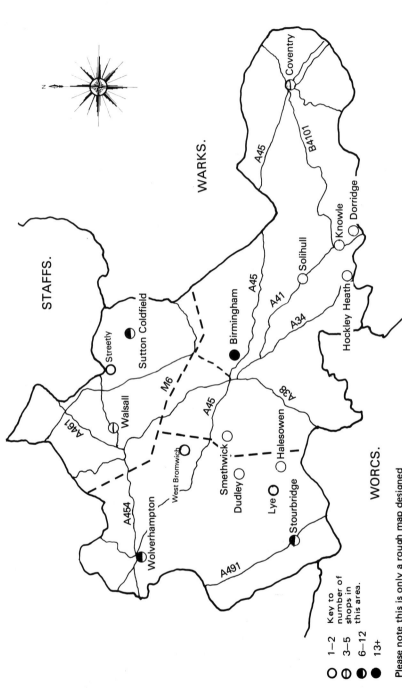

STAFFS.

WARKS.

WORCS.

Coventry

A45

B4101

Dorridge

Knowle

Solihull

Hockley Heath

A45

A41

A34

Birmingham

A38

Sutton Coldfield

Streetly

M6

Walsall

A45

A461

Smethwick

Halesowen

West Bromwich

Dudley

Lye

Stourbridge

Wolverhampton

A454

A491

Key to
number of
shops in
this area.

○ 1–2

◑ 3–5

● 6–12

● 13+

Please note this is only a rough map designed
to show dealers the number of shops in the
various towns, and is not necessarily totally
accurate.

BIRMINGHAM (021)

H. Abraham
246 Witton Rd. Open 11—5.30, Sat. 9.30—5. STOCK: General antiques. TEL: 523 8511.

Ashleigh House Antiques
Ashleigh House, 5 Westbourne Rd. (P. and R. Hodgson). Est. 1974. Open by appointment. SIZE: Large. STOCK: Furniture, £200— £5,000; clocks, £300—£2,000; oils and watercolours, £75—£1,500; objets d'art, £75—£2,000, all 1700—1880. LOC: From 5 ways Edgbaston take Calthorpe Rd. and bear right into Westbourne Rd., premises 150 yards on left. PARK: Easy. TEL: 454 6283; home — same. SER: Valuations; restorations (furniture and paintings); buys at auction. FAIRS: Most dateline, Midlands area. VAT: Stan/Spec.

Birmingham Antique Centre
141 Bromsgrove St. (Weller and Dufty Ltd.) Est. 1966. Open every Thurs. from 9 a.m., other times by appointment.There are about 30 dealers offering a wide range of general antiques. LOC: On the west side of city, off Bristol Rd. PARK: Meters; car park 200yds. TEL: 692 1414; stallholders — 622 2145. VAT: Stan/Spec.

Chesterfield Antiques
181 Gravelly Lane. (A.I. Beddard.) Est. 1977. Open 10—5.30. CL: Wed. STOCK: General antiques. TEL: 373 3876.

The City of Birmingham Antique Market
St. Martins Market, Edgbaston St. (Antique Forum (Birmingham) Ltd.) Est. 1976. There are approximately 300 dealers at this market which is open Mon. 7—2. SIZE: Large. STOCK: General antiques, art deco, 5p—£5,000. LOC: Adjacent to Bull Ring. PARK: Multi-storey nearby. TEL: (01) 624 3214. SER: Valuations.

Peter Clark Antiques   LAPADA
36 St. Mary's Row, Moseley. Open 9—5.30. SIZE: Small. STOCK: Furniture, mid-17th C to early 20th C, £175—£2,500; silver, early 19th C to early 20th C, £25—£100. LOC: Centre of Moseley. PARK: At rear. TEL: 449 8245. SER: Valuations; restorations (furniture). VAT: Stan/Spec.

Collecting World/Rings and Things
743 Bristol Rd., Selly Oak. (T. and J.B. Vincent). Est. 1975. Open 9.30—5.30. SIZE: Small and large. STOCK: Militaria, collectables, jewellery, 20th C, £5—£25. PARK: 200yds. TEL: 471 1645. SER: Valuations.

Birmingham continued

The Collectors Shop
63 Station St. (J. and T. Middleton.) Est. 1967. CL: Wed. p.m. Open 9—5.30. SIZE: Small. STOCK: Coins, militaria, secondhand jewellery, silver, small items. LOC: One minute from New St. Station. PARK: Nearby. TEL: 643 0571. SER: Valuations; buys at auction (coins). FAIRS: Most major coin. VAT: Stan/Spec.

R. Collyer
185 New Rd., Rubery. Open 9—5.30. STOCK: Clocks including longcase, watches, barometers, secondhand jewellery. LOC: 1 mile from Lydiate Ash roundabout. TEL: 453 2332. SER: Valuations; restorations.

Colmore Galleries Ltd.
5 Livery St. Est. 1954. Open 10—5.30, Sat. 10—1. STOCK: Paintings. TEL: 236 4284. SER: Valuations; restorations; framing. VAT: Stan/Spec.

Dalton Street Antiques
66 Dalton St. (M.L. Chandler.) Open 10.30—6. STOCK: General antiques, stripped pine, satinwood, fireplaces, beds, architectural items. TEL: 236 2479.

Edgbaston Gallery
42 Islington Row, Five Ways, Edgbaston. (I. Bethell.) Est. 1976. CL: Sat. and Sun. except by appointment. Open 12.30—5.30. SIZE: Medium. STOCK: Oil paintings and watercolours, £50—£1,000; small furniture, clocks, collectors' items; all 19th C. LOC: Junction of Islington Row and Frederick Rd. PARK: In Frederick Rd. TEL: 454 4244; home — 459 3568. SER: Valuations; restorations; framing; buys at auction (paintings).

Maurice Fellows
39 Broad St, Est. 1965. CL: Sat. Open 9—3. SIZE: Small. STOCK: General antiques, porcelain and silver. LOC: City centre. PARK: Easy. TEL: 643 5067. SER: Valuations; restorations.

Fine Pine
75 Mason Rd., Erdington. (H. Duignan.) Open 8.30—5.30. STOCK: Pine and satin walnut furniture, iron tiled fireplaces and surrounds, general antiques. TEL: 373 6321.

Format of Birmingham Ltd
269 Broad St. (P. Ireland, G. Charman and D. Vice.) Est. 1971. Open 10—5. STOCK: Coins, medals. PARK: Opposite. VAT: Stan/Spec.

Garratts Antiques
35 Stephenson St. Est. 1958. STOCK: Jewellery. TEL: 643 9507.

Gate Antiques
32 High St., Saltley. (R.G. Wyatt.) Est. 1975. Open 10—5.30. SIZE: Medium. STOCK: Pine, 19th C, £25—£200; oak, 19th—20th C, £5—£100. LOC: Near Gate public house. PARK: Easy. TEL: Home — Tamworth (0827) 285688.

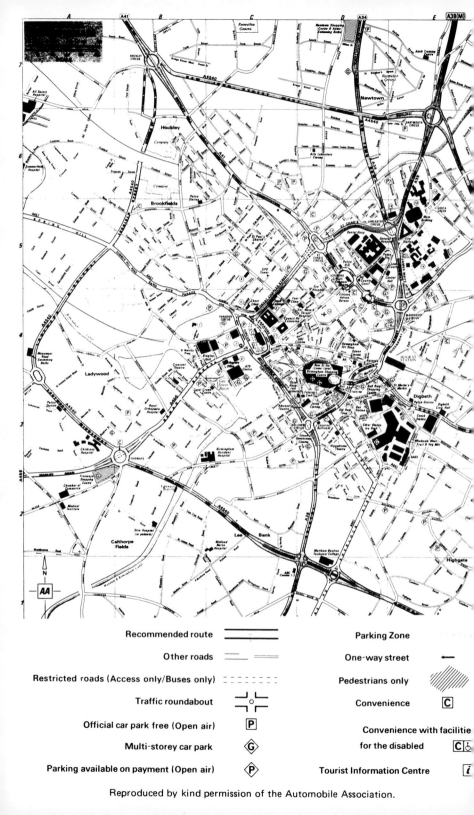

Legend

Recommended route	───────
Other roads	═ ═ ═
Restricted roads (Access only/Buses only)	─ ─ ─ ─ ─ ─ ─
Traffic roundabout	⌐○⌐
Official car park free (Open air)	P
Multi-storey car park	Ⓖ
Parking available on payment (Open air)	Ⓟ
Parking Zone	
One-way street	←
Pedestrians only	▨
Convenience	C
Convenience with facilities for the disabled	C &
Tourist Information Centre	i

Reproduced by kind permission of the Automobile Association.

BOB HARRIS & SONS Antiques

2071 Coventry Road, Sheldon, Birmingham 26
Tel. 021-743 2259

Showrooms and Warehouse

Antiques and Victoriana, General Trade and Shipping Goods

Birmingham continued

Genesis Antiques
222 Alcester Rd., Moseley. (M.K. Davis and C.A. Booth.) Est: 1977. CL: Mon. and Wed. Open 11—6. SIZE: Small. *STOCK: Furniture — walnut, pine, bamboo, satin walnut, oak and mahogany, Victorian and Edwardian, £35—£500; period clothing, accessories and furs, 1890—1950, £5—£50; art deco, prints and mirrors, 1880—1930, £5—£100; brass and iron beds, 1880—1920, £100—£350. LOC: At Moseley village turn right along Alcester Rd. (A435), shop 150 yards from village on left. PARK: Easy. TEL: 449 8820; home — same.*

Christopher Gordon Antiques
133 School Rd., Moseley. Est. 1974. CL: Wed. Open 10—5.30. *STOCK: Architectural and decorative items, £5—£500; early shop and pub fixtures and fittings; early advertising items, signs and mirrors, all 19th—20th C; pine, stained glass, fireplaces. LOC: 5 mins. from Moseley Village. PARK: Easy. TEL: 444 4644. SER: Courier.*

Perry Greaves Ltd.
1 Corporation St. (S. Preston.) Open 9—5.30. *STOCK: English silver and Old Sheffield plate, jewellery. TEL: 643 9305. VAT: Stan.*

Harborne Place Antiques
22—24 Northfield Rd., Harborne. CL: Sun. except by appointment. Open 9.30—5.30. *STOCK: Period and Victorian furniture, shipping goods and general antiques. TEL: 427 5788. SER: Restorations; re-upholstery; buys at auction. VAT: Stan/Spec.*

Birmingham continued

Bob Harris and Sons, Antiques   LAPADA
2071 Coventry Rd., Sheldon. (R.E. Harris.) Est. 1953. Resident. CL: Sun. except by appointment. Open 9—6. *STOCK: 18th—19th C furniture and general antiques. TEL: 743 2259. VAT: Stan/Spec.*

John Hubbard Antiques   LAPADA
224—226 Court Oak Rd., Harborne. Est. 1968. Open 9—6. SIZE: Medium. *STOCK: Furniture, 17th—19th C, £50—£5,000; paintings £50—£2,000. LOC: 3 miles from city centre. PARK: Easy. TEL: 426 1694. SER: Valuations; restorations; leather linings. VAT: Stan/Spec.*

James Architectural Antiques
15 Alcester Rd., Moseley. (P. and D. James.) Est. 1969. Open 1—6, mornings by appointment. SIZE: Medium. *STOCK: Fireplace and surrounds, 18th—19th C, £35—£300; stained glass, panels, 19th C, £10—£100; general architectural items, some 18th but mainly 19th C, to £400. LOC: Main Alcester road ½ mile from Moseley village. PARK: Easy. TEL: 449 6807; home — 444 4628. SER: Valuations; restorations (stripping, metal polishing); buys at auction (decorative and architectural items).*

Johnson Brothers (Treasure Chest Ltd.)
1267/69 Pershore Rd., Stirchley. Est. 1960. Open 8.30—6. *STOCK: General antiques, shipping furniture. TEL: 458 3705/459 4587.*

Jomarc Pianos U.K.
Unit 302, Jubilee Trades Centre, Pershore St. (P. Hoskinson.) Open by appointment. *STOCK: Pianos and furniture. TEL: 354 9078/622 1315.*

Birmingham continued

Kestrel House Antiques
72 Gravelly Hill North, Erdington. (E.C. Jones.) Est. 1865. Open 9—6. SIZE: Large. *STOCK: Oil paintings of all schools, 19th C; shipping furniture.* TEL: 373 2375. SER: Cleaning, relining and restoration for trade; framing. VAT: Stan.

G. and J. Lydiard
1571 Stratford Rd., Hall Green. CL: Wed. Open 10—5.30. *STOCK: Furniture, French clocks, watercolours, general antiques.* LOC: By the Robin Hood Parade and roundabout. PARK: Easy. TEL: 745 4354.

Manor Pine and Antiques
1616 Pershore Rd., Stirchley. Est. 1978. Open 9—5. SIZE: Medium. *STOCK: Stripped pine and satin walnut furniture, £5—£250.* PARK: Easy. TEL: 458 6982. SER: Stripping.

March Medals
22 St. Martins Place, off Broad St. (M.A. March.) Est. 1975. Open 10—4.30, Sat. 10—2, Sun. 10.30—1. SIZE: Small. *STOCK: Orders, decorations, campaign medals, militaria and military books.* LOC: 3rd road right from Hall of Memory, Broad St. PARK: Easy. TEL: 643 9990; home — 373 2020. SER: Valuations; buys at auction (medals and decorations). VAT: Stan/Spec.

Maxwells Book Shop
22 Shaftmoor Lane, Acocks Green. (M.L. and C.M. Prickett.) Open 10.30—5. *STOCK: Antiquarian and second-hand books.* TEL: 706 8379

Moseley Antiques
Unit 5 Woodbridge Rd., Moseley. (Mrs. H. Benstead.) Est. 1972. CL: Wed. Open 10—6. *STOCK: Furniture and clocks.* TEL: 449 6186.

The Moseley Gallery
Woodbridge Rd., Moseley. (M. Ashton and D. Griffiths.) Est. 1985. CL: Mon. Open 10—6, Sat. 9—5. *STOCK: Watercolours, 18th—20th C, £100—£2,000+.* LOC: Moseley Village, A435. PARK: Easy. TEL: 449 9456. SER: Valuations; restorations; buys at auction.

Nathan and Co. (Birmingham) Ltd.
31 Corporation St. Est. 1857. Open 9—5. SIZE: Medium. *STOCK: Silver and jewellery, £35—£25,000.* LOC: A31. PARK: New St. Station. TEL: 643 5225. SER: Valuations; restorations (silver and jewellery); buys at auction. FAIRS: British International (Birmingham). VAT: Stan/Spec.

Birmingham continued

The Old Clock Shop
32 Stephenson St. (M.L. and S.R. Durham.) Open 10.30—5. *STOCK: Clocks especially longcase, mantle and wall, £50—£1,000; scientific instruments, microscopes and sextants, £100—£1,000, all 18th—19th C; watches.* TEL: 632 4864. SER: Valuations; restorations (clocks). VAT: Stan/Spec.

Old Malt House
4 King Edwards Place, (off Broad St.) (G. Jones.) Open 9—5. TEL: 360 6603.

The Original Choice
1340 Stratford Rd., Hall Green. (J. Ellis.) Est. 1978. Open 11—6, warehouse Sat. 11—5. *STOCK: Architectural items, fireplaces, fenders, tiles, stained glass, mirrors and decorative items.* TEL: 778 3821; warehouse 778 5923.

Phoenix Pine and Antiques
634 Bristol Rd., Selly Oak. Est. 1967. Open 9.30—6 or by appointment. SIZE: Large. *STOCK: Stripped pine and satin walnut, £25—£500; general antiques.* LOC: A38, 4 miles south of city centre near university. PARK: Easy. TEL: 472 2399; home — 426 6090. SER: Restorations (door and furniture stripping).

Plumridge's   *Trade Only*
King Edward Place. (R.H. Plumridge.) Est. 1968. CL: Sat. Open 9—5. SIZE: Large. *STOCK: American and Continental shipping furniture, pianos.* LOC: Off Broad St., city centre. PARK: Easy. TEL: 643 5522; home — (0675) 70183. VAT: Stan.

S.R. Furnishing and Antiques
18 Stanley Rd., Oldbury. (S. Willder.) Est. 1975. *STOCK: General antiques.* TEL: 422 9788.

Stirchley Antiques
1257 Pershore Rd. (P. Boyce.) Est. 1970. Open Thur.—Sat. or by appointment. *STOCK: Period and decorative furnishings.* TEL: 459 2385.

J.T. Stirling
33 Clent Rd., Rubery. Open by appointment only. *STOCK: Antiquarian and rare books, fine prints.* TEL: 453 2238. SER: Catalogues.

Stratford House Antique Centre
Broad St. (M. Forman.) Est. 1954. CL: Fri. Open 9—5, Sat. 9—3, Sun. 10—1. SIZE: Large. There are 10 units are this centre. *STOCK: Furniture, £50—£500; general collectors' items, books, militaria, textiles, £50—£100; all 19th C.* PARK: At rear. TEL: 643 2057. VAT: Stan.

Birmingham continued

Stuart House Fine Art   LAPADA
123 Queens Park Rd., Harborne. Open 9—6.
SIZE: Small. *STOCK: Furniture, 17th to early
19th C, £100—£5,000; paintings, £200—
£2,000.* LOC: 3 miles from city centre. PARK:
Easy. TEL: 426 3300. SER: Valuations; restorations. VAT: Spec.

Treasure Trove
1852/4 Pershore Rd., Kingsnorton. CL: Wed.
p.m. Open 9.30—5.30. *STOCK: General
antiques, furniture and bric-a-brac.* PARK:
Easy. TEL: 458 2219. VAT: Stan.

The Twentieth Century Style
20 St. Martin's Place, Off Broad St. (R. Carter
and R. Butler.) Est. 1982. Open 11—5.30,
Sat. 10.30—5. SIZE: Small. *STOCK: Clothing
and accessories, 1900—1968, £5—£25.* LOC:
Next door to Stratford House Antiques. PARK:
Easy. TEL: 643 1267. SER: Hire for theatre,
television and film. VAT: Stan.

Victoria's Curios
287 Bearwood Rd., Bearwood, Warley. Open
9—5.30, Wed. 9—1. *STOCK: Small general
antiques including furniture.* TEL: 429 8661.

COVENTRY   (0203)

Barn Antiques
Binley Common Farm, Rugby Rd., Binley
Woods. (N. Green.) Open 7 days. *STOCK:
Stripped pine and satinwood, furniture and
bric-a-brac.* LOC: On A428. TEL: 453878 or
447628.

Memories Antiques
400A Stoney Stanton Rd. (R.D. Seymour.)
Est. 1964. CL: Wed. Open 10—4.30, Sat.
10—1. *STOCK: General antiques, especially
china; gold, silver and jewellery.* TEL: 687994.
SER: Buys at auction.

Milton Antiques   *Trade Only*
93 Dane Rd. (A.P. Ross.) Est. 1971. Open by
appointment. SIZE: Large. *STOCK: Furniture,
shipping goods.* Not stocked: Glass, china,
silver, pictures. LOC: Off A46. PARK: Easy.
TEL: 456285.

Spon End Antiques
115—116 Spon End. (Mrs. S. Halliday.)
*STOCK: General antiques, porcelain, glass,
crested and commemorative china, clothes,
lace, jewellery, textiles, postcards, prints.*
LOC: A4023, Knowle Rd. TEL: 28379.

Sports Programmes   *Postal Only*
P.O. Box 74, Chapel St. (A. Stanford.)
STOCK: Football programmes. TEL: 28672.

DORRIDGE, Nr. Solihull

Ashton Antiques
12 Arden Buildings, Station Rd. CL: Mon.
except by appointment. *STOCK: Furniture,
silver, pictures.* TEL: Knowle (05645) 3040.
SER: Restorations (furniture).

'Grange Antiques'
The Antiques Shop, 480 Station Rd. (T.
Pickering.) Est. 1950. Open 10—6. *STOCK:
General antiques, mahogany and oak furniture, silver and plate, jewellery, porcelain,
glassware, Staffordshire figures, oil paintings,
brass, copper, pewter, prints.* TEL: Knowle
(056 45) 3342.

DUDLEY   (0384)

Castle Antiques and Fine Art
2 Union St. Est. 1969. CL: Wed. Open 9—5.
*STOCK: Jewellery, porcelain, small collectors'
items.* Not stocked: Furniture. TEL: 52519.

HALESOWEN

Clent Books
Summer Hill. (I. Simpson.) Est. 1978. CL:
Wed. and Thurs. Open 10—4.30, Mon.
11—4.30, Sat. 9—5. SIZE: Small. *STOCK:
Antiquarian books, local history, history, topo-
graphy, £1—£100.* LOC: Town centre. PARK:
Opposite. TEL: (021) 550 0309; home —
Bewdley (0299) 401090. SER: Valuations.
FAIRS: Waverley Antique and Book (Organiser).

HOCKLEY HEATH, Nr. Solihull

Magpie House   *Trade Only*
2212 Stratford Rd. (D.P. Fair.) Est. 1958. CL:
Sat. except by appointment. SIZE: Medium.
STOCK: Shipping goods, £25—£700. LOC:
A34 to Stratford-on-Avon. PARK: Easy. TEL:
Lapworth (056 43) 2005. VAT: Stan/Spec.

KNOWLE   (056 45)

Chadwick Antiques
Chadwick End. (Mrs. P. Tibenham.) Resident.
Est. 1973. Open 10—5, also some Sun. SIZE:
Medium. *STOCK: Furniture, 18th—19th C;
collectors' items, general antiques.* Not
stocked: Oil paintings. LOC: A41. PARK:
Easy. TEL: Lapworth (056 43) 2096. SER:
Buys at auction.

IS YOUR ENTRY CORRECT?
If there is even the slightest
inaccuracy in your entry, *please* let us
know before 1st January 1987.
GUIDE TO THE
ANTIQUE SHOPS OF BRITAIN
5 Church Street, Woodbridge, Suffolk.

Knowle continued

Richard Lukeman Fine Art
1673-1675 High St. Est. 1980. Open 9.30—5.30, Sun. by appointment only. SIZE: Medium. *STOCK: Prints, drawings, water-colours and oil paintings, 19th C, £10—£2,000; furniture, including dry stripped pine, 18th C to Edwardian, £50—£1,500; porcelain, collectors' items, silver and jewellery, 19th C, £5—£1,000; garden ornaments.* LOC: Main Warwick/Birmingham road. PARK: Own and rear of premises. TEL: 4302. SER: Valuations; restorations (watercolours, oil paintings, drawings, prints and furniture), framing, hand- made English swept frames and washline mounts. VAT: Stan/Spec.

LYE   (4 fig. no.) (038 482)
                   (6 fig. no.) (0384)

The Lye Curios, Inc. Lye Antique Furnishings
17 Talbot St. (Mr. & Mrs. P. Smith.) Est. 1981. Open from 10 a.m. SIZE: Medium. *STOCK: Furniture, china, glass, clothing, from 1900, £5—£100.* LOC: Off High St. PARK: Easy. TEL: 7513; home — 7292. SER: Valuations.

Smithfield Antiques   *Mainly Export*
20 Stourbridge Rd. (R. Harling.) Open 9—5.30, other times by appointment. *STOCK: General antiques and shipping goods.* TEL: 7821.

SMETHWICK, Nr. Warley
Grannies Attic Antiques
                             Mainly Trade
437 Bearwood Rd. (B.A. Seymour.) Est. 1965. Open 10—5.30, Sat. 10—4.30 or by appointment to trade. SIZE: Medium. *STOCK: Dolls, oak, mahogany and walnut furniture, curios, art deco, Victorian and Edwardian clothes, porcelain, books, pictures, fans, toys, records, pre-1930, £5—£1,000.* LOC: Off Hagley Rd. PARK: Easy. TEL: (021) 429 4180; home — (021) 454 7507. SER: Valuations; buys at auction.

SOLIHULL
Geoffrey Hassall Antiques
20 New Rd. Est. 1972. CL: Mon. Open 9.30—1 and 2—5.30. SIZE: Small. *STOCK: Furniture, 18th—19th C.* Not stocked: Books, jewellery. PARK: Easy. LOC: Continuation of High St., past parish church. TEL: (021) 705 0068. SER: Restorations (furniture).

Renaissance
18 Marshall Lake Rd., Shirley. (S.K. Macrow.) M.G.M.C. Est. 1981. Open 9.30—6. SIZE: Small. *STOCK: General antiques.* LOC: Near Stratford Rd. TEL: (021) 745 5140. SER: Restorations (repairs, re-upholstery and polishing).

STOURBRIDGE   (0384)
Bridge Antiques
32A Market St. (D.P. and B. Deeley.) Est. 1976. Open Tues., Fri. and Sat. 10—5. SIZE: Small. *STOCK: General antiques, especially china — Prattware, Worcester, Doulton; small furniture, jewellery, glass and silver, £3—£1,000.* LOC: 1st right off ring road, 1st right into Market St. PARK: Nearby. TEL: 379495.

A turn of the century group where detail is at the half-way stage between realism and impressionism. From *Animals in Bronze* by Christopher Payne, published by the **Antique Collectors' Club**, 1986.

Thomas Coulborn & Sons

Vesey Manor Sutton Coldfield West Midlands B72 1QP
021 – 354 3974/3139

Antiques, Fine Arts, Fine Clocks, Silver and Works of Art

Fine George III mahogany inlaid sideboard of rare and unusual form and attractive mature colour and patination. Circa 1790. 5ft. 8ins.

Stourbridge continued

Curio Corner
32 Park St. (G.S. Pargeter.) CL: Thurs. Open 10—5. *STOCK: Jewellery and militaria.* TEL: 379652 or 394577.

D. and S. Antiques
33 High St., Amblecote. (D.R. and S.S. Waterfield.) Open 10—6. *STOCK: General antiques, especially glass.* PARK: Easy. TEL: 390586.

Falcon Antiques
210 Hagley Rd., Pedmore. (E. Jones.) Est. 1975. Open 10—5, or by appointment. *STOCK: Furniture, especially chairs, chaises, chests of drawers, brass, copper.* LOC: Main Hagley to Stourbridge Rd. PARK: Outside. TEL: 371603; home — 052 784 506.

Oldswinford Gallery
106 Hagley Rd., Oldswinford. (A.R. Harris.) Open 9.30—5. *STOCK: Oil paintings, water-colours and prints, 19th C.* TEL: 395577. SER: Restorations and framing.

Stourbridge continued

Robert Wilkes Antiques
2 Norton Rd. Est. 1867. Open Sat. 10—6. SIZE: Large. *STOCK: Furniture, shipping goods, bric-a-brac.* Not stocked: Weapons, coins. LOC: From M1/M5/M6, the Kidderminster to Birmingham rd. PARK: Easy. TEL: 393539. VAT: Stan.

STREETLY, Nr. Sutton Coldfield

Hardwick Antiques
Chester Rd. (R.J. Cassidy). CL: Wed. *STOCK: General antiques.* TEL: (021) 353 1489.

SUTTON COLDFIELD

Thomas Coulborn and Sons BADA
Vesey Manor, 64 Birmingham Rd. (P. Coulborn.) Est. 1939. Open 9—5.30. SIZE: Medium. *STOCK: General antiques, 1600—1830; English furniture, 17th—18th C; paintings and clocks.* Not stocked: 19th C bric-a-brac. LOC: From Birmingham A5127 through Erdington, premises on main road opposite cinema. PARK: Easy. TEL: (021) 354 3974 or (021) 354 3139. SER: Valuations; restorations (furniture and paintings); buys at auction. FAIRS: British International, Birmingham (Spring). VAT: Spec.

Sutton Coldfield continued

M. and A. Critchley Antiques
36b High St. Est. 1976. CL: Thurs. Open 9—5.30. *STOCK: General antiques and bric-a-brac.* TEL: (021) 355 1144 or (021) 329 2833.

Stancie Cutler Antique and Collectors Fair
Town Hall. Est. 1981. Open one Wed. monthly, usually 2nd, 11—8, trade 10—8. There are 70 stands at this fair offering *a wide variety of antiques from large furniture to thimbles, mostly pre-1940.* TEL: Home — Crewe (0270) 666802.

Driffold Gallery
78 Birmingham Rd. (D. Gilbert.) CL: Thurs. Open 10—6. *STOCK: Oil paintings, etchings and watercolours.* TEL: (021) 355 5433.

Gable End Fine Arts Ltd.
17 Belwell Lane, Four Oaks. Est. 1976. Open 10—6. *STOCK: General antiques, watercolours, porcelain, glass and books.* TEL: (021) 308 3773.

Ingestre Investment Antiques
60 Belwell Lane, Four Oaks. (Mrs. M.L. Wassall.) Est. 1974. CL: Mon. and Thurs. Open 10.30—5. *STOCK: 19th C English furniture, pictures, objets d'art, £10—£2,000.* TEL: (021) 308 5453. VAT: Stan/Spec.

Kelford Antiques
14a Birmingham Rd. (E.S. Kelsall.) Est. 1968. CL: Thurs. p.m. Open 9—5. *STOCK: General antiques, Georgian and Victorian furniture, silver, porcelain, Staffordshire figures, pot-lids, jewellery.* TEL: (021) 354 6607. VAT: Stan/Spec.

Osborne Antiques
91 Chester Rd., New Oscott. (C. Osborne.) Est. 1976. CL: Mon. Open 9—5, Sat. 9—3.30. *STOCK: Barometers, clocks and furniture.* TEL: (021) 355 6667. SER: Restorations; spares (clocks, barometers).

IS YOUR ENTRY CORRECT?
If there is even the slightest inaccuracy in your entry, *please* let us know before 1st January 1987.
GUIDE TO THE
ANTIQUE SHOPS OF BRITAIN
5 Church Street, Woodbridge, Suffolk.

Sutton Coldfield continued

H. and R.L. Parry Ltd. BADA
23 Maney Corner. (H. Parry.) Est. 1925. Open 10—5.30. SIZE: Medium. *STOCK: Furniture, silver and jewellery, all periods; metalware, paintings.* LOC: A38 from Birmingham into Sutton. Cinema on right, on corner of service road in which premises are situated. TEL: (021) 354 1178. SER: Valuations. VAT: Stan/Spec.

WALSALL (0922)

Caldmore Antiques
25 West Bromwich St. (J.A. Chambers.) Est. 1978. Open 9.30—6, or by appointment anytime. SIZE: Small. *STOCK: Furniture, £5—£1,000; clocks, porcelain, craft tools, collectors' items, photographic and scientific instruments, barometers, architectural items, fireplaces.* LOC: ¼ mile from Broadway (Ring road). PARK: Easy. TEL: 30843; home — Aldridge (0922) 51804. SER: Valuations; restorations (wood and clocks, upholstery). VAT: Stan/Spec.

Jewellery, Arts and Crafts
57 George St. (R. Nicholls.) Open 9—5. *STOCK: General antiques, especially jewellery.* TEL: 641081.

John Rutter Antiques
The Broadway. CL: Mon. and Thurs. Open 10.30—5.30, warehouse — 6 days. *STOCK: General antiques.* TEL: 611437; warehouse — 30829. VAT: Stan.

WEST BROMWICH

The Antique Shop
23B St. Michael St., West Bromwich Ringway. (Mrs. E. Watson.) Est. 1982. CL: Mon. Open 10—4.30. SIZE: Medium. *STOCK: General antiques, Victorian and Edwardian, £1—£500.* PARK: Easy. TEL: (021) 525 8133. SER: Valuations; restorations (mainly furniture).

Clover
50 New St. (J.T. and D. Carroll.) Open 10—5.30. *STOCK: General antiques, collectors items, furniture.* TEL: (021) 525 7897.

WOLVERHAMPTON (0902)

Baron Antiques
26 Queen Sq. (P., A. and M. Hackner.) Open 9—5.30. *STOCK: Victorian jewellery, silver, glass, china, watches.* TEL: 21818/28603.

Broad Street Gallery
16 Broad St. (J.E. and J.T. Hill.) Est. 1975. CL: Thurs. p.m. Open 9—5.30. *STOCK: Prints, watercolours, oils, £5—£1,000.* LOC: 3 minutes from St. Peter's Church. PARK: Easy. TEL: 24977. SER: Restorations; framing. VAT: Stan.

Wolverhampton continued

Collectors' Paradise Ltd.
56a Worcester St. (G. Hoppett and N.P. Stead.) Est. 1963. CL: Thurs. p.m. Open 9.30—5.30. *STOCK: Arms, armour, militaria, uniforms, collectors' items, bric-a-brac.* TEL: 20315.

Galata Coins Ltd.
Park House, 77 Albert Rd. (P. and B. Withers.) BNTA. Est. 1967. CL: Sat. Open 9—6.30, Sun. 3—5.30. SIZE: Small. *STOCK: Greek and Roman coins, 450 B.C. to 500 A.D., £10—£500; British coins, 800 A.D. to 1953, £5—£500; world coins, especially Scandinavian, 850 A.D. to 1960, £1—£1,000.* LOC: Near 'Halfway House' on Tettenhall Rd. (A41) towards Newport. PARK: Easy. TEL: 771118. SER: Valuations; buys at auction (coins). FAIRS: BNTA Coin, Europa Hotel. VAT: Stan/Spec.

Gemini Antiques
18a Upper Green, Tettenhall. (J. Pettitt.) Open 11—4. *STOCK: General antiques.* TEL: 742523; home — Sedgley (09073) 73334.

Martin-Quick   **LAPADA** Antiques Ltd.
323 Tettenhall Rd. Est. 1965. Open 9—5.30, Sat. 9.30—12.30 or by appointment. SIZE: Large. *STOCK: 18th—19th C furniture, shipping goods, architectural items, stripped pine.* Not stocked: Militaria, coins, silver. LOC: One mile from town centre on A41. PARK: Easy. TEL: 754703; Codsall (090 74) 3015. VAT: Stan/Spec.

Wolverhampton continued

Pendeford House Antiques
1 Pendeford Ave., Claregate, Tettenhall. (Mrs. B. Tonks.) Est. 1980. CL: Thurs. Open 11—6, Wed. 11—7.30, Sat. 10—6. SIZE: Medium. *STOCK: China and porcelain, £5—£500; furniture and clocks, £50—£1,500; oil paintings and watercolours, £50—£500; all 19th—20th C; glass, linen, brass and copper, jewellery and silver.* LOC: From main Tettenhall Rd., turn at traffic lights towards Codsall. At first small traffic island, take 3rd exit, shop next to Jet Garage. PARK: Easy. Tel: 756175; home — same.

Rainbow Antiques
76 Dudley Rd. Est. 1968. Open 10—6. *STOCK: General antiques.* TEL: 59800.

Rock House Antiques Centre
Rock House, The Rock, Tettenhall. (Mr. and Mrs. L. Avery.) CL: Mon. Open 10.30—5.30, Thurs. 10.30—8. There are 40 stallholders at this market selling *general antiques.* TEL: 754995.

Second Thoughts
1-3 Coalway Rd., Penn. (Mr. and Mrs. C.R. Turley.) Est. 1977. CL: Wed. Open 9.30—1 and 2—4.30, or by appointment. SIZE: Small. *STOCK: Furniture, 18th—19th C; porcelain, glass, watercolours and prints.* LOC: A449, ¾ mile from town centre. PARK: Easy. TEL: 337748 and 337366. SER: Valuations. VAT: Stan/Spec.

A.E. Wakeman   **LAPADA** and Sons Ltd.   *Trade Only*
140b Tettenhall Rd. Est. 1967. CL: Sat. Open 8.30—5.30. SIZE: Large. *STOCK: Furniture, 1840—1900, £5—£2,000; furniture, 1700—1830, £30—£2,000.* LOC: One mile from town centre on A41. PARK: Easy. TEL: 751166; home — Albrighton (090 722) 2991. VAT: Stan/Spec.

Engraving "Harvest Home" published by Robert Sayer. From "Rare Liverpool Enamel Plaques", in **Antique Collecting,** November 1985.

Wiltshire

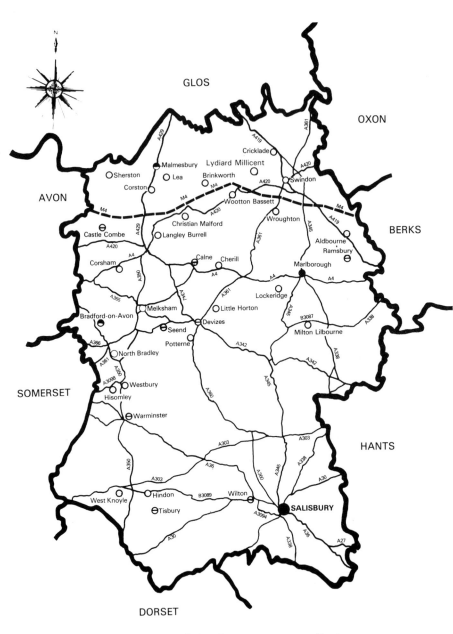

GLOS

OXON

AVON

BERKS

SOMERSET

HANTS

DORSET

Cricklade

Malmesbury
Lydiard Millicent
Sherston
Lea
Brinkworth
Corston
Swindon
Wootton Bassett
Wroughton
Christian Malford
Castle Combe
Langley Burrell
Aldbourne
Ramsbury
Corsham
Calne
Cherill
Marlborough
Lockeridge
Melksham
Little Horton
Bradford-on-Avon
Devizes
Milton Lilbourne
Seend
Potterne
North Bradley
Westbury
Hisomley
Warminster

West Knoyle
Hindon
Wilton
Tisbury
SALISBURY

A429
A419
A361
A420
A420
M4
M4
A429
A420
A4
A350
A365
A361
A344
A361
A4
A4
A345
A345
B3087
A338
A342
A338
A342
A345
A361
A366
A350
A3098
A360
A303
A303
A303
A36
A360
A345
A338
A30
A350
B3089
A360
A3094
A30
A338
A36
A27

Please note this is only a rough map designed to show dealers the number of shops in the various towns, and is not necessarily totally accurate.

Key to number of shops in this area.

○ 1–2
⊖ 3–5
◓ 6–12
● 13+

ALDBOURNE, Nr. Marlborough

R. and D. Coombes   LAPADA

The Old Priest House, West St. Est. 1972. Open any time by appointment. SIZE: Small. *STOCK: Oriental ceramics and works of art, also Japanese prints, 10th—19th C, £5—£500.* LOC: A419 between Swindon and Hungerford. PARK: Easy. TEL: Marlborough (0672) 40241. FAIRS: Midlands, British International (Birmingham), Chelsea and others. VAT: Spec.

BRADFORD-ON-AVON   (022 16)

Avon Antiques   BADA

26—27 Market St. (V. and A. Jenkins, B.A.) Est. 1960. Open 9.45—5.30, Sun. by appointment. SIZE: Large. *STOCK: English and Continental furniture, 1600—1880; metalwork, treen, clocks, barometers, some textiles, painted and lacquer furniture.* LOC: A363, main street of town. PARK: Opposite. TEL: 2052. VAT: Spec.

The China Hen

9 Woolley St. (Miss E. Stephenson.) Est. 1952. CL: Some Wed. p.m. Open 10—6. SIZE: Medium. *STOCK: Porcelain and pottery, 18th to early 19th C, £5—£250; furniture, 17th C to 1840, £20—£2,000; clocks, oils, watercolours, prints, late 18th to mid-19th C; jewellery.* Not stocked: Silver, guns, weapons. LOC: B3108. PARK: Easy. TEL: 3369. SER: Valuations; restorations (china); buys at auction. VAT: Spec.

Ray Coggins

The Old Brewery, Newtown. CL: Sat. Open 9—5.30, other times by appointment. *STOCK: Period pine furniture and architectural fittings.* TEL: 3431.

Harp Antiques

17 Woolley St. (H.A. and J. Roland-Price). Resident. Est. 1973. Open daily. SIZE: Medium. *STOCK: Furniture, £100—£3,000; silver, £5—£300; all 18th—19th C. Objects of vertue, 19th C, £50—£200.* LOC: B3107, 300yds. from town centre. PARK: Easy. TEL: 5770; home — same. SER: Valuations (silver, furniture); buys at auction (furniture and silver). VAT: Spec.

José Hornsey

3 Silver St. (P.S. and J. Hornsey.) Est. 1967. CL: Sat. Open 10—5.30 or by appointment. *STOCK: Country furniture, treen, metals, decorative items.* LOC: On mini roundabout on north side of town bridge. PARK: Nearby. TEL: 4333; home — Keevil (0380) 870764. SER: Interior decoration. VAT: Stan/Spec.

MOXHAMS ANTIQUES

Roger and Jill Bichard

**17 SILVER STREET
BRADFORD-ON-AVON
WILTSHIRE**

Tel. (022 16) 2789; evenings Seend (038 082) 677

*Five showrooms and a warehouse of period antiques: oak
and mahogany furniture, clocks, pottery and porcelain,
metalware, treen and some decorative items. French and
German spoken. Trade welcome.*

*Open 9 – 1, 2.15 – 5.30
or by appointment*

Bradford-on-Avon continued

Moxhams Antiques

17 Silver St. (R. and J. Bichard.) Est. 1966.
Open 9 – 1 and 2.15 – 5.30 or by appointment. SIZE: Large. *STOCK: English and Continental furniture, clocks, 1650 – 1830, £50 –
£15,000; European and Oriental pottery and
porcelain, 1700 – 1830, £10 – £1,500; metals,
treen, decorative items, 1600 – 1900, £1 –
£1,000.* PARK: Easy. TEL: 2789; home –
Seend (038 082) 677. SER: Valuations. VAT:
Stan/Spec.

Richard and Pamela Nadin

'Audleys', Woolley St. Est. 1970. Open
9.30 – 5.30 or by appointment. SIZE: Medium.
*STOCK: Unusual furniture and decorations,
carpets, fittings, needlework, 18th and 19th
C.* PARK: Easy. TEL: 2476. FAIRS: West
Kensington, Chelsea, Marlborough, Olympia.
VAT: Stan/Spec.

Rodney and Susan Otway

Dutch Barton Cottage, Church St. ABA. CL:
Wed. Open 10 – 1 and 2 – 5.30. *STOCK:
English literature, 17th – 19th C.* TEL: 3885.

BRINKWORTH (066 641)

North Wilts Exporters

Farm Hill House. (M. Thornbury.) Est. 1972.
Open Mon. – Sat. or by appointment. *STOCK:
American and Continental shipping goods,
pine, 18th – 19th C.* LOC: A4042. TEL: 423.
SER: Valuations and shipping. VAT: Stan.

CALNE (0249)

Calne Antiques

2a London Rd. (M. Blackford.) Open 9 – 5
including Sun. *STOCK: Furniture and shipping
goods, collectors' items.* TEL: 816311.

Calne continued

Clive Farahar and Sophie Dupré – Rare Books, Autographs and Manuscripts

14 The Green. Open by appointment. SIZE:
Small. *STOCK: Rare books on voyages and
travels, autograph letters and manuscripts,
15th – 20th C, £5 – £5,000.* LOC: Off A4 in
town centre. PARK: Easy. TEL: 816793;
home – same. SER: Valuations; buys at
auction (as stock). FAIRS: Universal Autograph Collectors' Club. VAT: Stan.

From "Bulb-Pots from Bristol" in **Antique
Collecting,** December 1985.

Calne continued

Hilmarton Manor Press
Hilmarton Manor. (H. Baile de Laperriere.) Est.
1967. Book on Silver Auction Records. Open
9—6. SIZE: Medium. *STOCK: New and out of
print art and photography reference books,
some antiquarian.* LOC: 3 miles from Calne on
A3102 towards Swindon. PARK: Easy. TEL:
Hilmarton (024 976) 208. SER: Buys at
auction.

CASTLE COMBE   (0249)
Nr. Chippenham

Combe Cottage Antiques   BADA
(B. and A. Bishop.) Est. 1960. Open 10—1
and 2—6. SIZE: Medium. *STOCK: Country
furniture, £20—£5,000; metalware, £10—
£2,000; both 17th to early 19th C; treen,
pottery, 18th—19th C, £5—£500; early lighting devices.* Not stocked: Mahogany furniture,
glass, silver, Victoriana. LOC: A420 from
Chippenham towards Bristol. After 3 miles
bear right on B4039. PARK: 20yds. TEL:
782250. SER: Valuations. Specialists in cottage furnishings. VAT: Spec.

Castle Combe continued

Michel Le Coz
High St. Est. 1960. Open 10—6. SIZE:
Medium. *STOCK: Antique and decorative
furniture, £300—£5,000.* LOC: Take Exit 17
from M4 for village. PARK: Easy. TEL:
782223.

Unicorn Gallery
The Street. (Mrs. N. Tresilian.) Est. 1962.
Open 9—1 and 2.15—5.30, most Sun. 3—5.
SIZE: Small. *STOCK: Pottery and porcelain,
£5—£300; small silver and furniture; all
Georgian to late Victorian.* Not stocked:
Pictures, firearms. LOC: West from Chippen-
ham on A420 and then B4039 at Castle
Combe sign. TEL: 782291; home — same.
VAT: Stan/Spec.

CHERHILL, Nr. Calne
P.A. Oxley   LAPADA
Antique Clocks and Barometers
The Old Rectory. Est. 1971. CL: Wed. Open
9.30—2.30, other times by appointment.
SIZE: Medium. *STOCK: Longcase and bracket
clocks, 18th—19th C, £300—£4,000.* LOC:
A4, not in village. PARK: Easy. TEL: Calne
(0249) 816227. VAT: Spec.

CHRISTIAN MALFORD
Nr. Chippenham
Harley Antiques   **LAPADA**
Trade Only
The Comedy. (G.J. Harley and G. Low.) Est. 1959. Open 9—6 or by appointment. SIZE: Large. *STOCK: Furniture, 18th—19th C, £150—£3,000; decorative objects, £30—£1,000.* LOC: A420. PARK: Own. TEL: Seagry (0249) 720112; home — same. VAT: Stan.

Harley Two   **LAPADA**
The Chimneys. Open by appointment. *STOCK: Country, pine and fruitwood furniture, baskets and country crafts.* TEL: Seagry (0249) 720112.

CORSHAM   (0249)
Robin and Matthew Eden
Pickwick Village. Resident. Est. 1947. SIZE: Large. *STOCK: 17th—18th C furniture, garden seats, statuary, pottery.* TEL: 713335. VAT: Spec.

CORSTON, Nr. Malmesbury
The Keyser Gallery
Quarry House. (C.P. Keyser.) Est. 1976. Open by appointment. *STOCK: Sporting and wildlife oils, watercolours and prints, 19th—20th C, £20—£8,000.* LOC: On A429. TEL: Malmesbury (066 62) 2429. SER: Valuations; restorations (paintings and prints); framing; buys at auction. FAIRS: Badminton; Game; Burghley. VAT: Stan/Spec.

CRICKLADE, Nr. Swindon
Cricklade Antique Shop
25 High St. (C. Wynn-Jones.) Est. 1973. Open Thurs., Fri. and Sat. 10—5. SIZE: Small. *STOCK: China, silver, Victorian jewellery and glass, small country furniture, 1800—1920, £5—£500.* PARK: Easy. TEL: Swindon (0793) 751236; home — same. SER: Valuations.

Eldred A.F. Gwilliam
Candletree House, Bath Rd. Est. 1976. Open by appointment. SIZE: Medium. *STOCK: Arms and armour, swords, pistols, long guns, £30—£10,000+.* PARK: Easy. TEL: Swindon (0793) 750241. SER: Valuations; buys at auction. FAIRS: Major arms. VAT: Stan/Spec.

DEVIZES   (0380)
H.W. and L.M. Barnett
49 Long St. Resident. Est. 1954. CL: Wed. and Sat. p.m. SIZE: Small. *STOCK: General antiques, mainly furniture.* TEL: 5519.

Devizes continued
Cross Keys Jewellers
18 Market Place. (D. and N. Pullen.) NAG. Est. 1967. CL: Wed. p.m. Open 9—5. *STOCK: Jewellery, silver.* LOC: Adjacent to cinema. PARK: Easy. TEL: 6293. VAT: Stan/Spec.

Saville Antiques
37 Long St. (P.M. Bruce.) Est. 1962. CL: Sun., except by appointment. Open 9—6, Sat. 9—1 or by appointment. SIZE: Small. *STOCK: Furniture, 17th to early 19th C, £50—£2,000; clocks, pictures, porcelain, objets d'art, 18th to early 19th C.* LOC: Near museum. PARK: Easy. TEL: 3559. SER: Valuations. VAT: Spec.

HINDON, Nr. Salisbury   (074 789)
Monkton Galleries   BADA
High St. (J. and B. Dempsey.) Resident. Est. 1967. CL: Sat. p.m. SIZE: Medium. *STOCK: Early oak and country furniture; metalware, longcase clocks.* PARK: Easy. TEL: 235. SER: Valuations; restorations (metalware, prints and pictures). VAT: Spec.

HISOMLEY, Nr. Westbury
D.J. and P.E. Thomas   *Trade Only*
"Hillview". Open anytime by appointment. *STOCK: General antiques especially country furniture.* TEL: Westbury (0373) 822593; home — same.

LANGLEY BURRELL
Nr. Chippenham
Fairfax Fireplaces
Langley Green House. (J. Fairfax.) Open by appointment only. *STOCK: Fireplaces, surrounds, inserts and grates, architectural and garden items.* TEL: Chippenham (0249) 652030. SER: Polishing; welding; blacksmithing; design consultancy.

LEA, Nr. Malmesbury
Relic Antiques at
Brillscote Farm
Brillscote Farm. (M. Gliksten and G. Gower.) Est. 1975. Open 9.30—5.30, Sat. and Sun. by appointment. SIZE: Large. *STOCK: Fairground animals, carvings, show fronts, old shop and pub fronts and interiors, doors, screens and bars, stained and engraved glass windows and architectural fittings, 19th C horse transport.* LOC: On Wootton Bassett Rd., turn left to Lea, 400yds. 2nd house on right. PARK: On premises. TEL: Malmesbury (066 62) 2332. SER: Valuations; buys at auction. VAT: Stan.

HARLEY ANTIQUES

THE COMEDY, CHRISTIAN MALFORD Nr. CHIPPENHAM, WILTSHIRE

Telephone: Seagry (0249) 720112

4 miles exit 17 M4

LARGEST COLLECTION OF SELECTED ANTIQUES AND DECORATIVE OBJECTS IN THE WEST COUNTRY

Resident on premises

LITTLE HORTON, Nr. Devizes

R.L. Cook
Belmont House. Est. 1950. Open by appointment. *STOCK: Antiquarian books.* TEL: Cannings (038 086) 214.

LOCKERIDGE   **(067 286)**

Robert Kime Antiques
Dene House. Est. 1968. Open 10—6, Sat. and Sun. by appointment. *STOCK: Decorative, period furniture.* TEL: 250. VAT: Spec.

LYDIARD MILLICENT Nr. Swindon

The Old Bakehouse Antiques
The Street. (Mrs. A.M. Wicks.) Est. 1978. CL: Mon. Open 10—5.30. SIZE: Medium. *STOCK: Furniture, porcelain, glass, collectables, £5—£1,000.* LOC: 3 miles from M4, junction 16. PARK: Easy. TEL: Swindon (0793) 771461; home — Swindon (0793) 770750. SER: Buys at auction (furniture, china, glass). FAIRS: Hallmark, Keynsham; Abbey Hall, Abingdon.

Monkton Galleries

(Joyce & Brian Dempsey)
HINDON, Nr. Salisbury
Wilts. (STD 074789) 235

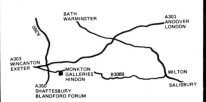

Specialists in
Early Oak & Country Furniture
Metalware & Pottery
Longcase, and other interesting clocks

Four showrooms of rapidly changing stock.

Resident on premises, trade welcome to call at any time.

MALMESBURY (066 62)

Antiques — Rene Nicholls
56 High St. (Mrs. R. Nicholls.) Est. 1980. Open 10—5.30, Sun. by appointment. SIZE: Small. *STOCK: English pottery and porcelain, 18th to early 19th C, £50—£900; small furniture.* PARK: Opposite. TEL: 3089; home — same.

Batstone Books
24 Gloucester St. (D. and M.E. Batstone.) Est. 1982. Open every day 10—1.30 and 2.30—6, until 5 on Mon. SIZE: Small. *STOCK: Books, some antiquarian, to £400.* LOC: Turn left top of High St., shop opposite spire near Abbey. PARK: Outside Bell Hotel. TEL: 3072. FAIRS: P.B.F.A.

Andrew Britten (Antiques)
48 High St. Resident. (T.M. Tyler and T.A. Freeman.) Est. 1975. Open 9.30—6, Sun. by appointment. SIZE: Medium. *STOCK: Furniture, 1700—1900, £50—£1,000; decorative brass, wood, glass and porcelain items, £5—£500.* Not stocked: Jewellery, militaria. PARK: Opposite. TEL: 3376. VAT: Spec.

Cross Hayes Antiques LAPADA
The Antique and Furniture Warehouse, 19 Bristol St. (D. Brooks.) Est. 1975. Open 10—5. SIZE: Warehouse. *STOCK: Georgian to 1920s furniture — oak, mahogany, walnut and pine; china, glass, copper, brass, books, frames, prints and bric-a-brac.* TEL: 4260; home — 2062. SER: Valuations. VAT: Stan/Spec.

J.P. Kadwell
The Gant and Silver St. Est. 1981. CL: Thurs. except by appointment. Open 8.15—5.30, Sun. by appointment. SIZE: Medium. *STOCK: General antiques, £5—£500.* PARK: Easy. TEL: 3589; home — same. SER: Restorations (wood); buys at auction. VAT: Stan/Spec.

Malmesbury Antique & Interiors
100 Lower High St. (P. Von Fullman.) Est. 1974. Open 9.30—1 and 2—5.30. SIZE: Medium. *STOCK: Furniture, 18th—19th C, £100—£1,500; lamps, paintings, fabrics and objects.* PARK: Nearby. TEL: 4656. VAT: Stan/Spec.

J.E. Randall
125 Lower High St. CL: Mon. Open 10—6. *STOCK: Giltwood, lacquer, papier mâché, small general items.* SER: Restorations (giltwood, oils and watercolours); bespoke frames. VAT: Stan.

MARLBOROUGH (0672)

The Antique and Book Collector
Katharine House, The Parade. (C.C. and Mrs. A. Gange.) Est. 1983. Open 9.30—5.30, Sun. by appointment. SIZE: Medium. *STOCK: Antiquities and Oriental items, 2000 BC to 1400, £30—£500; country furniture, 17th—18th C, £200—£1,000; glass, porcelain, pictures and silver, 18th—19th C, £20—£750; tribal art, mainly 19th C, £50—£300; books, modern first editions, travel, illustrated, mostly 20th C, £5—£500.* PARK: Easy. TEL: 54040; home — same. FAIRS: PBFA monthly; Town Hall quarterly; Oxfam annually. VAT: Stan/Spec.

Carousel Antiques
72 High St. Est. 1964. Open daily. *STOCK: Porcelain, glass, bric-a-brac, pictures, prints, some small furniture.*

Nigel Cracknell (Antiques) Ltd.
BADA
Cavendish House, 138 High St. Est. 1970. **Open 10—6; trade anytime. SIZE: Large.** *STOCK: English and Continental oak, walnut and mahogany furniture, 17th—19th C, £300—£15,000; brass, £50—£1,500; Masons ironstone.* **PARK: Easy. TEL: 52912. VAT: Stan/Spec.**

Dormy House Antiques
43 Kingsbury St. (D. and A. Bellerby.) Est. 1957. Article on lace-makers' bobbins. CL: Weekends. Usually open. SIZE: Medium. *STOCK: Lace-makers' bobbins, 19th C, £1—£150; glass, 18th C, £20—£700; furniture, 18th C, £20—£2,500.* Not stocked: Coins, weapons. LOC: From A4, turn right at Town Hall. TEL: 52703. SER: Valuations. VAT: Stan/Spec.

Lacewing Fine Art Gallery
124 High St. (N. James.) CL: Wed. Open 10—5.30. *STOCK: Paintings and watercolours, 16th—19th C, £200—£5,000.* TEL: 54580.

London House Antique Centre
End of High St. (R. and J. Watkins.) Est. 1964. Open 9.30—5.30, Sun. by appointment. SIZE: Large. *STOCK: Furniture, £100—£500; porcelain and pottery, £50— £1,000; clocks, £150—£1,500; silver, £30—£500; all 18th—19th C.* LOC: A4. PARK: Nearby. TEL: 52331; home — same. SER: Valuations; restorations; buys at auction. VAT: Stan/Spec.

Marlborough Antiques
18 The Parade. (M.E. Gray and L.J. Halliwell.) Est. 1963. Open 10—1 and 2—6, Sun. by appointment. SIZE: Small. *STOCK: Early oak, 16th—17th C, £500—£3,000; furniture, 18th—19th C, £300—£1,000; decorative items, £50—£500.* LOC: A4. PARK: Easy. TEL: 54818; home — 55165. SER: Restorations (furniture); buys at auction (furniture). VAT: Spec.

Marlborough continued

Marlborough Bookshop and Sporting Gallery

6 Kingsbury St. (R. Collens.) Est. 1977. CL: Mon. Open 10—5, Sun. by appointment. SIZE: Medium. *STOCK: Sporting oils, watercolours, £50—£1,000; sporting prints, £10—£500, all 1800—1950; books, 1750—1980, £3—£500.* LOC: Down hill below Town Hall. PARK: Easy. TEL: 54074. SER: Valuations; restorations (oils, watercolours, prints); buys at auction. FAIRS: Local. VAT: Spec.

The Marlborough Parade Antique Centre Ltd.

The Parade. (T. Page and R. Stenhouse.) Est. 1985. Open every day 10—5. There are 35 dealers at this centre selling a wide range of good quality *furniture, silver, porcelain, glass, clocks, jewellery, copper, brass and pewter, £5—£5,000.* LOC: Adjacent A4 in town centre. PARK: Easy. TEL: 55331. SER: Valuations; restorations (furniture, porcelain, copper, brass); buys at auction. VAT: Stan/Spec.

The Military Parade Bookshop

The Parade. (D. Gibbons.) *STOCK: Military history books, prints, medals, badges and militaria.* LOC: Next to The Lamb. TEL: 55470.

Rupert Gentle

*Dealer in Antiques and
Works of Art*

The Manor House,
Milton Lilbourne,
Pewsey, Wiltshire
SN9 5LQ

Telephone (0672) 63344

*17th and 18th century furniture, needlework
and all domestic accessories of the period.
Specialising in English and Continental
domestic brass, 1600-1800*

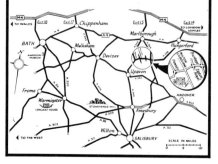

Marlborough continued

Objects
77 High St. (N. Mitchell.) Resident. Open 10—6. *STOCK: Furniture and decorative items, 18th—19th C, £5—£500.* TEL: 54563.

Principia Arts and Sciences
5 London Rd. (M. Forrer.) CL: Mon. Open 9.30—5.30. *STOCK: Collectors' items, scientific instruments, treen, small country furniture, pictures and clocks.* TEL: 52072.

Stuart Gallery
4 London Rd. (A.B. Loncraine.) Est. 1968. CL: Wed. Open 10—5. *STOCK: General antiques especially small collectables, watercolours, oils and prints, china, glass, interior design pieces, books, garden items.* PARK: Easy. TEL: 53593; home — 810694.

Annmarie Turner Antiques
22 Salisbury Rd. Est. 1960. Open 9—7, Sat 9—5, Sun. by appointment. SIZE: Large. *STOCK: Country and Welsh primitive furniture, £50—£1,000; English treen, kitchen and trade items, £10—£200; paintings and decorative items, £20—£400; all 17th—19th C.* Not stocked: Jewellery, silver and weapons. LOC: Left side of first roundabout approaching town from Hungerford on A4. PARK: Easy and at rear. TEL: 55396; home — same. SER: Valuations. VAT: Spec.

MELKSHAM (0225)
Alan Jaffray
16 Market Place. Est. 1956. Open 10—1 and 2—5, Sat. by appointment. SIZE: Large. *STOCK: Furniture and smalls, 18th—19th C, £50—£2,000.* LOC: Main Bath to Devizes Rd. PARK: Easy. TEL: 702269. VAT: Stan/Spec.

Tamaree Antiques
'Tamaree', 59 King St. (B. Gillet.) Resident. Est. 1965. CL: Wed. Open by appointment. SIZE: Small. *STOCK: Silver and jewellery, 19th—20th C; porcelain, pottery, glass, early Victorian to art deco.* LOC: 100yds. from Market Place. PARK: Easy. TEL: 703746. FAIRS: Local.

MILTON LILBOURNE, Nr. Pewsey
Rupert Gentle Antiques BADA
The Manor House. Est. 1954. Open 9.15—6. SIZE: Medium. *STOCK: Furniture, from £150; accessories, from £30; both early 18th C; especially English and Continental domestic brass, 16th—19th C.* LOC: From Hungerford on A4 take A338 for Pewsey. PARK: Easy. TEL: Marlborough (0672) 63344. SER: Valuations; buys at auction. VAT: Stan/Spec.

POTTERNE, Nr. Devizes
V.K. & R. Antiques
Dorcy House, 8 High St. (V. Morris.) Resident, usually available. SIZE: Small. STOCK: Oak furniture, 18th—19th C, £250—£500; chairs, metalware, brass. LOC: A360. PARK: Easy. TEL: Devizes (0380) 3933: home — same. VAT: Stan.

RAMSBURY, Nr. Marlborough
Heraldry Today
Parliament Piece. Est. 1954. Open 9.30—5; weekends by appointment. STOCK: Heraldic and genealogical books and manuscripts, 50p—£1,500. TEL: Marlborough (0672) 20617.

Inglenook Antiques
59 High St. (D. White.) Est. 1969. CL: Mon. p.m. Open 10—5.30, Sun. by appointment. STOCK: Longcase and wall clocks, fire irons, brass, copper, oil lamps, some furniture. LOC: 7 miles east of Marlborough off the A4. TEL: Marlborough (0672) 20261. SER: Restorations (longcase clock movements).

Bryan Mann Antiques
The Square. (B.K. Mann.) Est. 1973. SIZE: Medium. STOCK: Period and country, English and Continental furniture; decorative objects and unusual items. Not stocked: Coins, arms, glass. LOC: Approx. 4½ miles from Hungerford. PARK: Easy. TEL: Marlborough (0672) 20552. VAT: Stan/Spec.

SALISBURY   (0722)
Allum and Sidaway Ltd.
20 Queen St. Est. 1943. CL: Mon. Open 9—5.30. SIZE: Large. STOCK: Silver, Georgian and Victorian, £20—£2,000; other silver, £20—£1,500. LOC: City centre, Market Square. PARK: Opposite. TEL: 25907. SER: Valuations; restorations (silver); buys at auction. VAT: Spec.

Joan Amos Antiques
7a St. John St. Est. 1983. Open 9.30—12.30 and 1.30—5, Sat. 9.30—1. SIZE: Small. STOCK: Porcelain, 1900s, £20—£60; small furniture, late 19th C, £200—£500. LOC: On right hand side when entering city from south (A354). PARK: Limited. TEL: 330888; home — same.

The Avonbridge Antiques and Collectors Market
United Reformed Church Hall, Fisherton St. Open Tues. 9—4. There are fifteen dealers at this market selling a wide range of general antiques. LOC: Opposite hospital.

The Barn Book Supply
88 Crane St. (J. and J. Head.) Est. 1958. Open every day 9—4. STOCK: Antiquarian books on angling, shooting, horses, deerstalking. TEL: 27767.

Salisbury continued
D.M. Beach
52 High St. (A. Pearce.) Est. 1930. Open 9—5.30. SIZE: Large. STOCK: Antiquarian books, 1500—1972, 5p—£1,000; maps, prints, 1600—1900, to £500. LOC: From Bournemouth into city, take first possible turn left. Shop is on next corner. PARK: 120yds. down Crane St. TEL: 333801. SER: Valuations; restorations (leather bindings); buys at auction. FAIRS: U.S.A. and London.

Derek Boston Antiques   LAPADA
223 Wilton Rd., also warehouse at Wilton. Est. 1964. Open 9.30—5. SIZE: Large. STOCK: Furniture and decorative accessories. TEL: 22682; home — 24426. VAT: Stan/Spec.

Robert Bradley
71 Brown St. Est. 1970. CL: Sat. p.m. Open 9.30—5.30. STOCK: Furniture, 17th and 18th C; decorative items. TEL: 333677. VAT: Spec.

Castle Galleries
79 Castle St. (J.C. Lodge.) Est. 1971. Open 9.30—5, Wed. and Sat. 9.30—1. STOCK: General antiques, coins and medals. PARK: Easy. TEL: 333734. VAT: Stan/Spec.

Anne Davenport Antiques
61 Milford St. (Mrs. A. Davenport.) Est. 1959. CL: Wed. Open 10—1 and 2.30—5, Sat. 10—12.30. SIZE: Small. STOCK: Furniture, 1800—1900, £50—£300; brass and copper, general antiques, 1800—1870, £3— £100. Not stocked: Coins, stamps, weapons, jewellery. LOC: 200yds. city centre. PARK: Opposite, 30 mins. TEL: 336905.

A. de Saye Hutton Antiques
Est. 1963. By appointment only. STOCK: English porcelain especially New Hall, pottery, glass and prints, 18th—19th C. PARK: Easy. TEL: 20394.

The Farthing Gallery
7 St. John St. (J. and C. Wheeler.) Est. 1979. CL: Mon. Open 9.45—1 and 2.15—5.15. SIZE: Large. STOCK: Maps, prints, watercolours, oil paintings. LOC: From Bournemouth on right hand side of main road before entering town. PARK: 100yds., multi-storey. TEL: 26462. SER: Valuations; restorations; mount-cutting; framing. VAT: Stan.

Ian G. Hastie   BADA
46 St. Ann St. STOCK: English and Continental furniture, 17th and 18th C; decorative items, 19th C. TEL: 22957.

Salisbury continued

The Joiners Hall
St. Ann St. (G. and J. Warner Ltd.) Est. 1946. Books on collecting. Appointment essential. SIZE: Large. *STOCK: English furniture, 18th C; Oriental items including paintings.* PARK: Easy. Private by arrangement. TEL: 22842. SER: Valuations. VAT: Stan/Spec.

Memory Lane Antiques
34 Chipper Lane. (H.C. Golding, J.W. Cane.) Open 9.30—5.30. *STOCK: Antiquarian books, clocks, glass, china, collectors' items.* TEL: 337587.

Mr. Micawber's Attic
73 Fisherton St. (Mr. and Mrs. E.M. Johnson and others.) Est. 1981. CL: Wed. Open 9.30—5. SIZE: Large. There are approximately 14 stalls at this market selling a *wide range of general antiques including jewellery, silver, furniture, clocks, coins and medals, books, porcelain, art nouveau and art deco items, lace, linen and clothes.* LOC: 300yds. from railway station towards town centre. PARK: Opposite, behind shops. TEL: 337857. SER: Valuations; restorations (clocks and watches, jewellery). FAIRS: Local.

Patrick Mullins
St. Martin's House, 49 St. Ann St. CL: Sat. p.m. Open 9.30—5.30. *STOCK: Period furniture, porcelain.* TEL: 22570. VAT: Stan/Spec.

Richard Parker Ltd.   BADA
5 St. John St. (C.R.J., J.R.J. and Mrs. D.C.A. Parker.) Est. 1890. Open 9.30—1 and 2—6, Sun. by appointment. SIZE: Medium. *STOCK: Furniture, 1700—1850, £100—£5,000; objets d'art, 1700—1900, £50—£1,000.* LOC: Next to Kings Arms and White Hart Hotels. PARK: Easy. TEL. 28538; home — 337484. SER: Valuations; restorations. FAIRS: West of England, Olympia and Park Lane Hotel. VAT: Stan/Spec.

Chris Wadge Clocks
142 Fisherton St. CL: Mon. Open 9—5.30. *STOCK: Clocks especially anniversary.* TEL: 334467.

SEEND, Nr. Melksham   (038 082)
Antique Shop
High St. (K. and J. Adams.) Est. 1965. CL: Fri. and Sat. Open 10—6 or by appointment. SIZE: Small. *STOCK: Furniture and metalwork, pre-1830.* LOC: A361. On right on main rd. from Devizes. PARK: Easy. TEL: 434; home — same. SER: Restorations (furniture, metalwork, needlework). VAT: Spec.

Paul Wansbrough
Seend Lodge. Est. 1974. CL: Sat. p.m. Open 9.30—5.30, appointment advisable. SIZE: Medium. *STOCK: English furniture, £50— £2,500; small general items, objets d'art; all 18th to early 19th C.* LOC: On A361, on righthand side behind red brick wall. PARK: Easy. TEL: 213. SER: Buys at auction. VAT: Spec.

Winterbourne Antiques
Seend Green House. (Mrs. L.H. Thorpe.) Est. 1960. Open by appointment only. SIZE: Large. *STOCK: Glass, some prints, and decorative items.* LOC: First large house in Seend on the left-hand side, travelling on A361 from Devizes. PARK: Easy. TEL: 493.

SHERSTON
Sherston Antiques   LAPADA
Old Pharmacy House. (P.O. Hawkins.) Est. 1968. *STOCK: Porcelain, glass, silver, pictures, small decorative items.* TEL: Malmesbury (0666) 840291. VAT: Stan/Spec.

SWINDON   (0793)
Antiques and Old Pine
11 Newport St. (J.E. and M. Brown.) Resident. CL: Mon. and Wed. Open 10—1 and 2—5.30, or by appointment. SIZE: Medium. *STOCK: Lace and linen, pine, stripped satin walnut, general antiques.* LOC: From M4, follow signs to Old Town. PARK: 200yds. TEL: 20259. VAT: Stan/Spec.

Swindon continued
Victoria Bookshop
30 Wood St. (S. Austin.) Est. 1965. Open
9—5.30. SIZE: Large. *STOCK: Books, most
subjects, old postcards.* LOC: From Marlborough, Chippenham or M4, follow signs to
Old Town. PARK: 200yds. reached by
pedestrian way. TEL: 27364.

TISBURY   (0747)
Arundell Books
Arundell House, High St. Est. 1983. Open by
appointment. *STOCK: Antiquarian books on
Wiltshire and Cranborne Chase.* TEL: 870353.
SER: Buys at auction.

May and May Ltd.
Arundell House, High St. Est. 1963. Open by
appointment. *STOCK: Antiquarian music and
music literature.* TEL: 870353. SER: Buys at
auction.

Rectory Antiques
4 High St. (Mrs. G. Whitworth.) Resident. Est.
1965. CL: Mon. Open 10—5. *STOCK: Silver,
jewellery, glass, porcelain, small furniture.*
PARK: Easy. TEL: 870710.

WARMINSTER   (0985)
The Antique Warehouse
Furlong House, 61 East St. (P.A. and D. Gale.)
Open 8.30—5.30, other times by appointment. SIZE: Large. *STOCK: General antiques.*
TEL: 219460.

Barton-Booth Gallery
15 George St. Est. 1970. CL: Wed. p.m.
STOCK: Maps, prints. TEL: 215413. SER:
Restorations; mounting and framing; map and
print colouring. VAT: Stan.

Bishopstrow Antiques
55 East St. (A., J.M. and M. Stewart-Cox.)
Est. 1974. Open 10—1 and 2—5.30. SIZE:
Medium. *STOCK: Furniture including pine and
country; porcelain, boxes, small silver, interesting bygones, all 18th—19th C.* LOC: On left of
A36 leaving Warminster on Salisbury road,
opposite Esso garage. PARK: Easy. TEL:
212683; home — 214584. SER: Restorations
(furniture, frames, papier mâché). VAT: Stan/
Spec.

Britannia Antiques Exports
Furlong House, 61 East St. (M.T. Goodsman.)
Open 8.30—5.30, other times by appointment. SIZE: Large. *STOCK: General antiques.*
TEL: 219360.

Century Antiques
10 Silver St. (N. Giltsoff.) Open 10—5.30.
STOCK: General antiques. TEL: 217031.

Moulded salt-glazed teapot in the form of a camel, made in Staffordshire about 1745.
259mm high. From *A Collector's History of English Pottery* by Griselda Lewis,
published by the **Antique Collectors' Club,** 1985.

Warminster continued

Obelisk Antiques
2 Silver St. (P. Tanswell.) Open 10—1 and
2—5.30. *STOCK: English and Continental
furniture, 18th—19th C; decorative items,
objets d'art.* TEL: 216874.

Warminster Antiques
4a Silver St. (T. Mullen.) Est. 1967. Open
10—6. *STOCK: General antiques, English and
Continental small furniture, porcelain, decorative and Oriental items.* TEL: 212536. VAT:
Stan/Spec.

K. and A. Welch   *Trade Only*
1A Church St. Est. 1967. Open 8—6, Sat.
9—12. SIZE: Large. *STOCK: Shipping furniture, 18th—19th C, £10—£2,000.* LOC: A36
west end of town. PARK: Own. TEL: 214687;
home — 213433. VAT: Stan.

WEST KNOYLE

Sue Lawson Baker
Furze Patch. Open by appointment only.
STOCK: Watercolours, 1850—1950. TEL:
Mere (0747) 860351.

WESTBURY   (0373)

Bratton Antiques   LAPADA
Market Place. (J.A.W. and F.A. Hyde.) Est.
1976. Open 10.15—1 and 2.15—5, Sat.
10.15—1, Mon. and Wed. by appointment.
SIZE: Small. *STOCK: Staffordshire figures and
animals, furniture, both 18th—19th C;
country and domestic bygones.* Not stocked:
Jewellery, silver and weapons. LOC: Close to
A350. PARK: Easy. TEL: 823021. VAT: Stan/
Spec.

WILTON, Nr. Salisbury

Ian J. Brook,
Antiques and Picture Gallery
26 North St. Resident. Est. 1962. CL: Wed.
p.m. Open after hours to trade by appointment. *STOCK: Furniture, oil paintings and
watercolours, £5—£5,000.* TEL: Salisbury
(0722) 743392. VAT: Stan/Spec.

Constable Galleries Ltd.
25 North St. (L. and P. Constable.) Open
8.30—4.30, Sat. 9—12.30. *STOCK: Small
silver, furniture, paintings.* TEL: (0722)
744902.

Jamawar or gown (long)
shawl. Dogra period, late
19th century. From *The
Kashmir Shawl* by Frank
Ames, published by the
**Antique Collectors'
Club,** 1986.

Wilton continued

Earle
47 North St. (A. Earle.) Est. 1960. Open 9.30—5.30, Sun. 9.30—12.30, Wed. 9—1. SIZE: Small. *STOCK: 18th—19th C pistols, shotguns, swords; 19th—20th C revolvers, automatic pistols, rifles; all £5—£100; 18th C oak furniture and general antiques, £50—£100.* Not stocked: Large furniture. LOC: From market place turn directly into North St. PARK: Easy. TEL: Salisbury (0722) 743284. SER: Valuations (arms only); buys at auction (guns, swords and weapons). VAT: Stan/Spec.

Pamela Lynch
18 West St. Resident. CL: Wed. Open 10—5, Sat 10—1. *STOCK: Small furniture, needlework pictures, decorative items, objets de vertu.* TEL: (0722) 744113.

A.J. Romain and Sons
The Old House, 11 and 13 North St. *STOCK: Furniture, mainly 17th—18th C; early oak, walnut and marquetry; clocks; copper, brass and miscellanea.* TEL: Salisbury (0722) 743350. VAT: Stan/Spec.

Wealden House Antiques
25 North St. (L. Constable.) Open 8.30—4.30, Sat. 9—12.30. *STOCK: Porcelain.* TEL: (0722) 744902.

WOOTTON BASSETT

Stonedge Antiques
137 High St. (Dr. and Mrs. A. Stebbens.) Est. 1969. Open 9—5.30. SIZE: Small. *STOCK: Furniture, china, glass, copper, brass, some silver, 18th—19th C, £10—£100.* LOC: A420, opposite Post Office, 2 miles from interchange 16, M4. PARK: Easy. TEL: Swindon (0793) 853296.

WROUGHTON, Nr. Swindon

Wroughton Antiques
23 High St. (F.R. Kent.) Est. 1947. Open 9.30—1 and 2—5, Sat. 9—1, or by appointment. SIZE: Medium. *STOCK: Chests and bureaux, 18th C, £50—£1,000; general antiques, 19th C, £50—£100; bric-a-brac.* LOC: A361. PARK: Easy. TEL: Swindon (0793) 813232; home — Swindon (0793) 721286. SER: Valuations; restorations (furniture); buys at auction (furniture).

Yorkshire North

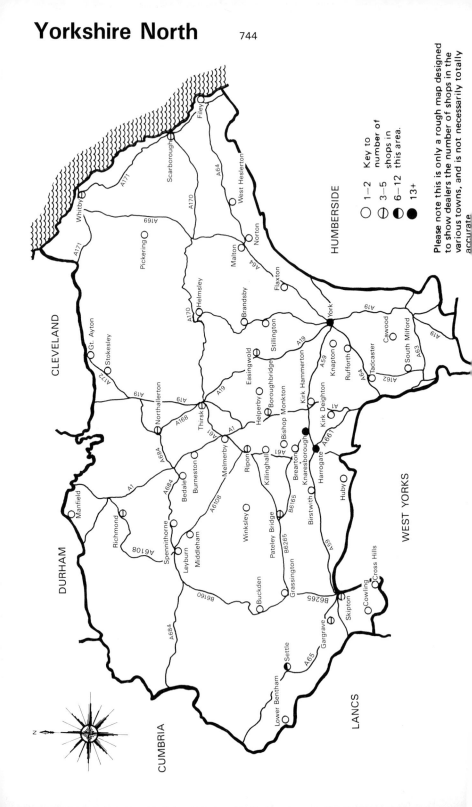

CLEVELAND

DURHAM

CUMBRIA

LANCS

WEST YORKS

HUMBERSIDE

Key to number of shops in this area.

- 1–2
- 3–5
- 6–12
- 13+

Please note this is only a rough map designed to show dealers the number of shops in the various towns, and is not necessarily totally accurate

Filey
Scarborough
Whitby
West Heslerton
Pickering
Norton
Malton
Flaxton
Helmsley
Brandsby
Gt. Ayton
Stokesley
Stillington
York
Cawood
South Milford
Tadcaster
Easingwold
Knapton
Rufforth
Northallerton
Helperby
Boroughbridge
Kirk Hammerton
Kirk Deighton
Thirsk
Bishop Monkton
Manfield
Melmerby
Ripon
Killinghall
Brearton
Knaresborough
Harrogate
Burneston
Bedale
Huby
Richmond
Winksley
Spennithorne
Leyburn
Middleham
Pateley Bridge
Birstwith
Buckden
Grassington
Cross Hills
Skipton
Cowling
Gargrave
Settle
Lower Bentham

A171
A170
A169
A64
A170
A172
A19
A684
A1
A6108
A684
A19
A168
A61
A1
A59
A19
A59
A64
A162
A63
A19
A61
B6165
A661
A59
B6265
B6160
A65

BEDALE (0677)
Thornton Gallery
Snape. (Mr. and Mrs. W.H. Turnbull.) Est. 1970. Open by appointment. SIZE: Small. STOCK: Oil paintings, £100—£1,000; watercolours, £45—£450; all 19th—20th C. Not stocked: Furniture, silver, pewter. LOC: 5 miles from A1 at Leeming Motel. PARK: Easy. TEL: 70318. SER: Valuations; restorations (oil paintings); buys at auction. VAT: Spec.

BIRSTWITH, Nr. Harrogate
John Pearson
Church Cottage. Est. 1978. Open by appointment. STOCK: Longcase, bracket and wall clocks, 18th C. LOC: Off A59. PARK: Easy. TEL: Harrogate (0423) 770828; home — same. SER: Restorations (clocks, cases, movements and especially dials).

BISHOP MONKTON
Nr. Harrogate
Pine Finds
The Old Cornmill. (G. and J. Pitt, G. and B. Harrison.) Est. 1979. Open 9—5, Sun. 10—5. SIZE: Large. STOCK: Pine and country smalls, 18th—19th C, £10—£1,000. LOC: 5 miles west of A1. TEL: Ripon (0765) 87159. SER: Restorations (pine). VAT: Stan.

BOROUGHBRIDGE (090 12)
Jeffery Bates Antiques
The Stone Yard, Fishergate. Est. 1966. Open Mon. 10—5, other times by appointment. SIZE: Small. STOCK: Small items and silver including snuff boxes and objets de vertu, £20—£350; pictures, £40—£500; furniture, £150—£1,000; medical and scientific instruments, £25—£500; all 18th—19th C. LOC: 1 mile from A1. PARK: Own. TEL: Home — Leeds (0532) 783306. SER: Valuations; buys at auction (silver and general antiques). FAIRS: Olympia; Heritage in the West End. VAT: Stan/Spec.

Country Antiques
High St. (J.P. and P.W. Raine). Est. 1969. CL: Thurs. and lunch times. SIZE: Medium. STOCK: Furniture, 17th to early 19th C, £10—£1,000; metalware, all periods; silver, 18th—20th C. PARK: Easy. VAT: Stan/Spec.

Joan Eyles Antiques BADA
The Stone Yard, Fishergate. (J.M. and J.C.H. Eyles.) Est. 1962. CL: Thurs. Open 11—5.30. STOCK: Pottery, furniture, general items, treen, sewing equipment, textiles. Not stocked: Weapons. PARK: Own. TEL: 3357; home — 2487. VAT: Spec.

Boroughbridge continued
R.S. Wilson and Sons
High St. Est. 1917. CL: Thurs. p.m. Open 9—5.30. STOCK: Furniture, 17th—19th C; porcelain and pottery. TEL: 2417; home — 2654. VAT: Stan/Spec.

BRANDSBY (034 75)
L.L. Ward and Son
Bar House. (R. Ward.) Est. 1970. Open 8—5, Sat. 10—12 and 1—5. STOCK: Old pine. TEL: 651. SER: Restorations (pine).

BREARTON, Nr. Knaresborough
C.J. Dennis (Books)
Sunnyside Farm. Open by appointment. STOCK: Field, sports and racing antiquarian books. LOC: On B6165, just off Ripley Rd. TEL: Harrogate (0423) 864707.

BUCKDEN, Nr. Skipton
Greystones Antiques
(S. Griffiths.) Usually open, appointment advisable. STOCK: Lace and linen, small furniture, collectors' items, copper, brass, Yorkshire Dales' paintings, model railways. TEL: Kettlewell (075 676) 847. SER: Repairs.

BURNESTON, Nr. Bedale
Simon Greenwood Antiques
(S. and C. Greenwood.) Est. 1976. Open by appointment. SIZE: Warehouse. *STOCK: General antiques, curios, china, paintings, shipping goods.* LOC: ¼ mile from A1. PARK: Easy. TEL: Home — Bedale (0677) 22554; Melmerby (076 584) 571. VAT: Stan/Spec.

W. Greenwood (Fine Art)   *Trade Only*
7 Church Wynd. Est. 1978. Open by appointment. *STOCK: Paintings and watercolours, 19th and 20th C, £100—£1,000; frames, £20—£200.* LOC: Take B6285 left off A1, village ½ mile. PARK: Easy. TEL: Bedale (0677) 24830. SER: Valuations; restorations (paintings), framing; buys at auction.

CAWOOD   (075 786)
The Pine Workshop
6 Old Rd. (D.J. Robinson.) Est. 1983. CL: Sat. Open 9—5 or by appointment. SIZE: Small. *STOCK: Stripped pine.* LOC: In centre of village. PARK: Easy. TEL: 243. SER: Restorations (pine).

COWLING, Nr. Keighley
Smith-Albany
60A Keighley Rd. Est. 1957. Open Mon., Wed. and Thurs. 10.30—3, other times by appointment. SIZE: Medium. *STOCK: Objets d'art, glass, furniture, £1—£1,000.* LOC: Midway between Colne and Cross Hills. PARK: Easy. TEL: Home — Gargrave (075 678) 516. SER: Valuations; buys at auction; courier service, container packing.

CROSS HILLS, Nr. Keighley (0535)
Heathcote Antiques
1 Aire St. (M. Webster.) Resident. Est. 1979. CL: Mon. and Tues. Open 10—5.30, Sun. 12.30—4. SIZE: Medium. *STOCK: Pine, Victorian furniture and small items, £5—£200.* PARK: Easy. TEL: 35250. SER: Valuations.

EASINGWOLD   (0347)
Chapman Medd and Sons
Market Place. Est. 1865. Open 8—12 and 1—5. Open at any time in summer. *STOCK: Country furniture, oak and mahogany.* TEL: 21370.

Pamela Davies
56/58 Long St. (P.A. Davies.) Est. 1970. Open 10—6, telephone call advisable. SIZE: Small. *STOCK: 18th—20th C oils and watercolours, £10—£1,500; 18th—19th C small furniture, £25—£800; objets d'art, books.* Not stocked: Automata, toys. LOC: Between York and Thirsk on A19. PARK: Easy. TEL: 21251. SER: Valuations; restorations (oil paintings and watercolours); buys at auction.

Mrs. B.A.S. Reynolds
42 Long St. *STOCK: General antiques, Victoriana.* TEL: 21078.

White House Farm Antiques
Thirsk Rd. (C. Hood.) Est. 1960. Resident. Usually open but prior 'phone call advisable. *STOCK: Kitchen and rural bygones, farm machinery, stone troughs, architectural reclamation and garden ornaments.* LOC: Two miles north of Easingwold, on A19. PARK: Easy. TEL: 21479 or 810872.

FILEY
Filey Antiques
1 Belle Vue St. (Mrs. E.M. Ridley.) Est. 1970. Open daily 10.30—4.30 in summer, 10.30—4 in winter, Thurs. to Sat. only. SIZE: Small. *STOCK: Small furniture, prints, china, bric-a-brac, jewellery.* Not stocked: Coins, militaria. LOC: Town centre, at corner of Belle Vue St. and West Ave. PARK: Easy. TEL: Scarborough (0723) 513440.

FLAXTON, Nr. York

Elm Tree Antiques
(R. and J. Jackson.) Est. 1975. Open 9—5, Sun. 10—5, until 7.30 in summer. SIZE: Large. *STOCK: Furniture, 17th C to Edwardian; small items £25—£100.* LOC: 1 mile off A64. PARK: Easy. TEL: Flaxton Moor (090486) 462; home — same. SER: Valuations; restorations (cabinet making, polishing and upholstery); buys at auction (furniture).

GARGRAVE   (075 678)

Andrew and Linda Blackburn
12 West St. Open by appointment. *STOCK: Georgian and Victorian furniture, metalware.* LOC: From Skipton turn right off High St. PARK: Easy. TEL: 403. SER: Valuations; containers; courier. VAT: Stan/Spec.

Bernard Dickinson   BADA
88 High St. Est. 1958. CL: Sat. p.m. *STOCK: English and Continental furniture, 17th—19th C.* TEL: 285 or 8257. SER: Repairs and restorations to the trade.

Myers Galleries   BADA
Endsleigh House, High St. (R.N. Myers and Son.) Est. 1890. Open 9—5.30 or by appointment. SIZE: Medium. *STOCK: Furniture, oak, mahogany, 17th to early 19th C; pottery, porcelain and metalware.* Not stocked: Victoriana, weapons, coins, jewellery. LOC: A65, Skipton— Settle road. PARK: Behind shop and opposite. TEL: 587. SER: Valuations. VAT: Spec.

GRASSINGTON, Nr. Skipton (0756)

Fairings
Lucy Fold. (Mrs. M.A. Byrne.) Est. 1979. CL: Thurs. SIZE: Small. *STOCK: Country antiques, including brass, copper, kitchenware, small furniture, pine, £1—£400.* LOC: Opposite Black Horse Hotel. PARK: Easy. TEL: 752755.

GREAT AYTON   (0642)

The Great Ayton Bookshop
47 High St. (M.S. Jones.) Est. 1978. CL: Mon. Open 10—6 (10—5 Oct.—Mar.), Wed. 10—2, Sun. 2—6. SIZE: Small. *STOCK: Books, antiquarian and secondhand, 50p—£100; postcards, pre-1930, 10p—£5; toys and games, pre-1960, prints and local maps, 10p—£50.* LOC: 7 miles south of Middlesbrough off Stokesley road. PARK: Easy. TEL: 723358. SER: Valuations. FAIRS: P.B.F.A. VAT: Stan.

HARROGATE   (0423)

Ann-tiquities
12 Cheltenham Parade. (Mrs. A. Wilkinson.) CL: Wed. Open 10—4. *STOCK: Bric-a-brac, linen, silver, brass, copper, small items.* TEL: 503567.

Antique Corner
25 Lower Market Hall. (N. Hare (Harrogate) Ltd.) Est. 1960. CL: Wed. Open 10—5. *STOCK: Silver plate, silver, china, pottery, jewellery, furniture.* PARK: Easy. TEL: 503761. VAT: Stan.

Antique Pine
Library House, Regent Parade. (M. Green.) Est. 1976. Open 8.30—6.30; Sun. by appointment. SIZE: Medium. *STOCK: Pine furniture, Georgian—Edwardian, £5—£1,000; kitchenalia and collectors' items.* LOC: Overlooking the Stray. PARK: Easy. TEL: 60452. SER: Valuations; restorations; stripping. VAT: Stan/Spec.

Antiques and Collectables
39 Cheltenham Crescent. (D. Nimmo.) Open 9.30—5.30. *STOCK: Jewellery, silver, watches, collectors' items.* TEL: 521897.

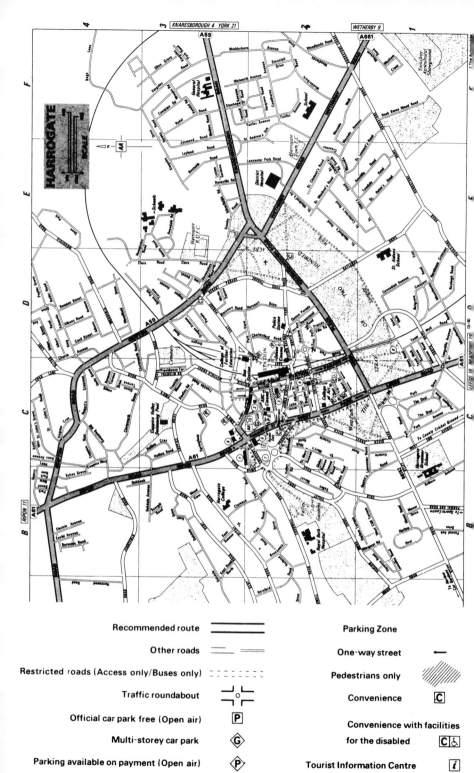

HARROGATE

Recommended route	━━━━━
Other roads	
Restricted roads (Access only/Buses only)	- - - - -
Traffic roundabout	
Official car park free (Open air)	P
Multi-storey car park	G
Parking available on payment (Open air)	P

Parking Zone	
One-way street	←
Pedestrians only	
Convenience	C
Convenience with facilities for the disabled	C &
Tourist Information Centre	i

Reproduced by kind permission of the Automobile Association

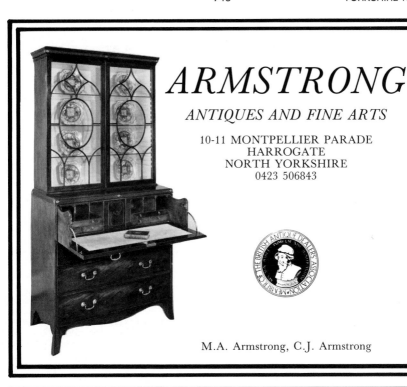
Harrogate continued

Armstrong Antiques

**BADA
LAPADA**

10—11 Montpellier Parade. (M.A. and C.J. Armstrong.) **Est. 1976. Open 10—6. SIZE: Medium.** *STOCK: Furniture, glass, decorative items, 17th to early 19th C.* **PARK: Easy. TEL: 506843. FAIRS: British International,** Birmingham; Park Lane. **VAT: Spec.**

Harrogate continued

Bill Bentley

16 Montpellier Parade. Open 9—5.30 by appointment. SIZE: Medium. *STOCK: Oak furniture, 1600—1800; country furniture, 1700—1800; metalwork, textiles, patchwork, samplers.* PARK: Easy. TEL: 64084 or 64564. SER: Restorations. VAT: Stan/Spec.

Harrogate continued

Bloomers
41 Cheltenham Crescent. (P.E. Llewellyn). Est. 1983. Open 10.30—5.30. SIZE: Small. STOCK: *Period clothes and accessories, costume jewellery, mainly pre-1940s; dolls.* LOC: Corner of King's Rd., almost opposite new conference centre. PARK: Nearby. TEL: 69389. SER: Valuations; restorations (re-beading of 20's dresses, re-stringing dolls).

Cheltenham Galleries
3 Cheltenham Parade. (L. Biffin.) Open 10.30—12.30 and 2.15—5.30. *STOCK: General antiques.* TEL: 60711.

Church View Antiques
34b Leeds Rd. (P. Bolton.) Open 9.15—5.30, Wed. 9.15—1.30. SIZE: Small. STOCK: *Furniture, clocks, silver and porcelain.* PARK: Easy. TEL: 502694. VAT: Stan.

Cold Bath Antiques
20 Cold Bath Rd. (Mrs. S.R. Houlgate.) Est. 1969. Open 9.30—5.30; but resident so usually available. SIZE: Medium. STOCK: *Small Victorian, Edwardian and some period furniture, interesting and unusual items.* Not stocked: Silver, coins and weapons. LOC: 400yds. south up hill from Crown roundabout. PARK: Easy. TEL: 62331. FAIRS: Local.

Cottage Antiques   LAPADA
3 Devonshire Place, Skipton Rd. (Mrs. S. Evans.) Open 10—5, other times by appointment. SIZE: Large. STOCK: *Period oak, pine, country furniture, 17th—19th C; country and dairy items, treen, brass, copper, pottery, 18th—19th C; domestic cast iron, 19th C.* LOC: A59, 100yds. from Westmoreland St. traffic lights. PARK: Easy. TEL: 68195; home — Collingham Bridge (0937) 72694. VAT: Stan/Spec.

Harrogate continued

Daleside Antiques
4 St. Peters Sq., Cold Bath Rd. Est. 1978. Open 8—12.30 and 1—5. Sat. and Sun. by appointment. SIZE: Large. STOCK: *Pine furniture, decorative items, architectural features and fittings, 18th—19th C, £50—£2,500.* LOC: At Crown Hotel roundabout turn into Cold Bath Rd., at Slip Inn on right, turn alongside at the Ginnel. TEL: 60286; home — 509618. SER: Containers. VAT: Stan.

Dragon Antiques
10 Dragon Rd. (G. Broadbelt.) Resident. Est. 1954. Open 9.30—6. Always available. SIZE: Small. STOCK: *Victorian art glass, £5—£100; art pottery, art nouveau, art deco.* LOC: 5 mins. from town centre. PARK: Easy. TEL: 62037.

Duncalfe Antiques   BADA
34 Montpellier Parade. (N.J. Duncalfe.) Open 9.30—5.30. STOCK: *Furniture, oak, walnut, mahogany, £100—£25,000; porcelain, pottery, £30—£1,000; paintings, 18th—20th C, £100—£20,000.* TEL: 521452. VAT: Spec.

Elizabeth Finlay
131 High St., Starbeck. (Mrs. Finlay.) Est. 1971. CL: Fri. Open 1—5. STOCK: *Furniture, small antiques.* LOC: Between Harrogate and Knaresborough. PARK: Easy. TEL: 886389 or 69759.

Fox's Antiques and Shipping
83 Knaresborough Rd. (M. and P. Fox and Son.) Est. 1958. CL: Sat. Open 9—1 and 2—5 or by appointment. SIZE: Medium and warehouse. STOCK: *General antiques and shipping goods.* LOC: A59. PARK: Easy. TEL: 888116; home — same. SER: Buys at auction. VAT: Stan/Spec.

DALESIDE ANTIQUES

SPECIALISTS IN OLD AND PERIOD PINE

4 ST. PETER'S SQUARE, COLD BATH ROAD
HARROGATE, NORTH YORKSHIRE
TELEPHONE (0423) 60286/509618

W.F. Greenwood & Sons Ltd.

2 & 3 Crown Place, Harrogate, N. Yorkshire HG1 2RY
Tel: (0423) 504467

*Fine, late 19th century ebony side cabinet with slate panels and
pietra dura ornament. Ormolu mounts, circa 1880,
length 78ins., height 45ins, depth 18½ins.*

Jewellers, Silversmiths and Antique Dealers
LICENSED VALUERS

Members of the British Antique Dealers' Association
Members of the National Association of Goldsmiths

A family business for over 150 years —
est. 1829

Harrogate continued

Galloway Antiques   LAPADA
4 Westmoreland St. (J. and D. Gay). Est.
1972. Open 9—1 and 2—5. SIZE: Large.
*STOCK: Furniture, £50—£1,000+; jewellery,
£5—£1,000, silver, £5—£700, both 18th and
19th C; general antiques £1—£1,000; porcelain £20—£2,000.* LOC: Off Skipton Rd.
TEL: 505298; home — 506719. FAIRS:
Northern, Midland, Southern, Dateline. VAT:
Spec.

W.F. Greenwood   BADA
and Sons Ltd.
**2 and 3 Crown Place. Est. 1829. CL: Wed.
p.m. Open 9—1 and 2.15—5.30. SIZE: Large.**
*STOCK: Furniture, 1660—1850, £25—
£15,000; pottery and porcelain, 1740—
1830, £15—£800; silver and jewellery,
£10—£3,500.* **TEL: 504467. SER: Valuations.
VAT: Stan/Spec.**

Harrogate continued

Grove Collectors Centre
Grove Rd. Open 9—5.30. There are approximately 8 dealers at this centre selling a wide
range of *general antiques including coins,
militaria, silver, collectables and furniture.* TEL:
61680.

The Harrogate Post Card Shop
38a Cold Bath Rd. (T.H.G. Mathews.) CL: Sat.
Open 12—4.30. *STOCK: Postcards, small
silver, Victoriana, small collectors' items.* TEL:
508501. SER: Approval (postcards only).

A strange little unsigned bronze of 1880-1900 that at first glance looks like the work
of the mid-19th century animalier school but may well be German imitating the Paris
style towards the end of the century. From *Animals in Bronze* by Christopher Payne,
published by the **Antique Collectors' Club**, 1986.

Harrogate continued

Irene Kelly Antiques

38 Forest Lane Head, Starbeck. CL: Tues. p.m. Open 10−5. SIZE: Small. *STOCK: Small furniture, £100−£1,000; needlework, porcelain, glass and objets d'art, all 18th−19th C; paintings and prints, 19th to early 20th C.* LOC: Adjacent to Harrogate Golf Club. PARK: Easy. TEL: 889832; home − 771058. SER: Valuations; restorations.

R.B. Kendal-Greene

Trade and Export Only
2A Chudleigh Rd. Est. 1964. *STOCK: General antiques.* TEL: 62497. VAT: Stan/Spec.

Rodney Kent   LAPADA

20 West Park. CL: Mon. Open 10−1 and 2.30−6. *STOCK: Paintings, drawings and watercolours, 18th−20th C; Oriental antiques; furniture.* TEL: 60352.

Harrogate continued

David Lawes

125 Cold Bath Rd. Est. 1962. Open 9−12 and 2−5.30, Fri. 9−11.45 and 2−5.30, Sat. 9−12.30. SIZE: Small. *STOCK: Philatelic items.* PARK: Easy. TEL: 68428. SER: Valuations.

David Love   BADA

10 Royal Parade. (Mr. and Mrs. D.A. Love.) Est. 1969. Open 9−1 and 2−6. SIZE: Large. *STOCK: Furniture, English, 17th−19th C; pottery and porcelain, English and Continental; decorative items, all periods.* **LOC: Opposite Pump Room Museum. PARK: Easy. TEL: 65797. SER: Valuations; buys at auction. VAT: Stan/Spec.**

Pew group of a lady with two suitors made of white salt-glazed stoneware with details picked out in dark brown stained clay. Made in Staffordshire, c.1730, 159mm high. From *A Collectors' History of English Pottery* by Griselda Lewis, published by the **Antique Collectors' Club**, 1985.

Harrogate continued

Charles Lumb and Sons Ltd. BADA
2 Montpellier Gardens. (F. and A.R. Lumb.) Est. 1920. Open 9—1 and 2—6. SIZE: Medium. *STOCK: Furniture, 17th to early 19th C, metalware, period accessories.* PARK: 20yds. immediately opposite. TEL: 503776; home — 863281. FAIRS: Harrogate. VAT: Spec.

McTague of Harrogate
17/19 Cheltenham Mount. (P. McTague.) CL: Wed. Open 9.30—1 and 2—5.30. SIZE: Medium. *STOCK: Prints, some oil paintings, drawings and watercolours, 17th—19th C.* LOC: From Conference Centre on Kings Rd., go up Cheltenham Parade and turn first left. PARK: Easy. TEL: 67086; home — 884400. SER: Valuations; restorations (oil paintings, prints, watercolours and drawings); buys at auction (paintings and prints). VAT: Stan/Spec.

D. Mason & Son
7/8 Westmoreland St. FGA, NAG. CL: Wed. p.m. Open 9—12.30 and 1.45—5. *STOCK: Victorian, Edwardian and second-hand jewellery; clocks.* TEL: 67305. SER: Repairs (clocks and jewellery.)

Mews Antiques
2 John St. Est. 1975. Open 9.30—5. SIZE: Medium. *STOCK: Period furniture, clocks, oil paintings, watercolours and prints; 18th C porcelain, glass, Oriental ceramics, collectors' items.* LOC: Behind Prospect Hotel. PARK: Easy. TEL: 507549; home — 883092.

Harrogate continued

Northern Fine Art Ltd.
Mowbray Square, Westmoreland St. CL: Sat. Open 8.30—4.30. *STOCK: Pictures, and mirrors.* TEL: 64224 and 770504.

Ogden of Harrogate Ltd. BADA
38 James St. Est. 1893. Open 9—5. SIZE: Large. *STOCK: English silver, Sheffield plate and jewellery, oil paintings, English and Continental, 19th C.* TEL: 504123. VAT: Stan/Spec.

The Old Cottage Shop
13 and 18 Lowther Arcade. (Mrs. M.R. Peveler.) Est. 1951. Open 1.45—5.45. *STOCK: Small general antiques.* TEL: 883942.

Omar (Harrogate) Ltd.
8 Crescent Rd. (R. Wolfe and P. McCormick.) Est. 1946. CL: Wed. p.m.; and Sun. except by appointment. Open 9—5.30. SIZE: Medium. *STOCK: Persian, Turkish, Caucasian rugs and carpets, £50—£5,000.* PARK: Easy. TEL: 503675. SER: Valuations; restorations (Oriental carpets); buys at auction. VAT: Stan.

Oriental Art Ware
12 Crescent Rd. (W. Christie.) Est. 1892. *STOCK: Oriental pottery, ivory, wood carvings; jewellery, some antique.* VAT: Stan/Spec.

Paul M. Peters Antiques
15a Bower Rd. Est. 1967. CL: Sat. p.m. Open 9.30—6. SIZE: Medium. *STOCK: Oriental, English and continental pottery and porcelain, art nouveau and art deco, scientific instruments, unusual small antiques, £25—£250; pewter, brass, copper, early metalware.* LOC: Town centre, at bottom of Station Parade. PARK: Easy. TEL: 60118. SER: Valuations. VAT: Stan/Spec.

A very rare Lowestoft salt, one of a pair from the Wallace Elliot and Colman Collections, 1⁴/₅ins. high, c.1770-5. From *Lowestoft Porcelains* by Geoffrey A. Godden, F.R.S.A., published by the **Antique Collectors' Club,** 1985.

Harrogate continued

Elaine Phillips Antiques Ltd. BADA
2 Royal Parade, and Horsemans Well, Felliscliffe. Open 9.30—5.30. By appointment at Horsemans Well. SIZE: Medium. *STOCK: Oak furniture, 1600—1800; country furniture, 1700—1800; period metal work and decoration.* LOC: Opposite Crown Hotel. PARK: Easy. TEL: 69745. SER: Restorations. VAT: Spec.

Regency Fine Art
123 Wetherby Rd. (G.B. Wright.) Resident. Est. 1966. Open by appointment. SIZE: Medium. *STOCK: English and Continental oil paintings, 18th—20th C, £100—£400.* PARK: Easy at rear. TEL: 883178. SER: Valuations; restorations. FAIRS: Bristol, Harrogate, Birmingham. VAT: Spec.

Renoir Galleries Ltd.
16 Crescent Rd. Open 9—5.30. *STOCK: Oil paintings; watercolours, signed limited editions.* TEL: 502998. SER: Framing; restorations (oil paintings, watercolours and prints); valuations.

Rippon Bookshop
1st Floor, 6 Station Bridge. (Mrs. A. Rawson.) Est. 1980. Open 10—5. SIZE: Medium. *STOCK: Antiquarian books — local history, £25—£150; local topography and general £5—£25.* LOC: Near Railway station and opposite Odeon Cinema. PARK: Nearby. TEL: 501835; home — Ripon (0765) 4848. SER: Valuations; restorations (book binding); finder. FAIRS: Harrogate.

The Saleroom
2 Grange Ave., Kings Rd. (F. and P.V. Curry.) Est. 1977. Open 9.30—5.30. SIZE: Large. *STOCK: General antiques, 19th—20th C, £50—£500.* LOC: Off Skipton Rd., turn left at National Westminster Bank, then first right. PARK: Easy. TEL: 64609; home — 504560. VAT: Stan/Spec.

F.B. Shaftoe *Trade and Export Only*
17—18 Regent Parade. Est. 1945. CL: Sun. except by appointment. Open 9—6. SIZE: Large. *STOCK: English furniture, 18th—19th C.* TEL: 502151. VAT: Stan/Spec.

Harrogate continued

Shaw Bros.
21 Montpellier Parade. (J. and C. Shaw.) CL: Wed. p.m. *STOCK: English and Continental porcelain, 18th—19th C; silver, jewellery, Meissen, Dresden vases and figures.* TEL: 67466.

G. Shaw
Omega St., off Ripon Rd., New Park. Est. 1948. Open Tues., Fri. and Sat. 1—4 or by appointment. SIZE: Small. *STOCK: Furniture, 18th—19th C, £20—£200.* Not stocked: Silver and jewellery. LOC: From Harrogate take the Ripon Rd., shop on right before junction of Skipton Rd. traffic lights. PARK: Easy. TEL: 503590. SER: Restorations (furniture).

Singing Bird Antiques
19 Knaresborough Rd. (A.M. Sagar.) Est. 1964. CL: Sat. Open 10.30—5. SIZE: Medium. *STOCK: Furniture, silver, pewter, 18th C; pottery, porcelain.* LOC: On A59, 1 mile out of Harrogate on left, just before pedestrian crossing. PARK: Easy. TEL: 888292; home — 885715.

Smith's ("The Rink") Ltd.
Dragon Rd. Est. 1906. Open 9—5.30. SIZE: Large. *STOCK: General antiques, 1750—1820, £150; Victoriana 1830—1900, £50.* LOC: From Leeds, right at Prince of Wales crossing, left at Skipton Rd. and left before railway bridge. PARK: Easy. TEL: 503217. VAT: Stan/Spec.

Snodgrass Antiques
4 Westmoreland St. (B. and E. Snodgrass.) Est. 1974. Open 9—5. *STOCK: Victorian and Georgian furniture, interesting small items.* TEL: 505298. SER: Buys at auction. VAT: Spec.

Sutcliffe Galleries BADA
8 Albert St. Est. 1952. CL: Wed. Open 10—5. *STOCK: Paintings, 19th C.* LOC: Opposite Prince's Square. TEL: 62976; home — Burnsall (075 672) 663. SER: Valuations; restorations; framing. VAT: Stan/Spec.

ELAINE PHILLIPS ANTIQUES LTD.

2 Royal Parade
Harrogate, North Yorkshire
Tel: Harrogate 69745

18th CENTURY OAK DRESSER AND RACK

Member of the British Antique Dealers Association.

Harrogate continued

Thorntons of Harrogate   LAPADA
1 Montpellier Gardens. Open 9.30—5.30.
*STOCK: 17th—18th C furniture, metalware,
clocks, pictures, porcelain, arms and armour,
scientific instruments.* TEL: 504118. VAT:
Spec.

Walker Galleries Ltd.   BADA
                                    LAPADA
6 Montpellier Gardens. Est. 1972. Open
9.30—1 and 2—5.30. SIZE: Medium. *STOCK:
Oil paintings and watercolours, 18th C furniture and Oriental ceramics.* TEL: 67933. SER:
Valuations; restorations; framing. FAIRS:
Chelsea, Harrogate, Kenilworth, British International, Birmingham, Northern (Harrogate).
VAT: Spec.

Christopher Warner   BADA
15 Princes St. (C.C. Warner and I.P. Legard.)
Est. 1770. Open 9.30—5. SIZE: Small.
*STOCK: Jewellery, 1740—1860, £50—
£4,000; silver, 1720—1850, £50—£3,500.*
PARK: Easy. TEL: 503617. SER: Valuations;
restorations (silver and jewellery); buys at
auction. FAIRS: Harrogate and British
International (Birmingham). VAT: Stan/Spec.

John Weatherell and Sons
                                    LAPADA
Westmoreland House, 13-19 Westmoreland
St. Est. 1961.Open 9—5.30. *STOCK: General
antiques.* TEL: 60038.

West Park Antiques Pavilion
20 West Park. CL: Mon. Open 10—5. TEL:
61758. Below are listed some of the dealers
at this centre.
  Shirley Baguley Antiques
  Stand 7. *Jewellery and silver.*
  Claud-Lee
  *Glass, porcelain, art deco, curios and small
  furniture.*
  Dove Antiques
  Smalls.
  Howarth Antiques
  Stand 5a. *Clocks.* SER: Restorations
  (clocks).
  Marquyn Antiques
  Blue and white pottery, small items.
  Mrs. B. Smith
  Porcelain and collectors items.
  Vogue Antiques
  Small china and prints.

Westmoreland Antiques
25/27 Westmoreland St. Est. 1965. Open
9—6, Sun. by appointment, Wed. 9—5. SIZE:
Medium. *STOCK: General antiques, £1—
£1,000.* LOC: High Harrogate, off Skipton Rd.
PARK: Easy. TEL: 506721; home — 504395.
SER: Valuations; restorations; buys at auction.
VAT: Stan.

HELMSLEY   (0439)
Ian Stephenson
Bondgate. Est. 1974. Open 9—5. *STOCK:
English 18th—19th C oak and country furniture, copper and brass, Royal Worcester and
Royal Crown Derby porcelain, £20—£2,000.*
LOC: 150yds. from Market Place on A170
towards Scarborough. TEL: 70351; home —
same. VAT: Spec.

York Cottage Antiques
7 Church St. (G. and E.M. Thornley.) Est.
1981. CL: Wed. Open daily July—Sept.
10—4. Open Fri. and Sat. only Oct—June,
other times by appointment. *STOCK: Metalware 18th—19th C. £10—£250; china
especially Ironstone, blue and white, Imari and
Victorian teaware; glass, especially coloured
Victorian and art glass; collectors' items.* LOC:
Opposite church. PARK: Adjacent. TEL: 70833;
home — same.

HELPERBY, Nr. York   (090 16)
Helperby Antiques   *Mainly Trade*
Main St. (K. Simpson.) Est. 1977. Open by
appointment. SIZE: Medium. *STOCK: General
antiques, Georgian, Victorian, Edwardian and
shipping furniture, clocks, small china, glass,
copper and brass.* PARK: Easy. TEL: 692.

HUBY, Nr. Leeds
Haworth Antiques
Harrogate Rd. (G. and J. White.) B.W.C.M.G.
Est. 1969. CL: Mon. Open 9—6 or by appointment. *STOCK: Clocks — wall, longcase and
bracket, 18th—20th C, £15—£1,000; small
furniture, collectors' items.* Not stocked:
porcelain, pottery and paintings. LOC: A658.
PARK: Own. TEL: Harrogate (0423) 74293.
SER: Restorations (clocks). VAT: Stan/Spec.

KILLINGHALL, Nr. Harrogate
Norwood Cottage Antiques
Ripon Rd. (Mr. and Mrs. J. Davies.) Est. 1981.
CL: Thurs. Open 10—6, other times by appointment. *STOCK: English mahogany, walnut and
rosewood furniture, 18th—19th C.* PARK:
Easy. TEL: Harrogate (0423) 56468. SER:
Valuations.

KIRK DEIGHTON, Nr. Wetherby
Elden Antiques
23 Ashdale View. (E. and D. Broadley). Est.
1970. Open 9—11.30 and 12.30—5.30, Sat.
12—5.30. SIZE: Small. *STOCK: General
antiques including small furniture.* LOC: Main
road between Wetherby and Knaresborough.
PARK: Easy. TEL: Wetherby (0937) 64770;
home — same. SER: Valuations.

KIRK HAMMERTON, Nr. York
Yorkshire Stripping Service
Mill Farm. (C. and K.M. Main.) Est. 1976. Open 9–5, Sun. by appointment to the trade only. SIZE: Large. *STOCK: Pine furniture, 18th–19th C, £100–£1,500; architectural pine, 19th–20th C, £50–£1,000; china and bric-a-brac, 18th–20th C, £5–£25.* LOC: 1½ miles off A59. PARK: Easy. TEL: (0901) 30451; home — same. SER: Restorations (pine); fitted kitchens. VAT: Stan.

KNAPTON, Nr. York
Garth Antiques
Burton Garth. (I. and J.I.F. Chapman.) Est. 1978. Open daily, Sun. by appointment. SIZE: Medium. *STOCK: Furniture and clocks, 18th–19th C, £50–£1,000; general antiques, 19th C, £1–£100.* LOC: Off A59 at Challis Garden Centre. PARK: Easy. TEL: York (0904) 790576. VAT: Stan/Spec.

KNARESBOROUGH
Robert Aagaard Ltd.   BADA
Frogmire House, Stockwell Rd. Est. 1952. Open 9–5, Sat. 9.30–12.30. SIZE: Medium. *STOCK: Chimney pieces, marble fire surrounds and interiors.* LOC: Town centre. PARK: Own. TEL: Harrogate (0423) 864805. VAT: Stan/Spec.

Knaresborough continued

H. and L. Bowkett
9 Abbey Rd. (E.S. Starkie.) Resident. Est. 1919. Open 9–6. SIZE: Medium. *STOCK: Chairs, small furniture, brass, copper, pot-lids, Goss, books.* LOC: By the river at the lower road bridge. PARK: Easy. TEL: Harrogate (0423) 866112. SER: Restorations (upholstery and small furniture). VAT: Stan/Spec.

Cheapside Antiques
4 Cheapside. (Mrs. M.E. Hanson.) CL: Thurs. Open 10–5. *STOCK: Furniture, porcelain, metalware and small collectors' items, 1750–1900.* TEL: Harrogate (0423) 867779. VAT: Spec.

Peter Hall Antiques
2 Cheapside. (P. Hall and P.P. Smith.) Est. 1977. CL: Thurs. Open 10–1 and 2–5. SIZE: Medium. *STOCK: Oak, mahogany and walnut furniture, £50–£2,000, oils, watercolours and prints, £25–£500; books, £2–£60; all 18th and 19th C; silver, 18th–20th C, £12–£400; bijouterie, 19th–20th C, £3–£200.* LOC: Corner premises with Gracious St. on York side of town. PARK: Nearby. TEL: Harrogate (04230) 868331; home — Tockwith (090 15) 453.

Knaresborough continued

Robert Hammond
6 Castlegate. Est. 1930. CL: Thurs. p.m.
Open 9—5.30. PARK: At side. TEL: Harrogate
(0423) 862047.

Milton Holgate   BADA
4 Market Square. Est. 1890. CL: Thurs. p.m.
Open 10—5. SIZE: Medium. *STOCK: Prints
and paintings.* PARK: Easy. TEL: Harrogate
(0423) 863205. VAT: Spec.

M.J. Holgate   *Mainly Trade*
36 Gracious St. Est. 1972. CL: Thurs. Open
9—5.30. SIZE: Small. *STOCK: Georgian furniture, longcase clocks and general antiques.*
PARK: Nearby. TEL: Harrogate (0423) 865219.
VAT: Mainly Spec.

The Home of Antiques
104—106 High St. (D. Lee.) Est. 1959. CL:
Thurs. Open 9—5.30. SIZE: Large. *STOCK:
Furniture, china, silver.* TEL: Harrogate (0423)
864563. SER: Valuations. VAT: Stan/Spec.

Kellys of Knaresborough
96 High St. (D.C. Kelly.) Est. 1969. CL: Thurs.
Open 10—5. SIZE: Large. *STOCK: Chandeliers, wall lights, oil lamps, candle sticks,
mainly 18—19th C; decorative glass.* Not
stocked: Silver, jewellery, weapons, pictures
and porcelain. LOC: A59. PARK: Own. TEL:
Harrogate (0423) 862041. SER: Restorations
(chandeliers); buys at auction. VAT: Stan/
Spec.

Terry and Sheila Kindon   LAPADA
Trade Only
St. John's House, Station Rd. CL: Sat. Open
8—6, other times by appointment. *STOCK:
Mainly furniture and pine.* TEL: Harrogate
(0423) 867554. SER: Container.

Lund and Bartholomew
23 Waterside. (J.E. Lund.) Resident. Est.
1977. Open Sat, Sun. and Wed. p.m., other
times by appointment. SIZE: Small. *STOCK:
Furniture, 19th C; paintings, 19th to early
20th C, both £50—£250; bric-a-brac and
brassware, 19th C, £5—£50; books, 19th to
early 20th C, £1—£100.* LOC: Turn off A59
at World's End Inn. PARK: Easy. TEL: Harrogate (0423) 864348 or 862389 (ansaphone).
SER: Valuations; restorations (furniture, paintings); framing; buys at auction (furniture,
paintings).

Knaresborough continued

The Gordon Reece Gallery — inc. Northern Kelim Centre
Finkle St. Est. 1981. CL: Thurs. Open
10.30—5, Sun. 2—5 or by appointment.
SIZE: Large. *STOCK: Furniture, carvings,
textiles, costume, artifacts, from non-
European tribal people and cultures, £5—
£1,000; tribal and nomadic flatweave rugs
and carpets.* LOC: Town centre. PARK: Own.
TEL: Harrogate (0423) 866219 or 866502;
home — same. SER: Exhibitions organised and
mounted; touring exhibitions. VAT: Stan.

Charles Shaw
12 Market Place. Est. 1981. Open daily
including Sun. p.m. SIZE: Medium. *STOCK:
Taxidermy, £25—£2,000; country and sporting pictures, £20—£5,000; both 19th—20th
C; out-of-print, country and sporting books,
£5—£500; small antiques and furniture,
18th—20th C, £5—£1,000; firearms.* LOC:
Off High St. A59. PARK: Easy and castle
grounds. TEL: Harrogate (0423) 867715;
home — same. SER: Valuations; buys at
auction. VAT Stan/Spec.

Swadforth House   LAPADA
Gracious St. (J. Thompson.) Est. 1968.
STOCK: General antiques. TEL: Harrogate
(0423) 864698. VAT: Spec.

The Workshop
Rear of 20 Finkle St. (G. Reece.) Est. 1982.
CL: Thurs. Open 10.30—5, Sun. 2—5. SIZE:
Medium. *STOCK: Mainly 17th C oak furniture
and carvings; country furniture, 18th C; treen,
metalware, provincial country pottery, 18th—
19th C; prints and textiles, 17th—19th C.*
LOC: Town centre. PARK: Own. TEL: Harrogate (0423) 866219 or 866502; home —
same. SER: Valuations; restorations (furniture,
treen); buys at auction (as stock); VAT: Stan/
Spec.

LEYBURN

Cottage Antiques
High St. (M. and S. Hardcastle.) Est. 1972.
CL: Tues., and Wed. SIZE: Medium. *STOCK:
Furniture, £45—£1,000; small items.* LOC:
A684. PARK: Easy. TEL: Wensleydale (0969)
23555.

LOWER BENTHAM

W.T. and J. Spencer
Arundel House. *STOCK: Stripped pine, oak,
mahogany, pottery, porcelain.* LOC: B6480.
TEL: Bentham (0468) 61058.

MALTON (0653)
Malton Antique Market
2 Old Maltongate. (Mrs. M.A. Cleverly.) Est. 1970. CL: Thurs. Open 9.30—12.30 and 2—5. SIZE: Medium. *STOCK: Furniture, Georgian to Victorian, to £500+; glass, bric-a-brac, porcelain, pottery, copper and brass.* LOC: From York take A64, shop is at main traffic light junction in Malton. PARK: 20yds. further. TEL: 2732. SER: Sells on commission basis.

Matthew Maw Antiques
18 Castlegate. CL: Thurs. Open 10—5. *STOCK: General antiques and shipping items.* LOC: A64. TEL: 4638. VAT: Stan/Spec.

MANFIELD, Nr. Darlington
Trade Antiques. D.D. White
Lucy Cross Cottage. Est. 1975. Open by appointment. *STOCK: Georgian, Victorian and export furniture.* LOC: B6275, Scotch Corner to Piercebridge road, 3½ miles after leaving A1. PARK: Easy. TEL: Piercebridge (032 574) 303. VAT: Stan/Spec.

MELMERBY, Nr. Ripon (076 584)
Simon Greenwood Antiques
23 Melmerby Industrial Estate, Green Lane. (S. and C. Greenwood.) Est. 1976. CL: Mon. Open 9.30—12.30, Sat. 9.30—12, other times by appointment. SIZE: Warehouse. *STOCK: Furniture, 17th—20th C., £5—£1,000; general antiques, furniture, decorative items and shipping goods.* LOC: From A1 take the A61 towards Ripon. PARK: Easy. TEL: 571; home — Bedale (0677) 22554. SER: Valuations; buys at auction. VAT: Stan/Spec.

MIDDLEHAM, Nr. Leyburn
White Boar Antiques and Books
Kirkgate. (J. and G. Armstrong.) Est. 1983. Open 10—6. Winter — closed Mon. Open 10—4.30 or by appointment. SIZE: Small. *STOCK: Furniture, clocks and porcelain, 18th—19th C, £500—£1,000; silver, copper, brass, pewter and glass, 19th C, £50—£150; books including antiquarian, 17th—20th C, £1—£450.* LOC: A6108 towards Leyburn. PARK: Easy. TEL: Wensleydale (0969) 23901; home — same. SER: Restorations (furniture and porcelain).

NORTHALLERTON (0609)
The Antique and Art
7 Central Arcade. (D.M. Willoughby.) Open 10—5. *STOCK: Porcelain, pottery, silver, glass, prints and paintings.* TEL: 2051; home — 2680.

Northallerton continued

Collectors Corner
145/6 High St. (J. Wetherill.) Est. 1972. Open Wed. and Fri. 10—4; Sat. 10—5; Tues. April—Oct; or by appointment. *STOCK: General antiques, collectors' items.* LOC: Opposite GPO. TEL: 5199. VAT: Stan.

'Coniscliffe Curios'
3 Weldons Yard, off High St. Open Wed.—Sat. 10—4. *STOCK: General antiques, curios.* TEL: Darlington (0325) 52256. SER: Repairs (furniture); french polishing and waxing; silver plating; dolls' hospital.

NORTON
L. Laborevics
81 Commercial St. Open 10—6 Thurs.—Sat. *STOCK: General antiques.* TEL: Malton (0653) 4505.

D. and M.H. Lindley
69 Commercial St. Est. 1958. CL: Thurs. p.m. Open 9—5. *STOCK: Furniture, china.* TEL: Malton (0653) 3220.

PATELEY BRIDGE
Cat in the Window Antiques
High St. (Mrs. S. Morgan.) *STOCK: Small furniture, silver, copper, brass, pewter, glass, ceramics, art nouveau, art deco, jewellery, ivory, amber, coral, jet, pictures, sewing items, linen, lace and collectors' items.* PARK: Easy. TEL: Harrogate (0423) 711343/780551.

Pateley Bridge continued

Brian Loomes
Calf Haugh Farm. Author of books on clocks. Est. 1966. Open 10–5, other times by appointment. SIZE: Medium. *STOCK: British clocks, especially longcase, wall, bracket and lantern, pre-1840, £200–£5,000.* Not stocked: Foreign clocks. LOC: From Pateley Bridge, first private lane on left on Grassington Rd. (B6265). PARK: Own. TEL: Harrogate (0423) 711163; home – same. VAT: Spec.

Archie Miles Bookshop
54 High St. (Mrs. C.M. Linsley.) *STOCK: Secondhand and antiquarian books, jewellery and bric-a-brac.* TEL: Harrogate (0423) 711294 or 711166.

PICKERING (0751)
John Hague
45 Market Place. Est. 1959. *STOCK: Furniture, porcelain and general antiques, prints and pictures.* TEL: 72829.

RICHMOND (0748)
Granny's Antiques
8 Newbiggin. Est. 1976. CL: Wed. Open 10.30–12 and 1–4.30; Sat. 10.30–12.30 and 1.30–4.30. SIZE: Small. *STOCK: Small furniture, Georgian, Victorian, Edwardian, £50– £800; pictures, general antiques.* Not stocked: Militaria, stamps. LOC: 2 mins. from Market Place. PARK: Easy. TEL: 2732 after 6 p.m.

Richmond continued

Newbiggin Antiques
Downholme. (G.L. and J. Pratt.) Est. 1967. Open by appointment. SIZE: Medium. *STOCK: 17th–20th C furniture, £50–£2,000; longcase and bracket clocks.* Not stocked: Coins, weapons, jewellery. PARK: Easy. TEL: 5454. SER: Valuations; buys at auction. VAT: Stan/Spec.

Richmond Pine
Unit 2 & 3 Greenbelt Holding, Borough Rd. Gallowfield Trading Estate. (M. smith, M. Bailes). Open 9–6, other times by appointment. *STOCK: Pine.* TEL: 3430. SER: Stripping.

St. Trinians Antiques
St. Trinians Hall, Easby. (T. and M. Bosman.) Est. 1982. CL: Sun. except by appointment. Open 10–5, Sat. 10–6. SIZE: Medium. *STOCK: Furniture, £50–£4,000; general antiques, all 17th–20th C.* LOC: On B6271, 1 mile from Richmond. PARK: Easy. TEL: 2560; home – same. SER: Valuations; buys at auction (furniture). VAT: Stan/Spec.

RIPON (0765)

Curiosity Shoppe
20 Westgate (G. and J. Hill). CL: Wed. Open 9.30—5. TEL: 701294. VAT: Stan/Spec.

Just Something
44 North St. (A. Halliday.) STOCK: Furniture, pine, small items, bric-a-brac. TEL: 2905.

Sigma Antiques and Fine Art LAPADA
Water Skelgate. (D. Thomson.) Est. 1963. Open 9—5.30. STOCK: Furniture, 17th—19th C; glass, paintings, 18th—19th C; jewellery, silver, European and Eastern pottery and porcelain; jades, ivories, fine objets d'art, bronzes; Continental furniture, ornaments, 18th—19th C, £1—£10,000. PARK: Nearby. TEL: 3163.

Skellgate Curios
2 Low Skellgate. (J.I. Wain and P.S. Gyte.) Est. 1974. CL: Wed. Open 10.30—5. STOCK: General antiques, silver, jewellery and curios. TEL: 701290; home — 85336 and 5345. VAT: Stan/Spec.

RUFFORTH, Nr. York

Rufforth Antiques
Ashville Farm, Wetherby Rd. (J. and B. Thacker.) Resident. Est. 1965. Open Sun., other times prior 'phone call advisable. SIZE: Medium. STOCK: Furniture, all periods, £1— £3,000; bric-a-brac. LOC: B1224, centre of village. PARK: Own. TEL: York (0904) 83741/ 33077. SER: Valuations; buys at auction. VAT: Stan/Spec.

SCARBOROUGH (0723)

Bar Antiques
14 Bar St. (C. Armstrong). Open 10—5. STOCK: Silver, porcelain and glass. TEL: 351487.

Gerards
14 Bar St. (H. Armstrong). Open 10—5. STOCK: Jewellery and bullion. TEL: 351487.

Lindy Lou Antiques
138 Victoria Rd. (J.B.J. Roberts.) Est. 1964. Open 9.30—5. SIZE: Large. STOCK: Glass, porcelain, silver, pictures, furniture, bronzes, jewellery, 1750—1930, £5—£350. Not stocked: Reproductions. LOC: A170 from Pickering or A64 from York. PARK: Easy. TEL: 363348; home — 862985.

M.A. Reynolds and Son
Hillcrest House Antiques, 157 Burniston Rd., Newby. Open 7 days 9am—10pm. STOCK: Trade and shipping goods. TEL: 375767.

SETTLE (072 92)

Jay Davis Antiques
Bishopdale Court. Est. 1975. CL: Sun., and Wed., except by appointment. STOCK: Period country furniture and associated items, needlework, base metalware, treen, pottery, some decorators' items. TEL: 2764. SER: Valuations; restorations; polishing, rushing. VAT: Spec.

David Dean Antiques   Mainly Trade
Church St., Bridge End. Est. 1966. Appointment advisable. SIZE: Small. STOCK: Furniture, 17th—19th C; unusual items. LOC: A65. PARK: Easy. TEL: 3702; home — 3660. SER: Valuations; buys at auction. VAT: Mainly Spec.

Devonshire House Antiques
Devonshire House, Duke St. (J.I. Cox.) CL: Mon. and Wed. except by appointment. STOCK: Pictures, prints, small furniture, glass and ceramics, 19th C. Not stocked: Militaria and coins. LOC: A65. In town centre. PARK: Easy. TEL: 2405.

H.I. Milnthorpe
Kirkgate. Est. 1974. CL: Wed. Open 9—12.30 and 1.30—5. SIZE: Medium. STOCK: English furniture, 17th to early 19th C, £100— £10,000; pottery and porcelain, pre-1840. Not stocked: Victorian furniture, guns, coins and jewellery. LOC: A65. PARK: Easy. TEL: 2331. SER: Valuations. VAT: Spec.

Mary Milnthorpe and Daughter
Antique Shop, Market Place. Est. 1958. CL: Sun. and Wed. Open 9.30—5. SIZE: Small. STOCK: Jewellery and silver, Georgian, Victorian and secondhand; pottery and porcelain, 18th—19th C. Not stocked: Guns, coins. LOC: Opp. Town Hall. PARK: Easy. TEL: 2331. VAT: Stan/Spec.

Nanbooks
Undercliffe Cottage, Duke St. (N.M. Midgley.) Resident. Est. 1962. Open Tues., Fri. and Sat. 11—12.30 and 2—5.30. SIZE: Small. STOCK: English pottery, porcelain, glass and pewter, 18th to early 19th C, clocks and watches, general small antiques, 17th—19th C; all under £150; bric-a- brac, 19th—20th C; some antiquarian books. Not stocked: Jewellery. LOC: Near Post Office. PARK: Easy. TEL: 3324.

The Pen-y-Ghent Antiques
Devonshire House, Duke St. (Mrs. A.M. Cox.) Est. 1975. CL: Mon. and Wed. except by appointment. STOCK: Country antiques, pottery, porcelain, glass. Not stocked: Militaria, coins. LOC: A65. In town centre. PARK: Easy. TEL: 2405.

Settle continued

R.M.S. Precious
King William House, High St. Resident. Est. 1972. CL: Wed. Open 10—5.30 or by appointment. SIZE: Medium. *STOCK: Oak, walnut, mahogany and country furniture, 17th—19th C, £30—£3,000; pottery, prints and paintings, 17th—20th C, £5—£1,500.* LOC: On the old High St., opposite Post Office. PARK: Easy. TEL: 3946. SER: Valuations. VAT: Stan/Spec.

E. Thistlethwaite
Corner of Duke St. and Station Rd. Est. 1972. CL: Wed. Open 9—5. SIZE: Small. *STOCK: Oak, 17th—18th C; country furniture, 18th C; early metalware, treen and country bygones.* LOC: A65. PARK: Nearby. TEL: 2460. FAIRS: Dateline. VAT: Spec.

Philip S. Walden
The Folly. Resident. Est. 1966. CL: Wed. Open 10—5 or by appointment. SIZE: Large. *STOCK: Furniture, 1750—1920, £25—£5,000; silver and porcelain, 1750—1900, £5—£1,500; paintings and watercolours, £20—£2,000.* LOC: Town centre. PARK: Nearby. TEL: 2312. SER: Valuations. VAT: Stan/Spec.

SKIPTON (0756)

Adamson Armoury
Newmarket St. (J.K. Adamson.) Est. 1975. Open 10—6, Sun. by appointment. SIZE: Small. *STOCK: Weapons, 18th—19th C, £10—£300; militaria, 19th—20th C, 50p—£50.* LOC: A65, 200yds. from town centre. PARK: Rear. TEL: 61355; home — same. SER: Valuations. FAIRS: Leeds.

Corn Mill Antiques
High Corn Mill, Chapel Hill. (Mrs. M. Hawkridge.) Est. 1984. CL: Tues. and Wed. Open 10—4. SIZE: Medium. *STOCK: Small furniture, £50—£500; porcelain, silver plate, prints, pictures, brass and copper, £5—£200; Victorian to 1930s.* Not stocked: Jewellery, gold and silver. LOC: From town centre, take Grassington road, shop on right, just across bridge. PARK: Easy. TEL: 2440; home — Airton (072 93) 489.

Craven Books
23 Newmarket St. (Miss K. Farey and Miss M.G. Fluck.) CL: Tues., and first and last Mon., every month. Open 9.30—12.30 and 1.30—5, Sat. 9—12.30 and 1.30—4. *STOCK: Northern topography, maps and prints.* TEL: 2677. SER: Finder.

Amy Egan
3 and 7 Mill Bridge, High St. Est. 1960. Open Wed. and Sat.; some Mon. and Thurs. in summer. SIZE: Medium. *STOCK: Jewellery and silverware, Victorian bric-a-brac and linens.* Not stocked: Large furniture. LOC: Adjacent to High St., turn left by Parish Church and Castle. PARK: In High St., 2 mins. walk. TEL: Home — Halifax (0422) 201203.

Skipton continued

Gadzooks
21 Otley St. (H. Blackburn.) Est. 1973. Open 9—5.30 or by appointment. SIZE: Large and warehouse. *STOCK: Furniture, all periods; clocks, pottery, porcelain, prints and metalware.* LOC: From church down High St., turn left at pedestrian crossing, shop 50yds. on left. PARK: Nearby. TEL: 3323; home — same. SER: Courier and shipping. VAT: Stan/Spec.

SOUTH MILFORD (0977)

Odyssey Antiques
Peckfield Lodge, Great North Rd. *STOCK: General antiques.* LOC: Near Selby Fork. TEL: 683904.

SPENNITHORNE, Nr. Leyburn

N.J. and C.S. Dodsworth
Thorney Hall. Est. 1973. Open by appointment. SIZE: Medium. *STOCK: Furniture, 17th—19th C; clocks, 18th C.* LOC: Off A684. TEL: Wensleydale (0969) 22277. VAT: Stan/Spec.

STILLINGTON

Manor Antiques
(D. and M. Law.) Est. 1970. CL: Wed. Open 9—5.30, Sun. 10.30—5.30. SIZE: Large. *STOCK: Regency tables, oak tallboys, wall and longcase clocks, oak and pine dressers, bureaux; copper and brass, porcelain, Victorian bric-a-brac.* LOC: B1363. PARK: Easy. TEL: Easingwold (0347) 810484. SER: Valuations; restorations (pine stripped, furniture repair). VAT: Stan/Spec.

Pond Cottage Antiques
Brandsby Rd. (C.M. and D. Thurstans.) Resident. Est. 1972. *STOCK: Pine, kitchenalia, country furniture, treen, metalware, brass, copper.* TEL: Easingwold (0347) 810796. SER: Pine stripping.

STOKESLEY (0642)

Three Tuns Antiques
2 Three Tuns Wynd. (E. and L.C. Payman.) Est. 1972. Open 10.30—5. *STOCK: Small furniture, jewellery, silver, general small antiques, ceramics, glass.* TEL: 711377; home — Gt. Ayton (0642) 724284.

TADCASTER (0937)

Lewis Hickson CMBHI
Antiquarian Horologist
(formerly Westgate Antiques)
9 Westgate. (L.E. Hickson.) Est. 1965. Open Thurs., Fri. and Sat. 9.30—5. SIZE: Small. *STOCK: Clocks, 17th—19th C.* LOC: Town centre. PARK: Easy. TEL: 833049. SER: Valuations; restorations (clocks).

THIRSK   (0845)

Cottage Antiques and Curios
1 Market Place. (Mrs. E.H. and S.R. Ballard.) Est. 1970. CL: Sun. except by appointment. Open 9—5. *STOCK: Victorian porcelain and glass, £5—£100; furniture, from 1750, £5—£1,000; brass, copper, silver and plated ware, £3—£300.* PARK: Easy. TEL: 22536 and 23212; home — 577461.

Kirkgate Picture Gallery
18 Kirkgate. (R. Bennett.) Est. 1979. Open Mon., Thurs. and Sat. 9.30—12.30 and 1.30—5 and by appointment. SIZE: Small. *STOCK: Oil paintings, £25—£1,000; watercolours, £15—£500; both 19th—20th C.* LOC: Joins Market Place. PARK: Nearby. TEL: 24085; home — same. SER: Restorations (oil paintings).

B. Ogleby   *Trade and Export Only*
35, 36 and 37 The Green. Open by appointment only. SIZE: Large. *STOCK: Furniture, 17th—20th C.* TEL: 22676. SER: Shipping and packing. VAT: Stan/Spec.

Potterton Books
The Old Rectory, Sessay. (C. Jameson.) Open 9.30—5.30. SIZE: Medium. *STOCK: Classic reference works on art, architecture and all aspects of antiques and collecting.* TEL: 401218. SER: Valuations; restorations; book search; decorative bindings; catalogues issued. FAIRS: Most London International.

WEST HESLERTON   (094 45)
Nr. Malton

Old Rectory Antiques and Pine
The Old Rectory. (J. and G. Wilson.) Resident. Est. 1980. Open 9—5, Sun. by appointment. SIZE: Large. *STOCK: Mahogany furniture, £50—£2,500; pine furniture, £20—£500; both Victorian; shipping items, 20th C, £5—£500.* LOC: A64. PARK: Easy. TEL: 364. SER: Valuations; restorations. VAT: Stan/Spec.

WHITBY   (0947)
'Bobbins'
Wesley Hall, Church St. (D. Hoyle.) Open 11—5 every day Easter to Christmas. SIZE: Large. *STOCK: Country furniture, rocking and rush seated chairs, spinning wheels, general antiques, clocks, oil lamps and fittings, 18th—20th C.* LOC: Between Market Place and Whitby Abbey. PARK: Nearby. TEL: 600585. SER: Repairs and spares (oil lamps). VAT: Stan.

Whitby continued

Coach House Antiques
Coach Rd., Sleights. (C.J. Rea.) Est. 1973. CL: Sun. and Thurs. except by appointment. Open 10—5. SIZE: Small. *STOCK: Porcelain, china, glass, £5—£200; furniture, £10—£500; silver, plate, £5—£100; 18th and 19th C; brass, copper, linen, paintings, pewter, Victorian prints, jewellery.* LOC: On A169, 3 miles south west of Whitby. TEL: 810313.

The Mount Antiques
Khyber Pass. (M. and B. Bottomley.) Est. 1970. *STOCK: General antiques, especially fireplaces.* TEL: 604516. VAT: Stan/Spec.

WINKSLEY, Nr. Ripon
Jeremy A. Fearn
The Old Rectory. Est. 1974. Open by appointment. SIZE: Large. *STOCK: English period furniture, 17th C to 1830, £200—£10,000+; furniture, Victorian and Edwardian; pictures, oils and watercolours, 19th C, £50—£1,000+.* LOC: Opposite church. PARK: Easy. TEL: Kirkby Malzeard (076 583) 625. SER: Valuations; restorations; buys at auction. VAT: Stan/Spec.

YORK   (0904)

Acomb Antiques
3 Westview Close, Boroughbridge Rd. (J.F. and A. James.) Est. 1969. SIZE: Large. *STOCK: Furniture, clocks and barometers, 17th—19th C, £50—£2,000; shipping goods.* LOC: Off Harrogate road, just outside York boundary. PARK: Easy. TEL: 791999.

Barbican Bookshop
24 Fossgate and Walmgate Bar. Est. 1961. Open 9—5.30. *STOCK: Antiquarian books.* TEL: 53643. VAT: Stan.

Barker Court Antiques and Bygones
44 Gillygate. (Mrs. D. Yates.) Est. 1970. CL: Sun. and Wed. except by appointment. Open 10.30—4.30. SIZE: Small. *STOCK: Pottery and porcelain, glass, plated items, Victorian to 1930, £3—£50.* LOC: 3 mins. walk from York Minster. PARK: Gillygate. TEL: 22611.

Barkes and Richardson
38 High Petergate. (P.R. Barkes and D.F. Richardson.) Est. 1978. Open 10—5.30. SIZE: Small. *STOCK: Japanese woodblock prints, 19th C, £10—£400.* LOC: 50yds. from Minster. PARK: 50yds. TEL: 51080. SER: Valuations; restorations (watercolours and prints); buys at auction. VAT: Stan/Spec.

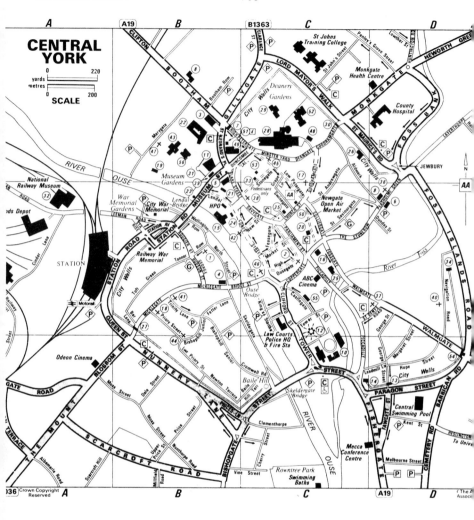

CENTRAL YORK

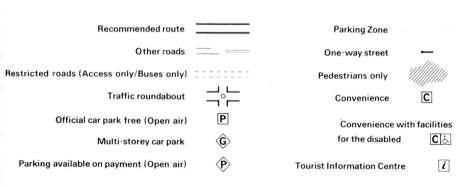

Recommended route	
Other roads	
Restricted roads (Access only/Buses only)	
Traffic roundabout	
Official car park free (Open air)	P
Multi-storey car park	G
Parking available on payment (Open air)	P
Parking Zone	
One-way street	
Pedestrians only	
Convenience	C
Convenience with facilities for the disabled	C
Tourist Information Centre	i

Reproduced by kind permission of the Automobile Association.

York continued

Blenheim House Antiques
47 Holgate Rd. (S. Johnson.) Est. 1977. CL: Sat. SIZE: Large. *STOCK: Jewellery, china, silver, brass, glass and furniture, 18th C to 1950, £1−£1,000.* LOC: Main Harrogate Rd. into York. PARK: Easy. TEL: 22905; home − same. VAT: Stan/Spec.

Coulter Galleries
90 Tadcaster Rd. Est. 1950. *STOCK: Watercolours and oils, pre-1900.* TEL: 706537/702101.

Discovery Fine Arts Ltd.
8 Minster Gates. (N. Wallace.) Est. 1970. Open 9.30−5.30. SIZE: Large. *STOCK: Antiquarian and secondhand books.* LOC: Opposite south door of York Minster. PARK: Nearby. TEL: 21812. SER: Valuations; restorations; book finding.

Gate Antiques
29 St. Saviourgate. (D. Butler.) Resident. Est. 1960. Open 10−5.30 or by appointment. *STOCK: Furniture, brass, china.* LOC: 500yds. from York Minster. TEL: 27035. SER: Valuations; restorations; re-upholstery; buys at auction, commission sales.

Henry Hardcastle Ltd.   BADA
51 Stonegate. Est. 1770. Open 9−5.30. *STOCK: Period English silver and plate; jewellery.* **TEL: 23401. VAT: Stan/Spec.**

R.K. Himsworth
28 The Shambles. Est. 1949. CL: Wed. Open 9−5. SIZE: Small. *STOCK: Victorian jewellery, 1820−1900, £10−£500; silver.* TEL: 25089; home − Green Hammerton (0901) 30105. VAT: Stan/Spec.

Holgate Antiques
Holgate Rd. (T. Betts.) Est. 1980. Open 10−6. *STOCK: General antiques, furniture, bric-a-brac.* TEL: 30005.

Daniel McDowell
3-5 Grape Lane. Est. 1972. Open 9−12.30 and 1.30−5. SIZE: Medium. *STOCK: Books, especially economics, science and medicine.* TEL: 22000.

Robert Morrison and Son   BADA
Trentholme House, 131 The Mount. (C. Morrison.) Est. 1890. Open 9−5.30, Sat. 9−12. SIZE: Large. *STOCK: English furniture, 1700−1900, porcelain and clocks.* **PARK: Easy. TEL: 55394. VAT: Stan/Spec.**

R.L. Morton Antiques   *Mainly Trade*
11 Green Lane, Acomb. Est. 1970. CL: Sat. Open 9.30−1 and 2−6. *STOCK: Victoriana, general antiques.* TEL: 799597. SER: Restorations; polishing. VAT: Stan/Spec.

York continued

O'Flynn Antiquarian Booksellers
35 Micklegate. Open 9−6. *STOCK: Antiquarian books on history, travel, natural history, sciences, poetry, biographies, literary criticism, general fiction and Scotland; original maps, prints and manuscripts.* TEL: 641404.

Ruddock Antiques
36 Stonegate. (G. Ruddock.) Est. 1970. *STOCK: Porcelain, especially Royal Worcester; silver, cutlery.* TEL: 22822. VAT: Stan.

Ken Spelman
70 Micklegate. (P. Miller and A. Fothergill.) ABA. Est. 1948. SIZE: Large. *STOCK: Secondhand and antiquarian books especially fine arts and literature, 5p−£1,000.* PARK: Easy. TEL: 24414. SER: Valuations; buys at auction (books). FAIRS: Bath, Oxford, York, Harrogate and London PBFA and ABA. VAT: Spec.

Taikoo Books Ltd.
29 High Petergate. (D. Chilton.) Open 10−5.30 but appointment advisable. *STOCK: Antiquarian and secondhand books especially on mountaineering, polar, Africiana, Oriental and big game hunting.* TEL: 641213.

Thacker's Antiques
42 Fossgate. Open 10−5. SIZE: Large. *STOCK: Furniture, £5−£5,000.* LOC: In city centre, next to Merchant Adventurers' Hall. PARK: Loading only. TEL: 33077 or 83741.

Trinity Antiques
Goodramgate. (G. and D. Thiel.) Usually available, or by appointment. *STOCK: Jewellery, commemorative china, clocks, watches, dolls, pewter.* TEL: 36673. VAT: Stan/Spec.

Inez M.P. Yates
5 The Shambles. Est. 1948. CL: Wed. Open 10.30−5. *STOCK: Furniture, porcelain, jewellery, unusual small collectors' items.* TEL: 54821; home − 422816.

Yesterdays Furniture
10 The Crescent, Blossom St. (M. Barrow.) Est. 1975. Open 9−6. SIZE: Medium. *STOCK: Stripped pine, Victorian and Edwardian furniture, pine doors, £20−£500; shipping furniture.* PARK: Easy. TEL: 641713 or 33974. SER: Restorations; stripping (pine).

Yon Antiques
Whip-ma-Whop-ma-Gate. (Next to The-Shambles.) (A.G. Macdonald.) Est. 1968. Open 9.30−6. SIZE: Small. *STOCK: General antiques, Georgian to art nouveau, £5−£25+.* Not stocked: Extra large furniture. LOC: Off Stonebow. PARK: Easy. TEL: 27928; home − Green Hammerton (0901) 30240. SER: Buys at auction.

York Antiques Centre
2 Lendal. Open 10−5.30. There are 35 dealers at this centre selling a wide range of *antiques, silver, dolls, medals and art deco.* PARK: Easy. TEL: 641582/641445.

Yorkshire South

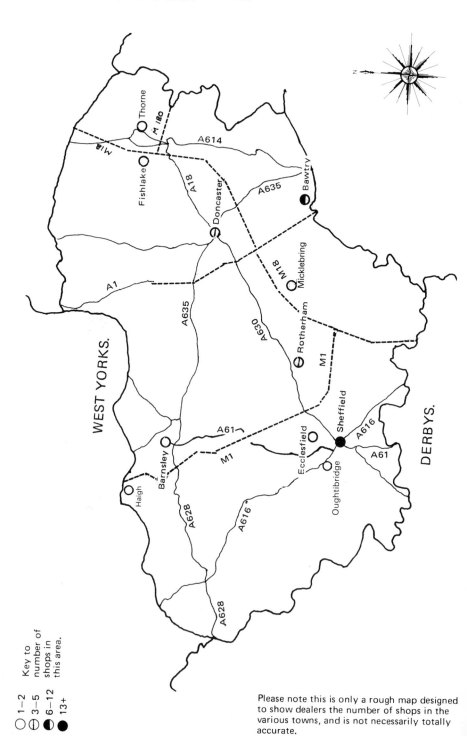

Thorne

M 180

A614

Fishlake

M18

A18

Doncaster

A635

Bawtry

Micklebring

M18

A635

A1

Rotherham

A630

M1

WEST YORKS.

Sheffield

A61

A616

Ecclesfield

Oughtibridge

A61

DERBYS.

A61

Barnsley

M1

Haigh

A628

A616

A628

Key to
number of
shops in
this area.

1–2 3–5 6–12 13+

Please note this is only a rough map designed
to show dealers the number of shops in the
various towns, and is not necessarily totally
accurate.

BARNSLEY (0226)

Charisma Antiques Trade Warehouse
St. Paul's former Methodist Chapel, Market St., Hoyland. (J.C. Simmons.) Est. 1980. Open 10—4. *STOCK: Furniture, shipping goods.* LOC: ½ mile off M1 exit 36. PARK: Easy. TEL: 747599; home — 790482. VAT: Stan/Spec.

Christine Simmons Antiques
St.Paul's Former Methodist Chapel, Market St., Hoyland. Est. 1976. Open 10—4. SIZE: Medium. *STOCK: Smalls.* LOC: ½ mile from exit 36, M1. PARK: Easy. TEL: 747599; home — 790482.

BAWTRY, Nr. Doncaster

Doyle Antiques
9a Swan St. (A.G. Doyle.) Est. 1974. Open Fri., Sat. and Sun., other times by appointment. SIZE: Medium. *STOCK: Country period oak furniture and collectors' items, £50—£6,000.* LOC: Just off A1. PARK: Easy. TEL: Evenings — Doncaster (0302) 710524. SER: Valuations. VAT: Spec.

Studio Antiques
34 Church St. (M. Adamson.) Est. 1970. CL: Mon. and Wed. Open 10.30—5. SIZE: Large. *STOCK: General antiques, furniture, prints, maps, studio ceramics, 1865—1960; collectable clothes, Victorian, Edwardian, to 1950s; shawls, table linen.* PARK: Easy. TEL: Evenings — Doncaster (0302) 536563.

Swan Antiques
4 Swan St. (G.J. Laywood.) Est. 1967. Open 9—5.30. *STOCK: Porcelain and pottery, silver and clocks, glass, oil paintings, watercolours, prints, early Victorian. Not stocked: Ivories, Oriental porcelain, antique weapons.* LOC: A638. PARK: Easy. TEL: Doncaster (0302) 710728.

Treasure House Antiques
M.J.M. Enterprises, 6 Swan St. Est. 1978. Open 7 days 10—5. SIZE: Large. *STOCK: Silver, porcelain, furniture, collectables.* PARK: Easy. TEL: Doncaster (0302) 710621; home — Worksop (0909) 732153.

Treasure House Antiques Centre
8—10 Swan St. Est. 1982. Open 10—5 including Sun. and Bank Holidays. SIZE: Large. The various dealers sell *silver, porcelain, scientific instruments, furniture, taxidermy and general antiques.* PARK: Easy. TEL: Doncaster (0302) 710621.

Timothy D. Wilson BADA
No. 1 Swan St. Est. 1926. Open 9—6, Sun. by appointment. SIZE: Large. *STOCK: English oak furniture, 17th—18th C; metalware.* PARK: Easy. TEL: Doncaster (0302) 710040. VAT: Spec.

DONCASTER (0302)

Antique and Bargain Stores
6 Sunny Bar, Market Place. CL: Thurs. Open 9.30—5. *STOCK: Dolls, toys, china, pistols, swords, small antiques.* TEL: 4857.

Bryan Bowden
199 Carr House Rd. Est. 1967. Open 9.30—1 and 2—5.30. SIZE: Medium. *STOCK: Porcelain and pottery, pre-1840; furniture, Georgian and Regency; paintings, pre-1895.* PARK: Easy. LOC: Near racecourse roundabout. TEL: 65353. SER: Valuations; buys at auction. FAIRS: Buxton. VAT: Spec.

Doncaster Sales and Exchange
20 Copley Rd. CL: Thurs. Open 9—5.30. *STOCK: General small antiques.* TEL: 4857. VAT: Stan.

Francis Sinclair Ltd.
39 Hallgate. Open 9.30—5.30, Thurs. 9.30— *STOCK: Clocks.* TEL: 67260.

Victoria Antiques
137 Balby Rd. (Mrs. E. Ducker.) Est. 1979. CL: Tues. Open 10.30—4, Sat. 10.30—1. *STOCK: General antiques.* TEL: 856546.

ECCLESFIELD, Nr. Sheffield

John R. Wrigley
185 The Wheel. Est. 1961. Postal only, catalogue issued monthly. *STOCK: Antiquarian books.* TEL: Sheffield (0742) 460275.

FISHLAKE

Wheelwright Antiques
Pinfold Lane. (M. Trimingham.) Resident. Est. 1972. Open 10—5 and Sun. p.m. and by appointment. SIZE: Medium. *STOCK: Rural furniture, especially stripped pine; clocks including longcase and wall clocks, Victorian to mid-19th C, £30—£1,000; small Victoriana — writing boxes, lamps, £3—£70; rural collectors' items — cartwheels, ploughs, wheelwright and carpenters' tools, 19th C, £1—£20.* LOC: Off A63. PARK: Own. TEL: Doncaster (0302) 841411. SER: Buys at auction.

HAIGH

Mallglade Antiques
Haigh Hall. CL: Sat. Open 10—5 or by appointment. SIZE: Medium. *STOCK: Georgian, Victorian, Edwardian furniture, £30—£3,000.* LOC: ¼ mile from exit 38, M1. PARK: Own. TEL: Bretton (092 485) 516. VAT: Stan/Spec.

MICKLEBRING, Nr. Rotherham
Robert Clark
Sunnyside House. (R.R. Clark.) Est. 1955. Open by appointment. *STOCK: English pottery and porcelain, silver spoons, furniture, metalware, prints and watercolours, 17th—19th C.* LOC: From M18 Junction 1 turn towards Maltby and Bawtry, take 2nd left over crossroads into village, 2nd building on left. PARK: Own. TEL: Rotherham (0709) 812540; home — same. FAIRS: Most major.

OUGHTIBRIDGE   (074 286)
Nr. Sheffield
Julie Goddard's
Cherry Tree Row. (Miss J.P. Goddard.) Est. 1982. Open 9.30—12.45 and 1.30—5.30, Fri. by appointment. *STOCK: Furniture—Victorian, £10—£1,000; Edwardian, £10—£500; Georgian/William IV, £150—£1,000.* Not stocked: Jewellery and silver. LOC: 12 minutes from M1, exit 36 towards Sheffield, shop situated in one-way system (A616). PARK: Easy. TEL: 2261. SER: Restorations (furniture — polishing, veneering, caning and re-rushing); buys at auction (furniture).

ROTHERHAM   (0709)
Roger Appleyard Ltd.   LAPADA
Trade Only
Fitzwilliam Rd., Eastwood Trading Estate. Open 8—6, Sat. 8—1. SIZE: Large. *STOCK: General antiques, £5—£1,500.* LOC: A630. PARK: Easy. TEL: 67670. SER: Packing and shipping. VAT: Stan/Spec.

John Mason (Rotherham) Ltd.
36 High St. CL: Thurs. Open 9—5.30. *STOCK: Silver, clocks, jewellery.* TEL: 382311. SER: Valuations; restorations. VAT: Spec.

Rawmarsh Hill Antiques
The Old Methodist Chapel, Parkgate. CL: Sat. Open 9.30—4.30. SIZE: Large. *STOCK: General antiques, £5—£5,000.* TEL: 522340. VAT: Stan.

South Yorkshire Antiques
88—94 Broad St. (A. Swindells.) Est. 1955. Open 9.30—4.30. *STOCK: General antiques and shipping furniture.* LOC: Rotherham—Swinton Rd. PARK: Easy. TEL: 585854/526514; 24 hr ansaphone 582688. SER: Valuations; restorations. VAT: Stan.

Philip Turner Furniture
94a Broad St. Open 9—5; Sat. 9—3. *STOCK: Shipping furniture, 1830—1930.* TEL: 524640.

Wellgate Antiques
Temperance Hall, Wellgate. SIZE: Large. *STOCK: Furniture, general antiques.* VAT: Stan/Spec.

Rotherham continued
Wickersley Antiques   LAPADA
3 Broad St., Parkgate. (N. and S. Butler.) Est. 1970. CL: Sun. Open 9—5.30, Sat. 10—5. SIZE: Large and warehouse. *STOCK: Furniture, 17th—19th C, £25—£1,000; oils and watercolours, 18th—20th C, £10—£1,000; general antiques, clocks, 18th—19th C, £25—£1,000; Victorian and Edwardian jewellery, export furniture including Victorian mahogany, walnut and oak; pianos.* LOC: 1 mile from Rotherham on A633 towards Barnsley. PARK: Easy. TEL: 525595; home — Sheffield (0742) 81486. SER: Valuations. VAT: Stan/Spec.

SHEFFIELD   (0742)
Bardwell Antiques
919 Abbeydale Rd. (R. Bardwell.) Open 8—4.30. *STOCK: General antiques.* TEL: 584669.

Broadfield Antiques
368 Abbeydale Rd. (S. Pennington.) Open 11—4. *STOCK: General antiques; antiquarian and secondhand books, postcards, jewellery.* TEL: 586611; evenings — 550130.

Canterbury Place Antiques
356 South Rd. (P. and J. Coldwell.) Open 9—5.30. SIZE: Warehouse. *STOCK: Stripped pine and general antiques.* TEL: 336103.

The Doll's House Antiques
659 Ecclesall Rd., Hunters Bar. (Mrs. S. Gray.) Est. 1960. CL: Sun. except by appointment, and Thurs. Open 2—6 and by appointment. SIZE: Small. *STOCK: Furniture, small general antiques, 18th to early 20th C, £5—£2,000; dolls, 19th to early 20th C; jewellery, Victorian and Edwardian clothes and accessories, collectors' items; oil paintings and watercolours.* Not stocked: Stamps, books, coins. LOC: A625, by Hunters Bar roundabout. PARK: Easy. TEL: Home — 360061. SER: Restorations (dolls, antique fabrics and garments, porcelain, silver, plate, jewellery, furniture, pictures); buys at auction.

Dronfield Antiques
375—377 Abbeydale Rd. (H.J. Greaves.) Est. 1968. CL: Thurs. Open 10.30—5.30. SIZE: Large. Also warehouses open by appointment. *STOCK: Victoriana; trade and shipping goods.* PARK: Easy. TEL: 550172 and 581821; home — 556024. VAT: Stan.

John Ellis
142 Whitham Rd. Est. 1943. Open 10—5.30. *STOCK: Oriental carpets, and rugs.* TEL: 662920. VAT: Stan.

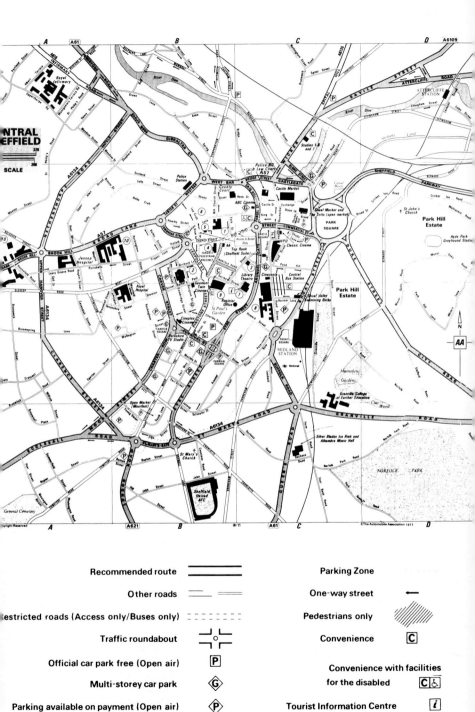

Recommended route

Other roads

Restricted roads (Access only/Buses only)

Traffic roundabout

Official car park free (Open air)

Multi-storey car park

Parking available on payment (Open air)

Parking Zone

One-way street

Pedestrians only

Convenience

Convenience with facilities
for the disabled

Tourist Information Centre

Reproduced by kind permission of the Automobile Association

Sheffield continued

Findley Antiques
314 Langsett Rd. (B. Findley.) Est. 1973. Open 9.30–5.30, Sun. by appointment. SIZE: Medium. *STOCK: Shipping items, 1900–1940, £25–£35; bric-a-brac, 1850–1950, £2–£10; general antiques, Victoriana, £100–£150.* LOC: 1 mile from city centre on A616. PARK: Easy. TEL: 346088; home – same. VAT: Stan.

Sheffield continued

G.W. Ford and Son Ltd.   BADA
290 Glossop Rd. (I.G.F. Thomson.) Est. 1900. Open 9–5.30, Sat. 10–5. SIZE: Large. *STOCK: Furniture, 18th–19th C, £50–£10,000; some porcelain, Old Sheffield plate, general accessories.* LOC: Near University and Hallamshire Hospital. PARK: Easy. TEL: 22082. SER: Valuations; restorations (furniture); buys at auction. FAIRS: British International (Birmingham) and Harrogate. VAT: Stan/Spec.

Fulwood Antiques
7 Brooklands Ave. (Mrs. H.J. Wills.) Est. 1977. Open Wed. and Fri. 10–5, Sat. 10–1. SIZE: Small. *STOCK: General small items, furniture, oil paintings and watercolours.* Not stocked: Very large furniture. LOC: From city centre towards Broomhill, Fulwood Rd., Nethergreen and straight on for Fulwood. PARK: Easy. TEL: 307387; home – 301346. SER: Valuations; restorations (ceramics, metal and pictures). FAIRS: Within 100 miles radius.

G.H. Green   *Trade Only Warehouse*
334–6 Abbeydale Rd. and warehouse, The Chapel, Broadfield Rd. Est. 1962. Open 9–5.30. *STOCK: Period and shipping goods.* TEL: 550881; home – 660494. VAT: Stan/Spec.

H. Hayden Antiques
477 London Rd. (Heeley Bottom.) Est. 1966. CL: Thurs. Open 10.30–5.30. SIZE: Small. *STOCK: Jewellery, silver, plate, porcelain, prints, paintings.* TEL: 556998.

Hibbert Bros.
117 Norfolk St. (P.A. Greaves.) Open 9–5.30. *STOCK: Oils and watercolours.* TEL: 22038.

Alan Hill Books, Sheffield
130 Whitham Rd., Broomhill. Est. 1980. Open 10.30–5.30, Sat. 10–5. *STOCK: Antiquarian books.* TEL: 665768.

Hinson Fine Paintings
679 Ecclesall Rd. Open 9.30–1 and 2–5. *STOCK: Oil paintings, watercolours, 19th C.* TEL: 665927. VAT: Spec.

Holme Antiques
144 Holme Lane, Hillsborough. (M.S. Maltby.) Est. 1980. Open 10.30–5.30. SIZE: Medium. *STOCK: General antiques, 19th C, £50–£100.* LOC: A61, turn left at traffic lights opposite Owlerton Sports Stadium, shop 1½ miles on right. PARK: Easy. TEL: 336698. SER: Valuations; restorations (furniture, clocks and watches, jewellery, re-plating).

Jacksons of Sheffield
223 Abbeydale Rd. (H. Jackson.) Est. 1947. Resident. Always open. SIZE: Small. *STOCK: Silver, 18th C to date.* PARK: Easy. TEL: 552101. VAT: Spec.

Sheffield continued

A.E. Jameson and Co.   LAPADA
257 Glossop Rd. (P. Jameson.) Est. 1883. CL:
Sat. p.m. Open 9—5.45. SIZE: Large. *STOCK:
Furniture, pre-1820, £20—£15,000; glass,
china, weapons.* LOC: A57. TEL: 23846;
home — 26189. SER: Valuations; restorations
(furniture); buys at auction. VAT: Stan/Spec.

Peter Kelsey
629/631 Abbeydale Rd. Est. 1973. CL: Thurs.
Open 10—5. *STOCK: Furniture, 18th—19th
C, silver, shipping goods.* TEL: 587288. SER:
Valuations. VAT: Stan/Spec.

Lynn's Antiques
351 Abbeydale Rd. (S. Walker.) Est. 1971.
Open 9—5. *STOCK: General antiques.* TEL:
581332. VAT: Stan/Spec.

Many Things
259 Fulwood Rd. (Mrs. J.H. Leslie.) Est.
1968. CL: Thurs. p.m. Open 10.30—1 and
2—5.30. SIZE: Medium. *STOCK: Furniture,
1750—1900; jewellery, ceramics, silver and
plate.* Not stocked: Books, coins, arms. LOC:
In Broomhill shopping centre on A57. TEL:
665459. VAT: Stan.

Milton Antiques
782 Ecclesall Rd. Est. 1970. Open 10.30—3.
*STOCK: Furniture, paintings, porcelain,
18th—20th C.* TEL: Home — Rotherham
(0709) 363071.

A.D. Moorhouse Ltd.   LAPADA
Trade and Export Only
2 Barmouth Court, Barmouth Rd., Abbeydale.
Est. 1972. CL: Sat. except by appointment.
Open 8.30—4.30 or by appointment. SIZE:
Large. *STOCK: Antique, Victorian, mahogany,
general shipping goods.* TEL: 582160;
evenings — 369801. SER: Container packing,
courier, buys at auction. VAT: Stan/Spec.

Olivant and Son
277/279 Ecclesall Rd. (G.M. Olivant.) Est.
1920. CL: Thurs. p.m. Open 9.30—6. SIZE:
Medium. *STOCK: Yew, oak and mahogany
furniture, copper and brass.* LOC: On Sheffield
to Buxton Rd. PARK: Easy. TEL: 661539.
VAT: Stan/Spec.

Oriel Antiques
185 Abbeydale Rd. (A. Black.) Est. 1970. CL:
Thurs. Open 9.30—5.30. SIZE: Small.
*STOCK: Pottery and porcelain, early 19th C;
copper and brass, 18th—19th C; all £5—£25.
Furniture, 17th—19th C, £5—£100.* LOC:
A621. PARK: Easy. SER: Buys at auction.

Sheffield continued

Paraphernalia
66/68 Abbeydale Rd. Est. 1972. *STOCK:
General antiques, stripped pine and lighting.*
TEL: 550203. VAT: Stan.

Persian Carpet Art
763 Abbeydale Rd. (A. Hazaveh.) Open
10—5. *STOCK: Rugs and carpets.* TEL:
589821.

Porter Prints (Broomhill)
205 Whitham Rd. *STOCK: Maps and prints.*
TEL: 685751.

Pot-Pourri
647 Ecclesall Rd., Hunters Bar. (Mrs. M.
Needham.) Est. 1972. Open 10—5.30.
*STOCK: Old and antique jewellery, silver,
plate including Sheffield.* TEL: 669790. VAT:
Stan.

Richards Furniture Sales
94 Abbeydale Rd. (R. Wardley.) Est. 1963.
CL: Thurs. Open 9—5.30. SIZE: Large.
STOCK: General antiques. LOC: On road
south out of Sheffield. PARK: Easy. TEL:
550720. SER: Valuations; restorations; re-
leathering; buys at auction. VAT: Stan.

N.P. and A. Salt Antiques LAPADA
Trade Only
Abbeydale House and Unit 1, Barmouth Rd.
CL: Sat. Open 9.30—4.30. *STOCK: Victorian
furniture, shipping goods.* TEL: 582672. SER:
Valuations; packing; shipping; courier.

Sheffield Pine Centre
9 Penistone Rd. (P. Coldwell.) Open 9.30—
5.30. SIZE: Medium. *STOCK: Stripped pine
and general antiques.* TEL: 464373.

Paul Ward Antiques
150 Abbeydale Rd. Est. 1976. Open 10—
3.30. SIZE: Medium. *STOCK: General antiques,
shipping goods, matched sets of Victorian
dining and kitchen chairs.* TEL: 583004; home
— 335980. VAT: Stan.

Wharf Antiques   LAPADA
Trade Only
85 William St. (M. Housley and R. Tamblyn.)
Est. 1967. Weekends by appointment. SIZE:
Large. *STOCK: Clocks, furniture, shipping
items, paintings, decorative and architectural
items.* LOC: City centre. PARK: Easy. TEL:
29321; home — 307639. SER: Valuations;
buys at auction. VAT: Stan.

THORNE, Nr. Doncaster   (0405)

Canterbury House
24 Finkle St. (J.R. Holgate.) Est. 1977. Open
8.45—5. *STOCK: General antiques, watches
and clocks.* TEL: 812102.

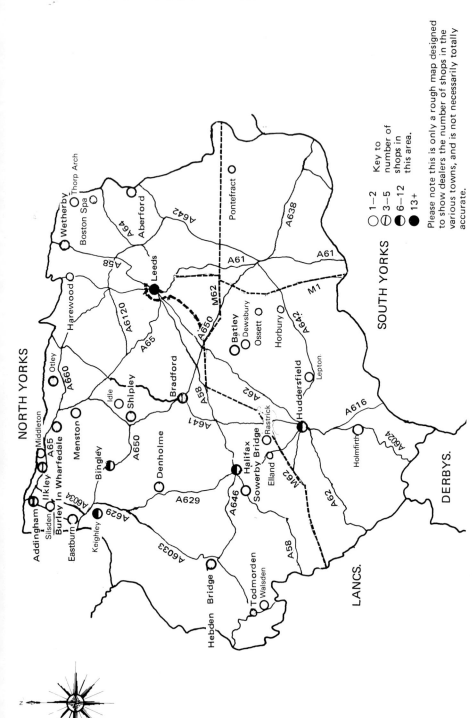

Key to number of shops in this area.

○ 1–2
◔ 3–5
◑ 6–12
● 13+

Please note this is only a rough map designed to show dealers the number of shops in the various towns, and is not necessarily totally accurate.

NORTH YORKS

SOUTH YORKS

LANCS.

DERBYS.

Thorp Arch
Wetherby
Boston Spa
Aberford
Pontefract
A642
A64
A638
A58
A61
A61
Harewood
Leeds
A6120
M62
M1
A65
A650
Batley
Dewsbury
Ossett
Horbury
A642
Otley
A660
Bradford
A58
Lepton
Huddersfield
A616
Idle
Shipley
Menston
A641
A62
A6024
Bingley
A650
Denholme
Rastrick
Holmfirth
Middleton
A65
Burley In Wharfedale
Halifax
Sowerby Bridge
Elland
Addingham
Silsden Ilkley
A6034
A629
A629
Eastburn
Keighley
A646
M62
A58
A92
A6033
Hebden Bridge
Todmorden
Walsden

ABERFORD
Aberford Antiques Ltd.
Hicklam House. (S.M. and J.W.H. Long.) Est. 1973. Resident. Open every day 9—5.30 or by appointment. SIZE: Large. STOCK: Stripped pine, Victorian and period, £10—£750; Victoriana, £5—£1,000; local prints and maps; Victorian oil paintings. LOC: Opposite Almshouses at entrance of village. PARK: Easy. TEL: Leeds (0532) 813209 and 813729. SER: Restorations (pine); French polishing; fitted pine kitchens, mahogany and oak furniture, all from old timber. VAT: Stan/Spec.

ADDINGHAM, Nr. Ilkley   (0943)
Addingham Antiques   LAPADA
70—72 Main St. (G.J. Estevez.) CL: Mon. and Wed. Open 10—5, Sat. 9—12. SIZE: Large. STOCK: Furniture, 17th—19th C; clocks, 18th—19th C; musical boxes; oil paintings, 19th—20th C; scientific instruments, Doulton studio pottery. LOC: A65. PARK: Opposite. TEL: 830788. SER: Restorations (clocks, musical boxes, furniture, paintings).

Manor Barn Pine
Burnside Mill, Main St. (Rose Farm Furniture Ltd.) Est. 1972. Open 8—5.30. SIZE: Warehouse. STOCK: Pine, 17th—19th C; shipping goods. PARK: Easy. TEL: 830176. VAT: Stan.

Village Antiques
102/104 Main St. (D. Norfolk.) Est. 1972. CL: Mon. Open 10—6, Sat. 10—5. SIZE: Large. STOCK: Furniture, clocks and barometers, 18th—19th C. LOC: A65. PARK: Easy. TEL: 831130; home — Rawdon (0532) 504987. SER: Valuations; restorations (furniture, clocks, barometers, upholstery).

BATLEY   (0924)
Leon Cooper   LAPADA
21 Commercial St. Est. 1952. CL: Sat. Open 9—5 by appointment. STOCK: Jewellery, watches, miniatures, clocks, weapons. LOC: Off B6124, near Hick Lane traffic lights. TEL: 475057. SER: Valuations. VAT: Stan.

BINGLEY
Bingley Antiques Centre
Keighley Rd. (J.B. and J. Poole.) Est. 1965. CL: Tues. p.m. Open 9.30—5. SIZE: Large. STOCK: Furniture, 18th—19th C; pottery, porcelain, shipping goods, garden furniture. LOC: On A650, opposite parish church. PARK: Easy. TEL: Bradford (0274) 567316; home — Bradford (0274) 880727. SER: Valuations. VAT: Stan/Spec.

E. Carrol
5 Ryshworth Hall, Keighley Rd., Crossflatts. Est. 1970. Open by appointment. SIZE: Small. STOCK: Oil paintings, watercolours. LOC: A650. PARK: Easy. TEL: Bradford (0274) 568800. VAT: Stan.

Curio Cottage
3 Millgate. (Mrs. W.J. Windle.) CL: Mon. and Tues. Open 2.30—5.30. SIZE: Small. STOCK: Victoriana, curios and stripped pine. TEL: Home — Bradford (0274) 612975.

Georgian House
88 Main St. (D. and E.M. Cowbourne) F.G.A. Est. 1960. Open Mon., Wed. and Thurs. 9—5, other times by appointment SIZE: Medium. STOCK: Period, Victorian and Edwardian furniture; silver, copper, brass, pottery, porcelain, collectors' items. LOC: A650 towards end of Main St. going north. PARK: Easy. TEL: Bradford (0274) 568883. SER: Valuations. VAT: Stan.

Harden's (of Bingley) Antiques
82—84 Main St., also 1—3 Millgate. (H.C. Harden.) Est. 1959. CL: Tues. Open 10—12 and 2—5. SIZE: Large. STOCK: Furniture, late Georgian and Victorian, to £6,000; pottery and porcelain, 19th—20th C, to £1,000; copper, brass, shipping goods. Not stocked: Pictures. LOC: A650, adjacent to 2nd set traffic lights going north. PARK: Easy. TEL: Home — Bradford (0274) 591040. SER: Valuations; buys at auction. VAT: Stan.

Jacques Van Der Tol B.V.

Specialists in restored
English and Continental
antique pine furniture and
reproduction pine furniture

HOLLAND
*40,000 sq. ft. wholesale
warehouse. Export
container packing and
courier service available*

ENGLAND
3,000 sq. ft. warehouse

	76—78
Energie St. 45,	**Old Main St.,**
1411 AS,	**Bingley,**
Naarden,	**Bradford,**
Holland	**West Yorkshire**
(02159) 44107	**(0274) 566188**

Bingley continued

J.V.T. Antiques
76—78 Old Main St. (J. Van Der Tol). Est.
1972. Open 9.30—5, Sun. by appointment.
SIZE: Medium. *STOCK: German and Austrian
pine, some reproduction.* PARK: Easy. TEL:
Bradford (0274) 566188. VAT: Stan.

Juliana
84 Main St. (J. and T. Capstick). CL: Tues.
Open 10—5. *STOCK: Silver, jewellery, small
collectors' items.* TEL: Bradford (0274) 562994.

BOSTON SPA (0937)
by Wetherby

**London House Oriental Rugs
and Carpets**
London House, High St. (M.A. and Mrs. I.T.H.
Ries.) CL: Mon. Open 9—6 including Sun.
SIZE: Medium. *STOCK: Caucasian, Turkish,
Afghan and Persian rugs, runners and carpets,
£50—£2,000; kelims, tapestries and textiles.*
LOC: Off A1, south of Wetherby. PARK: Easy.
TEL: 845123; home — same. SER: Valuations;
restorations (Oriental carpets and rugs); buys
at auction (Oriental carpets and rugs). VAT:
Stan/Spec.

BRADFORD (0274)
Collectors' Corner
5—7 Frizinghall Rd. (C. and G. Douthwaite.)
Est. 1970. CL: Thurs. Open 2—7, or by
appointment. *STOCK: Victoriana, bric-a-brac,
postcards.* PARK: Easy. TEL: 487098.

The Corner Shop
89 Oak Lane. (Miss Badland.) Est. 1961. Open
Tues. 2—5.30, Thurs. and Sat. 11—5.30.
*STOCK: Pottery, small furniture, clocks and
general items.*

Langley's (Jewellers) Ltd.
59 Godwin St. TEL: 722280. VAT: Stan.

Low Moor Antiques
233 and 234 Huddersfield Rd., Low Moor.
(J.A. Bowler.) Est. 1972. CL: Wed.; and Sat.
p.m. Open 9—12 and 2—5. *STOCK: Shipping
furniture, pine, silver plate and general
antiques.* TEL: 671047 and 673085.

BURLEY-IN-WHARFEDALE (0943)
Richard Greene Antiques
87 Main St. Est. 1977. CL: Wed. Open
10—5. SIZE: Small. *STOCK: Period furniture,
especially mahogany.* PARK: Easy. TEL:
862156; home — Bradford (0274) 591418.

DENHOLME, Nr. Bradford
Ye Olde Curiosity Shop
23 New Rd. (F. Weatherill.) Est. 1964. Open
11—5. SIZE: Medium. *STOCK: Curios, general
antiques, shipping goods.* LOC: 7 miles from
Bradford, via Thornton Rd. PARK: 20yds. on
side of main road. TEL: Home — Bradford
(0274) 42756.

DEWSBURY (0924)
Atkinson Antiques
Unit 4, Empire House, Wakefield Rd. (R.L.
Atkinson.) CL: Tues. Open 9.30—5.30.
STOCK: General antiques. TEL: 456988.

EASTBURN, Nr. Keighley
M. Kelly Antiques
41 Main Rd. Est. 1968. Open 9.30—5, Sun.
1.30—5. SIZE: Medium. *STOCK: English and
Continental pine, darkwoods and small items,
19th C, to £1,000.* PARK: Easy. TEL: Steeton
(0535) 53002; home — same. SER: Restorations (pine stripping). VAT: Stan.

ELLAND   (0422)
Andy Thornton Architectural Antiques Ltd.
Ainleys Industrial Estate. Est. 1973. Open 8—5; Sat. 9—12 by appointment. SIZE: Large. *STOCK: Architectural antiques — doors, stained, etched and cut glass windows, fireplaces, fittings for restaurants and public houses.* PARK: Easy. TEL: 78125; home — Huddersfield (0484) 712636. VAT: Stan.

HALIFAX   (0422)
Boulevard Reproductions
369 Skircoat Green Rd. (T. Bright.) Open 9.30—7 p.m., Sun. for viewing. *STOCK: Furniture.* TEL: 68628.

Jean Brear
19 Causeway Head, Burnley Rd. Est. 1955. *STOCK: Antiquarian books; maps, atlases, prints, oils, manuscripts, small antiques.* TEL: 66144.

Collectors Old Toys and Antiques
89 Northgate (J. Haley). Open 10—5. *STOCK: Collectors toys, general and shipping antiques, small items, china, glass, clocks.* TEL: 822148 or 60434.

Peter Gould
101 Northgate. CL: Mon. Open 10—1 and 1.45—4.30. SIZE: Medium. *STOCK: Oak furniture, 17th—18th C; metalware, 16th—18th C; decorative items, all periods.* LOC: Town centre near North Bridge. PARK: Easy. TEL: 69970; home — same. VAT: Spec.

Halez-Fax Antiques
12 Bull Green. (W. J. Rooth.) Open 9—5. SIZE: Medium. *STOCK: General antiques, furniture, porcelain, pottery, glass, collectors' items, curios.* LOC: Town centre. TEL: 68805. VAT: Stan.

Halifax Antiques Centre
Queens Rd. Open 10—5 Tues.—Sat. SIZE: Large and warehouse. There are 18 dealers at this centre selling *furniture, porcelain, silver, pictures, clocks, general antiques.* LOC: 1 mile from town centre, corner Queens Rd. and Gibbet St. PARK: Easy. TEL: 66657.

Hillside Antiques
Denholme Gate Rd., Hipperholme. (M. and J. Preston.) Est. 1981. CL: Wed. Open 10—12.15 and 2—5.15 Thurs. 10—12.15 and 2—4. SIZE: Small. *STOCK: Pottery, porcelain, small furniture, copper and brass, 1870—1940.* Not stocked: Linen, clothing and gold. LOC: A644, 150yds. north of Hipperholme crossroads. PARK: Easy. TEL: Home — 202744. FAIRS: Local.

King Cross Antiques
189 King Cross Rd. CL: Sat. p.m. *STOCK: General antiques, shipping goods, pine, longcase and wall clocks.* VAT: Stan/Spec.

Halifax continued
Scott and Varey
10 Prescott St. (W.B. Scott.) Est. 1963. Open 9—5. SIZE: Large. *STOCK: Furniture, 1740—1910; clocks, watercolours, oils, prints, cast iron, architectural fittings, chandeliers, tiles, silver, unusual brass, copper, pewter, writing boxes, art deco, pine.* LOC: Town centre near Halifax Building Society. PARK: Easy. TEL: 66928; home — 883388. VAT: Stan.

HAREWOOD, Nr. Leeds   (0532)
Harewood Cottage Antiques
26/27 Harrogate Rd. (D. Wilson.) CL: Sun., Mon., and Thurs. except by appointment. Open 10—6. *STOCK: Furniture, porcelain, collectors' items, 18th to early 20th C, £5—£2,000.* LOC: Opposite Harewood House Gates. PARK: At rear. TEL: 886327.

HEBDEN BRIDGE   (0422)
Nr. Halifax
Cornucopia Antiques
9 West End. (C. Nassor.) CL: Tues. Open 10—5, Mon., Wed. and Sun. 2—5. *STOCK: Pine, oak and mahogany furniture, art deco, kitchenware.* LOC: Town centre behind Pennine Information Centre. PARK: Easy. TEL: 844497.

HOLMFIRTH, Nr. Huddersfield
Chapel House Fireplaces
Netherfield House, St. Georges Rd., Scholes. CL: Mon. Open Tues. 9—8, Wed.—Fri. 9—5, Sat. 9—4. *STOCK: Restored antique and Victorian fireplaces and mantels.* TEL: Huddersfield (0484) 682275.

HORBURY, Nr. Wakefield
The Old Tithe Barn
16 Tithe Barn St. (J.S. Ingham.) Est. 1945. CL: Wed. Open daily. *STOCK: General antiques, especially furniture.* LOC: Between Ossett and Wakefield. PARK: Easy. TEL: Wakefield (0924) 274362; home — same. SER: Restorations (upholstery, French polishing, furniture repairs). VAT: Stan.

HUDDERSFIELD   (0484)
20th Century Antiques
23 Byram St. (S.J. Marten.) Est. 1970. SIZE: Large and warehouse. *STOCK: Furniture, export and shipping items, pianos and clocks, Georgian to 1920s, £5—£1,000.* LOC: Town centre near church. PARK: Easy. TEL: 515166. VAT: Stan/Spec.

Huddersfield continued

Almondbury Antiques
21-23 Westgate, Almondbury. (O. Furness.) Est. 1973. CL: Mon. Open 10.30—5. SIZE: Large. *STOCK: Victoriana, general antiques, crochet trimmed and embroidered linen, lace, costume and accessories, Victorian to 1930s.* LOC: ½ mile from A642. PARK: Easy. TEL: 548474 or 661203.

The Antique Shop
68 Westbourne Rd., Marsh. (P.T. Meal.) Est. 1938. CL: Wed., Thurs, and Sat. Open 11—12.30 and 2—5. SIZE: Small. *STOCK: English porcelain, 1880—1930, £20—£1,200; glass, Georgian and Victorian, £5—£250; small furniture, £30—£500.* Not stocked: Jewellery and militaria. LOC: ¾ mile from town centre (A640). PARK: Easy. TEL: 20952; home — 28136. SER: Valuations; buys at auction. FAIRS: Buxton and Stafford. VAT: Stan.

Beau Monde Antiques
343a Bradford Rd., Fartown. (R.M. Schofield.) Est. 1963. CL: Wed. p.m. Open 9.30—6, Sat. 9.30—5. SIZE: Medium. *STOCK: Furniture and general antiques, £5—£500.* LOC: On A641 1 mile from town centre. PARK: Easy. TEL: 27565.

Berry Brow Antiques
90/92 Dodds Royd, Woodhead Rd., Berry Brow. (M. Griffiths.) Est. 1972. Open 10.30—5.30, Sun. 12—6. SIZE: Medium. *STOCK: Pine, Victorian and Edwardian furniture, Victorian china, clocks, art deco, light fittings, bric-a-brac.* LOC: 2 miles from town centre on Holmfirth Rd. PARK: Easy. TEL: 663320. SER: Buys at auction.

Bygones
710 Manchester Rd., Cowlersley. (V. and H. Akroyd.) Est. 1973. CL: Sat. Open 10—4.30, Mon. and Fri. 1.30—4.30. *STOCK: General antiques, bric-a-brac, Victoriana, Doulton stoneware.* TEL: 842852.

IS YOUR ENTRY CORRECT?
If there is even the slightest inaccuracy in your entry, *please* let us know before 1st January 1987.
GUIDE TO THE
ANTIQUE SHOPS OF BRITAIN
5 Church Street, Woodbridge, Suffolk.

Huddersfield continued

Collectors Corner
13 Market Ave. Est. 1977. CL: Wed. Open 9—5. *STOCK: Jewellery, general antiques.* LOC: Opposite Boots, chemist. TEL: 28359. VAT: Stan/Spec.

Curio Corner Antiques
122 Westbourne Rd., Marsh. (D. Booth.) Est. 1957. Open 9—5.30. SIZE: Medium. *STOCK: Porcelain and pottery, £5—£500; furniture, £10—£1,500; clocks, £25—£1,750; brass and copper, £10—£200.* LOC: 1 mile from town centre on M62 approach road. PARK: Easy. TEL: 535535. VAT: Stan/Spec.

D.W. Dyson (Antique Weapons)
Holme Court, New Mill, Est. 1974. Open by appointment only. *STOCK: Antique weapons including cased duelling pistols, armour, rare and unusual items.* LOC: Off A616. PARK: Easy. TEL: 686578; home — same. SER: Valuations; buys at auction (antique weapons); advice on restoration. FAIRS: Dorchester Hotel, London; Dortmund, Stuttgart and other major foreign. VAT: Spec.

Fillans (Antiques)
2 Market Walk. (I. Fillan and G. Neary.) N.A.G. Est. 1852. Open 8.45—5.30. SIZE: Small. *STOCK: English silver, 1700—1900, to £1,000; Sheffield plate, 1760—1840, £10—£500; jewellery, £10—£5,000.* Not stocked: Other than above. PARK: Town centre multi-storey. TEL: 531609. SER: Valuations; restorations (silver); buys at auction (English silver and jewellery). VAT: Stan/Spec.

Huddersfield Antiques
170 Wakefield Rd., Moldgreen. (P. Lunn.) Est. 1971. Open 10.30—4.30, or by appointment. SIZE: Medium. *STOCK: Victoriana, bric-a-brac, collectors' items, postcards; warehouse of trade and shipping goods.* PARK: Easy. TEL: 539747. SER: Valuations; buys at auction.

Trinity Galleries
39 Market St., Paddock. (Mr. and Mrs. G.E. Haigh). Est. 1968. CL: Sat. Open 9.30—5.30. SIZE: Medium. *STOCK: Jewellery, silver, paintings and prints, £5—£500; clocks and plate, 19th—20th C, metalware, small furniture, pottery and porcelain, 19th C.* LOC: From A640 right at second roundabout, follow to 'T' junction then right. PARK: Easy. TEL: 536442; home — 20195. VAT: Stan/Spec.

IDLE, Nr. Bradford

R.E. and M. Jackson (formerly Messrs. Bethell Antiques. Est. 1880.)
9 Town Lane. Open by appointment. SIZE: Small. *STOCK: Small furniture, pottery, porcelain, 18th to early 19th C; glass, Victorian jewellery.* PARK: Easy. TEL: Bradford (0274) 618922.

ILKLEY (0943)

J.H. Cooper and Son (Ilkley) Ltd.
LAPADA
33—35 Church St., and 50 Leeds Rd. Est. 1910. Open 9—1 and 2—5.30 SIZE: Large. *STOCK: English furniture, pre-1830, £25—£1,000; porcelain and silver, pictures.* Not stocked: Post—1880 items. LOC: A65. PARK: Easy. TEL: 608020; workroom — 608942; home — 609932. SER: Valuations, restorations (furniture); buys at auction. VAT: Stan/Spec.

Pendragon Antiquarian Bookshop
10 Church St. CL: Wed. Open 10—6. *STOCK: Books, prints, pictures.* TEL: 607124; home — Harrogate (0423) 862312.

Jack Shaw and Co.
The Old Grammar School, Skipton Rd. Est. 1945. CL: Wed. Open 9.30—12.45 and 2—5.30. *STOCK: Silver, furniture.* TEL: 609467. VAT: Spec.

Ilkley continued

Simon
25 Church St. (S.G.H. Pratt.) SIZE: Medium. *STOCK: Furniture, 17th—20th C, £50—£3,500; longcase and bracket clocks.* Not stocked: Coins, weapons, jewellery. PARK: Behind shop. TEL: 602788. SER: Valuations; buys at auction. VAT: Stan/Spec.

Wharfedale Antiques
26 Leeds Rd. (I. and K. Richardson.) Est. 1974. CL: Wed. Open 9—5.30. SIZE: Medium. *STOCK: Jewellery, dolls, glass, furniture, Victoriana, crested china, commemorative ware.* PARK: In adjacent st. TEL: 600045.

KEIGHLEY (0535)

B.W. Antiques
Trade Only
Lees Mill, Lees Lane. (D.H. Buckley.) Est. 1973. Open 9—5, Sat. and Sun. by appointment. SIZE: Large. *STOCK: General antiques and shipping goods, 1850—1930, £50—£1,000.* LOC: Main road into Haworth. PARK: Easy. TEL: 43535; home — 662684. SER: Valuations; restorations (furniture). VAT: Stan.

Keighley continued

Barleycote Hall Antiques   LAPADA
2 Janet St., Crossroads. (R. Hoskins.) Resident. Est. 1968. CL: Mon. Open 11—5, trade may call evenings. *STOCK: Georgian and Victorian furniture, porcelain, metalwork, paintings, jewellery, Victorian and Edwardian clothing, clocks of all types, shipping goods.* LOC: A629, turn right towards Haworth, 600yds. on right. TEL: Haworth (0535) 44776. VAT: Stan/Spec.

Keighleys of Keighley
153 East Parade. (B. Keighley and Son.) Est. 1939. CL: Tues. Open 9—5. *STOCK: Furniture, jewellery, gold and silver, china.* LOC: Next to the Victoria Hotel. PARK: Easy. TEL: 663439; home — 607180. VAT: Stan.

Real Macoy
2 Janet St. (D. Seal.) CL: Mon., and Sat. Open 11—5 including Sun. *STOCK: Quilts, textiles, period clothing.* TEL: Haworth (0535) 44776.

Scar Top Antiques
Far Scar Top, Stanbury. (T. and S. Johnston.) Est. 1971. Open 9—5 seven days or by appointment. SIZE: Large. *STOCK: Pine, 18th—20th C; mahogany, oak.* LOC: Haworth/Colne road, alongside Ponden Reservoir. PARK: Easy. TEL: Haworth (0535) 46427 or 42585. SER: Stripping; timber reclamation. VAT: Stan.

Willow Bank
Riddlesden. (Mrs. F. Hutchinson.) Est. 1981. Open Tues. and Sat. 10—4, other times by appointment. SIZE: Small. *STOCK: Grand-daughter clocks, 1920—1930, £50—£100; Shelley teasets, small furniture.* LOC: A650. PARK: Easy. TEL: 602020; home — same. SER: Valuations; buys at auction (art deco). FAIRS: Bowman. VAT: Stan.

LEEDS   (0532)
Aladdin's Cave
19 Queens Arcade. (P. and S. Isaacs.) Est. 1954. CL: Mon. SIZE: Small. *STOCK: Jewellery, £15—£250; collectors' items; all 19th—20th C.* LOC: Town centre. PARK: 100 yards. TEL: 457903; home — 613151. SER: Valuations. VAT: Stan.

Leeds continued

Andrew's Antique Shop
inc. Exchange Jewellers
56 North St. (A.W.D. Rogers, K.A. Humphrey, B. Kerfoot.) Est. 1969. CL: Thurs. and Sat. p.m. Open 9.30—4.30. SIZE: Large and warehouse. *STOCK: General antiques, jewellery, shipping goods.* TEL: 445767 or 430870. VAT: Stan.

The Antique Exchange
400 Kirkstall Rd. (S. Wood.) Est. 1976. CL: Tues. and Wed. Open 10.30—3. SIZE: Medium. *STOCK: Furniture including pine, satin walnut and shipping, 19th—20th C, £100—£500.* LOC; Kirkstall Rd. is ½ mile west of Yorkshire Television Studios. PARK: Easy. TEL: 743513. VAT: Stan/Spec.

Antique Pine
197 North St., Sheepscar. (Miss A.H. Buckley.) Est. 1974. Open Thurs., Fri. and Sat. 11—3. SIZE: Small. *STOCK: Stripped pine, Victorian and 20th C.* LOC: Bottom of North St. right-hand lane into car park area. PARK: Easy. TEL: 444784; home — 661309. SER: Restorations (pine).

The Antique Shop
226 Harrogate Rd. (S.H. Revere.) Est. 1960. Open 9.30—5. *STOCK: Shipping goods, general antiques, weapons.* TEL: 681785.

Antiques & Reproductions
135 Green Lane. (D. Oddy.) Open seven days 10—5.30. *STOCK: Victoriana, furniture, copper, brass, silver, jewellery, paintings.* LOC: Just off Ring Rd. opposite Crossgates Railway Station. PARK: Easy. TEL: 643734; home — 649466.

Besbrode & Seals
Unit A, Holbeck New Mills, Braithwaite St. (M. Besbrode, B. Seals.) Open 9—5. *STOCK: General antiques and pianos.* TEL: 443685. SER: French polishing.

Bishops House Antiques
169 Town St., Rodley. (Mrs. J.M. Bishop.) Est. 1977. Open Sat. 2—5.30, or by appointment. *STOCK: General antiques, porcelain and glass.* TEL: Pudsey (0532) 563071.

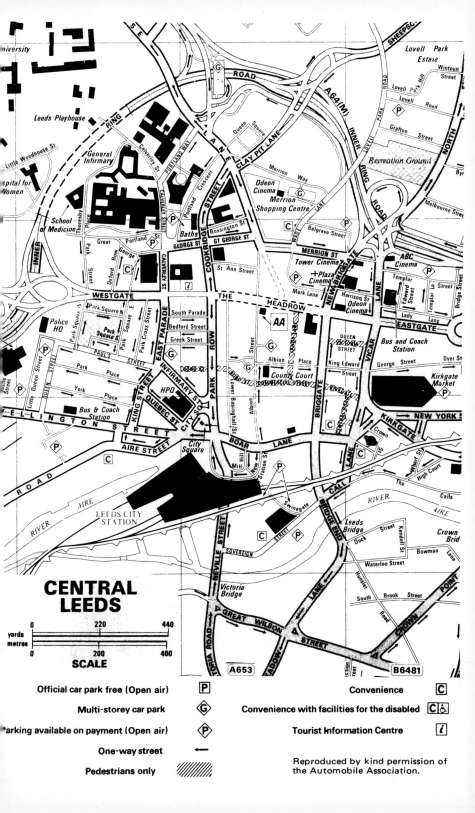

CENTRAL LEEDS

yards	0 220 440
metres	0 200 400

SCALE

Official car park free (Open air)	🅿	Convenience	C
Multi-storey car park	Ⓖ	Convenience with facilities for the disabled	C ♿
Parking available on payment (Open air)	Ⓟ	Tourist Information Centre	i
One-way street	←		
Pedestrians only	▨		

Reproduced by kind permission of
the Automobile Association.

Leeds continued

Boston Pine
Unit 3B, Globe Mills, Back Row. (Mrs. K. Harper, K. Burns.) Open 10—6; Sat 11—4. *STOCK: Pine.* TEL: 441650.

Clifton Antiques
854 Leeds Rd., Bramhope (A.S. Ambler.) Est. 1972. Open 9.45—6. SIZE: Medium. *STOCK: Furniture, china, pictures.* Not stocked: Stamps, medals and coins. LOC: A660. PARK: Easy. TEL: 673765; home — Otley (0943) 464801. VAT: Stan/Spec.

Geary Antiques
114 Richardshaw Lane, Stanningley, Pudsey. (J.A. Geary.) Est. 1933. CL: Wed. Open 10—5.30. SIZE: Large. *STOCK: Furniture, Georgian and Victorian; copper and brass, coloured glass; household contents, secondhand furniture, 20th C.* LOC: 50yds. off main Leeds/Bradford Rd. at Stanningley. PARK: Easy. TEL: Pudsey (0532) 564122. SER: Restorations (furniture). VAT: Stan/Spec.

William Goldsmith
23 County Arcade. (R.F. Chesterman.) Est. 1961. Open 9—5.30. SIZE: Medium. *STOCK: Jewellery, 19th—20th C, £50—£500; clocks, 19th C, £100—£1,000; samplers and prints, 18th—19th C, £25—£100.* LOC: Town centre. PARK: Nearby. TEL: 455161; home — 680275. SER: Valuations; restorations. VAT: Stan.

Leeds continued

Henson's Antiques
7a Chapel Place, North Lane, Headingley. (H.J.S. Henson.) Est. 1962. CL: Sat. p.m. Open 9—5.30, 4.30 on Fri. SIZE: Medium. *STOCK: Mostly furniture, curtain and upholstery materials.* LOC: At traffic lights at junction of Otley Rd. and North Lane, turn up North Lane, first turning on the right. PARK: Easy. TEL: 751914. VAT: Stan.

Hyde Park Rare Books
10 Headingley Lane. Est. 1966. Open by appointment only. *STOCK: Rare and antiquarian books on all subjects especially art reference and antiques; engravings, maps.* TEL: 782689. SER: Catalogues issued.

Kingsway Antiques
223 New Rd. Side, Horsforth. (T. Waddington.) Est. 1929. Open by appointment. *STOCK: General antiques, clocks, jewellery.* TEL: 587674. SER: Buys at auction.

Kirkstall Antiques
366 Kirkstall Rd. (S.R. and A. Gibson.) Est. 1973. CL: Wed. Open 10.30—3. SIZE: Medium. *STOCK: Stripped and painted pine, shipping goods, £5—£500; general small items, £1—£100.* LOC: A65. PARK: Easy. TEL: 757367. VAT: Stan/Spec.

Benjamin Herring, Senior. 'Three stallions fighting in a landscape.' 26½ins. x 40¼ins., signed and dated 1828. From *The Dictionary of British Equestrian Artists* by Sally Mitchell, published by the **Antique Collectors' Club**, 1985.

Leeds continued

L. Nathan & Sons
9 County Arcade. Open 9—5.30. *STOCK: Jewellery and curios.* TEL: 453444.

Parker Fine Arts
137 Kirkstall Lane. Open 10—4 Wed., and Sat., or by appointment. *STOCK: Oils and watercolours, 19th to early 20th C, £20—£500.* TEL: 742424; home — 657123.

Pianorama Antique Exports
Abbey Mill, Bridge Rd., Kirkstall. (C. Webster.) Open 9—5. *STOCK: General antiques and pianos.* TEL: 759351.

Rose's Jewellers
107—108 Briggate. (M. Rose.) Open 9—5.30. *STOCK: Victorian and antique gold jewellery, silver and watches.* TEL: 439767.

Taylor Antiques
30 Bradford Rd., Stanningway, Pudsey. (T.C. Taylor.) Est. 1975. Open 9—5, Sat. 10—4. *STOCK: Pine, general antiques and shipping goods.* TEL: Pudsey (0532) 569706.

T.L. Thirkill Antiques
Springfield Cottage, West End Lane, Horsforth. Est. 1963. *STOCK: Furniture, 19th C.* LOC: 10 mins. west of city centre. TEL: 589160.

Tomasso and Sons
Gledhow Hall, Gledhow Wood Rd. Est. 1898. Open by appointment. *STOCK: Italian and Dutch old masters' paintings and sculptures; Italian shipping items.* TEL: 654422.

Windsor House Antiques (Leeds) Ltd.   LAPADA
18—20 Benson St. (D.K. Smith.) Est. 1959. Open 9—5, Sat. 9—1. SIZE: Large. *STOCK: Furniture, 18th—19th C; metalware, silver and plate, porcelain, pottery, clocks, collectors' items.* PARK: Easy. TEL: 444666. VAT: Stan/Spec.

Year Dot
4/5 Boar Lane. (P. Davis.) Open 9.30—5.30. *STOCK: Oriental pottery and porcelain, paintings, clocks, barometers, glass, copper, brass, bric-a-brac.* TEL: 443522/460860.

Yorkshire Heritage Antiques
125/127 Roundhay Rd. Est. 1962. Open 10—5. SIZE: Small. *STOCK: Furniture, to Victorian, £5—£700; brass and copperware, pottery, china, glass, £5—£50; stripped pine.* LOC: From City follow signs for Wetherby (A1), on left past Gaiety Hotel. PARK: Easy. TEL: 491333; home — 813521. SER: Stripping; finishing.

LEPTON, Nr. Huddersfield
K.L.M. & Co. Antiques
The Antique Shop, Wakefield Rd. (K.L. & J. Millington.) Est. 1980. Open 10—5, other times by appointment. SIZE: Large and warehouse. *STOCK: Furniture, including stripped pine, to 1930s, £25—£1,000; pianos.* LOC: A642 Wakefield road from Huddersfield, shop opposite village church. PARK: Easy and at rear. TEL: Huddersfield (0484) 607763; home — Huddersfield (0484) 607548. SER: Valuations. VAT: Stan.

MENSTON   (0943)
Antiques
101 Bradford Rd. (W. and J. Hanlon.) Est. 1974. *STOCK: Small furniture, pottery, porcelain, art nouveau, art deco, silver, plate, jewellery, handworked linen, collectors items.* PARK: Forecourt. TEL: 77634; home — Otley (0943) 463693.

MIDDLETON
Wharfedale Galleries
1 Gilstead, 17 Rupert Rd. Open by appointment only. *STOCK: Mainly Victorian paintings.* TEL: Ilkley (0943) 602676.

OSSETT, Nr. Wakefield
Keith R. Oldroyd Antiques
68 Bank St. Est. 1979. Open 9—12.30 and 1.30—5.30, Sat. 9—4, Mon. and Wed. by appointment. SIZE: Small plus warehouse. *STOCK: Furniture, £5—£500; pottery and porcelain, £25—£500; stevengraphs, £25—£150; all 19th—20th C, clocks and mechanical music, 18th—20th C, £25—£500.* LOC: Town centre. PARK: Easy. TEL: Wakefield (0924) 261177; home — Wakefield (0924) 272163.

OTLEY, Nr. Leeds   (0943)
Butterchurn Gallery
32-36 Bondgate. (G.M. Dolan.) Est. 1980. Open 9—6. SIZE: Small. *STOCK: Stripped pine furniture, general antiques.* TEL: 462579. SER: Restorations (furniture); paint stripping.

H. and M. Suttle
18 Market Place. (D.M. Allott and S.M. Tankard.) Est. 1887. CL: Wed. Open 10—5. *STOCK: China, silver, jewellery, miniatures, coloured glass. Not stocked: Stamps, coins and postcards.* TEL: 462313. VAT: Stan/Spec.

PONTEFRACT   (0977)
Quality House
44 Front St. (T. Robinson.) Est. 1970. CL: Thurs. Open 10—5. SIZE: Medium. *STOCK: Clocks, 18th—19th C, £50—£2,000.* LOC: 2 miles from junction 32 off M62. PARK: Easy. TEL: 792507; home — 709658. VAT: Stan.

RASTRICK, Nr. Brighouse
Maps and Prints
Elder Lea, 14 Clough Lane. (J. Collins.) Est. 1980. Open by appointment. SIZE: Medium. *STOCK: Maps, 1600—1880; prints, 1700—1880; watercolours, 1800—1930.* LOC: From M62, junction 24, take Brighouse road, turn right at traffic lights, property on right 50yds. PARK: Easy. TEL: Brighouse (0484) 713531; home — same. SER: Valuations; restorations (framing); buys at auction (as stock). FAIRS: Yorkshire and Bedfordshire.

SHIPLEY
R. Bell and Son
37 Briggate. TEL: Bradford (0274) 582602.

SILSDEN   (0535)
Cobbeydale Pine
Waterloo Mill, Howden Rd. (D. & G. Cooper.) Open 9—5; Sat. 12—5, Sun. 12—4. *STOCK: Pine.* LOC: Opposite Toyota garage. TEL: 56280. SER: Stripping.

SOWERBY BRIDGE
Colin Greenwood
3 Wharf St. Est. 1962. CL: Sun. and Wed., and Sat. p.m. except by appointment. Open 9.15—12.30 and 2—5.45. SIZE: Small. *STOCK: Drinking glasses, from 1650, £5—£200; porcelain, from 1780, £1—£200; furniture, from 1600, £5—£750.* Not stocked: Coins, arms, armour, weapons, medals. PARK: At rear. TEL: Halifax (0422) 833939. SER: Buys at auction.

THORP ARCH, Nr. Wetherby
Mavis Daniel Antiques
The Green. (Mrs. M. Daniel.) Est. 1975. Open Thurs.—Sun. 2—5. SIZE: Small. *STOCK: Small furniture, brass, copper, lamps, porcelain, textiles, 19th C, £5—£500.* LOC: From Boston Spa turn into Bridge Rd., across river, the green is on right-hand side. PARK: Easy. TEL: Boston Spa (0937) 845843; home — Leeds (0532) 813650. SER: Valuations; restorations (brass). VAT: Spec.

TODMORDEN   (070 681)
Pennine Antiques
58/60 Burnley Rd. (K. and L. Chapman, K. Man.) CL: Mon., and Tues. Open 10.30—6, Sat. 11—5. *STOCK: Period, Victorian, Edwardian, country and upholstered furniture; stripped pine, shipping goods, clocks, metalware, paintings, prints, porcelain and pottery.* TEL: 3773.

Thistle Antiques
650a Halifax Rd., Eastwood. (Mrs. A. Williams.) Resident. Open every day. *STOCK: Country and decorative items.* TEL: 7505.

WALSDEN, Nr. Todmorden
Cottage Antiques (1984) Ltd.
788 Rochdale Rd. (G. and T. Slater.) Resident. Est. 1978. CL: Mon. Open daily, Tues. and Wed. by appointment. SIZE: Medium. *STOCK: Pine furniture, kitchenalia, 19th C, £5—£500; general antiques.* PARK: Easy. TEL: Todmorden (070 681) 3612. SER: Restorations; pine stripping.

WETHERBY   (0937)
Mitchell-Hill Gallery
2 Church St. (D.G. Mitchell-Hill.) Open 9—1 and 2—5, Wed. 9—1. *STOCK: Oils, watercolours and pastels from early 1800.* TEL: 65929.

Raymond Tomlinson (Antiques) Ltd.
LAPADA
(Wetherby Antiques)   *Trade Only*
Northfield Buildings, Northfield Place. Est. 1971. CL: Sat. Open 8—5 or by appointment. SIZE: Large. *STOCK: Furniture, £5—£5,000; clocks, £20—£3,000.* LOC: A1 Wetherby roundabout, Wetherby exit, take 8th turning left, warehouse on left behind "Fields" Joiners. PARK: Easy. TEL: 64866 or 64870. SER: Export; container packing; courier. VAT: Stan/Spec.

Wedgwood creamware mug. "Harvest Home." From "An Ebony Tea Caddy with Rare Liverpool Enamel Plaques", **Antique Collecting,** November 1985.

CHANNEL ISLANDS

(Channel Islands are exempt from V.A.T.)

Guernsey

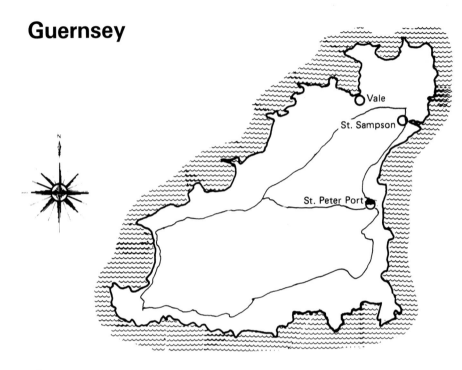

Jersey

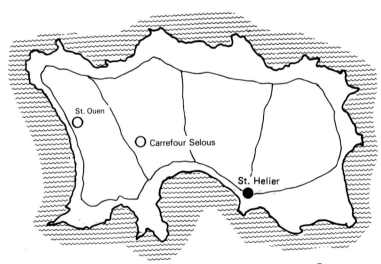

Please note this is only a rough map designed to show dealers the number of shops in the various towns, and is not necessarily totally accurate.

○ 1–2
⊖ 3–5
◑ 6–12
● 13+

Key to number of shops in this area.

GUERNSEY (0481)

ST. PETER PORT

Channel Islands Galleries Ltd.
Guernsey Craft Centre, Trinity Sq. (G.P. and Mrs. C. Gavey.) Est. 1967. CL: Thurs. p.m. Open 10−12.30 and 2−5, or by appointment. STOCK: Antique maps, sea charts and prints of the Channel Islands; oil paintings, watercolours, Channel Islands' books, illustrated, historical, social, geographical and natural history. Not stocked: General antiques. TEL: 23247; home − 47337.

Peter Cherry Antiques
17 Tudor House Shopping Centre, Mill St. Est. 1973. CL: Thurs. p.m. Open 10−12.30 and 2−5. SIZE: Large. STOCK: Period, Victorian and Edwardian furniture, longcase and wall clocks, nautical and marine items, metalware, oil lamps, items of local interest. LOC: Enter centre from Mill St. or from Le Bordage. PARK: Nearby. TEL: 26808; home − 711080.

Grange Antiques
7/8 The Grange. (K.M. Carré and A.C. Wilcox.) Est. 1968. CL: Sat. p.m., Thurs. and Sun., except by appointment. Open 9.30−5. SIZE: Medium. STOCK: Objets d'art, and small furniture, 18th−19th C, £25−£1,000; pottery and porcelain, 18th C to art deco, £5−£500; jewellery, antique and secondhand, £1−£500. LOC: One of main roads from harbour going inland, shop opposite the Elizabeth College. PARK: 50yds. on right. TEL: 21480. SER: Valuations; jewellery (re-threading); buys at auction.

J. and J. Hubbard
11a Mill St. (Mr. and Mrs. J. Hubbard.) Est. 1974. Open 10−12.30 and 2−5 or by appointment. SIZE: Small. STOCK: Japanese ivory and netsuke, lacquer, jade, Oriental porcelain, metalware and works of art. PARK: Easy. TEL: 28462 or 28540. SER: Valuations; buys at auction.

St. Peter Port continued

St. James's Gallery Ltd.
18-20 The Bordage. (A.P.H. and C.O. Whittam.) Est. 1945. CL: Thurs. p.m. and lunch times. SIZE: Large. STOCK: Furniture, £100−£20,000; porcelain, both 18th−19th C; paintings, 18th−20th C. PARK: Within 2 mins. walk. TEL: 20070; home − 23999. SER: Valuations; restorations (furniture, upholstery, pictures, framing); buys at auction.

Thesaurus
16 Tudor House, Mill St/Bordage. STOCK: Antiquarian and out of print books, maps and prints. LOC: Town centre. TEL: 20217.

ST. SAMPSON
The Old Curiosity Shop
Commercial Rd. Est. 1978. Open daily. STOCK: Old books, prints, paintings, small antiques, china, glass, silver, brass, furniture, £1−£5,000. TEL: 45324. SER: Valuations (books); bookbinding.

VALE
Geoffrey P. Gavey
Les Clospains, Rue de L'Ecole. Est. 1967. Open by appointment. STOCK: Maps, sea charts and prints of the Channel Islands; oil and watercolour paintings; Channel Islands books, illustrated, historical, social, geographic and natural history. Not stocked: General antiques. TEL: 47337.

A diamond brooch valued at about £1,500. From "Diamond Brooches, a comparison", **Antique Collecting,** December 1985.

This fine group by Alfred Barye, once again disproves his many critics. Certainly he was not as capable as his father but this model of Joan of Arc must rank amongst the top group of sculptures in Paris in the third quarter of the 19th century. From *Animals in Bronze* by Christopher Payne, published by the **Antique Collectors' Club,** 1986.

JERSEY (0534)

CARREFOUR SELOUS, St. Lawrence

David Hick Antiques
Alexandra House. Est. 1977. Open 10—5.
SIZE: Large and warehouse. STOCK: Furniture
and small items. TEL: 62965.

ST. HELIER

John Blench & Son
50 Don St. STOCK: Antiquarian books, fine
bindings, maps and prints. TEL: 25281; home
— 42674. FAIRS: Jersey.

Cameo Antiques
9 Union St. (Mrs. I. McQuaigue.) Est. 1868.
Open 9.30—5.30, Thurs. 9.30—1. STOCK:
Jewellery, silver, bronzes. TEL: 23899.

John Cooper Antiques
16 The Market. STOCK: General antiques.
TEL: 23600.

Dodo Antiques
23 Peter St. (J. Harvey.) Est. 1974. CL:
Thurs. p.m. Open 10—12.30 and 2—5.
STOCK: General small antiques, jewellery and
dolls, art deco, militaria. TEL: 71497.

Grange Gallery and Fine Arts Ltd.
39 New St. (G.J. Morris.) Est. 1974. CL: Sun.
except by appointment. Open 9—5.30. SIZE:
Medium. STOCK: Oil paintings, 18th and 19th
C, local prints, 19th C, £100—£9,000. LOC:
Antique area of St. Helier. PARK: Multi-storey
100yds. TEL: 20077. SER: Valuations; restorations (pictures); buys at auction; framing.

I.G.A. Old Masters Ltd.
Magdala Mount, Lower King's Cliff. (I.G. and
Mrs. C.B.V. Appleby.) Est. 1953. Open by
appointment. SIZE: Medium. STOCK: Old
Master paintings; 19th C paintings. LOC: Near
Queens Rd. PARK: Easy. TEL: 24226; home
— same.

St. Helier continued

John Rae Antiques
Savile St. Est. 1947. Open daily. STOCK:
General antiques, furniture, longcase clocks.
TEL: 32171.

The Selective Eye Gallery
50 Don St. (J. and P. Blench.) Est. 1958. CL:
Thurs. and Sat. p.m. Open 9.30—12.30 and
2—5. SIZE: Medium. STOCK: Oil paintings,
19th—20th C; maps, prints and antiquarian
books, 16th—18th C. Not stocked: General
antiques. LOC: Town centre. PARK: Multi-
storey 100yds. TEL: 25281; home — 42674.
SER: Valuations; restorations (pictures).
FAIRS: Jersey.

Shepherds Antiques
3 Burrard St. (J. Shepherd.) Est. 1967. Open
9—5. STOCK: General antiques. TEL: 22713.

Thesaurus (Jersey) Ltd.
26 Burrard St. (I. Creaton.) Est. 1973. Open
8.30—6. SIZE: Large. STOCK: Antiquarian
and out of print books, £1—£2,000; maps
and prints. Not stocked: General antiques.
LOC: Town centre. PARK: 100yds. TEL:
37045. SER: Buys at auction. VAT: Spec.

Union Street Antique Market
8 Union St. (A.L. Thomson.) Est. 1955. Open
9—6. SIZE: Large. There are several dealers at
this market selling a wide range of general
antiques. PARK: 150yds. TEL: 73805; home
— 22475. SER: Buys at auction.

ST. OUEN

St. Helier Galleries BADA
Les Ormes, Ville au Bas. (Mrs. R.S. du Feu,
J.H. and Mrs. M. Appleby.) Est. 1953. Open
by appointment. SIZE: Medium. STOCK:
Paintings, 15th—20th C, all schools; early
English watercolours, Continental and Colonial
drawings, prints from £80. LOC: From St.
Helier, turn right after St. Ouen church, first
house on left. PARK: Easy. TEL: 82332. SER:
Valuations; restorations (pictures); buys at
auction (fine art articles).

NORTHERN IRELAND

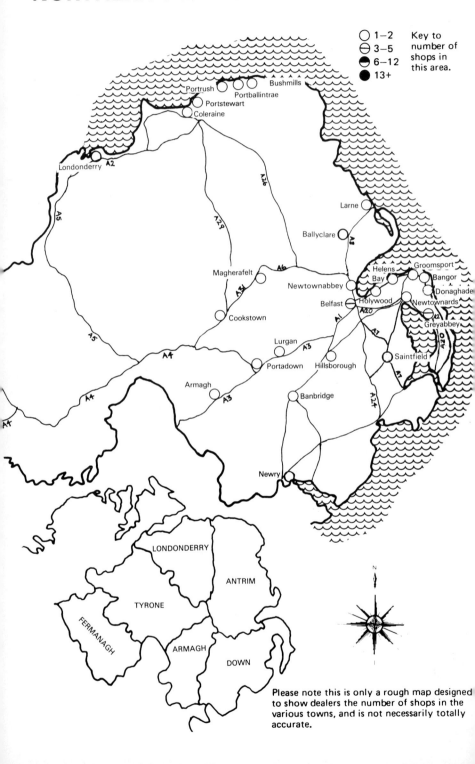

Key to number of shops in this area.

○ 1–2
⊖ 3–5
◑ 6–12
● 13+

Portrush
Portstewart
Portballintrae
Bushmills
Coleraine

Londonderry
A2
A5
A26
A29

Larne
Ballyclare
A2
A6
A54

Magherafelt
Newtownabbey
Helens Bay
Groomsport
Bangor
Donaghadee
Belfast
Holywood
Newtownards
A20
A2
Greyabbey
A20
Cookstown
A5
A1

Lurgan
A3
Saintfield
A4
Portadown
Hillsborough
A1
Armagh
A3
Banbridge
A24
A4

Newry

LONDONDERRY
ANTRIM
TYRONE
FERMANAGH
ARMAGH
DOWN

N

Please note this is only a rough map designed to show dealers the number of shops in the various towns, and is not necessarily totally accurate.

BELFAST (0232)

The Bell Gallery
13 Adelaide Park. (J.N. Bell.) Est. 1964. Open 10—6. SIZE: Medium. STOCK: British and Irish art, 19th—20th C. LOC: Off Malone Rd. TEL: 662998. SER: Valuations; restorations (paintings); buys at auction. VAT: Stan/Spec.

Emerald Isle Books
539 Antrim Rd. Est. 1966. Open by appointment. STOCK: Travel, Ireland, theology. TEL: 771798. SER: Catalogues available.

Charlotte and John Lambe
41 Shore Rd. CL: Sat. Open 10—5. STOCK: English and French furniture, 19th C; pictures and works of art. TEL: 777761.

Sinclair's Antique Gallery
19 Arthur St. Est. 1900. CL: Sat. Open 9—5.30. SIZE: Small. STOCK: Victorian jewellery, china, glass, £10—£1,000; silver, coins. LOC: 100yds. from city centre. TEL: 222335. SER: Valuations. VAT: Stan.

The Treasure House
123 University St. (T.H. Kearney.) Resident. TEL: 231055. SER: Restorations and upholstery. VAT: Stan.

County Antrim

BALLYCLARE (096 03)

Antique Shop
66 Main St. (T. Heaney.) Est. 1971. Open 10—5. STOCK: 18th—19th C, furniture and clocks, £20—£1,000; pottery, glass. TEL: 22719. SER: Restorations (clocks and furniture). VAT: Spec.

BUSHMILLS (026 57)

Dunluce Antiques
33 Ballytober Rd. (Mrs. C. Ross.) Est. 1978. Open 2—8, or by appointment. SIZE: Small. STOCK: Furniture, £50—£1,000; porcelain and glass, £1—£1,000; silver, £5—£500; all Georgian to Edwardian; paintings, mainly Irish, £50—£10,000. LOC: 1½ miles off Antrim coast rd. at Dunluce Castle. PARK: Easy. TEL: 31140. SER: Restorations (furniture and porcelain).

LARNE (0574)

Albert Graham Ltd. LAPADA
100 Main St. (A. and A. Graham.) Est. 1960. CL: Tues. Open 9.30—5.30 or by appointment. SIZE: Large + large warehouse. STOCK: Furniture, clocks, 18th—20th C, £25—£3,000. LOC: Beside Agnew St. car park. TEL: 76655/73134. VAT: Stan/Spec.

NEWTOWNABBEY

New Abbey Antiques BADA
Caragh Lodge, Glen Rd., Jordanstown. (A. MacHenry.) IADA. Est. 1964. Open 9.30—5.30 or by appointment. SIZE: Large. STOCK: General antiques, mostly furniture. LOC: 6 miles from Belfast to Whiteabbey village, fork left at traffic lights on dual carriageway; turn left into Old Manse Rd. and continue into Glen Rd. PARK: Easy. TEL: Whiteabbey (0231) 62036. SER: Valuations. FAIRS: Dublin, Belfast and Irish. VAT: Stan/Spec.

PORTBALLINTRAE
Nr. Bushmills

Brian R. Bolt, Collectors Antiques
88 Ballaghmore Rd. Business by post or appointment only. STOCK: Small and unusual silver, objects of vertu, snuff boxes, table silver, vesta cases, treen, tortoiseshell. TEL: Bushmills (026 57) 31129. SER: Catalogue available.

PORTRUSH (0265)

Alexander Antiques
108 Dunluce Rd. (R. and Mrs. Alexander.) Est. 1974. CL: Sun. except by appointment. Open 10—6. SIZE: Large. STOCK: Furniture, silver, porcelain, decorative items, 18th—20th C. Not stocked: Militaria, jewellery, coins. LOC: 1 mile from Portrush on A2 to Bushmills. PARK: Easy. TEL: 822783. SER: Valuations; buys at auction. VAT: Stan/Spec.

Seaview Antiques
110 Dunluce Rd. (Mrs. B. Macafee.) Est. 1981. CL: Sun. except by appointment. Open 2—5, Sat. 11—6; July and Aug. 11—6. SIZE: Small. STOCK: Small furniture, jewellery, silver and porcelain 19th—20th C. Not stocked: Militaria and coins. LOC: 1 mile from Portrush on A2 to Bushmills. PARK: Easy. TEL: Home — 823318.

County Armagh

ARMAGH (0861)

The Hole-in-the-Wall
Market St. (I. Emerson.) Est. 1953. STOCK: General antiques. LOC: City centre. VAT: Stan/Spec.

LURGAN (076 22)
Charles Gardiner Antiques
48 High St. Est. 1968. CL: Wed. Open 9—1 and 2—6. *STOCK: Clocks, furniture and general antiques.* PARK: Own. TEL: 3934. VAT: Stan/Spec.

PORTADOWN (0762)
Moyallon Antiques
54 Moyallon Rd. Est. 1975. Usually open. SIZE: Medium. *STOCK: Furniture, 19th C, £50—£500; pine and country furniture, 18th—19th C, £50—£250; ceramics and bric-a- brac, £5—£100.* LOC: Portadown—Gilford Rd., 1 mile from Gilford on right-hand side. PARK: Easy. TEL: 831615.

County Down

BANBRIDGE (082 06)
Cameo Antiques
41 Bridge St. (D. and J. Bell.) Est. 1966. VAT: Stan.

BANGOR (0247)
Phyllis Arnold Studio
(Fine Art Trade Guild)
7 Lowry Hill. Est. 1968. By appointment. *STOCK: Maps and prints of Ireland and Scotland; 19th and 20th C watercolours.* TEL: Helens Bay (0247) 853322. SER: Restorations (maps, prints); hand colouring. FAIRS: Culloden. VAT: Stan/Spec.

DONAGHADEE (0247)
Bow Bells Antiques
5 Bow St. (S.J. Henderson.) Est. 1974. Open 10—5. SIZE: Medium. *STOCK: Jewellery.* LOC: Town centre. PARK: Easy. TEL: 888612.

Furney Antiques
4 Shore St. (B. and I. Furney.) Est. 1976. Open Wed., and Thurs., 2—5.30, Fri. and Sat. 11—5.30 or by appointment. *STOCK: Georgian, Regency and early Victorian furniture; Victorian china, silver.* TEL: 883517.

GREYABBEY (024 774)
The Antique Shop
7 Main St. (M. McAuley.) Est. 1968. *STOCK: General antiques.* TEL: Home — Kircubbin (024 771) 333.

Greyabbey continued

Greyabbey Timecraft Ltd.
18 Main St. Est. 1976. CL: Sun. and Thurs., except by appointment. Open 2—5.30; Sat. open all day. SIZE: Small. *STOCK: Clocks and watches, 19th C, £100—£2,000; jewellery, 19th —20th C, £10—£500.* LOC: Opposite PO. PARK: Easy. TEL: 416; home — 252. SER: Valuations; restorations; buys at auction (clocks and watches).

Old Cross Antiques
3—5 Main St. (C.J. Auld.) Est. 1966. CL: Mon. a.m. and Thurs. Open 10.30—5.30, other times by appointment. SIZE: Medium. *STOCK: Silver, 1750—1920, £25—£800; porcelain and Staffordshire, 1800—1920, £5—£500; small furniture, 1800—1920, £10—£1,500.* Not stocked: Books, stamps, coins, medals. LOC: Village centre. PARK: Easy. TEL: 346, home — same.

GROOMSPORT
The Gallery
10 Bangor Rd. (J. and A. McFadden.) Est. 1946. CL: Thurs. SIZE: Small. *STOCK: Watercolours, 19th C, £20—£500; engravings and prints, 18th—20th C, £5—£500; oils, £50—£500.* LOC: Bangor to Groomsport Rd., take lower road to Groomsport, third last bungalow before reaching village. TEL: Bangor (0247) 464376; home — same. SER: Valuations; restorations; mounting mitring, picture framing; buys at auction (pictures).

HELENS BAY (0247)
Horse Rock
18 Grey Point. (Mrs. M.A. Kerr.) Est. 1875. Open by appointment only. *STOCK: Furniture, 18th C, £5—£100; china, glass, silver, brass, copper, pewter.* Not stocked: Edwardian furniture. PARK: Easy. TEL: Home — 853640.

HILLSBOROUGH (0846)
Stonewall Antiques
21 Lisburn St. Est. 1975. CL: Mon. Open 11—5. SIZE: Small. *STOCK: Porcelain, small furniture and silver, Victoriana, bric-a-brac, linens and lace.* TEL: 682117.

HOLYWOOD (023 17)
Hamilton Antiques BADA
19 Shore Rd. (Mr. and Mrs. H.D. Deering.) Est. 1908. CL: Mon. and Wed. Open 9.30—12.30 and 1.15—5. *STOCK: Porcelain, Irish glass, jewellery, silver, maps, furniture, 18th C.* Not stocked: Books, stamps. TEL: 4404 or 2863.

NEWRY (0693)
McCabes Antique Galleries
LAPADA
11–12 St. Mary's St. and 61-63 Downshire Rd. (H. and R. McCabe.) Est. 1910. Open 9.30–1 and 2–5.30, Wed., Sun. and evenings by appointment. SIZE: Large and warehouse. *STOCK: General antiques including furniture and porcelain, 18th–19th C, £50–£1,000.* PARK: Own. TEL: 2695; home — 5178. SER: Valuations; restorations (furniture). FAIRS: Conway Hotel, Lisburn; Drumkeen Hotel, Belfast. VAT: Stan.

NEWTOWNARDS (0247)
Fairfields Antique Cellars
12 Court St. (Mrs. J. Fairfield.) Est. 1968. CL: Thurs. Open 9.30–5.30. *STOCK: General antiques.* TEL: 813191.

SAINTFIELD (0238)
Albert Forsythe
Mill Hall, 66 Carsontown Rd. Resident. Usually open. *STOCK: Country pine, 18th–19th C.* TEL: 510398.

County Londonderry

COLERAINE (0265)
The Forge Antiques
24 Long Commons. (M.W. Walker.) Est. 1977. CL: Thurs. Open 10–5.30. *STOCK: General antiques, silver, clocks, jewellery, porcelain, paintings.* TEL: 51339. VAT: Stan.

LONDONDERRY (0504)
Richmond Antiques
Richmond Centre. (A. Fullam.) Open 9–5.30, Thurs. and Fri. 9–9, Sat. 9–6. *STOCK: Georgian and Victorian jewellery, furniture, linen, books, silver, china.* TEL: 260562; home — 52140.

MAGHERAFELT (0648)
K. and M. Nesbitt
21 Tobermore Rd. Est. 1976. Resident. Open by appointment. SIZE: Small. *STOCK: Clocks, 17th–19th C, from £200.* LOC: Private house 200yds. west of Rainey School. PARK: Easy. TEL: 32713. SER: Valuations; restorations (clocks and watches); buys at auction (clocks and watches).

PORTSTEWART (026 583)
The Forge Antiques
Cappagh, 182 Coleraine Rd. (Mrs. M.W. Walker.) Est. 1967. Open 2–6. SIZE: Large. *STOCK: Jewellery, 19th–20th C, £5–£4,000; furniture, silver, porcelain, Belleek, bric-a-brac.* LOC: Main road between Coleraine and Portstewart. PARK: Easy. TEL: 2209; home — Coleraine (0265) 2438. VAT: Stan.

County Tyrone

COOKSTOWN (064 87)
Cookstown Antiques
46 James St. (T.H. Jebb.) Est. 1976. CL: Wed. Open 9–5.30. SIZE: Small. *STOCK: Jewellery, silver, £10–£500; coins, £5–£100; pictures, ceramics and militaria, £5–£500; general items, all 19th and 20th C.* Not stocked: Large furniture. LOC: Opposite Post Office, in town centre. PARK: Easy. TEL: 65279; home — 62926. SER: Valuations; buys at auction. FAIRS: All Northern Ireland.

The Saddle Room Antiques
4 Coagh St. (C.J. Leitch.) Est. 1968. CL: Mon. and Wed. Open 10–6. *STOCK: China, silver, furniture, glass, jewellery.* TEL: 62033.

Scotland
NORTH

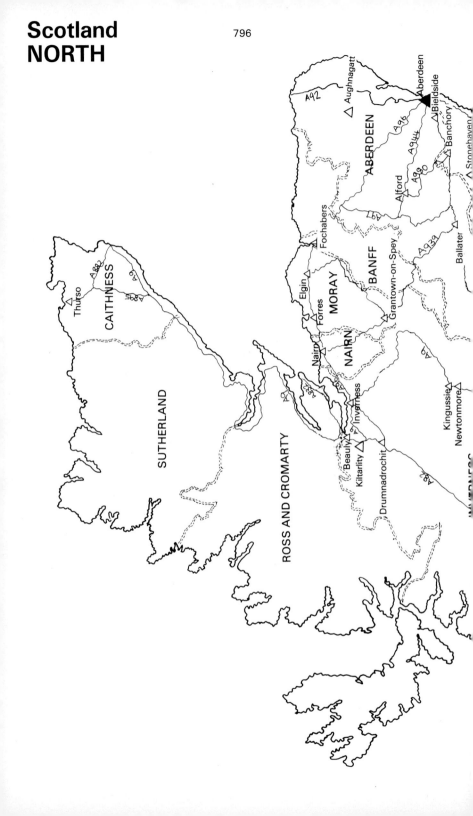

Scotland

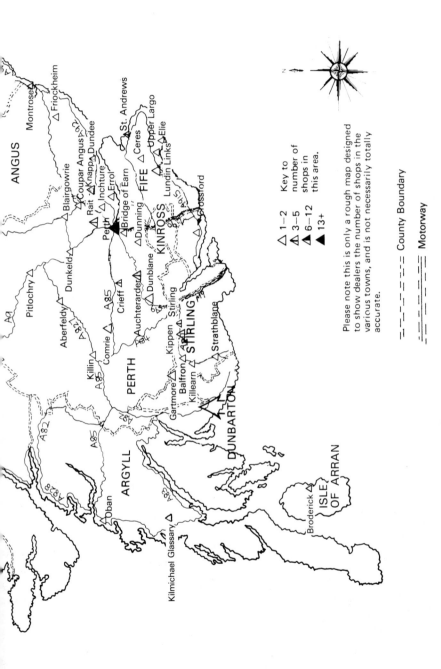

Key to
number of
shops in
this area.

△ 1–2
△ 3–5
▲ 6–12
▲ 13+

Please note this is only a rough map designed
to show dealers the number of shops in the
various towns, and is not necessarily totally
accurate.

–––––– County Boundary

––––––– Motorway

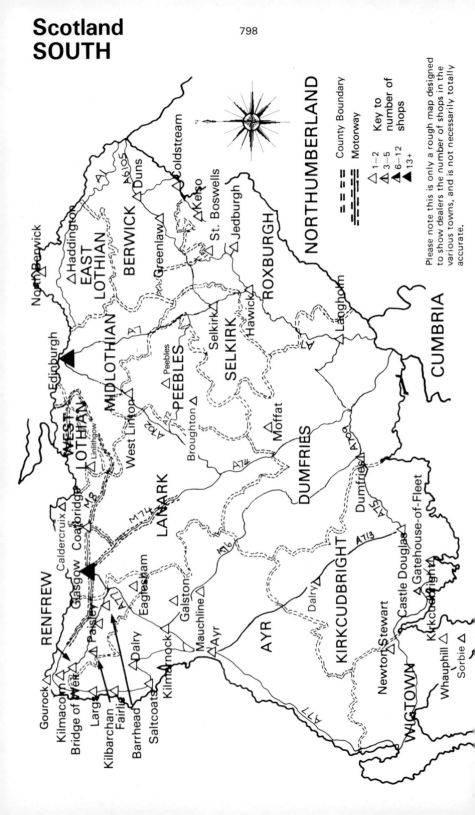

Scotland
SOUTH

SCOTTISH COUNTY BOUNDARIES

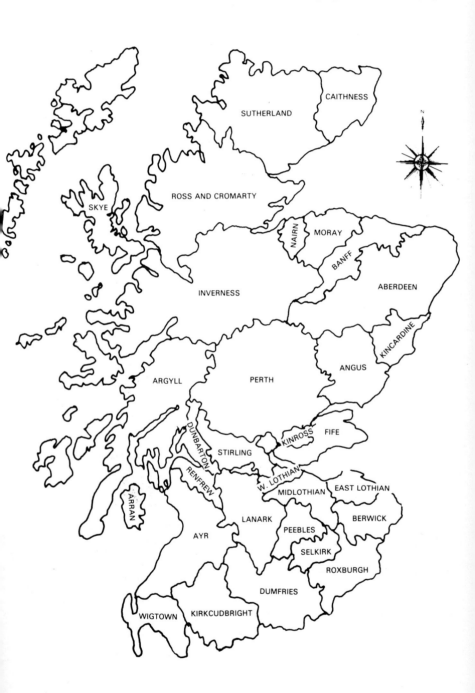

Please note the reorganised order of Scotland which is no longer broken down by counties. Towns throughout Scotland are arranged alphabetically with the county in brackets.

ABERDEEN   (0224)
(Aberdeenshire)

Atholl Antiques
322 Great Western Rd. Open 10.30−1 and 2.30−6, or by appointment. *STOCK: Scottish paintings and furniture.* TEL: 593547. VAT: Stan/Spec.

John Bell of Aberdeen Ltd.   BADA
Balbrogie by Blackburn, Kinellar. Est. 1899. CL: Sat. Open 9−5. SIZE: Large. *STOCK: Furniture, 18th C.* LOC: On A96, 8 miles from city centre. TEL: 79209. VAT: Stan/Spec.

James Benzie
651 George St. Est. 1953. Open 1−4. *STOCK: Small items, glass, china, pottery, copper, brass, silver, pictures.*

James G. Bisset Ltd.
99 High St., Old Aberdeen. Est. 1879. *STOCK: Antiquarian books.* TEL: 46102.

Gallery
41 Justice St. (J.H. Wells.) Est. 1981. Open 8.30−5.30, Sat. 9.30−4.30. SIZE: Small. *STOCK: Jewellery, post-1850; curios and Victoriana; paintings and prints, post-1800, £20−£80.* LOC: Between Castlegate and Beach Boulevard. PARK: Easy. TEL: 644909. SER: Valuations; restorations and repairs (jewellery); buys at auction. VAT: Stan.

McCall's (Aberdeen)
11 Castle St. (B. McCall.) Est. 1948. CL: Wed. p.m. PARK: Nearby. TEL: 591916. VAT: Stan.

McCall's Antique Shop
50 Upper Kirkgate. Open 9.30−6, Thurs. 9.30−7. *STOCK: Jewellery.* TEL: 643876.

The Rendezvous Gallery   LAPADA
100 Forest Ave. Est. 1973. CL: Fri. Open 10−1.30 and 2.30−6. SIZE: Medium. *STOCK: Art nouveau, art deco, glass, jewellery, bronzes, furniture, £100−£2,000; paintings, watercolours, Scottish School, £100−£2,000.* LOC: Just off Great Western Rd. to Braemar. PARK: Easy. TEL: 323247. VAT: Stan/Spec.

Mr. Reynolds
162/164 Skene St. Resident. *STOCK: General antiques.*

Thistle Antiques   LAPADA
28 Esslemont Ave. Est. 1967. TEL: 634692. VAT: Stan/Spec.

Aberdeen continued

Treasure House
560A, Holburn St. (W.G. Edwards.) Est. 1938. CL: Sat. p.m. and Wed. Open 10−12.20 and 2.30−5. SIZE: Small. *STOCK: Small furniture, jewellery, prints, curios, linen and collectors' items.* LOC: Main road from the South. PARK: Easy. TEL: 580219; home − 732241.

Elizabeth Watt
69 Thistle St. Est. 1976. CL: Mon. a.m. and Sat. p.m. Open 10−1 and 2.30−5. SIZE: Small. *STOCK: General antiques.* Not stocked: Large furniture. LOC: Off the west end of Union St. PARK: Easy. TEL: 647232. SER: Restorations (china, glass).

The Waverley Gallery
18 Victoria St. (A.F. Donaldson.) Open 10−5, Sat. 10−1. *STOCK: Oil paintings and watercolours, £50−£6,000; prints, £10−£200; etchings, £20−£400; all 18th−20th C.* LOC: Corner of Waverley Place. TEL: 640633. SER: Valuations; restorations (framing); buys at auction (paintings, watercolours). VAT: Spec.

Colin Wood (Antiques) Ltd.
25 Rose St. Est. 1968. Open 10−12.30 and 2.15−5, Sat. 10−12 and 2.15−4. SIZE: Medium. *STOCK: Furniture, 17th−19th C; works of art, Scottish paintings and silver.* PARK: Multi-storey in Chapel St. TEL: 643019; home − 640640. VAT: Stan/Spec.

J.H. Wood
2c Thistle St. CL: Sat. p.m. Open 10−5. *STOCK: Victoriana, bric-a-brac, copper, brass.* TEL: 645008.

Wm. Young (Antiques) Ltd.   BADA
1 Belmont St. Est. 1887. CL: Sat. p.m. *STOCK: Furniture, decorative items, Georgian to 19th C.* TEL: 644757.

ABERFELDY   (0887)
(Perthshire)

Denis Young Antiques
3 Kenmore St. (D.E. and Mrs. J.M. Young.) HADA. Est. 1979. CL: Mid-Oct−April and Wed., except by appointment. SIZE: Small. *STOCK: Oriental and English porcelain, pottery, glass, pre−1840; secondhand books especially children's; paintings, especially watercolours, pre−1900; small items.* LOC: By crossroads, 200 yards from Square. PARK: 20 yards. TEL: 20391; home − Glenlyon (08877) 232. SER: Valuations.

ALFORD (0336)
(Aberdeenshire)
R.S. Gordon (Antiques)
Main St. (R. and J. Gordon.) Est. 1959. CL: Mon. Open 9—5.30. *STOCK: General antiques; clocks, musical boxes, Victoriana, bric-a-brac.* LOC: Between Aberdeen and Huntly on the A944. TEL: 2404. VAT: Stan/Spec.

AUCHNAGATT, Nr. Ellon (035 83)
(Aberdeenshire)
Ye Olde Oak Chest
Elrick Lea. Open 7 days 2—5. *STOCK: Furniture, Dutch and English, 17th and 18th C; English and Chinese porcelain, artifacts, eastern rugs, interior decor items.* TEL: 336. VAT: Spec.

AUCHTERARDER (076 46)
(Perthshire)
Paul Hayes Gallery
71 High St. PADA. Est. 1962. *STOCK: Fine paintings, 18th—20th C, especially sporting, marine and Scottish post-impressionist.* TEL: 2320 or 3442. VAT: Spec.

Susan Procter
47/51 The Feus. *STOCK: Pottery, porcelain and decorative items.* TEL: 2532. VAT: Spec.

K. Stanley and Son
Regal Buildings, Main St. (Mr. and Mrs. Kasiewicz.) Est. 1957. Open 10—1 and 2—5.30. SIZE: Large. *STOCK: Furniture, porcelain, carpets, bric-a-brac; shipping goods.* VAT: Stan.

Stuart Antiques
4 High St. (I.H.C. and M.L. Stein.) Est. 1962. Open 9—1 and 2—5.30. SIZE: Large. *STOCK: Furniture, 18th—19th C; paintings, £50—£5,000; porcelain, glass, silver.* LOC: A9. PARK: Easy. TEL: 2410. SER: Valuations; insurance photography; buys at auction. VAT: Stan/Spec.

John Whitelaw and Sons Antiques
120 High St. Open 9—5.30. *STOCK: General antiques; furniture, 17th—19th C.* PARK: Easy. TEL: 2482. VAT: Stan/Spec.

AYR (0292)
(Ayrshire)
Antiques
39 New Rd. (T. Rafferty.) Est. 1970. Open 10—5. *STOCK: General antiques.* TEL: 265346.

Ayr continued

The Old Curiosity Shop
27 Crown St. (B.D. Kelly and D.S. Davie.) Est. 1970. Open 9—5 and 6.30 p.m.—9.30 p.m., Wed. 9—5, Sat. 10—5. SIZE: Small. *STOCK: Furniture and jewellery, 19th C; silver, 18th—19th C; all £50—£2,000.* LOC: Cross 'Auld Brig' leaving Ayr for Prestwick, 1st left after traffic lights. PARK: Easy. TEL: 280222; home — same. SER: Valuations; restorations (French polishing, re-upholstery). VAT: Stan/Spec.

BALFRON (0360)
(Stirlingshire)
Antiques
16—20 Buchanan St. (L. Ruglen.) Resident. Est. 1961. Open 10—5.30 and by appointment. SIZE: Large. *STOCK: General antiques, furniture, decorative items.* LOC: 18 miles north of Glasgow on A81 and A811 west of Stirling. TEL: 40329.

BALLATER (0338)
(Aberdeenshire)
The McEwan Gallery LAPADA
Bridge of Gairn. (D. and P. McEwan.) Est. 1968. Open all year (but November—April by appointment. SIZE: Medium. *STOCK: Oil paintings, watercolours and early miniatures, £50—£20,000; prints, £5—£100; all 18th—20th C; etchings, 17th—19th C, £5—£300; Scottish golf and natural history books.* LOC: First house on the east side of A939 after its junction with A93 outside Ballater. PARK: Easy. TEL: 55429. SER: Valuations; restorations (framing); buys at auction (paintings, watercolours, books). FAIRS: Buxton, Harrogate, Game, and exhibitions in Canada. VAT: Spec.

BANCHORY (033 02)
(Kincardineshire)
Sunfield Cottage Antiques
Inchmarlo. (H. and L. Henderson.) Est. 1974. Open 9—5.30, Sun. 1.30—5.30. SIZE: Small. *STOCK: 18th and 19th C china, glass, silver, brass, small furniture.* Not stocked: Large furniture, pictures, Oriental objets d'art. LOC: 3 miles west from Banchory, A93. PARK: Easy. TEL: 2703. SER: Restorations (clocks and watches).

BARRHEAD, Nr. Glasgow
(Renfrewshire)
P. and J. Antiques
1 Cochrane St. (Mr. Porterfield and W. Johnstone.) Est. 1965. CL: Tues. Open 10—5. SIZE: Medium. *STOCK: Brassware, furniture and curios, 19th—20th C, to £5,000.* PARK: Easy. TEL: (041) 881 5379. SER: Restoration (brass, copper, pewter); spare parts for oil lamps.

BEAULY (0463)
(Inverness-shire)
Iain Marr Antiques
3 Mid St. (I. and A. Marr.) HADA. Est. 1975. CL: Thurs. Open 10.30—5.30. *STOCK: Silver, jewellery, clocks, porcelain, scientific instruments, arms, oils, watercolours, small furniture.* LOC: Off Square, on left going north, beside Skillet restaurant. TEL: 782372. VAT: Stan/Spec.

BIELDSIDE
(Aberdeenshire)
Bieldside Antiques LAPADA
85 North Deeside Rd. (Mr. and Dr. I.E. James.) Author of "The Goldsmiths of Aberdeen". Est. 1970. CL: Sun. except by appointment. Open 9.30—5. SIZE: Medium. *STOCK: Porcelain, glass, £5—£200; small furniture, £25—£300; Scottish flatware, £20—£350; all 18th—19th C.* Not stocked: Coins and stamps. LOC: On Royal Deeside (A93) 5 miles from Aberdeen. PARK: Easy. TEL: Aberdeen (0224) 867339.

BLAIRGOWRIE (0250)
(Perthshire)
Roy Sim, Antiques
21 Allan St. PADA. Est. 1977. Open 9.30—1 and 2—5.30. SIZE: Large and warehouse. *STOCK: Furniture, jewellery, silver and plate, clocks, scientific and nautical instruments, weapons, brass and copper, oriental items, shipping furniture, £1—£2,000.* TEL: 3860; home — 3700. VAT: Stan/Spec.

BRIDGE OF EARN (0738)
(Perthshire)
Imrie Antiques LAPADA
Back St. (Mr. and Mrs. I. Imrie.) Est. 1969. Open 10—12.30 and 2—5.30. SIZE: Large. *STOCK: Victorian and 18th C shipping goods.* PARK: Easy. TEL: 812784. VAT: Stan.

BRIDGE OF WEIR (0505)
(Renfrewshire)
The Antique Shop
12 Castle Terrace. (C. Keen.) Est. 1964. CL: Wed., Sat. p.m. and Sun. a.m. Open 10.30—1 and 2.30—5. SIZE: Medium. *STOCK: Furniture, Victorian and Edwardian; brassware, china, glass, from Victorian.* Not stocked: Coins, books, stamps, weapons. LOC: From Glasgow via Paisley and Johnstone. PARK: Easy. TEL: 612670.

Castle Art and Antiques
4/5 Castle Terrace. (Mrs. L. Higgins.) *STOCK: Scottish marine oils, watercolours and etchings, silver and furniture.* PARK: Easy. TEL: 690951; home — Kilmacolm (050 587) 3450.

BRODICK (0770)
(Isle of Arran)
Kames Antiques
Kames Cottage, Shore Rd. (C. Mason.) Open 10—12.30 and 2—4.30. *STOCK: Bric-a-brac, collectables, objets d'art, gold and silver jewellery.* TEL: 2213.

BROUGHTON, Nr. Biggar (089 94)
(Peebles)
Wildman's at Merlindale
(P. Wildman.) Est. 1985. Open every day
10—4 or by appointment. SIZE: Small.
*STOCK: Silver, 1800—1950, £10—£1,000;
jewellery, 1800—1960, £5—£1,500; china,
1800—1950, £5—£800; furniture, 1800—
1850, £25—£1,500.* LOC: Off A701 on
B712 1 mile from Broughton. PARK: Easy.
TEL: 221; home — same. SER: Valuations.
VAT: Stan/Spec.

CALDERCRUIX (0236)
(Lanarkshire)
Newlife Antiques Ltd. *Trade Only*
175 Airdrie Rd. (J. Miller.) Est. 1968. Open
8—5, Sat. and Sun. by appointment. SIZE:
Large. *STOCK: Furniture, Georgian, Victorian
and shipping, £5—£1,000.* LOC: From M8
onto A73 then A89. PARK: Easy. TEL:
843292; home — 842720. SER: Restorations. VAT: Stan.

CASTLE DOUGLAS (0556)
(Kirkcudbrightshire)
Bendalls Antiques
221—223 King St. (R.A. Mitchell.) Est. 1949.
TEL: 2113. VAT: Stan.

Chapel Fine Art and Antiques
at McGill Duncan Gallery
231 King St. (A. Bradley.) Open 9—5.
STOCK: Small fine antiques and paintings.
TEL: 2468.

CERES (033 482)
(Fife)
Ceres Antiques
1 The Butts. (Mrs. Walker.) SIZE: Small.
STOCK: General antiques, china. PARK: Easy.
TEL: 384.

COATBRIDGE (0236)
(Lanarkshire)
Michael Stewart
Hornock Cottages, Gartsherry Rd. Est. 1968.
Open by appointment. *STOCK: Jewellery,
watches, clocks, barometers.* TEL: 22532 and
28964.

COLDSTREAM (0890)
(Berwickshire)
Coldstream Antiques
44 High St. (Mr and Mrs J. Trinder). Resident,
open daily. SIZE: Large. *STOCK: Furniture,
17th—20th C; general antiques, clocks, silver
and shipping goods, 17th—19th C.* LOC:
A697. TEL: 2552. VAT: Stan/Spec.

COMRIE (0764)
(Perthshire)
The Coach House
Dundas St. (Mrs. M. Chilcott.) Resident. Est.
1972. CL: Wed. Open 10.30—12.30 and
2.30—5.30. Outside hours and winter
months by appointment only. SIZE: Small.
*STOCK: Pottery and porcelain, £5—£100;
Sheffield plate, £30—£150; both early 18th
C; decorative items.* LOC: On main road to
Oban from Crieff. PARK: Easy.

COUPAR ANGUS
(Perthshire) (0828)
Henderson Antiques
35 Lintrose. Est. 1984. *STOCK: Furniture.*
TEL: 27450. VAT: Stan.

CRIEFF (0764)
(Perthshire)
Antiques and Fine Art
11 Comrie St. (Mrs. S. Drysdale.) CL: Wed.
p.m. Open 10—1 and 2—5. SIZE: Medium.
*STOCK: Furniture, paintings, silver, general
antiques, French paperweights.* Not stocked:
Shipping items. LOC: A85. PARK: Easy. TEL:
4496; home — 2653. VAT: Spec.

Crieff Antiques
Comrie Rd. (Mrs. J. Cormack.) Est. 1968. CL:
Wed. p.m. Open 10—12.30 and 2—4.30 and
some Sat. SIZE: Medium. *STOCK: Victorian
porcelain, paraffin lamps, £5—£150; music
boxes, clocks and small furniture, £10—£500;
motor mascots, lamps, badges, collectors
advertising items, enamel signs, 20th C, £5—
£300.* Not stocked: Large furniture. LOC: On
A85 next to West End Garage. PARK: Nearby.
TEL: 3322 and 3271.

Louis and Moira Di Marco
22—26 East High St. Est. 1971. Open 10—5,
Wed. 10—1; Sun. 2—5 during season.
*STOCK: Shipping goods, collectors' items and
general antiques.* TEL: 3155. VAT: Stan.

Strathearn Antiques
2 Comrie St. (R. Torrens.) Est. 1977. Open
10—1 and 2—5. SIZE: Medium. *STOCK:
General antiques and curios, Victoriana, £1—
£1,000; coins, medals, militaria, books, postcards, 10p—£1,000.* PARK: Easy. TEL: 4344;
home — 3592. SER: Valuations (coins, medals
and postcards). VAT: Stan.

CROSSFORD, Nr. Dunfermline
(Fife)
The Old Smiddy
66 Main St. (A. Sinclair.) Resident. Est. 1974.
Open Wed., Fri., Sat. and Sun. 10—6. *STOCK:
General antiques.* TEL: Dunfermline (0383)
22178.

DALRY
(Ayrshire)
Cartwheel Antiques
18 The Den, Barkip. (A. Thomson.) Est. 1960.
Open Sun. 2—5 or by appointment. *STOCK:
Victorian and Edwardian furniture including
pine, bric-a-brac.* LOC: A737 between Beith
and Dalry. PARK: Easy. SER: Valuations; buys
at auction. TEL: Evenings (041) 887 6446.

DALRY, Nr. Castle Douglas (06443)
(Kirkcudbright)
Boatknowe Antiques
(B. Farnell.) Open by appointment. *STOCK:
General antiques, clocks, silver plate, linens.*
LOC: On A713, 40 miles north of Castle
Douglas. TEL: 217.

DRUMNADROCHIT   (045 62)
(Inverness-shire)
Joan Frere Antiques
Drumbuie House. (Mrs. J. Frere.) Open daily
9—8 May—October, other times by appointment. SIZE: Medium. *STOCK: Furniture,
especially English oak, pre-1800, from £60.*
Not stocked: Victoriana, reproductions. LOC:
On Loch Ness just before Drumnadrochit
village, on A82. PARK: Easy. TEL: 210; home
— same.

DUMFRIES   (0387)
(Dumfriesshire)
I.G. Anderson
Gribton. Open by appointment only. *STOCK:
Antiquarian and secondhand books.* LOC:
From Dumfries, take B729 Moriaive road,
after 1¼ miles take Newtonairds road. First
entry on left. TEL: Newbridge (0387) 721071.

Dix Antiques
100 English St. (B. and M. Hughes.) Est.
1965. CL: Thurs. Open 10—4.30. SIZE: Small
and store. *STOCK: General antiques, £5—
£1,000.* LOC: Near cinema. TEL: 64234;
home — 65259.

Ye Olde Curio Shoppe
Midsteeple, High St. CL: Thurs. SIZE: Small.
*STOCK: Victorian and secondhand jewellery,
silver and collectors' items, linen, lace, christening gowns..* TEL: 63449; home — 55833.

DUNBLANE   (0786)
(Perthshire)
The Emporium
18 High St. (H. King.) Est. 1983. CL: In
summer Mon. and Wed; in winter Wed. Open
9.30—1 and 2—5.30, Sun. by appointment.
SIZE: Small. *STOCK: Small antiques and collectables, jewellery, linen, kitchenalia, 19th—
20th C, £5—£100.* LOC: Off A9. PARK: Easy.
TEL: 822030; home — 824063. SER: Valuations; restorations (pine stripping). FAIRS:
Local.

DUNDEE   (0382)
(Angus)
Angus Antiques
4 St. Andrews St. Est. 1964. *STOCK: Art
nouveau, art deco, advertising and decorative
items, tins, toys.* TEL: 22128.

Nethergate Gallery Ltd.   LAPADA
140 Nethergate. Est. 1975. Open 9—5 or by
appointment. SIZE: Large. *STOCK: Furniture,
silver, jewellery, general antiques, paintings,
shipping goods.* LOC: Main Dundee to Perth
and Glasgow Rd. PARK: Tay St. TEL: 21751;
home — 67454. SER: Buys at auction; USA
shipping; courier service. VAT: Stan/Spec.

DUNKELD   (035 02)
(Perthshire)
Dunkeld Interiors
14 Bridge St. (Mrs. B. Crowe.) Est. 1984. CL:
Mon. Open daily, Sat. and Sun. by appoint-
ment. *STOCK: Furniture, 18th—19th C,
£500—£2,500; prints, £30—£300; decora-
tive items, £25—£150; both 19th—20th C.*
LOC: 2 mins. off A9, Perth to Inverness road.
PARK: Easy. TEL: 582; home — same. SER:
Finder. VAT: Stan/Spec.

Sidlaw Antiques
Tay Terrace. (Mr. and Mrs. D. Dytch.) Est.
1979. Open 9.30—6.30, Thurs. 1—6.30,
Sat. and Sun. 9.30—7. By appointment in
winter. SIZE: Large. *STOCK: General antiques
especially Victorian and Edwardian oak;
stuffed animals and birds, 19th—20th C,
£5—£1,500.* LOC: Overlooking River Tay,
premises are a converted church. PARK: Easy.
TEL: 450; home — same. SER: Valuations;
buys at auction (clocks and furniture). VAT:
Stan/Spec.

K. Stanley and Son
High St. Est. 1962. *STOCK: General antiques,
Oriental carpets, bric-a-brac.* VAT: Stan.

DUNNING   (076 484)
(Perthshire)
Tron Antiques
Tron Sq. Est. 1984. Open daily 10—6. SIZE:
Small. *STOCK: Art nouveau, art deco, furni-
ture, pottery, pewter, glass.* LOC: Between
Perth and Auchterarder, 2 miles off A9. PARK:
Easy. TEL: 302.

DUNS   (0361)
(Berwickshire)   ✓
Country Shop Antiques
The Old Coach House, Murray Crescent. (T.P.
and K. Burns.) Est. 1965. *STOCK: Furniture,
period; musical boxes, dolls, paintings; clocks
— longcase, carriage and wall; jewellery,
silver.* TEL: 82240.

EAGLESHAM (035 53)
(Renfrewshire)

Eaglesham Antiques Ltd.
73 Montgomery St. (M.F. Finlay.) Est. 1966. CL: Mon. Open 12—5. *STOCK: Porcelain, silver, glass, objets d'art, paintings; furniture, Georgian, Regency, Victorian.* LOC: Original village past Eglington Arms Hotel. PARK: Easy. TEL: 2814.

EDINBURGH (031)
(Midlothian)

Another World
25 Candlemaker Row. (D. Harrison.) Est. 1974. Open Wed. and Fri. 10.30—4, Sat. 12—3 or by appointment. *STOCK: Netsuke and Oriental art.* TEL: 661 0723. VAT: Spec.

Antiques
38 Victoria St. (E. Humphrey.) Est. 1946. Open 10—4, Sat. 10—12.30 or by appointment. *STOCK: Paintings, glass, china, curios, postcards.* TEL: 226 3625.

'Artisan'
65A Dundas St. (R. Forrest.) *STOCK: Stripped pine furniture, general antiques, curios.* TEL: 556 4253.

Avarice Antiques
24 St. Stephen St. Open 11—4.30. *STOCK: Furniture, 18th to early 20th C; silver, ceramics.* TEL: 225 7237.

Edinburgh continued

Ballymenoch Antiques
22a Dundas St. (I. Murray.) Est. 1980. Open daily. SIZE: Medium. *STOCK: Furniture, £500—£2,500; porcelain, £50—£1,000; both 18th to early 19th C.* PARK: Easy. TEL: 556 2181; home — same. SER: Valuations; restorations (furniture). FAIRS: Bath Spring and Autumn; Olympia. VAT: Spec.

Behar Carpets
12a Howe St. (M. and Mrs P. Slater.) Est. 1920. Open 9—5.30. *STOCK: Oriental carpets and rugs, 19th C, from £200.* TEL: 225 1069. SER: Valuations; restorations (cleaning and repairs). VAT: Stan.

Joseph H. Bonnar. Jewellers
72 Thistle St. Open 10.30—5 or by appointment. SIZE: Medium. *STOCK: Antique and period jewellery.* LOC: Parallel with Princes St. PARK: Own. TEL: 226 2811. VAT: Stan/Spec.

Bourne Fine Art Ltd.
4 Dundas St. (P. Bourne.) Est. 1978. Open 10—6, Sat. 10—1. SIZE: Medium. *STOCK: British paintings, 1800—1950; decorative arts, 1860—1930.* PARK: Easy. TEL: 557 4050. SER: Valuations; restorations; buys at auction; framing. VAT: Stan/Spec.

Margaret Brown
14-16 St. Stephen St. Est. 1971. TEL: 225 9357.

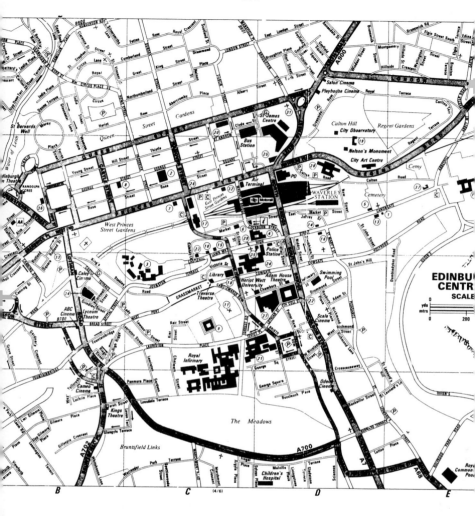

Recommended route	———
Other roads	—— ——
Restricted roads (Access only/Buses only)	= = = = =
Traffic roundabout	⊐⌐∘⌐⊏
Official car park free (Open air)	P
Multi-storey car park	◈
Parking available on payment (Open air)	◈
Parking Zone	
One-way street	←
Pedestrians only	
Convenience	C
Convenience with facilities for the disabled	C &
Tourist Information Centre	i

Reproduced by kind permission of the Automobile Association

Edinburgh continued

Calton Gallery
10 Royal Terrace (A. and S. Whitfield). Est. 1979. Open 10—6. SIZE: Large. *STOCK: Paintings and watercolours, £50—£10,000; prints, £5—£500, all 19th C to early 20th C; sculpture, 20th C, to £5,000.* PARK: Easy. TEL: 556 1010; home — same. SER: Valuations; restorations (oils, watercolours, prints and frames); framing; buys at auction (paintings). VAT: Stan/Spec.

Cinders
51 St. Stephen St. (A. Mutch.) CL: Mon. Open 1.30—5, Sat. 10—4. *STOCK: Period fireplaces.* TEL: 225 3793 or 556 6341 (evenings).

The Carson Clark Gallery
Scotia Maps — Mapsellers
173 Canongate, The Royal Mile. (A. Carson Clark). FRGS. Est. 1971. Open 10.30—5.30. *STOCK: Maps, atlases; topographic prints.* TEL: 556 4710. SER: Valuations.

The Collectors Shop
49 Cockburn St. (D. Cavanagh.) Est. 1960. Open 11—5. *STOCK: Coins, medals, militaria, cigarette and postcards, small collectors' items and jewellery.* Not stocked: Postage stamps. TEL: 226 3391. SER: Buys at auction.

Court Curio Shop
519 Lawnmarket. TEL: 225 3972.

Pauls Couts Ltd.   BADA
101-107 West Bow (Victoria St.). (B.P. Couts.) Est. 1959. Open 9—1 and 2.30—5, Sat. by appointment. SIZE: Large. *STOCK: Furniture, 18th C, £200—£20,000.* LOC: Ask for Grassmarket. PARK: Easy. TEL: 225 3238. FAIRS: Grosvenor House. VAT: Spec.

Eric Davidson (Antiques) Ltd.
4 Grassmarket. (E.C. Davidson.) Est. 1967. Open 8.30—5.30. SIZE: Large. *STOCK: Furniture, mostly period but also Edwardian and Victorian; porcelain and silver, oil paintings, 18th—19th C.* LOC: From West End of Edinburgh, straight along Kings Stable Rd. behind the castle. PARK: Easy. TEL: 225 5815. VAT: Stan/Spec.

Edinburgh continued

J. and J. Dewar
19 Brougham Place. Est. 1958. *STOCK: General antiques, curios.* TEL: 229 4157.

A.F. Drysdale
(J. Thomson and A. Williamson Ltd.)
20 and 35 North West Circus Place. Est. 1974. Open 10—1 and 2—5, Sat. 10—1. *STOCK: Small antiques, lamps, decorative furniture.* TEL: 225 4686. VAT: Stan.

George Duff Antiques   *Export Only*
254 Leith Walk. Open by appointment. *STOCK: Shipping goods, pre-1940.* TEL: 554 8164; home — 337 1422. VAT: Stan.

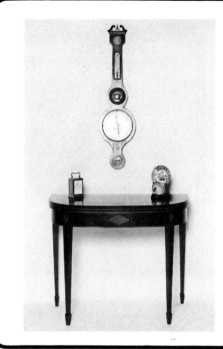
Edinburgh continued

Dunedin Antiques Ltd.
4 and 6 North West Circus Place. (D. Ingram, G. Niven.) Est. 1973. Open 9.30—5.30. SIZE: Large. *STOCK: Furniture, period items, chimney pieces, architectural fittings, 18th—19th C, £50—£5,000.* Not stocked: Porcelain and bronzes. LOC: From Princes St. down Frederick St. PARK: Easy. TEL: 226 3074 or 225 4874; home — 556 8140. SER: Valuations; buys at auction (furniture, weapons); interior design decoration. VAT: Stan/Spec.

Edinburgh Coin Shop
11 West Crosscauseway and 2 Polwarth Crescent. (T.D. Brown.) CL: Sun. Open 10—5. *STOCK: Coins, medals, badges, militaria, postcards, cigarette cards, jewellery, clocks and watches, general antiques, bullion dealers.* TEL: 668 2928 or 229 2915. VAT: Stan.

Donald Ellis Antiques
9 Bruntsfield Place. (D.G. and C.M. Ellis.) Est. 1970. *STOCK: Furniture, 18th to early 19th C, £20—£1,000; silver, porcelain, £5—£500; brass, copper, £1—£100.* LOC: Opp. Links Garage at Bruntsfield Links. PARK: Nearby. TEL: 229 1819.

Edinburgh continued

Tom Fidelo
49 Cumberland St. Open 2—6. *STOCK: Paintings, prints, maps, furniture, 17th—19th C.* LOC: Left at corner of Dundas St. and Cumberland St. PARK: Easy. TEL: 557 2444; home — 557 1881.

The Fine Art Society plc
12 Great King St. Est. 1876. Open 9.30—5.30, Sat. 10—1. SIZE: Large. *STOCK: British paintings, watercolours, drawings, sculpture, especially Scottish, from 1800.* TEL: 556 0305. VAT: Spec.

E.B. Forrest and Co. Antiques
2 and 3 Barclay Terrace. *STOCK: Jewellery, plate, cutlery, brass, copper, silver, china, art pottery, glass.* TEL: 229 3156. VAT: Stan.

Fyfe's Antiques
41 and 48 Thistle St. *STOCK: Furniture, oil paintings, silver, porcelain, Sheffield plate.* TEL: 225 4287. VAT: Stan/Spec.

Galloways (Edinburgh) Ltd.
Galloway House, Corner of St. Stephens St., Stockbridge. Est. 1949. CL: Sat. p.m. Open 9.30—1 and 2.15—5.30. SIZE: Large. *STOCK: Furniture, Victorian, Georgian and Regency, £100—£1,000; sundries, £10— £100.* LOC: From Forth Bridge, fork left at Blackhall for London Rd. Turn right in Princes St. for Frederick St. PARK: Easy. TEL: 225 3221. VAT: Stan.

R.B. Garriock
At the Edinburgh Antique Market, 64—78 St. Stephen St. Open daily 10—5.30. *STOCK: Furniture, porcelain, Victoriana, curios.* TEL: 669 4836.

Georgian Antiques   Trade Only
19 Windsor Place, Portobello. Est. 1976. Open by appointment. SIZE: Large. *STOCK: Furniture, Georgian, Victorian, inlaid, Edwardian; shipping goods, smalls, £10—£5,000.* LOC: Off Portobello High St. PARK: Easy. TEL: 657 3208; home — 661 0249. SER: Valuations; restorations; buys at auction; packing; shipping; courier. VAT: Stan/Spec.

Gladrags
17 Henderson Row. Est. 1977. Open Thurs., Fri. and Sat. 2—6. *STOCK: Period clothes, linen, lace, beadwork, shawls, costume jewellery, silks and satins.* TEL: 557 1916.

Goodwin's Antiques
15 Queensferry St. Est. 1952. Open 9.30— 5.30, Sat. 9.30—1. *STOCK: Jewellery, silver.* LOC: Off Princes St., West end. TEL: 225 4717. VAT: Stan/Spec..

Grange Bookshop ABA
186 Causewayside. (D. MacNaughton.) Open 10—5. *STOCK: Antiquarian books.* TEL: 667 2759.

John Grant Est. 1874
7 Dundas St. (I.R. and S. Grant.) CL: Mon. Open 9—5.30. SIZE: Medium. *STOCK: Scottish topographical prints, 1790—1870, £2—£170; maps, 1600—1800, £5—£300; original Scottish landscapes, £40—£300.* LOC: From Princes St. turn at Hanover St., straight down hill. Dundas St. is continuation of Hanover St. PARK: Easy. TEL: 556 9698. VAT: Stan.

Hand in Hand
3 North West Circus Place. (Mr. and Mrs. O. Hand.) Est. 1969. CL: Mon. Open 10—5.30. *STOCK: Victorian linen, embroidery, furnishings, lace, shawls (including Paisley), and period costume, 1800—1945.* TEL: 226 3598. VAT: Stan.

Tim Hardie Antiques
63 Frederick St. Open by appointment. *STOCK: Small decorative items and furniture.* TEL: 225 2169.

Michael Hart
30 St. Stephen St. Est. 1940. TEL: 226 3736.

Herrald Antiques
38 Queen St. Est. 1882. CL: Sat. p.m. Open 9—5. SIZE: Medium. *STOCK: Furniture, Persian rugs.* TEL: 225 5939. SER: Restorations. VAT: Stan.

Malcolm Innes Gallery
67 George St. Est. 1981. CL: Sat. *STOCK: Scottish landscape, sporting and natural history pictures.* TEL: 226 4151. SER: Valuations; restorations; buys at auction; framing. VAT: Spec.

Kenneth Jackson
66 Thistle St. Est. 1969. *STOCK: English and Continental furniture, 17th to early 19th C.* TEL: 225 9634. VAT: Stan/Spec.

Jacksonville Warehouse
83 Causewayside. (A.K.L. Jackson.) Est. 1974. Open 10—6, Sun. 12—5. SIZE: Large. *STOCK: Furniture, bric-a-brac, shipping goods, 1850—1950, £5—£500.* PARK: Easy. TEL: 667 0616; home — 667 3632. SER: Valuations. VAT: Stan.

Letham Antiques
20 Dundas St. (Mrs. J. Letham.) Est. 1966. CL: Mon. Open 10—5.30. SIZE: Medium. *STOCK: Furniture, late 18th to mid-19th C, £10—£1,500; jewellery, glass, pottery, porcelain, metalware, silver, 18th—19th C, £5—£500.* LOC: From Princes St., north along Hanover St. to Dundas St. PARK: Easy. TEL: 556 6565. SER: Buys at auction. VAT: Stan/Spec.

David Letham   BADA
17A Dundas St. Est. 1960. Open 11—6, Sat. 11—3. *STOCK: Furniture, objects, collectors' items.* TEL: 557 4466 or 225 7399. VAT: Spec.

Greig Linton Antiques
95 West Bow. Est. 1968. Open 10—5. *STOCK: Pictures, £15—£500; glass, bronzes, art nouveau, £10—£150; prints, ephemera, £1—£50.* LOC: Down Victoria St. on the way to the Grassmarket. PARK: Meters. TEL: 226 6946.

William MacAdam   BADA
86 Pilrig St. Est. 1976. Open by appointment only. SIZE: Small. *STOCK: Collectors drinking glasses, 17th—19th C, £50—£2,000; coloured glass, 18th—19th C, £15—£250; usable and pressed glass £5—£100; interesting and unusual items.* LOC: Off Leith Walk, halfway down. PARK: Easy. TEL: 553 1364. SER: Valuations. FAIRS: Most major. VAT: Spec.

Edinburgh continued

John McIntosh Antiques
60 Grassmarket. Est. 1935. CL: Sat. Open
10.30—3.30. *STOCK: General antiques.* TEL:
225 1165. VAT: Stan.

William Macintosh & Co.
5—5a Johnston Terrace. (P. and Mrs. J.
London.) Est. 1964. Open 10—6; Sun. 2—5
in summer. SIZE: Large. *STOCK: Brass architectural and light fittings, fenders, pine, panelling, mantelpieces, furniture, Victorian, £5—
£100.* LOC: Left at the top of Royal Mile.
PARK: Easy. TEL: 225 6113. VAT: Stan.

McNaughtan's Bookshop
3a Haddington Place. Est. 1957. CL: Mon.
Open 9.30—5.30. *STOCK: Antiquarian books.*
TEL: 556 5897.

May Mallinson
23 Grassmarket. *STOCK: General antiques.*

John R. Martin
96 West Bow. Est. 1968. CL: Sat. Open
10—4. *STOCK: Clocks, £3—£1,000; furniture, shipping goods, collectors' and decorators' items, £1—£1,000.* LOC: Halfway up
West Bow on right. TEL: 226 7190; home —
(062 082) 2769. VAT: Stan/Spec.

John Mathieson and Co.
48 Frederick St. Open 9—5.30, Sat. 9—4.30.
STOCK: Paintings, watercolours, prints. TEL:
225 6798. SER: Restorations (framing, gilding). VAT: Stan/Spec.

"The Modern Movement"
56 St. Stephen St. Est. 1978. Open
10.30—5. SIZE: Small. *STOCK: Art nouveau,
art deco, pottery, glass, pewter.* PARK: Meters.
TEL: 226 6450.

D. and N. Nairne   LAPADA
25a Dundas St. Est. 1964. Open 10—5.30,
Sat. 10—1, Sun. by appointment. SIZE:
Medium. *STOCK: Furniture, 17th—19th C,
£500—£1,500; ceramics, 18th—20th C,
£50—£1,000; paintings, £300—£1,500;
silver and plate, £20—£500; both 19th C.*
PARK: Easy. TEL: 557 0978; home — (0764)
70298. SER: Valuations. VAT: Spec.

John O. Nelson
22—24 Victoria St. Est. 1957. Open 10—12
and 1.30—5, Sat. 10—1. *STOCK: Antiquarian
maps, prints, watercolours.* LOC: First turning
off George IV Bridge on right, past Royal Mile.
Victoria St. leads down to Grassmarket.
PARK: Castle Terrace, west end. TEL: 225
4413; 667 5275 (evenings). VAT: Stan.

Edinburgh continued

Now and Then (Toy Centre)
7 and 9 West Crosscauseway. (D. Gordon.)
Open afternoons by appointment. SIZE: Small.
*STOCK: Tin and diecast toys, clockwork and
electric model trains, collectable mechanical
ephemera, automobilia, juvenilia, clocks, gold
and silver watches, small furniture, old
advertisements, bric-a-brac.* LOC: City centre
off A68. PARK: Nearby. TEL: 668 2927
(answer machine) or 226 2867. SER: Valuations; buys at auction.

Old Golf Shop Inc.
13 Albany St. (M.W. Olman.) Open by
appointment only. *STOCK: Pre-1910 wood-
shaft clubs, golf related items including oil
paintings, art work, books, bronzes, pottery,
silver, medals; tennis items.* TEL: 663 7647.

Osborne Antique Market
St. Stephens St. (R.A. Mitchel.) CL: Mon.
Open 10.30—12.30 and 2—5.30. TEL: 225
6016. VAT: Stan/Spec.

H. Parry
Castle Antiques, 330 Lawnmarket. *STOCK:
Silver, porcelain, English and Continental furni-
ture, clocks.* TEL: 225 7615.

Penny Farthing Antiques
8 Beaufort Rd. Open 10—12.30 and
2.30—5.30. PARK: Easy. TEL: 447 2410.
VAT: Stan.

Quadrant Antiques
5 North West Circus Place, Stockbridge. (M.
Leask.) Est. 1965. CL: Mon. Open 10.30—5.
SIZE: Medium. *STOCK: Nautical items,
general antiques including trade and shipping
goods, furniture, clocks, brass beds, 18th—
19th C.* PARK: Easy. TEL: 226 7282. VAT:
Spec.

Alan Rankin
72 Dundas St. Est. 1964. Open by appointment. SIZE: Small. *STOCK: Antiquarian books,
£5—£500; out-of-print scholarly books from
1850, £1—£40; prints, maps from earliest
times to 1860, £1—£200.* LOC: From Princes
St., down Hanover St. to first block on left
past Gt. King St. PARK: Easy. TEL: 556 3705;
home — same. SER: Valuaions; buys at
auction.

Chris Ratter Antiques
10 Bonnington Rd., Leith. CL: Sat. Open
9—5. *STOCK: General antiques.* TEL: 553
2564.

Royal Mile Curios
363 High St. (L. Bosi and R. Eprile.) Open
10.30—5. *STOCK: Jewellery and silver.* TEL:
226 4050.

Edinburgh continued

James Scott
43 Dundas St. Est. 1964. Open 10.30—1 and 2.30—5.30. *STOCK: Curiosities, unusual items, silver, jewellery, small furniture.* TEL: 332 0617. VAT: Stan.

The Scottish Gallery
94 George St. (W.C.M. Jackson.) Est. 1842. Open 9—5.30, Sat. 9—1. *STOCK: Paintings, Scottish engravings, lithographs, maps.* LOC: Off Princes St. TEL: 225 5955/6. VAT: Stan/ Spec.

Serendipity
118 West Bow. *STOCK: Small silver, plate, bijouterie, china, glass, prints.*

Daniel Shackleton
23 Dundas St. *STOCK: Paintings, water-colours, prints.* TEL: 557 1115. VAT: Spec.

The Silver Showcase   LAPADA
11 Douglas Crescent. (G. Fleming.) Open by appointment. *STOCK: Silver.* TEL: 346 0942. .SER: Valuations.

James Thin (Booksellers)
53-59 South Bridge. Est. 1848. Open Mon.— Sat. *STOCK: Antiquarian and secondhand books.* TEL: 556 6743. SER: Buys at auction.

This and That Antiques and Bric-a-Brac
22 Argyle Place. CL: Tues., and Wed. Open 2.30—5. *STOCK: Porcelain, silver, small furniture, Scottish pottery, bric-a-brac.* TEL: 229 6069; home — 447 1309.

The Thrie Estaits
49 Dundas St. Est. 1970. CL: Mon. *STOCK: Treen, pottery, porcelain, glass, tiles, small, decorative and collectors' items.* TEL: 556 7084. VAT: Stan.

Unicorn Antiques
65 Dundas St. (Mrs. N. Secchi.) Est. 1967. Open 1—5.30, Sat. 10.30—6.30. SIZE: Medium. *STOCK: Victoriana, (glass, china, curios), furniture, household items, prints, paintings, metalware, bric-a-brac, pre-1950, 10p—£500.* Not stocked: Guns, coins. LOC: From Princes St. turn into Hanover St. Dundas St. is a continuation of Hanover St. PARK: Easy. TEL: 556 7176; home — 332 9135.

West Bow Antiques
102 West Bow. Open 10—5.30. *STOCK: Paisley shawls, furniture, pottery, porcelain, glass, brass, decorative items.* TEL: 226 2852; home — 556 7935. VAT: Stan/Spec.

John Whyte
116b Rose St. Est. 1928. CL: Sat. p.m. Open 9.30—12 and 12.45—5.15. *STOCK: Jewellery, watches, silver.* TEL: 225 2140. VAT: Stan.

Edinburgh continued

Whytock and Reid
Sunbury House, Belford Mews. (J.C. and D.C. Reid.) Est. 1807. CL: Sat. p.m. Open 9—5.30. SIZE: Large. *STOCK: Furniture, English and Continental, 18th to early 19th C, £50—£10,000; furniture, £50—£3,000; Eastern rugs, £50—£6,000.* Not stocked: Victorian furniture. LOC: ½ mile from West End, off Belford Rd. PARK: Own. TEL: 226 4911. SER: Valuations; restorations (furniture, rugs); buys at auction. VAT: Stan/Spec.

Wildman's Antiques
48 St. Stephen St. (I. and M. Wildman.) Est. 1945. Open 10—4.30. SIZE: Small. *STOCK: General antiques, 19th—20th C, £5—£1,000.* LOC: Stockbridge area. PARK: Easy. TEL: 225 7310; home — 449 3038. SER: Valuations. VAT: Stan/Spec.

Aldric Young
49 Thistle St. *STOCK: General antiques; English and Continental furniture, paintings, 18th—19th C.* TEL: 226 4101. VAT: Spec.

Young Antiques
36 Bruntsfield Place. (T.C. Young.) Est. 1979. CL: Wed. p.m. Open 10.30—1.30 and from 2.30. SIZE: Medium. *STOCK: Victorian and Edwardian furniture, £50—£1,000; ceramics, £20—£2,000; Persian rugs, oils and water-colours, £50—£1,500.* LOC: Near Lothian Rd. PARK: Easy. TEL: 229 1361. SER: Valuations; buys at auction (Persian rugs, art pottery).

ELGIN   (0343) (Morayshire)

West End Antiques
35 High St. (F. Stewart.) HADA. Est. 1969. Open daily 9—5.30, Wed. 9—1. *STOCK: Silver, clocks and watches, Victorian jewellery, bric-a-brac.* TEL: 7531; home — 3216. VAT: Stan/Spec.

ELIE   (0333) (Fife)

Malcolm Antiques
5 Bank St. Est. 1965. *STOCK: Victoriana, collectors' items, curios, clocks.* TEL: 330405.

ERROL   (082 12) (Perthshire)

Errol Antiques
The Cross. (A. Knox.) PADA. Est. 1949. CL: Sat. and Sun. except by appointment. Open 8.30—12 and 1—4.30. SIZE: Small. *STOCK: Furniture, 18th—19th C, £50—£5,000; paintings, 17th—20th C, £25—£3,000.* Not stocked: Porcelain. LOC: 2 miles off A85. PARK: Easy. TEL: 391. SER: Valuations; restorations (cabinet making); buys at auction (furniture, paintings). VAT: Stan/Spec.

FAIRLIE   **(3 fig. no.) (047 556)**
(Ayrshire)   **(6 fig. no.) (0475)**
Antiques
86 Main Rd. (E.A. Alvarino.) Est. 1976. CL: Mon. Open 10.30—1 and 2—5.30. SIZE: Small. *STOCK: Bric-a-brac, £5—£100; small furniture, clocks and silver, £10—£500; all Victorian or Edwardian.* LOC: A78. PARK: 25yds. TEL: 613. SER: Valuations; buys at auction. VAT: Stan.

FOCHABERS   **(0343)**
(Morayshire)
Michael Low Antiques
64 High St. Est. 1967. TEL: 820238.

Pringle Antiques
High St. (G.A. Christie.) Est. 1983. Open 9.30—1 and 2—6 every day, closing at 5 p.m. in winter. SIZE: Medium. *STOCK: Furniture, Victorian, £20—£1,000; general antiques, pictures, brass, pottery, silver and jewellery.* Not stocked: Books and clothing. LOC: A96, premises are a converted church. PARK: Easy. TEL: 820362; home — 820599. VAT: Stan/ Spec.

George and Lesley Thom Antiques
89 High St. HADA. Est. 1980. Open 10—12.45 and 2—5. SIZE: Small. *STOCK: Furniture, £100—£500; china and earthenware, £5—£100; all 18th—19th C; etchings, silver and plate, 19th C, £10—£100.* LOC: A96. PARK: Easy. TEL: 821001; home — Spey Bay (034 387) 353. SER: Valuations; buys at auction. FAIRS: Aberdeen monthly. VAT: Stan/Spec.

FORRES   **(0309)**
(Morayshire)
Michael Low Antiques
45 High St. Est. 1967. TEL: 73696. VAT: Stan.

FRIOCKHEIM, Nr. Arbroath(024 12)
(Angus)
M.J. and D. Barclay
29 Gardyne St. Est. 1965. CL: Thurs. Open 10.30—1 and 2—5.30. SIZE: Small. *STOCK: General antiques.* Not stocked: Stamps, books, coins. PARK: Easy. TEL: 365. VAT: Stan.

IS YOUR ENTRY CORRECT?
If there is even the slightest inaccuracy in your entry, *please* let us know before 1st January 1987.
GUIDE TO THE
ANTIQUE SHOPS OF BRITAIN
5 Church Street, Woodbridge, Suffolk.

GALSTON   **(0563)**
(Ayrshire)
Window on the World
(incorporating Galleries de Fresnes)
Mainly Trade
Cessnock Castle. (The Baron de Fresnes,) D.A. (Glas). AIDDA. Est. 1934. Articles on drawings and paintings. Open 10—6. *STOCK: General antiques, to 1850; silver, glass, oil paintings, 20th C.* LOC: Approximately 600yds. on Sorn Rd. out of Galston 6 miles from Kilmarnock. PARK: Easy. TEL: 820314. SER: Valuations; restorations (paintings); buys at auction; courier for overseas traders.

GARTMORE, Nr. Aberfoyle
(Stirlingshire)
Robert and Vashti Lewis Antiques
Blairnabard Farm. Est. 1975. Resident — always open but prior telephone call advisable. SIZE: Medium. *STOCK: Pine, £25—£1,000; farm and kitchen items, £5—£100; all 18th— 20th C; general antiques, £5—£1,000.* LOC: First farm outside village on Drymen road, off A81. PARK: Easy. TEL: Aberfoyle (087 72) 374. SER: Valuations; restorations; pine stripping.

GATEHOUSE OF FLEET
(Kirkcudbrightshire)
R. and L. Hampshire Antiques
LAPADA
Rutherford Hall. Est. 1963. Open 9.30—5.30 or by appointment. *STOCK: General antiques especially furniture; shipping goods.* LOC: A75 west of Dumfries. PARK: Easy. TEL: Gatehouse (055 74) 616. SER: Valuations.

GLASGOW   **(041)**
(Lanarkshire)
A.A. Antiques   *Mainly Export*
Laurelbank Farm, 315 Hamilton Rd., Broomhouse. *STOCK: Shipping goods.* TEL: 773 2040 and 773 2917. SER: Export container loads to USA, Canada and Continent, specialist knowledge of USA.

Albany Antiques   **LAPADA**
1345-1351 Argyle St. (P.J. O'Loughlin.) Est. 1969. Open Mon.—Fri. or by appointment. *STOCK: Chinese and Japanese porcelain, Victorian and Edwardian furniture, shipping goods.* VAT: Stan/Spec.

M.A. Alexander Fine Arts Ltd.
LAPADA
147 Bath St. CL: Sat. *STOCK: Furniture, paintings, china, silver, plate, metalware.* TEL: 221 3539.

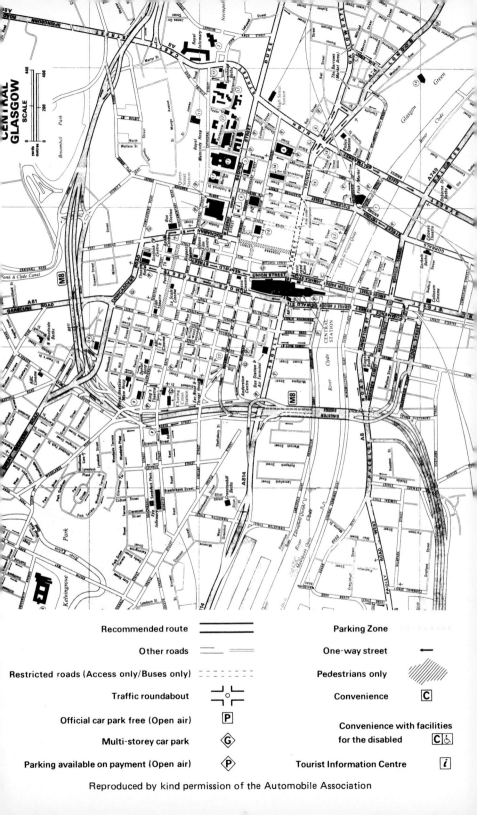

CENTRAL GLASGOW

SCALE

Recommended route		Parking Zone
Other roads		One-way street
Restricted roads (Access only/Buses only)		Pedestrians only
Traffic roundabout		Convenience
Official car park free (Open air)		
Multi-storey car park		Convenience with facilities
		for the disabled
Parking available on payment (Open air)		Tourist Information Centre

Reproduced by kind permission of the Automobile Association

Glasgow continued

Behar Carpets
11A Bath St. (M. and Mrs. P. Slater.) Est. 1920. Open 9−5.30. SIZE: Large. *STOCK: Oriental carpets and rugs, 19th C.* PARK: Multi-storey. TEL: 332 2858. SER: Valuations; restorations (cleaning and repairs). VAT: Stan.

Brown's Clocks Limited
203 Bath St. (A.M. and J. Wilson) FBHI. Est. 1933. CL: Sat. Open 10−5. SIZE: Medium. *STOCK: Longcase, wall and mantel clocks, £30−£3,000.* LOC: Town centre. TEL: 248 6760. SER:.Valuations; restorations; buys at auction. VAT: Stan/Spec.

Butler's Furniture Galleries Ltd.
24-26 Millbrae Rd., Langside. (L. Butler.) CL: Sat. Open 9.30−5.30 or by appointment. *STOCK: Furniture, Georgian−Edwardian; small items, paintings, silver, glass, Persian rugs.* TEL: 632 9853. SER: Valuations.

Corner House Antiques
217 St. Vincent St. (Mrs. V. Salvage and R. Flemming.) Est. 1979. Open 10−5. SIZE: Medium. LOC: Corner of Blythswood St., and St. Vincent St. PARK: Easy. TEL: 221 1000. VAT: Stan/Spec. Below are listed the dealers at this centre.

Fraser Antiques
Furniture, porcelain and general antiques.
C. Henderson
Small furniture and general antiques.
Martiniques
General antiques and collectors' items.
G.E. Moncur
Silver.
Victoria
General antiques, collectables, postcards.

The Den of Antiquity
61 Dixon Ave., Crosshill. Est. 1960. CL: Sat. and Sun., except by appointment. Open 10−5. *STOCK: General antiques.* TEL: 423 0375; 637 4434 (evenings). VAT: Stan/Spec.

The Fine Art Society plc
134 Blythswood St. Est. 1876. Open 9.30−5.30. Sat. 10−1. SIZE: Large. *STOCK: British paintings, watercolours, drawings, sculpture, especially Scottish, from 1800.* TEL: 332 4027. VAT: Spec.

James Forrest and Co. (Jewellers) Ltd.
105 West Nile St. Est. 1957. CL: Sat. p.m. *STOCK: Silver, jewellery, ivories, bric-a-brac.* LOC: City centre. TEL: 332 0494. VAT: Stan.

George and Helen Gardiner Antiques and Decorative Objects
105 West Regent St. CL: Sat. Open 10−5.30. *STOCK: Decorative and county furniture, treen,textiles, Paisley shawls, primitive pictures.* TEL: 332 1264; evenings (0236) 825286.

Glasgow continued

P. Graham Antiques
48 Park Rd. CL: Mon. Open 10−5. *STOCK: General antiques, curios, shipping items.* TEL: 357 2922.

David Gray Antiques   LAPADA
284 Woodlands Rd. Est. 1978. Open 10−4 Tues., Wed. and Thurs. or by appointment. SIZE: Small. *STOCK: Decorative items, art objects, pictures, 19th C, £50−£500.* LOC: Charing Cross turn-off M8, 200yds. to Glasgow University. PARK: Easy. TEL: 334 3047; home − (0360) 22244. SER: Valuations. VAT: Stan/Spec.

Jocelyn Antiques Scotland
Jocelyn (Clock Restoration)
Jocelyn Service Agencies, 161 West George St. Est. 1969. (J.T.B. McChesney.) Open 9−5. *STOCK: Clocks, furniture, brassware, bric-a-brac, shipping goods.* LOC: City centre. TEL: 248 3024. SER: Restorations (clocks, barometers and furniture); import and export − packaging, documentation, shipping. VAT: Stan.

Keep Sakes
27 Gibson St. (Mrs. R. Currie.) Est. 1971. Open 10−5, Mon. 10−2. *STOCK: General antiques, jewellery.* TEL: 334 2264. SER: Repairs (jewellery). VAT: Stan.

The Kelvin Gallery
117 Bath St. *STOCK: Oil paintings, watercolours, 19th C; prints; contemporary works.* TEL: 221 1367. SER: Restorations (paintings); framing.

A. and I. Loudon   *Trade Only*
1 Burnpark Ave., Uddingston. Resident. Est. 1946. Warehouse in Glasgow open by appointment, contact at above address. *STOCK: Victorian furniture, silver plate, china and brass, £5−£1,000.* LOC: ½ mile from end of M74 off Blantyre Farm Rd. PARK: Easy. TEL: Uddingston (0698) 812472; warehouse− 552 0514. VAT: Stan/Spec.

I.E. Lovatt Antiques   LAPADA
100 Torrisdale St. Est. 1963. CL: Sat. SIZE: Large. *STOCK: General antiques, Victoriana, shipping goods.* LOC: Adjacent Queen's Park railway station. TEL: 423 6497; home − 638 0302. SER: Valuations; buys at auction. VAT: Stan/Spec.

IS YOUR ENTRY CORRECT?
If there is even the slightest inaccuracy in your entry, *please* let us know before 1st January 1987.
GUIDE TO THE
ANTIQUE SHOPS OF BRITAIN
5 Church Street, Woodbridge, Suffolk.

Glasgow continued

Jean Megahy
481 Great Western Rd. (F.G. Halliday.) CL: Sat. p.m. Open 10—5. *STOCK: Furniture, brass, silver, Oriental items.* TEL: 334 1315. VAT: Stan/Spec.

Mercat Antiques
246 West George St. (J. Jack, P. Hughes.) *STOCK: Watches, jewellery, clocks, furniture, brass, glass, porcelain and trade items.* TEL: 204 0851.

Muirhead Moffat and Co.
182 West Regent St. (D.J. Brewster and J.D. Hay.) Est. 1896. CL: Sat. and Sun. except by appointment. Open 10—12.30 and 1.30—5. SIZE: Medium. *STOCK: Period furniture, barometers and jewellery; clocks, silver, weapons, porcelain, tapestries and pictures.* LOC: Off Blythswood Sq. PARK: Easy. TEL: 226 4683 and 226 3406. SER: Valuations; restorations (furniture, clocks, barometers and jewellery); buys at auction. VAT: Stan/Spec.

Glasgow continued

Nice Things Old and New
1010 Pollokshaws Rd. (J.E. Lake.) Est. 1961. Open 10.30—6. *STOCK: Interesting and unusual pieces.* LOC: Facing Langside Halls and Marlborough House (Shawlands). TEL: 649 3826.

Nithsdale Antiques   *Trade Only*
103 Niddrie Rd., Queens Park. (W. McDonald.) Est. 1935. CL: Sat. Open 9.30—5. *STOCK: General antiques.* TEL: 424 0444. SER: Buys at auction.

John Smith and Son (Glasgow) Ltd.
57—61 St. Vincent St. Est. 1751. Open 9—5.30. SIZE: Medium. *STOCK: Antiquarian books.* LOC: City centre. TEL: 221 7472. SER: Buys at auction (antiquarian books); out of print book search.

K. Stanley and Son
86 Maryhill Rd. Est. 1955. *STOCK: General antiques.* TEL: 881 0452. VAT: Stan.

The Palladian Bridge at Wilton House. From *Gardens in Edwardian England* published by the **Antique Collectors' Club,** 1985.

Glasgow continued

The Victorian Village

53 and 57 West Regent St. (J.D. McArdle.) Open 10—5, Sat. 10—1. LOC: Near Renfield St. PARK: Meters. TEL: 332 0703 and 332 0808. VAT: Stan/Spec. Below are listed some of the 30 dealers at this market.

Maria Bidnarack
Jewellery and clothing.
Terry Black
Silver, plate, jewellery.
John Cavanagh
Jewellery and furniture.
The Foxy Lady
Napery, jewellery, art nouveau.
Glenburn Antiques
General antiques, furniture.
Martha Hooper
Stamps and accessories.
Mrs Hutton
Unusual objects.
Sheila Lind
Jewellery.
Mackinnon
General furniture and small items.
Mrs. C. McLay
Napery, jewellery.

The Victorian Village continued

Mandersons
Small items.
Rosamund Rotherford
Jewellery, clothing.
Jeremy Sniders
Jewellery.
Lloyd Strang
Jewellery and furniture.
Karen Thom
Jewellery.
Weaver Antiques
Small antiques.
Yesteryear Antiques
(R. Devlin.) *Porcelain.*

Vintage and Value

220—224 Woodlands Rd. (S.K. Asiedu.) Open 10.30—7. *STOCK: General antiques.* TEL: 332 0495. VAT: Stan.

Virginia Antique Galleries

31/33 Virginia St. (Off Argyle St.) (M. Robinson.) Open 10—5, Sun. 12—5. There are 20 dealers here selling *furniture, glass, jewellery, silver, porcelain and brass.* TEL: 552 2573/8640; office — 552 5840. SER: Restorations; french polishing.

Glasgow continued
Douglas Weir
374 Byres Rd. and 193 Hyndland Rd. Est.
1960. CL: Tues. p.m. *STOCK: Furniture, bric-
a-brac.* TEL: 339 5673 and 334 4514. SER:
Restorations; polishing; upholstery; clock
repairs. VAT: Stan.

Tim Wright Antiques   LAPADA
147 Bath St. (T. and J. Wright.) Est. 1971.
Open 9.30—4.45, Sat. and Sun. by appointment. *STOCK: Porcelain, pottery and glass,
continental, British and Oriental, some 18th
but mainly 19th C, £25—£1,500; brass and
metalware, £20—£500; small furniture and
collectors items, £50—£2,000; silver and
plate, £20—£1,500.* LOC: On opposite corner
to Christie's, Glasgow. PARK: Multi-storey
opposite. TEL: 221 0364. SER: Valuations;
buys at auction (as stock). VAT: Mainly Spec.

GOUROCK   (0475)
(Lanarkshire)
McIntosh Antiques
The Bay Hotel, Pierhead. (G.B. Robertson.)
SIZE: Small. *STOCK: Silver, jewellery and
coins, 18th C, £5—£1,000+.* LOC: A8.
PARK: Easy. TEL: 31244; home — same.
VAT: Stan.

GRANTOWN-ON-SPEY   (0479)
(Morayshire)
Spey Valley Antiques
The Square. (Mr. and Mrs. L.W.A. Weurman.)
HADA. Est. 1977. Open 10—5, Tues.—
Thurs. 10—1. Winter open by appointment.
SIZE: Small. *STOCK: China, silver plate, brass,
copper, glass, paintings and prints, £25—
£500.* LOC: A95. PARK: Easy. TEL: 2340;
home — (0463) 223583. SER: Valuations.

GREENLAW   (036 16)
(Berwickshire)
Greenlaw Antiques
(Mr. and Mrs. A. Brotherston.) Est. 1970.
Open Mon. to Fri. and by appointment. SIZE:
Large. *STOCK: General antiques, £5—£500.*
PARK: Easy. TEL: 220. VAT: Stan/Spec.

Greenlaw Antiques
The Town Hall. (Mr. and Mrs. A. Brotherston.)
Open Sun. only 2—5. *STOCK: General
antiques, £5—£500.*

HADDINGTON   (062 082)
(East Lothian)
Elm House Antiques
The Sands, Church St. (Mrs. I. MacDonald.)
Est. 1972. Open daily, appointment advisable,
and Sat. 10—1 and 2—5. SIZE: Small.
*STOCK: English porcelain and pottery, 18th
and 19th C, £10—£300; blue and white
earthenware, Scottish pottery, £5—£150;
boxes, furniture, £10—£800.* LOC: Off A1,
end of High St. PARK: Easy. TEL: 3413; home
— same.

Leslie and Leslie
CL: Sat. Open 9—1 and 2—5. *STOCK:
General antiques.* TEL: 2241. VAT: Stan.

HAWICK   (0450)
(Roxburghshire)
Burlington House Antiques
25 North Bridge St. (J. and M. Turnbull.) Est.
1966. CL: Sat. and Sun. except by appointment. Open 9—5.30. SIZE: Medium. *STOCK:
Georgian and Victorian furniture, paintings,
silver, china, glass, shipping goods, £5—
£5,000.* PARK: Easy. TEL: 72984. VAT:
Stan.

INCHTURE   (0828)
(Perthshire)
C.S. Moreton Antiques
Inchmartine House. (P.M. Stephens.) PADA.
Est. 1922. Open 9—5.30. *STOCK: Furniture,
£50—£10,000; carpets and rugs, £50—
£3,000; ceramics, metalware; all 16th C to
1860; silver and plate, paintings, weapons.*
LOC: A85 from Perth, entrance on left at
Lodge. PARK: Easy. TEL: 86412; home —
same. SER: Valuations. VAT: Stan/Spec.

INVERNESS   (0463)
(Inverness-shire)
The Attic
Market Close, 34 Church St. (P. Gratton.)
HADA. Est. 1976. CL: Wed. Jan.—Mar.
closed Mon. and Wed. Open 10.30—1 and
2.15—5. SIZE: Small. *STOCK: Linen, textiles,
period clothes, Victorian to pre-1940s, from
£5; art deco, china.* PARK: Station Sq. TEL:
Home — 240224. SER: Valuations. FAIRS:
Inverness.

Frasers (Auctioneers)
28/30 Church St. Est. 1900. Open 9—12.45
and 2—5.30, Sat. 9—5. SIZE: Small. *STOCK:
Furniture, from 1800; oil paintings, prints,
£50—£1,000; china, brass, copper, £5—
£500.* LOC: Follow one-way traffic to Union
St., turn right, then right again into Church St.
PARK: Restricted. TEL: 232395. SER: Valuations; buys at auction. VAT: Stan.

JEDBURGH (0835)
(Roxburghshire)

R. and M. Turner LAPADA
(Antiques and Fine Art) Ltd.
34/36 High St. Est. 1965. CL: Sun. except by appointment. Open 10—5.30. SIZE: Large. STOCK: Furniture, clocks, porcelain, paintings, silver, jewellery, 17th—20th C. LOC: On A68 to Edinburgh. PARK: Own. TEL: 63445, 63349. SER: Valuations; restorations (furniture, pottery, porcelain); packing and shipping. VAT: Stan/Spec.

KELSO (0573)
(Roxburghshire)

The Curiosity Shop
27 Horsemarket. (H. and B.V. Cox.) Est. 1970. CL: Wed. p.m. Open 9.30—5. SIZE: Small. STOCK: General antiques, small furniture, jewellery, curios, watercolours and oil paintings. LOC: Near Kelso Sq. PARK: Easy. TEL: 24541. VAT: Stan.

Christopher Wood
Harlaw House. Est. 1968. Open by appointment. STOCK: Marine and pocket chronometers, regulators, clocks, longcase and bracket, 17th—19th C; scientific and navigational instruments. TEL: Stichill (057 37) 321. VAT: Stan.

KILBARCHAN (050 57)
(Renfrewshire)

Corrigan Antiques LAPADA
10 The Cross. Est. 1945. Open 10—5, weekends by appointment. SIZE: Medium. STOCK: General antiques and decorative items. LOC: 12 miles from Glasgow. TEL: 2229. SER: Valuations. VAT: Stan/Spec.

Gardner's The Antique Shop
LAPADA
Wardend House. (D.F., G.D. and R.K.F. Gardner.) Est. 1950. Open to the trade 7 days a week. Retail 10—1 and 2—6, Sat. 10—1. SIZE: Large. STOCK: General antiques. LOC: 12 miles from Glasgow, at far end of Tandlehill Rd. 10 mins. from Glasgow Airport. TEL: 2292.

Steeple Antiques
25 Steeple St. (J.N. Kinniburgh.) Est. 1959. CL: Mon., Wed. and Sat. Open 10—1 and 2—6, Sun. 2—5. STOCK: General antiques. TEL: 3623; home — Johnstone (0505) 28456. SER: Hire or sale to film and television industry. VAT: Stan.

KILLEARN (0360)
Nr. Glasgow (Stirlingshire)

Country Antiques
(Lady J. Edmonstone.) Est. 1975. SIZE: Small. STOCK: Small antiques, silver, brass, ceramics, Victoriana. LOC: A81. In main st. PARK: Easy. TEL: Home — 70215.

KILLIN (056 72)
(Perthshire)

Maureen H. Gauld
Cameron Buildings, Main St. Est. 1975. CL: Sun. from mid-Sept. Open every day 10—5.30. SIZE: Small. STOCK: Victoriana, £5—£500; general antiques, silver and paintings. PARK: Easy. TEL: 475; home — 605. SER: Buys at auction.

KILMACOLM (050 587)
(Renfrewshire)

Kilmacolm Antiques
Stewart Place. (H. Maclean.) Est. 1973. CL: Sun. and Wed. except by appointment. Open 10—12.30 and 2.30—5. SIZE: Medium. STOCK: Furniture, 18th—19th C, £50—£2,000; objets d'art, 19th C, £5—£50; jewellery, £5—£500; paintings, £5—£1,000. LOC: First shop on right when travelling from Bridge of Weir. PARK: Easy. TEL: 3149. SER: Restorations (furniture, silver, jewellery, porcelain). FAIRS: Hopetown House, Perth, Roxburghe, Edinburgh. VAT: Stan/Spec.

KILMARNOCK (0563)
(Ayrshire)

Iain and Margaret MacInnes Antiques
116 Galston Rd., Hurlford. Est. 1973. Resident, always available. STOCK: General antiques. TEL: 23688.

KILMICHAEL GLASSARY
By Lochgilphead (Argyllshire)

Rhudle Mill
(D. Murray.) Est. 1979. Open daily, winter weekends by appointment. SIZE: Medium. STOCK: Furniture, 18th C to art deco, £50—£3,000; small items and bric-a-brac, £10—£100. LOC: Signposted 3 miles south of Kilmartin on A816 Oban to Lochgilphead road. PARK: Easy. TEL: Dunadd (054 684) 284; home — same. SER: Restorations (furniture); French polishing; buys at auction.

Gardners

"THE ANTIQUE SHOP"
WARDEND HOUSE, KILBARCHAN

10 minutes from Glasgow Airport   20 minutes from Glasgow Centre
Telephone Kilbarchan 2292

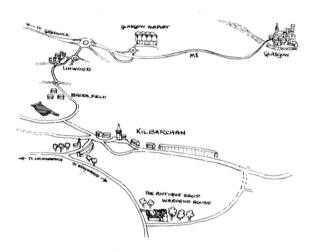

Large stock of
furniture, porcelain, silver, pictures
Shipping goods

KILTARLITY, By Beauly (046 374)
(Inverness-shire)
Old Pine Furniture and Jouet
Fuaranbuie, 8 Kinerras. (J. and A. Jeorrett.) Open by appointment. *STOCK: Stripped pine, £30—£600.* TEL: 261.

KINGUSSIE (054 02)
(Inverness-shire)
Colin Murdoch
56 High St. HADA. Est. 1968. CL: Wed. p.m. Open 9.30—1 and 2.15—5.30. In winter by appointment. SIZE: Small. *STOCK: Oil and watercolour paintings, 18th—20th C; prints and maps, books, some furniture.* LOC: Main St., signposted from new A9. PARK: Easy. TEL: 552; home — 300. SER: Valuations; buys at auction. VAT: Stan.

KIPPEN (078 687)
(Stirlingshire)
Robert Ainslie
"Glenora", Main St. Est. 1949. Resident. SIZE: Large. *STOCK: Furniture, brass, copper, shipping goods.* LOC: 9 miles from Stirling. PARK: Easy. TEL: 368. VAT: Stan.

KIRKCUDBRIGHT (0557)
(Kirkcudbrightshire)
Chapel Antiques
Chapel Farm. (A. Bradley.) Est. 1981. Open 9—5 and by appointment. SIZE: Small. *STOCK: China, small and shipping furniture, silver, brass and copper, 18th—20th C, £5—£1,000.* LOC: 200yds. off A75 between Ringford and Twynholm on A762, 2½ miles from Kirkcudbright. PARK: Easy. TEL: Ringford (055 722) 281.

Osborne
41 Castle St. (R.A. Mitchell.) Est. 1948. CL: Thurs. p.m. and Sat. p.m. Open 9—12.30 and 1.30—5. TEL: 30441. VAT: Stan/Spec.

KNAPP
(Perthshire)
Templemans — Wholesale Antiques
Trade Only
Mill Hill House. PADA. Est. 1967. Open 9—9. *STOCK: Furniture, 1750—1895, £50—£10,000; rugs and small items.* Not stocked: Coins and militaria. PARK: Easy. TEL: (0828) 86268. SER: Valuations. VAT: Stan/Spec.

LANGHOLM (0541)
(Dumfriesshire)
The Antique Shop
High St. (R. and V. Baird.) Est. 1970. Open daily 10.30—6. SIZE: Small. *STOCK: China, glass, pictures, 18th—20th C; jewellery, rugs, 19th—20th C; also Trade Warehouse of furniture, shipping goods, nearby.* LOC: 20 miles north of Carlisle on A7. PARK: 100yds. TEL: 80238. VAT: Stan/Spec.

LARGS (0475)
(Ayrshire)
S. Winestone and Son Ltd.
2 May St. Est. 1900. CL: Sat. Open 8.30—5 or by appointment. *STOCK: General antiques.* TEL: 672672. SER: Restorations (furniture, china).

Narducci Antiques
Mainly Trade and Export
12 Waterside St. (G. Narducci.) Open 10—1 and 2.30—5.30 or by appointment. SIZE: Warehouse. *STOCK: General antiques and shipping goods.* TEL: 672612. SER: Packing; export.

LINLITHGOW (0506)
(West Lothian)
Heritage Antiques
222 High St. (Mrs. A.G. Dunbar.) CL: Wed. Open 10—5. *STOCK: China, glass, small furniture, medals, silver, collectors' items.* TEL: 847460.

LUNDIN LINKS (0333)
(Fife)
Robb Antiques
19 Leven Rd. Est. 1968. SIZE: Small. *STOCK: General antiques.* PARK: Easy. TEL: 320266.

MAUCHLINE
(Ayrshire)
Bruce Marshall
Glenstang, Stair. Open by appointment. *STOCK: Antiquarian books on early travel, and natural history; atlases, colour plate books, fine bindings.* TEL: Ayr (0292) 591283.

MOFFAT (0683)
(Dumfriesshire)
T.W. Beaty LAPADA
22 Well St. Open 9.15—5; trade any time by appointment. SIZE: Large and warehouse. *STOCK: Furniture, 17th—20th C, £5—£5,000; china, glass, brass, 18th—19th C, £5—£3,000; pictures, 19th—20th C, £5—£15,000.* TEL: 20380. VAT: Stan/Spec.

Moffat continued

Harthope House Antiques
Church Gate. (Mrs. M. Owens.) Est. 1979.
CL: Wed. Open 10—5.30. *STOCK: Furniture,
general antiques especially Victorian jewellery.*
TEL: 20710.

MONTROSE   (0674)
(Angus)
Red Rose Antiques
47 Ferry St. (R. Noller.) Est. 1969. CL: Sun.
except by appointment. Open 10—5. *STOCK:
General antiques, smalls and furniture.* Not
stocked: Coins, stamps. LOC: 1 block south,
3½ blocks east of Montrose Steeple. PARK:
Easy. TEL: 73076; home — same.

Mrs. Margaret Smith
55 Murray St. *STOCK: General antiques.* TEL:
73730.

NAIRN   (0667)
(Nairnshire)
Highland Antiques
2 Bridge St. (J. Hesling.) HADA. Est. 1962.
CL: Wed. p.m. in summer Wed. all day in
winter. Otherwise open. SIZE: Small. *STOCK:
Furniture, £50—£500; paintings, £20—£500,
both 19th C; general antiques, 18th—19th C,
£5—£200; books.* LOC: Main Inverness—
Aberdeen Rd. PARK: Easy. TEL: 53614; home
— Daviot (046 385) 250. SER: Valuations;
buys at auction. VAT: Stan/Spec.

NEWTON STEWART   (0671)
(Wigtownshire)
Brown's Antique Shop
44, 51, 53 Queen St. (M.B. Brown.) Est.
1947. *STOCK: General antiques.* TEL: 2052.
SER: Valuations; restorations; re-upholstery,
repairs, auctioneers (furniture). VAT: Stan.

NEWTONMORE   (054 03)
(Inverness-shire)
The Antique Shop
Main St. (E. Campbell.) HADA. Est. 1964.
Open 9.30—1 and 2.30—5. SIZE: Medium.
*STOCK: Small furniture, £20—£500; glass,
china, silver, plate, copper, brass.* Not
stocked: Firearms. LOC: On A86 opposite
Mains Hotel. PARK: Easy. TEL: 272; home —
Kingussie (054 02) 487.

NORTH BERWICK   (0620)
(East Lothian)
Fraser Antiques
119 High St. Est. 1968. CL: Thurs. Open
10—5. SIZE: Large. *STOCK: Chinese and
English porcelain, English glass, pictures,
silver, small furniture.* LOC: From Berwick-on-
Tweed via A1 follow A198 4 miles north of
Dunbar. PARK: Easy. TEL: 2722. SER: Restorations (paintings, clocks, furniture).

OBAN   (0631)
(Argyllshire)
Campbell-Gibson Fine Arts
Star Brae. (R.A. Campbell-Gibson.) Est.
1973. Open 9.30—5.30. *STOCK: Victorian
watercolours and oil paintings, £15—£3,500;
engravings and prints, 1780—1920, £1—£45.*
TEL: 62303. SER: Restorations, framing; buys
at auction; heat sealing.

PAISLEY
(Renfrewshire)
Heritage Antiques
Walker St. (C.W. Anderson.) Est. 1963. Open
9.30—5, Sat. 10—2.30, Sun. by appoint-
ment. SIZE: Large. *STOCK: Furniture, late
18th—19th C; small items.* LOC: Off High St.
PARK: Own. TEL: (041) 889 3661 (24 hrs.).
SER: Valuations; restorations. VAT: Stan/
Spec.

Paisley Fine Books
17 Corsebar Crescent. (Mr. and Mrs. B.
Merrifield). Est. 1985. Open by appointment.
SIZE: Small. *STOCK: Books on architecture,
art, antiques and collecting.* TEL: (041) 884
2661; home — same. SER: Free book search;
catalogues issued.

PEEBLES   (0721)
(Peeblesshire)
Ancient and Modern
25 High St. (Mrs. D. Scott.) Est. 1981. Open
9.30—5.30, some Sundays 12—4.30. SIZE:
Small. *STOCK: China, glass, and crystal,
19th—20th C, £5—£25; furniture, mainly
20th C, £5—£100.* PARK: Easy. TEL: 20625;
home — Selkirk (0750) 20768. SER: Buys at
auction.

PERTH   (0738)
(Perthshire)
Aldgate Antiques (Perth) Ltd.
(D.J. Cameron.) Est. 1974. CL: Sat. p.m.
Open by appointment. SIZE: Small. *STOCK:
Furniture, £10—£1,000; brass, copper, £5—
£100; china, £1—£100; all 18th—19th C.*
Not stocked: Edwardiana. PARK: Meters. TEL:
20107. VAT: Stan/Spec.

Perth continued

W.S. Beaton BADA
75 Kinnoull St. (W.M.Y. Beaton.) PADA. Est. 1932. CL: Sat. p.m. Open 9.30—1 and 2—5.30. SIZE: Medium. *STOCK: Furniture, porcelain, metalware and paintings, mainly pre-1830.* Not stocked: Victoriana. PARK: Easy. TEL: 28127. VAT: Spec.

Beveridge (Antiques) BADA
1-2 South St. John's Place. (B. Beveridge.) PADA. Est. 1973. Open 10—1 and 2—5. SIZE: Medium. *STOCK: Furniture, 17th—18th C, £200—£5,000; Scottish paintings, 18th—19th C, £500—£10,000.* LOC: City centre. PARK: Easy. TEL: 35055; home — (030786) 212 or 209. VAT: Spec.

Coach House Antiques Ltd.
77 Kinngull St. (J. Walker.) PADA. Est. 1971. Open 9.30—5.30. SIZE: Large. *STOCK: Furniture, furnishings and decorative items, 18th—19th C; sporting prints; £20—£5,000.* PARK: Nearby. TEL: 29835; home — 828627. VAT: Spec.

A.S. Deuchar and Son
10—12 South St. (A.S. and A.W.N. Deuchar.) CL: Sat. p.m. Open 9.30—1 and 2—5.30. SIZE: Large. *STOCK: Victorian shipping goods, furniture; 19th C paintings; china, brass, silver plate.* LOC: Glasgow to Aberdeen Rd., near Queen's Bridge. PARK: Easy. TEL: 26297; home — 51452. VAT: Stan/Spec.

Forsyth Antiques
8 St. Paul's Sq. (A. McDonald Forsyth). Est. 1961. Open 10—5. SIZE: Medium. *STOCK: Silver, 18th—19th C, £5—£1,000; jewellery, 19th—20th C, £5—£750; Monant glass, 20th C, £5—£500.* LOC: Behind St. Paul's Church, junction of High St. and Methven St. PARK: Easy. TEL: 22173; home — (08214) 570. SER: Valuations; buys at auction (silver). VAT: Stan/Spec.

Hardie Antiques
25 St. John St. (T.G. Hardie.) PADA. Est. 1980. Open 9.30—5.15, Sat. 10—1. SIZE: Medium. *STOCK: Jewellery and silver, 18th—20th C, £5—£5,000.* PARK: Nearby. TEL: 33127; home — 51764. SER: Valuations. VAT: Stan/Spec.

Henderson
5 North Methven St. (J.G. Henderson.) Est. 1935. CL: Wed. p.m. Open 9—5.30. SIZE: Small. *STOCK: Porcelain, glass, 1720—1900, £5—£50; silver, jewellery, 1800—1900, £2—£200; coins, medals and stamps, £1—£100.* Not stocked: Furniture. LOC: On A9. PARK: Easy. TEL: 24836; home — 21923. SER: Valuations. VAT: Stan.

Perth continued

Thomas Love and Sons Ltd.
51—53 South St. CL: Sat. p.m. Open 9—5.30. *STOCK: Furniture, ceramics, glass, silver, pictures, clocks.* TEL: 24111. VAT: Stan.

Ian Murray Antiques Warehouse
21 Glasgow Rd. CL: Sat. Open 9—5. There are 8 dealers at this warehouse selling *a wide range of general antiques, Victorian, Edwardian and shipping items.* TEL: 37222. VAT: Stan/Spec.

Robertson and Cox Antiques
60 George St. PADA. CL: Wed. p.m. and Sat. p.m. Open 9.30—1 and 2—5. SIZE: Medium. *STOCK: Furniture 18th and 19th C; paintings, porcelain, Oriental rugs. smalls.* TEL: 26300; home — 32519. VAT: Spec.

John Scott-Adie
16 St. John St. Est. 1968. CL: Wed. p.m. Open 10.15—12.30 and 2—5. *STOCK: Paintings — Scottish, landscapes, £500—£15,000; watercolours, both 19th C.* LOC: City centre. TEL: 25550; home — (082 886) 320. VAT: Spec.

The South Street Gallery
19 South St. (M. Hardie). PADA. CL: Wed p.m. Open 9—1 and 2—5. *STOCK: Oil paintings and watercolours, especially Scottish artists, late 19th to early 20th C.* TEL: 38953.

Tay Street Gallery
70 Tay St. (I.C. Ingram.) Est. 1972. Open 9.30—1 and 2—5, Sat. till 4, other times by appointment. SIZE: Small. *STOCK: Furniture, mostly Georgian, £100—£3,000; pictures and prints, £100—£2,000; china, glass, metalware, decorative items, £10—£2,000.* LOC: Overlooking River Tay. PARK: Easy. TEL: 20604. VAT: Stan/Spec.

PITLOCHRY (0796)
(Perthshire)

Blair Antiques
30 Bonnethill Rd. (A.C. Huie.) PADA. Est. 1976. CL: Thurs. p.m. Open 9—5. *STOCK: Period furniture, Scottish oil paintings, silver — some provincial, curios, clocks, pottery and porcelain.* LOC: Beside Scotlands Hotel, on A9 to Inverness. TEL: 2624. SER: Valuations; buys at auction. VAT: Stan/Spec.

When in Scotland......

Carse Antiques
Rait, by Perth
Tel: 08217 205

Four Showrooms

RAIT   (082 17)
(Perthshire)
Carse Antiques
(Mr. and Mrs. M. Murray Threipland). PADA.
Est. 1983. CL: Sun., except by appointment.
Open 10—1 and 2—5.30. SIZE: Large.
*STOCK: Furniture, 17th—19th C, £25—
£25,000; decorative items, 17th—20th C,
£5—£500.* Not stocked: Silver and jewellery.
LOC: 1 mile north of A85 between Perth and
Dundee. PARK: Easy. TEL. 205; home —
227. VAT: Stan/Spec.

David Keith Antiques
Est. 1979. Open 9—5, Sun. by appointment.
SIZE: Medium. *STOCK: Furniture and clocks,
18th—19th C, £500—£3,000.* LOC: ¾ mile
off A85 midway between Perth and Dundee.
PARK: Easy. TEL: 339; home — 245. SER:
Valuations; restorations (furniture); buys at
auction (furniture, clocks and decorative
items). VAT: Stan/Spec.

Rait continued
Rait Antiques
Rait Steading. (D. and Mrs. J. Pickett.) Est.
1981. Open 9.30—6, Sun. and other times by
appointment. SIZE: Medium. *STOCK: Furniture including desks, bureaux and sofas, late
18th to early 19th C, £500—£3,000; tables,
chairs, Oriental porcelain, £50—£1,000; porcelain, brass, copper and bronze, £15—£150.*
LOC: A85 between Perth and Dundee. PARK:
Easy. TEL: 287; home — same. SER: Restorations (furniture); buys at auction (furniture).
VAT: Stan/Spec.

ST. ANDREWS   (0334)
(Fife)
Circa 1900
211 South St. (C. McDonald Craig.) Est.
1978. Open 10—1.30 and 2.30—5. SIZE:
Medium. *STOCK: General antiques, mainly
British Victoriana, 1830—1910, £5—£500.*
Not stocked: Postcards, crested china,
militaria and weapons. PARK: Limited and 100
yards. TEL: 76798.

MAINHILL GALLERY

Half Time
FEDERIGO ANDREOTTI, born Florence 1847
Exhibited, R.A. 1879 - 1883
12 x 10 ins., Oil on Canvas, Signed.
Full Gallery details are on pp

CHARLESFIELD
ST. BOSWELLS : ROXBURGHSHIRE
TEL. ST. BOSWELLS (0835) 23628/23788

St. Andrews continued

Dauphin Antiques
68 South St. (C. and Mrs. E. Jobson). Est. 1985. Open 9.30—1 and 2—5.30, Mon. 10—1 and 2—5.30, Thurs. 9.30—1. SIZE: Small. *STOCK: Furniture, to Victorian, £50—£3,000; general smalls, £5—£200.* LOC: Near town hall. PARK: Easy. TEL. 75849. VAT: Stan/Spec.

Old St. Andrews Gallery
9 Albany Pl. (Mr and Mrs. D.R. Brown). Est. 1973. CL: 1—2 daily. SIZE: Medium. *STOCK: Golf memorabilia, 19th C, £100—£500; silver and jewellery 19th—20th C, £100—£200; general antiques, from 18th C, £50—£100.* LOC: Main street. PARK: Easy. TEL. 77840. SER: Valuations; restorations (jewellery, silver); buys at auction (golf memorabilia). VAT: Stan.

ST. BOSWELLS (0835)
(Roxburghshire)

Mainhill Gallery
Mainhill. (W. and D. Bruce.) Est. 1981. CL: Sat. p.m. Open 10.30—5.30 (prior 'phone call advisable) and by appointment. SIZE: Medium. *STOCK: Oil paintings and watercolours, 19th—20th C; some prints; £50—£5,000.* Not stocked: Abstract paintings. LOC: ¼ mile south of village, 300yds. from A68. PARK: Easy. TEL. 23788. SER: Valuations; buys at auction. VAT: Spec.

SALTCOATS (0294)
(Ayrshire)
Narducci Antiques   *Mainly Trade and Export*
57 Raise St. (G. Narducci.) Est. 1972. Open 10—1 and 2.30—5.30, or by appointment. *STOCK: General antiques and shipping goods.* TEL: 61687 or 67137. SER: Packing, export.

SELKIRK (0750)
(Selkirkshire)
Heatherlie Antiques
6/8 Heatherlie Terrace. (A.F.D. Scott.) Est. 1979. CL: Sat. p.m. Open 9—12.30 and 1.30—6. SIZE: Medium. *STOCK: Furniture, £50—£100; pottery and porcelain, general antiques, brass, bric-a-brac and copper, £5—£25; all 19th—20th C.* LOC: Leave A7 at Selkirk market place and take Moffat/Peebles road for ½ mile. PARK: Easy. TEL: 20114. VAT: Stan/Spec.

SORBIE, (098 885)
Nr. Newton Stewart
(Wigtownshire)
R.G. Williamson & Co
Old Church. Est. 1965. Open 1—4, mornings by appointment. SIZE: Large. *STOCK: Furniture, from 1700, £50—£100; small items, from 18th C, £5—£25.* LOC: A75. PARK: Easy. TEL: 275; home — same. SER: Valuations; buys at auction. VAT: Stan/Spec.

STIRLING (0786)
(Stirlingshire)
Antiques
31 Baker St. (Mrs. J. Blewitt.) Est. 1945. CL: Wed. Open 10—1 and 2.30—5. SIZE: Medium. *STOCK: General antiques.* LOC: On road to Stirling Castle. PARK: 100yds. TEL: 61976; home — 63611. SER: Valuations.

Stirling continued

Monument Antiques
75 Wallace St. (Mr. and Mrs. G. Oddy.) CL: Wed. Open 11.30—5. *STOCK: General antiques especially clocks.* TEL: 70317.

Elizabeth Paterson Antiques
LAPADA
1A Main St., Bannock Burn. (E. and J. Paterson.) Est. 1976. CL: Sat. and Sun. except by appointment. Open 8.30—5.30. SIZE: Large. *STOCK: Furniture including pine, 1790—1930, £15—£900; Oriental porcelain, 1820—1870, £50—£600.* LOC: A9 Stirling to Edinburgh Rd. PARK: Easy. TEL: 816392; home — 823779. SER: Valuations; restorations (cabinet-work); export and packing worldwide.

STONEHAVEN
(Kincardineshire)
Quair Cottage Antiques
9 Bridgefield. (Mr. and Mrs. Ratcliffe.) Est. 1984. CL: Mon. Open 11—4, Sat. 10.30—4.30. SIZE: Small. *STOCK: Stripped pine, £20—£500; brass and copper, Georgian to mid-1930s, £10—£300; militaria, arms, pre-1939, £1—£1,000.* Not stocked: Large furniture, clocks. LOC: Main road. PARK: Easy. TEL: 63790; home — (033 044) 677.

STRATHBLANE
(Stirlingshire)
Whatnots
16 Milngavie Rd. (F. Bruce.) Est. 1965. *STOCK: Furniture, paintings, jewellery, silver and plate, clocks, small items, shipping goods, horse drawn and old vehicles.* LOC: 25 miles from Stirling and 10 miles from Glasgow. PARK: Easy. TEL: Blanefield (0360) 70310 or Killearn (0360) 50673. VAT: Stan/Spec.

THURSO   (0847)
(Caithness)
The Ships Wheel
2 Traill St. (A.H. and Miss H.E. Munro.) HADA. Est. 1949. CL: Thurs. p.m. Open 9—12.30 and 2—5; Oct.—March. CL: Thurs. Open 10—12.30 and 2—4. SIZE: Medium. *STOCK: Furniture, £50—£1,000; china, glass, £5—£500; all 18th—19th C; prints, 17th—19th C, £15—£150.* Not stocked: Coins, stamps. LOC: A836. PARK: 150yds. rear of shop. TEL: 62485; home — 62018. SER: Valuations. FAIRS: Aberdeen, Perth, Glasgow, Edinburgh, Inverness, Bath. VAT: Stan/Spec.

Thurso continued

Thurso Antiques
Drill Hall, Sinclair St. (G. and J. Atkinson.) HADA. Est. 1971. Open 10—1 and 2—5, Thurs. 10—1. SIZE: Small. *STOCK: Porcelain, 1700—1920, £5—£1,500; jewellery, 1700—1930, £25—£1,000; silver, 1750—1900, £25—£1,000; coins, 1500—1900, £2—£500; paintings, 1750—1920, £25—£1,500; fiddles, 1740—1930, £50—£1,000; medals.* LOC: Near Post Office. PARK: Easy. TEL: 63291; evenings — 66202. SER: Valuations; restorations; cleaning (paintings); silver, jewellery and fiddle repairs.

UPPER LARGO
(Fife)
Largo Antiques (Mrs. S. Bayne)
Main St. Est. 1970. Open 2—5.30 every day in summer, Sat. and Sun. only in winter, other times by appointment. SIZE: Large. *STOCK: 18th—19th C furniture and furnishings, £5—£500; 18th—20th C silver (including Scottish provincial), glass, porcelain, £2—£100; 19th C Scottish pottery, £2—£250.* Not stocked: Arms, books. LOC: A915, 3 miles east of Leven on coast rd. PARK: Easy. TEL: Home — (0333) 320219. SER: Valuations; buys at auction.

WEST LINTON   (0968)
(Peeblesshire)
Alex. M. Frizzell
Castlelaw. Open by appointment. *STOCK: Scottish books, typography and antiquarian.* TEL: 60450.

WHAUPHILL, Nr. Newton Stewart
(Wigtownshire)
Galloway Clocks
Woodlea Croft. (J. Carter.) Est. 1961. CL: Sun. a.m. SIZE: Small. *STOCK: Clocks, 18th—19th C, £50—£1,000; paintings, 19th C, £50—£300.* LOC: A714 to Port William. PARK: Easy. TEL: Kirkinner (098 884) 626; home — same. SER: Valuations; restorations (clocks); buys at auction (clocks).

IS YOUR ENTRY CORRECT?
If there is even the slightest inaccuracy in your entry, *please* let us know before 1st January 1987.
GUIDE TO THE
ANTIQUE SHOPS OF BRITAIN
5 Church Street, Woodbridge, Suffolk.

WALES

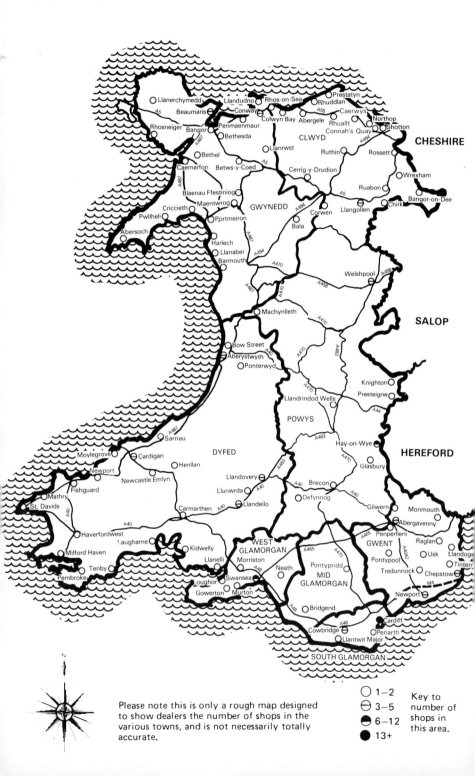

Please note this is only a rough map designed to show dealers the number of shops in the various towns, and is not necessarily totally accurate.

Key to number of shops in this area.

○ 1—2
⊖ 3—5
◑ 6—12
● 13+

WALES

Clwyd

ABERGELE (0745)
G.H. Jenkins and Son
Liverpool House, Market St. Est. 1937. STOCK: Clocks, china, jewellery, pottery, furniture, pictures and prints. TEL: 823170. VAT: Stan.

BANGOR-ON-DEE (0978)
Nr. Wrexham
Mr. Pickwicks
(Mrs. D.P. Whiteley.) Est. 1974. Open Sun. and Wed. 2—5; Thurs 10—12.30 and 2—4.30, Fri. 2—4.30. SIZE: Medium. STOCK: Furniture, £100—£200; silver and plate, £20—£50; jewellery and porcelain, £5—£25; all Victorian. LOC: A525 midway between Wrexham and Whitchurch. PARK: Easy. TEL: Wrexham (0978) 780026; home — Wrexham (0978) 840681.

The Old Smithy Antiques
The Old Smithy, Whitchurch Rd. (R.J.R. Ellington.) Open 9.30—7 including Sun. and Bank Holidays or by appointment in evenings. SIZE: Medium. STOCK: Period oak furniture, £100—£350; Victorian and Edwardian furniture, £25—£250; pottery, brass, copper, Staffordshire ware, glass, pictures and prints, stripped pine furniture, £5—£100; all 18th—20th C. LOC: On A525 in centre of village. PARK: Easy. TEL: 780620. SER: Valuations; restorations (furniture, pictures). FAIRS: Chester, Stafford, Nantwich.

CAERWYS, Nr. Mold (0352)
Tom Lloyd-Roberts
Old Court House. Est. 1967. STOCK: Antiquarian books, £2—£2,000. TEL: 720276.

CERRIG-Y-DRUDION (049 082)
Nr. Corwen
M. and A. Main
The Old Smithy. Resident. Open 8—4.30, Sat. 8—1 or by appointment. SIZE: Large. STOCK: Period doors, fire surrounds, balustrades, panelling, stained glass and other architectural items. LOC: Centre of village. PARK: Easy. TEL: 491. VAT: Stan.

CHIRK (0691)
Seventh Heaven
Chirk Mill. (Mr. and Mrs. J.J. Butler.) Est. 1971. Open 9—1 and 2—5, Sat. 10—1 and 2—5, Sun. 10—1 and 2—4.30. SIZE: Large. STOCK: Brass and iron bedsteads, 19th C, £85—£1,000. LOC: On A5 as it crosses Welsh border. PARK: Easy. TEL: 777622 or 773563. VAT: Stan.

COLWYN BAY (0492)
North Wales Antiques —
Colwyn Bay LAPADA
56-58 Abergele Rd. (F. Robinson.) Est. 1971. Open 9—5. SIZE: Large warehouse. STOCK: Shipping items, Victorian, early oak, mahogany and pine. LOC: On A55. PARK: Easy. TEL: 30521 or 516375. VAT: Stan.

CONNAH'S QUAY
Arnold Matthews Antiques Ltd.
Spring St. Open 9—5. SIZE: Warehouse. STOCK: Georgian, Victorian and Edwardian furniture. LOC: On A548, 1½ miles from Queensferry. TEL: Deeside (0244) 813629; evenings — Deeside (0244) 814989. SER: Containers, shipping, packing, courier, export. VAT: Stan.

CORWEN (0490)
Mrs. H. Kewley
Dee Valley Antiques
Bryn Meirion, Carrog Rd. Open by appointment. STOCK: Staffordshire, blue and white, copper and brass, small furniture. TEL: 2213. FAIRS: Portmeirion.

LLANGOLLEN (0978)
M. Gallagher (Antiques)
Hall St. Open by appointment. STOCK: General antiques. TEL: 860655.

J. and R. Langford
12 Bridge St. (P. and M. Silverston.) Est. 1960. CL: Thurs. p.m. and 1—2 daily. SIZE: Medium. STOCK: Furniture, £100—£1,000; pottery and porcelain, £50—£200; silver, general antiques, clocks, brass and paintings, £20—£400; all 18th—19th C. LOC: Turn right at Royal Hotel, shop on right. PARK: Easy. TEL: 860182; home — 860493. SER: Valuations. VAT: Stan/Spec.

Oak Chest Jewellers
1 Oak St. Est. 1950. STOCK: Victorian jewellery and silver. TEL: 860095. VAT: Stan.

Llangollen continued

Passers Buy (Marie Evans)
10 Chapel St. (Mrs. M. Evans.) Est. 1970. Open 10—5, Sun. by appointment. SIZE: Medium. STOCK: Pottery and porcelain, to £200; small furniture, copper and brass. LOC: Just off A5. Junction of Chapel St. and Oak St. PARK: Easy. TEL: 860861. FAIRS: Portmeirion Autumn.

Village Pine
15 Bridge St. (Mrs. J. Glenie.) Est. 1981. CL: Thurs. Open 10—5.30, Sun. by appointment. SIZE: Medium. STOCK: Pine furniture, pre-1901, £25—£400; country items, earthenware, frames, jelly moulds, Victorian, £10—£35; country kitchen items, £5—£25. LOC: Turn right in town centre towards Ruthin, turn 2nd right. PARK: Nearby. TEL: 861105; home — same.

NORTHOP, Nr. Mold (035 286)
James H. Morris and Co.
Old Village School, The Green. Appointment advisable. STOCK: Furniture, clocks. LOC: A55. TEL: 508. SER: Valuations.

PRESTATYN (074 56)
The Antique Shop
126 High St. (R. Conway.) Est. 1963. CL: Thurs. p.m. Open 10—5. STOCK: General antiques, furniture, clocks, porcelain, pottery, trade goods. TEL: 3369; home — 4435. VAT: Stan.

RHOS-ON-SEA
Dolwen Antiques
11 Everard Rd. (P.S. Roberts.) Open 10—4.30. STOCK: Furniture, porcelain vases and figures, brass, copper, oil lamps, clocks. TEL: Colwyn Bay (0492) 44728; home — Colwyn Bay (0492) 518417. VAT: Stan/Spec.

Shelagh Hyde
11 Rhos Rd. Est. 1960. CL: Wed. p.m. Open 9.30—5.30. STOCK: Trade selection of general antiques; furniture, porcelain, glass. TEL: Colwyn Bay (0492) 48879.

RHUALLT, Nr. St. Asaph
John Trefor Antiques
Rhuallt Hall Farm. Est. 1967. Open 9—6, and trade any time by appointment. SIZE: Large. STOCK: Oak, walnut and mahogany furniture and unstripped pine, £15—£2,000; longcase clocks, £250—£2,500; Victoriana, metalware, paintings, £10—£1,000; shipping goods. Not stocked: Jewellery, cards and medals. LOC: On A55, 7 miles west of Holywell, on right next to village shop. PARK: Easy. TEL: St. Asaph (0745) 583604. VAT: Stan/Spec.

RHUDDLAN (0745)
Rhuddlan Antiques
High St. (J. Griffiths.) CL: Mon. Open 10—4. SIZE: Medium. STOCK: General antiques, furniture, silver, brass, collectables, £5—£500. LOC: 3 miles from Rhyl towards Denbigh. TEL: 590705; home — Prestatyn (074 56) 6222.

ROSSETT, Nr. Wrexham (0244)
Times Past Antiques
Rossett Cottage. (Mrs. I.D. Peckham.) Est. 1953. Open every day. SIZE: Medium. STOCK: Small general antiques, paintings, bric-a-brac. Not stocked: Guns, coins. LOC: 4 miles from Chester, on Chester — Wrexham Rd. PARK: Own. TEL: 570516.

RUABON, Nr. Wrexham (0978)
Kings Head Antiques
Providence Chapel, Tan-y-lan. (P. Grassie.) Est. 1972. Open 8—6. STOCK: Pine shipping goods, oak. TEL: 824202.

Prospect Antiques
10 High St. (J.C. Hardy.) Est. 1974. Open 10—6. STOCK: Furniture, including pine, general antiques, some shipping goods. LOC: Next to Wynnstay Hotel. PARK: Easy. Next to shop. TEL: 820792.

RUTHIN (082 42)
Northeast Wales Antiques
LAPADA
15 Well St. (H.J. and Mrs. I.F. Northeast). Est. 1975. Open 9.30—5.30. SIZE: Small. STOCK: Furniture, 18th to early 20th C, £100—£3,000; oil paintings, 19th—20th C, £100—£1,500; silver, 18th—20th C, £25—£750. LOC: In main street. PARK: Nearby. TEL: 2782; home — 2154. SER: Restorations (furniture, silver, oil paintings); upholstery. FAIRS: Castle. VAT: Stan/Spec.

Old Tyme Antiques
21 Clwyd St. (G. and J. Vaughan.) CL: Thurs. p.m. Open 10—5. STOCK: Wall and mantel clocks; British, European and Oriental porcelain, Imari ware, cranberry, gaudy Welsh china, brass, silver, jewellery, linen, postcards, lace and bric-a-brac. LOC: 100yds. from town square. PARK: Nearby. TEL: Home — 2902. VAT: Stan.

SHOTTON

Angharad's Antiques
106 Chester Rd. West. (Mrs. J. Buckley.) Est. 1972. CL: Mon. and Wed. Open 10−5. SIZE: Small. *STOCK: Weapons, vintage air guns, model cannon, keys and collectors' items; portrait miniatures, £100−£500; small furniture, 19th C, £10−£100; brass, china, silver, bric-a-brac, 19th C, £5−£100.* Not stocked: Large furniture. LOC: A548, 1 mile from Queensferry roundabout. PARK: Easy. TEL: Deeside (0244) 812240.

WREXHAM   (0978)

Smith Antiques
2 New Rd., Rhosddu. (Mrs. J. Price.) *STOCK: Collectors and shipping items, needlework, 19th C furniture.* SER: Clock repairs; buys at auction. VAT: Stan.

Dyfed

ABERYSTWYTH   (0970)

Karen Axford
White Horse Corner, Terrace Rd. CL: Wed. p.m. Open 10.30−1 and 2.30−5. *STOCK: Jewellery, maps, prints, small furniture.* TEL: 4141.

The Furniture Cave
33 Cambrian St. (S. Bingley and P. David.) Est. 1975. Open 9−5, Wed. 9−4, Sat. 10−4. *STOCK: Pine, 1860-1920, £100−£200; general antiques, Victorian and Edwardian, £30−£300; small items, 19th C, £10−£50.* LOC: First right off Terrace Rd., at railway station end. PARK: Nearby. TEL: 611234. SER: Restorations. VAT: Stan/Spec.

Howards of Aberystwyth LAPADA
10 Alexandra Rd. Open 10−5.30. *STOCK: Furniture, jewellery, Welsh and copper lustre pottery, Staffordshire, blue and white, cranberry glass, prints and maps of Cardiganshire, collectables.* TEL: 4973.

BOW STREET

Garn House Antiques
Garn House. (Mrs. M. Hagarty.) Est. 1969. Open six days a week, but to the Trade any time. *STOCK: General antiques, furniture, Victoriana, copper, brass, porcelain, glass, collectors' items and Victorian jewellery.* TEL: Aberystwyth (0970) 828562 and 828885.

CARDIGAN   (0239)

Bayvil House Antiques
39 High St. (R.L.V. and G.V. Smith.) Est. 1940. CL: Wed. p.m. Open 9−5.30. *STOCK: Furniture, especially oak and mahogany, 18th−19th C; pottery, porcelain, copper and brass.* LOC: First shop on right when entering town from river bridge. TEL: 612654. VAT: Stan/Spec.

Cardigan Book Centre
1 Royal Oak, Quay St. (F. Mason.) Open by appointment. *STOCK: Antiquarian books, maps and prints especially theology, childrens, Welsh and British history.* TEL: 612704.

Pantywylan Antiques
By the Bridge. (H.G. Stubbs.) Est. 1969. Open daily 10−5. *STOCK: General antiques, collectors' items.* TEL: 613332; home − Crosswell (023 979) 606. VAT: Stan/Spec.

CARMARTHEN   (0267)

Bridgeview Antiques
Penfarn. *STOCK: Furniture, pine, oak, mahogany and shipping, collectables.* TEL: 231250.

Cwmgwili Mill
Bronwydd Arms. (R.C. Eden.) Est. 1950. Open 9−1 and 2−6, Sat. 9−1, Sun. by appointment. SIZE: Large. *STOCK: Furniture, oak, mahogany and country including dressers, coffers, long tables, and court cupboards, 17th−18th C, £50−£1,000.* PARK: Easy. TEL: 231500; home − Nantgaredig (026 788) 549. VAT: Spec.

FISHGUARD   (0348)

Hermitage Antiquities
10 West St. (J.B. Thomas.) Est. 1976. CL: Wed. and Sat. p.m. Open 9.30−1 and 2−5.30. SIZE: Small. *STOCK: Arms, armour and militaria − full suits of armour, 16th−17th C; military long-guns, pistols, swords; cased pistol sets, military headgear, ethnographica, 16th−19th C, £50−£5,000.* LOC: 50yds on right after leaving Square on Harbour road (West St.) PARK: 300yds. TEL: 873037; home − 872322. SER: Valuations; restorations (arms and armour, inlay work on wheel locks, flintlock parts re-built, wordwork repairs); buys at auction (arms and armour). VAT: Spec.

HAVERFORDWEST   (0437)

Gerald Oliver Antiques
14 Albany Terrace, St. Thomas Green. Est. 1957. CL: Thurs. p.m. Open 9.30−1 and 2−5. SIZE: Small. *STOCK: Furniture, pre-1881, £5−£2,000; ceramics, metalwork, small silver, from £5; unusual and decorative antiques, some shipping goods.* LOC: Via by-pass and up Merlins Hill to St. Thomas Green. PARK: Easy. TEL: 2794. SER: Valuations. VAT: Spec.

HENLLAN, Nr. Newcastle Emlyn

Richard Lloyd
Trade Only
Dolhaidd Mansion. Est. 1969. Open 9—6. SIZE: Large. *STOCK: Country furniture, shipping goods, general antiques, bygones.* LOC: On A484, 2 miles Newcastle Emlyn. TEL: Velindre (0559) 370791. VAT: Stan/Spec.

Tortoiseshell Antiques
Trebedw Guest House. (Mrs. P. Taylor.) Open every day. *STOCK: Carved ivory, coral, Georgian jewellery, objets d'art, fans, textiles and antiquities, lustre jugs, Welsh items.* TEL: Velindre (0559) 370943.

KIDWELLY (0554)

Country Antiques LAPADA
The Bridge and Old Castle Mill. (R. and L. Bebb.) CL: Mon. Open 10.15—5.15, or by appointment. SIZE: Large. *STOCK: Stripped pine, Welsh oak, Victorian and shipping furniture; interior decorators' items; china, brass and bygones.* Not stocked: Militaria. LOC: On A484. PARK: Easy. TEL: 890534. SER: Valuations. VAT: Stan/Spec.

LAUGHARNE (099 421)

Neil Speed Antiques
The Strand. Est. 1975. Open most days 10.30—5.30 in summer. Fri. and Sat. 10.30—5 in winter or by appointment. *STOCK: General antiques, country furniture.* TEL: 412.

LLANDEILO (0558)

Jim and Pat Ash
The Warehouse, 5 Station Rd. Est. 1977. Open 9.30—5. SIZE: Large. *STOCK: Furniture, oak, pine and mahogany, 18th—19th C; unusual and collectors' items; shipping furniture.* LOC: 50yds. off A40. PARK: Easy. TEL: 823726; home — Llandybie (0269) 850119. SER: Valuations; buys at auction. VAT: Stan/Spec.

Fine Feathers Antiques
7 King St. (P. and M. Halfpenny.) Est. 1967. CL: Thurs. and Sat. p.m. Open 10—1 and 2—5. SIZE: Small. *STOCK: Brass and copper, £20—£100; Victorian oil lamps, £40—£100, both 19th C; small furniture, small silver and clocks.* LOC: Opposite church. PARK; Easy. TEL: Home — Llandybie (0269) 850561.

Jones Antiques
1 Quay St. (Mrs. J.H. Jones.) Est. 1965. Always open. *STOCK: Period oak, trade and shipping items, longcase clocks.* TEL: 822748.

Llandeilo continued

Glyn Jones Antiques
Caebach Villa, Penybanc. Est. 1979. Open Tues.—Sun. 9 a.m.—10 p.m., Mon. 2—10, Mon. a.m. by appointment. SIZE: Medium. *STOCK: Pine and shipping furniture, from 19th C, £5—£1,000; oak furniture, from 18th C, £5—£5,000.* LOC: Off A40. PARK: Easy. TEL: 822043; home — same. SER: Restorations; stripping (pine); container packing; buys at auction (pine furniture).

LLANDOVERY (0550)

The Curiosity Shop
High St. (J.B. Luffman and Sons.) Est. 1959. Open 9.30—5, Sun. 10—4. SIZE: Medium. *STOCK: Country furniture, clocks, paintings, militaria, £5—£7,000.* LOC: A40 between Brecon and Llandeilo. PARK: Easy. TEL: 20390. SER: Valuations; buys at auction (militaria and paintings). VAT: Spec.

Dyfri Antiques
11 High St. (B. Leach.) Est. 1968. SIZE: Small. *STOCK: Small general antiques, china, pottery, collectors' items, old dolls.* TEL: 20602.

Ovell Prints Ltd.
1 Kings Rd. Open 9—5. *STOCK: Antiquarian maps and prints.* TEL: 20928, 21013.

LLANELLI (0554)

Alice's Antiques
24 Upper Park St. (Mrs. A. Davies.) Est. 1940. CL: Tues. p.m. Open 10—1 and 2—6. SIZE: Small. *STOCK: General antiques, 1850—1950, £5—£50; paintings, 1700, silver, Georgian and Victorian, china, metalware.* LOC: On main road in town centre. PARK: At rear. TEL: 773045. SER: Valuations; buys at auction. VAT: Stan.

LLANWRDA

Maclean Antiques
Tiradda, Llansadwrn. (D.J. Thorpe.) Resident. Est. 1972. Open 9.30—6.00. *STOCK: Period oak, pine and country furniture, 18th—19th C.* TEL: Llangadog (0550) 777509.

MATHRY

Cartrefle Antiques
(M. Hughes and Y. Chesters.) Open in summer 10.30—5.30; in winter Tues.—Sat. 10.30—4, evenings by appointment. *STOCK: General antiques especially jewellery.* PARK: Easy. TEL: Croesgoch (03483) 591.

MILFORD HAVEN (06462)

Milford Haven Antiques
Robert St. Est. 1968. Open 9.30—5.30. *STOCK: General antiques.* TEL: 2152.

MOYLEGROVE   **(023 986)**
Nr. Cardigan
Dibley Antiques
'Ffynnon Watty'. (J. and P. Dibley.) Est.
1971. Open by appointment only. *STOCK:
Silver, porcelain, pottery, 18th—19th C,
£5—£500.* LOC: Cardigan—Fishguard road,
turn right and take St. Dogmaels road, sign-
posted from St. Dogmaels (4 miles). PARK:
Easy. TEL: 668; home — same. SER:
Valuations.

NEWCASTLE EMLYN   **(0239)**
Castle Antiques
Sycamore St. (A. and E. Jones.) Est. 1962.
CL: Wed. p.m. and Sun. except by appoint-
ment. Prior 'phone call always advisable. SIZE:
Large. *STOCK: General antiques, furniture,
Welsh oak, stripped pine and mahogany;
clocks, oil lamps.* PARK: Easy. TEL: 710456.
VAT: Stan.

NEWPORT   **(0239)**
Newport Antiques
Llysmeddyg, East St. (R.W. and A. Atkinson.)
Est. 1970. *STOCK: Small furniture, pine,
silver, plate, brass, copper, porcelain and
jewellery.* LOC: A487. PARK: Easy. TEL:
820351.

PEMBROKE   **(0646)**
Northgate Antiques   **LAPADA**
10 Northgate St. (J.P. and J. Howells.) Est.
1956. CL: Wed. p.m. Open 10—5. *STOCK:
Furniture, oak, mahogany, 18th—20th C;
general antiques, copper, brass, china and
jewellery.* TEL: 684416; home — Lamphey
(0646) 672388. VAT: Stan.

PONTERWYD,   **(097 085)**
Nr. Aberystwyth
Doggie Hubbard's Bookshop
Ffynnon Cadno. (C.L.B. Hubbard.) ABA. Est.
1946. Open 10—5, Sun. by appointment.
SIZE: Medium. *STOCK: Rare books on dogs,
16th—19th C, £50—£500; scarce books on
dogs, 19th—20th C, £25—£100; other books
on dogs, 20th C, £5—£25.* LOC: ½ mile from
Ponterwyd westwards on A44. PARK: Easy.
TEL: 224; home — same. SER: Valuations;
buys at auction (rare dog books). FAIRS: New
York and Boston.

ST. DAVID'S   **(0437)**
Ramsey Island Shop
28 High St. (J.G. and A. Freeman.) Open
10—1 May—Sept. otherwise by appointment.
STOCK: Maps, prints. TEL: 720648.

SARNAU, Nr. Llandysul
Fyfnnon Las
(P. and G. Palmer). Est. 1971. Open at any time, prior 'phone call advisable. SIZE: Small. STOCK: Hand painted furniture, 19th to early 20th C, £50—£250; stripped pine and walnut, £65—£600; kitchenalia, £5—£25. LOC: Off A487 9 miles north of Cardigan, down track. PARK: Easy. TEL: (023978) 648; home — same.

TENBY (0834)
Audrey Bull
15 Upper Frog St. CL: Wed. Open 10—5. STOCK: Period and Welsh country furniture, general antiques, especially jewellery and silver. TEL: 3114; home — Saundersfoot (0834) 813425. VAT: Spec.

Mid. Glamorgan

BRIDGEND
Bridgend Antiques
Dunraven House, Riverside Buildings. (A. and M. Williams.) Open 9—5. STOCK: General antiques, Victoriana and shipping goods. TEL: 2468 and 2056.

PONTYPRIDD (0443)
P.J. Jones
Plas-y-Derwyn, 31 Tyfica Rd., Graigwen. Open 9—6.30, Sat. 9—12. STOCK: Shipping goods. TEL: 406563 or 401486. SER: Container packing and shipping.

South Glamorgan

CARDIFF (0222)
Adam Antiques
12 Sneyd St. (Mr. and Mrs. R. Davies.) Est. 1970. Open 9.30—6, Sat. 10—1. SIZE: Medium. STOCK: Furniture, 17th—19th C, £20—£1,000; silver and plate, 18th—19th C, £5—£500; copper, brass, clocks, 18th—19th C. LOC: From Cardiff Castle towards Cowbridge through traffic lights and first right after St. Davids Hospital. PARK: Easy. TEL: 40022; home — Caerphilly (0222) 883415. SER: Valuations; restorations (furniture); buys at auction. VAT: Stan/Spec.

Alice Lighting and Antiques
3 Wellfield Rd. (Mrs. A. Lewith.) Est. 1968. CL: Wed. p.m. Open 9—5.30. STOCK: Victorian and period furniture and lighting. TEL: 499156. VAT: Stan.

Cardiff continued

Antiques Unlimited
34 Church Rd., Whitchurch. (B. Williams.) Est. 1958. Open by appointment only. SIZE: Small. STOCK: Jewellery, silver, small antiques. TEL: 693748. SER: Valuations. FAIRS: Cardiff, Bristol.

Archway Antiques
182 Kings Rd. (G. Rich.) Open 10.30—5.30. STOCK: General antiques including country items. TEL: 388397; evenings Cowbridge (044 63) 2746.

Arlington Galleries Ltd.
253 Cyncoed Rd. Est. 1965. Open by appointment only. STOCK: Paintings. TEL: 752863. SER: Restorations (pictures). VAT: Stan/Spec.

Broadway Antiques   LAPADA
185—187 Broadway, Roath. (S. Hughes.) STOCK: Furniture, Georgian and Victorian; Welsh oak, longcase clocks, Victoriana, glass, metalware, Oriental and English porcelain, paintings, silver. TEL: 484470.

A. Burge Antiques
54 Crwys Rd. CL: Wed. Open 9—5.30. STOCK: General antiques including clocks. TEL: 383268.

Charlotte's Wholesale Antiques
129 Woodville Rd., Cathays. (P.G. Cason.) Open 9.30—4. SIZE: Large and warehouse. STOCK: Shipping goods, general antiques, period furniture. TEL: 759809, 24632, 627526.

Cottage Antiques   LAPADA
9 Kings Road, Canton. (P. Grimwade.) Est. 1965.Open 9—1 and 2—5. Wed. and Sat. p.m. by appointment only. SIZE: Medium. STOCK: Furniture, paintings, 1620—1940, £5—£2,000, jewellery, silver, small items. LOC: Second right after Cardiff castle. PARK: Easy. TEL: 24484; home — 565378. SER: Valuations. VAT: Stan.

W.H. Douglas   Trade Only
161 Cowbridge Rd. East. STOCK: General antiques, Victoriana, trade and shipping goods. TEL: 24861.

Heritage Antiques and Stripped Pine
83 Pontcanna St. (D. Gluck.) Est. 1974. Open 9—6. SIZE: Medium. STOCK: Pine and general antiques, 19th C, £50—£500. LOC: 1st turning by shops at top end of Cathedral Rd. PARK: Easy. TEL: 390097. SER: Restorations (mainly pine). FAIRS: Sophia Gardens, Cardiff. VAT: Stan.

Jacobs Antique Market
West Canal Wharf. Open Thurs. and Sat. 9.30—5. SIZE: Large. There are 55 dealers at this market selling general antiques, stripped pine and furniture. LOC: 2 mins. from main railway and bus stations. PARK: 100yds. TEL: Thurs. and Sat. only 382871. SER: Valuations; restorations; buys at auction.

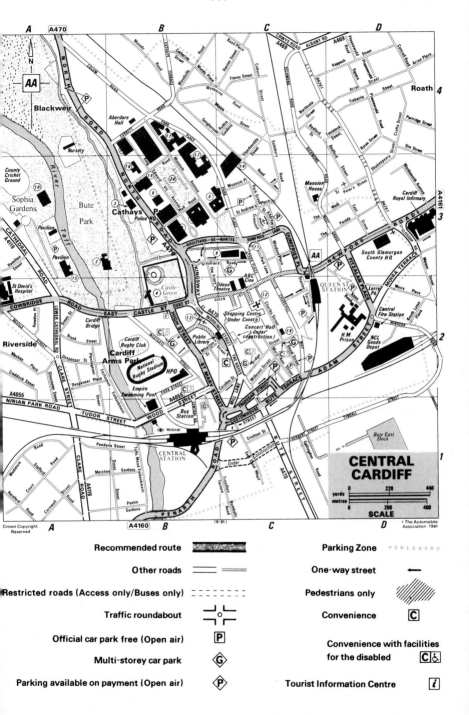

CENTRAL CARDIFF

yards 0   220   440
metres 0   200   400
SCALE

© The Automobile
Association 1981

Recommended route		
Other roads		
Restricted roads (Access only/Buses only)		
Traffic roundabout		
Official car park free (Open air)	P	
Multi-storey car park	Ⓖ	
Parking available on payment (Open air)	Ⓟ	
Parking Zone		
One-way street		
Pedestrians only		
Convenience	Ⓒ	
Convenience with facilities for the disabled	Ⓒ♿	
Tourist Information Centre	ⓘ	

Cardiff continued

Kings Antiques
Llandaff Rd. (P.W. Lichtenberg.) Open by appointment. STOCK: General antiques for trade and shipping. TEL: Home — 382110.

The Light Brigade and Penylan Antiques
110 Albany Rd. (R. and J. Stockton.) STOCK: General antiques especially lighting items, mainly Victorian and Edwardian. LOC: 5 minutes from Cardiff centre. TEL: 483927; home — 485321. VAT: Stan.

Llanishen Antiques
26 Crwys Rd., Cathays. (Mrs. J. Boalch.) CL: Wed. except by appointment. Open 10.30 — 4.30. STOCK: Furniture, silver, china, glass, bric-a-brac. TEL: 397244.

Llewelyn Antiques
64 Monthermer Rd., Cathays. Est. 1981. STOCK: General antiques and bric-a-brac. TEL: 43367.

Manor House Fine Arts
75 Pontcanna St., Pontcanna. (S.K. Denley-Hill.) Est. 1976. CL: Mon., Wed. and Sun. except by appointment. Open 10.30 — 5.30. SIZE: Medium. STOCK: Watercolours, oil paintings and prints, 1780-1960, £10 — £1,000; general antiques, 19th C, art nouveau and art deco, £5 — £800. LOC: Pontcanna St. is at north end of Cathedral Rd. PARK: Easy. TEL: 27787. SER: Valuations; restorations; framing and mounting; buys at auction. VAT: Stan/Spec.

Miles Antiques
151 Albany Rd. (Mrs. W. Miles.) Open 9 — 1 and 2 — 5, Wed. 9 — 1. STOCK: General antiques including furniture. TEL: 493485; evenings — 626959.

John Owen Gallery
20 Salisbury Rd. Est. 1970. Open 10 — 6, Sat. 10 — 5. STOCK: Oils and watercolours, 18th — 20th C. TEL: 45868. SER: Restorations; framing.

J. Parker
150 Penylan Rd. Est. 1954. Open by appointment. STOCK: Antiquarian books, pre-1850. Not stocked: Theology books. LOC: Near Roath Park. PARK: Lower down road. TEL: 486678. SER: Valuations.

Peter Philp
77 Kimberley Rd., Pen-y-lan. (P.M. and D.A. Philp.) Resident. Est. 1880. Books on furniture and pottery. Open preferably by appointment. SIZE: Medium. STOCK: English and Continental furniture, £50 — £3,000; metalware and unusual items, £10 — £250; all 1600 — 1850; pottery, porcelain, paintings, prints, objets d'art, 1700 — 1900, £10 — £500. Not stocked: Jewellery, coins, books. PARK: Easy. TEL: 493826. VAT: Stan/Spec.

Cardiff continued

San Domenico Stringed Instruments
175 Kings Rd., Canton. (H. Morgan.) CL: Sat. p.m. Open 10 — 1 and 2 — 5.30. SIZE: Small. STOCK: Violins, violas, cellos and bows, mainly 18th — 19th C, £100 — £5,000 +. LOC: Off Cathedral Rd. or Cowbridge Rd. PARK: Easy. TEL: 35881; home — 777156. SER: Valuations; restorations; buys at auction. VAT: Stan/Spec.

Time on your Hands
The Old Post Office, Penywain Rd., Roath Park. (Capt. and Mrs A.C. Enos). Est. 1983. CL: Mon. and Wed. Open 10 — 3. SIZE: Small. STOCK: Longcase clocks, 19th C, £500 — £1,500; wall and mantel clocks, 19th — 20th C, £50 — £500; Victoriana. LOC: Parallel to Ninian Rd. PARK: Easy. TEL: 496715; home (0446) 730891. SER: Valuations; restorations. VAT: Stan.

Paul Wanger Antiques
2d Wellfield Rd. Est. 1968. CL: Wed. p.m. Open 10 — 5. STOCK: Furniture, 18th — 19th C; paintings, china, glass, copper, brass, small silver. TEL: Home — 485446.

COWBRIDGE (044 63)
Brenin Porcelain and Pottery
Old Wool Barn, Verity's Court. (Mrs. S. M. King.) Est. 1984. Open Thurs., Fri. and Sat. p.m. or by appointment. SIZE: Small. STOCK: Porcelain and pottery, especially Welsh, 18th — 19th C. LOC: Off A48. PARK: 200 yds. TEL: 3893; home — (0443) 223553. FAIRS: Antiques in Britain.

Jenny Wren Antiques
23 High St. (Mrs. A. Roberts.) Est. 1976. CL: Wed. p.m. Open 10 — 1 and 2 — 5.30. SIZE: Medium. STOCK: Furniture, copper and brass, silver, jewellery, all Georgian and Victorian. LOC: Off A48. PARK: 50yds. TEL: 4165; home — 2118. VAT: Stan/Spec.

Renaissance Antiques
Old Wool Barn, Verity's Court. (R. and J. Barnicott). Est. 1984. CL: Wed. Open 10.30 — 1 and 2 — 5, other times by appointment. SIZE: Small. STOCK: Small furniture, Georgian, Victorian and Edwardian, £50 — £1,500; brass, copper, plate, decorative ceramics, objets d'art, 18th to 20th C, £5 — £200. Not stocked: Coins, militaria, reproductions. LOC: Down cobbled alley off main street. PARK: 200 yards. TEL: Home — 4656.

LLANTWIT MAJOR (044 65)
Clover Antiques
9 Church St. Est. 1966. Open 10 — 5. STOCK: Furniture, general antiques, silver, jewellery. PARK: Nearby. TEL: 6667; home — Rhoose (0446) 710662.

PENARTH (0222)

Grove Antiques
8 Grove Pl. (S. Wilson.) Open 10—5.30.
STOCK: General antiques. PARK: Easy. TEL:
709554.

West Glamorgan

GOWERTON (0792)

Yates Antiques
2 Brynmor Rd. (R. Yates.) Est. 1965. Open
9.30—5.30, Sat. p.m. and Sun. by appointment. SIZE: Large. STOCK: Furniture, mahogany and inlaid, sets of chairs, bookcases and
clocks, Victorian, from £50; oak furniture,
dressers and presses, 18th C, £500—£1,000;
shipping goods, Edwardian, from £25. TEL:
Swansea (0792) 875022; home — Swansea
(0792) 299924. VAT: Stan.

LOUGHOR, Nr. Gorsienon

John Carpenter
169 Glebe Rd. Est. 1973. SIZE: Large.
STOCK: Musical instruments, pianos, furniture, small items. LOC: Off M4 through
Gorsienon. PARK: Easy. TEL: 892141; home
— same. SER: Buys at auction.

MORRISTON, Nr. Swansea

Aaron Antiques
62-66 Martin St. (A. Davies.) Est. 1971. Open
10—5. STOCK: Furniture, longcase clocks,
shipping goods. TEL: Swansea (0792) 73271;
home — Swansea (0792) 53500. VAT: Stan.

MURTON, Nr. Swansea

West Wales Antiques   LAPADA
18 Manselfield Rd. (W.H. and J.I. Davies.) Est.
1956. Open 10—1 and 2—5. STOCK: Porcelain, 18th C, £20—£800; Welsh porcelain,
1814-1820, £20—£1,000; dolls, 1880—
1920; 18th—19th C furniture, silver, pottery,
glass, jewellery and collectors' items. LOC:
M4—A4067—B4436, entrance to Gower
Peninsula. TEL: Bishopston (044 128) 4318;
home — Neath (0639) 4379. VAT: Stan/
Spec.

NEATH (0639)

Peter R. George
64 Briton Ferry Rd. CL: Sat. Open 2—5.
STOCK: 17th—19th C furniture; porcelain,
Victorian jewellery. TEL: 4677.

SWANSEA (0792)

Antique Centre
21 Oxford St. Open 10—5 although dealers'
times vary. TEL: 466854. Below are listed
some of the 18 dealers at this centre:

Antiques
(C.G. Roberts.) Furniture, china and silver.
TEL: 466840.

John Carpenter
Musical instruments, pianos, furniture and
small items. TEL: 892141.

Collections
(Mrs. P. Elson.) General antiques —
jewellery, linen, silver, porcelain and glass,
mainly 19th—20th C, £5—£250. TEL:
Home — Gower (0792) 390332 and
390333.

Pauline Dicker
General antiques, 1850—1950, £5—£50.
TEL: Home — (0792) 66363.

Goldcraft
(C. and W. Davies.) Jewellery, coins and
general antiques.

Magpie Antiques
(H. and M. Hallesy.) Doulton figurines,
character jugs and series ware £10—£500;
general including Swansea pottery and
porcelain, small furniture. TEL: Home —
864514.

Past Times
(G. Richards.) Porcelain, china, postcards,
coins and curios, jewellery, 19th—20th C,
£5—£100. TEL: Home — 466840.

Timberstrip
(J. McCarthy.) Stripped and polished pine
furniture, 19th to early 20th C, £20—
£500. TEL: 465240.

Philip Davies
Swansea Antiques Centre, 21 Walter Rd.
STOCK: British watercolours and oil paintings,
1850—1950, £50—£1,500. TEL: 61766
(24hrs). SER: Valuations; restorations (paintings and frames).

Dylan's Bookshop
Salubrious Passage. (J.M. Towns.) Open
10—5. STOCK: Antiquarian books on Welsh
history and topography, Anglo/Welsh literature and general books. TEL: 55255.

Elizabeth Hughes Antiques
76 St. Helens Rd. Est. 1977. CL: Sat. p.m.
Open 10—5. STOCK: Pine and oak furniture,
wooden and marble mantels, cast-iron grates,
general antiques. TEL: 54697, home —
69899.

Roger Hughes Antique Gallery
13 Dillwyn St. CL: Thurs. Open 9.30—4.30.
STOCK: Period furniture, paintings, porcelain,
pewter, objets d'art. TEL: 52584. VAT: Stan/
Spec.

Swansea continued

Anne and Colin Hulbert   Trade Only
(Antiques and Firearms)
17 Approach Rd., Manselton. Est. 1962. CL: Sun. p.m. SIZE: Small. *STOCK: Shipping goods and general antiques.* PARK: Easy. TEL: 53818; home — same. SER: Valuations; buys at auction (furniture).

The Old Clock Shop
49 St. Helen's Rd. (L. Arnold.) Est. 1976. CL: Sat. Open 10—5. *STOCK: Clocks and general antiques.* TEL: 53334.

Swansea Antique Centre
21 Walters Rd. Open 9—5.30. There are 8 dealers at this centre selling *a wide range of general antiques.* TEL: 51446.

Swansea County and W.P. Ltd.
49 St. Helens Rd. Est. 1960. Open 10—5. *STOCK: Coins, medals; clocks, especially carriage, longcase and wall.* LOC: Town centre. TEL: 53334. SER: Antique auctioneers and valuers. VAT: Stan.

Thicke Galleries, Swansea LAPADA
Trade Only
26 St. Andrews Close, Mayals. (T.G. Thicke.) Est. 1981. Open by appointment, preferably Mon., Tues. or Wed. SIZE: Small. *STOCK: Oils and watercolours, 19th C, to £500; drawings, engravings and etchings, some early oils and watercolours, to £1,500.* LOC: Coast road to West Swansea. PARK: Easy. TEL: 401656; home — same. SER: Valuations; restorations (oils and watercolours); buys at auction (oils and watercolours). FAIRS: British International, Birmingham; Olympia, Castle. VAT: Spec.

Gwent

ABERGAVENNY   (0873)

Brecon Road Antiques
34 Brecon Rd. (M., H., P., S. and P. Morris.) CL: Thurs. p.m. Open 10—5 or by appointment. *STOCK: Period furniture, glass, militaria, shipping goods and bric-a-brac.* TEL: Crickhowell (0873) 810246.

Henry H. Close
36 Cross St. (Mr. and Mrs. H. Close.) Est. 1968. Open 9—5, and by appointment. *STOCK: 18th—19th C furniture, porcelain, pottery, glass, brass, copper, jewellery, silver, prints.* TEL: 3583. VAT: Stan/Spec.

H.K. Lockyer
Priory Bookshop, Milford House, Monk St. Open 9.30—5.30. *STOCK: Pottery, porcelain, silver, antiquarian books.* PARK: Opposite. TEL: 5825. VAT: Stan/Spec.

Abergavenny continued

Tower Antiques
11 Market St. (P. and A. Long.) Est. 1964. CL: Thurs. p.m. *STOCK: General antiques especially unusual items; books, paintings, porcelain, furniture.* LOC: Side of town hall. PARK: Own. TEL: 4283; home — 2146.

CHEPSTOW   (029 12)

John F. Davies   LAPADA
12 St. Mary St. Est. 1963. CL: Wed. Open 10—5.30. SIZE: Large. *STOCK: Furniture, 17th—20th C, £25—£2,000; general antiques, shipping goods.* PARK: Easy. TEL: 5957; home — (060083) 343. SER: Valuations; buys at auction. VAT: Stan/Spec.

Glance Back
17 Upper Church St. (Donner Ltd.) Resident. Open 10—5.30, Sun. by appointment. SIZE: Medium. *STOCK: Books, 40p—£400; prints, maps and engravings, £7—£75; stamps, coins, medals, badges, 10p—£100; postcards, pre 1930, 10p—£10.* LOC: Town centre. PARK: Easy. SER: Valuations; restorations; framing; buys at auction.

Esther Jones Antiques
(Puzzle House Antiques)
16a St. Mary's St. Resident. Est. 1974. Open 9.45—5.15, Sat. 11—4.30. *STOCK: Furniture, 1700—1930, £20—£2,000; boxes, 1780—1900; decorative items, 1800—1920; bric-a-brac.* PARK: Opposite. TEL: 3314. VAT: Stan/Spec.

Philip Morris Antiques
11, Lower Church St. Est. 1974. Open 10—4. *STOCK: Furniture, mahogany and walnut; brass and copper, bric-a-brac, collectors' items.* TEL: 6500. VAT: Stan/Spec.

Nash Antiques
5—6 Lower Church St. (C. and D. Huish.) *STOCK: Furniture, period and shipping.* TEL: 4150 or 4220.

GILWERN   (0873)
Nr. Abergavenny

Gilwern Antiques
Powell Bros. Main Rd. Est. 1968. *STOCK: General antiques especially clocks.* LOC: Leave A465 at Aberbaiden Caravan Park roundabout, ½ mile along A4077 to top end of Gilwern. PARK: Nearby. TEL: 830276/830384.

LLANDOGO
Llandogo Antiques
The Old Post Office. (R. and J. Hall.) Resident. Est. 1965. CL: Tues. Open 10—1 and 2—5.30. SIZE: Small. *STOCK: Ceramics, silver, jewellery, general antiques.* Not stocked: Furniture. LOC: Last shop in village going south A466. PARK: 50yds. TEL: Dean (0594) 530213.

MONMOUTH   (0600)
Monmouth Antiques   LAPADA
Dixton Lodge, Hadnock Rd. Est. 1971. Open 9—12.30 and 4—7, Sun. and other times by appointment. SIZE: Small. *STOCK: Furniture, £50—£1,000; clocks; all 18th—19th C.* LOC: Across Wye Bridge from town centre, turn left at Hadnock Rd., Dixton Lodge ¼ mile on right. PARK: Easy. TEL: 6568. SER: Valuations; restorations (furniture and clocks). VAT: Spec.

NEWPORT   (0633)
Antiques of Newport
84 Chepstow Rd. (Mr. and Mrs. D.G. Morgan.) Est. 1953. CL: Thurs. Open 9.30—5.30. *STOCK: Furniture, pottery, porcelain, silver, jewellery, maps and prints.* TEL: 59935. VAT: Stan.

D.S. Hutchings
The Annexe, 210 Chepstow Rd. Est. 1949. Open by appointment. *STOCK: Period furniture; English and Welsh porcelain, especially Swansea and Nantgarw.* TEL: 65511. VAT: Stan/Spec.

The Old County Hall Antiques Centre
3 Queens Hill. (Mrs. P.A. Johnson.) Est. 1980. Open Thurs., Fri. and Sat. 9.30—4.30 or by appointment. SIZE: Large. *STOCK: Furniture, mainly 19th C, £5—£1,000; ceramics, jewellery, 19th—20th C, £5—£500.* LOC: Off M4 junction 26, along Malpas road, right at first roundabout, shop at top of Queen's Hill. PARK: Nearby. TEL: Home — Dean (0594) 562804 (ansaphone). SER: Valuations; restorations (furniture); buys at auction. FAIRS: Cwmbran; Newport; Winchcombe; Croome Court, Worcs; Malvern and Thornbury, Avon.

Ryan Richards — Charles Street Antiques
34-35 Charles St. Est. 1973. Open 8—6, Sun. by appointment. SIZE: Small. *STOCK: 17th—19th C furniture, £50—£2,000; jewellery.* PARK: Easy. TEL: 55530; home — 64777. SER: Valuations; restorations (furniture and jewellery); buys at auction; jewellery design. VAT: Stan.

PENPERLLENI, Nr. Pontypool
Maurice and Nancy Willson
Court-y-Monos. Open by appointment. *STOCK: General antiques especially Oriental items, pendulum clocks and porcelain.* LOC: A4042 midway between Abergavenny and Pontypool. TEL: (0873 880) 589. SER: Valuations; restorations; commission on European and international basis.

PONTYPOOL   (049 55)
Pontypool Antiques
8 Wern Terrace, High St. (L.M. Brean.) Open 9—5.30. SIZE: Medium. *STOCK: General antiques, shipping goods and stripped pine furniture.* PARK: Easy. TEL: 52256. SER: Stripping.

RAGLAN   (0291)
Raglan Antiques
High St. (W. and M. Phillips.) Est. 1954. CL: Thurs. Open 9.30—8 or by appointment. SIZE: Small. *STOCK: Furniture and clocks, 17th—18th C; early glass, porcelain, blue and white china including Delft, silver, jewellery, pewter, metalware, smokers' pipes, paintings, prints.* LOC: A40. PARK: Easy. TEL: 690327. SER: Valuations; buys at auction. VAT: Stan/Spec.

TINTERN   (029 18)
Abbey Antiques
(D. and H. Ford.) FGA. CL: Fri. Open daily including Sun. SIZE: Large and warehouse. *STOCK: Jewellery, silver, country oak, pine and mahogany, shipping furniture, longcase and wall clocks.* LOC: A466, opposite Tintern Abbey. TEL: 233.

TREDUNNOCK   (063 349)
Betty Williams
Tyr Eglwys. Est. 1975. Open by appointment only. *STOCK: 19th and 20th C watercolours.* TEL: 301.

USK   (029 13)
Castle Antiques
41 Old Market St. (S. Lockyer.) Open 12—6 or by appointment. *STOCK: General antiques, especially English and Welsh pottery, porcelain, blue and white transfer ware.* TEL: 2424; home — Little Mill (049 528) 286.

Old Market Antiques
37 Old Market St. (V. Price.) Est. 1969. Tues., Thurs. and Fri. Open 10—5 or by appointment. SIZE: Medium. *STOCK: Pre-1830 furniture; 18th—19th C paintings and watercolours; Swansea, Nantgarw and Derby porcelain.* LOC: Opposite old Town Hall. PARK: Easy. TEL: 2813. SER: Restorations (paintings). VAT: Spec.

Gwynedd

ABERSOCH (075 881)
Annteaks (Antiques)
Main St. (H. Duke.) Est. 1946. Open 9—8. Always open to the Trade. *STOCK: General antiques from collectors' items to shipping goods; statuary figures.* LOC: Opposite Midland Bank. TEL: 2353. SER: Buys at auction.

BALA (0678)
Charlesworth Brothers Antiques Ltd.
Druid House. (D.J. and R.S. Charlesworth.) Est. 1924. CL: Wed. p.m. Open 10—6. SIZE: Large. *STOCK: General antiques, 50p—£1,500.* LOC: Left off A5, one mile out of Corwen, on A494. PARK: Easy. TEL: 520219; home — same.

BANGOR (0248)
David Windsor Gallery
201 High St. Est. 1970. CL: Wed. Open 10—5. *STOCK: Oils and watercolours, 18th—20th C; maps, engravings, lithographs.* TEL: 364639. SER: Restorations; framing; mounting. VAT: Stan/Spec.

BARMOUTH (0341)
Porters Lodge Antiques
Church St. (B.K. and J.M.H. Porter.) Est. 1973. Open 10—5. SIZE: Medium. *STOCK: Small items, furniture and collectors' postcards, pre-1930s, to £450.* PARK: In front and nearby. TEL: 280950; home — 280050. FAIRS: Bingley Hall, Birmingham, Charnock Richard, Stockport.

Tyn-y-Coed
High St. (E. Evans and J.G. Walter.) Est. 1945. CL: Wed. p.m. Open 10—12 and 2—5.30. SIZE: Small. *STOCK: China, glass, £5—£25; jewellery; prints, engravings.* Not stocked: Furniture. LOC: Centre of High St. PARK: At side. TEL: 280538. VAT: Stan.

BEAUMARIS (0248)
Elizabeth Bradley
1 West End. Open by appointment. *STOCK: Samplers, woolwork including pictures and cushions, and quilts.* TEL: 811055. FAIRS: Olympia, Ravenscott, Chelsea Town Hall, West Kensington.

Beaumaris continued
Museum of Childhood
1 Castle St. *STOCK: Childrens' toys.* TEL: 810448.

Tudor Rose and Mona Antiqua
31 and 32 Castle St. (H. and K. Lek.) RCA. Est. 1945. CL: Wed. p.m. Open 9—1 and 2—5.30; June—August open 9—5.30 Mon.—Sat. SIZE: Large. *STOCK: 16th C to Victorian prints, maps, china, glass, paintings, furniture, brass, copper, treen, domestic items, £2—£700; paintings, drawings including those by Karel and Hendrik Lek; prints.* Not stocked: Reproductions. LOC: In main st. PARK: Easy. TEL: 810203. SER: Valuations. VAT: Stan.

BETHEL, Nr. Caernarfon
W.W. Griffiths
Ivy Cottage. Est. 1978. Resident, prior telephone call advisable. *STOCK: Clocks, £300—£1,500; furniture, metalware, porcelain, some shipping goods.* LOC: After entering village from Caernarfon, turn left 200 yds. then 1st right. TEL: Port Dinorwic (0248) 670556. SER: Valuations. VAT: Stan/Spec.

BETHESDA (0248)
Ogwen Antiques
10 High St. (R. and J. Ostle.) Est. 1970. CL: Sun. except by appointment. Open 10—6. SIZE: Small. *STOCK: Victoriana, prints (topographical including North Wales), clocks, glass, china; art deco and art nouveau, paintings, 1800—1930; stripped pine, bottles, militaria, Railwayana, postcards, advertising, old tools, photographs, brass, copper.* LOC: On A5 to Betws-y-Coed. PARK: Easy. TEL: 600460; home — 600549. SER: Valuations; restorations (pictures); clock repairs.

BETWS-Y-COED (069 02)
Gwynedd Galleries
at Henllys (Old Court) Hotel. (N. W. Pritchard.) Est. 1973. Usually available but appointment advisable. SIZE: Large. *STOCK: Oil paintings and watercolours, 17th to early 20th C, £50—£1,000; small silver and collectors' items, mainly 19th C, £20—£500.* LOC: 1st right on A5 after Waterloo Bridge coming from south, then 200yds. on right. PARK: Easy. TEL: 534; home — same. SER: Valuations. VAT: Spec.

BLAENAU FFESTINIOG (0766)
The Antique Shop
74A Manod Rd. (Mrs. R. Roberts.) Est. 1971. *STOCK: Victoriana, furniture, brass and copper, oil lamps, clocks.* TEL: 830629.

CAERNARFON (0286)

Caernarfon Antiques LAPADA
18 Bangor Rd. (Mrs. E.C.P. Dyson.) Est. 1973. CL: Thurs. Open 10.15−5. SIZE: Medium. *STOCK: Jewellery, £25−£500; porcelain and silver, furniture, £25−£1,000; all Victorian.* LOC: Main road from Bangor. PARK: Easy. TEL: 5739; home − Port Dinorwic (0248) 670264. SER: Valuations; restorations (furniture); buys at auction (jewellery). FAIRS: Nantwich, Chester Northgate, Chester Grosvenor Hotel. VAT: Spec.

CONWAY (049 263)

Black Lion Antiques
11 Castle St. (M.A. Wilks-Jones.) Est. 1957. CL: Wed. p.m. Open 10−5.30. SIZE: Small. *STOCK: Small furniture, including stripped pine, china, coloured glass, Victoriana, books, brass, shipping goods, metalware.* LOC: A55. PARK: Easy. TEL: 2470. FAIRS: 3-day dateline.

Paul Gibbs Antiques
25 Castle St. Open 10−5. *STOCK: Period furniture, porcelain, pottery, pictures, objets d'art, decorative arts, 1880−1940; Royal Doulton figurines and character jugs.* TEL: 3429.

Pieces of Eight
8 Castle St. (P. Drury.) Resident. CL: Wed. and Sun. out of season. Open from 10 a.m. daily in season. *STOCK: Country furniture.* TEL: 6688.

Silcocks Fine Arts
Glyn Bach, Tyn-y-Groes. (P.W. Silcocks). Est. 1979. Open by appointment. SIZE: Small. *STOCK: Watercolours and oil paintings, sculptures, 18th C−20th C, £100−£2,000.* Not stocked: Prints and all other antiques. LOC: Turn right 3 miles south of Conway Castle on B5106, drive is 400 yards on left. PARK: Easy. TEL: Tyn-y-Groes (049 267) 269; home − same. SER: Valuations; buys at auction (as stock).

CRICCIETH (076 671)

Dorothy Harrison Antiques
1 Castle Sq. Est. 1963. CL: Wed. and Sat. Open 9−5. SIZE: Medium. *STOCK: Furniture and porcelain, 18th C.* TEL: 2955.

Eifiona Hughes
The Antique Shop, High St. Est. 1963. CL: Wed. and Sat. Open 10−12.30 and 2−5. SIZE: Small. *STOCK: Glass, 18th to early 19th C, £20−£150; small furniture, 18th C, £50−£300; ceramics and pottery, 18th−19th C, £10−£300; watercolours and oil paintings, £30−£400.* PARK: Easy. TEL: 2160.

HARLECH (0766)

Bartons Antiques for Investment
Blue Lion Yard. (J.R. and A.R. Barton.) Est. 1946. Usually open. SIZE: Medium. *STOCK: Furniture, silver, porcelain.* LOC: Opposite Plas Café. PARK: Easy. TEL: 780382/780076.

LLANABER, Nr. Barmouth

Ron Jones Antiques
Tri Brynwcws. Est. 1956. *STOCK: Welsh oak and general antiques.* LOC: 3 miles from Barmouth (on Harlech road.) TEL: Barmouth (0341) 280691.

LLANDUDNO (0492)

The Antique Shop
24 Vaughan St. (C.G. Lee.) Est. 1938. Open 9−5.30. SIZE: Medium. *STOCK: Jewellery, silver, porcelain, glass, ivories, metal goods, from 1700; period furniture, shipping goods.* LOC: Near promenade. PARK: Easy. TEL: 75575. SER: Valuations.

Madoc Antiques and Art Gallery
48 Madoc St. (H. and L. Aldridge.) Est. 1975. SIZE: Medium. *STOCK: English watercolours, 18th−20th C, £50−£500; furniture, Edwardian, Victorian and Georgian, £100−£4,000; porcelain, silver, pre-1930, £2−£600; longcase clocks, £450−£3,000.* PARK: Opposite. TEL: 79754; home − 79760. SER: Valuations; restorations (clocks). VAT: Stan/Spec.

LLANERCHYMEDD (024 876)

Andrew and Cusack
8 High St. (T. Andrew and M. Cusack.) Est. 1976. CL: Mon. Open 10−6 including Sun. SIZE: Small. *STOCK: Signed limited edition prints by Charles Tunnicliffe; furniture.* LOC: Centre of Isle of Anglesey. PARK: Easy. TEL: 204; home − same. SER: Framing; buys at auction.

LLANRWST (0492)

Snowdonia Antiques LAPADA
(J. Collins.) Est. 1968. CL: Thurs. p.m. Open 10−5. SIZE: Medium. *STOCK: Period furniture especially longcase clocks.* LOC: Turn off A5 just before Betws-y-Coed on to A496 for 4 miles. PARK: Easy. TEL: 640789. SER: Restorations (furniture); repairs (grandfather clocks).

MAENTWROG (076 685)

Harvey-Owen Antiques
The Old School (Mr. and Mrs. J. Harvey.) Est. 1972. Open 10−5. *STOCK: General antiques and shipping goods.* TEL: 310. VAT: Stan.

PENMAENMAWR   (0492)
Gay's Art Gallery
Ynys-Las, Conway Rd. (T. Johns.) Est. 1968. Open 9—6. SIZE: Large. *STOCK: Oil paintings and watercolours, £40—£1,500; Persian carpets; clocks, from 1750; blue and white and Oriental pottery, and porcelain.* Not stocked: Furniture, coins, guns, medals, swords. LOC: On A55, look for art gallery sign. PARK: Easy. TEL: 622850. SER: Valuations; restorations (clocks and oil paintings); buys at auction.

PORTMEIRION
Angel Arcade
(Portmeirion Ltd.) Est. 1960. CL: Oct. 30th to Easter unless by appointment. Open 11—5.30. SIZE: Medium. *STOCK: Staffordshire figures, ceramics; small furniture.* LOC: 1 mile from Penrhyndeudraeth. PARK: Easy. TEL: Penrhyndeudraeth (0766) 770453; home — Penrhyndeudraeth (0766) 770338. VAT: Stan.

PWLLHELI   (0758)
Rodney Adams Antiques
Hall Place, 10 Penlan St. Resident. Est. 1965. CL: Sun. except by appointment. *STOCK: Period furniture, especially longcase clocks, pine, shipping goods.* TEL: 613173; evenings — 614337. SER: Deliveries to Continent. VAT: Stan/Spec.

RHOSNEIGR   (0407)
Fan-Fayre Antiques
High St. (S. Richards.) APAT. Est. 1976. Open 10—5.30 every day. SIZE: Small. *STOCK: Jewellery, porcelain, silver, collectable items, 19th C, £25—£500.* LOC: 5 miles off A5 from the Holyhead Rd., on Anglesey Island. PARK: Easy. TEL: 810580; home — same. SER: Valuations. FAIRS: St. Martins, Birmingham; Portmeirion; Wales; Newark and Nottinghamshire Showground, Chester Northgate Arena.

Powys

BRECON   (0874)
Maps, Prints and Books
7 The Struet. (Mr. and Mrs. D.G. Evans.) Est. 1961. CL: Wed. Open 9—1 and 2—5. SIZE: Large. *STOCK: Books, maps, prints, 17th C, £5—£500.* LOC: A438, near Boots the Chemist. PARK: Opposite. TEL: 2714. VAT: Stan.

Ship Street Galleries
14 Ship St. (T.R. and C. Constantinescu.) Est. 1974. Open by appointment only. *STOCK: Period furniture, pine, shipping goods; glass, 18th—19th C; general antiques.* TEL: 3926.

DEFYNNOG, Nr. Brecon
Country Antiques
The Old School. (B. and J. Cayless.) Est. 1977. Open 9.30—5.30. SIZE: Medium. *STOCK: Original painted and stripped pine, 19th C, £25—£500; some country and oak furniture, treen and kitchenalia.* Not stocked: Mahogany, china, glass, shipping items, jewellery. LOC: Fork left off A40 towards Swansea (A4067), shop in village near Tanners Arms. PARK: Easy. TEL: Sennybridge (087482) 8155; home — Sennybridge (087482) 8855. VAT: Stan/Spec.

GLASBURY   (04974)
Mark Westwood Antiquarian Books
Little Mill. (M. and C. Westwood.) ABA. Est. 1976. Open by appointment only. SIZE: Small. *STOCK: Antiquarian books especially on science and medicine, 16th—20th C, £50—£100.* PARK: Easy. TEL: 436; home — same. SER: Valuations; buys at auction (antiquarian books). VAT: Stan.

HAY-ON-WYE   (0497)
Allott Abrahams & Son
The Bear, Bear St. Open 10—5. SIZE: Medium. *STOCK: English and French clocks; small furniture.* PARK: Easy. SER: Valuations; restorations; buys at auction. VAT: Stan/Spec.

Richard Booth's Bookshop
The Limited Bookshop, The Print Shop and Hay Castle Barn. Est. 1974. Open 9—8 including Sun. SIZE: Large. *STOCK: Books.* LOC: Centre of town. TEL: 820322.

The Corner Shop
5 St. John's Place. (E. Okarma.) CL: Tues. p.m. Open 10—5 May—Sept. other times appointment advisable. *STOCK: Prints and watercolours, 19th—20th C.* TEL: 820045. SER: Framing. VAT: Stan.

The Hay Galleries Ltd.   LAPADA
4 High Town. (J. Blunt.) Est. 1973. CL: Sun. except by appointment. Open 9—5.30. SIZE: Large. *STOCK: Stripped pine, country furniture, decorative china, textiles, metalware, treen.* Not stocked: Mahogany, shipping goods. LOC: Next to Post Office. PARK: Easy. TEL: 820356; home — 820852. SER: Restorations (oak, pine). VAT: Stan/Spec.

Hebbards of Hay
7 Market St. (G.B. Hebbard.) Est. 1958. Open 10—5. SIZE: Small. *STOCK: Furniture, pottery and porcelain.* LOC: A438, opp. the Post Office. PARK: Own. TEL: 820413.

Ye Olde Curiosity Shoppe
High Town. Est. 1975. CL: Tues. Open 10.30—1 and 2.30—5.30. *STOCK: Chinese curios, cloisonné, soapstone and wood carvings, china figures.* TEL: 820485.

Julian Blunt

THE
HAY GALLERIES LTD

4 High Town
Hay-on-Wye
Hereford HR3 5AE
Telephone 0497 820356

KNIGHTON   (0547)
Walkmill Antiques
7 High St. (A.J. Beirne.) Est. 1968. CL: Wed.
Open 10—5. SIZE: Small. *STOCK: Small furniture, Staffordshire pottery, pictures, prints; small collectable items.* LOC: Nr. Clock Tower. TEL: 528002. VAT: Stan/Spec.

LLANDRINDOD WELLS   (0597)
**Euston House Galleries and
Roma Antiques**
1, 2 and 3 High St. (A.H. Helliwell.) Est. 1969. CL: Wed. p.m. Open 9—9. SIZE: Medium. *STOCK: Cottage antiques, country furniture, metal implements, arms and silver.* LOC: Near County Hall, off A483. PARK: Easy. TEL: 2046.

MACHYNLLETH   (0654)
Colin Spencer Hughes
36 Penrallt St. Est. 1956. Open daily 9—6. SIZE: Medium. *STOCK: Oak, 18th C, £50—£2,000; mahogany, walnut, 18th—19th C; Victoriana, shipping goods, some pine.* LOC: Behind War Memorial. PARK: Easy. TEL: 2363. SER: Valuations. VAT: Spec.

PRESTEIGNE   (0544)
Min Lewis Antiques
8 High St. (Mrs. M. Lewis.) Est. 1969. Open by appointment. *STOCK: Clocks, furniture, dolls, toys, pictures and small items.* PARK: Easy. TEL: 267310.

WELSHPOOL   (0938)
F.E. Anderson and Son   LAPADA
5—6 High St. (D. and I. Anderson.) Open daily. *STOCK: Furniture, 17th—18th C; English and Chinese ceramics, glass, silver, paintings, early metalware.* TEL: 3340; home — 3324.

Horley Antiques
19 High St. (C. Darnell.) Est. 1970. Open 9.30—1 and 2.15—5, Sat. 9.30—1 and 2.15—4. SIZE: Small. *STOCK: Paintings, 19th C, £5—£500; general, mainly small, items.* PARK: Easy. TEL: 2421; home — 2213.

Waterloo Antiques   LAPADA
1 Waterloo Place, Salop Rd. (R. and N. Robinson.) Est. 1979. Open most days. SIZE: Medium. *STOCK: Porcelain, furniture, jewellery, silver, copper, brass, cast iron.* LOC: On A483 on entering town from the east. PARK: Easy. TEL: 3999; home — same. VAT: Spec.

Index of Packers and Shippers: Exporters of Antiques (Containers)

LONDON

Anglo Pacific (Fine Art) Ltd.
Units 1 and 2, Bush Industrial Estate, Standard Rd., NW10. Tel. 01 965 1234 or 01 965 0667. *(Packers and shippers of antiques, fine art, household effects and cars. All destinations).*

Baker Britt and Co. Ltd.
70/77 Cowcross St., EC1M 6ER. Tel. 01 253 3011. Telex. 21940. *(Freight forwarders, overseas removals.)* VAT: Stan.

Bartlett Packaging
12 Rosebery Ave. EC1R 4TD. Tel. 01 278 3476. Telex. 23279. (Corbet G.). *Export packing, warehousing and freight forwarding.)*

James Bourlet & Sons Ltd.
(See entry under Gtr. London.)

Davies Turner Removals Ltd.
334 Queenstown Rd., SW8 4NG. Tel. 01 622 4393. Telex. 8956479. *(Fine art and antiques packers and shippers. Courier and finder service. Full container L.C.L. and groupage service worldwide. In house travel and insurance depts.)*

London continued

Eurocrat Transport International Ltd.
The Clergy House, Mark St., EC2A 4ER. Tel. 01 739 8094. *(Antiques and fine art packing and shipping. European Van service. Storage.)*

Featherston Shipping Ltd.　　　　**LAPADA**
24 Hampton House, 15-17 Ingate Place, SW8 3NS. Tel. 01 720 0422. Telex. 24637. *(Antiques and fine art packed and shipped or airfreighted worldwide.)*

C.R. Fenton and Co. Ltd.
Beachy Rd., Old Ford., E3 2NX. Tel. 01 533 2711/18. Telex. Fenton G. 8812859. *(Packers and shippers.)*

Frate Movements
Cornwall Cottage, Leven Rd. E14 0LL. Tel. 01 987 4221. *(Shippers.)*

Gander and White Shipping Ltd.
21 Lillie Rd., SW6 1UE. Tel. 01 381 0571. Telex 917434. *(Specialist packers and shipper of antiques and works of art.)*

A silver "leaping carp" vase, late 19th century, 20.5cm high. From "Chinese Export Silver c.1760-1900" in **Antique Collecting**, January 1986.

Davies Turner

Antiques shipping since 1870

Davies Turner have been skilled packers and shippers of antiques and fine art since 1870. Our full and part-load container services run worldwide, and we have in-house insurance specialists.

Couriers and finders make buying much easier, and our own travel agency completes the service.

John Walsh
Davies Turner & Co. Ltd.
Spedition House
Queenstown Road
London SW8 4NG
Phone: 01 622 4393 Telex: 8956479

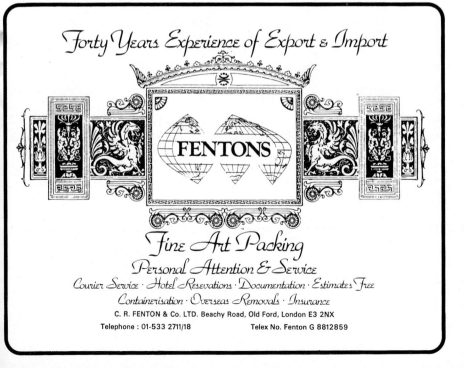

London continued

Gander and White Shipping Ltd.
14 Mason's Yard, Duke St., St. James's, SW1Y 6BU. Tel. 01 930 5383. Cables: Gandite.
Giltspur
Bullens Transport Services Ltd., Unit 9 Cranford Way, Tottenham Lane, Hornsey N.8. Tel. 01 272 6671.

London continued

Hedleys Humpers Ltd.   **LAPADA**
157-159 Iverson Rd., West Hampstead, NW6. Tel. 01 624 6874; 01 624 6981; 01 624 5904; 01 624 2306. Telex. 25229, and 33 Liddell Rd., Maygrove Rd. NW6. Tel. 01 625 4551/2. *(Weekly deliveries, door-to-door service to Europe, and part load shipments by air and sea to U.S.A.)*

London continued

Interdean Ltd.
3/5 Cumberland Ave., NW10 7RU. Tel. 01 961 4141; Telex: 922119. *(Antiques and fine art packed, shipped and airfreighted worldwide. Storage and international removals. Full container L.C.L. and groupage service worldwide.)*

Lockson Services Ltd.
29 Broomfield St., Limehouse, E14 6BX. Tel. 01 515 8600. Telex. 884222. And at Humber Works, Cricklewood, NW2. Tel. 01 452 3454. *(Full service to the antique trade including shipping, packing, insurance and couriers.)*

Masterpack Ltd.
Albion House, 860 Coronation Rd., Park Royal, NW10 7PU. Tel. 01 961 1222. Telex. 8813271 GECOMS G. *(Fine art packers and shippers. Personal service guaranteed.)*

Mat Transport Ltd.
Arnold House, 36-41 Holywell Lane, EC2P 2EQ. Tel. 01 247 6500. Telex. 886051. *(International freight forwarders and transport operators.)*

London continued

Stephen Morris Shipping Ltd.
89 Upper St., N1 ONP. Tel. 01 354 1212. Telex. 261707. *Worldwide shippers and packers. Groupage services to U.S.A. and Australasia.)*

Nelson Shipping
7 Glasshouse Walk, Vauxhall, SE11 5ES. Tel. 01 587 0265. *(Expert export and packing service.)*

Pitt and Scott Ltd.
20/24 Eden Grove, N7 8ED. Tel. 01 607 7321. Telex. 21857. *(Packers and shippers of antiques and fine art. Shipping, forwarding and airfreight agents. Comprehensive service provided for visiting antique dealers. Insurance arranged.)*

L.J. Roberton Ltd.   **LAPADA**
Marlborough House, Cooks Rd., Stratford, E.15. Tel. 01 519 2020. Telex. 8953984.

Scott Packing and Warehousing Co. Ltd.
Stephenson St. Canning Town. E.16. Tel. 01 474 1500. Telex. 897325. *(Packers and shippers — 12 offices throughout U.K.)*

Stekelman Art Services Ltd.

237 Alexandra Park Road
London N22 4BJ
Telephone: 01-881 8731

Fine Art Consultants
Antique Packing and Shipping · Freight Forwarders
Overseas Removals

Insurance Export and Import Agents

London continued

Stekelman Art Services Ltd.
237 Alexandra Park Rd., N22 4BJ. Tel. 01 881 8731. Telex. 893104. *(Fine art packers, shippers & freight forwarders worldwide. Import/export documentation, insurance. Specialised Spanish service.)*
Stephenson & Ephgrave Limited.
Est. 1921. Service House, Croft St., Deptford, SE8. Tel. 01 237 0101.
Trans-Euro Worldwide Movers
Fine Art Division, Drury Way, Brent Park, NW10 OJN. Tel. 01 459 8080. *(Worldwide shipping; courier, storage and finance services.)*
Wingate and Johnston Ltd.
78 Broadway, Stratford, E15 1NG. Tel. 01 555 8123 and 01 519 3211. Telex 897666. *(Specialists in the international movement of antiques and fine arts for over a hundred and fifty years — services incorporate all requirements from case making to documentation and insurance. Air freight groupage specialists.)*

GREATER LONDON

Airfreight Worldwide Samfreight Ltd.
Technicolour Estate, Bath Rd., Harmondsworth, West Drayton, Middx. Tel. 01 759 6011. Telex 22197. *(I.A.T.A. approved cargo agents, complete collection, packing and documentation service. Discount freight rates to all major destinations.)*
James Bourlet and Sons Ltd.
3 Space Waye, Pier Rd., Feltham, Middlesex, TW14 0TY. Tel. 01 751 1155. Telex. 935242. *(Fine art packing, freight forwarding and transport. Full responsibility undertaken for the complexities of shipments at all stages.)*
Martells International
Cubitts St., Purley Way, Croydon. Tel. 01 642 9551/681 5711. Telex. 946305. *(International removers, export packers and shippers.)* VAT: Stan.

Greater London continued

Phelps Ltd. **LAPADA**
133-135 St. Margarets Rd., Twickenham. Tel. 01 892 1778/7129.

AVON

Blatchpack Ltd.
22-24 Smyth Rd, Ashton, Bristol, BS3 2BX. Tel. 0272 665996. *(International fine art packers and shippers.)*
A.J. Williams Shipping
Griffen Court, 19 Lower Park Row, Bristol. TEL: 0272 297754/835223.

BEDFORDSHIRE

Yesterdays Pine
13 Dunstable St., Ampthill. Tel. 0525 402260. *(Shipping and container packing.)*

BUCKINGHAMSHIRE

Goyabam Translocations
108 Suffield Rd., High Wycombe. Tel. (0494) 446383. *(Worldwide container shipping & packing.)*

CHESHIRE

A. & S. Antiques of Chester
Unit 6B, Hartford Way, Sealand Industrial Estate. Tel. (0244) 375664.
The Rocking Chair
Unit 3/6, St. Peters Way, Warrington. TEL: (0925) 52409.

DORSET

Allan Franklin Transport
Unit 8, 27 Black Moor Rd., Ebblake Industrial Estate, Verwood. Tel. (0202) 826539/888138.

ESTABLISHED 1828

INTERNATIONAL SHIPPERS TO THE FINE ART AND ANTIQUES WORLD

JAMES BOURLET & SONS LIMITED

LONDON
3 Space Waye
Feltham
Middlesex TW14 OTY
Telephone: 01-751 1155
Telex: 935242

PARIS
Art Transport Counseil
Sarl.,
13 Boulevard Ney
Paris.
Telephone: 42 38 8417
Telex: 214548

NEW YORK
156 William Street
New York
N.Y. 10038
Telephone: 212 285 2340
Telex: WU1 62485

 **Alan Franklin Transport**

**UNIT 8, 27 BLACK MOOR ROAD,
EBBLAKE INDUSTRIAL ESTATE, VERWOOD,
DORSET, ENGLAND. BH21 6AX.
Telephone (0202) 826539, 826394 and 827092**

Specialist Carriers of Antiques and Fine Arts

Our door to door weekly service throughout
Europe is well known and very reliable

Container services, packing and shipping worldwide.

ESSEX

Victor Hall Antique Exporters, Packers and Shippers
The Old Dairy, Cranes Farm Rd., Basildon. Tel. 0268 289545/6.

HAMPSHIRE

Colin Macleod's Antiques Warehouse
139 Goldsmith Ave., Southsea, Portsmouth. Tel. 0705 816278.

KENT

Rod Hoyle & Son Ants.
Unit 24, Laundry Rd., Minster. Tel. (0843) 822334.
Mike Palmer Shipping
Brimsole Farm, Brimstone Hill, Meopham; Tel. (0474) 813768. *(Courier service, collections, packing and shipping.)*

LANCASHIRE

Alan Butterworth (Antiques) Ltd.
Union Mill, Albert St., Horwich, Bolton. Tel: 0204 693733; after hours 68094.
Anthony Walmsley Antiques
93 Montagu St., Blackburn. Tel. 0254 698755.

LEICESTERSHIRE

Kimbell and Co. Shipping Ltd.
Riverside, Market Harborough, LE16 7PT. Tel: 0858 33444. *(Container packers and shippers. Speedy despatch — competitive rates.)*

MERSEYSIDE

John Mason (Wavertree)
127 High St., Liverpool, L15 8JT. Tel. 722 2352. *(Specialist packer, full and part container loads.)*

OXFORDSHIRE

Cantay Group Ltd.
36-39 Park End St., Oxford. OX1 1JE. Tel. Freefone 'Cantay' (Antique and Fine Art Shippers). *(Removers and shippers.)*
J.N. Oakey.
Unit 1, Crawley Mill Industrial Estate, Crawley, Near Witney. Tel. 0993 5659/3264. (Nationwide haulage, removals and storage — household goods, antiques and fine art.)

SOMERSET

Colin Dyte Exports Ltd.
Huntspill Rd., Highbridge. Tel. 0278 788590.
Woodgates Packing and Shipping Ltd.
Station Rd., Bruton. BA10 OEH. Tel. (0749) 812417. Open 8.30—6, Sat. 8.30—12.30. *(Specialised collection, valuation, packing, shipping and export service worldwide especially U.S.A., Canada, Australia, South Africa.)*

SUSSEX

Anglo American Shipping Co. Ltd.
School Close, Burgess Hill, West Sussex, RH15 9RX. Tel. (04446) 45928. Telex. 87688. *(Shippers and freight forwarders.)*
British Antique Exporters Ltd.
Queen Elizabeth Avenue, Burgess Hill, West Sussex, RH15 9RX. Tel. 044 46 45577. *(Packers and shippers. Also exporters of container-loads with money back guarantee.)*
Lou Lewis
Avis Way, Newhaven, East Sussex, BN9 ODP. Tel. 0273 513091. *(Fine art and antique packers and shippers. Freight forwarders. World wide service.)*

Sussex continued

London and Southern Shipping Ltd.
The Warehouse, Gladstone Rd. Portslade, BN4 1LJ. Tel. 0273 420154. Telex 07323/LASS. Open Mon.—Fri. 8—5.30, or by appointment. *(Specialists in packing and shipping of antiques, works of art and household effects throughout the world. Container or groupage movement, export documentation, full insurance cover and destination services. Immediate quotations.)*

WARWICKSHIRE

Scott Packing and Warehousing Co. Ltd.
Unit 9, Ratcliffe Road Industrial Estate, Ratcliffe Rd., Atherstone, CV9 1JA. Tel. 08277 4631.

WILTSHIRE

P.A. and D. Gale
Furlong House, 61 East St., Warminster. Tel. 0985 219460.

YORKSHIRE

H. and A.M. Blackburn
21 Otley St., Skipton. Tel. (0756) 3323 or Gargrave (0756 78) 403. *(Export, packers, shippers, courier service.)*

SCOTLAND

Dial-a-Van
112 Crown St., Aberdeen. Tel. 0224 586001. *(Packers and shippers.)*

Elizabeth Paterson Antiques, Shipping and Packing
1A Main St. Bannockburn, Stirling, FK7 8LZ. Tel. 0786 816392. *(Packing, shipping and export service worldwide.)*

Scott Packing and Warehousing Co. Ltd.
Beaverbank Place, Edinburgh, EH7 4ET. Tel. 031 557 2000. *(Packers and shippers.)*

Scott Packing and Warehousing Co. Ltd.
Kilsyth Rd., Kirkintilloch, Glasgow, G66 1TJ. Tel. 041 776 5194. Telex. 778940. *(Packers and shippers.)*

WALES

James and Patricia Ash
The Warehouse, Station Rd., Llandeilo, Dyfed. Tel. 0558 823726. *(Shipping and container service. Supply and packing for overseas clients.)*

Index of Auctioneers

LONDON

Bloomsbury Book Auctions
3 and 4 Hardwick St., EC1R HRY. Tel. 01 833 2636/7 and 01 636 1945. *Twenty sales per year of books, manuscripts, maps, prints and especially disposal of academic libraries. Sellers commission 10% (trade 7½%); buyers premium 10%.*

Bonhams
Montpelier Galleries, Montpelier St., Knightsbridge, SW7 1HH. Tel. 01 584 9161. Telex 916477 Bonham G. *Tuesdays: silver (fortnightly); Wednesdays: Watercolours (monthly); Prints (bi-monthly); books and manuscripts (periodically); furs (monthly Oct.—April. Late night viewing Mon. until 7p.m.). Thursdays: Oil paintings (weekly); furniture (fortnightly); Oriental rugs and carpets (bi-monthly); Fridays: European and Oriental ceramics and works of art (monthly); clocks, watches, barometers and scientific instruments (bi-monthly); jewels and objects of vertu (monthly); textiles, costumes and dolls (bi-monthly). All sales are on view the two workdays prior. Late night viewing on Tuesdays until 7p.m. Catalogues are available at the Galleries or by post and regular subscriptions to catalogues can be arranged. Also at 65—69 Lots Rd., London SW10. Tel. 01 352 0466. Regular auctions of furniture and carpets on Mondays; ceramics, pictures and prints on Fridays.*

London continued

Camden Auctions
The Saleroom, Hoppers Rd., Winchmore Hill, N.21. Tel. 01 886 1550. *Sales alternate Thursdays at 10.30a.m. Viewing on Wednesdays from 9.30a.m. to 8p.m. and from 9a.m. on day of sale. Sellers commission 10%, buyers premium 5%.*

Christie's
8 King St., St. James's, SW1Y 6QT. Tel. 01 839 9060. *Porcelain, pottery, objets d'art and miniatures, pictures including Old Masters, English, Victorian, continental, impressionist, contemporary, prints, drawings, watercolours, art deco, art nouveau; Japanese and Chinese, Islamic and Persian works of art; glass, silver, jewellery, books, modern guns, arms and armour. Furniture, carpets, tapestries and wine. Other specialist sales periodically. Christie's are the oldest fine art saleroom in the world.*

Chattels Auctioneers and Valuers

Jackson-Stops & Staff

Contents of House Sales conducted throughout the British Isles

Valuations for Insurance, Probate, Family Division and any other purposes

14 Curzon Street, London W1Y 7FH
Telephone: 01-499 6291

ALSO IN: CHELSEA · FULHAM · CHESTER · CHICHESTER · CHIPPING CAMPDEN · CIRENCESTER · DARLINGTON · EXETER · MIDHURST · NEWMARKET · NORTHAMPTON · YEOVIL · YORK · DUBLIN ·

London continued

Christie's South Kensington Ltd.,
85 Old Brompton Rd., SW7 3LD. Tel. 01 581 7611. No buyer's premium. *Sales of jewellery; silver; pictures; watercolours, drawings and prints; antique furniture and carpets; ceramics and works of art; printed books; costume, textiles and embroidery; fortnightly. Toys and games; dolls; wines; art nouveau and art deco; cameras monthly. Periodic sales of automata, mechanical music and talking machines and records; photographs; scientific instruments and vintage machines; motoring and aeronautical items including car mascots; Staffordshire portrait figures, pot-lids and Goss; miniatures; antiquities and ethnographica; cigarette cards and post-cards.*

Dowell Lloyd and Co. Ltd.
118 Putney Bridge Rd., Putney, SW15 2NQ. Tel. 01 788 7777. *Two sales a week of general antique and modern items. VAT: Stan.*

Forrest and Co.
79–85 Cobbold Rd., Leytonstone, E11 3NS. Tel. 01 534 2931. *Sales of antique and quality furniture, china, glassware, clocks, clock sets and works of art at fortnightly intervals.*

Stanley Gibbons Auctions Ltd.,
399 Strand, WC2R OLX. Tel. 01 836 8444. *About 13 sales each year in London and overseas venues including popular general collections especially Gt. Britain, British Empire and Postal History. Catalogue subscription £15 p.a. (£18 overseas). Postal bidding service available through catalogues, which also provide current market prices.*

Glendining and Co.
Blenstock House, 7 Blenheim St., New Bond St., W1Y 9LD. Tel. 01 493 2445. *About 15 sales each year of coins; about 3 sales each year of military medals.*

London continued

Harmers of London Stamp Auctioneers Ltd.,
91 New Bond St., W1A 4EH. Tel. 01 629 0218. *The London division of the Harmer organisation of London, New York and San Francisco. Sales of postage stamps, postal history and associated material held normally monthly from September to July. Fully illustrated catalogue produced for each sale. Philatelic insurance. "Guarantee" scheme for vendors.*

Harvey's Auctions Ltd.
14-18 Neal St., WC2H 9LZ. Tel. 01 240 1464. *Sales of antique and general furniture, silver, ceramics, glass and paintings, held weekly on Wednesday at 10.30. Viewing Tuesday 9.30a.m.–3.30p.m.*

Jackson-Stops & Staff
14 Curzon St., London, W1Y 7FH. Tel. 01 499 6291. *Sales of contents of private houses conducted on the premises. SER: Valuations.*

IS YOUR ENTRY CORRECT?
If there is even the slightest inaccuracy in your entry, *please* let us know before 1st January 1987.
GUIDE TO THE
ANTIQUE SHOPS OF BRITAIN
5 Church Street, Woodbridge, Suffolk.

Est. 1979

LOTS ROAD CHELSEA AUCTION GALLERIES

71 Lots Road (off Kings Road Chelsea)
LONDON SW10
**Tel: 01-351 7771 or
01 352 2349**
ENGLAND'S HERITAGE
under the hammer
EVERY MONDAY EVENING

6.30 p.m. Oriental rugs, Textiles ...... (40 lots)
7 p.m. Paintings and Prints .... (60 lots)
7.30 p.m. Ceramics, Silver, Objets d'art,
clocks etc. .... (100 lots)
8 p.m. Selected Furniture .... (150 lots)

**4 DAYS VIEWING EVERY WEEK
Fridays 9−4
Saturdays & Sundays 10−1
Mondays 9−6**

Send SAE for Catalogue to dept. GASB
Quality items always accepted

London continued

Lots Road Chelsea Auction Galleries
71 Lots Rd., Chelsea, SW10 0RN. (Roger
Ross). Est: 1979. TEL: 01 351 7771/2/3.
Open Monday 9-10.30p.m., Tuesday 9-7p.m.,
Wednesday 9-6p.m., Thursday and Friday
9-5p.m. *Auction sales every Monday evening
at 6.30p.m., approx. 400 lots of antique,
traditional and modern furniture, Oriental rugs
and carpets, paintings, china, glass, silver,
objets d'art, textiles, mirrors, musical instruments, metal-ware, collectables, clocks,
books and boxes. On view Fridays 9-4,
Saturdays and Sundays 10-1 and Mondays
9-6. Items accepted Monday-Friday 9-5.
(Settlement within one week of sale).* LOC:
Off King's Rd, Worlds End. PARK: Easy.
Valuers and consultants: carrier service. VAT
registered.
Phillips
Blenstock House, 7 Blenheim St., New Bond
St., W1Y 0AS. Tel. 01 629 6602. *Furniture,
carpets, works of art: two sales a week.
Pictures, collectors' items, ceramics and glass,
silver, weekly. Many specialist sales covering
all aspects of art, antiques and collectors'
items at frequent intervals, mostly monthly.*
Phillips Marylebone Auction Rooms
Hayes Place, NW1 6UA. Tel. 01 723 2647.
*Sales of furniture, ceramics, pictures and
objects on Friday at 10 a.m. Viewing
Thursdays.*

London continued

Phillips West 2
10 Salem Rd., W2 4BU. Tel. 01 221 5303.
*Sales of furniture, porcelain and works of art
weekly on Thursday at 10a.m. Viewing
Wednesdays. A modern, custom-built saleroom with good parking facilities. Buyer's
premium 10% plus V.A.T.*
Rippon Boswell and Co.
The Arcade, South Kensington Station, SW7
2NA. Tel. 01 589 4242. *International
specialist auctioneers of old and antique
Oriental carpets. Approx. two auctions a year
in London. Also in Germany, Switzerland,
U.S.A. and Far East.*
Robson Lowe at Christies.
47 Duke St., St. James's, SW1Y 6QX. Tel.
01 839 4034/5. (Also at the Auction House,
39 Poole Hill, Bournemouth. Tel. 0202
295711 and in New York, Zurich and other
world centres.) *80−100 auctions a year in
the major centres listed above, all for postage
stamps and associated items. Most sales
begin at 10.30 or 11a.m. and continue
throughout the day. Viewing three or four
days before the sale.*
Sotheby's
34−35 New Bond St., W1A 2AA. Tel. 01
493 8080. *Mondays: books, antiquities,
Russian works of art, Japanese works of art,
miniatures and objects of vertu. Tuesdays:
books, Japanese works of art, Chinese works
of art, arms and armour, porcelain, glass.
Wednesdays: paintings, wine. Thursdays:
silver, jewels, coins, medals, drawings and
watercolours, prints, works of art, musical
instruments, clocks and watches. Fridays:
furniture, rugs and carpets.*
Sotheby's
Bloomfield Place, Off New Bond St. W.1.
*Sales Monday, Tuesday and Friday weekly, of
books, manuscripts, coins, medals and
jewellery.*
Southgate Antique Auction Rooms
rear of Southgate Town Hall, Green Lanes,
Palmers Green, N13. Tel. ·01 886 7888.
*Weekly sales of antique smalls and furniture
on Fridays at 6.30 p.m.*
Waltham Forest Auctions
101 Hoe St., Walthamstow, E17. Tel. 01 520
2998. *Wednesday sales of general antiques
and jewellery.*

GREATER LONDON

Abridge Auction Rooms and Antique Centre
Market Place, Abridge, Romford, RM4 1UA. *3
weekly sales a month at 7pm. (No sale on last
Wed. of month).*
Bonsor Penningtons
82 Eden St., Kingston, Surrey. Tel. 01 546
0022. *Sales every fortnight on a Thursday at
10a.m. Viewing previous Tuesday 2.30p.m.−
8p.m. and Wednesday 9a.m.−4p.m.*
Croydon Auction Rooms (Rosan and Co.)
144/150 London Rd., Croydon. Tel. 01 688
1123/4/5. *Collective sales every Saturday
10a.m.*

Greater London continued

Parkins
18 Malden Rd., Cheam, Surrey. SM3 8SD.
Tel. 01 644 6633 and 01 644 6127 (Auction
Room). *Weekly sales of Victorian, Edwardian
and modern furniture and effects on Mondays
at 10a.m. Viewing Friday 2—4 and Saturday
10—4p.m. Special antique and collectors
sales first Monday in month.*

AVON

Aldridges, Bath
The Auction Galleries, 130—132 Walcot St.,
Bath, BA1 5BG. Tel. 0225 62830 and 62839.
*Sales are held on Tuesdays and are broken
down into specialist categories: Antique furniture to include clocks and Oriental carpets;
silver and porcelain including glass and metalware; paintings and prints; Victorian and
general furniture. Viewing Saturday mornings
and Mondays until 7.30p.m. Catalogues
available upon annual subscription. Large
clients' car park.*

Blessley Davis
42 High St., Chipping Sodbury, Bristol, BS17
6AH. Tel. 0454 312848/313033. *Monthly,
except for July and December, collective sales
of antique and modern furniture; house sales
as instructed. Qualified chattels valuer on
staff.*

Hoddell Pritchard (Est. 1785)
Clevedon Salerooms, Sixways, Clevedon.
BS21 7NT. Tel. 0272 876699. *Bi-monthly
auctions of antique furniture, fine art and
collectors items. Fortnightly sales of Victorian,
Edwardian and general furniture and effects.
Occasional specialist sales and sales held on
vendors property. Valuations given. No
buyer's premium.*

Lalonde Bros. and Parham
71 Oakfield Rd., Clifton, Bristol, BS8 2BE. Tel.
0272 734052. *Quarterly specialist antiques
sales. General sales alternate Wednesdays at
Bristol and alternate Tuesdays at Station Rd.,
Weston-super-Mare.*

Osmond, Tricks
Regent Street Auction Rooms, Clifton, Bristol,
BS8 4HG. Tel. 0272 73201. *Six major sales
per year with sections reserved for brass,
copper, pewter, bronze and other metalware;
European, Oriental and British ceramics; glassware, plated ware; silver; oil paintings; watercolours; jewellery; objets d'art; ethnography;
models; clocks; furniture, rugs and carpets,
and musical instruments. View day prior to
sale from 10a.m. to 7p.m. and on day of sale
from 9a.m. until sale commences at
10.30a.m. Special sales of pictures and prints.
Sales of wine and vintage port. Catalogue
subscription service. No buyer's premium.*

Avon continued

Phillips and Jollys Auction Rooms of Bath
1 Old King St., Bath, BA1 1DD. Tel. 0225
310609 and 310709. *Members of the Phillips
Auction Group. Regular specialised sales of
antique furniture, clocks, Oriental rugs, porcelain, silver, paintings, and collectors' sales.
Programme of future sales sent on request.*

Taviner's Auction Rooms
Prewett St., Redcliffe, Bristol, BS1 6PB. Tel.
0272 25996. *Specialist sales monthly, antiques, and collectables; books. General furniture and effects every Friday.*

Woodspring Auctions
Churchill Rd. Weston-super-Mare. Tel. 0934
28419. *Fortnightly sales of Victorian, Edwardian and general household furniture, brass,
copper, glass, china, coins, medals and bric-a-
brac.*

BEDFORDSHIRE

Adelaide Auction Rooms
79-81 Windsor Walk, Luton. *Sales of antiques
and general held at 7 p.m. every Wednesday.*
Tel. 0582 28616/423809.

Peacock
The Auction Centre, 26 Newnham St.,
Bedford, MK40 3JR. Tel. 0234 66366.
*Antique sale first Friday of every month.
Viewing Thursday prior 9a.m.—6p.m. General
sales every Saturday at 1.30a.m. SER: Buys
at auction.*

Thorne Reeks and Co. (Auctioneers)
7 King St., Luton. Tel. 0582 27641.

BERKSHIRE

Chancellors Hollingsworths
31 High St., Ascot, SL5 7HG. Tel. 0990
27101. *Six weekly two days sales of antique
English and Continental furniture, porcelain,
china, clocks, glass, silver and plate, oil
paintings, watercolours, jewellery. Approx.
1,500 lots per sale.*

Dreweatt's
Donnington Priory, Donnington, Newbury.
RG13 2JE. Tel. 0635 31234, Telex 848580.
*Saleroom sales held fortnightly (general
antiques once a month). Household furnishings once a month. Specialist sales of silver,
jewellery, books, paintings and prints held
quarterly. Private house sales between the
above. Members of the Society of Fine Art
Auctioneers. Buyer's premium, 6% inc. VAT.*

Holloways
12 High St., Streatley, Reading. RG8 9HY.
Tel. 0491 872318. *Sales of antique furniture,
ceramics, paintings etc., at Goring Village Hall.
Approx. every five weeks.*

Martin and Pole
5a and 7 Broad St., Wokingham. Tel. 0734
790460. *Auctions of antiques and collectables held on third Wednesday every month at
Wokingham Auction Galleries, Milton Rd.*

Berkshire continued

Thimbleby and Shorland
31 Great Knollys St., Reading, RG1 7HU. Tel.
0734 508611. *Collective sales of antique and
modern furniture and effects held at Reading
Cattle Market approx. every 6/7 weeks. Also
4 specialist sales of horse-drawn vehicles,
harness, horse brasses, driving sundries,
whips and lamps etc.*

Duncan Vincent Fine Art & Chattel Auctioneers
105 London St., Reading. Tel. 0734 589502.
*About 8 collective sales of antique, Victorian
and all good quality modern furniture and
effects, about 700 lots, during the year at
Memorial Hall, Shiplake and the Village Hall,
Woodcote. No buyers premium.*

BUCKINGHAMSHIRE

Barnard and Learmount
18 Bathhurst Walk, Iver. Tel. (0753) 652024.
*Book auctions held at the above address,
furniture sales at 14 Bathurst Walk.*

Downer Ross (Auctioneers)
Silbury Court, 382 Silbury Boulevard, Milton
Keynes, MK9 2AF. Tel. 0908 679900. Sales
every 4—6 weeks.

W.S. Johnson and Co.
10 Market Sq., Buckingham. Tel. 0280 81
2120.

Hetheringtons Pretty and Ellis
The Amersham Auction Rooms, 125 Station
Rd., Amersham, HP6 5BD, and Turret House,
Station Rd., Amersham, HP6 5BD, and Turret
House, Station Rd., Amersham. Tel. 02403
29292. *Weekly sales of general antiques,
collectors' items and good quality household
effects. Monthly selected antique sales. Sale
day Thursday at 12.30p.m. Viewing on sale
day and previous Wednesday 10.30a.m.—
7p.m.*

CAMBRIDGESHIRE

Cheffins, Grain and Chalk
The Cambridge Saleroom, Cherry Hinton Rd.,
Cambridge. Tel. 0223 358721 (10 lines).
*Regular quarterly and other specialist sales of
furniture, clocks, books, sporting items, wine,
rural and domestic bygones.*

Comins
25 Market Place, Ely, CB7 4NP. Tel. 0353
2265. *Sales of antique furniture, silver, china,
glass, bric-a-brac etc., at Ely Maltings every
2—3 months (approx. 4 sales per annum).
Also weekly (Thurs.) sales of household
furniture.*

Ekins Dilley and Handley
The Salerooms, The Market, St. Ives,
Huntingdon. Tel. 0480 68144. *Sales of
antique furniture, fine art, pictures and silver
held once a month on Tuesdays at 10a.m.
General sales fortnightly on Saturday
mornings.*

Cambridgeshire continued

Grounds and Co.
2 Nene Quay, Wisbech, PE13 1AG. Tel. 0945
585041/2. *Two specialist two day sales a
year. Each sale comprises approx. 1,600 lots.*

Hammond and Co.
Cambridge Place, Cambridge. Tel. 0223
356067. *Weekly sales of furniture, smalls and
antiques on Fridays from 10 a.m.*

Norman Wright and Hodgkinson
Abbey Road, Bourne, PE10 9EE. Tel. 0778
422567. *Monthly auctions at Cheyne Lane
Auction Centre, Stamford and quarterly at The
Corn Exchange, Bourne.*

CHESHIRE

Andrew, Hilditch and Son
19 The Square, Sandbach, CW11 0AT. Tel.
093 67 2048 and 7246. *Sales of antique,
Victorian and general furnishings, paintings,
clocks and effects held every three to four
weeks.*

Brocklehursts
(Part of the Longden & Cook partnership.)
Brocklehurst House, King Edward St.,
Macclesfield. SK10 1AL. Tel. 0625 27555.
Fortnightly general sales.

Jackson — Stops and Staff
25 Nicholas St., Chester CH1 2NZ. Tel. 0244
28361. *Sales of private house contents held
on the premises. SER: Valuations.*

Frank R. Marshall and Co.
Marshall House, Church Hill, Knutsford,
WA16 6DH. Tel. 0565 53284. *Regular sales
of antique furniture, objets d'art, silver,
pewter, glassware, porcelain, pictures, brass
and copper. Monthly household collective
sales including bric-a-brac. Specialised sales at
The Knutsford Auction Salerooms.*

Phillips in Chester
New House, Christleton Rd., Chester, CH3
5TD. Tel. 0244 313936 (4 lines). *Auction
rooms at Chester and Colwyn Bay.*

Reeds Rains
Trinity House, 114 Northenden Rd.,
Manchester M33 3HD. Tel. 061 962 9237.
*Regular sales of antique jewellery, clocks,
watches, scientific instruments, paintings and
watercolours; Period, Victorian and modern
furnishings; Chinese and Japanese furnishings,
porcelain, collectors' items. Auctions held
Wednesday and Thursday commencing 2p.m.
and 10a.m. respectively. Viewing previous
and same day.*

Sotheby's
Booth Mansion, 28 Watergate St. and Saltney,
Chester. CH1 2NA. Tel. 0244 315531.
*Specialist sales of silver, jewellery, ceramics,
furniture, pictures and collectors' items fort-
nightly.*

Cheshire continued

Wright Manley
Beeston Sales Centre, Beeston Castle Smithfield, Tarporley. Tel. 0829 260318. *Fortnightly general sales and bi-monthly fine art and furniture sales.*

CLEVELAND

Ralph Appleton and Hall
22 High St., Stockton-on-Tees. TS18 1LS. Tel. 0642 675555. *Occasional antiques sales.*
Norman Hope and Partners
2 South Rd., Hartlepool. TS24 7SG. Tel. 0429 67828. *Periodic sales of antique and reproduction furniture, glass, china, silver, oils and watercolours.*

CORNWALL

Button, Menhenitt & Mutton Ltd.
Belmont Auction Rooms, Wadebridge. PL27 7NY. Tel. 020 881 2131. *Sales of general antiques, collectors items, books and stamps every 12 weeks.*
Jose Collins and Harris
The Auction Rooms, The Parade, Trengrove Way, Helston. TR13 8ER. Tel. 03265 63363. *Auctions held on first Wednesday monthly. Office — 29 Coinagehall St., Helston.*
W.H. Cornish
Central Auction Rooms, Castle St., Truro. Tel. 0872 72968. *Sales of general antiques every six to eight weeks.*
John Gorst, F.R.I.C.S.
50 Fore St., Copperhouse, Hayle. TR27 4DX. Tel. 0736 752400.
W.H. Lane and Son
Fine Art Auctioneers and Valuers. 64 Morrab Rd., Penzance, TR18 2QT. Tel. 0736 61447/8. *Twelve sales each year of antiques and objets d'art. Two specialist book sales per year. Four picture sales per year. Two coin, medal and stamp sales per year. Frequent house sales and other specialist sales.*
Lambreys
incorporating R.J. Hamm A.S.V.A., The Platt, Wadebridge. Tel. 020 881 3593. *Fortnightly sales of antiques and objets d'art. Illustrated catalogues issued.*
David Lay A.S.V.A.
The Auctioneer Offices, 7 Morrab Rd., Penzance. TR18 4EL. Tel. 0736 61414. *Sales of Fine Art, antiques and collectors' items every six weeks.*
Miller & Company
Lemon Quay Auction Rooms, Truro, TR1 2LW. Tel. 0872 74211. Telex. 45684. *Antique and selected sales every two months. Victorian, Edwardian and household sales every fortnight.*
Phillips Cornwall (formerly the Auction Rooms of May, Whetter and Grose)
Cornubia Hall, Par, PL24 2AQ. Tel. 072 681 4047. *Selected monthly Tuesday sales of antiques. Weekly Thursday sales of Victorian, pine and general household furnishings. Collectors sales, Feb., April, Aug., Dec.*

Cornwall continued

Pooley and Rogers
Regent Auction Rooms, Abbey St. Penzance. Tel. Office — 0736 3816/7 or 0736 795451. Saleroom — 0736 68814. *Bi-monthly sales of antique furniture. objets d'art, silver and jewellery.*
Rowse Jeffery and Watkins
5 Fore St., Lostwithiel. PL22 0BP. Tel. 0208 872245. *Sales approx. every fortnight. Viewing on the Tuesday and morning of sale. All sales commence at 10.30.*

CUMBRIA

Mossops
Loughrigg Villa, Kelsick Rd., Ambleside. LA22 0BZ. Tel. 0966/33015. *Collective sales of antiques, works of art and older style country furnishings at intervals throughout the year. Also catalogue sales on premises. Full valuation service.*
James Thompson
64 Main St., Kirkby Lonsdale, LA6 2AJ. Tel. 0468 71555. *Monthly sales of general antiques (with special picture sales four times a year).*
Thomson, Roddick and Laurie Ltd.
24 Lowther St., Carlisle. CA3 8DA. Tel. 0228 28939 and 39636. *Bi-monthly catalogue sales of antiques and collectors' items at Dumfries and Carlisle, Cumbria. Occasional specialist sales at Carlisle and Dumfries, particularly antiquarian books, sporting guns, silver and pictures. Monthly general furniture sales at Wigton, Brampton (Cumbria) and Annan, Dumfriesshire.*
Tiffen King Nicholson
12 Lowther St., Carlisle. CA3 8DA. Tel. 0228 25259. *Catalogue sales in Carlisle saleroom approx. every six to eight weeks. Regular monthly sales also at Keswick.*

DERBYSHIRE

Noel Wheatcroft and Son.
Matlock Auction Gallery, Old English Rd., off Dale Rd., Matlock. Tel. 0629 4591. *Monthly sales antiques and general.*

DEVON

Bearnes
Rainbow, Avenue Rd., Torquay TQ2 5TG. Tel. 0803 26277. *Regular sales of antique furniture, works of art, silver, jewellery, collectors' items, clocks and watches, paintings, ceramics and glass, carpets and rugs. Illustrated catalogues published 3 weeks prior to sale.*
Bennetts Fine Art and Chattel Auctioneers
The Auction Rooms, Alexandra Rd., Torquay. Tel. 0803 27796. *Monthly sales of antiques, works of art, collectors' items.*
Peter J. Eley, F.S.V.A.
Western House, 98-100 High St., Sidmouth, EX10 8EF. Tel. 039 55 252. *Sales of antiques, silver, pictures and china every 4—5 weeks.*

Devon continued

Gribble, Booth and Taylor
Head Office, West St., Axminster, EX13 5NU. Tel. 0297 32323. *Antique and general sales held at Axminster.*

Charles Head and Son
113 Fore St., Kingsbridge. TQ 1BG. Tel. 0548 2352. *General auction sales of antique and modern furniture and effects approx. each five weeks.*

Michael G. Matthews
The Devon Fine Art Auction House, Dowel St., Honiton. EX14 8LX. Tel. 0404 41872.

Michael Newman Central Auction Rooms
Kinterbury House, St. Andrews Cross, Plymouth. PL1 2DQ. Tel. 0752 669298. *Collective antique sales second Tues. of each month. Three picture sales, three coin sales and three book sales per year.*

Phillips
Alphin Brook Rd., Alphington, Exeter. EX2 8TH. Tel. 0392 39025/6. *Four types of sales held every other Thursday: — antique and reproduction furniture and furnishings; oil paintings, watercolours and good quality prints; silver, silver plate and jewellery; porcelain and glass, Victoriana and objets d'art. Book sales and sporting and collectors' items about three times a year.*

Potburys of Sidmouth
The Auction Rooms, Temple St., Sidmouth. EX10 8LH. Tel. 03955 2414/5/6. *Twice monthly plus private house sales.*

Rendells
Stone Park, Ashburton. Tel. 0364 53017. *Regular sales of antique furniture, silver, porcelain, books, coins, glass, clocks, stamps, miscellanea.*

John Smale and Co. Chartered Surveyors
19 Cross St., Barnstaple. EX31 1BD. Tel. 0271 42000 or 42916. *Intermittently throughout the year. Private house sales only.*

Spencer-Thomas and Woolland
27 Harbour Rd., Seaton. Tel. 0297 22453. *General household and antique auctions held every 4—6 weeks.*

Taylor's
Honiton Galleries, 205 High St., Honiton. Tel. 0404 2404. *Sales of paintings and prints, antiques, silver, books, porcelain every seven weeks.*

Taylor, Lane and Creber
The Western Auction Rooms, 38 North Hill, Plymouth. PL4 8EQ. Tel. 0752 670700.

Ward and Chowen
1 Church Lane, Tavistock. Tel. 0822 2458.

Whitton and Laing
32 Okehampton St., Exeter. Tel. 0392 52621. *Antique auctions monthly. Book auctions quarterly. Coins, silver, jewellery, every six weeks. General weekly.*

DORSET

S.W. Cottee and Son
The Market, East St., Wareham. Tel. 092 95 2826. *Furniture and effects every two weeks.*

Hy. Duke and Son
Fine Art Salerooms, Weymouth Ave., Dorchester. DT1 1DG. Tel. 0305 65080. *Sales every six weeks including specialist sections of silver and jewellery, Oriental and English porcelain, English and Continental furniture, pictures, books, or Oriental rugs. Also at Weymouth Furniture Saleroom, St. Nicholas St., Weymouth. Tel. 0305 783488. Sales of Victorian and later shipping furniture and effects.*

House and Son
Lansdowne House, Christchurch Rd., Bournemouth, BH1 3JW. Tel. 0202 26232. *Sales fortnightly of selected furniture, pictures, books, silver, porcelain and glass. Catalogues 50p inc. postage.*

John Jeffery and Son Auctioneers
Minster House, The Commons, Shaftesbury, SP7 8JL. Tel. Shaftesbury 3331-2. *Regular sales of antique furniture and effects.*

Riddetts of Bournemouth
Richmond Hill, Bournemouth Sq., Bournemouth, BH2 6EJ. Tel. 0202 25686. *Sales fortnightly including fine antiques, jewellery, silver, plate, pictures. Illustrated sale programme free. Catalogue subscription £20p.a.*

COUNTY DURHAM

G.H. Edkins and Son
122 Newgate St., Bishop Auckland, DL14 7HE. Tel. 0388 603095. *Fortnightly general sales in Auckland auction rooms. Special antique sales from time to time. Private house sales as instructed.*

G. Tarn Bainbridge and Son
North Rock House, High Row, Darlington, DL3 7QN. Tel. 0325 462633 and 462553. *Three to four collective sales per year and regular country house sales.*

Thomas Watson and Son
Northumberland St., Darlington, DL3 7HJ. Tel. 0325 462559/5 (two lines). *Sales of shipping furniture and house contents held every Wednesday and Thursday. Catalogue sales, including antiques, held monthly.*

ESSEX

Ambrose
149 High Rd., Loughton. IG10 4LZ. Tel. 01 508 2121. *Sales held on last Thursday of month.*

Cooper Hirst
Goldlay House, Parkway, Chelmsford, CM2 7PR. Tel. 0245 58141. *Regular sales every six weeks of antiques and weekly Friday sales of Victoriana, bric-a-brac etc. at The Granary Saleroom, Victoria Rd., Chelmsford. Catalogue subscription scheme.*

Essex continued

Elam's
15 West Rd., Westcliffe-on-Sea. Tel. 0702 34804. *Antiques sale first Monday of every month.*

Paskell and Cann
11-14 East Hill, Colchester. Tel. 0206 868070. *Weekly sales of antique and modern furniture, china, glass, silver and decorative items.*

Reemans
Headgate Auction Rooms, 12 Headgate, Colchester. Tel. 0206 574271/2. *Sales held every Wednesday. Viewing 9−7 Tuesday prior.*

Simon H. Rowland
Chelmsford Auction Rooms, 42 Mildmay Rd., Chelmsford. CM12 0DZ. Tel. 0245 354251. *Regular sales by order of the Sheriff of Essex and private vendors.*

John Stacey and Sons
Leigh Auction Rooms, 86-90 Pall Mall, Leigh-on-Sea, SS9 1RG. Tel. 0702 77051. *Monthly auctions of furniture, works of art and collectors items. Catalogue subscription scheme £12p.a.*

Edwin Watson and Son
1 Market St., Saffron Walden. CB10 1JB. Tel. 0799 22058. *Sales of antique and fine furniture, antique effects and objets d'art, held every month.*

J.M. Welch and Son
Old Town Hall, Great Dunmow. CM6 1AU. Tel. 0371 2117/8. *Quarterly sales of selected antique furniture and effects. Monthly sales of collectables and household furniture. No buyers premium. Catalogue subscription service available.*

GLOUCESTERSHIRE

G.H. Bayley and Sons
Vittoria House, Vittoria Walk, Cheltenham, GL50 1TW. Tel. 0242 521102. *Established in 1846 and specialising in private house sales of antique and other contents in the North Gloucestershire and South Worcestershire area. 5 to 7 sales each year with occasional collective sales.*

Bruton, Knowles and Co.
Albion Chambers, 111 Eastgate St., Gloucester, GL1 1PZ. Tel. 0452 21267. *Fine art auctioneers and valuers. House and collective sales held throughout the year. Valuations and inventories prepared.*

Cheltenham Galleries
1A Crescent Place, Cheltenham, GL50 3PH. Tel. 0242 584310. *Monthly sales of general antiques.*

Frazer, Glennie and Partners
The Old Rectory, Siddington, Cirencester. Tel. 0285 3938. *Monthly sales of antiques, other furniture and collectors' items.*

R.E. Graham & Son
City Chambers, 4/6 Clarence St., Gloucester, GL1 1EA. Tel. 0452 21177. *Sales of general antiques, household and outdoor effects, books, objets d'art and collectables every 4−6 weeks.*

Gloucestershire continued

Mallams
Auctioneers of Antiques, 26 Grosvenor St., Cheltenham. Tel. 0242 35712. *Monthly sales of antiques and works of art. Bi-monthly special sales.*

Moore, Allen and Innocent
33 Castle St., Cirencester. GL7 1QD. Tel. 0285 2862. *Monthly: collective sales of over 1,000 lots of antique and other furniture. Bi-annual specialist picture sales. Fridays at 10a.m.*

Sandoe Luce Panes
Wotton Auction Rooms, Wotton-under-Edge, GL12 7EB. Tel. 0453 844733. *Regular collective sales of quality antiques, furniture and effects. Catalogues issued. Valuations undertaken.*

Specialised Postcard Auctions
12 Suffolk Rd., Cheltenham. GL50 2AQ. Tel. 0242 580323/583314. *Postcard auctions at Cheltenham (1a Crescent Place) every 6 weeks.*

Tetbury Auctions
41 Church St., Tetbury, GL8 8JG. Tel. 0666 52756.

HAMPSHIRE

Austin and Wyatt
79 High St., Fareham. PO16 7AX. Tel. 0329 234211/4 also at Bishop's Waltham, Southampton, Hythe and Winchester. *Occasional private house sales and periodic sales of oil paintings, watercolours and prints in Winchester.*

Beales Furniture and Fine Art Dept.
13a The Hundred, Romsey. (Consultant − Michael G. Baker, F.S.V.A.) Tel. 0794 513331. The Romsey Auction Rooms, 86 The Hundred, Romsey. *Silver sales in January, March, May, July, September and November. Antique, Victorian and Edwardian furniture and effects February, April, June, August, October and December. Regular bi-monthly sales of household goods, etc. House clearance facilities available.*

Elliott and Green
40 High St., Lymington, SO4 9ZE. Tel. 0590 77045. *Fortnightly sales of antique and modern furniture and effects held at The Auction Sale Room, Emsworth Rd., Lymington. Special quarterly sales of antique and reproduction furniture, pottery and porcelain, silver and plated items, paintings, etc. Occasional house contents sales.*

Fox and Sons
5 and 7 Salisbury St., Fordingbridge, SP6 1AD. Tel. 0425 52121. *Monthly sales of antique furniture and effects. Quarterly sales of silver, porcelain, jewellery, pictures etc. Also at 30-34 London Rd., Southampton, SO9 2LP. Tel. 0703 25155.*

Hampshire continued

Hants and Berks Auctions
40 George St., Kingsclere. Tel. 0635 298181. *Monthly sales at Heckfield Village Hall, on Saturday at 10.30a.m. Viewing on previous day 11a.m. — 9p.m. Sales include antiques, reproduction and household furniture, clocks, porcelain, glass, silver, pictures, etc. Occasional specialist sales. Catalogues available. No buyer's premium.*

Jacobs and Hunt
Lavant St., Petersfield. GU32 3EF. Tel. 0730 62744/5. *General antique sales every 6/8 weeks on Fridays.*

Martin and Stratford
The Auction Mart, Market Sq., Alton. GU34 1EX. Tel. 0420 84402.

May and Son
18 Bridge St., Andover, SP10 1BH. Tel. 0264 23417 and 63331. *Monthly sales of antique furniture and effects at Penton Mewsey Village Hall. (Lots from private sources only.) Private house contents sales.*

D.M. Nesbit and Co.
7 Clarendon Rd., Southsea, PO5 2ED. Tel. 0705 864321. *Monthly sales of antique furniture, silver, porcelain, and pictures.*

Pearsons
54 Southampton Rd., Ringwood. Tel. 042 54 3333. *Monthly auctions.*

Pearsons
Walcote Chambers, High St., Winchester. SO23 9AB. Tel. 0962 64444. *Monthly sales of good quality antiques and fine art, and periodic specialised auctions of silver, jewels, objets vertu, books and paintings. Sales held at Tower House Sale Rooms, Tower St., Winchester and at Pinewood Chambers, 1-3 Fleet Rd., Fleet. Tel. 02514 29211.*

Whiteheads
111-113 Elm Grove, Southsea. PO5 1JT. Tel. 0705 82071. *Regular antique and fine arts and specialist sales. 40 offices in Hants., Sussex and Kent.*

HEREFORD AND WORCESTER

Banks and Silvers
Fine Art Dept., 66 Foregate St., Worcester. Tel. 0905 23456. *Sales of antiques and other furnishings conducted on the premises and at Oakhampton Saleroom. Weekly sale of household goods at Kidderminster Market Auctions. Tel. 741303.*

Blinkhorn and Co.
41-43 High St., Broadway, WR12 7DP. Tel. 0386 852456. *Collective antique and modern furniture sales held bi-monthly. Specialist sales of silver and porcelain twice yearly.*

Hereford and Worcester continued

Coles, Knapp and Kennedy
Georgian Rooms, Ross-on-Wye. HR9 5HL. Tel. 0989 62225/63553. *Twice monthly auctions on Wednesdays at 10.30a.m. as advertised.*

Andrew Grant, F.R.I.C.S.
59/60 Foregate St., Worcester. Tel. 0905 52310. *Monthly general fine art auctions including: bygones and household accessories; brass, copper, pewter, bronze, etc; china and glass, oil paintings; watercolours, prints and books; jewellery, watches and clocks; silver; furniture and carpets. Occasional specialist wine auctions. House contents auctions at least monthly. SER: Buys at auction.*

Arthur G. Griffiths and Son
57 Foregate St., Worcester. Tel. 0905 26464.

Lear and Lear
46 Foregate St., Worcester, WR1 1EE. Est. 1751. Tel. 0905 25184. *Fine art auctions at 46 Foregate St. Worcester and antique sales at 71 Church St., Malvern (tel: 65235). Specialists in the sales of contents of country property and Worcester porcelain (single items or collections.) Valuations.*

Phipps and Pritchard
Bank Buildings, Kidderminster, DY10 1BU. Tel. 0562 2244/5/6 and 2187. *Regular monthly sales of antique furniture; watercolours and oil paintings; copper, brass and glassware, china and porcelain; stamps; coins and weapons etc. Private house sales also conducted.*

Russell, Baldwin and Bright
The Fine Art Saleroom, Ryelands Rd., Leominster. HR6 8SG. Tel. 0568 3897. *Specialist sales held once a month. Book and picture sales held three times a year. Four two-day sales of fine antiques held per year. General collective sales held every week.*

Stooke, Hill and Co. Antiques, Fine Art and Chattels Auctioneers and Valuers
24 Widemarsh St., Hereford. Tel. 0432 272413. *Salerooms at Portland St., Hereford. Sales every other Monday commencing at 11 a.m. — general antiques, furniture, pictures, books and household effects. Special antique sales held last Monday in every month.*

HERTFORDSHIRE

Brown & Merry
41 High St., Tring. Tel. 044282 6446. *Fortnightly Saturday sales held at The Cattle Market, Brook St., Tring.*

George Jackson and Son
Paynes Park House, Paynes Park, Hitchin. Tel. 0462 55212. *Sales of antique and modern furniture and effects every fortnight. No buyer's premium.*

Established 1846

Regular Specialist Sales:

RUSSELL, BALDWIN & BRIGHT

FURNITURE
WORKS of ART
PORCELAIN & POTTERY
SILVER
PEWTER
CLOCKS
MUSICAL BOXES
BRONZES
BOOKS and PICTURES
BYGONES
ORIENTAL CARPETS

VALUATIONS for all purposes carried out by our qualified staff
SALES by AUCTION of the contents of Town and Country Houses conducted throughout the West Midlands and Wales
Enquiries: The Fine Art Saleroom, Ryelands Road, LEOMINSTER (Tel. 0568 3897), Herefordshire

---

Hertfordshire continued

Norris and Duvall — Furniture and Fine Art Auctioneers and Valuers
106 Fore St., Hertford, SG14 1AH. Tel. 0992 52249. *Monthly sales of 18th and 19th century furniture and effects at Castle Hall, Hertford. Selected entries invited from private customers, details to be received at least a fortnight before each sale. Annual catalogue subscription £12.*

Pamela and Barry Auctions
Antiques and collectors auctions held fortnightly at Village Hall, Sandridge, St. Albans, AL4 9ST. Tel. 0727 61180 *for details.*

G.E. Sworder and Sons
Chequers, 19 North St., Bishops Stortford. Tel. 0279 52441. *Six weekly sales on Tuesdays of antique and selected items, weekly sales of household items. On view Saturday prior to sale 10.30a.m.—12.30p.m. Monday prior to sale 10a.m.—4.30p.m. General sales on Thursdays, viewing morning of sale. Catalogues available on request.*

Watson's
Water Lane, Bishops Stortford, CM23 2JZ. Tel. 0279 52361/4. *Every six weeks — selected antique furniture and objets d'art, antique, modern and household furniture. Five times a year — special sales of pictures, jewellery, silver and plate. On view Saturday prior to sale 9.30—12.30p.m. Monday prior to sale 10a.m.—4p.m. Catalogues available on request.*

HUMBERSIDE NORTH

Gilbert Baitson, F.S.V.A.
"The Edwardian Auction Galleries", 194 Anlaby Rd, Hull, HU3 2RJ. Tel. Hull 223355/6. *Sales of antique and modern furnishings every Wednesday at 10.30a.m. Viewing, day prior until 8p.m.*

Broader and Spencer
18 Quay Rd., Bridlington. YO15 2AP. Tel. 0262 670355/6. *Weekly auctions of general items. Special regular antique sales.*

Humberside North continued

Dee and Atkinson
14 North Bar St., Beverley. Tel. 0482 869389. *Regular sales of general antiques. Victorian, silver, jewellery, etc. Sales at 10.30a.m. Viewing 2 days prior. Also at The Exchange, Driffield, YO25 7LJ. Tel. 0377 43151. Bi-monthly antique sales, silver, jewellery etc. at 10.30a.m.*

H. Evans and Sons
1 St. James's St., Hessle Rd., Hull. Tel. 0482 23033. *Six antiques sales per annum, monthly general furniture and effects.*

HUMBERSIDE SOUTH

Dickinson, Davy and Markham
10 Wrawby St., Brigg, DN20 8JH. Tel. 0652 53666. *General fine art and antique auctions held 10 times per annum. Country house sales in Lincolnshire and South Humberside as instructed. Catalogue subscription service available. Buys at auction.*

ISLE OF WIGHT

Watson, Bull and Porter
Auction Rooms, 79-81 Regent St., Shanklin, PO37 7AP. Tel. (098386) 3441. *Monthly auctions of antique furniture.*

Way, Riddett and Co.
Town Hall Chambers, Lind St., Ryde, PO33 2NQ. Tel. 0983 62255. *Bi-monthly sales of general antiques, furniture, paintings, silver, porcelain, etc. Monthly sales of antique and modern furnishings.*

KENT

Albert Andrews Auctions and Sales
Maiden Lane, Crayford, Dartford. DA1 4LX. Tel. 0322 528868. *Weekly auctions on Wednesdays at 10.00a.m. — viewing Tuesdays 4.30p.m.—8.30p.m. — including antiques, Victorian and Edwardian furniture, bric-a-brac, paintings, clocks etc.*

Geering & Colyer
A Black Horse Agency

REGULAR SALES BY AUCTION
and
SALES ALSO HELD ON OWNERS' PREMISES AND VALUATIONS PREPARED FOR ALL PURPOSES

Fine Art Auctioneers and Estate Agents
22/24 High Street, Tunbridge Wells, Kent Tel: (0892) 25136
Further details, and catalogues (£1.30 by post) available from the Auctioneers

---

Kent continued

Baldwin and Partners
Medway Auction Rooms, 26 Railway St., Chatham. ME4 4JT. Tel. 0634 400121. *First Wednesdays monthly.*

Bracketts
27-29 High St., Tunbridge Wells, TN1 1UU. Tel. 0892 33733. *Weekly sale of antiques and general household furniture on Fridays. Special sales of antiques and sales on the premises.*

Butler and Hatch Waterman
102 High St., Tenterden. Tel. 058 06 3233/2083. 86 High St., Hythe. Tel. 0303 66022/3. *Monthly general sales of good quality antique furniture and effects. Special contents sales at private residences in the county.*

Cobbs, Burrows and Day
39/41 Bank St., Ashford, TN23 1DJ. Tel. 0233 24321. *General collective sales at monthly intervals. Specialised sales of antiques and collectors' items every three months.*

Geering and Colyer
22/24 High St., Tunbridge Wells, TN1 1XA. Tel. 0892 25136. *Collective sales at regular intervals and house sales held on the premises. Valuations. Catalogues available (£1.30 posted.)*

Hobbs Parker
Romney House, Ashford Market, Ashford, TN23 1PG. Tel. 0233 22222. *Monthly sales of antiques and household furniture.*

John Hogbin and Son
53 High St., Tenterden, TN30 6BG. Tel. 058 06 3200. *Antique and modern furniture and effects in the first Wednesday of each month. Evening sales of antiques, pictures, porcelain, silver, objets d'art, etc., on the second Wednesday of each month. Also fine art sales at Cranbrook announced in the press.*

Ibbett, Mosely, Card and Co.
125 High St., Sevenoaks, TN13 1VT. Tel. 0732 452246. *Antiques and objets d'art.*

Kent continued

Kent Sales
Kent House, New Rd., South Darenth, DA4 9AR. Tel. 0322 864919. *Specialist sales of militaria, antique weapons, Napoleonic collectables, Imperial German and 3rd Reich memorabilia. Sales of varied theatrical costume, general antiques.*

Parsons, Welch and Cowell
49 London Rd., Sevenoaks. TN13 1AR. Tel. 0732 451211/4. *Monthly sales of antiques and collectors' items.*

Phillips
Bayle Place, 11-13 The Bayle Parade, Folkestone, CT20 1SQ. Tel. 0303 45555. *Monthly fine art sales.*

Messrs. Stewart, Gore
100/102 Northdown Rd., Margate, 137 Canterbury Rd., Westbrook, 191 Northdown Rd., Cliftonville and 95 High St., Broadstairs. Auction Rooms: Clifton Place, Margate. Tel. 0843 221528/9. *Monthly collective sales of antiques. Specialist sales according to demand. Private house sales.*

Ward and Partners
16 High St., Hythe, CT21 5AT. Tel. 0303 67473/4. *Monthly auctions held on Saturday at 5 High St. from 9.30.*

Worsfold's
40 Station Rd. West, Canterbury. Tel. 0227 68984. *Monthly antiques sales.*

LANCASHIRE

Artingstall and Hind
378-380 Deansgate, Knott Mill, Manchester 3 4NA. Tel. 061 834 4559. *Weekly sales on Tuesdays and periodic specialist sales on Thursdays.*

Capes Dunn and Co.
The Auction Galleries, 38 Charles St., Manchester, M1 7DB. Tel. 061 273 6060. *Fine Art Auctioneers founded 1826. Catalogues of fortnightly specialist sales available on request.*

Lancashire continued

Entwistle Green
The Galleries, Kingsway, Ansdell, Lytham St. Annes, FY8 1AB. Tel. 0253 735442. *Sales of antique, reproduction and modern furnishings and appointments held fortnightly on Tuesday and Wednesday. Average 700—1000 lots commencing 10.30a.m. each day. View Saturday morning before noon and Monday to 4p.m.*

McKennas, Auctioneers and Valuers
Bank Salerooms, Harris Court, Clitheroe, BB7 2DP. Tel. 0200 25446/22695. *Antique and older furniture, bric-a-brac, bygones. Regular monthly auction sales held on Thursdays commencing at 10a.m. Fine art, silver, bronzes, specialist sales held quarterly.*

J.R. Parkinson Son and Hamer Auctions
The Auction Room, Rochdale Rd., Bury. Tel. 061 761 1612/7372. *Specialised auctions of antiques, Victoriana and Edwardiana on a 6/8 week basis throughout the year.*

John E. Pinder and Son
Stone Bridge, Longridge, Preston, PR3 3AH. Tel. 077 478 2282/3838. *Mixed antique and period furnishings on alternative Thursdays. Commencing 9.30a.m. Viewing Wednesday prior noon till 7p.m.*

LEICESTERSHIRE

Freckeltons
1 Leicester Rd., Loughborough. LE11 2AE. Tel. 0509 214564. *Monthly sales of general antiques.*

Gilding (Fine Art)
Gumley, Market Harborough, LE16 7RU. Tel. 053753 2847. *Monthly sales of fine art and general items.*

Walker Walton Hanson
4 Market Place, Oakham, LE15 6DT. (Office) 0572 3377. South St., Oakham (Saleroom) 0572 2681. *General sales fortnightly (alternate Thursdays). Special sales of antique furniture, silver, china, jewellery etc. every 6 weeks.*

Warner, Sheppard and Wade
The Warner Auction Rooms, 16/18 Halford St., Leicester, LE1 1JB. Tel. 0533 21613. *Regular sales of antiques, pictures, porcelain, silver, etc., in our rooms; outside sales by arrangement.*

Wolfenden and Britton Auctions Ltd.
Cottontree Sales Rooms, Trawden, Colne. Tel. (0282) 869565. *Monthly sales.*

LINCOLNSHIRE

William H. Brown
Westgate Hall, Grantham, NG31 6LT. Tel. 0476 68861. *Monthly antique and fine art sales. Occasional specialist and house contents sales. Monthly sales of general household furniture and effects.*

A.E. Dowse and Son
89 Mary St., Scunthorpe. Tel. 0724 842039. *Monthly sales of general antiques and collectors' items.*

Lincolnshire continued

Earl and Lawrence
55 Northgate, Sleaford, NG34 7AB. Tel. 0529 302946. *Regular antique and general sales at Northgate Hall, Sleaford (usually every 3 weeks).*

James Eley and Son
1 Main Ridge West, Boston. Tel. 0205 61687. *Regular sales at Boston and Skegness.*

Escritt and Barrell
Elmer House, Grantham. Tel. 0476 65371. *Monthly sales.*

Lyall and Co.
Market Place, Bourne Salerooms, Spalding Rd., Bourne. Tel. 0778 422686 or 0778 422431. *Antiques sales every two months. Antique and modern furniture sales every three weeks.*

Thomas Mawer and Son
63 Monks Rd., Lincoln, LN2 5HP. Tel. 0522 24984. *General sales every fortnight. Catalogued antique sales monthly.*

Henry Spencer Vergettes
38 St. Mary's St., Stamford. PE9 2DS. Tel. 0780 52136. *Antique and fine art sales. Also general furniture sales. Buys at auction on commission.*

MERSEYSIDE

Ball and Percival
Salerooms at 21 Hoghton St., Southport. PR9 0AD. Tel. Southport 36900. *Sales of antique, reproduction and modern furnishings held every three weeks. Average 300/400 lots commencing 10a.m. View day prior to sale.*

Robert I. Heyes & Associates
9 Hamilton St., Birkenhead, L41 6DL. Tel. 051 647 9104/5. Also at 24 Cooks Rd., Crosby, Liverpool. Tel. 051 931 4118. *Fortnightly sales of shipping and other furniture and effects. Monthly fine art sales of antique furniture, porcelain, silver, jewellery, coins, metalware, paintings, rugs. Regular sales of antiquarian books, maps, postcards. Ser: Valuations for insurance or probate.*

Kingsley and Co. Auctioneers
3/4 The Quadrant, Hoylake, Wirral, L47 2EE. Tel. 051 632 5821. *Sales every Tuesday of antiques, fine art and general chattels.*

Outhwaite and Litherland
"Kingsway Galleries", Fontenoy St., Liverpool, L3 2BE. Tel. 051 236 6561/3. *Victorian, Edwardian and modern furnishings — weekly Tuesday. General antiques and fine quality reproductions — fortnightly Wednesday. Fine art sales including all works illustrative of the fine arts — monthly Wednesday. Specialist sales of books, wines, stamps etc. — periodically. Members of The Society of Fine Art Auctioneers.*

KEYS OF AYLSHAM

Norfolk's and one of East Anglia's leading Fine Art Auctioneers.

Conducting regular Sales of Antiques

Periodic Picture and Book Sales at

AYLSHAM SALEROOMS

Weekly Sales of Shipping and Household Furniture and Effects.

Valuations for Probate, Insurance, Family Division and many other purposes.

6 Offices in North Norfolk.

G.A. Key
Incorporated Auctioneers
and Valuers
8 Market Place
Aylsham, Norwich, Norfolk
NR11 6EH
Telephone 0263 733195

NORFOLK

Noel D. Abel
32 Norwich Rd., Watton. Tel. 0953 881204. *Auction of period furniture, silver and art etc., held on the last Friday in every month. Annual catalogue subs. £5.00.*

Clowes, Nash and Thurgar
6 Tombland, Norwich. Tel. 0603 627261. *Antiques and general furniture every fortnight.*

Ewings
Market Place, Reepham, Norwich, NR10 4JJ. Tel. 0603 870473. *Periodic sales of antique and modern furniture and effects.*

Thos. Wm. Gaze and Son
10 Market Hill, Diss, IP22 3JZ. Tel. 0379 51931. *Weekly (Fridays 11.30) sales of antique and cottage furniture, together with special country house sales.*

Charles Hawkins and Sons
Lynn Rd., Downham Market. Tel. 0366 382112/382113. *Sales of antique and modern household furniture and effects etc., held on 2nd Wednesday in each month at 11a.m. at our Downham Market Repository. Fixture card of dates for the year available.*

Nigel F. Hedge
28B Market Place, North Walsham, NR28 9BS. Tel. 0692 402881. *Monthly general and antique sales.*

Norfolk continued

Hilham's
44 Baker St., Gorleston-on-Sea, NR31 6QT. Tel. 0493 662152/600700/604104. *Art auctions held regularly. Antiques and Victoriana sales every month.*

James — Norwich Auctions Ltd.
(Member of the James Group)
Head Office — 33 Timberhill, Norwich NR1 3LA. Tel. 0603 24817. Auctioneer of antiques, and collectors' items. Regular sales, catalogues.

G.A. Key
Incorporated Auctioneers, 8 Market Pl., Aylsham, NR11 6EH. Tel. 0263 733195. *Sales operating from Aylsham salerooms. Three weekly sales of period antique, Victorian furniture, silver, porcelain, etc. Bi-monthly pictures sales for all classes of oils, watercolours, prints, etc. Periodic book sales. Weekly sales of shipping and secondhand furniture. Further details of all sales from auctioneers' offices as above.*

Long and Beck
2 Oak St., Fakenham. MR21 9EB. Tel. 0328 2231. *Weekly sales of antique and other furniture every Thursday at 11a.m. at the Corn Exchange, Fakenham. Annual evening picture sale around the end of March. Country house sales as instructed.*

Hanbury Williams
1 Upper King St., Norwich. Tel. 29691 and 34 Church St., Cromer, NR27 9ES. Tel. 0263 513247. *3-weekly sales at Cromer on a Friday of antique and modern furniture, bric-a-brac, porcelain, silver, etc. (No entries from dealers or manufacturers.) Periodic sales at Norwich.*

NORTHAMPTONSHIRE

Goldsmith and Bass
15 Market Pl., Oundle. Tel. 08327 2349. Approximately bi-monthly.

Heathcote Ball & Co
Old Albion Brewery, Commercial St., Northampton. Tel. 0604 37263/4. *Regular fine art and antiques sales, weekly general sales, specialist sales. Mailing subscription £7 per annum.*

R.L. Lowery and Partners
24 Bridge St., Northampton. NN1 1NT. Tel. 0604 21561. *Country and town house sales. Collective sales mainly to wind up estates. Approx. eight sales p.a. Fine art valuations for probate and family division.*

T.W. Arnold Corby and Co.
30/32 Brook St., Raunds. Tel. 0933 623722/3. *Victoriana and antiques catalogue sales approximately every six weeks.*

Southams
Corn Exchange, Thrapston, Nr. Kettering, NN14 4JJ. Tel. 08012 4486. *Sales of antiques and superior furniture, silver, silver plate, copper, brass, fine china, glass, Oriental rugs, oil paintings, watercolours and prints. Catalogues 70p incl. p. & p. Yearly subscription £7 incl. p. & p. First Thursday each month. Viewing Wednesday 9.30a.m. to 8p.m.*

Northamptonshire continued

H. Wilford Ltd.
Midland Rd., Wellingborough, NN8 1NB. Tel. 0933 222760/222762. *Weekly sales of antique and modern furniture, shipping goods, jewellery, etc. every Thursday.*

NOTTINGHAMSHIRE

Edward Bailey and Son
17 Northgate, Newark, NG24 1EX. Tel. 0636 703141 and 77154. *Monthly sales of antique and Victorian furniture, oil paintings, silver etc. Weekly sales of early 20th C and general household furniture etc.*

Arthur Johnson and Sons Ltd. (Auctioneers)
The Cattle Market, London Rd., Nottingham. Tel. 0602 869128. *About 1,000 lots weekly on Saturday at 10a.m. of antique and shipping furniture, silver, gold, porcelain, metalwares and collectables.*

Neales of Nottingham
192 Mansfield Rd., Nottingham, NG1 3HX. Tel. 0602 624141. *Monthly sales of paintings, drawings, prints and books; European and Oriental furniture, works of art, ceramics and glass; silver, jewellery and bijouterie; decorative arts, 1880-1940. Weekly sales of antiques, Edwardian and reproduction furnishings and decorative arts. Bi-monthly sales of postcards, cigarette cards and ephemera, stamps, coins and medals. Sales in-situ of contents and town and country properties.*

John Pye and Sons
Furniture and General Auctions, Corn Exchange, Cattle Market, London Rd., Nottingham. Tel. 0602 866261/865238.

C.B. Sheppard and Son
The Auction Gallery, Chatsworth St., Sutton-in-Ashfield. Tel. 0773 872419. *Saledays, Mansfield 0623 556310. Monthly sales of antiques, collectors' items, jewellery and works of art. No buyers premium.*

Henry Spencer and Sons — Fine Art Auctioneers
20 The Square, Retford, DN22 6DJ. Tel. 0777 708633. *Specialist sales of furniture, carpets, ornamental items, works of art; paintings, drawings and prints; porcelain and glass. Silver, jewellery and bijouterie. Monthly non-specialist sales of furniture and effects. Sales on the premises at town and country houses.*

Walker Walton Hanson
Byard Lane, Bridlesmith Gate, Nottingham, NG1 2GL. Tel. 0602 586161. *General sales every 2 weeks on Wednesday; fine art and antiques, 3 monthly.*

OXFORDSHIRE

Green and Co.
33 Market Pl., Wantage, OX12 8AL. Tel. 023 57 3561/2. *Regular sales of antiques and other furniture, copper, brass, china, glass, silver and plate, clocks and objets d'art, both in private houses and at salerooms.*

Oxfordshire continued

Holloways
49 Parsons St., Banbury, OX16 8PF. Tel. 0295 53197. *Regular sales on first and third Tuesday of the month.*

Mallams
Fine Art Auctioneers, 24 St. Michael's St., Oxford. Tel. 0865 241358. *Monthly sales of antiques and works of art. Bi-monthly specialist sales.*

Messenger's
Pevensey House Salerooms, Manorsfield Rd., Bicester, OX6 7JF. Tel. 0869 252901. *Antique furniture and effects each month. Specialist sales of carpentry tools, collectors items and domestic bygones.*

Phillips inc. Brooks
39 Park End St., Oxford, OX1 1JD. Tel. 0865 723524. *Regular specialist sales of antique furniture and works of art, ceramics and glassware, silver and jewellery, Eastern rugs and carpets, paintings, books and collectors' items. Quarterly sales of fine wines.*

SHROPSHIRE

Cooper and Green
3 Barker St., Shrewsbury. Tel. 0743 50081 and at 4 Church St., Ludlow. Tel. 3721.

Hall, Wateridge and Owen
Welsh Bridge Salerooms, Shrewsbury. Tel. 0743 60212. *Regular Victoriana and household (Fridays). Regular special antiques. And at Bridge Road Salerooms, Wellington, Telford. Tel. Telford 54242. Fortnightly household and general (Tuesday).*

Nock Deighton and Son
10 Broad St., Ludlow. Tel. 0584 2364/3760.

Perry and Phillips
Newmarket Salerooms, Newmarket Buildings, Listley St., Bridgnorth, WV16 4AW. Tel. 074 62 2248. *Weekly sales of good quality household furniture and effects. Monthly sales of antique furniture, Victoriana, china, porcelain, pictures etc. Regular specialist sales and house contents sales.*

SOMERSET

Cooper and Tanner Ltd.
Salerooms at: 14 North Parade, Frome, BA11 1AU. Tel. 0373 62045. 41 High St., Glastonbury, BA6 9DS. Tel. 0458 31077. 44A Commercial Rd., Shepton Mallet, BA4 5DN. Tel. 0749 2607. *Collective monthly sales of antique and modern furniture and effects, including china, brass, silver, carpets, pictures and prints. Sales are held on a regular basis as follows: Glastonbury auction rooms 1st Friday in the month; Frome Market Salerooms 2nd Friday in the month; Shepton Mallet auction rooms 3rd Friday in the month. Each sale commences at 11a.m. Auctioneers delivery service.*

Somerset continued

Jackson-Stops and Staff
30 Hendford, Yeovil, BA20 1UA. Tel. (0935)
74066. *Sales of private house contents held
on the premises. SER: Valuations.*

Lawrence Fine Art of Crewkerne
South St., Crewkerne TA18 8AB. Tel. 0460
73041. *Specialist auctioneers and valuers.
Regular sales of antiques and fine art.*

The London Cigarette Card Co. Ltd.
Sutton Rd., Somerton, TA11 6QP. Tel. 0458
73452. *Suppliers of thousands of different
series of cigarette and trade cards, and special
albums. Publishers of catalogues, reference
books, and monthly magazine. Regular
auctions in London. S.A.E. for details. Mail
order, open by appointment.*

Nuttall Richards and Co.
The Town Hall, Axbridge, BS26 2AR. Tel.
732969. *Six-weekly sales of privately entered
fine art and selected antiques of all categories.
Extra sales conducted on owners premises
when instructed. SER: Valuations; inventories
prepared.*

Phillips, Sanders and Stubbs
32 The Avenue, Minehead, TA24 5AZ. Tel.
0643 2281/2/3. *Regular sales every three
weeks of antique and other furniture and
effects at Mart Road Salerooms, Minehead.
Occasional house clearance sales.*

Priory Saleroom
Winchester St., Taunton, TA1 1RN. Tel. 0823
77121. *Monthly sales of antique and good
quality modern furniture, silver, plate, copper
and brass, china and glassware, pictures and
prints etc. Catalogues subscription £8 p.a.*

Tamlyn and Son
56 High St., Bridgwater, TA6 3BN. Tel. 0278
458241/2.

Wellington Salerooms
Mantle St., Wellington, TA21 8AR. Tel. 082
347 4815. *Fortnightly sales of general
antiques and shipping goods, preceded by
selected modern furnishings.*

STAFFORDSHIRE

Bagshaws
17 High St., Uttoxeter. Tel. 088 93 2811.
*Monthly collective sales of antique and house-
hold furniture. Special house sales and farmhouse sales on the premises as required.*

John German
The Rotunda, Burton-on-Trent, DE14 1LN.
Tel. 0283 42051. *Occasional sales of major
house contents; specialist fine art valuation
department.*

Hall and Lloyd, Auctioneers. Est. 1882
7 Church Lane, Stafford. ST16 2DZ. Tel.
0785 58176. *Regular fortnightly sales at
South St. auction rooms of antique and
general household furniture and effects.
1,000 or more lots every other Thursday.
Special catalogued sales of antiques held
quarterly.*

Staffordshire continued

Louis Taylor and Sons
Percy St., Hanley, Stoke-on-Trent, ST1 1NF.
Tel. 0782 260222. *Approx. four special fine
art sales each year which include all classes of
fine art, furniture, pictures, china, pottery,
silver and objets d'art. Specialist Royal
Doulton auctions.*

Wintertons
St. Mary's Chambers, Lichfield, WS13 6LQ.
Tel. 054 32 23256. *Monthly sales of antiques
and fine art of various specialised categories
and monthly sales of general furniture and
effects.*

SUFFOLK

Abbotts (incorporating) Spear & Sons
The Hill, Wickham Market, nr. Woodbridge,
IP13 0QX. Tel. 0728 746321. *Sales every
Monday, except some Bank Holidays, at
12.45p.m. at Wickham Market salerooms
situated at Campsea Ashe, comprising 300
lots; antique and cottage furniture, Victoriana
and bric-a-brac. Monthly sales in new saleroom comprising 400 lots; Georgian and other
antique furniture, porcelain, pictures, silver
and objets d'art. Viewing Saturdays 9a.m. –
11a.m. for Monday sales. Monthly sales
normally Wednesday, viewing Monday before
2p.m. – 8p.m. SER: Buys at auction.*

H.A. Adnams
The Auction Room, 98 High St., Southwold.
Tel. 0502 723292.

Boardman – Fine Art Auctioneers
Station Road Corner, Haverhill, CB9 0EY. Tel.
0440 703784. *Large sales held bi-monthly
specialising in furniture, alternating oak and
mahogany. The largest special sales of oak
furniture in Great Britain.*

Diamond Mills and Co.
117 Hamilton Rd., Felixstowe, IP11 7BL. Tel.
0394 282281 (2 lines). *Auctions at The
Orwell Hall, Orwell Rd., Felixstowe, approx.
every 3 weeks.*

Durrant's
10 New Market, Beccles. Tel. 0502 712122.
*Antique and general furniture auctions every
Friday at own showrom Gresham Rd.,
Beccles.*

Charles Hawkins
Notleys Salerooms, Royal Thoroughfare,
Lowestoft. Tel. (0502) 2024. *Regular auction
sales (catalogued) of antiques, pictures, silver
and jewellery. Periodic special evening sales.*

Jackson-Stops and Staff
168 High St., Newmarket. CB8 9AJ. Tel
0638 662231. *Sales of private house contents
held on the premises. SER: Valuations.*

James – In Suffolk
St. John's Antique Centre, 30 St. John's St.,
Bury St. Edmunds, IP33 1SN. Tel. 0284
702415.

Shoulder mantle, Afghan, c.1805, 137cm x 304cm. From **The Kashmir Shawl** by Frank Ames, published by the **Antique Collectors' Club,** 1986.

Suffolk continued

Lacy Scott (Fine Art Dept.)
10 Risbygate St., Bury St. Edmunds, IP33
3AA. Tel. 0284 63531. *Quarterly sales of fine art including antique and decorative furniture, silver, pictures, ceramics, etc. on behalf of executors and private vendors. Regular (every three weeks). Sales of Victoriana and general household contents. Also bi-annual sales of working steam scale models and annual sales of fine wines.*

Neal Sons and Fletcher
26 Church St., Woodbridge, IP12 1DP. Tel.
2263. *Four to five special mixed antiques sales per year. Individual specialised sales and complete house contents sales as required. Household furniture sales monthly.*

Olivers
23/24 Market Hill, Sudbury. CO10 6EN. Tel.
0787 72247. *Weekly sales of antique and household furniture and shipping goods. Regular sales of good quality antiques. Illustrated fine arts review published annually. Enquiries to: James Fletcher, F.R.I.C.S. Furniture and Fine Art Dept.*

Phillips inc. Garrod Turner
Dover House, Wolsey St., Ipswich. Tel.
(0473) 55137, and Garrod Turner Salerooms,
50 St. Nicholas St., Ipswich. Tel. (0473)
54664. Office no. (0473) 55137. *Three specialist sales per month.*

Tuohy and Son
Denmark House, 18 High St., Aldeburgh. Tel.
072885 2066. *Collective sales 6 times a year or by arrangement. Jan., Mar., May, July, Sept., Nov. Antique sales by arrangement.*

H.C. Wolton and Son
6 Whiting St., Bury St. Edmunds. IP33 1PB.
Tel. 0284 61336. *High class sales of selected antiques. 60 years experience of Fine Art sales.* SER: Valuations.

SURREY

Clarke Gammon
45 High St., and Bedford Rd., Guildford. GU1
3EF. Tel. 0483 572266/66458.

Lawrences' — Fine Art Auctioneers
Norfolk House, 80 High St., Bletchingley. Tel.
0883 843323. *Monthly fine art auctions.*

Messenger May Baverstock
93 High St., Godalming. Tel. 048 68 23567.
Fine art at 93 High St. General and shipping goods at Bridge St., Godalming. SER: Valuations.

Wentworth Auction Galleries
21 Station Approach, Virginia Water. GU25
4DW. Tel. 09904 3711. *Antique and general sales every four to six weeks.*

Surrey continued

Harold Williams Bennett and Partners
2/3 South Parade, Merstham, Redhill, RH1
3EG. Tel. 073 74 2234/5 and at Redhill, Reigate, Caterham, Godstone, Croydon and Westminster. *Monthly sales of antique, reproduction and modern furniture and effects, silver and plate, bronze, copper and brass, ornamental china and glass, pictures and jewellery. Private house sales.*

P.F. Windibank
18—20 Reigate Rd., Dorking. RH4 1SG. Tel.
0306 884556. *General antique sales held each calendar month. Specialised picture, book sales at certain intervals.*

SUSSEX EAST

Burstow and Hewett
Abbey Auction Galleries and Granary Sale Rooms, Battle TN33 0AT. Tel. 04246
2302/2374. *Monthly sales of antique furniture, silver, jewellery, porcelain, brass, rugs, etc., at the Abbey Auction Galleries. Also monthly evening sales of pictures, coins, books and stamps. At the Granary Sale Rooms — monthly sales of furniture, china, silver, brass, etc.*

Clifford Dann Auction Galleries
Fine Art Auction Galleries, 20-21 High St., Lewes. BN7 2LN. Tel. 0273 477022. *General sales of period furniture, oil paintings, watercolour drawings, porcelain, carpets, silver, jewellery, books, etc. every six weeks on Tuesdays.*

Fryer's Auction Galleries
Terminus Rd., Bexhill-on-Sea. Tel. 0424
212994. *Fortnightly sales of collective household goods including shipping goods. Antiques and collectors' items sold every six weeks.*

Gorringe's Auction Galleries
15 North St., Lewes. Tel. 0273 472503.
Sales approx. every 6 weeks of period furniture, Oriental carpets and rugs, oil paintings, watercolour drawings and prints, decorative china, glass, silver plate, jewellery etc.

Graves, Son and Pilcher
71 Church Rd., Hove, BN3 2GL. Tel. 0273
735266. *Monthly sales of fine art including antique furniture, pictures, silver, Oriental carpets and rugs and ornamental items. Specialised sales of primitive art, coins, books and jewellery.*

Edgar Horn
Auction Galleries, 46/50 South St., Eastbourne, BN21 4XB. Tel. 0323 22801/2/3.
Approx. ten sales per year, each including antique furniture, porcelain, glass and collectors' items, Oriental rugs and carpets. Specialist sales of silver and jewellery, oil paintings and watercolours, prints, etc.

Raymond P. Inman
The Auction Galleries, 35 and 40 Temple St., Brighton. BN1 3BH. Tel. 0273 774777.
Monthly collective sales, including silver and jewellery.

Sussex East continued

Lewes Auction Rooms (Julian Dawson)
56 High St., Lewes, BN7 1XE. Tel. 0273 478221. *Antique and reproduction furniture and effects every six weeks. General furniture and bric-a-brac every Monday.*
Vidler and Co.
Rye Auction Galleries, Cinque Ports St., Rye, TN31 7AL. Tel. 0797 222124. *Sales on first Friday each month 10a.m.*
Wallis and Wallis
West Street Auction Galleries, West St., Lewes, BN7 2NJ. Tel. 0273 473137. *Nine annual sales of arms and armour, militaria, coins and medals. Specimen catalogue £1.50. Current combined catalogues £4.25.*

SUSSEX WEST

T. Bannister and Co. (Est. 1866)
The Market Salerooms, Haywards Heath, RH16 1DH. Tel. 0444 412402. *Auctions of antique and reproduction furniture and effects. Annual subscription £6.50 for catalogues. No buyers premium.*
R.H. Ellis and Sons
44/46 High St., Worthing, BN11 1LL. Tel. 0903 38999. *Monthly specialist auctions of antique, Victorian and Edwardian furniture, porcelain, silver and paintings.*
Fox and Sons Worthing Auctions
41 Chapel Rd., Worthing, BN11 1EL. Tel. 0903 205565. *Weekly general antique furniture sales, viewing Mondays, sale Tuesdays at 31 Chatsworth Rd. commencing 9.30a.m. Easter week viewing Tuesdays, sale Wednesdays.*
Garth Denham and Associates
Horsham Auction Galleries, The Carfax, Horsham. Tel. 0403 53837. *Two day antique sales. Monthly on Wed. sales of good furniture of all periods, silver, jewellery, European and Oriental ceramics and collectors' items, paintings, drawings, prints and bronzes, metalware, and Oriental carpets and rugs, general antiques, modern and shipping furniture. Periodic sales of books, stamps, coins and medals, arms and armour and specialist collections as advertised.*
Jackson-Stops and Staff
37 South St., Chichester, PO19 1EL. Tel. 0243 786316. *Sales of private house contents held on the premises. SER: Valuations.*
G. Knight and Son
West St., Midhurst, GU29 9NG. Tel. 073081 2456/7/8. *General sales of antique and modern furniture and effects every 6−8 weeks.*

Sussex West continued

Sotheby's in Sussex
Summers Place, Billingshurst, RH14 9AD. Tel. 040381 3933. Telex Gavel 87210. *Fortnightly specialist sales of paintings, furniture, carpets, clocks, ceramics, glass, silver, jewellery, weapons, toys, books and Oriental items.*

Stride and Son
Southdown House, St. John's St., Chichester, PO19 1XQ. Tel. 0243 782626/780207. *Last Friday of each month — antiques and general sales.*
Sussex Auction Galleries
59 Perrymount Rd., Haywards Heath, RH16 3DS. Tel. 0444 414935. *Selected furniture, ceramics, silver, jewellery, clocks, Persian rugs, Victoriana.*
Turner, Rudge and Turner
29 High St., East Grinstead. Tel. 0342 24101/3. *Offices also at Uckfield, Crawley and Crawley Down.*
Wyatt and Son
59 East St., Chichester, PO19 1HN. Tel. 0243 786581. *Sales twice per month. Tuesday sales of household furniture and effects. Thursday sales of antique and reproduction furniture, clocks, paintings, Persian and other carpets. Sales commence at 10a.m. View day prior to sale. Also sales of silver and porcelain.*

TYNE AND WEAR

Anderson and Garland
Fine Art Salerooms, Anderson House, Market St., Newcastle-upon-Tyne, NE1 6XA. Tel. 0632 326278. *Monthly sales of antique furniture and effects.*

Boldon Auction Galleries
24a Front St., East Boldon. NE36 OSJ. Tel. 0783 372630. *Quarterly antique auctions.*

Thomas N. Miller
18—22 Gallowgate, Newcastle-upon-Tyne, 1. Tel. 0632 325617/8. *Auctions of antiques every Wednesday and every other Thursday.*

WARWICKSHIRE

John Briggs and Calder
Chartered Surveyors, 133 Long St., Atherstone. CV9 1AD. Tel. 082 77 68911. Also at Clinton House, Coleshill, Birmingham. Tel. Coleshill 62355 and 62805, and 1 Victoria Rd., Tamworth (Staffordshire). Tel. Tamworth 61144. *Auctions on clients' instructions.*

Colliers, Bigwood and Bewlay
The Old School, Tiddington, Stratford-upon-Avon, CV37 7AW. Tel. 0789 69415. *Regular auction sales held every Friday. Specialist sales monthly. Catalogue subscription rates available on request.*

Thomas Hemming and Son
Tudor House, 18 Church St., Alcester. Tel. 0789 762712. *Occasional sales.*

Henley in Arden Auction Sales Ltd.
The Estate Office, Warwick Rd., Henley-in-Arden. B95 5BH. Tel. 05642 3211. *Regular Saturday sales of antique and modern furniture and effects.*

Locke and England
1 and 2 Euston Place, Leamington Spa, CV32 4LW. Tel. 0926 27988. Salerooms: Walton House, 11 The Parade, Leamington Spa. *Antique furniture, porcelain, pictures, silver, etc., each month. Shipping goods, Victorian and Edwardian furniture, household and effects. Weekly Thursdays at 11a.m. house contents sales. Phone for full details.*

Seaman of Rugby
132 Railway Terrace, Rugby, CV21 3AW. Tel. 0788 2367. *Regular specialist antique and house contents auctions.*

Warwick and Warwick Ltd.
Arbon House, 21 Jury St., Warwick, CV34 4EH. Tel. 0926 499031. *Philatelic auctioneers and private treaty specialists. Auctions normally held on the first Wednesday of every month with philatelic material covering the whole world, also picture postcards and ephemera.*

WEST MIDLANDS

Biddle and Webb
Ladywood Middleway, Birmingham, B16 OPP. Tel. 021 455 8042. *Fine art sales first Friday of every month, antique sales on second Friday of every month, silver and jewellery sales on fourth Friday of every month, quarterly sales of antique photographica and scientific instruments at 11a.m. Also specialist sales periodically. Weekly sales of Victoriana and collectables. Tuesdays at 10.30a.m.*

Cecil Cariss and Son
20/22 High St., Kings Heath, Birmingham 14. Tel. 021 444 5311. *General sales of antique furniture, chattles, etc., and periodical specialist sales.*

Codsall Antique Auctions
Codsall Village Hall, Nr. Wolverhampton. Tel. Willenhall 0902 66728. *Alternate Wednesday evening sales of Victorian antiques and shipping goods.*

Fellows and Sons
Bedford House, 88 Hagley Rd., Edgbaston, Birmingham, B16 8LU. Tel. 021 454 1261/1219. *Auctioneers of antique and modern jewellery, silver, objets vertu and fine art.*

James and Lister Lea, Est'd. 1846
11 Newhall St., Birmingham, B3 3PF. Tel. 021 236 1751. *Approx. four sales a year of contents of country and town houses as required. All sale items are from private sources with an emphasis on the more unusual collectors' items. No buyer's premium.*

Johnson Brothers (Treasure Chest Ltd.)
1267/69 Pershore Rd., Stirchley. B30 2YT. Tel. 021 459 4587/458 3705.

Phillips
The Old House, Station Rd., Knowle, Solihull, B93 0HT. Tel. 056 45 6151. *Specialised weekly sales of (a) furniture and works of art, (b) silver and jewellery, (c) Victoriana, (d) paintings and watercolours, (e) Collectors' items, (f) ceramics, (g) books. Free sales programme available on request.*

Weller and Dufty Ltd.
141 Bromsgrove St., Birmingham, B5 6RQ. Tel. 021 692 1414. *Ten sales per annum, approximately every five weeks, all consisting of antique and modern firearms, edged weapons, militaria, etc. Postal bids accepted. Illustrated catalogue available.*

WILTSHIRE

Allen and Harris
The Plank Auction Rooms, Old Town, Swindon. Tel. 0793 615915/615916. *Weekly auctions of antique furniture, shipping goods, china, glass and collectors' items on Saturdays. Antique sales on last Thursday in month.*

Wiltshire continued

Berry, Powell and Shackell
46 Market Pl., Chippenham, SN15 3HU. Tel.
0249 653361. *Sales of antique and modern
furniture, silver, pictures, ceramics, collectables etc., approx. once a month on
Wednesday at 10.30a.m.*

Dennis Pocock and Drewett
20 High St., Marlborough, SN8 1AA. Tel.
0672 53471/2. *Antique and quality furniture
and effects sales on first Wednesday in each
month, general household furniture and
effects on second Wednesday each month.*

Woolley and Wallis
The Castle Auction Mart, Salisbury, SP1 3SU.
Tel. 0722 21711. *Monthly sales of antique
furniture, porcelain, and pottery, glass and
metalwork. Special sales of Eastern carpets
and rugs, books and maps, also paintings,
watercolours and prints. Quarterly sales of
silver and plated items, jewellery, objects of
art, etc.*

YORKSHIRE NORTH

Boulton and Cooper Ltd.
St. Michaels House, Market Pl., Malton, YO17
0LR. Tel. 0653 2151. Members of S.O.F.A.A.
*Monthly general sales. Bi-monthly antiques
sales at Malton, Seamer and Stokesley. Bi-
monthly brocante sales at Pickering and
Seamer.*

H.C. Chapman and Son
The Auction Mart, North St., Scarborough,
YO11 1DL. Tel. 0723 372424. *Members of
S.O.F.A.A. Monthly special sales of antiques
and fine art. Monthly sales of Victorian,
Edwardian and later shipping furniture and
bric-a-brac. Sales held on Tuesdays. Viewing
for antique sales Friday 2p.m. — 9p.m.,
Saturday 10a.m.—4p.m. Monday 9a.m.—
12noon. Catalogues annual subscription £12.*

James Johnston
The Square, Boroughbridge, YO5 9AS. Tel.
090 12 2382. *Occasional private dispersal
sales.*

Lawson, Larg
St. Trinity House, King's Square, York, YO1
2BH. Tel. 0904 21532. *Sales of antiques and
general contents. Periodic catalogue and
country house sales.*

Morphets of Harrogate
4 Albert St., Harrogate, HG1 1JL. Tel. 0423
502282. *Thursday sales embracing antiques,
works of art and related items. Catalogue
subscription scheme.*

Renton and Renton
Fine Art Auctioneers and Valuers, 16 Albert
St., Harrogate. Tel. 0423 61531. *Weekly
general sales of antiques and miscellanea.
Frequent catalogue sales of period furniture,
objects of art, porcelain, pictures, silver and
jewellery.*

Yorkshire North continued

M. Philip H. Scott
Church Wynd, Burneston, Bedale, DL8 2JE.
Tel. 0677 23325. *Specialist fine art
auctioneers holding four or five sales per
annum in Northallerton These collective
catalogue sales comprise period furniture, fine
clocks, silver, porcelain, pottery, glassware,
period metalware and Victoriana. Buyer's
premium 5.75%. Vendor's commission scaled
to value of individual items.*

Stephenson and Son
43 Gowthorpe, Selby, YO8 0HE. Tel. 0757
706707. *Six sales annually of antique and
Victorian furniture, silver and paintings.*

G.A. Suffield and Co.
27 Flowergate, Whitby. YO21 3AX. Tel.
0947 603433. *Monthly antiques sales. VAT:
Stan.*

Geoffrey Summersgill, A.S.V.A.
8 Front St., Acomb, York, YO2 3BW and at
Market Pl., Easingwold. Tel. 0904 791131
and 0347 21366. *Monthly auctions of
antiques and household effects. Collectors'
items.*

Tennant's
26/27 Market Pl., Leyburn, DL8 5AS. Tel.
0969 23451. *Sales held every other Saturday
at Middleham Salerooms (antiques and later
residual house contents — approx. 600 lots.)
No catalogues. View Fridays. Catalogue sales
held at Richmond Salerooms, with major sales
every April and November. Sales frequently
held on vendors' premises during summer
months.*

YORKSHIRE SOUTH

A.E. Dowse and Son
Cornwall Galleries, Scotland St., Sheffield.
Tel. (0742) 25858. *Monthly sales of antiques
and collectors' items.*

Eadon Lockwood and Riddle
Western Saleroom, Crookes, Sheffield S10
1UA. Tel. 0742 686294. *General sales each
month. Occasional collective antique sales.*

Stanilands
28 Nether Hall Rd., Doncaster, DN1 2PW. Tel.
0302 67766 or 27121 ext. 43. *Monthly sales
of miscellanea, Victorian and Edwardian items
and shipping goods. Bi-monthly catalogue
sales. Periodic ephemera, stamp, coin sales.*

YORKSHIRE WEST

Armitage, Hewitt and Hellowell
32 Queen St., Huddersfield. Tel. 0484
26118. *Occasional antique sales.*

Butterfield's
The Auction Galleries, Riddings Rd., Ilkley,
LS29 9LU. Tel. 0943 603313. *Monthly antique, specialist and collectors items. Sporting
sales.*

Dacre, Son and Hartley
1-5 The Grove, Ilkley, LS29 8HS. Tel. 0943
600655. *Twenty-five furniture sales per year
including approx. six good antique sales at the
Ilkley salerooms, and in country houses.*

Stand, ebonised and inlaid wood, made by George Bullock in 1816 for Abbotsford. The silver neoclassical urn of 'Attic' bones presented by Lord Byron to Sir Walter Scott in 1815 was placed on this in the library.
From *Regency Furniture* by Frances Collard, published by the **Antique Collectors' Club,** 1985.

Yorkshire West continued

Ernest R. de Rome
12 New John St., Bradford. Tel. 0274 734116/9. *Weekly sales.*

Eddisons
Auction Rooms, 4/6 High St., Huddersfield, HD1 2LS. Tel. 0484 33151. *General sales every three weeks. Special catalogue sales of antiques, silver and pictures held quarterly.*

Garside, Waring and Robinson
Harrison House, 15 Harrison Rd., Halifax. HX1 2AF. Tel. 0422 53527/62138.

Laidlaws
Crown Court Salerooms, off Wood St., Wakefield, WF1 2SU. Tel. 0924 375301. *Auctions bi-monthly.*

Phillips at Hepper House
17A East Parade, Leeds. Tel. 0532 448011. *Monthly sales of antique furniture and objects of art and regular speciality sales of pictures, ceramics, silver/jewellery, books, etc.*

John H. Raby and Son
Salem Auction Rooms, 21 St. Mary's Rd., Bradford, BD8 7QL. Tel. 0274 491121. *Sales of antique furniture and pictures every 4–6 weeks.*

CHANNEL ISLANDS

Langlois Ltd
Don St., St. Helier, Jersey. Tel. 0534 22441. *Quarterly antique sales.*

F. Le Gallais and Sons
(Auctioneers and Valuers), Bath St., Jersey. Est. 1825. Tel. 0534 30202. *Sales held every Wednesday and Friday. Items accepted for regular antiques sales, and regular collections from the mainland. No buyers premium. No V.A.T.*

SCOTLAND

John Anderson Auctioneers
33 Cross St., Fraserburgh, Aberdeens. Tel. 0346 28878. *Weekly furniture sales held Tuesday evenings at Strichen.*

Christie's and Edmiston's Ltd.
164-166 Bath St., Glasgow, G2 4TG. Tel. 041 332 8134/7. Telex 779901. *Christie's Scottish saleroom holding regular sales of jewellery, silver, porcelain, furniture and paintings, together with specialist sales and those of particular Scottish interest.*

Frasers (Auctioneers)
28-30 Church St., Inverness. IV1 1EH. Tel. 0463 232395. *Sales every two weeks on Thursday and Friday.*

Thomas Love and Sons Ltd.
South St. John's St., Perth, Perthshire PH1 5SU. Tel. 0738 24111. *General weekly sales of household furniture, etc. on Fridays (10.30a.m.). Sales of antique and reproduction furniture, silver and plate, paintings, Eastern rugs and carpets quarterly.*

Scotland continued

Lyon and Turnball
51 George St., Edinburgh, Midlothian. Tel. 031 225 4627..

John Milne
9 North Silver St., Aberdeen, AB1 1RJ. Tel. 0224 639336. *Weekly general sales, regular catalogue sales of antiques, silver, paintings, books, jewellery and collectors' items.*

Robert Paterson and Son
8 Orchard St., Paisley, PA1 1UZ, Renfrewshire. Tel. 041 889 2435. *Every second Tuesday.*

Phillips in Scotland
98 Sauchiehall St., Glasgow, G2 3DQ. Tel. 041 332 2286. *Oil paintings, watercolours, furniture, British Oriental and Continental ceramics, silver and jewellery – all monthly. Collectors items – bi-monthly; modern furniture and carpets – weekly. And at 65 George St., Edinburgh, EH2 2JL. Tel. 031 225 2266. Oil paintings, furniture, Oriental rugs, objets d'art, silver, British Oriental and Continental ceramics – all monthly; rare and modern books, watercolours and prints, jewellery – bi-monthly; dolls and lace – quarterly.*

L.S. Smellie and Sons Ltd.
Within The Furniture Market, Lower Auchingramont Rd., Hamilton, ML3 6BB. Tel. 0698 282007. *Extensive sales of household furniture, antiques, etc., every Monday at 10.00a.m.; also quarterly sales of fine antiques all held within the Furniture Market, Lower Auchingramont Rd., Hamilton.*

Taylor's Auction Rooms
11 Panmure Row, Montrose, Angus, DD10 8HH. Tel. 0674 72775. *Antique sales held every second Saturday.*

Thomson, Roddick and Laurie Ltd.
60 Whitesands, Dumfries. Tel. 0387 55366.

WALES

Dodds Property World
Victoria Auction Galleries, Mold, Clwyd, CH7 1EB. Tel. 0352 2552. *Weekly auctions of general furniture, shipping goods on Wednesdays at 10.30a.m. Bi-monthly auctions of antique furniture, silver, porcelain and pictures etc. on Wednesday evenings at 6p.m. Catalogues available.*

John Francis, S.O.F.A.A. Chartered Surveyors
Curiosity Sale Rooms, King St., Carmarthen, SA31 1BS. Tel. 0267 233456/7. *Antique sales every six weeks. Household sales at regular intervals.*

King Thomas, Lloyd Jones and Co.
Bangor House, High St., Lampeter, Dyfed. Tel. 0570 422550/422855. *Monthly sales of general antiques. No buyer's premium.*

Harry Ray and Co.
Lloyds Bank Chambers, Welshpool, SY21 7RR. Tel. 0938 2555. *Fortnightly country sales.*

Rennie
1 Agincourt St., Monmouth, NP5 3DZ. Tel. 0600 2916. *Monthly sales of antique furniture and effects, usually on Thursday.*

ALPHABETICAL LIST OF TOWNS AND VILLAGES WITH THE COUNTIES UNDER WHICH THEY APPEAR IN THIS GUIDE

A

Abbots Bromley, Staffs.
Aberdeen, Aberd., Scot.
Aberfeldy, Perths., Scot.
Aberford, W. Yorks.
Abergavenny, Gwent, Wales.
Abergele, Clwyd, Wales.
Abersoch, Gwynedd, Wales.
Aberystwyth, Dyfed, Wales.
Abingdon, Oxon.
Abinger Hammer, Surrey.
Abridge, Essex.
Accrington, Lancs.
Adderley, Shrops.
Addingham, W. Yorks.
Addlestone, Surrey.
Albrighton, Shrops.
Alcester, Warks.
Aldbourne, Wilts.
Aldbury, Herts.
Aldeburgh, Suffolk.
Alderley Edge, Cheshire.
Aldsworth, Glos.
Alford, Aberd., Scot.
Alfreton, Derbys.
Alfriston, E. Sussex.
Allonby, Cumbria.
Alnwick, Northumb.
Alresford, Hants.
Alrewas, Staffs.
Alsager, Cheshire.
Alton, Staffs.
Altrincham, Cheshire.
Alum Bay, Isle of Wight.
Alverstoke, Hants.
Ambergate, Derbys.
Ambleside, Cumbria.
Amersham, Bucks.
Ampthill, Beds.
Ancaster, Lincs.
Angarrack, Cornwall.
Angmering, W. Sussex.
Annfield Plain, Durham.
Anstey, Leics.
Appleby-in-Westmorland, Cumbria
Appleton, Cheshire.
Ardingley, W. Sussex.
Armagh, Co. Armagh, N. Ireland.
Arnesby, Leics.
Arreton, Isle of Wight.
Arundel, W. Sussex.
Ash Priors, Somerset.
Ash Vale, Surrey.
Ashbourne, Derbys.
Ashburton, Devon.
Ashby de la Zouch, Leics.
Ashfield, Suffolk.
Ashley, Northants.
Ashtead, Surrey.

Ashton-under-Lyne, Lancs.
Askham, Notts.
Aslockton, Notts.
Aspley Guise, Beds.
Aston Upthorne, Oxon.
Atcham, Shrops.
Atherstone, Warks.
Attleborough, Norfolk.
Auchnagatt, Aberd., Scot.
Auchterarder, Perths., Scot.
Avening, Glos.
Aveton Gifford, Devon.
Axbridge, Somerset.
Axminster, Devon.
Aylesbury, Bucks.
Aylsham, Norfolk.
Ayr, Ayr., Scot.

B

Babworth, Notts.
Bakewell, Derbys.
Bala, Gwynedd, Wales.
Balcombe, W. Sussex.
Baldock, Herts.
Balfron, Stirlings., Scot.
Ballater, Aberd., Scot.
Ballyclare, Co. Antrim, N. Ireland.
Bamburgh, Northumb.
Bampton, Devon.
Banbridge, Co. Down, N. Ireland.
Banbury, Oxon.
Banchory, Kincard., Scot.
Bangor, Co. Down, N. Ireland.
Bangor, Gwynedd, Wales.
Bangor-on-Dee, Clwyd, Wales.
Banwell, Avon.
Barmouth, Gwynedd, Wales.
Barnard Castle, Durham.
Barnet, Gtr. London.
Barnoldswick, Lancs.
Barnsley, Glos.
Barnsley, S. Yorks.
Barnstaple, Devon.
Barnt Green, Hereford and Worcs.
Barrhead, Renfrews., Scot.
Barrow-in-Furness, Cumbria.
Barrow-on-Soar, Leics.
Bartlow, Cambs.
Barton, Cheshire.
Basildon, Essex.
Basingstoke, Hants.
Baslow, Derbys.
Bath, Avon.
Bathealton, Somerset.
Batheaston, Avon.

Batley, W. Yorks.
Battle, E. Sussex.
Battlesbridge, Essex.
Bawdeswell, Norfolk.
Bawtry, S. Yorks.
Beaconsfield, Bucks.
Beaminster, Dorset.
Beaulieu, Hants.
Beauly, Inver., Scot.
Beaumaris, Gwynedd, Wales.
Beccles, Suffolk.
Beckenham, Gtr. London.
Bedale, N. Yorks.
Bedford, Beds.
Bedingfield, Suffolk.
Beeston, Notts.
Belchamp Otten, Essex.
Belfast, N. Ireland.
Belper, Derbys.
Bembridge, Isle of Wight.
Benson, Oxon.
Bentley, Hants.
Berkeley, Glos.
Berkhamsted, Herts.
Berwick-on-Tweed, Northumb.
Bethel, Gwynedd, Wales.
Bethesda, Gwynedd, Wales.
Betley, Staffs.
Betws-y-Coed, Gwynedd, Wales.
Beverley, N. Humberside.
Bewdley, Hereford and Worcs.
Bexhill-on-Sea, E. Sussex.
Bexley, Gtr. London.
Bicester, Oxon.
Bideford, Devon.
Bidford-on-Avon, Warks.
Bieldside, Aberd., Scot.
Bildeston, Suffolk.
Billericay, Essex.
Billingham, Cleveland.
Bilstone, Leics.
Bingham, Notts.
Bingley, W. Yorks.
Birchington, Kent.
Birdbrook, Essex.
Birdham, W. Sussex.
Birkenhead, Merseyside.
Birley, Hereford and Worcs.
Birmingham, W. Mids.
Birstwith, N. Yorks.
Bishop Monkton, N. Yorks.
Bishops Castle, Shrops.
Bishops Cleeve, Glos.
Bishop's Stortford, Herts.
Bishops Sutton, Hants.
Bishops Waltham, Hants.
Bisley, Glos.
Blackburn, Lancs.
Blackmore, Essex.

Blackpool, Lancs.
Bladon, Oxon.
Blaenau Ffestiniog, Gwynedd, Wales.
Blairgowrie, Perths., Scot.
Blakeney, Norfolk.
Blandford Forum, Dorset.
Blaydon, Tyne and Wear.
Bletchingley, Surrey.
Blewbury, Oxon.
Blockley, Glos.
Boddington, Glos.
Bognor Regis, W. Sussex.
Bolton, Lancs.
Bolton-by-Bowland, Lancs.
Bordon, Hants.
Boreham Street, E. Sussex.
Boroughbridge, N. Yorks.
Bosham, W. Sussex.
Boston, Lincs.
Boston Spa, W. Yorks.
Botley, Hants.
Bottesford, Leics.
Boughton, Kent.
Bourne, Lincs.
Bournemouth, Dorset.
Bourton-on-the-Water, Glos.
Bow Street, Dyfed, Wales.
Bowness-on-Windermere, Cumbria.
Boxford, Suffolk.
Brackley, Northants.
Bradford, W. Yorks.
Bradford-on-Avon, Wilts.
Bradiford, Devon.
Braintree, Essex.
Brampton, Cambs.
Brampton, Cumbria.
Brancaster, Norfolk.
Brancaster Staithe, Norfolk.
Brandsby, N. Yorks.
Branksome, Dorset.
Brasted, Kent.
Braunton, Devon.
Brearton, N. Yorks.
Brecon, Powys, Wales.
Brentwood, Essex.
Brereton, Staffs.
Bressingham, Norfolk.
Brewood, Staffs.
Bridge of Earn, Perths., Scot.
Bridge of Weir, Renfrews., Scot.
Bridgend, Mid. Glam. Wales.
Bridgnorth, Shrops.
Bridlington, N. Humberside.
Bridport, Dorset.
Brierfield, Lancs.
Brighton, E. Sussex.
Brill, Bucks.
Brinkworth, Wilts.
Bristol, Avon.
Brixham, Devon.
Broadway, Hereford and Worcs.

Brobury, Hereford and Worcs.
Brockdish, Norfolk.
Brodick, Isle of Arran, Scot.
Bromley, Gtr. London.
Bromsgrove, Hereford and Worcs.
Bromyard, Hereford and Worcs.
Brookland, Kent.
Brough, Cumbria.
Brough, N. Humberside.
Broughton, Peebles, Scot.
Bruton, Somerset.
Buckden, N. Yorks.
Buckfastleigh, Devon.
Buckingham, Bucks.
Buckminster, Leics.
Bucks Green, W. Sussex.
Bude, Cornwall.
Budleigh Salterton, Devon.
Bulkington, Warks.
Bungay, Suffolk.
Bures, Suffolk.
Burford, Oxon.
Burgess Hill, W. Sussex.
Burgh-le-Marsh, Lincs.
Burghfield Common, Berks.
Burley-in-Wharfedale, W. Yorks.
Burneston, N. Yorks.
Burnham Market, Norfolk.
Burnham-on-Crouch, Essex.
Burnham-on-Sea, Somerset.
Burnley, Lancs.
Burscough, Lancs.
Burton-on-Trent, Staffs.
Burwash, E. Sussex.
Burwell, Cambs.
Bury, Lancs.
Bury, W. Sussex.
Bury St. Edmunds, Suffolk.
Bushey, Herts.
Bushmills, Co. Antrim, N. Ireland.
Buxton, Derbys.

C

Cadeby, Leics.
Cadnam, Hants.
Caernarfon, Gwynedd, Wales.
Caerwys, Clwyd, Wales.
Caldbeck, Cumbria.
Caldercruix, Lanarks., Scot.
Callington, Cornwall.
Calne, Wilts.
Camberley, Surrey.
Camborne, Cornwall.
Cambridge, Cambs.
Cambridge, Glos.
Canterbury, Kent.
Capel, Surrey.
Cardiff, S. Glamorgan, Wales.

Cardigan, Dyfed, Wales.
Carlisle, Cumbria.
Carlton Curlieu, Leics.
Carlton-on-Trent, Notts.
Carmarthen, Dyfed, Wales.
Carnforth, Lancs.
Carrefour Selous, Jersey, C.I.
Carshalton, Gtr. London.
Cartmel, Cumbria.
Cassington, Oxon.
Castle Bytham, Lincs.
Castle Cary, Somerset.
Castle Combe, Wilts.
Castle Douglas, Kirkcud., Scot.
Castle Hedingham, Essex.
Castleton, Derbys.
Castletown, Isle of Man.
Castor, Cambs.
Caton, Lancs.
Catsfield, E. Sussex.
Caversham, Berks.
Cawood, N. Yorks.
Ceres, Fife, Scot.
Cerne Abbas, Dorset.
Cerrig-y-Drudion, Clwyd, Wales.
Chagford, Devon.
Chalfont St. Giles, Bucks.
Chalfont St. Peter, Bucks.
Chalgrove, Oxon.
Charing, Kent.
Charlecote, Warks.
Charlton Horethorne, Somerset.
Charlton Marshall, Dorset.
Charndon, Bucks.
Chatham, Kent.
Cheadle, Cheshire.
Cheadle Hulme, Cheshire.
Cheam, Gtr. London.
Checkley, Staffs.
Cheddleton, Staffs.
Chelmsford, Essex.
Cheltenham, Glos.
Chepstow, Gwent, Wales.
Cherhill, Wilts.
Chesham, Bucks.
Chessington, Gtr. London.
Chester, Cheshire.
Chesterfield, Derbys.
Chichester, W. Sussex.
Chiddingfold, Surrey.
Chiddingstone, Kent.
Chilham, Kent.
Chilton, Bucks.
Chipping Campden, Glos.
Chipping Norton, Oxon.
Chirk, Clwyd, Wales.
Chislehurst, Gtr. London.
Chobham, Surrey.
Chorley, Lancs.
Christchurch, Dorset.
Christian Malford, Wilts.
Chulmleigh, Devon.
Church Broughton, Derbys.
Church Enstone, Oxon.

Church Over, Warks.
Church Stretton, Shrops.
Churt, Surrey.
Cinderford, Glos.
Cirencester, Glos.
Clacton on Sea, Essex.
Clanfield, Hants.
Clare, Suffolk.
Claydon, Suffolk.
Claygate, Surrey.
Clayton, W. Sussex.
Clayton-le-Moors, Lancs.
Clevedon, Avon.
Cleveleys, Lancs.
Clitheroe, Lancs.
Clutton, Avon.
Coalville, Leics.
Coatbridge, Lanarks., Scot.
Cobham, Surrey.
Cockermouth, Cumbria.
Codicote, Herts.
Codsall, Staffs.
Coggeshall, Essex.
Colchester, Essex.
Coldstream, Berwicks., Scot.
Coleford, Glos.
Coleraine, Co. Londonderry, N. Ireland.
Colne, Lancs.
Colsterworth, Lincs.
Coltishall, Norfolk.
Colwyn Bay, Clwyd, Wales.
Colyton, Devon.
Combe Martin, Devon.
Comberton, Cambs.
Compton Abbas, Dorset.
Comrie, Perths., Scot.
Congleton, Cheshire.
Coniston, Cumbria.
Connah's Quay, Clwyd, Wales.
Consett, Durham.
Conway, Gwynedd, Wales.
Cookham, Berks.
Cookstown, Co. Tyrone, N. Ireland.
Corby Hill, Cumbria.
Corfe, Somerset.
Corfe Castle, Dorset.
Corse Lawn, Glos.
Corsham, Wilts.
Corston, Wilts.
Corwen, Clwyd, Wales.
Cosgrove, Northants.
Costessey, Norfolk.
Coughton, Warks.
Coulsdon, Gtr. London.
Coupar Angus, Perths., Scot.
Coventry, W. Mids.
Cowbridge, S. Glamorgan, Wales.
Cowes, Isle of Wight.
Cowfold, W. Sussex.

Cowling, N. Yorks.
Cranborne, Dorset.
Cranbrook, Kent.
Cranham, Glos.
Cranleigh, Surrey.
Craven Arms, Shrops.
Crawley, W. Sussex.
Crayford, Gtr. London.
Cremyll, Cornwall.
Crewkerne, Somerset.
Criccieth, Gwynedd, Wales.
Cricklade, Wilts.
Crieff, Perths., Scot.
Cromer, Norfolk.
Crook, Durham.
Crossford, Fife, Scot.
Cross Hills, N. Yorks.
Croughton, Northants.
Crowmarsh Gifford, Oxon.
Croydon, Gtr. London.
Cuckfield, W. Sussex.
Cuerdon, Lancs.
Culloden Moor, Inver., Scot.
Cullompton, Devon.

D

Dalry, Ayr., Scot.
Dalry, Kirkcudbright, Scot.
Dalton-in-Furness, Cumbria.
Darlington, Durham.
Dartington, Devon.
Dartmouth, Devon.
Darwen, Lancs.
Datchet, Berks.
Dawlish, Devon.
Deal, Kent.
Debenham, Suffolk.
Deddington, Oxon.
Defynnog, Powys, Wales.
Denham Village, Bucks.
Denholme, W. Yorks.
Derby, Derbys.
Desborough, Northants.
Devizes, Wilts.
Dewsbury, W. Yorks.
Disley, Cheshire.
Diss, Norfolk.
Ditchling, E. Sussex.
Doddington, Cambs.
Doddington, Kent.
Donaghadee, Co. Down, N. Ireland.
Doncaster, S. Yorks.
Donington-on-Bain, Lincs.
Donyatt, Somerset.
Dorchester, Dorset.
Dorchester-on-Thames, Oxon.
Dorking, Surrey.
Dorney, Berks.
Dorridge, W. Mids.
Dorrington, Shrops.
Douglas, Isle of Man.

Dover, Kent.
Dowlish Wake, Somerset.
Driffield, N. Humberside.
Droitwich, Hereford and Worcs.
Drumnadrochit, Inver., Scot.
Dudley, W. Mids.
Duffield, Derbys.
Dulverton, Somerset.
Dumfries, Dumfries., Scot.
Dunblane, Perths., Scot.
Dunchurch, Warks.
Dundee, Angus, Scot.
Dunkeld, Perths., Scot.
Dunmow, Essex.
Dunning, Perths., Scot.
Duns, Berwicks., Scot.
Dunstable, Beds.
Dunster, Somerset.
Durham, Durham.
Duxford, Cambs.

E

Eachwick, Northumb.
Eaglesham, Renfrews., Scot.
Earl Shilton, Leics.
Earsham, Norfolk.
Easingwold, N. Yorks.
East Bridgford, Notts.
East Budleigh, Devon.
East Dereham, Norfolk.
East Grinstead, W. Sussex.
East Hagbourne, Oxon.
East Harling, Norfolk.
East Horsley, Surrey.
East Molesey, Surrey.
East Peckham, Kent.
East Pennard, Somerset.
East Preston, W. Sussex.
Eastbourne, E. Sussex.
Eastburn, W. Yorks.
Eastergate, W. Sussex.
Eastleach, Glos.
Eastry, Kent.
Eastwood, Notts.
Eccles, Lancs.
Ecclesfield, S. Yorks.
Eccleshall, Staffs.
Edenbridge, Kent.
Edenfield, Lancs.
Edgware, Gtr. London.
Edinburgh, Midloth., Scot.
Egham, Surrey.
Elgin, Moray., Scot.
Elie, Fife, Scot.
Elland, W. Yorks.
Ellastone, Staffs.
Ellesmere, Shrops.
Elstow, Beds.
Ely, Cambs.
Endmoor, Cumbria.
Enfield, Gtr. London.

Epping, Essex.
Epsom, Surrey.
Epworth, S. Humberside.
Errol, Perths., Scot.
Esher, Surrey.
Eton, see Windsor and
  Eton, Berks.
Eversley, Hants.
Eversley Cross, Hants.
Everton, Notts.
Evesham, Hereford and
  Worcs.
Ewell, Surrey.
Ewhurst, Surrey.
Exeter, Devon.
Exmouth, Devon.
Exton, Somerset.
Eyam, Derbys.
Eye, Suffolk.
Eynsham, Oxon.

F

Failsworth, Lancs.
Fairford, Glos.
Fairlie, Ayr., Scot.
Fakenham, Norfolk.
Falmouth, Cornwall.
Fareham, Hants.
Faringdon, Oxon.
Farnborough, Gtr. London.
Farnborough, Hants.
Farndon, Cheshire.
Farnham, Surrey.
Farnham Common, Bucks.
Farningham, Kent.
Faversham, Kent.
Felixstowe, Suffolk.
Felmingham, Norfolk.
Felpham, W. Sussex.
Felsted, Essex.
Felton, Northumb.
Fencehouses, Tyne &
  Wear.
Fen Ditton, Cambs.
Feniscowles, Lancs.
Ferndown, Dorset.
Fernhill Heath, Hereford
  and Worcs.
Fernhurst, W. Sussex.
Ferryhill, Durham.
Filey, N. Yorks.
Finchingfield, Essex.
Finedon, Northants.
Fishguard, Dyfed, Wales.
Fishlake, S. Yorks.
Flamborough, N.
  Humberside.
Flaxton, N. Yorks.
Fleet, Hants.
Flimwell, E. Sussex.
Flore, Northants.
Fochabers, Moray., Scot.
Folkestone, Kent.
Fordham, Cambs.
Fordingbridge, Hants.
Forest Row, E. Sussex.

Formby, Merseyside.
Forncett St. Mary, Norfolk.
Forres, Moray., Scot.
Four Elms, Kent.
Fowlmere, Cambs.
Framlingham, Suffolk.
Frampton, Lincs.
Freiston, Lincs.
Frensham, Surrey.
Freshford, Avon.
Freshwater, Isle of Wight.
Frinton-on-Sea, Essex.
Friockheim, Angus, Scot.
Frome, Somerset.
Fulbeck, Lincs.
Fyfield, Hants.
Fyfield, Oxon.

G

Gainsborough, Lincs.
Galston, Ayr., Scot.
Gants Hill, Gtr. London.
Gargrave, N. Yorks.
Gartmore, Stirlings., Scot.
Gatehouse of Fleet,
  Kirkcud., Scot.
Gateshead, Tyne and
  Wear.
Gazeley, Suffolk.
Gedney, Lincs.
Gerrards Cross, Bucks.
Gillingham, Dorset.
Gillingham, Kent.
Gilwern, Gwent, Wales.
Glasbury, Powys, Wales.
Glasgow, Lanarks., Scot.
Glastonbury, Somerset.
Glossop, Derbys.
Gloucester, Glos.
Godalming, Surrey.
Godmanchester, Cambs.
Godstone, Surrey.
Gomshall, Surrey.
Gosberton, Lincs.
Gosforth, Tyne and Wear.
Gosport, Hants.
Goudhurst, Kent.
Gourock, Lanarks., Scot.
Gowerton, W. Glamorgan,
  Wales.
Grampound, Cornwall.
Grantham, Lincs.
Grantown-on-Spey, Moray.,
  Scot.
Grasmere, Cumbria.
Grassington, N. Yorks.
Gravesend, Kent.
Grays, Essex.
Great Ashfield, Suffolk.
Great Ayton, N. Yorks.
Great Baddow, Essex.
Great Bardfield, Essex.
Great Bookham, Surrey.
Great Chesterford, Essex.
Great Horkesley, Essex.
Great Malvern, Hereford
  and Worcs.

Great Missenden, Bucks.
Great Ponton, Lincs.
Great Shefford, Berks.
Great Urswick, Cumbria.
Great Wakering, Essex.
Great Waltham, Essex.
Great Yarmouth, Norfolk.
Greatford, Lincs.
Greenlaw, Berwicks., Scot.
Greyabbey, Co. Down, N.
  Ireland.
Greystoke, Cumbria.
Grimsby, S. Humberside.
Groomsport, Co. Down, N.
  Ireland.
Grundisburgh, Suffolk.
Guildford, Surrey.
Guilsborough, Northants.
Guisborough, Cleveland.
Gunthorpe, Notts.

H

Hacheston, Suffolk.
Haddenham, Bucks.
Haddington, E. Loth., Scot.
Hadleigh, Essex.
Hadleigh, Suffolk.
Hadlow, Kent.
Haigh, S. Yorks.
Haisthorpe, N. Humberside.
Hale, Cheshire.
Halesowen, W. Mids.
Halesworth, Suffolk.
Halifax, W. Yorks.
Halstead, Essex.
Hambridge, Somerset.
Hampton, Gtr. London.
Hampton Hill, Gtr. London.
Hampton Wick, Gtr.
  London.
Handcross, W. Sussex.
Hanford, Staffs.
Harbertonford, Devon.
Harewood, W. Yorks.
Harle Syke, Lancs.
Harlech, Gwynedd, Wales.
Harleston, Norfolk.
Harlington, Beds.
Harlow, Essex.
Harpenden, Herts.
Harpford, Devon.
Harpole, Northants.
Harrogate, N. Yorks.
Harrow, Gtr. London.
Harston, Cambs.
Hartley, Kent.
Hartley Wintney, Hants.
Harwell, Oxon.
Harwich and Dovercourt,
  Essex.
Haslemere, Surrey.
Haslingden, Lancs.
Hastings, E. Sussex.
Hatch Beauchamp,
  Somerset.
Hatfield, Herts.

Hatfield Broad Oak, Essex.
Hatherleigh, Devon.
Hatton Heath, Cheshire.
Havant, Hants.
Haverfordwest, Dyfed,
    Wales.
Hawick, Roxbs., Scot.
Hawkhurst, Kent.
Hay on Wye, Powys,
    Wales.
Haydon Bridge, Northumb.
Hayle, Cornwall.
Hayling Island, Hants.
Haynes, Beds.
Haywards Heath, W.
    Sussex.
Hazel Grove, Cheshire.
Heacham, Norfolk.
Headington, Oxon.
Heath and Reach, Beds.
Heathfield, E. Sussex.
Hebden Bridge, W. Yorks.
Helens Bay, Co. Down, N.
    Ireland.
Helmsley, N. Yorks.
Helperby, N. Yorks.
Hemel Hempstead, Herts.
Hempstead, Essex.
Henfield, W. Sussex.
Henley-in-Arden, Warks.
Henley-on-Thames, Oxon.
Henllan, Dyfed, Wales.
Hereford, Hereford and
    Worcs.
Hermitage, Berks.
Herne Bay, Kent.
Herstmonceux, E. Sussex.
Hertford, Herts.
Hessle, N. Humberside.
Heswall, Merseyside.
Heversham, Cumbria.
Hexham, Northumb.
High Halden, Kent.
High Wycombe, Bucks.
Highbridge, Somerset.
Highcliffe, Dorset.
Highleadon, Glos.
Hillsborough, Co. Down, N.
    Ireland.
Hindhead, Surrey.
Hindon, Wilts.
Hinton Waldrist, Oxon.
Hisomley, Wilts.
Hitchin, Herts.
Hockley Heath, W. Mids.
Hollingbourne, Kent.
Hollinwood, Lancs.
Holme, Cumbria.
Holmfirth, W. Yorks.
Holt, Norfolk.
Holywood, Co. Down, N.
    Ireland.
Honiton, Devon.
Hook, Hants.
Hookwood, W. Sussex.
Hooton, Cheshire.
Horbury, W. Yorks.
Horncastle, Lincs.

Horndean, Hants.
Horrabridge, Devon.
Horsebridge, E. Sussex.
Horsham, W. Sussex.
Horwich, Lancs.
Hounslow, Gt. London.
Hoylake, Merseyside.
Huby, N. Yorks.
Huddersfield, W. Yorks.
Hull, N. Humberside.
Hungerford, Berks.
Hunstanton, Norfolk.
Hursley, Hants.
Hurst, Berks.
Hurst Green, E. Sussex.
Hurstpierpoint, W. Sussex.
Husbands Bosworth, Leics.
Husborne Crawley, Beds.
Hyde, Cheshire.
Hythe, Kent.

I

Ibstock, Leics.
Ickleton, Cambs.
Iddesleigh, Devon.
Idle, W. Yorks.
Ilchester, Somerset.
Ilford, Gtr., London.
Ilfracombe, Devon.
Ilkeston, Derbys.
Ilkley, W. Yorks.
Ilminster, Somerset.
Inchture, Perths., Scot.
Indian Queens, Cornwall.
Ingatestone, Essex.
Ingoldsby, Lincs.
Inverness, Inver., Scot.
Iping, W. Sussex.
Ipswich, Suffolk.
Ironbridge, Shrops.
Isleworth, Gtr. London.
Islip, Northants.
Ivybridge, Devon.
Ixworth, Suffolk.

J

Jedburgh, Roxbs., Scot.
Jesmond, Tyne and Wear.
Jurby, Isle of Man.

K

Keighley, W. Yorks.
Kelso, Roxbs., Scot.
Kelvedon, Essex.
Kemerton, Hereford and
    Worcs.
Kempsford, Glos.
Kempston, Beds.
Kendal, Cumbria.
Kennington, Kent.
Kesgrave, Suffolk.
Kessingland, Suffolk.

Keswick, Cumbria.
Kettering, Northants.
Kew, Gtr. London.
Kew Green, Gtr. London.
Kibworth Beauchamp,
    Leics.
Kidderminster, Hereford
    and Worcs.
Kidwelly, Dyfed, Wales.
Kilbarchan, Renfrews.,
    Scot.
Killamarsh, Derbys.
Killearn, Stirlings., Scot.
Killin, Perths., Scot.
Killinghall, N. Yorks.
Kilmacolm, Renfrews.,
    Scot.
Kilmarnock, Ayr., Scot.
Kilmichael Glassary, Argyll,
    Scot.
Kiltarlity, Inver., Scot.
Kimpton, Herts.
Kineton, Warks.
Kings Langley, Herts.
Kings Lynn, Norfolk.
Kingsbridge, Devon.
Kingston-upon-Thames,
    Gtr. London.
Kingussie, Inver., Scot.
Kintbury, Berks.
Kinver, Staffs.
Kippen, Stirls., Scot.
Kirdford, W. Sussex.
Kirk Deighton, N. Yorks.
Kirk Hammerton, N. Yorks.
Kirk Michael, Isle of Man.
Kirkby Lonsdale, Cumbria.
Kirkby-on-Bain, Lincs.
Kirkby Stephen, Cumbria.
Kirkcudbright, Kirkcud.,
    Scot.
Kirton, Lincs.
Knaphill, Surrey.
Knapp, Perths., Scot.
Knapton, N. Yorks.
Knaresborough, N. Yorks.
Knebworth, Herts.
Knighton, Powys, Wales.
Knipton, Leics.
Knowle, W. Mids.
Knutsford, Cheshire.

L

Lake, Isle of Wight.
Laleham, Surrey.
Lamberhurst, Kent.
Lancaster, Lancs.
Lancing, W. Sussex.
Landbeach, Cambs.
Langar, Notts.
Langford, Avon.
Langford, Notts.
Langholm, Dumfries., Scot.
Langley Burrell, Wilts.
Langley Moor, Durham.
Langport, Somerset.

Lapworth, Warks.
Largs, Ayr., Scot.
Larne, Co. Antrim, N.
  Ireland.
Laugharne, Dyfed, Wales.
Launceston, Cornwall.
Lavenham, Suffolk.
Layer-de-la-Haye, Essex.
Layer Marney, Essex.
Lea, Wilts.
Leamington Spa, Warks.
Leavenheath, Suffolk.
Lechlade, Glos.
Ledbury, Hereford and
  Worcs.
Leeds. W. Yorks.
Leedstown, Cornwall.
Leek, Staffs.
Leicester, Leics.
Leigh, Kent.
Leigh-on-Sea, Essex.
Leighton Buzzard, Beds.
Leiston, Suffolk.
Leominster, Hereford and
  Worcs.
Lepton, W. Yorks.
Letchmore Heath, Herts.
Lewes, E. Sussex.
Leyburn, N. Yorks.
Lichfield, Staffs.
Limington, Somerset.
Limpsfield, Surrey.
Lincoln, Lincs.
Lindfield, W. Sussex.
Linlithgow, West Lothian,
  Scot.
Linslade, Beds.
Liskeard, Cornwall.
Liss, Hants.
Litcham, Norfolk.
Little Baddow, Essex.
Little Brickhill, Bucks.
Little Budworth, Cheshire.
Little Haywood, Staffs.
Little Horton, Wilts.
Little Shefford, Beds.
Little Walsingham, Norfolk.
Little Weighton, N.
  Humberside.
Littleborough, Lancs.
Littledean, Glos.
Littleport, Cambs.
Litton Cheney, Dorset.
Liverpool, Merseyside.
Llanaber, Gwynedd, Wales.
Llandeilo, Dyfed, Wales.
Llandogo, Gwent, Wales.
Llandovery, Dyfed, Wales.
Llandrindod Wells, Powys,
  Wales.
Llandudno, Gwynedd,
  Wales.
Llanelli, Dyfed, Wales.
Llanerchymedd, Gwynedd,
  Wales.
Llangollen, Clwyd, Wales.
Llanrwst, Gwynedd,
  Wales.

Llantwit Major, S.
  Glamorgan, Wales.
Llanwrda, Dyfed, Wales.
Lockeridge, Wilts.
Londonderry, Co.
  Londonderry, N. Ireland.
Long Buckby, Northants.
Long Crendon, Bucks.
Long Eaton, Derbys.
Long Hanborough, Oxon.
Long Melford, Suffolk.
Long Stratton, Norfolk.
Long Sutton, Lincs.
Longfield, Kent.
Longton, Lancs.
Looe, Cornwall.
Lostwithiel, Cornwall.
Loudwater, Bucks.
Loughborough, Leics.
Loughor, W. Glamorgan,
  Wales.
Loughton, Essex.
Louth, Lincs.
Low Fell, Tyne and Wear.
Lower Bentham, N. Yorks.
Lower Halstow, Kent.
Lower Kingswood, Surrey.
Lower Kinnerton,
  Cheshire.
Lowestoft, Suffolk.
Lubenham, Leics.
Ludford, Lincs.
Ludlow, Shrops.
Lundin Links, Fife, Scot.
Lurgan, Co. Armagh, N.
  Ireland.
Luton, Beds.
Lyddington, Leics.
Lydford, Devon.
Lydiard Millicent, Wilts.
Lydney, Glos.
Lye, W. Mids.
Lymington, Hants.
Lyndhurst, Hants.
Lynton, Devon.
Lyonshall, Hereford &
  Worcs.
Lytchett Minster, Dorset.
Lytham, Lancs.

M

Macclesfield, Cheshire.
Machynlleth, Powys,
  Wales.
Maentwrog, Gwynedd,
  Wales.
Magherafelt, Co.
  Londonderry, N. Ireland.
Maiden Newton, Dorset.
Maidencombe, Devon.
Maidenhead, Berks.
Maidstone, Kent.
Maldon, Essex.
Malmesbury, Wilts.
Malpas, Cheshire.
Malton, N. Yorks.

Malvern Link, Hereford
  and Worcs.
Manchester, Lancs.
Manfield, N. Yorks.
Manningtree, Essex.
Mansfield, Notts.
Manton, Leics.
March, Cambs.
Margate, Kent.
Market Bosworth, Leics.
Market Deeping, Lincs.
Market Drayton, Shrops.
Market Rasen, Lincs.
Market Harborough, Leics.
Market Weighton, N.
  Humberside.
Marlborough, Wilts.
Marlow, Bucks.
Marnhull, Dorset.
Marple, Cheshire.
Martlesham, Suffolk.
Martock, Somerset.
Marton, Cleveland.
Matching Green, Essex.
Mathon, Hereford and
  Worcs.
Mathry, Dyfed, Wales.
Matlock, Derbys.
Mattingley, Hants.
Mauchline, Ayr., Scot.
Mawnan Smith, Cornwall.
Mayfield, E. Sussex.
Mayland, Essex.
Medbourne, Leics.
Melbourn, Cambs.
Melbourne, Derbys.
Melksham, Wilts.
Melmerby, N. Yorks.
Melton, Suffolk.
Menston, W. Yorks.
Meonstoke, Hants.
Merrow, Surrey.
Merstham, Surrey.
Meshaw, Devon.
Methwold, Norfolk.
Mevagissey, Cornwall.
Micheldever Station,
  Hants.
Micklebring, S. Yorks.
Middle Wallop, Hants.
Middleham, N. Yorks.
Middlesbrough, Cleveland.
Middleton, Lancs.
Middleton, N. Yorks.
Middleton, W. Yorks.
Middleton St. George,
  Durham
Midhurst, W. Sussex.
Midsomer Norton, Avon.
Milburn, Cumbria.
Mileham, Norfolk.
Milford, Staffs.
Milford, Surrey.
Milford Haven, Dyfed,
  Wales.
Milford-on-Sea, Hants.
Milnthorpe, Cumbria.
Milton Keynes, Bucks.

Milton Lilbourne, Wilts.
Milverton, Somerset.
Minchinhampton, Glos.
Minster, Kent.
Minsterley, Shrops.
Misterton, Notts.
Modbury, Devon.
Moffat, Dumfries, Scot.
Monks Risborough, Bucks.
Monmouth, Gwent, Wales.
Montacute, Somerset.
Montrose, Angus, Scot.
Monyash, Derbys.
Morchard Bishop, Devon.
Morden, Gtr. London.
Morcombelake, Dorset.
Moreton-in-Marsh, Glos.
Moretonhampstead, Devon.
Morriston, W. Glamorgan,
   Wales.
Mountsorrel, Leics.
Mousehole, Cornwall.
Moylegrove, Dyfed, Wales.
Much Hadham, Herts.
Much Wenlock, Shrops.
Murton, W. Glamorgan,
   Wales.

N

Nailsworth, Glos.
Nairn, Nairn., Scot.
Nantwich, Cheshire.
Naphill, Bucks.
Navenby, Lincs.
Nayland, Suffolk.
Neath, W. Glamorgan,
   Wales.
Neatishead, Norfolk.
Needham Market, Suffolk.
Nelson, Lancs.
Neston, Cheshire.
Nether Stowey, Somerset.
Nettlebed, Oxon.
New Bolingbroke, Lincs.
New Mills, Derbys.
New Romney, Kent.
New York, Lincs.
Newark, Notts.
Newbold on Stour, Warks.
Newbury, Berks.
Newby Bridge, Cumbria.
Newcastle Emlyn, Dyfed,
   Wales.
Newcastle-under-Lyme,
   Staffs.
Newcastle-upon-Tyne,
   Tyne and Wear.
Newhaven, E. Sussex.
Newmarket, Suffolk.
Newnham-on-Severn,
   Glos.
Newport, Dyfed, Wales.
Newport, Essex.
Newport, Gwent, Wales.
Newport, Isle of Wight.
Newport, Shrops.

Newry, Co. Down, N.
   Ireland.
Newton Abbot, Devon.
Newton Stewart,
   Wigtowns., Scot.
Newtonmore, Inver., Scot.
Newtown, Chesire.
Newtown Linford, Leics.
Newtonabbey, Co Antrim,
   N. Ireland.
Newtownards, Co. Down,
   N. Ireland.
Ninfield, E. Sussex.
Nonington, Kent.
Norham, Northumb.
Normanton on Trent,
   Notts.
North Berwick, E. Loth.,
   Scot.
North Bradley, Wilts.
North Petherton,
   Somerset.
North Petherwin,
   Cornwall.
North Shields, Tyne &
   Wear.
North Shoebury, Essex.
North Walsham, Norfolk.
Northallerton, N. Yorks.
Northampton, Northants
Northchapel, W. Sussex.
Northiam, E. Sussex.
Northlew, Devon.
Northolt, Gtr. London.
Northop, Clwyd, Wales.
Norton, Suffolk.
Norton. N. Yorks.
Norwich, Norfolk.
Nottingham, Notts.
Nuneaton, Warks.
Nutley, E. Sussex.

O

Oadby, Leics.
Oakamoor, Staffs.
Oakham, Leics.
Oakley, Hants.
Oban, Argyll., Scot.
Ockbrook, Derbys.
Ockley, Surrey.
Odiham, Hants.
Okehampton, Devon.
Old Hunstanton, Norfolk.
Oldham, Lancs.
Ollerton, Notts.
Olney, Bucks.
Ombersley, Hereford and
   Worcs.
Orford, Suffolk.
Ormskirk, Lancs.
Orpington, Gtr. London.
Orsett, Essex.
Orwell, Cambs.
Osbournby, Lincs.
Osgathorpe, Leics.
Ossett, W. Yorks.

Oswestry, Shrops.
Otford, Kent.
Otley, W. Yorks.
Ottery St. Mary, Devon.
Oughtibridge, S. Yorks.
Oundle, Northants.
Outwell, Cambs.
Oxford, Oxon.

P

Padstow, Cornwall.
Painswick, Glos.
Pailton, Warks.
Paisley, Renfrews., Scot.
Parkstone, Dorset.
Parwich, Derbys.
Pateley Bridge, N. Yorks.
Patrington, N.
   Humberside.
Pattishall, Northants.
Paulerspury, Northants.
Peasenhall, Suffolk.
Peebles, Peebles., Scot.
Peel, Isle of Man.
Pembroke, Dyfed, Wales.
Pembury, Kent.
Penarth, S. Glamorgan,
   Wales.
Pendlebury, Lancs.
Penmaenmawr, Gwynedd,
   Wales.
Penn, Bucks.
Penperlleni, Gwent,
   Wales.
Penrith, Cumbria.
Penryn, Cornwall.
Penshurst, Kent.
Penzance, Cornwall.
Perranarworthal, Cornwall.
Pershore, Hereford and
   Worcs.
Perth, Perths., Scot.
Peterborough, Cambs.
Petersfield, Hants.
Petworth, W. Sussex.
Pevensey, E. Sussex.
Pevensey Bay, E. Sussex.
Pickering, N. Yorks.
Pill, Avon.
Pinchbeck, Lincs.
Pinner, Gtr. London.
Pitchcombe, Glos.
Pitlochry, Perths., Scot.
Plaitford, Hants.
Playden, E. Sussex.
Plumley, Cheshire.
Plymouth, Devon.
Pockington, N.
   Humberside.
Polegate, E. Sussex.
Pontefract, W. Yorks.
Ponteland, Northumb.
Ponterwyd, Dyfed, Wales.
Pontypool, Gwent, Wales.
Pontypridd, Mid Glam.,
   Wales.

Poole, Dorset.
Port Erin, Isle of Man.
Port Isaac, Cornwall.
Portadown, Co. Armagh, N. Ireland.
Portballintrae, Co. Anrim, N. Ireland.
Portmeirion, Gwynedd, Wales.
Portrush, Co. Antrim, N. Ireland.
Portscatho, Cornwall.
Portslade, W. Sussex.
Portsmouth, Hants.
Portstewart, Co. Londonderry, N. Ireland
Potterne, Wilts.
Potterspury, Northants.
Poulton-le-Fylde, Lancs.
Powick, Hereford & Worcs.
Poynton, Cheshire.
Prestatyn, Clwyd, Wales.
Prestbury, Cheshire.
Presteigne, Powys, Wales.
Preston, Lancs.
Princes Risborough, Bucks.
Priors Marston, Warks.
Puckeridge, Herts.
Puddletown, Dorset.
Pulborough, W. Sussex.
Pulford, Cheshire.
Pulham Market, Norfolk.
Pulham St. Mary, Norfolk.
Pulloxhill, Beds.
Purley, Gtr. London.
Puttenham, Surrey.
Pwllheli, Gwynedd, Wales.

Q

Quarndon, Derbys.
Queen Camel, Somerset.
Quenilborough, Leics.
Quorn, Leics.

R

Radlett, Herts.
Radstock, Avon.
Raglan, Gwent, Wales.
Rainford, Merseyside.
Rainham, Kent.
Rait, Perths., Scot.
Ramsbottom, Lancs.
Ramsbury, Wilts.
Ramsdell, Hants.
Ramsey, Cambs.
Ramsey, Isle of Man.
Ramsgate, Kent.
Rastrick, W. Yorks.
Ravenstonedale, Cumbria.
Rawcliffe, N. Humberside.
Rawtenstall, Lancs.
Rayleigh, Essex.
Reach, Cambs.
Read, Lancs.

Reading, Berks.
Redbourn, Herts.
Reddish, Cheshire.
Redditch, Hereford and Worcs.
Redhill, Surrey.
Redmarley D'Abitot, Glos.
Redmile, Leics.
Redruth, Cornwall.
Reepham, Norfolk.
Reigate, Surrey.
Retford, Notts.
Reymerston, Norfolk.
Rhosneigr, Gwynedd, Wales.
Rhos-on-Sea, Clwyd, Wales.
Rhuallt, Clwyd,Wales.
Rhuddlan, Clwyd, Wales.
Ribchester, Lancs.
Richmond, Gtr. London.
Richmond, N. Yorks.
Rickmansworth, Herts.
Ridgewell, Essex.
Ringway, Cheshire.
Ringwood, Hants.
Ripley, Surrey.
Ripon, N. Yorks.
Risby, Suffolk.
Riverhead, Kent.
Robertsbridge, E. Sussex.
Rochdale, Lancs.
Rochester, Kent.
Rolvenden, Kent.
Romsey, Hants.
Rossett, Clwyd, Wales.
Ross-on-Wye, Hereford and Worcs.
Rothbury, Northumb.
Rotherham, S. Yorks.
Rottingdean, E. Sussex.
Royston, Herts.
Royton, Lancs.
Ruabon, Clwyd, Wales.
Rufforth, N. Yorks.
Rugby, Warks.
Rugeley, Staffs.
Ruskington, Lincs.
Rumford, Cornwall.
Runcorn, Cheshire.
Rushden, Northants.
Ruthin, Clwyd, Wales.
Ryde, Isle of Wight.
Rye, E. Sussex.

S

Sabden, Lancs.
Saddleworth, Lancs.
Saffron Walden, Essex.
St. Albans, Herts.
St. Andrews, Fife, Scot.
St. Anne's-on-Sea, Lancs.
St. Austell, Cornwall.
St. Boswells, Roxburgh., Scot.
St. Davids, Dyfed, Wales.

St. Helier, Jersey, C.I.
St. Ives, Cambs.
St. Ives, Cornwall.
St. Just, Cornwall.
St. Leonards-on-Sea, E. Sussex.
St. Margaret's Bay, Kent.
St. Mawes, Cornwall.
St. Neots, Cambs.
St. Ouen, Jersey, C.I.
St. Peter Port, Guernsey, C.I.
St. Sampson, Guernsey, C.I.
Saintfield, Co. Down, N. Ireland
Salcombe, Devon.
Sale, Cheshire.
Salisbury, Wilts.
Saltburn, Cleveland.
Saltcoats, Ayr., Scot.
Sandbach, Cheshire.
Sanderstead, Gtr. London.
Sandford, Devon.
Sandgate, Kent.
Sandhurst, Berks.
Sandiacre, Derbys.
Sandwich, Kent.
Sarnau, Dyfed, Wales.
Sarratt, Herts.
Sawbridgeworth, Herts.
Saxmundham, Suffolk.
Scarborough, N. Yorks.
Scarthoe, S. Humberside.
Scunthorpe, S. Humberside.
Seaford, E. Sussex.
Seaham, Durham.
Seaton, Devon.
Seaton Ross, N. Humberside.
Seaview, Isle of Wight.
Sedburgh, Cumbria.
Sedlescombe, E. Sussex.
Seend, Wilts.
Seighford, Staffs.
Selkirk, Selks., Scot.
Settle, N. Yorks.
Sevenoaks, Kent.
Shaftesbury, Dorset.
Shaldon, Devon.
Shalford, Surrey.
Shanklin, Isle of Wight.
Sharrington, Norfolk.
Shawforth, Lancs.
Sheffield. S. Yorks.
Shefford, Beds.
Shenfield, Essex.
Shepperton, Surrey.
Shepshed, Leics.
Shepton Mallet, Somerset.
Sherborne, Dorset.
Shere, Surrey.
Sheringham, Norfolk.
Sherston, Wilts.
Shifnal, Shrops.
Shillingstone, Dorset.
Shipdham, Norfolk.

Shingle Street, Suffolk.
Shipley, W. Yorks.
Shipston-on-Stour, Warks.
Shipton-under-Wychwood, Oxon.
Shirley, Gtr. London.
Shoreham, Kent.
Shoreham-by-Sea, W. Sussex.
Shottermill, Surrey.
Shotton, Clwyd, Wales.
Shrewsbury, Shrops.
Sible Hedingham, Essex.
Sibsey, Lincs.
Sidcup, Gtr. London.
Sidmouth, Devon.
Sileby, Leics.
Silk Willoughby, Lincs.
Silsden, W. Yorks.
Skegness, Lincs.
Skipton, N. Yorks.
Slad, Glos.
Smeeth, Kent.
Smethwick, W. Mids.
Snettisham, Norfolk.
Snodland, Kent.
Soham, Cambs.
Solihull, W. Mids.
Somerford Keynes, Glos.
Somerton, Somerset.
Sorbie, Wigtown, Scot.
South Brent, Devon.
South Lopham, Norfolk.
South Milford, N. Yorks.
South Molton, Devon.
South Ockendon, Essex.
South Shields, Tyne & Wear
South Walsham, Norfolk.
Southampton, Hants.
Southborough, Kent.
Southend-on-Sea, Essex.
Southport, Merseyside.
Southwell, Notts.
Southwold, Suffolk.
Sowerby Bridge. W. Yorks.
Spalding, Lincs.
Sparkford, Somerset.
Sparkwell, Devon.
Spennithorne, N. Yorks.
Spilsby, Lincs.
Sproughton, Suffolk.
Stafford, Staffs.
Staines, Surrey.
Staithes, Cleveland.
Stalham, Norfolk.
Stamford, Lincs.
Standlake, Oxon.
Stanford Dingley, Berks.
Stanford-le-Hope, Essex.
Stansted, Essex.
Stapleford, Lincs.
Staunton Harold, Leics.
Staveley, Cumbria.
Steeple Claydon, Bucks.
Steyning, W. Sussex.
Stiffkey, Norfolk.
Stillington, N. Yorks.

Stirling, Stirlings., Scot.
Stock, Essex.
Stockbridge, Hants.
Stockbury, Kent.
Stockland, Devon.
Stockport, Cheshire.
Stockton Heath, Cheshire.
Stockton-on-Tees, Cleveland.
Stoke Ferry, Norfolk.
Stoke Golding, Leics.
Stoke Goldington, Bucks.
Stoke-on-Trent, Staffs.
Stokenchurch, Bucks.
Stokesley, N. Yorks.
Stone, Staffs.
Stonehaven, Kincardine, Scot.
Stonham Parva, Suffolk.
Storrington, W. Sussex.
Stourbridge, W. Mids.
Stourport, Hereford & Worcs.
Stowmarket, Suffolk.
Stow-on-the-Wold, Glos.
Stradbroke, Suffolk.
Stratford-upon-Avon, Warks.
Strathblane, Stirlings., Scot.
Streatley, Berks.
Streetly, W. Mids.
Stretton, Cheshire.
Stroud, Glos.
Stroud, Hants.
Studley, Warks.
Sturminster Newton, Dorset.
Sturry, Kent.
Sudbury, Suffolk.
Suffield, Norfolk.
Sunbury, Surrey.
Sunderland, Tyne and Wear.
Sundridge, Kent.
Surbiton, Gtr. London.
Sutton, Gtr. London.
Sutton Bonington, Notts.
Sutton Bridge, Lincs.
Sutton Coldfield, W. Mids.
Sutton-on-Sea, Lincs.
Sutton-on-Trent, Notts.
Sutton Valence, Kent.
Swaffham, Norfolk.
Swanage, Dorset.
Swansea, W. Glamorgan, Wales.
Swanton Abbot, Norfolk.
Swindon, Wilts.

T

Tadcaster, N. Yorks.
Takeley, Essex.
Tamworth, Staffs.

Tanworth-in-Arden, Warks.
Tattershall, Lincs.
Taunton, Somerset.
Tavistock, Devon.
Teddington, Gtr. London.
Teignmouth, Devon.
Temple Sowerby, Cumbria.
Tenby, Dyfed, Wales.
Tenterden, Kent.
Tern Hill, Shrops.
Terrington St. Clement, Norfolk
Tetbury, Glos.
Tewkesbury, Glos.
Teynham, Kent.
Thame, Oxon.
Thames Ditton, Surrey.
Thatcham, Berks.
Thaxted, Essex.
Theydon Bois, Essex.
Thirsk, N. Yorks.
Thornaby, Cleveland.
Thornage, Norfolk.
Thorne, S. Yorks.
Thornton Heath. Gtr. London.
Thorp Arch, W. Yorks.
Thorpe-le-Soken, Essex.
Thrapston, Northants.
Thurlton, Norfolk.
Thurnby, Leics.
Thurso, Caithness, Scot.
Ticknall, Derbys.
Tideswell, Derbys.
Tilbury, Essex.
Tillington, W. Sussex.
Tilston, Cheshire.
Timberscombe, Somerset.
Tingewick, Bucks.
Tintern, Gwent, Wales.
Tisbury, Wilts.
Titchfield, Hants.
Tiverton, Cheshire.
Tiverton, Devon.
Toddington, Beds.
Todmorden, W. Yorks.
Tonbridge, Kent.
Tonge, Leics.
Topsham, Devon.
Torquay, Devon.
Totnes, Devon.
Towcester, Northants.
Tredunnock, Gwent, Wales.
Tregony, Cornwall.
Trent, Dorset.
Tring, Herts.
Trumpington, Cambs.
Truro, Cornwall.
Tunbridge Wells, Kent.
Tutbury, Staffs.
Tuxford, Notts.
Twickenham, Gtr. London.
Twyford, Berks.

Twyford, Hants.
Tynemouth, Tyne and
  Wear.

U

Uckfield, E. Sussex.
Uley, Glos.
Ullenwood, Glos.
Ulverston, Cumbria.
Upham, Hants.
Upholland, Lancs.
Upminster, Gtr. London.
Upper Beeding, W. Sussex.
Upper Boddington,
  Northants.
Upper Largo, Fife, Scot.
Uppingham, Leics.
Upton-upon-Severn,
  Hereford and Worcs.
Usk, Gwent, Wales.
Usworth, Tyne and Wear.
Uttoxeter, Staffs.
Uxbridge, Gtr. London.

V

Vale, Guernsey, C.I.
Ventnor, Isle of Wight.
Virginia Water, Surrey.

W

Waddesdon, Bucks.
Wadebridge, Cornwall.
Wadhurst, E. Sussex.
Wainfleet, Lincs.
Wakes Colne, Essex.
Wallasey, Merseyside.
Wallingford, Oxon.
Wallington, Gtr. London.
Walsall, W. Mids.
Walsden, W. Yorks.
Walton on Thames, Surrey.
Walton-on-the-Hill and
  Tadworth, Surrey.
Wangford, Suffolk.
Wansford, Cambs.
Wantage, Oxon.
Warboys, Cambs.
Warburton, Cheshire.
Wardley, Tyne and Wear.
Wareham, Dorset.
Wargrave, Berks.
Warminster, Wilts.
Warnham, W. Sussex.
Warrington, Cheshire.
Warwick, Warks.
Washington, W. Sussex.
Washington, Tyne and
  Wear.
Watchet, Somerset
Watford, Herts.
Watton, Norfolk.
Wedmore, Somerset.

Weedon, Bucks.
Weedon, Northants.
Weldon, Northants.
Wellingborough, Northants.
Wellington, Somerset.
Wells, Somerset.
Wells-next-the-Sea, Norfolk.
Welshpool, Powys, Wales.
Welwyn, Herts.
Wembley Park, Gtr.
  London.
Wendover, Bucks.
West Bridgford, Notts.
West Bromwich, W. Mids.
West Felton, Shrops.
West Haddon, Northants.
West Heslerton, N. Yorks.
West Kirby, Merseyside.
West Knoyle, Wilts.
West Linton, Peebles, Scot.
West Malling, Kent.
West Monkton, Somerset.
West Peckham, Kent.
West Stour, Dorset.
Westbourne, W. Sussex.
Westbury, Wilts.
Westcliff-on-Sea, Essex.
Westcott, Surrey.
Westerham, Kent.
Weston-in-Gordano, Avon.
Weston-super-Mare, Avon.
Wetherby, W. Yorks.
Weybridge, Surrey.
Weymouth, Dorset.
Whaley Bridge, Derbys.
Whalley, Lancs.
Whauphill, Wigtown, Scot.
Wheathampstead, Herts.
Whimple Devon.
Whissendine, Leics.
Whitby, N. Yorks.
Whitchurch, Bucks.
Whitchurch, Hants.
Whitchurch, Shrops.
White Colne, Essex.
White Roding, Essex.
White Waltham, Berks.
Whitefield, Lancs.
Whitegate, Cheshire.
Whitehaven, Cumbria.
Whitley Bay, Tyne and
  Wear.
Whitstable, Kent.
Whittington, Shrops.
Whittlesey, Cambs.
Whittlesford, Cambs.
Whyteleafe, Surrey.
Wickham Market, Suffolk.
Widegates, Cornwall.
Wigan, Lancs.
Williton, Somerset.
Wilmslow, Cheshire.
Wilshamstead, Beds.
Wilton, Wilts.
Wimborne Minster, Dorset.
Wincanton, Somerset.
Winchcombe, Glos.
Winchelsea, E. Sussex.

Winchester, Hants.
Windermere, Cumbria.
Windsor and Eton, Berks.
Winforton, Hereford &
  Worcs
Wingham, Kent.
Wingrave, Bucks.
Winkleigh, Devon.
Winksley, N. Yorks.
Wisbech, Cambs.
Wisborough Green. W.
  Sussex.
Witham, Essex.
Withersdale, Suffolk.
Witney, Oxon.
Wiveliscombe, Somerset.
Woburn, Beds.
Woburn Sands, Bucks.
Woking, Surrey.
Wokingham, Berks.
Wolseley Bridge, Staffs.
Wolverhampton, W. Mids.
Wonersh, Surrey.
Woodbridge, Suffolk.
Woodbury, Devon.
Woodchurch, Kent.
Woodford Green, Gtr.
  London.
Woodlands, Hants.
Woodstock, Oxon.
Woodville, Derbys.
Wooler, Northumb.
Woolhampton, Berks.
Woolpit, Suffolk.
Woore, Shrops.
Wootton, Isle of Wight.
Wootton Bassett, Wilts.
Worcester, Hereford and
  Worcs.
Worfield, Shrops.
Worksop, Notts.
Worsley, Lancs.
Wortham, Suffolk.
Worthing, W. Sussex.
Wotton-under-Edge, Glos.
Wragby, Lincs.
Wraysbury, Berks.
Wrentham, Suffolk.
Wrexham, Clwyd, Wales.
Wrington, Avon.
Wroughton, Wilts.
Wroxham, Norfolk.
Wye, Kent.
Wymeswold, Leics.
Wymondham, Norfolk.

Y

Yarm, Cleveland.
Yarmouth, Isle of Wight.
Yatton, Avon.
Yazor, Hereford and Worcs.
Yealand Conyers, Lancs.
Yeovil, Somerset.
York, N. Yorks.
Yoxall, Staffs.
Yoxford, Suffolk.

DEALERS' INDEX
ALPHABETICAL LIST OF SHOPS AND DEALERS
AND THE NAME OF THE TOWN AND COUNTY
UNDER WHICH THEY APPEAR IN THIS GUIDE

In order to facilitate reference to dealers, this index lists separately both the names of dealers and their trade names, i.e. the name of their shop or business, as well as the towns and counties under which they are to be found in this Guide. Thus A.E. Jones and C. Smith of High St. Antiques will be indexed under

Jones, A.E., Town, County
Smith, C., Town, County
and High St. Antiques, Town, County

Where there are a large number of dealers in one town, the shop name has been added in brackets after the dealer, i.e.

A.E. Jones, Town, County (High Street Antiques).

Stallholders at markets are indicated by abbreviations after their listing.

i.e.   Smith, J., London, W.8. Ant. Hyp.

=   J. Smith is to be found as a stallholder under entry for Antique Hypermarket, London, W.8.

Market Abbreviations

Alf. Ant. Mkt.	=	Alfies's Antique Market.
Ant. Ant. Mkt.	=	Antiquarius Antique Market.
Ant. C.	=	Antique Centre.
Ant. Mkt.	=	Antique Market.
B. Ant. Mkt.	=	Bath Antique Market.
B. L. Ant. C.	=	Butter Lane Antique Centre.
B. St. Ant. C.	=	Bond Street Antique Centre.
B. St. Silv. Galls.	=	Bond Street Silver Galleries.
Ber. Ant. Whse.	=	Bermondsey Antique Warehouse.
Bex. Ant. C.	=	Bexhill Antique Centre.
Chen. Gall.	=	Chenil Galleries.
Clift. Ant. Mkt.	=	Clifton Antique Market.
G. Ant. Mkt.	=	Grays Antique Market.
G. Mews	=	Grays Mews Antique Market.
G. Port	=	Grays Portobello.
Gt. West. Ant. C.	=	Great Western Antique Centre.
Gt. West. Ant. C.		
Wed. Mkt.	=	Great Western Antique Centre Wednesday Market.
Ham. Ant. Emp.	=	Hampstead Antique Emporium.
L. Arc.	=	The Lamb Arcade.
L. Ant. Mkt.	=	Leominster Antique Market.
Lon. Silv. Vts.	=	London Silver Vaults.
Mid. Ant. Mkt.	=	Midhurst Antique Market.
N. A. Ant. C.	=	Newton Abbot Antique Centre.
N.W. Ant. C.	=	North Western Antique Centre.
Royal Ex. S.C.	=	Royal Exchange Shopping Centre.
S. Ant. C.	=	Sandgate Antiques Centre.
Smith St. A.C.	=	Smith Street Antique Centre.
Str. Ants.	=	Strand Antiques.
Tor. Ant. C.	=	Torquay Antique Centre.
Vict. Vill.	=	The Victorian Village.
W. Pk. Ant. Pav.	=	West Park Antiques Pavilion.
Wob. Ab. Ant. C.	=	Woburn Abbey Antiques Centre.

A

7 The Arcade, Worthing, W. Sussex.
20th Century Antiques, Huddersfield,
W. Yorks.
20th Century Gallery, London, S.W.6.
23 Squadron, Wallasey, Merseyside.
39 Antiques, London, N.1.
50's Clothes, Surbiton, Gtr. London.
53 Ledbury Road, London, W.11.
"55" Antiques, Hull, N. Humberside.
634 Kings Road, London, S.W.6.
A1A Antiques, Ulverston, Cumbria.
A.A. Antiques, Glasgow, Lanarks., Scot.
A.A.A., London, W.1. G. Ant. Mkt.
A. and B. Antiques of London and Henry
Block, London, W.1. B. St. Ant. C.
A-B Gallery Salcombe, Devon.
A.C. Antiques, Altrincham, Cheshire.
A. & D. Antiques, Blandford Forum, Dorset.
A.D. Antiques, Doddington, Cambs.
A.D.C. Heritage Ltd., London, W.1.
A. & F. Partners, Faringdon, Oxon.
A. & G. Antiques, London, W.1. G. Ant.
Mkt.
A.N. Antiques, Eye, Suffolk.
A.S. Antiques, Manchester, Lancs.
A Thing of Beauty, Farnham Common,
Bucks.
Aagaard Ltd., Robert, Birstwith, N. Yorks.
Aagaard Ltd., Robert, Knaresborough,
N. Yorks.
Aalders, M. and E., London, W.5.
Aaron Antiques, Morriston, W. Glam.,
Wales.
Aaron Antiques, Snodland, Kent.
Aaron Gallery, London, W.1.
Aaron (London) Ltd., Didier, London, S.W.1.
Aaron, M. & D., London, W.1.
Aarquebus Antiques, St. Leonards-on-Sea,
E. Sussex.
Abacus, Hitchin, Hertfordshire.
Abacus Antiques, London, W.1. G. Ant.
Mkt.
Abacus Antiques, Stroud, Hants.
Abbas—Combe Pine, Bristol, Avon.
Abbey Antique Shop, Whalley, Lancs.
Abbey Antiques, Birkenhead, Merseyside.
Abbey Antiques, Carlisle, Cumbria.
Abbey Antiques, Glastonbury, Somerset.
Abbey Antiques, Hastings, E. Sussex.
Abbey Antiques, Hollinwood, Lancs.
Abbey Antiques, Ickleton, Cambs.
Abbey Antiques, Market Harborough, Leics.
Abbey Antiques, Ramsey, Cambs.
Abbey Antiques, Tewkesbury, Glos.
Abbey Antiques, Tintern, Gwent, Wales.
Abbey Antiques and Arts, Hemel
Hempstead, Herts.
Abbey Galleries, Bath, Avon.
Abbey House, Derby, Derbys.
Abbots House, Glastonbury, Somerset.
Abbott Antiques, A., Ipswich, Suffolk.
Abbott, C. and A., Hartley Wintney, Hants.
Abbott, H., East Molesey, Surrey.
Abbott and Holder, London, S.W.13.
Abbott, J.L., East Molesey, Surrey.

Abbott Antiquarian Horologist, Leon, Esher,
Surrey.
Abbott, Nicholas, Hartley Wintney, Hants.
Abbott, S. & R., Needham Market, Suffolk.
Aberford Antiques Ltd., Aberford, W. Yorks.
Abingdon House Antiques, Honiton, Devon.
Abington Books, London, N.W.5.
Abode, Stratford-upon-Avon, Warks.
Abraham, H., Birmingham, W. Mids.
Abramov, Eli, London, W.1. B. St. Ant.C.
Abrehart, S. and F.T., Beccles, Suffolk.
Abridge Antique Centre, Abridge, Essex.
Accossato, G., London, S.W.3., Chen. Gall.
Accurate Trading Co., London, W.1. B. St.
Ant. C.
Ace Antiques, Oldham, Lancs.
Acevedo, A., London. S.W.3., Chen. Gall.
Ackermann and Son Ltd., Arthur, London,
W.1.
Ackrill, B.D. and B.G., Tetbury, Glos.
Ackroyd, J.L., Haslemere, Surrey.
Acomb Antiques, York, N. Yorks.
Acorn Antiques, Evesham, Hereford &
Worcs.
Acorn Antiques Hitchin, Herts.
Acorn Antiques, London, S.E.21.
Acorn Antiques, Towcester, Northants.
Acquisitions (Fireplaces) Ltd., London,
N.W.1.
Actino Antiques, London, S.E.13.
Adam Antiques, Burnham-on-Sea, Somerset.
Adam Antiques, Cardiff, S. Glam., Wales.
Adam, D., Edenbridge, Kent.
Adamas Antiques, Manchester, Lancs. Royal
Ex. S.C.
Adams, London, W.1.
Adams Antiques, Chester, Cheshire
Adams Antiques, London, N.W.1.
Adams Antiques, London, S.W.6.
Adams Antiques, Redhill, Surrey.
Adams Antiques, St. Ives, Cambs.
Adams, B.J., Holt, Norfolk.
Adams, B. and T., Chester, Cheshire.
Adams, D., London, W.1. (Tooley, Adams &
Co. Ltd.)
Adams, Eleanor, Guildford, Surrey. Ant. C.
Adams Antiques, Gil, London, S.W.6.
Adams, K. and J., Seend, Wilts.
Adams, Mr. and Mrs. L., London, W.1.
Adams, M., Bath, Avon (Tassles). Gt. West.
Ant. C.
Adams Ltd., Norman, London, S.W.3.
Adams, N.W. and S.M., Weston-super-Mare,
Avon.
Adams, P., Ipswich, Suffolk. (Country
Bygones and Antiques)
Adams Antiques, Rodney, Pwllheli,
Gwynedd, Wales.
Adams Room Ltd., Antiques, and Adams
Gallery, London, S.W.19.
Adams Bygones Shop, Tony, Ipswich,
Suffolk.
Adamson, Alexander, Kirkby Lonsdale,
Cumbria.
Adamson Armoury, J.K., Skipton, N. Yorks.
Adamson, M., Bawtry, S. Yorks.
Addingham Antiques, Addingham, W.
Yorks.

Addison Antiques, Michael, Purley, Gtr. London.
Addison, M. and N. Purley, Gtr. London.
Addison-Ross Gallery, London, S.W.1.
Adler, L. and M., Tunbridge Wells, Kent (Hadlow Antiques).
Adrienne, London, S.W.3. Ant. Ant. Mkt.
Affordable Arts, Bristol, Avon.
Agace, J., London, W.1 (Johnson Walker & Tolhurst Ltd.).
Ager, A. & A., Ashburton, Devon.
Ages Ago, London, S.E.26.
Agincourt House, Dartmouth, Devon.
Agnew and Son Ltd., Thomas, London, W.1.
Ahuan (U.K.) Ltd., London, S.W.1.
Aindow, H.P., A.O., and R.A., Kendal, Cumbria.
Ainslie, Robert, Kippen, Stirls., Scot.
Aird, P.S., Stockport, Cheshire.
Airdale Antiques, Eversley, Hants.
Aitchison, Mrs. S., Reepham, Norfolk.
Akroyd, V. and H., Huddersfield, W. Yorks.
Al Mashreq Galleries, London, W.8.
Aladdin of Buckingham, Buckingham, Bucks.
Aladdin's Cave, Ambleside, Cumbria.
Aladdin's Cave, Great Malvern, Hereford and Worcs.
Aladdin's Cave, Leeds, W. Yorks.
Aladics, Janos, Weedon, Northants.
Alan Ltd., Adrian, Brighton, E. Sussex.
Albany Antiques, Glasgow, Lanarks., Scot.
Albany Antiques Ltd., Hindhead, Surrey.
Albany Gallery, London, S.W.1.
Albion Fine Art, London, W.11.
Albuquerque, Jane, Wallingford, Oxon. L.Arc.
Alcock, Mr. and Mrs. D., Tunbridge Wells, Kent. (York Gallery.)
Aldeburgh Antiques, Aldeburgh, Suffolk.
Alderley Antiques, Alderley Edge, Cheshire.
Alderson and Alderson, Bath, Avon.
Alderson, C.J.R., Bath, Avon.
Aldgate Antiques (Perth) Ltd., Perth, Perths., Scot.
Aldiss, Grace, Fakenham, Norfolk. Ant. C.
Aldred, L.J., Cambridge, Cambs. (Dolphin Antiques).
Aldridge, H. and L., Llandudno, Gwynedd, Wales.
Alexander Antiques, Henfield, W. Sussex.
Alexander Antiques, Manchester, Lancs. Royal Ex. S.C.
Alexander Antiques, Portrush, Co. Antrim, N. Ireland.
Alexander and Berendt Ltd., London, W.1.
Alexander, G., London, S.W.3. Ant. Ant. Mkt.
Alexander, Molly, Seaford, E. Sussex.
Alexander Fine Arts Ltd., M.A., Glasgow, Lanarks., Scot.
Alexander, Richard, Seaford, E. Sussex.
Alexander, R. and Mrs., Portrush, Co. Antrim, N. Ireland.
Alexander, Robert R., Fleet, Hants.
Alexandrena, Fakenham, Norfolk. Ant. C.

Alfano and Bostock, London, W.1. B. St. Ant. C.
Alfies Antique Market, London, N.W.8.
Alfred's Old Curiosity Shop, Mr., incorporating James Morris, Fine Art Dealer, Southampton, Hants.
Alfriston Antiques, Alfriston, E. Sussex.
Ali Baba, Bristol, Avon. Clift. Ant. Mkt.
Ali Baba, Guildford, Surrey.
Alice Lighting and Antiques, Cardiff, S. Glam., Wales.
Alice's, London, W.11.
Alice's Antiques, Llanelli, Dyfed, Wales.
All Things Bright and Beautiful, St. Just, Cornwall.
Allam, Miss W.E., London, N.21.
Allan, C., Cheadle Hume, Cheshire.
Allan, Gwyneth, Glasgow, Lanarks., Scot. Vict Vill.
Allan Gallery, Richard, London, S.W.10.
Allan's Antiques, Cheadle Hume, Cheshire.
Allbrook, A.F., Theydon Bois, Essex.
Allbrook, R.L. and M.F., Theydon Bois, Essex.
Allen, A.P. and D.A., Lytham, Lancs.
Allen and Co., Alfred S., South Ockendon, Essex.
Allen Avery Interiors, Haslemere, Surrey.
Allen, F.J. and G. J., Tutbury, Staffs.
Allen and Co., J.A., London, S.W.1.
Allen Antiques Ltd., Peter, London, S.E.15.
Allen, P.L., Chertsey, Surrey.
Allen, Trevor, London, S.W.3. Ant. Ant. Mkt.
Allen, T.W., Eye, Suffolk.
Allen, W. and M.E., Ashby-de-la-Zouch, Leics.
Allens Antiques, Newark, Notts.
Allen's Antiques, Stapleford, Lincs.
Allen's (Branksome) Ltd., Branksome, Dorset.
Allford, Col. and Mrs. J., Withersdale, Suffolk.
Allison and Sons, C.W., Preston, Lancs. N.W. Ant. C.
Allison Antiques, Donald, Preston, Lancs.
Allison, J. and P., Hull, N. Humberside.
Allison, P., Hull, N. Humberside.
Allison, P. and P., Preston, Lancs. N.W. Ant. C.
Allison, R., Preston, Lancs. N.W. Ant. C.
Allison, S.R., East Dereham, Norfolk.
Allison's, London, W.1. G. Mews.
Allnutt Antiques, Topsham, Devon.
Allom and Co. Ltd., P.G., Ramsey, I. of Man.
Allott Abrahams and Son, Hay-on-Wye, Powys, Wales.
Allott, D.M., Otley, W. Yorks.
Alloway, Nicholas, London, S.W.3., Chen. Gall.
Allport, E., Coltishall, Norfolk.
Allport, (Corner Antiques), Elizabeth, Coltishall, Norfolk.
Allsop, Duncan M., Warwick, Warks.
Allsop, K. and G., Alfreton, Derby.

Allsopp, Mrs., London, N.W.6.
Allsopp Antiques, John, London, S.W.1.
Allsorts Antiques, Uppingham, Leics.
Allum and Sidaway Ltd., Salisbury, Wilts.
Alma Antiques, Lindfield, W. Sussex.
Alma Street Warehouse, Worcester,
  Hereford and Worcs.
Almond, K., Darwen, Lancs.
Almondbury Antiques, Huddersfield,
  W. Yorks.
Alpha Antiques, Checkley, Staffs.
Alpha Omega, London, W.1. G. Ant. Mkt.
Alps, R. & V., Westcliff-on-Sea, Essex.
Alresford Clocks Ltd., Alresford, Hants.
Alresford Gallery, Alresford, Hants.
Alston, E., Hexham, Northumb.
Alston, R.P., Long Melford, Suffolk.
Altfield, B., London, W.8.
Altfield Fine Arts, London, W.8.
Alvarino, E.A., Fairlie, Ayr., Scot.
Alverstoke Antiques, Alverstoke, Hants.
Alvin Antiques, Plymouth, Devon.
Alyn House, North Shields, Tyne and Wear.
Amati, E., London, S.W.1 (Antiquus).
Amato, L., London, N.W.1.
Amazing Grates, London, N.2.
Ambassador Marketing Ltd., London, S.W.6.
  (M. Pauw Antiques)
Ambler, A.S., Leeds, W. Yorks.
Amend Antiques, Stokenchurch, Bucks.
Amend, B., Stokenchurch, Bucks.
Amini-Persian Carpet Gallery, M., Petworth,
  W. Sussex.
Amor Ltd., Albert., London, S.W.1.
Amor, M., Princes Risborough, Bucks.
Amos, C.M., Sandgate, Kent.
Amos and Sons, George, London, E.C.2.
Amos Antiques, Joan, Salisbury, Wilts.
Amos, Richard, Folkestone, Kent.
Amos Antiques, Tony, Portsmouth, Hants.
Ampthill Antiques Centre, Ampthill, Beds.
Amstad, R., Bexhill-on-Sea, E. Sussex. Bex.
  Ant. C.
"An Englishman's Home", Bristol, Avon,
Ancestors, Bath, Avon. Gt. West. Ant. C.
Anchor Antiques Ltd., London, W.C.2.
Ancient and Modern, Barnstaple, Devon.
Ancient and Modern, Blackburn, Lancs.
Ancient and Modern, Colne, Lancs.
Ancient and Modern, Peebles, Peebles.,
  Scot.
Ancient and Modern, St. Austell, Cornwall.
And So To Bed, Whitley Bay, Tyne and
  Wear.
And So To Bed Ltd., London, S.W.6.
Anderman, S., East Molesey, Surrey.
Andersen, G. and V., London, W.8 (The
  Lacquer Chest).
Anderson, Mr. and Mrs. A., Bath, Avon
  (Trimbridge Galleries).
Anderson, C. J., Loughton, Essex.
Anderson, C.W., Paisley, Renfrews., Scot.
Anderson, D. and I., Welshpool, Powys,
  Wales.
Anderson and Son, F.E., Welshpool, Powys,
  Wales.
Anderson, I.G., Dumfries, Dumfries., Scot.
Andipa Icon Gallery, Maria, London, S.W.3.

Andrade Ltd., Philip, South Brent, Devon.
Andreae, E.J., Eversley, Hants.
Andrea, K., London, S.W.3., Chen. Gall.
Andrew and Cusack, Llanerchymedd,
  Gwynedd, Wales.
Andrew, Tony, Llanerchymedd, Gwynedd,
  Wales.
Andrew's Antique Shop, Leeds, W. Yorks.
Andrew's Gallery/Norman Hall, Beccles,
  Suffolk.
Andrews Antiques, Michael, Bournemouth,
  Dorset.
Andrews Antiques, Michael, Milford, Surrey.
Andrews, R., Thrapston, Northants.
Andwells, Hartley Wintney, Hants.
Andy's Antiques, Ilkeston, Derbys.
Angel Antiques, Brighton, E. Sussex.
Angel Arcade, London, N.1
Angel Arcade, Portmeirion, Gwynedd,
  Wales.
Angel, P., Brighton, E. Sussex.
Angel Shades, Petworth, W. Sussex.
Angela Antiques, Chester, Cheshire.
Angela John, Witney, Oxon.
Angeli, Mrs., London, W.1., G. Mews.
Angharad's Antiques, Shotton, Clwyd,
  Wales.
Anglia Antique Exporters, North Walsham,
  Norfolk.
Anglia Antiques, East Dereham, Norfolk.
Anglo-Persian Carpet Co., London, S.W.7.
Angloam Warehouse, Eastbourne, E. Sussex.
Angus Antiques, Dundee, Ang., Scot.
Ann Teak, Lowestoft, Suffolk.
Annal, E. and M., Glossop, Derbys.
Annalicia Antiques, Wallingford, Oxon.
  L.Arc.
Anne Tique — Curio Jewellers, Lancaster,
  Lancs.
Annesley, F., London, N.1.
  (Commemoratives.)
Annexe Antiques, Tunbridge Wells, Kent.
Annick Antiques, Kimpton, Herts.
Annie's Antiques and Clothes, London, N.1.
Annique Antiques, Tunbridge Wells, Kent.
Anno Domini Antiques, London, S.W.1.
Ann's Antiques, Stoke-on-Trent, Staffs.
Annteaks (Antiques) Abersoch, Gwynedd,
  Wales.
Ann-tiquities, Harrogate, N. Yorks.
Another World, Edinburgh, Midloth., Scot.
Ansari, London, W.1. G. Ant. Mkt.
Ansell's, Brighton, E. Sussex.
Anson, Stephen, London, W.14.
Anstee, P., London, S.W.1. (Bayly's Gallery
  Antiques)
Anstey, Mrs. J.M., Poole, Dorset.
Antediluvian and Ark Antiques, Blackpool,
  Lancs.
Antelope Antiques, Woburn, Beds. Wob.
  Ab. Ant. C.
Anthony James Antiques, Whimple, Devon.
Antica, Bromley, Gtr. London.
Antica, Orpington, Gtr. London.
Antichi, G., London, W.11.
Antics, Cobham, Surrey.
Antiquarian Prints, London, W.1. G. Ant.
  Mkt.

Arbiter, Wallasey, Merseyside.
Arbour Antiques Ltd., Stratford-upon-Avon, Warks.
Arca, London, W.1. G. Ant. Mkt.
Arcade Antiques, Wallasey, Merseyside.
Arcade Gallery Ltd., London, W.1.
Arcadia Antiques, Woodstock, Oxon.
Arcadia Gallery, Southport, Merseyside.
Archbold — Violins, Robert, Hexham, Northumb.
Archbold, S.N., Hexham, Northumb.
Archer Antiques, Penrith, Cumbria.
Archer, K., Penrith, Cumbria.
Archer, R.G., Lavenham, Suffolk.
Architectural Antiques, South Molton, Devon.
Archway Antiques, Cardiff, S. Glam. Wales.
Archway Antiques, Keswick, Cumbria.
Archway Antiques, Towcester, Northants.
Archway Antiques, Upper Boddington, Northants.
Archways, Tavistock, Devon.
Arden Antiques, Stratford-upon-Avon, Warks.
Arden, Mrs. B., Tiverton, Cheshire.
Arden Gallery, Henley-in-Arden, Warks.
Arden and Clouds Gallery, Keith, Much Hadham, Herts.
Arden-Davis, M., Much Hadham, Herts.
Ardingly Antiques, Ardingly, W. Sussex.
Arditti, A. and J.L., Christchurch, Dorset.
Arditti, J.L., Christchurch, Dorset.
Arditti, L.J., Tunbridge Wells, Kent.
Arena Billi, London, S.W.3. Ant. Ant. Mkt.
Arenski, London, W.1.
Argent Gallery, Tetbury, Glos.
Argentum Antiques, Bexley, Gtr. London.
Argosy Antiques, London, S.E.1 Ber. Ant. Whse.
Argyll House Antiques, Felsted, Essex.
Arieta, Valerie, London, W.11. G. Port.
Aristo-Cat, Gerrards Cross, Bucks.
"Ark Angel", The, London, N.1.
Arkea Antiques, Bath, Avon.
Arlidge, N.J., Axbridge, Somerset.
Arlington Galleries Ltd., Cardiff, S. Glam., Wales.
Armada Antiques, London, W.1. G. Ant. Mkt.
Armada Exports, Cheltenham, Glos.
Armand Antiques, London, W.1. G. Mews.
Armelin, Antiques, Karin, London, S.W.6.
Armett, C.H. Burton-on-Trent, Staffs.
Armitage, London, W.1.
Armitage, Mrs. M., Chester, Cheshire (Richmond Galleries).
Armour-Winston Ltd., London, W.1.
Armoury Antiques, London, W.1. G. Ant. Mkt.
Armson Antiques Ltd., Michael, Berkhamsted, Herts.
Armson, Roger t/a Armson, J.C.E. & N.I., Yoxall, Staffs.
Armstrong Antiques, Harrogate, N. Yorks.
Armstrong, C., Scarborough, N. Yorks.
Armstrong, H., Scarborough, N. Yorks.
Armstrong, J., London, W.1. (Folli Follie) B.St. Ant. C.

Armstrong, J. and G., Middleham, N. Yorks.
Armstrong, M.A. and C.J., Harrogate, N. Yorks. (Armstrong Antiques.)
Armstrong-Davis Gallery, Arundel, W. Sussex.
Arndale Antiques, Poole, Dorset.
Arnold Antiques, Hugh, Nayland, Suffolk.
Arnold, L., Swansea, W. Glam., Wales.
Arnold Gallery, Peter, Wingrave, Bucks.
Arnold Studio (Fine Art Trade Guild), Phyllis, Bangor, Co. Down, N. Ireland.
Arnold, Roy, Needham Market, Suffolk.
Arnold-Brown, A.S. &. J.L., Salcombe, Devon.
Arnsby, A.D., Ludlow, Shrops.
Arrow Antiques, Newark, Notts.
Arsenic & Old Lace, Manchester, Lancs. Royal Ex. S.C.
Art and Antiques, Beccles, Suffolk.
Art and Antiques, Bridlington, N. Humberside.
Art and Antiques (Wadhurst), Wadhurst, E. Sussex.
Artake, S., London, S.W.3, Ant. Ant. Mkt.
Art-Antica, London, W.1. B.St. Ant. C.
Artbry's Antiques, Pinner, Gtr. London.
Artemesia, Alresford, Hants.
Artemis Fine Arts (U.K.) Limited, London, S.W.1.
Arthy, D., Hythe, Kent.
Artifact, London, W.1. G. Mews.
Artintorias, London, N.W.2.
Artisan, Edinburgh, Midloth., Scot.
Artisan Antiques & Collectables, Cambridge, Cambs.
Arts and Antiques (Oxford) Ltd., Wantage, Oxon.
Arts of Living, Bath, Avon.
Arundel Antiques and Collectors Market, Arundel, W. Sussex.
Arundel Antiques Market, Arundel, W. Sussex.
Arundell Books, Tisbury, Wilts.
Arwas, V., London, W.1 (Editions Graphiques Gallery).
Arzeni, Emidia, London, S.W.3., Ant. Ant. Mkt.
As Time Goes By, London, N.1.
Ash House, Ramsgate, Kent.
Ash, Jim and Pat, Llandeilo, Dyfed, Wales.
Ash (Rare Books), J., London, E.C.3.
Ash Tree Antiques, Halesworth, Suffolk.
Ashburton Marbles, Ashburton, Devon.
Ashby Antiques, Ashby-de-la-Zouch, Leics.
Ashby Antiques, London, S.W.6.
Ashby Antiques, Derek, St. Leonards-on-Sea, E. Sussex.
Ashleigh House Antiques, Birmingham, W. Mids.
Ashley Antiques, Hungerford, Berks.
Ashley Antiques, Long Melford, Suffolk.
Ashley House Antiques, Alrewas, Staffs.
Ashton Antiques, Dorridge, W. Mids.
Ashton, D., Shirley, Gtr. London.
Ashton, K., Gants Hill, Gtr. London.
Ashton, M., Birmingham, W. Mids. (The Moseley Gallery).
Ashton, R., Brighton, E. Sussex.

Ashton's Antiques, Brighton, E. Sussex.
Ashworth-Jones, Paddy, Fakenham, Norfolk. Ant.C.
Asiedu, S.K., Glasgow, Lanarks., Scot. (Vintage and Value).
Aspidistra, The, Hitchin, Herts.
Aspidistra, Bath, Avon.
Aspinall Antiques, Walter, Sabden, Lancs.
Aspley, J., Leek, Staffs.
Aspleys Antique Market, Leek, Staffs.
Aspleys Antique Market, Uttoxeter, Staffs.
Asprey p.l.c., London, W.1.
Asprey and Co. (City Branch) Ltd., London E.C.3.
Asprey Ltd., Maurice, London, S.W.1.
Assad, E., London, W.1. G. Mews.
Asser Fine Arts, Chichester, W. Sussex.
Asser, R., Chichester, W. Sussex.
Asta, J. and V., Long Crendon, Bucks.
Astarte Gallery, London, W.1.
Astill Antiques, John, Bridgnorth, Shrops.
Astill, P.H.K., Nottingham, Notts.
Astley Bridge Antiques, Bolton, Lancs.
Astley House — Fine Art, Moreton-in-Marsh, Glos.
Astley's, London, S.W.1.
Aston, C.D. and Mrs. I., Fordingbridge, Hants.
Aston, C.R.C., London, W.1 (Tessiers Ltd.).
Atfield and Daughter, Ipswich, Suffolk.
Atfield, D.A. and Miss S.F., Ipswich, Suffolk.
Atfield, D.J., Bournemouth, Dorset (Antiques and Curios).
Athena Antiques Centre and Peel Common Stamps, Gosport, Hants.
Atholl Antiques, Aberdeen, Aberd., Scot.
Atkin, Miss D.J., Nantwich, Cheshire.
Atkins, T., Taunton, Somerset.
Atkinson Antiques, Dewsbury, W. Yorks.
Atkinson, C.W.R., Hoylake, Merseyside.
Atkinson, G. and J., Thurso, Caith., Scot.
Atkinson Gallery, James, Sandwich, Kent.
Atkinson, Keith J., Croydon, Gtr. London.
Atkinson, R.J. and S.M.R., Sandwich, Kent.
Atkinson, R.L., Dewsbury, W. Yorks.
Atkinson, R.W. and A., Newport, Dyfed, Wales.
Atlantic Bay Carpets, London, S.W.6.
Atlantis Bookshop Ltd., London, W.C.1.
Atrium Antiques, Guisborough, Cleveland.
Atrium Antiques, Woburn, Beds.
Attic, The, Baldock, Herts.
Attic, The, Inverness, Inver., Scot.
Attic, The, Wallington, Gtr. London.
Attic Antiques, Brighton, E. Sussex.
Attic Antiques, Penzance, Cornwall.
Attic Antiques, Wisbech, Cambs.
Attic Gallery, Wisbech, Cambs.
Attic (Sevenoaks) Ltd., A.B.A., The, Brasted, Kent.
Atticus Books, Southend-on-Sea, Essex.
Aubyn Antiques, London, S.W.6.
Audraw Ltd., Soham, Cambs.
Audus L., Soham, Cambs.
Augill Castle Antiques Ltd., Brough, Cumbria.
Auld, C.J., Greyabbey, Co. Down, N. Ireland.

Auld, Ian, London, N.1.
Aune Valley Antiques, Aveton Gifford, Devon.
Austen, Mrs. R.A., Basingstoke, Hants.
Austen, S.T. & R.J., Rayleigh , Essex.
Austin, A.D. and E., Whalley, Lancs.
Austin, G., Winchester, Hants.
Austin and Sons Ltd., G., London, S.E.15.
Austin, H., A., D. and V., London, S.E.15.
Austin, S., Leicester, Leics.
Austin, S., Swindon, Wilts.
Autograph Shop, The, Hounslow, Gtr. London.
Avakian Oriental Carpets Ltd., London, W.1.
Avarice Antiques, Edinburgh, Midloth., Scot.
Avery, Mrs. E.B., Chiddingstone, Kent.
Avery, Mr. and Mrs. L., Wolverhampton, W. Mids.
Avon Antiques, Bradford-on-Avon, Wilts.
Avon Gallery, The, Moreton-in-Marsh, Glos.
Avon Lodge Antiques, Fordingbridge, Hants.
Avonbridge Antiques and Collectors Market, The, Salisbury, Wilts.
Avril Antiques, Bath, Avon, Gt. West. Ant. C.
Awad, Mrs. L.G. London, S.W.1. (Belgravia Gallery Ltd.)
Axford, Karen, Aberstwyth, Dyfed, Wales.
Axia, London, W.11.
Ayers, J.A., Felmingham, Norfolk.
Ayliffe, L., Tetbury, Glos.
Aylwin, Mrs. R., Coggeshall, Essex.
Ayres, M., London, W.C.1.
Ayston House Antiques, Uppingham, Leics.
Aytac, Osman, London, W.1. G. Ant. Mkt.
Aytag, G., London, S.W.3. Ant. Ant. Mkt.

B

B.B.C. Antiques, Catsfield, E. Sussex.
B.B.M. Jewellery and Antiques, Kidderminster, Hereford and Worcs.
B. and C. Antiques, Newbold-on -Stour, Warks.
B.C. Metalcrafts Ltd., London, N.W.9.
B.G.R. Silver, Wisbech, Cambs.
B. and J. Antiques (Curio Corner), Herne Bay, Kent.
B.P. Antiques, London, N.W.1.
B.S. Antiques, East Molesey, Surrey.
B. and T. Antiques, London, W.11.
B.W. Antiques, Keighley, W. Yorks.
Bacchus Antiques — In the Service of Wine, Hale, Cheshire.
Bacchus Antiques — In the Service of Wine, Heversham, Cumbria.
Bach, Mr. and Mrs., London, S.W.3., Ant. Ant. Mkt.
Bachmann, Mrs. J.P., Romsey, Hants.
Bacon, D., London, W.1 (G. Heywood Hill Ltd.).
Baddiel, Colin, London, W.1., G. Mews.
Baddiel Golfiana, London, W.1., G. Mews.
Baddow Antique and Craft Centre, Gt. Baddow, Essex.
Badger, The, London, W.5.

Badger Antiques, Colchester, Essex.
Badgery, R.A., Plymouth, Devon.
Badir, R. and R., London, W.1. G. Ant. Mkt.
Badland, Miss, Bradford, W. Yorks.
Badman, J.A., Glastonbury, Somerset.
Baggott Church Street Ltd., Stow-on-the-
Wold, Glos.
Baggott Duncan J., Stow-on-the-Wold, Glos.
Bagnall Antiques, W., Chulmleigh, Devon.
Bagpuss, London, W.1. G. Ant. Mkt.
Bagshawe, N., London, S.W.3. (Walker-
Bagshawe.)
Baguley Antiques, Shirley, Harrogate, N.
Yorks. W. Pk. Ant. Pav.
Bail, A. and I., Ash Vale, Surrey.
Baile de Laperriere, H., Calne, Wilts.
Bailes, M., Richmond, N. Yorks.
Bailey, Ann, Bath, Avon, Gt. West. Ant. C.
Bailey, Elizabeth, Beeston, Notts.
Bailey Antique Clocks, John, Mayland,
Essex.
Bailey, M., Manchester, Lancs. Royal
Ex.S.C.
Bailey, M. and S., Ross-on-Wye, Hereford &
Worcs.
Baileys Architectural Antiques, Ross-on-Wye,
Hereford & Worcs.
Bailie Antiques, Alexander, London, W.1.
Baillache, Serge, London, W.11.
Bain, Cdr. and Mrs. H.E.R., Albrighton,
Shrops.
Bainbridge, P.G., London, S.W.10.
Baines, Henry, Southborough, Kent.
Baird, R. and V., Langholm, Dumfries, Scot.
Bakehouse Antiques, Bridgnorth, Shrops.
Baker Antiques, Anthony, Alderley Edge,
Cheshire.
Baker, C.J. and B.A.J., Lavenham, Suffolk.
Baker, David, London, W.11. G. Port.
Baker Antiques, G., Dover, Kent.
Baker Oriental Works of Art, Gregg, London,
W.1.
Baker, J., London, N.W.8. Alf. Ant. Mkt.
Baker Antiques, John, Newbury, Berks.
Baker, J. and J., Lavenham, Suffolk.
Baker, K.R., Woking, Surrey.
Baker, Michael and Margaret, Merstham,
Surrey.
Baker, N.V., Spalding, Lincs.
Baker, Sue Lawson, West Knoyle, Wilts.
Baker, T., Langford, Notts.
Bakers of Maybury Ltd., Woking, Surrey.
Balchin, C.B., Brighton, E. Sussex.
Balchin and Son, H., Brighton, E. Sussex.
Balcombe Galleries, Balcombe, W. Sussex.
Balcombe Galleries, London, S.W.10.
Baldwin and Sons Ltd., A.H., London,
W.C.2.
Baldwin, G.E. and J.E., London, W.11.
Baldwin, Michael, Bournemouth, Dorset.
Baldwin, M., Tunbridge Wells, Kent.
(Mission Antique Centre.)
Baldwin Antiques, Michael G., Caversham,
Berks.
Baldwin, P.J., Exeter, Devon.
Baldwin, R.J.S., London, S.W.3. (Green and
Stone).
Balfour-Lynn, A., London, W.C.1.

Ball Antiques, David, Luton, Beds.
Ball Antiques & Fine Art, David, Leighton
Buzzard, Beds.
Ball, D. & J., Leighton Buzzard, Beds.
Ball, Mr. and Mrs. G., Tattershall, Lincs.
Ball, Mrs. J., Bristol, Avon. Clift. Ant. Mkt.
Ball, W.M., Retford, Notts.
Ballard, Mrs. E.H. and S.R., Thirsk, N.
Yorks.
Ballard, F. & Mrs. J., Weymouth, Dorset.
Ballinger, J., Ruskington, Lincs.
Ballroom Antiques, Petworth, W. Sussex.
Ballymenoch Antiques, Edinburgh, Midloth.,
Scot.
Bamber and Son Ltd., Richard, Preston,
Lancs.
Bampton Antiques, Bampton, Devon.
Banbury Bookshop, Banbury, Oxon.
Banbury Fayre, London, N.1.
Bandini, L., London, W.1 (Eskenazi Ltd.).
Bangs, Christopher, London, S.W.11.
Banham, K., London, W.1 (Grimaldi).
Banham, Sue, London, S.W.3. (Sue
Biddulph.) Ant. Ant. Mkt.
Bank House Gallery, The, London, N.W.7.
Banks, A., London, N.1. (Quaker Lodge
Antiques).
Banks, B.A. and G., Sherborne, Dorset.
Banks, D. and S. Finedon, Northants.
Banks, P.M.L., London, S.W.15.
Banks, R., Leigh-on-Sea, Essex.
Banner Antiques, St. Leonards-on-Sea,
E. Sussex.
Bannister, Mrs. A., Stratford-upon-Avon,
Warks.
Bannister, David, Cheltenham, Glos.
Bar Antiques, Scarborough, N. Yorks.
Barbara Antiques, London, N.W.8. Alf. Ant.
Mkt.
Barber, B., Mrs., London, W.3 (Yours and
Mine).
Barber, P.M., Stratford-upon-Avon, Warks.
Barbers Picture Framing, Woking, Surrey.
Barbic, Natasha, London, S.W.3. Ant. Ant.
Mkt.
Barbic, N., London, S.W.3. (M. Parker.) Ant.
Ant. Mkt.
Barbican Antique Market Ltd., Plymouth,
Devon.
Barbican Bookshop, York, N. Yorks.
Barbieri, Anthony and Daniel Nelson,
London, S.W.3. Chen. Gall.
Barcbourne Ltd., London, N.1 (Mall Antiques
Arcade).
Barclay Antiques, Bexhill-on-Sea, E. Sussex.
Barclay Antiques, Headington, Oxon.
Barclay, C. & B., Headington, Oxon.
Barclay, Mr. & Mrs. K., London, N.W.8.
Barclay, M.J. and D., Friockheim, Ang.,
Scot.
Barclay, R. and M., Bexhill-on-Sea, E.
Sussex.
Barclay, T.H. and J., King's Lynn, Norfolk.
Bardawil, Eddy, London, W.8.
Bardawil, E.S., London, W.8.
Barden House Antiques, Tonbridge, Kent.
Barder Antiques, Richard, Hermitage, Berks.
Barder, R.C.R., and P.A., Hermitage, Berks.

Bardwell Antiques, Sheffield, S. Yorks.
Bardwell, C. and N., Barnoldswick, Lancs.
Bardwell, R., Sheffield, S. Yorks.
Bargain Box, Luton, Beds.
Barham, A.E., Plymouth, Devon.
Barham Fine Art, London, W.11.
Barham, M., London, S.W.3. Ant. Ant. Mkt.
Barham, P.R., London, W.11.
Baring, R.W., West Peckham, Kent.
Barker Antiques, Leicester, Leics.
Barker, Mrs. B., London, S.W.3. Ant. Ant. Mkt.
Barker, B., Swanage, Dorset.
Barker Court Antique and Bygones, York, N. Yorks.
Barker, D., Beaconsfield, Bucks.
Barker, I. & R., Pocklington, N. Humberside.
Barker-Mill, C., London, W.8. (Bohun & Busbridge).
Barkes, P.R., York, N. Yorks.
Barkes and Richardson, York, N. Yorks.
Barklem Ltd., David, N.1.
Barklem, D.N., London, N.1.
Barley Antiques, Robert, London, S.W.6.
Barley, R.A., London, S.W.6.
Barleycote Hall Antiques, Keighley, W. Yorks.
Barling of Mount Street Ltd., London, W.1.
Barlow, A., Grantham, Lincs.
Barlow Antiques, Anne, Letchmore Heath, Herts.
Barlow, Anne, London, W.11. G. Port.
Barlow, E., London, S.W.1. (General Trading Co. Ltd.)
Barlow, J., Alderley Edge, Cheshire.
Barlow Ltd., K., London, W.1.
Barn, The, Bicester, Oxon.
Barn, The, Petersfield, Hants.
Barn, The, Risby, Suffolk.
Barn Antiques, Coventry, W. Mids.
Barn Book Supply, The, Salisbury, Wilts.
Barn End Antiques and Firearms, Hadleigh, Suffolk.
Barn Gallery, The, Powick, Hereford and Worcs.
Barnard Gallery, The, Everton, Notts.
Barnard, J., Ilminster, Somerset.
Barnard, Thomas, Uxbridge, Gtr. London.
Barnes, D., Dover, Kent.
Barnes, F. & P., Clitheroe, Lancs.
Barnes, H., Stafford, Staffs.
Barnes House Antiques Centre, Wimborne Minster, Dorset.
Barnes Antiques, R.A., London, S.W.15.
Barnes, Mrs. V., Hemel Hempstead, Herts.
Barnet Antiques and Fine Arts, Barnet, Gtr. London.
Barnet Antiques and Fine Art, London, N.20.
Barnett, H.W. and L.M., Devizes, Wilts.
Barnett, J.P., London, W.11 (S. Lampard & Son Ltd.).
Barnett, Mr. and Mrs. K.D., London, S.W.6 (And So To Bed Ltd.).
Barnett, Roger, Windsor and Eton, Berks.
Barnicott, R. and J., Cowbridge, S. Glam., Wales.
Burnt Green Antiques, Burnt Green, Hereford and Worcs.

Barntiques, Colchester, Essex.
Barometer Shop, Leominster, Hereford and Worcs.
Baron Antiques, The, Manchester, Lancs.
Baron Antiques, Wolverhampton, West Mids.
Baron, Mrs. C., Winchester, Hants.
Baron, H., London, N.W.2.
Baroq Antiques, Little Brickhill, Bucks.
Barr, Mrs. E., Bungay, Suffolk.
Barr, G.W., Croydon, Gtr. London.
Barr, K., Bath, Avon. B. Ant. Mkt.
Barr, R., Merstham, Surrey.
Barragan, A., London, N.W.8. Alf. Ant. Mkt.
Barratt, N. and J., Warrington, Cheshire.
Barrett and Co., C., London, W.1.
Barrett, I. and B., Widegates, Cornwall.
Barrett, P.R. and S.M., Seaford, E. Sussex.
Barrett, P.S., Weymouth, Dorset.
Barrett's Furniture Workshop, Ian, Widegates, Cornwall.
Barrie, K., London, N.W.6.
Barrie, P. and M., Cheltenham, Glos.
Barrie's Bookshop, Cheltenham, Glos.
Barrington, David, Brasted, Kent.
Barrington, D. and J., London, N.1. (Yesterday Child).
Barron and Sons, J., Mevagissey, Cornwall.
Barronfield Gallery, Preston, Lancs.
Barrow, M., York, N. Yorks. (Yesterday's Furniture).
Barrow Antiques, Richard, Tring, Herts.
Barrows, R., N. and J.S., Ollerton, Notts.
Barrows and Son, T.S., Ollerton, Notts.
Barry, John, Nailsworth, Glos.
Barrymore & Co., J., Honiton, Devon.
Barrymore, David, London, W.11. G. Port. (Anita Vandenberg).
Barsley Antiques, Douglas, Eastbourne, E. Sussex.
Barter, Mrs. P.M., Navenby, Lincs.
Bartlett, Nigel A., London, S.E.1.
Bartlett, R.G., Redhill, Surrey.
Barlett Street Antique Centre, Bath, Avon.
Bartman, F., London, S.W.1 (Anno Domini Antiques).
Barton, B.A., P.G. and G.S., Leamington Spa, Warks.
Barton House Antiques, Stanford-le-Hope, Essex.
Barton, J.R. and A.R., Harlech, Gwynedd, Wales.
Barton, Robert Budleigh Salterton, Devon.
Barton, R. and C., Watford, Herts.
Barton, Roy, Pulborough, W. Sussex.
Barton-Booth Gallery, Warminster, Wilts.
Barton's Antiques for Investment, Harlech, Gwynedd, Wales.
Bartram, Albert, Chesham, Bucks.
Bartrick, Douglas J., Gloucester, Glos.
Barwick, T., London, N.1 (Old Woodworking Tools).
Basile, N., Frinton-on-Sea, Essex.
Baskett and Day, London, W.1.
Bass, B., Cheltenham, Glos. (Montpellier Clocks).
Bassett, G. and H., Codsall, Staffs.
Bassett, M. & G., Ashbourne, Derbys.

Bastasian, Esther, London, W.1. G. Mews.
Bastillo, J., London, S.W.6. (Just a second Antiques Ltd.)
Bate, A.C., London, W.1 (Scarisbrick & Bate Ltd.).
Bate, C.J. and J.A., London, S.W.14.
Bateman, Don, Pulham St. Mary, Norfolk.
Bateman, Jean A., Stratford-upon-Avon, Warks.
Bateman Antiques, J. and R., London, S.W.15.
Bateman, W., Hoylake, Merseyside.
Bates, E.R., High Wycombe, Bucks.
Bates & Sons, Eric, Coltishall, Norfolk.
Bates & Sons, Eric, North Walsham, Norfolk.
Bates Antiques, Jeffery, Boroughbridge, N. Yorks.
Bates, J.S., Esher, Surrey.
Bates, S., Stowmarket, Suffolk.
Bates, T. and P., Tavistock, Devon.
Bateson Antiques, David, Bressingham, Norfolk.
Bateson, D. and P., Bressingham, Norfolk.
Bath Antique Market, Bath, Avon.
Bath Chair, The, Woolhampton, Berks.
Bath Coin Shop, Bath, Avon.
Bath Galleries, Bath, Avon.
Bath Saturday Antiques Market, Bath, Avon.
Bathurst, Tony, Guildford, Surrey. Ant. C.
Batley, J., Bath, Avon. Gt. West. Ant. C.
Batsford, L., Weedon, Northants.
Batstone Books, Malmesbury, Wilts.
Batstone, D. and M.E., Malmesbury, Wilts.
Battersby Antiques, Botley, Hants.
Battlesbridge Antique Centre, Battlesbridge, Essex.
Batty, Mrs. L.A., Datchet, Berks.
Baumkotter Gallery, London, W.8.
Baumkotter, Mrs. L., London, W.8. (Baumkotter Gallery).
Bawden, L.J. and S., Wareham, Dorset.
Baxter, A.L., London, W.8.
Baxter and Sons, H.C., London, S.W.3.
Baxter, R.C., T.J., M., J. and G.J., London, S.W.3.
Bay House, Uppingham, Leics.
Bayley, C., London, W.8.
Baylis, M.S., Wallingford, Oxon.
Bayliss, D.W. and A.B., Ludlow, Shrops.
Bayliss, J.H. Leominster, Hereford & Worcs. L. Ant. Mkt.
Bayly's Gallery Antiques, London, S.W.1.
Bayne-Powell, H., West Peckham, Kent.
Baynton-Williams, R.H. & S.C., Arundell, W. Sussex.
Bayntun, George, Bath, Avon.
Bayntun-Coward, C.M., and H.H., Bath, Avon.
Bayntun-Coward, H.H., Bath, Avon (George Gregory).
Bayvil House Antiques, Cardigan, Dyfed, Wales.
Bazaar, The, Bedford, Beds.
Beach and Co. Antiques, Bridport, Dorset.
Beach, D.M., Salisbury, Wilts.
Beacon Gallery, Woburn, Beds. Wob. Ab. Ant. C.
Beaker Antiques, Ludlow, Shrops.

Beal, A.S., London, W.1. B. St. Ant. C.
Beaminster Antiques, Beaminster, Dorset.
Beamish, Mrs. S., London, W.4 (Mangate Gallery).
Beare, John and Arthur, London, W.1.
Beasley, P.T. and R., Farningham, Kent.
Beaton, W.M.Y., Perth, Perths., Scot.
Beaton, W.S., Perth, Perths., Scot.
Beau Monde Antiques, Huddersfield, W. Yorks.
Beaubush House Antiques, Sandgate, Kent.
Beaufort Gallery, Hexham, Northumb.
Beaulieu Fine Arts, Beaulieu, Hants.
Beaumont Antiques, Michael, Hempstead, Essex.
Beaver, A.G. and H.L., Hereford, Hereford and Worcs.
Beaver Coin Room, London, S.W.5.
Beazor and Son Ltd., John, Cambridge, Cambs.
Bebb, R. and L., Kidwelly, Dyfed, Wales.
Beccles Gallery, Beccles, Suffolk.
Beck, Claudia, London, W.1. B. St. Ant. C.
Beck, P., Lavenham, Suffolk.
Beckenham Antique Market, Beckenham, Gtr. London.
Becker, A.G. and M.S., Attleborough, Norfolk.
Becker, O.M., London, S.W.3 (The Purple Shop).
Becker, P.C. and C.C., Lindfield, W. Sussex.
Becker, Susan, London, S.W.15.
Beckfoot Antiques, Kirkby Stephen, Cumbria.
Beckman, Patricia, London, N.W.3.
Beckwith and Son, Hertford, Herts.
Bed Bazaar, Framlingham, Suffolk.
Bed of Roses, Cheltenham, Glos.
Bedale, David, Knutsford, Cheshire.
Beddard, A.I., Birmingham, W. Mids. (Chesterfield Antiques)
Bede Antiques, Hexham, Northumb.
Bede Antiques Ltd., Newcastle-upon-Tyne, Tyne and Wear.
Bedford, Pat, London, W.11. G. Port.
Bedford Place Antiques, Southampton, Hants.
Bedford, W., Hexham, Northumb.
Bedford p.l.c., William, London, N.1.
Bedford, W. and J., London, N.1.
Bedi Antiques, Margaret, Billingham, Cleveland.
Bee, Linda, London, W.1. G. Mews.
Beech Antiques, Clevedon, Avon.
Beech, Nicolas, London, S.W.8.
Beech, N.A., London, S.W.8.
Beech, Ron, Brighton, E. Sussex.
Beech, R., Parwich, Derbys.
Beech, R.E., Brighton, E. Sussex.
Beechdean Bygones, High Wycombe, Bucks.
Beedham Antiques Ltd., W.H., Bakewell, Derbys.
Beedles, P., London, S.W.3. Ant. Ant. Mkt.
Beer, Courtney, Brixham, Devon.
Beer, John, London, N.6.
Beercock, S., Hessle, N. Humberside.
Beerts, R., London, W.11 (Rodger's Antique Galleries).

Beese, M., Bristol, Avon (Michael's Antiques).
Beet, Brian, London, W.1.
Beet, B.H., London, W.1.
Beetles Ltd., Watercolours and Paintings, Chris, London, S.W.1.
Beetles Ltd., Watercolours and Paintings, Chris, London, W.9.
Begbie, A.J.S., Bristol, Avon. Clift. Ant. Mkt.
Behan, R., London, S.E.15.
Behar Carpets, Edinburgh, Midloth., Scot.
Behar Carpets, Glasgow, Lanarks., Scot.
Beider, Mrs. J., London, W.1. B. St. Ant. C.
Beiny, Mrs. R., London, W.1. (Antique Porcelain Co. Ltd.)
Beirne, A.J., Knighton, Powys, Wales.
Belcher, P.A., London, W.1. (Grimaldi).
Belgrave Gallery, London, S.W.1.
Belgravia Gallery Ltd., London, S.W.1.
Bell Antiques, Grimsby, S. Humberside.
Bell Antiques, Romsey, Hants.
Bell Book and Radmall, London, W.C.2.
Bell and Collett, London, W.1. G. Mews.
Bell, D. and J., Banbridge, Co. Down, N. Ireland.
Bell, Elaine, Cockermouth, Cumbria.
Bell Gallery, Belfast, N. Ireland.
Bell House Antiques, Cambridge, Glos.
Bell Harry Books, Canterbury, Kent.
Bell, H.J., Saddleworth, Lancs.
Bell, I., London, E.2.
Bell Antiques, J. and H., Castletown, I. of Man.
Bell, J.N., Belfast, N. Ireland.
Bell of Aberdeen Ltd., John, Aberdeen, Aberd., Scot.
Bell, K.E., Alresford, Hants.
Bell of Boscombe, Bournemouth, Dorset.
Bell, Mrs. P., Lechlade, Glos.
Bell Passage Antiques, Wotton-under-Edge, Glos.
Bell Fine Arts, Peter, Lechlade, Glos.
Bell, Mrs. R., Long Melford, Suffolk.
Bell, R., Southport, Merseyside.
Bell and Son, R., Shipley, W. Yorks.
Bell Antiques, Tim, Lavenham, Suffolk.
Bellamy, Robin, Witney, Oxon.
Belle Vue Antiques, Bristol, Avon.
Bellerby, D. and A., Marlborough, Wilts.
Bellinger Antiques, C., Barnet, Gtr. London.
Bellis Antiques, Mary, Hungerford, Berks.
Belmont-Maitland, R., London, W.1 (Tradition Military Antiques).
Below Stairs, Hungerford, Berks.
Below Stairs, Kendal, Cumbria.
Belsten, Roger, Stiffkey, Norfolk.
Belton, Anthony, London, W.8.
Benardout and Benardout, London, S.W.7.
Benardout, N., London, S.W.7.
Benardout, Raymond, London, S.W.1.
Benardout Antiques Ltd., Raymond, London, S.W.1.
Bend, J.C, Moreton-in-Marsh, Glos.
Bendall, R.D.J. and L.D.M., Liss, Hants.
Bendall's Antiques, Castle Douglas, Kirkcud., Scot.
Bendon, H.V., Buckfastleigh, Devon.

Benedict Jewellers, Amersham, Bucks.
Benet Gallery, Cambridge, Cambs.
Beney, D., Beaminster, Dorset.
Bengue, Francoise, London, W.1. G. Mews.
Benjamin Antiques, Ronald, London, E.C.1.
Benjamin/Szramko, London, W.1. G. Ant. Mkt.
Benjamin, S., London, W.1 (Halcyon Days).
Benjamin, S., London, E.C.3.
Bennett, A., Truro, Cornwall.
Bennett Antiques, Newton Abbot, Devon. N.A. Ant. C.
Bennett, B.M., Orford, Suffolk.
Bennett and Sons, C., Bournemouth, Dorset.
Bennett, D. and C., Bath, Avon. Gt. West. Ant. C.
Bennett, D.G., Blackburn, Lancs.
Bennett, F.R., Shipston-on-Stour, Warks.
Bennett, G., Alderley Edge, Cheshire.
Bennett (Antiques), Julia, Stansted, Essex.
Bennett, N. and P., Plymouth, Devon.
Bennett, N.P.J., Plymouth, Devon.
Bennett, Paul, London, W.1.
Bennett, R., Thirsk, N. Yorks.
Bennett, W.C., Amersham, Bucks.
Bennetta, M., Bath, Avon. Gt. West. A. C. Wed. Mkt.
Bennetts, Bath, Avon. Gt. West. Ant. C.
Bennison, London, S.W.1.
Benson Antiques, Cheltenham, Glos.
Benson Antiques, Woburn, Beds. Wob. Ab. Ant. C.
Benson, H.F. & F., Cheltenham, Glos.
Benstead, Mrs. H., Birmingham, W. Mids. (Moseley Antiques).
Bental, Miss B., London, S.W.3. Ant. Ant. Mkt.
Bental, Brenda, London, S.W.3. Ant. Ant. Mkt.
Bentley, Bill, Harrogate, N. Yorks.
Bentley and Co. Ltd., London, W.1.
Bentley, M.R., Knutsford, Cheshire.
Bentley, Peter, London, W.2.
Bentley, S.R., London, S.W.3 (P. Colleck).
Bently Antiques, Pat, Ampthill, Beds.
Benton, J.G., Cheltenham, Glos. (Manor House Antiques)
Benton, P.A., Alrewas, Staffs.
Benzie, James, Aberdeen, Aberd., Scot.
Beresford, E. and B., Alderley Edge, Cheshire.
Beresford-Clark, London, S.W.6.
Beresiner, Y., London, N.1. (Intercol London).
Berge, I., London, W.8. (Little Winchester Gallery)
Berkeley Antiques, Berkeley, Glos.
Berkeley Galleries Ltd., London, S.E.3.
Berkeley, Mrs. S., Heath and Reach, Beds.
Berkeleys, West Bridgford, Notts.
Berkshire Metal Finishers Ltd., Sandhurst, Berks.
Berktay, Y., Somerton, Somerset.
Bermondsey Antique Market, London, S.E.1.
Bermondsey Antique Warehouse, London, S.E.1.
Bermondsey Antiques, London, S.E.1.
Bernard, L.S., London, S.W.3 (Chelsea Rare Books).

Bernards Heath Antiques, St. Albans, Herts.
Berrows House Antiques, Hereford, Hereford and Worcs.
Berry Brow Antiques, Huddersfield, W. Yorks.
Berry, F.E., Disley, Cheshire.
Berry, L., Alcester, Warks.
Berry, Mrs. L., Flamborough, N. Humberside.
Berry Antiques, Lesley, Flamborough, N. Humberside.
Berryman Music Boxes, Shelagh, Wells, Somerset.
Besbrode, M., Leeds, W. Yorks.
Besbrode and Seals, Leeds, W. Yorks.
Beslali, London, W.1. G. Mews.
Best Antiques, Ray, Ilminster, Somerset.
Best, R. and W., Ilminster, Somerset.
Beszant, A., Evesham, Hereford & Worcs.
Bethell, I., Birmingham, W. Mids. (Edgbaston Gallery).
Bethge, J., London, W.8. (The Winter Palace).
Bethney, P.W. and J.A., Knaphill, Surrey.
Betley Court Gallery, Betley, Staffs.
Bett, H., London, W.1 (Maggs Bros. Ltd.)
Betts, T., York, N. Yorks. (Holgate Antiques).
Bevan, Mrs. M., Whitchurch, Hants.
Beveridge (Antiques), Perth, Perths., Scot.
Beveridge, Barbara, Perth, Perths., Scot.
Beverley, London, N.W.8. Alf. Ant. Mkt.
Beverley Brook Antiques, London, S.W.13.
Bevins, E.A. and J.R., Ulverston, Cumbria.
Bexfield Antiques, A.B., Hitchin, Herts.
Bexhill Antiques Centre, Bexhill-on-Sea, E. Sussex.
Bhaduri, A. and B., London, W.11 (Elgin Antiques).
Bichard, R. and J., Bradford-on-Avon, Wilts.
Bick, Cheltenham, Glos.
Bickersteth, David, Cambridge, Cambs.
Biddle, Mrs. M.E.P., Bath, Avon. (Colleton House Gallery).
Biddle, Mrs. M.E.P. Tetbury, Glos.
Biddulph, Sue, London, S.W.3. Ant. Ant. Mkt.
Bidnarack, Maria, Glasgow, Lanarks, Scot. Vict Vill.
Bieganski, Z., Woburn, Beds.
Bieldside Antiques, Bieldside, Aberd., Scot.
Biffin, L., Harrogate, N. Yorks. (Cheltenham Galleries).
Big Ben Antique Clocks, London, S.W.6.
Bigden, C., Debenham, Suffolk.
Bigden, C., Martlesham, Suffolk.
Biggs, Newton Abbot, Devon. N.A. Ant. C.
Biggs, A.C., Worthing, W. Sussex.
Biggs, David, Exeter, Devon. (Exeter Antique Wholesalers).
Biggs of Maidenhead, Twyford, Berks.
Biggs, P., Bath, Avon. Gt. West. Ant. C.
Biggs, P. and J., Bideford, Devon.
Biles, J., Hartley Wintney, Hants.
Billings, J., Kelvedon, Essex.
Bilson, Madeleine, Dorking, Surrey.
Binder, D., London, N.W.8. Alf. Ant. Mkt.
Bingham Antiques, Brian, Chesterfield, Derbys.

Bingham, Tony, London, N.W.3.
Bingley Antiques Centre, Bingley, W. Yorks.
Bingley, S., Aberystwyth, Dyfed, Wales.
Binks, Peter, London, W.1. G. Ant. Mkt.
Binning, R., Penshurst, Kent.
Binsted Antiques, Teddington, Gtr. London.
Birbeck Antiques, Torquay, Devon.
Birbeck, H., Torquay, Devon.
Birbeck, H.S. and K., Torquay, Devon.
Birch, C. & H., Leicester, Leics.
Birch, E., Shrewsbury, Shrops.
Birches Art Deco Shop, Leicester, Leics.
Birchington Antiques, Birchington, Kent.
Birchmore, John, London, N.1.
Bird Antiques, Bryan, Minsterley, Shrops.
Bird, Annette Puttnam, John, Brighton, E. Sussex.
Birdcage Antiques, The, Windermere, Cumbria.
Birkinshaw, N., Sutton-on-Sea, Lincs.
Birmingham House Antiques, Shipston-on-Stour, Warks.
Birmingham Antique Centre, Birmingham, W. Mids.
Biscoe, A., Worthing, W. Sussex.
Bishop, B. and A., Castle Combe, Wilts.
Bishop Beveridge House, Barrow on Soar, Leics.
Bishop, Constance, Manchester, Lancs.
Bishop, G.W. and N.S., Swanage, Dorset.
Bishop, J.A., Leominster, Hereford and Worcs.
Bishop, J.H. and M.M., Cheltenham, Glos. (Bick).
Bishop, Mrs. J.M., Leeds, W. Yorks.
Bishop Antiques, Micheal, Haisthorpe, N. Humberside.
Bishop (Marlow) Ltd., Marlow, Bucks.
Bishop, M. & S., Haisthorpe, N. Humberside.
Bishop, P. and L., Marlow, Bucks.
Bishop's Antiques, Basildon, Essex.
Bishops House Antiques, Leeds, W. Yorks.
Bishop's of Swanage, Dorset.
Bishopstrow Antiques, Warminster, Wilts.
Bisset Ltd., James G., Aberdeen, Aberd., Scot.
Bits and Pieces, Brighton, E. Sussex.
Bits and Pieces, Farnham, Surrey.
Bizarre, London, N.W.8.
Black, A., Sheffield, S. Yorks. (Oriel Antiques).
Black Ltd., Arthur, London, W.1. B. St. Silv. Galls.
Black Boy (1677), Appleby-in-Westmorland, Cumbria.
Black Oriental Carpets, David, London, W.11.
Black, Mrs. J., Warwick, Warks.
Black, J.M., Dunmow, Essex.
Black Lion Antiques, Conway, Gwynedd, Wales.
Black, Roy D., London, W.1. B.St.Ant.C.
Black Terry, Glasgow, Lanarks., Scot. Vict. Vill.
Blackburn, Andrew and Linda, Gargrave, N. Yorks.
Blackburn, E.M., Tunbridge Wells, Kent. (Pantiles Antiques).

Boodle and Dunthorne Ltd., Liverpool, Merseyside.
Boodle and Dunthorne Ltd., Manchester, Lancs.
Book House, The, Ravenstonedale, Cumbria.
Book in Hand, The, Shaftesbury, Dorset.
Book Shelf, The, Mansfield, Notts.
Bookcellar, Edinburgh, Midloth., Scot.
Booker, Lee, Bath, Avon. B. Ant. Mkt.
Bookham Galleries, Great Bookham, Surrey.
Bookham Galleries, London, S.W.6.
Bookroom (Cambridge), The, Cambridge, Cambs.
Books Afloat, Weymouth, Dorset.
Books Etc., Stamford, Lincs.
Books and Things, Great Wakering, Essex.
Books and Things, London, W.11.
Bookshop, The, Sandiacre, Derbys.
Boon, Janet, Fakenham, Norfolk. Ant. C.
Booth, A.E., Ewell, Surrey.
Booth, C.A., Birmingham, W. Mids. (Genesis Antiques).
Booth, C.M., Rolvenden, Kent.
Booth, D., Huddersfield, W. Yorks.
Booth, Joanna, London, S.W.3.
Booth, Joanna, London, S.W.3. Ant. Ant. Mkt.
Booth, J., Princes Risborough, Bucks.
Booth, T., London, W.1. (Antiques Corner). G. Ant. Mkt.
Booth, T.J., Rye, E. Sussex.
Boothferry Antiques, Brough, N. Humberside.
Booth's Bookshop, Richard, Hay-on-Wye, Powys. Wales.
Bord (Gold Coin Exchange) M., London, W.C.2.
Border Booksellers, Bungay, Suffolk.
Border Bygones, Lyonshall, Hereford & Worcs.
Border Sporting Gallery, Wooler, Northumb.
Bornoff, Claude, London, W.2.
Borton Fine Arts, Peter, Hindhead, Surrey.
Bosch, Milena, London, S.W.3. (Natasha Barbic) Ant. Ant. Mkt.
Bosham Antiques, Bosham, W. Sussex.
Bosi, L., Edinburgh, Midloth., Scot. (Royal Mile Curios.)
Bosman, T. and M., Richmond, N. Yorks.
Boss Antiques, Petworth, W. Sussex.
Bosson Antiques, Peter, Wilmslow, Cheshire.
Boston Antiques, Derek, Salisbury, Wilts.
Boston Antiques Centre, Boston, Lincs.
Boston Pine, Leeds, W. Yorks.
Bothy Antiques, Market Rasen, Lincs.
Botting, Mrs. E., Canterbury, Kent.
Botting Antiques, John, Polegate, E. Sussex.
Bottles and Bygones, Cheltenham, Glos.
Bottomley, Mrs. G.J., Wymeswold, Leics.
Bottomley, M. and B., Whitby, N. Yorks.
Boulevard Reproductions, Halifax, W. Yorks.
Boulton, N., Torquay, Devon.
Bourdon-Smith Ltd., J.H., London, S.W.1.
Bourne Antiques, Bourne, Lincs.
Bourne Fine Art, London, S.W.1.
Bourne Fine Art Ltd., Edinburgh, Midloth., Scot.

Bourne Gallery, Reigate, Surrey.
Bourne Mill Antiques, Farnham, Surrey.
Bourne, P., Edinburgh, Midloth., Scot. (Bourne Fine Art Ltd.).
Bourne, Mrs. P., Ramsey, Isle of Man.
Bournemouth Gallery Ltd., The, Poole, Dorset.
Bousfield, Guy, Windsor and Eton, Berks.
Boutell, Mrs., Newton Abbott, Devon. N.A. Ant. C.
Boutique Fantasque, London, N.1.
Bow Bells Antique, Donaghadee, Co. Down, N. Ireland.
Bow Cottage Antiques, Stratford-upon-Avon, Warks.
Bow House Antiques, Hungerford, Berks.
Bow Window, Frinton, Essex.
Bow Windows Book Shop, Lewes, E. Sussex.
Bowden Antiques, Welwyn, Herts.
Bowden, Bryan, Doncaster, S. Yorks.
Bowden, J.A., Scunthorpe, S. Humberside.
Bowden, J. and B., Scunthorpe, S. Humberside.
Bowden, R. & C., Welwyn, Herts.
Bowdery, M.J., Hindhead, Surrey.
Bowdler, M.A., Shrewsbury, Shrops.
Bowen, Mrs. S., Wilshamstead, Beds.
Bowes, R.L., Dartmouth, Devon.
Bowkett, H. and L., Knaresborough, N. Yorks.
Bowlby, Nicholas, Uckfield, E. Sussex.
Bowle, R., Dover, Kent.
Bowler, J.A., Bradford, W. Yorks.
Bowler, Mrs. R., Woodville, Derbys.
Bowley Antiques at Imogen Graham, Audrey, London, S.W.6.
Bowman Antiques, Thatcham, Berks.
Bowood Antiques, Wendover, Bucks.
Bowring, Mrs. S., Dunmow, Essex.
Bowry, Stanhope, London, W.1. G. Ant. Mkt.
Box House Antiques, London, S.W.1.
Box Shop, The, London, S.W.3. Chen. Gall.
Boyce, P., Birmingham, W. Mids. (Stirchley Antiques).
Boyer, R., Nantwich, Cheshire.
Boylan, M. and A., Market Bosworth, Leics.
Boyle (Booksellers) Ltd., Andrew, Worcester, Hereford and Worcs.
Boyle, B., Ashton-under-Lyne, Lancs.
Boyle, B., Manchester, Lancs. (Tameside Antiques).
Boyle & Co., John, London, S.W.10.
Boyle, T., Luton, Beds.
Boyle, Mrs. T.B., Cobham, Surrey.
Boyle's Furniture, Luton, Beds.
Boyne House Antiques, Leominster, Hereford and Worcs.
Boyne, T., Bournemouth, Dorset (Antiques and Furnishings).
Boys, Rob, London, W.11. G. Port.
Bracewell, J. and E., Shawforth, Lancs.
Bradbourne Gallery, Sevenoaks, Kent.
Bradbury, R., Coltishall, Norfolk.
Bradgate Antiques, Newtown Linford, Leics.
Bradley, A., Kirkcudbright, Kirkcud., Scot.
Bradley, Elizabeth, Beaumaris, Gwynedd, Wales.

Bradley, Mrs. P., Stockbridge, Hants.
Bradley, P. and V., Bletchingley, Surrey.
Bradley, Robert, Salisbury, Wilts.
Bradley, Mrs. S., Claydon, Suffolk.
Bradshaw, Mrs. E., Blaydon, Tyne & Wear.
Bradshaw, R., Leominster, Hereford & Worcs. L. Ant. Mkt.
Bradshaw, S.J. and V.J., Buckfastleigh, Devon.
Braemar Antiques Ltd., White Waltham, Berks.
Bragg Antiques, John, Lostwithiel, Cornwall.
Bragge Antiques, Lesley, Petworth, W..Sussex.
Bragge, N.H. and J.R., Rye, E. Sussex.
Bragge and Sons, Rye, E. Sussex.
Braham Ltd., Maurice, London, W.8.
Braithwaite, Mrs. C., Hexham, Northumb.
Bramhall, D.H., Modbury, Devon.
Bramhall, D.H., Totnes, Devon.
Brampton Mill Antiques, Brampton, Cambs.
Bramwell, Penzance, Cornwall.
Bramwell, Derek, Woodstock, Oxon.
Bramwell, R.H., Cambridge, Cambs. (Dolphin Antiques).
Brancaster Staithe Antiques, Brancaster Staithe, Norfolk
Brand Antiques, Colin, Stow-on-the-Wold, Glos.
Brand, Mrs. D.V., Wotton-under-Edge, Glos.
Brand, L.B., Boston, Lincs.
Brandl — Paintings, Erika, London, S.W.6.
Brandler Galleries, Brentwood, Essex.
Brandler, J., Brentwood, Essex.
Brandt Oriental Antiques, London, S.W.6.
Brandt, R., London, S.W.6. (Brandt Oriental Antiques).
Branklin-Frisby, M.J., Carlton Curlieu, Leics.
Branksome Antiques, Branksome, Dorset.
Brass Cannon, The, Highcliffe, Dorset.
Brass & Son, Lawrence, Bath, Avon.
Brasted Antiques, Brasted, Kent.
Bratton Antiques, Westbury, Wilts.
Braund, J.F., Thaxted, Essex.
Braverman, B., Runcorn, Cheshire.
Bray, Ltd., H.H., Warwick, Warks.
Brayne Court Gallery, Littledean, Glos.
Brazil Antiques Ltd., Croydon, Gtr. London.
Breakspeare Antiques, A.M., Tetbury, Glos.
Breakspeare Antiques, M. and S., Tetbury, Glos.
Brean, L.M., Pontypool, Gwent, Wales.
Brear, Jean, Halifax, W. Yorks.
Breck Antiques, Nottingham, Notts.
Brecon Road Antiques, Abergavenny, Gwent, Wales.
Breeden Antiques, Roy, Dorking, Surrey.
Breeze, G.E. and R.G., London, S.E.15.
Bremner, Mr. and Mrs. C., Maidstone, Kent.
Brenchley Antique Jewellery, Julie, Jesmond, Tyne and Wear.
Brenin Porcelain and Pottery, Cowbridge, S. Glam., Wales.
Breton Antiques, Colchester, Essex.
Brett and Sons Ltd., Arthur, Norwich, Norfolk.
Brett, M. & T., Newport, I. of Wight.
Brett, Simon, Moreton-in-Marsh, Glos.

Brett, V.M., Hadleigh, Suffolk.
Brewer, Ann, Wallingford, Oxon. L. Arc.
Brewer, Michael, Lincoln, Lincs.
Brewer, M.N., Lincoln, Lincs.
Brewster, Avril, Fakenham, Norfolk. Ant. C.
Brewster, Brian, Fakenham, Norfolk. Ant. C.
Brewster, B.D., Fakenham, Norfolk. Ant. C.
Brewster, D.J., Glasgow, Lanarks., Scot. (Muirhead Moffat and Co.).
Brian Antiques, Addlestone, Surrey.
Brian Antiques, Luigi, London, W.C.2. Lon. Silv. Vaults.
Bric-a-Brac, Ilford, Gtr. London.
Bric-a-Brac, The, Whitley Bay, Tyne and Wear.
Bric-a-Brac Hall, Stiffkey, Norfolk.
Bric-a-Brac Shop, The, Boston, Lincs.
Brice, Robin, Newton Abbot, Devon. N.A. Ant. C.
Bridge Antiques, Durham, Durham.
Bridge Antiques, Stourbridge, W. Mids.
Bridge Antiques, Sutton Bridge, Lincs.
Bridge Antiques, Wingham, Kent.
Bridge, Christine, London, W.1. G. Mews.
Bridge End Antiques, Berwick-on-Tweed, Northumb.
Bridge House Antiques, Cranbrook, Kent.
Bridge House Antiques, Nantwich, Cheshire.
Bridge House Antiques, Penshurst, Kent.
Bridge Street Antiques, Bungay, Suffolk.
Bridge Street Antiques, Nailsworth, Glos.
Bridgeman Coins, J., Accrington, Lancs.
Bridgend Antiques, Bridgend, M. Glam., Wales.
Bridges, P., Scarthoe, S. Humberside.
Bridgeview Antiques, Carmarthen, Dyfed, Wales.
Briere, Gilbert and Edna, Fakenham, Norfolk. Ant. C.
Briere, G. and E., Suffield, Norfolk.
Briere Antiques, R., Kirton, Lincs.
Briggs, D., Ipswich, Suffolk (Majors Galleries).
Briggs Ltd., F.E.A., London, W.11.
Briggs, S., St. Neots, Cambs.
Brigham, R. Loftus, London, W.13.
Bright Antiques, Carl, Stockport, Cheshire.
Bright, T., Halifax, W. Yorks.
Brighton Antique Wholesalers, Brighton, E. Sussex.
Brighton Antiques Gallery, Brighton, E. Sussex.
Brill Antiques, Brill, Oxon.
Brimsmore House Antiques, Yeovil, Somerset.
Brindle, T. and D., Blackburn, Lancs.
Brindle-Wood-Williams, D., Haslemere, Surrey.
Brindle-Wood-Williams, D.M., Midhurst, W. Sussex. Mid. Ant. Mkt.
Brinn, D.M., Bath, Avon. Gt. West. A.C. Wed. Mkt.
Briscoe, J.I. and S., Craven Arms, Shrops.
Briscoe, J.I. and S., Ludlow, Shrops.
Brise, J., London, S.W.6. (Pryce & Brise Antiques).
Brisigotti Antiques Ltd., London, S.W.1.
Bristol Antique Market, Bristol, Avon.

Bristol Guild of Applied Art Ltd., Bristol, Avon.
Bristol Trade Antiques, Bristol, Avon.
Bristow (Antiques), Bordon, Hants.
Bristow, A. and P., Tetbury, Glos.
Bristow, D.R., Bordon, Hants.
Bristow Antiques, J. and M., Tetbury, Glos.
Bristow, M., London, S.W.3. Chen. Gall.
Bristow, M.J. and J.A., Tetbury, Glos.
Britannia, London, W.1. G. Ant. Mkt.
Britannia Antiques, Manchester, Lancs.
Britannia Antique Exports, Warminster, Wilts.
British Antique Exporters Ltd., Burgess Hill, W. Sussex.
Britten Antiques, Andrew, Malmesbury, Wilts.
Britton, Mrs., Radlett, Herts.
Britton's Jewellers, Nelson, Lancs.
Broad, M., Tunbridge Wells, Kent. (Annexe Antiques).
Broad Street Antiques, Bungay, Suffolk.
Broad Street Gallery, Wolverhampton, W. Mids.
Broadbelt, G., Harrogate, N. Yorks. (Dragon Antiques).
Broadbridge, G.M. Alderley Edge, Cheshire.
Broadfield Antiques, Sheffield, S. Yorks.
Broadhurst and Co. Ltd., C.K., Southport, Merseyside.
Broadley, E. and D., Kirk Deighton, N. Yorks.
Broadwater Bookroom, Worthing, W. Sussex.
Broadway Antiques, Cardiff, S. Glam., Wales.
Broadway Antiques, Shifnal, Shrops.
Broadway Antique Arcade, Broadway, Hereford and Worcs.
Broadway Studios, Burton-on-Trent, Staffs.
Brobury House Gallery, Brobury, Hereford and Worcs.
Brocante Antiques, Cheltenham, Glos.
Brocantiques, London, N.W.10.
Broccardi-Schelmi, (Fine Arts) (Belmont Galleries Ltd.), Aldo, Wadhurst, E. Sussex.
Brockdish Antiques, Brockdish, Norfolk.
Brocklehurst, Aubrey, London, S.W.7.
Brod Gallery, London, S.W.1.
Broe, Magnus, and Samuel Orr, Hurstpierpoint, W. Sussex.
Bromley Antique Market, Bromley, Gtr. London.
Brook, Alexis, Kettering, Northants.
Brook, Mrs. A., Kettering, Northants.
Brook, Erol, Warwick, Warks. Smith St. A.C.
Brook Antiques and Picture Gallery, Ian J., Wilton, Wilts.
Brook Lane Antiques, Alderley Edge, Cheshire.
Brooke Antiques, Rodney, London, S.W.18.
Brooke, S., Brighton, E. Sussex. (Gloucester Road Antiques)
Brooke, T.C.S., M.A. and S.T., Wroxham, Norfolk.
Brooker Antiques, Mary, Sandgate, Kent.
Brookes, R., Ross-on-Wye, Hereford and Worcs.

Brookfield Gallery, Colyton, Devon.
Brook-Hart, Mrs M., Lymington, Hants.
Brookland Antiques, Brookland, Kent.
Brooks, A., London, W.C.1.
Brooks, David, Malmesbury, Wilts.
Brooks, Mr. Temple, London, N.W.6.
Brooks-Court, A., Wareham, Dorset.
Brooks-Rex, J., Wareham, Dorset.
Brookstone, J. and M., London, S.W.3. (Julian Simon Fine Art.) Ant. Ant. Mkt.
Broome, P., Witney, Oxon.
Broomfield, G.H., Newcastle-under-Lyme, Staffs.
Brosinovich, S., Bath, Avon. Gt. West. Ant. C.
Brotherston, Mr. and Mrs. A., Greenlaw, Berwicks., Scot.
Brotherton Gallery Ltd., The, London, S.W.3.
Broughton Antiques, Church Broughton, Derbys.
Brower Antiques, David, London, W.8.
Brown, Mrs. Newton Abbot, Devon. N. A. Ant. C.
Brown, A., Bath, Avon. (Avril Antiques.) Gt. West. Ant. C.
Brown, A., London, S.W.3. Chen. Gall.
Brown, Mrs. A.F., Mayfield, E. Sussex.
Brown, A.G., Arundel, W. Sussex.
Brown, D., Darlington, Durham.
Brown, D. & C., St. Just, Cornwall.
Brown, Mr. and Mrs. D.R., St. Andrews, Fife, Scot.
Brown, Prof. G.N. and Dr. F., Betley, Staffs.
Brown House Antiques, Newport, Essex.
Brown, H. and K., Bletchingley, Surrey.
Brown, H. and M.F., Sandgate, Kent.
Brown, I. and J.L., London, S.W.6.
Brown Ltd., I. and J.L., Hereford, Hereford and Worcs.
Brown Antiques, John, Ashbourne, Derbys.
Brown Antiques, Judy, Darlington, Durham.
Brown, Mrs. J.A., Darlington, Durham.
Brown, J.A., Gloucester, Glos.
Brown, J.E. and M., Swindon, Wilts.
Brown, J.H., Midhurst, W. Sussex.
Brown, J. & M., Cheltenham, Glos. (Bottles and Bygones).
Brown, Margaret, Edinburgh, Midloth., Scot.
Brown, M., North Shoebury, Essex.
Brown, M.B., Newton Stewart, Wigtowns., Scot.
Brown, R., Bexhill-on-Sea, E. Sussex. Bex. Ant. C.
Brown, Mrs. M.R., Hawkhurst, Kent.
Brown, R., Lewes, E. Sussex.
Brown, R., Southampton, Hants.
Brown, R.G., Broadway, Hereford and Worcs.
Brown, Sue, London, W.1. G. Mews.
Brown, S., Cosgrove, Northants.
Brown, Miss S., Newtown Linford, Leics.
Brown and Sons, S., The Popular Mart, Darlington, Durham.
Brown, Teddy, London, N.W.8. Alf. Ant. Mkt.
Brown, T.D., Edinburgh, Midloth., Scot. (Edinburgh Coin Shop).

Brown, T.P. and P.M., Brighton, E. Sussex (Robinson's Bookshop Ltd.)
Brown, Mrs. V.M., Tewkesbury, Glos.
Brown, William, London, S.W.3. Ant. Ant. Mkt.
Brown, W.R., Ilfracombe, Devon.
Browne, M., Battle, E. Sussex.
Brownhouse Antiques, Claydon, Suffolk.
Browning and Son, G.E., Glastonbury, Somerset.
Brownings Antiques, Cheltenham, Glos.
Brown's Antique Shop, Newton Stewart, Wigtowns., Scot.
Brown's Number Three Ltd., Arthur, London, S.W.6.
Brown's Clocks Ltd., Glasgow, Lanarks., Scot.
Browns of West Wycombe, High Wycombe, Bucks.
Brownsells Granary, Wiveliscombe, Somerset.
Browse, Stafford, Staffs.
Browse and Darby Ltd., London, W.1.
Browzers, Manchester, Lancs.
Bruce, F., Strathblane, Stirls., Scot.
Bruce Antiques, Paul, Ipswich, Suffolk.
Bruce, P.M., Devizes, Wilts.
Bruce, W. & D., St. Boswells, Roxburghs., Scot.
Bruford and Heming Ltd., London, W.1.
Bruford and Son Ltd., Wm., Eastbourne, E. Sussex.
Bruford and Son Ltd., Wm., Exeter, Devon.
Brunel Antiques, Bath, Avon. Gt. West. Ant. C.
Brunel Antiques, Bristol, Avon.
Brunner, K., London, S.W.3. Ant. Ant. Mkt.
Brunning, M. and J., Redbourn, Herts.
Brunsveld, Mr., Manchester, Lancs. (The Baron Antiques).
Brunswick Antiques, Hull, N. Humberside.
Brunswick, Gary, London, N.W.8. Alf. Ant. Mkt.
Bruschweiler (Antiques) Ltd., F.G., Rayleigh, Essex.
Bruton, Brighton, E. Sussex.
Bruton Gallery, Bruton, Somerset.
Bruton, H.B. and B.C., Sherborne, Dorset.
Bryan, Mr. and Mrs. D.R., Cranbrook, Kent.
Bryan, Mr. and Mrs. V.C., Endmoor, Cumbria.
Bryan-Peach Antiques, N., Wymeswold, Leics.
Bryant, A.D.P., Debenham, Suffolk.
Bryant, E.H., London, S.W.14.
Bryden, D., Stow-on-the-Wold, Glos.
Brydon, R.and J., Brasted, Kent.
Bryers Antiques, Bath, Avon.
Bryers, S., Bath, Avon.
Brynolf, S., London, S.W.3. Ant. Ant. Mkt.
Bubley, S., London, S.W.3. Chen. Gall.
Buchan, I. and R., Brookland, Kent.
Buchan, K.S., Leigh-on-Sea, Essex.
Buchanan, A.R., Lincoln, Lincs.
Buck, Mrs. B., Chalfont St. Giles, Bucks.
Buck and Payne Ltd., London, N.1.
Buck, R., London, W.11. (Rod's Antiques).
Buck, W.F.A., Stockbury, Kent.

Buck, W.M., London, N.1.
Bucke, A.P., Crewkerne, Somerset.
Buckie, G.McC., and P.R., Cambridge, Cambs.
Buckie, K.W., Swaffham, Norfolk.
Buckie's, Cambridge, Cambs.
Buckingham, Mr. and Mrs., London, S.W.6.
Buckingham Books, Buckingham, Bucks.
Buckingham, C.W., Cadnam, Hants.
Buckingham, C.W., London, S.W.6.
Buckland, A.G.J., Shottermill, Surrey.
Buckland, Lorraine, London, S.W.3.
Buckle, Evelyn, Redmile, Leics.
Buckle, Mrs. R.N., Redmile, Leics.
Buckle Ltd., T.F. London, S.W.10.
Buckley, Miss A.H., Leeds, W. Yorks.
Buckley, D.H., Keighley, W. Yorks.
Buckley, Mrs. J., Shotton, Clwyd, Wales.
Buckminster Antiques, Buckminster, Leics.
Bucks House, Chalfont St. Giles, Bucks.
Budd, J., Nottingham, Notts.
Bude Antiques, Bude, Cornwall.
Budhu, H.P., London, S.W.3. (B. O'Brien). Ant. Ant. Mkt.
Bugle Antiques, The, Chipping Norton, Oxon.
Bulka, S., London, W.C.2. Lon. Silv. Vts. (David S. Shure and Co.).
Bull, Antiques, The, Husborne Crawley, Beds.
Bull, Audrey, Tenby, Dyfed, Wales.
Bull (Antiques) Ltd., John, London, W.11.
Bull (Antiques) Ltd., John, London, W.1. B. St. Silv. Galls.
Bull, M., Eynsham, Oxon.
Bull, M., London, S.W.15.
Bull, M. Oxford, Oxon.
Bull, S. London, W.1 (Bobinet Ltd.).
Bull and Son (Cirencester) Ltd., Walter, Ciren- cester, Glos.
Bull, Wilfred, Coggeshall, Essex.
Bullard, S., Ipswich, Suffolk (Spring Antiques).
Bulldog Antiques, Manchester, Lancs.
Bullivant Antiques, Gt. Ashfield, Suffolk.
Bullivant, Michael, Winchester, Hants.
Bullivant, P.T., Gt. Ashfield, Suffolk.
Bullock, G., Worcester, Hereford and Worcs.
Bunce, N.P.J., Hertford, Herts.
Bunn, R.J. and E.R., Evesham, Hereford and Worcs.
Bunting, Miss J.L., Belper, Derbys.
Bunzl, Tony and Zal Davar, London, S.W.3.
Burden Antiques, Anthony, Dartmouth, Devon.
Burden, Clive A., Rickmansworth, Herts.
Burden Ltd., Clive A., London, W.C.2.
Bures Antiques, Bures, Suffolk.
Burfield P., Lake, I. of Wight.
Burford Antiques, Burford, Oxon.
Burford Gallery, The, Burford, Oxon.
Burford, L., Rochester, Kent.
Burgan, Mrs. S.E.M., Yatton, Avon.
Burge Antiques, A., Cardiff, S. Glam., Wales.
Burgess, Bridget, Great Horkesley, Essex.
Burgess, D.J., Parkstone, Dorset.
Burke, H. and M.J., Worsley, Lancs.

Burkinshaw, David, Lindfield, W. Sussex.
Burlington Gallery Ltd., London, W.1.
Burlington House, Preston, Lancs. N.W. Ant. C.
Burlington House Antiques, Hawick, Roxbs., Scot.
Burlington Paintings Ltd., London, W.1.
Burlington, R.W. and M.V., Southport, Merseyside. (Churchtown Antiques).
Burman Antiques, Stratford-upon-Avon, Warks.
Burn, J., March, Cambs.
Burne (Antique Glass) Ltd., W.G.T., London, S.W.3.
Burne, W.G.T., Mrs. G., R.V. and A.T.G., London, S.W.3.
Burnett, C.A., London, N.7.
Burnett, D.H., Finedon, Northants.
Burnett Antiques, Jean, Finedon, Northants.
Burnett, L. and G., London, W.10.
Burnley Antiques and Fine Arts Ltd., Burnley, Lancs.
Burns and Graham, Winchester, Hants.
Burns, G., Bourne, Lincs.
Burns, G.H., Stamford, Lincs.
Burns, K., Leeds, W. Yorks.
Burns, K., Southport, Merseyside.
Burns, T.P. and K., Duns, Berwicks., Scot.
Burrell, V.S., Abinger Hammer, Surrey.
Burrough, R.J., Exmouth, Devon.
Burrows, David E., Quorn, Leics.
Bursig, R.H., Arundel, W. Sussex.
Burton Antiques, Burton-on-Trent, Staffs.
Burton, A. and D., Bridport, Dorset.
Burton, C.V., Colne, Lancs.
Burton, D. and A., Felton, Northumb.
Burton Fine Art, Pailton, Warks.
Burton, J., Ipswich, Suffolk. (John's Antiques.)
Burton Antiques, Jasper, Sherborne, Dorset.
Burton, Mr. and Mrs. S., London, W.1. ('Young Stephen' Ltd.)
Burton-Garbett, A., Morden, Gtr. London.
Bury, Mrs. I., Long Melford, Suffolk.
Bury Street Gallery, London, S.W.1.
Busato, G., Preston, Lancs. N.W. Ant. C.
Busby Ltd., Guy, Nantwich, Cheshire.
Busby, J., East Molesey, Surrey.
Busek, A., South Molton, Devon.
Busek, N., Bristol, Avon. ("An Englishman's Home . . . '')
Bush, A., London, N.1 (Bushwood Antiques).
Bush and Partners, A.E., Attleborough, Norfolk.
Bushe Antiques, London, N.1.
Bushwood Antiques, London, N.1.
Butcher, F.L. and N.E., Sherborne, Dorset.
Butcher, Mrs. S., Nottingham, Notts.
Butchoff Antiques, London, S.E.15.
Butchoff, I.M., London, S.E.15.
Butler and Co., Cheltenham, Glos.
Butler, D., York, N. Yorks. (Gate Antiques).
Butler Antiques, Donald, Thame, Oxon.
Butler, D.J., Cheltenham, Glos.
Butler, H., Beckenham, Gtr. London.
Butler, J., Merstham, Surrey.
Butler, John, Weston-super-Mare, Avon.

Butler, Mr. and Mrs. J.J., Chirk, Clwyd, Wales.
Butler, J.J., Honiton, Devon.
Butler, L., Glasgow, Lanarks., Scot. (Butler's Furniture Galls. Ltd.)
Butler, N. and S., Rotherham, S. Yorks.
Butler, O.E.M., Liss, Hants.
Butler, R., Birmingham, W. Mids. (The Twentieth Century Style.)
Butler, R., Blandford Forum, Dorset.
Butler, Robin, Bristol, Avon.
Butler, Roderick P., Honiton, Devon.
Butler, Mrs. S.A., London, S.E.23.
Butler and Wilson, London, S.W.3.
Butler's Furniture Galleries Ltd., Glasgow, Lanarks., Scot.
Butt Antiques, Anthony, Baldock, Herts.
Butterchurn Antiques, Poole, Dorset.
Butterchurn Gallery, Otley, W. Yorks.
Butterwalk House, Totnes, Devon.
Butterworth (Antiques) Ltd., Alan, Horwich, Lancs.
Butterworth, C., London, S.W.3. Ant. Ant. Mkt.
Butterworth, J.A., Beckenham, Gtr. London.
Butterworth, J.A., London, S.E.5.
Butterworth, J.A., London, S.W.9.
Butterworth, J.W., Potterspury, Northants.
Butterworth, R., Oldham, Lancs.
Button, K., Mountsorrel, Leics.
Button Queen, The, London, W.1.
Button-Stephens, (formerly Old Curiosity Shop), Christopher J., Honiton, Devon.
Buxton Interiors, Caroline, Brighton, E. Sussex.
Buxton Antiques, Helen, London, W.11.
Bye Antiques, Ann, Reading, Berks.
Bygone Days Antiques, Tiverton, Devon.
Bygone Ways, Pinchbeck, Lancs.
Bygones, Angmering, W. Sussex.
Bygones, Benson, Oxon.
Bygones, Fakenham, Norfolk.
Bygones, Huddersfield, W. Yorks.
Bygones, London, S.W.3. Ant. Ant. Mkt.
Bygones, Sidcup, Gtr. London.
Bygones by the Cathedral, Worcester, Hereford, and Worcs.
Bygones Ltd., Peel, Isle of Man.
Bygones (Worcester), Worcester, Hereford and Worcs.
Byles, Robert, Bampton, Devon.
Byrne, Mrs. M.A., Grassington, N. Yorks.
Byrne, Patricia, London, W.1. G. Ant. Mkt.
Byron, R., Royton, Lancs.
Byskou, R., Worthing, W. Sussex.

C

C.K. Antiques, Woburn, Beds. Wob. Ab. Ant. C.
Cabral, J., Canterbury, Kent.
Caddy, I., Morcombelake, Dorset.
Cadogan Gallery, London, S.W.1.
Caelt Gallery, London, W.11.
Caernarfon Antiques, Caernarfon, Gwynedd, Wales.
Caesar, S., Liss, Hants.

Caffell Management Services, Tetbury, Glos.
Cain, H., Carlisle, Cumbria.
Caira and Co., Frank L., London, N.20.
Caira, F.L. and I.D., London, N.20.
Caldmore Antiques, Walsall, W. Mids.
Caldwell, Ian, Walton on the Hill and
    Tadworth, Surrey.
Cale Antiques, (Gerald Freeman), London,
    S.W.6.
Caledonian Antiques, Glasgow, Lanarks.,
    Scot. Regent Antiques.
California Art Galleries, London, S.W.1.
Callan, J.R. and D.A., Norwich, Norfolk.
    (Maddermarket Antiques.)
Calleja, L., Redmarley D'Abitot, Glos.
Callingham Antiques, D. and A., North
    Chapel, W. Sussex.
Callingham, S. and N., Kirdford, W. Sussex.
Calne Antiques, Calne, Wilts.
Calton Gallery, Edinburgh, Midloth., Scot.
Calvert Antiques, Endmoor, Cumbria.
Camberwell Antiques Market, London,
    S.E.5.
Camborne Junktion, Camborne, Cornwall.
Cambridge Antiques, Romsey, Hants.
Cambridge Fine Art Ltd., Little Shelford,
    Cambs.
Cambridge, T., Romsey, Hants.
Cambridge, T.R., Romsey, Hants.
Camden Antiques and Collectors Market,
    London, N.W.1.
Camden Lock Antiques Centre, The,
    London, N.W.1. (Relic Antiques.)
Camden Passage Antiques Centre, London,
    N.I.
Came, S., Henley-on-Thames, Oxon.
Camel Antiques, Newton Abbot, Devon. N.
    A. Ant. C.
Camelot Antiques, Boreham Street, E.
    Sussex.
Cameo Antiques, Banbridge, Co. Down,
    N. Ireland.
Cameo Antiques, Bath, Avon. Gt. West.
    Ant. C.
Cameo Antiques, Milford-on-Sea, Hants.
Cameo Antiques, St. Helier, Jersey, C.1.
Cameo Antiques/China Doll, Cheltenham,
    Glos.
Cameo Corner, Worthing, W. Sussex.
Cameo Corner at Liberty's, London, W.1.
Camerer Cuss and Co., London, S.W.1.
Cameron Antiques, Ingatestone, Essex.
Cameron, D.J., Perth, Perths., Scot.
Cameron, M., Paulerspury, Northants.
Cameron, N.S., Southend-on-Sea, Essex.
Cameron, Peter, Londdon, W.1.
Campbell, A., Midhurst, W. Sussex.
Campbell, C., Cowes, I. of Wight.
Campbell, C., Yarmouth, I. of Wight.
Campbell, D., Perranarworthal, Cornwall.
Campbell, E., Newtonmore, Inver., Scot.
Campbell, Gerard, Lechlade, Glos.
Campbell, G., Middleton, Lancs.
Campbell, Mrs. J., Colyton, Devon.
Campbell, J. and G., Lechlade, Glos.
Campbell, Jean, Saxmundham, Suffolk.
Campbell, Picture Frames Ltd., John,
    London, S.W.3.

Campbell, Meg, Southampton, Hants.
Campbell, Mrs. M., London, S.W.3. Ant.
    Ant. Mkt.
Campbell Antiques, Peter, Faringdon, Oxon.
Campbell, R. & S., Camberley, Surrey.
Campbell, Sally, Bexhill-on-Sea, E. Sussex.
    Bex. Ant. C.
Campbell Walchli Antiques, Midhurst,
    W. Sussex.
Campbell-Gibson Fine Arts, Oban, Argylls.,
    Scot.
Campbell-Gibson, R.A., Oban, Argylls., Scot.
Campbell-Macinnes, A.,Bath, Avon. (Lantern
    Gallery.
Campion, London, S.W.13.
Campion, R.J., London, S.W.6. (Old World
    Trading Co.).
Candle Lane Books, Shrewsbury, Shrops.
Cane, J.W., Salisbury, Wilts.
Canham, Mr. and Mrs. H., Cranbrook, Kent.
Cannell Antiques, M.D., Thurlton, Norfolk.
Cannell, R.H., Ampthill, Beds.
Cannon Antiques, Bristol, Avon.
Cannon, Elizabeth, Colchester, Essex.
Cannon Hill Antiques, Bude, Cornwall.
Cannon Hill Antiques, Torquay, Devon. Tor.
    Ant. C.
Canonbury Antiques, London, N.1.
Canonbury Antiques Ltd., London, W.11.
Cantabrian Antiques & Architectural
    Furnishing, Lynton, Devon.
Canterbury House, Thorne, S. Yorks.
Canterbury Place Antiques, Sheffield,
    S. Yorks.
Canterbury Rostro, Canterbury, Kent.
Canterbury Weekly Antique Market,
    Canterbury, Kent.
Capital Clocks, London S.W.8.
Capon, Ann, Castleton, Derbys.
Capon, Patric, London, N.1.
Capricorn Antiques Ltd., London, N.1..
Capstick, J. and T., Bingley, W. Yorks.
Cardigan Book Centre, Cardigan, Dyfed,
    Wales.
Careless Cottage Antiques, Much Hadham,
    Herts.
Carey, Gary, Manchester, Lancs. Royal Ex.
    S.C.
Carey, N., Bexhill-on-Sea, E. Sussex. Bex.
    Ant. C.
Carillon Antiques, Loughborough, Leics.
Caris, Gordon, Hexham, Northumb.
Carleton, Michael, London, N.W.3.
Carling Antiques, Long Melford, Suffolk.
Carling, R., Long Melford, Suffolk.
Carlton House Antiques, Cheltenham, Glos.
Carlton House Antiques, Pershore, Hereford
    and Worcs.
Carlyon-Gibbs, A.S., Egham, Surrey.
Caroline's Pine — Antiques, Sevenoaks,
    Kent.
Carmichael, P., Brighton, E. Sussex.
Carnell, Paul, London, W.11. G. Port.
Carnival Antiques, Bristol, Avon.
Carousel Antiques, Derby, Derbys.
Carousel Antiques, Marlborough, Wilts.
Carousel Antiques, Middleton St. George,
    Durham.

Carousel Antique Centre, T/A Goodbuys, Boston, Lincs.
Carpenter, F., Lincoln, Lincs.
Carpenter, John, Loughor, W. Glam., Wales.
Carpenter, John, Swansea, W. Glam., Wales. Ant. Centre.
Carpenter, S., Hartley Wintney, Hants.
Carr Antiques, Harry, Washington, Tyne and Wear.
Carr, J., Royston, Herts.
Carré, K.M., St. Peter Port, Guernsey, C.I.
Carrie's Antiques, Cheltenham, Glos.
Carronade Antiques, Craig, Painswick, Glos.
Carrington Antiques, Craig, Painswick, Glos.
Carrington and Co. Ltd., London, W.1.
Carritt Limited, David, London, S.W.1.
Carrol, E., Bingley, W. Yorks.
Carroll Bros. Antiques, Brighton, E. Sussex.
Carroll, J.J., J.N. and B.P., Brighton, E. Sussex.
Carroll, J.T. and D., West Bromwich, W. Mids.
Carroll, Mrs. V., London, S.W.3. Ant. Ant. Mkt.
Carronade Antiques, Glasgow, Lanarks., Scot. Regent Antiques.
Carruthers, C., Carlisle, Cumbria.
Carruthers, J., C. and F.E., Carlisle, Cumbria.
Carse Antiques, Rait, Perths., Scot.
Carshalton Antique Galleries, Carshalton, Gtr. London.
Carter (Canada), A.W., London, W.1. (Bluett and Sons Ltd.)
Carter, D.R., Woolhampton, Berks.
Carter, J., Whauphill, Wigtowns., Scot.
Carter, J.F., M.F., R. and A.E., Kirkby-on-Bain, Lincs.
Carter, K., London, W.11 (Alice's).
Carter, L., London, S.W.3. Chen. Gall.
Carter, M. and P.A., Taunton, Somerset.
Carter, M.J., Wells, Somerset.
Carter, N.S., Farnborough, Hants.
Carter, R., Birmingham, W. Mids. (The Twentieth Century Style.)
Carter, R.A., Bicester, Oxon.
Carter Gallery, Simon, Woodbridge, Suffolk.
Carthew, Olwen, London, S.E.26.
Cartmell, T. and J., Tring, Herts.
Cartographia Ltd., London, W.C.2.
Cartrefle Antiques, Mathry, Dyfed, Wales.
Cartwheel Antiques, Dalry, Ayr., Scot.
Cartwright and Co., Craven Arms, Shrops.
Cary Antiques Ltd., Castle Cary, Somerset.
Carysforth, S., Blackburn, Lancs.
Casey, F.G. and A.P., Wilmslow, Cheshire.
Cashmore Antiques, G. and E., Chipping Norton, Oxon.
Casimir Ltd., Jack, London, W.11.
Cason, P.G., Cardiff, S. Glam., Wales. (Charlotte's Wholesale Antiques).
Caspall Antiques, J. and J., Stow-on-the-Wold, Glos.
Casque and Gauntlet Antiques Ltd., Farnham, Surrey.
Cassidy, P., Bakewell, Derbys.
Cassidy, R.J., Streetly, W. Mids.
Cassio Antiques, London, W.11.
Castle, The, Sandgate, Kent.

Castle Antiques, Bletchingley, Surrey.
Castle Antiques, Cheltenham, Glos.
Castle Antiques, Clitheroe, Lancs.
Castle Antiques, Newark, Notts.
Castle Antiques, Newcastle Emlyn, Dyfed, Wales.
Castle Antiques, Orford, Suffolk.
Castle Antiques, Peel, I. of Man.
Castle Antiques, Rochester, Kent.
Castle Antiques, Stoke-on-Trent, Staffs.
Castle Antiques, Tunbridge Wells, Kent.
Castle Antiques, Usk, Gwent, Wales.
Castle Antiques, Wallingford, Oxon. L. Arc.
Castle Antiques, Woodford Green, Gtr. London.
Castle Antiques and Fine Art, Dudley, W. Mids.
Castle Antiques Ltd., Deddington, Oxon.
Castle Antiques — Warwick's Art Deco Shop, Warwick, Warks.
Castle Art and Antiques, Bridge of Weir, Renfrews, Scot.
Castle Bookshop, Colchester, Essex.
Castle Galleries, Salisbury, Wilts.
Castle Gallery, Lincoln, Lincs.
Castle Gate Antiques, Shrewsbury, Shrops.
Castle Gate Antiques Centre, Newark, Notts.
Castle Lane Books, Torquay, Devon.
Castle Lodge, Ludlow, Shrops.
Castle, Simon, London W.8.
Castlegate Antiques, Berwick-on-Tweed, Northumb.
Castleton Country Furniture, Sherborne, Dorset.
Cat in the Window Antiques, Pateley Bridge, N. Yorks.
Cater, D.B., London, S.E.1. Ber. Ant. Whse.
Cater Antiques, Paul, Moreton-in-Marsh, Glos.
Cater, P.J.C., Moreton-in-Marsh, Glos.
Cathay Antiques, London, W.8.
Cathedral Gallery, Norwich, Norfolk.
Catley, B.R., London, S.W.3. (W.J. Sparrow.) Chen. Gall.
Cato, L.P., Brighton, E. Sussex. (Lennox Antiques).
Caudwell, Doreen, Woodstock, Oxon.
Causey Antique Shop, Gosforth, Tyne & Wear.
Cavanagh, D., Edinburgh, Midloth., Scot.
Cavanagh, John, Glasgow, Lanarks., Scot. Vict. Vill.
Cave, F. and C.H., Northampton, Northants.
Cave, G., Northampton, Northants.
Cave and Sons Ltd., R.G., Ludlow, Shrops.
Cavendish, John, London, S.W.3. Ant. Ant. Mkt.
Cavendish, Odile, London, S.W.1.
Cavendish Rare Books, London S.W.1.
Cavendish Antiques, Rupert, London, S.W.6.
Cawthorn, Elaine, Fakenham, Norfolk. Ant. C.
Cayless, B. and J., Defynnog, Powys, Wales.
Cayley, D., Cambridge, Cambs. (Lensfield Antiques.)
Cazalet Ltd., Lumley, London, W.1.
Cedar Antiques, Hartley Wintney, Hants.

Cekay Antiques, London, W.1. G. Ant. Mkt.
Celia, London, N.W.8. Alf. Ant. Mkt.
Celia Charlottes, Lewes, E. Sussex.
Cellier, N., Dorking, Surrey.
Centaur Gallery, London, N.6.
Century Antiques, Warminster, Wilts.
Century Antiques and Art Gallery,
Windermere, Cumbria.
Century Galleries, Bideford, Devon.
Cerberus, London, W.1. G. Ant. Mkt.
Ceres Antiques, Ceres, Fife, Scot.
Cerne Antiques, Cerne Abbas, Dorset.
Chadwick Antiques, Knowle, W. Mids.
Chadwick, Mrs. A.C., Arundel, W. Sussex.
Chalcraft, J.N., Brighton, E. Sussex (The
Shop of the Yellow Frog).
Chalk, H. and E., South Lopham, Norfolk.
Chalkwell Antiques, Leigh-on-Sea, Essex.
Challis Ltd., A.R., Portsmouth, Hants.
Challis Ltd., A.R., Sevenoaks, Kent.
Challis, R., London, S.E.10.
Chalmers, A.F.M., Pulborough, W. Sussex.
Chalon, N., M. and T., Hambridge,
Somerset.
Chalon UK Ltd., Hambridge, Somerset.
Chamberlin Galleries Ltd., Torquay, Devon.
Chambers, Mrs. B.C., Boreham Street,
E. Sussex.
Chambers, D., Stratford-upon-Avon, Warks.
Chambers, J.A., Walsall, W. Mids.
Chan, K.L., London, S.W.3. Ant. Ant. Mkt.
Chancery Antiques, Debenham, Suffolk.
Chancery Antiques, Thrapston, Northants.
Chancery Antiques, Tiverton, Devon.
Chancery Antiques Ltd., London, N.1.
Chancery Lane Antiques, Bridport, Dorset.
Chanctonbury Antiques, Washington,
W. Sussex.
Chandler, M.L., Birmingham, W. Mids.
(Dalton Street Antiques.)
Chandlers, Bideford, Devon.
Channel Islands Galleries Ltd., St. Peter Port,
Guernsey, C.I.
Channer, C., Hucknall, Notts.
Chanteau, Madame Y., London, S.W.10.
Chanter Antiques, Julian, Blandford Forum,
Dorset.
Chanter, J.P. and A.M., Blandford Forum,
Dorset.
Chanticleer Antiques, London, W.11.
Chantry Galleries, London, W.11.
Chantry Galleries, West Stour, Dorset.
Chantry House Antiques, Stow-on-the-Wold,
Glos.
Chapel Antiques, Battle, E. Sussex.
Chapel Antiques, Glossop, Derbys.
Chapel Antiques, Nantwich, Cheshire.
Chapel Antiques Ltd., Woburn, Beds. Wob.
Ab. Ant. C.
Chapel Collectors Centre, Castor, Cambs.
Chapel Fine Art and Antiques at McGill
Duncan Gallery, Kirkcudbright, Kirkcud.,
Scot.
Chapel House Fireplaces, Holmfirth, W. Yorks.
Chapel Place Antiques, Tunbridge Wells,
Kent.
Chaperlin Antiques, Mary, Woburn, Beds.
Wob. Ab. Ant. C.

Chaplefield Antiques, Warwick, Warks. Smith
St. A. C.
Chaplin, P., Bures, Suffolk.
Chaplin, R.M. and S.V., Coggeshall, Essex.
Chapman, A., Matlock, Derbys.
Chapman and Davies Antiques, London, N.1.
Chapman, F.N.L., Painswick, Glos.
Chapman, Hilary, London, S.W.6.
Chapman. I. and J.I.F., Knapton, N. Yorks.
Chapman, K. and L., Todmorden, W. Yorks.
Chapman, M., Petworth, W. Sussex.
Chapman Medd and Sons, Easingwold,
N. Yorks.
Chapman, P., Bristol, Avon. Clift. Ant. Mkt.
Chapman Antiques, Peter, London, N.1.
Chapman, P.J., London, N.1.
Chapman, R., Bury St. Edmunds, Suffolk.
Chapman, R.A., Hythe, Kent.
Chapmann, J., London, S.W.11.
Chappell Antiques and Fine Art, K., Bakewell,
Derbys.
Chappell Antiques and Fine Art, K., Baslow,
Derbys.
Chappell, P., Hertford, Herts.
Chappelow, M., Leominster, Hereford &
Worcs.
Charisma Antiques Trade Warehouse,
Barnsley, S. Yorks.
Charisma Curios and Antiques, Chorley,
Lancs.
Charles Antiques, Romsey, Hants.
Charles Antiques, Stephen, Leigh-on-Sea,
Essex.
Charles Fairs, Stephen, Orsett, Essex.
Charles International Antiques, Maidstone,
Kent.
Charles, S. and M., Halstead, Essex.
Charleston, Peter, Preston, Lancs. N.W.
Ant. C.
Charlesworth Brothers Antiques Ltd., Bala,
Gwynedd, Wales.
Charlesworth, D.J. and R.S., Bala, Gwynedd,
Wales.
Charlesworth, J., London, W.9.
Charleville Gallery, London, W.14.
Charley Farleys, Billericay, Essex.
Charlick, J.B., London, S.W.6. (Fergus
Cochrane Antiques.)
Charlotte's Wholesale Antiques, Cardiff,
S. Glam., Wales.
Charlton, E. and M., Eachwick, Northumb.
Charlton Fine Art and Porcelain, E. and N.R.,
Marton, Cleveland.
Charlton, W. and F., Leamington Spa, Warks.
Charltons Antiques, Leamington Spa, Warks.
Charman, G., Birmingham, W. Mids. (Format
of Birmingham Ltd.).
Charnwood Gallery, The, Anstey, Leics.
Chart House, The, Shenfield, Essex.
Charterhouse Antiques, Heath and Reach,
Beds.
Charterhouse Antiques, Teignmouth, Devon.
Chatal Ltd., London, N.W.3.
Chate, Katy, Wargrave, Berks.
Chateau Briand Antique Centre, Burwash,
E. Sussex.
Chatelaine, The, Atherstone, Warks.
Chater-House, A., Long Melford, Suffolk.

Chater-House Gallery, Long Melford, Suffolk.
Chattels, Callington, Cornwall.
Chattels, Woking, Surrey.
Chattels of Church Hill, Loughton, Essex.
Chaucer Bookshop, Canterbury, Kent.
Chaucer Fine Arts Inc., London, S.W.1.
Chawner, John, Chatham, Kent.
Cheapside Antiques, Knaresborough,
   N. Yorks.
Checker Books, Abingdon, Oxon.
Cheek, P.F., London, W.C.1.
Cheese Hill Antiques, East Harling, Norfolk.
Chelsea Antique Market, London, S.W.3.
Chelsea Bric-a-Brac Shop Ltd., London,
   S.W.19.
Chelsea Clocks, London, S.W.3. Ant. Ant.
   Mkt.
Chelsea Clocks and Antiques, London,
   S.W.6.
Chelsea House Antiques, Stowmarket,
   Suffolk.
Chelsea Oriental Carpets, London, S.W.3.
   Chen. Gall.
Chelsea Rare Books, London, S.W.3.
Cheltenham Antique Market, Cheltenham,
   Glos.
Cheltenham Galleries, Harrogate, N. Yorks.
Cheneviere, A., London, W.1. (Tzigany Fine
   Arts).
Cheney Antiques, Derek J., Sandgate, Kent.
Chenil Galleries Fine Art and Antique Centre,
   London, S.W.3.
Cheriton Antiques, Worthing, W. Sussex.
Cherrington, T.A., Southampton, Hants.
Cheriton Antiques, Worthing, W. Sussex.
Cherrington, T.A., Southampton, Hants.
Cherry Antiques, Hemel Hempstead, Herts.
Cherry Antiques, Peter, St. Peter Port,
   Guernsey, C.I.
Cherub Antiques, Wells, Somerset.
Cheshire Antiques, London, S.W.3. Chen.
   Gall.
Cheshire Antiques, Macclesfield, Cheshire.
Cheshire, E.M., Bingham, Notts.
Cheshire, Mrs. E.M., Woburn, Beds. Wob.
   Ab. Ant. C.
Chest of Drawers, The, Tetbury, Glos.
Chester Antique Hypermarket, Chester,
   Cheshire.
Chester Antiques, Chester, Cheshire.
Chester Furniture Cave, Chester, Cheshire.
Chester, J. and P., North Shields, Tyne and
   Wear.
Chesterfield Antiques, Birmingham, W. Mids.
Chesterfield Antiques Centre, Chesterfield,
   Derbys.
Chestergate Antiques, Stockport, Cheshire.
Chesterman, R.F., Leeds, W. Yorks.
Chester-Master, R., Fairford, Glos.
Chester-Master, Mr. and Mrs. R.T.G.,
   Cirencester, Glos.
Chesters, B., Rawtenstall, Lancs.
Chesters and Co., Rawtenstall, Lancs.
Chesters, N.E., Ampthill, Beds.
Chesters, N.E., Woburn, Beds.
Chesters, Y., Mathry, Dyfed, Wales.
Chesterton, Mrs. Margaret, St. Austell,
   Cornwall.

Chesterton-North, R.G., Lincoln, Lincs.
Chesterton-North, R.G., Wragby, Lincs.
Chestnuts Antiques, Kineton, Warks.
Chevertons of Edenbridge Ltd., Edenbridge,
   Kent.
Chibnall, C., Leicester, Leics.
Chichester Gallery, Chichester, W. Sussex.
Chilcott, Mrs. M., Comrie, Perths., Scot.
Child, J.C. and E.A., Morchard Bishop,
   Devon.
Child, P., London, N.1. (Swan Fine Art).
Child, Rachel, London, W.1.
Child and Son, S.G., Smeeth, Kent.
Chilham Antiques Ltd., Chilham, Kent.
Chiltern Antiques International, Dunstable,
   Beds.
Chiltern Collectables, London, W.1. G. Ant.
   Mkt.
Chiltern Jewellery & Coins, Dunstable, Beds.
Chilton, B.J., London S.W.3. Chen. Gall.
Chilton, C. and I., Long Melford, Suffolk.
Chilton, D., York, N. Yorks. (Taikoo Books
   Ltd.)
Chilver, M., Canterbury, Kent.
Chimera Books, Hurstpierpoint, W. Sussex.
Chimes, The, Reepham, Norfolk.
China Hen, The, Bradford-on-Avon, Wilts.
China Locker, The, Lamberhurst, Kent.
China Repairers, incorporating Mair and
   Drayson Antiques, London, N.W.8.
Chiodo, F.A., London, N.1 (Franco's
   Antiques).
Chislehurst Antiques, Chislehurst,
   Gtr. London.
Chiswick Antiques, London, W.4.
Chiswick Fireplaces, London, W.4.
Chitty, R.L. and R.A., Cheltenham, Glos.
   (Cameo Antiques).
Chizumi, Nonaka, London, S.W.3. Ant. Ant.
   Mkt.
Chloe Antiques, Worthing, W. Sussex.
Chobham Antiques Market, Chobham,
   Surrey.
Christchurch Carpets, Christchurch, Dorset.
Christensen, H.O., London, S.W.1. (Watts
   and Christensen).
Christie, G.A., Focabers, Morays., Scot.
Christie, J., London, W.1.
Christie, Mrs. M.J. and P.S., London, W.1.
Christie Antiques, S.E., Macclesfield,
   Cheshire.
Christie, W., Harrogate, N. Yorks. (Oriental
   Art Ware).
Christophe, J., London, W.1 (Harcourt
   Antiques.)
Christophers, W.J., Canterbury, Kent.
Christopher-Walsh, Mr. and Mrs. E.,
   Modbury, Devon.
Chugg, Mrs. M., Braunton, Devon.
Chulmleigh Antiques, Chulmleigh, Devon.
Church End Antiques, Dunmow, Essex.
Church House Antiques, Weybridge, Surrey.
Church Street Antiques, Hadleigh, Suffolk.
Church Street Antiques, Market Deeping,
   Lincs.
Church Street Galleries Ltd., London W.8.
Church Street Gallery, The, Saffron Walden,
   Essex.

Church Street Gallery, The, Stow-on-the-Wold, Glos.
Church View Antiques, Harrogate, N. Yorks.
Church View House Antiques, Kirk Michael, I. of Man.
Churchtown Antiques, Southport, Merseyside.
Ciancimino Ltd., London, S.W.1.
Cider House Galleries Ltd., The, Bletchingley, Surrey.
Cinders, Edinburgh, Midloth., Scot.
Cinema Bookshop, London W.C.1.
Circa, London, W.1. G. Mews.
Circa 1900, St. Andrews, Fife, Scot.
Circa Antiques, Bushey, Herts.
Circa Fine Art, Plymouth, Devon.
Cirencester Antique Market, Cirencester, Glos.
Cirencester Antiques Ltd., Cirencester, Glos.
City Clocks, London, E.C.1.
City of Birmingham Antique Market, Birmingham, W. Mids.
Clare Collector, The, Clare, Suffolk.
Clare Gallery, Tunbridge Wells, Kent.
Clare Hall Co. Ltd., The, Clare, Suffolk.
Clare, J. and A., Tunbridge Wells, Kent.
Clare, Marjorie, Micheldever Station, Hants.
Clare, Mr. and Mrs. M.E., Stockton Heath, Cheshire.
Clare, Mr. and Mrs. M.E., Stretton, Cheshire.
Clare, R.A., London S.W.19.
Clarence House Antiques, Watchet, Somerset.
Clarendon Gallery, London, W.1.
Clarges Gallery, London, S.W.3.
Clark, Mrs. A., Dawlish, Devon.
Clark, A., Carson, Edinburgh, Midloth., Scot. (The Carson Clark Gallery — Scotia Maps).
Clark B., Oxford, Oxon.
Clark and Bell Antiques, Sandgate, Kent.
Clark, B.E., Walton-on-Thames, Surrey.
Clark, B.J., London, N.W.1. (Country Pine Ltd.)
Clark Gallery, Scotia Maps — Mapsellers, Carson, Edinburgh, Midloth., Scot.
Clark, D., London S.E.6.
Clark, D.E., Brampton, Cambs.
Clark Antiques Ltd., Elias, Bletchingley, Surrey.
Clark Antiques Ltd., Gerald, London N.W.7.
Clark, G.J. and J., London N.W.7.
Clark, H., Moretonhampstead, Devon.
Clark, H.M., Southend-on-Sea, Essex.
Clark, J., East Molesey, Surrey.
Clark, L.D. and J.M., Bletchingley, Surrey.
Clark, Malcolm G., Cambridge, Cambs.
Clark Antiques, Peter, Birmingham, W. Mids.
Clark, P.B. & A.L., Penrith, Cumbria.
Clark, R., Faringdon, Oxon.
Clark, Reg, London, W.11. G. Port.
Clark, Roy, London, W.11. G. Port. (Rob Boys).
Clark, Robert, Micklebring, S. Yorks.
Clarke, A.T., Walton-on-the-Hill and Tadworth, Surrey.
Clarke Antiques, Christopher, Stow-on-the-Wold, Glos.
Clarke, C.J., Stow-on-the-Wold, Glos.

Clarke, Miss D., Brighton, E. Sussex (Bits and Pieces).
Clarke, F.J., Lancaster, Lancs.
Clarke, H., Hyde, Cheshire.
Clarke, Janet, Freshford, Avon.
Clarke, J.E., Camberley, Surrey.
Clarke, M., Warboys, Cambs.
Clarke, O., London, S.W.20.
Clarke, R.A., Oakham, Leics.
Clarke, R.A. and A.M., Oakham, Leics.
Clarke, R.J., Nuneaton, Warks.
Clarke-Hall Ltd., J., London, E.C.4.
Clarke's Antiques (Camberley), Camberley, Surrey.
Classic Art, Billericay, Essex.
Claud-Lee, Harrogate, N. Yorks. W. Pk. Ant. Pav.
Clay, John, London, S.W.6.
Clay, P., Peterborough, Cambs.
Clayton Antiques, Jesmond, Tyne and Wear.
Clayton, Mrs. J.D., Hexham, Northumb.
Clayton, Teresa, London, W.1. G. Mews.
Cleeve Antiques, Bristol, Avon.
Cleeve Picture Framing, Bishops Cleeve, Glos.
Clegg, J., Ludlow, Shrops.
Clegg, W. and S., Nettlebed, Oxon.
Cleland, M.A. and J.O., Benson, Oxon.
Cleland, Robert, London, N.W.8. Alf. Ant. Mkt.
Clement House Antiques, Burford, Oxon.
Clements, James W., Carlisle, Cumbria.
Clements, V. and R., Plumley, Cheshire.
Clent Books, Halesowen, W. Mids.
Clermont Antiques, Watton, Norfolk.
Clevedon Fine Arts Ltd. (with Clevedon Books.), Clevedon, Avon.
Cleveland, William, London, W.11.
Cleverly, M.A., Malton, N. Yorks.
Clewett, Mrs. P., Oxford, Oxon.
Clewlow, Miss J., Nantwich, Cheshire.
Cliffe Antiques Centre, Lewes, E. Sussex.
Clifford and Son Ltd., T.J., Bath, Avon (Paragon Antiques and Collectors Market).
Clifton Antiques, Leeds. W. Yorks.
Clifton Antiques, Lytham, Lancs.
Clifton Antiques Market, Bristol, Avon.
Clifton House Antiques, Haslingden, Lancs.
Clifton House Antiques, Weston-super-Mare, Avon.
Clingly Antiques, Antony, Fencehouses, Tyne and Wear.
Clink, D., Haslingden, Lancs.
Clisby at Andwells Antiques, Bryan, Hartley Wintney, Hants.
Clock Clinic Ltd., The, London, S.W.15.
Clock House, Leavenheath, Suffolk.
Clock Investment, Orpington, Gtr. London.
Clock Shop, The, Hoylake, Merseyside.
Clock Shop, The, Southport, Merseyside.
Clock Shop, The, Weybridge, Surrey.
Clock Shop Antiques, The, Boughton, Kent.
Clock Shop Antiques, The, Topsham, Devon.
Clock Shop — Phillip Setterfield of St. Albans, The, St. Albans, Herts.
Clock Tower Antiques, Newmarket, Suffolk.

Clock Tower Antiques, Tregony, Cornwall.
Clockcraft Antiques, Bridlington,
N. Humberside.
Cloisters, Canterbury, Kent.
Cloisters Antiques Fair, Norwich, Norfolk.
Close Antiques, Winchester, Hants.
Close, Henry H., Abergavenny, Gwent,
Wales.
Clovelly Antiques, Newton Abbot, Devon.
N.A. Ant. C.
Clover, West Bromwich, W. Mids.
Clover Antiques, Llantwit Major, S. Glam.,
Wales.
Clover Antiques, B.R., Framlingham,
Suffolk.
Clow, M.R., Finedon, Northants.
Clunes Antiques, London, S.W.19.
Clutter, Uppingham, Leics.
Clutterbank, Mrs. F., Hythe, Kent.
Clyde Antiques, Patrington, Hull,
N. Humberside.
Coach House, The, Comrie, Perths., Scot.
Coach House, The, Costessey, Norfolk.
Coach House Antiques, Canterbury, Kent.
Coach House Antiques, Hastings, E. Sussex.
Coach House Antiques, Whitby, N. Yorks.
Coach House Antiques, Wisbech, Cambs.
Coach House Antiques Ltd., Perth, Perths.,
Scot.
Coach House Gallery, Wedmore, Somerset.
Coakley, Tony, London, S.W.3. Chen. Gall.
Coakley, T., London, N.W.8. Alf. Ant. Mkt.
Coast, G., Portsmouth, Hants.
Coates of Malvern, Joan, Great Malvern,
Hereford and Worcs.
Coats, A., London, W.8. (Coats Oriental
Carpets and Co. Ltd.)
Coats Oriental Carpets and Co. Ltd.,
London, W.8.
Cobblers Hall Antiques, Toddington, Beds.
Cobbles Antiques, The, Bishops Castle,
Shrops.
Cobbydale Pine, Silsden, W. Yorks.
Cobham Galleries, Cobham, Surrey.
Cobra and Bellamy, London, S.W.1.
Cochrane Antiques, Fergus, London, S.W.6.
Cochrane, F.V., London, S.W.6.
Cockburn Antiques, P., Glasgow, Lanarks.
Scot. Vict. Vill.
Cockermouth Antique Market, Cockermouth,
Cumbria.
Cockram, A., Lincoln, Lincs.
Cocoa, Cheltenham, Glos.
Cocozza Antiques, London, W.11.
Cocozza, G., London, W.11 (Cocozza
Antiques).
Coe — English Paintings and Watercolours,
Peter, Shepton Mallet, Somerset.
Coexistence, London, N.1.
Coggins, Mr. and Mrs. G., Painswick, Glos.
Coggins, Ray, Bradford-on-Avon, Wilts.
Cohen and Sons, B., London, S.W.1.
(Trafalgar Galleries)
Cohen, Edward, London, S.W.1.
Cohen, Eliaho, London, S.W.3. Ant. Ant. Mkt.
Cohen, M., London, W.11.
Cohen and Pearce (Oriental Porcelain),
London, W.11.

Cohen, Mr. and Mrs. S., Manchester, Lancs.
(The Connoisseur).
Cohn, George and Peter, London, W.C.1.
Coin and Stamp Centre, The, Colchester,
Essex.
Coins of Canterbury, Canterbury, Kent.
Coke, P., Sharrington, Norfolk.
Cold Bath Antiques, Harrogate, N. Yorks.
Coldstream Antiques, Coldstream,
Berwicks., Scot.
Coldwell, P., Sheffield, S. Yorks. (Sheffield
Pine Centre).
Coldwell, P. and J., Sheffield, S. Yorks.
(Canterbury Place Antiques).
Cole (Fine Paintings) Ltd., Christopher,
Beaconsfield, Bucks.
Cole, J., London, N.1. (House of Steel
Antiques).
Cole at Twenty-Eight Camden Passage,
Judy, London, N.1.
Colefax and Fowler, London, W.1.
Coleman Antiques, Aubrey, J., London,
W.8.
Coleman, B., Liverpool, Merseyside. (Savoy
Antiques).
Coleman, Daphne, Fakenham, Norfolk. Ant.
C.
Coleman, G.D. & G.E., London, W.8.
(Aubrey J. Coleman Antiques).
Coleman, Harry, London, W.1. G. Ant. Mkt.
Coleman Antiques, Nigel, Brasted, Kent.
Coleman, Pat, Bath, Avon. B. Ant. Mkt.
Coleman, Robin and Jan, Bath, Avon.
Coleman Antiques, Simon, London, S.W.13.
Colemans W. and B., Clayton-le-Moors,
Lancs.
Coles, D.A., Bristol, Avon. (Beech Antiques.)
Coles, J., Woodstock, Oxon.
Coles, Mrs. P., Bristol, Avon. Clift. Ant.
Mkt.
Coles, S., Bristol, Avon. Clift. Ant. Mkt.
Collard, B., Totnes, Devon.
Collard's Books, Totnes, Devon.
Colleck Ltd., Philip, London, S.W.3.
Collectables, Tunbridge Wells, Kent.
Collecting World/Rings and Things,
Birmingham, W. Mids.
Collection, London, W.1. B. St. Ant. C.
Collection Antique Shop, The, Mountsorrel,
Leics.
Collections, Swansea, W. Glam. Wales. Ant.
Centre.
Collector, The, Barnard Castle, Durham.
Collectors Centre, Cambridge, Cambs.
Collectors' Corner, Bradford, W. Yorks.
Collectors' Corner, Callington, Cornwall.
Collectors' Corner, Huddersfield, W. Yorks.
Collectors' Corner, Newton Abbott, Devon.
N.A. Ant. C.
Collectors' Corner, Northallerton, N. Yorks.
Collectors' Corner, Waddesdon, Bucks.
Collectors' Corner Antiques, Chatham, Kent.
Collectors' Corner Antiques, Croydon,
Gtr. London.
Collectors' Corner — Militaria, London,
S.E.22.
Collectors Gallery, The, Caversham, Berks.
Collectors' Market, Cambridge, Cambs.

Collectors Old Toys and Antiques, Halifax, W. Yorks.
Collectors' Paradise Ltd., Leigh-on-Sea, Essex.
Collectors' Paradise Ltd., Wolverhampton, W. Mids.
Collectors Shop, The, Bath, Avon. Gt. West. Ant. C.
Collectors' Shop, The, Birmingham, W. Mids.
Collectors' Shop, The, Edinburgh, Midloth., Scot.
Collectors Shop, The, Hungerford, Berks.
Collectors' Trail, The, Indian Queens, Cornwall.
Collectors' Treasures Ltd., Wendover, Bucks.
Collens R., Marlborough, Wilts.
Colleton House Gallery, Bath, Avon.
Colleton House Gallery, Tetbury, Glos.
Collet's Chinese Gallery, London, W.C.1.
Colley, A.J., Bristol, Avon.
Collie, B., London, S.W.3. Ant. Ant, Mkt.
Collier, Mrs. D.E., Sheringham, Norfolk.
Collier, Mark, Fordingbridge, Hants.
Collings, C.J. and M., Ashton-under-Lyne, Lancs.
Collings, John H., Banwell, Avon.
Collingwood of Conduit St., London, W.1.
Collino, Julie, London, S.W.7.
Collins, A., Wallingford, Oxon. L. Arc.
Collins Antiques (F.G. and C. Collins Ltd.), Wheathampstead, Herts.
Collins, B.L., London, W.C.2. Lon. Silv. Vts.
Collins and Clark, Cambridge, Cambs.
Collins, E., Leominster, Hereford and Worcs.
Collins Antiques, Frank Beccles, Suffolk.
Collins Antiques, Frank, London, W.11.
Collins Antiques Ltd., Jimmy, Wigan, Lancs.
Collins, Joan and Clive, London, W.11.
Collins, J.G., Cambridge, Cambs.
Collins, J.J., Wigan, Lancs.
Collins, J., Rastrick, W. Yorks.
Collins, J., Llanrwst, Gwynedd, Wales.
Collins and Son, J., Bideford, Devon.
Collins, Noel, Dorking, Surrey.
Collins, N., Shifnal, Shrops.
Collins (Fine Books), Nigel, Shifnal, Shrops.
Collins, P., Balcombe, W. Sussex.
Collins, Peter, London, S.W.6.
Collins, P. and G., London, S.W.10.
Collins, Sylvia, London, W.1. B. St. Ant. C.
Collins, S., Richmond, Gtr. London.
Collins, S.J. and M.C., Wheathampstead, Herts.
Collins, W.E. Brighton, E. Sussex (South Coast Antiques Ltd.)
Collister, S.A., London, N.W.3. Ham. Ant. Emp.
Collister, S.A., Wembley Park, Gtr. London.
Colliton Antique and Craft Centre, Dorchester, Dorset.
Collyer Antiques, Jean, Boughton, Kent.
Collyer, Mrs. J.B., Boughton, Kent.
Collyer, R., Birmingham, W. Mids.
Colman, J., Royston, Herts.
Colman, Wing Cmdr. M.H.J., Cromer, Norfolk.

Colmans, Hexham, Northumb.
Colmans of Hexham (Saleroom and Antique Fair), Hexham, Northumb.
Colmore Galleries Ltd., Birmingham, W. Mids.
Colmore Galleries Ltd., Henley-in-Arden, Warks.
Colnaghi and Co. Ltd., P. and D., London, W.1.
Colt, R., Farnham, Surrey.
Coltishall Antiques Centre, Coltishall, Norfolk.
Coltsfoot Gallery, Leominster, Hereford and Worcs.
Colystock Antiques, Stockland, Devon.
Combe Cottage Antiques, Castle Combe, Wilts.
Comberton Antiques, Comberton, Cambs.
"Commemoratives", London, N.1.
Commin's Antiquarian Bookshop, Bournemouth, Dorset.
Complete Automobilist, The, Greatford, Lincs.
Compton-Dando (Fine Arts) Ltd., Long Melford, Suffolk.
Compton-Dando (Fine Arts) Ltd., White Colne, Essex.
Conisbee, Mr., London, W.2 (Connaught Galleries).
Coniscliffe Curios, Northallerton, N. Yorks.
Connaught Galleries, London, W.2.
Connaughton, J., North Walsham, Norfolk.
Connell, J., Wargrave, Berks.
Connoisseur, The, Manchester, Lancs.
Connoisseur Gallery, The, London, S.W.1.
Connolly, J., London, N.W.3.
Connor, John G., London, S.W.3. Ant. Ant. Mkt.
Conquest House Antiques, Canterbury, Kent.
Constable, C., St. Albans, Herts.
Constable, J., Shifnal, Shrops.
Constable Galleries Ltd., Wilton, Wilts.
Constable, L., Wilton, Wilts.
Constable, L. and P., Wilton, Wilts.
Constant Reader Bookshop, The, London, S.W.6.
Constantinescu, T.R. and C., Brecon, Powys, Wales.
Constantinidi, P., London, W.1. (Eskenazi Ltd.)
Continuum, Joy, London, W.1. G. Ant. Mkt.
Conway, R., Prestatyn, Clwyd, Wales.
Cook, E.J. and C.A., Gloucester, Glos.
Cook and Son Antiques, E.J., Gloucester, Glos.
Cook, Mr. and Mrs. E.W., Ottery St. Mary, Devon.
Cook, K.J., Rochester, Kent.
Cook, M.E. and T.E., Ipswich, Suffolk (College Gateway Bookshop).
Cook Antiques, Rodney, Twickenham, Gtr. London.
Cook, R.L., Little Horton, Wilts.
Cook and Son, S.A., London, N.W.3.
Cook, Susan and James, Cuerdon, Lancs.
Cook, W., East Budleigh, Devon.
Cooke, D., Playden, E. Sussex.

Cooke, F.G., Ironbridge, Shrops.
Cooke, J.E. & M.G., Hatch Beauchamp, Somerset.
Cooke Antiques Ltd., Mary, London, S.W.1.
Cooke, R., Bath, Avon. B. Ant. Mkt.
Cooke, S., Long Melford, Suffolk.
Cooke, S.M., Thatcham, Berks.
Cookson, Mr. and Mrs. F., Beaulieu, Hants.
Cookson, R., Leominster, Hereford and Worcs.
Cookstown Antiques, Cookstown, N. Ireland.
Coombe Farm Antiques, Litton Cheney, Dorset.
Coombe House Antiques (Georgian Town House), Lewes, E. Sussex.
Coombes, J. and M., Dorking, Surrey.
Coombes, R. and D., Aldbourne, Wilts.
Coombes, R. and D., London, W.14.
Coombes, S. and R., Burnham-on-Sea, Somerset.
Coombs, A. and L., Richmond, Gtr. London.
Coombs, L., Walton-on-the-Hill and Tadworth, Surrey.
Cooper, B., Bath, Avon. Gt. West. Ant. C. Wed. Mkt.
Cooper, B.S., Launceston, Cornwall.
Cooper, C., Bath, Avon. (The French Connection).
Cooper, C., Glastonbury, Somerset.
Cooper, D., Bath, Avon. Gt. West Ant. C.
Cooper, D. and G., Silsden, W. Yorks.
Cooper Antiques, Eileen, Braunton, Devon.
Cooper, E. and R., Great Missenden, Bucks.
Cooper, E.T., Gosport, Hants.
Cooper, G., Sale, Cheshire.
Cooper Antiques, John, St. Helier, Jersey, C.I.
Cooper and Son (Ilkley) Ltd., J.H., Ilkley, W. Yorks.
Cooper, J.P., Disley, Cheshire.
Cooper, J.S., Bourton-on-the-Water, Glos.
Cooper, Leon, Batley, W. Yorks.
Cooper, S.M., Bath, Avon. (Sheila Smith Antiques.)
Cooper, T. & M., Stockport, Cheshire.
Cooper and Son, William, Walton-on-the-Hill and Tadworth, Surrey.
Coote Antiques, Belinda, London, W.8.
Cope, M.J. and I., Alton, Staffs.
Cope-Brown, S.J., Gazeley, Suffolk.
Copeman Antiques, Duncan, Bath, Avon. Gt. West. Ant. C.
Coppage, J, Canterbury, Kent.
Coppelia Antiques, Plumley, Cheshire.
Copper Kettle Antiques, Watford, Herts.
Copperfield Antiques, Loughborough, Leics.
Copperfield, Robert, Macclesfield, Cheshire.
Copperfields, Sidmouth, Devon.
Coppers, Bexhill-on-Sea, E. Sussex.
Corbitt (Numismatists) Ltd., J.H., Newcastle-upon-Tyne, Tyne and Wear.
Cordas, Mrs. S., London, S.W.3. Ant. Ant. Mkt.
Cordell Antiques, Sonia, Ipswich, Suffolk.
Cordon, D., Stowmarket, Suffolk.
Corder, J., Coggeshall, Essex.
Corfield of Lymington Ltd., Lymington, Hants.

Corinium Antiques, Kempsford, Glos.
Corke, G.N., Bath, Avon. (Pineside Studios.) Gt. West. Ant. C.
Corkhill, Miss V., Ramsey, Isle of Man.
Cormack, Mrs. J., Crieff, Perths., Scot.
Corn Exchange Antiques, Tunbridge Wells, Kent.
Corn Mill Antiques, Skipton, N. Yorks.
Corner Cabinet, Thornton Heath, Gtr. London.
Corner Cottage Antiques, Leicester, Leics.
Corner Cottage Antiques, Market Bosworth, Leics.
Corner Cupboard, The, Boxford, Suffolk.
Corner Cupboard, The, London, N.W.2.
Corner Cupboard Curios, Cirencester, Glos.
Corner Gallery, The, Lindfield, W. Sussex.
Corner House Antiques, Glasgow, Lanarks., Scot.
Corner House Antiques, St. Ives, Cornwall.
Corner Portobello Antiques Supermarket, London, W.11.
Corner Shop, Bradford, W. Yorks.
Corner Shop, Eye, Suffolk.
Corner Shop, The, Hay-on-Wye, Powys, Wales.
Corner Shop Antiques, Bury St. Edmunds, Suffolk.
Cornerways, Penrith, Cumbria.
Cornish, James R., Langford, Avon.
Cornmarket Antiques, Romsey, Hants.
Cornucopia, London, S.W.1.
Cornucopia Antiques, Hebden Bridge, W. Yorks.
Cornwell, I., Royston, Herts.
Coronel, H.S., London, S.W.6.
Corrall, I., Mountsorrel, Leics.
Corridor Antiques and Perdy's Junk Shop, Lichfield, Staffs.
Corridor Stamp Shop, Bath, Avon.
Corrigan Antiques, Kilbarchan, Renfrews., Scot.
Corrin Antiques, John, Douglas, I. of Man.
Corry, E.I., Derby, Derbys.
Corson, Margaret, Neatishead, Norfolk.
Cosmo Antiques, Westerham, Kent.
Cosmos, O. M., Westerham, Kent.
Cosmos, P., Westerham, Kent.
Cosmos, Peter and Maggie, Tenterden, Kent.
Cossa Antiques, Gabor, Cambridge, Cambs.
Costiff, Mrs. M.W., London, S.W.3. Ant. Ant. Mkt.
Cotham Galleries, Bristol, Avon.
Cotswold Curios, Stroud, Glos.
Cotswold Galleries, The, Stow-in-the-Wold, Glos.
Cotswold House, Broadway, Hereford and Worcs.
Cottage Antique Shop, The, Eccleshall, Staffs.
Cottage Antiques, Beaminster, Devon.
Cottage Antiques, Cambridge, Cambs.
Cottage Antiques, Cardiff, S. Glam., Wales.
Cottage Antiques, Harrogate, N. Yorks.
Cottage Antiques, Kendal, Cumbria.
Cottage Antiques, Langford, Avon.
Cottage Antiques, Leyburn, N. Yorks.

Cottage Antiques, Ringway, Cheshire.
Cottage Antiques, Southampton, Hants.
Cottage Antiques, Woburn, Beds. Wob. Ab. Ant. C.
Cottage Antiques, Worcester, Hereford and Worcs.
Cottage Antiques (1984) Ltd., Walsden, W. Yorks.
Cottage Antiques and Curios, Thirsk, N. Yorks.
Cottage Crafts Antiques, Congleton, Cheshire.
Cottage Curios, Allonby, Cumbria.
Cottage Style Antiques, Rochester, Kent.
Cotton, A., Lincoln, Lincs.
Cotton, B.D., Eastleach, Glos.
Cotton (Antiques), Joan, West Bridgford, Notts.
Cotton, J.S. and Mrs., London, W.1. (The Curio Shop).
Cotton Antiques and Fine Art, Nick, Watchet, Somerset.
Cottrell, A. & Mrs. A.E., Godalming, Surrey.
Cottrell Galleries, Andrew, Godalming, Surrey.
Coughton Galleries Ltd., Coughton, Warks.
Coulborn, P., Sutton Coldfield, W. Mids.
Coulborn and Sons, Thomas, Sutton Coldfield, W. Mids.
Coulson — Antiques, Peter, Fulbeck, Lincs.
Coulter Galleries, York, N. Yorks.
Country Antiques, Boroughbridge, N. Yorks.
Country Antiques, Defynnog, Powys, Wales.
Country Antiques, Kidwelly, Dyfed, Wales.
Country Antiques, Killearn, Stirling, Scot.
Country Antiques, Long Melford, Suffolk.
Country Antiques, Maiden Newton, Dorset.
Country Antiques, Market Bosworth, Leics.
Country Antiques Centre, Ilminster, Somerset.
Country Bygones and Antiques, Ipswich, Suffolk.
Country Clocks, Tring, Herts.
Country Cottage Bedsteads, Fyfield, Hants.
Country Cottage Furniture, Modbury, Devon.
Country Cottage Furniture, Totnes, Devon.
Country and Eastern, Norwich, Norfolk.
Country Furniture, Charlecote, Warks.
Country Furniture Shop, Penn, Bucks.
County House Antiques, Bungay, Suffolk.
Country House Antiques, Ludlow, Shrops.
Country Kitchen Antiques, Takeley, Essex.
Country Life Antiques, Bushey, Herts.
Country Life Antiques, Ludford, Lincs.
Country Life Antiques, Market Rasen, Lincs.
Country Life Antiques, Stow-on-the-Wold, Glos.
Country Life by Bursig, Arundel, W. Sussex.
Country Pine, Poulton-le-Fylde, Lancs.
Country Pine and Antiques, Sherborne, Dorset.
Country Pine Antiques (Pearce's Pieces), Thorpe-le-Soken, Essex.
Country Pine Ltd., London, N.W.1.
Country Pine Shop, The, West Haddon, Northants.
Country Seats, Cirencester, Glos.
Country Shop Antiques, Duns, Berwicks., Scot.

Country Shop Antiques, Walton-on-the-Hill and Tadworth, Surrey.
Country Style, Deal, Kent.
County Antiques, Sandgate, Kent.
Coupe, J. and J., Tuxford, Notts.
Course, Jane, London, S.W.3. Ant. Ant. Mkt.
Court Antiques (Richmond), Richmond, Gtr. London.
Court Curio Shop, Edinburgh, Midloth., Scot.
Court Gallery, The, East Molesey, Surrey.
Court House Antiques, Methwold, Norfolk.
Courtenay, R.W., Ramsey, I. of Man.
Courtney and Sons, Phillip, Hooton, Cheshire.
Courtney Ltd., Richard, London, S.W.3.
Courtney and Son, William, Birkenhead, Merseyside.
Courtyard Antiques, Hitchin, Herts.
Cousins and Son, E.W., Ixworth, Suffolk.
Cousins, S., Hereford, Hereford and Worcs.
Couts, B.P., Edinburgh, Midloth., Scot.
Couts Ltd., Paul, Edinburgh, Midloth., Scot.
Coutts, A.C., London, W.1. (Under Two Flags).
Cove, A., Windsor and Eton, Berks. (Studio 101).
Covent Garden Flea Market, London, W.C.2.
Coventry, R., Preston, Lancs. N.W. Ant. C.
Cowan, J., London, S.W.3. Ant. Ant. Mkt.
Cowan Antiques, Philip, Liverpool, Merseyside.
Cowan Antiques, Philip, Prestbury, Cheshire.
Coward Fine Silver, Timothy, Braunton, Devon.
Cowden Antiques, Tunbridge Wells, Kent.
Cowderoy Antiques, John, Eastbourne, E. Sussex.
Cowderoy, J.H., R., D.J. and R.A., Eastbourne, E. Sussex.
Cowe, Mrs. B., Dunkeld, Perths., Scot.
Cowell, J., Bath, Avon. (D. Howard) Gt. West. Ant. C.
Cowell and Sons, W.J., Preston, Lancs.
Cowfold Clocks, Cowfold, W. Sussex.
Cowley, I.H.R., Sandiacre, Derbys.
Cowley's Book Shop, Heather, Nottingham, Notts.
Cowling, Martin, Woburn, Beds. Wob. Ab. Ant. C.
Cowpland, Mr. and Mrs. D., Bexhill-on-Sea, E. Sussex.
Cox, Mrs., Leominster, Hereford and Worcs. L. Ant. Mkt.
Cox, A.H., Heath and Reach, Beds.
Cox, Mrs. A.M., Settle, N. Yorks.
Cox, A.T., Newark, Notts.
Cox, C., Bridport, Dorset.
Cox, Charles, Exeter, Devon.
Cox at College Gateway Bookshop, Claude, Ipswich, Suffolk.
Cox, C.D., Gillingham, Kent.
Cox, H. and B.V., Kelso, Roxburghs., Scot.
Cox, J., Colne, Lancs.
Cox, J., London, S.W.3. Chen. Gall.
Cox, Jane, Stamford, Lincs.
Cox, J.I., Settle, N. Yorks.
Cox, O.M. and R.D., Stamford, Lincs.

Crowther and Son Ltd., T., London, S.W.6.
Croydon and Sons Ltd., Ipswich, Suffolk.
Crozier, F.W. and G.R., Bishops Stortford, Herts.
Cruickshank, E.A., London, S.W.3. (Clarges Gallery).
Cry for the Moon, Haslemere, Surrey.
Cryer, J. and W. Newcomb, Berkeley, Glos.
Crypt Antiques, The, Burford, Oxon.
Crystal Ball, Carlisle, Cumbria.
Csakys Antiques, London, S.W.15.
Cubby Hole, The, Tunbridge Wells, Kent.
Cubitt, Mrs. A.B., Norwich, Norfolk.
Cubitt, Charles, Norwich, Norfolk.
Cull Antiques, Petersfield, Hants.
Cull, Phillip, London, W.1. B. St. Silv. Galls.
Cullen, A. and R.S., Hemel Hempstead, Herts.
Cullimore, Jill, Bath, Avon. Gt. West. Ant. C. Wed. Mkt.
Culverwell, C.T., Burnham-on-Sea, Somerset.
Cumberland Pine, Penrith, Cumbria.
Cumbley, G.R., King's Lynn, Norfolk
Cumming, A.J., Lewes, E. Sussex.
Cumming, J., London, W.C.1.
Cummings, R., Preston, Lancs. N.W. Ant. C.
Cunningham Antiques, E., Falmouth, Cornwall.
Cupboard Antiques, The, Amersham, Bucks.
Cura Antiques, London W.11.
Cura, D., London W.11.
Curbishley, John O., Knutsford, Cheshire.
Curbishley, John S., Stockport, Cheshire.
Curbishley, Peter A., Sandbach, Cheshire.
Curd, S., Goudhurst, Kent.
Curio Corner, Stourbridge, W. Mids.
Curio Corner Antiques, Huddersfield, W. Yorks.
Curio Cottage, Bingley, W. Yorks.
Curio Shop, The, London, W.1.
Curio Shop, Teignmouth, Devon.
Curios (St. Annes), St. Annes-on-Sea, Lancs.
Curiosites, Lancing, W. Sussex.
Curiosity, Ollerton, Notts.
Curiosity, Stockport, Cheshire.
Curiosity Antiques, Portscatho, Cornwall.
Curiosity Corner, Hacknall, Notts.
Curiosity Shop, The, Kelso, Roxbs., Scot.
Curiosity Shop, Lichfield, Staffs.
Curiosity Shop, The, Llandovery, Dyfed, Wales.
Curiosity Shop, The, Padstow, Cornwall.
Curiosity Shop, The, South Shields, Tyne & Wear.
Curiosity Shop, Wallington, Gtr. London.
Curiosity Shop & Alfreton Piano Co., Alfreton, Derbys.
Curiosity Shop, The, Military and Curio Supplies, Gloucester, Glos.
Curiosity Shoppe, Ripon, N. Yorks.
Curiotique, Leicester, Leics.
Currie, A., Edinburgh, Midloth., Scot. (Curio Corner).
Currie, Mrs. R., Glasgow, Lanarks., Scot. (Keep Sakes).
Curry, F. and P.V., Harrogate, N. Yorks. (The Saleroom.)

Curtis, D. and M., Bath, Avon. B. Ant. Mkt.
Curtis, G., Cheltenham, Glos. (Montpellier Clocks.)
Curtis, George, Cheltenham, Glos.
Curtis, Mrs. J., Maiden Newton, Glos.
Curtis, P. and Mrs. R., Torquay, Devon.
Cusack, M., Llanerchymedd, Gwynedd, Wales.
Cuss Clock Co. Ltd., The, London, S.W.1.
Cutler Antique & Collectors Fairs, Stancie, Alsager, Cheshire.
Cutler Antique and Collectors Fairs, Stancie, Nantwich, Cheshire.
Cutler Antique and Collectors Fairs, Stancie, Sutton Coldfield, W. Mids.
Cutler Street Antique Market, London, E.C.1.
Cutting, R. and M., Winchester, Hants.
Cutting, Mrs. T., Bury St. Edmunds, Suffolk.
Cwmgwili Mill, Carmarthen, Dyfed, Wales.

D

D. & G. Antiques, Newark, Notts.
D.J. Jewellery, Parkstone, Dorset.
D.M. Jewellers Ltd., Highcliffe, Dorset.
D. and S. Antiques, Stourbridge, W. Mids.
D. and V. Antiques, Newark, Notts.
Dade Antiques, A.F., Brighton, E. Sussex.
Dade, P.V., Redhill, Surrey.
Dades of Redhill, Redhill, Surrey.
Daedalus, London, S.E.7.
Dahl, R., Great Missenden, Bucks.
Dahl and Son, Great Missenden, Bucks.
Dahl, T., Great Missenden, Bucks.
Dalby, Mrs. J., London, S.W.3. Ant. Ant. Mkt.
Dalby, R., Wallasey, Merseyside.
Dale, John, London, W.11.
Dale Ltd., Peter, London, S.W.1.
Daleside Antiques, Harrogate, N. Yorks.
D'Alessandro and Bessant, London, W.8. Ant. Hyp.
D'Allesandro, Rocco, London S.W.6.
Dallas and Sons Ltd., Anthony, London, W.1.
Dalloe, Mrs. M., Husbands Bosworth, Leics.
Dalton Street Antiques, Birmingham, W. Midlands.
Daly, Peter, Winchester, Hants.
Dam Mill Antiques, Codsall, Staffs.
D'Amico Antiques Ltd., Norwich, Norfolk.
D'Amico Antiques Ltd., Terrington St. Clement, Norfolk.
Dando, Andrew, Bath, Avon.
Dando, G., Bath, Avon.
Daneby House Antiques, Priors Marston, Warks.
Danelagh Estates Ltd., Chobham, Surrey.
Daniel, A., London, N.1. (Heritage Antiques).
Daniel, A. and M., Harewood, W. Yorks.
Daniel Antiques, Clive, London, N.W.3.
Daniel, F., Maidenhead, Berks.
Daniel, Mrs. M., Thorp Arch, W. Yorks.
Daniel Antiques, Mavis, Thorp Arch, W. Yorks.
Daniell, J., Upton-on-Severn, Hereford and Worcs.

Day, Miss J.L., Farnham, Surrey.
Day and Son (Exports) Ltd., K.C. Burford, Oxon.
Day, M., London, W.1. (Burlington Paintings Ltd.)
Day Antiques, Michael, Eastbourne, E. Sussex.
Day Antiques, Michael, Stamford, Lincs.
Day, R.J., Eastbourne, E. Sussex.
Day, S., Burford, Oxon.
Day Ltd., Shirley, London, S.W.1.
Dazeley, R.A., Norwich, Norfolk. (Norwich Antique and Collectors Centre).
D'Este, Mrs. R., London, W.1. B. St. Ant. C.
De Courcy-Ireland, Polly, Winchester, Hants.
De Fresnes, The Baron, Galston, Ayr., Scot.
De Grey Antiques, Hull, N. Humberside.
De Havilland, Adele, London, W.1. B. St. Ant. C.
De Havilland (Antiques) Ltd., London, S.W.1.
De Jaeger, A., Canterbury, Kent.
De Juan, C., London, N.5.
De Kort, E.J., Bembridge, Isle of Wight.
De la Fuerte, London, N.W.8. Alf. Ant. Mkt.
De Lotz, P.G., London, N.W.3.
De Lucy Antiques, Alresford, Hants.
De Lucy Antiques, Alresford, Hants.
De Molen Ltd., Blackpool, Lancs.
De Montfort, Robertsbridge, E. Sussex.
De Monti Ladds, Margaret, Woburn, Beds. Wob. Ab. Ant. C.
De Rin, V., London, S.W.3 (Rogers de Rin).
De Saye Hutton Antiques, A., Salisbury, Wilts.
Deacon, Gerald, Bath, Avon.
Deacon, S., London, W.1. B. St. Ant. C.
Deakin, J.R., Seaford, E. Sussex.
Dean, Mrs. B., Spalding, Lincs.
Dean Antiques, David, Settle, N. Yorks.
Dean Gallery, The Newcastle-upon-Tyne, Tyne and Wear.
Dean, M. and H., London, W.C.1.
Dean Antiques, Margery, Colchester, Essex.
Dean, R. and S., Castle Bytham, Lincs.
Deane Antiques, Taunton, Somerset.
Deane Antiques, Whaley Bridge, Derbys.
Deane Antiques, Graham, Brighton, E. Sussex.
Dean's Antiques, Spalding, Lincs.
Dearden, M. and S., East Pennard, Somerset.
Deasy Ltd., Mike, Brighton, E. Sussex.
Deasy, M. and P., Brighton, E. Sussex.
Decor Galleries, Southport, Merseyside.
Deeley, D.P. and B., Stourbridge, W. Mids.
Deeley, R., Stow-on-the-Wold, Glos.
Deering, Mr. and Mrs. H.D., Holywood, Co. Down, N. Ireland.
Deerstalker Antiques, Whitchurch, Bucks.
Deeva, London, W.1. B. St. Ant. C.
Defferary, Guy, Sturry, Kent.
Defresne, P., London, S.W.3. Ant. Ant. Mkt.
Defty, G.H., Hertford, Herts.
Deighton, Bell and Co., Cambridge, Cambs.
Deja Vu, Macclesfield, Cheshire.
Del Grosso, Joe, London, N.W.8. Alf. Ant. Mkt.

Delaney Antiques, London N.1.
Delaney, W., London N.1.
Dela-Ware, Bath, Avon.
Dela-Ware, Radstock, Avon.
Delawood Antiques, Hunstanton, Norfolk.
Delehar, London, W.11.
Delehar, Peter, London, W.11.
Delf Antiques, Sandwich, Kent.
Delieb Antiques Ltd., London, N.W.11.
Delieb, E., London, N.W.11.
Delightful Muddle, The, London, S.W.1.
Dell, O.J., Cheltenham, Glos. (Cocoa).
Dellar, R., Rye, E. Sussex.
Dellow, H., Bath, Avon. (Dela-Ware.)
Dellow, H., Radstock, Avon.
Delmas, Hurst Green, E. Sussex.
Delomosne and Son Ltd., London, W.8.
Delta Antiques, Liverpool, Merseyside.
Demas, London, W.1.
Demetzy Books, London, W.11.
Dempsey, J. and B., Hindon, Wilts.
Den of Antiquity, Glasgow, Lanarks., Scot.
Den of Antiquity, The, Hythe, Kent.
Den of Antiquity, London, S.W.20.
Den of Antiquity, Nether Stowey, Somerset.
Dench, J.W., Worksop, Notts.
Denham Gallery, John, London, N.W.6.
Denis, Rose, Sheringham, Norfolk.
Denisa, the Lady Newborough, London, W.1.
Denison Antiques, Manchester, Lancs.
Denley-Hill, S.K., Cardiff, S. Glam. Wales. (Manor House Fine Arts).
Denney, L., London, W.11. G. Port. (Lorenz John).
Denning Antiques, Guildford, Surrey.
Dennis, A., Newark, Notts.
Dennis, A.T., Y.M. and S.T., Hastings, E. Sussex.
Dennis (Books), C.J., Brearton, N. Yorks.
Dennis, P. and R., Berkeley, Glos.
Dennis, Richard, London, W.8.
Dennison, Beverley Patrick, Ambleside, Cumbria.
Dennison, D.H., Lewes, E. Sussex.
Dennison and Son, H.P., Lewes, E. Sussex.
Denny Ltd., Colin, London, S.W.3.
Denton Antiques, London S.E.26.
Denton Antiques, London, W.1.
Denton (Antiques) J., Luton, Beds.
Denton, M. and M., London, W.1.
Denton-Ford, A.H., Long Melford, Suffolk.
Denver House Antiques & Collectables, Burford, Oxon.
Denver Antiques, Peter, Bournemouth, Dorset.
Derby Antique Centre, Derby, Derbys.
Derby Antiques Market, Derby, Derbys.
Derby House Antiques, Torquay, Devon.
Derbyshire Antiques Ltd., Poynton, Cheshire.
Derbyshire, R.C. and M.T., Poynton, Cheshire.
Derbyshire Clocks, Glossop, Derbys.
Dereham Antiques, East Dereham, Norfolk.
Derham Ltd., John, Earsham, Norfolk.
Derwent Antiques, Cockermouth, Cumbria.
Designs on Pine, Lincoln, Lincs.
Desire Attire, Bournemouth, Dorset.

Desk Shop, The, Oxford, Oxon.
Desmonde, Kay, London, W.8.
Deuchar, A.S. and A.W.N., Perth, Perths.,
  Scot.
Deuchar and Son, A.S., Perth, Perths., Scot.
Deutsch Antiques, H. and W., London, W.8.
Deverall, Ivan, R., Uckfield, E. Sussex.
Devereux, J., Oxford, Oxon.
Deveson, T. and H., Kingston-upon-Thames,
  Gtr. London.
Devlin, R., Glasgow, Lanarks., Scot.
  (Yesteryear Antiques), Vict. Vill.
Devon House Clocks, Warwick, Warks.
Devonshire Gallery, The, Torquay, Devon.
Devonshire House Antiques, Bath, Avon.
Devonshire House Antiques, Settle, N. Yorks.
Dew, Roderick, Eastbourne, E. Sussex.
Dewar, J. and J., Edinburgh, Midloth., Scot.
Dewar, R.W. and E.V., Clacton-on-Sea,
  Essex.
Dewart, Glen, London, S.W.3. Chen. Gall.
Dewdney, J.M., Farnborough, Gtr. London.
Dewdney, Mrs. V., Bristol, Avon. (Antique
  Beds).
Dewenny, Mrs. M., London, S.W.3. Ant.
  Ant. Mkt.
Dharia, P. and N., Wingham, Kent.
Di Marco, Louis and Moira, Crieff, Perths.,
  Scot.
Di Michele, E., London, W.11. (E. and A.
  Antiques).
Dial House Antiques, Kelvedon, Essex.
Dial House Antiques, Marnhull, Dorset.
Dial Marylebone, The, London, W.1.
Diamond and Son., Harry, Brighton,
  E. Sussex.
Diamond, R. and H., Brighton, E. Sussex.
Dias, S.A., Whyteleafe, Surrey.
Dibley Antiques, Moylegrove, Dyfed, Wales.
Dibley, J. and P., Moylegrove, Dyfed,
  Wales.
Dick, G., Hull, N. Humberside.
Dickens Antiques, Gillingham, Kent.
Dickens Curios, Frinton, Essex.
Dickenson, A.S.R., Ashtead, Surrey.
Dickenson, Bill, Ironbridge, Shrops.
Dickenson and Thomas (Antiques),
  Stamford, Lincs.
Dicker, Pauline, Swansea, W. Glam., Wales.
  Ant. Centre.
Dickins, F.N. & J.B., London, W.1.
Dickins, H.C., London, W.1.
Dickinson, Bernard, Gargrave, N. Yorks.
Dickinson, D., Manchester, Lancs.
  (Dickinson Deansgreen Gallery).
Dickinson, D. and B., Bath, Avon.
Dickinson Deansgreen Gallery, Manchester,
  Lancs.
Dickinson, Mrs. E.C., Stoke Golding, Leics.
Dickinson, S.G., D., N.W. and Mrs. E.M.,
  Bath, Avon.
Dickson, R., Bath, Avon. (Abbey Galleries).
Dickson Antiques Ltd., Robert, London,
  S.W.3.
Diddy Box, The, London, N.W.6.
Digby, Richard, London, W.1.
Dike, L., Bristol, Avon. (Bristol Trade
  Antiques).

Dilger, C., Oakham, Leics.
Dilliway, B. and J, Tunbridge Wells, Kent.
  (White Horse Antiques).
Dimmer, I.M. and N.C.S., Cheltenham, Glos.
  (Martin and Co. Ltd.)
Dimoch, Annette, London, N.W.8. Alf. Ant.
  Mkt.
Dining Room Shop, The, London, S.W.13.
Dinitto, D., London, S.W.10.
Dinnis, C., Felsted, Essex.
Directmoor Ltd., Oakamoor, Staffs.
Dis and Dat, Market Weighton,
  N. Humberside.
Discoveries, Hampton Wick, Gtr. London.
Discovery Fine Arts Ltd., York, N. Yorks.
Disley, T.H. and M.G., Coggeshall, Essex.
Diss Antiques, Diss, Norfolk.
Ditheridge, C.L. & J.K., Burgh-le-Marsh,
  Lincs.
Dix Antiques, Dumfries, Dumfries., Scot.
Dix, S., London, S.W.6. (Spice.)
Dixon, A.C.J. and B.M., London, W.11.
Dixon Ltd., C.J. and A.J., Bridlington,
  N. Humberside.
Dixon, C.P., Bridgnorth, Shrops.
Dixon, J. and R., London, S.W.14.
Dixon, K.M., L.A., P. and C., Stow-on-the-
  Wold, Glos.
Dixon, P., London, S.W.6. (Chelsea Clocks
  and Antiques).
Dixon, T.C., Bamburgh, Northumb.
Dixon's Antique Market, London, S.W.14.
Dobbs, R.H. and R.J., Hertford, Herts.
Dobie Antiques Ltd., J., Grantham, Lincs.
Doble, I., Exeter, Devon.
Dobney, D.A., Ingoldsby, Lincs.
Dockerill Ltd., A. and R., London, S.W.15.
Dodd, J., London, W.8.
Dodd, Maurice, Carlisle, Cumbria.
Dodd, Peter and Daniele, London, W.11.
Doddington House Antiques, Doddington,
  Cambs.
Dodge, S., Sherborne, Dorset.
Dodge and Son, Sherborne, Dorset.
Dodington Antiques, Whitchurch, Shrops.
Dodo Old Advertising, London, W.11.
Dodo Antiques, St. Helier, Jersey, C.I.
Dodson Antiques, Rodney, Portsmouth,
  Hants.
Dodsworth, N.J. and C.S., Spennithorne,
  N. Yorks.
Doe, M., Liss, Hants.
D'Offay, Anthony, London, W.1.
Doggett, F.C., Somerton, Somerset.
Dolan, G.M., Otley, W. Yorks.
Dolby, A. and S. McGurk, London, W.1.
  G. Mews.
Dolleris, A.J., London, S.W.15.
Dollin and Daines, Bath, Avon.
Doll's House, The, Ambergate, Derbys.
Doll's House Antiques, The, Sheffield,
  S. Yorks.
Dolls House Toys Ltd., The, London, W.C.2.
Dolls and Toys of Yesteryear, Hungerford,
  Berks.
Dolphin Antiques, Cambridge, Cambs.
Dolphin Antiques, St. Albans, Herts.
Dolphin Arcade, London, W.11.

Dolphin Coins, London, N.W.3.
Dolphyn, Coggeshall, Essex.
Dolton, Mrs. R., Hemel Hempstead, Herts.
Dolwen Antiques, Rhos-on-Sea, Clwyd, Wales.
Dombey, Philip and Bernard, London, W.8.
Dome Antiques (Exports) Ltd., London, N.1.
Domus, Castle Cary, Somerset.
Donaldson, A.F., Aberdeen, Aberd., Scot.
Donay Antiques, London, N.1.
Donay, N., London, N.1.
Doncaster, A.B., Colchester, Essex.
Doncaster Sales and Exchange, Doncaster, S. Yorks.
Donelly, J., Whaley Bridge, Derbys.
Donn Gallery, Henry, Whitefield, Lancs.
Donnelly, D.E., Colchester, Essex.
Donnelly, R.M., London, S.W.3 (Ledger Antiques Ltd.).
Donner Ltd., Chepstow, Gwent, Wales.
Donoghue, C., London, S.W.3. (Nina) Ant. Ant. Mkt.
Donohoe, London, W.1. G. Mews.
Donovan, J., London, W.11 (A.M. Web).
Dorchester Antiques, Dorchester, Dorset.
Dorchester Galleries, Dorchester-on-Thames, Oxon.
Dorking Antiques, Dorking, Surrey.
Dorking Desk Shop, The, Dorking, Surrey.
Dorling, T., Truro, Cornwall.
Dormy House Antiques, Marlborough, Wilts.
Dorosti, R., Ramsgate, Kent.
Dorothy's Antiques, Sheringham, Norfolk.
D'Orsai Ltd., Sebastian, London, W.C.1.
Doubleday, S., Colchester, Essex.
Douch, A., London, W.1.
Dougall, R., Bath, Avon. Gt. West. Ant. C.
Douglas, G., Marple Bridge, Cheshire.
Douglas, R.M., Dorking, Surrey.
Douglas, W.H., Cardiff, S. Glam., Wales.
Douglass, Mrs. A.G., Hythe, Kent.
Douthwaite, C. and G., Bradford, W. Yorks.
Douwes Fine Art, London, S.W.1.
Douwma (Prints and Maps) Ltd., Robert, London, W.C.2.
Dove Antiques, The, Debenham, Suffolk.
Dove Antiques, Harrogate, N. Yorks. W. Pk. Ant. Pav.
Dove Antiques, London, S.W.13.
Dove House Antiques, Cambridge, Cambs.
Doveridge House of Neachley, Albrighton, Shrops.
Dower House Antiques, Kendal, Cumbria.
Dowling and Bray, Looe, Cornwall.
Dowlish Wake Antiques, Dowlish Wake, Somerset.
Down, G., Barnstaple, Devon.
Downes, A., Southampton, Hants.
Downes, A.G. and E.A., Wallasey, Merseyside.
Downes Antiques, Brian and Angela, Bath, Avon.
Downes, L. and D.W., Lincoln, Lincs.
Downing, Peter, Shingle Street, Suffolk.
Downworth, D., Ashton-under-Lyne, Lancs.
Downworth, D., Manchester, Lancs. (Tameside Antiques.)
Downworth, M., Bath, Avon. Gt. West. A. C. Wed. Mkt.

Dowzall, Mrs., London, W.1. B. St. Ant. C.
Doyle Antiques, Bawtry, S. Yorks.
Doyle, A.G., Bawtry, S. Yorks.
Doyle, F.A., Bedford, Beds.
Doyle Antiques, James R., Brighton, E. Sussex.
D'Oyly, N.H., Saffron Walden, Essex.
Dragon Antiques, Harrogate, N. Yorks.
Dragon Antiques, Petersfield, Hants.
Dragons of Walton St. Ltd., London, S.W.3.
Drake, B., Harrogate, N. Yorks. W. Pk. Ant. Pav.
Drake Fine Prints, Christopher, Northlew, Devon.
Drake, L., Weymouth, Dorset.
Drawers, Buckfastleigh, Devon.
Drawing Room, The, Lewes, E. Sussex.
Draycott, J., London, W.C.2.
Draysey, Robert L., London, S.E.1.
Drayson, A., London, N.W.8.
Drayton, M., Formby, Merseyside.
Dreams, London, N.W.1.
Drecker, L.C.M., London, W.11 (The Witch Ball).
Dreezer, Alan & Karen Mendelsohn, London W.1. G. Mews.
Dress the Part, Billericay, Essex.
Driffold Gallery, Sutton Coldfield, W. Mids.
Dring, C. and K.E., Lincoln, Lincs.
Driver, Mrs. B., Arundel, W. Sussex.
Dronfield Antiques, Sheffield, S. Yorks.
Drop Dial Antiques, Bolton, Lancs.
Drown, William R., London, S.W.1.
Drucker, Leon, London, N.W.2.
Drummer Antiques, South Molton, Devon.
Drummer's Antique Centre, South Molton, Devon.
Drummond, D.B., London, W.C.2 (Pleasures of Past Times).
Drummond, J.N., London, N.W.8.
Drummond-Hoy, C. & M., Nottingham, Notts.
Drury, John, Colchester, Essex.
Drury, P., Conway, Gwynedd, Wales.
Drury, Mrs. P., Longfield, Kent.
Dryburgh, B., Wells next-the-Sea, Norfolk.
Dryden Ltd., Peter, Teignmouth, Devon.
Drysdale, A.F., (J. Thomson and A. Williamson Ltd.,) Edinburgh, Midloth., Scot.
Drysdale, Mrs. S., Crieff, Perths., Scot.
Du Cros, Mr. and Mrs. J., Liss, Hants.
Du Cros Antiques, J., Liss, Hants.
Du Feu, Mrs. R.S., St. Ouen, Jersey, C.I.
Du Monceau, A., Cirencester, Glos.
Dubiner, M., London, W.1 (Paul Bennett).
Ducker, Mrs. E., Doncaster, S. Yorks.
Duckworth, V.K., N. and M., Preston, Lancs.
Duckworths Antiques, Preston, Lancs.
Dudley, A.F. and J.A., Newmarket, Suffolk.
Dudley, A.F. and J.A., Reach, Cambs.
Dudley's Antiques and Home Interiors, Newmarket, Suffolk.
Dudley's Antiques and Home Interiors, Reach, Cambs.
Duff Antiques, George, Edinburgh, Midloth., Scot.
Duffield Antiques, Duffield, Derbys.

Duffy Antiques, A.M., Wallasey, Merseyside.
Duffy Country Style, London N.W.8. Alf. Ant. Mkt.
Duffy, J.L., Bath, Avon. Gt. West. A. C. Wed. Mkt.
Dugdale, J.V., Mawnan Smith, Cornwall.
Dugdale, P. and T., London, N.1.
Dugdale's Antique Warehouse, London, N.1.
Duggan, J.A., Blackburn, Lancs.
Duggan, J.J., Ipswich, Suffolk (R.W. Paul).
Duggans, Blackburn, Lancs.
Duigan, H., Birmingham, W. Mids. (Fine Pine.)
Duke, H., Abersoch, Gwynedd, Wales.
Duke, H.P., Newport, Essex.
Duke Mrs. R., Lewes, E. Sussex.
Dukeries Antiques, Tuxford, Notts.
Dulverton Antique Centre, Dulverton, Somerset.
Dunbar, Mrs. A.G., Linlithgow, West. Loth., Scot.
Duncalfe Antiques, N.J., Harrogate, N. Yorks.
Duncan, G.P., Birkenhead, Merseyside.
Duncan House Antiques, Woburn, Beds. Wob. Ab. Ant. C.
Duncan, W., Camborne, Cornwall.
Dunedin Antiques Ltd., Edinburgh, Midloth., Scot.
Dunford, C., and J., Uckfield, E. Sussex.
Dunkeld Interiors, Dunkeld, Perths., Scot.
Dunkley Carpets and Pictures, Liss, Hants.
Dunlinson, Barry, St. Leonards-on-Sea, E. Sussex.
Dunluce Antiques, Bushmills, Co. Antrim, N. Ireland.
Dunn, A., Bath, Avon. Gt. West. A.C. Wed. Mkt.
Dunn, G.J., Bath, Avon. B. Ant. Mkt.
Dunn, Mark, London, N.W.8. Alf. Ant. Mkt.
Dunsdale Lodge Antiques, Westerham, Kent.
Dunster, Mrs. C., Guildford, Surrey.
Dunster Antiques, K.W., Staines, Surrey.
Dunworth, M., Dulverton, Somerset.
Dunworth, M., Taunton, Somerset.
Dupont Galleries, Brighton, E. Sussex.
Dupont and Fils, Madame J., London, W.C.2.
Dupré, Sophie, Calne, Wilts.
Duran, S., London, N.1. (Sekmet Galleries.)
Durante and Ephrain Garcia, Anthony, London, S.W.3. Ant. Ant. Mkt.
Durham Furniture, Langley Moor, Durham.
Durham, M.L. and S.R., Birmingham, W. Mids. (The Old Clock Shop.)
Duriez, L., Exeter, Devon.
Durn, J.D., South Molton, Devon.
Durose Antiques, Ilkley, Derbys.
Durose, M.D., Ilkeston, Derbys.
Durrant, D. and E., Stockport, Cheshire.
Durrant, Mrs. M., Bristol, Avon. Clift. Ant. Mkt.
Dusty Corner, Middleton, Lancs.
Dutch Connexion, Manchester, Lancs.
Duveen Antiques, Fordingbridge, Hants.
Dwyer, Miss S., London, S.W.3. (T. Giorgi.) Ant. Ant. Mkt.

Dycheling Antiques, Ditchling, E. Sussex.
Dyer and Follett Ltd., Alverstoke, Hants.
Dyer, W.G., Hayle, Cornwall.
Dyer and Sons, W., Hayle, Cornwall.
Dyer and Son, W., Redruth, Cornwall.
Dyfri Antiques, Llandovery, Dyfed, Wales.
Dyke Antiques, Peter, Boughton, Kent.
Dylan's Bookshop, Swansea, W. Glam., Wales.
Dymond, J., Meshaw, Devon.
Dyson and Sons, C.G., Market Weighton, N. Humberside.
Dyson (Antique Weapons), D.W., Huddersfield, W. Yorks.
Dyson, Mrs. E.C.P., Caernarfon, Gwynedd, Wales.
Dyson, F.H., Burton-on-Trent, Staffs.
Dyson, K., London, S.W.13.
Dyson, S., Ollerton, Notts.
Dytch, Mr. and Mrs. D., Dunkeld, Perths., Scot.
Dyte Exports Ltd., Colin, Highbridge, Somerset.
Dyte Antiques, T.M., Highbridge, Somerset.

E

E. and A. Antiques, London, W.11.
E. and A. Antiques, Woburn, Beds. Wob. Ab. Ant. C.
E.H.W. and Co. Ltd., London, W.C.1.
Eagle House, Wallingford, Oxon.
Eagle House Antiques Market, Midhurst, W. Sussex.
Eaglesham Antiques Ltd., Eaglesham, Renfrews., Scot.
Ealing Gallery, London, W.5.
Eames, L., E. and S., Hemel Hempstead, Herts.
Eardisley Antiques, Leominster, Hereford and Worcs. L. Ant. C.
Earl, P. and R., Halstead, Essex.
Earl Shilton Antiques, Earl Shilton, Leics.
Earle, A., Wilton, Wilts.
Easden, G. and M.H., Chislehurst, Gtr. London.
Easdens Antiques, Chislehurst, Gtr. London.
East Bridgford Antiques Centre, East Bridgford, Notts.
East, F., Anstey, Leics.
East Gates Antiques, Colchester, Essex.
East Gates Antiques, London, N.W.8. Alf. Ant. Mkt.
East-Asia Co, London, N.W.1.
East Kent Antiques, New Romney, Kent.
Eastbourne Antique Market, Eastbourne, E. Sussex.
Eastbourne Fine Art, Eastbourne, E. Sussex.
Easterby, Betty, Longton, Lancs.
Eastgate Antique Centre, Lincoln, Lincs.
Easton, F.M. and A., Reading, Berks.
Eaton (Booksellers) Ltd., Peter, London, W.11.
Eaton (Booksellers) Ltd., Peter, Weedon, Bucks.
Eaton, P. and P., Windsor and Eton, Berks.
Eatons of Eton Ltd., Windsor and Eton, Berks.
Eavis, Caroline, London, S.W.3. Ant. Ant. Mkt.

Eccles Used furniture and Antique Centre, Eccles, Lancs.
Eccleston, D. and P., Manchester, Lancs.
Eckersley, D., Woolhampton, Berks.
Eddelin, Mrs. A.M., Southend-on-Sea, Essex.
Eddelin, F.H., Southend-on-Sea, Essex.
Eddy, P. and S.N., Leominster, Hereford and Worcs.
Eddy, V.A., St. Ives, Cornwall.
Ede Ltd., Charles, London, W.1.
Edelstein at Robin Symes, Annamaria, London, S.W.1.
Eden, Robin and Matthew, Corsham, Wilts.
Eden, R.C., Carmarthen, Dyfed, Wales.
Eden, R. and M., Woodstock, Oxon.
Edgar Gallery, Owen, London, S.W.1.
Edgbaston Gallery, Birmingham, W. Mids.
Edge, Bryan, Leominster, Hereford and Worcs. L. Ant. Mkt.
Edgington, A. and D., Blandford Forum, Dorset.
Edgware Antiques, Edgware, Gtr. London.
Edinburgh Coin Shop, Edinburgh, Midloth., Scot.
Editions Graphiques Gallery, London, W.1.
Edmonds Ltd, D.H., Brighton, E. Sussex.
Edmonstone, Lady J., Killearn, Stirling, Scot.
Edmunds, Andrew, London, W.1.
Edmunds, V. and J., Bury St. Edmunds, Suffolk.
Edward and Victoria Antiques, London, S.E.10.
Edwardian Antiques, Newton Abbot, Devon. N.A. Ant. C.
Edwardian Shop, The, Ipswich, Suffolk.
Edwards, B., Bradiford, Devon.
Edwards Antique Exports, Brian, Lower Kinnerton, Cheshire.
Edwards, B.H. Lower Kinnerton, Cheshire.
Edwards, D., Long Melford, Suffolk.
Edwards, Mrs. J., Dunchurch, Warks.
Edwards, K., London, W.1. B. St. Ant. C.
Edwards Antiques, Keith D., Kendal, Cumbria.
Edwards, Martin, London, W.11.
Edwards, Mrs. M.D., Worthing, W. Sussex.
Edwards, M.G., Lyonshall, Hereford and Worcs.
Edwards, R., Upminster, Gtr. London.
Edwards, W.G., Aberdeen, Aberd., Scot.
Edwick, Peter and Audrey, Layer Marney, Essex.
Eekhout Gallery, Brockdish, Norfolk.
Eekhout, R.S., Brockdish, Norfolk.
Egan, Amy, Skipton, N. Yorks.
Egan, T.M., Leicester, Leics.
Eichler, R.J. and Mrs. Whitchurch, Bucks.
Eisler, R.J. and D.M., Wendover, Bucks.
Ekstein, L., London, S.W.1.
Ekstein Ltd., M., London, S.W.1.
Elden Antiques, Kirk Deighton, N. Yorks.
Eldridge, B., London, E.C.1.
Eldridge Antiques, Edmund, Tonbridge, Kent.
Eldridge, E.A.W., Tonbridge, Kent.
Eldridge London and Co., London, E.C.1.
Eleanor Antiques, Warwick, Warks. Smith St. A.C.
Elefantessa, London, W.1. G. Mews.

Elena and Peter, London, N.W.8. Alf. Ant. Mkt.
Elgin Antiques, London, W.11.
Elian, C., London, W.1. (Jadis.)
Elias Antiques, J.G., Dorking, Surrey.
Elicha, Jacqueline, London, W.1. G. Ant. Mkt.
Elichaoff Oriental, London, N.5.
Eliot Antiques, Stanford Dingley, Berks.
Elithorn, A. and S., London, N.W.5.
Elizabethans, Fareham, Hants.
Elizabeth's & Son, Ulverston, Cumbria.
Elkington Antiques, Doreen, Adderley, Shrops.
Elkington, Mrs. D.E., Adderley, Shrops.
Ellesmere House Antiques, Whitchurch, Shrops.
Ellington, R.J.R., Bangor-on-Dee, Clwyd, Wales.
Ellingworth, M.K. and J.S., Pershore, Hereford and Worcs.
Elliot, R.J., Southampton, Hants.
Elliott, C., Alcester, Warks.
Elliott, Colin, Cheltenham, Glos.
Elliott, C.R., Eastbourne, E. Sussex.
Elliott, E., Hexham, Northumbs.
Elliott, L., Bath, Avon. Gt. West. A.C. Wed. Mkt.
Elliott, Mrs. P., Glastonbury, Somerset.
Elliott and Scholz Antiques, Eastbourne, E. Sussex.
Ellis Antiques, Donald, Edinburgh, Midloth., Scot.
Ellis Antiques, D.G. and C.M., Edinburgh, Midloth., Scot.
Ellis, D.W., London, W.11.
Ellis, J., Birmingham, W. Mids. (The Original Choice.)
Ellis, John, Sheffield, S. Yorks.
Ellis Antiques, Tony, London, N.5.
Elm House Antiques, Haddington, E. Loth., Scot.
Elm Tree Antiques, Flaxton, N. Yorks.
Elmarko, London, W.1. G. Mews.
Elmerside Ltd., London, S.W.1.
Elmes Antiques, Margaret, Denham Village, Bucks.
Elmore, Petersfield, Hants.
Elphick, P. and E., Reepham, Norfolk.
Elsies Antiques (and Junk), Bishops Waltham, Hants.
Elsom Antiques, Pamela, Ashbourne, Derbys.
Elson, Mrs. P., Swansea, W. Glam., Wales. Ant. Centre.
Elton, D.L., Littleborough, Lancs.
Elton, S.P., Beckenham, Gtr. London.
Elwin, A., Dorchester, Dorset.
Elwood, Mrs. S., Lowestoft, Suffolk.
Emanouel Antiques Ltd., London, W.1.
Emanuel, D., London, S.W.13.
Embden, K.B., London, W.C.2 (Anchor Antiques Ltd.).
Emerald Isle Books, Belfast, N. Ireland.
Emerson, I., Armagh, Co. Armagh, N. Ireland.
Emerson, S., London, S.W.3. Ant. Ant. Mkt.
Emery, Valérie, London, W.C.2 (Travis and Emery).

Emperor Antiques Centre, Bexley, Gtr. London.
Empire Antiques, Sandwich, Kent.
Emporium, The, Dunblane, Perths., Scot.
Emporium of Age and Art, Annfield Plain, Durham.
Emscote Antiques, Warwick, Warks.
Ena Antiques, London, N.W.8. Alf. Ant. Mkt.
Enchanted Aviary, The, Long Melford, Suffolk.
End of Day, London, N.W.6.
Endeavour Antiques, Saltburn, Cleveland.
Enfield Corner Cupboard, Enfield, Gtr. London.
England and Sons, A.W., Stroud, Glos.
England, F.J. and S., Leek, Staffs.
England's Gallery, Leek, Staffs.
English Heritage, Bridgnorth, Shrops.
English Street Furniture Company, The, Redhill, Surrey.
English, Toby, Wallingford, Oxon. L. Arc.
Enloc Antiques, Colne, Lancs.
Enos, Capt and Mrs. A.C., Cardiff, S. Glam., Wales. (Time on Your Hands).
Enstone, G., Deddington, Oxon.
Epping Galleries, Epping, Essex.
Epping Saturday Market, Epping, Essex.
Eprile, R., Edinburgh, Midloth., Scot. (Royal Mile Curios.)
Erbrick, T., London, N.W.8. Alf. Ant. Mkt.
Errington Antiques, Newcastle-under-Lyme, Staffs.
Errington, G.K., Newcastle-under-Lyme, Staffs.
Errol Antiques, Errol, Perths., Scot.
Eskenazi, J.E., London, W.1.
Eskenazi Ltd., London, W.1.
Esme's Antiques, Alsager, Cheshire.
Essenhigh, Mrs. J., Hexham, Northumb.
Essex Antiques, Richard, Bristol, Avon.
Ester Antiques, London, N.5.
Estevez, G.J., Addingham, W. Yorks.
Estling, Mrs. G., Dowlish Wake, Somerset.
Etceteras Antiques, Seaton, Devon.
Etheridge, B., Burford, Oxon.
Etherington, G., Hull, N. Humberside.
Ethos Gallery, Clitheroe, Lancs.
Etna Antiques, London, W.8.
Eton Antique Bookshop, Windsor and Eton, Berks.
Eton Gallery Antiques, Windsor and Eton, Berks.
Eureka Antiques, Sale, Cheshire.
Euston House Galleries and Roma Antiques, Llandrindod Wells, Powys, Wales.
Evans, B. and Mrs. P., Burford, Oxon.
Evans, Mr. and Mrs. D.G., Brecon, Powys, Wales
Evans, D. and N. Alresford, Hants.
Evans and Evans, Alresford, Hants.
Evans, E., Barmouth, Gwynedd, Wales.
Evans, Mrs. M., Llangollen, Clwyd, Wales.
Evans, Mollie, Richmond, Gtr. London.
Evans, M., Stratford-upon-Avon, Warks.
Evans, Patricia, London, S.W.3. Ant. Ant. Mkt.
Evans, Mrs. S., Harrogate, N. Yorks. (Cottage Antiques.)

Evans, Stewart, Malpas, Cheshire.
Evans, S.J., Reading, Berks.
Evanson, P., London, S.W.6.
Eve, J., Cambridge, Cambs. (Gabor Cossa Antiques.)
Eve, S., Sudbury, Suffolk.
Evenden, R., Eastbourne, E. Sussex.
Eve's Lace, London, S.W.3. Ant. Ant. Mkt.
Everitt, E.J., Norton, Suffolk.
Evers, Georgina, Frome, Somerset.
Everyday Antiques, Laleham, Surrey.
Eves Casket, Wareham, Dorset.
Evonne, London, W.1. G. Ant. Mkt.
Ewart, A.J. and Mrs. G., Stow-on-the-Wold, Glos.
Ewart, Gavina and A.J., Broadway, Hereford and Worcs.
Ewen, D., London, W.11.
Ewer, William, London, W.1. G. Ant. Mkt.
Ewhurst Gallery, Ramsdell, Hants.
Ewing, J.F., London, S.W.19.
Exeter Antique Wholesalers, Exeter, Devon.
Exeter Rare Books, Exeter, Devon.
Extence Antiques, Teignmouth, Devon.
Extence, T.E. and L.E., Teignmouth, Devon.
Eyles Antiques, Joan, Boroughbridge, N. Yorks.
Eyles, J.M. and J.C.H., Boroughbridge, N. Yorks.
Eyre, G., London, W.1. (Eyre and Greig)
Eyre and Greig Ltd., London, W.1.

F

Faber, E., London, W.C.1.
Facade, The, London, W.11.
Fagin, Mr., London, E.11.
Fagin's Antiques, Exeter, Devon.
Fagin's Antiques, Exmouth, Devon.
Fagin's Phonograph Emporium, London, N.5.
Fair Deal Antiques, Mansfield, Notts.
Fair, D.P., Hockley Heath, W. Mids.
Fairbairn, Mrs. R., Berwick-on-Tweed, Northumb.
Fairbarns, M.B., Cranbrook, Kent.
Fairclough, L., Preston, Lancs. N.W. Ant. C.
Fairfax Antiques, London, S.W.6.
Fairfax Fireplaces, Bath, Avon. Gt. West. Ant. C.
Fairfax Fireplaces, Langley Burrell, Wilts.
Fairfax, Miss J., Bath, Avon. Gt West Ant. C.
Fairfax, J., Langley Burrell, Wilts.
Fairfax, J., London, S.W.6, (Fairfax Antiques.)
Fairfield, Mrs. J., Newtownards, Co. Down, N. Ireland.
Fairfields Antique Cellars, Newtownards, Co. Down, N. Ireland.
Fairhurst Gallery, London, S.W.6.
Fairhurst Gallery, The, Norwich, Norfolk.
Fairhurst, M., London, S.W.6.
Fairings, Grassington, N. Yorks.
Fairings, The, Harrogate, N. Yorks.
Fairman (Carpets) Ltd., Jack, London, W.11.
Faithfull Antiques, Philip, Boughton, Kent.
Fakenham Antique Centre, Fakenham, Norfolk.

Forman Piccadilly Ltd., London, W.1.
Format of Birmingham Ltd., Birmingham,
W. Mids.
Formby Antiques, Formby, Merseyside.
Forrer, M., Marlborough, Wilts.
Forrest and Co., E.B., Edinburgh, Midloth.,
Scot.
Forrest and Co. (Jewellers) Ltd., James,
Glasgow, Lanarks., Scot.
Forrest and Son, P.H., London, S.E.1. Ber.
Ant. Whse.
Forrest, R., Edinburgh, Midloth., Scot.
(Artisan)
Forster, B., London, S.W.1. (M. Ekstein
Ltd.)
Forster, J.D. and M.W., Eversley Cross,
Hants.
Forster, J.D. and M.W., Hook, Hants.
Forster Ritchie, Eversley Cross, Hants.
Forster Ritchie, Hook, Hants.
Forster, Tony, Arnesby, Leics.
Forster, W., London, N.16.
Forsyth Antiques, Perth., Perths., Scot.
Forsyth, A. McDonald, Perth, Perths., Scot.
Forsyth, W., Cheltenham, Glos.
Forsythe, Albert, Saintfield, Co. Down,
N. Ireland.
Fort Antiques, Petersfield, Hants.
Forte's, Ipswich, Suffolk.
Fortescue, S. and M., Ipswich, Suffolk
(Forte's).
Fortnum and Mason p.l.c., London, W.1.
Fortunate Finds, Torquay, Devon.
Fortunoff Silver Sales Incorporated, London,
W.1. B. St. Silv. Galls.
Forty Eight Walton St., London, S.W.3.
Forty Nine, Manningtree, Essex.
Fosse Gallery, Stow-on-the-Wold, Glos.
Fosse House Antiques, Moreton-in-Marsh,
Glos.
Foster, A. and E., Naphill, Bucks.
Foster Antiques, Gene and Sally, Bath,
Avon.
Foster and Son, J., Radlett, Herts.
Foster Ltd., Kate, London, S.W.1.
Foster, Michael, London, S.W.3.
Foster, Mrs. M., Market Rasen, Lincs.
Foster, M. Odell, Wonersh, Surrey.
Foster of Putney, London, S.W.15.
Foster, P., Dorking, Surrey.
Foster, Miss P.I. and Keith A., Lewes,
E. Sussex.
Foster, R.W., Weybridge, Surrey.
Foster, Miss S., Bristol, Avon. Clift. Ant.
Mkt.
Fothergill, A., London, S.W.3. Ant. Ant.
Mkt.
Fothergill, A., York, N. Yorks. (Ken
Spelman)
Foulger, P.L. and W.B., Bungay, Suffolk.
Fountain Antiques, Honiton, Devon.
Four Seasons Antiques, Woodstock, Oxon.
Fournier, Ginette, Guildford, Surrey. Ant. C.
Fowle, A.C., London, S.W.16.
Fowle, A. and J., London, S.W.16.
Fowler, John, London, W.1 (Sibyl Colefax
and John Fowler).
Fowler, L., Ferndown, Dorset.

Fowler, S.G., Boughton, Kent.
Fox Antiques, Sidmouth, Devon.
Fox, B. and H., Stockbridge, Hants.
Fox and Co., Yeovil, Somerset.
Fox House, Woodstock, Oxon.
Fox House Antiques, Stow-on-the-Wold,
Glos.
Fox, Judy, London, W.11.
Fox and Son, M. and P., Harrogate, N.
Yorks.
Fox, Pauline, London, S.W.3. Chen. Gall.
Fox Antiques, Peter, Diss, Norfolk.
Fox and Pheasant Antique Pine, White
Colne, Essex.
Fox's Antiques and Shipping, Harrogate,
N. Yorks.
Foxy Lady, The, Glasgow, Lanarks., Scot.
Vict. Vill.
Foye Gallery, Luton, Beds.
Foyle Ltd., W. and G., London, W.C.2.
Fradley, P.J., Ellastone, Staffs.
Frampton, Mrs. T.P.F., Beaminster, Dorset.
Franca Antiques, Tunbridge Wells, Kent.
Frances, London, N.W.8. Alf. Ant. Mkt.
Francis, H. and R., Colchester, Essex.
Francis, Peter, London, W.C.1.
Francis, Mrs. P.B., Puckeridge, Herts.
Franco's Antique Warehouse, London, N.1.
Franco's Antiques, London, N.1.
Franfam Ltd., Moreton-in-Marsh, Glos.
Frankham Gallery, Tunbridge Wells, Kent.
Frankl, G., London, N.W.4.
Frankland, B.A., Doddington, Cambs.
Franklin, R., London, S.E.5.
Franklin Antiques, Thomas, Hungerford,
Berks.
Franklins, Camberwell Antique Market,
London, S.E.5.
Franklyn, S., London, W.11. (The Antique
Textile Company).
Franks Book Shop, Manchester, Lancs. R.
Ex. S.C.
Franks, Dorothy, Uttoxeter, Staffs.
Franks, Douglas, Frensham, Surrey.
Franks, I., London, W.C.2. Lon. Silv. Vts.
Franks Ltd., J.A.L., Brighton, E. Sussex.
Franks Ltd., J.A.L., London, S.W.1.
Franks Ltd., J.A.L., London, W.C.1.
Franks, Renee, Manchester, Lancs. Royal
Ex. S.C.
Franses, J. and S., Moreton-in-Marsh, Glos.
Franses, M. and P., London, W.9.
Franses and Sons, Robert, London, N.W.8.
Franses Ltd., S., London, S.W.1.
Franses Ltd., S., London, W.2.
Franses Gallery, Victor, London, S.W.1.
Fraser Antiques, Glasgow, Lanarks., Scot.
(Corner House Antiques).
Fraser Antiques, North Berwick, E. Loth.,
Scot.
Fraser Antiques, Alastair, West Bridgford,
Notts.
Frasers (Auctioneers), Inverness, Inver.,
Scot.
Frazer, A., Cosgrove, Northants.
Frazer Antiques, Malcolm, Cheadle,
Cheshire.
Frazer, Mrs. S., Macclesfield, Cheshire.

Fredericks and Son, C., London, S.W.3.
Fredericks and Son, J.A., London, W.1.
Fredericks, J.A. and C.J., London, W.1.
Fredericks, R.F., London, S.W.3.
Freedman — Cale Antiques, Gerald, London, S.W.6.
Freedman, Mrs. H., London, N.21.
Freedman, S., London, W.1 (C. Barrett and Co.).
Freeman, Stow-on-the-Wold, Glos.
Freeman, C., Bath, Avon. Gt. West. Ant. C. Wed. Mkt.
Freeman, C., St. Mawes, Cornwall.
Freeman and Son, I., Simon Kaye Ltd., London, W.1.
Freeman, J., London, W.11.
Freeman, J.G. and A., St. Davids, Dyfed, Wales.
Freeman, K., Sandgate, Kent.
Freeman and Lloyd Antiques, Sandgate, Kent.
Freeman, R.H. and E.M., Stow-on-the-Wold, Glos.
Freeman, S., Cheltenham, Glos. (Carrie's Antiques).
Freeman, T.A., Malmesbury, Wilts.
Freeman, Vincent, London, N.1.
Freestone, E., London, S.W.3. Ant. Ant. Mkt.
Freestone, F., Manningtree, Essex.
Freestone, Mrs. J.C., Bournemouth, Dorset. (Desire A'ttire)
French, C., Eastbourne, E. Sussex.
French Connection, The, Bath, Avon.
French-Greenslade, S., Tilston, Cheshire.
French-Greenslade, S.H., Nantwich, Cheshire.
Frenches Farm Antiques, Kings Langley, Herts.
Frere Antiques, Joan, Drumnadrochit, Inver., Scot.
Friar Antiques and Collectors Centre, Nottingham, Notts.
Friars Gate Antiques, Worcester, Hereford and Worcs.
Friars Walk Antiques, Lewes, E. Sussex.
Friary Antiques, Quarndon, Derbys.
Friary Cabinet Makers, Derby, Derbys.
Friedner, M., London, W.C.2. (Linden and Co. (Antiques) Ltd.). Lon. Silv. Vts.
Friend Antiques, David, Manchester, Lancs.
Friend, J., London, N.1 (Camden Passage Antiques Centre).
Frings, S., Leicester, Leics.
Frinton Antiques, Frinton-on-Sea, Essex.
Frith Antiques, H.A. and Mrs. M.A., Petworth, W. Sussex.
Frith, T. and M., London, W.1 (The Button Queen).
Fritzi, London, N.W.8. Alf. Ant. Mkt.
Frizzell, Alex. M., West Linton, Peebles., Scot.
Frocks Antiques, Bristol, Avon.
Frognal Rare Books, London, W.C.2.
Front Parlour, The, Hythe, Kent.
Frossard, C.P. and E.M., Penzance, Cornwall.
Frost, C.C., Long Melford, Suffolk.

Frost, E., Bath, Avon. Ant. Mkt.
Frost, Paddy, London, S.W.3. Ant. Ant. Mkt.
Frost, R.F., Debenham, Suffolk.
Frost, R.F., Martlesham, Suffolk.
Frost and Reed Ltd., London, W.1.
Fry, C. and S., London, S.W.1.
Fry Gallery, London, S.W.1.
Fry, M., London, N.W.2.
Fry, M., London, N.W.6.
Frydman, O., London, W.1. B. St. Silv. Galls.
Fryer Antiques, Chris, Bexhill-on-Sea, E. Sussex.
Fryer, F., Ross-on-Wye, Hereford and Worcs.
Fryer Antique Lighting, Fritz, Ross-on-Wye, Hereford and Worcs.
Fryer, M., Southport, Merseyside. (Arcadia Gallery).
Fryer, S.A., Southport, Merseyside. (Bobbins.)
Fuke, I., Hitchin, Herts.
Fulda Gallery, The, Manchester, Lancs.
Fulda, M.J., Manchester, Lancs.
Fullam, A., Londonberry, Co. Londonderry, N. Ireland.
Fuller, Nina, London, N.W.8. Alf. Ant. Mkt.
Fulwood Antiques, Sheffield, S. Yorks.
Furness, O., Huddersfield, W. Yorks.
Furney Antiques, Donaghadee, Co. Down, N. Ireland.
Furney, B. and I., Donaghadee, Co. Down, N. Ireland.
Furniture Cave, The, Aberystwyth, Dyfed, Wales.
Furniture Cave, London, S.W.10.
Furniture Fair, London, N.W.8.
Furniture Mart, Margate, Kent.
Furniture Store, The, London, N.W.6.
Furniture Store, The, London, N.W.8. Alf. Ant. Mkt.
Furniture Vault, London, N.1.
Furze, M., Much Hadham, Herts.
Fyfe's Antiques, Edinburgh, Midloth., Scot.
Fylde Antiques, Preston, Lancs. N.W. Ant. C.
Fyson Antiques, Jonathan, Burford, Oxon.
Fyson Antiques, Jonathan, Cassington, Oxon.
Fyson, J.R., Burford, Oxon.
Fyson, J.R., Cassington, Oxon.

G

G.G. Exports, Middleton, Lancs.
G.M.S. Antiques, Wotton-under-Edge, Glos.
G.W. Antiques, Lancaster, Lancs.
Gabie, A.E., Liss, Hants.
Gable End Fine Arts Ltd., Sutton Coldfield, W. Mids.
Gadsby Stores, Ashtead, Surrey.
Gadsden, P., Hindhead, Surrey.
Gadsden, P., Petersfield, Hants.
Gadzooks, Skipton, N. Yorks.
Gage, J. and E., Topsham, Devon.
Gahlin Ltd., Sven, London, W.1.
Gainsborough House Antiques, Sidmouth, Devon.

Gainsborough House Antiques, Tewkesbury, Glos.
Gainsborough Street Gallery, Sudbury, Suffolk.
Galata Coins Ltd., Wolverhampton, W. Mids.
Galaxy Art, Plymouth, Devon.
Gale, P.A. and D., Warminster, Wilts.
Gale, E. and S., Portscatho, Cornwall.
Gale, H., Carlisle, Cumbria.
Galerias Segui, Cowes, I. of Wight.
Galerie 360, London, S.W.6.
Galerie 1900, London, N.W.1.
Galerie Appenzell, Newport, Essex.
Galerie George, London, W.1.
Galerie George, Kensington, London, W.8.
Galerie Harounoff, London, W.1. G. Mews.
Galerie Lev, Woodford Green, Gtr. London.
Gallagher (Antiques), M., Llangollen, Clwyd, Wales.
Galleon, The, Bath, Avon.
Galleon Antiques, Hastings, E. Sussex.
Galleon Antiques, St. Leonards-on-Sea, E. Sussex.
Galleries de Fresnes, Galston, Ayrs., Scot. (Window on the World)
Gallery, Aberdeen, Aberd., Scot.
Gallery, The, Bexhill-on-Sea, E. Sussex.
Gallery, The, Groomsport, Co. Down, N. Ireland.
Gallery, The, Knaresborough, N. Yorks.
Gallery, The, Portsmouth, Hants.
Gallery, The, Yarmouth, Isle of Wight.
Gallery 2, London, W.5
Gallery 25, London, S.W.1.
Gallery 77, Bolton, Lancs.
Gallery 922, Bournemouth, Dorset.
Gallery Antiques Ltd., Winchester, Hants.
Gallery Kaleidoscope, London, N.W.6.
Gallery Laraine Ltd., Eastbourne, E. Sussex.
Gallery Lingard, London, S.W.1.
Gallery of Antique Costume and Textiles (incorporating Topfloor.), The, London, N.W.8.
Gallery and Things, The, South Lopham, Norfolk.
Gallery Three, March, Cambs.
Gallie, F., Battlesbridge, Essex.
Gallie, J.F., Battlesbridge, Essex.
Galloway Antiques, Harrogate, N. Yorks.
Galloway Clocks, Whauphill, Wigtowns., Scot.
Galloway and Porter Ltd., Cambridge, Cambs.
Galloways (Edinburgh) Ltd., Edinburgh, Midloth., Scot.
Gamble, A.F.H., Plymouth, Devon
Game Advice, London, N.W.5.
Gander, Michael, Hitchin, Herts.
Gange, C.C. and Mrs. A., Marlborough, Wilts.
Gannon, R.J. and M.T., Bishops Castle, Shrops.
Gant, Elizabeth, Thames Ditton, Surrey.
Gapp, B., Bath, Avon. Gt. West. A. C. Wed. Mkt.
Garcia, Mr. and Mrs. Sulaiman, London, S.W.3. Ant. Ant. Mkt.
Garcia, D., Portsmouth, Hants.

Garcia, Ephrain, London, S.W.3. Ant. Ant. Mkt. (Anthony Durante)
Gardiner Antiques, Charles, Lurgan, Co. Armagh, N. Ireland.
Gardiner Antiques and Decorative Objects, George and Helen, Glasgow, Lanarks., Scot.
Gardner, A.J., London, S.W.3 (The Purple Shop).
Gardner, Mrs. B., Loughborough, Leics.
Gardner Antiques, C.B., Chipping Norton, Oxon.
Gardner Antiques, Doreen, Woodlands, Hants.
Gardner, D.F., G.D. and R.K.F., Kilbarchan, Renfrews., Scot.
Gardner, Mrs. H., Ledbury, Hereford and Worcs.
Gardner, J., Bishops Cleeve, Glos.
Gardner, P., Bexhill-on-Sea, E. Sussex. Bex. Ant. C.
Gardner, T.J., Ludford, Lincs.
Gardner, T.J., Market Rasen, Lincs.
Gardner's The Antique Shop, Kilbarchan, Renfrews., Scot.
Garn House Antiques, Bow Street, Dyfed, Wales.
Garner, John, Uppingham, Leics.
Garner Antiques, P.R., Landbeach, Cambs.
Garrard and Co. Ltd., (The Crown Jewellers), London, W.1.
Garrard, Steve, Colchester, Essex.
Garratt, A.W., Canterbury, Kent.
Garratt (Fine Paintings), Stephen, London, S.W.3.
Garratts Antiques, Birmingham, W. Mids.
Garrett, L., Bath, Avon. Gt. West. A. C. Wed. Mkt.
Garrett Antiques, Robert, Stratford-upon-Avon, Warks.
Garrett (Auctioneers) Ltd., Robert, Stratford-upon-Avon, Warks.
Garrick Bookshop, The, Stockport, Cheshire.
Garrick Antiques, Philip, London, W.11.
Garriock, R.B., Edinburgh, Midloth., Scot.
Garry Anne, London, N.W.8. Alf. Ant. Mkt.
Garth Antiques, Knapton, N. Yorks.
Garton and Cooke, London, W.1.
Gasquet, J.P., London, S.W.3. Chen. Gall.
Gasson, Herbert Gordon, Rye, E. Sussex.
Gastrell House, Tetbury, Glos.
Gate Antiques, Birmingham, W. Mids.
Gate Antiques, York, N. Yorks.
Gatehouse, Nottingham, Notts.
Gatehouse Antiques, Macclesfield, Cheshire.
Gates, Diana, Deddington, Oxon. Ant. C.
Gates, Mrs. M.A.B., Hartley Wintney, Hants.
Gates, Mrs. M.A.B., London, N.1. (Boutique Fantasque).
Gatward Fine Arts, Haynes, Beds.
Gauld, Maureen H., Killin, Perths., Scot.
Gaunt, P., Outwell, Cambs.
Gauntlett Antiques, Midhurst, W. Sussex.
Gavey, Geoffrey P., Vale, Guernsey, C.I.
Gavey, G.P. and Mrs. C., St. Peter Port, Guernsey, C.I.
Gay, J. and D., Harrogate, N. Yorks.
Gay, M. and B.M., Romsey, Hants.

Glaisyer, D. and N., Moreton-in-Marsh, Glos.
Glaisyer, R. and C., Stow-on-the-Wold, Glos.
Glamour City, London, S.W.6.
Glamour City, London, S.W.11.
Glance Back, Chepstow, Gwent, Wales.
Glanfield, R.W., Lowestoft, Suffolk.
Glasby and Son, A.W., Leedstown, Cornwall.
Glasby, D.E., Leedstown, Cornwall.
Glass and Son, G., London, W.1. B. St. Silv. Galls.
Glass, H., London, W.1. B. St. Silv. Galls.
Glass, Richard, Whaley Bridge, Derbys.
Glassman, Miss R., Brighton, E. Sussex (The Witch Ball).
Glasspole Fine Art, M.P., Folkestone, Kent.
Glazebrook, A., Richmond, Gtr. London.
Gleave, Mrs. J., Hungerford, Berks. (Pandora's Box.)
Glenburn Antiques, Glasgow, Lanarks., Scot. Vict. Vill.
Glencorse Antiques, Kingston-upon-Thames, Gtr. London.
Glendale Antiques, Wooler, Northumb.
Glendale, M. and R., London, W.1.
Glen-Doepel, Mrs. D., Lincoln, Lincs.
Glenie, Mrs. J., Llangollen, Clwyd, Wales.
Glenville Antiques, Yatton, Avon.
Gliksten, M., Lea, Wilts.
Gliksten, M., London, N.1. (Relic Antiques at Camden Passage).
Gliksten, M., London, N.W.1 (Relic Antiques at Camden Lock).
Gloria and Eamon, London, N.W.8. Alf. Ant. Mkt.
Gloucester House Antiques Ltd., Fairford, Glos.
Gloucester Road Antiques, Brighton, E. Sussex.
Glover, F.D., Southport, Merseyside. (Decor Galleries).
Glover (Antiques), J.K., Haslemere, Surrey.
Gluck, D., Cardiff, S. Glam., Wales (Heritage Antiques and Stripped Pine).
Glydon and Guess Ltd., Kingston-upon-Thames, Gtr. London.
Glynn Interiors, Knutsford, Cheshire.
Gnome Cottage Antiques, Stroud, Glos.
Goble, Paul, Brighton, E. Sussex.
Goddard, J. and A., Christchurch, Dorset.
Goddard, Miss J.P., Oughtibridge, S. Yorks.
Goddard's, Julie, Oughtibridge, S. Yorks.
Goddard-Smith, Lisa and Stuart, Ashburton, Devon.
Godden Chinaman, Geoffrey, Worthing, W. Sussex.
Godden, G.A., Worthing, W. Sussex.
Godden of Worthing, Worthing, W. Sussex.
Godfrey Antiques, Howard, Sandgate, Kent.
Godfrey, Jemima, Newmarket, Suffolk.
Godfrey's Old Newspaper Shop, David, London, S.W.1.
Godsell, A.A. and C.M.J., Ridgewell, Essex.
Godson and Coles, London, S.W.3.
Goff Galleries, The, Long Melford, Suffolk.
Gold and Silver Exchange, Exeter, Devon.
Goldband, D. and T., London, W.C.2 (Old Curiosity Shop).

Goldcraft, Swansea, W. Glam., Wales. Ant. Centre.
Golden Cage, The, Nottingham, Notts.
Golden Drop Antiques, The, Warboys, Cambs.
Golden Goose Books, Lincoln, Lincs.
Golden Oldies, Holt, Norfolk.
Golden Oldies, Leicester, Leics.
Golden Past, The, London, W.1.
Golden Sovereign, Great Bardfield, Essex.
Golder, Gwendoline, Coltishall, Norfolk.
Golding, D., London, W.C.2. Lon. Silv. Vts.
Golding, Eric, Wisbech, Cambs.
Golding, H.C., Salisbury, Wilts.
Golding and Co., Jules, London, W.C.2. Lon. Silv. Vts.
Golding, M.F., S.P. and N.M.J., Stow-on-the-Wold, Glos.
Golding, Pat, Arundel, W. Sussex.
Golding and Sons, South Molton, Devon.
Goldmark Bookshop, Uppingham, Leics.
Goldmark, M.M., Uppingham, Leics.
Goldney, C., Saffron Walden, Essex.
Goldscheider, Gaby, Windsor and Eton, Berks.
Goldsmith, Mrs. G., London, S.W.1 (Loot).
Goldsmith & Perris, London, N.W.8. Alf. Ant. Mkt.
Goldsmith, William, Leeds, W. Yorks.
Goldstein and M. Druks, Roma, London, N.W.8. Alf. Ant. Mkt.
Goldstone and Son, Maurice, Bakewell, Derbys.
Goldthorpe, P. and J., Godalming, Surrey.
Golfiana Miscellanea Ltd., Brighton, E. Sussex.
Gommers, H.T.M., West Felton, Shrops.
Gomshall Gallery, Gomshall, Surrey.
Gonzales, F., London, S.W.3. Ant. Ant. Mkt.
Good Fairy Open Air Market, The, London, W.11.
Good Hope Antiques, Beaminster, Dorset.
Good, Mrs. K., Waddesdon, Bucks.
Goodacre Engraving Ltd., Long Eaton, Derbys.
Goodall and Co., Ltd., London, W.4.
Goodall, C.R., London, W.4.
Goodall, Peter, Guildford, Surrey. Ant. C.
Gooday, Peter and Debbie, Richmond, Gtr. London.
Gooday, R., East Molesey, Surrey.
Gooday Shop and Gooday Studio, The, East Molesey, Surrey.
Goodban, P.M., Oxford, Oxon.
Goodbrey, B., Framlingham, Suffolk.
Goodbrey, R. and M., Framlingham, Suffolk.
Goodbreys, Framlingham, Suffolk.
Goode, J.V.S., Newton Abbot, Devon.
Goode, J.V.S., Torquay, Devon.
Goode and Co. (London) Ltd., Thomas, London, W.1.
Goode, Vyvyan, Newton Abbot, Devon. N.A. Ant. C.
Goodfellow, R., Berwick-on-Tweed, Northumbs.
Goodfellow (Antiques), William, Carnforth, Lancs.

Gooding Clocks, G. Buxton, Lapworth, Warks.
Goodinge, Mrs. J.A., Henfield, W. Sussex.
Goodlad, A.D., Chesterfield, Derbys.
Goodland, D. and Mrs. C., Spilsby, Lincs.
Goodman, K., Bath, Avon. Gt. West. Ant. C. Wed. Mkt.
Goodman, K.E., Torquay, Devon.
Goodman of Holt, Holt, Norfolk.
Goodman, P., Reymerston, Norfolk.
Goodman, P. and L., Beverley, N. Humberside.
Goodman, R.J., Snodland, Kent.
Goodsman, M.T., Warminster, Wilts.
Goodson, R. and C., Warwick, Warks.
Goodson's (Ragamuffin) Antiques, Warwick, Warks.
Goodwin, E., Great Bardfield, Essex.
Goodwin, G.A. and A.M., London, N.W.2.
Goodwin, M., Alderley Edge, Cheshire.
Goodwin Exports, Nick, Guilsborough, Northants.
Goodwin, P., London, S.W.6.
Goodwin, Peter, London, S.W.7.
Goodwin & Wadhwa, London, S.W.6.
Goodwins Antiques, Edinburgh, Midloth., Scot.
Gooley, P., London, W.9.
Gooseman, S. and G., Sundridge, Kent.
Goosens-Berg, Barbara, London, S.W.3. Chen. Gall.
Gordon, London, W.1. G. Mews.
Gordon, A. and F., London, W.1.
Gordon, Brian, London, S.W.3. Chen. Gall.
Gordon Antiques, Christopher, Birmingham, W. Mids.
Gordon, D., Edinburgh, Midloth., Scot. (Now and Then (Toy Centre)).
Gordon, Lord Douglas, Stockbridge, Hants.
Gordon Antiques, Douglas, Stockbridge, Hants.
Gordon, D.S., Fordingbridge, Hants.
Gordon, G., London, N.W.3.
Gordon, G., London, N.W.8.
Gordon, Janet, Wakes Colne, Essex.
Gordon, Mr. and Mrs. J.F., Newton Abbot, Devon.
Gordon, M., Torquay, Devon.
Gordon, Mrs. P., Ardingley, W. Sussex.
Gordon, R. and J., Alford, Aberd. Scot.
Gordon (Antiques), R.S., Alford, Aberd., Scot.
Gore-Langton, Grenville, Alresford, Hants.
Goslett Gallery, Roland, Richmond, Gtr. London.
Gosnell, R., Chislehurst, Gtr. London.
Goss and Crested China Ltd., Horndean, Hants.
Gothic Cottage Antiques, London, S.W.13.
Gottlieb, M., London, W.1 (Libra Design).
Gottschald, P.W., D.J. and C.R., Ambergate, Derbys.
Gouby, M., London, W.8 (Michael Coins).
Gough, Mr., Leicester, Leics.
Gough, B.A., Carshalton, Gtr. London.
Gough, L.G., Wigan, Lancs.
Gough Books, Simon, Holt, Norfolk.
Gould and Sons (Antiques) Ltd., A.E., East Horsley, Surrey.

Gould, D. and P., East Horsley, Surrey.
Gould, Peter, Halifax, W. Yorks.
Gould, Patrick and Susan, London, W.1. G. Mews.
Gould, Valentine, Bath, Avon.
Goulding, S.J., Middleton, Lancs.
Gover, V.B. and C.D.P., Sandgate, Kent.
Gower, G., Lea, Wilts.
Gower, G., London, N.1. (Relic Antiques at Camden Passage).
Gower, G., London, N.W.1 (Relic Antiques at Camden Lock).
Grafton Country Pictures, Oakham, Leics.
Graham, A. and A., Larne, Co. Antrim, N. Ireland.
Graham Ltd., Albert, Larne, Co. Antrim, N. Ireland.
Graham, A.P., Newcastle-upon-Tyne, Tyne and Wear. (The Dean Gallery).
Graham Gallery, David, London, N.1.
Graham Gallery, Burghfield Common, Berks.
Graham Gallery, Gavin, London, W.11.
Graham, Imogen, London, S.W.6.
Graham, J., Ross-on-Wye, Hereford and Worcs.
Graham, Mrs. M.L.D., Whitehaven, Cumbria.
Graham and Oxley (Antiques) Ltd., London, W.8.
Graham Antiques, P., Glasgow, Lanarks., Scot.
Graham, R.A. and M.V., Durham, Durham.
Graham, Mr. and Mrs. R.M. Maxtone, Hythe, Kent.
Graham, Mr. and Mrs. R.M. Maxtone, Sandwich, Kent.
Graham, W.N., Bournemouth, Dorset. (Sterling Coins and Medals).
Grahame, Eila, London, W.8.
Grahamslaw, Alex, London, S.W.6.
Granary Galleries, The, Ash Priors, Somerset.
Grandad's Photography Museum, Colchester, Essex.
Grange Antiques, Dorridge, W. Mids.
Grange Antiques, St. Peter Port, Guernsey, C.I.
Grange Bookshop, Edinburgh, Midloth., Scot.
Grange Court Antiques, Corfe, Somerset.
Grange Gallery, The, Withersdale, Suffolk.
Grange Gallery and Fine Arts Ltd., St. Helier, Jersey, C.I.
Grannies Attic, Market Weighton, N. Humberside.
Grannie's Attic, Shottermill, Surrey.
Grannie's Attic Antiques, Smethwick, W. Mids.
Grannie's Goodies, London, S.W.3. Chen. Gall.
Grannie's Parlour, Hull, N. Humberside.
Grannie's Treasures, Hull, N. Humberside.
Granny's Antiques, Richmond, N. Yorks.
Granny's Attic, Clare, Suffolk.
Granny's Attic, Nottingham, Notts.
Granny's Treasures, Wimborne Minster, Dorset.
Granshaw, M. and D., Shalford, Surrey.
Grant, A., London, S.W.3 (J.P. Gasquet). Chen. Gall.

Grant Antiques, Denzil, Long Melford,
Suffolk.
Grant Fine Art, Droitwich, Hereford and
Worcs.
Grant, I.R. and S., Edinburgh, Midloth.,
Scot.
Grant, J., Avening, Glos.
Grant, John, Est. 1874, Edinburgh, Midloth.,
Scot.
Grant, K.N., London, W.1. G. Ant. Mkt.
Grant, Mrs. P., London, S.W.1 (Ning Ltd.).
Grant Antiques, Stephanie, Barnard Castle,
Durham.
Grant, Sylvia, Woburn, Beds. Wob. Ab.
Ant. C.
Grant, Mrs. V., Waddesdon, Bucks.
Granville Antiques, Eastergate, W. Sussex.
Granville Antiques, Woburn, Beds. Wob. Ab.
Ant. C.
Granville, P., London, N.W.8.
Grassie, P., Ruabon, Clwyd, Wales.
Grater, Sally, Billericay, Essex.
Gratton, P., Inverness, Inver., Scot.
Graus Antiques, London, W.1.
Graus, E. and H., London, W.1.
Gravener Antiques, Wm. J., Mayfield,
E. Sussex.
Graves, G.P.H. and Mrs. A.E., Walton-on-
the- Hill and Tadworth, Surrey.
Gray, Mr. and Mrs. A., Penrith, Cumbria.
Gray Antiques, Tunbridge Wells, Kent.
Gray Antiques, Ann, Limpsfield, Surrey.
Gray, A.E., London, W.1. (Hudson and
Williams)
Gray, B., London, N.W.8. Alf. Ant. Mkt.
Gray, B.D., Tunbridge Wells, Kent.
Gray, C. Anthony, London, W.1. G. Mews.
Gray Antiques, David, Glasgow, Lanarks.,
Scot.
Gray, E.B., Bath, Avon. Gt. West. Ant. C.
Gray, F., Oakham, Leics.
Gray, G.C.M., Hertford, Herts.
Gray, Mrs. J., Cirencester, Glos.
Gray Antiques, Jay, Cirencester, Glos.
Gray, Kuniko, London, W.1. G. Ant. Mkt.
Gray, Marion, London, N.4.
Gray, M.E., Marlborough, Wilts.
Gray, Mrs. S., Sheffield, S. Yorks. (The
Dolls House Antiques).
Gray, Solveig and Anita, London, W.1.
G. Ant. Mkt.
Grays Antique Market, London, W.1.
Grays Mews, London, W.1.
Great Ayton Bookshop, The, Great Ayton,
N. Yorks.
Great Brampton House Antiques Ltd.,
Hereford, Hereford and Worcs.
Great Malvern Antiques Arcade, Great
Malvern, Hereford and Worcs.
Great Western Antique Centre Ltd. - The
Wednesday Market, Bath, Avon.
Great Western Antique Centre Ltd., Bath,
Avon.
Greaves, A., London, W.1. G. Mews.
Greaves, H.J., Sheffield, S. Yorks. (Dronfield
Antiques).
Greaves, P.A., Sheffield, S. Yorks. (Hibbert
Bros.)

Greaves Ltd., Perry, Birmingham, W. Mids.
Green Gallery, David, E., London, S.E.26.
Green, D.M., London, S.W.3. Ant. Ant.
Mkt.
Green, D.S., Hartley Wintney, Hants.
Green, Ena, London, N.W.8. Alf. Ant. Mkt.
Green, E.M., London, W.1. (Garrard and Co.
Ltd.)
Green, Gladys, Cheltenham, Glos.
Green, G.H., Sheffield, S. Yorks.
Green, Mrs. J., Chilham, Kent.
Green Antiques, Jonathan, Fordingbridge,
Hants.
Green and Son, J., Queniborough, Leics.
Green, M., Harrogate, N. Yorks. (Antique
Pine).
Green, Norah, Bexhill-on-Sea, E. Sussex.
Bex. Ant. C.
Green, N., Coventry, W. Mids.
Green, N., London, S.W.3. (Linwick
Minerals.) Chen. Gall.
Green Parrot, The, London, S.E.10.
Green, Richard, London, W.1.
Green, R., Queniborough, Leics.
Green (Fine Paintings), Richard, London, W.1.
Green, Ron, Towcester, Northants.
Green, Renée and Roy, Lewes, E. Sussex.
Green, S., London, W.8.
Green and Stone, London, S.W.3.
Green, T. and A., Wallingford, Oxon. L. Arc.
Green, W., London, S.W.3. Ant. Ant. Mkt.
Greenaway, A., Canterbury, Kent.
Greenaway, A., Maidstone, Kent.
Greenaway, T., London, W.1 (Blunderbuss
Antiques).
Greenbury Antiques, Royston, Herts.
Greene, B.G., Highcliffe, Dorset.
Greene, E. and I., Castle Hedingham, Essex.
Greene Antiques, Richard, Burley-in-
Wharfedale, W. Yorks.
Greenfield, A.G. and T.S., Canterbury, Kent.
Greenfield and Son, H.S., Canterbury, Kent.
Greenfield, K., London, W.1. B. St. Ant. C.
Greengrass Antiques, Derek, Windsor and
Eton, Berks.
Greenhalgh and Son, Syd, Dalton-in-Furness,
Cumbria.
Greenhouse Antiques, Painswick, Glos.
Greenland, R. and E., Dorchester, Dorset.
Greenlaw Antiques, Greenlaw, Berwicks.,
Scot.
Greenman, Irene, Woburn, Beds. Wob. Ab.
Ant. C.
Greenman, S., London, N.12.
Green's Antique Galleries, London, W.8.
Greensleeves Galleries, Gerrards Cross,
Bucks.
Greenwall Antiques, Jonathan, Sandgate,
Kent. S. Ant. C.
Greenway Antiques, Colin, Witney, Oxon.
Greenwich Antiques Market, London,
S.E.10.
Greenwich Chimes, London, S.E.10.
Greenwold, L., Stow-on-the-Wold, Glos.
Greenwood, Mrs. B., Little Budworth,
Cheshire.
Greenwood, Colin, Sowerby Bridge, W.
Yorks.

Greenwood, Judy, London, S.W.6.
Greenwood Antiques, Simon, Burneston, N. Yorks.
Greenwood Antiques, Simon, Melmerby, N. Yorks.
Greenwood, S. and C., Burneston, N. Yorks.
Greenwood, S. and C., Melmerby, N. Yorks.
Greenwood (Fine Art), W., Burneston, N. Yorks.
Greenwood and Sons Ltd., W.F., York, N. Yorks.
Greenwoods of Oulton Mill, Little Budworth, Cheshire.
Greer, Robin, London, S.W.3.
Greg, Meriel de M., Bath, Avon. B. Ant. Mkt.
Gregory, A., Castle Cary, Somerset.
Gregory, Bottley and Lloyd, London, S.W.6.
Gregory, Mrs. D., Bristol, Avon. Clift. Ant. Mkt.
Gregory, D., Dulverton, Somerset.
Gregory, George, Bath, Avon.
Gregory, Henry, London, W.1. G. Ant. Mkt.
Gregory, J., London, S.W.6. (C. Kent (Fireplaces))
Gregory, J., London, N.W.8. Alf. Ant. Mkt.
Gregory, M., London, W.9.
Gregory Gallery, Martyn, London, S.W.1.
Gregory Gallery, Noel, Farnham Common, Bucks.
Gregory, R.A.W., Deddington, Oxon.
Greig, C., London, W.1. (Eyre and Greig)
Grenville Art Gallery, Manchester, Lancs. Royal Ex. S.C.
Grenville Street Bookshop, Stockport, Cheshire.
Gres (David Gill), London, W.1. G. Ant. Mkt.
Gresham, R.A., Bath, Avon. Gt. West. Ant. C.
Gretton, K., London, S.W.11.
Greville Antiques and Design Ltd., Aspley Guise, Beds.
Grey House Antiques, Tiverton, Devon.
Greyabbey Timecraft Ltd., Greyabbey, Co. Down, N. Ireland.
Grey-Harris and Co., Bristol, Avon.
Greyhound Gallery Ltd., The, Wincanton, Somerset.
Greyhound Lodge Antiques, White Colne, Essex.
Greystoke Antiques, Sherborne, Dorset.
Greystoke Antiques, Castle Bytham, Lincs.
Greystones Antiques, Buckden, N. Yorks.
Gridley, Gordon, London, N.1.
Griffin Antiques, Petworth, W. Sussex.
Griffin Gallery, Windsor and Eton, Berks.
Griffin, G.E., Croydon, Gtr. London.
Griffin, R., Bath, Avon. Gt. West. Ant. C. (Roy's Watches).
Griffin Antiques Ltd., Simon, London, W.1.
Griffin, S.J., London, W.1.
Griffith, A., London, S.W.6 (Singing Tree)
Griffith, C. and J., Southampton, Hants.
Griffith, J., Canterbury, Kent.
Griffiths, London, N.W.8. Alf. Ant. Mkt.
Griffiths, D., London, N.1 (Number Nineteen).

Griffiths, D., Birmingham, W. Mids. (The Moseley Gallery.)
Griffiths, F., Rochdale, Lancs.
Griffiths, J., Bath, Avon (Bath Galleries).
Griffiths, J., Rhuddlan, Clwyd, Wales.
Griffith's Antiques Highbridge Antique Galleries, Keith, Highbridge, Somerset.
Griffiths, M., Huddersfield, W. Yorks.
Griffiths, R. and W., Southport, Merseyside.
Griffiths, S., Buckden, N. Yorks.
Griffiths, W. and B., Burscough, Lancs.
Griffiths, W.W., Bethel, Gwynedd, Wales.
Griffons Court, Newbury, Berks.
Grigor-Taylor, B., London, S.W.1. (Cavendish Rare Books).
Grimaldi, London, W.1.
Grimes House Antiques, Moreton-in-Marsh, Glos.
Grimwade, P., Cardiff, S. Glam., Wales. (Cottage Antiques).
Grindley, Nicholas, London, S.W.3.
Grinling, Mrs. M., Lewes, E. Sussex.
Grogan, F.J., Littledean, Glos.
Grogan, Major and Mrs. R., Dorking, Surrey.
Gross, Colin, London, W.11. G. Port.
Grosschild, Teresa, London, N.W.8. Alf. Ant. Mkt.
Grosvenor Antiques, Leek, Staffs.
Grosvenor Antiques Ltd., London, W.8.
Grosvenor House Interiors, Beaconsfield, Bucks.
Grosvenor, K. and S., Leek, Staffs.
Grosvenor Antiques of Chester, Chester, Cheshire.
Grosvenor, Norman, Leek, Staffs.
Grosvenor Prints, London, W.C.2.
Groucott, M., Peterborough, Cambs.
Group 3, London, W.1. G. Ant. Mkt.
Grout-Smith, S.A., Petersfield, Hants.
Grove Antiques, Penarth, S. Glam., Wales.
Grove Antiques, Wallasey, Merseyside.
Grove Collectors Centre, Harrogate, N. Yorks.
Grove Galleries, Deddington, Oxon.
Grover, R., Brighton, E. Sussex. (Victorian Interiors.)
Groves, M.A. and A. Uttoxeter, Staffs.
Grozier, W.B.T., Hull, N. Humbs.
Grupman, Joan, Manchester, Lancs. Royal Ex. S.C.
Gubb, J. and A.H., Southampton, Hants.
Gubbins, R., London, S.W.3. Ant. Mkt.
Guelfano, Mrs. L., London, S.W.3. Ant. Ant. Mkt.
Guerra Antiques, L., London, W.11.
Guest, G., London, S.W.6. (20th Century Gallery)
Guildhall Antiques, Whittlesford, Cambs.
Guildhall Bookshop, The, Twickenham, Gtr. London.
Guildhall Fair, Chester, Cheshire.
Guildhall Gallery, Bury St. Edmunds, Suffolk.
Guildhall Street Antiques, Bury St. Edmunds, Suffolk.
Guillemot, Aldeburgh, Suffolk.
Guinevere Antiques, London, S.W.6.
Gulliver's, Bath, Avon. Gt. West. Ant. C.
Gun Powder House Antiques, Faversham, Kent.

Gunn, Mrs. B., London, S.W.3. Ant. Ant. Mkt.
Guns and Tackle, Scunthorpe, S. Humberside.
Gunson, P.M., Kendal, Cumbria.
Gunter Fine Art, London, N.W.2.
Gurl, Bath, Avon. Gt. West. Ant. C.
Guthrie, L.W. and R.M., Shipston-on-Stour, Warks.
Guy, A.R. and D.E., Amersham, Bucks.
Guy, A., Risby, Suffolk.
Guymer, H., Bath, Avon. Gt. West. Ant. C.
Gwatkin, R., Ludlow, Shrops.
Gwilliam, D.L., Bath, Avon (The Galleon).
Gwilliam, Edred A.F., Cricklade, Wilts.
Gwynedd Galleries, Betws-y-Coed, Gwynedd, Wales.
Gwyneth Antiques, London, S.W.1 (Antiques).
Gyles, D.E., Bath, Avon. Gt. West. A. C. Wed. Mkt.
Gyte, P.S., Ripon, N. Yorks.

H

H.L.B. Antiques, Bournemouth, Dorset.
HQ 84, Gloucester, Glos.
Haas, Otto, (A. and M. Rosenthal), London, N.W.3.
Hackett, R. and B., Frome, Somerset.
Hackner, P.A. and M., Wolverhampton, W. Mids.
Hadfield, G.K., Shepshed, Leics.
Hadji Baba Ancient Art, London, W.1.
Hadlee, R. and J., London, E.C.3.
Hadley, Denis, Woburn, Beds. Wob. Ab. Ant. C.
Hadley, G.A., Chester, Cheshire. (Chester Furniture Cave).
Hadley, R., Bournemouth, Dorset. (The Antique Centre).
Hadlow Antiques, Tunbridge Wells, Kent.
Hagarty, Mrs. M., Bow Street, Dyfed, Wales.
Hagen Ltd., Richard, Broadway, Hereford and Worcs.
Hague Antiques, Leamington Spa, Warks.
Hague, John, Pickering, N. Yorks.
Hague, J., Leamington Spa, Warks.
Hahn, S., London, W.1
Hahn and Son Fine Art Dealers, London, W.1.
Haig, H. and M., Woodstock, Oxon.
Haigh, Mr. and Mrs. G.E., Huddersfield, W. Yorks.
Haig-Harrison, A.G., Bristol, Avon. (Frocks Antiques).
Haillay, Mrs. C.L., Lechlade, Glos.
Haines Antiques Ltd., John, London, S.W.13.
Haines, J. and S.D., London, S.W.13.
Haines, T.E., Trent, Dorset.
Hakeney Antiques, David K., Hull, N. Humberside.
Hakim, M., London, W.1.
Halcyon Days, London, W.1.
Halcyon Days, London, E.C.3.

Haldane, J., London, N.W.5.
Hale, M.F., Heathfield, E. Sussex.
Hale, P., Uckfield, E. Sussex.
Hales Antiques Ltd., Robert, London, W.8.
Halewood and Sons, Preston, Lancs.
Haley, J., Halifax, W. Yorks.
Halez-Fax Antiques, Halifax, W. Yorks.
Halfpenny, P. and M., Llandeils, Dyfed, Wales.
Halifax Antiques Centre, Halifax, W. Yorks.
Halkes, H. Sidmouth, Devon.
Hall, Anthony C., Twickenham, Gtr. London.
Hall, A.J. and N., Beccles, Suffolk.
Hall, A.R. and J.M., Ash Priors, Somerset.
Hall Antiques, Barbara, Stamford, Lincs.
Hall, B.J. and H.M., Crewkerne, Somerset.
Hall, D., Hexham, Northumb.
Hall Ltd., Douglas, Brighton, E. Sussex.
Hall Ltd., F., Chesterfield, Derbys.
Hall Antique Clocks, Henry, Westerham, Kent.
Hall, J., Leominster, Hereford and Worcs.
Hall Antiques and Prints, John, London, S.W.6.
Hall, J.H., Earl Shilton, Leics.
Hall, L.M., Great Malvern, Hereford and Worcs.
Hall, P., Forest Row, E. Sussex.
Hall Antiques, Peter, Knaresborough, N. Yorks.
Hall Antiques, Rob, Bath, Avon. Gt. West. A. C. Wed. Mkt.
Hall, R., Ash Priors, Somerset.
Hall, Robert, London, W.9.
Hall, R. and J., Bath, Avon. Gt. West. A. C. Wed. Mkt.
Hall, R. and J., Llandogo, Gwent, Wales.
Hall Antiques, Victor, Basildon, Essex.
Hall-Bakker, Lis, Woodstock, Oxon.
Hallah, S., Crewkerne, Somerset.
Hallam Antiques, Michael, Norwich, Norfolk.
Hallam, M.J., Norwich, Norfolk.
Hallesy, H. and M., Swansea, W. Glam., Wales. Ant. Centre.
Halliburton, A., Wallingford, Oxon. L. Arc.
Halliday, A., Ripon, N. Yorks.
Halliday, F.G., Glasgow, Lanarks., Scot. (Jean Megahy).
Halliday, Mrs. S., Coventry, W. Mids.
Halliday's Antiques Ltd., Dorchester-on-Thames, Oxon.
Halliday's Carved Pine Mantelpieces Ltd., London, S.W.3.
Halliwell, L.J., Marlborough, Wilts.
Hallmarks, Brighton, E. Sussex.
Halloway, Mrs. P.W., Annfield Plain, Durham.
Hall's Antiques, Ash Priors, Somerset.
Hall's Bookshop, Tunbridge Wells, Kent.
Hallstile Antiques, Hexham, Northumb.
Hallstroem, Micky, London, S.W.3. Ant. Ant. Mkt.
Halo Antiques, Altrincham, Cheshire.
Halsby, J. and M., London, N.6.
Halsby, M. and J., London, N.1. (Highgate Gallery)
Halsey, Kingsbridge, Devon.
Halsey, London, S.W.1.

Halsey, M. and R., Sandford, Devon.
Halstead Antiques, Halstead, Essex.
Halstow Antiques, Lower Halstow, Kent.
Ham, M.D., Powick, Hereford & Worcs.
Hamadani, Mrs. B., London, S.W.3. Ant. Ant. Mkt.
Hamand Antiques, Painswick, Glos.
Hamilton Antiques, Holywood, Co. Down, N. Ireland.
Hamilton Antiques, London, W.C.2. Lon. Silv. Vts.
Hamilton Antiques, Woodbridge, Suffolk.
Hamilton, D., Sherborne, Dorset.
Hamilton, G., Bath, Avon. Gt. West. A. C. Wed. Mkt.
Hamilton, P., and Schiff, London, W.1. G. Mews.
Hamilton, Rosemary, London, S.W.1.
Hamilton, S., Fernhurst, W. Sussex.
Hamilton, S., Midhurst, W. Sussex.
Hamilton, S., Merrow, Surrey.
Hamlyn, M.G., Rainham, Kent.
Hammer, Mrs. P., Wimborne Minster, Dorset.
Hammerbeck, Dunmow, Essex.
Hammersley, Mrs. B.A., Abbots Bromley, Staffs.
Hammersley Galleries, Harpenden, Herts.
Hammersley, S.V., Harpenden, Herts.
Hammond, Carol, London, N.W.8. Alf. Ant. Mkt.
Hammond Ltd., Charles, London, S.W.1.
Hammond Antiques, Jeffery, Twyford, Hants.
Hammond, J. and E., Twyford, Hants.
Hammond, Peter, Thornage, Norfolk.
Hammond, P.M.C., Gosberton, Lincs.
Hammond, Robert, Knaresborough, N. Yorks.
Hampshire Gallery, Bournemouth, Dorset.
Hampshire, P. and Mrs. S., Honiton, Devon.
Hampshire, P. and Mrs. S., Ottery St. Mary, Devon.
Hampshire Antiques, R. and L., Gatehouse of Fleet, Kirkcud., Scot.
Hampshires of Dorking, Dorking, Surrey.
Hampstead Antique Emporium, London, N.W.3.
Hampton Court Antiques, East Molesey, Surrey.
Hampton Court Revival Antique Market, East Molesey, Surrey.
Hampton, G., Christchurch, Dorset.
Hampton Gallery, Minchinhampton, Glos.
Hampton Hill Gallery Ltd., Hampton Hill, Gtr. London.
Hampton Wick Antiques, Hampton Wick, Gtr. London.
Hamptons, Christchurch, Dorset.
Hanborough Antiques, Long Hanborough, Oxon.
Hanbury, Mrs. D., Chobham, Surrey.
Hanbury, R. and A., Bartlow, Cambs.
Hanbury Antiques Ltd., Rupert, Bartlow, Cambs.
Hancock, G., Shrewsbury, Shrops.
Hancock Gallery, London, W.11.
Hancock, M.L., Chichester, W. Sussex.

Hancock Antiques, Peter, Chichester, W. Sussex.
Hancocks and Co. (Jewellers) Ltd., London, W.1.
Hancox, G., Wansford, Cambs.
Hancox, G. and D., Little Haywood, Staffs.
Hancox, G. and D., Wolseley Bridge, Staffs.
Hand, Elizabeth, Petworth, W. Sussex.
Hand in Hand, Edinburgh, Midloth., Scot.
Hand, Mr. and Mrs. O., Edinburgh, Midloth., Scot. (Hand in Hand).
Handbury-Madin, R. and G., Shrewsbury, Shrops.
Handcross Antiques, Handcross, W. Sussex.
Handford Antiques, William, London, S.W.10.
Hankinson, N. and M., Bristol, Avon. (Affordable Arts).
Hanks, P.C., Rochester, Kent.
Hanlin, London, N.W.3. Ham. Ant. Emp.
Hanlon, W. and J., Menston, W. Yorks.
Hannant, M., Folkestone, Kent.
Hannent, Donna and Jean, Norwich, Norfolk.
Hanness, M., London, W.4.
Hanreck, Mrs. M., Hadleigh, Essex.
Hansen, Mrs. A., Great Missenden, Bucks.
Hansen Antiques, S., Boughton, Kent.
Hansen Chard Antiques, Pershore, Hereford and Worcs.
Han-Shan Tang Ltd., London, S.W.6.
Hanson, Mrs. M.E., Knaresborough, N. Yorks.
Hansord, David J., Lincoln, Lincs.
Harari and Johns Ltd., London, S.W.1.
Harborne Place Antiques, Birmingham, W. Midlands.
Harby, Diane, London, W.1. G. Ant. Mkt.
Harcourt Antiques, London, W.1.
Harcourt, P., London, W.1. (Maggs Bros. Ltd.)
Hardcastle Ltd., Henry, York, N. Yorks.
Hardcastle, M. and S., Leyburn, N. Yorks.
Hardcastle, R., Lancester, Lancs.
Harden, H.C., Bingley, W. Yorks.
Harden's (of Bingley) Antiques, Bingley, W. Yorks.
Hardie Antiques, Tim, Edinburgh, Midloth., Scot.
Hardie Antiques, T.G., Perth, Perths., Scot.
Hardiman, M. and G.A., Melbourn, Cambs.
Hardiman, P.N., Melbourn, Cambs.
Harding, Mrs. J., Duffield, Derbys.
Harding, Mrs. J., Long Melford, Suffolk.
Harding Antiques, Keith, London, N.7.
Harding, R., London, W.1. (Maggs Bros. Ltd.)
Harding, W.K., London, N.7.
Harding-Hill, M. and D., Chipping Norton, Oxon.
Hardman, A., Forest Row, E. Sussex.
Hardwick Antiques, Streetly, W. Mids.
Hardwick, Mrs. P., Churt, Surrey.
Hardy and Co., James, London, S.W.3.
Hardy Antique Shop, John, Oadby, Leics.
Hardy, J.C., Ruabon, Clwyd, Wales.
Hardy Pine and Country Furniture, Joyce, Hacheston, Suffolk.

Hare (Harrogate) Ltd., N., Harrogate,
N. Yorks. (Antique Corner).
Harewood Cottage Antiques, Harewood,
W. Yorks.
Harker, P.G., Bridlington, N. Humberside.
Harkins, Brian, London, W.1. G. Mews.
Harlequin Gallery, Lincoln, Lincs.
Harlequin, Lancaster, Holland Antiques,
London, W.1. G. Ant. Mkt.
Harley Antiques, Christian Malford, Wilts.
Harley, G.J., Christian Malford, Wilts.
Harley Two, Christian Malford, Wilts.
Harling, R., Lye, W. Mids.
Harman Antiques, Robert, Woburn, Beds.
Wob. Ab. Ant. C.
Harman Antiques, Robert, Ampthill, Beds.
Harman, J.D., Ruskington, Lincs.
Harmandian, G., Bath, Avon (Arkea
Antiques).
Harmer, Michael, Pevensey Bay, E. Sussex.
Haros Antiques, London, N.W.3. Ham. Ant.
Emp.
Harp Antiques, Bradford-on-Avon, Wilts.
Harper, B. and I., Warwick, Warks.
Harper, Erica and Hugo, Chester, Cheshire.
Harper, Mrs. K., Leeds, W. Yorks.
Harper, M. and D., Checkley, Staffs.
Harper, M.R., Bristol, Avon. (Bristol Ant.
Mkt.)
Harper, Mrs. N.C., Guildford, Surrey.
Harper, Mr. and Mrs. R.B., Temple
Sowerby, Cumbria.
Harper's Antiques, Guildford, Surrey.
Harper's Antiques, Temple Sowerby,
Cumbria.
Harpers Hill Farm Antiques, Stoke Golding,
Leics.
Harries, C., Bladon, Oxon.
Harriman, D. and E., Sarratt, Herts.
Harris, Mrs. A., Bristol, Avon. Clift. Ant.
Mkt.
Harris, A.R., Stourbridge, W. Mids.
Harris, B., Cinderford, Glos.
Harris, Mrs. B., Hungerford, Berks.
Harris Antiques, Bibi, Hungerford, Berks.
Harris, B.C. and R.H., London, W.1.
(S.H. Harris and Son (London) Ltd.).
Harris and Sons Antiques, Bob, Birmingham,
W. Mids.
Harris, Essie C., London, E.C.1.
Harris, E.C. and D., London, E.C.1.
Harris and Fergie, Bath, Avon. Gt. West.
Ant. C. Wed. Mkt.
Harris, F.J., Stansted, Essex.
Harris, F.J.H., Stansted, Essex.
Harris, I., London, W.1 (N. Bloom and Son
Ltd.).
Harris, Jonathan, London, W.8.
Harris, J., Petworth, W. Sussex.
Harris, J.F., London, W.4 (Chiswick
Antiques).
Harris, Leon and Rowena, Fakenham,
Norfolk. Ant. C.
Harris and Sons, M., London, S.W.1.
Harris, Nicholas, London, W.1.
Harris, R., Bath, Avon. Gt. West. Ant. C.
Harris, R., Bath, Avon. Gt. West. Ant. C.
Wed. Mkt.

Harris, R.E., Birmingham, W. Mids.
Harris, R.M., London, S.W.1.
Harris, Sylvia, Berkeley, Glos.
Harris, S., Deal, Kent.
Harris and Son (London) Ltd., London, W.1.
Harris, Mrs. S.J., Berkeley, Glos.
Harrison, Mrs., Letchmore, Herts.
Harrison Antiques, Miss, Carlisle, Cumbria.
Harrison Fine Antiques, Anna, Gosforth,
Tyne and Wear.
Harrison and Son, A.A., Sevenoaks, Kent.
Harrison, B.R.C., East Grinstead, W. Sussex.
Harrison, D., Edinburgh, Midloth., Scot.
(Another World).
Harrison Antiques, Dorothy, Criccieth,
Gwynedd, Wales.
Harrison, G. and B., Bishop Monkton,
N. Yorks.
Harrison, J.E., Sevenoaks, Kent.
Harrison, L.J., Bath, Avon. Gt. West. Ant. C.
Harrison, Marguerite, London, W.11. G.
Port. (Anne Barlow)
Harrison, O.E., Carlisle, Cumbria.
Harrison, Miss P., Lewes, E. Sussex.
Harrison, R., Sevenoaks, Kent.
Harrison, Mrs. T., Dorking, Surrey.
Harrison, Tim, Warwick, Warks.
Harrods Ltd., London, S.W.1.
Harrogate Post Card Shop, The, Harrogate,
N. Yorks.
Harrop Fold Clocks, Bolton-by-Bowland, Lancs.
Hart, Mrs. B., Marnhull, Dorset.
Hart, E., London, N.1.
Hart, Joe, Warwick, Warks. Smith St. A.C.
Hart, J.A. and N., Bletchingley, Surrey.
Hart, M., Hadleigh, Suffolk.
Hart, Michael, Edinburgh, Midloth., Scot.
Hart, Rosemary, London, N.1.
Hart and Rosenberg, London, N.1.
Hart, Steve, London, N.W.8. Alf. Ant. Mkt.
Hart Antiques, Sheila, London, N.1.
Harthope House Antiques, Moffat,
Dumfries., Scot.
Hartley Antiques, Hartley, Kent.
Hartley Antiques Ltd., J., Ripley, Surrey.
Hartley, M., Cockermouth, Cumbria.
Hartley, S.N., Birchington, Kent.
Hartley, S.N., Wingham, Kent.
Hartnell Antiques and Victoriana, Dorothy,
Sidmouth, Devon.
Hartnoll, Julian, London, S.W.1.
Harvesters Barn, Four Elms, Kent.
Harvey, A.D., London, N.W.1.
Harvey, C.S., Ludlow, Shrops.
Harvey and Gore, London, W.1.
Harvey, I.P., Lower Halstow, Kent.
Harvey, J., St. Helier, Jersey, C.I.
Harvey, Mr. and Mrs. J., Maentwrog,
Gwynedd, Wales.
Harvey, J.M., Aylesbury, Bucks.
Harvey, J.M., Gt. Malvern, Hereford and
Worcs.
Harvey Antiques, Morton, Aylesbury, Bucks.
Harvey, S. and N., Shoreham-by-Sea,
W. Sussex.
Harvey, W., London, S.W.3. Ant. Ant. Mkt.
Harvey and Co. (Antiques) Ltd., W.R.,
London, W.1.

Harvey and Co. Ltd., W.R., London, N.W.1.
Harvey, W.R., G.M. and A.D., London, N.W.1.
Harvey, W.R., G.M. and A.D., London, W.1.
Harvey-Jones, A., Melton, Suffolk.
Harvey-Morgan, R., Stratford-upon-Avon, Warks.
Harvey-Owen Antiques, Maentwrog, Gwynedd, Wales.
Harwood, A., Weston-super-Mare, Avon. Mkt.
Harwood, Mrs. J., Ambleside, Cumbria.
Harwood West End Antiques, Weston-super-Mare, Avon.
Hasel-Britt Ltd., Radlett, Herts.
Haskins, B.J., Ashtead, Surrey.
Haslam, Betty, Faringdon, Oxon.
Haslam and Whiteway, London, W.8.
Hassall Antiques, Geoffrey, Solihull, W. Mids.
Hastie, Ian G., Salisbury, Wilts.
Hastings-Spital, K., Bath, Avon. (Quiet St. Antiques)
Hatcher, Sherry, London, N.1.
Hatchwell Antiques, Simon, Brighton, E. Sussex.
Hatherleigh Antiques, Hatherleigh, Devon.
Hattam D., P. and W., Newcastle-upon-Tyne, Tyne and Wear.
Hattam's Antiques, Newcastle-upon-Tyne, Tyne and Wear.
Hatton, N.J., Benson, Oxon.
Haughey Antiques, D.M., Kirkby Stephen, Cumbria.
Haughton Antiques, Brian, London, W.1.
Havard, T. and P., Harpole, Northants.
Havemann-Mart, M.K., Chipping Campden, Glos.
Haven Gallery, The, Great Yarmouth, Norfolk.
Havenplan's Architectural Emporium, Killamarsh, Derbys.
Haverstock Antiques, London, N.W.3.
Haw, S., Haslemere, Surrey.
Hawker, Mr. and Mrs. P.M. Halliday, Corfe, Somerset.
Hawkey, V., Grimsby, S. Humberside.
Hawkins, Mr., Barnet, Gtr. London.
Hawkins, Mr., London, N.20.
Hawkins Antiques, Brian, London, N.1.
Hawkins Antiques, Brian, Loughton, Essex.
Hawkins (Brighton) Ltd., David, Brighton, E. Sussex.
Hawkins, G. and J., Cambridge, Glos.
Hawkins, J.A.S., Kingsbridge, Devon.
Hawkins, P.O., Sherston, Wilts.
Hawkins, R., Finedon, Northants.
Hawkridge, Mrs. M., Skipton, N. Yorks.
Hawley, John and Carol, Clevedon, Avon.
Hawley, Ray, Beverley, N. Humberside.
Haworth Antiques, Huby, N. Yorks.
Haworth, Fine Paintings (Cumbrian Fine Art Galleries) Peter, Kirkby Lonsdale, Cumbria.
Hay Galleries Ltd., Hay-on-Wye, Powys, Wales.
Hay, J.D., Glasgow, Lanarks, Scot. (Muirhead Moffat and Co.).

Hay Loft Gallery, Broadway, Hereford and Worcs.
Hay, Rachael, Fakenham, Norfolk. Ant. C.
Hay, S., R. and A., London, W.1. (Portman Carpets).
Haybarn and Bridgebarn Antiques Centre, Battlesbridge, Essex.
Hayden Antiques, H., Sheffield, S. Yorks.
Haydon Bridge Antiques, Haydon Bridge, Northumb.
Haydon House Antiques, Woburn Sands, Bucks.
Hayes, Miss M.L., North Shields, Tyne and Wear.
Hayes and Newby Antique Warehouse, Gloucester, Glos.
Hayes, P. and A., Gloucester, Glos.
Hayes Gallery, Paul, Auchterarder, Perths., Scot.
Hayes, Tim, Pulham Market, Norfolk.
Hayhurst Fine Glass, Jeanette, London, W.1.
Hayloft Antiques, Callington, Cornwall.
Hayman, Mrs. M.C., London, S.W.3. Ant. Ant. Mkt.
Hayter, Mrs. M., London, S.W.3. (T. Coakley) Chen. Gall.
Hayter, R.W. and F.L., Ryde, I. of Wight.
Hayters, Ryde, I. of Wight.
Hayton Antiques and Crafts., Sybil, Chessington, Gtr. London.
Hayward, Patricia, Deddington, Oxon. Ant. C.
Haywood, J. and M., Chester, Cheshire (Look Around Antiques).
Hazareh, A., Sheffield, S. Yorks. (Persian Carpet Ant.)
Hazel Cottage Clocks, Eachwick, Northumb.
Hazlitt, Gooden & Fox Ltd., London, S.W.1.
Heacock, J.A., Stockport, Cheshire.
Head, J. and J., Salisbury, Wilts.
Head, P., Liss, Hants.
Heads 'n' Tails, Milverton, Somerset.
Healey, J.P. and Mrs. I., London, S.W.3. Ant. Ant. Mkt.
Healey, T., Newark, Notts.
Heaney, T., Ballyclare, Co. Antrim, N. Ireland.
Hearne, E.W.A. and R.E.W., Beaconsfield, Bucks.
Hearne, R.E.W. and P.A., High Wycombe, Bucks.
Heath Antiques, Reigate, Surrey.
Heath, A.R., Bristol, Avon.
Heath, B., London, E.C.1.
Heath, K.W. and Y.F., Moreton-in-Marsh, Glos.
Heath-Bullock, Godalming, Surrey.
Heath-Bullock, A.H. and R.J., Godalming, Surrey.
Heathcote Antiques, Crosshills, N. Yorks.
Heather Antiques, London, N.1.
Heather, J.C., Woolpit, Suffolk.
Heatherlie Antiques, Selkirk, Selkirks., Scot.
Heathfield Antiques Centre, Heathfield, E. Sussex.
Heawood, A.M., Horncastle, Lincs.
Hebbard, D.L., Titchfield, Hants.

Hebbard, G.B., Hay-on-Wye, Powys, Wales.
Hebbards of Hay, Hay-on-Wye, Powys, Wales.
Hedge, G., Oxford, Oxon.
Hedingham Antiques, Sible Hedingham, Essex.
Hedley, E., Maldon, Essex.
Hedley, J.A. and T., Hexham, Northumb.
Heelis, J. and J., Milburn, Cumbria.
Heffer, W., Cambridge, Cambs. (Antiques Etc.).
Heffle Corner Antiques, Heathfield, E. Sussex.
Hefford, Mrs. R., Carlisle, Cumbria.
Heian Gallery, London, W.1. G. Mews.
Heigham, T., Sudbury, Suffolk.
Heim Gallery, London, S.W.1.
Heinsen, P. and M., Linslade, Beds.
Heirloom and Howard Ltd., London, W.1.
Helendean Antiques, Bath, Avon. B. Ant. Mkt.
Helius Antiques, London, S.W.14.
Heller, Mrs., London, N.W.8. Alf. Ant. Mkt.
Helliwell, A.H., Llandrindod Wells, Powys, Wales.
Hellmers, P., Epping, Essex.
Helperby Antiques, Helperby, N. Yorks.
Helton Antiques, Heath and Reach, Beds.
Hemmings, F.K., St. Ives, Cambs.
Hencotes Antiques and Books, Hexham, Northumb.
Henderson, Perth, Perths., Scot.
Henderson, Mrs., Arundel, W. Sussex.
Henderson, Mrs. A., Grays, Essex.
Henderson Antiques, Coupar Angus, Perths., Scot.
Henderson, B., Tunbridge Wells, Kent (Corn Exchange Antiques).
Henderson, C., Glasgow, Lanarks., Scot. (Corner House Antiques).
Henderson, F.M., Cowfold, W. Sussex.
Henderson, H. and L., Banchory, Kincard, Scot.
Henderson, J.G., Perth, Perths., Scot.
Henderson, Milne, London, W.1.
Henderson, J. and S. Milne, London, W.1.
Henderson, S.J., Donaghadee, Co. Down, N. Ireland.
Hendrika Antiques, Newton Abbot, Devon. N.A. Ant. C.
Heneage, Thomas, London, S.W.1.
Heneage, Thomas, London, S.W.4.
Henderson, G., London, W.1. (Clarendon Gallery.)
Henham (Antiques), Martin, London, N.2.
Henley House Antiques, Rumford, Cornwall.
Henley Antiques, R. and J.L., Canterbury, Kent.
Hennell Ltd., (incorporating Frazer and Haws (1868) and E. Lloyd Lawrence (1830)), London, W.1.
Hennessy, C. and G.C., Beaminster, Dorset.
Henning, Tina, London, N.W.8. Alf. Ant. Mkt.
Henson, D. and T., West Bridgford, Notts.
Henson, H.J.S., Leeds, W. Yorks.
Henson, R., London, S.W.3. Ant. Ant. Mkt.
Henson's Antiques, Leeds, W. Yorks.

Hepburn, T. and N., Beaconsfield, Bucks.
Hepner, R.P., Knutsford, Cheshire.
Hera Fine Art, Hythe, Kent.
Heraldry Today, London, S.W.3.
Heraldry Today, Ramsbury, Wilts.
Heraty, P., Hartley Wintney, Hants.
Heraz, London, S.W.1.
Herbert, N.R., Newmarket, Suffolk.
Hereward Antiques, Woburn, Beds. Wob. Ab. Ant. C.
Herford, H.W. and D.M., Kemerton, Hereford and Worcs.
Heritage Antiques, Linlithgow, West Loth., Scot.
Heritage Antiques, London, N.1.
Heritage Antiques, Paisley, Renfrews., Scot.
Heritage Antiques and Gallery Six, Salcombe, Devon.
Heritage Antiques and Restorations Ltd., Great Missenden, Bucks.
Heritage Antiques and Stripped Pine, Cardiff, S. Glam., Wales.
Heritage Interiors, Upper Beeding, W. Sussex.
Herman Antiques, Petworth, W. Sussex.
Herman, N. and S., Petworth, W. Sussex.
Herman, R., Milford-on-Sea, Hants.
Hermitage Antiques, London, S.W.1.
Hermitage Antiquities, Fishguard, Dyfed, Wales.
Heron, H.N.M., Mrs. J., and Mrs. E.M., Yoxall, Staffs.
Heron and Son Ltd., H.W., Yoxall, Staffs.
Herrald Antiques, Edinburgh, Midloth., Scot.
Herring, W., North Petherwin, Cornwall.
Herrington, D.M., Hungerford, Berks. (Dolls and Toys of Yesteryear).
Herrington, L.R., Hungerford, Berks. (Bow House Antiques).
Hersheson, J., Brighton, E. Sussex. (Hallmarks).
Hersheson, J.J., Brighton, E. Sussex (Kingsbury Antiques).
Hershkowitz Ltd., Robert, London, S.W.7.
Herts. and Essex Antique Centre, The, Sawbridgeworth, Herts.
Heskia, London, W.1.
Hesling, J., Nairn, Nairn., Scot.
Hester, Mrs. B.M., Indian Queens, Cornwall.
Hetreed, D.M., Gillingham, Dorset.
Hewes, P.N., Bury St. Edmunds, Suffolk.
Hewlett Gallery, Richard, London, S.W.3.
Hewlett, T.A, London, W.11.
Hewson, Mrs. K., Woodchurch, Kent.
Hex, Mrs. A., Uppingham, Leics.
Hexham Antiques, Hexham, Northumb.
Hext, D., Coniston, Cumbria.
Heyday, Saddleworth, Lancs.
Heyday Antiques, Wallingford, Oxon. L. Arc.
Heyes, A., Poulton-le-Fylde, Lancs.
Heyward, Pat, Wallingford, Oxon. L. Arc.
Heywood Antiques, J., Glastonbury, Somerset.
Heywood, E., London, S.W.3. (Monro Heywood Ltd.)
Hibbert Bros., Sheffield, S. Yorks.
Hick Antiques, David, Carrefour Selous, Jersey, C.I.

Hickford, T.K. and W.E., Grundisburgh, Suffolk.
Hickley, Maurice, London, S.W.3. Ant. Ant. Mkt.
Hickman, Tom, Frome, Somerset.
Hickmott, J.R., Tunbridge Wells, Kent.
Hicks-Bolton Galleries, Jo, Newton Abbot, Devon. N.A. Ant. C.
Hicks, K., London, N.W.8. Alf. Ant. Mkt.
Hicks, M.B. and I.F., North Walsham, Norfolk.
Hicks, M.B. and I.F., Stalham, Norfolk.
Hickson, Lewis, CMBHI, Antiquarian Horologist formerly Westgate Antiques, Tadcaster, N. Yorks.
Hickson, L.E., Tadcaster, N. Yorks.
Hidden Gem, Macclesfield, Cheshire.
Higbee, W. and N., Chichester, W. Sussex.
Higgins, B.R., Brighton, E. Sussex (Yellow Lantern Antiques Ltd.).
Higgins, Mrs. L., Bridge of Weir, Renfrews., Scot.
High Street Antiques, Alcester, Warks.
High Street Antiques, Bisley, Glos.
High Street Antiques and Decor, Falmouth, Cornwall.
Highgate Antiques, Kendal, Cumbria.
Highgate Gallery, London, N.1.
Highgate Gallery, London, N.6.
Highland Antiques, Nairn, Nairn., Scot.
Highmoor, Mrs. E.M., Cambridge, Cambs. (Collectors Market).
Highway Gallery, The, Upton-on-Severn, Hereford and Worcs.
Hilbery House, Leominster, Hereford and Worcs. L. Ant. Mkt.
Hilden, Mrs. C., Canterbury, Kent.
Hildreth, Ltd., W., London, W.11.
Hill, Mrs., Newton Abbot, Devon, N.A. Ant. C.
Hill Books, Alan, Chesterfield, Derbys.
Hill Books, Alan, Sheffield, S. Yorks.
Hill, A.R., Bristol, Avon. (The Oriental Carpet Centre)
Hill, B., Shipton-under-Wychwood, Oxon.
Hill, B.E., Pinner, Gtr. London.
Hill, Mrs. C., Canterbury, Kent.
Hill, Mrs. C., London, N.1.
Hill, David, Kirkby Stephen, Cumbria.
Hill, D., Macclesfield, Cheshire.
Hill, D. and M., Long Melford, Suffolk.
Hill, G., London, S.W.3. (Past Times.) Chen. Gall.
Hill, G. and J., Ripon, N. Yorks.
Hill Ltd., G. Heywood, London, W.1.
Hill, G., M., and J., London, S.W.3. (Jeremy Ltd..).
Hill House, Pulborough, W. Sussex.
Hill, J.E. and J.T., Wolverhampton, W. Mids.
Hill, M.A., Chichester, W. Sussex.
Hill Antiques, Peter, Bedford, Beds.
Hill Rise Antiques, Richmond, Gtr. London.
Hill, R.I., Burgh-le-Marsh, Lincs.
Hill, R.M., Bulkington, Warks.
Hill and Sons, W.E., Great Missenden, Bucks.
Hillair Antiques, Theydon Bois, Essex.

Hilliard, J., London, W.11. G. Port. (Lorenz John)
Hillman Antiques, M., Macclesfield, Cheshire.
Hills Antiques, Macclesfield, Cheshire.
Hills and Partners Ltd., Richard, Plymouth, Devon.
Hillside Antiques, Lindfield, W. Sussex.
Hillside Antiques, Halifax, W. Yorks.
Hillyers, London, S.E.26.
Hilmarton Manor Press, Calne, Wilts.
Hilson, A. and B., Tewkesbury, Glos.
Hilton Antiques, Sidmouth, Devon.
Hilton, Simon, Dunmow, Essex.
Himsworth, R.K., York, N. Yorks.
Hind, M., Langford, Avon.
Hinde Fine Art, Sheila, Kirdford, W. Sussex.
Hinde, P., Richmond, Gtr. London.
Hindle and Son, W., Wigan, Lancs.
Hines, J., Costessey, Norfolk.
Hingston's, Southampton, Hants.
Hingstons, N., Southampton, Hants.
Hinson Fine Paintings, Sheffield, S. Yorks.
Hinton Gallery, The, Hookwood, W. Sussex.
Hirsbrunner, Mr. and Mrs. R.B., Christchurch, Dorset.
Hirsch and Braun, London, W.1. G. Mews.
Hirschler, B., London, N.16.
Hirst Antiques, Christchurch, Dorset.
Hirst Antiques, London, W.11.
Hirst, Mrs. S.M., Alnwick, Northumb.
His Nibs, London, W.C.2.
Hitchcox, P. and R., Chalgrove, Oxon.
Hitchcox, P. and R., Oxford, Oxon.
Hitchin Antiques Gallery, Hitchin, Herts.
Hoad, G.A.J., Poole, Dorset.
Hoare, Oliver, London, S.W.1 (Ahuan U.K. Ltd.).
Hoare Ltd., Peter, Tunbridge Wells, Kent.
Hobart, A. and M., London, S.W.1 (Pyms Gallery).
Hobbs, Carlton, London, S.W.10.
Hobby Horse Antiques, Bridport, Dorset.
Hobhouse Ltd., London, S.W.1.
Hobhouse, N., London, S.W.1. (Hobhouse Ltd.)
Hobson Antiques, Diana, Sandgate, Kent. S. Ant. C.
Hockin (Antiques) Ltd., Keith, Stow-on-the-Wold, Glos.
Hockley Coins, Nottingham, Notts.
Hockley Antiques, William, Cranleigh, Surrey.
Hockley Antiques, William, Petworth, W. Sussex.
Hodge, Jean, Worcester, Hereford and Worcs.
Hodge, Sarah, Worcester, Hereford and Worcs.
Hodges Antiques, Tony, Harbertonford, Devon.
Hodges, T.A.R., Harbertonford, Devon.
Hodgkins and Co. Ltd., Ian, Slad, Glos.
Hodgkins, Z., Brighton, E. Sussex. (Dupont Galleries).
Hodgkinson, B. and J., Newport, Essex.
Hodgkinson, P.M. and P.A., Hertford, Herts.
Hodgson, J., Great Shefford, Berks.

Hodgson, Joy, London, N.W.8. Alf. Ant. Mkt.
Hodgson, P. and R., Birmingham, W. Mids. (Ashley House Antiques).
Hodsoll, Christopher, London, S.W.1.
Hoevelmann, H., Eastbourne, E. Sussex.
Hoff Antiques Ltd., London, W.8.
Hoff, Mrs. R., London, W.8.
Hoffman Antiques, London, W.1. G. Ant. Mkt.
Hoffman, J.E., Ashley, Northants.
Hofgartner, S. and L., Hungerford, Berks. (Below Stairs).
Hofman Antiques, George, Stockbridge, Hants.
Hofmann and Freeman Ltd., Otford, Kent.
Hogarth, M., Brough, Cumbria.
Hogg, David, London, W.1. G. Ant. Mkt.
Hogg Antiques, Michael, London, S.W.3.
Holborough, D., Eynsham, Oxon.
Holden, Mrs. A., Capel, Surrey.
Holden Ltd., Esmond, Reigate, Surrey.
Holden, K.E., Reigate, Surrey.
Holden, L.J., Hastings, E. Sussex.
Holder, D., London, W.C.1.
Hole-in-the-Wall, The, Armagh, Co. Armagh, N. Ireland.
Hole-in-the-Wall Antiques, Stockport, Cheshire.
Holgate Antiques, York, N. Yorks.
Holgate, J.R., Thorne, S. Yorks.
Holgate, Milton, Knaresborough, N. Yorks.
Holgate, M.J., Knaresborough, N. Yorks.
Holland Bros. Antiquarian Booksellers, Ledbury, Hereford and Worcs.
Holland, Guy, Eastleach, Glos.
Holland and Holland Ltd., London, W.1.
Holland, N., Tunbridge Wells, Kent. (Annique Antiques.)
Holland Press Ltd., The, London, W.2.
Hollander, E., London, S.W.3.
Hollard, S.A., Langport, Somerset.
Hollens Antiques, David, Brentwood, Essex.
Holleyman and Treacher Ltd., Brighton, E. Sussex.
Hollings Antiques, Irene, Woburn, Beds. Wob. Ab. Ant. C.
Hollingshead and Co., London, S.W.6.
Hollingshead, D., London, S.W.6.
Hollington Antiques, Long Crendon, Bucks.
Holloway Antiques, Topsham, Devon.
Holloway, J.M., Dorchester, Dorset.
Holloways Antiques, Burton-on-Trent, Staffs.
Hollowood, G., Daventry, Northants.
Holly Style Antiques, Chobham, Surrey.
Hollywood Road Antiques, London, S.W.10.
Hollywood Road Gallery, London, S.W.10.
Holme Antiques, Sheffield, S. Yorks.
Holme Fires, Holme, Cumbria.
Holme, Mrs. P., Bures, Suffolk.
Holmes Antiques, Keswick, Cumbria.
Holmes, Brian and Lynn, London, W.1. G. Ant. Mkt.
Holmes Antiques, B. and T., Sandgate, Kent. S. Ant. C.
Holmes, C., Keswick, Cumbria.
Holmes, D., London, W.8.
Holmes, D., Port Isaac, Cornwall.
Holmes House Antiques, Sedlescombe, E. Sussex.

Holmes, J., Perranporth, Cornwall.
Holmes Antique Maps and Prints, Julia, Haslemere, Surrey.
Holmes, Ltd., London, W.1.
Holochwast, V., Bath, Avon. Gt. West. Ant. C. Wed. Mkt.
Holt Antiques Centre, Holt, Norfolk.
Holt, M.K., Bath, Avon. Gt. West. A. C. Wed. Mkt.
Holt and Co. Ltd., R., London, E.C.1.
Holtom, J. and J. Burman, Stratford-upon-Avon, Warks.
Holyome, A.C., London, N.1 (Canonbury Antiques).
Holzgrawe, W. and A.M., Cirencester, Glos.
Holzgrawe Antiques, W.W., Cirencester, Glos.
Home Features, Dartington, Devon.
Home Features Ltd., Dartington, Devon.
Home of Antiques, The, Knaresborough, N. Yorks.
Homer, J.P.J., Cheltenham, Glos.
Homer Oriental Rugs, Cheltenham, Glos.
Homewood Antiques, Hythe, Kent.
Homewood, D.C. and R.A., Hythe, Kent.
Hone, Angela, Beaconsfield, Bucks.
Honiton Antiques, Honiton, Devon.
Honiton Lace Shop, The, Honiton, Devon.
Hooberman, E., London, S.W.10.
Hood and Broomfield, Newcastle-under-Lyme, Staffs.
Hood, C., Easingwold, N. Yorks.
Hood and Co., Helena, Bath, Avon.
Hood, J., Newcastle-under-Lyme, Staffs.
Hood, Mrs. L.M., Bath, Avon.
Hoodeners Antiques and Collectors Market, Canterbury, Kent.
Hook, Anthony J., Westerham, Kent.
Hook, I., Norwich, Norfolk (The Little Gallery).
Hooke and Son, John, London, W.11.
Hooper Antiques, David, Leamington Spa, Warks.
Hooper, Martha, Glasgow, Lanarks., Scot. Vict. Vill.
Hooper and Purchase, London, S.W.3.
Hooper, P., Worcester, Hereford and Worcs.
Hope Chest, The, Bath, Avon. Gt. West. Ant. C.
Hope and Glory, London, W.8.
Hope, Howard, London, W.1. G. Mews.
Hope, June, Deddington, Oxon. Ant. C.
Hope, June, Weston-super-Mare, Avon.
Hope, Mrs. J., Weston-super-Mare, Avon.
Hope, Mrs. J.P., Deddington, Oxon. Ant. C.
Hopkins (Antiques) Ltd., J., Brighton, E. Sussex.
Hoppen Ltd., Stephanie, London, S.W.3.
Hoppett, G., Wolverhampton, W. Mids.
Hopwell Antiques, Paul, West Haddon, Northants.
Hopwood, D. and R., Windermere, Cumbria.
Hopwood, J., Windermere, Cumbria.
Horley Antiques, Welshpool, Powys, Wales.
Horn Antiques, Churt, Surrey.
Horn at the Golden Past, Dorothea, Peel, Isle of Man.
Hornbeam Antiques, Wymeswold, Leics.

Horne, Jonathan, London, W.8.
Hornsby, E., Wallingford, Oxon. L. Arc.
Hornsby, P.R.G., and J.M., Witney, Oxon.
Hornsey Ltd., Adrian, Buckingham, Bucks.
Hornsey, José, Bradford-on-Avon, Wilts.
Hornsey, P.S. and J., Bradford-on-Avon, Wilts.
Horological Workshops, Guildford, Surrey.
Horse Fair Antiques, Chipping Norton, Oxon.
Horse Market Antiques, Barnard Castle, Durham.
Horse Rock, Helens Bay, Co. Down, N. Ireland.
Horsebridge Antiques Centre, Horsebridge, E. Sussex.
Horseshoe Antiques and Gallery, Burford, Oxon.
Horsman, P. and M., London, W.1. (Neptune)
Horswell, E.F. and J., London, W.1 (The Sladmore Gallery).
Horswill Antiques, Helen, West Kirby, Merseyside.
Horswill, J.O., West Kirby, Merseyside.
Horton, E. and R., Hertford, Herts.
Horton, G.B., Henley-in-Arden, Warks.
Horwit, J.I. (Henry Faber Ltd.), London, W.C.1.
Horwood, R., Bristol, Avon (Sedan Chair Antiques).
Hosains Books and Antiques, London, W.2.
Hoskin, C., Padstow, Cornwall.
Hoskin, R., Ewhurst, Surrey.
Hoskins, R., Keighley, W. Yorks.
Hoskinson, P., Birmingham, W. Mids. (Jomarc Pianos U.K.)
Hotspur Ltd., London, S.W.1.
Houchen, B., King's Lynn, Norfolk.
Houghton Hall Antiques, Market Weighton, N. Humberside.
Houlgate, Mrs. S.R., Harrogate, N. Yorks. (Cold Bath Antiques)
Houlton, N., Bristol, Avon. (Triangle Antiques)
Hour Glass Antiques, Ramsey, Isle of Man.
House (Mitre Antiques), Bernard G., Wells, Somerset.
House of Antiques, Brighton, E. Sussex.
House of Antiques, The, Hull, N. Humberside.
House of Antiques, The, Petersfield, Hants.
House of Buckingham (Antiques), London, E.C.1.
House of Christian Antiques, Ash Vale, Surrey.
House of Mallett, Surbiton, Gtr. London.
House of Mirrors, London, S.W.6.
House of Steel Antiques, London, N.1.
House, Sonia, Bath, Avon. Gt. West. A.C.
Housley, M., Sheffield, S. Yorks. (Wharf Antiques)
Houston Gallery, Wells, Somerset.
Houston, M., Bath, Avon. Gt. West. Ant. C.
How, Mrs. G.E.P., London, S.W.1.
How of Edinburgh, London, S.W.1.
Howard Antiques, London, W.1.
Howard Antiques, London, W.1. G. Ant. Mkt.
Howard Antiques, Oundle, Northants.

Howard, D. and J. Cowell, Bath, Avon. Gt. West. Ant. C.
Howard, David, Cheltenham, Glos.
Howard, Derek, London, S.W.3. Chen. Gall.
Howard, D.S., London, W.1 (Heirloom and Howard Ltd.).
Howard, Elizabeth, Bath, Avon. B. Ant. Mkt.
Howard, J., Felsted, Essex.
Howard, Jonathan G., Chipping Norton, Oxon.
Howard, Kerry, Bath, Avon. Gt. West. Ant. C.
Howard, K.C., Much Wenlock, Shrops.
Howard, The Hon. Maurice, Cirencester, Glos.
Howard, M., Much Hadham, Herts.
Howard Books, Peter, Croydon, Gtr. London.
Howard Antiques, Stuart, Much Hadham, Herts.
Howard-Jones, H., London, W.8.
Howards of Aberystwyth, Aberystwyth, Dyfed, Wales.
Howarth Antiques, Harrogate, N. Yorks. W. Pk. Ant. Pav.
Howarth, G.H., Lichfield, Staffs.
Howarth, Mrs. M.K., Lytham, Lancs.
Howarth Fine Paintings, Peter, Kirkby Lonsdale, Cumbria.
Howe, Christine, London, S.W.3. Ant. Ant. Mkt.
Howell, F.G. and P.B., Hereford, Hereford and Worcs.
Howell, M., Bournemouth, Dorset. (Gallery 922)
Howells, J.P. and J., Pembroke, Dyfed, Wales.
Howes Bookshop, Hastings, E. Sussex.
Howes Gallery, Petworth, W. Sussex.
Howes, R., Horrabridge, Devon.
Howkins, Antiques, Barry, Gt. Yarmouth, Norfolk.
Howkins, John, Great Yarmouth, Norfolk.
Howkins, Peter, Gt. Yarmouth, Norfolk.
Howlett, P., London, S.W.6. (White and Howlett)
Howlett, Peter, London, W.11. G. Port (Richard White)
Hoy Antiques, Windsor and Eton, Berks.
Hoyle, D., Whitby, N. Yorks.
Hoyle and Son Antiques, Rod, Ramsgate, Kent.
Hoyles Antiques and Collectors Bazaars, Warburton, Cheshire.
Hoysted, Anna, Mattingley, Hants.
Hubbard Antiques, Leominster, Hereford and Worcs.
Hubbard Antiques, Ipswich, Suffolk.
Hubbard, C.L.B., Ponterwyd, Dyfed, Wales.
Hubbard, J., Canterbury, Kent.
Hubbard, J. and J., St. Peter Port, Guernsey, C.I.
Hubbard Antiques, John, Birmingham, W. Mids.
Hubbard's Bookshop, Doggie, Ponterwydd, Dyfed, Wales.
Huckett, A.G. and N.E., Toddington, Beds.
Huckvale, C. and G., Battle, E. Sussex.

Huddersfield Antiques, Huddersfield, W. Yorks.
Hudes, Eric, Braintree, Essex.
Hudes, Eric, London, W.11.
Hudson, Barry, Preston, Lancs. N.W. Ant. C.
Hudson, Barbara, St. Albans, Herts.
Hudson, Lady Cathleen, Stanford Dingley, Berks.
Hudson, D. and B., Misterton, Notts.
Hudson, E.A., Ditchling, E. Sussex.
Hudson, F.R., London, N.1. (Capricorn Antiques Ltd.)
Hudson, J., Farnham, Surrey.
Hudson, M.A., Saffron Walden, Essex.
Hudson, Thomas and Pamela, Cirencester, Glos.
Hudson and Williams, London, W.1.
Huetson Antiques, Gordon, Market Weighton, N. Humberside.
Hufton, M. and C., Nottingham, Notts.
Hugall, G., Jesmond, Tyne and Wear.
Huggett and Son, L.J., Honiton, Devon.
Hugh Evelyn Picture Shop, The, London, N.W.8.
Hughes, A., Wisborough Green, W. Sussex.
Hughes, B. and M., Dumfries, Dumfries., Scot.
Hughes, Colin Spencer, Machynlleth, Powys, Wales.
Hughes, D., London, S.W.1. (Whitford and Hughes).
Hughes, Doreen, Rye, E. Sussex. Str. Ants.
Hughes, Eifiona, Criccieth, Gwynedd, Wales.
Hughes Antiques, Elizabeth, Swansea, W. Glam. Wales.
Hughes, J. Dunstable, Beds.
Hughes, M., Mathry, Dyfed, Wales.
Hughes, M.A. and D.A., Bath, Avon.
Hughes, P., Glasgow, Lanarks., Scot. (Mercat Antiques).
Hughes, P., Lymington, Hants.
Hughes, Textiles, Paul, London, W.2.
Hughes Antique Gallery, Roger, Swansea, W. Glam., Wales.
Hughes, S., Cardiff, S. Glam., Wales. (Broadway Antiques).
Hughes, Mrs. S., Cobham, Surrey.
Hughes and Smeeth Ltd., Lymington, Hants.
Hughes-Reckitt, S., Sproughton, Suffolk.
Huie, A.C., Pitlochry, Perths., Scot.
Huish, C. and D., Chepstow, Gwent, Wales.
Hulbert, (Antiques and Firearms), Anne and Colin, Swansea, W. Glam., Wales.
Hull, Major J. G. and Mrs. P., Budleigh Salterton, Devon.
Hulme, J. Alan, Chester, Cheshire.
Humble Antiques, Mac, Bath, Avon.
Humble, Owen, Jesmond, Tyne and Wear.
Humble, W. McA., Bath, Avon.
Humbleyard Fine Art, Holt, Norfolk.
Hume, Dudley, Brighton, E. Sussex.
Humphrey, C. and D., Manchester, Lancs. (Crown Antiques)
Humphrey, E., Edinburgh, Midloth., Scot. (Antiques).
Humphrey, K.A., Leeds, W. Yorks. (Andrew's Antique Shop).

Humphreys, R., London, N.1. (The Shop on the Corner).
Humphry Antiques, J. and M., Petworth, W. Sussex.
Humphrys, Brian, Penzance, Cornwall.
Hunaban, R.S. and E.A., Great Malvern, Hereford and Worcs.
Hunger, J., London, W.1. (Sac Freres).
Hungerford Arcade, Hungerford, Berks.
Hunka, Winifred, Fakenham, Norfolk. Ant. C.
Hunnings, P.J.M., Penn, Bucks.
Hunt, B., Newton Abbot, Devon, N.A. Ant. C.
Hunt, R.J., Burgess Hill, W. Sussex.
Hunt, Mrs. S., Bolton, Lancs.
Hunter, Mrs., Weymouth, Dorset.
Hunter Antiques, Weymouth, Dorset.
Hunter, Mrs. A.E.C., Norwich, Norfolk (Charles Cubitt).
Hunter and Patrick Seale Fine Art, Sally, London, S.W.1.
Hunter, T., London, S.W.1. (Cobra and Bellamy).
Hunter-Smith, J., S.W.3. Ant. Ant. Mkt.
Huntingdon Antiques, Nottingham, Notts.
Huntington Antiques Ltd., Stow-on-the-Wold, Glos.
Hunwick, J., Herstmonceux, E. Sussex.
Hunwick, P.F., Hungerford, Berks. (The Old Malthouse).
Hurdle, N., Bladon, Oxon.
Hursley Antiques, Hursley, Hants.
Hurst, A.H.B., Woodbridge, Suffolk.
Hurst Antiques, Anthony, Woodbridge, Suffolk.
Hutchin, D., Chesham, Bucks.
Hutchings, D.S., Newport, Gwent, Wales.
Hutchings Antiques, Edward, Sandgate, Kent. S. Ant. C.
Hutchins, Mrs. A.M., Market Harborough, Leics.
Hutchins, E.H., Oakley, Hants.
Hutchinson, Mrs. F., Keighley, W. Yorks.
Hutchinson, P. and M., London, W.11.
Hutchinson-Shire, Mr. and Mrs. N.A., Endmoor, Cumbria.
Hutchison, J. and C., Hythe, Kent.
Hutton, Mrs., Glasgow, Lanarks., Scot. Vict. Vill.
Hutton Antiques, Shrewsbury, Shrops.
Hutton (Jewellers and Silversmiths), Eleanor, Dorking, Surrey.
Hutton, J. and J., Berkhamsted, Herts.
Hutton, Martin, Ninfield, E. Sussex.
Hutton, Mrs. P.I., Shrewsbury, Shrops.
Hutton-Clarke, J. and H., Painswick, Glos.
Huyton, E., Ramsey, Isle of Man.
Hyde, J.A.W. and F.A., Westbury, Wilts.
Hyde, M., Romsey, Hants.
Hyde Park Antiques, London, W.11.
Hyde Park Rare Books, Leeds, W. Yorks.
Hyde, R., Exeter, Devon.
Hyde, Shelagh, Rhos-on-Sea, Clwyd, Wales.
Hyder, Steven, London, W.11. G. Port.
Hymore-Hodson, London, S.W.3. Chen. Gall.
Hyron Antiques, Sandgate, Kent.
Hythe Antique Centre, Hythe, Kent.
Hythe Galleries, Hythe, Kent.

I

I.G.A. Old Masters Ltd., St. Helier, Jersey, C.I.
I. and S., Antiques, Ludlow, Shrops.
Ibba, A., London, W.11.
Ibbitson, J.M., Stratford-upon-Avon, Warks.
Iconastas, London, S.W.1.
Idears of Diss incorporating Benton Antiques Ltd., Diss, Norfolk.
Idler's Alley Antiques, North Shoebury, Essex.
Igel, M., Kingston-upon-Thames, Gtr. London.
Iglesis, D., London, S.W.1 (Gallery '25.)
Ilchester Antique Pine, Ilchester, Somerset.
Iles Family, The, Rochester, Kent.
Iles, Francis, Rochester, Kent.
Iles Gallery, Richard, Colchester, Essex.
Iles, P., Worfield, Shrops.
Iles, R. and C., Colchester, Essex.
Il Libro, London, S.W.3. Chen. Gall.
Ilsley, R., London, N.W.3.
Imperial Antiques, Hull, N. Humberside.
Imperial Antiques, Stockport, Cheshire.
Impressions and Alexandra's Antiques, St. Margaret's Bay, Kent.
Imrie, Mr. and Mrs. I., Bridge of Earn, Perths., Scot.
In Retrospect, Pocklington, N. Humberside.
Ing, J., Wisbech, Cambs.
Ingestre Investment Antiques, Sutton Coldfield, W. Mids.
Ingham, J.S., Horbury, W. Yorks.
Inglenook Antiques, Harpole, Northants.
Inglenook Antiques, Ramsbury, Wilts.
Inglis, Brand, London, S.W.1.
Ingram, D., Edinburgh, Midloth., Scot. (Dunedin Antiques Ltd.).
Ingram, I.C., Perth, Perths., Scot.
Ingrams, C., Haslemere, Surrey.
Inheritance, London, N.1.
Innes Gallery, Malcolm, London, S.W.3.
Innes Gallery, Malcolm, Edinburgh, Midloth., Scot.
Intercol London, London, N.1.
Ion, J.E., London, W.6.
Iona Antiques, London, W.1. Grays A. M.
Iona Antiques, London, W.8. Ant. Hyp.
Irani, M.Z., London, S.W.1. (The Connoisseur Gallery.)
Ireland, P., Birmingham, W. Mids. (Format of Birmingham Ltd.)
Ironbridge Antiques, Exeter, Devon.
Ironbridge Antique Centre, Ironbridge, Shrops.
Irons, Mr. and Mrs. C.A., Coalville, Leics.
Irving Antiques, Manchester, Lancs. Royal Ex. S.C.
Irving, Giulia, Woodstock, Oxon.
Irwin, C. and M., Ravenstonedale, Cumbria.
Isaacs, P. and S., Leeds, W. Yorks.
Isbell, S., Bath, Avon. (Queen's Parade Antiques Ltd.)
Isenberg, M., Bushey, Herts.
Islington Artefacts, London, N.1.
Ison, Mr. and Mrs. P., Swaffham, Norfolk.
It's About Time, Westcliff-on-Sea, Essex.
Ivanhoe Antiques, Ashby-De-La-Zouch, Leics.
Ivelet Books Ltd., Redhill, Surrey.

Ives Bookseller, John, Twickenham, Gtr. London.
Ives, K.C. and Mrs., Baldock, Herts.
Ivy House Antiques, Abbots Bromley, Staffs.
Ivy House Antiques, Brasted, Kent.
Ivy House Antiques, Gt. Shefford, Berks.
Ivy House Antiques, Shillingstone, Dorset.
Ivy Lane Antique Centre, Canterbury, Kent.

J

J.C. Antiques, London, E.17.
J. and G. Antiques, London, S.W.3. Ant. Ant. Mkt.
J.J. Antiques, Wallingford, Oxon. L. Arc.
J.N. Antiques, Redbourn, Herts.
J.P. Antiques, Deddington, Oxon.
J. and P. Antiques, London, N.W.8. Alf. Ant. Mkt.
J.T. Antiques, London, S.W.11.
J.V.T. Antiques, Bingley, S. Yorks.
Jack, J., Glasgow, Lanarks., Scot. (Mercat Antiques).
Jackdaw Antiques, The, Haslemere, Surrey.
Jackdaw Antiques, The, Rothbury, Northumb.
Jackman, F.T. and S., Jesmond, Tyne and Wear.
Jackman, Mr. and Mrs. J., Brighton, E. Sussex (Minutiques).
Jack's Antiques, Egham, Surrey.
Jackson, A., Leamington Spa, Warks.
Jackson, Miss A.E., Chesham, Bucks.
Jackson, A.K.L., Edinburgh, Midloth., Scot. (Jacksonville Warehouse)
Jackson, B., London, S.W.1. (Northfield Antiques (Belgravia).)
Jackson, B.M., Wimborne Minster, Dorset.
Jackson Antiques, Charles, Penzance, Cornwall.
Jackson, G.T.M., Penzance, Cornwall.
Jackson, H., Sheffield, S. Yorks.
Jackson, H.N.B., Penzance, Cornwall.
Jackson, Kenneth, Edinburgh, Midloth., Scot.
Jackson, Metcalfe, Wimborne Minster, Dorset.
Jackson, N.W., Quarndon, Derbys.
Jackson, Olivia, London, W.11.
Jackson, P., London, S.W.3. (O.F. Wilson Ltd.).
Jackson, P., Windsor and Eton, Berks. (Times Past Antiques Ltd.)
Jackson Antiques, Peter and Heather, Brackley, Northants.
Jackson, R. and J., Flaxton, N. Yorks.
Jackson, R.E. and M., Idle, W. Yorks.
Jackson, T.C. and Mrs., Newbury, Berks.
Jackson, W.C.M., Edinburgh, Midloth., Scot. (The Scottish Gallery).
Jackson, W.R., Bampton, Devon.
Jackson-Grant Antiques, Teynham, Kent.
Jackson-Grant, D.M., Teynham, Kent.
Jacksons of Sheffield, Sheffield, S. Yorks.
Jacksonsville Warehouse, Edinburgh, Midloth., Scot.

Johnson, D., Oakamoor, Staffs.
Johnson, D.E., Clacton-on-Sea, Essex.
Johnson, Mr. and Mrs. E.M., Salisbury,
Wilts.
Johnson Antiques, George, London, W.11.
Johnson and Son (Shaftesbury) Ltd., G.E.,
Shaftesbury, Dorset.
Johnson, Mrs. I.A., London, S.W.3. Ant.
Ant. Mkt.
Johnson, Mrs. J.A., Hale, Cheshire.
Johnson, Mrs. J.A., Heversham, Cumbria.
Johnson, Mrs. M., Bath, Avon. Ant. Mkt.
Johnson, N.R. and J.J., Sherborne, Dorset.
Johnson Ltd., Oscar and Peter, London,
S.W.1.
Johnson, Mrs. P.A., Newport, Gwent,
Wales.
Johnson, P. and J., Stone, Staffs.
Johnson, Robert, London, W.1. G. Ant.
Mkt.
Johnson, S., London, S.W.3. Ant. Ant. Mkt.
Johnson, S., Newton Abbot, Devon. N.A.
Ant. C.
Johnson, S., York, N. Yorks. (Blenheim
House Antiques).
Johnson, T.L., Maidenhead, Berks.
Johnson, Walker and Tolhurst Ltd., London,
W.1.
Johnsons of Sherborne Ltd., Sherborne,
Dorset.
Johnsons of Stone, Stone, Staffs.
Johnston, A.A., Somerton, Somerset.
Johnston, A.W., Wimborne Minster, Dorset.
Johnston Antiques, Paul, Gedney, Lincs.
Johnston, T. and S., Keighley, W. Yorks.
Johnston, William, Radlett, Herts.
Johnstone, W., Barrhead, Renfrews., Scot.
Joiners Hall, The, Salisbury, Wilts.
'Jolie', Westerham, Kent.
Joly, Ruth, London, S.W.1.
Jomarc Pianos U.K., Birmingham, W. Mids.
Jon David (Fine Furniture) Ltd., Hoylake,
Merseyside.
Jones, A., Colchester, Essex.
Jones, A., Sproughton, Suffolk.
Jones Antiques, Llandeilo, Dyfed, Wales.
Jones Antiques, Alan, Okehampton, Devon.
Jones Antiques, Alan, Sparkwell, Devon.
Jones, A. and E., Newcastle Emlyn, Dyfed,
Wales.
Jones, B.J., Litcham, Norfolk.
Jones, D.J., Kendal, Cumbria.
Jones Ltd., D.L., Lyddington, Leics.
Jones, E., Chester, Cheshire.
Jones, E., Stourbridge, W. Mids.
Jones Antiques, Esther, (Puzzle House
Antiques), Chepstow, Gwent, Wales.
Jones, E.C., Birmingham, W. Mids. (Kestrel
House Antiques).
Jones and Son Antiques, E.D., Ryde, I. of
Wight.
Jones, E.P., Liverpool, Merseyside.
Jones, G., Birmingham, W. Mids. (Old Malt
House.)
Jones, G., Leicester, Leics.
Jones Antiques, Glyn, Llandeilo, Dyfed,
Wales.
Jones, Howard, London, W.8.

Jones, H. and I., Billericay, Essex.
Jones, Jenny, Manchester, Lancs. Royal
Ex. S.C.
Jones, J., Towcester, Northants.
Jones, J., Warwick, Warks.
Jones, J. and G., London, W.11.
Jones, Mrs. J.H., Llandeilo, Dyfed, Wales.
Jones, K., Bath, Avon. Gt. West. Ant. C.
(Tassles.)
Jones, L., Ludlow, Shrops.
Jones, Jeweller, Michael, Northampton,
Northants.
Jones, M.R.T. and Mrs. J.A., Cromer,
Norfolk.
Jones, M.S., Great Ayton, N. Yorks.
Jones, Paul, London, S.W.3. Ant. Ant. Mkt.
Jones, P., Watton, Norfolk.
Jones Antiques, Paul, Chalfont St. Peter,
Bucks.
Jones, P. and A., Nantwich, Cheshire.
Jones, P.J., Pontypridd, Mid. Glam., Wales.
Jones Antiques, Ron, Llanaber, Gwynedd,
Wales.
Jones, R., Bristol, Avon. Clift. Ant. Mkt.
Jones, R., London, W.8. (R. and J. Jones)
Jones, R. and J., London, W.8.
Jones, R.T., London, S.E.13.
Jones, T. and S., Chipping Norton, Oxon.
Jones, W.A. and E.S., Bromyard, Hereford
& Worcs.
Jones, Z., Exmouth, Devon.
Jordan, P.A. and W.E., Farnham, Surrey.
Jordan, P. and B., Farnham, Surrey.
Jordan, R.A., Barnard Castle, Durham.
Jordan, S., Great Missenden, Bucks.
Jordan (Fine Paintings), T.B. and R., Yarm,
Cleveland.
Jorgen Antiques, London, S.W.15.
Joseph, A. and B., Southport, Merseyside.
(Jays Fine Art Dealers).
Joseph, E., London W.1.
Joseph, John, London, W.1. G. Ant. Mkt.
Joseph, S., London, W.8. Ant. Hyp.
Joslin, Richard, London, W.14.
Joslyn, J.H., London, S.E.22.
Jouques, P., Bath, Avon. Gt. West. Ant. C.
Joy, Mrs. N., Hadlow, Kent.
Joyce, Beryl, Guildford, Surrey. Ant. C.
Joynt Antiques, Hereford, Hereford &
Worcs.
Joynt, P.F. and B.F., Hereford, Hereford &
Worcs.
Jubb, Mrs. M., Bristol, Avon, Clift. Ant.
Mkt.
Jubilee, London, N.1.
Jubilee Antiques, Southampton, Hants.
Jubilee Antique Cellars and Collectors
Market, Brighton, E. Sussex.
Jubilee Books, Burford, Oxon.
Judith Antiques, Sandygate, Kent. S. Ant.
C.
Judd, W.S., Highcliffe, Dorset.
Juett, A.H.C. and D.C., Shillingstone,
Dorset.
Jukes, Mr. and Mrs. G., St. Leonards-on-
Sea, E. Sussex.
Julian Antiques, Hurstpierpoint, W. Sussex.
Julian Antiques, London, N.1.

Kinver Antiques, Kinver, Staffs.
Kippax, G.W., Hitchin, Herts.
Kirdford Antiques, Kirdford, W. Sussex.
Kirkby Antiques Ltd., Kirkby-on-Bain, Lincs.
Kirkby, J., Greystoke, Cumbria.
Kirkgate Picture Gallery, Thirsk, N. Yorks.
Kirkland, G., London, S.W.6. (Whiteway & Waldron Ltd.).
Kirkland, Mr. and Mrs. L.R., Petersfield, Hants.
Kirkstall Antiques, Leeds, W. Yorks.
Kirson, Mrs. B., London, S.W.3. Ant. Ant. Mkt.
Kirton Antiques, Kirton, Lincs.
Klaber, Mrs. B. and Miss P., London, W.8.
Klaber and Klaber, London, W.8.
Klein, M., London, S.W.3. Ant. Ant. Mkt.
Klein, M., Margate, Kent.
Knaphill Antiques, Knaphill, Surrey.
Knight and Partners, Mrs. B.R., St. Ives, Cambs.
Knight and Son, B.R., St. Ives, Cambs.
Knight, D., London, S.W.3. (Cheshire Antiques) Chen. Gall.
Knight, D., Macclesfield, Cheshire.
Knight, John C., Luton, Beds.
Knight, Peter, Kennington, Kent.
Knight, P. and V., Bridport, Dorset.
Knight Ltd., W.F., Wellingborough, Northants.
Knights' Gallery, Luton, Beds.
Knights, P.H., Norwich, Norfolk (Oswald Sebley).
Knightsbridge Coins, London, S.W.1.
Knightsbridge Pine, Coulsdon, Gtr. London.
Knipe, D., Dorchester-on-Thames, Oxon.
Knowles Rare Toys and Fine Dolls, Anthea, London, N.8.
Knowles, R., Callington, Cornwall.
Knox, A., Errol, Perths., Scot.
Knutsford Gallery Antiques, Knutsford, Cheshire.
Knutsford Road Antiques, Wilmslow, Cheshire.
Kollectarama, Arreton, I. of Wight.
Kollect-o-Mania, Brighton, E. Sussex.
Kook, N. and J., Stow-on-the-Wold, Glos.
Koopman and Son Ltd., E. and C.T., London, W.C.2. Lond. Silv. Vts.
Koopman and Son Ltd., E. and C.T., Manchester, Lancs.
Kopriva, A., London, S.W.6. (Pageant Antiques).
Korbon, H., London, W.1. (Jadis.)
Korn, E., London, N.W.5.
Korn, M.E., London, N.W.5.
Korniczky, London, N.W.8. Alf. Ant. Mkt.
Krasine, Miss A., Gomshall, Surrey.
Krell, Mrs. V., London, S.W.3. Chen. Gall. Wear.
Krios Gallery, London, S.W.3.
Krolick, H., Newcastle-upon-Tyne, Tyne and Wear.
Krolle, Mrs. D., Amersham, Bucks.
Krucker, S., Stroud, Glos.
Kruml, Richard, London, W.1.
Krystyna Antiques, London, W.11.
Kurzelewska, K., London, W.11.

Kydd, P., Bristol, Avon (Cannon Antiques).
Kyte, J., London, W.1. (Bolsover Gallery)

L

L. and D. Antiques, Lincoln, Lincs.
L. and M. Antiques, London, N.W.8. Alf. Ant. Mkt.
La Barre Ltd., P., Leominster, Hereford and Worcs.
La Chaise Antiques, Faringdon, Oxon.
Laborevics, L., Norton, N. Yorks.
Laburnum Antique Galleries, Torquay, Devon.
Lace, Stratford-upon-Avon, Warks.
Lacewing Fine Art Gallery, Marlborough, Wilts.
Lacquer Chest, The, London, W.8.
Lacy Gallery, Henley-in-Arden, Warks.
Lacy Gallery, London, W.11.
Ladd, D. and M., London, W.8 (Peel Antiques).
La-di-da, Stratford-upon-Avon, Warks.
Lady Bountiful Antiques and Objets d'Art, Hampton Hill, Gtr. London.
Lady Bountiful Two Antiques and Objets d'Art, East Molesey, Surrey.
Ladygate Antiques, Beverley, N. Humberside.
Lafrance and Weber, Bournemouth, Dorset.
Laidlaw, Bill and Fiona, London, N.W.8. Alf. Ant. Mkt.
Laidlaw Antiques, Fiona and Bill, London, W.8.
Laidlaw, Mr. and Mrs. W., London, W.8.
Laidler Antiques, G.J. and M., Staveley, Cumbria.
Lain, H.J. and V.J., Westbourne, W. Sussex.
Lain, L.M. and M.D., Bosham, W. Sussex.
Lake Antiques, Lake, I. of Wight.
Lake, J.E., Glasgow, Lanarks., Scot. (Nice Things Old and New).
Lake, J.R. and I.D., Dorchester, Dorset.
Laker, I.A. and E.K., Somerton, Drayton, Somerset.
Laklia, L.T., Bexley, Gtr. London.
Laleham Antiques, Laleham, Surrey.
Lamari, R., London, S.W.3. Ant. Ant. Mkt.
Lamas, A., London, N.1 (Vane House Antiques).
Lamb Arcade, The, Wallingford, Oxon.
Lamb, Barry, Swanage, Dorset.
Lamb Antiques, Michael, Minster, Kent.
Lamb, Mrs. J., Virginia Water, Surrey.
Lambe, Charlotte and John, Belfast, N. Ireland.
Lambert, John, Preston, Lancs. N.W. Ant. C.
Lambert, P.M. and A.M.F.T., Halesworth, Suffolk.
Lambert's Barn, Woodbridge, Suffolk.
Lambourn-Brown, M., Cambridge, Cambs. (Artisan Antiques and Collectables.)
Lamont Antiques, Totnes, Devon.
Lamont Antiques Ltd., London, S.E.1.
Lamont, N., London, S.E.1.

Lampard and Sons, L.E., Horsham, W. Sussex.
Lampard and Son Ltd., S., London, W.11.
Lampert, B., London, W.C.2. Lon. Silv. Vts.
Lancashire Bygones, Upholland, Lancs.
Lancaster Antiques, Don, Brighton, E. Sussex.
Lancastrian Antiques, Lancaster, Lancs.
Lancefield Antiques, David, Sandgate, Kent. S. Ant. C.
Lanchester, N., Debenham, Suffolk.
Landau, A., London, N.W.6.
Landau Antiques, Buxton, Derbys.
Lane Antiques, Stockbridge, Hants.
Lane Antiques, Barbara, Chiddingstone, Kent.
Lane Antiques, David, Compton Abbas, Dorset.
Lane, E.K., Stockbridge, Hants.
Lane Fine Art Ltd., London, S.W.1.
Lane, Mrs. N., London, W.5.
Lane, R., Horsebridge, E. Sussex.
Lane Antiques, Russell, Warwick, Warks.
Lane, R.H.G., Warwick, Warks.
Langer and Collins, London, W.1. G. Mews.
Langford, J., Shrewsbury, Shrops.
Langford, J. and R., Llangollen, Clwyd, Wales.
Langford, L.L., London, W.C.2.
Langford, L.L. and M.V., London, W.C.2.
Langfords, London, W.C.2.
Langfords Silver Galleries, London, W.C.2. Lon. Silv. Vts.
Langham, Marion, London, W.1. G. Ant. Mkt.
Langhorn Antiques, Outwell, Cambs.
Langley Antiques, Corby Hill, Cumbria.
Langley Galleries, Rochester, Kent.
Langley, J.A. and K., Uppingham, Leics.
Langley's (Jewellers) Ltd., Bradford, W. Yorks.
Langold Antiques Ltd., West Peckham, Kent.
Langran, Mrs. J., St. Austell, Cornwall.
Langton Gallery, London, S.W.10.
Langton, M., Hull, N. Humberside.
Langton, N., Mrs. V.M. and Miss N.S., Chorley, Lancs.
Lanham, Miss A., Newmarket, Suffolk.
Lanham, R., Teddington, Gtr. London.
Lankester Antiques and Books, Saffron Walden, Essex.
Lankester, J. and P., Saffron Walden, Essex.
Lankshear, M.I., Christchurch, Dorset.
Lansdown Antiques, Bath, Avon.
Lantern Antiques, Shrewsbury, Shrops.
Lantern Gallery, Bath, Avon.
Lantern Shop, The, Sidmouth, Devon.
Lapwing Antiques, Lyddington, Leics.
Lapwing Antiques, Woburn, Beds. Wob. Ab. Ant. C.
Larcombe, M. and P., Bucks Green, W. Sussex.
Large Gallery, George, Woburn, Beds.
Large, W.R., Painswick, Glos.
Largo Antiques (Mrs. S. Bayne), Upper Largo, Fife, Scot.
Larner, P., Cirencester, Glos.
Larri Clocks and Junk, South Brent, Devon.

Lascelles, R., London, S.W.6. (Big Ben Antique Clocks).
Lasher, C., London, W.1. (M. and L. Silver Co. Ltd.)
Laski, Irina, London, W.8 (John Jesse and Irina Laski Ltd.)
Lassalle (Antiques) Ltd., Leonard, Tunbridge Wells, Kent.
Lassco Heavy Materials Dept., London, E.15.
Lasseters, Arundel, W. Sussex.
Lasson Gallery, London, S.W.1.
Lasson, Z., London, S.W.1.
Lassota, M., London, S.W.6.
Last Drop Antique and Collectors Club, Bolton, Lancs.
Lastlodge Ltd., London, W.11 (Wynyards Antiques.)
Latford, J., Colchester, Essex.
Latham, J. and D., Hexham, Northumb.
Latham Antiques, R.H., Blackpool, Lancs.
Latham Antiques, R.H. Preston, Lancs.
Lathbury Antiques, Jean, Ashton Upthorpe, Oxon.
Latimer, E., Bicester, Oxon.
Laura's Bookshop, Derby, Derbys.
Laurence Corner Militaria, London, N.W.1.
Laurence Ltd., Victor, London, N.W.1 (Laurence Corner Militaria.)
Laurens Antiques, G.A., Whitstable, Kent.
Lauretta Jewellers, Blandford Forum, Dorset.
Laurie, John, London, N.1.
Lavender Antiques Ltd., D.S., London, W.1.
Laver, F.W., Glastonbury, Somerset.
Laverick Hall Antiques, Wardley, Tyne and Wear.
Lavian, Joseph, London, N.W.5.
Law, D., Woking, Surrey.
Law, D. and M., Stillington, N. Yorks.
Law, J., Worthing, W. Sussex.
Law, P. and I., Herne Bay, Kent.
Lawes, David, Harrogate, N. Yorks.
Lawrence Antiques, London, S.E.18.
Lawrence and Sons, F.G., Redhill, Surrey.
Lawrence, John, Newton Abbot, Devon. N.A. Ant. C.
Lawrence, L., Eastbourne, E. Sussex.
Lawrence, L.D., London, N.6.
Lawrence R., London, S.W.1. (Gallery 25).
Lawson and Co., E.M., East Hagbourne, Oxon.
Lawson Antiques, F. and T., Richmond, Gtr. London.
Lawson, Mrs. V., Hungerford, Berks. (The Collectors Shop).
Lawson, W.J. and K.M., East Hagbourne, Oxon.
Layfield, Mrs. C., Nottingham, Notts.
Layte, J.D., Holt, Norfolk.
Layton, Lady, Richmond, Gtr. London.
Layton Antiques, Richmond, Gtr. London.
Laywood, Anthony W., Knipton, Leics.
Laywood, G.J., Bawtry, S. Yorks.
Lazarell, London, W.1. G. Ant. Mkt.
Lazarus Antiques, D., Hartley Wintney, Hants.
Lazarus, S., London, N.W.8. Alf. Ant. Mkt.
Le Centre Antiques, Richmond, Gtr. London.

Le Coz, Michel, Castle Combe, Wilts.
Le Marchant, M., Bruton, Somerset.
Le Rougetel, B. and P., Chester, Cheshire.
  (Filkins Antiques).
Le Soken Antiques, Thorpe-le-Soken, Essex.
Leach, B., Llandovery, Dyfed, Wales.
Leach, R., Canterbury, Kent.
Leadenhall Gallery, Canterbury, Kent.
Leadenhall Gallery, Maidstone, Kent.
Leading Lady, London, W.1. G. Mews.
Leadlay, Gallery, Warwick, London, S.E.10.
Lear, J., Staines, Surrey.
Leaside Antiques, Luton, Beds.
Leask, M., Edinburgh, Midloth., Scot.
  (Quadrant Antiques).
Leath-Butler, P., Hythe, Kent.
Leatherland Antiques, P.D., Reading, Berks.
Lechmere, R.A.H., Great Malvern, Hereford
  and Worcs.
Ledger Antiques Ltd., London, S.W.3.
Ledger, B.A., Exeter, Devon.
Ledger, D.G., London, S.W.3.
Ledger, M. and A., Stockport, Cheshire.
Ledger, P., Long Eaton, Derbys.
Lee, C.G., Llandudno, Gwynedd, Wales.
Lee, D., Knaresborough, N. Yorks.
Lee, David and Dorothy, Southwold,
  Suffolk.
Lee, J. Morton, Hayling Island, Hants.
Lee Antiques, Peter, Wiveliscombe,
  Somerset.
Lee, P. and A., Wiveliscombe, Somerset.
Lee (Fine Arts) Ltd., Ronald A., London,
  W.1.
Lee, R.A. and C.B., London, W.1.
Lee and Stacy, London, N.W.3. Ham. Ant.
  Emp.
Lees, J.A., Glossop, Derbys.
Lees and Sons, M., Worcester, Hereford and
  Worcs.
Leete R.L., Lubenham, Leics.
Lefevre Gallery, London, W.1.
Lefevre Ltd., London, W.1.
Legard, I.P., Harrogate, N. Yorks.
  (Christopher Warner).
Leger Galleries Ltd., The, London, W.1.
Leger, H., London, W.1.
Legg and Son, E.C., Somerford Keynes,
  Glos.
Legg, E.M.J., Dorchester, Dorset.
Legg, Michael, Dorchester, Dorset.
Legg of Dorchester, Dorchester, Dorset.
Legg, W. and H., Dorchester, Dorset.
Leggatt Brothers, London, S.W.1.
Leggatt, H., London, S.W.1.
Legge, C.T., Oxford, Oxon.
Leicester Antique Centre Ltd., Leicester,
  Leics.
Leicestershire Sporting Gallery, Lubenham,
  Leics.
Leigh and Son, G.E. and J.E., Reddish,
  Cheshire.
Leigh and Son, G.E., Reddish, Cheshire.
Leigh, H., Bath, Avon. Gt. West. Ant. C.
Leigh Antiques, Laurie, Oxford, Oxon.
Leigh, L., D., and W., Oxford, Oxon.
Leigh, P.K. and R.H., Grimsby,
  S. Humberside.

Leighton, L., Leominster, Hereford and
  Worcs. L. Ant. C.
Leinster Antiques, London, W.2.
Leiston Trading Post, Leiston, Suffolk.
Leitch, C.J., Cookstown, Co. Tyrone,
  N. Ireland.
Leitch, C. and W., Great Bardfield, Essex.
Leith's Brocanterbury, Nan, Canterbury,
  Kent.
Lek, H. and K., Beaumaris, Gwynedd,
  Wales.
Leloup, Diane, London, W.11. G. Port.
Lemkow, Sara, London, N.1.
Lenda Antiques, Gloucester, Glos.
Leni, London, N.W.8. Alf. Ant. Mkt.
Lennard Antiques, Tingewick, Bucks.
Lennard Antiques, Woburn, Beds. Wob. Ab.
  Ant. C.
Lennard, Pat, London, W.1. G. Ant. Mkt.
Lennox Antiques, Brighton, E. Sussex.
Lennox Antiques, Bromyard, Hereford &
  Worcs.
Lensfield Antiques, Cambridge, Cambs.
Lenson, Nellie and Smith, Roy, London, N.1.
Leo, R., Bournemouth, Dorset. (Victorian
  Chairman)
Leominster Antiques, Leominster, Hereford
  and Worcs.
Leominster Antiques Market, Leominster,
  Hereford and Worcs.
Leon Antiques Ltd., London, W.C.2. Lon.
  Silv. Vts.
Leon, Mrs. N., London, S.W.3. (Miss E.
  Pollock) Ant. Ant. Mkt.
Leonard Antiques, Alan, Liverpool,
  Merseyside.
Leong, London, W.1. G. Mews.
Leopard, The, Brighton, E. Sussex.
Leppard, A. and A., Brighton, E. Sussex
  (The Leopard.)
Leroy, D., London, N.1. (The Ark Angel).
Lesley's Antiques, Hull, N. Humberside.
Leslie, Mrs. J.H., Sheffield,S. Yorks. (Many
  Things).
Leslie, K. J., Southampton, Hants.
Leslie and Leslie, Haddington, E. Loth., Scot.
Leslie Antiques, R.K., Southampton, Hants.
Leslie, Stanley, London, S.W.3.
Leslie's, Portsmouth, Hants.
Lester, Orientalist, A., London, S.W.3.
  Chen. Gall.
Lester, O., London, S.W.3. Chen. Gall.
Letham, David, Edinburgh, Midloth., Scot.
Letham Antiques, Mrs. J., Edinburgh,
  Midloth., Scot.
Letty's Antiques Ltd., Leicester, Leics.
Lev, Mrs., London, W.8.
Lev (Antiques) Ltd., London, W.8.
Levene Ltd., M.P., London, S.W.7.
Leverington Hall Antiques, Wisbech, Cambs.
Leverington Hall Gallery, Wisbech, Cambs.
Leveson-Gower, M., Standlake, Oxon.
Levine, B.L., Little Weighton, N.
  Humberside.
Levine, D. and L., Norwich, Norfolk.
Levine and Co., Henry, Norwich, Norfolk.
Levine, Jenny, London, W.11. G. Port.
Levy Antiques, London, E.C.1.

Levy, G.J., M.P. and W.Y., London, W.1
  (H. Blairman and Sons Ltd.)
Levy, J., London, E.C.1.
Levy, M., London, S.W.3. Ant. Ant. Mkt.
Lewes Antiques Centre, Lewes, E. Sussex.
Lewis, Arthur, S., Corse Lawn, Glos.
Lewis, Mrs. B., London, W.11.
Lewis, Gerald, Montacute, Somerset.
Lewis Antiques, Gerald, Woburn, Beds.
  Wob. Ab. Ant. C.
Lewis, G. and B., Montacute, Somerset.
Lewis, Mrs. H., Southwell, Notts.
Lewis Antique and Fine Art Dealers, Ivor
  and Patricia, Peterborough, Cambs.
Lewis, J.D. and P.C., Reigate, Surrey.
Lewis and Lloyd (Reigate) Ltd., Reigate,
  Surrey.
Lewis, M., Truro, Cornwall.
Lewis, Mrs. M., Presteigne, Powys, Wales.
Lewis Antiques, Michael, London, N.1.
Lewis Antiques, Min, Presteigne, Powys,
  Wales.
Lewis Oriental Carpets and Rugs, Michael
  and Amanda, Bristol, Avon.
Lewis — Oriental Carpets and Rugs, Michael
  and Amanda, Wellington, Somerset.
Lewis, M. and D., London, W.11.
Lewis Gallery, Michael, Bruton, Somerset.
Lewis, N., London, N.1. Ang. Arc.
Lewis Antiques, Robert and Vashti,
  Gartmore, Stirlings., Scot.
Lewis, V. and L.R., Bristol, Avon (Victoria's
  Emporium).
Lewith, Mrs. A., Cardiff, S. Glam., Wales.
  (Alice Lighting and Antiques).
Lewzeye, J.A., Woolhampton, Berks.
Lexton, M., London, S.W.3. Ant. Ant. Mkt.
Leycester Map Galleries Ltd., Arnesby,
  Leics.
Li, Wan, London, N.1.
Lianos, A., London, S.W.3. Ant. Ant. Mkt.
Liberati, L., Preston, Lancs. N.W. Ant. C.
Liberty Retail plc., London, W.1.
Libra Antiques, London, W.8.
Libra Designs, London, W.1.
Lichtenberg, P.W., Cardiff, S. Glam., Wales.
  (Kings Antiques).
Liddell, D., Seaham, Durham.
Liddiard Antiques, Susan, Pill, Avon.
Liddiard, V.A., Woolhampton, Berks.
Lievesley, Mrs. E.E., Hartley, Kent.
Light Brigade and Penylan Antiques, The,
  Cardiff, S. Glam., Wales.
Lightbody, P., Callington, Cornwall.
Lighthouse Ltd., The, London, S.W.19.
Liley, E., Deal, Kent.
Liliana, Gigi, London, S.W.3. Chen. Gall.
Lillicrap, P.J., Bexley, Gtr. London.
Lillistone, C., Ipswich, Suffolk (A. Abbott
  Antiques).
Lime Tree Antiques, Burwash, E. Sussex.
Limner Antiques, London, W.1. B. St.
  Ant. C.
Limpsfield Watercolours, Limpsfield, Surrey.
Linaire Antiques, Hemel Hampstead, Herts.
Lincoln Fine Art, Lincoln, Lincs.
Lind, Sheila, Glasgow, Lanarks., Scot. Vict.
  Vill.

Linden and Co. (Antiques) Ltd., London,
  W.C.2. Lon. Silv. Vts.
Linden, H. and F., London, W.C.2. Lon. Silv.
  Vts.
Linden House Antiques, Stansted, Essex.
Linden, S., London, W.C.2.
Lindfield Galleries Ltd., Lindfield, W. Sussex.
Lindley, D. and M.H., Norton, N. Yorks.
Lindley, P., Hemel Hampstead, Herts.
Lindsay Antiques, London, W.8.
Lindsay, Muriel, Winchcombe, Glos.
Lindsay-Stewart, G., Balcombe, W. Sussex.
Lindsell Chairs, Coggeshall, Essex.
Lindsey Fine Arts Ltd., John, Stow-on-the-
  Wold, Glos.
Lindum Antiques, Donington-on-Bain, Lincs.
Lindy Lou Antiques, Scarborough, N. Yorks.
Line, J., Westcliff-on-Sea, Essex.
Lineham, Andrew, London, S.W.3. Ant.
  Ant. Mkt.
Lineham and Sons, Eric, London, W.8.
Linen and Lace, Manchester, Lancs. Royal
  Ex. S.C.
Linfield, Helen, Petworth, W. Sussex.
Lingard, Ann, Rye, E. Sussex.
Lingard, T.P., London, S.W.1. (Gallery
  Lingard.)
Link Gold Ltd., Epsom, Surrey.
Link Gold Ltd., Kingston-upon-Thames,
  Gtr. London.
Link Gold Ltd., Staines, Surrey.
Linnets Nest Antiques, Rugby, Warks.
Linnett, E., Derby, Derbys.
Linslade Antiques and Curios, Linslade,
  Beds.
Linsley, Mrs. C.M., Pateley Bridge, N. Yorks.
Linstead, A., Tunbridge Wells, Kent
  (Cowden Antiques).
Linton Antiques, Greig, Edinburgh, Midloth.,
  Scot.
Linwick Minerals, London, S.W.3. Chen Gall.
Lion Antiques, Coggeshall, Essex.
Lion Gallery and Bookshop, Knutsford,
  Cheshire.
Lions and Unicorns, Appleton, Cheshire.
Lipitch Ltd., J., London, W.11.
Lipitch, Michael, London, S.W.3.
Lipitch Ltd., Peter, London, S.W.3.
Lipka Ltd., W., London, W.11. Corn. Port.
  Ant. Sup.
Lipman, Louis, Brentwood, Essex.
Lipton, Sanda, London, S.W.5.
Lipton, Mrs. S., London, S.W.5.
Lis, J., London, S.W.5.
Liss Antiques, Liss, Hants.
Liss Bookshop and Gallery, The, Liss, Hants.
Liss Pine Warehouse, Liss, Hants.
Lisseter, D., Bicester, Oxon.
Lisseter of Bicester, Bicester, Oxon.
Little Antique Shop, The, Hanford, Staffs.
Little Bric-a-Brac Shop, Morcombelake,
  Dorset.
Little Curiosity Shop, The, London, N.21.
Little Gallery, The, Norwich, Norfolk.
Little Gem, The, Shrewsbury, Shrops.
Little Lantern Shop, The, Sidmouth, Devon.
Little, N., Bexhill-on-Sea, E. Sussex. Bex.
  Ant. C.

Little Raven Antiques, Oswestry, Shrops.
Little Shop, The, Corfe Castle, Dorset.
Little Shop, The, Leamington Spa, Warks.
Little Shop Antiques, Newport, Essex.
Little Winchester Gallery, London, W.8.
Little Window, The, Moreton-in-Marsh, Glos.
Littlebury Antiques — Littlebury Restorations Ltd., Saffron Walden, Essex.
Littleton, Richard, London, W.1. B. St. Ant. C.
Liu, Mrs., London, W.11. G. Port.
Liu, Mrs. M-C., Riverhead, Kent.
Livani, P., Bath, Avon. Gt. West. Ant. C.
Liverpool Coin and Medal Co., Liverpool, Merseyside.
Livesley, Mrs. N., Ribchester, Lancs.
Livesley, W.H., Macclesfield, Cheshire.
Livingstone, J., Methwold, Norfolk.
Liz, London, N.W.8. Alf. Ant. Mkt.
Llandogo Antiques, Llandogo, Gwent, Wales.
Llanishen Antiques, Cardiff, S. Glam., Wales.
Llewellyn, P.E., Harrogate, N. Yorks. (Bloomers)
Llewellyn, F., London, S.E.1.
Llewelyn Antiques, Cardiff, S. Glam., Wales.
Lloyd, A., London, W.1. (Burlington Paintings Ltd.)
Lloyd, A.S., London, W.1. (Burlington Gallery Ltd.).
Lloyd, C.L., Gomshall, Surrey.
Lloyd, D., Kew, Gtr. London.
Lloyd, D.S., Bournemouth, Dorset. (Victorian Parlour)
Lloyd, Mrs. P., Chester, Cheshire (Grosvenor Antiques of Chester.)
Lloyd, M.R., Sandgate, Kent.
Lloyd Antiques, Rachel, Canterbury, Kent.
Lloyd, Richard, Henllan, Dyfed, Wales.
Lloyd Antiques, Robin, Ross-on-Wye, Hereford and Worcs.
Lloyd, R.J., Bideford, Devon.
Lloyd Antiques Ltd., Vera, Gomshall, Surrey.
Lloyd, W.M., London, W.1. (Burlington Gallery Ltd.).
Lloyd-Roberts, T., Caerwys, Clwyd, Wales.
Lloyd's Bookshop, Wingham, Kent.
Lloyds of Kew, Kew, Gtr. London.
Lo, Monty, London, W.1. G. Ant. Mkt.
Lock, Mrs., Newton Abbot, Devon. N.A. Ant. C.
Lock, J., Ashtead, Surrey.
Locke, G.W. and R.M., Surbiton, Gtr. London.
Locke, M., Ashbourne, Derbys.
Locks, E. and J., Mevagissey, Cornwall.
Lockyer, H.K., Abergavenny, Gwent, Wales.
Lockyer, S., Usk, Gwent, Wales.
L'Odeon, London, S.W.3.
Lodge Furniture, Southport, Merseyside.
Lodge House Antiques, Grays, Essex.
Lodge, Mrs. J., Cirencester, Glos.
Lodge, J.C., Salisbury, Wilts.
Lodge, Rose, Petworth, W. Sussex.
Lodge, Mrs. R., Petworth, W. Sussex.
Lodge Road Antiques, Southampton, Hants.
Lodge-Mortimer, A., Exton, Somerset.

Loewenthal Antiques, Tillington, W. Sussex.
Loft Antiques, Dorking, Surrey.
Loft Antiques, Newton Abbot, Devon. N.A. Ant. C.
Loft, S.F. Oliver and Son, The, Weldon, Northants.
Loman Ltd., David, London, S.W.13.
Lomas Antique Shop, Colyton, Devon.
Lomas W.J., Colyton, Devon.
Loncraine, A.B., Marlborough, Wilts.
London Apprentice Antiques, St. Austell, Cornwall.
London Architectural Salvage and Supply Co. Ltd., London, E.C.2.
London Cigarette Card Co. Ltd., The, Somerton, Somerset.
London House Antique Centre, Marlborough, Wilts.
London House Oriental Rugs and Carpets, Boston Spa, W. Yorks.
London International Silver Co. Ltd., London W.11.
London, P. & Mrs. J., Edinburgh, Midloth., Scot. (William Macintosh & Co.)
London Postcard Centre, London, W.11.
London Silver Vaults, The, London, W.C.2.
London and Sussex Antiquarian Book and Print Services, Eastbourne, E. Sussex.
London-West Exports, Westcliff-on-Sea, Essex.
Long Hall Antiques & Design, Wareham, Dorset.
Long, J., Manchester, Lancs.
Long Melford Antiques Centre, Long Melford, Suffolk.
Long, P. and A., Abergavenny, Gwent, Wales.
Long, Stephen, London, S.W.10.
Long, S.M. and J.W.H., Aberford, W. Yorks.
Longfield Antiques, Longfield, Kent.
Longley, J., Castle Cary, Somerset.
Longley's Antiques, Castle Cary, Somerset.
Longmire Ltd., Paul, London, S.W.1.
Longporte Antiques, Portsmouth, Hants.
Longthorne, A.M., Brighton, E. Sussex (Douglas Hall Ltd.)
Lonsdale Antiques, Southend-on-Sea, Essex.
Look, Winchester, Hants.
Look Around Antiques, Chester, Cheshire.
Look-In Antiques, The, Tewkesbury, Glos.
Loomes, Brian, Pateley Bridge, N. Yorks.
Loot, London, S.W.1.
Lord Antiques, Alan, Folkestone, Kent.
Lord, A.G. and J.A., Folkestone, Kent.
Lord, Derek R., Stratford-upon-Avon, Warks.
Lord, E., Portsmouth, Hants.
Lord, Moira, Sherborne, Dorset.
Lord, R. and R., Godmanchester, Cambs.
Lord's Gallery, London, N.W.8.
Lorelle Art and Antiques, Callington, Cornwall.
Lorenz, John, London, W.11. G. Port.
Lorie, S.C. and E., London, W.8. (Grosvenor Antiques Ltd. and Lories Ltd.).
Losh, M., Cheltenham, Glos. (Bed of Roses).
Lott-32, London, N.W.1.
Lott, G.E., Faringdon, Oxon.

M

McBain and Sons, Ian, Exeter, Devon. (Exeter Antique Wholesalers.)

Macbeth, Jan and Don, Bath, Avon. Gt. West. Ant. C.

McCabe, H. and R., Newry, Co. Down, N. Ireland.

McCabe's Antique Galleries, Newry, Co. Down, N. Ireland.

McCall, B., Aberdeen, Aberd., Scot.

McCall's (Aberdeen), Aberdeen, Aberd., Scot.

McCall's Antique Shop, Aberdeen, Aberd., Scot.

McCarthy Ltd., F.J., Normanton-on-Trent, Notts.

McCarthy, Ian and Diane, Clutton, Avon.

McCarthy, J. Swansea, W. Glam., Wales. Ant. Centre.

McCaw, N.A. and S.E., Caldbeck, Cumbria.

McChesney, J.T.B., Glasgow, Lanarks., Scot. (Jocelyn Antiques Scotland and Clock Restoration Ltd.)

McClaren, J., Gosport, Hants.

Macclesfield Antiques, Macclesfield, Cheshire.

McCloy Pine, Margaret, Kingston-upon-Thames, Gtr. London.

McCollum, D.C. & S.J., Stockland, Devon.

MacConnal Mason Gallery, London, S.W.1.

MacConnal Mason Gallery, London, W.1.

McConnell, Mr. and Mrs. A., Great Malvern, Hereford and Worcs.

McCormick, N., London, S.W.13.

McCormick, P., Harrogate, N. Yorks. (Omar (Harrogate) Ltd.)

McCreery, Jonathan, Newbury, Berks.

McCrory and Conlon, Middlesbrough, Cleveland.

McCrudden Gallery, D., Rickmansworth, Herts.

McCulloch Antiques, John, Felixstowe, Suffolk.

MacDonald, A.G., York, N. Yorks. (Yon Antiques).

MacDonald, A. and Mrs. M., Amersham, Bucks.

MacDonald, Mrs. I., Haddington, E. Loth., Scot.

McDonald, Joy, London, S.W.13.

MacDonald, J., Tunbridge Wells, Kent. (John Thompson)

McDonald, W., Glasgow, Lanarks., Scot. (Nithsdale Antiques)

MacDonnell, Finbar, London, N.1.

McDougall, R.J.R., London, S.W.3 (Clarges Gallery).

McDowell, Daniel, York, N. Yorks.

McEvoy, Mrs. M., Comberton, Cambs.

McEwan Gallery, The, Ballater, Aberd., Scot.

McEwan, P. and D., Ballater, Aberd., Scot.

McFadden, J. and A., Groomsport, Co. Down, N. Ireland.

MacGillivray, G., Whitchurch, Shrops.

McGrane, I.A., Stroud, Glos.

McGrath, S., Farnham, Surrey.

MacGregor, P.A., Framlingham, Suffolk.

McGregor, V., Halstead, Essex.

McGuire, J. and A., Olney, Bucks.

McGurk, S., London, W.1. (A. Dolby). G. Mews.

MacHenry, A., Newtownabbey, Co. Antrim, N. Ireland.

McHugh, Helen, Guildford, Surrey. Ant. C.

MacInnes Antiques, Iain and Margaret, Kilmarnock, Ayr., Scot.

McIntosh Antiques, Gourock, Lanarks., Scot.

McIntosh and Company, Derek, Hungerford, Berks.

McIntosh Antiques, John, Edinburgh, Midloth., Scot.

Macintosh & Co., William, Edinburgh, Midloth., Scot.

McIntyre, R. and C., Bridlington, N. Humberside.

Mack Antiques, David, Branksome, Dorset.

McKay, Mrs. E., Burnham-on-Crouch, Essex.

McKenzie, J.W., Ewell, Surrey.

Mackenzie-Smith, P., Bristol, Avon. Clift. Ant. Mkt.

McKinley, D. and A., Milverton, Somerset.

MacKinnon, Glasgow, Lanarks., Scot. Vict. Vill.

MacKinnon, Miss J., Cambridge, Cambs. (The Antique Seeker).

McKnight, E.W., Bury St. Edmunds, Suffolk.

McLay, Mrs. C., Glasgow, Lanarks., Scot. Vict. Vill.

Maclean Antiques, Llanwrda, Dyfed, Wales.

Maclean Gallery, The, London, S.W.10.

Maclean, H., Kilmacolm, Renfrews., Scot.

McLennan, Rodd, London, S.W.1.

MacLennon, J.C., Whyteleafe, Surrey.

MacLeod's Antique Centre, Colin, Portsmouth, Hants.

McManus, Mr., Bath, Avon (Smith and Bottrill).

McMaster, John, Tenterden, Kent.

McMullan, C., Burnham-on-Crouch, Essex.

McNally, C., Amersham, Bucks.

McNaughtan's Bookshop, Edinburgh, Midloth., Scot.

MacNaughton, D., Edinburgh, Midloth., Scot. (Grange Bookshop).

McNeill Fine Art, Agnes, London, S.W.3. Chen. Gall.

MacNeill Press Ltd., London, S.E.1.

MacNeill's Art and Antique Warehouse, London S.E.1.

McPherson Antiques, A.L., Peel, I. of Man.

McPherson, I. and H., Coalville, Leics.

MacPherson, John, Fakenham, Norfolk. Ant. C.

McPherson, Mrs. J., Woburn, Beds. Wob. Ab. Ant. C.

McQuaigue, Mrs. I., St. Helier, Jersey, C.I.

Macrow, S.K., Solihull, W. Mids.

Mac-Smith, Bristol, Avon. Clift. Ant. Mkt.

Mactaggart Books, Yeovil, Somerset.

Mctaggart, Richard, Bath, Avon. Gt. West. A.C.

McTaque of Harrogate, P., Harrogate, N. Yorks.

McVay, Mrs. J., Sutton Bonington, Notts.

MacWhirter, Rob, Petworth, W. Sussex.

Mad Hatter, Weymouth, Dorset.

Madden Galleries, London, W.1.

Madden, Sue, London, S.W.3. Ant. Ant. Mkt.
Maddermarket Antiques, Norwich, Norfolk.
Made of Honour, Chester, Cheshire.
Madeira Antiques, V. and C., Weedon, Northants.
Madeira, V.M.R., Weedon, Northants.
Madelaine of Taunton, Taunton, Somerset.
Madoc Antiques and Art Gallery, Llandudno, Gwynedd, Wales.
Magee, D.A., Canterbury, Kent.
Magee, D.A., Eastry, Kent.
Magee, D.A., London, N.1.
Magee, D.A., Sandwich, Kent.
Maggie May's Plantiquity, North Shields, Tyne and Wear.
Maggs Antiques, Liverpool, Merseyside.
Maggs Bros. Ltd., London, W.1.
Maggs, John, Falmouth, Cornwall.
Maggs, J.F. and B.D., London, W.1.
Magna Carter Antiques, London, S.W.3. Ant. Ant. Mkt.
Magna Gallery, Oxford, Oxon.
Magpie, Whitstable, Kent.
Magpie Antiques, Battle, E. Sussex.
Magpie Antiques, Stoke Goldington, Bucks.
Magpie Antiques, Swansea, W. Glam., Wales. Ant. Centre.
Magpie House, Hockley Heath, W. Mids.
Magpie Jewellers and Antiques, Evesham, Hereford and Worcs.
Magpies Nest, The, Warrington, Cheshire.
Mahboubian Gallery, London, W.1.
Mahboubian, H., London, W.1.
Mahoney, Mrs. H., Kempsford, Glos.
Mahy, J.V., Stockbridge, Hants.
Mahy Ltd., Victor, Stockbridge, Hants.
Main, C. & K.M., Kirk Hammerton, N. Yorks.
Main, M. and A., Cerrig-y-Drudion, Clwyd, Wales.
Mainhill Gallery, St. Boswells, Roxburghs., Scot.
Mainline Furniture, Kesgrave, Suffolk.
Mainstream, Penryn, Cornwall.
Mair, P., London, N.W.8.
Major, A.H., London, W.8.
Major (Antiques) Ltd., C.H., London, W.8.
Major, Mrs. N.V., Cambourne, Cornwall.
Majors Galleries, Ipswich, Suffolk.
Maker, J.P., Camborne, Cornwall.
Malcolm Antiques, Elie, Fife, Scot.
Maldon Antiques and Collectors Market, Maldon, Essex.
Malik, David, London, W.8.
Malik Antiques, S.H., Oldham, Lancs.
Mall Antiques Arcade, The, London, N.1.
Mall Galleries, The, London, S.W.1.
Mall Gallery, The, Bristol, Avon.
Mall Jewellers, The, Bristol, Avon.
Mallett at Bourdon House Ltd., London, W.1.
Mallett, K., Surbiton, Gtr. London.
Mallett and Son (Antiques) Ltd., London, W.1.
Mallglade Antiques, Haigh, W. Yorks.
Mallinson, C., Tavistock, Devon.
Mallinson, May, Edinburgh, Midloth., Scot.

Mallory and Son Ltd., E.P., Bath, Avon.
Malmed, G., London, S.W.1 (California Art Galleries).
Malmed, Mrs. V., London, S.W.1 (Old London Gallery).
Malmesbury Antiques and Interiors, Malmesbury, Wilts.
Malone, Peggy, London, W.1. G. Ant. Mkt.
Maloney, John, Failsworth, Lancs.
Maltby, M.S., Sheffield, S. Yorks. (Holme Antiques).
Malthouse Antique Centre, Alcester, Warks.
Malthouse Arcade, Hythe, Kent.
Maltings Market, Farnham, Surrey.
Malton Antique Market, Malton, N. Yorks.
Malvasi, T., London, W.11.
Malvern Bookshop, Great Malvern, Hereford and Worcs.
Malvern Studios, Great Malvern, Hereford and Worcs.
Mammon, C. and T., London, W.C.2. Lon. Silv. Vts.
Mammon Antiques, J., London, W.C.2. Lon. Silv. Vts.
Man, Henry, London, S.W.3. Ant. Ant. Mkt.
Man, K., Todmorden, W. Yorks.
Manchester Antique Hypermarket, Manchester, Lancs.
Manchester Coin & Medal Centre, Manchester, Lancs. Royal Ex. S.C.
Mandarin Gallery, Riverhead, Kent.
Mandell's Gallery, Norwich, Norfolk.
Mander, J.P., London, E.2.
Mandersons, Glasgow, Lanarks., Scot. Vict. Vill.
Mandey's Antiques, Brasted, Kent.
Mandrake Stephenson Antiques, Ibstock, Leics.
Manfield, G. and J.E., Chelmsford, Essex.
Mangate Gallery, London, W.4.
Mangham, J. and J., London, N.1.
Mangion Antiques, A.J., London, S.E.15.
Manheim (Peter Manheim) Ltd., D.M. and P., London, W.1.
Manheim, P. and P., London, W.1.
Manion Antiques, Ashbourne, Derbys.
Manion, Mrs. V.J., Ashbourne, Derbys.
Mankovitz, Jonathan, London, W.11. G. Port. (David Baker)
Mankowitz, Daniel, London, W.2.
Mankowitz/Wilbourg, London, W.1. G. Mews.
Manley Antique Jewellery, Pamela, Titchfield, Hants.
Manley, J., Windsor and Eton, Berks.
Mann Antiques, Bryan K., Ramsbury, Wilts.
Mann, David, Stiffkey, Norfolk.
Mann and Sons Ltd., David, Cranleigh, Surrey.
Mann Antiques, Frank, Merstham, Surrey.
Mann Antiques, Kathleen, Harrow, Gtr. London.
Mann Antiques, W. and I.E., Hyde, Cheshire.
Manning, M., Darwen, Lancs.
Manor Antiques, Stillington, N. Yorks.
Manor Antiques, Westerham, Kent.
Manor Antiques, Wilshamstead, Beds.

Marsh, J. & P., Tetbury, Glos.
Marsh, J.B. and P.R.J., Henley-in-Arden, Warks.
Marsh Militaria, Martin, Whaley Bridge, Derbys.
Marsh, Simon, Bletchingley, Surrey.
Marshall, A.R., Kirton, Lincs.
Marshall, Bruce, Mauchline, Ayrs., Scot,
Marshall, E.M., Carshalton, Gtr. London.
Marshall, J., Tiverton, Devon.
Marshall, N., London, S.W.13.
Marshall, P. and B., Alnwick, Northumb.
Marshall, S., Lavenham, Suffolk.
Marsbeck Antiques, Lavenham, Suffolk.
Marshfield Antiques, Wells-next-the-Sea, Norfolk.
Marston, B.F. and H.M., Hadleigh, Suffolk.
Martelli, A. and G., Bridport, Dorset.
Marten, S.J., Huddersfield, W. Yorks.
Martin Antiques, Alan, Olney, Bucks.
Martin, A.D., Olney, Bucks.
Martin, Barbara, Deddington, Oxon. Ant. C.
Martin, B., London, N.2.
Martin and Co. Ltd., Cheltenham, Glos.
Martin, D., Bath, Avon. Gt. West. Ant. C. (Vintage Sound).
Martin, D., London, S.W.3. Chen. Gall.
Martin Antiques, Greg, Gravesend, Kent.
Martin, J., Farnborough, Hants.
Martin Antiques, John, Castle Cary, Somerset.
Martin, John R., Edinburgh, Midloth., Scot.
Martin, L.M., Bournemouth, Dorset. (Blade and Bayonet)
Martin and Parke, Farnborough, Hants.
Martin Antiques, Peter, Bognor Regis, W. Sussex.
Martin, P.E., Bath, Avon. Gt. West. Ant. C. Wed. Mkt.
Martin, Peter J., Windsor and Eton, Berks.
Martin, Robin, London, W.11.
Martin, R.E., Honiton, Devon.
Martin, Tony, Looe, Cornwall.
Martin, T.J.L., Coggeshall, Essex.
Martin, W., Deal, Kent.
Martiniques, Glasgow, Lanarks., Scot. (Corner House Antiques.)
Martin-Quick Antiques Ltd., Wolverhampton, W. Mids.
Martin-Taylor, David, London, S.W.6.
Martlesham Antiques, Martlesham, Suffolk.
Martock Gallery, The, Martock, Somerset.
Martom Antiques, Bexhill-on-Sea, E. Sussex.
Marton Galleries (Antiques), Blackpool, Lancs.
Marvin, J., Seaford, E. Sussex.
Maryan and Daughters, Richard, London, S.W.19.
Maskell, D., Wadhurst, E. Sussex.
Maskell, R.E. and L.J., Branksome, Dorset.
Maskell, R.E. and L.J., Sturminster Newton, Dorset.
Mason, A.A., Wimborne Minster, Dorset.
Mason, C., Brodick, I. of Arran, Scot.
Mason, C., Kettering, Northants.
Mason, D., Kelvedon, Essex.
Mason & Son, D., Harrogate, N. Yorks.
Mason, F., Cardigan, Dyfed, Wales.

Mason (Rotherham) Ltd., John, Rotherham, S. Yorks.
Mason, J.F., Wimborne Minster, Dorset.
Mason, Oriental Art, Jeremy J., London, W.1.
Mason, P., London, W.9.
Mason, Gallery, Paul, London, S.W.1.
Mason, T.H. and J., Gillingham, Kent.
Mason-Pope, C., Woodstock, Oxon.
Massada Antiques, London, W.1.
Massey and Son, D.J., Alderley Edge, Cheshire.
Massey & Son, D.J., Cheadle, Cheshire.
Massey and Son, D.J., Hazel Grove, Cheshire.
Massey & Son, D.J. Macclesfield, Cheshire.
Massey, P., London, S.W.6. (Gil Adams Antiques).
Massey's Antiques, Coalville, Leics.
Massingham, R., New Romney, Kent.
Mathaf Gallery Ltd., London, S.W.1.
Mather, D. and Mrs. P., Corby Hill, Cumbria.
Mather, J.J. and P., Whalley, Lancs.
Matheson, I., Daventry, Northants.
Mathews, Mrs. B., Cranborne, Dorset.
Mathews, Lt. Col. I.G. and Mrs., Ross-on-Wye, Hereford and Worcs.
Mathews, Michael, R., Berkeley, Glos.
Mathews, T.H.G., Harrogate, N. Yorks. (The Harrogate Postcard Shop).
Mathias, G.S., London, S.W.3. Ant. Ant. Mkt.
Mathieson and Co., John, Edinburgh, Midloth., Scot.
Mathon Gallery, London, S.W.3.
Mathon Gallery, Mathon, Hereford and Worcs.
Matsell Antiques Ltd., Nottingham, Notts.
Matsell, B. and P., Nottingham, Notts.
Matson, J., Liverpool, Merseyside (Theta Gallery).
Mattar Antique Galleries, Wincanton, Somerset.
Mattar Arcade Antique Centre, Sherborne, Dorset.
Mattar, S. and M., Sherborne, Dorset.
Mattar, S. and M., Wincanton, Somerset.
Mattey Antiques, David, Bury, W. Sussex.
Matthews Antiques Ltd., Arnold, Connah's Quay, Clwyd, Wales.
Matthews, Graham, London, N.W.8. Alf. Ant. Mkt.
Matthews, G., Norwich, Norfolk. (St. Giles Antiques).
Matthews, L., Brasted, Kent.
Matthews, R., Stourport, Hereford & Worcs.
Matthews, Stallbrass and Carter, London, S.W.3. Ant. Ant. Mkt.
Matthey, P., Burford, Oxon.
Matthiesen Fine Art Ltd. and Matthiesen Works of Art Ltd., London, S.W.1.
Maude, R.M.C., London, S.W.15.
Maude Tools, Richard, London, S.W.15.
Maufe, J., Burnham Market, Norfolk.
Maund, Mr., Leominster, Hereford and Worcs. L. Ant. Mkt.
Maw Antiques, Matthew, Malton, N. Yorks.
Mawby's International, Church Over, Warks.

Moggach Antiques, Ian, London, S.W.6.
Mokhtarzadeh, M., London, W.1 (Mansour
Gallery).
Molano, A., Bath, Avon. Gt. West. Ant. C.
Mole Antique Exports, Geoffrey, Hull,
N. Humberside.
Mole Hall Antiques, Aldeburgh, Suffolk.
Molloy, P., Southport, Merseyside.
Molloy's Furnishers Ltd., Southport,
Merseyside.
Molony, J., London, W.1. (The Richmond
Gallery)
Momtaz Gallery, Persian and Islamic Art,
London, W.11.
''Mon Galerie'', Amersham, Bucks.
Mona Antiqua, Beaumaris, Gwynedd, Wales
(Tudor Rose).
Monarch Antiques, Glastonbury, Somerset.
Moncur, G.E., Glasgow, Lanarks., Scot.
Corner House Antiques.
Money (Antiques) Ltd., Lennox, London,
S.W.1.
Money, L.B., London, S.W.1.
Monmouth Antiques, Monmouth, Gwent,
Wales.
Monge, F.B., Cranbrook, Kent.
Monk Bretton Books, Cirencester, Glos.
Monk and Son, D.C., London, W.8.
Monkton Galleries, Hindon, Wilts.
Monro Heywood Ltd., London, S.W.3.
Monro, J., London, S.W.3. (Monro
Heywood Ltd.)
Monro Ltd., Mrs., London, S.W.7.
Montacute Antiques, Montacute, Somerset.
Montagu-Williams, Peter, Tanworth-in-Arden,
Warks.
Montgomery, Anne, Dumfries, Dumfries.,
Scot.
Montgomery, J., Sidmouth, Devon.
Montilla, A., London, S.W.3. Ant. Ant. Mkt.
Montpellier Clocks, Cheltenham, Glos.
Monument Antiques, Stirling, Stirlings., Scot.
Moody, L., Southampton, Hants.
Moolham Mill Antiques, Ilminster, Somerset.
Moon, Michael, Whitehaven, Cumbria.
Moon, M. and S., Whitehaven, Cumbria.
Moon, Pauline, Bexhill-on-Sea, E. Sussex.
Bex. Ant. C.
Mooney, Riro, D., Duxford, Cambs.
Moor, J.R., Pocklington, N. Humberside.
Moor, M. and A., Middlesbrough, Cleveland.
Moordown Antiques, Bournemouth, Dorset.
Moore, A.E., Leiston, Suffolk.
Moore, B., Norwich, Norfolk.
Moore, Eric, T., Hitchin, Herts.
Moore, J.I., Melbourn, Cambs.
Moore Antiques, Michael, Clare, Suffolk.
Moore, M.D. and M., Bristol, Avon (Clifton
Antiques Ltd.).
Moore, N. and E., Tynemouth, Tyne and
Wear.
Moore Ltd., Stephen, Lewes, E. Sussex.
Moores, H. and P., Leicester, Leics.
Moores and Son, Walter, Leicester, Leics.
Moorhead and Son, F.B. and M.J., Brighton,
E. Sussex (Attic Antiques).
Moorhead Antiques, Patrick, Brighton,
E. Sussex.

Moorhen Antiques, The, Walton-on-the-Hill
and Tadworth, Surrey.
Moorhouse Ltd., A.D., Sheffield, S. Yorks.
Morchard Bishop Antiques, Morchard
Bishop, Devon.
Morden, L. and J., White Colne, Essex.
Moreton Antiques, C.S., Inchture, Perths.,
Scot.
Morgan, Mr. and Mrs., D.G., Newport,
Gwent, Wales.
Morgan, Dr. and Mrs. D.H., Wymondham,
Norfolk.
Morgan, H., Cardiff, S. Glam., Wales. (San
Domenico Stringed Instruments).
Morgan, R., Arreton, I. of Wight.
Morgan, R.E., Bournemouth, Dorset (R.E.M.
Antiques.)
Morgan, Mrs. S., Pateley Bridge, N. Yorks.
Morley, B. & J., Catsfield, E. Sussex.
Morley Antiques, David, Twickenham,
Gtr. London.
Morley Galleries, London, S.E.13.
Morley, Patrick and Gillian, Warwick, Warks.
Morley, P.P., Kenilworth, Warks.
Morley Antiques, William, West Monkton,
Somerset.
Morley, W.H., West Monkton, Somerset.
Morrell, D., Bath, Avon. Gt. West. Ant. C.
Morrill Ltd., W.J., Dover, Kent.
Morris, Alan, Redditch, Hereford and Worcs.
Morris Antiques and Bygones, Wickham
Market, Suffolk.
Morris, B., Leamington Spa, Warks.
Morris Fine Art, Stockport, Cheshire.
Morris, G.J., St. Helier, Jersey, C.I.
Morris, Ian, Chesterfield, Derbys.
Morris, J., Tetbury, Glos.
Morris, J., Torquay, Devon.
Morris Ltd., John G., Petworth, W. Sussex.
Morris and Co., James H., Northop, Clwyd,
Wales.
Morris, J.M., Stockport, Cheshire.
Morris, John, Morton, London, S.W.1.
Morris, M., H., P., P. and S., Abergavenny,
Gwent, Wales.
Morris, Pearl, London, N.1.
Morris Antiques, Philip, Chepstow, Gwent,
Wales.
Morris Antiques, Richard, London, S.W.6.
Morris Antiques, R.R., Abingdon, Oxon.
Morris, S., Westerham, Kent.
Morris, T.W., Stow-on-the-Wold, Glos.
Morris, V., Potterne, Wilts.
Morris, William, Stow-on-the-Wold, Glos.
Morrish, K.W., Reigate, Surrey.
Morrison, Mrs., Bristol, Avon. Clift. Ant.
Mkt.
Morrison, Mrs., London, S.W.3. Ant. Ant.
Mkt.
Morrison, C., York, N. Yorks.
Morrison, Guy, London, S.W.1.
Morrison, Mrs. J., Wingham, Kent.
Morrison Ltd., J.A., Thurnby, Leics.
Morrison, M., Warwick, Warks.
Morrison, P.H., Kirk Michael, Isle of Man.
Morrison, R.J., Whyteleafe, Surrey.
Morrison and Son, Robert, York, N. Yorks.
Morrow, P. and H., Bungay, Suffolk.

Morse and Son Ltd., Terence, London, W.11.
Morten, Eric J., Manchester, Lancs.
Mortens Bookshops Ltd., Macclesfield, Cheshire.
Mortens of Macclesfield, Macclesfield, Cheshire.
Mortimer, A.C., Altrincham, Cheshire.
Mortimer, Brian, Exeter, Devon.
Mortimer and Sons, C. & J., Great Chesterford, Essex.
Mortimer, Mr. and Mrs. L.G., Petersfield, Hants.
Mortimer, M.C.F., London, W.8 (Delomosne and Son Ltd.)
Mortimore-Hooper, A.J., London, S.W.3 (Hooper and Purchase).
Mortlake Antiques, London, S.W.14.
Morton Morris and Co., London, S.W.1.
Morton Antiques, R.L., York, N. Yorks.
Mosdell, Newton Abbot, Devon. N. A. Ant. C.
Mosdell, G., Ashburton, Devon.
Moseley Antiques, Birmingham, W. Mids.
Moss, A., London, N.1 (Annie's Antiques and Clothes).
Moss, B. and R., London, W.4.
Moss Galleries, London, W.4.
Moss, P.G. and E.M., London, W.1.
Moss, R.A. and B.A., Baldock, Herts.
Moss, Ralph and Bruce, Baldock, Herts.
Moss Ltd., Sydney L., London, W.1.
Moss, Z., Bath, Avon. Gt. West. Ant. C.
Mostly Boxes, Windsor & Eton, Berks.
Mostly Furniture, Windsor and Eton, Berks.
Mostyn-Joyner, T., Bembridge, I. of Wight.
Mote, H.C., London, S.W.3. (H.W. Newby)
Mott, G.W., Trent, Dorset.
Mott, J.G. and D.M., Lavenham, Suffolk.
Mottershead, Mr. and Mrs. J.K., Manchester, Lancs. (The Ginnel Gallery).
Mottershead, D., and Mrs., Long Eaton, Derby.
Mottishaw, R.J., Babworth, Notts.
Mottram Antiques, Nantwich, Cheshire.
Mottram, F. and A., Nantwich, Cheshire.
Motts of Lavenham, Lavenham, Suffolk.
Mouat, J.W.L., Whitchurch, Hants.
Mould Ltd., Anthony, London, W.1.
Moulin Antiques, Ipswich, Suffolk.
Moult Antiques, Richard, Stow-on-the-Wold, Glos.
Moulton, J., West Bridgford, Notts.
Moulton's Antiques, West Bridgford, Notts.
Mount, The, Woore, Shrops.
Mount Antiques, The, Whitby, N. Yorks.
Mount Gallery, Wembley Park, Gtr. London.
Mount Gallery, London, N.W.3. Ham. Ant. Emp.
Mount Street Galleries, London, W.1.
Movie Shop, The, Norwich, Norfolk.
Mowatt, D. and V., Nonington, Kent.
Mowe, C. and J., Seighford, Staffs.
Moxhams Antiques, Bradford-on-Avon, Wilts.
Moy, R.F., London, S.E.10.
Moyallon Antiques, Portadown, Co. Armagh, N. Ireland.

Muccio, L. and P., Bromley, Gtr. London.
Muckle, M.A., Market Harborough, Leics.
Muddiman, A.R.T., Chesham, Bucks.
Mudlark (Collectors Shop) The, Barnard Castle, Durham.
Muggeridge Farm Warehouse, Battlesbridge, Essex.
Muggleton, Mrs. R., London, S.W.3. Chen. Gall.
Muirhead Moffat and Co., Glasgow, Lanarks., Scot.
Mulberry House Galleries, Pulborough, W. Sussex.
Mulcare, R., Lindfield, W. Sussex.
Mulder, Frederick, London, N.W.3.
Mullarkey, T. and N., Maidstone, Kent.
Mullarkey, T. and N., Sutton Valence, Kent.
Mullen, T., Warminster, Wilts.
Mullett, G. and A., London, S.W.6. (The Constant Reader Bookshop).
Mulligan, A.J., and F., Whimple, Devon.
Mullin, D., Hollinwood, Lancs.
Mullins, Patrick, Salisbury, Wilts.
Mulvaney, L.M., Woodford Green, Gtr. London.
Mummery Ltd., Kenneth, Bournemouth, Dorset.
Munday, G.S., Windsor & Eton, Berks.
Mundey, Richard, London, W.1.
Munro, A.H. and Miss H.E., Thurso, Caiths., Scot.
Murdoch, Colin, Kingussie, Inver., Scot.
Murdoch, P.G., Nottingham, Notts. (Nottingham Antique Centre).
Murfin and Sons, A.W., New York, Lincs.
Murphey, C., East Budleigh, Devon.
Murphy, B. and S., Newton Abbot, Devon, N. A. Ant. C.
Murphy, I., Portsmouth, Hants.
Murphy, T.H., London, N.1. (Terry Antiques).
Murphy, T.H., London, N.19.
Murray, D., Kilmichael Glassary, Argyll, Scot.
Murray, I., Edinburgh, Midloth., Scot. (Ballymenoch Antiques)
Murray Antiques Warehouse, Ian, Perth, Perths., Scot.
Murray Antique Export, Peter, Bruton, Somerset.
Murray-Brown, London, S.W.1.
Murray-Brown, G. and J., London, S.W.1.
Murray's Ltd., Leicester, Leics.
Museum Bookshop, Woodstock, Oxon.
Museum of Childhood, Beaumaris, Gwynedd, Wales.
Museum of Clocks, Alum Bay, I. of Wight.
Music, Anne, London, W.1. B. St. Ant. C.
Music Centre, The, Billericay, Essex.
Music, Graham, London, N.W.8. Alf. Ant. Mkt.
Mussenden and Son Antiques, Jewellery and Silver, G.B., Bournemouth, Dorset.
Mutch, A., Edinburgh, Midloth., Scot. (Cinders).
Myers, Fiandaca, London, W.1. G. Ant. Mkt.
Myers Galleries, Gargrave, N. Yorks.

Myers, P., Bushey, Herts.
Myers, R. and H., Bath, Avon. Gt. West.
Ant. C.
Myers and Son, R.N., Gargrave, N. Yorks.
Myers (Autographs) Ltd., W.A., London,
W.C.2.
Myland, Mrs. M., Merstham, Surrey.
Mynott, Mrs. C., Warwick, Warks.
Mynott, R.H., Warwick, Warks.
Myriad Antiques, London, W.11.
Myrtle House Antiques, Tregony, Cornwall.
Mytton Antiques, Atcham, Shrops.

N

N., Mr., London, N.W.8. Alf. Ant. Mkt.
Nadin, Harold, Grantham, Lincs.
Nadin, Richard and Pamela, Bradford-on-
Avon, Wilts.
Naghi, E., London, W.1 (Emanouel Antiques
Ltd.).
Nagioff (Jewellery), I. and R., London,
W.C.2. Lond. Silv. Vts.
Nahum, Peter, London, S.W.1.
Nairne, D. and N., Edinburgh, Midloth.,
Scot.
Naisby and Son Ltd., G.R., Stockport,
Cheshire.
Nakota Curios, Hastings, E. Sussex.
Namdar, V., London, W.1. G. Mews.
Nanbooks, Settle, N. Yorks.
Nangle, C., Babworth, Notts.
Nanson Antiques, Geoffrey, Brampton,
Cumbria.
Nanson, J. and D.B., Kendal, Cumbria.
Nantwich Antique Centre, Nantwich,
Cheshire.
Nanwani and Co., London, E.C.3.
Napier House Antiques, Halstead, Essex.
Napier Ltd., Sylvia, London, W.11.
Napier-Fox, J. and B., Sidmouth, Devon.
Narbeth, B. and L., Uley, Glos.
Narducci Antiques, Largs, Ayr., Scot.
Narducci Antiques, Saltcoats, Ayr., Scot.
Narducci, G., Largs, Ayr., Scot.
Narducci, G., Saltcoats, Ayr., Scot.
Nares, M.A. and E.A., Atcham, Shrops.
Nash Antiques, Bath, Avon.
Nash Antiques, Chepstow, Gwent, Wales.
Nash Antiques, London, W.11. (Barry
Davies Oriental Art).
Nash Antiques & Interiors, John, Redmarley
D'Abitot, Glos.
Nash, P., London, S.E.1. Ber. Ant. Whse.
Nash Antiques, Paul, Tetbury, Glos.
Nash, P.L. and A.S., Gifford, Tetbury, Glos.
Nassor, C., Hebden Bridge, W. Yorks.
Nat Leslie Ltd., London, W.C.2. Lon. Silv.
Vts.
Nathan and Co. (Birmingham) Ltd.,
Birmingham, W. Mids.
Nathan Antiques, John, Exeter, Devon.
Nathan & Sons, L., Leeds, W. Yorks.
Nathan, M.A., Hemel Hempstead, Herts.
Naves, Ann, Bexhill-on-Sea, E. Sussex. Bex.
Ant. C.
Naxos Art Ltd., London, W.1.

Naylor, Mrs. M., Mountsorrel, Leics.
Neal, B.A., Branksome, Dorset.
Neal, B.A., Sturminster Newton, Dorset.
Neal Cabinet Antiques, Isabel, Coltishall,
Norfolk.
Neal, Mr. and Mrs. N.W., Salcombe, Devon.
Neale Antiques, Hertford, Herts.
Neale, A.J. and S.C., Hertford, Herts.
Neale, A.N., B.J. and I.J., London, W.1
(Holmes Ltd.)
Neale, P., Rumford, Cornwall.
Neame Ltd., Kenneth, London, W.1.
Neary, G., Huddersfield, W. Yorks.
Neath, P., Bournemouth, Dorset. (Antiques
and Furnishings)
Necus, R.S. and S., London, S.W.3. Ant.
Ant. Mkt.
Needham, A. and A., Buxton, Derbys.
Needham, K., Cobham, Surrey.
Needham, Mrs. M., Sheffield, S. Yorks. (Pot
Pourri).
Needham Antiques, Victor, Stockbridge,
Hants.
Neill, F. and J., White Roding, Essex.
Neilson, H.C. and Mrs. A.B., Sturminster
Newton, Dorset.
Nello, London, N.W.8. Alf. Ant. Mkt.
Nelson, Daniel, London, S.W.3. Chen. Gall.
(Anthony Barbieri)
Nelson, H. and K., Langley Moor, Durham.
Nelson, J.M., Balcombe, W. Sussex.
Nelson, John O., Edinburgh, Midloth., Scot.
Nelson and Spurling, Bath, Avon. Gt. West.
Ant. C.
Neptune, London, W.1.
Nesbitt, K. and M., Magherafelt, Co.
Londonderry, N. Ireland.
Nethercott, A., Bath, Avon. Gt. West. A. C.
Wed. Mkt.
Nethergate Gallery Ltd., Dundee, Angus,
Scot.
Netherley Cottage Antiques, Milburn,
Cumbria.
Nettleton, S.M., Patrington, N. Humberside.
Neumann, P., Hexham, Northumbs.
Nevill Antiques, R., Shrewsbury, Shrops.
Nevill, Miss S.M., Budleigh Salterton,
Devon.
Neville Antiques, Howard, London, W.1. G.
Ant. Mkt.
Neville Antiques, Robert, Leicester, Leics.
Nevill's Antiques, Woburn Sands, Bucks.
New Abbey Antiques, Newtownabbey, Co.
Antrim, N. Ireland.
New Gallery, Budleigh Salterton, Devon.
New Grafton Gallery, London, S.W.13.
New Malthouse, The, Herstmonceux,
E. Sussex.
New, S., Chester, Cheshire.
New Street Antique Centre, Plymouth,
Devon.
New Street Antiques, Altrincham, Cheshire.
New Street Antiques, Holt, Norfolk.
New Street Antiques, Penzance, Cornwall.
Newark Art and Antique Centre, Newark,
Notts.
Newark, Gordon and Muriel, Deddington,
Oxon. Ant. C.

Norman Antiques and Restorations, Peter, Burwell, Cambs.
Norman, P.G., Flore, Northants.
Norman, R.O., and J.I., Eye, Suffolk.
Norman, Sue, London, S.W.3. Ant. Ant. Mkt.
Normandy House Antiques, Salcombe, Devon.
Norris, M., Snettisham, Norfolk.
Norris, P., Preston, Lancs. N.W. Ant. C.
North, Amanda and Desmond, East Peckham, Kent.
North Parade Antiques, Eynsham, Oxon.
North London Clock Shop Ltd., London, N.5.
North Parade Antiques, Oxford, Oxon.
North Wales Antiques, Colwyn Bay, Clwyd, Wales.
North Walsham Antique Gallery, North Walsham, Norfolk.
North Western Antique Centre, Preston, Lancs.
North Wilts Exporters, Brinkworth, Wilts.
Northam, E. and J., Long Sutton, Lincs.
Northeast, H.J. and Mrs. I.F., Ruthin, Clwyd, Wales.
Northeast Wales Antiques, Ruthin, Clwyd, Wales.
Northend Antiques, Batheaston, Avon.
Northern Fine Art Ltd., Harrogate, N. Yorks.
Northfield Antiques (Belgravia), London, S.W.1.
Northgate Antiques, Canterbury, Kent.
Northgate Antiques, Pembroke, Dyfed, Wales.
Northgate Antiques, Rochester, Kent.
Northiam Antiques, Northiam, E. Sussex.
Northumbria Pine, Whitley Bay, Tyne and Wear.
Northwold Gallery, Newmarket, Suffolk.
Northwood Maps Ltd., Rickmansworth, Herts.
Norton Antiques, Beaconsfield, Bucks.
Norton House Antiques, Henfield, W. Sussex.
Norton, M.S., N.E.L., J.P. and F.E., London, W.1. (S.J. Phillips Ltd.)
Norton, N., Leicester, Leics.
Norton Galleries, Pauline, Bridgnorth, Shrops.
Norwell Antiques, Southwell, Notts.
Norwich Antique and Collectors Centre, Norwich, Norfolk.
Norwood Cottage Antiques, Killinghall, N. Yorks.
Nostalgia, Stockport, Cheshire.
Nosworthy, P. and R., Grampound, Cornwall.
Not Cartier, Bath, Avon. Gt. West. Ant. C.
Not Just Silver, Cobham, Surrey.
Noton Antiques, Finedon, Northants.
Nott, E.J., Bath, Avon. (Pioneer). Gt. West. Ant. C.
Nottingham Antique Centre, Nottingham, Notts.
Nottingham Stamp Exchange, West Bridgford, Notts.
Now and Then, East Grinstead, W. Sussex.
Now and Then Antiques, Chiddingfold, Surrey.

Now and Then (Toy Centre), Edinburgh, Midloth., Scot.
Nowell, Edward A., Wells, Somerset.
Number Nineteen, London, N.1.
Number 26, London, S.W.11.
Number Ten, Oxford, Oxon.
Number Ten Antiques, Sutton-on-Sea, Lincs.
Nunan, M.P., Bath, Avon. (Mark's Antiques). Gt. West. Ant. C.
Nuneaton Antiques, Nuneaton, Warks.
Nunn, K., St. Leonards-on-Sea, E. Sussex.
Nunn and Son, W.C., Long Melford, Suffolk.
Nuttall Antiques, David, Hollinwood, Lancs.
Nuttall, Miss H., Oldham, Lancs.
Nutter, Simon W., Stow-on-the-Wold, Glos.
Nutting Antiques, Brenda, Brackley, Northants.
Nye, Pat, London, W.11.
Nyman and Co. Ltd., Chas. L., London, N.W.1.

O

Oak Chest Jewellers, Llangollen, Clwyd, Wales.
Oak Tree Antiques, Blackpool, Lancs.
Oakes and Son Bolton Ltd., G., Bolton, Lancs.
Oakes, H. & S., Stoke-on-Trent, Staffs.
Oakham Antiques, Oakham, Leics.
Oakley, L.G., London, W.1 (Wilberry Antiques).
Oasis Antiques, Brighton, E. Sussex.
Oasis Fine Arts Ltd., Ormskirk, Lancs.
Obelisk Antiques, Warminster, Wilts.
Objects, Marlborough, Wilts.
O'Brien, B. Budhu, H.P., London, S.W.3. Ant. Ant. Mkt.
O'Brien, R. and J., Oldham, Lancs.
O'Callaghan, J., London, W.1. G. Mews.
Ockbrook Antiques, Ockbrook, Derbys.
O'Connor Brothers, Windsor and Eton, Berks.
O'Connor, R., London, W.11.
Oddiquities, London, S.E.23.
Oddity Shoppe, The, London, S.E.23.
Odds 'n' Ends Antiques, Guildford, Surrey.
Oddy, D., Leeds, W. Yorks.
Oddy, Mr. and Mrs. G., Stirling, Stirlings., Scot.
O'Dell, F. and M., Shefford, Beds.
Odgers, J.W., Harwich and Dovercourt, Essex.
Odin Antiques, London, S.W.3. Chen. Gall.
O'Donnell, A., London, S.E.13.
O'Donnell, A.J., Sale, Cheshire.
O'Donnell, L., Wallingford, Oxon.
O'Donnell, Steven, London, W.1. G. Ant. Mkt.
O'Dwyer, J.P. and E., London, N.W.3. Ham. Ant. Emp.
Odyssey Antiques, South Milton, N. Yorks.
O'Farrell, G., Stow-on-The Wold, Glos.
Off the Rails, Bath, Avon. Gt. West. Ant. C.
O'Flynn Antiquarian Booksellers, York, N. Yorks.
Ogden, J. and M., Honiton, Devon.

Ogden of Harrogate Ltd., Harrogate, N. Yorks.
Ogden Ltd., Richard, London, W.1.
Ogden, S., Cockermouth, Cumbria.
Ogleby, B., Thirsk, N. Yorks.
Ogwen Antiques, Bethesda, Gwynedd, Wales.
Okarma, E., Brobury, Hereford and Worcs.
O'Karma, E., Hay-on-Wye, Powys, Wales.
O'Keefe, B., Hadleigh, Suffolk.
Okolski, Z.J., London, W.3.
Old Bakehouse, Whissendine, Leics.
Old Bakehouse Antiques, The, Lydiard Millicent, Wilts.
Old Bakery, The, East Budleigh, Devon.
Old Bakery, The, Woolhampton, Berks.
Old Bakery Antiques, Cranbrook, Kent.
Old Bakery Antiques, Jurby, I. of Man.
Old Barn, The, Wolseley Bridge, Staffs.
Old Barn Antiques, Church Stretton, Shrops.
Old Barn Antiques, Exeter, Devon.
Old Barn Antiques, The, Perranarworthal, Cornwall.
Old Barn Antiques Co., Trent, Dorset.
Old Brass Kettle, Moretonhampstead, Devon.
Old Button Shop, The, Lytchett Minster, Dorset.
Old Chair and Wheel Antiques, Cambourne, Cornwall.
Old Chapel Antiques, Uley, Glos.
Old Chapel Antiques and Collectors Centre, Ferndown, Dorset.
Old Clock Shop, The, Birmingham, W. Mids.
Old Clock Shop, The, Swansea, W. Glam., Wales.
Old Clock Shop, The, West Malling, Kent.
Old Coach House, The, Arundel, W. Sussex.
Old Coach House, Long Stratton, Norfolk.
Old Coffee House Antiques, The, Launceston, Cornwall.
Old Cottage Antiques, The, Upminster, Gtr. London.
Old Cottage Shop, The, Harrogate, N. Yorks.
Old Cottage Things, Romsey, Hants.
Old Country Hall Antiques Centre, Newport, Gwent, Wales.
Old Cross Antiques, Greyabbey, Co. Down, N. Ireland.
Old Curio Shop, Bowness-on-Windermere, Cumbria.
Old Curiosity Shop, The, Ayr, Ayr., Scot.
Old Curiosity Shop, Bath, Avon.
Old Curiosity Shop, Beaconsfield, Bucks.
Old Curiosity Shop, The, Bristol, Avon.
Old Curiosity Shop, Frome, Somerset.
Old Curiosity Shop, London, W.C.2.
Old Curiosity Shop, Manchester, Lancs. Royal Ex. S.C.
Old Curiosity Shop, The, Mevagissey, Cornwall.
Old Curiosity Shop, The, St. Sampson, Guernsey, C.I.
Old Curiosity Shop (Antiques), The, Axminster, Devon.
Old Dolls House Antiques, Fordingbridge, Hants.

Old Drawings Gallery, London, S.W.1.
Old Drury, The, London, W.C.2.
Old Farmhouse Furniture, Parwich, Derbys.
Old Firm, The, Newport, I. of Wight.
Old Forge, The, Hollingbourne, Kent.
Old Forge, The, Long Melford, Suffolk.
Old Forge, The, Swanage, Dorset.
Old Forge Antiques, Godstone, Surrey.
Old Forge Antiques, Hartley Wintney, Hants.
Old Forge Antiques, Hatch Beauchamp, Somerset.
Old George Antiques, Long Melford, Suffolk.
Old Golf Shop Inc., Edinburgh, Midloth., Scot.
Old Granary Antique and Collectors Centre, Kings Lynn, Norfolk.
Old Granary Antique & Craft Centre, The, Battlesbridge, Essex.
Old Granary Studio, Kings Lynn, Norfolk.
Old Hall Bookshop, The, Brackley, Northants.
Old Hall Gallery Ltd., Morden, Gtr. London.
Old Hall (Sphinx Gallery), Brasted, Kent.
Old Hall (Sphinx Gallery), Sundridge, Kent.
Old Hat, Radlett, Herts.
Old House, The, Pembury, Kent.
Old House, The, Seaford, E. Sussex.
Old House Gallery, The, Oakham, Leics.
Old London Gallery, London, S.W.1.
Old Malt House, Birmingham, W. Mids.
Old Malthouse, The, Hungerford, Berks.
Old Man Antiques, The, Coniston, Cumbria.
Old Manor House Antiques, Brasted, Kent.
Old Maps and Prints, London, S.W.1.
Old Market Antiques, Usk, Gwent, Wales.
Old Mermaid Antiques, Sherborne, Dorset.
Old Mint House, The, Pevensey, E. Sussex.
Old Paint Shop, The, Alfriston, E. Sussex.
Old Pine Furniture and Jouet, Kiltarlity, Inver., Scot.
Old Pine Loft, The, Luton, Beds.
Old Pine Seller, The, Warwick, Warks.
Old Pine Shop, The, Congleton, Cheshire.
Old Pine Shop, The, Lancing, W. Sussex.
Old Pine Shop, Ross-on-Wye, Hereford and Worcs.
Old Post House Antiques, Playden, E. Sussex.
Old Post House Antiques, Woolhampton, Berks.
Old Post House, The, Penzance, Cornwall.
Old Reading Room Antiques, The, Wrentham, Suffolk.
Old Rectory Antiques and Pine, West Heslerton, N. Yorks.
Old Red Lion, The, Bedingfield, Suffolk.
Old Road Antiques Centre, Frinton-on-Sea, Essex.
Old Rose Gallery (Antiques Market), The, Sandgate, Kent.
Old Saddlers Antiques, Goudhurst, Kent.
Old St. Andrews Gallery, St. Andrews, Fife, Scot.
Old School Antiques, Cambridge, Cambs.
Old School Antiques, The, Dorney, Berks.
Old School House, The, Cassington, Oxon.
Old School House Antiques, Lower Kinnerton, Cheshire.

Old Smiddy, The, Crossford, Fife, Scot.
Old Smithy, Feniscowles, Lancs.
Old Smithy Antique Centre, The, Merstham, Surrey.
Old Smithy Antiques, Bangor-on-Dee, Clwyd, Wales.
Old Soke Books, Peterborough, Cambs.
Old Solent House Galleries, Lymington, Hants.
Old Stores Antiques, The, Chichester, W. Sussex.
Old Tithe Barn, The, Horbury, W. Yorks.
Old Town Hall Antique Centre, The, Needham Market, Suffolk.
Old Treasures, Newton Abbot, Devon.
Old Vicarage Gallery, Worfield, Shrops.
Old Warehouse, The, Shoreham-by-Sea, W. Sussex.
Old Woodworking Tools, London, N.1.
Old World Trading Co., London, S.W.6.
Old Zion Chapel, Somerton, Somerset.
Olde Englande, Hoylake, Merseyside.
Olde Shoulder Curiosity Shop, Hadleigh, Suffolk.
Olde Tyme Antiques, Ruthin, Clwyd, Wales.
Oldfield, Southampton, Hants.
Oldfield Cottage Antiques, Saddleworth, Lancs.
Oldfield, N.E., Preston, Lancs.
Oldham Antique Centre, Oldham, Lancs.
Oldham, Mrs. J.A., Castle Cary, Somerset.
Oldroyd Antiques, Keith R., Ossett, W. Yorks.
Oldswinford Gallery, Stourbridge, W. Mids.
Olink, Mrs. J., High Wycombe, Bucks.
Olivant, G.M., Sheffield, S. Yorks.
Olivant and Son, Sheffield, S. Yorks.
Olive Antiques, Alverstoke, Hants.
Olive Branch Antiques, Broadway, Hereford and Worcs.
Oliver Antiques, West Kirby, Merseyside.
Oliver, A., London, W.8 (Oliver-Sutton Antiques).
Oliver and Sons, G., Guildford, Surrey.
Oliver Antiques, Gerald J., Haverfordwest, Dyfed, Wales.
Oliver, H.R., Guildford, Surrey.
Oliver and Co., John, Diss, Norfolk.
Oliver, Patrick, Cheltenham, Glos.
Oliver, R.A. and Mrs. K.A.G., Brighton, E. Sussex. (Rodney Arthur Classics).
Oliver, R.R., Egham, Surrey.
Oliver, S.F. and C.H., Weldon, Northants.
Oliver, Tony L., Windsor and Eton, Berks.
Oliver-Sutton Antiques, London, W.8.
Olliff, Jonathan, London, W.11. G. Port.
Olman, M.W., Edinburgh, Midloth., Scot. (Old Golf Shop Inc.)
Olney Antique Centre, Olney, Bucks.
Olney, A. and D., Ampthill, Beds.
Olney Antique Porcelain Co., Olney, Bucks.
O'Loughlin, P.J., Glasgow, Lanarks., Scot. (Albany Antiques).
Olschki, Leo S., Belchamp Otten, Essex.
Omar (Harrogate) Ltd., Harrogate, N. Yorks.
Omell Galleries, London, S.W.1.
Omell, N.R., London, S.W.1.
Omniphil, London, W.1. G. Ant. Mkt.

Omniphil Ltd., Chesham, Bucks.
O'Neill, C., London, S.W.3. (Past Times) Chen. Gall.
O'Neill, Michael J., Petworth, W. Sussex.
O'Nians, Hal, London, S.W.1.
Onions, A.J. and L. — White Cottage Antiques Tern Hill, Shrops.
Onions, D. & D., Mayfield, E. Sussex.
Onions, Mrs. E., Shifnal, Shrops.
Onslow Clocks, Twickenham, Gtr. London.
Onslow-Cole, M., Twickenham, Gtr. London.
Oola Boola Antiques London, London, S.E.1.
Oppenheimer, M. and I., London, W.1 (The Golden Past).
Oqyer Antiques, Stockport, Cheshire.
Oracle Antiques, St. Leonards-on-Sea, E. Sussex.
Oram, R., Ilchester, Somerset.
Orbell House Gallery, Castle Hedingham, Essex.
Orchard Antiques, London, W.2.
Orchard House, Oriental Rugs, Reepham, Norfolk.
Orchard, R., London, W.2.
Organ, G.H. and S.M., Bath, Avon (Corridor Stamp Shop).
Organ, R., Bristol, Avon. (Triangle Antiques).
Oriel Antiques, Hindhead, Surrey.
Oriel Antiques, Sheffield, S. Yorks.
Oriental Art Ware, Harrogate, N. Yorks.
Oriental Carpets, Oxford, Oxon.
Oriental Carpet Centre, The, Bristol, Avon.
Oriental Rugs, Swanton Abbot, Norfolk.
Original Architectural Heritage, The, Boddington, Glos.
Original Choice, The, Birmingham, W. Mids.
Original State Ltd., Bicester, Oxon.
Original Victorian Furniture Co., The, Exeter, Devon.
Orman, R., Newnham-on-Severn, Glos.
Ormonde, F., London, W.11. (Ormonde Gallery).
Ormonde Gallery, London, W.11.
Orpin, J., M. and N., Stansted, Essex.
Orr Fine Art, A. and R.M., London, N.W.4.
Orr, Samuel, Hurstpierpoint, W. Sussex.
Orsett Hall Antiques Fair, Orsett, Essex.
Orton, R.J., London, N.4.
Orton Antiques, Stephen, London, N.1.
Orten, S.C., London, N.1.
Osbaldiston, V.W., Manchester, Lancs. (Constance Bishop).
Osborne, Kirkcudbright, Kirkcud., Scot.
Osborne Antiques, Sutton Coldfield, W. Mids.
Osborne Art and Antiques, Jesmond, Tyne and Wear.
Osborne Antiques and Jewellery, Portsmouth, Hants.
Osborne Antique Market, Edinburgh, Midloth., Scot.
Osborne, C., Sutton Coldfield, W. Mids.
Osborne Gallery, London, W.1.
Osborne, T.N.M., London, W.8. (Delomosne and Son Ltd.).
Osbournby Antiques, Osbournby, Lincs.
Oscar's, Crewkerne, Somerset.
O'Shea Gallery, London, S.W.1

Osman, Aytac, London, S.W.3. Ant. Ant. Mkt.
Ossowski, Alec, London, S.W.1.
Ossowski, Alec, London, S.W.6.
Ostle, R. and J., Bethesda, Gwynedd, Wales.
O'Sullivan, Miss, Bristol, Avon. Clift. Ant. Mkt.
O'Sullivan, D., London, S.E.26.
O'Sullivan, D.J., Parkstone, Dorset.
Othen, John, Fakenham, Norfolk. Ant. C.
Otter Antiques, Honiton, Devon.
Otti, Mrs., London, N.W.8. Alf. Ant. Mkt.
Otto, Rudolph, Stow-on-the-Wold, Glos.
Ottrey Antiques, Mike, Dorchester-on-Thames, Oxon.
Ottrey, M.J., Dorchester-on-Thames, Oxon.
Ottrey and Son, W.J., Wallingford, Oxon.
Otway, Rodney and Susan, Bradford-on-Avon, Wilts.
Oulton, Major & Mrs. P., Altrincham, Cheshire.
Out of Time Antiques, Ashbourne, Derbys.
Ovell Prints Ltd., Llandovery, Dyfed, Wales.
Overland, C. and J., Olney, Bucks.
Owen, Mrs. A., Cambridge, Cambs. (Cottage Antiques).
Owen Antiques, Rochdale, Lancs.
Owen, F., Windsor and Eton, Berks.
Owen, G. and J., Penzance, Cornwall.
Owen Gallery, John, Cardiff, S. Glam., Wales.
Owen, J.G.T., Rochdale, Lancs.
Owen, M., Nelson, Lancs.
Owen, N., Ringwood, Hants.
Owen Antiques, Tom, Preston, Lancs.
Owen, Aquarius Antiques Tom, Blackpool, Lancs.
Owen's Jewellers, Newcastle-upon-Tyne, Tyne and Wear.
Owens, Mrs. M., Moffat, Dumfries, Scot.
Oxenhams, Wellington, Somerset.
Oxford Antiques Omnibus, Oxford, Oxon.
Oxford House — Victorian Skip and Basket Works, Hyde, Cheshire.
Oxfordshire County Council, Woodstock, Oxon.
Oxley Antiques and Fine Arts, Eyam, Derbys.
Oxley, L., Alresford, Hants.
Oxley, N.S., Eyam, Derbys.
Oxley Antique Clocks and Barometers, P.A., Cherhill, Wilts.

P

P. and D. Antiques, Newton Abbot, Devon. N.A. Ant. C.
P.D.R. Pine, Ingoldsby, Lincs.
P. and J. Antiques, Barrhead, Renfrews., Scot.
P. & J. Antiques, London, W.1. G. Mews.
P. and O. Carpets Ltd., London, W.1.
Packer House Antiques, Chipping Norton, Oxon.
Packet Quays Gallery, Falmouth, Cornwall.
Packshaw, Louise, London, S.W.3. Ant. Ant. Mkt.

Padgett, G.R., Hull, N. Humberside.
Padgetts Antiques, Photographic and Scientific, Hull, N. Humberside.
Paessler, S.D. and R.J., Wendover, Bucks.
Page Antiques, Stockport, Cheshire.
Page Antiques, Angela, Tunbridge Wells, Kent.
Page, A. and H., London, S.W.7.
Page, A.J., Maidstone, Kent.
Page, B., Walton-on-the-Hill and Tadworth, Surrey.
Page, Mr. and Mrs. B., Walton-on-the-Hill and Tadworth, Surrey.
Page Antiquarian Books, Colin, Brighton, E. Sussex.
Page, C.G., Brighton, E. Sussex (Colin Page Antiquarian Books).
Page, D.R.J. and S.J., London, W.11 (J. Fairman (Carpets) Ltd.)
Page, F., Bath, Avon. ('Kimino' Antiques).
Page & Hawkes, Brighton, E. Sussex.
Page, Jane and Neil, Honiton, Devon.
Page, Mrs. K., Bath, Avon (Kimono).
Page Oriental Art, Kevin, London, N.1.
Page, T., Marlborough, Wilts.
Pageant Antiques, London, S.W.6.
Pain, B, Cambridge, Cambs. (Artisan Antiques & Collectables).
Pain Gallery, Jean, Cambridge, Cambs.
Painswick Antiques, Painswick, Glos.
Paisley Fine Books, Paisley, Renfrew., Scot.
Paisnel Gallery Ltd., London, S.W.6.
Paisnel, S., London, S.W.6.
Palace Gallery Antiques, Charing, Kent.
Palfrey, M., Brockdish, Norfolk.
Pall Mall Antiques, Leigh-on-Sea, Essex.
Palmer, B., Topsham, Devon.
Palmer Antiques, Dermot and Jill, Brighton, E. Sussex.
Palmer, D. and M., Bicester, Oxon.
Palmer, F.G. and H.G., Bude, Cornwall.
Palmer, G.I., Martock, Somerset.
Palmer, H.J. and Miss J., London, S.W.3. Ant. Ant. Mkt.
Palmer Ltd., J. and J., Grantham, Lincs.
Palmer Antiques, Mary, Stradbroke, Suffolk.
Palmer Antiques, P.E., Ringwood, Hants.
Palmer, P. and G., Sarnau, Dyfed, Wales.
Palmer, R., Ramsbottom, Lancs.
Pam Antiques, Petworth, W. Sussex.
Pamela Furs and Things, London, S.W.3. Ant. Ant. Mkt.
Pandora's Box, Brighton, E. Sussex.
Pandora's Box, Hungerford, Berks.
Pandora's Box Antiques and Gifts, Buxton, Derbys.
Pandora's Bric-a-Brac, Oxford, Oxon.
Panormo, S.V., Gosport, Hants.
Pantelli, A., London, N.1 (Inheritance).
Pantiles Antiques, Tunbridge Wells, Kent.
Pantywylan Antiques, Cardigan, Dyfed, Wales.
Paolo, London, N.W.8. Alf. Ant. Mkt.
Paradise, J., Nottingham, Notts.
Paragon Antiques and Collectors Market, Bath, Avon.
Paraphernalia, Sheffield, S. Yorks.
Parasol Antiques, Ventnor, I. of Wight.

Pardoe, Stuart, London, W.11.
Pargeter, G.S., Stourbridge, W. Mids.
Parikian, D., Oxford, Oxon.
Park Antiques and Fine Arts, Nottingham, Notts.
Park Antiquities, Weymouth, Dorset.
Park Galleries, Brighton, E. Sussex.
Park Galleries, London, N.3.
Park Galleries Antiques, Fine Art and Decor, Bolton, Lancs.
Park House Antiques, Bladon, Oxon.
Park House Antiques, Stow-on-the-Wold, Glos.
Park, N., Tiverton, Devon.
Park Street Antiques, Berkhamsted, Herts.
Parker, C.R.J., J.R.J. and Mrs. D.C.A., Salisbury, Wilts.
Parker, Elizabeth, Moreton-in-Marsh, Glos.
Parker Fine Art, Leeds. W. Yorks.
Parker Antiques Ltd., Geoff, Freiston, Lincs.
Parker Gallery, The, London, W.1.
Parker, J., Cardiff, S. Glam., Wales.
Parker, J. and E., Blackpool, Lancs.
Parker, L., Canterbury, Kent.
Parker, Mrs. M., London, S.W.3. Ant. Ant. Mkt. (J. Feleyuska)
Parker, M. and Barbic, N., London, S.W.3. Ant. Ant. Mkt.
Parker Antiques, Michael and Margaret, London, S.W.7.
Parker, Philip, London, S.W.6.
Parker Ltd., Richard, Salisbury, Wilts.
Parker Ltd., Thomas H., London, W.1.
Parker-Williams, Canterbury, Kent.
Parkhouse Antiques and Jewellery, Mark, Barnstaple, Devon.
Parkhouse and Wyatt Ltd., Southampton, Hants.
Parkin, D.T., Ingoldsby, Lincs.
Parkin, J., Derby, Derbys.
Parkin Fine Art Ltd., Michael, London, S.W.1.
Parkinson, E. & D., Chalfont St. Giles, Bucks.
Parkinson-Large, P., Woburn, Beds.
Parks of Dover, Dover, Kent.
Parkside Antiques, Nottingham, Notts.
Parnaby, J.H., Stockbridge, Hants.
Parr, R., Westleton, Suffolk.
Parrington Fine Art, Bishops Sutton, Hants.
Parrington, J. and Mrs. E., Bishops Sutton, Hants.
Parriss, J.H., Sheringham, Norfolk.
Parry, H., Edinburgh, Midloth., Scot.
Parry Ltd., H. and R.L., Sutton Coldfield, W. Mids.
Parry, R., Exeter, Devon.
Parry (Old Glass), S.W., London, W.2.
Parry (Old Glass), S.W., London, W.11.
Parsons, A.L. and R.F., London, W.1. (Tessiers Ltd.)
Parsons, Mrs. B.D., Tonbridge, Kent.
Parsonson, N.C., Launceston, Cornwall.
Parsonson, R.S., Launceston, Cornwall.
Particles of Time, Boston, Lincs.
Partington, C., Shrewsbury, Shrops.
Partner and Puxton, Colchester, Essex.
Partner, S.H., M. and J.G., Colchester, Essex.

Partridge (Fine Arts) Ltd., London, W.1.
Partridge Antiques, L., Hertford, Herts.
Partt, J., Bath, Avon. Gt. West. Ant. C.
Pascoe, M., Truro, Cornwall.
Passers Buy (Marie Evans), Llangollen, Clwyd, Wales.
Passing Time, Barrow-in-Furness, Cumbria.
Past for Sale, The, Brighton, E. Sussex.
Past and Present, Burnham-on-Crouch, Essex.
Past and Present, Cromer, Norfolk.
Past and Present, Husbands Bosworth, Leics.
Past and Present, Leigh-on-Sea, Essex.
Past and Present, Seaham, Durham.
Past Times, London, S.W.3. Chen. Gall.
Past Times, Swansea, W. Glam., Wales. Ant. Centre.
Pastiche, Virginia Water, Surrey.
Pataky Antiques and Reproductions, Victoria, West Malling, Kent.
Patchwork Dog, The and The Calico Cat Ltd., London, N.W.1.
Paterson Antiques, Elizabeth, Stirling, Stirlings., Scot.
Paterson, E. and J., Stirling, Stirlings., Scot.
Patina, Bath, Avon. Gt. West. Ant. C.
Patina Antiques, Clacton-on-Sea, Essex.
Patricia Antiques, Ramsgate, Kent.
Patrick, W., Folkestone, Kent.
Patrickson, E., Seaham, Durham.
Patten, R., Westcliff-on-Sea, Essex.
Patterson, A., Manningtree, Essex.
Patterson Antiques, David, Lostwithiel, Cornwall.
Patterson Antiques, Jo., Crook, Durham.
Patterson, J.G., Oxford, Oxon.
Patterson, J.W.B., Crook, Durham.
Patterson, T. and P., Sible Hedingham, Essex.
Patterson Fine Arts Ltd., W.H., London, W.1.
Patterson, W.H. and P.M., London, W.1.
Pattersons Antiques, North Shields, Tyne & Wear.
Pattison, Fenwick, Coniston, Cumbria.
Paul and Daughters, Barbara, Maldon, Essex.
Paul, Mrs. E., London, W.1 (Demas).
Paul, R.W., Ipswich, Suffolk.
Paull, Janice, Warwick, Warks. Smith St. A.C.
Pauw Antiques, M., London, S.W.6.
Pawsey and Payne, London, S.W.1.
Pay, D., London, S.W.3 (E. Hollander).
Payman, E. and L.C., Stokesley, N. Yorks.
Payne, Mrs., Newton Abbot, Devon. N. A. Ant. C.
Payne, C., London, W.11.
Payne, D.M., G.N., E.P. and J.D., Oxford, Oxon.
Payne, J. and M., Hemel Hempstead, Herts.
Payne Antiques, Martin, Warwick, Warks.
Payne, M.H., London, N.1.
Payne, P., Alcester, Warks.
Payne and Son (Goldsmiths), Ltd., Oxford, Oxon.
Payton, F.B. and S., Mansfield, Notts.

Payton Antiques, Mary, Chagford, Devon.
Peache, N. and M., Honiton, Devon.
Peacock Antiques, Chilham, Kent.
Peacock, Carol, Wallingford, Oxon. L. Arc.
Peacock, R., Bournemouth, Dorset. (Gallery 922)
Pead, L.W., Aylsham, Norfolk.
Peake, D.T., Nottingham, Notts.
Peake, N.B., Norwich, Norfolk (The Scientific Anglian Bookshop).
Pearce, A., Salisbury, Wilts.
Pearce, B. and A., Ombersley, Hereford and Worcs.
Pearce, D.G. and H.J., Ludlow, Shrops.
Pearce, F.G., Parkstone, Dorset.
Pearce, G. and J., Fordingbridge, Hants.
Pearce, P., Hexham, Northumb.
Pearce, R., London, W.11 (Cohen and Pearce).
Pearl Cross Ltd., London, W.C.2.
Pearse, Mrs. N.P., Chichester, W. Sussex.
Pearse, Robert D., Diss, Norfolk.
Pearson Antiques, Hull, N. Humbs.
Pearson Antiques, Mrs. J., Altrincham, Cheshire.
Pearson, John, Birstwith, N. Yorks.
Pearson, J. and D., Nottingham, Notts.
Pearson, Mrs. J.A., Appleton, Cheshire.
Pearson Ltd., John A., Windsor and Eton, Berks.
Pearson, P.S., Castle Cary, Somerset.
Peasenhall Art and Antiques Gallery, Peasenhall, Suffolk.
Peckham, Mrs. I.D., Rossett, Clwyd, Wales.
Peckham Rye Antiques, London, S.E.15.
Peckwater Pine and Antiques, Charing, Kent.
Peddie, Mrs., Newton Abbot, Devon. N.A. Ant. C.
Pedlar, The, Navenby, Lincs,
Pedlars, Chipping Campden, Glos.
Pedlar's Pack, Stockbridge, Hants.
Pedlar's Pack (Beckenham), The, Beckenham, Gtr. London.
Pedlar's Pack (Hadlow), The, Hadlow, Kent.
Pedler, R.S., London, S.W.15. (The Clock Clinic Ltd.)
Peek, G., Gillingham, Kent.
Peel Antiques, London, W.8.
Peett Antiques, Dalton, London, S.W.6.
Peett, S. and M., London, S.W.6.
Pegg, R., Ipswich, Suffolk. (Victoria House Antiques).
Pegler, W.H., Gloucester, Glos.
Pegler's Antiques, Gloucester, Glos.
Pelham Galleries, London, S.W.3.
Pelican Antiques, Greystoke, Cumbria.
Pelly, William, Fairford, Glos.
Pelly, W.R.B., Fairford, Glos.
Pelter/Sands Fine Paintings, Bristol, Avon.
Pembery, M., Bakewell, Derbys.
Pembleton, Mrs. A., Nottingham, Notts.
Pembleton, S., Nottingham, Notts.
Penandrea Gallery, Redruth, Cornwall.
Pendeford House Antiques, Wolverhampton, W. Mids.
Pendlebury, J.M. and M.L., Lancaster, Lancs.

Pendragon Antiquarian Bookshop, Ilkley, W. Yorks.
Penn Barn, Penn, Bucks.
Pennard House, East Pennard, Somerset.
Pennine Antiques, Todmorden, W. Yorks.
Pennington, S., Sheffield, S. Yorks. (Broadfield Antiques)
Pennink and Owers, Tunbridge Wells, Kent.
Penny Farthing Antiques, Edinburgh, Midloth., Scot.
Penny Farthing Antiques, Southend-on-Sea, Essex.
Penny Farthing Antiques Arcade, London, S.E.1.
Penny Farthing Antiques and Pretty Things, Chobham, Surrey.
Pennyfarthing, Crowmarsh, Gifford, Oxon.
Penny-Farthing Antiques, Clacton-on-Sea, Essex.
Penoyre Antiques, Pershore, Hereford and Worcs.
Penrith Coin and Stamp Centre, Penrith, Cumbria.
Penrose Antiques, Sarratt, Herts.
Penryn Antiques and Pictures, Penryn, Cornwall.
Pen-y-Ghent Antiques, The, Settle, N. Yorks.
Pen-y-Ghent Gallery, Settle, N. Yorks.
Pepper, M.E. and Mrs. G.J., Bury St. Edmunds, Suffolk.
Pepper, T.G., Luton, Beds.
Pepper's Antique Pine, Seaford, E. Sussex.
Peppers Period Pieces, Bury St. Edmunds, Suffolk.
Pepys Antiques, Beckenham, Gtr. London.
Percik, B. & L.M., Sidmouth, Devon.
Percival, A.N.W., and Mrs. E.M., Litton Cheney, Dorset.
Percy's, London, W.C.2. Lon. Silv. Vts.
Peretz Antiques, Pauline, Long Melford, Suffolk.
Perez, Maria, London, S.W.3. Chen. Gall.
Period Brass Lights, London, S.W.7.
Period Furniture Showrooms, Beaconsfield, Bucks.
Periwinkle Press, Doddington, Kent.
Perkins Antiques, Bryan, Wellingborough, Northants.
Perkins, B.H. and J., Wellingborough, Northants.
Perkins, Mr. and Mrs. G., Church Enstone, Oxon.
Perovetz, H., London, W.C.2. Lon. Silv. Vts.
Perovetz Ltd., H., London, W.C.2.
Perret, J.B., London, W.8 (Delomosne and Son Ltd.)
Perrott House Antiques, Pershore, Hereford and Worcs.
Perry, A. and C., Woking, Surrey.
Perry Antiques, Christopher, St. Albans, Herts.
Perry Antiques, Christopher, Woburn, Beds. Wob. Ab. Ant. C.
Perry, L., Pendlebury, Lancs.
Perry, Ron, Woburn, Beds. Wob. Ab. Ant. C.
Perry, R.J., Hitchin, Herts.
Perry Antiques, R.J., Hitchin, Herts.

Persian Carpet Art, Sheffield, S. Yorks.
Persian Market, London, N.1.
Persian Rugs, West Peckham, Kent.
Persiflage, London, S.W.3. Ant. Ant. Mkt.
Peston, D., London, N.W.1.
Peter, London, N.W.8. Alf. Ant. Mkt.
Peter John Antiques, St. Neots, Cambs.
Peter Pan's Bazaar, Gosport, Hants.
Peter Pan's of Gosport, Gosport, Hants.
Peters, A., Tiverton, Devon.
Peters, Mrs. D., Worthing, W. Sussex.
Peters, D.J., Great Missenden, Bucks.
Peters, Mrs. P., Batheaston, Avon.
Peters Antiques, Paul M., Harrogate, N. Yorks.
Petersfield Bookshop, Petersfield, Hants.
Peterson Antiques, Torquay, Devon. Tor. Ant. C.
Pethick, K.J. and Mrs., Frinton-on-Sea, Essex.
Petkowski, J.H.O., London, S.W.3. Ant. Ant. Mkt.
Petre, N. and P., Hertford, Herts.
Petrie, M., Rochester, Kent.
Petticombe Manor Antiques, Bideford, Devon.
Pettifer Ltd., David, London, S.W.3.
Pettitt, J., Wolverhampton, W. Mids.
Pettitt, J.P., Battlesbridge, Essex.
Petworth Antique Market, Petworth, W. Sussex.
Petworth Antiques Warehouse, Petworth, W. Sussex.
Peveler, Mrs. M.R., Harrogate, N. Yorks. (The Old Cottage Shop).
Peyton-Jones, Miss P., Wendover, Bucks.
Pheazey, G.B., Haynes, Beds.
Phelps Ltd., Twickenham, Gtr. London.
Phelps Antiquarian Books, Michael, London, S.W.15.
Phelps, W.J. and R.C., Twickenham, Gtr. London.
Philby, W., Herne Bay, Kent.
Philip and Sons Ltd., Trevor, Brighton, E. Sussex.
Phillips, Mrs. A., Altrincham, Cheshire.
Phillips Antiques Ltd., Elaine, N. Harrogate, Yorks.
Phillips and Sons, E.S., London, W.11.
Phillips, Henry, London, W.8.
Phillips, Howard (Antique Glass), London, W.1.
Phillips, John F.C., London, S.W.12.
Phillips, Mary, Burford, Oxon.
Phillips, M. and J., Hitchin, Herts.
Phillips of Hitchin (Antiques) Ltd., Hitchin, Herts.
Phillips, R.J., Milford, Staffs.
Phillips Ltd., Ronald, London, W.1.
Phillips Ltd., S.J., London, W.1.
Phillips, W. and M., Raglan, Gwent, Wales.
Phillips and Sons, Cookham, Berks.
Phillipson, M., Leominster, Hereford and Worcs.
Philp, Miss F.M., Broadway, Hereford and Worcs.
Philp, Peter, Cardiff, S. Glam., Wales.
Philp, P.M. and D.A., Cardiff, S. Glam., Wales.

Philp, R., London, W.11.
Philpot, P., Stoke Ferry, Norfolk.
Phipps and Co. Ltd., London, S.W.3 (Mathon Gallery.)
Phipps and Co. Ltd., Mathon, Hereford and Worcs.
Phoenix Antiques, Fordham, Cambs.
Phoenix Antiques, London, W.11 (Philip and Paul Allison Antiques Ltd.)
Phoenix Green Antiques, Hartley Wintney, Hants.
Phoenix Pine and Antiques, Birmingham, W. Mids.
Pianoland incorporating Cradle Well Antiques, Newcastle-upon-Tyne, Tyne and Wear.
Pianorama Antique Exports, Leeds, W. Yorks.
Piccadilly Antiques, Bath, Avon (Stuart King.)
Piccadilly Gallery, London, W.1.
Pickard, P.M., Saffron Walden, Essex.
Pickering, B., Allonby, Cumbria.
Pickering and Chatto Ltd., Incorporating Dawsons of Pall Mall, London, W.C.1.
Pickering, Ernest, Eastbourne, E. Sussex.
Pickering T., Dorridge, W. Mids.
Pickett, D. and Mrs. J., Rait, Perths., Scot.
Pickwick Antiques, London, N.W.3. Ham. Ant. Emp.
Pickwick Antiques, Mr., London, S.E.1. Ber. Ant. Whse.
Pickwicks, Mr., Bangor-on-Dee, Clywd, Wales.
Pic's Bookshop, Bridport, Dorset.
Picture House, London, W.14.
Pieces of Eight, Conway, Gwynedd, Wales.
Pierce, P.J., Deal, Kent.
Pierpoint Gallery, Hereford, Hereford and Worcs.
Pigeon House Antiques, Hurst Green, E. Sussex.
Pigney, L. and J., Stanford-Le-Hope, Essex.
Pike, David, Weston-super-Mare, Avon.
Pilling, D. and P., Boston, Lincs.
Pillory House, Nantwich, Cheshire.
Pinches, Mrs. R., London, S.W.3 (Heraldry Today).
Pine Antiques, Uttoxeter, Staffs.
Pine Cellars, The, Winchester, Hants.
Pine Company, Ringwood, Hants.
Pine and Country Antiques, North Petherwin, Cornwall.
Pine and Country Antiques — Sandhill Barn, Washington, W. Sussex.
Pine and Design, Balcombe, W. Sussex.
Pine Finds, Bishop Monkton, N. Yorks.
Pine House, The, London, W.8.
Pine Merchants, The, Great Missenden, Bucks.
Pine Mine, The, (Crewe-Read Antiques), London, S.W.6.
Pine, N.J., Horndean, Hants.
Pine, P.D.R., Grantham, Lincs.
Pine Place, Manchester, Lancs. Royal Ex. S.C.
Pine Shop, The, Bury St. Edmunds, Suffolk.
Pine Shop, The, Fernhurst, W. Sussex.

Pine Shop — Launceston, The, Launceston, Cornwall.
Pine Shop, The, Merrow, Surrey.
Pine Village, The, London, S.W.6.
Pine Warehouse, The, Midhurst, W. Sussex.
Pine Workshop, The, Cawood, N. Yorks.
Pineapple, Bath, Avon.
Pinecrafts, Bishops Waltham, Hants.
Pineside Studios, Bath, Avon. Gt. West. Ant. C.
Pinfold Antiques, Ruskington, Lincs.
Pinkerton, M. Ockley, Surrey.
Pinn, K.H. and W.J., Sible Hedingham, Essex.
Pinn and Sons, W.A., Sible Hedingham, Essex.
Pinner Antiques, Pinner, Gtr. London.
Pinner, Mrs. E., Bexhill-on-Sea, E. Sussex.
Piombo and Partners, S., London, W.8. (Traditio Antiques).
Pioneer, Bath, Avon. Gt. West. Ant. C.
Pipe, J. and W., Wrentham, Suffolk.
Pirouette, Exeter, Devon.
Pitcher, J., Southend-on-Sea, Essex.
Pitman, J.T. and C., Weymouth, Dorset.
Pitt, G. and J.., Bishop Monkton, N. Yorks.
Pitt, Mrs. J.R. & Miss S.A., Broadway, Hereford & Worcs.
Pivnick Gallery, London, W.11.
Pivnick, S., London, W.11.
Place Antiques, Peter, London, S.W.6.
Plaitford House Gallery, Plaitford, Hants.
Plant, M., Hitchin, Herts.
Plantenga, Janet, Market Weighton, N. Humberside.
Plantenga, Pieter, Market Weighton, N. Humberside.
Plater, K.W. and J.M., Tamworth, Staffs.
Platt, E., Faversham, Kent.
Platt Antiques, Keith, Chipping Norton, Oxon.
Platt, K. and J., Warwick, Warks.
Platts-Martin, G.P. & E., Bognor Regis, W. Sussex.
Pleasures of Past Times, London, W.C.2.
Plough, The, Eastry, Kent.
Plough, The, Iping, W. Sussex.
Pluck, Mrs. A., Bristol, Avon. Clift. Ant. Mkt.
Plume of Feathers Antiques, Dorchester, Dorset.
Plumridge, R.H., Birmingham, W. Mids.
Plumridge's, Birmingham, W. Mids.
Pocock, K., North Petherton, Somerset.
Pocock, P., Weybridge, Surrey.
Podlewski, J. and Daniel, P., London, W.C.2. Lon. Silv. Vts.
Podmore Antiques, N., London, W.1. G. Ant. Mkt.
Pointer, S., London, S.W.3. (The Map House).
Polak Gallery, London, S.W.1.
Poldark Antiques, St. Austell, Cornwall.
Poley Antiques, D.T. and A.G., Alrewas, Staffs.
Pollak, Dr. P.M., South Brent, Devon.
Pollington, P.B., Wadhurst, E. Sussex.
Pollitt, J., Pershore, Hereford and Worcs.

Pollock Antiques, Jane, Penrith, Cumbria.
Pollock, Miss E. and Leon, Mrs. N., London, S.W.3. Ant. Ant. Mkt.
Pollock, M., Nottingham, Notts.
Polly, A., London, S.E.10.
Polyera Antiques, Middlesbrough, Cleveland.
Polyviou, N., London, N.W.1. (Galerie 1900.)
Pomeroy Antiques, Torquay, Devon. Tor. Ant. C.
Pomfret, J. and J.D., Cheltenham, Glos.
Pond Antiques, Walton-on-the-Hill and Tadworth, Surrey.
Pond Cottage Antiques, Stillington, N. Yorks.
Ponsford Antiques, A.J., Cirencester, Glos.
Ponsford, A.J. and R.L., Cirencester, Glos.
Ponsonby, Mrs. A.M., Ashfield, Suffolk.
Ponteland Antiques, Ponteland, Northumb.
Pontypool Antiques, Pontypool, Gwent, Wales.
Poole, J., Truro, Cornwall.
Poole, J.B. and J., Bingley, W. Yorks.
Poole, P., London, W.C.2. (His Nibs).
Poole, P.E., St. Leonards-on-Sea, E. Sussex.
Pope, D and D., Buckfastleigh, Devon.
Pope and Hunts Antiques Ltd., John, London, S.W.7.
Pope, R. and A., Croydon, Gtr. London.
Popper, Madeline, London, W.1. G. Mews.
Popular Mart, The, Darlington, Durham.
Porcelain Collector, The, Shoreham, Kent.
Porcupines Bookshop and Toy Museum, Barnstaple, Devon.
Pordes Remainders Ltd., London, N.W.3.
Pordes Books Ltd., Henry, London, W.C.2.
Porter, Arthur G.R., Baldock, Herts.
Porter and Son, A.W., Hartley Wintney, Hants.
Porter, B.K. and J.M.H., Barmouth, Gwynedd, Wales.
Porter, D., Shoreham, Kent.
Porter, I.B., Towcester, Northants.
Porter Antiques, James, Sandwich, Kent.
Porter, M.A., Hartley Wintney, Hants.
Porter Prints (Broomhill), Sheffield, S. Yorks.
Porter, R.E., Bournemouth, Dorset.
Porter, Fine Antique European Arms and Armour, Terence H., Steeple Claydon, Bucks.
Porter-Davison, J., Bath, Avon. (Wye Knot Antiques). B. Ant. Mkt.
Porterfield, Mr., Barrhead, Renfrews., Scot.
Porters Lodge Antiques, Barmouth, Gwynedd, Wales.
Portique, Bournemouth, Dorset.
Portland Gallery, London, W.11.
Portman Carpets, London, W.1.
Portmeirion Antiques, London, S.W.13.
Portmeirion Ltd., Portmeirion, Gwynedd, Wales.
Portobello Antiques, Bradiford, Devon.
Portobello Silver Co., London, W.11.
Portsmouth Stamp Shop, Portsmouth, Hants.
Posnett, D., London, W.1 (The Leger Galleries Ltd.).
Post House Antiques, Bletchingley, Surrey.

Postcard Corner (Mr. & Mrs. Brown), Newton Abbot, Devon. N.A. Ant. C.
Pot of Gold Antiques, Ramsbottom, Lancs.
Potashnick Antiques, David, Coulsdon, Gtr. London.
Pot-Pourri, Sheffield, S. Yorks.
Potter, B.C., Bristol, Avon.
Potter Antiques, David and Carole, Nottingham, Notts.
Potter, H. and E., Laleham, Surrey.
Potter Ltd., Jonathan, London, W.1.
Potter, Mrs. M., Bristol, Avon. Clift. Ant. Mkt.
Potter, N.C., London, W.1. (Burlington Gallery Ltd.).
Potter and Son, W.G., Axminster, Devon.
Potters Antiques and Coins, Bristol, Avon.
Potterton Books, Thirsk, N. Yorks.
Potts, Mrs. R., Saddleworth, Lancs.
Poulter and Son, H.W., London, S.W.10.
Poulter Antiques, Irene, Old Hunstanton, Norfolk.
Poulton, Sheila, London, W.1. B. St. Ant. C.
Pound, Mrs. M.F., Cobham, Surrey.
Pout Antiques, Ian, Witney, Oxon.
Pout, I. and J., Witney, Oxon.
Powell Bros., Gilwern, Gwent, Wales.
Powell, John, Reigate, Surrey.
Powell (Hove) Ltd., J., Portslade, W. Sussex.
Powell, P., Leamington Spa, Warks.
Powell Antiques, Steve, Clayton, W. Sussex.
Powling, L.G., Southend-on-Sea, Essex.
Powlings, Southend-on-Sea, Essex.
Poynter, F.B. and R., Everton, Notts.
Poynter, P., Brasted, Kent.
Poyser, G.A., Derby, Derbys.
Pratt, A., Hythe, Kent.
Pratt, G.L. and J., Richmond, N. Yorks.
Pratt, Mrs. G.S., Church Broughton, Derbys.
Pratt, J., Ramsgate, Kent.
Pratt and Son, Leo, South Walsham, Norfolk.
Pratt, M. and J., Burford, Oxon.
Pratt Antiques, Rosemary, Woburn, Beds. Wob. Ab. Ant. C.
Pratt, R. and Mrs. E.D., South Walsham, Norfolk.
Pratt, S.G.H., Ilkley, W. Yorks.
Precious, R.M.S., Settle, N. Yorks. Worcs.
Preece, J., Tewkesbury, Glos.
Preiss, Shaushana, London, N.W.8. Alf. Ant. Mkt.
Prescott, C., West Bridgford, Notts.
Pressman, Mrs. R., London, E.18.
Prest, R., Bath, Avon. Gt. West. A. C. Wed. Mkt.
Prestbury Antiques, Prestbury, Cheshire.
Prestige Antiques, John, Brixham, Devon.
Preston, Mrs., Duffield, Derbys.
Preston Antiques Ltd., Antony, Stow-on-the-Wold, Glos.
Preston Book Co., Preston, Lancs.
Preston, M. and J., Halifax, W. Yorks.
Preston, Mr. and Mrs. N., Launceston, Cornwall.

Preston, S., Birmingham, W. Mids. (Perry Greaves Ltd.)
Pretty Chairs, Portsmouth, Hants.
Price Antiques, Graham, Polegate, E. Sussex.
Price, G.D.A., Alderley Edge, Cheshire.
Price, Mrs. J., Wrexham, Clwyd, Wales.
Price, M. & A. Harlington, Beds.
Price, R., West Bridgford, Notts.
Price Antiques, Sandy, Warwick, Warks. Smith St. A. C.
Price, V., Usk, Gwent, Wales.
Prichard Antiques, K.H. and D.Y., Winchcombe, Glos.
Prickett, M.L. and C.M., Birmingham, W. Mids.
Priddy, W.R., Portsmouth, Hants.
Pride Oriental Rugs, Eric, Cheltenham, Glos.
Prides of London, London, S.W.3.
Pridham, Newton Abbot, Devon. N. A. Ant. C.
Pridham, B., Newton Abbott, Devon. N. A. Ant. C.
Priest, M.G. and A.C., Thame, Oxon.
Priestly, M., London, W.8 (The Antique Home).
Priests Antiques and Fine Arts, Thame, Oxon.
Primrose Antiques, Moreton-in-Marsh, Glos.
Princedale Antiques, London, N.7.
Princedale Antiques, London, W.11.
Principia Arts and Sciences, Marlborough, Wilts.
Pringle Antiques, Fochabers, Morays., Scot.
Pringle, T., London, W.1. (The Richmond Gallery)
Print Room, The, Deal, Kent.
Print Room, The, London, W.C.1.
Printed Page, Winchester, Hants.
Prior, R., Brighton, E. Sussex (The Sussex Commemorative Ware Centre).
Priory Antiques, Bridlington, N. Humberside.
Priory Antiques, Godalming, Surrey.
Priory Antiques, Litcham, Norfolk.
Priory Antiques, London, E.C.1.
Priory Gallery, The, Bishops Cleeve, Glos.
Pritchard, J., Dorking, Surrey.
Pritchard, Mary, London, S.W.3 (Mr. Gill.) Ant. Ant. Mkt.
Pritchard, N.W., Betws-y-Coed, Gwynedd, Wales.
Probsthain, Arthur, London, W.C.1.
Procter, M.J., Lancing, W. Sussex.
Procter, Susan, Auchterarder, Perths., Scot.
Proctor, A. and H., Windsor and Eton, Berks. (Windsor Antiques and Design).
Proctor, C.D. & H.M. Puddletown, Dorset.
Proctor, Lucidgate, J.J., London, S.W.3. Ant. Ant. Mkt.
Proops, Joanna, Bath, Avon. B. Ant. Mkt.
Prospect Antiques, Ruabon, Clwyd, Wales.
Prospect Antiques, Studley, Warks.
Prosser, D., Sutton-on-Sea, Lincs.
Prothero, P. and M., Neston, Cheshire.
Providence House Antiques, Blakeney, Norfolk.
Provincial Antique Silver Co., London, W.C.2. Lon. Silv. Vts. (E. and C.T. Koopman).

Pruskin Gallery, London, S.W.3. Chen. Gall.
Pruskin, M. and J., London, S.W.3. Chen. Gall.
Pryce and Brise Antiques, London, S.W.6.
Pryce, N., London, S.W.6.
Prydal, B.S., Kingston-upon-Thames, Gtr. London.
Pryor and Son, E., Liverpool, Merseyside.
Pugh Antiques, Christopher, Chester, Cheshire.
Pugh, J. and J., Layer de la Haye, Essex.
Pugh, Robert, London, W.8.
Pughs' Porcelains, Layer de la Haye, Essex.
Pullen, D. and N., Devizes, Wilts.
Pullen, Antiques, David and Sarah, Bexhill-on- Sea, E. Sussex.
Pullen Jeweller, Richard, Lincoln, Lincs.
Pullen, Sylvia, Guildford, Surrey. Ant. C.
Pulliblank, I., Cerne Abbas, Dorset.
Pulton, J.J.A. and D.A., London, S.W.6 (Through the Looking Glass Ltd.).
Purchase, S., London, S.W.3 (Hooper and Purchase).
Purdon, R., Cirencester, Glos.
Purple Shop, London, S.W.3.
Purple Shop, The, London, S.W.3. Ant. Ant. Mkt.
Putnam, London, N.W.8. Alf. Ant. Mkt.
Putnam, R. and M., Farnham, Surrey.
Putnams Antiques, London, N.W.6.
Puttenham Gallery Antiques, Puttenham, Surrey.
Puttick, M.J., London, S.W.1. (Heraz).
Puttnam, Annette, Brighton, E. Sussex (John Bird.)
Puyenbroek, Mr. and Mrs. N. Sunbury, Surrey.
Puzzle House Antiques, Bath, Avon. B. Ant. Mkt.
Puzzle House Antiques, Cinderford, Glos.
Pye, Mrs. N. Hull, N. Humberside.
Pyke — Fine British Watercolours, Beverley, Totnes, Devon.
Pym Antiques, Craven Arms, Shrops.
Pym, J. and S., Craven Arms, Shrops.
Pyms Gallery, London, S.W.1.
Pynn, J. Debenham, Suffolk.
Pyrmont Antiques, Sibsey, Lincs.

Q

Quadrangle Gallery, Oxford, Oxon.
Quadrangle Gallery Warehouse, Chalgrove, Oxon.
Quadrant Antiques, Edinburgh, Midloth., Scot.
Quair Cottage Antiques, Stonehaven, Kincard., Scot.
Quaker Lodge Antiques, Finedon, Northants.
Quaker Lodge Antiques, London, N.1.
Quality House, Pontefract, W. Yorks.
Quaradeghini, T., London, N.W.1. (Regent Antiques).
Quaritch Booksellers Ltd., Bernard, London, W.1.
Quarter Jack Antiques, Sturminster Newton, Dorset.

Quartlet Art, London, N.W.8. Alf. Ant. Mkt.
Quastel, P., Bromley, Gtr. London.
Quay Antiques, Burnham-on-Sea, Essex.
Quay Antiques, Ramsey, Isle of Man.
Quay Gallery, The, Exeter, Devon.
Quayle, F., Peel, Isle of Man.
Quayles Emporium, Septimus, Hawkhurst, Kent.
Queen Anne House, Chesham, Bucks.
Queens Parade Antiques Ltd., Bath, Avon.
Quentin, Paul, Manchester, Lancs.
Quest Antiques, London, W.13.
Quest Antiques and Pine, Bath, Avon.
Quested, A., Surbiton, Gtr. London.
Quested Antiques, Surbiton, Gtr. London.
Questor, Woburn, Beds.
Questor Antiques, London, W.6.
Quevedo, London, W.C.2.
Quick, J.C. and R.B., Liskeard, Cornwall.
Quiet Street Antiques, Bath, Avon.
Quill Antiques, Bletchingley, Surrey.
Quill Antiques, Deal, Kent.
Quilter, Michael, Amersham, Bucks.
Quinn Antiques, Barrie, London, S.W.6.
Quinn, B.J., London, S.W.6.
Quinn, N.J., London, W.4. (Stratton-Quinn Antiques Etc.).
Quinney's, Bristol, Avon.
Quinney's, Budleigh Salterton, Devon.
Quinto Bookshop, Brighton, E. Sussex.
Quinto of Cambridge, Cambridge, Cambs.
Quinton, E.A., Bath, Avon. (Queens Parade Antiques Ltd.)
Quirke, Mrs. M.M., Seaton Ross, N. Humber- side.
Quorn Antiques, Leicester, Leics.

R

R.B.R. Group, London, W.1. G. Ant. Mkt.
R.E.M. Antiques, Bournemouth, Dorset.
R. and L. Coins, Blackpool, Lancs.
R. and R.'s Gold and Silver Exchange, London, N.W.4.
Rabbitz, London, W.11.
Rabi Gallery, London, W.1.
Rackham, Mrs. P.M., Lichfield, Staffs.
Radcliffe, J., Hastings, E. Sussex.
Radford Antiques and Interiors, Dorothy, Trumpington, Cambs.
Radford, Mrs. P.J., Alfriston, E. Sussex.
Radio Vintage, Hythe, Kent.
Radman, T. and B., Burford, Oxon.
Radnor House, Grampound, Cornwall.
Radosenska, Mrs. E., Bath, Avon (Bladud House Antiques.)
Rae Antiques, John, St. Helier, Jersey, C.I.
Raeymaekers, F., London, W.1. (A.D.C. Heritage).
Rafferty, T., Ayr, Ayr., Scot.
Raffety and Huber, London, W.8.
Raglan Antiques, Raglan, Gwent, Wales.
Rainbow Antiques, Wolverhampton, W. Mids.
Raine Antiques, Harry, Consett, Durham.
Raine, J.P. and P.W., Boroughbridge, N. Yorks.

Reigate Galleries Ltd., Reigate, Surrey.
Reilly, K., London, S.W.3. Ant. Ant. Mkt.
Reily-Collins, E.M. and S.A., Dorchester-on-Thames, Oxon.
Reindeer Antiques Ltd., Potterspury, Northants.
Relcy Antiques, London, S.E.10.
Relic Antiques at Brillscote Farm, Lea, Wilts.
Relic Antiques at Camden Lock and The Camden Lock Antiques Centre, London, N.W.1.
Relic Antiques at Camden Passage, London, N.1.
Relic Shop, The, Needham Market, Suffolk.
Relics Antiques, Southampton, Hants.
Relph, S., Bath, Avon. (Off the Rails). Gt. West. Ant. C.
Remember When, London, W.1. G. Mews.
Remember When, London, S.W.13.
Remember When, London, S.W.14.
Remington, Reg and Philip, London, W.C.2.
Renaissance, Solihull, W. Mids.
Renaissance Antiques, Cowbridge, S. Glam., Wales.
Renaissance Antiques, Tynemouth, Tyne and Wear.
Renate, London, W.1. G. Ant. Mkt.
Rendall Antiques, London, S.W.6.
Rendall, R. and L., London, S.W.6.
Rendell, Eunice, Warwick, Warks. Smith St. A.C.
Rendezvous Gallery, The, Aberdeen, Aberd., Scot.
Rendlesham and Dark, London, S.W.10.
René Antiques and Art, Derek Ashby Antiques, St. Leonards-on-Sea, E. Sussex.
Renoir Galleries Ltd., Harrogate, N. Yorks.
Repind Ltd., Newark, Notts.
Resners', London, W.1. B. St. Ant. C.
Resonia Antiques, Matlock, Derbys.
Restall Brown and Clennell Ltd., Cosgrove, Northants.
Restoration Workshops, Bristol, Avon. Clift. Ant. Mkt.
Retford Pine, Babworth, Notts.
Retrospect Antiques, Combe Martin, Devon.
Revell, Miss, Newton Abbot, Devon, N. A. Ant. C.
Revere, S.H., Leeds, W. Yorks. (The Antique Shop).
Reville and Rossiter, London, W.1. G. Mews.
Revival Pine Stripping, Ormskirk, Lancs.
Revivals, Great Malvern, Hereford and Worcs.
Rex Antiques, London, W.11.
Reynold, A., London, W.C.2.
Reynolds, Mr., Aberdeen, Aberd., Scot.
Reynolds, B.A.S., Easingwold, N. Yorks.
Reynolds, Mrs. C., Tonge, Leics.
Reynolds and Son, M.A., Scarborough, N. Yorks.
Reynolds, Peter, London, S.W.6.
Reynolds, S.H. and W.P., Bournemouth, Dorset.
Rhodes Antiques, Colin, Plymouth, Devon.
Rhodes, Isobel, Hadleigh, Suffolk.
Rhodes, Patricia, London, S.W.3. Chen. Gall.

Rhuddlan Antiques, Rhuddlan, Clwyd, Wales.
Rhudle Mill, Kilmichael Glassary, Argyll, Scot.
Ribbons, James, Somerton, Somerset.
Ribchester Antiques, Ribchester, Lancs.
Rice Antiques, Leigh, Bristol, Avon.
Rice, R.J., Great Malvern, Hereford and Worcs.
Rich, G., Cardiff, S. Glam., Wales. (Archway Antiques)
Richards, Mrs., Newton Abbot, Devon, N.A. Ant. C.
Richards Antiques, Rainford, Merseyside.
Richards, D., Penzance, Cornwall.
Richards, D.M., Rainford, Merseyside.
Richards and Sons, David, London, W.1.
Richards Furniture Sales, Sheffield, S. Yorks.
Richards, G., Swansea, W. Glam., Wales. Ant. C.
Richards and Son Antiques, G.E., Hereford, Hereford and Worcs.
Richards, H., Felsted, Essex.
Richards and Son, H.J., Burton-on-Trent, Staffs.
Richards, J., London, S.W.13.
Richards, L., London, W.11 (Mercury Antiques).
Richards, M., H. and E., London, W.1.
Richards, Paul, London, S.W.6.
Richards — Charles Street Antiques , Ryan, Newport, Gwent, Wales.
Richards, S., Rhosneigr, Gwynedd, Wales.
Richardson, B., Bristol, Avon (Quinney's).
Richardson, D.F., York, N. Yorks. (Barker and Richardson).
Richardson, I. and K., Ilkley, W. Yorks.
Richardson, M., Westerham, Kent.
Richardson, P., Bristol, Avon. (Quinney's).
Richardson, P., Haslemere, Surrey.
Richardson, Pat, London, W.1. G. Mews.
Richardson, Ronald, Darlington, Durham.
Richardson, S. and E., Blewbury, Oxon.
Richardson, W.L. and M.G., Guisborough, Cleveland.
Riches, Pulloxhill, Beds.
Riches, L., Hythe, Kent.
Richmond Antiques, Littleport, Cambs.
Richmond Antiques, Londonderry, Co. Londonderry, N. Ireland.
Richmond Antiquary, The, Richmond, Gtr. London.
Richmond Galleries, Chester, Cheshire.
Richmond Gallery, The, London, W.1.
Richmond, Margaret, Wallingford, Oxon. L. Arc.
Richmond Pine, Richmond, N. Yorks.
Richmond Traders, Richmond, Gtr. London.
Rickett and Co. Antiques, Shepperton, Surrey.
Ricketts, D.G., Eastbourne, E. Sussex.
Ridgeway Antiques, Newnham-on-Severn, Glos.
Ridgewell Crafts and Antiques, Ridgewell, Essex.
Ridler, P.W., Pershore, Hereford and Worcs.
Ridley, Mrs. E.M., Filey, N. Yorks.
Ridout, S.J., Hindhead, Surrey.

Ries, M.A. and Mrs. I.T.H., Boston Spa, W. Yorks.
Rievel Antiques, Mansfield, Notts.
Riley, Mrs. G.M., London, S.W.3. Ant. Ant. Mkt.
Riley, J.M. Chichester, W. Sussex.
Riley, M. and L., Ludlow, Shrops.
Riley, P. and S., Broadway, Hereford and Worcs.
Rimmer, E.J. and A., Southport, Merseyside. (The Clock Shop).
Ringles Cross Antiques, Uckfield, E. Sussex.
Ripley Antiques, Ripley, Surrey.
Rippon Bookshop, Harrogate, N. Yorks.
Risdale, Mrs. M., Bristol, Avon. Clift. Ant. Mkt.
Ritchie, A.M.F. and Mrs., Teignmouth, Devon.
Ritchie, G.M. and V., Kendal, Cumbria.
Ritchie, J., Weymouth, Dorset.
Riverdale Hall Antique and Bric-a-Brac Market, London, S.E.13.
Rivers, John D., Cirencester, Glos.
Riverside Antiques, Hungerford, Berks.
Riverside Lodge Antiques, Retford, Notts.
Rivett, Mrs. S., Fakenham, Norfolk.
Rivett, T. and M., Bath, Avon. Gt. West. Ant. C.
Robb Antiques, Lundin Links, Fife, Scot.
Robbies Antiques, Wallasey, Merseyside.
Roberts, Windsor and Eton, Berks.
Roberts, A., Bath, Avon. Gt. West. A. C. Wed. Mkt.
Roberts, Mrs. A., Cowbridge, S. Glam., Wales.
Roberts Antiques, Ann, Ampthill, Beds.
Roberts, C., Bath, Avon. (No.12 Queen St.)
Roberts, C.G., Swansea, W. Glam., Wales. Ant. C.
Roberts, D., Nantwich, Cheshire.
Roberts Antiques, David, Leominster, Hereford and Worcs.
Roberts Antiques, Derek, Tonbridge, Kent.
Roberts, D.G., Bletchingley, Surrey.
Roberts, I.W. and I.E., Bolton, Lancs.
Roberts Bookshop, John, Bristol, Avon.
Roberts, J. and B., Leicester, Leics.
Roberts, J. and B., Market Bosworth, Leics.
Roberts, J. B. J., Scarborough, N. Yorks.
Roberts, J.T., Bristol, Avon (John Roberts).
Roberts, N.P., Petworth, W. Sussex.
Roberts Antiques, Peter, Moreton-in-Marsh, Glos.
Roberts, P.S., Rhos-on-Sea, Clwyd, Wales.
Roberts, Mrs. R., Blaenau Ffestiniog, Gwynedd, Wales.
Roberts, T.J., Lubenham, Leics.
Robertson and Cox Antiques, Perth, Perths., Scot.
Robertson, D.W., Newcastle-upon-Tyne, Tyne and Wear. (Owen's Jewellers).
Robertson, E., Woburn, Beds. Wob. Ab. Ant. C.
Robertson, G.B., Gourock, Lanarks., Scot.
Robertson, J., Reigate, Surrey.
Robertson, Mrs. J., Bath, Avon (Quest Antiques and Pine).
Robertson Antiques, Leon, Penryn, Cornwall.

Robertson, Michael, Shrewsbury, Shrops.
Robertson, R.D.A., London, S.W.6 (David Alexander Antiques).
Robins, Guy, London, W.11. G. Port.
Robinson, London, N.W.8. Alf. Ant. Mkt.
Robinson, London, W.1. G.M. Ant. Mkt.
Robinson, A., Bishops Waltham, Hants.
Robinson, Mrs. A., Monyash, Derbys.
Robinson, B.A. and S.A., Upper Boddington, Northants.
Robinson, C., London, N.W.8. Alf. Ant. Mkt.
Robinson, D.J., Cawood, N. Yorks.
Robinson, D. and M., Chipping Norton, Oxon.
Robinson, E.J.H. Croydon, Gtr. London.
Robinson, Mrs. E.N., Cleveleys, Lancs.
Robinson, F., Bolton-by-Bowland, Lancs.
Robinson, F., Colwyn Bay, Clwyd, Wales.
Robinson, Mrs. J., Chiddingfold, Surrey.
Robinson, Jonathan, London, W.1. G. Mews.
Robinson Antiques, John, Wigan, Lancs.
Robinson, K., Bristol, Avon. Clift. Ant. Mkt.
Robinson Antiques, Keith, Worcester, Hereford and Worcs.
Robinson, K.B., Worcester, Hereford and Worcs.
Robinson, M., Glasgow, Lanarks., Scot. (Virginia Antique Galleries)
Robinson, Peter, Heacham, Norfolk.
Robinson, R. and N., Welshpool, Powys, Wales.
Robinson, Mrs. S., Brighton, E. Sussex.
Robinson, T., Pontefract, W. Yorks.
Robinson, T.E., Bath, Avon.
Robinson, V., London, S.W.6. (Han-Shan Tang Ltd.)
Robinson (Newcastle) Ltd., W., Newcastle-upon-Tyne, Tyne and Wear.
Robinson-Tara Antiques, Wendy and Alan, London, W.1. G. Mews.
Robinson Yates Ltd., London, W.8. (Kensington Furniture)
Robinson's Bookshop Ltd., Brighton, E. Sussex.
Robson, P. and P. K., Barnard Castle, Durham.
Robson, T., Sunderland, Tyne and Wear.
Robson, Tom, Usworth, Tyne and Wear.
Roch, J., London, S.W.3. Ant. Ant. Mkt.
Rochefort Antiques Gallery, London, N.21.
Rochester Antiques and Flea Market, Rochester, Kent.
Rochester, D., Sudbury, Suffolk.
Rochford, Michael, Hertford, Herts.
Rock House Antiques Centre, Wolverhampton, W. Mids.
Rocking Chair, The, Warrington, Cheshire.
Rockman, A.C., London, N.W.8. Alf. Ant. Mkt.
Rockman, B.M., London, N.W.8. Alf. Ant. Mkt.
Rodber, J., Bridport, Dorset.
Rodd, Brenda, Rye, E. Sussex. Str. Ants.
Rodgers, J.F.T., London, W.C.2 (Quevedo).
Rodney Arthur Classics, Brighton, E. Sussex.
Rodriguez, A., London, W.C.1.

Rod's Antiques, London, W.11.
Rodwell, Mrs. E.A., Hitchin, Herts.
Roe, B.F., Crawley, W. Sussex.
Roe, Mr. and Mrs. J., Islip, Northants.
Roe Antiques, J., Islip, Northants.
Roe, P.S., London, S.W.1 (Trove).
Roebuck, C. and J., Great Malvern, Hereford and Worcs.
Roffe, V., London, W.1 (Vigo-Sternberg Galleries).
Roger, J., London, W.8.
Roger (Antiques) Ltd., J., London, W.8.
Rogers Antique Gallery, London, W.11.
Rogers Antiques and Rogers Antique Interiors, Cheam, Gtr. London.
Rogers, A.W.D., Leeds, W. Yorks. (Andrew's Antique Shop).
Rogers, C.F., Bath, Avon. (N.S. Woodbridge)
Rogers, C. and M., Cheam, Gtr. London.
Rogers Oriental Rugs, Clive, Brighton, E. Sussex.
Rogers de Rin, London, S.W.3.
Rogers, Eva, Ampthill, Beds.
Rogers, Eva, Kempston, Beds.
Rogers, N.G., Radlett, Herts.
Rogers of Alresford, Alresford, Hants.
Rogers Turner Books Ltd., London, S.E.10.
Rogers, T. and V., Alresford, Hants.
Rogerson, P.R., Bridlington, N. Humberside.
Rogerson, T.H. and B.A., Whitegate, Cheshire.
Rolandi, C., London, S.W.6. (The Pine Mine (Crew-Read Antiques))
Roland-Price, H.A. and J., Bradford-on-Avon, Wilts.
Rolleston, B.T.W., London, W.8 (The Antique Home).
Romain and Sons, A.J., Wilton, Wilts.
Romer, J., London, W.1. G. Mews.
Romic, Hertford, Herts.
Romsey Medal and Collectors Centre, Romsey, Hants.
Ronay, Edina, London, S.W.3. Ant. Ant. Mkt.
Root, J. and H., Williton, Somerset.
Rooth, W.J., Halifax, W. Yorks.
Roper's Pine Shop, Chris., Leicester, Leics.
Ropers Hill Antiques, Staunton Harold, Leics.
Rose, B., London, N.W.1. (Galerie 1900).
Rose Cottage Antiques, Highleadon, Glos.
Rose Court Studio Antiques, Olney, Bucks.
Rose, Dorothy, London, S.W.15.
Rose, D.H. and Mrs. C., Carlton-on-Trent, Notts.
Rose Farm Furniture Ltd., Addingham, W. Yorks.
Rose Antiques, Glenys, Tutbury, Staffs.
Rose, Mrs. G.E., Tutbury, Staffs.
Rose Ltd., Geoffrey, London, S.W.1.
Rose, M., Leeds, W. Yorks.
Rose Antiques, Marilyn, Newport, I. of Wight.
Rose, P. Chatham, Kent.
Rose, R.E., London, S.E.9.
Rose, Sally, Ilford, Gtr. London.
Rose, W., Yeovil, Somerset.
Rosemary and Time, Thame, Oxon.

Rosenberg, C., Heswall, Merseyside.
Rosenberg, H., London, N.1 (Hart and Rosen- berg).
Rosenthal Ltd., A., Oxford, Oxon.
Rose's Jewellers, Leeds, W. Yorks.
Roslyn House Galleries Ltd., Hitchin, Herts.
Ross, A.P., Coventry, W. Mids.
Ross, Mrs. C., Bushmills, Co. Antrim, N. Ireland.
Ross, D. and C., Bridport, Dorset.
Ross, D. and T., Wooler, Northumb.
Ross, H., Bisley, Glos.
Ross Hamilton Ltd., Antiques, London, S.W.1.
Ross, J., Laleham, Surrey.
Ross Antiques and Decoration, Jane, Sevenoaks, Kent.
Ross, Mrs. J.E., Farnham, Surrey.
Ross and Co. Ltd., Louise, Bath, Avon.
Ross, L.J., Liverpool, Merseyside (Liverpool Coin and Medal Co.).
Ross, M., London, S.E.1.
Ross Antiques, Marcus, London, N.1.
Ross, N.P., London, S.W.15.
Ross, T.C.A. and D.A.A., London, S.W.1. (Addison-Ross Gallery).
Ross-Durrant, D., Stockport, Cheshire.
Rosser-Rees, E., Bath, Avon. (Ancestors). Gt. West. Ant. C.
Rossinyol Antiques, Guildford, Surrey.
Rosson, J., London, E.C.1.
Rossu, London, N.W.8. Alf. Ant. Mkt.
Rota Ltd., Bertram, London, W.C.2.
Rotchell, P., Godalming, Surrey.
Rote, R. and D., London, N.1 (Chancery Antiques Ltd.).
Roth, M., Market Deeping, Lincs.
Rothera, D., London, N.1 (Antique Trader).
Rotherford, Rosamund, Glasgow, Lanarks. Scot. Vict. Vill.
Rothman, A.P.F., Winchester, Hants.
Rothwell, Mrs. C., Dulverton, Somerset.
Rothwell, Mrs. C., Taunton, Somerset.
Rothwell and Dunworth, Dulverton, Somerset.
Rothwell and Dunworth, Taunton, Somerset.
Round-A-Bout Antiques, Whyteleafe, Surrey.
Rourke, J.L., Tilbury, Essex.
Rowan, M. and P., Blockley, Glos.
Rowan, Pamela, Blockley, Glos.
Rowden Antiques, Wendy, Chichester, W. Sussex.
Rowe, Mrs. A., Falmouth, Cornwall.
Rowe, A.T., Wootton, I. of Wight.
Rowe, J., Great Bookham, Surrey.
Rowe, J.H. and J., London, S.W.6 (Bookham Galleries.)
Rowell and Son Ltd., Oxford, Oxon.
Rowlands, K., Preston, Lancs. N.W. Ant. C.
Rowlands, Mrs. M., London, S.W.14.
Rowlett, A.H., Lincoln, Lincs.
Rowlett, Mrs. R.B., Brasted, Kent.
Rowlett's, Lincoln, Lincs.
Rowley, J., Stoke-on-Trent, Staffs.
Roxburgh, E., Sherborne, Dorset.
Royal Exchange Art Gallery, London, E.C.3.
Royal Exchange Shopping Centre, Manchester, Lancs.

Royal Mile Curios, Edinburgh, Midloth., Scot.
Royal Thoroughfare Gallery, Lowestoft,
　Suffolk.
Royall, E. and C., Medbourne, Leics.
Royall Antiques, E. and C., Uppingham,
　Leics.
Royall, H., Aldeburgh, Suffolk.
Royle, Mrs. M., Beaconsfield, Bucks.
Roy's, Bath, Avon. Gt. West. A. C.
Royston Antiques, Royston, Herts.
Ruane, A., Southport, Merseyside.
Ruben, Jorgen, London, W.11. G. Port.
Rubin, E.W. and A., London, S.W.3 (Pelham
　Galleries).
Ruddock Antiques, York, N. Yorks.
Ruddock, G., York, N. Yorks.
Rudge Books, Loudwater, Bucks.
Rudkin Antiques, G.D. and Z., Grantham,
　Lincs.
Ruff, J., Newton Abbot, Devon. N. A.
　Ant. C.
Ruffell, J., Portsmouth, Hants.
Rufforth Antiques, Rufforth, N. Yorks.
Rugeley Antique Centre, Brereton, Staffs.
Ruglen, L., Balfron, Stirls., Scot.
Rumble, R.J. and V., Highbridge, Somerset.
Rumble, R.V. and C., East Molesey, Surrey.
Rumble, S.R., Cambridge, Cambs. (Old
　School Antiques).
Rumens, Olivia, Ludlow, Shrops.
'Run of the Mill', Sproughton, Suffolk.
Rundells Antiques, Harlow, Essex.
Rundle, J., New Bolingbroke, Lincs.
Rupert's Early Wireless, London, W.13.
Rush, Mrs. F.R., Yoxford, Suffolk.
Rushton, E. and B., Pulford, Cheshire.
Ruskin Gallery Ltd., The, Stratford-on-Avon,
　Warks.
Russell, C., Needham Market, Suffolk.
Russell, Miss C.C., Lewes, E. Sussex.
Russell, G., Bournemouth, Dorset (Fine
　Arts).
Russell, H.S., Great Malvern, Hereford and
　Worcs.
Russell, Leonard, Newhaven, E. Sussex.
Russell, M. and J., Yazor, Hereford and
　Worcs.
Russell, P., Tunbridge Wells, Kent.
Russell, T.A., London, S.E.15.
Russell-Funnel, D.P., Wincanton, Somerset.
Russells (Antiques) Ltd., Torquay, Devon.
Rust Antiques, Benjamin, Cromer, Norfolk.
Rust, G., Eccles, Lancs.
Rust, Mr. and Mrs. R.S., Kesgrave, Suffolk.
Rusthall Antiques, Tunbridge Wells, Kent.
Rutherford, A., Cockermouth, Cumbria.
Rutherford, J.L., Eccleshall, Staffs.
Rutherford and Son, J.T., Sandgate, Kent.
Rutherford Ltd., Stella, Darlington, Durham.
Rutherford's Antiques, Cockermouth,
　Cumbria.
Rutland Antiques, Brighton, E. Sussex.
Rutland Coins and Antiques, Oakham, Leics.
Rutland Gallery, London, W.1.
Rutland Gallery Workshop, The, Rutland,
　Leics.
Rutter, F.J., and A. Fagiani, London, S.E.15.
Rutter Antiques, John, Walsall, W. Mids.

Ryan-Wood Antiques, Liverpool, Merseyside.
Ryburgh House Antiques, Carlisle, Cumbria.
Ryce, L.R., Winkleigh, Devon.
Ryder, Sue, Shaftesbury, Dorset.
Rye Antiques, Rye, E. Sussex.
Ryland, B.R., Henley-on-Thames, Oxon.
Ryles, J., Saffron Walden, Essex.
Ryte Lynes Antiques, Leicester, Leics.
Rytham Antiques, Seaton Ross,
　N. Humberside.

S

SPCK Bookshops, Winchester, Hants.
S.R. Furnishing and Antiques, Birmingham,
　W. Mids.
S. and S. Antiques, Northolt, Gtr. London.
S.W. Antiques, Pershore, Hereford and
　Worcs.
Saadat, R. Tadj, London, W.1 (Armitage).
Saalmans, J.A. and K.M., Grasmere,
　Cumbria.
Sabin Galleries Ltd., London, W.8.
Sabin, S.F. and E.P., London, W.8.
Sabine, Antiques, C.E., Stock, Essex.
Sac Freres, London, W.1.
Sachser, M., Leominster, Hereford and
　Worcs.
Sackett Antiques, Les, Ramsgate, Kent.
Sackie, Mrs. N., London, N.W.1 (Country
　Pine Ltd.).
Saddle Room Antiques, The, Cookstown,
　Co. Tyrone, N. Ireland.
Saddlers Antiques, Cowfold, W. Sussex.
Sadler, Newton Abbot, Devon. N.A. Ant. C.
Sadler, M., Clare, Suffolk.
Sadler Antiques, M. and R., Macclesfield,
　Cheshire.
Sadler, R. and Mrs. H., Macclesfield,
　Cheshire.
Saffell, M.E., Bath, Avon. Gt. West. A. C.
　Wed. Mkt.
Sagar, A.M., Harrogate, N. Yorks. (Singing
　Bird Antiques).
Sage Antiques and Interiors, Ripley, Surrey.
Sage, H. and C., Ripley, Surrey.
Sagers, C. and Y., Blackpool, Lancs.
Sailmakers Barn, Wells-next-the-Sea,
　Norfolk.
Sainsbury, Barry, London, S.W.1.
Sainsbury, Barry M., Wincanton, Somerset.
Sainsbury. M., Bath, Avon.
Sainsburys of Bournemouth and New World
　Export Co., Bournemouth, Dorset.
St. Albans Antique Market, St. Albans, Herts.
St. Breock Gallery, Wadebridge, Cornwall.
St. Clare, M., London, N.1. (Get Stuffed).
St. Edmunds Antiques Centre, Bury St.
　Edmunds, Suffolk.
St. Elphege's Church Hall, Wallington,
　Gtr. London.
St. George, P., London, N.W.6.
St. George's Antiques, Perranporth,
　Cornwall.
St. George's Antiques, Stamford, Lincs.
St. George's Antiques Centre, Winchester,
　Hants.

Saint George's Gallery Books Ltd., London, S.W.1.
St. Giles Antiques and Period Fashion, Norwich, Norfolk.
St. Helier Galleries, St. Ouen, Jersey, C.I.
St. James Antiques, Manchester, Lancs.
St. James's Gallery Ltd., St. Peter Port, Guernsey, C.I.
St. John Foti, C., Norwich, Norfolk. (The Antique Textile Shop).
St. John-House, C., Hull, N. Humberside.
St. John's Collection, London, S.W.3. Chen. Gall.
St. John's Studio, Coleford, Glos.
St. Jude's Antiques, London, W.8.
St. Leonards Antiques, Ludlow, Shrops.
St. Leonards Clocks, St. Leonards-on-Sea, E. Sussex.
St. Mary's Galleries, Stamford, Lincs.
St. M. Morgan, B.J., London, W.1 (Bluett and Sons Ltd.)
St. Nicholas Galleries (Antiques and Jewellery), Carlisle, Cumbria.
St. Nicholas Galleries (Antiques) Ltd., Carlisle, Cumbria.
St. Ouen Antiques, Puckeridge, Herts.
St. Peters Organ Works, London, E.2.
St. Trinians Antiques, Richmond, N. Yorks.
Sale Ltd., Charles, Beaconsfield, Bucks.
Sale, W.A. and E.D., Beaconsfield, Bucks.
Saleroom, The, Harrogate, N. Yorks.
Salisbury, R. and J., Edenfield, Lancs.
Salmagundi, Maidstone, Kent.
Salmon, David, London, S.W.3 (David Tremayne Ltd.)
Salt Antiques, N.P. and A., Sheffield, S. Yorks.
Salter Antiques, F.D., Clare, Suffolk.
Saltgate Antiques, Beccles, Suffolk.
Salti, Edward, London, W.9.
Saltisford Pine Antiques, Warwick, Warks.
Salvage, Mrs. V., Glasgow, Lanarks., Scot. (Corner House Antiques).
Samiramis Ltd.,London, W.1. G. Mews.
Samman Antiques, Maidenhead, Berks.
Samne, H., London, W.C.2 (Anchor Antiques Ltd.)
Samovar Antiques, Hythe, Kent.
Sampson, Anthony, Moreton-in-Marsh, Glos.
Sampson Antiques inc. Tobias Jellinek Antiques, Alistair, London, S.W.3.
Sampson, A.H., London, S.W.3.
Sampson, M. and M., Coulsdon, Gtr. London.
Sampson, P. and J., Wardley, Tyne and Wear.
Samuel, P.J.E., London, S.W.6. (Ashby Antiques).
Samuels and Sons Ltd., C., Exeter, Devon.
San Domenico Stringed Instruments, Cardiff, S. Glam., Wales.
Sandberg, Mrs., Colchester, Essex.
Sandberg Antiques, Patrick, London, S.W.6.
Sandberg, P.C.F., London, S.W.6.
Sanders, Marian, Woburn, Beds., Wob. Ab. Ant. C.
Sanders of Oxford Ltd., Oxford, Oxon.
Sanders, T., London, S.W.6 (Singing Tree).

Sanders Antiques, Tony, Penzance, Cornwall.
Sandgate Antiques Centre, Sandgate, Kent.
Sandleton-Edwards, Littleborough, Lancs.
Sandra, London, W.1. G. Ant. Mkt.
Sandringham Antiques, Hull, N. Humberside.
Sands, J. and M.M., Stow-on-the-Wold, Glos.
Sands, R., London, W.1. (M. and R. Glendale)
Sandy's Antiques, Bournemouth, Dorset.
Sansom, K.W., Leicester, Leics.
Sanson, C., Four Elms, Kent.
Santer, N., London, W.11 (Portobello Silver Co.)
Santer, N. and C.F., London, W.11 (London International Silver Co. Ltd.)
Santos, A.V. and M.R., London, W.8.
Saracen Antiques, Ulverston, Cumbria.
Saracens Head Inn, Warburton, Cheshire.
Saracen's Lantern, The, Canterbury, Kent.
Sarel, D., London, S.W.3. (L'Odeon).
Sargeant, A.W. and K.M., Stansted, Essex.
Sargeant, Denys, Westerham, Kent.
Sarti Antiques Ltd., G., London, W.11.
Sarum Antiques, Benson, Oxon.
Satchell, S., Kendal, Cumbria.
Satoe, London, W.1. G. Ant. Mkt.
Satterthwaite, Mrs. D., Ulverston, Cumbria.
Sattin Ltd., Gerald, London, W.1.
Sattin, G. and M., London, W.1.
Saunders, A.J. and A.K., Weybridge, Surrey.
Saunders, D. and T., Leominster, Hereford and Worcs.
Saunders, E., Weedon, Northants.
Saunders, E.A. and J.M., Weedon, Northants.
Saunders, Lester, London, W.1. G. Mews.
Saunders, R., Weybridge, Surrey.
Saunders, R.A., Bristol, Avon.
Saunders, Terry, Penzance, Cornwall.
Savage Antiques, Ian, Bath, Avon. B. Ant. Mkt.
Savage, M.J., Northampton, Northants.
Savage and Son, R.S.J., Northampton, Northants.
Savage Antiques, Sam, Ticknall, Derbys.
Savage, S. and M., Ticknall, Derbys.
Savile, Hon. C.A. and Mrs., London, S.W.3. (The Map House).
Savile Pine, London, S.W.6.
Saville Antiques, Devizes, Wilts.
Savitsky, Mrs. J.M., Hitchin, Herts.
Savoy Antiques, Liverpool, Merseyside.
Saw, D.F., Brighton, E. Sussex (Shelton Frames and Prints.)
Sawers, Robert G., London, W.1.
Sawyer, Chas. J., London, W.1.
Sawyer, R.E.B. and G., London, W.1.
Saxton House Gallery, Chipping Campden, Glos.
Sayer, Mrs. J., Dorking, Surrey.
Scadgell, M., Cowes, I. of Wight.
Scadgell, M., Pulborough, W. Sussex.
Scales, R., London, S.E.1.
Scallywag, Beckenham, Gtr. London.
Scallywag, London, S.E.5.

Scallywag, London, S.W.9.
Scar Top Antiques, Keighley, W. Yorks.
Scaramanga Antiques, Anthony, Witney, Oxon.
Scarisbrick and Bate Ltd., London, W.1.
Scarthoe Antiques, Scarthoe, S. Humberside.
Schanzer, R.P., London, N.W.1. (This and That (Furniture)).
Schapira, Mrs. M., London, W.1. (Bond St. Carpets).
Schraverien, L. and G., London, W.1. B. St. Ant. C.
Schein, A. and B., Stamford, Lincs.
Scheregate Antiques, Colchester, Essex.
Schidlof Galleries, London, W.14.
Schiff, London, W.1. (P. Hamilton), G. Mews.
Schloss, E., Edgware, Gtr. London.
Schneider, Mrs. P., Abingdon, Oxon.
Schofield, G.M., St. Leonards-on-Sea, E. Sussex.
Schofield, R.M., Huddersfield, W. Yorks.
Schofield, Miss S.A., Padstow, Cornwall.
Scholar, London, N.W.8. Alf. Ant. Mkt.
Scholz, K.V., Eastbourne, E. Sussex.
Schotten, M., Burford, Oxon.
Schrager, G.R. and H.J., London, W.11. (Schredds of Portobello).
Schredds of Portobello, London, W.11.
Schuster, Thomas E., London, S.W.1.
Schwager, R.O. and E.M., Stow-on-the-Wold, Glos.
Schwartz, N., Lindfield, W. Sussex.
Schwier, D.W., Wimborne Minster, Dorset.
Scientific Anglian (Bookshop), The, Norwich, Norfolk.
Sciville, A.J., Ludlow, Shrops.
Scobie, W.D.L., Wallasey, Merseyside.
Scope Antiques, London, N.W.6.
Scorpio Antiques, London, N.W.3. Ham. Ant. Emp.
Scott, A., Westerham, Kent.
Scott Antiques, Bath, Avon.
Scott Antiques, Walton-on-the-Hill and Tadworth, Surrey.
Scott, A.F.D., Selkirk, Selkirks., Scot.
Scott, A. and L., Cambridge, Cambs. (Dove House Antiques).
Scott, Mrs. D., Peebles, Peebles., Scot.
Scott House Antiques, West Malling, Kent.
Scott, Miss J., London, S.W.3. Ant. Ant. Mkt.
Scott, James, Edinburgh, Midloth., Scot.
Scott, R., Nottingham, Notts.
Scott Antiques, Richard, Holt, Norfolk.
Scott, R.G., Margate, Kent.
Scott and Varey, Halifax, W. Yorks.
Scott, W.B., Halifax, W. Yorks.
Scott-Adie, John, Perth, Perths., Scot.
Scott-Cooper Ltd., Cheltenham, Glos.
Scottish Gallery, The, Edinburgh, Midloth., Scot.
Scratchley, K.S., Sidmouth, Devon.
Scudder Antiques, Terry, Woburn, Beds. Wob. Ab. Ant. C.
Scull, T. and S.E., Bristol, Avon (Cleeve Antiques).

Seabrook Antiques, Long Melford, Suffolk.
Seaby Ltd., B.A., London, W.1.
Seafords Barn Collectors Market and Studio Book Shop, Seaford, E. Sussex.
Seager, A.A., London, W.8.
Seager Antiques Ltd., Arthur, London, W.8.
Seago, A.E., Cromer, Norfolk.
Seago, B. and C., Cuckfield, W. Sussex.
Seago, D.C., Cromer, Norfolk.
Seal, D., Keighley, W. Yorks.
Seal, T., London, S.E.1. Ber. Ant. Whse.
Seale Fine Art, Patrick, London, S.W.1. (Sally Hunter and Patrick Seale Fine Art).
Seals, B., Leeds, W. Yorks.
Searle and Co. Ltd., London, E.C.3.
Searle, E.A., Cambridge, Cambs. (The Bookroom (Cambridge)).
Searle, G.R., Bungay, Suffolk.
Sears, M.D., London, W.1. (M. and R. Glendale)
Seaton, E.W. and Mrs. V., Barnard Castle, Durham.
Seaview Antiques, Portrush, Co. Antrim, N. Ireland.
Seaview Antiques, Seaview, I. of Wight.
Sebley, Oswald, Norwich, Norfolk.
Secchi, Mrs. N., Edinburgh, Midloth., Scot. (Unicorn Antiques).
Seccombe, Mrs. J., Charlecote, Warks.
Second Hand Rose, Hindhead, Surrey.
Second Thoughts, Wolverhampton, W. Mids.
Secondhand Alley, Shefford, Beds.
Sedan Chair, The, Ryde, I. of Wight.
Sedan Chair Antiques, Bristol, Avon.
Sedan Chair House, Bath, Avon. Gt. West. Ant. C.
Seddon, A.E. and M., Manchester, Lancs. (Browzers).
Sedler, H., London, S.W.3. Ant. Ant. Mkt.
Sedman Antiques, Bridlington, N. Humberside.
Sedman, R.H.S. and M.A., Bridlington, N. Humberside.
Seeley, G., Northolt, Gtr. London.
Sefton Antiques for the Country Home, Sidmouth, Devon.
Seidler, Chris, London, W.1. G. Ant. Mkt.
Sekmet Galleries, London, N.1.
Selected Antiques, London, W.1. G. Ant. Mkt.
Selective Eye Gallery, The, St. Helier, Jersey, C.I.
Self, W., Appleby, Cumbria.
Seligmann, M. and D., London, W.8.
Sellefyan, Mrs. F., London, S.W.3. Ant. Ant. Mkt.
Selwoods, Taunton, Somerset.
Selwyn, W., Bath, Avon. Gt. West. Ant. C. (Mendip Antiques).
Semus Antiques, Brighton, E. Sussex.
Semus Ltd., Frank, Brighton, E. Sussex.
Semus, F. and I., Brighton, E. Sussex.
Semus, P. and R., Brighton, E. Sussex.
Senior, M., London, S.W.3 (Krios Gallery.)
Sensation Ltd., London, S.W.6.
Serendipity, Deal, Kent.
Serendipity, Edinburgh, Midloth., Scot.

Serendipity, Oxford, Oxon.
Serendipity, Ross-on-Wye, Hereford and
Worcs.
Serendipity Antiques, Arundel, W. Sussex.
Serpentine Antiques, Bowness-on-
Windermere, Cumbria.
Setterfield of St. Albans, Philip, St. Albans,
Herts.
Sevenoaks Furniture Gallery, Sevenoaks,
Kent.
Seventh Heaven, Chirk, Clwyd, Wales.
Severn, D., Truro, Cornwall.
Severn Fine Art, Shrewsbury, Shrops.
Sewell (Antiques) Ltd., Jean, London, W.8.
Sewell R. and J., London, W.8.
Seyfried Antiques, David, London, S.W.6.
Seymour, B.A., Smethwick, W. Mids.
Seymour Galleries, Glossop, Derbys.
Seymour, P., Glossop, Derbys.
Seymour, R.D., Coventry, W. Mids.
Shabby Tiger Antiques, Stroud, Glos.
Shackleton, Daniel, Edinburgh, Midloth.,
Scot.
Shadowfox Antiques, Finedon, Northants.
Shaftesbury Antiques, Clacton-on-Sea,
Essex.
Shaftesbury Antiques, Gillingham, Dorset.
Shaftoe, F.B., Harrogate, N. Yorks.
Shaikh, M., London, W.1.
Shaikh and Son (Oriental Rugs) Ltd.,
London, W.1.
Shakeshaft, R.A. and S.D., Castor, Cambs.
Shalloe, A.W. and S., Preston, Lancs.
Shamoon, S., London, S.W.7.
Shanclare Antiques, Hadleigh, Essex.
Shand, George G., Wallingford, Oxon.
Shand, L., London, W.8. (Lindsay Antiques).
Shanks, M., Berkhamsted, Herts.
Shans-Nia, Roger, London, N.W.8. Alf. Alf.
Mkt.
Shapero, Bernard, London, W.1. G. Ant.
Mkt.
Shapiro and Co., London, W.1. G. Ant.
Mkt.
Shapland, R.S.C., London, W.C.1.
Sharp, Mrs., Bristol, Avon. Clift. Ant. Mkt.
Sharpe Antiques, John, Gravesend, Kent.
Sharpe, J. and E., Aveton Gifford, Devon.
Sharrington Antiques, Sharrington, Norfolk.
Shave, K.J., Cheltenham, Glos. (Armada
Exports).
Shave, K.J. Cheltenham, Glos. Chelt. Ant.
Mkt.
Shaw Antiques, Spilsby, Lincs.
Shaw Bros., Harrogate, N. Yorks.
Shaw, Charles, Knaresborough, N. Yorks.
Shaw, D., Congleton, Cheshire.
Shaw, G., Harrogate, N. Yorks.
Shaw, J., Bakewell, Derbys.
Shaw and Co., Jack, Ilkley, W. Yorks.
Shaw, J. and C., Harrogate, N. Yorks.
Shaw, Mrs. J.M., Spilsby, Lincs.
Shaw Antiques, Laurence, Horncastle, Lincs.
Shaw, Nona, Ditchling, E. Sussex.
Shaw Antiques, Robert, Brighton, E. Sussex.
Shawforth Antiques, Shawforth, Lancs.
Shaw's Bookshop Ltd., Manchester, Lancs.
Sheaf Street Antiques, Daventry, Northants.

Sheargold, E., Wigan, Lancs.
Sheffield Pine Centre, Sheffield, S. Yorks.
Shelagh Antiques, London, N.W.3. Ham.
Ant. Emp.
Sheldon's, London, S.W.7.
Shelkin, Henry, London, N.W.3. Ham. Ant.
Emp.
Shelley, A. and J., Lewes, E. Sussex.
Shelton Frames and Prints, Brighton,
E. Sussex.
Shelton, Miss S., London, S.W.3. Ant. Ant.
Mkt.
Shenton Antiques, Hexham, Northumb.
Shenton, Rita, Twickenham, Gtr. London.
Shepherd, J., St. Helier, Jersey, C.I.
Shepherd Antiques, Peter, Hurst, Berks.
Shepherds Antiques, St. Helier, Jersey, C.I.
Shepherds Antiques Ltd., Cobham, Surrey.
Shepherds Arcade, London, W.11.
Sheppard, C.B., Chesterfield, Derbys.
Sheppard and Cooper Ltd., London, W.1.
Sheppard, J., Christchurch, Dorset.
Sheppard Antiques, John B., Mansfield,
Notts.
Sheppard, J.E., Thaxted, Essex.
Sheppard, P., Baldock, Herts.
Sheppard, P.G., Lyonshall, Hereford and
Worcs.
Sheppard, Sylvia, London, W.8.
Sheradon Craft Workshop, Poole, Dorset.
Sheraton Antiques Ltd., London, W.11.
Sheraton Galleries, Rickmansworth, Herts.
Sheraton House, Torquay, Devon.
Sherborne Antiques Ltd., Sherborne, Dorset.
Sheredays Antiques Centre, Billericay,
Essex.
Sheridan's Bookshop Hampton, Ian,
Hampton, Gtr. London.
Sherlock, George, London, S.W.6.
Sherman, M., Great Wakering, Essex.
Sherman, M., Leigh-on-Sea, Essex.
Sherman, P., Newton Abbot, Devon. N.A.
Ant. C.
Sherman and Waterman Associates Ltd.,
London, W.C.2.
Sherman and Waterman Assoc. Ltd.,
Brighton, E. Sussex (Jubilee Antique
Cellars and Collectors Market.)
Sherston Antiques, Sherston, Wilts.
Sherwood (Antiques) Ltd., D.W., Rushden,
Northants.
Shield and Allen Antiques, London, S.W.6.
Shield Antiques, Robin, Ferryhill, Durham.
Shield, W.R. and P.E., Ferryhill, Durham.
Shillingford, B.C., Maidstone, Kent.
Shindler, A., Chester, Cheshire (Watergate
Antiques).
Shine, Mr. and Mrs., London, S.W.3. Ant.
Ant. Mkt.
Shiner, G.F. and J.E., Chelmsford, Essex.
Ship Street Galleries, Brecon, Powys, Wales.
Shippeys' of Boscombe, Bournemouth,
Dorset.
Ships Wheel, The, Thurso, Caiths., Scot.
Shiraz Oriental Antiques and Carpets,
Exeter, Devon.
Shire Antiques, J. and B., Newby Bridge,
Cumbria.

Shires, P., Rickmansworth, Herts.
Shirley Antiques, Shirley, Gtr. London.
Shirley's Antiques, Langport, Somerset.
Shop of the Yellow Frog, Brighton, E. Sussex.
Shop on the Corner, The, London, N.1.
Shop Upstairs, The, Glastonbury, Somerset.
Shorborn, N. and S., London, S.W.3. Ant. Mkt.
Shorn, D., London, S.W.3. Ant. Ant. Mkt.
Short, C., Upper Beeding, W. Sussex.
Short, M. and K., Deal, Kent.
Shotter Collectors Centre, Keith, Shanklin, I. of Wight
Shotton Antiquarian Books and Prints, J., Durham, Durham.
Showcase, Merstham, Surrey.
Shrewsbury Antique Centre, Shrewsbury, Shrops.
Shrewsbury Antique Market, Shrewsbury, Shrops.
Shrubsole, C.J., London, W.C.1.
Shrubsole Ltd., S.J., London, W.C.1.
Shulman, H. and S., Manchester, Lancs.
Shulman of Manchester, Manchester, Lancs.
Shure and Co., David S., London, W.C.2. Lon. Silv. Vts.
Shuttleworth, J.M., Preston, Lancs. N.W. Ant. C.
Sidaway, E., Barnard Castle, Durham.
Sidbury Galleries, Liskeard, Cornwall.
Sidders, P.J.K., Tunbridge Wells, Kent (The Cubby Hole).
Siden, G.T. London, S.W.1. (Old Drawings Gallery).
Sidgwick Antiques, Antony, Cirencester, Glos.
Sidlaw Antiques, Dunkeld, Perths., Scot.
Sidmouth Antiques Market, Sidmouth, Devon.
Siggie's Antiques Centre, Walton-on-Thames, Surrey.
Sigma Antiques and Fine Art, Ripon, N. Yorks.
Silbert, C., London, S.W.6 (The Gallery).
Silcocks, Joan, Pitchcombe, Glos.
Silcocks, Mrs. J.M., Pitchcombe, Glos.
Silcocks Fine Arts, Conway, Gwynedd, Wales.
Silcocks, P.W., Conway, Gwynedd, Wales.
Silk Road, Shrewsbury, Shrops.
Silstar, London, W.C.2. Lond. Silv. Vts.
Silver, Alan, London, N.W.8. Alf. Ant. Mkt.
Silver Mouse Trap, The, London, W.C.2.
Silver Shop, Newton Abbot, Devon. N. A. Ant. C.
Silver Shop, The, Torquay, Devon. Tor. Ant. Ant. C.
Silver Showcase, The, Edinburgh, Midloth., Scot.
Silver Sixpence, London, S.E.6.
Silver Stall, The, Bristol, Avon. Clift. Ant. Mkt.
Silver, S.M. and J.A., Barrow-in-Furness, Cumbria.
Silver Thimble, The, Kendal, Cumbria.
Silverdale Antiques, Torquay, Devon. Tor. Ant. C.

Silverman, B., London, W.C.2. Lon. Silv. Vts.
Silverman, S. and R., London, W.C.2. Lon. Silv. Vts.
Silverston, P. and M., Llangollen, Clwyd, Wales.
Silvester and Sons Ltd., A.T., Warwick, Warks.
Silvester, S., Lichfield, Staffs.
Silvester, S.K., Y.M. and C.A., Warwick, Warks.
Silvesters, Birchington, Kent.
Silvesters, Wingham, Kent.
Silv's, London, W.1. G. Mews.
Sim, Michael, Chislehurst, Gtr. London.
Sim Antiques, Roy, Blairgowrie, Perths., Scot.
Simeon, London, W.1.
Simmonds, R.M., Southampton, Hants.
Simmons and Son, A.W.J., Croydon, Gtr. London.
Simmons Antiques, Christine, Barnsley, S. Yorks.
Simmons, J.C., Barnsley, S. Yorks.
Simmons, L.M. and S.L., Brighton, E. Sussex.
Simmons and Simmons, London, W.1. G. Mews.
Simmons Antiques, S. and L., Brighton, E. Sussex.
Simms, Mrs. L., Midhusrt, W. Sussex.
Simms, L., Newport, Essex.
'Simon', Ilkley, W. Yorks.
Simons, Jack (Antiques) Ltd., London, W.C.2. London Silv. Vts.
Simpson, D., London, S.W.3 (A. Lianos.) Ant. Ant. Mkt.
Simpson, D. and E., Liverpool, Merseyside.
Simpson and Son Ltd., D., Liverpool, Merseyside.
Simpson and Sons Jewellers (Oldham) Ltd., H.C., Oldham, Lancs.
Simpson, I., Halesowen, W. Mids.
Simpson, K., Helperby, N. Yorks.
Simpson Antiques, M.R., Highcliffe, Dorset.
Simpson, Oswald, Bildeston, Suffolk.
Simpsons Pine Mirrors, London, W.14.
Sims, N., Stratford-upon-Avon, Warks.
Sims, Robin, London, N.1.
Sims, Reed and Fogg Ltd., London, S.W.1.
Sinai Antiques Ltd., E. and M., London, W.8.
Sinclair, A., Crossford, Fife, Scot.
Sinclair, F.J., Stamford, Lincs.
Sinclair Ltd., Francis, Doncaster, S. Yorks.
Sinclair, Gloria, London, N.W.8. Alf. Ant. Mkt.
Sinclair, John, Stamford, Lincs.
Sinclaire, H.A., Brighton, E. Sussex (M. Fields and H.A. Sinclaire Antiques).
Sinclair-Hill, Mrs. J.C., Windsor and Eton, Berks. (John A. Pearson Ltd.).
Sinclair's Antique Gallery, Belfast, N. Ireland.
Sinfield Gallery, Brian, Burford, Oxon.
Singer, A.J., London, W.1 (South Audley Art Galleries Ltd.).
Singing Bird Antiques, Harrogate, N. Yorks.
Singing Tree, The, London, S.W.6.

Sinnott, I.R., Bristol, Avon. (Abbas-Combe Pine).
Sitch, H., London, W.1 (W. Sitch and Co. Ltd.)
Sitch and Co. Ltd., W.; London, W.1.
Sjovold, A., London, S.W.3. Chen. Gall.
Skeaping Gallery, Lydford, Devon.
Skeel Antiques, Keith, London, N.1.
Skeel Antiques Warehouse, Keith, London, N.1.
Skellgate Curios, Ripon, N. Yorks.
Skipwith, W.G., Winchester, Hants.
Skirving (Fine Art), Andrew, Langar, Notts.
Skoob Books Ltd., London, W.C.1.
Skoulding, P.M., Hadleigh, Suffolk.
Slade, Bristol, Avon. Clift. Ant. Mkt.
Slade, David, Cheltenham, Glos.
Slade, Mrs. M. and Miss N., Bristol, Avon. Clift. Ant. Mkt.
Sladmore Gallery, The, London, W.1.
Slater, David, London, W.11.
Slater, G. and T., Walsden, W. Yorks.
Slater, M. and Mrs. P., Edinburgh, Midloth., Scot. (Behar Carpets.)
Slater, M. and Mrs. P., Glasgow, Lanarks., Scot. (Behar Carpets.)
Slater, N., Barnt Green, Hereford and Worcs.
Slim, R.T., Worcester, Hereford and Worcs.
Sloane, E.D. and A.A., Robertsbridge, E. Sussex.
Sloane, Peter, London, W.11. G. Port.
Sloane, Peter and Sara Jane, London, W.1. G. Mews.
Small, Mrs. K., Dorking, Surrey.
Smeeth, A.G., Leavenheath, Suffolk.
Smeeth, S., Lymington, Hants.
Smith, A., Bristol, Avon (Triangle Antiques).
Smith, A., Ludlow, Shrops.
Smith Antiques, Wrexham, Clwyd, Wales.
Smith and Bottrill, Bath, Avon.
Smith, Mrs. B., Harrogate, N. Yorks. W. Park Ant. Pav.
Smith Antiques, David, Manton, Leics.
Smith, D.K., Leeds, W. Yorks. (Windsor House Antiques (Leeds) Ltd.).
Smith, D.R. and G.B., Ringwood, Hants.
Smith, E., Stone, Staffs.
Smith, E.B. and E.M., Hungerford, Berks (The Fire Place (Hungerford) Ltd.)
Smith (Leicester) Ltd., E., Leicester, Leics.
Smith, Mrs. G., Riley, Swanton Abbot, Norfolk.
Smith and Sons (Peterborough) Ltd., G., Peterborough, Cambs.
Smith, Hammond, Leicester, Leics.
Smith Sons and Daughters, H. and D., Thame, Oxon.
Smith, H.W. and P.E., Leigh-on-Sea, Essex.
Smith, I., Witney, Oxon.
Smith, I.E., Torquay, Devon.
Smith and James, London, W.1. B. St. Silv. Galls.
Smith, Joyce, Warwick, Warks. Smith St. A.C.
Smith, J., Windsor and Eton, Berks. (Eton Gallery Antiques).
Smith Antiques, John, Coggeshall, Essex.

Smith, John Carlton, London, S.W.1.
Smith, J. and J., Haydon Bridge, Northumb.
Smith, J.P., Coggeshall, Essex.
Smith, J.P.D., London, S.W.1 (Trove).
Smith and Son (Glasgow Ltd.), John, Glasgow, Lanarks., Scot.
Smith, J.R. and T., Eastbourne, E. Sussex.
Smith, J.S. and S.D., Hatfield, Herts.
Smith, J.T., Stroud, Glos.
Smith, K., St. Neots, Cambs.
Smith, K.J., Amersham, Bucks.
Smith, L.G., London, S.E.7.
Smith, L. Royden, Lichfield, Staffs.
Smith, M., Bexhill-on-Sea, E. Sussex.
Smith, Mrs. Margaret, Montrose, Angus, Scot.
Smith, M., Richmond, N. Yorks.
Smith, M., West Malling, Kent.
Smith, M.A., London, S.W.13.
Smith Antiques, Michael, Shrewsbury, Shrops.
Smith, M.C., Stratford-upon-Avon, Warks.
Smith, M. and J., Cambridge, Cambs. (Michaels Antiques).
Smith, N., Wortham, Suffolk.
Smith, P., Brough, N. Humberside.
Smith, Pam, Bath, Avon. Gt. West. A. C. Wed. Mkt.
Smith, Paul, Ludlow, Shrops.
Smith, Mr. and Mrs. P., Lye, W. Mids.
Smith, Pauline, Bath, Avon. Gt. West. Ant. C. Wed. Mkt.
Smith, P., Staines, Surrey.
Smith Antiques, Peter, Sunderland, Tyne and Wear.
Smith, P. and B., Ludlow, Shrops.
Smith (Bookseller), Peter Bain, Cartmel, Cumbria.
Smith Antiques, P. and D., Gosforth, Tyne and Wear.
Smith, P.P., Knaresborough, N. Yorks.
Smith, Raymond, Eastbourne, E. Sussex.
Smith, Roy, London, N.1. (Nellie Lenson and Roy Smith).
Smith, R., Penryn, Cornwall.
Smith, R. and Mrs. B., London, S.W.16.
Smith, R. and J., Ramsey, Cambs.
Smith (Antiques), Raymond J., Brighton, E. Sussex.
Smith, R.L.V. and G.V., Cardigan, Dyfed, Wales.
Smith, R. Morley, Rottingdean, E. Sussex.
Smith, R.W., Fowlmere, Cambs.
Smith, Sandra, Deddington, Oxon. Ant. C.
Smith Antiques, Sheila, Bath, Avon.
Smith, S. and A., Rochester, Kent.
Smith, Stanley, and Fawkes, Keith, London, N.W.3.
Smith Street Antique Centre, Warwick, Warks.
Smith Antiques, Tom, Ipswich, Suffolk.
Smith Antiques, Tom, Lavenham, Suffolk.
Smith, Miss T.A., Windermere, Cumbria.
Smith, T.J., Guildford, Surrey.
Smith (Booksellers) Ltd., William, Reading, Berks.
Smith-Albany, Cowling, N. Yorks.
Smith-Carrington, Philip, London, S.W.3.

Smithells, Mrs. A., Iping, W. Sussex.
Smithfield Antiques, Lye, W. Mids.
Smithies, Witney, Oxon.
Smith's Antiques, Bridlington, N. Humberside.
Smith's (The Rink) Ltd., Harrogate, N. Yorks.
Smithson Master Drawings, Andrew, London, S.W.3.
Smurthwaite, T. and S., Holme, Cumbria.
Smyth, J. and N., London, S.W.6 (Aubyn Antiques).
Smyth — Antique Textiles, Peta, London, S.W.1.
Sneath, J.H., Pinchbeck, Lincs.
Sniders, Jeremy, Glasgow, Lanarks., Scot. Vict. Vill.
Snodgrass Antiques, Harrogate, N. Yorks.
Snodgrass, B. and E., Harrogate, N. Yorks.
Snook, T.B. and H.J., Caversham, Berks.
Snoopers Paradise Bric-a-Brac Market, Worthing, W. Sussex.
Snow, M., Thaxted, Essex.
Snowdonia Antiques, Llanrwst, Gwynedd, Wales.
Snow's, Thaxted, Essex.
Snuff Box, The, Ryde, I. of Wight.
Snyder, B., London, W.1. (Spring Antiques).
Soleimani, R.R., London, W.1 (Hadji Baba Ancient Art.)
Soleymani, R. and V., London, W.1 (Rabi Gallery).
Solus Marketing (Norfolk), Felmingham, Norfolk.
Somers, R.P.W., Gt. Malvern, Hereford and Worcs.
Somerset, B., London, W.1. (The Dial Marylebone).
Somervale Antiques, Midsomer Norton, Avon.
Somerville and Simpson, London, W.1.
Something Old, Donyatt, Somerset.
Something Old, Hertford, Herts.
Something Old, Southport, Merseyside.
Something Particular, Whitchurch, Hants.
Sonmez, N., London, S.W.3. Chen. Gall.
Soper, J., London, S.W.3. Ant. Ant. Mkt.
Sotheran Ltd., Henry, London, W.1.
Soul, R.F. and D.F., Olney, Bucks.
Soul, T., London, W.11. G. Port.
Source Enterprises Ltd., The, Chorley, Lancs.
Soutergate Antiques, Ulverston, Cumbria.
South Audley Art Galleries Ltd., London, W.1.
South Bar Antiques, Stow-on-the-Wold, Glos.
South Coast Antiques Ltd., Brighton, E. Sussex.
South Molton Antiques, South Molton, Devon.
South Street Gallery, The, Perth, Perths., Scot.
South Yorkshire Antiques, Rotherham, S. Yorks.
Southall, G., Northampton, Northants.
Southard, G. and G., Exeter, Devon.
Southdown Antiques, Lewes, E. Sussex.

Southdown House Antique Galleries, Brasted, Kent.
Southdown House Antiques, Nonington, Kent.
Southend Pine, Southend-on-Sea, Essex.
Southern, J., Bath, Avon. Gt. West. Ant. C.
Southgate Gallery, Shifnal, Shrops.
Southgate, P., Maldon, Essex.
Southworth, S. and R., Staunton Harold, Leics.
Sovereign Art, Woburn, Beds. Wob. Ab. Ant. C.,
Spa Antiques, Leamington Spa, Warks.
Spackman, R., Peterborough, Cambs.
Spafford Art Deco, London, N.W.8. Alf. Ant. Mkt.
Span Antiques, Woodstock, Oxon.
Sparks, C., London, S.W.6. (Galerie 360).
Sparks Ltd., John, London, W.1.
Sparks, T., Rickmansworth, Herts.
Sparrow Antiques, Woburn, Beds. Wob. Ab. Ant. C.
Sparrow, R. and P., Stroud, Glos.
Sparrow, W.J. and Catley, B.R., London, S.W.3. Chen. Gall.
Sparth House Antiques, Clayton-le-Moors, Lancs.
Speakman, P., Haslingden, Lancs.
Speakmans, Haslingden, Lancs.
Spearing, B., Wrentham, Suffolk.
Special Edition, Wallingford, Oxon. L. Arc.
Speed (Maps), John, Bilstone, Leics.
Speed Antiques, Neil, Laugharne, Dyfed, Wales.
Speelman, Alfred, London, W.1.
Speelman Ltd., Edward, London, W.1.
Speight, Mrs. A., Bristol, Avon. Clift. Ant. Mkt.
Speight, Connie, London, W.1. G. Ant. Mkt.
Spellman, D. and S., London, W.1 (The Wel- beck Gallery).
Spelman, Ken, York, N. Yorks.
Spence, G., Twyford, Berks.
Spencer, A.L., Shepperton, Surrey.
Spencer Theatre Gallery, Charles, London, W.1.
Spencer, Don, Warwick, Warks. Smith St. A.C.
Spencer Decorations Ltd., George, London, S.W.1.
Spencer, W.T. and J., Lower Bentham, N. Yorks.
Spencer-Brayn, N., Winchester, Hants.
Spendlove, Mrs. B., Ulverston, Cumbria.
Spero, Simon, London, W.8.
Sperr, J.R., London, N.6.
Spey Valley Antiques, Grantown-on-Spey, Morays., Scot.
Spice, London, S.W.6.
Spicker, Rosalynd and Carole, Newcastle-upon-Tyne, Tyne and Wear.
Spiers, Aubrey, London, S.W.3. Chen Gall.
Spigard, A., London, N.W.1.
Spillers Ltd., H.J., London, W.1.
Spilsby Antiques, Spilsby, Lincs.
Spindles, The, Tonge, Leics.
Spindley, D.A., Louth, Lincs.
Spink and Son Ltd., London, S.W.1.

Spinning Wheel, The, Beaconsfield, Bucks.
Spinning Wheel, The, Mawnan Smith, Cornwall.
Spinning Wheel, Port Erin, Isle of Man.
Spinning Wheel, The, Southport, Merseyside.
Spinning Wheel Antiques, St. Annes-on-Sea, Lancs.
Spon End Antiques, Coventry, W. Mids.
Spooner, J.G., Dorking, Surrey.
Spooner, K.L. and J.S., Leek, Staffs.
Spooner, P.J., Dorking, Surrey.
Sport and Country Gallery, Bulkington, Warks.
Sporting Paintings Ltd., Carlton Curlieu, Leics.
Sports Programmes, Coventry, W. Mids.
Sprake, R.H., Lowestoft, Suffolk.
Spratt Antiques, Jack, Newark, Notts.
Spratt Watercolours, Michael, Shalford, Surrey.
Spread Eagle Antiques, London, S.E.10.
Spring Antiques, Ipswich, Suffolk.
Spring Antiques, London, W.1.
Spring Park Jewellers, Shirley, Gtr. London.
Spurrier-Smith Antiques, Ashbourne, Derbys.
Spurrier-Smith, I., Ashbourne, Derbys.
Spyer and Son (Antiques) Ltd., Gerald, London, S.W.1.
Squires Antiques, Altrincham, Cheshire.
Squires, A., Faversham, Kent.
Squires Antiques, Faversham, Kent.
Squirrel Antiques, Stratford-upon-Avon, Warks.
Squirrel Collectors Centre, Basingstoke, Hants.
Squirrels, Ottery St. Mary, Devon.
Stable Antiques, Osgathorpe, Leics.
Stable Antiques, Sedbergh, Cumbria.
Stable Enterprises, Weston-super-Mare, Avon.
Stables, The, Grasmere, Cumbria.
Stables Antiques, The, Dorking, Surrey.
Stables Antiques, Ombersley, Hereford and Worcs.
Stables, K., Bath, Avon. (No.12 Queen St.).
Stacey, G.M.St.G., Wotten-under-Edge, Glos.
Stacey and Sons, John, Leigh-on-Sea, Essex.
Stacy-Marks Ltd., E., Eastbourne, E. Sussex.
Stage Door Prints, London, W.C.2.
Stair and Co. Ltd., London, W.1.
Stait, T.G., Painswick, Glos.
Stalham Antique Gallery, Stalham, Norfolk.
Stalker, J.E., Bexhill-on-Sea, E. Sussex.
Stallabrass, Mrs. S.G., Princes Risborough, Bucks.
Stamp, F.R. and M.H., Twyford, Berks.
Stamp, J., Bungay, Suffolk.
Stampantique Ltd., Egham, Surrey.
Stancomb, J.A., Ilminster, Somerset.
Standishgate Antiques, Wigan, Lancs.
Standley, M.E. and J.E., Wymondham, Norfolk.
Standley, R.C., Wymondham, Norfolk.
Stane Street Antiques, Ockley, Surrey.
Stanford, A., Coventry, W. Mids.

Stanford, Miss M.A., Farnham, Surrey.
Staniland (Booksellers), Stamford, Lincs.
Staniland, M.F. and M.G., Stamford, Lincs.
Stanley and Son, K., Auchterarder, Perths., Scot.
Stanley and Son, K., Dunkeld, Perths., Scot.
Stanley and Son, K., Glasgow, Lanarks., Scot.
Stanley, Mrs. P., Brentwood, Essex.
Stanley Studios, London, S.W.10.
Stanton, E., Worthing, W. Sussex.
Stanton, Louis, London, W.11.
Stanton, L.R. and S.A., London, W.11.
Stanworth, Mr. and Mrs. G., Cadeby, Leics.
Stanworth (Fine Arts), P., Cadeby, Leics.
Staplegate Antiques, Canterbury, Kent.
Staplegrove Lodge Antiques, Taunton, Somerset.
Stapleton, D.H., Bedford, Beds.
Stapleton's Antiques, Bedford, Beds.
Starkey, James H., Beverley, N. Humberside.
Starkie, E.S., Knaresborough, N. Yorks.
Starks, E.M., Bishops Waltham, Hants.
Station Antiques, Burgh-le-Marsh, Lincs.
Station Pine Antiques, Nottingham, Notts.
Staton Antiques, Alanna, Cobham, Surrey.
Staton, Mr. and Mrs., Cobham, Surrey.
Status Antiques, London, N.W.3. Ham. Ant. Emp.
Stead, Geoffrey, Cheltenham, Glos.
Stead, N.P., Wolverhampton, W. Mids.
Stebbens, Dr. and Mrs. A., Wootton Bassett, Wilts.
Stebbing Ltd., P.M., Bournemouth, Dorset.
Steed-Croft Antiques, Brancaster, Norfolk.
Steedman, R.D., Newcastle-upon-Tyne, Tyne and Wear.
Steeds, J., Burghfield Common, Berks.
Steel, N., London, N.1. (Banbury Fayre)
Steel, Mrs. V., London, N.2.
Steele, W.G., Stoke-on-Trent, Staffs.
Steenson, M., London, W.11. (Books and Things).
Steeple Antiques, Kilbarchan, Renfrews., Scot.
Steers, D. and D., Shoreham-by-Sea, W. Sussex.
Stein, I.H.C. and M.L., Auchterarder, Perths., Scot.
Stein, M.W., Bristol, Avon. Clift. Ant. Mkt.
Stellas Antiques Art Deco, London, N.W.8. Alf. Ant. Mkt.
Stenhouse, R., Marlborough, Wilts.
Stent, J., Amersham, Bucks.
Stephens, P.M., Inchture, Perths., Scot.
Stephenson, Miss E., Bradford-on-Avon, Wilts.
Stephenson, Ian, Helmsley, N. Yorks.
Stephenson, Robert, London, N.W.6.
Steppes Hill Farm Antiques, Stockbury, Kent.
Sterling Books, Weston-super-Mare, Avon.
Sterling Coins and Medals, Bournemouth, Dorset.
Stern Gallery, London, W.11.
Stern, H., London, W.C.2. Lon. Silv. Vts. (Silstar).

Stern, M., London, W.11.
Sternberg, C., London, W.1 (Vigo-Sternberg Galleries).
Sternshine, A., Manchester, Lancs. (A.S. Antiques).
Stevens, D., Burford, Oxon.
Stevens Booksellers, E. and J., London, N.W.6.
Stevens, Geoffrey G., Guildford, Surrey.
Stevens Antiques, J.E., St. Albans, Herts.
Stevens, R. and C., Ilford, Gtr. London.
Stevens-Wilson, L.W. and Mrs., London, N.21.
Stevenson, E. and W., Whissendene, Leics.
Stevenson, I. and A., Brighton, E. Sussex. (Oasis Antiques).
Stevenson, P. and T., Wainfleet, Lincs.
Stewart, F., Elgin, Moray., Scot.
Stewart Gallery, Eastbourne, E. Sussex.
Stewart, J. and D., Norham,-Northumb.
Stewart — Fine Art, Lauri, London, N.2.
Stewart, Michael, Coatbridge, Lanarks., Scot.
Stewart Antiques, Michael, Leominster, Hereford and Worcs.
Steward, Paul, London, S.W.3. Ant. Ant. Mkt.
Stewart-Cox, A., J.M. and M., Salisbury, Wilts.
Steyne House Antiques, Seaford, E. Sussex.
Stickland, W.T. and B., Moreton-in-Marsh, Glos.
Stiffkey Lamp Shop, The, Stiffkey, Norfolk.
Stimpson, J., Brasted, Kent.
Stimpson, P.D., Hurst Green, E. Sussex.
Stirchley Antiques, Birmingham, W. Mids.
Stirling Antiques, Abinger Hammer, Surrey.
Stirling, J.T., Birmingham, W. Mids.
Stobo, Constance, London, W.8.
Stock, Colin, Rainford, Merseyside.
Stockbridge Antiques, Stockbridge, Hants.
Stocker, C.J., Harston, Cambs.
Stocker, J., Chipping Campden, Glos.
Stocker, Philip, Bexhill-on-Sea, E. Sussex.
Stockham at Images, Peter, London, W.C.2.
Stockland, M., Hungerford, Berks. (Riverside Antiques).
Stockman, Paul, Newton Abbot, Devon. N.A. Ant. C.
Stockman, P. and D., Newton Abbot, Devon. N. A. Ant. C.
Stockspring Antiques, London, W.1. G. Mews.
Stockton, R. and J., Cardiff, S. Glam., Wales (The Light Brigade and Penylan Antiques.)
Stodart, T.A. and Mrs., Pulborough, W. Sussex.
Stodel, Jacob, London, W.8.
Stodel, S. and J., London, W.C.2. Lon. Silv. Vts.
Stodgell, C., Torquay, Devon.
Stoker, D., Leigh-on-Sea, Essex.
Stokes, Mr. and Mrs. J., Worksop, Notts.
Stokes, Mrs. S., Wallington, Gtr. London.
Stokes, William H., Cirencester, Glos.
Stokesay Antiques, Craven Arms, Shrops.
Stone Antiques, Alan, London, S.W.15.

Stone, A.B., Tunbridge Wells, Kent (Rusthall Antiques.)
Stone Antique Centre, Stone, Staffs.
Stone, A.H., Basingstoke, Hants.
Stone, Barbara, London, N.W.8. Alf. Ant. Mkt.
Stone, Cyril, Brighton, E. Sussex.
Stone Hall Antiques, Matching Green, Essex.
Stone House Antiques, Painswick, Glos.
Stonecourt Antiques, Eastwood, Notts.
Stonedge Antiques, Wootton Bassett, Wilts.
Stones Antiques, Dick, Farndon, Cheshire.
Stones, Mrs. M. Palmer, Stradbroke, Suffolk.
Stones, Mrs. S., Wisbech, Cambs.
Stonewall Antiques, Hillsborough, Co. Down, N. Ireland.
Stone-Wares Antiques, Stone, Staffs.
Stoodley, Dinah, Brasted, Kent.
Storer, Mr. and Mrs. M., Nottingham, Notts. (Trade Wind Antiques).
Stores, The, Great Waltham, Essex.
Storey, Harold T., London, W.C.2.
Storey, M. and J., London, S.W.1. (The Delightful Muddle).
Storrington Antiques, Storrington, W. Sussex.
Stour Gallery, Blandford Forum, Dorset.
Stove Shop, The, London, W.C.1.
Stowaway (U.K.) Ltd., Horncastle, Lincs.
Strachie, Julie, Wallingford, Oxon. L. Arc.
Strain Antiques, David R., Tynemouth, Tyne and Wear.
Strait Antiques, The, Lincoln, Lincs.
Strand Antiques, Bromsgrove, Hereford and Worcs.
Strand Antiques, London, W.4.
Strand Antiques, The, Rye, E. Sussex.
Strang, Lloyd, Glasgow, Lanarks., Scot. Vict. Vill.
Strange, D., London, W.C.2 (Pearl Cross Ltd.).
Strange, Sheila B., Newton Abbot, Devon. N. A. Ant. C.
Stratford Antique Centre, Stratford-upon-Avon, Warks.
Stratford House Antique Centre, Birmingham, W. Mids.
Strathearn Antiques, Crieff, Perths., Scot.
Stratton-Quinn Antiques Etc., London, W.4.
Stratton-Shaw, Mrs. C.M., Ambergate, Derbys.
Strawson's Antiques, Tunbridge Wells, Kent.
Streamer Antiques, J., Leigh-on-Sea, Essex.
Streatham Traders and Shippers Market, London, S.W.16.
Streatham Village Antiques, London, S.W.16.
Streather, Pamela, Chilton, Bucks.
Streather, Pamela, London, S.W.1.
Street, H., London, N.W.8.
Street, J.R. and D.J., Colchester, Essex.
Streeter and Daughter, Ernest, Petworth, W. Sussex.
Stretton Antiques, Church Stretton, Shrops.
Strickland and Dorling, Truro, Cornwall.
Strickland, G., Portsmouth, Hants.
Strickland, P., Truro, Cornwall.

Strike One (Islington) Ltd., London, N.1.
Strong, C.J., Exeter, Devon.
Strong, C.J., Exmouth, Devon.
Stroud, Louise, London, S.W.3.
Stroud of Southwell (Antiques), Southwell,
  Notts.
Stroud Antiques, Peter, Chipping Norton,
  Oxon.
Stroud, V.N. and J., Southwell, Notts.
Stroud's of Taunton, London, S.W.3.
  (Louise Stroud)
Strover Antiques, B.J. and L., Fen Ditton,
  Cambs.
Struwwelpeter, Cheltenham, Glos.
Stuart Antiques, Auchterarder, Perths., Scot.
Stuart Antiques, D.C., Bournemouth, Dorset.
Stuart Gallery, Marlborough, Wilts.
Stuart House Fine Art, Birmingham, W.
  Mids.
Stuart, J. and V., Shere, Surrey.
'Stuart Martin', London, N.6.
Stuart, R.S., London, S.W.10.
Stuart-Mobey, Alan, Woodstock, Oxon.
Stuart-Mobey and Daughter, A. and J.,
  Oxford, Oxon.
Stubbs, H.G., Cardigan, Dyfed, Wales.
Studio, The, London, N.1.
Studio 41, Southport, Merseyside.
Studio 101 and Turk's Head Antiques,
  Windsor and Eton, Berks.
Studio Antiques, Bawtry, S. Yorks.
Studio Antiques, Peterborough, Cambs.
Studio Antiques Ltd., Bourton-on-the-Water,
  Glos.
Studio Bookshop and Gallery, Alresford,
  Hants.
Studio One Gallery, Oxford, Oxon.
Studium, London, W.1. G. Mews.
Stuff, Dover, Kent.
Stuff and Nonsense, London, N.W.8. Alf.
  Ant. Mkt.
Sturgeon, J.A. and Mrs. J., Sandhurst,
  Berks.
Sturton, J., London, S.E.1. Ber. Ant. Whse.
Stutchbury, Mr. and Mrs. D., Newark,
  Notts.
Styles, P. and D., Hungerford, Berks.
Su and Son, Burford, Oxon.
Suckling, J. and D., Wallingford, Oxon.
  L. Arc.
Su and Son, Burford, Oxon.
Sulaiman, Mr., London, S.W.3. Ant. Ant.
  Mkt. (Mr. Garcia)
Sulford-Smith, Mrs. C., Sevenoaks, Kent.
Sullivan, Mrs., Bristol, Avon. Clift. Ant. Mkt.
Sullivan, B., Southport, Merseyside.
Sullivan, J., Nottingham, Notts.
Sullivan, Mrs. V., Ingatestone, Essex.
Summerfield, R.E., Cheltenham, Glos.
Summers, Davis and Son Ltd., Wallingford,
  Oxon.
Sumner Antiques, Janet, Bath, Avon. Gt.
  West. A. C. Wed. Mkt.
Sumner, Mrs. Jane, Saffron Walden, Essex.
Sumner, M.C., Uppingham, Leics.
Sumner, N.F. and M.A., Ormskirk, Lancs.
Sumner, N.J., Bath, Avon. Gt. West. A. C.
  Wed. Mkt.

Sun H.... Antiques, Long Melford, Suffolk
Sun Street Clock Shop, Lancaster, Lancs.
Sundial Antiques, Amersham, Bucks.
Sundridge Antiques, Bromley, Gtr. London.
Sundridge Antiques, Sundridge, Kent.
Sunfield Cottage Antiques, Banchory,
  Kincard., Scot.
Surbiton Bookhouse, Surbiton, Gtr. London.
Surpass Coins, London, W.1. G. Ant. Mkt.
Surrey Antiques Centre, Chertsey, Surrey.
Surrey Clock Centre, Haslemere, Surrey.
Surrey Pine, Godalming, Surrey.
Susands, M. and M., London, S.W.15.
Sussex Commemorative Ware Centre, The,
  Brighton, E. Sussex.
Sutcliffe Galleries, Harrogate, N. Yorks.
Sutcliffe, Gordon, Hadleigh, Suffolk.
Sutcliffe, Ralph A., Harle Syke, Lancs.
Sutcliffe, Steve, Market Drayton, Shrops.
Sutcliffe Antiques, Tony and Anne,
  Southport, Merseyside.
Suthburgh Antiques, Long Melford, Suffolk.
Sutherland Antiques, Chester, Cheshire.
Suthurland, Alistair, Newton Abbot, Devon.
  N. A. Ant. C.
Suttle, H. and M., Otley, W. Yorks.
Sutton Antiques, Uppingham, Leics.
Sutton, J.A., Uppingham Leics.
Sutton, L., Great Malvern, Hereford and
  Worcs.
Sutton, L. and M., London, W.11.
Sutton P., London, W.8 (Oliver-Sutton
  Antiques).
Sutton and Sons, Frome, Somerset.
Sutton Valence Antiques, Maidstone, Kent.
Sutton Valence Antiques, Sutton Valence,
  Kent.
Suzie-Q Antiques, London, N.W.3. Ham.
  Ant. Emp.
Swadforth House, Knaresborough, N. Yorks.
Swaffer, Spencer, Arundel, W. Sussex.
Swaffham Antiques Centre, Swaffham, Norfolk.
Swaffham Antiques Supplies, Swaffham,
  Norfolk.
Swag, Preston, Lancs.
Swain, E.R.A., A.L. and J.R., Doddington,
  Kent.
Swainbank, R., Liverpool, Merseyside.
Swainbank's Ltd., Liverpool, Merseyside.
Swan Antiques, Bawtry, S. Yorks.
Swan Antiques, Chipping Campden, Glos.
Swan Antiques, Cranbrook, Kent.
Swan Antiques, Dorking, Surrey.
Swan Antiques, Manchester, Lancs. Royal
  Ex. S. C.
Swan Fine Art, London, N.1.
Swan Gallery, Burford, Oxon.
Swan Lane Antiques (Antique Centre),
  Warwick, Warks.
Swann Galleries, Oliver, London, S.W.3.
Swansea Antiques Centre, Swansea,
  W. Glam., Wales.
Swansea County and W.P. Ltd., Swansea,
  W. Glam., Wales.
Swanson Antiques, London, S.W.6.
Swanson, D. and N., London, S.W.6.
Sweeney, K. and E., Bridlington,
  N. Humberside.

Temple, R.C.C., London, S.W.3.
Templemans — Wholesale Antiques, Knapp, Perths, Scot.
Tempus Antiques Ltd., London, N.6.
Tempus Fugit, Halstead, Essex.
Tempus Fugit, Shaldon, Devon.
"Tequesta", Caton, Lancs.
Terry Antiques, London, N.1.
Terry Antiques, London, N.19.
Terry, Jean, London, S.W.3. Ant. Ant. Mkt.
Tessiers Ltd., London, W.1.
Tetbury Antiques, Tetbury, Glos.
Tewkesbury Antique Centre, Tewkesbury, Glos.
Textile Gallery, The, London, W.9.
Thacker, J. and B., Rufforth, N. Yorks.
Thacker's Antiques, York, N. Yorks.
Thackray, Mrs., Newton Abbot, Devon. N. A. Ant. C.
Thame Antique and Art Galleries, Thame, Oxon.
Thames Gallery, Henley-on-Thames, Oxon.
Thatched Barn Antiques, The, Ombersley, Hereford and Worcs.
Thaxted Galleries, Thaxted, Essex.
Thesaurus (Jersey) Ltd., St. Helier, Jersey, C.I.
Thesaurus, St. Peter Port, Guernsey, C.I.
Theta Gallery, Liverpool, Merseyside.
Thicke Galleries, Swansea, W. Glam., Wales.
Thicke, T.G., Swansea, W. Glam., Wales.
Thiel, G. and D., York, N. Yorks. (Trinity Antiques).
Thiele, A.C., Epsom, Surrey.
Thiele, A.C., Kingston-upon-Thames, Gtr. London.
Thiele, A.C., Staines, Surrey.
Thimble Society, London, W.1. G. Ant. Mkt.
Thin (Booksellers), James, Edinburgh, Midloth., Scot.
Thirkill Antiques, T.L., Leeds, W. Yorks.
Thirty Eight Antiques, Weedon, Northants.
This and That Antiques and Bric-a-Brac, Edinburgh, Midloth., Scot.
This and That (Furniture), London, N.W.1.
Thistle Antiques, Aberdeen, Aberd., Scot.
Thistle Antiques, Todmorden, W. Yorks.
Thistlethwaite, E., Settle, N. Yorks.
Thom Antiques, George and Lesley, Fochabers, Morays, Scot.
Thom, Karen, Glasgow, Larnarks., Scot. Vict. Vill.
Thomas, Alan G., London, S.W.3.
Thomas, Clare, Deddington, Oxon. Ant. C.
Thomas (Fine Arts), Carole, Hitchin, Herts.
Thomas and Dymond, Meshaw, Devon.
Thomas, D.J. and P.E., Hisomley, Wilts.
Thomas, Mrs. E., London, W.1.
Thomas, I., London, N.1. (Garrick House Antiques).
Thomas, J.B., Fishguard, Dyfed, Wales.
Thomas, M. and V., Penn, Bucks.
Thomas Antiques, Nicholas, London, W.11.
Thomas Fine Paintings, Paul, Wokingham, Berks.
Thomas, Philip, J.L., Ashburton, Devon.
Thomas, R., Thornton Heath, Gtr. London.

Thomas, Lt. Col. R.C.W., London, S.W.3. Ant. Ant. Mkt.
Thomas, R. and D., Brasted, Kent.
Thomas, Wing Cdr. R.G., Midsomer Norton, Avon.
Thomas, R.N., Meshaw, Devon.
Thompson, A., Luton, Beds.
Thompson, A. and G., Wisbech, Cambs.
Thompson Antiques formerly Ships and Sealing Wax, Winchester, Hants.
Thompson, B., London, N.1 (Antique Trader).
Thompson, D., Dunchurch, Warks.
Thompson, D. and P., Alresford, Hants.
Thompson, D. and Mrs. S., Ipswich, Suffolk.
Thompson, John, Tunbridge Wells, Kent.
Thompson, J., Knaresborough, N. Yorks.
Thompson, Mrs. J., Ulverston, Cumbria.
Thompson, J.A., London, W.11.
Thompson, J. and S., Aldeburgh, Suffolk.
Thompson, L.E., Stockport, Cheshire.
Thompson, M., Long Melford, Suffolk.
Thompson Antiques, Michael, Aslockton, Notts.
Thompson, M. and M., Aslockton, Notts.
Thompson, M. and M., East Bridgford, Notts.
Thompson, N., Tunbridge Wells, Kent (John Thompson.)
Thompson, N.F., Tideswell, Derbys.
Thompson, R., Warwick, Warks.
Thompson, R.E., Long Buckby, Northants.
Thompson, Sue and Allan, London, S.W.3. Ant. Ant. Mkt.
Thompson-Bone, R., Puttenham, Surrey.
Thompson's, Ipswich, Suffolk.
Thompson's Antiques, Ipswich, Suffolk.
Thompson's Gallery, Aldeburgh, Suffolk.
Thomson, A., Dalry, Ayr., Scot.
Thomson Antiques, A.D. and S., Ivybridge, Devon.
Thomson, A.L., St. Helier, Jersey, C.I.
Thomson, Mrs. C., Stratford-upon-Avon, Warks.
Thomson, D., Ripon, N. Yorks.
Thomson, I.G.F., Sheffield, S. Yorks. (G.W. Ford and Son Ltd.)
Thomson Ltd., Murray, London, W.8.
Thomson Ltd., Murray, London, W.11.
Thomson, R.N. and J., Blackpool, Lancs.
Thomson, W.B., London, S.W.1.
Thorn, David J., Budleigh Salterton, Devon.
Thornberry, R.C., London, W.1 (Wilberry Antiques).
Thornborough Galleries, Cirencester, Glos.
Thornbury, M., Brinkworth, Wilts.
Thorne, S., Hursley, Hants.
Thornhill Galleries Ltd., London, S.W.6.
Thornhill Galleries Ltd., London, S.W.15.
Thornhill, J., Shrewsbury, Shrops.
Thornley, G. and B., Monks Risborough, Bucks.
Thornley, G. and E.M., Helmsley, N. Yorks.
Thornton Architectural Antiques Ltd., Andy, Elland, W. Yorks.
Thornton Gallery, Bedale, N. Yorks.
Thornton, J., London, S.W.6 (634 Kings Road.)

Thornton, J., Ulverston, Cumbria.
Thornton Antiques, Joseph, Windermere, Cumbria.
Thornton and Son, J., Oxford, Oxon.
Thornton Antiques Supermarket, J.W., Bowness-on-Windermere, Cumbria.
Thorntons of Harrogate, Harrogate, N. Yorks.
Thorp, Thomas, St. Albans, Herts.
Thorp, Bookseller, Thomas, Guildford, Surrey.
Thorpe, A., Dorking, Surrey.
Thorpe Antiques, Finedon, Northants.
Thorpe, D.J., Llanwrda, Dyfed, Wales.
Thorpe and Foster Ltd., Dorking, Surrey.
Thorpe, Mrs. L.H., Seend, Wilts.
Thorpe, Simon, London, S.W.3 (Patricia Rhodes.) Chen. Gall.
Thorpe, S., Newton Abbot, Devon, N.A. Ant. C.
Thorpe, T., Epworth, S. Humberside.
Thorpe's Antiques and Curio Shop, Epworth, S. Humberside.
Three Gables Antiques, Nutley, E. Sussex.
Three Tuns Antiques, Stokesley, N. Yorks.
Threipland, Mr. and Mrs. M. Murray, Rait, Perths., Scot.
Thrie Estaits, The, Edinburgh, Midloth., Scot.
Throckmorton, Lady Isabel, Coughton, Warks.
Throp, R. Brasted, Kent.
Through the Looking Glass Ltd., London, S.W.6.
Thrower, D. and V., Cranleigh, Surrey.
Thrower, D. and V., Petworth, W. Sussex.
Thuillier, William, London, S.W.1.
Thurlow, K., London, S.W.6 (David Alexander Antiques).
Thurso Antiques, Thurso, Caith., Scot.
Thurstans, C.M. and D., Stillington, N. Yorks.
Thurston, Mrs. W., Newmarket, Suffolk.
Thwaites and Co., Julian, Bushey, Herts.
Tibenham, Mrs. P., Knowle, W. Mids.
Tibetan Shop, London, W.1. G. Mews.
Tiernan, Eugene, London, W.1. G. Mews.
Tiffin's Antiques, Framlingham, Suffolk.
Tilings Antiques, Brasted, Kent.
Till, M., London, N.1 (Vane House Antiques).
Tillbrook, P., Theydon Bois, Essex.
Tillett, James and Ann, Norwich, Norfolk.
Tillett, M., London, S.E.8.
Tillett, M., London, S.E.10.
Tilley, A.G.J. and A.A.J.C., Chesterfield, Derbys.
Tilley, Mrs. P., Macclesfield, Cheshire.
Tilley's Bookshops, Chesterfield, Derbys.
Tilly's Antiques, Rayleigh, Essex.
Tilston, G., Hatton Heath, Cheshire.
Tilston-Woolley Antiques, Hatton Heath, Cheshire.
Timberstrip, Swansea, W. Galm., Wales. Ant. Centre.
Time in Hand, Shipston-on-Stour, Warks.
Time on Your Hands, Cardiff, S. Glam., Wales.

Timecraft, St. Ives, Cambs.
Times Past, Pershore, Hereford and Worcs.
Times Past Antiques, Rossett, Clwyd, Wales.
Times Past Antiques Ltd., Windsor and Eton, Berks.
Timmis and Son, B., Eccleshall, Staffs.
Timm's Antiques, Woburn, Beds. Wob. Ab. Ant. C.
Timms Antiques Ltd., S. and S., Ampthill, Beds.
Timms Antiques, S. and S., Woburn, Beds. Wob. Ab. Ant. C.
Timothy, P., London, E.C.1.
Tincknell, R., Bath, Avon. Gt. West. Ant. C. Wed. Mkt.
Tincknell, R.C. and L., Bath, Avon. Gt. West. Ant. C.
Tinder Box, The, Stoke-on-Trent, Staffs.
Tinderbox, Great Malvern, Hereford and Worcs.
Tinne, G., Bath, Avon. Gt. West. Ant. C. (Not Cartier)
Tipping, Brian, London, S.W.3. Ant. Ant. Mkt.
Titchfield Antiques Ltd., Titchfield, Hants.
Titles Old and Rare Books, Oxford, Oxon.
Titmuss, E.L., London, W.8. (Hope and Glory).
Toby Antiques, Brighton, E. Sussex.
Tociapski, Igor, London, W.11.
Tod, W. and S.J., Salcombe, Devon.
Todd, A., Stockport, Cheshire.
Todd and Austin Antiques of Winchester, Winchester, Hants.
Todd, G. Uppingham, Leics.
Todd, M.S., Nether Stowey, Somerset.
Todd, W., Winchester, Hants.
Token House Antiques, Ewell, Surrey.
Toll House, Sturminster Newton, Dorset.
Toller, C., Datchet, Berks.
Toller, C. and J., Datchet, Berks.
Tollett, B., Witney, Oxon.
Tolley, T.M., Worcester, Hereford and Worcs.
Tolley's Galleries, Worcester, Hereford and Worcs.
Tollgate Antiques Bicester, Oxon.
Tomasso and Sons, Leeds, W. Yorks.
Tomkinson, J. and B., Clitheroe, Lancs.
Tomlin, D.S., London, N.5.
Tomlin, Mrs. J., London, S.W.3. Ant. Ant. Mkt.
Tomlinson and Son, F., Stockport, Cheshire.
Tomlinson, R., — (Antiques) Ltd., (Wetherby Antiques), Wetherby, W. Yorks.
Tonks, A.R. and T.A., Gosport, Hants.
Tonks, Mrs. B., Wolverhampton, W. Mids.
Tontine Antiques Ltd., Folkestone, Kent.
Toogood, R.G., Lincoln, Lincs.
Tooke, M.D., Guildford, Surrey.
Tooley, Adams and Co. Ltd., London, W.1.
Tooley, M.V., Great Missenden, Bucks.
Toop, Rosemary, Wallingford, Oxon. L. Arc.
Top Hat Antiques Centre, Nottingham, Notts.
Top Hat Exhibitions Ltd., Nottingham, Notts.
Top Shop, Wallingford, Oxon. L. Arc.

Troman, C.G. and J.A., Newmarket, Suffolk.
Tron Antiques, Dunning, Perths., Scot.
Tron (Antiques) Ltd., David, London, S.W.3.
Trotman, C., Sidmouth, Devon.
Trotter, G., London, S.W.3. Ant. Ant. Mkt.
Trouthouse Antiques, Eastleach, Glos.
Trove, London, S.W.1.
Trower, Mrs. V.G., Guildford, Surrey.
Trudgett, I.S., Winchester, Hants.
Trueman, H., Berkeley, Glos.
Truro Antique Centre, Truro, Cornwall.
Truscott, Christina, London, W.11.
Tryon, Mrs. J.P., Congleton, Cheshire.
Tryon and Moorland Gallery, The, London, W.1.
Tubbs, (Old Parsonage Gallery), Michael, Little Baddow, Essex.
Tucker, F.H. and S.M., Charing, Kent.
Tucker, F.S., London, S.W.6. (Savile Pine)
Tucker, Jean, Rye, E. Sussex. Str. Ants.
Tucker, Kim, Rye, E. Sussex. Str. Ant.
Tucker and Langs, Dorking, Surrey.
Tucker, Mrs. S., Charing, Kent.
Tudor Antiques, Hatfield Broad Oak, Essex.
Tudor Antiques, Long Melford, Suffolk.
Tudor Antiques, Monks Risborough, Bucks.
Tudor Antiques, Woburn, Beds. Wob. Ab. Ant. C.
Tudor Cottage Antiques, Shoreham-by-Sea, W. Sussex.
Tudor Cottage Antiques Centre, Tonbridge, Kent.
Tudor Gallery, Dorchester, Dorset.
Tudor House Antiques, Bridport, Dorset.
Tudor Rose Antiques, Carlton-on-Trent, Notts.
"Tudor Rose" and "Mona Antiqua", Beaumaris, Gwynedd, Wales.
Tuffs, C., Wraysbury, Berks.
Tugwell and Thomas, London, W.1. G. Ant. Mkt.
Tullison, N.S., London, S.W.3. Chen. Gall.
Tunnicliffe, A.J., Stoke-on-Trent, Staffs.
Tunnicliffes Antiques, Stoke-on-Trent, Staffs.
Tunstall, T., Newark, Notts.
Tupman, David, London, N.W.8. Alf. Ant. Mkt.
Turbibilles, J. and F., Dorchester, Dorset.
Turl, Mrs., Kimpton, Herts.
Turley, Mr. and Mrs. C.R., Wolverhampton, W. Mids.
Turley, S.J. and N.V., Brasted, Kent.
Turn of the Century Antiques, Hexham, Northumb.
"Turn On" Ltd., London, N.1.
Turnbull, J.F., Hexham, Northumb.
Turnbull, J. and M., Hawick, Roxburgh., Scot.
Turnbull, Mr. and Mrs. W.H., Bedale, N. Yorks.
Turner Antiques, Annmarie, Marlborough, Wilts.
Turner, A., Shrewsbury, Shrops.
Turner, Mrs. D., Rye, E. Sussex.
Turner, J., Cheltenham, Glos. (Antiques Cheltenham).
Turner, L.D. and M.W., Wickham Market, Suffolk.

Turner, Mrs. M., Loughborough, Leics.
Turner (Antiques) Ltd., Philip, London, W.1.
Turner Furniture, Philip, Rotherham, S. Yorks.
Turner Antiques and Fine Art Ltd., R. and M., Jedburgh, Roxbs., Scot.
Turner, Sally, Haddenham, Bucks.
Turner, W.A., London, W.13.
Turpin Ltd., M., London, S.W.7.
Turpin's Antiques, Thaxted, Essex.
Turret House, Wymondham, Norfolk.
Turtle Antiques, Cheltenham, Glos.
Turtons Antiques, Warwick, Warks. Smith St. A. C.
Tushingham, M.E., London, S.W.3. (O.F. Wilson Ltd.)
Tutbury Mill Antiques, Tutbury, Staffs.
Twemlow and Co. Ltd., Nottingham, Notts.
Twentieth Century Style, The, Birmingham, W. Mids.
Twenty-One Antiques, Westerham, Kent.
Twitchett, J., Eynsham, Oxon.
Twyford Antiques, Twyford, Hants.
Twyford Antiques Centre, Twyford, Berks.
Tyler, T.M., Malmsesbury, Wilts.
Tyndall, J.G.R., Long Melford, Suffolk.
Tyn-y-Coed, Barmouth, Gwynedd, Wales.
Tyrrell Bookshop and Gallery, Ringwood, Hants.
Tyrrell, G. and M., Woburn Sands, Bucks.
Tyzack Ltd., R., High Wycombe, Bucks.
Tzigany Fine Arts, London, W.1.

U

Udall, R., Sedbergh, Cumbria.
Uden, Penelope, London, W.1. G. Mews.
Ullmann Ltd., A.R., London, E.C.1.
Ullman, J.S., London, E.C.1.
Ulverston Point, Ulverston, Cumbria.
Umezawa (M.C.N.), London, W.1. G. Ant. Mkt.
Under Two Flags, London, W.1.
Underhill Gallery, Leigh, London, N.1.
Underwood Antiques, Woburn, Beds. Wob. Ab. Ant. C.
Underwood, B. and C., Newbold-on-Stour, Warks.
Underwood Antiques, Clive, Colsterworth, Lincs.
Unicorn Antiques, Edinburgh, Midloth., Scot.
Unicorn Books, London, N.W.3. Ham. Ant. Emp.
Unicorn Gallery, Castle Combe, Wilts.
Union Antiques, Newton Abbot, Devon. N.A. Ant. C.
Union Antiques, Southport, Merseyside.
Union Street Antique Market, St. Helier, Jersey, C.I.
Upchurch, Kenneth, Ashbourne, Derbys.
Upcraft, A. and T., Wangford, Suffolk.
Upper Court, Kemerton, Hereford and Worcs.
Upstairs, Downstairs, Newcastle-under-Lyme, Staffs.
Upstairs, Downstairs Antiques, Dorking, Surrey.

Upton Lodge Galleries, Avening, Glos.
Urbach, A., London, W.C.2. Lon. Silv. Vts.
Urch, D., Brill, Oxon.
Ursula, London, S.W.3. Ant. Ant. Mkt.
Ursula, London, S.W.3. Chen. Gall.
Usher and Son Ltd., James, Lincoln, Lincs.
Usher Antiques, Richard, Cuckfield,
  W. Sussex.
Usher, R.N., Bury St. Edmunds, Suffolk.
Utopia Antiques Ltd., Holme, Cumbria.

V

V.K. and R. Antiques, Potterne, Wilts.
Valcke, Francois, London, S.W.6.
Vale Antiques, London, W.9.
Vale Stamps and Antiques, London, S.E.3.
Valerie, London, N.W.8. Alf. Ant. Mkt.
Valley Antiques, Royton, Lancs.
Vallis, A., Farnham, Surrey.
Valls, Rafael, London, S.W.1.
Valmar Antiques, Stansted, Essex.
Van Beers, Jan, London, W.1. G. Mews.
Van Broek Antiques, Sunbury, Surrey.
Van Dam, J.D., Lancing, W. Sussex.
Van Den Bussche, L., Brasted, Kent.
Van Den Bussche, L., Sundridge, Kent.
Van Der Tol, J., Bingley, W. Yorks.
Van Haeften Ltd., Johnny, London, S.W.1.
Van Haeften, J. and S., London, S.W.1.
Van Kuijk, H., Hythe, Kent.
Van Praagh, J. and B., Ryde, I. of Wight.
Van Riemsdijk, Mrs. B., Stow-on-the-Wold,
  Glos.
Van Riemsdijk Fine Art, Stow-on-the-Wold,
  Glos.
Van Vredenburgh, Edric, London, S.W.1.
Van Zwanenberg, M., Timberscombe,
  Somerset.
Vanbrugh House Antiques, Stow-on-the-
  Wold, Glos.
Vandekar Antiques, London, W.1. G. Mews.
Vandekar, Betty and Vera, London, W.1.
  G. Mews.
Vandekar of Knightsbridge Ltd., Earle D.,
  London, S.W.3.
Vandeleur Antiquarian Books, London,
  S.W.14.
Vandenberg, Anita, London, W.11. G. Port.
Vander (Antiques) Ltd., C.J., London, E.C.1.
Vanderkar G.B., and Sabin and Vanderkar
  (Fine Paintings) Ltd., London S.W.1.
Vane House Antiques, London, N.1.
Vanity Fayre, Mousehole, Cornwall.
Varnham, H.J. and R.P., London, S.E.3.
Vartuli, Salvador, London, S.W.3. Ant. Ant.
  Mkt.
Vaseroy, London, W.1. B. St. Ant. C.
Vaughan, London, S.W.15.
Vaughan, G. and J., Ruthin, Clwyd, Wales.
Vaughan, Joan, Bath, Avon. Gt. West.
  Ant. C.
Vaughan, J. and J., Deddington, Oxon.
Vaughan Antiques and Jewellery, Michael,
  Exmouth, Devon.
Vaughan, M.J. and Mrs. L.M., London,
  S.W.15.

Vaughan, Robert, Stratford-upon-Avon,
  Warks.
Vaughan, R. and C.M., Stratford-upon-Avon,
  Warks.
Vecchi and Sons, V.C., London, S.W.1.
Vectis Fine Arts Gallery, Bembridge, I. of
  Wight.
Venables Antiques, Jeremy, Warwick,
  Warks.
Vendy Antiques, Market Harborough, Leics.
Vendy, D.R., T.W. and Mrs. V.R., Market
  Harborough, Leics.
Veness, K., Yoxford, Suffolk.
Venn, Edward, Williton, Somerset.
Venn, J. and D., Worcester, Hereford and
  Worcs.
Venners Antiques, London, W.1.
Ventura-Pauly, M., London, W.1. G. Ant.
  Mkt.
Venture, The, Felsted, Essex.
Venture, The, Woking, Surrey.
Verey, Denzil, Barnsley, Glos.
Verney, J., Clare, Suffolk.
Vernon, R., Bath, Avon.
Verrall and Co., Brian R., London, S.W.17.
Very Small Shop, The, Teignmouth, Devon.
Veryard, D.J., Northampton, Northants.
Vetta, S., Oxford, Oxon.
Vicary Antiques, Lancaster, Lancs.
Vice, D., Birmingham, W. Mids. (Format of
  Birmingham Ltd.).
Vickers, John, London, N.W.8. Alf. Ant.
  Mkt.
Vickery, S. and A., Burwash, E. Sussex.
Victoria, Glasgow, Lanarks., Scot. (Corner
  House Antiques).
Victoria Antiques, Doncaster, S. Yorks.
Victoria Antiques, Windsor and Eton, Berks.
Victoria Bookshop, Swindon, Wilts.
Victoria and Edward Antiques Centre,
  Dorking, Surrey.
Victoria Gallery, Camborne, Cornwall.
Victoria House Antiques, Ipswich, Suffolk.
Victoria House Antiques, Tunbridge Wells,
  Kent.
Victoria Pine, Wickham Market, Suffolk.
Victorian Chairman, Bournemouth, Dorset.
Victorian Interiors, Brighton, E. Sussex.
Victorian Parlour, Bournemouth, Dorset.
Victorian Village, The, Glasgow, Lanarks.,
  Scot.
Victoriana, Wimborne Minster, Dorset.
Victoriana Dolls, Reigate, Surrey.
Victoria's Bedroom, Hungerford, Berks.
Victoria's Curios, Birmingham, W. Mids.
Victoria's Emporium, Bristol, Avon.
Victory, The, Rochester, Kent.
Vieux-Pernon, B., London, S.W.1 (Heritage).
Vigo Carpet Gallery, London, W.1.
Vigo-Sternberg Galleries, London, W.1.
Viladech, T.M.V., London, S.W.3. Ant. Ant.
  Mkt.
Village Antique Market, The, Weedon,
  Northants.
Village Antiques, Addingham, W. Yorks.
Village Antiques, Bexhill-on-Sea, E. Sussex.
Village Antiques, Newton Abbot, Devon.
  N.A. Ant. C.

Village Antiques and Gallery, Truro, Cornwall.
Village Furniture Co., Manchester, Lancs.
Village Gallery, The, Brasted, Kent.
Village Gallery, London, W.11.
Village Green Antiques, Hertford, Herts.
Village Pine, Farnham, Surrey.
Village Pine, Llangollen, Clwyd, Wales.
Vince, N.B., Bawdeswell, Norfolk.
Vince, D. and I., Maldon, Essex.
Vincent, H., Barrow-in-Furness, Cumbria.
Vincent, H.M. and V.J., Bungay, Suffolk.
Vincent, T. and J.B., Birmingham, W. Mids. (Collecting World/Rings and Things)
Vinci Antiques, London, W.1. B. St. Ant. C.
Vindolanda Antiques, Hexham, Northumb.
Vine Cottage Antiques, Streatley, Berks.
Vine House Antiques, Neston, Cheshire.
Vine House Antiques, Princes Risborough, Bucks.
Viney, Elizabeth, Stockbridge, Hants.
Vintage, London, W.1. G. Ant. Mkt.
Vintage Antique Market, The, Warwick, Warks.
Vintage Antiques, Crawley, W. Sussex.
Vintage Cameras Ltd., London, S.E.26.
Vintage Fishing Tackle Shop and Angling Art Gallery, Shrewsbury, Shrops.
Vintage Pine, Nottingham, Notts.
Vintage Sound, Bath, Avon. Gt. West. Ant. C.
Vintage and Value, Glasgow, Lanarks., Scot.
Vintage Wireless Co. Ltd., The, Bristol, Avon.
Vintagevale Ltd., Shrewsbury, Shrops.
Virginia Antique Galleries, Glasgow, Lanarks., Scot.
Vitos, London, W.1. G. Ant. Mkt.
Vivian Antiques, C., Nuneaton, Warks.
Vogue Antiques, Harrogate, N. Yorks. W. Pk. Ant. Pav.
Voke, Joanna, Guildford, Surrey. Ant. C.
Voke, Mrs. J.S.A., Guildford, Surrey. Ant. C.
Von Dahlen, Baroness, V., Long Melford, Suffolk.
Von der Berg, C., London, S.W.6. (Han-Shan Tang Ltd.).
Von Fullman, Paul, Malmesbury, Wilts.
von Hunersdorff, Richard, London, S.W.10.
Von Westenholz, P., London, S.W.1. (Westenholz Antiques)
Vosburgh, B., London, N.1 (Jubilee).
Vosper, R.J., Michinhampton, Glos.
Voss, A.G., Woodbridge, Suffolk.

W

W.13 Antiques, London, W.13.
W.H.E.A.P. Antiques, Worcester, Hereford and Worcs.
Waddington Antiques, John, Rawcliffe, N. Humberside.
Waddington, T., Leeds, W. Yorks. (Kingsway Antiques).
Wade Galleries, Deal, Kent.
Wade Antiques, Ray, Preston, Lancs.

Wade Antiques, Ray, Preston, Lancs. N.W. Ant. C.
Wade, Valerie, London, S.W.1.
Wadge Clocks, Chris, Salisbury, Wilts.
Wadham, Peter, Exeter, Devon.
Wadhwa, M., London, S.W.6.
Waggoner, J. and J., Bath, Avon (Aspidistra Antiques).
Wagstaff, Sue, Bath, Avon. Gt. West. Ant. C.
Wagstaff, William, Bath, Avon. Gt. West. Ant. C.
Wain, C.T. and M., Buckminster, Leics.
Wain, J.I., Ripon, N. Yorks.
Wain Antiques, J. and P., Tetbury, Glos.
Waite, C., Westcliff-on-Sea, Essex.
Wajzner, John, Southport, Merseyside. (The White Elephant).
Wake, Mrs. P., Uppingham, Leics.
Wakefield, R., London, S.W.15. (Thornhill Galleries Ltd.)
Wakelin, Michael and Helen Linfield, Petworth, W. Sussex.
Wakeman and Sons Ltd., A.E., Wolverhampton, W. Mids.
Wakeman Brothers, Redhill, Surrey.
Wakeman and Co. Ltd., D.J., Dorrington, Shrops.
Wakenham, Keith, Fakenham, Norfolk. Ant. C.
Walchli, S., Midhurst, W. Sussex.
Walcot Reclamation, Bath, Avon.
Walden Antique Jewellery, Catherine, Ingatestone, Essex.
Walden, Philip S., Settle, N. Yorks.
Waldy, J. and P., Petworth, W. Sussex.
Wale, B.C., Teignmouth, Devon.
Wale Ltd., Percy F., Leamington Spa, Warks.
Waley, Antony, Reigate, Surrey.
Waley, S. and A., Hookwood, W. Sussex.
Walford, G.W., London, N.1.
Walker, Mrs., Ceres, Fife, Scot.
Walker, Mrs., Newton Abbot, Devon. N. A. Ant. C.
Walker, A.C., Rainham, Kent.
Walker, C., London, S.W.3. (Walker-Bagshawe)
Walker, Mrs. D., Ewell, Surrey.
Walker, Miss Gay, Birley, Hereford and Worcs.
Walker Galleries Ltd., Harrogate, N. Yorks.
Walker Galleries Ltd., London, S.W.3.
Walker, G.R., Penrith, Cumbria.
Walker, H., Tetbury, Glos.
Walker, J., Perth, Perths., Scot.
Walker Antiques, John, Jesmond, Tyne and Wear.
Walker Gallery, Meldrum, London, S.W.6.
Walker, M. and D., Meldrum, London, S.W.6.
Walker, M.W., Coleraine, Co. Londonderry, N. Ireland.
Walker, Mrs. M.W., Portstewart, Co. Londonderry, N. Ireland.
Walker, P., Burford, Oxon.
Walker, R.K., Chipping Norton, Oxon.
Walker, S., Sheffield, S. Yorks. (Lynn's Antiques)

Wathew, Mrs. V.J., Taunton, Somerset.
Watkins Books Ltd., London, W.C.2.
Watkins, R. and J., Marlborough, Wilts.
Watling Antiques, Crayford, Gtr. London.
Watson, Mrs., Terrington St. Clement, Norfolk.
Watson, B., Bexhill-on-Sea, E. Sussex. Bex. Ant. C.
Watson, B.G., London, S.E.1. Ber. Ant. Whse.
Watson, Mrs. E., Norwich, Norfolk. (Yester-year).
Watson, Mrs. E., West Bromwich, W. Mids.
Watson, G.D., London, S.W.3. (Lewis M. Kaplan Associates Ltd.)
Watson, H. and P., Warwick, Warks.
Watson, J., Bath, Avon. Gt. West. Ant. C.
Watson, Mrs. L., Brighton, E. Sussex. (Kingsbury Warehouse).
Watson, M.E., Market Weighton, N. Humberside.
Watson, Paul, Sparkford, Somerset.
Watson, P. and E., Lymington, Hants.
Watt, Mrs. C., Gainsborough, Lincs.
Watt, Mrs. Elizabeth, Aberdeen, Aberd., Scot.
Watts, Chris, Cowes, I. of Wight.
Watts and Christensen, London, S.W.10.
Watts, C.E.H., London, S.W.1.
Watts, P.J., St. Austell, Cornwall.
Watts, S., Cheltenham, Glos. (Mirrors).
Watts, T.J., Norwich, Norfolk (The Whatnot).
Waveney Antiques, London, S.E.15.
Waveney Antiques Centre, Beccles, Suffolk.
Waverley Gallery, The, Aberdeen, Aberd., Scot.
Way, Mrs. J., Bures, Suffolk.
Way, R.E. and G.B., Newmarket, Suffolk.
Waymouth, A., Milverton, Somerset.
Waymouth, Joyce and Hay, Rachael, Fakenham, Norfolk. Ant. C.
Wayne, M., Bolton, Lancs.
Wayne, The Razor Man, Neil, Belper, Derbys.
Wayne Fine Art, Wylma, London, W.1.
Wayside Antiques, Duffield, Derbys.
Wayside Antiques, Tattershall, Lincs.
Weald Gallery, The, Brasted, Kent.
Wealden House Antiques, Wilton, Wilts.
Wearn and Son Ltd., R., London, S.W.3.
Weatherell and Sons, John, Harrogate, N. Yorks.
Weatherhead, N.F., Aylesbury, Bucks.
Weatherheads Bookshop Ltd., Aylesbury, Bucks.
Weatherill, F., Denholme, W. Yorks.
Weaver Antiques, Woburn, Beds. Wob. Ab. Ant. C.
Weaver Antiques, Glasgow, Lanarks., Scot. Regent Antiques.
Weaver, J., Gunthorpe, Notts.
Weaver, L., Aldeburgh, Suffolk.
Weaver, P., Aldeburgh, Suffolk.
Weaver, Trude, London, W.11.
Web, The, Cranborne, Dorset.
Web, A.M., London, W.11.
Webb, Graham, Brighton, E. Sussex.

Webb, J., Leigh-on-Sea, Essex.
Webb, J.V., London, N.1.
Webb, L., Guildford, Surrey.
Webb, Mrs. M., Winkleigh, Devon.
Webb, P.A., and V.K., Yarmouth, I. of Wight.
Webb, Roy, Wickham Market, Suffolk.
Webster, Tuxford, Notts.
Webster, A., Tuxford, Notts.
Webster, A. and S., Teignmouth, Devon.
Webster, E.T., Stonham Parva, Suffolk.
Webster, E.W., Bickerstaffe, Lancs.
Webster, G., Liverpool, Merseyside (Maggs Antiques).
Webster, M., Crosshills, N. Yorks.
Webster, M., Great Waltham, Essex.
Webster-Speakman, S.J., Cambridge, Cambs.
Weedon Antiques, Weedon, Northants.
Weightman, J., Bowness-on-Windermere, Cumbria.
Weijand, Karel, Farnham, Surrey.
Weiner, G., Brighton, E. Sussex.
Weiner aus Wien Military Antiques, Brighton, E. Sussex.
Weinreb Architectural Books Ltd., B., London, W.C.1.
Weinreb Ltd., B., London, W.C.1.
Weir, Abingdon, Oxon.
Weir, Douglas, Glasgow, Lanarks., Scot.
Weir Antiques, Gerald, Ipswich, Suffolk.
Weiss, A. and G., London, W.C.2. Lon. Silv. Vts.
Weiss Gallery plc., The, London, W.1.
Weiss, Peter K., London, W.C.2. Lon. Silv. Vts.
Welbeck Gallery, The, London, W.1.
Welbourne, Stephen and Sonia, Brighton, E. Sussex.
Welch, K. and A., Warminster, Wilts.
Weldon Antiques and Jewellery, Southport, Merseyside.
Weldon, H.W. and N.C., Southport, Merseyside.
Well House Antiques, Ewell, Surrey.
Well House Antiques, Tilston, Cheshire.
Wellard, Mary, London, W.1. G. Ant. Mkt.
Wellby Ltd., H.S., Haddenham, Bucks.
Wellby, C.S., Haddenham, Bucks.
Weller and Dufty Ltd., Birmingham, W. Mids. Birm. Ant. Centre.
Weller and Son, W.H., Eastbourne, E. Sussex.
Wellgate Antiques, Rotherham, S. Yorks.
Welling Antiques, Anthony, Ripley, Surrey.
Wellingham, Helga, London, W.1. G. Mews.
Wellington Gallery, London, N.W.8.
Wells, G., Wallingford, Oxon.
Wells, J., Crewkerne, Somerset.
Wells, J.H., Aberdeen, Aberd., Scot.
Wells, L., London, W.1. G. Mews.
Wells, L.I., East Dereham, Norfolk.
Wells, M.B., Tunbridge Wells, Kent (Frankham Gallery).
Wells, P.F., Buxton, Derbys.
Wells, William, G., Norwich, Norfolk.
Wellsthorpe, Mrs. V., London, W.11.
Wellsthorpe, Mrs. V., West Stour, Dorset.

Welsh, P., Brasted, Kent.
Welsh, R., Sandgate, Kent.
Wendover Antiques, Wendover, Bucks.
Wengraf, P., London, W.1 (Arcade Gallery Ltd.).
Wenlock Antiques, Much Wenlock, Shrops.
Wensum Antiques, Norwich, Norfolk.
Wentworth, J., London, W.11. (The Antique Textile Company).
Wertheim, Mr. and Mrs. C.D., London, W.8 (Japanese Gallery).
West, B., Canterbury, Kent.
West Bow Antiques, Edinburgh, Midloth., Scot.
West Country Antiques and Collectors Fairs, Ashburton, Devon.
West, C. and J., Hull, N. Humberside.
West End Antiques, Elgin, Moray, Scot.
West End Galleries, Buxton, Derbys.
West Farm Antiques, Orwell, Cambs.
West Felton Antiques, West Felton, Shrops.
West, J., St. Ives, Cornwall.
West Lancs. Antiques, Burscough, Lancs.
West London Antiques, London, W.4.
West Street Antiques, Dorking, Surrey.
West-Cobb Antiques Ltd., Mark J., London, S.W.19.
West-Cobb Antiques Ltd., Mark J., London, N.1.
West Park Antiques Pavilion, Harrogate, N. Yorks.
West, T., Whitehaven, Cumbria.
West Wales Antiques, Murton, W. Glam. Wales.
Westbourne Antiques, Westbourne, W. Sussex.
Westcott Antiques, Westcott, Surrey.
Westenholz Antiques, London, S.W.1.
Westerham Antique Centre, Westerham, Kent.
Westerham Galleries, Westerham, Kent.
Western Antiques, Shoreham-by-Sea, W. Sussex.
Westfield Antiques, Chesterfield, Derbys.
Westgarth Antiques, Mark, Lynton, Devon.
Westgarth, M.W., Lynton, Devon.
Westgate Street Antiques, Long Melford, Suffolk.
Westle, D. and J., Jesmond, Tyne and Wear.
Westley, D. and J., Uxbridge, Gtr. London.
Westley, John, Uxbridge, Gtr. London.
Westminster Group, London, W.1. G. Ant. Mkt.
Westmoreland Antiques, Harrogate, N. Yorks.
Weston Ltd., David, London, S.W.1.
Weston, D.A., London, S.W.1.
Weston, J., Oswestry, Shrops.
Weston, R. and P., Harrow, Gtr. London.
Weston Gallery, William, London, W.1.
Westrope, I., Birdbrook, Essex.
West-Skinn, R., Lincoln, Lincs.
West-Skinn, W., Lincoln, Lincs.
Westward Country Pine, Launceston, Cornwall.
Westwood Antiques, Cirencester, Glos.
Westwood, F., Petersfield, Hants.

Westwood Antiquarian Books, Mark, Glasbury, Powys, Wales.
Westwood, M. and C., Glasbury, Powys, Wales.
Wetherill, J., Northallerton, N. Yorks.
Weurman, Mr. and Mrs. L.W.A., Grantown-on-Spey, Morays., Scot.
Weybridge Antiques, Weybridge, Surrey.
Weysom, John, London, W.1. (Sue Brown) G. Mews.
Whadcock, B., Anstey, Leics.
Whaley, C.J.R., Great Pontin, Lincs.
Whaley, Roberson, Great Pontin, Lincs.
Whalley, Mrs. O.M., Eye, Suffolk.
Wharfe Antiques, Sheffield, S. Yorks.
Wharfedale Antiques, Ilkley, W. Yorks.
Wharton Antiques, Tim, Redbourn, Herts.
What the Dickens, London, E.11.
Whatnot, The, Norwich, Norfolk.
Whatnots, Strathblane, Stirls., Scot.
Whay, K. and D., Hoylake, Merseyside.
Wheatley Antiques, London, W.1. G. Ant. Mkt.
Wheatley, R., Kibworth Beauchamp, Leics.
Wheatley, Rodney and Michael, Gt. Yarmouth, Norfolk.
Wheeldon, Mrs. D., Ellesmere, Shrops.
Wheeldon, R.W. and E.H.G., Bridlington, N. Humberside.
Wheeler, G. and S., Stone, Staffs.
Wheeler, J. and C., Salisbury, Wilts.
Wheellock Arms and Armour, Herne Bay, Kent.
Wheelwright Antiques, Coggeshall, Essex.
Wheelwright Antiques, Fishlake, S. Yorks.
Wheldon and Wesley Ltd., Codicote, Herts.
Whitby Antiques, Peter, Lechlade, Glos.
White, London, N.W.8. Alf. Ant. Mkt.
White, A.W., Exeter, Devon.
White Boar Antiques and Books, Middleham, N. Yorks.
White, B.B., London, E.C.1.
White Cottage Antiques, Tern Hill, Shrops.
White D., Ramsbury, Wilts.
White Antiques, David, Godalming, Surrey.
White, D.D., Manfield, N. Yorks.
White, D. and Y., Godalming, Surrey.
White, E., Derby, Derbys.
White Elephant, The, Southport, Merseyside.
White, E. and B., Brighton, E. Sussex.
White Hart Gallery, Aylsham, Norfolk.
White Horse Antiques, Tunbridge Wells, Kent.
White House Antiques, The, High Halden, Kent.
White House Antiques, Princes Risborough, Bucks.
White House Farm Antiques, Easingwold, N. Yorks.
White and Howlett, London, S.W.6.
White, John, London, N.W.8. Alf. Ant. Mkt.
White, J., Wiveliscombe, Somerset.
White, J.C., White Waltham, Berks.
White, J. and G., Huby, N. Yorks.
White, J.I., Bridgnorth, Shrops.
White Lion Antiques, Ellesmere, Shrops.
White, P., Cranborne, Dorset.
White, P. Denver, Bournemouth, Dorset. (Peter Denver Antiques)

White, R., London, S.W.6. (White and Howlett)
White, Richard, London, W.11. G. Port.
White Roding Antiques, White Roding, Essex.
White, Rosemary and David, Charlton Horethorne, Somerset.
White, R.S., Cranbrook, Kent.
White, W., South Shields, Tyne and Wear.
Whitehall Antiques, Darwen, Lancs.
Whitehart Rare Books, F.E., London, S.E.23.
Whitehead, D. and V., Newark, Notts.
Whitehead, W.S.H., and Mrs. M.M., Lewes, E. Sussex.
Whitehouse Antiques Ltd., Worthing, W. Sussex.
Whitehouse, J.H. and J.P., Loughton, Essex.
Whitelaw and Sons Antiques, John, Auchterarder, Perths., Scot.
Whiteley, Mrs. D.P., Bangor-on-Dee, Clwyd, Wales.
Whiteside, R.J., Pershore, Hereford and Worcs.
Whitestone, S., London, W.1 (Bobinet Ltd.).
Whiteway, M., London, S.W.6. (Whiteway and Waldron Ltd.).
Whiteway, T.M., London, W.8 (Haslam and Whiteway).
Whiteway and Waldron Ltd., London, S.W.6.
Whiteway-Wilkinson, G.A., Maidencombe, Devon.
Whitfield, A. and S., Edinburgh, Midloth., Scot. (Calton Gallery).
Whitfield, P.C., London, W.1 (Tessiers Ltd.).
Whitfield, R.J., London, S.E.1. Ber. Ant. Whse.
Whitfield Antiques, William, Bromley, Gtr. London.
Whitford and Hughes, London, S.W.1.
Whitgift Galleries, Croydon, Gtr. London.
Whitmore, Great Malvern, Hereford and Worcs.
Whitney, R., Whitchurch, Shrops.
Whittaker, E., Henley-on-Thames, Oxon.
Whittaker, R.A. and Mrs. L.R., Angmering, W. Sussex.
Whittam, A.P.H. and C.O., St. Peter Port, Guernsey, C.I.
Whittingham, A., Bath, Avon. (Bath Saturday Antiques Mkt.).
Whittingham, E.N. and M., Bath, Avon. Gt. West. A. C. Wed. Mkt.
Whittington Galleries, Sutton, Gtr. London.
Whittock, P.E., Tingewick, Bucks.
Whitton, A.T., Exeter, Devon.
Whitworth, Mrs. G., Tisbury, Wilts.
Whitworth and O'Donnell Ltd., London, S.E.13.
Whotnots, Christchurch, Dorset.
Whybrow, John, Thatcham, Berks.
Whyte, John, Edinburgh, Midloth., Scot.
Whytock and Reid, Edinburgh, Midloth., Scot.
Wickens, Mrs. P., Sandwich, Kent.
Wickersley Antiques, Rotherham, S. Yorks.
Wickham, K., Wallasey, Merseyside.
Wickins, A. and M., Peasenhall, Suffolk.

Wickins, Mrs. C.J., Farnham, Surrey.
Wicks, Mrs. A.M., Lydiard Millicent, Wilts.
Wicks, Fiona, London, N.W.8. Alf. Ant. Mkt.
Widcombe, Antiques and Pine, Bath, Avon.
Widmerpool House Antiques, Maidenhead, Berks.
Wieliczko, J. and D., London, N.6.
Wiffen, C.A., Parkstone, Dorset.
Wiffen's Antiques, Parkstone, Dorset.
Wigdor, David, Brighton, E. Sussex.
Wigdor, D., London, W.1. G. Mews.
Wigek, Z., London, S.W.6. (House of Mirrors).
Wigg, B.K., Petworth, E. Sussex.
Wiggins and Sons Ltd., Arnold, London, W.9.
Wiggins, Peter, Chipping Norton, Oxon.
Wiggs, S.M., Poole, Dorset.
Wigington and Partners, Henry, Shipston-on-Stour, Warks.
Wigington, James, Stratford-upon-Avon, Warks.
Wigington, R.J., Stratford-upon-Avon, Warks.
Wiglesworth, Mrs. J.C., Kineton, Warks.
Wigmore's Ltd., Hindhead, Surrey.
Wigram, Francis, Penn, Bucks.
Wilberry Antiques, London, W.1.
Wilbourg, London, W.1. (Mankowitz). G. Mews.
Wilby, D.G. and M., Donington-on-Bain, Lincs.
Wilby Gallery, The, Northampton, Northants.
Wilcox, A.C., St. Peter Port, Guernsey, C.I.
Wild Goose Antiques, Modbury, Devon.
Wild, W.M., Long Melford, Suffolk.
Wilde, Sue, Sidmouth, Devon.
Wildenstein and Co. Ltd., London, W.1.
Wilding, Mr., Liverpool, Merseyside (E. Pryor and Son).
Wildish, Lt. Col. V. and Mrs. A., Dorney, Berks.
Wildman, I. and M., Edinburgh, Midloth., Scot.
Wildman, K., Bushey, Herts.
Wildman, P., Broughton, Peebles, Scot.
Wildman's Antiques, Edinburgh, Midloth., Scot.
Wildman's at Merlindale, Broughton, Peebles, Scot.
Wiles, Bret, Woodstock, Oxon.
Wiles, Courtney, Woburn, Beds. Wob. Ab. Ant. C.
Wiles Antiques Ltd., Courtney, Chardon, Bucks.
Wilkes, M. and Mrs. G. , London, N.W.1. (Lott-32).
Wilkes Antiques, Robert, Bath, Avon.
Wilkes Antiques, Robert, Stourbridge, W. Mids.
Wilkin, G.F., Honiton, Devon.
Wilkins, B. and M., London, W.1.
Wilkins, C.A., Holt, Norfolk.
Wilkins, D., Woking, Surrey.
Wilkins, Mrs. J., Witney, Oxon.
Wilkins Antiques, Joan, Witney, Oxon.
Wilkins and Wilkins, London, W.1.

Wilkinson, Mrs. A., Harrogate, N. Yorks.
(Ann-tiquities).
Wilkinson, A., Newhaven, E. Sussex.
Wilkinson Antiques, H.V., Windermere,
Cumbria.
Wilkinson, Mrs. P., Osgathorpe, Leics.
Wilkinson, P.J. and Mrs. J., Holme,
Cumbria.
Wilkinson and Son, R., London, S.E.23.
Wilkinson, S., London, W.11 (Chanticleer
Antiques.)
Wilkinson, S.P. and H.S., Lancaster, Lancs.
Wilkinson, Wynyard, R.T., East Dereham,
Norfolk.
Wilks-Jones, M.A., Conway, Gwynedd,
Wales.
Willan, David H., Kirkby Lonsdale, Cumbria.
Willatt, Mr. and Mrs. R.F., Heathfield,
E. Sussex.
Willcocks Antiques, London, S.W.3. Chen.
Gall.
Willcox, Michael, London, W.1. G. Mews.
Willder, S., Birmingham, W. Mids. (S.R.
Furnishing and Antiques).
Williams, Mrs. A., Todmorden, W. Yorks.
Williams, A.J., Bristol, Avon (Carnival
Antiques).
Williams, Mrs. A.L., Bournemouth, Dorset.
(Antiques Trade Warehouse).
Williams, A. and M., Bridgend, M Glam.,
Wales.
Williams, B., Cardiff, S. Glam., Wales.
(Antiques Unlimited).
Williams, Mrs. B., Gloucester, Glos.
Williams, Betty, Tredunnock, Gwent, Wales.
Williams, C., Bournemouth, Dorset (The
Antique Centre.)
Williams Antiquarian Bookseller, Christopher,
Bournemouth, Dorset.
Williams Antiques, Catherine, London,
S.W.3. Ant. Ant. Mkt.
Williams, E., Canterbury, Kent. Wales.
Williams, Frank, Burford, Oxon.
Williams, Jacqueline, Bath, Avon. B. Ant. Mkt.
Williams, J. and B., Gloucester, Glos.
Williams, John L., Haslemere, Surrey.
Williams Gold and Silversmiths, J. and S.,
Brighton, E. Sussex.
Williams, K., Much Hadham, Herts.
Williams, L., Eastbourne, E. Sussex.
Williams, Margaret, Woburn, Beds. Wob.
Ab. Ant. C.
Williams, R., London, S.W.1.
Williams, R.G. and J.R., London, W.1.
Williams, R. and Y., Coniston, Cumbria.
Williams and Son, London, W.1.
Williams, S.E., Bromley, Gtr. London.
Williams, S.N. and I.C., Merstham, Surrey.
Williams, Temple, London, W.8.
Williams Antiques Ltd., Thomas, Bideford,
Devon.
Williams, Winifred, London, S.W.1.
Williamson, I.A., Lynton, Devon.
Williamson and Co., R.G., Sorbie,
Wigtowns., Scot.
Willis (Antique Silver), Henry, London, W.1.
Willis Antique Clocks, Matthew,
Glastonbury, Somerset.

Willis Antiques and Curios, R., South
Shields, Tyne and Wear.
Williton Antiques, Williton, Somerset.
Willott Antiques, J., Leek, Staffs.
Willoughby, D.M., Northallerton, N. Yorks.
Willow Antiques, Ledbury, Hereford and
Worcs.
Willow Antiques, Oswestry, Shrops.
Willow Bank, Keighley, W. Yorks.
Willow Farm Antiques, Harlington, Beds.
Wills, C.J., Teddington, Gtr. London.
Wills, Mrs. H.J., Sheffield, S. Yorks.
(Fulwood Antiques).
Willson, Anthony, Hartley Wintney, Hants.
Willson, E., Hungerford, Berks. (Mary Bellis
Antiques).
Willson, Maurice and Nancy, Penperlleni,
Gwent, Wales.
Willy, London, W.1. G. Mews.
Wilsher, Miss M., Frinton, Essex.
Wilshire, J. and S., Great Missenden, Bucks.
Wilson, A., Woodstock, Oxon.
Wilson, A.M. and J., Glasgow, Lanarks.,
Scot. (Brown's Clocks Limited)
Wilson, D., Harewood, W. Yorks.
Wilson, Derick, Newton Abbot, Devon. N.A.
Ant. C.
Wilson, G., Lamberhurst, Kent.
Wilson and Son, H., Worthing, W. Sussex.
Wilson, H. Woods, London, W.1.
Wilson Antiques, Ian, London, S.E.15.
Wilson, Jeff, Leominster, Hereford and
Worcs. L. Ant. Mkt.
Wilson (Autographs) Ltd., John, Eynsham,
Oxon.
Wilson, J. and A.M., Glasgow, Lanarks.,
Scot. (Browns of Argyle Street Ltd.).
Wilson, J. and G., West Heslerton, N.
Yorks.
Wilson, J.M., Keswick, Cumbria.
Wilson, K., Ickleton, Cambs.
Wilson, M., Bath, Avon. Gt. West. A. C.
Wed. Mkt.
Wilson, M.J., Brancaster Staithe, Norfolk.
Wilson, N., New Romney, Kent.
Wilson, Nancy, Sandwich, Kent.
Wilson Ltd., O.F., London, S.W.3.
Wilson, O. and M.E., Bideford, Devon.
Wilson, P., Nayland, Suffolk.
Wilson Old, Antique and Reproduction Pine,
Paul, Hull, N. Humberside.
Wilson, Roger, Middle Wallop, Hants.
Wilson, R. and C., Petworth, W. Sussex.
Wilson and Sons, R.S., Boroughbridge,
N. Yorks.
Wilson, R.T., Chester, Cheshire.
Wilson, S., Fyfield, Hants.
Wilson, S., Penarth, S. Glam., Wales.
Wilson, Timothy D., Bawtry, S. Yorks.
Wilson, Wellesley, Chester, Cheshire.
Wilson, Mrs. W.F., Uckfield, E. Sussex.
Wilton House Gallery, Pocklington,
N. Humberside.
Wilton, K., Newton Abbot, Devon. N.A.
Ant. C.
Wiltshire, D.K. and R.M., Hurst Green,
E. Sussex.
Wimbledon Pine Co., London, S.W.19.

Wimborne Antiques, Wimborne Minster, Dorset.
Wimsett, G.R., Pembury, Kent.
Wimsett, P., Ramsgate, Kent.
Winchester House Antiques, Alresford, Hants.
Winchester, P., Newton Abbot, Devon. N.A. Ant. C.
Winckworth, Newton Abbot, Devon. N. A. Ant. C.
Windebank, R., Bath, Avon. (Quiet St. Antiques)
Windermere Antiques, Windermere, Cumbria.
Windermere and Bowness Dollmaking Co., Windermere, Cumbria.
Windhill Antiquary, The, Bishops Stortford, Herts.
Windle, Mrs. W.J., Bingley, W. Yorks.
Windley, R.A., Westcott, Surrey.
Windmill, The, Gateshead, Tyne and Wear.
Windmill Antiques, Bembridge, I. of Wight.
Windrush Antiques, Witney, Oxon.
Windsor Antique Gallery, Windsor and Eton, Berks.
Windsor Antiques Market and Fleamarket, Windsor and Eton, Berks.
Windsor Gallery, Lowestoft, Suffolk.
Windsor Gallery, David, Bangor, Gwynedd, Wales.
Windsor House Antiques (Leeds) Ltd., Leeds, W.Yorks.
Windsor, Mrs. L., Rugby, Warks.
Windsor Street Antiques Centre, Leamington Spa, Warks.
Window on the World, Galston, Ayr., Scot.
Winestone and Son Ltd., S., Largs, Ayr., Scot.
Winikus, J. and F., Sandgate, Kent.
Winkworth Antiques, Richard, Penryn, Cornwall.
Winkworth Antiques, Richard, Redruth, Cornwall.
Winkworth Antiques, Richard, Truro, Cornwall.
Winlove, A. and H.V.H., Kings Lynn, Norfolk.
Winlove, C., Kings Lynn, Norfolk.
Winram, J. and R., Middleton St. George, Durham.
Winstanley, T., Hindhead, Surrey.
Winston Galleries, Harrow, Gtr. London.
Winston Mac (Silversmith), Bury St. Edmunds, Suffolk.
Winstone, D., Bath, Avon. Gt. West. Ant. C.
Winstone Stamp Co. and S.D. Postcards, Bath, Avon. Gt. West. Ant. C.
Winter, Eveline, Rugeley, Staffs.
Winter, Mrs. F.J., Bath, Avon (Widcombe Antiques and Pine).
Winter Palace, The, London, W.8.
Winterbourne Antiques, Seend, Wilts.
Winterbourne, M., Harwell, Oxon.
Winterburn, Tony, High Wycombe, Bucks.
Winterdown Books, Folkestone, Kent.
Winters' Antiques, Weston-super-Mare, Avon.

Winters, R.N. and L.B., Weston-super-Mare, Avon.
Wirral Antiques, West Kirby, Merseyside.
Wirth, J. and P., London, S.W.19.
Wisborough Green Antiques, Wisborough Green, W. Sussex.
Wise, Mrs. D., Nottingham, Notts.
Wise, Mary, London, W.8.
Wise Owl Book Shop, The, Bristol, Avon.
Wisehall, Michael, Knutsford, Cheshire.
Wishing Well, Lancaster, Lancs.
Wiskin Antiques, Stansted, Essex.
Wiskin, K. and M, Stansted, Essex.
Witch Ball, The, Brighton, E. Sussex.
Witch Ball, The, London, W.11.
Witham Antiques, Witham, Essex.
Witham, Norman, Beckenham, Gtr. London.
Withers of Leicester, Leicester, Leics.
Withers, P. and B., Wolverhampton, W. Mids.
Witney Antiques, Witney, Oxon.
Witsend Antiques, Gunthorpe, Notts.
Witting, Lt. Col. and Mrs. D.W. Church Stretton, Shrops.
Woburn Abbey Antiques Centre, Woburn, Beds.
Woburn Fine Arts, Woburn, Beds.
Wolf Antiques Ltd., H. and B., Droitwich, Hereford and Worcs.
Wolf, H.G. and B.J., Droitwich, Hereford and Worcs.
Wolfe (Jewellery), London, W.C.2. Lond. Silv. Vts.
Wolfe, Mark B., Bath, Avon.
Wolfe, R., Harrogate, N. Yorks. (Omar (Harrogate) Ltd.).
Wolfers, D., London, S.W.13.
Wolff and Son Ltd., J., London, N.W.1.
Wolff and Son Ltd., J. Woburn, Beds. Wob. Ab. Ant. C.
Wood, A.P., Nailsworth, Glos.
Wood, Christopher, Kelso, Roxburgh., Scot.
Wood (Antiques) Ltd., Colin, Aberdeen, Aberd., Scot.
Wood Gallery, Christopher, London, S.W.1.
Wood, D.V., Brighton, E. Sussex (Zyzyx.)
Wood Antiques, Jonathan, Cartmel, Cumbria.
Wood Fine Art, Jeremy, Petworth, W. Sussex.
Wood House Antiques, Wiveliscombe, Somerset.
Wood, J.H., Aberdeen, Aberd., Scot.
Wood, Mrs. J.R., London, E.17.
Wood, J. and S., Cartmel, Cumbria.
Wood Antiques, Lilian, Great Urswick, Cumbria.
Wood, Mrs. M.A., Donyatt, Somerset.
Wood, Pat, Leek, Staffs.
Wood, P.W., Tregony, Cornwall.
Wood Antiques, Russell, London, S.E.10.
Wood, R.M. and P.A., Hatfield Broad Oak, Essex.
Wood, R.R. and Mrs., Westerham, Kent.
Wood, S., Leeds, W. Yorks. (The Antique Exchange)
Wood, S., London, W.3.
Wood, S., Osbournby, Lincs.

Wyrardisbury Antiques, Wraysbury, Berks.

X

Xanthus Gallery, Reymerston, Norfolk.

Y

Yacobi, B. and C., London, W.1 (Massada Antiques.)
Yandell, Mrs. A., Cambridge, Cambs. (Cottage Antiques).
Yardley, K.A.C., London, E.17.
Yardy, S., London, W.14.
Yarwood, Mr. and Mrs. G.E., Stoke-on-Trent, Staffs.
Yates Antiques, Gowerton, W. Glam., Wales.
Yates, Mrs. C.A., St. Annes-on-Sea, Lancs.
Yates, Mrs. D., York, N. Yorks. (Barker Court Antiques and Bygones).
Yates, Inez M.P., York, N. Yorks.
Yates, R., Gowerton, W. Glam., Wales.
Ye Olde Curio Shoppe, Dumfries, Dumfries., Scot.
Ye Olde Curiosity Shop, Denholme, W. Yorks.
Ye Olde Curiosity Shope, Aldeburgh, Suffolk.
Ye Olde Curiosity Shoppe, Godalming, Surrey.
Ye Olde Curiosity Shoppe, Guildford, Surrey.
Ye Olde Curiosity Shoppe, Hay-on-Wye, Powys, Wales.
Ye Olde Junk Shoppe, Shipton-under-Wychwood, Oxon.
Ye Olde Oak Chest, Auchnagatt, Aberd., Scot.
Ye Olde Saddlers Shoppe, Horrabridge, Devon.
Year Dot, Leeds, W. Yorks.
Yeates, Winston, Warwick, Warks. Smith St. A.C.
Yellow Lantern Antiques Ltd., Brighton, E. Sussex.
Yeo Antiques, Tetbury, Glos.
Yeo, G.A., Hazel Grove, Cheshire.
Yeo, W.B., Plaitford, Hants.
Yeoman, M.C., Salcombe, Devon.
Yesterday, London, W.1. G. Mews.
Yesterday Antiques, Tideswell, Derbys.
Yesterday Child, London, N.1.
Yesterdays, East Molesey, Surrey.
Yesterdays Antiques, Bushey, Herts.
'Yesterdays Furniture', York, N. Yorks.
Yesterday's Pine, Ampthill, Beds.
Yesterday's Pine, Shere, Surrey.
Yesterday's Pine, Woburn, Beds.
Yesteryear, Norwich, Norfolk.
Yesteryear Antiques, Glasgow, Lanarks., Scot. Vict. Vill.
Yewdale Antiques, Coniston, Cumbria.
Yewman, J.S. and F.M., Abridge, Essex.
Ying, W., London, W.8 (Cathay Antiques).
Yistelworth Antiques, Isleworth, Gtr. London.

Yon Antiques, York, N. Yorks.
York Antiques Centre, York, N. Yorks.
York Cottage Antiques, Helmsley, N. Yorks.
York Court Antiques, Southport, Merseyside.
York Galleries, Twickenham, Gtr. London.
York Gallery (Tunbridge Wells) Ltd., Tunbridge Wells, Kent.
York House Antiques, Ledbury, Hereford and Worcs.
York, J., Quorn, Leics.
Yorke, J.H., London, S.E.15.
Yorkshire Heritage Antiques, Leeds, W. Yorks.
Yorkshire Shipping Service, Kirk Hammerton, N. Yorks.
Young Antiques, Billericay, Essex.
Young, Aldric, Edinburgh, Midloth., Scot.
Young Antiques, Edinburgh, Midloth., Scot.
Young, A.E. and D.D., Coleford, Glos.
Young, A.R., Deal, Kent.
Young Antiques, Denis, Aberfeldy, Perths., Scot.
Young, D.E., and Mrs. J.M., Aberfeldy, Perths., Scot.
Young, J.S., Henfield, W. Sussex.
Young and Son (Antiques), John, Keswick, Cumbria.
Young, K. and R., Norwich, Norfolk.
Young Antiques, Lionel, Lewes, E. Sussex.
Young, Mavis, Newton Abbot, Devon. N.A. Ant. C.
Young Antiques, Peter, Darwen, Lancs.
Young Antiques, Peter, Saddleworth, Lancs.
Young Antiques, Robert, London, S.W.11.
Young Antiques, Robert, Norwich, Norfolk.
Young, Sue, Plymouth, Devon.
'Young Stephen' Ltd., London, W.1.
Young, T.C., Edinburgh, Midloth., Scot. (Young Antiques).
Young (Antiques) Ltd., Wm., Aberdeen, Aberd., Scot.
Yours and Mine, London, W.3.
Yoxford Antiques and Country Things, Yoxford, Suffolk.
Yoxford Bazaar, Yoxford, Suffolk.

Z

Zadah Persian Carpet Ltd., London, W.1.
Zafer, R.D., Twickenham, Gtr. London.
Zambrzycki, M., Bath, Avon. Gt. West Ant. C.
Zammit and Sons, G., Manchester, Lancs. (Britannia Antiques).
Zebra, London, N.W.6.
Zeno Booksellers and Publishers, London, W.C.2.
Zentner, F., London, W.C.1.
Zinni-Lask, J., London, N.W.1. (The Patchwork Dog and The Calico Cat Ltd.)
Zwan Antiques, Timberscombe, Somerset.
Zwemmer Ltd., A., London, W.C.2.
Zwolinska, Zophie, London, W.11. G. Port.
Zyzyx, Brighton, E. Sussex.

SPECIALIST DEALERS

Most antique dealers in Britain sell a wide range of goods from furniture, through porcelain and pottery, to pictures, prints and clocks. Much of the interest in visiting antique shops comes from this diversity. However, there are a smaller number of dealers who obtain their livelihood by specialising, and the following is a list of these dealers. Most of them will always have in stock a representative selection of the items under their classification.

The figure appearing after the name of the dealer indicates the page on which his entry lies in the Guide. The full address of the dealer, together with his telephone number, can be found from the entry. Again, we would like to repeat the advice given in the introduction that, if readers are looking for a particular object, they would be well advised to telephone around before making long journeys.

CLASSIFICATIONS

Antique Centres
Antiquities
Antiquarian Books (see Books)
Architectural Items
Arms and Militaria
Art Deco and Art Nouveau
Barometers
Books (Antiquarian)
Brass (see Metalwork)
Bronzes
Carriages and Cars
Carpets and Rugs
Chinese Art (see Oriental Art)
Clocks and Watches
Coins and Medals
Dolls and Toys
Furniture
   Country
   Georgian
   Oak
   Pine
   Victorian
Garden Furniture (see Sculpture)
Glass
Horn Items
Icons
Japanese Art (see Oriental Art)
Jewellery (see Silver and Jewellery)
Lighting
Maps and Prints
Metalwork
Miniatures

Mirrors
Musical Instruments and Literature
Nautical Instruments (see Scientific Instruments)
Needlework (see Tapestries)
Netsuke (see Oriental Art)
Oil Paintings
Oriental Art
Photographs and Equipment
Playing Cards
Porcelain
Pottery (see also Porcelain)
Prints (see Maps)
Rugs (see Carpets)
Russian Art (see Icons)
Scientific Instruments
Sculpture
Shipping Goods and Period Furniture for the Trade
Silver and Jewellery
Sporting Items and Associated Memorabilia
Sporting Paintings and Prints
Stamps
Tapestries and Needlework
Tools (including Needlework and Sewing)
Toys (see Dolls and Toys)
Trade Dealers (see Shipping Goods)
Treen
Vintage Cars (see Carriages and Cars)
Watercolours
Wholesale Dealers (see Shipping Goods)
Wine Related Items

Antiques Centres

Art Deco and Art Nouveau

Editions Graphiques Gallery, London, W.1 — 41
Libra Designs, London, W.1 — 51
'Young Stephen' Ltd., London W.1 — 62
John Jesse and Irena Laski Ltd., London, W.8 — 68
Joan and Clive Collins, London, W.11 — 75
Jones, London, W.11 — 78
Cobra and Bellamy, London, S.W.1 — 88
Lewis M. Kaplan Associates Ltd., London, S.W.3 — 107
L'Odeon, London, S.W.3 — 108
The Studio, London, N.1 — 143
Tadema, London, N.1 — 143
Lyons Gallery, London, N.W.6 — 152
Peter and Debbie Gooday, Richmond, Gtr. London — 171
Brunel Antiques, Bristol, Avon — 188
Hirst Antiques, Christchurch, Dorset — 351
Armstrong-Davis Gallery, Arundel, Sussex West — 693
Castle Antiques, Warwick, Warks — 717
The Modern Movement, Edinburgh, Scotland — 810

Barometers (Most clock dealers also sell barometers)

Grimaldi, London, W.1 — 47
John Carlton Smith, London, S.W.1 — 97
E. Hollander, London, S.W.3 — 107
Patric Capon, London, N.1 — 138
Strike One Ltd., London, N.1 — 143
The Old Malthouse, Hungerford, Berks — 205
Anthony Baker Antiques, Alderley Edge, Cheshire — 231
Derek Rayment Antiques, Barton, Cheshire — 231
The Antique Shop, Stockton Heath, Cheshire — 243
Antiques Etc., Stretton, Cheshire — 243
Peter Bosson Antiques, Wilmslow, Cheshire — 243
Castle Antiques, Cheltenham, Glos — 386
Saxton House Gallery, Chipping Campden, Glos — 389
Gastrell House, Tetbury, Glos — 406
Bryan Clisby, Hartley Wintney, Hants — 414
Gerald E. Marsh (Antique Clocks), Winchester, Hants — 426
Nigel Coleman Antiques, Brasted, Kent — 467
Bernard G. House, Wells, Somerset — 619
Edward A. Nowell, Wells, Somerset — 620
Suthbrough Hall, Long Melford, Suffolk — 646
A.E. Gould and Sons (Antiques) Ltd., East Horsley, Surrey — 659
Adrian Alan Ltd., Brighton, Sussex East — 676
P. Carmichael, Brighton, Sussex East — 678
P.A. Oxley Antique Clocks, Cherhill, Wilts — 733

Books (Antiquarian)

M. & R. Glendale, London, W.1 — 43
G. Heywood Hill Ltd., London, W.1 — 49
E. Joseph, London, W.1 — 50
Maggs Bros. Ltd., London, W.1 — 51
Marlborough Rare Books Ltd., London, W.1 — 52
Jonathan Potter Ltd., London, W.1 — 56
Bernard Quaritch Ltd., London, W.1 — 56
Robert G. Sawers, London, W.1 — 57
Chas J. Sawyer, London, W.1 — 57
Henry Sotheran Ltd., London, W.1 — 58
The Holland Press Ltd., London, W.2 — 62
Hosains Books and Antiques, London, W.2 — 62
D. Mellor and A.L. Baxter, London, W.8 — 70
Demetzy Books, London, W.11 — 76
Peter Eaton (Booksellers) Ltd., London W.11 — 76
J. Allen and Co., London, S.W.1 — 84
Cavendish Rare Books, London, S.W.1 — 87
Pickering and Chatto Ltd., London, S.W.1 — 96
Saint George's Gallery Books Ltd., London, S.W.1 — 96
Thomas E. Schuster, London, S.W.1 — 96
Sims, Reed and Fogg Ltd., London, S.W.1 — 97
Spink and Son Ltd., London, S.W.1 — 97
Chelsea Rare Books, London, S.W.3 — 104
Robin Greer, London, S.W.3 — 107
Heraldry Today, London, S.W.3 — 107
Stephanie Hoppen Ltd., London, S.W.3 — 107
Alan G. Thomas, London, S.W.3 — 109
Thomas Heneage, London, S.W.4 — 109
John Boyle and Co., London, S.W.10 — 120
Richard von Hünersdorff, London, S.W.10 — 121
Harriet Wynter Ltd., London, S.W.10 — 122
Vandeleur Antiquarian Books, London, S.W.14 — 124
The Warwick Leadley Gallery, London, S.E.10 — 130
Rogers Turner, London, S.E.10 — 131
F.E. Whitehart Rare Books, London, S.E.23 — 132
J. Ash (Rare Books), London, E.C.3 — 136
J. Clarke-Hall Ltd., London, E.C.4 — 136
Intercol London, London, N.1 — 141
G.W. Walford, London, N.1 — 144
Keith Harding Antiques, London, N.7 — 145
Barrie Marks Ltd., London, N.10 — 145
East-Asia Co., London, N.W.1 — 148
Leon Drucker, London, N.W.2 — 149
P.G. de Lotz, London, N.W.3 — 150
The Flask Bookshop, London, N.W.3 — 150
Otto Haas, London, N.W.3 — 150
Clifford E. King, London, N.W.3 — 151
Frederick Mulder, London, N.W.3 — 151

Blackwell's Rare Books, Fyfield, Oxon — 574

D. Parikian, Oxford, Oxon — 578

A. Rosenthal Ltd., Oxford, Oxon — 578

J. Thornton and Son, Oxford, Oxon — 579

Titles Old and Rare Books, Oxford, Oxon. — 579

Robin Waterfield Ltd., Oxford, Oxon. — 579

Museum Bookshop, Woodstock, Oxon. — 586

R.G. Wragg, Cheddleton, Staffs — 624

Claude Cox at College Gateway Bookshop, Ipswich, Suffolk — 639

Thomas Thorp Antiquarian Books, Guildford, Surrey — 664

Charles W. Traylen, Guildford, Surrey — 664

Robinson's Bookshop Ltd., Brighton, Sussex East — 681

Howes Bookshop, Hastings, Sussex East — 685

Rodney and Susan Otway, Bradford-on-Avon, Wilts — 732

Clive Farahar and Sophie Dupré, Calne, Wilts. — 732

Hilmarton Manor Press, Calne, Wilts — 733

Ronald Cook, Little Horton, Wilts — 735

Heraldry Today, Ramsbury, Wilts — 739

The Barn Book Supply, Salisbury, Wilts — 739

D.M. Beach, Salisbury, Wilts — 739

Victoria Bookshop, Swindon, Wilts — 741

Great Ayton Bookshop, Great Ayton, Yorkshire North — 747

Rippon Bookshop, Harrogate, Yorkshire North — 758

Archie Miles Ltd., Pateley Bridge, Yorkshire North — 764

Potterton Books, Thirsk, Yorkshire North — 767

Barbican Bookshop, York, Yorkshire North — 767

Discovery Fine Arts Ltd., York, Yorkshire North — 769

McDowell, Daniel, York, Yorkshire North — 769

Ken Spelman, York, Yorkshire North — 769

Taikoo Books Ltd., York, Yorkshire North — 769

John R. Wrigley, Ecclesfield, Yorkshire South — 771

Alan Hill Books, Sheffield, Yorkshire South — 774

John Blench and Son, St. Helier, Jersey, C.I — 791

Thesaurus (Jersey) Ltd., St. Helier, Jersey, C.I — 791

I.G. Anderson, Dumfries, Scotland — 804

James Thin (Booksellers), Edinburgh, Scotland — 811

John Smith and Son (Glasgow) Ltd., Glasgow, Scotland — 815

Glance Back, Chepstow, Gwent, Wales — 836

Richard Booth's Bookshop, Hay-on-Wye, Powys, Wales — 840

Brass (See Metalwork)

Bronzes

J. Christie, London, W.1 — 40

The Sladmore Gallery, London, W.1 — 58

Claude Bornof, London, W.2 — 62

Victor Franses Gallery, London, S.W.1 — 89

Rodd McLennan, London, S.W.1 — 93

Peter Nahum, London, S.W.1 — 94

Gerald Spyer and Son (Antiques) Ltd., London, S.W.1 — 97

Trove, London, S.W.1 — 97

Anthony James & Son Ltd., London, S.W.3 — 107

Apollo Galleries, Croydon, Greater London — 166

West End Galleries, Buxton, Derbys — 316

Armstrong-Davis Gallery, Arundel, Sussex West — 693

John G. Morris Ltd., Petworth, Sussex West — 701

Carriages and Cars

Brian R. Verrall and Co., London, S.W.17 — 126

Carpets and Rugs

Avakian Oriental Carpets Ltd., London, W.1 — 35

Attilio Gilberti, London, W.1 — 42

Hadji Baba Ancient Art, London, W.1 — 48

C. John (Rare Rugs) Ltd., London, W.1 — 50

Alexander Juran and Co., London, W.1 — 50

Kennedy Carpets and Kelims, London, W.1. — 50

Mayfair Carpet Gallery Ltd., London, W.1 — 54

P. and O. Carpets Ltd., London, W.1 — 55

Portman Carpets, London, W.1 — 56

Rare Carpets Gallery, London, W.1 — 56

Shaikh and Son (Oriental Rugs) Ltd., London, W.1 — 57

Vigo Carpet Gallery, London, W.1 — 60

Vigo-Sternberg Galleries, London, W.1 — 60

Zadah Persian Carpets Ltd., London, W.1 — 62

S. Franses Ltd., London, W.2 — 62

M.L. Waroujian, London, W.6 — 64

Bohun and Busbridge, London, W.8 — 65

Coats Oriental Carpets and Co. Ltd., London W.8 — 66

The Textile Gallery, London, W.9 — 72

Clive Loveless, London, W.10 — 74

David Black Oriental Carpets, London, W.11 — 74

Chantry Galleries, London, W.11 — 75

J. Fairman (Carpets) Ltd., London, W.11 — 77

Benardout, Raymond, London, S.W.1 — 86

S. Franses (Carpets) Ltd., London, S.W.1 — 89

Victor Franses Gallery, London, S.W.1 — 89

Anglo Persian Carpet Co., London, S.W.7 — 119

Benardout and Benardout, London, S.W.7 — 119

Elichaoff Oriental, London, N.5 — 144

Y. and B. Bolour, London, N.W.5 — 151

Joseph Lavian, London, N.W.5 — 152

M. and M. Oriental Gallery Ltd., London, N.W.5 — 152

Robert Stephenson, London, N.W.6 — 153

Robert Franses and Sons, London, N.W.8 — 156

Arts of Living, Bath, Avon — 177

J.L. Arditti, Christchurch, Dorset — 351

Orbell House Gallery, Castle Hedingham, Essex — 364

Homer Oriental Rugs, Cheltenham, Glos — 388

Eric Pride, Oriental Rugs, Cheltenham, Glos. — 388

Thornborough Galleries, Cirencester, Glos — 392

Dunkley Carpets and Pictures, Liss, Hants — 417

Desmond and Amanda North, East Peckham, Kent — 471

Orchard House Oriental Rugs, Reepham, Norfolk — 542

Oriental Carpets, Swanton Abbot, Norfolk — 545

Oriental Carpets, Oxford, Oxon — 578

Lindfield Galleries Ltd., Lindfield, Sussex West — 698

Omar (Harrogate) Ltd., Harrogate, Yorkshire North — 756

London House Oriental Rugs and Carpets, Boston Spa, Yorkshire West — 778

Whytock and Reid, Edinburgh, Scotland — 811

Chinese Art (See Oriental Art)

Clocks and Watches

Asprey p.l.c., London, W.1 — 35

N. Bloom and Son (Antiques) Ltd., London, W.1 — 36

Bobinet Ltd., London, W.1 — 36

Garrard and Co. Ltd. (The Crown Jewellers), London, W.1 — 42

Graus Antiques, London, W.1 — 43

Grimaldi, London, W.1 — 47

Ronald A. Lee (Fine Arts) Ltd., London, W.1 — 50

Mallett at Bourdon House Ltd., London, W.1 — 52

The Badger, London, W.5 — 64

Philip and Bernard Dombey, London, W.8 — 67

Raffety and Huber, London, W.8 — 70

Camerer Cuss and Co., London, S.W.1 — 87

E. Hollander, London, S.W.3 — 107

Hymore-Hodson, London, S.W.3 (Chenil Gall.) — 105

Aubrey Brocklehurst, London, S.W.7 — 119

Capital Clocks, London, S.W.8 — 120

The Clock Clinic Ltd., London, S.W.15 — 124

R.E. Rose, London, S.E.9 — 130

Ronald Benjamin Antiques, London, E.C.1 — 134

City Clocks, London, E.C.1 — 134

As Time Goes By, London, N.1 — 136

Bushe Antiques, London, N.1 — 137

Patric Capon, London, N.1 — 138

Strike One Ltd., London, N.1 — 143

North London Clock Shop Ltd., London, N.5 — 145

Keith Harding Antiques, London, N.7 — 145

Mr. Temple Brooks, London, N.W.6 — 151

Michael Sim, Chislehurst, Gtr. London — 166

Apollo Galleries, Croydon, Gtr. London — 166

Clock Investment, Orpington, Gtr. London, — 170

Onslow Clocks, Twickenham, Gtr. London — 174

John Croft Antiques, Bath, Avon — 180

Quiet St. Antiques, Bath, Avon — 186

Smith and Bottrill, Bath, Avon — 186

John and Carole Hawley, Clevedon, Avon — 192

James R. Cornish, Langford, Avon — 192

Richard Barder Antiques, Hermitage, Berks — 204

Times Past Antiques Ltd., Windsor and Eton, Berks — 211

Wyrardisbury Antiques, Wraysbury, Berks — 211

Norton Antiques, Beaconsfield, Bucks — 214

Period Furniture Showrooms, Beaconsfield, Bucks — 214

M.V. Tooley, Great Missenden, Bucks — 215

Market Place Antiques, Olney, Bucks — 217

Alan Martin Antiques, Olney, Bucks — 217

Rodney T. Firmin, Cambridge, Cambs — 224

S. J. Webster-Speakman, Cambridge, Cambs — 224

Timecraft, St. Ives, Cambs — 227

Adams Antiques, Chester, Cheshire — 232

Boodle and Dunthorne Ltd., Chester, Cheshire — 232

Chester Antiques, Chester, Cheshire — 232

Cheshire Antiques, Macclesfield, Cheshire — 237

Chapel Antiques, Nantwich, Cheshire — 239

Coppelia Antiques, Plumley, Cheshire — 240

The Antique Shop, Stockport, Cheshire — 241

The Antique Shop, Stockton Heath, Cheshire — 243

Antiques Etc., Stretten, Cheshire — 243

The Antiques Shop, Whitegate, Cheshire — 243

Peter Bosson Antiques, Wilmslow, Cheshire — 245

Paul Jennings Antiques, Angarrack, Cornwall — 247

Charles Jackson Antiques, Penzance, Cornwall — 250

Coins and Medals

Georgian (1714—1830)

Adams Antiques, St. Ives, Cambs — 227

The Golden Drop Antiques, Warboys, Cambs — 228

Richmond Galleries, Chester, Cheshire — 234

The Old Pine Shop, Congleton, Cheshire — 234

Greenwoods of Oulton Mill, Little Budworth, Cheshire — 237

Stewart Evans, Malpas, Cheshire — 239

Westward Country Pine, Launceston, Cornwall — 249

David Patterson Antiques, Lostwithiel, Cornwall — 249

Pine and Country Antiques, North Petherwin, Cornwall — 250

All Things Bright and Beautiful, St. Just, Cornwall — 251

Utopia Antiques, Holme, Cumbria — 304

Cumberland Pine, Penrith, Cumbria — 308

Old Farmhouse Furniture, Parwick, Derbys — 321

Drawers, Buckfastleigh, Devon — 325

Country Cottage Furniture, Modbury, Devon — 331

Daniels House Antiques, Beaminster, Dorset — 345

Castleton Country Furniture, Sherborne, Dorset — 354

Wye Antiques, Stow-on-the-Wold, Glos — 404

Paul Wilson Old and Antique Pine, Hull, N. Humberside — 457

Enloc Antiques, Colne, Lancs — 492

Christopher Roper's Pine Shop, Leicester, Leics — 505

Richard Kimbell Antiques, Market Harborough, Leics. — 507

John Dereham, Earsham, Norfolk — 534

Richard Kimbell Antiques, Desborough, Northants — 548

The Farmhouse, Oxford, Oxon — 576

Ye Olde Junk Shoppe, Shipton-under-Wychwood, Oxon — 579

The Antique Shop, Wallingford, Oxon — 580

Domus, Castle Cary, Somerset — 610

Pennard House, East Pennard, Somerset — 612

Chalon U.K. Ltd., Hambridge, Somerset — 613

Anvil Antiques, Leek, Staffs. — 625

Directmoor Ltd., Oakamoor, Staffs — 626

Michael Moore Antiques, Clare, Suffolk — 632

Joyce Hardy Pine and Country Furniture, Hacheston, Suffolk — 635

Pine and Design, Balcombe, Sussex West — 694

Pine and Country Antiques, Washington, Sussex West — 704

Pine Finds, Bishop Monkton, Yorkshire North — 745

Daleside Antiques, Harrogate, Yorkshire North — 750

James and Pat Ash, Llandeilo, Dyfed, Wales — 830

The Hay Galleries Ltd., Hay-on-Wye, Powys, Wales — 840

Victorian (1830-1901)

Connaught Galleries, London, W.2 — 62

Zal Davar, London, S.W.6 — 114

Furniture Cave, London, S.W.10 — 120

A. and J. Fowle, London, S.W.16 — 125

Bermondsey Antiques, London, S.E.1 — 127

Tower Bridge Antique Warehouse Ltd., London, S.E.1 — 128

Butchoff Antiques, London, S.E.15 — 131

Tony Ellis Antiques, London, N.5 — 144

Keith Atkinson, Croydon, Gtr. London — 166

Brazil Antiques Ltd., Croydon, Gtr. London — 166

Phelps Ltd., Twickenham, Gtr. London — 174

Mendip Antiques, Bath, Avon (Gt. West Ant. C.) — 183

Haughey Antiques, Kirkby Stephen, Cumbria — 306

Louis Lipman, Brentwood, Essex — 364

Pretty Chairs, Portsmouth, Hants — 420

Dudley Hume, Brighton, Sussex East — 679

Geary Antiques, Leeds, Yorkshire West — 784

A.S. Deuchar and Son, Perth, Scotland — 822

See also Shipping Goods and Period Furniture for the Trade.

Garden Furniture (See Sculpture)

Glass

Arenski, London, W.1 — 35

Denton Antiques, London, W.1 — 41

Thomas Goode and Co. (London) Ltd., London, W.1 — 43

Jeanette Hayhurst, London, W.1 — 49

Howard Phillips, London, W.1 — 56

S.W. Parry (Old Glass), London, W.2 — 63

Delomosne and Son Ltd., London, W.8 — 67

Eila Grahame, London, W.8 — 67

W.G.T. Burne (Antique Glass) Ltd., London, London, S.W.3 — 104

Pryce and Brise Antiques, London, S.W.6 — 117

R. Wilkinson & Son, London, S.E.23 — 132

Mark J. West — 144b Antiques Ltd., London, N.1 — 144

Somervale Antiques, Midsomer Norton, Avon — 192

Todd & Austin Antiques of Winchester, Hants — 427

J. and J. Hutton, Berkhamsted, Herts. — 445

Sun House Antiques, Long Melford, Suffolk — 646

The Rendezvous Gallery, Aberdeen, Scotland — 300

William MacAdam, Edinburgh, Scotland — 809

Horn Items

Horn Antiques, Churt, Surrey — 656

Icons
The Mark Gallery, London, W.2 — 63
Maria Andipa Icon Gallery, London, S.W.3 — 99
Temple Gallery, London, S.W.3 — 109

Japanese Art (See Oriental Art)

Jewellery (See Silver and Jewellery)

Lighting
W. Sitch & Co. Ltd., London, W.1 — 57
David Malik, London, W.8 — 70
Jones, London, W.11 — 78
Christopher Wray, London, S.W.6 — 119
Period Brass Lights, London, S.W.7 — 119
M. Turpin Ltd., London, S.W.7 — 119
R. Wilkinson & Son, London, S.E.23 — 132
Oddiquities, London, S.E.23 — 132
Ian & Dianne McCarthy, Clutton, Avon — 192
Jeanne Temple Antiques, Milton Keynes, Bucks, 216
The Lantern Shop, Sidmouth, Devon — 336
Kellys of Knaresborough, Knaresborough, N. Yorks — 762
Alic Lighting & Antiques, Cardiff, S. Glam., Wales — 832

Maps and Prints
Baskett and Day, London, W.1 — 36
Burlington Gallery Ltd., London, W.1 — 40
Lumley Cazalet Ltd., London, W.1 — 40
Andrew Edmunds, London, W.1 — 41
Garton and Cooke, London, W.1 — 42
Omniphil (Grays A. Mkt.), London W.1 — 44
Jonathan Potter Ltd., London, W.1 — 56
Spring Antiques, London, W.1 — 58
Tooley, Adams and Co. Ltd., London, W.1 — 58
Peter Loveday Prints, London, W.11 — 78
Old London Gallery, London, S.W.1 — 94
Old Maps and Prints, London, S.W.1 — 94
Paul Mason Gallery, London, S.W.1 — 94
O'Shea Gallery, London, S.W.1 — 96
Thomas E. Schuster, London, S.W.1 — 96
Richard Hewlett Gallery, London, S.W.3 — 107
The Warwick Leadlay Gallery, London, S.E.10 — 130
J. Ash (Rare Books), London, E.C.3 — 136
Intercol, London, N.1 — 141
Finbar MacDonnell, London, N.1 — 142
Sebastian D'Orsai Ltd., London, W.C.1 — 158
The Print Room, London, W.C.1 — 158
Waterloo Fine Arts Ltd., London, W.C.1 — 159
Clive A. Burden Ltd., London, W.C.2 — 160
Cartographia Ltd., London, W.C.2 — 160
Robert Douwma (Prints and Maps) Ltd., London, W.C.2 — 160
Grosvenor Prints, London, W.C.2 — 161
Lantern Gallery, Bath, Avon — 186
Omniphil Ltd., Chesham, Bucks — 215
Penn Barn, Penn, Bucks — 218
Collectors Treasures Ltd., Wendover, Bucks — 219

Benet Gallery, Cambridge, Cambs — 221
Jean Pain Gallery, Cambridge, Cambs — 224
Attic Gallery, Wisbech, Cambs — 229
Richard A. Nicholson, Chester, Cheshire — 234
John Maggs, Falmouth, Cornwall — 247
C. Samuels & Sons Ltd., Exeter, Devon — 328
The Little Lantern Shop, Sidmouth, Devon — 336
Oldfield, Southampton, Hants — 423
Leycester Map Galleries Ltd., Arnesby, Leics — 502
Leicestershire Sporting Gallery, Lubenham, Leics — 506
Grafton Country Pictures, Oakham, Leics — 508
Harlequin Gallery, Lincoln, Lincs — 518
Lyver & Boydell Galleries, Liverpool, Merseyside — 526
Anthony Reed, Norwich, Norfolk — 540
The Barnard Gallery, Everton, Notts — 559
Magna Gallery, Oxford, Oxon — 576
Sanders of Oxford Ltd., Oxford, Oxon — 579
Steve Sutcliffe, Market Drayton, Shrops — 604
Newmarket Gallery, Newmarket, Suffolk — 648
Horn Antiques, Churt, Surrey — 656
Julia Holmes, Antique Maps and Prints, Haslemere, Surrey — 664
Reigate Galleries Ltd., Reigate, Surrey — 668
The Old Paint Shop, Alfriston, Sussex East — 675
The Witch Ball, Brighton, Sussex East — 683
Ivan R. Deverall, Uckfield, Sussex East — 691
D.M. Beach, Salisbury, Wilts — 739
The Farthing Gallery, Salisbury, Wilts — 739
Barton-Booth Gallery, Warminster, Wilts — 741
McTague of Harrogate, Harrogate, Yorkshire North — 756
Craven Books, Skipton, Yorkshire North — 766
Porter Prints (Broomhill), Sheffield, Yorkshire South — 775
John Grant Est. 1874, Edinburgh, Scotland — 809
Ovell Prints Ltd., Llandovery, Dyfed, Wales — 830
Glance Back, Chepstow, Gwent, Wales — 836
Tudor Rose and Mona Antiques, Beaumaris, Gwynedd, Wales — 838
Maps, Prints and Books, Brecon, Powys, Wales — 840

Metalwork
Maurice Braham Ltd., London, W.8 — 65
Jack Casimir Ltd., London, W.11 — 75
Alistair Sampson Antiques, London, S.W.3 — 108
Christopher Bangs, London, S.W.11 — 122

House of Steel, London, N.1 — 141
Cannon Antiques, Bristol, Avon — 188
Christopher Sykes Antiques, Woburn, Beds
— 199
Berkshire Metal Finishers Ltd., Sandhurst,
Berks — 207
Sundial Antiques, Amersham, Bucks — 213
Albert Bartram, Chesham, Bucks — 214
A. and E. Foster, Naphill, Bucks — 217
Margaret Bedi Antiques, Billingham,
Cleveland — 245
Stable Antiques, Sedbergh, Cumbria — 309
Paul Cater Antiques, Moreton-in-Marsh, Glos
— 396
J. and J. Caspall Antiques, Stow-on-the-
Wold, Glos — 400
Country Life Antiques, Stow-on-the-Wold,
Glos — 401
Keith Hockin (Antiques) Ltd., Stow-on-the-
Wold, Glos — 402
Huntington Antiques Ltd., Stow-on-the-
Wold, Glos — 402
Prichard Antiques, Winchcombe, Glos —
409
Arthur Brett and Sons Ltd., Norwich,
Norfolk — 539
Peter Norden Antiques, Burford, Oxon —
569
Key Antiques, Chipping Norton, Oxon —
571
Mike Ottrey Antiques, Dorchester-on-
Thames, Oxon — 573
Robin Bellamy, Witney, Oxon — 582
Pine and Country Antiques, Washington,
Sussex West — 704
Rupert Gentle Antiques, Milton Lilbourne,
Wilts — 738
Windsor House Antiques (Leeds) Ltd.,
Leeds, Yorkshire West — 785
Peter Philp, Cardiff, S. Glam., Wales — 834

Miniatures
Limner Antiques, London, W.1 (B. St. Ant.
C.) — 38
Maurice Asprey Ltd., London, S.W.1 — 84
Simon Brett, Moreton-in-Marsh, Glos — 395
Angharad's Antiques, Shotton, Clwyd,
Wales — 829

Mirrors (Most furniture dealers also sell Mirrors)
Anno Domini Antiques, London, S.W.1 —
84
Fernandes and Marche, London, S.W.1 —
89
Alec Ossowski, London, S.W.1 — 96
Gerald Spyer, London, S.W.1 — 97
Norman Adams Ltd., London, S.W.3 — 99
Anthony James, London, S.W.3 — 107
Clifford Wright, London, S.W.3 — 109
House of Mirrors, London, S.W.6 — 116
P.L. James, London, S.W.6 — 116
Alec Ossowski, London, S.W.6 — 116
Through the Looking Glass Ltd., London,
S.W.6 — 118
Ferenc Toth, London, S.W.6 — 118
Dahl and Son, Great Missenden, Bucks —
215

Mirrors, Cheltenham, Glos — 388
Rudolph Otto, Stow-on-the-Wold, Glos —
402

Musical Instruments and Literature
John and Arthur Beare (J. and A. Beare
Ltd.), London, W.1 — 36
William Reeves Bookseller Ltd., London,
S.W.16 — 125
Morley Galleries, Robert Morley and Co.
Ltd., London, S.E.13 — 131
H. Baron, London, N.W.2 — 149
David Miles, London, N.W.1 — 149
Tony Bingham, London, N.W.3 — 150
Travis and Emery, London, W.C.2 — 163
Dollin and Daines, Bath, Avon — 180
W.E. Hill and Sons, Great Missenden, Bucks
— 215
Mayflower Antiques, Harwich and
Dovercourt, Essex — 371
Arthur S. Lewis, Corse Lawn, Glos — 392
Julian Thwaites and Co., Bushey, Herts —
446
Chester and Co., Rawtenstall, Lancs. —
499
Norfolk Polyphon and Clock Centre,
Bawdeswell, Norfolk — 531
Richard Archbold — Violins, Hexham,
Northumb — 555
Laurie Leigh Antiques, Oxford, Oxon — 576
Graham Webb, Brighton, Sussex East —
682
Jomarc Pianos U.K., Birmingham, West
Midlands — 723
May and May Ltd., Tisbury, Wilts — 741
San Domenico Stringed Instruments, Cardiff,
S. Glam., Wales — 834

Nautical Instruments (See Scientific Instruments)

Needlework (See Tapestries)

Netsuke (See Oriental Art)

Oil Paintings
Arthur Ackermann and Son Ltd., London,
W.1 — 34
Thomas Agnew and Sons Ltd., London,
W.1 — 34
Bolsover Gallery, London, W.1 — 36
Browse and Darby Ltd., London, W.1 — 40
Burlington Paintings Ltd., London, W.1 —
40
Clarendon Gallery, London, W.1 — 40
P. and D. Colnaghi and Co. Ltd., London,
W.1 — 40
Anthony Dallas and Sons Ltd., London, W.1
— 41
Anthony d'Offay, London, W.1 — 41
Fine Art Society p.l.c., London, W.1 — 42
Frost and Reed Ltd., London, W.1 — 42
Galerie George, London, W.1 — 42
Christopher Gibbs Ltd., London, W.1 — 42
Iona Antiques, London, W.1 (Grays Ant.
Mkt.) — 44
Richard Green (Fine Paintings), London W.1
— 47

Oriental Art

Mandarin Gallery, Riverhead, Kent — 477
Ribchester Antiques, Ribchester, Lancs —
447
De Montfort, Robertsbridge, Sussex East —
688
Ringles Cross Antiques, Uckfield, Sussex
East — 691
R. and D. Coombes, Aldbourne, Wilts — 731
Oriental Art Ware, Harrogate, Yorkshire
North — 756
Walker Galleries Ltd., Harrogate, Yorkshire
North — 760
Sigma Antiques and Fine Art, Ripon,
Yorkshire North — 765
Albany Antiques, Glasgow, Scotland — 812
Gay's Art Gallery, Penmaenmawr, Gwynedd,
Wales — 840

Photographs and Equipment
Christopher Wood Gallery, London, S.W.1
— 99
Robert Hershkowitz, London, S.W.7 — 119
Jubilee, London, N.1 — 141
Vintage Çameras, London, S.E.26 — 134

Playing Cards
Intercol, London, N.1 — 141

Porcelain
Antique Porcelain Co. Ltd., London, W.1 —
34
Thomas Goode and Co. (London) Ltd.,
London, W.1 — 43
Harcourt Antiques, London, W.1 — 48
Brian Haughton Antiques, London, W.1 —
49
Heirloom and Howard Ltd., London, W.1 —
49
D.M. and P. Manheim (Peter Manheim) Ltd.,
London, W.1 — 52
Gerald Sattin Ltd., London, W.1 — 57
Venners Antiques, London, W.1 — 60
David Brower, London, W.8 — 65
Delomosne and Son Ltd., London, W.8 —
67
H. and W. Deutsch Antiques, London, W.8
— 67
Graham and Oxley (Antiques) Ltd., London,
W.8 — 67
Grosvenor Antiques Ltd., London, W.8 —
67
Hoff Antiques Ltd., London, W.8 — 68
Hope and Glory, London, W.8 — 68
R. and J. Jones, London, W.8 — 68
Klaber and Klaber, London, W.8 — 68
Eric Lineham and Sons, London, W.8 — 69
J. and J. May, London, W.8 — 70
St. Jude's Antiques, London, W.8 — 71
Jean Sewell (Antiques) Ltd., London, W.8
— 72
Edward Salti, London, W.9 — 72
Mary Wise, London, W.8 — 72
Mercury Antiques, London, W.11 — 79
Albert Amor Ltd., London, S.W.1 — 84
Kate Foster, London, S.W.1 — 89
Winifred Williams, London, S.W.1 — 99
Aubrey Spiers, (Chenil Galleries) London,
S.W.3 — 106

Ledger Antiques, London, S.W.3 — 108
H.W. Newby (A.J. Waller) and H.C. Mote,
London, S.W.3 — 108
Earle D. Vandekar of Knightsbridge Ltd.,
London, S.W.3 — 109
Gerald Freedman — Cale Antiques, London,
S.W.6 — 114
Susan Becker, London, S.W.15 — 124
Rochefort Antiques Gallery, London, N.21 —
147
Gerald Clark Antiques Ltd., London, N.W.7
— 153
Whittington Galleries, Sutton, Gtr. London
— 172
Andrew Dando, Bath, Avon — 180
Gerald Deacon, Bath, Avon — 180
The Old School Antiques, Dorney, Berks —
203
Old Malthouse, Hungerford, Berks — 205
Crispin Antiques, Amersham, Bucks — 213
Baroq Antiques, Little Brickhill, Bucks — 216
Olney Antique Porcelain Co., Olney, Bucks
— 217
Gabor Cossa Antiques, Cambridge, Cambs
— 222
A.D. Antiques, Doddington, Cambs — 224
Gallery Three, March, Cambs — 226
Sydney House Antiques, Wansford, Cambs.
— 228
Peter A. Crofts, Wisbech, Cambs — 229
E. and N.R. Charlton Fine Art and Porcelain
Marton, Cleveland — 245
London Apprentice Antiques, St. Austell,
Cornwall — 252
Augill Castle Antiques Ltd., Brough, Cumbria
— 301
Kendal Studio Pottery, Kendal, Cumbria —
305
P.W. Gottschald, Ambergate, Derbys — 313
Westfield Antiques, Chesterfield, Derbys —
318
David J. Thorn, Budleigh Salterton, Devon
— 326
Mary Payton Antiques, Chagford, Devon —
326
The Lantern Shop, Sidmouth, Devon — 336
Philip Andrade, South Brent, Devon — 336
Pamela Rowan, Blockley, Glos — 384
Studio Antiques Ltd., Bourton-on-the-Water,
Glos — 384
Mrs. M.K. Nielsen, Moreton-in-Marsh, Glos
— 396
Hamand Antiques, Painswick, Glos — 398
L. Greenwold, Stow-on-the-Wold, Glos —
401
F.W. Taylor, Tewkesbury, Glos — 408
Goss and Crested China, Horndean, Hants
— 416
Todd and Austin Antiques of Winchester,
Winchester, Hants — 427
Gavina Ewart, Broadway, Hereford and
Worcs — 429
H. and B. Wolf Antiques Ltd., Droitwich,
Hereford and Worcs — 430
M. Lees and Sons, Worcester, Hereford and
Worcs — 443
W.W. Warner (Antiques) Ltd., Brasted, Kent
— 468

The Porcelain Collector, Shoreham, Kent — 480

Steppes Hill Farm Antiques, Stockbury, Kent — 480

Dunsdale Lodge Antiques, Westerham, Kent — 486

Burnley Antiques and Fine Arts Ltd., Burnley, Lancs — 491

Timothy Kendrew Antiques, Stamford, Lincs — 523

Elizabeth Allport (Corner Antiques), Coltishall, Norfolk — 532

T.C.S. Brooke, Wroxham, Norfolk — 545

Peter and Heather Jackson Antiques, Brackley, Northants — 547

David John Ceramics, Eynsham, Oxon — 574

Bill Dickenson, Ironbridge, Shrops — 594

Teme Valley Antiques, Ludlow, Shrops — 604

Castle Gate Antiques, Shrewsbury, Shrops — 605

Dowlish Wake Antiques, Dowlish Wake, Somerset — 611

A. Lodge-Mortimer, Exton, Somerset — 612

P. and B. Jordan, Farnham, Surrey — 661

Barclay Antiques, Bexhill-on-Sea, Sussex East — 675

Geoffrey Godden Chinaman, Worthing, Sussex West — 705

Bridge Antiques, Stourbridge, West Midlands — 726

The China Hen, Bradford-on-Avon, Wilts — 731

A. de Saye Hutton, Salisbury, Wilts — 739

Myers Galleries, Gargrave, Yorkshire North — 747

Armstrong Antiques, Harrogate, Yorkshire North — 749

W.F. Greenwood and Sons Ltd., Harrogate, Yorkshire North — 752

David Love, Harrogate, Yorkshire North — 754

Shaw Bros., Harrogate, Yorkshire North — 758

Ian Stephenson, Helmsley, Yorkshire North — 760

Bryan Bowden, Doncaster, Yorkshire South — 771

Robert Clark, Micklebring, Yorkshire South — 772

The Antique Shop, Huddersfield, Yorkshire West — 780

Dunluce Antiques, Bushmills, Co. Antrim, N.I. — 793

Ballymenoch Antiques, Edinburgh, Scotland — 805

D. and N. Nairne, Edinburgh, Scotland — 810

Tim Wright Antiques, Glasgow, Scotland — 817

Elm House Antiques, Haddington, Scotland — 817

Dibley Antiques, Moylegrove, Dyfed, Wales — 831

Brenin Porcelain and Pottery, Cowbridge, S. Glam., Wales — 834

West Wales Antiques, Murton, S. Glam., Wales — 835

D.S. Hutchings, Newport, Gwent, Wales — 837

Castle Antiques, Usk, Gwent, Wales — 837

Old Market Antiques, Usk, Gwent, Wales — 837

Pot-Lids

Oliver-Sutton Antiques, London, W.8 — 70

Gavina Ewart, Broadway, Hereford and Worcs — 429

Kollectarama, Arreton, Isle of Wight — 462

The Old Forge, Hollingbourne, Kent — 475

Steppes Hill Farm Antiques, Stockbury, Kent — 480

Ivanhoe Antiques, Ashby-de-la-Zouche, Leics — 503

Pottery (See also Porcelain)

Brian Haughton Antiques, London, W.1 — 49

D.M. and P. Manheim (Peter Manheim) Ltd., London, W.1 — 52

Richard Dennis, London, W.8 — 67

Graham and Oxley (Antiques) Ltd., London, W.8 — 67

Jonathan Horne, London, W.8 — 68

Lindsay Antiques, London, W.8 — 69

J. and J. May, London, W.8 — 70

Oliver-Sutton Antiques, London, W.8 — 70

M. and D. Seligmann, London, W.8 — 71

Mercury Antiques, London, W.11 — 79

Ledger Antiques Ltd., London, S.W.3 — 108

Rogers de Rin, London, S.W.3 — 108

Alistair Sampson Antiques, London, S.W.3 — 108

Earle D. Vandekar of Knightsbridge Ltd., London, S.W.3 — 109

Gerald Freedman — Cale Antiques, London S.W.6 — 114

John Hall Antiques & Prints, London, S.W.7 — 115

Gerald Clark Antiques Ltd., London, N.W.7 — 153

Andrew Dando, Bath, Avon — 180

Baroq Antiques, Little Brickhill, Bucks — 216

Olney Antique Porcelain Company, Olney, Bucks — 217

Christopher Pugh Antiques, Chester, Cheshire — 234

J. Milner Antiques, Marple, Cheshire — 239

Mary Payton Antiques, Chagford, Devon — 326

Trevor Micklem Antiques Ltd., Iddesleigh, Devon — 330

Philip Andrade Ltd., South Brent, Devon — 336

Rogers of Alresford, Alresford, Hants — 411

Close Antiques, Winchester, Hants — 425

W.W. Warner (Antiques) Ltd., Brasted, Kent — 468

Burnley Antiques and Fine Arts Ltd., Burnley, Lancs — 491

Peter and Heather Jackson, Brackley, Northants — 547

Barclay Antiques, Bexhill-on-Sea, Sussex East — 675

Leonard Russell, Newhaven, Sussex East — 688

Geoffrey Godden Chinaman, Worthing, Sussex West — 705

Moxhams Antiques, Bradford-on-Avon, Wilts — 732

Bratton Antiques, Westbury, Wilts — 742

W.F. Greenwood and Sons Ltd., Harrogate, Yorkshire North — 752

Myers Galleries, Gargrave, Yorkshire North — 747

Bryan Bowden, Doncaster, Yorkshire South — 771

Robert Clark, Micklebring, Yorkshire South — 772

Brenin Pottery and Porcelain, Cowbridge, S. Glam., Wales — 834

West Wales Antiques, Murton, S. Glam., Wales — 835

Prints (See Maps)

Rugs (See Carpets)

Russian Art (See Icons)

Scientific Instruments

Grimaldi, London, W.1 — 47

Mayfair Microscopes Ltd., London, W.1 — 54

Eila Grahame, London, W.8 — 67

Peter Delehar, London, W.11 — 76

Rod's Antiques, London, W.11 — 81

Arthur Davidson Ltd., London, S.W.1 — 88

David Weston Ltd., London, S.W.1 — 99

Peter Goodwin, London, S.W.7 — 119

Harriet Wynter Ltd., London, S.W.10 — 122

Vintage Cameras Ltd., London, S.E.26 — 134

Arthur Middleton, London, W.C.2 — 162

Christopher Sykes Antiques, Woburn, Beds — 199

Malcolm Frazer Antiques, Cheadle, Cheshire — 232

Mike Read Antique Sciences, St. Ives, Cornwall — 252

Galaxy Art, Plymouth, Devon — 334

Mayflower Antiques, Harwich and Dovercourt, Essex — 371

Country Life Antiques, Stow-on-the-Wold, Glos — 401

Padgett's Antiques, Hull, Humberside North — 457

Hadlow Antiques, Tunbridge Wells, Kent — 474

David T. Hansord, Lincoln, Lincs — 518

Pinfold Antiques, Ruskington, Lincs — 521

Humbleyard Fine Art, Holt, Norfolk — 536

Turret House, Wymondham, Norfolk — 545

Bernard G. House, Wells, Somerset — 619

Trevor Philip and Son, Brighton, Sussex East — 681

Paul M. Peters Antiques, Harrogate, Yorkshire North — 756

Roy Sim Antiques, Blairgowrie, Scotland — 802

Quadrant Antiques, Edinburgh, Scotland — 810

Christopher Wood, Kelso, Scotland — 818

Sculpture

Barling of Mount Street Ltd., London, W.1 — 36

Crowther of Syon Lodge, London, W.1 — 41

Anthony d'Offay, London, W.1 — 41

Ted Few, London, W.1 — 42

The Fine Art Society p.l.c., London, W.1 — 42

Madden Galleries, London, W.1 — 51

Mallett at Bourdon House Ltd., London, W.1 — 52

Sladmore Gallery, The, London, W.1 — 58

Philp, London, W.11 — 80

Edric Van Vredenburgh, London, S.W.1 — 98

Mathon Gallery, London, S.W.3 — 108

T. Crowther and Son Ltd., London, S.W.6 — 112

Crowther of Syon Lodge Ltd., Isleworth, Gtr. London — 168

Mathon Gallery, Mathon, Hereford and Worcs — 438

Manor Farm Antiques and Garden Ornaments, Swaffham, Norfolk — 544

Bruton Gallery, Bruton, Somerset — 610

D.E. Granshaw, Shalford, Surrey — 670

Armstrong-Davis Gallery, Arundel, Sussex West — 693

Shipping Goods and Period Furniture for the Trade

Peter and Daniele Dodd, London, W.11 — 76

Lamont Antiques Ltd., London, S.E.1 — 128

MacNeill's Art and Antique Warehouse, London, S.E.1 — 128

Oola Boola Antiques, London, S.E.1 — 128

Bushwood Antiques, London, N.1 — 137

Just Desks, London, N.W.8 — 156

Brocantiques, London, N.W.10 — 157

Phelps Ltd., Twickenham, Gtr. London — 174

The Woburn Abbey Antiques Centre, Woburn, Beds — 199

Syd Greenhalgh and Son, Dalton-in-Furness, Cumbria — 303

Exeter Antique Wholesalers, Exeter, Devon — 327

Alan Jones Antiques, Okehampton, Devon — 334

R.A. Swift and Sons, Bournemouth, Dorset — 348

David Mack Antiques, Branksome, Dorset — 350

Tower Antiques, Cranborne, Dorset — 351

Antiquatat Antiques, Wimborne Minster, Dorset — 356

Jo Patterson Antiques, Crook, Durham — 360

S. Brown and Sons 'The Popular Mart', Darlington, Durham — 360

Rundells Antiques, Harlow, Essex — 371

F.G. Bruschweiler (Antiques) Ltd., Rayleigh, Essex — 376

Valmar Antiques, Stansted, Essex — 379

Armada Exports, Cheltenham, Glos — 386

Silver and Jewellery

Treasure House Antiques, Bawtry, Yorkshire South — 771

John Mason (Rotherham) Ltd., Rotherham, Yorkshire South — 772

H. Hayden Antiques, Sheffield, Yorkshire South — 774

Many Things, Sheffield, Yorkshire South — 775

Fillans (Antiques), Huddersfield, Yorkshire West — 780

Goodwins Antiques, Edinburgh, Scotland — 809

Letham Antiques, Edinburgh, Scotland — 809

James Forrest and Co. (Jewellers) Ltd., Glasgow, Scotland — 814

Ryan Richards, Newport, Gwent, Wales — 837

Sporting Items and Associated Memorabilia

Simon Brett, Moreton-in-Marsh, Glos — 395

Sports Programmes, Coventry, West Midlands — 725

Old Golf Shop Inc., Edinburgh, Scotland — 810

Sporting Paintings and Prints

Arthur Ackermann and Son Ltd., London, W.1 — 34

Richard Green (Fine Paintings), London, W.1 — 47

The Tryon and Moorland Gallery, London, W.1 — 59

Lacy Gallery, London, W.11 — 78

Paul Mason Gallery, London, S.W.1 — 94

Malcolm Innes Gallery, London, S.W.3 — 107

The William Marler Gallery, Cirencester, Glos — 391

Border Sporting Gallery, Wooler, Northumb. — 557

Sally Mitchell Fine Paintings, Askham, Notts — 559

Malcolm Innes Gallery, Edinburgh, Scotland — 809

Stamps

J.A.L. Franks, London, W.C.1 — 158

Stanley Gibbons, London, W.C.2 — 161

Corridor Stamp Shop, Bath, Avon — 178

Portsmouth Stamp Shop, Portsmouth, Hants — 420

Stampantique, Egham, Surrey — 660

Glance Back, Chepstow, Gwent, Wales — 836

Tapestries and Needlework

C. John (Rare Rugs) Ltd., London, W.1 — 50

Alexander Juran and Co., London, W.1 — 50

Mallett and Son (Antiques) Ltd., London, W.1 — 52

Vigo-Sternberg Galleries, London, W.1 — 60

Daniel Mankowitz, London, W.2 — 63

Belinda Coote Antiques, London, W.8 — 66

Victor Franses Gallery, London, S.W.1 — 89

Mayorcas Ltd., London, S.W.1 — 94

Yistelworth Antiques, Isleworth, Gtr. London — 169

Blyth Antiques, Bath, Avon — 178

Scaramanga Antiques, Witney, Oxon — 585

Elizabeth Bradley, Beaumaris, Gwynedd, Wales — 838

Tools (including needlework and sewing)

Richard Maude Tools, London, S.W.15 — 125

Sheila Smith, Bath, Avon — 186

Filkins Antiques, Chester, Cheshire — 232

Woolmarket Antiques, Chipping Campden, Glos — 390

Country Antiques, Long Melford, Suffolk — 644

Roy Arnold, Needham Market, Suffolk — 647

Horn Antiques, Churt, Surrey — 656

Toys (See Dolls and Toys)

Trade Dealers (See Shipping Goods)

Treen

Halcyon Days, London, W.1 — 48

Simon Castle, London, W.8 — 65

Arthur Seager Antiques Ltd., London, W.8 — 71

M. and D. Seligman, London, W.8 — 71

Wynyards Antiques, London, W.11 — 83

Robin Butler, Bristol, Avon — 188

Charles Toller, Datchet, Berks — 203

A. and E. Foster, Naphill, Bucks — 217

Denzil Verey, Barnsley, Glos — 383

Paul Cater Antiques, Moreton-in-Marsh, Glos — 396

Huntington Antiques Ltd., Stow-on-the-Wold, Glos — 402

Prichard Antiques, Winchcombe, Glos — 409

Polly de Courcy-Ireland, Winchester, Hants — 426

Barclay Antiques, Bexhill-on-Sea, Sussex East — 675

Vintage Cars (See Carriages and Cars)

Watercolours

Thomas Agnew and Sons Ltd., London, W.1 — 34

Bolsover Gallery, London, W.1 — 36

P. and D. Colnaghi and Co. Ltd., London, W.1 — 40

H.C. Dickins, London, W.1 — 41

The Fine Art Society p.l.c., London, W.1 — 42

Frost and Reed Ltd., London, W.1 — 42

Galerie George, London, W.1 — 42

Garton and Cooke, London, W.1 — 42

Richard Green (Fine Paintings), London, W.1 — 47

E. Joseph, London, W.1 — 50

The Leger Galleries Ltd., London, W.1 — 51

Maas Gallery, London, W.1 — 51

Osborne Gallery, London, W.1 — 55

Hood and Broomfield, Newcastle-under-Lyme, Staffs — 626

Andrew's Gallery/Norman Hall, Beccles, Suffolk — 629

Cransford Gallery, Bungay, Suffolk — 630

Guildhall Gallery, Bury St. Edmunds, Suffolk — 630

Peasenhall Art and Antiques Gallery, Peasenhall, Suffolk — 648

The Grange Gallery, Withersdale, Suffolk — 649

Simon Carter Gallery, Woodbridge, Suffolk — 651

The Falcon Gallery, Wortham, Suffolk — 653

Stampantique, Egham, Surrey — 660

Limpsfield Watercolours, Limpsfield, Surrey — 665

Bourne Gallery, Reigate, Surrey — 667

Michael Spratt, Shalford, Surrey — 670

Edward Cross, Weybridge, Surrey — 673

Howes Gallery, Petworth, Sussex West — 700

Fine-Lines (Fine Art), Shipston-on-Stour, Warks — 716

Ashleigh House Antiques, Birmingham, West Midlands — 721

The Moseley Gallery, Birmingham, West Midlands — 724

Ian J. Brook, Wilton, Wilts. — 742

Thornton Gallery, Bedale, Yorkshire North — 745

E. Carrol, Bingley, Yorkshire West — 777

The Rendezvous Gallery, Aberdeen, Scotland — 800

The Waverley Gallery, Aberdeen, Scotland — 800

The McEwan Gallery, Ballater, Scotland — 802

The Calton Gallery, Edinburgh, Scotland — 807

Fine Art Society plc., Edinburgh, Scotland — 808

Campbell-Gibson Fine Art, Oban, Scotland — 821

Mainhill Gallery, St. Boswells, Scotland — 824

David Windsor Gallery, Bangor, Gwynedd, Wales — 838

Wholesale Dealers (See Shipping Goods)

Wine Related Items

Richard Kihl Wine Antiques and Accessories, London, N.W.1 — 148

Robin Butler, Bristol, Avon — 188

Christopher Sykes Antiques, Woburn, Beds — 190

Bacchus Antiques in the Service of Wine, Hale, Cheshire — 235

Bacchus Antiques in the Service of Wine, Heversham, Cumbria — 304

STOP PRESS AND AMENDMENTS

London W.1 (01)

Aux Menus Plaisirs
23 Grafton St. (B.B. Steinitz.) CL: Sat. Open 9—6. *STOCK: French furniture and objets d'art, Louis XIV to Louis XVI.* TEL. 493 5512

Deborah Gage Ltd.
35 Piccadilly, Suites 101—110. Est. 1982. Open by appointment only. *STOCK: Fine European works of Art, 18th C, from £5,000.* LOC: Entrance is in Swallow St., off Piccadilly. TEL: 727 7971; messages — 439 8985. SER: Valuations; restorations; buys at auction (as stock). VAT: Stan/Spec.

Christopher Hull Gallery
17 Motcomb St. Open 10—6, Sat. 10—1. *STOCK: British paintings.* TEL: 235 0500.

London W.2

Craven Gallery Trade Only
30 Craven Terrace. (C. & A. Quaradeghini.) Est: 1974. Open Sat. 3—7, other times by appointment. SIZE: Large and warehouse. *STOCK: Silver and plate, 19th—20th C; furniture, china and glass, Victorian, all from £15.* LOC: Off Bayswater Rd. PARK: Easy. TEL: 402 2802; home — 960 0557. SER: Valuations. VAT: Stan.

London W.8

Abingdon Antiques
87 Abingdon Road., Kensington. (Mrs. J. de Sousa Macedo.) CL: Sat. a.m. Open 11—6.30, Fri. 11—7, Mon. 4.30—6.30, Sat. 2—6.30, other times by appointment. SIZE: Medium. *STOCK: English and Continental pottery and porcelain, £5—£700; small furniture, glass and general items, £5-£500; all 18th—19th C; Oriental ceramics, 15th—19th C, £10—£500.* Not Stocked: Silver, jewellery, weapons. LOC: At junction of Abingdon Rd. and Scarsdale Villas. PARK: Easy. TEL: 937 4118. SER: Valuations; buys at auction.

London W.11

Frank Hastwell & Michael Howard Antiques
65 Portobello Rd. Open Sat. 7—3, other times by appointment. *STOCK: Period metalware and furniture.* TEL: 769 6207.

Themes and Variations
231 Westbourne Grove. (L. Fawcett, G. Medda.) Open 10—6. *STOCK: Decorative items, furniture, glass, ceramics, carpets, lamps, jewellery, art nouveau, art deco and 1950s.* TEL: 727 5531.

London S.W.1

I.J. Mazure and Co. Ltd. BADA
90 Jermyn St. *STOCK: Gold, objets de vertu, Russian works of art including Faberge.* TEL: 839 3101/2.

London S.W.6

The Artisan
72 New King's Rd. (A.L. Estadieu.) Est. 1975. Open 10—5.30. SIZE: Large. *STOCK: Furniture including painted, 17th—20th C, £100—£1,500; studio glass, 20th C, £50—£150; paintings, £50—£500.* PARK: Easy. TEL: 736 3336. SER: Restorations. VAT: Stan.

Cooper Fine Arts Ltd.
768 Fulham Rd. (J. Hill-Reid.) Est. 1976. Open 10—6.30. SIZE: Medium. *STOCK: Oils and watercolours, £200—£5,000; bronzes, £200—£1,000; all 1820—1950.* LOC: Putney Bridge end of Fulham Rd. PARK: Easy. TEL: 731 3421; home — same. SER: Valuations; restorations; framing; buys at auction. VAT: Stan/Spec.

Plot 13 Warehouse
The Warehouse, Kempson Rd. Open 9.30—1 and 2—5.30, Sat. 9.30—1, Sat. p.m. by appointment. SIZE: Medium. *STOCK: General antiques, 17th—19th C, £10—£10,000; art deco, 20th C, £50—£5,000.* LOC: Close to New King's Rd. PSRK: Easy. TEL: 731 6474. SER: Valuations; buys at auction. VAT: Stan/Spec.

Ranelagh Antiques Ltd.
25 Waterford Rd. (C.A. Joll.) Est. 1986. Open by appointment only. SIZE: Medium. *STOCK: Pairs of decorative objets d'art, Louis XV to William IV, £500—£5,000; engravings, £10—£100; small furniture, £500—£1,500; both 18th—19th C.* Not stocked: Chandeliers, paintings and large furniture. LOC: Close to New King's Rd. PARK: Easy. TEL: 736 9618; home — same. SER: Buys at auction (objets d'art); finder.

Swanson Antiques
186 Wandsworth Bridge Rd., Fulham. (D. and N. Swanson.) Est. 1976. Open 9.30—6, Sun. 10—4. SIZE: Medium. *STOCK: Oak, fruitwood, pine and country furniture, 17th C to early 19th C, £100—£5,000.* LOC: 2 minutes from New King's Rd. PARK: Easy. TEL: 736 5802. SER: Valuations; restorations. VAT: Stan/Spec.

London S.W.15

Seago
16 Lower Richmond Rd. (T.P. and L.G. Seago.) Open 9.30–5.30. *STOCK: Garden and decorative furniture; statuary 17th-19th C.* TEL: 785 7155.

London S.E.1

Bermondsey International Traders
Trade Only
212 Bermondsey St. (R. Tindall and E. Hoogeveen.) Est. 1976. CL: Sat. Open Thurs. 9–6, Fri. 9–4, other times by appointment. SIZE: Medium. *STOCK: Shipping goods, 19th-20th C, £10–£200.* LOC: Adjacent to Bermondsey market. TEL: 407 0235; home — (0702) 217326. SER: Valuations; restorations (brass polishing). VAT: Stan.

London, E.C.1

R.I. McKay   LAPADA
Trade Only
88/90 Hatton Garden. Est. 1951. Open by appointment only. SIZE: Small. *STOCK: Jewellery, all periods, from £100.* LOC: Centre of Hatton Garden. PARK: Easy and multi-storey nearby. TEL: 405 7544. VAT: Stan/Spec.

London   N.I.

Antique Dealers International
57-58 Upper St., Islington. (Antique Dealers International p.l.c.) Open 9.30–5.30. *STOCK: English and Continental furniture, to 1850; works of art, bronzes, paintings and porcelain.* TEL: 354 0766. LOC: Opposite Camden Passage. SER: Valuations; restorations (furniture and pictures); buys at auction. VAT: Stan/Spec.

London W.C.2

The London Silver Vaults
53-65 Chancery Lane. Please note that I.J. Mazure and Co. Ltd. are no longer trading from Vault 9. Their business address is now 90 Jermyn St., London W.1. (See entry above).

Greater London

RICHMOND (Surrey)
Palmer Antiques
10 Paved Court. (C.D. and V.J. Palmer.) Est. 1984. Open 10–5. SIZE: Medium. *STOCK: Furniture, 19th C, £100–£1,000; prints, watercolours and engravings, 19th–20th C, £50–£300.* PARK: Richmond Garden. TEL: (01) 948 2668; home — (01) 998 0901. VAT: Stan/Spec.

RUISLIP (Middx.)   (08956)
Stephenson Brothers
34 High St. (R.R. Hutchinson.) Est. 1951. CL: Wed. p.m. SIZE: Medium. *STOCK: Furniture, 19th C, £50–£500; bric-a-brac, early 20th C, £5–£50; pianos, 20th C, £200–£600.* LOC: Approx. 2 miles north of Polish war memorial junction on Western Ave. TEL: 32651. SER: Valuations; restorations (pictures, clocks); French polishing. VAT: Stan/Spec.

Avon

BRISTOL   (0272)
Alan Bailey Antiques Ltd.   LAPADA
14a Alma Vale Rd., Clifton. Est. 1959. Open 9–5, Sat. 9–12, Sun. by appointment. SIZE: Medium. *STOCK: General antiques, 1920s furniture, porcelain, silver and pictures.* LOC: Off Pembroke Rd., turn by C. of E. church. PARK: Easy. TEL: 735778; home — 629263. SER: Valuations; buys at auction. VAT: Stan/Spec.

Buckinghamshire

CHESHAM   (0494)
Chess Antiques   LAPADA
85 Broad St. (M. Wilder.) Open 9–5.30, Sat. 10–1. *STOCK: Furniture, 18th C and Victorian; clocks.* TEL: 783043. SER: Restorations.

MARLOW   (062 84)
Collectors Treasures Ltd.   LAPADA
4 Liston Court. (R.J. and D.M. Eisler, S.D. and R.J. Paessler.) Open 9.30–5.30. *STOCK: Maps and prints, 16th-20th C, £3–£2,000; antique wallpaper roller lamps.* TEL: 73424. SER: Valuations; framing and mounting (maps). VAT: Stan.

Buckinghamshire continued

PRINCES RISBOROUGH   (084 44)
Bell Street Antiques Centre
20/22 Bell St. (J. Booth and R. Howard.) Est. 1976. CL: Wed. Open 9.30—6, Sun. by appointment. SIZE: Medium. *STOCK: Furniture, 18th—-19th C, £40—£4,000; porcelain, glass, collectables, pewter, copper, brass, 19th C, £5—£100.* LOC: A4010. PARK: Easy. TEL: 3034; home — 2198. SER: Valuations; buys at auction. VAT: Spec.

Cambridgeshire

BOTTISHAM
Cambridge Pine
Hall Farm, Lode Rd. (Mr. and Mrs. D. Weir.) Est. 1980. Open seven days. SIZE: Medium. *STOCK: Pine, 18th—19th C, £25—£800; doors and fireplaces, 19th C, £20—£200; old pine kitchens.* LOC: Midway between Bottisham and Lode, near Angelsey Abbey. PARK: Easy. TEL: Cambridge (0223) 811208; home — same. SER: Stripping, sanding and polishing.

Cheshire

CHESTER   (0244)
A. & S. Antiques of Chester
Trade Only
Unit 6b, Hartford Way, Sealand Industrial Estate. Open 8.30—5.30. SIZE: Warehouse. *STOCK: General antiques, Edwardian—1930.* TEL: 375664.

St. Peters Fine Art Gallery Ltd.
St. Peters Churchyard, Northgate St. (D. Hellon, L. Walker.) Est. 1984. Open 10—5.30, Sun. by appointment. SIZE: Medium. *STOCK: Watercolours and oil paintings, 19th to early 20th C, £250—£20,000.* LOC: In city centre off Northgate St. and Watergate St. PARK: Nearby. TEL: 45500. SER: Valuations; restorations; buys at auction (oil paintings and watercolours). VAT: Spec.

MACCLESFIELD   (0625)
G. Bagshaw Antiques
74 Mill Lane. Est. 1971. CL: Wed. Open 10—5.30. SIZE: Small. *STOCK: General antiques.* LOC: On Leek Rd. PARK: Easy. TEL: 21642; home — 72000.

Cornwall

ST. KEW, Nr. Wadebridge
Tim and Clare Belton Pine
Maidenland. Est. 1981. Open 8—1 and 1.30—5, Sat., Sun. and other times by appointment. SIZE: Large. *STOCK: Pine, from early 19th C, £15—£700.* LOC: ½ mile from A39. PARK: Own. TEL: St. Mabyn (020 884) 242; home — same. SER: Restorations. VAT: Stan.

Derbyshire

BARLOW, Nr. Sheffield
Hackney House Antiques
Hackney Lane. (Mrs. J.M. Gorman.) Open 9—6, seven days. *STOCK: General antiques.* TEL: Sheffield (0742) 890248.

BRAMPTON, Nr. Chesterfield
Cottage Curios
209 Chatsworth Rd. (P. Coleman.) Est. 1981. Open Thurs. and Fri. 10—5, Sat. 2—5. SIZE: Small. *STOCK: General antiques and curios, late 19th C to 20th C, £5—£500.* LOC: A619. PARK: Easy. TEL: Chesterfield (0246) 202225. SER: Picture framing.

DRONFIELD   (0246)
Bardwell Antiques
51 Chesterfield Rd. (S. Bardwell.) Open 10—5. *STOCK: General antiques.* TEL: 412183.

The Fanshaw Gallery
High St. (R.H. Long.) Est. 1969. CL: Wed. Open 10—5. *STOCK: Paintings and frames, 18th—19th C.* TEL: 418959.

WHALEY BRIDGE   (066 33)
Nimbus Antiques
139 Buxton Rd., and 5 Lower Macclesfield Rd. (L.M. and H.C. Brobbin.) Est. 1978. Open 9—6, Sun. 2—6. SIZE: Large. *STOCK: Furniture, mainly mahogany provincial, some country, £500—£1,000; longcase and wall clocks, £200—£1,000; all 18th—19th C; desks and beds, 19th C, £250—£1,000.* LOC: A6. PARK: Easy. TEL: 4248; home — 3332. SER: Valuations; restorations (furniture). VAT: Stan/Spec.

Devon

CULLOMPTON   (0884)
Sunset Strip
The Old Forge, Higher Mill Lane. (N. Miller and R. Reeves.) Est. 1981. CL: Sat. p.m. and lunch times. SIZE: Medium. *STOCK: English stripped pine, £50—£250; country furniture, £25—£150; bric-a-brac and kitchenalia, £5—£25; all 19th C.* LOC: M5, junction 28. Behind Kings Head public house on left hand side at top of High St. PARK: Easy. TEL: 32689; home — 32890 or 33051. SER: Valuations; restorations (stripping and furnishing pine).

PAIGNTON   (0803)
Portobello Surplus Store
373-377 Torquay Rd. (K.J. Prestwood, T.V. Martin.) Open 9—5.30. *STOCK: General antiques.* TEL: 524955. SER: Shipping.

TORQUAY   (0803)
Portobello Surplus Store
59 Market St. (K.J. Prestwood, T.V. Martin.) Open 9—5.30. *STOCK: General antiques.* TEL: 27149. SER: Shipping.

Dorset

BOURNEMOUTH   (0202)
Richard Batsford Antiques
798A Christchurch Rd., Boscombe. Open 9.30—5.30. *STOCK: General antiques and shipping furniture.* TEL: 303706.

BRIDPORT   (0308)
Westdale Antiques
4a St. Michael's Trading Estate. (D. Westover and D. Dale.) Est. 1981. CL: Mon. Open 9—5. SIZE: Medium. *STOCK: Restored pine furniture, linen, lace and textiles, 19th C, £1—£150; general antiques, £1—£200.* LOC: Follow signs from West St. bus station. PARK: Nearby. PARK: Nearby. TEL: 27271 (24 hours). SER: Restorations.

Gloucestershire

MORETON-IN-MARSH   (0608)
Chandlers and Bow Antiques
High St. (I. Kellam, J. Kitcat and P. Grout.) Open 9.30—1.30 and 2.30—5.30. *STOCK: Pottery, porcelain, glass, silver, small furniture and general antiques.* TEL: 51347.

Hampshire

STOCKBRIDGE
Dorothea Fitzgibbon
Open by appointment. *STOCK: 19th—20th C watercolours.* TEL: Romsey (0794) 301242.

Hertfordshire

CODICOTE
Antiques Fair
Peace Memorial Hall. Est. 1975. Open first Sat. monthly 9—4. There are 25 dealers at this market selling *a wide range of general antiques.* TEL: Welwyn (043 871) 6892.

North Humberside

DRIFFIELD   (0377)
Carlton Gallery
60A Middle St. South. (B. Nichols.) Est. 1983. CL: Wed. Open 10—4.30. SIZE: Medium. *STOCK: Pictures, 18th—20th C, £25—£1,000.* LOC: Town centre. PARK: Easy. TEL: 44087; home — 43321. SER: Valuations; buys at auction (pictures).

HOWDEN   (0430)
Minster Antiques
34 Market Pl. (A. and J. Dundas.) Est. 1982. Open 9.30—5, Thurs. and Sun. by appointment. SIZE: Medium. *STOCK: Stripped pine, mahogany, bric-a-brac and pictures, 19th C, £50—£100.* LOC: 10 mins. from M62. PARK: Easy and rear of premises. TEL: 31677; home — Bubwith (075 785) 535. SER: Restorations (pine, mahogany and oak); stripping (pine); buys at auction (furniture).

South Humberside

GRIMSBY   (0472)
Equipage
54 Pasture St. (R. and C. Richardson.) Est. 1982. Open 10—6. SIZE: Small. *STOCK: General antiques including collectors items, gold, silver and plate, pre-1920; brassware, pre-1900; military items, sporting guns, from 1700, all £5—£500; general small furniture, pre-1914, £25—£200.* LOC: Near end of M180. PARK: Easy and opposite. TEL: 45438; home — same.

Grimsby continued

Goodman Gold
43 Pasture St. (S.N. Goodman.) Est. 1978. Open 10.15—5 seven days. SIZE: Small. *STOCK: Jewellery, £25—£50; smalls, £5—£25; furniture and bric-a-brac, £5—£50; all mainly 19th—20th C.* LOC: Town centre just off Victoria St. PARK: Opposite. TEL: 41301; home — 360740. SER: Valuations (jewellery); buys at auction. FAIRS: Memorial Hall, Cleethorpes and local.

Simon Antiques
Trade Only
7 Saunders St. (S.N. Goodman.) Open by appointment only. *STOCK: Jewellery, smalls, furniture and bric-a-brac, mainly 19th—20th C, £5—£50.* TEL: 360740. SER: Valuations (jewellery); buys at auction. FAIRS: Memorial Hall, Cleethorpes and local.

Kent

FARNBOROUGH (0689)
Pembroke Antiques Ltd.
3 Church Rd. Open 10—1 and 2.30—5.30. *STOCK: Fine period furniture, 17th to early 19th C; period artifacts.* LOC: Just off A21, 10 minutes from M25. PARK: Easy. TEL: 62846. VAT: Stan/Spec.

MARGATE
Manor House Antiques
45 Arlington Sq. (D. and G.G. Rimington.) Open 10—3 during winter, 10—6 including Sun. in summer. *STOCK: China, porcelain, small furniture, copper and brass.* TEL: Thanet (0843) 295025.

Katherine L. Pugh
95a King St. Open 9—5, other times by appointment. *STOCK: Pine and china.* TEL: Thanet (0843) 294703.

SANDGATE
Dench Antiques
32 High St. (Mr. and Mrs. J.W.G. Elcombe.) Est. 1980. Open 10—5. SIZE: Medium. *STOCK: Continental and English furniture, decorator's items, both 18th—19th C, £250—£5,000.* PARK: Easy. TEL: Folkestone (0303) 30824; home — (0622) 685807. SER: Buys at auction. VAT: Stan/Spec.

Lancashire

BOLTON (0204)
Corner Cupboard
2 Hawarden St. (Mrs. E. Pratt.) Open Tues., Thurs. and Fri. 9.30—5.30, Sat. 9.30—2. *STOCK: Bric-a-brac.* TEL: 58948.

COLNE (0282)
Wot the Dickens
73-75 North Valley Rd. (J. and L. Semple.) Resident. CL: Mon. and Tues. Open 10—5.30, Sat. 10—12. SIZE: Small. *STOCK: Shipping furniture and jewellery, late 19th C to early 20th C, £5—£100; ceramics, £5—£50.* LOC: Left after railway station coming from the west. PARK: Adjacent. TEL: 869216. FAIRS: Park Hall, Charnock Richard; Newark and Birmingham Trade.

GARSTANG, Nr. Preston (099 52)
J.C. Jewellery
Thomas's Shopping Centre. (J. Critchley.) Est. 1980. CL: Mon. and Wed. *STOCK: Jewellery, from 1900, £50—£100.* LOC: Off High St. PARK: Nearby. TEL: 4059. SER: Valuations; restorations; buys at auction (jewellery).

HORWICH (0204)
T. & J. Antiques
156 Chorley New Rd. (T. Grounds.) CL: Wed. Open 10—6. *STOCK: General antiques.* TEL: 695324.

LEIGH (0942)
Leigh Coins, Antiques and Jewellery
4 Queens St. (R. Bibby.) Open 9.30—5.30, Wed. 9.30—12.30. *STOCK: General antiques and jewellery.* TEL: 607947.

LYTHAM ST. ANNES
Pine Mine Antiques
33 St. Andrews Rd. South. (N. and T. Shaw.) Open 10.30—5.30. *STOCK: Pine, some oak.* TEL: Lytham (0253) 720492.

MANCHESTER (061)
Albion Antiques
643 Stockport Rd., Longsight. (A. Collins.) Est. 1971. Open 9—6, Sat. by appointment. SIZE: Medium. *STOCK: Furniture, £25—£1,000.* LOC: A6. PARK: Easy. TEL: 225 4957; home — 224 7429. SER: Valuations (furniture, architectural and nautical items); restorations (furniture).

Antiques & Curios
1090 Stockport Rd., Levenshulme. (D. McMullan.) Open 10—7, Sat. 10—6. *STOCK: Fireplaces and some furniture.* TEL: 431 8075.

Family Antiques
245 Bury Old Rd., Prestwich. (J. & J. Ditondo.) Open daily. *STOCK: General antiques.* TEL: 798 0036.

Mrs. S.J. Rigg
Gazebo, 106 Burton Rd., Withington. Open 9—6. *STOCK: Clothes, linen and lace.* TEL: 445 3802.

Manchester continued

Village Antiques
416 Bury New Rd., Prestwich. (R. Weidenbaum.) Est. 1981. Open 10−5, Wed. 10−1. SIZE: Medium. *STOCK: Ornaments and pottery, 19th C, £5−£100; glass, 18th C, porcelain, 18th−19th C, both £50−£100; furniture, 18th to early 20th C, £100−£500.* LOC: Village centre, 2 minutes from M62. PARK: Easy and opposite. TEL: 773 3612. FAIRS: Chester, Wilmslow, Stockport and Blackpool.

ROCHDALE (0706)
Antiques and Bygones
100 Drake St. (K. and E. Bonn.) Est. 1983. CL: Tues. Open 10.15−4.15. *STOCK: Pottery, 19th to early 20th C, £5−£25; jewellery, collectors' items, late 19th to 20th C, £5−£50.* PARK: Opposite. TEL: 48114; home − Whitworth (070 685) 2137. SER: Valuations.

SADDLEWORTH, (045 77)
Nr. Oldham
Isolde Antiques
14 King St., Delph. (J. Healey.) Est. 1984. CL: Tues. and Wed., also Thurs. in winter. Otherwise open, evening by appointment. SIZE: Medium. *STOCK: Furniture including tables, desks, bookcases and chests of drawers, 18th−19th C, £200−£400.* LOC: Off A62 in village centre. PARK: Easy. TEL: 71579; home − same. SER: Valuations; buys at auction.

WORSLEY
Wayside Antiques
32 Seddon St., Off Cleggs Lane, Little Hulton. (V. Partington.) Est. 1983. CL: Tues. and Wed. SIZE: Large. *STOCK: Furniture, £100−£1,000; porcelain, £25−£250; both 19th C. Pictures, 19th−20th C, £100−£400.* LOC: Midway between Salford and Chorley on A6, 300yds left, off Cleggs Lane. PARK: Easy. TEL: (061) 790 3211; home − same. SER: Valuations; buys at auction. FAIRS: Park Hall, Charnock Richard; Stafford; Last Drop (Bolton); Stockport.

Leicestershire

ASHBY-DE-LA-ZOUCHE (0530)
The Pine Gallery
Old Mission, Derby Rd. (M.A. Hemus.) Est. 1971. Open daily. SIZE: Large. *STOCK: Pine, mahogany and walnut, 18th−19th C, £25−£5,000.* LOC: 200yds from town centre. PARK: Easy. TEL: 416614. SER: Valuations; restorations (furniture); buys at auction (furniture). VAT: Stan.

LEICESTER (0533)
Betty's
9 Knighton Fields Rd. West. (A. Smith.) Est. 1968. Open 9.30−5. SIZE: Small. *STOCK: Satinwood and pine items, brass and copper, pictures.* LOC: Off Saffron Lane. PARK: Easy. TEL: 839048; home − 538694. SER: Valuations; buys at auction.

MARKET HARBOROUGH (0858)
St. Mary's Mart
3 St. Mary's Rd. (P. Bowley and J. Clarke.) Est. 1985. Open 9.30−5.15, Wed. 9−2, Sat. 9.30−5, Sun. by appointment. SIZE: Medium. *STOCK: Porcelain and pictures, 19th C, £50−£100; general antiques, 19th to early 20th C, £5−£200.* LOC: A6. PARK: Nearby. TEL: 34554; home − 33234.

Lincolnshire

HORNCASTLE (065 82)
Chapman and Witney Antiques
47a East St. (E. Chapman and A. Witney.) Est. 1973. Open 9−5. SIZE: Large. *STOCK: Furniture, £5−£500; smalls, to £200; bygones, all to 1930.* LOC: A158. PARK: Easy. TEL: 3287; home − 7704 or Alford (05212) 3530. SER: Restorations (cane and rush work, furniture). FAIRS: Newark Showground.

LINCOLN (0522)
Dorrian Lambert Antiques
64 Steep Hill. (R. Dorrian and R. Lambert.) Est. 1981. CL: Wed. Open 10−5, Sat. 10−12.30 and 2−5. SIZE: Medium. *STOCK: Furniture including longcase clocks, partner desks and chairs, from 1790, to £1,000.* PARK: Loading only or nearby. TEL: 45916; home − 37293 or (042784) 686. SER: Valuations; restorations (clocks). FAIRS: Newark Showground.

Old Chapel Antiques
The Old Chapel, Croft St. (M. Frith.) Est. 1979. Open daily, Sun. by appointment. SIZE: Large. *STOCK: Furniture, collectors' items, 19th−20th C, £5−£200; pine, 19th C, £30−£300.* LOC: Near Thos. Mawer Auction Rooms. PARK: Easy. TEL: 33998; home − same. SER: Valuations; buys at auction (shipping goods and Continental items). FAIRS: Whittaker, Newark Showground; Granby Hall, Leicester; Lincoln Showground; Doncaster Racecourse. VAT: Stan.

SCOTTON, Nr. Gainsborough
W.F. Sargent
5 Eastgate. Open by appointment only. *STOCK: General antiques.* TEL: (0724) 762726.

Oxfordshire

WALLINGFORD (0491)
MGJ Antiques LAPADA
1A St. Martins St. (Mrs. M. Jane.) Est. 1971. Open 9.30—4.30, Sat. 9.30—5. SIZE: Small. *STOCK: Jewellery, Victorian and secondhand, £100—£1,000.* LOC: Town centre. PARK: Nearby. TEL: 34336; home — (0235) 848444. SER: Valuations. VAT: Stan/Spec.

Shropshire

CHURCH STRETTON (0694)
Stretton Antiques Market
36 Sandford Ave. (J. Briscoe and L. Alger.) Est. 1986. Open 9—5, Sun. 10.30—4.30. Winter and Bank Holidays open 10.30—4.30, Sun. 2.30—4.30. SIZE: Large. There are 30 dealers at this centre selling *a wide range of general antiques, shipping items and collectables.* LOC: Town centre. PARK: Easy. TEL: 723718; home — 722689 and (058 84) 374. SER: Valuations; restorations; buys at auction. VAT: Stan/Spec.

WELLINGTON, Nr. Telford
Haygate Gallery
40 Haygate Rd. (Mrs. M. Kusnierz.) Open 9.30—5.30, Sat. 9.30—1. *STOCK: Victorian oils and watercolours.* TEL: Telford (0952) 48553.

Somerset

BRUTON (0749)
Harlequin Antiques
Bruton Arcade, High St. Open 9—5.30, Sat. 9—1. *STOCK: Decorative and small items.* TEL: 813653.

WINCANTON (0963)
Roger Coon Antiques Trade Only
8 Bennetts Field. (R. & N. Morland-Coon.) Est. 1920. Open 8.30—5.30, Sat. and Sun. by appointment. *STOCK: Furniture and metalwork, 17th—18th C, £100—£10,000; silver, £100—£2,500; paintings, £250—£5,000; both 18th—19th C.* LOC: Just off A303 to industrial estate. PARK: Easy. TEL: 34256. SER: Valuations. VAT: Spec.

Staffordshire

LEEK (0538)
Country Cottage Interiors
The Old Co-op, 31 Compton. (J. and L. Salmon.) Est. 1972. Open 10—5. SIZE: Medium. *STOCK: Pine, mainly Victorian, £5—£500; kitchenalia, 25p—£100.* LOC: On Stone road on left from town centre. PARK: Easy. TEL: 386621; home — Cheadle (0538) 754762. SER: Pine stripping.

Gemini Trading Trade Only
Limes Mill, Abbotts Rd. (T.J. Lancaster and Mrs. Y.A. Goldstrow.) Est. 1981. Open daily, appointment preferred. SIZE: Large. *STOCK: Pine, £25—£300; bric-a-brac, £5—£25; both 19th C.* LOC: Turn off A53 along Abbotts Rd. before town centre. PARK: Easy. TEL: 387834; home — 371840 and 381478. VAT: Stan.

Surrey

BOXHILL, Nr. Dorking
Barbara Rubenstein Fine Art
Flint Cottage. Open by appointment. *STOCK: English watercolours, 18th—19th C, £250—£5,000.* LOC: Turn off A24 at the Burford Bridge Hotel. PARK: Easy. TEL: Dorking (0306) 887342; home — same. SER: Buys at auction (watercolours).

East Sussex

FOREST ROW (034 282)
Cygnet Antiques
(Mrs. M. Erskine-Hill.) Est. 1979. CL: Sat. p.m. and Wed. Open 10—1 and 2.30—5. SIZE: Small. *STOCK: General antiques especially porcelain.* LOC: A22. TEL: 3029; home — 2549.

RYE (0797)
Rope Walk Antiques LAPADA
62 Cinque Port St. (A. Lingard.) Open 9—1 and 2—5.30, Sun. shippers by appointment. SIZE: Medium. *STOCK: Pine furniture, kitchenalia and general antiques.* LOC: Opposite Conduit Hall, corner of Rope Walk. PARK: Nearby. TEL: 223486. VAT: Stan/Spec.

West Sussex

SHOREHAM (0273)
The Old Warehouse
15/16 Western Rd. (L. and M. Mills.) Open mornings only. SIZE: Large. *STOCK: Furniture, bric-a-brac and collectables.* TEL: 453504.

West Midlands

BIRMINGHAM (021)
The Halcyon Gallery
59 Birmingham Shopping Centre. (L., P. and R. Green.) Open 9—5.30. *STOCK: Victorian watercolours and some oils.* TEL: 643 4474.

North Yorkshire

RICHMOND (0748)
Five Owls Bookshop
28 Victoria Rd. (B. and V. Alderson.) CL: Mon. Usually open but prior telephone call advisable. *STOCK: Antiquarian and secondhand books.* TEL: 3648.

RIPON (0765)
Yesteryear
Ripon Small Shops, Duckhill (off Kirkgate). (J. Rowlay.) CL: Wed. Open 10.30—4.30. *STOCK: General antiques.* TEL: 701281.

South Yorkshire

BARNSLEY (0226)
Angela Charlesworth Antiques
99 Dodworth Rd. (A. and B. Charlesworth.) Est. 1971. CL: Mon. a.m. and Thurs. Open 10—5. SIZE: Small. *STOCK: English pottery and porcelain especially Yorkshire factories, 18th to early 19th C, £25—£200; small furniture, 18th—19th C, £100—£750; collectors' items, 18th C to 1900s, £5—£100.* LOC: Exit 37, M1, follow Barnsley signs for approximately 1 mile on main road. PARK: Easy. TEL: 282097; home — 203688. FAIRS: Buxton; Kedelston Hall, Derby; Dyson Perrins Museum, Worcester; Crown Hotel, Harrogate and Harrogate Fine Art.

SHEFFIELD (0742)
Ancient and Modern
226 City Rd. (H. Farrar.) Open 9—4.30. *STOCK: General antiques.* TEL: 750167.

West Yorkshire

LEEDS (0532)
John Browne Antiques
St. Andrews Parsonage, 67-67a Burley St. Open 10—5, Sat. and Sun. by appointment. *STOCK: Shipping goods, Victorian and Edwardian, £50—£150; pianos, £100—£350; modern marble figures, urns and fountains, £50—£1,000.* LOC: Continuation of Burley Rd. PARK: Easy and at rear. TEL: 430610. SER: Buys at auction. VAT: Stan.

NORTHERN IRELAND
County Down

HILLSBOROUGH (0846)
Period Architectural Features and Antiques
5 The Square. (J. Cousans.) Est. 1966. Open 9.30—6. SIZE: Large. *STOCK: Marble chimney pieces, early 18th to late 19th C, £5—£1,000; period panelling and pine pews, stained glass, Victorian bathrooms, wide range of decorative architectural items.* LOC: Main Belfast/Dublin road. PARK: Easy. TEL: 683703. SER: Valuations; restorations (marble); pine stripping; French polishing; buys at auction. VAT: Stan.

SCOTLAND

GLASGOW (041)
(Lanarkshire)
Barclay Lennie Fine Art   LAPADA
203 Bath St. (S.B. Lennie.) Open 10—5, Sat. 10—1. *STOCK: Oil paintings and watercolours.* TEL: 226 5413.

WALES
Gwynedd

PWLLHELI (0758)
Mayfair Antiques   LAPADA
11a Goal St. (Mrs. E. and I. Jones-Roberts, K. Bowers-Jones.) Open 10—5. *STOCK: Ceramics, brass and copper, 19th C.* TEL: 613033.

Dealers' Index — Stop press

Leigh Coins, Antiques and Jewellery, Leigh, Lancs.
Lennie Fine Art, Barclay, Glasgow, Scotland.
Lennie, S.B., Glasgow, Scotland.
Lingard, A., Rye, E. Sussex.
Long, R.H., Dronfield, Derbys.
MGJ Antiques, Wallingford, Oxon.
McKay, R.I., London, E.C.1.
McMullan, D., Manchester, Lancs.
Manor House Antiques, Margate, Kent.
Martin, T.V., Paignton, Devon.
Martin, T.V., Torquay, Devon.
Mayfair Antiques, Pwllheli, Gywnedd, Wales.
Mazure & Co. Ltd., I.J., London, S.W.1.
Mazure & Co. Ltd., I.J., London, W.C.2.
Medda, G., London, W.11.
Meyer, Tuggy, London, W.8.
Miller, N., Cullompton, Devon.
Mills, L. & M., Shoreham, W. Sussex.
Minster Antiques, Howden, N. Humberside.
Morland-Coon, R. & N., Wincanton, Somerset.
Nichols, B., Driffield, N. Humberside.
Nimbus Antiques, Whaley Bridge, Derbys.
Old Chapel Antiques, Lincoln, Lincs.
Old Warehouse, The, Shoreham, W. Sussex.
Paessler, S.D. & R.J., Marlow, Bucks.
Palmer Antiques, Richmond, Gtr. London.
Palmer, C.D. & V.J., Richmond, Gtr. London.
Partington, Victor, Worsley, Lancs.
Pembroke Antiques Ltd., Farnborough, Kent.
Period Architectural Features and Antiques, Hillsborough, Co. Down, N. Ireland.
Pine Gallery, The, Ashby-de-la-Zouch, Leics.
Pine Mine Antiques, Lytham St. Annes, Lancs.
Plot 13 Warehouse, London, S.W.6.
Portobello Surplus Store, Paignton, Devon.
Portobello Surplus Store, Torquay, Devon.
Pratt, Mrs. E., Bolton, Lancs.
Prestwood, K.J., Paignton, Devon.
Prestwood, K.J., Torquay, Devon.
Pugh, Katherine L., Margate, Kent.
Quaradeghini, C. & A., London, W.2.
Ranelagh Antiques Ltd., London, S.W.6.
Reeves, Rob, Cullompton, Devon.
Richardson, R. & C., Grimsby, S. Humberside.
Rigg, Mrs. S.J., Manchester, Lancs.
Rimington, D. & G.G., Margate, Kent.
Rope Walk Antiques, Rye, E. Sussex.
Rowlay, J., Ripon, N. Yorks.
Rubenstein Fine Art, Barbara, Boxhill, Surrey.
St. Mary's Mart, Market Harborough, Leics.
St. Peter's Fine Art Gallery Ltd., Chester, Cheshire.
Salmon, J. and L., Leek, Staffs.
Sargent, W.F., Scotton, Lincs.
Seago, London, S.W.15.
Seago, T.P. and L.G., London, S.W.15.
Semple, J. and L., Colne, Lancs.
Shaw, N. & T., Lytham St. Annes, Lancs.
Simon Antiques, Grimsby, S. Humberside.
Smith, A., Leicester, Leics.
Steinitz, B.B., London, W.1.
Stephenson Bros., Ruislip, Gtr. London.
Stretton Antiques Market, Church Stretton, Shrops.
Sunset Strip, Cullompton, Devon.
Swanson Antiques, London, S.W.6.
Swanson, D. and N., London, S.W.6.
T. & J. Antiques, Horwich, Lancs.
Teignmouth & Son, Pamela, London, W.8.
Teignmouth, P., London, W.8.
Themes and Variations, London, W.11.
Tindall, R., London, S.E.1.
Village Antiques, Manchester, Lancs.
Walker, L., Chester, Cheshire.
Wayside Antiques, Worsley, Lancs.
Weidenbaum, R., Manchester, Lancs.
Weir, Mr. & Mrs. D., Bottisham, Cambs.
Westdale Antiques, Bridport, Dorset.
Westover, D., Bridport, Dorset.
Wilder, M., Chesham, Bucks.
Witney, A., Horncastle, Lincs.
Wot the Dickens, Colne, Lancs.
Yesteryear, Ripon, N. Yorks.

**FOR THE 1988 EDITION OF THIS GUIDE
THIS FORM MUST BE RECEIVED BY
1st JANUARY, 1987**

FOR EXISTING ENTRIES — If in general, the entry given for your shop or gallery is correct, please sign the declaration given below and post back before 1st January. If no notification is received from you we shall not automatically repeat the entry in this Guide and it may be necessary to revert to a short entry.

The entry given in this Guide for my establishment is correct and you should repeat it in the next edition. (If there are any minor alterations please note them on the space provided below.) I understand this is entirely free of charge.

Name of shop...

Address ....

....

....
BLOCK CAPITALS PLEASE

Date...................................Signed...................................
Proprietor/Manager/Owner/Director

Minor Alterations

Please attach a letter heading or use your official company or shop stamp.

Please complete and return to: *Guide to the Antique Shops of Britain, Church Street, Woodbridge, Suffolk.*

FOR A NEW OR SUBSTANTIALLY ALTERED ENTRY USE THIS FORM

Please complete and return this form; there is no charge.

Name of shop..

Address of shop ....

....
full address including actual county (not postal area)

Name (or names) and initials of proprietor(s) ....
(Mr/Mrs/Miss/or title)

Previous trading address (if applicable) ....

....

State whether "Trade Only" (Yes or No)...

BADA (Yes or No)..

LAPADA (Yes or No) ....

Year Established ....

Are you resident on the premises (Yes or No) ....

Telephone Number: Business..

Home...
(only if customers can ring for appointments outside business hours)

Which V.A.T. scheme do you operate — Standard/Special/Both ....

Hours of Opening: (One entry, e.g. "9.30 — 5.30" if open all day or part day. Two entries, e.g. "9.30 — 1.00, 2.00 — 5.30" if closed for lunch)

Please put 'CLOSED' and 'BY APPT.' where applicable

	Morning	Afternoon
Sunday......		
Monday		
Tuesday		
Wednesday		
Thursday		
Friday......		
Saturday......		

Size of Showroom: Small (under about 600 square feet) ....

Medium (about 600 to 1,500 square feet) ....

Large (over 1,500 square feet) ....

OF WHAT DOES YOUR STOCK CHIEFLY CONSIST?

(A) Please list in order of importance	(B) Approximate period or date of stock shown in Column A	(C) Indication of average price range of stock in Column A, e.g. £50—£100 or £5—£25
1. (Principal stock)		
2.		
3.		
What do you normally refrain from stocking?		

HOW TO GET TO YOUR SHOP (BUSINESS)

Brief helpful details from the nearest well-known point:

....

....

....

Number of road on which shop is situated (e.g. A30): ....

IS PARKING *OUTSIDE* YOUR SHOP (BUSINESS) Easy (Yes or No) ....

If not give directions and distance to nearest parking place ....

....

SERVICES OFFERED:

Valuations (Yes or No)..

Restorations (Yes or No) ....

Type of work ....

Buying specific items at auction for a commission (Yes or No)...............................

Type of item ....

At which fairs (if any) do you normally exhibit?...

....

....

CERTIFICATION:

The information given above is accurate and you may publish it in the Guide. I understand that this entry is entirely free.

Signed...

Date...

CONFIDENTIAL INFORMATION — NOT FOR PUBLICATION

If you know of any recent changes concerning dealers in your area it would be helpful if you would list these below (open, closed, etc. beside each name).

....

....

....

....

....

....

....

....

....

....

....

....

....

....

....

....

....

....

....

....

NOTES